Encyclopedia of

AMERICAN
LITERATURE

Encyclopedia of
AMERICAN
LITERATURE

STEVEN R. SERAFIN
General Editor

Alfred Bendixen, Associate Editor

CONTINUUM · NEW YORK

1999

The Continuum Publishing Company
370 Lexington Avenue, New York, NY 10017

Printed in the United States of America

Library of Congress Cataloging-in-Publication Data

Encyclopedia of American literature / Steven R. Serafin, general
   editor ; Alfred Bendixen, associate editor.
      p.   cm.
   Includes bibliographical references and index.
   ISBN 0-8264-1052-9 (hardcover : alk. paper)
    1. American literature—Encyclopedias.   I. Serafin, Steven.
  II. Bendixen, Alfred.
  PS21.E53   1999
  810'.3—dc21   98-46391
                                                         CIP

Introduction

The history of American literature is what Van Wyck Brooks terms the story of its "makers and finders," those responsible for creating an "American" literature and those who provide meaning and understanding to the creative process. It is the story of a literature coming of age in search of definition and affirmation, extending many centuries from Native American oral and pictorial tradition to the literary expression of a new millennium. It is both reflection and representation of past and present: from exploration and discovery to settlement and colonization; from rebellion and independence to growth and maturity; from slavery and abolitionism to civil war and restoration; from expansion and industrialization to immigration and naturalization; from world war and recovery to nuclear capability and global diplomacy. Most importantly, it is the story of the American author shaping the scope and perception of American presence, purpose, and identity.

From oral history to the written word, literature originated with a utilitarian purpose—to record deed and event so that others would acknowledge and appreciate the act of accomplishment and benefit from the wisdom of experience. With the infusion of narrative voice, the telling of the story itself was enhanced with depth and personality and the artistry of the storyteller gained in both popularity and importance. Evolving as a progression from the earliest storyteller to the most recent, the historian and biographer to the poet and novelist, the "making" of American literature is in effect the story of its "makers": Puritan visionaries such as William Bradford and Increase and Cotton Mather; voices of creative intuition such as Anne Bradstreet, Royall Tyler, and Phillis Wheatley; masters of the American Renaissance—Ralph Waldo Emerson, Henry Wadsworth Longfellow, Henry David Thoreau, Nathaniel Hawthorne, Herman Melville, Emily Dickinson, Walt Whitman; realists and naturalists—William Dean Howells, Henry James, and Edith Wharton; Stephen Crane, Frank Norris, and Jack London; writers of the Harlem Renaissance such as Jean Toomer, Zora Neale Hurston, Langston Hughes, and Richard Wright; modernists such as Ezra Pound, T. S. Eliot, Eugene O'Neill, Robert Frost, William Faulkner, Wallace Stevens, and William Carlos Williams; writers of the Lost Generation—Gertrude Stein, F. Scott Fitzgerald, and Ernest Hemingway; Fugitive/Agrarians such as John Crowe Ransom, Allen Tate, and Robert Penn Warren; Beat writers—Allen Ginsberg, William S. Burroughs, Jack Kerouac, Gregory Corso, Gary Snyder, Lawrence Ferlinghetti, Kenneth Rexroth, and Michael McClure; the Black Mountain school—Charles Olson, Denise Levertov, Robert Duncan, Paul Blackburn, Robert Creeley, and Ed Dorn; the New York school—Kenneth Koch, Frank O'Hara, John Ashbery, James Schuyler, Barbara Guest; postmodernists from Donald Barthelme, Ishmael Reed, John Hawkes, Robert Coover, and Thomas Pynchon to Kathy Acker, Richard Powers, and William Gibson.

Inherent within the making of American literature is a sense of place—from the vast wilderness of a New World to the forging of a new nation; from township and village to city, state, and country. Serving as a means to enhance identity, place tends to define the individual as well as the community. Consequently, places both real and imagined have informed the landscape of American literature: from places that sound of discovery and settlement—Plymouth, Providence, Jamestown—to places that serve as testimony to history—Concord and Bunker Hill, Virginia City, Shiloh and Gettysburg, Birmingham, Dallas, Wounded Knee and Kent State, Haight-Ashbury and Three Mile Island; from places that acquire a literary identity—Henry David Thoreau's Walden, Carl Sandburg's Chicago, William Carlos Williams's Paterson, and Woody Allen's Manhattan—to fictional places that become part of American culture—William Faulkner's Yoknapatawpha County, Edgar Lee Master's Spoon River, Sinclair Lewis's Gopher Praire, Sherwood Anderson's Winesburg, Thorton Wilder's Grover's Corners, and Garrison Keillor's Lake Wobegon. The association of individual and place is further evident in relation to American regionalism—from the New England of Emerson, Thoreau, Hawthrone, Robert Frost, and Galway Kinnell to the South of Faulkner, Robert Penn Warren, Flannery O'Connor, Eudora Welty, and Lee Smith. Writers of the Midwest are contrasted with Southwestern writers, writers of the Pacific Northwest, East Coast writers and West Coast writers.

The study of American literature details the lives and works of its makers and finds the means by which to digest and appreciate its importance. It is the study of genres and forms; the study of trends and movements—from Puritanism to nationalism, transcendentalism to realism, naturalism to expressionism, modernism to nihilism, postmodernism to deconstruction; it is the study of critical theory and application; the study of its interrelationship with history, politics, music, religion, and science; it is the study of race, ethnicity, and gender—from the Black Aesthetic to El Teatro Campesino, from Jewish American tradition to Asian American tradition, from the revisionist impact of feminist theory to the significance of gay male and lesbian literatures. It is the study of a literature maturing from its infancy in colonial America to a literature in the twentieth century of international importance. In 1930, Sinclair Lewis became the first American to be awarded the Nobel Prize in literature, followed in 1936 by Eugene O'Neill; in 1938 by Pearl S. Buck, the first American woman to win the award; in 1948 by American-born T. S. Eliot; in 1949 by William Faulkner; in 1962 by John Steinbeck; in 1976 by Canadian-born Saul Bellow; in 1978 by Isaac Bashevis Singer, born in Poland; in 1987 by Joseph Brodsky, born in Russia; and in 1993 by Toni Morrison, the first African American to win the award.

American literature is by nature a literature that reflects the multiplicity of a people united by a common bond and diversified by region, ethnicity, religion, social and economic status, political conviction, and cultural identity. Seeking to provide insight and understanding to the quality of American life and the realities of existence in society, the American author has from the beginning explored the boundaries of human depth and perception. Inheriting the legacy of commonality and diversity, the contemporary American author continues to broaden the underlying prospect of heritage: Paul Auster and Amy Tan; Cristina Garcia and Vikram Seth; N. Scott Momaday and Ricardo Pau Llosa; Bharati Mukhergee and Ai; Yosef Komunyakaa and Israel Horovitz; Jade Snow Wong and T. Coraghessan Boyle; Wendy Wasserstein and Louis Chu; Edwidge Danicat and Dana Gioia; Wakako Yamashita and Ntozake Shange.

The *Encyclopedia of American Literature* is envisioned as a comprehensive survey of the growth and development of literature that is by definition American in scope or origin. Incorporating entries for authors from colonial times to the present with a cross-section of topical articles pertaining to genre, period, ethnicity, and discipline, the *Encyclopedia* represents the most extensive single-volume treatment of its subject available for the general and scholarly reader alike. A decade in the making, the *Encyclopedia* represents a collaborative effort involving over 300 contributors from across the United States and

Canada. Consisting of more than 1,100 entries, the *Encyclopedia* serves as both guide and companion to the study and appreciation of American literature.

Bases of Selection: The selection of authors for individual *Encyclopedia* entries is based primarily on assessment and evaluation of the author's literary contribution and role in relation to the growth and development of literature in the United States. The process was designed to provide appropriate representation and balance to the volume within the constraints of length. The *Encyclopedia* includes entries for authors of international stature as well as authors noteworthy for regional or historical significance. Additional consideration was given to lesser-known authors who were instrumental in the emergence of ethnic American literatures.

Omissions: Despite the scope of the *Encyclopedia,* it is inevitable that authors of merit have been underrepresented or omitted from the volume. Although every effort has been made for the *Encyclopedia* to be as comprehensive as possible, the limitations of a single-volume edition impacted on the selection process. Wherever possible, references to authors of merit who did not receive individual entries are incorporated into the text of the most relevant topical articles.

Entries—Organization and Data: Individual author entries are arranged in three parts: a headnote that contains vital statistics concerning birth and death; a body that incorporates brief biographical information and a critical overview of the author's work and achievement; and a final section, titled *Bibliography,* comprising selective bibliographical material concerning the author and his or her work. A list of abbreviations used for periodicals cited is included in the front of the volume, and an index to the edition, with author dates, concludes the work.

Cross-References and Pseudonyms: Cross-references to other authors and related topics appear whenever appropriate in the texts of all entries. Where a writer with an individual entry is cited in another entry, at the first mention his or her last name appears in small-capital letters. Likewise, where a topic with a separate entry in the volume is cited in another entry, at the first mention the topic appears in small-capital letters.

Author entries are arranged alphabetically by last name. Authors known primarily by their pseudonym will be cross referenced within the edition to the appropriate entry (e.g., under Twain, Mark, or Mark Twain, will be found "See Clemens, Samuel Langhorne").

The Contributors: These have been drawn from a wide sphere of literary authorities from the United States and Canada. Each author entry and topical article in the *Encyclopedia* appears over the signature of the individual contributor or joint contributors.

ACKNOWLEDGMENTS

The General editor wishes to express his appreciation, first, to the numerous individuals whose contributions have helped to make the *Encyclopedia* a reference work of distinction, and as well to Werner Mark Linz, publisher of Continuum, and Evander Lomke, managing editor.

Assisting the general editor, Madeline D. Murray was the senior editor and production coordinator. Production editors were Sonya Collins, Victoria Eng, and Matthew Miller. Technical assistance was provided by Enercida Guererro, Ana Angelillo, and Harlan Cayetano. Editorial assistance was provided by Carina Garcia, Bonnie MacSaveny, Denise Galang, Sean O'Hanlon, Christine Cifra, Michelle Gonzalez, Anna DeGrezia, Francesco Fiore, Rebecca Lawson, Jill Bauer, Lisa Butler, Michelle Cutler, Julie Miele, Anna Gross, Karma Cloud, Nancy Moore, Joseph Weissman, Rose Sung, Jason Berner, and Greta Wagle.

STEVEN R. SERAFIN
HUNTER COLLEGE OF THE CITY UNIVERSITY OF NEW YORK

Guide to Topical Articles

Abbreviations for Periodicals

AAR	African American Review
AHI	American History Illustrated
AHJ	Atlanta Historical Journal
AIQ	American Indian Quarterly
AJGLL	American Journal of Germanic Linguistics and Literature
AL	American Literature: A Journal of Literary History, Criticism, and Bibliography
ALR	American Literary Realism
AL&C	American Letters & Cometary
AmerasiaJ	Amerasia Journal
AmerP	American Poetry
AmerR	American Review
AmerS	American Studies
AmRev	The Americas Review: A Review of Hispanic Literature and Art of the USA
AppalJ	Appalachian Journal: A Regional Studies Review
APR	The American Poetry Review
AQ	American Quarterly
AR	The Antioch Review
ArkHQ	Arkansas Historical Quarterly
ArkQ	Arkansas Quarterly
ArQ	Arizona Quarterly
ASch	The American Scholar
ATQ	The American Transcendental Quarterly: A Journal of New England Writers
BALF	Black American Literature Forum

BB	Bulletin of Bibliography
BR/RB	The Bilingual Review/La Revista Bilingüe
Callaloo: A Black South Journal of Arts and Letters	
CanL	Canadian Literature
CCur	Cross Currents: A Yearbook of Central European Culture
CentR	The Centennial Review
ChiR	Chicago Review
ChildL	Children's Literature: An International Journal, Inc. Annual of the Modern Language Association Division on Children's Literature Association
CLAJ	College Language Association Journal
CLC	Columbia Library Columns
CollL	College Literature
ComM	Communications Monographs
ConL	Contemporary Literature
ConP	Contemporary Poetry: A Journal of Criticism
Costerus: Essays in English and American Language and Literature	
CP	Concerning Poetry
Crit	Critique: Studies in Modern Fiction
CritI	Critical Inquiry
CultCrit	Cultural Critique
CurL	Current Literature
DLB	Dictionary of Literary Biography
DQ	Denver Quarterly

DrS	Drama Survey	*KenR*	Kennesaw Review
EAL	Early American Literature	*KPR*	Kentucky Philological Review
EAS	Essays in Arts and Sciences	*KR*	The Kenyon Review
EJ	The English Journal	*LALR*	Latin American Literary Review
FSt	Feminist Studies	*L&P*	Literature and Psychology
GaR	The Georgia Review	*LCrit*	The Literary Criterion
GettR	Gettysburg Review	*LitP*	Literature in Performance
GHQ	Georgia Historical Quarterly	*LitR*	Literary Review: An International Journal of Contemporary Writing
HC	The Hollins Critic		
HemR	Hemingway Review	*MarkhamR*	Markham Review

Hispania: A Journal Devoted to the Interests of the Teaching of Spanish and Portuguese

		MAWAR	MAWA Review
HPLR	High Plains Literary Review	*MD*	Modern Drama
HRev	Harvard Review		

MELUS: The Journal of the Society for the Study of the Multi-Ethnic Literature of the United States

HSRL	Harvard Studies in Romance Languages	*MFS*	Modern Fiction Studies
HTR	Harvard Theological Review	*MHSP*	Massachusetts Historical Society Proceedings
HUB	Harvard University Bulletin		

Midamerica: The Yearbook of the Society for the Study of Midwestern Literature

HudR	The Hudson Review		
IJAS	Indian Journal of American Studies	*MinnR*	The Minnesota Review
IowaR	The Iowa Review	*MissR*	The Missouri Review
ISAL	Indian Studies in American Literature	*MissQ*	Mississippi Quarterly: The Journal of Southern Culture
JAC	Journal of American Culture	*MLS*	Modern Language Studies
JAmS	Journal of American Studies	*MMisc*	Midwestern Miscellany
JBA	Jewish Book Annual	*MPS*	Modern Poetry Studies
JCH	Journal of Contemporary History	*MQ*	Midwest Quarterly
JCL	The Journal of Commonwealth Literature	*MQR*	Michigan Quarterly Review
		MR	Massachusetts Review: A Quarterly of Literature, the Arts, and Public Affairs
JES	Journal of European Studies		
JEthS	The Journal of Ethnic Studies	*NAR*	North American Review
JJQ	James Joyce Quarterly	*NCHR*	North Carolina Historical Review
JPC	Journal of Popular Culture	*NConL*	Notes on Contemporary Literature
JPFT	Journal of Popular Film and Television	*NDQ*	North Dakota Quarterly
JSH	Journal of Southern History		
KanQ	Kansas Quarterly	*NEQ*	The New England Quarterly: A Historical Review of New England Life and Letters
KFQ	Keystone Folklore		

NER	New England Review and Bread Loaf Quarterly
NewC	The New Criterion
NHSQ	Nevada Historical Society Quarterly
NLH	New Literary History: A Journal of Theory and Interpretations
NYRB	New York Review of Books
NYT	New York Times
NYTBR	New York Times Book Review
NYTMag	New York Times Magazine
Obsidian II: Black Literature in Review	
OntarioR	Ontario Review
PMHB	The Pennsylvania Magazine of History and Biography
P&W	Poets & Writers
Paintbrush: A Journal of Poetry, Translations, and Letters	
PAPA	Publications of the Arkansas Philological Association
Parnassus: Poetry in Review	
PLL	Papers on Language and Literature
PM	Pembroke Magazine
PR	Partisan Review
Proteus: A Journal of Ideas	
PrS	Prairie Schooner
PSt	Prose Studies
PULC	Princeton University Library Chronicle
RCF	The Review of Contemporary Fiction
RCL	The Review of Contemporary Literature
RC-R	Revista Chicano-Riqueño
RFI	Regionalism and the Female Imagination
RLA	Romance Languages Annual
RQ	Riverside Quarterly
SAD	Studies in American Drama

SAF	Studies in American Fiction
SAGE: A Scholarly Journal on Black Women	
Sagetrieb: A Journal Devoted to Poets in the Pound—H. D.—Williams Tradition	
SAIL	Studies in American Indian Literature
SAJL	Studies in American Jewish Literature
SALit	Chu-Shikoku Studies in American Literature
SAQ	South Atlantic Quarterly
SAR	Studies in the American Renaissance
SatR	Saturday Review
SCR	South Carolina Review
SCRev	South Central Review
SDR	South Dakota Review
SFQ	Southern Folklore Quarterly
SHR	Southern Humanities Review
SLAPC	Studies in Latin American Popular Culture
SLH	Studies in Literary Humor
SLitI	Studies in the Literary Imagination
SLJ	Southern Literary Journal
SNNTS	Studies in the Novel
SoAR	South Atlantic Review
SoQ	The Southern Quarterly: A Journal of the Arts in the South
SoR	The Southern Review
SoSt	Southern Studies
SR	Sewanee Review
SSF	Studies in Short Fiction
SSMLN	Society for the Study of Midwestern Literature Newsletter
StAH	Studies in American Humor
StPC	Studies in Popular Culture
StWF	Studies in Weird Fiction
SUS	Susquehanna University Studies
SWR	Southwest Review

TCL	Twentieth Century Literature: A Scholarly and Critical Journal	*UTQ*	University of Toronto Quarterly: A Canadian Journal of the Humanities
TCW	Turn-of-the-Century Women	*VQR*	Virginia Quarterly Review: A National Journal of Literature and Discussion
TDR	The Drama Review		
TennQ	Tennessee Quarterly	*VV*	Village Voice
TexP	Textual Practice	*W&Lang*	Women and Language
TLS	[London] Times Literary Supplement	*WAL*	Western American Literature
		WascanaR	Wascana Review
TRev	Translation Review	*WHR*	Western Humanities Review
TriQ	TriQuarterly		
TSE: Tulane Studies in English		*WLT*	World Literature Today: A Literary Quarterly of the University of Oklahoma
TSL	Tennessee Studies in Literature		
TSLL	Texas Studies in Literature and Language: A Journal of the Humanities	*WLWE*	World Literature Written in English
		WMQ	The William and Mary Quarterly. A Magazine of Early American History and Culture
TSWL	Tulsa Studies in Women's Literature		
UBS	The University of Buffalo Studies		
UDR	University of Dayton Review		
UHSL	University of Hartford Studies in Literature: A Journal of Interdisciplinary Criticism	*WS*	Women's Studies: An Interdisciplinary Journal
		YES	Yearbook of English Studies
UMB	University of Maine Bulletin	*YR*	The Yale Review

Encyclopedia of

AMERICAN
LITERATURE

A

ABBEY, Edward
b. 29 January 1927, Home, Pennsylvania; d. 14 March 1989, Tucson, Arizona

Called "the Thoreau of the West," A. is the preeminent natural history writer of the Southwestern deserts. His twenty-three novels, essay collections, travel books, and journal extracts constantly reiterate a poetics of wilderness, one in which undeveloped land is America's best and most sacred resource. A. has claimed that he "would rather kill a man than a snake"; the inverted logic of this statement, as well its brash humor and its break with conventional anthropomorphism, all make it a signature "Abbeyism."

His best-known and most widely admired book is a tightly crafted nonfiction journal, *Desert Solitaire* (1968), which recounts his field experiences as a seasonal ranger in Arches National Park. Part rhapsody, part diatribe, the episodic narrative describes typical chores—cooking over a campfire, exploring remote canyons, recovering the body of a lost hiker—but often slides away into digressive, sometime furious considerations of the physical environment and man's relationship to it. A. has a master's degree in philosophy from the University of New Mexico, and although he adopts the persona of a redneck crank, his erudition sneaks out here and there, rather like his pet bull snake—which, coiled around his belly, startles tourists by poking its head out from between the buttons of his ranger's uniform.

The value of the book comes not from A.'s presentation of land-use issues, such as paving roads versus leaving them dirt, nor from his irascible yet hilarious descriptions of the park visitors, but from his ability to make his readers see the desert as he does, which is with passion, ecstasy, and unabashed acceptance. The "Down the River" chapter recounts a float trip on the Colorado River through Glen Canyon, prior to the completion of Glen Canyon Dam. Alternately awed by natural splendor and exasperated by unquestioned social norms, A. and his companion resemble Huck and Jim on their river: nature is a moral constant, while civilization is a dubious force at best, something that corrupts us from our better selves.

Glen Canyon appears again in the novel *The Monkey Wrench Gang* (1975). Advocating radical politics, the book has become most closely linked to the environmental group Earth First!; it also popularized the expression "monkeywrenching"—carefully planned acts of eco-sabotage. Based on composites of people A. knew, it tells the story of four neo-Luddites who plot to blow up Glen Canyon Dam. Their target is not just a random piece of civilization, but—to many activists, not just A.—stands as a symbol for all that is short-sighted and destructive in the West. In the course of the book, as the characters perfect their plans, they pull out road survey stakes and burn down rural billboards and perform other minor acts of vandalism, all of which A. portrays as being justifiable acts of civil disobedience. In essence, *The Monkey Wrench Gang* is a modern, high-stakes retelling of the Boston Tea Party myth, with a few *Lone Ranger* episodes thrown in. As literature, with its one-dimensional characters and a lurid plot, the novel makes a poor showing, but as with Edgar Rice BURROUGHS's *Tarzan* or other popular works, the book remains constantly in print, never quite a best-seller, but never quite forgotten. Many critics agree with Wendell BERRY that it would be easier to dismiss if it weren't so much fun to read.

None of his other fiction has achieved the status of *The Monkey Wrench Gang*. *The Brave Cowboy* (1960) and *Fire on the Mountain* (1962) both feature iconoclastic loners who in climactic scenes try to hold off the 20th c. at gunpoint; in *The Fool's Progress* (1988), Henry Holyoak Lightcap, a thinly disguised stand-in for A. himself, travels east from Tucson to die in his childhood home in Appalachia. Among other prejudices, the protagonist's misogyny reveals a central problem in A.'s writing: his fiction is weak because he can't escape himself, yet his essays are strong because they are so completely himself, or rather are so consistently the crabby "Cactus Ed" persona, a figure with greater luster and depth than anybody found in his novels.

A. represents a postwar generation of essayists who defend the rights of untamed things and unappreciated habitats, and of these he remains, as A. said of Henry David THOREAU, "an unpeeled man. A man with the bark still on him."

BIBLIOGRAPHY: Bishop, J., *Epitaph for a Desert Anarchist: The Life of E. A.* (1994); Hepworth, J., and G. McNamee, eds., *Resist Much, Obey Little: Remembering E. A.* (1989); McCann, G., *E. A.* (1977); Ronald, A., *The New West of E. A.* (1982)

                                              CHARLES HOOD

ABISH, Walter
b. 24 December 1931, Vienna, Austria

Although A. began his literary career with a volume of poetry entitled *Duel Site* (1970), he secured his reputation as an important postmodern writer with his innovative short stories and novels. A.'s middle-class family left Austria when Adolf Hitler annexed the country in 1938; they first settled in Nice, but fled again to Shanghai just ten days before Germany invaded France. In 1949, the family immigrated to Israel where A. served in the army, studied architecture, and began writing poetry in English. He married Cecile Gelb, an American photographer, and they moved to New York in 1957. In 1960, A. became a U.S. citizen.

A.'s first novel, *Alphabetical Africa* (1974), challenges traditional narrative form and emphasizes the artificial nature of fiction. The first chapter uses only words beginning with the letter *A,* the second chapter uses words beginning with *A* and *B,* until finally, chapter twenty-six may contain words beginning with any of the letters, including *Z.* The novel then moves back down the alphabet subtracting letters one by one—therefore deconstructing itself—until the last chapter, like the first, is composed only of words beginning with *A.* The characters—Alex, Allen, Alva, and Queen Quat—are little more than names, and the plot is a concoction of jewel robberies, travels across Africa, and an invasion by army ants. Despite its comic tone and outlandish plot, *Alphabetical Africa* is a serious novel. In addition to illustrating the artificial nature of fiction, the novel satirizes a number of Western stereotypes about Africa and Africans.

A. continues his experiments with narrative form in his collections of short fiction: *Minds Meet* (1975), *In the Future Perfect* (1977), and *99: The New Meaning* (1990). "Minds Meet," the title story of the first collection, is a tale in which a number of messages are lost or ignored by various characters. The message of "Minds Meet" is that communication is improbable if not impossible. *In the Future Perfect* opens with "The English Garden," a story that questions contemporary Germany's relationship to its past. The narrator of "The English Garden" is an American writer who travels to Germany to visit the newly constructed town of Brumholdstein. Brumholdstein is named after a famous philosopher, and it is built upon the ruins of a concentration camp. "The English Garden" sketches several themes detailed more fully in the novel *How German Is It* (1980). Most notably, the story implies that beneath the veneer of normality that is contemporary Germany there lies a monstrous spirit that has yet to be completely exorcised. *99: The New Meaning* is an experimental work in which A. makes use of selected segments of published texts by other authors to construct narrative fragments that carry emotional charges.

It was not until publication of *How German Is It* that A. obtained a wide readership and a reputation as a major contemporary author. *How German Is It* is far less experimental than A.'s other work, but it exhibits the deft style and the accumulation of short narrative snapshots that have become his trademark. The novel is also set mainly in Brumholdstein and follows the sexual and professional exploits of two brothers who are members of Germany's new cultural elite: Ulrich Hargenau, a novelist, and Helmuth Hargenau, a famous architect. The brothers are special Germans because their father was shot in 1944 for plotting against Hitler. Most of the characters—with the exception of a crazy waiter named Franz who builds a model of the concentration camp—are happy to forget the recent past and pursue materialism, but the horror of the past lies beneath the familiar surface of the newly constructed German reality. The buried past literally haunts Brumholdstein when a sewer line breaks and repair men dig up a mass grave—a remnant of the concentration camp.

Eclipse Fever (1993) is A.'s least experimental work. Thematically, the novel is an exploration of political, economic, and cultural corruption in contemporary Mexico. Among the characters are a literary critic named Alejandro and his wife Mercedes. Mercedes leaves Alejandro to live with an American novelist. The novelist's teenage daughter, Bonnie, runs away and becomes entangled with Emilio, a dealer in stolen pre-Columbian artifacts. Much of the story follows Bonnie's adventures—sexual and otherwise. Other characters include Pech, an art dealer, Preston, a wealthy American, and Rita, his oversexed wife. Like *How German Is It, Eclipse Fever* is concerned with the past—in this case, the less savory elements of Mexico's history—and its relationship to the present.

BIBLIOGRAPHY: Klinkowitz, J., "W. A. and the Surfaces of Life," *GaR* 35 (Summer 1981): 416–20; Martin, R., "W. A.'s Fictions: Perfect Unfamiliarity, Familiar Imperfections," *JAmS* 17 (1983): 229–41; Van Delden, M., "W. A.'s *How German Is It:* Postmodernism and the Past," *Salmagundi* 85–86 (Winter-Spring 1996): 172–94

DAVE KUHNE

ABOLITIONISM

The term "abolitionism" was probably born into language as a malediction coined by opponents of the antislavery movement, and was only later defiantly worn as a badge of moral integrity by those whom it was first intended to stigmatize. Perhaps because it originated in polemic, rather than in airy discourse among philosophers, abolitionism unambiguously denoted the radical wing of the antislavery movement, as opposed to the moderate one that advanced a variety of compromises and gradualist approaches—the moderates constituting always a powerful, although usually not as vocal, a faction, especially in the British colonies of North America and the fledgling U.S.

Due in part to the fact that the majority of 19th-c. American authors who have been deemed American masters by early and mid-20th-c. American criticism were at least loosely associated with the transcendentalist movement, TRANSCENDENTALISM has perennially been considered a more fruitful and necessary concern of literary scholarship than abolitionism. The imaginative writers who were active in the abolitionist movement—John Greenleaf WHITTIER, James Russell LOWELL, and Harriet Beecher STOWE—were deemed minor by the 20th-c. critics who did most to establish the American literary canon, because the movement was championed mainly and most effectively in the nonbelletristic works, and in the political actions, of writers predominantly of nonfiction—William Lloyd GARRISON, Frederick DOUGLASS, Theodore PARKER, Lydia Maria CHILD, William Wells BROWN—and in the unpreserved or imperfectly preserved speeches of orators and politicians—Wendell Phillips, Charles Sumner, Gerrit Smith, Lucretia Mott. Abolitionism was conceded as a topic mainly for the historians of U.S. sectionalism and of the Civil War, which relative disinterest led to the somewhat simple understanding in 20th-c. American literary scholarship of abolition-

ism as a movement that, however consequential it might have been in the social sphere, produced relatively little worthy of modern critical attention.

The recent rise in interest in cultural studies, in feminist criticism and women's studies, and in African American studies may, however, be in the process of transforming abolitionism from a footnote to American literature into a topic that demands major attention from contemporary American literary scholarship. Expansion of the canon is by now no longer a controversial proposition but a fact of both higher and secondary education in the U.S., and many of the previously neglected antebellum 19th-c. writers and works that are in the process of being let into contemporary anthologies and curricula of American literature were at least as connected to abolitionism as America's traditional literary masters were connected to transcendentalism. Now that race and gender have become prime concerns, and now that the discrimination between the subliterary and the genuinely literary is being suspected as class-, race-, and gender-biased, abolitionism may bid to equal, or even to surpass, transcendentalism as one of the main currents of 19th-c. American thought.

The evolution of abolitionism is contained in outline in every standard reference to American history. More complete histories are of course available in specialized studies—although something of a trend reaching back at least to the antebellum and Civil War scholarship of the 1960s has been to concentrate more on factors other than abolitionist agitation in seeking out the causes and describing the playing out of sectional rivalries in the emerging nation. The deemphasizing of the significance of abolitionism does not so much contradict as extend the conventional wisdom that abolitionists managed to win the public relations campaign in the North—defining as an antislavery crusade a war many of whose principal agents, including even Abraham LINCOLN, either sought to avoid or sought to incite based on considerations quite other than the ethics of chattel slavery. Long before revisionist histories of the Civil War were being written late in the 20th c., even some abolitionists, themselves, had become cynical and discouraged about the real underlying motives of Northern leadership—Child, for example, went so far as to denounce the Emancipation Proclamation itself as "merely a war measure." Stephen CRANE in *The Red Badge of Courage,* the novel still celebrated as the most realistic, and the sole truly masterful, fictional depiction of the Civil War in American literary history, also casts doubt on the impact of the abolitionist movement: Henry Fleming considers hundreds of things while trying to justify either his loyalty to or his principled desertion from the Union Army, before, during, and after being drawn into the battle patterned closely on the battle of Chancellorsville; however, never once is Henry shown by Crane to consider slavery, which word appears not once in the entirety of the novel.

Other, similar, paradoxes confront contemporary literary scholarship that would take abolitionism seriously, suggesting the existence of conflicts between literary interest and abolitionist orthodoxy. Garrison's abolitionist credentials are probably the most impeccable of all: he repudiated an early advocacy of repatriating manumitted slaves to a colony in Africa; he spent time in jail in 1830 for libeling slave traders; he founded an antislavery society in New England in 1832, whose membership included both lower-class African Americans and members of Boston's economic and cultural elite; his life was threatened by antiabolitionist riots in Boston in 1835; he publicly burned a copy of the U.S. Constitution in 1854 in protest against the transparent euphemisms that afforded the highest U.S. statutory foundation for slave owning. However, his voluminous writings have not been judged to rise above relatively simple polemic, even by modern scholars most respectful of his inflexible moral zeal.

After enjoying a not inconsiderable commercial success with her early novels, Child jeopardized her entire career with the publication in 1833 of *An Appeal in Favor of That Class of Americans Called Africans,* and was still selflessly committed enough to the cause much later, in 1859, when she wrote the governor of Virginia requesting permission to personally nurse John Brown in prison after the Harpers Ferry raid. Her abolitionist writings, including *An Appeal* and *Romance of the Republic,* published in 1837, that followed Stowe in attempting to fictionalize slavery and the Civil War from an abolitionist perspective, receive little notice today, even from those who have become interested in recuperating Child as early, protofeminist, advocate of sentiment and the domestic sphere. Whittier, hailed by Douglass as "the slave's poet," was, like Child, ostracized because of the constancy and radicalism of his abolitionist views, and divided his career equally between poetry and public service. He was elected to the Massachusetts Assembly on an abolitionist platform, and he always considered himself one of the founders of the Republican Party. However, although ranked by his contemporaries as an equal of William Cullen BRYANT and Henry Wadsworth LONGFELLOW, he is read today—when he is read at all—for his regional nature poems. *Voices of Freedom,* Whittier's collection of abolitionist poetry, and "Massachusetts to Virginia," probably his most famous single abolitionist poem, remain today almost entirely forgotten.

The two writers who would seem to combine firm ties to the abolitionist movement with the kind of literary value whose interest to contemporary literary scholars remains not only secure but growing are of course Stowe and Douglass. But although the personal dedication of each to the abolitionist movement is undeniable, and although the abolitionist intent of the most famous work of each is unmistakable, the role of abolitionism in Stowe's *Uncle Tom's Cabin* and *Narrative of the Life of Frederick Douglass, an American Slave, Written by Himself* can be seen not so much to enable as to trouble a contemporary literary critical retrospect eager to claim Stowe as a protofeminist theorist of gender, and to claim Douglass as a proto-Afrocentric theorist of race.

Although it would still be premature to claim for the Stowe equal status in contemporary literary scholarship with the 19th-c. male authors canonized by F. O. Mattheissen in *American Renaissance* (1941), the coincidence of the publication of *Uncle Tom's Cabin* in the middle of the same decade *mirabilus* that saw publication of the most famous works by Ralph Waldo EMERSON, Henry David THOREAU, Nathaniel HAWTHORNE, Herman MELVILLE, and Walt WHITMAN, and the irony of *Uncle Tom's Cabin* having outsold them all put together—having outsold, in all probability, any other single book in publication history, excepting the Bible—are by now noted as more than mere curiosities, or mere confirmation of the shortsightedness of contemporary literary fashion. *Uncle Tom's Cabin* is increasingly being taken up by contemporary literary scholars as being of lasting, even seminal, theoretical importance. The problem of the book's undeniable condescension to blacks is for the most part elided by these contemporary studies, which do not converse with contemporary African American scholarship, and so the issue of Stowe's abolitionism infrequently comes up in them. There is above all the uncomfortable realization that "the little lady who started this great big war," as Lincoln famously greeted Stowe, with perhaps a bit more exasperation than irony, did so by writing a book the affective power and political efficacy of whose abolitionist sentiment is inseparable from its racist stereotyping of blacks as dependents toward whites as both stewards—externally of power, which is responsible for ensuring that dependents be treated justly, and internally of sentiment, which is capable of pitying dependents being treated unjustly—and as masters, not exclusively for worse, but potentially for better, as well. If the efficacy of *Uncle Tom's Cabin* as abolitionist literature depends on its racism, then what is called into question is the whole image of abolitionism as a signal and early example of the dominant culture in the U.S. at least desiring to do the right thing, and thus at least trying to expiate one of the two great crimes that haunt the founding of the nation.

Douglass was of course during the Civil War, and especially in the aftermath of the Civil War, often impatient with the white conscience of America, which had allowed slavery to persist long enough past its time contrasted to the histories of the "enlightened" nations of the world to become a peculiar institution, indeed, the virtual equivalent in the mid-19th c. of South African apartheid in the late 20th c. Although Douglass's first work, which remains still today his most widely read and studied, was written expressly at the behest of Wendell Phillips to reinforce the effectiveness of Douglass's abolitionist oratory by substantiating the veracity of Douglass's identity as former slave, it can be seen in many ways to depart from the aims of white abolitionists, and even at times to contradict them.

After the publication of his autobiography, Douglass fled to Europe, at the suggestion of his abolitionist allies, who warned him that the candor of the book exposed him to recapture. But the rhetoric of his work, which in its skill and extravagance does little or nothing to answer anti-abolitionist charges that so eloquent an orator as Douglass could never have been a slave, coupled with its several implications that white allies in the North and institutions can be relied upon only to betray their supposed African American beneficiaries, combine to suggest that Douglass may have had almost as much to fear from his white Northern as from his white Southern masters. Abolitionism, which in so many obvious ways creates the conditions that make the writings of both Stowe and Douglass possible, in several less obvious ones also constrains their writings, and does so in ways that speak directly to contemporary literary scholarly interests. The intellectual history of abolitionism may have become a tired subject; however, the theoretical implications of abolitionism in the writings of hitherto unread or underread antebellum American writers may be a subject that is just now in the process of coming into its own.

BIBLIOGRAPHY: Baker, H. A., Jr., *Long Black Song: Essays in Black Literature and Culture* (1972); Lowance, M. I., Jr., E. E. Westbrook, and R. C. De Prospo, eds., *The Stowe Debate: Rhetorical Strategies in "Uncle Tom's Cabin"* (1994); Quarles, B., *Black Abolitionists* (1969); Showalter, E., *The New Feminist Criticism* (1985)

R. C. DE PROSPO

ACKER, Kathy

b. 1948, New York City; d. 30 November 1997, Tijuana, Mexico

As a conceptual artist, A. directed textual space to provoke and jar her audience as she violated law, convention, and morality both in substance and construct. Her texts experiment with sexual identity to the point of being labeled pornographic, and her novels counter a linear structure in their fragmented, deconstructed forms, in which chaos replaces order. A. was politically subversive—called by critics a punk postmodern writer. Framed within a radical feminist discourse, similar to performance artists like Karen Finley, A. aggressively showed the sadomasochistic relationship between men and women and, in so doing, intentionally manipulates woman's body to display the insidiousness of the culture's perversion and festishization of it; thus, A. used the system to break the system. Her work received critical acclaim, but its provocative nature made A. the subject of controversy and debate.

Influenced by William S. BURROUGHS and by artists such as Sherrie Levine and David Salle, A. infused dream and fantasy into her narratives while playing with the referential I; as she states: "the I became a dead issue because I realized that you make the I and what makes the I are texts . . . If there's no problem with the I, then in terms of text there was no self and other, I could use everyone else's writing." A. lets go of identity, centrality, and ownership so that knowledge is only an experience framed within juxtapositions and recontextualized within different spaces; no idea is owned, only temporarily copyrighted.

While living in the Haight Ashbury area of San Francisco in the early 1970s, A. took the pseudonym of the Black Tarantula (because she liked its sensuality and the misconception of danger that surrounds it) and used the name for several of her books. In *The Childlike Life of the Black Tarantula* (1975), which is largely autobiographical, A. takes each chapter to work with a distinct dimension of identity, ranging from the child to the sexual being to violent anger. After attending Brandeis and the University of California, San Diego, A. returned to New York to write poetry, while supporting herself as a sex-show stripper and actor. At this time, she began exploring the multidimensional personae of the text, appropriating the stories of other strippers, alongside her own experience. She was then unaware of the French school of criticism—later she discovered Michel Foucault and deconstruction—but was driven by her own desire to lose herself in text in a kind of schizophrenia, as she called it.

Playing with narrative identity became the trademark of A.'s writing and is constant throughout the body of her work. Where initially she took the stories of unknown individuals, A. quickly moved on to experimenting with authorial manipulation—pirating the writings of such authors as Sigmund Freud, the Marquis de Sade, Jean Genet, Charles Dickens, and Miguel de Cervantes—and within those settings remapping the traditional bildungsroman into a woman's journey.

For example, in A.'s *Don Quixote* (1986), it is a woman who, after having an abortion, fantasizes that she is on a quest to combat the evil found within contemporary right-wing America, confronting the power figures of Niccolo Machiavelli and Jesus Christ, and sexually exploiting men to get revenge. In *Pussy, King of the Pirates* (1995), which vaguely echoes Robert Louis Stevenson's *Treasure Island,* the tale becomes a sexual maze of dreams that include pirate girls loving girls, discovering a murdered mother, and searching for a father. A. began experimenting with narrative myths, particularly de Sade's version of Oedipus in *Empire of the Senseless* (1988), because myth allowed her to explore what she calls the "strange worlds" of antiquity that were tied to concepts such as destiny.

While there was philosophical, political, and artistic embodiment to her act of stealing and rearranging, it also lent itself to her outlaw—Genet-like—persona; in *Pussy, King of the Pirates,* she states, "I only love poets who are criminals." A. liked breaking boundaries, creating violence in text (which included the taking and cutting up of other texts), moving into dangerous territory, and shocking her audience. Her concept was to break into the taboos of the culture that inscribe themselves within the body. A. invested all libidinal energy in purging the frozen God within, slashing idols, reclaiming myths that set man above all. Her radical approach, throwing the reader against the opposing wall of rationality and law, positioned her in such extreme that inadvertently a dichotomy was kept within her work and categorizations of another kind—warring, decentered, and outlandish women descending on society—produced a farcical dimension.

BIBLIOGRAPHY: Deaton, R., "K. A. Interviewed," *TexP* 6 (Summer 1992): 271–82; Redding, A. F., "Bruises, Roses: Masochism and the Writing of K. A.," *ConL* 35 (Summer 1994): 281-304; special A. issue, *RCF* 9 (Fall 1989)

LISA TOLHURST

ACKERMAN, Diane

b. 7 October 1948, Waukegan, Illinois

A. initially achieved fame as a lyric poet, but is now perhaps more widely known as an essayist. This distinction is one of genre only—both her poems and her essays are marked by a lush lyricism, an attention to evocative detail, and a mingling of the worlds of science and poetry.

A. is first and foremost a love poet: she writes as one who is deeply in love with the world and its manifold contents. Her desire for knowledge is not analytic but passionate. Her open, accessible poetry speaks primarily from and to the heart. This is not to say that there is not an intellect at work in the poems, but rather that her concerns as a writer lie in the realms of emotion, lived experience, and passionate attachments. As such, they do not lend themselves well to the detachment, irony, and self-reflection that mark another dominant strand of contemporary poetry: this is either a blessing or a curse (or both), depending on one's point of view. Her poems are likewise not confessional, in the usual sense of the term. A.'s self-consciousness is a consciousness of how experience impinges on the body, rather than an ironic view of the poet-in-space.

Her first book of poems, *The Planets: A Cosmic Pastoral* (1976), deals primarily in astronomy. In it, she makes rich use of science in a variety of ways: as metaphor, as an instance that evokes a response, or as something to relate to—a kind of sounding-board of otherness. These uses of science continue in *Wife of Light* (1978), in which A. also adds an element of history—dramatic monologues by George Sand and Anne Donne, for instance. There is also more of a focus on a specifically female sensibility. *Lady Faustus* (1983) carries on these additional themes; the major change is in a move from astronomy and physics to the natural sciences. *Reverse Thunder* (1988) is an intriguing book, a long dramatic poem in the persona of Sister Juana Ines de la Cruz, a 14th-c. South American poet and scholar, and perhaps not coincidentally, a woman interested in both poetry and science. *Jaguar of Sweet Laughter* (1991) contains both new poems and a selection of her earlier works. The new poems are generally more mature in style, and show a wide variety of topics, including addresses to famous poets, poems on the Amazon and the Antarctic, and more domestic pieces.

A. is one of the few contemporary poets who have managed to reach a broad audience—in order to do so, she had to switch genres from poetry to prose. *On Extended Wings* (1985) consists of her memoirs of being a student pilot. Her most widely read book is *A Natural History of the Senses* (1990), which is a collection of essays that explore the biological and cultural nature of the senses; it is perhaps the site that brings her scientific/lyric style into its best realization. Keeping with her turn to natural history, *The Moon by Whale Light* (1991) deals with rare and endangered species. *A Natural History of Love* (1994) and *The Rarest of the Rare* (1995) seem inevitable, given the overall shape of A.'s career and her approach to life—she is investigating the biology and cultural history of her own prime mover, the force that creates and sustains an interesting and diverse body of work.

BIBLIOGRAPHY: Alford, J. G., "D. A.," in Gwynn, R. S., ed., *DLB,* vol. 120, *American Poets since World*

War II (1992): 3–9; Velsany, K., "A Conversation with D. A.," *Creative Nonfiction* 3 (1995): 91–102

ROBERT C. SPIRKO

ACOSTA, Oscar Zeta
b. 8 April 1935?, El Paso, Texas

Chicano political activist, lawyer, and author, A. is a controversial and enigmatic figure who insisted that readers view his life as his work. His two autobiographical novels, *The Autobiography of a Brown Buffalo* (1972) and *The Revolt of the Cockroach People* (1973), recount his life, from an alienated boyhood in central California to his ethnic activism during the volatile 1960s and 1970s in Los Angeles, then suddenly the story ends and A. is gone. He disappeared into Mexico in the early 1970s and is presumed to be dead.

For A., the line between fact and fiction was always blurred. He wrote about himself in a style that drew upon the Beat writers and gonzo journalism. His language, subject matter, and sense of humor work to engage readers and bring them on a wild odyssey of self-discovery. His central concern is his Mexican American ethnicity and its influence on his self-concept, but the quest for identity is universal.

The Autobiography of a Brown Buffalo is a fictionalized version of A.'s struggle for self. As a boy, the young protagonist is frustrated in his attempts to assimilate into dominant Anglo culture. In school, he is taught to feel inferior. Later, he works for an antipoverty agency and becomes a Chicano activist, yet still lacks a sense of identity. Drug-addled and on the brink of nervous collapse, he takes to the road to find himself. Along the way, he ponders the different ways in which experience is interpreted depending on social context. He understands that one's worldview is inextricably linked to one's culture and language. He embraces his ancestry, yet his model of interpreting experience remains troubling to him as its logical conclusion is that objective reality does not exist. In his travels, he meets a journalist—a thinly veiled Hunter S. Thompson—who will later immortalize A. as Dr. Gonzo, the three-hundred-pound Samoan attorney in *Fear and Loathing in Las Vegas* (1972). At the end of *The Autobiography of a Brown Buffalo,* the main character takes the name Zeta and proclaims ethnicity the basis of his identity and commitment to social change.

The Revolt of the Cockroach People picks up where the previous book left off and follows Zeta into the political arena in Los Angeles. The lawyer-activist Zeta Brown recounts day-to-day life during the revolutionary period in which challenges are raised against religion, the courts, and the educational system. It

is a time of increasing Latino consciousness in Los Angeles, the Southwest, and America as a whole. Zeta is completely committed to the movement. As the story progresses, he finds that not all Chicanos think alike. Some care little for their ancestry. He also discovers that Chicano groups have been infiltrated by police. As a result, he becomes disillusioned and feels personally betrayed.

A. remains an important, though controversial figure in Chicano circles. His commitment to and zeal for the cause of social justice and equality is unquestioned, but some critics take issue with his reversed discrimination and portrayal of women as little more than sources of ego gratification. As an anthropologist of sorts, he may not have been entirely objective—he never meant to be so. As a gonzo journalist, he records among his philosophical musings and political idealism his many faults and foibles.

BIBLIOGRAPHY: Rodriguez, J. D., "O. Z. A.," in Lomelí, F. A., and C. A. Shirley, eds., *DLB,* vol. 82, *Chicano Writers* (1989): 3–10; Smith, N. D., "Buffalos and Cockroaches: A.'s Siege at Aztlán," *LALR* 5 (Spring-Summer 1977): 85–97

JASON MCMAHON

ADAMS, Alice
b. 14 August 1926, Fredericksburg, Virginia

A. is one of the only contemporary writers of fiction to suffer the charge that she is too nice to her characters. Critics have pointed out her generosity in both her short stories and novels, especially in the case of Daphne Mathiesson, heroine of the aptly entitled *Rich Rewards* (1980). A. cares for the characters she creates, but she creates likable people. These amiable characters have helped her to acquire a popular audience, while receiving acclaim for her well-crafted, controlled yet vivid prose from those same critics who fault her for being generous.

A. has achieved that difficult balance of critical and popular success in the genres of both novels and short stories. She won the National Book Critics Circle Award in 1975 for the novel *Families and Survivors* (1974), and her 1984 novel *Superior Women* was a popular best-selling paperback. Her short stories have appeared in women's publications such as *Redbook, McCalls,* and *Mademoiselle,* but also in literary magazines such as the *Paris Review,* the *Atlantic,* and the *New Yorker.* She has been represented nearly continuously since 1971 in the yearly O. Henry Award anthologies for best short fiction, receiving an O. Henry Special Award for Continuing Achievement in 1982.

Both A.'s novels and short fiction usually center on female characters in contemporary settings, women caught in a fluctuating world but longing for stability without personal compromise. They often find this stability in a balance between love—familial, romantic, or friendly—and fulfilling work. In addition to *Families and Survivors,* her early works included the novel *Careless Love* (1966), *Listening to Billie* (1978), and *Beautiful Girl* (1979), both collections of stories. In the novel *Rich Rewards,* the fortunate Daphne Mathiesson is not handed a happy ending easily. She spends many years of her life either entangled in unhealthy relationships or examining herself for the flaw that makes her unable to mend these relationships. She builds a career slowly and deliberately from what she discovers to be her own talent.

Many other characters in A.'s fiction follow Daphne's pattern of fulfillment through love and work. Both Stuart and Martha in "A Jealous Husband" from *Beautiful Girl* learn the need for this balance, though each learns this lesson from a different perspective. Jessica Todd of the Todd series of stories in the same collection finds relief from her stagnant marriage through her work and friendships in her bookstore. By following the lives of four different women in *Superior Women,* A. reveals the many ways personal and professional successes and failures affect the self-images of women. She followed *Superior Women* with a series of novels, *Return Trips* (1985), *Second Chances* (1988), *After You've Gone* (1989), and *Caroline's Daughters* (1991). In the midst of these mobility-oriented titles, she produced a book of travel writings, *Mexico: Some Travels and Some Travellers There* (1990).

Travel is often a factor in the development of A.'s female characters. Moving for a purpose, a new job, as Daphne Mathiesson does, can be a solution to a bad situation. In the novel *A Southern Exposure* (1996), the first two characters of the ensemble are introduced as they drive south to escape a variety of impending personal and professional disasters. A.'s characters are this way: they are eminently tactful and they know when to leave. A. makes a journey of her own in *A Southern Exposure.* She describes the Chapel Hill, North Carolina of her youth in a full novel with a wide range of characters including the most interesting men ever to appear in her fiction. Her previous novels tend to be placed in contemporary, metropolitan settings; *A Southern Exposure* is set in a small Southern university town in the 1930s. Its tone and setting bear a resemblance to the Hilton of the Todd stories, a group A. has identified as closest to her childhood memories of home.

A.'s technical skills are perfection. Her ear will tolerate no harshness of sound; each word and phrase is placed with an exactness more like poetry than prose. Her Southern settings are often the most satisfying merely because her dialect writing is so accurate and natural. It is for her expert craftsmanship that A. has won consistent praise from critics and especially from other writers.

BIBLIOGRAPHY: Flora, J. M., and R. Bain, eds., *Contemporary Fiction Writers of the South* (1993); Upton, L., "Changing the Past: A. A.'s Revisionary Nostalgia," *SSF* 26 (Winter 1989): 33–41

NICOLE SARROCCO

ADAMS, Harriet Stratemeyer

b. 11 December 1892, Newark, New Jersey; d. 27 March 1982, Pottersville, New Jersey

A. is best known as author and producer of the Nancy Drew books, movies, and television series. However, her connection with popular children's books extended far beyond Nancy Drew since she was the daughter of Edward STRATEMEYER and guided the Stratemeyer Syndicate from her father's death in 1930 until her own death in 1982. She graduated from Wellesley College in 1914 and had done some writing for publication during her college years. She had little contact with the operation of the Syndicate, however, since her father did not approve of women working outside the home. Since her father had about thirty active juvenile series in print at the time of his death, there was a major concern about the future of the Syndicate. Together with her sister, Edna Stratemeyer, A. assumed the responsibilities of running the business and continuing such popular Syndicate series as the Hardy Boys, Tom Swift, the Bobbsey Twins, and Nancy Drew. During the Depression era, they continued to create new series, to modify and develop existing series, and to cancel older and less successful series. Edna became inactive in 1942, leaving A. as the active partner, who continued to provide story outlines and detailed guidelines for the contract writers who wrote the stories. After World War II, A. expanded the number of Syndicate series. She introduced a Tom Swift, Jr. series in 1954, a modern science fiction series featuring the children of the first Tom Swift. Tom Swift, Jr. was mainly authored by James Duncan Lawrence and the thirty-three titles proved to be among the most popular of the later series.

Many of the older series—the Bobbsey Twins started in 1904, the Hardy Boys in 1927, and Nancy Drew in 1930—contained ethnic stereotypes or dated plots and dialogue. In 1959, A. began the process of updating these series. A. recognized the influence of Syndicate series on young people and made a conscious effort to maintain a conservative moral code in her books. In the guidelines to her writers, she warned against profanity, sex, and violence. She felt that her Syndicate books were accurate and educational although they also emphasized mystery and contained lots of action. The books were not written as great literature but as clean, entertaining, and action-filled stories for the young.

A. spent over fifty years with the Stratemeyer Syndicate. An unanswered question is still how many of the Nancy Drew mysteries she actually authored and how many were written by contract authors. Her importance, however, rests on the impact of her Stratemeyer Syndicate books on the attitudes and belief of American children. The Nancy Drew books, with which her name is particularly associated, are believed to have been the most widely published and most popular children's books of the 20th c. The merits of the Stratemeyer series books have been challenged by educators and librarians from the founding of the Syndicate but their popularity has continued. Young people identify with Tom Swift and Nancy Drew and the Hardy Boys. In the process, they may also absorb, as A. wished, the Syndicate's emphasis on clean living, fair play, independence, and success through hard work.

BIBLIOGRAPHY: Billman, C., *The Secret of the Stratemeyer Syndicate* (1986); Dizer, J. T., *Tom Swift and Company* (1982); Dyer, C. S, and N. T. Romalov, eds., *Rediscovering Nancy Drew* (1995); Plunkett-Powell, K., *The Nancy Drew Scrapbook* (1993)

JOHN T. DIZER

ADAMS, Henry [Brooks]

b. 16 February 1838, Boston, Massachusetts; d. 27 March 1918, Washington, D.C.

The fourth-generation member of the nation's most distinguished political family, A. stands in the shadows of American history, an observer and dissenter but never a leader. Yet his voice remains authentically American—even when, as so often, he raises doubts about results and leaves his questions unanswered. In fact, A. is an uncomfortable fit in the national pantheon, a writer too important to ignore because his ideas cut a path for his readers to the core of the American character. At both an individual and a representative level, A.'s lifelong search identified our national quest.

In his life, A. broke with the family conventions of political leadership and turned his back on the examples of John and John Quincy Adams. In his writing, A. rejected almost as much, by crossing the lines between

familiar materials and forms and refining his techniques until the accepted literary definitions no longer applied.

Until recently, A. owed his popular reputation to a single publication, *The Education of H. A.* (1907), which after being privately printed appeared in published form just after its author had died in 1918 and made the writer famous. It was awarded the Pulitzer Prize in 1919, thus providing an ironic commentary on the unsuspected loss to national letters occasioned by the author's death. Yet in a far more serious way, the fame of this one book put into critical eclipse the substantial body of literary work that A. had accomplished earlier in essays, biographies, novels, letters, and especially in a magisterial nine-volume historical study of the presidencies of Thomas JEFFERSON and James Madison—a classic of American historiography. In the years since 1919, that shadow has largely disappeared, and a more fair-minded sense of A.'s proper place in the cultural history of the late 19th and early 20th cs. has gradually emerged. With the passage of time, we have come to see that A. stands apart even while he belongs to his age; as an artist and a man, he must be understood in terms that remain uniquely his own—those of an independent observer, yet a man of his time.

A. was born into the special world of the Massachusetts Adamses as the third son of Charles Francis Adams, the grandson of President John Quincy Adams and the great-grandson of another president, John Adams. This was hardly an inauspicious beginning. All three illustrious forebears exemplified the principle of duty before pleasure, especially political duty to their state and nation. But each one of the Adamses, as their heir soon learned, was habitually committed to the equally demanding role of lifelong authorship—to be writers almost as much as politicians and statesmen. From their collective efforts has emerged the remarkable four-generation record of diary-keeping, document-drafting, and letter-writing that is known as the Adams Papers. As we have come to understand only recently—but as A. must have known almost from birth—the Adamses were a literary as much as a political family. Along with a political name, he inherited a duty to celebrate, explain, demand, and often to justify in simple words the complex experiences that were his life.

The earliest surviving evidence of A.'s attempts to satisfy this family demand for authorship dates from his years as a student at Harvard College (1854–58). His undergraduate essays on such subjects as the reading habits of his fellow students were printed in the *Harvard Magazine,* and they helped to establish for A. a college popularity that led to his election as class orator for 1858. After graduation and the usual grand tour of Europe, he took up residence in Berlin, to begin the study of civil law and of the German language. In 1859 and 1860, A. moved around Europe, touring in northern Italy with his vivacious sister, Louisa Adams Kuhn, and later taking advantage of an unusual opportunity to interview Garibaldi, the most popular revolutionary figure of the moment. Based on these experiences, A. wrote colorful travel letters that found their way back home to the Boston *Daily Courier,* thus marking A.'s initiation into the adult world of newspaper journalism.

Returning to Massachusetts in 1860, A. was soon recalled to family duty. He packed up and moved to Washington, where he served a double function: private secretary to his father, now Congressman Charles Francis Adams, and Washington correspondent for the Boston *Daily Advertiser.* Once settled in the national capital, A. found that his varied round of activities seemed to satisfy both the political and literary demands of his complex nature. Certainly, he took to Washington with rare enthusiasm. In fact, A. never recovered from Potomac fever, as the city played an important role in the long remainder of his life.

In 1861, President Abraham LINCOLN appointed A.'s father to be Minister to the Court of St. James, and A. reluctantly moved his residence to London as the Civil War commenced. There he remained, an unhappy but especially well-informed spectator, until 1868—an accident of time and place that A. later insisted cost him a role in the most historic single event of his lifetime. During these London years, the young private secretary made good literary use of his time, however, as he wrote often on politics, history, and science, especially in the essay form. His most ambitious pieces, better than mere journalism, appeared in the prestigious *North American Review:* "Captain John Smith" (1867) and an extended essay-review of Sir Charles Lyell's tenth edition of *Principles of Geology,* a key text in evolutionary theory. Returning to Washington after the Civil War, A. continued his career as an essayist, writing now in a more popular style a series of political studies aimed at practical reform. These essays began appearing in periodicals during 1869–70, and they were later collected in *Chapters of Erie* (1871), along with similar efforts written by A.'s brother, Charles Francis Adams II. Both of the fourth-generation sons were at this moment dedicated to the task of shaping a practical force of public opinion, one they hoped would prove sufficiently powerful to effect reform in American political life.

Soon disillusioned by a failure to achieve any real results, and with strong encouragement from his family, A. moved back to Boston and Harvard in 1870 to become both an instructor in history at the College

and editor of the prestigious *North American Review.* His marriage in 1872 to Marian "Clover" Hooper, a young lady he had met first in London and a member of proper Boston society, led next to a lengthy wedding journey to England, continental Europe, and Egypt. The newlyweds carried with them written introductions to political and intellectual leaders in the countries they would visit, and some of the resulting friendships lasted throughout their lives. Back at Harvard, A. took up his work with new seriousness; he taught courses in medieval and American history, introduced within the University the first graduate seminars organized on the German model, and published the historical writing of his best graduate students along with some of his own in *Essays in Anglo-Saxon Law* (1876). A.'s chief contribution, the essay, "Anglo-Saxon Courts of Law," stands as an impressive demonstration that the academic instructor had mastered traditional techniques for scholarly research and publication. In December 1876, A. gave further evidence of his versatility as he presented a carefully prepared paper on "The Primitive Rights of Women" to a popular audience at the Lowell Institute.

Valuable fruits of his work in American history began to appear in 1877 under the title *Documents Relating to New England Federalism, 1800–1815.* Although it was not apparent at the time, this spirited defense of his grandfather, John Quincy Adams, against the old attacks from Federalist Party loyalists also signaled the end of A.'s academic career. He resigned his appointment at Harvard during 1877, and once again he moved to Washington, where he began to sort through the private papers of Albert Gallatin, Secretary of the Treasury in the Cabinet of President Thomas Jefferson. A.'s scholarly work soon made itself known to the public. In 1879, both *The Writings of Albert Gallatin* and *The Life of Albert Gallatin* appeared to justify his literary and editorial efforts in Washington. Both books were massively documented, and each seemed somewhat old-fashioned in form and style, as if the author-editor had joined the times of his subject. At the moment of publication, however, A. was using the fruits of his work on Gallatin to announce a new sense of high purpose in a developing literary career. Henceforth, A. would owe his life to the pursuit of letters rather than to society, higher education, business, or even politics.

Finishing the biography of Gallatin, A. felt confident enough to extend his range and to begin a far more ambitious historical study, which would appear finally to the general public between 1889 and 1891 as the *History of the United States during the Administrations of Thomas Jefferson and James Madison.* This nine-volume work mixes social, diplomatic, and intellectual history of the period 1800–17. In A.'s day, it remained unmatched in breadth and power, and it still represents one of the most significant literary achievements in his entire career. The *History* is, in fact, a true classic in American historical writing. The research used for the book—undertaken, organized, and paid for by its author—was extensive, especially in the archives of England, France, Spain, and America. In many cases, A. brought into public view for the first time archival materials that he had been able to see and use only because he was an Adams and the great-grandson and grandson of American presidents. Once he had gained access to these treasures, the historian worked with copyists, translators, and personal secretaries to construct a really massive documentary foundation, one that could support a deep yet broad reconsideration of a crucial period in the development of his own nation. Organized in this peculiar way and completed on the grand scale of scientific national inquiry, the *History* came to represent in A.'s mind less another title to be added to his bibliography than an obligatory act of familial and patriotic duty.

Yet, while he was at work on the *History,* A. also found time to sharpen his literary skills and also to use writing as a pleasurable diversion for both his wife and himself when he turned his attention to critical biography and fiction. His vitriolic attack on an earlier Southern politician, in the short biography, *John Randolph* (1882), remains even today compelling reading. The book was highly seasoned by its author's clear dislike for his subject—an opposite feeling from the one he had entertained for Gallatin—and the result was an enduring portrait of an unattractive, enigmatic man, a picture that demanded correction by Randolph's more sympathetic biographers. In this book, A. was trying out in public a biographical style quite different from the one he had used in *The Life of Albert Gallatin*. Now, fresh from his archival researches for the *History,* he could draw upon new materials to fashion a powerful critique of Randolph, one that would later be incorporated into the larger work. In *John Randolph,* A. made the most of his opportunities, but both books show their author learning the difficult art of literary biography.

Striking off in another literary direction, A. also added to his skills by writing, more for fun than financial gain, his two novels, *Democracy: An American Novel* (1880) and *Esther: A Novel* (1884). Neither of these fictional works displayed its author's real name; instead, A. sought to protect his reputation as a serious historian and man of letters, at least until the appearance of the *History,* on which his real literary hopes were staked.

Of the two novels—all that A. ever wrote—*Democracy* has enjoyed the greater reputation. Set in post-Civil War Washington, the book stands as an extension into fiction of its author's persistent interest in political reform. The chief characters in the novel—often identified with real-life counterparts, people whom A. knew in Washington—play out the moral and ethical dramas of personal and national right and wrong, set against a backdrop of political reconciliation in the historical period just after the Civil War. As the lessons of politics and life are taught to the heroine, Madeleine Lee, they also become available to the reading audience. Now, instead of relying on didactic essays, A. attempted to teach his countrymen a series of lessons by means of his novel, using character portrayal as a primary artistic device. Senator Ratcliffe, the political villain from the American West, and Carrington, the noble but impecunious Southerner who was once a Confederate soldier but never a secessionist, engage in a romantic contest for the hand of the widowed Mrs. Lee, an attractive and intelligent woman who has come to Washington to learn political and human truths at first hand. In the end, Mrs. Lee recoils at what she does find—pragmatism instead of patriotic idealism and personal corruption in the men (and perhaps even the women) who determine our national destiny. Confronted by the virtuous Mrs. Lee, Ratcliffe pursues his ambitions unreformed, although not untouched by the admirable feminine principles she represents. No matter what her charms, however, he cannot renounce American politics-as-usual, with its blandishments of POWER. To the end of the book, nonetheless, the hope of something better remains, as the author continues to insist that a more idealistic solution to the problems of democracy must be possible. His faith has been shared by the many readers who have ranked it among the best ever written about the nation's capital.

Made uncomfortable by journalistic speculations concerning the authorship of *Democracy,* A. sent a second novel to press with the pseudonym Frances Snow Compton on the title page. That book was *Esther,* another "problem" novel with a heroine as the central figure, but a story that focuses on religion rather than politics. Here, a host of male characters surround Esther Dudley, trying their best to help the heroine find a usable personal philosophy that will get her through life. She searches for a set of modern—scientifically, aesthetically, and religiously up-to-date—ideas that will provide answers to her old-fashioned questions about human experience. In fact, Esther's personal needs are sympathetically defined; like the author, she desperately hopes to function as a forceful, effective human being in a post-Darwinian world. Yet, writing about her plight, A. acknowledges his own limitations. To Esther, in her particular dilemma as a woman, the novelist brings only what help he can find around him, faint help from the conventional tradition of romantic love, but also what seems more substantial from the worlds of art, science, and religion. None of these aids proves adequate for Esther's personal adjustment to life, however. Her own solution is to flee the complications of her dilemma—an attractive literary escape that would later prove congenial to the author of this fiction, who obviously included much of his own experience in his novel.

A. would later claim, with some justice, that *Esther* and, to a lesser extent, *Democracy* owed their best qualities to the influence of his high-spirited wife. Still, it is also true that both novels display largely autobiographical characteristics. Of course, when he developed the most feminine traits of his heroines, A. knew that he was using his fiction to compliment his wife and to repay the interest she had shown in his own writing. In the novels, A. also tested the first rough outlines of his emerging theory of feminine force—the hypothesis that he would later develop more fully in *Mont-Saint-Michel and Chartres* (privately printed in 1904 and published in 1913) and *The Education of H. A.* In another important way, the novels signaled a new freedom in A.'s art. In them, he showed that he could write well without relying on the discipline of historical scholarship or bowing to traditional family demands for serious nonfiction and political didacticism. Just as he had moved his home from Boston, A. had transferred his mind to Washington and points beyond. For him, there would be no turning back.

Aside from writing during the 1880s, A. enjoyed planning for the elegant new house he and his wife would jointly occupy just across Lafayette Park from the White House. Their lives seemed the best that financial security and select Washington society could offer. But before *History* was finished or the new house completed, A.'s life was shattered by his wife's suicide. He could never recover fully from this blow, as his letters and books remind us. At that time, however, A. appeared to continue in the normal patterns of his married life, moving into the new house on H Street, spending time with friends, finishing the writing of *History,* and traveling whenever he found opportunity and good companionship available to him.

A.'s *History of the United States during the Administrations of Thomas Jefferson and James Madison* was the first important example of scientific history written in the U.S. Borrowing something from both German and English history and even more from what A. knew of the scientific method used in geology, biology, and physics, the historian attempted to study the presidential years of Jefferson and Madison as an experiment crucial to the fate of American democracy. Between the framing chapters at the beginning and end of his nine volumes—a frame that painted in con-

trasting colors two grand pictures, the U.S. in 1800 and again in 1817, and using an ambitious form of social and intellectual history—A. sought to recount a sixteen-year story of the American nation with something approaching scientific precision by arranging facts in their sequence. Just such facts, A. believed, were the proper business of the historian, who should write history as a way of inviting others to observe and compare their conclusions with his own. Thus, A.'s reader must accept the role of a student who views this scientific demonstration with the purpose increasing his personal understanding. This reader does not exist merely to be entertained. Yet, even as A. was setting down his facts about the lives and thoughts of Jefferson, Gallatin, John Quincy Adams, Randolph, and others, his historical sequence took on the coloration of his own prejudices and limitations in understanding, so that the objectivity he prized and aimed to achieve inevitably escaped from his artistic grasp.

For later readers, who have been inclined to deny any real possibility of scientific history, at least of the kind that A. sought in this work and in later essays, the limitations of *History* are less remarkable than are its achievements. By skillful handling of original source materials in several languages, effective portrayal of character and personality, breadth of historical vision, and more, A. turned the most ambitious literary project that he ever undertook into a personal triumph, creating a milepost on the road to modern historical writing. Not surprisingly, his most appreciative readers have been professional scholars rather than members of a more general public; but this fact does not diminish his overall achievement. A. succeeded beyond question in changing an old-fashioned narrative form into something quite different by writing a new kind of history that consciously challenged every serious reader to improve upon the author's findings. In a personal way, moreover, A. could point to *History* as his first literary work that demonstrated a full use of his mature abilities and talents.

In his life, except for an extension of travels and a deeper cultivation of his platonic relationship with Elizabeth Cameron, A. after 1885 seemed to withdraw increasingly into a private existence. Publication of the final volumes of *History* in 1891—along with a companion volume, *Historical Essays,* to complete the ten-volume set—brought significant professional recognition but no public acclaim. The author was elected president of the American Historical Association, but he did not receive an important ambassadorship nor a presidential nomination to become a Cabinet member. Rather than appear in person to read his presidential address to the Historical Association, A. had it printed and sent to the members. In that seminal paper, published in 1894 as "The Tendency of History," the author drew upon his personal experiences with *History* and ended by inviting his colleagues to find new and better ways to teach and write their own versions of history, both ancient and modern. Meanwhile, from his magnificent point of vantage in Washington, across the park from the White House, A. watched his friend John HAY become Minister to the Court of St. James—the same position A.'s father had occupied during the Civil War—and later Secretary of State (following, after many years, John Quincy Adams). Whatever the ironics A. might have derived from the flight of real political power from his family during the course of American history, he managed to keep silent. Yet, in the troubled years that followed his wife's death, his mind and pen remained active, as he turned away from political subjects, to use his considerable skills in writing two important works of private rather than public history. In fact, these two titles distinguish the final decade of A.'s complete mental and physical capabilities, a decade that ended with partial paralysis caused by the cerebral thrombosis that afflicted him in 1912.

In that final decade of performance—if not life—A. wrote the two best known of all his works, *Mont-Saint-Michel and Chartres* and *The Education of H. A.* In a less ambitious way, A. also brought forth several essays and two memorial volumes for friends who had died: *Letters of John Hay and Extracts from Diary* (3 vols., 1908) and *The Life of George Cabot Lodge* (1911). These works remain largely unread, and neither has contributed much to A.'s fame. On the other hand, along with *History,* both *Mont-Saint-Michel and Chartres* and *The Education of H. A.* have gained general acceptance as pillars of A.'s modern reputation as a man of letters.

Even so, the special attractions of *Mont-Saint-Michel and Chartres* remain difficult to define in any fully satisfactory way. The book is less an attempt to write either serious or popular history than a compelling invitation to travel and enjoy (as the author so obviously does) the aesthetic and emotional benefits of immersion in medieval life and culture. Where the pedant might have written a history textbook for classroom use, A. casts himself in a different role. As tour guide, he insists good-naturedly on leading a procession of favorite nieces in wishes along a path to appreciation based on knowledge. Despite objections from serious-minded historians who want their history straight, testimonials to the artistic success of the book abound. It has captured readers who feel sympathetic toward a kindly uncle, and who know that history as a cultural exercise can offer something more than mere instruction, just as religion is more than catechism and art something more than gallery-hopping. In its own ineffable way, *Mont-Saint-Michel and Chartres* invites those who pick it up to participate in a reading experience which is greater than the sum of its critical parts.

Most complex and problematical of all A.'s writings, *The Education of H. A.* stands alone in method and message. It is the most often cited—and all too frequently the only—work of A. used by commentators as a basis for broad generations about its author, and even about the world of his time. Given its sophisticated narrative method, one product of A.'s mature literary art, the work easily falls victim to such simplistic treatment. In fact, the full measure of his accomplishment in the book deserves our admiration: *The Education of H. A.* is at once an accounting for a single private life, written in a tradition of great autobiography that includes St. Augustine, Jean Jacques Rousseau, Benjamin FRANKLIN, and Henry David THOREAU, and a panoramic representation of one man's version of American history. For A., that highly personalized history—which, in the telling, nevertheless owes a debt to *Mont-Saint-Michel and Chartres* and *History*—began with the optimistic phrases of Jefferson and John Adams and ended in the moral decadence of Grantian politics. A. represents as a kind of American Everyman, decline and fall seem to provide the only possible moral of "Education." Yet the richness of A.'s art and his reluctance to accept pessimism as a working philosophy lead him to explore every alternative. Whenever we hear his private voice, the author insists that all human experience is dense and complex, and that living—for an Adams and for Everyman—may not be simple or easy. If history showed a decline in human capacity (for whatever reasons), and that fact proved unappealing to the fourth-generation heir of presidents and statesmen, what was left to A. was yet an unqualified legacy of intelligence and talent. Finally, *The Education of H. A.* justified that combination as more than sufficient for A.'s time.

Along with *Mont-Saint-Michel and Chartres, History,* and the best of A.'s few poems and many letters, *The Education of H. A.* provides us with ample evidence to rank their author outstanding in wit, range, and depth. If over four generations his family had suffered a loss in political distinction, A.'s writings—while remaining highly individualized in method and message—used perceptive thought and literary skill to more than compensate the American public.

BIBLIOGRAPHY: Dusinberre, W., *H. A.: The Myth of Failure* (1980); Harbert, E. N., ed., *Critical Essays on H. A.* (1981); Harbert, E. N., *The Force So Much Closer Home* (1977); Hochfield, G., *H. A.: An Intro-*

duction and Interpretation (1962); Jordy, W. H., *H. A.: Scientific Historian* (1952) Levenson, J. C., *The Mind and Art of H. A.* (1957); Mane, R., *H. A. on the Road to Chartres* (1971); Samuels, E., *The Young H. A.* (1948); Samuels, E., *H. A.. The Middle Years* (1958); Samuels, E., *H. A.: The Major Phase* (1964)

EARL N. HARBERT

ADAMS, Léonie [Fuller]
b. 9 December 1899, Brooklyn, New York; d. 27 June 1988, New Milford, Connecticut

A.'s poems reveal a mind hard at work with a Georgian elegance. In tightly controlled, formal verse, she would call up images from the natural world that glitter and burn, blossom, or wither. Early critics have described her work as metaphysical; incorporating language play and finely wrought syntax. Like Wallace STEVENS, A. also calls upon the imagination to see and hear the reality of nature. In her first book, *Those Not Elect* (1925), A. chooses animals, seasons, the moon, and trees to comment about aspects of human passion. Her angels fall, laugh, eat, and taste forbidden fruit. Written when A. was in her twenties, *Those Not Elect* may seem superficial and overly sentimental for the contemporary reader's taste. However, with her second book, *High Falcon and Other Poems* (1929), A. relinquishes angels, dust, wings, and heaven—which clutter the first book—and appears ready to take on real people in real houses.

In the 1940s and 1950s, A. spent most of her time teaching and editing. As a teacher, A. was insistent that the students know form and meter before choosing to abandon them. Unlike her friend and fellow poet, Louise BOGAN, there is little biographical data available. A. was married to the editor William Troy, and she busied herself in preserving his writings. However, her body of work did not go unrecognized. In 1954, she won the Harriet Monroe Award from the literary journal *Poetry;* in the following year, she won the Shelley Memorial Award and shared the Bollingen Prize with Bogan.

Much has been made of A.'s use of nature, but her use is less innocent than the romantic poets. She does not chronicle the seasons as a means of person afflatus; there are no hints of immortality. Her best poems evoke winter as bringing death as well as gusts and hail. The great birth cycle in nature is a vehicle for chance, change, and ultimate loss. Nature is useful to depict the whole creative process, but sometimes comes to nothing, a notion farmers, teachers, and poets know in grand measure, as illustrated in the poem "The Wood" from *Poems: A Selection* (1954). She shows a great willingness to explain chance and

change and to recognize death in an unsentimental way. Death is the great dispassionate spoiler that takes everything away. In the end, beauty, greatness, and the held-out miracle all dissolve. A.'s affinity to William Butler Yeats can be felt in the central number of poems that are variations of the sonnet dealing with meditative themes that rely on the metaphor of the falcon in the second book. A. speaks of memory, dreams, and the associative effects, a fact critics seemed to have overlooked. In these poems, she challenges language—stretching and shaping until all the philosophical notes are fixed inside her words. Death—that "cool lord of chances"— takes the past and uses up memory until everything that once moved, felt, loved is consumed. Death makes a mockery of innocence. Many of her later poems speak of farewells or dirges, with an acceptance of what was once is now lost.

BIBLIOGRAPHY: Deutsch, B., *Poetry in Our Time* (1963); Redd, T. N., "L. A.," in Quartermain, P., ed., *DLB,* vol. 48, *American Poets, 1880–1945* (1986): 3–9

HARRIET SUSSKIND

ADE, George
b. 9 February 1866, Kentland, Indiana; d. 16 May 1944, near Brooke, Indiana

A. was a Hoosier comedian who made his mark in late-19th- and early-20th-c. Chicago, a rich place and period for newspaper writing that included Theodore DREISER, Eugene FIELD, and Finley Peter DUNNE as well. Reared in a small town in Indiana, A. went from Purdue University to Chicago, where he soon found his niche as a daily columnist producing a feature called "Stories of the Streets and of the Town" for the *Chicago Record*. Like Charles Dickens, who also began with newspaper sketches, A. soon turned to fiction; his book-length *Artie* (1896), *Pink Marsh* (1987), and *Doc' Horne* (1899) were episodic anthologies of stories and tales arranged around a central character—and first published in the column.

In 1897, A. published "The Fable of Sister Mae Who Did as Well as Could Be Expected" in his column. He had invented his own special contribution to American letters, the "Fables in Slang." The first collection, *Fables in Slang* (1900), and its successors—collections of fables appearing every year or two, ten collections in all—made A. immensely popular and quite wealthy as well.

His recipe for a fable was "one portion of homely truth, one pinch of satire, a teacupful of capital letters, well-spliced with up to date slang, and garnished with woodcut drawings." Modern readers will likely be most struck by the capital letters; the slang is muted, and consists of striking comparisons and a deadpan tone: "Once there was a man who wore a Six Hat and had a Head shaped like an Egg Plant" begins a typical fable. They are often fairly cynical; the "moral" appended to each is usually irrelevant.

A. had another career as successful author of musical comedies for Broadway, notably *The College Widow* (1904) and his best play *The Sultan of Sulu* (1902). However, his popularity as a playwright began to wane even during his lifetime. His lasting mark on the American language and literature is limited to his impact on later writers and to the best of his "Fables in Slang," which are still funny and even fresh.

BIBLIOGRAPHY: Coyle, L., *G. A.* (1964); DeMuth, J., *Small Town Chicago: The Comic Perspective of Finley Peter Dunne, G. A., and Ring Lardner* (1980); Kelly, F. C., *G. A.* (1947); Kelly, F. C., ed., *The Permanent A.* (1947)

MERRITT MOSELEY

AFRICAN AMERICAN LITERATURE

Each period within the history of African American literature contains its own agenda. In each period, however, most African American authors have sought to provide at least a glimpse into the diverse experiences of African Americans. A cursory glance at the breadth of African American literature reveals two facts: First, African American experiences have varied widely from the point that Africans were forcibly brought to the Americas; second, these experiences are bound by the eternal desires of African Americans to continue surviving and thriving in the Americas. This desire stems primarily from the long and extremely difficult period of indentured servitude and chattel slavery, the systems under which most African Americans lived and struggled until the abolition of slavery in the U.S. in 1865 after the Civil War.

Appropriately, then, the first two centuries of the African diaspora's sojourn in the U.S. were marked by the dominance of the SLAVE NARRATIVE and African American FOLKLORE, both of which continued to flourish and influence African American literature and politics long after the end of slavery. This does not mean, however, that these two creative forms represented the totality of African American literature. Phillis WHEATLEY is generally considered one of the first important American poets. Though Wheatley's contemporaries, including Thomas JEFFERSON, criticized her verses as being derivative and overly sentimental, they were also a beacon and foundation for burgeoning early American literary aspirations, inasmuch as she achieved national and international recognition despite the predominant biases against the fact

of the ingenuity of black people in general. Moreover, Wheatley's verses were arguably no less developed than those of other early American writers.

The slave narrative and various forms of folklore, however, maintain the most imposing presence on the horizon of African American literature until the late 19th c. In the first case, this is due to the slave narrative's past and present political importance. The vast majority of slave narratives were originally published to aid the cause of abolitionists, but the political strategies put forth in these narratives are still important to African Americans today. In addition, a substantial portion of African American folklore not only contains dominant themes found throughout African American literature, but is every bit as politically, socially, and culturally important as any other literary form.

Though thousands of slave narratives were published, ranging from short anecdotes to long, formal autobiographies, a few authors had an indelible impact upon American politics. *Narrative of the Life of Frederick Douglass, an American Slave, Written by Himself* is almost universally hailed as one of the most powerful and well crafted of the slave narratives, as is Harriet JACOBS's *Incidents in the Life of a Slave Girl*. Other important slave narrative authors include William Wells BROWN, Olaudah EQUIANO, Mary Prince, Sojourner Truth, Denmark Vesey, David Walker, and Booker T. WASHINGTON. The antebellum slave narratives' primary purposes were to expose the truths and horrors of American slavery in order to speed along its abolition, whereas postbellum narratives such as Washington's *Up from Slavery* were indeed to posit economic and social programs for the formerly enslaved and their descendants.

African American folklore yields further insights into African American thought inasmuch as folk culture is an integral base of African American culture. African American folk and vernacular forms, as products of African folk culture and the experiences of Africans in America, display both subtle and overt ironic stances toward natural and man-made adversities, such as slavery and other forms of racism. Folklore serves numerous purposes, but its primary uses were and are for subtly socializing its audience and for criticizing and easing the personal or social tensions slavery and racism engender. These were the primary purposes of trickster tales, including such perennial favorites as the different versions of the "Br'er Rabbit" tales that provide ironic insights into American historical events and period lifestyles that only folklore can provide. Unfortunately, the folklorists, teachers, and scholars who collected the tales of enslaved Africans and their free descendants, such as Joel Chandler HARRIS, despite often arduous and diligent work, did not always have the advancement of African American art and culture foremost in their minds. Many early collections of black folklore are corrupted both in their diction and content by common beliefs in black cultural inferiority and white supremacy, to which these collectors were often susceptible.

Neither fiction nor poetry, however, were ignored during slavery. Such novelists and short story authors as William Wells Brown, Martin R. Delany, Harriet Wilson, Victor Sejour, and Frances E. W. HARPER, were noted pioneers of prose fiction, while Harper, George Moses HORTON, Lucy Terry, and James M. Whitfield maintained and developed the poetic tradition spearheaded by Wheatley. Though each author's subject matter necessarily differs from the others, realistic and often autobiographical portrayals of the complexities and frequent frustrations and horrors of enslaved and free life, albeit fictional, bear many similarities to the nonfictional slave narratives and predominate their work. Most significant of this group are Brown, the author of *Clotel,* published in England, and the first novel written by an African American, while Delany and Wilson, whose respective novels *Blake* (1859) and *Our Nig; or, Sketches from the Life of a Free Black* (1859) are the first African American novels originally published in the U.S.

Antebellum works were the natural forebears of the literary tradition that emerged during Reconstruction and subsequent years. The 1880s and 1890s witnessed the rise of Charles W. CHESNUTT, whose highly successful "Conjure Woman" stories blended the conventions of the "local color" genre, with its emphases on the quaintness of provincials and their concomitant dialects, and African American folklore. Less successful were Chesnutt's later novels and nondialect short works, primarily because they tended to confront contemporary racial issues in ways that were offensive to white sensibilities of the time.

Chesnutt's contemporary, Paul Laurence DUNBAR, is considered the most significant poet in the African American tradition after Wheatley and before the Harlem Renaissance of the 1920s and 1930s. His best-known collections, *Majors and Minors* and *Lyrics of Lowly Life,* sold very well, helping him to earn an international reputation as the "Poet Laureate of the Negro race," an appellation coined by Booker T. Washington. Dunbar's poetry, such as "We Wear the Mask," "Sympathy," "When Malindy sings," and "The Colored Soldiers," written in both African American dialect and standard English, alternately celebrate sensuous pleasures of black life, recall black history, and criticize the ways in which black life was officially and unofficially circumscribed. Dunbar's novels and short stories reflect the same alternating pattern of concern with African American cultures, though most of his novelistic output spent little time dealing with

black characters, with the notable exception his final *Sport of the Gods,* which deals with the problem of black migration from the South to the North.

On the other hand, James Weldon JOHNSON's remarkable *The Autobiography of an Ex-Coloured Man,* published anonymously in 1913, deals directly with the problems of racial classification, racism, and intraracial politics that Chesnutt attempted to delineate with limited success in his novels. This work is arguably the first important novel by an African American in the 20th c., inasmuch as it had a deep influence upon younger writers of the later Harlem Renaissance. Johnson's total contributions to African American literature are legion. His edition of *The Book of American Negro Poetry* (1922; rev. ed., 1931) is one of the strongest poetry anthologies of the time; his own poetic works, collected in *God's Trombones* and elsewhere, follow in the thematic footsteps of Dunbar, though Johnson demonstrates a richer understanding of the black vernacular tradition and less ambivalent sentiments against racial inequality.

A criticism frequently leveled against Chesnutt's and Dunbar's works, as well as those of Johnson, James D. Corrothers, and other writers, is whether each author's use of black dialect and inclusion of stereotypical black characters qualified as acquiescence to the generally ugly racial climate of the years between Reconstruction and the Harlem Renaissance. The issue was a deeply political one, closely related to the ongoing debates over the direction and strategies of African American political, economic, and social progress that began in antebellum times. The era's most prominent political voices were Washington, founder and president of Tuskegee Institute in Alabama and one of the most powerful African American leaders ever; W. E. B. DU BOIS, the "father of sociology" and the most prolific African American activist, essayist, and scholar of the 20th c.; and Ida B. Wells-Barnett, an investigative journalist and activist.

Washington's rise to fame and power, narrated in his autobiography, *Up from Slavery,* was fueled by his accommodationist stance vis-à-vis black progress and legal segregation. Washington's stance, particularly its delineation in his famous speech at the Atlanta Exposition in 1895, known as the "Atlanta Compromise," is often said to have contributed to the conditions that allowed the landmark 1896 *Plessy v. Ferguson* Supreme Court decision, thus ushering in a period of legal segregation that did not begin to crumble until 1954. On the other hand, Washington was also instrumental in improving the state of black colleges and institutions and in garnering power for selected black leaders.

Du Bois's many political and sociological writings, the most prominent being the classic *The Souls of*

Black Folk, opposed some aspects of Washington's accommodationist program, arguing instead for a strong and sustained push for social equality and civil rights; it also included the important essay, "Of Our Spiritual Strivings," in which Du Bois introduced the concept of "double-consciousness," the "sense of always looking at one's self through the eyes of others, of measuring one's soul by the tape of the world that looks on in amused contempt and pity." The metaphor of double-consciousness is but one Du Bois employs to argue that the "problem of the 20th c. is the problem of the color-line," an idea that informs all of his early work and has influenced sociologists, writers, critics, and activists to this day. In addition, Du Bois's early activist work eventually laid the groundwork for the National Association for the Advancement of Colored People, which was the most radical civil rights organization in the U.S. for at least the first half of the 20th c.

Wells-Barnett's tireless literary campaign against lynching and other inequalities were among the strongest protests against racism, rivaling those of Du Bois. The debate between the camps of Du Bois and Wells-Barnett, on the one hand, and Washington on the other, were continuations of the conflict between forces arguing for civil rights and the immediate integration of African Americans into the American mainstream and those arguing for a separatism that would allow African Americans to achieve economic parity with whites with relatively little concern for civil rights. This debate found earlier manifestations in the arguments between Frederick DOUGLASS and David Walker; it would achieve the spotlight again during the Harlem Renaissance, as Du Bois squared off against black nationalist Marcus Garvey and in the 1960s, as Martin Luther King, Jr.'s work was opposed by Elijah Muhammad, Malcolm X, and other nationalists.

Despite the groundwork laid by earlier generations, though, African American literature still lacked a clearly definable coterie of creative writers whose narrative forms reflected the broad range of African American life. The Harlem Renaissance was the event that engendered one of the most prolific and artistically sound collections of literature by and about African Americans to date, surpassed only but the flowering of black literature and arts since the 1960s. The intellectual exchanges during the Harlem Renaissance resulted in a wider dissemination of the full scope of African American political thought, reaching beyond Harlem and into mainstream American discourse, albeit to a limited degree.

Like most literary flourishes, the period we presently call the Harlem Renaissance did not carry that name while it was occurring; rather, it was called the "New Negro Renaissance." Unlike previous flourishes, however, the writers of the Harlem Renaissance were fully conscious of the cultural significance of their entreé into American letters. This consciousness was not a product of the simple historical fact that black writers had been repeatedly excluded from the literary marketplace; rather, the Harlem writer's awareness was largely the product of an era in which black cultures, particularly those within Harlem, were undergoing sharp changes in their makeup and economy that managed to sweep African Americans and a gaggle of curious white patrons into a new appreciation of numerous embodiments of black life.

African Americans returned from the battlefields of World War I decorated with impressive military achievements and, perhaps most importantly, a glimpse of a life not circumscribed by legal segregation and lynchings in European countries. Coincidentally, a substantial number of African Americans migrated from the South to the North in order to escape overt racial discrimination. The convergence of these conditions as well as those that gave rise to MODERNISM in literature led the writers of the Harlem Renaissance to gain a new sense of the African American's history and potential fortune in America and to defy white's and middle-class blacks' definitions of "acceptable" black behavior. Harlem occupied a singular place in the African American imagination in the early 20th c. owing to its status as a black community in which decent housing was affordable, where employment and social opportunities for black residents abounded in comparison to the South, and as a locus that attracted and contained many of the preeminent black institutions, such as the NAACP, the Urban League, Marcus Garvey's nationalist Universal Negro Improvement Association, Father Divine, and virtually every denomination of black church. Although not all major artists of the Harlem Renaissance resided in Harlem itself or even in New York City throughout the movement, its status as a cultural locus helped to loom large over the literary and political landscape.

Alain Locke's literary and critical anthology *The New Negro* (1925) was one of the first Harlem Renaissance texts to attempt to navigate the complicated terrain of African America and Harlem's location upon its map. In his essay "The New Negro," Locke posits the audaciously powerful argument that a greater consciousness spurred by racial progress is supplanting previous thoughts and images about black people. In the same volume, Charles S. Johnson describes the transformation in black culture as an evolutionary process in which the new form of life is "a city Negro" who is "being evolved out of those strangely divergent elements of the general [that is, rural] background." The shift from a focus on rural to city life in the early part of the century additionally affected the frequency with which black people came into contact with each other; whereas the black church was the most frequent locus of black political and social activity, cities and communities like New York and Harlem had astonishing varieties of organizations devoted to those purposes. Into this variety entered not only talented black artists but also rich whites who patronized black artists and contributed to the Renaissance's literature themselves. This racial admixture helped introduce black artists to the marketplace and, simultaneously, pushed understanding of inter-and intraracial politics forward.

Although not all of the Harlem Renaissance's artists and intellectuals agreed with the notion of the "New Negro" as put forth by Locke, Johnson, and Jessie Redmond FAUSET (one of "the midwives of the Harlem Renaissance" via her edition of the NAACP's *Crisis* magazine and her career as a novelist in her own right), they did draw upon the financial support to publish an impressive body of richly variegated works. The protest verses, novels, and autobiographies of Claude MCKAY complemented the surrealism of Jean TOOMER, the historical perspective of Arna BONTEMPS, and the "folk realism" of Zora Neale HURSTON's novels. The blues-derived verses of Langston HUGHES and Sterling A. BROWN stood in contrast to the traditionalism and ambivalence of Countee CULLEN and Nella LARSEN, while the political writings of Du Bois and Garvey were countered by the satirical barbs and comedic humor of George S. Schuyler, Rudolph Fisher, and Wallace THURMAN. This loosely aggregated stable of authors attained unprecedented access to mainstream publishing houses, publicity and underwriting, thanks in part to their patrons and a nationwide curiosity about and fascination with black culture that helped the wave of black creativity to crest. If the "Roaring Twenties" was a hedonistic decade, African Americans were perceived as symbols and sources of that hedonism.

Consequently, the Harlem Renaissance is often thought to have reached its apex prior to the onset of the Great Depression in 1929. Although the quantitative output of and publicity for the Renaissance's most prominent artists clearly declined as interest in black culture faded with the hedonistic spirit of the 1920s, it is important to note that many of its most mature works were published well into the Depression years. We have but to consider Schuyler's *Black No More* (1931), Hurston's extended works—most notably *Their Eyes Were Watching God*—and Richard WRIGHT's early works, including "The Ethics of Living Jim Crow" and the stories within *Uncle Tom's Children* in order to see that not all of the Renaissance's creative energy dissipated after 1929.

In fact, black literature continued to flourish after the Harlem Renaissance, though not with the same

spectacular publicity. The late 1930s and early 1940s comprise the period of NATURALISM in African American literature, in which Richard Wright published his greatest novel *Native Son*. Wright and *Native Son* shifted the paradigm for African American writing irrevocably. *Native Son*'s themes of protest and naturalism—use of theories espoused by the Chicago school of sociology regarding the marginalization of African Americans within American society, open confrontation of the hypocrisies of American racial thinking, and support for Marxist thought—helped make it a Book-of-the-Month Club selection and catapulted Wright to the top of the mountain of African American writers. Wright wielded an enormous influence on his contemporaries and protégés, especially novelists Chester HIMES, James BALDWIN, Ralph ELLISON, and Ann PETRY, as well as on poet and personal friend Margaret WALKER.

Each of these authors explored inter-and intraracial discourse before and after World War II, which was perhaps one of the most crucial catalysts for critical discourse on race in the 20th c. Prior to the war, such political ideologies as socialism, Marxism, and communism gained new popularity and acceptance among African American intellectuals and, to a far lesser extent, the African American masses, fueled partially by the promises of jobs and political organization different radical groups offered. The Great Depression cooled much of this political ardor, though the idealism and social programming of President Franklin D. Roosevelt's New Deal maintained some hope that social justice waited in the wings for African Americans. The protest fiction of Wright, Himes, and Walker served notice that the New Deal, despite its promises, still fell far short of the needs of African Americans and had to become even more radical. The alternatives were for African Americans to turn to the activists and politics of communism and socialism, alternatives that Wright advocated most strongly as a member of the Communist Party, which he eventually parted with on ideological grounds.

World War II only served to heighten the hopes raised in the early days of the New Deal, as the war effort created new demands for labor and consequently greater success to these jobs for African Americans. The excellent performance of African Americans in the military during the war revived the hopes that bloomed in the African American mind after World War I, in which, as noted above, black servicemen and laborers performed well. These successes emboldened both those African Americans on the American homefront and those returning from military service to demand full suffrage and other rights long denied them. Unfortunately, the voicing of these demands met a response similar to that following World War I: increased suppression of black rights and horrific racial violence. Himes protests these forms of oppression in Los Angeles via his pair of powerful early novels, *If He Hollers Let Him Go* and *Lonely Crusade.* Each of these novels is nearly as strong as Wright's *Native Son,* though not nearly as well known. Himes later turned his creative energies toward a series of popular detective potboilers featuring Coffin Ed Johnson and Gravedigger Jones; the best known of these is *Cotton Comes to Harlem.*

Unlike the post-World War I era, however, African Americans maintained a solid and relatively consistent struggle for civil rights that led to the dramatic legal gains of the 1950s and 1960s. Underlying that hue and cry, though, were the literary efforts of African America's intelligentsia. Ralph Ellison's phenomenal *Invisible Man,* which started out as a war novel itself, created a new respect for black authorship that would extend into the next few decades, due to Ellison's highly nuanced views of race and its problematic relationship to the idealistic principles upon which America was founded and by which it operates. Centered around the picaresque adventures of its anonymous narrator, *Invisible Man* drew upon, parodied, and paid homage to Ralph Waldo EMERSON—Ellison's namesake—and TRANSCENDENTALISM, Herman MELVILLE, black folklore, American pragmatism, black colleges, modernism, the blues, Sigmund Freud, and the entire history of African America. This tour de force novel's artistic achievement earned it a National Book Award in 1952, an award that would not be bestowed upon another African American author until Charles JOHNSON earned it in 1990 for his novel *Middle Passage.* Moreover, *Invisible Man* is widely recognized as the finest novel in most canons of African American and American literature. Ellison died before he could complete the manuscript for his second novel, but his essay collections, *Shadow and Act* and *Going to the Territory,* are excellent examples of literary and cultural criticism.

Although *Invisible Man* towered over African American literature in the 1950s, it was by no means alone. Baldwin, who had been a protégé of Wright, emerged as a powerful novelist in the 1950s, owing to the success of two early works, *Go Tell It on the Mountain* and *Giovanni's Room.* The former is a largely autobiographical narrative of Baldwin's relationship with his father and family and the power of redemption; the latter takes a look at homosexuality that was very frank for the 1950s. Baldwin's greatest achievements, however, are arguably his critical essays, which are scathing in the condemnation of racism's perfidy. Many of Baldwin's most complex essays, such as "Many Thousands Gone" and "Everybody's Protest Novel," are collected in *Notes of a Native Son* and *Nobody Knows My Name: More Notes of a Native Son.* Baldwin's most controversial extended essay, *The Fire Next Time,* is a damning condemnation of America's reluctance to embrace racial justice and equality.

No less impressive during the post-World War II era were the poetic works of Gwendolyn BROOKS and Robert HAYDEN. Brooks's Pulitzer Prize-winning *Annie Allen* and *The Bean Eaters* set new standards in modernist poetry. Her *Selected Poems* is perhaps the best introduction to her work, which Brooks writes primarily in order to reach and inspire black audiences to action. Brooks's early work also includes the novel *Maud Martha,* one of relatively few successful novels written by a black woman after the Harlem Renaissance. Hayden's work also stands as a landmark in highly symbolic, modernist poetry. Hayden was largely influenced by the poets and prose writers of the Harlem Renaissance and W. H. AUDEN, who was his teacher at the University of Michigan. Though Hayden believed that black experiences could clarify general human problems, he came under fire later in his career for not subscribing to nationalist politics. Despite this controversy, little doubt remains that the poems collected in such volumes as *The Lion and the Archer, Ballad of Remembrance,* and *The Night-Blooming Cereus* reveal a consistent love of intricate symbolism and personal exploration.

If the 1950s and early 1960s were a time in which African American authors honed and perfected their craft, the mid-to late-1960s was a period of expansion, of fascinating experimental writing that may be called revolutionary. The 1960s brought with them a comprehension, by both blacks and whites, of black American politics and culture that had not been paralleled since the height of Garvey's influence in the 1920s and 1930s. The civil rights movement was in full swing and being continually debated by the American public in all of the most dominant media by white and black integrationists, black nationalists and/or separatists (most notably the Nation of Islam and its chief spokesman, Malcolm X), white segregationists and racists, white moderates, and every other group or position that had a stake in the preservation or elimination of accepted racial categories and stratifications. Nowhere did these debates rage more hotly than within the black community itself, which was forced to redefine its own parameters when faced with the possibility that national *de jure* segregation might actually be eliminated through the efforts of civil rights activists and presidential administrations that at least appeared to be sympathetic to the social plight of black Americans.

The terms of the intraracial debate over racial/cultural identity and the course of black political organizing and action—as well as the parties and organizations who argued for and against specific terms and actions—were remarkably similar to those of earlier decades. Significantly, the type of support given to particular positions could be mapped out along class lines as well; a great deal of black nationalism's support came from the disenfranchised (and often urban) component of black communities, whereas integration appealed most often to middle-class black people, though many blacks of the working class and below lent their political support to integration as well.

In the writings and work of black artists in particular, though, 1960s debates centered on questions of images and aesthetics that were, according to Hoyt W. Fuller, "about the business of destroying those images and myths that have crippled degraded black people, and the institution of new images and myths that will liberate them." This business was called the "Black Aesthetic," which reviled the notion that black culture was forever inferior to or dependent on European-derived aesthetics. Such a notion, Fuller argues, fed practices that would cause black people to detest, and perhaps even destroy, themselves. According to critics such as Addison Gayle, Amiri BARAKA, and Larry Neal, the responsibility of the black artist was to use the word, to use language as a tool invested with the power to transform ideas generated by black people into action, especially revolutionary action. This was the ideological foundation of the Black Aesthetic/Black Arts movement.

The new set of narratives inspired by the Black Aesthetic was devoted to elevating the most valuable and cherished aspects of the African American and criticizing those who would stand in the way of black progress and empowerment. In essence, then, the Black Aesthetic movement perceived itself as a direct advocate of the black masses and a staunch adversary to any agency that upheld oppressive stereotypes, whether that agency originated within or outside of black communities. Not every African American author, however, subscribed to all the tenets of the Black Aesthetic. Ralph Ellison was perhaps the most famous author to refuse to embrace it, a refusal that brought him a great deal of scorn from younger authors. But the politics that spawned the Black Aesthetic did influence a wide sampling of black artists, young and old. Such younger poets as Nikki GIOVANNI, Sonia SANCHEZ, Haki R. MADHUBUTI, Carolyn M. Rodgers, Etheridge KNIGHT, and Jayne CORTEZ worked to represent the pains of black ghetto life and black life in general, while Brooks's poetry took on a somewhat more nationalistic tone in the late 1960s. In addition, novelist William Melvin KELLEY also incorporated nationalistic politics more openly into his novels; Baraka, who had begun his career as the bohemian Beat poet LeRoi Jones, embraced black nationalism and

then Marxism as his muse evolved, establishing himself as one of the premier poets, playwrights, critics, and essayists in contemporary American literature.

The decades following the passage of the civil rights legislation of the 1960s and 1970s witnessed enormous and unprecedented transformations in the composition of the African American and mainstream American communities and their respective politics. Economists, political scientists, and sociologists have documented at length the changes within African American communities as *de jure* civil rights and racial integration allowed African Americans greater—though limited—access to mainstream institutions, professions, and corporations through Equal Opportunity and Affirmative Action programs. These new forms of access helped empower a significant portion of African Americans, who quickly found themselves endowed with increased purchasing power and with the help of antidiscriminatory housing laws the means to move to the neighborhoods of their choice and send their children to better schools at the primary, secondary, and college levels in greater numbers than ever before. Thus a new, ever-expanding middle class was created within African American communities. This class's existence, combined with the decidedly antibourgeois slant of black nationalism, forced African Americans to face the challenge of articulating a new meaning for "race" and this definition's subsequent effects upon black political and economic life, since that life was no longer legally circumscribed, at least not openly.

To the extent that African American literature is a reflection of black politics at a particular moment in time, it has had to absorb these changes in the black political landscape as often and as radically as black people themselves have. Since 1970, African American literature has witnessed the influx of a new cadre of black women authors, who have helped propel African American literature as a whole into a new era where black literature is more acceptable as popular reading material while almost becoming a staple of many American university curricula and the subject of far more critical studies than ever before. It is possible to argue, with considerable evidence, that African American literature now possesses a core canon, although like other literary canons, it is constantly in flux and subject to change in both political climates and taste.

Not surprisingly, the establishment of a canon of sorts has transformed the Black Aesthetic established in the mid-1960s and early 1970s, though it has not necessarily invalidated all of its claims. While the original Black Aesthetic, as the artistic branch of black nationalism, was supposed to reflect "black community," this particular purpose became more complicated in a black nation that had fractured into several class-divided states. As Madhu Dubey argues, without the "sheer possibility of blackness" that came out of nationalist thought, the focus of contemporary black authors on black community would be rendered moot; a contemporary text's foregrounding of previously neglected issues more often than not argues for a cohesive black community, though the glue that would hold black community together varies from text to text. In the works of Alice WALKER, for example, we may find examples of her "womanist" aesthetic, which essentially calls for "black women, especially those most marginalized by race, caste, and class, to have their voices heard and their histories read" via literature and other forms of creative discourse. In pursuit of this aesthetic, Walker was instrumental in reviving the novels of Zora Neale Hurston in the early 1970s, catapulting *Their Eyes Were Watching God* to a new height of celebration for its close attention to women's concerns. Walker's own novels and womanist aesthetic, as well as novels by other black women, especially Toni MORRISON, Toni Cade BAMBARA, Ntozake SHANGE, Maya ANGELOU, Audre LORDE, Jamaica KINCAID, Gloria NAYLOR, and J. California Cooper, have helped expand general notions about what black literature is.

In 1993, Morrison received the Nobel Prize in literature, the first African American ever to be so honored. Her best-selling novels—*The Bluest Eye, Sula, Song of Solomon, Tar Baby, Beloved,* and *Jazz*—combine the symbolic virtues of modernism with the politics of the Black Aesthetic and a rich lyricism. Morrison has become one of the most frequently discussed African American authors in history, due in large part to *The Bluest Eye* and *Beloved.* Her work as an author and critic has helped inspire the career of Gloria Naylor; in addition, as an editor at Random House in the 1970s, Morrison helped bring the work of younger African American authors, especially women authors, into published form.

African American male authors have been no less productive in the decades since 1970. Equally as influenced by the Black Aesthetic as African American women authors, a new coterie of authors whose work may be described in any number of ways—including such labels as modernist, postmodernist, or Afrocentric—entered into literary canons and found new respectability in academia. Cecil Brown and John Oliver KILLENS provided humorous outlooks on black politics in the early 1970s, while Ishmael REED, Clarence MAJOR, and John Edgar WIDEMAN are three authors whose work, however widely divergent, has often been described as postmodern, usually due to their tendency to undermine the genres in which they write, whether as poets or novelists. Charles Johnson, David BRAD-

LEY, and Ernest J. GAINES write in more traditional styles, but their most famous novels, *Middle Passage, The Chaneysville Incident,* and *The Autobiography of Miss Jane Pittman,* respectively, have been cited often as paradigm-shifting landmarks in African American letters. In other areas, Samuel R. Delany and Octavia Butler are both award-winning authors of science fiction whose work is discussed as part of the tradition of African American writing all too seldom; August WILSON is considered one of the major playwrights in the U.S. today.

Finally, the 1990s yielded a number of new authors whose work, whether influenced by the work of previous generations of African American and white writers or such cultural phenomena as Hip-Hop, was already carving out a new niche in the African American literary tradition. Trey Ellis, Bebe Moore Campbell, Darryl Pinckney, Walter Mosley, Yusef KOMUNYAKAA, Terry MCMILLAN, Darius James, Tina McElroy Ansa, Paul Beatty, and Rita DOVE—named poet laureate of the U.S. in 1993—have all had a part in reshaping contemporary African American literature. McMillan and Mosley's popular fiction alone has helped spur widespread interest in African American fiction, thus feeding what some critics are calling a "New Renaissance" in African American art.

If anything is certain about the African American literary tradition, it is that it has always been richly varied, in both ideology and form. But as African Americans have slowly entered into the mainstream of American life, that variety has only bloomed. The shape the tradition shall take is not written in stone, but it shall certainly be great enough to encompass an extended family of voices, as it has always done.

BIBLIOGRAPHY: Baker, H. A., Jr., *Blues, Ideology and Afro-American Literature: A Vernacular Theory* (1984); Bell, B. W., *The Afro-American Novel and Its Tradition* (1987); Cruse, H., *The Crisis of the Negro Intellectual* (1967); Dubey, M., *Black Women Novelists and the Nationalist Aesthetic* (1994); Dundes, A., ed., *Mother Wit from the Laughing Barrel: Readings in the Interpretation of Afro-American Folklore* (1973); Gates, H. L., Jr., *Figures in Black: Words, Signs, and the "Racial" Self* (1987); Gates, H. L., Jr., *The Signifying Monkey: A Theory of African-American Literary Criticism* (1988); Gayle, A., Jr., ed., *The Black Aesthetic* (1971); Levine, L. W., *Black Culture and Black Consciousness: Afro-American Folk Thought from Slavery to Freedom* (1977); Roberts, J. W., *From Trickster to Badman: The Black Folk Hero in Slavery and Freedom* (1989); Watkins, M., *On the Real Side: Laughing, Lying, and Signifying—the Underground Tradition of African-American Humor That Transformed American Culture, from Slavery to Richard Pryor* (1994); Zafar, R., *We Wear the Mask: African Americans Write American Literature, 1760–1870* (1997)

DARRYL B. DICKSON-CARR

AGEE, James [Rufus]

b. 27 November 1909, Knoxville, Tennessee; d. 16 May 1955, New York City

As a poet, journalist, film critic, screenwriter, and novelist, A. wrote out of deeply felt moral convictions in order to confront the reader with ethical and social issues. His account of the lives of three Alabama tenant-farming families, *Let Us Now Praise Famous Men* (1941), is the best example of such literary translation of his moral impulse and is the work for which he is most celebrated. His novel *A Death in the Family* (1957) won the Pulitzer Prize in fiction in 1958, and in recent years his essays on film have brought him renewed praise.

After the trauma of his father's accidental death in 1916, A. attended a primary and secondary boarding school, St. Andrew's, run by an Episcopalian monastic order in his hometown of Knoxville. There he met Father James Harold Flye, whose lifelong friendship helped form his intellectual and religious attitudes. A. went on to the Phillips Exeter Academy where he began writing. At Harvard, he was deeply influenced by I. A. Richards, from whom he drew his commitment to disciplined, concrete language and to active, first-person narration. Richards, as well as S. Foster Damon and Robert FROST, encouraged A. to write poetry.

A. published a volume of poems, *Permit Me Voyage* (1934), of variable merit. The more skilled examples experiment with religious themes and traditional forms; the collection now seems rather mannered and "literary." His short stories, sampled in *The Collected Short Prose of J. A.* (1968), also treat religious and ethical problems.

From 1932 to 1948, A. worked as a journalist. Convinced that writers had the duty to reveal "truth," a much-repeated and uncompromising ideal for him, he felt ambivalent about the inevitable commercial bias of journalism. Nevertheless, it was *Fortune* that sent him to Alabama to research *Let Us Now Praise Famous Men* with photographer Walker Evans. He lived with the farm families, scrupulously cataloging their meager possessions and recording the tenor of their lives. The ambitious book that resulted is complexly structured, drawing on elements of drama, music, liturgy, and poetry. The work is as much a tormented meditation on A.'s motives for invading the curious purity of his subjects' poverty as it is reportage.

A. wrote for and about the movies for a more sustained period than he devoted to any other art form. His film reviews for *Time* and *The Nation,* collected in *A. on Film: Reviews and Comments* (1958), reveal a subjective but earnest concern for film's capacity for honesty, as well as a contagious enthusiasm for the medium. *A. on Film, Volume II: Five Film Scripts* (1960) contains *The African Queen,* written with John Huston, *The Night of the Hunter,* and adaptations of Stephen CRANE short stories and Paul Gauguin's journal. Two original film scripts are included in *The Collected Short Prose of J. A.* (1968).

A. also produced two loosely autobiographical novels. *The Morning Watch* (1951) takes place on the night and early morning of Good Friday and is suffused with Christian imagery. It tells of the young hero's struggle to find an identity, either within the church or among the more callow boys at his Episcopal school. *A Death in the Family* was not quite complete when A., who had serious heart trouble, died of a heart attack. The novel is about a young boy, Rufus, who must come to terms with his father's sudden death and with subsequent revelations about familial love and animosity that have become clear only over time to the older Rufus who is telling the story. The editors of the manuscript placed several narrative fragments that had been left unrelated to the frame of the plot in italics, so that the first-person narrator is able to move freely back and forth between innocence and enlightenment. The result is one of A.'s finest achievements.

BIBLIOGRAPHY: Bergreen, L., *J. A.: A Life* (1984); Larsen, E., *J. A.* (1971); Ohlin, P. H., *A.* (1966); Lofaro, M. A., ed., *J. A.: Reconsiderations* (1992); Lowe, J., *The Creative Process of J. A.* (1994); Madden, D., *Remembering J. A.* (1974)

ROBIN BEATY

AI

b. 21 October 1947, Albany, Texas

The narrators of A.'s poems—male and female, famous and anonymous, white and black—reveal the dark side of human nature—violence, cruelty, sin, love, and death. Perhaps A. is interested in the commonality beneath the surface of ethnic, gender, or social veneer because of her own background—born Florence Anthony, A. is African American, Japanese, Choctaw, and Irish. After the ethnic cultural awakening in the 1960s, A. began to explore themes of life from different cultural perspectives that were sometimes in conflict.

A. definitely operates on two levels, even in her choice of pseudonym. A.'s name means love in Japanese. Yet she has described it as the sound of grief. Her poems often wrestle with two sides of a social issue or the story behind the story.

Her poems, which are dramatic monologues, act as masks for voices taken from everyday life, current events, and history. Described as page turners and the equivalent of a talk show without a host, A. cuts beneath the glamor and the myth to the bare bones, using razor-sharp objects as reoccurring images. Her narrators bleed with violence, lust, cruelty, and sex; these are the elements that bind all her narrators.

Anonymous narrators are as strong as those with names we recognize. An abused mother, a child murderer, a priest, and a journalist speak out on incest, jealousy, pride, and temptation. "Priest's Confession," in *Sin* (1986), is an example of one narrator's torment. As the priest chronicles his struggle with temptation, the beautiful Rosamund grows and develops into a woman. He gives into this temptation, knowing full well the sin he is committing, and ultimately pays for one sin with another by taking his own life.

Some of the famous voices—John and Robert Kennedy, Jimmy Hoffa, Lyndon Johnson, James Dean, and Elvis Presley—speak out on eroticism, politics, religion, and other obsessions. A. takes real life, looks behind the glitter of the fame, and cuts the line between myth and reality, public image and private obsessions.

The anonymous voice of "Riot Act, April 29, 1992," in *Greed* (1995), one of the living dead of South Central, Los Angeles, rises to take what is his to take. A. blends the headlines of the Los Angeles riots, combines it with references from movies and brand names, as if the act were part of myth, part of popular culture. This treatment further strips the speaker of his identity and any reason or reality for his actions, making his life all the more hollow, all the more stereotypical. This and A.'s later poetic monologues start moving into the realm of the docudrama monologue written by Anna Deveare Smith in *Twilight: Los Angeles, 1992.*

It is through her many voices that A. tells what lies beneath the current events, what will live on as history and sometimes myth; with her themes of greed, sin, violence, and fate, she paints a landscape of contemporary America.

BIBLIOGRAPHY: Field, C. R., "A.," in Gwynn, R. S., ed., *DLB*, vol. 120, *American Poets since World War II* (1992): 10–17; Mintz, S. B., "A Descent toward the Unknown in the Poetry of A.," *Sage* 9 (Summer 1995): 36–46

KATHLEEN MOTOIKE

AIKEN, Conrad [Potter]

b. 5 August 1889, Savannah, Georgia; d. 17 August 1973, Savannah, Georgia

A. is a formidable figure in 20th-c. American letters. As a poet, novelist, short story writer, and critic, he has exercised an important influence upon his contemporaries and successors.

After the murder/suicide of his parents in 1901, A. was taken to Massachusetts to live with relatives. He attended Harvard and, for several years, lived in England. His later years were divided between New England and Georgia, and, as a result, his writing often displays elements of the regional as well as the cosmopolitan and international.

As an undergraduate, in 1911, he composed a lengthy narrative poem, *The Clerk's Journal* (published in 1971), which exhibits the influence of John Masefield and Edwin Arlington ROBINSON. The romantic exoticism of Theophile Gautier had its effect upon him, and he translated Gautier's "La Morte Amoureuse" while still in college and later used its plot in a poem. He read Lafcadio HEARN to good effect and studied John Gould FLETCHER's experimental "Colour Symphonies." The poems of his Harvard classmate, T. S. ELIOT, affected him powerfully; he was prominent in having "The Love Song of J. Alfred Prufrock" accepted and published.

A. was a practicing critic for about half a century; from the outset of his career, he wrote book reviews for many of the leading journals, including the *New Republic, The Dial, Criteron,* the *Yale Review,* and *Poetry.* While living in England during the 1930s, he contributed a "London Letter" to the *New Yorker.* Many of the pieces represent A.'s studied attempt to come to terms with the writing of his time and to move the conservative publishers toward the new experimental writing of the 1920s. Earlier than that, however, he had gathered a selection of his critical writings in *Scepticims: Notes on Contemporary Poetry* (1919). Here, he attacked the conventional anthologies that annually appeared and praised the work of D. H. Lawrence. Substantial essays on poetic technique appeared in later years, and A. displayed a keen eye for what was worth preserving in the work of contemporaries such as Eliot and William FAULKNER. As editor of *The Dial,* Marianne MOORE characterized him as "the perfect reviewer, Diogenes' one honest man, fearing only to dispense himself." A large collection, *A Reviewer's ABC* (1958), edited by Rufus A. Blanshard, contains much of what A. wished preserved from his critical writings. As an editor, he brought out a survey collection of American poetry with the intent of revising commonly held opinions about the major figures; successive editions of the volume did establish new patterns of thinking about the subject. A collection of modern poetry, for the Modern Library, served as competition to Louis Untermeyer's critical anthologies. For English readers, A. edited a selection of Emily DICKINSON's poems in 1924.

As a poet, A. began with a couple of inconsequential volumes; he thought little of them, himself, and rejected them from his collected poems. But during the later teens and early twenties, he published a series of poetic "symphonies," long poems in which he attempted to substitute a contrapuntal musical method of composition to replace linear narrative. Of the six symphonies, the most effective are "Senlin: A Biography" (1918) and "Changing Mind" (1925). Publication of the whole series of symphonies in a volume called *The Divine Pilgrim* (1949), and subsequently in *Collected Poems* (1953; rev. ed., 1970) allows the reader to see their relationships as they explore the themes of nympholepsy, wish fulfillment, the evolution of consciousness, and the desire for knowledge, even inconclusive knowledge. Later narrative and dramatic poems include *Punch: The Immortal Liar* (1921), which explores the theme of the puppets in the classic puppet show being manipulated by a mountebank, himself a puppet figure in a deterministic universe; *John Deth: A Metaphysical Legend* (1930), an allegorical treatment of life and death; and *The Coming Forth by Day of Osiris Jones* (1931), derived from the Egyptian *Book of the Dead,* as the inventory of the life of an ordinary man.

Although the long poems commanded attention, A. composed a number of excellent brief poems during the 1920s—"The Road," "Deaf Leaf in May," "Sea Holly," and "The Room"—and these led to his composition of his most important work, a long series of short lyric, dramatic, and narrative poems that form a coherent sequence. The 169 "preludes," as he called them, spread themselves over two volumes, *Preludes for Memnon* (1931) and *Time in the Rock* (1936). Because of the varied forms, they are not constricting, as a sonnet cycle might be, as they analyze the modern consciousness that is despairing and lost to religious or philosophical consolations, but still attempting to discover a *modus vivendi.*

For more than twenty years, A. expended serious effort upon the novel and the short story. The longer works have been characterized as picaresque novels of the psyche, and *Blue Voyage* (1927) fits this designation well. It is the tale of a man's journey across the Atlantic Ocean and the inward probing of his spiritual pain as he seeks self-knowledge. In *Great Circle* (1933), the hero, having discovered his wife's adultery, plunges into a series of interior monologues that relive his youth. A.'s perceptive use of psychoanalytic techniques makes the book attractive; Freud considered

this novel a masterpiece and often recommended it. *King Coffin* (1935) has a Dostoevskian protagonist, a megalomaniac who plots a perfect crime that he intends to commit as a gratuitous act, completely unmotivated. He is a criminal of the type of Honoré de Balzac's Vautrin, Dostoevsky's Stavrogin, or André Gide's Lafcadio; his disinterested plan of murder is fastened upon an ordinary stranger. The *Collected Novels* (1964), with an introduction by R. P. BLACKMUR, makes these books, along with A.'s other two novels, *A Heart for the Gods of Mexico* (1939) and *Conversation; or, Pilgrim's Progress* (1940), readily available.

A.'s short stories, first published in magazines, were collected in *Bring! Bring! and Other Stories* (1925) and *Costumes by Eros* (1928), and then brought together, with a preface by Mark Schorer, in *The Collected Short Stories* (1950). They are uneven, but several of the stories are excellent, and two, "Mr. Arcularis" and "Silent Snow, Secret Snow," have become much-reprinted fantasy classics. But A.'s finest venture into prose remains *Ushant* (1952), an autobiography, individual in its conception, and written as an "essay" that employs stream-of-consciousness narrative and musical devices in its development.

The poems of A.'s later years are gathered in a number of volumes, including *Skylight One* (1949), *A Letter from Li Po and Other Poems* (1955), *Sheepfold Hill* (1958), and *The Morning Song of Lord Zero* (1963). Each of these volumes has memorable poems that display the mastery gained by long years of poetic practice, among them "Mayflower," "Halloween," "A Letter from Li Po," "The Crystal," "Herman Melville," and "Oneiromachia."

BIBLIOGRAPHY: Butscher, E., *C. A.: Poet of White Horse Vale;* Hoffman, F. J., *C. A.* (1962); Martin, J., *C. A.: A Life of His Art* (1962); Peterson, H., *The Melody of Chaos* (1931); Seigel, C. F., *The Fictive World of C. A.* (1993); Spivey, T. R., *The Writer as Shaman: The Pilgrimages of C. A. and Walker Percy* (1986); Spivey, T. R., and A. Waterman, *C. A., A Priest of Consciousness* (1988)

DOUGLAS ROBILLARD

AKINS, Zoë
b. 30 October 1886, Humansville, Missouri; d. 29 October 1958, Los Angeles, California

Poet, actress, screenwriter, novelist, and essayist, A. is known primarily as a playwright. Although considered a major playwright of the 1920s, A.'s dramatic works of upper-class society have reaped mixed critical reaction. Her plays are praised for presenting engaging characters who communicate in keen, incisive dialogue. Dominating negative evaluations, however, are comments criticizing A. for effectively failing to probe the depths of contemporary social issues in addition to structural and technical weaknesses and an excess of sentimentality. Most damning is the accusation that she fails to adopt a point of view. Certainly, A. concentrates on the fashionable levels of European and East Coast society, rejecting her Midwestern background. But within these contexts, she explores woman's position in the society of her day, subtly commenting on man's supposed dominance while providing actresses such as Ethel Barrymore and Laurette Taylor with rare opportunities to portray complex leading roles.

Generally, A.'s early work is considered her best, and of these *Daddy's Gone A-Hunting* (1923) represents a peak level of achievement. In this play, A. recounts the all-too-familiar story of a woman who sacrifices her personal ambitions to assist her husband in furthering his career as an artist. Absorbed by the need to attend to the domestic chores as well as provide for financial stability of their family, the woman loses contact with the world into which her husband is moving. Predictably, he is unfaithful to her and eventually abandons her. A. was accosted for the stark realism with which she presents the situation, although most critics responded to the genuine emotion of a realistic tragedy.

The Texas Nightingale—alternatively entitled *Greatness* (1923)—ranks highly as well. Again, the character portrayal is what commands attention, but for its comedy, generated by the unpredictable moods of its female opera star, rather than its anguish. *The Texas Nightingale* is considered by many to be a superior work because of its dialogue and three-dimensional character portrayal.

Déclassée (1923), the story of the social destruction of Lady Helen Haden due to her exposure of a cheat, was the production that first brought A. to the attention of New York audiences and critics. Edward Thayer retaliates by revealing her past indiscreet letters to him, forcing her out of her marriage and her social circle. She lives by selling her valuables until she accepts the proposal of Rudolph Solomon, a kind and wealthy New York Jew, even though she still loves Edward, her betrayer. When he abruptly appears at Solomon's house, Solomon breaks the engagement to free her. Thinking, however, that Solomon has rejected her, she runs away and is hit by a taxi in the street in front of the house. The play established for A. a reputation for cosmopolitan characters and topics.

The Old Maid (1935), a dramatization of Edith WHARTON's novel, was awarded a Pulitzer Prize, but not without the controversy that usually attended A.'s

works. It is the poignant story of a woman who gives birth to an illegitimate daughter, gives her to her married cousin to rear, and then, when the now grown daughter is about to wed, decides to tell her daughter the truth. When she ultimately lacks the courage to reveal herself, her cousin generously steps in to share the wedding moment with the true mother.

Divided critical opinion of the play itself was forgotten in the virtually universal disbelief when the play was awarded the Pulitzer Prize. The incident was a key factor in the founding of the New York Drama Critics Circle, which began to award its own prizes.

Although labeled by some as pretentious in both her personal and professional lives, A. nevertheless wrote from her abiding belief in the power of drama to expose and correct social ills. Her commentaries could perhaps have scrutinized more closely the issues she raised, but she did indeed raise them.

BIBLIOGRAPHY: Bradley, J., "Z. A. and the Age of Excess: Broadway Melodrama in the 1920s," in Schlueter, J., ed., *Modern American Drama: The Female Canon* (1990): 86–96; Hughes, G., *A History of the American Theatre, 1700–1950* (1951)

BEVERLY BRONSON SMITH

ALBEE, Edward
b. 12 March 1928, Washington, D.C.

A. has been called "the American Absurdist," conferring upon him a status in the modern theater equivalent, categorically at least, to Samuel Beckett, Eugène Ionesco, Jean Genet, and Harold Pinter. Such classification, especially attached to geography, to say nothing of valuation, is in itself absurd, but functions fine as a synecdoche pointing to A.'s genius as a dramatist within a prominent and, as the designation suggests, playful literary historical lot. Critical appreciation of A.'s work has always broken divisively along tediously predictable fault lines: squandered/redeemed promise, original work versus adaptations, before and after *Who's Afraid of Virginia Woolf?* (1962). A. has contributed to this dialectic in commentary in the media and on occasion from the stage, but his arguments and manifestoes can be seen in a broader perspective as one of the responsibilities adopted in a life devoted to realizing a theatrical vision—as, like directing, part of the job.

A.'s early career appears in retrospect a progression of successes, experimental one-acts of dramatic savvy and anthologizable literary merit. *The Zoo Story* (1960) was first produced, on a double bill with Beckett's *Krapp's Last Tape,* in Berlin in 1959, establishing A.'s reputation in Europe, where critical appreciation has been more readily and regularly forthcoming than in America. The first American production the next year began a relationship with the director Alan Schneider, most famous for his direction of American productions of Beckett's plays. In *The Zoo Story,* A. discovers several fundamental features of his dramatic sensibility: Jerry, the angry young American, is derived from the British post-World War II "angry young man" dramas in which the conflict gains psychological significance and attitude from the fact that the antagonist is the protagonist; despite being capable of crisp exchanges of dialogue, A.'s characters—in this case, Jerry—display a natural talent for storytelling; both Jerry and Paul, the entire *dramatis personae,* demonstrate A.'s openly representative characterization, affording them symbolic, satiric, and expressionistic potential; A.'s talent for finding the apt twist on the conventions of theater that dramatizes, to satiric, surreal, or existential effect, the collapse of social conventions—in this case Jerry's suicide/murder—generates a den--ment powerful both in its narrative and theatrical effects.

The Sandbox (1960) and *The American Dream* (1961) share characters and themes, the latter work elaborating in variations upon the former, though both plays provide such vivid stage pictures and inherent ambiguities that they mark individual achievements in A.'s career. They both present a symbolic typology of American family life and of characters that will recur in many of A.'s plays: Mommy is the model of the harridan wife that will drive the action in some of A.'s most vital drama; Daddy is the type of the weak-willed husband, the dramatic foil to Mommy; Grandma is the antic wisdom and embarrassment of age in a culture greedy for appearance and youth; the Young Man/Angel of Death is that thoughtless, history-less innocence of appearance that is so winning and so destructive; the American family is a power structure dedicated to the exploitation and oblivion of the weak. A. demonstrates in these pieces a theatricality of broad strokes, bold colors, and Brechtian tones that vigorously and effectively serves his theme.

How highly developed A.'s technique and talent had become was evident in his next major work, *Who's Afraid of Virginia Woolf?* A mature masterpiece, it entertained without fail for three demanding, exhausting acts, offering audiences, in its long run on Broadway, recurrent revivals, and film version, every theatrical payoff, from guilty pleasure to shocking affront to authentic catharsis. George and Martha are at once a demonic parody of the first First Family, George and Martha Washington, an implied symbolic irony, while recapitulating Daddy as a failed and dangerously bitter intellectual and Mommy as a monumentally self-deluded shrew. Yet they each achieve by the long evening's end a piteously individual pain,

and their endlessly inventive vituperation and pointedly vicious storytelling resolve in a postapocalyptic calm and a shared existential strength.

It can be the bane of a playwright's career to turn out a "classic" at age thirty-five, but over the next three decades A. answered with major works in decidedly diverse dramatic keys. *Tiny Alice* (1965) puts surreal stress on its symbols and typed characters (the Cardinal, Lawyer, Butler, "Brother" Julian), and, according to A., responding to charges of obscurantism, must happen to an audience, like a religious experience. Its concern with abstraction as a dangerously dynamic shadow of reality suggests that it is a self-referential meditation, a dream of the power of theater. *A Delicate Balance* (1966), which won the 1967 Pulitzer Prize, seems to domesticate the types of the harridan wife and harried husband and the host-guest antagonism of *Who's Afraid of Virginia Woolf?* in the monied, mannered White-Anglo-Saxon-Protestant milieu in which A. was reared, but the existential terror and breakdown of social forms that menace all A.'s drama cannot be escaped, and, in fact, are finally welcomed. For only the third time in his original dramas, all the characters have names, but the nameless dread that haunts them neither friends nor family, norms nor habit, be it drinking, shopping, or divorcing, can dispel. In this company the 1975 Pulitzer Prize-winning *Seascape* (1975) appears whimsical, with its odd couple of couples, the standard-issue upper-middle-class, self-important, angst-ridden seaside picnickers and a pair of human-sized, sentient, name-bearing amphibians, poking and prodding each other and each other's species-bound presumptions. The clash of cultures is manifest in the slippage of styles from naturalistic to surrealistic, the resultant cognitive dissonance setting the unsettlingly comic tone. A. was awarded still another Pulitzer Prize in 1994 for *Three Tall Women* (1995), which bears stylistic traits recognizable as A.'s: the title characters are named A, B, and C, storytellers all; in the first, naturalistic act they are three different women, while in the second, surrealistic act they are three ages of the same woman; A is reminiscent of the Grandma-type; the elegantly disturbing stage-center image of the dying, bedridden A which visually dominates the second act reminds us of A.'s starkly efficient use of stage pictures throughout his career.

Critical opinion is so widely varied on A.'s other original works that any selection for discussion would necessarily raise controversy, but a few examples will show the range and vitality of his dramatic imagination. *Box* and *Quotations from Chairman Mao Tse-Tung* (1969) are interrelated experiments with vocality and musical structure; *Counting the Ways* (1977) is billed as "A Vaudeville" and applies Brechtian technique to sketch comedy on the themes of death and loss, performed by He and She; its companion piece and counterpoint, *Listening: A Chamber Play* (1977) originally written for the radio, presents the problem of communication as a grim power struggle between the sexes and the generations. A.'s many stage adaptations include the libretto for an opera of Herman MEL-VILLE's *Bartleby, the Scrivener,* and dramatizations of prose fiction, notably Carson MCCULLERS's *Ballad of a Sad Café,* James PURDY's *Malcom,* Truman CAPOTE's *Breakfast at Tiffany's,* and Vladimir NABOKOV's *Lolita,* all of which, in their dark depictions of the modern family or their existential core thematics, fit A.'s sensibility but apparently failed to engage his full imaginative capabilities, as they failed critically and at the box office. As a director he has dedicated himself to revivals and premieres of his own work, and the plays of Samuel Beckett.

The themes of unstable identity and the lost son would seem to relate directly to A.'s personal history as an adopted child, but other themes—madness, the bankruptcy of institutions, sexual politics, the stage as a borderland, to name but a few—call up as impassioned a commitment and insightful a vision. His talent for entertaining while troubling his audience has helped him endure, but his engagement with the most intractable mysteries and brutalities of modernity has tempered his talent in integrity's fires. America's absurdist is one of the modern theater's major figures.

BIBLIOGRAPHY: Bigsby, C. W. E., *E. A.: A Collection of Critical Essays* (1975); Bloom, H., ed., *E. A.: Modern Critical Views* (1987); Hayman, R., *E. A.* (1973); Roudane, M., *Understanding E. A.* (1987)

DENNIS PAOLI

ALCOTT, Amos Bronson

b. 29 November 1799, Spindle Hill, Connecticut; d. 4 March 1888, Boston, Massachusetts

Educator, philosopher, reformer, conversationalist, and poet, A. epitomized the stereotypical extremes of idealism and impracticality associated with TRAN-SCENDENTALISM. In his own day, he was frequently the lightning rod for ridicule directed at the movement; today he is still regarded as a second-rate writer, but his educational and reform theories and his important transcendentalist friendships, which he chronicled, have won him a measure of critical respect.

Peddling was a means for young A. to escape rural Connecticut poverty, but he was no shrewd Yankee. A thoroughgoing idealist, he was a gifted and innovative teacher, first formulating his theories in *Observations on the Principles and Methods of Infant Instruction*

(1830). His most notable teaching experiment was at the Masonic Temple in Boston. Believing that children are innately good and intelligent, and possess a spark of divinity, he refused to use corporal punishment. He sought instead to draw out the potential in his students through Socratic questioning. But controversy surrounded the Temple School and the theories A. put forth in *Conversations with Children on the Gospels* (2 vols., 1836–37), and A. moved to Concord to try farming and to bask in the more congenial company of his friends Ralph Waldo EMERSON and Henry David THOREAU.

A.'s most enduring—and notorious—writings are the "Orphic Sayings," published in *The Dial* (1840–41). Brief, oracular utterances on themes ranging from "Immortality" to "Vocation," from "Mysticism" to "Identity and Diversity," from "Originality" and "Beauty" to "Prometheus," the "Sayings" are based on A.'s assumption that "your heart is an oracle." In keeping with his long-held educational theories, he advocates self-reliance as opposed to convention, intuition over science. Sometimes sounding Emersonian, often impenetrably Platonic, he emphasizes the innocence of the soul, believing that flux and spirit pervade reality. Though some of the "Orphic Sayings" betray a streak of originality, they were the object of public laughter and critical mockery, and today are regarded essentially as dense, vapid curiosities.

Hoping to realize the ideal of transcendental economy, A. took his family to Harvard, Massachusetts, and with English reformer Charles Lane founded the Fruitlands utopian community in June 1843; by January the scheme had failed. In *Transcendental Wild Oats,* A.'s daughter Louisa May ALCOTT immortalized the venture—and the long-suffering family's ordeal in coping with a well-meaning but otherworldly father. Visionary and financially inept, A. was a constant burden and source of exasperation to family and friends. Yet he was universally beloved as a kind, genial soul, by none more so than by his patron and neighbor Emerson, who called him "a pail of which the bottom is taken out."

A sincere but clumsy poet, A. devoted considerable effort to that most transcendental genre, his journal. And he memorialized his transcendental friendships in such appreciative and insightful works as *Emerson* (1865; reissued as *Ralph Waldo Emerson,* 1882) and *Concord Days* (1872). Tapping the talent that had made him an effective, if unsuccessful, teacher, A. achieved some fame (and money) in the 1850s for his "Conversations." This kind of talk, which enjoyed a brief fashionableness, was based on the transcendentalist notion of inspiration, aiming to give expression to the spontaneous flow of truth. By definition ephemeral, the "Conversations" have survived only in scattered fragments recorded by auditors, many of them unsympathetic to either A. or the genre.

A more lasting legacy was the Concord School of Philosophy, which A., with the help of Franklin SANBORN, founded at Orchard House in 1879 as a forum for transcendentalism in its twilight. The school is often cited as the first sustained program of "adult education" in America. Though A.'s writing style has seldom been considered worthy of intensive critical study, scholars now recognize the importance of his contributions to education and reform and acknowledge his vital role in stimulating the thought of other transcendentalists. Emerson, while somewhat bemused by this "Peripatetic philosopher," admired his "singular gifts for awakening contemplation and aspiration in simple and in cultivated persons."

BIBLIOGRAPHY: Dahlstrand, F. C., *A. B. A.* (1982); Herrnstadt, R. L., ed., *The Letters of A. B. A.* (1969); McCuskey, D., *B. A., Teacher* (1940); Sanborn, F. B., and W. T. Harris, *A. B. A.* (2 vols., 1893); Shepard, O., *Pedlar's Progress* (1937); Shepard, O., *The Journals of B. A.* (1938)

WESLEY T. MOTT

ALCOTT, Louisa May

b. 29 November 1832, Germantown, Pennsylvania; d. 6 March 1888, Boston, Massachusetts

A prolific writer of over 270 poems, plays, short stories, novels, and sketches, A. is best known as the author of *Little Women* (1868) and other realistic yet sentimental fiction about Victorian family and domestic life. Less well known until recently is A.'s considerable body of sensational adult fiction, published pseudonymously in the early part of her career. These writings, as well as Civil War fiction, feminist tracts, and stories of women artists pursuing their own careers, reveal a subversive side of A. Viewed as a whole, then, her work is complex—often conflicted—with sunny depictions of feminine domesticity and submissiveness countered by unreconciled darkness and rebellion.

The second of four daughters, A. was reared in Concord, Massachusetts, and Boston. Her mother, Abagail (Abba) May Alcott, was from an established Boston family and was an unpublished writer, social worker, and ardent mother for whom A. felt great affection. Her father, Amos Bronson ALCOTT, was a brilliant but impractical reformer whose radical but mismanaged transcendental projects led the family into poverty. Following their reformist philosophies, both parents shared in child rearing, fostering imagination in A., who showed early signs of artistic talent.

The fiery temper and independent spirit that she inherited from her mother often clashed with her father's insistence on obedience, however, laying the foundation for a lifelong conflict between self-sacrificing duty to others and pursuit of her own goals.

When financial straits required that A., her mother, and sisters take jobs to support the family, A. worked as a domestic servant, took in sewing, taught school, edited a children's magazine called *Merry's Museum,* and turned her pen to popular domestic fiction, thus beginning her habits of satisfying others' literary tastes at the expense of her own. She never married, once saying, "liberty is a better husband than love to many of us," and she lived at home except for a brief stint as a Civil War nurse, cut short by typhoid fever, and two trips to Europe: one in 1865–66 when she served as a lady's companion, and another in 1870–71, after the success of *Little Women*. A. doggedly committed herself to an ethos of work and self-sacrifice, faintheartedly awaiting reward that never came. "Shall never live my own life," she remarked in a late journal entry.

A. began writing theatrical melodramas, poems, and short stories. Her first poem was published in 1851 in *Peterson's Magazine* under the pseudonym Flora Fairchild. In 1855, she published *Flower Fables* (1855), a didactic collection of fairy tales written for Ralph Waldo EMERSON's daughter that espouse selflessness, control of temper, and "the power of love to overcome obstacles and reform obdurate sinners." During the same period, however, and through the 1860s, A. secretly published intricately plotted sensation stories and gothic thrillers like "V. V.," "The Marble Woman," and "Pauline's Passion." The best of these stories, which deal with drug addiction, murder, and insanity and feature doomed women bent on deception, manipulation, and revenge, is "Behind a Mask," published in 1866 under the pseudonym A. M. Barnard. A livid answer to woman as child and victim, it both indicts patriarchal culture and reveals its author's own repressed and conflicted self. A. also published *A Modern Mephistopheles* in 1877 in Roberts Brothers's "No Name Series," reusing the title of an earlier unpublished and lurid story. A Faustian tale, it parallels A.'s sense that she herself had sold her soul for popularity and commercial success.

In 1863, A. published *Hospital Sketches,* based on her Civil War experiences. A commercial success, it reveals A.'s search for a legitimate female voice, her sensitivity to wounded men, and her outrage at hospital incompetence and mismanagement. "My Contraband," an abolitionist story also published in 1863, is set in a Civil War hospital and introduces class and racial conflicts, with the subtext of interracial love. In this and other fiction, A. sublimates her sexual attraction for men with motherly affection. Perhaps encouraged by favorable critical reception, she published *Moods* in 1865, her first serious adult novel. An Emersonian and too-frank treatment of marriage and divorce for the time, it was poorly received. A. revised it into a moralistic tale of adulterous longing and return to one's husband in an 1882 version.

In 1868, at the prodding of her father and publisher, A. published the first volume of *Little Women,* an instant critical and commercial success. She published the second half in 1869 with the same acclaim. Although sometimes charged with sentimentality, moralizing, and blindness to class issues, this popular Victorian novel is a realistic depiction of New England life and a celebration of female community. It also established a new standard for children's fiction. Patterned on John Bunyan's *Pilgrim's Progress, Little Women* refrains from preaching, instead presenting social and moral doctrine through the examples of fully drawn characters: Marmee, the firm but compassionate Victorian mother and moral guide inspired by A.'s own mother; Mr. March, the absent but loving father and Civil War preacher; and the four March sisters, Jo, Meg, Beth, and Amy, modeled after A. and her three sisters. Jo stands alone in the novel as the ambitious, independent young writer—obviously A. herself—ever renewing her resolutions to curb temper and conform to expected female roles. A. refuses a typically romantic ending for Jo, marrying her to a fatherly professor supportive of her work.

Little Women brought A. fame as a children's author and pressure to produce more fiction of the same kind, a demand she obliged with dozens more children's stories and novels, two of which are sequels to *Little Women: Little Men* (1871) and *Jo's Boys* (1886). Although some of this fiction continues to explore domestic and moral issues of young people with freshness, much of it—*An Old-Fashioned Girl* (1870), *Under the Lilacs* (1878), and *Jack and Jill* (1880), for example—is imitative and mechanical, more deserving of the label, "moral map for the young," that A. so disparagingly used to refer to her own work. Some children's writings, however, express A.'s more feminist stances on coeducation, women's rights, and dress reform, notably *Eight Cousins* (1875) and its sequel *Rose in Bloom* (1876).

Written for adults, *Work* (1873) is A.'s most feminist work, revising *Little Women* with a Jo-like character who leaves home to make her way in the world and experience various traditional and nontraditional vocations. "Transcendental Wild Oats" (1873) is a biting satire of the failed community Fruitlands established by her father. Exonerating her father, it nevertheless exposes the sexism and impractical idealism of the male transcendentalists. In works such as "A Modern

Cinderella" (1860), and "Psyche's Art" (1868), as well as the unfinished four-chapter *Diana and Persis* (begun in 1878), A. writes what might be called her masterplot: because of circumstances, a talented artist forgoes her own aspirations in order to serve others.

A. wrote prodigiously until her death—"I can do two [short stories] a day and keep house between times," she commented, but her later works show marked decline. Deteriorating health caused by a mercury cure given her for typhoid and continued family responsibilities including nursing her dying mother, supporting an orphaned niece, and caring for her father continued to press her. A. died two days after her father died, the minister suggesting in a joint eulogy that even in heaven the father had need of his daughter's help. In some of A.'s works, talented women artists do find nurturance in loving female communities, but always a conflict between art and love, duty to self and duty to others, remains. A.'s writing is valuable for the varied insight it gives into these still unresolved questions.

BIBLIOGRAPHY: Elbert, S., *A Hunger for Home: L. M. A. and Little Women* (1984; rev. ed., 1987); Keyser, E. L., *Whispers in the Dark: The Fiction of L. M. A.* (1993); Payne, A. J., *L. M. A.: A Reference Guide* (1980); Saxton, M., *L. M.: A Modern Biography of L. M. A.* (1977); Stern, M. B., *L. M. A.* (1950); Stern, M., ed., *Critical Essays on L. M. A.* (1984); Strickland, C., *Victorian Domesticity: Families in the Life and Art of L. M. A.* (1985)

CAROL J. SINGLEY

ALDRICH, Thomas Bailey
b. 11 November 1836, Portsmouth, New Hampshire; d. 19 March 1907, Boston, Massachusetts

Humorist, editor, war correspondent, poet, novelist, dramatist, and essayist, A. was a prolific writer, who endeavored to emulate and to be accepted among the genteel intellectuals of Boston society. Seldom delving beyond the superficial in his works, he rarely treated issues of an ideological, sociological, or psychological nature. A. did not regard himself a realist and found Gustave Flaubert and Émile Zola especially harsh. He is best known for *The Story of a Bad Boy* (1870), a fictionalized autobiography, and "Marjorie Daw" (1873), an epistolary short story.

A.'s short stories are intricately plotted and known for their originality and humor. The author of approximately twenty-eight stories, A. is often credited with "reformulating and reapplying" Edgar Allan POE's theories and principles of the short story in his works. "Marjorie Daw" first appeared in the *Atlantic Monthly* and was regarded as a prototype for comparable works by Brander Matthews and Frank R. STOCKTON. In a series of letters, A. captivates his reading audience with the depiction of Marjorie Daw, a woman who embodies the essence of the style and grace of New York society. John Fleming is confined to his home because of illness, and, in an effort to cheer his friend, Edward Delaney soothes Fleming with news of Daw, his irresistible, fictional neighbor. After Fleming falls in love with Marjorie, he discovers, via a surprise ending, that she does not exist.

The Story of a Bad Boy is a children's novel set in Portsmouth, New Hampshire, reminiscing A.'s New England boyhood. This work was praised by William Dean HOWELLS and influenced Samuel Langhorne CLEMENS in his treatment of boys in *The Adventures of Tom Sawyer* and *Adventures of Huckleberry Finn.* In the opening sentences, A. qualifies his use of "bad boy" as just being a real human boy. Told in retrospect, the novel is a bildungsroman portraying the escapades of Tom Bailey. Bailey, the narrator, is basically a type; he functions largely to reveal A.'s attitude toward youth. Using a loosely organized episodic structure, A. chronicled his life with his grandfather Thomas Darling Bailey, alias Grandfather Nutter, in a small New England town during the middle of the 19th c. Initially, the story ran for a year in *Our Young Folks,* a magazine published in 1869. Considered lacking in theme and development, the novel is praised for its graphic detail. A.'s other novels, *Daisy's Necklace* (1857), *Prudence Palfry* (1874), *The Queen of Sheba* (1877), and *The Stillwater Tragedy* (1880), are considered weak in plot structure.

A. achieved national acclaim with the publication of his poem "The Ballad of Babie Bell," first included in the *Journal of Commerce* (1855) and reprinted in newspapers throughout the country. Most of his first poems were sentimental and contrived in form and rhyme. His lyric poetry prior to 1870 comprises his best work. A. wrote carefully constructed society verse which adhered to the tenets of the genteel tradition. Later in his career, he published fifteen volumes of poetry in addition to his first collection entitled *Poems* (1897).

BIBLIOGRAPHY: Greenslet, F., *The Life of T. B. A.* (1908); Samuels, C. E., *T. B. A.* (1966); Tarpley, J. D., "T. B. A.," in Riley, S. G., ed., *DLB*, vol. 79, *American Magazine Journalists, 1850–1900* (1988)

CHARLENE TAYLOR EVANS

ALGER, Horatio, Jr.

b. 13 January 1832, Chelsea, Massachusetts; d. 18 July 1899, Natick, Massachusetts

Few American writers enjoy the cultural cachet of A., whose more than one hundred juvenile books have been credited with defining the American myth of success. The phrase "H. A. hero" has obtained popular currency in the language as a metaphor of economic triumph. The writer's modern reputation as an apologist for capitalism was epitomized by the establishment in 1947 of the H. A. Awards, conferred annually on "living individuals who by their own efforts had pulled themselves up by their bootstraps in the American tradition."

A Phi Beta Kappa graduate of Harvard College in 1852, A. also completed a three-year course at the Harvard Divinity School in 1860. After moving to New York following his dismissal from the Unitarian ministry in 1866 on charges of pederasty, he began to earn his living exclusively as a writer. His most popular juvenile novel, *Ragged Dick; or, Street Life in New York,* was serialized in 1867 and issued as a book by the Boston publisher A. K. Loring in 1868. In it, a bootblack gradually improves his station by acquiring a rudimentary education and genteel habits, a reformation signaled by his chanting names—Ragged Dick to Dick Hunter to Richard Hunter, Esq. In this story, too, A. introduced the basic elements of his juvenile formula: a young disadvantaged hero rises form rags to middle-class respectability through the intercession of an adult patron and is given a job as well as a new suit of clothes and/or a watch in a symbolic rite of passage.

Between 1867 and 1873, at the height of his career, A. wrote a total of eighteen didactic novels, including the multivolume "Ragged Dick" and "Luck and Pluck" series of books. Never abandoning his ambition to write for adults, he also collaborated with his cousin William Rounseville Alger on the authorized biography of the actor Edwin Forrest; he published a collection of his magazine verse, *Grand'ther Baldwin's Thanksgiving with Other Ballads and Poems* in 1875; and he wrote an adult nouvelle entitled *The New Schoolma'am; or, A Summer in North Sparta,* issued without signature in 1877. These experiments were only modest critical and commercial successes, however, and in the end, A. was compelled by the demands of the literary market to specialize in juvenile writing for his livelihood. In the late 1870s, he made two trips to the West to research his more sensational "Pacific series" of stories for boys, including *Joe's Luck* (1878) and *The Young Miner* (1879), and in the early 1880s he wrote juvenile biographies of Daniel Webster, Abraham LINCOLN, and James Garfield.

A liberal Republican, A. often indicted, especially in his late fiction, corrupt business practices, unscrupulous investment, and wage-slavery. In *The Store Boy* (1883), for example, he condemned Jay Gould, James R. Keene, and other "robber barons" for manipulating the price of stock in the Union Pacific railroad for their profit, and in *Luke Walton* (1887) he endorsed usury laws to protect the working poor from loan sharks. That is, despite his modern reputation as a capitalist ideologue, A. celebrated such virtues as fidelity, honesty, and piety, and his novels may be more fairly read as moral fables prompted by humanitarian impulse whose appeal was fundamentally nostalgic than as stories of economic triumph or tools of social control wielded by an entrenched ruling class. His heroes almost never worked in factories; indeed, his settings were typically preindustrial. The evolution of A.'s reputation—from didactic writer for boys to economic mythmaker and capitalist idealogue—seems to have been dictated less by the content of his books than by the context in which they were appropriated in the 20th c.

BIBLIOGRAPHY: Bennett, B., *H. A., Jr.: A Comprehensive Bibliography* (1980); Nackenoff, C., *The Fictional Republic: H. A. and American Political Discourse* (1994); Scharnhorst, G., and J. Bales, *H. A., Jr.: An Annotated Bibliography of Comment and Criticism* (1981); Scharnhorst G., with J. Bales, *The Lost Life of H. A., Jr.* (1985)

GARY SCHARNHORST

ALGREN, Nelson

b. 28 March 1909, Detroit, Michigan; d. 9 May 1981, Sag Harbor, New York

A. wrote raw, unforgiving fiction and prose poetry that championed the down-and-out segment of America from the Great Depression through the Richard Nixon era. A latecomer to the Chicago school of American social realism, he introduced a rare slangy poetic voice, a radical sense of alienation that appealed to contemporary existentialist writers, and, occasionally, a gentle dark humor.

Although he traveled widely through America, riding boxcars through the Southwest with hobos during the Great Depression and later spending much time on the East Coast, A. lived much of his life in Chicago and his work is associated with its urban streets. He called Chicago "the most American of cities" because he believed that the social and moral forces which had shaped the nation were closest to the surface there: forces embodied by swindlers and suckers, sinners and would-be saviors, the rich and the poor—all of whom share a dual innocence and guilt. Simone de Beauvoir, with whom A. had a long, stormy affair, called him "Division Street Dostoevsky" after the street on which much of the city's vice was centered.

Most of his writing concerns characters who live in the tough Chicago neighborhoods that he too called home. He based his first novel, though, on people he met while traveling by boxcar. *Somebody in Boots* (1935) is a Marxist picaresque protest novel focusing on Cass McCay, a young man lacking education and job skills, displaced and adrift in the American social landscape of the early 1930s. A rough first novel, it nonetheless introduces concerns that would preoccupy him throughout his life's work.

After participating in the WPA Federal Writers' Project in the late 1930s, A. wrote *Never Come Morning* (1942), a novel that is rooted in the same naturalism as *Somebody in Boots,* but develops a new moral and psychological complexity. This novel, which Ernest HEMINGWAY praised as "about the best book to come out of Chicago," tells the story of Bruno Bicek, a brutal, lower-class Polish-American young man, whose own viciousness has been determined by a vicious urban environment and by the social leaders who have fostered that environment. "The source of the criminal act," A. writes in the book's preface, "is not the criminal but the righteous man: the man too complacent ever to feel that he—even *he*—belongs to those convicts and prostitutes himself."

This theme, in one form or another, dominates much of the rest of A.'s work. It is central to *The Neon Wilderness* (1947), his first collection of short stories. It is central also to his best-known novel, *The Man with the Golden Arm* (1949), a book set once again in Chicago. Telling a story of obsessive dependence involving morphine addict Franky Machine, his crippled wife Zosh and his mistress Molly, the novel extends A.'s interest in individual characters' moral and psychological conditions. Remaining solidly naturalistic in style, it dispenses with most of the sentimentalism and didacticism that inflected his earlier work. The novel won the first National Book Award and was made into a movie directed by Otto Preminger, starring Frank Sinatra.

Following this popular success, A. published a long prose poem, *Chicago: City on the Make* (1951), which addresses the city's dual history of sin and innocence, evil and good. The poem personifies Chicago as a woman with a face of chastity by day and the face of a prostitute by night. While A. views that fused personality as grounds for sharp social criticism, he also sees it as a powerful stimulus to love. The city is terribly flawed, but it is his own.

In *A Walk on the Wild Side* (1956), his last well-known novel, A. rewrites *Somebody in Boots,* replacing Cass McKay with Dove Linkhorn, eliminating the Marxist rhetoric, and introducing a strong strain of dark humor. In critical opinion, the book is a mixed success: while some have seen it as a masterpiece opposing 1950s social conformity, others have faulted it for departing from realism and developing overblown characters. This book, too, was made into a movie.

The decade between 1947 and 1956 saw the publication of much of A.'s best and most important work. Later, he published travel accounts and short stories. Just before his death, he completed a new novel, *The Devil's Stocking* (1983), about the boxer Rubin "Hurricane" Carter who was railroaded into a conviction on homicide charges.

During the twenty-five years that followed the publication of *A Walk on the Wild Side,* A. suffered a diminution in popularity and reputation, partially rectified in the last year of his life by his election to the American Academy of Arts and Letters and posthumously by the republication of his works.

BIBLIOGRAPHY: Bruccoli, M. J., *N. A.: A Descriptive Bibliography* (1985); Cox, M. H., and W. Chatterton, *N. A.* (1975); Drew, B., *N. A.: A Walk on the Wild Side* (1989); Shay, A., *N. A.'s Chicago* (1988)

MICHAEL WILEY

ALLEN, [William] Hervey [Jr.]

b. 8 December 1889, Pittsburgh, Pennsylvania; d. 28 December 1949, Coconut Grove, Florida

Educated at the U.S. Naval Academy and the University of Pittsburgh, A. was seriously wounded in World War I. Settling in Charleston, South Carolina, in 1919, he met DuBose HEYWARD, and they, along with Ohio-born John Bennett, established the influential Poetry Society of South Carolina, one of the earliest manifestations of the Southern Literary Renaissance.

After graduate study at Harvard from 1920 to 1922, A. returned to Charleston to teach high school English. He later lectured on American literature at Columbia University and Vassar College and on modern poetry at Bread Loaf. He served also on the original staff of *Saturday Review.*

A devotee of the works of Edgar Allan POE, A. published *Israfel: The Life and Times of Edgar Allan Poe* (2 vols., 1926) and, with renowned Poe scholar Thomas Ollive Mabbott, *Poe's Brother* (1926). While these books have been surpassed by more recent biographies, they are still recognized as important contributions to Poe scholarship.

Anthony Adverse, a picaresque romance and A.'s best-known work, appeared in 1933. Until the publication of Margaret MITCHELL's *Gone with the Wind* three years later, *Anthony Adverse* had been the best-selling novel of the decade.

A.'s output was significant and varied. His other writings include collections of poetry, *Ballads of the Border* (1916), *Wampum and Old Gold* (1921), *The Bride of Huitzal* (1922), *Carolina Chansons* (1922, with DuBose Heyward), *Earth Moods* (1925), *New*

Legends (1929), and *Sarah Simon* (1929); the novels *Action at Aquila* (1938), *It Was like This* (1940), *The Forest and the Fort* (1943), *Bedford Village* (1944), *Toward the Morning* (1948), and *The City in the Dawn* (1950, published posthumously); and the autobiographical *Toward the Flame* (1926), and account of his military service during World War I.

A. was a trustee of the University of Miami and a member of the National Institute of Arts and Letters, as well as Great Britain's Royal Society of Arts. Although his writings are little read nowadays, he was during his lifetime regarded as a significant voice in American literature. Perhaps a trifle too elegant for contemporary tastes, A.'s style is lyrical and graceful, reminiscent of the literature of an earlier age.

BIBLIOGRAPHY: Hart, P. L., "H. A.," in Quartermain, P., ed., *DLB,* vol. 45, *American Poets, 1880–1945* (1986): 23–26; Rubin, L., Jr., *The Curious Death of the Novel: Essays in American Literature* (1967)

HARRY MCBRAYER BAYNE

ALLEN, James Lane

b. 21 December 1849, Lexington, Kentucky; d. 18 February 1925, New York City

Popular in his lifetime as the producer of a body of literature portraying the Kentucky of his birth as the home of contented slaves and gentle masters, A. is sometimes seen as one more purveyor of decayed romanticism about the South. However, a second look shows this assessment to be overly simplistic. For example, he published for each tale of life on the old plantation a corresponding historical sketch that attempts to put the story into perspective. The tales are collected in *Flute and Violin* (1891), and the sketches in *The Blue Grass Region of Kentucky* (1892). A. insisted that the Kentucky aristocrats he pictured were not merely idealistic fantasies but very real types, and that it was the duty of the historian to record them faithfully. But although he regarded this view of Kentucky as no more than accurate, he was well aware of the weakness in an unalloyed romantic view of life. In his fiction, A. sometimes achieves an expert balance between realism and romance; sometimes he fails, and lapses into sentimentalism.

Probably his best novel, *A Kentucky Cardinal* (1894), is the love story of Adam Moss and Georgiana Cobb. She watches from her window as he works in his garden, but she is decidedly not a dreamy Southern belle. Adam, not Georgiana, is the dreamy idealist. He tames the birds to his hand; he is an admirer of Henry David THOREAU. Georgiana, on the other hand, admires John James Audubon, who killed the birds to study them. The climax of the story comes when Georgiana hints that, as a love-test, Adam might cage a cardinal for her, which has come to trust him. He does so, and the bird dies. Adam suffers a remorse and revulsion of feeling toward Georgiana that drive them apart, but Georgiana refuses to apologize. She says she never meant for the bird actually to be caged; she had just wanted Adam's assurance that he cared more for her than for his birds. In the end, their passion for each other tells, and they decide to marry; however, the final words of the novel reveal Adam's deep uneasiness and foreboding, and achieve for the author a delicate balance between the possible oversweetness of a love story set in a garden and the possibly sinister facts of real life. Unfortunately, after this skillful balancing act, the sequel novel, *Aftermath* (1895), sinks the story to a bathetic ending.

One of A.'s best short stories is "Miss Locke" (1925), strongly reminiscent of Henry JAMES's "The Beast in the Jungle," with its theme of the deceptive and destructive power of idealistic obsession—A.'s novel *The Nettle of the Pasture* (1903) has also been called Jamesian, for its intense scrutiny of character. In "Miss Locke," a jaded old woman advises the young Gridley, who is caught in such an obsession, that life is not like the opposite banks of a river: a bank of the actual on which we stand, and a bank of the ideal to which we gaze across. Life is the river itself, with the actual and ideal inextricably commingled. A. attempts in his fiction to mingle actual and ideal faithfully, and sometimes, in his best work, he succeeds.

BIBLIOGRAPHY: Bottorff, W. K., *J. L. A.* (1964); Knight, G. C., *J. L. A. and the Genteel Tradition* (1935)

CECELIA LAMPP LINTON

ALLEN, Woody
b. 1 December 1935, Brooklyn, New York

Hailed as a premier funny man in the 1960s, former joke-writer and stand-up comedian, A. has become one of America's most thoughtful humorists and astute observers of contemporary life in literature and film. Born Allen Stewart Konigsberg in Flatbush, Brooklyn and reared in a religious Jewish home, A. disliked Midwood High School and enrolled for only two college courses; these he seldom attended and never completed. His early experiences left him skeptical of both organized religion and organized education; however, he respects genuine "religious sensibility," and he is an avid, disciplined reader, especially of philosophy.

A. is best known for his award-winning comic and seriocomic films that portray the trials of anxious nebbish characters suffering various identity crises in urban settings; however, he honed his screenwriting skills as a joke-writer, essayist, playwright, and short story writer. A. is the author of two long-running Broadway plays, *Don't Drink the Water* (1967) and *Play It Again, Sam* (1969); his darker drama *The Floating Lightbulb* (1982) was presented at Lincoln Center in New York. A.'s essays and short stories have appeared in the *New Yorker,* the *New Republic, Playboy,* the *Evergreen Review,* and the *Kenyon Review.* A number of A.'s essays, short stories, and short plays such as "God" and "Death" have been collected in *Getting Even* (1971), *Without Feathers* (1975), and *Side Effects* (1980).

"The Metterling Lists," "Selections from the A. Notebooks," "The Whore of Mensa," and other writings of the 1960s and 1970s established A. as a gifted parodist in a variety of genres. While the earliest pieces, like his first films, are frequently elaborate jokes, born out of his beginnings as a stand-up comic and writer of one-liners, subsequent pieces such as "The Kugelmass Episode" are distinguished—as are his films after *Annie Hall*—by a greater concern for characterization, narrative technique, and thematic depth. A. claims his work is more psychological and philosophical than political; all his work, he says, has to do with love, death, and the meaning of life.

A. has been accused of narcissism and insularity because of the apparently self-confessional, autobiographical quality of his writings and films that often feature middle-class New Yorkers like himself, and of being too self-deprecating in the depiction of his central, beleaguered characters; however, he insists that although he writes about what he knows, his characters are fictional. His conscience-ridden "schlemiels" who manage to survive are indebted to Jewish humor as well as to the American "little man" comic tradition of *New Yorker* humorists such as Robert BENCHLEY and S. J. PERELMAN, who created ordinary people perplexed by the ambiguities and indeterminacies of modern living. A.'s texts extend and modify the traditions, reflecting a postmodern critical sensibility to language and context; they intermingle self-conscious artifice, dense intertextual references, and other metafictional devices with "realistic" images of everyday life. A. frequently produces reflexive, surreal effects that combine the pleasures of transparent storytelling with defamiliarization and deconstruction. Although his early films and writings contained sexist jokes and one-dimensional female figures, his work increasingly involves more complex female characters and female perspectives.

A.'s most recent writings and films are not simply parodic; they are less concerned with debunking history than with understanding the importance of memory and the past. They frequently humanize and dramatize the philosophical dialogues between moral relativity and ethical choice, subjectivity and meaning, loyalty and betrayal, innocence and sophistication (or decadence), freedom and determinism that A. once only joked about. Since the 1970s, A. has shown signs of becoming a profound humorist in the manner of the later Charlie Chaplin or Mark TWAIN; his texts combine the comic and the pathetic; they question how integrity and humanity can survive amid dehumanizing conditions; they put popular audiences in touch not only with personal anxieties but with the fundamental issues and absurdities of their times.

BIBLIOGRAPHY: Adler, B., and J. Feinman, *W. A.: Clown Prince of American Humor* (1975); Brode, D., *W. A.: His Films and Career* (1985); Hirsch, F., *Love, Sex, Death and the Meaning of Life* (1981); Lax, E., *On Being Funny: W. A. and Comedy* (1975); Lax, E., *W. A.: A Biography* (1991); Pogel, N., *W. A.* (1987); Yacowar, M., *Loser Take All: The Comic Art of W. A.* (1979; rev. ed., 1991)

NANCY POGEL

ALMANACS AND YEARBOOKS

The tendency to approach American popular culture with the same degree of seriousness that American literature has traditionally been approached mounts yearly in current literary scholarship. But this tendency has not yet extended to include any major scholarly or pedagogical attention to one phenomenon of contemporary popular print culture in the U.S. that rivals tabloids and romance novels in popularity: the yearly editions of the *Old Farmer's Almanac,* the oldest continuously published almanac in America, which has a current readership of over nine million, not to mention the *Farmer's Almanac,* the *Readers Digest Almanac,* and about a dozen other major contemporary U.S. almanacs.

Contemporary almanacs are descended from the enhanced calendars—supplemented with astrological data, prognostications, and other quotidia—that date back to the 15th c. in northern European culture, to classical and neoclassical antiquity in ancient Greece and Rome, and at least to the reign of Ramses II around 1200 B.C.E. in even-more-ancient northern African culture. The literary study of almanacs and yearbooks in the U.S. is slight, and thus far has been confined mainly to the study of almanacs produced in the 17th and 18th cs. in the British colonies of North America and the early U.S. During this period, almanacs—along with early newspapers, sermons, and accounts of European colonists held captive by Indians—were the early American equivalent of mass media.

Considering the contemporaneous popularity of early American almanacs, as well as the efforts of early American literary scholarship to keep pace with other American area studies in expanding and democratizing the early American literary canon, it is somewhat surprising that early American almanacs have enjoyed almost no scholarly attention—especially in contrast to attention paid to so-called captivity narratives. Of course early almanacs were quintessentially ephemeral, literally designed for obsolescence, and so of course no formal and institutional efforts efforts were made to preserve almanacs by the 17th-and 18th-c. readers who consumed them so avidly, nor even by almanac makers, for whom their own achievements, at the moment these achievements were completed and published, instantly lost all value.

The ephemerality of early American almanacs represents no necessary or significant barrier to modern scholarship, however; so many 17th- and 18th-c. American almanacs were printed that a relatively large sampling of them survives, especially relative to the scarcity of surviving early editions of so-called captivity narratives. Having been "read to death" (a phrase that recurs in virtually all contemporary studies of early American accounts of Indian captivity, less as a hindrance than as an inducement to ever greater contemporary scholarly efforts somehow to restore the early accounts of captivity), early American almanacs would seem at least potentially an attractive subject for more current scholars eager to get beneath records of the official culture of early America—voluminously and carefully preserved, especially in the New England colonies—to discover glimmers of ordinary colonial American lives. The only trace that has been found to date of the first edition of Mary ROWLANDSON's 1692 account of her captivity among the Algonquins during King Phillip's War in Massachusetts Bay Colony is a tiny fragment, which happened to survive only because it was ripped out and recycled as a book-cover for what was clearly considered at the time far more worthy of preservation: a copy of the 18th-c. Puritan minister Samuel Willard's sermon, "Covenant Keeping." The uncertain provenance of Rowlandson's text extends to doubts about its authenticity, since, as the wife of a minister and as a prime candidate for the early American Puritan's meticulously Protestant version of sainthood, her account was almost certainly silently vetted by others, others who were almost certainly more pious, who were certainly more formally educated, and who were incontestably male; it can also inspire legitimate questions even over its original title. None of this has prevented Rowlandson's captivity narrative from becoming currently the most widely read, the most widely studied, and the most widely anthologized text of early American popular print culture.

The earliest almanac known to have been produced in English in the new world was compiled in 1638 and was to be the first printing of the press at Harvard College: *An Almanac for New England for the Year 1639*. Attributed to "William Pearce, Mariner," it inaugurated the yearly appearance, until nearly the end of the 18th c., of almanacs produced by Harvard graduates, self-styled "philomaths," whose almanacs by the middle of the 17th c. in the British colonies of North America would be distinguished by their "pedantry." Miscellaneous materials in the Harvard almanacs were restricted solely to the subjects of natural philosophy—what would today be called science—and religion. Virtually no preeminence has been granted to this series in contemporary American literary scholarship, probably because the earliest series contains little evidence of what is commonly assumed by this scholarship to be a new, distinctively American, character—that is, the greater secular-mindedness, in particular the irreverence, that emerges in later 17th- and 18th-c. almanacs in Massachusetts Bay and Pennsylvania colonies.

Well known today among later American almanacs are those inaugurated by Daniel Leeds in Philadelphia in 1687 and by Nathaniel Ames in Dedham, Massachusetts Bay Colony, in 1725. Leeds, calling himself "a student of Agriculture," was perhaps deliberately distinguishing his almanacs as a more democratic alternative to those of the Harvard "philomaths," and both Leeds's and Ames's series certainly contained plenty of practical, in addition to educational, and also entertaining, in addition to edifying, marginalia. The most famous early almanac maker by far for posterity would be "Richard Saunders" or "Poor Richard," better known as Benjamin FRANKLIN, whose *Poor Richard's Almanack* began publishing in 1733 in Philadelphia by feeding off the nearly half-century's success of the Leeds series. Franklin's almanac remained the greatest rival of the Leeds series in Pennsylvania Colony and would eventually, long after its competition with the Leeds series becomes a footnote of publishing history, become the most famous almanac of all time. Although vastly overshadowed by the *Memoirs* and by other occasional writings—in particular the "Articles of Faith and Principles of Religion" and the speech before the Constitutional Convention—at least a token one or two of "Poor Richard's" proverbs, originally published in the almanac, usually make it into the Franklin section of contemporary anthologies of American literature.

It is doubtful that almanacs will ever attain the status of captivity narratives in the modern scholarship of early American literature, mainly because the challenges with which early American almanacs confront modern scholarship—uncertain attribution, slipshod production, apparently baffling heterogeneity, and, last but not least, only sporadic efforts to differentiate themselves as containing some authentically American improvements on their European models—are not balanced by sufficient promise of the opportunity to discover in them at least hints of the indigenously American; there is no equivalent in early American almanacs of those famous representations—no matter how scant proportionately, how corrupted by European prejudice, nor how narratively underdeveloped—of the early encounters of European explorers, conquerors, and settlers with America's virgin land and its aboriginal inhabitants that have made the captivity narratives such a cynosure of early American literary scholarship.

Maybe the only hope today of mainstreaming early American almanacs in the prevailing currents of early American culture for modern retrospect lies in somehow redefining those prevailing currents, and thereby converting what seem now the deficiencies of early American almanacs into advantages. There may be some future, for example, in recuperating the anonymous and polynomial status of early American almanac makers as more than a stigma of the primitive conditions of early American almanac production. Perhaps uncertain attribution can be connected to an anonymity, or a paleonymity, that dates back to the times of medieval craftsmen, and that may signify a very unfamiliar underlying conception of selfhood, so strange a conception to a modern retrospect immersed in a culture of self as to seem the absence of any real conception of selfhood whatsoever.

For example, there was Benjamin West, known also as the borrowed, Swiftian "Isaac Bickerstaff," an obscure Massachusetts Bay almanac maker who allowed his individuality to dissolve not only in the rough-and-tumble commercial role of almanac maker, but also in the much more refined, scientific, dignified role of contributor to international learned societies. During two major collective astronomical efforts, the first mounted in 1769 to observe the passage of the planet Venus across the sun, the second mounted in 1781 to observe the eclipse of the sun, West set aside his primary employment as almanac maker to write accounts of both the transit and the eclipse—both of which have been conclusively attributed by modern scholarship to West's hand alone. But West's individuality in these two writings is as obscure as it is in his almanacs, and in these two more formal writings much more explicitly obscure, in continual reminders that individuality must defer—that individuality is fundamentally antagonistic—to a power that might seem beside the point in the midst of West's apparently purely secular literary and scientific labors. Not only does West take pains always modestly to minimize the individual significance of his own astrological achievements—they will attain value only when combined with countless other anonymous indistinguishable achievements of countless other anonymous indistinguishable observers—he betrays an almost Puritan ministerial fastidiousness about regularly reminding natural philosophers like himself and his readers that no amount of experiential justification of the works of God to man is sufficient to convert sinners, which, properly to be considered a miracle, must be left to God's supernatural work alone.

Maybe when a regularity joining the piety of early American religious writers to the non-authoritative authorship of early American almanac makers is seen to evidence a main current of early American culture—a single, massive, integral, strange *episteme*—then, perhaps, almanacs will be taken up by the modern scholarship of early American literature. However, although partisans of the new when seeking new world innovations in early American literature, most contemporary scholars of early American literature remain very skeptical of innovations in the theorizing of their subject; Northrop Frye, pondering the related issue of the timeliness of literary theoretical change in general, predicted that those who seek it will have to wait a long time.

BIBLIOGRAPHY: Drake, M., *Almanacs of the United States* (1962); Levernier, J. A., et. al, eds., *American Writers before 1800* (1983); Sagendorph, R. H., *America and Her Almanacs* (1970); Stowell, M. B., *Early American Almanacs: The Colonial Weekly Bible* (1977)

R. C. DE PROSPO

ALVAREZ, Julia
b. 27 March 1950, New York City

A. is one of a number of culturally diverse female writers in the U.S. to achieve critical acclaim and popular success in the late 20th c. Drawing on her native homeland, the Dominican Republic, A. weaves fact and fiction and the political and the personal to create the vivid plots and passionate characters in her much celebrated novels, *How the García Girls Lost Their Accents* (1991), *In the Time of the Butterflies* (1994), and *¡Yo!* (1997).

A. gained national recognition with the publication of her first novel, *How the García Girls Lost Their Accents,* a series of fifteen loosely autobiographical interconnected stories that narrate the lives of four Dominican adolescent sisters forced for political reasons to migrate to the U.S. in the 1960s. With the return of the youngest sister, Yolanda García, to the Dominican Republic, *How the García Girls Lost Their Accents* begins in the adult present and moves back in time lyrically unfolding the poignant and often humorous experiences of each young woman coming of age. Winner of the 1991 PEN Oakland/Josephine Miles Book Award for works that present a multicultural perspective, *How the García Girls Lost Their Accents* captures what it means to be growing up in two culturally distinct worlds.

Nominated for the 1995 National Book Critics Circle Award, *In the Time of the Butterflies* affirmed A. as a popular transnational novelist. *In the Time of the Butterflies* is based on the 1960 historical account of the Mirabal sisters, four strong and defiant young rebels who risked their lives to overturn the thirty-one-year-old regime of Trujillo, the Dominican Republic's notorious dictator. A. crawls into the minds and hearts of these four unique spirits, whose political name was Las Mariposas (The Butterflies), and skillfully invents the details of their lives. Emotional, vibrant, and stunning, *In the Time of the Butterflies* speaks of the dangers of oppression and empowers both men and women of all cultures.

¡Yo!, a sequel to *How the García Girls Lost Their Accents,* centers around the character of Yolanda García—"Yo" is short for Yolanda and translated as "I" in Spanish—and is presumably modeled after A.'s own life. Yolanda is a writer who has just received widespread recognition for her novels, which are based on the lives of her Dominican family, and everyone is in an uproar. From her mother who wants to file a lawsuit to her former lovers, husbands, writing teacher, and landlady, everyone has a story to tell about the independent female writer who had entered and touched their lives in some significant way. Playful and poignant, poetic and passionate, *¡Yo!* blurs the lines between fact and fiction; it is a modern-day portrait of the artist as a young woman.

A. has also published several collections of poetry: *Homecoming* (1984), *The Housekeeping Book* (1984), and *The Other Side* (1994). A.'s themes include the Latina experience in the U.S.; the immigrant's return to the native homeland; woman's value and self-empowerment; and the sensuality and intimacy of love. A., however, is recognized most for her fiction. Both *How the García Girls Lost Their Accents* and *In the Time of the Butterflies* have been translated into A.'s native Spanish.

BIBLIOGRAPHY: Miller, S., "Caught between Two Cultures," *Newsweek* 20 April 1992: 78-79; Oliver, B., "From Tangents to Trespasses," *NER* 15 (Summer 1993): 208–12

SALINDA LEWIS

AMERICAN ADAM

The term "American Adam" refers to a mythic concept considered by some critics and scholars to be the central, definitive element of American literature. Its fundamental premise is based on the view of European colonists who saw the New World not only as a haven from religious persecution but also as a metaphoric garden, a latter day Eden. For these early colonists, heavily influenced by their belief in the Judeo-Christian Bible as a divinely ordained guide for human behavior, their sojourn to the New World was gradually perceived as a sort of spiritual "second chance." This second garden offered a new beginning, free of the collective error that had pervaded the world since the failure of the first spiritual experiment in that original garden where Adam had succumbed to evil and lost his innocence.

By the late 18th c., the religious premise of the Adamic myth had largely given way to a more general metaphor, one that suggested a distinctively heroic entity thought to be the quintessence of the American character—the American in dramatic contrast to his European forebears. In his *Letters from an American Farmer,* J. Hector St. Jean de CRÈVECOEUR defined this new inhabitant of the New World not as a European expatriate exiled to a distant colony, but as an *American,* "a new man" who acts upon new principles; he must therefore entertain new ideas and form new opinions. In Europe, the legacy had been "involuntary idleness, servile dependence, penury and useless labor"; America offered "toils of a very different nature, rewarded by ample subsistence." This view of man set down by providence in a garden of agrarian independence, of a freshly minted American characterized by virtuous promise and self-reliance, became the foundation of the Adamic myth.

An allusive figure, one not definitively expressed anywhere in American literature, the American Adam is nonetheless an intrinsic part of American cultural tradition. In his earliest form, he is the optimistic innocent exemplified by Ralph Waldo EMERSON, Henry David THOREAU, and Walt WHITMAN. He is the authentic man, the figure referred to by Emerson as "the plain old Adam, the simple genuine self against the whole world." Free of the constraints of the past and of limitations imposed by centuries of tradition, he is centered on the future and the promise inherent in the very "newness" of America. At the same time, that determining innocence is the very heart of his vulnerability. Innocence by its very nature cannot maintain its pristine condition, and the innocence of the American Adam is inevitably shaped and altered by experience. This confrontation of Adamic innocence with transforming experience is at the core of the works of Nathaniel HAWTHORNE, Herman MELVILLE, Stephen CRANE, William FAULKNER, and Ernest HEMINGWAY.

Emerson succinctly expressed this innocence/experience dichotomy in what he termed the "party of Hope" and the "party of Memory," and was an articulate advocate for the former. In America, according to the "Hope" credo, man has begun anew, facing forward to a bright future from the perspective of an optimistic present. Most notably, he is free of the enduring legacy of original sin. Sin for Emerson was not a burdensome spiritual reality; it was a subjective concept: "the evils of the world are such only to the evil eye." On the other hand stood the party of Memory. In their most extreme form, they held to the adamant Calvinist orthodoxy that sin and corruption remained intrinsic to the heritage of humanity. Melville, among others, took issue with Emerson's somewhat ingenuous view. In his reading of *Spiritual Laws,* Melville noted in his own copy of Emerson's essay the author's admonition to "trust men and they will be true to you." In the margin, the author of *Moby-Dick* appended: "God help the poor fellow who squares his life according to this." Melville was philosophically somewhere between the party of Memory and what R. W. B. Lewis, in his definitive study of the American Adam, identifies as a third party, the party of Irony. This third party held to a certain tragic optimism, a paradox that maintained the view that a unique spiritual strength can arise from the inevitable clash of innocence with experience, if only as an object lesson for the reader.

For idealists of the party of Hope such as Emerson, Thoreau, and Whitman, experience remained only the gray shadow of reality intermittently threatening to overshadow the bright vision of a future unencumbered by the past. If the new Adam could keep his perspective fresh and new, free of the traditional and conventional, he would come into full possession of authentic existence. No one followed this course with greater commitment than Emerson's most famous disciple, Henry David Thoreau. In the experiment that became *Walden,* Thoreau's masterpiece, the author became a literal Adam, leaving Concord to enter the more edenic surroundings of Walden Pond. There in solitude he was determined to "live deliberately, to confront only the essentials of life." From Emerson, Thoreau had learned to reject tradition and historical Christianity, and to look instead to natural surroundings, to the nature of things that had not yet been encroached upon by civilization. Although he remained quite deliberately within hearing distance of the Concord Clock tower and had built his small cabin only a short walk from the railroad tracks that connected Boston with Fitchburg, Thoreau effectively distanced himself from the corrupting influences that he believed characterized 19th-c. New England. His purpose was not to ignore them, but to supplant them with rediscovered values of greater importance. Unlike its old testament predecessor, the garden of *Walden* imposed no restrictions on partaking of the tree of knowledge. In establishing his own eden in proximity to the genteel, conventional civilization of Concord, Thoreau suggests that the essential innocence of the new American Adam can be both recovered and maintained by genuine introspection, by discovery and examination of the essentials of life that are inherent in both human nature and the nature of wilderness. *Walden,* which begins with the limitations imposed on personal freedom by such conventions as property and the responsibilities of ownership, ends with the coming of spring, marking the new dawn that awaits the enlightened Adam.

In poetry, Whitman, the primary representative of Emerson's party of Hope, not only felt this sense of affirmation, he lived it. Where Thoreau recognized that some (perhaps many) might not respond to his call for an awakening, Whitman's subjective view seemed to allow for no such consideration. All negatives became positives for this personification of the American Adam who moved with total confidence through a world in which the new dawn of promise became an unending sunny day. In poems such as "I Sing the Body Electric," part of the *Children of Adam* series, Whitman celebrates innocent, natural, and seemingly unlimited virtue and vitality. This state is not a recovery of primal perfection, since in Whitman's subjectively ordained cosmos there is no fall to recover from. Man is self-created in the present, and exults in the perfection of his innocent, confident creation. He inhabits a universe in which beauty and human energy are the one enduring truth.

Such optimistic idealism could not withstand the progress and growth of a new nation. Whitman's vision of unassailable innocence was gradually dispelled by the experience and reality of what America had become and perhaps always was. The late-19th-c. American Adam frequently began his journey in innocent optimism; just as frequently it ended in tragic frustration. Crane's Henry Fleming in *The Red Badge of Courage* moves innocently and confidently forward into battle only to have his enthusiasm and his idealism destroyed by the traumatic experience of war. The Adamic illusion is abruptly dispelled by the sudden awareness of his own animalism, which reflexively turns him from the virtue of courage to the instinct of self-preservation. The title character of Frank NORRIS's *McTeague,* a brutish innocent who has instinctively moved west with the growth of the nation, finds himself trapped by civilization and progress in San Francisco, where the westward movement had come to a decisive end. McTeague is an aberrant Adam, a crea-

ture of nature overwhelmed by the modern world where his descent ends in murder. More intuitive than intelligent, he seeks to escape but cannot find direction. Ironically, he dies on the arid floor of Death Valley, fleeing civilization and seeking the sanctuary of a primitive world, a figurative lost garden.

In the 20th c., the Adamic figure without locus or direction, the innocent battered by experience, has become a definitive mainstay of American literature; Hemingway's Nick Adams, Ralph ELLISON's nameless protagonist in *Invisible Man,* and J. D. SALINGER's Holden Caulfield in *Catcher in the Rye* are among the more prominent. Perhaps the most poignant of the Adamic figures who illustrate Lewis's party of tragic optimism is F. Scott FITZGERALD's Jay Gatsby in *The Great Gatsby,* who struggles to keep alive the incorruptible dream of primal innocence even as he is overwhelmed by a world of corruption and moral cynicism.

BIBLIOGRAPHY: Chase, R. V., *The American Novel and Its Tradition* (1957); Gunn, G., "The Myth of The American Adam," in Dorsone, R. M., ed., *Handbook of American Folklore* (1983): 79–85; Lewis, R. W. B., *The American Adam: Innocence, Tragedy, and Tradition in the Nineteenth Century* (1955); Smith, H. N., *Virgin Land: The American West as Symbol and Myth* (1950); York, A. D., "From Biblical Adam to the American Adam: Evolution of a Literary Type," *UDR* 21 (Spring 1992): 103–24

RICHARD KEENAN

AMMONS, A[rchie] R[andolf]
b. 18 February 1926, Whiteville, North Carolina

Of the major American poets coming into maturity since World War II, A. is among the most prolific and comprehensive. He is known for his vision, his careful attention to the concrete world, his boldly experimental forms, his whimsy, and his penetrating examination of the epistemological, scientific, and philosophical issues of the postmodern era. A.'s prominence came late in his career: the National Book Award in 1973 and 1993, the Bolingen Prize 1973–74, a MacArthur Prize in 1981, and a National Book Critics Circle Award in 1981. He is a master of the short lyric, the narrative, comic verse, parodies, experimental forms, and long philosophical poems. His work explores our relationship with the natural world, the role of language and art, the desire for absolutes, and the mysteries of identity, entropy, and ecology.

A. is a nature poet with a scientist's eye for minutiae. He was reared on a pinewoods farm in eastern North Carolina, later studied science at Wake Forest, attended the University of California at Berkeley, and from 1952 to 1961 was an executive for a biologic glassware firm. A.'s detailed observation of nature is unrivaled. He often focuses on peripheries: weeds, gulches, desert places, bugs, and garbage. His precise visual notations are combined with verbal virtuosity into philosophical inquiries of the natural world. His subject matter is often the quotidian, from which he seeks not transcendence but the lessons of stones and the example of nature's whirlwind into nothingness.

A.'s first book, *Ommateum with Doxology* (1955), was highly structured, rhetorical, and melodramatic. He assumed the stance of a lonely figure, Ezra, seeking transcendence but ignored by the indifferent wind and sand. With *Expressions of Sea Level* (1963), *Corson's Inlet* (1965), and *Northfield Poems* (1966), A. changed direction. He examined the complex interdependence of humanity and nature and our limited comprehension of nature but refused to draw distinctions between objective and subjective realities, saying, "in nature there are few sharp lines." In these books, gathered into *Collected Poems, 1951–1971* (1972), A. avoids seeking order, seeking instead "to fasten into order englarging grasps of disorder," acknowledging that his vision will be incomplete and that he will have to begin again.

During this same period, A. began to experiment with form, voice, and tone, especially in long poems. *Tape for the Turn of the Year* (1965) was an experimental long poem composed on adding machine tape as a poetic journal from December 6, 1963, to January 10, 1964. In this poem, as in his other long poems, A. exhibits a dizzying variety of voices and moods, rapidly cutting from slang to epistemology, testing the reader's tolerance of unpoetic material and then opening out exquisitely into what Helen Vendler calls the "mind of the universe." *Garbage* (1993), a major poem like William Carlos WILLIAMS's *Patterson* and T. S. ELIOT's *The Waste Land,* tallies up the 20th c. by examining our detritus and finding not just decay and meaninglessness but a regenerative and spiritual power that promises meaning in the 21st. A.'s other long poems include *Sphere: The Form of a Motion* (1974), *The Snow Poems* (1977), and *Six Piece Suite* (1978), as well as "Pray without Ceasing," "Essay on Poetics," "Extremes and Moderation," and "Hibernaculum," collected into *Selected Longer Poems* (1980), plus "The Ridge Farm," in *Sumerian Vistas* (1987), and "Summer Place," in *Brink Road* (1996).

A.'s free verse lines are usually enjambed, running over stanzas and even larger segments such as cantos. He has made the colon his trademark, like Emily DICKINSON's dash, and his use of dialect, ribaldry, slang, complex scientific jargon, and syntactical ambiguity characterize his expansive poetics.

BIBLIOGRAPHY: Bloom, H., ed., *A. R. A.* (1986); Holder, A., *A. R. A.* (1978); Schneider, S., *A. R. A. and Poetics of Widening Scope* (1994); Vendler, H., *The Music of What Happens* (1988)

NEWTON SMITH

ANAYA, Rudolfo [Alfonso]
b. 30 October 1937, Pastura, New Mexico

In twenty-five years of writing fiction that reflects his Chicano heritage, A. has achieved both a national and regional reputation as a writer who explores the magic in realism. He writes out of his own early life on the plains of Pastura, New Mexico and later in the city of Albuquerque. Critics express some ambivalence about A.'s mixture of fantasy and realism, yet acknowledge that his novels, especially his first and most widely acclaimed novel, *Bless Me, Ultima* (1972), resemble the contemporary American novel in the realistic treatment of his characters and their sense of their history and place.

In his trilogy of the 1970s, consisting of *Bless Me, Ultima, Heart of Atzlan* (1976), and *Tortuga* (1979), A. narrates the attachment of his characters to the land and to the myths and legends of New Mexico and creates shamanlike figures—Ultima, Crispin, and Salomon respectively—who guide a young boy toward a maturity that encompasses a vision of reconciliation and harmony. In his first novel, described as romance by one critic, seven-year-old Antonio Juan Marez y Luna, learns lessons in life from Ultima, an old curandera or healer who comes to live with the family. In rapid succession, Antonio experiences the brutality of men and women against each other, the horror of evil embodied in the Trementino family, doubts about his traditional Catholic faith, and death. Ultima's presence offers him a vision of the myth of pastoral stability that assaulted by the chaotic mass culture of the outside world can offset the effect of World War II on his brothers and the loss of harmony among people. With the death of Ultima, Antonio follows not his father's wish that he become a free-spirited vaquero or his mother's wish that he lead the quiet agricultural life. Instead, he turns to art in the form of the writing of the recurring clashes between good and evil that he witnesses in the history and myths of New Mexico.

In *Heart of Atzlan,* the Chavez family for financial reasons must sell their land in Guadalupe and move to the Albuquerque barrio of Barelas where the once solid family begins to disintegrate. The father and one son follow the path shown by Crispin, a mystical poet with a magical blue guitar, to work among the unemployed Chicanos of their community. In *Tortuga,* Salomon, a wise, shamanlike figure, introduces the crippled young narrator to the magic mountain whose recuperative waters are piped to the patients in the hospital. The connection between land and patients restores them to health within A.'s magical-mythical vision.

As these novels extol the individual and collective necessity for relationship to land, A.'s four novels of the 1990s—*Alburquerque* [sic] (1992); *Zia Summer* (1995); *Rio Grande Fall* (1996); and *Jalamanta: A Message from the Desert* (1996)—focus on the city as a place where people must forge loving and spiritual relationships with each other like the people's connection with the land depicted earlier. In these urban-based novels, A. still creates the fantastic figures and symbols of New Mexican folklore and Native American mythology to function side by side with the "real" characters that act out the conflict between ethnic diversity and expanded urbanization and the pastoral cultural purity of village life. However, *Alburquerque, Zia Summer,* and *Rio Grande Fall,* the latter two narrated in the form of detective fiction, rely more on plotting than on the kind of characterization that would signify how to make solid relationships in an environment of bigotry, materialism, and power struggles. In *Alburquerque,* it is the artist Abran Chavez, the new Chicano, born of the Mexican father and Anglo mother, who will draw the two worlds together to express artistically a common ground for community within the diversity of ethnic heritage that threatens to tear apart not only a city but by implication the U.S. In *Jalamanta,* the protagonist, emerging from a thirty-year exile in an unnamed desert, returns unrepentant, still trying to convey his message of how to create harmony among urban people. A.'s attempted articulation of Jalamanta's philosophy to the city's people is so dense that the novel lacks dramatic tension.

Winner of a Kellogg Foundation Fellowship (1984), A. composed his travel notes on China into a journal, *A Chicano in China* (1986), in which he claims to have connected his own rural cultural background with that of the Chinese. As a short story writer and compiler of Hispanic tales and legends, he has gained a reputation as a developer of Chicano literary history. His best-known short story, "B. Traven is Alive and Well in Cuernavaca," is collected in *Cuentos Chicanos* (1984). His collection of ten stories entitled *The Silence of the Llano* (1982), which includes selections from his first three novels, not only connects their themes with those in his short stories, but also continues his fictional exploration of Christian, Mexican, and Mayan sources of belief and myth and of the universal riddles of adolescence, marriage and family, and rituals surrounding death. A.'s works highlight the challenge of a visionary writer like himself emerging from a traditional culture and translating that vision

to both everyday circumstances and storytelling systems.

BIBLIOGRAPHY: Sharma, R. S., "Interview with R. A.," *PrS* 68 (Winter 1994): 177–87; Vassalo, P., ed., *The Magic of Words: R. A. A. and His Writings* (1982)

CHARLOTTE S. MCCLURE

ANDERSON, Frederick Irving

b. 14 November 1877, Aurora, Illinois; d. 24 December 1947, Sandisfield, Connecticut

Renowned from the 1920s into the 1950s, through the *Saturday Evening Post* and like magazines, A. is now emerging from temporary obscurity. His metier, the crime story, coupled with general scarcity of his works, militated his reconditeness. Many features place his writings within mainstream American literature, however, and thus they merit attention. A. had established himself in newspaper journalism, chiefly for the *New York World,* then brought out scientific articles and two agricultural books, *The Farmer of Tomorrow* (1913) and *Electricity for the Farm* (1915), as well as experiments in fiction, when his crime stories initially drew attention.

A creator of series characters, A. imbued his first sleuth, Mr. White, with oddities traditional among literary detectives from Edgar Allan POE onward. To the fore soon came Deputy Parr, of the New York Police Force, however, who remained A.'s principal detective. Parr depended upon his friend Oliver Armiston, an "extinct author"—extinct from police orders: his crime stories had inspired actual crimes. Parr's subordinates, handsome Morel and shabby little Pelts, also rendered much assistance. Two antagonists repeatedly tantalizing this group were a master rogue, the Infallible Godahl, and, as his feminine counterpart, the infuriating but endearing Sophie Lang. Three Sophie Lang films appeared in the 1930s.

Brisk narration and lively dialogue furnish vehicles for manifesting American literary traditions of alienated beings, con men, and wily women. Lines separating good guys from criminals often blur, making these stories akin to those by Poe or Jorge Luis Borges. A. used narrative techniques that are now much praised, along with storytellers whose stances toward their tales remain wonderfully ambiguous.

A.'s stories often feature rural New England settings. As such, in combination with the outwitting of urban characters by the rural folks, these stories rank with the oft-repeated use of the city mouse-country mouse themes found in much other American literature. One illuminating comparison might team A.'s crime fiction with Edith WHARTON's *Ethan Frome,* in which an educated outsider, who has been assigned to work in rural New England, manifests increasing interest in a triangular love situation that encompasses both physical and—more intense—emotional tragedy. The outsider-narrator's imperfect comprehension of the events related enhances the thematic ambiguity. Several of Wharton's short stories also incorporate similar New England locale and bewildering pyschological intrigues, and thus both A.'s and Wharton's rural New England stories carry on traditions of American humor established in the 19th c. Violence, sexuality, and subtle touches of seeming supernatural enrich the texture of their fiction. Unfortunately, A.'s work has been too frequently overlooked, doubtless because so much of it was never collected from magazines. His crime story collections are *Adventures of the Infallible Godahl* (1914), *The Notorious Sophie Lang* (1925), and *The Book of Murder* (1930).

BIBLIOGRAPHY: Fisher, B. F., Jr., *F. I. A. (1877–1947): A Bibliography* (1987); Kunitz, S. J., and H. Haycraft, eds., *Twentieth Century Authors* (1942; rev. ed., 1944)

BENJAMIN FRANKLIN FISHER IV

ANDERSON, [James] Maxwell

b. 15 December 1888, near Atlantic, Pennsylvania; d. 28 February 1959, Stamford, Connecticut

Even in the 1930s, when A.'s reputation was at its zenith, he was considered an oddity. Resisting the realism that dominated the American theater, he turned out neoromantic dramas, often in blank verse, suffused with nostalgia for past ages and lost causes. With *Elizabeth the Queen* (1930), *Mary of Scotland* (1933), *Joan of Lorraine* (1946), and *Anne of the Thousand Days* (1948), A. combined pageantry, heightened diction, and the techniques of the well-made play, gaining critical respect as America's leading tragedian. His attempts to apply this dramaturgy to crime melodramas of contemporary life in *Winterset* (1935) and *Key Largo* (1939) sparked lively debates about the appropriateness of putting blank verse into the mouths of gangsters and corrupt policemen. Today, his plays have all but vanished from the stage and no longer enjoy the esteem of critics. A. is now largely dismissed as an aesthetic reactionary whose verse is pedestrian and merely decorative, and whose attempts at tragedy resemble 19th-c. costume drama more than Sophocles or Shakespeare.

Although his first stage success *What Price Glory?* (1924, with Laurence STALLINGS) was a contemporary drama noted for its colloquial vigor rather than a historical verse drama, it shows the deep distrust of institutions and celebration of individualism that marks A.'s later work. Set during World War I, it condemns the bureaucratic squandering of life at the front, while idealizing the soldiers, both for their stoic heroism and their boisterous comraderie. Uninterested in detailed political analysis, A. presents his soldiers as vital individuals sacrificed to a senseless system.

A. views governments with suspicion and scorn, and reserves his most venomous attacks for those who pursue power; there is little difference between the autocratic Emperor Franz Joseph in *The Masque of Kings* (1937), the corrupt Judge Gaunt in *Winterset,* and the gangster Murillo in *Key Largo.* In a lighter vein, congressional logrolling and pork barrel spending are the objects of satire in *Both Your Houses* (1933), while the New Deal meets similar treatment in the musical comedy, *Knickerbocker Holiday* (1938, music by Kurt Weill). Only with World War II did A. temper his pacifistic and libertarian convictions. *The Eve of St. Mark* (1942)—which almost reads as a repudiation of *What Price Glory?*—praises chastity, obedience, and self-sacrifice for a greater social good.

In his theoretical essays, A. argues that a play should inspire audiences by showing the moral improvement of its protagonist, and the victory of good over evil. Even in tragic defeat, the hero triumphs. This insistence on ennoblement tends to heighten the pathos of A.'s tragedies. In *The Wingless Victory* (1936), a retelling of the Medea myth, its protagonist commits suicide with her children, rather than flying off unrepentant in a dragon chariot. The defeat of noble protagonists at the hands of a corrupt and small-minded world is often so total, however, that the plays appear darker than A.'s theories would have them. The suicide of Prince Rudolph in *The Masque of Kings* not only ends his life, but also any hopes for the liberalization of the Austro-Hungarian empire. The gangland shooting of the star-crossed lovers in *Winterset* seems more gratuitous cruelty than tragic inevitability. It is in his pessimism that A. often appears most modern.

BIBLIOGRAPHY: Hazelton, J. J. D., and K. Krauss, eds., *M. A. and the New York Stage* (1991); Horn, B. L., *M. A.* (1996); Shivers, A. S., *The Life of M. A.* (1983)

ROBERT F. GROSS

ANDERSON, Robert [Woodruff]

b. 28 April 1917, New York City

A. is primarily known for his ability to communicate strong feeling in his plays, most of which are to some degree autobiographical. The death of his wife from cancer, his relationship with his father, his feelings about aging and failure—all have found a place in his writing. Winning prizes for his work even as a schoolboy, four of his plays have been selected for inclusion in either the *Best American Plays* or *Best Plays* series; two filmscripts have received Academy Award nominations—*The Nun's Story* (1959) and *I Never Sang for My Father* (1970). A. has also written for radio and television, including Theatre Guild of the Air, Studio One, and Cavalcade of America. An important part of his work has been sharing his expertise with the next generation by teaching playwriting in venues such as the American Theatre Wing, the Actor's Studio, the Salzburg Seminar in American Studies, the University of North Carolina, and the University of Iowa. A. has said about his work that "every play I've ever written is me. I am Naked when I finish." His approach is a blatant attempt to stimulate his audiences to respond.

Tea and Sympathy (1953), A.'s Broadway breakthrough, is set in a New England boys' school, where a student's extreme shyness marks him as distinct. The boy begins to question the differences he finds within himself, but he is unable to turn to his unsympathetic father or to the headmaster, who places a high value on all things masculine. Only the headmaster's wife seems to understand, even to the point of offering to help him prove his manhood. Typical of A.'s plays, *Tea and Sympathy* is character driven rather than plot driven, although A. provides enough forward movement to maintain audience interest in finding out more about these characters. While A.'s own prep school experiences provide the background for this piece, in one of his many essays he stresses that the audience members must interpret for themselves. A. also wrote the screenplay for the film version.

You Know I Can't Hear You When the Water's Running (1967), four one-act plays, also enjoyed a lengthy run on Broadway. *The Shock of Recognition* portrays an anxious actor auditioning for a part requiring nudity; the shock is that of the playwright holding the auditions. *The Footsteps of Doves* turns to a frequent A. topic, marriage, when the wife upsets established sleeping habits, prompting her husband's infidelity. Marriage is again at issue in *I'll Be Home for Christmas* as a couple realize that the only topic they have in common is their children. In the final piece, *I'm Herbert,* the details of long ago romances prove amusingly elusive to an elderly couple. A. masterfully explores in these pieces how superficial incidents initiate wrenching, although in this case comedic, self-examination.

I Never Sang for My Father, published in 1968, is unquestionably A.'s most personal play, with himself as the model for the narrator Gene Garrison, his mother the basis for Margaret Garrison, and his own wife Phyllis the prototype for the writer/teacher wife of the main character. The soul-exposing meat of this work is clearly A.'s account of his attempts to sort out his relationship with his own father. This play, along with two others, *All Summer Long* (1955), about the struggle of a family to keep their home, and *Silent Night, Lonely Night* (1960), about strangers who fall in love on Christmas Eve, played limited runs in New York. His first published work of fiction was the novel *After* in 1973.

A.'s writing is distinguished by its highly personal and evocative intelligence. He deals with issues that are the substance of humanness—growing older and watching those we love pass away from us, relationships or the lack of them, dreams and the failure to realize them. He is a writer always conscious of the play as a performance vehicle, providing his audiences with an experience both for the moment and for future contemplation.

BIBLIOGRAPHY: Adler, T. P., *R. A.* (1978); Witkoski, M., "R. A.," in MacNicholas, J., ed., *DLB,* vol. 7, part 1, *Twentieth-Century American Dramatists* (1981): 35–45

BEVERLY BRONSON SMITH

ANDERSON, Sherwood

b. 13 September 1876, Camden, Ohio; d. 8 March 1941, Colon, Panama

A.'s literary reputation has been eclipsed by those of his one-time followers, including William FAULKNER, Ernest HEMINGWAY, Thomas WOLFE, and John STEINBECK. A. himself assessed his talent, observing, "For all my egotism I know I am but a minor figure." Despite A.'s self-deprecating evaluation and the uneven quality of his work, A.'s mark upon American literature has proven indelible. In a 1956 interview, Faulkner acknowledged A.'s role as a creative progenitor, noting that his friend was "the father of my generation of American writers and the tradition of American writing which our successors will carry on." A. was a pioneer in American MODERNISM, recording the cultural change upon Midwestern small-town life as technology replaced craftsmanship, as a sense of community became increasingly elusive, as standardization and materialism invaded American society. He was an innovator, no less than Washington IRVING, Edgar Allan POE, and Nathaniel HAWTHORNE, in the short story form, moving away from plot and chronology to an evocation of a mood, an impression. He was a trailblazer in recognizing sexuality as a significant force in people's lives. And always, whether in novels, plays, stories, poems, sketches, newspaper articles, or fictionalized autobiography, A.—following in the footsteps of his father—was a consummate storyteller, one especially compelled to relate the lives of the lonely, the repressed, the misunderstood, and the obsessed.

A.'s sensitivity to suffering humanity emanated from his own upbringing, for he grew up amidst poverty and hardship. His father was a dreamer who was never able to adjust to the changes brought by industrialization. He moved the family from one small Ohio town to another in search of work, eventually settling in Clyde, an agricultural town of puritanical moralism that eventually became his son's model for *Winesburg, Ohio* (1919). His mother symbolized for A. defeated aspirations and loneliness and yet inner beauty, courage, and wisdom that flowers forth from deprivation. As a child, A.—humiliated by his family's destitution—worked so hard delivering newspapers, running errands, and taking on any temporary employment he could find that he earned the nickname "Jobby." In the early 1900s, determined not to follow the fate of his parents, A. began to climb the ladder to success, working as an advertising salesman and writer in Chicago, then as president of United Factories Company, a mail-order firm in Cleveland, and eventually going into business for himself in Elyria, Ohio. A respectable married life, a country club membership, and a wide circle of successful friends seemed to indicate the achievement of the American Dream, but in November 1912 A. suffered a nervous breakdown. While dictating a letter to his secretary, he broke off in mid-sentence, walked out of the office to the railroad tracks heading toward Cleveland, where he was found several days later wandering about and muttering incoherently. Despite the apparent happiness of his life, A. was tormented by a divided soul in which the desire for commercial success and middle-class family life warred with the deeper desire to be a writer and to attain a freedom from stultifying routine and oppressive responsibilities. Ultimately, an inherent small town idealism defeated vaulting materialistic ambition. Thus, A. chose to devote himself to the life of the intellect and the imagination and to become the voice for the grotesques, those isolated individuals whose pathetic lives have an inner sweetness like twisted apples overlooked in an orchard.

Such devotion produced *Winesburg, Ohio,* A.'s greatest critical success and most widely read book today. This volume represents A.'s discovery of the power of the short story, which he describes in his *Memoirs* (1942): "There were people everywhere, thousands, millions of people wanting their stories told . . . It was as though one of these began to speak through me. The pen began to run over the paper. I did not seek for words. They were there. They seemed to leap out from my hand to the paper."

In relating the haunting stories of the grotesques in *Winesburg, Ohio,* A. explores problems of the decline of handicrafts and of rural life, sexual suppression, and loneliness, usually caused by the failure to communicate. He also creates a bildungsroman focusing upon the character of George Willard, who in the course of the book grows up through experiencing sex, love, and the death of his mother, and who in absorbing himself in the lives of others realizes that his destiny is to be a writer. Moreover, the book reveals A.'s lessons learned from literary and artistic masters. From Ivan Turgenev he learned to substitute lyrical insight for action. From Gertrude STEIN, he developed a style that values repetition and simple syntax and rejects artificial literary rhetoric. From Edgar Lee MASTERS, he conceived of presenting thematically related sketches of small-town inhabitants. The postimpressionist painters, whose paintings A. saw at the 1914 exhibition in the Chicago Armory, influenced him to compose a narrative based upon a flow of feelings, thoughts, and impressions rather than upon events in chronological time. James Joyce taught him the value of symbols and recurrent images as unifying devices and the significance of epiphanies, renderings of the inner life of a character during a moment of insight.

The results of such lessons may also be seen in A.'s subsequent short story collections *The Triumph of Egg* (1921), *Horses and Men* (1923), and *Death in the Woods* (1933), which, as with their predecessor, focus upon isolated, sensitive individuals entrapped in unfulfilled lives. Also notable in these collections are A.'s stories of adolescents, the best of which are "I Want to Know Why," " I'm a Fool," and "The Man Who Became a Woman." Influenced by Mark TWAIN's *Adventures of Huckleberry Finn,* A. combines comedy and pathos as he relates these tales from a first-person retrospective point of view in which the narrator reveals an initiation into the complexity and corruption of life.

In explaining the development of his career, A. wrote in his *Memoirs,* "If *Winesburg, Ohio* tried to tell the story of the defeated figures of an American individualistic small town life, then my later books have been but an attempt to carry these same people forward into the new American life, into the whirl and roar of modern machines." *Poor White* (1920) examines the dire consequences when the inventor Hugh McVey attempts to bring progress to the town of Bidwell, Ohio. *Many Marriages* (1923), attesting to the influence of D. H. Lawrence and Henry ADAMS upon A., offers the pure reverence and expression of sexuality as a panacea for sterile PURITANISM and worship of the false idols of mechanization. Reflecting his reading of James Joyce's *Ulysses* and Lawrence's *Lady Chatterley's Lover,* A.'s *Dark Laughter,* his only best-selling work at the time of publication, celebrates primitivism and sexual freedom.

To a large degree A. tells the same tale, whether in short story collections, novels, or autobiographical works, such as *Tar: A Midwest Childhood* (1926), *A Story Teller's Story* (1924), and his *Memoirs*. It is a tale exposing the limitations of small town life while cherishing a preindustrial innocence, revealing that the promises of big city life are disappointing, and celebrating the writer's mystical illumination of beauty in the lives of people futilely struggling to achieve harmony and wholeness.

BIBLIOGRAPHY: Anderson, D., ed., *Critical Essays on S. A.* (1981); Burbank, R. J., *S. A.* (1964); Chase, C. B., *S. A.* (1927); Howe, I., *S. A.* (1951); Papinchak, R. A., *S. A.: A Study of the Short Fiction* (1992); Rideout, W. B., ed., *S. A.: A Collection of Critical Essays* (1974); Schevill, J., *S. A.: His Life and Work* (1951); Townsend, K., *S. A.* (1987); Weber, B., *S. A.* (1964); White, R. L., ed. *The Achievement of S. A.* (1966); Williams, K. J., *A Storyteller and a City: S. A.'s Chicago* (1988)

                                    LYNNE SHACKELFORD

ANGELOU, Maya
b. 4 April 1928, St. Louis, Missouri

A. is an extremely prolific black American woman writer whose greatest achievement is her series of autobiographical novels in which the A. persona moves from age three to her mid-thirties, from 1928 to the mid-1960s. Published in 1970, *I Know Why the Caged Bird Sings* was followed by *Gather Together in My Name* (1974), *Singin' and Swingin' and Gettin' Merry like Christmas* (1976), *The Heart of a Woman* (1981), and *All God's Children Need Traveling Shoes* (1986). A. has also written lyric poetry that has been published in several volumes: *Just Give Me a Cool Drink of Water 'fore I Diiie* (1971); *Oh Pray My Wings Are Gonna Fit Me Well* (1975); *And Still I Rise* (1978); *Shaker Why Don't You Sing?* (1983); *Now Sheba Sings the Song* (1987, with art by Tom Feelings); and *I Shall Not Be Moved* (1990). Generally, this poetry is of less interest than A.'s other work. She has also accomplished much in drama, having produced, directed, and written a number of plays and screenplays. In addition to all of these achievements, A. has been a successful dancer, singer, and university teacher. Part of her importance is clearly the verve, creativity, and drive that she has displayed in so many different creative roles.

In terms of her literary importance, A.'s contribution will be her addition to the autobiographical tradi-

tion, a tremendously important genre in the African American literary historical tradition. In the 18th and 19th cs., thousands of slave narratives were written. These were autobiographical "captivity narratives" that detailed the narrators' reaction to slavery. Many of these stories were written by women who experienced the oppression of white racism and sexism within their own communities. Nevertheless, for both male and female writers, the significance of their work depended on the extent to which they, as writers, could separate themselves from their narrators's subjectivity and mediate between the experience of the personal self and the experience of the larger group. At its best, A.'s work speaks for more than her narrator's subjective experience so that she becomes the spokesperson for a race and a gender.

This inclusiveness is found in A.'s most effective work, *I Know Why the Caged Bird Sings,* in which the narrator claims to write about herself as the "black female" who is assaulted by male prejudice, white racism, and black lack of power. In the middle autobiographies, A. loses this focus as her narrator falls into obsessive insecurity. This is manifested in a tendency to romanticize her relationships with men and to direct her most important actions by this tendency. Only in *All God's Children Need Traveling Shoes* does the narrator again speak for a larger group. Here the author tells of her narrator's journey to Africa, a spiritual home where she will be judged on her own qualities rather than on the basis of her race or her gender.

If A.'s fictive and developing self is to be viewed from the perspective of all her books, her achievement must be analyzed more closely. The self that is recounted is an insecure child leaving a broken home, separated from parents, and insecure about her beauty. She is raped at age eight by her mother's boyfriend and then suffers guilt and feelings of worthlessness well into her adult years, at least as recorded in the books. Still, this journey through childhood and young adulthood is remarkable because it testifies to the narrator's ability to suffer some of life's worst experiences and still survive to become tremendously successful. In the second volume, the narrator slides into helpless failures, but in the third and fourth volumes she becomes a talented dancer and singer, thereby gaining the attention and success that provide further opportunities to meet others who notice her singing and her literary talent. Together, the books are a paean to the human ability to rise above circumstances that textbook wisdom tells us do irremediable harm to the personality.

I Know Why the Caged Bird Sings is an account of the narrator's life from the age of three, when she was sent to Arkansas to live with her paternal grandmother, to the age of sixteen when she gave birth to her son. During this time, the narrator stresses the influence of her grandmother, an immensely strong woman, entrepreneur, and survivor in a racist society. During a visit to her mother in St. Louis, the A. character was raped by her mother's boyfriend, who was then found murdered. Because she felt responsible for the man's murder, the young narrator did not speak for five years, and when she did it was with the help of a kind neighbor who taught her the importance of herself and of words. The novel shows the corrosion of racism, family disruption, and the violation of a young woman. But set against this corrosion is the saving power of strong relationships in A.'s life, particularly with her brother Bailey, her mother Vivian Baxter, and her grandmother Annie Henderson. "Momma" Henderson especially gave A. a sense of the importance of hard work, order, discipline, and courage.

A.'s masterful selection of the incidents that will become part of her story leads up to the violation of her narrator, after the first third of the story, and then away from this violence toward a healthier sense of self in the second and third parts of the novel. Many of the scenes are humorous, and A.'s use of language is skillfully metaphoric when she attempts to convey the larger issues in the novel. For instance, she compares her character's understanding of displacement as the "rust on the razor" held at the throat of blacks, an unnecessary insult added to the wounds of discrimination. There is also a distinct separation between the author and the character mediated by the narrator who is able to analyze the meaning of the character's experiences.

In the later books, the selection of detail is not as controlled, the language is not as expressive, and the anecdotes are not as humorous. But the persona has survived and emerged a success by any standards. In charting this journey through the various volumes, A.'s narrator reveals the life of black women in a way that is both instructional and empowering. The narrator reveals a great deal about the pressures, particularly those experienced through the broken family and white racism, that confront many black women. The cumulative force of the books is the argument that no outside force is as important as the ability to value oneself alone, without even the aid of romantic relationships. Such an awakening would have been welcome earlier than the fifth volume, but A. is writing about a narrator who was victimized by rape and by fantasies of bourgeois security that were made impossible by the same white society that concocted them.

Gather Together in My Name presents the nadir of the narrator's reported experience. In this novel, the A. persona reports her life from age sixteen, when she gives birth to her son, to the age nineteen. This is a very lonely time of her life. The character feels guilty for having had a child outside of marriage and for living in her mother's house without contributing to expenses. She finds a job cooking creole food, but soon afterward allows herself to become the lover of a thirty-one-year-old man who warns her that he is engaged. In her disappointment at his desertion, the narrator moves to Los Angeles to live with her uncles, but they cruelly, on her arrival, ask her when her train is leaving. Because her father had little interest in her life, A. moves to San Diego but takes a job as a waitress. She exploits two lesbian lovers whom she sets up as prostitutes and then flees when trouble occurs. She becomes infatuated with L. D. Tolbrook who claims to be a gambler but whose real occupation is pimping. He entreats her to be a prostitute, for a short time, to help him out of his gambling debts. Only the threats of her brother Bailey save the narrator from becoming trapped in her role.

The troubling part of this account is the narrator's rationalization of prostitution as a respectable occupation. At no time in the novel does the author dispute or analyze such logic. And at the end of the novel the narrator makes the same mistake of falling in love with another dangerous man. This time her lover, who is a heroin addict, takes her to a junkie hit joint to show her what life as a user would be like. The A. persona states at the end of this scene that her "innocence" reasserted itself and saved her from drug use. But her escape from self-destruction is only lucky. A different attitude in her lover would have led her to heroin addiction. In the final pages of the novel, the narrator still has learned nothing from her experiences. As she watches a pimp anxiously waiting for his prostitute so that he can receive a fix, the narrator remarks that she saw nothing wrong with this because they were "a couple and depended on each other." Reading this novel is disappointing and saddening. It is as if no real sense of self had been formed during the years recorded in *I Know Why the Caged Bird Sings*. Perhaps in the rush to make abstract assertions of affirmation at the end of the first volume, A. repressed the genuine wrestling with demons of self-hatred and guilt that must have been the result of the difficult experiences in her first sixteen years.

Fortunately, *Singin' and Swingin' and Gettin' Merry like Christmas* narrates the A. persona's discovery of her talents for singing and dancing. She appears at several nightclubs, the well-known Purple Onion, and finally in the cast of Gershwin's opera *Porgy and Bess*. The narrator's tour with the cast through Europe and Africa helps to develop her sense of success and her relief at having escaped the dangers of her past. Even in this volume, however, the narrator retains an obsession with men on whom she becomes dependent.

She recounts her first marriage to a man who attempts to keep her and her son shut off from the rest of society. The sense of pride in herself that one finds in this novel comes only from her talent in the opera. Thus the major flaw of the book is that there is so little analysis of the saving artistic talents of the narrator and so much emphasis on her destructive personal relationships.

The fourth volume, *The Heart of a Woman,* follows the persona's account of seven years (1957–63), a time that meshed with the civil rights movement. The narrator moves to New York City and begins to meet with the Harlem Writers Guild where she finds friendship and encouragement for writing. She also becomes the Northern coordinator of Martin Luther King, Jr.'s Southern Christian Leadership Conference. The description of these and other important political events is cut short by further intrusion of romantic fantasies. The persona quits her job with SCLS to marry a man she had known for two weeks. While he lives beyond their means and is unfaithful, both in the U.S. and Africa, the narrator concludes the novel with her decision to remain in Africa because it offers her a sense of home that she never felt in the U.S. Despite the story of betrayal, the narrator's commitments to literary and political concerns show a widening, and a stronger sense of self emerges in this work.

All God's Children Need Traveling Shoes presents the four years the narrator lived in Ghana. During this time, she writes freelance articles for the *Ghanaian Times* and for the Ghanaian Broadcast Corporation in Accra. She was also an administrator at the University of Ghana. Of great interest is her description of the black American expatriates in Africa and of their reception by the Ghanaians. Although there is some suspicion of them because they are foreigners and American, many begin to fell that they have found a community in which racism is not an issue. Significantly, the narrator no longer feels pressured to prove herself through a dependent relationship. Instead, the narrator presents as subplot her distress when her nineteen-year-old son begins to seek independence from his mother and to make his own life. These issues raise this volume above all but the first of the autobiographies and indicate a maturity in the A. persona and in the author's literary sophistication. Too often critics have stated that the A. narrator has begun to fly at the end of *I Know Why the Caged Bird Sings,* that one can suffer defeats but can never become defeated. While the other volumes eventually bear out this affirmation, they also testify to the amount of talent, suffering, and time this takes—a full twenty years—before the narrator's difficulties and triumphs

can be presented objectively and without false optimism.

BIBLIOGRAPHY: Cudjoe, S. R., "M. A. and the Autobiographical Statement," in Evans, M., ed., *Black Women Writers (1950–1980): A Critical Evaluation* (1984): 6–24; Elliot, J. M., *Conversations with M. A.* (1989); O'Neale, S., "Reconstruction of the Composite Self: New Images of Black Women in M. A.'s Continuing Autobiography," in Evans, M., ed., *Black Women Writers (1950–1980): A Critical Evaluation* (1984): 25–36; Smith, S. A., "The Song of a Caged Bird: M. A.'s Quest after Self-Acceptance," *SHR* 7 (Fall 1973): 365–75

LAURA NIESEN DE ABRUNA

APPLE, Max
b. 22 October 1941, Grand Rapids, Michigan

Best known for his humorous and satirical short stories, A. is often compared to such writers as John BARTH, Philip ROTH, Robert COOVER, and Woody ALLEN. His caricatures of real people fill his parables with spoof (which has a special Midwestern ring to it), gentle irony, and a touch of absurdity that distinguishes his writing from a more erudite satire. His language is accessible without requiring hidden associations to real meanings. Having early developed a taste for pop culture, A. incorporates into his fiction the visual message of the cartoonist and the juxtaposed imagery of the collagist to mine and scrap the depths and surfaces of the American consciousness.

A. often uses real names and historical figures in his stories. In what many consider his signature piece, the title story from *The Oranging of America and Other Stories* (1976), the protagonist is restaurant franchiser Howard Johnson, who is first encountered at the Los Angeles International Airport in a brontosaurian Cadillac limousine. Not forgetting that ice cream was the cornerstone of his empire, Johnson has equipped the car with a freezer that contains eighteen flavors of ice cream. Millie, a secretary-turned-traveling companion, and a former busboy, Otis, share in the tastings of ice cream. With a Waspish taste unmotivated by flavor, Johnson eats only vanilla and is addicted to it. They spend most of their time on the road, and perhaps due to a diet of ice cream, develop a sixth sense, their bodies tingling upon divining a new location to erect a Howard Johnson's restaurant. A. weaves wordplay and wit to bring symbolic references to the saga of Western civilization that includes the "oranging" of the map with dots as well as the "oranging" of the landscape with new logos and architecture. The themes of greed and avarice—prominent in many of A.'s early stories—would be further expanded in A.'s first novel, *The Profiteers* (1987).

In the story "Walt and Will" from his collection entitled *Free Agent* (1984), A. introduces a person whom one would never expect Ezra POUND to have acclaimed as one of the greatest geniuses in American art—Walt Disney. Studying the way ants move with as much intensity as one would expect from J. Henri Fabre or Remy de Gourmont when they focused on the world of insects, the character of Walt fixates on the idea of motion, which later becomes the principle behind his genius for animation. Fantasy, reality, absurdity, and seriousness merge as one of the great artistic spirits and one of the great entrepreneurial spirits—Walt and his brother Will—combine forces to make the dreams of the worldwide Disney empire materialize.

A. has deservedly enjoyed critical acclaim and popularity, but in an age where cultural references are as immediate as the medium waves, it is difficult to assess A.'s importance as an author. A. may not yet have escaped postmodernism, and—like other writers—he has to deal openly or secretly with Pound's hauntingly simple definition: "Literature is news that stays news."

BIBLIOGRAPHY: Vorda, A., "An Interview with M. A.," *MQR* 27 (Winter 1988): 69–77; Wilde, A., "M. A. And the American Nightmare," *Crit* 30 (Fall 1988): 27–47

CHARLES PLYMELL

ARNOW, Harriette [Louisa Simpson]
b. 7 July 1908, Wayne County, Kentucky; d. 22 March 1986, Ann Arbor, Michigan

One of A.'s major thematic concerns, the rural Southerner who moves to the urban North, reflects A.'s own life: Kentucky-born, she spent most of her life in Michigan. Her major novels—*Mountain Path* (1936), *Hunter's Horn* (1949), and *The Dollmaker* (1954), together known as her Kentucky trilogy—examine the plight of the uprooted individual who must adapt to an alien culture.

The Dollmaker, her best-known work and for which A. won numerous awards, is the story of Gertie Nevels, who surrenders her dream of owning a Kentucky farm in order to follow her husband to Detroit, where he takes a wartime factory job. Gertie has a talent for woodcarving, and brings with her a block of cherry wood in which she sees a figure of Christ awaiting release through her art. But Gertie is forced to adjust to the impersonal, industrial society of Detroit, and sacrifices her art to economic necessity: at the end of the novel she chops up the cherry wood to mass-produce carved dolls so that her family can eat. The novel, which was adapted for television in 1984, indicts a mechanized and materialistic society that destroys humanity and individuality.

In *Seedtime on the Cumberland* (1960) and *Flowering of the Cumberland* (1963), A. turned from fiction to social history. Both books, chronicles of the Cumberland Valley during the 18th and 19th cs., are "scrapbooks" of information culled from diaries, letters, court records, deeds, and wills; A. lets the facts speak for themselves, venturing little opinion. As a result, A. presents a vivid picture of rural Kentucky life.

With *The Weedkiller's Daughter* (1970), A. deliberately turned from the rural South to the middle-class urban North. She wished to contrast the America of the pioneer with the America of the 1950s and 1960s, as well as to avoid such literary labels as regionalist or naturalist. The novel, her least successful in terms of characterization, explores the destruction of nature and the corrupting of the children by their nouveau riche parents. A.'s final books, *The Kentucky Trace: A Novel of the American Revolution* (1974) and *Old Burnside* (1977), a childhood memoir and social history, return to the familiar milieu of the South.

A.'s work, which includes short stories and essays along with her novels and histories, are dominated by a concern with the disappearance of rural life, the destruction of the natural world, and the displacement of individuals. *The Dollmaker,* in which A. skillfully unifies all of her thematic concerns, is at once her masterpiece and her most representative work.

BIBLIOGRAPHY: Eckley, W., *H. A.* (1974); Hobbs, G., "Starting Out in the Thirties: H. A.'s Literary Genesis," in Bogardus, R. F., ed., *Literature at the Barricades: The American Writer in the 1930s* (1982): 144–61; Hobbs, G., "H. A.'s Kentucky Novels: Beyond Local Color," in Toth, E., ed., *Regionalism and the Female Imagination: A Collection of Essays* (1985): 83–92

JUDITH E. FUNSTON

ARRINGTON, Alfred W.
b. 17 September 1810, Iredell County, North Carolina; d. 31 December 1867, Chicago, Illinois

Born in North Carolina, A. moved with his family to Indiana, where he became a child preacher until 1832, when he renounced religion and lectured on agnosticism. In the same year, he moved to Arkansas, where he worked as a Methodist circuit rider. A. possessed a commanding physical presence and repeated charges of sexual impropriety followed him. By 1834, he was married and teaching school. In 1838, he joined the Christian (Campbellite) movement and began the practice of law. A. was active in the Whig Party, serving in the legislature and as a presidential elector. His career failed to blossom, especially when no one would accept his challenges to duel. In 1844, he removed to Texas, abandoning his first wife. Three years later, he appeared in New York, associated with Ralph Waldo EMERSON and Henry David THOREAU, married again, and published his first book, *The Desperadoes of the South-West,* using the pseudonym Charles Summerfield. This was followed by *Duelists and Duelling in the South-West* (1847). Returning to Texas, he served as a district judge and wrote a number of short stories for the newspapers. *Rangers and Regulators of the Tanaha* (1856) is an autobiographical novel and unusual in that the villain's career closely resembles the author's. After relocating briefly at Madison, Wisconsin, A. settled in Chicago, attaining considerable legal recognition prior to his death in 1867. One of his last poems, a panegyric to John Wilkes Booth, was not well received.

In both his life and writing, A. was something of an original. His first works, although labeled as fiction, purport to be factual accounts. Apparently, some parties protested, for in later editions slight variations in the spelling of names appear. *Rangers and Regulators of the Tanaha,* a full-fledged novel, is far less effective, being greatly inferior to similar work by William G. SIMMS. His short stories, which have never been collected, are valuable social documents on frontier legal life.

A.'s works can be called the precursors of the dime novels of the post-Civil War era—*Duelists and Duelling in the South-West* actually sold for fifteen cents. His argument, that the desperado, although bad, possessed badness in such a large degree as to obtain heroic stature, prepared the way for the later fascination with Billy the Kid and other outlaws. W. H. Rhodes's *The Case of Summerfield* (1907) is a novel in which A. appears as the major character.

BIBLIOGRAPHY: Durham, P., "The Desperado as Hero," *ArkHQ* 14 (Winter 1955): 340–58; Worley, T. R., "The Story of A. W. A.," *ArkHQ* 14 (Winter 1955): 315–39

MICHAEL B. DOUGAN

ARTHUR, T[imothy] S[hay]

b. 6 June 1809, near Newburgh, New York; d. 6 March 1885, Philadelphia, Pennsylvania

A magazine editor and tremendously prolific writer of moral works, A. was one of the most widely known and best-selling literary figures of his day. He wrote more than 150 novels and story collections—he is said to have composed over six percent of all American

fiction published during the 1840s—and sold more books in the U.S. in the 1850s than any author except Harriet Beecher STOWE. Throughout his career, A. held that literature should be used for what was to him its highest purpose, the moral uplift of the reader. This motive appealed to the emerging middle-class female readership that would form his most loyal audience. He was also critically popular: reviewers in the 19th c. held that the works of this "friend of virtue" were likely to become classics. However, A. is now chiefly remembered as the author of just one book, *Ten Nights in a Bar-Room and What I Saw There* (1854), a popular temperance novel that was adapted for the stage and is still occasionally performed in repertory.

A.'s youth offered little indication of the path his career would take. His health prevented him from receiving formal schooling until the age of nine, and even then he showed little talent for scholarship. He left school and began an apprenticeship, probably with a tailor, which severely damaged his eyesight. Forced to abandon his trade, he worked for a time in a countinghouse and then for a banking company while struggling to educate himself and beginning to write. The banking concern's failure in 1833 cost him his job, but his association with a literary group in Baltimore led to an offer to coedit a weekly literary magazine, the *Baltimore Athenaeum and Young Men's Paper.* Three years later, he founded the critically successful *Baltimore Literary Monument.*

In 1836, A. married Eliza Alden and published his first book, *The Young Wife's Book: A Manual of Moral, Religious and Domestic Duties.* This marked the beginning of his work focusing on the domestic sphere. He also published repeatedly in *Godey's Lady's Book* on home-related issues.

A. acquired a second literary magazine, the *Baltimore Saturday Visiter,* in 1837, employing his acquaintance Edgar Allan POE. A. published the *Monument* until 1839 and the *Visiter* until 1840, when he began to edit the *Baltimore Merchant,* a political organ for William Henry Harrison. For the *Baltimore Merchant,* he covered meetings of the Washington Temperance Society and developed a lifelong passion for their cause. *Six Nights with the Washingtonians,* his first full-length contribution to movement literature, appeared in 1842.

A. moved to Philadelphia in 1841 and three years later began a new magazine, the *Ladies' Magazine of Literature, Fashion and Fine Arts,* which merged with *Godey's* in 1846. In 1850, he launched his most successful periodical, *A.'s Home Gazette,* later called *A.'s Home Magazine.* Circulated through subscribers' clubs, as was common for women's magazines, the *Home Magazine* developed a loyal readership and finally outlived its creator. The publication also provided a forum for many of the best-known female writers of the era.

In 1854, A.'s novel *Ten Nights in a Bar-Room* found wide acceptance among adherents of the fast-growing temperance movement, the cause most closely associated with his name. However, A. also articulated positions on a wide variety of other issues. Between 1840 and 1860, he wrote scores of opinionated novels and stories, advocating proper etiquette in *Anna Milnor, the Young Lady Who Was Not Punctual* (1845), advising against speculation in *The Debtor's Daughter; or, Life and Its Changes* (1850), addressing the subject of divorce in *The Hand but Not the Heart; or, The Life-Trials of Jessie Loring* (1855), and praising socialism in *The Good Time Coming* (1855). During the Civil War, his publication urged its readers to support Abraham LINCOLN when most other women's magazines remained neutral.

In his later years, A. published one of the first children's magazines and wrote voluminously for the young under the pseudonym "Uncle Herbert." He also continued to edit the *Home Magazine,* even when his always-weak eyesight began to fail, until illness confined him to his home a month before his death in 1885.

A.'s focus on virtue and domesticity seems somewhat quaint today. His works, often didactic and of widely varying quality, may even appear to justify his present obscurity. But by addressing the concerns of women and families, A. contributed to the recognition of issues frequently neglected in the public sphere.

BIBLIOGRAPHY: Endres, K. L., "T. S. A.," in Riley, S. G., ed., *DLB,* vol. 79, *American Journalists, 1850–1900* (1989): 33–43

CAROLYN LENGEL

ASCH, Sholem

b. 1 November 1880, Kutno, Poland; d. 10 July 1957, London, England

In the 1940s and early 1950s, A. was perhaps the best-known Yiddish novelist and dramatist living in America. In 1936, Ludwig Lewisohn included A. in his list of the world's "Ten Outstanding Jews" then living, a distinction he shared with Albert Einstein, Sigmund Freud, Henri Bergson, and Martin Buber, among others. He was a prolific writer, at the time the most translated Yiddish writer in the West, and perhaps most significantly, his writings were enjoyed by Jews and non-Jews alike. Yet when A. died in London in 1957, his funeral was sparsely attended. Today, he is nothing more than in footnote in most anthologies of American literature.

The discrepancies underlying A.'s reputation, the highs of popular and critical recognition and the lows of obscurity, may best be explained by his position as an ethnic writer living in the U.S. Like Isaac Bashevis SINGER, A. grew up in a Polish shtetl, returned to his roots as a source for much of his fiction, wrote in Yiddish, and in his time was a widely read author. Yet unlike Singer, his reputation has suffered greatly since his last years, especially within the Jewish community. Perhaps more than any other writer living in America, A. and his legacy has been uncomfortably caught between Jewish ethnic identification and Western literary acceptance.

By the 1930s, A. was already an American citizen and at the peak of his creative powers. He became increasingly popular as translations of his work began to appear in English, notably *America* (1918), *Uncle Moses* (1920), *Chiam Lederer's Return* (1938), and *Judge Not* (1938), which all deal with Jewish life transplanted to the new world. His Russian Revolution trilogy, translated as *Three Cities* (1933), is an expansive work on the scale of Tolstoy's *War and Peace* or Thomas Mann's *The Magic Mountain,* and is one of the first to take him largely outside the Jewish shetl. *Salvation* (1934) is A.'s attempt to counter the reports that were coming from Europe and demonstrate the moral superiority of the Jews over the Nazis, and *The War Goes On* (1936) is a plea for tolerance set in the post-World War I Jewish communities of Germany. All of these novels, their enlightened tone and their humanity, solidly secured his reputation both within Jewish literary circles and the nation at large.

However, his Christological novels, *The Nazarene* (1939), *The Apostle* (1943), and *Mary* (1949), brought mixed results. Not only did they bring him more fame and a wider audience, but they also brought hostile attacks from the Jewish community. Numerous Jewish critics, the most notable of which were Abraham Cahan and his colleges at the *Jewish Daily Forward,* accused him of apostasy, of courting Christian favor, and of selfishly denying his own people in hopes of obtaining a Nobel Prize. His *East River* (1946) can in many ways be seen as A.'s reply to these criticisms. It is the story of both Jews and Christians living close together in New York, and demonstrates an attitude that he had attempted to portray in his Christological novels: that there is more that Jews and Christians have in common than not.

His subsequent works, *Moses* (1951) and *A Passage in the Night* (1953), can be read as novels that attempt to come to terms with his strained relationships with both Jewish America and the country at large—A. had come under attack by Senator Joseph McCarthy and the House Committee on Un-American Activities. But by 1953, discontent with life in the U.S. and traumatized by the Holocaust, A. chose to live the last of his productive years first in Europe, and then in Israel. A.'s controversial literary life, caught between cultures, was both a challenge and testimony to his place as a writer.

BIBLIOGRAPHY: Lieberman, C., *The Christianity of S. A.* (1953); Liptzin, S., *The Flowering of Yiddish Literature* (1963): 178–89; Niger, S., *S. A.: His Life and His Work* (1960); Roback, A. A., *Contemporary Yiddish Literature* (1957): 29–34; Siegel, B., *The Controversial S. A.* (1976)

DEREK PARKER ROYAL

ASHBERY, John [Lawrence]
b. 28 July 1927, Rochester, New York

Often accused by critics of being the academic "darling" among contemporary American poets, A. was never himself an academician. He did postgraduate work briefly at New York University from 1957 to 1958, worked in publishing, then went to France from 1960 to 1965 as an art critic for the Paris edition of the New York *Herald-Tribune* and *Art News,* of which he subsequently became an editor. In 1965, he returned to New York City.

A.'s first book, *Turandot and Other Poems,* was published by the Tibor de Nagy Gallery in 1953; despite this previous publication, he won the first book award of the Yale Series of Younger Poets for *Some Trees* in 1956. Subsequent collections include *The Poems* (1960), *The Tennis Court Oath* (1962), *Rivers and Mountains* (1966), *Selected Poems* (1967, published in London), *The Double Dream of Spring* (1970), *Three Poems* (1972), *The Vermont Journal* (1975), *As We Know* (1979), *A Wave* (1984), *Hotel Lautreamont* (1992), *And the Stars Were Shining* (1994) and *Girls on the Run* (1999).

Although many critics have complained about the difficulty of A.'s work, it is not at all certain that, as one critic says, A.'s poetry is "almost indecipherable." If one critic is categorical in his rejection of A., there is an ambivalence in the attitude of another, almost as though he were abashed to like the poetry and unable to understand why he should do so against all reason. But A. does not want to attach a "program" to his poetry, as composers have done on occasion to their musical compositions. He wants to achieve in language the mysterious pleasures of music by using abstract syntax, word order that follows the form of a thought in the mind of the poet but without defining that thought. Thus, the poet does not provide the reader with landmarks in the landscape of his mind, but A.'s

choice of words, and his way of putting them together, are at once mysterious and entrancing.

A.'s method of composition may explain something about how his poems manage to gather mystery to themselves. As A. has stated in an interview, "I write down phrases and ideas on pieces of paper which I then can't keep track of. I put them in a drawer, and sometimes I can't find them, and sometimes I use ones I've already used before and then I have to do something about that. I don't keep any journal. I write down things that seem suggestive to me when they occur and I think might be usable later on. Then if I can't find them, that's all right too because meanwhile I will have already started to think about something else." Despite the fact that his syntax is "abstract" and his methodology removed from the mechanical or even the rational, A.'s approach to versifying is neither "ludic and whimsical" nor "academic," nor is it entirely without "architectonic structure."

The poet is supposed to make leaps of the imagination that surprise the reader and to make associations that others perhaps would not have made. It is evident that the difficulty readers have with A. and other members of the New York school is that they jump from one association to another without intervening transitions—a modernist technique that Ezra POUND discovered in the original draft of T. S. ELIOT's *The Waste Land* by editing out those transitions and leaving only the fragments and abstract syntax that mirror the fragmentation and technological leaps of the 20th c. It is a technique from which Wallace STEVENS forged a career of writing poetry for himself, not for readers, but that some readers loved anyway. What is certain is that A. writes his poems in an abstract "musical syntax," and this syntax is sometimes to be found bottled in traditional lyric verse forms.

BIBLIOGRAPHY: Bellamy, J. D., ed., *American Poetry Observed: Poets on Their Work* (1984): 9–20; Holden, J., *Style and Authenticity in Postmodern Poetry* (1986); Lehman, D., *Beyond Amazement: New Essays on J. A.* (1980); Shapiro, D., *J. A.: An Introduction to the Poetry* (1979)

LEWIS PUTNAM TURCO

ASIAN AMERICAN LITERATURE

In its broadest sense, Asian American literature encompasses the oral and written literary traditions of Asian immigrants in North America, of American-born generations of Asian ancestry, and of Asian and Pacific Islander populations living in U.S. territories. The cultural texts of this last group have a long history predating the founding of the U.S.; prior to Captain

James Cook's "discovery" of the Hawaiian islands in 1778, the myths and legends of Pacific Islanders were told in the chanted poetry of the *mele* and *oli*. Yet, most accounts of Asian American literature begin with the migration histories of East and Southeast Asians to the U.S. and Hawai'i as miners and plantation workers from the mid-19th c. onward. Chinese emigrated to the U.S. from the late 1840s through the early 1880s attracted by the Gold Rush in California. Japanese, Koreans, and Filipinos came first to Hawai'i in the 1880s as contract laborers to the sugar plantations and later to the continental U.S. as farmworkers, domestics, and cannery workers. South Asians, mostly Sikhs from the Punjab region, migrated through Canada, finding work in the lumber, railroad construction, and farming industries. Some of these early Asian immigrants expressed their great hopes for America as well as the hardship of their experiences in folk rhymes sung in their native languages. Such vernacular oral and written traditions were ethnically specific and often geographically localized. Marlon K. Hom's *Songs of Gold Mountain* (1987) records the Cantonese folk songs circulating in San Francisco's Chinatown in the early 20th c. Janice MIRIKITANI's *Ayumi* presents translated versions of prose and poems published in U.S.-based Japanese language newspapers from 1927 onward, and the two Canadian volumes, *Maple* (1975) and *Paper Doors* (1981), contain selected works of Japanese poets in Canada, many of whom established *tanka* and *haiku* circles prior to World War II.

At the same time these local literary efforts were circulating within individual ethnic communities, stories by and about Asian immigrants were gaining a foothold in the popular publishing industry. The *Independent* published a series of autobiographical sketches of ethnic Americans, including one by Lee Chew, a Chinese businessman in New York (1903), another by Fomoaley Ponci, an Igorot from the Philippines (1905), and yet another by a nameless Japanese servant (1905)—all of which were reprinted in a volume edited by Hamilton Holt in 1906. In 1909, the same journal published a memoir by Sui Sin Far, the pen name of Edith EATON, a Eurasian journalist who devoted her life to portraying the Chinese in America as a dignified and complex community. Sui Sin Far published sketches of the Chinese from 1888 to 1914 in various popular magazines, contributing to traditions of Western local color and of urban, immigrant social protest. The mass marketing of exotic literary pieces benefitted her sister, Winnifred EATON, who adopted the pen name Onoto Watanna and wrote fanciful romances set in Japan. Presses such as the D. Lothrop Publishing Company also helped manufacture the public's desire for Orientalia by soliciting early Asian American autobiographies, for instance, Lee

Yan Phou's *When I Was a Boy in China* (1887) and New Il-Han's *When I Was a Boy in Korea* (1928). Likewise spurred on by an American magazine publisher was Etsu Sugimoto whose *Daughter of the Samurai* (1925) was a best-seller. Other popular self-ethnographies include Yung Wing's *My Life in China and America* (1909), Lin Yutang's *My County and My People* (1937), and Younghill KANG's *The Grass Roof.* These early texts are part bildungsroman, part Asian ethnography, detailing the customs, lifestyles, living habits, family structures, education, village relations, rituals, and holidays of the author's Asian homeland. Such early works later became a negative model for Asian American writers of the 1970s who insisted that Asian American culture was not about Asia but about a creolized culture particular to Asians born in the U.S.

Also at the turn of the century, two upper-class, cosmopolitan intellectuals, Yone Noguchi and Sadakichi HARTMANN, published poetry, critical essays, and drama in a high art tradition written for a bohemian elite audience. Rather than writing about themselves, these two authors took "art" as their subject. Hartmann also wrote what might be considered the first Asian American dramatic works in English, *Christ, Buddha,* and *Confucius,* with Gladys Li's *The Submission of Rose Moy* (1924) being one of the earliest known dramatic works written by an Asian American woman.

Beginning in the 1930s, several Asian American writers published works, again in a semiautobiographical vein, that focused on their entry and incorporation into American life. Kang's second novel, *East Goes West,* rather than a reminiscence of his former homeland, details the Korean immigrant protagonist's desire not merely to make a living in America but to embrace it intellectually and socially. Other notable novels of this period include Pardee Lowe's *Father and Glorious Descendent* (1943), Jade Snow WONG's *Fifth Chinese Daughter,* Lin Yutang's *Chinatown Family* (1948), Monica SONE's *Nisei Daughter,* Diana Chang's *Frontiers of Love* (1956), and C. Y. Lee's *Flower Drum Song* (1957), all of which touch upon the schism between an older, more traditional Asian generation and their more Westernized children.

Also in the late 1930s, Carlos BULOSAN, heavily influenced by the literary left movement, was publishing poetry evocative of a coming socialist revolution. His collections of poetry, *Letter from America* and *The Voice of Bataan,* were well received at a time when Filipinos were being hailed as war-time allies. Yet his autobiographical novel, *America Is in the Heart,* also exposes the horrors of prejudice against Filipinos who were neither citizens nor aliens but "nationals" migrating from the colonial outpost to the imperial core—following the annexation of the Philippines by the U.S. Interweaving patriotic sentiment with collectivist labor politics, Bulosan's novel depicts the heroism of Filipino American migrant workers in the decade following the Great Depression. Likewise memorializing the tenderness and nostalgia of the Filipino oldtimers, Bienvenido SANTOS crafted short stories based on his memories of this generation, collected in *You Lovely People, The Day the Dancers Came,* and *Scent of Apples.*

During the postwar period, Asian American short fiction writers produced a rich body of works, with N. V. M. Gonzalez publishing his stories about life in the remote forests of Mindoro in both Philippine and American journals, and with Toshio Mori and Hisaye YAMAMOTO crafting tales devoted to the inner lives of Japanese Americans living in more or less insular communities. The achievement of these latter two writers is quite remarkable considering the antipathy directed toward Japanese Americans during World War II. Mori's stories—scheduled for release in 1941—suffered from an eight-year delay in publication, finally appearing as *Yokohama, California* in 1949. That same year, Yamamoto's "Seventeen Syllables" came out in *Partisan Review* and shortly thereafter her "Yoneko's Earthquake" was selected as one of the *Best American Short Stories.*

The harsh treatment of Japanese Americans during World War II greatly affected the literary production of Japanese Americans. The shock of war, the dislocation of internment, the feelings of shame and helplessness experienced by the *issei,* and the effects of the military draft are themes poignantly explored in John OKADA's *No-No Boy;* Wakako YAMAUCHI's "And the Soul Shall Dance"; Jeanne Wakatsuki Houston and James Houston's *Farewell to Manzanar* (1973); Mitsuye YAMADA's *"Camp Notes" and Other Poems* and *Desert Run;* Lawson Fusao Inada's *Before the War: Poems as They Happened* (1971) and *Legends from Camp* (1992); Edward Miyakawa's *Tule Lake* (1979); and Yoshiko Uchida's *Journey to Topaz* (1971) and *Desert Exile* (1982). Joy Kogawa's *Obasan* (1981) details the brutal experiences of Japanese Canadians forcibly removed from British Columbia. Kazuo Miyamoto's *Hawai'i: End of the Rainbow* (1964) chronicles the saga of a Japanese immigrant to Hawai'i and his internment in an American camp.

Milton Muryama's *All I Asking for Is My Body* (1959), set in the decade prior to the entry of the U.S. into the war, dwells only briefly on the conditions of martial law after the bombing of Pearl Harbor and focuses primarily on the oppressions of both the plantation economy and the Japanese family system. Other novels of immigration and family life on the islands include Shelley Ota's *Upon Their Shoulders* (1951), Margaret Harada's *The Sun Shines on the Immigrant* (1960), and Patsy Saiki's *Sachie: A Daughter of*

Hawai'i (1977). Murayama's work is notable for its combining standard English narration with dialogue rendered in Hawai'i's pidgin, following the example of Philip K. Ige in his short story, "The Forgotten Flea Powder" (1946). This stylistic hallmark reappears in the works of more recent "local" prose writers of Hawai'i, such as Darrell H. Y. LUM, Gary PAK, and Lois-Ann Yamanaka. The revivifying of local culture in the "Hawaiian Renaissance" also saw a flourishing of poetry in the late 1970s and early 1980s in the works of Larry Kimura, Eric Chock, Juliet Kono, Wing Tek Lum, Cathy SONG—whose *Picture Bride* won the Yale Series of Younger Poets Award—and Diane Mei Lin Mark, among others. Recent scholarship on Hawaiian literary culture has also sought to reinterpret late-19th-c. *mele* and *oli* in terms of a protest literature against the U.S. annexation of the islands in 1898.

The resurgence of pride in Hawaiian local culture coincided with a broader movement of ethnic revival on the mainland. In the late 1960s, Asian American student activists, demanding that their history and culture be represented in college curricula, helped solidify a pan-Asian American identity. With renewed pride in their Asian cultural heritage, Asian Americans writers, tired of being stereotyped as Fu-Manchus and Charlie Chans, explicitly confronted the racism of American society. The Combined Asian Resources Project (CARP) worked to uncover neglected Asian American texts, such as Louis CHU's portrait of New York's Chinese bachelor community in *Eat a Bowl of Tea.* In 1974, Frank CHIN, Jeffrey Paul Chan, Lawson Fusao Inada, and Shawn Wong published the landmark anthology *Aiiieeeee!* in which they delineated a cultural nationalist agenda. Two years later, Maxine Hong KINGSTON's best-seller, *The Woman Warrior,* was awarded the National Book Critics Circle Award. This text, along with Kingston's second and third novels, *China Men* and *Tripmaster Monkey,* brought mainstream recognition to Asian American writing as had no other work of fictional prose in the latter half of the 20th c., except perhaps for Amy TAN's *The Joy Luck Club.* The feminist tones of Kingston's first book, however, drew sharp critiques from some members of the community troubled by the author's representation of Asian American men. Debates over the gender politics and authenticity of *The Woman Warrior* became as much a part of Asian American literary culture throughout the 1980s and 1990s as the work itself.

On the theatrical front, Los Angeles's East-West Players, founded in 1965, galvanized Asian American playwriting by actively seeking out and developing dramatic material by and about Asian Americans. East-West, along with San Francisco's Asian American Theater Company, Seattle's Northwest Asian American Theater Company, and New York's Pan

Asian Repertory, created auspicious conditions for plays such as Momoko Iko's *Gold Watch* (1993), Frank Chin's *Chickencoop Chinaman* and *Year of the Dragon,* Wakako Yamauchi's *And the Soul Shall Dance* (1990) and *The Music Lessons* (1993), David Henry HWANG's *FOB* and *Family Devotions,* Genny Lim's *Paper Angels* (1993), Philip GOTANDA's *A Song for a Nisei Fisherman, The Wash,* and *Fish Head Soup,* and Velina Hasu HOUSTON's *Asa Ga Kimashita, Dreams,* and *Tea* to emerge. Interweaving themes of cross-dressing and cross-culturalism, Hwang's Broadway hit, *M. Butterfly,* won a Tony Award for best play in 1988.

Asian American poetry also flourished in this period, with certain authors impressing their writings with ethnically specific markers and others, such as José Garcia Villa and John Yau, making little reference to the social conditions of Asians in America. Poets publishing in the 1970s and 1980s include Mei-Mei Berssenbrugge's *Fish Souls* (1971) and *Summits Move with the Tide* (1974), Jessica HAGEDORN's *Dangerous Music,* Meena Alexander's *The Bird's Bright Ring* (1976) and *House of a Thousand Doors* (1988), Arthur Sze's *Two Ravens* (1976), Nellie WONG's *Dreams in Harrison Railroad Park* and *The Death of Long Steam Lady,* Eric Chock's *Ten Thousand Wishes* (1978), Janice Mirikitani's *Awake in the River* and *Shedding Silence,* Alan Lau's *Songs for Jadina* (1980), Garrett HONGO's *Yellow Light* and *The River of Heaven,* Al Robles's *Kayaomunggi Vision of a Wandering Carabao* (1983), Kitty Tsui's *The Words of a Woman Who Breathes Fire* (1983), John Yau's *Corpse and Mirror* (1983), Vikram SETH's *Golden Gate,* and Wing Tek Lum's *Expounding the Doubtful Points* (1987).

Multiauthor collections of poetry continued to appear in the late 1980s and early 1990s. Filipino poets from the Kearny Street Workshop, an Asian American collective of artists and writers, published their work in the anthology *Without Names* (1985). Garrett Hongo's *The Open Boat* included works by both established and upcoming writers, while Walter Lew's *Premonitions, The Kaya Anthology of New Asian North American Poetry* (1995) focused on experimental, often overlooked texts. A new generation of poets also published their own volumes from the mid-1980s onward, most notably Li-Young LEE's *Rose* and *The City in Which I Love You,* Agha Shahid Ali's *The Half-Inch Himalyas* (1987), Marilyn Chin's *Dwarf Bamboo* (1987), Chitra Divakaruni's *Dark like the River* (1987) and *The Reason for Nasturtiums* (1990), Sesshu Foster's *Angry Days* (1987), Jeff Tagami's *October Light* (1987), Juliet Kono's *Hilo Rains* (1988), Carolyn Lau's *Wode Shuofa* (1988), Kimiko Hahn's *Air Pocket* (1989), and David Mura's *After We Lost Our Way* (1989).

Although American literary historians often use "postwar era" to refer to the decades immediately following World War II, Asian American literature tells a different story of this same period, one that emphasizes the massive decolonization of Asian territories, the rise of Third World nationalisms, and the struggles for political power within these regions. Richard KIM's *The Martyred* and *The Innocent* dwell on the clashes between military and civilian populations during and after the Korean War. Hua-ling Nieh's *Mulberry and Peach* (1981) details a Chinese woman's continual fugitive status, punctuated by the Sino-Japanese War, the Communist revolution, China's conflict with Taiwan, and immigrant dislocation in the U.S. Wendy LAW-YONE's *The Coffin Tree* focuses on Burma (Myanmar) after British decolonization. Theresa CHA's *Dictee,* a tour de force of stylistic experimentation, also records the heroines and martyrs of Korean resistance. Autobiographies, such as Ved Mehta's *The Ledge between the Streams* (1984) and Sara Suleri's *Meatless Days* (1989), and novels, such as Bapsi Sidhwa's *Cracking India* (1991) and Rohinton Mistry's *Such a Long Journey* (1991), recall the partitioning of India in 1947 and the later separatist movement of Bangladesh from Pakistan. Autobiographical and historically based fiction of the post-Vietnam War era continues to reflect on the shifting grounds of post- and neocolonial Asia, as in Ninotchka Rosca's *State of War* (1988), Hagedorn's *Dogeaters,* and Le Ly HAYSLIP's *When Heaven and Earth Changed Places.*

The popularity of fiction focusing on an American landscape also swelled in the 1980s and early 1990s in short story collections such as Bharati MUKHERJEE's *"The Middleman" and Other Stories* and David Wong Louie's *Pangs of Love* (1991), and in exemplary novels such as Mukherjee's *Wife* and *Jasmine,* Ronyoung's KIM's *Clay Walls,* Cynthia Kadohata's *The Floating World* (1989), Frank Chin's *Donald Duk,* Gish Jen's *Typical American* (1991), Gus Lee's *China Boy* (1991), Shawn Wong's *Homebase* (1991), Bapsi Sidhwa's *An American Brat* (1993), and Fae Myenne Ng's *Bone* (1993). Memoirs and fiction devoted, in part, to the "return" of Asian Americans to "homelands" that they oftentimes have not yet seen include Peter Bacho's *Cebu* (1991), David Mura's *Turning Japanese* (1991), and Lydia Minatoya's *Talking to High Monks in the Snow* (1992). Expanding the thematic terrain of Asian American literature southward, both Zulfikar Ghose and Karen Tei Yamashita set their fiction in Brazil.

As with any living literature, Asian American prose, poetry, and drama continue to expand and diversify, in keeping with the post-1965 influx of new Asian immigrants from Southeast Asia and South Asia.

Definitions of Asian American literature have undergone massive revision, initially emphasizing the function of the literary works to effect social change, later encompassing a broader-based thematic coalition pertinent to a variety of texts, and most recently delving into the continuities between Asian American literature and the cultural artifacts of scattered Asian diasporas across the globe. Influenced by contemporary theories of poststructuralism and postcolonialism, the topics of Asian American literature continue to range from immigration, biculturalism, generational conflicts, problems in language and voice, and heroism in a racialized society to the possibilities and limits of multiethnicity and of relationships with other minorities, the hardship of migration, exile and diaspora, the specific circumstances of war and of refugee status, the experience of being reared Asian American, and the continual battle against Orientalism.

BIBLIOGRAPHY: Cheung, K., and S. Yogi, *Asian American Literature* (1988); Kim, E. H., *Asian American Literature: An Introduction to the Writings and Their Social Context* (1982); Lin, S. G., and A. Ling, *Reading the Literatures of Asian America* (1992); Ng, F., *The Asian American Encyclopedia* (1995); Sumida, S., *And the View from the Shore: Literary Traditions of Hawai'i* (1991); Wong, S., *Reading Asian American Literature: From Necessity to Extravagance* (1993)

RACHEL LEE

ASIMOV, Isaac
b. 2 January 1920, Petrovichi, Russia; d. 6 April 1992, New York City

When A. died in 1992, he left behind a literary legacy of nearly five hundred books published during his lifetime. His works combined fiction and nonfiction, but almost all related in some way to the popularization of science.

While still a young child, his family moved from Russia to Brooklyn, New York. Much of A.'s "free" time as a child was spent helping out in the family-run candy store, and the availability of new magazines for sale in the store sparked A's interest in pulp fiction—and especially in the still-fledgling genre of SCIENCE FICTION. Eventually, A. received a Ph.D. in biochemistry, but he continued to have very eclectic tastes in reading matter—and the pull of speculative fiction proved especially attractive.

In 1938, A. met John W. Campbell, Jr., the new editor of *Astounding Science-Fiction* and the most important editor of science fiction in the 1930s and the 1940s. As with most science fiction writers, A. began first as an enthusiast—joining the Futurians, one of the earliest science fiction fan clubs and whose membership included Damon Knight and Frederick

Pohl, among others. In 1939, A.'s first short story, "Marooned off Vesta" was accepted for publication—later collected in *The Best of I. A.* (1973). The story was considered derivative and lacking a good sense of dialogue; however, it added elements of mystery to the science fiction genre and incorporated the theme of something going wrong that "couldn't" go wrong as would be seen in A.'s later Robot stories.

The first of these stories entitled "Robbie" was published as "Strange Playfellow" in 1940, which, along with eight other Robot stories, was included in the collection *I, Robot* in 1950. "Robbie," which centers on a robot that is purchased to serve as a nursemaid to a young child, introduced what has come to be known as the "Three Laws of Robotics," a series of directives programmed into all robots: a robot may not injure a human being, or, through inaction, allow a human being to come to harm; a robot must obey the orders given it by human beings except where such orders would conflict with the First Law; a robot must protect its own existence as long as such protection does not conflict with the First or Second Law. These "laws" have had a major impact on science fiction, finding their way into the works of other authors in the genre as well as works of science fiction on film and television—as if they were indeed scientific law.

Even more than for the Robot stories, A. is best known in the field of fiction writing for his "Foundation" series. This series, set in a far-distant future, pivots on the idea of the science of psychohistory, a field developed as a tool to predict mass behavior. A mathematical tool such as this one becomes particularly useful in an alternate universe composed of twenty-five million separate worlds and civilizations. However, psychohistory ultimately fails as a "perfect" tool, for it cannot predict the independent actions of individuals who may be responsible for drastic changes in the course of history.

Apart from these two fiction series about two very distinct universes (which, incidently, are brought together in some of A's later novels), A was also a prolific mystery writer, an author of fiction and nonfiction books for children, an essayist, a textbook writer, and an author of popular treatments of science fact in such areas as astronomy, physics, and chemistry. The plotting and narrative structures of A's fiction grew more sophisticated and complex throughout his forty-year writing career, but the depth of character and emotional impact that one might have wished to find in his later works never moved far beyond what could be found in his earliest works. However, A. himself always considered fiction little more than a hook upon which to hang ideas. And ideas were certainly what A. gave to the world.

BIBLIOGRAPHY: Fiedler, J., *I. A.* (1982); Gunn, J. E., *I. A.: The Foundations of Science Fiction* (1982); Patrouch, J. F., *The Science Fiction of I. A.* (1974); Touponce, W. F., *I. A.* (1991)

ELIZABETH HADDRELL

ATHERTON, Gertrude [Franklin Horn]

b. 30 October 1857, San Francisco, California; d. 14 June 1948, San Francisco, California

On the jacket cover of Emily W. Leider's biography, *California's Daughter: G. A. and Her Times* (1991), the California-born novelist whose writing career extended from 1888 to 1948 is portrayed as a puzzle with a piece missing. That missing piece is an image not only of A.'s camouflaged idealized version of herself but also her depiction in fiction of the varying social, cultural, and geographical backgrounds of her major character, the Western American New Woman, who, she believed, might cause a change in Western civilization. In over thirty novels, collections of short stories, and three histories of California and her native San Francisco, A. strove to be accepted by the prevailing Eastern literary establishment. Having by the first years of the 20th c. produced eleven novels and two volumes of short stories in her favored romantic-realistic vein, she felt confident enough to challenge publicly in a *North American Review* article (1904) the "timid realism" of William Dean HOWELLS. Admiring Henry JAMES's writing for his own specific group of readers, A. identified her audience of self-restricted middle-class women whose imaginations she hoped to stimulate with psychological dramas of her fictional woman's quest for self-identity and for a life purpose within and beyond her procreative function.

Throughout her career, A. narrated the adventures and internal conflict between nature and heredity of this evolving "Woman of Tomorrow." Placing her in California, the Midwest, and New York, in England, Munich, and ancient Athens, A. imagined that her aristocratic-spirited character would work out a new resolution of the nature-nurture question. In portraying her New Woman up to the years preceding World War II, during which time women's ambitions and talents generally had few outlets, A. used gender as a perspective on American society. As a social historian who wrote novels, A. told stories wittily, though often undecorously, on some controversial aspects of American civilization as she saw them. Long out of print, her works began to be reprinted and studied in the late 1960s.

A. claimed *The Doomswoman* (1892), the first portrait of her idealized Western woman, began her career. *Patience Sparhawk and Her Times* (1897) depicts the blossoming of a poor California Ranch girl into an independent-spirited, self-supporting woman in New York; its unjudgmental acknowledgment of woman's sexuality antedates Kate CHOPIN's The *Awakening* (1899). In *The Californians* (1898), A.'s romantic Hispanic-Anglo-Saxon heroine and her realistic depiction of San Francisco in the expansive 1880s create A.'s finest expression of her perception of California and the Bay City as a fool's paradise, a theme she explores further in *Ancestors* (1907), *The Sisters-in-Law* (1921), and the short stories of The *Splendid Idle Forties* (1902). Considered her first novel of the American middle class, *Perch of the Devil* (1914) features the rivalry of an aristocratic lady and a rising working woman for the love of a mining engineer in Montana, the underground mines providing a metaphor of the characters' unprobed depths as well as a setting for the author's praise of her engineer's heroic stand for competitive Western capitalism in its struggle with the growing strength of labor unions.

Although a popular author, A.'s only best-seller—a commercial success that outstripped Sinclair LEWIS's *Babbitt*—was *Black Oxen* (1923). In it, she narrates a story of a three-generation gap among upper-class women of New York who try to cope with aging, the loss of sexual ambition, and the frivolity of the flapper crowd. The tremendous response by women readers to *Black Oxen* showed A.'s heroine's choice of power over love exploded the motive force of romance—a fool's paradise—behind the happy endings in marriage in popular fiction. Two years later in *The Immortal Marriage* (1925), A. demonstrated her versatility as a historian-fictionist in re-creating the famous love story of Aspasia and Pericles, in which she exercises her invention of a biographical novel, utilizing the methods of fiction as she did in her highly successful biography of Alexander Hamilton in *The Conqueror* (1902). *The House of Lee* (1940) brings her social history of San Francisco in fiction up to the eve of World War II. She narrates the effect of social, economic, and political changes on three generations of women who strive to be independent yet loving in a society that in A.'s view still limited opportunities for women.

A.'s autobiography, *Adventures of a Novelist* (1932), published when she was seventy-five, provides few clues to the missing piece of her life puzzle. Writing candidly and ironically about herself and the many people she had known, she portrays herself as the adventurous, feisty, aloof, and beautiful California heroine of her novels.

BIBLIOGRAPHY: Leider, E. W., *California's Daughter: G. A. and Her Times* (1991); McClure, C. S., *G. A.* (1979)

CHARLOTTE S. MCCLURE

ATTAWAY, William [Alexander]

b. November 1911, Greenville, Mississippi; d. 17 June
1986, Los Angeles, California

Born in a small Mississippi town and migrating to
Chicago at an early age with his physician father and
school teacher mother, A. deserves critical recognition
primarily for his two novels, *Let Me Breathe Thunder*
(1939) and *Blood on the Forge* (1941). In both works,
A. renders with stunning success, through his skillful
interfusion of raw realism and poetic lyricism, the
emotional and psychological realities of working-class
migrants caught between the socioeconomic aftermath
of the Great Depression and the hard-driving industrial
ethos dominating the American imagination after
World War I. However, it is in his second novel *Blood
on the Forge,* in which he chronicles the psychological,
emotional, and spiritual odyssey of the Moss brothers—who escape poverty and racism in the South only
to find backbreaking tragedy and death in the steel-
mill towns of western Pennsylvania—that A.'s artistic
genius rivals that of Richard WRIGHT's in *Native Son.*
In his brilliant interpretation of the "Great Black Migration" of the late 1890s, A. has contributed to American literature nothing less than a classic.

A.'s first novel, *Let Me Breathe Thunder,* rendered
through a first-person narrator, received favorable notices from the critics, impressed by the twenty-five-
year-old black novelist's ability to convey with intriguing accuracy and an uncanny perceptiveness the
nuanced gestures, language, and thoughts of two
young white, hard-boiled box-car wanderers, Ed and
Step, who forge a paternal bond with a homeless Mexican boy as they all drift across America, hopping
freight trains, picking berries in Washington, and
working the land in California just to stay alive. Remarkable as well was A.'s gift for tempering the stark
reality of his story—the violence, the primitive sexuality—with an emotional poignancy not unlike that
found in John STEINBECK's *Of Mice and Men.* Drawing
on his experiences as a hobo, a lifestyle undertaken
after the death of his father and in anticipation of his
career as a writer, A., displaying his mastery of the
understated style of Ernest HEMINGWAY—the bareness
of speech, the clean powerful lines—captures the wanderlust, the sense of impermanence and yet the longing
in the soul to take root somewhere that characterized
many young drifters during the post-Depression years.

In *Blood on the Forge,* A. shifts from first-person
narrator to omniscient narrator in homage to the epic
nature of his tale—the story of the great migration of
Southern blacks who in the late 19th c. abandoned
their share-cropping existence in the killing fields of
the South in search of a promised salvation in the
North. But for many, like the Moss brothers, what

they found at the end of the journey was another
Hell—the killing fires of the Northern steel mills. A.'s
novel, clearly influenced by Wright in its Marxian
interpretation of the destructive transformational
power of capitalism as it alienates individuals from
the land and each other, tells the story of the Mosses—Melody, Chinatown, and Big Mat—brothers who
are tragically and permanently scarred when they are
abruptly uprooted from their land in the barren hills
of Kentucky because Big Mat, the oldest and the
strongest, has struck an overseer whose cruelty
snatches even the possibility of mere subsistence from
them. But amid the hopelessness of their impoverished
lives in the mountains of Kentucky, A. argues for the
primacy of the soil. In Kentucky, Melody—the guitar-
playing brother—composes and sings; Chinatown—the simple-minded brother, attracted to outward symbols—finds happiness and a kind of dignity
in his gold tooth that smiles at him; and Big Mat reads
his Bible and awaits the baby his wife Hattie will
probably never bring forth. But after being seduced
North as strikebreakers, forced to ride in a dark, filthy,
sealed boxcar—a journey emblematic of the Middle
Passage—they are violently transfigured by the giant
hearths, blast furnaces, and smoking chimneys that
symbolize the ugliness of their altered existence. Their
new way of life exacts a price as the men are systematically debased. A. is impressive in conveying the degraded life surrounding the steel mills through a proliferation of perverted pastimes such as whoring and
watching dog fights. In *Blood on the Forge,* race is
secondary, as A. reveals that Eastern Europeans, who
work side by side with black men at the mills and live
in shanties that litter the surrounding landscape, are
devoured as well by the steel. Their children inevitably
fall into fornication and prostitution as an inescapable
way of life.

There are undeniable similarities between *Blood
on the Forge,* a work that failed commercially after
winning critical acclaim, and Wright's *Native Son,*
published one year earlier and perhaps responsible for
eclipsing much of the popularity of A.'s book. Like
Wright's, A.'s novel is shaped by a proletarian vision—taking into account the lives of working people
and their struggle against a powerful hostile force.
Like Wright, too, A. is adept at interpreting the psychological and emotional landscape of his characters while
arguing the apocalyptic consequences of a choking
capitalism. But unlike *Native Son* (1940), where the
folk have no voice, A. throughout *Blood on the Forge*
not only embeds within the fabric of his work the rich
Kentucky dialect spoken by the brothers, but he infuses
effectively placed lyrical interludes throughout his
story, consistently superimposing the memory of the
green Kentucky countryside against the ugliness of

the North. And it is in this evocation, a tragic reminder of where they have come from—"a fall from glory"—and that fact that they will never return, that *Blood on the Forge* attains an emotional depth and sense of epic proportion that *Native Son* never realizes.

BIBLIOGRAPHY: Baker, H. A., and P. Redmond, eds., *Literary Study in the 1990s* (1989); Barthold, B. J., *Black Time: Fiction of Africa, the Caribbean, and the United States* (1981); Bell, B. W., *The Afro-American Novel and Its Traditions* (1987); Campbell, J., *Mythic Black Fiction: The Transformation of History* (1986)

BARBARA L. J. GRIFFIN

AUCHINCLOSS, Louis

b. 27 September 1917, Lawrence, New York

A. is America's most accomplished novelist of manners since Edith WHARTON. Related to several families prominent in New York society, he studied at Groton, Yale, and the University of Virginia Law School. For most of his adult life, he has been a partner in a New York law firm as well as a prolific writer. Drawing upon both his social and business experiences as materials for his fiction, A. examines life in the Park Avenue drawing room and in the downtown board room.

In publishing his first novel, *The Indifferent Children* (1947), A. used the pseudonym Andrew Lee. Sprawling and at times improbable, this book documents the war experiences of several younger members of New York society. Two subsequent novels focus sympathetically on the problems of women. *Sybil* (1952) portrays a woman who is prominent in society but deeply dissatisfied with her lot, and *A Law for the Lion* (1953) examines the efforts of Eloise Dilworth to find a true identity within her various assigned roles. Two other early novels display males who are unable to conform to the expectations of family and society. The main character in *The Great World and Timothy Colt* (1956) abandons his idealism and suffers punishment for professional misconduct. In *Venus in Sparta* (1958), Michael Farish fails as a banker and husband, runs away to Mexico, and eventually commits suicide.

Some of A.'s best novels are sagas of family life spanning several generations. *The House of Five Talents* (1960) examines a robber baron's acquisition of wealth and the effects of this inherited fortune on his five children. *Portrait in Brownstone* (1962) covers fifty years in the life of the Denison family—apparently based on A.'s own relatives, the Dixons. Here Ida Trask Hartley is a formidable force of unity in a slowly disintegrating clan.

Often identified as A.'s most accomplished book, *The Rector of Justin* (1964) is a study of Francis Prescott, the recently deceased headmaster of a private school. By giving incomplete and sometimes inconsistent recollections from his wife, daughter, students, and alumni, A. shows the difficulty in arriving at the truth about any character. This narrative strategy is reminiscent of Henry JAMES but also suggests a lawyer carefully weighing the testimony of various witnesses. A. uses a similar technique in *The Embezzler* (1966), a story of crime recounted from three different perspectives, and again in *The Book Class* (1984), an account of the late founder of a women's book club told by its surviving members.

Two of A.'s more recent novels deal with contemporary political and social issues. *Honorable Men* (1986) examines the values of leaders who formed and executed public policy during the Vietnam War era. *Diary of a Yuppie* (1987) is the story of Robert Service, a self-serving lawyer intent on succeeding in a realm of corporate brutality. Service ironically reveals his crass values through his own diary entries. Along with these very contemporary stories A. has also written several historical novels. *The Cat and the King* (1981) is an account of life at Versailles under the rule of Louis XIV, and *Exit Lady Masham* (1983) is the fictional memoir of an attendant to England's Queen Anne.

In his collections of interrelated short stories, A. continues his emphasis on multiple perspectives and frequently blurs the distinction between story and novel. In *Skinny Island* (1987), for example, he presents several distinct but overlapping versions of Manhattan society. *Powers of Attorney* (1963) analyzes the dynamics of a large law firm in twelve connected stories. The fourteen stories in *The Partners* (1974) examine personal and professional crises among the members of a different but similar law firm. Particularly noteworthy in this collection is the story entitled "The Novelist of Manners," where a writer reminiscent of A. comments ironically on his limited popularity among reviewers and readers. *The Winthrop Covenant* (1976) is a story collection with a broader historical scope that examines the force of Puritan values in New England society from 1630 to the present time.

A. has also written biographies and literary criticism. His most notable works in these areas—*Edith Wharton: A Woman in Her Time* (1972) and *Reading Henry James* (1975)—focus on writers he admires and imitated. As a historian, A. has examined French culture in *False Dawn: Women in the Age of the Sun King* (1985) and 19th-c. New York in *The Vanderbilt Era: Profiles of a Gilded Age* (1989).

Some critics have regarded A.'s fiction as overly intellectual and deficient in human feeling. His focus on an increasingly outmoded way of life has diminished his reception by critics and his popularity among readers. He contends, however, that his emphasis is not so much on society—the requirements of class—as on individual psychology—a character's preoccupation with self-image. A. calls himself a Jacobite, and in the tradition of James he provides penetrating analyses of characters confronted with social crises or ethical dilemmas.

BIBLIOGRAPHY: Bryer, J. R., *L. A. and His Critics* (1977); Dahl, C. C., *L. A.* (1986); Gelderman, C., *L. A.: A Writer's Life* (1993); Piket, V., *L. A.: The Growth of a Novelist* (1991)

ALBERT WILHELM

AUDEN, W[ystan] H[ugh]
b. 21 February 1907, York, England; d. 29 September 1973, Vienna, Austria

Although A. made his reputation in England, he spent most of his creative years as an American citizen. A. was a mentor and example to other poets even as an undergraduate at Corpus Christi College, Oxford, and during the 1930s, he was at the center of a group of young, mostly leftist English writers that included Stephen Spender, Louis MacNeice, and Christopher Isherwood. He helped shape the attitude of all of them both to the craft of writing and to the world, which he then viewed through the lenses of political commitment and Freudian psychology. After losing faith in political action and moving to America in 1939, A. returned to Christianity as a means of understanding the world and became the focal point of group of American poets, including James MERRILL, who shared his devotion to poetry as craft.

A.'s early published work *Poems* (1930) was written in the shadow of T. S. ELIOT and shares the obscurity of much of the first generation of modernist poetry. Although A. never abandoned the surreal or imagistic entirely, his writing became more and more accessible as he began exploring different forms and genres. His more surreal work began to take the form of the folktale or the ballad, and he achieved real conversational clarity, as well as a perfect mastery of meter, in long, almost didactic poems, such as "Letter to Lord Byron"—part of his contribution to the travel book he wrote with MacNeice entitled *Letters from Iceland* (1937)—and *New Year Letter* (1941).

Some of the work from the 1930s dealt explicitly with politics. "Spain" (1937) addresses the Spanish Civil War and was first printed in a series whose proceeds supported the Republican cause. But A.'s own experience in Republican Spain, where he was shocked to see churches closed and to hear of priests tortured and executed, led him to reevaluate his involvement in politics and his rejection of religion. After traveling to war-torn China with Isherwood—and contributing a series of sonnets to *Journey to a War* (1939), published about their journey—A. decided not to return to England. In the face of a good deal of criticism from his compatriots, he chose to spend the war years in America. Almost as a farewell to political engagement, he wrote "September, 1939" as the war began. Soon afterward, he wrote in one of his greatest works, "In Memory of W. B. Yeats," that "poetry makes nothing happen." His days as an engagé poet were over.

In later years, A. allowed neither "Spain" nor "September, 1939" to be republished, believing that their feeling was dishonest. Instead of political verse, he wrote a series of long poems that deal with guilt and ambiguity from an explicitly Christian, but thoroughly ironic, perspective. *For the Time Being: A Christmas Oratorio* (1944) retells the story of Christmas, both the first Christmas and the annual, disappointing reenactment. *The Sea and the Mirror* is at once a commentary on Shakespeare's *The Tempest* and a meditation on art itself. *The Age of Anxiety* (1947), which is written for the most part in alliterative verse reminiscent of Old English, reveals both A.'s interest in Sören Kierkegaard and his perception of the isolation of modern Americans.

Besides individual poems on many subjects, A. wrote a number of poetic sequences that show both his continuing interests and his constant exploration of new poetic forms. In "Horae Canonicae," A. explores the nature of society and the guilt that is its basis by describing the events of Good Friday with a poem on each of the canonical hours of prayer. In "Thanksgiving for a Habitat," from *About the House* (1965), he devotes a poem to each room in his summer house in Austria. The real subject, though, is the domestic life, especially as embodied in A.'s own relationship with Chester Kallman, which lasted from 1939 to his death.

In the last two decades of his life, during which he divided his time between New York and summer homes, first in Italy and then in Austria, A. sought to be a "man of letters" in the largest sense. He wrote occasional poems to mark many events, both public and private. He fitted his interests, which ranged from music to microbes, to complicated poetic forms. He edited many collections of poetry. *The Dyer's Hand* (1962), which includes some of A.'s addresses as Professor of Poetry at Oxford, and *Forewords and Afterwords* (1973) contain some of the most readable criticism of the time. During the final year of his life, he left New York to take up residence as an honorary fellow of Christ Church College at Oxford.

Throughout his career, A. had a strong interest in drama. In the 1930s, he wrote a number of plays with Isherwood, including *The Dog beneath the Skin* (1936) and *The Ascent of F.6* (1937). He also worked on several musical pieces with Benjamin Britten, notably the operetta *Paul Bunyan,* produced in 1941. From the late 1940s onward, opera became one of his central interests, and he wrote a number of important libretti with Kallman. The first, *The Rake's Progress,* was written for Stravinsky, and the resulting piece may be the most successful of modern operas. A.'s other libretti, set by Hans Werner Henze, *Elegy for Young Lovers* and *The Braisards* have not held the stage but are fascinating to read.

Critical reaction to A.'s work has been divided. Some readers prefer the early, political work, some the later disengaged or religious work. Evaluation is complicated because of the irony that is present even in A.'s most accessible work. In many of A.'s books, the tone veers constantly from earnestness to flippancy—and in his endless revisions of his work, A. sometimes substituted one for the other. Nevertheless, in his constant attention both to his poetic craft and to the moral qualities of his work, he was an example for the generations of poets that succeeded him.

BIBLIOGRAPHY: Carpenter, H., *W. H. A.: A Biography* (1981); Hecht, A., *The Hidden Law: The Poetry of W. H. A.* (1993); Johnson, W. S., *W. H. A.* (1990); Spender, S., ed., *W. H. A.: A Tribute* (1975)

BRIAN ABEL RAGEN

AUSTER, Paul
b. 3 February 1947, Newark, New Jersey

A.'s fiction and essays call into question the grand design of existence as lives are undermined by unexpected turns, and the intuitive dance between individuals is as rigorous and defining as the spoken word. A. is a master at relating the subtleties that transform, and chance and coincidence play as real a role in his fiction as they do in the everyday, which is brilliantly depicted in his personal essays, particularly "The Red Notebook"—included in *The Art of Hunger* (1992) and *Why I Write* (1996).

Influenced by Miguel de Cervantes, Franz Kafka, and Samuel Beckett, A. is attracted to secrecy and so are his characters who often lead themselves into the absurd, but simultaneously the very real. Since A. is so concerned with what is concealed, within the individual, and within this, the play between illusion and fact, it is not surprising that his early fiction falls

into the mystery genre, as is the case in the New York trilogy, including the three novels *City of Glass* (1985), *Ghosts* (1986), and *The Locked Room* (1986), which pay homage to Raymond CHANDLER and film noir. *City of Glass* presents a labyrinth of circumstance and identity as Quinn, a detective writer, takes on the role of his detective pseudonym Max Work, after receiving a wrong number from someone looking for a detective agency. The last volume, the most critically celebrated book in this trilogy, *The Locked Room,* continues with the theme of stolen identity as the narrator invades the life of a dead man, Fanshawe, whose unpublished writings are left in his care.

A. often illuminates a universe that alienates people and in the New York trilogy, he presents a city that is severe and ungiving. This environment is heightened in *The Country of Last Things* (1987), in which his character Anna Blume faces an apocalyptic urban 20th-c. world that is violent and amoral. In *The Music of Chance* (1990), A. leaves the metropolitan nightmare but replaces it with a rural one: Nashe leaves behind his past and with a small inheritance takes to the road only to find himself imprisoned on the grounds of wealthy gamblers to whom he has lost his money and his soul.

A. looks to his own past to unravel identity in his memoir *The Invention of Solitude* (1982), in which he plays with narrative outlook. In segment one, "Portrait of an Invisible Man," written in the first person, A. reacts to the death of his father by searching for truths of him; in segment two, "The Book of Memory," he switches the focus onto himself and shifts, as well, in narrative style to the third person, constructing a distance between "self" and "writer." This theme reappears in *Moon Palace* (1989), in which Fogg, an orphan, takes to the road seeking keys to his past. Looking toward the future rather than the past, A. creates Walt, in *Vertigo* (1994), a young boy, who learns to fly and begins his ascent in life, reflecting in his later life that despair—and the emptiness it creates within the individual—rather than his master's teaching was responsible for lifting him off the ground.

A. is a superb storyteller particularly owing to his innate and finely tuned awareness of life, which he reports with refreshing simplicity; thus, the story is never swallowed by the language in which it is carried. His earlier writing in "The Red Notebook" relates life stories that highlight, among other things, the strange, the unexplainable; in one case, A. tells of an adult friend who had never met his father but on his daughter's third birthday was driven to search for him—later finding out that his father had left him and his mother when he was three years old.

In "Pages for Kafka," part of A.'s collection of critical essays from *The Art of Hunger* (a title referring both to Kafka and Knut Hamsun), his words express the human dilemma and convey A.'s philosophy and what is at the heart of his fiction: "He wanders toward the promised land . . . he moves from one place to another, and dreams continually of stopping. And because this desire to stop is what haunts him, is what counts most for him, he does not stop. He wanders. . . . And by the blindness of the way he has chosen, against himself, in spite of himself, with its veerings, detours, and circlings back, his step, always one step in front of nowhere, invents the road he has taken. . . . And yet on this road he is never free. For all he has left behind still anchors him." Here we find many of A.'s personae and understand better such characters as Nashe, reinventing his life only to become imprisoned by the turn of chance; Fogg, looking behind to find answers, and Walt, whose magical ascent begins in flight.

A. has received several fellowships and awards including a nomination for the 1990 PEN/Faulkner Award for *The Music of Chance* and the 1993 Prix Medicis Etranger for *Leviathan* (1992). At the 1995 Berlin Film Festival, his screenplay for the movie *Smoke* was awarded the Silver Bear; Special Jury Prize; the International Film Critics Circle Award; and the Audience Award for Best Film. A.'s early work includes several collections of poetry, including *Disappearances: Selected Poems* (1988) and critical essays. He is known for his translations of such French authors as Maurice Blanchot and Stéphan Mallarmé. A. has also received both public and critical acclaim, as well, for his two screenplays, *Smoke* and *Blue in the Face,* both released in 1995.

BIBLIOGRAPHY: Barone, D., ed., *Beyond the Red Notebook: Essays on P. A.* (1995); Baxter, C., "The Bureau of Missing Persons: Notes on P. A.'s Fiction," *RCL* 14 (Spring 1994): 40–43; McCaffery, L., "An Interview with P. A.," *ConL* 33 (Spring 1992): 1–23

LISA TOLHURST

AUSTIN, Mary Hunter
b. 9 September 1868, Carlinsville, Illinois; d. 13 August 1934, Santa Fe, New Mexico

A. was a member of the transitional generation of American women writers who wrote at the turn of and into the 20th c., and who gave voice to the concerns of the then-burgeoning feminist movement. However, A.'s style and subject matter transcend time periods and movements, and contemporary readers will respond to the searching tone of her concise, honest, and oftentimes enormously funny voice, and will relate to the issues she found important: how to balance love and work, how to nurture one's creativity as well as one's family, and how to preserve and celebrate the spiritual impulses that arise from landscape and live in harmony with nature.

A. published over twenty books and hundreds of articles on a remarkable range of subjects, including fiction, natural history, art, anthropology, and philosophy. Born in the Midwest, an environment she found suffocating and provincial as she details it in her autobiography *Earth Horizon* (1932), she moved with her family to Owens Valley, California when she was twenty. A. found the Southwestern landscape and its indigenous cultures tremendously inspirational, and she was a political leader in preserving the Native American and Hispanic art and architecture that she so appreciated.

A.'s great talent lies in her work as a cultural historian and critic, both in her fiction and her nonfiction. Her first collection of sketches, *The Land of Little Rain* (1903), depicts the stretch of land between the Sierra Nevada Mountains and Death Valley, a place A. found mystical. In this classic of American nature writing, A. draws lyrical portraits of the Paiute and Shoshone Indians, of the miners, the animals, the domestic ritual of white, Native American, and Hispanic women, and most importantly, of the land itself. Landscape and culture infuse and inform each other in these sketches, and always A.'s perceptive and ironic voice gives life to what she sees. For example, in "The Basket Maker," one of the most beautiful sketches in the collection, A. writes about the Paiute woman Seyavi and shows how the land has given shape to her life as a woman, and to her art as a basket maker. However, amidst her lovely descriptions of Seyavi's baskets is a biting critique of white society: "In our kind of society, when a woman ceases to alter the fashion of her hair, you guess that she has passed the crisis of her experience. If she goes on crimping and uncrimping with the changing mode, it is safe to suppose she has never come up against anything too big for her."

Perhaps her best novel, *A Woman of Genius* (1912), has the same cultural criticism underlying it. In this largely autobiographical kunstlerroman, A. details the life of Olivia Lattimore, a talented actress who is first thwarted by and then triumphs over the narrow views of small-town America. As a social history, *A Woman of Genius* shows the shift from the 19th-c. cult of true womanhood and its virtues of purity, piety, and domesticity to the New Woman of the 1890s who values independence, a profession outside the home, and feminist politics. The novel never answers its central question—can a woman be married and be an artist too?—a question that A. contemplates in her autobiography as well. *A Woman of Genius* and *Earth*

Horizon are companion pieces, fascinating social history and commentary from a deeply talented and artistic woman who wrote truthfully about her time.

BIBLIOGRAPHY: Church, P. P., in Armitage, S., ed., *Wind's Trail: The Early Life of M. A.* (1990); Graulich, M., ed., *Western Trails: A Collection of Short Stories by M. A.* (1987); Pearce, T. M., *M. H. A.* (1966); Stineman, E. L., *M. A.: Song of a Maverick* (1989)

ANNE M. DOWNEY

AUSTIN, William
b. 2 March 1778, Lunenburg, Massachusetts; d. 27 June 1841, Charlestown, Massachusetts

From among A.'s few creative productions, his fame rests primarily on a single short story, "Peter Rugg, or the Missing Man," published first in the *New England Galaxy* (September 10, 1824; September 1, 1826; and January 19, 1827). "Peter Rugg" quickly won immense popularity, with notable appeal for Nathaniel HAWTHORNE and Henry Wadsworth LONGFELLOW, and it remains a perennial anthology piece. A. domesticated legends of the Wandering Jew and the Flying Dutchman into new England circumstances, much as Washington IRVING had done with Knickerbocker materials in "Rip Van Winkle."

A.'s narrative method of recounting Rugg's situation by means of one narrative nested within another is sophisticated. The frame storyteller, Jonathan Dunwell, presents events that transpire chiefly during 1820, although A. distorts time to heighten ambiguities along borders of reality and supernaturalism. Importuned to spend a stormy night with friends in Concord, Rugg, a man given to violent tempers, responds that if he does not reach home in Boston that night he hopes he may never see it. Thereafter, he and his young daughter Jenny, always precursors of storms (like the older Flying Dutchman), travel continuously in what by 1820 is an antiquated carriage. These wanderers furnish models for the 1950s popular song, "The Man Who Never Returned," by the Kingston Trio.

Much negative opinion has been directed toward the so-called crude narrative method in "Peter Rugg," but, viewed from current literary perspectives, that disjointed procedure serves as a means of enriching the supernatural-psychological qualities and of foregrounding the psychological makeup of the narrator. A.'s second great success in transmuting folklore into literary substance occurs in "The Man with the Cloaks: A Vermont Legend," first published in the *American Monthly Magazine* (January 1836), a reworking of the old theme of a penalty meted out to a self-centered person whose egotism will not permit him to assist someone more needy than he. Refusing to give warmth to another, the protagonist is condemned never to be warm himself again. This tale represents another treatment of the wanderer character who was to gain increasing hold upon the American literary imagination. Likewise, "The Late Joseph Natterstrom," which originally appeared in the *New England Magazine* (July 1831), furnished a specimen of the Orientalism that had been and continued to be popular among American creative writers. With its Hawthornesque element of identity loss, this story, too, offers an example of A.'s exploration of character creation that others such as Henry JAMES, William FAULKNER, and Thomas PYNCHON, would hone with greater subtlety.

BIBLIOGRAPHY: Austin, W., *W. A., the Creator of Peter Rugg* (1925); Hall, D. G., "W. A.," in Kimbel, B. E., ed., *DLB*, vol. 74, *American Short-Story Writers before 1880* (1988): 15–20

BENJAMIN FRANKLIN FISHER IV

AUTOBIOGRAPHY

From Benjamin FRANKLIN's *Autobiography* to *The Autobiography of Malcolm X* (1964), from *The Education of Henry Adams* to *Hunger of Memory: The Education of Richard Rodriguez* (1982), from John G. NEIHARDT's *Black Elk Speaks* to Maxine Hong KINGSTON's *The Woman Warrior,* American autobiography has been characterized by a tendency toward the blending of fiction and nonfiction, which has produced a rich tradition of individual lives narrated in a wide variety of forms. Autobiography has moved from its origins as an almost nonliterary form of record keeping, through a period when the genre was thought of as a subtype of biography—useful mainly for providing inspiration and additional information about authors—to its current status as a literary genre in its own right, worthy of being taught and analyzed as any other work of literature for its inherent aesthetic value as well as its historical interests, for its insights into individual lives and its ability to explain the struggle all people have with seeing patterns in their lives.

Although autobiography has been a part of American literature from the beginning, an exact definition of the genre has been almost impossible to attain. At first the word seems simple enough, its three Latin roots breaking down cleanly into self (*autos*), life (*bios*), and writing (*graphe*), so that autobiography becomes self life writing, of biography of the self. The immediate problem with this simple etymology is determining exactly what we mean by self, life, and writing. *Self* has been thought of as identity, personality, "I," and persona, and further amplified into child-

hood self, female self, American self, and other qualifications. *Life* has been treated as life history, life span,
religious or spiritual life, sexual life, and so on. *Writing*
has been given a full range of distinctions, from the
autobiographical occasion and the autobiographical
act as a performative speech act, to case history, self-
analysis, confession, discovery and self-invention.
More recently, critics have challenged the idea that
autobiographies have to be written, expanding the
genre to include other forms, such as oral history,
autobiography in the form of photography, and autobiography of those using American Sign Language.

What distinguishes autobiography from other
forms of life writing is difficult to be certain about
because the genre is defined not by form but by content, and because writers have often chosen to combine
various forms of life writing into one document. Autobiographies, like individual American lives, can take
any form they wish. Generally, critics agree that memoir focuses not so much on an individual person's life-
story as on historical events to which the memoirist
was an eye witness, while diary and journal are more
personal and historical records, meant not to get at
the author's life seen in retrospect as a complete narrative, but as daily records, usually not intended for
publication. In contrast, autobiography is generally
thought of as the story of a person's life, told in retrospect, by the person who lived it, focusing primarily
on the internal life.

For some readers and critics, Walt WHITMAN's *Song
of Myself,* Nathaniel HAWTHORNE's *The Scarlet Letter,*
and the confessional poems of Robert LOWELL or Sylvia PLATH are all autobiography, while for others only
works of nonfiction prose can be labeled *autobiography.* Some writers argue that autobiography is clearly
different from autobiographical novels like Thomas
WOLFE's *Look Homeward, Angel* or fictional autobiographies like Ernest J. GAINES's *The Autobiography of
Miss Jane Pittman* because autobiography is nonfictional. But for some of autobiography's theorists, that
distinction is not so easy to maintain as first thought.
Many poststructuralists argue that autobiography is
neither nonfiction nor any more referential than any
other form of writing; instead, they see autobiography
as merely another mode of writing, one that depicts
a constructed self's life as a narrative.

Although the usual distinctions between fiction and
nonfiction would seem to apply to autobiography,
these terms have by the 1980s begun to blur as authors
discover that writing about themselves is no longer
necessarily a completely nonfictional act, and that the
unwritten rule that autobiography could only be written by the famous was not necessarily true. For many
authors, the autobiographical form of writing possesses a peculiar kind of truth through a narrative

composed of the author's metaphors of self attempting
to reconcile the individual events of a lifetime by
using a combination of memory and imagination—all
performed in a unique act rooted in what really happened, but including some invention, and judged both
by the standards of truth and falsity and by the standards of success as an artistic creation.

Although current autobiographical theorists have
worked through the whole issue of autobiographical
truth and arrived at the conclusion that the proper
question to ask about autobiography is not how much
it reproduces the life that a biographer might write of
its subject, or what its researchable fidelity quotient
is, many readers are attracted to the genre because it
has a strong sense of referentiality: autobiographers
are real people, even if their autobiographical characters are not always completely accurate.

Nearly everyone who has ever attempted an autobiography realizes that turning a life into a narrative
necessarily requires shaping, selecting, and structuring
the life so that it becomes as much how the present
writer views his or her life in retrospect. Virtually all
critics acknowledge that memory is unreliable, and
therefore autobiography often tells us more about what
a person remembers than what really happened. But
often we discover in autobiography that what is literally true is less helpful in explaining a life than what
is figuratively true. We become what, in a sense, we
remember we were in the past.

From the colonial period to the present, American
autobiography has been less concerned with absolute
factual accuracy and more interested in creating or
inventing a mythic version of the self. Colonial autobiographies, for instance, although they have roots in
historical accounts such as William BRADFORD's *Of
Plymouth Plantation,* or Captain John SMITH's *The
General History of Virginia, New England, and the
Summer Isles,* or in travel journals like Christopher
Columbus's *The Journal of the First Voyage* (1827),
were mainly written, not to give a historical record of
individual lives, but to achieve the specific purpose
of establishing the theological goals of the Puritans.
Early autobiographies were intended to provide an
exemplar of the individual whose life would be both
a model of the new American and an attraction for
those in Europe considering coming to the new land.
Among the earliest full Puritan spiritual autobiographies was Thomas SHEPARD's "My Birth and Life,"
which is characteristic of the type. Spiritual autobiographies told those portions of people's lives that demonstrated their conversion from sin and selection by
God as the recipients of grace; individual lives were
shaped to reflect the needs of the community and to
provide good examples for the generations to come.
Great emphasis was placed on the experience of emi-

grating to America, an experience often compared to a spiritual rebirth.

Classic examples of the spiritual autobiography include Jonathan EDWARDS's *Personal Narrative,* Increase MATHER's autobiography, neither of which were published during the author's lifetime, and the *Journal of John Woolman,* this last a Quaker, rather than a Puritan autobiography, with the result that Woolman's emphasis is less on conversion and more on living a spiritual life within the New England Quaker community. Both the Puritan and the Quaker versions of the spiritual autobiography have influenced autobiographies that followed. Franklin's famous *Autobiography* turned both traditions in practical, secular directions, presenting his life through the metaphor of a book with errata, and constantly equating his life with the life of America. Influences of the spiritual autobiography in the 20th c. include Norman MAILER's *Armies of the Night.*

The spiritual autobiography evolved into two variations with important ramifications, the INDIAN CAPTIVITY NARRATIVE and the SLAVE NARRATIVE. The first type, exemplified by *A Narrative of the Captivity and Restoration of Mrs. Mary Rowlandson,* featured a personal account of white settlers captured by Indians, which had the advantage of allowing graphic details of adventures and hardships among the "savages," contrasted with the superior spiritual life of the authors, whose eventual return to civilization, presented as evidence of God's special providence toward the newly arrived Europeans, was often compared to the captivity of the Israelites by the Egyptians. So popular were captivity narratives that soon fictional versions began to appear, like James Fenimore COOPER's *The Last of the Mohicans,* leading eventually to the popular WESTERN novel, featuring capture and torture by exotic Indians. The slave narrative is exemplified by such books as *The Interesting Narrative of the Life of Olaudah Equiano; or, Gustavus Vassa, the African; Narrative of the Life of Frederick Douglass, an American Slave, Written by Himself;* and Harriet JACOBS's *Incidents in the Life of a Slave Girl, Written by Herself.*

These autobiographical accounts of life under African American slavery, and subsequent escape and deliverance, were originally intended by abolitionists as propaganda, which explains the insistence on white introductions and authentifications. Like the stories of being captured by native Indians, slave narratives included the spiritual autobiography's emphasis on life before and after conversion, and soon emerged as important literary works in their own right. Many writers realized the potential for fictionalizing the authentic slave narrative by combining that form with the sentimental novel. The result was such books as Harriet Beecher STOWE's *Uncle Tom's Cabin* and Harriet Wilson's *Our Nig; or, Sketches from the Life of a Free Black* (1859).

The influence of the captivity and slave narratives has been pervasive in 20th-c.-autobiography. A number of black autobiographies use the basic structure—enumeration of physical and mental tortures of slavery, escape to the North, followed by spiritual conversion, and rebirth as an individual. This pattern can be seen clearly in *The Autobiography of Malcom X,* which includes the slave narrative's characteristic ambiguity about authorship in the relationship between Malcom X and Alex HALEY, to whom the story was told.

Classic 19th-c. autobiographies continue the confusion of genre, blending journalism, diary, TALL TALE, almanac, and other literary forms with fiction. Whether Henry David THOREAU's *Walden,* for instance, is autobiography or nature writing or philosophy, depends on whether his focusing on a short period of his life—truncating two actual years into one—and turning himself into a mythic figure satisfies autobiography's call for a retrospective account of a life and historical authenticity. That *Walden* combines many elements of both the Puritan and the Quaker spiritual autobiography is clear enough, but should we stretch the definition of autobiography to include Whitman's *Song of Myself?* For readers who think of autobiography as prose, Whitman's poem is autobiographical but not autobiography; however, for others, his way of turning himself into a sort of American everyman, a fictional persona not always directly connected to the actual author, is a classic example of the Emersonian ideal of the self, resulting in a classic American autobiography.

Similar generic problems abound. Hawthorne, for example, deliberately confused his fictional and non-fictional prefaces, sometimes referring to himself in the third person, a characteristic of two major autobiographies of the 20th c.: *The Education of Henry Adams* and Gertrude STEIN's *The Autobiography of Alice B. Toklas.* Although Henry ADAMS's book seems at first to be more history than autobiography, its emphasis on his intellectual life places it squarely in the spiritual tradition of confession. Unlike Franklin, who saw himself as an example of the self-made man rising through ingenuity and industriousness to success, Adams saw his own life as a failure because of his inability to reconcile the tension between the intellectual and spiritual life in which he believed deeply, and the powerful force of science for which his education had not prepared him. Taking an opposite stance, Stein's autobiographical persona projected herself, through the supposed words of Alice B. TOKLAS, as a genius. Stein's trick of writing her life story by pretending to be writing Toklas's autobiography is made more complex by the fact that the book is not actually in the form of Toklas's autobiography so much as Toklas's biography of Stein.

Autobiographies in the 20th c. are as diverse as 20th-c. Americans. Particularly strong examples have emerged from various ethnic groups. Noteworthy African American autobiographies include W. E. B. DU BOIS's *Dusk of Dawn*, Richard WRIGHT's *Black Boy*, Maya ANGELOU's *I Know Why the Caged Bird Sings*, and *All God's Dangers: The Life of Nate Shaw*, a personal narrative fashioned by Theodore Rosengarten out of tape-recorded conversations. A somewhat similar collaborative effort produced *Black Elk Speaks*, an autobiography "as told through" John G. Neihardt, which follows the tradition of the spiritual autobiography in relating the author's life directly to a journey in search of God. Other valuable ethnic autobiographies include Carlos BULOSAN's *America Is in the Heart*, Ernesto Galarza's *Barrio Boy* (1971), N. Scott MOMADAY's *The Names*, Eva Hoffman's *Lost in Translation* (1989), Sara Suleri's *Meatless Days* (1989), and Frank McCourt's *Angela's Ashes* (1996).

Toward the end of the 20th c., the distinction between autobiography and the autobiographical novel was increasingly harder to maintain. James Weldon JOHNSON's *The Autobiography of An Ex-Colored Man*, a novel, was so often taken for a real autobiography that the author was forced to write in compensation *Along This Way*, a nonfictional account of his life. In addition, there have been numerous autobiographical books that deliberately stand on the border. From their titles and subtitles alone, we can see basic problems inherent in such books as Herbert GOLD's *Fathers*, subtitled "A Novel in the Form of a Memoir," Gore VIDAL's *Two Sisters*, subtitled "A Memoir in the Form of a Novel," or Frederick EXLEY's *A Fan's Notes*, subtitled "A Fictional Memoir," or John BARTH's *Once Upon a Time*, which he describes as a memoir bottled in a novel.

What are we to make of such books as Frank Conroy's *Stoptime* (1967), parts of which were originally published as fiction, Paul THEROUX's *My Other Life*, which features a writer named Paul Theroux whose books have the same titles as the actual Theroux's, or Philip ROTH's *My Life as a Man*, a book he calls mock-autobiography and divides into two parts: Peter Tarnopol's autobiographical narrative "My True Story" and this fictional hero's "fictional fiction" called "Useful Fictions"? Adding to the confusion, Roth's *The Counterlife* tells us that Nathan Zuckerman, protagonist of the three Roth novels collected as *Zuckerman Bound*, is a literary character invented by Tarnopol, while Zuckerman's fictional fiction includes thinly disguised parodies of Roth's *Portnoy's Complaint*.

Roth's apparently nonfictional *The Facts: A Novelist's Autobiography* is bracketed by a letter from Roth to Zuckerman and a reply from Zukerman to Roth.

Questions generated by such blurring of distinctions between genres are not always academic nitpicking. Failure to realize the nature of autobiography, its emphasis on what is remembered over the historical record, often results in misreading. For example, two of our most important autobiographers, Mary MCCARTHY and Lillian HELLMAN, became embroiled in a lawsuit because of McCarthy's claim that Hellman's autobiographies were filled with lies. McCarthy's charge of lying is odd, when we consider that in her *Memories of a Catholic Girlhood*, a book filled with confessions of fictionalizing the past, the inability to tell the truth becomes the author's major metaphor of self. Hellman's four autobiographies, *An Unfinished Woman*, *Pentimento*, *Scoundrel Time*, and *Maybe*, have as a common argument the increasing difficulty of relying on memory for an accurate portrait of the past. Both writers illustrate a common thread that runs through American autobiography from beginning to end: American autobiographers, while usually hesitant to write about themselves, wish to tell their own stories as examples of the value of the individual in a democracy. In telling about themselves, they stress story over history, personal myth over absolute fact, and individual style over generic requirements.

BIBLIOGRAPHY: Adams, T. D., *Telling Lies in Modern American Autobiography* (1990); Andrews, W. L., *To Tell a Free Story: The First Century of Afro-American Autobiography, 1760–1865* (1986); Andrews, W. L., *African American Autobiography* (1993); Benstock, S., *The Private Self* (1988); Braxton, J., *Black Women Writing Autobiography* (1989); Brumble, H. D., *American Indian Autobiography* (1988); Cooley, T., *Educated Lives: The Rise of Modern Autobiography in America* (1976); Couser, G. T., *American Autobiography: The Prophetic Mode* (1979); Eakin, P. J., *Fictions in Autobiography* (1985); Kaplan, L., ed. *A Bibliography of American Autobiography* (1961); Krupat, A., *For Those Who Came After: A Study of Native American Autobiography* (1985); Olney, J., ed. *Autobiography: Essays Theoretical and Critical* (1980); Payne, J. R., ed., *Multicultural Autobiography* (1992); Shea, D. B., *Spiritual Autobiography in Early America* (1968); Smith, S., *A Poetics of Women's Autobiography* (1987); Stone, A. E., ed. *The American Autobiography: A Collection of Critical Essays* (1981); Stone, A. E., *Autobiographical Occasions and Original Acts* (1982); Taylor, G. O., *Chapters of Experience* (1983); Wong, H., *Sending My Heart Back across the Years* (1992)

TIMOTHY DOW ADAMS

B

BACA, Jimmy Santiago
b. 2 January 1952, Sante Fe, New Mexico

Like many Southwestern writers, B. identifies with the land around him and the myths that are part of his culture. And like Joy HARJO, B. seeks transformation "to make sense of a terrible, terrible history." For B., that terrible history is both personal and cultural. Identified as a mestizo, a person with both Spanish and Native American heritage, B. perceives himself as an outsider in much of his work. Abandoned as a child, B.'s life is seared with a punishing past, which includes incarceration in an Arizona prison, where he found salvation in language and the power of poetry to transform oneself. His first major collection of poems, *Immigrants in Our Own Land* (1979), centers around his prison experience. His poems reveal an honest, passionate voice and powerful imagery full of the dark jewels of the American Southwest landscape (llanos, mesas, and chiles) and the chaotic urban landscape (nightclubs, rusty motors, and bricks) woven into a rich lyricism sprinkled with Spanish. It is this style and careful attention to language that won him an American Book Award in poetry from the Before Columbus Foundation in 1988 for *Martín and Meditations on the South Valley* (1987).

B.'s semiautobiographical *Martín and Meditations on the South Valley* follows the journey of a "detribalized Apache" in much the same way Leslie Marmon SILKO's novel *Ceremony* follows the journey of the Native American character, Tayo. For Tayo, returning to his Native American traditions and beliefs restores and guides him back to his genuine self. B.'s Martín hungers for the stories of his relatives much in the way Native Americans understand that storytelling is a powerful way to remain connected to one's culture and history. It is through stories and returning to his native land, "Burque" (Albuquerque, New Mexico), that Martín, like Tayo, finds a sense of restoration and peace although B. always reminds us that the American Dream remains out of reach for most Chicanos and Native Americans.

In *Black Mesa Poems* (1989), B. becomes a voice for a larger circle of the disenfranchised who work the fields, who push to keep a life going from day to day, who edge near violence daily, and who have almost forgotten the rich roots of their culture. Ironically, it is in B.'s storytelling that these lives will be remembered and their history recorded. In his collection of essays, *Working in the Dark* (1992), which won the 1993 Southwest Book Award, B. directly discusses his troubled history, the power of language, and the loss of dignity among Chicanos. In an article from that collection, "Chicanismo: Destiny and Destinations," B. eloquently and poignantly portrays himself as someone who aches to lead his people to freedom much with the sweeping exuberance of Walt WHITMAN or dark determination of Martin Luther King, Jr.

While B.'s work has cultural and sociological significance to American studies at the end of the 20th c., it also belongs among a growing number of works written by men who, inspired, empowered, or perhaps enraged by the women's movement of the 1970s, have sought to redefine their role as a man. Some of these writers include Robert LOWELL, Robert BLY, and James WRIGHT. One of B.'s poems that addresses this issue is "El Gato," a mournful and dynamic wail about a young boy whose life spirals further into violence each day. At the end of the poem, B. urges all men to learn to "cry" to undo the old wounds of the past and the suffocating thinking they have inherited as men.

The search for a genuine identity is a common theme in American literature. B.'s journey in his poetry for his genuine identity is an especially critical one because as Rudolfo ANAYA and others have recognized, until all the voices of the nation are heard, we will not know the true literature of the U.S.

BIBLIOGRAPHY: Cochran, S., "The Ethnic Implications of Stories, Spirits, and the Land in Native American

Pueblo and Aztlan Writing," *MELUS* 20 (Summer 1995): 69–91; Coppola, V., "The Moon in J. B.," *Esquire* 119 (June 1993): 48–56; Keene, J., "'Poetry Is What We Speak to Each Other,' An Interview with J. S. B.," *Callaloo* 17 (Winter 1994): 52–61

CATHERINE HARDY

BALDWIN, Faith

b. 18 March 1893, New Rochelle, New York; d. 18 March 1978, Norwalk, Connecticut

A prolific and successful writer of "light fiction" from 1921 until 1977, B. claimed to have begun her writing career with a play at the age of six. She married Hugh H. Cuthrell, the president of Brooklyn Union Gas Company in 1920, with whom she reared four children. Many of her romances deal with women who attempt to balance family with career, the personal with the professional, notably *Rosalie's Career* (1928), *Men Are Such Fools!* (1936), *He Married a Doctor* (1944), and *A Job for Jenny* (1945). In addition to over sixty books, including two written under the pen name Amber Lee, B. wrote hundreds of short stories, novellas, and articles as well as a column published in *Woman's Day* from 1958 to 1965. She was also the founder and director of the Famous Writers School in Westport, Connecticut.

B. was particularly popular during the Great Depression. Every book that she wrote during that period was a national best-seller; many of them were serialized or made into movies, including *Skyscraper* (1931), *Week-End Marriage* (1932), and *Beauty* (1933). Her explanation for her success during this period was that "People had to have some escape hatch, some way to get out of themselves, especially during the Depression. . . . When we got into the war nothing was more exciting than the headlines. After that I was still successful, but it was all different, because the world was different. Escape wasn't as important then."

When *American Family* was published in 1935, the *New York Times* noted that the novel was "solidly conceived" and firmly established B.'s claim to be considered a serious novelist. B. herself dismissed serious intentions, despite the book's historical background, stating: "*American Family* is just a story. It propounds no problems and sets no match to controversial tinder . . . I have in no way attempted to draw accurate or serious portrait of the fifty-five years which this story embraces. If I have omitted significant trends or erred in the cut of a gown or the curling of a tress of hair, I am sorry. But I am no historian, I am merely a teller of tales."

Although B.'s novels are largely romance novels, praised faintly by mainstream newspapers and magazines, much of her work subverts the expectations of the traditional romance novel, even as they rely on them. Marriage as a complicated contractual agreement is a frequent theme in B.'s novels, and as she stated in a 1974 interview, "Marriages founder more often because of trivia than trauma."

B. created a fictional community, Little Oxford, where she set a number of her novels, including *Station Wagon Set* (1939), *Any Village* (1971), *No Bed of Roses* (1973), *Time and the Hour* (1974), and *Thursday's Child* (1976). The Little Oxford books create a charming village setting for romance, but the subject matter—divorce, career and family, infidelity—remains relentlessly modern. B.'s portrayal of undying love is always tied to more mundane concerns, particularly financial ones. Her novels reflect her belief that even true love is tested by day-to-day reality.

JILL JONES

BALDWIN, James

b. 2 August 1924, New York City; d. 1 December 1987, St. Paul-de-Vence, France

Along with Richard WRIGHT, Ralph ELLISON, Zora Neale HURSTON, and Toni MORRISON, B. is not only an eminent African American writer but one of the most influential 20th-c. American novelists. Unlike that of his contemporaries, B.'s range of writing encompasses various genres: as novelist, essayist, playwright, and civil rights activist, he has attracted a large audience in America and abroad.

As his first novel *Go Tell It on the Mountain* (1953) shows, B.'s early life was replete with personal, familial, racial, and social turmoils. Despite and perhaps because of the adversity he experienced in Harlem, his gift as writer manifested itself. Even before he became a teenager, he published a short story in a church newspaper. While watching over his younger step brothers and sisters, B. devoured books borrowed from school and local libraries. At fourteen, he learned French from Countee CULLEN at Frederick Douglass High School. Cullen, one of the most celebrated poets of the Harlem Renaissance, was also a literary club advisor and inspired him to write and travel to France and other countries. Of his reading, *A Tale of Two Cities* and *Uncle Tom's Cabin* made lasting impressions for Charles Dickens's romantic portrayal of the French Revolution and Harriet Beecher STOWE's discourse on antislavery, respectively.

As apprentice in writing fiction, B. emulated Dostoevsky for his dialectic technique and Henry JAMES for his impressionism. Among African American books, B. held in the highest regard Wright's *Black Boy* and Ellison's *Invisible Man*. While holding a series of menial jobs and writing reviews and brief pieces for some literary magazines, B. met Wright, who, reading part of the manuscript of *Go Tell It on the Mountain,* encouraged him. This novel, much like *Black Boy,* is an autobiographical portrait of John Grimes, an African American youth in search of identity in racist society. Distinct from *Black Boy,* however, B.'s work concerns, in particular, the protagonist's sexual identity and guilt as well as his ambivalent relationships with his parents. In Paris, B. also befriended his American contemporaries such as William STYRON and Norman MAILER.

His second novel, *Giovanni's Room* (1956), like *Go Tell It on the Mountain,* is his major achievement. Although *Giovanni's Room* was not written in the tradition of literary naturalism, it represents the author's attempt to write a Zolaesque experimental novel. B. focuses on real characters taken from life: David, bisexual white American; his fiancée Hella, white American; and Giovanni, David's male homosexual lover. The story thrives on Hella's painful discovery of a mystery of human sexuality. *Another Country* (1962), a controversial novel, is nonetheless B.'s most ambitious work. Whereas his experiment in *Giovanni's Room* concerns only white characters and society, *Another Country* conducts an experiment on a variety of interracial sexual relationships. *Another Country* comprises the four narratives interrelated at certain points in the novel: the black man Rufus Scott and the white woman Leona; the black woman Ida Scott and the white bisexual man Vivaldo Moore; the white man Richard and the white woman Cass Silenski; the white homosexual man Eric Jones and the homosexual man Yves. Most of the events are perhaps too carefully arranged, but Rufus's tragic suicide and Vivaldo's and Ida's reconciliation are depicted with great compassion and understanding.

Two of B.'s later novels, *Tell Me How Long the Train's Been Gone* (1968) and *If Beale Street Could Talk* (1974), both explore the life of an African American artist. *Tell Me How Long the Train's Been Gone* is autobiographical and lacking in precipitous events and actions, but through flashbacks subtly conveys harrowing experiences of a middle-aged actor, Leo Proudhammer: Leo's worship of his brother, the failure of his relationship with a white actress, and his love for a young African American revolutionary man. *If Beale Street Could Talk,* unlike B.'s other novels, reflects his attempt to explore heterosexuality. This novel celebrates the genuine love relationship of an African American couple. Fonny, a young sculptor and an intellectual, consciously aware of the primacy of love over any racial or social obstacles, is able to

revive that relationship and attain his deliverance. The ultimate domain of love, as B. has shown throughout his work, is governed by the subjectivity of two individuals' deepest emotions that transcends their sexual orientation. His work has demonstrated that homosexuality is just as normal as is heterosexuality.

B. had earlier established his reputation as a premier social and literary critic. His essay collections, such as *Nobody Knows My Name* (1961), *The Fire Next Time* (1963), and *No Name in the Street* (1972), eloquently address various issues of race, slavery, American society, the South, and politics. His most influential social and literary criticisms are collected in *Notes of a Native Son* (1955). Focusing on the problems of race in American society, he discusses literature of antislavery from Harriet Beecher Stowe to Wright, as well as his own experiences in America and Europe. Earlier B. regarded Wright as his mentor but soon rebelled against him. Calling Bigger Thomas, the hero of Wright's *Native Son,* a descendant of Uncle Tom, B. argues that *Native Son* "suggested a revolution of racial conflict that was merely the liberal dream of good will in which blacks would obliterate their personalities and become as whites." B. disagrees with Wright's use of violence, which he calls "gratuitous and compulsive because the root of the violence is never explained." B. appreciates Wright's courageous representation of the African American "rage," but to him the novelist must analyze raw emotion and transform it into an identifiable human experience.

BIBLIOGRAPHY: Harris, T., *Black Women in the Fiction of J. B.* (1985); Kinnamon, K., ed., *J. B.: A Collection of Critical Essays* (1974); Porter, H. A., *Stealing the Fire: The Art and Protest of J. B.* (1989); Pratt, L. H., *J. B.* (1978); Standley, F. L., and N. V. Burt, eds., *Critical Essays on J. B.* (1988); Standley, F. L., and L. H. Pratt, eds., *Conversations with J. B.* (1989); Weatherby, W. J., *J. B.: Artist on Fire: A Portrait* (1989)

YOSHINOBU HAKUTANI

BAMBARA, Toni Cade

b. 25 March 1939, New York City; d. 9 December 1995, Philadelphia, Pennsylvania

Best known for short stories set in the urban landscape of her youth, B.'s fiction and criticism are informed by her work as educator, social worker, and activist. While her only novel, *The Salt Eaters* (1980), received mixed reviews, her short story collections, *Gorilla, My Love* (1972) and *The Sea Birds Are Still Alive* (1977), are highly regarded for their astute representations of the inner struggles of the young, their skilled synthesis of social and political themes with inquiries into the nature of identity and community, and B.'s dexterous use of language in evoking the cadences and nuances of African American life. B.'s documentation and celebration of the inner lives and struggles of ordinary African Americans and her challenge to consider the responsibilities inherent in transforming one's life constitute a singular contribution to American literature.

B. first received critical attention with the publication of two anthologies she edited, *The Black Woman* (1970) and *Tales and Stories for Black Folks* (1971). *The Black Woman,* the first anthology of its kind to be published in the U.S., grew out of B.'s impatience with the dearth of literature directly relevant to black women. B.'s contributions to the anthology, "On the Issue of Roles" and "The Pill: Genocide or Liberation," are cogent interrogations of the impact of sexism on the struggle for black liberation. *The Black Woman* contains essays by students, mothers, and community workers, as well as work by such writers as Alice WALKER, Nikki GIOVANNI, and Audre LORDE. Similarly, *Tales and Stories for Black Folks* combines stories by established authors with those of students in B.'s creative writing course at Livingston College whom she had instructed to create works that would be "useful" to someone. B.'s commitment to providing "usable lessons" to the African American community—which she believed to be "at war" with a dominant society orchestrated to oppress it—led her to prefer the economy of the short story form to the novel, a choice she acknowledged limited her commercial success.

The stories in *Gorilla, My Love* articulate determining moments in the lives of ordinary people—always African American, usually female, often young or elderly—with an accuracy of diction and depth of understanding that evidence B.'s connection to and concern for her community. Perhaps B.'s best-known work is the widely anthologized title story from the collection. Narrated by Hazel, an audacious little girl determined to confront life's injustices head on, "Gorilla, My Love" is remarkable for the authenticity of the child's voice, which B. manages to capture without condescension, and for its layered structure, through which B. gives voice to the pain of an unrequited first love while subtly interrogating the indifference with which adults, as individuals and as institutions, betray children.

The "lessons" imparted through other stories in *Gorilla, My Love* cover a wide range of themes: the folly of rejecting homegrown values and everyday caring for nationalist posturing ("My Man Bovane"); the exhilaration and empowerment inherent in celebrating and sharing the best of oneself ("Raymond's

Run"); the consequences of unexamined rage ("Talkin Bout Sonny"); the sustaining power of close friendship ("The Johnson Girls"). While acknowledging the ravages of racism, sexism, and neglect, characters in B.'s stories offer a spectrum of responses to oppression that lies beyond the rage, recrimination, and superficial self-aggrandizement upon which many of B.'s contemporaries built their reputations.

Published after visits to Cuba in 1973 and Vietnam in 1975, and set in a variety of geographical locations, the stories in *The Sea Birds Are Still Alive* also underscore B.'s belief in the self as the main instrument of social transformation. These stories present protagonists exhibiting fissures in their resolve to revise their realities; they are battle-worn revolutionaries and novice organizers, self-made women and refugees under fire. Probing their personal triumphs and concessions, B. critiques disconnections in communities under siege and their implications for the individual who resists oppression.

The Salt Eaters broadens this exploration. Set in the beleaguered community of Claybourne, Georgia, the novel attempts to capture the social, political, and spiritual tenor of the 1980s. *The Salt Eaters* draws from B.'s short story "Broken Field Running," focusing on the emotional breakdown of a tireless community worker, Velma Henry. While the main plot of the novel centers on Velma's healing session with community elders—led by "swamphag" Minnie Ransom—and occurs in the space of two hours, B. uses flashback, stream-of-consciousness and digression to reveal Claybourne's history, to project possible futures for it, and suggest a model for the community's recovery that synthesizes the energies of its "healers" and its "warriors." In *The Salt Eaters,* B. attempts to use the narrative voice as a medium through which the action of the plot is channeled rather than merely observed. Some critics take issue with the novel's somewhat difficult structure; others admire the breadth of its scope and B.'s ambitious attempt to reposition the narrative stance.

Throughout her career, B. struggled to make language accommodate a worldview that questions assumed patterns. To better articulate her vision, B. turned to video and filmmaking in the mid-1980s and wrote and produced a number of acclaimed documentaries, including *The Bombing of Osage Avenue* and *W. E. B. Du Bois: A Biography in Four Voices.*

Deep Sightings and Rescue Missions: Fiction, Essays and Conversations, a collection of B.'s fiction, criticism, and interviews, was edited by Toni MORRISON and published posthumously in 1996. Morrison, who had been B.'s editor at Random House, wrote in the preface to the volume, "There was no doubt whatsoever that the work she did had work to do. She always knew what her work was for."

BIBLIOGRAPHY: Byerman, K. E., "Women's Blues: The Fiction of T. C. B. and Alice Walker," *Fingering the Jagged Grain: Tradition and Form in Recent Black Fiction* (1985): 104-128; Deck, A. A., "T. C. B.," in Davis, T. M., and T. Harris, eds., *DLB*, vol. 38, *Afro-American Writers After 1955: Dramatists and Prose Writers* (1985): 12–22; Kelley, M. A., "'Damballah is the First Law of Thermodynamics': Modes of Access to T. C. B's *The Salt Eaters*," *AAR* 27 (1993): 479–93; Morrison, T., "City Limits, Village Values: Concepts of the Neighborhood in Black Fiction," in Jaye, M. C., and A. C. Watts, eds., *Literature and the Urban Experience: Essays on the City and Literature* (1981): 35–43; Traylor, E. V., "Music as Theme: The Jazz Mode in the Works of T. C. B.," in Evans, M., ed., *Black Women Writers (1950–1980): A Critical Evaluation* (1984): 58–70; Vertreace, M. M., "T. C. B: The Dance of Character and Community," in Pearlman, M., ed., *American Women Writing Fiction: Memory, Identity, Family, Space* (1989): 155–71

MADELINE D. MURRAY

BANGS, John Kendrick

b. 27 May 1862, Yonkers, New York; d. 21 January 1922, Ogunquit, Maine

In his genial way, B. amused the masses not with regional dialect and local color, but with pleasant wit and irony. His vast output, consisting of light verse, humorous sketches, novels, and plays, wittily poke fun at social mores. Never reaching the misanthropic stages of writers like Mark TWAIN, B. was considered an entertainer, not a reformer. He tended to avoid altogether the dark aspects of humor and struck at social follies of the natural and supernatural with a quill, not an axe. Although B. achieved great popularity during his lifetime, his work is presently ignored.

B.'s first work appeared in a collegiate literary magazine, *Acta Columbia,* under the pseudonyms Shakespeare Jones, T. Carlyle Smith, and the Collegiate Vituperator. As his career progressed, he wrote for virtually every major periodical of the time and edited the humor department of both *Harper's Magazine* and *Harper's Bazaar* from 1888 to 1889, as well as *Harper's Weekly* (1899–1903) and *Puck* (1904–7). Most of the magazine sketches were later compiled, as in B.'s first book, *The Lorgnette* (1886), a collection of satires concerning, among other things, money worship and anglomania. After 1907, B. took to the lecture platform and with lectures like *Salubrities I Have Met* became one of the most popular and sought-after

comic speakers. His most popular works were comic treatments of the supernatural. *The Water Ghost* (1894) and *Ghosts I Have Met* (1898) mock Gothic tradition, while his books on Hades present an unlikely gathering of shades attempting to entertain themselves for eternity. *The House-Boat on the Styx* (1896), his most interesting book, portrays imaginary confrontations between Hamlet and Shakespeare in which a remake of the tragic play, to be called "Irving," is contemplated. Doomed Dr. Johnson is forever fleeing from Boswell, who is inevitably thrown into the muckish river by the rest of the shades. Others who haunt the pages of this charmingly witty book are Nero, Lucrezia Borgia, Confucious, Charon (as "janitor"), and Xanthippe and Mrs. Noah, who, after masterminding the mutiny of the houseboat in the final pages, are kidnapped by Captain Kidd. In the book's sequel, *The Pursuit of the House-Boat* (1897), Sherlock Holmes's ghost is obtained to track the missing spouses. As Holmes becomes involved in a dialogue of endless theorizing, Kidd quickly grows weary of the women's chatter and attempts to leave them on an eternal Parisian shopping spree. By chance, they all are reunited in the end.

B.'s love of myth, folklore, and fairy tale is illustrated in his juvenile collections, *Tiddledywink Tales* (1891) and *Half-Hours with Jimmieboy* (1893). His books for adults include a mock biography, *Mr. Bonaparte of Corsica* (1895), and farcical looks at current celebrities in *Peeps at People* (1899).

BIBLIOGRAPHY: Bangs, F. H., *J. K. B.* (1941); Nelson, J. A., "J. K. B.," in Riley, S. G., ed., *DLB*, vol. 79, *American Magazine Journalists, 1850–1900* (1989): 50–55

MICHAEL J. PETTENGELL

BANKS, Russell

b. 28 March 1940, Newton, Massachusetts

B. is one of America's most powerful moralists of postmodern fiction. His writing addresses the raw edges of contemporary life: poverty, abuse, violence, guilt, loss, greed, uprootness, blue collar despair, and inexplicable fate. His voice is one of the most persistent ones in publishing; every book he has published since 1975 has been reissued. Unlike other postmodern novelists, B. has focused his attention on the despair and struggle of the lower classes, not on the ironies and anxieties of the affluent middle class. Consequently, his work, though often humorous, tends toward moral outrage. His early work experimented with contemporary novelistic techniques and language. His later work follows traditional realistic forms but utilizes unconventional narrators, who, like intimate companions or storytellers with their arms around their reader's shoulders, comment on the characters and sometimes address the reader directly.

The early collections of stories, *Searching for Survivors* (1975) and *The New World: Tales* (1978), combine experimental and traditional narrative techniques with extraordinary and everyday elements. Both are about people attempting to recover meaning in a world where all the heroes—Henry Hudson, Ernesto "Ché" Guevara, Simón Bolívar, and others—are dead leaving ordinary people the task of rescuing memory and sorting illusions. B. first major novel, *Hamilton Stark* (1978), parodies biographies, memoirs, mysteries, and itself by having family, friends, and a narrator, who is himself writing a novel, present their versions of Stark, an unlikable alcoholic who never actually appears in the novel.

The novel *The Book of Jamaica* (1980), a compelling moral exploration of poverty, race, and class, is the story of a New Hampshire college professor involved with the Maroons and Rastafarians of Jamaica where he has gone to finish a novel. *Trailerpark* (1981), a masterful collection of thirteen interrelated stories taking place in a down-at-the-heels trailer park, examines the lives of lonesome, uneducated characters, wanting something better than their misery and vain hopes. *Success Stories* (1986), another remarkable collection of stories, looks at the world from underneath with narrators depicting the ugly bruises of life, recounting how they got there and who or what is to blame.

With *Continental Drift* (1985), his most accomplished novel, B. achieved commercial and critical success. The plot brings together Bob Dubois, a repairman who moves from New Hampshire to Florida looking for a better life, and Vanise, a Haitian woman who has lost almost everything in a world manipulated by voodoo spirits. The tragedy is as searing and unstoppable as a wrenching tectonic collision. B.'s next novel, *Affliction* (1989), explores how loss, pain, fear, and a sense of fragility in a small town cop in New Hampshire, erupts into rage, self-destruction, and mayhem.

In *The Sweet Hereafter* (1991), also produced as a film, B. examines the character of a town trying to make sense of a bus accident where fourteen children die. The story, told by the bus driver, a drunken mechanic, a girl paralyzed by the accident, and a negligence lawyer, reveals how we create scapegoats, blame, and symbols to rationalize the fact that life is out of human control. B. again demonstrates that he is one of our major moral storytellers. *Rule of the Bone* (1995), is B.'s popular but unromanticized *Catcher in the Rye,* examining a seventh-grade drugged-out

dropout trying to escape a miserable childhood who gets involved with a Jamaican mystic and a drug deal gone bad. This unflinching but funny picture of blue-collar America demonstrates B.'s mastery of his subject and art.

BIBLIOGRAPHY: Niemi, R., *R. B.* (1997); Pfeil, F., "Head of the Class," *VLS* 78 (September 1989): 25–26; Vandersee, C., "R. B. and The Great American Reader," *Cresset* 53 (December 1989): 13–17; Lee, D., "About R. B.," *Ploughshares* 19 (Winter 1993–94): 209–13

NEWTON SMITH

BARAKA, Amiri [Everett LeRoi Jones]
b. 7 October 1934, Newark, New Jersey

Early in his career, with the publication in 1960 of his collection of poems entitled *Preface to a Twenty Volume Suicide Note*—followed by *The Dead Lecturer* (1964), *Black Art* (1966), *Black Magic: Poetry 1961–1967* (1969), and *It's Nation Time* (1970)—B. established his characteristic themes of distrust and hatred toward the Caucasian world. By the publication in 1972 of *Spirit Reach,* LeRoi Jones had become "Imamu Amiri Baraka" and was well established as the leading black militant of the world of poetry, but he was also establishing himself as a playwright; in addition, he had written a novel and a collection of short stories, and he had edited or written many other titles, most of them on social issues.

B. inspired more scholarship since 1973 than any other black poet in the U.S. He never wrote formal poetry like that of such contemporaries as Langston HUGHES, Robert HAYDEN, or Gwendolyn BROOKS. His earliest work was line-phrased prose, and as he matured B. sometimes treated prose in the manner of Walt WHITMAN and Allen GINSBERG, writing in grammatical parallels.

Despite his rejection of white associations, B. was deeply influenced and associated with the Black Mountain school, in particular by the poetry and preachments of its founder, Charles OLSON. In this respect, B.'s primary literary influences were those of a renegade white academy rather than those of his black contemporaries who worked out of a tradition of formalism deriving from, on the one hand, mainstream English literature and, on the other, black musical forms such as gospel, blues, and jazz.

A comparison of B.'s early work with his late shows, in the opinion of some critics, an improvement. Unfortunately, B. did not transform Olson's prosodic peculiarities and poeticisms into his own style as successfully as Hayden and Brooks combined black ethnic traditions with formal techniques to make a poetry as effective as any written during the period of protest.

His novel *The System of Dante's Hell* (1966) was followed by a collection of short stories entitled *Tales* (1967). In addition, B. has published or produced over three dozen plays, including *A Good Girl Is Hard to Find* (1958), *The Slave* (1964), *A Black Mass* (1966), *The Death of Malcolm X* (1969), *Four Black Revolutionary Plays* (1971), and *Black Power Chant* (1972). B. has also written screenplays, notably *Dutchman* (1967), *Black Spring* (1967), *A Fable* (1971), and *Supercoon* (1971). B.'s nonfiction includes *Blues People: Negro Music in White America* (1963), *A Black Value System* (1970), *National Liberation and Politics* (1974), *The Autobiography of LeRoi Jones/A. B.* (1984), and *The Music: Reflections on Jazz and Blues* (1987), written with his wife, Amina Baraka.

Very little changes in B.'s world, either in the way he perceives his historical environment or in the way he writes. If he is typecast as an experimental writer, the fact is that very little that he does in his poetry is much different from either Olson or Ezra POUND. If Pound was an extremist of the fascist right, B. is his mirror image on the extreme left. In a peculiar way, B.'s situation has made him a salable entity in the world of academe where B. has always made his living as a college professor. However, there is no denying that B. has made a significant impact among young readers and writers of color.

BIBLIOGRAPHY: Benston, K. W., *B.: The Renegade and the Mask* (1976); Harris, W. J., *The Poetry and Poetics of A. B.* (1985); Hudson, T., *From LeRoi Jones to A. B.: The Literary Works* (1973); Reilly, C., ed., *Conversations with A. B.* (1994)

LEWIS PUTNAM TURCO

BARKER, James Nelson

b. 17 June 1784, Philadelphia, Pennsylvania; d. 9 March 1858, Philadelphia, Pennsylvania

B.'s plays show vital developments within early American drama, and his critical history of drama maintains value. Of a prominent Philadelphia family aligned with the Democratic party, he rose to high national political office, but such public service diminished his creative pursuits. His sketch of his literary career in William DUNLAP's *History of the American Theatre* bears witness to frustrated dramatic endeavors.

Four of B.'s surviving plays are important. *Tears and Smiles* (1808), a comedy, dramatizes the then-familiar theme of American superiority over European customs and tastes. Nathan Yank, a stage rustic of the type originated by Royall TYLER in *The Contrast*, demonstrates B.'s advances upon previous renderings of vernacular speech. *The Indian Princess* (1808), another comedy, an "operatic melo-drame" because of its interspersed songs, was the first performed play about American Indians by an American playwright, and it was the first to draw upon the Pocahantas story. It proved popular on both counts, and, despite occasionally stilted dialogue, it neatly blends American history with dramatic interest. *Marmion* (1816), deriving in part from Sir Walter Scott's famous narrative poem, offers traditional Gothicism in its high-pitched characters amidst an atmosphere of mystery, intrigue, and impending doom. B.'s innovation is the subtle unfolding of Marmion's guilt about consequences of his misdeeds. Sexuality is also more realistically treated here than in the early Gothic works.

B.'s most significant play, and one of the most important plays from early 19th-c. American drama, *Superstition* (1826), offers compelling perspectives upon warped psychology against a background of New England religious intolerance yoked with witchcraft scares, Indian warfare, and regicides connected with the death of England's King Charles I. The clergyman Ravensworth intends to exterminate Isabella and her son Charles. Both have offended because of what Ravensworth deems their insufficient regard for his office. Charles, moreover, is a threat because he loves the clergyman's daughter Mary. Ravensworth, in a dramatic trial scene, cleverly shifts his accusation of sorcery to one of murder, rape, and dealing with the devil. Playing upon superstitious fears of the villagers, Ravensworth manages to hurry off Charles to execution. In turn, Mary's death occurs because her constitution can no longer bear the intense trauma. Melodramatics in *Superstition*—the terrible storm that accompanies the trial and catastrophe of double death; or revealing the "Unknown," the devil according to Ravensworth, as the regicide Goffe and the father of Isabella, and now pardoned—serve functional purposes in this drama of actual and psychological warrings, mysteries in identity, and overriding turmoil. B.'s use of New England history anticipates that by James Fenimore COOPER in *The Wept of Wish-ton-Wish* and Nathaniel HAWTHORNE in "The Gray Champion" (1835), although the pioneer has no mean artistic hand. B.'s other writings include biographical sketches of renowned Americans, verse published in annuals, and most significant, "The Drama," an eleven-part series in the Philadelphia *Democratic Press* (December 1816-February 1817), which together constitute a thoughtful history of drama and critical perceptions about contemporaneous plays and players by a writer of experience and considered opinions.

B. significantly modified traditions for American playhouses. His decided turn to nationalistic themes and types marks him singly during a period when many other American writers clung to foreign inspirations. His use of colloquial language, his subordination of Gothic luridness to realistic settings and credible characterizations, and his employment of American history manifest a pioneering into areas later given additional currency by dramatists such as Eugene O'NEILL, Arthur MILLER, Thornton WILDER, and Tennessee WILLIAMS.

BIBLIOGRAPHY: Meserve, W. J., *An Emerging Entertainment* (1977); Moody, R., *America Takes the Stage* (1955); Musser, P. H., *J. N. B.* (1929); Quinn, A. H., *A History of the American Drama from the Beginnings to the Civil War,* 2nd ed. (1943)

BENJAMIN FRANKLIN FISHER IV

BARLOW, Joel
b. 24 March 1754, Redding, Connecticut; d. 21 December 1812, Zarnowiec, Poland

Poet and revolutionary, B. was one of the Connecticut Wits, famous for his ambition to write the great American epic and for his radical pro-revolution pamphlets that are second in importance only to those of Thomas PAINE. B. graduated as class poet from Yale in 1778. Although his commencement poem, "The Prospect of Peace," looked forward to a new era of republican peace, prosperity, and progress, the war against England was still on and B., aged twenty-four, joined the fight as chaplain in the Third Massachusetts Brigade. Later, he edited the *American Weekly,* published in Hartford from 1784 to 1785 and notable for its anti-slavery views. As one of the Connecticut Wits, who were Calvinist in religion and Federalist in politics, B. brought out an influential edition of the Psalms, *Doctor Watt's Imitation of the Psalms* (1785), and from 1886 to 1887 helped write the Federalist satire *The Anarchiad.* This marks the high point of his early conservative career.

In 1787, B. published *The Vision of Columbus,* an epic in nine books of heroic couplets on the history of America. The poem begins with the despairing Columbus in prison at the end of his life, and consists of Columbus's vision of the New World's future as an outgrowth of its native past. B.'s intellectual radicalism is shown by his avoidance of Homeric, Miltonic, and biblical mythology, and by his founding the civilization of the New World on South American myth, on the advent and teachings of the legendary Peruvian demigods Manco Capek and Mama Oella.

B.'s daringly indigenous pan-American epic has never had the attention it deserves.

In 1788, B. went to France on a private commercial venture. He was quickly converted from Federalist to Jeffersonian democratic ideas, from Calvinism to Deism in religion, and he became a leading spokesman for the French Revolution, remaining in France for the next eighteen years. His *Advice to the Privileged Orders* (part 1, 1792; part 2, 1793) ranks with Thomas Paine's *Rights of Man* as an answer to Edmund Burke's *Reflections on the French Revolution.* B.'s *Letter to the National Convention* (1793) called for the French to abandon their first try at a revolutionary constitution and devise a more radical one along American lines. B. advocates elimination of the monarchy, abolition of the National Church, elimination of property qualifications for voting, and instituting annual elections. He was made an honorary citizen of France for this book, and he actually ran for election to the National Convention. It was while running for office in Savoy that B. was unexpectedly served a meal of hasty pudding—New England's corn meal mush—which led him to write a mock epic *The Hasty Pudding* (1796), his most popular poem.

Returning to the U.S. in 1805, B. called for the creation of a National University in Washington, D.C., to set standards and coordinate public education. Put forth in his *Prospectus of a National Institution* (1806), B.'s idea of a university was ahead of its time in the high place given to the humanities and to political science. In 1807, a much revised but not much improved version of his epic was published as *The Columbiad.* B.'s verse—often mannered, inflated, or dull—is strongest when denouncing aristocracy, inequality, kingship, and, especially, priestcraft. *The Columbiad,* and much of B.'s prose, marks the high tide of militant deism in America, and B. is a major American proponent of natural religion. He also has a strong satiric gift, evident in his prose, in *The Hasty Pudding,* and in his last poem, "Advice to a Raven in Russia," which he wrote in the last year of his life, when, as American Minister to France, he vainly chased Napoleon across Northern Europe on the terrible retreat from Moscow in 1812, trying to get a treaty signed. While on this final mission B. died of pneumonia in Poland, where he still lies buried.

BIBLIOGRAPHY: Bottorff, W., and A. Ford, eds., *The Works of J. B.* (2 vols., 1970); Howard, L., *The Connecticut Wits* (1943); Miller, V. C., *J. B.: Revolutionist London, 1791–1792* (1932); Todd, C. B., *Life and Letters of J. B.* (1880); Woodress, J., *A Yankee Odyssey: The Life of J. B.* (1859); Zunder, T., *The Early Days of J. B.* (1934)

ROBERT D. RICHARDSON, JR.

BARNES, Djuna [Chappell]

b. 12 June 1892, Cornwall-on-Hudson, New York; d.
18 June 1982, New York City

Admired by contemporary writers and long widely considered by scholars to be a stylistically intriguing but minor modernist novelist, poet, and playwright, B. has recently received increasing attention from critics who praise her dense verse, intricate prose, explorations of women's relationships, and radical critiques of masculine domination of family and culture.

During the years in New York City, B. worked as an illustrator and began the journalism she continued through the 1930s, some of which is collected in *Interviews* (1985). Her Beardsleyesque drawings complemented her decadent early poetry in *The Book of Repulsive Women* (1915). The Provincetown Theater produced three of her complex one-act plays. Some of her deterministic sketches are collected in *Smoke and Other Early Stories* (1982).

In Paris during the 1920s, B. continued to produce poems, stories, plays, and drawings, a selection of which were published as *A Book* (1923). This was revised, with additions and deletions, and retitled for one of the stories as *A Night among the Horses* (1929), and again as *Spillway* (1962). Her first extended work, *Ryder* (1928), was briefly a best-seller until the small first edition sold out. Much of the novel is in bawdy, mock-18th-c. style, and it incorporates verse, drama, soliloquies, biblical parody, and illustrations in a somewhat naive style influenced by illustrations B. found in Paris. Many of the brief chapters are devoted to narratives or topics only tangentially or thematically related to the story of the novel's eponymous household, consisting of the matriarch Sophia Grieve Ryder, her irresponsible son Wendell, dedicated to populating the planet, his wife Amelia de Grier, his mistress Kate-Careless, and their children. Wendell's sexuality is scandalous to the townspeople, oppressive to his mates, threatening to his children, and a lascivious dark joke to the narrator. His power in the family has been granted to him by Sophia, who finally oversees his downfall and Amelia's expulsion from the family.

In the same year, B. privately printed and circulated a small edition of the humorous *Ladies Almanac* (1928), which displays similar virtuosity. Through verse, music, illustrations, double columns of text, retellings of myths, and non-narrative meditations the book examines multiple definitions of woman and relations among women. Between digressions, it describes a female community reputedly based on the Natalie Barney circle, and including, besides Dame Evangeline Musset (Barney), Patience Scalpel (Mina Loy), and Lady Buck-and Balk and Tilly Tweed-in-Blood (Una Troubridge and Radclyffe Hall). Repeatedly seen as antilesbian, the book has been reclaimed by critics who recognize its celebration of female sexuality and see its satire as emerging from a sympathetic position within a women's community.

B.'s best known work is *Nightwood* (1936), completed in England and titled by T. S. ELIOT. The novel, a critique of Western religious moralities, theories of sexual inversion, and femininity, revolves around the mysterious Robin Vote, a figure of female sexuality and otherness. Lacking in self-knowledge and outside social regulations, the amoral Robin is exploited by her pretentious husband Felix Volkbein and deceitful lover Jenny Petherbridge, and obsessively misread by her lover Nora Flood, the character most available to realistic reading. The novel's baroque syntax repeatedly displaces Robin through extended metaphors that dwarf or displace her from the subject position. More stylistically unified than B.'s earlier books, the novel digresses only within metaphor and in the monologues of the voluble Doctor Matthew O'Connor (also the family doctor in *Ryder*), a transvestite invert and vehicle for much of the book's indictment of the puritanism that creates the notion of depravity and alienates women from themselves and each other.

Although it was little appreciated in the U.S., B.'s verse drama entitled *The Antiphon* (1958) was enthusiastically received when first performed in Stockholm in 1961 in a translation by Dag Hammarskjold. Most of the play is in densely imagistic blank verse, with some rhyme and variation of line length; it has been compared to Greek, Elizabethan, and Jacobean tragedy. Set in the crumbling Burley family seat in 1939 England, the play brings together the elderly widow Augusta Burley Hobbs, her brother Jonathan, her businessmen sons Dudley and Elisha, and her estranged daughter, Miranda. Augusta has been invited to Burley by her estranged son Jeremy, disguised in the play as "Jack Blow," a coachman. The action concerns the gradual revelation of the crimes of Augusta's husband, Titus Higby Hobbs, a polygamist with delusions of religious grandeur, guilty of attempting to rape his young daughter, and, with his wife's complicity, of arranging her rape. Critics have particularly praised the final third act's fatal confrontation between mother and daughter. The elaborate obliquity of the language tends to lure the audience into complicity with the family's denial of the past.

BIBLIOGRAPHY: Broe, M. L., ed., *Silence and Power: A Reevaluation of D. B.* (1991); Field, A., *D.: The Formidable Miss B.* (1985); Herring, P., *D.: The Life and Work of D. B.* (1995); Kannenstine, L. F., *The Art of D. B.: Duality and Damnation* (1977)

FRANN MICHEL

BARNES, Margaret Ayer

b. 8 April 1886, Chicago, Illinois; d. 25 October 1967, Cambridge, Massachusetts

Born into a prominent Chicago family, B. received her education at Bryn Mawr only to return home, marry a wealthy native Chicagoan, and settle into Chicago society. This was the familiar terrain she carefully chronicled in a collection of short stories, *Prevailing Winds* (1928), and five novels, *Years of Grace* (1930), *Westward Passage* (1931), *Within This Present* (1933), *Edna His Wife* (1935), and *Wisdom's Gate* (1938). Her work focuses on the lives of upper-middle-class Chicagoans, tracing the changes in a small number of families over the course of several generations, from the turbulent 1890s through World War I and the Great Depression. This historical sweep allowed her to explore her deep ambivalence over both the traditions that constrained earlier generations and what was lost when later generations discarded these traditions to pursue individual interests and desires.

B. began her career collaborating with the playwright Edward SHELDON on several plays, including an adaptation of Edith WHARTON's *Age of Innocence,* but her first novel, *Years of Grace,* which won the Pulitzer Prize in 1931, suggests the themes that would exercise her throughout her career. The novel spans the life of Jane Ward, from her adolescence through her fifties. The early chapters of the novel recount Jane's first open confrontation with the timid and hidebound values of her family and class. When her relationship with a young bohemian Frenchmen, Andre Duroy, leads to a proposal of marriage, her family, uneasy with and disdainful of the unconventional Duroy family, insists that Jane and Andre wait until she is twenty-one to renew their relationship. In the meantime, she attends Bryn Mawr for two years, returning home when her older sister marries. There she meets and marries Stephen Carver, son of a wealthy banking family. Much of the novel describes Jane's gradual accommodation to the demands of motherhood—they have three children—and as wife to a socially prominent banker. In a brief rebellion against the stultifying round of dinner parties, summers with Stephen's family, and charitable work, she falls in love with the husband of her longtime friend and Bryn Mawr roommate, the roguish Jimmy Trent, but stays with Stephen, whom she still loves. The final chapters focus on Jane's painful realization that her children's lives are not all she hoped they would be—her son has too quickly taken up the sedate life of his father, her daughter Cicily has left her husband for Albert, the husband of her childhood friend.

The novel at its best offers a series of quiet but intense reflections on where and when individual de-

sires should be sacrificed to the larger interests of the family or society. Both her attraction for Jimmy Trent and her children's lives bring this issue into sharp focus. In her farewell to Jimmy, she argues that despite her tendency to ridicule her parents for their "Victorian views," she now realizes that it "isn't right for married people, happily married people, to leave their homes and children for their own individual pleasure," not when "they trusted us, once for all, with their life happiness." She expresses these same views when her daughter Cicily contemplates a divorce, and yet the issue is complicated by Jane's awareness that the candor and self-confidence of her daughter's generation are welcome antidotes to her own generation's silence and hesitation in these matters.

Jane's own conflict is sharpened in the next generation, and *Wisdom's Gate,* B.'s final novel, picks up the thread of Albert and Cicily's marriage after their respective divorces at the end of *Years of Grace.* When the novel opens, Albert has just resigned from the foreign service and returned with Cicily and their children to Chicago to join his stepfather's advertising agency. The novel dramatizes their marital problems, as Cicily struggles to reconcile herself to Albert's affairs, one of which leads him to be cited in a divorce suit. Cicily's predicament, like her mother's, takes the form of weighing "what seems to be most decent" for all concerned, including their children, against her immediate need to flee the pain and suspicion.

This predicament is especially acute for B.'s female protagonists, all of whom are suspended in this leisure sphere. Wealth has relieved them of most of the duties of wives and mothers, college has enlarged their interests and tastes and given them a glimpse of meaningful work beyond the domestic sphere, and yet they remain strangely inert. We see this in Jane Ward, who is bemused by her own passivity as she listens to President M. Carey Thomas exhort Bryn Mawr students to lead accomplished lives. We see this as well in Olivia Van Tyne Ottendorf, the protagonist of *Westward Passage,* whose anxieties about becoming middle-aged and an affair with her ex-husband, the writer Nick Allen, cloak her real fears about not having accomplished much in her idle, comfortable marriage to a wealthy stockbroker.

B.'s anatomy of the plight of the upper-middle-class wife continues in *Edna His Wife.* The novel traces the marriage of Edna Losser and Paul Jones, an ambitious lawyer whose single-minded pursuit of wealth and respectability takes them from their Chicago working-class origins to a secure place among New York's most prominent families. But while Paul quickly adapts to the social demands of each new circle, artless Edna's progress is awkward and halting. As the title of the novel suggests, her identity is largely defined as "his wife." What makes the novel interesting is that it is told almost entirely from Edna's perspective, and we see her loneliness, her quiet acquiescence in her husband's ambitions, and her bewilderment as her husband and two children effortlessly assimilate the tastes and values of the upper middle class. In the end, her childlike candor and simplicity serve to unmask the pretensions and cruelties of those around her, including her husband and daughter.

Like Wharton's, B.'s work discloses a deep awareness of how the wealthy use things to carefully mark off their place in the social hierarchy. Thus, one of the most effective and compelling ways to reconstruct their lives was to describe the things they surrounded themselves with, and she does this painstakingly. In *Edna His Wife,* for example, B. represents the couple's rise in a series of symbolic moves from four-room flat to suburban house to New York brownstone and then penthouse. Along the way, the author describes in great detail the furnishings that are embraced and then cast off with each move. Her social commentary, while not, like Wharton's, satirical, reveals nonetheless how and where the national ferment in the early decades of the 20th c. intersected private lives.

BIBLIOGRAPHY: Mainiero, L., ed., *American Women Writers* (1989); Taylor, L. C., Jr., *M. A. B.* (1974); Wagenknecht, E., *Chicago* (1964)

MARY V. MARCHAND

BARRY, Philip [James Quinn]

b. 18 June 1896, Rochester, New York; d. 3 December 1949, New York City

Like many playwrights of his generation, B. experimented with myriad dramatic forms though his arena was the Broadway stage. Beginning with *You and I* (1923) and ending with the posthumously produced *Second Threshold* (1951), B. wrote twenty-one plays. He is chiefly identified with his successful social comedies, but B. also created a body of symbolic drama that explored cosmic and moral themes, often in departures from realism. Through most of his work, however, he stresses the importance of individual freedom and responsibility.

The comedies examine youthful revolt, social climbing, materialism, and the limitations of conventional marriage among the upper classes. His central characters often find themselves unfulfilled as each play's action centers around search for completion in a superficially beautiful world. B. enraptured audiences with *Paris Bound* (1927), a comedy in which a theoretical open marriage stumbles when put to the test.

He further assaulted the bounds of matrimony with *The Animal Kingdom* (1932) by pitting a healthy, unconventional relationship against an ailing traditional one. At the height of America's financial boom, *Holiday* (1928) posed free-spirited youth and individualism versus tradition and big business. In this verbal romp, the hero, afraid of being entombed alive, desires to retire at age thirty. The longest running play of B.'s career, *The Philadelphia Story* (1939), centered on divorce and confusion of romantic priorities. After confronting her own human weakness, the proud heroine forgives failure in the man she loves.

Although B. was much more earnest about them, his philosophical plays usually failed to find an audience. In *White Wings* (1926), a satirical fantasy on resistance to change, B. symbolized tradition versus progress with the horse and automobile. Considered esoteric at the time, *Hotel Universe* (1930) depicted searching, disturbed people who are free but without purpose. The characters are allowed to reenact significant traumatic experiences and find release from their past that is their albatross in the present. In *Here Come the Clowns* (1938), an allegory on the nature of good and evil, a stagehand, confronting a troupe of misfit performers, searches for God and the mystery behind suffering in the world. At his moment of death, he recognizes that it is only people who create evil in the world and determine their own destiny.

Whatever the genre of play, B. explored many of the same themes throughout his career, but enjoyed much more critical and popular success when placing his ideas inside a comic structure. This frustrated him repeatedly, but he persevered with serious plays until his end.

BIBLIOGRAPHY: Krutch, J. W., *The American Dream since 1918* (1957); Meserve, W. J., *An Outline History of American Drama* (1965); Roppolo, J. P., *P. B.* (1965)

RONALD H. WAINSCOTT

BARTH, John [Simmons]

b. 27 May 1930, Cambridge, Maryland

The publication of Robert Scholes's *The Fabulators* (1967) marked the first appreciation of B.'s talent as a writer and the first genuine understanding of B.'s concern with the nature of reality as mutable and linguistically based. As Scholes points out, the defining feature of all of B.'s fiction is the play of language, a joy in orchestrating words on the page, of developing ideas and clashing them one against the other. This joy displays itself partly as humor and partly as sheer exuberance in the arrangement of B.'s knowledge of history, mythology, and literature.

B.'s more serious concern is the inability of contemporary philosophy to ascertain the nature of reality. Given this problem, B. believes that an author must create his or her own reality through language, and usually also through myth or philosophy. The process of creating this reality is also a legitimate theme in fiction. Thus, B.'s work is characteristically marked by a metafictional concern with the process of writing itself. Writing becomes a major theme in B.'s fiction, which he characterized in his influential *Atlantic Monthly* article (1967) as the proper response to an age producing the "Literature of Exhaustion." Since all narrative possibilities have been used up, the postmodern author is forced to review the old stories from a new perspective. It would be futile to pretend that art and life are seamless, so B. chooses to emphasize the artificial element in art, and to make the use of artifice part of his story. In this process, B. joins the postmodern movement because he seeks to dislocate his readers and to force them to realize that they are perceiving words rather than life itself.

While most of B.'s fiction seeks to create its own world rather than mirror the nonfictional world, his first two novels, *The Floating Opera* (1956; rev. ed., 1967) and *The End of the Road* (1958; rev. ed., 1967), were philosophical yet mimetic fiction. In *The Floating Opera,* B. poses the question, through the character Todd Andrews, whether in the absence of absolute values if values less than absolute (he does not use the word "relative") might not be acceptable. Although B. eschews a traditional plot for a narrative line that floats on the tide of his narrator's imagination, the bulk of the story follows the events in one day of Todd's life as he decides not to commit suicide. His ultimate judgment is that there is no final reason for committing suicide—or for living. One might regard oneself as a rabbit shot on the run, condemned to death but not yet dead, and with some minutes left to consider the best course of action.

Although the novel ends with the image of the rabbit, the consideration of "values less than absolute" is taken up in *The End of the Road,* in which Jacob Horner, a nihilist, questions the value of any action at all. An instructor of prescriptive grammar at Wicomico State Teachers' College, Jake begins a triangular relationship with his friends Joe and Rennie Morgan. Jake's inertia is pitted against Joe's conviction that some values, like his marriage, are not absolute but are at least worthy of one's energy. When Jake finds that Rennie is pregnant, he arranges an abortion during which Rennie chokes on food and dies. This grisly ending makes B.'s point that neither Morgan's cold

rationalism nor Jake's inertia and pessimism is the proper response to an irrational and mutable world.

This novel brought B.'s interest in the questions of values and mimetic fiction to their own cul-de-sac. After writing *The End of the Road,* B. took a deeper turn into the postmodern concerns with the process of writing and with the search to "re-orchestrate" old narratives by telling them from a new perspective. *The Sot-Weed Factor* (1960; rev. ed., 1967) parodies the 18th-c. poem of Ebenezer COOKE, "The Sot-Weed Factor," which satirizes colonial Maryland. In his novel, B. initiates what became a characteristic pattern: framing his novel with his own distorted historical documents, a liberty he takes because he considers all historical documents themselves distortions of reality. Deliberate distortion of the attempt to produce mimetic fictions is continued in *Giles Goat-Boy* (1966; rev. ed., 1967), an extremely long allegory of the world as the university in which God (the Grand Tutor) must rise from humble beginnings to reprogram the computer and usher in the New Revised Syllabus (Bible). Although the novel is more comic than satiric, there are some serious philosophical issues debated, especially the familiar dilemma of values. Despite its length and heavy-handed allegory, the novel was a popular success and allowed B. the financial freedom to continue writing fiction and to revise his first three novels.

Resting from the exertion of writing long novels, B. spent four years working on shorter fiction, which he placed in two collections of short stories. *Lost in the Funhouse* (1968) is an extended experiment with the possibilities of narrative. This collection of fourteen fictions is interrelated through each story's metafictional concern with the processes of writing (for the author) and perceiving (for the audience). In the "prefatory note to the book," B. states that each story has an appropriate medium: *Fiction for Print, Tape,* or *Live Voice.* For a framing device, B. uses the Moebuis strip to suggest that his fiction ends where it begins. In this popular collection, B. was experimenting with narrative conveyed with the voice rather than through the printed page. Moving back to print, B. found another way to relieve the exhaustion of narrative by going back to classical mythology. B. revived classical stories by treating them realistically rather than looking at them for clues to present reality. The result was *Chimera* (1972), a volume of three novellas. The first, "Dunyazadiad," was inspired by the story of Scheherazade in *The Thousand and One Nights.* This story, as well as the second and third novellas, "Bellerophoniad" and "Perseik," are all concerned with the relationship of the author to the reader and the possibility of engendering new fiction by lending a new perspective to old stories. Both concerns are related, since the metaphor of the writing block is used in the novellas to indicate the author's problem in finding new material.

After receiving the National Book Award in 1973 for *Chimera,* B. went back to writing long fiction and produced *Letters* (1979), an epistolary fiction in which seven narratives are threaded through the larger narrative by means of letters the characters write to one another and to the author, who is himself a character. Many of these correspondents come from B.'s earlier fiction, a usage that results from his habit of looking to old material for new stories. B.'s characters include Lady Amherst, Todd Andrews, Jacob Horner, A. B. Cook, Jerome Brady, Ambrose Mensch, and "The Author." In his novel *Sabbatical* (1982), B. returns to the academic setting and places a college professor on a long trip with her husband, who is trying to write a novel. In 1984, B. published *The Friday Book: Essays and Other Nonfiction* followed by the novels *The Tidewater Tales* (1987) and *The Last Voyage of Somebody the Sailor* (1991), as well as a collection of short stories entitled *On with the Story* (1996).

B. is a major voice in the postmodern era of experimental fiction in the U.S. He merits this ranking through the virtuosity of his narrative experiments and his ability to find something new in the age of the "Literature of Exhaustion." While some critics—usually book reviewers looking for a "realistic" story—have found B.'s fiction too long, too tedious, and too self-reverential, they have usually not considered the integrity of B.'s refusal to ignore the status of fiction in the half-century after James Joyce brought the novel to the end of its technical road. Instead of avoiding this problem and pretending that art mirrors reality, B. chooses to foreground the artificial element in fiction. Readers are reminded that they are not reading mimetic art. In addition to his clear stand on the state of fiction, B. must be commended for his technical experiments. Most notable among these is his use of framing devices to dislocate the reader from assumptions of historical truth and his use of mythology—not as a modernist starting point for contemporary application—but as discrete narratives that should be retold from a different perspective—the perspective of the author who is doing the telling. Consistently praised for his brilliance, sometimes condemned for obscurity and pedantry, B. has written important fiction that explores the postmodern perspective on the teller and the tale.

BIBLIOGRAPHY: Harris, C. B., *Passionate Virtuosity: The Fiction of J. B.* (1983); Tharpe, J., *J. B.: The Comic Sublimity of Paradox* (1974); Waldmeir, J. J., ed., *Critical Essays on J. B.* (1980)

LAURA NIESEN DE ABRUNA

BARTHELME, Donald

b. 7 April 1931, Philadelphia, Pennsylvania; d. 23 July 1989, Houston, Texas

Widely acclaimed as one of the more influential postmodern writers, B. defies easy categorization. On the one hand, he is a radical innovator noted for his self-conscious metafiction, but on the other hand, his work also displays traces of ROMANTICISM. B.'s fiction is deeply and intensely humorous; while he strains the bounds of conventionality at every step, he remains, at the most fundamental level, a very funny writer.

The romantic and the cynic are in constant tension in B.'s writings. His body of work includes three novels, a National Book Award-winning children's book entitled *The Slightly Irregular Fire Engine; or, The Hithering Thithering Djinn* (1971), and more than one hundred short stories. Constant interplay between a quest for spiritual transformation and the harsh, tawdry modern reality that intrudes on this quest is at the center of B.'s work. The interaction of these two forces is often manifested in a collagelike presentation of plots, themes, and characters. His fiction is intensely, relentlessly, and defiantly superficial; fragments of contemporary experience are treated as worthy in their own right, rather than as degraded pieces of an elusive higher unity.

Although B. war reared in Texas, both his life and his work became intimately connected with New York City where he lived and worked much of his adult life. Many of his short stories appeared in the *New Yorker,* and many more are infused with a subtle background of late-20th-c. urban life. Nevertheless, childhood experiences left their mark on B.; he has attributed his talent for unusual visual perspectives and startling verbal pyrotechnics to the influence of his father, a well-known architect. B. won a Guggenheim Fellowship in 1966, the National Institute of Arts and Letters Award in 1972, and both the PEN/Faulkner Award in fiction and the Los Angeles Times Book Prize in 1982 for *Sixty Stories* (1981).

B.'s longer works are best represented by *Snow White* (1967). This retelling of the classic fairy tale is typical of his work in that it contrasts the power of myth with the empty, unsatisfactory tenor of contemporary culture. After "tending the vats" in an apparently aimless manner for the duration of the novel, Snow White's seven lovers finally take their leave at the conclusion of the tale, departing "in search of a higher principle." The absurd, chaotic circumstances leading to this departure give little hope that the anticipated quest for a "higher principle" will be successful.

B. published eight separate collections of short stories, beginning with *Come Back, Dr. Caligari* (1964). The lead story in this anthology, "Florence Green Is

81," is typical of B.'s short fiction. Superimposed on the general stream-of-consciousness flow of this story is an intricate web of digressions from a variety of viewpoints and perspectives. Florence's final plaintive request—"I want to go somewhere where everything is different"—might well express the author's own desire to break free from the conventional bonds of fiction.

Perhaps B.'s most representative collection is *Sixty Stories*. In stories such as "The Balloon" and "Glass Mountain," B. places incongruous and wholly unlikely objects in a familiar urban setting. In both cases, the juxtaposition between the absurd and the familiar is the engine driving the story. The traditional literary mechanisms of plot, character, and theme are aggressively shoved to the background by the demands of a ludicrous scenario pitting "normal" humans against extraordinary cultural artifacts. Critical response to these artistic artifacts is also parodied—the balloon, for example is described as having "monstrous pourings" and "warm, soft lazy patches."

Stories like "At the Tolstoy Museum" from *City Life* (1970) illustrate B.'s abiding concern with the fragmentary nature of modern experience. The collagelike story is broken up by the insertion of various graphic exhibits, such as portraits of Tolstoy at different stages of his life, as well as a monstrous head of the author looming among his artifacts. Apparently, conventional literary forces, symbolized here by the legacy of Tolstoy, can be resisted, but never entirely vanquished.

B.'s fiction is highly representative of the postmodern approach to literature. Breaking free from the modernist commitment to subjective reality and interpretative mythologies, B.'s stories range across the chaotic American landscape with alternately grim and hilarious determination illuminated by a poignant awareness of the absurdity of existence. Rarely, however, does this awareness lead to the despair one might expect; instead, B.'s characters are typically rescued from the precipice by the absurd humor injected by the author.

But while B. can be seen primarily as a humorist, he should nevertheless not be regarded as "only" a humorist. That is, his importance to modern literature lies not just in his frequently delightful responses to the absurdist condition, but also in his innovative manipulation of the tools and conventions of fiction in order to achieve effects not previously realized or even imagined.

BIBLIOGRAPHY: Molesworth, C., *D. B.'s Fiction: The Ironist Saved from Drowning* (1982); Patterson, R. F., ed., *Critical Essays on D. B.* (1992); Roe, B. L., *D. B.: A Study of the Short Fiction* (1992); Trachtenberg, S., *Understanding D. B.* (1990)

HENRY L. WILSON

BARTHELME, Frederick
b. 10 October 1943, Houston, Texas

Before finally settling into his career as a writer, B. did many things, including working as an artist. The materials for his sculptures were often the stuff of everyday life, collected and gathered into new configurations that led viewers to see the parts and the whole of the quotidian in new ways. While still in career flux, he produced his first novel, *Rangoon,* published in 1970, which consists of text cobbled together with drawings and photographs by the author and his friends. His second novel, *War and War,* came out the next year; it too is filled with artwork from friends as well as letters, autobiographical detail both real and invented, and thoughts on the process of writing fiction. After earning his second M.F.A., this time not in studio art but in writing, B. focused more exclusively on his writing and established a more mainstream style that still reflects his early visual art work. In two short story collections and five novels produced after those early efforts, B. has continued to display an ability to re-create in living detail the stuff of everyday life, and to cobble it together with a distinctive prose style and cockeyed approach that makes the world appear strange and familiar at once.

For setting much of his fiction in the South and in suburbia, and for a somewhat stripped-down style and sensibility that bears some debt to Ernest HEMINGWAY, B. has often been spoken of in the same breath as Raymond CARVER, Ann BEATTIE, and other "minimalist" writers who became prominent in the 1980s. His work also suggests a debt to the postmodern fiction of which his older brother Donald BARTHELME was one of the better-known practitioners, in his close attention to the ways in which popular culture, especially its media manifestations, saturates American consciousness. From *Second Marriage* (1984) to *Tracer* (1985), from *The Brothers* (1993) to *Painted Desert* (1995), B. has painted landscapes and characters crowded not just with physical junk but with cultural junk as well. The haphazard courses of his stories, the unseen twists and turns, are played out against a backdrop insistently buzzing with these undigested cultural products, suggesting the difficulty of comprehending and ordering one's life in a world so filled with what Don DELILLO called "white noise."

Despite the overwhelming information with which B.'s characters must deal, there is a kind of order to the chaos. Plots and characters are repeated from story to story and novel to novel: *Tracer* and *The Brothers* share the story of a divorced man traveling South and getting entangled with the sibling of an ex-spouse, in the former novel, or the spouse of a sibling, in the latter. Del Tribute and his girlfriend Jen appear in *The Brothers* and reappear in *Painted Desert.* More important than the order that this repetition presents in B.'s oeuvre is the order his characters try to make for themselves. In *The Brothers,* Jen puts together a newsletter of bizarre stories culled from the Internet; Del has a Ph.D. in communications, and is as interested in the way inanimate roadside junk talks to people as he is in the way people talk to people. In *Painted Desert,* Del and Jen's fascination with media coverage of accidents, disasters, and murders turns to the Los Angeles riots and the O. J. Simpson case, and they set off cross country to see the famous streets—Florence and Normandie, Rockingham Drive—where these things were shown to have happened, over and over again, on television. In his portrayal of his characters' fascination with the world as filtered through wires and their redeeming encounter with the physical world they meet on their way to Los Angeles, B. presents us both with our own slack-jawed acceptance of technologically mediated information and with a kind of alternative.

BIBLIOGRAPHY: Brinkmeyer, R. H., Jr., "Suburban Culture, Imaginative Wonder: The Fiction of F. B.," *SLitI* 27 (Fall 1994): 105–14; Peters, T., "80s Pastoral: F. B.'s Moon Deluxe Ten Years On," *SSF* 31 (Spring 1994): 175–85

SAM COHEN

BARTRAM, William

b. 9 February 1739, Philadelphia, Pennsylvania; d. 22 July 1823, Philadelphia, Pennsylvania

B. was a botanist, ethnographer, and natural scientist, whose enduring importance has been foremost literary. The full title of his only major published work indicates the scope of his concerns, but little hints at the work's lasting effect on imaginative writing: *Travels through North & South Carolina, Georgia, East & West Florida, the Cherokee Country, the Extensive Territories of the Muscogulges, or Creek Confederacy, and the Country of the Chactaws; Containing an Account of the Soil and Natural Productions of Those Regions, Together with Observations on the Manners of the Indians* (1791). Written with an empiricist's attention to detail and a romantic's eye for sublime yet ultimately benign nature, the book satisfied a transatlantic desire for a landscape at once real and ideal. Written and read during years of American and European revolution and war, B.'s book revealed an alternative mode of existence in which the terrific forces of nature conspired to produce a pastoral utopia.

B. was the son of another eminent botanist, the Quaker John Bartram, who in 1722 founded America's first botanical garden. While John Bartram associated with Benjamin FRANKLIN, Thomas JEFFERSON, and other central political figures of 18th-c. America, B. generally refrained from direct political or social commentary, focusing instead on the plants, animals, and people he encountered far from the conflicts faced by his readers. After early failures as a merchant in Philadelphia and North Carolina and as a plantation operator in Florida, in 1772 B. received a commission to collect flora, make drawings, and record observations in Florida. He wandered through the region from 1773 to 1778, and his *Travels* are his account of his experiences.

While B.'s ostensible purposes were scientific and while he contributed important discoveries to known plant varieties and animal species as well as knowledge about 18th-c. Native Americans, historians long have debated the scientific reliability of his account. *Travels* consistently reveals as much about B.'s enthusiasm as a beholder of nature as about the objects he beheld. Rather than purely scientific, the pleasures and value of the book are narrative and aesthetic. More than a catalogue of naturalist descriptions, *Travels* includes a harrowing escape from man-eating alligators, an eroticized meeting with Cherokee maidens in an Arcadian strawberry field, and painterly descriptions of the landscape and its inhabitants. Nine copperplate illustrations of plants, animals, and the King of the Seminoles enhance both the descriptions and the narrative.

Travels was published in London in 1792 and almost immediately had a great impact on the British romantics. Images and scenes from it reappear in Samuel Taylor Coleridge's "Kubla Khan" (1798), and William Wordsworth's "Ruth" (1800) and *The Prelude* (1805). Robert Southey, Felicia Hemans, Charles Lamb, and Percy Bysshe Shelley, among others, also cite B.'s images and ideas in their writing.

Anglo-European concepts of natural nobility and pastoral society had influenced B. in his representations of nature. In turn, B.'s book was perhaps as responsible as any other for the late-18th-and 19th-c. Anglo-European literary image of America. In a letter to Ralph Waldo EMERSON, Thomas Carlyle, seeing in the book a mythopoeic testament to America's origins, suggested that all American libraries should retain a copy as "a future biblical article." Although less well known today, *Travels* remains a foundational American literary text.

BIBLIOGRAPHY: Earnest, E. P., *John and W. B.: Botanists and Explorers, 1699–1777* (1940); Fagin, N. B.,

W. B.: Interpreter of the American Landscape (1933); Slaughter, T. P., *The Natures of John and W. B.* (1996)

MICHAEL WILEY

BEATTIE, Ann

b. 8 September 1947, Washington, D.C.

B. established herself as an important observer of a cross section of American culture in her early short stories, many of which, beginning in 1974, originally appeared in the *New Yorker*. Her first novel, *Chilly Scenes of Winter,* and a collection of short stories, *Distortions,* were both published in 1976. She was hailed as chronicler of idealists of the 1960s who found themselves unable or unwilling to cope with the apathy surrounding them a decade later. B. herself strongly objects to having her work categorized in this manner, claiming that it is reductive.

Nonetheless, her early work was widely praised and she was thrust into the literary limelight. Contemporary critics agree that it is important to trace her development as a far more diversified and accomplished writer through the five novels and five collections of short stories she has published during these years. Although her work has always been primarily character-driven and is often short on plot, her evolution has led to more fully developed characters and a narrative voice that exhibits a deeper understanding of and concern for her characters. However, most of her novels suffer, at least in part, from a lack of structure. Her strongest work is still in the form of the short story or novella.

Characters in the early works tend to be passive dropouts, many of whom have become shiftless and consumed by vague fears. Like B.'s prose style, their lives are flat and formless. There is little action and rarely any form of resolution. But B. is a master of dialogue and the telling detail; indeed her simple, clipped sentences, often rendered in the present tense, rely far more on conveying meaning through an accumulation of detail rather than through building on traditional narrative structure.

Many of the characters in her next three short story collections, *Secrets and Surprises* (1978), *Jacklighting* (1981), and *The Burning House* (1982), indicate a slight shift in B.'s style. While still for the most part aimlessly drifting from place to place and in and out of relationships, they begin to be more fully realized and treated with less irony and somewhat more sympathy. A number of stories in *Where You'll Find Me* (1986) and in *What Was Mine* (1991) contain characters who are older. Many are married; some have even moved to the suburbs and have children. The ironic distance of earlier works is tempered by a denser prose style that takes on adult problems of lives more fully

realized. Time has more fullness. No longer do people merely stagnate in the present tense. Characters have pasts that affect their present situations and influence their decisions regarding their futures. Issues concerning death, old age, family, and social relationships are treated with a far more complex sensitivity.

The novels *Falling in Place* (1980) and *Love Always* (1985) show similar changes in B.'s development of her characters. Although there are indications that she has become more interested in structure, the longer works still have been criticized for lack of form. Indeed, the fact that B. still begins writing with no plan, no plot or outline, may account in part for the perceived problems. B. has acknowledged that her approach to her work has changed over the years. She no longer writes as quickly or as often as she had. Her early stories were often written in one sitting, and the first draft of *Chilly Scenes of Winter* was completed in three weeks. *Picturing Will: A Novel* (1989) took almost three years to finish.

In a 1995 interview in *Ploughshares*, B. discussed her growing frustration with the publishing business and her difficulty in placing her short stories with magazines. She also commented on a crisis she encountered while working on the novel *Another You* (1995). She had written over three hundred pages before she realized that she had serious problems with the momentum. That and a lack of deep feeling about the characters caused her to scrap almost all of the original version. The published novel received mixed reviews as did *My Life, Starring Dara Falcon* (1997). In both works, there is, on the positive side, more assessment of characters' motivations and a deeper exploration of their ethical and moral lives. But the structural and thematic problems still exist. She is criticized for choppy dialogue, for being stuck in the 1970s and obsessed with pop culture references.

The issue of B.'s problems with longer works has become paramount as she herself recognizes. The publishing industry has changed; writers cannot count on the future resembling the past. Her strongest medium is the shorter work of fiction, which received less critical attention in late-20th-c. American literature.

BIBLIOGRAPHY: Lee, D., "About A. B.," *Ploughshares* 21 (Fall 1995): 231–35; Montresor, J. B., ed., *The Critical Response to A. B.* (1993); Plath, J., "Counternarrative: An Interview with A. B." *MQR* 32 (Summer 1993): 359–79

MARGARET D. SULLIVAN

BEHRMAN, S[amuel] N[athaniel]

b. 9 June 1893, Worcester, Massachusetts; d. 9 September 1973, New York City

Although his works are now seldom revived or studied, B. was among the most important and successful

American playwrights of the 1920s and 1930s and enjoyed a versatile writing career spanning four decades. His works showcased such notable actors as Ina Claire, Alfred Lunt, Lynne Fontanne, and Laurence Olivier, and frequently ran for several hundred performances on Broadway. His urbane, witty prose style and his social consciousness distinguished him as the leading practitioner of the genre usually known as "high comedy," also associated with, among others, Philip BARRY and Paul Osborn. Yet his seemingly light and genteel Depression-era plays often strained the conventional limits of comedy, persistently exploring issues of class conflict, generational strife, ethnic bigotry, and the threat of global fascism.

Like Barry, Eugene O'NEILL, and Sidney HOWARD, B. studied playwriting with the eminent teacher George Pierce Baker at Harvard, from which he graduated in 1916. But in 1911, B. had already toured on the vaudeville circuit, performing in his own skit, "Playing a Part"; in 1915, he published a short story in H. L. MENCKEN's *Smart Set,* and sold several more stories in 1917. B. earned a master's degree at Columbia in 1918, but on the advice of his close mentor Daniel Asher he rejected an academic career to remain in New York and focus on his writing. Always ready to form valuable connections, B. began his career by collaborating with other playwrights, including the Pulitzer Prize-winning Owen Davis, and later wrote essays for Harold Ross at the *New Yorker* and contributed to the screenplays of several major Hollywood films of the 1930s. Following a highly successful association with the Theatre Guild, in 1938, at the height of his success, B. joined Howard, Elmer RICE, Maxwell ANDERSON, and Robert E. SHERWOOD to form the Playwrights' Company, a cooperative production group.

Frequently criticized for their indifferent plotting, B.'s plays emphasize character and situation. Rather than resolving problems or neatly restoring a disrupted order, B.'s characters typically achieve a larger understanding of themselves and their relations to the world beyond the confines of the summer house or well-appointed parlor. Though such early plays as *The Second Man* (1927) and *Serena Blandish* (1929) are romantic comedies relatively free of serious themes, with the onset of the Great Depression a new tone of socioeconomic critique became conspicuous in his writing. B.'s knack for bright, entertaining dialogue about the most menacing issues largely accounts for his success. He managed to address the need for reform and action without threatening his audience's middle-class values.

Perhaps his most prescient concern, as early as 1929 in *Meteor,* was the emerging problem of authoritarian right-wing power in the hands of self-styled "superior" men of wealth or accomplishment. Several of B.'s plays, including *Biography* (1952), *Rain from Heaven*

(1934), *End of Summer* (1936) and *The Talley Method* (1941), pit younger leftist radicals against reactionary, sometimes monomaniacal older men. Though B.'s sympathies usually lie with the young revolutionaries, he rejects uncompromising ideologies of all kinds in favor of humane tolerance, a sensibility often expressed by strong, liberated female characters such as Marion Froude of *Biography* and Lael Wyngate of *Rain from Heaven.* In the latter play, B. also began to show increasing artistic self-consciousness about his Jewish heritage and the genocidal program of the new Nazi regime in Germany.

After World War II, B. continued writing plays, essays, and fiction, enjoying one of his greatest commercial successes with his only musical play, *Fanny* (1954). If his wit and sensibility fail to interest producers and directors today, his ability to confront the most serious ideological problems of the time with grace and humane understanding assures his place in the history of American playwriting.

BIBLIOGRAPHY: Fearnow, M., *The American Stage and the Great Depression* (1997); Gross, R. F., *S. N. B.* (1992); Rabkin, G., *Drama and Commitment* (1964); Reed, K., *S. N. B.* (1965)

KURT EISEN

BELKNAP, Jeremy

b. 4 June 1744, Boston, Massachusetts; d. 20 June 1798, Dover, New Hampshire

Congregational minister, patriot, and founder of the Massachusetts Historical Society (1791), B. wrote two significant histories and one satirical fiction. His three-volume *The History of New-Hampshire* (1784, 1791, 1792) served as a model for early American historians. In the two-volume *American Biography* (1794), B. pioneered biographical art in this country. *The Foresters, An American Tale: Being a Sequel to the History of John Bull the Clothier. In a Series of Letters to a Friend* (1792; rev. ed., 1796) is the single important American fiction of its time concerned with history.

B.'s reputation rests not on a single work, but on his belief in the value of history. *The History of New-Hampshire* and *American Biography* are, for their day, scholarly, evenhanded studies. They detail the difficulties and triumphs of explorers and settlers and the creation of viable societies and institutions. Though a minister, B. emphasizes human effort in history, not God's providence. In the "Author's Advertisement" to *American Biography,* B. stresses the "utility" of his work. Indeed, his life was dedicated to utility, to the creation of historical consciousness and understanding in a new nation whose people ignored the past.

B. referred to *The Foresters* as an "historical allegory." Both a "usable" satire and a patriotic fiction, *The Foresters* attacks the degeneracy and villainy of the English, the Old World, and American Tories while praising the fortitude and common sense of New World settlers and patriots. In *The Foresters,* as in his histories, B. masters a lucid, vigorous style; as a result, his prose retains its appeal.

BIBLIOGRAPHY: Kirsch, G. B., *J. B.: A Biography* (1982); Tucker, L. L., *Clio's Consort: J. B. and the Founding of the Massachusetts Historical Society* (1990)

JOHN ENGELL

BELL, James Madison
b. 3 April 1826, Gallipolis, Ohio; d. 1902

B. is a minor 19th-c. African American orator and poet. Although he spent many years residing in various parts of Canada and California, he finally settled in Toledo, Ohio, the city on the Maumee River. In his youth, B. lived in Cincinnati, Ohio, where he was trained as a plasterer. He usually worked at his trade during the summer and fall months. Very early in his life, he acquired a strong desire to obtain an education; and thus when a school for blacks was established, B. took advantage of the slack winter seasons in his trade to attend night classes. It was while being schooled that his mind and heart were opened up to the sentiments of the antislavery crusade.

B. moved to Canada in 1854, where he resided until 1860. While in Canada, he became a friend to the abolitionist John Brown, who in 1859 asked B. to assist him in organizing the raid on the arsenal at Harpers Ferry, West Virginia. After the attack failed and Brown was executed, B. left for California and remained there for over five years.

Before and after the Civil War, B. was sought after on the lecture circuit because of his ability to give stirring deliveries of his long abolitionist and political poems. While being praised for his high moral stance in the struggle for human rights and freedom, B. was admired also for his poetry and honored with the titles of the "Bard of the Maumee" and the "Poet of Hope." However, today's reader finds B.'s work dull and prosaic and too imitative of the styles of such poets as Alexander Pope, Sir Walter Scott, William Cullen BRYANT, and Alfred, Lord Tennyson.

Much of B.'s poetry is commemorative and occasional and was written to be delivered at public events celebrating the anniversaries of the emancipation of slavery in the British West Indies and in the U.S. In 1870, he published a poem observing the final ratification of the Fifteenth Amendment to the U. S. Constitu-

tion. However, his most popular work was "Modern Moses, or 'My Policy' Man," which presents a harsh satire of President Andrew Johnson's handling of Reconstruction programs and policies. This long poem of rhymed couplets contains many topical references to political events, persons, and places; and it is shot through with graphic images of Johnson's treacherous and clownish dealings in government affairs.

In later years, B.'s interest centered on themes dealing with nature, Christianity, and the problem of moral evil. In 1901, the year before B. died, his close friend Bishop B. W. Arnett persuaded him to publish the collection, *The Poetical Works of J. M. B.*, which included Arnett's biographical sketch of the poet.

During his life, B. also was praised for writing several short poems commemorating emancipation and the great leaders who fought for freedom, especially those verses honoring British abolitionist William Wilberforce, insurrectionist John Brown, and President Abraham LINCOLN. However, most of his poetry is too lengthy, two of his works run to over a thousand lines. The poems consist of numerous metrical and style shifts and contain too many lifeless and boring passages. Today's readers may appreciate the courage and commitment to human rights that B. displayed in his oratorical-sounding verse, but the literary value of his work is minimal at best. However, critical historian Eugene B. Redmond has stated that B. "is important in a continuing chronicle of the mind and creative development of the Afro-American poet."

BIBLIOGRAPHY: Redding, J. S., *To Make a Poet Black* (1939); Redmond, E. B., *Drumvoices* (1976). Sherman, J. R., *Invisible Poets: Afro-Americans of the Nineteenth Century* (1974)

ANGELO COSTANZO

BELL, Madison Smartt
b. 1 August 1957, Nashville, Tennessee

While still in his thirties, B. published eight novels and two collections of short stories. However, it was not until *All Souls Rising* (1995), his seventh novel, that the literary community recognized him as a major figure in contemporary fiction.

B. began writing fiction during high school and attended Princeton University (A.B., 1979), where he studied with George GARRETT. After living in New York City for several years, B. earned his M.A. at Hollins College (1981) where he wrote his first novel, *Washington Square Ensemble* (1983).

In his early novels there is a strong undercurrent of Judeo-Christian philosophy. The major conflict in *Washington Square Ensemble* is one that takes place between the traditions of Islam and Santeria. *Waiting*

for the End of the World (1985) has an Eastern Orthodox slant on Christianity at the core of the text. In
Straight Cut (1986), the underlying tradition invoked
is a philosophical Christianity peppered with Sören
Kierkegaard. *The Year of Silence* (1987), a novel predominantly about suicide, decidedly takes place in
lives that are devoid of religion, which is a religion
in itself: existentialism. B.'s next novel, *Soldier's Joy*
(1988), returns again to primitive Christianity. While
Doctor Sleep (1991) at first appears to turn from this
religious trend, the themes of faith and hermetic Gnos-
ticism are clearly present. *Save Me, Joe Louis* (1993)
reads more like a comedy of errors. There is no apparent or underlying religious theme.

All Souls Rising's inception can be traced back to
B.'s earlier research on Santeria for *Washington
Square Ensemble*. Because Santeria is often paired
with Voodoo, B. found himself looking into the latter
subject to some length. This was, at least, the beginning of B.'s interest in the history of Haiti. The politics
of Haiti, being indelibly intertwined with the country's
religion, caught B.'s attention and thus began this
work.

To date, *All Souls Rising* is B.'s masterpiece. Intended as the first in a trilogy, it is a historical novel
that focuses on several true life characters. The time
line of the novel is four years. It begins in 1791, the
beginning of slave rebellion, through 1794, the burning
of the capital city of Haiti. In the center of the novel
is Toussant L'Ouverture, a second generation African
slave. His view lends a detailed, intricate voice to the
narration as a whole.

Ten Indians (1996), written concurrently with *All
Souls Rising,* takes place in contemporary Baltimore.
Its focus is Mike Devlin, a white, middle-aging, child
psychologist, who decides to open a Tae Kwon Do
school in a black ghetto in the city. In this, B. moves
further towards a tone present in earlier works of a
no-rules, meaningless kind of existence.

In B.'s relatively short career thus far, his interests
and themes have reached across a broad spectrum.
With the last two volumes of his Haitian trilogy expected, he is sure to continue being a force in American fiction.

BIBLIOGRAPHY: Sanderlin, R. R., "M. S. B.," in Flora,
J. M., and R. Bain, eds., *Contemporary Fiction Writ-
ers of the South* (1993): 46–53; Weaks, M. L., "An
Interview with M. S. B.," *SoR* 30 (Winter 1994): 1–12

                                    MARIKA BRUSSEL

BELL, Marvin [Hartley]
b. 3 August 1937, New York City

In each of his numerous volumes, B. makes insight
accessible and experience meaningful. B.'s poems are
by turns humorous and heartrending; often, a poem
will modulate from one to the other, creating a single,
unified image. While some of his early poems tested
the credibility of such modulations, B. has developed
the ability to express emotional depth with precision.
A perceptive listener and reader, B. is as important a
teacher of poetry as he is a poet whose carefully voiced
poems are often disarming in their simplicity, beauty,
and lyricism.

Following Ezra POUND's mandate to "make it new,"
B. writes to make his language and knowledge new
in each poem: he admits being a poet of ideas, learning
what he knows by writing what he feels. Although
he has learned much from William Carlos WILLIAMS,
Theodore ROETHKE, and James WRIGHT, B. is always
original in his expression, seamlessly joining the unrelated. Based on free verse and the rhythms of speech,
B.'s method stresses the phrase over the line, insisting
that a poem must "listen" to itself to create unity,
clarity, and spontaneity.

B. began writing poetry seriously after his father's
death in 1959. His father, an immigrant from the
Ukraine, figures prominently in B.'s early work, most
memorably in "Treetops," first published in *Things
We Dreamt We Died For* (1966), and "You Would
Know," the thirteen-poem sequence from *Residue of
Song* (1974). In "Treetops," the speaker attempts to
formalize his memories by imagining his father hunting; however, the circuitous third sentence reveals that
all is a dream, for the father is floating in a coffin.
The last line of the poem provides the title for B.'s
first major collection, *A Probable Volume of Dreams*
(1969), a book of clever turns about loss and the poet's
own Russian-Jewish heritage. In "You Would Know,"
B. continues to grapple with his father's death, using
images of snow and distance to describe the weight
of memory and physical absence, a weight which leads
the son to question identity: "You who were / are no
longer and what I was I'm not. / Am I to know myself,
except as I was?"

With *Stars Which See, Stars Which Do Not See*
(1977), his first widely acclaimed volume, B. achieves
a more mature language in quiet meditation. "The Self
and the Mulberry" introduces problems of seeing the
self in nature, testing metaphors, and challenging nature to do the same. But, in the title poem, the poet
realizes that, while a breeze may shatter our perceptions of a thing, the thing itself remains. "Trinket"
expands these ideas by locating the self not in the
ocean—"too many / presences for any / to absorb"—but in a slight trickle of water from a crack
in a fern pot. Such precision of focus underlies the
entire volume, with "The Mystery of Emily Dickinson" and "Gemwood" exemplifying how single im-

ages develop from perceptions registered through time and space.

In *These Green-Going-to-Yellow* (1981), B.—using shorter, terser lines—examines mortality and mutability, focusing on temporal changes of the self in "Late Naps" and "Letters from Africa." In contrast, B. lengthens lines and experiments with prose in *Drawn by Stones, by Earth, by Things That Have Been in the Fire* (1984), elegizing metaphor, as in "Trees as Standing for Something," and searching for childlike wonder in adult experiences, as in "To Be."

B.'s more recent work challenges the limits of language. In *Iris of Creation* (1990), B. dramatizes the creative act, drawing attention to the malady of the quotidian ("A Man May Change"), positing identity against past-tense expressions of self ("Dark Brow"), and searching for a poem in the flowering of its thought ("Tie-Down of a Bonsai"). The volume ends with a long poem, "Initial Conditions," a meditation on the determinant and indeterminable *now* of the poem, tracing "the blows of the pencil-point / against the grain of a page," finding that "At impact, a purity / is born from the attraction and repulsion of an instant." Such contraries inspire *The Book of the Dead Man* (1994), as B., redefining perceptions by turning images to anti–images, continues to seek knowledge in poems of discovery.

BIBLIOGRAPHY: Jackson, R., "Containing the Other: M. B.'s Recent Poetry," *NAR* 280 (1995): 45–48; McGuiness, D., "Exile and Cunning: The Recent Poetry of M. B.," *AR* 48 (1990): 353–61; Oberg, A., "M.B.: 'Time's Determinant / Once I Knew You,'" *APR* 5 (1976): 4–8

TODD VERDUN

BELLAMANN, Henry

b. 28 April 1882, Fulton, Missouri; d. 16 June 1945, New York City

A musician, educator, poet, critic, and novelist, B. is remembered principally as the early champion of avant-garde American composer Charles Ives and as the author of a popular novel, *Kings Row* (1940), made into a 1942 motion picture starring, among others, Ronald Reagan.

Born Heinrich Hauer Bellaman, B. grew up in the college town of Fulton, Missouri, reared by his autocratic but adoring maternal grandmother, in whose sheltered household he spoke only German. In 1900, he enrolled at Westminster College in Fulton, but left after a year of undistinguished study. He then moved on to Denver, where he took music courses at the

University of Denver's conservatory, but returned to Fulton in 1904.

From 1905 to 1907, B. taught music in schools in Tennessee, Alabama, and Texas. In 1907, he married singer and voice teacher Katherine McKee Jones in her hometown of Carthage, Mississippi, and began with her a life devoted to the fine arts. For the next seventeen years, the couple taught at Chicora College (moved from Greenville to Columbia, South Carolina, in 1915), during which time they studied abroad, and B.—who anglicized his first name, dropped his middle name, and added an "n" to his surname during World War I—published two volumes of poetry, *A Music Teacher's Notebook* (1920) and *Cups of Illusion* (1923). B. also joined the prestigious Poetry Society of South Carolina and was the initial encourager of writer Julia PETERKIN, whose *Scarlet Sister Mary* won a Pulitzer Prize in fiction.

In 1924, B. accepted a post with the Juilliard Musical Foundation in New York; other teaching jobs at Vassar College and Philadelphia's Curtis Institute of Music followed. At the same time, his literary output increased: he served as book reviewer and fine arts editor of the *Columbia Record* (1923–29) and the *State* (1929–32) in Columbia, South Carolina, and of the *Charlotte* (North Carolina) *Observer* (1934–37); produced another poetry collection, *The Upward Pass* (1928); and the novels *Petenera's Daughter* (1926), *Crescendo* (1928), *The Richest Woman in Town* (1932), *The Gray Man Walks* (1936), *Kings Row, Floods of Spring* (1942), and *Victoria Grandolet* (1943). At the time of his death, he was at work on *Lonesome Waters,* a sequel to *Kings Row,* which appeared in 1948 as *Parris Mitchell of Kings Row*—having been completed by his widow—herself a poet and the author of two other novels, *My Husband's Friends* (1931) and *The Hayvens of Demaret* (1951).

B.'s current reputation is small, perhaps undeservedly so. A keen critic—he was among the first to recognize in print the Southern Literary Renaissance—and an imaginative writer, B. authored a number of learned articles on a variety of topics and published many Imagist poems in journals and little magazines in the 1920s and 1930s. Although most of his novels are not memorable, *The Gray Man Walks* is a better-than-average murder mystery set on the South Carolina coast, and the semiautobiographical *Kings Row* boldly deals with such issues as incest, mental illness and psychoanalysis, homosexuality, and medical malpractice. Apart from these contributions, however, B.'s name is usually the subject of little more than arcane footnotes.

BIBLIOGRAPHY: Bayne, H. M., "H. M.'s "Madame Arndt," *UMSE* 10 (1992): 204–12; Bayne, H. M., and

B. F. Fisher, IV, "A Neglected Detective Novel: B.'s *The Gray Man Walks*," *Mystery Fancier* 12 (Fall 1990): 3–19

HARRY MCBRAYER BAYNE

BELLAMY, Edward
b. 26 March 1850, Chicopee Falls, Massachusetts; d. 22 May 1898, Chicopee Falls, Massachusetts

A few studies of B.'s early fiction have appeared, and the impact of his best-known work, *Looking Backward* (1888), continues to attract attention. The latter interest is not surprising. Only Harriet Beecher STOWE's *Uncle Tom's Cabin* surpassed *Looking Backward* in sales during the 19th c.; new journals, including the *Nationalist* and *New Nation* (edited by B.), were inspired by *Looking Backward;* B. and Nationalist Clubs formed nationwide; and socialist and labor groups in Europe and Asia championed B.'s ideas. Despite this understandable interest in impact, the primary concern of most recent B. scholarship is the book itself: the nature of the utopia envisioned and the literary forms and conventions B. used to make this utopia accessible to his readers.

Several characteristics of B.'s life suggest the origins and nature of his utopia. His small, industrial town background helps us to understand his longings for lifestyles simpler than competitive urban rat-races and to comprehend his awareness of industrial problems, especially inequality. The strong religious overtones of *Looking Backward,* emphasized more clearly in its sequel *Equality* (1897), can be related to B.'s powerful conversion experience in 1864 and to his essay "Religion of Solidarity' (wr. 1873–74, pub. 1940) with its emphasis on the transcendence above selfish identities. B.'s anxieties about a career choice—for example, he left the legal profession after experiencing one eviction case—found fictional resolutions in the rigid authoritarian structure, meritocracy, and security of his utopia's economic equality and industrial army. Clearly B.'s journalism and fiction contributed to his utopia. The journalism (e.g., *Springfield Daily Union*) helped him to conceive of a socialist state achieved by evolution from private to public trusts. His stories, many of which were collected in *The Blindman's World* (1898), and his novels, notably *The Duke of Stockbridge,* published in serial form in 1879 and as a book in 1900, *Dr. Heidenhoff's Process* (1880), and *Miss Ludington's Sister* (1884), taught him the skills of historical interpretation and social and psychological speculation necessary for the creation of a utopia and its confused visitor.

Of course, biography cannot fully explain *Looking Backward,* just as the economic traumas and the tech-nological and reform hopes of the period cannot explain the book's popularity. We must also appreciate how B. made his utopia disturbingly reassuring. His tale of an insomniac aristocrat (Julian West) who sleeps for 113 years and awakens in C.E. 2000 represents a reaffirmation and modification to conventional utopian narratives. There are familiar elements: a wise guide (Dr. Leete), his sympathetic daughter (Edith), and visitor-guide dialogues. Still, B. invigorated the conventions by inverting the usual sleeper-awakes episode (West dreams that he returns to 1887, then reawakens in the future), and, most of all, by having West experience traumas that go far beyond the typical visitor responses and invite readers to sympathize with his experience. B.'s use of familiar Christian motifs and of popular domestic novel conventions—the domestic focus, the angelic heroine, the love story, and the emotional appeals—helped make his radical economic ideas less threatening and more meaningful for his contemporaries. For these readers the provocative criticisms and socioeconomic models of *Looking Backward* were disturbingly exciting and could encourage new perceptions of reality and future potentiality. And yet, the familiar elements made these provocations reassuring. B. created a utopia of familiar estrangement.

BIBLIOGRAPHY: Bowman, S. E., *The Year 2000: A Critical Biography of E. B.* (1958); Bowman, S. E., *E. B. Abroad: An American Prophet's Influence* (1962); Bowman, S. E., *E. B.* (1986); Griffith, N. S., *E. B.: A Bibliography;* (1986) Lipow, A., *Authoritarian Socialism in America: E. B. and the Nationalist Movement* (1982); Morgan, A. E., *E. B.* (1944); Patai, D., ed., *Looking Backward, 1988–1888: Essays on E. B.* (1988); Thomas, J. L., *Alternative America: Henry George, E. B., Henry Demarest Lloyd, and the Adversary Tradition* (1983); Widdicomb, T., *E. B.: An Annotated Bibliography of Secondary Criticism* (1988)

KENNETH M. ROEMER

BELLOW, Saul
b. 10 June 1915, Lachine, Quebec

B. is without question the most honored of living American novelists. The recipient of three National Book Awards, a Pulitzer Prize, the international Prix Littéraire, and the 1976 Nobel Prize in literature, he enjoys a reputation distinct from that of writers like Joseph HELLER and Philip ROTH, whose novels of Jewish manners possess a comic fury similar to his own. Indeed, while Jewish novelists were drawing attention to their work as an exploration of Jewish identity and becoming a force in the literary establishment, B. persistently identified himself as an American rather than a Jewish writer. Such literary independence is typical of him. Most contemporary novelists understand themselves as heirs of MODERNISM, but B. finds his antecedents in Gustave Flaubert and Theodore DREISER. While the majority of serious novelists today emphasize the irrational element in human behavior, he writes densely thoughtful novels about persons committed to thought. In effect, thought is both the subject and the strategy of B.'s fiction. "There is nothing left for novelists to do but think," he pronounced unfashionably upon receiving the National Book Award in 1965.

This orientation of B.'s fiction is evident in his first novel, *Dangling Man* (1944), the journal of a young man named Joseph who dangles between the civilian and military worlds during World War II as the result of bureaucratic red tape. Although affecting to dispose this status, Joseph savors it for its metaphoric adaptability to larger problems of consciousness. He fancies himself an intellectual, dangling between intelligence and will, theory and experience, composure and irascibility. Actually, he is a self-deluded poseur. Joseph is a standard Bellovian character in that his dealings with the world tend to be irrationally passionate, but *Dangling Man* is not otherwise typical of B.'s work. Almost painfully mandarin, it approaches crabbedness in both style and plot.

The Victim (1947) is a more successful novel. The story of Asa Leventhal and his interaction one summer in New York City with a man named Kirby Allbee, it evokes the world of Nazi Germany through allusions to a Jewish business conspiracy, ethnic persecutions, and near-death in a gas oven. Instead of the humanistic outrage one might expect, B. offers the reader an array of ironic meanings that calls into question conventions of thinking about victims and oppressors, particularly in ethnic and religious contexts, and particularly in relation to Jews. Leventhal, he suggests, is Allbee's oppressor as much as he is Allbee's victim, and it is even a possibility that Allbee is Leventhal's unconscious creation—a Doppelgänger. B. fails to resolve that lurid possibility within the realistic framework of his story, however. As a consequence, his plot fails to support its weight of historical evocation. If the novel is successful in its play of characterization against stereotype, it is memorable chiefly for its richly detailed New York setting.

In writing *The Adventures of Augie March* (1953), B. abandoned the claustrophobically inward mode of *Dangling Man* and *The Victim* in favor of a loosely picaresque form better able to contain his meditative excursions, his elaborate inventories of the physical world, and the expressionistic dislocations of scene and psychology that tend to explode his realistic story

lines. Augie March is an impoverished young man who journeys from the Chicago slums to more exotic climes and from youth to a specious maturity, resisting those who would make him over in their own image and spreading *joie de vivre* all the way. We gradually come to realize that Augie's cheeriness is a feint—the repression of a gathering angst—and the novel takes on chiaroscuric depths of light and shadow in consequence. With a fine doubleness of effect, the extravagant catalogues in the narrative are not only stylistic tour de force but symptoms of the narrator's mania. Few novels of its kind have articulated so powerfully as *Augie March* the drift into despair of a spirit resolutely blithe.

The picaresque looseness of *Augie March* has proved to be B.'s most successful mode, but he has continued to employ the tautly disciplined style of the early novels in the majority of his short fiction. The most important of these stories is the novelette *Seize the Day* (1956), the story of a Dangling Man named Tommy Wilhelm who is mean-spirited and hypocritical—understandably, even forgivably so, yet not quite forgiven. Fine short stories collected in *Mosby's Memoirs* (1968) and *Him with His Foot in His Mouth* (1984) sound a similar note of moral equivocation, and within their restricted forms they render forcefully the same density of experience and the same enigmas of the heart as the novels. Particularly notable are the fine stories "Leaving the Yellow House," "Cousins," and "What Kind of Day Did You Have?" Equally notable are two novellas, "A Theft" and "The Bellarosa Connection," published in the collection *Something to Remember Me By* (1991).

Henderson the Rain King (1959) is the most engaging of B.'s novels in the picaresque mode. Eugene Henderson, its narrator and protagonist, is another Dangling Man, alternately sensitive and boorish, thoughtful and impulsive, whose talent for mishap makes him one of the most interesting rogues in modern literature. A spiritual quester, he journeys to darkest Africa, where he lives among the Arnewi and Wariri tribes and hacks energetically through the intellectual underbrush of the 1950s in search of primal unity. He discovers instead that everything in the world consorts jauntily with its opposite. The Arnewi and Wariri tribes mirror his inner duality; the Sancho Panzas that he meets are ideological Don Quixotes; Freudians betray themselves as functional Reichians; Africa is ultimately the expressionistic landscape of his soul. B.'s joke is to substitute unresolvedness and relativism for the neat resolutions and absolute values of traditional quest literature and thereby to parody the genre. His audacity is to render Henderson's journey into the "Heart of Darkness" as a boldly colorful tale.

Herzog (1964) is a darker and more disturbing novel than *Henderson*—indeed, the most daunting of all B.'s novels. Like its immediate predecessor, it is a picaresquely spacious and psychologically frenetic work, as crammed with disquisitions as with characters, but it draws in an important way upon the claustrophobic inwardness of B.'s early novels, too. Moses Herzog is a university professor who composes imaginary letters of general social observation to real persons living and dead in a manic attempt to deal with the chaos of his personal life. Surprisingly, he reaches at the end of his impassioned struggle a momentary accommodation with reality. Like Henderson before him, he embraces experience as unresolvable, thus skirting mental breakdown and tempering his aggressive intelligence. The letters have been his bulwark against the complexities of experience, and he can finally, eloquently, be silent.

Mr. Sammler's Planet (1970) is the most undervalued of B.'s major novels. Septuagenarian Artur Sammler is almost a Tiresias figure—half-blind, a survivor of the worst horrors of modern history, living now in a New York City that emblemizes for him a planetary malaise. He greets the excesses of life in New York City with a mildness born in part of weariness with the human fray, in part by a preference for ideas over reality. Particularly distasteful to him is the manner in which life seems to be transformed everywhere into a theater of sensibility. But accidental engagements with the New York scene make inroads into Sammler's dispassion and break down the distinction he values between lawless vitality and the disciplines of humanistic culture. Gradually he is forced to realize that he has evaded the involvements required by his "human contract." *Mr. Sammler's Planet* lacks the imaginative energy of *Henderson the Rain King* and the winsome charm of *Augie March,* but it substitutes for those qualities an intricate architecture of ironies that invigorates the old, humanist questions about man's tenure upon earth. Generally dismissed as a splenetic indulgence of B.'s distaste for the Vietnam years in America, it is more properly esteemed as a part of his continuing meditation on the place of intellect in modern consciousness.

Humboldt's Gift (1975) is to some extent a *roman à clef,* inasmuch as the eponymous Von Humboldt Fleisher bears a resemblance to the poet Delmore SCHWARTZ, who was once B.'s friend. The novel is more fundamentally the story of Charlie Citrine, another Dangling Man. Like Herzog, Citrine is afflicted with too much awareness and a Proustian amplitude of memory. He recalls a veritable rogues' gallery of characters: the manic-depressive Humboldt, an inept gangster named Renaldo Cantabile, an uninhibited seductress named Renata Koffritz, and other characters highly colored and vastly entertaining. Memory serves Citrine as a distraction from the suspicion that he is somehow less substantial than these characters, and his frequent allusions to Rudolf Steiner's anthroposophy suggest a wish to escape from the insufficiency of his ego into a world of spirit. He suffers, ultimately, B.'s familiar dialectic: the unending struggle of mind to deal with an obdurately physical world. There is never question of victory or transcendence in the struggle, for that way lies the madness of Von Humboldt Fleisher and the near-madness of Henderson and Herzog. For Charlie, there is only the continuing effort to validate his ego.

Albert Corde of *The Dean's December* (1982) is still another Dangling Man. Less traumatized by his dangling between alternative realities than other Bellovian questers, he actively seeks experiences of a dialectic kind in the hope of discovering some ultimate synthesis. His search involves him in both college administration and muckraking journalism and in marriage to an astrophysicist whose temperament and interests are the opposite of his own. Against a group of men who seek his downfall in Chicago, he posits a "love community" of women who cosset him in Bucharest. More completely than any other of B.'s Dangling Men, Corde seems to achieve a lasting accommodation with dividedness. That his accommodation has to be inferred by the reader may seem a weakness of the novel, but Corde himself is unaware of the moment of accommodation, and through this double opacity B. makes the point that such adjustments are accomplished mysteriously in some process beyond cerebration's reach. It is a more serious weakness of *The Dean's December* that Corde does not suffer a mental distress commensurate with the magnitude of his self-appointed task. The greater traumas of Henderson and Herzog as they struggle with their dividedness make Corde's success seem inadequately earned.

In *More Die of Heartbreak* (1987), B.'s narrator is thirty-five-year-old Kenneth Trachtenberg, who tells the story of his beloved Uncle Benn, a world-famous botanist who has married an adventuress twenty years younger than he. Kenneth has an inordinately complex relationship with Benn, for he superimposes upon the uncle/nephew relationship a parent/child relationship that reverses the parent/child roles of an unhappy relationship with his real parents. Benn's marriage serves as an occasion for Kenneth to explore this tangle further, but his dialectics and his analogies resist imposition upon the relationship because all his understandings are cross-purposed. Nothing hinders his volubility, however. Kenneth is in part a parody of the academic who lectures compulsively whatever his grasp of the subject, but he is also a Bellovian figure in that he must deal with a reality too complex for satisfactory analysis. There is no overarching Truth of experience in *More Die of Heartbreak;* as in other of B.'s novels, there are only moments of chameleon perception, each with its own validity. In 1989, B. published both *The Bellarosa Connection* and *A Theft* followed by *Something to Remember Me By: Three Tales* (1991), *It All Adds Up: From the Dim Past to the Uncertain Future* (1994), and *The Actual* (1997).

So steadily has this series of novels examined the place of ideas in modern consciousness, so crammed are they with speculation and allusion, that B. is regarded today as an intellectual writer almost without peer in America. His characters are updated Quixotes who know the vanity of their commitment to mind but choose to cling to ideas as if to flotsam in a shipwreck. Like Cervantes's masterpiece of realism, the novels derive a characteristic urgency from that sense of intellectual shipwreck, and like the *Quixote* they succeed less as treatises than as novels—as dramatized skirmishes with the anarchy of experience. B. is among our most serious and commanding novelists because, almost alone, he writes of the attempt to salvage a role for mind in a world overburdened with consciousness. Indeed, he is preeminently the modern novelist of that subject.

BIBLIOGRAPHY: Bradbury, M., *S. B.* (1982); Cohen, S. B., *S. B.'s Enigmatic Laughter* (1974); Fuchs, D., *S. B.: Vision and Revision* (1984); Kiernan, R. F., *S. B.* (1989); Miller, R., *S. B.: A Biography of the Imagination* (1991); Newman, J., *S. B. and History* (1984)

ROBERT F. KIERNAN

BENCHLEY, Robert [Charles]

b. 15 September 1889, Worcester, Massachusetts; d. 21 November 1945, New York City

B. is best known as a prolific author of short comic pieces, published in magazines and then in books, in which a carefully crafted persona tangled unsuccessfully with the intricacies of manners, politics, technology, social affairs, and the many other ills of modern life. Later in life B. began to appear in movies and eventually appeared in some forty-five short films. But it is as a comic writer that he is chiefly remembered.

His career began at Harvard, where he wrote for the *Lampoon* and appeared on stage giving fuddled talks—like "Through the Alimentary Canal with Gun and Camera"—that foreshadowed later essays like his confused "Treasurer's Report." On graduation he wrote for *Life* (then a humor magazine), *Vanity Fair,* the New York *Tribune* and *World,* contributed subtitles for films, and wrote and acted in stage productions.

At this time he was producing an enormous amount of copy, writing theater reviews for the newspapers, *Vanity Fair,* and *Life,* and writing humor both under his own name and as a paid contributor to the F.P.A. column in the *Tribune.*

During the 1920s, B. was close to Dorothy PARKER and Robert E. SHERWOOD, with whom he belonged to the Algonquin Round Table. In 1927, B. began contributing to the *New Yorker* (founded in 1925). His twelve years writing for that magazine have overshadowed the rest of his career, perhaps unfairly, but it was then that he began publishing in the best outlet for humor of the times. He also became associated with E. B. WHITE, James THURBER, and other writers publishing in the same magazine.

B.'s first book, *Of All Things!,* was published in 1921; others appeared every year or two until his death, bearing titles such as *My Ten Years in a Quandary, and How They Grew* (1936) and *After 1903—What?* (1938). These books are all collections of humorous pieces first published in periodicals.

The typical B. essay is two or three pages on some topic either unimportant—such as waking people up in the morning or getting candy wrappers opened—or important but misunderstood—such as war or diplomacy. Though fiction in the usual sense sometimes appears, and B. writes a good deal of very fine parody, his best essays feature his own persona, one based on himself but more incompetent, more nervous, and more prone to suffer from life's absurdities.

B. once complained that S. J. PERELMAN had bested him in his own *metier,* "the *dementia praecox* field." The continuing tributes of writers like Perelman and Thurber and the obvious influence on contemporaries such as Woody ALLEN and Veronica Geng show B.'s lasting centrality to the tradition of the American comic essay.

BIBLIOGRAPHY: Altman, B., *Laughter's Gentle Soul: The Life of R. B.* (1997); Benchley, N., *R. B.* (1955); Benchley, N., ed., *The B. Roundup: The Best of B.* (1954); Ernst, G., *R. B.: An Annotated Bibliography* (1995); Rosmond, B., *R. B.: His Life and Good Times* (1970); Yates, N. Y., *R. B.* (1968)

MERRITT MOSELEY

BENÉT, Stephen [Vincent]

b. 22 July 1898, Bethlehem, Pennsylvania; d. 13 March 1943, New York City

The strongest influence on B.'s development as a major prize-winning author—the last fifteen years of his life represented his most successful period—seems to have been his family, which on the paternal side had come from the Spanish island of Minorca. His paternal grandfather, Brigadier General Stephen Vincent Benét, fought in the Civil War, and B.'s father, Colonel James Walker Benét, also devoted most of his professional service to the military. However, this strong disciplinarian and caring parent read widely and was steeped in English poetry. He had writing talent and produced a lengthy, though unpublished, autobiography. B.'s mother, whose own father had also fought in the Civil War—but for the Confederacy—was an occasional writer of verse, and his brother and sister were poets.

Like his brother William Rose Benét, B. was originally intended for a military career; however, the traumatizing abuse he sustained from bullying schoolmates led him to direct his energies toward literary self-expression. Here the family's military experiences, as well as its concern with American history and culture, stood him in good stead. B. the well-traveled "Army brat" with keen poetic sensibility was able to combine letters with service to his country in a satisfactory manner, displaying, in John Griffith's words, "a sympathetic observer's interest in America's regional cultures, and an old-fashioned devotion to domestic and patriotic values."

B. wrote in many genres, including poetry, novels, operettas, plays, articles, and radio scripts for the U.S. Government during World War II to aid in the American war effort against the Axis Powers. Among his various awards for literary excellence were two Pulitzer Prizes in poetry—in 1929 for the quasi-epic *John Brown's Body* (1928) and posthumously in 1944 for his unfinished opus *Western Star* (1943). These two ambitious works constitute his major contributions to American literature, although certain of his short stories, particularly "The Devil and Daniel Webster" (1936) will long be remembered and appreciated.

His biographer Parry E. Stroud considers *John Brown's Body* as giving B. his best claim to a permanent place in American literary history. Aside from historical and biographical works consulted, B. drew on the Official Records of the Civil War, and personal letters, autobiographical accounts, and memoirs of a number of the leaders in that tragic drama. Of the 385-page *John Brown's Body,* B. wrote that it was "not a history," it was "a long poem dealing with some of the things that happened in our Civil War and how they affected various kinds of Americans." He wanted to show, in their exclusively American forms, "certain realities, legends, ideas, landscapes, ways of living, faces of men."

Most importantly, the face of the violent abolitionist leader John Brown, whose attack on the Federal arsenal at Harpers Ferry, Virginia in 1859 served as prelude to the Civil War, is indirectly evoked, to be imagined by the reader. In the cyclorama of B.'s retrospective

of that era, comprising poetry—deliberately, as B. explained, "written in a variety of meters"— dialogue, narrative, and documentary material, there is a good deal of beautiful writing. One example is the long requiem for Brown, opening with the familiar ballad line "John Brown's body lies a-mouldering in the grave," which closes the book. Aside from the book's namesake there are other historic figures in the cast of characters.

One major storyline highlights the Southern perspective, through the fictive adventures of the quasi-aristocratic Clay Wingate, whose family owns a plantation, and who joins the Black Horse Troop to fight against the North. As a counterpart, the Northern perspective is given through the story of a Connecticut Yankee abolitionist named Jack Ellyat, who sees action in important battles: Bull Run, Shiloh, Gettysburg. B. added a third region, the West and the Border States, exemplified by transplanted Easterners: John Vilas, his wife, and his daughter Melora, with whose lives Ellyat becomes involved when he flees his Confederate captors after the Union defeat at Shiloh and the Vilas family gives him sanctuary. Among the other fictional characters are a Southern mountaineer named Luke Breckinridge, Sally Dupré (Wingate's future wife), and three of the Wingate slaves—Aunt Bess (the mammy), Cudjo (the loyal, skillful mainstay of Wingate Hall), and a fieldhand named Spade. A complicated pattern of symbols and images runs through the entire saga. Foremost is an ornamental figure on a clock: the mythological charioteer Phaeton driving his "horses of anger." *John Brown's Body,* despite its lack of focus, remains eminently worth reading, and deserves being grouped with other American poetic sagas such as Walt WHITMAN's *Song of Myself* and William Carlos WILLIAMS's *Paterson.*

Western Star, which might have become as great a poetic-drama achievement as *John Brown's Body,* if not an even greater one, was barely gotten underway before B.'s other activities, including his wartime work for the U.S. Government, and finally his failing health, prevented his going on with the enterprise. What was published in 1943 as *Western Star* was only book 1 of many projected books, chronicling America's immigrants and pioneers—real and fictitious, landing, and colonizing, and then migrating westward, ever westward. In this early section, dealing with the Virginia and Massachusetts colonizers, B.'s characters follow the "Western Star," described by B. through a series of beautiful metaphors. "Star in the West, fool's silver of the sky, / Desolate lamp above the mountain pass / Where the trail falters and the oxen die, / Spiked planet on the prairie of wild grass, / Flower of frost, flower of rock and ice, / Red flower over the blood sacrifice." And, "Star-rocket, bursting when the dawn was grey, / Will-o'-the-wisp that led the riflemen / Westward and westward, killing down the day."

While B.'s handful of novels, like most of his short poems, have not made a lasting impression on American readers generally, this is not the case with a number of his short stories. "The Devil and Daniel Webster" presents a great court trial in which the soul of a poor farmer, sold to the devil, is at stake, and the famous orator and statesman Daniel Webster (for the defense) is pitted against the devil himself in an attempt to convince the jury of hellish sinners that his client deserves to reclaim his soul. "A Tooth for Paul Revere" (1937), with its motif of the rustic innocent seeking a person of eminence in a colonial town, suggests Nathaniel HAWTHORNE's classic tale, "My Kinsman, Major Molineux." B. provided ethnic and racial diversity, albeit stereotypically, in the story of a Jewish peddler: "Jacob and the Indians" (1938), the narrative of a runaway Negro slave: "Freedom's a Hard-Bought Thing" (1940), and—less effectively—an Irish folktale involving a leprechaun, "O'Halloran's Luck" (1938).

"By the Waters of Babylon" (1937), drawing apparently on the Bible story of Sodom and Gomorrah, as well as on popular lore of the increasingly war-cloudy 1930s, describes a native wandering amid, and barely comprehending, the ancient ruins of what once was New York. "Johnny Pye and the Fool-Killer" (1937), which adds a menacing footnote to Shakespeare's Puck's observation ("What fools these mortals be"), is one of B.'s morbid tales, at core, suggesting dim hope and inevitable death. "No Visitors" (1940), about a dying hospital patient, and "The Land Where There Is No Death" (1942)—which suggests a region reachable "only through living and dying," belong in this category. "Doc Mellhorn and The Pearly Gates" (1936) is a lighthearted, feel-good treatment of the subject, verging on a spoof. Given B.'s generally benevolent, humanitarian attitude toward our great nation, and good people, his "The Story About the Anteater" (1928)—based on a degrading racial joke treated, in the final analysis, positively—is an unsavory and out of place anomaly.

Though B.'s stories were by and large written for the mass-circulation magazine market, such as that of the *Saturday Evening Post,* the better short fictions show great imaginative powers and an old-fashioned love of language for oral transmission of the long ago and the here and now. Together with his ambitious poetic sagas of the trials, tribulations, and triumphs in the making of our modern nation, they justify his continued claim to a secure position in 20th-c. American literary history.

BIBLIOGRAPHY: Fenton, C. A., *S. V. B.: The Life and Times of an American Man of Letters, 1898–1943* (1958); Griffith, J., "S. V. B.," in Quartermain, P., ed., *DLB,* vol. 45, *American Poets, 1880–1945* (1986): 9–19; Roache, J., "S. V. B.," in Kimbel, B. E., ed., *DLB,* vol. 102, *American Short-Story Writers, 1910 1945* (1991): 11–19; Stroud, P. E., *S. V. B.* (1962)

SAMUEL I. BELLMAN

BERGER, Thomas
b. 20 July 1924, Cincinnati, Ohio

B. is a highly accomplished and prolific writer who has earned a lasting place in American letters. His 1983 novel, *The Feud,* a stunningly unattractive picture of Middle America in the 1930s, was nominated for a Pulitzer Prize, but he is probably best known for *Little Big Man* (1964). In 1965, this novel, whose main character observes the Battle of the Little Bighorn from both the white man's and the Indian point of view, was awarded the Western Heritage Award and the Richard and Hinda Rosenthal Award from the National Institute of Arts and Letters. Both *Little Big Man* and *Neighbors* (1981), in which an innocent suburbanite's life is shattered by his new neighbors, were made into films in 1970 and 1981 respectively. To date, B. has published twenty novels, two plays, and numerous short stories. Often called America's satirist, B. is masterful at myth bashing, but the enormous range his novels cover defies easy generalizations. His work has been widely and favorable reviewed, yet his novels are so different from one another that critics find it impossible to locate B.'s cannon within a recognizable movement or genre.

His writing has been described as scathing social commentary, but B. claims he is far more interested in exploring the creative possibilities of language itself rather than in trying to parody the ills of society. He will often take well-established tales and twist them just enough to create his own version—often imbued with large helpings of farce, underscoring rather than mediating the strange feel of the landscape and the characters who inhabit it. In B.'s *Robert Crews* (1994), a present-day version of Daniel Defoe's Robinson Crusoe, the hero is a middle-aged alcoholic completely unprepared for a life in the wild when his private plane crashes in a small lake in the backwoods. *Orrie's Story* (1990) is the Oresteia writ small, set in an American city at the end of World War II, with Agamemnon as a failed businessman called Augie Mencken.

B. does not see himself as a writer of comedy. He is, in fact, rather annoyed that readers find his novels funny. In discussing *Meeting Evil* (1992), he claimed, "I've been trying in recent years to be grimmer and grimmer and grimmer. I wanted to write a book no one could call comic." However, B. has also commented that "my way of looking at things, which is not humorless, no doubt tends to mislead the careless." And misleading the careless—as well as the not-so-careless—is in good part what fuels B.'s work. Because the language of his novels is accessible and his themes are at first glance familiar, he is able to draw the reader in, consistently disproving expectations and shaking preconceived notions. This is not to say that his prose style is simple; he writes with grace and precision and many sentences are constructed to surprise and challenge the reader.

Language may present and represent reality, but it can also be used to blur, to misrepresent and to obscure. Thus, the importance of Kafka's influence on B.: viewed from a slightly different perspective, framed in somewhat different language, reality shifts and the seemingly mundane and everyday suddenly, without warning, turns sinister. In *Meeting Evil,* a doorbell rings at breakfast time one Monday morning and an ordinary middle-class citizen in a medium-sized American town finds himself thrown headlong into a nightmare of mayhem and murder. B. is expert at manipulating the entirely plausible aspects of what might ordinarily be considered insanity. *Suspects* (1996) begins with the brutal killing of a mother and daughter, but what seems to be a conventional murder mystery slowly unwinds into something far more bizarre.

One of B.'s champions, the critic Richard Schickel claims that B. accepts free enterprise as the basis of Western civilization, on an economic level and on a spiritual level as well. He sees the free-enterprise system as the only viable way to organize both the self and society, given that man is a greedy and fallen creature. Indeed, clues to the philosophical underpinnings of B.'s novels may be found in his conviction that life is not responsive to any "cure." He believes in "fundamental reciprocity, which maintains the principle of constant damage in the universe."

BIBLIOGRAPHY: Landon, B., *T. B.* (1989); Madden, D. W., ed., *Critical Essays on T. B.* (1995)

                              MARGARET D. SULLIVAN

BERRY, Wendell [Erdman]

b. 5 August 1934, Henry County, Kentucky

The prolific author of over thirty books, B. is currently recognized as an able regional novelist, insightful environmental essayist, and astute social philosopher, though his sustained literary reputation will likely depend on the distinguished poetry he has produced over the past forty years.

After unhappy prep school years at Millersburg Military Institute, then B.A. and M.A. degrees in English from the University of Kentucky, B. was awarded a Wallace Stegner Fellowship at Stanford, where he studied creative writing with classmates Ernest J. GAINES, Ken KESEY, and Larry MCMURTRY. Numerous awards followed, including Rockefeller and Guggenheim Fellowships, leading B. to France, Italy, and finally New York University, where dissatisfaction with city and academic life turned him homeward. Except for a hiatus from 1977 to 1987, B. has taught at the University of Kentucky since 1964.

Leading a lifestyle reminiscent of the Amish, whom he admires, B. now uses draft animals to farm seventy-five acres in his birthplace of Henry County, Kentucky. A Bible-quoting nondenominationalist, B. would feel right at home with his younger contemporary Sydney LEA's backwoods Christianity. And, although he writes with a pencil and doesn't own a television, B. is no neoprimitive kook. As he says in *What Are People For?* (1990), computers are not bringing people one step closer to anything that matters: "peace, economic justice, ecological health, political honesty, family and community stability, good work."

In *A Continuous Harmony: Essays Cultural and Agricultural* (1972), B. notes that the relationship between "culture" and "agriculture" is not merely etymological. His belief that only a sense of community can cure the ills of industrial society aligns him with Jeffersonian ideals as well as the Agrarian tenets espoused in *I'll Take My Stand* (1930). His spiritual kinship to Henry David THOREAU is detectable in the themes of his novels: self-reliance, rapport with nature, the communal interdependence of country people, the mystical connection of all things, and loyalty to family and locale.

Just as William FAULKNER made his fictional real estate manageable by founding Yoknapatawpha County, B. created his fictional town of Port William and populated it with characters who appear and reappear in his four novels—*Nathan Coulter* (1960), *A Place on Earth* (1967), *The Memory of Old Jack* (1974), and *Remembering* (1988)—all of which draw on his personal experience and dramatize not only the agonies and ecstasies but also the drudgery of farm life.

Among the concerns of B.'s nonfiction books are the atomic bomb, governmental antipoverty programs that perpetuate the problems of the poor, the mass media's responsibility for declining sexual morality, and his usual topics: strip mining, solar energy, topsoil preservation, organic fertilizers, and the socioeconomic hazards of mechanized, monocrop farming. B. is especially dissatisfied with institutional Christianity's complicity in the destruction of the environment due in part to its emphasis on the next world. Other books offer solutions to the problems resulting from the government's treatment of land and rivers as economic commodities and resources: *The Unsettling of America* (1977), *The Gift of Good Land* (1981), *Home Economics* (1987).

As a social critic, B. addresses America's legacy of violence in *November Twenty Six Nineteen Hundred Sixty Three* (1964), a poem about the assassination of President John F. Kennedy, while *The Hidden Wound* (1970) is a reflection on the lingering problems caused by slavery and racism.

As literary critic, B. has decried the egocentric nihilism of so many younger poets, whose malady he attributes to their disconnection from a grounding community with a historical memory that would give them a sense of identity, continuity, and, ultimately, purpose.

B.'s most likely chance for lasting literary fame lies in his poetry, which has been compared to the verse of Gary SNYDER and A. R. AMMONS. His tonally muted, usually short-lined poems tend towards formality and rhyme in his later volumes. B.'s conversational style is spiced by aphoristic wisdom, startling phrases, and the wit and charm of country idioms. Not surprisingly, B.'s poems commemorate the workaday world of farmers: planting and harvest, seasonal changes, the flora and fauna of river, wood, and field, putting a new roof on a house, hog butchering, worthwhile work done well, the bliss of hard-earned rest, and the wonder of the natural world, for example, of trees as "weighty creatures made of light."

B.'s most memorable poetic creation is his spunky Mad Farmer, who first appears in *Farming: A Handbook* (1970). A contrarian whose wisdom seems madness to the uninitiated, the Mad Farmer resembles W. B. Yeats's Crazy Jane. Through this eccentric persona, who functions as a ventriloquist's dummy for the poet's ideology, B. is able to propagandize without sounding pushy, as when the Mad Farmer says, "The finest growth that farmland can produce is a careful farmer."

B. exercises his special talent, the elegy, on the deaths of friends, public figures, and even animals and trees. Perhaps B.'s most accomplished lyric is "The Peace of Wild Things," in which the fear of nuclear destruction is balanced by the beauty of nature, so that by poem's end the persona finds a Frostian "momentary stay against confusion."

Throughout B.'s poetry, one hears echoes of Yeats. The title essay of *The Long-Legged House* (1969) recalls not only the sanctuary of Thoreau's cabin but also the grace of Yeats's long-legged fly. Like Yeats, too, B. has composed his own epitaph, in "Testament," from *The Country of Marriage* (1973): "Beneath this stone a B. is planted/In his home land, as he wanted."

The passage epitomizes two of B.'s major themes: the lifelong marriage of a person to a place, and the ultimate recycling—finding one's end in one's beginning.

BIBLIOGRAPHY. Angyal, A. J., *W. B.* (1995); Merchant, P., *W. B.* (1991)

NORMAN GERMAN

BERRYMAN [Smith], John
b. 25 October 1914, McAlester, Oklahoma; d. 7 January 1972, Minneapolis, Minnesota

B. is usually grouped with the writers who became prominent after World War II under the rubrics the Middle Generation and the confessional poets. This group includes Randall JARRELL, Robert LOWELL, Theodore ROETHKE, and Sylvia PLATH. They have been so designated because of the frankness and urgency with which they rehearsed in their work the often self-destructive turbulence of their lives. Such poetry characteristically confesses and confides strife with spouses and parents, lovers and friends, dead and living; bouts with alcoholism, depression, and various manias; anxiety over the quality and the reception of their work. B. articulated the principle underlying confessional poetry by claiming that any ordeal, as long as it didn't kill him, was terrific for him as a writer. His major confessional work and his most lasting contribution to American writing were the "Dream Songs" he published between 1964 and 1969. A posthumous collection of Dream Songs, *Henry's Fate and Other Poems,* appeared five years after B. killed himself in 1972 after struggling against alcoholism for several years.

B.'s harrowing and fascinating life and the daring of his poetry often obscure his balanced wide-ranging accomplishments as a man-of-letters—an accomplished and prolific writer of fiction and criticism, on figures as diverse as Thomas Nashe, Miguel de Cervantes, Matthew "Monk" Lewis, Isaac Babel, Anne Frank, as well as several 20th-c. British and American writers. In 1950, B. published a pioneering critical biography of Stephen CRANE. Four years earlier, the eminent English Shakespeare editor, W. W. Greg, praised B.'s efforts to establish an authoritative text of *King Lear*. Seldom separating his intellectual interests from personal attachments, B. sought and served several literary apprenticeships. Some psychoanalytically minded biographers speculate that B.'s habit of apprenticing himself to more established writers represented a search for the father whose suicide B. witnessed at age eleven. Mark VAN DOREN, B.'s primary mentor during his undergraduate years at Columbia College, recalled how the young B. "walked with verse as if in a trance." While studying in England as a graduate fellow at Clare College, Cambridge, B. befriended Dylan Thomas, a fellow reveler B. came to regard as a kindred spirit. The high point for B. of his British sojourn was meeting Yeats whom B. emphatically claimed as his most important influence. This reverence for W. B. Yeats that B. shared with Delmore SCHWARTZ—a close friend and an influential early mentor—was part of their program of resistance to the influence of T. S. ELIOT, especially his doctrine of poetic impersonality, which they deemed perniciously hegemonic.

B.'s poetry also shows this erudite, self-conscious, and often programmatic literariness. It is most pronounced in his early work—a sonnet sequence written in the forties and published in 1967 and *Homage to Mistress Bradstreet,* an extended dramatic meditation on the origins and the predicament of the poet in America, first published in *Partisan Review* in 1953. A calculated vulgarity that modulates and undercuts his omnivorously polymath erudition marks B.'s late work. In *The Dream Songs* (1969), B. voices his Whitmanesque omnivorousness through a learned, iconoclastic, self-mocking, and rhetorically polymorphous alter-ego named Henry Bones. Throughout *The Dream Songs,* erudite discussions of art and culture follow and lead into frank confessions of lust, drunkenness, madness, infidelity, and paternal anxiety. Elegies on dead friends and colleagues, lamentations over lost loves, lost powers, and lost opportunities pervade *The Dream Songs* which, the poet announces at the outset, constitute a response to some irreversible loss. B.'s distinctive idiom in *The Dream Songs* compounds learned euphuism, which approaches pedantry at times, with baby talk and minstrel patois, often strained through irregular grammar and syntax.

The same manic succession of voices, from plodding pedant to enraged or enraptured wild man, pervades B.'s other late work: *Love and Fame* (1970; rev. ed., 1972)—a self-consciously provisional autobiographical sequence reminiscent of Lowell's *Notebook*—and the posthumous *Delusions, Etc.* (1972). These poems, however, lack the focus that a central and continuing dramatic speaker provides in *The Dream Songs.*

The autobiographical protagonists of B.'s most memorable fiction, "Wash Far Away' (1975) and the incomplete novel *Recovery* (1973), also test the obsessive bookishness that characterized B.'s life and his poetry, along with the other obsessive appetites that sometimes crippled and sometimes empowered him. Like much of B.'s poetry, his fiction also draws on B.'s many years as a professor, mostly at the University of Minnesota where he began teaching, through the efforts of his friend Allen TATE, in 1954 and where

he spent the rest of life. B. taught at several other colleges, including Harvard, Wayne State, Bread Loaf (Middlebury), the University of Iowa, and Princeton, where he worked with R. P. BLACKMUR, Saul BELLOW, and Delmore Schwartz. Among B.'s students who went on to achieve literary renown in their own right: Frederick Buechner, Edward HOAGLAND, Donald JUSTICE, W. D. SNODGRASS, W. S. MERWIN.

BIBLIOGRAPHY: Arpin, G., *The Poetry of J. B.* (1978); Bloom, J. D., *The Stock of Available Reality: R. P. Blackmur and J. B.* (1984); Conarroe, J., *J. B.: An Introduction to the Poetry* (1977); Haffenden, J., *J. B.: A Critical Commentary* (1978); Haffenden, J., *The Life of J. B.* (1982); Kelly, R., ed., *We Dream of Honor: J. B.'s Letters to His Mother* (1988); Kelly, R., and A. Lathrop, eds., *Recovering B.: Essays on a Poet* (1993); Linebarger, J. M., *J. B.* (1974); Mariani, P., *Dream Song: The Life of J. B.* (1990); Matterson, S., *B. and Lowell: The Art of Losing* (1988); Mazzaro, J., *Postmodern Poetry* (1980); Pinsky, R., *The Situation of Poetry* (1976); Simpson, E., *Poets in Their Youth* (1982); Thomas, H., ed., *B.'s Understanding: Reflection on the Poetry of J. B.* (1988); Vendler, H., *Part of Nature, Part of Us* (1980); Vendler, H., *The Given and the Made: Strategies of Poetic Redefinition* (1995)

JAMES D. BLOOM

BESTER, Alfred

b. 18 December 1913, New York City; d. 30 September 1987, Doylestown, Pennsylvania

B. has received critical acclaim for his innovations in the field of SCIENCE FICTION and for the care with which he develops his plots and characters. He is also considered a master stylist. Besides this critical recognition, however, he is regarded as one of the most popular science fiction writers ever. His many short stories and novels have garnered literally dozens of honors, including the prestigious Hugo Award for the best science fiction novel of the year in 1953, awarded by the Science Fiction Writers of America, and his writing has been reprinted in numerous major collections of science fiction. B.'s influence on the genre has been extraordinary, as demonstrated in critical reactions to his work, and his peers in the field constantly attest to the impact that he has had on science fiction in general and on themselves individually. To some extent this is due to the fact that he writes well about significant themes that transcend his genre. Interestingly, B. has also written nonfiction and articles for journals such as *Holiday, Show, Venture,* and *Rogue,* and for about twenty years he served as an editor at *Holiday* and did very little science fiction writing. In the final analysis, B.'s place among the best and most important science fiction writers of all time is assured by his two outstanding novels, *The Demolished Man* (1953) and *The Stars My Destination* (1957). His standing was recognized by his being named Grand Master by *Nebula* in 1987.

As is true with many science fiction writers, B. first became enamored with the genre as a young fan. He read the classical works of H. G. Wells and others whose writing later would affect his own style—authors whose works appeared in Hugo Gernsback's *Amazing* magazine and John W. Campbell, Jr.'s *Astounding;* Stanley Weinbaum, A. E. Van Vogt, Robert HEINLEIN, and Lewis Padgett were foremost among those whom he admired. He also benefitted from the tutelage of Mort Weisinger and Jack Schiff, editors of *Thrilling Wonder,* and Horace Gold, editor of *Galaxy Science Fiction*—the psychologically oriented magazine that was considered the top journal in its field. In addition, B. had considerable experience in writing for comic strips (*Superman, Batman,* and *Green Lantern*) and radio scripts (for *Nick Carter, Charlie Chan,* and *The Shadow*), and this helped him hone his style.

The Demolished Man, published in serial form in *Galaxy* (January-March 1952) and then as a novel in 1953, is B.'s first significant science fiction novel. The plot revolves around a murder, the ultimate antisocial act: businessman Ben Reich kills his business rival, Craye D'Courtney. At the base of B.'s work is a carefully developed philosophy of how humanity must evolve, given his specific, detailed, image of the contemporary world that underlies his philosophical assumptions. Thus, he creates a mystery story in which his protagonist, Lincoln Powell, is a representative of society, the prefect of police, and B. focuses not on the traditional chase element but rather on the psychological puzzle of motivation. Powell is endowed with the extrasensory perception ability to read minds, but while he can prove who the murderer is, he cannot demonstrate what the motive was because the killer himself is unaware of his motivation. The situation is complicated by Powell's love for Barbara D'Courtney, the victim's daughter and Reich's half sister.

The symbolic Man with No Face who stalks Reich represents the novel's theme, for B. is concerned with the dual nature of man (who embodies both good and evil impulses). Ultimately, B. suggests that humankind is essentially good and capable of improvement. Extrasensory perception is seen as a possible means of evolving to a more nearly perfect state for it reveals that "there is nothing in man but love and faith, courage and kindness, generosity and sacrifice. All else is only the barrier of . . . blindness." Reich's maturation, then,

is a microcosmic view of how the entire race can develop.

In representing his tale, B. effectively extends the concepts of mankind's duality, a traditional literary subject, and the motivation of revenge. By using a mystery story to do so, he is following the path of Anthony Boucher. B. employs literary techniques such as stream of consciousness and the imaginative use of print (following the lead of Laurence Sterne in *Tristram Shandy*). Still, *The Demolished Man* is a unique creation, and this last device is used imaginatively—in spelling (1/4 maine for Quartermaine) and in utilizing italics to graphically represent mind-to-mind communications.

The Stars My Destination, like its predecessor, was published serially as *Tiger! Tiger!* in *Galaxy* (October 1956-January 1957) and then in novel form, first as *Tiger! Tiger!* (1955) and then republished as *The Stars My Destination* (1957). In a number of ways, this novel reflects B.'s maturing as an author. To some extent this is made possible by the fact that where the main characters in *The Demolished Man* were upper class, many of those in *The Stars My Destination* are lower class. This allows the author a wider perspective in his story, which is appropriate because although he is focusing on society in *The Demolished Man,* in this case his subject is the continued evolution of humankind as a species.

The protagonist, Gulliver Foyle, an unskilled Mechanic's Mate on the 24th-c. spaceship *Nomad* is marooned in space for 170 days by the forces of the Outer Planets. The attack, it is later revealed, was instigated for financial reasons. The event that initiates Gully's development is not the attack itself, however, but his reaction when a second ship, which could have rescued him, leaves him to die. Enraged at the actions of the second ship, Gully determines to seek revenge on those who have deserted him. In order to survive he is forced into a special awareness of himself which in turn permits him to develop supernormal powers. An insensitive egoist at the beginning of the novel, by its conclusion he has come to represent the next evolutionary development of the human race.

Gully's evolution into a kind of Shavian superman, driven by a compelling life-force, comes about because his desire for revenge is delayed. Two factors complicate his plan. The first is the fact that humanity has discovered a limited form of teleportation called jaunting. The second is the existence of a material called PyrE, a secret cargo carried by the *Nomad* that can be detonated by thought.

As he seeks his revenge, Gully comes into contact with a number of people, the majority of whom are eager to betray or even murder anyone who might keep them from achieving their goals. These include

Saul Dagenham, a radioactive superpatriot; Robin Wednesbury, a telepath who can transmit thoughts but who cannot receive them; Presteign, a stereotypical businessman, unsentimental and manipulative in nature; Olivia Presteign, his daughter, who can see only in the infrared spectrum and who is more ruthless than her father; and Captain Peter Y'ang-Yeovil, a mixed-race detective who uses body language as a means of communication. The novel ends when Gully, after confronting all of these characters in a series of deadly adventures, gives the secret of PyrE to the human race so that no one person or group can use the power of this material to control all of humanity. With the knowledge of this element and the ability to transport it telepathically, the human race, like Gully, will be forced to rise to its next evolutionary stage in order to survive.

B.'s idea for *The Stars My Destination* came from two sources, one historical and one literary. In World War II, German submarines sometimes set traps by leaving shipwreck victims where they could be found so that other ships might be lured to the site—sometimes the survivors were simply left to die, as Gully was. B. also incorporated the plot line from Alexander Dumas's *The Count of Monte Cristo* in this novel.

Stylistically, *The Stars My Destination* is probably B.'s most ambitious work. The most obvious device is the use of different fonts (type faces) to replicate the sensory effect of synaesthesia. Dialogue and imagery are also utilized to reenforce the thematic elements. B. invented a language for Gully to speak that reflects his social status—and that becomes increasingly more intellectually subtle as Gully matures. The hideous tiger-mask that is tatooed on Gully's face and the reappearing image of The Burning Man reveal the emotional states that separate Gully from the rest of humanity and simultaneously provide a benchmark against which his development can be measured. These two images coalesce in the quote of the opening quatrain of William Blake's poem "The Tyger." The significance lies in the literary allusion: Blake's poem is contained in his *Songs of Experience*, which demonstrate that innocence is a matter of choice; an individual can only become innocent when options are known and can be rejected or embraced. Finally, the frame created by the repetition of the novel's opening paragraph and the end of the story suggests that Gully's transformation, and by extension the evolution of the human race, is ongoing and eternal.

BIBLIOGRAPHY: Aldiss, B. W., and H. Harrison, eds., *Hell's Cartographers: Some Personal Histories of Science Fiction Writers* (1976); Godshalk, W. L., "A. B.," in Cowart, D., and T. L. Wymer, eds., *DLB*, vol. 8, *Twentieth-Century Science-Fiction Writers* (1981): 30–36; Riggenbach, J., "Science Fiction as Will and Idea: The World of A. B.," *RQ* 5 (August 1972): 168–77; Scholes, R., and E. S. Rabkin, *Science Fiction: History, Science, Fiction* (1977); Spinrad, N., ed., *Modern Science Fiction* (1974); Wendel, C., *A. B.* (1980)

STEVEN H. GALE

BEVERLEY, Robert
b. ca. 1673, Middlesex County, Virginia; d. 21 April 1722, Middlesex County, Virginia

Although he published *A Ballad Address'd to the Reverend Members of the Convocation* (1704) and *An Abridgement of the Public Laws of Virginia* (1722), B. owes his literary reputation almost exclusively to his historical and naturalistic account of his homeland: *The History of Present State of Virginia* (1705), the first extended history of Virginia by a native-born Virginian.

B. divides his work into four books. In the first he treats briefly the exploration and settlement of Virginia from the efforts of Raleigh beginning in 1583 through "the present Time." The second is a naturalistic description of the land and its commodities; the third describes the physical characteristics and the customs of the native Indians; and the fourth considers the "present State" of the colony, its government, alterations, and husbandry.

Written in response to the author's dissatisfaction with another account of the same subject, this history in part perpetuates the myth of Virginia as a paradisiacal garden. nevertheless B.'s account is unique in its plain style and its forceful repudiation of the colonial governors—a repudiation deleted in the revised edition, published in 1722. The imagery throughout is of the lushness of the land, the plenty of fruit and fish, and the beauty and pristine simplicity of the Native Americans. But the history is plagued, like its subject, with the hint of a serpent in the garden. Though the Indians are Edenic figures, for example, they can be resentful and violent; though the harbors are inviting, worms eat at the ships' hulls; though the land is fertile, its very fruitfulness causes sloth among the inhabitants. Thus, B.'s history is an important contribution to American literature both in its depiction of early Virginia and in its thematic insistence on the dichotomy between a new world Eden and old world problems.

BIBLIOGRAPHY: Marx, L., *The Machine in the Garden: Technology and the Pastoral Ideal in America* (1964); Small, J. J., "R. B. and the New World Garden," *AL*

55 (1983): 525–40; Wright, L. B., *The First Gentlemen of Virginia* (1940)

LEE SCHWENINGER

BIDART, Frank

b. 27 May 1939, Bakersfield, California

Although he has written in various forms, B. is best known for his harrowing depiction of psychologically disturbed characters and the innovative prosody of his dramatic monologues. Influenced by Ezra POUND's *Cantos* and Robert LOWELL's *Life Studies,* B. positions his work between traditional forms and free verse, developing a post-confessional mode in these monologues to dramatize the sexuality and psychosis of an individual. A B. poem looks like no other: he uses capital letters, italics, and punctuation to mark the volume and intensity of the speaking voice, and he may combine sections of prose with variously indented short lines so that a line's meaning depends on semantics, spatial position, and formatting. These visual indicators attempt to direct the voice, or, as B. says, to "fasten the voice to the page." Such an original form, along with the intensity of character he creates, has secured B.'s place among American poets in the late 20th c.

In his acclaimed first volume, *Golden State* (1973), B. demonstrates his poetic range by testing the meter and rhymes of a Shakespearean sonnet in "Self-Portrait, 1969" and offering a partial translation of Virgil's *Aeneid.* However, the book is dominated by autobiographical impulses, with the poet exploring his relationship with his father and questioning his past. The volume begins with the first of B.'s disturbing monologues, "Herbert White," a confession of the child killer, rapist, and necrophiliac that aims to shock from the opening line: "When I hit her on the head, it was good." Such a demonic impulse persists through the poem, as the speaker, echoing Milton's Satan, attempts to reconcile his self-image with the reality of his actions: "Hell came when I saw / MYSELF."

In *The Book of the Body* (1977), B. dramatizes the mind/body dualism by scripting conflicts between the self and the body: the self denying then accepting the body's history, as in "The Arc" and the self annihilating the body for the sake of the self, as in "Ellen West." With "Ellen West," B. expands the dramatic monologue to a psychological case study, including journal entries and medical notes that resituate the speaking voice of West, a famous anorexic patient of Ludwig Binswanger. From cover to cover, the volume develops this obsession of the body, with the self "Wanting to cease to feel," as the repeated lines in the

villanelle "Envoi" confirm: "If it resists me, I know it's real. / I feel too much. I can't stand what I feel."

B.'s technique gained wider acceptance with *The Sacrifice* (1983), which attracted a larger readership. The volume features B.'s most famous poem, "The War of Vaslav Nijinsky," winner of the *Paris Review*'s first Bernard F. Conners Prize for a long poem. A tour de force for the poet's method, the poem uses the full range of B.'s prosody to examine the psyche of the modernist choreographer and one-time principal male dancer of the Ballets Russes. The poem focuses on Nijinsky's self-consciousness about his neurosis and sexuality, using both the speaking voice and prose sections derived from biographical sources to dramatize his attempt to join his own guilt to the world's guilt over World War I by dancing a sacrifice. Such themes dominate the entire volume, which posits sacrifice as the only means of expiating sin, ending with a new prosodic rendering of the creation story in Genesis 1–2:4, precursor to the Fall which introduces guilt in the Judeo-Christian worldview.

B. has been criticized for his melodramatic impulses, for his overformatted words that shout from the page, for his obsessions, and for his fragmented lines and halting statements. Despite these criticisms, many readers admire his inventiveness and intensity, with his monologues providing the best forum for his dramatic originality and psychological insight.

BIBLIOGRAPHY: Crenshaw, B., "The Sin of the Body: F. B.'s Human Bondage," *ChiR* 33 (Winter 1983): 57–70; Gray, J., "'Necessary Thought': F. B. and the Post-Confessional," *ConL* 34 (Winter 1993): 714–39

TODD VERDUN

BIERCE, Ambrose [Gwinnett]

b. 24 June 1842, Meigs County, Ohio; d. 1914?, Mexico

B. has long had an international reputation of being a classic short story writer but is still in the process of being recognized as an author of considerable depth as well as power.

He has not been well served by literary scholarship. Most criticism of his work has been amateur or impressionistic, fixing on some perceived stylistic feature of a small sample of his writing and generalizing without regard to history, biography, or even chronology. On slender evidence, he has been accused of imitation, usually of Edgar Allan POE. Much of what passes for biographical criticism is fruitless speculation about his mysterious disappearance into Mexico in 1914 and treats B. more as a colorful personality than as a gifted author. In contrast, the most useful works of criticism are characterized by close textual analysis in the context of a familiarity with his work, life, and times.

B. was one of the few 19th-c. American authors of note who served in the Civil War. Of that small number, he served the longest and saw the most action. After the war, B. moved to San Francisco where he quickly won respect for his integrity and journalistic ability. His hatred of crime, cruelty, incompetence, and sham was inexhaustible and always fresh, and he raised to an art form the witty satire of his sharp epigrams with which he fearlessly skewered his targets wherever he found them. Of one of his enemies, for example, he wrote the following epitaph: "Here lies Frank Pixley—as usual." Of some politician much in the news: "[He] has acquired the exposure habit and, like the red lobster, does not prosper out of hot water." In his *Devil's Dictionary* he mocked with cynical definitions such pieties as "applause, *n.* The echo of a platitude"; "befriend, *v.t.* To make an ingrate"; and "marriage, *n.* The state or condition of a community consisting of a master, a mistress and two slaves, making in all, two."

When William Randolph Hearst bought the San Francisco *Examiner* in 1887, B. was one of the first journalists he hired. Though B. despised Hearst, he remained with the Hearst organization as a feature writer until 1909 because he was left free to write whatever he wished, and was paid well. He usually wrote a column of matter each week; normally it was commentary on the news but sometimes he substituted short stories.

The Civil War was a seminal experience for B., for he lost his youthful naivete in the carnage, and terribly vivid memories of the war haunted him for the rest of his life. It took him close to twenty-five years of constant reflection on the war before he was ready to express his deepest thoughts on it. When he finally began framing these thoughts in fictional form, he had come to regard war—in both its extended as well as its literal sense—as a more accurate representation of life than peace. This view led him to place a high but ambivalent value on reason. B. saw it as man's most potent weapon of self-defense, but also as one that was never good enough, deceptive, and indifferent to love and happiness. A recurrent motif in his work is how human attempts to use reason to live up to high standards or even for protection ironically bring suffering or destruction.

This can be best discerned in the stories of his major anthology, *Tales of Soldiers and Civilians* (1891). "A Horseman in the Sky," for example, one of B.'s most famous stories, leads up to the unbearable decision its protagonist has to make. At the outset of the Civil War, Carter Druse joined the Union army out of conviction, his father the Confederate. The father's last word to Carter was the admonition to do what he conceived to be his duty. One day, while serving as a sentinel, Carter took aim at a mounted Confederate scout positioned on a cliff overlooking a valley in which a Union force was camped. Suddenly, Carter realized that the scout was his father. Either Carter had to shoot or let the man escape. Carter lowered his sights from the rider to the horse and shot it. The horse plunged off the cliff, bringing sure death to the father and maddening grief to Carter.

This story thus allegorizes a no-win conflict between incompatible notions of duty. Only the pitiful gesture of Carter's slightly lowering rifle—a "compromise" which made no practical difference—outwardly reflects the civil war that ravaged Carter's spirit and left him numb.

A counterpart of this story on a less emotional plane is "Haïta the Shepherd," which utilizes the pastoral tradition to allegorize the tantalizing nature of happiness. When the young shepherd Haïta resolved one day to stop inquiring for knowledge the gods withheld and henceforth to concern himself only with doing his duty, he was suddenly visited by a maiden of surpassing beauty. When he tried to know her, she vanished. She reappeared to him several times, gladdening his heart, but then immediately devastated him by abrupt and inexplicable disappearances. When Haïta complained to a holy hermit that because she vanished as soon as he expressed curiosity, doubt, or misgiving, he had had her each time only for a single instant, the hermit identified her as Happiness and explained, "Unfortunate youth! . . . but for thine indiscretion thou mightst have had her for two."

This story does not deny the value of happiness, but describes it as deriving only from the unreflective carrying out of duty and as being incompatible with the effects of reason: curiosity, doubt, and misgiving. Although the story may appear playful, it is basically a serious analysis of one of the greatest goods of life and is as satisfactory an explanation of the evanescence of happiness as one is likely to find.

Like Jonathan Swift, to whom he is strikingly similar, B. often cloaked his compassion in satire or irony. Critics who interpret B. as misanthropic or gratuitously bitter or cynical fundamentally misunderstand how sensitive he was to pain and suffering and how deeply he hated whatever or whoever caused it needlessly. He mocked only the villains of his stories; for the innocent victims he had empathy.

Having lost his faith in doctrinal Christianity and its certainties, B. was attracted to the forms and humanistic philosophies, especially Stoicism, of classicism. Stoicism did not completely satisfy, however; he understood that while, negatively, it might inure to pain it did not foster the creative and positive goods of happiness and love. But he accepted as accurate description its doctrine of *vivere est militare*—to live is to be a soldier.

In addition to being a talented author with a penchant for concision and accuracy, B. was also psychologically sensitive to both his characters and his readers, as is borne out by such stories as "An Occurrence at Owl Creek Bridge." Nevertheless, the entire corpus of his writing, his journalism as well as his fiction, is rooted in a stark military morality tensed between tragedy and Stoicism. He saw man as fatally pitted from birth against other men, Nature, and even himself. Complaint and lament were futile. B.'s response was that man should be a good soldier and serve truth and justice with the best that was in him.

BIBLIOGRAPHY: Berkove, L. I., ed., *Skepticism and Dissent: Selected Journalism, 1898–1901* (1980; rev. ed., 1986); Davidson, C. N., ed., *Critical Essays on A. B.* (1982); Grenander, M. E., *A. B.* (1982); McWilliams, C., *A. B.: A Biography* (1929)

LAWRENCE I. BERKOVE

BIOGRAPHY

From the spoken to the written word, the inherent nature of biography combines an inventive mixture of people, places, and events in the process of telling or retelling the story of a person's life. Fact or fiction, the interpretation of the story serves as a representation of the individual; consequently, our understanding and appreciation of the life is dependent on the ability and credibility of the narrator. Biographical writing has from the beginning been a fundamental aspect of American literature, but as a genre onto itself biography was slow to emerge, superseded by more clearly defined literary endeavors. As suggested by Native American pictorial and oral tradition, biography in its earliest forms was intended to illustrate or record specific events or to acknowledge the deeds, accomplishments, or contributions of certain individuals from within the group. The storyteller/narrator performed the same function as the later historian/biographer, evinced by the mid-17th c. with the arrival of colonists to the New World.

Descending from the British tradition of providing a utilitarian purpose, biographical writing in America served as a means to supplement the writing of history and chronicle. Perceived as a craft rather than a literary form, biography was intended to enhance the documentation of what would evolve as American history. From colonial times to the present, the writing and rewriting of history has played an instrumental role in the growth and development of our cultural heritage

as well as our national literature. Early 17th-and 18th-c historical tracts such as Captain John SMITH's *The Generall Historie of Virginia, New-England, and the Summer Isles,* published in 1624, William BRADFORD's *Of Plymouth Plantation,* written in 1630–50 and published in 1856, and Jeremy BELKNAP's three-volume *The History of New-Hampshire* paved the way for later literary historians such as William Hickling PRESCOTT, John Lothrop MOTLEY, and Francis PARKMAN who reflect the maturity of historical scholarship in the 19th c. Similarly, the scope and magnitude of such pivotal works as George Bancroft's twelve-volume *History of the United States,* published from 1834 to 1882, and Henry ADAMS's *History of the United States during the Administrations of Jefferson and Madison,* published in 1889–91, were instrumental in formulating the expectations and accomplishments of 20th-c. historians. Of most importance is that throughout the course of historical writing there exists an interrelationship between history and biography, between the making of history and the makers of history

Early colonial literature was dominated by Puritan New England authors intent upon glorifying as well as preserving the public virtues and innate spirituality of their preeminent religious, political, and judicial leaders. The objective of the biographer as well as the historian was to articulate the experience of life in the New World as the enactment of divine providence. Illustrated as well in personal narrative, in the form of diary or AUTOBIOGRAPHY, literature was intended as spiritual record for the edification of posterity. Didactic in purpose and eulogistic by design, biographical writing like history was more appropriately a form of moral instruction. Less concerned with factual detail and more toward presentation and image, the majority of biographical writing was either commemorative or hagiographic. The earliest known Puritan biography to appear in print is John Norton's life of English-born clergyman and author John Cotton entitled *Abel Being Dead Yet Speaketh,* published in 1658. Drawing in part upon Cotton's diaries and letters, Norton provides an account of Cotton's coming to the New World, comparing the experience to a spiritual exodus of biblical proportion. In effect, Norton established a precedent for future biographers to follow, illustrated by Increase MATHER's biography of his father, *The Life and Death of That Reverend Man of God, Mr. Richard Mather,* published in 1670, and further illustrated—with evidence of the increasing secularization within Puritan New England—by the publication in 1724 of Cotton MATHER's biography of Increase. However, Cotton Mather's most important contribution to biographical writing is his *Magnalia Christi Americana.* Written between 1694 and 1698 and published in 1702 in London, *Magnalia Christi Americana* was intended as a comprehensive account of the Puritan experience in New England. Incorporating elements of historical, biographical, and autobiographical writing, Mather created a document of lasting importance that in many ways marks a transition in the development of American literature.

In the aftermath of the Revolutionary War, the birth of an independent republic initiated an unprecedented sense of NATIONALISM. In an effort both to ratify and to justify the act of independence, it fell to the historian to chronicle the founding of the nation and to the biographer to write the lives of its founders. While the 17th and 18th cs. were dominated by historical rather than biographical accounts, biography gradually developed as a distinctive genre as readers—perhaps more familiar with the story itself—became more interested in the makers of history. The public demand in the first half of the 19th c. for biographies of America's statesmen and patriots produced a significant contribution to the development of the genre, as illustrated by Mason WEEMS's life of George Washington, published in 1800, and Benjamin FRANKLIN, published in 1815, John Marshall's life of Washington (5 vols., 1804–7), William Wirt's life of Patrick Henry (1817), William Tudor's life of James Otis (1823), Jared SPARKS's life of Franklin, and George TUCKER's life of Thomas JEFFERSON. Simultaneously, readers became increasingly drawn to the lives of those who personified the emerging American spirit, which produced biographies of such legendary figures as Davy CROCKETT and Daniel Boone to Sam Houston and Kit Carson.

By the mid-19th c., biography attracted the attention of more established writers. In 1852, Nathaniel HAWTHORNE produced *The Life of Franklin Pierce,* followed by Washington IRVING's five-volume *The Life of George Washington,* published from 1855 to 1859. The development of the genre was further enhanced by the increasing recognition at home and abroad of a distinctive American literary canon. In effect, the makers of American literature now became the substance of literature as reader demand in the second half of the 19th c. produced biographical treatments of the major transcendentalist and American Renaissance authors, illustrated by such works as Thomas R. Lounsbury's life of James Fenimore COOPER (1882), Oliver Wendell HOLMES's life of Ralph Waldo EMERSON, published in 1885, George E. Woodberry's life of Edgar Allan POE (1885), and Charles W. CHESNUTT's life of Frederick DOUGLASS, published in 1899.

In the late 19th and early 20th c., American biography began to mature into a more analytical and evaluative genre, under the guidance of such respected authors as George Edward Woodberry, Van Wyck BROOKS, and Gamaliel BRADFORD. In conjunction with a distinguished career as a literary scholar, Woodberry produced biographies of American subjects—Poe, Emerson, Wendell Phillips, Hawthorne—as well as non-American subjects—A. C. Swinburne, Mary Wollstonecraft—indicative of the increased breadth and recognition given to American literary scholarship. In additon to such highly significant critical studies as *America's Coming-of-Age,* published in 1915, and *The Flowering of New England* (1936), the first of a five-volume series entitled Makers and Finders, Brooks wrote lives of Emerson, Washington Irving, Mark TWAIN, and William Dean HOWELLS; British writers John Addington Symonds and H. G. Wells; the painter John Sloan; and the educator Helen Keller.

Following World War I, biography became increasingly influenced by Freudian techniques that emphasized the internal elements that informed personality, which impacted on biographer's interpretation of the individual. The Freudian dominance of biography in the 1920s and 1930s also impacted on the revisionary nature of biography, illustrated in such works as Bradford's psycobiographies and Lewis MUMFORD's life of Herman MELVILLE (1929). During this same period, the Southern Agrarians turned to biography as a means to reflect on the accomplishments of men of importance to the South, illustrated in Allen TATE's biographies of Stonewall Jackson and Jefferson Davis, Robert Penn WARREN's life of John Brown, and John Crowe RANSOM's *God without Thunder,* as well as Douglas Southall Freeman's Pulitzer Prize-winning life of Robert E. Lee.

The 1950s represents a "golden age" of American biography, a period that produced an unprecedented array of distinguished life writing, both of literary figures—Newton Arvin's life of Melville (1950), Arthur Mizener's life of F. Scott FITZGERALD (1951), Edgar Johnson's two-volume life of Charles Dickens (1952), James L. Clifford's life of Samuel Johnson (1955), Gordon N. Ray's two-volume life of Thackeray (1955–58), Gay Wilson Allen's life of Walt WHITMAN (1955), Edwin H. Cady's two-volume life of Howells (1956–58), and most noteworthy the introductory volume in 1953 of Leon Edel's five-volume life of Henry JAMES, Leslie A. Marchand's three-volume life of Byron, and Richard Ellmann's life of James Joyce (1959)—and nonliterary figures—from John F. Kennedy's Pulitzer Prize-winning *Profiles in Courage* (1956) to Erik Erikson's psychological study of Martin Luther, published in 1958.

In the second half of the 20th c. biography solidified itself as a genre of both popular and critical importance. As a means to satisfy curiosity as well as reader demand, popular biography is generally identified with subjects of current interest or celebrity status—often focusing on sensational or controversial speculation rather than factual information. Scholarly biography, on the other hand, implies a more introspective analysis and evaluation of its subject with the intent to create a literary work of art. Nonetheless, all biography follows the basic premise of telling the story of a person's life. Biographies turn to the past—often resurrecting or revising our perceptions of their subjects—or the present—often with the accompaniment of terminology such as "authorized" or "unauthorized." Throughout the course of its development, biography has transformed from its humble beginnings to one of the most widely read forms of American literature.

BIBLIOGRAPHY: Clifford, J. L., *Biography as an Art: Selected Criticism, 1569–1960* (1962); Honan, P., *Author's Lives: On Literary Biography and the Art of Language* (1990); Iles, T., ed., *All Sides of the Subject: Women and Biography* (1992); Kendall, P. M., *The Art of Biography* (1965); Meyers, J., *The Biographer's Art* (1989); Meyers, J., ed., *The Craft of Literary Biography* (1985); Oates, S. B., ed., *Biography as High Adventure* (1986); O'Connor, U., *Biographers and the Art of Biography* (1991); Veniga, J., ed., *The Biographer's Gift: Life Histories and Humanism* (1983); Weintraub, S., *Biography and Truth* (1967)

STEVEN R. SERAFIN

BIRD, Robert Montgomery

b. 5 February 1806, New Castle, Delaware; d. 23 January 1854, Philadelphia, Pennsylvania

B. lived primarily in Philadelphia where he studied and practiced medicine and briefly served as a professor at the Pennsylvania Medical College. Though he published poetry, B. was best known for two consecutive literary careers: playwright from 1830 to 1834; romancer and novelist from 1834 to 1839. Several of his fictions retain their appeal. The border romance *Nick of the Woods; or, The Jibbenainosay. A Tale of Kentucky* (1837) contains a character among the most memorable in American fiction—Nathan Slaughter.

B. wrote his popular verse plays, the tragedies *The Gladiator* and *Oralloossa,* produced in 1831 and 1832 respectively, and the domestic drama *The Broker of Bogata,* produced in 1834, for Edwin Forrest, then the premier American actor. *The Gladiator* ennobles the revolt of Roman slaves. *Oralloossa* mourns the destruction of an Indian nation. Both are melodramatic spectacles crammed with bombast; both are explicitly democratic and implicitly patriotic. *The Broker of Bogata,* set like *Oralloossa* in South America, contains less posturing and more psychological motivation. None of B.'s plays could withstand revival.

B.'s reputation therefore rests on his fiction. He wrote two romances of the conquest of Mexico, *Calavar* (1834) and *The Infidel* (1835); two American historical romances, *The Hawks of Hawk Hollow* (1835) and *Nick of the Woods;* and two satirical novels of American life, *Sheppard Lee* (1836) and *The Adventures of Robin Day* (1839). The Mexican romances, carefully researched and occasionally powerful, sink under plot contrivances and stylistic excesses. *The Hawks of Hawk Hollow* is an uninspired Revolutionary War tale.

The two satires, however, are amusing, even trenchant. In *Sheppard Lee,* B. employs an extraordinary device to explore contemporary American society. Through metempsychosis the narrator, Sheppard, successively enters six bodies, leading six lives: rich squire, young reprobate, old moneylender, Quaker philanthropist, slave, and dyspeptic southern gentleman. Sheppard hates each life; he returns to his humble, honorable estate. Though B.'s condemnation of greed, dissipation, misguided philanthropy, and abolitionism is obvious, his device and humor make *Sheppard Lee* a fine satire. *Robin Day,* more traditionally picaresque, contains several hilarious scenes, especially when Robin fights mistakenly for the British during the War of 1812.

Nick of the Woods and Nathan Slaughter are B.'s great creations. *Nick of the Woods* is a disturbing American historical romance. Slaughter, a Quaker, honestly professes nonviolence. But by night he is a "Nick" or "Jibbenainosay" haunting the forests, stalking Indians, killing them brutally, and carving a cross on their chests. Slaughter's family has been murdered by Indians before his eyes; his life as "Nick" is his sublimated, schizophrenic response. In his greatest romance, B. unveils the primitive, terrifying implications of frontier experience. None of B.'s contemporaries, except John NEAL, was willing or able to explore the dark psychological depths found in *Nick of the Woods.*

BIBLIOGRAPHY: Dahl, C., *R. M. B.* (1963); Foust, C. E., *The Life and Dramatic Works of R. M. B.* (1971)

JOHN ENGELL

BISHOP, Elizabeth

b. 8 February 1911, Boston, Massachusetts; d. 6 October 1979, Boston, Massachusetts

While long respected among other contemporary poets, as well as literary critics, B. is finally coming to be recognized as not merely one of the finest 20th-c. American poets, but as one of the great poets of our era. In her lifetime, her work won considerable recognition—most notably the Pulitzer Prize for *Geography*

III (1976). However, more recently her work has been regarded with increasing seriousness, so that at least according to some critics she ranks with Wallace STEVENS, Robert FROST, and Marianne MOORE. Her reputation is destined to increase even further as the linguistic subtlety and the feminist politics of her verse become more fully understood.

B.'s father died only a few months after she was born, and her mother was permanently institutionalized five years later for a mental breakdown. Thereafter, B. lived with her grandparents in Nova Scotia before being sent to live with her aunt in Massachusetts as a young teenager. This lack of home, of a "center" in both the metaphorical and metaphysical senses, permeates B.'s verse from the early poems, through *Questions of Travel* (1965), to the "crypto-dream-house" of one of her late poems. Even Robinson Crusoe as rendered in her textual tour de force "Crusoe in England" is a person without a home when returned to his homeland. While attending Vassar College, B. met Marianne Moore, who served as an early mentor. Later, just as her first book, *North & South* (1946), was published, she became good friends with Robert LOWELL. Despite such personal alliances, however, B. traveled extensively, as if in search of a home, living briefly in Europe, Mexico, Key West, and for nearly twenty years in Brazil before returning to the U.S. to teach at Harvard. Her preoccupation with places, with "questions of travel," and most crucially with the arbitrary but necessary distortion which occurs as we chart or describe our experience manifests itself as one of her most consistent themes—from "The Map" which opens her first volume to the "watery, dazzling dialectic" of "Santarém" (written the year she died).

Among her early critics, B. has been perhaps most famous for her realistic detail (as in the frequently anthologized "The Fish") and for her tone—reticent, decorous, and witty. And while, at least superficially, B.'s tone is that of a slightly amused, reserved New England woman, it is far more critical and political than has been previously recognized. As scholars are beginning to see, B. uses a quintessentially "feminine" voice, modest and reserved, in a very feminist way, denouncing consistently the social "scripting" (or "conscripting") of women, not only in such poems as "Sestina" or "In the Waiting Room," but also in her prose pieces as well, like "In Prison." In this regard, she is much more akin to Emily DICKINSON than to Wallace Stevens (that poet with whom she has been most often compared).

Far more than most major poets of this century, B. uses traditional poetic forms such as sestinas, sonnets, ballads, and villanelles, a fact which contributes to her seeming reticence. However, in the hands of Bishop the traditional poetic forms, as in the poem

entitled "Sestina," become ironic critiques of the deformations which occur as life becomes literally contextualized within the traditions of (any) society. Not surprisingly perhaps, B.'s poetic critique extends to politics as well—as in "In the Waiting Room" and the prose/poem "12 O'Clock News," both of which reticently indict, even as the instantiate, the conditions leading to World War I and the Vietnam War, respectively. Despite this facet of her verse, however, B.'s verse remains unusually witty, deceptively reassuring in its friendliness—always, as it were, civilized.

It is worth noting that B.'s verse matured as she did, so that her late work is her best. In addition to *Geography III, The Complete Poems, 1927–1979* (1983) contains previously uncollected late poems such as "Santarém," "North Haven" (her elegy to Lowell), and "Sonnet," published posthumously and that ironically serves as her own brilliant epithet.

BIBLIOGRAPHY: Bloom, H., ed., *E. B.* (1985); Brogan, J. V., "*E. B.: Perversity* as Lyric Voice," *AmerP* 7 (1990): 31–49; Parker, R. D., *The Unbeliever: The Poetry of E. B.* (1988); Stevenson, A., *E. B.* (1966); Travisano, T. J., *E. B.: Her Artistic Development* (1988)

JACQUELINE VAUGHT BROGAN

BLACKBURN, Paul

b. 24 November 1926, St. Albans, Vermont; d. 13 September 1971, Cortland, New York

B. is loosely associated with both the Black Mountain and the Beat writers of the 1950s and early 1960s, but he is best understood as a poet whose work in the lyric is characterized by its revivifying variety and independence from schools of thought.

After his mother, Frances Frost, was selected for the Yale Younger Poets Series in 1929, she abandoned her family and left four-year-old B. for her elderly parents to raise. His reconciliation with her at the age of fourteen profoundly influenced his own developing interest in reading poetry. After a brief and domestic stint in military service during the closing days of World War II, B. began his formal reading of poetry, and especially the poems of Ezra POUND, with M. L. Rosenthal at New York University. B. transferred to the University of Wisconsin in 1949, where he continued the correspondence he had begun with Pound, even hitchhiking cross-country to visit him during his confinement at St. Elizabeths Hospital. Forty years before, Pound had declared song to be the fundamental condition of modern poetry and traced the lyrical form to the songs of the troubadours of the Middle Ages. His translations from their extant songs, *Proensa* (1953), became his first book. *Proensa* and the first collection of his own poems, *The Dissolving Fabric* (1955), were published by Robert CREELEY's Divers Press in Mallorca. It had been at Pound's urging that B. contacted Creeley, who was to be his introduction to the Black Mountain poets.

B. used a 1954–55 Fulbright Fellowship to travel to Provence and immerse himself in both the archives and the countryside of the troubadours, and also to explore Spain, where he began a lifelong practice of translating the poems of Federico García Lorca. The poet of *The Dissolving Fabric* announces himself, at the beginning of his career, among the foremost postmodern practitioners of the poem sung in "the common tongue" or *vulgari eloquentia*. The harmony of play that resonates within the musical intervals of these lines from "The Hawser" is typical: "The lovers disembarrass / themselves (meaning 3.), startled, / their legs are uneasy, blare of whistle, in- / sistent, making fun, makes / them laugh at last. The tug / comes in to water up." The narrative technique of the persona, a speaker who is at once mindful of himself and the culture he finds himself in, is the showcase for B.'s keen ear for speech; although the journal poems of his last period—beginning with his European travel poems in late 1967 and continuing through his hospital journals—drop the persona in favor of the urgency of a private notation seeking form.

The publishing history of *Sixteen Sloppy Haiku and a Lyric for Robert Reardon* (1966) suggests a poet ahead of his times. Printed by White Rabbit Press in an edition of forty-four copies, half of the run was confiscated by the Cleveland, Ohio police for what was considered in those days to be offensive cover art. Subsequently, the poems were never circulated and most readers had to wait for his *Collected Poems,* which appeared in print fourteen years after the poet's death. On the other hand, some gender-sensitive readers today find B.'s characterizations of women to be dated and dehumanizing. In the poems "The Once-Over" and "Clickety-Clack," a voyeur male narrator vividly fantasizes about the bodies of women he encounters randomly while riding the subway. But B.'s authentic mode is historical, not prophetic; he "makes new" the troubadors' love lyric. His narrator is oftentimes the singer, as in the poem "The Dissolving Fabric," who feels himself wounded by the remoteness of his lady as he experiences the modern world's version of unrequited love. In other poems, like "Definition," an omniscient watcher narrates a scene in which the male, here a swimmer, distances himself from the female, who displays an animalistic sexuality on the beach. One of B.'s editors hints that he had worked out a desire to control women in poems in part because his mother had abandoned him for poetry and a lesbian

lover. In a successful lyric like "The Continuity," B. seems to artlessly record the overheard conversation of urban speakers, but the page develops into a mini-libretto about how stories come to us, across centuries and cultures, in a continuity that is reenacted in everyday events like gossip on a city bus and a paperboy writing down his sales.

B. was a prolific translator, and he continues to be valued for the sensitivity of his renderings of works by García Lorca, Pablo Picasso, Antonio Jiménez-Landi, Guillaume IX (Duke of Aquitaine), Julio Cortázar, and others. Among B.'s most lasting influences has proved to be the poetry reading programs he helped establish and popularize, including the ongoing St. Mark's Poetry Project in New York.

BIBLIOGRAPHY: Conte, J. M., "Against the Calendar: P. B.'s Journals," *Sagetrieb* 2 (Fall 1988): 35–52; Perloff, M., "On the Other Side of the Field," *Parnassus* 2 (1988): 197–214; Sorrentino, G., "Singing Virtuoso," *Parnassus* 2 (1976): 57–67; Sturgeon, T., "Doing That Medieval Thing," *Sagetrieb* 1–2 (Spring-Fall 1990): 147–68; Woodward, K. M., *P. B.: A Checklist* (1980)

RICHARD L. BLEVINS

BLACKMUR, R[ichard] P[almer]

b. 21 January 1904, Springfield, Massachusetts; d. 2 February 1965, Princeton, New Jersey

B. belongs to the generation of influential critic-poets, including John Crowe RANSOM, Allen TATE, and Yvor WINTERS, who carried the message and example of T. S. ELIOT's MODERNISM into literary studies at American universities under the loose doctrine that came to be known as New Criticism. As a founding and contributing editor of *Hound and Horn* (1927–34) and in his contributions to such journals as the *New Republic* and *Partisan Review,* B. also pioneered in the explication of such other challenging modernist masters as Wallace STEVENS, Hart CRANE, Marianne MOORE, and W. B. Yeats whose influence, along with Eliot's, pervades B.'s own poetry, published in three volumes between 1937 and 1947. Today, however, B. is remembered mostly as a critic and as the high school dropout sage-in residence at Princeton, where he taught from 1941 until his death.

During his lifetime and in the years immediately after his death, B.'s reputation rested on his work as a close reader of modern poetry. Recently, however, literary theorists, such as Edward W. Said (B.'s student) and Geoffrey H. Hartman, have adopted B. as one of the pioneers in the antinomian skepticism that American academic literary criticism now demands. These critics tend to look favorably upon B.'s later essays. Published after 1950, these olympian meditations on cultural politics, on the novel, and on European novelists B. knew only in translation were widely dismissed as obscure and convoluted and were often contrasted unfavorably with B.'s earlier, more concrete and particular essays on poets and their poems. Much of the authority, as well as the difficulty, in B.'s essays, early and late, can be ascribed to his early and formative affinities for Henry JAMES and Henry ADAMS, both of whom, Denis Donoghue argues, inhabited and inhibited B. A prolific essayist, B. never published a book-length work of criticism, though he worked for over thirty years to complete his comprehensive study of Adams and published thirteen essays on James between 1934 and 1964.

BIBLIOGRAPHY: Bloom, J. D., *The Stock of Available Reality* (1984); Boyers, R., *R. P. B., Poet-Critic* (1980); Fraser, R. A., *A Mingled Yarn: The Life of R. P. B.* (1981); Jones, J. T., *Wayward Skeptic: The Theories of R. P. B.* (1986)

JAMES D. BLOOM

BLEECKER, Ann Eliza [Schuyler]

b. October 1752, New York City; d. 23 November 1783, Tomhanick, New York

Although B. lived a short life and apparently destroyed much of her work, the small amount remaining establishes her as an innovator. She wrote the earliest known frontier romance and the first highly personal lyrics.

B.'s aristocratic family encouraged her writing, but she married at sixteen and moved to Tomhanick, New York, a frontier village continually threatened by hostile Indians or British soldiers. Several terrifying experiences, one leading to the death of a daughter, made B. ill and melancholic. Before her death she wrote, "I am charmed with the lovely scene the spring opens around me.—Alas! the wilderness is within."

This split between the garden and the wilderness appears in all B.'s work, from *The History of Maria Kittle* (1797), a fictionalized captivity narrative that juxtaposes idyllic rural scenes with a bloody Indian attack and violent earthquake, to her poems and her vivid letters to her family. The poems tend to be light and humorous, like the playful verses addressed to Mr. L, or grim and despairing, like the poems on the death of her daughter. Much of B.'s poetry is occasional and takes the form of letters to friends and family members. Her writings were published only after her death, presumably by her daughter, Margaretta Faugères, in *New York-Magazine* and then *The Posthumous Works of A. E. B.* (1793).

Until recently B. was dismissed as "sentimental" and "imitative." However, *The History of Maria Kittle* was not acknowledged as the first in a genre, "The Story of Henry and Anne" mistakenly said to be about noble savages, and some "sentimental" poems not recognized as parodies. A modern critic, Emily Stipes Watts, finds B. the best lyric poet of her time.

BIBLIOGRAPHY: Ellison, J., "Race and Sensibility in the Early Republic: A. E. B. and Sarah Wentworth," *AL* 65 (September 1993): 445–74; Faugères, M. B., "Memoirs of Mrs. A. E. B.," in *The Posthumous Works of A. E. B.* (1793); Freibert, L. M., and B. A. White, eds., *Hidden Hands* (1985); Giffen, A., "'Till Grief Melodious Grow': The Poems and Letters of A. E. B.," *EAL* 28, 3 (1993): 222–41; Watts, E. S., *The Poetry of American Women from 1632 to 1945* (1977)

BARBARA A. WHITE

BLOOM, Harold

b. 11 July 1930, Bronx, New York

B. has established himself as the leading American critic of his day, much to the suspicion and displeasure of his contemporaries in the academy, with whom his battles form a long and arresting record of achievement. He has come to be the predominant contrarian on the critical scene, even achieving some notoriety through his appearances on television and through his reviews in such widely distributed notices of the literary and journalistic moment as the *New York Times Book Review,* the same journal's editorial page, the *New York Review of Books,* and over the years, numerous publications in academic journals. He writes a book almost yearly, and his range includes textual commentary, literary theory, an experimental novel, biblical exegesis, social comment on the American religious scene, a defense of the literary classics as the most appropriate subject of study in English departments, and his 1996 heterodox autobiography, *Omens of Millennium: The Gnosis of Angels, Dreams, and Resurrection.* He is author or editor of some six hundred titles; many in the last few years are collections of critical essays on significant writers in European and Anglo-American culture.

B.'s first books were commentary, but of a signal independence: works on Percy Bysshe Shelley, William Blake, and other English authors of the romantic revolution, then W. B. Yeats, followed by the critically unique and unsurpassed *The Anxiety of Influence: A Theory of Poetry* (1973, 1997), then a critical exegesis of Wallace STEVENS, a poet whom B. read daily for two decades. All of this major work (including *A Map of Misreading* [1975], the often-overlooked *Kabbalah and Criticism* [1975], and *Poetry and Repression* [1976]) remains a record of unparalleled accomplishment. His first book, *Shelley's Mythmaking* (1959), was encouraged by Frederick A. Pottle, whose 1952 essay, "The Case of Shelley," helped turn favorable attention to this most contemptuously reviled of the major poets of the 19th c.

B.'s chief critical distinction is his rejection of both the myths of Christianity and the enlightened expectation of some forms of Judaism, both of which, in his view, exercise dubious influence on literary commentary. Most criticism, he asserts, has been but slightly disguised religion, and he quickly dismissed the spectrum of critics from T. S. ELIOT, Northrop Frye, F. R. Leavis, Cleanth BROOKS, and others of lesser note. B. rejects the notions of a synthesized Roman and Christian culture—and defines the major works in literature as the working of creative radicalism. As such, he also rejects the normative limits of "influence," the thesis of a good deal of literary commentary in the 20th c. He defines the greatest works of literature as massive "mis-readings" or a synergistic appropriation of cultural memory that is bent and broken to form works of creative innovation.

The greatest works of literature, in his view, do not exist independently of their creators, but are graphic records of artists' dialectical struggles, their eventual rejections of past models in a series of contests often recorded in the works themselves. The greatest artists finally triumph over their own earlier and derivative work. This creative process is not achieved through assimilation in a familial, supportive craft. Rather, the mentor is discarded, if not annihilated; progenitors are recognized, if at all, in distorted alteration.

One of the models for this process is John Milton, an overt heretic, B. asserts, even though he is a poet conventional critics have smoothed and rounded into a difficult but still recognizable proponent of normative orthodoxies. Instead, Milton's major poetry is that of a gnostic rebel, and the first lines of book 3 of *Paradise Lost* syntactically conceal a self coexistent with the first spirit of creation itself: Milton's poetic being is itself a divine creator, finally released in the apostrophe of the creative agent, a self-apotheosis. This heterodoxy is, for B., the impulse of the highest orders of poetic creation—and may be discovered in such diverse writers as William Wordsworth, Ralph Waldo EMERSON, Walt WHITMAN, or Stevens.

B.'s forays into commentary in *The American Religion: The Emergence of the Post-Christian Nation* (1992) and the autobiographical revelation of his heterodoxy in *Omens of Millennium* have not been critically welcomed. B. would view pious approbation, were it to visit him, with alarm—a contradiction of his essential, subversive purpose. To be "well received"

would ignore his intent. In his view, America has no "religion" that may be categorized as such: conventional belief is a synthesis of self-interest and economic profit, its landscape littered with New Age verbal salad and other psychological detritus. Both the critical and creative selves must operate against any received wisdom, repeated too casually, that becomes inane custom.

The most controversial of his recent books concerns "the canon," the literary refuge, depending on the antagonistic political camp, of sexual, class, and ethnocentric bias as well as manifold sins against the wronged and dispossessed. B. holds that such judgments are of doubtful validity. They attack the aesthetic foundations of high culture, substitute nothing of artistic value, and degrade the sites of learning. He is pessimistic about the survival—or more accurately, the revival—of humanistic learning in an increasingly politicized and trade-driven academy. In addition to its polemical stance, *The Western Canon* (1994) is thus far the most impressive and eloquent of B.'s aesthetic commentary. B. further enhanced his critical reputation with the publication in 1998 of *Shakespeare: The Invention of the Human*.

BIBLIOGRAPHY: Abrams, M. H., "How to Do Things with Texts," *PR* 46 (1979): 566–88; Handelman, S. A., *The Slayers of Moses* (1982); Moynihan, R., *A Recent Imagining* (1986); O'Hara, D. T., *The Romance of Interpretation* (1985); Salusinszky, I., *Criticism in Society* (1987)

ROBERT MOYNIHAN

BLY, Robert [Elwood]
b. 23 December 1926, Madison, Minnesota

B. is one of the most prominent and influential living American poets. A prolific writer, editor, and translator, B. has been held in high esteem since his first book of poetry, *Silence in the Snowy Fields,* published in 1962, and with the National Book Award in 1968 for his second book of poetry, *The Light around the Body,* B.'s literary reputation was firmly and undeniably established. Consequently, he has had the rather unique experience of being in critical favor throughout his long and extremely productive career. Moreover, B. has certainly achieved a unique stature in contemporary society: he is a recognizable public figure, and his poetry has managed to attract both a public as well as an academic audience.

B.'s poetry and writing generally falls into three distinctive and chronological categories: "deep image" poetry; public-political poetry; and public-interpersonal poetry or essays. B. is often discussed in relationship with the deep image poets, who included

Louis SIMPSON, James WRIGHT, and Donald HALL. These poets emphasized the unconscious as the wellspring of inspiration for a range of images that are juxtaposed with one another. B. names this poetic technique "leaping" whereby the poem literally leaps from image to image through what seems to be an associational chain or through random sequencing. The poetic effect is often provocative and startling, but it has prompted some to criticize the coherence of the poems. While such a technique certainly draws upon Sigmund Freud's geography of the unconscious, B.'s poetic technique is more indebted to the surrealist and expressionist writers and especially Federico García Lorca and Pablo Neruda—two poets who figure largely in B.'s poetic genealogy. B.'s deep image poems are also marked by an emphasis upon solitude, an insistence upon a simple, opaque language, as well as a meticulous detailing of attention. B.'s early work—especially his first two books—share much with the verbal precision and reflective style of Eastern poetry, which he has translated.

During the late 1960s, B. reconsidered his stance that poetry must be a solitary act in order to create a public poetry capable of addressing his disdain over the Vietnam War. In the essay "Whitman's Line as a Public Form," from *The Teeth Mother Naked at Last* (1970), B. discusses his perceived need to create a poetry of rhetorical power that eschews subjective introspection: "I think we all want poetry that can at times embody public speech, a way of writing that is not introverted." B. modeled his poetry after the political force of Walt WHITMAN and Pablo Neruda, and he strove to create a poetry that was a public performance capable of presenting a sophisticated, poetic protest. At that time B. also moved away from the lyric and focused his attention upon the prose poem, which he considered a more apt and flexible form for a more public poetry.

While B.'s writing has always been romantic in its concern with the spiritual elements in the relationship of the conscious and the unconscious as well as the dynamic of "male" and "female" aspects, *Iron John: A Book about Men* (1990) marks an important turn in B.'s career. The book became the cornerstone of the men's movement, and it placed B. in the position of the wise sage. Not only did *Iron John* become a national best-seller, but suddenly B. became a recognizable public figure, and he drew upon his stature to proselytize about human relationships—thereby blending the inner and outer person. B.'s poetry also began to explore his own interpersonal world. *From Loving a Woman in Two Worlds* (1985) onwards, B.'s poetry has focused upon his relationships with his mother, father, wife, and children, and in more recent works like *Meditations on the Insatiable Soul* (1994),

B. continues to use his poetry as a public forum. But instead of political injustices, his poetry brings into relief the cruelty and injustice present in the everyday lives of men, women, and children. Subsequently, his writing is often looked to as a guide to rectify the ills of contemporary American society. In this regard, B. has achieved the role of the public poet-guide-shaman.

BIBLIOGRAPHY: Daniels, K., and R., Jones, eds., *Of Solitude and Silence: Writings on R. B.* (1982); Davis, W. V., ed., *Critical Essays on R. B.* (1992); Howard, R., *Alone with America* (1969; rev. ed., 1980); Nelson, H., *R. B.: An Introduction to the Poetry* (1984)

DAVID W. CLIPPINGER

BODENHEIM, Maxwell

b. 26 May 1892 or 1893, Hermanville, Mississippi; d. 6 or 7 February 1954, New York City

By contemporary standards, B. can seem somewhat out of focus as well as out of fashion. He was born Maxwell Bodenheimer, but the date of his changing of his surname is uncertain, as are the year and place of his birth and day of his death. The best evidence supports May 26, 1892, as his date of birth and Hermanville, Mississippi, as his birthplace, but a measure of doubt can be raised about almost every detail of his early history. What is not much in doubt is the pathos of his decline from a young poet of brilliant promise to a besotted derelict scraping by in a hand-to-mouth existence that became a ghastly caricature of the liberated life of bohemian artists in Greenwich Village.

B.'s wretched life was haunted by prophecy. While still in his twenties, he was pickled in the strange formaldehyde of F. Scott FITZGERALD's *This Side of Paradise*. In book 2, chapter 2, the hero Amory Blaine is much amused by his decadent friend Tom D'Invilliers, whose "Boston Bards and Hearst Reviewers" begins, "So, / Walter Arensberg, / Alfred Kreymborg, / Carl Sandburg, / Louis Untermeyer, / Eunice Tietjens, / Clara Shanafelt, / James Oppenheim, / M. B., / Richard Glaenzer, / Scharmel Iris, / Conrad Aiken, / I place your names here / So that you may live / If only as names, / Sinuous, mauve-colored names, / In the Juvenalia / Of my collected editions." Carl SANDBURG and Conrad AIKEN are remembered as poets of secondary importance, and Louis Untermeyer remains known as an influential anthologist, but the rest have fulfilled the prophecy of the undergraduate satirist.

During the 1920s, some identified B. with Christopher Marlowe and even addressed him by the name of the Elizabethan genius, who, he remarked, was murdered in a brawl. B. would be murdered, if not in a brawl at least in circumstances violent and squalid. His own patently autobiographical poem "Simple Account of a Poet's Life," published in 1922, predicts death at age seventy, which turned out to be eight years late: "In 1892 / When literature and art in America / Presented a mildewed but decorous mien, / He was born. . . . / In 1962 / He died with a grin at the fact / That literature and art in America / Were still presenting a mildewed, decorous mien.

In his day—and at his best—B. was an effective lyric poet, a capable novelist, and a critic of enough discernment to discover the eighteen-year-old Hart CRANE well before anyone else got around to it. He began friendships with many writers—Ben HECHT, Eugene O'NEILL, William Carlos WILLIAMS, Alfred KREYMBORG, among others—but they tended to come apart under the corrosion of B.'s complex personality. Untermeyer wrote the introduction to B.'s first book of poetry and included him in the early editions of *Modern American Poetry;* but the new and enlarged editions after 1950 dropped B. Crane, who began as a sympathetic reviewer of that same first book, later dismissed and ridiculed B. Kreymborg and Hecht stood by their old associate as much as they could—even Williams and Ezra POUND spoke and wrote in support—but finally B. cast himself beyond the reach of anybody's help.

The wartime symposium-anthology *Seven Poets in Search of an Answer,* edited by Thomas Yoseloff, contains work by B., Kreymborg, and Langston HUGHES but is of little interest today except to devotees of C. S. Lewis, since another contributor was Joy Davidman (Gresham), the American poet who married Lewis in 1956.

B. remains a peripheral figure in the histories of the Chicago Renaissance, the Provincetown Players, Greenwich Village. He was published by all the best magazines, including *Poetry, New Yorker, The Dial,* and *Esquire.* But it seems unlikely that any talent could persist under the successive insults and abuses that B. dealt to his for such a long time. He must have been sturdy and lucky to survive for as long as he did.

BIBLIOGRAPHY: Kreymborg, A., *Troubadour* (1925); Moore, J. B., *B.* (1970)

                                    WILLIAM HARMON

BODMAN, Manoah
b. 28 January 1765, Sunderland, Massachusetts; d. 1 January 1850, Greenfield, Massachusetts

The prose of B.'s two broadsides, two booklets, and one book, which is all the work of B. that we know of, is the product of a mystic who had verbal communi-

cation with visions of various kinds all his life, and of an Enthusiast who was deeply affected by the so-called "Second Great Awakening" of religion in America. However, though his prose is long-winded, turgid, and expository of his religious obsessions, his poems are curiously modern in their diction, predating the poetry of Emily DICKINSON.

B. stands between Philip FRENEAU and William Cullen BRYANT, but his works in no way resemble either the Augustan or pre-romantic modes of Freneau, or the romantic mode of Bryant. Rather, B. is an idiosyncratic product of rural New England and of the Second Great Awakening; autobiographical narratives in his *Oration on Death* (1817) tell of both visions and painless seizures that are symptomatic of epilepsy. However, it would be better to say, not that B. was a bridge in time between Freneau and Bryant, but that he is a link between Edward TAYLOR and Walt WHITMAN in a chain of American poets that would later be called "visionary" or "Emersonian" by some scholars.

There were two strong fibers in B.'s character. One was his religious conviction, but the first to surface was his militant patriotism, surely derived from his being eleven years old in 1776 and full of the fervor of preadolescence when the American Revolution broke out. The first two of his publications were patriotic, not religious.

Only in *Oration on Death,* published when B. was thirty-five, and in one broadside are there examples of B.'s poetry; the poems of the latter publication are really merely rewritings of hymns by Isaac Watts, one of these clearly expressing abolitionist sentiments. Scattered among the pages of prose are several verses—B. had disassembled poems in order to use stanzas from them for purposes of illustrating his prose text—and the book concludes with four long poems. His structures are naive, when they are not idiosyncratic, and they are easily identifiable as his on both counts, for all these pieces are highly individual and curious manifestations of early American poetry in what was later to be called the transcendentalist tradition.

BIBLIOGRAPHY: Turco, L., "M. B.: Poet of the Second Awakening," *Costerus* 8 (1973): 219-31; Turco, L., *Visions and Revisions of American Poetry* (1986)

                                    LEWIS PUTNAM TURCO

BOGAN, Louise
b. 11 August 1897, Livermore Falls, Maine; d. 4 February 1970, New York City

Though her forty years of activity as poet, translator, editor, and critic now place her firmly in the first rank of 20th-c. literary artists, B.'s work immediately after her death was overlooked by critics, principally because her poetry does not fit easily into the categories used to classify verse written between 1920 and 1970. Not fundamentally imagist, modernist, nor confessional, but displaying at times characteristics of each of these movements, B.'s compact, highly structured lines have their deepest roots in the demanding meters and subtle conceits of such 17th-c. metaphysical poets as George Herbert, John Donne, and Henry Vaughan. A formalist writing at a time when free-verse experimentation was taking poetry by storm, B. in a letter to Theodore ROETHKE declared that her artistic goal was pure music: "My aim is to sound so pure and so liquid that travelers will take me across the desert with them, or to the North Pole, or wherever they are going."

Her poems are as densely packed thematically as they are metrically, often disturbingly so. B.'s mother's affairs and frequent abandonments rocked the poet's childhood and B.'s own fractured marriages (the first of which led to the birth of a daughter when B. was twenty), and her mental breakdowns and subsequent therapy in 1930 and 1931 surface obliquely in her writing. B. chose to write about these personal griefs in an impersonal, stoic manner which some critics complained was too severe. Her fellow artists deeply admired her work, however: in 1941, W. H. AUDEN's list of important American poets included only B., T. S. ELIOT, and Marianne MOORE. Her collections include *Body of This Death* (1923), *Dark Summer* (1929), *The Sleeping Fury* (1937), *Poems and New Poems* (1941), *Collected Poems, 1923–1953* (1954), and *The Blue Estuaries: Poems, 1923–1968* (1968).

B.'s contribution to American letters on the critical front was also impressive. Her *Achievement in American Poetry, 1900–1950* (1951) succinctly documents how poetry in English rose from the flaccid moralism and sentimentality of the 19th c. (at the close of which both Walt WHITMAN and Emily DICKINSON had slipped into obscurity) to the sophistication, diversity, and experimentation of the early 1950s. Her work as a poetry editor at the *New Yorker* from 1931 until her death in 1970 shaped not only the public's literacy in poetry but the magazine's exacting standards for verse as well. She also translated Johann Wolfgang von Goethe, Jules Renard, Yvan Goll, and Ernst Jünger, compiled with William Jay SMITH an excellent anthology of poetry for children entitled *The Golden Journey* (1965), and wrote penetrating literary criticism, collected in *A Poet's Alphabet: Reflections on the Literary Art and Vocation* (1970), edited by Robert Phelps and Ruth Limmer. Her additional critical work included *Selected Criticism* (1955); *Emily Dickinson: Three Views* (1960), written with Archibald MACLEISH

and Richard WILBUR; and an afterword for Virginia Woolf's *A Writer's Diary*.

BIBLIOGRAPHY: Frank, E., *L. B.: A Portrait* (1985); Limmer, R., ed., *What the Woman Lived: Selected Letters of L. B. 1920–1970* (1973); Maxwell, W., and C. McGrath, eds., *A Final Antidote: From the Journals of L. B.* (1991); Ridgeway, J., *L. B.* (1984)

GORDON JOHNSTON

BOKER, George Henry
b. 6 October 1823, Philadelphia, Pennsylvania; d. 2 January 1890, Philadelphia, Pennsylvania

Though most often remembered as the U.S. ambassador to Turkey, B. was a prolific poet and playwright unfortunately ignored in his age and today. Raised in genteel Philadelphia the son of a prominent banker, B. attended the College of New Jersey (Princeton) where he cofounded the *Nassau Monthly*. His numerous contributions and their high quality demonstrated his literary aspirations and an unusual maturity of thought, though his first volume of lyric and narrative verse, *The Lesson of Life* (1848), did not meet with financial success nor critical acclaim. In *Calaynos* (1848), however, B. showed his power as a playwright.

A blank verse tragedy set in medieval Spain, *Calaynos* presents a romantic and typical hero who is pitted against the traditional Spanish hatred of Moorish blood. B. attempts to demonstrate how the weight of social convention will destroy a person who opposes it, though the individual be superior to the destructive force. The celebration of the individual is a theme which B. would explore throughout his plays, notably in *Anne Boleyn* (1850) and *Leonor de Guzman* (perf. 1853, pub. 1856), and his admiration and veneration of the stubborn soul who rises above the conventional law doubtless provided him with a small matter of satisfaction when critics attacked his work. At a time when American literary experts called for American themes, B. stubbornly asserted that all the world and all history were his material. He deplored the commercialism of the emerging American mass culture and was saddened by the dearth of legend in the new republic; thus, B. looked to the past and other lands for artistic inspiration, most notably in *The Betrothal* (perf. 1850, pub. 1856), *The World a Mask* (perf. 1851, pub. 1940), *The Podesta's Daughter and Other Poems* (1852), and *Königsmark, The Legend of the Hounds and Other Poems* (wr. 1853, perf. 1855, pub. 1856).

B. found the story for his greatest artistic achievement, *Francesca da Rimini* (1853), in 13th-c. Italian history. Employing the story of Francesca and Paolo, wife and brother of Prince Lanciotto of Rimini, who loved each other and died by his hand, B. created an arresting romantic tragedy considered by many critics to be the best of the 19th-c. American stage. B.'s success with *Francesca* comes from his delicate and sensitive treatment of Lanciotto who though a strong and fierce leader in battle is gentle and emotional in life; B.'s Lanciotto is a brooding and philosophical character whose alternating moods of tenderness and passion are exhibited in rich soliloquies. B.'s superior writing, however, did not guarantee his play's production and it was three years after its completion that *Francesca* finally found the stage. Short-runs, critical reviews, and mediocre productions kept B.'s plays from receiving the praise justly due them.

B. did find some financial and critical success in lyric and narrative poetry. He had a gift for the sonnet on public affairs though his love verses are also worthy of note. B. combined his love of poetry and his strong patriotic sentiments in *Poems of the War* (1864), his most popular and successful work. B. used ballad form and long narrative settings to report events from the Civil War, often drawing attention to individual acts of heroism and the splendor of sacrifice. Of note within this volume are his touching "Dirge for a Soldier," his noble "Ode to America," and the ideologically and racially motivated "Black Regiment." His pro-Union sentiments garnered him considerable acclaim, and for his efforts he was awarded a diplomatic post to Turkey in 1871. His literary career was suspended for nearly fifteen years while serving abroad. His last two plays *Nydia* (wr. 1885, pub. 1929) and *Glaucus* (wr. 1885–86, pub. 1940), both blank verse tragedies, went unpublished for years, and only *Glaucus* received a short performance. With his death a few years later, B. slipped into obscurity noted only for his minor contributions to the American stage and able service to American foreign policy.

BIBLIOGRAPHY: Bradley, E. S., *G. H. B.: Poet and Patriot* (1927); Evans, O. H., *G. H. B.* (1984)

ANDREW J. LEWIS

BONTEMPS, Arna[ud Wendell]

b. 13 October 1902, Alexandria, Louisiana; d. 4 June 1973, Nashville, Tennessee

When B. set out for New York City in 1924, he did not know that he would land in the middle of the literary movement that was to become known as the Harlem Renaissance. There he would launch a writing career and become one of the group's most prolific authors; form associations that included a lifelong warm friendship with Langston HUGHES; and eventually go on to become librarian of Fisk University and director of the Afro-American program at Yale. All

this he did not know, but he did remember the advice his father had given him as he had gone off to high school: "don't go acting colored." Here in Harlem, it seemed, nobody would mind if one "acted colored"; the young writers of the Harlem Renaissance were excited about racial themes and motifs in their work. However, when B. brought out his first novel, *God Sends Sunday* (1931), he was disappointed; it was received coolly by the black critics, particularly W. E. B. DUBOIS, who pronounced it sordid and immoral. B. felt that his novel had been misunderstood. Based on the life of his favorite uncle, *God Sends Sunday* is a frankly unapologetic sketch of a high-rolling, loose-living jockey who rises to riches and sinks back to oblivion by playing for the highest stakes and taking no thought for the consequences. In this novel, one feels, B. hits exactly the right note in his characterization; his hero is immanently believable. Unfortunately, Little Augie was not a model of good behavior for anyone who was looking for such in black literature in the 1930s. After the novel's poor reception, B. changed his style. For all of a long life, he continued to write and edit: poetry, children's fiction, biographies and histories written for children, anthologies of African American poetry and folklore, novels, short stories, and history. But B. never wrote another novel like *God Sends Sunday*.

His next and best-known novel, *Black Thunder* (1936), is a fictionalized version of an uprising led by the slave Gabriel Prosser in Virginia in 1800, which was rendered impotent by a tremendous storm and by treachery among the rebelling slaves. The novel's plot has abiding interest, and it uses well such themes as the innate human hunger for freedom, the ambivalence among the slaves towards the white masters, and the eerie, almost magic power of nature to stop human enterprises. At the same time, the characterization is not B.'s best, and the details sometimes fail. For example, Juba, Gabriel's woman in the novel, is a flat character introduced only for the love-interest; and the slaves speak a dialect more like that of the French-influenced English of B.'s native Louisiana than like any dialect of Virginia. The character Gabriel, so different from the happy-go-lucky Augie, still does not quite attain the mythical stature that the novel seeks for him. *Black Thunder* received more attention after its second printing, in 1963, during the civil rights movement, than after its first publication. Respected as documentary fiction, it has never been a best-seller.

Between the disorderly Little Augie and the somber Gabriel, the typical B. character is black, homely, dignified, friendly—in short, ordinary and realistic. Many readers probably know the author best from one short story, the widely anthologized "A Summer Tragedy," about Jeff and Jennie Patton, an old couple who choose suicide with dignity rather than the further depredations that age and poverty are sure to bring upon them.

B. is well respected for his significant contributions to integration through his nonfiction, particularly his efforts at teaching children about the contributions of African Americans to our culture. *God Sends Sunday* was an early attempt to teach that same lesson through his fiction. Perhaps, unlike those of the 1930s, critics of today could endure the knife fights and the general air of low caste in Augie's milieu for the sake of the beautifully detailed fancy strut balls, cake walks, and courting rituals in the gambling society of late-19th and early-20th-c. Louisiana. In his essay "Why I Returned" (1965), B. tells what he likes about the South. Among other things, he mentions that today, and in fact ever since the world at large picked up the cake walk and it became the rage, everyone who stands up on a dance floor starts "acting colored" immediately. Maybe it is time to give Little Augie another chance.

BIBLIOGRAPHY: Fleming, R. E., *James Weldon Johnson and A. W. B.: A Reference Guide* (1978); Jones, K. C., *Renaissance Man from Louisiana* (1992); Nichols, C., ed., *A. B. and Langston Hughes Letters* (1980); Sundquist, E. J., *The Hammers of Creation* (1992)

CECELIA LAMPP LINTON

BOTTOMS, David

b. 11 September 1949, Canton, Georgia

B.'s first full-length book of poetry, *Shooting Rats at the Bibb County Dump* (1980), was chosen by Robert Penn WARREN as the winner of the 1979 Walt Whitman Award from the Academy of American Poets; from this auspicious beginning, B.'s poetry has continued to be highly esteemed and valued for its poetic craftsmanship, thematic vision, and descriptive imagery. Other prize-winning collections are *In a U-Haul North of Damascus* (1983) and *Under the Vulture-Tree* (1987), and new poems plus selections from his earlier volumes appear in *Armored Hearts* (1995). B. is also a short story writer and the author of two novels, *Any Cold Jordan* (1987) and *Easter Weekend* (1990), which deal with many of the same subjects as his poems.

While all of B.'s earlier work reflects his southern heritage, later work that appears in *Armored Hearts* draws upon recent experiences in Montana, but B. successfully utilizes the same techniques and selected focus on subject matter for both locales, proving he is no mere regionalist. Variously humorous or disturbing in tone, the majority of his poems are short, open-form, first-person narratives in which the action builds from concrete images and simile to the conclusion. B.'s considerable descriptive powers and his smooth use of alliteration give the experience contained in a poem a heightened sense of reality; and one of B.'s major themes, that moments of universal recognition are contained in specific encounters, is accentuated by this technique. By the resolution, the reader is able to connect the specific, external world of experience to a more all-encompassing metaphoric realization.

B.'s subject matter often concerns the self-contained cultures of the small town or ranch or the lives of modern suburban dwellers. Within these settings, B. focuses on specific subcultures: the world of "country-and-western" musicians and honky tonks, fishing and hunting, truck drivers and waitresses, fundamentalists and faith healers, family members and family memories, divorce and death. Many of the narrators and characters in the works are eccentrics, so-called rednecks, but B.'s attention to the universal validity of these individuals' experiences in matters of loss, disillusionment, alienation, and redemption keeps his work well above the level of stereotype. In his use of wilderness settings and human encounters with wildlife, B. excels. From southern swamps of cottonmouths, catfish, gators, and copperheads to suburbia with its possums, bees, and rats to the wolves and eagles of the Montana mountains, B. examines the delicate, often dangerous relationship we have with animals and the ultimate realities we share. One concept that B. explores is the idea of humankind's repressed animal nature: in the rare moments that humans recognize this affinity with other creatures, we gain greater insights into ourselves. Otherwise, we remain just as destructive and as trapped as the animals in the shrinking natural environment.

Both of B.'s novels utilize aspects of the southern characters, settings, and themes that appear in his poems. The novels, however, are more ironic in tone and violent in plot. *Any Cold Jordan,* set in Florida, draws from B.'s own experiences as a bluegrass and country singer. Jack, the disillusioned protagonist disheartened by his wife's infidelity and the commercialization of country music, reluctantly becomes involved in the world of drugs. *Easter Weekend,* set in Georgia, details a botched kidnapping; Connie Holtzclaw, an ex-boxer and small-time loser, joins his brother in the plot to kidnap a rich local college student. Attempting to escape unfulfilling lives, both Jack and Connie are forced into destructive crises where they must face and conquer their own irresponsibilities. While his excursions into fiction have been well received, B.'s reputation as a major voice in contemporary American literature comes from his poetry and his ability to draw extraordinary insights form the lives of ordinary people and their surroundings.

BIBLIOGRAPHY: Cass, M., "Danger and Beauty: D. B.'s 'In a U-Haul North of Damascus,'" *SR* 20 (Summer

1984): 743–45; Rider, E., "An Interview with D. B.," *ChatR* 12 (Fall 1991): 79-89

LYNN RISSER

Dolman Press B. (1964); Walsh, T., *The Career of D. B.* (1915)

EDMUND M. HAYES

BOUCICAULT, Dion

b. 27 December 1820, Dublin, Ireland; d. 18 September 1890, New York City

Actor and playwright, author of over 120 plays (many adaptations of novels or other plays), B. is remembered today for his social satire *The Poor of New York* (1857), *The Octoroon* (perf. 1859, pub. 1953), his Irish plays *The Colleen Bawn* (perf. 1860, pub. 1953), *Arrah-na-Pogue* (1865), and *The Shaughraun* (perf. 1874), and his version of *Rip Van Winkle* for Joseph Jefferson (perf. 1865). He was also important for his efforts to secure a copyright law to protect American authors, and his introduction of the traveling company.

B. often set his plays in "real" locales or shaped the action according to some recent or contemporary event—the 1837 financial panic for *The Poor of New York* or abolitionists' activities for *The Octoroon*. He was capable of strong social criticism as in *The Octoroon* or *The Poor of New York* where he has one character remark bitterly, "Wall Street is a perch, on which a row of human vultures sit." He often devised impressive themes: the conflict between the Fenian Brotherhood and the British in *The Shaughraun,* class difference that leads to attempted murder in *The Colleen Bawn,* and slavery and miscegenation in *The Octoroon*. Many of his characters are strongly conceived and developed (Father Dolan in *The Shaughraun* and Salem Scudder in *Octoroon*), and his Irish rogues (Myles-Na-Coppaleen, Conn, the Shaughraun) are appealing theatrical creations who inspired his conception the vagabond Rip Van Winkle.

B., however, was not a realist; he constantly sought to please audiences by giving them romantic pieces that were flawed with melodramatic and sensational events with the result that his plays have lost their power and impact. *The Octoroon,* for example, would be a stronger play had B. dealt with the issues of slavery and miscegenation without murder, a purloined letter, and a steamboat explosion. Although the play reflects his sympathetic insight into the problems facing the blacks and Indians in a so-called white man's world, he was limited by the prejudices of his times. On balance, he was a versatile and energetic playwright who remained an important force in the theater for many years.

BIBLIOGRAPHY: Fawkes, R., *D. B.: A Biography* (1979); Hogan, R., *D. B.* (1969); Krause, D., ed., *The*

BOURJAILY, Vance [Nye]

b. 17 September 1922, Cleveland, Ohio

As an editor, journalist, novelist, playwright, and teacher, B. has proven himself to be one of the most astute chroniclers of post-World War II America. His work—like Ernest HEMINGWAY's, Randall JARRELL's, and James DICKEY's—has documented the development of the American mind in the wake of the "just" war. While his novels have not garnered the popular acclaim his technique might warrant, they have nonetheless established B. as a master of detail and characterization with a diverse pallet of interests.

Many of the fundamental characteristics of B.'s work stem from his early life in Cleveland, Ohio. His eye for detail is no doubt inherited from his father Monte Ferris Bourjaily, a noted newspaper editor and publisher, and his strong relationship with the outdoors exhibits itself throughout B.'s fiction and in his book on hunting, *The Unnatural Enemy* (1963). More importantly, the four years of military service that interrupted his education at Bowdoin College provide content for most of his early work. Since graduating college, B. has edited a literary journal, worked as a television dramatist, and taught at the Writers Workshop of the University of Iowa and in the Creative Writing Program at Louisiana State University in Baton Rouge, where he currently resides.

B.'s first four novels explore the effects of war on American culture from a variety of contexts. His first novel, *The End of My Life* (1947), tracks the eventual disillusionment of a young soldier, Skinner Galt. B. follows Galt from the careless immunity of youth through the horrible reality of man's vulnerability and impotence in the face of war. Galt's final realization that war ruins and disrupt lives in isolated and temporary bursts forces him to withdraw from life. *The Hound of Earth* (1955) contradicts this view of war as spasmodic. The novel revolves around Al Barker, a man who is unable to reconcile himself to the fact that he helped to develop the atomic bomb. B.'s second novel is far less concerned with the direct horrors of war, choosing to focus on the moral responsibilities of those who participate in it. The novel finally has Barker maintaining that war is a permanent characteristic of society. B.'s third novel, *The Violated* (1958), examines war as the fulfillment of personal aggressions. His four main characters—Ellen, Tom, Guy, and Eddie—suffer from all of the traits of society that cause/necessitate war—inability to communicate, to love, to respect others, and to create. Technically, B.'s adventurous interweaving of plot, his use of story within story, and his intricate characterizations make *The Violated* a foreshadowing of the rest of his career. *Confessions of a Spent Youth* (1960) continues in this vein to become B.'s most experimental work. Organized loosely around the initiation experiences of the novel's narrator, Quince, *Confessions* illustrates scene by scene the war's numbing effect on an entire generation of Americans. Quince's introduction to sex, drugs, and crime combine to produce a vague fear of what will come of our culture having survived the war.

B.'s later work abandons the disaffected victims of war and their search for meaning in our society for the "wars" adults face every day in America. Arguably B.'s most famous piece, *The Man Who Knew Kennedy* (1967), is built around the assassination of President John F. Kennedy, an act of senseless violence analogous to the death of American innocence. The novel focuses on the perilous nature of life and the inadequacy of luck to see us through. *Brill among the Ruins* (1970) offers hope in the form of companionship and spiritual growth. A return to nature and the fundamental values of American life enable the main character, Robert Brill, to escape moral corruption and to put his life back together. The novel is characterized by B.'s finely written descriptions of nature. The same can be said of B.'s novel *Old Soldier* (1990), which unites the themes of the preceding novels and attacks contemporary battle fronts including AIDS, broken homes, and cultural prejudice against homosexuality. *Old Soldier* is vaguely reminiscent of Hemingway's "Big Two-hearted River" in its subtle handling of its narrator's struggle to come to grips with his own war-torn past, the trials of his AIDS-stricken brother, and the legacy of hope represented by his nephew.

B.'s work offers a sensitive and accurate view of the development of the American culture that survived World War II. Each novel becomes increasingly more involved in its handling of American concerns, and the technique and craft of each piece ensure B.'s place in the canon of contemporary writers.

BIBLIOGRAPHY: Aldridge, J. W., *After the Lost Generation* (1951); Stringfellow, H., "V. B.," in Helterman, J., and R. Layman, eds., *DLB,* vol. 2, *American Novelists since World War II* (1978): 56–60

JACK B. BEDELL

BOURNE, Randolph Silliman
b. 30 May 1886, Bloomfield, New Jersey; d. 22 December 1918, New York City

Beginning in 1911 B.'s essays "marked the literary voice of young America," according to his friend and editor Waldo FRANK. B.'s reports, polemics, and exhortations in *The Dial,* the *New Republic,* the *Seven Arts,* the *Masses,* the *Menorah Journal, Scribner's,* and the *Atlantic* set much of the agenda for American cultural criticism in the twentieth century. Especially influential, his autobiographical "History of a Literary Radical" (1918) stresses the role of generation gaps in politics and the arts; promotes, describes, and coins the phrase "cultural revolution"; and unmasks the effects on literature of academic canon-formation. In B., Van Wyck BROOKS found "[Ralph Waldo] Emerson's 'American Scholar' at last, but radiating an infinitely warmer, profaner, more companionable influence than Emerson had ever dreamed of, an influence that savored rather of [Walt] Whitman and William James."

B. was deformed by obstetric malpractice at his birth into a long-established but financially straitened New Jersey family and was dwarfed by spinal tuberculosis at four. At twenty-one, he entered Columbia College on a scholarship, after six years of clerical and factory work. Influenced by Columbia professors John Dewey and Charles Beard, B. became a leader and ultimately a legendary embodiment of the agnostic yet idealistic youth revolt that marked American culture in the years preceding and following the U. S. entry into World War I. A militant pacifist, B. broke with many of his fellow radicals, including his mentor Dewey and his colleagues at the *New Republic,* over the war. Killed by the war-borne influenza epidemic of 1918, B. never lived to complete any book-length work.

BIBLIOGRAPHY: Abrahams, E., *The Lyrical Left* (1986); Lasch, C., *The New Radicalism in America 1889–1963* (1965); Vitelli, J., *R. B.* (1981)

JAMES D. BLOOM

BOWLES, Jane [Sidney Auer]
b. 22 February 1917, New York City; d. 4 May 1973, Malaga, Spain

Poorly received in the U.S. both commercially and critically, B.'s work was greeted favorably in England and was enthusiastically praised by contemporary writers including John ASHBERY, Truman CAPOTE, Carson MCCULLERS, Tennessee WILLIAMS, and B.'s husband, Paul BOWLES.

Like many of B.'s works, the novel *Two Serious Ladies* (1943) has an elliptical style that forces the reader to make connections left unstated in the text, and focuses on characters who feel compelled to do things precisely because they don't want to. The wealthy Christina Goering, obsessed with sin and absolution, renounces luxury. Frieda Copperfield fears change but finds happiness by leaving her husband for a Central American prostitute. The book's humor comes from the precise formality of the characters's statements about their squalid lives and from the juxtaposition of the profound and the frivolous.

B.'s play *In the Summer House* (1953) treats murderous sibling rivalry and the potentially crippling mutual dependency in mother-daughter relations. The first act concentrates on the tension between Molly and her mother Gertrude Eastman Cueva's surrogate daughter Vivian Constable, Molly's dependence on her mother, and Mrs. Constable's devotion to her daughter. The second act reveals Mrs. Eastman Cueva's dependence on Molly and culminates with her recognition of her jealousy of her own sister. A Mexican family provides comic relief.

The title story of the collection *Plain Pleasures* (1966) dramatizes the tense and tentative interactions of two solitary neighbors, Alva Perry and John Drake, and ends with Mrs. Perry's tender feelings towards Drake after her rape by a hotel proprietor. Probably the best story in the collection, "Camp Cataract" presents the power struggle between two middle aged sisters, Sadie and Harriet, and their separate fears and guilty desires to leave familiar and protected environments. The story climaxes with Sadie's long and deceptively realistic hallucination prompted by a conviction that secrecy provides absolution.

In the later, unfinished works, B. pursued the themes of morality and sexuality, but attempted to forgo her earlier terse and oblique style in favor of a more descriptive psychological realism. The posthumous *Feminine Wiles* (1976) collects selected fragments from these works and six letters. B.'s selected letters, *Out in the World* (1985), further reveal her humor and her belief in the moral weight of all decisions, describe her life in Tangier, Morocco, and comment on her work and on the writer's block that plagued her from the 1950s.

BIBLIOGRAPHY: Dillon, M., *A Little Original Sin: The Life and Work of J. B.* (1981); Dillon, M., ed., *Out in the World: The Selected Letters of J. B., 1935–1970* (1985)

FRANN MICHEL

BOWLES, Paul
b. 30 December 1910, New York City

B.'s literary reputation rests on his prose fiction: four novels, collected short stories, and a volume of historical vignettes. His artistic efforts, however, have also included music composition, poetry, travel writing, autobiography, translation, and for a short time painting. He became serious as a writer, he has said, due to the influence of his wife, the novelist Jane BOWLES, who showed him a "new approach, psychologically." B.'s subsequent novels and stories have been called existentialist, the finest American version of the mid-20th-c. French literary vision. Yet, as Joyce Carol OATES has noted, "American-ness" is practically "invisible" in B.'s writing. An expatriate since the age of twenty-one, B. has lived since 1947 mainly in Tangier, Morocco. No American writer has been such a compulsive wanderer, particularly in "exotic" locales that challenge and affront Western sensibilities. B.'s great theme is the disintegration of "civilized" consciousness in pitiless alien environments.

The Sheltering Sky (1949) establishes the pattern. A married couple, Port and Kit, journey with their friend Tunner into the "famous silence of the Sahara"—metaphorically an encounter with "the inner desert of the spirit." What follows is infidelity, separation, death for Port, and (at the novel's controversial closing) madness and sexual slavery for his wife Kit. Similar motifs of fantasy, self-destructiveness, and sexual ambiguity appear in *Let It Come Down* (1949) and *The Spider's House* (1955), both also set in North Africa, and in *Up Above the World* (1956), set in Latin America. B.'s short stories, particularly those collected in *The Delicate Prey* (1950), are perhaps even more extreme in their mixtures of exotic locale and unspeakable behavior. "A Distant Episode" tells of an American linguistics professor turned into a freakish attraction for a tribe of nomads, while "A Delicate Prey" is a story of drug madness, multiple murder, and torture. B.'s theme of marital treachery is seen again in "Call at Corazón," where a husband "smiling[ly]" abandons his wife in a remote port. "Pages from Cold Point" deals explicitly with homosexuality and incest; in recent years, critics have increasingly interpreted B.'s (and his wife's) writings in terms of gay sensibility.

Some readers have found B.'s fiction ultimately monotonous in its themes. What saves his work is its stylistic distinction. According to the critic Stephen Koch, strangeness of content is balanced by "precise, incisive" use of language: this produces a unique combination of the "classic" and the "unspeakable." Paradoxically, this kind of linguistic control is not found in B.'s own poetry, which he has called "surrealist" and claimed to have composed of "words and phrases as they came into my head." But in *Points of Time* (1982), B. created a kind of prose poetry, a series of evocative cultural and historical vignettes about Morocco. This work, along with superb translations from the Arabic, distinguish the later part of his long career.

Recent years have seen a flowering of interest in B. and his writings. This is due in part to the growth of gay literary criticism, which has emphasized autobiographical complexities that give his fiction a richness it does not have when seen primarily as existentialist parables. It seems likely, however, that B.'s lasting reputation will derive mainly from his accomplishments as a prose stylist.

BIBLIOGRAPHY: Bertens, J., *The Fiction of P. B.* (1979); Caponi, G. D., *P. B.* (1994); Green, M., *Dream at the End of the World* (1991); Hibbard, A., *P. B.* (1993); Pounds, W., *P. B.* (1985); Stewart, L., *P. B.* (1974)

GLEN M. JOHNSON

BOYESEN, H[jalmar] H[jorth]

b. 21 September 1848, Fredrikvaern, Norway; d. 2 October 1895, New York City

In 1869, B. moved from Norway to the U.S., where he hoped to fulfill his aspiration to make a living as a writer. He published twenty-five books, both of fiction and criticism, and while many of them have descended into obscurity, he was, during his lifetime, an avid and important participant in literary debates that characterized the late 19th c.

When William Dean HOWELLS published B.'s first novel, *Gunnar* (1874), as a serial in the *Atlantic* in 1873, it began a long literary association. Howells also helped B. secure a teaching job, and when he eventually taught at Columbia University as a professor of German, he wrote influential studies of Scandinavian and European literature in English, including *Goethe and Schiller: Their Lives and Works* (1879) and *A Commentary on the Lives of Henrik Ibsen* (1894). Although Howells was well known as a public defender of literary REALISM during "the realism wars" fought in the magazines and newspapers during the late 19th c., B. exceeded even Howells's ardor for the genre by writing apologies such as "The Great Realist and the Empty Story-Tellers" in prominent publications such as *Harper's, Critic, Forum, Cosmopolitan,* and *McClure's.* As critic Robert S. Fredrickson writes, "What was a sophisticated literary method to Howells was a key to ultimate truth to B."

In fact, B. was deeply persuaded by the popular theories of evolutionary progress such as Social Darwinism, and his understanding of its tenets is dramatically explicated in his last three novels: *The Mammon of Unrighteousness* (1891), *The Golden Calf* (1892), and *Social Strugglers* (1893). B. writes in the preface to *The Mammon of Unrighteousness,* a political novel, "I have disregarded all romantic traditions, and simply asked myself in every instance, not whether it was amusing, but whether it was true to the logic of reality—true in color and tone to the American sky, the American soil, the American character." Despite these general claims, the novel succeeds because it closely

observes how trivial aspirations poison entire lives. Horace and Aleck Larkin, sons of the president of a college in upstate New York (widely believed to be based on Cornell University, where B. taught briefly), are moral foils; Horace is a shrewd political careerist, while Aleck leaves the law to become a writer. Characters such as Aleck and his artist-wife Gertrude seeking an authentic, substantial way of life are rewarded, while the characters who debase ideals are duly punished.

Social Strugglers proceeds from B.'s own conviction that American fiction must focus on the city, and follows the myriad of "strugglers" in New York, especially ruthless women such as Mrs. Buckley, whose single-minded interest in social standing is set against the social work of Warburton. These novels indicate that B. clung to the expectation that women were responsible for buttressing a moral culture with self-effacing ideals, and while this makes his work difficult to admire from our contemporary vantage point, it also makes it an instructive testimony to the late-19th-c. longing for moral order in an age of radical change.

BIBLIOGRAPHY: Cady, E., *The Realist at War* (1958); Fredrickson, R. S., *H. H. B.* (1980); Seyersted, P., *H. H. B.: From Norwegian Romantic to American Realist* (1984)

MONIQUE DUFOUR

BOYLE, Kay

b. 15 February 1902, St. Paul, Minnesota; d. 27 December 1992, San Francisco, California

In 1929, the avant-garde literary magazine *transition* published a manifesto calling for a new movement in literature. The undersigned authors of "The Revolution of the Word," mostly expatriate Americans inspired by the recent work of James Joyce and Gertrude STEIN, sought to claim for themselves a new originality and imagination, and called for liberation from "existing grammatical and syntactical laws." Their interest was in creativity as opposed to the "propagation of social ideas," and they rebuked the "plain reader." Although in her later life and work she would contradict many of these tenets, B.'s name was first on the undersigned list. Her willingness to participate, however, probably resulted not only from the close relationship she shared with other writers in the group, but also from her impulse to reform, to correct wrongs, whether literary, political, social or personal. This impulse was the driving force in her art, which included short fiction, novels, poetry, essays, and translations.

B.'s destiny was determined from the beginning by her mother, who was convinced that her daughter would become a great writer. Over dinner table discussions during her early years, B.'s passion for social justice and artistic integrity developed as she observed her mother's intense debates with her father and grandfather, conservative businessmen. In 1923, she left for Europe with her first husband. She would remain there for most of the next two decades, developing her individual philosophies of art and social awareness, separate from the American society she viewed as constricting: "I am too proud and too young to need the grandeur of physical America which one accepts only at the price of one's own dignity." Her contacts and experiences in Europe became fuel for her work, which contained much autobiographical material. During this time of heightened experience, her first novels and short stories appeared, often to favorable critical notice; writers like Katherine Anne PORTER and William Carlos WILLIAMS saw her as a fresh talent with great potential. She placed her first story in the *New Yorker* in 1931, the beginning of an extended relationship with the magazine. B. is credited with the invention of "the *New Yorker* story," a style characterized by close focus on a single significant incident involving a protagonist whose life is altered irrevocably. This incident usually dramatizes a moral point, usually clarifying or crystallizing a view held by the protagonist, the author, and, according to the tone of the narrative, presumably the reader as well. This form suited B.'s definition of the instructional responsibilities of the artist, although at times this somewhat allegorical method would be insufficient for her purpose and she would turn to the essay instead.

B.'s publication career began in 1929, the year of her departure for France, with *Short Stories.* For the next decade, collections of short stories alternated with novels. The first novel, *Plagued by the Nightingale,* appeared in 1931, and was followed by *Year before Last* (1932), *Gentlemen, I Address You Privately* (1933), *My Next Bride* (1935), *Death of a Man* (1936), *Monday Night* (1938), and *The Crazy Hunter: Three Short Novels* (1940). Story collections during these years included *Wedding Day and Other Stories* (1930), *The First Lover and Other Stories* (1933), and *The White Horses of Vienna and Other Stories* (1936). Though her first novel earned critical praise, it was her stories that continued to generate the most attention. She won the O. Henry Award for best short story of the year in 1934 for "The White Horses of Vienna" and in 1941 for "Defeat." An anthology, *Thirty Stories,* was published in 1946; two more collections, *The Smoking Mountain: Stories of Postwar Germany* (1951) and *Nothing Ever Breaks Except the Heart* (1966), appeared before the definitive collection, *Fifty Stories,* came out in 1980. The novels continued through the 1940s and 1950s: *Primer for Combat*

(1942), *Avalanche* (1944), *A Frenchman Must Die* (1946), *1939* (1948), *His Human Majesty* (1949), *The Seagull on the Step* (1955), and *Generation without Farewell* (1960). In 1975, the novel *Underground Women* emerged from D.'s own brushes with the law during war protests. Although several of the novels fell out of print over the years, many new editions began appearing in the 1980's and are now available, some revised by the author.

B.'s political activism continued throughout her life. Her outspokenness prompted an intense investigation during the McCarthy era, and protests of the Vietnam War led to an arrest and jail term. She spoke for students' rights during her days as a professor at San Francisco State, and she voiced her objections to the bombing of Libya by the U.S. *Words That Somehow Must Be Said: Selected Essays of B., 1927–1984* (1985) illustrates her deep convictions, their wide range and scope. B.'s body of work included poetry, translations, and children's literature; she was an editor and ghost writer for many of her friends, including the father of her first child, the poet Ernest Walsh. A collaboration with friend Robert MCALMON, *Being Geniuses Together* (1968), chronicles the life and work of that expatriate society of the twenties which helped shape hers and so many others' literary futures. By the time of her death in 1992, B. numbered among her may honors two Guggenheim Fellowships, two O. Henry Awards, the California Literary Medal Award, the Before Columbus Foundation American Book Award, the Robert Kirsch Award from the *Los Angeles Times,* the French-American Foundation Translation Prize, a National Endowment for the Arts Fellowship, and the *Los Angeles Times* Book Award in poetry, for *This Is Not a Letter and Other Poems* (1985). Several of her stories, including "The Crazy Hunter," "The Ballet of Central Park," and "Maiden, Maiden" have been adapted for film and television.

BIBLIOGRAPHY: Mellen, J., *K. B.: Author of Herself* (1994); Spanier, S. W., *K. B.: Artist and Activist* (1986); special B. issue, *TCL* 34 (Fall 1988)

NICOLE SARROCCO

BOYLE, T[homas] Coraghessan
b. 2 December 1948, Peekskill, New York

For a writer of many styles and subjects, responsible for five story collections and six novels in the space of less than two decades, B. is thought of surprisingly often in one of two ways: either as a postmodern Dickens with a keen ear and a devastatingly satirical eye, or as a technically proficient but perpetually underachieving yarn-spinner whose work lacks depth. In many ways, these evaluations are two sides of the same coin: what readers react to in B. is his combination of verbal inventiveness and social awareness, whether they think these elements result in broad-canvassed and sharp social satire or superficial, even mocking blitheness. The strength of these reactions is itself an indication of the importance of B. to the contemporary fiction scene.

Published in 1977, *Descent of Man and Other Stories* established B. as an innovative storyteller, a reputation further enhanced by *Greasy Lake and Other Stories* (1985), *If the River Was Whiskey* (1989), and *Without a Hero and Other Stories* (1994). All have been marked by a wildly various mix of settings, subjects, and sensibilities; all could also be said to have only two kinds of stories, broadly defined: comic romps through a contemporary society ripe for satire, and quieter, more psychological explorations of family and other intimate human entanglements. Praised for both kinds of stories, B. didn't reach a broader audience until the success of his third novel, *World's End* (1987). Following in the footsteps of *Water Music* (1981), a long, rollicking tale very loosely based on the life of Scottish explorer Mungo Park, and *Budding Prospects: A Pastoral* (1984), set in the pastures of a Northern California pot farmer, *World's End* encompasses four hundred years' worth of the history of three families in the lower Hudson Valley as well as the bleak, drug-filled present of one of their descendants. The novel won a PEN/Faulkner Award in 1988 and brought a wider audience to B.'s fiction.

The preternaturally prolific B. followed with *East Is East* (1990), a novel about a Japanese seaman who washes up on the shores of Georgia and is taken in by an aspiring young writer at an artists' colony. In the novel, B. manages to poke fun at the cultures of the South, Japan, and writers' colonies and at the same time approach some insights about the difficulties of cross-cultural understanding and the ironic similarities in the way members of different worlds deal with these difficulties. His next novel, *The Road to Wellville* (1993), chooses as its target the turn-of-the-century American fascination with physical health, focusing on the Battle Creek sanitarium of real-life guru John Kellogg. Fixating on the enema as a central element as few novels have, *The Road to Wellville* follows three principle characters—Kellogg, sanitarium patient Will Lightbody, and doomed entrepreneur Charlie Ossining—along the course of their involvement with the sanitarium and the surrounding fascination with the eating of breakfast cereal and with what goes on at the other end of the alimentary canal. This reduction

of humans to ambulant digestive tracts is exposed as folly in the novel; ironically, what some readers criticized the novel for most was what they perceived as B.'s own deterministic reduction of his characters to animals and their world to a jungle.

B. followed *Without a Hero and Other Stories* with the novel *The Tortilla Curtain* (1995), which follows a double plotline that intersects at crucial moments, chronicling the lives of a Mexican illegal immigrant couple and a yuppie couple in Southern California. And again, as with many of his novels, *The Tortilla Curtain* can be praised for its sharp eye and stinging wit and criticized for the shallowness and hopelessness of its vision. More successful portraying its first, victimized couple than its second, merely contemptible one, the novel is also more successful at skewering society than it is at making sympathetic the individuals of whom society consists.

BIBLIOGRAPHY: Adams, E., "An Interview with T. C. B.," *ChiR* 37 (1991): 51–63; Pope, D., "A Different Kind of Post-Modernism," *GettR* 3 (Autumn 1990): 658–69; Schenker, D., "A Samurai in the South: Cross-Cultural Disaster in T. C. B.'s *East Is East*," *SoQ* 34 (Fall 1995): 70–80

SAM COHEN

BOYLE, Virginia Frazer

b. 14 February 1863, near Chattanooga, Tennessee; 13 December 1938, Memphis, Tennessee

Admired in the late 19th and early 20th cs. for maintaining traditions of plantation literature akin to those of Thomas Nelson PAGE, B. also served as poet laureate of the Confederacy. A Tennessee writer, like Mary Noailles MURFREE, she readily employed local color from that state. Experimenting with several genres, she reached her zenith in short stories, which appeared in leading literary periodicals of the day, among them the *Century, Atlantic,* and *Harper's New Monthly* magazine. From *Harper's,* stories of black folklore were collected as *Devil Tales* (1900), a book that reveals deft drawing of superstitions into literary sophistication. Along with stories from the *Century* in particular, these merit greater currency than they have been given, although much else of value remains uncollected.

The stories of slave life were originally told to the young B. by her black nurse, Ellen. They contribute significantly to larger issues of supernatural fiction, notably in presenting devil figures, and they link as well with Southwest humor. These stories demonstrate subtle transmission of oral lore into literary art. Although B. incorporated kindred elements into her novels, especially *Serena* (1905), the brief treatments of these materials are better sustained. As is the case with Julia PETERKIN, she has been overlooked in favor of other delineators of black character.

BIBLIOGRAPHY: Gaines, F. P., *The Southern Plantation* (1924); Puckett, N. N., *Folk Beliefs of the Southern Negro* (1924)

BENJAMIN FRANKLIN FISHER IV

BRACKENRIDGE, Hugh Henry

b. 1748, Kintyre, Scotland; d. 25 June 1816, Carlisle, Pennsylvania

B. was the first important American satiric novelist. Volumes of *Modern Chivalry,* his only book-length fiction, appeared from 1792 to 1819. This sprawling, episodic narrative relates the adventures of Captain John Farrago and his Irish manservant Teague O'Regan as they wander through Pennsylvania, primarily on the western frontier. B. uses their travels to satirize innumerable social attitudes and institutions.

Like most writers of his age, B. was a public figure. After receiving degrees at Princeton, where he befriended Philip FRENEAU and supported independence, B. served as a teacher on the eastern shore of Maryland, a chaplain in Washington's army, the editor of the *United States Magazine* in Philadelphia, and after the Revolution as a lawyer in Pittsburgh and judge in western Pennsylvania. And like most writers of his age, B. employed many forms. His poems include a blank verse "Progress Piece" (with Freneau), two heroic dramas, satirical Hudibrastics, and Scottish doggerel. His prose ranges from a farcical adventure tale (with Freneau) to sermons, newspaper essays, political treatises, legal miscellanies, and an *apologia pro vita sua.*

The current reputation of B. rests on *Modern Chivalry,* which contains hundreds of episodes but only three developed characters: Farrago, Teague, and B. as intrusive third-person narrator. Farrago is an educated, naive, quixotic American searching for a republic of virtuous men. Teague is a rascally, stupid, self-serving bogtrotter searching for the main chance. In early volumes of *Modern Chivalry* (part 1, published from 1792 to 1807) the satiric pattern repeats. Farrago and Teague arrive at a new place. Because the citizens are foolish and Teague is sly, he gains social or political eminence. Farrago remonstrates with Teague but never changes his character. Eventually they leave, or are forced to leave. As narrator, B. employs irony to emphasize his social and moral lesson: America must

become a virtuous republic; but without just laws, liberal education, and common sense, the mob will make men like Teague its leaders.

In later volumes of *Modern Chivalry* (part 2, published from 1804 to 1819), the pattern of satiric episodes laced with ironic commentary disappears. Farrago and Teague enter the wilderness where the Captain attempts to establish a utopia. He fails. B., too, fails as narrator. He develops few humorous episodes; he abandons irony and becomes didactic. Thus B. satirically contrasts the vulgar and genteel, the virtuous and villainous, the ideal and real. But as moralist, reformer, and proponent of a virtuous republic, B. despairs when these opposites remain unreconciled. *Modern Chivalry* introduces the subjects of later American satire and humor, then descends to didacticism.

BIBLIOGRAPHY: Ellis, J. J., *After the Revolution: Profiles in Early American Culture* (1979); Engell, J., "B., *Modern Chivalry,* and American Humor," *EAL* 22 (Spring 1987): 43–62; Newlin, C. M., *The Life and Writings of H. H. B.* (1932)

JOHN ENGELL

BRADBURY, Ray

b. 22 August 1920, Waukegan, Illinois

B. is often proclaimed "the world's greatest living science fiction writer," and, indeed, if one were asked to name the premier 20th-c. science fiction writer, the response would likely be either B. or Isaac ASIMOV. But while Asimov was the more prolific author—producing hundreds of books, as well as innumerable short stories and articles on a plethora of topics—B. set the standard for artistry. Primarily a short story writer, B. is noteworthy for his constant celebration of the human spirit. His works are, truly, not SCIENCE FICTION at all; they are first and foremost philosophical/psychological stories dealing with human beings and human issues. Advanced technology or fantastic settings are often employed, but B. always writes primarily about people.

B.'s most famous work is probably *The Martian Chronicles* (1950). This short story collection gathers previously published works, dealing with—as the title implies—man's attempts to colonize the red planet. But it must be emphasized that B.'s Mars bears no resemblance to the actual planet (for example, it has a breathable atmosphere and a native population). In the stories, Earthmen journey to Mars and often encounter villages much like the small towns they left behind (and like the ones in which B. was reared). But, as critics have pointed out, B. makes the argument that too much fondness for the past—too great an attempt to transfer the structures and values of Earth to the surface of Mars—is dangerous. And in stories such as "Mars Is Heaven" (1948), collected in *The Martian Chronicles* as "The Third Expedition," and "The Earth Men" (1948)—where Earthling explorers meet their dooms through an inability to let go of preconceived (literally, "earthbound") notions—B. suggests that a lack of vision coupled with advanced technology is a lethal combination.

This theme is taken up again in a different manner in the story "A Sound of Thunder" (1952), whose basic plot has become something of a science fiction cliché. A time traveler journeys back to the age of dinosaurs. He is counseled to remain on the path indicated by the time travel agency, lest there be dire consequences for the future. Predictably, he steps off the path and crushes a butterfly underfoot. Upon returning to his "present," he finds the world he had known transformed into a brutal dictatorship. "There Will Come Soft Rains" (1950) presents another bleak portrait of the world of high technology, as a fully automated house goes about its daily chores despite the fact that the human owners are dead, victims of an apparent nuclear holocaust. "The Veldt" (1950), originally entitled "The World the Children Made," also warns against overreliance on technology, as parents fall victim to the depredations of their children's holographic "playroom." Yet it should be stressed that B. is in no way a Luddite. One of his most beloved stories, "I Sing the Body Electric!" (1969), originally entitled "The Beautiful One Is Here"—about a robotic "grandmother"—celebrates the positive potential of technology to enrich people's lives.

In addition to short stories, B. has published several novels. Probably his most famous novel, *Fahrenheit 451* (1953), deals with a dystopia wherein so-called Firemen no longer extinguish fires; they start them—specifically, by burning books. This is B.'s eloquent attack on censorship. In this future world, reading is forbidden; instead, ubiquitous television screens broadcast vacuous entertainment to the passive population. The protagonist, Guy Montag, is a Fireman who comes to see the flaws of his society and who ultimately leaves behind his living-dead wife and the society of which she is emblematic in favor of a group of rebellious outcasts who keep literature alive. The year after the publication of *Fahrenheit 451,* B. received an award from the National Institute of Arts and Letters for his contribution to American literature. B.'s other major novels include *Dandelion Wine* (1957)—really a collection of related short stories—which is a sort of memoir of his childhood; *Something Wicked This Way Comes* (1962), which developed out of the short story "The Black Ferris" (1948), deals with a sinister traveling carnival and its satanic ringmaster.

B.'s interests and his writings are not limited to the fantastic. He has always been interested in Mexican art and artifacts, and he has written numerous stories about Mexico, as in "The Next in Line" (1947) and "Calling Mexico" (1980). Ireland is another popular setting for B.'s stories, notably "The Anthem Sprinters" (1963), originally entitled "The Queen's Own Invaders," "The Terrible Conflagration at the Place" (1969), and the autobiographical *Green Shadows, White Whale* (1992), about B.'s experiences in Ireland while he was working on the screenplay for Herman MELVILLE's *Moby-Dick* (1956, with George C. Johnson).

It is primarily as a fantasist, however, that B. will be remembered. His is ultimately an optimistic vision of man's future, and his "Mars" must be ranked alongside C. S. Lewis's "Narnia" and J. R. R. Tolkien's "Middle Earth" as one of the most fully realized and memorable imaginary worlds. In 1977, B. was presented with the World Fantasy Award for life achievement; in the years since then, he has continued to contribute to that genre and to the world of literature in general.

BIBLIOGRAPHY: Greenberg, M. H., and J. D. Olander, eds., *R. B.* (1980); Johnson, W. L., *R. B.* (1980); Mogen, D., *R. B.* (1986); Miller, W. J., *R. B.'s "The Martian Chronicles": A Critical Commentary* (1987); Nolan, W. F., *The R. B. Companion* (1975); Slusser, G. E., *The B. Chronicles* (1977)

JASON BERNER

BRADFORD, Gamaliel [VI]

b. 9 October 1863, Boston, Massachusetts; d. 11 April 1932, Wellesley Hills, Massachusetts

A descendant of the Pilgrim governor William BRADFORD, B. was a lifelong semi–invalid who essayed almost every type of literary composition in vogue in his time—fiction (*Between Two Masters,* 1906); poetry (*A Pageant of Life,* 1904); drama (*Unmade in Heaven,* 1917)—but owes his reputation almost entirely to his "psychographs." He coined the word independently but later learned that C. A. Sainte-Neuve, the most important literary influence upon his work, had used it before him, though without devising a psychographic method. Psychography is a form of biographical writing organized topically, not chronologically, which concentrates upon an analysis of the subject's character and personality rather than the outer events of his life.

B. made his first success as a psychographer with *Lee the American* (1912), which enjoyed a long vogue, especially in the South, inspired at the outset by delighted surprise that a Yankee could be so sympathetic toward the great Southerner, to which he promptly added *Confederate Portraits* (1914) and *Union Portraits* (1916). Sixteen other volumes of psychographs followed. Four concerned women: *Portraits of Women* (1916); *Portraits of American Women* (1919); *Wives* (1925); and *Daughters of Eve* (1930), while religious faith and doubt formed the subject matter of *Darwin* (1926), *D. L. Moody, A Worker in Souls* (1927), and the nonpsychographic *Life and I* (1928), which B. called "An Autobiography of Humanity." Only in *The Quick and the Dead* (1931) did he attempt to apply his methods to still living persons.

American Portraits, 1875–1900 (1922) was designed as the first volume of a series covering representative figures of American history, proceeding backwards in time, but this plan was aborted by the popularity of *Damaged Souls* (1923), both serially in *Harper's Magazine* and as a book, which directed its author's energies toward rather livelier and more varied subjects. During the 1920s, B. was one of the "stars" of all the quality magazines and was often mentioned along with such contemporary biographers Lytton Strachey, André Maurois, and Emil Ludwig. How much of this was due to the fact that he was the only American biographer who devised a new form of biographical writing is speculative, for the term "psychography" never caught on, and only the present writer has used his methods in a succession of books.

B. was a phenomenal linguist and a man of rich culture and amazingly wide reading. His rapid production during his last years was facilitated by his ability to draw at will upon the accumulated riches of a lifetime. He planned his work in advance in such detail that he never needed to revise. Though warmly admired by H. L. MENCKEN, he had no sympathy with the "debunking" tendencies popular in the biography and criticism of his time and once wrote that "in every character I have portrayed so far it has been my endeavor to find the good rather than the evil, to set the figure firmly on its common human basis, but at the same time to insist that if the human heart were not worth loving, my work would not be worth doing." But his sympathy was neatly balanced by a clear, sharp eye, and he was never sentimental.

BIBLIOGRAPHY: Brooks, V. W., ed., *The Journal of G. B., 1883–1932* (1933); Brooks, V. W., ed., *The Letters of G. B., 1913–1921* (1934); Wagenknecht, E., *G. B.* (1982)

EDWARD WAGENKNECHT

BRADFORD, Roark [Whitney Wickliffe]

b. 21 August 1896, Lauderdale County, Tennessee; d. 13 November 1948, New Orleans, Louisiana

A direct descendant of William BRADFORD, colonial governor of Massachusetts, B. was born in Lauderdale

County, Tennessee, trained soldiers in ballistics in World War I, and wrote for newspapers in Atlanta and New Orleans in the 1920s.

All his fiction, beginning with an award-winning series of stories published by the *New York World* in 1927, and reissued in book form as *Ol' Man Adam an' His Chillun* (1928), deal with Southern blacks, portraying them as simple, carefree, humorous characters. *Ol' Man Adam* was later adapted as a successful Pulitzer prize-winning play and motion picture, *Green Pastures,* by Marc CONNELLY.

B.'s other published works include *This Side of Jordan* (1929), *Ol' King David an' the Philistine Boys* (1930), *How Come Christmas* (1934), *John Henry* (1931), *Kingdom Coming* (1933), *Let the Band Play Dixie and Other Stories* (1934), *The Three-Headed Angel* (1937), *John Henry* (1939, play version, with music by Jacques Wolf), and *The Green Roller* (published posthumously, 1949).

He served in the Navy during World War II and afterwards lectured at Tulane University on fiction writing. He died at his New Orleans home in 1948, the victim of an amoebic infection he had contracted in West Africa in 1943.

B.'s writings range from the patronizing to the racist, although current readers must make themselves aware of the historical context in which they were written. Artistically, he was a gifted storyteller with a rare talent for capturing black speech accurately.

BIBLIOGRAPHY: Hall, W., "R. B.," in Kimbel, B. E., ed., *DLB,* vol. 86, *American Short-Story Writers, 1910–1945* (1989): 43–48; Simpson, L. P., "R. B.," in Rubin, L. D., Jr., ed., *A Bibliographic Guide to the Study of Southern Literature* (1969): 159–60

HARRY MCBRAYER BAYNE

BRADFORD, William

b. March 1590, Austerfield, Yorkshire, England; d. May 1657, Plymouth, Massachusetts

Among the best known of the 17th-c. New England colonists, B. is highly regarded as a leader and a historian of the Pilgrim settlement of Plymouth. Every historical or literary assessment of early American colonial culture must come to terms with B.'s legacy.

B. was largely self-educated and eventually worked in the cloth trade. In 1608, he emigrated to Holland to escape religious persecution, and in 1620 he emigrated with the Pilgrims to the New World. A signer of the "*Mayflower* compact," B. became the second governor of the Plymouth colony in 1622, a position he continued to hold, with the exception of five years, to the end of his life.

B.'s first published writing is believed to be included in *A Relation or Journal of the Beginning and Proceedings of the English Plantation Settled at Plymouth in New England* (1622), authored principally by Edward Winslow. Just what B. contributed is uncertain, but probably he wrote the first section describing the Pilgrims's initial arrival in winter at Cape Cod. This section is rich in detail, but it does not achieve the grace and sweep of B.'s next work.

This second work, *Of Plymouth Plantation* (wr. 1630–50, pub. 1856), is B.'s masterpiece, a work whose style reflects the influence of the language of the Geneva Bible. For a long while later readers thought that it was a work of impeccable truth because other colonial historians seemed to verify B.'s observations. Eventually, however, it was disclosed that these subsequent historians had in fact relied on B.'s work in manuscript. Moreover, the scene of the Pilgrims first coming ashore at Cape Cod differs markedly from the same scene in the *Relation,* a fact that has led some readers to suspect that in *Of Plymouth Plantation* B. heightened episodes for dramatic effect.

Most of this work evidences a controlling theme that shapes its narrative and influences especially B.'s selectivity of detail: the colonists' repetitive experience of a decline in fortune, followed by a recognition of fault and a submission to God, followed by a new ascent in the welfare of the colony. Time and again the episodes B. emphasizes conform to this biblical thematic architectonic. Eventually, however, in the later parts of his book, only the steady decline of the colony is recorded, as if God no longer would raise up the colony. This later emphasis coincides with the transition from B.'s sense of his book as a public document asserting a special vision of history to, by the end of his book, his sense of it as a private journal trying to ascertain the meaning of history, which has become ambiguous to him. Sadly intimating B.'s despair over his sense of the colony's religious and social decline, the history ends in silence, with merely two dates listed without any commentary.

B.'s changing view of the history of the Pilgrims also emerges clearly in his treatment of the concept of necessity. Whereas at the start of his book B. uses the word *necessity* to refer to a divine communication urging the colonists to change direction, at the end of his book *necessity* is reduced to mean only a clever argument for the desires of the corrupt wills of the colonists. In the early part of the book necessity refers to those dire circumstances that force, or necessitate, the Pilgrims to change their present situation; at first, the problem seems bad indeed, but later with hindsight the now comfortable Pilgrims see that the necessity to which they were forced to respond was really a way that God, their divine taskmaster, communicated to them to improve their condition. This same argument based on a divinely goading necessity occurs in 1623, when against his better judgment and against the colony's charter B. grants land for private use. By 1632, B. clearly knows that the land arrangements of nine years before have been a terrible mistake, for the colony is breaking apart as people leave to acquire more and more land. Near the end of his life he reread his history, and in a note he then appended to an early page of his text he specifically remarks how he and the colonists were fooled by the "fair pretenses of necessity."

If B. only eventually suggests that history and the idea of necessity are ambiguous, from the beginning to the end of *Of Plymouth Plantation* he characterizes the colonists in a way that suggests that human motives and behavior are too ambiguous for any fellow human to assess. With such few exceptions as Thomas Morton, who is presented as evil, and John Robinson, who is presented as virtuous, the cast of characters in B.'s book reveal a fall-and-rise pattern similar to the structure of the narrative itself: a decline of religious, economic or social security that leads to a recognition of fault and a submission to God, followed by the attainment of renewed security. B. usually is extremely charitable about human foibles, wisely refuses to pass sentence on people, and explicitly leaves the judgment of them to God.

Also concerned with the Plymouth colonists, especially their decline in piety, are two works by B., both entitled *A Dialogue* (wr. 1648, pub. 1841; wr. 1652, pub. 1871). Written as historical and theological discussions between younger and older New England colonists, these tedious and repetitive works were designed to instill in an apparent apathetic younger generation of the colony something of the religious fervor which inspired their parents. The first dialogue discusses the origin of Congregationalism, whereas the second advances a case of the Congregationalist form of church government as the closest to primitive Christianity and therefore as superior to the Roman Catholic, Episcopal and Presbyterian forms.

In the 1650s, B. wrote seven awkward, unartistic and didactic poems, such as "On the Various Heresies" and "A Word to New Plymouth," which also attempt to move the younger generation toward greater piety and moral purpose. In "Epitaphium Meum," B. portrays himself as a man of sorrows waiting for the relief of death. If in his old age, as this poem and *Of Plymouth Plantation* suggest, B. had not given up on his faith and on his Moses-like role in reminding the young of their mission, he apparently had just about given up on his fellow colonists.

BIBLIOGRAPHY: Daly, R., "W. B.'s Vision of History," *AL* 44 (January 1973): 557–69; Scheick, W. J., *Design in Puritan American Literature* (1992); Smith, B.,

B. of Plymouth (1951); Wenska, W. P., "B.'s Two Histories: Pattern and Paradigm in *Of Plymouth Plantation*," *EAL* 13 (Fall 1978): 151–64; Westbrook, P., *W. B.* (1978)

WILLIAM J. SCHEICK

BRADLEY, David

b. 7 September 1950, Bedford, Pennsylvania

B.'s literary reputation rests on two novels, the second of which, *The Chaneysville Incident* (1981), won the PEN/Faulkner Prize and also garnered considerable other critical attention. Yet his first novel, *South Street* (1975), written while its young author was an undergraduate at the University of Pennsylvania, is in many ways a remarkable precursor of the talent that he was to display in his second work, and certainly worthy of more attention than it has received. Focusing on a ghetto in Philadelphia, the novel has a main storyline involving an African American poet and occasional bartender named Adlai Stevenson Brown, as well as several subsidiary storylines involving other colorful denizens of the neighborhood. B. adeptly captures the mood of urban despair implied in his setting through the descriptiveness of his writing and the accuracy of his dialogue. He also skillfully weaves together the various threads of his narrative in a manner impressive in a writer so young, thereby reflecting the fragmented, dissolute, but highly energetic world of which he writes.

The novel's flaws—Brown's romance with 'Nessa, a stock character who is a prostitute, and its lack of thematic unity, as not all of the storylines are reflective of the same ideas—are amply compensated for in his successful second novel, which took him some ten years to write. *The Chaneysville Incident* is about a young African American history professor named John Washington, and his efforts to determine both why his father chose to commit suicide and a group of runaway slaves elected to have their lives ended upon the realization that their attempts to win their freedom via the Underground Railroad were to prove fruitless. The story involving the slaves, with which B. had long been fascinated, and which he had researched, like his protagonist, had long been the subject of popular mythology in the Bedford area of Pennsylvania in which B. had been reared. B. is more successful in integrating the secondary storylines with the main one than in his previous work, on the level of theme as well as narrative. The whole is a complex, densely analytical meditation on subjects that clearly preoccupy him—primarily the belief that the present can only be understood through exploring the past in a

society whose persisting racial divisions continue to exert considerable hold over it members.

B. is also an accomplished essayist whose work has appeared in the *Village Voice* and numerous other publications. In spite of the intellectual manner of his writing, his essays can be popular in terms of both subject matter and appeal, as one of his essays, "How TV Drew Our Family Together—In Spite of Its Messages," reveals. At turns humorous, insightful, sentimental, and scathing, the essay is a recapitulation of B.'s childhood memories involving his father, mother, and grandmother, viewed through the prism of one of America's most notorious pastimes. B. is reputed to be at work on several full-length book projects. One can only regret that the tradeoff for the high quality of his books is the amount of time it takes for him to produce them, necessitating that they appear at such lengthy intervals.

BIBLIOGRAPHY: Bonetti, K. "An Interview with D. B.," *MissR* 15 (1992): 69–88; Brigham, C., "Identity, Maculinity, and Desire in D. B.'s Fiction," *ConL* 36 (Summer 1995): 289–316; Wilson, M., "The American American Historian: D. B.'s *The Chaneysville Incident*," *AAR* 29 (Spring 1995): 97–107

MICHAEL MANDELKERN

BRADSTREET, Anne [Dudley]

b. ca. 1612, Northampton, England; d. 16 September 1672, Andover, Massachusetts

Although she played the role of a dedicated Puritan and a dutiful daughter and wife, B. often expressed ambivalence about the male authorities in her life, including God, her father, and her husband, and the literary critics and authors whose models she initially copied. On one hand, she very much wanted their approval and, on the other, she was angered by their denial of the value of her experience and abilities. In her dedication of *The Tenth Muse* (1650) to her father Thomas Dudley, B. assumes the persona of the obedient daughter: she wrote "From her that to your self, more duty owes / Then water in the boundless Ocean flows," and she describes her work as "lowly," "meanly clad," and "ragged" in contrast to the soaring strength of her male mentors. In the "Prologue" to the volume, B. persists in her strategy of self-deprecation, describing her muse as "foolish, broken, blemished" in her effort to conceal her ambition.

In dramatic contrast to her declarations of weakness is B.'s eulogy honoring the "Happy Memory" of Queen Elizabeth, the only poem in *The Tenth Muse* that contains no apologies. Here she expresses her unqualified admiration for the queen as an exemplar of female prowess: "Who was so good, so just, so learn'd so wise / From all the Kings on earth she won the prize. / Nor say I more then duly is her due, / Millions will testifie that this is true. / She hath wip'd off th' aspersion of her Sex, / That women wisdome lack to play the Rex."

These assertive lines claim for Elizabeth what B. dared not claim for herself—power, judgment, wisdom, achievement. Certainly it was less stressful and less dangerous to make this bold declaration praising female abilities in a historical context than it would have been for B. to publicly proclaim the worth of her own work. Although B. was an educated woman, a child of one colonial governor and the wife of another, this privileged status alone could not protect her against the scorn and persecution visited upon women who stepped beyond their deferential role in Puritan society. Only by careful execution of her prescribed responsibilities could she escape the fate of Anne Hutchinson and her own sister Sarah Keayne who had both been excommunicated from the church and ostracized by the community for speaking their minds in public. Certainly, B.'s life and work illuminate the conflict that American women writers have traditionally experienced between a need for intellectual and emotional autonomy and a desire for recognition and acceptance from male authorities.

Near the end of her life, weakened by chronic illness and saddened by the deaths of her loved ones and the destruction of her home, her library, unpublished manuscripts, and most of her household effects by fire, B. finally appeared to take genuine comfort in the promise of an afterlife. Nevertheless, her penultimate poem, an elegy for her month-old grandson written three years before her own death, reveals deep reservations about the wisdom of God's decisions: "With dreadful awe before him let's be mute, / Such was his will, but why, let's not dispute, / With humble hearts and mouths put in the dust, / Let's say he's merciful as well as just."

B.'s forced resignation barely conceals her anguished rage about a death that seems to her to be arbitrary and unfair. Unlike some of her male contemporaries—John WINTHROP, Samuel SEWALL, and Thomas SHEPARD—who accepted the deaths of their family members as afflictions intended to correct their own sins, B.'s response was not so self-centered. For example, when his son dies at four months, Thomas Shepard does not grieve for the infant but laments the fact that his sinfulness caused "the Lord to strike at innocent children for my own sake." And even his *wife's* death is subsumed by this devouring conscience: "He took away my dear, precious, meek and loving wife in childbed . . . this affliction was very heavy to me, for in it the Lord seemed to withdraw his tender

care for me and mine which he graciously manifested by my dear wife." In contrast to Shepard's egocentric conviction that God has singled him out for punishment, B. is shocked by the apparently wanton demonstration of divine power. These polarized responses of mastery and nurturance mirror traditional masculine and feminine emotional patterns.

B. was not always able to sustain her faith during periods of severe testing; her doubt was, at times, overwhelming. Her despair even prevented her from sleeping: "By night when others soundly slept, / And had at once both ease and Rest, / My waking eyes were open kept, / And so to lye I found it best." The ambiguity created by "lye" in the last line underscores B.'s misgivings about the promise of salvation and eternal life. Her wavering belief resulted in more than one dark night of the soul: "I have often been perplexed that I have not found that constant Joy in my Pilgrimage and refreshing which I supposed most servants of God have . . . Yet have I many Times sinkings and droopings, and not enjoyed that felicity that sometimes I have done."

Although the preparationists stressed the difficulty of the journey, cautioning of obstacles intended to test faith that required continual renewal—each moment necessitated reaffirmation of commitment to God's will—there were dramatic differences in the spiritual experience of the individual members of the New England congregations. The diaries of B.'s male counterparts reveal a certainty of God's love that she did not experience. Even though suffering was seen as proof of divine testing, it did not guarantee salvation. Nevertheless, the men tended to count themselves among the elect. In contrast to B.'s agonizing uncertainty, John Winthrop's diary indicates that he emerged from his spiritual trial more assured of regeneration than she did. After undergoing a process of humiliation and preparation, Winthrop reports that he received confirmation of his faith: he said "The good spirit of the Lord breathed upon my soule, and said that I should live." Winthrop experienced the emotional turmoil of the preparatory stage of conversion—that is conviction and repentance—prior to receiving sanctification. Unlike B., however, he seems not to have felt abandoned by his Savior: "Hee left mee not till hee had overcome my heart to give up it selfe to him, and to bid farewell to all the world, and until my heart could answer, Lord, what wilt thou have mee to doe?" Although, as Edmund Morgan has observed, the soul's testing never ceased, permitting no rest of the Puritan conscience, Winthrop seems to have felt comforted and sustained by God in his moments of doubt and adversity; he is more certain of redemption than B., and he is more assured that the denial of the body brings forth spiritual life: he wrote "And the more I grew thus acquainted with the spirit of God, the more were my corruptions mortifyed, and the new man quickened." Here Winthrop emphasizes regeneration and freedom from the body's bondage, and although the reshaping of his consciousness is arduous, he is convinced that he is ultimately transformed by God.

Thomas Shepard also believed that conversion did not happen in an instant of illumination but was a gradual process involving much moral backsliding; he too sees his unworthiness as a sign of his redemption: "I found the Lord helping me to see my unworthyness of any mercy, and that I was worthy to be cast out of his sight, and to leave myself with him to do with me what he would; and then, and never until then, I found rest, and so my heart was humbled."

Fifty years later, Cotton MATHER's account of his soul's testing demonstrates that he also shared Winthrop's confidence in God's love. In his diary, Mather recorded an occasion full of doubt when he lay prostrate lamenting his "Loathesomeness" until he was overwhelmed "by a Flood of Tears, that ran down upon the floor ... This Conversation with Heaven, left a sweet, a calm, a considerate, a sanctifying, an Heavenly Impression upon my Soul." Interpreting his self-loathing as a sign of ultimate worthiness, Mather assumes that he has received God's grace. Mather was so sure of God's concern for him that he even prayed for three days for the death of his son-in-law and was gratified, but not surprised, when the healthy man died suddenly. Likewise, B.'s contemporary Edward TAYLOR wrote poetry that reveals a masochistic certainty that God has broken his heart, his spirit, and his will in order to redeem him. In contrast to these confident men who emerged reassured from their spiritual turmoil, B.'s faith in God's grace was the result of *willed resolution:* "But when I have been in darkness and seen no light, yet have I desired to stay myself upon the Lord." Her determination to submit to the authority of the church and to resist temptation enabled her to accept spiritual and physical affliction as God's "tender mercies."

Ultimately, B.'s need for assurance triumphed over her desire for autonomy, but her faith was based on a profound desire to remain connected to life, whether in this world or the next. Repeatedly, she observes that if it were not for death and decay, earth would be heaven. Two hundred years later, Emily DICKINSON decided that "heaven was superfluous" and found paradise on earth instead of looking for earth in heaven as B. had done.

BIBLIOGRAPHY: Cowell, P., and A. Stanford, eds., *Critical Essays on A. B.* (1983); Rosenmeier, R., *A. B.*

Revisited (1991); White, E. W., *A. B.: "The Tenth Muse"* (1971)

WENDY MARTIN

BRAUTIGAN, Richard [Gary]

b. 20 January 1935, Spokane, Washington; d. September 1984 (body discovered 25 October), Bolinas, California

For a brief time in the late 1960s and 1970s, B. was a literary idol. The generation of hippies, Woodstock, and Haight Ashbury adored his highly imaginative style that blended optimism with satire and outrageous situations. His books were bought with the same enthusiasm as the music of the era. After his popularity declined in the U.S., he was much admired in Japan and France.

B. began his literary career in 1957 with *The Return of the Rivers,* a book of poetry. He was a marginal figure hanging around the Beat literary scene in San Francisco, an acquaintance of Allen GINSBERG, Lawrence FERLINGHETTI, and Jack KEROUAC, though he never accepted their sullen outlook. Before *Trout Fishing in America* (1967), the novel that made him famous, he published with little notice four books of poetry and the novel, *A Confederate General from Big Sur* (1964).

Trout Fishing in America altered the shape of fiction in America and was one of the first popular representatives of the postmodern novel. The novel involves the narrator, his female companion, and their child wandering from one trout stream to another while witnessing scenes of violence and decay. The narrative is episodic, almost a free association of whimsy, metaphors, puns, and vivid but unconventional images. *Trout Fishing in America* is, among other things, a character, the novel itself as it is being written, the narrator, the narrator's inspirational muse, a pen nib, and a symbol of the pastoral ideal being lost to commercialism, environmental degradation, and social decay.

Early reviews of the novel focused on the naive pastoral optimism of the narrator, overlooking the pervasive themes of violence, death, and decay. Current criticism maintains that B.'s novel was not a pastoral romance but a statement that the pastoral ideal no longer worked. Again and again his characters try trout fishing but then turn to their imaginations as a way of accepting and transcending the ugly and violent facts of life.

In the postmodernist tradition, B.'s books are not mimetic but are self-conscious literary texts full of allusions to authors such as Benjamin FRANKLIN, Thomas JEFFERSON, Henry David THOREAU, Herman

MELVILLE, Walt WHITMAN, Mark TWAIN, Ernest HEMINGWAY, Henry MILLER, and others. *A Confederate General from Big Sur,* constructed in much the same manner as *Trout Fishing in America,* is the story of a character in Big Sur who imagines himself to be a general in the Confederate army, told by a narrator working on a textual analysis of the punctuation of *Ecclesiastes.*

In Watermelon Sugar (1967), B.'s third and most serious novel, his parable for survival in the 20th c., is the story of a successful commune called iDEATH whose inhabitants survive in passive unity while a group of rebels live violently and end up dying in a mass suicide. The book can be seen as a metafiction about the act of writing a novel and reflects B.'s interest in Eastern religions.

The Pill Versus the Springhill Mine Disaster (1968), B.'s most successful poetry publication, collected most of his early poems. The poems are brief and whimsical with bizarre metaphors, inventive language, and a casual tone, focusing on transforming everyday events into art. Subsequent poetry publications were criticized for their off-handed style and slight content.

During the 1970s, B. published six novels, each representing a different genre. The novels were clever parodies of their genre but were poorly received by the critics who continued to view B. as an aging hippie. This series includes *The Abortion: An Historical Romance, 1966* (1971); *The Hawkline Monster: A Gothic Western* (1974); *Willard and His Bowling Trophies: A Perverse Mystery* (1975); *Sombereo Fallout: A Japanese Novel* (1976); *Dreaming of Babylon: A Private Eye Novel, 1942* (1977); and *The Tokyo-Montana Press* (1980).

BIBLIOGRAPHY: Abbot, K., *Downstream from Trout Fishing In America: A Memoir of R. B.* (1989); Barber, J., *R. B.: An Annotated Bibliography* (1990); Boyer, J., *R. B.* (1987); Chenetier, M., *R. B.* (1983); Malley, T., *R. B.: Writers for the Seventies* (1972)

NEWTON SMITH

BRODKEY, Harold [Roy]

b. 25 October 1930, Staunton, Illinois; d. 26 January 1996, New York City

With the exception of his last novel, *Profane Friendship* (1994), B.'s slim but impressive output meticulously chronicles his early life. His short stories in *First Love and Other Sorrows* (1957) and *Stories in an Almost Classical Mode* (1988) and his novel *The Runaway Soul* (1991) delineate his Midwestern roots,

his unique family situation, and his transplantation from Midwest to East.

Born Aaron Roy Weintraub to an illiterate junkman and a bright but uneducated mother who died before he was two, B. was sold by his father to Joseph and Doris Brodkey. In his collection *Women and Angels* (1985), B. writes about his birth mother in the story "Ceil," where he idealizes a mother pieced together from fragments revealed to him by people who knew her. As a child ruminating about what his mother must have been, his skill at interweaving fragments of information about her turned him into a close observer and successful creator of characters.

The Brodkeys had adopted B. at the insistence of Doris, a self-absorbed woman, who, separated from her husband shortly before the adoption, was seeking to stabilize her foundering marriage. Doris appears variously as Leila, Leah, and Lila in B.'s stories; Joseph appears as S. L. Silenowicz. Their dysfunctional daughter, suspected of killing two infant brothers, is Nonie.

B.'s writing is an odyssey of sexual development that stems from memories of his post-World War II childhood, of his growing up first in the Midwest, then in the East, where his autobiographical character, Wiley Silenowicz, like B., goes to attend Harvard.

Death and loss permeate B.'s fiction. The loss of his own mother before he had the opportunity to know her forever haunted him. His adoptive father suffered disabling strokes when B. was eight and died five years later. His adoptive mother was diagnosed with cancer when B. was twelve and died shortly before he left for Harvard. B. manufactures his stories around these events, particularly the title story in *Stories in an Almost Classical Mode,* whose title suggests the generational repetition of family behaviors.

In many of his stories, the adoptive mother, with her omnipresent contradictions of personality, tacitly competes against B.'s idealization of his lost mother, now exempt from the human frailties of Doris/Lila/Leila/Leah. The history of his family and of B.'s relationship to it is spun out in *The Runaway Soul.*

Shortly after his AIDS diagnosis, B. wrote an essay "To My Readers," in which he revealed the diagnosis and reflected on his feelings about death. In 1992, while he was spending a year in Italy as the guest of the city of Venice, he wrote his final novel, *Profane Friendship,* a homosexual novel that reveals better than his earlier work his longing for a different kind of love than society usually condones. His final book, a memoir about his experience with AIDS, is *This Wild Darkness* (1996).

Among the most notable features of B.'s writing are his involved but clear sentence and paragraph structure and his almost tyrannical use of punctuation, particularly colons, semicolons, and parentheses. In the carpentry of his sentences, he masters punctuation as the pegs and dowels that successfully hold together his intricate rhetorical structures.

BIBLIOGRAPHY: Rothstein, E., "Look Homeward, Angel," *NYRB* 37 (15 February 1990): 36–41; Woodward, R., "B.," *Mirabella* (October 1991): 90–100

R. BAIRD SHUMAN

BRODSKY, Joseph [Josif Alexsandrovich]

b. 24 May 1940, Leningrad, U.S.S.R. (now St. Petersburg, Russia); d. 28 January 1996, Brooklyn, New York

Recognized by many as the preeminent Russian poet of the modern era, B. is also acknowledged as one of the most significant authors in the 20th c. to write in English. After emigrating in 1972 to the U.S., where he continued to write poetry while working as a professor in various colleges and universities, B. was awarded the Nobel Prize in literature in 1987. He was later named the U.S. Poet Laureate in 1991.

Born and reared in the former Soviet Union, B. was of Jewish origin. He dropped out of high school but worked at English and Polish on his own and tried his hand at poetry, falling in with a circle of poets with connections in the Russian literary underground. His friends introduced him to poet Anna Akhmatova, who became an ardent supporter. Eventually, in 1963, he was condemned as a social parasite (as a poet he could not give ample enough evidence to the state of gainful employment) and sentenced to five years in an arctic prison camp. Akhmatova commented, "What a biography they're creating for our redhead! You'd think he's hired them." Ironically, B. claimed to have enjoyed the regimen of manual labor that left him free at night to read volumes of poetry. But one of the first visible victims of the crackdown under Nikita Khrushchev that replaced the growing leniency the Soviet government had begun to view as dangerous to the state, his cause was taken up internationally and B. was released after eighteen months. He was invited to participate in literary conferences throughout the world, but didn't attend. He was twice invited to emigrate to Israel, and upon turning down these offers he was questioned by the soviets before being expelled in 1972. The expulsion was dramatic: his papers were seized and he was interrogated by KGB agents who came to his apartment. Eventually he was put on a plane to Austria, forced to leave behind his parents and friends.

Fortunately for B. his persecution as well as his poetry had won him influential foreign friends. In Austria, he was met by a poet he admired greatly W. H. AUDEN, and a suggestion by a professor of Russian literature at the University of Michigan brought B. to Ann Arbor. After that, he held several university positions, at Mount Holyoke and Queens College, even returning, at one point, to the University of Michigan. He was a dedicated teacher, and, despite his international recognition, remained humble, by most accounts.

Of the four books puplished in Russian, only *Selected Poems* (1973) was translated into English. Although B. was influnced and inspired by many poets in English such as Auden, Robert FROST, T. S. ELIOT, and Robert LOWELL, like many exiles—James Joyce, for example—B. remained stepped in the lore and language of the country he left behind. In fact, B. wrote a lot of his poetry in Russian, sometimes translating it himself into English, and in translations tried to remain true to Russian metrics and rhyme. Like Joyce too, however, despite his allegiance to his mother tongue and its linguistic tradition, B. was a truly global writer. Some critics fault him for too slavish faithfulness to the orginal Russian version of his poems; others fault him for his ultimate lack of allegiance to Russian literature. But he often used references to the Roman empire as analogies to the Soviet bloc. Classical references as well as biblical allusions abound in his poetry. He also has links to the English metaphysicals and neometaphysisals, as his admiration for Auden and his "Elegy for John Donne" in *Elegy for John Donne and Other Poems* (1967) would suggest.

Despite his knowledge of English poetry and tradition, B. has links to a modern Russian, specifically Leningradian, influence, a school of thought called "Acmeism." Akhmatova was a member of that school, as well as Osip Mandelstam, whom B. admired. Acmeists held allegiance, in fact, to a world culture that was classical and traditional. This was, of course, frowned upon by Soviet authorities.

Disregarding this international influence, some critics argue that B. was too faithful an imitator of Russian poetics in his rhyme and metrics. He had severe standards for translations, and when he translated his own poems he often strove—critics say strained—to retain a similar rhyme scheme in the English version. There are certain intrinsic differences between the Russian and the English languages that make this kind of attempt at fidelity to the original Russian awkward. The inflected endings, for instance, of Russian words make for an abundance of feminine rhymes that is more difficult to achieve in English, and the heavy consonant sound patterns of Russian are difficult to reproduce in English. Sometimes, as in "1972" from *A Part of Speech* (1980), the feminine rhymes of, to name one example, "senility" and "chilly tea" strike critics such as Anthony Astrachan as downright ludicrous.

Other translators are also guilty of similar faults. *A Part of Speech* again, in some critics' views, notably the poet Robert HASS, also strains too hard to achieve rhyming and metrical effects. The title poem and "Lullaby of Cape Cod" are two of B.'s most celebrated poems. However, the tone of the latter poem is sometimes inappropriate, and the diction is not conversational but forced. This latter characteristic could be another consequence of linguistic differences between English and Russian, for in B.'s mother tongue word order is more flexible. However, B. himself condemned use of the vernacular in poetry: "I think we have all been brainwashed in this c. into believing that a poet should employ the language of the street," he said in an interview in the *Economist*. Another critique is that his poems tend to overuse the genitive case, a consequence of forcing iambic rhythm. However, "A Part of Speech," translated by B. himself, is a poem that has won almost universal praise.

The volume *A Part of Speech* is divided into two sections, the first, entitled "A Song to No Music," seventeen poems written before B. left the Soviet Union, and the section "A Part of Speech" consisting of poems written in exile. Of course, the theme of exile is one of the most prominent in B.'s works. But for B., the condition of being exiled was not confined to his personal experience as Soviet expatriate, but applies to the human condition generally. Nonetheless, his own expulsion from the Soviet Union was traumatic. In a letter to the Communist Party's then general secretary, Leonid Brezhnev, he protested his exile: "I am bitter to have to leave Russia. I was born here, grew up here, lived here, and everything I have in my soul I owe to it. . . . Once I stop being a citizen of the U.S.S.R. I will not stop being a Russian poet. I believe I will return; poets always return—in the flesh or on paper." He never actually went back to his homeland, even after the dissolution of the Soviet Union. Going back to a mother country that was no longer home, he said, was an absurdity that he couldn't imagine committing.

To Urania (1988) was, for some critics (among them Derek Walcott), final proof of B.'s mastery of the English language and literary tradition. Some poems were translated from his original Russian collections of poetry, *Chast'rechi* (1976) and *Uraniia* (1987), but some poems were originally written in English. His use of literary allusion and sheer eruditeness impressed some as evidence of the revitalization of poetry written in English, while others condemned the volume as mere doggerel.

Perhaps his essays have too much of the conversational style his poetry lacks. In contrast to so much of his poetry, the essays were, for the most part, written in English, and have a breezy tone. *Less Than One* (1986) focuses on a range of topics. "The Keening Muse" focuses on his Russian mentor, Akhmatova, and there is a version of his lecture "On 'September 1, 1939'" by Auden, both of which were singled out for praise. B. was called a "stunning essayist," and his essays on literary subjects in the volume were deemed "excellent criticism." *Watermark* (1992), a book about B.'s beloved city of Venice, also received high praise for its vivid and lyrical prose. *On Grief and Reason* (1995), another collection of essays, was less well received, but "Spoils of War," his reminiscences of World War II, and "Altra Ego," which focuses on the poet and love, received accolades, and "The Condition We Call Exile, or Acorns Aweigh" is extremely provocative not only in its relationship to B. himself. The title essay, "On Grief and Reason," is a close reading of two Frost poems, and "Wooing the Inanimate," an essay on the modernist tendencies in the poetry of Thomas Hardy, is brilliant.

Ironically, since B.'s main early influence was a woman, Anna Akhmatova, feminist critics condemned his apparent condescending attitude to women in his writing. The critic Jessica Greenbaum, reviewing *On Grief and Reason* in *The Nation,* condemns his "overt sexism": "the poet is male, the muse female . . . The reader, too, is presumed male." However, a transcript of one of B.'s classes recorded by Susan Jacoby around 1973 represents him as well liked by his students and, in one interaction with a female student, respectful. His American students' knowledge of what he had suffered in his home country made them respect not only B., but the cause for which he suffered, literature: "It's inspiring to study with a man who has actually endured something for the sake of words. We don't know about that kind of endurance in this country. You place moral value on the integrity of words when you are reminded that they can cost a man dearly." B. himself observed, "for a writer only one form of patriotism exists: his attitude toward language . . . Bad literature, for example, is a form of treason."

B. the exile often took the guise of solitary observer in his poetry. A good summation of his physical rootlessness but final grounding in language and literature is a statement he made in an interview with the *Economist:* I don't know any more what earth will nurse my carcass. Scratch on, my pen: Let's mark the white the way it marks us."

BIBLIOGRAPHY: Astrachan, A., "A Murder Is / A Murder," *The Nation* 231 (4 October 1980): 323–25; Bethea, D. M., *J. B. and the Creation of Exile* (1994); Polukhina, V., *J. B.: A Poet for Our Time* (1989);

Remnick, D., "Perfect Pitch," *New Yorker* 71 (12 February 1996): 38–45

JOSEPHINE A. MCQUAIL

BROMFIELD, Louis
b. 27 December 1896, Mansfield, Ohio; d. 18 March 1956, Columbus, Ohio

Although B.'s nonfiction books on experimental farming ended up outselling his novels by the end of his writing career, most of his fiction achieved bestseller success and he won the Pulitzer Prize for his third novel, *Early Autumn* (1926). He wrote a total of nineteen novels, five short story collections, and seven nonfiction books, in addition to a dozen Hollywood screenplays—all in a prose style that ignored the innovations of the modernists. However, he was perhaps most widely known as a farmer and conservationist whose farming methods were controversial in his day. B.'s response to a decade of economic depression and Hitler's threat in Europe was to buy up, in 1939, three failed farms in the Western Reserve region near his boyhood home of Mansfield and return from France to make his living on the land and at his desk. His farm, Malabar Farm, is now a state park in central Ohio.

B. was born Louis Brumfield; his name was misspelled in the printing of his first novel, the "u" becoming an "o," and he kept the changed spelling for the rest of his writing career. But B. never succeeded in distancing himself from the profound effects of his parents on his character and work. B.'s ability to depict strong women characters, such as Julia and Lily Shane in his first published novel *The Green Bay Tree* (1924) and Olivia Pentland in *Early Autumn* (1926), was no doubt influenced by his own strong-willed mother, Annette Coulter Brumfield. In fact, he depicted her as Hattie Tolliver in his first two novels—*The Green Bay Tree* and *Possession* (1925)—and again she is the model for the character Emma Downes in *A Good Woman* (1927), his fourth novel. As if consciously wishing to terminate her influence on his thinking while announcing the modernist theme of the social transition from rural to urban life, B. indicates in his foreword to *A Good Woman* that his first four novels "might be considered as a single novel with the all-encompassing title *Escape.*" She lived on at the Malabar Farm. His father, Charles Brumfield, who failed at farming and county politics, instilled in B. a deep and abiding love for the land and a curiosity about people and their acts. *A Modern Hero* (1932) was dedicated to his father, "who has always known the things that count." B.'s career was also strongly defined by his business manager, editor, and confidante of nineteen years, George Hawkins, who moved to Malabar Farm from New York City. *Mr. Smith* (1951),

which was published after Hawkins's unexpected death in 1948, was the least successful and last fiction that B. wrote before devoting his energies exclusively to increasingly pedantic nonfiction books with titles like *A New Pattern for a Tired World* (1954) and *Animals and Other People* (1955).

The experience of Malabar Farm acted as a source for B.'s last two decades of writing in two distinct ways. His experiments in farming the one thousand acres in Pleasant Valley inspired a decade, from 1945 to 1955, of writing about subsistence agriculture and especially soil conservation. His practice of the so-called New Agriculture is characterized by crop rotation, contour plowing of the hillsides and setting aside the steepest grades in permanent bluegrass crop, wood lot management, and a practical minded balance between organic and chemical fertilizers. And from the constant feast of company he loved to host, including Hollywood stars and starlets as well as intellectuals and naturalists who had come to Malabar for scotch and vegetables and talk, he was supplied a table of characters for the novels and stories of the 1940s.

BIBLIOGRAPHY: Anderson, D. D., *L. B.* (1964); Brown, M., *L. B. and His Books* (1957); Carter, J. T., *L. B. and the Malabar Farm Experience* (1995); Geld, E. B., *The Heritage: A Daughter's Memories of L. B.* (1962); Ward, H. J., *L. B.* (1956)

JOANN BLEVINS and RICHARD L. BLEVINS

BRONER, E[sther] M[asserman]
b. 8 July 1930, Detroit, Michigan

Like other Jewish women writers such as Grace PALEY, Cynthia OZICK, Anne Roiphe, and Norma Rosen, B. explores Jewish tradition and issues from a woman's perspective. Yet B.'s fiction is in many ways more overtly and more radically feminist in nature, subverting traditional patriarchal forms—both social and literary—and reordering them to reflect the perspectives of women.

A common theme in B.'s writings is the weight of the past, and how that history can be both a defining inheritance as well as a restrictive curse. Many of her protagonists struggle to find a place for themselves within a less than accommodating tradition, and define themselves through those struggles. B. herself could serve as a prototype to such heroines. She has co-authored a woman's Haggadah, holds an annual woman's seder, and regularly speaks on the religious persecution of women within various patriarchal traditions. Given the religious nature of B.'s activism, it is easy to see how the quests of her characters are not only political and psychological, but spiritual as well.

Her first book, *Summer Is a Foreign Land* (1966), is a verse drama that centers on a Russian Jewish matriarch and how she uses magical wishes to bring her family to America. She followed that up with *Journal/Nocturnal and Seven Stories* (1968), the title novella of which is an early feminist work of experimental form. The text is divided into two columns, each one depicting the double-mindedness of a woman divided between her husband and her lover, and paralleling this, torn between her opposition to the Vietnam War and her defense of it. In this short work, she manages not only to represent an America divided by war, but to compare that war to the crimes against female subjectivity.

B.'s first novel, *Her Mothers* (1975), explores one of her most prominent themes: the relationship between mothers and daughters. Beatrix, a middle-aged woman, searches for her missing daughter, Lena, and along the way reminisces on her own past as a daughter. It is a nontraditional narrative that inverts patterns of the quest romance and reorders chronological sequence. *A Weave of Women* (1978), for which B. is perhaps best known, works within the utopian literary tradition but does so from a feminist perspective. Set in the old city of Jerusalem, it is the story of an eclectic community of women who attempt to envision an ideal woman's society, and in doing so challenge cultural and biblical precepts. It is an innovative work that, as the title suggests, weaves together the strands of fifteen women's lives into a narrative of triumphant self-discovery and solidarity.

In *Ghost Stories* (1995), B. once again turns to the relationship between mother and daughter. This collection of stories centers around a dying mother who returns to her daughter after her death, and tells the daughter stories about herself that she never told while alive. It attests to the bond between mothers and daughters and the need for women to create their own histories, two themes in which B.'s writings abound.

BIBLIOGRAPHY: Hoy, N. J., "Of Holy Writing and Priestly Voices: A Talk with E. B.," *MR* 24 (Summer 1983): 254–60; Robson, R., "A Conversation with E. M. B.," *Kalliope* 7 (1985): 51–57; Shapiro, A. R., "The Novels of E. M. B.: A Study in Secular Feminism and Feminist Judaism," *SAJL* 10 (Spring 1991): 93–103

DEREK PARKER ROYAL

BROOKS, Cleanth

b. 16 October 1906, Murray Kentucky; d. 10 May 1994, New Haven, Connecticut

As a formidable literary critic and one of the founders of the school of New Criticism, B. was a scholar and university professor who was motivated primarily by a desire to teach a viable and practical approach to poetry and literature. He was the Gray Professor and later Emeritus Professor of Rhetoric at Yale University, where he was a faculty member from 1947 to 1975. He served as a cultural attaché at the U.S. Embassy in London from 1964 to 1966. Despite B.'s reputation and achievements as scholar and author, some considered him a dangerous and threatening actor in schisms over literary theory played out in modern universities and, by extension, culture. Nevertheless, several generations of American undergraduate students as well as literary critics were taught by the formalist principles of New Criticism, so widely disseminated were his ideas and practices immediately prior to and especially after World War II, and even today.

B. received a preparatory education at the McTyeire School in the west Tennessee town of McKenie before attending Vanderbilt University from 1924 to 1928, where he first met Robert Penn WARREN, his lifelong friend and collaborator. He was a Rhodes scholar at Oxford from 1929 to 1932, and received his first teaching job at Louisiana State University upon his return to the U.S. It was at LSU in 1935 that Warren was approached by its president, James Monroe Smith, about founding a literary and critical quarterly that became the *Southern Literary Review.* Warren and B. served as managing editors from 1935 to 1942, the journal's entire existence. The *Review's* lifespan may have been relatively brief, but it was enormously influential not just in its effect, but in the fact that the collaboration between B. and Warren would continue in various manifestations until Warren's death. The *Southern Literary Review* reflected the views of the Agrarians, but their emphasis on formal aesthetic qualities of literary works was a precursor to New Criticism.

B., like Warren, was a creative writer of sorts himself, having written and published poetry early on in his career in, among other places, the *Sewanee Review.* However, he judged himself, as posterity judges him, also, to be a better critic than a poet. Perhaps, though, his own early ambition as a creative writer was the reason for his passionate belief in the inherent validity of the writer's stylistic choices when evaluating a work. The original motivation of B.'s and Warren's textbooks was not polemics so much as the feeling that their students did not understand how to read literature: as creative writers, in addition to being teachers, themselves, a belief in the viability of literature motivated their critical pursuits. Their first textbook, *An Approach to Literature: A Collection of Prose and Verse with Analysis and Discussions* (1936)—a book that would remain in print for fifty years—had as its precursor "The Sophomore Poetry Manual," an informal handout the two prepared to help students read, evaluate and judge poetry while developing their imaginations. B. and Warren continued to expand their methodology in *Understanding Poetry* (1938) and *Understanding Fiction* (1942). In these works, the dominant voice was B.'s, as it remained in the final attempt to expand New Critical approaches to the remaining genre of literature, *Understanding Drama* (1948), cowritten this time with Robert B. Heilman. These books applied the tenets of what became known as New Criticism to these various genres, and all emphasized the formal aspects of the works themselves rather than historical or textual backgrounds.

The close textual analysis that exemplified New Criticism was also a predominant feature of B.'s *Modern Poetry and the Tradition* (1939) and *The Well Wrought Urn* (1947). Both works emphasize the predominance of wit and irony in poetry. In the former, B. emphasized that idea and image are one, and metaphor, despite its dismissal by neoclassical poets, is vital. He also asserted that poetry does not necessarily espouse a particular ideology and that a great poet need not have a belief system at all. In *The Well Wrought Urn*, B. argues that the author's biography is immaterial, echoing Robert Browning in his essay entitled "Keats's Sylvan Historian" in "Ode on a Grecian Urn" that it matters not "What porridge had John Keats." Here, too, B. states his distrust of the critic's ability to adequately paraphrase a work of literature, but, as many critics have noted, this is largely what he does in his book, despite an entire chapter devoted to "The Heresy of Paraphrase." The works discussed are themselves relegated to an appendix where they are quoted in full, which itself symbolizes what rankles New Criticism's detractors: criticism has become more important than the literature itself.

B., of course, would argue otherwise. He sees meaning revealed in the structure of the poem itself and the tension created between conflicting elements in the poem, and thus this search for meaning demands a close reading of the poem or work. Despite the charge that B. and New Critics neglect history in their analyses (a claim his supporters deny), one valuable feature of *The Well Wrought Urn* to many would be the fact that it to some degree traces the history of British poetry, since it starts with, and, according to B. himself, represents every significant period since Shakespeare.

In *The Hidden God* (1963), B. concentrates on modern British and American writers—T. S. ELIOT, Ernest HEMINGWAY, William FAULKNER, W. B. Yeats, and Warren—but his attempt to try to fit them into an explicitly Christian tradition seems mistaken to many critics. He admires Eliot and Yeats perhaps most among modern poets, but to look past their essential humanism and religious doubt misses the point of the main body of their writings. Here, he essentially ignores his emphasis in earlier works: poetry need not express ideology. These writers offer a philosophy that serves as a substitute for formal religion in the 20th-c., but may not satisfy the needs of the dogmatically Christian reader B. seems to address in *The Hidden God*, and his tone is defensive throughout. However, this is a theme that he returns to in his last collection of essays, *Community, Religion, and Literature* (1995), where he argues that literature is not just pure language, as some modern critics believe, but like religion provides people with a community and offers the truth about human beings. In the later collection, B. argues again that literature also affords values to modern humanity.

Following his study of Faulkner and other prose writers in *The Hidden God*, B. devoted a few books to William Faulkner exclusively, though he returned to poetry in others of his works of the 1970s. *William Faulkner: The Yoknopatawpha Country* (1963) received much praise for its refreshing and insightful analysis of Faulkner's works set in the fictional county. David Littlejohn called it "the most sensible, most valuable book on Faulkner ever written." B.'s approach varies depending on the work of Faulkner's discussed, but he tried to account for formal features while assuming that the form itself is the most significant element. *William Faulkner: Toward Yoknopatawpha and Beyond* (1974) was less widely successful, partly, perhaps, because it covers less significant works by Faulkner in addition to some of the more standard works like *Absalom Absalom*, but B. still generated praise and appreciation.

In *A Shaping Joy* (1971), B. protested the label of "close reader" and suggested that an apter title than New Criticism would be "structural" or "formal" criticism, but these terms have already been coopted by the structuralists and the formalists of the early 20th-c. B.'s title refers to a poem by Yeats which praises the power of the artist. Like many of his books, it started as lectures that he revised into a collection of essays.

B. may have begun chaffing against the labels bestowed on him through the years, but he was still interested in the same basic critical issues and features of literature, as his later works reveal. He always believed that the author was "right" in the sense that the work speaks for itself and great art needs no defense—every feature has a significance. One of his last books, *The Poetry of Tension* (1972), recurs to a feature of literary works that had fascinated him before, the contrasting of qualities in literature, especially poetry.

John Crowe RANSOM called B. "one of our best readers." A prolific writer as well, B. did much to emphasize the value of literature in itself. His dedication to literature and commitment to teaching is also remarkable in a university professor, who, like Warren, never completed his doctorate.

BIBLIOGRAPHY: Blackmur, R. P., *New Criticism in the United States* (1959); Crane, R. S., ed., *Critics and Criticism: Ancient and Modern* (1952); Graft, G., *Poetic Statement and Critical Dogma* (1970); Grimshaw, J. A., "A Singular Association: The Brooks Warren Literary Correspondence," *SoR* 31 (Spring 95): 239–51; Gunton, S. R., ed., "C. B.," *CLC* (1973): 101–17; Littlejohn, D., *Interruptions* (1970); Ransom, J. C., *The New Criticism* (1941); Simpson, L., *The Possibilities of Order: C. B. and His Work* (1976)

JOSEPHINE A. MCQUAIL

BROOKS, Gwendolyn
b. 7 June 1917, Topeka, Kansas

Although born in Kansas, B. went to Chicago with her parents as an infant, and it is the Chicago environs that provide the background for much of her acclaimed work. After a short career in journalism, B. devoted herself chiefly to poetry. While her sensibility has always been "black," as critics have recently discovered, B.'s poems seek to find the universal in the individual. The individuals she most often represents tend to come from the ranks of the urban poor, especially black women, and these people have remained her constant subject, even as her political views and her ideas of her audience have changed in the course of her career.

B. became interested in poetry at a young age, keeping notebooks of her work. She later studied the modernist poets at a local community center. Unlike many of her contemporaries, she often chose to work within the confines of structured, traditional poetic forms, such as the sonnet, even as she wrote about Chicago's South Side ghetto known as Bronzeville. Her first collection of poetry, *A Street in Bronzeville* (1945), introduced a gifted lyric poet. Her pithy, spare style nevertheless allows her to express the speech patterns of the people she writes about, with the result that her poems are conversational, yet not a word is wasted. *Mademoiselle* magazine named her one of its ten Women of the Year after this first book.

In 1949, B. followed up with *Annie Allen,* a collection that won her a Pulitzer Prize in poetry in 1950. She published one novel, *Maud Martha,* in 1953, and produced a new collection of poetry, *Bronzeville Boys and Girls,* in 1956.

During the early part of her career, B.'s political views were akin to the integrationist ideal expressed by older Harlem Renaissance writers, and much of her support came from a white audience. Then B. attended the 1967 Second Black Writers' Conference at Fisk University, where she met militant young poets. She came away determined to aim her writings more specifically toward African American readers. In an effort to win over an audience less interested in traditional poetry, she began to work in free verse, noting in her autobiography, *Report from Part One* (1972), that she wanted not to imitate the young black poets but to adapt her own voice. Her free-verse output has been more slender, and her repeated revision of some of this later poetry suggests that she is less satisfied with the material.

B. has continued to address important contemporary issues in poetry throughout her career. She has written about famous public figures such as Winnie Mandela and Jane Addams while never losing sight of the extraordinary in the lives of ordinary people. B. was inducted into the National Women's Hall of Fame in 1988 and received a Lifetime Achievement Award from the National Endowment for the Arts in 1989. She has also become a much-studied poet. An anthology of her collected works published in honor of her seventieth birthday entitled *Blacks* (1987) is a reminder of the heartfelt concerns and thematic unity of B.'s poetry.

BIBLIOGRAPHY: Kent, G. E., *A Life of G. B.* (1989); Madhubuti, H. R., *Say That the River Turns: The Impact of G. B.* (1987); Melham, D. H., *G. B., Poetry and the Heroic* (1987); Miller, R. B., *Langston Hughes and G. B.: A Reference Guide* (1978)

CAROLYN LENGEL

BROOKS, Van Wyck
b. 16 February 1886, Plainfield, New Jersey; d. 2 May 1963, Bridgewater, Connecticut

Shortly after completing his college career at Harvard in 1907, B. sailed for England, intent on becoming a serious writer and on exposing himself to the high culture that America lacked and only Europe could provide. The contrast between Europe and the U.S., however, became markedly different and provided the groundwork for his lifelong analysis of America's problem with its literary and cultural identity. The work of B. might best be described as a probing and extended analysis of what he perceived to be a pervasive illness afflicting American literature and culture from its earliest beginnings. He addressed the definitive characteristics of this disorder in his first book,

The Wine of the Puritans (1908), written shortly after his graduation from Harvard. He maintained that there was a flaw in the nascent American character, a malady that had developed in the moral shadow of Calvinistic PURITANISM and the essential division it imposed between the "ideal," the all-encompassing will of the deity, and the "real," the practical and social concerns of what would increasingly become a secular society. In B's view, the emergent American culture began its formative growth at the end of the 18th c. around a rift that became intrinsic to its very nature, and led to a collective inferiority complex that influenced and largely defined American arts and letters in the 19th c.

His view was far from objective. As an impressionable undergraduate, B. became convinced that an American who seriously wished to be a writer must leave America behind at the earliest opportunity and make his way to Europe. The distancing from America, however, softened his convictions and he gradually recognized the writer's need to draw sustenance from his native environment. Since America in the post-Jacksonian era was generally thought to have no recognizable cultural tradition comparable to Europe, the serious writer was faced with a dilemma. The answer was to discover what B. termed a "usable past," to reexamine and reevaluate American literature by studying its social and cultural history, thereby bringing to light its latent and disparaged tradition.

His critical reputation grew with the publication of *America's Coming of Age* (1915) and *Letters and Leadership* (1918), which combined his study of the Puritan duality in American literary history with an optimistic heralding of a new age of American writers. The duality, however, was not easily dismissed. *The Ordeal of Mark Twain* (1920), for example, presented a view of Mark TWAIN in which the celebrated author in his later years all but destroyed his talent by succumbing too readily to native traditions and an insularity that included vestiges from puritanism that emphasized the natural depravity of man. *The Pilgrimage of Henry James* (1925) offered the opposite view, the author who separated himself through willful deracination and completely lost touch with his own people. B. would later offer similar indictments of Henry ADAMS and T. S. ELIOT. In *The Life of Emerson* (1932), B. found the necessary fulcrum to balance the diverse oppositions of American literature. It was Emerson who overcame the strictures of moribund Puritanism, discovered and enhanced an intellectual circle in Concord, put European culture in proper perspective and, in essays such as "The American Scholar," inspired a renewed literary culture.

In the 1930s and 1940s, B.'s eminently readable combinations of literary history, biography, and criticism were highly popular with the general public.

The Flowering of New England (1936) won both the Pulitzer Prize and the National Book Award for 1937. *New England: Indian Summer, 1865–1915* (1940) was also enormously popular, although some critics objected to an undue emphasis on social and cultural environment at the expense of a more thorough literary criticism. Both were part of a five-volume series entitled *Makers and Finders: A History of the Writer in America, 1800–1915* and were followed by *The World of Washington Irving* (1944), *The Times of Melville and Whitman* (1947), and *The Confident Years* (1952). B.'s general premise in the series celebrates the ascendancy of democracy and the Jeffersonian ideals of a liberal, progressive, essentially native tradition. Walt WHITMAN is the central figure of the late 19th c., the radical democrat who fully incarnated every healthy strain of distinctively American life.

B. further identified Thomas JEFFERSON, Whitman, Abraham LINCOLN, the early Herman MELVILLE and Twain, and William Dean HOWELLS as liberal and progressive cultural leaders who encouraged an organic, native tradition while also recognizing what was of value in the old world. In the opposite camp were the Federalist Alexander Hamilton, Nathaniel HAWTHORNE, Edgar Allan POE, Henry JAMES, and Eliot, all of whom B. identified as conservative and aristocratic, preoccupied with the Calvinist view of man's natural depravity, and culturally focused on the old world.

B.'s ultimate accomplishment was to recover a literary tradition from neglect and indifference and to demonstrate that it had quality, character, and a past on which subsequent writers could build in the future.

BIBLIOGRAPHY: Hoopes, J., *V. W. B.: In Search of American Culture* (1977); Nelson, R., *V. W. B.: A Writer's Life* (1981); Wasserstrom, W., *The Legacy of V. W. B.: A Study in Maladies and Motives* (1971)

RICHARD KEENAN

BROUGHAM, John
b. 9 May 1810, Dublin, Ireland; d. 7 June 1880, New York City

Called by Laurence Hutton an "American Aristophanes," B. was a prolific playwright and actor-manager who specialized in comedy, especially burlesque. He wrote deliberately for performance and not for a reading audience. Dublin born and trained in the London theater, B. moved to the U.S. in 1842 where he performed and wrote until 1879. Although he created 126 plays of varying forms—farces, burlesques, Irish plays, melodramas and adaptations—B. repeatedly delighted in deriding attempts by Americans to write serious drama.

His most effective burlesques, which attacked the American vogue for plays celebrating the noble savage, are *Po-Ca-Hon-Tas; or, The Gentle Savage* (1855) and *Metamora; or, The Last of the Polywogs* (1857). These two plays are usually credited with terminating the "Indian" play's popularity. *Metamora* is a spoof of Edwin Forrest and his bombastic performances of the romantic hero of John Augustus Stone's *Metamora. Po-Ca-Hon-Tas* also satirized political and social subjects while ridiculing the Indian play even more effectively than *Metamora*. This minor masterpiece of parody, replete with puns, remained a standard on the American stage for nearly thirty years.

Other of his most popular comic pieces include *Row at the Lyceum* (1851), a rehearsal play in which a "Quaker" planted in the audience attempts to stop the play when he spies his daughter on the stage; an outrageous burlesque on Christopher Columbus entitled *Columbus El Filibustero* (1857); *Ye Devil and Dr. Faustus* (1851), a satire on New York City authorities; and the hybrid *Much Ado about a Merchant of Venice* (1858).

With such plays as *Temptation; or, The Irish Immigrant* (1856) B. joined Dion BOUCICAULT in popularizing the Irish hero in American drama. He also wrote sensational melodrama such as *The Lottery of Life* (1868), and local-color plays about city life. *Life in New York; or, Tom and Jerry on a Visit* (1856), for example, satirized English travelers abroad through a visitor attempting to write a book on America. B. was also a major adaptor of Charles Dickens, most significantly in *Dombey and Son* (1849) for William E. Burton and *Little Nell and the Marchioness* (1867), adapted from *The Old Curiosity Shop* for Lotta Crabtree.

Like many playwrights of his period who really made their living as actors or theater managers, B. usually wrote with little revision in getting his plays quickly to the stage. It is not surprising that his surviving plays display unevenness amidst the topical humor.

BIBLIOGRAPHY: Keese, W. L., *A Group of Comedians* (1901): 43–60; Lalor, E. J., *The Literary Bohemians of New York City in the Mid-Nineteenth Century* (1977); Rourke, C., *American Humor: A Study of the National Character* (1931)

RONALD H. WAINSCOTT

BROWN, Alice

b. 5 December 1857, Hampton Falls, New Hampshire; d. 21 June 1948, Boston, Massachusetts

B. had a long and prosperous writing career that continued until four years before her death, and her reputation rests on her mastery of the "local color" New England tale. Praised for her realistic rendering of small, New England farming communities and her ability to utilize this background in combination with rich characterization, particularly in the consideration of universal human qualities, B. ranks with contemporaries Sarah Orne JEWETT and Mary E. Wilkins FREEMAN.

B. wrote what she knew. She left New Hampshire only in her adulthood, after attending Robinson Academy in Exeter, New Hampshire and teaching in a country school. In 1880, she moved to Boston and joined a literary circle that included Jewett, William Dean HOWELLS, and Louise Imogen GUINEY. She and Guiney became close friends, traveling together and encouraging other women travelers in their magazine, *Pilgrim Scrip* (1892). B. worked for several magazines, and, between 1890 and 1920, she published over 130 stories in popular periodicals. In addition to tales, she published novels, criticism, biographical studies, poetry, and plays. She won the 1914 Winthrop Ames Prize, which brought her play *Children of the Earth: A Play of New England* to Broadway. This play treats some typical themes for B., such as intergenerational conflict, spiritual and familial attachment to the land, examination and praise of the moral value of country life as opposed to city life, and reflection on life after one's middle age.

Her New England stories center on the fictional location "Tiverton" and can be found in several collections, including *Meadow-Grass* (1895), *Tiverton Tales* (1899), and *The Country Road* (1906). "Farmer Eli's Vacation" and "A Day Off" have been anthologized frequently. For her stories, B. typically uses village settings, eccentric middle-aged or elderly individualists speaking local dialects, and forceful, natural surroundings. Like many local colorists, B. valued strong community relations based on service to others and founded on a love of the land. This basis gave residents a firm, moral foundation. As characters like Farmer Eli face spiritual crises, their perspectives tend toward mysticism, although they almost always reach resolutions that combine mystical awareness with practical resolutions to build better relations with others through love, duty, and service. John Raven, in her novel *Old Crow* (1922), achieves this kind of self-growth, and the *New York Times* recognized *Old Crow* as one of B.'s best novels. B.'s many novels, including *Margaret Warrener* (1901), *My Love and I* (1912), and *John Winterbourne's Family* (1910), deal with themes found in her stories yet lack the same degree of realistic detail. B. realized that her stories could offer sociological as well as artistic contributions; "America should multiply these homely records of a time now becoming fugitive before a strenuous and complex civilization."

Despite the moralistic tone of her writing, her stories record fine observations of human nature.

BIBLIOGRAPHY: Baker, M. A., "A. B.: A Bibliography of Books and Uncollected Prose," *ALR* 17 (Spring 1984): 99–115; Fisken, B., "A. B. (1857–1948)," *Legacy* 6 (Fall 1989): 51–57; Toth, S., "A. B. (1857–1948)," *ALR* 5, 2 (Spring 1972): 134–43; Walker, D., *A. B.* (1974)

TAIMI OLSEN

BROWN, Charles Brockdon
b. 17 January 1771, Philadelphia, Pennsylvania; d. 21 February 1810, Philadelphia, Pennsylvania

B. is generally regarded as the first professional novelist in America. In form, the four major works on which his reputation largely rests—*Wieland* (1798), *Ormond* (1799), *Arthur Mervyn* (1799) and *Edgar Huntly* (1799)—blend elements from William Godwin's novels of purpose, Samuel Richardson's sentimental romance, and Ann Radcliffe's tales of terror. Hastily written, B.'s novels suffer from complicated and sometimes confusing plots, with frequent clumsy digressions and segments lifted from one work and patched into another. B. was also not a careful observer of either social or physical detail, and his characters, therefore, tend to be flat, almost obsessive or grotesque in their representation of certain ideas. His style, typical of the genre of terror, is frequently overwrought and prolix. Much of the fascination of his works derives from the use of the Gothic to explore psychological themes, but B. was also interested in radical social and political issues. Most of his novels, in fact, are constructed as tests in which such ideas as universal benevolence, human perfectibility, and the moral efficacy of the understanding or reason are identified with individual characters and evaluated through action. B.'s work, thus, is characterized by an ambiguous mix of philosophical argument and dark psychological exploration, a tension between the rational and the irrational, the conscious and the subconscious, the practical and the imaginative, that anticipates the direction American literature would take in such writers as Edgar Allan POE, Nathaniel HAWTHORNE and Herman MELVILLE.

To some degree, these tensions in B.'s fiction have biographical sources. His fascination with terror and the dark, mysterious tone of his novels have sometimes been attributed to a melancholic disposition coupled with a youthful tendency to bookish isolation. Other psychological and moral concerns of his work would appear linked to the Quaker faith of his parents, particularly his treatment of characters motivated by nonrational "inner lights" and tormented by the use of violence, even in self-defense. More certainly, as he grew to manhood in Philadelphia during the Revolutionary and early national periods, B. was stimulated by the contemporary debates over rationalist philosophy and radical politics. His father brought Godwin's *Political Justice* and Mary Wollstonecraft's *French Revolution* into the home, and later, through his friendship with a young deist and physician, Elihu Hubbard Smith, he joined in frequent discussions of current issues with a group of New York professionals who met in the 1790's as the Friendly Club. In part, B.'s giving up the study of law to pursue a literary career was fired by his interest in rationalist ideas, and his first published work, *Alcuin* (1798), is a dialogue in which practical education and political equality for women and even the abolition of marriage are advocated by the central characters. B.'s career choice may be the most significant source of psychological tension in his work for it pitted him against his family as well as against an unreceptive culture. B.'s efforts to establish himself as a man of letters in America, which included the editing of three short-lived journals and writing several political and scientific pamphlets in addition to the fiction, were part of a crusade for the emergence of an American literature generally, but these efforts were largely unrewarded, the struggle as frustrating as it was brief.

The mix of dark psychology and rationalist ideology is clearly illustrated by *Wieland,* B.'s first novel. It is the story of a melancholy young man, Theodore Wieland, who kills his wife and children and attempts to murder his sister, Clara, because he believes he has heard heavenly voices directing him to these acts. However, most of these voices are the work of a ventriloquist, Carwin, the first of several intelligent, altruistic, artistic, but dangerously self-willed villains in B.'s work. The novel's central concern is the reliability of the senses and the value of the "enlightened" education the Wieland children receive after their fanatically religious father dies of "spontaneous combustion." Carwin's ability to dupe the senses clearly challenges Clara's faith in the understanding or reason, informed by the senses, to act as a reliable moral guide, and Theodore's desire to find a rational basis for his religious belief is similarly undermined by Carwin and by his own unreasonable and uncontrollable melancholy. Thus, the antirationalist arguments are balanced against an image of the irrational at once fascinating but clearly evil, and the role of the imagination in Carwin's art and Clara's own narration is similarly ambiguous, powerfully evocative but morally uncertain.

Although with fewer elements of terror, *Ormond* explores themes similar to those in *Wieland.* It is basically a seduction novel in which the seducer, Ormond, another high-minded, strong-willed, European political and social radical, uses his special "art" of disguise and concealment to gain power over others. The threatened maiden, Constantia Dudley, is an exemplar of the value of useful education for women, and it is precisely her practical knowledge and strong moral character that see her through the ordeal of caring for her blind father, even during the worst of a plague. But, the real test is her ability to see through Ormond's wiles and eventually resist his attempted rape. Here as in *Wieland,* B.'s point is ambiguous, for Constantia's rationality makes her both attractive to Ormond and susceptible to his appeals to her mind. He, in turn, like Carwin, is a mix of benevolent purposes, fascinating powers and a tyrannizing ego. Also like *Wieland,* the novel points to the heroine's lack of formal religious training as the most serious defect in her education, suggesting the strain of orthodoxy in B.'s work that becomes more pronounced in his last (and weakest) novels, *Clara Howard* (1801) and *Jane Talbot* (1801).

Whereas *Wieland* owes some of its success to its relatively simple plot and consistent narration, *Arthur Mervyn* is a labyrinth of tales within tales and shifting points of view. The plot may be summarized as the hero's misadventures trying to make his way in the world after he is driven out of his country home, a pattern of the "young man from the provinces," the confrontation of a rural innocence with urban evil and experience. However, *Arthur Mervyn* is most noted for its memorable plague scenes based on B.'s firsthand experiences. He was, therefore, more successful in this novel than he had been earlier in grounding his fiction in actual scenes and events of American life.

Edgar Huntly is also noted for its use of native materials for Gothic effects—particularly Indians, rugged mountain scenery, a panther, and a cave. Its central theme is similar to *Arthur Mervyn*'s insofar as the central characters in both novels are obsessed with benevolent intentions that seem invariably to lead to disaster. Huntly's obsessive behavior is even more pronounced and its implications darker in that, like Clithero Edny, the man he believes to be his friend's murderer, Huntly becomes a sleepwalker and, eventually, a killer. *Edgar Huntly* is, in many ways, B.'s most intensely psychological work, and, therefore, along with *Wieland,* the most fascinating for modern readers. The novel's mixture of benevolence and madness, of an optimistic idealism foundering on something dark and submerged in the human psyche appears in each of B.'s major novels. Rather than reflecting a private torment, this tension may grow out of his instinctive response to the emerging conditions of American culture and, therefore, suggest his most significant role as literary pioneer.

BIBLIOGRAPHY: Axelrod, A., *C. B. B., An American Tale* (1983); Christophersen, B., *The Apparition in the Glass: C. B. B.'s American Gothic* (1993); Clark, D. L., *C. B. B., Pioneer Voice of America* (1952); Grabo, N. S., *The Coincidental Art of C. B. B.* (1981); Ringe, D. A., *C. B. B.* (1966); Warfel, H. R., *C. B. B., American Gothic Novelist* (1949); Watts, S., *The Romance of Real Life: C. B. B. and the Origins of American Culture* (1994)

JOHN LAWRENCE CLEMAN

BROWN, Rita Mae

b. 28 November 1944, Hanover, Pennsylvania

B. is a prolific author whose reputation as a strongly feminist, lesbian spokesperson was established with her first novel, *Rubyfruit Jungle* (1976). B.'s outspoken positions in that novel were made acceptable to a wide audience because of the humor and directness with which she treated her controversial subject matter. B. has sought to escape the label of feminist lesbian and gain wider acceptance as a Southern woman writer by experimenting with a wide range of genres.

Molly Bolt, the protagonist of *Rubyfruit Jungle,* is a semiautobiographical character whose wise-cracking intelligence and self-determination allow her to succeed in a world that erects barriers to the type of direct expression of passion and love that B.'s protagonists always seek. After the surprise success of *Rubyfruit Jungle,* B.'s second novel, *In Her Day* (1976), was a disappointment because it exhibited B.'s tendency to allow her message to dominate character and plotting. *Six of One* (1978) was more successful as the town of Runnymede, straddling the Maryland-Pennsylvania border, becomes the focus of the almost slapstick presentation of two generations of women whose supportive relationships enable them to survive World War I, the Roaring Twenties and the Great Depression. This novel initiates an important concern of B.'s, the ways in which the past informs the present and shapes the future. It also marks the beginning of her almost exclusive concern with depicting Southern life, especially the life of a small, closed community.

The historical presentation of a group in a closed, Southern community is also the focus of *Southern Discomfort* (1982), with the added issues of miscegenation and incest. Miscegenation is a minor element of B.'s Civil War novel *High Hearts* (1986), which has as its primary focus the varying roles of women in the war. B. revisits Runnymede in *Bingo* (1988).

With *Wish You Were Here* (1990), B. enters the world of the mystery novel in the first of the Mrs. Murphy Mysteries, coauthored by her cat Sneaky Pie Brown. These stories, including *Rest in Pieces* (1992), *Murder at Monticello; or, Old Sins* (1994), *Pay Dirt; or, Adventures at Ash Lawn* (1995), and *Murder, She Meowed* (1996) feature Mary Minor Haristeen, known

as Harry, the postmistress of Crozet, Virginia, whose
central position in the small community puts her right
in the middle of the plots and scandals that occasion the
murder and mayhem with which she and her faithful
companions, the cat Mrs. Murphy and the dog Tee
Tucker, come in contact. Sneaky Pie's fine paw is no
doubt responsible for the dialogue among the animals
to which readers are privileged as the four footed
sleuths discover and lead the humans to important
clues. These mysteries have brought a wider audience
to B.'s works.

B. revisits the historical novel with *Dolley: A Novel
of Dolley Madison in Love and War* (1994) and with
Riding Shotgun (1996). The former explores American
history in 1814. The latter uses the popular device of
time travel to bridge the present to colonial Virginia
as the protagonist Pryor "Cig" Blackwood travels back
to colonial times to learn lessons that enable her to
cope more effectively in the present.

In addition to the fiction for which she is best
known, B. has also written poetry, essays, screenplays,
notably *Starting from Scratch: A Different Kind of
Writers' Manual* (1988) and *Rita Will: Memoir of a
Literary Rabble-Rouser* (1997). The theme that dominates her work is the right of the individual to assert
her or himself, a right that can only be developed
through genuine love and support among members of
the human community to overcome the barriers erected
by confining social restrictions based on race, class,
and gender.

BIBLIOGRAPHY: Chew, M., "R. M. B.: Feminist Theorist and Southern Novelist," *SoQ* 22 (Fall 1983):
61–80; Ladd, B., "R. M. B.," in Flora, J. M., and R.
Bain, eds., *Contemporary Fiction Writers of the South*
(1993): 67–75; Ward, C. M., *R. M. B.* (1993)

HARRIETTE C. BUCHANAN

BROWN, Sterling A[llen]

b. 1 May 1901, Washington, D.C.; d. 13 January 1989,
Takoma Park, Maryland

B. was an experimentalist in American poetry and an
important, sensitive interpreter of the black experience. Early in his life, B. recalled his mother reading
to him poems of such diverse writers as Robert Burns,
Alfred, Lord Tennyson, Henry Wadsworth LONGFEL-
LOW, and Paul Laurence DUNBAR. On the Howard
University campus where he was reared, he was surrounded by black intellectuals and writers, and at Dunbar High School his teachers included writers Jessie
FAUSET and Angelina Weld GRIMKÉ. At Williams College, where he was elected to Phi Beta Kappa, he
continued the writing he had begun in high school.

While the poems he wrote then were mainly conventional, he experimented with other forms. After receiving a M.A. degree from Harvard University in 1923,
he went South to teach. It was there that he found the
wealth of material that would enrich his writing.

The poetic renaissance that occurred during the
second decade of the 20th c. in America brought with
it poetry that inspired B., especially the works that he
described as "people's poetry." Among the poets of
this period were Carl SANDBURG, Robert FROST, Edwin
Arlington ROBINSON, and Edgar Lee MASTERS, who
were writing about specific areas—Chicago, New England, Tilbury Town, and Spoon River.

Also having an impressive effect on B. was the
literature of the black experience, especially the poetry,
produced in the 1920s during the period known as the
Harlem or New Negro Renaissance. Some of these
writers include Claude MCKAY, Jean TOOMER, Langston
HUGHES, and James Weldon JOHNSON.

The life of ordinary people attracted B., and he
wanted to explore it in his writing—in all its complexity and depth. He became deeply interested in the folk
speech that had been missing from popular plays and
fiction about African Americans because of the dominant use of comic stereotypes. He discovered in the
speech of black folk tonic shrewdness, irony, and
double-edged humor, stemming from the people's
sharp observation of life. In the South, he listened to
the yarns, spirituals, and tales of the "great old liars."
The essence of these people is what he wanted to
capture in his poems.

One of the people B. met was a wandering black
guitarist named Calvin "Big Boy" Davis who is the
inspiration for such poems as "Odyssey of Big Boy,"
"Long Gone," and "When de Saints Go Ma'ching
Home." Railroad lore learned from "Big Boy" appears
in "Long Gone" and in other poems by Brown. Mrs.
Bibby, a student's mother, inspired the poem "Sister
Lou" and the contrasting poem "Virginia Portrait."
These portraitures were the beginning of a long series
of poetic masterpieces.

B. spent sojourns in Virginia, Missouri, Tennessee,
Georgia, and Washington, D.C., mainly as an educator,
but always gathering material as a writer. In Missouri,
he listened to the Ma Rainey story and in a blues
ballad he portrays this blues singer and captures the
effect she had on her people. A number of poems
came from his Missouri experience, including the Slim
Greer series inspired by a waiter. While teaching at
Fisk University in Nashville, Tennessee, B. encountered Gillie, a valuable yarnspinner who owned a barber shop and who also added to the tall tales of Slim.
From Washington, D.C., B. remembered from his
youth a strutting peacock of a man who became the
subject of his poem "Sporting Beasley."

In 1932, three years after B.'s arrival at Howard University as a professor, *Southern Road,* his first volume of poetry, was published and its importance lauded by the critics. It was described by some critics as the beginning of a new era in African American poetry. To James Weldon Johnson, who wrote the preface, B., Toomer, McKay, Hughes, and Countee CULLEN were the five most outstanding young poets of that period. The poetry in *Southern Road* is both literary and folk, but it is the folk-inspired poetry that is most remarkable. In this poetry, B. breaks with the pastoral idyllic mood in the treatment of the rural black. He uses both standard and experimental poetic forms. Though the sonnet, free verse, and the quatrain stanzaic form are present, the poetry is filled with chants and chain-gang songs, blues and ballads, dance beats and guitar rhythms. His poetry is deceptively simple, sometimes economic, always sure of itself. B. writes of mythic black characters and common people, of their bittersweet lives, their tragedies and joys, dignity and pride, and, above all, resilience, the power to endure. The strong move on, despite adversity. B. not only lyrically affirms life, but shows the possibilities of the human spirit.

Throughout his professional life, in addition to his poetry, B. wrote valuable critical essays on a variety of subjects, including black folklore and music and the treatment of blacks in American literature. *Negro Poetry and Drama* (1937) and *The Negro in American Fiction* (1937) are seminal critical works, panoramic surveys, of African Americans in American poetry, drama, and fiction. He was one of a triad of editors of *The Negro Caravan* (1941), an anthology of writings by blacks from 1760 to 1941. Forty-three years after the publication of *Southern Road,* B.'s second volume of poetry, *The Last Ride of Wild Bill and Eleven Narrative Poems* (1975), appeared and continued his explorations of the black experience. In 1980, *The Collected Poems of S. A. B.* was published and won deserving critical accolades and awards, notably the 1980 Lenore Marshall/Saturday Review Poetry Prize, given annually to the outstanding book of poems published in the U.S. In "Songs of a Racial Self," published in the *New York Times Book Review* (11 January 1981), Henry Louis GATES, Jr., wrote that B. was "not only the Afro-American Poet Laureate, he is a great poet." Closest to B.'s heart always was the interpretation of the lives of his people.

BIBLIOGRAPHY: Gabbin, J. V., *S. A. B.: Building the Black Aesthetic Tradition* (1985); Smith, G., "The Literary Ballads of S. A. B.," *CLAJ* 32 (June 1989): 393–409; special B. issue, *Callaloo* 5 (February-May 1982); special B. section, *AAR* 31 (Fall 1997)

                                    JEANNE-MARIE A. MILLER

BROWN, William Hill
b. November 1765, Boston, Massachusetts; d. September 1793, Murfreesborough, North Carolina

B. has been known primarily as the author of the first American novel, *The Power of Sympathy* (1789), although he also wrote numerous poems and essays that were published pseudonymously in popular periodicals of Massachusetts and North Carolina.

In *The Power of Sympathy,* B. follows the formal traditions and thematic concerns of English epistolary novels of seduction by such writers as Samuel Richardson, carefully couching within the narrative a scandal of adultery and incest which rocked 18th-c. Boston. From the late 19th c. until very recently, most B. scholars classified the epistolary novel as worthy of attention merely as a chronological demarcation in American literary history—a point of origin—rather than as a fictional work meriting attention due to its artistic achievement or its political force. They focused on historical evidence rather than artistic merit: proving B. was author of the "anonymous" work, churning up biographical information about him, and exploring a possible suppression of sales as cause of the work's failings by financial standards.

Formally, however, the novel's multiple narrative voices invite readers to participate in the construction of meaning as they absorb the correspondence of several characters—siblings, parents, and confidants. The plot becomes entangled and resolved as we learn Harrington and Harriot, who wish to be wed, are half-siblings due to a father's infidelity. Both hero and heroine die, Harriot brokenhearted and Harrington driven in his grief to suicide.

Although B. claimed the purpose didactic—the preface explains, "the dangerous Consequences of SEDUCTION are exposed, and the Advantages of FEMALE EDUCATION set forth and recommended"—the text's significant "meanings" are not so obvious. With analysis such contemporary concerns as the societal role of reading in the new nation emerge. And, as critic Anne Dalke has asserted, B.'s novel provides a glimpse of political and familial concerns in a time of "flexible social arrangements." It establishes a trajectory followed by best-selling American authors Susanna ROWSON and Sally S. B. K. WOOD as it shows us characters who "long, not merely for fathers who will perform their duties more prudently, but for a benevolent, protective upper class, for a clearly defined and clearly responsible social structure that will minimize the effects of misbehavior and the disruption it causes."

Thus, when examined for more than its contextual accuracy, its publishing history, and its formal innovations, B.'s novel may be seen as more than the receptacle of the seeds which flowered during the American

Renaissance—it reminds us of the power of multiple, fictional voices both to create and reinforce social codes.

BIBLIOGRAPHY: Dalke, A., "Original Vice: The Political Implications of Incest in the Early American Novel," *EAL* 23 (1988): 188–201; Ellis, M., "The Author of the First American Novel," *AL* 4 (1932–1933): 359–68; Walser, R., "Boston's Reception of the First American Novel." *EAL* 17 (1982): 65–74

ETTA M. MADDEN

BROWN, William Wells

b. ca. 1814, near Lexington, Kentucky; d. 6 November 1884, Boston, Massachusetts

One of the leading abolitionist and temperance orators of his day, B., a former slave, was the first African American to write a published novel, the first to write a published play, and the first to write a travel book; in addition, he was probably the first African American to earn a living as a writer. Most of his works were intended, above all, to be propaganda pieces dedicated to proving the inherent worth of the African American race and the inherent evils of slavery, and they were effective as such. Whether they are equally effective as works of literature is a subject that has been much debated in literary scholarship.

B.'s propaganda work seems to have begun with the narrative of his own life, of which he wrote at least three different versions. These differ in facts of his early life, his birth year, and his parentage. He was certainly born a slave in Kentucky, and very likely his father was white. He escaped to freedom in Ohio in 1834, aided by a Quaker named Wells Brown, whose name he adopted; thereafter, he improved upon the basic literacy skills he had acquired working for a newspaper as a "hired out" slave. B. worked at several types of jobs with success before moving to Buffalo, New York, and meeting William Lloyd GARRISON, who recognized his value as an abolitionist speaker.

His first publication was his autobiography in 1847. Its success encouraged B. to collect songs for abolitionist meetings and publish them as *The Anti-Slavery Harp* (1848). As his fame grew, his former master contacted B.'s friends with an offer to sell him to them. B. publicized this information and firmly declined the offer. He departed for Europe in 1849, a delegate to the International Peace Congress in Paris where he was befriended by such important literary figures as Victor Hugo and Alexis de Tocqueville. B. remained in Europe, traveling, lecturing, and writing, for five years, and in 1852 he published his travel book, *Three Years in Europe; or, Places I Have Seen and People*

I Have Met. In England, he brought out the first edition of his most famous work, the novel *Clotel; or, The President's Daughter* (1853).

Clotel features a beautiful mulatto heroine, Thomas JEFFERSON's daughter by a slave mistress, who in spite of her aristocratic lineage is sold as chattel. The original version of the first African American novel, in which every horror of slavery is proven by elaborate documentation, is more closely related to B.'s abolitionist speeches than to a genuine work of fiction. Although the Jefferson connection caused a mild scandal, the book attracted little attention from reviewers. This work would go through three revisions in the next fourteen years, during which *Clotel* became *Miralda; or, The Beautiful Quadroon* (1861–62) in a newspaper serial, then *Clotelle: A Tale of the Southern States* (1864), and finally *Clotelle; or, The Colored Heroine* (1867). The heroine's presidential relation no longer figures in these versions; some critics believe that B. was more inclined to appease Northerners with each successive edition. Clotelle remains a "tragic mulatto," a woman who looks white and is therefore designed more to implicate the institution of slavery than to arouse sympathy for the blacks who suffered under it. Even in the final version, the book is recognizably a pastiche of factual antislavery material and sentimental fiction.

B.'s soft-sell approach to the political issues surrounding slavery in his revisions of *Clotel* belies the increasingly black nationalist sentiments of his orations shortly before the Civil War. During the 1850s, he also wrote two plays. The first, now lost, was a satire entitled *The Doughface Baked; or, How to Give a Northern Man a Backbone,* poking fun at Northern pro-slavery clergymen. The second was a drama, *The Escape; or, A Leap for Freedom,* published in 1858. In the years following the war, he devoted himself to biographical and historical essays designed to demonstrate the importance of black contributions to American culture.

BIBLIOGRAPHY: DeVries, J. H., "The Tradition of the Sentimental Novel in *The Garies and Their Friends,*" *CLAJ* 17 (December 1973): 241–49; Ellison, C. W., and E. W. Metcalf, Jr., *W. W. B. and Martin R. Delany: A Reference Guide* (1978); Hemenway, R., ed., *The Black Novelist* (1970); Whitlow, R., *Black American Literature: A Critical History* (1973)

CAROLYN LENGEL

BROWNE, Charles Farrar

b. 26 April 1834, Waterford, Maine; d. 6 March 1867, Southampton, England

B.'s unparalleled fame as a humorist during the Civil War era came from his creation of a series of letters written by the fictitious "Artemus Ward," the loquacious circus showman whose correspondence commented on the foibles of his time. B.'s place is most significant in the evolution of American humor as he helped transform a once provincial and unpolished brand of humor into a sophisticated art form. His was a blend of Down East humor—characterized by the use of understatement, overstatement, malapropisms, and comic misspellings—and the Southwestern variety which was replete with sensationalized facts and incidents. Artemus Ward traveled across the U.S. and abroad reporting in a phonetic dialect and exaggerated style the world's goings on.

B.'s career in newspapers and magazines began on the printing staffs. He worked a variety of places learning the business and probably got to write some occasional filler. Still in his teens, he was given the opportunity to write short humor pieces for the *Carpet Bag,* a Boston weekly. He later moved on to become local editor of the Toledo-based *Commercial.* This position required substantial writing and his skills further developed. His success at the *Commercial* led to an editorial position at the much larger *Plain Dealer* in Cleveland. B. was responsible for a small column, "City Facts and Fancies," which entailed covering minor local happenings. B. livened up the column with jokes, witty commentary, and mock letters and answers. A letter from a boastful huckster with a traveling show consisting of "a Californy Bare two snakes tame foxies &c also wax works." and other "nateral curiosities" created a buzz among B.'s readers. For B., the Artemus Ward character was a matter of course, but public demand led to the appearance of twenty more Ward letters in the next two years. In 1860, B. became managing editor of *Vanity Fair* and produced the letters at the rate of two or three per month.

Artemus Ward, His Book, a collection of the comic letters and other B. writings, was published in 1862, followed by *Artemus Ward, His Travels* (1865). Though prone to extravagance and exaggeration, B. does some responsible reporting and social commentary. He includes burlesque romances, mocking the traditional variety's characteristic flowery prose and escapist fantasy.

Even by today's standards, the letters are genuinely funny—he writes of the newly elected Abraham LINCOLN as being "surrounded by a perfect swarm of orfice seekers"—but the additional value of B.'s humor, critic Robert E. Abrams writes "lies in its unprecedented cosmopolitanism . . . its willingness, in sum, to open its mid-century audience, still somewhat regional and provincial, to the follies and absurdities of the nation and the world at large." Although his satire may be too topical to attract modern readers, and his comic devices out of fashion, B. is still worth

reading for those interested in the rise and maturation of American humor.

BIBLIOGRAPHY: Abrams, R. E., "C. F. B.," in Trachtenberg, S., ed., *DLB,* vol. 11, *American Humorists, 1800–1950* (1982): 429–34; Austin, J. C., *Artemus Ward* (1964); Williams, S. T., "Artemus the Delicious," *VQR* 28 (Spring 1952): 214–27

JASON MCMAHON

BROWNSON, Orestes Augustus

b. 16 September 1803, Stockbridge, Vermont; d. 17 April 1876, Detroit, Michigan

Restless and outspoken, B. was passionately and prominently engaged in the major political, theological, philosophical, reform, and literary issues of his time. Raised by a Congregationalist family, he became a Presbyterian, a Universalist, a Unitarian, and then a leading Transcendentalist before converting to Catholicism in 1844. His career thus has served as a useful touchstone in the rise of TRANSCENDENTALISM as well as an important critique of the movement.

Author of the progressive *New Views of Christianity, Society, and the Church* (1836) and an original member of the Transcendental Club, B. edited the *Boston Quarterly Review* (1838–42) and from this platform vigorously defended Ralph Waldo EMERSON in the wake of the Divinity School Address controversy. In the October 1838 issue B. called the address "remarkable" and praised Emerson's courage and character. A conservative strain in B.'s thought is already evident in his reservations about Emerson's style and lack of philosophical rigor. But he recommends the former minister for "induc[ing] men to think for themselves on all subjects."

Though he would always admire Emerson, B. stressed the social, economic, and political implications of the new idealism. His controversial "Laboring Classes" essays (1840), which warned of class violence, are often viewed as forerunners of Karl Marx, though B. considered himself fundamentally a democrat and a Christian.

B.'s conversion to Catholicism was the logical result of his deep sense that transcendentalism emphasized intuition and individualism at the expense of involvement in history, society, and an organic church. He continued to speak out in *B.'s Quarterly Review* (1844–64, 1873–75) and wrote for many other periodicals, including Isaac Hecker's *Catholic World.* His autobiographical *The Convert* (1857) tells the story of his religious odyssey in typical B. fashion: with an intensity that is sometimes poetic, often combative, but always unafraid and uncompromising. His most ambitious work was the still-admired *The American*

Republic: Its Constitution, Tendencies, and Destiny (1865). Significant not only as a disaffected Transcendentalist, B. was an independent, vigorous, and influential controversialist.

BIBLIOGRAPHY: Brownson, H. F., ed., *The Works of O. A. B.* (20 vols., 1982–87); Gilhooley, L., *Contradiction and Dilemma* (1972); Lapati, A. D., *O. A. B.* (1965); Myerson, J., ed., *The Transcendentalists* (1984); Maynard, T., *O. B.* (1943); Ryan, T. R., *O. A. B.* (1976); Schlesinger, A. M., Jr., *O. A. B.* (1939; rev. ed., 1966)

WESLEY T. MOTT

BRYANT, William Cullen

b. 3 November 1794, Cummington, Massachusetts; d. 12 June 1878, New York City

The poetry of B. expresses a vision of life much like that to be found in the landscape paintings of Thomas Cole and the descriptions of nature in the novels of James Fenimore COOPER. Derived from the theories of such Scottish associationist philosophers as Dugald Stewart, Thomas Reid, and Archibald Alison, whose works were widely read in American colleges during the early 19th c., this view of reality posited an ordered nature that stood as an intermediary between the human perceiver and the God who created it. Through nature the qualities of the Creator could become known to men; in nature those principles were revealed by which men could guide their lives; from nature the artist could derive both the philosophic basis for his themes and the means by which he could communicate them most effectively to his readers. Fundamental to an understanding of the natural landscape were two qualities which served as a kind of given to the artist: the spaciousness of the untamed American landscape and the depths of time through which it had been developing.

B. did not, of course, begin his poetic career with so comprehensive a worldview. Under the influence of his maternal grandfather, Ebenezer Snell, a rather strict Calvinist, he versified passages from the Old Testament, while under his more liberal father, Doctor Peter Bryant, himself a writer of verses, he read a great deal of English poetry, especially that of the Augustan age. In 1808, at the age of thirteen, young B. published his first book, *The Embargo,* a satire in rhymed couplets on Thomas JEFFERSON and his policies. The poem was so successful when it appeared in Boston that the young poet produced a second and enlarged edition the following year. Indeed, it was not until around 1815, when he began to write the poems by which he is still best known, that he developed the

sense of space and time that characterize his mature poetry. "To a Waterfowl" (1815) evokes space on a continental scale, and the early version of "Thanatopsis" that appeared in the *North American Review* for September 1817 develops its theme through the suggestion of both vast space and deep time, aspects of nature that B. emphasized even more when he enlarged the poem for the edition of his poetry that appeared in 1821.

Since men can learn the qualities of the Creator through contemplation of his works, we find B. stressing in "A Forest Hymn" (1825) the "boundless power / And inaccessible majesty" that primitive man discerned in untouched nature and the "Grandeur, strength, and grace" that still bespeak the similar qualities of God. Indeed, the poet even reads "The lesson of [God's] own eternity" in the recurring cycles of growth and decay among the forest trees throughout "the flight of untold centuries." The psychological reaction experienced by the perceiver in such a presence is two-fold. He may feel humility, for the poet seems "Almost annihilated" by the size of the trees among which he stands. But paradoxically, he may also feel an expansion of the spirit at the sight of so much grandeur and beauty. Such is the reaction B. describes in "Monument Mountain" (1824), where the "expanding heart" of the observer feels "kindred with that loftier world" to which he is translated and partakes "The enlargement of [his] vision." So too in "The Prairies" (1832), where, at the contemplation of "the encircling vastness," the poet's "heart swells" as his "dilated sight" takes in the great expanse of the Illinois prairies.

Not everyone reacts so appropriately to the grandeur of the external landscape. The order and harmony are frequently broken by the passions of men. As the poet makes clear in "Inscription for the Entrance to a Wood" (1815), B. believed in a fallen human race, and he turned to nature at times to escape the "sorrows, crimes, and cares" of a guilty and miserable world. Here, and in "Green River" (1818), man can find solace in the calm of the landscape. For those who will not learn to still their passions, however, the violent storms of "A Forest Hymn" and "A Hymn of the Sea" (1842) are designed to teach willful men who rules the elements. In the former poem, the tumult of the heavens—the "tremendous tokens of [God's] power"—should teach erring men to still their pride and lay their "strifes and follies by." Indeed, B. concludes his hymn with the prayer that he and his not "need the wrath / Of the mad unchained elements to teach / Who rules them." He hopes their lot will be "to meditate, / In these calm shades, [God's] milder majesty, / And to the beautiful order of [his] works / Learn to conform the order of our lives."

B. used time in his poems to suggest a more social theme. Like many in his generation, B. subscribed to a cyclical theory of history that saw civilizations pass through a process of growth, maturity, and decay. He developed this idea in "The Ages" (1821), the Phi Beta Kappa poem he delivered at Harvard, and he gave it an American emphasis in poems like "The Prairies" and "The Fountain" (1839). In the former, he develops a Ruins of Empire theme in which the mound builders, thought in his day to be a pre-Indian people, give way to the Indian tribes, who are in turn supplanted by the white men. The logic of the poem suggests that American civilization too may one day suffer a similar fate. B. develops this theme explicitly in "An Indian at the Burial-place of His Fathers" (1824). To the eyes of the Indian who narrates the poem, the changes in the landscape wrought by the white settlers threaten the destruction of the natural environment. To cut the forests is to lower the water table and cause the streams to run "With lessening current." If the process continues unchecked, the Indian concludes, the white men may yet turn the continent into "a barren desert."

Not all of B.'s poems develop such broad philosophic themes. Some very effective pieces are short personal lyrics developed through the use of analogy. "To a Waterfowl," "The Yellow Violet" (1814), and "To a Fringed Gentian" (1829) are excellent examples of this aspect of B.'s poetry. All are based upon the correspondence that B. perceived between the things of the moral and the natural worlds. The "certain flight" of the waterfowl suggests to the poet a fundamental truth: the divine power that guides the bird unerringly to its destination will also "lead [his] steps aright." That he ignores the yellow violet, a flower of early spring, when later blooms appear brings to his mind the tendency of those who acquire wealth to forget old friends. And the blooming of the fringed gentian late in the year evokes the wish that hope will so blossom in his heart when his own death approaches. Close, indeed even scientific, observation of nature leads the poet to truths that in his view transcend the physical, and he attempts to win the assent of the reader to his themes by the accuracy of his description.

B. is sometimes criticized for the narrowness of his range and for the fact that he did not develop significantly as a poet. He found his themes and mode of expression early—probably by 1815—and his period of greatest productivity was during the 1820s. Thereafter his poetic production fell off markedly. Most of his life was spent in nonliterary activities. For half a century he edited the New York *Evening Post,* and he was a significant force in journalism and politics. He also wrote, however, three volumes of travel

letters and translated both *The Iliad* (1870) and *The Odyssey* (1871–72). Yet B.'s poetic voice is authentically American and deserves to be heard today. If his poetry seems old fashioned, it is characteristic of his age, and one need only learn to read it sympathetically to perceive that, like other artists in his generation, he saw value in the American landscape just at the time that the westward movement was transforming it forever. Though B. is not much read today, his response to the natural world and his warning to his countrymen that their despoilation of nature would have dire consequences for the future are matters that should still be of interest to thoughtful Americans.

BIBLIOGRAPHY: Brown, C. H., *W. C. B.* (1971); Bryant, W. C., II, and T. G. Voss, *The Letters of W. C. B.* (6 vols., 1975–92); McLean, A., Jr., *W. C. B.* (1964; rev. ed., 1989); Ringe, D. A., *The Pictorial Mode* (1971)

DONALD A. RINGE

BUCK, Pearl S[ydenstricker Walsh]

b. 26 June 1892, Hillsboro, West Virginia; d. 6 March 1973, Danby, Vermont

B. is one of the most popular of American novelists, here and abroad. *The Good Earth* (1931) was translated into more than thirty languages, and her later books were also widely translated. For all her popularity, her critical reputation was at best mixed, even at the peak of her career, and until recently she received little attention. This refusal to take her seriously persists despite her Pulitzer Prize in 1932 and the William Dean Howells Medal for Distinguished Fiction (1935). She was openly criticized when she won the Nobel Prize in 1938, but was defended by Sinclair LEWIS, Henry Seidel Canby, Malcolm COWLEY, and Oscar Cargill. Her biographer Paul A. Doyle dismisses her fiction after 1940 as inferior, but this appraisal is based on a misconception of the central thrust of her work.

The daughter of missionaries Absolom and Caroline Sydenstricker, B. was exposed to Buddhist, Taoist, and Confucian influences and to the lives of Chinese peasants and city dwellers. At Randolph-Macon Women's College, a Methodist institution in Lynchburg, Virginia, she honed writing skills demonstrated in childhood. After graduating in 1914, she returned to China and in 1917 married John Lossing Buck, an agricultural expert with whom she toured northern China for five years before settling as an English teacher at the University of Nanking. In 1925, she visited the U.S. seeking treatment for her retarded child and earned an M.A. from Cornell University. B. moved to the U.S. in 1934 and the following year divorced her husband and married Richard Walsh, president of her publishing firm. B. wrote over one hundred books, nearly half of them fiction. China remained her favorite subject, but she also dealt with American themes, especially the roles of women, racial issues, and American attitudes toward the Far East.

Her first novel, *East Wind: West Wind* (1930), foreshadows a lifelong preoccupation with the clash of cultures—East and West—and with the clash of generations—traditional and modern. A traditionally educated Chinese woman copes with the tensions of marriage to a Western-educated doctor and with her complex relationship with an American sister-in-law. In *The Good Earth,* the traditionalist consciousness is Wang Lung, who rises from peasant farmer to wealthy landowner and ends his life pleading fruitlessly with his adult sons to preserve his values. *Sons* (1932) and *A House Divided* (1935) complete the trilogy *House of Earth* and detail the painful, inevitable transition from traditional to modern China.

Two of her nonfiction works, biographies of her mother, *The Exile* (1936), and father, *Fighting Angel* (1936), weighed heavily with the Nobel Committee. Carie (B.'s mother Caroline) marries a missionary to China, only to discover he merely wants a housewife. Dying after years of dutiful hardship, she refuses to see her husband and regrets the wasting of her life. Andrew (B.'s father Absolom) is a dedicated missionary, avid for danger and oblivious to his family's needs.

Although the peasants of *House of Earth* come to mind whenever B.'s fiction is mentioned, many of her later novels follow the pattern set by her first—the crisis of the middle class in transition. Of these the most notable is *Pavilion of Women* (1946) where forty-year-old Madame Wu is forced from a fastidious refusal of her essential humanity to a recognition that she is a feeling human being. Her sublimated relationship with Father André, the unfrocked priest who is English tutor to her son, becomes her gateway to self-awareness; in the context of lessons in western culture, she acknowledges her existence as a person and responsibility for her inhumane treatment of dependents.

In *Peony* (1948), the clash is not with modernity but with another powerful tradition. The moribund mid-19th c. Jewish community in Kaifung is finally completely assimilated into the majority culture. *Imperial Woman* (1956) brings the clash of tradition with modernity to a climax when the "Old Buddha" is forced by political expediency to allow Westernization of her Empire.

Between 1945 and 1953, B. published five "American" novels under the name John Sedges: *The Townsman* (1945), *The Angry Wife* (1947), *The Long Love* (1949), *Bright Procession* (1952), and *Voices in the House* (1953). She chose a masculine pen name, she said, to avoid difficulties faced by women writers.

B.'s John Sedges novels, dramatic writing, children's books, and sociopolitical works are virtually forgotten, and traditional critics regard her as merely "popular." But more recently, as reviews of reprints in the *New York Times* and elsewhere indicate, critics find her work more compelling than her reputation as a merely superficial Far Eastern regionalist would.

BIBLIOGRAPHY: Doyle, P. A., *P. S. B.* (1965; rev. ed., 1980); Lipscomb, E. J., and F. E. Webb, eds., *The Several Worlds of P. S. B.* (1994); Stirling, N. B., *P. B.: A Woman in Conflict* (1983)

MARYJEAN GROSS and DALTON GROSS

BUKOWSKI, [Henry] Charles [Jr.]

b. 16 August 1920, Andernach, Germany; d. 9 March 1994, Los Angeles, California

B.'s popularity was a result of his anti-authoritarian and obstinate philosophy, which advocated all things contrary to polite and middle-class life. He was among the most cynical of American writers and a literary outsider. He shunned all literary movements, which he felt would confine his creative impulse, and he rejected American culture, which he considered facile. He choose to be fiercely independent and free of all constricting rules and regulations. He discovered his romantic utopia on Los Angeles's skid row, where he lived for a decade as a bohemian bum and where he formulated and fashioned his hardboiled literary persona and attitude. He transported his tough and outrageous views into more than sixty books of prose and poetry, which were translated into more than a dozen languages. B. remains an underground literary cult hero and is one of the most imitated of American poets.

B.'s short stories and novels are slightly modified, first-person, autobiographical narratives, which depict the tumultuous life of a hard drinking, tough talking, and working-class poet, who is satirical, ironic, romantic, and antisocial. *Notes of a Dirty Old Man* (1969) is a collection of vignettes that foreshadows B.'s picaresque novels. *Post Office* (1971) reveals his awkward and confrontational life as a postal employee. *Ham on Rye* (1982) is a memoir of B.'s childhood. *Factotum* (1985) documents the wandering of his young manhood. B.'s fictional hero and alter ego is Henry Chinaski. He is unbending, uncompromising, and original: a Dostoevskian, modern American underground man. He is a self-proclaimed coward who takes extreme pleasure in the most basic human functions: imagination, creation, defecation, copulation and intoxication. He lives in a derelict American society by choice rather than circumstance, trading normalcy and mediocrity for self development and leisure. While he is a rebel, a form of middle-aged Huck Finn, Chinaski has a strong, almost Yankee spirit. He is single-minded, hardheaded, judgmental, intolerant, self-reliant, and opportunistic. Chinaski's endless problematic predicaments make him a fascinating American antihero. Through his exploits the ridiculous in American society is exposed.

Among the many lauded collections of poetry B. published were *The Days Run Away like Wild Horses over the Hills* (1969), *Burning in Water Drowning in Flame* (1974), *Love Is a Dog from Hell* (1977), *Dangling in the Tournefortia* (1981), and *The Roominghouse Madrigals* (1988). B.'s first book of poetry was the tiny *Flower Fist and Bestial Wail* (1960), which contained only fourteen poems. For B., poetry was a record or journal of literary and philosophical maxims and insights as well as a forum from which he could critically comment upon society, art, faith, and people in general. In poetry, B. examined and developed his various propositions from various points of view and in various poetic forms. The manipulation of form was never important to B. His philosophical attitude was most important. His poetry emerges from a set of preordained artistic laws and commandments, which were the ingrained limits in which his poetic imagination functioned. B. disliked what he considered false poetry, which was communally regulated, craft-ridden, and artistically aloof from the tragic humdrum of life. As an alternative to premeditated and regulated poetry, he offered a form of naturalistic poetry that could not be separated intellectually from instinctual drives and desires. B. understood poetry to be a spontaneous act of naturalistic imagination.

In *The Last Night of the Earth Poems* (1992), the last book published before his death, B. brings into focus the themes of regeneration and rebirth and death, which were the extremes of his writing. After a lifetime of orgy in words and idea and a strictly cynical stance, B. offers several sentimental love poems. He confronts his own mortality and testifies that writing for only writing's sake was his raison dêtre. Writing for B. was a passionate activity. It aided his survival, kept death at bay, and was for him a constant spiritual rebirth. Developing and exposing his often sublimated romantic themes reveals that B. was a romantic poet engaged in the spiritual cycles of death and rebirth. As a resolution to his eventual death, B. recognized himself as a part of the cosmic whole and the poems in his last book temper the extremes that were his literary hallmarks.

BIBLIOGRAPHY: Brewer, G., *C. B.* (1997); Cherkovski, N., *Hank: The Life of C. B.* (1991); Harrison, R., *Against the American Dream: Essays on C. B.* (1994); Locklin, G., *C. B.: A Sure Bet* (1995)

                                    MICHAEL BASINSKI

BULLINS, Ed

b. 2 July 1935, Philadelphia, Pennsylvania

Though B. has written fiction, poetry, and essays, he is best known as a playwright. As a playwright, he has been described as prolific, influential, and talented. He was an important presence in the Black Arts movement of the late 1960s and early 1970s in the U.S.

B. grew up in a rough neighborhood in Philadelphia and admittedly lived the life of a street person. He served in the navy from 1952 to 1955 and in 1958 moved to California. In 1961, while a part-time student at Los Angeles City College, he started writing seriously. Several years later in San Francisco, he began writing plays because he believed that this form was the most effective for communicating with black people. Influenced by the early plays of LeRoi Jones (now Amiri BARAKA), B. nevertheless developed his own style and voice. In his plays, he writes about the black experience, but embraces what he calls a "theater of reality."

In California, B. was one of the organizers of a militant cultural-political group called Black House, which included some future leaders of the Black Panther Party. For a brief time, B. was the minister of culture for the Black Panther Party. He split with Black House because of a conflict in ideology. The artists in the group believed that art should lead to cultural awakening, whereas the revolutionaries believed in coalition with white radicals and thought that art should inspire people to militant action.

In 1967, B. joined the New Lafayette Theater, a black theater located in the Harlem section of New York City. This move proved to be important, for it was in New York that his plays became known nationally and internationally. In 1968, the New Lafayette Theater produced three one-act plays by B.: *A Son, Come Home; The Electronic Nigger;* and *Clara's Ole Man*—published in 1969 with *Goin' a Buffalo* and *In the Wine Time*. As a result, B. won the Vernon Rice Drama Desk Award for that year. In the same year, this theater premiered B.'s *In the Wine Time,* a full-length work. This play is a part of his "20th-c. cycle," which concerns the lives of a group of African Americans. Because of B.'s interest in common or ordinary folk, in his cycle of plays, he focuses on some of these people—their lifestyles and strategies for survival and happiness as they see them. Some of the characters reappear, and the plays seem to be episodes in a single text. In addition to *In the Wine Time,* the completed plays in this planned twenty full-length play cycle are *The Duplex* (1970); *In New England Winter* (1971), which received an Obie Award; *The Fabulous Miss Marie* (1971), which also was awarded an Obie; and two unpublished works, *Home Boy* (perf. 1976) and *Daddy!* (perf. 1977).

In the Wine Time, the first play in the Cycle, begins with a lyrical prologue, really Ray's short story, symbolic in nature, which tells of his almost silent love affair one summer with a mysterious young woman whom he saw each day on the Avenue. On the last day of his wine time on Derby Street, she came to tell him of her love and her going away. When he is ready, she tells him, he can come to find her. "But where?" Ray asks. She responds—"Out in the world." When he is ready to leave this place, she will be waiting. All he needs to do is search.

The major characters in the play are black, and the principals are Cliff Dawson, a failed U.S. Navy sailor, who philosophizes as he drinks cheap wine; Lou, his wife; and Ray, their nearly sixteen-year-old nephew. The action takes place on a sultry August evening in the early 1950s on Derby Street, for the most part, a short side street of a large Northern American industrial city. The Avenue and other places on Derby Street are viewed from the Dawson's front stoop. A radio blares, simultaneous monologues take place, and verbal games such as the dozens are played, the language often crude.

In the Wine Time, a slice-of-life drama, one that uses a naturalistic motif, depicts the weariness of some of the lives of black ghetto dwellers, but also depicts their dreams and hopes for a better world. Lou's father had accepted his lowly place; Cliff will not, but the future—the changes that will be meaningful—rests in the hands of Ray and his contemporaries. Through a noble act, Cliff, Ray's mentor, makes it possible for his young nephew to live so that he can forge a better world. During a night of drinking and fun, violence erupts. A filthy trick played on Ray by a friend who has stolen Ray's girlfriend leads to a fight in which the friend is killed. The violence occurs offstage. Cliff accepts the responsibility for the murder so that Ray can continue his quest for manhood.

Along with his plays of the black experience, B. also wrote black revolutionary plays. As Leslie Sanders points out, B. usually differed from other black artists in the writing of these plays. Sanders relates that B.'s "plays depicting revolution were objects of concern in themselves, and typically his plays examine the implications of both revolutionary rhetoric and physical violence." For example, in *Dialect Determinism* (1965), B. criticizes the black revolutionary movement, particularly the political opportunist and the empty rhetoric. In *Death List* (1970), Black-

woman unsuccessfully tries to persuade Blackman not to kill the sixty blacks who signed a *New York Times* statement in support of Israel. Each person on the death list has been designated an "Enemy of the Black People."

The author of numerous plays, B. has used many styles, including realism, naturalism, surrealism, satire, farce and absurdist and other avant-garde techniques. In addition to plays employing a more traditional form or variations on this form, he has written black rituals, street-theater plays, and agitprop dramas.

Overall, B. has been praised by theater critics, although some are not at ease with the structure of his plays. In 1982, Genevieve Fabre wrote that B. along with Amiri Baraka was perhaps the most important African American dramatist of the last twenty years. She adds that no other "playwright better demonstrates how drama can alternate between political commitment and ethnic expression free from the constraints of ideology." As such, B. remains one of America's finest playwrights.

BIBLIOGRAPHY: Fabre, G., *Drumbeats, Masks, and Metaphor: Contemporary Afro-American Theater* (1983); Hay, S. A., *African American Theater: A Historical and Critical Analysis* (1994); Sanders, L. C., *The Development of Black Theater in America: From Shadows to Selves* (1983)

JEANNE-MARIE A. MILLER

BULOSAN, Carlos
b. 24 November 1913, Binalonan, Philippines; d. 13 September 1956, Seattle, Washington

Among the most celebrated of Filipino American writers was B., whose poetry, short stories, and autobiographical history, *America Is in the Heart* (1946), remain vital texts for scholars of Asian American literature and class struggle alike. Known as much for his activism as for his writing, B.—who never returned to the Philippines—made the uplift of his countrymen in America his principal cause during his lifetime.

B. was one of the first Filipinos to write in English while in America, and achieved nominal fame as a writer of poems and stories. *Who's Who* listed him in 1932, only two years after his arrival in Seattle. "Freedom from Want" (1943), an essay published in the *Saturday Evening Post* and illustrated by Norman Rockwell, expressed B.'s ultimate faith in American democracy, an ideal that would alternately trouble and encourage him throughout his life. One story, "The End of the War" (1944), published in the *New Yorker,* drew charges of plagiarism. Though the claim was settled out of court, B. and his reputation suffered from the publicity. *Laughter of My Father* (1944), a collection of stories serialized in the *New Yorker,* was misinterpreted by critics as a humorous work. B. had tried satire to convey the hardship of Filipino peasant life, a convention he decided to eschew in his personal history.

Look magazine recognized *America Is in the Heart* as one of the fifty most important American books ever published. It documents the period beginning with the narrator's childhood in the Philippines through his time in the American West searching for work and organizing Filipino laborers. Though it celebrates minor triumphs, the book focuses upon the disillusionment and tremendous brutality suffered by the narrator and his acquaintances at the hands of a racist America. Perhaps to eliminate any further doubt over his disposition as a writer, B. features the injustices of an unsympathetic system, explicitly detailing the violence visited upon the narrator because of his race and union sympathies. Still, moments of kindness from strangers rescue him from total despair and also keep the narrative from turning into polemic. Critics have described the book's style as uneven—perhaps owing to B.'s belief that he was dying as he was writing it—with the author himself recognizing its fragmentary quality.

Controversy continued to follow B., as Filipino intellectuals questioned the veracity of his life account. The narrator could not possibly have experienced everything claimed, they argued: B. must have fabricated certain events to elevate his own stature. Since the author most likely appropriated the experiences of others, *America Is in the Heart* is more accurately regarded as a collective autobiography instead of as B.'s own. Still, since B. saw his writing as a means toward winning equality for all Filipino laborers, he must have felt himself bound less by convention than by the strictest need to voice their common protest. His work remains the logical introduction to Filipino American literature for all students of the field.

BIBLIOGRAPHY: Evangelista, S., *C. B. and His Poetry* (1985); Morantte, P. C., *Remembering C. B.: His Heart Affair with America* (1984); San Juan, E., Jr., *C. B. and the Imagination of the Class Struggle* (1972)

DAVID SHIH

BURKE, Kenneth

b. 5 May 1897, Pittsburgh, Pennsylvania; d. 19 November 1993, Andover, New Jersey

For much of the 20th c., one of the most formidable and provocative mavericks on the American cultural scene, B. did his most impressive work in a series of remarkable books of literary, social, and cultural

criticism beginning with *Counter-Statement* (1931). In this book, whose contents originated as early as the mid-1920s, B.'s interests are more narrowly literary than they would be later; in fact, some of the essays in the book rank among the classics of literary formalism. Yet his was from the beginning a formalism with a difference. Rather than focusing on the literary work as an autonomous aesthetic object, B. saw form as the creation and ultimate satisfaction of appetites in the auditor.

The introduction of the auditor into the equation suggests an opening to the sociology of literature, and indeed to still broader sociocultural considerations that characterize B.'s later work, although B. never abandons his interest in literature. The difference is that the literary work becomes for B. one of the most important of many forms of human action, specifically of what he comes to call "symbolic action"; B. moves beyond the formalist tendency to valorize what distinguishes literature from the rest of human behavior to a determination that literature must be seen as a part of human behavior. The implication for critical method is that the formalist tendency to bar from criticism such "extrinsic" interests as the biographical, the historical, the ethical, the political, will now be seen as an unacceptable narrowing of the critical act, which, for B., must use all that is available.

The exploration of symbolic action in all its implications that is a principal motif of B.'s work in the 1930s broadens in the 1940s and 1950s toward a system, the "dramatism" unfolded in *A Grammar of Motives* (1945) and *A Rhetoric of Motives* (1950). A related third volume, a "Symbolic of Motives," was announced but never appeared. Critics differ on whether dramatism, which would study the full range of human relations through the analogy of drama, is the fully achieved and coherent synthesis that B. was aiming for, but the effort generated more insights, revelations, and intellectual provocations than most critics produce in a lifetime.

While engaged in system-building and in applying his system to interests that ranged far beyond the "literary," in the narrow sense, B. remained a perceptive and illuminating reader of texts. His readings, however, are for the most part also exercises in an evolving critical method and are offered in part as examples of the method. A consequence is that B. is rarely in his practical criticism concerned exclusively with the uniqueness of the work before him, even though he would certainly not deny that uniqueness.

Dramatism is deeply concerned with the function of linguistic forms, including literary forms, in society at large. In the 1960s, B., while never abandoning his earlier attitude, began to place a greater emphasis on the ways in which "nonverbal" reality is determined by the verbal. B. christened this new emphasis "logology," and in *The Rhetoric of Religion: Studies in Logology* (1961) B., whose work has more than once been compared to a secularized Christianity, explores the relations of logology and theology, considering such matters as the likeness between words about words—one way of defining "logology"—and words about the Word—one way of defining "theology."

At his best B. suggested ways beyond the destructive dichotomies of criticism. He demonstrated that a sensitivity to literary form can coexist with, indeed is essential to, an understanding of the social functions of literature. He also encouraged us to "read" society with the sensitivity a fine critic brings to a literary text. We can now appreciate the degree to which he anticipated the interests and insights of structuralism and deconstruction years before either of those terms had become current, and his work has not been superseded by the later fashions. Much of B.'s placing of literature within its sociocultural context, including his emphasis on the relation of literature to power, foreshadows the concerns of the New Historicism as well. Recent commentators have noted that the B. who so eloquently and ingeniously developed the definition of form in terms of appetites of the auditor was doing reader-response criticism before there was a word for it. In its essentials, B.'s accomplishment retains its significance and relevance.

BIBLIOGRAPHY: Behr, M., *Critical Moments in the Rhetoric of B.* (1996); Brock, B. L., *B. and Contemporary European Thought* (1995); Bygrave, S., *B.: Rhetoric and Ideology* (1993); Carter, C. A., *B. and the Scapegoat Process* (1996); Henderson, G., *K. B.: Literature and Language as Symbolic Action* (1988); Kimberley, C. R., *K. B.'s Dramatism and the Popular Arts* (1982); Knox, G., *Critical Moments: K. B.'s Categories and Critiques* (1957); Simons, H., and T. Melia, eds., *The Legacy of B.* (1989); Wess, R., *B.: Rhetoric, Subjectivity, Postmodernism* (1996); White, H., and M. Bruce, eds., *Representing K. B.* (1982)

W. P. KENNEY

BURNETT, Frances Hodgson

b. 24 November 1849, Manchester, England; d. 29 October 1924, Plandome, New York

Remembered today primarily for three children's classics, B. was also a popular and prolific writer of adult fiction. The enduring popularity of *Little Lord Fauntleroy* (1886), *A Little Princess* (1905), and *The Secret Garden* (1911) has overshadowed B.'s other achievements.

The events of B.'s childhood prefigure many elements of her fiction. After her father's death, the family's financial difficulties led them to move first to a more working-class neighborhood in Manchester, then to Tennessee to live with relatives. The desire to improve the family finances led to the publication of her first story in *Godey's Lady's Book* in 1868. She continued to publish formulaic love stories in fashionable magazines in the following years.

One of B.'s earliest attempts at longer and more serious fiction was *That Lass o' Lowrie's* (1877), set in a Lancashire mining district with a pit-girl heroine. *Surly Tim and Other Stories* (1877) also used Lancashire dialect and featured working-class characters. Both sold well in England and the U.S. and won B. high praise, including comparison to Elizabeth Cleghorn Gaskell and George Eliot.

B. turned to American characters and themes with novels like *Louisiana* (1880) and *A Fair Barbarian* (1881), in which a young Nevada woman wins over her relatives in England. *Through One Administration* (1883), possibly B.'s best achievement in adult realist fiction, features a woman trapped in an unhappy marriage, painted against the background of the political life of Washington, D.C., which B. had witnessed firsthand during the early 1880s. This book, which some critics have compared to Henry JAMES's *Portrait of a Lady,* represents both the climax of B.'s efforts at REALISM and the close of that phase of her career.

The enormously successful *Little Lord Fauntleroy,* the story of an American boy heir to a British title and fortune, marked a turning point in B.'s career and established themes that would be important to her other children's fiction. *Little Lord Fauntleroy* was a best seller, a successful dramatic production, and a merchandising bonanza. Following this success, B. produced more children's fiction, most notably *A Little Princess* and *The Secret Garden.* These three landmark works share important themes: reversals of fortune, loss of family members, the formation of new family groups, and the ability of a child's innocence to reform adults.

B. also continued to write fiction for adults. Although the early efforts at realism are not as apparent in these later works, they share many features with her earlier fiction: regionalism, as in *In Connection with the De Willoughby Claim* (1899); Anglo-American relations, as in *The Shuttle* (1907); and changes of economic fortune, as in *T. Tembarom* (1913).

Although B.'s children's classics clearly deserve their reputation, her contributions to realism also deserve the attention of critics. Her career as a whole perhaps has been neglected because of the difficulty of categorizing her unusual blend of realism and ROMANCE.

BIBLIOGRAPHY: Bixler, P., *F. H. B.* (1984); Burnett, V., *The Romantick Lady* (1927); Laski, M., *Mrs. Ewing,*

Mrs. Molesworth, and Mrs. H. B. (1950); Thwaite, A., *Waiting for the Party: The Life of F. H. B., 1849–1924* (1974)

ANGELA VIETTO

BURROUGHS, Edgar Rice

b. 1 September 1875, Chicago, Illinois; d. 19 March 1950, Encino, California

B. is one of the most popular writers of the 20th c.; his work has been translated into over thirty languages, and sales of his novels exceed one hundred million copies. However, despite his success as a science fiction writer and as the creator of the Tarzan novels, critics have only recently given B the attention he deserves.

The twenty-four novels in the Tarzan cycle represent only a third of B.'s literary output, but they are largely responsible for his popularity. *Tarzan of the Apes* (1912) is the first, best, and most important of the Tarzan books. Abandoned on the coast of West Africa, Tarzan's parents, Lord Greystoke and his wife Alice, build a tree house in the jungle and wait for rescue. When they die, the infant Tarzan is adopted by Kala—an ape who has recently lost her own baby. Tarzan is raised by the apes and eventually becomes leader of the ape tribe. The plot of *Tarzan of the Apes* is typical of many B. novels; the hero overcomes numerous challenges to win the heroine. Outsiders, including Jane Porter, invade Tarzan's jungle domain. Jane must be rescued from villains—both human and animal—and Tarzan must use his strength and cunning to banish the invaders. The novel concludes with Tarzan's visit to Baltimore where he wins Jane's hand and is informed that his identity as Lord Greystoke has been confirmed. Although films have portrayed him as monosyllabic, Tarzan teaches himself to read and write English by examining books he finds in his father's tree house, and he rescues an explorer named D'Arnot who teaches him to speak French. Moreover, Tarzan is able to communicate with apes, lions, elephants, and other animals.

Themes found in the Tarzan novels—appearance versus reality, the nature of science and technology, religion, Darwinism, and eugenics—are also features of B.'s science fiction, which critics have divided into three groups, depending on the setting of the novels. There are eleven books set on Mars, five books set on Venus, and six books set at the center of the earth.

B. began his writing career with works set on Mars—*A Princess of Mars* (1912), *The God of Mars* (1913), and *The Warlord of Mars* (1913)—and the Mars books are the most representative of his science fiction. The Mars cycle details the exploits of John Carter, a Virginia gentleman who is transported to the red planet at the moment of his death in an Arizona cave. As Carter goes about rescuing heroines such as Dejah Thoris from various villains, details about Martian civilization and about numerous dead Martian cities are released. B. also uses the Mars novels to speculate about such concerns as genetic engineering and organ transplantation. Death, both of individuals and of cultures, is an important theme in the Mars novels.

B. wrote his Venus novels relatively late in his career, beginning with *Pirates of Venus* (1932), and they are considered inferior to the novels in the Mars cycle. The hero of the Venus books is Carson Napier, a rather flat character who, after arriving on the strange and sometimes hostile planet, is put to a variety of tests as he searches for Duare, Princess of Vepaja. In these novels, social corruption often leads to political corruption, and the hero must fight to overthrow evil leaders.

B. wrote the Pellucidar cycle over a period of thirty-five years, but the best of these novels, *At the Earth's Core* (1914) and *Pellucidar* (1915), came early in his career. The Pellucidar novels are based on the notion that a counterworld exists at the center of the earth. Evolution is a major theme of these stories; for instance, on earth reptiles are considered lowly, but in Pellucidar they are the ruling species.

B. was an extremely prolific writer who produced novels for more than three decades. Unfortunately, many of his works are inferior to *Tarzan of the Apes* and the early Mars novels. Because he wrote genre fiction and because he was so prolific, for many years B. was dismissed as a pulp writer who did not merit serious discussion. Recently, however, critics have begun to appreciate the inventiveness of his science fiction, and some have discovered classical Greek and Latin influences in the Tarzan books.

BIBLIOGRAPHY: Holtsmark, E. B., *E. R. B.* (1986); Holtsmark, E. B., *Tarzan and Tradition: Classical Myth in Popular Literature* (1981); Lupoff, R. A., *E. R. B.* (1968); Porges, I., *E. R. B.: The Man Who Created Tarzan* (1975)

DAVE KUHNE

BURROUGHS, William S[eward]

b. 5 February 1914, St. Louis, Missouri; d. 2 August 1997, Lawrence, Kansas

Through his association with the Beat writers and the avant-garde and from his own chronicles of drug addiction and personal tragedies, B. has achieved celebrity status as much for his eccentric lifestyle as for his innovative literature. Nonetheless, his novels and his nonfiction work continue to receive critical praise and analysis, and B. is considered by many to be one of the major writers of the 20th c. The grandson of the inventor of the Burroughs adding machine, B. attended courses at Harvard and Columbia and traveled in prewar Europe before moving in 1943 back to New York where he met Allen GINSBERG and Jack KEROUAC. Although a generation older than the young men who would later become known as the Beats, B. identified with their unconventional, antimainstream attitudes and found encouragement to begin a serious writing career. Through Ginsberg's connections, B.'s first novel, *Junkie,* was published in 1953, followed by *The Naked Lunch,* published in Paris in 1959. When Grove Press brought out an American edition entitled *Naked Lunch* in 1962, the work was prosecuted as obscene by the state of Massachusetts. By the time the Massachusetts Supreme Court declared in 1966 that the book was not obscene, *Naked Lunch* had become a notorious, widely reviewed success for B. and is still the novel most immediately associated with him.

Many of the themes, images, and stylistic devices of *Naked Lunch* first appear in *Junkie*—later published as *Junky* (1977)—the nature of addiction, the drug subculture, bizarre insect and crustacean forces, and B.'s view of time as defined by action. *Junkie* follows a traditional, chronological narrative of the events of B.'s life as an addict. *Naked Lunch* is B.'s attempt to break from this traditional form, and the theme that dominates this work as well as much of his later works—the theme of the manipulation of language and other means of control of the individual by the industrialized power complexes of the world—becomes the basis for the innovative technique and style of *Naked Lunch.* In this novel, B. established his position as the comic satirist; what many readers often miss is that B.'s works are playful and funny. In "routines," episodic sketches of a variety of characters and voices that sometimes depict graphic, almost hallucinogenic homosexual relations, B. proves the power of language to shock and, therefore, to control. *Naked Lunch* also features B.'s use of the mythology of other cultures, particularly Mayan, to develop his own private symbols for the struggle of the individual against the agents of control. While B. remains thematically well within the definition of MODERNISM in *Naked Lunch,* in later works further experiments with language and technique point to B.'s role as a transitional writer between modernism and postmodernism.

For the composition of the trilogy consisting of *The Soft Machine* (1961), *The Ticket That Exploded* (1962), and *Nova Express* (1964), B. drew from his experiments conducted with Brion Gysin concerning the selective use of the cut-up or the fold-in to generate literature. This approach rearranges the words of the text by cutting or folding the pages into sections and then reorganizes the sections to create new passages

which reveal subliminal, non-Aristotelian, interrelated realities. For *The Wild Boys* (1971), B. added film techniques, particularly the montage theory of film editing. Point of view is established by camera angle, each episode appears as a script or a scene, and each character is an actor able to slip across time and space to change identity. Many readers believe that *The Wild Boys* is B.'s most successful and perhaps most accessible novel. Humorous and imaginative, it chronicles the rise of a violent and isolated cult of young boys who wage guerrilla warfare against all that stand in their path and who ultimately destroy what remains of the existing Western power structures.

In works following *The Wild Boys,* B. draws from SCIENCE FICTION, pulp detective and adventure stories, cowboy novels, WESTERN films, and an even more eclectic use of world mythologies to continue his search for means to overthrow the clerical, political, and military powers that overwhelm and subjugate the individual. His depiction of surreal subcultures unbound by time or space have influenced the more recent generation of cyberpunk writers, notably William GIBSON. While his works have left many mainstream readers bewildered and offended, B.'s writings continue to attract literary critics and contemporary audiences. His collaboration with rock artists, his appearances in independent films and documentaries, and the production of the movie *Naked Lunch* in 1993 attest to his popularity and influence.

BIBLIOGRAPHY: Lydenberg, R., *Word Cultures: Radical Theory and Practice in W. S. B.'s Fiction* (1987); Lydenberg, R., and J. Skerl, eds., *W. S. B. at the Front: Critical Reception, 1959–1989* (1991); Morgan, T., *Literary Outlaw: The Life and Times of W. S. B.* (1988); Mottram, E., *W. B.: The Algebra of Need* (1977); Skerl, J., *W. S. B.* (1985)

LYNN RISSER

BUTLER, Robert Olen
b. 20 January 1945, Granite City, Illinois

Throughout the 1980s, B. attracted a devoted audience on the strength of his six published novels. However, by his own admission, he was a mid-level author living in Lake Charles, Louisiana, and teaching at McNeese State University. His standing was lifted considerably with the publication of his collected short stories, *A Good Scent from a Strange Mountain* (1992), which earned him the 1993 Pulitzer Prize in fiction.

B. grew up in a small, culturally diverse steel-mill town near Cahokia State Park in Illinois, the former center of a vast, ancient Indian civilization that he excavates for symbolic importance in his fiction. He has worked in the blast furnace operation at Granite

City Steel, studied theater and playwriting at North-western University, served in the army as a linguist during the Vietnam War, and from 1975 to 1985 created and edited *Energy User News,* an investigative business newspaper for industrial consumers and users of energy.

In a 1994 interview, B. revealed that the "ravishingly sensual experience" of being in Vietnam in 1971 illuminated his future to be an artist. Three of his first four novels, in fact, loosely comprise a Vietnam trilogy as Clifford Wilkes in *The Alleys of Eden* (1981), Wilson Hand in *Sun Dogs* (1982), and David Fleming in *On Distant Ground* (1985) serve together in an army intelligence unit when Hand is taken prisoner by the Viet Cong. Seeking his rescue changes their lives: Wilkes becomes a deserter, Hand dies ten years later on a mountain ledge near Alaska's North Slope, and Fleming, after being court-martialed for aiding the enemy, returns to Saigon and rescues his firstborn son in the final hours before the city's collapse. In a later novel *The Deuce* (1989), B. adopts the personae of a seventeen-year-old Amerasian, the son of a Saigon prostitute and American GI, who lives with his father in New Jersey and is coming of age in the generation immediately following the war. Vo Dinh Thanh/Tony Hatcher runs away from Point Pleasant and discovers that being a street kid in New York City has uncanny similarities to his earlier years as one of the "children of dust" in Vietnam. Unlike Mark TWAIN's Huck Finn and J. D. SALINGER's Holden Caulfield, his most famous literary predecessors, "the Deuce" searches across two cultures for his identity, and while doing so, Thanh/Tony first befriends an alcoholic Vietnam veteran and then avenges his murder. Sometimes criticized for being melodramatic, B. takes risks in the depths of human desire. His characters might fail in their initial responsibilities, but they are afforded second chances in which to redeem or honestly confront themselves. Their Vietnam experiences surpass war's absurdity and enlighten them about simple, yet life-enduring principles of decency, compassion, sacrifice, loyalty, and forgiveness.

B. probes dimensions of violence within other specific historical contexts. In *Countrymen of Bones* (1983), a university archeologist is pitted against an army physicist working for the Manhattan Project in the weeks leading to the first atomic detonation on the morning of 16 July 1945. In *Wabash* (1987), Deborah and Jeremy Cole struggle to reconnect after the death of their daughter as company thugs seek to fracture "Red" infiltration at Wabash Steel, for whom Jeremy works during the Great Depression. Although these narratives are set in America's troubled past, B. addresses contemporary issues such as rape, prejudice, blue-collar exploitation, and the threat of global nu-

clear catastrophe. As war and brutality resurrect themselves, he advocates love as a profound healing force.

B. credits his theater training for helping him to project the first-person voices in *A Good Scent from a Strange Mountain.* His Vietnamese refugees living in southwest Louisiana range from the quite young to the very old Dao, who nearing death at age one hundred is visited not only by his relatives, but also by the ghost of his former friend Ho Chi Minh. In "Mid-Autumn," a pregnant woman talks to her unborn baby girl about the young man whom she was to wed before he was killed in a battle in the mountains. In "A Trip Back," a successful businessman goes to Houston to pick up his wife's grandfather who is so lost in the past that he has no memory of her. Throughout these fifteen stories, B.'s characters reach through religion and folklore, distance and time, and the loss of country and home to "learn about the suffering that comes from desire."

They Whisper (1994), B.'s most controversial novel, is a serious literary work about human sexuality written as a stream-of-consciousness exploration into the thoughts of thirty-five year-old Ira Holloway, a public-relations man and lover of women. Ira recounts, from the age of ten to the present scene in Puerto Vallarta in 1980, all of the inner voices of women who have whispered only to him of their intimate secrets. His wife's voice is both heart-rending and frightening. Fiona was sexually abused as a child, and she believes she must return to God, bringing her husband and son with her, if she is to survive. To protect his son, John, from religious obsession, Ira stays in a marriage that demands his fullest sexual sacrifice.

B. has made his reputation by writing about the nature of love, nostalgia, kinship, and human connection. "If you're an artist," he says in *They Whisper,* "you have to live completely in your body." Whether it is set in the present or past, in Alaska or Saigon, his multilayered fiction is praised for its precision, sensual detail, and emotional clarity. Because his craft has matured in stride with his vision, B. ranks among the most imaginatively daring and lyrical novelists to emerge since the Vietnam War.

BIBLIOGRAPHY: Beidler, P. D., *Re-Writing America: Vietnam Authors in Their Generation* (1991); Steinberg, S. S., "R. O. B.," *PW* 241 (3 January 1994): 60–61

JOE NORDGREN

BYLES, MATHER

b. 15 March 1707, Boston, Massachusetts; d. 5 July 1788, Boston, Massachusetts

The grandson of Increase MATHER, B. trained for the ministry at Harvard College (A.B., 1725; M.A., 1728), moving to his living at Hollis Street Congregational Church in 1732. He was dismissed in 1776 because of his allegiance to the British. While political problems persisted, he remained in Boston out of the public eye. Various sermons had been published, showing a baroque style and elaborate artifice, and eschewing theological or political issues. B. evidences a strong Anglican tendency, and thus his children's choice of religion is understandable. What this is symptomatic of, of course, is the change in economic, social, and intellectual stratifications after the first hundred years of the Massachusetts colony. B. reflects British aristocratic culture and attitudes, and this is manifest in his poetry. He was married twice and fathered nine children, six with his first wife and three with his second, of whom only a son and two daughters survived him.

A prolific author, his prose and poetry are of a piece: he was concerned with the writing process and its results, he was aware of and influenced by other sermonists and poets, and while continuing to employ typologies, he stressed the revelation of God through nature. He had begun to publish his poetry while in college, and with Governor William Burnet and Thomas Prince was one of the writers of the *New-England Weekly Journal* (1727–41), which generally offered *Spectator*-like essays. *A Collection of Poems by Several Hands* (1744) includes besides his work poems by friends who often praise him and liken him to such authors as John Milton. *Poems on Several Occasions* (1744) makes clear his poetic derivation from Isaac Watts, Alexander Pope, James Thomson, and Milton. *A Poem on the Death of His Late Majesty, King George, of Glorious Memory, and the Succession of our Present Sovereign, King George II, to the British Throne* (1727) is in heroic couplets with Miltonic apostrophes, diction, and language; *To His Excellency Governor Belcher, on the Death of His Lady, An Epistle* (1736) and *On the Death of the Queen, A Poem. Inscribed to His Excellency Governor Belcher* (1738) iterate what has been said of taste, influence, and style.

The range of subgenre is neoclassic: the ode, the hymn, the verse epistle, the encomium, the elegy, stanzaic and nonstanzaic verse; the meters are usually the heroic couplet, at times the ballad, upon occasion blank verse. While many allusions in his writings indicate his classical education, he also records contemporary events, such as the earthquake on November 18, 1755, which gives rise to a sermon on God's "Divine Power and Anger Displayed" and his long and well-received poem *The Conflagration, Applied to that Grand Period or Catastrophe of Our World, When the Face of Nature Is to Be Changed by a Deluge of Fire, as Formerly It Was by That of Water. The God of Tempest and Earthquakes.* While his poetry is not individualis-

tic, it represents the polished verse of England as well as what was being produced by many in America. It has been pointed out, for example, that Phillis WHEATLEY's 1773 *Poems on Various Subjects, Religious and Moral* owes much to B. in the choice of literary forms, meters, language, and arrangement, while reflecting Pope's and Thomson's poetry. His "Written in Milton's *Paradise Lost*" (1774), a frequent topic, not only praises the epic by use of blank verse, invocations, language and imagery, but suggests his awareness of his limitations: "His mighty Numbers tow'r above thy Sight, / Mock thy low Musick, and elude thy Strains."

BIBLIOGRAPHY: Eaton, A. W. H., *The Famous M. B.* (1914); Franklin, V. B., ed., *M. B.'s Works* (1978)

JOHN T. SHAWCROSS

BYNNER, [Harold] Witter

b. 10 August 1881, Brooklyn, New York; d. 1 June 1968, Sante Fe, New Mexico

During his long career, between 1907 and 1960, B. produced thirty volumes of poetry and prose. Yet his name is more known for the Witter Bynner Foundation for Poetry and for the Spectra hoax, a spoof on 20th-c. literary fads like imagism and vorticism, which he perpetuated with his friend, Arthur Davidson FICKE, under the respective pseudonyms "Emanuel Morgan" and "Anne Knish." The reasons for this relative obscurity for such a prolific writer as B. are multifaceted and perhaps rising out of his unconventional views on life and art. Overshadowed throughout his lifetime by modernist giants like Ezra POUND, T. S. ELIOT, and Wallace STEVENS, B., openly homosexual, living in New Mexico, removed from literary circles found in cities, was an early champion of women's rights and of African American writers, who geared his poetry to have a definite non-Western orientation, incorporating Native American, Hispanic American, and especially Chinese literature into his own aesthetic. Yet he maintained at points of his life fascinating relationships with the writers of his generation: Stevens, W. B. Yeats, D. H. Lawrence, Henry JAMES, and Edna St. Vincent MILLAY, his Santa Fe house becoming a sort of literary salon of the American Southwest.

The zestful unconventionality of his life and worldview inevitably was expressed in his writing, which has been described with a gamut of adjectives: effusive, descriptive, non-symbolic, idealistic, irreverent, endearing, sharp, witty, intuitive, pure, outlandish, comic, eclectic, urbane, expressive, playful, democratic, laconic, dreamlike, malicious, accepting, broad, silly, unreal, and serious.

For a man who experimented with a variety of different forms—odes, plays, verse portraits, nonsense jingles, canticles, shih octaves, hoax poems, propaganda pieces, visions, confessions, dream compositions—such a mixed grab bag of responses is not so unwarranted. It suggests if nothing else a Protean and original talent.

For twenty-one-year-old B., the three great constellations in the literary heavens were Walt WHITMAN, and the British authors George Meredith and A. E. Housman. Having visited the elderly Meredith in England in 1902, B. paid homage to Whitman early on in a youthful poem bout the Mount Auburn Cemetery and then fully in his second collection, *The New World* (1915). The book is haunted by a mysterious woman named Celia, whom the poet loves and who renders the worldly sounds of everyday experience into another continent of poetry, while the Great Bard along with the unnumbered dead, spiritually entering, mediates between them a commingling of earth and heaven. B. later claimed that Celia was a real person. The poems, despite an internal cadence and rhetoric, offer, according to Richard WILBUR, a fervent but naive experiment in humanitarian vision mingled with an irregularly felt Christian faith, largely because of an unsustained technique and a static argument.

If *The New World* was overtly artificed and idealistically ambitious, *Grenstone Poems* (1917) is unassuming and direct. It offers many fine lyrics of simple self-expression. In "The Dead Loon," the poet eerily identifies his voice with that of a dead loon, equating its voiceless fate with the fate of the poet. an in "Shasta," the poet when gazing at a western landscape ponders his future work, asks for what divine experiment he would be ready to be used anew, and what figure of divinity would he conceive for himself in the gathering infinity. The poem introduces B.'s identification with the mythic locale of America, the land where he saw a place for his poet persona. This rootedness of self, a stranger, older intimacy with a place is developed in the poem, "Breath," in which the remote circumference of breath ifs the final achievement—the sighting, the harvest as well the unburdening of the self in relation to all others and all things. B.'s idea of a master poet was one who can "so use language that a whole vast sky of words seems simple as a petal . . . to condense a novel or symphony to even eight lines, the great machinery of Greek purgation gathered into a dewdrop."

In 1917, B. took his first trips to Asia, and when he returned, he met Chinese scholar Kiang Kang-hu at Berkeley, and thus commenced ten years of translating classical Tang poetry—a formidable task which reaped the *Jade Mountain* (1929). Of his translations, it has been said that they generally embodied the virtue of the original and were a groundbreaking achievement. The translation work influenced B.'s own poetry, and there are evidences of this in almost all of his later collections, beginning with The *Beloved Stranger* (1919) with the images of white phoenixes and the blue roofs of Nankow appearing in "The Wall." *A Canticle of Pan* (1920) brims over with polished imitations of Chinese poems, as well as original pieces that exude the spare suggestiveness of haiku, where the images never strike for attention, argument or explication, but rather stand brazenly alone as parts in the flow of thought. In his essay, "The Persistence of Poetry" (1929), B. argues (and he is referring specifically to the "Age of Eliot") that Western poetry, with its overcultured, jaded, self-conscious, strained intellectual meanings, is estranged from poetry's true simple source, which the Chinese poets embraced completely: the whole of expression, seldom only one portion; no departure into exaggeration or fantasy; acceptance of the world as is; abstention from superfluous comment; hard selectiveness; and perfectly colloquial language. Adopting the Chinese view, B. wants to achieve a poetry that has the beauty of frozen jade in what he called the soft English tongue.

Pins for Wings (1920) is fabulously witty departure into the art of poking fun at famous literary figures, with "E. E. Cummings" heaving much ado about the alphabet, "Harriet Monroe" as Mother Superior considering lingerie, and "Ezra Pound," a book-worm donning tights. *Caravan* (1925) in contrast is a darker collection of stark poems that develop primal, elemental themes. In "O Hunted Huntress," a figure flees a black boar while pursuing the white fawn before it too becomes black. The symbolic suggestion is that pursuit of beauty is under the risk of being overtaken by death, the primal darkness, and that the slender barbs of language, even of poetry, are useless in defense. The collection also contains a negative portrait of D. H. Lawrence, who had gone to Mexico with B., depicting the novelist as smothering in his uncouth primitivism.

Indian Earth (1929) is considered B.'s best book, and it is saturated with the local color of Chapala, Mexico, where B. had a house, and descriptions of native people and customs: the barefoot fellows who come to town to sell on "Market Day," bringing broad-woven hats, leafy baskets of cheese, oranges, limes, zarapes, and earthenware. The picture is almost Homeric in its detail and pageantry. the book also has octets or groups of octets, each focusing on a figure or a local scene or an item, like a spider web, a reed, or a calendar, each focused image a departure to other subtler realities. "In Mescala" depicts a requiem for the Spanish dead performed on a drum and a morning-glory-pipe by two old sages with Asian faces and

Indian hats in tumbled plaza. these poems show that B. was a grand surveyor of life around him.

BIBLIOGRAPHY: Kraft, J., ed., *The Works of W. B.* (5 vols., 1981); Kraft, J., *Who Is W. B.: A Biography* (1995)

H. S. YOON

BYRD, William, II

b. 28 March 1674, Westover, Virginia; d. 26 August 1744, Westover, Virginia

B. was American literature's most important Southern writer in the years preceding the American revolution. In contrast to the didactic sermons, religious treatises, and soul searching diaries that characterized the writing of his contemporaries in Puritan New England, B.'s diary and travel journals present a richly diverse and temporal view of life on an early-18th-c. Virginia plantation that is unavailable anywhere else in the literature of the period. The diary in particular covers roughly some thirty years of formative history of the region that would supply so many of the leaders of a new nation. It combines political affairs in the operation of the Virginia colony with the everyday details of plantation manners, customs, and economics.

B.'s *Secret Diary* was written intermittently, in three phases of his life. The first phase, 1709–12, followed his inheritance of Westover plantation after his father's death in 1705. The second and third phases, 1717–21 and 1734–41, were apparently interrupted by extended visits to London. If B. continued to write in his diary during the missing years, the entries have never been found. The diary, first published in 1939, has subsequently been designated "secret" because B. wrote it in a special shorthand code. Clearly he did not wish that it be published or read by anyone other than himself. His observations and introspection, though brief, are candid and unselfconscious in a manner highly atypical of an 18th-c. document intended for publication.

The entries follow a consistent pattern. B. begins with the hour he arose from bed, the classic literature he read every morning (frequently Hebrew and Greek), the meager breakfast that followed (frequently "boiled milk," occasionally "milk hot from the cow"). This is generally followed by the curious reference, "I danced my dance," a statement that puzzled scholars for many years, particularly in the work of a man given to writing in code. It is now believed to refer to some form of calisthenics. His dinner was invariably limited to one main dish, usually meat. The typical entry concludes with reference to his prayers or his omission of them, and by his thanking God for "good health, good thoughts, and good humor." Interspersed throughout this recurring pattern are brief statements that cover diverse activities, including plantation business, politics, punishing slaves, sexual activity with his wife, dreams that troubled him, and petty fits of bad temper.

His *History of the Dividing Line Run in the Year 1728,* unpublished until 1841, is a combination travel journal and official record of the Virginia Commission's survey and establishment of the dividing line between Virginia and North Carolina. It is in many ways a more interesting work, decidedly less repetitive than the *Diary.* Incidents are enlarged into anecdotes, there are extended observations on nature and topography, and his contempt for the natives of the North Carolina back country is presented with a wry and satirical humor.

Together the *Diary* and the *History* reveal the writer as two persons, fused by will and necessity into one. On his frequent trips to England and in social interaction with his contemporaries in Williamsburg, B. was the cultured, aristocratic Anglican gentleman of colonial Virginia; witty, urbane, passionate, and risque, a well-read rationalist whose library of some 3,600 volumes was generally recognized as the largest in America, with the possible exception of Cotton MATHER's. In the daily operations of Westover plantation, he was the moderate, disciplined, steadfast entrepreneur, creating, maintaining, and constantly expanding a viable commercial enterprise on the edge of the 18th-c. American wilderness. That the two aspects of his character, the cavalier gentleman and the industrious American farmer, so effectively blend together attests to the richness and diversity of his personality.

BIBLIOGRAPHY: Lockridge, K. A., *The Diary and Life of W. B. II of Virginia* (1987); Marambaud, P., *W. B. of Westover, 1674–1744* (1971); Wright, L. B., and M. Tinling, eds., *The Secret Diary of W. B. of Westover, 1709–1712* (1941)

RICHARD KEENAN

CABELL, James Branch

b. 14 April 1879, Richmond, Virginia; d. 5 May 1958, Richmond, Virginia

Best known as a writer of ROMANCE and high comedy, C. was also a genealogist, as his fictions reflect. A true Virginian, he published under his full name, acknowledging both the maternal and paternal lines of his distinguished lineage. His major life's work, the eighteen volumes of "The Biography of the Life of Manuel," portrays the life of Manuel, a swineherd who set out to make a name for himself, and the lives of Manuel's descendants. As a comic writer, C. was interested in patterns, in repetitions—hence, the appropriateness of genealogy to his work. From his lowly beginnings, Manuel eventually reigned over C.'s mythical Poictesme, and Manuel's descendants eventually migrated from medieval Poictesme to Virginia. Thus, C.'s works range over a broad canvas. Although the earliest of his novels, set in contemporary Virginia, are realistic, the most distinguished are set in Poictesme and are more fantasy than novel. Emerging from C.'s skillful blending of myth and fairy tales, they reveal his tendency to make dream and individual consciousness the most important realities.

The most famous character in Manuel's line in Jurgen. Through him, C. profoundly influenced the Southern Literary Renaissance, for *Jurgen* (1919) was a pronounced departure not only from C.'s earlier work, but from the prevailing standards both in the South and in the nation. In a body restored to the full vigor of youth, forty-year-old Jurgen wanders Odysseus-like in pursuit of his missing wife Lisa, encountering along the way the women of his past as well as numerous enchantresses of mythology. With Rabelaisian zest, C. balances parody and irony as he narrates Jurgen's picaresque journey.

Before *Jurgen,* C.'s reputation was modest. But on January 14, 1920, John Sumner, executive secretary for the New York Society for the Suppression of Vice, assured C. of national attention by pressing charges against Guy Holt of McBride's for publishing an obscene book. In October 1922 the work was exonerated in a famous trial important to freedom of expression in America. Meanwhile, a host of defenders were discovering C. One of his most vocal defenders was H. L. MENCKEN. With Mencken, C. became one of the chief symbols for rebellion against the genteel tradition and for new directions in life and art.

Although counted an iconoclast, C. did not write primarily from that motive. Essentially a private person, he was, like Manuel, intent on following his own destiny, creating books as fine as he could make them, his eye on an ideal audience—readers as demanding as himself. He was a meticulous stylist, though he would be faulted as an aesthete in the 1930s, a period that saw his reputation wane dramatically.

Meanwhile, C. followed *Jurgen* with the major romances on which his reputation chiefly rests: *Figures of Earth* (1921), *The High Place* (1923), *The Silver Stallion* (1926), and *Something about Eve* (1927). *Figures of Earth* narrates the life and death of Manual the Swineherd who eventually ruled Poictesme. *The Silver Stallion,* in part a parody of the Acts of the Apostles, recounts the lives of Manuel's roundtable following his death: Manuel achieves apotheosis as Manuel the Redeemer. Florian de Puysange, protagonist of *The High Place,* is a 17th-c. descendant of Manuel living a licentious life in southern France, but searching for perfect beauty in the Princess Melior. In *Something about Eve* the protagonist is Gerald Musgrave, a descendant of Manuel who lives in early-19th-c. Virginia. A poet, Gerald protests naturalistic reductionism and looks for beauty and meaning in poetry, though he, too, makes his compromises. In general, C.'s protagonists, in seeking to control their destinies and affirm their importance, consider three approaches or attitudes to life: the Chivalric (man is a worshiping creature who serves his Maker through service to a beautiful woman); the Gallant (doubtful of the ultimate reality behind Chivalry, man lives for the moment, playing pleasantly with many women); the Poetic (man finds beauty and meaning in poetry, living life "as if" he can find permanent meanings). C. defines these attitudes in *Beyond Life* (1919), the fullest statement of his artistic credo.

For the Storisende Edition (1927–30), C. revised all of his work, modifying his earlier Virginia novels to fit the scheme of the "Biography" and incorporating as well his short fictions and poetry. Because the "Biography" is arranged chronologically according to the time it portrays, C.'s weaker work comes at the last volumes of the Storisende Edition. The best of the works dealing with contemporary Virginia, as C. and his critics have agreed, is *The Cream of the Jest* (1917). Felix Kennaston, the protagonist and an author, discovers through a magic talisman (in reality the lid of his wife's cold cream jar) that his dream life can be immeasurably more satisfying than the humdrum of his daily life, enabling him to reside in mythic Poictesme and to visit with personages who helped mold the history of the Western world. In writing *The Cream of the Jest,* C. discovered his *métier.*

Following completion of the "Biography," C. undertook other ambitious work. The trilogy "The Nightmare Has Triplets" is concerned with the dream life of a Virginia novelist. Similar to James Joyce's *Finnegans Wake, Smirt* (1934), *Smith* (1935), and *Smire* (1937) attempt to render with Zolaesque completeness nocturnal dream life. The trilogy "Heirs and Assigns" deals with political machinations and fierce competition for power. *Hamlet Had an Uncle* (1940), *The King Was in His Counting House* (1938), and *The First Gentleman of America* (1942) are set in diverse times and countries; through them C. was commenting on the darker side of human nature that had engulfed the world in war. "It Happened in Florida," the last of C.'s trilogies to include fictions, is lighter in spirit, touching on the lore of Florida (where the Cabells wintered) and echoing C.'s earlier explorations of man's questing, restless spirit. C. coauthored the first book of that trilogy, *The St. Johns* (1943), with A. J. Hanna for the Rivers of America Series. The fictional volumes were C.'s own: *There Were Two Pirates* (1946) and *The Devil's Own Dear Son* (1949).

C. also wrote a memorable autobiographical trilogy, "Virginians are Various," emphasizing his Southern roots and revealing much about his private nature: *Let Me Lie: Being in the Main an Ethnological Account of the Remarkable Commonwealth of Virginia and the Making of Its History* (1947), *Quiet, Please* (1952), and *As I Remember It: Some Epilogues in Recollection* (1955). The pun of the first title underscores his essential playfulness, the last his tentativeness—his willingness to play with possibilities, as he does throughout his fictions. In *Some of Us* (1930) C. took a look at literary figures of the 1920s, creating epitaphs for writers like himself who no longer seemed of the moment. C.'s skills as essayist are also richly demonstrated in the trilogy "Their Lives and Letters": *These Restless Heads* (1932), *Special Delivery* (1933), and *Ladies and Gentlemen* (1934). In the first, and best, of these, C. identifies with an aging Prospero, more concerned with his magic than with the politics of this world. In the second, C. presents a series of letters he would like to have sent to correspondents, but did not. In *Ladies and Gentlemen* C. writes letters to real and imaginary dead persons, including his own Jurgen.

Sometimes too narrowly identified with *Jurgen,* C. is a writer with impressive range. Edmund WILSON's important essay "The J. B. C. Case Reopened" in the *New Yorker* (April 21, 1956) called attention to C.'s distinction, then too easily overlooked. Although C. has not again achieved the position of dominance that he held in the 1920s, scholars and readers have increasingly paid attention to his works, both for their importance to that period and for their own merits.

BIBLIOGRAPHY: Davis, J. L., *J. B. C.* (1962); Inge, M., and E. MacDonald, *J. B. C.: Centennial Essays* (1983); MacDonald, E., *J. B. C. and Richmond-in-Virginia* (1993); Mencken, H. L., *J. B. C.* (1927); Riemer, J., *From Satire to Subversion: The Fantasies of J. B. C.* (1989); Tarrant, D., *J. B. C.: The Dream and the Reality* (1967); Van Doren, C., *J. B. C.* (1932); Wells, A. R., *Jesting Moses: A Study in Cabellian Comedy* (1962)

JOSEPH M. FLORA

CABLE, George Washington

b. 12 October 1844, New Orleans, Louisiana; d. 31 January 1925, St. Petersburg, Florida

C. is often identified as a local color writer who mined the picturesque qualities of his native New Orleans to produce a few exotic short stories and one significant novel, *The Grandissimes* (1880). Typical of most of the local color writing of his day, C.'s early fiction has thinly romantic plots, flat characters and rich texture—abundant with accurate renditions of Creole, Black and other dialects, with the variety of regional character types, with the details of Louisiana history and folkways and with vivid images of bayou and delta landscapes, of balconies, shuttered windows and iron grill-work. Even his style, a whimsical mix of intimacy and irony, of luxuriant description and sometimes spare, oblique, mystifying narration, seems part of the milieu. However, C.'s best work also evidences his strong moral and social conscience, and, thus, in his fidelity to social and historical detail, especially in his honest treatment of the themes of racial injustice, violence, miscegenation, and caste, C. is recognized as one of the first Southern realists.

C.'s ability to write critically about the South was due partly to his being enough southerner to understand and care for the region, but enough northerner in sensibility to question some of its most cherished values. Born in New Orleans, his father a native Virginian and his mother an Indianian descended from New Englanders, C. supported the Southern cause by enlisting in the Confederate army. Later, reasoning from a careful reading of the Declaration of Independence, the Constitution, and the Bible, he rejected the conservative Southern argument on race and defended the freedman's claim to equal rights. Concern with the wrongs of slavery and the plight of blacks in the post–Civil War South not only figured in his early fiction, but also appeared increasingly in a number of periodical essays, most notably "The Freedman's Case in Equity" (1885). C.'s forthright arguments on race may have endeared him to some in the North, such as William Dean HOWELLS and Samuel Langhorne CLEMENS who joined with C. in a celebrated 1884 reading tour—but his views also helped alienate him from many of his friends and neighbors in the South. In 1885, he moved his family to Northampton, Massachusetts, where for a time he continued his involvement in various public issues and wrote and published fiction into the second decade of the twentieth c.

The group of stories that first appeared in the pages of *Scribner's Monthly* in the 1870s and were collected as *Old Creole Days* (1879), including the novelette, "Madame Delphine," in editions after 1883, are notable for their artistry in evoking the atmosphere of early 19th-c. New Orleans. In several of the tales, C. uses this atmosphere to establish themes or suggest features of Creole culture and character: the Creole's ancestral pride, their resistance to change, their muffled pasts are figured in signs of architectural decay and ornamental splendor and the exclusiveness and mystery of walled gardens, closed shutters and overhanging balconies. While mostly melodramatic or sentimental in treatment, the stories do involve such serious social themes as miscegenation and the culture conflict between the Creoles and the new immigrant populations. Thus, in both "Madame Delphine" and "'Tite Poulette" quadroon mothers are forced to deny their maternity so that their daughters may marry white gentlemen. The theme of culture conflict appears most interestingly in "Jean-ah Poquelin," in which an old Creole indigo planter and slave trader, somewhat like William FAULKNER's Emily Grierson, becomes an object of mystery, fear, hatred and some veneration to his neighbors in the community by living proudly and fiercely alone in a grand house, surrounded by swamps, at the edge of town. The community's growth and civic improvements drain the swamp and break down his isolation, until at his death the mystery of his life is exposed: the younger brother the community had supposed dead, possibly killed by Jean-ah, is a leper living in the house, protected by Jean-ah's isolation. Perhaps the strongest of the stories, "Jean-ah Poquelin" ends like others on a sentimental note, and the moral-thematic issues raised by Jean-ah's slave trading and the *Américain* community's identity with progress are never resolved.

In *The Grandissimes,* C. again utilizes picturesque settings and romantic characterizations, especially the faithful transcription of dialect, to create the atmosphere of New Orleans around the time of the 1803 Louisiana Purchase. The sense of mystery, of a closed, insular world with dark secrets, ancient myths and legends behind the walls and shutters, is heightened and deepened by the narrative technique in which main events are presented in glimpses and broken pieces to Joseph Frowenfeld, an American of German ancestry and recent immigrant to New Orleans. As a man of science and an outsider to the Creole past and culture, Frowenfeld is a suitable center of consciousness, eager to learn and make sense of his new environment, but able also to evaluate it critically. The romantic main plot centers on the love tribulations of Honoré Grandissime and Aurora Nancanou, the most attractive and noble representatives of two feuding aristocratic families. However, the more important thematic conflict is between the old Creole and new American cultures, or, by implication, between the hold of the past and the need for change in the post–Civil War South.

The penalty of the Creoles's resistance to change, their perversely clinging to outworn codes of honor, to ancestral loyalties, to rigid systems of racial exclusion and caste, is partly measured in the negative portrayal of such characters as the family patriarch, Agricola Fusilier. It is measured more significantly in their clinging also to an outworn economic system that threatens to ruin them. Thus, Honoré's attempts to rescue the failing Grandissime fortunes through progressive business enterprise are met with the family's suspicion and hostility. The most serious barrier to change, however, is not economics, but race, "The shadow of the Ethiopian" that Honore agrees "blanches . . . ow whole civilization." The mistreatment of such characters as Clemence and Palmyre depicts some of the injustices of slavery, and their anger and hatred toward their oppressors, whether hidden and insidious or open and murderous, provides a measure of the consequences. The story of Bras-

Coupé, an African prince and Palmyre's husband, who is beaten, hamstrung, and killed because he refuses to work as a slave, seems almost an archetype of the wrongs C. is indicting. A more complex wrong, and more germane to the time of the novel's publication, is the situation of Honoré Grandissime's half brother, Honoré *f. m. c.* (free man of color), who, despite his refinement, Paris education, property holdings and birthright as a Grandissime, is driven into a shadowy, marginal existence by the limits of his race and caste.

In *Dr. Sevier* (1884) and *John March, Southerner* (1894), C. continued to address social and political issues of the post reconstruction South, but both novels lack the rich evocation of history and milieu in C.'s earlier fiction and, therefore, seem stiff and preachy. "The Haunted House in Royal Street," collected in *Strange True Stories of Louisiana* (1889), recounts effectively two separate incidents of racial injustice linked to a well-known landmark in the Vieux Carrè. It offers one of C.'s most succinct indictments of both the "peculiar institution" and segregation. Also, because of their moral and rational lucidity, his essays on civil rights collected in *The Silent South* (1885; rev. ed., 1889) and *The Negro Question* (1890) remain as powerful and relevant critiques of America's history of race relations. These and other social concerns appear in varying degrees in C.'s later work, but in ways that either seem dated or are diminished in significance by the primary concern with romance. Only in *The Grandissimes* did C. create a satisfying artistic whole by developing his social themes through a convincing and fully rendered sense of time and place.

BIBLIOGRAPHY: Butcher, P., *G. W. C.: The Northampton Years* (1959); Cleman, J., *G. W. C. Revisited* (1996); Ekström, K., *G. W. C.: A Study of His Early Life and Work* (1950); Petry, A. H., *A Genius in His Way: The Art of C.'s "Old Creole Days"* (1988); Rubin, L. D., Jr., *G. W. C.: The Life and Times of a Southern Heretic* (1969); Turner, A., *Critical Essays on G. W. C.* (1980); Turner, A., *G. W. C.: A Biography* (1956)

JOHN LAWRENCE CLEMAN

CAIN, James M[allahan]

b. 1 July 1892, Annapolis, Maryland; d. 27 October 1977, University Park, Maryland

In the words of novelist-critic David Madden, C. was "the twenty-minute egg of the hardboiled school." C.'s seventeen novels are the toughest of the "tough-guy" crime fiction, modeled stylistically on Ernest HEMINGWAY, that flourished in the 1930s and 1940s. C. turned to fiction in his forties after a career in journalism,

notably as an editorial writer on the *New York World* and as a contributor to early issues of the *American Mercury* and the *New Yorker*. He lived in Hollywood from 1931 to 1947, the period when he wrote his best novels. He was unsuccessful as a scriptwriter but saw three classic movies made from his works—*The Postman Always Rings Twice* (1934), filmed in 1946, *Mildred Pierce* (1941), filmed in 1945, and *Double Indemnity* (1943), filmed in 1944. Eventually, nine of his novels were filmed.

The success of C.'s novels, in both media, derives from their strong plots, moving toward inevitable fatality. Sex is the driving force, usually the perverse relationship of two archetypal American figures: a tough-talking loner and a beautiful, ruthless seductress. In *The Postman Always Rings Twice*, a drifter, Frank Chambers, conspires with Cora Papadakis to murder her husband, owner of a gas station and lunchroom; in *Double Indemnity*, insurance salesman Walter Huff is seduced by Phyllis Nirdlinger into a plot to murder her husband for money. In both novels, the murderous plans succeed, but the destructive passion—what C. called the "love rack"—leads the guilty lovers to destroy each other. Fate is most perverse in *The Postman Always Rings Twice*, where Frank is to be executed for Cora's murder—which was in fact accidental. *Serenade* (1937) presents C.'s sexual themes at their most perverse: Jack Sharp, an opera singer, loses his voice after homosexual advances by his conductor. Jack becomes involved with Juana, a Mexican Aztec prostitute, who ends up murdering the conductor; having witnessed this, Jack is once again unable to sing. The female characters in these novels are caricatures, but in *Mildred Pierce*, C. depicted with insight the career of a suburban housewife who, driven by financial need and a weak husband, works and schemes her way to wealth, only to lose almost everything because of a destructive relationship with the daughter she sought to put forward in the world.

C.'s settings capture the drab suburban world of America during the Great Depression. His plots and characterizations reflect the anomie and fatalism of middle-and working-class Americans during those years. And his style is powerful in its spare, stark qualities. His successful novels are all written in the first person. His narrators and characters speak a terse, unaffected language punctuated by bizarre outbursts.

C.'s best writing was done in California, before World War II. In 1947, he returned to his native Maryland, where he continued to publish until the year before his death. C. has had many admirers among his fellow writers, but his critical reputation has been modest, largely because he focused his efforts on a limited, highly stylized sub-genre. The very starkness of his writing has kept it from aging, however, and his best novels are perennially popular with readers.

BIBLIOGRAPHY: Hoopes, R., *C.* (1982); Madden, D., *C.'s Craft* (1985); Madden, D., *J. M. C.* (1970)

GLEN M. JOHNSON

CALDWELL, Erskine

b. 17 December 1903, Newman, Cowetta County, Georgia; d. 11 April 1987, Paradise Valley, Arizona

The C. canon includes twenty seven novels/novellas, nine collections of stories, and eleven works of nonfiction. Receiving strong critical approval early in his career from distinguished critics like Malcolm COWLEY, Kenneth BURKE, and Joseph Wood Krutch, C. is today regarded as a writer of limited appeal whose fame rests primarily on two novels, *Tobacco Road* (1922) and *God's Little Acre* (1933).

The author's milieu is distinctly Southern, rooted, by and large, in the Wrens, Georgia, area thirty-five miles south of Augusta. It was just outside Wrens that C. became familiar with the "tobacco roads" where hogsheads of tobacco were rolled down to the Savannah River and where so many impoverished tenant farmers, the models for his fiction, lived. Despite what seems a love of Southern life and people, C., as noted by Wayne B. Mixon, was out of step with the most influential school of Southern literary thought, the AGRARIANS, who felt he wrote about "people who did not fit into their schema of a pastoral Southern whose values were nobler than those of a grasping North."

C.'s portrayal of Southern poverty from a liberal point of view, however, is one of the great strengths of his fiction. His philosophic determinism includes an emphasis on sex in his comic moments and the tragic or near-tragic implications of poverty manifest in the grotesqueries of pellagra, harelips, voyeurism, and impotence. Often, the earth serves as metaphor or symbol for his men and women, both clearly exhausted. In the social justice views of his two novels of rural America, C. fuses his knowledge of both Freud and Marx into a dark, relentless view of Southern humanity.

Sociologically, the motivation for the overwhelming poverty of *Tobacco Road* recalls, in large part, C.'s career as lecturer at the New School for Social Research in New York. Behind his fictional narrative lies a keen interest in unionization, wage scales, and collective bargaining. C.'s best known, his most successful comic grotesques are Jeter Lester in *Tobacco Road* and Ty Ty Walden in *God's Little Acre,* both exponents for C.'s call to reform.

The curious intermingling of the tragic and the comic in the former novel creates highly effective rhetorical tension. Too poor during the Depression to buy seed and fertilizer to bring life to his sterile farm, Jeeter Lester finds little comfort, on the other hand, in his sixteen-year-old hare-lipped daughter Ellie May or his eighteen-year-old married son Dude. Both Jeeter and his wife Ada are consumed in the fires of their own ignorance: the flames he ignites to burn over his own fields by day ignite by night to destroy him and his family. The conflagration symbolizes both the dehumanization of man and a wasteland of modern inertia and ignorance.

Ty Ty Walden, an obsessive poor white, digs for gold for fifteen years on his farm, accelerating the devastating sterilization of his own earth. *God's Little Acre* reveals a strong theme of castration and effective symbolic primitive fertility rites. After Will, for example, sleeps with his sister-in-law, he turns on the power at the local mill, which has remained idle by labor disputes and strikes.

Both *Trouble in July* (1940) and *Tragic Ground* (1944) display the author's deep interest in social justice. The sheriff in *Trouble in July* ignores a lynching in order to hold on to his job and apartment above the jail. *Tragic Ground* moves to an urban shanty town on the Gulf coast and is sharply critical of the government for luring the rural poor to work in a munitions plant and then closing the plant down to leave the employees in poverty.

BIBLIOGRAPHY: Arnold, E. T., ed., *E. C. Reconsidered* (1990); Cook, S. J., *E. C. and the Fiction of Poverty: The Flesh and the Spirit* (1991); Devlin, J. E., *E. C.* (1984); MacDonald, S., ed., *Critical Essays on E. C.* (1981); Miller, D. B., *E. C.* (1995); Mixon, W. B., *The People's Writer* (1995)

GEORGE LONGEST

CALISHER, Hortense

b. 20 December 1911, New York City

Although C. wrote no fiction until she was almost forty, she has subsequently published six collections of novellas and short stories and twelve novels. Four of her stories have won O. Henry prizes, and two books have received nominations for the National Book Award. Highly varied in content but always complex in style and intellectually challenging, her work has provoked mixed reviews.

In the preface to her *Collected Stories* (1975), C. defines the short story as "an apocalypse, served in a very small cup." Such a description shows her proclivity for dramatic psychological revelation within a compact and well-crafted narrative. Many of C.'s early stories are autobiographical. Her father was a kindly Southern gentleman and her mother a demanding European immigrant. C. grew up within upper middle-class Jewish society in New York City and later studied English and philosophy at Barnard. Her stories about the Elkin family mirror her own urban coming of age. C. affirms that both Hester and Kinny Elkin are manifestations of herself as they confront adult sexuality in "The Pool of Narcissus" or the death of a relative in "A Box of Ginger." Critics have also praised the Elkin family stories as elegant miniatures of social history—revealing glimpses of one particular melting-pot family.

Although rites of passage are a persistent concern in C.'s fiction, several less obviously autobiographical stories explore other significant themes. The title story of her first collection, "In the Absence of Angels," dramatizes the conflict between art and ideology after a totalitarian power has conquered the U.S. "The Scream on Fifty-Seventh Street" reveals the horrible isolation of modern urban life.

Less favorably received than C.'s short stories, her novels also focus on moments of insight and personal growth. In C.'s first novel, *False Entry* (1961), a middle-aged encyclopedia compiler tries to narrate the chaotic events of his past. The false entry of the title refers to his peripheral involvement in the lives of others, but in the act of writing he establishes a real identity that permits true entry into the life of Ruth Mannix, the woman he loves. *The New Yorkers* (1969) is a companion novel that reveals the history of Ruth. Having murdered her mother in an act of adultery, Ruth grows up in the company of an odd assortment of misfits whose individual stories inflate and complicate her own. The novella *Tale for the Mirror* (1962) focuses on a lawyer who in the process of exposing a fake doctor begins to comprehend his own fraudulence. *Textures of Life* (1963) is a more conventional novel about a rebellious couple who grow to appreciate the commonplace comforts of marriage and parenthood.

C. has proclaimed herself a feminist, and several works offer sensitive treatment of the problems of women. In the novella *The Railway Police* (1966), a middle-aged social worker flaunts traditional expectations for women by publicly displaying her baldness. *On Keeping Women* (1977) gives voice to a wife and mother of four who lies naked on the bank of the Hudson River and tries to discover meaning in the many tasks of women that society fails to value.

Critics have categorized two of C.'s novels as SCI-ENCE FICTION, but she rejects this label. *Journal from Ellipsia* (1965) does portray an alternate world, but C. regards the book as a social satire in the tradition of Samuel Butler's *Erewhon* and Jonathan Swift's *Gulliver's Travels*. When a young anthropologist named Janice Jamison goes to a remote star to escape messy emotions, C. uses this otherworldly venue as a means of satirizing contemporary male-female relationships and portraying human displacement in an era of science. A later novel, *Mysteries of Motion* (1983), depicts the expedition of the first all-civilian crew to inhabit a space station. C.'s main concern as a self-proclaimed humanist is not so much the mysteries of science as the moral implications of such a dramatic change in perspective.

Critics have compared C. to writers as diverse as Franz Kafka and Henry JAMES. Her characters are frequently offbeat, but they remain psychologically engaging. C.'s detractors find her style excessive and cryptic, but her adherents see it as an apt vehicle for her explorations of complex social and philosophical questions.

BIBLIOGRAPHY: Snodgrass, K., "Coming Down from the Heights: Three Novels by H. C.," *TSLL* 31 (Winter 1989): 554–69; Snodgrass, K., *The Fiction of H. C.* (1993)

ALBERT WILHELM

CANADA

The line between Canadian and American identity is often a blurred one—much to the dismay of our neighbors to the north, especially if they perceive insensitivity or indifference on the part of those from the south. In the U.S., the feeling often seems to be that if you speak, act, and look like us, then you must be one of us. These are feelings that fail to take into account that there is a different culture to the north, in a land that specifically chose two hundred years ago not to break away from the mother country. Nonetheless, the list of those born in Canada but absorbed into American culture is seemingly endless—from "America's sweetheart," the silent film actress Mary Pickford, to the Nobel laureate in literature Saul BELLOW. It is more than likely that unless Canadians identify themselves as Canadians on a regular basis, then they are considered by many to be Americans.

This state of affairs obviously is not a recent one. Certain citizens on both sides of the border are descended from the same European founding nations, and in earlier times some from English-and French-speaking groups roamed throughout North America. French names sprinkled across the maps—Dubuque, Pierre, Coeur d'Alene, Des Moines, Detroit, Saint Louis, Terre Haute, Versailles—remind us of the French presence of yesteryear and help explain why

French Canadians could feel at ease in certain centers of the U.S.—writers such as Pamphile Lemay and Louis Fréchette in Chicago, for example, and Honoré Beaugrand, in New Orleans, St. Louis, and Fall River, Massachusetts. In addition, many journalists moved to New England in the 19th and early 20th cs. to be leading spirits behind French-language newspapers, Ferdinand Gagnon who founded Worcester's *Le Travailleur* being one of many. Although such centers no longer are prominently Francophone, the closeness to the border has often been a sufficient welcome—Calixa Lavallée, the composer of "O Canada," lived in Boston, as did Louis Dantin, the poet, novelist, and literary critic. Olivar Asselin, the essayist, studied in Rimouski and then Fall River, where he began his career in journalism. He joined the U.S. Army and became an American citizen, but eventually returned to Canada and regained his Canadian citizenship.

The reverse type of situation also occurred: Jules-Paul Tardivel, born in Covington, Kentucky, went to Quebec to learn French in 1868, became a journalist and promoter of French Canadian nationalism, and remained in Canada for the rest of his life. Ironically, his only novel, *Pour la patrie* (1895), takes place in 1995 and discusses political tensions between Anglophones and Francophones. But proximity need no longer be a prerequisite, as can be seen in Gaëtan Brulotte, residing in Florida, for example, and the visits of such writers as Jacques Godbout and Jacques Poulin in California, as reflected in their novels, *Une histoire américaine* (1986) and *Volkswagen Blues* (1984). In an earlier era, when immigration was easier, many Francophones crossed over to neighboring states; indeed, hundreds of thousands of them came to New England in the second half of the 19th c. and the beginning of 20th. Métis leader and writer Louis Riel is an example of one of many who moved from one country to the other—born in the Northwest Territories, educated in Montreal, lived in Montana, established American citizenship in 1883, died in Regina. One famous American writer from this group, born in Massachusetts, Jack KEROUAC, spoke only French until he attended school. Many Quebeckers see him as one of their own who made good in the U.S. by, among other things, living North American adventures in the spirit of the *coureur de bois*.

The same situation obviously obtained, and on an even grander scale, for Anglophones: Thomas D'Arcy McGee worked as a journalist for a number of years in the U.S. before moving on to Montreal; Mary Anne Madden Sadlier, of Irish origin, promoted Catholicism and Irish culture in North America, living first in the U.S. and then in Canada; Edward William Thompson, the author of *Old Man Savarin Stories: Tales of Canada and Canadians* (1895; rev. ed., 1917), fought for the Union during the Civil War, and worked in Boston for ten years before returning to Canada; Bliss Carman, one of Canada's most revered poets, went to Harvard in the 1880s and remained in New England a good number of years until the end of his life; Merrill Denison, one of Canada's first important playwrights, was born in Detroit because his mother went there to give birth, wanting him to be born in a republic. He remained a U.S. citizen but worked on both sides of the border all his life. Ernest Thompson Seton, who wrote many books on animals, including *Wild Animals I Have Known* (1898), often worked in New York in the 1880s and 1890s and finally settled in New Mexico, becoming an American citizen in 1931. Norman Duncan, who wrote many stories about Newfoundland, lived and worked in New York and became a professor of rhetoric in Pennsylvania; Martha Ostenso, born in Norway, the author of *Wild Geese* (1925), lived on both sides of the border, from 1915 to 1921 in Manitoba, but in the U.S. from 1929 on; Margaret Marshall Saunders, whose *Beautiful Joe: The Autobiography of a Dog* (1893), was the first book by a Canadian author to sell over a million copies, spent many years in the U.S. before going to Toronto permanently; Charles G. D. Roberts, the writer of animal stories, lived in New York for many years before settling in Toronto; John Coulter, Belfast-born, worked for CBS in New York before becoming successful in Canada with his play *Riel* (1962); Brian Moore, the Belfast-born author who became a Canadian citizen, the author of *The Great Victorian Collection* (1975) and *Black Robe* (1985) among other works, relocated to California; and more recently, Bruce McCall, who has been attached to the *New Yorker,* published his autobiography, *Thin Ice, Coming of Age in Canada* (1997), in which he discusses becoming a U.S. citizen..

When artists from both countries find themselves living side by side abroad, the national distinction can be difficult to make. For example, Canadians Morley Callaghan and John Glassco lived in Paris at the same time as Ernest HEMINGWAY and F. Scott FITZGERALD. When they work for the same groups (Hemingway for a Toronto newspaper, for example), publish in the same language, on similar topics, in the same magazines or with the same publishers, it becomes increasingly difficult to keep national identities separate. Callaghan, for example, published his first novel, *Strange Fugitive* (1928), and his first collection of short stories, *A Native Argosy* (1929), in New York, and subsequently published in the *New Yorker, Atlantic Monthly,* and *Esquire.* The same could be said of Mavis Gallant, born in Montreal, who has chosen to live in Paris for decades, but who has published many of her works in the *New Yorker.*

In academic circles, there is a constant interchange, a blurring of the categories of Canadian and American. Canadian authors Gérard Bessette taught at Duquesne, Hubert Aquin at SUNY Buffalo, Paul Morin at Smith College and the University of Minnesota, Robert Choquette at Smith College, Arthur J. M. Smith, the poet and compiler of *The Oxford Book of Canadian Verse* (1960) and *Modern Canadian Verse* (1967), at Michigan State, Robert Kroetsch at SUNY Binghampton, Margaret Atwood at the University of Alabama, Michael Ondaatje—made famous recently for his Booker Prize-winning *The English Patient,* but who derived early success for his book on an "American" topic, *The Collected Works of Billy the Kid* (1970)—at the University of Hawai'i and Brown. Marshall McLuhan, author of *The Medium is the Massage* (1961) and *Gutenberg Galaxy* (1962), at the University of Wisconsin and the University of St. Louis before continuing his career at St. Michael's College, University of Toronto. And of course numerous Canadians have pursued studies at American institutions of higher learning: Stephen Leacock at the University of Chicago; Philip Child, author of the *Village of Souls* (1933), at Harvard; Louis Dudek at Columbia; Hugh MacLennan, the author of *Two Solitudes* (1945) who married an American writer, Dorothy Duncan, at Princeton; and Jack Ludwig at UCLA.

In certain very popular areas of literature, Canadians have been successful throughout all of North America: Anna Leonowens, whose *The English Governess at the Siamese Court* (1870), written while she taught in Staten Island, is the basis for *Anna and the King of Siam;* Lucy Maud Montgomery for her *Anne of Green Gables* (1908); Arthur Stringer is behind the *Perils of Pauline;* Robert Service,"the poet of the Yukon," is known for his colorful poems such as "The Cremation of Sam McGee"; Leslie McFarlane wrote a number of Hardy Boys books; Arthur Hailey has achieved celebrity for *Hotel* (1965) and *Airport* (1968); and of course Harlequin romances are a Canadian product.

Similarly, many Americans have had experiences in Canada, some, like Joyce Carol OATES went and came back, while others living and writing in Canada have published works which grow out of their American experiences: Jane Rule, author of such works as *A Hot-Eyed Moderate* (1986) known for her involvement with lesbian topics, was born in New Jersey and lived in the U.S. until moving to Canada in 1956 and becoming a Canadian citizen; Leon Rooke, novelist and writer of short stories, was brought up and educated in North Carolina, moved to British Columbia in 1969, and has pursued his career in Canada; Audrey Thomas, whose book *Songs My Mother Taught Me* (1973) gives evidence of her Binghampton, New York

background, has taught at different Canadian universities; and Carol Shields, author of the 1995 Pulitzer Prize-winning novel *The Stone Diaries,* received an M.A. from the University of Ottawa and has taught at the Universities of Ottawa, British Columbia, and Manitoba.

The Iowa Writers' Workshop has been important for many Canadian writers: Robert Harlow, Robert Kroetsch, W. P. KINSELLA, Dave Godfrey, Clark Blaise, and Bharati MUKHERJEE. Kinsella has written on topics such as baseball, *Shoeless Joe Jackson Comes to Iowa,* a collection of stories, and the novel *Shoeless Joe,* which inspired the film *Field of Dreams.* Blaise and Mukherjee illustrate how a "Canadian" background can fulfill itself in the U.S.. In his books, the collection of stories in *A North American Education* (1973) and his novel *Lunar Attractions* (1979), among others, Blaise describes his early years spent growing up in the U.S. Born in North Dakota, with a French Canadian father and an English Canadian mother, he has long identified himself with Canada and is considered to be a Canadian writer. His wife, Bharati Mukherjee, born in India, discusses the problems awaiting those from other cultures as they try to develop a life in a country in which they are aliens, in Canada, for example. She herself found life difficult there and chose to further her career in the U.S., among other places at the University of California. Her husband has recently continued to be attached to the University of Iowa, heading the International Writing Program. With these and many others mentioned here, the reader is hard-pressed to identify a Canadianness in certain of their works.

For many years, Canadian writers sometimes felt that they had to look to the U.S. From a purely financial point of view, this attitude is understandable: with a readership over ten times that of Canada, the U.S. opens up greater financial rewards. For many years, what was produced in the U.S., as Bruce McCall reminds us, just seemed to be better and more exciting. Over the last decades, Canadians have taken stock of the value of their literary efforts, helped along by government grants that supported Canadian works of art, and the attitude has become that Canada has indeed produced a literature reflecting its own version of North American culture, both in French and in English, a literature worth studying for its own sake and not because it is the younger sibling of the world power to the south. For decades, as Pierre Berton has pointed out in his study of the image of Canada in the movies, Canada was viewed as a "cityless" land of forests, mountains, and near constant snows, populated by heroic Mounties and French-speaking woodsmen. Things have changed. Writers in French, such as Anne Hébert, Jacques Godbout, Marie-Claire Blais, and Réjean Ducharme are known in the French-speaking world as well as in Quebec. Writers and literary critics such as Robertson Davies, Northrop Frye, Margaret Atwood, and many others who write in English remind us that there is much more to Canada than Hollywood's stereotypical image and show us at the same time that they have not had any need of an American identification to be successful in the U.S.

BIBLIOGRAPHY: New, W. H., *A History of Canadian Literature* (1989); Pevere, G., and G. Dymond, *Mondo Canuck, A Canadian Pop Culture Odyssey* (1996); Story, N., ed., *The Oxford Companion to Canadian History and Literature* (1967); Toye, W., ed., *Supplement to The Oxford Companion to Canadian History and Literature* (1973); Wilson, E., *O Canada, an American's Notes on Canadian Culture* (1965)

                                        PAUL BARRETTE

CAPOTE, Truman

b. 30 September 1924, New Orleans, Louisiana; d. 25 August 1984, Los Angeles, California

An arresting personality and respected stylist, C. rose quickly in the world of American letters, producing his best work in the two decades following World War II. His work ranges from gothicism of *Other Voices, Other Rooms* (1948) to the meticulous reportage of *In Cold Blood* (1965). Most critics praise his technical brilliance but are less certain about the value and depth of his focus. He was interested in peripheral elements of American culture—eccentric characters alienated from the mainstream by deprivation or wealth. The obvious appeal of his fiction is in its glimpses into international society and the criminal demimonde. More subtly, his fiction characteristically concerns personal emptiness.

C.'s mother's affection was volatile and undependable. Born Streakfus Persons, he was shunted among unfeeling or mildly dotty relatives in the rural South before being summoned to live in New York. He claims to have known as a child that he was a writer and worked steadily throughout adolescence to perfect his craft.

His first novel, *Other Voices, Other Rooms,* like his early short stories, relies on psychological horror and creepy atmospheric touches to sustain the reader's interest in young Joel Knox's search for identity. Though overwritten, it is memorable for its distinct rendering of children and childlike adults. The controversy that greeted the book owed as much to a provocative jacket photo of C. as to its homosexual theme.

A Tree of Night (1949) combined sinister tales with lighter, comic stories. *Local Color* (1950) is a Euro-pean travel record focusing on everyday social life. His next novel, *The Grass Harp* (1951), about a group of misfits who dream and bicker in a treehouse, is a fable celebrating human diversity. During the 1950s, C. also produced dramatizations and screenplays, notably *Beat the Devil* (1954) with John Huston. But perhaps his most popular effort was *Breakfast at Tiffany's* (1958), the story of an insouciant playgirl, as seen through the eyes of a wistful young writer.

The decade also saw the beginning of C.'s most important work, the genre of the "nonfiction novel" he claimed to have invented. In 1955, he accompanied the cast of *Porgy and Bess* when they performed in Russia. His widely praised account of the tour, *The Muses Are Heard* (1956), acutely but sympathetically observes the politics and personalities involved. He reveals human foibles without the malice of his later portraits. The work's attempt "to produce a journalistic novel, something on a large scale that would have the credibility of fact, the immediacy of film, the depth and freedom of prose, and the precision of poetry" established ambitious formal goals for the large projects to follow.

Although its merit was fiercely debated when it appeared, *In Cold Blood* is now regarded by most critics as his major work. C. spent six years investigating the murder of a family in western Kansas by two disturbed drifters. His account of the crime, trial, and execution is riveting, although critic Stanley Kauffmann's dig that "this isn't writing, it's research" makes a serious point about the work's genre.

In Cold Blood brought C. fame and wealth. He planned a novel to be called *Answered Prayers* that would break new literary ground, but most of his energy in the next ten years went into cultivating the socialites whose lives would be the subject of the new work. He produced two charming but slight memoirs, *A Christmas Memory* (1966) and *The Thanksgiving Visitor* (1967), and a collection of earlier work, *The Dogs Bark* (1973). The tide of his popularity turned disastrously when, in 1975–76, he published four chapters of the long-awaited book in *Esquire.* The chief literary innovation of these gossipy and rather mean-spirited stories was his use of real characters, often named and all identifiable to the initiated.

Thereafter, his health deteriorated and he grew dependent on drugs and alcohol. In the preface to *Music for Chameleons* (1980), a collection of new nonfiction articles in a style increasingly brittle and anecdotal, he discussed the "creative crisis" of trying to combine techniques from different forms. The tone of the preface is hopeful, but work on *Answered Prayers* remained stymied. Four years later, C. died of liver disease and drug intoxication. Three chapters of *An-*

swered Prayers, unaltered since 1976, were published posthumously in 1988.

BIBLIOGRAPHY: Clarke, G., *C.* (1988); Clarke, G., *T. C. : A Biography,* Garson, H. S., *T. C.* (1980); Grobel, L., *Conversations with C.* (1985); Nance, W., *The Worlds of T. C.* (1970)

ROBIN BEATY

CARRUTH, Hayden
b. 3 August 1921, Litchfield, Connecticut

Known less as a formalist than as a versatile poet who worked in numerous metrical and free-verse forms, C. interweaves late romantic and existentialist worldviews into a grim yet steadfastly hopeful rendering of mankind experiencing nature, love, and the most humble everyday pastimes. He has published over twenty books of poetry and one novel. As an editor, critic, and anthologist, he has been a vital presence in American poetry for fifty years. The reception for his *Collected Shorter Poems, 1946–1991,* published in 1992 and winner of the National Book Critics Award, accorded C. central status. He argues that poetry must be political and espouses a "nonviolent radical anarchism." Yet his writing is only indirectly so, typically registering the plight of the individual confronting the utter bleakness of existence.

In 1953, C. was hospitalized for a brief time in a psychiatric setting, the subject of *The Bloomingdale Papers* (1975), poems published twenty-two years after he wrote them in the asylum; he later worked for years as a hardscrabble farmer in Vermont and portrayed his impoverished neighbors in the persona idylls included in *The Clay Hill Anthology* (1970), *Dark World* (1974), and *Brothers, I Loved You All* (1978). Hardship and depression are integral to C.'s writing. However, his existential elegies are given balance and grace by the classical devices he draws from the Greeks and Latins. C. uses classical structures to endow his raw, volatile world with an ennobling aesthetic architecture, rendering the mind as on a journey towards "pure subjectivity."

After attending the University of North Carolina at Chapel Hill and serving in World War II, C. earned a master's degree from the University of Chicago. He was editor of *Poetry* from 1949 to 1950 and, some time later, poetry editor for *Harpers.* He had taken up residence in Vermont when he published his first books, *The Crow in the Heart* (1959) and *The Norfolk Poems* (1962). These poems are written in the academic, formally dense style prevalent during the 1940s and 1950s. In later collections, including *From Snow and Rock, from Chaos* (1973), *If You Call This Cry*

a Song (1983), and *Asphalt Georgics* (1985), C. experimented with more open verse forms while steadfastly maintaining the need for a formalist principle.

In 1965, C. published a philosophical fiction, *After the Stranger: Imaginary Dialogues with Camus,* in which several characters, including the French writer, meet to discuss his novel. With *Contra Mortem,* a long, breakthrough poem, published in 1967, C. displayed his own honed existentialist aesthetic. It is structured according to what C. called "paragraphs," which read as a sequence of verbal gazings: "The Mountain Fastness," "The Trees," "The Beings as Memory," and "The Moment." Whether describing the threatening quiet of a coming snowfall or an ecstatic vision of dawn, C. employs the improvisational technique he learned from jazz. Improvising within a fixed form, the jazz soloist transcends the objective world and becomes a "free, undetermined sensibility"—what C., in a subtle rebuke of T. S. ELIOT, terms "personality" in his essay "The Act of Love: Poetry and Personality." The poems' focus shifts from the ego to its relation to the larger world. That "paragraph" originally meant "outside the writing," the letter "p" that medieval scribes put in their margins, implies how C.'s "paragraphs" intuit an experience beyond the margins of the conscious subject—"beyond bounds," in Blake's nonrationalist sense. C.'s gesture of self-extension is undeniably romantic, but it is romanticism chastened by the existentialist conviction of the void.

C. continued to employ paragraphs in later poems, especially in "Paragraphs," published in *Brothers, I Loved You All,* arguably his finest work, and the 124-stanza sequence *The Sleeping Beauty* (1982), a discursion on the spirit of romance in Western cultural life. "Paragraphs" looks at a Vermont violated by commercial development. Its locals articulate the "nothingness" of being. And yet the poem concludes with the redemptive boisterousness of a 1944 Manhattan recording session played by black and Jewish jazz artists. *The Sleeping Beauty* is a romantic poem about the paradox of the romantic impulse—that the drive to love and the "lust for the idea" have perversely fostered massive destruction. However, love proves its own antidote.

As a journeyman critic who often supported himself by freelancing, C. has generated a substantial output, selections from which are reprinted in five books—*Working Papers* (1982), *Effluences of Sacred Caves* (1983), *Sitting In* (1986), *Suicides and Jazzers* (1992), and *Selected Essays and Reviews* (1996). Impassioned but blunt, he can excoriate Henry David THOREAU, point to defects in Robert FROST and Robert LOWELL, vaunt against "academicism," advocate a poetry of autobiogenis, and pay homage to his masters—Ezra POUND, Albert Camus, Paul GOODMAN, and various jazz musicians. He tirelessly connects aesthetic issues to the real world, arguing for the inextricability of art and life, poetry and morality, form and political consciousness.

BIBLIOGRAPHY: DePiero, W. S., "A Note on H. C. and Personality," *Shooting the Works: On Poetry and Pictures* (1996): 54–58; Flint, R. W., "The Odyssey of H. C.," *Parnassus* 11 (Spring-Summer 1983): 17–32; Kizer, C., "Others Call it God: H. C.," *Proses: On Poems and Poets* (1993): 139–45

DAVID WOLF

CARSON, Rachel [Louise]

b. 27 May 1907, Springdale, Pennsylvania; d. 14 April 1964, Silver Springs, Maryland

While C. was not the first writer to be concerned with the environment, her 1962 book *The Silent Spring,* has done more than any other to raise the public consciousness about the indiscriminate use of pesticides. Still in print, and frequently excerpted for anthologies, its impact has been compared to Harriet Beecher STOWE's *Uncle Tom's Cabin* and Upton SINCLAIR's *The Jungle.* Part of C.'s success is in her literate and graceful prose, coupled with a compelling vision of the dynamic interconnection of all natural phenomena, a vision that unifies all of her writings on biology. In this she anticipates the tenets of much of contemporary Ecofeminism.

C.'s early education focused on literature and writing. Originally an English major at Pennsylvania College for Women (now Chatham College), she switched to biology at the encouragement of her teacher, Mary Scott Skinker. This led to study at the Woods Hole Marine Biological Laboratory and graduate work at Johns Hopkins University, initiating a career in marine biology. Even at an early stage, C. combined her literary and scientific backgrounds, writing radio scripts for the U.S. Bureau of Fisheries and articles for popular magazines. Her 1937 article "Undersea" for the *Atlantic Monthly* became the core of her first book *Under the Sea Wind* (1941). Published shortly before the Japanese attack on Pearl Harbor, the book received little attention. Nevertheless, it anticipates many of her themes. It presents a scientific discussion of the cycles of birth and death in the sea, organized around the narrative account of bird and fish migrations. In this way, the sea becomes a nearly eternal organic whole.

In 1948, C. became editor-in-chief of the Fish and Wildlife Information Division, beginning work on *The Sea around Us.* Serialized excerpts first appeared in the *New Yorker,* followed by publication in 1951. The book was an immediate success, winning a National Book Award (1951) and the John Burroughs Medal (1952), and bringing C. fame and independence that allowed her to resign from the Fish and Wildlife Service to work full-time on her writing. A classic of modern popular writing on natural science, *The Sea around Us* synthesizes a vast knowledge of contemporary geography, geology, meteorology, and biology to present a vivid and comprehensive portrait of the ocean. Beginning with the origins of the sea, she traces its interconnected movements and cycles through time and across it, from its surface to its depths. Aiming for a literate general reader, she paints poetic images such as those of the sperm whale and the giant squid, or the great movements of tides, that nonetheless have interest to the scientist as well. While more recent deep sea explorations of the ocean floor and the theories of plate tectonics have developed our understanding, C.'s book remains a powerful vision of the unity and interconnection of the seas and everything in them, themes she developed in the subsequent *The Edge of the Sea* (1956) and *The Sense of Wonder* (1965).

C.'s most controversial work was *The Silent Spring,* though her concern with pesticides predates it. As early as 1945, she proposed an article on the effects of DDT to the *Reader's Digest.* The offer was rejected. The interim delay coupled with the subsequent success of her other books, however, lent scientific depth and authority to her warning and indictment. In 1958, she picked up the topic again, agreeing to do an article on DDT for the *New Yorker.* The idea for this article grew into the book published in 1962, an excerpt of which also appeared in the *New Yorker.* Taking her title from a vision of life stripped of life, C. presents a rigorous survey and analysis of the cumulative effects of pesticides on the web of natural connections. While the subject matter and angry tone differ from her earlier work, *The Silent Spring* represents not a break with her past work, but a culmination.

BIBLIOGRAPHY: Gartner, C. B., *R. C.* (1983); Jamison, A., and R. Eyerman, *Seeds of the Sixties* (1994); McCay, M. A., *R. C.* (1993); Sterling, P., *Sea and Earth: The Life of R. C.* (1970)

THOMAS L. COOKSEY

CARUTHERS, William Alexander

b. 23 December 1802, Lexington, Virginia; d. 29 August 1846, near Marietta, Georgia

C. was one of the first important Virginia romancers, a distinction unappreciated at the time. Concluding his first novel, *The Kentuckian in New York; or, The Adventures of Three Southerns* "By a Virginian"

(1834), he wrote: "there is evidently a current in American literature, the fountain-head of which lies north of the Potomac, and in which a Southern is compelled to navigate up the stream if he jumps in too far South." But in spite of his professed difficulty in matching James Fenimore COOPER's impact, during his short life he nonetheless published three noteworthy novels that idealize Virginia or Virginians. In these romances, the "Chronicler of the Cavaliers," as his biographer calls him, assumes his place in literary history chiefly for helping to mythologize these dashing aristocrats, "the fox-hunting, horse-racing, and jovial race of Virginians."

At the time he wrote *The Kentuckian in New York; or, The Adventures of Three Southerns,* C. himself was living in New York, practicing medicine, and frequenting Gotham's literary gatherings. His first fiction is largely and epistolary work that compares notes of three college friends: two South Carolinians who, in company with an eccentric Kentuckian, journey north to New York City and the third, a Virginian, who tours the deep South. Both parties record their uncertain fortunes in love and more finely observed insights on each region—the cruel but necessary system of slavery, the poverty of rural North Carolina, the destitution and the sophistication of New York City. C.'s chief motive in this first novel was not to glorify his native state or even the three lively young Southerners, but to show that each region needs better to understand its ways and that, to fully mature into gentlemen, the three need to acquire a knowledge of good and evil. Indeed, the metaphysical theme often seems to predominate, for, as one hero asks, "is it man's singular destiny, that all sensations should be born of contrasts? That all pleasures should be born of pains, and that our ideas should be but the combined representatives of these?" So in learning to love—through pain—and in learning to appreciate contrasting regions—the declining South, the mercantile North, and, through the Kentuckian, the raucous West—the students mature into men, into Southern gentlemen.

This first novel concludes with a vision that predominates in his two other works; in the West "the spirit of the age is working out a gradual revolution, which, in its onward career, will sweep away the melancholy vestiges of a former and more chivalrous and generous age beyond the mountains." In effect, he here announces the subject of his second and most influential novel, *The Cavaliers of Virginia, or The Recluse of Jamestown. An Historical Romance of the Old Dominion* (1835). C. turns to a historic 1676 "revolution" that captures this tension between the aristocratic East and the democratic West, Bacon's Rebellion. But as the above quotation suggests, C.'s

sympathies are somewhat divided. On the one hand, his hero, Nathaniel Bacon, is a "symbol of manifest destiny and national unity," a dashing young Westerner who champions the popular cause and defeats the hostile Indians. On the other, C. glorifies the chivalrous age that passes, in part through his delineation of the colonial governor, William Berkeley, and in part through Bacon's own dash and allure. C., like other Southern writers of his era, acknowledged the passing of the Cavalier at the same time that he ennobled and preserved him in fiction.

Having published two novels with Harper and Brothers in two years, C. moved South again, first to Lexington and then, in 1837, to Savannah, Georgia, where he continued to practice medicine and to pursue his literary career. For the next few years, he wrote for local periodicals; published in the *Knickerbocker Magazine* what became a celebrated firsthand account of a college friend's exploit, "Climbing the Natural Bridge" in Virginia; and researched and completed another historical romance, *The Knights of the Golden Horse-shoe* (1841). Showing marked improvement in dialogue, characterization, and plot development, this last novel focuses on the planning and execution of lieutenant Governor Spotswood's 1716 expedition to the Shenandoah Valley, "that garden spot of land." Many pages of this complex plot are given over to romance, and here, as in the earlier books, C. the romantic historian reveals his penchant for cloaked figures, mistaken identities, and melancholy maidens. But of the greatest historical and literary importance is the final quarter of the novel, the telling of the trip itself. Here Spotswood is elevated to the Knight who leads his band across the mountain; here appears one of C.'s most convincing characters, Natty Bumppo's fictional cousin, Joe Jarvis; and here also C. captures some of Cooper's skill at recounting the adventuresome trek. And in his most accomplished prose, he records the moment of discovery and reiterates the theme that runs throughout this novel, manifest destiny: when he gazes into the Valley for the first time, "Governor Spotswood carried his thoughts into the future, and imagined the fine country which he beheld, peopled and glowing under the hands of the husbandman."

The writer who helped create the mythic Cavalier—the accomplished and daring, yet never self indulgent gentleman—was himself equally inspired by another American myth, the promise of the West. The tension between Virginia's glorious past and America's glorious future gave C. his fictional voice.

BIBLIOGRAPHY: Davis, C. C., *Chronicler of the Cavaliers: A Life of the Virginia Novelist Dr. W. A. C.* (1953); Davis, R. B., *Literature and Society in Early*

Virginia, 1608–1840 (1973); Fishwick, M. W., *Virginia: A New Look at the Old Dominion* (1959); Watson, R. D., Jr., *The Cavalier in Virginia Fiction* (1985)

SUSAN SHILLINGLAW

CARVER, Raymond

b. 25 May 1938, Clatskanie, Oregon; d. 2 August 1988, Port Angeles, Washington

Born into a blue-collar household in the Pacific Northwest, C. experienced early on the problems, including unemployment, alcoholism, and anomie, that afflict his characters. This, he often claimed, led to the affection and understanding he invested in the often feckless characters of his fiction. By describing their struggle to confront and understand the limitations of their lives, his work explores their search for humanity. Groping toward some meaning, however slight or brief, his characters demonstrate an instinct for survival and, especially in his later work, a desire for stability and hope in their often bleak worlds. In his finely wrought narratives, C. suggests that only by confronting the results of their insular lives—failed marriages, alcoholism, alienation—can they stumble towards perception and ultimately transcend their fates.

Exploring the sense of loss and lack of humanity that afflicts contemporary man, his early short story collections, including *Will You Please Be Quiet, Please?* (1976), *Furious Seasons* (1977), and *What We Talk about When We Talk about Love* (1981), are peopled with characters, often couples, who can't or won't communicate, and who lack the knowledge and energy to master their fates. In "Neighbors" (1976), Bill and Arlene Miller are briefly awakened from their emotional torpor after agreeing to watch—and becoming obsessed with—the apartment of another, more successful, couple. The story highlights the inherent sterility of their voyeurism when they lock themselves out of the apartment and are again faced with the barrenness of their own lives. Emotional distance similarly dominates Stuart and Claire's relationship in "So Much Water So Close to Home" (1981). Stuart and a group of friends discover a dead girl on the first day of a fishing trip, and instead of going directly to the police, decide to continue fishing. Back home, Stuart cannot understand why this delay in notifying the police would affect his wife. With its undercurrent of sexual violence, the story illustrates C.'s obsession with the dangers caused by the lack of communication and insularity of modern life. This emotional lassitude also afflicts the characters in "What We Talk About When We Talk About Love" (1981). Faced with a loss of sensibility, the couples in this story can no longer

feel or respond to the world around them. Lacking empathy, they cannot appreciate the substance and stability love offers. Their conversation, like their lives, trails away into darkness.

The importance of conversation becomes clear in his later works, where dialogue leads to emotional fulfillment. Unlike his earlier collections, the characters in these stories often come to grips with their situations and achieve, if not a state of grace, an enlightened acceptance of their lives. In *Cathedral* (1983) and *Where I'm Calling From* (1988), C., as he made clear in several interviews, made a conscious movement away from the compressed diction and sparse narrative of his previous work, to a fuller, more expansive fiction, still infused with suffering, but leavened with healing. By establishing connections, however tenuous, with others, the characters in these stories move from isolation to consolation, finding, often through the simple act of conversation, a measure of hope and affirmation. As he explained in *Fires* (1983), a collection of essays, poems, and short stories, this hope is evinced not in highly wrought narratives or sentimental tales, but in deceptively modest stories, rendered in simple, direct language.

In "Cathedral" (1983), his best-known story, the unnamed narrator slowly realizes the emptiness of his life through the gentle questioning of Robert, his wife's blind friend. Only after closing his eyes—or empathizing and fully appreciating Robert's world—does he tentatively move toward enlightenment. In "A Small Good Thing" (1983), conversation figures more prominently, as a disaffected baker rediscovers hope, and a couple grieving the loss of their son finds solace through the simple act of sharing bread and, most importantly, their stories.

His poetry, in *Winter Insomnia* (1970), *At Night the Salmon Move* (1976), *Fires, Where Water Comes Together with Other Water* (1985), and *Ultramarine* (1986), explores the same terrain as his fiction. Using the same spare, simple language which lends his fiction its immediacy and strength, his poems are short, still vignettes, often detailing, with seemingly innocuous images such as the breaking of eggs into a skillet in "Morning, Thinking of Empire" (1983), that moment of insight when characters realize the futility of their lives. Other poems, such as "Forever" (1983), show his acceptance of the inevitability of life and death, lending the same note of affirmation which illuminates his later fiction.

Eschewing the novel, C. concentrated on developing a terse narrative voice, which lent a poetic precision to his fiction, and initiated a stream of imitators. Considered the father of "minimalist" fiction (a label he abhorred), his insistence on investing commonplace language with emotional significance, and on finding drama in the lives of the working class, led to a renaissance of the American short story.

BIBLIOGRAPHY: Gentry, M. B., and W. L. Stull, eds., *Conversations with R. C.* (1990); Nesset, K., *The Stories of R. C.* (1995); Saltzman, A. M., *Understanding R. C.* (1988)

DAVID BORDELON

CASEY, John
b. 18 January 1939, Worcester, Massachusetts

C.'s *Spartina* (1989) won the National Book Award in fiction. Its winning was due, at least in part, to its sounding some of the major themes in the tradition of American fiction: Man against Nature, Man in and out of Society. Interestingly, it also enacts one of the major critical arguments about that tradition: the characterization of American fiction in terms of romance and realism.

C.'s first novel titled *An American Romance* (1977) centers around the romance between the hero and heroine, Mac and Anya, and it also makes a number of allusions to the romance tradition in American letters, likening Mac and Anya to the heroes and heroines of Nathaniel HAWTHORNE and James Fenimore COOPER. If, as one reviewer noted, the title was a bit tongue-in-cheek, the story of love in the academy and the satire of life in the academy are still wrapped in this distinctly American paper. The novel won critical praise for the romance of its main characters and the hint of the romance in the Hawthorne sense, as well as for its sharp puncturing of the pretensions of university life. *Testimony and Demeanor* (1979) was less well received. Composed of three short stories and a novella, the collection centers on young men and women pursuing careers and each other.

With *Spartina,* C. removes his tongue from his cheek and writes a powerful, affecting book with an element of romance. Dick Pierce, his wife May, and his two boys, Charlie and Tom, live on a small island off the coast of Rhode Island that the Pierce family once owned in entirety but has since sold off piece by piece. Dick barely gets by hiring himself out as a hand on fishing boats and making the occasional, just bearable run out to sea with rich men, but his heart is with the boat in his backyard, which he will finish as soon as he can get the money together. The difficulty in securing this money is part of his bitterness, as is his status as a member of a once-proud trade that is now more a quaint remnant of times gone by than a viable industry. Other difficulties with which the crusty, taciturn, and sometimes sympathetic Dick must deal include his affair with Elsie Buttrick, young Fish and Wildlife officer who feels for the sea as he does, his peripheral involvement with drug-running, his now

completed boat's surviving a hurricane, and his threatened marriage.

The sea, Dick's struggles, and the central metaphor of spartina, a hardy marsh grass, lend the novel its air of romance. The attention to the details of the social world and to the interrelation of characters in this world give the novel its realism. The traditional characterization of American fiction as producing romance over realism often explains this production as the result of America's youth, which denies its writers the embedded social matrices available to European writers of realism but provides fertile ground for the kind of symbolic, mythic tales of Hawthorne and Herman MELVILLE. More recently, critics have questioned both the characterization of American society and that of American fiction. The realism and naturalism of the late 19th c. has been brought back into the canon and reexamined for the ways in which it goes beyond reportage and creates worlds; the traditional romances have been looked at in the light of their arising out of a complex, changing social ground. And the division between romance and realism itself has been scrutinized. Contemporary novels like *Spartina* that combine the lyrical, symbolic aspects of the romance with close attention to society do more than combine disparate elements: when they are as artistically successful and critically praised as *Spartina* (in spite of potential quibbles with the sophistication of Dick's voice, quibbles which ignore the workings of generic convention), they question the very distinction itself, not just in the reading of contemporary fiction but retrospectively, in the way readers think about novels as different as Melville's *Moby-Dick* and William Dean HOWELL's *The Rise of Silas Lapham.*

BIBLIOGRAPHY: Bellamy, J. D., *Literary Luxuries* (1995): 193–95; Kenney, S., "Man Meets Boat Meets Hurrican," *NYTBR* 25 June 1989: 1; Sage, L., "The End of Fun," *NYTBR* 5 April 1998: 1

SAM COHEN

CASTILLO, Ana [Hernandez Del]
b. 15 June 1953, Chicago, Illinois

Born to Mexican American parents and raised in Chicago, C. has distinguished herself as a prolific Chicana writer, editor, essayist, and teacher who has greatly contributed to 20th-c. American literature. She began writing poetry at the age of nine and in 1975 published her first collection, a chapbook of poetry entitled *Zero Makes Me Hungry.* Her following collections include *i close my eyes (to see)* (1976), *Otro canto* (1977), *The Invitation* (1979), *Women Are Not Roses* (1984), and *My Father Was a Toltec: Poems* (1988). C.'s poems speak of the despair, loneliness, and isolation that comes from gender and class oppression.

Like her poetry, C.'s prose fiction proves her to be a compelling writer. Her first novel, *The Mixquiahuala Letters* (1986), is an epistolary novel composed of forty letters written over a ten year period by Teresa, a Chicana from California, to Alicia, her Anglo friend. In the table of contents, the author provides the reader with three different combinations of the order in which the letters may be read: for the "Conformist," the "Cynic," and the "Quixotic." Each order arrives at a different conclusion. The novel recounts the lives and experiences of the two characters, their friendship, their travels together, their personal lives and their relationships with men. It examines gender conflict and critiques both Anglo and Hispanic cultural ideology and fixed gender identity.

C.'s second novel, *Sapogonia: An Anti-Romance in 3/8 Meter* (1990), continues to explore gender identity and conflict. The story is filtered through the perspective of Máximo Madrigal, in alternating first and third person narration. It recounts the destructive love affair between the obsessive mestizo male character, Máximo, and the woman he is unable to fully possess, Pastora Aké. Máximo, a native of the make-believe Sapogonia, is a man struggling to reconcile his chaotic present with his mythical heritage. As critics have noted, he is torn between his position as both conqueror and conquered.

C.'s third novel, *So Far From God* (1993), examines the experience of being a woman part of a minority group. This novel explores the trials and tribulations and the survival of a Hispanic family of women composed of the mother Sofía and her four daughters: Esperanza, Fe, Claridad, and La Loca. It provides the reader with a keen account of the feminine condition. This novel confirms her as one of the major Chicana writers of the late 20th c.

For her contributions, C. has won recognition not only in the U.S. but in Mexico and Europe as well. Her awards include the Before Colombus Foundation American Book Award for her novel, *The Mixquiahuala Letters* in 1986, the National Endowment for the Arts Fellowship in poetry in 1990, and the Carl Sandburg Literary Award in 1993 for her third novel *So Far From God*. In addition, she served as a coeditor to *This Bridge Called my Back: Writings by Radical Women of Color* (1988) and to *Third Woman, Vol. IV: The Sexuality of Latinas* (1989). In 1995, she saw the publication of her collection of Chicana feminist essays entitled *Massacres of the Dreamers: Reflections on Mexican-Indian Women in the U.S.; 500 Years After the Conquest* and in 1996 a collection of short stories by the name of *Loverboys*. Throughout her entire career, C. has shown a persistent interest in minority and feminist issues and has greatly contributed to the canon of Chicana writers.

BIBLIOGRAPHY: Gómez-Vega, I., "Debunking Myths: The Hero's Role in A. C.'s *Sapogonia*," *AmRev* 22 (Spring-Summer 1994): 244–58; Torres, H. A., "Story, Telling, Voice: Narrative Authority in A. C.'s *The Mixquiahuala Letters*," in Herrera-Sobek, M., and H. M. Viramontes, eds., *Chicana (W)rites on Word and Film* (1995): 125–45

CONSTANZA GOMEZ

CATHER, Willa
b. 7 December 1873, Back Creek (now Gore), Virginia; d. 24 April 1947, New York City

During the C. centennial celebration at the University of Nebraska, Henry JAMES scholar Leon Edel predicted about C.'s reputation, "I think the time will come when she'll be ranked above Hemingway. . . . But I've got her below Faulkner." Because William FAULKNER is our great novelist since Henry James, this accolade is significant, especially coming from a male critic. Harold BLOOM, in an introduction to a recent collection of essays on C., echoes Edel in crediting her with six "permanent" novels, "a remarkable number for a modern American writer; I can think only of Faulkner as C.'s match in this respect, since he wrote six truly enduring novels." With the possible exception of Edith WHARTON, no other female American novelist approaches C. in stature. But recognition was a long time coming, as delayed a process as C.'s novel-writing career, which crowned twenty years of apprentice writing—short stories, hundreds of reviews of novels, poetry, stage plays, music, and art—years of teaching Latin and English and of editing magazines, including the celebrated *McClure's*. C. was the contemporary of Stephen CRANE, Jack LONDON, and Frank NORRIS, as her early short stories reveal, with a strong anti-Howellsian penchant for violence and the romantic. But her delayed major career grouped her with Faulkner, Sinclair LEWIS, F. Scott FITZGERALD, and Ernest HEMINGWAY, since she produced her best work between the late teens and the early 1930s. During the Lost Generation era, she preserved Jamesian sensibility and an appreciation of aesthetic and religious traditionalism.

The most effective introduction to C. is through her lucid and lyrical prose. Even casual and brief exposure to C. criticism will confirm in the memory scenes like Jim Burden's introduction to the Nebraska prairie in *My Ántonia* (1918), his discovery of "nothing but land: not a country at all, but the material out of which countries are made. . . . Between that earth and sky I felt erased, blotted out." The aging Jean Latour, protagonist of *Death Comes for the Archbishop* (1927), has a love affair with the "bright edges of the world," the plains and deserts, where one could dissolve into "something soft and wild and free," become released "into the blue and gold, into the morning, into the morning!" When Alexandra Bergson, the Amazonian heroine of *O Pioneers!* (1913), turns her radiant face toward the "rich and strong and glorious" land, "the great, free spirit which breathes across it, must have bent lower than it ever bent to a human will before." There are also ecstatic moments when civilization is uncovered in empty places. Tom Outland beholds the city of stone in *The Professor's House* (1925) in "silence and stillness and repose—immortal repose. That village sat looking down into the canyon with the calmness of eternity. The falling snow flakes, sprinkling the pinons, gave it a special kind of solemnity. I can't describe it." In *The Song of the Lark* (1915) the inexpressible dawns for Thea Kronborg as she bathes deep within another Southwestern canyon after having collected Indian pottery fragments: "The stream and the broken pottery: what was any art but an effort to make a sheath, a mold in which to imprison for a moment the shining, elusive element which is life itself—life hurrying past us and running away—too strong to stop, too sweet to lose?" *Shadows on the Rock* (1931) filters the swift and sweet element through the order of faith. The courageous nuns inhabit a particular worldview, "this all-important earth, created by God for a great purpose, the sun which he made to light it by day, the moon which he made to light it by night,—and the stars, made to beautify the vault of heaven like frescoes, and to be a clock and compass for man."

And the best of C.'s narratives are as liberating as these passages, their characters monumental, moving through landscapes scantily marked by humankind, pursuing some adventure or ideal, either in solitude or with a beloved companion. C.'s uprooting in 1883, at the age of nine, from the hill-enclosed, green world of Virginia and her introduction to a Nebraska as bare as a square of sheet metal motivated story after story, as bleak landscape was either pitted against or blended with civilization from the East and Europe. Her unique variation on the Jamesian theme of Europe and America, the New and Old Worlds, lies at the heart of her three major novels—*My Ántonia, The Professor's House,* and *Death Comes for the Archbishop*—and her three great minor ones—*O Pioneers!, A Lost Lady* (1923), and *Shadows on the Rock*.

Narrator Jim Burden's account of his childhood adventures with Ántonia Shimerda is C.'s most popular story. Jim becomes the voice of C. describing her rather jarring introduction to Nebraska and subsequent exploration of the prairie during her first year there. The prototype for the title character, Annie Pavelka, C. knew in Red Cloud, Nebraska, as the hired girl of a neighboring family. Jim and Ántonia's experiences range from lyricism to violence and include the discovery of arching sky and limitless land, dramatic seasonal changes, story-telling and candy making, a snake killing and an attempted rape, the suicide of Ántonia's father, and so on. Since no romantic love develops between Jim and Ántonia, some readers feel emptiness at the heart of the novel. However, if we approach it as Jim's reconstruction of a rich childhood for therapeutic reasons during middle age, after achieving a successful career but then having his childless marriage fail, then we realize that the emptiness is intended.

Taking the midlife crisis approach to *My Ántonia* prepares us for *The Professor's House* and a protagonist in his fifties so spiritually distanced from his wife, daughters, and career that he wants to die. Rather than reconstructing his own boyhood story, Professor St. Peter relives the adventures of Tom Outland, his brilliant student killed in the Great War. Tom's story is real-life explorer Richard Wetherill's, the discovery of the honeycomb of cliff dwellings at Mesa Verde, Colorado. The center of the novel transports us from the materialistic clutter of contemporary life to the breathtaking Southwestern landscape for a complex story of egoism and treachery that mirrors the problems of the St. Peter family. C.'s forced resolution of the professor's story in the third part prevents the novel from reaching the level of her other two major novels, although it is strategic for understanding a mentality plagued by and in need of human relationships yet substituting bleak solitude for them.

Solitude is the key to the story of Jean Marie Latour in *Death Comes for the Archbishop;* however, "it is not a solitude of atrophy, of negation, but of perpetual flowering," the "solitariness of love in which a priest's life could be like his Master's." As in *My Ántonia* friendship and landscape are fused, here in the journeys of the missionary companions in the New Mexico diocese, where "the very floor of the world is cracked open into countless canyons and arroyos, fissures in the earth which are sometimes ten feet deep, sometimes a thousand." The major conflict is twofold: of reclaiming a wayward native clergy and neglected and isolated Catholics and of sacrificing companionship to accomplish this work. Bishop Latour's particular agony is surrendering Father Joseph Vaillant, his dear friend, to the missions in Arizona and Colorado, and depriving himself of his emotional need for Joseph. As befits transcendental fiction, the landscapes and the lives of the heroes assume other-worldly dimensions, from Latour's contemplation of Christ's passion before a cross-shaped juniper tree at the opening, to the legendary appearance of the Holy Family in the desert to renowned California missionary Junipero Serra near the end. C.'s pioneer priests are based on historical figures—Jean Baptiste Lamy of New Mexico inspired Latour, and Joseph Priest Machebeuf of Colorado is the prototype of Vaillant—but her method transfigures them into legend.

The great minor novels duplicate the major ones: *O Pioneers!* and *A Lost Lady* anticipate and repeat, respectively, *My Ántonia,* while *Shadows on the Rock* continues many of the themes of *Death Comes for the Archbishop.* Alexandra Bergson in *O Pioneers!* is C.'s first great pioneer heroine. A farm manager rather than tiller of the fields, a somewhat sexless spinster into her forties, and a fair-haired Scandinavian rather than dark Czech, she is a foil for the more famous Ántonia. Alexandra's maternal capacities are evident in her attentions to her younger brother Emil, her love needs pallidly suggested in her long friendship with Marie Shabata, the torrid Bohemian neighbor who falls in love with Emil. The climactic love and murder episode, with its shades of Keats and Dante, is a rare concession in C. to the conventional, although it is set within an original cosmic landscape pulsating with the creative energy of Whitman's poetry.

In *A Lost Lady* Niel Herbert's relationship with Marian Forrester duplicates certain aspects of the Jim-Ántonia relationship in *My Ántonia.* Niel's ascetic worship of Mrs. Forrester, the youthful wife of an aged pioneer railroad builder, is challenged by his discovery of her extra-marital sexual exploits. Discomfort with sex characterizes Niel as it had Jim Burden when he was forced to admit Ántonia's sexual nature. C.'s attempt to make Niel's disillusionment with Marian tantamount to disillusionment with the decline of the West fails to obscure the essential intimacy of the story, and the novel remains less historically evocative than the very best of C.

However, in *Shadows on the Rock* C. successfully universalized a slight domestic story of a father and daughter in late-17th-c. Quebec City. Middle-aged Euclide Auclair is a combination of Professor St. Peter and Bishop Latour, a contemplative widower with reclusive tendencies but very devoted to his young daughter, Cecile. French-born Cecile's growth and eventual marriage in the Epilogue to a Montreal-born woodsman becomes Canada's coming of age, and her many sons the Canadians of the future. C. was able to combine the best of French civilization, which she revered throughout her life, with the overpowering impact of nature in the New World. The culture through which nature filters, as in *Death Comes for the Archbishop,* is a Catholic one of religious devotion, miracles, mystical asceticism, and courageous missionary priests and nuns.

Decidedly lesser but of importance in the C. canon are *The Song of the Lark,* a favorite novel of feminist critics for tracing the growth of the female artist, and *One of Ours,* awarded the 1922 Pulitzer Prize, which sends the Jim Burden-Niel Herbert character off to war in France, where in his idealism he discovers a superior culture to replace the growing materialism of prairie life back home. *My Mortal Enemy* (1926), the shortest and bleakest of the novels, presents the unforgettable tragedy of the dying Myra Henshawe, whose love-hate relationship with her husband and her Irish Catholic past serves as a bridge between the abortive religious themes in *The Professor's House* and their flowering in *Death Comes for the Archbishop.* The story of Sapphira and Henry Colbert in C.'s final novel, *Sapphira and the Slave Girl* (1940), resembles Myra and Oswald Henshawe's, that of a dying tyrannical wife and her mild-mannered husband, although the Virginia setting of C.'s early childhood gives it historical significance, enabling her to address freedom, slavery, and racial issues. *Alexander's Bridge* (1912), C.'s adolescent attempt in her late thirties to ape James and Wharton on their terrain, the drawing rooms of the Northeast and Europe, rather than her own, can be chalked up as the product of inexperience, while *Lucy Gayheart* (1935), the affair of a girly girl and a vapid middle-aged singer, is the result of exhaustion. Yet all these novels are well-written, serious literature. There are no bombs among C. novels, and beyond the three major books there is room for disagreement in classifying them according to importance and quality.

C. did her bad writing in her short stories, most of it before she published her first novel but a surprising amount into the 1920s, while she was writing flawless novels like *Death Comes for the Archbishop* and *A Lost Lady.* However, of approximately sixty published stories, at least ten may be ranked among the best American short stories: "Paul's Case"; "Neighbour Rosicky"; "The Sculptor's Funeral"; "Coming, Aphrodite!"; "The Best Years"; "Two Friends"; "The Enchanted Bluff"; "Old Mrs. Harris"; "Before Breakfast"; "The Joy of Nelly Deane."

Several themes and subjects appear over and over in C.'s fiction. However, the relationship of nature and culture is her major theme, inherent in the development of farms and towns on the Nebraska prairie, the revival of Catholicism in New Mexico, the extension of France in the arctic Canadian forest, and the discovery of mesa civilizations in the Southwest. The energy to civilize displaces sexual energy in C.'s fiction, as in novel after novel heterosexual love either turns sour, fails to develop beyond friendship, or is replaced by same-sex companionship devoted to civilizing and artistic accomplishment.

C. has generated a rapidly growing body of criticism—recently three to four books and twenty-five to thirty articles annually—that clearly divides into two seldom intermingling streams. The earlier camp originated at the University of Nebraska during the 1960s with the gathering and publication of three volumes of turn-of-the-century magazine nonfiction, *The Kingdom of Art* (1966) and *The World and the Parish* (2 vols., 1970)—reviews of contemporary fiction and essays on literary figures as diverse as George Eliot and Walt WHITMAN, Ivan Turgenev and Robert Burns, William Dean HOWELLS and Paul Verlaine. Here, indeed, was evidence of the significant breadth of C.'s reading, and veteran critic Bernice Slote proclaimed that "C.'s work has not been accurately read . . . in part because [this magazine writing] has been unknown . . . and [due to] the neglect of clues and allusions within the work that in T. S. ELIOT's *The Waste Land* would have drawn forth tomes of analysis." Slote led a generation of scholars into studies of C.'s use of the pastoral and epic modes, myth, classical drama, explorations of her experiments in structure (especially in *The Professor's House*), and her development of the unfurnished novel (of which *My Mortal Enemy* is the extreme example). This work supplemented earlier considerations of place and local history by Mildred R. Bennet, founder of the Willa Cather Pioneer Memorial in Red Cloud.

Since C. never married and her strongest attachments were to other women, questions of sexual preference, conspicuously avoided by Nebraska critics and their proteges, began to surface by the C. centennial. There is insufficient evidence to answer these questions satisfactorily, but this has not discouraged gender theorists who have contributed interesting, if highly speculative, revisions, like viewing C.'s priest companions as substitutes for herself and Isabelle McClung, whom she loved, or Edith Lewis, with whom she lived, or interpreting Jim Burden's feelings for Ántonia as expressive of C.'s fascination for Annie Pavelka or some other woman. The most accomplished of gender critics is Sharon O'Brien, for whom C.'s fiction traces a search for a mother (C. was neglected by her own mother according to this theory) complicated by lesbian fears of loss of identity to another female. This theory illuminates many of the apprenticeship stories as well as *My Ántonia* and *A Lost Lady,* novels in which C. assumes a male persona. Although such an approach risks making the work of a writer who jealously guarded her privacy an encoded sexual biography for her reading public, it poses new and exciting challenges for more traditional critics. There is need for cooperation between these critical camps, a case in point being the two outstanding 1987 books on C.: O'Brien's study and James Woodress's "definitive" biography. Where O'Brien reduces C.'s fiction by too rigorous application of her gender thesis, Woodress's meticulous general scholarship suffers from failure to probe where O'Brien's insistently dwells.

Challenging for all of us is the significance of C.'s involvement of Czechs and Scandinavians in America's story while rendering them superior to their WASP counterparts; her celebration of America's Hispanic, Franco, and Indian heritages by making her saints Mexican Catholic instead of Yankee Puritan; her transforming of Winthrop's city on a hill to French Quebec, "gleaming above the river like an altar with many candles, or like a holy city in an old legend, shriven, sinless, washed in gold." It took boldness and originality of vision, allowing these "others" to revise the standard rendition of America's story.

BIBLIOGRAPHY: Bennett, M. R., *The World of W. C.* (1961); Gerber, P. L., *W. C.* (1975) Murphy, J. J., ed., *Critical Essays on W. C.* (1984); O'Brien, S., *W. C.: The Emerging Voice* (1987); Rosowski, S. J., *The Voyage Perilous: W. C.'s Romanticism* (1986); Wagenknecht, E., *W. C.* (1994); Woodress, J., *W. C.: A Literary Life* (1987)

JOHN J. MURPHY

CATHERWOOD, Mary Hartwell

b. 16 December 1847, Luray, Ohio; d. 26 December 1902, Chicago, Illinois

C. rooted her works in local color, and she is one of the earliest and best American writers of that bent, though now for the most part neglected. She gained popularity in the 1890s by adding the historical dimension, melodramatic incident, and sentimentalism to produce popular historical romances about the French in North America.

C. was the first woman novelist born west of the Alleghenies and, a graduate of Granville Female College, the first prominent college-educated one. She began writing when a school teacher and soon supported herself by writing for periodicals. When she married and moved to a small town in Indiana, C. turned to writing realistic stories and novels of Midwestern life, rich in local color, and published them in the Kokomo *Weekly Dispatch*. She became well acquainted with Indianapolis writers like James Whitcomb RILEY and Eugene FIELD and began to infuse much of her fiction with sentimentalism, melodrama, or both. Her work was published in such periodicals as *Lippincott's Magazine, Atlantic Monthly,* and *C. Magazine.* Late in life, she lived in Chicago, summered on Mackinac Island, and wrote mostly historical romances, publicly defending her mode against Hamlin GARLAND and his "veritism."

Comparing "A Little God" (1878), published in the Kokomo newspaper, with its reworking in *The Spirit of an Illinois Town* (1897) reveals how C. softened some of the bitter realism of the earlier story with sentimentalism and melodrama, most notably in the description of the heroine's funeral. Here, the shock of her death and the other destruction a violent cyclone has brought effect a reconciliation among competing factions in the raw Illinois boomtown. In "The Career of a Prairie Farmer," published in *Lippincott's Magazine* (June 1880), C. successfully subordinates touches of sentimentalism and a melodramatic incident or two to the realistic story of the long struggle of a young pioneer to farm a section of Illinois prairie. The title story and "The Stirring-Off" in *The Queen of the Swamp and Other Plain Americans* (1899) are successful, humorous stories of courtship in rural mid-19th-c. Ohio because C. creates realistic characters and relationships in communities rich in frontier folklore and dialect. In *Mackinac and Lake Stories* (1899), "The King of Beaver" and "Beaver Lights" center on a splinter Mormon settlement on Beaver Island in Lake Michigan and its leader, James Strang; both show mature craftsmanship in plot, incident and characterization. However, other stories in both collections are overly sentimental.

In *Lazarre* (1901), representative of her nine historical romances, C. utilizes the "lost dauphin" theme and quest motif. Raised by the Iroquois near Lake Champlain, Eleazar Williams ("Lazarre") undertakes the missions of discovering his true identity and winning the beautiful Eagle de Ferrier. His quest takes him from New York to France and Russia, and then to Ohio and Wisconsin, where he finally settles, united with Eagle. By making Lazarre the narrator, C. maintains tantalizing ambiguity regarding his identity, but most of the other characters lack complexity. C. usually stretched her talents too far in the novels, but some of her short stories are excellent.

BIBLIOGRAPHY: Price, R., "Mrs. C.'s Early Experiments with Critical Realism," *AL* 17 (May 1945): 140–51; Treece, P. B., "A Hidden Woman of Local Color: Mrs. M. H. C.," *MMisc* 3 (1975): 24–31; Wilson, M. L., *Biography of M. H. C.* (1904)

KENNETH A. ROBB

CERVANTES, Lorna Dee

b. 6 August 1954, San Francisco, California

C.'s poetry voices the experience of being a Chicana in Anglo-American society. Actively involved in the Chicano cultural and literary movement of the 1970s, she began reading her poetry in public as early as 1974 at the Quinto Festival de los Teatros Chicanos in Mexico City. Throughout the years, she has gained recognition writing poetry that expresses the feelings of alienation and frustration born from the sense of not belonging to either the American or the Mexican culture, and from the experience of marginalization by white Anglo society. She writes as a woman, as a member of the Chicano community, and as a poet. Her poetry is at once clear, direct, powerful, narrative, descriptive, and lyrical.

The title of C.'s first collection, *Emplumada* (1981), embodies the main themes of the work; it combines *emplumada* ("plumed") with an echo of *plumada* ("pen flourish"). This combination not only points to the use of bird metaphors throughout the book but also to C.'s concern with writing as a liberating and empowering tool. Further, the allusion to Quetzalcóatl, the plumed serpent and Mexican god of wisdom, indicates C.'s concern to connect with her mythical heritage as a way to overcome feelings of fragmentation.

Emplumada is divided into three sections, each containing a brief title, the third of which carries the name of the collection as a whole. The first presents the portrait of a woman growing up in her *barrio*. It recounts the child's experiences as she grows and discovers the grim reality of abuse and violence that surrounds her and her woman-centered household. The second section tackles the problems of language, writing, and oppression as well as the sense of alienation felt by the woman in her inability to reconcile her heritage, her tradition, and her utopian ideals with the modern Anglo-American world that surrounds her. The poems of the third section become increasingly more lyrical, with abundant bird imagery, and may be described as love poems. Here the voice belongs to a mature woman who has found a sense of harmony and wholeness.

Like the title of her first book, the title of her second embodies the main themes of the work as a whole. Many of the poems in *From the Cables of Genocide: Poems on Love and Hunger* (1991) are addressed to an absent lover or husband. These poems speak of death, love, hunger, alienation, and absence while continuing to recount the experience of a Chicana living in the western U.S.

This collection is divided into four sections. The poems of the first section range from long narrative-like ones to the last which is formally constructed in the shape of a half-heart. The heart as symbol prevails in this section with its most obvious association to love. However, feelings of absent love prevail, as do feelings of separation, emptiness, isolation, and absence. Likewise the theme of absence is present in section two and is ironically conveyed by means of food imagery; food does not provide fulfillment but, as in "On Love and Hunger," points to lack and therefore to hunger: "I feed you / as you hunger. / I hunger as you feed / and refuse / the food I give." Finally, sections three and four recollect all of her main images. Section three speaks of oppression and resistance and section four, concluding the book, is filled with water imagery and all the connotations associated with it: danger, death, horror, desire, rebirth, and hope.

If *Emplumada* gained her the recognition she so much deserves, *From the Cables of Genocide* confirms her as one of the most powerful voices of 20th-c. poetry. She provides us with works that recount an experience that is at once personal and collective.

BIBLIOGRAPHY: Sánchez, M. E., *Contemporary Chicana Poetry* (1985); Seator, L., "*Emplumada:* Chicana Rites-of-Passage," *MELUS* 11 (Summer 1984): 23–37

CONSTANZA GOMEZ

CHA, Theresa Hak Kyung
b. 4 March 1951, Pusan, Korea; d. 5 November 1982, New York City

C.'s *Dictee* (1982) is the most well-known publication of experimental writing by an Asian American writer. A visual, video, and performance artist as well as a writer and an editor of a volume of film theory entitled *Apparatus* (1980), C.'s art is distinctive in its crossing boundaries of genre. Her multimedia work has been exhibited by the University Art Museum at the University of California at Berkeley (1990), as well as the Whitney Museum of American Art in New York (1992–93). Works in these exhibitions included mixed-media pieces made of materials such as ink, paper, cloth, rubber stamps, glass or porcelain jars, and plywood; artist's books; photograph negatives; videos; poems; and performance documentation.

The form of *Dictee* reflects this multimedia sensibility. *Dictee* is a collage text that juxtaposes prose, poetry, photographs, handwritten drafts, historical documents, biographical excerpts, letters, translation exercises, diagrams, maps, charts, and other "found" texts in what critic Lisa Lowe calls a "discontinuous weave." A chart resembling a table of contents leads the reader to assume that the book is organized into nine sections, each named after one of the nine Muses. However, elements of the text before and after these nine sections unsettle the reader's expectation that the book may be contained and understood within this paradigm. This unsettling of its own method of organization is characteristic of C.'s aesthetic, in which form and content are constantly shifting.

C. was especially interested in treating language as an object rather than a medium, of representation. Experimental syntax and sentence construction are characteristic of her work: sentences and phrases are frequently fragmented, inverted, or repeated. Linked to C.'s questioning and manipulation of elements of language are her concern with exile and displacement, as well as the problems of memory and history. One might consider her uprooting and transplanting of words and phrases from one context to another an allegory for cultural and geopolitical displacement—a process explicitly referred to in sections of *Dictee.*

Dictee is a text that is heavily populated by female characters—not only a mother figure, St. Theresa of Lisieux, Joan of Arc, and the Korean resistance leader Yu Guan Soon, but also references to unnamed or abstract female figures, signaled only by the pronouns "she" or "her." Rather than reinforcing an essential or foundationalist female identity, however, C.'s invocation of multiple named and unnamed women is in keeping with her aesthetic of shifting and displacement, so that gender identification is fluid rather than fixed.

The critical reception of C.'s work has had varied locations: her work has been read within the frameworks of conceptual art, experimental writing, film studies, poetry studies, poststructuralism, feminism, psychoanalysis, new historicism, Korean and Korean American nationalism, postcolonialism, and critical race studies. This appreciation of C. by critics with such different orientations and investments attests to the richness and profundity of her writing and art. Her work has been described by many as haunting, beautiful, and deeply intelligent. As interest in C.'s work continues to grow, she will be established as one of the major visionaries of her time.

BIBLIOGRAPHY: Kim, E. H., and N. Alarcón, eds., *Writing Self, Writing Nation* (1994); Spahr, J. M., "Postmodernism, Readers, and T. H. K. C.'s *Dictee,*" *CollL* 23 (October 1996): 23–43; Wolf, S., "T. C.: Recalling Telling Retelling," *Afterimage* 14 (Summer 1986): 11–13

JULIANA CHANG

CHAMBERS, Robert W[illiam]
b. 26 May 1865, Brooklyn, New York; d. 16 December 1933, New York City

After an early period of studying art in New York and Paris, and serving as an illustrator for various American magazines during the 1890s, C. turned to fiction and began a career as an immensely popular and prolific writer who was always sensitive to public tastes. Several of his novels and volumes of short stories fall in the general category of SCIENCE FICTION; more properly, they are tales of fantasy, the SUPERNATURAL, and horror. The stories in *The King in Yellow*

(1891) and the novel *The Maker of Moons* (1895) sometimes haunt as well as deal with haunting. Contemporary fascination with prehistory and specimen collecting, psychic phenomena, and eugenics and women's rights are reflected—always together with a sentimental love plot—in the satire of *In Search of the Unknown* (1904), *The Green Mouse* (1910), and *The Gay Rebellion* (1913), respectively. A lost race figures into the adult fantasy of *The Slayer of Souls* (1920).

Another genre in which C. excelled was the historical romance. Rousing action and effective description, if not historical accuracy, mark his tetralogy on the Franco-Prussian War. During the turn-of-the-century vogue for books about the American Revolution, he produced the first three of six novels on that conflict in New York state: *Cardigan* (1901), *The Maid-at-Arms* (1902), and *The Reckoning* (1905). The series continued with *The Hidden Children* (1914), *The Little Red Foot* (1921), which belongs before *The Reckoning* in plot sequence, and *America* (1924). Typical of the period in tone as well as subject matter, and despite dealing with "independence" from England, these romances express, as C. noted in the preface to *America,* a conservative and xenophobic pride in "all English speaking peoples." C.'s conventional Civil War novels include *Special Messenger* (1909) and *Ailsa Paige* (1910).

A third group of novels by C. treat salient aspects of modern American society, from alcoholism to the new morality and divorce: *The Fighting Chance* (1906) and *The Danger Mark* (1909), *The Younger Set* (1907) and *The Firing Line* (1908), among others. If produced to formula, intended for a mass market and responsive to its demands, C.'s fiction does possess the virtues of exciting plots and a competent though uninspired style, and has the additional value of serving as an indicator of middle-class tastes of the time. As much entertainer as interpreter, C. molded a career as a novelist that parallels his earlier one as a popular illustrator.

BIBLIOGRAPHY: Murray, W., "Lovecraft, Blackwood, and C.: A Colloquium of Ghosts," *StWF* 13 (Summer 1993): 2–8; Weinstein, L., "R. W. C.," in Franklin, B. E., ed., *Supernatural Fiction Writers: Fantasy and Horror* (1985), vol. 2: 739–45

BENJAMIN S. LAWSON

CHANDLER, Raymond

b. 23 July 1888, Chicago, Illinois; d. 26 March 1959, La Jolla, California

Finding himself middle-aged and unemployed in the middle of the Great Depression, C. embarked on a literary career, of sorts. Although the product of a classical education who had in fact committed some poetry in his youth, C. turned his attention and hopes to the pulp magazines, whose penny a word pay scale might provide him with something resembling an income. The pulps had for a full decade been publishing hardboiled detective stories alongside the straight action and adventure yarns meant to appeal to a predominately male working class audience. In the work of a few writers, notably Dashiell HAMMETT, the hardboiled story was acquiring some measure of literary respectability. Hammett's novel *The Maltese Falcon,* published in 1930, was hailed by many sophisticated readers as a serious novel, transcending genre considerations. Hard-boiled detective fiction, then, might have seemed to C. a kind of commercial fiction an educated and sensitive man like himself need not be ashamed to write.

He prepared himself for his first submission by carefully studying representative samples of this fiction, especially as he found them in *Black Mask,* the most respected of the pulps. In all, C. spent five months writing his first story, "Blackmailers Don't Shoot," which appeared in *Black Mask* in December 1933; C. was then forty-five.

Having thus committed himself, C. would champion the artistic value of hard-boiled detective fiction throughout his career, most eloquently in the essay, "The Simple Art of Murder," first published in the *Atlantic Monthly* in December 1944. Here he celebrates in particular the work of Hammett, although, for C., Hammett suggests possibilities beyond those he managed to realize. In C.'s much quoted formulation, "Down these mean streets a man must go who is not himself mean. . . . He is the hero, he is everything." The hero contributes to the "quality of redemption" in "everything that can be called art."

In Philip Marlowe, the detective protagonist of his novels, C. provides his version of the hero, a more complex figure than the code heroes created by Hammett. Where Hammett emphasized surfaces in a relentlessly objective prose, C. insists upon the psychological and, above all, ethical richness of the inner life of Marlowe. In his role as narrator, Marlowe constantly comments on, judges, and searches for hints of redemption in, the mean streets. C.'s hero, unlimited by a clearly defined class position, moves freely and perceptively within the existing class structure, permitting him to explore a fictional world of considerable range and complexity that is also a stylized but incisive portrait of Southern California as it sprawls toward midcentury. The tension between the romantic sensibility of the hero and the demands of survival in the threatening world C. depicts generates both the celebrated C. style, swinging from tough talk to baroque simile off the American plain style, and the moral tension between the detective's need to know the world as it is and the idealist's desire to see the world as it might be.

The tensions that characterize C.'s best work are most fully in play in his first two novels, *The Big Sleep* (1939) and *Farewell, My Lovely* (1940). *The High Window* (1942) falls below the level established in these two novels, but C. is back in form in *The Lady in the Lake* (1943). The later work is on the whole inferior. The sixth novel in the series, *The Long Goodbye* (1953), has its admirers, but the tensions of C.'s best work have collapsed as Marlowe slides into a cynicism and self-pity from which the author does not succeed in distancing himself.

If Hammett was the most important influence in the definition of the hard-boiled detective story, C. has been as important in its development. His detective hero has served as the point of departure for countless later writers, while his style and the range and sharpness of his social observation redefined standards in the hard-boiled idiom. His inclusion in the *Library of America* series may be taken to mark his admission to the American literary canon. Some would say he transcended his genre. Perhaps it is more accurate to say that he revealed its possibilities.

BIBLIOGRAPHY: Luhr, W., *R. C. and Film* (1982); Mac-Shane, F., *The Life of R. C.* (1976); Marling, W., *R. C.* (1986); Speir, J., *R. C.* (1981); Wolfe, P., *Something More Than Night: The Case of R. C.* (1985)

W. P. KENNEY

CHANNING, William Ellery
b. 7 April 1780, Newport, Rhode Island; d. 2 October 1842, Bennington, Vermont

In American cultural and literary studies, C. is recognized primarily for his liberal theological teachings and his formulation of theological ideas that ultimately resulted in the founding of Unitarianism in America; for his indirect influence on New England literary TRANSCENDENTALISM, most notably in the works of 19th-c. American romantic writers such as Ralph Waldo EMERSON, Henry Wadsworth LONGFELLOW, James Russell LOWELL, and Henry David THOREAU; and for his participation in social reform movements, particularly abolition, in early 19th-c. America. In his rhetorically impassioned "Remarks on National Literature" (1823), C. called for a "literary Declaration of Independence," an independence he believed could be achieved through the development of a theologically and democratically inspired national literature. Since America, C. declared, had already been created for a new kind of man, then its writers must create a

"higher literature," one not merely imitative or conforming to any prior literary or intellectual heritage, but rather directed toward a progressive and new understanding of human destiny. In similarly stirring terms, C.'s "Self-Culture" (1838) calls upon his fellow Americans to promote "self-culture," a concept adapted in part by Emerson in "Self-Reliance." C.'s writings were consistently linked to his theological commitments, and he relied heavily on biblical analogy and metaphor to further his arguments. In "Self-Culture," for example, C. explains in short, emphatic, and theologically impassioned phrases how the national potential in the U.S. could be achieved through the liberal, religious, and literary education of its citizens and also through the progressive, self-reliant, intellectual, and self-motivated striving of the individual.

Although New England transcendentalism ideologically differed from New England Unitarianism, C.'s complex, varied, and fervent sermons, public speeches, argumentative treatises, and published editorial letters were successfully utilized by intellectuals aligned with both intellectual movements. Despite his indirect influence on the New England transcendentalist movement, C. never aligned himself with it, and most of his writings or speeches were focused on theological issues explicitly related to Christianity, or, more specifically, Unitarianism. Yet C.'s concerns ranged from those displayed in theological treatises, such as "The Moral Argument against Calvinism" (1820), to those in literary or cultural ones, such as "Remarks on the Character of Writings of John Milton" (1825), to those in political or social ones, such as "The Duty of the Free States" (1842). In the first treatise, C. argues against the Calvinistic idea of man's essential depravity; in the second, he presents a stirring testimony to the spiritually "unapproachable" and literary greatness of Milton; and in the third, he redefines the religious parameters of his uncompromising political and moral commitment against slavery.

Literary critics after 1970 tend to treat C. as a less significant figure in the development of major 19th-c. American literary transcendentalism or ROMANTICISM; and with the development of the feminist critique of New England transcendentalism, C.'s critique of religious dogma, his liberal ideas regarding social and national reform, his often impassioned abolitionist stance, and his general exclusion of commentary of women's reform issues have been cited as both contributing to and inhibiting the development of 19th-c. FEMINISM. Nevertheless, C.'s significance to the development of American literary culture and of early 19th-c. literary variations on American romanticism continues to reside in his uncompromising and impassioned defense of the political, social, and theological rights of all humans.

BIBLIOGRAPHY: Delbanco, A., *W. E. C.: An Essay on the Liberal Spirit in America* (1981); Douglas, A., *The Feminization of American Culture* (1977); Edgell, D. P., *W. E. C.: An Intellectual Portrait* (1955); Patterson, R. L., *The Philosophy of W. E. C.* (1952)

B. A. HUME

CHANNING, William Ellery, II

b. 29 November 1817, Boston, Massachusetts; d. 23 December 1901, Concord, Massachusetts

C.'s greatest contributions to American literature are the unrecorded conversations between himself and two of the major figures of the transcendentalist movement, Henry David THOREAU and Ralph Waldo EMERSON. To each, C. was sympathetic intellectually and emotionally, a trusted critic, and a friend of unusual proportions. Their walks with C. through the woods around Concord provided Thoreau and Emerson with a sounding board for their theories about nature, poetry, and literature. For both men, C. was an under acknowledged resource, in part responsible for their evolution in thought and the person in whom their ideas of friendship, love, and genius were brought into immediate, familiar experience.

As a literary figure himself, however, C. was ignored in his lifetime and is nearly forgotten today. Reared in Boston, the son of a preeminent physician and Harvard professor, C. left college after only a few weeks to pursue a life as a poet. His first published poem "The Spider" appeared in the *New England Magazine* in 1835 and suggested a promising career. From then until his death sixty-six years later, he produced a steady stream of poetry and some prose, publishing in periodicals, gift books, biographies, church Christmas annuals, or any other publication that would accept his work. He published seven volumes of verse during his lifetime, of which no book was a financial success, most notably *Poems* (1845), *Poems: Second Series* (1847), and *The Woodman, and Other Poems* (1849). C.'s other works of poetry include *Near Home* (1858), *The Wanderer* (1871), *Eliot, a Poem* (1885), and *John Brown and the Heroes of Harper's Ferry* (1886).

The reasons for this are clear: a great deal of the poetry he wrote was third rate; his artistic production was more quantitative than qualitative. A transcendentalist, C. possessed a love of nature, individualism, and self-reliance; he rebelled against technology, venerated the emotional life, and made his verses show a skeptical urban audience how their lives were being wasted. Though he could not resist the temptation to

indulge in occasional youthful melancholy, his poetry is mostly optimistic; it reflects the refreshment he found in nature and attempts to capture the sense of awe realizable only in the natural world. These beliefs C. attempted to portray in his verse; unfortunately, most of his poems failed. C.'s poems too often suffer from lackluster metaphors and images; his routine descriptions often rob his poems of a real imaginative vitality. Sadly, C. employs vague abstractions and murky phrases; he was never receptive to the possibilities of symbolism nor the joy of using language in fresh, precise ways. Added to these limitations are the techniques that so often fail him: he inverts words for rhymes that become strained; he adds to and takes feet from his lines in an erratic, obtrusive attempt to avoid monotony. And though a champion of freedom in verse, his poems show a consistent deference to established practices—notably sonnet form, blank-verse monologue, and four and five beat rhythms.

It was in prose, however, that C. garnered his greatest acclaim. His biography of his longtime friend, *Thoreau: The Poet Naturalist* (1873), was an honest attempt to portray the author's life in all its attractiveness. In this work, C. exhibited the characteristics that marked much of his prose—his comic sensibility and bitingly satiric voice; however, these qualities were reserved for prose, a literary form C. deprecated, but one in which he still attempted to grapple with the larger transcendentalist issues. In ways more successful than in his poetry, C.'s prose captured the moods of New England and his transcendentalist friends, an achievement for which he should be remembered and studied.

BIBLIOGRAPHY: Hudspeth, R. N., *E. C.* (1973); McGill, F. T., *C. of Concord* (1967)

ANDREW J. LEWIS

CHAPPELL, Fred

b. 28 May 1936, Canton, North Carolina

Among the most accomplished, versatile, and intellectually adept of contemporary American writers and critics, C. is a Southern poet and novelist whose rich depictions of his native North Carolina and its people resonate with universal human emotion and conflict. This resonance has earned him the respect of fellow writers—southern novelist Lee SMITH has called him the "one truly great writer we have among us"—and international recognition, including a Prix de Milleur de Livres Etrangers from the Académie Française (1971).

With its striking sophistication, music, and variety, C.'s poetry is his most original work. *Midquest* (1981), a tetralogy universally praised by critics, brings together four previously published volumes—*River, Bloodfire, Wind Mountain,* and *Earthsleep*—each of which is based on one of the four essential elements of water, fire, air, and earth. Each volume contains eleven poems spoken at the Dantean midpoint of the poet's life—his thirty-fifth birthday. Moving freely between poetic forms and voices and between description and introspection, *Midquest* includes dialogue, narration, direct address, and meditation. Though free verse and blank verse predominate, as C. notes in his useful preface to the book, intervals of terza rima, rhymed couplets, elegiacs, chant royal, and Yeatsian tetrameter keep the book's music various and startling. C. acknowledges in his preface to the book that his model for it was the sampler, with each poetic form standing for a "different fancy stitch." In his next collection, *Castle Tzingal* (1984)—a "political fairy tale" according to the book's dust jacket—the poet uses the form of the Elizabethan revenge tragedy to create an offbeat, tightly plotted dramatic poem driven by strong characterization. In *Spring Garden: New and Selected Poems* (1995), rather than follow the usual chronological approach of the new and selected poems, C. divides the collection into seven sections, each with a theme and prologue of its own. Together, these sections comprise a loose narrative in which C. picks and chooses carefully among twenty-five years' worth of work.

In his prose depictions of the North Carolina Appalachians and their people in *It Is Time, Lord* (1963), *Moments of Light* (1980), and *I Am One of You Forever* (1985), C. has pursued the darker, less nostalgic faces of his homeland as well as its more redeeming aspects. In *The Gaudy Place* (1972), a novel light in tone but heavily freighted with sociological questions and implications about the webs formed by crossing human fates, C. explores what happens when characters from seedy, whore-haunted Gimlet Street collide with those from a liberal, moral, family-based middle class. *Dagon* (1968) narrates the moral and mental disintegration of Peter Leland, a minister whose academic interest in the pagan god Dagon entangles him with Mina, a sadistic teenaged nymphomaniac who leads him to murder his wife before eventually torturing Leland to death. At the opposite extreme from these dark novels, *I Am One of You Forever* bears witness story by story to the first-person narrator's gradual initiation into the joys, sorrows, and ambiguities of the adult world. His six novels and two collections of short fiction have received mixed reviews, but each—with the exception of *It Is Time, Lord*—was declared a masterpiece by

one critic or another, and C.'s reputation as a stylist of the first rank seems secure.

Also a demanding critic, C. has written reviews for such prominent literary journals as the *Georgia Review, Sewanee Review,* and the *Saturday Evening Post*. His essays on poetry are collected in *Plow Naked* (1993).

BIBLIOGRAPHY: Dillard, R. H. W., "Letters from a Distant Lover: The Novels of F. C.," *HC* 10 (April 1973): 1–15; Makuck, P., "C.'s Continuities: First and Last Words," *VQR* 68 (Spring 1992): 315–22; Taylor, H., *Compulsory Figures: Essays on Recent American Poets* (1992)

GORDON JOHNSTON

CHAVEZ, Denise
b. 15 August 1948, Las Cruces, New Mexico

Recognized as one of the leading Chicana writers—a member of "Las Girlfriends," a small group of Latina authors and friends, including Julia ALVAREZ, Sandra CISNEROS, and Ana CASTILLO—C. began her career as a playwright. She has since gained popularity with the publication of two major works, *The Last of the Menu Girls* (1986) and *Face of an Angel* (1994), which focus primarily on the lives of women, notably Chicanas, who live in the U.S. Southwest.

The Last of the Menu Girls is a collection of seven, closely-related short stories, which C. refers to as "dramatic vignettes." The stories form a bildungsroman, focusing on the coming of age of Rocio Esquibel, a Mexican American college student, who, in the title story, delivers menus to patients in a New Mexico hospital. It is through the encounters and interactions with the various patients in the hospital as well as people in her neighborhood that young Rocio grows into maturity. Rocio is further influenced by her mother, who encourages her to become a writer. Heeding her mother's advice, Rocio provides a voice for the traditionally unheard Mexican Americans who surround and shape her life. As such, *The Last of the Menu Girls* is the result of Rocio's craft as a writer. The work was well received, and critics praised C.'s insightful characterizations and revealing dialogues. Rudolfo ANAYA heralded C.'s *The Last of the Menu Girls* for contributing richly to the canon of Chicano/a literature: "The feminine voice adds a new vision and dimension to the literature of this community. Clearly, a new vanguard is here, and its name is woman."

In her first novel, *Face of an Angel* (1994), C. continues to write about Mexican American womanhood, this time focusing on the life of Soveida Dosamantes, a divorced and widowed waitress, who finds solace and strength while working at El Farol Mexican Restaurant in the fictitious town of Agua Oscura, New Mexico. Soveida is the latest of a long line of suffering women in a patriarchal culture. The novel offers readers an account—often zany, often tragic—of Soveida's adventures in Agua Oscura and the memorable characters who touch her life. *Face of an Angel* illustrates beautifully the strength and perseverance of the Mexican American woman. C. even produces Soveida's own writings in the novel, a handbook for waitressing, which asserts the value and dignity of women's work in a male-dominated world. *Face of an Angel* further offers a revealing and bitter portrait of its male characters, men who tend to perpetuate the oppression of women in their culture. Although Soveida's mother warns her against Mexican men ("I don't have anything against our own, except that they don't make good husbands"), she seems destined to be trapped in a cultural, vicious circle of relationships with unsuitable men. Perhaps C.'s greatest triumph as a writer is her skillful ability to convey value and voice to the struggles of Chicanas who must balance identity and gender roles in a bicultural world.

C. has also written three children's plays and has edited an anthology of plays by Latinas, *Shattering the Myth: Plays by Hispanic Women* (1992). Her writings have been acclaimed, earning her several prestigious awards: Best Play from the University of New Mexico for *The Wait* (1970), the Steele Jones Fiction Award for her story "The Last of the Menu Girls," two fellowships from the National Endowment for the Arts, a Rockefeller Foundation Fellowship, and a Creative Writing Arts Fellowship from the Cultural Arts Council of Houston.

BIBLIOGRAPHY: Eysturoy, A. O., "D. C.," in Balassi, W., et al., eds., *This Is about Vision: Interviews with Southwestern Writers* (1990): 157–69; Heard, M. E., "The Theatre of D. C.: Interior Landscapes with 'sabor nuevomexicano," *AmRev* 16 (Summer 1988): 83–91; Kanellos, N., *The Hispanic Almanac: From Columbus to Corporate America* (1994)

JOSEPH M. VIERA

CHAYEFSKY, [Sidney] Paddy
b. 29 January 1923, New York City; d. 1 August 1981, New York City

Even among historians of television's "Golden Age," the era when he first achieved fame in the 1950s, C. today is perceived mostly as an historical figure. His Hollywood writing, principally *Marty (*1955), *The Goddess* (1958), *The Hospital* (1972), and *Network*

(1976), although still sometimes cited as significant, seems neglected. And apart from *The Tenth Man* (1959), his writing for the theater has become practically unknown.

His dramatic vision evolved from a type of sentimentalized realism, exemplified in *Marty,* through the heightened naturalism of *The Goddess,* to the quasi-historical, quasi-realism of *Gideon* (1961), to a type of mild absurdism, as in *The Latent Heterosexual* (1967). He deserved the widespread esteem that was his for more than twenty years. Yet once he had departed from dramatizing the nominal insider preoccupied with the vagaries of conjugal love, as in *Bachelor Party* (1953) and *Middle of the Night* (1954)—having envisioned the relationship between a transcendent religious faith and daily life, as in *The Tenth Man;* having, that is, refocused his concern from illuminating the life of the postwar, middle-class urban America, and shifted from the little screen to stage to film—C. returned to play writing in the mid-1960s with a very different subject matter only to meet rejection, the reasons for which seem obvious—and mistaken.

Neither of his mid-1960s plays, *The Passion of Josef D.* (1964) and *The Latent Heterosexual,* proceed linearly. In *The Passion of Josef D.,* the 1917 Russian Revolution is humanized, while *The Latent Homosexual* offers a comic but disturbing account of the reach of the corporate sensibility into individual and social identity. As long as C. had restricted himself to ethnic characters and plots or to plotting the lives of so-called common men and women, both audience and critics were generally favorable. But the serious elaboration of class conflict, of complex sexuality, or of the implication of inherited or otherwise superimposed codes of conduct and personal fulfillment seem to have compromised his appeal. The majority of C.'s scripts are well-made, but *The Passion of Josef D.* and especially *The Latent Heterosexual* contain dramatic energy and power of an order which invites not merely rereading but reproduction.

C.'s dialogue—continually sharp, intelligent, active, and specific—assumes in these late plays greater precision and point, its articulation of character and circumstances becoming ever more adept. But the climate of opinion, always an element in media priorities, must have preferred diffidence toward both the former Soviet Union and homosexuality when these plays were written and premiered. Making Stalin somewhat sympathetic, enlivening the vital distinction between his code of conduct and Lenin's, and ultimately offering reasons to heighten our awareness of the human side of the Soviet Union—such choices were quixotic at the height of the Cold War. And then, next time out as dramatist, to create the compellingly theatrical gay protagonist, John Morley, a protagonist who, moreover, becomes in act 2 an extremely successful but unattractive and pitiable incorporation of heterosexuality, C. dramatizes dynamic interrelations among capitalism, geopolitics, self-knowledge, personal contentment, and social conscience. What the 1960s disdained to appreciate, however, the post-Stonewall gay civil rights movement, the dissolution of the Soviet Union and the reaction to the widely-publicized profiteering of the 1980s may well have positioned *The Passion of Josef D.* and *The Latent Homosexual,* indeed much of C.'s work, to be understood and appreciated more clearly.

BIBLIOGRAPHY: Cohen, S. B., ed., *From Hester Street to Hollywood: The Jewish-American Stage and Screen* (1983); Considine, S., *Mad as Hell: The Life and Work of P. C.* (1994)

THOMAS T. APPLE

CHEEVER, John

b. 27 May 1912, Quincy, Massachusetts; d. 18 June 1982, Ossining, New York

One of modern American literature's preeminent short story writers and novelists, C. is also the principal chronicler of suburban malaise. Next to John O'HARA, C. published more short stories in the *New Yorker* than any other writer (120 of them). He also published in *Esquire, Playboy,* the *Saturday Evening Post* and many other mainstream magazines. Though his short stories became models for many younger writers during the 1950s, 1960s, and 1970s, his novels made him both rich and famous, especially *The Wapshot Chronicle* (1957), *The Wapshot Scandal* (1964), and *Falconer* (1977). *Falconer* became a best-seller and the *Stories of John Cheever* (1978) won him a Pulitzer Prize and a National Book Critics Circle Award in 1979, along with an honorary doctorate from Harvard University in 1981.

One of the early traumas in young C.'s life was his expulsion from the prestigious Thayer Academy in nearby South Braintree, Massachusetts, for poor grades when he was seventeen. C. wrote a short story about it called "Expelled," and sent it to the editor of the *New Republic,* Malcolm COWLEY, who published it in October 1929. Rather than returning to school, C. decided to go to New York City and try to publish his stories. After several fallow years, and with Cowley's help, he began to publish them in *Hound & Horn, Pagany, Collier's,* the *Yale Review, Story,* and the *New Yorker.* In 1938, he also worked for the Federal Writers' Project—part of President Franklin Delano Roosevelt's WPA projects—as a writer and editor.

At age twenty-seven, C. met and married Mary Winternitz, the daughter of two well-known physicians: her mother was the first woman in America to earn a medical degree and her father eventually became Dean of the Yale University Medical School. Just as the young couple was settling down, World War II broke out and C. enlisted in the army. Thanks to the publication of his first critically acclaimed short story collection, *The Way Some People Live* (1943), his military superiors sent him to work with fellow writers at the Signal Corps in New York City to work on anti-Fascist propaganda films, a move that probably saved his life since well over half of his infantry unit were killed in Europe. Many of the stories in *The Way Some People Live* dealt with victims of the Great Depression, the separation of young married couples due to the war, and the isolation and loneliness of marginalized middle-and lower-middle-class individuals. Though many of C.'s stories were autobiographical, they are autobiographical in the patterns of his experiences rather than a literal presentation of actual events. Throughout his writing life, C.'s fictive treatments of these events create rather than document what those experiences meant to him.

After the war, C. began a novel about the fall of a respected New England family named Wapshot, a family that greatly resembled his own. Though it took him twenty years to finish what would become *The Wapshot Chronicle,* his short stories established him as one of America's most innovative fiction writers. The publication of *The Enormous Radio and Other Stories* in 1953 established him as a sophisticated writer using mythic patterns in the title story and "Torch Song," stories which evoke deep mythic resonance by presenting the woman in "Torch Song" as a veiled form of the Greek goddess Hecate, and the couple in "The Enormous Radio" as the fall of a pair of innocents into the painful knowledge of the reality of their own lives. Many of his stories explored the love/hate relationship between brothers, a problem he himself had with his brother, Fred, throughout their lives. His stories also become longer and more psychologically complex. After winning a Guggenheim Fellowship in 1951, the C. family moved to Westchester County and C.'s stories concerned themselves with the lives of bored suburbanites who drank too much and had extramarital affairs whenever they had an opportunity. He established a pattern of mythologizing the commonplace with his prize-winning story "The Country Husband," the novel *The Wapshot Scandal,* and the story collection, *The Brigadier and the Golf Window* (1964). With the establishment of fictive communities such as St. Botolphs, Shady Hill, Proxmire Manor, and Bullet Park, C. created mythopoeic communities comparable to William FAULKNER's Yoknapatawpha County. Within these Westchester-like communities, C. presents his primary themes for the rest of his writing career: alcoholic obsessiveness, sexual desperation, the necessity of illusion, the fear of financial ruin, and the failure of wealth and position to bring permanent happiness. These themes were also the dark core of C.'s own life and enabled him to transform them into the recurring subject matter of his best fiction. His picture appeared on the cover of *Time* in 1964, calling him "Ovid in Ossining."

Because C.'s drinking forced him to quit his teaching position at Boston University in 1974, he did sober up at the Smithers Alcohol Rehabilitation Center in Manhattan and immediately began his most successful novel, *Falconer,* the idea of which came from his teaching at Sing Sing Prison in his hometown of Ossining, New York. The critics were universal in their praise of *Falconer;* his picture appeared on the cover of *Newsweek* in March 1977. *Falconer* also explored in depth the most important topic in all of his books: the conflict of brothers. The publication of *The Stories of J. C.* by Knopf in 1978 won him a Pulitzer Prize in 1979 and the American Book Award in 1981.

BIBLIOGRAPHY: Donaldson, S., *J. C.* (1988); Hunter, G. W., *J. C.: The Hobgoblin Company of Love* (1983); Meanor, P., *J. C. Revisited* (1995)

PATRICK MEANOR

CHESEBRO' [or CHESEBROUGH], Caroline

b. 30 March 1825, Canandaigua, New York; d. 16 February 1873, Piermont, New York

C. contributed to magazines such as *Atlantic Monthly, Galaxy, Harper's, Knickerbocker, Lippincott's,* and *Putnam's.* Her novels readily found publishers, and the better critics approved her work. But critical acclaim and publication of about twenty volumes of fiction—short stories and novels, some for young adults—did not make C.'s bold thought and unorthodox style popular. Current scholars are examining her work with new interest.

Born in Canandaigua, New York, where she attended the Canandaigua Seminary, C. began writing stories and articles for *Graham's* and *Holden's Dollar Magazine* in about 1848. Biographers neither identify the source of the unusual ideas presented in C.'s works of the 1850s nor account for her later conservatism. In her last eight years, she taught rhetoric and composition at the Packer Collegiate Institute in Brooklyn, New York.

C.'s first book, *Dream-Land by Daylight* (1851), collects previously published stories. The *Harper's*

reviewer found in her work "unmistakable evidence of originality of mind," but thought her lack of grace and fluency would make C. unpopular.

In her novels, as in her stories, C. boldly examined a variety of religious experiences and created a new kind of woman who recognized her right to enjoy a fulfilling life, though not necessarily in a conventional marriage. *Isa, a Pilgrimage* (1852) follows Isa Lee, an orphan reared in a devout household, as she develops into a freethinker, turns to socialism and feminism, and rejects the marriage contract. *The Children of Light* (1853), which contrasts orthodoxy and transcendentalism, traces the experiences that bring together to a mutual lifetime commitment Asia Phillips, a poor, aspiring actress betrayed by her mentor-lover, and Vesta Maderon, a wealthy friend, herself rejected by a clergyman in favor of a childlike parishioner. *In Victoria, or the World Overcome* (1856) Maud Saltonstall, a child of nature, falls victim to an accusation of witchcraft brought by highly educated and envious Hope Rossitur. The novel indicts Puritan-based culture as particularly destructive to women.

Peter Carradine (1863), considered C.'s best-written novel, belongs to the conservative period in which her vision for women had narrowed markedly. Through a conflict with Carradine, Miranda Roy, a spirited teacher, loses her position—thus her independence. Eventually she marries the minister who converted her. Mercy Fuller, who replaces Roy, marries Carradine as a way of participating in the moral government of the world.

BIBLIOGRAPHY: Baym, N., *Woman's Fiction* (1978): 208–230; Brown, H. R., *The Sentimental Novel in America, 1789–1860* (1940); Freibert, L. M., "C. C.," in Knight, D. D., ed., *Nineteenth-Century American Women Writers: A Bio-Biographical Critical Sourcebook* (1997): 36–41

LUCY M. FREIBERT

CHESNUT, Mary Boykin Miller

b. 31 March 1823, Camden, South Carolina; d. 22 November 1886, Camden, South Carolina

Although she tried her hand at essays and novels, C. excelled as a diarist, writing mostly about the Civil War and her life in Camden, South Carolina. Her childhood on a plantation gave her firsthand knowledge of slavery, planters, and Southern politics, but her family opened other windows for her by placing her in Madame Talvande's French School for Young Ladies in Charleston. Her C. learned not only French and developed a keen interest in Gallic culture but also German. Here she grew to admire French novelists and here she formed social ties to some of the South's best families, one of which was the Chesnut clan of Camden. Shortly after reaching her seventeenth year, she became the bride of James Chesnut, Jr. His role in politics eventually led to his election to the U.S. Senate, an office he resigned to throw his energies behind the Confederacy.

His association with Confederate leaders and politics, in particular Jefferson Davis, took him and his wife to the center of Confederate activities. It is from this position that C. recorded her impressions of Confederate leaders, the women in their lives, and the battles they waged on the field and in the drawing rooms and legislative chambers of Montgomery and Richmond. And she did her recording with keen eyes, sharp ears, and a clear mind, leaving portraits of men and women whose lives are played out against a war begun in high hopes and ending in bitter defeat and painful straits. Robert Penn WARREN was to say of her work: "As an intimate view of actors and actions of great consequence and as a human picture—tender, outraged, comic—of a great war, there is nothing quite like [her] book."

That book was not to appear in her lifetime and not in its entirety until 1981, when C. Vann Woodward published *Mary Chesnut's Civil War,* which won the 1982 Pulitzer Prize in history. Before that, her work had appeared in edited extracts, the best known version of which was Ben Ames Williams's edition called *A Diary from Dixie* (1949).

With the publication of Williams's edition, C.'s reputation started to flourish. She now stands as an accomplished writer, one who cared about style, content, structure, ideas, and human passions, one who revealed a clear understanding of what forces moved Southern society and Southern institutions.

BIBLIOGRAPHY: DeCredico, M. A., *M. B. C.: A Confederate Woman's Life* (1996); Muhlenfeld, E., *M. B. C.: A Biography* (1981)

JOHN L. IDOL, JR.

CHESNUTT, Charles W[addell]
b. 20 June 1858, Cleveland, Ohio; d. 15 November 1932, Cleveland, Ohio

C. brought conventional fictional modes to bear on black protest themes better than any writer before him. C. combined the themes and techniques of the late 19th c. American Plantation Tradition and the themes and techniques of late-19th-c. ROMANTICISM, SENTIMENTALITY, and melodrama with black protest; he very skillfully addressed the racial issues in the American South near the end of the 19th c. and in the early 20th c. C. was especially talented as a short story

writer. C.'s stature and reputation have grown over recent decades. Critics and readers now accept him as a good writer who was restricted by the extreme pressures affecting black writers of his time; they see him as a writer who courageously and effectively worked to overcome these pressures.

C. devoted much of his early short fiction in the 1880s and 1890s, when publishers did not reveal his race for fear of adverse reactions from white readers, to developing his craft and preparing himself for the time when he would publish his first book, a collection of stories entitled *The Conjure Woman* (1899).

In *The Conjure Woman,* which is set in the antebellum South, C. uses the conventional plantation tradition form, as used by white writers like Joel Chandler HARRIS, as the primary outer frame for his stories, and manipulates and changes the characters and themes inside the large conventional frame. C. appeases his largely white audience by giving it plantation tradition humor, sentiment, and nostalgia. The more subtle story told by Uncle Julius, the main character in each piece, reveals the savagery, brutality, and inhumanity of slavery, however.

In *The Wife of His Youth and Other Stories of the Color Line,* another collection of stories published in 1899, C. cloaks his racial protest in romantic feeling and sentiment, and uses melodramatic techniques to hold together his plots and bring his themes to fruition. The statement against racism is more direct and trenchant than it is in *Conjure,* though. The best story, which attains the level of brilliance, is entitled "The Passing of Gandison," in which C. largely eschews romanticism, sentimentality, and melodrama and shocks and surprises the reader through the device of irony. "Baxter's Procrustes," an uncollected short story with all white characters, also attains the level of brilliance because of C.'s deft use of irony.

The House behind the Cedars (1900) is C.'s first novel. The main character Rena Walden is a mulatto who is light enough to pass for white, like C. was. Also like C., she is intelligent, accomplished, and sophisticated. Through Rena, C. revealed his strong interest in other blacks like himself who were trapped between the races, pushed out of the sphere of most blacks by their near whiteness and educational attainments, but refused entry into white society because of their black ancestry. Romanticism, sentimentality, and melodramatic techniques cushion the impact of the very realistic statements C. is making about racism in *The House behind the Cedars,* but in this book, C. moves closer than he was in *The Wife of His Youth* to a direct, explicit attack on racism.

C.'s next novel, *The Marrow of Tradition* (1901), continues his development and progress toward a more direct treatment of Southern racism. Violence and virulent white racism permeate the book, and its realistic content stands out clearly over the masking or muting effect of any conventional literary forms.

The Colonel's Dream (1905) does not have the racial conflict that *The Marrow of Tradition* has, but it presents a very realistic assessment of the grim condition of race relations in the South. C. did not publish a novel after *The Colonel's Dream*. His early short fiction had achieved popular success, but his novels had made him increasingly controversial. By the time he published *The Colonel's Dream*, C. knew he could not go any further with his fictional assault on racism.

BIBLIOGRAPHY: Andrews, W., *The Literary Career of C. W. C.* (1980); Chestnutt, H., *C. W. C.* (1952); Render, S. L., *The Short Fiction of C. W. C.* (1974)

JAMES W. COLEMAN

CHESTER, Alfred

b. 7 September 1928, Brooklyn, New York; d. 1 August 1971, Jerusalem, Israel

C. is one of those intriguing minor writers who could fall through the cracks if more critical attention is not paid to him. From his birth in Brooklyn to his death at the age of forty-two in Jerusalem, C. sought frantically to find a place which would accept him the way he was. His literary production, while not vast, is certainly significant for its daring and inventiveness. He may, in fact, speak more to our times than his own. In his life and work, he boldly and openly displayed the operation of homosexual desire—in a pre-Stonewall era. His minor masterpiece *The Exquisite Corpse* (1967) is, along with William S. BURROUGHS's *Naked Lunch,* an early instance of a style which has subsequently come to be known as "postmodern."

At the age of seven, C. suffered the traumatic loss of body hair due to a case of scarlet fever. The wig he wore most of his life to cover that loss has become legendary. The very title of Cynthia OZICK's *New Yorker* essay "A. C.'s Wig" dramatically calls attention to the hairpiece. The real focus of Ozick's essay, however, is her own literary rivalry with C. when the two—along with the poet and long-time C. champion Edward FIELD—were students at Washington Square College in the late forties.

In 1951, C. left for Paris to make a break from a repressive puritan culture and to begin his writing career. His early stories—a handful of which were collected in a volume called *Here Be Dragons* (1955)—first appeared in European-based literary journals such as *Merlin,* the *Paris Review,* and *Botteghe Oscure.* While in Paris, he published a pornographic novel, *The Chariot of Flesh* (1955), under the pseudonym of Malcolm Nesbit as well as his first serious novel, *Jamie Is My Heart's Desire* (1957). Written in a scintillating style reminiscent of James PURDY or Ronald Firbank, *Jamie* is narrated by a funeral parlor employee named Harry. The story revolves around an absent enigmatic figure, Jamie, to whom all the other characters, particularly a young man named Mark, apparently Jamie's lover, seem devoted. All the time the reader is left wondering who Jamie is, or what is his significance.

In the early 1960s, back in New York, C. made a name for himself as a sharp and savage critic. In the pages of *Commentary,* the *New York Review of Books,* and *Partisan Review* he took on some of the major figures of his day: Burroughs, Norman MAILER, J. D. SALINGER, Truman CAPOTE, Edward ALBEE, Mary MCCARTHY, John RECHY, Vladimir NABOKOV, and Jean Genet. These essays are collected in *Looking for Genet* (1992) edited by Field. From this time, too, come his groundbreaking "gay" stories, "From the Phoenix to the Unnameable, Impossibly Beautiful Wild Bird," "Ismael," and "In Praise of Vespasian," included in his collection of stories, *Behold Goliath* (1964). Among those in C.'s intimate circle of friends during this time in New York were Susan SONTAG, Maria Irene FORNÉS, and Denis Selby.

C. went to Tangier in 1963, at the suggestion of Paul BOWLES whom he had met at a party in New York the previous year. His sojourn in Morocco—before he was asked to leave by Moroccan authorities because of his disruptive conduct—proved to be the climax of his life and career, from which he began a downward spiral into a madness from which he never recovered. In the Atlantic fishing village of Asilah, C. met and struck up an intimate relationship with a young Moroccan, Driss el Kasri, to whom he dedicates his novel, *The Exquisite Corpse,* written in Morocco. The novel is wonderfully bizarre. Characters shift names, genders, and places without any warning. Ira Cohen, who knew C. in Tangier, describes the novel as "a homo masterpiece born in the Bronx, made hairless by x-ray treatments, lovers with burnt marshmallow faces, a changeling born of lesbian frankfurter love taken away by angels with frosted toilet glass wings, broken telephone booths in the middle of the forest."

The last years of C.'s life were tragic, as he darted here and there, trying to find his bearings. Finally, he ended up in Israel. In his brilliant essay, "Letter From the Wandering Jew," written just before his death (apparently suicide), C. tells of his hopes for life in this young country made for the Jewish people; he also tells of the utter disillusionment and despair he suffered upon encountering the reality.

BIBLIOGRAPHY: Field, E., "Among the Tangerinos: The Life, Madness and Death of A. C.," *NYTBR* 15 September 1991: 15–16; Green, M., *The Dream at the End of the World* (1991); Ozick, C., "A. C.'s Wig," *New Yorker* 68 (30 March 1992): 79–98

ALLEN HIBBARD

CHILD, Lydia Maria [Francis]

b. 11 February 1802, Medford, Massachusetts; d. 20 October 1880, Wayland, Massachusetts

C. was a leading abolitionist, an early feminist, a lifelong advocate of Native American rights, and a prolific popular writer of transcendentalist fiction. Widely influential in her own time, her views often made her controversial. Recently renewed interest in her life, her work, and her impact is revealing her to have been a major figure in 19th-c. reform movements.

Born Lydia Francis in Medford, Massachusetts, she was the youngest of the six children of Susanna Rand and David Convers Francis, a baker. Largely self-educated, in contrast to her brother Convers (who went to Harvard, became a Unitarian minister, then a professor at Harvard Divinity School and the senior founding member of the Transcendentalist Club), she moved after her mother's death to the house of a sister in Norridgewock, Maine, and then to a teaching job in Gardiner, Maine. In 1824, she rejoined her brother and his new wife, moved to Watertown, Massachusetts, changed her name by adding "Maria," and wrote her first book, *Hobomok*. In this novel, based loosely on a long poem *Yamoyden* (1820) by James Wallis Eastburn and Robert Charles Sands, C. weaves a romance around a historical figure, Hobomok, associated with Squanto and Plymouth. Mary Conant, daughter of an austere Puritan, falls in love with, and eventually marries, the Indian Hobomok. Although Hobomok cedes his claim to Mary to her other, white, suitor at the very end, the romance depends on C.'s bold exploration of mixed marriage and her theme of assimilation.

In 1828, C. married David Child, who was interested both in radical abolition and in saving the Cherokees. By 1831, she had been completely won to the former cause by William Lloyd GARRISON, and in 1833 she wrote *An Appeal in Favor of That Class of Americans Called Africans*. The book had considerable impact, advocating immediate emancipation, opposing laws prohibiting mixed marriages, and arguing for the intellectual and moral equality of races. By now C. was a well-known name. She had brought out a homemaker's book for women of modest means in 1829 and biographies of Madame de Staël and Madame Roland in 1832. Her antislavery book made her no longer acceptable to polite society and meant the end of her popular *Juvenile Miscellany*, an attractive children's magazine she had started in 1826. In 1835 she published a pioneering *History of the Condition of Women, in Various Ages and Nations*, which served as a basis for later work by Sarah Moore GRIMKÉ, and in 1836 she published *Philothea*, a philosophical romance set in ancient Greece. The title character, an intellectual woman with strong moral and idealist views, is meant to stand for a pure and natural monotheism, a pre-Christian world view strongly marked by womanly qualities.

C. moved to New York in 1841 to edit the *National Anti-Slavery Standard*. She published *Letters from New York* in 1843, full of reform views and lively writing. The book was praised as literature by Margaret FULLER. C. continued to produce important work. Her *Progress of Religious Ideas, through Successive Ages* (1855) was a major work of religious liberalism, part of a new ecumenical nontheological approach to the history of religions. Her *Correspondence between Lydia Maria Child and Gov. Wise and Mrs. Mason of Virginia* (1860) championed the cause of John Brown. In 1861 she edited, and helped publish, Harriet JACOB's *Incidents in the Life of a Slave Girl*. Her *Appeal for the Indians* (1868) was a vigorous return to her old theme of justice for Native Americans. C. died at the age of seventy-eight. Her later years were, like her earlier ones, marked by radical interest in reform, long-sustained adherence to causes, and personal courage. Her writing at its best—often in dialogue or reported dialogue—is imaginative, lively, and colloquial.

BIBLIOGRAPHY: Baer, H. G., *The Heart is Like Heaven: The Life of L. M. C.* (1964); Clifford, D. P., *Crusader for Freedom: A Life of L. M. C.* (1992); Holland, P. G., M. Meltzer, and F. Krasno, eds., *L. M. C.: Selected Letters, 1817–1880* (1982); Holland, P. G., et al., eds., *The Collected Correspondence of L. M. C., 1817–1880* (1980); Karcher, C. L., *The First Woman in the Republic: A Cultural Biography of L. M. C.* (1994); Meltzer, M., *Tongue of Flame: The Life of L. M. C.* (1965); Mills, B., *Cultural Reformations: L. M. C. and the Literature of Reform* (1994); Osborne, W. S., *L. M. C.* (1980)

ROBERT D. RICHARDSON, JR.

CHILDREN'S LITERATURE

As Leslie A. FIEDLER proclaimed in *Love and Death in the American Novel*, "There is a real sense in which our prose fiction is immediately distinguishable from that of Europe, though this is a fact difficult for Americans to confess. The great works of American fiction [*Adventures of Huckleberry Finn, The Last of the*

Mohicans, the tales of Poe, *The Red Badge of Courage*] are notoriously at home in the children's section of the library." It is the embarrassment that is peculiar to the U.S. In Great Britain, the field of children's literature has long enjoyed respectability among scholars, probably because of children's authors who were also Oxford dons: Lewis Carroll, C. S. Lewis, and J. R. R. Tolkien. In Germany, as well as in most European and Scandinavian countries, the situation is similar: the study of children's literature has been regarded seriously because of its connection with folkloric pursuits.

Until recently, however, American scholars have not regarded their nation's children's literature as a serious subject and, in general, abandoned the field to lady librarians, school educators, and antiquarian book collectors. If this last statement smacks of sexism, there is probably something to that. Much of the effort to win respectability for American literary scholarship has been connected to the history of the novel and its similar bid to be regarded seriously as art—an enterprise that came to mean dissociating the novel from its reputation as the domestic reading of women and children.

In the last few decades, however, the study of children's literature in American universities has begun to enjoy a higher status. Scholars have started to come to terms with the relationship between our literary history and audiences of women and children, and with the "shameful" connection between America's masterpieces and children's literature. Even the titles of these studies are revealing: Russel Nye's *The Unembarrassed Muse: The Popular Arts in America* (1970) briefly surveyed American children's literature and the leading journal in the field was for a time called the *Great Excluded* (now *Children's Literature* and published by Yale University Press).

In recent years, in other words, some American scholars have begun to regard children's literature as their European counterparts do: as a literary genre available (like women's literature, say, or black literature) to scholarly study and as no less serious (simply because of its association with children) than, say, its medical analogue of pediatrics. Scholarship continues to appear with increasing frequency. But there is, as yet, no single, comprehensive and widely acknowledged volume to turn to for the history of this nation's children's literature.

Though it was printed in England, John Cotton's *Spiritual Milk for Boston Babes* (1646) was probably the first book prepared for North America's youth. Along with Isaac Watt's poems and other selections, this catechism was often an entry in the *New England Primer,* America's most popular educational work (more than six million copies were printed between 1680 and 1830). *The Primer* was part catechism and part schoolbook, as the beginning of its alphabet suggests: "In *A*dam's fall, / We sinned *a*ll."

But American children did not have to depend only on native fare. Folktales and other stories in the oral tradition were a shared inheritance. And they were not cut off from literature on the other side of the Atlantic. Chapbooks and reprints were routinely imported: the fairy tales of Perrault and the fables of Aesop, stories of Cock Robin and Dick Whittington, and those novels not necessarily intended for them but which juveniles came to especially like, such as Daniel Defoe's *Robinson Crusoe,* John Bunyan's *Pilgrim's Progress,* and Jonathan Swift's *Gulliver's Travels.* Moreover, American publishers routinely pirated British works for children or conjured close variants.

Cotton MATHER published what was probably the first work printed in America for minors, *A Token for the Children of New England* (1700). Mather's work, like countless others in the first half of the 18th c., presented what can be called the "Protestant Pieta": biographical accounts of juvenile saints who die prematurely, but not before lecturing others who surround the deathbed or providing pious example to young readers.

By the mid-18th c., however, John Locke's ideas about child-rearing had gained currency and turned prior Protestant practices on their head: instead of original sin, Locke stresses the vision of the child as *tabula rasa;* instead of Mather's sickrooms, he championed the outdoors; instead of prayer and secret fasting, he advocated fresh air and exercise; and instead of exemplary biography with tearful accounts of youthful martyrs, Locke endorsed Aesop's fables as a way of inculcating ethics.

This shift is evident in the anonymous *A New Gift for Children* (1750), perhaps America's first secular storybook, and its Aesop-like tales of children who are good and merit rewards, and tales of children who are otherwise and receive their deserts. Most noticeable is the fact that justice does not wait for the afterlife but is immediate and Aesopian: when George snubs a poor boy in the morning in *The Grateful Return* (1796), he cannot share in the gift the boy brings that very afternoon; "You should have recollected," his brother tells him, "the Fable you read this morning of the Mouse that released the Lion from the net."

This development of a juvenile literature emphasizing secular morality continued unabated through the first half of the 19th c. Mason Locke WEEMS's famous biography *The Life of Washington the Great,* published in 1806, can serve as an example. The celebrated anecdote about the chopping of a cherry tree taught a lesson about honesty, but it did so by substituting a civil saint into the role otherwise reserved for a pious Protestant ephebe.

The American view of childhood was changing. The lassies of Lydia Maria CHILD's *The Girl's Own Book,* published in 1831, or a globetrotting lad like Jacob Abbott's Rollo in the series that bears his name, beginning in 1835, give the impression that children exist to learn lessons, about anger and disobedience, about history and geography. Even "Sunday school" books—those small volumes of the American Sunday School Union (1824–60) and similar organizations (e.g., the American Tract Society) by which countless Americans learned to read—offered lessons that were temporal: boys who fail to go to church on Sunday morning are struck by lightning in the afternoon; and those who climb trees to steal apples, inevitably fall and break their arms.

If readers were impressed by young George Washington's example of honesty, writers seem to have been struck by the very appearance of Washington in a book. American history was approaching mythic status. Samuel Griswold Goodrich would have a grandfatherly veteran fall into recollective bliss and tell children about the French Indian Wars and the Revolution in *The Tales of Peter Parley about America* (1827). Washington IRVING would write about Dutch settlers named Rip Van Winkle and Ichabod Crane in tales that were soon to become favorites. And if others felt America really didn't yet have its own myths, then the classics could at least be co-opted and retold to children in a Massachusetts setting, as Nathaniel HAWTHORNE did in his *Wonder Book* (1852) and *Tanglewood Tales* (1853).

This same kind of appropriation was occurring in the world of verse with the entirely spurious claim made at the time that Mother Goose was actually a dame who lived in 17th-c. Boston; by this piece of invented history, all nursery rhymes were, retrospectively, made American. In a similar vein, Clement Clarke Moore's "The Night before Christmas" (1823) appropriated Dutch customs; in fact, few other poems have had such a wide influence on American culture since Moore's lines are generally credited with adding Santa and gift-giving to the celebration of what had otherwise been a solemn religious holiday.

As all this begins to suggest, it is difficult to underestimate the role children have had in determining this country's literary patrimony. To a certain extent, this was the result of inspired anthologists who created 19th-c. textbooks for a growing public-school movement—such works, for example, as William Holmes McGuffey's *First Eclectic Reader* (1836). Instead of today's jejune textbook tales, trimmed down for phonetic reasons and spruced up to suit someone's agenda for social change, America's children were given liberal doses from the works of Shakespeare and Dickens, and from what was slowly being recognized as their national literature.

A wide familiarity with this literature, its preservation and its recognition as distinctly "American," was largely due to youthful readers who were, for example, learning their history while memorizing "passages" from Henry Wadsworth LONGFELLOW: "This is the forest primeval" ("Evangeline"), "By the shore of Gitchee Gumee" ("The Courtship of Miles Standish"), and "One, if by land, and two, if by sea" ("Paul Revere's Ride"). It was the children, too, who committed to national memory such set pieces as John Greenleaf WHITTIER's "Snow-Bound," Edgar Allan POE's "The Raven," and William Cullen BRYANT's "Thanatopsis."

American children were no different from others in adopting books not particularly intended for the young. Following upon Weems's life of George Washington, historical works were unusually popular: James Fenimore COOPER's *The Last of the Mohicans, The Life of David Crockett* (1834), Daniel P. Thompson's *The Green Mountain Boys* (1839), and Richard Henry DANA, Jr.'s *Two Years before the Mast.* From these national adventure stories would arise the "boy's book"—inaugurated perhaps in the novels of the "Oliver Optic" series, beginning in 1855, written by William Taylor Adams, and furthered by the incredible success encountered by Irwin Beadle who first offered mass-market fiction as "dime novels" in 1860.

The "girl's book" took shape differently. If the boy's book was concerned with the outdoors, the girl's book was, instead, domestic fiction. If the boy's book was concerned with adventure, the girl's book was concerned with moral development. In this way the roots of the girl's book were not in historical fiction, but in the Sunday School story and (behind that) the juvenile martyrology of early American offerings. A concern with touching sentiment and tearful contrition in these novels—Susan WARNER's *The Wide, Wide World,* Maria Susanna CUMMINS's *The Lamplighter,* and Martha FINLEY's *Elsie Dinsmore*—would lead scholars to refer to their authors as the "lachrymose ladies," an injudicious sobriquet. Instead, these books should be thought of as kin to *Uncle Tom's Cabin,* a novel with which they shared best-seller status and which also became a favorite among the young.

The so-called "Golden Age of Children's Books" (1865–1914) was a remarkable time. It was an era when "the majors wrote for minors"; when the very best authors on both sides of the Atlantic, writers with worldwide reputations, addressed themselves to juveniles—Samuel Langhorne CLEMENS, for example, or Stevenson and Kipling. It was a time when children's books headed the adult best-seller lists and "Children's Books" was not some satellite department, but the very center of publishing houses. And it was an age in America that produced such timeless childhood classics as Louisa May ALCOTT's *Little Women,* Clemens's *The Adventures of Tom Sawyer,* L. Frank Baum's *The Wonderful Wizard of Oz,* Edgar Rice BURROUGHS's *Tarzan of the Apes,* and Frances Hodgson BURNETT's *The Secret Garden.*

If much of modern American literature was encouraged by the existence of magazines which paid well, American children's literature flourished during this period for the same reason and because of such popular periodicals as the *Youth's Companion* (1827–1929), *Our Young Folks* (1865–73), the *Riverside Magazine for Young People* (1867–70), and *Harper's Young People* (1879–99). Foremost among those was *St. Nicholas* (1873–1943), ably edited by Mary Mapes Dodge and whose contributors included virtually every literary notable of the time.

Besides her editorial skills, Dodge is best known for her story about a hard luck Dutch family in her *Hans Briner, or the Silver Skates* (1865). "The Pathetic Family," a title Louisa May Alcott once entertained before she decided upon *Little Women,* accurately describes both novels. They are examples of the "family story," a genre continued in Margaret Sidney's *The Five Little Peppers* (1881) and Alice Caldwell Hegan's *Mrs. Wiggs of the Cabbage Patch* (1901), and with a comic twist in Lucretia Peabody HALE's *The Peterkin Papers.*

Hans Briner and *Little Women* are also novels about the control of emotions. The Dutchboy who keeps his finger in the leaking dike is a symbol of Hans's steadfast resistance to the tidal waves of emotions. The "bosom enemies" of the March sisters (Meg, Jo, Beth, and Amy) are feelings (vanity, anger, shyness, and envy).

This emphasis on sentiment is conspicuous in the girls' books which seem, in retrospect, secularized versions of the earlier religious stories. Now, instead of sin, children wrestled with character flaws; instead of winning salvation, the subject is personality growth in Kate Douglas WIGGIN's *Rebecca of Sunnybrook Farm* and Jean Webster's *Daddy Long-Legs* (1912); and instead of juvenile martyrs, there is a long line of injured girls from Beth March dying of scarlet fever to the immobilized girls of Susan Coolidge's *What Katy Did* (1872) and Eleanor H. Porter's *Pollyanna* (1913).

In these latter-day pietas the question is not whether children will resist temptation, but whether they will lose their high spirits and succumb to darker moods. *The Secret Garden* (1911) presents this choice, and its spirited advocacy of the power of positive thinking makes it clear Frances Hodgson Burnett has in mind a secularized version of Christian Science. Likewise,

behind *Pollyanna*'s notorious optimism is evangelical Christianity.

If girls' books rewrote the religious story, boys' books deliberately undermined it. This was Clemens's intention when he wrote *The Adventures of Tom Sawyer,* and it was a motive shared in other "bad-boy novels": Thomas Bailey ALDRICH's *The Story of a Bad Boy,* George W. Peck's *Peck's Bad Boy* (1883), and Booth TARKINGTON's *Penrod.* To be sure, there were books meant to inculcate lessons of industry, Horatio ALGER's novels, beginning in 1868 with *Ragged Dick,* or provide examples of goodwill and good manners, *Little Lord Fauntleroy* in 1885. But readers seem to remember James Otis's *Toby Tyler* (1881) more for the fun to be had in running away to join the circus, than the contrition the author stresses that Toby repeatedly feels. In fact, as the *Adventures of Huckleberry Finn* indicates, it's when a boy doesn't listen to his conscience that good results.

Instead of sentiment, boys' books embraced primitivism. Clemens's prince in *The Prince and the Pauper* is a better ruler because of his vernacular education among the *sans culottes,* and during the interim and interregnum the pauper demonstrates his own natural nobility because he has risen from the *hoi polloi.* Other authors would descend further into primitivism by crossing naturalist Ernest Thompson Seton's nonfiction account of *Wild Animals I Have Known* (1898) with Charles Darwin to arrive at Jack LONDON's *The Call of the Wild* and *White Fang* and Burroughs's *Tarzan of the Apes.*

Thriving apart from either domestic fiction or the adventure story, the girls' or boys' book, was America's minor tradition—fantasy, which would become most visible in 1900 with the publication of *The Wonderful Wizard of Oz.* But there was ample activity before then, evident in the fairy tales of Frank R. STOCKTON or the folk tales of Joel Chandler HARRIS's *Uncle Remus.*

In retrospect, much of America's early fantasy seems English and Pre-Raphaelite. This is suggested by the eminence of the visual in the work of authors who were also illustrators, Palmer Cox, for example, or Howard Pyle, and in their subject matter—which ranged from the fantastical in Cox's *The Brownies* (1887) to Olde Englande in Pyle's *The Merry Adventures of Robin Hood* (1883) or *King Arthur and his Knights* (1903). If American illustrators differed from their English counterparts, it was in their emphasis upon whimsy, something which is characteristic of W. W. Denslow's pictures for *The Wonderful Wizard of Oz* or Gellett Burgess's amusing *Goops and How To Be Them* (1900). Even so, American artists who provided illustrations in the high style for British books—N. C. Wyeth memorably in Stevenson's *Trea-*

sure Island, for example, or Maxfield Parrish in Grahame's *Dream Days*—gave hints at the possibility of a new genre, something beyond simply illustrating the words on the facing page, a symbiotic equality of art and text in that special *objet* known as the picture book.

Besides identifiably native fare, such as Virginia Lee Burton's *Mike Mulligan and His Steam Shovel* (1938) and Watty Piper's *The Little Engine That Could* (1947), many of the best picture books by Americans in the early 20th c. seemed foreign: stories about an Eastern European peasant couple in Wanda Gag's *Millions of Cats* (1928), a Parisian mischiefmaker in Ludwig Bemelmans's *Madeline* (1938), or a Spanish bull in Munro Leaf's *Ferdinand* (1936). Or perhaps they really were "foreign" because, during a jingoistic period between the wars, they questioned competitiveness and stupid uniformity or (in the story of a bull content to smell the flowers) advocated pacifism. Whatever the case, each work showed, respectively, how art had left the museum and entered the book: in Gag's brilliant kinetic designs of a page into handlettered text and folk pictures; in Bemelmans's Picasso-like sketches of Paris; in Robert Lawson's amusing visual commentary upon Leaf's *Ferdinand,* for example, sitting under a cork tree.

The picture book also provided a new venue for children's poetry, a field that had seemed aged and short of breath near the end of the 19th c. when genius was stretched thinly between Eugene FIELD's "Wynken, Blynken and Nod" and Ernest Lawrence Thayer's "Casey at the Bat." Now there was Margaret Wise Brown's *Goodnight Moon* (1947) and DR. SEUSS's *The Cat in the Hat.* Since then, the picture book has also provided a venue for psychological insight—in such works as Maurice Sendak's *Where the Wild Things Are* (1963) and William Steig's *Sylvester and the Magic Pebble* (1969)—and, often, a showcase for genuine artistic genius.

By the mid-20th c., taxonomists working in publishing house and libraries had divided longer children's books into a bewildering number of phylae and species—including, historical fiction, "problem novels," information books, YOUNG ADULT LITERATURE, animal stories, nonfiction, social realism, and BIOGRAPHY. In truth, the best of modern American children's literature seems to fit nearly all those categories. One need only think of Laura Ingalls WILDER's *Little House* books, beginning in 1932.

But what these categories do suggest are modern emphases. More than before, the problems of adolescence became a subject, from the awkward courtships of William Sylvanus Baxter in Booth Tarkington's *Seventeen* to the moody depressions of Holden Caulfield in J. D. SALINGER's *The Catcher in the Rye.* Often in extended monologues, readers were offered the

problematics of a solipsist's entrance into a community—particularly in girls' books from Dorothy Canfield's *Understood Betsy* (1917) to Louise Fitzhugh's *Harriet the Spy* (1964). And frequently, the work was "realistic"—historical, regional, and informative: about cowboy life in Will James's *Smoky, the Cowhorse* (1926); about pioneer life in the *Little House* books; about the Florida scrub country in Marjorie Kinnan RAWLINGS's *The Yearling* or Lois Lenski's *Strawberry Girl* (1945); about California Indians in Scott O'Dell's *Island of the Blue Dolphin* (1960).

It is only in the field of fantasy, perhaps, that change has been so dramatic that the first half of the century does not seem consonant with the second half. Johnny Gruelle's *Raggedy Ann Stories* (1918) and Carl SANDBURG's *Rootabaga Stories* (1922) seem simple nonsense compared to contemporary high fantasy and SCIENCE FICTION of today by Lloyd Alexander, Jane Yolen, Eleanor Cameron, Madeline L'Engle, and Ursula LE GUIN.

Like the 19th c., the 20th c. has had its "dime novels" and series fiction—the Bobbsey Twins, the Hardy Boys, Nancy Drew—but what is perhaps the most conspicuous difference between literature of the two centuries is film. Purists would object and, unwilling to concede that story on celluloid is still story, have hastily dismissed the productions of Walt Disney Studios, for example, in unthinking prejudice. Still, it has been Disney, in particular—not only in animated masterpieces like *Snow White,* but in live-action films like *Pollyanna* and *Toby Tyler*—who has both preserved and defined what are the classics of children's literature in America. Since Disney, less historically minded filmmakers—especially George Lucas in his *Star Wars* trilogy—have taken the aficionados of story even deeper into fantasy and the future.

Even so, the farther this essay, itself, travels into the 20th c., the more this writer feels like the king in the fairy tale "The Sleeping Beauty" who, after listing twelve, overlooked the thirteenth fairy and was filled with trepidation and remorse. Perhaps, like the fairy tale, one hundred years need to elapse before we can tell how many of our choices were correct and how much the pattern discovered in the carpet was really the impression of our own foot.

Perhaps, a hundred years from now, readers will feel our own time too roughly criticized, say, Judy Blume; or didn't pay enough attention to, say, Virginia Hamilton; or wrongly ignored, say, D. Mancus Pinkwater. Perhaps, in the next century, too, readers will have solved a dilemma of our own era: that canonical lists need to be balanced by racial, gender and ethnic diversity; and vice versa.

If there is any consolation in the interim, it is that during the next one hundred years we and children will have the company of Isaac Bashevis SINGER and Russell Hoban, E. B. WHITE's *Charlotte's Web* and Randall JARRELL's *The Animal Family*. As Jarrell himself says in his poem "Children Selecting Books in a Library": Read meanwhile . . . / And find one cure for Everychild's diseases / Beginning: *Once upon a time there was.*"

BIBLIOGRAPHY: Attebery, B., *The Fantasy Tradition in American Literature* (1980); Griswold, J., *Audacious Kids Coming of Age in America's Classic Children's Books* (1992); Griswold, J., *The Classic American Children's Story: Novels of the Golden Age* (1996); Jordan, A. M., *From Rollo to Tom Sawyer* (1948); Kiefer, M., *American Children through Their Books* (1948); MacLeod, A. S., *A Moral Tale* (1975); Meigs, C., ed., *A Critical History of Children's Literature* (1969); Rosenbach, A. S. W., *Early American Children's Books* (1966)

JERRY GRISWOLD

CHILDRESS, Alice

b. 12 October 1920, Charleston, South Carolina; d. 14 August 1994, New York City

Though she wrote in other literary forms such as the novel, C. considered herself to be essentially a playwright. One of the most talented black authors emerging in the 1960s, C. was a pivotal figure in the development of FEMINISM in plays by African American women.

In an article entitled "A Woman Playwright Speaks Her Mind" (1966), C. outlines the plight of the black woman in the United States, from slavery to freedom and beyond, and discusses the black woman's depiction in American literature, most frequently as an "empty and decharacterized faithful servant." To C., however, the black woman is the most heroic figure to emerge in America. Her beliefs are reflected in her dramas, at the heart of which is usually an "ordinary" black woman, whose life is uneventful until circumstances force her to rise to the fullness of her strength. She comes to grips with human problems and rises victorious over them, however small the triumph. Here the black woman not only transcends her own personal predicaments but often functions as a catalyst for change in those whose lives she touches.

In *Florence* (1950), C.'s first published play, Mrs. Whitney, an African American mother in the South, en route to bringing her struggling actress daughter home from New York, has a chance meeting with a white woman in the hometown railroad station. They are separated from each other by the symbolic railing and signs that distinguish the blacks from the whites in the racially segregated waiting room. The railing and the signs are also mental barriers. After listening to the bigoted views of the white woman who believes that the rightful place of blacks is in menial jobs, the mother sends her own travel money to her daughter Florence with an encouraging note, "Keep trying." Transformed by the white woman's remarks, she now wishes to aid her daughter in succeeding in the career that she has chosen for herself.

The structure of the Obie Award-winning play *Trouble in Mind* (1971) enabled C. to use the American theater as a metaphor in exploring racial prejudice in the U.S. A metadrama, *Trouble in Mind* employs a play within a play. Wiletta Mayer, a black veteran actress, has earned a living in the theater by playing stereotypical roles on the stage and by behaving in the passive manner required in life if she is to succeed in her career. In rehearsal for a new play, "Chaos in Belleville," written, directed, and produced by whites, she is so disturbed by the action of the character she is playing—a black mother who sends her innocent son out to a mob to be lynched—that she denounces it. She labels this image of an African American mother as false and contradictory of reality. Wiletta also exposes the hypocrisy of the director who masquerades as a liberal. She does all this, knowing that her assertiveness and her correction of the misinterpretation of the black experience, particularly that of the woman, will cause her to be dismissed from the cast.

Julia Augustine, the protagonist in *Wedding Band* (1973), takes her place as one of C.'s strong women who are determined to live life as they see fit. She is one of C.'s most finely drawn and tragic characters. Set in 1918 in South Carolina, *Wedding Band,* which also could be read as wedding "ban," treats the forbidden love between a black woman and a white man in a state that has strict laws against miscegenation. In the community of women in which Julia lives, all are struggling to survive. Through all of the unpleasantness resulting from her ten-year interracial romance, Julia, who has pride, dignity, and inordinate strength, stays with Herman, her lover, until his death from influenza parts them forever.

In *Wine in the Wilderness* (1969), Tomorrow Marie continues C.'s exploration of the unsung ordinary black woman who, despite many obstacles, has carved out a respectable life for herself. She grants the wish of a black middle-class artist to have her portrait painted as part of a triptych of black women, but learns accidentally that in the painting she is to symbolize the degraded black woman, the woman beyond redemption. The other parts of the painting, already completed, are innocent black girlhood and perfect black womanhood or "Wine in the Wilderness." Tomorrow Marie teaches valuable lessons to the artist and his friends. Their concerns are with the superficial accessories of life rather than with its interior—with human worth. With far fewer privileges than theirs, the protagonist has learned who she is—"a woman that's a real one and a good one"—one who has come through hardships with her head held high. Regardless of their differences in class, she reminds them that all blacks are the victims of racism. She also challenges the myths of black womanhood.

In *When the Rattlesnake Sounds* (1975), a one-act children's play, C. treats an imaginative episode in the life of Harriet Tubman, who is reduced from mythic proportions and made just a human being, though a heroic one. When one of the women working with her in a laundry to earn money to support the Underground Railroad, a network of aid given to escaping slaves, expresses fear, Harriet assures her that fear is a natural trait. She preaches black unity. Women should contribute to the freedom struggle, which transcends class and sex, and should act to improve the conditions of their race.

Critics of C.'s dramas usually praise her works, but note that despite their excellence, they are underproduced. Doris E. Abramson wrote that C. was "a crusader and a writer who resists compromise." Elizabeth Brown-Guillory stated that in C.'s efforts to find "new and dynamic ways of expressing old themes in an historically conservative theater," she paved the way for other black playwrights, especially Lorraine HANSBERRY and Ntozake SHANGE, "to make dramaturgical advances."

In C.'s best-known work of fiction, *A Hero Ain't Nothin' But a Sandwich* (1973), she focuses on Benji Johnson, a thirteen-year-old drug addict. The novel contains twenty-three short narratives and presents in their own voices the attitudes of others, such as teachers, drug pushers, parents, and friends, about a young drug addict. The novel won several awards, among them, the Jane Addams Honor Award in 1974 for a young adult novel.

In her fiction, C. wrote about the black experience and issues; in her dramas, she concentrated on racism, classism, and sexism, using traditional dramatic forms with some modifications. With a vision that was both black and feminine, she contributed to the literature of America, particularly that of the American theater.

BIBLIOGRAPHY: Abramson, D. E., *Negro Playwrights in the American Theater, 1925–1959* (1969); Brown-Guillory, E., *Their Place on the Stage: Black Women Playwrights in America* (1988); Harris, T., "A. C.," in Davis, T. M., and T. Harris, *DLB,* vol. 38, *Afro-American Writers after 1955: Dramatists and Prose Writers* (1985): 66–79

JEANNE-MARIE A. MILLER

CHIN, Frank [Chew, Jr.]
b. 25 February 1940, Berkeley, California

Undoubtedly one of the most outspoken, controversial, and important Asian American writers today is C., known also as the "Chinatown cowboy" both for his iconoclasm and stylistic attachment to the American West. An award-winning playwright, novelist, short story writer, and essayist, C. has been instrumental in bringing Asian American literature to the attention of the academy. In doing so, he has also set himself apart from his Asian American contemporaries, not hesitating to criticize their literary efforts as ultimately detrimental to the image of Asian Americans.

One of C.'s first major projects was the 1974 anthology of Asian American literature, *Aiiieeeee!,* which he coedited with Jeffery Paul Chan, Lawson Inada, and Shawn Wong. In this volume, the editors selected pieces that they felt best represented an authentic Asian American sensibility and left out works they deemed informed by racist American popular opinion. This theme of cultural authenticity would go on to define C.'s position within the field and become the central message of his works.

When it opened at the American Place Theatre, *The Chickencoop Chinaman* (1972) owned the distinction of being the first major Asian American play produced in New York. Its protagonist, Tam Lum, is the prototype of the author's tragic hero—a misunderstood Chinese American artist who struggles with his projects among an unsympathetic circle of acquaintances. Fred Eng, the next avatar of C.'s hero in *The Year of the Dragon* (1974), attempts to balance familial pressure to succeed with his own desires. His conscious surrender of personal integrity to material need—he is a Chinatown tour guide—generates the keen tragedy of this drama. The play's setting of Chinatown becomes C.'s milieu of choice for his fiction as he explores its destructive and enervating effects upon its citizens.

The Chinatown Pacific & Frisco R.R. Co. (1988), which won the American Book Award, is a collection of short stories linked in narrative through a common protagonist known as Dirigible. Depicted in near-naturalistic quality, his Chinatown is a decaying site populated by equally decrepit old people—a place from which any young person would want to leave. The opposition of filial responsibility and youthful ambition emerges as the author's signal *leitmotif.* As in his plays, C.'s prose is unyielding and lyrical, demanding of the reader. Rich with historical allusion, it borrows multiple images from the iconography of the transcontinental railroad. Like C. himself was, Dirigible is a brakeman, and as such, claims the American West as a legitimate legacy. C.'s first novel, *Donald*

Duk (1991) explores the mythic possibilities of this image system in a tale ostensibly targeted for children.

Despite his impressive body of work, C. may be remembered best for his quarrel with Maxine Hong KINGSTON over her memoir, *The Woman Warrior.* Citing her book as an example of "fake" Asian American literature, he railed against creative interpretation in autobiography that ignored historical fact as basis. This debate, known as "the real and the fake," has remained a current topic in the field, and no doubt contributed to the rise in interest in Asian American literature since the 1980s.

BIBLIOGRAPHY: Cheung, K., "The Woman Warrior Versus the Chinaman Pacific: Must a Chinese American Critic Choose between Feminism and Heroism?," in Hirsch, M., and E. F. Keller, eds., *Conflicts in Feminism* (1990): 234–51

DAVID SHIH

CHIVERS, Thomas Holley
b. 18 October 1809, Washington, Georgia; d. 19 December 1858, Decatur, Georgia

Edgar Allan POE, perceptive as usual in his reading of literature, characterized C. as "one of the best and one of the worst poets in America." Publishing his works in the face of general public neglect, C. has managed little more than claiming a minor place in histories of Southern writing. Much of his poetry and all of his plays have been dismissed or deplored, but a few of the poems do continue to receive some favorable attention.

Trained as a physician, C. drew upon a congeries of influences: Emanuel Swedenborg, Chateaubriand, and the available writings on the American Indian, and the poems of Milton, Byron, Shelley, Keats, and Tennyson. For a time, he and Poe were friends who read each other's poems and corresponded. some of C.'s compositions border upon plagiarism; but he claimed that Poe stole from him and there is some evidence that the better-known poet did profit from reading C.'s magazine verse and drama.

C.'s speculations about poetry were often expressed in prefaces, letters, and poems, and they constitute a fairly consistent romantic view. He holds that poetry is the soul of Nature and that the poet, through divine inspiration, is the voice of God and the echo of Nature, so that poetry holds ethical as well as aesthetic value. In verses about Byron, Shelley, and Poe, C. often expresses his idolatry of his great contemporaries.

Publication, always difficult in the 19th c., was achieved mostly at the poet's expense. C.'s first volume, *The Path of Sorrow* (1832), dealt with his unhappy first marriage. Later volumes of poems include

The Lost Pleiad (1845), *Eonchs of Ruby* (1851), *Memoralia* (1853), and *Virginalia* (1853). The subjects of the poems are motley; there are verses on the woes of marriage, songs on the deaths of children, celebrations of divinity and angelology, intimations of an earthly Eden, and declamatory patriotic lines on the destiny of America. The poetic technique veers wildly between the nearly excellent and the merely gauche. C. composes passable blank verse, competent sonnets, and a serviceable nine-line stanza. Some poems are weighted with exotic learning, epigraphs, elaborate similes, and annoying refrains. The diction is marked by a sometimes curiously pleasing use of obsolete words such as *obsecration* and *reboantic,* or neologisms like *eonch,* as well as Coleridgean resonant names like *Cydonian, Chrysomelian,* and *Conchimarian.* Thus, it is easy to ridicule C.'s poetic excesses. But in some instances, as in "The Poet of Love," "The Voice of Thought," and "Apollo," they conjoin properly into dignified and even noble poetic utterances.

C. was a failed but tenacious dramatist. In 1834, he published *Conrad and Eudora; or, the Death of Alonzo,* a poetic tragedy based upon the Kentucky murder of Colonel Sharp by Jeroboam Beauchamp. This was a theme that would attract literary compositions by Poe, William Gilmore SIMMS, and others, but C.'s version is overwritten and unactable. A revision, *Leoni, or the Orphan of Venice* (wr. 1839, pub. 1980), improves upon the original in its plotting, characterization, and verse. *The Sons of Usna* (1858) is an early version of the Gaelic legend of Deirdre. Persisting in the face of indifference, C. completed *Count Julian, Osceola,* and *Charles Stuart,* all of which lay unpublished until the issuance of *Unpublished Plays* in 1980. Another drama, *Tacon,* is still in manuscript.

Drawing upon his friendship and knowledge of Poe, C. wrote a biography that remained unpublished until 1952. Unfortunately, he put himself into the untenable position of declaring that some of his poems had priority and that Poe was guilty of plagiarism, a claim that has invited derision as well as some careful but inconclusive studies.

BIBLIOGRAPHY: Chase, E. L., and L. F. Parks, eds., *The Correspondence of T. H. C.* (1957); Damon, S. F., *T. H. C., Friend of Poe* (1930); Lombard, C. M., *T. H. C.* (1979); Watts, C. H., *T. H. C.: His Literary Career and Poetry* (1956)

DOUGLAS ROBILLARD

CHOPIN, Kate [O'Flaherty]
b. 8 February 1850, St. Louis, Missouri; d. 22 August 1904, St. Louis, Missouri

Regarded in the first half of the 20th c. only as a minor writer of Louisiana local color, C. is now recognized as the author of both a major realist American novel of female identity and an impressive body of short fiction.

A native of St. Louis, C. grew up in a multigenerational household of women, her father having died in a railroad disaster when she was five. At twenty she married Oscar Chopin, a young Louisiana cotton factor. The couple settled in New Orleans and soon commenced a family—five sons and a daughter by 1879. That year, her husband's business failing, they moved to Cloutierville, a tiny village near Natchitoches, whose environs and inhabitants became a staple of C.'s later fiction. After her husband's death in 1882, C. returned to St. Louis, where a few years later she began what was to be a relatively brief but highly productive literary career, resulting in two novels, several essays and poems, and nearly a hundred short stories.

Although C. experimented with other settings and fictional styles, the ready market for her Louisiana stories established her commercial niche. Her early fiction is largely in the tradition of Southern local color, relying for effect on the unique settings of New Orleans and central Louisiana, and on their colorful inhabitants: French-speaking Acadians, aristocratic Creoles, African Americans, Native Americans. C. presents an adroit range of dialects with a minimum of phonetic distortion. As *Bayou Folk* (1894), her first and most popular collection, suggests, her early themes were likewise typical of reconstruction fiction. There are tales tracing the effects of the Civil War, like "Ma'ame Pélagie" (1893), sketches of loyal ex-slaves and tragic mulattoes, like "La Belle Zoraide" (1894), and variations on conventional romance, like "Madame Célestin's Divorce" (1894), or "In Sabine" (1894).

But C. disdained the merely conventional; and she distinguishes her use of these materials in several ways. First, in contrast to most other Southern local colorists, she prefers the reality of the present to the nostalgic myths of antebellum life. Even a story with a rare pre-war setting like her justly famous "Désirée's Baby" (1893) treats that era with a characteristically unsentimental realism. This tragic tale of mixed blood—a standard motif of Southern local color—is superbly crafted, building suspense and developing its ironies through a deft use of setting, imagery, and point of view. The compressed tragedy of Armand Aubigny's haughty fall and the passive "victimhood" of Désirée tap deeply felt issues of race and gender. The exquisite surprise ending was a technique C. learned from Maupassant, who was a major influence on her work and who exemplified her creed of realism, writing, as she explained, "life, not fiction."

The realistic bent of C.'s adaptations of local color motifs and strategies is also manifest in her explorations of psychology and perspective. In "Beyond the Bayou" (1893), for example, C.'s matter-of-fact treatment of the manic effects of a wartime trauma gives depth and sympathy to LaFolle, an otherwise generic type, the loyal ex-slave. Likewise characteristic is C.'s use of landscape to image LaFolle's perspectives as she moves from neurotic isolation to an accepting community beyond the bayou.

Thematically, however, male and female relationships were a more constant element of C.'s fiction than the types of reconstruction. "At the 'Cadian Ball" (1892) typifies both that focus and her distinctive Louisiana flavor. The tale knots and unravels interlocking love stories of two Creoles, Alcee and Clarisse, and two 'Cadians, Calixta and Bobinot. Central here is the way that class and social conventions limit individual choices, particularly those of women, and especially in their expression of passion. Neither Calixta nor Clarisse can act directly in achieving her desires because the role of the lady confines them both, one by her conformity to it, the other by her recalcitrance in it. This complex interaction between selfhood and social roles recurs in many of C.'s stories, from her first, "Wiser than a God" (1889), in which a young musician must choose between art and love, to one of her last, "Charlie" (1900), in which a youthful tomboy must learn to relinquish her androgynous role.

C.'s growing independence from local color, which she well understood to be the vehicle and not the substance of lasting art, was clearly bolstered by the critical success of *Bayou Folk*. "The Story of an Hour" (1894), which immediately followed the collection's publication, is a masterpiece of condensed storytelling and a brilliant evocation of 19th-c. marriage for women. Louise Mallard, hearing of her husband's sudden death, retreats to her room to weep, only to experience the unfamiliar thrill of freedom that his loss now promises. As she returns downstairs, however, Brently Mallard enters the door, his death a mistake, but hers now its shocking consequence. C.'s subtle handling of detail and point of view, entering Louise Mallard's consciousness and then withdrawing to the doctors's final misreading of her death, deftly unfolds the story's radical challenge to conventional marriage and its suppression of female selfhood. In exploring that selfhood, C. insisted on both its natural bases—as from Louise Mallard's open window—and its sensuous dimensions. But she also recognized the complexities of its realization in a society with limiting notions of both women and sexuality. For C. to possess oneself was often a consequence of acknowledging the body and one's connectedness to nature. But the romance of that wholeness was always shadowed by the reality of the social institutions and the human relationships on which every individual must depend.

This dual awareness, together with her psychological interests, marks many important stories from C.'s second collection, *A Night in Acadie* (1897), as well as those of her unpublished third collection, "A Vocation and a Voice." In stories like "Lilacs" (1896), "Regret" (1895), "A Pair of Silk Stockings" (1897) or "The Storm" (1898), awakening to sensuality or the consequences of its repression are focal concerns, while conventional morality, or characters's—often unwitting—adherence to it, represent the obstacles to self-realization.

Characteristically, these oppositions between self and society, between sensuousness and discipline, are left unresolved or ambivalent, highlighting both the dualism of C.'s perspectives and the obstinance of her realism.

C.'s most extended reflection, before *The Awakening* (1899), on the connections between selfhood and sensuality and the ambivalent part that motherhood and marriage play for women occurs in "Athénaise" (1896). After only two months of wedlock, Athénaise Miché flees home to her parents and eventually to New Orleans. There she attracts the courtly attentions of Gouvernail, who patiently waits for her to respond. But when Athénaise learns she is pregnant, her sensuality is awakened and she returns abruptly to her waiting husband, Cazeau. Both marriage and romance are scrutinized in this tale, the former as an oppressive institution and the latter, more obliquely, as a screen for the disillusioning realities of sex and lost identity in marriage. Neither Cazeau nor Gouvernail wish to force Athénaise, by law or by affection; each waits for her to act freely, to know her own mind. But that awaited autonomy is revealed to Athénaise paradoxically in her incipient motherhood—through the body whose powers and sensuality she now apprehends, and whose apprehension has given her the limited but real freedom of self-possession, of ratifying the choices decreed by custom and biology. The complexity of C.'s vision—her cognizance of the repressiveness of marriage for women, of the powerful relationship between sensuality and selfhood, and of the deep physical satisfactions of motherhood—is particularly evident in this fine story, which directly anticipates the yet more complex conflicts in *The Awakening*.

C. only published two novels, having destroyed a third early in her career. *At Fault* (1890), like much of her early fiction, is closely associated with the local color movement in its techniques and themes. The cultural clash of Northern industrialism and Southern agriculture is embodied both in the central characters—David Hosmer, a Yankee sawmill operator and the young Creole widow, Therese Lafirme—and in the dual settings of bustling, mercantile St. Louis and the placid communal life of a Louisiana plantation.

The melodramatic plot and subplots, designed to bring these opposites together, are often unconvincing, as are several of the characters. However, the novel is distinctive on other counts: its lack of sentimentality, its realistic dialect and settings, its examination of individualism, and its unusual neutrality toward divorce, as one of the first American novels to treat the issue without moralistic judgement. The insistence in *At Fault* on the difficulty of moral certainty in human life recurs throughout C.'s canon, perhaps most eloquently in *The Awakening,* written seven years and virtually a career later.

The Awakening traces the erratic path to self-discovery of Edna Pontellier, a Kentuckian woman of twenty-eight, married to Léonce, a New Orleans businessman. Stirred to a vague restlessness by a languid Gulf summer, Edna is romantically drawn first to Robert Lebrun, a young Creole bachelor, and eventually into a half-hearted affair with a local rake, Alcée Arobin. Unsatisfied by the latter and abandoned by the former, she returns in despair to Grande Isle, discarding her clothes on the beach and swimming alone out to her death.

Not surprisingly *The Awakening* draws on many of the themes and techniques developed in C.'s career as a short-story writer. Its richly etched images of the sensuous Gulf and the intriguing Vieux Carre, its economically drawn characters, its subtle narrative, were all techniques perfected in her short fiction. The evocative prose, with its disarming simplicity and detached irony—a means of suspending authorial judgment—derives as much from such early sketches as "Ripe Figs" (1893) as from later experiments with the prose poem, such as "Two Portraits: The Wanton and the Nun" (1895) and "An Egyptian Cigarette" (1900). Briefly popular at the turn of the century, the prose poem drew upon many of the French influences that shaped C.'s style, especially Alphonse Daudet and Charles Baudelaire. Adapting it to the novel and to her markedly realistic themes of sexuality and the self in society, C. anticipates an essentially modern form, the poetic novel.

From its first appearance, *The Awakening* has unsettled its readers, and critics remain divided over the significance of Edna's troubling awakening and death. A complex character, Edna is both reserved and sensuous, headstrong and romantic, and like many of C.'s strong-minded young women, not fully prepared for either the advent or the consequences of self-possession. Edna's emerging sense of selfhood is heralded by an awakening sensuality: first the unaccustomed languor of the Gulf and Creole society, then the romantic indulgences with Robert, and eventually the passionate caresses of Alcée, which brings her, like Athénaise's pregnancy, to a new consciousness of self and an awakening to its powers. But for Edna the control of those powers is ephemeral. Neither the pigeon-house to which she retreats from Leonce's possessiveness, nor the splendid dinner she arranges to celebrate her departure enable her to redirect her life from the courses she had blindly chosen in marrying Leonce—and, more importantly, in bearing her two sons. Even her decision to choose Robert, to abandon her empty marriage, is pointedly interrupted by her friend Adele's reminder to think of the children. Whether weak or immature or overpowered, Edna cannot realize the self she has belatedly recognized. Indeed, it has already been betrayed by the patterns society and biology have decreed for women. When Edna finally understands her dilemma, she relinquishes the unessential, sacrificing her life rather than her newly awakened self to the choices of the past and the rigors of social convention.

Richly symbolic, as befits the economy of a poetic novel, *The Awakening* interweaves significant characters, events, and imagery. Primary among these are Edna's contrasting confidantes, Adele Ratignolle and Mlle. Reisz. Like other "mother-women" or the indistinguishable lovers at the beach, Adele has willingly silenced her individuality to socially prescribed roles; Mlle. Reisz, on the other hand, like the pious, solitary woman in black, has forfeited her place in the community and her sexuality to her individuality as an artist. Neither of these roles suits Edna, but having discarded them both like ill-fitting garments, she is unable to imagine any other for herself.

Other such metaphoric patterns, like the clothing imagery, intimate the unconscious depths of Edna's confusion: from the grassy field of her childhood or the naked figure on a rock evoked by Mademoiselle's music, to the crippled bird above the beach or, above all, the ambivalent embraces of the sea. Such textures sustain the novel's psychological realism and its challenging mythic dimensions, foremost of which are myths of gender, which inflect much of C.'s fiction. The social realities to which Edna finally succumbs are, in fact, patriarchally defined, while her desire, as well as her ambivalent struggle towards selfhood, is profoundly female. C.'s poetic articulation of that multivalent opposition is at the heart of the novel's power.

The Awakening was not well received. Praised for its elegant style and searching insight into character, it was also roundly rebuked for its articulation of female passion and its failure to condemn Edna's pursuit of sexual and social freedom. The unanimity of the criticism evidently caught C. by surprise. *The Awakening* was her most penetrating fiction, but it had emerged directly from the short stories which had won her the audience that now chastised her work. Indeed, the

confidence of her vision is evident in a short story she had written while awaiting the novel's appearance. "The Storm: A Sequel to the 'Cadian Ball" provides Alcée and Calixta with an unexpected occasion to renew and consummate their lingering desire. Exquisitely matching the progress of a summer storm with the rhythms of their passion, the story is remarkable for its positive and frank portrayal of sexuality, presenting even adulterous passion as a natural and satisfying encounter, refreshing the lives of everyone involved.

C. never even tried to publish this daring tale and, after the furor over *The Awakening,* seems to have gradually lost faith in her vision altogether. Her health failing, she wrote relatively few, largely conventional, stories after 1899 and published still fewer. After her death, her reputation faded and for many years she was remembered only as a minor writer of local color. Then, at mid-century, the revival of *The Awakening* as an early realistic novel and as a powerful portrait of women's struggle for selfhood gave her work a new audience and a fuller appraisal. The coincidental reemergence of the women's movement, for which the novel was often a touchstone, contributed to C.'s reputation. The poetic prose and compelling themes of *The Awakening* are the marks of excellence; and its endurance, like those of C.'s stories, from which the novel emerged and whose full appreciation remains underway, seems assured.

BIBLIOGRAPHY: Bloom, H., ed., *K. C.* (1987); Ewell, B., *K. C.* (1986); Seyersted, P., *K. C.: A Critical Biography* (1969); Toth, E., *K. C.* (1990)

BARBARA C. EWELL

CHU, Louis [Hing]
b. 1 October 1915, Toishan, China; d. 2 March 1970, New York City

Along with Carlos BULOSAN and John OKADA, C. is held as one of the seminal figures in the tradition of Asian American prose narrative. His only novel, *Eat a Bowl of Tea* (1961), received minimal notice during C.'s lifetime, but has enjoyed renewed attention since the mid-1970s. Today, he is considered one of the first Chinese American novelists.

C. did not earn his living by his writing, but remained a popular public figure during his lifetime. An immigrant from China as a boy of nine, C. grew up in Newark and later served the Chinese immigrant community in New York City as a radio personality and social worker. *Eat a Bowl of Tea* is set in just such a postwar Chinatown community, one whose characters comically negotiate the changes brought into their lives by relaxed immigration restrictions. In doing so, it documents a watershed moment in Chinese American history.

The novel is a satire of manners opposing the ideals and behavior of a younger Chinese American population with the strict mores of the previous generation. The immigrant community is largely composed of aging "bachelors," whose wives remain in China due to legislation barring their entry into the country. Unused to the influence of women in their bachelor society, the old men scramble to maintain their control in the face of a rapidly changing gender dynamic. C. characterizes his bachelors through their language, which is a literal translation of the Sze Yup dialect. Authentic phrases such as "you dead boy" and "you many-mouthed bird" led contemporary reviewers to balk at what they regarded as unpolished prose. C. later earned respect as a realistic writer of Chinatown life with his decision to remain faithful to the vernacular in place of an expected and flowery—yet inauthentic and ultimately damaging—speech.

Just as its language marked the novel as amateurish to its first readers, so too did its plot seem unremarkable. Yet *Eat a Bowl of Tea* rewards the careful reader familiar with the historical circumstances surrounding its action. Because the novel is not explicitly political, its treatment of the inequities of historical exclusion may be unappreciated, when in fact it lends the narrative its greatest complexity. The efforts of the Chinatown fathers Wah Gay and Lee Gong to manage Ben Loy's and Mei Oi's marriage is less comic when considering that their ineffectiveness is a result of an enforced isolation from the mainstream and from women. They dispense advice that seems outdated because they are products of an artificial and aging construct—old Chinatown itself—and are without any meaningful agency beyond its boundaries. As a native American citizen, the son born to the young couple represents the birth of a new, enfranchised Chinese American community.

Recent critical readings of the novel point out the problematics of an extant patriarchal system only renewed by the birth of Kuo Ming. This viewpoint is consistent with other treatments of early Asian American literature that have begun to address the gender relations within the culture, in addition to the race and class issues without. To reduce *Eat a Bowl of Tea* to simply another exercise of patriarchal control, however, would be to diminish its historical significance and artistic achievement. C.'s single contribution to the American canon remains important foremost for its nuanced handling of social inequity.

BIBLIOGRAPHY: Hsiao, R., "Facing the Incurable: Patriarchy in *Eat a Bowl of Tea*," in Lim, S. G., and A. Ling, eds., *Reading the Literatures of Asian America* (1992): 151–62; Ling, J., "Reading for Historical Specificities: Gender Negotiations in L. C.'s *Eat a Bowl of Tea*," *MELUS* 20 (Spring 1995): 35–51

DAVID SHIH

CHURCHILL, Winston

b. 10 November 1871, St. Louis, Missouri; d. 12 March 1947, Winter Park, Florida

Born and reared in St. Louis and educated at the Naval Academy, C. became one of the most well-known novelists of his day. After a brief stint as a journal editor, C. married and turned to a writing career in 1895, producing several short stories and *The Celebrity* (1898), a predictably plotted first novel satirizing the idle rich. Very popular between the Spanish-American War and World War I, C.'s ensuing series of best-selling novels reflected and influenced contemporary social and intellectual trends. In an order which illustrates cultural fashions of the times, C. turned from the historical novel to the political novel to the novel of social and religious reform.

C.'s fame was established by the American Revolutionary War romance *Richard Carvel* (1899). Describing the lives of aristocrats in both Maryland and London and lauding an Anglo-American tradition, the novel presents a hero who nonetheless eventually catches some nationalistic fervor from the example of John Paul Jones. The panoramic and patriotic *The Crossing* (1904), although not technically a sequel, carries the saga of American pioneering from the Revolution to the Louisiana Purchase (on the centennial of which the book appeared). The three sections of the novel trace the fortunes of David Ritchie from the Appalachians through Charleston and Kentucky to New Orleans, portraying in his career the image of a national manifest destiny. C.'s other historical novel, *The Crisis* (1901), is notable for its depiction of the Civil War's effects on the border city of St. Louis and its characterizations of Abraham LINCOLN, Ulysses S. Grant, William T. Sherman, and John Charles Frémont. As in his other romances, the requisite conventional and sentimental love story concludes happily despite initially divisive ideological, social and political loyalties. Most critics attribute the success of these books in part to C.'s meticulous historical research and frequent revisions.

C.'s serving as a New Hampshire state legislator and lobbyist, and his unsuccessful attempt to become the Republican nominee for governor, furnished him material for his fictional treatments of American political life. His critiques of contemporary public and private life combine the subjects of William Dean HOWELLS with the tone of the genteel tradition. Written from a moderate Rooseveltian Progressive point of view, these novels are not greatly different from the historical fiction in their old-fashioned idealism. *Coniston* (1906) presents a memorable picture of a state party boss along with the corruptions of the railroad interest. Humphrey Crewe's gubernatorial campaign in *Mr. Crewe's Career* (1908) reveals to him the ruthless muckraking-era manipulations of corporations, lobbyists, and lawyers. C.'s usual answer to these troubles lies in individual ethical change and a return to earlier American values.

In the first and least discursive of C.'s problem novels, *A Modern Chronicle* (1910), men's preoccupation with business and finance and women's with social status have created the painful reality of divorce. *The Inside of the Cup* (1913) became the most controversial of his books because of its criticism of the materialism and hypocrisy of organized religion, its lengthy doctrinal debates, and its promoting the social gospel. Several months spent in Berkeley and reading economics, sociology, psychology, and religion affected his treatment of these themes in *A Far Country* (1915). The last of C.'s novels, *The Dwelling-Place of Light* (1917), centers around the Lawrence mill strike and is the novelist's most radical in its mild naturalism and implication that something may be wrong with the economic system itself. After writing a second play and articles on the American fleet and the European and home fronts during 1917–19, C. settled down to a life of painting and carpentering, developing a personal version of a scientific and enlightened Christianity which became the subject of his final book, *The Uncharted Way* (1940).

BIBLIOGRAPHY: Quinn, A. H., *American Fiction: An Historical and Critical Survey* (1936): 496–501; Titus, W. I., *W. C.* (1963); Walcutt, C. C., *Compromise in the Novels of W. C.* (1951)

BENJAMIN S. LAWSON

CHUTE, Carolyn
b. 14 June 1947, Portland, Maine

C.'s first novel, *The Beans of Egypt, Maine* (1985), instantly established her as a uniquely American writer, comparable to William FAULKNER, Alice WALKER, and Erskine CALDWELL for her subjects and use of language, and with Charles Dickens and Samuel Langhorne CLEMENS for her own working-class roots. The book was given an urgency and sense of authority by C.'s assertion that the poverty and social marginalization within its pages had been "involuntarily researched" during her life as a struggling single parent in rural Maine. It polarized critics with one of two equally strong judgments: C.'s fiction was either the coarse-tongued, vulgar attempt to put a Faulknerian twist on a New England town, or it was the intensely if uncomfortably accurate literary representation of the economic class that is the most overlooked, silenced constituency of the American public.

The Beans of Egypt, Maine is narrated in part by Earlene, who has grown up watching the Bean clan's squalid trailer camp disapprovingly, only to find that adolescent hormones and social despair draw her into their violent, incestuous web. It is a tribute to C.'s skill that over the course of the novel, generations of wildly fertile, and equally brutal Beans take on a humanity, and their actions begin to make sense in the context of their limited choices and foreshortened horizons.

C. withstood significant criticism for her blunt depictions of social and sexual practices found, at the very least, distasteful to the middle-class literary market. She presented these practices without judgment, sentimentality, or cries for social reforms, but with raw, gritty language and remarkable humor. The novel bore all the ingredients of what was to become C.'s stylistic signature: strong women, desperate men, episodic narration, and a lyricism of description that gives dimensionality to characters and a lifestyle that could easily be flattened and exploited for pathos.

Ten years after its original publication, C. released *The Beans of Egypt, Maine: The Completed Version* (1995), which contained changes and a postscript in which she directly responded to what she perceived as critical misinterpretations of the first version. She also expressed disappointment with the critical reception of her subsequent novels: *Letourneau's Used Auto Parts* (1988), which charts the further adventures of Big Lucien, first introduced in *The Beans of Egypt, Maine,* and the sprawl of his ex-wives, children, and sundry relatives; and *Merry Men* (1993), an epic of nearly seven hundred pages that is anchored by four shifting narrators and openly valorizes farmers and the self-protecting insularity of rural life. While *Letourneau's Used Auto Parts* was praised as a more powerful and confident use of her talent for composing a portrait out of disjointed scenes, some found an authorial distancing from the characters that prevented the reader's development of strong emotional attachment to any one of them. *Merry Men* fared even more poorly; critics accused her third novel of being preachy and C. of having lost her trademark sense of humor. Again set in Egypt, *Merry Men* employs four narrators to take on the divisive issues of attempts at so-called social progress and the limitations and ethics of individual gain in the face of corporate exploitation.

While C.'s short fiction and poems are increasingly anthologized, she has recently turned some of her energies to both social commentary and a political activism which underscore the economic and political positions found in her most recent novel. Unapologetically patriotic and pro-labor, her stance against big government and big business has won her considerable support from the living communities that constitute the realistic counterparts for C.'s fictional Egypt.

BIBLIOGRAPHY: Christopher, R., "Lower-class Voices and the Establishment: The Reception of C. C.," *AL& C* 5 (1993): 106–21; Lesser, E., "An Interview with C. C.," *NER* 8 (Winter 1985): 158–77; Wright, N. H., "Of Pomerleaus and Pumpkins: Christianity and Paganism in *The Beans of Egypt, Maine*," *KPR* 2 (1987): 13–20

ELIZABETH BLEICHER

CIARDI, John [Anthony]

b. 24 June 1916, Boston, Massachusetts; d. 30 March 1986, Edison, New Jersey

Poet, translator, editor, and teacher, C. exemplifies that generation of mid-20th-c. American poets such as Richard WILBUR, Muriel RUKEYSER, Karl SHAPIRO, Robert LOWELL, Randall JARRELL, and Elizabeth BISHOP, who came into prominence after World War II. Still working in the aesthetic shadow of T.S. ELIOT and Ezra POUND, they represented a highly personal vision coupled with a more diverse and democratic spirit.

Poetry was C.'s career. Publishing over twenty books of original poetry, as well as another twelve books of poetry for children, C.'s work draws on his personal experiences as the son of Italian immigrant parents, growing up around Boston, as a veteran of the World War II, and as an academic, to represent and trace the development of the American consciousness from the 1940s to the early 1980s. From his first volume, *Homeward to America*, published in 1940—a work begun as an undergraduate at Tufts College and completed in graduate school at the University of Michigan, where it won the Hopwood Award for poetry—to his *Selected Poems* (1984) and *The Birds of Pompeii* (1985), C.'s poetry is marked by a concern for craftsmanship, discipline, and technical mastery, while employing vivid, colloquial language. His imagery is highly personal, though not private, drawn from the common events of everyday life. Much of his earlier poetry is concerned with the theme and identity of the father. His own father died in an automobile accident when C. was three; in turn, C. was concerned with his cultural and artistic identity as an Italian American Catholic writing poetry in an Anglo-American medium. Later volumes, such as *I Marry You* (1958) and *The Little That Is All* (1974) explore his own role as husband and father. Throughout, his language struggles to find the means appropriate to the passions and feelings it tries to express. C.'s poetry is also marked by its wit and playfulness. These, coupled with his concern for language and craftsmanship, are especially evident in his several volumes of limericks as well as his many fine books of children's poetry.

As a poet, C.'s influence is now perhaps most immediately present in his translation of Dante's *Divine Comedy*. The *Inferno* appeared in 1954, followed by *The Purgatorio* in 1961, *The Paradiso* in 1970, and a complete version in 1977. Aspiring to capture Dante's pace and realism, C. was less concerned with a literal rendition of Dante's formal features, such as the *terza rima*. The result is a work that stands not only as a translation, but as a poem.

C. also exercised a profound influence on modern American poetry as an editor and literary journalist. In 1949, he became poetry editor for Twayne Publishers, bringing out his influential anthology *Mid-Century American Poets* (1950). From 1955 to 1977, C. was associated with Norman Cousins and the *Saturday Review* as poetry editor and the regular contributor of often controversial reviews and columns. His textbooks, *How Does a Poem Mean?*, first published in 1959 and revised with Miller Williams in 1975, and *Poetry: A Closer Look* with James M. Reid and Laurence Perrine in 1963, shaped the understanding, reading, and study of poetry for a generation of American students.

Combining passion and wit with the scholarly and the earthy, and coupled with a resonant baritone voice, C. was a natural teacher. He taught at the University of Kansas City, Missouri, Harvard, and Rutgers University. He joined the Bread Loaf Writers' Conference in 1947 and directed the program from 1955 to 1972. In 1961–62, he hosted the educational program *Accent* on CBS television, and toward the end of his life contributed regular commentaries on language and etymology to National Public Radio. These essays were collected in his *A Browser's Dictionary* (1980), *A Second Browser's Dictionary* (1983), and *Good Words to You* (1987).

If C. is perhaps not the most widely read poet of the second half of the 20th c., his efforts as a translator, editor, and teacher have made him one of the most influential.

BIBLIOGRAPHY: Clemente, V., ed., *J. C.: Measure of the Man* (1987); Krickel, E., *J. C.* (1980); Southworth, J. G., "The Poetry of J. C.," *EJ* 50 (1961): 583–89; Williams, M., ed., *The Achievement of J. C.* (1969)

THOMAS L. COOKSEY

CISNEROS, Sandra
b. 20 December 1954, Chicago, Illinois

Once known primarily as a poet, with her first novel, *The House on Mango Street* (1984), as well as *Woman Hollering Creek and Other Stories* (1991), C. has transcended that label.

Born in Chicago of Mexican American heritage, C. attended Loyola University of Chicago, where she earned her B.A. (1976), and went on to study at the graduate level at the Iowa Writers' Workshop, where she received an M.F.A. in 1978. She has won numerous awards and fellowships, including two National Endowment for the Arts Fellowships in poetry and fiction and the 1991 Lannan Literary Award in fiction.

In her first book of poetry, *Bad Boys* (1980), C. introduced themes that become prevalent throughout her work: Chicana strength and independence, depicted with pride and lyricism.

The House on Mango Street is relayed through series of connecting narrative vignettes. Told from the perspective of Esperanza, a young girl in Hispanic Chicago, it is a novel of hope set against the difficult realities of growing up amid violence, racism, and oppression. Although the issues are familiar, the work itself is distinctive, not only from other narratives, but from C.'s earlier poetry. Many of the stories are told with what could be called an experimental edge. C.'s prose does not follow a conventional, linear, storytelling frame.

My Wicked Wicked Ways (1987), C.'s second collection of poetry, fuses the narrative voice of *The House on Mango Street,* with the more worldly voice of the poet. Separated into titled sections, the collection seems to move forward in time and place: from Chicago to Texas to "Other Countries"; from child to woman.

Woman Hollering Creek and Other Stories is a collection of stories in a variety of voices that span countries. Many of the stories are more short prose pieces told by narrators with extremely distinctive voices. The first section, "My Lucy Friend Who Smells Like Corn," includes seven short pieces. These are stories told from a child's point of view, with both a child's voice and perspective: honest and cutting. As the collection moves forward, the stories themselves grow: in length and by the age of the narrators. The title story in the collection, a third-person narrative, is indicative of C.'s primary interests. Cleofilas Enriquita DeLeon Hernandez, the protagonist, is taken. Presumably, she has gone from Mexico to Texas where she, who has waited her entire life to be married, is wed to an abusive man. C. tells these tales in the lyrical tone of her earlier prose, though the work is influenced by her poetic accomplishments.

With *Loose Woman* (1994), C. moves again to the poetic format. In this collection, the child's voice has been eclipsed by the certain, passionate voice of the author. *Loose Woman* is an introspective and risqué collection of celebration. The poems, both in English and spanish, reveal love and eroticism, womanhood and feminism in a playful and serious manner.

Although still in a relatively early stage of her career, C.'s work has already achieved both popular and scholarly recognition. Her poems have been translated into many languages, including Bengali. The strength in the thematic context of her work and the studied sureness of her language, assure that C.'s growing body of work will be welcomed long into the next c.

BIBLIOGRAPHY: Elías, E. F., "S. C.," in Lomelí, F. A., and C. R. Shirley, *DLB,* vol. 122, *Chicano Writers* (1992): 77–81; Ganz, R., "S. C.: Border Crossings and Beyond," *MELUS* 19 (Spring 1994): 19–29; Satz, M., "Returning to One's House: An Interview with S. C.," *SWR* 82 (Spring 1997): 166–85

MARIKA BRUSSEL

CITY AND LITERATURE, The

Ever since the settlers of the Massachusetts Bay Colony envisioned themselves in 1630 as building an ideal "city upon a hill," American writers have been engaged in a debate over the value of urban civilization. Some have pictured the city as a New Jerusalem, a heavenly metropolis capable of redeeming the wilderness surrounding it. Others, seeing the worldly city's dedication to power and wealth, have characterized it as a decadent Babylon, bent on self-destruction. But whether seeking the celestial city or condemning the infernal one, writers have relied on the dynamic confrontation of urban and natural spaces as a means of exploring the imaginative potential of American life.

Both Puritans and profiteers saw early on that the New Jerusalem's reuniting of Edenic garden and postlapsarian urban world offered a compelling model for the making of America. The aspirations of the young republic were often couched in terms of an urban-pastoral harmony: Walt WHITMAN in "The Prairie States" (1880) envisioned the American continent as a "newer garden of creation" that would be "iron interlaced," filled with "modern, populous millions, cities and farms." Whitman expresses a view popular in American culture at large, but most writers were more skeptical about the possibility of such an ideal synthesis.

In his *Autobiography,* Benjamin FRANKLIN provides an influential secular version of the *Pilgrim's*

Progress: hard work and perseverance lead him to success in the prosperous town. Much of the popular fiction in subsequent periods, such as the rags-to-riches novels of Horatio ALGER, Jr. follow Franklin in extolling the opportunities of the American city. Urban prospects and self-importance rise so high in youthful Manhattan that Washington IRVING satirizes its pretensions to Homeric and biblical stature in his mock-epic *A History of New York.*

But the letters of Thomas JEFFERSON toward the end of the 18th c., and James Fenimore COOPER's Leather-Stocking novels early in the 19th, warn that the unchecked expansion of urban industry threatens the moral and political benefits of pastoral American life. Moreover, the best-known characters in 19th-c. fiction—Natty Bumppo, Hester Prynne, Ishmael, and Huckleberry Finn—decisively turn their backs on the city, contributing to the impression that "classic" American literature is fundamentally anti-urban in outlook. In his pioneering account of the big city's impenetrable anonymity, "The Man of the Crowd" (1840), Edgar Allan POE concludes that his obsessed urbanite is "the type and the genius of deep crime."

Yet the very range of complaints and the extent of urban dissatisfaction suggest that writers are attempting more than a mimetic portrayal of an alienating environment. Rather, they use urban life as a metaphor for their own complex relation to a culture that the city embodies in concrete form. Thus, Puritan sermons of the later 17th c. castigate Boston for its sinful backsliding, while in *The Scarlet Letter,* Nathaniel HAWTHORNE denounces the same town and era for its authoritarian repression. In many of Hawthorne's works, city and country represent competing aspects of human nature, and journeys between the two worlds become efforts to understand the relation between the needs of individuals and those of a society that inevitably constrains them. "My Kinsman, Major Molineux," for example, sets the country-bred illusions of a naive narrator against the experience, both nightmarish and promising, of revolutionary Boston. With a similar purpose the rurally inspired meditations of Ralph Waldo EMERSON's *Nature* and Henry David THOREAU's *Walden* analyze the forces that lead people to settle on farms or in cities, and they call for a more organic society that can reconcile natural man to the artificial metropolis he has created.

Far less optimistic, Herman MELVILLE assesses America's relentless drive for economic gain by measuring its human cost. When the hero of *Pierre* leaves his idyllic village, he sees New York as a Dantesque city of the damned: conforming, commercial, and callous. And in "Bartleby, the Scrivener," Melville reveals "Wall Street" as a double-edged metaphor that delineates the crippling moral effects of laissez-faire capi-

talism. For not only is Bartleby's Wall Street the nation's economic center; it also represents the physical and psychological barriers that the city erects between its citizens. In contrast, Walt Whitman's poems celebrate the human fellowship underlying social or geographical differences. In "Song of Myself" and "Crossing Brooklyn Ferry" he announces that for the expansive soul there are no divisions between city and self, town and country. His imaginative synthesis of poet, reader and passerby—"myself disintegrated, every one disintegrated yet part of the scheme"—proposes a startling personal intimacy amid the burgeoning industrial city.

Later in the century, the question of how to live in the city draws the attention of realists like William Dean HOWELLS and psychological novelists such as Henry JAMES and Edith WHARTON. In *The Rise of Silas Lapham* and *A Hazard of New Fortunes,* Howells voices common fears about the anonymity and amorality of big city life by exploring their effects on representative middle-class families. James, on the other hand, balances his treatment of the American city as hypocritical and constricting (*Washington Square* and *The Bostonians*) against the cultural and social sophistication of Europe. But from James's earliest works such as *The American, Daisy Miller,* and *The Portrait of a Lady,* to the latest such as *The Wings of the Dove* and *The Golden Bowl,* the seductive capitals of Europe spell decadence, corruption, and even death for American expatriates. Similarly, the upper-class protagonists of Wharton's novels *The House of Mirth* and *The Age of Innocence* are torn between the moral compromise of fleeing to Europe and the soul-destroying respectability of social life in turn-of-the-century New York.

As the Western frontier closed and growing concern for the city's poor gave rise to modern sociology, many writers conducted their own investigations into the ways that the spreading urban environment determines the lives of ordinary people. Stephen CRANE's *Maggie, A Girl of the Streets* traces the passage of a slum child from romantic innocent to prostitute, and in *Sister Carrie,* Theodore DREISER analyzes the economic laws and sexual trade-offs that condition a working girl's struggle to rise in Chicago and New York. Upton SINCLAIR's *The Jungle* exposes the sordid brutality of Chicago stockyards and slums. Although in *The Four Million,* O. HENRY usually softens his depiction of urban hardships with surprise endings, his stories matter-of-factly note the grinding poverty of shop girls, clerks, and laborers. Somewhat later, Sinclair LEWIS records the debilitating results of complacent materialism on small town life in *Main Street* and *Babbitt.*

With the advent of MODERNISM, the city emerges as a territory of almost infinite artistic potential, although in economic and human terms it may remain as inhospitable as before. John DOS PASSOS's *Manhattan Transfer* is the first American novel to place the random, disjunctive quality of urban life itself in the foreground, using techniques such as narrative discontinuity and interior monologue. the fragmentation of the city plays and equally central role, both formally and thematically, in T. S. ELIOT's *The Waste Land*. Although set in London, the poem undertakes a characteristically American quest that turns from the "unreal city" of modern life to the desert beyond, searching for a regenerative path that will revivify both natural and urban worlds. A similar tension between a contemporary urban wasteland and the Edenic garden that the New World once promised animates F. Scott FITZGERALD's *The Great Gatsby*. Under Gatsby's spell, the narrator Nick Carraway temporarily forgets the valley of ashes, the barren fruit of the city's wealth, and discovers a gleaming Manhattan where America's past hopes can be recreated from its dreams: "The city seen from the Queensboro Bridge is always the city seen for the first time, in its first wild promise of all the mystery and the beauty of the world."

Hart CRANE's epic poem *The Bridge,* intended in part as a positive response to *The Waste Land,* also joins America's urban present to its mythic rural past. Using the symbol of Brooklyn Bridge as a link between the vision of Columbus and the subsequent history of the continent, Crane, like Whitman, fuses personal and national destinies in a moment of urban transcendence. William Carlos WILLIAMS's early reaction to New York is largely aesthetic, but by the time of his long collage-poem *Paterson* he too concentrates on the relation between the natural and man-made environments. From the "disembodied roar" of his New Jersey town and the cataract that crashes beside it, he strives to create an articulate language that will reveal "the city / the man, an identity." All these works symbolically oppose some version of a pastoralized New Jerusalem, what Eliot calls "the city over the mountains," to the falling towers of misguided Babylon.

After World War II, an important variation appears in the basic pattern of American writing about the city. Recasting their narratives in exclusively urban terms, many authors abandon the physical journey toward nature and the frontier. Instead, their characters seek salvation within the city's metaphoric wilderness, and the pilgrim's progress out of Babylon is charted on a vertical rather than horizontal axis. Literal and figurative undergrounds blend in such works as Richard WRIGHT's "The Man Who Lived Underground" (1944) and Jack KEROUAC's *The Subterraneans;* subways and skyscrapers become the indicators of spiritual status in Norman MAILER's *An American Dream;* and in *Invisible Man,* Ralph ELLISON's narrator follows an intricate symbolic route between basement and rooftops, between the white city downtown and black Harlem uptown.

In the work of postwar Jewish and black writers, for whom the city had been held out as a promised land, there often seems to be no world beyond the city limits. Second-generation autobiographers like Alfred KAZIN (*A Walker in the City*) recall their search for fulfillment in terms of the journey from Brooklyn to Manhattan, much as earlier Jewish writers such as Abraham Cahan, Anzia Yezierska, and Henry ROTH had recorded the trials and rewards of immigrant experience in New York's Lower East Side. While the shattering of the American dream of urban success has been the concern of novelists such as Bernard MALAMUD (*The Assistant* and *The Tenants*) and Saul BELLOW (*The Victim* and *Seize the Day*), their characters find no solace in the suburbs or the countryside further west.

If works produced by the Harlem Renaissance were not so much about the city as born of it, the next generation of black writers focuses closely on life in the expanding Northern ghettos. Set in Chicago, Wright's *Native Son* uncompromisingly portrays the frustration and rage of blacks denied freedom in the white city that exploits them. James BALDWIN's *Go Tell It On the Mountain* and *Another Country* trace the troubled passage toward black identity in New York, while Ann PETRY's *The Street* details the devastating effects of the Harlem environment upon a young mother. In *Browngirl, Brownstones,* Paule MARSHALL describes the aspirations of more hopeful Barbadian immigrants in Brooklyn.

Two of the major movements in postwar poetry have been urban in inspiration: the Beats, which included Allen GINSBERG, Gregory CORSO, and Lawrence FERLINGHETTI; and the New York school, comprising Frank O'HARA, Kenneth KOCH, and John ASHBERY, among others. The hallucinatory intensity of Ginsberg's *Howl* and the surreal serendipity of O'Hara's *Lunch Poems* stand in contrast to the quieter urban meditations of Robert LOWELL, Elizabeth BISHOP, and James MERRILL.

Finally, several classics of the modern American theater, including Clifford ODETS's *Awake and Sing!,* Eugene O'NEILL's *The Iceman Cometh,* Tennessee WILLIAMS's *A Streetcar Named Desire,* Arthur MILLER's *Death of a Salesman,* and Amiri BARAKA's *Dutchman* use urban settings to dramatize the psychological conflicts of their characters.

As metropolitan areas continue to expand, American life and literature have become ever more urban in character. Among the many other important chroniclers of the city are Thomas WOLFE, James T. FARRELL, Dorothy PARKER, Mary MCCARTHY, J. D. SALINGER,

Grace PALEY, Sylvia PLATH, John CHEEVER, William S. BURROUGHS, Hubert SELBY, Jr., and Donald BARTHELME. Despite new interest in regional centers, exemplified by William KENNEDY's "Albany Cycle," since the 1960s the dominant literary cities have been New York and, increasingly, Los Angeles. New York's economic swings and baffling complexity feature in novels by Saul BELLOW, Don DELILLO, Jay MCINERNEY and Tom WOLFE, while the formlessness of Los Angeles metaphorically grounds works by Alison LURIE, Joan DIDION, and Brett Easton ELLIS. Apocalyptic in Nathanael WEST's *The Day of the Locust,* maddeningly enigmatic in Thomas PYNCHON's *The Crying of Lot 49,* Los Angeles is emerging as the latest city of American destiny. Amid the labyrinth of freeways, Pynchon confronts the semiotic overload of the postmodern metropolis: "Behind the hieroglyphic streets there would either be a transcendent meaning," or none at all, "only the earth." The spiritually charged quest in contemporary American literature to read the illegible city, or to comprehend its myriad voices, suggests that biblical archetypes will continue to shape the writer's response to the city—although the most common comparison is no longer to Babylon, but Babel.

BIBLIOGRAPHY: Bercovitch, S., M. Jehlen, and L. Marx, eds., *Ideology and Classic American Literature* (1986); Gelfant, B., *The American City Novel* (1954); Jaye, M. C., and A. C. Watts, eds., *Literature and the Urban Experience* (1981); Siegel, A., *The Image of the American City in Popular Literature, 1820–1870* (1981); Stout, J. P., *Sodoms in Eden: The City in American Fiction before 1860* (1976); White, M., and L. White, *The Intellectual Versus the City* (1962)

WILLIAM CHAPMAN SHARPE

CLAMPITT, Amy [Kathleen]

b. 15 June 1920, New Providence, Iowa; d. 10 September 1994, Lenox, Massachusetts

Although C. after her graduation from Grinnell College has subsequently worked as an editor and in other positions associated with publishing, it was only a few years ago that her first collection of poetry, *The Kingfisher* (1983) was published. This was followed by *What the Light Was Like* (1985) and *Archaic Figure* (1987).

C.'s poetry is relatively new on the literary scene, but it is obvious that hers is an important voice. Her first book was praised highly for its mastery of demanding poetic forms, for her lavish use of inventive language and for her challenging thought. Her subse-

quent books have born out its promise, and have further illustrated her wit and the depth of her intellect.

C.'s poetry belongs to the school of the New Formalism; Mona VAN DUYN has compared her work to what might emerge if Marianne MOORE had married Gerard Manley Hopkins and produced a child with both their talents. Her poems are almost shockingly rich in their subject matter, using a remarkable knowledge of wild life—it is no surprise that she was once the reference librarian for the National Audubon Society. Landscape also inspires her, not only her native Midwest, but Maine, Europe, and especially Greece. In her latest book she mines the myths of that country, turning them inside out to find part of the genesis of women's ambivalent place in the world, doing this through metaphors of headache, drowning and terror. She is fearless in juxtaposition of allusions, setting Lawrence Durrell's travel account of a Greek island side by side with an Iowa tornado. Her references are so complicated that she has included a set of notes in each volume.

Her poems are equally rich in technique. She frequently uses slant rhymes or visual rhymes and except as a concluding device, seldom uses obvious ones. She is a tamer of those two big cats, assonance and consonance, making them jump through her hoops. The musical quality in her work comes primarily from these devices, especially her masterly use of assonance. In the headlong rush of her particularly realized objects, she attempts a synthesis of sound, metaphor, and narrative, all toward a new meaning. Edmund WILSON finds, however, that she does not truly use narrative but rather superimposes image upon image in an attempt to make the poem move. Using formal techniques that are formidable, she is primarily a poet of ideas. Although her first book was published when she was of an age when many other people are considering retirement, she is just beginning a new and illustrious career.

BIBLIOGRAPHY: Howard, R., "The Hazardous Definition of Structures," *Parnassus* 11 (Spring-Summer 1983): 271–75; Vendler, H., "On the Thread of Language," *NYRB* 3 March 1983: 19–21; White, E., "Poetry as Alchemy," *The Nation* 236 (16 April 1983): 485–86

ANN STRUTHERS

CLARK, Walter Van Tilburg

b. 3 August 1909, East Orland, Maine; d. 10 November 1971, Reno, Nevada

On the strength of three novels and a modest number of short stories, C. ranks among the most important

of writers from the American West. Many writers from
the West have been exceedingly prolific, notably Zane
GREY and Louis L'Amour are obvious examples, but
few brought to their craft the grounding in the arts
that C. did. His mother was a musician; his father an
academic, for twenty years president of the University
of Nevada in Reno. C. grew up surrounded by books
and the arts. After earning two master's degrees in
English, he taught high school in New York state for
over a decade. Back in the West, for most of the
remainder of his life he taught creative writing at the
collegiate level in Nevada, Oregon, California, and
Montana. Although he counted himself a man of the
desert, he was decidedly an educator as well. This
tension may account for central conflicts in his work
and also explain the small body of work. C.'s published
writing was done in a little over a decade. Although
he continued to write, he published no fiction in his
last two decades. At his death, he left two novels
completed but did not judge them worthy of publication. Although many Western writers have ignored or
scorned the critics, C. could not. Critics aside, C.
brought a very high standard to his work.

C. did his apprenticeship work in poetry; his first
M.A. thesis was a verse presentation of the Tristam
story, the second a study of the poet Robinson JEFFERS.
His first book was *Ten Women in Gale's House and
Shorter Poems* (1932), but his true metier was fiction.
His first novel, *The Ox-Bow Incident* (1940), made
him famous. Made into an acclaimed film in 1942,
the novel has never gone out of print; it ranks with
the great novels of the West, an American classic.

Sometimes called an anti-Western, *The Ox-Bow
Incident* reverses many of the features of the prototypical Western. It is a novel without a hero: no one is
strong enough to stop the lynching of three innocent
men charged with cattle rustling and a killing that
never happened, though some try. The novel's publication occurring just before the U.S. entered World War
II, C. described an American brand of fascism, showing that it can happen here, has happened here. The
nature of evil is central to all of C.'s work. It is a
revealing feature of *The Ox-Bow Incident* that the
intellectual (one narrates the novel) is no force in the
counter effort at the Ox-Bow lake; his role is but to
"tell" later, a special kind of action.

The city of *The City of the Trembling Leaves*
(1945), C.'s second novel, is Reno. As the title suggests, its focus is not the city of gambling, the quick
divorce and the quick marriage. Rather C. depicts other
rhythms. The novel is a bildungsroman, describing the
city C. knew growing up. The narrator is named Walt
Clark, but the author finds reflection in other characters
as well, certainly in Timothy Hazard, the young musician protagonist. Hazard's best friends is a painter who

deplores bourgeois society. The girl Hazard loves is
also not at ease with the world of people. Reviewers
faulted the novel for the failings common to the bildungsroman.

The Track of the Cat (1949) is the favorite among
C. scholars. Complex and intense, the novel explores
the major C. themes—man's relationship to man and
his relationship to the natural world—keeping at bay
the sentimentality that sometimes marred C.'s bildungsroman. Dream and nightmare structure C.'s study of
the Bridges, a family of Nevada ranchers. The action
begins when Arthur Bridges discovers a mountain lion
has been killing his cattle. After the lion kills Arthur,
his brother Curt seeks revenge on the lion, who has
become as much mythical as real. In his pursuit of
the lion, Curt falls off a cliff to his death. Eventually,
Harold, the younger brother, and the old Indian Joe
Sam succeed in killing the lion. Although *The Track
of the Cat* was made into a movie in 1954, the novel
has not had the popular appeal of *The Ox-Bow Incident,* and it is no longer in print.

Several of C.'s short stories have been anthologized, though increasingly compilers now bypass C.
"The Portable Phonograph" is probably the most famous of his stories. An ominous study of man's relationship to man, it ends with an image of civilized,
artistic man reduced to his "natural" self—ready to
kill to maintain ownership of his phonograph. "Hook"
is another favorite. Jeffers-like, it celebrates the majesty and power of the natural world. The protagonist
is a great hawk who takes his death, a consequence
of man's gun, with dignity and beauty.

BIBLIOGRAPHY: Gorrell, R., "W. V. T. C. and Trembling
Leaves: A Review Essay," *NHSQ* 35 (Fall 1992):
149–61; Laird, C., ed., *W. V. T. C.: Critiques* (1983);
Lee, L. L., *W. V. T. C.* (1973); Westbrook, M. R., *W. V.
T. C.* (1969)

JOSEPH M. FLORA

CLEMENS, Samuel Langhorne
b. 30 November 1835, Florida, Missouri; d. 21 April
1910, Redding, Connecticut

Better known by his famous pen name, "Mark Twain,"
C. ranks among the most esteemed and influential
authors the U.S. has produced and is widely regarded
as our premier literary humorist. His adaptable talents
enabled him to master a wide range of literary forms,
including sketches, essays, short stories, travel narratives, and novels. C.'s *The Innocents Abroad* (1869)
scoffs impudently at tourist sights in Europe and the
Holy Land, his *Roughing It* ((1872) appeals to all
lovers of the American West, and *A Connecticut Yan-*

kee in King Arthur's Court (1889) retains its satiric force; however, it is his writings about the Mississippi River, particularly *The Adventures of Tom Sawyer* (1876), *Life on the Mississippi* (1883), and C.'s masterpiece, *Adventures of Huckleberry Finn* (1884), which have earned him the admiration of writers and readers of the modern era.

The circumstances of C.'s birth and boyhood did not augur for immense fame and literary immortality. He was born in the hamlet of Florida, Missouri (today the site of the Mark Twain Birthplace and Museum), to a less-than-prosperous mother and father who had moved westward (their families originally from Kentucky and Virginia, respectively), hoping for better opportunities. His father was speculating unsuccessfully (as he had already done in Tennessee) on the possibility of a land boom, but again John Marshall Clemens, a merchant and lawyer, had to concede defeat and in 1839 move his family to another location. Yet the Florida vicinity would leave a vital imprint on C., for he returned there each summer to what he later termed "a heavenly place for a boy," his Uncle John Quarles's farm, where C. heard the dialect and tales of black slaves and learned the pleasures of swimming holes, forest paths, and country schools.

The family's next stop—five children were then living of the original seven, C. being next to the youngest—was Hannibal, Missouri. (The family's residence at 206 Hill Street has been preserved as the Mark Twain Boyhood Home and Museum.) Hannibal, too, might seem like an unpromising locale for a future writer, since it was only an overgrown village in 1839 and had many swelling competitors up and down the Mississippi River. Nevertheless, in Hannibal young C. witnessed the periodic spectacle of a gaudy steam packet approaching the city wharf, black smoke billowing ("all in a twinkling the dead town is alive and moving," C. would recall). "The great Mississippi, the majestic, the magnificent Mississippi, rolling its mile-wide tide along, shining in the sun," as C. once pictured it, transported slave-traders, minstrels, confidence men, and gamblers, along with plantation-owners and other river passengers. In Hannibal, too, C. first became acquainted with the printing trade, working for Joseph Ament's newspaper and printing firm after John Marshall Clemens died in debt in 1847. C. thus had little classroom education; print shops served as his high school, and newspaper and magazine offices functioned as the equivalent of his college.

Assisting his older brother Orion in a newspaper venture (the Hannibal *Journal*), C. contributed facetious sketches, humorous poems, and factual reports for several years, beginning in 1851. In 1852, C. placed his first piece in a national periodical—a short sketch titled "The Dandy Frightening the Squatter," which appeared in Benjamin P. SHILLABER's weekly Boston *Carpet-Bag.*

Wanderlust seized C. in 1853, and at the age of seventeen he departed from Hannibal, never really to return. A preference for frequent travel would characterize the rest of his days. After sojourns in St. Louis, New York City, Philadelphia, and Cincinnati (and a visit to Washington, D.C.), cities where he earned a subsistence wage as a printing compositor and utilized the libraries available to those of the printers's guild, he returned for a time to help his brother with further print—shop enterprises in Muscatine and Keokuk, Iowa. Then C. took the most consequential step of his life: he persuaded a steamboat pilot, Horace Bixby, to teach him the fundamentals of that vocation. In 1857, C. set about the task of learning a set of multitudinous details about the Mississippi River between St. Louis and New Orleans, and in April 1859 he became a full-fledged, licensed pilot. This was a much-envied profession with a handsome income ($250 per month)—and showy enough to suit even the spotlight-seeking C. He once wrote that he "loved the profession far better than any I have followed since," and proudly recalled that "a pilot, in those days, was the only unfettered and entirely independent human being that lived in the earth." The piloting experiences also afforded him crucial exposure to the varieties of humanity who swarmed aboard steamboats traversing the heart of the nation, and C. would testify that "when I find a well-drawn character in fiction or biography, I generally take a warm personal interest in him, for the reason that I have known him before—met him on the river." Only the death of C.'s younger brother Henry, who received fatal burns in a steamboat explosion near Memphis in 1858, marred these blissful years.

The outbreak of Civil War hostilities in 1861 promptly closed commercial navigation on the river, and C.—owing to his friendships with both Southern and Northern sympathizers—felt too ambivalent to participate more than a few weeks in the hurriedly formed Confederate militia unit he impetuously joined. He subsequently told several versions of this episode, including "The Private History of the Campaign That Failed" (1885). Orion Clemens having received an appointment as Secretary of the Territory of Nevada, C. welcomed an opportunity to go west and wait out what many people presumed would be a short war. In 1861 the two young men took a jarring stagecoach journey to Carson City, Nevada, and C. later amusingly described in *Roughing It* his unprofitable stints as a gold and silver prospector and his decision to enter the field of newspaper journalism to support himself. In the summer of 1862 he became a salaried reporter for Joseph T. Goodman's Virginia City *Territorial Enterprise.* The comic lecturer and author Charles Farrar BROWNE ("Artemus Ward"), visiting Virginia City in December 1863, encouraged C. by singling him out from the other newspaper writers as someone with special promise.

Eventually, C. relocated in California, where he joined the staffs of the San Francisco *Morning Call* and a literary journal, *The Californian.* On November 18, 1865, C.'s acclaimed story of "The Celebrated Jumping Frog of Calaveras County" made its appearance in a New York City weekly magazine, under the pen name C. had adopted on February 2, 1863—"Mark Twain" (two fathoms, i.e., twelve feet, the river-navigational term denoting a "safe" depth of water for a steamboat). This early masterpiece, based on a campfire tale that C. heard in California, contained several elements C. would employ in subsequent stories: a distracted narrator with a deadpan delivery (Simon Wheeler), an impatient frame narrator who resents Wheeler's long-winded, vernacular monologue, and a series of improbable occurrences related as verifiable local history. In "The Celebrated Jumping Frog," an inveterate gambler, who bets on every conceivable animal contest and specializes in wagers involving his dog Andrew Jackson and frog Dan'l Webster, eventually meets his match when a confidence man swindles him by filling the frog with lead pellets. Following C.'s return from the Hawaiian Islands, where he was a traveling correspondent for the Sacramento *Union,* he launched a lecture-circuit career. His initial platform performance in San Francisco on October 2, 1866 was advertised with characteristic ingenuity: THE TROUBLE BEGINS AT 8 O'CLOCK warned the humorous handbills. Gradually he perceived that the potential for his literary reputation and earnings could not be fulfilled in the West Coast milieu of the 1860s.

After C. took a voyage to Europe and the Holy Land aboard the *Quaker City* in 1867, his travel letters to the San Francisco *Alta California* and the New York *Tribune* elicited an invitation from the American Publishing Company of Hartford, Connecticut for him to fashion the correspondence into a book. The resulting narrative represented something entirely fresh in travel literature: a witty American tourist tells of his pilgrimage to obligatory Continental museums and Biblical sites, but, while duly impressed by certain scenes—Milan, Venice, St. Peter's, Pompeii, Athens, the ruins of Baalbec, the oasis of Damascus, the Pyramid of Cheops, the Sphinx—he refuses to kowtow to officious European guides or admire every Middle Eastern shrine. "Is he dead?" he and his light-hearted companions nonchalantly ask a chagrined guide who shows them ancient artifacts in Italy. Turkish coffee and the Turkish bath are vastly overrated by most guidebooks, he warns. And while he displays a reverence for Christ's life and teachings, he pokes fun at his

pious fellow passengers and scoffs at some pilgrims's hypocrisy in forcing their horses to gallop to the next destination in the Holy Land in order to avoid traveling on the Sabbath. The large sales of *The Innocents Abroad* addicted C. to a lucrative type of publishing known as the "subscription" method: a publisher hired thousands of agents to canvass door-to-door, and the book was printed only after orders were already placed by customers. The profits—and the author's royalty payments—were much larger and more secure than those produced by the "retail bookstore" system.

Buoyed by visions of the wealth ahead of him, C. paid court to a young woman who had grown up in Elmira, New York, Olivia L. Langdon, whose brother Charles Jervis Langdon had sailed on the *Quaker City* excursion. C.'s infatuated glimpse of a miniature painting of Olivia had led him to seek an introduction to her in December 1867. The pair were wed on February 2, 1870, and thereafter C. never ceased to idolize "Livy," whose literary judgment he often sought (though he sometimes disagreed with her about the work of other writers). After abandoning the pretense of becoming a conventional newspaper editor and publisher of the Buffalo *Express* in Buffalo, New York (and an assistant editor of the *Galaxy,* a New York City monthly), C. moved in 1871 to Hartford, Connecticut, where he would reside for twenty years. He often spent summers in Elmira, however, writing at Quarry Farm, the rural home of his wife's relatives. (This Victorian farmhouse and its grounds on East Hill, overlooking Elmira and the Chemung River valley, were donated to Elmira College and its Center for Mark Twain Studies in 1983; C.'s small octagonal study, originally situated on a promontory at Quarry Farm, has been moved to the nearby campus.) In addition to these summer sojourns, C. left Hartford to live abroad in 1873, 1878–79, and other years.

In November 1874, C. and his wife took possession of a sumptuous nineteen-room house (restored today as the Mark Twain House) in Nook Farm, a suburb of Hartford, commencing a halcyon epoch when C. became a respected civic figure and met and entertained countless American and English authors. The intellectual climate of New England seemed conducive to C.'s genius, and the literary periodicals of Boston and New York City—influenced by his close friend, eminent author-critic William Dean HOWELLS—proved receptive to C.'s writings. In Hartford, and at Quarry Farm during the summers, he produced most of the literary works for which he is best remembered. In 1872, C. and his family lost their infant son Langdon to illness, but three daughters, Susan ("Susy"), Clara, and Jane ("Jean") were born in 1872, 1874, and 1880, respectively.

Besides chronicling C.'s experiences in the Far West, *Roughing It* offered memorably vibrant accounts of Western outlaws, Mormons, Carson City, Virginia City, Lake Tahoe, the Sierra Nevada mountains, San Francisco, and Honolulu. Like C.'s other travel narratives, this one has numerous self-contained stories and tall tales, among which may be mentioned "Bemis' Buffalo Hunt," "A Genuine Mexican Plug," "Lost in the Snow," " Buck Fanshaw's Funeral," "Jim Blaine and His Grandfather's Ram," and "Dick Baker and His Cat." *Roughing It* was followed by C.'s first novel, *The Gilded Age* (1873), a work written in collaboration with Charles Dudley WARNER that appropriately named the decades following the Civil War. A frantically paced satire, *The Gilded Age* is set in small Missouri towns, St. Louis, Philadelphia, Washington, and other locations. Its most interesting characters are Colonel Beriah Seller, a speculator, and promoter who, rewritten as the quixotic Mulberry Sellers, supplied a successful stage vehicle for actor John T. Raymond in the title role of *Colonel Sellers* (1874); Laura Hawkins, stunningly beautiful but callous, who eventually murders the man who seduced and left her; and Senator Abner Dilworthy, a political hack and bribe-dispenser supposedly typical of the Reconstruction-era Congress. C.'s shorter pieces were collected in *Sketches, New and Old* (1875). His moving indictment of slavery, "A True Story, Repeated Word for Word as I Heard It," appeared in an *Atlantic Monthly* issue in 1874; the story chronicles with unabashed sentiment a black mother's separation from and miraculous reunion with one of her slave children. William Dean Howells's journal also published C.'s farcical "Facts Concerning the Recent Carnival of Crime in Connecticut" (1876), a clever account of one man's battle with (and permanent victory over) his nagging conscience that is reminiscent of Edgar Allan POE's "William Wilson" and anticipatory of Robert Louis Stevenson's stories about alter egos.

Possibly inspired by the success of Thomas Bailey ALDRICH's *The Story of a Bad Boy*, C. wrote *The Adventures of Tom Sawyer,* his first extended use of his memories of ante-bellum Hannibal, Missouri. Though *Tom Sawyer* has a serious, even morbid plot—Tom and his chum Huckleberry Finn witness a murder in a graveyard, Tom testifies against Injun Joe, and Tom and Becky Thatcher subsequently encounter this villain in McDougal's Cave—the horrific events significantly take place outside the town limits of sun-drenched, idyllic St. Petersburg, which perches scenically on the Mississippi River. Therefore most readers primarily recall the boyish antics that made *Tom Sawyer* the best in a line of American "bad-boy" books: Tom's playing hookey, whitewashing the fence, trading Sunday-school tickets, playing Robin Hood on

Cardiff Hill, camping out on Jackson's Island with Huck and Joe Harper (and alarming the townspeople, who believe they have drowned), returning to his own funeral service, digging for buried treasure. Although C. soon commenced a sequel, *Adventures of Huckleberry Finn,* several difficulties of plot kept him from completing the novel until 1884. In the interim, he exploited his recent European travels for another anecdotal mixture of factual matter and comedy, *A Tramp Abroad* (1880). On a pedestrian tour of Germany, Switzerland, and Italy, C.'s narrator, as usual in his travel works, ridicules European guidebooks and antiquity while introducing miscellaneous tales, character sketches, local legends, and self-mocking accounts of his mountain-climbing attempts and other stunts. Included in the book are extractable stories such as "Jim Baker's Bluejay Yarn."

During this period, C. also brought out *The Prince and the Pauper* (1881), a historical romance set in 16th-c. England that involves an exchange of identities between Tom Canty and the youth who was to rule as Edward VI. C. took satisfaction in learning that this work found approval with a genteel circle of New England readers, but those people who valued the vigor of C.'s less refined fiction were far less favorably impressed. Conceivably C. chaffed in his emerging role as the agreeable "family" author; at any rate, in 1880 he authorized the publication of a mildly off-color fragment of Tudor court conversation, *1601,* and periodically thereafter he amused all-male audiences with ribald speeches, sketches, and poems.

In 1882, C. refreshed his recollections of his piloting days by revisiting the Mississippi River, traveling by steamboat from St. Louis to New Orleans, and then returning north as far as Minneapolis-St. Paul. Already the efficient, reliable, crisscrossing railroad lines had effectually closed the chapter of American steamboating, and in praising the prosperity of the middle and northern river towns, C. recognized as well that he was witnessing the final days of his once-glorious profession of river-piloting. The immediate result of this nostalgic journey was *Life on the Mississippi,* which depicted the history, scenery, characters, and steamboat-lore of the Mississippi River region. The most evocative passages occur in chapters four through seventeen (already published serially in the *Atlantic Monthly* in 1875 as "Old Times on the Mississippi"), which recounted C.'s cub-pilot experiences and his growth from a romantic boy fascinated with the river and piloting to a young man familiar with the dangers hiding beneath surface beauty and the demands of adult responsibility.

Even better, the stimulation of the Mississippi River trip in 1882 enabled C. to complete his greatest work: *Adventures of Huckleberry Finn* finally appeared in

England in 1884 (in the U.S. not until 1885, owing to the sabotage of a malicious engraver, who turned one of E. W. Kemble's energetic drawings into an obscene illustration of Uncle Silas Phelps exposing himself). This first-person narrative of a fleeing boy invigorated the American Realism movement and forever enlarged the possibilities for fictional points of view. Huckleberry Finn merely reports passively on adult life observed in the towns and on the farms he visits in traveling down river with a runaway slave; as a child with no social standing, he feels utterly inconsequential, and indeed ceases to exist as himself after he symbolically stages the "murder" of Huckleberry Finn in chapter seven. Nevertheless, Huck's actions are often critical in the narrative, as when he dissuades two slave-hunters from boarding the raft by playing on their fears of smallpox. Huck's integrity and sense of wonder endow his folkspeech expressions with such compression and originality that his phrasing becomes poetically lyrical. "Next we slid into the river and had a swim, so as to freshen up and cool off," writes Huck Finn in chapter nineteen; "then we . . . watched the daylight come. Not a sound, anywheres—perfectly still—just like the whole world was asleep, only sometimes the bull-frogs a-cluttering, maybe."

Tom Sawyer's antics in the first three and last ten chapters of this novel provided the familiar elements of bad-boy books and literary burlesques for which C. was already known, though commentators have often decried the presence of these elements as incongruous in this context. Literary critics unanimously esteem the central section of the novel, in which Huck escapes from alcoholic, abusive Pap Finn, flees to Jackson's Island, and meets Miss Watson's black slave Jim, who is fleeing from St. Petersburg. Huck and Jim travel together toward Cairo, Illinois and the Ohio River, but they miss this landmark and their raft floats farther south into the region C. knew thoroughly from his river-piloting days; Huck explores a wrecked steamboat, lives with the Grangerfords (witnessing the bloody conclusion to that family's feud with the Shepherdsons), takes aboard two rapscallions who style themselves a King and a Duke, participates in these rascals's schemes to fleece the river villages, and betrays their plan to defraud Mary Jane Wilks and her sisters of an inheritance. Along the way, Huck and Jim develop mutual respect and affection for each other, so the reappearance of Tom Sawyer (and his pranks) at Silas Phelps's farm in Arkansas seems disappointing to many critics (though others point out that this reversion to the lighter bad-boy mode is not entirely complete, for now Huck resists Tom's commands at crucial junctures; moreover, the conclusion confers an aesthetically satisfying, framing symmetry

on the book). C.'s masterwork, whether marred or not, satirizes human gullibility, sham religion, racial prejudice, social pretension, superstition, avarice, and cruelty; it celebrates the innocence and glory of youth, the saving power of truthfulness, the fulfilling bond of genuine friendship.

Adventures of Huckleberry Finn became (and remains) a controversial book partly because of C.'s audacious experiment in reproducing the vernacular speech of the son of a town drunkard. And Huck Finn's nonchalant acceptance of the vocabulary of Southern slavery—including racial stereotypes and the demeaning colloquialism "nigger"—disturbed a number of late-20th-c. readers as much as Huck's dialectal grammar and carefree morals disgusted the Concord, Massachusetts Free Public Library, which banned the novel in 1885. C. himself was relatively liberal on the "race question" for his time, and implicit themes in *Huckleberry Finn* presume the sacredness of human aspirations and emotions, white or black, and insist upon the inherent, transcending equality of all people.

C.'s next novel, *A Connecticut Yankee in King Arthur's Court,* further revolutionized American prose style by introducing another "colloquial" narrator—a brash, slang-slinging industrial foreman from Hartford, Connecticut named Hank Morgan ("when I make up my mind to hit a man, I don't plan out a love-tap; . . . as long as I'm going to hit him at all, I'm going to hit him a lifter"). Morgan, hurled backward into 6th-c. England through some inexplicable means of time-travel, resolves to elevate Arthur's kingdom by conferring on it the gifts of 19th-c. progress. In denouncing the uncouthness and superstition he encounters in this medieval kingdom, the Yankee inadvertently nullifies the worshipful portrayals of peerless Round Table knights penned by British authors like Sir Thomas Malory and Alfred, Lord Tennyson; on the other hand, Hank Morgan's assumptions and deeds implicitly call into question some cherished notions of American civilization. For one thing, commentators have pointed out that this version of medieval England resembles the antebellum American South as much as it does Arthur's kingdom; slave-trains move morosely through the streets (even the King and his advisor Morgan are inadvertently sold into bondage, in one of C.'s many fictional incidents of mistaken identity), feudal lords hold sway over the economy, and tournaments with elaborate pageantry, dominated by chivalric traditions C. insistently associated with the historical writings of Sir Walter Scott, decide issues by personal combat. Despite the Yankee's introduction of stock market exchanges, railroads, factories, schools, baseball games, electric power plants, merciful punishments, and other supposed benefits, human fallibility and the machinations of the Church officials doom his utopia; the Arthurian knights perish in the dreadful battle described by Malory, and survivors of the conflict march against Hank Morgan, who electrocutes, drowns, and blows up tens of thousands of them in an apocalyptic ending. Nothing avails, however; these rotting corpses destroy the victors, and Merlin casts a spell that transports Hank Morgan away from his wife Sandy and the ruins of the age he sought to improve before its time, and forward into the 19th c. he once enjoyed but now cannot abide.

In the mid-1880s, C.'s writing projects began to have two ominous competitors for his time and enthusiasm: his ambition to preside over his own subscription-publishing firm, and his fascination with financial investments, beginning with successful speculations like the "Mark Twain Self-Pasting Scrapbook," but culminating in his disastrous faith in James W. Paige's typesetting machine. Awed by the mechanical ingenuity of Paige's typesetter, which employed 18,000 intricate parts, and encouraged by Paige's repeated assurances that the machine would soon be marketable, C. poured at least $190,000 into this venture between 1881 and December 1894, when the futility of further outlays became obvious even to C. As it happened, C.'s publishing firm, crippled by the financial Panic of 1893, had declared bankruptcy on April 18, 1894. Thus, in January 1895, a dazed C. suddenly found himself a publicly embarrassed man, unable to repay his creditors and the object of a newspaper campaign for charitable contributions (a solution he declined). Only the financial counsel of Standard Oil Company vice-president Henry H. Rogers, and the calming prophecy of a palm-reader named Cheiro, offered C. any hope as he faced his tribulations.

Struggling with his mounting business problems in the 1890s, C. somehow managed to produce a flawed but engaging detective novel set in the village of Dawson's Landing, another version of early-day Hannibal. In *Pudd'nhead Wilson* (1894), C., like William FAULKNER after him, instinctively identified racial prejudice as the most divisive and enduring issue in American history. This bizarre novel, set in Dawson's Landing, Missouri, on the Mississippi River, features yet another instance of switched identities—in this case, a black slave's infant boy and a prominent white couple's son. David Wilson, the bookish attorney from New York state whom the townspeople foolishly brand a "pudd'nhead," sorts out this exchange of children and dramatically solves a murder at the conclusion of the novel. An intertwining farce, *Those Extraordinary Twins* (1894), distracted C. and had a vitiating effect on his composition method. Far less readable than either story, however, was an oddly constructed novel titled *The American Claimant* (1892), principally a vehicle for an extravagantly impractical character,

Colonel Mulberry Sellers. In 1895, C. published a rare venture into literary criticism, "Fenimore Cooper's Literary Offenses," as unfair to Cooper as it is delightful to college students. C. turned to historical sources—always for him a revelatory, therapeutic pastime—to write *Personal Recollections of Joan of Arc* (1896), which he thought well of but which literary critics have seldom applauded.

C. worried about his financial security during the rest of his life, but with the shrewd advice of Rogers (who instructed him to place the copyright of his books in his wife's name to protect this asset from his creditors) he regained and even surpassed his former standard of living. This recuperation was hastened in 1895–96, when he undertook a much-publicized voyage around the world, lecturing in Australia, India, South Africa, and elsewhere, and then recounted these travel experiences in *Following the Equator* (1897). That work is the least-respected of his travel books, but it contains occasional nuggets of well-told anecdotes, and like *Pudd'nhead Wilson,* it offers as chapter headings a collection of pithy maxims deserving to be ranked with the wise sayings of Benjamin Franklin's Poor Richard or the sardonic definitions of Ambrose Bierce: "Truth is the most valuable thing we have. Let us economize it"; "It could probably be shown by facts and figures that there is no distinctly native American criminal class except Congress"; "It is by the goodness of God that in our country we have those three unspeakably precious things: freedom of speech, freedom of conscience, and the prudence never to practice either of them."

By 1898, rescued by book royalties and lecture income, C. was solvent again and his creditors had been repaid. But his personal life had begun to suffer other buffets of fate. His eldest and favorite daughter, Susy, left behind in the U.S. during the global lecture tour on which Livy and Clara accompanied him, died of meningitis on August 18, 1896. Only some neighbors and a housekeeper, Katy Leary, were with Susy as she mumbled deliriously about being "Mark Twain's daughter" in the empty Hartford house, reopened at her request. Blaming himself for her death (as he had earlier condemned himself for the deaths of his brother Henry and his infant son Langdon), C. was reluctant to return to the U.S. from London, and he lived nomadically in Vienna and elsewhere in Europe for several years. Stories such as "The Man That Corrupted Hadleyburg" (1899), recounting a practical joke that embarrasses the smug civic leaders of a pious town by unmasking their greed, testified to C.'s determination to seek solace in creative activity.

When he did come back to his native land, it was a triumphant occasion. Newspaper and magazine reporters were on hand to copy down his remarks, day or night; he had become an American icon, and his quips were front-page copy, usually accompanied by a photograph of the white-maned author. He had captured much newspaper coverage in 1897 by casually assuring a reporter that "the report of my death was an exaggeration." Enjoying this attention from the press, C. adopted habits to embellish his legendary image: he smoked cigars or pipes whenever a photographer was in sight, granted interviews while lazily lying abed in the mornings, and commenced (in 1906) wearing unconventional white suits, whatever the season, that gave him a stunning appearance. He also took advantage of this idolatry to register his cynical criticisms of U.S. foreign policies—especially the American occupation of the Philippine Islands.

By other measures, however, the best times had passed. In 1903, C. and his wife sold their beloved Hartford house, now associated with Susy's pathetic death. His wife had developed a heart condition that no amount of medical attention or travel for climate (they moved to Florence, Italy in 1903) was able to ease; she died on June 5, 1904, to C.'s immense grief. The youngest daughter, Jean, would die on December 24, 1909, after suffering an epileptic seizure in her bath. Only Clara, who in 1909 married pianist-conductor Ossip Gabrilowitsch, survived her father.

C. alternated between moods of despair and gaiety, but continued to dictate his (voluminous but fragmented) autobiography and write stories and essays almost until the end. Increasingly these productions revolved around his belief that all human motives are ultimately selfish. A tedious dialogue titled "What Is Man?" (1906) argues that all human acts are predetermined, that free will is an illusion. During these last years he undertook a series of transitory crusades—moral and political—assailing King Leopold's policies in the Belgian Congo, animal vivisection, bullfighting, Mary Baker Eddy's claims for Christian Science, "city hall" corruption, the Russian Czar, American lynchings, foreign missionaries, and other targets. C.'s religious skepticism, detectable periodically throughout his life, became much more visible in the final years. Sometimes this tendency toward freethinking produced readable literature. "Extracts form Captain Stormfield's Visit to Heaven" (1909) amusingly satirizes conventional Christian notions of Paradise; a sea captain reports on his arrival in, and gradual comprehension of, Heaven and its wonders. "Letters from the Earth" (1962) presents eleven letters to archangels Michael and Gabriel from C.'s ultimate mysterious stranger visitant, Satan. Exiled from Heaven, Satan idly investigates life on earth; he is alternately amused and disgusted by what he discovers about Christianity as it is practiced—its pride in man as God's noblest creation, its absurd notions of Heaven,

its illogical Bible. Satan dissects the Book of Genesis at length, pointing out improbabilities and contradictions, and execrating God's cruelties and inconsistencies and his foolish design for mankind.

C. succumbed to heart disease in 1910, having lived, as he predicted, to witness the next appearance of Halley's comet. Like the rest of the family, he was buried in Elmira, New York. He left behind a newly built Italianate-villa mansion, which burned in 1923, in Redding, Connecticut; a growing income for the Mark Twain Estate; numerous unpublished manuscripts such as "Which Was the Dream?" and "Tom Sawyer's Conspiracy" (most of these now part of the Mark Twain Papers in the Bancroft Library at the University of California, Berkeley, and many of them issued in print by the Mark Twain Project); and a gloomy but eerily appealing tale—which exists in three versions, collectively called *The Mysterious Stranger* (1916)—about a Satanic visitor who shares his supernatural knowledge with a few selected villagers. A variant titled "No. 44, the Mysterious Stranger" (1969), set in Austria toward the end of the Middle Ages, is the best-known version of this moral fable.

Biographers and literary critics in the 1960s, 1970s, and 1980s conventionalized a view of C.'s life and outlook as shadowed, obsessed, even tragic. His later, deterministic works, neglected in the decades following his death, have since been elevated to a status that some critics contend they do not deserve. The truth about C.'s life and art lies somewhere between the perceptions of him as a merry, enviable jester and a brooding, pitiable King Lear. C., after all, gratified most of his youthful longings, finding a devoted wife, earning financial wealth, traveling internationally, receiving literary and social fame. The premature deaths of his son and daughters, common bereavements in the 19th c., assuredly were adverse blows, and his wife's lingering illness understandably made him apprehensive. But his existence in its entirety was hardly a lamentable ordeal. His financial fortunes, for example, were soon restored by a celebrated lecture tour around the world. Most of his personal sadness was basically confined to the last fifteen of his seventy-four years.

C. was a man of warm friendships, but was also capable of temperamental outbursts against perceived enemies such as Bret HARTE, Edward M. House, and Whitelaw Reid. As he matured, he seemed increasingly divided within himself, susceptible to contradictory impulses and alienated from the insouciant "Mark Twain" mask he had originated for the purpose of humor.

In spite of such tendencies, he succeeded in devising a prose style whose loose rhythms, written to gratify the ear, give the impression of real speech. He accomplished the difficult task of writing books that appeal to both children and adults. Ernest HEMINGWAY acknowledged that "all modern American literature comes from . . . *Huckleberry Finn*." And C. employed undeniably effective techniques of burlesque to slash at the complacent pride that disgusted him about his human race.

In C.'s own day, he was better known as a platform lecturer than as a serious novelist, and the popularity of actor Hal Holbrook's impersonations of C. (and countless performances of Holbrook's numerous imitators) in the latter half of the 20th c. showed that C.'s words and mannerisms are still capable of entertaining mass audiences. In such respects, C.'s assumed name, public image, and literary works have become pervasively identified with U.S. history and culture.

BIBLIOGRAPHY: Budd, L. J., *Our Mark Twain: The Making of His Public Personality* (1983); Cox, J. M., *Mark Twain: The Fate of Humor* (1966); Doyno, V. A., *Writing Huck Finn: Mark Twain's Creative Process* (1991); Emerson, E., *The Authentic Mark Twain: A Literary Biography of S. L. C.* (1984); Gale, R. L., *Plots and Characters in the Works of Mark Twain* (1973); Hill, H., *Mark Twain: God's Fool* (1973); Kaplan, J., *Mr. C. and Mark Twain: A Biography* (1966); LeMaster, J. R., and James D. Wilson, eds., *The Mark Twain Encyclopedia* (1993); Rasmussen, R. K., *Mark Twain A to Z* (1995); Smith, H. N., *Mark Twain: The Development of a Writer* (1962); Skandera-Trombley, L., *Mark Twain in the Company of Women* (1994); Steinbrink, J. *Getting to Be Mark Twain* (1991); Wilson, J. D., *A Reader's Guide to the Short Stories of Mark Twain* (1987)

ALAN GRIBBEN

CLIFF, Michelle

b. 2 November 1946, Kingston, Jamaica

C. is part of the postcolonial movement of the 1980s, a time in which African and Caribbean writers stripped bare the colonized spaces, that had clothed their cultures in European ideology. In this context, C.'s writing is set within the fracture of language and culture, that resulted from British rule of her homeland, Jamaica, but paradoxically, it is through the severed pieces that she offers the possibility of wholeness.

Being a light-skinned Jamaican, C. says that she "received the message of anglocentrism," and "internalized it." In her early work of prose and poetry, *Claiming an Identity They Taught Me to Despise* (1980), C. began to explore this ambivalence as she awakened to, as she states, "a feminist consciousness

and a rapidly evolving consciousness of colonialism, and a knowledge of self hatred." In *The Land of Look Behind* (1985), a collection of essays, C. explains how the idealized model of Western intellect—Milton, Wordsworth, and Keats—crippled the imagination and initiative of her people. Those were the Gods that, as she tells, "were held before us with an assurance that we were unable, and would never be enabled, to compose a work of similar correctness." C. subverts this prescription, remembering, through her fiction, her country's once prohibited language—patois—its African roots, and, most importantly, the pieces of her own individuality.

After writing her dissertation, C. realized that she did not know who she was: "I could speak fluently, but I could not reveal." She had mastered an "eloquent linear prose," that mimicked, but she wanted to learn a different language, one that would offer itself to her anger, passion, and to the real Jamaica, which she loved: "As my writing developed longer and deeper into this part of myself, I began to dream and imagine. I was able to clearly envision Nanny, the leader of a group of guerilla fighters known as the Windward Maroons, as she is described: an old Black woman naked except for a necklace made from the teeth of whitemen. I began to love her."

Reclaiming these legendary images as a vital part of Jamaican identity, C. wrote *Abeng* (1984), a novel set in Jamaica, which profiles the West Indian battle for freedom and the history of African slaves brought to its land. C. begins her story with the reconstruction of the historical figure, Nanny, and continues to weave in the stories of women, like the light-skinned Inez, who is continually raped by the judge on his plantation: a man, who rationalizes that his slaves must not be freed because they would become a "plague" on the land; and the slave Mma Alli, a powerful obeah woman, who guides her people and names herself "a one-breasted warrior woman," representing "a tradition which was older than the one which had enslaved them."

In *Abeng,* C. stays centered in the emotional, spiritual, and intellectual journey of a young girl, Clare Savage, who begins to awaken to the reality of Jamaica and thus the conflict that lies within her: she is as much connected to the Maroons who fought the English for their independence as she is to the history of Jamaica's oppression, living with the knowledge that her great-great-grandfather killed his hundred slaves the day before their liberation. This split in identity is emphasized in C.'s explicit use of the African word, abeng (translated as conch shell), which serves as the title of the novel and as its motif. In Africa, the abeng was used as a means for amplified communication; however, in Jamaica, it became an object of dissimulation: slaveowners used it to call slaves to the canefields while the Maroon guerrillas used it as a necessary means of intercommunication in the resistance.

C. has stated that she was deeply influenced by Ghanaian writer Ama Ata Aidoo in her novel *Our Sister Killjoy; or, Reflections from a Black-eyed Squint* (1977), in which the dislocation of the protagonist, living in the "inbetween" of Europe and Ghana, is reinforced by the fragmented narrative, incorporating epistolary, fictive and poetic devices. C. intentionally draws from this technique, in *No Telephone to Heaven* (1987), particularly in her attendance to disrupting linear narrative. In this novel, C. continues with Clare Savage's story, which, as C. states, echoes her own childhood experience, but, here, C.'s rage and protest deepen as does her portrait of Jamaica, which is beautifully personified through a merging of lyricism and naturalism.

C. now resides in the U.S. and has continued to show a profound understanding of her environment in her writing. *Bodies of Water* (1990), a collection of stories and prose, is set in America about American life, bringing in such current and past issues as the Vietnam War, AIDS, slavery, and the Holocaust. Her most poignant work in this selection is the title story "Bodies of Water," in which she digs deep into the experience and the consciousness of an old woman, struggling to survive in a culture that alienates her and threatens her autonomy. In this piece, C. shows the richness of human life, regardless of the circumstances that entangle the spirit, as well as her exquisite ability to write the words and images that impart the truth of a culture and its people.

BIBLIOGRAPHY: Gikandi, S., *Writing in Limbo* (1992); Cudjoe, S. R., *Caribbean Women Writers* (1990)

LISA TOLHURST

CLIFTON, [Thelma] Lucille [Sayles]
b. 27 June 1936, Depew, New York

Author of nine volumes of poetry, some twenty children's books, and the memoir, *Generations* (1976), C. is the only poet to have had two collections—*Good Woman: Poems and a Memoir, 1969–1980* (1987) and *Next: New Poems* (1987)—nominated for the Pulitzer Prize in the same year. Poet Laureate of Maryland from 1979 to 1982, C. has been awarded fellowships from the National Endowment for the Arts, the Juniper Prize, and the Coretta Scott King Award, among others. Criticism of C.'s work often focuses on its place in the African American and feminist literary traditions. However, C.'s cogent considerations of the human condition—though often filtered through the

particulars of her own experience—have rendered a complex, layered body of work, and secured C.'s place among the major poets—of any race or either gender—in American literature.

C. uses simple language and achieves precise portraiture in brief stanzas of short lines that witness the grace of ordinary lives, contemplate the paradoxes of human consciousness, and interrogate nuances of power. Critics note a connection to Emily DICKINSON as evidenced by C.'s use of domestic images and the Christian optimism that mark her work. Raised in a large extended family in Buffalo, New York, much of C.'s work draws from her family's history and, like that of Gwendolyn BROOKS, focuses on the everyday lives of working-class African America, particularly its women. C.'s close examinations of family and community relationships and of her life as a poet yield models of creative endurance and uncompromising clarity.

C. is sometimes associated with the Black Arts movement of the 1960s and 1970s. Indeed, in her first volumes of poetry, *Good Times: Poems* (1969) and *Good News about the Earth* (1972), C. combines taut imagery and an unfailing ear for the rhythms of black vernacular speech to reveal the close family ties, fierce self-respect, and long collective memory that undergird the harsh urban lives her poems depict. In *Good Times,* poems like "The 1st" and "Still" vividly illustrate how these realities are not only survived but transcended, while others, notably, "The Discoveries of Fire," "Pity this Poor Animal," and "The White Boy," critique the presumed moral supremacy of mainstream Western culture.

Good News about the Earth (1972) parallels C.'s personal passage through a 1940s childhood marred by the frustration of "trying to be white" with African America's collective journey into black power consciousness. In addition to offering praise songs to the personal and cultural heroes who make such passages possible in poems such as "Daddy" and "Apology (To the Panthers)," in "The Bodies Broken On" and "After Kent State," C. connects the atrocities of America's past to the turbulent times in which these poems were written. Throughout, C.'s accessible diction and familiar images serve to intensify the power of her observations. In the "Some Jesus" section of the collection, C. recasts biblical characters as black folk—a technique she will use in subsequent works—to personalize the mythic possibilities of these archetypes and delineate connections between their lives and those of modern readers. In "Daniel," for example, the speaker has learned that "when a man / walk manly / he don't stumble / even in the lion's den." Yet while *Good Times* and *Good News about the Earth* impart the same cultural pride and social disquiet to which C.'s contemporaries Sonia SANCHEZ, Nikki GIOVANNI, and Amiri BARAKA give voice, these volumes are set apart by their suggestion of the broader themes C. treats in later work. For example, in "Earth," "Later I'll Say," and "For the Bird Who Flew against Our Window One Morning and Broke His Natural Neck," C. illuminates the ambiguities that complicate existence, and reminds us that human action carries with it not only social and political repercussions, but moral implications as well.

C.'s concern with the ambiguities of experience is strikingly evident in *An Ordinary Woman* (1974) in which she contemplates the kaleidoscopic nature of black women's lives. While this volume also contains poems that reconsider America's past, honor black women's heroism and endurance, and celebrate the promise of the young, C.'s focus narrows in *An Ordinary Woman* to claim the tensions that emerge as the "ordinary" events of a woman's life unfold. With uncompromising honesty, C. catalogues the losses, contradictions, and ironies peculiar to the roles of daughter, mother, and poet. A series of poems in which the Hindu goddess Kali is the central metaphor confronts the intimate connection between violence and birth. But these harrowing interrogations, with their images of blood and bone, ultimately prove affirming as the speaker reconciles chaos and creativity, expectation and disappointment, integrating them into a wisdom born of clarity.

In *Generations,* C. underscores the connections between the paradigms that have shaped the woman she has become with a tapestry of brief anecdotes, each introduced with a portrait of the family member for whom it is named and an epigraph from Walt WHITMAN's *Song of Myself. Generations* traces C.'s family's history from the remarkable story of her paternal great-great grandmother, Caroline Donald to the death of her parents, Thelma and Samuel Sayles. Without evading the ironies and betrayals that punctuate every family's story, C. demonstrates how "our lives are more than the days in them, our lives are our line and we go on." C.'s meditation on this theme is extended in the collections following the publication of her memoir: *Two-Headed Woman* (1980), *Next* (1987), *Quilting* (1991), *The Book of Light* (1993), and *The Terrible Stories* (1996). As C. chronicles her life, witnesses history's lessons, and celebrates the possibilities of the future, readers are gently instructed to see the eternal and the universal in the details of ordinary lives.

The mother of six, C.'s gentle instruction is no less evident in her works for children. Her children's books treat similar themes to those addressed in her work for adults. *The Black BC's* (1970) and *All Us Come Cross the Water* (1973), for example, are designed to foster the black child's pride in and understanding of

African American history and heritage. In *Good Says Jerome* (1973) and the highly acclaimed Everett Anderson series, C. tenderly examines difficult issues that confront young children, while celebrating the joys they can experience by just being themselves. C.'s respect and affection for children allow her to render characterizations of them that neither deny their humanity nor insult their intelligence, and the verse written for them is as rich and insightful as her work for adults.

BIBLIOGRAPHY: Lazar, H., "Blackness Blessed: The Writings of L. C.," *SoR* 25 (July 1989): 760–70; McCluskey, A. T., "Tell the Good News: A View of the Works of L. C.," in Evans, M., ed., *Black Women Writers (1950–1980): A Critical Evaluation* (1984): 137–49; Peppers, W. R., "L. C.," in Harris, T., and T. M. Davis, eds., *DLB,* vol. 41, *Afro-American Poets since 1965* (1985): 55–60; White, M. B., "Sharing the Living Light: Rhetorical, Poetic, and Social Identity in L. C.," *CLAJ* 40 (March 1997): 288–304

MADELINE D. MURRAY

COATES, Robert M[yron]

b. 6 April 1897, New Haven, Connecticut; d. 8 February 1973, New York City

Despite a brief critical reappraisal shortly following his death in 1973, C. is essentially a minor writer of the Lost Generation. As one of the American expatriates living in Paris in the 1920s, C. associated with such writers as Gertrude STEIN, James THURBER, Malcolm COWLEY, and Ernest HEMINGWAY and was strongly influenced by Dadaism; indeed, his first novel, *The Eater of Darkness* (1926), was called the first American Dadaist novel. Dadaist elements of surrealism, displacement, and warped time along with a highly subjective and self-reflexive point of view are hallmark features of his longer works. His short stories, noted for their intensely macabre or bizarre ironic twists, treat the themes of alienation and lack of feeling in modern times, reflecting the derangement of normal feelings in urban settings and the decay of old ways of life in rural ones. His early experimentations in style and intensely subjective mood presaged much work of the late 20th c., yet his works themselves remain largely unrecognized.

C. graduated from Yale University in 1919 and, after a brief stint as an aviation cadet at the end of World War I, sailed to Europe in 1921 where he met some of the prominent artists of the era, and wandered among the "workaday streets" of French towns, settling in Giveny and later in Paris. *The Eater of Darkness* was published with the help of Stein in a limited edition in Paris, and three years later in New York. The novel concerns the adventures of Charles Dograr, centering on his involvement with the inventor of an x-ray death machine capable of mass murder. The plot includes elements of SCIENCE FICTION, ROMANCE, and murder mystery and features both accidental and planned murder, impersonation, and bizarre love triangles. Its surreal images, nonsequitur plot, and unconventional narrative structure led critics to impatiently dismiss the novel as "extravagantly difficult to follow."

C. returned to New York in 1926 where he would spend the next forty years as art critic and contributor at the *New Yorker.* Following the nonfiction *The Outlaw Years: The History of the Land Priates of the Natchez Trace* (1930) came C.'s next, and most highly acclaimed novel, *Yesterday's Burden* (1933). Consisting of a series of events related at times only by the overarching presence of the narrator, the novel intertwines a first-person account of C.'s lifestyle with the story of the fictional protagonist, Henderson. *Yesterday's Burdens* again features Dadaist qualities of time inversion and a blurring of the real and the imaginary. C.'s identification with the perspectives of both Henderson and the narrator further blurs the distinction between external reality and subjective perception as well as accentuates his theme of alienation. Like C.'s first novel, *Yesterday's Burden* received little critical appreciation when it was published, but received renewed interest when it was reprinted in the Lost American Fiction series (1975).

C. continued working at the *New Yorker,* publishing little over the next ten years. In 1943, he published his first collection of short stories, *All the Year Long,* which features vignettes alternating between city and country life. C.'s themes of isolation and alienation remain constant, but his intensely subjective point of view is tempered somewhat in these stories by a more straightforward narrative style. Another semiautobiographical work, *The Bitter Season,* appeared in 1946, followed two years later by C.'s most popular novel, *Wisteria Cottage* (1948). With a style more akin to his short stories, and less subjective in mood than his earlier novels, *Wisteria Cottage* became a near bestseller and was even considered for purchase by a motion picture company. However, C. followed this burst of success with a seven-year dry spell before publishing anything else.

C.'s next novel, *The Farther Shore* (1955), was similar in style to *Wisteria Cottage.* This was followed by another book of short stories, *The Hour after Westerly* (1957), marking a return to a Dadaist style, which, according to C., always meant a spirit of playful gaiety. While less grim than his earlier collection, the bizarre and often macabre twists of stories in *The Hour after* *Westerly* can only be considered "playful" in the most ironic way.

A trio of nonfiction works—a book of personal reminiscences, *The View from Here* (1960), and two travel books, *Beyond the Alps* (1961) and *South of Rome* (1965)—and a final collection of stories, *The Man Just Ahead of You* (1964), brought C.'s career to a close on a personal, self-reflective note.

Although prolific, and well liked by publishers, C. never achieved serious critical success. Throughout most of his career, he was pegged as a *New Yorker* writer, sophisticated and urbane, but, ultimately, trivial. This assessment is not entirely unfair, especially in regard to the short stories; however, C.'s own lifestyle and his personal aversion to fame may account for his failure to pursue success more aggressively. Indeed, he saw himself in the aristocratic tradition and fancied himself a modern-day Sir Philip Sydney, preferring to share his works primarily with a small circle of friends rather than embrace a worldwide audience.

BIBLIOGRAPHY: Eisinger, C., *Fiction of the Forties* (1963); Messer, R., "R. M. C.," in Kimbel, B. E., ed., *DLB,* vol. 102, *American Short-Story Writers, 1910–1945* (1991): 43–47

GRETA WAGLE

COBB, Irvin S[hrewsbury]

b. 23 June 1876, Paducah, Kentucky, d. 10 March 1944, New York City

C. was one of the most successful men of letters in American literature. After a twenty-year career in journalism as editor, reporter, and war correspondent in his native Kentucky and in New York, he turned his talents to short stories, novels, plays, essays—even to film acting—and scored successes in all of them. In addition, he was a popular lecturer and oral humorist, and, like his friend Will ROGERS became a famous public figure. With his portly build, his bushy eyebrows, several chins, and ubiquitous cigar, he was a favorite subject for cartoonists.

C.'s formal education ended when he was sixteen and quit school in his hometown of Paducah, Kentucky, in order to help support his family as a cub reporter for the local *Evening News.* In 1900, he married Laura Spencer Baker of Savannah, Georgia, and in 1904 he moved to New York in quest of fame and fortune. He found both, first as a writer for the *Evening Sun* and later as a contributor and World War I correspondent for the *Saturday Evening Post.* In 1922, he began contributing to *Cosmopolitan Magazine,* in which he published a story or article in every issue for a decade. By 1930, he was one of the highest paid short story writers in the world, receiving up to four thousand dollars for a single story. Before his death in 1944, he had published more than three hundred short stories and sixty books. During his lifetime, probably more of his stories were anthologized than those of any other living American writer.

In 1934, filmmaker Hal Roach invited C. to Hollywood, where he consulted on the making of several movies about the Old South. He also appeared in several films, including *Steamboat Round the Bend,* based on a novel by his fellow Kentuckian Ben Lucien Burman. In 1935, he was master of ceremonies for the Academy Awards, and in 1936 he starred in his own radio show "Paducah Plantation."

His "down-home" fiction, set in a small Southern town, featured aged, benevolent plantation owners and other people he knew as a boy: lawyers, merchants, ministers, physicians, and black servants. His most popular creation was Judge William Pitman Priest, a genial Confederate veteran who was based on a real circuit court judge in western Kentucky. The 1934 movie, *Judge Priest,* based on his popular stories, was directed by John Ford and starred Will Rogers, with Stepin Fetchit and Hattie McDaniel as the properly obedient servants. C. intended his local color stories, he said, as a correction to the stereotypes of southerners as either proud and poor colonels or sorry white trash. Unfortunately, his fiction tended to confirm the South as a triumphantly unrepentant society, unwilling to recognize defeat and prepare for change. In his novel, *J. Poindexter, Colored* (1922), a happy, faithful black servant accompanies his white employer to New York, where he lectures members of his race on how to respect their white superiors.

In his tales of mystery and terror, however, he demonstrated that his talent could transcend popular taste and regional prejudices. In such stories as "Fishhead," "The Belled Buzzard," and "Snake Doctor," he plumbs the psychology of suspicion, murder and guilt. He was also more successful in such light essays as "Speaking of Operations," a gentle satire on doctors and hospitals which he based on his experience as a patient. Originally published in a 1915 issue of the *Saturday Evening Post,* it was reprinted as a sixty-four-page booklet and quickly sold more than half a million copies.

C.'s reputation has declined considerably since his death. Many of his contemporaries deemed him worthy to be in the company of Samuel Langhorne CLEMENS and Bret HARTE. In praising him, however, the critic Robert H. Davis, showed his weakness by citing his facile virtuosity. C., he said, "writes in octaves, striking instinctively all the chords of humor, tragedy, pathos and romance with either hand." Indeed,

he found it easy to please a large and uncritical public with superficial characters, loosely constructed plots and a florid style.

As a writer, C. exactly suited and reflected the tastes of his time. He once used these words to describe his vocation as a writer: "I did not set out to do anything by my writing except to amuse and interest, or both, and to get money for it." Indeed, he accomplished those goals, but in setting his sights so low, he achieved a literary reputation that hardly survived his death. His niche in American literary history is reserved for those writers who are content to court superficial popularity.

BIBLIOGRAPHY: Cobb, E., *My Wayward Parent, I. S. C.* (1945); Davis, R. H., *I. S. C., Storyteller* (1924); Lawson, A., *I. S. C.* (1984)

WADE HALL

COFFIN, Robert [Peter Tristram]
b. 18 March 1892, Brunswick, Maine; d. 20 January 1955, Portland, Maine

Few American authors have brought to their calling the energy, enthusiasm, and versatility of C. Though known primarily as a poet—sixteen volumes of his own poems appeared during his lifetime—and as a poetry editor, he also published several volumes of fiction, criticism, essays, history, biography, and genealogy. C. was also known for his personal promotion of poetry and was famed for his public readings. His tireless advocacy carried him to college and university campuses in many parts of the U.S. to lecture on poetic topics and to recite poems for ceremonial occasions.

The descendant of a whaling family with roots extending from early-17th-c. Nantucket, C. was reared on a saltwater farm on the Maine coast. Following his graduation from Bowdoin in 1915 and a year of graduate study at Princeton (A.M., 1916), he attended Oxford as a Rhodes Scholar (B.A., 1920; B.Litt., 1921). He taught at Wells College from 1921 to 1934 and held various visiting professorships; however, the greater part of his academic career (1934–55) was spent at Bowdoin .

Although C. occasionally ventured into non-American subjects, notably with *Laud, Storm Center of Stuart England* (1930) and *The Dukes of Buckingham* (1931), the primary subject of his work, both in poetry and prose, was his native Maine. It proved both an asset and a limitation. On the one hand, the richness of this milieu—its history, legends, landscape, natives, and family traditions—provided a fecund array of subjects. Many of these are captured in the lyrics of the Pulitzer Prize-winning collection *Strange Holiness* (1935) as well as those of *Saltwater Farm* (1937) and

Maine Ballads (1938). Maine subjects are also the basis of *Portrait of an American* (1931), a biography of the author's father; of the autobiographical *Lost Paradise* (1934); of the novel *Red Sky in the Morning* (1935); of *Kennebec: Cradle of America* (1937); and of the essays in *Yankee Coast* (1947).

On the other hand, viewed in retrospect, much of C.'s work seems topical and dated, which may partially explain why it has not proven more durable or deserving of attention from modern-day critics. His poetic subjects, for all their appeal as examples of colorful provincialism, often tend toward the quaint and genrelike. Structurally, his forms are derivative of the English poetic tradition, with regular quatrains and a predictable pattern of rhyme predominating. C. was a defender of the New England poetic tradition—the Turnbull lectures he gave at Johns Hopkins University formed the basis of *The New Poetry of New England: Frost and Robinson* (1938). However, his own verse tends to lack the more profound, parable-like dimensions of that of his contemporary, Robert FROST. In 1932, Frost himself stated some of C.'s strengths and weaknesses in an unpublished letter to his friend when, after calling him "one of my accepted few" among living poets, and "full of sure-fire figures," he observed that he considered his work uneven.

In an introduction prepared for an enlarged edition of his *Collected Poems* (1948), C. attempted to summarize his own approach to writing poetry, as well as some personal observations on the nature of the art form itself. He noted that poetry might be defined as a rearrangement, by the poet, of the best possible elements, derived, ideally, from a vast and diverse array of sources. Although far from original, this definition is nevertheless rooted in the Western critical tradition and echoes the sentiments of critics such as Wordsworth, Shelley, and Matthew Arnold. However, in defining the object of poetry, C. veers sharply from these antecedents. "I have another way of saying what poetry is," he continued, "it is the art of making people feel well about life." This candid admission, despite its lofty intentions, may effectively summarize the major limitation of C.'s poetry: that its appeal is mainly to a democratic, as opposed to an intellectual, aesthetically sophisticated, readership.

BIBLIOGRAPHY: Peabody, B., "R. P. T. C.," in Quartermain, P., ed., *American Poets, 1880–1945* (1986): 29–94

WELFORD DUNAWAY TAYLOR

COLWIN, Laurie

b. 14 June 1944, New York City; d. 24 October 1992, New York City

Distinguishing C.'s fiction is the unlikely pairing of wry, often dark humor with a concern for the state of domesticity and home life in the modern world. C.'s characters are sensitive to the stress and cruelty of the fast-paced professional worlds they inhabit as successful people. Therefore, the domestic is often their retreat from chaos; home, food, and maternal instinct are all solid and dependable, though perhaps not as exciting. Throughout *Goodbye without Leaving* (1990), C.'s best-known work, and in her last, *A Big Storm Knocked It Over* (1994), the central female characters evaluate the differences between their professional and domestic roles.

Beginning with C.'s first book, *Passion and Affect,* published in 1974, her characters struggle to balance home, work and love. Two novels followed, *Shine On, Bright and Dangerous Object* (1975), and *Happy All the Time* (1978). *The Lone Pilgrim* (1981), and *Another Marvelous Thing* (1986), although collections of stories, interrelate so as to read like novels in installments. These two books were separated by *Family Happiness* (1982), a novel.

In *Goodbye without Leaving,* the central figure reflects on her experiences as the only white female backup singer on tour with a rhythm and blues act, a contrast to her later, rather normal home life. In *A Big Storm Knocked It Over,* Jane Louise describes with deadpan wit the various flamboyant figures surrounding her at her job in a high-pressure publishing house. At the same time, she cultivates a stable home life with her new husband and, eventually, a new baby. Motherhood is an essential grounding factor in the lives of C.'s women; even Billie in *Another Marvelous Thing* justifies her affair with Francis by calling him her "substitute child."

C.'s sense of humor emerges in her characters' remarks as they compare their public and private worlds. Being in love, Francis notes to himself in *Another Marvelous Thing,* is "rather like having a bird trapped in one's hair." Half economist, half lover, he struggles to quantify an emotion he cannot control. They often see themselves as an outsider to both sides, mocking contrived sophistication in professionals, but also displaying bewilderment at perfect homemakers. Even the professions of her characters seem to hover between so-called high and low arts; they are book jacket designers, nature writers, pop singers and chefs. C. herself was a columnist for *Gourmet* and wrote two cookbooks, *Home Cooking: A Writer in the Kitchen* (1988) and *More Home Cooking: A Writer Returns to the Kitchen* (1993). The titles themselves reflect her interest in the role of professional identity in a traditionally nonprofessional context.

Reviewers praise C. for her cleverness and keen sense of dialogue, attributes which have drawn comparisons to Jane Austen. Her characters seem to share a sharp sense of irony along with great timing. That wit seems to have been an extension of C.'s own sense of humor; her anecdotes in the cookbooks seem to be told in the droll voice of one of her own characters.

C.'s twenty-year career included novels, short stories and nonfiction works. She earned a loyal following of readers and received enthusiastic reviews for her books, but little critical study has been published on the subject of her career. Her last novel, *A Big Storm Knocked it Over,* was in publication at the time of her death from a heart attack in 1992. Her popularity continues to grow; recently her novels and short story collections have all been redesigned and reprinted in trade paperback form.

BIBLIOGRAPHY: Richlin, A, "Guilty Pleasures: The Fiction of L. C.," *NER* 13 (Spring-Summer 1991): 296–309

NICOLE SARROCCO

CONFIDENCE MAN, The

The American version of a universal comic figure, the Trickster, got its name in 1849 when William Thompson (a.k.a. Samuel Willis) began accosting strangers in New York City streets asking them if they would "have confidence in me to trust your watch until tomorrow." Incredibly, they did. But tomorrow never came, and when no watches were returned, Mr. Thompson's whereabouts became a matter of some concern. Once apprehended, he was quickly asked to retire to a cell in Ossining, and the term "confidence man" has stuck.

Up until Mr. Thompson's scam, America's tricksters, humbugs, and swindlers had been called "diddlers" after the British knave Jeremy Diddler in James Kenney's stage production *Raising the Wind* (1803). The currency of that term is evident in the fact that Edgar Allan POE, himself a hoaxer and diddler, dashed off a journal piece with the same title, subtitled "Diddling Considered as One of the Exact Sciences," in 1843. But the roots of this character type go back as far as Eden and penetrate into every culture. Native Americans have the larcenous Coyote; Eastern Indians have the monkey; black slaves invented Br'er Rabbit. In European culture, we find scores of mountebanks including Arlecchino and Scapino, Tartuffe and Volpone, Munchaussen and the big bad wolf. There are as well tricksters who do good: such wise and clever (although morally problematic) trimmers as Ulysses, Falstaff, Becky Sharp, and Huck Finn survive by their wits and the injudicious presumptions of their enemies.

Whatever the specific name or characterization given to this type, the confidence man has had an enduring appeal, especially in primitive, emergent, and repressive societies. While actual con men continue to be a felonious nuisance in malls and on Wall Street, the fictionalized confidence man has enjoyed almost heroic stature in humor and comic literature. The trickster amuses us by violating taboos, working against or around the system, and enticing powerful fools to expose their follies. Thus, an identification with the con man is the expression of a covert desire to undo the strings and laces of law, order, convention, tradition, and culture. In America's formative decades, the con man appeared as the cagey Yankee Peddler, eager to sell you a wooden nutmeg, or the flamboyant gamecock woodsman, boasting, lying, and conning listeners into believing his tall tales. If the frontier exhibited Nature as a deadly and deceptive force (Is that an Indian or a hoot owl?), then it required a mind capable of discerning truth and illusion, and such a mind could be sharpened by the comic and safe exposure to tall tales and fictionalized con men. By observing con games in humor, one might be better prepared for more serious con games in the woods, or even downtown. For this reason we laugh at and with the confidence man, but do so nervously, wondering whether we may not become victims ourselves to the ever-present rapacity of man and nature. In a sense, P. T. Barnum's popularity rested squarely on the fact that he was an acknowledged con man whose petty scams ("This way to the Egress") delighted patrons of his American Museum in New York City because such hijinx openly tested their gullibility. Frontier evangelists like Lorenzo Dow also acted as tricksters for God luring sheep into the fold with their amusing camp meeting cons. Herman MELVILLE knew well the aesthetic potential of America's Diddler, Dow, Barnum, and Thompson, and in 1857 his comic masterpiece *The Confidence-Man* explored the metaphysical, social, political, and religious implications of making belief into a game of confidence. But it was Samuel Langhorne CLEMENS's work that introduced con men and artistry more successfully into American fiction. With such characters as Jim Smiley in "Jumping Frog," Huck, Tom Sawyer, the Duke and King in the *Adventures of Huckleberry Finn,* Hank Morgan in *Connecticut Yankee,* and Philip Traum in "Mysterious Stranger," Clemens gave readers a lifetime of con men: benign, innocent, malicious, self-deluding, and cosmic. These characters have their antecedents in a host of comic liars drawn by America's best 19th-c. yarnspinners and literary comedians: Augustus Baldwin LONGSTREET, Thomas Bangs THORPE, Thomas Chandler Haliburton ("Sam Slick"), James Clover Baldwin ("Ovid Bolus"), Johnson J. HOOPER ("Simon Suggs"), David Ross LOCKE ("Petroleum V. Nasby"), George Washington HARRIS ("Sut Lovingood"), and Charles Farrar BROWNE ("Artemus Ward").

The 20th c. has come to see Barnum's games refined into the subtler arts of advertizing, public relations, and televangelism. Our liars have become bigger and more sophisticated, and the need for the fictionalized depiction of con men has not lessened. Accordingly we find con games, flim-flams, and stings in Henry JAMES's later works, Sinclair LEWIS's *Elmer Gantry,* Nathanael WEST's *A Cool Million,* various tales and novels by William FAULKNER and F. Scott FITZGER-ALD, Joseph HELLER's *Catch 22,* Thomas PYNCHON's *V* and *The Crying of Lot-49,* and the recent plays and films of David MAMET. In all likelihood, the literary convention of the confidence man will last as long as there are knaves to perpetrate lies, and fools who will perpetuate them.

BIBLIOGRAPHY: Blair, W., and H. Hill, *America's Humor* (1978); Bryant, J., *Mellville and Repose: The Rhetoric of Humor in the American Renaissance* (1993); Halttunen, K., *Confidence Men and Painted Women* (1982); Hauck, R. B., *A Cheerful Nihilism* (1971); Lindberg, G., *The Confidence Man in American Literature* (1982); Rourke, C., *American Humor* (1931); Wadlington, W., *The Confidence Game in American Literature* (1975); Wonham, H. B., *Mark Twain and the Art of the Tall Tale* (1993)

JOHN BRYANT

CONNELL, Evan S., Jr.
b. 17 August 1924, Kansas City, Missouri

C. has had a various and accomplished career as novelist, short story writer, and poet. He is best known for his diptych of novels on Mr. and Mrs. Bridge, a prototypical Midwestern couple.

C.'s poetry is almost universally neglected; however, it is probably the most ambitious portion of his entire literary enterprise. *Points from a Compass Rose* (1973) is a book-length poem composed wholly of pearl-like fragments of erudition. At once erudite journal and lapidary bricolage, the poem's vast learning and "purple prose" would surprise many readers familiar with C. only as a middle-class chronicler. Although the poem occasionally seems like only a series of disparate lumps of novels, there are common themes: many of the facts pertain to European exploration of other continents, and C. seems to emphasize both the thrill of exploring unknown lands and the tragedy of the exploitative colonialism that followed upon the European voyages of discovery. *Notes from a Bottle Found on the Beach at Carmel* (1963) is a similar effort: historical and geographical lore are displayed side-by-side with outrage over the Vietnam War. In both these books, there is a kind of sidewise self-awareness that collecting data is an only partially authentic exercise. C.'s poems are laden with an awareness of the ambiguous situation of the voyeur or con-

noisseur, a theme that reverberates in his work in other forms and may well be the common denominator that characterizes his artistry.

Two little-known books of prose essays, *A Long Desire* (1979) and *The White Lantern* (1980), also take up the theme of exploration, with particular emphasis on a "diffusionist" model—where, for example, the Phoenicians came to America before Columbus. Although C. might offend readers who feel that to claim a nonindigenous origin for Native American culture is racist, the essays are informative and also reveal a deep authorial sensibility. C.'s novel *Son of the Morning Star* (1984) was far more heralded. A stark and curiously low-key retelling of the story of General Custer's defeat in 1976, C.'s treatment revealed a feeling for the western landscape and a sense of the ignoble nature of the white man's effacement of Native American nationhood.

Mrs. Bridge (1959) and *Mr. Bridge* (1969) are C.'s most prominent works of fiction. Together, they chronicle the lives of a successful Kansas City lawyer and his wife in the 1920s and 1930s. The *Bridge* novels are unchallenged in their description of the daily routine of an average American life. Though written from a perspective that sees beyond the Midwestern conformity of their characters, the novels are not just satirical of middle American life in the manner of Sinclair LEWIS. While recognizing and exploring the sadness and limitations of their protagonists, they empathize with and, occasionally, honor the goals for which they lived. Unfailingly evocative of Kansas City (C. is one of the few writers to put Kansas City on the literary map), the novels gain in strength as their sociological milieu passes out of living memory and into the archive. C., himself born in Kansas City but who early on chose an artistic lifestyle that led him to live largely in California and the Southwest, produces more than a sophomoric reaction to boyhood constraints; he puts the world of his youth into a time capsule to be studied and experienced by future readers. The closing scene of *Mrs. Bridge,* where the title character, whose first name is, incongruously, "India," is trapped in a snow-bound car, is a powerful metaphor for the isolation and emotional confinement that permeate the *Bridge* novels.

The *Bridge* novels are not completely traditional narratives. They are structured in small parts, rarely lasting more than a few pages, and thus resemble the chiseled segments of C.'s poetry. Indeed, Mr. Bridge himself, at the end of his namesake novel, lets loose a riff on the ancient Nabataean city of Petra that seems far more characteristic of a cosmopolitan aesthete than an unimaginative businessman. *The Alchymist's Journal* (1991) is also told in segments; this tale of seven renaissance alchemists mixes C.'s narrative and eso-teric interests.

C.'s short stories, collected in *The Collected Stories of E. S. C.* (1996), are anecdotal rather than epiphanic. They do not build any extravagant artistic effects within themselves, but tell stories in an understated and finely crafted manner that lets the reader draw the implications of what is related. The often anthologized "The Fisherman from Chihuahua" (1952) gives a glimpse of the relation between ordinary and extraordi-nary experience, and "The Cuban Missile Crisis" (1993) deals wittily with the sometimes unbalanced relation between the public and the private in mod-ern life.

C. has received little critical treatment. The reasons for this are mystifying, perhaps having to do with his not publishing any novels during the 1980s and thus not consolidating his reputation. Nonetheless, C.'s lit-erary career has been an accomplished one.

BIBLIOGRAPHY: Heller, D. A., *Family Plots: The De-Oedipalization of Popular Culture* (1995); Shapiro, G., "E. S. C.: A Profile," *Ploughshares* 13 (1987): 11–25

NICHOLAS BIRNS

CONNELLY, Marc[us Cook]

b. 13 December 1890, McKeesport, Pennsylvania; d. 21 December 1980, New York City

Although perhaps more commonly known for the plays written in collaboration with George S. KAUF-MAN, C. demonstrated his finest work on his own in his adaptation of a series of Bible stories into the successful, albeit controversial, *The Green Pastures* (1930). He was a humorist, prankster, director, actor, traveler, and charter member of the so-called Algon-quin Round Table. His experiments with form and function contributed to the vitality of theatrical produc-tion in the 1920s and 1930s.

Starting as a reporter to support himself, C. soon formed a partnership with fellow newspaperman Kauf-man. Together they wrote five plays: *Dulcy* (1921), *To the Ladies* (1923), *Merton of the Movies* (1925), *The Deep Tangled Wildwood* (perf. 1923), and *Beggar on Horseback* (1924). *Dulcy* and *To the Ladies* were opposite views on the same theme—a wife's influence on her husband's career. In the first, a naive and foolish Dulcy seems only to cause trouble in her efforts to promote her husband's business deals. She sets up a weekend retreat designed to clinch a contract, but her meddling creates a series of ludicrous situations. The formula is inverted in *To the Ladies,* where an inven-tive and sparking wife saves her bumbling husband's

career. In both plays, the comedy is sharpened by wit and energy in the dialogue and pertinence to contem-porary affairs. Both plays were generally well received by the critics.

The team's next effort, *Merton of the Movies,* was one of the first New York plays, and ultimately one of the best, to take on Hollywood. A small-town clerk is fired because of his constant mooning over dreams of stardom and his mail-order acting classes. Taking this as a sign, Merton sets out for the movie capital, where he is overwhelmed by the vulgarity under the glamour. His insistence on playing his comic roles with solemn earnestness eventually makes him a star.

C. and Kaufman attempt an expressionist style in *Beggar on Horseback,* their last work together. The dream sequence in which Neil succumbs through mar-riage to his desire for wealth and position, only to sacrifice his artistic talent, is a humorous yet pointed comment on the contemporary state of art versus eco-nomics, creativity versus conformity. The stifling of Neil's talent causes him in his dream to murder all of his in-laws, but the nightmare continues at his trial, where he is consigned to write formula music. Upon wakening, Neil realizes his true happiness lies in his talent.

The Green Pastures, C.'s solo effort based on Roark BRADFORD's *Ol' Man Adam and His Chillun,* represents the fulfillment of his potential as a play-wright. Awarded the Pulitzer Prize, the play's engaging innocence and virtuous vigor charmed audiences and critics alike. C. strove for authenticity in his choice of the spirituals that connected the scenes and in the dialect and colloquialisms, which he personally re-searched in Louisiana.

The production was not without controversy, how-ever. C., who directed himself, worried over the play's reception at a time when black actors on Broadway were not common, theology was a touchy issue, and depicting a black God was considered by many the extreme of sacrilegiousness. C. need not have been concerned about America's reaction, but the play was banned in England. The attention caused by this action was directly related to the demise of a congressional bill on federal censorship.

C. uses comedy to hold contemporary society up for scrutiny. His wit was pointed yet mild, universal, and self-revealing.

BIBLIOGRAPHY: Engle, R., and T. L. Miller, eds., *The American Stage: Social and Economic Issues from the Colonial Times to the Present* (1993); Hughes, G., *A History of the American Theater, 1700–1950* (1951); Nolan, P. T., *M. C.* (1969)

BEVERLY BRONSON SMITH

COOKE [or COOK], Ebenezer
b. 1667?, London, England; d. 1732?, Maryland

Though long relegated to literary obscurity, C. deserves better; he was the most popular of America's early Southern poets, he helped establish the tradition of Southern literary humor, and he holds the position of the first great American satirist. Fortunately, John BARTH's novel *The Sot-Weed Factor* has helped to promote a reevaluation of C.'s place in American letters.

Details of C.'s life are, at best, speculative. The self-appointed laureate of colonial Maryland was probably born in London around 1667. Records show he was in Maryland in 1694, but returned to London around 1700 and again about 1708, and that he was deputy of Maryland's receiver general in 1720. He probably worked as a land agent and was admitted to the bar sometime before 1700. His poems provide the only record of his life after 1722; his last poem, written in 1732, gives the best estimate of his death.

C.'s greatest poem, "The Sot-Weed Factor" (1708), offers an ironic and satiric view of the manners and mores of colonial Maryland in the early 1700s. Published in 1708, although probably written much earlier, it established him as an major colonial poet. The poem's protagonist, an English sot-weed factor (tobacco merchant) is confronted by contradictory views of the colonies: a new Edenic paradise and a place offering endless possibility for economic exploitation. The poor and unhappy merchant sails to America anticipating both an earthly paradise and financial gain. What he finds instead are drunken lawyers, dishonest planters, debased women, and demonic Indians. A variety of thieves and con artists take the little wealth he has, and the poem ends with his return to England after cursing a colony "where no Man's Faithful, nor a Woman Chast." The 1731 edition, which omits this curse, is referred to by the printer as the third edition; however, there is no other record of a second edition. Recent critical analysis of the poem focuses on C.'s use of the comic character type of the disgruntled merchant adventurer, and on specific images and motifs—misogyny, animal imagery, sexual metaphors, savagery, and the curse—used in the poem.

C.'s "Sotweed Redivivus; or, The Planter's Looking-Glass" (1730) is, like "The Sot-Weed Factor," a hudibrastic poem. It employs a variety of Horatian allusions to discuss problems in Maryland: the single crop system, absentee landlords, English taxes, and the burgeoning slave trade. Unlike the earlier work, C. seems more interested in offering political and economic advice than satire.

His final satire, "The History of Colonel Nathaniel Bacon's Rebellion in Virginia" (1731), uses mock-epic conventions to relate Bacon's 1676 skirmishes against the British governor. Again, C. presents a vision of Americans that focuses on an assortment of liars, thieves, and scoundrels. C. also wrote a series of elegies, including the first example of belletristic writing published in the colonial South (1726).

BIBLIOGRAPHY: Arner, R. D., "C.: Satire in the Colonial South," *SLJ* 8 (Fall 1975): 153–64; Coers, D. V., "New Light on the Composition of E. C.'s *Sot-Weed Factor*," *AL* 49 (1978): 604–5; Cohen, E. H., *C.: The Sotweed Cannon* (1975)

KENNETH L. MITCHELL

COOKE, John Esten
b. 3 November 1830, Winchester, Virginia; d. 27 September 1886, Boyce, Virginia

C.'s earliest publications, such as *The Virginia Comedians* (1854), and *The Youth of Jefferson* (1854), demonstrate that he had already begun on his ambitious task of doing for his home state of Virginia what James Fenimore COOPER, William Gilmore SIMMS, Washington IRVING, and Nathaniel HAWTHORNE had done for their respective regions. C.'s background as a member of an old Virginia family gave him an interest in the lore of the Old Dominion which never waned. When Virginia joined the Confederacy, C. went eagerly to war, serving in J. E. B. Stuart's Horse Artillery; this experience provided him with a rich new mine of stories about Virginia. His writing took on the quality almost inevitable in fictionalized firsthand accounts of history: it is difficult to know where fact leaves off and fiction begins. His technique of having his narrator frequently speak directly to the reader, attesting to the accuracy of his account, intensifies the overlapping. Seeing C.'s obvious lack of objectivity, his emotional involvement in his accounts, critics have frequently dismissed him as one more maker of myths about the South.

C. sometimes uses the device of pretending that his story has been unearthed in the form of an old manuscript by his narrator. Particularly interesting is the use of this technique in *My Lady Pokahontas* (1885), which purports to a biography of Pocahontas by one of her intimates. In this fictionalized "biography," the Lady Pokahontas is shown to be the lifelong devoted lover-from-afar of Captain John SMITH; she marries John Rolfe only because she has been told that the captain is dead. The story culminates in a final meeting of Smith and Pokahontas just before her death, in which they reveal their faithful devotion to each other. It is interesting to speculate as to how much influence this version of the story may have had on the current widespread perception of Pocahontas and Smith as a romantic couple. C. must have known the facts of the case, as he was a historian of Virginia; this fictional version illustrates his penchant for romanticizing history.

His best-known war novels are *Surry of Eagle's Nest* (1866) and *Mohun* (1869). The first concentrates on narration of battle scenes, emphasizing the valor and insouciance of the Confederates; the sequel, *Mohun,* begins in 1863 and ends with the surrender in 1865. Not surprisingly, the picture of the Confederacy, as it moves towards its doom, is sober; the prevailing theme in this novel is endurance amid suffering. In both books, Mordaunt and Mohun, the protagonists, are dashing and romantic heroes. Such portrayal is to be expected, but the entire picture is not to be lightly contemned, coming as it does almost directly from the battlefields where the author fought. In fact, C.'s biography of Stonewall Jackson, published in 1863, was actually written between campaigns. C. wrote also a biography of Robert E. Lee, published in 1871, and several volumes of sketches, essays, and short stories.

BIBLIOGRAPHY: Beaty, J. O., *J. E. C., Virginian* (1922); Wegelin, O., *A Bibliography of the Separate Writings of J. E. C. of Virginia* (1941)

CECELIA LAMPP LINTON

COOKE, Rose Terry

b. 17 February 1827, Hartford, Connecticut; d. 18 July 1892, Pittsfield, Massachusetts

C., along with her sister Connecticut writer Harriet Beecher STOWE, pioneered the American local color short story. The uncompromising realism seen in many C. stories furthered its growth in American literature. Her accomplishment includes several neglected masterpieces. Enthusiastic admirers included Samuel Langhorne CLEMENS, Sarah Orne JEWETT, James T. Fields, William Dean HOWELLS, and Bliss Perry.

Rose Terry (C. was her married name, which she assumed in 1873) was born on a farm near Hartford into a distinguished family. Much of her fiction is set in rural western Connecticut. In 1843 she graduated from the Hartford Female Seminary, founded in 1823 by Catharine Beecher and attended also by Harriet Beecher Stowe. It was undoubtedly at this school, which promoted a liberal "feminized" Christianity, that C.'s anti-Calvinism was fostered. This became a central theme in her fiction. According to Harriet Prescott SPOFFORD, C.'s first published story appeared in *Graham's Magazine* in 1845. If so, it was under a pseudonym (probably "Emma Duval," and the story "Cousin Matthew"). Jean Downey, however, in her

authoritative bibliography, lists C.'s first story as "The Mormon's Wife," which appeared in 1855 in *Putnam's* under "Rose Terry" (the name by which she published until her marriage). Two years later, C. provided the lead story, "Sally Parson's Duty," for the first issue of the *Atlantic Monthly* (November 1857).

C. was a prolific writer, partly because she needed the income. She published nearly two hundred stories, more than two hundred poems, and two novels. Her best stories are included in three collections: *Somebody's Neighbors* (1881), *The Sphinx's Children and Other People's* (1886), and *Huckleberries Gathered from New England Hills* (1891). A modern selection is available in *"How Celia Changed Her Mind" and Selected Stories* (1986).

C.'s genius lies in her acutely realistic use of authentic regional characters, setting, and dialect. Unlike some local colorists, C. did not fetishize such details; rather she incorporated them into a larger, moral design. In addition to her critiques of the inhuman strictures of Calvinism, C. also returned continually to the theme of the oppression of wives in marriage and conversely to the relative liberty of the spinster. One of her greatest characters, Polly Mariner, is an entrepreneurial spinster who manages to survive and triumph by her own resources. "Folks's luck," she believed, "is generally their own makin'," a clear endorsement of a philosophy of salvation by works rather than by predestination.

Polly appears in a series of stories, the most important of which are "Polly Mariner, Tailoress" (1870), "Clary's Trial" (1880), and "How Celia Changed Her Mind" (1891). C.'s critical treatment of the tyrannical conditions under which many married women lived is the central theme of "Freedom Wheeler's Controversy with Providence" (1877), "Squire Paine's Conversion" (1878), and "Mrs. Flint's Married Experience" (1880).

"Alcedama Sparks; or, Old and New" (1859) and "Too Late" (1875) are C.'s most devastating depictions of the destructiveness of rigid Calvinism; in these and other stories C. anticipated the grim vision of New England mores seen in the works of Mary E. Wilkins FREEMAN, who was undoubtedly influence by C. Unlike some of the other local colorists, notably Stowe and Jewett, who emphasized the utopian aspects of rural life, in her best stories C. saw its dark side: a world of "hard labor . . . [with] a soil bitter and barren" where women had to endure "the daily dullness of work, the brutality, stupidness, small craft, and boorish tyranny of husbands." "What wonder," she asked in "The West Shetucket Railroad" (1872), "that a third of all the female lunatics in asylums are farmers' wives?"

BIBLIOGRAPHY: Donovan, J., *New England Local Color Literature: A Women's Tradition* (1983); Downey, J., "R. T. C.: A Bibliography," *BB* 21, 7 (May-August 1955): 159–63; 21, 8 (September-December 1955): 191–92; Pattee, F. L., *The Development of the American Short Story* (1923); Toth, S. A., "R. T. C. (1827–1892)," *ALR* 4 (Spring 1971): 170–76; Warren, J. W., ed., *The (Other) American Traditions: Nineteenth-Century Women Writers* (1993)

JOSEPHINE DONOVAN

COOPER, James Fenimore

b. 5 September 1789, Burlington, New Jersey; d. 14 September 1851, Cooperstown, New York

Although C. is most widely known for his Leather-Stocking (or Leatherstocking) tales—five romances of the American frontier—his range is much wider and his accomplishment greater than what is suggested by his most famous work. He wrote other frontier romances, tales of the sea, fiction set in Europe, and novels of contemporary America. He wrote satire, history, and other nonfiction, including books on American principles and five travel volumes on society as he found it during his seven year sojourn in Europe. Yet despite the diversity of his work—he wrote thirty-two novels and at least a dozen volumes of nonfiction—there runs through it all a consistent thematic thread. Central to his works is his moral view of man, frequently embodied in the action of the novels and in the great land-and seascapes that abound in them. His moral position forms the basis for his criticism of both European and American societies so that C. the *moraliste* and C. the social critic are one. His works, like the poetry of William Cullen BRYANT and the paintings of Thomas Cole, are the profound exposition of a great moral vision.

C. did not publish his first book until he was thirty-one, but he soon found his characteristic themes and mode of expression. Though *Precaution* (1820) is a weak imitation of a British manners novel, his next three books, *The Spy* (1821), *The Pioneers* (1823), and *The Pilot* (1824), are thoroughly American in subject matter and theme. Two are concerned with the American Revolution and use the physical setting to define the meaning. In *The Spy,* set on the neutral ground between the American and British forces in New York in 1780, he plays out a drama of moral ambiguity and divided loyalty in which both sides have their heroes and villains and choices are difficult to make. In *The Pilot,* set partly on the ocean off the British coast, he explores the conflict between freedom and authority as it bears upon the young American revolutionaries who serve under John Paul Jones. A ship cannot function without strict obedience to the commanding officer, yet these men are trying to create

a state which allows the individual to do as he sees fit. Far from being patriotic celebrations of the American Revolution, therefore, both probe the serious questions raised by that conflict.

In *The Pioneers,* C. turned for the first time to the American wilderness and set his book at the foot of Otsego Lake, where Judge Marmaduke Temple is establishing the community of Templeton, a village modeled on Cooperstown, where the novelist was reared. Here the problem is the conflict between the values of civilization, represented by the Judge, and those of the wilderness, embodied in Natty Bumppo, here called Leather-Stocking, an aging frontiersman. Judge Temple is bringing American civilization to the wilderness, but at a terrible cost: the wanton destruction of trees, the slaughter of game and fish, and the displacement of the Indian. Although he is a conservationist who wants to establish laws for the use of resources, Judge Temple cannot restrain the wasteful settlers—or indeed, even himself. Leather-Stocking protests that one should take from nature only what he can use, but he falls into the meshes of the law for killing one deer out of season, is tried and convicted for the offense, and eventually heads west, opening the way, ironically, for the very settlers he opposes. In this novel, C. examines the costs of the westward movement, a theme he would continue to develop in subsequent books.

For the next half dozen years, C. continued to write on American subjects. After the unsuccessful *Lionel Lincoln* (1825), an historical novel with strong Gothic elements set during the siege of Boston in 1775–76, he revived the character of Leather-Stocking in two more tales of the American wilderness: *The Last of the Mohicans* (1826) and *The Prairie* (1827). The first of these books, perhaps the most popular that C. wrote, is an exciting tale of chase, capture, and escape set during the old French War of 1757, when rival armies of distant kings fought for possession of the continent. Caught up in the struggle is a small group of white characters who are all but engulfed by the wilderness they have penetrated. They are present at the massacre at Fort William Henry, an episode that speaks volumes about the irrelevance of the white man's code of honorable war in the wilderness. The forest and hills still belong to the red man, and even Leather-Stocking, here called Hawkeye, must rely on his Indian friends, Chingachgook and Uncas, to survive. Indeed, the white men succeed only because the tribes are divided and Indian is set against Indian—a foreshadowing of what is to recur as the white men push the frontier westward.

The Prairie carries the series forward to 1804–5, when Lewis and Clark are crossing the continent. The wholesale destruction of the wilderness is in full swing, and Leather-Stocking, here called the trapper, is an aged man who has been driven to the Great Plains to die. In this book, C. examines the various attitudes toward nature held by his countrymen: the despoilers, Ishmael Bush and his tribe, who wastefully take what they want from nature; the scientific rationalists, represented here by Dr. Bat, who in their arrogance assume the dominion of man over the natural world; and the conservers, embodied in the trapper, who see the natural world as the creation of God, who remain humble before the power of the Creator, and who treat the natural world with respect. With the death of the trapper, the series comes to a close. In the first three Leather-Stocking tales, C. had shown the development of the westward movement from the 1750s to the beginning of the 19th c., and he had explored the problems entailed by the settlement of the wilderness, especially the despoliation of the landscape to make way for a civilization that already contained the seeds of its destruction.

C. completed *The Prairie* in Paris, where he had taken his family in 1826, and as he enjoyed the social life of Europe and observed the political scene, he brought the first phase of his career to a close with three additional novels using American materials. Two continue the line of development he had begun in *The Pilot. The Red Rover* (1827) and *The Water-Witch* (1830) are exciting tales of the sea in which C. indulged his most romantic bent. The Rover, a gentleman pirate, is his most Byronic character, and the ship in *The Water-Witch*, commanded by a gentleman smuggler, is full of romantic trappings, including strong suggestions of the supernatural. Both books are set in colonial days, and both captains are allowed to have patriotic motives for their attitudes and actions. Between these novels, C. wrote the utterly different *Wept of Wish-ton-Wish* (1829), a somber wilderness tale of Puritan New England. In it, he carries his treatment of the American settlement back into the 17th c. and develops it in terms of a conflict between settlers and Indians that eventually leads to King Philip's War.

C.'s experience in Europe was crucial. He soon learned that many Europeans had mistaken ideas about the U.S. and that many Americans took too favorable a view of Europe. He wrote *Notions of the Americans* (1828), a book that paints a glowing picture of American society, to correct the erroneous opinions of the Europeans, and he turned to fiction to warn American readers of the dangers they faced if they did not have an accurate view of European society. *The Bravo* (1831), the best of the three books with European settings, shows that an aristocratic reality can be concealed behind republican forms as it had been in Venice, while *The Heidenmauer* (1832), set in Reformation Germany, and *The Headsman* (1833), laid in

18th-c. Berne, reveal the evils inherent in aristocratic societies. C. detested aristocracy and feared that a moneyed class in the U.S. might establish itself like the oligarches of Venice, or, more immediately, the aristocracies he saw in Great Britain and France. The issue was so important to him that he would spend nearly a decade warning his countrymen of the danger and warding off the attacks of those among the Whig party in America who did not like his message.

C. was not surprised that European conservatives should attack him for affirming American principles in a book like *The Bravo*. What angered him was that his fellow Americans did not come to his support, but repeated the unfavorable European criticism. He advised Carey and Lea, his American publisher, therefore, that he would end his career as a novelist with *The Headsman*. Yet when he returned to America in 1833, he brought with him the unfinished manuscript of *The Monikins*, a satire on England, France, and the U.S., projected through a race of monkeys living near the South Pole, and he apparently also had plans for a series of travel volumes on his European experience. C. did not stop writing. He published *The Monikins* in 1835, and between 1836 and 1838, five volumes of European travel describing the scenery and commenting upon the society of France, England, Switzerland, Italy, and the Rhine as he had experienced them between 1826 and 1833. The books on Switzerland and Italy are the most picturesque, those on England and France the most sharp in their social commentary. In addition, he issued in 1838 *The American Democrat*, a concise little book on American principles that was intended as a kind of school text.

On his return to America, C. was shocked to discover the change that had taken place in American society during his absence. In his eyes, the old republican social and political virtues were being submerged in an uninformed, leveling democracy, and the tone of American life had lowered. This perception was only confirmed by the controversy which developed between him and his neighbors in Cooperstown over Three Mile Point, a piece of land on Otsego Lake. The conflict soon led to personal attacks on him in the Whig press, and C.'s famous series of lawsuits followed. The literary result was a pair of novels, *Homeward Bound* and *Home As Found*, both published in 1838, which contain a good deal of social criticism on both British and American society, but which also added fuel to the flames of controversy. Indeed, the conflict even spilled over to his fine historical work, *The History of the Navy of the United States of America* (1839), a book which is still respected by naval historians, but which became embroiled in C.'s war with the press when some Whigs took issue with

C.'s treatment of the Battle of Lake Erie. The struggle continued in the courts well into the 1840s.

C.'s publishers were understandably concerned with the direction his career had taken, and Richard Bentley, in London, had urged him to write the tale of forest and sea that had been in C.'s mind for years. C.'s next novel was just such a book. In *The Pathfinder* (1840), he reintroduced the character of Leather-Stocking, now called Pathfinder, set the scene on Lake Ontario a year or so after the action of *The Last of the Mohicans,* included incidents on both land and water, and showed the frontiersman in love. The following year he concluded the Leather-Stocking Tales with *The Deerslayer* (1841), a romance set at Otsego Lake, the scene of *The Pioneers.* It presents Leather-Stocking, here named Deerslayer, as a very young man on his first warpath during the 1740s. Between these books, to be sure, C. wrote the stilted *Mercedes of Castile* (1840), a dull account of the discovery of America, but in the new Leather-Stocking novels, C. made clear to his public that his creative powers were not dead. He had taken up old material without repeating himself and launched his career as a novelist in a new and interesting direction.

For the last two Leather-Stocking tales are quite different in theme from those which preceded them. They are, of course, both set in the almost untouched wilderness of upstate New York and contain the usual exciting episodes of chase, escape, and encounter with the Indians, but *The Pathfinder* is also a deeply social book, and *The Deerslayer* a religious one. Though the central problem in the former is the marriage of the heroine, Mabel Dunham, among whose suitors is Pathfinder, a larger issue concerns the need for human beings to recognize both their strengths and their limitations so that they may do what their background, talents, and education best fit them for. C. plays a number of variations upon this theme, for much of the trouble the characters face comes about when men step out of their proper roles and attempt to do things for which they are unsuited. Even Pathfinder errs in this matter. He allows the attraction of Mabel to keep him in the fort when he should be scouting for enemies. He has been drawn from his customary path and must in the end return to the wilderness life for which he has special gifts.

In *The Deerslayer,* on the other hand, C. develops a religious theme not only through the actions of his characters, but also through their relation to an almost idyllic setting. The Glimmerglass (Otsego Lake) and the surrounding hills reflect a holy calm that Deerslayer, alone among the characters, is fully able to appreciate. The values implicit in nature are lost on violent men like Tom Hutter and Hurry Harry—the one an ex-pirate, the other a self-centered frontiersman—who would even kill women and children for the bounty on their scalps. At the moral center of the book are Deerslayer and Hetty Hutter, Tom's simple minded daughter. Other characters, the beautiful but tarnished Judith, Hetty's sister, as well as Hutter and Harry, are measured against the standard of value that they represent: Christian principles, which Hetty takes literally and attempts to preach to the Indians, and the practical adaptation of Christian virtue that Deerslayer is forced to make if he is to survive among violent men. In the course of the novel, he kills his first Indian, but only in self-defense. The violence is thrust upon him. He tries to avert it, but when he cannot do so, he reluctantly takes the other's life.

After *The Deerslayer,* C.'s novels become increasingly concerned with the question of values, and his major characters not only struggle with conflicting principles but often fail to solve their problems. Admiral Bluewater, in *The Two Admirals* (1842), is torn by competing loyalties, one of which he must betray because the times—the Stuart rising in Great Britain in 1745—demand that he act. Ghita Caraccioli, a Roman Catholic in *The Wing-and-Wing* (1842), cannot fulfill her love for Raoul Yvard, a French Revolutionary atheist, because their philosophical differences are irreconcilable. Captain Willoughby, a retired British officer in *Wyandotté* (1843), tries to remain neutral during the American Revolution and is destroyed by his refusal to take sides. Only Miles Wallingford, in the double novel *Afloat and Ashore* and *Miles Wallingford,* both published in 1844, manages to resolve his conflict. He leaves the security of his Hudson River farm for an adventurous life at sea and in the course of time risks everything in an attempt to make his fortune in trade. Only when he is brought low by the apparent loss of all he holds dear does he learn where his true well-being and happiness lie, on the farm he almost lost in his pursuit of wealth.

C. had always seen the landed gentry as the foundation of American society, and he feared that if the values they represented should be lost, money would become the only measure of distinction among men. For this reason he was deeply concerned when the Anti-Rent controversy broke out in New York, for he saw the tenants' attempt to force the landlords to sell them the farms they rented as an attack upon the very basis of society. In response, he wrote three novels, the Littlepage series, to show the trouble and expense to which the landlords had gone to establish settlements in the wilderness and the threats to their property that they had had to meet and overcome: the incursion of French and Indians in 1758 in *Satanstoe* (1845) and the theft of their timber by lawless squatters just after the Revolution in *The Chainbearer* (1845). Finally, in *The Redskins* (1846) he presents the attempt by unprincipled levelers to seize the Littlepage lands in the mid-1840s and the specious arguments they use to justify their actions. *Satanstoe* is the best of the group as a novel, but the other books are important for their analysis of the issues as C. perceived them.

C.'s remaining novels record the decay of principle he saw in American society and suggest a return to traditional religious belief as the only cure. Though *The Crater* (1847) is set on Pacific islands colonized by Americans, the rise and ultimate destruction of their society is clearly intended to suggest the fate which, in C.'s view, Americans faced if they did not recover their sense of values. Two other novels detail more immediate problems. *Jack Tier* (1848) presents an American sea captain who traffics with the enemy during the Mexican War for gain; *The Ways of the Hour* (1850) questions the ability of the common man to arrive at truth through the use of reason. The religious theme, on the other hand, is most apparent in *The Oak Openings* (1848), C.'s last wilderness tale, and *The Sea Lions* (1849), his last romance of the sea. Both are strong in their affirmation of Christian belief. Although this theme had become explicit in C.'s work with *The Deerslayer,* it receives an unusual emphasis in these books in the remarkable conversion of major characters, the one an Indian chief in Michigan in 1812, the other an American sailor trapped in an antarctic winter.

But if C.'s late novels are more explicitly religious than his previous ones, it must not be assumed that they mark a radical departure from his early fiction. They are, rather, a natural development out of it. From the very beginning of his career, C. had always affirmed American principles and was quick to criticize his fellow countrymen when he believed that they had erred. The religious view of the world had also been present from the beginning, implicit in the descriptions of the natural landscape in his wilderness tales, or subscribed to by the democratic gentlemen who figure so largely in his depictions of society. In C.'s view, the U.S. had changed for the worse over the course of his life, and it was perhaps to be expected that he should seek to counter the materialism and ignorant self-assertion so prevalent in American society during his later years with a strong affirmation of traditional religious values. Through it all he remained the American patriot, whose love of country, despite its manifest faults, was a driving force behind his long and distinguished career as a writer of fiction.

BIBLIOGRAPHY: Axelrad, A. M., *History and Utopia* (1978); Beard, J. F., ed., *The Letters and Journals of J. F. C.* (1960–1968); Dekker, G., *J. F. C. the Novelist* (1967); Franklin, W., *The New World of J. F. C.* (1982); Grossman, J., *J. F. C.* (1949); House, K. S., *C.'s Americans* (1965); Long, R. E., *J. F. C.* (1990); McWilliams, J. P., Jr., *Political Justice in a Republic* (1972); Nevius, B., *C.'s Landscapes* (1976); Peck, H. D., *A World by Itself* (1977); Philbrick, T., *J. F. C. and the Development of American Sea Fiction* (1961); Railton, S., *F. C.* (1978); Ringe, D. A., *J. F. C.* (1962); Ringe, D. A., *The Pictorial Mode* (1971); Spiller, R. E., *F. C.: Critic of His Times* (1931); Walker, W. S., *J. F. C.* (1962); Wallace, J. D., *Early C. and His Audience* (1986)

DONALD A. RINGE

COOVER, Robert

b. 4 February 1932, Charles City, Iowa

John BARTH, Donald BARTHELME, Thomas PYNCHON, and C. are the four metafictionists who most influenced both the practice and the reputation of American fiction in the 1960s and 1970s. Inspired by the early postmodernists Samuel Beckett and Jorge Luis Borges, as well as the protometafictionist Miguel de Cervantes and magic realist Gabriel García Márquez, C. wittily and exhaustively uses fiction to explore fiction, or more specifically the fiction-making process; his critical but also comical deconstruction of narrative conventions and forms is part of a larger postmodernism premised on a liberating loss of faith in the idea of metanarrative. Growing out of 1960s iconoclasm, C.'s writing examines the "naked" individual's and more especially the culture's unwise reliance on "used-up" fictions, on cultural myths that are, as Larry McCaffery has demonstrated, ideological rather than ontological in nature: contingent and historical rather than essential and eternal.

These concerns and interests are evident in his first book publication, *The Origin of the Brunists* (1966), in which C. "paid his dues" to the realist novel. Set in the Midwest, where C. grew up, the novel concerns a small community's attempt to make sense of a mining disaster by transforming a brain-damaged survivor into a Christ-figure. More than an irreverent parody of Christianity in general and American millenarianism in particular, *The Origin of the Brunists* examines the myth-or fiction-making process from anthropological and sociological, as well as narrative, perspectives, thus setting the stage for C.'s later explorations of American sports, politics, films, and other pop culture forms—the conjoining of televised presidential campaigns and DR. SEUSS books in *A Political Fable* (1980), originally published as "The Cat in the Hat for President." Many of the short narratives in his most overtly metafictional book *Pricksongs and Descants* (1969) recycle old forms in postmodern ways, creating (as the book's title suggests) a narrative counterpoint (pricksongs and descants being two terms for what is essentially the same contrapuntal musical form). Like Barthelme in *Snow White* or Angela Carter in *The Bloody Chamber,* C. rewrites familiar folk—and Bible—stories, most exhaustively in *Briar Ruse* (1997), teasing out and highlighting their sexual content, addressing in "The Hat Act" the writer-reader relationship even more directly.

C.'s second novel, *The Universal Baseball Association, J.* Henry Waugh, Prop. (1968), represents metafiction at its most rewarding and least reductive. Its protagonist is a postmodern Walter Mitty, a lonely as well as vulnerable accountant by day, creator (Jahweh/ Jehovah) of a parlor baseball game by night, who finds fulfillment in fantasy. Slowly, the game becomes his life, taking on a life of its own, its author (Henry) disappearing altogether, consumed by his own fiction. In a sense, C. nearly suffered the same fate while writing his next novel *The Public Burning* (1977). What began as a one-act play about Julius and Ethel Rosenberg, executed as Russian spies in 1953, slowly developed over nine years into C.'s best and most ambitious as well as most controversial novel, indeed one of the finest and most important novels of the c. C.'s exhaustively researched yet wildly fantastical treatment of the Rosenberg case opens out to encompass not only J. Edgar Hoover, Dwight Eisenhower, and then Vice President Richard Nixon (the novel's chief clown and one of its two narrators) but the peculiarly American preoccupation with a divinely ordered national destiny and the reductive manicheanism upon which it (in its virulent anti-communist phase) is based. Legal matters first delayed publication then drove the novel that one conservative columnist assailed as "a cowardly lie" out of print for nearly twenty years.

An embittered C., claiming that in America books are sold the way condoms are, began writing fiction that seemed designed to address, even assault, a relatively small and select audience. *Spanking the Maid* (1981), originally published as "A Working Day," brilliantly and perversely deals with (among other things) the writer-reader relationship in sadomasochistic terms. *Gerald's Party* (1986), an even more hilariously punishing work, pushes C.'s love of exhausting a single image or metaphor further still, taking it and the reader through all its permutational possibilities. His spectacular, relentless proliferation and fusion of material, his "clogging" of the narrative at every level—sentence, page, paragraph, party—anticipate his more recent experiments in computer writing and hypertext at Brown University, where C. was "Professor of Electronic Fiction."

An intertextual extravaganza for amateur and hardcore cineastes alike, *A Night at the Movies* (1987) looks back, parodically reworking specific films and film genres, teasing out and playing with various cinematic conventions while at the same time underscoring the reality of film and overturning film's effect on filmgoers all too willing to suspend their disbelief. *Pinocchio in Venice* (1991) harks back even further, reimagining Carlo Collodi's puppet-turned-boy as an aging professor of art history back in Venice to write his magnum opus. In C.'s ribald novel, the pseudonymous Collodi is combined with the contemporary Italian writer Italo Calvino, the carnivalesque play of the commedia dell'arte with the pedant's Chaplinesque pratfalls as well as *Death in Venice*—both Thomas Mann's novella and Luchino Visconti's film version. More than a bit of self-indulgent postmodern play, C.'s novel does not so much deface Carlo Collodi's story as rescue it from the sanitized, sentimentalized Disney version. *John's Wife* (1996) plays a different kind of game with the reader, its title character little more than a narrative ploy, one of Hitchcock's MacGuffins, a Derridean absent presence: the enticing but illusory center. As the story's setting, a small Midwestern town, develops into a small metropolis, C.'s novel develops, less in plot than in texture, the sentences themselves getting longer and more involved, the pages thickening with type, then circle and bowing out, leaving bits and pieces of Robert Staughton Lynd and Helen Merrell Lynd's Middletown, Sherwood ANDERSON's Winesburg, and Edgar Lee MASTERS's Spoon River in its quintessentially postmodern wake.

BIBLIOGRAPHY: Cope, J. I., *R. C.'s Fictions* (1986); LeClair, T., *The Art of Excess: Mastery in Contemporary American Fiction* (1989); McCaffery, L., *The Metafictional Muse: The Works of R. C., Donald Barthelme and William Gass* (1982)

ROBERT A. MORACE

CORN, Alfred
b. 14 August 1943, Bainbridge, Georgia

C. is considered one of the most eloquent and far-reaching American poets of his generation. He is especially known for his long poems that combine emotional expansiveness with aesthetic precision.

Born in Georgia, C. came to New York City to do graduate work at Columbia in the 1960s; he has lived in New York ever since. His poetic breakthrough occurred with *A Call in the Midst of the Crowd* (1978), a rhapsodic evocation of New York City similar in effect to Hart CRANE's "Bridge" poems. Interspersing soaring urban praise-songs and evocations of the pace of everyday life in the city with prose excerpts from previous literary and historical descriptions of New York, C.'s poem dramatically impressed critics with its declaration that ambition and extravagance were by no means dead in the American poetry of the 1970s. The poems in *The Various Light* (1980) have a metaphysical complexity that makes reading them a strenuous, though rewarding, intellectual exercise. In "Reading *Pericles* in New London," C. interweaves Shakespeare's play with a car ride through eastern Connecticut; he notes the temporal irony and displacement of the conjunction, but concludes the poem with a democratic acceptance of the American present as a fit time in which to read, and produce, significant literature. "The Outdoor Amphitheater" is an autobiographical narrative which richly chronicles C.'s Georgia boyhood during the 1950s.

Autobiography surged to the forefront in *Notes from a Child of Paradise* (1984). This book-length narrative poem tells the story of C.'s personal odyssey and that of his entire generation. Structured around C.'s youthful marriage to a woman named Ann, the poem takes a panoramic view of the political unrest, cultural ferment, and transcendental hopes of the American 1960s. C.'s poem tacitly argues that this decade, despite its aura of antiestablishment rebellion, was characterized by an optimism, a kind of last romanticism that aspired to redeem the fallen American spirit. This quest is figured in the poem by a cross-country trip C. and Ann take that retraces the route of Lewis and Clark's expedition, reinvigorating the spirit of American newness that C. perhaps naively contrasts to European traditionalism at the beginning of the poem. But the poem's celebration of freedom is gradually overtaken by irony and loss. The utopian tendencies of the decade become corroded; the expedition into the heart of America yields no ultimate meaning; and C. and Ann's marriage ends as C. discovers his homosexuality and begins a relationship with a man named Walter. But the spirit of American optimism is resonantly alive in the texture of the poem itself, and surely helped C.'s book to become that rarest of things, a "poetry best-seller."

There seemed to be the possibility that C. would define himself exclusively as an "American" poet, a position which had its pitfalls in light of the increasingly plural nature of American society and identity. Fortunately, C. chose a different path with his next book, *The West Door* (1988), perhaps the peak of his poetic achievement. The intricately beautiful lyrics of this book are memorable; C.'s painstaking yet passionate evocations of objects, places, and situations seize the reader with their aptness and skill. A poem retelling the story of the Prodigal Son with an important new character—a taken-for-granted sister—stands out, as does a description of the *Irish Book of Kells* which delights in both the craftsmanship and spirituality of the medieval manuscript. The interest in Christianity displayed in these poems was further shown when C., who had become an Episcopalian as an adult, edited *Incarnation* (1990), an important collection of reflections on the New Testament by prominent writers.

Autobiographies (1992) is a partial sequel to *Notes from a Child of Paradise;* much of the volume's main long poem, "1992," is devoted to recalling the poet's travels with Walter in the early 1970s. Unlike the earlier autobiographical poem, though, C. interpolates other voices into his narratives; by listening to people he meets or by imagining the lives of strangers fleetingly encountered, he makes the poem a network of different voices in which the poet's is crucial but not dominant. With each section of the poem titled by the date of the events it chronicles, "1992" ranges through time as it ruminates on evidence of both personal and social history. *Present* (1997) contains more autobiographical poems, covering youth, travel, and current relationships, as well as "Musical Sacrifice," a complicated long poem juxtaposing the figures of Bach and Kafka. *Part of His Story* (1997) is a venture into the novel form, concerning a gay American dramatist in London who falls in love with a working-class Irishman. *The Poem's Heartbeat* (1997) is a manual of prosody that displays C.'s continuing interest in poetic form. Occasionally, C.'s portraits are stilted, and his populism seems a bit willed. But passages such as the brilliant evocation of C.'s boyhood visit to St. Augustine, Florida at the beginning of the poem once again demonstrate that C. has one of the most eloquent, indeed magniloquent, voices of any poet writing in the 1990s.

BIBLIOGRAPHY: Martin, R., *The Homosexual Tradition in American Poetry* (1979); Murray, G. E., "In the Place of Time," *Parnassus* 11 (Spring-Summer 1983): 277–85

NICHOLAS BIRNS

CORSO, Gregory
b. 26 March 1930, New York City

In the introduction to C.'s second volume of poems, *Gasoline* (1958), Allen GINSBERG described C. as a "scientific master of mad-mouthfuls of language." Although the epithet refers mainly to the C. who helped his friends Ginsberg and Jack KEROUAC found the Beat movement, it can be applied to the later C. as well, as he continues to combine conversational idioms with a frenetic and occasionally surrealistic sense of movement and image.

C.'s early life was difficult. He spent much of his childhood in orphanages, and was imprisoned for theft at age sixteen. While in prison, however, C. made up for his brief formal education by reading Fyodor Dostoevsky, Stendhal, Percy Bysshe Shelley, Thomas Chatterton, and Christopher Marlowe. He also studied a 1905 dictionary, obtained from one of the inmates, which may account for the mixture in many of his poems of archaic English idioms and Beat generation slang.

His first volume, *The Vestal Lady on Brattle and Other Poems* (1955), uses Beat slang copiously, mixed with what some see as residual poetic diction from his studies of English poetry. One of the best known poems in the volume, "Requiem for 'Bird' Parker, Musician," is a tribute to Charlie Parker, whom C. had met. *Happy Birthday of Death* (1960) contains several protest poems, the most famous of which is "Bomb," an antinuclear poem itself shaped like a mushroom cloud. The poem refuses to preach directly about the evils of nuclear war, but ironically suggests that the bomb is responsible for the death of God in the line, "O Bomb thy BOOM his tomb." In a similarly ironic vein, the poem "Marriage" considers the question: "Should I get married? Should I be good? / Astound the girl next door with my velvet suit and faustus hood?" and shows C.'s occasional attraction to rhyme, though almost all of his poems are free verse. The poem continues by picturing newlyweds, "All streaming into cozy hotels," with the poet losing his patience with what he sees as a beehive of empty ritual, finally "Screaming: I deny honeymoon! I deny honeymoon! / running rampant into those almost climactic suites / yelling Radio belly! Cat shovel!" This poem earned C. the Longview Poetry Award and is probably one of his best known.

When Kerouac died in 1969, C.'s book *Elegiac Feelings American* (1970) meditated on the loss of his friend in the leading poem of the same title. In the course of the poem, C. symbolically associated many of the ills then facing America with the death of Kerouac. This attempt to translate private pathos into public symbol, which some of his later poems also do, has led one critic to remark that C. can sometimes "mistake cant for inspiration," since many of his poems blur the boundaries between private reflection and social criticism.

His next collection, *Herald of the Autochthonic Spirit* (1981), shows an increasing interest in questions about childhood and religion, as does *Mindfield: New and Selected Poems* (1989). The poem "Hi," for example, whimsically asks "How can there be a god . . . When chickens eat hard boiled eggs / and when Gregorys are called Gregs." The fact that C. has not won the recognition and money enjoyed by Ginsberg and Lawrence FERLINGHETTI surfaces in "Poet Talking to Himself in the Mirror," where he considers the price of fame: "Ain't got no agent / can't see poets having

agents / Yet Ginsy, Ferl, have one." The question is resolved emphatically in the last lines: "Maybe I should get an agent? / Wow! / No way, Gregory, stay / close to the poem!!!" C. again asserts in his own idiom what he sees as the immediate and authentic over the commercially lucrative.

BIBLIOGRAPHY: Gregory, S., *Exiled Angel: A Study of the Work of G. C.* (1989); Selerie, G., *G. C.* (1982)

R. A. BENTHALL

CORTEZ, Jayne
b. 10 May 1936, Arizona

Although C. has fashioned one of the more singular voices in late-20th-c. American poetry, her unrestrained use of a sometimes profane vernacular, her commitment to political positions often sharply critical of standard social assumptions and her ingenious investigations of the possibilities of a surrealistic vision of experience have resulted in a somewhat marginal position in the literary landscape. In accordance with what might be regarded as a personal credo, C. in the closing poem of her collection *Somewhere in Advance of Nowhere* (1996) insists, "Find your own voice & use it / use your own voice & find it"—an assertion of independence and individual merit indicative of the people and values she celebrates and supports in her work.

One of the crucial components of C.'s voice is her employment of elements of the blues in her poetry. In addition to a series of recordings with jazz musicians demonstrating her ability to participate effectively in performance presentations of the rich musical tradition, she has—as Nikki GIOVANNI puts it—"got inside the music and the people who create it." Poems that honor the work of such masters as Duke Ellington or Miles Davis such as "Rose Solitude" from *Mouth on Paper,* (1977) and "A Miles Davis Trumpet," effectively recreate the moods and characteristic signatures of these artists in structural arrangements which contribute to an ethos evocative of their playing. Her thorough knowledge of the history of jazz is the basis for her compelling catalogue/tribute to 20th-c. poets, painters, and musicians ("States of Motion") whose deaths are depicted as a kind of transcendence toward the eternal engineered by a vehicle shaped by the spirit of their lives, while her "If the Drum Is a Woman," from *Firespitter* (1982), uses a familiar motif from an Afrocentric folk-saying to castigate men who have abused the women they claim to respect and appreciate.

The forceful feminist declarations of some of C.'s poems—encouraging and supporting women under attack in "Rape," or enumerating a kind of male emotional coldness in "She Got He Got"—are examples of strength built on a specifically woman's experience, but C.'s sources of power includes a particular political philosophy not dependent on gender. Her critique of the dominant modes of Western political systems is an outgrowth of the Black Consciousness movement developed during the 1960s and it includes an admiration for post-colonial and/or Third World cultural orientations which to C. seem more humane and less destructive than the "greedy mouth of imperialism" which "will try to exploit you / absorb you confine you / disconnect you isolate you / or kill you" as she says in "There It Is." Her responses to the forces she identifies as the agents of destruction and blight, however, are distinctive not as much for their adversarial perspective but for the inventive imagery with which C. constructs a surreal collage of striking dimensions.

Her admiration for the French Caribbean poet Aimé Césaire, who, as she expresses in her poem "At a Certain Moment in History," "fired up words that revolted like / overheated cockroaches," is consistent with her own fascination with and imaginative use of aspects of surrealism not generally associated with a black blues motif. The intertwining of elaborate, unusual juxtapositions of objects, ideas, emotions and graphic images with the rhythms and sonic effects of blues variants enables C. to present views of a world in which a hard-edged, even hardboiled depiction of society merges with the extravagant metaphysics of a cosmos defined by parameters beyond the traditions of realism. This unique fusion has kept C.'s poetry on the fringes of public awareness but has also led to a body of work which will remain striking when more conventional writing has begun to seem bland and muted.

BIBLIOGRAPHY: Melham, D. H., "A MELUS Profile and Interview: J. C.," *Melus* 21 (Spring 1996): 71–79; Woodson, J., "J. C.," in Harris, J. and T. M. Davis, eds., *DLB,* vol. 41, *Afro-American Poets since 1955* (1985): 69–74

LEON LEWIS

COUNTERCULTURE AND LITERATURE

The term "counterculture," perhaps paradoxically, is deeply engrained in American literature, from what many recognize as the first original voices of the country to the present. Ralph Waldo EMERSON, often called the father of American literature even though he wrote well into the 19th c., and the transcendentalists, of which he was a founding member, were the first to

significantly challenge established American culture, protesting the limitations of organized religion and established government, objecting in particular to slavery and unjust wars like the Mexican-American War of 1846–48. American literature, then, in a sense has its roots in an independence of spirit and character. Early American writers associated with TRANSCENDENTALISM like Emerson, Henry David THOREAU, Nathaniel HAWTHORNE, Amos Bronson ALCOTT, and Margaret FULLER, as well as less-known figures such as Frederic Henry Hedge, William Ellery CHANNING, and James Freeman Clarke challenged the norm and sought to break free of tradition. Emerson's lecture "The American Scholar" gave voice to an impulse to express a unique and original American spirit in scholarship and letters. This essay had a great influence on Thoreau, who famously went so far in "Resistence to Civil Government" to call for passive resistance tactics to combat government injustice, and himself refused to pay his poll tax, for which he was jailed. Thoreau's tactics would inspire such 20th-c. figures as Mahatma Gandhi and Martin Luther King, Jr.

The abolitionists overlapped the transcendentalists, and agreed with them in abhorring slavery. Among the first works to protest against the institution of slavery was Harriet Beecher STOWE's *Uncle Tom's Cabin*. Abraham LINCOLN was to greet her as "the little lady who made this big war!," referring to the Civil War, but although an early feminist, Stowe was still quite conventional in her view of Negroes, evident in the creation of the enduring stereotype, Uncle Tom. Her books *My Wife and I*, a fictional account of a marriage, and its sequel *We and Our Neighbors* were feminist declarations, but Stowe was to offend the escaped slave Harriet JACOBS when the latter approached Stowe about treating her life story, which Jacobs eventually did herself after being angered by racist and indecorous remarks from Stowe.

Jacobs did find an editor in another famous female abolitionist, Lydia Maria CHILD, who is most famous for her poem "Over the River and through the Wood," but she also wrote novels and children's books. *Hobomok, A Tale of Early Times,* is a novel about a Puritan woman who marries a Native American. She also started the first children's periodical in America, the *Juvenile Miscellany.* Stowe's *Uncle Tom's Cabin* and Jacobs's at least somewhat fictionalized autobiography *Incidents in the Life of a Slave Girl* effectively argued against the fugitive slaves law of 1850 which mandated the arrest and return of fugitive slaves to their owners even if apprehended in a free state. Surely this was a law that demanded disobedience, in the eyes of these writers.

William Lloyd GARRISON was a radical abolitionist who effectually split the movement with the schism of the American Anti-Slavery Society in 1840. He started the Anti-Slavery Society in 1831, the same year he began publication of the journal the *Liberator*. Abolitionists who followed his precepts—which included advocating the dissolution of the U.S. as early as the 1840s—became known as Garrisonians. Garrison himself was a nonresistant, a pacifist opposed to any kind of violence, including government action (although Garrison could still thrill at the violent actions of Nat Turner and John Brown). Abolitionist literature is counterculture primarily in the sense of being protest literature. Frederick DOUGLASS, a spokesman for the abolitionist and former escaped slave whose *Narrative of the Life of Frederick Douglass, An American Slave* was pivotal to the cause, worked with Garrison on the abolition lecture circuits, but Garrison felt betrayed by Douglass when the latter made in 1846 the decision to start a paper called the *North Star*. Though Douglass explained that he felt it was important to have a paper that was directly controlled and directed by "immediate victims of slavery and oppression," and Garrison publically gave his support, because his cause would suffer from any open rift with a prominent black American, a certain resentment remained. Despite the well-meaning intent of the abolitionists, the sometimes extreme stances of leaders like Garrison alienated the general public. Sometimes they can be accused of using blacks as spokespeople as in the novel *Our Nig; or, Sketches from the Life of a Free Black* (1859), by the black writer Harriet E. WILSON, in which the beleagured heroine of the book, Fado, marries a man named Samiel who professes to be a fugitive slave, only to abandon her while she is pregnant with the news that "his illiterate harangues were humbugs for hungry abolitionists" and he never was a slave or even a resident of the South.

William Wells BROWN was another black spokesperson and writer for the antislavery movement, and his book *Clotel; or, The President's Daughter,* the first novel by a black American, benefited in turn from the enormous success of *Uncle Tom's Cabin,* published a year earlier. Brown was an extremely versatile writer, also penning the first black author's play (*The Escape; or, A Leap for Freedom*), the first black book of travel (*Three Years in Europe*), as well as the first history of black soldiers in the Civil War (*The Negro in the American Rebellion*).

Of course, while FEMINISM was often intertwined with ABOLITIONISM, suffragists were to be immensely disappointed when women were not accorded the vote along with black makes during Reconstruction (although the black make vote, like other supposed rights granted to Negroes, was soon effectually blocked). The feminist cause continued to be espoused by such writers as Charlotte Perkins GILMAN, whose story "The

Yellow Wallpaper" showed the maddening effect of male oppression on women, and Kate CHOPIN whose novel *The Awakening* caused a sensation with its depiction of liberated woman, but the extreme censure of Chopin showed the cost of speaking out in those conservative times.

The feminist cause reemerged with the granting to women the vote in America in 1920. Mary AUSTIN was a writer of the American far West and Southwest who popularized American Indian tales. She was fascinated with the stories and the oral patterns of Native American lore and advocated the adoption of Indian ways. She was an emergent female writer in what was still a man's world. Despite her friendship with the writer Jack LONDON, her militant indictments of men got her into trouble, and *A Woman of Genius* was withdrawn four months after publication. Austin contended that the novel's frank treatment of a woman's life—dealing with such issues as sexuality, motherhood, and birth control—was not received well by the patriarchal publishing industry or press.

Another prominent woman, Josephine HERBST, a radical journalist, has been compared to John DOS PASSOS. She was also a Communist Party member, a left wing novelist, and in the eyes of her biographer Elinor Langer, a feminist martyr. Three parts of her posthumous memoirs, *The Starched Blue Sky of Spain* chronicle her triumphs and struggles; her *A Year of Disgrace* (1961), recalling the 1920s; "Yesterday's Road" was published in 1968 in *New American Review*. Her trilogy of the Midwestern Trexler family from the Civil War through the Great Depression, *Pity Is Not Enough, The Executioner Waits,* and *Rope of Gold* culminates in an account of the break up of a marriage and lesbian affairs modeled on the dissolution of her own marriage.

Edna St. Vincent MILLAY, poet, dramatist, political activist and feminist, won the Pulitzer Prize in 1923 for her volume of poetry *Ballad of the Harp-Weaver*. She was a self-proclaimed revolutionary and in her poetry advocated emotional and sexual liberation for women. Genevieve TAGGARD was a poet and college professor who also wrote a biography of Emily DICKINSON and published more than ten volumes of verse, beginning with *For Eager Lovers,* and anthologies of English and American poetry.

Proletarian writers were active primarily during the Depression. Tillie OLSEN worked as a domestic servant and incorporates much of her own and her originally working class family's experience into her works. She was a member of the Young Communist League and was active in the San Francisco labor movement in the 1930s. As a woman, she provided a perspective that male proletarian writers could not in works such as *Yonnondio*. But other proletarian writers like the black homosexual Claude MCKAY also gave an alternate take on mainstream society. He used the Petrarchan and Shakespearean sonnet forms while protesting racism and promoting black pride. *Songs of Jamaica* and *Constab Ballads* were early works, but it was not until *Harlem Shadows* that his fame was definitely established. He has been criticized for his preference of traditional forms for his angry diatribes because of the limiting effect of formal control versus boundless anger.

W. E. B. DU BOIS organizer of the Niagra Movement (1905), which was eventually to merge with the NAACP in 1909, was really the father of Black American studies in the U.S. In 1888 he received a B.A. from Fisk University, and another B.A. and M.A. from Harvard in 1890 and 1891, finally earning a Ph.D. in history in 1895. His dissertation was published as a debut to the series of Harvard Historical Studies. His most famous book, *The Souls of Black Folk* was a daring mixture of scholarship and popular culture that expounded on the schizophrenic double consciousness of being at once black and American in this society, and points out that race was a huge problem in early 20th-c. America. Du Bois's observations proved prophetic: race remained a problem throughout the 20th c., and Ralph ELLISON would explore the same double consciousness in the metaphor of invisibility in the *Invisible Man*. Like the black expatriate writer Richard WRIGHT, though, Du Bois found answers to the problems faced by American blacks in Marxist and communist ideologies.

Expatriate writers became legion in the late 19th and early 20th cs. Edith WHARTON one of the earliest expatriates, was from a prominent New York family, and was educated in the U.S. and abroad, moving to France in 1907. America was the subject of her writing, as in the Pulitzer Prize–winning *The Age of Innocence,* and she exposed the hypocrisies and drawbacks of upper and middle-class American society.

Another female expatriate was Gertrude STEIN, who went abroad in 1902 after getting a degree from Radcliffe in 1897. Stein, who coined the term lost generation for the era, is famous for her stylistic experimentation and the influence she exercised on other writers, especially Sherwood ANDERSON and Ernest HEMINGWAY. The visual arts, including the cubist painters she came to know and patronize in Paris, and the cinema, very much influenced her style. *Three Lives* and *Tender Buttons* are her best-known works besides her own autobiography disguised under the title *Autobiography of Alice B. Toklas,* TOKLAS being her secretary and her life partner, but Stein's *Lectures in America* addresses her literary style. Stein's *Four Saints in Three Acts,* staged by Virgil Thomson, with its all black cast, had a major influence on theater.

Despite Stein's influence on it, the lost generation gave a mixed view of female liberation. The female figures were great examples of liberated women, but the men seemed to show a certain resistance to the New Woman of the 1920s. One example of this misogyny, and an imporant spokesman for the lost generation, is of course Ernest Hemingway. The collection of short stories *In Our Time,* linked by vignettes that qualify it as a sort of experimental novel giving a composite view of his generation, was followed up by *The Sun Also Rises,* about American and British expatriates, and a novel that also typifies the lost generation. Hemingway was an activist in and correspondent during the Spanish Civil War, the favorite cause of American liberals in the 1930s and 1940s, and an issue he addresses in his novel *For Whom the Bell Tolls.* Hemingway won the Pulitzer Prize in 1953 and the Nobel Prize in 1954.

Martha Gellhorne was a foreign correspondent for *Collier's* magazine from 1937 to 1945 whose descriptions of the Spanish Civil War as well as war in Finland, China, and Europe in World War II were published in *The Face of War* (1959). She was notorious as the third wife of Ernest Hemingway, with whom she spent time in Spain during its civil war as a reporter. She was a published writer before her marriage to Hemingway (which only lasted from 1940 to 1945); besides a novel, she published a collection of short stories *The Trouble I've Seen* (1936) about the plight of workers during the Great Depression.

Robert MCALMON was another member of the lost generation, who, for the most part, in France had published several volumes of free verse. His autobiography *Being Geniuses Together* was used as a springboard for the memoirs of Kay BOYLE, another expatriate, in her edition of McAlmon's autobiography published in 1938.

Djuna BARNES also lived abroad. *Nightwood,* an experimental novel about disconnected characters which contains a lesbian affair, is a fitting prose work from someone who was a friend of James Joyce. Barnes eventually returned to New York City where she was supported in her increasing eccentricity by patrons including Samuel Beckett, and eventually the National Endowment for the Arts.

Anaïs NIN acknowledged the influence of Barnes on her own lyrical writing style. Besides her voluminous *Diaries* (published as *The Diary of Anaïs Nin 1931–1966* in seven volumes, 1966–80) Nin wrote a series of novels called collectively the *Cities of the Interior.* She met Henry MILLER while both were writing studies of D. H. Lawrence. Appropriately (like Lawrence) both believed sexuality gave access to a power that modern humanity had lost in sublimation. Both Nin and Miller experimented with sexual taboos in their lives and writings. Miller's autobiographical novels *Tropic of Cancer, Tropic of Capricorn,* and *Black Spring*—all originally published in France—would even be banned as obscene in the U. S. until the 1960s, and, still, in 1963, the Supreme Court of the U.S. had to rule that *Tropic of Cancer* was not obscene for his work to continue being published in America.

Miller was a major influence on the Beat movement. In fact, an entire issue of the beat magazine *The Beat Book* was dedicated to him. The Beat movement primarily emanated from New York and San Francisco, the word "beat" was applied to the movement by Herbert Huncke who borrowed it from Chicago fringe elements (carnival workers, hustlers, jazz afficionados) who used it to describe the typical condition of the itinerants on the road. A mentor to many of the Beat poets was the University of California-Berkeley English professor Josephine MILES. A poet in her own right, she was open to the new free form style, and encouraged her students to experiment with it, rather than stifling them, as many other academics tended to do. She met Allen GINSBERG and considered his work when he informally asked her advice on whether he should become a graduate student at Berkeley. It was Miles who passed along a copy of Ginsberg's "Howl" as an example of Bay Area writing to a visitor from New York, Richard EBERHART, who wrote a favorable piece for the *New York Times,* solidifying Ginsberg's reputation. Not just Ginsberg but most of the beats were, like the transcendalists, very critical of the U.S., yet also idealistic about their country. Ginsberg was certainly an icon for this. "Howl" and "America" (both published in *Howl and Other Poems*) were both indictments of American culture, and the homosexuality and homosexual encounters important for many of the group, not only Ginsberg, but William S. BURROUGHS and Peter Orlovsky, were part of the rebellion against mainstream values. As Amiri BARAKA (then known as LeRoi Jones) commented, the honesty with which the beats wished to live their lives was a factor in coming out so openly, and certainly made the movement a forerunner to gay rights.

Although the beats were not famous for their feminism, there were some women who came out of the movement. For instance, Anne Waldman, a beat poet, said she found valuable freedoms in the movement and the new consciousnesses its practitioners were exploring. City Lights books published her *Fast Speaking Woman* (1975), and she became in 1974 a founder and teacher at the Naropa Institute, the Jack Kerouac School for Disembodied Poets as it was called by Ginsberg and his cohorts. Hettie Jones was both a prose and poetry writer, married for some time to Baraka, who has not only made her own original contributions to the movement, but has devoted herself as well to holding writing workshops for homeless people and women in prison. Her memoir, *How I Became Hettie Jones* (1990) was received with much interest.

The modern environmental movement can be said to have started at the same time as the Beats (although it can also be traced as far back as transcendentalism), for Rachel CARSON, a zoologoist famous for her muckraking *Silent Spring,* definitely raised the awareness of modern Americans. *Silent Spring* warned of the effect that pesticides were having on nature, and Carson also wrote about the ocean. Gary SNYDER is an environmental writer who was also a participant in the Beat movement, having studied oriental languages at University of California–Berkeley. Like Ginsberg, he embraced Buddhism as an alternative to what he saw as failed Western traditions. Snyder won the Pulitzer Prize in 1979, for *Turtle Island,* a combination of poetry and prose expounding upon his philosophy and world view. Edward ABBEY, a writer of the American West, was passionately committed to preserving the Western landscape he loved. A nonfiction paen to the American Southwest, *Desert Solitaire,* was an elegant defense of the region. His novel *The Monkey Wrench Gang* inspired the environmental group Earth First! Distrustful of government and industry, including forest rangers whom he saw as betrayers of nature, he advocated a nonviolent type of ecoterrorism in his novel that became the modus operandi of Earth First!

New feminist writers, like the beats, started writing in the reactionary period of the 1950s. Certainly Sylvia PLATH must be counted among them, with her outraged condemnation of patriarchy in such poems as "Daddy" and "Lady Lazarus." Adrienne RICH started out as a poet with very traditional models (among them Yeats, Auden, and Stevens, as well as Donne), but poems like "Aunt Jennifer's Tigers" foreshadow her future development artistically and philosophically. Her life was at first very traditional, too; she was married, with three sons. But in the 1960s she and her husband became involved in anti–Vietnam War activities. In the 1960s, she ended her marriage and eventually became a lesbian. Her volumes of poems *Diving Into the Wreck* won the National Book Award, which Rich rejected as an individual but accepted on behalf of all women. She has figured importantly in feminism's second wave.

Rita Mae BROWN was another spokeswoman for lesbian sexual liberation. Her *Rubyfruit Jungle* (1974), about a lesbian's coming of age in a sexually repressive society, was a trailblazing novel upon which her subsequent works have elaborated.

Norman MAILER has authored many works that challenged the status quo: *Barbary Shore* was a novel that explored liberal and conservative elements in the U.S.; *The Deer Park* posited Hollywood as a microcosm of America during the era of the Red Scare; and, of course, *Armies of the Night,* for which he won a Pulitzer Prize, was his report on a march on the Pentagon to protest the Vietnam War, what can be said to be the first of his "nonfiction novels."

Thomas PYNCHON attended Cornell University in the 1950s, and studied physics for a time, but graduated in 1959 with a degree in English. His writings, especially *The Crying of Lot 49, Gravity's Rainbow,* and *Vineland* prove him to be a product of his generation, but his eclectic and wide-ranging imagination helps to align his work with James Joyce's in terms of complexity and allusiveness. His works are anti-authoritarian and subversive of order, narrative and societal. "Entropy," published in the *Kenyon Review,* was composed like a fugue, but later works draw on popular culture—songs, detective stories, comics, films, actual history and science—as much as Joyce's do.

Music, literature, and graphic arts were very much intertwined during the 1960s and 1970s. Just as counterculture literature borrowed from and impinged on music and other arts in its history—the expatriate Gertrude Stein collected and was inspired by early-20th-c. painting, and black writers W. E. B. Du Bois and Ralph Ellison incorporated elements of jazz music into their works—so too did the Beat literature of the 1950s shape the music of the sixties' artists and the free form counterculture music shape such avant garde works as that of Thomas Pynchon. The most obvious beneficiaries of the Beat literary legacy in terms of musicians were Bob DYLAN and the Grateful Dead. Dylan (born Robert Zimmerman), of course, most likely named himself after the Welsh poet Dylan Thomas, and his literary legacy in the early 1960s were the traditional ballads he and other "folkies" sang. That was to change when he switched from acoustic to electric guitar and electrified the world. Dylan, an eloquent and powerful lyricist, has mesmerized and inspired audiences for over three decades.

The Grateful Dead, with primary lyricists John Barlow and Robert Hunter, has been a similarly long-lived musical phenomenon. Born in 1965, the band dissolved as a single entity at least in 1995 with the death of Jerry Garcia. Associated with Ken KESEY and the Merry Pranksters, their legendary concert tours and peripatetic fans known as Deadheads continued in the spirit of the beat vagabond writers, poets and personalities. Tour songs like "Truckin,'" with the refrain of "What a long strange trip it's been" summed up the experience of several nonconformist generations. But, like Dylan's music, the repertoire of the Dead was firmly rooted in, in fact largely consisted of, American and English traditional ballads, as evi-

denced by the songs "Goin' Down the Road Feeling Bad," a ballad politicized by Woody Guthrie in the 1930s, and "Peggy-O," also performed by Dylan, another traditional ballad. However, there's no denying the originality of lyrics by Dylan, Hunter, or Barlow, and their songs will be considered as contributions to American literature, as, indeed, they are already, which their study in literature classes in public schools and universities today attests.

Philip Glass in music and Twyla Tharp in dance are from the same generation as the original psychedelic or hippy movement that Dylan, the Beats, and the Grateful Dead were part of, and transformed classical opera, ballet and music with their performance art. This new music also arose in the 1960s, but was far from the improvisational noodling of psychedelic music. Glass's repetitive vocals and notes are sometimes reported to be the bane of singers and musicians, but in pieces like *Einstein on the Beach* (1975), *Satyagraha* (1980) about Gandhi, and *The Photographer* (1982) (about the pioneer photographer Eadweard Muybridge) he seeks out heroes for contemporary times. Tharp choreographed dances to every kind of music creating a fusion of modern dance and ballet. She worked with Mikhail Baryshnikov and the American Ballet Theatre from 1987 to 1989, when he left. Both Glass and Tharp have recently been working with rock singers on pieces, Glass with David Bowie and Tharp with Laurie Anderson.

As for drama, the modern American theatre can be traced back to Eugene O'NEILL. His early experiments in NATURALISM included *Anna Christie* for which he won a Pulitzer Prize. In the 1920s he also experimented with expressionism, epitomized by *The Hairy Ape. Strange Interlude,* which also won a Pulitzer Prize, took his experiment with form as far as stream of consciousness. O'Neill won a posthumous Pulitzer Prize (the first time the award was given posthumously) for *A Long Day's Journey into Night.* David MAMET is known for his naturalistic dialogue, particularly in *Sexual Perversity in Chicago* and *American Buffalo.* Sam SHEPARD won the Pulitzer Prize in drama for his play *Buried Child,* but like Mamet, finds his theatrical reputation overshadowed by his film work.

Art Spiegelman came out of the underground comic phenomenon of the 1960s, writing for *RAW,* and thus the counterculture shaped his identity as artist. Spiegelman's comic books point out the difficulties of categorizing genres. His representation of his father's experience during the Holocaust in comic strip form through mice and other animals in *Maus: A Survivor's Tale* (1986) resulted in a sequel, *Maus II* (1991), at which point Spiegelman requested that the book be moved from the fiction to the nonfiction section of the *New York Times* best-seller list, in spite of calling it a "comic-book novel." The tension between the subject matter and form in *Maus* is notable, and Spiegelman to a large extent subverts the form, showing up the sense in which modern mechanical society is indifferent to the horrors of the genocide which he describes, as the stripes of his father's uniform fade into the UPC bar code of volume 2 of the work (Doherty). Robert Crumb, editor of *ZapComix,* is famous as the creator of Mr. Natural and his disciple Flakey Foont, and Fritz the Cat among other counterculture icons, some of which were ruled obscene in 1970. Crumb illustrated a 10th anniversary edition of Abbey's *The Monkey Wrench Gang.*

Perhaps the designation "counterculture literature" is itself a misnomer, since Transcendentalism is now recognized as the foundation of canonical American literature, and thus the anti-establishment becomes the fundament. Gary Snyder made a comment in an interview about the term "subculture" saying it is actually "the main line and what we see around us is the anomaly." In the same way, perhaps the literature of counterculture is in itself the mainstream, an outgrowth of the questioning and self-critical American spirit that is the ideal.

BIBLIOGRAPHY: Bell, P. K., "Josephine Herbst," *New Republic* 191 (17 September 1984): 30–33; Bellini, J. D., "Up to Heaven's Gate, Down in Earth's Dust: The Politics of Judgment in *Uncle Tom's Cabin*," *AL* 65 (June 1993): 275–95; Clausen, J., "The Starched Blue Sky of Spain," *The Nation* 253 (11 November 1991): 594–96; Doherty, T., "Art Spiegelman's 'Maus': Graphic Art and the Holocaust. Write Now: American Culture in the 1980s and 1990s," *AL* 68 (March 1996): 69–85; Gish, R., "The Land of Journey's Ending," *AIQ* 16 (Fall 1992): 596–99; Jones, R. T., ed., *Music by Philip Glass* (1987); Harold, S., *The Abolitionists and the South, 1831–1861* (1995); Knight, B., *Women of the Beat Generation* (1996); Langlois, K. S., "Mary Austin's *A Woman of Genius:* The Text, the Novel, and the Problem of Male Publishers and Critics and Female Authors," *JAC* 16 (Summer 1992): 279–87; Mendolson, E., ed., *Pynchon: A Collection of Critical Essays* (1978); Merrill, W. M., *Against Wind and Tide: A Biography of William Lloyd Garrison* (1963); Orr, E., "On the Side of the Mother: *Yonnondio* and *Call It Sleep*," *SAF* 21 (Autumn 1993): 209–24; Stafford, T., "In Reluctant Praise of Extremism," *Christianity Today* 36 (26 October 1992): 18–21

JOSEPHINE A. MCQUAIL

COWLEY, Malcolm

b. 24 August 1898, Belsano, Pennsylvania; d. 28 March 1989, New Milford, Connecticut

The American writers who form the Lost Generation have a group identity in literary history largely because of the work of C., who was one of them himself, leaving America for France during World War I and again during the glory days of Paris in the 1920s, returning home to face the political questions posed by the Great Depression, and then finding himself a lionized man of letters in the last decades of his life. More importantly, he was his generation's chronicler. In *Exile's Return* (1934; rev. ed., 1951) and other books, he vividly recalls the world of the expatriate writers. C. was also extremely influential as an editor and reviewer. He has been credited with forming the reputations of several writers, most notably that of William FAULKNER.

In 1917, C. interrupted his studies at Harvard to go as a volunteer to France, where he found himself driving a munitions truck for the French Army instead of the ambulance he had expected. After returning home to serve in the U.S. Army and complete his degree, he spent several more years in France, where he moved in both French and American expatriate literary circles. He received a diploma from the Universite de Montpellier, published a pamphlet on Racine, and began a series of translations of French authors. Despite his friendship with European intellectuals, especially Louis Aragon, the central focus of his attention remained American writers, especially American writers who had shared his experience of war and exile.

After leaving France in 1923, C. moved in Greenwich Village literary circles that included Allen TATE, Caroline GORDON, and Hart CRANE. Thanks in part to Crane's encouragement, C. published his first collection of poems, *Blue Juniata,* in 1929. The poems in that collection, like those in *The Dry Season* (1941) and the final version of *Blue Juniata* (1968), show a great deal of skill and received critical praise. C.'s true métier, however, was the critical essay and, even more, the memoir.

From his undergraduate days onward, C. worked as an editor and book reviewer. In 1929, he joined Edmund WILSON at the *New Republic,* and his reviews became extremely influential, many of which are collected in *Think Back on Us . . . A Contemporary Chronicle of the 1930s* (1967). During this period, C. devoted a great deal of attention to political activities and became involved in several leftist organizations.

C. devoted several chapters to politics in the first version of *Exile's Return,* his memoir of the 1920s. Describing the experiences of the lost generation, both in Paris and in New York, *Exiles's Return* became the starting point for every later critical account of many writers. It is also a fascinating and very readable autobiography. C. made the book much stronger both as criticism and as a narrative when he revised it in 1951, changing the subtitle from *A Narrative of Ideas* to *A*

Literary Odyssey of the 1920s. C. eliminated chapters and passages that presented pat, leftist opinions, and expanded the account of Hart Crane. It remains the best book ever written on writers of the 1920s.

As the revisions of *Exile's Return* indicate, C. turned more from politics to literature itself after the 1930s. His work as critic or essayist advanced the careers of a number of his contemporaries. As editor of *The Portable Faulkner* (1946), for example, he made it clear that Faulkner's great achievement is the creation of the whole world of Yoknapatawpha County. However, in many ways, the most productive period of C.'s career was not the 1920s or 1930s, but the 1970s, when he returned to his characteristic mixture of criticism and memoir. *Second Flowering: Works and Days of the Lost Generation* (1973), *And I Worked at the Writer's Trade* (1978), and *The Dream of the Golden Mountains: Remembering the 1930s* (1980) are at once continuations of *Exile's Return* and meditations on the whole idea of literary generations. Having traced his generation's progress from its eager youth onward, it was fitting that the last book he published, *The View from Eighty* (1980), explored what it was like to be one of "the old old."

BIBLIOGRAPHY: Faulkner, D. W., "M. C. and American Writing," *SR* 98 (Spring 1990): 222–35; Kempf, J. M., *The Early Career of M. C.: A Humanist among Moderns* (1985)

BRIAN ABEL RAGEN

COZZENS, James Gould

b. 19 August 1903, Chicago, Illinois; d. 9 August 1978, Stuart, Florida

C. holds the curious distinction of being one of America's foremost novelists of manners and, at the same time, one of the least read and studied writers of the 20th c. Although C. began writing his first novel, *Confusion* (1924), as a prep school student in Kent, Connecticut, publishing it during his second year at Harvard, he would wait twenty-five years and nine novels later before receiving critical recognition for his Pulitzer Prize-winning *Guard of Honor* (1949). C.'s literary star appeared to be rising with *By Love Possessed* (1957), a number one best seller and William Dean Howells Medal recipient, but critics remained sharply divided over its literary merits and its politics. After reviewers overwhelmingly denounced *Morning Noon and Night* (1968), C. stopped writing fiction, realizing "work of mine's all out of season."

Scorning fame and the East coast literary establishment, C. acknowledged he wrote, not with an eye toward popular audiences, but with an ideal reader in mind: an intelligent, learned "grown-up" who would appreciate his dense, classical style and detached, unsentimental approach to the problem of exercising power and authority in situations where moral absolutes are ill-suited to the purpose of preserving a community's peace and order. Particularly in his later, most important novels, C.'s fictional world concerns itself with society's elite—middle-aged professional men of Anglo-Saxon Protestant stock who hold positions of power and leadership based on their commitment to public service and profound respect for social traditions and a professional code of ethics. Excepting the irascible, unrestrained Doctor Bull in *The Last Adam* (1933) C.'s protagonists—Ernest Cudlipp, Abner Coates, Colonel Ross and Arthur Winner—privilege rational thought, contemplation, and pragmatism in deciding how best to lead their communities through periods of disorder and crisis. However, such men of reason find that human limitations and life's contingencies require compromise between their moral principles and doing the "right" thing. While society is never perfectible, then, C.'s fiction does not subscribe to bleak naturalism. As Colonel Ross puts it in *Guard of Honor:* "Downheartedness was no man's part. A man must stand up and do the best he can with what there is. . . . A pattern should be found; a point should be imposed."

His most commercially successful novel, *By Love Possessed,* exemplifies C.'s intricate, tightly constructed narratives, which evolve from single events to richly textured webs of cause and effect relationships. The novel begins with Arthur Winner, a prominent lawyer, offering to defend his secretary's brother on a rape charge. Over the next two days, Winner becomes entangled in his partner's personal problems with his alcoholic wife and grapples with a moral dilemma involving another partner's "innocent" embezzlement of trust funds. Human emotion—being possessed by love in its multifarious forms—seemingly causes much of the self-deception and unhappiness in Winner's small city; thus he seeks to impose a rational design on human existence, which, tempered by pragmatic concerns, restores equanimity to his community.

More in keeping with British novelists of manners, C.'s work was consistently out-of-step with his literary contemporaries. He derided the introspective, alienated idealists of the Lost Generation, ignored the class analysis of social realism, and regarded postwar liberalism as sentimental. In turn, the social conservatism of his later novels—respect for cultural continuity, unproblematic acceptance of a stratified society and ambivalence toward racial and ethnic minorities—was denounced by liberal critics. But for some scholarly interest following the posthumous publication of *Just*

Representations (1978), a collection of essays, short stories, and excerpts from novels, C.'s literary merits remain overlooked by those who stress his political standpoint.

BIBLIOGRAPHY: Bracher, F. G., *The Novels of J. G. C.* (1972); Bruccoli, M. J., *J. G. C.: A Life Apart* (1983); Mooney, H. J., *J. G. C.: Novelist of Intellect* (1963)

JANE E. HENDLER

CRANE, [Harold] Hart

b. 21 July 1899, Garrettsville, Ohio; d. 27 April 1932, at sea

In the past two decades, C.'s poetry has been rescued from the unsympathetic rumblings of his early critics to take its place within major American poetry of the 20th c. C.'s tempestuous life and suicide at thirty-three did nothing to ingratiate him with many of his first critics, who turned their often scathing rhetoric on his flaws, some real and some imagined. More recent critics, noting the incompatibility of C.'s approach to poetry with that of T. S. ELIOT and his modernist followers, have appreciated C. on his own terms. Although some prefer the difficult, highly compressed, linguistically experimental poetry of C.'s first collection, *White Buildings* (1926), it is C.'s more accessible epic poem sequence, *The Bridge* (1930), which will, despite the brevity of his career, ensure him a place in the very tradition his contemporaries accused him of abandoning.

C. lived a life resonant with the symbolism of his poetry, often described by his critics as strongly "personal." C.'s education was largely informal, encouraging his detractors to criticize his ignorance in an era that emphasized, in Eliot's terms, the relationship between tradition and the individual talent. Yet C. was a voracious if somewhat eclectic reader, whose work critics have found to be influenced by writers ranging from Plato to William Blake to Herman MELVILLE, from the romantics to the imagists, as well as by visual artists and composers. Despite travels in the U. S., the Caribbean, and Mexico, C.'s home base was New York, which offered him the stimulation of a group of literary and artistic friends, including Malcolm COWLEY, Allen TATE, Gorham Munson, Kenneth BURKE, Alfred Stieglitz, and Waldo FRANK.

White Buildings, C.'s only published collection, introduces C.'s major themes: the redemptive power of love in a fragmented, "waste land" world, and the special mission of the poet in translating the vision of wholeness and continuity which love has vouchsafed him. Both within individual poems and in the sequence of poems appears a pattern of despair followed by reassurance that would typify C.'s work throughout his career and dramatize his struggle with Eliot's *The Waste Land.*

These poems also exemplify C.'s reliance on what he called a "logic of metaphor,' which C. characterized by an appeal to the reader's "pure sensibility" in constructing metaphors that could not be rationally analyzed. At times, however, C. admitted that the connections he made in his highly compressed metaphoric language were obscure and inaccessible even to a sensitive reader. As in his American predecessor Emily DICKINSON, a poet C. admired, the difficulty in C.'s poetry most frequently derives from compression, as well as from C.'s extensive and varied vocabulary. These poems evidence C.'s love of language, his affection for obscure words and startling juxtapositions.

Although the freedom of the visionary experience is the object of the poet's quest—freedom from despair and disorder, freedom from the entrapment of time and space—C. did not attempt freedom from poetic structure. Instead he accepted the necessity of defining freedom within the context of structure, a principle noted in several of his poems and letters. Much of his poetry uses conventional meter and regular stanzas, and sometimes regular rhyme schemes. Only rarely did C. experiment, as his friend E. E. CUMMINGS did, with unusual typography or spatial arrangement.

Two notable poem sequences end *White Buildings.* "For the Marriage of Faustus and Helen" prepares the way for *The Bridge* by recasting a literary myth of the past in contemporary terms and employing an ideal of feminine beauty in the pursuit of transcendence: the protagonist encounters Helen in a streetcar, and her subsequent seduction ends with the Great War. Section 2 of this poem demonstrates C.'s attempt to translate jazz into poetry, an experiment in which he was keenly interested. In the final lines of the poem, the speaker-poet praises the imaginative power that permits him to transform the myth and redeem destruction through its message of transcendent beauty.

"Voyages" is a series of love poems thought by some to be C.'s finest achievement. It describes a sexual voyage of lovers who entrust their love to a sea described as cruel in "Voyages I," but ultimately indulgent. In "Voyages V," the lovers part, but in "Voyages VI" the poet describes the vision he has attained, the assurance of an order that transcends the shifting vagaries of human love. C. captures the intimacy of a speaking voice throughout the "Voyages" with blank verse; in "Voyages VI," he translates his vision of order into regular four-line stanzas and a regular rhyme scheme.

The poems of *Key West: An Island Sheaf,* a collection C. had prepared before his death, and other late poems published posthumously in *Collected Poems*

(1933) are similar to the poems in *White Buildings,* although many have tropical settings, and some experiment with spatial arrangement. C.'s last published poem, "The Broken Tower," describes the poet in a "broken world,' unsure of his vision and his power to articulate it; although the poem ends with a description of healing love, many find the ending compromised by the power of the opening stanzas.

The imagery of the short poetry—its towers and spans, serpents and seas—and its themes—memory and desire, words and the Word—are echoed in C.'s masterwork, *The Bridge.* C. wanted *The Bridge* to be "an epic of modern consciousness" built upon a revitalized "Myth of America." The symbol which dominates the poem is Brooklyn Bridge, symbolically a bridge between earth, water and sky; past, present, and future; time and eternity, space and infinity; and myth and reality. C.'s opening "proem," "To Brooklyn Bridge," is one of his most breathtaking lyrics, a powerful balancing act of striking metaphor and directness, a successful demonstration of his poetic virtuosity.

From this opening, *The Bridge* moves back and forth across the continent, and back and forth in time in an attempt to attain a mythic transcendence of time and space. The protagonist returns to the beginnings of the white man's history in America through Columbus's monologue in "Ave Maria," and to the dawn of Indian history through the ritual of the dance in "The Dance." The connection to Native American myth is mediated by a lover, Pocahontas, metaphorically the body of the American continent, and the protagonist must become, like the modern Rip Van Winkle of "Van Winkle" and like Pocahontas herself, "time's truant." Similarly, the modern subway of "The Harbor Dawn" becomes transformed into a train and then a river, the Mississippi, in "The River," before reappearing in the subway of "The Tunnel." Maritime history is recaptured in "Cutty Sark,' the history of aviation in "Cape Hatteras." In the latter, however, the protagonist calls upon the great American optimist, Walt WHITMAN, to redeem through new vision that history from the destruction of war in which it has eventuated. After attaining the geographic height of "Quaker Hill," where the vista is of an American ideal tarnished by commercialism, the poem descends to "The Tunnel," where Edgar Allan POE replaces Whitman as the presiding spirit—the protagonist's epic descent into hell, and the poem's descent, both stylistically and thematically, into Eliot's waste land. Poem and protagonist emerge in "Atlantis," where vision is drawn upward to the bridge, symbol of cosmic unity and freedom from despair. The poem begins in the cold dawn of winter, passes through the spring of "The Dance" and the autumn of "Quaker Hill" to the spring night of "Atlantis."

Critics have evaluated *The Bridge* as myth, as epic, as American history, as philosophic diatribe, as mystic vision, and as unified poem, and often found it wanting. Yet, as others have pointed out, measuring it against any single definition, even one C. himself may have used, misses the point and diminishes its achievement. The poem, like its central symbol, bridges all of these impulses. Like any long poem, it has weak links, but given the number of themes and corresponding images it assimilates, it is a remarkably unified and consistent whole. Finally, at its best, *The Bridge* attests to C.'s felicitous command of diction and meter in service to his vision, to his lyric power as a visionary poet.

BIBLIOGRAPHY: Horton, P., *The Life of An American Poet* (1937); Lewis, R., *The Poetry of H. C.* (1967); Trachtenberg, A., *H. C.: A Collection of Critical Essays* (1982); Unterecker, J., *Voyager: A Life of H. C.* (1969); Weber, B., ed., *The Complete Poems and Selected Letters and Prose of H. C.* (1966)

LYNETTE CARPENTER

CRANE, Stephen

b. 1 November 1871, Newark, New Jersey; d. 5 June 1900, Badenweiler, Germany

C., more even than most literary geniuses who die young, burst into the pantheon of letters like a firework, brilliant, fascinating, finished. He had, however, a shaping history. Born into a professionally religious family—his father, the Reverend Doctor Jonathan Townley Crane, being the highest ranking Methodist elder in the district, and his mother, Mary Helen Peck Crane, coming from a New York line of Methodist preachers—he would rebel against institutional, devotional religion, while scrutinizing moral issues in his art. The family's move to Port Jervis, New York, provided C. with a small town upbringing remembered acutely in later fiction, and his father's death when he was seven complicated his social and spiritual life with struggle. He attended seminary and military schools, but his accomplishments were less bookish than boyish, his captaincy in the Claverack College cadet corps and success on the Syracuse University baseball team being the highlights of his academic career. If he was well read, it appears to have been in the popular literature of the period, primarily the magazines.

The moral seriousness of language he learned from his family, and the experience of testing skills and character through sport and playing soldier, prepared him for his writing career, which he began with collegiate, then professional journalism. The tradition in

American literature of writing as a manly activity, an adventure in itself that required in its highest calling courage, craft, and dedication, runs directly through C. He was soon in trouble for testing the limits of reporting, his blend of observation and generalization causing offense and costing him a job. The fundamental irony of publishing politics, that "reporting" is often expected, if not required, to rationalize reality in conformation with a public or publisher's agenda, became, as applied to the rationalizing impulse of individual desire, thematically central to C.'s art, tempering without extinguishing his romanticism, deconstructing while demanding a cardinal realism. That these strains of sensibility sometimes resolved themselves in a radical, literary impressionism does not define C. as belonging exclusively to any particular school but demonstrates his strict attention to the literary historical moment and his experimenting imagination.

Fiction presented itself as more amenable, in part because it was more challenging, than journalism to this stylistic debate, which resonates between and within his works and is always materially present in the themes and drama of his fiction. His first important narrative work, the novella *Maggie: A Girl of the Streets* (1893), was a product of his close observation of Bowery life in New York City, and its initial image—a "very little boy" atop "a heap of gravel" engaged in a particularly vicious game of King of the Mountain with a stone-throwing pack of "howling urchins" for the "honor" of his neighborhood gang—introduces many of the characteristics of his art: the theme of childhood, though not necessarily of innocence; the dead-on dialogue of carefully reproduced dialect; the startling prose style of finely observed, aptly chosen imagery contesting with bold abstractions; the deft juggling of third-person limited viewpoint, creating ironic crosscurrents among a cross section of starkly drawn *dramatis personae;* and the thematic conceit of life, even in pathos or parody, as in essence a battle, a war. Also typical of his talents, to their and *Maggie*'s disadvantage, is C.'s failure with female characters, except as shrewish gossips, narrow moralists, or superficial beauties. This failing can be considered to express the limitations of the age in affording choices to women, but the poignancy and moral corrosion of their circumstances is not appreciated in anywhere near the detail or nuance of his fiercely ambivalent portraits of the double-bind of manly virtues and vices.

Lack of publisher interest led C. to have *Maggie* printed privately, though he could ill afford it, living, as he was, off Bohemian friends in lower Manhattan and his brothers in New Jersey and upstate New York. Nearly starving, he got an idea for an historical novel writ small, the Civil War from a soldier's personal perspective. He read deeply in relevant memoirs, recalled his cadet days, and applied his considerable, nearly full-blown art to the task, and in a year had created a masterpiece, *The Red Badge of Courage* (1895). Its predominant style, the ultimate point of its irony, the genesis of its sensibility—these major artistic issues have been debated for a century without resolution. But that it is the great novel, short as it is, of the most dramatic event in American history is a cultural given. That it was written wholly from the imagination of a twenty-two-year-old astonished the literary world, and still does. The story of two days in the life of Union soldier Henry Fleming, it records the drudgery and petty resentments of army duty as well as the numb fury and exhausting din of battle. The protagonist's swings from romantic notions to self-conscious doubt to self-serving rationalizing to unprocessed emotion give the novel's realism a psychological dimension, and the peremptory imagery gives it a physical presence. But what is the point of the novel? Does Fleming redeem himself? Is there any such thing as heroism? The title itself is clearly ironic, but what is the value system that grounds the irony? And does the imagery cohere in a symbolism that supports an ideology? C., despite his disaffection from authority and his compassion for the poor, seems an almost perfectly apolitical, agnostic author. His focus on individual experience within a small social group grappling with large social problems generates ironies that define as they dissect the culture but then refocus on individual behavior, often with near-tragic effect, revealing heroism to be by nature ambivalent.

When C. insisted that the publisher of *The Black Riders* (1895), his first volume of poetry, leave in "all the ethical sense," "[a]ll the anarchy," it was as close as he would come in his career to a ideological stand, though he would also run afoul of the New York City Police for testifying in defense of a young Bowery woman suffering harassment at their hands. His poems—he called them his "pills"—encapsulate, in minidramas, mental monologues, and free-verse versions of Blakean rhetoric, an "anarchy" that is more metaphysical than political. Written over roughly the same period in which he wrote *The Red Badge of Courage,* the poetry of *The Black Riders,* like that in the later volume, *War Is Kind* (1899), is "prosaic" in the same sense that his fictional prose is "poetic," utilizing stylistic contrast to highlight intellectual and/or emotional conflict. His verse, like his fiction, is so original as to be uncategorizable.

With the success of his poetry and first novel, C. got journalistic work, traveling to the West and Mexico, to Greece, and to Cuba, in the last two cases to cover wars. Confronted with armed conflict, he was gratified to find that his imaginative descriptions of battle had been accurate, and, though a noncombatant, he proved courageous under fire. From these travels, and the resultant journalism, came his later major literary works, his short stories. His most well-known and successful stories, "The Blue Hotel" and "The Bride Came to Yellow Sky," are set in the West and explore the ironies, comic and deadly, of its myths; "Death and the Child" draws an episodic, symbolic contrast between war and child's play, a Greek's dream of glory and his disillusionment, the pastoral and the pathetic; and "The Open Boat," considered his finest story, recounts in spare, fictional form the perils C. and three comrades faced when shipwrecked off the Florida coast on a filibustering mission to Cuba. The *Whilomville Stories* (1900) recall the author's youth in Port Jervis; as in several of his Mexican and Bowery tales, characters recur, but the irony is applied with a much lighter touch. The central irony in the novella *The Monster* (1900), also set in Whilomville, is perhaps C.'s cruelest, indicting every group and individual in town, the entire society, in a conspiracy of moral cowardice.

The unalloyed virtues in C.'s work—courage, understanding, forgiveness—are also unorganized, and most often overwhelmed by vice, hypocrisy, denial, and delusion. But they stand, against war and nature, like the "Marines Signaling under Fire at Guantanamo," one of C.'s few first-person narratives. At the age of twenty-nine, living in England, where critical reception of his work was even more effusive than in America, and where he was not harassed by the police, the accumulated hardships of travel, usually to rugged, war-torn territory, and of survival by the pen, contributed to the tubercular attacks that finally killed him. He died in a sanitarium in the Black Forest and was buried in his native New Jersey.

BIBLIOGRAPHY: Berryman, J., *S. C.* (1950); Bloom, H., ed., *S. C.: Modern Critical Views* (1987); Bloom, H., ed., *S. C.'s The Red Badge of Courage: Modern Critical Interpretations* (1987); Cady, E. H., *S. C.* (1980); Nagel, J., *S. C. and Literary Impressionism* (1980); Stallman, R. W., *S. C.: A Biography* (1968)

DENNIS PAOLI

CRAPSEY, Adelaide

b. 9 September 1878, Brooklyn, New York; d. 8 October 1914, Rochester, New York

Had it not been for the efforts of Claude Bragdon, a family friend, C.'s cinquains, concise and precise poetic snapshots, might have been consigned to obscurity. The posthumous publication of *Verse* (1915) introduced the poetry of a reticent and retiring young woman to the younger generation of the early 1920s, and its second edition, published in 1922, ensured that recognition of C.'s poetry would continue throughout the 20th c.

C., whose reticent life style and poetry are most often compared to those of Emily DICKINSON, spent her brief life in the glow of more famous relatives and friends. Her father, the Reverend Algernon Crapsey, was a radical, and therefore infamous, Episcopal priest whose social gospel gave rise to formal charges of heresy. Her best friend, novelist and dramatist Jean Webster, enjoyed popular acclaim. During her first twenty years, C. lived quietly in support of family members and friends. Her literary pursuits during this period were typical of an aspiring and educated woman of the period: newspaper editorials, yearbook poems, and college skits and plays. It was while she attended Vassar College that C. became fascinated by the relationship between the structures of poems, particularly their syllables and stresses, and their meanings.

A series of teaching positions in private women's schools offered the solitude C. needed to pursue a distinctive syllabic study of English prosody. Cut short by encroaching tuberculosis, her investigations evolved into the creation of tightly structured cinquains, patterned after the Japanese haiku and tonka forms. The unrhymed pattern, which C. felt was as condensed as a poetic idea in English could be, depended on stresses incrementing by one in each of the first four lines and abruptly returning to a single stress in the final line. The distillations of idea and sensation that resulted from such control anticipated the British imagist movement espoused by T. E. Hulme, F. S. Flint, Ezra POUND, and Hilda DOOLITTLE. C.'s increasing debility motivated her to focus ever more tightly on an examination of the physical alterations she was experiencing and of the imminence of her own death, and the tightly controlled cinquain form required that her experiences be isolated from emotionalism and melodrama that characterized much of contemporaneous poetry.

Some of the cinquains that have been judged most successful at marrying the message with the form include: "November Night," "The Warning," "Niagara," and "Night Winds," which capture single moments in sound; "Triad" and "The Guarded Wound," which are metaphors for pain and death; "Amaze," "Madness" and "Trapped," which focus on the enigma of change. While the content of the cinquains is always serious and colored by the poet's deteriorating health, they are not morose. Two longer, autobiographical poems provide more detailed glimpses of C.'s sense of humor and her indomitable spirit: "Lines Addressed to My left Lung" and "To the Dead in the Grave-Yard under My Window."

Ironically, other than the early, less mature efforts that appeared in the *Kemper Hall Kodak, Vassar Miscellany,* and *Vassarion,* all of C.'s works were published posthumously. The first edition of *Verse,* poems selected by the author herself, appeared the year following her death. Seven years later, Bragdon edited an expanded edition of *Verse,* for which Jean Webster wrote a preface. *A Study in English Metrics,* C.'s unfinished linguistic study of English poems, appeared in 1918. To further illustrate and illuminate C.'s values and attitudes, the poet's letters have been combined with the collected poems in a single comprehensive edition.

BIBLIOGRAPHY: Alkalay-Gut, K., *Alone in the Dawn: The Life of A. C.* (1988); Butcher, E., *A. C.* (1979); Smith, S. S., ed., *The Complete Poems and Collected Letters of A. C.* (1976)

TERESA K. LEHR

CRAWFORD, F[rancis] Marion

b. 2 August 1854, Bagni di Lucca, Italy; d. 9 April 1909, Sorrento, Italy

The author of forty-four novels, four plays, three volumes of history, two travel books, thirty-two articles, and twenty miscellaneous pieces, C. was viewed as the quintessential American man of letters in the last two decades of the 19th and the first decade of the 20th c. On a lecture tour across the U.S. in 1898, he was hailed by the New Orleans *Daily Picayne* as "the greatest living American novelist." The San Francisco *Chronicle* concurred, calling C. "the first novelist of America." The *Atlantic Monthly* claimed that his novel *Corleone* (1897) was "difficult to overpraise," and the public shared the enthusiasm. *A Cigarette-Maker's Romance* (1891) sold over 150,000 copies in England and still more in America; *Cecilia: A Story of Modern Rome* (1902) sold nearly 100,000 copies. *The White Sister* (1909) was dramatized and twice made into a motion picture, in 1923 with Lillian Gish and Ronald Colman, and a decade later with Helen Hayes and Clark Gable. Although virtually all of C.'s work remains in print, his critical reputation has sharply declined since his death.

C.'s late-20th-c. status as a minor figure is largely the consequence of his approach to fiction. In response to William Dean HOWELL's *Criticism and Fiction,* which defended the realist movement, C. published *The Novel: What It Is* (1893), expressing his preference for romance. "The first object of the novel is to amuse and interest the reader," C. wrote, and C. believed that the novel best achieved that aim by representing the world "in such a way as to make it seem more agreeable and interesting than it actually is."

Rejecting the social concerns of Howells and the psychological explorations of Henry JAMES, C. filled his book with incident, much of it set in exotic locations, and ideal characters. Even in his own day, C. recognized that he represented an older tradition, writing to Isabella GARDNER, "The old fashioned novel is really dead, and nothing can revive it or make anybody care for it again" (May 18, 1896).

Exoticism came easily to C., who drew heavily on his own experiences. His first novel, *Mr. Isaacs: A Tale of Modern India,* grew out of a story that C. had told his uncle about an encounter with Alexander M. Jacob, whom the author had met at Simla, in the Himalayan Mountains, while editing the *India Herald* in Allahabad on the Ganges River. Nearly half of C.'s novels are set in Italy, where he was born and where he lived most of his life. On November 29, 1908, C. wrote to Gardner of *The Primadonna* (1908), "Of course, there is fiction in the stories, but there is more truth and many of the scenes are taken, whole, from life." Paul Griggs, who appears in this and several other of C.'s novels, is largely autobiographical. C.'s Catholicism to which he converted about 1880 also colors his work.

While his fiction was thus grounded in reality, he added a strong dose of melodrama. *Paul Patoff* (1887) is filled with improbable incidents ranging across Germany, England, and Turkey, beginning with Alexander Patoff's disappearance from the gallery of the mosque of Agia Sofia. He subtitled *The Witch of Prague* (1891) "A Fantastic Tale," as it is, with hypnotism, mistaken identity, and attempts to embalm the living. *Corleone* depends on mistaken identity and the confidentiality of the confessional.

In addition to his books with contemporary settings drawn on his own wide travel, C. wrote historical fiction. Though he had begun his first historical novel, *Zoroaster* (1885), in 1883, his 1898 lecture tour demonstrated a large audience for history, and C. responded with a spate of novels and nonfiction based on solid research. At the time of his death, C. was working on a history of Rome between the 13th and 16th cs. He had hoped that this project, which he believed would run to ten volumes, would insure his literary fame, but no volumes were published.

Though C.'s fame has been eclipsed by Howells, James, Samuel Langhorne CLEMENS, and naturalist writers like Stephen CRANE, whose approach to fiction C. rejected, his works delighted tens of thousands of readers in his own day. The enduring popularity of the romance suggests that despite the critics, readers continue to enjoy the kind of fiction that C. produced and championed.

BIBLIOGRAPHY: Elliot, M. H., *My Cousin, F. M. C.* (1934); Moran, J. C., *An F. M. C. Companion* (1981); Pilkington, J., *F. M. C.* (1964)

JOSEPH ROSENBLUM

CREELEY, Robert
b. 21 May 1926, Arlington, Massachusetts

Following a somewhat diverse path as a chicken farmer, Harvard student sans degree, fugitive publisher, and ambulance driver in Burma during World War II, C. found his metier as a theoretician of the possibilities of language when he was invited by his then epistolary friend the poet Charles OLSON to edit the *Black Mountain Review* in 1953. Olson was the rector of the now legendary Black Mountain College, and in his company C. began an exploration of the poetics of what Olson called "Projective Verse," or composition in an open field in which traditional elements of form and structure were augmented by a conviction that, as C. put it, "there's an appropriate way of saying something inherent in the thing to be said."

His first major collection, *For Love* (1962), is a reflective expression of several very intense erotic relationships, the "love" that C. calls "like nothing else on earth," but which generated—as the poet-publisher Cid Corman called them—some of the "unhappiest love poems of our time." A taut form, intense but tentative utterance, moods of frustration mingled with an almost poignant vulnerability and moments of dark humor marked poems actualizing C.'s conviction that Ezra POUND's observation, "Only emotion endures," could be realized in terms of radically new organizations of poetic syntax.

The exploration of language as a concentration on its most fundamental components was carried further in *Words* (1967), which attempted to intersect the processes of the mind at the instant of creative perception, while *Pieces* (1969) collected, as in an extended journal, the almost daily, especially nonreflective writing C. had done over a period of time without any specific ordering or organizing strategy. Because they respected his seriousness and obvious capability, some conventional critics were disturbed by what they regarded as the excessively minimalist nature of this volume, but C. used their pieces as a necessary preparation for *Later* (1979), a book which indicated a ripening and widening of the poet's sensibility and style.

C. returned to the power of an individual poem in *Later*, but his characteristic expression of a moment of intense thought or feeling was tempered by an awareness of the poet's life as an accumulation of significant occasions. The next collection, *Mirrors* (1983), continued C.'s use of a pared-down, almost elliptical mode of utterance, a spare and urgent lyricism often conveying a kind of "luminous austerity" but one balanced by a degree of acceptance that suggested a kind of coming to terms with the poet's intense responses to the patterns of his life. C. continued this

mode in *Windows* (1990), where his moods of quiet, almost meditative reflection on the central circumstances of an often strained life are mingled with what are clearly ineradicable doubts about the nature of existence. The range of poetry in this collection is a testament to C.'s virtuosity, offering many examples of his structural expertise, recalling work from earlier books but in inventive, original variations.

In *Echoes* (1994), his sense of time's passage and the accumulated associations of familiar places informs the poems with a gravity that effectively conveys the effects of age and the span of the poet's life, but the often bristling energy that pulses through C.'s work is also evident here, a function of his continuing, characteristic capacity for the location of carefully chosen, individual words in a very specific position in the poem. At this point in the poet's writing life, it is apparent that what critic Charles Molesworth calls the "hard-won specificity of his voice, its timbre, its tremors" is unique—an impressive accomplishment in an era of unparalleled poetic production. C.'s poetry is distinguished by the manner in which the placement of words—themselves familiar as part of the American vernacular—resonate and interact within the form of the poem in a continuing exploration of the unfolding potential of poetic syntax.

BIBLIOGRAPHY: Clark, T., *R. C. and the Genius of the American Common Place* (1993); Edelberg, C. D., *R. C.'s Poetry: A Critical Introduction* (1978); Ford, A. L., *R. C.*, 1978; Terrell, C. F., ed., *R. C.: The Poet's Workshop* (1984); Wilson, J., ed., *R. C.'s Life and Work: A Sense of Increment* (1987)

LEON LEWIS

CREVECOEUR, Michel-Guillaume Jean de
b. 31 January 1735, Caen, France; d. 12 November 1813, Sarcellas, France

C., better known as J. Hector St. John de Crevecoeur, is one of the most influential interpreters of American life in the 18th c. In his classic work, *Letters from an American Farmer* (1782), C. attempts to explain for his readers the essence of "that new man," the American. Although C.'s vision is ambiguous and sometimes contradictory and his prose style is, to modern tastes, frequently overwrought, his portrait of the life of the American farmer became part of the European myth of the new world and was incorporated into later American attempts at national self-definition.

C.'s life and literary career were filled with vicissitudes. Born into the minor nobility of France, educated in France and England, C. sailed for America in 1755 and served with the French army during the French and Indian War. For reasons that remain unclear, C.

abruptly resigned his commission in 1759 and sailed to the British colonies of North America. There he adopted the name of J. Hector St. John and traveled widely along the sea coast and in the wilderness—though just how extensive his travels were remains a matter of dispute—before marrying and settling on a farm in Orange County, New York. From 1769 to 1779, C. lived the life of an American farmer; during these years he also found time to write a series of essays and sketches about America which became the basis for his major work. When C. left America in 1779 for England and, later, France, he took a trunk full of these sketches with him. A selection of them, published in England as *Letters from an American Farmer,* gained rapid and widespread popularity.

In France, C. associated with the intellectuals surrounding Madame d'Houdetot, reacquainted himself with the French language and current literary tastes, gained the attention of Benjamin FRANKLIN, and was appointed French consul to New York. He also published a French version of his book, *Lettres d'un Cultivateur Americain* (1784); a revised, expanded *Lettres* appeared in 1787. C.'s diplomatic career was brought to a halt by the French Revolution, and he spent most of the latter part of his life living quietly in retirement. During these years, he completed a final attempt to interpret the significance of the American experiment, *Voyage dans la Haute Pensylvanie et dans l'Etat de New York (1801).* He died leaving a number of unpublished manuscripts, some of them evidently written during his years in America. In the 20th c., a selection of these previously unpublished essays and sketches was published under the title *Sketches of Eighteenth-Century America* (1925).

Although C.'s central work, *Letters from an American Farmer,* was widely read and much translated in the 18th c., it was all but forgotten in the next as new accounts of America superseded it. In the 20th c., its popularity revived, and it is now viewed as a classic work of colonial American literature. In the *Letters,* C. interprets for his contemporaries the significance of the creation in America of a new society. The first few letters create an idyllic portrait of the bucolic life of the work's invented narrator, Farmer James. Farmer James is a minimally educated, native American farmer who ascribes his happiness to the mild laws under which he lives in America, to the absence in America of extremes of wealth and poverty, and especially to his ownership of and closeness to the soil which he farms. Although the portrait of James's felicity contains a few jarring notes, the dominant impression in the early letters is of ideal harmony between the American farmer and the natural world in which he lives.

In the work's crucial letter, "What is an American," C. attempts to provide a theoretical explanation of the sources of the happiness of the American farmer. Building upon neo-Lockean theory, C. argues that humanity is the product of its environment. Given easy ownership of land and a mild government, European immigrants can, if they are industrious, be transformed into that "new man," the American farmer. When men escape European evils and prejudices to start anew, they can be regenerated by the independence and rewards of owning and farming American land. Although C. places limits on America's regenerative powers, his central vision in the early letters is optimistic. He looks forward to a future in which European immigrants, freed from the religious, class and political evils of Europe, will be melted into a harmoniously prosperous and tolerant society. Later letters introduce serious doubts about Farmer James's optimism. Confronted with the evils of slavery on a visit to South Carolina, the narrator despairs of mankind and sees the earth as a place of punishment rather than felicity. The *Letters* end with Farmer James, unnerved and terrified by the violence of the American Revolution, planning to join the Indians beyond the frontier in a desperate attempt to reestablish the idyll that war has destroyed. The disparities in Farmer James's responses to America remain unresolved in the *Letters.*

Early commentators on the *Letters* viewed the work as a naive, impromptu response to American experience. More recent critics have emphasized the conscious artistry and the ambiguity of the work. Current critical debate focuses on the issue of whether the pessimism of some of the later letters is designed to undermine and destroy the optimistic vision of earlier ones or whether the two visions of America simply remain in unresolved suspension. C.'s other works offer no resolution of this dilemma. The late *Voyage* provides both idealistic and pessimistic visions of American experience, and the works published posthumously in the *Sketches,* while they throw light on C.'s loyalist sympathies during the Revolution, do not present a unified vision. C.'s *Letters* remains a significant work in American literature in part because of the intensity with which it conveys its author's conflicting interpretations of the American experience.

BIBLIOGRAPHY: Mitchell, J. P., *St. J. de C.* (1916); Philbrick, T., *St. J. de C.* (1970)

DAVID M. LARSON

CREWS, Harry
b. 7 June 1935, Bacon County, Georgia

In his memoir, C. recounts the circumstances surrounding his birth and beginnings in rural Bacon

County, Georgia. C. has drawn on this rich legacy in his work, especially as a mimic of rural speech, throughout a long career as an essentially Southern writer and storyteller, a career that has earned him a place in the first rank of contemporary Southern writers. Retired in 1996 after nearly three decades as a writing teacher at Florida, C. has suffered and stormed his way through a lifetime of extremes that has provided the material for his major works: thirteen novels, the autobiography, and two volumes of collected nonfiction. Following a stint in the Marine Corps and an aborted career as a student at Florida, C. embarked on a rowdy motorcycle odyssey that occasioned the unpublished *There's Something about Being Straddle of a Thing*. Over the years, C.'s legendary exploits and public persona have created a cult of personality comparable in weight to his literary reputation.

C.'s work reveals a concern with the individual's relationship to his personal past, and represents that relationship in the context of a present moment severed by poverty, progress, or human falsity from values capable of sustaining hope. Two gigantic obsessions inhabit C.'s work: the grotesque and the masculine. A consuming interest in the grotesque—"freaks" visibly misshapen and characters deformed by inner demons and drives—characterizes his novels. C.'s world abounds in cruelty and violence—with men and women seeking an elusive sense of the "rightness of things"—and characters often in the grip of an impossible love. A brooding observer of mob psychology and an unblinking chronicler of human suffering, C. is nevertheless recognized as a talented comic novelist.

His first novel, *The Gospel Singer* (1968), contains C.'s most significant treatment of race in the South through the intertwined narratives of the "Gospel Singer" and Willalee Bookatee Hull, a poor black accused of the rape and murder of the white MaryBell Carter. The novel begins C.'s career long examination of the grotesque in the depiction of a traveling carnival of freaks, and ends with a symbolic double lynching of Willalee and the title character. An early masterpiece, *Naked in Garden Hills* (1969), confirms him as a master of the grotesque in the tale of "Fat Man," the 600-pound heir to the devastated industrial landscape of Garden Hills, Florida, and Jester, an unusually diminutive black jockey. C. brilliantly realizes the agrarian/industrial conflict in the South, and satirizes the post-industrial world emerging from the ashes of modernity. In *This Thing Don't Lead to Heaven* (1970), Jeremy Tetley confronts death without religion, and Jefferson Davis Monroe gropes after an improbable love.

Karate is a Thing of the Spirit (1971) marks C.'s first sustained depiction of a physical discipline, a motif that characterizes much of his later work, in the story of John Kaimon, a Mississippian who joins a bizarre karate cult seeking the order and meaning modern life has failed to deliver. *Car* (1972) depicts Herman Mack's comical effort to eat an automobile, but is also an eccentric love story in the C.'s manner. In *The Hawk is Dying* (1973), George Gattling attempts to make sense of his life and the death of his nephew by training hawks, finding in birds of prey an antidote to emotional need and ambiguity. The narrator of *The Gypsy's Curse* (1974), Marvin Molar, is a trademark C. freak, a paraplegic performance artist who makes a living balancing on his hands and fingers for crowds. It is a story of both love and obsession, much like C.'s finest literary work, *A Feast of Snakes* (1976), which chronicles the descent into despair of Joe Lon Mackey. Macabre and cruel, the novel is also a compelling meditation on love, with a shockingly violent and ambiguous resolution to the narrative action.

The next ten years saw three works of nonfiction appear. *A Childhood: The Biography of a Place* (1978), is a hauntingly beautiful achievement of autobiography and the storyteller's art. C.'s essays from various magazines were published in two main collections, *Blood and Grits* (1979), and *Florida Frenzy* (1982). The books form a study in C.'s immersion in the cult of masculinity, including interviews, studies of American bloodsports, writing, cars, and sexual politics.

All We Need of Hell (1987), a sequel to *A Feast of Snakes,* narrates the existential ordeal and breakthrough of Duffy Deeter. *The Knockout Artist* (1988) mines a masochistic vein in the story of a failed boxer, Eugene Biggs, who knocks himself out for money in the seedy New Orleans underworld. *Body* (1990) is notable for its female protagonist, Dorothy Turnipseed, a poor white refugee on the verge of success as a female bodybuilder. Another of C.'s "grit" heroes, Pete Butcher, finds healing and salvation in Scar *Lover* (1992). C.'s novel *The Mulching of America* (1995) follows traveling salesman Hickum Looney in a satire on big business and the failed cultural promise of America.

BIBLIOGRAPHY: Jeffrey, D. K., *A Grit's Triumph: Essays on the Works of H. C.* (1983); Hargraves, M., *H. C.: A Bibliography* (1986); Noble, D. R., "The Future of Southern Writing," in Rubin, L. D., Jr., et al., eds., *The History of Southern Literature* (1985): 578–88; Sauve, D., *The H. C. Website and Bibliography* (1996)

VINCENT J. BREWTON

CRICHTON, [John] Michael
b. 23 October 1942, Chicago, Illinois

C. supported himself through medical school by writing thrillers under the pseudonyms John Lange and

Jeffery Hudson. One of the novels he wrote during this period, *A Case of Need* (1968), received an Edgar Award from the Mystery Writers of America. And although C. did, in fact, receive his M.D. in 1969, he realized that his true passion lay in writing, and he devoted himself to a literary career. Since that time, he has established himself as a popular novelist—primarily of SCIENCE FICTION and suspense novels—an engaging nonfiction writer, and a screenwriter and film director.

The strength of C.'s novels lies in their pacing and verisimilitude. While his characters are generally unmemorable—basically two-dimensional vehicles for advancing the storyline—his plots are riveting; the action moves along at a nonstop pace, and the characters are forced to deal with one seemingly insoluble problem after another. C.'s medical training and his inquisitive mind have led him to read extensively in a variety of fields, and—although he claims to do no special research for his novels—this reading manifests itself in the air of reality that infuses his fiction. Whether his novels deal with a train robbery in Victorian England or about the cloning of dinosaurs, the fantastic details are presented with such precision that many readers have wondered just how much is fiction and how much reality. As C. has said, his writing is often "a game of trying to be true to what you *can* know, and trying to give the impression you weren't making up very much, when you were, in fact, making up everything."

C.'s first novel written under his own name, *The Andromeda Strain* (1969), deals with the attempts of a team of scientists to halt the spread of a deadly virus from outer space. This was the first of many suspense novels to deal with science and technology. *The Terminal Man* (1972) is, according to C., a sort of modern reworking of the Frankenstein story. *Congo* (1980) deals with a team of explorers and their "talking" gorilla, Amy, who speaks in sign language, searching through the jungle for a cache of rare diamonds. *Sphere* (1987) is about the underwater recovery of an alien spacecraft. And *Jurassic Park* (1990) and its sequel, *The Lost World* (1995), resurrect dinosaurs through the technology of cloning. What all these science fiction novels, as well as the more "realistic" *The Great Train Robbery* (1975), have in common are tightly constructed plots and a focus on the problem-solving skills of the central characters.

While C.'s interest in technology has continued unabated, two recent novels have moved "out of the laboratory" and into the world of corporate America. *Rising Sun* (1992) is a murder mystery that also deals with issues of international trade; a call girl is killed in the American headquarters of a major Japanese corporation, and the detective investigating the case must deal with difficulties caused by the cultural differences between the U.S. and Japan. In *Disclosure* (1994), C. investigates the controversial topic of sexual harassment, but he turns the tables as it is a man who accuses a woman of harassment. Once again, however, the social issue is explored against the backdrop of a high-tech thriller.

C. has produced significant nonfiction, including *Five Patients: The Hospital Explained* (1970), which deals with the medical establishment; *Electronic Life: How to Think about Computers* (1983), an early attempt to make computers "accessible" to the average person; and *Travels* (1988), an autobiographical work. C. has also written extensively for film, producing screenplays of his own novels *The Great Train Robbery* (1978), *Rising Sun* (1993, with Philip Kaufman and Michael Backes), and *Jurassic Park* (1993, with David Koepp), as well as *Coma* (1977), based on the novel by Robin Cook, and original screenplays, notably *Looker* (1981) and *Runaway* (1984). He has also directed movies and was the co-creator of the television series *ER*.

C.'s novels are not great literature, but they are undeniably entertaining. His use of technological details and his lucid and engaging explications of scientific theory have made him one of the most popular novelists in contemporary American fiction.

BIBLIOGRAPHY: See, F. G., "'Something Reflective': Technology and Visual Pleasure," *JPFT* 22 (Winter 1995): 162–71; Trembley, E. A., *M. C.: A Critical Companion* (1996)

JASON BERNER

CROCKETT, Davy [David]
b. 17 August 1786, Greene County, Tennessee; d. 6 March 1836, the Alamo, San Antonio

C., man and myth, has had a profound influence on American humor. Born in Greene County, Tennessee, C. rose from humble origins to eventually serve in the U.S. Senate (1827) and his actions, both real and apocryphal, have served to illustrate the essence of the American backwoods character. Although several works were attributed to him during his lifetime, C.'s larger-than-life quality blossomed with the publication of the *C.'s Almanacks* (1835–56). It has become increasingly difficult to separate the real from the fantastic in the writings of C., but it seems clear that the man whose motto was, "Be always sure you're right—THEN GO AHEAD!", influenced the style of Thomas Bangs THORPE, George Washington HARRIS, and among others, Samuel Langhorne CLEMENS.

C., after spending his youthful years as a laborer, married early, and between 1813 and 1815 served as an occasional scout during the Creek War under the command of Andrew Jackson, one who would later become his political opponent. First elected to the Tennessee Legislature in 1821, C. was reelected in 1823, and then on a campaign based on humor and common sense was elected to the U.S. Senate. C.'s talent for public speaking triggered an enthusiastic response from journalists, making him a national heroic, as well as comic, figure.

In 1833, the first of C.'s books (probably written by Matthew St. Claire), *The Life and Adventures of Colonel D. C. of West Tennessee,* was published. It contains many of C.'s favorite anecdotes and tales of the campaign trail. Four other books were attributed to C., including a fanciful biography of Martin Van Buren (1835) and a posthumously released work, *Col. C.'s Exploits and Adventures in Texas* (1836), actually written by Richard Penn Smith in an effort to capitalize on C.'s recent demise at the Alamo. Interestingly, *Exploits* was purported to have been found on his body after the battle. These publications did much to turn the historical C. into legend, a task completed by the *Almanacks,* whose content ranges from out-and-out plagiarism to incredibly vivid tall tales. Other books attributed to C. are *A Narrative of the Life of D. C. of the State of Tennessee* (1834, by C. and Thomas Chilton) and *An Account of Col. C.'s Tour to the North and Down East* (1836, probably written by Augustin Smith Clayton).

BIBLIOGRAPHY: Clark, W. B., "D. C.," in Trachtenberg, S., ed., *DLB,* vol. 11, part 1, *American Humanists, 1800–1950* (1982): 89–94; Shackford, J. A., *D. C., the Man and the Legend* (1956)

MICHAEL J. PETTENGELL

CROTHERS, Rachel
b. 12 December 1870, Bloomington, Illinois; d. 6 July 1958, Danbury, Connecticut

C. participated as playwright and director in many of the important developments in American drama during the early 20th c. Having moved to New York from Bloomington, Illinois to study acting at the age of seventeen, she made her professional acting debut in 1897, had her first Broadway production as a playwright with *The Three of Us* in 1906, and directed her own *Myself Bettina* in 1908. Her first literary success was in the writing of discussion plays about the issues arising from the emergence of the "New Woman" at the turn of the century. *A Man's World* (1910) was recognized as a powerful attack on the

double standard, and her discussion of the conflicts arising from the demands of a career and the demands of marriage and a family in *He and She* (1912) was substantial enough for the play to be revived in 1920 and again in 1973.

During the early 1920s, C. turned from the serious discussion play to social comedy, and through this vehicle made some telling criticisms of the Jazz Age and its values in *Nice People* (1921), *Expressing Willie* (1924), and *Let Us Be Gay* (1929). C.'s concern with marriage and its abuses was perennial, and received effective treatment throughout her career. In *Mary the Third* (1923), she produced a comedy pervaded by discussion of the differing views of marriage held by the generations of the young flapper Mary and her mother and grandmother, exposing the unhappiness that could arise from all three. In *When Ladies Meet* (1932), she wrote one of the first American comedies in which divorce, not marriage, is treated as the desired outcome for the characters. Her last produced play, *Susan and God* (1937), was a light satire on the underlying social attitudes that made society ladies into converts to the so-called Oxford movement.

BIBLIOGRAPHY: Flexner, E., *American Playwrights, 1918–1938* (1939); Gottlieb, L., *R. C.* (1979); Lindroth, C., and J. Lindroth, *R. C.: A Research and Production Sourcebook* (1995); Murphy, B., *American Realism and American Drama* (1987)

BRENDA MURPHY

CRUZ, Victor Hernandez
b. 6 February 1949, Aguas Buenas, Puerto Rico

Through the syncretic use of *salsa* musical rhythms and Spanish syntax, the poetry and prose of C. creates a transformation and revitalization of literary English. His works explore the relationship between the environments—both natural and cultural—of the U.S. urban milieu and the rural setting of island life in Puerto Rico while frequently exhibiting the influence of minimalism and concrete poetry.

C. moved from the village of Aguas Buenas, Puerto Rico to New York's Lower East Side when he was five years old. Yet the tastes, smells, sounds, and rhythms of his home remained stitched firmly within his heart and serve as a continuous source of inspiration. He published his first collection of poems, *Snaps* (1968), at nineteen and gained immediate national attention. The poems in this collection display the rhythm of jazz poetry and the political optimism of a young man beginning to test his power and place in the U.S. The speaker in these mostly narrative poems often uses street talk and surrealist humor to depict the culturally diverse Lower East Side of Manhattan. *Snaps* thematically focuses on the tension and/or interplay between the paved city and a natural world of mangoes and mountains, on the power of *salsa* music, and on travel, especially within the city via subways, car, and foot. These themes remain prominent in the poet's successive works.

In *Mainland* (1973), the theme of travel is expanded from intracity travel to interstate and ultimately international migrations. The settings of these poems move from New York to the Midwest, California, the Southwest, and then to Puerto Rico, which for C. represents a mythical return to origins. The collection ends back in New York, signifying a recentering of the self in the reality of New York urban life. One of the most notable poems in this collection, "The Man Who Came to the Last Floor," exemplifies C.'s characteristic use of surrealist humor in its description of an Anglo New York City policeman who found himself with a mango tree growing out of his head. This image communicates C.'s underlying poetics of a revitalization of the urban scape which both originates from and depends upon the Latino community in the U.S.

Tropicalization (1976) continues to bring much of the Caribbean to New York through image and rhythm. Many of these poems are more lyric than his previous works, and the collection also includes some of his first published prose poems.

The works in *By Lingual Wholes* (1982) signify a growing sophistication in C.'s language use and wordplay. The title itself exemplifies this sophistication, both in the phrase "by lingual," a sound-alike for "bilingual," and in the choice of "wholes," which can mean totality or, as in, "holes," absence. The wordplays and double meanings found throughout the book function as yet another way for C. to explore the themes of migration and the commingling of cultures. Specific techniques used to achieve this effect include writing Spanish sayings in English and using Spanish/English sound-alikes. These techniques set C. apart from the oppositional linguistic dialectic prevalent in the earliest bilingual poetry of U.S. Latinos. Just as cultures converge in *By Lingual Wholes,* so do the past and present, achieving a sense of cultural empowerment through a living connection to history.

C. presents his most overtly political poems, criticizing the Puerto Rican government and the CIA, in "Islandis: The Age of Seashells," a book-length section appearing in *Rhythm, Content and Flavor: New and Selected Poems* (1989). "Islandis" also continues to juxtapose and interweave images of nature with the urban.

The sense of spontaneity, the barrio language and the irony that characterizes C.'s earlier works is tempered in *Red Beans* (1991) by a more mature, reflective voice. The resulting poems contain denser, more carefully crafted language while retaining the sensual beauty and allure of C.'s tropical sensibilities. *Red Beans* also contains prose pieces rich with poetic language. The color "red," a favorite symbol of C.'s which appears in even his earliest poems, takes center stage in *Red Beans* as an emblem for mood, vitality, urgency, and indigenism. In this book, a connection to the indigenous shines through the Spanish and Afro-Caribbean overlay, as though C. had caught the Taino pictographs in the Puerto Rican rocks singing to the accompaniment of African drums and Spanish *guitarras*. The poems in *Red Beans* regularly employ the use of synaesthesia to express the interlinking of these three ethnicities in the Caribbean person's life.

With the recent publication of *Panoramas* (1997), a collection of new poetry, C. continues to act as a major force in what he himself has termed the ongoing "tropicalization" of American culture. His poetry has evolved from the fragmented, violent images of urban life in *Snaps* through a dynamic expression of multiculturalism in *By Lingual Wholes* to a resurrection of the native elements of his background in *Red Beans.* While one could fault C. for his repeated description of women as merely fragments of persons (skirt, eyes, dress), he has undeniably done much valuable work to diversify and thereby energize American literature through a sensuous commingling between mainstream American culture and Caribbean culture. C.'s works illuminate the benefits to mainstream America of this commingling and so deny a state of victimization to Puerto Rican immigrants and U.S. Latinos in general, placing them instead in a position of importance, value, and power.

BIBLIOGRAPHY: Aparicio, F. R., "Salsa, Maracas and Baile: Latin Popular Music in the Poetry of V. H. C.," *MELUS* 16 (Spring 1989): 43–58; Moyers, B., *The Language of Life* (1995); Waisman, S. G., "The Body as Migration," *BR/RB* 19 (1 May 1994): 188–92

MARIA MELENDEZ

CUBISM

While narrowly defined as a school in the visual arts led by Pablo Picasso and Georges Braque in Paris (ca. 1907–25), cubism may well be the most important aesthetic development in the 20th c., influencing not only painting and sculpture, but cinematography, architecture, and literature as well. In terms of American literature, the impact of cubism can be seen most clearly in much of the avant garde work produced during the two world wars—although it can still be felt today, illustrated by the Language poets. At least during certain phases of their careers, Gertrude STEIN, William Carlos WILLIAMS, T. S. ELIOT, Mina Loy, William FAULKNER, Ezra POUND, E. E. CUMMINGS, and Wallace STEVENS could all be described as cubist writers.

Given this diversity, it is useful to remember that even within the visual arts, cubism was an extremely complex movement that developed rapidly through almost contradictory stages. Beginning as an art movement committed to analyzing form (in part as a reaction against the amorphous quality of impressionism), cubism quickly evolved into an aesthetic mode that fractured form, shattered traditional linear perspective (through multiple points of view), and challenged the very idea of *representation* itself (most acutely through the use of *collage* and *papier collé*). Somewhat oversimplified, the difference between the early and late forms of cubism can be summarized as "analytic" cubism (which alternately accents or dissects the inherent geometrical forms of objects) and "synthetic" cubism (in which fragments of forms are reincorporated as a new aesthetic object). In this regard, Cézanne is the most immediate precursor of analytic cubism, whereas Surrealism is the descendant of synthetic cubism.

Given this complexity, it is likely that such diversity (even seeming contradictions) would appear in cubist literature as well, as various authors responded to different facets or techniques of cubism. Thus, Williams's "The Red Wheelbarrow" or Stevens's "Thirteen Ways of Looking at a Blackbird" (both of which are constructed by small cubelike stanzas thematically focused on the question of perception itself) may be accurately called analytic cubist poems, whereas Pound's *Cantos* or Eliot's *The Waste Land* (both of which are characterized by temporal disruption and multiple voices—including fragments from other texts and languages) can be seen as verbal counterparts to synthetic cubism. George OPPEN's *Discrete Series* falls somewhere in between analytic and synthetic interpretations of verbal cubism, as does Faulkner's *The Sound and the Fury.*

Nevertheless, it is important to admit that the terms *cubist literature* and *cubist poetry* are still open to critical debate. In part because of the theoretical problems of transferring a term used to define one medium to another (Picasso precluded the possibilities of cubist mathematics, music, and psychoanalysis as well), and in part because such writers as Apollinaire and Cummings denied being cubist poets, several critics have rejected the possibility of cubist literature in general and cubist poetry in particular. Still, it is worth noting that as a term *cubist literature* was accepted critically as early as 1941 (in Georges Edouard Lemâitre's *From Cubism to Surrealism in French Literature*) and popu-

larly as early as 1928 (Dorothy Sayers describes one of her characters as a "cubist poet") and has subsequently gained increasing critical acceptance. Wendy Steiner has even argued that cubism most accurately describes the 20th-c. critical temperament.

However, in the most specific terms, the impact of cubism on the American scene can be traced most directly to the famous Armory Show of 1913 (shown in New York and subsequently in Chicago and Boston), to the emigration of such cubist painters as Francis Picabia and Marcel Duchamp during World War I, and even before that to the reproduction of some Picasso's drawings in Alfred Stieglitz's *Camera Work* in 1911 (and the showing of the same works in corresponding Secession Gallery). While the critical reception of these books was quite hostile (one New York critic described Picasso as demonic), Steiglitz in particular tried repeatedly to introduce and defend this new artistic development to the American audience. Most importantly here, he printed Gertrude Stein's prose piece "Picasso," noting that she was doing *with* the verbal medium what Picasso was doing with the visual one. This heightened sense of language as a medium, to be manipulated as an object (especially typographically, and therefore, visually), is one of the first marks of cubist literature in America that rapidly began to be explored in a number of small magazines. In addition to Steiglitz's famous *291* (which specifically discusses the problem of achieving in language the kind of "simultanism" achieved in cubism), *Others* was founded in 1915 and printed some of the most experimental and earliest cubist poetry written in this country. One issue in particular, which notably includes Stevens's "Thirteen Ways of Looking at a Blackbird," is specifically called "For the Mind's Eye / Not to Be Read Aloud." In addition to Stevens and Williams, Mina Loy (though British-born) published early cubist poems in *Others*—most notably, her volume-length *Songs to Joannes.*

The "revolution of the word"—as it would be called in a special issue of the Paris journal *Transition* some years later—encouraged by these early works had an almost immediate and extensive impact on American literature. The poetry published in *The Dial* and the *Little Review,* for example, became much more avant garde (both journals introducing visual art as well). In fact, *The Dial* first published Cummings (that most quintessentially cubist poet) in 1920. Of all the American journals, however, perhaps *Blues,* published between 1929 and 1930, most consistently prints cubist poets, including Louis ZUKOFSKY, Parker Tyler, Kenneth REXROTH, Gertrude Stein, and William Carlos Williams, among others. *Pagany,* founded only a couple of years later, proves to be a close cousin, publishing almost exactly the same poets, though with somewhat more variety.

Still, it is ultimately impossible to discuss American cubist literature without mentioning its on-going international involvement. In addition to such writers as Eliot and Pound, whose expatriation makes them somewhat difficult to label as American, many American authors of this period (such as Ernest HEMINGWAY and Faulkner), traveled in Europe extensively—both absorbing and influencing aesthetic developments. Perhaps more intriguing is the fact that even for writers who remained in America (such as Williams and Stevens), the international aspect of this new aesthetic was unavoidable through the means and modes of publication itself. Pound, for example, served as the foreign editor to Margaret Anderson's the *Little Review* for a number of years (introducing *Ulysses* in serial form). Alfred KREYMBORG, who had founded *Others,* began the well-known *Broom* with Harold Loeb only two years after *Others* folded. Published in Italy for economic reasons, *Broom* printed poems, stories, essays, and reproductions of visual art by a wide array of artists, including Joseph Stella, Stein, Cummings, Williams, and Stevens—as well as Juan Gris, Apollinaire, Picasso, and Jacques Lipchitz, among others. Similarly, *Secession,* though founded by American Gorham Munson, was first produced in Australia, printing a range of authors from Tristan Tzara to Williams. Most of the American journals which published cubist poetry also published European authors as well. In general, not only are media and genre distinctions (as in the visual poem and the prose/poem) broken down by the cubist movement, but, appropriately, national boundaries are fractured as well.

BIBLIOGRAPHY: Brogan, J. V., *Part of the Climate: American Cubist Poetry* (1990); Fry, E., *Cubism* (1978); Golding, J., *Cubism: A History and an Analysis, 1907–1914* (1988); Gray, C., *Cubist Aesthetic Theories* (1953)

JACQUELINE VAUGHT BROGAN

CULLEN, Countee
b. 30 May 1903, Louisville, Kentucky; d. 9 January 1946, New York City

C., one of the major writers of the Harlem Renaissance, emerges today a deeply confounding figure. Heaped with praise in his spectacularly successful youth by mainly white critics, he was disdained by the African American critics of the 1960s, a critical deestimation that lingers in the general current view of C. as a central yet frustratingly naive and derivative poet of

his moment. He was an exemplum of the "Négritude" of the Harlem Renaissance—the quest to reclaim the power of a mythic mother Africa—and yet his major poetic influence was John Keats; in fact, he observed, in the forward he wrote to the poetry anthology he edited, "Caroling Dusk," that "[a]s heretical as it may sound, Negro poets may have more to gain from the rich background of English and American poetry than from any nebulous atavistic yearnings toward an African inheritance." And yet the poet made this "nebulous" reaching for an "African inheritance" a central component of his work, however problematically or ambivalently treated.

After being passed around among relatives, C. was eventually adopted, in 1918, by the Reverend Frederick Asbury Cullen and Carolyn Mitchell Cullen of the Salem Methodist Episcopal Church in Harlem. The Cullen household—given the fact that the Cullens were both devoutly religious and actively political (the Reverend Cullen was president of the Harlem chapter of the NAACP)—and the atmosphere of World War I-era New York City—where many blacks had migrated to fill positions left vacant by white soldiers—both deeply shaped the young C.'s poetic sensibility. In 1923, the precociously gifted C. won second place in the national Witter Bynner Poetry Contest for a poem he had written while a sophomore at New York University, "The Ballad of the Brown Girl." This is an emblematic poem in the C. oeuvre—dealing with nobility and miscegenation, eroticism and death—whose titular figure is descended from royal African lineage. When C. graduated from New York University—headed for Harvard and the M.A. he would get there—in 1925, he had won many prizes and was awaiting the publication of his first book of poems, "Colors."

A smashing success, "Colors" led the way to C.'s appointment as assistant editor to Charles S. Johnson at *Opportunity* magazine and the republishing of "The Ballad of the Brown Girl." Two more books of poetry followed, "Copper Sun" and "The Black Christ and Other Poems," as did his high-profile marriage to the daughter of W. E. B. DU BOIS's daughter, Nina Yolande. It's safe to say that this was C.'s shining period.

But the marriage terminated in divorce in 1930, and, with it, the seeming flawlessness of C.'s aesthetic and personal success. Many have conjectured that C. was homosexual, which may account for the failure of his marriage. But was there a spillover from the failed marriage into his aesthetic output? The poet seems to have lost his footing after the marriage ended. His attempt at a novel, the satiric and politically ambitious "One Way to Heaven" (1932), was and is considered a failure. His collaboration with Arna BONTEMPS, the play "St. Louis Woman," in addition to being a commercial failure, received lukewarm reviews and generated an enormous amount of controversy in the black intelligentsia, many of whom advised C. to abandon the play. He died shortly before its opening.

Though the black critics of the 1960s attacked C. as a race sell-out, this judgment is not borne out by the often strikingly multi-layered early poems. In his famous "Heritage," the poet struggles with the complexities of an African inheritance: "Africa? A book one thumbs / Listlessly, till slumber comes." Enigmatically, the poem offers both a depiction of Africa as a text the reader cannot stop reading until slumber overtakes him, or one that itself produces slumber in the reader. Whichever interpretation one makes, the Africa of the poet is rendered quirkiliy, complexly, and unpredictably, all of which are qualities characterizing C.'s work at its best. Perhaps it is C.'s very uncategorizability that has hampered just treatments of his work. Though he may have been overpraised in his youth, C. wrote uneven yet memorable poetry, as evinced by these oft-quoted lines from "Yet Do I Marvel": "Yet do I marvel at this curious thing: / To make a poet black, and bid him sing!" So bidden, the poet sang discordant yet affecting songs.

BIBLIOGRAPHY: Baker, H. A., *A Many-Colored Coat of Dreams: The Poetry of C. C.* (1974); Ferguson, B. E., *C. C. and the Negro Renaissance* (1966); Shucard, A. R., *C. C.* (1984)

DAVID GREVEN

CUMMINGS, E[DWARD] E[STLIN]
b. 14 October 1894, Cambridge Massachusetts; d. 3 September 1962, Joy Farm, New Hampshire

Although extraordinarily prolific in various literary and art forms, and although also a significant satirist in the Juvenalian mode, C. will chiefly be known as the foremost American lyric poet of his generation. If by "lyric" is meant not simply the short poem but also that type of short poem embodying the songful expression of universal feelings associated with the individual, nature, love, and growth, then C. is unique among major modernist poets in English because of his willingness to focus on these traditionally more "romantic" themes—and without the constant protection of irony. Indeed, this focus and method of treatment are the source of both his strengths and his weaknesses, and are responsible for much of the critical debate about his importance in the canon.

C.'s role in the history of modern poetry is, in fact, complex. While he was an innovator in rhetoric, tone, syntax, and vocabulary, as well as in modernist incorporations of "unpoetic" language and subject matter,

his poetry is sometimes seen to lack the characteristic ambivalence and intellectual knowingness that mark the work of other notable poets of his time, and that is why he has had difficulty in finding acceptance among academic critics—although he is quite well regarded, for a serious artist, by the general reading public. Despite the fact that he himself came from an academic background and was a highly cultured and highly educated intellectual, he quite early on made a deliberate choice to adopt the mask of the naive observer from another culture, the sharp-eyed clown, the spontaneous child—as in his exuberant "let's live suddenly without thinking."

This mask is a brilliant literary device for exposing the emptiness of conventional society—"this little bride & groom are," for example—and for embodying the expression of love and growth as remedies for that emptiness—"anyone lived in a pretty how town"—but if it is taken literally, the entire enterprise can easily be misunderstood. Thus C. has been accused of being the perpetual adolescent, the child who never grew up. To retain the freshness of the child's vision does not necessarily entail the rejection of adult responsibilities, and shouldering adult responsibilities does not necessarily involve the adoption of bourgeois values, but that these attitudes sometimes become confused in criticism of C. is due in part to some uncertainty in his own handling of this mask and in part to imperceptiveness on the side of the critics.

C.'s difficulty with his mask is that he tended to identify himself too exclusively with it, perhaps rebelling against the pieties of his respectable background, as satirized in "the Cambridge ladies who live in furnished souls," and needing to define himself as different. Thus there is an occasional note of impatience and petulance in work that is otherwise mature and accomplished.

The bias of his detractors, however, is another matter. Because he worked within the tradition of romantic TRANSCENDENTALISM, a tradition that, although it is still more central and generative than is commonly acknowledged, has met with a mixed reception among modern critics, the salience of C.'s underlying faith in the organic processes of growth—as in "O sweet spontaneous / earth," for example—remains invisible when seen through the lenses of the more pessimistic contemporary philosophical systems. His tradition goes back, in America, to Ralph Waldo EMERSON, Walt WHITMAN, and Henry David THOREAU, and its vision perceives the world as the garment of God, the seen as the signature of things unseen, and it deplores those things that cloud over that vision—custom, commercialism, and mere intellectualism.

Hence C.'s emphasis on feeling, both sensuous and emotional, and his Swiftian attacks on thinking, politics, and business, as well as on clichés and stereotypes of all kinds—see "POEM, OR BEAUTY HURTS MR. VI- NAL," one of the rare C. poems with a title, here with obvious satiric intent. And hence his techniques—ex- periments in typography, grammar, syntax, diction, rhythm, and structure, representing various ways of breaking up the familiarity of language to achieve freshness, but without systematically breading up the language *itself* to the extent that, say, Gertrude STEIN or James Joyce did.

C. spent his childhood and youth in Cambridge. His father was a prominent Unitarian minister and social reformer, who taught sociology at Harvard. Es- tlin, as he was known to his family and friends because his father's name was also Edward, was educated at the Cambridge Latin school and at Harvard, receiving his B.A. in 1915 and his M.A. in 1916. At college, he studied literature and languages, was associated with the campus literary magazines, and made a num- ber of important friends—such as Scofield Thayer and James Sibley Watson (who later became editors of *The Dial* and firm supporters of C.'s career), S. Foster Damon, and John DOS PASSOS.

C.'s genius and love for poetry—and for drawing, sketching, and painting as well—manifested them- selves even when he was a child, but it was during his college years that he began to approach his art and craft in a disciplined and professional way. Although his first literary models and influences were tradi- tional—Keats was chief among them—and his early poetry was naturally derivative, he soon became caught up in the early excitement of modernism that was stirring around him while he was still a student.

World War I was to intervene, however, and like many idealistic young men of his time—notable artists and writers among them—C. hastened his entry into the war. He joined the Norton-Harjes Ambulance Corps in 1917 and was shipped to France, where he first discovered Paris before being sent to the front. He and his friend Slater Brown, however, whom he had met on the way over to the Continent, wrote letters home that were critical of the conduct of the war—initial idealism souring to disillusionment in the face of blundering and waste—and so they attracted the notice of the overly apprehensive French mili- tary censors.

Ironically, they were rounded up for interrogation by the authorities of the very nation they were serving and ultimately sent to a detention center, La Ferté- Macé in Normandy, where they were held on suspi- cion—apparently for refusing to say that they hated the Germans—to await the arrival, under miserable conditions, of the sentencing commission that came through once every three months. Thus it was three months or more before they were released, thanks to

C.'s father's frantic wire-pulling, and sent back home, much the worse for wear. This terrible experience did not prevent C. from being drafted into the U.S. Army not long after, and he was stationed at Camp Devens, some thirty-five miles northwest of Cambridge and not far from Emerson's Concord and Thoreau's Wal- den, until shortly after the Armistice was signed in 1918.

Meanwhile, he continued to write and paint, and after the war he settled permanently in New York City's Greenwich Village to devote himself to his dual artistic career. He received *The Dial* Award in 1925, traveled to Europe frequently, and in 1931 visited Stalinist Russia, remaining for about a month, meeting artists and writers, and seeing the sights.

Known chiefly in the 1920s and 1930s as an avant- gardist and *enfant terrible,* by the 1940s and 1950s C. acquired a more established reputation and received a number of additional honors and awards, including two Guggenheim Fellowships, a Fellowship of the American Academy of Poets, the Charles Eliot Norton Professorship at Harvard, the National Book Award, the Bollingen Prize, and the Boston Arts Festival Award. He was also in great demand to give poetry readings, visiting many lecture halls and college cam- puses around the country. His reputation at the time of his death had never been higher.

C.'s career as a writer may be seen in terms of the four major decades of his creative output. He published half a dozen works during the 1920s. *The Enormous Room* (1922), often miscalled a "novel," is in reality a highly impressionistic account, based loosely on Bunyan's *Pilgrim's Progress* for its structure and sym- bolism, of his imprisonment at La Ferté-Macé. It was here that he first began to explore his distrust of gov- ernments and his corresponding love for the individ- ual, and to become aware of the transcendence of time into timelessness—as he said, when one is imprisoned under an indefinite sentence, one must learn to live in the present or go mad. When seen in relation to more recent concentration camp literature, this early work—which was praised by Dos Passos, T. E. Law- rence, and Robert Graves, among others—has proven to be remarkably prescient and remains one of C.'s most widely-known books.

His first book of poems was called *Tulips and Chim- neys* (1923), the title possibly referring to poems of nature and poems of the city, or perhaps to freely spaced poems and conventionally arranged poems. But after this, his book titles become more idiosyncratic (indeed, as suggested above, he soon stopped using titles for poems altogether): *&,* and *XLI Poems* in 1925, and *is 5*—rejecting the "logic" of two times two is four—in 1926. His main characteristics—liveliness, concreteness of image, and an inexhaustible curiosity about both language and the world—reflect C.'s role in the modernist "project" of expanding the language and subject matter of poetry.

Climaxing his entry into the literary arena in the 1920s was his play entitled *HIM*—the only "name" given to the hero, the heroine being called, correspondingly, "ME." A poetic and surrealistic portrait of a young playwright struggling to reconcile the apparently conflicting claims of love and art, it aroused a storm of protest because of its experimental nature when it was published in 1927 and performed in 1928.

Publishing six books within five years is a brilliant and startling beginning, but C. surpasses himself in the 1930s, publishing no fewer than eight separate works. [*No Title*]—C. called it "a book without a title"—a book of dadaesque prose sketches with accompanying drawings, was published in 1930, as was his next play, *Anthropos,* a brief exemplum portraying the Artist *versus* the Mob in an antediluvian setting. The next book of poems, *W* [*ViVa*], appeared in 1931, and it focuses his transcendental vision by increased use of his unique conceptual vocabulary, based on such grammatical shifts as making nouns out of verbs and adverbs, as in "devout am" or "deeplyness," and suggesting movement in stasis *via* verb-meaning out of noun-function. *is 5* and *W* also contain two of the most superb love poems in English of the modern period—"since feeling is first" and "somewhere i have never traveled, gladly beyond." A collection of art works entitled *CIOPW* (charcoal, ink, oil, pencil, and watercolor) came out in the same year.

In 1933, C. published *EIMI* (Greek for "I am," pronounced A as in "made," ME as in "me," accent on "me"), an account—this time structured along the lines suggested by Dante's *Divine Comedy*—even more impressionistic than *The Enormous Room* of his Russian trip, during which he saw once again with great prescience the soulless state oppose the alive individual. He brought out in 1935 a scenario for a ballet based on Harriet Beecher STOWE's *Uncle Tom's Cabin,* entitled *Tom,* which showed the transcendence of the hero through suffering, and his next volume of poems, *No Thanks,* "dedicated" to the fourteen publishers who had rejected it. This volume culminates his first two decades of experimentation, and his deservedly popular *Collected Poems* of 1938 (in fact a *selection*) beautifully rounds off this phase of his career.

In the next quarter-century—more than half of his creative life—C. continued his multifaceted productivity and perforce became engaged in dealing with the consequences of his fame and consolidating (and in some ways retrenching) his art and vision. He brought out *50 Poems* in 1940, which reveals a trend toward greater typographical regularity together with an increased use of his conceptual vocabulary. The subsequent book of poems, *1 x 1* [*One Times One*] (1944), develops this trend further, the title referring to one of its poems, "if everything happens that can't be done," wherein love is celebrated as the equation 1 x 1 = 1. In 1946, he published his fourth work for the stage, *Santa Claus,* a very affecting allegorical verse play involving Death, the Mob, Santa Claus, and a little girl looking for her father.

In the 1950s, the final full decade of his life, C. published the last three volumes he was the send to the printer. *XAIPE* (pronounced "hi-ruh," with a throaty initial "h," Greek for "Greetings!" or "Rejoice!"), his next volume of poems, came out in 1950 and reveals a greater concern for dealing with the pain of life, thereby broadening and deepening his transcendental vision. C. was honored by his *alma mater*'s invitation to deliver the Charles Eliot Norton Lectures during 1952–53, and since, as he said, he was not a teacher, he chose to take an autobiographical approach, presenting his own view of his development as a man and artist—thus the title, *i: SIX NONLECTURES,* published in 1953. In 1958, he issued *95 Poems.*

After C.'s death in 1962, two new volumes appeared: *Adventures in Value* (1962) is a book of photographs by C.'s wife (Marion Morehouse), a photographer's model and professional photographer herself, with accompanying writings—some of them epigrammatic captions—by the poet; and *73 Poems* in 1963. Four *Fairy Tales* appeared in 1965, although they were written much earlier; *Complete Poems: 1913–1962* came out in 1972; *Etcetera: The Unpublished Poems of E. E. Cummings* appeared in 1983; and *E. E. Cummings: Complete Poems, 1904–1962,* published in 1989, promises to be the definitive edition.

Much unpublished material is on deposit at the libraries of Harvard, Yale, and the Universities of Virginia and Texas, and a series devoted to the publication of all of the poet's major works, published and unpublished—with the poetry and poetic prose in "typescript editions"—has been inaugurated under the editorship of G. J. Firmage. Many translations have been made, and several children's books with illustrations to accompany certain C. poems have been created by Heidi Goennel (1988) and Deborah Kogan Ray (1989).

The fact that C. does not fit neatly either into the category of merely popular verse or into that of academically favored poetry neither surprised nor dismayed him, for he looked with suspicion at categories in the first place—*vide* "all worlds have halfsight, seeing either with." As an authentic and innovative modernist poet, he continues to absorb the interest of a number of professorial critics; and as a poet of hope, prayer, and health, as in "i thank You God for most this amazing," he is read and quoted spontaneously at weddings and in movies and plays and memorized by young children. He always concerned himself deeply with love, death, mortality, and time-lessness—"being to timelessness as it's to time"—and he always treated them deeply and inventively, yet he was at the same time rarely abstruse, difficult, or pedantic. He was, that is to say, strictly himself.

One final note: the proper way to print C.'s name is with standard capitalization and not, as is often done, with lowercase letters. While it is true that he became famous—even notorious—for using the lowercase "i" instead of the usual "I" for the first-person singular pronoun, and also for experimenting with capital and lowercase letters in his writings, it is not true that he used lowercase for his name.

BIBLIOGRAPHY: Cohen, M. A., *Poet and Painter* (1987); Dendinger, L. N., ed., *E. E. C.: The Critical Reception* (1981); Friedman, N., *E. E. C.: The Growth of a Writer* (1964), Friedman, N., ed., *E. E. C.: A Collection of Critical Essays* (1972); Friedman, N., *(Re) Valuing C.* (1996); Kennedy, R. S., *Dreams in the Mirror* (1980); Kennedy, R. S., *E. E. C. Revisited* (1994); Norman, C., *The Magic Maker* (1958); Rotella, G. L., ed., *Critical Essays on E. E. C.* (1984)

NORMAN FRIEDMAN

CUMMINS, MARIA [SUSANNA]

b. 9 April 1827, Salem, Massachusetts; d. 1 October 1866, Dorchester, Massachusetts

Throughout the latter half of the 19th c., C. enjoyed significant popularity here and abroad, her first novel *The Lamplighter* (1854) reportedly selling 40,000 copies in two months, 70,000 in the first year. Her other three novels, though structurally better, did not equal *The Lamplighter* in sales.

Contemporary critics have recalled sporadically that Nathaniel HAWTHORNE included C. among the "d----d mob of scribbling women," asking peevishly, "What is the mystery of these innumerable editions of the Lamplighter [sic]?" They have remembered, too, that James Joyce parodied *The Lamplighter* in the Gerty MacDowell section of *Ulysses*. Now, scholars are reevaluating C.'s work in light of canon revision.

Born into a well-to-do Massachusetts family, C. lived in Salem and later in Dorchester. She attended the school run by Mrs. Charles Sedgwick, sister-in-law of author Catharine Maria SEDGWICK. Financially secure and free from family responsibilities, the unmarried C. wrote at her own leisure.

Although generally classified as sentimental and/or domestic, C.'s novels fit other categories more pre-

cisely. *The Lamplighter* and *Mabel Vaughan* (1857) belong to what Nina Baym calls woman's fiction. In the former, which takes its title, opening passage, and lamplighting motif from Susan WARNER's *The Wide, Wide World,* the rebellious orphan Gerty, aided by the lamplighter Trueman Flint and the blind Emily Graham, develops into the self-sufficient paragon Gertrude Amory. The heroine of *Mabel Vaughan,* on the contrary, begins with economic, social, and educational advantages. When financial reverses and other family problems test her moral and psychological fiber, she transcends circumstances and, like Warner's Fleda Ringgan, helps restore family stability. *El Fureidis* (1860), a romance, set in the Near East, follows the travels of Robert Meredith through Palestine and Syria into Lebanon, where he meets the courageous Havilah Trefoil. *Haunted Hearts* (1864), a mystery set in New Jersey, depicts the moral growth of Angie Cousin, although its protagonist is George Rawle.

BIBLIOGRAPHY: Baym, N., *Woman's Fiction* (1978); Devlin, K., "The Romance Heroine Exposed: 'Nausicca' and *The Lamplighter,*" *JJQ* 22, 4 (Summer 1985): 383–96; Kelley, M., *Private Woman, Public Stage* (1984); Smith, C. S., "Joyce's *Ulysses,*" *Explicator* 50, 1 (1991): 37–38

LUCY M. FREIBERT

CUNNINGHAM, J[ames] V[incent]

b. 23 August 1911, Cumberland, Maryland; d. 30 March 1985, Marlborough, Massachusetts

C. was an important poet and literary critic. Initially, he tried to write in the style of the modernist poets who had been popular since the early 20th c., notably Wallace STEVENS and William Carlos WILLIAMS. However, C. was ill-suited to the modernist style that was so much in vogue during his younger years both by personal and poetic temperament. Though clearly able to write convincingly about emotions such as love, he was by nature reserved and methodical. Therefore, he was uncomfortable with the emphasis in modernism on spontaneous bursts of feeling which had been derived from British ROMANTICISM. C. was also essentially a metrical poet. Most of his poems are precisely written with regard to the length of lines and rhythm, making him an anomaly so long as he attempted to write in a style known more for its emphasis on imagery and metrical freedom.

In spite of some obvious strengths which are indicative of future promise, these weaknesses were evident in C.'s first collection of poetry, *The Helmsman,* which was published in 1942. It is interesting that C. himself examined the problems contained in his early writing in *The Quest of the Opal,* his most important work of criticism, which appeared in 1950. In that work, C. shows a keen ability to analyze modern poetry as well as his own work, belying D. H. Lawrence's assertion that the artist can never be trusted when it comes to assessing his own art. Indeed, C. identified another problem in his work: the learned nature of the allusions rendered it incapable of being understood by any but the most educated reader, whose learning was equal to C.'s.

C.'s next volume of poetry, *The Judge Is Fury* (1947), which consisted mostly of new material but some older poems that had not been included in his first collection, was more successful. In it, he first demonstrated his command of that direct, precise, and witty style for which he would gain recognition. Notable is the fact that it was his first book to contain examples of the epigram, a form at which he would greatly distinguish himself, so much so that he was to become thought of primarily as a practitioner of it. In one poem titled "History of Ideas," C. writes, "God is love. Then by conversion / Love is God, and sex conversion." It is interesting to note that, like a number of significant epigrammists before him, C. was not averse to using the form to write on the subject of death. In a particularly lyrical epigram from this period, he writes, "My dear, though I have left no sigh / Carved on your stone, yet I still cherish / Your name,

and your flesh will not die / Till I and my descendants perish."

C. must have realized his proficiency at the form, for his next two works, *Doctor Drink: Poems* (1950) and *Trivial, Vulgar and Exalted* (1957), consisted exclusively of epigrams. They were followed by a poetic "sequence"—or series of poems linked together by a unifying idea—*To What Strangers, What Welcome* (1964). The framing device for C.'s sequence is a journey to the western U.S. and back.

C.'s *Collected Poems and Epigrams* was published in 1971. It was followed by *The Collected Essays of J. V. C.* in 1976. *The Poems of J. V. C.,* published in 1997, includes most of the material contained in the former, along with some poems which C. had written during his later years and his translations of the Latin poets, including Martial, an epigrammist to whom he obviously owed an enormous debt. Indeed, these splendid translations reveal C. for what he was: a poet who was more at ease in the world of the ancient poets than of his modernist contemporaries.

BIBLIOGRAPHY: Fraser, J., "Heroic Order in the Poetry of J. V. C.," *SoR* 23 (Winter 1987): 68–83; Pinsky, R., "The Poetry of J. V. C.," *ChiR* 35 (1985): 4–14; Steele, T., "Interview with J. V. C.," *IowaR* 15 (Fall 1985): 1–24

MICHAEL MANDELKERN

D

DAHLBERG, Edward
b. 22 July 1900, Boston, Massachusetts; d. 27 February
1977, Santa Barbara, California

D. is one of the most enigmatic, eccentric, and provocative writers of the 20th c. He began by establishing
the genre of the proletariat novel. Later, he became a
curmudgeonly literary critic. He then examined the
philosophy of sex and sensuality, wrote one of the
most powerful autobiographies in American letters,
gained critical acclaim for his poetry and essays, and
through correspondence with Herbert Read, Charles
OLSON, and others, profoundly influenced the development of modern and postmodern literature. Critics
have never known what to make of D.'s style which
ranges from coarse realism to a baroque amalgam of
quotations, allusions, archaic diction, and street slang.
Yet his striking insights, vituperative moralizing, poignant epithets, and unflinching realism make him a
rich, unforgettable voice in American letters.

D.'s early life became the material for his novels,
his autobiography, and his reinterpretation of American literature and culture. Shortly after D.'s birth, his
father stole his mother's money and abandoned the
family. She moved from city to city, finally settling in
Kansas City. At twelve, D. was placed in an orphanage
where he endured a grim life until seventeen. He became a day laborer, drover, and a hobo but graduated
from Columbia University in 1925 and set out for
Europe where he joined expatriates, Hart CRANE, Robert MCALMON, and Richard Aldington.

His first novel, *Bottom Dogs* (1929), published with
a lengthy introduction by D. H. Lawrence, was a departure from any novel to that point because of its harsh,
graphic description of the hopelessness of society's
bottom dogs. The imagery was repulsive and the language, D. admitted, was a "rough, bleak idiom" which
dates the book for current readers. The book and its
sequels, *From Flushing to Calvary* (1932), about slum

life in New York City, and *Those Who Perish* (1934),
about the treatment of American Jews, follow the lives
of Lorry and Lizzie Lewis, modeled on D. and his
mother. These novels became the prototype for the
social realism/proletariat novels of the 1930s.

D. later repudiated these "mediocre manipulations"
of his childhood in a series of essays about modern
culture collected in *The Flea of Sodom* (1950). His
reexamination of American literature and the classics
was accompanied by a reshaping of his prose style.
The result, *Do These Bones Live* (1941; rev. as *Can
These Bones Live,* 1960), is as original and oracular
as Lawrence's critique of American writers. His impatience with contemporaries, T. S. ELIOT, Ezra POUND,
and William FAULKNER, reveals his suspicion of erudition without experience. His *The Sorrows of Priapus*
(1957) explores the mind/body dichotomy in Greek,
Hebrew, and pre-Columbian cultures, and *The Carnal
Myth* (1968) examines sensuality in classical literature.

For many, his autobiography, *Because I Was Flesh*
(1964), is D.'s crowning achievement. The combination of its realism, his archaic style, the allusiveness,
and powerful aphorisms shape his life, his mother's,
and American culture into a powerful tale of mythic
power. Late in life, D. turned to poetry, publishing
Cipango's Hinder Door (1966) and *The Leafless
American and Other Writings* (1967), again mythologizing American history and his life. During this period
he collected his letters, wrote a comic novel, published
a commentary on modern literature with Read, collected his aphorisms, and wrote a book of reminiscences. His correspondence with Olson influenced the
Black Mountain writers and continues to affect postmodern literature.

BIBLIOGRAPHY: Billings, H., ed., *E. D.: American Ish-
mael of Letters* (1968); Cech, J., *Charles Olson and
E. D.: A Portrait of a Friendship* (1982); DeFanti,
C., *The Wages of Expectation: A Biography of E. D.*

(1978); Moramarco, F., *E. D.* (1972); Williams, J., ed., *E. D.: A Tribute* (1971)

NEWTON SMITH

DALY, [John] Augustin

b. 20 July 1838, Plymouth, North Carolina; d. 7 June 1899, Paris, France

Foremost impresario of the 19th-c. American theater, D. formed the leading American theater company, in part due to his clever adaptations and original sensation dramas. He is known for having introduced a more subtle, realistic style of acting to the American stage that militated against the firmly entrenched "star system" and enabled the psychological REALISM that dominated 20th-c. drama. His own plays and adaptations, while adhering to the melodramatic conventions of the era's theater, also contributed to this change in dramatic style.

D. had a hand in every aspect of theater production, working as critic, press agent, manager and producer as well as author and adapter. In 1867, he held the post of dramatic critic at five newspapers simultaneously; in 1869, he opened his first theater. As a manager, he was known as a martinet who didn't put up with "stars," insisting on hard work and discipline from an ensemble company. Although known for elaborate staging, he encouraged "natural" acting rather than the highly conventional, declamatory style of the era. Fashionable society admired the understated elegance of the new style, but the "gallery gods"—patrons who paid less for seats much farther away—thought it simply a lack of acting. Nevertheless, the subtler acting style encouraged the development of plays that relied on psychological realism, rather than sensational plots, for dramatic effect.

D.'s repertory consisted largely of novel adaptations, reworked English, French, and German plays, and versions of Shakespeare prettified by critic William Winter. He did most of his own adaptations, and also wrote original plays in popular genres. His melodramas *Under the Gaslight* (1867), *A Flash of Lightening* (1885) *The Red Scarf* (perf. 1868), and *The Under Current* (perf. 1888), were unabashed "sensation dramas": intricately plotted potboilers in which each act's curtain dropped on a hair-raising spectacle. D.'s sensation scenes included a man tied to a log about to be halved by a sawmill, an Indian raid on a moving barge, and, famously, *Under the Gaslight*'s locomotive bearing down on the play's bound hero while the heroine chops her way out of a signal shed to save him. D. sued Dion BOUCICAULT for copyright infringement when the latter's *After Dark* included a

similar scene; the case was an important milestone in theatrical copyright law.

Similar questions of authorship haunt D.'s own work, particularly his adaptations. Lax copyright laws meant that even after hiring a translator to make a "literal translation," then a hack writer to adapt it, D. published his adaptations under his own name. Furthermore, he seems to have collaborated regularly with his brother Joseph, a prominent attorney, whose contributions were substantial.

Regardless of authorship, the most original plays attributed to D. were contemporary issue plays. *Horizon* (1885) was a frontier drama assembled from contemporary events, current literature, music hall sketches, and other popular plays, and partaking in the cultural interest in Native American issues during the 1870s. Similarly topical were *Round the Clock* (perf. 1872), *Roughing It* (perf. 1873), and *The Dark City and Its Bright Side* (perf. 1877), all "local color" spectacles that used realistic scenes and locations to take audiences on a "low-life" tour of the city's seamier side.

It has been argued that the addition of such realistic effects prolonged the reign of melodrama on the American stage, postponing the emergence of a literary, realistic drama. More recent critics have rejected the absolute distinction between melodrama and realism. D.'s contributions, while unabashedly commercial, moved American drama in the direction later artists would take.

BIBLIOGRAPHY: Felheim, M., *The Theater of A. D.* (1956); Kauffman, S., "Two Vulgar Geniuses: A. D. and David Belasco," *YR* 76 (Summer 1987): 496–513

GINGER STRAND

DALY, Thomas Augustine

b. 28 May 1871, Philadelphia, Pennsylvania; d. 4 October 1948, Philadelphia, Pennsylvania

Essentially a journalist, D. worked for a series of Philadelphia newspapers: the weekly *Catholic Standard and Times,* the *Philadelphia Record,* and finally the *Philadelphia Evening Bulletin.* He published a number of books, mostly humorous and sentimental verse, either new or reprinted from his newspaper columns; *Canzoni* (1906), for instance, went to a twelfth edition in 1916 with a run of 50,000 copies. Other titles include *Songs of Wedlock* (1916), *McAroni Ballads and Other Verse* (1919), *McAroni Medleys* (1932)—in both, an Italian word is revealingly transformed into an Irish name—and *Selected Poems of T. A. D.* (1936). He attended Villanova and Fordham Universities and later received honorary doctoral degrees from Fordham,

Notre Dame, and Boston College. D. lived and worked exclusively in and around Philadelphia.

The difficulty in assessing D.'s literary production stems from his writing mostly in dialect, chiefly Italian American and Irish American. Although technically skillful, he writes lightly, often preferring the cute and the pathetic, exemplified in "Da Comica Man," published in *Canzoni*. When he writes in his own voice, the subject is usually home life, as in "Night in Bachelor's Hall," published in *Canzoni*, or love life, as in "Ballade of Summer's Passing," published in *Madrigali* (1912), both of which he treats with great yet superficial tenderness.

But if one would know something outside the news items about the sensibility of the news-reading public, or about the matters typically assumed to be subjects for poetry, or the styles in which poetry could become widely and immediately influential, then D.'s work seems an excellent source. Journalistic verse is meant to appeal to a various and numerous audience; when D. turns out column after popular column—and volume after popular volume of poems—he must be saying appealing things about appealing subjects. Moreover, D. wrote within a solid, albeit minor genre in which the more famous Eugene FIELD and James Whitcomb RILEY composed.

Coming from Irish ancestry, D. belonged to a group whose numbers increased greatly during the mid-19th c. By the early 1890s, when D. began reporting for the *Philadelphia Record*, the Irish had become well established in the U.S. His Italian American verse would appear, therefore, as a vehicle in which a more mainstream host introduces a less mainstream guest to "strangers." His Irish American verse is self-reflexively nostalgic. The cultural iconography, the reliance on a dialect which he presumably did not speak, and the domestic routines celebrated in his non dialectical verse categorize D. as a lyric poet of impersonal experience. Read sociologically, D.'s writing becomes an aperture through which relations between vocabulary, syntax, and pronunciation can be seen to inform class and ethnic distinctions. D. also types the ways that self- and group-consciousness must be reconfigured in learning new words and new references in new circumstances. That an Irish American newspaperman would undertake commercially to write not simply of things Irish American but also of and, in some sense, for a less-well assimilated ethnic minority points to a little-known moment in our national heritage.

BIBLIOGRAPHY: Perkins, D., *A History of Modern Poetry: From the 1890s to the High Modernist Mode* (1976); Williams, P. O., "T. A. D.," in Trachtenberg, S., ed., *DLB*, vol. 11, part 1, *American Humorists, 1800–1950* (1982): 100–102

THOMAS T. APPLE

DANA, Richard Henry, Sr.
b. 15 November 1787, Cambridge, Massachusetts; d. 2 February 1879, Boston, Massachusetts

DANA, Richard Henry, Jr.
b. 1 August 1815, Cambridge, Massachusetts; d. 6 January 1882, Rome, Italy

A poet and essayist who rejected the strictures of Lockean epistemology, D., Sr. published works in the 1820s that anticipated subsequent interest in romantic subjectivism. "The Buccaneer" (1827), a lengthy supernatural poem, won praise from the *Blackwood's* critic "Christopher North" and influenced Edgar Allan POE. In essays in the *North American Review* and in other periodicals, he presented the theory, then quite controversial, that Shakespeare's genius surpassed that of the Augustan poets. His work was collected in the two-volume *Poems and Prose Writings* (1833; rev. ed., 1850).

Educated at Harvard and trained for the law, D., Sr. pursued a career of modest literary output that included editing, and lecturing. During a term as associate editor of the *North American Review*, his acceptance of William Cullen BRYANT's "Thanatopsis" initiated a friendly correspondence that continued throughout D., Sr.'s life. His attempt in 1821 to publish his own periodical, the *Idle Man*, lasted only six months. After a fairly extensive lecture tour from 1839–40, ill health forced D. into semiretirement.

By contemporary standards, Bryant has been relegated to a second tier among American poets. In the 1840s, however, D., Sr. and Bryant, along with Henry Wadsworth LONGFELLOW, Charles Sprague, and Fitz-Greene HALLECK, were known as the "Copperplate Five," a five-member Establishment enshrined on the frontispiece of Rufus Griswold's influential *The Poets and Poetry of America* (1842). This anthology, testimony to D., Sr.'s prominence at the time, represented an early attempt to codify an American poetic canon.

During his lengthy period of inactivity, D., Sr.'s literary reputation was eclipsed by that of his son and namesake, the author of *Two Years before the Mast* (1840). This vivid and popular account of sea life strictly belongs to the genre of autobiography and travel writing, but its narrative techniques influenced writers of maritime fiction, notably Herman MELVILLE. Unlike his father, who abandoned law for literature in his twenties, D., Jr. remained active as a jurist by participating in the antislavery movement. *The Sea-*

man's Friend (1841) reflected D., Jr.'s interest in maritime law, a subject that occupied him until his death.

BIBLIOGRAPHY: Hunter, D. H., *R. H. D., Sr.* (1987); Wilson, J. G., *Bryant and His Friends* (1886)

KENT LJUNGQUIST

DANTICAT, Edwidge
b.14 June 1969, Port-au-Prince, Haiti, West Indies

At the age of twenty-seven, D. had already published one novel, *Breath, Eyes, Memory* (1994), and one collection of short stories *Krik? Krak!* (1995). This achievement is equaled only by the fact that D. writes with clarity, insight, and breadth of vision well beyond her years. Her accomplishment as a writer is all the more noteworthy when one realizes that until she joined her parents in the U.S. when she was twelve, the author, who had been living with her aunt in Haiti, spoke no English.

As a creative writer, D. is part of a burgeoning group of Caribbean American women writers, such as Paule MARSHALL, Rosa GUY, Jamaica KINCAID, who are attempting to come to terms with the complexities inherent in their bicultural heritage by exploring in their fiction many aspects of cultural ambivalence that occur within the family and the community. This concern is further developed in D.'s second novel entitled *The Farming of Bones*, published in 1998.

Set in Haiti and the U.S., *Breath, Eyes, Memory* is an unforgettable account of the complexities in the lives of Haitian women of different generations, as they struggle in their relationships with one another, in a society that grants them little or no economic independence. This is a society that often subjects them to sexual oppression and violence, while paradoxically demanding of them "sexual purity." Such is the setting of this partly autobiographical first novel featuring the Caco women of four generations.

Specifically, *Breath, Eyes, Memory* is the story of Sophie Caco; her mother, Martine; her aunt, Atie; her grandmother, Ife. Sophie's baby daughter, Brigitte, takes the women to the fourth generation. The text challenges blind adherence to tradition by revealing the Caco women from generation to generation participating, however unwittingly, in their own sexual subjugation. Mothers of unmarried daughters are expected to physically "test" their daughters to ensure their sexual purity. This tradition goes unchallenged among the Caco women until Sophie, now living with her mother in New York, rebels, with dire consequences to herself. These well-intentioned women can only justify their actions by claiming that they simply do to their daughters what their mothers had done to them.

Two years after D. arrived in the U.S., she started publishing her short stories. *Kirk? Krak!* is a collection of nine stories; seven of the nine are set in Haiti; two, in New York. Perhaps, because the collection comprises some of the earlier stories juxtaposed with the later and more sophisticated, some critics think this collection is somewhat uneven. Written in clear lyrical prose and influenced strongly by the oral tradition of storytelling in the Caribbean, these stories compel the reader to confront some very painful issues. Dominant among these issues is the omnipresent political corruption that leads to sexism, classism, and unspeakable violence against the citizens, especially women who have the least power. With the skillful use of folklore and history, D. circumvents one-dimensional portrayals and characterizations, as she creates multilayered vignettes that resonate with myth, legend, and folklore.

Thus, in the second story of the collection, "Nineteen Thirty-Seven," myth and reality come together with tragic and deadly consequences for women. Utilizing a well-known African Caribbean folk belief that there are women who have the power to change their physical form at nights, exchange their breasts for wings and fly, D. highlights the plight of these Haitian women. Ironically, these women are victimized for supernatural powers with which the culture has endowed them and for which they are punished with imprisonment and death. Just as this myth of the women's power to defy gravity can be read as a symbol of female bonding, so are all the disenfranchised Haitians linked to each other through their common kinship with the sea, as reflected in the story, "Children of the Sea." This common kinship with the sea unites all the people, those who started the Middle Passage but did not complete it, those who elected to make the water their road back to Africa once they arrived in the New World and foresaw the future, as well as those who attempt to journey to Miami on the "death boats."

In her New York stories, "New York Day Women" and "Caroline's Wedding," D. returns to her earlier theme of tradition versus modernity when she positions traditional Haitian culture against contemporary metropolitan values. In "New York Day Women," mother and daughter realize that they are of different worlds but can accept their differences with grace and a certain amount of humor. And in "Caroline's Wedding," the mother attempts to share all the richness of the Haitian culture with her two daughters with mixed results. Finally, D. convinces her readers that these women, young and old, do not have to continue at odds with each other, for each has much to teach and learn from the other.

BIBLIOGRAPHY: Mead, R., "Queen Creole," *New York* 28 (20 November 1995): 50–51; Shea, R. H., "The

Dangerous Job of E. D.: An Interview," *Callaloo* 19 (1996): 382–89

LEOTA S. LAWRENCE

DARGAN, Olive Tilford

b. 11 January 1869, Grayson County, Kentucky; d. 22 January 1968, Asheville, North Carolina

D. remains best noted for her social novels written during the Great Depression that detail the exploitation of Southern mountain people as they became urban millworkers. D. established her career as a poet and lyrical dramatist, but achieved wide recognition largely through her local color anecdotes and stories set in the South. Her works have not been the subject of continued critical attention, although her use of a female heroine's explorations of women's traditional social roles in her two best novels appear to offer fertile ground for more contemporary feminist scholarship.

Reared in Kentucky and Missouri by parents who were both schoolteachers, D. pursued her education vigorously. After graduating from Peabody College in Nashville, Tennessee and devoting some time to teaching, D. continued her studies for a year at Radcliffe College. There she met and later married Pegram Dargan, and their increasingly unhappy marriage in New York, punctuated by the death of an infant daughter in 1907, undoubtedly contributed to D.'s turn to the causes of women's rights and social activism. She developed close friendships with Rose Pastor Stokes, a founding member of the American Communist Party (an organization which D. actively supported but never officially joined) and Alice Stone Blackwell, daughter of Lucy Stone, a leader of the suffrage movement and editor of the *Women's Journal*. Settling in Asheville, North Carolina after the death of her husband in 1915, D. divided her time between social causes and writing. She established a women's shelter in North Carolina in 1927, and her friendship with Edwin August Björkman, a Swedish American novelist, critic, and editor of the *Asheville-Citizen,* opened to her a literary community in Asheville which read widely from world literature. Many details of D.'s personal life and political thoughts and actions remain unknown due to D.'s insistence on privacy, as well as to the burning of the bulk of her papers on three separate occasions.

D.'s early writings in New York were divided between poetry and verse drama. *Semiramis and Other Plays* (1904), *Lords and Lovers and Other Dramas* (1906), and *The Mortal Gods and Other Dramas* (1912) contain plays of archaic form set in such disparate locales as ancient Greece, Asia Minor during the later Crusades, 13th-c. England, and peasant Russia during the rumblings of revolution. At best, these dramas reveal D.'s lyrical idealism and sympathy for the downtrodden. They contain only hints of D.'s major thematic concerns, however, and have had no lasting impact on drama or poetry. Her volume of verse, *Lute and Furrow* (1922), contains an overt indication, especially in the poem "Burning Bridges," of D.'s desire to branch out in new personal and artistic directions. *Highland Annals* (1925) marks such a change in D.'s literary medium. The work contains anecdotes and stories of mountain folk in North Carolina and reveals her considerable talents in mastering narrative.

The cotton mill workers' strike in Gastonia, North Carolina in 1929 provided the background for D.'s finest novel, *Call Home the Heart* (1932). Written under the pseudonym Fielding Burke, *Call Home the Heart* is often regarded as the best of six novels of the early 1930s, including Mary Heaton Vorse's *Strike!* (1930), which drew their inspiration from this event. The central character of the novel, Ishma, is a poor white woman torn between the traditions of family and mountain life and a desire for social and personal awakenings. Ishma deserts her family for a lover, and in their new industrial environment she becomes a politicized Marxist. The character remains particularly noteworthy in her reevaluation of women's traditional roles and in her pursuit of personal independence, a feature which contemporary critics ignored in favor of commenting on the novel's overall communist sympathy and regional characters. D. suggests that Ishma's final retreat back to her husband and family reflects more her own personal failures, particularly due to her racial prejudices toward her black coworkers, than any attempt to restore traditional domestic values. A subsequent novel, *A Stone Came Rolling* (1935), returns to the characters of Ishma and her husband Britt. Although Ishma rededicates her life to revolutionary causes, she does so at great personal expense due to Britt's untimely death. Critics unfavorably compared this novel to *Call Home the Heart,* citing their displeasure over the increasing didacticism and sentimentality of the writing and the subordination of characterization to coincidental plotting. Many critics, however, praised D.'s well-drawn, minor characters, as well as her more detailed understanding of the overall social milieu of the organized labor movement, especially in the role played by religion in the worker's struggle. Taken together, both novels outline the sacrifices demanded of a remarkably courageous woman who seeks fulfillment in both domestic and political arenas.

D.'s later works are less strident in political ideology, and she finished her literary career with a final collection of anecdotal stories, *Innocent Bigamy* (1962), at the age of ninety-three. Her strengths as a fiction writer were in her compassion for her working-class characters and her flair for capturing the language and customs of her regional subjects.

BIBLIOGRAPHY: Cook, S., "O. T. D.," in Mainiero, L., ed., *American Women Writers* (1979), vol. 1: 456–58; Rideout, W. B., *The Radical Novel in the United States, 1900–1954* (1956)

JERRY DICKEY

DAVENPORT, Guy

b. 23 November 1927, Anderson, South Carolina

D.'s fiction has attracted a small but dedicated following, a fact that tells us as much about contemporary American reading preferences as it does about an author who for all his erudition and formal innovation often writes about those who have not lost their sense of childlike wonder. "The century's mystery," as one of his characters puts it, "is that intelligent children become teenage louts, who grow up to be pompous dullards." D.'s writing—his essays and translations no less than his extraordinary stories—is always intelligent but never pompous or dull. Flouting narrative conventions and displaying an astonishing range of reference, D.'s fiction resembles not only the poetry of Ezra POUND to which it is most frequently compared—Pound's *Cantos* was the subject of D.'s doctoral dissertation—but the music of Charles Ives. The amazing thing about Ives's music, D. has noted, is that one actually has to listen to it; it cannot merely be heard playing in the background.

D.'s art, equally "Daedalian," requires active reading rather than passive perusal; it uses cunning craftsmanship to "elicit complexities of meaning beyond inherited styles" in order to reinvest even the most commonplace reality with meaning and mystery. Juxtaposition—"architectonic arrangement of images"—is one of D.'s chief means for "generating significance" and for enabling the reader (as hunter/forager) to see with "prehistoric eyes." His collages, or what he more accurately prefers to call "assemblages of fact and fiction," may seem disjointed to those who read narratives the way they listen, or rather don't listen, to music but in fact possess or rather evoke a surprising sense of imaginative wholeness. They attempt to rescue the past in general and the archaic in particular from the ravaging forgetfulness of the modern—as opposed to modernist—sensibility. "Behind all this passion for the archaic," he has noted, "is a longing for something lost, for energies, values, and uncertainties unwisely abandoned by an industrial age."

D.'s method is inventive in a double sense, as concerned with finding as with making. He combines fact and fantasy (the Kafka who wrote "The Aeroplanes of Brescia" crossing paths at the same airshow with not only Wittgenstein and Bleriot but also Pinocchio), daunting erudition and an almost childlike sense of intellectual play. A single story or sentence can seem at once serious and lyrically sensuous, simple yet wondrously precise description transformed into dizzying and delightful tour de force. "The Daimon of Sokrates" in *Eclogues* (1981), for example, is "a kind of translation" of Plutarch with "embellishments" drawn from a variety of sources. The novella-length "Apples and Pears" (1984), D.'s longest single work, gathers together and muses on many of his favorite subjects: art, philosophy, nature, sexual exploration and play, and theories of social harmony (especially those of Charles Fourier). The story has the aptly open, narratively peripatetic form of the journal kept by a Dutch philosopher—a recurrent figure in D.'s fiction.

The title story of the earlier *Tatlin!* (1974), arguably D.'s finest assemblage, focuses on the Russian constructivist artist Vladimir Tatlin and his hope for combining art, politics, and technology in one utopian whole. D.'s cubistlike story heeds Tatlin's advice, that "all must be kept kinetic, fluid, revolutionary." Its chief trope is flying: soaring, gliding, defeating gravity, including the heaviness of linear plot and the weight of history that manifests itself in the story both temporally (the eve of Stalin's purges) and spatially (the repetition of D.'s full-page bannerlike drawings of Lenin and Stalin hauntingly rendered in deadening social realist style). *DaVinci's Bicycle* (1979), D.'s best collection, travels allusively through time and space, from South Carolina to Dogon myth, rescuing, among others, C. Musonius Rufus and Robert Walser (the proto-Kafka), juxtaposing the imaginative, inventive brilliance of DaVinci and the singular yet strangely representative dullness of the Nixon who "opened" China.

The collections that followed: *Eclogues; Trois Caprices* (1981); *Apples and Pears; The Jules Verne Steam Balloon* (1987)—although marked by the same "sheer precision and uncompromising artistry"—otherwise seem less successful than either the earlier ones or the two much discussed collections of essays D. published during this same period, *The Geography of the Imagination* (1981) and *Every Force Evolves a Form* (1987). A third collection, *The Hunter Gracchus,* appeared in 1996 and a selection of previously published fiction, *Twelve Stories,* the following year. The ten "stories" in *A Table of Green Fields* (1993), with its three pages of reader-friendly "Author's Notes," evidence D. back in top form, the intricate and inviting lead assemblage, "August Blue," in particular. It is unlikely that D.'s fiction will, even with appended notes, prove any more successful in restoring a sense of cultural and imaginative wholeness than did the poems and novels of the modernist writers D. so admires; indeed it may even serve to increase most readers' sense of alienation. But for those less constrained by convention, more inquisitive than acquisitive, his astonishing assemblages will prove a source of imaginative as well as intellectual wonder and delight, their aesthetic riches nicely balanced by their utopian aspirations.

BIBLIOGRAPHY: Morace, R. A., "Invention in *Da-Vinci's Bicycle*," *Crit* 22 (April 1981): 71–87; Olsen, L., *Circus of the Mind in Motion: Postmodernism and the Comic Vision* (1990); Schöpp, J. C., "Perfect Landscape with Pastoral Figures": G. D.'s Danish Eclogue à la Fourier," in Ziegler, H., ed., *Facing Texts: Encounters between Contemporary Writers and Critics* (1988): 128–39

ROBERT A. MORACE

DAVIDSON, Donald [Grady]

b. 18 August 1893, Campbellsville, Tennessee; d. 25 April 1968, Nashville, Tennessee

D.'s professional life comprised three roles, poet, critic, and scholarly professor, with each role being guided by a poetic sensibility grounded in D.'s unerring understanding of himself as a small-town Tennessean. Though understandable, it is still frustrating to some readers that D. and his work have not become better known and more widely discussed over the years, for in both his literary and social criticism and his poetry are found a rare artistic talent and perhaps an even rarer gift for graceful and forceful prose that few mid-20th-c. American essayists can equal.

One can attribute D.'s general lack of notoriety today to his reputation as one of the Nashville Agrarians. This categorization is in itself all-too-often reductive and misunderstood, and, too, it has had the effect of placing D. in unjustified competition with his lifelong friends and Agrarian colleagues and collaborators Robert Penn WARREN, Allen TATE, and John Crowe RANSOM. Careful study, however, suggests that D. stands very well on his own not only as an accomplished artist, but also as a developer of a rigorous artistic aesthetic rooted in a regionally-based social vision, a vision serves to shed light on the work of his Southern contemporaries and, more importantly, on the work of any regionally inspired American art.

Still, it must be admitted that D. acquired his Agrarian reputation honestly. As one of the most demonstrably regionally driven thinkers and poets contributing to *I'll Take My Stand* (1930), D. seems to embody what the "Twelve Southerners" meant by Agrarian, although part of that image is attained only in retrospect. As other Agrarian essayists left the South, D. dug deeper into it, wrestling with and exposing the problems and tensions he saw in the disappearance of his region's traditional past in the wake of a progressive, technologically based and modern present. Hints of the theme of tradition versus progress are already evident in *An Outland Piper* (1924), his first collection of poems, and it achieves clearer expression and power in his next collection, *The Tall Men* (1927). In the years between these works, D. honed his artistic skills and sharpened his sensibilities through his teaching at Vanderbilt (where he remained as an English professor from 1922 to 1964), but more significantly through his involvement in the informal poetry reading group whose members gained notoriety through their publication the *Fugitive*. Most scholars agree with Randall Stewart's assessment of D. as the primary mover of the Fugitive poets' publishing efforts.

D.'s work with the short-lived but influential *Fugitive* helped him develop an intensely discerning critical eye for poetry and kept him in constant contact and correspondence with some of the finest American poets of the day. This period in the late 1920s of high-pitched aesthetic discussions produced the artistic germ for the social criticism of the Nashville Agrarians in the early 1930s. In *I'll Take My Stand*, D. produced his first essay dealing with the difficulties of producing Art in the modern age; "A Mirror For Artists" continues to merit serious consideration by scholars, and not only for its insightful and unnervingly prophetic discussion of the difficulties produced federally funded art programs.

The subsequent Agrarian publication, *Who Owns America?* (1938), was less than successful, and its discussions of regional-and folk-based economies, although its perceived nationalistic leanings were neither particularly well understood nor well received by an economically depressed nation in a world moving toward military crisis. Nevertheless, D. maintained and worked to clarify his belief that understanding one's regional identity is the only sure way for an individual to maintain a sense of self. This sense of self becomes synonymous with the individual's understanding and preservation of a traditional past in the fragmented, modern world. The culmination of D.'s thoughts on these subjects appeared in two 1938 collections, one of poetry—*Lee in the Mountains and Other Poems*—and the other of essays—*The Attack on Leviathan*, which has recently been reprinted under its original subtitle *Regionalism and Nationalism in the United States.*

The poems from the 1938 volume are remarkable examples of the power of D.'s poetry at its best. The title piece, "Lee in the Mountains," is his most anthologized work and arguably one of the very finest, if most overlooked, great American poems. In its subject matter, a long interior monologue and reflection by Robert E. Lee, D. finds the objective correlative he seeks but often seems just to miss in other poems. But in the poem, D. captures what he came to describe as the Agrarians' purpose, "to seek the image of the South which [one] could cherish with high conviction and to give it . . . the finality of art in those forms fictional, poetical, or dramatic, that have the character of myth." This same purpose can as easily be applied to D.'s own art and efforts.

D.'s other major works include *The Tennessee,* a two-volume history of the Tennessee River and world along its banks. A second collection of essays, most reprinted from earlier publications, appeared in 1957 under the title *Still Rebels, Still Yankees.* A 1957 Lamar Lecture series appeared that same year under the title *Southern Writers in the Modern World.* And three publications were printed in the years just before his death: *The Long Street* (1961), his fourth volume of poetry that contains both older and some newer very fine works; *The Spyglass* (1963), a collection chiefly of reviews published in the Nashville *Tennessean;* and finally *Poems: 1922–1961* (1966). D.'s only novel, *The Big Ballad Jamboree* (1996), was published post-humously.

What remains so compelling about the whole of D.'s work—his poetry, criticism, even his composition textbooks—is that it forms a cohesive and unswerving effort to understand the 20th-c. American South, and in that singleness of purpose reflects a cohesive vision of one of America's, certainly one of the South's, most refined men of letters who, though he never moved far from his point of origin, found in his local surroundings the stuff of universally applicable art and thought.

BIBLIOGRAPHY: Hill, R. W., "D. D.," in Quartermain, P., ed., *DLB,* vol. 45, *American Poets, 1880–1945* (1986): 94–107; Rubin, L. D., et al., eds., *The History of Southern Literature* (1985); Young, T. D., and M. T. Inge, *D. D.* (1971)

JOHN V. GLASS

DAVIS, H[arold] L[enoir]

b. 18 October 1894, Rone's Mill, Oregon; d. 31 October 1960, San Antonio, Texas

D. began his literary career as a poet; he later had financial and critical success as a short story writer. His greatest popularity, however, came from his five novels set in the American West in the late 19th and early 20th cs. The first of these, *Honey in the Horn* (1935), won D. a Pulitzer Prize.

D. was the son of a country schoolteacher who moved frequently from job to job in Oregon. D.'s experiences gave him a thorough familiarity with the rural areas of the state where he spent his youth and, after high school, worked as an assessor and a surveyor for several years. He went away to Stanford University when he had saved some money, but he soon returned to Oregon when the funds ran out.

In 1918, he was drafted and served three months before he was discharged. During this brief military career, he sent poems to Chicago's *Poetry* magazine, whose editor praised and published them. The work was also admired by Carl SANDBURG and Robinson JEFFERS. After his discharge, D. returned to Oregon and wrote poetry while working at various jobs. In 1926, he attracted the interest of H. L. MENCKEN, who urged him to turn to fiction. First, however, he created a stir with a literary manifesto, *Status Rerum* (1927), coauthored by James Stevens, which criticized the Northwest's literary establishment, including the writing programs at the Universities of Oregon and Washington.

D.'s first short story appeared in 1928. By 1941, he had published twenty-five short stories and ten sketches, most dealing with rural Oregon life, a topic his poetry had also explored. His use of vernacular language and humor have caused some of these works, notably the sketches "Team Bells Woke Me" and "A Town in Eastern Oregon" and the stories "Old Man Isbell's Wife," "Homestead Orchard," and "Open Winter," to be increasingly admired, though his short prose was not collected until 1953.

He was able to earn a living by writing during this period. D. also earned a Guggenheim Fellowship to write an epic poem in Mexico; however, he instead produced his first novel. *Honey in the Horn,* a humorous tale of a young orphan on a wandering, at times picaresque journey in the West, attempts to show the universal human experience at the heart of the western myth. Not all critics appreciated this: some praised the novel only for its western scenery and dialects, some dismissed it as a pulp adventure story, and some criticized the lack of individuality in the main character—a critique whose validity D. later acknowledged. Nevertheless, *Honey in the Horn* was the Harper Prize Novel in 1935 and won a Pulitzer Prize the following year.

While embroiled in a dispute with his publishers over the rights to his second novel, D. allowed the company to release a volume of collected poetry in 1942. He took his second novel, *Harp of a Thousand Strings* (1947), to a new publisher. A less comical work integrating three separate story lines moving from Tripoli to Oklahoma, *Harp of a Thousand Strings* was given a fairly good critical reception. D.

then began to rework an earlier manuscript which became his third novel, *Beulah Land* (1950). Another journey is featured in this book's depiction of a mixed-race woman looking for a place to belong in the West. This novel, a more purely realistic work than the previous two, was considered evidence of D.'s maturing talent.

Some critics regard D.'s fourth novel as his finest. *Winds of Morning* (1952), again set in Oregon, combines Christian symbolism and folk humor in a more controlled structure than *Honey in the Horn*. The novel depicts another journey on which the young narrator accepts his responsibilities and his older companion reconciles with his past. *Winds of Morning* was extremely successful with critics and the public alike.

From 1953 until the end of his life, D. worked on a series of essays about the Pacific Northwest for *Holiday* magazine. A collection of short prose appeared in 1953. D.'s health, long precarious, worsened in 1956; acute arteriosclerosis necessitated the amputation of his left leg. In 1957, his last novel, *The Distant Music,* appeared, but was considered too ambitious in scope and, finally, less successful than the previous four. A short story published in 1959 was intended to be the beginning of a sixth novel, which he did not live to complete. While visiting Texas in 1960, he suffered a heart attack on his birthday and remained hospitalized until a second attack less than two weeks later caused his death.

D.'s reputation as a literary artist exploring the Western experience has increased in the intervening years. The seriousness of his subject is no longer in doubt, and the best of his novels and short stories have earned a place in the American literary canon.

BIBLIOGRAPHY: Bain, R., *H. L. D.* (1974); Bryant, P. T., *H. L. D.* (1978); Bryant, P. T., "H. L. D.," in Martine, J. J., ed., *DLB*, vol. 9, part 1, *American Novelists, 1900–1945* (1981): 188–92

CAROLYN LENGEL

DAVIS, Rebecca [Blaine] Harding

b. 24 June 1831, Washington, Pennsylvania; d. 29 September 1910, Mount Kisco, New York

As an author emerging in the latter half of the 19th c., D. was shaped by a richly paradoxical set of influences. She was a devout Christian, and her religious sensibility finds varied expression in work that creatively merges popular sentimentalism as well as competing strains of ROMANTICISM, REALISM, and NATURALISM. In narratives such as "Life in the Iron Mills" and *Margret Howth: A Story of Today* (1862), D. integrates a variety of ethical and religious concerns.

She has emerged from the dimly lit back shelves of literary history as an author concerned with the historical experience of the industrial revolution. Her work negotiates between the ideals and utopian hopes of TRANSCENDENTALISM, the ascetic impulses of Christianity, and an increasing awareness of the dark and sordid reality that many Americans were forced to endure. Through her powers of observation and expression, she balanced these tensions in a series of brief but distinctive narratives that capture the multifaceted character of her region and her nation.

D. spent her first five years in Huntsville, Alabama and moved to Wheeling, West Virginia in 1836. Valuing education highly, her parents provided her with private tutors, through which she was exposed to John Bunyan, Maria Edgeworth, Sir Walter Scott, Charles Dickens, and particularly Nathaniel HAWTHORNE. She concluded her formal education at the Washington Female Seminary in Washington, Pennsylvania. Her writing career began some years later with the *Atlantic Monthly* and the publication of "The Life in the Iron Mills." As a young woman of genteel birth in Pennsylvania, D. observed from a comfortable distance the brutal conditions experienced by the working poor in the industrial North. Employing a realistic technique in physical description, she portrayed the dark descent of a sensitive and delicate mill worker, Hugh Wolfe. In its preoccupation with the psychological transformative power of physical experience, "Life in the Iron Mills" anticipates later naturalists and prefigures such works as Stephen CRANE's *Maggie*.

"Life in the Iron Mills" was tremendously well received, and as a result, James T. Fields, editor of the *Atlantic Monthly,* requested more fiction from D. She responded with *Margret Howth: A Story of Today* and with it secured her reputation. As a result of her literary success, D. exchanged ideas with Hawthorne, Louisa May ALCOTT, Ralph Waldo EMERSON, and Oliver Wendell HOLMES. She continued writing, focusing upon the Civil War as a primary subject, exploring in detail the effects of the war upon both participants and those who waited at home. D.'s Civil War stories include "John Lamar" (1862), "David Gaunt" (1862), and "Paul Blecker" (1863). These brief works are indebted to Hawthorne and the psychological romance, since they focus on the transformative role of experience in shaping and reshaping the human mind. D.'s work at this stage in her career, in spite of a romantic preoccupation with the psychological and personal, came to exemplify the emerging realism of the period. This literary practice continues in *Waiting for the Verdict* (1868), a novel dealing with the black experience in America, and *John Andross* (1874), a work about political corruption in Pennsylvania. She wrote several other novels, an autobiography, and a number of short stories collected in *Silhouettes of American Life* (1892).

D.'s work is a channel through which the diverse influences of a changing intellectual culture merge and reconstitute themselves. She combines the fervent optimism of Emerson and Walt WHITMAN, the cautious skepticism of Hawthorne and Herman MELVILLE, and the seething wry cynicism of Samuel Langhorne CLEMENS. "Life in the Iron Mills" best exemplifies these tensions. Like later authors such as Crane, Theodore DREISER, Frank NORRIS, Jack LONDON, and JOHN STEINBECK, D. powerfully portrays the stark and dramatic dichotomies of American history and literature.

BIBLIOGRAPHY: Harris, S. M., *R. H. D. and American Realism* (1991); Lungford, G., *The Richard Harding Davis Years: A Biography of Mother and Son* (1961); Quinn, A. H., *American Fiction: An Historical and Critical Survey* (1936); Rose, J. A., *R. H. D.* (1993)

STEVEN FRYE

DAVIS, Richard Harding

b. 18 April 1864, Philadelphia, Pennsylvania; d. 11 April 1916, Mount Kisco, New York

More than any other writer of the fin-de-siècle generation, D. epitomized the genteel man of letters. A celebrated war correspondent and popular fiction writer, D. was also a tireless self-promoter who well understood the importance of publicity to literary reputation.

Son of the novelist Rebecca Harding DAVIS, he early developed a sentimental and impressionistic style of journalistic writing. An indifferent student, D. withdrew from Lehigh University in 1885 without completing a degree. During his apprenticeship as a reporter for several Philadelphia and New York newspapers, he earned a reputation for human interest writing. He also won renown for such travel books as *The West from a Car Window* (1892), *Our English Cousins* (1894), and *About Paris* (1895), in which he assumed a polite if slightly jaundiced narrative perspective. A pioneering sportswriter, D. was also paid the unprecedented sum of $500 to cover the 1895 Yale-Princeton football game for the Hearst syndicate of newspapers. Best known for founding the "glamourboy" school of war correspondence, he reported the exploits of Theodore ROOSEVELT's Rough Riders for the *New York Herald* during the Spanish-American War. Later, however, he was disappointed by the assumptions of Anglo superiority during the Boer War, as he explained in *With Both Armies in South Africa* (1900), and he was disgusted by German atrocities during World War I, as he detailed in *With the Allies* (1914).

As a writer of popular fiction, D. specialized in mechanical or formulaic plots centering on a gentleman-adventurer with whom he was often identified. As in his journalism, D.'s fiction was marked by glib turns of phrase, as when he wrote in "The Mind Reader" (1912) that there were only "two kinds of men who succeed in writing fiction—men of genius and reporters." The sophisticated Courtland Van Bibber, the hero of many of his best tales, betrays the decisive influence of Rudyard Kipling and Robert Louis Stevenson. His most popular story "Gallegher" (1890) recounts how a stringer for the *Philadelphia Press* solves a murder case the police have been unable to break. "An Unfinished Story" (1891) and *Soldier of Fortune* (1897) argue for the superiority of literary romance over realism. The latter text, the critical and commercial highlight of his career, also defends American economic interests abroad. In such late stories as "My Buried Treasure" (1911), D. still pleaded the case for a chivalric code, albeit less earnestly than in his earliest stories. He also tried to exploit his popularity as the author of such theatrical farces as *The Dictator* (1904) and *The Galloper* (1906), the first about the affairs of the state in a fictional Latin American republic, the second based on his reportage of the Greco-Turkish war. In all, D.'s chief claim to modern fame is as a forerunner of the "virile" or "muscular" school of writers that includes Jack LONDON, Stephen CRANE, Ernest HEMINGWAY, and Norman MAILER.

BIBLIOGRAPHY: Eichelberger, C. L., and A. M. McDonald, "R. H. D. (1864–1916): A Check List of Secondary Comment," *ALR* 4 (1971): 313–89; Lubow, A., *The Reporter Who Would Be King: A Biography of R. H. D.* (1992); Osborn, S. C., and R. L. Phillips, Jr., *R. H. D.* (1978)

GARY SCHARNHORST

DAY, Clarence [Shepard, Jr.]

b. 18 November 1874, New York City; d. 28 December 1935, New York City

Remembered primarily for his autobiographical work *Life with Father* (1935), D. began his career with the publication of *This Simian World* (1920), an elegantly written serio-comic essay on the origins of the human race. After speculating about alternative evolutionary paths had humankind descended from ants, snakes, cats, or elephants, D. reflects on such simian traits as curiosity and a distractible brain. Because of simian fears, there is "too urgent need of religion" and a god "who drops any cosmic affair at short notice . . . to notice a fellow when he is going to bed." The success of this light-hearted, humanistic essay caught the attention of *New Yorker* editor Harold Ross, who recruited D. to write for the magazine. Virtually all of D.'s later publications originally appeared as articles in the *New Yorker.*

Thoughts without Words (1928), a collection of D.'s drawings was, by his own admission, a "horrible failure" commercially and led him to turn to his own childhood for new subject matter. Following the moderate success of *God and My Father* (1932), D. continued to portray his Victorian New York childhood in *Life with Father,* one of the most popular books of the period. In a deceptively simple, almost conversational prose style, D. humorously recounts the petty tyrannies and tantrums of his father as well as the more subtle and effective challenges of his mother. In 1940, *Life with Father* was transformed by Howard Lindsay and Russel Crouse into a play that ran for six years on Broadway, and a later film version adapted by Donald Ogden STEWART (1947) was also successful. Two subsequent volumes of D.'s autobiographical writings—*Life with Mother* (1937) and *Father and I* (1940)—were edited by his wife and published posthumously. As a result of the quiet wit that punctures the image of heavy masculine domination, D.'s comic memoirs continue to attract new readers.

BIBLIOGRAPHY: Schwartz, R. A., "C. D.," in Trachtenberg, S., ed., *DLB,* vol. 11, part 1, *American Humorists, 1800–1950* (1982): 108–13; Yates, N. W., *The American Humorist: Conscience of the Twentieth C.* (1964)

RICHARD NORDQUIST

DE FOREST, John W[illiam]

b. 31 March 1826, Humphreysville (now Seymour) Connecticut; d. 17 July 1906, New Haven, Connecticut

D. was born in Connecticut and lived in New Haven for most of his life. He prepared for the Yale University entrance examinations, but illness prevented his attempting a college education. Instead, to improve his health, he was sent abroad and spent several years in the Middle East and in Europe.

He began a half-century writing career with nonfiction by publishing a useful *History of the Indians of Connecticut* (1851). His travels gave him the materials for *Oriental Acquaintance* (1856) and *European Acquaintance* (1858), unpretentious, gossipy accounts of ordinary scenes and sights. During the Civil War, he served as a Union officer and chronicled his experiences in letters home and in a series of articles for *Harper's New Monthly Magazine* and the *Galaxy.* In his later years, he formed these materials into a book, but the manuscript was not published until 1946 as *A Volunteer's Adventures.* In a plain style, he recorded the facts of war and military duties, the emotional stresses of the soldier, and the coarseness of day to day army existence. D. spent some postwar years of service in South Carolina and wrote articles about these experiences, which he later converted into a book manuscript intended as a second volume in his planned *Military Life.* Again he was unsuccessful in gaining publication and the book finally appeared in 1948 as *A Union Officer in the Reconstruction.* His duties in the Freedman's Bureau provided him with first hand information about the problems of Reconstruction and of the new relationships between black and white citizens. He came to know the people of his district well, and the book is a vivid realization of a portion of the country's history.

These journalistic writings displayed D.'s natural inclination toward the realistic portrayal of persons, scenes, and events. At the same time, he was widely read in the fiction of REALISM; he knew the works of Balzac, Stendhal, Dickens, Thackeray, and George Eliot and found much to approve in their works. In an interesting magazine article, "The Great American Novel" (1868), he used their works to point out the difference between the mature literary culture of Europe and that of our country.

D. began writing fiction early in his career. In 1856–57, his first novel, *Witching Times,* was serialized in *Putnam's Monthly Magazine;* it did not reach book publication in his lifetime. The story offers a rational account of the witchcraft trials in Salem, mixing its fictional characters with some of the historical personages who took part in the events. A second novel, *Seacliff* (1859), a contemporary mystery story, is a slighter work.

During his military service, D. wrote the novel that has secured his posthumous reputation, *Miss Ravenel's Conversion from Secession to Loyalty* (1867). The book is a study of the divided loyalties of citizens in the period just before the Civil War, a love story that deals with the tensions of Northern and Southern feelings, and a panoramic picture of some of the battles in the war. The battle scenes are presented realistically and are different in kind from what had gone before in American literature; they owe some of their force, perhaps, to D.'s reading of Stendhal. Despite its excellence, the novel did not attract the attention it deserved, and William Dean HOWELLS, a warm advocate of his friend's work, guessed that a reason for its failure might be its inability to appeal to a female audience. War was the province of men's literature and the portrayal of Lily Ravenel was felt to be too unsympathetic.

Attempts to reach a popular audience did not serve D. well, and he scattered his talents by trying too many things. Two novels, *Della; or, The Wild Girl* and *Annie Howard,* serialized in *Hearth and Home* in 1870, have never appeared as books. A Western adventure, *Overland* (1871), dealing with potentially interesting material, has a dime novel plot calculated to appeal to boys. Another try at a mystery novel, *The Wetherall Affair* (1873) was a failure. At the same time, a fair number of shorter magazine stories have made little impression.

However, the author did produce some fiction that should interest the modern reader. In *Kate Beaumont* (1872), he draws a careful picture of prewar life in South Carolina. Two satirical novels, *Honest John Vane* (1875) and *Playing the Mischief* (1875), present a perceptive analysis of corruption in Washington during the Grant administration.

Critical opinion is divided about *Irene the Missionary* (1879), a study of life in Syria, based upon D.'s earlier travels. *The Bloody Chasm* (1881), set just after the war, gives an account of the effects of the war and of Reconstruction upon citizens of South Carolina, another subject for which D. could draw upon the fund of his experiences. After a long interval during which he gave up the practice of fiction, D. wrote a final novel, *A Lover's Revolt* (1898), set during the American Revolution and offering portraits of historical personages and the battles of Lexington and Bunker Hill.

With the exception of *Miss Ravenel's Conversion,* D.'s novels have received little attention in the 20th c. In his study of the literature of the Civil War, *Patriotic Gore* (1962), Edmund WILSON offered a long account of D.'s career and tried to account for the writer's unpopularity. The novelist, he asserted, has a "curiously dull and chill touch" in his treatment of characters and scenes and his novels "never quite come off." Wilson's judgment is a perceptive one and probably accounts for D.'s troubles with the reading public. He certainly had the materials available to write important novels, and, at least once in his career, was able to do so. His broad range of interests allowed him to treat a significant part of American history, from colonial times to the late 19th c., and his characterizations are of a large and varied gallery of persons.

After giving up fiction, D. turned to writing poetry and proved himself an amateurish and uninteresting poet. At his own expense, he published *The Downing Legends* (1901) and *Poems: Medley and Palestina* (1902). The legends were what he called them in his preface, rhymed magazine stories and extravaganzas, while the medley was made up of short poems, mostly religious.

BIBLIOGRAPHY: Bergmann, F., *The Worthy Gentleman of Democracy: J. W. D. and the American Dream* (1971); Garango, J. W., ed., *Critical Essays on J. W. D.* (1981); Hijiya, J. A., *J. W. D. and the Rise of American Gentility* (1988); Light, J. F., *J. W. D.* (1965)

DOUGLAS ROBILLARD

DELAND, Margaret

b. 28 February 1857, near Allegheny, Pennsylvania;
d. 13 January 1945, Boston, Massachusetts

Tensions between old and new customs and mores and between contrasting values drive D.'s novels and short stories. D., who lived from before the Civil War to the last year of World War II, saw tremendous changes in America, and her fiction reported those changes to great popular success. Her prolific writings were so eagerly read and widely admired that she earned an international reputation, four honorary doctorates, and the distinction in 1926 of being one of the first women—along with Edith WHARTON—to be inducted into the National Institute of Arts and Letters. But perhaps because the issues in her works were so compelling in her time, some of those concerns now seem dated, and her former fame is considerably diminished.

D. was born Margaretta Wade Campbell, named for her mother, who died at her birth. Orphaned at four, D. was raised by an aunt on a wealthy estate in Manchester, Pennsylvania; she fictionalized this town as "Old Chester" in her first published short story, "Mr. Tommy Dove," which appeared in the *Atlantic Monthly* in January 1889.

D. quickly proved herself an unusually independent woman. In 1875, she moved to New York, alone, to study art and design at Cooper Union. She was hired as an assistant instructor in drawing and design at Girls' Normal School (now Hunter College) the following year. In 1880, she married Lorin Deland of Boston. The couple's shared social vision led them to open their home to unwed mothers and their infants. These experiences convinced her of the need for sex education and birth control, although the childless D. retained an almost sentimental respect for the redeeming possibilities of maternal love. To help support the household, D. began to write poetry. She published in magazines beginning in 1885, and in 1886, when Houghton, Mifflin published a collection, *The Old Garden and Other Verses,* the first printing sold out in a week.

Raised a strict Presbyterian, D. began to question the tenets of her faith, and she and her husband later became Episcopalians. Her doubts are reflected in her first published novel, *John Ward, Preacher* (1888), which draws sympathetic portraits of both the strict Calvinist Ward and his beloved liberal wife. This book and two later novels, *Philip and His Wife* (1890) and *Sidney: The Story of a Child* (1892), aroused controversy; some critics denounced her works as immoral, while others praised her rejection of religious orthodoxy.

But if some of her subject matter was overtly controversial, D. could also charm a wide audience. Her most popular fiction continued to detail the lives of Old Chester's citizens. Recurring characters from the town appeared in several short stories, which became part of the Old Chester collections *Old Chester Tales* (1899), *Dr. Lavendar's People* (1903), *Around Old Chester* (1915), and *New Friends in Old Chester* (1924). In these character studies, D. shows morality to be relative and complex by approaching the same ethical dilemmas again and again through different characters and presenting the varying outcomes of their decisions.

After achieving widespread fame, D. also wrote some nonfiction. She published articles on one of her favorite social issues, the status of women in American society—a subject on which she was surprisingly, and perhaps contradictorily, elitist. In addition, she wrote two autobiographical works, *If This Be I, As I Suppose It Be* (1938) and *Golden Yesterdays* (1941), and a collection of pieces about her experiences in war-torn France, collected as *Small Things* (1919).

Once a household name, D. has become much less well known since her death. Her concern with the societal issues of her time makes much of her work seem outmoded. D.'s once-controversial positions on religion and sex are now of interest chiefly as a window into an earlier era in American life. But her best works, especially the finest Old Chester materials, address universal human qualities and thus transcend their time.

BIBLIOGRAPHY: St. Andrews, B. A., "M. D.," in Kimbel, B. E., ed., *DLB,* vol. 78, *American Short-Story Writers, 1880–1910* (1989): 147–53; Reep, D. C., *M. D.* (1985)

                                        CAROLYN LENGEL

DELILLO, Don
b. 20 November 1936, New York City

D. has emerged as one of the most important and consistently interesting American novelists of the late 20th c. His ten novels—along with a handful of short stories, essays, and plays—comprehend the vast surface of contemporary American life while plumbing the depths of anomie and obsession lurking below. D. writes both about his age and against it and "its facile knowledge-market." Although far more verbal than visual, his novels possess a cinematic quality. Giving the impression of being edited rather than linearly and causally developed, they create a sense of disjunction and dislocation. Readers and characters experience what it is like to be lost in the perpetual present of postmodern space and to face the contemporary crises of identity and "referentiality," the split between word and world. D.'s prose is perfectly suited to his vision: flattened, often disembodied dialogue, barely fleshed out characters, edgy humor. Yet what makes his "terrific comedy" so unnerving is the way in which D. invests his depiction of "the way we live now" with an almost prophetic quality, each of his novels serving as an early warning system for the seismic social disturbances to follow.

D.'s novels evidence his interest in the ways in which technology changes man's relation to reality, consumerism makes people lonely and the world increasingly inaccessible, and "desperate men give their solitude a purpose and a destiny." Technological change, social disintegration, paranoia and conspiracy breed the restlessness, the pervasive transience of his fiction, a sense of drift on the one hand and paranoid, obsessive plot on the other. In D.'s world, the more denatured reality becomes—the more artificial and man-made—the more inhuman it appears and the greater his characters' need for some means for obsessively ordering and controlling it.

D. discovered his essential subject early. "This is America. Bad as it is we have to learn to live with it." For the main character of *Americana* (1971), a twenty-eight-year-old television executive, this means leaving his job and "realizing the strangest, darkest, most horrifying idea" of his life: making a film "somewhere out there among the lost towns of America." D. found his distinctive style in his second novel, the leaner, eerier *End Zone* (1972), in which Logos College in Texas—"built out of nothing in the middle of nowhere"—becomes a microcosm of the country and football one means among many for artificially ordering and controlling "the overflowing world." In *Great Jones Street* (1973), rock star Bucky Wunderlich withdraws from fame, fans, "sensory overload," and a world increasingly ruled by corporate giant Transparanoia only to find himself in a plot involving a drug produced by the government to silence troublemakers. If Bucky is a latter-day Holden Caulfield, then Billy Twillig is D.'s Alice in a Wonderland of rarefied mathematics. More ambitious than successful, *Ratner's Star* (1976) focuses on secret scientific efforts to decode a message from space which turns out to have originated from earth thousands of years earlier, sent by a civilization just as advanced, self-deluded and self-destructive as Billy's. *Players* (1977) and *Running Dog* (1978) rehearse several of the major themes that receive fuller and more complex treatment in *The Names* (1982), whose main character follows his estranged wife and their son to Greece, takes a job in Athens as a "risk analyst" for a transnational company with links to the CIA and becomes interested in a murderous, quasi-religious cult of Abecedarians, one of the many Middle Eastern groups that "burn with a clear vision" of a design outside time, their alternative to the drift and abstraction of Western consumerism and information gathering.

White Noise (1984) was D.'s breakthrough novel, reaching a wider audience and published to greater critical acclaim than any of his previous works. This book club selection and winner of an American Book Award offers D.'s fullest (and funniest) look at postmodern life, American style: the restructuring of family, the nature of higher education, the pervasiveness of mediation and simulation, the constant low-level panic, the denaturing of life and death, the enfeebling of the self, the growing toxicity (cultural as well as chemical), and the growing reliance on therapeutic services, tabloid fantasies, and of course plots. Plot is central to *Libra* (1988), which deals directly with what is in effect the subtext of all D.'s fiction, the assassination of John F. Kennedy. If the assassination is, as D. has said, "a story about our uncertain grasp on the world," then *Libra* offers less an explanation than "a way of thinking about the assassination without being constrained by half-truths or overwhelmed by possibilities, by the tide of speculation that widens with the years." For D., the assassination is neither an isolated act nor part of a conspiracy but instead a sign of the times, much like the international terrorism in *Mao II* (1991), which makes its J. D. SALINGER/Thomas PYNCHON-like author Bill Gray feel and be increasingly marginalized. Although only half as long as *Libra, Mao II* both sums up and extends D.'s densely textured and deeply disturbing depiction of contemporary life in an age of televised "blur and glut" and of pop icons, from Andy Warhol and Reverend Moon to Chairman Mao and the Ayotollah Khomeini. No one writes better about the "blur and glut" of postmodern life or about "what happens to all the unexpended faith" when "the old God leaves the world."

BIBLIOGRAPHY: Keesey, D., *D. D.* (1993); LeClair, T., *In the Loop: D. D. and the Systems Novel* (1988); Lentricchia, F., ed., *Introducing D. D.* (1991); Tabbi, J., *Postmodern Sublime: Technology and American Writing from Mailer to Cyberpunk* (1995)

ROBERT A. MORACE

DEMBY, William
b. 25 December 1922, Pittsburgh, Pennsylvania

D. is known primarily for his existentialist novels. Set in the U.S. and in Europe, most of his stories scrutinize the black experience of the 1950s and 1960s. He appeared on the literary scene as a new talent in 1950

with a very good first novel entitled *Beetlecreek,* which draws upon his experiences as a youth growing up in West Virginia. It was followed fifteen years later by the experimental work, *The Catacombs,* which reflects D.'s long immersion in the Roman world of art and film.

During World War II, D. joined the U.S. Army and served in Italy and in North Africa. Returning to the U.S. after the war, he enrolled at Fisk University; however, upon graduation the pull of Europe drew him back to Italy to study art. For the next twenty years he wrote screenplays and scripts for Italian film and television productions. Much of what he learned about cinema technique at this time found its way into his literary work.

It was while he was abroad that he began work on *Beetlecreek,* a starkly realistic depiction of evil and stagnation among men and women in the black community of a West Virginia mining town during the Great Depression. The protagonist is the young black man Johnny Johnson who teams up with his uncle in befriending Bill Trapp, a white hermit. However, the perverse pressures of the black society force Johnny and his uncle to turn against Trapp; whereupon, for the purpose of gaining membership in the community's black gang, Johnny tries to burn down Trapp's house. The general theme of human alienation is conveyed through means of cinematic devices that focus on visual objects and activities suggesting larger meanings and moral ambiguities. D. portrays both black and white characters as morally deficient persons who demonstrate negative traits of narrowmindedness, prejudice, and violent evil. He makes his book serve as an indictment of the whole of human society.

In D.'s second and most critically acclaimed work, *The Catacombs,* he places himself as a character in the story who is writing a novel in Rome about a black woman named Doris with whom at times he is having a love affair. Demby has introduced Doris to an Italian count, and she has begun a two-year liaison with the Count while still continuing to meet with Demby. Doris becomes pregnant with the Count's or Demby's child, but the baby is born dead. The novel ends in the Catacombs of Rome where the Count has taken Doris to view the site of the ancient Christian martyrs. There the Count loses her and frantically searches the dank, winding underground passages while calling out Doris's name.

By making himself the central character and unifying force in the story, D. is able to bring all the novel's loose ends and experimental devices together for their full effect. Here he uses a stream-of-consciousness technique that permits the reader to probe the writer's innermost thoughts and deepest sense of awareness. Most of these musings focus on historical incidents and major events, such as the death of Pope John XXIII, the Cuban Missile Crisis of 1962, and the assassination of President John F. Kennedy. Many of D.'s thoughts are evoked by the actual headlines and news items of contemporary happenings that he literally presents in the novel. Related to these devices is D.'s overall view of reality derived from the Cubistic artists who conceived of all time and all strands of life as existing in a state of simultaneity.

The Catacombs is another work of death and passivity, but here D. presents a counterforce. While the Count represents the decadence of Western society, Doris expresses the life force. In addition, she is associated with a dynamic African heritage that can revitalize the catacombs of the West. Both the Count and Doris symbolize the opposing struggles within the mind and heart of D. The fact that the novel begins and ends during the Easter season and that Demby decides to return to the U.S. on Easter Monday demonstrates the work's theme of resurrection.

In 1969, D. began his long teaching career at the College of Staten Island of the City University of New York. He wrote two other novels, *Love Story Black* (1978) and *Blueboy* (1979), but this later writing is more conventional and not as successful as his early work. *Love Story Black* analyzes three levels of love experienced by its narrator and main character, named Edwards, who undergoes two unfulfilling relationships. However, a third one proves to be somewhat Edenic and most rewarding. D.'s themes related to myth and race are still evident in these literary expressions.

BIBLIOGRAPHY: Berry, J. R., "The Achievement of W. D.," *CLAJ* 26 (June 1983): 434–51; Bone, R., *The Negro Novel in America* (1965); Bone, R., "W. D.'s Dance of Life," *TriQ* (Spring 1969): 127–41; Margolies, E., *Native Sons: A Critical Study of Twentieth-Century Negro American Authors* (1968)

ANGELO COSTANZO

DERLETH, August [William]
b. 24 February 1909, Sauk City, Wisconsin; d. 4 July 1971, Sauk City, Wisconsin

D. was a phenomenally prolific writer who wrote or edited more than 150 books, the best of which are focused on his hometown of Sauk City, Wisconsin, and its companion town of Prairie du Sac. Writing under a variety of pseudonyms—Stephen Grendon, Tally Mason, Eldon Heath, Simon West, Michael West, Kenyon Holmes, Will Garth, and Romily Devon—D. merged the names and historical events of these two towns to create his fictive village of "Sac Prairie," a

Wisconsin village whose inhabitants he described in thirty-eight volumes of poetry, short stories, novels, and prose sketches known collectively as the "Sac Prairie Saga."

The Sac Prairie Saga focuses on the everyday lives of real people in a small German farming community, some of whom D. knew so well as a boy that he could walk into their homes without knocking or ringing the doorbell. D. presented the lives of these people (and their forbears) with such an insightful blend of understanding, humor, and nostalgia that he achieved a permanent if minor place as a successful regional writer.

Educated in the country ways of Sauk City and at the University of Wisconsin, D. worked for several months as an editorial assistant in Minneapolis before turning his back on the city and returning to Sauk City to stay. Like two of his literary heroes, Henry David THOREAU and Ralph Waldo EMERSON (both of whom were the subject of D. biographies), D. found village life sufficient to his needs. He was also influenced by the poems of Walt WHITMAN, Robert FROST, and Edgar Lee MASTERS, and the prose writings of Sinclair LEWIS, whose stories of small-town life resulted in both a lasting friendship as well as a lasting influence.

Most of D.'s best writings came near the beginning of his career in such Sac Prairie novels as *Wind over Wisconsin* (1938) and *Evening in Spring* (1941), as well as in two volumes of verse, *Hawk on the Wind* (1938) and *Man Track Here* (1939). A collection of short stories, *Country Growth,* published in 1940, also enjoyed critical acceptance. In that same year D. began enlarging upon the narrow focus of his Sac Prairie Saga with his "Wisconsin Saga," five novels dealing with the state history of Wisconsin. Like the volumes in his earlier series, each of the new books was meant either to stand alone or to be read collectively as a part of a larger series. Works in the Wisconsin Saga were less well received by critics and reviewers, many of whom found the details of pioneer life dull and repetitive. Of the five novels in this series, *The Hills Stand Watch* (1960) is closest in spirit to the common folk discussed in the other series.

D.'s chief strength and preoccupation was his ability to show the individual's relation to the village, and to the natural environment surrounding it. He was fascinated to the end of his days with natural phenomena, and many of his works show an encyclopedic knowledge of Wisconsin's plant life.

His shortcomings began to be evident after World War II as village life slowly waned in importance while D. continued to chronicle it. His novels were described as too lengthy and detailed, his verse as only a mirror of nature, and lacking in insights commonly found in better poets. His short stories enjoyed better treatment, and some of those in *Sac Prairie*

People (1948) and *Wisconsin in Their Bones* (1961) may prove to be lasting.

Parallel to his Sac Prairie and Wisconsin sagas, D. also worked on two mystery series. His "Solar Pons" mysteries are among the frankest imitations of Sir Arthur Conan Doyle's stories of Sherlock Holmes, but they are well done, and many readers have enjoyed *In Re: Sherlock Holmes, The Adventures of Solar Pons* (1945), *Mr. Fairlie's Final Journey* (1968), and others. A second series, the Judge Peck mysteries, features a kindly country judge who works with authorities to solve murders in books such as *The Seven Who Waited* (1943) and *Death by Design* (1953).

D. maintained a lifelong interest in science fiction and fantasy and in 1939 helped establish the publishing firm of Arkham House, which disseminated the works of a variety of writers, including those of supernaturalist H. P. LOVECRAFT. D. also published four histories (three of which dealt with Wisconsin) and numerous books for juveniles. He also edited more than two dozen books of poetry and prose. In 1961, D. published the best of his later Sac Prairie works, *Walden West,* a prose setting forth of his fascination with nature and village life: "From my post in Sac Prairie I fished in the wider stream that flowed past my private Walden and eddied outward to the stars. . . . Sac Prairie was the microcosm which reflected the macrocosm."

D. is not much read today, but his Sac Prairie Saga remains an important regional assessment. D.'s village is not so well known as Masters's Spoon River, Lewis's Gopher Prairie, or Sherwood ANDERSON's Winesburg, but it is a permanent part of America's literary landscape, and a significant achievement for one who once said that he wanted most of all simply "to wander in his private Walden."

BIBLIOGRAPHY: Bishop, Z. B., "A Wisconsin Balzac: A Profile of D.," in *The Curse of Yig* (1953): 153–75; Dyke, B., ed., *Remembering D.: All about Augie, 1909–1971* (1988); Roberts, J. P., ed., *Return to D., Selected Essays* (1993); Schroth, E. M., *The D. Saga* (1979); Wilson, A. M. *D.: A Bibliography* (1983)

                                    HERBERT K. RUSSELL

DETECTIVE STORY, The

The detective story is a form of fiction in which a protagonist solves a criminal problem, usually murder, by observation, investigation, and deduction, and unmasks the antagonist at its denouement. Because of the infinite number of variations that can be successfully grafted onto this basic formula, the detective story sometimes appears as a "Gothic," a "cozy," a "techno-thriller," a "police procedural," a novel of espionage

or "pursuit," a "hard-boiled" or "private eye" novel, or, more loosely, a "mystery novel." In all its guises, certain story elements—surveillance, eavesdropping, disguise, tracking, research, code-breaking, interrogation, evasive tactics, entrapment, disinformation, and the whole bagful of intelligence and counterintelligence tricks—occur frequently enough to identify it immediately as "detective" in spirit. In some of its variations a detective as such may not even appear, although there is always a surrogate who acts like a detective in deducing unseen facts from visual evidence.

One of the most important attributes of the detective story, over and above its ability to enlighten and entertain, is its capacity to comment sociologically, psychologically, politically, and even philosophically on contemporary life. This element in its makeup helps account for its remarkable longevity.

Credit for the first detective story goes to Edgar Allan POE, whose "The Murders in the Rue Morgue" and "The Purloined Letter" featured C. Auguste Dupin as an armchair detective who solves crimes through analysis of clues and logical reasoning. Anna Katharine Green expanded Poe's short form into the detective novel, the best known of which was *The Leavenworth Case* (1878), employing Poe's basic literary techniques. Melville Davisson Post's Uncle Abner detective stories, substituting a down-to-earth American puzzle solver for Poe's French intellectual, enjoyed great popularity at the turn of the century.

By now, the detective format was fairly well established, honed and reshaped by Wilkie Collins in England, Émile Gaboriau in France, and later the incomparable A. Conan Doyle, stressing the puzzle and its solution. In a specific closed milieu a murder victim is discovered, a group of suspects is interrogated by a detective, and eventually through deductive logic the protagonist solves the crime, revealing the details and identifying the criminal.

The focus of interest was now shifting from the puzzle to the protagonist, inspired undoubtedly by the tremendous international success of Doyle's Sherlock Holmes, Agatha Christie's Miss Marple, and Dorothy L. Sayers's Lord Peter Wimsey. On the American scene, S. S. Van Dine's Philo Vance was a gifted amateur after Dupin; Ellery Queen's "Ellery Queen" was an amateur detective and the son of a New York detective inspector; Earl Derr Biggers's Charlie Chan was a Chinese detective inspector on the Honolulu, Hawai'i police force; Erle Stanley GARDNER's lawyer Perry Mason threaded his triumphant way through labyrinthine plots to unmask murderers in countless courtroom denouements.

Enter Dashiell HAMMETT and his colleagues who opened the format's closed milieu and put murder out into the streets. Directed by deductive logic, the detective seeks out suspects one by one in hard-boiled confrontations rather than in sedate and low-keyed interviews. The revelation element typically becomes subordinated to the actual search for and final show-down with the killer, although the murderer is usually identified in the final phase of narration. For his pro-tagonist, Hammett chose himself: a working private detective (he had been a Pinkerton operative as a young man). On the surface cool and taciturn, Hammett's Continental Op spoke in terse, sparse, but colorful language, a far cry from the carefully turned diction of the earlier gifted amateur sleuth. Action was re-ported in down-to-earth terms. The particular genius of this new departure was the blending of the detective format and its literary elements with those of the "all-American" Western genre, rooted in James Fenimore COOPER's Leather-Stocking Tales, where Natty Bump-po plays a kind of frontier knight errant. It was Owen WISTER's *The Virginian* that established the classic Western in 1902, the main character a nameless fron-tier figure who sets wrongs to right. Hammett's modi-fied white knight, originally as nameless as Wister's Virginian, was tough and hard-boiled, the prototypical "private eye"—the word "eye" a play on "I" of "Inves-tigator" but also hinting broadly at the unwinking eye of the Pinkerton Agency's logotype. *Red Harvest*, Hammett's first novel, follows the traditional Western format almost slavishly: the Continental Op visits a desert town, finds it corrupt, and cleans it up, solving crimes as he does so. Later, Hammett polished up the format and named his protagonists in *The Maltese Falcon* and *The Thin Man*.

Following Hammett's lead, Raymond CHANDLER created Philip Marlowe, debuting in *The Big Sleep*—another white knight riding the urban jungle (Marlowe = Malory?)—to set right a corrupt and law-less urban milieu. Rex STOUT had the best of both traditional and hard-boiled worlds by creating in *Fer-de-Lance* a detective duo: Nero Wolfe, an updated armchair detective and Archie Goodwin, a mobile action-oriented street-smart muscle-man.

The cataclysm of World War II, with the introduc-tion of new mid-century technologies, upscaled meth-ods of communication and transportation, advances in all branches of science including psychology and sociology, the advent of the Cold War, and, in particu-lar, a much more sophisticated reading public, saw the fractionation of the detective novel into a number of interesting variations.

A result of the war itself was the novel of pursuit involving espionage and wartime activities. An early practitioner was Dorothy B. Hughes, writing during the hostilities, followed by Helen MacInnes and others. This variation resurged later in the 1960s as the cold-

war novel, and then, in a slightly altered form, as the novel of international intrigue, practiced by writers as disparate in temperament and craft as Robert Ludlum, Ross Thomas, James Grady, the author of *Six Days of the Condor* (1974), and Tom Clancy, author of *Patriot Games* (1987). In this modification, murder and revelation usually make up only a minor part of the general structure, the main elements being the cat-and-mouse game played by protagonist and antagonist until resolution. Disguise, deception, and duplicity predominate up to the final unmasking and showdown. In some cases the detective story's critical ele-ment—revelation of the criminal identity at the very end of the work—may be violated.

The immediate postwar years also inspired a return to Émile Gaboriau's 19th-c. *roman policier* ("police novel"), rechristened the "police procedural." Inaugu-rated in the prewar years by such writers as Lawrence Treat, it was taken up after World War II by Hillary Waugh and Ed McBain (pseudonym of Evan HUNTER), whose 87th Precinct became celebrated not only in print but on television as well. Joseph Wambaugh, an ex-police officer, capped the police procedural in the 1970s, with *The New Centurions* (1970) and novels that spawned numerous television series in the past two decades such as *Hill Street Blues, Cagney and Lacey, Miami Vice, NYPD Blue,* and *Homicide.*

The police procedural hewed closely to the estab-lished Poe-Gaboriau formula, occasionally turning it inside out in the "caper" variation, concentrating ex-clusively on the criminal or criminals in the progress of a crime, or even following both criminal and detec-tive as the search narrows, thus violating the main precept of the detective-story format but employing most of its story elements. The caper variation found its roots in the early 16th-c. picaresque novel, the adventures of the *picaro,* or wily rogue. It is not un-usual for the modern caper to involve humorous or farcical elements. Donald Westlake, an established master of the comical caper, was in top form in *Castle in the Air* (1980).

Yet another early mystery form, the 18th-c. Gothic, made a dramatic and dichotomous reappearance in the last third of the 20th c.: first in a resurgence of the Gothic's alter ego, the "romantic suspense" novel; and second in the development of the "fantasy-horror" novel.

A word about the Gothic form, a favorite of the innovator of the detective story, Edgar Allan Poe: in spite of his important achievement in introducing this new genre, he was in his lifetime more popular as a writer of horror and fantasy stories. His inspiration and mentor was Charles Brockden BROWN, an American whose stories of romance, intrigue, and crime followed the Gothic formula of Mrs. Ann Radcliffe in England, rooted in Horace Walpole's *The Castle of Otranto,* Matthew Gregory Lewis's *The Monk* , and Mary Wollstonecraft Shelley's *Frankenstein.* It was this popular genre, Americanized from the 19th-c. "Bronte" Gothic, updated through Daphne du Maurier's *Rebecca* (1938), that was revived as the romantic suspense novel in the 1960s, establishing Phyllis A. Whitney as its American champion, as in *Spindrift* (1975). She and her colleagues confined their plots to its basic "woman in jeopardy" theme, with mysterious happenings to be solved, exotic locales predominating, and "supernatural-but-scientifically explained" horrors revealed at the end, following the Radcliffe precept. Mary Higgins Clark, author of *Where Are the Children?* (1975), shifted the Gothic setting from moldering castles and exotic villas to the dark city streets to create a chilling urban/suburban Gothic bristling with suspense, terror, violence, and larded with sexual angst.

In the modern "fantasy-horror" Gothic—the Poe-type terror story—supernatural became the new norm; no longer were phenomena "scientifically explained." Shirley JACKSON experimented by introducing ghosts in *The Haunting of Hill House;* Ira Levin came on with *Rosemary's Baby* (1967), a story of a devil cult and its attempt to breed a new Antichrist; and William Peter Blatty followed with *The Exorcist* (1971), the story of a young girl possessed by the devil. These were only precursors to the arrival of Stephen KING. In *Carrie* and titles that followed he fine-tuned the 20th-c. tale of horror (and detection), complete with spirit possession, witchcraft, psychokinesis, ESP, thought control, paranoia—usually with a criminal problem to be solved by deduction and climaxed in flight and pursuit. In some hands the supernatural or ghost story is *not* a detective story, but only a distant cousin despite identical roots. Detection by deduction must be present to keep it within the genre.

Another most successful postwar variation of the detective formula was the "psychological" mystery. Particularly effective in this category were Margaret MILLAR, Patricia Highsmith, Helen Eustis, author of *The Horizontal Man* (1946), Dorothy Salisbury Davis, and Lucy Freeman. The writing tends to focus on psychological elements: Freudian symbolism may prove important in clues; the motivation of a crime may be more important than the identity of its perpetrator; the victim or killer may be psychotic, allowing the writer to plunge deeply into the wellsprings of motivation to probe *reasons;* the stress falls on the "why" of the murder or crime rather than the "who."

Another modification was the detective story in which the motivational elements were fixed in the external sociopolitical world. Most representative of this modification was Carolyn G. Heilbrun, writing under the pseudonym "Amanda Cross," whose university-oriented mystery novels, nicely balanced between conversation, literary allusions, and detection, were deliberately constructed as comedies of manners with classic detective subplots.

Many American writers have consistently preferred to follow the "true" detective novel; Mary Roberts RINEHART, John Dickson Carr, Craig Rice, Mignon G. Eberhart, Hugh Pentecost (pseud.: Judson Philips), Aaron Marc Stein, up through Tony Hillerman, Emma Lathen (pseuds.: Mary J. Satsis and Martha Henissart), Martha Grimes, Patricia Cornwell, and Elizabeth George worked successfully within the parameters. Many others deserve attention but are too numerous to list.

The private-eye variation continued strong and unabated from World War II on, with one major aberration—the story of sex, violence, and vengeance. Mickey Spillane's Mike Hammer not only identified, but tried, judged, condemned, and, in the end, executed the killer in a plethora of blood and gore, as in *I, the Jury* (1947). In the true Hammett-Chandler vein, Ross MACDONALD continued with Lew Archer. So did William Campbell Gault, Brett Halliday with Mike Shayne, John D. MacDonald with Travis McGee, Lawrence Block, and many others, right up to one of the most derivative and yet imaginative of the "new" private-eye writers: Robert B. PARKER.

Parker's "Spenser," introduced in *The Godwulf Manuscript* (1974), was so close to Philip Marlowe—both names came out of English literature—that differences were difficult to detect; yet the milieu of Spenser's Boston differed radically from the milieu of Marlowe's Los Angeles. Also, half a century separated them. Parker saw people in his fictional world in shades of gray, unlike Chandler, who knew who wore the white hat and who the black. Spenser's world was one of ambiguity and crosscurrents of social tension.

Contemporary with Parker was another innovator who looked back not to the creations of Hammett and Chandler but to the Western genre. Elmore LEONARD chose the surrogate drifter for his protagonist, and the fringes on the darker side of society for his settings. His "hero," or "anti-hero," usually lived on the raw edge of life—an outlaw drifter—with a morality in no way black or white, and an inborn need to live existentially from one moment to the next, making up the rules as he went along. Although no "private eye," the Leonard hero was definitely a member of the "hard-boiled" school; if no detective, he acted like one and the lives he touched and the stories he lived were "detective" in spirit; *LaBrava* and *Get Shorty* are vintage Leonard.

In the 1970s and 1980s through the 1990s, a viable variation of the detective story appeared and flourished: the woman private investigator. The hard-boiled elements were there: tough prose and terse diction. Sue Grafton and Sarah Paretsky are representative.

From its birth in Poe, the detective story continued to attract readers all through the 19th and 20th cs., depending on the vagaries of the publishing world, with the ingenious Stanley Ellin and the prolific Edward D. Hoch proving the versatility and durability of the short form.

Detective story writers are constantly rediscovering thematic and stylistic literary devices to elaborate the human condition. No one knows how the genre will reinvent itself, or turn out next. It will always prove an exceptionally effective literary vehicle, one in which there is usually something of value for everyone, to interpret and illuminate the times, the people, and the lives they lead.

BIBLIOGRAPHY: Ball, J., *The Mystery Story* (1976); Benstock, B., *Art in Crime Writing: Essays on Detective Fiction* (1983); Haycraft, H., *The Art of the Mystery Story: A Collection of Critical Essays* (1946); Murch, A. E., *The Development of the Detective Novel* (1958); Nevins, F. M., *The Mystery Writer's Art* (1971); Symons, J., *Bloody Murder: From the Detective Story to the Crime Novel* (1985); Winks, R. W., *Modus Operandi: An Excursion into Detective Fiction* (1982); Woeller, W., and B. Cassiday, *The Literature of Crime and Detection: An Illustrated History* (1987)

BRUCE CASSIDAY

DEUTSCH, Babette

b. 22 September 1895, New York City; d. 13 November 1982, New York City

Seeing herself primarily as a poet, D. nevertheless made significant contributions as a critic, translator, novelist, and author of children's books. As a poet, D. was highly regarded by her peers. Robert FROST, Louise BOGAN, William Carlos WILLIAMS, John Wain, and Marianne MOORE were among those who spoke glowingly of her work. Since her death, however, she has fallen into obscurity, selections from her poetry rarely appearing in contemporary anthologies. For the most part, her name survives as the author of two critical studies, *Poetry in Our Time* (1952; rev, ed., 1963) and *Poetry Handbook: A Dictionary of Terms* (1957), which for years were standard texts in American universities.

Born in New York City, D. remained a New Yorker throughout her life, receiving her B.A. at Barnard College (1917), teaching at the New School for Social Research (1933–35) and Columbia University (1944–71), and drawing upon her native city for many of her poetic materials. Her first volume of poetry, *Banners* (1919), reflects the influence of the imagist movement and of the atmosphere of turbulent change generated by the Russian Revolution. Poems such as "Death of a Child," "Ombres Chinoises," and "Ballet School" announce subjects—children, cityscapes, the arts—that she would explore more fully as her career unfolded. Subsequent volumes display D.'s wide-ranging interests, presenting poems on such themes as love, marriage, motherhood, animals, and broad historical and philosophical questions: *Honey Out of the Rock* (1925), *Fire for the Night* (1930), *Epistle to Prometheus* (1931), and *One Part Love* (1939). Two volumes are notable for poems that express her outrage at the destructiveness of World War II: *Take Them, Stranger* (1944) and *Animal, Vegetable, Mineral* (1954). With *Coming of Age: New and Selected Poems* (1959), D. began to select, revise, and reprint her best poems, continuing with *Collected Poems: 1919–1962* (1963) and *The Collected Poems of B. D.* (1969).

The final volume reveals D.'s technical skills in both formal and free verse. Prominent in it are poems recording her reactions to artists, composers, and to other writers, such works no doubt a reflection of a life spent in a culturally rich urban environment. Accompanying these, however, are many landscapes and seasonal poems. Nearly all of D.'s poems are marked by the "impersonality" prized by the generation of modernists to which she belonged.

D. published numerous translations of Russian and German verse, often in collaboration with her husband, Avraham Yarmolinsky. Collections such as *Modern Russian Poetry* (1921; rev. ed., 1927) and *Contemporary German Poetry* (1923) rendered into English important and, in many cases, previously untranslated works of European literature. She also wrote four novels: *A Brittle Heaven* (1926), *In Such a Night* (1927), *Mask of Silenus: A Novel about Socrates* (1933), and *Rogue's Legacy: A Novel about Francois Villon* (1942). Particularly revealing among these is the first, which semiautobiographically depicts a woman juggling the roles of writer, wife, and mother. Among D.'s works for juveniles the most noteworthy is *Walt Whitman: Builder for America* (1941), which was awarded the Julia Ellsworth Ford Foundation Prize.

Even though they are an illuminating index to the modernist movement, D.'s writings have not received the attention they deserve. The critical neglect of her poetry would seem to stem far less from problems with quality than from the forces of gender politics.

BIBLIOGRAPHY: Drake, W., *The First Wave: Women Poets in America, 1915–1945* (1987); Gould, J.,

American Women Poets: Pioneers of Modern Po-etry (1980)

DONALD D. KUMMINGS

DE VRIES, Peter

b. 27 February 1910, Chicago, Illinois; d. 28 September 1993, Norwalk, Connecticut

British novelist Kingsley Amis called D. "the funniest serious writer to be found either side of the Atlantic." Probably there is no better way to describe this author of twenty-four novels and scores of short stories. Over a fifty-year career, he successfully mixed earnest theology with borderline blasphemy, lust with love, life with death, disasters with delights, happiness with sorrow. He turned all forms of grave and farcical opposites into witty, ironic fiction that carries a sting but never a painful one. He was a relentless punster, a master of repartee, a skillful satirist, and the originator of memorable epigrams, as well as a specialist in the non sequitur and double entendre.

Even the titles of his books often reflect the comic streak that lightens their underlying gravity: *The Tents of Wickedness* (1959) and *Forever Panting* (1973), about marital infidelity; *I Hear America Swinging* (1976), about the sexual revolution; *Slouching towards Kalamazoo* (1983), about a teenage boy's maturation and sexual aspirations; and *The Prick of Noon* (1985), about the misfortunes of a pornographer. Recognized as a writer who could make the reader laugh out loud, D. was immensely popular both in the U.S. and Great Britain.

A native of the American Midwest, D. grew up in a strict Dutch Calvinist home and graduated from Calvin College in 1931 with an English degree. He then worked at odd jobs and attempted to support himself as a freelance writer before becoming an editor in 1938 at Chicago-based *Poetry* magazine. In 1944, at the prodding of James THURBER, he joined the *New Yorker* as a staff member, and continued his association with the magazine until his death in 1993. Disowning the three novels he published during the early 1940s, D. first met success in 1954 with *The Tunnel of Love*. This tale of a struggling neophyte in the publishing community became a best-seller, was adapted for the stage in 1957 by D. and Joseph Fields, and after a successful Broadway run was turned into a film.

One of D.'s early novels and one of his funniest, *The Mackerel Plaza* (1958), contains most of the stylistic elements, subjects, and themes that he developed and refined in subsequent work. Concern with the role of religion and the trials surrounding romance and marriage, as well as the gentle indictment of human pretensions and foibles, all emerge in this account of the Reverend Andrew ("Holy") Mackerel's personal and spiritual plight. His saintly wife recently deceased, he faces opposition from his ultra-liberal congregation when he expresses a desire to remarry. Typically short on plot but long on comic development, *The Mackerel Plaza* offers a delectable account of the pastor and congregants of the People's Liberal Church, whose members are planning a shopping center, to be called "Mackerel Plaza," in memory of the church's beloved, former first lady. Meanwhile the Reverend pursues his "bit of fluff," dodges the attentions of his housekeeper named Hester, hassles street evangelists, and demands that the city remove a signboard emblazoned with "Jesus Saves," which distracts him during sermon preparation. But even as the fun goes on, the narrative takes a serious turn when it focuses on Reverend Mackerel's apostasy, which could best be described as Calvinistic anti-Calvinism.

Usually considered D.'s finest novel, *The Blood of the Lamb* (1962) recounts a father's struggle to accept the death of his child. In 1960, D. himself had grappled with a similar loss when his youngest daughter died from leukemia. Perhaps through this fictional account of personal tragedy, D. set out to define his own doubts and religious beliefs. *The Blood of the Lamb,* incongruous as it may seem considering its somber subject, once more displays the rare ability to blend comedy with tragedy.

Although D. spent his career reminding readers of the absurdity and contradictions surrounding marriage, organized religion, society's restrictions and demands, personal relations, and humankind in general, his work is neither consistently cynical nor funny for its own sake. He is a writer who explored and exploited the thin line that separates comedy and tragedy as he stubbornly pursued answers to life's unanswerable questions.

BIBLIOGRAPHY: Bowden, J. H., *P. D.* (1983); Davis, M., "Fools for Christ's Sake: A Study of Clerical Figures in D., Updike, and Buechner," *SLH* 6 (1983): 60–72; Sanders, D., *Contemporary Novelists* (1991): 242–44

ROBERT L. ROSS

DICKEY, James

b. 2 February 1923, Atlanta, Georgia; d. 19 January 1996, Columbia, South Carolina

A prolific poet, essayist, and novelist, D. employed resonant and disturbing imagery to create a private mythos rooted in the Southern Gothic tradition of violence, identification with nature, and stoic endurance. While not strictly autobiographical, his poetry and fiction often transmute his experiences as a Southerner, college athlete, World War II bomber, and advertising executive into the imagery and subjects of his poetry and fiction.

His early poetry, including *Into the Stone* (1960), *Drowning with Others* (1962), *Helmets* (1964), and *Buckdancer's Choice* (1965), which received the National Book Award in poetry in 1966, set out his primary themes. Exploiting the imaginative possibilities of art, the poems, often unrhymed narratives portraying surreal or exaggerated scenarios, depict, with hallucinatory clarity, the connections between the visible world and the natural or spiritual world, as well as man's capacity for violence and animal sexuality.

In "The Performance" (1960), D. re-creates the beheading of a World War II airman, Donald Armstrong, captured by the Japanese, and transforms a brutal execution into a celebration of Armstrong's love of life. The mysticism of "Drinking from a Helmet" (1964), initiated by a sip of water from the helmet of a recently killed soldier, transports a seventeen-year-old narrator from a war ravaged island, to the green fields of an imagined heaven. In this vision, the dead soldier's spirit commingles with the narrator's, lending him the wisdom earned only through death. "The Sheep Child" (1967) also employs a dream vision, in this case from a mythic half-sheep half-man beast, to illustrate another of D.'s recurring themes: the intersection between nature and modern man. The "Child," product of a bestial sexuality, symbolizes our attraction to nature, but its doomed fate—dying right after birth—illustrates our inability to fully embrace it.

The revelatory nature of these early poems represent an updated romanticism, an attempt to explain the rational and the irrational through the transitory links between the two worlds. Collected in *Poems, 1957–1967* (1967), his poetry gained him early recognition as a major literary figure.

His next work, after a collection of literary criticism, *Babel to Byzantium* (1968), links a romantic view of nature to man's capacity for brutality. *Deliverance* (1970), published to critical and public acclaim, attacks the sterility of modern life. In the novel, four suburbanites set out on a wilderness canoe trip to experience nature and instead discover their instinct for survival—and violence. Drawn into a baptism by blood through his friendship with Lewis Medlock, the narrator, Ed Gentry, discovers the power of his instincts. While the hunt figured in earlier poems, here it acts as an archetypal symbol for the rejuvenating spirit, the missing link in modern life. Made into a popular motion picture in 1973 with a screenplay by D., the novel, with its erotic overtones and celebration of male virility and nature, extends the themes of his poetry.

The philosophical backgrounds to these themes, and especially D.'s penchant for experimentation and imagination, are articulated in the prose ruminations *Self-Interviews* (1970) and *Sorties* (1971). His focus on the creative impulse leads him to assume a variety of voices and subjects in his later poetry and fiction. In the poem "The Eye-Beaters," from *The Eye-beaters, Blood, Victory, Madness, Buckhead and Mercy* (1970), a narrator describes a group of blind orphans who repeatedly strike their eyes to create, or so believes the narrator, ecstatic visions. The book-length poem *The Zodiac* (1976) offers, through the voice of a drunken poet, D.'s view of the poet as maker, deriving strength from the heavens. And while the poems in *The Strength of Fields* (1979) find D. working in more conventional themes and voices, *Puella* (1982) marks another imaginative leap for this most masculine of poets. Inspired by his wife, this series of poems explores the maturation of a young girl into womanhood.

These works were followed by *Night Hurdling* (1983), a collection of essays, interviews, and stories, and the novel *Alnilam* (1987). *Alnilam* recounts the investigation of a blind father, Ed Cahill, into the death of his son, Joel, killed in a mysterious plane accident at a World War II training camp in Georgia. Filled, like *The Zodiac,* with references to the stars and imbued with mysticism, the novel suggests the dangers and attractions in bridging the spiritual and material worlds.

His next two works, the poetry collection, *The Eagle's Mile* (1990), and a novel, *To the White Sea* (1993), both use bird imagery to illustrate the connections between man and nature. *To the White Sea* is the story of Muldrow, a tail gunner shot down over Tokyo in the waning days of World War II, who escapes to the northern islands of Japan. After killing his way through Japan, he is hunted down and shot, but envisions himself escaping death by becoming part of nature and transforming into the wind. Though implausible, the novel distills D.'s views of a mystic communion with nature, the hunt, and the instinct for survival.

While most critics agree that D.'s later poetry lacks the clarity and precision of his earlier work, the overall scope and range of his poetic aesthetic, collected in *The Whole Motion* (1992), illustrate an artist constantly working with his medium and experimenting with ways to communicate his vision. D.'s novels are prose extensions of his poetry, narratives which explore his impressions of the tenuous distinctions between man and beast and between reality and spirituality.

BIBLIOGRAPHY: Bloom, H., ed., *J. D.* (1987); Bowers, N., *The Poet as Pitchman* (1985); Bruccoli, M. J., and J. Baughman, *J. D.: A Descriptive Bibliography* (1990); Calhoun, R. J., and R. W. Hill, *J. D.* (1983)

DAVID BORDELON

DICKINSON, Emily [Elizabeth]

b. 10 December 1830, Amherst, Massachusetts; d. 15 May 1886, Amherst, Massachusetts

"Madder rhymes one has seldom seen—scornful disregard of poetic technique could hardly go farther—and yet there is about the book fascination, a power, a vision that enthralls you, and draws you back to it again and again" (Louise Chandler Moulson in the Boston *Sunday Herald,* November 23, 1890). Along with pointing out the idiosyncrasies of D.'s poetic language, this reviewer of the first published volume of her poems expresses an intensity of response that is common to D.'s readers. In *E. D.* (1986), Cynthia Griffin Wolff notes the unusually diverse readership, from schoolgirls to scholars, of the "undeniably cryptic author who nonetheless addresses some deep need in a wide variety of readers." Typically, people who love D.'s poetry feel a sense of personal relationship with the writer herself. D.'s own assessment for the reading and evaluation of poetry is apt for describing what happens to her readers: she knows that language is poetry, she said to the editor Thomas Wentworth HIGGINSON, when "I feel physically as if the top of my head were taken off." The combination of intimacy and broad applicability, of homeliness and rich complexity in D.'s writing leads to both the greatness of her art and the passionate devotion in which she is held.

D.'s life differed both from that of the typical poet and of the typical woman of her time. Unlike the literary men she knew, hers was in no way a public or professional life. It was private and domestic, centered in the home and in family affairs. However, unlike the life of most women of her social status, hers was a peculiarly private life—solitary and self-focused, in contrast to lives lived in the service of others—husband, children, or, in the case of unmarried women, parents and the families of relatives. Gradually withdrawing from even the wider world of women, of visits, church, and social events in a New England town, seeing fewer and fewer people within the confines of her own home except her immediate family, D. made a place for writing poems: 1,775 of them. Thus, when we speak of her life, we understand how its biographical facts outline an intense, sustained, and richly mined inner world. The experience which formed the subject matter of her poetry was not to be found in travel and adventure, if only because such public exposure was unacceptable for a lady. Rather, it was culled from the development and exploration of private, internal events—emotional, philosophical, spiritual—that took their impetus from external occurrences but attained a concomitant reality in the words into which she shaped them. D.'s poems are at the same time theoretical and topical, because their subject is the urgency and revelation of mental experience. Even as her poems as a whole write a biography of the life of the mind, so our own biographies of her quickly find their way to the poems and letters in order to detail the myriad events of her life.

D. was born on December 10, 1830, the middle child of Emily Norcross Dickinson and Edward Dickinson. Her older brother Austin was born in 1829; her younger sister Lavinia in 1833. Hers was one of the leading families in Amherst, Massachusetts. Her father was a prominent lawyer and treasurer of Amherst College, which her grandfather, Samuel Fowler Dickinson, had been instrumental in founding. Her mother centered her world around her husband and children.

From 1840 to 1847, D. attended the Amherst Academy, where she received an education as demanding as that of many colleges today. Amherst Academy was closely connected with Amherst College; many of its teachers were professors at the college, where its students often attended lectures. She studied languages, philosophy, and science. Under the aegis of Edward Hitchcock, professor of geology and moral theology and president of Amherst College from 1845 to 1854, she received a thorough grounding not only in the most modern scientific thought of the day but in its direct connection to religion, for Hitchcock believed that truth in every branch of learning manifested God's nature and will as revealed in the Bible. Hitchcock encouraged religious revivals, as did Mary Lyons, the founder of Mount Holyoke Female Seminary in nearby South Hadley, which Dickinson attended for two terms; for moral instruction and secular learning were not separate categories. However, D. found herself incapable of the commitment to Christ that her friends and family were making. Although conversion was necessary in order to become an "established Christian," D. never did make a profession of faith.

Thereafter, with the exception of three trips to Boston, two for eye treatment, in 1851, 1863, and 1864, and a trip to Washington, with stops in Baltimore and Philadelphia, in 1855, D. never left Amherst and its environs. Her life was centered in the family at the Homestead—father, mother, and sister Vinnie, who also never married and who served as practical and loyal helpmeet to Emily, taking the largest responsibility for household affairs. (D. baked and gardened—and wrote, though few realized it, much poetry.) Her adored brother Austin, also a lawyer, settled in the Evergreens next door, with his wife, Susan Gilbert Dickinson. With her keen intelligence and firm ambitions, Sue was originally D.'s closest girlhood friend. D.'s passionate attachment to her did not abate after her marriage; it only grew more complex, since Sue was now as well her sister-in-law.

D. had as well a circle of friends and relatives with whom she corresponded energetically: girlhood friends like Abiah Root Strong and Kate Turner Anthon; relatives like her cousin Lavinia Norcross and her daughters Louise and Frances, as well as her brother Austin, before he settled next door; and friends from public life—the editor and writer Josiah Gilbert Holland and his wife Elizabeth; the writer Helen Hunt JACKSON; the editor Samuel Bowles and his wife Mary; the Reverend Charles Wadsworth; Judge Otis Lord; the editor Thomas Wentworth Higginson. D. was drawn to men of authority, like her father—Bowles, Wadsworth, Lord, and Higginson, whom she sought out as a possible source of criticism and publication for her writing. On the other hand, her romantic desires were also aroused by women, such as Susan Gilbert Dickinson, with whom she corresponded ardently both before and after Susan came to reside next door. The strong feelings that these important relationships provoked became the occasion for many of her poems: poems which, however, focused not on some event but on its emotional impact and significance. Even as she rarely saw the people whom she loved but conducted her relationships through letters, through the written word, so her poems, too, brought control as well as distillation to her passions.

Her friends and family knew that she wrote poetry, for she often included poems in and with her letters to them, especially to Sue (with whom she often discussed her poetry); but no one had any idea of the extent of her writing. Ten of her poems appeared in print during her lifetime, but perhaps in response to the way these were altered to fit conventional standards and to Higginson's conservative treatment of her work, and probably because of her own reticence as well, D. stopped seeking publication and even refused some requests in later years. When she died of Bright's disease in 1886, her sister discovered hundreds of poems in her desk drawers, many of them carefully compiled and sewn together into small booklets or "fascicles." Others were less systematically organized, written on scraps of paper, the backs of recipes, on anything, it seems, that had been at hand for the purpose.

Although D. had stipulated that her letters and papers be burned upon her death, Vinnie decided that this mandate did not apply to the poems. Subsequently, Vinnie made it her goal to have the poems published. When her sister-in-law Sue initially turned her down, she turned to Mabel Loomis Todd, the wife of David Peck Todd, an astronomer at the College. Mabel Todd

was a women of literary aspirations herself, whose long-standing love affair with Austin Dickinson was an ill-kept secret. In turn, Mabel Todd enlisted the help of Higginson. The project, which involved transcribing the poems from D.'s handwritten versions, along with making editorial decisions about punctuation, line arrangement, and word-choice (for it was D.'s custom to provide alternatives for words or phrases) took several years. *Poems* was published in 1890. Thereafter, for a period of fifty-five years, subsequent volumes of poems and then letters were published not only by Mrs. Todd and Colonel Higginson and Mrs. Todd's daughter, Millicent Todd Bingham, but by Sue Dickinson's daughter Martha Dickinson Bianchi, for Sue had had in her own possession many hundreds of poems and letters. Animosity between all concerned made D.'s slow public appearance as much a matter of competition and rancor as it must have been of pride and pleasure.

In 1955, the scholar T. H. Johnson published in approximately chronological order a complete edition of the poems that seeks to replicate the form in which they were originally written. His variorum edition also includes D.'s variants, although the one-volume edition does not. Johnson also published the collected letters in 1958. In 1981, R. W. Franklin published *The Manuscript Books of E. D.,* a manuscript edition which arranges the poems in fascicle order. In the 1990s concern with D.'s own choices for presenting her writing has led to a greater focus on the manuscripts. Print as well as hypermedia editions of her manuscript writing are in process.

D.'s poetry is immediately identifiable because of its language: punctuated primarily with dashes, grammar and syntax often oddly altered, elliptical and condensed, highly metaphorical. No other poetry in the English language looks or sounds like D.'s. These peculiarities are admittedly a mark of her genius: her need to create a form suited to express the unique quality of her vision. Yet within these larger categories we can identify some specific constraints and opportunities that informed her choices, especially those determined by her identity as a woman. On the one hand, her privacy and isolation; on the other hand, her urge to communicate, to connect. On the one hand, her abstractness and desire to generalize; on the other hand, her concrete and colloquial familiarity. D.'s is at heart a language of privacy that seeks always for community, its characteristics contributing both to its obscurity and its astonishing insights. For private and public, privacy versus publicity, privation in contrast to publication, are responses to the cultural constructions of gender, creating not so much contradiction as complexity, a duplicity of consciousness and experience that itself demands expressive form. D. exaggerated her privacy to meet the demands of her personality and her art, versions of the same impulse towards self-realization. This brought her some degree of privation and, at last, publicity. Along the way it engendered a tension between participation and critique, between accepting cultural norms and definitions and challenging them, that accounts for the duplicity—a both/and rather than an either/or—of her vision and its expression in language.

Looking at the most apparent features of D.'s language, the capitalizations and dashes that her early editors more or less erased, we see this linguistic doubling in operation. On the one hand, they point to the private quality of her language. If we take the capitalizations as a form of emphasis—they seem to replace the underlinings with which D. so liberally sprinkled her letters—and the dashes as an abrogation of formal punctuation for the haste of utterance that is approximating speech (typical of both letters and diaries), we see how these poems seek for the intimacy, the conversationality, of private forms. D.'s poems have a powerful aural element. Read aloud, the strange punctuation and syntax helps with the movement, and the pauses, and what we hear are sounds less like song than urgent speech.

At the same time, those capitalizations and dashes foster other goals. Capitalizations serve to generalize the specific. One person's despair becomes everybody's Despair, and the experience of one isolated woman in a country town claims universal applicability. The dashes reinforce this gesture. For as much as they provoke energy and spark, they also and at the same time slow down the reading process by isolating and emphasizing individual words and phrases. Set off by dashes, these words become important, weighty.

Finally, the dashes assist in expressing tension between these two impulses, and this is the most characteristic tone in D.'s poetry. Ambiguity; indeterminacy; lack of direction rather than its specification. Punctuation is meant to point out the terms of a relationship, casual or contrastive. This the dash refuses to do, signifying that there is some connection between one phrase or line or version, and another, but never telling exactly what it is. The dashes are as much holes, or gaps, as they are arrows. These signs both give and take away, making the reader complicit in the meaning, even as D.'s refusal to choose between alternate word choices has the same effect. Because writing poetry is dangerous—a woman writing at all, a woman claiming self-importance and authority, especially when daring to question the status quo of religion or human values—D. withholds as much as she reveals. Ambiguity is as much self-protection as it is sophistication: especially, it is both.

Complementing the dashes are D.'s extraordinary figures of speech, which work to mend these holes by weaving meaning across categorical differences. For if the dashes cause moments of evasive reticence, of near-silence, the extravagant energy and unflagging inventiveness of her metaphors show her creating correspondences and connections in the teeth of such difficulties. Most of her poems are definitional in nature and intent: "Presentiment is—that long Shadow—on the Lawn"; "Delight is as the flight—." Commonly a matter-of-fact opening truism that, upon second look, seems more mysterious than obvious, is explicated by a series of parallel or appositional clauses, sentences, and stanzas that complicate as they clarify, especially because these phrases are largely constituted as analogies or metaphors for an original subject. D.'s poems tend to develop according to a principle of accrual rather than chronology or argument. These figures consistently work along an axis of concrete to abstract, with dramatic encounters between these two categories, so that concepts become tangible, and things reveal their abstract proclivities. Metaphor, or its relaxed form, analogy, is exactly capable of emphasizing the existence of separations and differences—between noon and night, life and death, human and God, female and male, solitude and society, mind and world, gain and loss, safety and danger—and at the same time mediating between them.

Ellipsis and grammatical irregularities are the other major characteristics of D.'s poetic language. D. rings changes upon conventional structure when it suits her, and this includes both altering it and condensing it. We should remember, however, that these irregularities, like her disruptions of the Protestant hymn meter which she regularly employed, are the exception rather than the rule. She relies on the conventional to highlight the unconventional; or, to put it another way, embeds the unconventional in the conventional. This is akin to her own position vis-à-vis cultural givens. When she uses an adjective as an adverb, or leaves out the subject of a verb, or causes an adverb to modify two different predicates, she is reshaping inherited language to accommodate to her individual needs. Frequently, such disruptions occur at tender places, as when she must take or abjure authority—in specific instances, as in personal relationships, or in general matters like the interpretation of observed phenomena. At times, however, these tactics result in the loss rather than discovery of meaning: her shorthand has left out a little too much. We cannot overlook the real holes in the fabric of her discourse, and we must take them into account when we propose meanings of our own.

D.'s poems are like telegraphic messages, each one as brief as it is tightly wound, about moments in the individual consciousness's encounter with its physical, social, and spiritual environments. Her Puritan heritage, and in particular the conversion-based nature of the Congregationalism in which she was raised, stressed the drama of introspection as it centered in each person's soul. There was a tradition for this kind of thing, but D.'s version, though equally spiritual, focused on her sense of difference from prevailing norms and ideals, her concomitant desires both to operate in relationship and to understand and maintain her own integrity. Often these goals were contradictory; usually they brought forth struggle—with God, with love, with time itself. D.'s poems are meditative throughout, but they are never calm.

For the original 1890 edition of *Poems,* Higginson proposed the categories Life; Nature; and Time, Death and Eternity. These indeed constitute the abiding subjects of D.'s concern, although in such a thematic inventory we may well want to add Self, Solitude, and Love. Especially, we need to recognize how these subjects inform one another in her poems, so that a "nature" poem is equally about death and the question of immortality, a "love" poem about the need for solitude. Taken together, D.'s poems constitute a diary of the internal life. And yet they are not at all consistent in their approach to or conclusions about any one of these subjects. One poem never does determine her position. Rather, they approach and surround an issue like points on a circle, a circumference, offering variations, alternatives, and complements. When we read a cluster of poems on love, for example, we get a sense, not of conclusions, but of the gestalt in which D.'s thinking operates.

D. told Higginson in a famous letter that her business was "Circumference." This suggestive phrase points to her circling kind of reasoning, but also to her daring. In a poem she depicts herself as "out upon Circumference—," and the edge of the circle, where she habitually situates her speaker, is a place of danger. In her exploration of life and death, D. pushes all things to the limits: feelings, be they painful or pleasurable, and ideas—the possibility of an afterlife, the possibility of union—in order to probe, test, and define them.

D.'s letters, like her poems, are characterized by elliptical phrasing and excessive figuration that grows more and more condensed through the years, their rhythms frequently forming sentences that, punctuated by dashes, are prose only in as much as they are not divided into verse lines. Especially because she both enclosed poems with and within her letters, used phrases from her letters in her poems and from her poems in her letters, and lineated the same phrases sometimes as verse and sometimes not, editors have since the beginning had difficulty determining what was "prose" and what was "poetry" in her letters. In recent years, the need to make this distinction has begun to seem more and more unnecessary. True, these are letters, writing addressed to specific individuals rather than to the world at large; yet D. rarely saw their recipients and tended to structure her relationships with them in terms of the written word. Although the letters do offer biographical information that readers continue to relish, for the poet kept no actual diary, and the details of her life remain shrouded by ignorance and myth, her letters bear a relation to that life that is similar to the poems. Emanating from it, surely, yet shaped and controlled by language so as to be an extension rather than a replication of it. Her letters are, finally, equally *literary,* and as such they join the constellation of writings that D. produced.

Reading D.'s writing is both satisfying and mysterious—and always exciting. These beautiful, highly charged, and brilliant utterances, because of both their gaps and leaps, demand the full participation of the reader to a degree that provokes a reciprocal passion. Yet these poems can be frustrating as well as illuminating, for often they provoke contradictory interpretations, both local and general, and even outright confusion. What are we to make of these difficulties in the midst of such gratification? Rather than persisting on, by some process of elimination, to determine the "right" meaning, or even an "overt" and a "covert" meaning, we might rather think about D.'s messages in terms of multiple meanings, acknowledging ideas and images as they overlap at crucial moments. Sometimes these multiple meanings are contradictory; sometimes they are complementary; but always, when taken together, they yield revelation. Multiplicity, then, *is* the meaning and not an impediment to it. It widens our own perceptions, when D.'s poems, as they so often do, make us feel physically as if the tops of our heads were taken off.

BIBLIOGRAPHY: Anderson, C., *E. D.'s Poetry: Stairway to Surprise* (1960); Franklin, R. W., ed., *The Manuscript Books of E. D.* (2 vols., 1979); Franklin, R. W., ed., *The Master Letters of E. D.* (1986); Johnson, T. H., ed., *The Poems of E. D.* (3 vols., 1955); Johnson, T. H., and T. Ward, eds., *The Letters of E. D.* (3 vols., 1958); Juhasz, S., *The Undiscovered Continent: E. D. and the Space of the Mind* (1983); Leyda, J., *The Years and Hours of E. D.* (2 vols., 1960); Miller, C., *E. D.: A Poet's Grammar* (1986); Porter, D., *The Art of E. D.'s Early Poetry* (1966); Seawall, R., *The Life of E. D.* (2 vols., 1974); Smith, M. N., *Rowing in Eden: Rereading E. D.* (1992); Stonum, G. L., *The D. Sublime* (1993); Wolff, C. G., *E. D.* (1986)

SUZANNE JUHASZ

DIDION, Joan
b. 5 December 1934, Sacramento, California

As both journalist and novelist, D. has become, since the 1960s, a major critic of American culture. Noted for a terse style replete with precise details, she has drawn numerous portraits of American cultural hegemony in ruins. Many of her essays, collected in *Slouching toward Bethlehem* (1968) *White Album* (1979), and *After Henry* (1992), focus primarily on the underside of California life, employing understatement and ironic juxtapositions to effect caustic commentary. At times, however, she reveals an almost sympathetic fascination with such phenomena as the Manson trials or drug culture in Haight-Ashbery communes.

While her Western locales and concern with the past have led some critics to see D. as a "frontier" writer, her attention to the grotesquery of California and, especially, Hollywood have led others to brand her a contemporary Nathanael WEST. Her most important California novel, *Play It as It Lays* (1970), is told from shifting points of view, by and about Maria Wyeth, a woman suffering nearly catatonic—some critics have called it existential—malaise. Her parents are dead; the desert town where she grew up is now a test site; her daughter, Kate, is institutionalized with severe brain damage. Fearing her estranged husband, Carter, will prevent her from seeing Kate, Maria submits to an abortion and then to a divorce at his direction. Thus cut off from her marriage, her progeny, and her past, she has trouble defining her identity amid an array of fragmented roles. The problem is exacerbated by the fact that she is a movie actress and Carter a director, the person who controls the final "cut," a word that connects Maria's abortion with aborted roles—child, wife, mother, friend, lover—she cannot play for lack of context or direction.

Abortions—actual and metaphoric—form a central motif in D.'s fiction, from her first novel, *Run River* (1963), to *The Last Thing He Wanted* (1996), in which the loose ends of aborted and redirected covert actions in Central America become the final legacy of a failed patriarch whose family forms the thematic matrix of the cold war era. That era is marked in D.'s work by the elision of the boundaries between fiction and reportage, personal history and national narrative. In her most important novel, *Democracy* (1984), the aborted past and future become jettisoned cargo, lost memory, and failed insurgencies in the narrative of American imperialism. That book typifies D.'s later fiction and nonfiction, both of which attempt to relate the fragmented loyalties, sense of arbitrary authority, lack of connection in American private lives and culture to America's global politics. These books assault the propriety of narrative, itself, suggesting that every teller may be a guilty bystander in an uncontrollable story. Such a character presents the narrative of *A Book of Common Prayer* (1977) set in an imaginary—but easy to imagine—Latin American dictatorship. D. herself plays this dubious narrator in both the nonfiction *Salvador* (1982), based on her visit to El Salvador, and *Democracy,* about a fictional family—a former presidential hopeful and his wife, who is part of an affluent Hawaiian family—at the time of America's withdrawal from Vietnam. The novel thus foregrounds D.'s inability to tell the story of the two families without implicating herself in the modes narrative authority that the book questions, as *Salvador* questions equally both the authority of official government narratives and the ability of journalism to penetrate them, and as the nonfiction *Miami* (1987) reveals the microcosmic American city of the 21st c. enmeshed in conflicting national narratives.

BIBLIOGRAPHY: Felton, S., ed., *The Critical Response to J. D.* (1994); Friedman, E. G., ed., *J. D.: Essays and Conversations* (1984); Henderson, K. U., *J. D.* (1981); Winchell, M. R., *J. D.* (1980; rev. ed., 1989)

ALAN NADEL

DILLARD, Annie [Doak]
b. 30 April 1945, Pittsburgh, Pennsylvania

D.'s first publication, and winner of the 1975 Pulitzer Prize in nonfiction, *Pilgrim at Tinker Creek* (1974), represents a late-20th-c. revision of Henry David THOREAU's *Walden* in the form of a year's sojourn in the Roanoke Valley of Virginia. A mix of personal revelation and intense examination of the natural world, *Pilgrim at Tinker Creek* is broadly Christian in its celebration of creation amid nature's violence, yet Emersonian in the particular mysticism evident in D.'s perspective of the relationship between the writer and the world. Her central subject, the process of seeing, and ability to explode commonplace observations of nature into fully realized and intricately detailed epiphanies, are evident in the powerful vision of the "tree with lights" surrounded by "grass that was wholly fire." This moment of perception, "utterly focused and utterly dreamed," is the typical theme of both a volume of poetry, *Tickets for a Prayer Wheel* (1974), and a later collection of essays, *Holy the Firm* (1977). The opening selection, "Newborn and Salted," echoes the highly poetic diction and cadence, as well as subject, of *Pilgrim:* "Every day is a god, each day is a god, and holiness holds forth in time. I worship each god, I praise each day splintered down, splintered down and wrapped in time like a husk, a husk of many colors spreading, at dawn fast over the mountains split." Likewise, personal narratives focused upon natural events (an eclipse or mirages), animals, or unusual sites (the Galapagos Islands or North Pole), extend D.'s range of interests in *Teaching a Stone a Talk* (1982).

In *Living By Fiction* (1982) D. examines traditional literary topics (character, point of view, symbol, narrative technique), as well as issues of current literary theory (as in "Does the World Have Meaning?"). *Encounters with Chinese Writers* (1984) is a result of D.'s participation in a U.S. Cultural Delegation to China in 1982 and her role as American Writers Delegate to the UCLA U.S.-China Writers Conference of that same year.

Her memoir, *An American Childhood* (1987), complements D.'s distinctive form of narrative nonfiction as she re-creates the 1950s Pittsburgh of her upbringing. She has commented, however, in "To Fashion a Text" (1987), that she is not the real subject of this work; rather, the narrative represents her first-person account of a "child's interior life" revealed through the connections between that interior "landscape" and the topography of "common history" created out of an American landscape. While D. rejects the label "social history" for this type of autobiography, *American Childhood* crosses generic categories as part autobiography, part cultural history, and part philosophy—the characteristic mix of all her works.

BIBLIOGRAPHY: Conahay, M. D., "'Into the Bladelike Arms of God': The Quest for Meaning Through Symbolic Language in Thoreau and A. D.," *DQ* 20 (Fall 1985): 103–16; Lavey, D. L., "Noticer: The Visionary Art of A. D.," *MR* 21 (1980): 255–70; Reimer, M. L., "The Dialectic Vision of A. D.'s *Pilgrim at Tinker Creek*," *Crit* 24 (Spring 1983): 182–91; Scheik, W. J., "A. D.: Narrative Fringe," *Contemporary American Women Writers: Narrative Strategies* (1985): 51–65

E. SUZANNE OWENS

DISCOVERY AND EXPLORATION ACCOUNTS

American literature has been quintessentially multicultural since the earliest New World writings. Contrary to the New England Puritan bias that has traditionally dominated early American studies, cultural pluralism originally characterized America. During the c. before the first permanent English settlements at Jamestown and Plymouth, the Spanish, French, Italian, and Portuguese explored, colonized, and reported the New World. Soon thereafter, the Dutch, Swedes, and Germans added their voices to mankind's greatest adventure story. Of course, in the 17th and 18th cs.,

writers in the booming British colonies all along the Atlantic seaboard chronicled the events and spirit of the dominant culture that became known as American.

Although often hit-or-miss and utilitarian, accounts of the New World were not only historical records and official logs, but also literary texts and dramatic narratives using rhetorical and anecdotal techniques for personal and promotional purposes. To promote their discoveries and to increase their glory, their stories stressed the uniqueness of their experiences, sometimes becoming fictive by exaggeration, invention, omission, and transposition. Having made the transoceanic journey and proven themselves heroes, the New World travelers were an extraordinary group, proud of their distinction, and many of them assumed "American" voices. Often avowing the indescribable nature of the wonders they witnessed, their written responses to the New World adapted Old World language and schema to evoke and interpret the unfamiliar scenes, and thus they heralded a literary tradition. Evoked with biblical analogies, mythological allusions, and classical tropes, the images recorded and created in the texts began to establish a national identity in the popular imagination that immigrated and evolved into the U.S. They initiated "the invention of America." In the literature of discovery and exploration first appear many concepts, themes, myths, motifs, values, and patterns of experience that came to be considered characteristically American: e.g., the new Eden and the cultivation of the wilderness; the inadequacy of language to describe the sublime grandeur of the American landscape; the landscape of golden opportunities and natural riches; the identity of white men as gods or God's chosen and red men as devils; the affirmation or regeneration of spiritual faith through wilderness suffering and violence; the possibility for common men to earn wealth and social status through courage, skill, and hard work; the self-reliant hero at home in the forest and on the frontier; the rebellion against authority and the chance for freedom. In addition to the significance of these writings to early English interest in America, as reflected by such promoters as Richard Hakluyt and Walter Raleigh, the literature of the New World remained popular and influential during the quest for literary independence by 19th-c. American writers, as demonstrated in such works as Washington IRVING's *A History of the Life and Voyages of Christopher Columbus* and Henry David THOREAU's *A Yankee in Canada*, where he writes, "I am not sure but I have most sympathy with that spirit of adventure which distinguished the French and Spaniards of those days, and made them especially the explorers of the American Continent."

Excluding the prehistoric Asian migrations and the 11th-c. Scandinavians, whose westward excursions from Greenland to Vineland are hinted at in the 13th-c. saga of Leif Ericsson, the earliest European travelers in America were the Spanish. Columbus's journals and letters are the first European records of America, but of course Columbus never saw mainland North America and in fact never understood his discovery, dying still believing that he had reached the Indies in Marco Polo's Golden East. Nonetheless, his interpretation of everything new based on his old preconceptions, his descriptions of paradise, his reports of gold and rich kingdoms, his increasingly hostile encounters with the heathen and, therefore, subhuman (although paradoxically innocent and beautiful) "Indians," his search for a passage through the newly discovered lands to Cathay, his misfortunes with nature and mutiny, his sense of religious purpose, his physical suffering and madness, his dreams and disillusionment and ultimate belief in his fulfillment of prophecy—all these features in Columbus's writings prefigure the early American explorers' experiences.

The earliest Spanish account of events on future U.S. soil is *The Narrative of Alvar Núñez Cabez de Vaca,* originally printed as *La Relación y Comentarios . . .* (1542), the first North American captivity narrative and one of the greatest testimonies of human endurance. It is a harrowing tale based on an eight-year trek (1528–36) through Texas, New Mexico, and Arizona by four men who survived by practicing faith healing and coming to identify with their Indian captors. Unlike most explorers, Cabeza de Vaca retained sympathy for the natives and became profoundly disillusioned with the Spanish conquistadores, thus losing his European identity. As in many wilderness survival and Indian captivity narratives, physical privation precedes a psychological loss of self and culminates in spiritual rebirth into a type of new American hero—self-reliant, elemental, godly. This heroic personality and the theme of survival in the wilderness recur not only throughout early American narratives, such as Mary ROWLANDSON's, but also in much classic American literature, perhaps most notably James Fenimore COOPER's Leather-Stocking Tales.

As a result of stories of rich cities that Cabeza de Vaca's party had heard, one of the most famous quests in early America was undertaken from 1540 to 1542 by Francisco Vásquez de Coronado, recorded by Pedro de Casteñeda in his memoirs, *Relación de la Jórnada de Cibola* (ca. 1565), and by Francisco López de la Gomara in *La Historia General de las Indias* (1552). His search for the mythic Seven Cities of Cibola is the first and best known of many such reports of Indian kingdoms of gold in North America, including also Jacques Cartier's Saguenay in Canada and Ralph Lane's Chaunis Temoatan in Virginia. Indeed, this dream of America as a land of cities paved with gold

is an enduring national myth, and the quest is an act of the imagination by Edgar Allan POE's "gallant knight . . . in search of Eldorado" ("Eldorado"). Seen from an opposite moral perspective, a treasure hunt after a similar Indian legend of the Crystal Hills in Maine is the subject of Nathaniel HAWTHORNE's allegorical tale of foolishness and greed, "The Great Carbuncle" (1837).

Besides these central texts by Cabeza de Vaca and Pedro de Casteñeda, many other Spanish accounts are notable. For example, the anonymous "Gentleman of Elvas," a Portuguese, chronicled Hernando de Soto's 1539–42 march from Florida to North Carolina and west to the Mississippi, where the conquistador's death and dramatic burial in the Father of Waters climaxed the account, *Relaçam Verdadeira . . .* (1557). Another account tells of Antonio de Espejo's expeditions in the Southwest from 1582 to 1583. In addition, there are the accounts of Hernando Cortes, who named California after a rich, exotic, fictional island of black Amazons in the popular chivalric romance, *Las Sergas del Virtuoso Cavallero Esplandian* (1525), and of its exploration by Juan Rodriguez Cabrillo. Typical of exploration narratives in all the languages, these Spanish accounts are simply organized chronologically but can be as confusing as the events they narrate. Because paragraph indentations and transitions are infrequent, sometimes the form seems shapeless, as though the events had rushed by too rapidly for the writer to discern any patterns or connections. The subject matter within the often interminable paragraphs can vary from natural resources, to ethnographic customs, to battles, in a series of unconnected, rambling sentences. It is as if the prose reflects the untamed land itself—multifarious, fulsome, undefinable, limitless, resistant to demarcation.

Like Columbus, the first French explorer was an Italian, Giovanni da Verrazano, whose 1524 "Letter to the King" describes his voyage up the North American coast. Among the classical allusions sprinkled throughout this unusually polished composition, Verrazano compares the idyllic southern landscape with Arcadia. This Renaissance convention—the pastoral ideal, the dream of an earthly paradise, the vision of a new Golden Age—shaped early responses to the New World and evolved into a cultural attitude that influenced the American writer's tendency to favor a withdrawal from civilized society to a life of hardy simplicity in an idealized landscape. Examples of this pattern in American literature range from Thoreau's *Walden; or, Life in the Woods* to Ernest HEMINGWAY's "Big Two-Hearted River." However, as Verrazano coasted northward, his descriptions of the forests and their inhabitants become disapproving and foreshadow the response of William BRADFORD nearly one hundred years later as he looked from the *Mayflower* on a "hideous and desolate wilderness" filled with hellish horrors. Another important feature of Verrazano's narrative is the conflict between experience and expectation, which prefigures one of the dominant themes in American literature, i.e., the experiential challenge to authoritative concept, the preference of observation over theory. Like Columbus, Verrazano expected to find a route to Asia as Ptolemy, Aristotle, and other ancients believed possible, but unlike Columbus, he recognized that the obstacle was a new land mass and accepted that the globe of the ancients was wrong.

The first French attempts to settle in this new earthly paradise were Jean Ribault's Huguenot colonies in Florida from 1562 to 1565. Their tragic history, including another search for Cibola, attempts at mutiny, depredations against the Indians, and a final massacre by the Spanish, was recorded by René Goulaine de Laudonniére in *L'histoire notable de la Floride* (1586). Laudonniére was anxious to warn his countrymen about the dangers of a half-hearted commitment to any colonial enterprise, even one in an Arcadian environment. Unfortunately, the English too would repeat Ribault's mistakes in their first attempt.

The first major explorer of the St. Lawrence, Jacques Cartier wrote reports, including his *Brief recit, et succincte narration, de la navigation faicte es yles de Canada . . .* (1545), boasting of America's wealth and justifying the risks he had taken to search for the Northwest Passage and then the fabled riches of Saguenay; however, the most important early French explorer to write reports of America was Samuel de Champlain. In particular, the 1613 edition of his vivid, detailed *Voyages* reports his mapping of New England and his memorable 1609 battle with the Iroquois near present-day Fort Ticonderoga. Champlain's objective descriptions of the Iroquois and his allies, the Hurons, Algonquians, and Montagnais, show understanding of both their admirable qualities and their semibarbarous traits. Such descriptions eventually led to the concept of the "noble savage" and to portrayals of the Western hero's faithful Indian companion. Although called the Father of New France, Champlain extensively explored today's northeastern U.S., such as during his trips through upstate New York in 1615, described in the 1627 edition of *Voyages et Descouvertures,* and he represents an archetypal American hero—the tough, pragmatic, self-reliant frontiersman—a progenitor of Natty Bumppo.

The most monumental collection of documents related to the French in North America is *The Jesuit Relations,* reports by 17th- and 18th-c. missionaries in the Great Lakes region, New York, Michigan, Illinois, Wisconsin, and Minnesota. Primarily reports of God's work inspired by religious zeal, they also record Indian life and lore, natural phenomena, and psychological insights into a fascinating group of scholars who sought and often gained martyrdom among savages. Foremost among them were Claude Jean Allouez, Jean de Brébeuf, Claude Dablon, Jérome Lalament, Paul Le Jeune, Jacques Marquette, Paul Ragueneau, and Barthélemy Vimont.

The competing religious order, the Franciscans, also had their writers, including Gabriel Sagard, "historian of the Hurons," who produced one of the first dictionaries of an Indian language, and whose *Histoire du Canada* (1636) documents Etienne Brulé's arrival in Michigan in 1619. Franciscan Recollect friars also accompanied La Salle during his explorations of the Mississippi. Accounts by Zenobius Membré and others, filled with the typical descriptions of natural abundance and divine providence, are compiled in Chrétien Le Clercq's *Premier etablissement de al foy dans la nouvelle France* (1691), but the most popular of these writers was Louis Hennepin, whose *Description de la Louisiane* (1683) and *Nouveau voyage* (1696) are perhaps most interesting for the way the narrator becomes the hero of the great American adventure.

The beginning of the story of the Dutch in America is told by an Englishman, Robert Juet, a sailor with Henry Hudson in 1609, but Dutch writers left their own record of New Netherland. Johann de Laet's *Nieuwe Wereldt, ofte Beschrijvinghe van West-Indien* (1625) was the first history of the Dutch colonies, but Adriaen van der Donck was a much more important and interesting writer. His *Vertoogh van Nieu-Neder-Land* (1650) is a vigorous remonstrance stating the grievances of the Hudson Valley tenant farmers against the despotism of Governor Peter Stuyvesant. His *Beschryvinge van Nieuw-Nederlant* (1655) is a reliable description of the Dutch province. Another vivid description of the people, manners, and natural beauty of the Hudson is by David Pieterszoon de Vries in *Korte Historiael* (1655). A later account of colonial New York is the journal of Jasper Danckaerts's travels in 1679–80. Among many modern attitudes and ideas it expresses, his critical yet sympathetic portrayal of Indian life demonstrates his outrage at Europeans's treatment of the Indians. The earliest English account of the area is Daniel Denton's *A Brief Description of New York: Formerly Called New Netherlands* (1670). In the travelogue tradition, Denton claims to be an eyewitness to all he describes, though he mentions Dutch and Indian hearsay of mineral wealth in the mountains. Generally, however, he replaces extravagant claims with realistic descriptions, while still concluding that the area could offer a haven of opportunities for the Old World poor. The Dutch legacy in the New World had its greatest impact on American literature through the works of Washington Irving and his persona Diedrich Knickerbocker.

The short-lived Swedish colony along the Delaware is also vividly reported by David Pieterszoon De Vries in *Korte Historiael* and by its own chroniclers. Peter Mårtensson Lindeström's account of his visit in 1653–54 is in his *Geographia Americae,* which remained in the original manuscript until 1925. Pastor Campanius Holm left journals and accounts by members of the original colony, from which his grandson, Tomas Campanius Holm, composed the first detailed report, *Kort Beskrifning om Provincien Nya Swerige* (1702). The Swedish accounts are characterized by religious zeal comparable to the English Puritans, but they were too late and too few to establish a place for themselves in British North America.

By compiling, translating, and editing a voluminous mass of documents from the discovery, exploration, and settlement of the New World, Richard Hakluyt was a prime agent in the gradual association of the American experience with the English language. As a publicist for British colonization, Hakluyt reprinted many non-British and early English reports in such collections as *Divers Voyages Touching the Discovery of America* (1582), *The Princiapp Navigations, Voiages, and Discoveries of the English Nation* (1589; rev. ed., 2 vols., 1598–1600), and *Virginia Richly Valued* (1609). Sometimes Hakluyt wrote the narratives himself based on eyewitness reports, as he did "The Famous Voyage of Sir Francis Drake into the South Sea, and There Hence About the Whole Globe of the Earth, Begun in the Year of Our Lord, 1577." This account includes Drake's five-week stay in northern California, where the Indians worshiped the sailors like gods and gave Drake their lands, which he named Nova Albion (the first "New England"). Such events, often interpreted as providential, were the usual scenario upon first contact and show the important role of the relative cultural myths in the conquest of America. Among the most remarkable of the earliest British accounts published by Hakluyt is "The Relation of David Ingram" (1582), whose sailor's yarn of a nine-month march in 1568 and 1569 from Mexico to Maine through a paradise dotted with crystal cities could be considered the first tall tale in the American tradition of exaggeration. Although eventually omitted from Hakluyt's collections because of "incredibilities," so says Samuel Purchas, Hakluyt's successor as compiler of additional accounts in *Hakluytus Posthumus; or, Purchas his Pilgrimes* (1625), Ingram's story influenced Sir Humphrey Gilbert's disastrous 1583 voyage to discover the land of the legendary golden city Norumbega on the Maine coast. Gilbert's tragic obsession with finding precious metals is recorded by Edward Hayes, and the legend of the Eldorado in New England entered American literature in John Greenleaf WHITTIER's "Norumbega" (1869), a narrative poem about a French explorer, and the sonnet "Norumbega Hall" (1886).

Excluding the narratives relating to Martin Frobisher's three voyages in search of goldmines and a Northwest Passage in the Canadian Arctic, the early British reports of America, particularly those promoting Walter Raleigh's dream of a colonial empire in Virginia, stressed the natural abundance and pastoral simplicity of the natives. Edenic imagery pervades Arthur Barlowe's glowing description of the fruitful, fragrant Carolina coast, "The First Voyage Made to the Coasts of America" (1584), and even the reports by Ralph Lane and Thomas Harriot, written during and after the first fiasco at Roanoke in 1585–86, are only slightly less enthusiastic. Typically self-justifying, like the reports of most disappointed explorers, Governor Lane's report to Raleigh confirms the existence of the rich mines and exploitable kingdoms that Raleigh had imagined and that Lane had wasted his time and resources seeking. Harriot's cautious promotional pamphlet, *A Briefe and True Report of the New Found Land of Virginia* (1588), the first published book about America by an English explorer, also contains unrealistic predictions that did not follow from his keen naturalistic observations. An Oxford scientist, Harriot used classification, categorical descriptions, and lists of practical commodities in an attempt to demonstrate that America was not a wild, fabulous world but a real land with bountiful natural resources which could be reduced to ordinary utility and which thus justified further investments in colonization. Unfortunately, the subsequent attempt was the infamous Lost Colony of Roanoke. Nonetheless, Harriot's cataloging techniques were employed by most later travelers to control their American material.

Following the two earliest, but otherwise undistinguished, British descriptions of the New England coast—John Brereton's *A Briefe and True Relation of the Discoverie of the North Part of Virginia* (1602) and James Rosier's *A True Relation* ... (1605)—a new type of early American account began to evolve from the promotional tract. As colonies were planted successfully, discovery and exploration reports merged into settlement histories. Still essentially promotional, such writings sought investors in long-term colonization projects rather than speculators in potentially profitable exploration voyages. British-America's first major author, Captain John SMITH exemplifies this change in his many books, particularly *A True Relation of Such Occurrences and Accidents of Note as Hath Happed in Virginia since the First Planting of that Colony; A Description of New England; New England's Trials; The Generall Historie of Virginia,*

New-England, and the Summer Isles; and *Advertisements for the Unexperienced Planters of New England, or Anywhere.* In them, the dream of sudden acquisition of riches by gentlemen adventurers is replaced by a vision of colonial development by hard working settlers. Although admitting the likelihood of mineral deposits among the land's resources, Smith satirized explorers like Raleigh who sought only gold and ignored the ready wealth in fish, furs, lumber, and farm crops. Smith stressed the hardships and necessities as well as opportunities for earning wealth and freedom. In his visionary proposals, he combined realistic objectivity, practical advice, caution, and enthusiasm for America's potential as a land of equal opportunity where the poor could earn a new social position by developing the abundant natural riches and where heroic self-made men could establish a new democratic society. Showing a sharp appreciation for the wonders of the new Eden and a pragmatic awareness of necessity, Smith saw the land as more than just an obstacle to sudden wealth or a satanic wilderness to convert to the New Canaan. He saw a land of freedom and opportunities for a new start on life unavailable in England. Smith's egalitarian and economic themes were as influential in creating the characteristic secular side of a national identity as were the oft-heralded Puritan origins of the complex American self.

Despite their overlap, settlement accounts and colonial advertisements are a subject beyond the scope of exploration literature, although many closely related texts deserve mention. The original New England histories are best known. Francis Higginson's *New-Englands Plantation* (1630), William Bradford's *Of Plymouth Plantation* (which remained in manuscript until 1856), Edward Johnson's *The Wonder-Working Providence of Sions Savior in New England,* and Nathaniel Morton's *New England's Memoriall* (1669) describe the first experiences of the Pilgrims as they explored and settled their new land. These accounts are filled with vivid details of early colonial life in the wilderness, but their main emphasis is of course to record God's work and to teach religious truth. They are the record of the Puritan foundations of the ecclesiastical and social framework that helped form the American character. In contrast, Thomas MORTON's riotous *New English Canaan,* published in 1637, criticizes Puritan intolerance and defends his rum and gun business at Merrymount as a legitimate free enterprise. Their clash became the subject of Hawthorne's short story "The Maypole of Merry Mount" (1836). More secular accounts of the natural features of New England include William Wood's *New England's Prospect* (1634) and John Josselyn's *New-Englands Rarities Discovered* (1672) and *An Account of Two Voyages to New-England* (1674), which is a blend of natural

history, herb lore, religious satire, romantic idealizations of Indian life, and tall tales.

Accounts of the settlement and exploration of the Middle Atlantic and Southern colonies are characterized by their practical advice and capitalist spirit. These writers were generally less introspective and meditative than the New Englanders, so they produced factual descriptions of the fruitful land and political histories of their agrarian society, often celebrating the life of pleasure and sport amid a vale of plenty, in striking contrast to the stern founding of the City upon a Hill in New England. Alexander Whitaker's *Good News from Virginia* (1613), one of the earliest of these promotional tracts, assures readers that they cannot starve in the New World as they do in the Old. The direct contrast between the plenty in America and the misery in England was a prominent promotional technique, used early by John Smith, later by Daniel Denton, and by many others, such as John Hammond in *Leah and Rachel; or, The Two Fruitful Sisters, Virginia and Maryland: Their Present Condition, Impartially Stated and Related* (1656). Two other Maryland accounts are Andrew White's *A Relation of . . . Lord Baltimore's Plantation in Maryland* (1634) and George Alsop's *A Character of the Province of Maryland* (1666), which argues that pioneer life in America, even for indentured servants, was preferable to poverty in England. This theme also enters Thomas Budd's *Good Order Established in Pennsylvania and New Jersey* (1685). Important early accounts of the south include William Hilton's *A Relation of a Discovery Lately Made on the Coast of Florida* [i.e. South Carolina] (1664), John Lederer's *The Discoveries of John Lederer in Three Several Marches from Virginia to the West of Carolina* (1672), Samuel Wilson's *An Account of the Province of Carolina* (1682), and Thomas Ash's *Carolina . . .* (1682). An especially entertaining account of an early attempt to demarcate and thereby control the wilderness is William BYRD's *History of the Dividing Line Run in the Year 1728,* a narrative of the survey of the Virginia-North Carolina boundary, filled with ironic, even sardonic, anecdotes of the back country. Originally a journal, Byrd's *History* reveals an adventurous American observer-participant interested in all phenomena of the environment and life, a Benjamin FRANKLIN-type Everyman.

In the 18th c., further changes evolved in the explorers' writings. John Lawson's *A Voyage to Carolina* (1709) is typical. Lawson claimed to aim at truth and accuracy, which he preferred to "falsities and hyperboles" for the sake of entertainment. Such 18th-c. reports differ in spirit from the romanticized idealized Elizabethan accounts. These are filled with factual, scientific observations and sober, moderate language. From them stemmed historiography and natural history, and their techniques were applied by the chroniclers of the subsequent exploration of the interior. An important example of this Enlightenment spirit is Thomas JEFFERSON's *Notes on the State of Virginia*, which combined sublime imagery with concrete facts to refute European misconceptions about the degenerative effects of the American environment. Perhaps the best known of this type of report are *Observations on the Inhabitants, Climate, Soil . . . Made by John Bartram in His Travels from Pensilvania to . . . Lake Ontario* (1751) and his son William BARTRAM's *Travels Through North and South Carolina, Georgia, East and West Florida . . . Containing an Account of the Soil of Those Regions, Together with Observations on the Manners of the Indians.* Bartram's *Travels* was the culmination of early scientific description. His work is remarkable for its artistic sensitivity to form and color, its rich vocabulary, its idyllic strain, its pantheistic philosophy, and its dramatic renderings of nonhuman consciousness. It is a masterpiece of early American ROMANTICISM.

Interior exploration in the 18th c. produced many chronicles of the expanding frontier and its ethos. The last important French account of central North America was the journal of Pierre Francois Xavier de Charlevoix, part of his *Histoire de la Nouvelle France* (1744). Imperialistic in perspective, Charlevoix expresses respect for natural man and for the hardy, courageous, self-reliant, capable pioneers, but he fails to foresee the inevitable loss of European control over the spreading free spirits on the American frontier. In contrast, written from the point of view of a frontiersman, is James Adair's *The History of American Indians, Particularly Those Nations Adjoining to the Mississippi, East and West Florida, Georgia, South and North Carolina, and Virginia* (1775). It is an important expression of the frontiersman's love of the forest, survival ethics, and contempt for the soft city-dweller. The first English account of exploration west of the Mississippi is Jonathan Carver's *Travels Through the Interior Parts of North America, in the Years 1766, 1767, and 1768* (1778), famous for its grandiose European vision of a westward moving empire, complete with palaces and temples in the places of Indian huts. A more American vision of this Manifest Destiny is John Filson's *The Discovery, Settlement, and Present State of Kentucke* (1784). Filson's book contains the story of Daniel Boone, as told to a schoolmaster by the illiterate woodsman and Indian fighter who led the way literally and imaginatively into the American frontier. This characteristic figure was invested with much significance and glamour in the popular mind during the early 19th c., and Boone left his mark on American literature in fictional portrayals like Cooper's Leather-Stocking.

After the Louisiana Purchase in 1803, America's literature of discovery and exploration began anew with the journals of Meriwether Lewis, William Clark, and their party, from which Nicholas Biddle compiled *History of the Expedition Under the Command of Captains Lewis and Clark to the Sources of the Missouri, Thence Across the Rocky Mountains and Down the River Columbia to the Pacific Ocean* (1814). The compact prose of the day-by-day narrative records the grandeur and newness of the Far West, and their movement from conjecture to knowledge. The amazing travelogue of Lewis and Clark inspired later literary authors, such as Cooper, and the narrator of Poe's *Narrative of Arthur Gordon Pym* is said to have read their account. In fact, Poe's interest in the West inspired him to write a fictional account of the first crossing of the Rocky Mountains, *Journal of Julius Rodman,* which drew from the Lewis and Clark accounts and later works. Lewis and Clark, "Julius Rodman," and the rest of the early explorers of the West repeatedly emphasized the strangeness and immensity of the often terrifying wilderness. However, in the terrible strangeness they also perceived beauty and freedom, and their writings express the rapture of romanticism.

A very early American report of the Mississippi Valley and the West is Zebulon Pike's *An Account of Expeditions to the Sources of the Mississippi, and Through the Western Parts of Louisiana to the Sources of the Arkansaw, Kans, La Platte, and Pierre Juan Rivers; Performed by Order of the Government of the U.S. During the Years 1805, 1806, and 1807* (1810). Pike wrote Elysian descriptions of the Kansas prairies and pictured them covered with domestic herds, but he exaggerated the sterility of the Great Plains. Two other contrasting early accounts of the Far West are Henry Marie Brackenridge's sentimental but shrewdly observant *Views of Louisiana, Together with a Journal of a Voyage Up the Missouri River in 1811* (1814), and Edwin James's scientific *Account of an Expedition from Pittsburgh to the Rocky Mountains Performed in the Years 1819, 1820, by. . . S[tephen] H. Long, of the U. S. Top Engineers* (1823). These accounts greatly stimulated interest in the West and were Cooper's sources for his romanticized depictions in *The Prairie.* Sharing this interest, Irving traveled west for firsthand knowledge and produced *A Tour on the Prairies,* but Irving also drew from the early accounts to write *Astoria; or, Anecdotes of an Enterprise Beyond the Rocky Mountains* (1836) and *The Rocky Mountains; Digested Form the Journal of Capt. B. L. E. Bonneville* (1837). A trip to the frontier for adventure became a kind of initiation experience for many American writers after Irving, for example Richard Henry DANA, Jr. (*Two Years before the Mast*), Walt WHITMAN (*Leaves of Grass*), Herman MELVILLE (*The Confidence Man*), Bret HARTE ("The Luck of Roaring Camp,"), Mark TWAIN (*Roughing It*), and even Thoreau, who traveled north instead of west to see life amid nature (*The Maine Woods*).

The numerous accounts of expeditions into New Spain along the Santa Fe Trail and into the Northwest along the Oregon Trail continued to stress the strangeness of the land and the heroism of its explorers. For example, *Report of the Exploring Expedition to the Rocky Mountains in the Year 1842* (1843) by John Charles Frémont appealed to the public excitement over Manifest Destiny, and its chivalric descriptions of the mountain-man guide Kit Carson, like Filson's Boone, contributed a figure to our national folklore. Earlier, less influential, and often belatedly published accounts of the northwestern frontier were written by fur trappers and early settlers too numerous to mention. Perhaps the best of these books is Lewis H. Garrard's *Wah-to-yah, and the Taos Trail* (1850), which records the rich metaphorical language and lore of the Mountain Men and their Indian companions in the Colorado Rockies. The initial American advance in the south was most vividly recorded by Josiah Gregg in *Commerce of the Prairies; or, The Journal of a Sante Fe Trader, During Eight Expeditions Across the Great Western Prairies, and a Residence of Nearly Nine Years in Northern Mexico* (1844), the narrative of a free loner traveling through the tranquil plains in the 1830s. Even the war with Mexico produced exploration accounts of a sort, such as George W. Kendall's *Narrative of the Texan Santa Fe Expedition* (1844), which documents the Americans's enthusiasm, courage, and confidence despite Indians, starvation, and initial failure, and John T. Hughes's *Doniphan's Expedition, Containing an Account of the Conquest of New Mexico* (1847), which describes the determination, endurance, independence, honor, and intelligence of the bearded, buck-skinned Westerners who won the war and embodied the frontier ideal.

The settlers and travelers who surged into the West during and after the California Gold Rush wrote prolifically. Each was an explorer in his own right, although not in the strictest sense since they were not covering new ground. Such works as Edwin Bryant's *What I Saw in California* (1848) and Alonzo Delano's *Life on the Plains and among the Diggings* (1854) are representative and readable. More literary but limited views of California appear in Bret Harte's stories. The integration of West and East became a major theme, expressed notably in *Eldorado; or, Adventures in the Path of Empire,* published in 1850, by Bayard TAYLOR, a correspondent for Horace Greeley and the New York *Tribune,* and by Greeley's own *An Overland Journey, from New York to San Francisco* (1860). Such observa-

tions by travelers peaked with Mark Twain's *Roughing It,* a classic assessment of frontier life and values. In addition, of course, actual exploration of the U.S. wilderness continued also in the second half of the 19th c., with important reports written by Clarence KING, John Wesley Powell, William Gilpin, and Clarence E. Dutton. In the 20th c., the subject of the Western wilderness evolved into the naturalistic writings of authors like John Muir and into Westerns like those of Louis L'Amour.

The age of discovery and its chroniclers have passed. America's frontiers have passed repeatedly from explorer and trapper and Indian fighter, to hunter and transient settler, to farmer developer, to capitalist and industrialist. Nonetheless, America's seemingly inexhaustible wilderness and newness allows a continual process of discovery, both natural and personal, by the loner living near a pond in Massachusetts, by the boy floating a raft down the Mississippi, by the shell-shocked modern hero fishing up in Michigan. Indeed, the wonder of discovery is perhaps the greatest legacy of the explorers to American literature. They led the way for major American authors to see a world that is excitingly and perpetually new.

BIBLIOGRAPHY: Franklin, W., *Discoverers, Explorers, Settlers* (1979); Fussell, E., *Frontier: American Literature and the American West* (1965); Honour, H., *The New Golden Land* (1976); Kolodny, A., *The Lay of the Land* (1975); Lewis, R. W. B., *The American Adam* (1955); Miller, P., *The New England Mind: The Seventeenth Century* (1939); Miller, P., *From Colony to Province* (1953); Morison, S. E., *The Great Explorers* (1978); Nash, R., *Wilderness and the American Mind* (1967; rev. ed., 1973); O'Gorman, E., *The Invention of America* (1961); Page, E., *American Genesis* (1973); Quinn, D. B., *North America from Earliest Discovery to First Settlements* (1977); Quinn, D. B., *New American World* (1979); Sanford, C. L., *The Quest for Paradise* (1961); Seelye, J., *Prophetic Waters: The River in Early American Life and Literature* (1977); Slotkin, R., *Regeneration through Violence* (1973); Smith, H. N., *The Virgin Land: The American West as Symbol and Myth* (1950); Turner, F. J., *The Frontier in American History* (1920); Turner, F. W., *Beyond Geography: The Western Spirit against the Wilderness* (1980); Todorov, T., *The Conquest of America* (1984)

RAYMOND F. DOLLE

DIXON, Stephen
b. 6 June 1936, Brooklyn, New York

D. is certainly the most prolific short story writer since John CHEEVER or John O'HARA; he has published well over four hundred short stories in magazines as varied as *Playboy, Harper's,* the *North American Review,* and *TriQuarterly,* to name only a few. He has also published several novels along with eleven short story collections. Both his *The Stories of S. D.* (1994) and his novel *Interstate* (1995) received the highest critical acclaim from the *New York Times, Time,* and writers such as Grace PALEY. And the fact that *The Stories* contained the same number of stories that *The Stories of John Cheever*—sixty—invites obvious comparisons between these two American masters of short fiction. D. is the busiest experimental realist in contemporary American literature.

His early stories won him the O. Henry Award and a Pushcart Prize in 1977 for "Mac in Love" from his book *No Relief* (1976). That story became the archetypal D. story, which begins with a spurned lover at the door of his girlfriend who simply wants him to go away. The more she tries to get him to leave, the more insistent he becomes, creating such a commotion that the police are summoned and he is forcefully removed. What began as a simple request ends in a neighborhood scandal, a typical D. scenario showing the way language complicates matters rather than clarifying them.

The agony of love relationships is a recurring theme throughout many of his novels and stories, as lovers try hopelessly to understand each other in the heat of passion, anger, and frustration. Communication breaks down the more they try to understand each other.

Language often drives lovers apart, as it creates information systems that become so complex that genuine human considerations become secondary. One of the gems in D.'s *14 Stories* (1980) "The Signing," shows a grief-stricken husband leaving the hospital after the death of his wife and refusing to sign the necessary documents an impersonal medical bureaucracy requires to dispose of the body. The husband wants immediate closure to the devastating event, but the administrative system forces him to confront the horror of consciousness and the memory of the past, traumas that drive him to attempt suicide. Resisting the system creates unbearable predicaments that exacerbate rather than comfort the grieving widower's agony.

D.'s stories also chronicle the relentless pressure of urban living in finding work, sustaining relationships and, in many cases, simply avoiding injury or death that mere chance may create. The story "The Student," from *All Gone* (1990), concerns a dental student casually driving a cab in New York city when he is taken hostage by a maniac who orders him at gunpoint to drive without stopping. Instead of being rescued by the police, the driver is convicted as the kidnapper and spends years in prison. The victim, then, is treated as the criminal because the system allows no other alternative.

Frog (1991) earned glowing critical praise and became a finalist for the National Book Award in 1992 for the brilliance of its postmodern arrangement of stories, novellas, novels, and fragments, all working together to reveal the character of its protagonist, Howard Tetch. One of *Frog's* most impressive stories, "Frog Dances" (1986), tells of how Howard Tetch decides to become a family man. Chance becomes fortuitous rather than lethal, as Howard is casually walking down a street in Manhattan and observes through a window a young father dancing around a room with his baby in his arms. The scene of perfect familial bliss drives Howard to begin searching for a wife so that he may become that young, happy father someday. After dating a variety of women, he finally marries one; the story concludes with Howard Tetch dancing around his living room with a baby boy.

One of the most accomplished stories in *The Stories of S. D.* is "Man, Woman and Boy" (1992), a story which shows why D. is considered one of the foremost postmodernist writers in America; it traces the psychological processes of the unnamed narrator as his memory regresses from one event to another, until he finds himself back in his mother's womb and, simultaneously, at the origins of his own consciousness.

D.'s novel *Interstate* (1995) garnered high praise as a chronicle of the terrifying minute-by-minute journey of a middle-class family driving along an interstate highway as they are relentlessly attacked by a car full of maniacs who fire guns at them with tragic results. *Interstate* shows D.'s capability of sustaining long narratives without the slightest diminution of interest.

No other contemporary American fiction writer combines so effortlessly and comically the diverse influences of Franz Kafka, the German writer Peter Handke, and Samuel Beckett as D. And no other writer has captured the authentic experience of life in America since the end of World War II.

BIBLIOGRAPHY: Klinkowitz, J., "S. D.," in Meanor, P., ed., *DLB,* vol. 130, *American Short-Story Writers since World War II* (1993): 124–32; Saltzman, A. M., "To See the World in a Grain of Sand: Expanding Literary Minimalism," *ConL* 31 (Winter 1990): 423–33

PATRICK MEANOR

DOCTOROW, E[dgar] L[awrence]
b. 6 January 1931, Bronx, New York

While D. has published one play, *Drinks before Dinner* (1978), a collection of short stories, a novella, *Lives of the Poets* (1984) and a book of essays, *Jack London, Hemingway, and the Constitution: Selected Essays,*

1977–1992 (1993), his critical acclaim rests primarily upon his nine published novels, especially *Ragtime* (1975), which received awards from both the American Academy of Arts and Letters and the National Book Critics Circle and which critics frequently use as a standard for evaluating D.'s other works.

D. sets his first novel, *Welcome to Hard Times* (1960), in the Dakota plains of the West and *Loon Lake* (1980) in the Adirondack Mountains during the Depression era. However, novels such as *Ragtime, World's Fair* (1985), *Billy Bathgate* (1989), and *The Waterworks* (1994) reflect the urban Jewish milieu of New York City, where D. grew up. Because D. has particularly relied on the Bronx as a setting in his works, has shown concern for the plight of Jewish immigrants to the U.S. at the turn of the c., and has given several of his characters his own first name, some critics have labeled his work autobiographical. Like his contemporary, writer Tim O'BRIEN, D. complicates his historical fiction by naming his characters after himself and other relatives. In *Drinks before Dinner, World's Fair,* and *The Waterworks,* for instance, the protagonists are named Edgar, and in *World's Fair,* the young Edgar's parents share the same first names as D.'s parents, Dave and Rose, and his brother the same name as D.'s brother, Donald, yet D. does not consider his works autobiographical.

A master of genre who possesses the enviable skill to make each of his works different, D. is well known for the numerous literary types that his fiction embodies. *Welcome to Hard Times,* a linear first person Western, has also been called a dystopian novel, an anti-Western, and an American parable, and his second novel, *Big as Life* (1966), a work of science fiction. *Lives of the Poets* consists of six short stories and a novella, their only apparent connection being the single character who authors them and who ends them in the middle of a sentence. *World's Fair* is part memoir, part oral history, part fictional narrative. *Loon Lake,* a mixture of blank verse and prose, moves abruptly back and forth between first and third person and ends with the protagonist's resume. Part thriller, part fairy tale, *Billy Bathgate* is both a picarcsque and a coming of age novel. D.'s ninth novel, *The Waterworks* has been categorized as Gothic horror fiction. *Welcome to Hard Times, The Book of Daniel* (1971), and *Ragtime* have also been called revenge tragedies and *The Book of Daniel, Lives of the Poets, Loon Lake,* and *Ragtime* political works. D.'s fiction has been complicated further by the use of multiple narration and abrupt, unexpected shifts in point of view, a trademark of D.'s writing.

Much of D.'s popularity derives from his historical fiction, which has earned him a reputation as a postnmodernist. *The Book of Daniel* is a plural text with three different endings, each in its own way valid, a kunstlerroman and a bildungsroman, and a fusion of newspaper excerpts, letters, family accounts, the protagonist's dissertation material, autobiography, biblical quotations, trial transcripts, fiction, and nonfiction. In *Ragtime,* also a combination of fiction, history, and biography, D. suggests that since life is "volatile . . . everything could as easily be something else." He thus introduces the theme of epistemological uncertainty, his interest in the ways of knowing, that permeates not only *Ragtime* but also many of his other novels. D.'s literary works confront a main epistemological dilemma: can historical events be distinguished from those which take place in the processes of human thought? Is there a historical truth that can be defined? "Facts," D. notes in *Ragtime,* "are as much of an illusion as anything else;" history is only as accurate as the points of view of those who record it.

D.'s historical revisionism, his skillful blend of fact and fantasy, his meshing of fictional characters with real historical figures, forces his readers to continually question the reality that he creates. An early example of D.'s historical experimentation can be found in *The Book of Daniel* where the fictional Daniel and Susan Lewin-Isaacson represent the children of the historical Julius and Ethel Rosenberg who were found guilty of espionage and executed in 1953. While D. retains some of the historical details of the Rosenberg case, he changes the dates of the trial and the sexes of the Rosenberg's children, lowers the family's social status, and renames the central characters. *Ragtime,* too, raises questions about the facts of its characters. Readers wonder if Houdini really found himself face to face with the Archduke Franz Ferdinand and if J. P. Morgan and Henry Ford and Emma Goldman and Evelyn Nesbit actually met each other in real life or only in D.'s novel. Similarly, is the anachronistic Coalhouse Walker, the African American ragtime pianist, a re-creation of an earlier literary figure like Heinrich von Kleist's protagonist, Michael Kohlhaas, from the 1808 novel of the same name, an actual historical figure, or solely a fictional creation of D.? Like *Ragtime, Billy Bathgate* merges historical and fictional figures, such as Walter Winchell, Thomas E. Dewey, and the infamous gangster Dutch Schultz, who may or may not have conspired to have Thomas E. Dewey murdered. D.'s open texts force the reader to participate actively in the process of creation in an effort to determine what is literary artifice and what is possible historical "truth."

In each of his works, D. tries to capture a particular era of American history, frequently the 1930s, his more specific concerns being capitalism and the elusiveness of the American Dream. Ironically, Billy Bathgate, who represents the criminal side of the American Dream, is the only D. character to really strike it rich. *Loon Lake* is set during the Great Depression, certainly one of the worst eras for achieving capitalistic success. Its protagonist, Joe, quests after the perfect woman, riches, and power, typical American pursuits that more often fail than succeed. *The Waterworks,* set in a urban industrial environment, shows the evils of corruption and slavery and the experiments of a scientist who uses young children and the elderly as Guinea pigs and steals the fortunes of dying men. In D.'s world, materialism more often breeds evil, not good, and the characters search for the truth, only to find it less than desirable.

BIBLIOGRAPHY: Fowler, D., *Understanding E. L. D.* (1992); Harter, C. C., and J. R. Thompson, *E. L. D.* (1990); Parks, J. G., *E. L. D.* (1991); Tokarczyk, M. M., *E. L. D.: An Annotated Bibliography* (1988); Trenner, R., ed., *E. L. D.: Essays and Conversations* (1983)

CATHERINE CALLOWAY

DOERR, Harriet
b. 8 April 1910, Pasadena, California

D. weaves stories about the lives of American expatriates and Mexicans living together in rural towns and villages. Her descriptions, unsentimental and nonjudgmental, unfold with detailed deliberateness, forcing the reader to adjust to the pace, to take in the sights and the sounds of her world.

Both of D.'s novels, *Stones for Ibarra* (1984) and *Consider This, Senora* (1993), are set in locales where the people live simply, often from day to day with only their faith to sustain them. She tells us a different story of Mexicans—not of the immigrants who come to America for economic opportunity, but the people who have chosen to stay behind.

It is the Americans who escape to Mexico for opportunity. For example, Richard and Sara Everton come to Ibarra with a dream built on a great aunt's memories before the revolution. Friends and relatives think they are mad. The residents of Ibarra, equally puzzled by the Evertons, observe them from a distance, often literally getting to know them by observing their day-to-day activities—when they leave for trips into town, when they take their meals, how they set up their household—by literally looking into their windows.

This is how D. contrasts the Mexican culture with the American, through the defining rituals of daily life. Ultimately, D. deals with a major cultural difference, the perspective of life and death. For the Americans, life is something to be held on to as long as possible, no matter the cost. It is by living with death that Sara, and the reader, observe the meaning of life. In Ibarra, death is an accepted part of life, an unsentimental fact. But it isn't as if the dead are forgotten. Death and other incidents of unfortunate fate are re-

membered by the placement of a stone, a custom from which D. names her novel.

Expanding on the theme of life, death, and fate, in *Consider This Senora,* Sue Ames, an artist running from a shattered marriage, and Bud Loomis, a businessman escaping from unpaid taxes, are unlikely partners in real estate. They buy land in Amapolas and sell off lots to other Americans: Fran Bowles, a writer who romanticizes Mexico in her travel book much the way she romanticizes love, and her mother, whom the citizens of Amapolas refer to simply as the Widow Bowles. Neither Sue Ames, Bud Loomis, nor Fran Bowles can escape their fates. It is only the Widow Bowles who finds what she seeks, a peaceful death in Mexico.

Both novels are episodic, short stories with the same characters woven together. The style is reminiscent of Katherine Anne PORTER and Amy TAN. Her reflective and lyrical prose is like the oral tradition of storytelling. The narrator controls the pace, slowing the reader down, just as her American characters, Sara Everton and Sue Ames, must slow down and become accustomed to the rhythm of life in rural Mexico.

BIBLIOGRAPHY: Pearlman, M., and K. U. Henderson, *Interview: Talks with America's Writing Women* (1990); Stegner, W. E., "H. D.," *Esquire* 110 (December 1988): 200–201

KATHLEEN MOTOIKE

DOIG, Ivan
b. 27 June 1939, White Sulphur Springs, Montana

As a journalist, historian, autobiographer, and novelist, D. has unified the great variety of his writing production, from freelance newspaper articles to award-winning novels, under his own personal vision of the West, particularly of Montana, his birth state. A thorough and meticulous researcher with a clear sense of broad historical and cultural contexts, D. situates his writing particularly, but always with an eye that looks beyond regionalism toward larger implications for the West, for America, and for the world. His multivoiced auto/biographies and fictions reflect his preoccupation with internal, as well as external, landscapes and his willingness to experiment with different narrative styles in each book. D.'s 1989 Distinguished Achievement Award from the Western Literature Association formalizes the place he has earned as a significant western American writer. D.'s novel *Bucking the Sun* (1996), which chronicles the experiences of the Duff family working on Montana's Fort Peck Dam Project during the New Deal era, reflects his continuing preoccupation with familial, historical, and regional themes.

This House of Sky: Landscapes of a Western Mind (1978) and *Heart Earth* (1993) represent D.'s autobiographical impulse. *This House of Sky,* a finalist for the 1978 National Book Award, first brought D. to national attention as an important voice in western studies. In the bildungsroman/künstlerroman tradition, it tells the story of his development from childhood growing up in the ranch world of his father, Charlie, after the death of his mother, Berneta, when he was only six; the failure of his father's second marriage; the uneasy alliance Charlie finally makes with his estranged former mother-in-law, Bessie Ringer, Berneta's mother; and young Ivan's decision to leave Montana for college and a nonagricultural career. *Heart Earth,* winner of the 1993 Evans Biography Award, fills in the blank space in *This House of Sky* by developing a narrative based on a collection of his mother's letters written over a six-month period in 1945 to her brother Wally. D. uses excerpts from her letters both to frame and to spark his own narrative, which seems part historical documentation and part memorial novelization. He meets his mother, not face-to-face, but text-to-text; the dialogue between the two makes *Heart Earth* engaging and productive, like a good conversation.

Dancing at the Rascal Fair (1987), *English Creek* (1984), and *Ride with Me, Mariah Montana* (1990) comprise the epic McCaskill family trilogy, which traces their immigration from Scotland and their settlement and continuing residence in Montana. Although *English Creek* was written first, *Dancing at the Rascal Fair* comes first chronologically and tells the story of Scot immigrant Angus McCaskill's life and times on what was still the Montana frontier. D. avoids cliched western myths and moral simplicities in his complex depiction of Angus, who is torn by his unrequited love for a married woman. *English Creek* tells the story of Angus's son, Varick, his wife, Beth, and their teenaged sons, Alec and Jick, during the summer of 1939. D. divides the novel into three main parts: June, with worries about drought and Alex's conflict with the family; July, with its Independence Day celebration; and August, with a forest fire and Alex's continuing estrangement. Like *English Creek, Ride with Me, Mariah Montana* is narrated by Jick, now a widower accompanying his daughter Mariah and her former husband, Riley Wright, on a 1989 centennial road trip across Montana. With Mariah's photographs and Riley's articles, they create a unique and fascinating look at the state and its inhabitants.

BIBLIOGRAPHY: Ahern, K. D., "I. D.'s Self-Narratives: The West, Wilderness, and the Prophetic Impulse," *SDR* 20 (Winter 1982–83): 7–22; Simpson, E., *Earthlight, Wordfire: The Work of I. D.* (1992)

PHILLIP A. SNYDER

DONLEAVY, J[ames] P[atrick]
b. 23 April 1926, Brooklyn, New York

Known primarily as the author of *The Ginger Man* (1955), D. received considerable acclaim on the publication of this novel, which first introduced readers to his characteristic techniques: an antiheroic protagonist at odds with social constraints; a frequently grotesque, ribald sense of humor mixed with an undercurrent of melodramatic loss and absurdist futility; and a loose plot structure indebted to the tradition of the picaresque novel. Readers also encountered a lively prose style marked by repeated shifts between third-person narration and Joycean stream-of-consciousness, a use of prepositional and participial sentence fragments in capturing the protagonist's thought, vivid displays of lyrical imagery, and a trademark use of short poetic lines to close certain chapters. After the late 1950s, however, the very attributes that established D.'s reputation subsequently weakened it: while his later novels have merit as surreal, satiric expressions of contemporary malaise, reviewers frequently regarded these works as flawed stylistic and thematic reworkings of his first novel. Although some critics have consequently given D. the dubious honor of being a "cult" figure, his fiction nevertheless serves to illustrate both the strengths and weaknesses of a modernist heritage in post-World War II literature.

The son of middle-class Irish immigrants, D. served in the navy during World War II, left the U.S. in 1946 to attend Trinity College in Dublin, and resided mostly in England and Ireland until becoming an Irish citizen in 1967. In *The Ginger Man,* D. drew on this background in creating the protagonist Sebastian Dangerfield, an ex-naval officer studying law at Trinity under the GI Bill. Throughout the novel, Dangerfield's life of drunken carousing and lustful intrigue conflicts with his responsibilities as a scholar and a married father, despite his aspirations for a successful, upper-class life. Disdaining the life of the lower class, Dangerfield does not idealistically reject materialistic values, but is simply unable to accept the sacrifices and compromises demanded by society. In this sense, he is the classic mid-20th-c. antihero—more misfit than martyr. In depicting the divided motives of this unseemly protagonist, D.'s oscillation between first-person and third-person narrative conveys a sense of psychological disorder that also suggests a complex relationship between the authorial voice and his fictional counterpart. This scenario, in which the vices or neuroses of a protagonist/narrator at once oppose and remain implicated by a bankrupt social order, offers a form of complex satire found in much post-World War II American fiction—particularly in such authors as Saul BELLOW, John UPDIKE, and Thomas

PYNCHON. This trait also links D.'s work with that of Franz Kafka, one of his avowed influences.

D.'s next two novels, *A Singular Man* (1963) and *The Saddest Summer of Samuel S* (1966), intensify this pattern of alienated protagonists. In the first novel, a wealthy eccentric's paranoid fear of the world leads him to construct a mausoleum containing all the conveniences of a modern home. Reminiscent of Howard Hughes, George Smith both reacts against the ills of modern, urban life in America, and symbolizes perhaps the ultimate extreme of a capitalistic system: an investment in death itself as individualistic "success." In the latter novel, the neurotic title character consults a psychiatrist in the hope of overcoming his morbid isolation from society, but finally remains unable to escape the mausoleum of his own consciousness. As in the case of George Smith, Samuel's fixation on death is reinforced by the loss of a loved woman—a pattern also seen in *The Ginger Man* and many of D.'s other novels.

Such parallels soon led to charges that D. remained stuck in the formula established in his first novel, although some critics argued that the subsequent novels pursued their themes with more depth and variety. Some of them notably play upon genre conventions, although they remain marked—and, for some, hampered—by D.'s style of fragmented syntax. In *The Beastly Beatitudes of Balthazar B* (1968), he offers an antibildungsroman in which a young French nobleman acquires an abrasive education through the forces of change and death. Offering a new variant of mannered, alliterative titles, *The Destinies of Darcy Dancer, Gentleman* (1977) fuses an 18th-c. picaresque plot with a contemporary setting. Dancer's misadventures also become the basis for the sequel *Leila* (1983). In *The Onion Eaters* (1971), the triple-testicled Clayton Claw Cleaver Clementine inherits an old Irish castle which soon comes under siege by a bizarre mob of unseemly, surreal grotesques. While *Schultz* (1979) would eventually mark a departure from his characteristic style, D.'s continued use of crude, burlesque humor remained out of sync with the contemporary critical sensibilities.

If the development of his work since *The Ginger Man* has admittedly displayed the unevenness of an offbeat creative temperament, D.'s unique blend of American black humor and an Irish comic tradition resulted in some of the more memorable allegories of the absurd to appear in the postwar period.

BIBLIOGRAPHY: Hassan, I. H., *Radical Innocence: Studies in the Contemporary American Novel* (1961); Masinton, C. G., *J. P. D.: The Style of His Sadness and Humor* (1975); Podhoretz, N., *Doings and Undoings* (1964); Sharma, R. K., *Isolation and Protest: A Case Study of J. P. D.'s Fiction* (1983)

CHAD TREVITTE

DONNELLY, Ignatius [Loyola]
b. 3 November 1831, Philadelphia, Pennsylvania; d. January 1901, Nininger, Minnesota

"The Sage of Nininger" was a forceful orator and influential politician who helped found the Populist Party. D. also gained recognition as the author of books characterized by his interest in unusual topics and viewpoints. *Atlantis* (1882) argued for the reality of the lost civilization described by Plato; *Ragnarok* (1883) linked the nature of the earth's surface to contact with a comet. Less popular but still of historical interest are *The Great Cryptogram* (1887), which presents Francis Bacon as the author of works attributed to Shakespeare, and *The Golden Bottle* (1892), which celebrates a Christian and Populist vision of utopia.

Caesar's Column (1890) sold approximately 60,000 copies within a year of its publication and is D.'s most important contribution to American literature. It combines apocalyptic warnings with foreshadowings of the 20th-c. dystopia. Toward the close of the 20th c., Gabriel Weltstein visits New York. At first he is impressed with the city's technological marvels and apparent prosperity. Soon he discovers, however, that beneath the "gorgeous shell" is a seething mass of humanity oppressed by a small monied class led by the likes of Prince Cabano and powerful bankers. A secret brotherhood, led by Caesar Lomellini and his associates, begins a revolution that runs amuck and destroys modern civilizaiton (Caesar's "column" is an enormous cement-covered pile of corpses). Gabriel and a few friends fly away from the destruction and seek refuge in an isolated Ugandan colony—an agrarian, Populist utopia. D.'s depictions of immigrants, Jews, and violence have stirred controversy. Like Mark TWAIN's *Connecticut Yankee in King Arthur's Court* (1889), *Caesar's Column* reveals in sensational images some of the era's most extreme ambivalences about technology, democracy, and reform.

BIBLIOGRAPHY: Anderson, D. D., *I. D.* (1980); Pfaelzer, J., *The Utopian Novel in America, 1886–1896* (1984): 112–40; Ridge, M., *I. D.* (1962)

KENNETH M. ROEMER

DOOLITTLE, Hilda
b. 10 September 1886, Bethlehem, Pennsylvania; d. 27 September 1961, Zurich, Switzerland

Ezra POUND gave D. her pen name in 1912, when he read her poems, wrote "H. D. Imagiste" on the page, and cited her as one of the first and best of the imagist poets. Pound recognized that D.'s work exemplified the qualities which he proposed for IMAGISM: that the poem should strive for direct treatment of the subject or the emotion, that there should be no superfluous words, and that poetic rhythms should be based on the phrase rather than the metronome.

Until the 1970s, D. was regarded principally as an Imagist poet and represented in anthologies by her early works, such as "Hermes of the Ways" and "Orchard," both published originally in 1913 in *Poetry* magazine. Since then, however, there has been renewed interest and reevaluation of D.'s voluminous literary output: her Imagist poetry, her later epic and mystical poetry, her novels, translations, and memoirs. Important biographies and critical studies of D. have been published, as have her previously unpublished or uncollected works, and many out-of-print works have been reissued. D.'s reputation is now secure among the pantheon of early modernist writers, including Pound, T. S. ELIOT, and Marianne MOORE.

D.'s early poetry, collected in *Sea Garden* (1916), reveals the influence of Pound and of the classical Greek poet Sappho, whose lean and lyrical poetry provided a model to the Imagist poets. Many of the poems in D.'s early volume play upon the contrast between a protected inland place and another place of danger and beauty, excitement and wind. Suggested in the imagery of such poems as "The Sheltered Garden" is D.'s move from her Moravian household in Bethlehem, Pennsylvania to London during the exciting early years of MODERNISM.

D.'s poetry written in the late teens and the twenties and gathered in *Collected Poems* (1925) shows her moving away from the imagist mode. Much of this work was influenced by her immersion in classical Greek literature, especially that of Euripides, as well as by her hardships in England during World War I, and by her literary and personal relationships. Although she writes through the masks of classical Greek heroes, she chronicles such personal experiences as her marriage and separation from Richard Aldington and her stormy alliances with Pound and D. H. Lawrence. The poem "Eurydice," for example, depicts the Greek heroine's loss when she was swept into hell by Orpheus's backward glance, but it also reveals D.'s bitterness over the loss of her friendship with Lawrence.

D.'s poetry of the 1930s and 1940s includes *Red Roses for Bronze* (1931), which continues the reliance on Greek masks, but also additional poems written in a more personal voice, most of which remained unpublished until Louis Martz's edition of D.'s *Collected Poems, 1912–1944* (1983). These poems were strongly influenced by D.'s psychoanalysis in the thirties by Sigmund Freud and by his urgings that she

find connections between her personal past and the wider cultural past. The poems thus begin D.'s search for forebears, particularly female forebears, in Christian as well as in Egyptian and classical Greek mythologies.

D.'s most ambitious poems, her epic *Helen in Egypt* (1961) and her Christian, mythical *Trilogy* (1973), attempt to find the pattern and the meaning of human life, and to express the layerings of human experience. In *Helen in Egypt* D. herself can be recognized as one version of the heroine, repeating the longings expressed by Helen of Troy, by the goddesses Isis and Aphrodite, by Thetis the mother of Achilles and by Mary the mother of Christ.

In addition to poetry, D. wrote many prose works, both fiction and essays. Her novels, all fictionalized accounts of her own life and relationships, are *Palimpsest* (1926), *Bid Me to Live* (1960), and *Asphodel* (1992) all based on D.'s travel to Europe and her London years; *HERmione* (1981), focusing on a young American woman's love for a man and for another woman; *The Gift* (1982), about the Moravian community of Bethlehem, Pennsylvania; and *Nights* (1935), written under the pseudonym John Helforth and exploring the theme of bisexuality.

D.'s nonfiction prose includes *Notes on Thought and Vision* and *The Wise Sappho* (1982), two essays which treat her esoteric mystical interests and her search for a female spiritual ancestor; *Tribute to Freud* (1956), a fascinating account of Freud, of psychoanalysis in the 1930s, and of D.'s discoveries about her personal and sexual identity; *End to Torment: A Memoir of Ezra Pound* (1979), her recollections of her long friendship with Pound.

D. also wrote several translations of the classics, especially of the dramas and choruses of Euripides. These tended to be transformations of the original, as in her version of Euripides's *Ion* (1937); D. rendered the Greek play into syncopated English free verse and made it essentially a new work.

BIBLIOGRAPHY: Broughn, M., *H. D.: A Bibliography* (1993); Friedman, S. S., *Penelope's Web: Gender, Modernity, H. D.'s Fiction* (1990); Friedman, S. S., *Psyche Reborn: The Emergence of H. D.* (1981); Fritz, A. D., *Thought and Vision: A Critical Reading of H. D.'s Poetry* (1988); Guest, B., *Herself Defined: The Poet H. D. and Her World* (1984); King, M., ed., *H. D.: Woman and Poet* (1986); Robinson, J., *H. D.: The Life of an American Poet* (1982)

LAURA JEHN MENIDES

DORN, Ed[ward Merton]
b. 2 April 1929, Villa Grove, Illinois

Known predominately for his extraordinary epic *Gunslinger* (1975), D. is one of America's best narrative poets. His works also include, lyrics of geography and history, political poems, love poems, hilarious parodies, fiction, translations, and critical essays. Educated at Black Mountain College where he came under the influence of Charles OLSON, D. incorporated the projective field poetics of that movement but soon staked out his own terrain: exploring how Americans come to terms, socially, linguistically, economically, and poetically with living on this continent. His poetry—ambitious, intense, experimental, detailed, comic, and lyrical—reminds one of a jazzman or the cowboy-gunslinger, living on the edge, attentive to everything.

With *Hands Up!* (1964), reprinted in his *Collected Poems* (1975), D. began his examination of the southwestern culture. In *From Gloucester Out* (1964), a tribute to Olson, D.'s lifelong geographical focus begins in earnest. *From Idaho Out* (1965) is a rambling travelogue of intense, short poems full of sharp detail expressed in a flat, clotted, severe style. In this collection, D. turns the reader and himself into discoverers instead of tourists, making the poem a means of intellection, a tool for discovering the particulars and topography of our place in the world.

D. spent time in England as a Fulbright lecturer (1965–67) and as a visiting professor (1967–68, 1974–75). While there, his poetry became intensely political beginning with *Geography* (1965), which harshly examines the quality of American life in a somewhat discursive, flat style. *North Atlantic Turbineü*(1967), a much more ambitious piece, is, according to Donald Wesling, "the most penetrating attempt any American poet has made at an inquiry . . . into the world system of trade, control, and oppression." The poem lyrically combines the language of soap operas, rock and roll, comic strips, and puns with allusions to such diverse topics as the Lone Ranger, Martin Heidegger, Claude Lévi-Strauss, the drug culture, and cybernetics.

D.'s masterpiece, *Gunslinger,* is the most exuberantly successful long poem of the postmodern period. The four-volume epic is a comic cowboy and Indian tale. Though the poem ranges the West, it explores interior as well as linear space. The characters include the Slinger as demigod hero, the poet narrator, a mysterious "I," a madam of a saloon, a talking horse named Claude Levi-Straus, and others, all searching for the cultural bad guy, Howard Hughes. Each character's dialect represents a metaphysical as well as a cultural perspective. The "I" disappears, signifying that the reader-observer and poet-narrator have merged into one consciousness where the drama unfolds. Language becomes the poem's dominant theme. D. uses an ecstatic combination of jingles, rhymes, ballad tunes, structuralist jargon, drug argot, bikers' talk, and the tough guy swagger of the West to illustrate how hard

it is to comprehend our place in the world using the chaotic yet creative jumble of speech of our time. At the end, the Slinger leaves saying he'll miss "this marvelous accidentalism."

BIBLIOGRAPHY: Davidson, M., "To Eliminate the Draw: E. D.'s Slinger," *AL* 53 (November 1981): 443–64; McPheron, W., *E. D.* (1988); Wesling, D., *Internal Resistances: The Poetry of E. D.;* Paul, S., *The Lost America of Love: Rereading Robert Creeley, E. D. and Robert Duncan* (1981)

NEWTON SMITH

DORRIS, Michael [Anthony]
b. 30 January 1945, Louisville, Kentucky; d. 11 April 1997, Cornish, New Hampshire

A wide-ranging writer often identified as a Native American and as a collaborator with wife Louise ERDRICH, D.'s short stories, essays, novels, and memoirs repeatedly return to the difficult lives of ordinary people. The importance and the complexity of family relationships are recurring themes in D.'s realistic fiction, but his subject matter varies widely from draft dodgers to indigenous peoples. Although a relatively minor figure, he established a reputation as a fine essayist and fiction writer in the last ten years of his life.

D. was formally educated as an anthropologist but began writing fiction during the early 1980s when he and Erdrich collaborated on a series of short stories, several of which were published under the pseudonym Milou North. Critics warmly greeted D.'s first novel *A Yellow Raft in Blue Water* (1987), but it was *The Broken Cord* (1989) that won him national attention. In his first book of creative nonfiction, D. weaves together the frightening statistics on Fetal Alcohol Syndrome (FAS) and his personal struggle to deal with developmental problems faced by his three adopted FAS and Fetal Alcohol Effect (FAE) children. Painfully honest and with the last chapter written by his then twenty-year-old son, who is also deceased, *The Broken Cord* was almost universally well received, focusing national attention on D. and the damaging effects of consuming alcohol during pregnancy. Notably, it received the 1989 National Book Critics Circle Award, was named Outstanding Academic Book by *Choice,* and won the Christopher Award and the Heartland Prize.

In 1989, D. and Erdrich coauthored *The Crown of Columbus.* Although melodramatic plot twists near the end detract from an otherwise well-written novel, it sold well. Following the evolving relationship of two academics who are concurrently searching for new perspectives of Christopher Columbus, the novel raises significant questions about constructions of history and the processes of myth making. Typical of both Erdrich and D.'s other work is a strong female protagonist who refuses to relinquish the past as she crafts her future.

Working Men (1993), a collection of short fiction, and *Paper Trail* (1994), a collection of essays, added to his reputation as an increasingly fine craftsman. *Working Men* includes some exceptional short stories, the finest of which is "The Benchmark."

D.'s last novel, *The Cloud Chamber* (1997), likewise increased his stature. Both a prequel and a sequel to his first novel, *The Cloud Chamber* traces a varied family history through four generations of betrayal. In the last chapter, D. returns to Rayona, the teenaged protagonist from *A Yellow Raft in Blue Water*. The youngest member of the family, Rayona gracefully weaves together her Irish American, African American, and Native American heritage. Like most of his fiction, this is a realistic but fragmented novel, which is dominated by first-person narratives.

In the midst of an acrimonious divorce from Erdrich and struggling with relationships with his two FAE children, D. committed suicide. At the time of his death, he was working on *A Matter of Conscience,* a follow-up to *The Broken Cord,* and a new children's book.

BIBLIOGRAPHY: Chavkin, A., and N. F. Chavin, eds., *Conversations with Louise Erdrich and M. D.* (1994); Rayson, A., "Shifting Identity in the Work of Louise Erdrich and M. D.," *SAIL* 3 (1991 Winter): 27–36; Thomas, M., "Exploring the Meaning of Discovery in *The Crown of Columbus,*" *NDQ* 59 (1991): 243–50

M. GENEVIEVE WEST

DOS PASSOS, John [Roderigo]

b. 14 January 1896, Chicago, Illinois; d. 28 September 1970, Baltimore, Maryland

D. was considered one of the foremost writers of his generation when the novels of the *U.S.A.* trilogy appeared in the 1930s exceeding the promise of *Three Soldiers* (1921) and *Manhattan Transfer* (1925). In that embattled decade this was the supreme political fiction; D.'s lifelong theme of the individual's struggle with the system developed in a portrait of the U.S. from the turn of the century to the beginning of the Great Depression. No one since Walt WHITMAN had attempted as inclusive a book about America, and, among many writers making the language new, D. had listened most closely to "the speech of the people," which, he wrote in the prologue to his trilogy, "the initials U.S.A. stand for most of all."

With *Adventures of a Young Man* (1939), D.'s reputation as a novelist declined abruptly, and, to the extent that such criticism was based on his anti-Communism rather than changes in his technique, he was judged unfairly. As an earnest conservative, he wrote popular histories of the Jeffersonian era and began to call his fiction "contemporary chronicles," as if to minimize his inventiveness. *U.S.A.* remains his undoubted achievement amidst glowing revaluation of earlier work or sharp disagreement over the merit of his later writings.

As the unrecognized natural son of a prominent attorney, D. spent his early childhood traveling abroad with his invalid mother. At Choate School he struggled to overcome his foreignness, but, according to his friend, E. E. CUMMINGS, "no one at Harvard looked less like an American." D.'s writing apprenticeship at Harvard and in the World War—with the Norton-Harjes Ambulance Service and later the U.S. Army Medical Corps—is recorded in *The Fourteenth Chronicle* (1973), the collection of his letters and wartime diaries that show him determined to follow Flaubert's and modern examples of finding the right word. His undergraduate poems and stories rarely meet his standards, but *One Man's Initiation—1917* (1920) shows vivid observations among the impressions its ambulance driver hero has of the war and his comrades. While this slender book sold fewer than a hundred copies, D.'s first novel, *Three Soldiers* was widely praised for realistic exposure of army life or condemned as a desecration of the recent American war effort. Its hero is a composer (an "art hero," in Malcolm COWLEY's phrase) who hopes to forget himself as part of a great cause only to find that the army isolates each man within a dehumanizing routine. In the famous last scene, leaves from John Andrews's tone poem rustle along the floor as he is led away by military police, arrested for desertion. The furor over this book reached D. in Beirut soon after he had taken a camel caravan from Baghdad to Damascus. He was by far the most traveled American writer of his time, and the collections of his travel writing are valuable records of experience that shaped his art and thought. In *Rosinante to the Road Again* (1922), he is drawn to the anarchistic spirit of Spanish villagers. *Orient Express* (1927) includes the camel caravan and a 1920 trip to the Soviet Caucasus, where, typically, he hoped for and doubted the success of the revolution at hand. *In All Countries* (1934) contains the 1928 scene, when, standing beside his departing train in Moscow, he was unable to answer precisely "yes" or "no" when Soviet students asked him whether he was for them or against them.

Streets of Night (1923) is a severe revision of part of the "great novel" D. had carried around through the war and put aside to write *Three Soldiers*. Set in

Cambridge and Boston, it is chiefly interesting as a psychological study of its hero, a suicide at odds with the memory of his father.

D. became a leading modernist with *Manhattan Transfer,* an astonishingly original work. Influenced by film technique more than by any literary precedent, it is a montage of many fictional lives linked to the central stories of an idealistic reporter and a calculating actress. It foreshadows *U.S.A.* by telling these stories against the historical background of New York from the beginning of the borough system to the rampant materialism of D.'s immediate observations. Typically of his best work, vivid images stand for his bitterest feelings—here, anger over the dehumanization of figures "rolled in gold foil . . . beckoning from skyscrapers." His own paintings for the dust jackets of this book and *Orient Express* confirm this acute visual imagination. His play, *The Garbage Man* (1926), is an attempt to dramatize similar themes, and, along with *Airways, Inc.* (1928) from his association with the New Playwrights, has always been compared unfavorably to his fiction.

In 1927, D. was deeply involved in the work of the Sacco and Vanzetti Defense Committee. His pamphlet, *Facing the Chair: The Americanization of Two Foreignborn Workmen* (1927), analyzes a Massachusetts society about to execute the anarchists in terms that anticipate the *U.S.A.* pronouncement, "all right we are two nations." *The 42nd Parallel* (1930) was even more singular than *Manhattan Transfer* with its discrete narratives, biographies, autobiography, and "Newsreels" eventually understood as the structure of *U.S.A.* Each narrative traces the existence of an ordinary, if not representative, American from cradle to grave or to the point where he has been finally compromised by the system. These bleak stories are enlivened by D.'s prodigious powers of observation and his satiric style—a character's fate told by a mocking voice using exact nuances of his own speech. The biographical "portraits," most widely read of all D.'s writings, are, T. K. Whipple noted, like "monuments" looming over everything else in the trilogy. Far more poetic than D.'s earlier published verse, the cadenced lines proclaim Eugene Debs a "lover of mankind" and Andrew Carnegie the philanthropist for peace, "except in time of war." The "Camera Eye" sections begin obscurely as someone's childhood memories, but soon take shape as a Joycean self-portrait of the writer. The "Newsreels" are collages of news story excerpts and song lyrics that D. actually pasted up and copied out. *The 42nd Parallel* ends with the nation going to war in 1917. The radical labor movement, followed in the narrative of Mac, the itinerant Wobbly, has been suppressed, while the growth of monopoly capital has been told in the career of publicist J. Ward Moorehouse

whose early real estate ads have led to his sonorous pronouncements as master of the new business of public relations.

1919 (1932), focused on two years of war and the Versailles conference, is at once D.'s bitterest and liveliest novel. In its compression it is the triumph of the method of *U.S.A.* Its most contemptible character is, as D. himself was, an ambulance driver and a Harvard poet, an irony made closer by "Camera Eye" scenes in the same frontline and Parisian settings. Merchant seaman Joe Williams, typical of the workmen "muckers" of D.'s fiction is killed in a barroom brawl on armistice night in a scene that provoked Jean-Paul Sartre's 1938 observation that D. was the "greatest living writer." Perhaps the most memorable *U.S.A.* portraits—the greatest images in D.'s historical writing—are "Meester Veelson," the President as tragic dupe at Versailles, and "Body of an American," the unknown soldier buried at Arlington, delegate at the close of this novel for the living as well as the dead. Influenced by Thorstein Veblen, *The Big Money* (1936) is D.'s novel of the twenties and the runaway hedonism and materialism that one character calls "the waste." Inevitably even more satiric than *The 42nd Parallel* or *1919,* its portraits of Rudolph Valentino and Isadora Duncan complement the narrative of Margo Dowling, a silent film star displaced by the talkies. Although the Wright brothers' moment at Kitty Hawk is portrayed undimmed by the drone of bombers in years to come, the longest narrative concerns another tinkering mechanic, Charley Anderson, chasing the big money to his violent, drunken death. In the general praise for the completed trilogy, politically astute readers observed that denunciations of the Sacco and Vanzetti trial in "Camera Eye" were balanced by the narrative of a radical expelled from the Communist Party for "exceptionalism."

In Madrid in 1937 while working on a film about the Republican war effort, D. learned that José Robles, his friend and translator, had disappeared from his government office, and when Robles's execution was unofficially confirmed, D. left Spain full of disillusionment recorded immediately in such articles as "Farewell to Europe" and pursued in his next novel and the historical essays collected as *The Ground We Stand On* (1941). From then on he was an unswerving anti-Communist devoted to what he called "the principle of selfgovernment." *Adventures of a Young Man* (1939) is the story of a labor organizer alienated within the movement and sent to a martyr's death in Spain. It was dismissed by sectarian critics as "Trotskyist agitprop" and by most other reviewers as a puzzling descent from *U.S.A.* Relatively ignored, *The Ground We Stand On* is D.'s attempt to write episodes of early American history as a prescription for political action in the 1940s. He reveals not only his dread of all European police states, but alarm over the growing power of the Franklin Roosevelt administration as well.

Adventures of a Young Man, Number One (1943), and *The Grand Design* (1949), published together as *District of Columbia* in 1952, depart sharply from the techniques of *U.S.A.* The first novel is a single sustained narrative lightened by a few caricatures of political types. *Number One,* while linked to characters in *Adventures of a Young Man,* is, in the story of the title character, another novel based on the career of the Louisiana politician, Huey Long. Lies, or the political misuse of language, are a notable theme in D.'s work since *One Man's Initiation,* here overshadow even the other machinations by which the demagogue is crushed by the steamroller in Washington. *The Grand Design* is D.'s *Vanity Fair* of the Roosevelt administration from the Hundred Days in 1933 to "the Level of the Leaders" at Yalta. It approaches the breadth of *U.S.A.* in stories of several betrayed and self-deluded characters, but the interpolated prose-poems bearing D.'s opinions are not as poetic as his earlier portraits and "Camera Eye."

Chosen Country (1951), a memorial to Katherine Smith Dos Passos, is a long love story developed through several generations of the fictionalized backgrounds of the writer and his first wife. Minor postwar novels include *Most Likely to Succeed* (1954) and *The Great Days* (1958). *Midcentury* (1961) was widely heralded as the writer's return to the level of his achievement in *U.S.A.* It most resembles the trilogy in portraits of Douglas MacArthur and the actor, James Dean. The only parallel to "Camera Eye" is a pair of sardonic meditations by a man walking his dog, while the song lyrics of *U.S.A.* newsreels give way to advertising copy. Based on labor violence, entrepreneurial failure, and credit-card consumption, *Midcentury* is, thematically, a sequel to *The Big Money.* D. had not revised or fully organized the materials published posthumously as *Century's Ebb* (1975), a book almost as overlooked as *One Man's Initiation* had been fifty-five years earlier. It continues D.'s fictional autobiography from *Chosen Country* into the Spanish Civil War and beyond, contains admiring portraits of Whitman and Orwell and ends with an enthusiastic report of the 1969 *Apollo 10* moon shot.

D.'s best historical narratives are lively accounts of the social consequences of ideas, although many historians have judged them short on interpretation. *The Men Who Made the Nation* (1957), widely praised, is a montage of the Constitutional period. *Mr. Wilson's War* (1962) recants nothing that D. had written earlier about Woodrow Wilson. Other historical writings include the often pigeonholed *Head and Heart of*

Thomas Jefferson (1954), *The Shackles of Power: Three Jeffersonian Decades* (1966), *The Portugal Story* (1969), and the full-page text of *Life's Picture History of World War II* (1950). D.'s World War II reporting is reprinted in *State of the Nation* (1944) and *Tour of Duty* (1946). Collections with revisions and retrospective comments include *Journey between Wars* (1938), *The Prospect before Us* (1950), *The Theme Is Freedom* (1956), and *Occasions and Protests* (1964); *Brazil on the Move* (1963) and *Easter Island* (1971) are later travel books. *The Best Times* (1966) is a memoir that stops in the 1930s. *Three Plays* (1934) adds the unperformed *Fortune Heights* to his dramatic canon. *A Pushcart at the Curb* (1922) is a collection of poems.

BIBLIOGRAPHY: Belkind, A., *D., the Critics, and the Writer's Intention* (1971); Carr, V. S., *J. D.: A Life* (1983); Landsberg, M., *D.'s Path to U.S.A.* (1973); Ludington, T., *J. D.: A Twentieth Century Odyssey* (1980); Pizer, D., *D.'s U.S.A.: A Critical Study* (1988); Rosen, R., *J. D.: Politics and the Writer* (1982); Sanders, D., *J. D.: A Comprehensive Bibliography* (1987); Wagner, L., *J. D.: The Artist as American* (1979)

DAVID SANDERS

DOUGLASS, Frederick

b. February 1818, Talbot County, Maryland; d. 20 February 1895, Washington, D.C.

D. was one of the most prominent black leaders of the 19th c. and his influence continues to be felt in the late 20th c. Born into slavery as Augustus Washington Bailey, he taught himself to read illegally and escaped to the North when he was twenty. D. became a successful author, orator, editor, and political advisor to two presidents, "a noble vindication of the highest aims of the American anti-slavery movement." Early in his life, D. learned the importance of literacy and it became a driving force behind his desire for and love of freedom; indeed, he chose his surname after the hero of Walter Scott's *The Lady of the Lake.*

After escaping from slavery in 1838, D. made his way to Massachusetts and became involved in William Lloyd GARRISON's abolitionist movement. He proved to be a moving speaker and was widely respected and admired as a leader of the black community. As his speaking abilities developed, D.'s language skills were honed into an eloquence that caused some members of the public to question his origins, so in 1845 he published *Narrative of the Life of F. D., an American Slave, Written by Himself.* The autobiography was a huge success but was so detailed that D. had to flee to

England to avoid recapture. His friends there "bought" him and then "allowed" him to return to the U.S. to carry on his work. The success of his narrative is partly due to its intended audience: white, middle-class Christians who were in a position to recognize the horror and evils of slavery and then to act upon their feelings to abolish the practice. The heartfelt, vivid descriptions of his life as a slave garnered his readers' sympathy when his accusations might have repulsed them.

When he returned to the U.S., D. moved to Rochester, New York where he established a newspaper, the *North Star,* continued his abolitionist activities, and was active in the women's rights conventions at Seneca Falls and Rochester in 1848. In 1852, he delivered his most poignant antislavery speech "What to the Slave is the Fourth of July" in which he makes it plain that while he and his mostly-white audience are all citizens of the same country, the holiday celebrating freedom is not his to share with them; the hypocrisy of the nation is evident while men are enslaved anywhere in America on the date of the nation's independence. The speech is a brilliantly constructed as D. begins with a gentle introduction and builds to a moving crescendo as he accuses his Christian audience, "YOUR HANDS ARE FULL OF BLOOD" while they say their prayers. D. ends with a matter-of-fact discussion of the Constitution which, he notes, contains not a single mention of the words "slave" or "slavery."

D. published a second version of his autobiography in 1855 entitled *My Bondage and My Freedom,* which expands upon the *Narrative* and offers some new, and sometimes contradictory, information. It is an important text because it shows how D. came to break from Garrison's type of abolition and formed his own brand that earned him the respect of northern blacks, once denied him because of his loyalty to Garrison. D. published a third and final autobiography, *The Life and Times of F. D.* in 1881. After the Civil War, during which he recruited black officers for the Union Army, D.'s writing decreased and he became politically active in Washington D.C., eventually representing the U.S. in Haiti.

For an audience at the end of the 20th c., D.'s work provides not only a keen insight into the life of a slave and his fight for freedom but also stands as a true text of the American Renaissance, detailing an individual's personal philosophy which teaches his audience a code from which it can only benefit. Critics continue to discuss D.'s work as a seminal slave narrative but, importantly, tend to compare it more to other contemporary works rather than only comparing it to other slave narratives. Discussing D.'s work within the context of his contemporary writers demonstrates his importance as an American writer. While his aim was to bring attention to the plight of the slaves and to move his audience to help them, D. created an oeuvre that delineates a crucial American experience. To understand the 19th c., we must try to understand slavery from the slave's perspective; through his autobiographies and other writings, D. portrays the slave experience with crucial, graphic detail while he also lays bare his development as a writer. Each of his texts is a study in rhetoric and eloquence: how to win the sympathy of an audience with a unique mixture of charm, truth, accusation, and common sense.

BIBLIOGRAPHY: Burke, R. K., *F. D.: Crusading Orator for Human Rights* (1996); McFeely, W. S., *F. D.* (1991)

MARCY L. TANTER

DOVE, Rita
b. 28 August 1952, Akron, Ohio

D. graduated summa cum laude from Miami University, Ohio in 1973, after which she spent one year studying in West Germany at the University of Tubingen. In 1977, she obtained an M.F.A. from the University of Iowa.

D.'s poetry is an ingression into world history, black culture, and inscriptions of gender. She is lauded for both her style and her varied thematic concerns; within a tightly woven lyric, she articulates the everydayness of life while also signaling the consequential milestones of human existence. Her poetry weaves images and sensual detail into language so charged that each word is a condensation of its many emotional and descriptive possibilities.

As early as 1974, her poetry gained prominence in literary publications, and D.'s initial books, including *The Only Dark Spot in the Sky* (1980), *The Yellow House on the Corner* (1980), and *Museum* (1983), distinguished her as a poet who combined history, culture, and poetic craft. From 1981 to 1984, D. taught creative writing at the University of Iowa, and in 1982 she was writer-in-residence at Tuskegee Institute, Alabama.

While *The Yellow House on the Corner* highlights family life and intimacy, enriching the commonplace with legendary elements, *Museum* explores histories of people around the world, including the poem "Parsley," which recounts the massacre of Haitian blacks by General Rafael Leonidas Trujillo because they had failed to clearly annunciate the letter "r" in perejil (parsley). D also brings her gift of language to prose in *Fifth Sunday* (1985), a collection of eight concise short stories that dig deeply into the subjectivity of her characters, ranging from an adolescent girl awakening to her sexuality amid the condemning eyes of fellow churchgoers to an old woman alienated from her family because grief and loneliness had once driven her into a brief incestuous relationship with her brother.

From 1984 to 1987, D. taught at the University of Iowa, and in 1987 she joined the faculty of Arizona State University. In that same year, D. became the second black woman to receive the Pulitzer Prize in poetry for *Thomas and Beulah,* which was sparked by her interest in her grandparents' history, spanning the years from 1919 to 1968. These linked poems, parts of which began in *Mandolin* (1982), are separated into two segments and perspectives—"Mandolin" is dedicated to Thomas and "Canary in Bloom" to Beulah. The underlying narrative is that of a black man striving to define himself and support his family under white domination and racism, and a black woman framed not only by racial bigotry but also by the men in her life: as a daughter, overshadowed by a domineering father and as a wife and mother, kept within the boundaries of the home. Thomas is greatly compromised as an African American, but he, as a man, moves freely, and his journey begins on a riverboat leaving Tennessee for the north, in the first poem, "The Event." As a woman, Beulah does not have this same mobility; hers is an inward journey toward the wisdom and insight she realizes in her later years. Overall, *Thomas and Beulah* is an epic lyric of sustained love between two people and the sacrifices they make to keep their family together, and as D. noted, "It's the way one handles sacrifices that's crucial."

Grace Notes (1989) is a collection of poems, many of which address the tension between the singular identity and the needs of the family and black community. In D.'s novel *Through the Ivory Gate* (1992), her vibrant descriptions impart the richness of life as she tells the story of Virginia, a talented cellist, puppeteer, and actress, who returns to her childhood home of Akron to accept a teaching position in her old elementary school. The novel begins with a prelude that implicates how the identity of this black woman has been influenced by the social norms of white culture: a young Virginia is mourning the loss of her much loved white silky red-haired doll that has been supplanted by her family with a black doll, to whom she cannot relate.

Since 1989, D. has been professor of English at the University of Virginia. In 1993, she became the first African American and the youngest poet to be appointed poet laureate. D.'s poetic vision unearths the duality of life's offering, finding strands of beauty in the hideous, possibilities of freedom in oppression, and fecundity in barren lands. She brings life to poetry and therefore people to life.

BIBLIOGRAPHY: Rampersad, A., "The Poems of R. D.," *Callaloo* 9 (Winter 1986): 52–60; Schneider, S., "R. D. and Steven Schneider in an Interview," *IowaR* 19 (Fall 1989): 112–23; Vendler, H. H., *The Given and the Made: Strategies of Poetic Redefinition* (1995)

LISA TOLHURST

DRAMA

For the first century and a half of English settlement in America, the prevailing attitudes were inhospitable to the drama and especially toward theatrical performance. Indeed, the earliest plays written and performed in North America were not English at all: a Spanish commedia by Capitán Marcos Farfán de los Godos was acted on the banks of the Río Grande in 1598, and a French masque, *Les muses de la nouvelle France,* by Marc Lescarbot raised the spirits of settlers at Port Royal in Acadia in 1606. The early English colonists, however, were mostly Puritans who left England to escape religious persecution in the decades before the Commonwealth, bringing with them their antipathy toward plays and players. Opposition was strongest in New England and also in areas settled by Quakers and Presbyterians; Virginia and Maryland were the only colonies in which theatrical performances were not prohibited by law. That prejudice against the staging of plays certainly inhibited the writing of plays.

The earliest known English-language play in America was William Darby's *Ye Bare and Ye Cubb,* which Darby and two other men presented in Acomac County, Virginia, in 1665. Although the text has not survived, the activity is documented in court records that show charges brought against the three. Ordered to repeat their performance, in costume, for the court, Darby and friends complied and were found "not guilty of fault." Another early, lost play is noted in the journal of the English actor Anthony Aston in 1703: "We arrived in Charles-Town, full of Lice, Shame, Poverty, Nakedness, and Hunger. I turned Player and Poet, and wrote one Play on the Subject of the Country."

America's first published play was actually a pointed, and even ribald, political satire in dialogue form. Written in 1714 by Robert Hunter, who was then governor of the province of New York, and entitled *Androboros* (Man-Eater), the three-act "Biographical Farce" apparently achieved its purpose of discrediting Hunter's obstructionist lieutenant governor. It was fifty years before the next surviving play appeared in print. In *The Paxton Boys* (1764), the anonymous author satirized Presbyterians as well as the gang of frontiersmen named in the play's title who bungled relations with Indians on the Pennsylvania border.

In contrast to the pernicious influence of plays, "dramatic dialogues" were considered an effective format for moral instruction as well as for exercising oratorical skills. Written by classically educated men, these short, plotless pieces were often presented at colleges, especially after the practice was encouraged by William SMITH, provost at the College of Philadelphia. In 1756, Smith adapted *The Masque of Alfred,* adding over two hundred lines of his own, for recitation by students. With Francis HOPKINSON, he wrote "An Exercise Containing a Dialogue and an Ode, Sacred to the Memory of his Late Gracious Majesty George II" for performance at commencement. The following year's commencement was Hopkinson's dialogue and ode "On the Accession of His Present Gracious Majesty George III." Patriotic dialogues soon appeared, most notably a three-character narration entitled "Poem on the Rising Glory of America" by Hugh Henry BRACKENRIDGE and Philip FRENEAU, presented at the College of New Jersey in 1771. At Dartmouth College, Professor John Smith promoted the Indians' plea for tolerance in "A Dialogue between an Englishman and an Indian" (1779) and offered a spirited comment on inflation in "A Little Teatable Chitchat" (1781).

Thomas GODFREY was the first American author to have a play professionally produced in an American theater. His five-act heroic tragedy, *The Prince of Parthia,* won that distinction only by chance, for the American Company had originally rehearsed Colonel Thomas Forrest's comic opera, *The Disappointment,* for presentation at Philadelphia's Southwark Theatre in April 1767, but the latter work was abruptly withdrawn as "unfit for the stage" due to "personal reflections." Godfrey's Shakespeare-inspired tragedy in verse was substituted, although the talented young author had died of a fever four years earlier.

Plays about Indians were popular well into the 19th c. The first of these was *Le Pere-Indien* (1753), written by LeBlanc de Villeneuve and performed by amateurs in New Orleans, but now lost. Major Robert Rogers, commander of "Roger's Rangers" in the French and Indian War, wrote the best of the pre-Revolutionary Indian plays. His *Ponteach; or, The Savages of America,* a sympathetic portrayal of the tragic-heroic title character (pronounced Pontiac) was published in London in 1766, but not performed in Rogers's lifetime.

The American Revolution inspired a number of plays on both sides, although only the British side had the energy and inclination to produce its morale-building drama. In fact, the Continental Congress passed an edict in 1774 recommending suspension of theatricals in order to conserve resources for the war effort. Among the American patriots who wrote "pamphlet plays" for publication but not performance was Mercy Otis WARREN, the wife of a general in

Washington's army and the close friend of John and Abigail Adams. *The Adulateur* and *The Group* are both vehemently patriotic, satiric attacks in verse on Tories like Massachusetts governor Thomas Hutchinson, who is lampooned in *The Adulateur* as the villainous Rapatio. That character appears also in *The Defeat* (1773), which is sometimes attributed to Warren. In response to General Burgoyne's mocking treatment of Americans in *The Blockade of Boston* (1775), an anonymous patriot published *The Blockheads; or, The Affrighted Officers* (1776). John Leacock served the cause of liberty with *The Fall of British Tyranny; or, American Liberty Triumphant, The First Campaign, A Tragi-Comedy of Five Acts* (1776). Tracing the Revolution from its causes in England to events of 1776, this immensely popular work is said to be America's first chronicle play. It is also the first of many plays in which George Washington appears as a character. Although several editions were published within the year, there is no evidence that it was produced.

The American patriots whose Revolutionary-period plays went against the grain were Hugh Henry Brackenridge and Colonel Robert Munford. Brackenridge's *The Battle of Bunker's Hill* (1776) and *The Death of General Montgomery* (1777) are unusual in that seriousness of tone had historical accuracy take precedence over satire and propaganda values. Munford's comedies—*The Candidates* and *The Patriots,* both written in the 1770s and published in 1798—are unusual in taking a strictly nonpartisan view of events, although Munford himself fought on the American side. *The Candidates* is signaled by Richard Moody as "the transitional step from commencement dialogues to a more conventional play form" and for its dignified portrayal of Ralpho, "the first Negro character in the American drama."

Royall TYLER's comedy, *The Contrast,* may be credited with several firsts: it was the first professionally produced play on an American subject, the first produced comedy by a native American, the first American play reviewed in the press, the first play to feature a "stage Yankee" character, and the first wholly successful, long-running American play. Perhaps most significantly, it is the earliest American play that still frequently finds a place in today's repertoire. And Walter J. Meserve credits it as the one literary work that, more than any other, helped to unify the new American nation in the difficult postrevolutionary years. It did this by pointing up, in humorous dialogue, clever twists of plot, and believable characterizations, the "contrast" between the pretentious affectations of Europeans and the straightforward honesty of Americans. The texts of Tyler's three other produced plays have not survived, while none of his four other extant plays was produced. His important place in American drama rests solely on *The Contrast.*

America's first professional dramatist was William DUNLAP, author of over fifty plays, about twenty of which were translations/adaptations of French and German melodramas and the rest original works. The quantity and range of his work—from sentimental comedy to historical tragedy—earned him the epithet "Father of the American Drama." He supplemented his play writing career with less-successful forays into theater management, and he wrote the first *History of the American Theater.* Among his most popular plays are *The Father; or, American Shandyism,* a moralizing comedy; *Darby's Return* (1789), a farcical sketch; *The Fatal Deception; or, The Progress of Guilt,* a romantic tragedy, which was published as *Leicester* in 1806; *André,* a historical tragedy in blank verse, which Dunlap later rewrote as *The Glory of Columbia—Her Yeomanry* (1803), a patriotic spectacle for Independence Day celebrations; and *A Trip to Niagara; or, Travelers in America,* a comedy-travelogue featuring stock ethnic characters and a moving panorama to illustrate its eighteen continuous scenes.

The most notable trend in early-19th-c. drama was plays that considered in one way or another what it meant to be an American. Susanna Haswell ROWSON paved the way with works like *The Female Patriot* and *Slaves in Algiers; or, A Struggle for Freedom.* The latter, a melodrama with songs, about American captives in Algiers, illustrates the thesis that "No man should be a slave." Irish-born John Daly Burk contributed *Bunker Hill; or, The Death of General Warren* (1797), a patriotic play renowned for the staging of its spectacular fifteen-minute battle scene without dialogue. The best of the seven plays by Mordecai M. Noah was a patriotic comedy, *She Would Be A Soldier; or, The Plains of Chippewa,* which is enlivened by the heroine's disguise in breeches, a noble Indian chief, and a Yankee plowboy. James Nelson BARKER drew upon colonial American history for his best work *Superstition; or, The Fanatic Father;* he also wrote the earliest surviving play about Pocahontas, *The Indian Princess; or, La Belle Sauvage.* A charming homespun paean to democracy, *The Forest Rose; or, American Farmers* by Samuel WOODWORTH held the stage for over forty years and definitively established the Yankee character as a mainstay of the American stage. In 1845, Anna Cora Mowatt RITCHIE reiterated the theme of Tyler's *The Contrast* in her perennially popular comedy of manners, *Fashion.*

ROMANTICISM invaded the American stage at about the same time as it swept Europe. John Howard PAYNE, the first American author to win a reputation abroad, approached a classical subject in a romantic vein with his blank-verse masterpiece, *Brutus; or, The Fall of Tarquin* (1818). After Edmund Kean premiered it at the Drury Lane, the historical tragedy became a long-running success with American actors like Edwin Forrest and Edwin Booth. Payne's first play, *Julia; or, The Wanderer,* had been produced at New York's Park Theater when he was fourteen, and he went on to write over sixty plays, including *Clari; or, The Maid of the Mill* (1832) for which he wrote the words to the song "Home, Sweet Home," and the popular comedy *Charles the Second; or, The Merry Monarch* (1824), on which he collaborated with Washington IRVING.

Two of the outstanding American romantic dramatists owed their recognition to actor Edwin Forrest who sponsored a series of nine play writing competitions to stimulate native drama and to create vehicles for himself. John Augustus STONE won the first prize with his powerful tragedy of the idealized Indian *Metamora; or, The Last of the Wampanoags.* It inspired, according to Richard Moody, thirty-five more such "noble savage" dramas in the next twenty years; *Metamora* was the most successful of some seventy-five Indian dramas of the 19th c. Robert Montgomery BIRD, author of four of Forrest's nine prize-winning plays, is best remembered for *The Gladiator* and *The Broker of Bogota.* Primarily a lyric poet, George Henry BOKER contributed eleven plays to the romantic movement, including the finest dramatization ever achieved of Dante's Paolo and Francesca story: *Francesca da Rimini* (1855).

Romanticism sensationalized for popular appeal, with special emphasis upon production values, best describes the genre that held the American stage for the second half of the 19th c. Among the more popular melodramas were W. H. Smith's *The Drunkard; or, The Fallen Saved* (1844, which is preserved fairly faithfully in W. C. Fields's *The Old-Fashioned Way* [1934]); *The Poor of New York* (1857); and *The Octoroon* by the prolific Irish-American actor-manager-playwright Dion BOUCICAULT, who also coauthored with actor Joseph Jefferson III the most successful dramatization of Washington Irving's *Rip Van Winkle;* Clifton W. Tayleure's dramatization of *East Lynne* (1863); *Under the Gaslight* by Augustin DALY; *The White Slave* (1882) by Bartley Campbell; *The Heart of Maryland* (1895) and *The Girl of the Golden West* (1905) by David Belasco. Most popular of all were the numerous dramatizations—all unauthorized—of Harriet Beecher STOWE's *Uncle Tom's Cabin,* the best of which, by George L. Aiken, appeared within seven months of the novel's publication. Even as late as the turn of the 19th c., some five hundred companies toured the country with productions of *Uncle Tom's Cabin.*

The gradual trend toward REALISM in the drama may be detected first in the increasingly realistic stage effects used in melodramas and, later, in melodramas with drawing room settings, or those exhibiting social concerns like the focus on American business practices in *The Henrietta* (1887) by Bronson Howard. Also exemplifying this transitional synthesis of melodrama and realism are plays like *Hazel Kirke* (1880) by Steele MacKaye; *In Mizzoura* (1893) by Augustus THOMAS; *Secret Service;* and *Sherlock Holmes* by actor William GILLETTE; *Way Down East* (1897) by Lottie Blair Parker; *The Great Divide* by William Vaughn MOODY; and *The City* by Clyde FITCH.

Ibsen's plays began to be produced in America in the 1880s, and this decade marks the rise of full-fledged realism in the drama. William Dean HOWELLS earned the epithet "Father of American Realism" for his novels and criticism, but he also wrote thirty-six plays in which he applied the same principles. Although these works have a great deal of charm for the modern reader, they were too subtle and low-key for audiences accustomed to melodrama. Far more successful in his day was James A. HERNE, "the American Ibsen," whose seriousness of purpose and sure craftsmanship is evident in plays like *Margaret Fleming* (1891) and *Shore Acres* (1892). Rachel CROTHERS also tackled social problems, especially relating to women's place in society, as in *A Man's World. The Nigger* and *The Boss* were unflinching realistic dramas from the cultivated pen of Edward SHELDON. One of the wittiest realistic plays of the period was a social comedy on the serious subject of divorce: *The New York Idea* (1906) by Langdon Mitchell. A variation on dramatic realism was the ethnic play, best exemplified by the "Mulligan Guard" plays of Edward HARRIGAN and Tony Hart . This was a series of warm-hearted comedies, written between 1878 and 1884, depicting the Lower East Side's mix of German, Irish, Italian, Jewish, and Negro characters.

Coinciding with the woman suffrage movement was the emergence of the woman playwright. Over a hundred women had their plays professionally produced in New York between 1890 and 1930. Martha Morton, author of popular comedies like *A Bachelor's Romance* (1897), was a particularly prolific trailblazer. She also organized a Society of Dramatic Authors with thirty women as charter members, since they were barred from the all-male American Dramatists' Club. Rida Johnson Young wrote over twenty-five plays and musical comedies as well as over five hundred songs; among her most popular were *Brown of Harvard* (1906), *Naughty Marietta* (1910), *Maytime* (1917), and *Little Old New York* (1920). Another very successful librettist-lyricist was Anne Caldwell, whose plays included *The Nest Egg* (1910). Anne Crawford Flexner succeeded with plays in a variety of styles, but may be best remembered for her dramatization

of *Mrs. Wiggs of the Cabbage Patch* (1903). Lillian Mortimer continued to win favor with her melodramas like *No Mother to Guide Her* (1905), long after their vogue had passed. Among the outstanding serious plays by women are Edith Baker Ellis's *Mary Jane's Pa* (1908), Josephine Preston PEABODY's poetic *The Piper,* Harriet Ford's *The Argyle Case* (1912, with Harvey O'Higgins), Alice BROWN's *Children of Earth,* Susan GLASPELL's one-act *Trifles,* Zoë AKINS's *Déclassé,* and Zona GALE's *Miss Lulu Bett.* Representative comedies include Margaret Mayo's *Polly of the Circus* (1907) and *Baby Mine* (1910); Marian Fairfax's *The Talker* (1912); Clare Kummer's *Good Gracious, Annabelle* (1916); Catherine Chisholm Cushing's *Jerry* (1914); Zelda Sears's *Lady Billy* (1920); and Anne Nichols's long-running *Abie's Irish Rose* (1922).

Although the Harlem Renaissance (1919–30) is perhaps best known for its musicals, it also generated a wealth of legitimate drama by African American playwrights. One of the first of such plays to be publicly presented by black performers, *Rachel* by Angelina Weld GRIMKÉ protested the widespread lynchings of black men that occurred all too frequently in the South. Other similar plays followed, many written by black women, including Georgia Douglas Johnson, Mary Burrill, and May Miller. The prolific Willis Richardson pioneered serious dramatizations of black life and folklore; his one-act *The Chip Woman's Fortune* (1923) premiered in Chicago and subsequently moved from Harlem to Broadway. The 1930s brought plays by Zora Neale HURSTON, Shirley Graham, and Langston HUGHES.

A lively, mass-market commercial theater stimulated an outpouring of plays of all kinds in those decades. George M. Cohan dominated Broadway beginning with his 1901 play *The Governor's Son* and continuing through such hits as *Little Johnny Jones* (1904) and *Broadway Jones* (1912). A husband-and-wife play writing team, Frederick and Fanny Hatton, captured the foibles and frivolities of the era with clever comedies like *Upstairs and Down* (1916). That same period, however, finally saw the emergence of an experimental drama, most notably the expressionistic works of Eugene O'NEILL and Elmer RICE. Rice shocked theatregoers with *The Adding Machine,* and went on to win the Pulitzer Prize for *Street Scene.*

Eugene O'Neill, America's only Nobel Prize-winning dramatist, was one of a generation of playwrights who were influenced by Harvard University's Professor George Pierce Baker. Baker pioneered the academic study of practical theater, including the famous 47 Workshop for production of student-written plays. His efforts helped to launch the "Little Theater" movement of the 1920s, an important stimulus to the writing of one-act plays. O'Neill's career was launched when some of his one-act "sea plays" were produced by the Provincetown Players beginning in 1916. He won his first of four Pulitzer Prizes in 1920 for *Beyond the Horizon.* Two expressionistic masterpieces, *The Emperor Jones* and *The Hairy Ape,* were followed by such major dramas as *Anna Christie, Desire Under the Elms,* and *Mourning Becomes Electra.* He wrote one comedy, *Ah! Wilderness,* but returned to his more characteristic tragic vision with *The Iceman Cometh* and the tortured, posthumously produced autobiographical drama *Long Day's Journey into Night.*

Social concerns came to the fore in serious drama of the 1930s, but two major trend-setters of hard-hitting realism appeared as early as 1924: Laurence STALLINGS's and Maxwell ANDERSON's war play, *What Price Glory?,* and Sidney HOWARD's uncompromising treatment of a "fallen woman" and her older, Italian husband, *They Knew What They Wanted.* Both Anderson and Howard continued to write important social dramas, although Anderson eventually turned to historical dramas in verse. Other prominent dramatists committed to examining social and moral issues were John Howard Lawson, Clifford ODETS, S. N. BEHRMAN, Sidney KINGSLEY, Robert E. SHERWOOD, and Lillian HELLMAN. A more upbeat, philosophical outlook characterized the work of Thornton WILDER, most notably in *Our Town,* and also William SAROYAN, best remembered for his affectionate portrayal of losers in *The Time of Your Life.*

Since World War II, two American dramatists have remained in the forefront and have earned a permanent place in the theatrical repertoire. Arthur MILLER succeeded in giving tragic stature to a very ordinary man in *The Death of a Salesman,* but his moral fervor has tended to overburden the human drama of his later plays. Tennessee WILLIAMS achieved the greatest number and variety of masterpieces of any American dramatist. Although criticized for "cinematic plotting," his plays—from the haunting *Glass Menagerie* to experimental gems like *The Two-Character Play*—have given the American drama a gallery of memorable characters and a unique, poetic stage language flavored with his Southern regionalism and enhanced by his skilled use of lighting, music, sound effects, scenic metaphor, and visual symbols. The best of his work includes *A Streetcar Named Desire, Camino Real, Cat on a Hot Tin Roof,* and *The Night of the Iguana.*

Williams and Miller continued to dominate the theater of the 1950s; indeed, two of Miller's finest plays are *The Crucible* and *A View from the Bridge.* William INGE also peaked in that decade with *Picnic, Bus Stop* and *The Dark at the Top of the Stairs.* Robert ANDERSON wrote *Tea and Sympathy,* a sensitive drama about adolescent sexuality. Alice CHILDRESS drew from her acting experience with the American Negro Theater to write *Trouble in Mind,* a provocative play with a theatrical setting. *A Raisin in the Sun* by Lorraine HANSBERRY was the first play by a black woman to reach Broadway.

Neil SIMON produced an unbroken string of commercially successful comedies following his 1963 hit *Barefoot in the Park* until the late 1970s; he rebounded in the 1980s with his bittersweet autobiographical trilogy: *Brighton Beach Memoirs, Biloxi Blues,* and *Broadway Bound.* Edward ALBEE began as an avant garde playwright but has been subjected to the critical expectations of mainstream drama ever since the 1962 success of *Who's Afraid of Virginia Woolf?.* His Pulitzer prize-winning plays are *A Delicate Balance, Seascape,* and *Three Tall Women.* Arthur KOPIT moved from the absurdism of *Oh Dad, Poor Dad, Mama's Hung You in the Closet and I'm Feelin' So Sad* to the social concern of *Indians* and to the personal drama of *Wings. Viet Rock* (1967) by Megan Terry has been signaled as the first play to question American involvement in Vietnam, as well as the first to use rock music. With *Funnyhouse of a Negro,* Adrienne KENNEDY began her long string of highly personal, dramatic departures from realism.

Lanford WILSON must be accounted the leading playwright of the 1970s with works that alternated between urban settings—such as *The Hot L Baltimore* and *Burn This*—and plays set in his native Lebanon, Missouri, which include *The 5th of July* and *Talley's Folly.* Sam SHEPARD, August WILSON, and David MAMET moved to the forefront in the 1980s. Mamet and Shepard excel in the use of simple, direct, yet often musically rhythmic language and strong stage images to powerful effect. Pulitzer Prizes went to Shepard's *Buried Child* and Mamet's *Glengarry Glen Ross.* Using richer and denser language, August Wilson began with *Ma Rainey's Black Bottom* to chronicle the black experience in 20th-c. America. Outstanding works in the cycle include *Joe Turner's Come and Gone, Fences, The Piano Lesson,* and *Seven Guitars.*

The birth of Off-Broadway in the 1950s and Off-Off-Broadway in the 1960s, as well as the rapid expansion of regional professional theaters since the 1960s, has encouraged a healthy pluralism in the American drama. In *M. Butterfly,* David Henry HWANG examined a cross-cultural encounter involving sexual ambiguity. Latino/a dramatists include Maria Irene FORNÉS, Luis VALDEZ, Migdalia Cruz, Eduardo Machado, and Carlos Morton. Other noteworthy contemporary playwrights include A. R. GURNEY, Jr., Romulus Linney, John GUARE, Terrence MCNALLY, Marsha NORMAN, Wendy WASSERTEIN, Beth HENLEY, and Tony KUSHNER. Finally, there are those who create their plays as much in images as in verbal language, so that the production is heavily dependent upon their own direction; chief among these are Richard Foreman, Lee Breuer, and Robert Wilson.

BIBLIOGRAPHY: Bigsby, C. W. E., *Critical Introduction to Twentieth-Century American Drama* (3 vols., 1982–85); Bogard, T., et. al., *The Revels History of Drama in English, Volume VIII: The American Drama* (1977); Churchill, A., *The Theatrical 20s* (1975); Cohn, R., *New American Dramatists: 1960–1980* (1982); Downer, A. S., *Fifty Years of American Drama, 1900–1950* (1966); Dukore, B. F., *American Dramatists, 1918–1945* (1984); Grimsted, D., *Melodrama Unveiled: American Theater and Culture, 1800–1850* (1987); Havens, D. F., *The Columbian Muse of Comedy: The Development of a Native Tradition in Early American Social Comedy, 1787–1845* (1973); Londré, F. H., and D. J. Watermeier, *The History of North American Theater* (1998); Meserve, W. J., *Heralds of Promise: The Drama of the American People in the Age of Jackson, 1829–1849* (1986); Meserve, W. J., *An Emerging Entertainment: The Drama of the American People to 1828* (1977); Meserve, W. J., *Outline History of American Drama* (1970); Moody, R., ed., *Dramas from the American Theater, 1762–1909* (1966); Vaughn, J. A., *Early American Dramatists: From the Beginning to 1900* (1981); Wegelin, O., *Early American Plays, 1714–1830* (1970)

FELICIA HARDISON LONDRÉ

DREISER, Theodore [Herman]
b. 27 August 1871, Terre Haute, Indiana; d. 28 December 1945, Hollywood, California

D. is recognized as a major novelist and the most thorough practitioner of naturalistic fiction in America. A native of Terre Haute, Indiana, his fiction reflects rather directly his upbringing in an impoverished family which moved about repeatedly, his early struggle to succeed as a journalist in Chicago, St. Louis, and Pittsburgh, his unhappy marriage, and his see-sawing battle in New York to establish himself on the national scene as a writer of prominence. Although he is best known as the author of eight novels, D. published plays, poetry, and short stories, and his nonfiction included essays and autobiographies. His early career was marked by critical attacks and by attempts, sometimes successful, to censor his controversial fiction. But D.'s impressive output has persisted in attracting admirers who see in his most typical work an accurate and truthful rendering of the American scene. His reputation has remained remarkably steady since his death; indeed, in recent years a noticeable upsurge of critical interest has been apparent. Born a Roman Catholic, the influence of the Church is apparent throughout D.'s writing, most often in a mood of rebellion against it. In 1894, he encountered Herbert Spencer's *First Principles,* a book which blew him to pieces intellectually and impressed on him its view of the world as a mechanism in which the hopes and dreams of men counted for very little. Later he came under the influence of Sigmund Freud, and during the last stage of his life was fascinated by Eastern philosophy.

D.'s first novel, *Sister Carrie* (1900), tells the story of Caroline Meeber, a Midwestern girl of eighteen who comes to Chicago in 1889 and finds that survival involves adaptation to a society in the throes of socio-economic adjustments caused by the post-Civil War industrialization of America. Lacking marketable skills, Carrie is forced to begin earning a living at the bottom of the heap, in a sweatshop. She suppresses her emotional life in order to survive and enters passionless attachments with a prosperous salesman, Charles Drouet, and then with George Hurstwood, manager of a popular restaurant-bar. Hurstwood takes Carrie to New York, embezzling money from his employer to finance his move, and when his funds are depleted, Carrie learns to make her way alone upon the musical-comedy stage. Eventually, and largely through happy accidents, she becomes a rich and celebrated star. Her rise and Hurstwood's simultaneous fall into poverty and suicide serve to illustrate D.'s theme of America as a scene of struggle where some succeed and many fail, a bewildering process upon which the individual is able to exert little or no control. *Sister Carrie* is recognized as one of D.'s most important books and has become a modern classic of our literature. *Jennie Gerhardt* (1911), D.'s second novel, tells of a quite different sort of girl, but one who emerges from the same Midwestern background as Carrie Meeber. Jennie pays little attention to the conventional emphasis upon Success, but her warm emotional life makes her rich in other ways. Seduced as a girl by an older man, who then dies, Jennie gives birth to a daughter and makes the girl's welfare a major aim in her life. Jennie forms an emotional bond with a wealthy lover, Lester Kane, and for years lives with him in direct transgression of society's strict marital codes. When Kane's family threatens him with disinheritance should he not leave Hennie, she gives him up, satisfied with devoting the remainder of her years to nurturing a pair of adopted children. In *Jennie Gerhardt* D. suggests that, societal decrees notwithstanding, one's success is best measured not in dollars-and-cents but in the quality of one's affective life.

D. based *The Financier* (1912) upon the career of Charles T. Yerkes, an ambitious, capable, cunning, and ruthless 19th-c. "Captain of Industry." *The Financier* tells of Yerkes's (here called Frank Cowperwood) dealings in Philadelphia, including his early success, his ruination, and his eventual resurgence. A sequel, *The Titan* (1914), takes Cowperwood to Chicago, where he creates a monopoly in street transportation but eventually falls victim to the onslaught of an enraged populace. A third novel, *The Stoic* (1947), published posthumously, completes what D. called *A Trilogy of Desire* and depicts the amoral Cowperwood as he invades London, intent on cornering the Underground system. Unexpectedly, death intervenes and the financier's grandiose plans come to naught; his properties are auctioned off to satisfy his creditors. The *Trilogy,* which stands high among works of fiction concerning business, demonstrates D.'s belief in Spenser's principle that all great forces affecting life undergo a process of growth called evolution, followed by a devolution which brings them low and leaves the universe fundamentally unchanged.

D.'s fifth published novel, *The "Genius"* (1915), is also his most thoroughly autobiographical. Although its hero, Eugene Witla, is disguised as a painter rather than a writer, his fictional story maintains close parallels to that of D.'s own career through his early struggles, his unhappy marriage, and up to the 1910 era when he lost his lucrative editorial position at the Butterick Company because of his imprudent love affair with a fellow employee's lovely young daughter, here called Suzanne Dale. From the first, critical response to *The "Genius"* has been mixed, but the lengthy novel does possess an accretive power and, in these later times, society is considerably more tolerant of the strong sexual content for which The New York Society for the Suppression of Vice successfully influenced D.'s publisher to withdraw the book from circulation.

Following D.'s unhappy experience with *The "Genius"* he did not produce another novel until 1925 when his monumental *An American Tragedy* appeared, became a huge critical and financial success, and made D. a candidate for the Nobel Prize in literature (an award that went instead to Sinclair LEWIS in 1930). *An American Tragedy* again treats the grossly exaggerated emphasis which American society places upon material Success. Based in spirit and in many of its details upon the 1906 murder of Grace Brown by Chester Gillette at Big Moose Lake in the New York Adirondacks, the novel portrays the fate of Clyde Griffiths, son of penniless street missionaries, who conducts a surreptitious love affair with Roberta Alden, a worker under his supervision in his uncle's shirt factory. Subsequently, Clyde perceives an opportunity to rise in the world through a liaison with Sondra Finchley, daughter of a wealthy manufacturer. But Roberta, who now is pregnant, refuses to let herself be abandoned. Pressures mount and the result is murder, the only option which the misguided and confused Clyde is

able to comprehend. A fumbling killer, he is soon tracked down, arrested, tried and convicted. He goes to his death not quite knowing for certain whether he truly bears personal guilt for Roberta's death or whether he is simply the latest victim of those huge chaotic forces which play through the universe, capriciously altering human destinies. Along with *Sister Carrie,* this emotionally compelling novel is recognized as being a D. masterpiece.

A project which D. held in reserve since 1914, *The Bulwark,* was completed only shortly prior to his death and not published until 1946. It is the story of a Quaker family whose philosophy of plain living is directly at odds with the increasing materialism of the society surrounding them. The father, Solon Barnes, attempts to preserve his sons and daughters from being corrupted by alien standards, but the pressures of the main society are too great, his efforts prove to be futile, and he dies knowing it. At his funeral, his daughter Etta weeps—not for Solon but "for *life,*" that mysterious, ironic, and unfathomable phenomenon which had often punished, sometimes rewarded, but never failed to intrigue D. since the days of his earliest youth.

D. recognized early on that he required a "large canvas" on which to depict his visions of human life and struggle, and this fact militated against his being successful with the short story form. His best tales resemble his novels in being records of an entire life, but highly condensed and more often than not narrated from a vantage point located at a late stage in that life. Collections of his stories are *Free* (1918) and *Chains* (1927), from which come his most successful efforts: "Convention," "Free," "Nigger Jeff," "The Old Neighborhood," "The Second Choice," and "Typhoon." Like "Married," another fine story, which concerns the belatedly discovered incompatibility of a husband and wife, D.'s superior stories are tied closely to events in his biography.

In other forms of *belles lettres,* D. produced works which easily matched the standards of his time but usually did not excel over them. His experiments with the short drama appeared in *Plays of the Natural and the Supernatural* (1916) and included his most admired one-act, *The Girl in the Coffin.* This play concerns the enmity between two labor leaders in the death, following an abortion, of the daughter of the one who is pregnant by the other. D.'s single full-length drama, *The Hand of the Potter* (1918), explores the guilt-innocence questions which later became central to *An American Tragedy* and has the distinction of standing among the very first American plays to reflect the influence of Freudian theory. The central figure of the drama, Isadore Bershansky, is deformed physically and twisted psychically and, driven by pressures he neither understands nor controls, he molests and then murders a neighbor girl in the New York slum where he resides. In Isadore is epitomized D.'s interest in the baleful effects on individual lives of great forces such as heredity, environment, and subconscious impulses. Considerably too grim for the audiences of its time, the play was not a commercial success. The free-verse movement which swept into vogue after 1912 inspired D. to try his hand at poems. Characteristically, once started, he wrote verse by the ream, publishing dozens of experiments in periodicals throughout the 1920s. His verses are based largely on vagrant thoughts and impulsive reactions to natural (or supernatural) phenomena, and they are capable of achieving memorable approximations of the grim and ironic philosophy dramatized in his fiction. A sizable collection of D.'s poetry, aptly entitled *Moods, Cadenced and Declaimed,* appeared in 1928.

In the various forms of nonfiction, D. was continually active and often successful. His work in the essay proper is best represented by the collection *Hey, Rub-A-Dub-Dub!* (1920), which informs a reader concerning wide areas of D.'s philosophical views. A unique mixture of the biographical sketch and the philosophical essay is achieved in *Twelve Men* (1919) and *A Gallery of Women* provides psychological analyses semidisguised as fiction of fifteen women whose paths crossed D.'s. Indirectly these volumes have much to suggest about the author, but for pure autobiography *A Book About Myself* (1922) (later called *Newspaper Days*) and *Dawn* (1931) are the best sources for a reader who wishes to have the subject's personal reflections on his life. Together they bring D.'s story from birth to the mid-1890s, being all that he finished of a projected multivolume complete biography. Random portions of the biographical record are filled in by D.'s report on his 1911–12 tour of Europe, *A Traveler at Forty* (1913) and by *Dreiser Looks at Russia* (1928), based on his 1927 tour of the former Soviet Union.

BIBLIOGRAPHY: Dudley, D., *Forgotten Frontiers: D. and the Land of the Free* (1932); Fisher, P., *Hard Facts* (1985); Gerber, P. L., *T. D.* (1964); Hussman, L. E., Jr., *D. and His Fiction* (1983); Kazin, A., and C. Shapiro, *The Stature of T. D.* (1955); Lingeman, R. R., *T. D.* (1986); Matthiessen, F. O., *T. D.* (1951); Pizer, D., *The Novels of T. D.* (1976); Swanberg, W. A., *D.* (1965)

PHILIP L. GERBER

DUBIE, Norman [Evans, Jr.]
b. 10 April 1945, Barre, Vermont

At once both lyric and scholarly, D.'s body of work engages a vast and various historical sensibility. D.

excels at invading the extraordinary minutiae of the everyday, and from such material—no matter whose everyday he invade—manages to construct realistic, disturbing, and compelling personae, creating peculiarly specific and subdued insights into prominent and influential historical figures throughout history. His voices range from Breughel and Beethoven to Einstein and Ibsen, from Virginia Woolf, Ovid, and Rodin to a young woman living her life in a leper colony in 1922.

D., author of fourteen volumes of poetry, received his education at Goddard College in Vermont and at the University of Iowa. He has won numerous awards, including the Bess Hokin Award of the Modern Poetry Association and fellowships from the National Endowment for the Arts, the John Simon Guggenheim Memorial Foundation, and the Ingram Merrill Foundation. A professor at Arizona State University, he has produced a substantial amount of work in the past three decades, has published with the most prestigious journals and publishing houses, and appears regularly in the most-used collections and anthologies of modern American poetry.

Often daunting and rarely slight, his poems challenge the reader on a number of levels, from presenting an often ambiguous point of view to implicitly questioning the reader's own historical and cultural literacy, yet never does the imagery descend into obscurity. Regardless of the reader's familiarity with the subject matter, in D.'s hands, these characters breathe, eat, fornicate, and evacuate like everyone else, their singular historical narratives unfolding into surprisingly familiar, refreshingly human meditations. D.'s lyric insight, clearly the progeny of at least one romantic—Robert Browning—as well as such moderns as T. S. ELIOT, Ezra POUND, and Wallace STEVENS, is ultimately less interested in educating readers than in enlightening them as to the universality of their condition. Having said this, it is also true that since D.'s first full volume of poems, *The Alehouse Sonnets* (1971), a sequence of imagined conversations with William Hazlitt, the ratio of more purely personal lyrics has gradually increased.

Moving through D.'s oeuvre, approaching his most recent volumes, *The Springhouse* (1986) and *Groom Falconer* (1989), the reader begins to recognize a trajectory in the corpus of his work similar to that which arcs through the individual poems. The closer one comes to the end, the more self-recognition becomes available. Nevertheless, the sense of specificity regarding obscure but important objects, a diamond-backed vacuum hose, a gold tooth, a brass makeweight, as well as D.'s obvious infatuation with the natural world, particularly in winter, never lets readers forget by whose well-crafted words they are held suspended.

When, in "The Funeral" and speaking of his youngest aunt, D. writes, "The cancer ate her like horse piss eats deep snow" or when he describes the mold that has grown on the bricks of butter in the springhouse as "ermine" on cheese, it does not matter that the reader has not lived D.'s life, or any others' for that matter. What matters is that one is transported to the cathartic moment when the distance between self and "other," between memory and history and even fiction vanishes.

BIBLIOGRAPHY: Green, J., "N. D.: *Groom Falconer,*" *APR* 18 (November-December 1989): 28–31; Slattery, W., "My Dubious Calculus," *AR* 52 (Winter 1994): 132–40; Wojahn, D., "Four From Prospero," *GaR* 43 (Fall 1989): 589–601

BRYAN D. DIETRICH

DU BOIS, W[illiam] E[dward] B[urghardt]
b. 23 February 1868, Great Barrington, Massachusetts; d. 27 August 1963, Accra, Ghana

D. died in Africa on the eve of the March on Washington for Jobs and Freedom in 1963. Through a long life D., who held degrees from Fisk University and Harvard, had been one of those most influential in preparing the way for such a gathering, and in establishing guidelines for the civil rights movement and for the Black Power movement that was soon to emerge. D. had been advocating a form of Black Power—the development of an independent, black-controlled economic structure—at least as early as 1928. Along the way, D. was one of the founders in 1909 of the National Association for the Advancement of Colored People and the editor of that organization's publication, the *Crisis,* from its inception in 1910 until 1934. His many roles included scholar, propagandist, artist, activist, candidate (in 1950) for the U.S. Senate, radical. He knew the sting of racism and was more than once the target of the nation's periodic red scares. D. was also involved in controversy within the black community, as an eloquent critic of what he regarded as the excessive accommodationism of Booker T. WASHINGTON, the demagoguery of Marcus Garvey, and the timidity of the NAACP. His joining the Communist Party in 1961 and his assumption of Ghanaian citizenship in 1962 reflect a late pessimism regarding reform in capitalist America, providing an ironic and melancholy context for the moment of mourning observed at the announcement of D.'s passing by the gathering of idealists in Washington.

The concerns of D. the man determine to a considerable extent his activities as a writer. He was awarded a Harvard doctorate in history, and his dissertation,

The Suppression of the African Slave Trade to the U.S. of America, was published in 1896 as the inaugural volume of the Harvard Historical Studies series. By 1935, when he published his *Black Reconstruction in America,* D. had become convinced that historical scholarship and advocacy, while not identical, could not be entirely separated. The later book is both responsible scholarship and conscious attempt to undo the harm perpetrated by white racist historians, who had portrayed Reconstruction as a mixture of scandal and farce, and to evoke a proper appreciation of the achievements of the black masses and of their political representatives in the years immediately following the end of the Civil War.

D.'s scholarly interests extended to sociology as well as history. His *The Philadelphia Negro: A Social Study* (1899), a pioneer work of ethnic and urban sociology, by examining with the objectivity of the social scientist the role of the environment in the shaping of character and conduct, makes a case against notions of innate racial inferiority. D.'s editorship from 1897 to 1910 of the Annual Publications of the Atlanta University Conferences, substantial contributions to the sociology of black America, enhanced his reputation as a social scientist.

D.'s five novels are not to today's critical taste, but they are not without interest. Critics have tended to prefer *The Quest of the Silver Fleece* (1911), which combines social realism and romance in its symbolic depiction of the southern cotton economy. His most ambitious undertaking in fiction is the *Black Flame* trilogy (1957–61), which follows four generations of a black family through the last quarter of the 19th c. and the first half of the 20th c.

Most critics would rate D.'s autobiographical *Dusk of Dawn: An Essay toward an Autobiography of a Race Concept* (1940) more highly than his novels as literature. As the subtitle suggests, D. is not concerned to provide us with intimate details of his life. Rather, the concept gives significance to the life. D.'s masterpiece remains *The Souls of Black Folk* (1903), a book of essays and sketches in which, by a combination of scholarship, personal reminiscence and reflection, and polemic, D. draws aside the veil of stereotype and bigotry that had rendered black America invisible and affirms the full humanity of his people.

As editor of the *Crisis,* in addition to publishing important black writers, D. worked to define the terms of a black American literature and to spell out the criteria by which such a literature might be judged. Although some critics regarded D. as incorrigibly genteel in his literary preferences, his practices as an editor and his pronouncements as a critic suggest that the truth was more complicated.

D. was for much of his life a man in intellectual motion. Only in the last years of his life, and not entirely even then, does his thought begin to harden into dogma. He remains a forceful critical presence in American culture.

BIBLIOGRAPHY: Andrews, W., ed., *Critical Essays on W. E. B. D.* (1985); Broderick, F., *W. E. B. D.: Negro Leader in a Time of Crisis* (1959); Byerman, K. E., *Seizing the Word: History, Art, and Self in the Work of W. E. B. D.* (1994); Clarke, J. H., ed., *Black Titan* (1970); Horne, G., *Black and Red: W. E. B. D. and the Afro-American Response to the Cold War, 1944–1963* (1986); Lewis, D. L., *W. E. B. D.: Biography of a Race, 1868–1919* (1993); Marable, M., *W. E. B. D.: Black Radical Democrat* (1985); Moon, H. L., ed., *The Emerging Thought of W. E. B. D.* (1972); Moore, J. B., *W. E. B. D.* (1981); Rampersad, A., *The Art and Imagination of W. E. B. D.* (1976); Rudwick, E., *W. E. B. D.: Propagandist of the Negro Protest* (1960); Zamir, S., *W. E. B. D. and American Thought, 1888–1903* (1995)

W. P. KENNEY

DUBUS, Andre

b. 11 August 1936, Lake Charles, Louisiana; d. 24 February 1999, Haverville, Massachusetts

If our society revered the short story as it does the novel, D. would be a household name. Although he has produced two novels—*The Lieutenant* (1967) and *Voices from the Moon* (1984)—in a career spanning four decades, D.'s forte has always been the short story. Often compared to Anton Chekhov, D. populates his fiction with ordinary people struggling to reconcile their disjointed lives with a higher order represented sometimes by the military, sometimes by the Roman Catholic Church, and sometimes by an unknown power. The mundane existence led by most of his characters is reflected in his locales: most of his fiction is set in the various towns in the Merrimack River Valley of Massachusetts, where he has lived since 1966. The region boasts a few upper-middle-class Boston bedroom communities, but many of the towns and cities are poor, the economic base having gone south with the textile mills and shoe factories in the first half of the 20th c. Thus, it is not surprising that his characters often turn to the military, the Church, or some other authority to find the solace unavailable to them in their everyday lives.

Perhaps his most successful work with critics, *The Times Are Never So Bad* (1983) features a novella and eight stories in which characters cope with divorce, infidelity, domestic violence, and tragic accidents. In the novella "The Pretty Girl," D. explores an ex-husband's rape of his former wife from both points of view. Polly's horror and revulsion at the ordeal is matched by Ray's satisfaction with his mastery over her. This work reflects D.'s ability to render credible a female perspective, something another master to whom he is compared, Ernest HEMINGWAY, never seemed quite capable of accomplishing. That D. can tell a story from the perspective of a twenty-five-year-old woman, an eighteen-year-old girl, or a twelve-year-old boy as convincingly as he can from the perspective of a forty-five-year-old man is testimony to both the sympathy he has for his characters and the skill he has honed in over thirty years of writing.

Of paramount significance to D., particularly in *The Times Are Never So Bad,* is the depth of his characters' spiritual identity. For example, Ray in "The Pretty Girl" has no true spiritual center to help him cope with the loss of Polly, and thus resorts to gradually escalating and ultimately self-destructive violence. Conversely, Luke Ripley in "A Father's Story" converses with God after concealing his daughter's killing a pedestrian while driving drunk. The spiritual satisfaction that settles over Luke at the end of the story involves neither denying nor rationalizing his sin; he accepts the spiritual consequences of his act as wholeheartedly as he refuses to feel remorse for it. Similarly, a married man in "Bless Me, Father" is dismayed that the priest to whom he confesses an adulterous affair recognizes only the sin against the wife, and not that against the "other woman." The complex moral questions surrounding sexual behavior turn up frequently in D.'s work, particularly in *Adultery and Other Choices* (1977), and *Finding a Girl in America* (1980) These characters' search for a spiritual center rarely results in an endorsement of traditional precepts of organized religion.

Other characters in D.'s fiction find their spiritual center in the military, particularly the Marine Corps. Himself a Marine veteran, D. recognizes the appeal of the regimentation, order, and masculine solidarity of military life. Paul in "Cadence" from *Adultery and Other Choices* and "Goodbye," from *The Times Are Never So Bad,* finds in the Corps a refuge from the loveless marriage of his parents. And Harry in "The Captain," from *The Times Are Never So Bad,* returning home from a four-year stint in the Marines at age twenty-two, reenlists as soon as his father informs him that a job in the foundry is waiting for him.

By the mid-1980s, D. had, through seven books, established his reputation as a writer with a keen appreciation of the social and spiritual complexities of contemporary life. Then, in 1986, his life was shattered: Stopping to help at the scene of a freeway accident north of Boston, D. was himself hit by an automobile. The accident cost him one leg, the use of the other, and finally his family—he lost custody of his two youngest children when his wife divorced him. Unable to write fiction after the accident, D. finally published *Broken Vessels* in 1991, a collection of nonfiction, much of it dealing with the accident and its aftermath. With the publication of this work he expanded his themes to include the effects of crippling—physical, emotional, and spiritual. He then went on to write fourteen new stories, published in 1996 in the collection *Dancing after Hours.* Similar to his previous work in setting and atmosphere, these stories nonetheless bear witness to the powerful hold his physical condition has over him—many of the characters in these stories are themselves cripples (D. prefers this term over other euphemisms), either physically or spiritually. The title story recounts one evening of comradely drinking, during which a quadriplegic's observations on his everyday life entertain and inspire a group of friends, acquaintances, and bartenders. In another story, "Out of the Snow," a housewife successfully and violently resists two would-be rapists, only to discover that she relished the battle, fighting not for the sake of her family, but for her own life. These stories of survival reflect the wisdom of a writer who has been forced to come to terms not simply with his mortality, but with the far more frightening prospect of living life as a cripple.

In 1996, D. added to his 1985 NEA Fellowship, 1988 MacArthur Award, and other acknowledgments the Rea Short Story Award for *Dancing after Hours.* Always thematically autobiographical, his recent work holds the promise that he will continue to mine his physical, personal, and spiritual struggles, creating new landscapes and new characters, but hauntingly familiar human stories.

BIBILIOGRAPHY: Kennedy, T. E., *A. D.: A Study of the Short Fiction* (1988); Yarbrough, S., "A. D.: From Detached Incident to Compressed Novel," *Crit* 28 (Fall 1986): 19–27

KATHLEEN SHINE CAIN

DUGAN, Alan

b. 12 February 1923, Brooklyn, New York

With *Poems* (1961), winner of the Yale Series of Younger Poets Award, the Pulitzer Prize and the National Book Award, D. immediately carved a niche for himself on the margins of American literature, often characterized by his own term, "Dugan's Edge." Subsequent collections, from *Poems 2* (1963) and *Poems 3* (1967) through *New and Collected Poems, 1961–1983* (1983) and *Poems 6* (1989), have only

confirmed his reputation as an urbane, caustic, self-deprecating commentator on modern American life.

Aesthetically, philosophically, and politically, D.'s work remains unaffiliated with any contemporary creed or school, so critics have dubbed him an anarchist, a "confirmed angel-wrestler," a poet of "bitter eloquence" with "an intensely private, almost a claustrophobic vision," and even "the clown of nihilism." D., however, rejects the label of nihilist, responding in an interview, "If I were a nihilist, I wouldn't bother to write poetry." In fact, D.'s poems are fixated on the pragmatic problem-solving of everyday life. His abiding concerns include landing or keeping a job, the agonies of sex, the obsession with money, the suffering caused by class differences, heavy drinking, the absurdities of war and politics, the pitfalls of urban life, the inanities of faith and nature, and aging. Rare among contemporary poets as an uncompromising satirist, he poses as the patent outsider. Yet while he refuses to approach any subject (including himself) sympathetically or compassionately, behind the polemical veneer lies an inherently classical sensibility, like that of the Roman satirists he echoes. Although offering no redeeming or transcendent hopes, his remains a fundamentally moral vision. Throughout his career, he has been criticized for not developing his style or varying his focus, but considered chronologically, his work becomes less frantic and more subtle, if relentlessly vitriolic.

Stylistically idiosyncratic, a D. poem might begin with a dilemma, then scavenge its material for a response, as in "Love Song: I and Thou" or "Winter: For an Untenable Situation." Its diction can be oddly abstruse, its mood frenetic yet austere. Usually D. employs a recognizable rhythm—often roughly tetrameter or pentameter—and a conversational syntax that render his poems immediately accessible, despite ironic surprises that erupt throughout. Lines and stanzas tend to be short, as are most poems; though he challenges a reader's intelligence, he is rarely obscure, and never dull, as his poems have a polished, sometimes celebratory rhetoric. Like Samuel Beckett, D. often uses rational language to demonstrate the shortcomings of reason itself. Telling titles are everywhere: "Funeral Oration for a Mouse," "Tribute to Kafka for Someone Taken," "For Masturbation," "Adultery," "On Rape Unattempted," "On Being a Householder," "Teacher's Vacation Lament in the Country," "On Shields: Against World War III." Other poems are called simply "Poem" or "Untitled Poem."

D. attended Queens College, served in the U.S. Army Air Force during World War II, graduated from Mexico City College, and worked in advertising, publishing, and model making. After *Poems,* fellowships allowed him to turn full-time to writing and teaching.

Since 1971, he has been associated with the Provincetown Fine Arts Work Center. Though lacking the notoriety of many contemporaries, D. has created a distinctive place for himself by virtue of his sheer candor and iconoclastic wit.

BIBLIOGRAPHY: Boyers, R., "A. D.: The Poetry of Survival," in Boyers, R., ed., *Contemporary Poetry in America* (1974): 339–47; Gery, J., "'Pieces of Harmony': The Quiet Politics of A. D.'s Poetry," in Sorkin, A. J., ed., *Politics and the Muse* (1989): 206–21; Heines, D., "A Conversation with A. D.," *MR* 22 (Summer 1981): 285–300

JOHN GERY

DUNBAR, Paul Laurence

b. 27 June 1872, Dayton, Ohio; d. 9 February 1906, Dayton, Ohio

Most critics today agree that D. was talented, but do not find much of high quality in his overall literary output of six volumes of poetry, four collections of short stories, and four novels. They see D. as a good study in the way that the racial pressures of early-20th-c. America could control, debilitate, and devastate a black writer.

The desires of white publishers and readers to see late-19th-c. plantation tradition portrayals of infantile, contented, sentimentalized antebellum slaves speaking in Negro dialect controlled and limited the quality of much that D. wrote. D. was aware of his accommodation to white racism, and also aware that this accommodation limited his literary achievement. But the tortured soul wrought by this awareness, and pained by the knowledge while he was still in his twenties that he was incurably ill with tuberculosis, also poured forth some of his best poetry. This poetry does break from the prescriptions of the time for black portrayals and express some of D.'s true feelings about his role as a black writer and the role white society forced black people to play. Further, his best novel to some extent breaks conventional plantation tradition prescriptions and makes direct statements about racism in the framework of literary NATURALISM.

D.'s conventional, accommodationist plantation tradition poetry and fiction well portray various aspects of black culture, including black folk speech, but they also ignore the hardships of black antebellum life and consequently the skill and ability of blacks in coping with these hardships. The fact that this poetry and fiction captured authentic aspects of black culture is overshadowed by the fact that D.'s black portrayals failed to acknowledge the harsh realities of black life and, instead, soothed guilty, racist white consciences

in the postbellum period. Only one of D.'s short stories, "The Lynching of Jube Benson," sets forth a realistic portrayal of racist Southern acts of violence, and this story is not a strong denunciation of racist violence.

Two of D.'s best and best-known poems, "We Wear the Mask" and "Sympathy," are written in standard English. "We Wear the Mask" expresses the deep anguish and pain of both D. and black Americans because white racism forces blacks to hide their true selves behind degrading, stereotypical masks. The persona in "Sympathy" empathizes with the desperate plight of a caged bird who futilely beats his bruised, bloodied wing against his bars. D. is probably talking about the restrictions on him as a black man and black poet, and perhaps also the restrictions on his spirit imposed by his physical infirmities.

The Sport of the Gods (1902) is D.'s only novel with a main focus on black characters. The novel clearly exposes white, Southern racism, but also shows the evils of the urban North and the bad fortune of black characters in the hand of callous fate. Racism forces the black family that *Gods* focuses on out of the South, but the heads of the family, the mother and father, return to the South after the hard life of New York City ravages the family. The South and its racism are not the main culprits after all.

BIBLIOGRAPHY: Brawley, B., *P. L. D.: Poet of His People* (1936); Cunningham, V., *P. L. D. and His Song* (1947); Gould, J., *That D. Boy: The Story of America's Famous Negro Poet* (1958); Lawson, V., *D. Critically Examined* (1941)

JAMES W. COLEMAN

DUNBAR-NELSON, Alice [Moore]

b. 19 July 1875, New Orleans, Louisiana; d. 18 September 1935, Philadelphia, Pennsylvania

D.-N. is recognized today, as she was in her own lifetime, as a respected writer and critic, newspaper columnist, and activist for the rights of African Americans, particularly African American women. Although she was a generation older than the writers and artists of the Harlem Renaissance, her critical reviews of their works brought many, like Langston HUGHES, their first public acclaim. Throughout her career, she wrote numerous articles and columns for many of the major black and white publications of her day, but only two volumes of her poetry and fiction, *Violets and Other Tales* (1895) and *The Goodness of St. Rocque and Other Stories* (1899), were published in her lifetime. Her early literary fame coincided with the somewhat celebrity status of her brief marriage to and separation from the poet Paul Laurence DUNBAR. Later years were full of struggle. Nonetheless, she continued her involvement in current affairs and to write poetry, scholarly articles, sociological essays, novels, and even scenarios for film. D.-N. received renewed critical attention with the publication of her collected diaries, *Give Us Each Day* (1984). Written during the stressful times of the 1920s and 1930s, the diaries reveal the very human concerns of D.-N.'s private life, her views on her work, her relationship with her family, her sexuality, and the local and national politics of the time.

Violets and Other Tales is often classified as mere juvenilia, but the work does establish certain literary themes and concerns that D.-N. will return to in more mature works. The romantic image of a bouquet of violets that is first developed in the title story will appear twenty years later in a more mature poem, "Violets" (1917). In the earlier tale, a young girl in love presses her Easter bouquet of violets and other flowers as a memento for her lover and their future. The second part of the story indicates that the girl is dead, and the lover, now married to a cold woman, finds the bouquet by accident and seems to regret the life he chose. The poem similarly deals with romantic disappointment and the contrast between the memory of the natural sweetness of true love and the "deadened" world of the present.

The sentimentality of D.-N.'s first work is tempered somewhat in the stories presented in *The Goodness of St. Rocque*. While similar to Grace KING's Creole tales, *The Goodness of St. Rocque* examines in a subtle and almost secondary manner the close interrelationship among the races of the New Orleans and bayou cultures on a level ignored by King. In "When the Bayou Overflows," the romance between the French Cajun Sylves with the brown-skinned Louisette is tender and equal and lacks the melodramatic theme of miscegenation of so many works of the period. The title story, "The Goodness of St. Rocque," is set in New Orleans and shows D.-N.'s skill in combining standard English and Creole dialect in the story of the struggle of the dark-eyed Manuela to pry her lover away from the blue-eyed Claralie through the exotic combination of voodoo and good Catholic prayers to St. Rocque. While D.-N. privately deplored Paul Laurence Dunbar's use of black dialect to popularize his works, the stories in this anthology show that she was just as adept as he in capturing speech patterns and Southern cultures.

Primarily known for these two early volumes, D.-N. continued to write throughout the rest of her life. The drafts of three unfinished novels are now available in recent volumes of her works issued by the Schomburg Library of 19th-c. Black Women Writers. Many of her scholarly articles and sociological essays such as

"Wordsworth's Use of Milton's Description of Pandemonium" (1909), "People of Color in Louisiana" (1917), and "The Negro Looks at an Outworn Tradition" (1928) also deserve attention for the characteristic clarity and thoroughness that D.-N. brought to studies of literature, history, and current affairs.

BIBLIOGRAPHY: Hull, G. T., *Color, Sex, and Poetry: Three Women Writers of the Harlem Renaissance* (1987); Williams, O., *An A. D.-N. Reader* (1979)

LYNN RISSER

DUNCAN, Robert [Edward]
b. 7 January 1919, Oakland, California; d. 3 February 1988, San Francisco, California

As a writer, D., created one of our strongest mythopoetics, claiming his intellectual birthright from the modernist poets Hilda DOOLITTLE and Ezra POUND. He was an informing intelligence in two formative schools of poetry, the San Francisco Renaissance and the Black Mountain writers. Born Edward Howard Duncan, he first edited and published under his adopted name, Robert Edward Symmes, before 1941. His experiments in open forms, especially the serial poem and the collage, helped to define the practice of a defiantly non-academic yet highly intellectual poetry in the U.S. following World War II.

D.'s contribution is unique because his writing keeps alive, against the grain of our era, humanistic traditions of the mystical. Whereas Charles OLSON, D.'s contemporary, announced a new poetics with his recognition that open poetic form is an extension of contents, D.'s work is a reminder that language makes sense beyond the poet's control or technical mastery, so the act of writing can mean a personal reenactment of a higher order. To D., "the poet desires to penetrate the seeming of style and subject matter to that most real where there is no form that is not content, no content that is not form." His is a poetry that "enacts in its order the order of first things," first things to include the Adamic act of naming the things in his world, the experience of erotic love, and the mysteries of his own birth. Working from Olson's argument for a fundamentally open-ended poetry, D. imagines his "Passages" poems belonging "to a series that extends in an area larger than my work in them. I enter the poem as I entered my life, moving between an initiation and a terminus I cannot name." His first success in writing serial form came with *Medieval Scenes* (1950), ten discrete yet interrelated poems written over ten consecutive evenings in 1947. "Passages" and his other long-running serial poem "The Structure of Rime" were sustained in the books that established his reputation—*The Opening of the Field* (1960), *Roots and Branches* (1964), and *Bending the Bow* (1968)—through the poetry of his last stage, *Ground Work: Before the War* (1984) and *Ground Work II: In the Dark* (1987). In poems like "The Fire: Passages 13," D.'s epistemology of starting from primordial acts is not a hermetic practice but one that generates contemporary political commentary.

Starting in 1936, D. enrolled in classes at the University of California, Berkeley, long enough to come under the influence of medievalist historian Ernst Kantorowicz. Following a lover east, he emerged in New York as a precocious genius in the circle of Anaïs NIN. Dismissed from Army boot camp during the war as a "sexual psychopath," he went on to write the position statement "The Homosexual in Society" (1944) that is among his first important publications. After the war, he hitchhiked across the country to visit Pound at St. Elizabeths Federal Hospital and corresponded with Doolittle. A year after meeting Olson, he had already experimented in open form in "The Venice Poem." D. lived in Mallorca during parts of 1955 and 1956, where Robert CREELEY's Divers Press published the original edition of *Caesar's Gate.* In 1956, while an instructor at Black Mountain College, he launched into the writing of the poems he had begun in London for *The Opening of the Field,* an early masterpiece of what Olson had termed "composition by field." The late 1950s saw him reunited with poets Jack SPICER and Robin Blaser and the community of artists known as the San Francisco Renaissance.

A self-proclaimed "derivative" poet by method, D. named influences as diverse as Igor Stravinsky, Edith Sitwell, Jean Cocteau, St. John of the Cross, Louis ZUKOFSKY, Laura RIDING, Mary Butts, Helen Adam, and Dante. His imitations of Gertrude STEIN in the volume *Writing Writing* (1953) and the poems of *A Seventeenth-Century Suite* (1973) are his most direct homages, and "The H. D. Book" is a book-length meditation on a poetry of influence. But in D.'s art, even the product of derivation must show the process of an inclusive and grander design. "The great art of our time is the collagist's art," he explains, "to bring all things into new complexes of meaning." For one of D.'s most striking collages, in the third section of "The Poem beginning with a line from Pindar," he parallels the tale of Psyche sorting her seeds and the tragedy of Pound at Pisa, in this way appropriating ancient and modern myths of the impossible task and nature's coming to man's aid. The painter and collagist Jess Collins, D.'s long-time companion, strongly influenced his life's work in "the grand collage."

Instinctively a lyrical poet, D. is the singer of the songs we hear most purely in poems like "Often I Am Permitted to Return to a Meadow" and "My Mother Would Be a Falconress." His arrangements of passages by collage, and poems in series, present one of postmodernism's most successful solutions to the difficulty—inherited from the poetics of Pound's *Pisan Cantos,* William Carlos WILLIAMS's *Paterson* and Doolittle's "The War Trilogy"—of sustaining the long poem while valuing the concrete image.

BIBLIOGRAPHY: Bertholf, R. J., and I. W. Reid, eds., *R. D.: Scales of the Marvelous* (1979); Faas, E., *Young R. D.: Portrait of the Poet as a Homosexual in Society* (1983); Johnson, M., *R. D.* (1988); Paul, S., *The Lost America of Love: Rereading Robert Creeley, Edward Dorn, and R. D.* (1981)

RICHARD L. BLEVINS

DUNLAP, William

b. 19 February 1766, Perth Amboy; d. 28 September 1839, New York City

The "Father of American Drama," D. rather uncustomarily combined theater management with play writing. Adapting instead of translating literally, he enterprisingly introduced plays by August von Kotzebue, Friedrich Schiller, Heinrich Zschokke, and other Europeans to Americans. His original dramas on American themes offered innovations in established modes or else fresh material, and he pioneered in American Gothicism. His *History of the American Theatre* (1832), biographies of George Frederick Cooke (1813), Charles Brockden BROWN (1815), and a *History of the Rise and Progress of the Arts of Design in the United States* (1834) maintain value. His three-volume, incomplete edition of his own plays (1806–16) is among the few such collections by an early American dramatist.

Inspired by knowledge about theater gained during his years in London to study painting with Benjamin West, D. returned to America, where, impressed by acclaim for Royall TYLER's comedy *The Contrast,* he determined to become a playwright. His first work to be staged, also a comedy, *The Father* (1789; rev. as *The Father of an Only Child,* 1806), featured ordinary Americans speaking colloquial language. Here, and in like plays, his methods anticipated later vernacular accomplishments in drama. D.'s final play, *A Trip to Niagra* (perf. 1828, pub. 1830), included the first serious role of a black character in American drama. Job Jerryson, a waiter, speaks in accents unlike those of comic blacks from bygone American popular culture. Another type-figure, a stage Yankee, Jonathan Doolittle, did appear. Atypically shady, he is also the first stage Yankee to tell tall tales. D.'s work with American materials is, for many, at its best in *André* (1798), his initial experiment in American tragedy. Major André's story was familiar, so action opened after he had been condemned, and interest centered in efforts to save his life. The inclusion of George Washington also doubtless appealed to Americans. Narrative instead of dramatic technique prevailed; therefore, *André* never achieved great theatrical successes.

Another major accomplishment, D.'s Gothic drama, has too often been neglected. *Fatal Deception, or the Progress of Guilt* (perf. 1794, pub. as *Leicester,* 1806), *Fontainville Abbey* (perf. 1795), and *The Mysterious Monk* (perf. 1796, pub. as *Ribbemont; or, The Feudal Baron,* 1803), may be inspired by British models, but the first two manifest a virtuosity uncommon in such plays. All contain typical eerie architectural settings, mysteries of identity, overwhelming remorse, considerable violence, and rampant sexuality. D.'s poetics, however, enhance artistic unity. The motifs of light-dark, of storms-calm, and of imprisonment-flight symbolize emotional and physical conditions in the dramatis personae. Few other playwrights of D.'s time attained such art, or cared about it, in their eagerness to serve out thrilling entertainments alone. Actual supernaturalism is absent; thus we see here the beginnings of an American rational Gothicism in contrast to a European predilection for the inexplicable. Significantly, these plays precede Charles Brockden Brown's novels by some years, so D. should be credited with initiating American Gothicism. Although he did not abandon his muse of terror, he wrote no more wholly Gothic dramas. His adaptation of Zschokke's *Abaellino, the Great Bandit* (1801), for example, typifies the "robber play," another Gothic offshoot. Later, in several stories for the *New-York Mirror,* D. ridiculed gullible reception of absurdities rife in unrefined Gothic works. Such literary hoaxing places him with James Kirke PAULDING, Washington IRVING, Edgar Allan POE, and others who readily discerned the exaggerations to which Gothicism was prone.

More plays of varied excellences came from D.'s pen, at times betraying a sacrifice of art to financial gain. His endeavors, however, promoted the cause of drama in America, despite his own shortcomings. The *History of the American Theater,* along with James Nelson BARKER's "The Drama," in the Philadelphia *Democratic Press* (December 1816-February 1817), supplies one of a few substantial early documents about American drama. Moreover, whatever crudities might reside within his own plays, he could draw, creatively and easily, on a heritage from Renaissance and classical drama or on colloquial expression from his own era.

BIBLIOGRAPHY: Canary, R. H., *W. D.* (1970); Coad, O. S., *W. D.* (1917); Fisher, B. F., IV, "W. D.," in Magill, F. N., ed., *Critical Survey of Drama: English Language Series* (1985), vol. 1: 526–34; Moody, R., *America Drama of the American People to 1828* (1977)

BENJAMIN FRANKLIN FISHER IV

DUNNE, Finley Peter

b. 10 July 1867, Chicago, Illinois; d. 24 April 1936, New York City

D., an Irish American who grew up in Chicago, began his long career as a newspaperman in 1884. By the time he was twenty-one he was city editor of the *Chicago Times.* His real fame began, though, when he began to write humorous sketches in Irish dialect. He first created a spokesman called Colonel McNeery, modeled on a living Chicagoan who eventually complained. Then he created the wholly imaginary Martin J. Dooley, who debuted in the *Chicago Post* in 1893.

"Mr. Dooley," D.'s spokesman, eventually became his public *alter ego* so that people who have never heard of D. still quote Mr. Dooley. Martin Dooley was presented as an unmarried, middle-aged bartender who presided over his saloon on "Archey Road" in the Irish section of Chicago, a working-class section of rolling mills and factories, saloons and Roman Catholic churches. The standard Mr. Dooley essay has him speaking at length, usually to his friend Jawn Hinnessy, on some subject of current interest; originally D. used the Dooley essays to comment on Chicago politics, but eventually he expanded his scope, and many of his best efforts are about national politics, war, and U.S. imperialism. His imagined account of Admiral Dewey's activities in Cuba was read—during a news blackout—as the closest thing to reportage.

The essays are distinguished by a remarkably clear-sighted outlook on human affairs. The use of Mr. Dooley as narrator is in the tradition of ARTEMUS WARD or Ring LARDNER—an uneducated savant comments sagaciously in demotic, vernacular language. The comments are often biting: "Mr. Dooley" paraphrased Theodore ROOSEVELT's account of his own exploits in Cuba as "Th' Biography iv a Hero be Wan who Knows" and "Th' Darin' Exploits iv a Brave Man be an Actual Eye Witness." The usual targets of Mr. Dooley's deflating humor are windbags, imperialists, pretentious politicians, and malefactors of great wealth.

Mr. Dooley's performances usually have a form imposed by their newspaper origins, and a shape which leads from some preliminary discussion with Mr. Hinnessy to an aphoristic conclusions. Some of his sayings are still current: "Thrust ivrybody, but cut the cards," he said, and "no matter whether th' constitution follows th' flag or not, th' supreme coort follows th' iliction returns." To Mr. Hinnessy's declaration that we are a great people, Mr. Dooley responds: "We ar-re that. An' the best iv it is, we know we ar-re."

D., like many writers strongly identified with one mode or one character, grew tired of writing as Mr. Dooley. After achieving national acclaim, he moved to New York in 1900 and became first a magazine editor and then a newspaper proprietor. He wrote for the *New York Morning Telegraph, Collier's, Mc-Clure's,* and the *American Magazine.* He produced Mr. Dooley essays until 1916. His career continued after that date, but his national influence, and his literary importance, were as the creator of Mr. Dooley.

BIBLIOGRAPHY: Bander, E., *Mr. Dooley and Mr. D.: The Literary Life of a Chicago Catholic* (1981); Dunne, P., ed. *Mr. Dooley Remembers* (1963); Eckley, G., *F. P. D.* (1981); Ellis, E., *Mr. Dooley's America: A Life of F. P. D.* (1941); Fanning, C., *F. P. D. and Mr. Dooley* (1978); Hutchinson, R., ed. *Mr. Dooley on Ivrything and Iverybody* (1963); Nordloh, D., *F. P. D.* (1981); Schaff, B., *Mr. Dooley's Chicago* (1977)

MERRITT MOSELEY

DUNNE, John Gregory

b. 1 May 1932, Hartford, Connecticut

After reviewing his life in his autobiographical *Harp* (1989), D. concludes that he became an author because writing is a license to be curious: "I, for example, am interested in how things work, in how a creative movie deal is structured, how a conglomerate is formed. . . . How a geologist pinpoints a possible oil strike, how an immunologist isolates a virus. . . . How Fernando Valenzuela throws a screwball." This "childish curiosity," he continues, "inexorably draws the writer to his own past." D.'s interweaving of these interests—his gleeful explorations of the experiences, the accomplishments and especially the vices of others, combined with mercilessly confessional self-absorption—shapes all of his work as a journalist, a novelist, and a screenwriter.

D. graduated from Princeton in 1954. He later regretted choosing the most socially elitist and class-conscious of the Ivy League schools, recalling his undergraduate preoccupation with aping the manners of his wealthier classmates. He thanks the Army for drafting him and separating him from what was becoming a career as the "quintessential Princeton prig." And yet, when he describes a frightening health crisis, a syncopal episode that occurred when he was in his fifties, he recalls that he was at the time wearing exercise togs marked with the Princeton colors. His feelings about his Irish-Catholic background are similarly

mixed. As a journalist and novelist, he has caustically scrutinized American Irish-Catholicism, frequently using his own family as a case study. This subject grounds his first best-selling novel, *True Confessions* (1977), which he and his wife, novelist and journalist Joan DIDION, rewrote as an award-winning 1981 film. *True Confessions* shows D.'s interest in the underside of things, as he explores the flawed characters behind the public facades of two morally compromised Irish-Catholics: a police detective and his brother, a priest. Similarly unblinking but less parochial examinations of major and minor villainies lend coherence to two anthologies of D.'s journalistic reports, interviews, and character sketches, *Quintana & Friends* (1978) and *Crooning: A Collection* (1990).

D.'s continuing and specific attraction to the workings of the Irish-Catholic personality directed his choice of subject in his novel *Dutch Shea, Jr.* (1982), the story of a philosophically broken lawyer who defends the irredeemably guilty, and joins their club when he becomes an embezzler. D. creates another Irish-Catholic family in *Red, White and Blue* (1987), a family which includes another flawed priest, his reporter/screenwriter brother, and their rebelliously promiscuous sister: all the characters are guilty of vocational or personal prostitution to an exploitative institution. But D.'s indictment of Irish American frailties has been "catholic" in the most capacious sense of the word. While D. can be exasperatingly introspective, he never stops seeking the external analog, the larger cultural context for the individual subject. In *Delano: The Story of the California Grape Strike* (1969), D.'s obsessive documentation of England's exploitation of the Irish—his own marginalized forebears—is turned to chronicling a similar conflict between California's Anglo management and Chicano labor force. In his novel *Vegas: Memoir of a Dark Season* (1974), D.'s own Irish American sensibility again significantly colors his view of Nevada's lounge lizards, deviants, and criminals, but what he terms his "mining" of his own individual sensibility ultimately shows us a dankly shadowed Las Vegas as the fermenting Id of the larger, collective American psyche.

Critics have cited D.'s personal involvement in his nonfiction reportage to enroll him in 1960s school of participatory reportage called the New Journalism. In *The Studio* (1969), D. reports on the filmmaking business as an outsider, but he proves to be only the most complicitous sort of observer. By 1971, when he and his wife collaborated on the screenplay for *Panic in Needle Park,* a grimly chiaroscuro portrait of New York junkies, D. was himself a major player in the Hollywood scene. D. and Didion worked on the scripts for *Play It As It Lays* (1972), *A Star Is Born* (1976), *Hills like White Elephants* (1990), *Broken Trust*

(1995), and *Up Close and Personal* (1996). D. details this resume in his memoir, *Making It off the Big Screen* (1997), where he again savages the industry he has observed "up close and personally" for the past quarter of a century.

D.'s favorite subject is not so much himself as a more generalized *homo fabricans:* man the maker. He examines crafted things to see how they work, and then examines the craftsmen. He is especially interested in the makers of personae, whether these be intended for the page, the screen, or for the craftsman's personal use. Some readers disdain D.'s unconstrained obscenities and his attraction to the lurid and/or venal; some find his New Journalistic subjectivity self-indulgent. Others enjoy D.'s vitriolic humor, his eye for detail, and his graceful mastery of the "demotic discourse" he finds most appropriate to his personal worldview.

BIBLIOGRAPHY: Lahr, J., "Entrepreneurs of Anxiety," *Horizon* 24 (January 1981): 36–39;; Plimpton, G., "The Art of Screenwriting, Part II: J. G. D.," *Paris Review* 38 (April 1996): 282–309; Winchell, M. R., *J. G. D.*, (1986)

GWEN CRANE

DWIGHT, Timothy
b. 14 May 1752, Northampton, Massachusetts; d. 11 January 1817, New Haven, Connecticut

Best known in literary studies as the author of "Greenfield Hill" and as a member of the Yale-educated poetic circle, the Connecticut Wits, D. wrote numerous other works of prose and poetry. These generally uphold his Christian millennial vision, following the traditions of his grandfather, Jonathan EDWARDS, great-grandfather Solomon STODDARD, and great-great-grandfather Thomas HOOKER. Among students of the history and prose of early America, D.'s expansive *Travels in New England and New York* (4 vols., 1821–22) is second only to Thomas JEFFERSON's *Notes on the State of Virginia* for the insights it provides to the life and ideology of a leader in the early Republic.

D.'s works emerge as important when we consider his influence and power as a Congregationalist minister, putting forth Calvinist and Federalist conservatism in a time when Christian armenianism, deism, and Jeffersonian politics were more popular. During his twelve-year clerical appointment in Greenfield, Connecticut, and during his lengthy term as president of Yale (1795–1817), D. influenced not only his parishioners but also many of the new nation's religious and political leaders; his written works have influenced countless others in the years since his death.

"Greenfield Hill," written last and considered by many to be "best" among D.'s poetic works, has been overshadowed by the belles lettres of his contemporaries Phillis WHEATLEY, Joel BARLOW, and Philip FRENEAU, whose concerns with race, use of humor, and romantic sensibility, respectively, have appealed more to late-20th-c. readers. Formally and thematically, "Greenfield Hill" lacks innovation. D. follows the epic and oratorical conventions of his Puritan forebear, John Milton, but he chooses the heroic couplets of the 18th-c. Augustan poets Alexander Pope and Oliver Goldsmith rather than Milton's blank verse. At the time of his writing, both modes were well worn; in addition, D.'s "Dissertation on the History, Eloquence, and Poetry of the Bible" (1782), asserting the Bible as the model of the best poetry (1782), and his poem "The Critics" (1791), castigating Europeans who fail to understand the concerns and development of American verse, have led him to be labelled a conservative reactionary railing against the romantic emphasis on individualism and the sublime and dialectical natures of true art.

Yet because D. informs readers from the start that "Greenfield Hill" is autobiographical—the speaker is minister of Greenfield—we should be all the more understanding of the poet's impressive vision, oratory, and prophecy. The force of these, the closing section demonstrates, convinces the citizens of Greenfield, converts them to Christ, and unifies the community. The seven-part epic opens with the speaker's vision of the land, followed by his vision of the inhabitants of the "flourishing village," which is destroyed by the British. The colonists, in turn, deploy destruction against the Pequods. With a move from these observations to "advice" in the final sections, the clergyman warns the people to turn "attention to the truths and duties of religion." A farmer's secular advice to good conduct follows, with the explanation that such behavior contributes to a better life on this earth. Thus, following the pattern of colonial jeremiads and Cotton MATHER's *Bonifacius,* D.'s work reinforces a theme to which New England prose writers of the 19th c. would return—the sketch of a New England town as a blueprint for the nation.

In *Travels in New England,* D. also focuses on his visions of the land and the people—the seeds of a millennial utopia—which distinguish America from other countries. Following the traditions of exploration and travel literature, and comprised of letters written "to fictive British gentlemen," the four volumes mimic Hector St. Jean de CREVECOEUR's *Letters from an American Farmer,* as the provincial writer instructs foreigners with the purported "truth" rather than exaggerations about the young nation.

Recent analyses of D.'s works have explored the ambivalent nature of these overtly didactic and oratorical pieces, acknowledging the leader's internal and less explicit concerns with societal and religious changes and his openness to discovering new truths. As Jane Kamensky as argued, when reflecting on "unimproved," unsettled, and chaotic landscapes, Dwight appears to be "delighting in possibilities." Finally, however, D.'s works are, as Peter Kafer has written, controlled by his public, didactic, and conservative persona; his personal sensibilities only occasionally and all too rarely "punctuate and disrupt" them.

BIBLIOGRAPHY: Dowling, W. C., *Poetry and Ideology in Revolutionary Connecticut* (1990); Elliott, E., *Revolutionary Writers* (1982); Kafer, P., "The Making of T. D.," *WMQ* 47 (April 1990): 189–209; Kamensky, J., "'In These Contrasted Climes, How Chang'd the Scene,'" *NEQ* 63 (March 1990): 80–108

ETTA M. MADDEN

DYLAN, Bob
b. 24 May 1941, Duluth, Minnesota

D., born Robert Allen Zimmerman, is one of America's most inventive and influential lyricists. Equal parts Elvis Presley and Arthur Rimbaud, Hank Williams and William Blake, D. bridges the intellectual excesses of the Beat poets and popular culture. He has brought a more self-conscious literary manner to traditional folk and urban-blues-based song writing. In this way, D.'s transformative approach differs from the work of Stephen Foster, Cole Porter, Ira Gershwin, and Woody Guthrie, his only peers among American songwriters.

Reared in a middle-class Jewish home, from childhood in Hibbing, D. early on developed a keen sense of racial and economic inequalities in American society. His early literary models included John STEINBECK and Dylan Thomas, the latter being the most plausible source for the spelling of his professional name. Dropping out of the University of Minnesota, D. both impressed and alienated those on the burgeoning Minneapolis–St. Paul folk scene before heading for New York City, where he soon created new artistic possibilities for young singer–songwriters. D.'s rapid rise as writer–composer and enigmatic personality helped capture the attention of millions in the early 1960s: "Blowin' in the Wind" (1962), "A Hard Rain's a-Gonna Fall" (1963), "The Times They Are a-Changin'" (1963), and "Mr. Tambourine Man" (1964 [1965]) galvanized a generation. D.'s evolution to rock 'n' roll in the mid-1960s, in degree under the tutelage of Allen GINSBERG, is highlighted by "Subterranean Homesick Blues" (1965), his masterpiece "Like a Rolling Stone" (1965), and "Visions of Johanna" (1965 [1966]).

A motorcycle accident in 1966 changed the course of D.'s career. Out of his convalescent retreat came a renewed concentration on the traditional roots of American music: *The Basement Tapes* (released in 1975) and *John Wesley Harding* (1968). D.'s only novel, *Tarantula,* was published in 1971 to mostly negative notices. Several collections of lyrics and drawings have also been published, along with many songbooks. A return to a more personal folk and blues idiom *(Blood on the Tracks,* 1975), and brief associations with Jacques Levy and Sam SHEPARD in the mid-1970s (Shepard, again, in the mid-1980s) was followed by a spiritual conversion to Christianity ("Gotta Serve Somebody," 1979; "Every Grain of Sand," 1981; and "Foot of Pride," 1983 [1991] are notable), a faith D. continues to embrace and reflect in his music, as often as not, to this day (e.g., the moody *Oh Mercy* [1989]). In 1997, D. suffered the cardiac effects of histoplasmosis and was reported near death, which he once again cheated: himself now roughly between the age that it had taken his "last idol," Woody Guthrie, in October 1967 and his father, Abraham, in June 1968. Later in 1997, D. performed for the Pope and released *Time out of Mind,* a critical success that earned D. three Grammy Awards in 1998.

Although many question D.'s lasting contribution to literature, his unique song-writing and performing style mark a revival of the ancient oral tradition of the bard as well as new levels of individual expression and social thought in American lyricism.

BIBLIOGRAPHY: McGregor, C., ed., *B. D.: A Retrospective* (1972); Scaduto, A., *B. D.: An Intimate Biography* (1971); Shepard, S., *Rolling Thunder Logbook* (1977); Shelton, R., *No Direction Home: The Life and Music of B. D.* (1986)

EVANDER LOMKE

EASTLAKE, William [Derry]

b. 14 July 1917, Brooklyn, New York; d. 1 June 1997, Cuba, New Mexico

In outline, there appear to have been two stages to E.'s career. The first produced four novels whose complexities have led us to speak of them either as pieces of Western regionalism—they are all set in New Mexico and are peopled with "cowboys and Indians"—or to regard them as avant-garde forays into modernist black humor. The three novels of his second stage—similar in style to those of his first—are set against the backdrop of war.

Ironically, E. did not turn to his war novels directly after having served in the infantry, where, incidentally, he suffered a wound in the Battle of the Bulge. E. came back to the subject of war by a circuitous route. After a season of literary expatriotism or bohemianism in postwar France, E. seems to have jumped dramatically to New Mexico. He quite deliberately chose the state not only for his home, but also for his subject matter—because, as he suggested in interviews, he believed that our storytellers had neglected the Southwest and that by moving boldly he could pretty much have the virgin territory all to himself.

But then, having delivered himself of his Western novels, he turned back to his war experiences for his fuel. Ensconced on his New Mexican ranch, whose rehabilitation he has spoken of as the best of his accomplishments, he perhaps sought to see further through his writing and took on the war theme that has transcended even the largest regions: E. began to explore what it is in mankind that drives it to attempt the mass killings of those who in their difference are taken as enemies.

As a young man, E. knocked around a good deal, both in the U.S. and in Mexico, before landing in Los Angeles, where he found a job clerking at Stanley Rose's Book Store that would profoundly influence his future course. A well-known hangout for artists of all sorts, the store served to help him meet, among others, Clifford ODETS, Nathanael WEST, and Theodore DREISER, who, in their turn, helped to initiate E. into an apprenticeship under editors whose guidance was to shape E.'s decidedly avant-garde tone or style.

Comic surrealism marks every milepost of E.'s oeuvre, notably in *Go in Beauty* (1956), *The Bronc People* (1958), and *Portrait of an Artist with Twenty-Six Horses* (1963). *Dancers in the Scalp House* (1975) is actually E.'s sixth novel; he wrote this last New Mexican novel while in the middle of his run of war novels. In its absurdist humor, *Dancers in the Scalp House* reads as though he had never turned his attention away from what he had been doing in his regional stories. Dam building is the central theme of the novel, which is to result in flooding what has always been an arid reservation. The Indians can hardly imagine such a fate for themselves, and the story turns on their comic attempt to escape it.

The war stories have generally ranked behind the New Mexican stories; however, E.'s first war novel, *Castle Keep* (1965), won enough recognition that the Filmway Company shot and released a version of it starring Burt Lancaster. It tells the story of American soldiers in World War II trying to hold a castle wherein a duke keeps a priceless art collection. Each of the characters narrates a chapter, as is also the technique in William FAULKNER's *As I Lay Dying;* however, E. effects the satire of his story by finally bringing the soldiers together to appreciate moments of music and art and thus to observe moments of peace.

The Bamboo Bed (1969) is the title of both the novel set in Vietnam and of a rescue helicopter. The problem is that this "bed" rescues nobody; it is sent only to recover the remains of Alpha Company. Otherwise, the copter is a bed in the sense that its pilot takes nurses up, and there, hanging in the air, trysts with them, far above the turmoil of the war. Evidently, this device of carrying his characters up above a war appealed to E., for in *The Long Naked Descent into Boston* (1977), he has journalists observe the American Revolution from one of the first hot air balloons. The "naked" part of it is that they have to burn their clothes to stay up but are nonetheless greeted back on the ground as heroes.

E. was also a prolific short story writer and magazine journalist whose work appeared in some forty anthologies and in thirteen foreign language editions. Among the highlights of his career was that he had traveled as a correspondent for *The Nation* during the Vietnam War. His last publication was a collection of stories entitled *Jack Armstrong in Tangier* (1984).

BIBLIOGRAPHY: Lewis, L. K., "W. E.," *BB* 41 (March 1984): 6–11; special E. issue, *RCF* 3 (Spring 1981)
                                        J. RUSSELL BURROWS

EASTMAN, Charles Alexander
b. February 1858, Redwood Falls, Minnesota; d. 8 January 1939, Detroit, Michigan

One of the late-19th-c.'s principal exhibits in the case for cultural evolutionism and social Darwinism, E. "rose" from the traditional life of a Plains Indian to become a medical school graduate. Though he did not spend much time as a practicing physician, E. demonstrated the capacity of the "savage" for the "civilized" life of the Euro-American through a variety of endeavors, including the production of nine books.

The most important books written by E. were two autobiographies. The first of these, *Indian Boyhood,* came out in 1902. It begins with the Minnesota Sioux Uprising in 1862, when E.'s father was presumably killed and the future physician, then known as Hakadah, "The Pitiful Last," accompanied a band led by his uncle into the Turtle Mountains of Manitoba. A series of vignettes of traditional Plains Indian life aimed at young readers, *Indian Boyhood* deals with the life of Ohiyesa, "The Winner" (a name that the young E. acquired from his community's victory in a lacrosse game), through 1873, when his father, now known as Jacob Eastman, reappeared and took the young man to Flandreau, South Dakota. The book romanticizes the life of pre-reservation Native Americans, but also acknowledges the cultural gradations that figured into contemporary social theory. Writing from the perspective of someone socialized into the values of Euro-American society, E. saw his people, the Santee Sioux, as representing the highest level of pagan, uncivilized humanity. His own experience showed how smooth the transition to civilized Christianity could be made.

In 1916, E. published *From the Deep Woods to Civilization,* which takes up his life from the time of his reunion with his father. The volume recounts his formal education beginning at the Santee Normal School in Nebraska and continuing through the reception of a baccalaureate degree from Dartmouth College and his graduation from Boston University Medical School. Upon receiving his medical diploma, E. assumed the post of agency physician on the Pine Ridge Reservation in South Dakota. In that capacity, he was on the scene shortly after the Wounded Knee Massacre in 1890, an experience that concludes this second volume of autobiography. Though he expresses no explicit regrets, E. was much less enthusiastic about Euro-American culture by the time he came to write this book than he had been in *Indian Boyhood.* Partially disillusioned, he perceives that the life of his "savage" forebears had many humane features lacking in Euro-American life. While accepting the tenets of Christianity, he recognizes that many Euro-Americans gave only lip service to those tenets.

In addition to these works dealing with his own experience, E. produced several books that aimed to familiarize Native American life and lore to his Euro-American readers. With his wife, Elaine Goodale (to whom some commentators assign collaborator's credit on most of his works), he published *Wigwam Evenings* (1909), a collection of Sioux folktales that he had learned during his childhood from the storyteller Smokey Day. This book intended to make available for Euro-American readers, especially young ones, the same oral literary heritage that E. had encountered in his own youth.

E.'s interpretation of Sioux spirituality, which he apparently assumed to be pan-Native American, appeared as *The Soul of the Indian* in 1911. He also wrote a series of short biographies of Plains Indian leaders that were collected as *Indian Heroes and Great Chieftains* in 1918. E.'s commitment to educating America's youth about Native American ways resulted in *Indian Scout Talks,* published in 1914, and in his advocacy of the scouting movement and the YMCA. He and his family also ran a summer camp in New Hampshire.

The two autobiographies that he produced remain E.'s most important contribution to American literature. Read together, they reflect his dynamic attitude toward his cultural identity, which changed from acceptance of the superiority of Euro-American civilization to serious reservations about it. E.'s disillusionment with Euro-American ways increased throughout the rest of his life, the last fourteen years of which he lived in an isolated cabin in the Ontario wilderness.

BIBLIOGRAPHY: Brumble, H. D., *American Indian Autobiography* (1988); Copeland, M. W., *C. A. E.*

(Ohiyesa) (1978); Wilson, R., *Ohiyesa: C. E., Santee Sioux* (1983); Wong, H. D., *Sending My Heart Back across the Years: Tradition and Innovation in Native American Autobiography* (1992)

WILLIAM M. CLEMENTS

EASTMAN, Max [Forrester]

b. 4 January 1883, Canandaigua, New York; d. 25 March 1969, Bridgetown, Barbados

Though active as a conservative writer, critic, and corresponding editor for *Reader's Digest* during the last thirty years of his life, E.'s reputation rests largely on his radical political activities during the early decades of the 20th c. A professor of philosophy at Columbia University (1907–11), editor of the socialist periodical the *Masses* (1912–17) and later the *Liberator* (1918–22), an organizer of the early feminist and pacifist movements, publisher of Lenin's deathbed testament and translator of the works of the exiled Leon Trotsky, E. was at the center of key movements in early-20th-c. radical thought.

E.'s body of writings offers a guide, alternately humorous and caustic, to the dominant events and cultural opinions of his time. The *Masses* and the *Liberator* combined radical journalism, social commentary, satire, poetry, and experimentation with modernist forms, including promotion of the "ash can" school of art—realistic, socially conscious depictions of working-class life. In the company of contributors that included Art Young, John Sloan, John Reed, and Randolph BOURNE, the young E. was an unapologetic fighter of left-wing causes: ardent supporter of women's rights, advocate of free love and open marriage, and compelling defender of civil liberties.

An early enthusiast of the Russian Revolution, E. visited the Soviet Union for two years in the early 1920s to observe the effects of the revolution firsthand and undertake a biography of Trotsky. He returned convinced that the noble intentions of the October Revolution had been subverted by corrupt leaders. E. expressed his initial disillusionment in *Since Lenin Died* (1925), detailing how Trotsky's authority had been undermined by Stalin. As a result, E. found himself increasingly alienated from his old colleagues on the militant left, most of whom continued to endorse Stalin. The devolution of his radical beliefs continued throughout the 1930s, expressed in such works as *Artists in Uniform* (1934), *The End of Socialism in Russia* (1937), and *Stalin's Russia and the Crisis in Socialism* (1940), which concludes with a call for a "new scientific party" and the "equivalent to an abandonment of socialism" as a viable social ideal.

Through his one, largely forgotten novel, *Venture* (1927), E. attempted to transform his own political experiences into fiction. For the contemporary reader, however, E. endures as the prototype for the character of Brimmer in *The Last Tycoon*, F. Scott FITZGERALD's last, unfinished novel. Like E., the attractive journalist Brimmer is a disillusioned radical, a socialist whose ideals have been challenged following a visit to Stalin's Russia and first-hand encounters with the oppression of free expression in art, science, and literature. Judged by Leslie A. FIEDLER to be the least convincing communist in American literature, Brimmer—like E.—embodies Fitzgerald's familiar theme of stricken idealism.

The best introduction to E. remains his two works of autobiography, *Enjoyment of Living* (1948) and *Love and Revolution: My Journey Through an Epic* (1965). A lucid study of metaphor, *The Enjoyment of Poetry* (1913) is the best known of his critical works. Overall, however, E.'s generally superficial literary judgments will be of little more than historical interest to the contemporary reader. His reactionary critique of literary MODERNISM in *Love and Revolution* and his condescending dismissal of such figures as T. S. ELIOT, Ernest HEMINGWAY, William FAULKNER, and James Joyce are neither intellectually persuasive nor rhetorically very interesting. In "The Swan-Song of Humane Letters," for instance, he attempts to expose Eliot's "ignorance" through a succession of brief quotations taken out of context from a number of Eliot's own critical essays. Indeed, for the most part E. simply reworks sentiments that he had first articulated decades earlier in the essays collected in *The Literary Mind* (1931). In the end, it appears that E.'s legacy resides not in his ample collection of writings (almost all of which are out of print) but in his iconic status as the disillusioned American radical.

BIBLIOGRAPHY: Aaron, D., *Writers on the Left: Episodes in American Literary Communism* (1961); Diggins, J. P., *Up from Communism* (1994); Eastman, C., *On Women and Revolution* (1978); O'Neill, W. L., *The Last Romantic: The Life of M. E.* (1978)

RICHARD NORDQUIST

EATON, Edith Maude

b. 15 March 1865, Macclesfield, England; d. 7 April 1914, Montreal, Canada

Throughout her life, E. crossed many physical and psychological borders. Writing under a pseudonym that asserted her half-Chinese ancestry, Sui Sin Far, E. produced sympathetic portrayals of Chinese immigrant communities. As a child, she immigrated with her British father, Chinese mother, and siblings from her birthplace in England to New York, and afterwards, to Montreal, Canada. As an adult, E. never married or settled down. Between temporary visits to Montreal, she lived and worked in various American cities, including San Francisco, Seattle, and Boston; she also lived in Jamaica where she worked briefly as a journalist. In 1914, *Mrs. Spring Fragrance,* the only collection of her short stories, was published.

Critics praise E. for her realistic portrayals of Chinese immigrant experience and her attempts to expose American racial bias. Rather than focusing on male laborers, her stories and essays depict immigrant families of all classes. By describing different relationships between spouses, siblings, and parents and children, E. contradicts stereotypes and draws similarities between all Americans regardless of color. Despite the worthiness of her Chinese characters, they are subject to the indignities of unfair treatment. "In the Land of the Free" documents the trials of Hom Hing and his wife, Lae Choo, when their newborn son is detained by immigration officials. After paying exorbitant fees, the couple get him back; however, in the ten months the son has been gone, he has forgotten who his parents are. Through this description of a family's loss, E. exposes the fundamental absurdity of America's monocultural bias and the unfairness of laws that restricted Chinese immigration.

In addition to race, E.'s stories belie a concern with issues of gender. Indeed, she continually draws parallels between the degradation of Chinese immigrants in America and the subjugation of woman. The title character in "Mrs. Spring Fragrance," for example, exposes the contradiction between her husband's desire for racial equality and his attempts to subjugate women. Wou Sankwei in "The Wisdom of the New" similarly tries to control his wife, Pau Lin. Transforming her increasing alienation into a fear of American culture, she kills her son who is becoming more "Americanized." E., however, partially absolves her of blame by indicting patriarchy and American culture. The husband and his American female friends have given Pau Lin few choices by keeping her in an inferior position.

While focusing on E.'s concern with gender and attempts to overturn negative Chinese stereotypes, critics tend to overlook her obvious concern with issues of mixed-race identity. The autobiographical essay "Leaves from the Mental Portfolio of An Eurasian" (1909), which traces her life from age four to forty, challenges racial hierarchies while discussing her efforts to unite the diverse aspects of her dual racial ancestry. Presenting herself as a "connecting link," E. draws similarities rather than oppositions between races.

During her lifetime, E. never gained popular recognition. In an era of extreme anti-Chinese sentiment, she was never able to earn much writing about Chinese Americans. She is finally receiving the recognition she deserves.

BIBLIOGRAPHY: Dong, L., and M. K. Hom, "Defiance or Perpetuation," *Chinese America: History and Perspectives* (1987): 139–168; Ling, A., *Between Worlds* (1990); Solberg, S. E., "Sui Sin Far/E. E.," *MELUS* 8, 1 (1981): 27–39; White-Parks, A., *Sui Sin Far/E. M. E.: A Literary Biography* (1995)

LINDA TRINH MOSER

EATON, Winnifred [Babcock Reeve]

b. 21 August 1875, Montreal, Canada; d. 8 April 1954, Butte, Montana

Although she was of Chinese and European ancestry, E. assumed a Japanese-sounding pen name under which she published works using Japanese characters and settings. As Onoto Watanna, E. gained a large and devoted audience. Her first novel, *Miss Nume of Japan* (1899), was favorably reviewed by the *New York Times;* it was followed by fourteen others, including *The Wooing of Wisteria* (1902), *The Heart of Hyacinth* (1903), *Tama* (1910), *Cattle* (1923), and *His Royal Nibs* (1925). William Dean HOWELLS praised her second novel, *A Japanese Nightingale* (1901), which went through several editions and was adapted into a Broadway play (1903). Later in her career, E. ventured from Japanese motifs. *Diary of Delia* (1907) depicts the romance of an Irish American maid, while *Me* (1915) and *Marion* (1916) describe the lives of two biracial sisters who immigrate to America. Her literary reputation led to work as chief scenarist for Universal Studios in Hollywood from 1925 to 1932. Despite her success, the life and work of E. is scarcely mentioned today.

Most of E.'s novels take place entirely in Japan. Filled with lengthy descriptions of kimono-clad geishas, blooming cherry trees, and samurai legends, E.'s fiction relies on stereotypes that romanticize and exoticize rather than accurately depict or explain Japanese culture. The tendency to focus on negative aspects of E.'s "Japanese" masquerade and depictions obscures historical definitions of race and the reality of American hostility towards Asians. For E., "passing" as Japanese was a viable response to turn-of-the-century American racism. By disguising her own ethnicity, E. avoided animosity toward Chinese immigrants while at the same time capitalizing on general ignorance about Japan. E.'s readers did not realize that her pseudonym, Onoto Watanna, only sounded Japanese, nor did they recognize her novel's Western sources. Although they seem "Japanese," the star-crossed lovers from feuding families in *The Wooing of Wisteria* (1902) and *The Honorable Miss Moonlight* (1912) are versions of Shakespeare's *Romeo and Juliet;* the Japanese princess who changes places with a poor look-alike half-sister in *Daughters of Nijo* (1904) is reminiscent of Samuel Langhorne CLEMENS's *Prince and the Pauper.*

While never overtly concerned with racism, E.'s work typically challenges gender and class stereotypes. Her female protagonists are not in positions of social power; however, they are never passive when faced with adversity. In *Me: A Book of Remembrance* (1915), an autobiographical novel, Nora Ascough overcomes poverty and resists gender oppression to find success as a writer. The work also touches upon racial attitudes, especially when describing a brief stay in Jamaica. Despite E.'s refusal to reveal her Chinese ancestry, some of her fiction belies concern about racial attitudes in America. The last of E.'s "Japanese" novels, *Sunny-San* (1922), subtly protests systems of racial classification used to restrict Asian immigration. Published in the year following well-publicized hostility to the immigration of Japanese picture brides, *Sunny-San* ironically focuses on the immigration experience of a Japanese woman and addresses issues faced by Asians in the U.S.

Critics generally interpret E.'s manipulation of Japanese culture as an indifference to the reality of Asian life in America; however, her professional choices reflect important attitudes about race in early-20th-c. America. As the first successful novelist of Chinese ancestry to be published in America, her life and work deserve further attention.

BIBLIOGRAPHY: Ling, A., *Between Worlds* (1990); Moser, L. T., Afterward to *Me: A Book of Remembrance* (1997); White-Parks, A., *Sui Sin Far/E. M. E.: A Literary Biography* (1995)

LINDA TRINH MOSER

EBERHART, Richard

b. 5 April 1904, Austin, Minnesota

Like many poets of modernism's "middle generation" born between 1900 and 1920, E. is often overshadowed by T. S. ELIOT and Ezra POUND. Although a writer of verse plays and screenplays, E. is most noted for his lyric poetry and earned the Pulitzer Prize in 1966 for his *Selected Poems, 1930–1965* and the National Book Award (1977) for *Collected Poems, 1930–1976.*

A poet firmly grounded in the idealist tradition, E. is perhaps modernism's most loyal neoromantic poet. Like William Blake, he fashions language to his purpose; the reader will not be surprised to find his work

teeming with sleep, death, the supernatural, divine madness, and spirituality. Like Samuel Taylor Coleridge, he revels in mystery and illusion—poetic moments that strive toward reverie. Like William Wordsworth, he writes to re-create childhood, memory, the self and is often torn by his subject: he is a poet half trying to remain in the corporeal world, half trying to transcend it. In his later work, he shares Percy Bysshe Shelley's dream of an age when there is power *in* poetry, rather than poetry and power, and he comes to terms with John Keats's notion that truth exists only in the uncertainty of the world around us.

Critical assessments of E.'s work generally fall into two camps: first, those who praise his poetry for its risks, experimentation, and independence from the New Critical tenets that he confronted in his early career; the second group sees this departure as gauche, resulting in rough, awkward diction and a voice that is ineffectual. Regardless, E.'s best work has endured in anthologies and is proof, as is Gerard Manley Hopkins's verse, that a poet's incongruity with his contemporaries may well become the basis for his notoriety.

Several key formative experiences have inevitably influenced E.'s work. Like Carl SANDBURG, he worked blue-collar jobs in his youth (including a slaughterhouse in New York) before making his artistic debut in Harriet MONROE's literary journal *Poetry*. The result is a latent populist theme that is resurrected throughout his work, especially in poems like "Half-Bent Man," "The Clam Diggers and Diggers of Sea Worms," and "Death in the Mines." Like Randall JARRELL, E. is a poet deeply effected by World War II, during which he served as Naval aerial gunnery instructor. He responds to the destructiveness of battle and the loss of human life in such poems as "The Fury of Aerial Bombardment," "An Airman Considers His Power," "Brotherhood of Men," "At the End of War," and most notably, "Dam Neck, Virginia," a poem whose ironic symbolism acknowledges the dreamlike beauty of antiaircraft tracers in the night sky, while concurrently lamenting the loss that war brings to the collective human spirit.

Other well-known E. poems include "For a Lamb," "The Cancer Cells," and "The Horse Chestnut Tree," yet "The Groundhog" is his single most famous piece. This poem confronts the notoriously romantic notions of death (the inevitable fate that all living beings share) and immortality (the way in which those beings may continue to live on). The speaker reports finding a decaying groundhog in a summer field and his revisiting of it in the autumn to measure its decomposition. In returning he finds merely a skeleton, the poem's central image, and in a Wordsworthian "spot of time" recognizes the balance that necessarily exists between mortality and immortality.

E. is admittedly uncomfortable as a critic, but he is a euphonious spokesman of the poet's craft and a valuable historian of the memory of many of his contemporaries, whom he knew personally. His retrospective essays on W. B. Yeats, Wallace STEVENS, Theodore ROETHKE, Robert FROST, and W. H. AUDEN, as well as interviews and testaments of his own poetics are collected in *Of Poetry and Poets* (1979).

BIBLIOGRAPHY: Engle, B. F., *The Achievement of R. E.* (1968), Engle, B. F., *R.. E.* (1971); Mills, R. J., Jr., *R. E.* (1966); Roache, J., *R. E.: The Progress of an American Poet* (1971)

R. A. WEST

EDWARDS, Jonathan

b. 5 October 1703, East Windsor, Connecticut; d. 22 March 1758, Princeton, New Jersey

Among colonial American writers, E. is often considered the greatest intellect of his period, a man of genius who labored valiantly to arrest the decline of Puritanism during the 18th c. More than any other Puritan author, he has received serious attention from historians, theologians, psychologists and literary critics, albeit there is at the moment no consensus about E.'s sources, beliefs or influence.

Born in frontier East Windsor, Connecticut, E. was the son of Timothy and Esther [Stoddard] Edwards. In 1720, he graduated from Yale College, which also awarded him an M.A. in 1723 (while he served a small Presbyterian church in New York City) and hired him as a tutor from 1724 to 1726. He then became an associate of his controversial grandfather, Solomon STODDARD in Northampton, Massachusetts, where he married Sarah Pierrepont in 1727 and became minister of that parish when Stoddard died in 1729. In 1734–35, E. headed a religious revival in his parish, and particularly in the 1740s, he became a leading figure in the Great Awakening, a time of intense religious awareness that spread throughout the colonies. When he attempted to reinstate anti-Stoddardian conservative practices, particularly concerning admission to the Lord's Supper, he was to his dismay dismissed by his congregation in 1750. He then reluctantly accepted a post in Stockbridge, Massachusetts, a place of virtual exile for him among a small parish that included Native Americans. While there during the 1750s, E. wrote his major works, and in 1757, he reversed his earlier decision to decline the presidency of the College of New Jersey (later Princeton University). Within three months of his arrival in Princeton, he died of a small-pox inoculation, his career and his writings abruptly left unfinished.

E.'s youthful writings are neither as original nor as seminally influenced by John Locke as some critics have asserted, but they are interesting in their emphasis on orthodoxy and on the mind, a stress that becomes particularly pronounced in his later, more accomplished works of philosophical idealism. Included in these early documents are a series of notes called "The Mind," a composition entitled "Of Insects," and a short essay on being, all of which argue that creation exists only in the mind of the deity, whose voluntary will alone supports existence. The human mind is featured in the extant portion of a diary E. kept from 1722 to 1735, which focuses on the deceits of the heart, particularly how pride can disguise itself as reason.

Reason was a key concern in E.'s writings because at the time of his ministry, the Age of Reason, there was among many articulate cultural spokesmen a trust in the potentiality of human thought as the curative of human imperfection on earth. Many of the literary techniques E. used in his early sermons were designed to counter this presumptuous trust in reason in his parishioners, some of whom apparently derived comfort about their salvation from their reasoning about the self-sufficiency of their proper behavior. E.'s first published work, *God Glorified in the Work of Redemption* (1731), reminds his parish of the absolute sovereignty and (from a human perspective) arbitrariness of divine will, and in this work, he uses images of the moon and the planets as types for the inner realm of the mind in such a way as to vex his hearers' sense of natural phenomena as real (it is only a divine idea) and to confound their related sense of external reality as a secular basis for secure identity. *A Divine and Supernatural Light* (1734), a sermon on the difference between common grace (that detectably affects reason) and special or saving grace (that undetectably affects will), relies at times on a slowly expanding repetitive rhetorical formulation of words placed close together in a paragraph; this formulation becomes incantatory, even hypnotic in communicating its message (about an intuitive sense of saving grace) beyond the level of a merely rational comprehension of the words (the level of common grace, which is not sufficient for salvation).

"The Excellency of Christ," a sermon delivered sometime in the 1730s about humanity's inability to comprehend the deity, also assails any sense of religious security based on reason alone. Chief among E.'s literary devices in this sermon is a passage in which a series of images ascends from the earthly realm of kings and lords, through the sky or heavens, to the realm of angels, at which point his hearers would have anticipated the next step in the progression: some comment about the deity. But this rational expectation is frustrated as E. abruptly returns the listener to the beginning of the imagistic series, which again ascends and again fails to fulfill the expectation it engenders even more emphatically than the first time. This second progression, however, contains similes attached to the images, and these similes convey a reverse progression as they descend from worms, through dust, to "nothing." This technique not only frustrates rational expectations based on a ladder-like series of analogies, but also cancels the very terms of the progression through mind-baffling paradox (the juxtaposition of images of ascent and descent). E. apparently wanted to leave the hearer contemplating "nothing," an emptiness of mind confuting any sense of security based on reason and, as well, conveying an intuitive impression of the sermon's theme, that no one can comprehend the deity, least of all in the matter of one's salvation.

Without ceasing to attack confidence based on reason, E. also tried to encourage a new, tentative confidence, one based on certain orthodox Puritan images that seemed to him to be free from iconic transgression and immune to the vicissitudes of time. In *A Faithful Narrative of the Surprising Work of God* (1737), the image of the well-ordered family serves as a conservative central symbol for the successful religious community and provides a structural motif for the work, the theme of which is that conversion (the work of special grace) usually occurs in an appropriate environment, especially the renewed family unit. In *A History of the Work of Redemption* (wr. 1739, pub. 1774), he resorts to conventional Puritan images of streams and oceans as metaphors for humanity and the deity, respectively, in order to reinforce his theme that (just as all steams flow into an ocean) all temporal life flows into eternity in God's grand design. E. augments these orthodox images by expanding their usual reference to the individual soul and making them refer to all of history, which becomes for him an allegory of the spiritual progress of the saint and thereby an image of hope, like that of the family, for the sinner.

About 1739, E. wrote "Personal Narrative," a curious document that at first seems to be a formulary spiritual autobiography, but that on reflection seems to be artfully managed instruction for a presumed audience. Concerned with the subtle deceits of the heart, even the heart of a prominent minister like E., this work assails rational expectations in its readers, expectations fostered by an elusive corruption E. detected in any common association that gives comfort to the unwary (and therefore possibly damned) soul, which ideally should always remain uneasy before the mystery of divine will. E. creates this uneasiness through his account by presenting a narrator who remains baffled by the apparent phases of his spiritual growth; the narrator makes three separate attempts to ascertain the time when his experiences really evinced a sign of his salvation. Each of these three attempts is abruptly halted, as the narrator turns upon himself (and implicitly upon his audience, who has been sharing in a similar rational expectation of an emerging sense of spiritual security in the narrator), and even the very end of the narrative is left as a mere inconclusive fragment disappointing a reader's anticipation of a neat finish. The narrative suggests that there can be no rational security in the matter of assessing one's spiritual state, only process in time that one hopes is indeed progress. Faith is required, not presumptuous reason.

E.'s most famous sermon, *Sinners in the Hands of an Angry God* (1741), was delivered several times during the Great Awakening and is replete with imagery designed to undercut his audience's sense of spiritual security. These images, when consolidated subliminally in the hearer's mind, often tell stories, such as how the sinner is a rebel plotting insurrection but achieving only punishment and how the wicked lose their natural families and become the children of Satan. The web motif in the sermon is among the best of E.'s literary techniques; introduced obliquely, the audience first hears of the web as something by which a person dangles a loathsome insect over a fire (as if he were in control of fate, the thread of life), then encounters the image as if he and the insect shared something in common, and then finally finds himself described as an insect hanging from the thread of life held over the fires of hell by the hands of God (the true force of fate in human life). This expanding imagistic web is reinforced by an incantatory rhetorical parallelism similar to the technique in *A Divine and Supernatural Light*. This manner functions by slowly expanding what it includes within its rhetorical formula; at first it implies that the audience is at some distance from the depicted horrors of hell, but steadily it moves the viewer closer until he is directly over the flames of perdition. These literary techniques, influenced by execution sermons, certainly affected E.'s audience, which was more susceptible to being moved deeply by the force of rhetoric and imagery than we are today, for reports of his contemporaries document the emotional impact of this sermon.

Neither *Distinguishing Marks of a Work of the Spirit of God* (1741), refuting the idea that conversion must occur in certain steps, nor *Some Thoughts Concerning the Present Revival* (1743), defending enthusiasm as often a proper response to grace, nor *An Humble Inquiry into the Rules of the Word of God* (1749), arguing for a return to first-generational Congregational practices in admitting communicants to the Lord's Supper, evidence E.'s experimentation with literary techniques to reinforce his message. *A Treatise Concerning Religious Affections* (1746), perhaps E.'s most influential text in his time, focuses on such expressions of the will as fear, hope and love, and returns to a concern in *A Divine and Supernatural Light,* the difference between rational understanding and spiritual knowledge. Coupling his attack on reason once again with a devaluation of the reality of external phenomena, E. applies a few images (especially the stream/ocean metaphor he used earlier) to augment his argument, but basically he devotes his literary energy to clarity of conception and expression.

The best-seller among E.'s books, *An Account of the Life of the Late Reverend Mr. David Brainerd* (1749), is a most peculiar document. Comprised principally of the journals of Brainerd, a missionary to Native Americans, this work gives a peek into E.'s mind unlike anything else he published. Uncomfortable with Brainerd's liberalism in admitting Native Americans to the Lord's Supper, E. simply deleted whatever displeased him in the document concerning this matter—the whole point of Brainerd's mission—and emphasized only "the inward exercises" of Brainerd's mind. Yet this silent editing is prefaced with a statement by the editor that God meant for him to make the journals public. If the design of providence is behind the publication of these journals, by what authority did E. edit them so severely to conform to his own views of conversion and of admission to the Lord's Supper? Whatever its other implications, E.'s handling of this document perhaps provides a personal clue to his sense of himself beyond even his prophetic stance in his preceding works.

In *A Farewel-Sermon* (1751), E. sadly, without vindictiveness, resorts to the image of the family, that orthodox symbol he used earlier, to communicate a warning about disorder in the Northampton community, which has just expelled him (as its spiritual father) from the pulpit. The disorder of rebellious childlike Arminian heretics, who despise "their fathers with such magisterial assurance" and who exhibit a spiritual malaise in their theology of rational capability, figures as well in *A Careful and Strict Enquiry into the Modern Prevailing Notions of That Freedom of the Will* (1754), a major work defending the doctrine of predestination and also revealing E.'s earlier tendency to internalize images of nature as a means of reminding his readers that phenomenal existence is only an idea in the deity's mind. It is doubtful that the image of the family in this book affected its audience with any of the power it once had in Puritan culture, perhaps even as late as the publication of *A Faithful Narrative.*

Retreating ever deeper into conservative orthodoxy, E. buttressed his case against free will by attacking directly certain 18th-c. concepts of the essentially good innate nature of humanity, both assaults designed again to refute a trust in secular reason. In *The Great Christian Doctrine of Original Sin Defended* (1758), the last work he published during his life, E. argues relentlessly that the human heart is naturally corrupt. In this

work, he sometimes fashions analogies that combine empirical reasoning (so favored by his opponents) and traditional religious imagery (so favored by him); for example, in his illustration of a ship that survives most of a trip but fails finally to make port as typical of the sort of faulty arguments made by his opponents on behalf of the progress of human perfection, he stresses the empirical fact about the failure of the ship and implicitly infuses this example with the traditional image of the Christian pilgrim as a mariner sailing the seas of life toward the port of heaven.

At the time of his death, E. left numerous documents, though none apparently of a personal nature. Many have been posthumously published, or are planned for future publication, but perhaps the most important of these works is "The Nature of True Virtue," which was included in *Two Dissertations* (1765). Differentiating between particular beauty (anything appearing beautiful when it is viewed within a limited purview, as humanity sees it) and general beauty (anything appearing beautiful when viewed comprehensively and universally, as the deity sees it), E. again emphasizes that the natural world is only an idea in the deity's mind, internalizes external reality in images depicting features of the human mind and stunningly refutes the capacity of humanity to do anything of a truly virtuous nature. Whether directly through his work or indirectly through the New Divinity, Edwardsean arguments for predestination find resonance, if not mere acceptance, in the work of such 19th-c. American writers as Nathaniel HAWTHORNE and Herman MELVILLE, among others, who seem to have been equally fascinated by the Edwardsean refutation of human virtue.

BIBLIOGRAPHY: Cherry, C., *The Theology of J. E.: A Reappraisal* (1966); Conforti, J. A., *J. E., Religious Tradition, and American Culture* (1995); Davidson, E., *J. E.: The Narrative of a Puritan Mind* (1966); Elwood, D. J., *Philosophical Theology of J. E.* (1960); Fiering, N., *J. E.'s Moral Thought and Its British Context* (1981); Heimert, A., *Religion and the American Mind from the Great Awakening to the Revolution* (1966); Lesser, M. X., *J. E.: A Reference Guide* (1981); McDermott, G. R., *One Holy and Happy Society: The Public Theology of J. E.* (1992); Miller, P., *J. E.* (1949); Scheick, W. J., *The Writings of J. E.: Theme, Motif, and Style* (1975)

WILLIAM J. SCHEICK

EGGLESTON, Edward

b. 10 December 1837, Vevay, Indiana; d. 3 September 1902, Lake George, New York

E.'s best-known book is *The Hoosier School-Master: A Story of Backwoods Life in Indiana* (1871), the first of E.'s novels describing his native Midwest. Despite numerous literary flaws—stereotyped characters, creaky plot, multitudinous author asides, relentless moralizing, and embarrassing sentimentality—the book retains a certain charm, particularly in the Flat Crick schoolroom and spelling bee sections. The protagonist schoolmaster, young Ralph Hartsook, frustrates a pupil lockout, resists the wiles of simpering Mirandy Means, wins over her brother Bud to good deeds, gains the hand of the attractive bond girl Hannah Thomson, frees Hannah's mother from the poorhouse, is declared innocent of trumped-up charges of nightriding, and wins the admiration of poor little Shocky, Hannah's brother. Ralph does all this while resisting Pete Jones's harsh philosophy of education: "Lay it on good. Don't do no harm. Lickin' and la'rnin' goes together. No lickin', no l'arnin'!"

The Hoosier School-Master set off a vogue for spelling bees and encouraged the growth of local color fiction. A younger Midwestern author, Hamlin GAR-LAND, referred to it as a "milestone in my literary progress as it is in the development of distinctive Western fiction."

In depicting teaching, E. had only a few weeks of experience to draw on plus the troubles of his brother George Cary Eggleston in running a district school. In treating religion, a favorite subject, E. could draw on a more extensive acquaintance. Over his lifetime, he saw religion differently: first as a Methodist circuit rider in the Ohio River valley; later as a Methodist clergyman in frontier Minnesota; then as a writer for religious publications in Chicago; still later as the pastor of a nondenominational church in Brooklyn; and finally as an agnostic cultural historian.

E.'s next novel, *The End of the World: A Love Story* (1872), shared most of its predecessor's faults but yet conveyed the particulars of Midwestern pioneer life, ranging from an attempted lynching to a boisterous shivaree. The main title refers to the Millerite delusion that the world would end in 1843; the subtitle to the love story of August Wehle, a handsome young "Dutchman" (German), and Julia Anderson, a match held up by prejudice against German immigrants. Another religious novel, *The Circuit Rider: A Tale of the Heroic Age* (1874), tells of Morton Goodwin's conversion to Methodist fervor and a career as a circuit rider after youthful indulgence in drinking and gambling. His love, Patty Lumsden, a rich Episcopalian heiress, rejects Morton and Methodism until the fiery sermon of a Methodist preacher cured her of such vanities as the wearing of jewelry and returned her to Morton.

Roxy, the protagonist of *Roxy* (1878), finds Methodism central to her life in an Ohio River town in the 1840s. Her husband, a wealthy and politically ambitious lawyer, commits adultery with Nancy Kirtley, a poor white Cleopatra, and fathers her child. Horrified, Roxy leaves her husband but later sees her duty as Christian forgiveness and decides to raise the child as her own. Though lacking the exuberance of *The Hoosier School-Master*, *Roxy* is much more smoothly written.

Lest E. be seen only as a Midwestern local colorist, there exists his last novel, *The Faith Doctor: A Story of New York* (1891), portraying the anguish caused by faith healing in the nation's metropolis. Its two chief characters and lovers are a sophisticated young banker and the aristocratic, religiously active daughter of a deceased Presbyterian minister. Other works by E. include the thickly didactic juvenile *The Hoosier School-Boy* (1883) and *The Graysons* (1888), a novel in which Abraham LINCOLN appears.

E.'s last years were devoted to the writing of American cultural history. Though E. never became a major novelist, his work merits attention for its understanding of frontier Midwestern dialect and customs and for its religious insights.

BIBLIOGRAPHY: Cowie, A., *The Rise of the American Novel* (1951); Eggleston, G. C., *The First of the Hoosiers* (1903); Randel, W., *E. E.* (1963); Randel, W., *E. E.: The Author of the Hoosier School-Master* (1946)

ROBERT L. COARD

EISELEY, Loren [Corey]
b. 3 September 1907, Lincoln, Nebraska; d. 9 July 1977, Philadelphia, Pennsylvania

A professor of anthropology who published the first of his thirteen books at age fifty, E. has been credited by Annie DILLARD with "restoring the essay's place in imaginative literature' and extending the "symbolic capacity" of the essay form. That first book, *The Immense Journey* (1957), has been translated into more than a dozen languages and contains several of the most frequently anthologized essays—"How Flowers Changed the World," "The Judgment of the Birds," "Man of the Future"—in the second half of the 20th c.

Though variously characterized as a philosophical naturalist, a literary anthropologist, and a poetic scientist, both E. and his writings resist neat taxonomies. E. himself once described his chosen genre as "the concealed essay, in which personal anecdote was allowed gently to bring under observation thoughts of a more scientific nature." Influenced by writers as diverse as Ernest Thompson Seton, G. K. Chesterton, and Henry David THOREAU, E. exploited the broad territory of the essay in short pieces that range from sermons and polemics, such as "How Human Is Man" and "The World Eaters," to poetic meditations ("The Star Thrower") to tall tales ("The Dance of the Frogs").

Even his poetry—collected in *Notes of an Alchemist* (1972); *The Innocent Assassins* (1973); and *Another Kind of Autumn* (1977)—might be categorized as a poetic species of the essay: except for their layout on the page, E.'s poems are nearly indistinguishable from his more lyrical prose.

In addition to the scientific subject matter of his writings, the lyrical essayistic voice and the artistically shaped persona of E. may be the primary defining characteristics of his work. In "The Slit," the opening essay in *The Immense Journey,* E. defines this persona as "a man preoccupied with time" who can "at best report only from my own wilderness." Just as significantly, he invites the reader's identification with this persona: "We have joined the caravan, you might say, at a certain point; we will travel as far as we can." The image of the journey yoking writer and reader is both a favored metaphor and an implicit rhetorical strategy that reappears frequently in the later essays as well—those collected in *The Unexpected Universe* (1969), *The Invisible Pyramid* (1970), *The Night Country* (1971), and *The Star Thrower* (1978)—as well as in E.'s autobiography, *All the Strange Hours* (1975). Poet William E. STAFFORD observed that throughout E.'s autobiography "the reader feels the presence of the narrator, a helpful presence, a knowing presence, but also a companion for the reader's questioning and puzzlement and fear." The exploratory journey of writer and reader is, of course, one of Montaigne's definitions of the essay form itself.

E.'s contributions to literature cannot be separated from his significant roles in the modern environmental movement and the history of science. With Elliot Porter, he wrote the Sierra Club's seminal volumes on the redwoods and the Galapagos Islands entitled *Galapagos* (1968), thus launching the group's campaign for an Earth Natural Park. Shortly afterwards, he articulated the philosophic basis of an ecologic ethic in *The Unexpected Universe.* In addition, E. established himself as a creditable—and controversial—historian of science in *Darwin's Century* (1958), winner of the Phi Beta Kappa prize for best book in science, and in the posthumously published *Darwin and the Mysterious Mr. X: New Light on the Evolutionists* (1979).

BIBLIOGRAPHY: Angyal, A. J., *L. E.* (1983); Gerber, M. E., and M. McFadden, *L. E.* (1983); Heidtmann, P., *L. E.* (1991)

RICHARD NORDQUIST

ELIOT, T[homas] S[tearns]
b. 26 September 1888, St. Louis, Missouri; d. 4 January 1965, London, England

"The first half of the 20th c. will probably be known . . . as the age of E.," Allen TATE suggested in 1973,

"as the mid-18th c. was the age of Johnson. But Samuel Johnson came at the end of the neoclassical period and summed it up; whereas E., as critic and poet, created his age." Tate's view has long been disputed, but E.'s stature is apparent as much in the zeal of his detractors, notably Harold BLOOM and Richard Poirier, as in the fervor of his admirers. The most quotable and quoted of recent English and American critics, poets, and dramatists, E. is securely placed as a founder of the modernist movement. When reading his manuscript poems in 1914, Ezra POUND noted that E. had already "modernized himself," unaided by such revolutionists as Pound himself. A case in point was "The Love Song of J. Alfred Prufrock," written in 1910–11 while E. was still a student at Harvard. Self-mocking yet soul-searching, the poem is sharply imaged, dramatic, antiromantic in mood, and urban in setting. A gulf yawns between high society and low in the speaker's disturbing life. The poem was a response to E.'s exhilarating discovery of Charles Baudelaire, Jules Laforgue, and other French symbolists, who taught him that certain attitudes toward the sordid or disgusting" in modern life could awaken his own voice in poetry. Only after 1927 did he gradually acknowledge that positive responses to beauty and joy were equally authentic in the experience of living poets.

E.'s education was literary, classical, and philosophical—at Smith Academy in St. Louis, at Milton, and then at Harvard where he studied from 1906 to 1914, beginning graduate work in 1910. He had two traveling fellowships, to attend Henri Bergson's lectures in Paris (1910–11), and in 1914 to write his doctoral thesis on F. H. Bradley's "Idealist" philosophy in Marlburg, Oxford, and London. As an undergraduate, E. had been an editor of the *Harvard Advocate* and a member of the literary Signet Club. Some of his poems appeared in the *Advocate* (though not "Prufrock"), and a lively group of friends, including Conrad AIKEN, criticized one another's fledgling efforts. Soon, however, after E.'s Harvard teacher Irving Babbitt sparked his interest in Oriental thought, he decided to pursue doctoral studies in ancient and modern philosophies. He read Sanskrit and Pali scriptures under Charles Lanman and others, but the teachers who most influenced his thesis were Josiah Royce, William JAMES, George SANTAYANA, and Bertrand Russell. In Royce's seminar, E. took up the problem of interpreting primitive religions by modernist methodologies. He long remembered Santayana's lectures on the philosophical poems of Lucretius, Dante, and Goethe, but he was equally impressed by James's empiricist approaches to psychology and religion. As a visiting professor at Harvard in early 1914, Russell taught a seminar on physical realism, later remembering Eliot as his "most promising student." Nevertheless E. found the field of philosophy and university education in general disappointing. When the outbreak of war fortuitously drove him to England from his studies in Germany, he fitted easily into Pound's international circle of avant-garde artists and writers. In 1915, he finished his thesis, *Knowledge and Experience in the Philosophy of F. H. Bradley,* published in 1964, and impulsively married Vivienne Haigh-Wood after a three-month courtship. Vivacious, passionately interested in E.'s poetry as well as her own writing, she had an immeasurable influence on his creative work, no less so as she became increasingly unstable mentally and was confined to hospitals for many of the years before her death in 1947.

From 1915 to 1920, E. gradually enlarged a sheaf of poems earlier sketched, publishing a few in little magazines before collecting them in two volumes: *Prufrock and Other Observations* (1917) and *Poems* (1920). This was originally entitled *Ara Vos Prec* and included "Ode," which was later dropped for "Spleen" in *Poems.* Several of these early poems (like "Gerontion") are pungent interior monologues, philosophically troubling, the speaker deriding his own effeteness as he fantasizes on outworn grandeurs and falls back in tedium on the squalid circumstances of his actual life. Other poems are simply "observations" of country or city scenes in New England and Europe, touching on known figures like La Rochefoucauld and Madame H. P. Blavatsky, or else invented types like Sweeney, Burbank, and Bleistein. The Christian Church is recurrently lampooned in the 1920 poems: for example, as a hippopotamus that can both sleep and feed (itself and its young) at once; or as a bee-like swarm of epicene panderers, propagating their own kind.

Also between 1915 and 1922, E. demonstrated his paradoxical principle that while his poems expressed the "actuality" of his experience, his prose conveyed his "ideals" in various fields, including philosophy, music, and all the literary arts. Explaining his "program for the métier of poetry" in his most famous essay, "Tradition and the Individual Talent" (1919), he said that a great poet always writes with "the whole" of his own literature and cultural history in his mind but that such traditions "cannot be inherited." They must be obtained "by great labor." Furthermore, tradition exists only when kept alive by "the really new," for whatever merely conforms cannot "be a work of art." Paradoxically too, in this essay, E. argues that the uniqueness of great art lies in the complete "separation" of the poet's personal feelings and emotions from the "new compound" of feeling and emotion in the finished poem. This separation is achieved when the poet extinguishes his own personality "as he is at the moment" in favor of "something which is more valuable." The essay's famous "Impersonal theory" of

poetry ranges E. (along with T. E. Hulme, Pound, and James Joyce) on the side of "classicism" against "romanticism," and it also set him on the way toward what he would call the "mythical method" in an essay of 1922 on Joyce's *Ulysses.* Tradition reaches the individual best through conscious and unconscious transmissions of history, fable, romance, and ritual, many of which survive in illegible fragments, telling of a vanished world of meanings lost in the "panorama" of futility and anarchy which is contemporary history." To resuscitate the vitality of early religions was impossible, E. thought at the time, but through continuous parallels with ancient myths, modern poetry could remind us at least of our losses, thereby appealing for renewed coherence in cultural life. Poetry could recover intensities dulled in the "ruminative" poetry of the Victorian era, moreover, by reconstituting the poetic elements denatured when writers and critics claimed that poets should look into their hearts and write. Praising John Donne and the metaphysical poets of his school in an essay of 1921, E. said that going to "the heart" was not deep enough: "One must look into the cerebral cortex, the nervous system, and the digestive tracts." In other words, poetry should not only express and distinguish among emotions but should also represent thought, unwilled impulses, and physiological functions.

E.'s attention to these processes (evident in his poems) is central in his finest essays. In "Hamlet and His Problems" (1919), he suggests that Shakespeare's own psychic problems, inaccessible to the transmutations of art, prevented his discovery of an "objective correlative" sufficient to account for Hamlet's disgust with life. Such personal difficulties of the author's thus rendered *Hamlet* less successful than, for instance, Shakespeare's late romances, which E. elsewhere cites for their power to objectify intense emotions and thought. Even at this early stage, as in his later two essays on Dante, E. revealed that biographical and cultural information will necessarily aid in the interpretation of literature. Those who have placed him among the midcentury's New Critics rightly focus on his statement in "Tradition and the Individual Talent" that criticism must deal with the "emotion which has its life in the poem and not in the history of the poet." Yet by insisting too much on the separation of the poet's personal experience from the poem, readers (and E. himself) often ignored the persistently autobiographical impetus in his own work as well as that of most great poets. This became a celebrated issue after his publication of *The Waste Land* in 1922.

At first blush, the long poem (430-odd lines in varying meters and rhyme schemes) appeared to be an "impersonal" medley of many voices. From the beginning through part four, the Sibyl and Tiresias

speak apocalyptically in counterpoint to desperate socialites and cheap seducers of both sexes. In the fifth
and last section, those voices are succeeded by the
anxious monologue of a brooding quester after water
and emotional relief. Associated with the Buddha, this
voice finally erupts into polyglot fragments of European poetry, then quiets itself with chanting "Shantih"
(Peace) from the Hindu Upanishads. In the original
"Notes," E. compared this ultimate peace to the "feeble" echo of it in Christ's "Peace that passeth all understanding."

Understandably, in view of E.'s "Impersonal theory," *The Waste Land* was greeted as a representation
of his entire generation's disillusionment over the recent war and the breakdown of Western civilization,
seen from one of its noblest cities ("London Bridge
is falling down . . ."). But the poem is equally concerned with the failure of marital love and a personal
sense of all-pervading sterility, waste, futility, and horror. E.'s personal life was a shambles at the time. His
father had recently died, and had pointedly excluded
E.'s wife from his legacy. His mother's visit to London
in 1921 and her silent awareness of Vivienne's disorder, the actual drought in Europe that summer, and
his doctor's warning of a complete nervous breakdown
if E. did not let up on work, all figure directly or
obliquely in the poem. When I. A. Richards praised the
poem as a corrective to autobiographical and religious
poetry of the last century, and as a poem without belief,
E. reacted with surprising animus. First he insisted
that his "scepticism" in *The Waste Land* was a kind
of belief. But before long, in a series of new poems,
letters, and essays, he pointedly expressed the torments
of a life without belief in a definite and reliable source
of truth.

In "The Hollow Men" (1925), *Ash-Wednesday*
(1930), and the "Ariel Poems" (1927–31), E. shifted
from his earlier resistance to "the first voice of poetry"
(as he termed it in 1953), the poet directly expressing
himself in his poems, he showed a continuing mastery
of the "second voice" or dramatic monologue—as in
"A Song for Simeon," "The Journey of the Magi,"
and "Marina," each perhaps a rehearsal for the fully
dramatized (or "third") voice of poetry soon to be
expressed in his plays. The poems of the late twenties
also displayed his renewed interest in Dante's depictions of Hell, Purgatory, and Paradise. Though Dante's
precision of imagery, simplicity of diction, and philosophical range had always appealed to E., he now
began to appreciate the *Paradiso* in ways earlier impossible, he said, because before 1925 Beatrice and
Heaven had seemed too "cheerful" and also were
spoiled by such poems of the Dante cult as Rossetti's
"The Blessed Damozel." Intermediary women like
Beatrice now appeared increasingly in E.'s own

poems—in *Ash-Wednesday* (dedicated to his wife), in
"Marina" (1930), and in the verse dramas that initiated
a new phase of his career from 1934 on. He now
believed that the literature of disillusionment was immature. This new interest in connecting himself with
Dante's legacy was clear from his 1928 essay on
Dante, where a long note decisively rejected Richards's theory that personal religious belief is irrelevant
to, or even an imposition on, the writing and enjoyment
of poetry. In 1926, E. had delivered the Clark Lectures
at Cambridge University, describing Dante as the
greatest of "metaphysical poets." These eight lectures
traced the gradual disintegration of the intellect and the
"increasing separation of sound, image, and thought"
from Dante to the present. E. now assigned a lower
place to Donne as poet than in his 1921 essay, "The
Metaphysical Poets." There Donne had appeared as
the supreme example of an intellectual poet, for whom
poetic thought and feeling were one response. Here
Donne is a great poet but imprisoned in his feelings,
unable to unify experiences of the body with those of
the soul, owing to his century's increasing "psycholo-
gism" and philosophical incoherence. In the year following the Clark Lectures, E. asked to be received in
the Anglican Church and became a British citizen. At
Babbitt's urging he also declared himself in the preface
to *For Lancelot Andrewes* to be "a classicist in literature, royalist in politics, and Anglo-Catholic in religion." His wife, among others, was appalled at this
turn, and in 1932—after a particularly bitter exchange—while E. was lecturing in America, he moved
to separate from her legally. She did not blame him
for the choice and continued to sign herself "Mrs. T. S.
E." until her death fifteen years later.

The lectures in America (Harvard's Norton Lectures and the Page-Barbour Lectures at the University
of Virginia) were published as *The Use of Poetry and
the Use of Criticism* (1933) and *After Strange Gods:
A Primer of Modern Heresy* (1934). Another lecture
series, on metaphysical poetry—similar to the Clark
Lectures and like them never published, was delivered
at Johns Hopkins University (the Turnbull Lectures).
The Norton lectures ranged from Elizabethan drama
through Dryden, Wordsworth and Coleridge, Shelley
and Keats, to Matthew Arnold, concluding with a commentary on "the modern mind" (once more engaging
with Richards as antagonist). The Virginia lectures,
never republished, dealt with such "heretics" (radical
individualists) in literature as Hardy, Lawrence, and
Pound. This book was used often to type E. as a
"fascist," but early in the 1930s he foresaw the crises
emerging in what he called the new paganism of totalitarian regimes, and he attempted to dramatize the confrontation of the Christian against state power in *Mur-*

der in the Cathedral (1935), the first of five plays that occupied him in the last phase of his career.

E. had long considered the theater to be the ideal medium for poetry, answering a psychological need of the audience and also of the poet, both together seeking reconciliations and the resolution of conflicts, public as well as personal. When E. Martin Browne urged him to submit a play on St. Thomas à Becket for the Canterbury Festival of 1935, E. wrote his first completed poetic drama on the conflict between political expediency and individual responsibility, between action and suffering, between the clamor of the crowds and the silence of God. His next play, *The Family Reunion* (1939), had a contemporary setting, as did all the later plays, but all "crisscrossed" the modern theme with references to a classical play underlying it. In this play, Aeschylus' *Eumenides* (with its band of Furies) adumbrated E.'s story of a husband's self-torture over the death of his wife. Euripides' *Alcestis* underlay *The Cocktail Party* (1948), about the return of a wife "from the dead," also paralleling the journey of a saintly woman to life through martyrdom. Euripides's *Ion* was a pattern for *The Confidential Clerk* (1952), whose comedy of misidentified children reflects Gilbert and Sullivan's in *Pinafore,* as well as Oscar Wilde's in *The Importance of Being Earnest* and earlier comedies, back to Plautus. The play also seriously tests the authenticities of parenting and the make-believe worlds we construct, allowing real vocations to slip from our hold. E.'s last play, *The Elder Statesman* (1958), has Sophocles' *Oedipus at Colonus* as a starting point, and looks back to the medieval *Everyman* as well. All three plays celebrate the crisis of an eminently successful man as he faces death and only then for the first time begins to live. Plainly E. was himself taking stock of his life and was prepared when this play (like the previous one) was criticized as neither poetry nor prose, the work of a tired laureate. He had, however, deliberately sought a verse language for the theater that would be colloquial and unobtrusive while also having the compression and universality of poetry. His five plays have yet to be written off as unprofitable and may still find directors equal to their demands. As "Sagittarius" pseudonymously said, this "metaphysical mime / That should have been / The most distinguished failure of all time / Proves quite the opposite" in *The Cocktail Party,* and maybe in at least three of the other plays as well.

When England declared war in 1939 and the theaters were closed, E. interrupted his career as playwright to concentrate on a long reflective poem. He then saw that the five-part "Burnt Norton" (1936) could become the first of four "quartets"—a long reflective poem (with intense lyric interludes) on time, time as history and time as the impetus to spiritual quest—a meditation both for nations and for the individual self. E. would come to see *Four Quartets* as his masterpiece, the work on which his reputation should stand or fall. The first Quartet deals with time that "might have been." Beginning in the rose garden of an English manor that E. visited once in 1934, the Quartet presents a vision of perfect happiness fulfilled only in an imagined past, which yet points to the same "end" as does completed time. The second Quartet, "East Coker," has the actually completed past as its focus, appropriately dwelling on the town in England where E.'s ancestor, Andrew Eliot, departed for America around 1669, the town where E. had decided his own burial place would be. In the third Quartet, "The Dry Salvages," E.'s birthplace on the Mississippi and his boyhood memories of a New England fishing village on the coast of Cape Ann become the locales for images of imperfect time: fearful voyaging without certain destination (which yet is a phase in all voyages of discovery). The last Quartet, "Little Gidding," has its place in the present time, the scene being partly in war-torn London and partly at an English prayer house (Little Gidding) established in the 17th c., now again for E. a place of pilgrimage, recollection and reconciliation. Each of the Quartets has a Heraclitean "element" and a season of the year: first air and spring, then earth and summer, then water and autumn; finally fire and the strange spring that often comes in mid-winter. Each Quartet (except the American Quartet oddly) also has a reflection on the perfecting of a language for poetry. And in all the quartets, there are sections on the soul's descent into darkness, its moments of grace and light, and the evidence both in history and in private life that all will finally be "well," when the many "ends" imaged by fire and roses will become one in the foretold end of time.

Until his death in 1965, E. maintained his British citizenship and his chief residence in London. He continued to serve as a director of Faber and Faber, the publishing firm he had joined in 1925. He corresponded extensively with other writers, especially younger poets as the years went by. Always needing, and wishing, to have regular employment apart from his creative work, he had briefly tried school teaching and extension lecturing, then for several years kept regular hours at Lloyd's Bank, where he became an expert on the settlement of pre-World War I Anglo-German debts. From 1925 on, his editorial work for Faber's was also backed by his seventeen years (1922–39) as editor of the *Criterion,* a literary review in the broadest and most international sense. Hitler's invasions depressed him so deeply in 1939 that he discontinued the review, which had described itself as devoted to rebuilding European solidarity after World War I. In 1940, he published the first of two short books on political philosophy, *The Idea of a Christian Society* (1939) and *Notes toward a Definition of Culture* (1948).

E. received both the Order of Merit from Queen Elizabeth II and the Nobel Prize in literature in 1948. His prestige counted for much when he joined with other writers in an appeal to the U.S. Government for Ezra Pound's release from St. Elizabeths Federal Hospital, where Pound was confined for treasonably supporting the Axis powers in World War II. E. had also defended Pound in the controversy over the Bollingen Prize, awarded to Pound in 1949 for his *Pisan Cantos.*

In 1957, E. married Valerie Fletcher, a much younger fellow worker at Faber and Faber. He credited her with bringing to his last eight years the happiness that (his poems suggest) he had seldom known. After his death, she edited his letters and helped to produce the popular musical *Cats,* based on the finest of his light verses, *Old Possum's Book of Practical Cats* (1939). She also helped produce the best documentary film on E.'s life, "The Mysterious Mr. Eliot" (1973).

When E. was interviewed in his last years, he declared his poetry to be American in its life sources and emotional springs. He was nonetheless to be given a memorial in Westminster Abbey, and his ashes were to remain in England, in the church at East Coker where his name reads simply THOMAS STEARNS ELIOT, POET.

BIBLIOGRAPHY: Bergonzi, B., *T. S. E.* (1972); Browne, E. M., *The Making of T. S. E.'s Plays* (1963); Drew, E., *T. S. E.: The Design of His Poetry* (1949); Frye, N., *T. S. E.* (1963); Gardner, H., *The Art of T. S. E.* (1949); Gardner, H., *T. S. E. and the English Poetic Tradition* (1965); Gordon, L., *E.'s Early Years* (1977); Hay, E., *T. S. E.'s Negative Way* (1982); Howarth, H., *Notes on Some Figures Behind T. S. E.* (1965); Kenner, H., *The Invisible Poet: T. S. E.* (1959); Margolis, J. D., *T. S. E.'s Intellectual Development, 1922–1939* (1972); Matthiessen, F. O., *The Achievement of T. S. E.* (1935; rev. ed., 1947); Moody, A. D., *T. S. E., Poet* (1979); Rajan, B., Spender, S., *The Overwhelming Question: A Study of T. S. E.* (1976); Smith, C. H., *T. S. E.'s Dramatic Theory and Practice* (1963); Smith, G., *T. S. E.'s Poetry and Plays* (1956)

ELOISE KNAPP HAY

ELKIN, Stanley [Lawrence]

b. 11 May 1930, New York City; d. 31 May 1995, St. Louis, Missouri

Even in a literary age of oddity and innovation, E.'s writing, his voice and vision, was truly distinctive. E.

never enjoyed the degree of popular and critical acclaim bestowed on fellow Jewish American writers Phillip ROTH and Saul BELLOW, even though his fiction shares the narrative outrageousness of the one and the quasi-spiritual yearning of the other. Of course, E.'s ten novels, three collections of short stories, two of novellas, and one of essays are not conventionally Jewish American; indeed they are not conventional at all. His plots do not develop; they accrete, following a rhythm of tension and release wherever his muse, Serendipity, leads. His characters are in fact grotesques, generally little more than the sum total of their tics and quirks, their occupations and grievances. Most are businessmen (as E.'s father was); all feel passed-over and second-rate. None is particularly likeable, yet all are strangely sympathetic. They are sad clowns, garrulous and grieving, part Pagliacci, part Ancient Mariner—as Helen Vendler has said of E. himself. E. transforms their tragicomic griefs and grievances into furiously funny prose, the "fierce, energetic language" of an obsessional and highly stylized art of excess produced at the painstaking rate of a page a day.

E.'s unusual yet in most ways utterly commonplace characters grapple with indignity in all its forms, including disease and death. But the death they face is always physical, never (as in Bellow) metaphysical. Their pains—the various slings and arrows of outrageous fortune it has been their bad luck or worse genes to suffer—are versions of E.'s own, the multiple sclerosis that led E. to think of style as a form of revenge and to contend that "All books are the Book of Job." E.'s slapstick Jobs exist in a modern mode, outside faith, in an existential—or rather post-existential, postmodern—absurd. Advised to be a strong man, the titular hero in *Boswell* (1964) becomes a pro wrestler (losing of course to the Grim Reaper). Department store owner Leo Feldman in *A Bad Man* (1967) goes to jail for giving people what they want, in effect for following the inexorable logic of his nature as a salesman. Dick Gibson's odyssey, in *The Dick Gibson Show* (1971), takes him from radio station to radio station across America, living the itinerant life of pure apprenticeship, broadcasting at one point to no one at all and at another to listeners just as obsessive as himself. Ben Flesh in *The Franchiser* (1976), E.'s finest, funniest, most furious creation, is a version of Arthur MILLER's equally eponymous Willy Loman. Ben is the culture, the word "America" made flesh. Heir to the prime rate, the franchiser is a kind of Johnny Appleseed, "addressing need itself," "speaking some Esperanto of simple need, answering appetite with convenience food" and One Hour Martinizing. Less than he seems—not a franchiser at all, merely a franchisee—he "lives the franchised life under the logo of others" until the onset of both MS and the energy crisis of 1970s brings him down. The deaths of his eighteen godcousins, each the result of his or her weirdly funny life-long malady, lead Ben to realize that "there are no ludicrous deaths . . . only ludicrous life, screwball comedy, goofy being."

The injustice of ludicrous life is particularly evident in *The Living End* (1979). Ellerbee, a truly good man, is shot and killed in a holdup, arrives at the pearly gates (heaven is a theme park made up of cliches) only to be told to go to hell, "the ultimate inner city" but also a kind of nightclub for a God made in the image of a stand-up comic, whining about never having gotten any respect, never having found his audience. The protagonist of *George Mills* (1982), on the other hand, is E.'s most passive hero—and ironically the one that brought E. the critical acclaim he long deserved: a National Book Award. In this, he resembles Jerry Korngold in *The Rabbi of Lud* (1987), whose fear of life is so great he takes up residence in a necropolis as clergy-in-residence: better the boredom, anonymity, and death-in-life in Lud, he feels, than the risks he would run anywhere else. *The Magic Kingdom* (1985) is E.'s riskiest book: a comic novel about terminally ill children. For all its grotesque humor, the novel is deeply affecting, brilliantly balancing two of Elkin's most important themes: that "Death, not health, was at the core of things" and that commitment to life is necessary, no matter how ridiculous the life or absurd the commitment. Suffering no fatal illness, over-the-hill streets commissioner Robert Druff in *The Mac-Guffin* (1991) tries to compensate for his joke life with paranoid fantasies. "If nothing happened to you, you had to fall back on your character, spinning your life out of whole cloth, disaffiliate from the world." The protagonist of *Mrs. Ted Bliss* (1995) is the last of E.'s disaffiliates: older, less verbally extravagant, a woman of small grudges, petty vanities, and lifelong effacement—first as wife, then as widow. Alone and helpless, she discovers what so many E. characters do, that even after all the losses and indignities, there is still the sense of obligation, for her to others, for E. to writing well.

BIBLIOGRAPHY: Bailey, P., *Reading S. E.* (1985); Bargen, D., *The Fiction of S. E.* (1980); Dougherty, D. C., *S. E.* (1990)

ROBERT A. MORACE

ELLIOTT, William

b. 27 April 1788, Beaufort, South Carolina; d. 3 February 1863, Charleston, South Carolina

E.'s reputation as writer rests largely upon a single work, *Carolina Sports by Land and Water* (1846), a well-loved volume that holds the distinction of being among the first books of sporting adventure in America and one of the very few that has stayed in print without interruption. It contains sketches, tales, and essays in a bold, manly prose, works that vigorously recount rattling good adventures and hair-raising exploits in a finely polished style. They come from an intellect whose acute powers of discernment and masculine control are never in question, and whose genial good sense and bantering tone are among the volume's greatest strengths. E. uses baroque flourishes, mock-heroic burlesques, colloquialisms, and classical references in Latin and Greek in stories that blend effectively the fruits of an excellent classical training with Southern folklore and the oral yarn. For example, his tale of the white spectre buck that cannot be killed is an old legend of his area.

The paradox of a style that mates ruggedness with grace and charm is explained by understanding the chivalric ideals of the Southern aristocracy to which E. belonged, a class whose gentlemanly code prescribes brave, forceful action, but in graceful and elegantly simple form. Such it is with E.'s style, and so it was with his life. In his case, truly, the style was the man. As sportsman, he was known for daring escapades under the roughest conditions; but as sensitive lover of elegance and beauty, he gloried in the special roses around his manor house—in a garden that covered no less than ten acres. His was a life of opulence, comparable to the European grand style, which he knew from extensive travels. Thus, it is small wonder that *Carolina Sports* mirrors well the high culture of the society that produced it, and in doing so, is a luxuriously rich evocation of time and place, particularly in the "Chee-ha" plantation sketches. That time is largely the decade of the 1830s; and that place is the fields, swamps, tidal waters, and ocean about the southern tip of South Carolina. Through his code of gentlemanly behavior and honor, and his good family connections, E. is an excellent representative of the planter class at its best and is among those men in America who have highest claim to the title "aristocracy."

E. first began publishing the sketches that were to become *Carolina Sports* in the *American Turf Register* in 1829. "Fishing Extraordinary" appeared there in December of that year; and in 1831, the sketch "Drum Fishing" greeted the public. From April 1837 to May 1838, he published much of what was to be *Carolina Sports* in an excellent new Charleston magazine, the *Southern Literary Journal*. These pieces were "A Wild Cat Hunt in Carolina," "A Day at Chee-ha," "Another Day at Chee-ha," "Devil-Fishing," and "A Business Day at Chee-ha," stories that establish his position as an important predecessor of the school of local color. By 1838, more than half of the volume had been penned, and in subsequent years leading to publication in 1846, he filled out his volume. He augmented his sketches on his piscatorial efforts for drum and devil-fish with pieces on bass and sheepshead fishing. To the "Chee-ha" series, he added "The Last Day at Chee-ha," then rounded off his volume with "The Fire Hunter," "Of the Animals of Chase in South-Carolina," "Of the Birds Which Are the Objects of Sport," and, finally, "Random Thoughts on Hunting." When the new revised edition of 1859 was published, he included one additional chapter, "The Sea-Serpent."

E. chose the American scene as his setting, a decision in itself commendable in 1829, when many "American" writers still yearned toward Europe. Although these stories report some extraordinary and almost unbelievable events (such as riding the back of a devil-fish and killing two bears with one discharge), E. assured his readers that they were "sketches from life." He was foremost a realist and portrayed life accurately. Although he makes use of the magical-beast folk motif in writing of the devil-fish, sea-serpent, and spectre buck, and does engage in some infrequent mild spoofing, his work does not fall primarily into the tall-tale genre in which Southern authors of his day were beginning to excel. E.'s credo was that he must write only from true and unembellished concrete experience, for that which the author has himself "seen or done" is precisely that which makes "the liveliest impression, . . . and with none other . . . should he attempt the difficult task of interesting the reader." Critics have accordingly praised his ability to sustain interesting narrative, his enthusiasm for the subject that creates dramatic effect, and his skill at conveying the dash of the chase. A bold and almost reckless man of courage, who was at the same time capable of the most severe control, his actions on land and sea generate involvement even in those who are not sportsmen. On the subject of the morals of the hunt, he says in the concluding chapter of *Carolina Sports* that he is in favor of such sport as a means of siphoning off "animal passions" which might otherwise be destructive. Further, true sportsmen must be *of* the place, not city men who "marshal their forces for a week's campaign" and who "go so far and get so little for their pains." Conservation must be practiced to perpetuate the pastime, which he considers "noble."

E. was accurate in assessing his several publications when he chose *Carolina Sports* as that which would have the best chance to live and "be a sort of legacy of honor to my posterity." William Gilmore SIMMS, in the best contemporary review of the volume, agreed on its likelihood of permanence. The descriptions of a people's sport, Simms wrote, "will continue to command attention when graver volumes, on what may seem to be more important subjects, have been long

forgotten. The sports of a country are somewhat akin to its ballads, and are more important than its laws." In E.'s case, both men's statements have proved prophetic. All in all, *Carolina Sports* is a remarkable book, much bigger than its 172 pages. Its value goes beyond its charm and the realistic picture it creates of the Carolina aristocracy at play. The tangible world that it presents and the personal relationships that it portrays are not milked of life by rendering them into abstract "meaning." They possess "meaning" enough in themselves in true Southern fashion. There is no doubt that *Carolina Sports* will continue to delight and become more valuable to us in an age of abstraction, and as the modern industrial world and its technology rob us ever more steadily of a basic, necessary need for the contact with nature that will help insure the preservation of our humanness.

BIBLIOGRAPHY: Jones, L., "W. E., South Carolina Non-Conformist," *JSH* 17 (August 1951): 361–81; Scafidel, B., "W. E., Planter and Politician," *Southern Carolina Journal and Journalists* (1975): 109–19; Wimsatt, M. A., and R. Phillips, "Antebellum Humor," in Rubin, L., ed., *The History of Southern Literature* (1985): 146–47

                                    JAMES EVERETT KIBLER, JR.

ELLIS, Bret Easton
b. 7 March 1964, Los Angeles, California

E. was twenty-one and a student at Bennington College in Vermont when his first book, *Less than Zero* (1985), was published by Simon & Schuster, startling the literary world with its depiction of youths interested only in drugs, sex, material possessions, and music videos. Like his second novel, *Rules of Attraction* (1987), it portrays disaffected middle-class youth of the 1980s.

It is natural for a successful book penned by one so young as E. was at the time of *Less than Zero*'s publication to garner attention. In E.'s case, the grisly subject matter, music video style, and detached prose made his book the center of a debate that literary critics and readers are still engaged in about the writer. If E. is indeed the voice of his generation, it is a cynical, decadent, and materialistic generation.

E. denies that *Less than Zero* is autobiographical. Nonetheless, references to real Los Angeles hot spots abound and its setting is a suburban section of Los Angeles not unlike that in which E. was reared, the son of a real estate investment banker and a homemaker. At the center of the tale is Clay, who returns to Los Angeles for Christmas vacation and whose mild disgust at the life he finds his friends leading provides the only counterbalance to the blasé, detached tone of the narrator, a tone maintained to describe even dead bodies and the gang rape of a twelve-year-old girl on heroin.

In E.'s second novel, *The Rules of Attraction,* the story moves East, but the characters' ages, interests, and alienation from the real world change little from the first book. And like the first book, it is filled with references to brand names, fashion designers and expensive cars, driving home the author's interest in exposing the materialistic nature of our culture. The plot involves a love triangle between Paul, a homosexual, Sean, the bisexual object of Paul's desire, and Lauren, the woman Sean wants.

A minor character in *The Rules of Attraction* became the main character in E.'s third book, *American Psycho* (1991), published by Vintage Books, a division of Random House. If *Less than Zero* stirred controversy, *American Psycho* boiled the stew. In a novel so graphically violent that Simon & Schuster withdrew its agreement to publish it, Patrick Bateman is a morally bankrupt investment banker, businessman by day, brutal killer by night. As in the first novel, the dispassionate narrative adds to the disturbing quality of the book. The reader finds no remorse in the voices of the character or the narrator as they describe grotesque, violent scenes and actions. It is this flat tone that has led many critics to accuse E. of writing novels with no moral context.

American Psycho was followed by *The Informers* (1994), a book of linked short stories with themes similar to that of the novels.

Admittedly influenced as much by television, music, and films as by books, E.'s style has changed little from one book to the next, offering short visual vignettes of the *cinéma-vérité* sort—a peek at a disturbing world. Whether it is a world he invents or merely exposes, like the *cinéma-vérité* filmmaker he is responsible for selecting and arranging the material. That said, it appears that E. anticipates readers with short attention spans who are so desensitized to violence that only the most shocking descriptions can keep them awake.

BIBLIOGRAPHY: Freccero, C., "Historical Violence, Censorship, and the Serial Killer: The Case of *American Psycho,*" *Diacritics* 27 (Summer 1997): 44–58; Sahlin, N., "'But This Road Doesn't Go Anywhere': The Existential Dilemma in *Less Than Zero,*" *Crit* 33 (Fall 1991): 23–42

                                        JENNIFER WHEELOCK

ELLISON, Harlan

b. 27 May 1934, Cleveland, Ohio

E. began his writing career in the 1950s, after being dismissed from Ohio State University due to an argument with a writing instructor who accused E. of having no talent. From this inauspicious beginning followed one of the great American literary careers of the late 20th c. For the last forty years, E. has been a prolific writer of short stories, essays, screenplays, teleplays, and criticism.

Although generally considered a writer of SCIENCE FICTION, E. rejects that label. He describes his writing as "magic realism." In an interview, E. stated that he explains "the world through which we move by reflecting it through the lens of fantasy turned slightly askew, so that you can see it from a new angle." In fact, many of E.'s best works would most accurately be described as realistic. The short story collection *Gentleman Junkie and Other Stories of the Hung-up Generation* (1961)—which brought E. a measure of fame when it was favorably reviewed by Dorothy PARKER—consists of such fiction. Other notable examples of E.'s realism include the novels *Web of the City* (1958), based on E.'s experiences with a teen gang in New York, and *Spider Kiss* (1961), about a rockabilly musician; the short stories "Daniel White for the Greater Good" (1961) and "A Prayer for No One's Enemy" (1966)—two of E.'s many explorations of the consequences of racial and religious hatred; and the novella "The Resurgence of Miss Ankle-Strap Wedgie" (1968), a story of Hollywood.

His success in other genres notwithstanding, however, the majority of E.'s most memorable works fall into the category of fantasy. Arguably his two most famous short stories are "Repent, Harlequin! Said the Ticktockman" (1965) and "I Have No Mouth and I Must Scream" (1967). The former, which won both Hugo and Nebula Awards, is set in a future where time is of the essence; everything is rigidly scheduled, and any indiviual deviations from the master schedule result in time being "deducted" from one's life. The Harlequin, a rebellious figure, sets about to disrupt the system, much to the consternation of the Master Timekeeper—(the "Ticktockman." This story exemplifies E.'s lifelong battle against complacency and mindless conformity. "I Have No Mouth and I Must Scream," winner of the Hugo Award for best short story, is a chilling postapocalyptic vision. After the last great war, the last five people on Earth are kept alive in the belly of AM, a supercomputer that has, in effect, become the world. AM has developed self-awareness and, with it, an unimaginable hatred for the race that created him. He keeps his five captives alive perpetually, tormenting them endlessly. "I Have No Mouth and I Must Scream" is a Dantesque vision of Hell updated to fit the technological worldview of the late 20th c.

Another postapocalyptic story "A Boy and His Dog" (1969) tells the story of a teenager and his telepathic dog. This novella, which also won Hugo and Nebula Awards, is one of E.'s more controversial works. Its basic themes are love and loyalty, but the main character's attitude toward women and the story's grisly denouement have led several critics to interpret the novella and its author as sexist. Similar charges have been leveled against "Croatoan" (1975), which deals with abortion.

E.'s other major stories include "Delusion for a Dragon-Slayer" (1966), which argues that our fantasies may come true, but only if we are worthy of them; "The Deathbird" (1973), an experimental story about the "true" nature of God and mankind's place in the universe; "The Whimper of Whipped Dogs" (1973), inspired by the true story of Kitty Genovese, who was murdered outside her New York apartment building while her neighbors looked on and did nothing; and the hilarious "I'm Looking for Kadak" (1974), about a Jewish alien's attempt to gather a *minyan* (a group of ten Jewish men) in order to provide a proper funeral for one of his co-religionists.

In addition to short stories, E. has produced screenplays and teleplays, perhaps most notably the as-yet unproduced *I, Robot* (1994), based on Isaac ASIMOV's classic short stories. E. has also produced a large body of television and film criticism—collected in such volumes as *The Glass Teat* (1970), *The Other Glass Teat* (1975), and *H. E.'s Watching* (1989)—and essays on numerous topics, many of which have been collected in *Sleepless Nights in the Procrustean Bed* (1984), *An Edge in My Voice* (1985), and *The H. E. Hornbook* (1990). As an editor, E. compiled *Dangerous Visions* (1967) and *Again, Dangerous Visions* (1972), two seminal collections of original "magic realism" stories. In all his literary endeavors—whether as writer or editor—E. has consistently been an eloquent, unapologetic, and uncompromising critic of mediocrity and conformity and a champion of the most notable instincts of mankind.

BIBLIOGRAPHY: Porter, A., ed., *The Book of E.* (1978); Slusser, G. E., *H. E.: Unrepentant Harlequin* (1977); Swigart, L. K., *H. E.: A Bibliographical Checklist* (1973)

JASON BERNER

ELLISON, Ralph [Waldo]

b. 1 March 1914, Oklahoma City, Oklahoma; d. 16 April 1994, New York City

Perhaps no 20th-c. novelist has achieved so great an impact and acquired so solid a reputation on the basis of one book as has E. for his 1952 novel, *Invisible Man*. Although he had published some essays and short fiction earlier, and subsequently some excerpts from an as yet unfinished second novel as well as two collections of essays, his claim as a major American author rests deservedly on the powerful surreal novel that won the thirty-eight-year-old E. the National Book Award.

E. had come to New York in the summer of 1936, in the hope of earning tuition to complete his senior year at Tuskegee Institute, where he was majoring in music. Instead of returning to Tuskegee, he found himself involved in black and leftist literary and cultural circles, befriended and encouraged by such people as Alain Locke, Langston HUGHES, and, perhaps most influential in that early period, Richard WRIGHT, who encouraged E. to write his first short story and to study technique as employed by such writers as Henry JAMES, Joseph Conrad, and James Joyce. During the winter of 1937, E. studied closely those writers along with Ernest HEMINGWAY and Gertrude STEIN, even to the point of copying passages from Hemingway by hand. He, Joyce, and Eliot remained E.'s greatest stylistic influences.

Although E.'s movement from adolescence to adulthood, from the segregated South to the Harlem of the 1930s and 1940s, from educational institutions to political, forms the basis for *Invisible Man*'s plot, it can be termed autobiographical only in the very loosest sense. In many ways, the nameless narrator's coming of age is as much modeled on Stephen Dedalus's biography as on E.'s. Like Dedalus, the invisible man moves toward an aesthetic perspective on what emerges as the motifs of his life. The motifs are as deeply embedded and carefully orchestrated in the imagery of *Invisible Man* as they are, for example, in Joyce's *A Portrait of the Artist* or T. S. ELIOT's *The Waste Land*.

The book's interweaving of theme and motif, however, relies on the model of improvisational jazz—especially the "blues"—rather than European musical forms. And this emphasis on American paradigms is, itself, one of the book's central themes. By interweaving slave folk tales with Greek myths, for example, or African American spirituals with Emersonian oratory, Freudian dreams with Faulknerian monologues, antebellum artifacts with revisionist histories, Communist rallies with Christian allegories, the book asserts that the unique quality of American culture is the way it reflects its inextricable connection to black culture, even as it attempts to erase the signs of that connection. This willful failure of the 20th-c. American establishment to acknowledge this source of America's power and diversity, of its artistic innovation and moral imperative, creates the blindness that makes E.'s narrator "invisible."

That narrator, in telling his tale from the temporal distance of some twenty years and the physical distance of a clean, well-lighted place in subterranean Harlem, provides a symbolic story of black Americans moving from the 19th c. to the 20th, the South to the North, and the soil to the city. Characters that bear uncanny resemblances to one another, and recurrent images—of eyes, lights, blindness, and blindfolds; of reds, whites, blues, and blacks; of trickster rabbits and duped bears; of phoney documents and deceitful papers—give the novel its dreamlike quality. Because each episode mirrors the preceding one in its pattern of duplicity, violence, and catastrophe, the dream consists of a series of nightmares each managing another way to "keep this nigger boy running." And thus the novel comprises one cumulative cultural nightmare the theme of which is that its dreamer is invisible.

Through an elaborate body of allusions, *Invisible Man* provides a focused critique of the American literary canon. Although the black, according to E., served as the symbol of humanity in 19th-c. American literature, 20th-c. revisionist history and criticism had overlooked the important role the black played in the conscience of American authors. In order to make visible that oversight, E. constructed detailed allusions to works by Ralph Waldo EMERSON, Herman MELVILLE, Walt WHITMAN, Mark TWAIN, William FAULKNER, as well as parodies of literary criticism by such authors as Lewis MUMFORD, Granville Hicks, and Leslie A. FIEDLER.

Over a forty-year period, E. made these same points more directly in an array of occasional essays, reviews, speeches, and interviews, collected in three volumes, *Shadow and Act* (1964) and *Going to the Territory* (1986), and the more comprehensive posthumous volume, *The Collected Essays of R. E.* (1995). Some find these essays to be more polished and sophisticated than E.'s short fiction, collected in *Flying Home and Other Stories* (1996). Although the collection contains numerous signs of E.'s stylistic brilliance and social incisiveness, as a group the essays are eloquent works that seamlessly combine autobiographical details with critical insights. They not only comment extensively on E.'s influences and on the themes and structures in *Invisible Man,* but also comprise an extended argument for an integrated view of American culture based on an understanding of its art, music, literature, and history, which reveals the folly, paradox, and pain involved in trying to sort black from white. This viewpoint has opened E. to some criticism, especially during the late 1960s and early 1970s, when black separatism was at its peak of militancy. Nevertheless, E. has continued to be a cogent and, in some ways, prophetic cultural critic.

BIBLIOGRAPHY: Benston, K. W., ed., *Speaking for You* (1987); Bishop, J., *R. E.* (1988); Bloom, H., ed., *R. E.* (1986); Gates, H. L., Jr., and K. A. Appiah, eds., *R. E.: Critical Perspectives Past & Present* (1994); Hersey, J., ed., *R. E.* (1974); List, R. N., *Dedalus in Harlem* (1982); Nadel, A., *Invisible Criticism* (1988); O'Meally, R. G., *The Craft of R. E.* (1980)

ALAN NADEL

EMERSON, Ralph Waldo
b. 25 May 1803, Boston, Massachusetts; d. 27 April 1882, Concord, Massachusetts

When Matthew Arnold visited Boston in December 1883 to lecture Americans on the true merits of their most highly regarded sage, E., he presumably had little notion of the flap his objective and well-reasoned assessment of E.'s work would cause. Arnold insisted on comparing E.'s poetry and philosophy to the lofty standards of Milton and Plato, and as Arnold saw it, in that company E.'s thought and writing seemed to pale. What Arnold and many other critics have missed in the century since the first dispassionate estimates of E.'s worth are the special circumstances of American culture that are indispensable to any consideration of E.'s value and his significant contribution as the intellectual midwife of American cultural identity. Principally through his essays and lectures, E. gave clear expression to what had up to his time been vague yearnings and partially submerged American themes. E.'s writings served to inspire and anger and, above all, to liberate a specifically American consciousness and perspective so that its potential might be realized.

E.'s family circumstances shaped what he would become. He was a patrician by birth, heir to a family tradition of religious and public service. His grandfather stood with the Minutemen at Concord in 1775, and his father, William, held the prestigious pulpit of Boston's First Church (Unitarian) and was a founding member of the Anthology Society, a precursor of the Boston Athenaeum. But when William Emerson died in 1811, the family was left in poverty. It depended to a great extent on the charity of friends, and E. received financial help to attend Harvard, where he did little to distinguish himself as a scholar. The experience at Harvard was, however, important to E. in other ways. Formally, he did excel in the rhetoric classes of Edward Tyrrel Channing, and he did demonstrate an affinity for Socratic philosophy, winning a Bowdoin Prize for an essay on Socrates in 1821, but he showed little interest in the empirical philosophies of John Locke and the Scottish Common-Sense philosophers, then the heart of the Harvard curriculum and the conceptual base of Unitarian theology. Instead, he seemed most interested in European romantic literature and the sacred writings of India. That he did not do well with empirical philosophy boded ill for the course he would soon pursue. In part to fulfill family expectations, E., after graduating from Harvard in 1821 and serving a stint as a school teacher, entered the Harvard Divinity School in 1825. A mysterious malady of the eyes that had dogged him through his undergraduate days flared up and forced him to withdraw. He returned to the Divinity School in 1828 and despite continued ill health was finally ordained in 1829 during a period of radical change in his life. He accepted the post of junior pastor of Boston's Second Church, and he married the daughter of a wealthy Boston merchant, Ellen Tucker. However, things began to sour quickly. E., while an eloquent pulpit orator, was not gifted with the interpersonal skills that the duties of pastoral care required, and Ellen, tubercular and in frail health from the beginning of her relationship with E., declined rapidly. Her death in 1831 began another transitional phase in E.'s life that saw him resign his pastorate in 1832 and immediately set out for Europe.

The decade from E.'s graduation from Harvard to his return from Europe was one of increasing maturity and intellectual growth. He continued his study of European romantic literature, preached a theology that was quickly identified with the liberal wing of the Unitarian Church under the leadership of William Ellery CHANNING, read in manuscript the treatises of Sampson Reed, who was interpreting the thought of the Swedish mystic, Emanuel Swedenborg, for an American audience, and became acquainted with the philosophy of Samuel Taylor Coleridge, whose *Aids to Reflection* was published in this country in 1829. These disparate influences merged in the crucible of E.'s intellect with an abiding interest in British literary periodicals and the political, social, and economic turmoil of Jacksonian America. This volatile mix was only stirred by his 1832–33 trip to Europe, a journey that allowed him to test his own growing sense of self against the acknowledged great minds of his age, notably Walter Savage Landor, William Wordsworth, Coleridge, and, perhaps most important, Thomas Carlyle, whose *Sartor Resartus,* which E. was responsible for publishing in America, served as a sort of blueprint for E.'s continuing intellectual growth and literary aspirations. It is in the shipboard journal entries on E.'s return from Europe in 1833 that one begins to sense the self-direction and power that would be made concrete in his great essays and lectures of the late 1830s.

One also senses in the events that followed E.'s return from Europe a new assertiveness over the circumstances of life. In 1834, he delivered in Boston the first of the series of lectures that would sustain him intellectually and financially for the rest of his life. In 1835, he married Lydia Jackson of Plymouth,

bought a house and established himself as a country squire in his ancestral village of Concord, Massachusetts, and he published his first literary work, the *Historical Discourse,* which he delivered at the bicentennial celebration of the founding of Concord. In 1836, he helped establish a discussion group of disaffected Unitarian ministers that came to be known as the Transcendental Club. But for E. (and perhaps for American culture in general), the most momentous event of 1836 was the publication of his slim book *Nature.*

The prevailing critical approach to E. for nearly a half-century has been to see his work within a teleology or pattern that represents his writing and thinking of the late 1830s and early 1840s as inherently powerful and confident because it manifests an unquestioned faith in mankind's unlimited potential and the inevitability of realizing that potential. As this theory would have it, in the mid-1840s, perhaps as a result of the deaths of his first wife, two gifted younger brothers, and his young son Waldo, E. entered a period of skepticism that eventually became, in the 1850s. a spiritual acquiescence to the circumstances and natural forces that control individuals and leave them powerless. Thus proponents of this approach argue that E.'s thought and career prefigure the intellectual movement of the 19th c. in general, beginning with the idealism and romanticism that had emerged in response to 18th-c. empiricism and rationalism and moving toward a deterministic naturalism, which was itself a response to the scientific and industrial revolutions of the early 19th c. But the problem with such reductive thinking is that it transforms the complexity of E. to a formula and robs his writing of its greatest value as an expression of the ineffable human response to the dynamism, surprise, and awe of life itself.

There is no better representative of this value among all of E.'s work than *Nature* (1836), which is a distillation of his intellectual growth during the preceding decade. As such, it narrates the evolution of a new type of consciousness that ran counter to Lockean empiricism in its advocacy of the inherent power of intuitive knowledge and its optimistic statement of the essential dignity of all human life. E.'s style was gnomic and his structural principle essentially that of the sermon with its formal introduction of themes, quasi-rational development of central ideas, and passionate conclusion or peroration. But E. managed to achieve an important variation of this basic structural principle by suggesting through his organization the aspiration that is the heart of his message in *Nature.* Thus, through his organization, which treats the uses of nature sequentially from its lowest use as a commodity, an objective thing to be molded by mankind for its own benefit, to its highest use as a repository of the same universal spirit that is the essence of both nature and man, E. argues implicitly for the ultimate value of human integration with nature, suggests the evolutionary character of mankind's relationship with the natural world, and notes the implication of that relationship on human growth toward spirit. Man may be "a god in ruins," as E's Orphic Poet says in the "Prospects" section of *Nature,* but the natural world, as a revelation of the same omnipotent force that resides in man, holds the key for man's eventual recognition of and reconciliation with that spirit, a reconciliation that will ultimately empower mankind to realize its fullest potential.

Fundamental to this realization is the method of seeing and knowing nature that E. delineates. In the "Idealism" section of *Nature,* he elaborates on the importance of seeing familiar things in new ways. "Turn the eyes upside down, by looking through your legs," he counsels, "and how agreeable is the picture, though you have seen it any time these twenty years." This simple action that creates a different perception of the physical world is analogous to apprehension through the faculty that E. denotes, following Coleridge, as "Reason." This intuitive faculty has nothing to do with rationality, which is more properly the function of the empirical faculty of Understanding. "Reason" can enable one to see beyond the surfaces of material forms in the natural world and to pierce to the flowing reality of the spirit that underlies all things—an experience that E. dramatizes in the famous "Transparent Eyeball" passage of *Nature,* describing himself as pure spirit without material form and as "part or parcel" of God through whom "the currents of the Universal Being circulate." We might, then, see Emersonian "Reason" as the means through which an individual's integration with nature may be accomplished. As such it is also the means through which humans can most fully realize themselves and their individual potentials to create the world they live in from the source of the universal spirit they share with nature. "Every spirit builds itself a house, and beyond its house a world, and beyond its world a heaven," E. proclaims in his stirring conclusion. "Know then that the world exists for you. For you is the phenomenon perfect."

Nature has been accurately described as E.'s cosmology, his theory of the way in which the universe works, and his next two important publications build upon that theory and carry it into areas of more immediate concern to E. and his contemporaries. On the surface, *An Oration, Delivered before the Phi Beta Kappa Society, at Cambridge* (1837), popularly known as "The American Scholar," is a call for American cultural independence quite in keeping with the expected theme of such graduation addresses. But the main thrust of E.'s argument is his theory of the

scholar, a concept at least in part occasioned by the socioeconomic turmoil of the spring of 1837. The scholar as E. sees him (and himself) exists within a society but is intellectually apart from it because he is singularly attuned to the universal, intuitive truth of Reason. Because of this source of inspiration, E. argues that all of the duties of the scholar can be reduced to just one—"self-trust"; that is, the scholar, influenced by nature, the past, and action (or more properly interaction with the world outside himself) will gain access to universal truth through the intuitive faculty of Reason. This intuition, an epiphany of the essence of both self and otherness, must be trusted because it will invariably lead the scholar to intellectual and moral positions counter to those held by society in general, which functions merely on the level of Understanding. In its elaboration of the idea of self-reliance as social doctrine, "The American Scholar" is a key document that informs other works by E., including the address on "Education" that he delivered at the opening of the Greene Street School in Providence in June 1837; the address delivered at Dartmouth College in July 1838, "Literary Ethics"; the seminal essay "Self-Reliance," and E.'s theory of biography, which he developed in an 1835 lecture series and ultimately used as the basis for *Representative Men* (1850).

The concept of self-reliance, this time as it impinges upon religion, is also the topic of *An Address Delivered before the Senior Class in Divinity College, Cambridge* (1838). Convinced that the religion of his fathers had become what he characterized as "corpse-cold Unitarianism" because of its reliance on 18th-c. rationalism and Lockean psychology, E. took his call for an intuition-based reform to Unitarianism's inner sanctum—the Divinity School at Harvard. There, during a period of intensified political and religious oppression in Boston, E. called for a religion that is at "one with the blowing clover and the falling rain"; that is, a religion based upon individual revelation of an innate divinity—E. called it "the infinitude of man"—rather than a formal system of belief tied to prophets and institutions. This so-called "Divinity School Address" earned E. the scorn of the Unitarian establishment and Brahmin Boston. For a time in the fall of 1838, he doubted whether people would pay to hear him lecture, and he sank into a depression, no doubt brought on by public ostracism of him and his ideas.

But this experience presumably helped E. to realize that his destiny lay not so much in the ministry as in a sort of secular priesthood akin to that he articulated in "The American Scholar" and that he would restate even more forcefully in the mid-1840s in "The Poet." Even though he continued to supply Unitarian pulpits into the early 1840s, he began to identify his future more and more as that of philosopher and poet rather than minister. Some of this change might be attributed to new friendships with other intellectuals such as Amos Bronson ALCOTT, Margaret FULLER, or Henry David THOREAU, all of which were formed in the mid-1830s; or to the wide-ranging discussions of the Transcendental Club; or even to his association with the *Dial,* the transcendentalist periodical that he helped found in 1841 and which he edited in 1843–1844. Whatever the immediate reason for change, however, the fruits of it are apparent in a lecture schedule that increased dramatically in the late 1830s and began to include venues outside New England by 1842–43. Yet another and more lasting effect of E.'s change was the publication of two series of essays: *Essays* (1841) and *Essays: Second Series* (1844).

Both of these collections spring from the same source—the journals in which E. recorded the ideas that were subsequently melded into lectures and then refined into published essays. *Essays* is structured by pairing complementary or contrasting topics, suggesting E.'s fondness for interpreting experience as dualism. Thus, in the first series of essays, for instance, we are presented with "Love" and "Friendship" and "Prudence" and "Heroism." Certainly, the most famous essay from the first collection is "Self-Reliance," a rhapsodic, self-motivational monologue that has, in the 20th c., come to epitomize all of E.'s thinking. But despite that essay's drawing together of many of the themes of E.'s thought in the late 1830s, and especially his emphasis on a fierce individualism, it means more when read with the essay that precedes it in the collection—"History"—a theoretical exercise in which E. obliterates the notion of chronological history and invests the power of the historical process in the present moment through the individual. Other essays in this first collection, notably "Compensation," "The Over-Soul," and the enigmatic "Circles," support the individualistic message of the first two essays and flesh out the principal aspects of E.'s philosophical agenda. *Essays: Second Series,* on the other hand, is a more eclectic collection that contains E.'s great essays, "The Poet," a literary manifesto that rivals "The American Scholar" in its powerful call for a poet who can sing the greatness of America, and "Experience," an essay in part motivated by the death of E.'s young son, Waldo, in 1842, that suggests a pragmatic tempering of the idealism so characteristic of E.'s thought in the 1830s.

E.'s first-known composition at the age of ten was a poem entitled "Fortus," and his interest in poetry never flagged. After the publication of *Essays: Second Series* in 1844, he turned his attention to a collection of poetry and the result was *Poems,* published in late

1846. Despite his pronouncement in the essay "The Poet" that poetry "is not metres, but a metre-making argument," meaning that the form of a poem should develop organically from its theme, E.'s unmusical ear and the ineradicable influence of neoclassical poetics make his poetry problematic. Unlike Walt WHITMAN, who early in his career called E. his "Master," E. was never able to free himself from an understanding of poetry that was incapable of containing his vision. Yet, E.'s best poetry from *Poems* and the 1867 collection, *May-Day and Other Pieces,* is distinguished by the same freshness of language and power of vision and expression that is the hallmark of his prose.

By the time of the publication of *Poems,* E. had developed an international reputation and, at the invitation of a young journalist, Alexander Ireland, in Manchester, England, he set off in late 1847 on an extended lecture tour of England. This second visit to Europe during the crucial year of 1848, which witnessed the Chartist demonstrations in England and revolutions in Italy and France, was a key experience in E.'s self-definition. After being lionized by the British, meeting Dickens, Tennyson, and other British literary lions on more or less equal footing, and being feted with honorary memberships to several London clubs, E.'s outlook on the world underwent a significant change, and he returned to America more pragmatic and, ironically, more materialistic than when he left. The literary fruit of his second European sojourn was realized in *Representative Men,* a collection of biographical essays based on lectures delivered in England and focusing on an idea that E. had been toying with since his biographical lecture series of 1835; that is, the notion that important historical personages transcend their physical existence by coming to embody the principal ideas of their ages. Thus, Plato *represents* the philosophical worldview of the classical world, Montaigne the skepticism of the late renaissance, and Napoleon the materialism of the 19th c. The other product of E.'s stay in England was *English Traits* (1856), a work intended to show that America was heir to the glories of English culture, which E. thought had reached its apogee in the work of Sir Francis Bacon. But it is difficult not to recognize in *English Traits* E.'s often grudging admiration for the pragmatism, traditions, and earthiness of the English. Perhaps the most neglected of all of E.'s works, *English Traits* deserves more attention as a key text in understanding the origins and implications of the pragmatic shift of E.'s thought in the 1850s.

The work that has traditionally been used to note that shift is the collection of essays E. published in late 1860, *The Conduct of Life.* The essays in this volume were developed from lectures first delivered by E. in 1851–52, but the restrained and often dour tone of essays such as "Fate" and "Illusions" seems much more suitable to the late 1850s, capturing as they do a sense of a nation about to make war upon itself. Perhaps even more pertinent is the implicit constriction of E.'s optimism in *The Conduct of Life,* an implication that some have linked to the growing influence of science upon culture, and particularly to the theories of Charles Darwin, whose *Origin of Species* also appeared in 1859. Others view that constriction as E.'s "acquiescence" to the pervasive control of natural law over human life and the more or less logical outcome of the tempering of E.'s early optimism that began in the 1840s.

However we wish to view the phenomenon of *The Conduct of Life,* it was the last major publication of E.'s career. It is as though the only proper response to his realization that man is not so much a god in ruins as a Prometheus bound was silence, and so the work of the next twenty years became for E. an opportunity not for blazing new intellectual trails but for revisiting paths he had marked much earlier in his career. Thus *Society and Solitude* (1870) lacks the intellectual vigor of earlier collections, as does *Letters and Social Aims* (1876), despite its fine opening essay, "Poetry and Imagination," which some have seen as a theoretical blueprint for E.'s anthology of poetry, *Parnassus* (1875). The posthumously published *Lectures and Biographical Sketches* (1884), *Miscellanies* (1884), and *The Natural History of Intellect* (1893) are all composed of early fugitive pieces collected by his son, Edward Waldo Emerson, or his literary executor, James Elliot Cabot.

As the beginning of E.'s career as an author was marked by a trip to Europe, so is its end. In 1872, E.'s Concord home burned. Funds for its rebuilding were collected by friends and well-wishers, and E. was whisked away on a trip to Europe with his daughter, Ellen. However, the shock of the house burning was too much for E. who, from that moment on, suffered from an increasingly severe loss of memory. When he died peacefully of pneumonia in Concord on April 27, 1882, his passing was mourned by the entire country, and he was eulogized in countless newspapers, as in the *Springfield Republican,* as "the most spiritual of American poets and all poets born in the 19th c."

BIBLIOGRAPHY: Allen, G. W., *W. E.* (1981); Bishop, J., *E. on the Soul* (1964); Buell, L., *Literary Transcendentalism* (1973); Buell, L., *New England Literary Culture* (1986); Burkholder, R. E., and J. Myerson, *E.: An Annotated Secondary Bibliography* (1985); Lewis, W. B., *The American Adam* (1955); Matthiessen, F. O., *American Renaissance* (1941); Myerson, J., *R. W. E.: A Descriptive Bibliography* (1982); Packer, B. L., *E.'s Fall* (1982); Porte, J., *E. in His Journals* (1982); Porte, J., *Representative Man* (1979); Rusk, R. L., *The Life of R. W. E.* (1941); Slater, J., *The Correspondence of E. and Carlyle* (1964); Whicher, S. E., *Freedom and Fate* (1953)

ROBERT E. BURKHOLDER

ENGLE, Paul [Hamilton]

b. 12 October 1908, Cedar Rapids, Iowa; d. 22 March 1991, Chicago, Illinois

Perhaps because he attempted generally to be a popular rather than a literary writer, as many of his titles attest, E. was never a celebrated poet; nevertheless, he played a major part in the postmodernist world of poetry, for his workshops at the University of Iowa provided the archetype for nearly every creative writing program in the U.S. The writers who passed through his hands academically, either as graduate students or faculty, include nearly everyone of consequence in American literature during the latter half of the 20th c..

E. attended Coe College in his home town where he studied for the Methodist ministry and preached in a local church, but it became apparent to him that he had no calling; therefore, he instead took an M.A. from the University of Iowa in 1932. In that same year, he published what may have been the first creative thesis ever submitted anywhere for a graduate degree, *Worn Earth,* which appeared as a volume in the prestigious Yale Series of Younger Poets. Leaving his native state at last, he did graduate work at Columbia University and subsequently traveled to England, where he studied at Oxford University on a Rhodes Scholarship and took another set of degrees.

Returning to the University of Iowa in 1937 as a faculty member, E. at last discovered his destiny, for he eventually became director of the Writers' Workshop, and under his leadership it became world famous as a training ground for young writers. He never abandoned writing for teaching, however, and over the decades he published many collections of poems, including *American Song* (1934), *Break the Heart's Anger* (1936), *Corn* (1939), *New Englanders* (1940), *West of Midnight* (1941), *American Child* (1945), *The World of Love* (1951), *Book and Child* (1956), *Poems in Praise* (1959), *Christmas Poems* (1962), *A Woman Unashamed and Other Poems* (1965), *Embrace: Selected Love Poems* (1969), and *Images of China: Poems Written in China, April-June 1980* (1981). His tribute, *To Praise a Poet: Robert Frost,* appeared in 1982.

Although literarily E. wished to be known as a writer of poetry, he did not limit himself to that genre. He was the author of two scripts—both productions with music by Philip Bezanson. The first was *For the Iowa Dead* (1956); the second, *Golden Child,* was televised in 1960 and published as a novel in 1962. His first novel was *Always the Land* (1941). Other books were *A Prairie Christmas* (1960); a children's book, *Who's Afraid?* (1963); *An Old-Fashioned Christmas* (1964); *Portrait of Iowa* (1974, with photographs by John Zielinski); and *Women in the American Revolution* (1976).

E. was the editor of many other books as well, including *Midland: Twenty-Five Years of the Iowa Writers' Workshop* (1961), which he prepared with Henri Coulette and Donald JUSTICE, both his former students, *Poet's Choice* (1962), with Joseph Langland, also a Workshop graduate, *On Creative Writing* (1964), *Midland 2* (1970), and *The World Comes to Iowa: The Iowa International Anthology,* with two collaborators including Hualing Nieh Engle, his second wife. This latter collection was the showcase for another of E.'s major academic projects, the Translation Workshop of the University of Iowa, in the directorship of which he collaborated with Hualing Nieh Engle.

Although E. and his workshops were accused by critics of many things, including "turning out" too many faceless replicas of the typical "Iowa Workshop hack," he stood stolidly in the line of fire to take the hits, a good many of them of the sour grapeshot variety, for E. did not "turn out" writers. Rather, what he did was to encourage talented young people to attend Iowa. In this encouragement, he was a good deal more than merely successful.

BIBLIOGRAPHY: Ward, R., "The Poetry of P. E.: A Voice of the Midwest," *Midamerica* 16 (1989): 94–102; Wilson, J., "P. E.," in Quartermain, P., ed., *DLB,* vol. 48, *American Poets, 1880–1945* (1986): 159–66

LEWIS PUTNAM TURCO

EPIC, The

That nearly every generation of American writers, from the Revolution to the present, has produced at least an attempt at an epic is unsurprising given that the subjects of the major epics of Western literature—war, adventurous voyage or spiritual journey, the creation of a culture or a consciousness—are seminal themes and recurring historical features of the American enterprise. The attempts themselves have been epic: in their struggle with and within literary movement after literary movement—TRANSCENDENTALISM, NATURALISM, impressionism, IMAGISM, MODERNISM, postmodernism—seemingly inimical to epic expression; in their effort to negotiate the cross-currents and vortices of

American self-representation; in the fury of their righteousness, polemical and promotional. If William Wordsworth and James Joyce transformed the epic into a modern genre, the catastrophic innovations and redefinitions that bred and bore that transformation follow a similar passage to—indeed, many follow from—the shifts of sensibility and discontinuities of culture that drive and derive from what has proved over two centuries to be the fundamental nature of the American character, its genius for reinventing itself.

The question that reiterates across the history of the genre in American letters is, "Is a failed epic still an epic?" Joel BARLOW's *The Columbiad* has been the measure of "epic failure" for American poets since its first publication as *The Vision of Columbus* in 1787, a mere six years after the surrender at Yorktown. The poem's federalist principles and international idealism were soon and summarily dismissed as outdated by a generation of poets whose equally self-conscious epics in praise of "manifest destiny" were soon outdated in turn. Modern critics are friendlier to Barlow's politics, but they universally dismiss his poetry. His heroic couplets fall flat and bare his ambition before his real but limited talent.

With Barlow, the imitative method of writing an epic sunk into disrepute, clearing the way for modern forms. If Milton was no longer the model, America's populist ethos could adopt a more popular, contemporary shape. The 18th-c. English novel had declared itself epic, at least parodically so with Henry Fielding's *Tom Jones,* and the unprecedented popularity of Walter Scott's historical novels made the progression to prose inevitable. James Fenimore COOPER's Leather-Stocking tales, five novels published between 1823 and 1841 featuring the heroic adventures of Natty Bumppo from youth to death, have, taken together—as posterity grants Homer to have gathered the orated tales of his heroes—the scope and landscape of epic. Always at the frontier, where the ambivalence between warrior culture and civilization is fiercest, Cooper's tales of the crises and cost of geo-/ethno-political expansion express the American character in, and as, continuous change—except in two critical literary aspects, the character of the hero and narrative form. Bound by romance convention, Bumppo/Leather-Stocking/Hawkeye/Pathfinder/Deerslayer changes name more than mind and is stalwart to a novelistic fault, failing to demonstrate Cooper's epic theme in his foursquare heroism, as the plots of the tales ultimately fix to a formula no less imitative than that which inspired to the point of inhibiting Barlow.

The two major contenders for the title of "*the* American epic" were published in the 1850's: Herman MELVILLE's *Moby-Dick* and Walt WHITMAN's *Leaves of Grass.* Both, however, challenge the general conception of an epic as a sacred text, essentially, or at least referentially, scriptural. While Puritan influences are readily found in each, the novel explores and the poetry expounds a new, modern covenant—of the ego. Melville's bardic voice, adopted from Shakespeare, is fundamentally different from Whitman's, defining the difference in their perspectives, dramatic and ecstatic, but both locate the sacerdotal in the bardic. Encyclopedic, they express the culture; experimental, they extend it. If neither embraces their culture's conventions of the sacred, it is because those conventions no longer imbue the culture. The theocratic character of the original colonies, proclaimed in Cotton MATHER's ecclesiastical epic, *Magnalia Christi Americana,* was no longer available to Melville and Whitman. The closest they could come was the profoundly philosophical, the authentically poetic, the capital "R" Romantic.

The intriguing mystery that troubles any study of the American epic is why the next generation did not produce one. Two of the momentous, "epic" events of the nation's history, the Civil War and the settling of the West, offered unparalleled opportunities to the literary imagination. Literary historical accident can be cited, as the novel gained greater prominence just as the novelistic sensibility "moved" toward realism. Epic themes and features can be found in numerous works from *Huckleberry Finn* to *The Red Badge of Courage,* but the form became progressively naturalistic and impressionistic. Not until the 20th c., in such "sprawling" novels as Margaret MITCHELL's *Gone with the Wind* and Larry MCMURTRY's *Lonesome Dove,* both Pulitzer Prize-winners, do novelists afford epic scope to the war and the expansion west. But these works are more romances, bourgeois reimaginings of the bygone, bringing to mind Lew WALLACE, who fought in the Civil War and who wrote, while territorial governor of New Mexico, the historical romance, *Ben Hur,* to which "epic" can be applied only as an adjective.

Not that naturalism could not accommodate the epic. Frank NORRIS's turn-of-the-century novels *The Octopus* and *The Pit* comprise two-thirds of a projected trilogy called "Epic of the Wheat" that was left unfinished at his death. The war rendered here, that shaped the culture of the country for next century and spurred its spiritual journeys, is the class war. Three decades later, John DOS PASSOS would write his trilogy of novels, *U.S.A.,* in which he experiments with a multiform novel in an effort to create a panorama. The friction of the parts—short fictional narratives of "average" Americans contrasted with short biographies of VIPs, swatches of popular culture contrasted to interludes of poetic stream-of consciousness—creates a dissonance that defines the culture of the first third of the century. But Dos Passos's political pessimism, even if its purpose is to inspire social

protest, defeats epic design, since it cannot express the dominant character of the nation, and demonstrates the dissociation of the sacred from epic form in modern fiction. Is nature the modern epic muse? Is social justice?

American poets of the 20th c. proved aggressive in their attitudes and approaches to the epic. From T. S. ELIOT's *The Waste Land* and *Four Quartets* to James MERRILL's *The Changing Light at Sandover,* many of the finest examples of the modern long poem are written by Americans. And for most critics that's what they are, "long poems," not epics. Ezra POUND's *Cantos,* Hart CRANE's *The Bridge,* William Carlos WILLIAMS's *Paterson,* John BERRYMAN's *Dream Songs,* Allen GINSBERG's *Howl*—all have epic aspirations, and while all innovate, all imitate Whitman, to their diminishment. Where Whitman was confident the bardic could achieve the sacerdotal, as in ancient cultures—*Leaves of Grass* proclaiming itself to be the "great psalm of the republic"—modern poets are insistent that the bardic substitute for the sacerdotal, a difference that can wither epic at the root. At times, instead of speaking for America, they lecture to it; in giving themselves full voice, they verbalize their alienation, not as the doubt of a quester, but as the judgment of a warrior king. This puts them in the role of Achilles, not Homer, and undoes the democratic ethos they profess. The frustrations of speaking to the spiritual in a materialistic culture leads them to speak *for* the spiritual *against* the culture, or to speak in dreams, or through a Ouija board. Yet the benefit of following Whitman is clear in the considerable achievements of these poets, in their epic assumption that a single voice can fill a vision, in their sense of working in an epic tradition. Working in a different tradition, Stephen Vincent BENÉT had different problems when he took as his poetic project the Civil War. *John Brown's Body* peoples the conflict with historical and fictional characters that do not serve a vision but must add up to one; critics consider this effort, too, a "long poem." At his death he had begun an epic of westward expansion, but *Western Star* got him only to the shores of the first colonies.

"Epic drama" is an interesting idea, in that the provenance of epic is oral storytelling and the modern form most amenable to epic may be the cinema. The drama of Eugene O'NEILL gives evidence of epic intention, pushing plays out of shape—the nine acts of *Strange Interlude,* the trilogy *Mourning Becomes Electra,* the plan for an eleven-play sequence following a family from colonial times to the present—to reach to the core of the American character, in barrooms and barnyards, in the aftermath of the Civil War, in the immigrant experience. O'Neill did not have many followers in an epic American theater, but

Angels in America by Tony KUSHNER reaches high and low across class, east and west across the continent, from night to night through two plays to tell its millennial tale. From D. W. Griffith's *Birth of a Nation* to Orson Welles's *Citizen Kane* to the television miniseries of Alex HALEY's *Roots,* American cinema has ever had epic pretensions, and a case can be made for the visual language of film being so efficient a medium for narrative that it can spread to express a story writ large, like an epic, without compromising the story or the form. The film industry, though, will always compromise the aesthetic to the economic, and film history is principally the study of the application of technology to the presentation of romances, illustrated by *Gone with the Wind.* When William Cody, Buffalo Bill, helped invent "the show business" by translating his authentic frontier experience into melodrama, he set the historical stage for Hollywood and may have ruined the form for epic expression. Though melodramatic romance is the characteristic fictional form of the sentimental capitalist ethos of America as a European imperial culture in its rhetorically inevitable progress from colony to empire, the romance, by the middle of the 19th c., had become formally reductionist, its sensibility, even if it were epic, reduced to a sentiment.

The strategy of the "local epic," focusing on a family across generations, the long life of a significant individual, and/or the history of a specific locality, fits the novel well. Over several books, as with William FAULKNER's Yoknapatawpha County, or in one big one, as in Ross LOCKRIDGE, Jr.'s *Raintree County,* the novel and epic develop a metonymic relation, as if there were two imaginations at work, the novelistic in relief against the suggestion of a longer history and tangle of relationships beyond itself, the epic operating within the bound text, reminding the reader of/with its novel's spine. The metonymy unmakes the epic, though, in a way in which it does not unmake the novel: a novel may, by a tour de force, assume epic proportion and significance; an epic reimagined as a novel loses dimension. The regional nature of the narrative has less to do with the question of epic size than its genre distinction. Similarly, the question of location has less to do with whether an epic is "American" than does the question of character. Take the works of Thomas PYNCHON, for example. Is *Mason and Dixon* more "American" than *V.?* Technically, Charles Mason and Jeremiah Dixon were Englishmen, but the geography they defined has an American character, like Gettysburg or the Great Plains. There are plenty of Americans in *V.,* but the novel's Europeans, Levantines, and Afrikaners are imagined just as finely, Manhattan is no more central to the story than Malta, and the reader is left nationalizing the novel according to the author's nationality. For that matter, what is

American in *Moby-Dick?* Does the multicultural crew represent an immigrant-rich America, or the world? Does it matter that the setting is the sea, and that the climactic confrontation occurs in the ocean off the East Indies? Is the nationality of the controlling characters—Ahab, the mates, the narrator—determinate? How do we recognize the national character of an imagination?

The principal problems in redefining the epic for modernity—the translation between and transvaluation of the traditional and original, the imitative and innovative, the spiritual and secular, the heroic and existential—at once drive and undermine American epic literature. William Wordsworth's *Prelude* could still draw on English and European traditions as it revolutionized them, placing the poet's consciousness in the hero's role, making his spiritual-psychological struggle the narrative structure. James Joyce made a metonymy of the epic and mock-epic, besides the novel, so his theme would resonate with each oscillation between genres, but the culture he gave expression to in *Ulysses* was among the most tradition-bound of its time. The politics and demographics of American history, its wars of expansion and self-definition, insured that by the time any epic had expressed American culture, the culture had changed, the change accelerating with the invention and distribution of new technologies, especially information technology, in the development and exploitation of which America was, and is, preeminent.

There are American epics outside this history: for example, the Navaho tale of the Twin Warriors, a central myth in one of the major Native American cultures, and central to Joseph Campbell's study of comparative mythology. The journey and adventures of these twin gods of war is heroic and holy, traditional and oral; their tale is in every classical respect epic. And there are American epics unwritten, or unrecognized: consider *The Declaration of Independence.* Beginning with an invocation of Nature and Necessity, the great 18th-c. gods of the Enlightenment, the document proceeds to a catalogue of oppressions perpetrated by the British Crown, "a history of repeated injuries and usuprations," on land and sea, employing armies, foreign mercenaries, and Indians, tyrannies imposed upon a heroic "People" resolved to oppose "with manly firmness" these "invasions," an opposition that must end, as the declaration does, with freedom for the colonies and the creation of "the UNITED STATES OF AMERICA." The narrative of the America's founding—its re-imagining of itself as a nation—is there in outline, declaring the character of the new nation's political culture in principle for perpetuity. Thomas JEFFERSON could, with the "General Congress Assembled," frame their action in heroic, epic terms, because they were pledged—"our Lives, our Fortunes and our sacred Honor"—to act out the epic. Like the development of the individual psyche and its trials of survival in the culture of urban materialism, America itself is a modern epic project.

BIBLIOGRAPHY: Dickie, M., *On the Modernist Long Poem* (1986); Fiedler, L. A., *The Inadvertent Epic* (1979); McWilliams, J. P., *The American Epic* (1989); Safer, E., *Contemporary American Comic Epic* (1988); Walker, J., *Bardic Ethos and American Epic* (1989)

DENNIS PAOLI

EQUIANO, Olaudah

b. ca. 1745, Essaka, Nigeria; d. 31 April 1797, England

Known as Gustavus Vassa, E. was the author of the first African American slave narrative about America, a document contributing firsthand documentation for the growing abolitionist movement. While *A Narrative of the Uncommon Suffering and Surprising Deliverance of Briton Hammon, a Negro Man* appeared in Boston in 1760 and *A Narrative of the Lord's Wonderful Dealings with John Marrant* in 1785 (its continuation as a journal was published in 1790), they stress captivity narrative or religious conversion rather than slavery. *The Interesting Narrative of Olaudah Equiano of Gustavus Vassa, The African, Written by Himself* (London, 1789) was published eight times between 1789 and 1794. Related are his birth in eastern Nigeria, his abduction by slave-runners at eleven, his purchase first by British naval Lt. Michael H. Pascal and service in the Seven Years' War, then by James Doran, a sea captain, and by Robert King, a Quaker, to whom he owed his education. King reneged on his promise to free E., who was finally able to acquire sufficient money from various menial employments to buy his freedom. He migrated to England, where, after a stint in the West Indies, he studied further, and as assistant to Dr. Charles Irving, made trips to the Arctic, to Turkey, and to other Mediterranean lands. He returned to Philadelphia in 1785, married Susanna Cullen of Ely in 1792, and worked to suppress the slave trade until his death.

The authorship of the *Narrative* has been questioned in the past, apparently because of prejudicial attitudes that such an informed, cultured, and well composed work would not be possible from an African American. The work is presented in a "novel" form, within a frame: chapter 1 sets forth a popular view of the African American and levels of slavedom, concluding with the still pertinent questions, "When they come among Europeans, they are ignorant of their language, religion, manners, and customs. Are any pains taken to teach them these? Are they treated as men? Does not slavery itself depress the mind, and extinguish all its fire and every notable sentiment?" Chapter 12 begins, "Such were the various scenes which I was a witness to, and the fortune I experienced until the year 1777. Since that period, my life has been more uniform, and the incidents of it fewer, than in any other equal number of years preceding; I therefore hasten to the conclusion of a narrative which I fear the reader may think already sufficiently tedious," and ends, after quotation of various documents, with an adaptation of *Paradise Lost* (12.561–73), Adam's conclusion which will develop the "Paradise Within": "After all, what makes any event important, unless by its observation we become better and wiser, and learn 'to do justly, to love mercy, and to walk humbly before God'?" The *Narrative,* seeking the relief of his suffering countrymen, is presented as a dialectic between acts of prejudice and the means to be free. Like most novels of the 18th c., the account frequently quotes others' poetry as well as the author's religious musings, "Miscellaneous Verses," in chapter 10, in tetrameter quatrains with couplet rhyme. The significance of quotation may be seen in chapter 5, which ends by adapting *Paradise Lost* (2.332–40) as answer to his questions, "Why do you use those instruments of torture? Are they fit to be applied by one rational being to another? And are ye not struck with shame and mortification, to see the partakers of your nature reduced so low? . . . Are you not hourly in dread of an insurrection?" The quotation details Satan and his cohorts' justification of their revolt against God, and we see E. thus employing a motif which emerges in various poems of the period, Satan/colonists against God/the English, and in various romantic views from William Godwin's *Political Justice* onward.

The effects of the Great Awakening upon E. (he had heard George Whitefield in Philadelphia) can be read throughout the *Narrative.* The inadequacies of the religion of the Quakers, the Roman Catholics, and the Jews, led him "to reflect deeply on [his] eternal state" and to study the Bible, and to conclude the hypocrisy of "nominal Christians": "might not an African ask you—Learned you this from your God, who says unto you, Do unto all men as you would men should do unto you?" In emotive and cadenced prose he cries out against inhumanity: "Surely, this is a new refinement in cruelty, which, while it has no advantage to atone for it, thus aggravates distress, and adds fresh horrors even to the wretchedness of slavery."

BIBLIOGRAPHY: Costanzo, A., *Surprising Narrative: O. E. and the Beginnings of Black Autobiography*

(1987); Edwards, P., ed., *The Life of O. E.* (2 vols., 1969)

JOHN T. SHAWCROSS

ERDRICH, Louise [Karen]

b. 6 July 1954, Little Falls, Minnesota

Versatile and innovative, E. has been well received and respected as an author since she began publishing in 1984. That year saw not only the publication of *Jacklight,* a collection of forty-four poems, but also of *Love Medicine,* the first of E.'s six novels and the recipient of a National Book Critics Circle Award. Since then, she has established herself as a mainstream writer of short stories and nonfiction essays as well as a poet and a novelist. A main influence on E.'s writing was Michael DORRIS, her husband and collaborator on all of her writing projects, with whom she coauthored one novel, *The Crown of Columbus* (1991), and shared the Nelson Algren Award for a work of short fiction.

E. abandons traditional realism for more innovative forms and techniques, such as multiple narration and intertextuality. *Love Medicine,* for instance, features seven speakers, all members of the Turtle Mountain Chippewa community but not necessarily Native Americans, who alternate as the narrators of fourteen linked stories in the 1984 edition and eighteen in the 1993 expanded edition. *The Beet Queen* (1986) is more segmented than *Love Medicine,* moving not only from one speaker to another, but also shifting time frames back and forth between 1932 and 1972. The novels are further complicated by the presence of an omniscient outside voice who speaks when the main characters do not and who grants us knowledge about both major and minor characters. Chronologically, *Tracks* (1988), while published after *The Beet Queen,* takes place before its predecessor and alternates between two narrators, Nanapush and Pauline, who were characters in *Love Medicine.* Lipsha Morrissey, also from *Love Medicine,* narrates ten of the twenty-seven chapters in *The Bingo Palace* (1994) and an outside narrator the remaining ones. In all of these works, however, it is the voices that E. creates that are so significant, not merely the chronology in which events are narrated. The voices serve to characterize each individual speaker and to capture the flavor of the Midwestern region in which the stories are set.

Of German American and Native American descent, E. has made her North Dakota Chippewa heritage the subject of many of her works, which explore the lifestyles of the residents of the Turtle Mountain Community. Two Native American families, the Lamartines and the Kashpaws, occur and reoccur in four of E.'s novels: *Love Medicine, The Beet Queen, Tracks,* and *The Bingo Palace,* bridging gaps and providing an intertextual frame from one novel to another. *Love Medicine,* for example, gives background information about Adelaide, a woman who deserts her children in *The Beet Queen.* Dot Adare, a central figure and a narrator in *The Beet Queen,* is only a minor figure in *Love Medicine. Tracks,* E.'s third novel, reveals that one relationship in *Love Medicine* was incestuous and tells the story of Fleur Pillager, a descendant of both the Native Americans and the white race, who is related to characters from *Love Medicine.* In *The Bingo Palace,* E. focuses on Fleur's great-grandson, Lipsha Morrissey, also a figure from her first novel. Other characters from previous works, notably Fleur Pillager, Lulu Lamartine, and Lyman Lamartine, play important roles as well. Characters such as Sister Leopolda from *Love Medicine*—who goes by the name Pauline in *Tracks*—and Lyman Lamartine reappear in a fifth novel *Tales of Burning Love* (1996). E.'s intertwining of tales through recurring characters, themes, and motifs has led critics to compare her writing techniques to those of William FAULKNER and her Turtle Mountain Community to Faulkner's Yoknapatawpha County.

E.'s works reveal the tension between the Native American people and the white race that threatens the destruction of Chippewa culture and heritage and the conflicts between family members within the Native American world. In a nonjudgmental way, she treats the Native American weakness toward the excessive consumption of alcohol and the compulsion toward gambling, addictions introduced by the white world, in addition to such topics as the thinning of the Chippewa bloodline due to intertribal and interracial marriages and relationships and the loss of native ground due to the encroachment of a nonnative society that blatantly disregards Native American culture and property. In *Tracks,* for instance, E. reveals how characters such as Fleur Pillager leave the community rather than succumb to the intrusion of the white world on the Chippewa tribe. However, E. handles the subject of the integration of the white and Native American worlds well, showing how the Chippewa tribe must mix with the white world in order to survive. *The Bingo Palace* especially demonstrates that survival means the embracing of both the old and the new worlds. There, Fleur Pillager, a strong believer in and practitioner of the old ways, drives a big white Pierce-Arrow, Marie Kashpaw resides in a senior citizen's apartment, not with one of her tribesmen, and Lipsha Morrissey uses spiritual powers to help him win an American van in a Bingo game. E. advocates that in order for the Chippewa people to survive they must gradually integrate the old ways with modernized ones.

The theme of transformation is also evident in E.'s works in the many characters who lack definite identities. Pauline in *Tracks,* a half-breed who has grown up in the Chippewa tradition, longs to be white, not a mixture of bloodlines, and thinking herself saintlike, eventually becomes a nun after her efforts to give birth to a dead child fail. Mary and Karl Adare in *The Beet Queen* struggle to find their identities after their mother abandons them, as does Lipsha Morrissey of *The Bingo Palace,* whose mother left him to drown after his birth. The characters must reestablish their connections with the past and their Native American heritage in order to find out who they really are.

One means of achieving this transformation is through storytelling. E.'s novels are as much about telling stories as they are composed of stories themselves. In *Love Medicine,* Albertine Johnson and Lipsha Morrissey seek out stories about their heritage, their ancestry, while searching for their identities. Nanapush in *Tracks,* who believes stories have the power to heal, tells stories to Lulu, not only to reunite her with her estranged mother, Fleur, but also to reconcile the Chippewa family unit and give it a future, the dissolution of family being another of E.'s themes. In *Tales of Burning Love,* four women, all of whom have at some point have been married to the same man, Jack Mauser, rely on the healing power of storytelling to save them when they are trapped together in a blizzard. The stories of burning love that Eleanor, Candice, Marlis, and Dot tell save them emotionally as well as physically. It is clear that for E. storytelling involves a spiritual dimension, one that grants individual characters survival, a traditional culture, and hopefully a future.

BIBLIOGRAPHY: Bonetti, K., "An Interview with L. E. and Michael Dorris," *MissR* 11 (1988): 79–99; Chavkin, A., and N. F. Chavkin, eds., *Conversations with L. E. and Michael Dorris* (1994); Rainwater, C., "Reading Between Worlds: Narrativity in the Fiction of L. E.," *AL* 62 (September 1990): 405–22; Van Dyke, A., "Questions of the Spirit: Bloodlines in L. E.'s Chippewa Landscape," *SAIL* 4 (Spring 1992): 15–27

CATHERINE CALLOWAY

ERSKINE, John
b. 5 October 1879, New York City; d. 2 June 1951, New York City

E. was a best-selling fiction writer, poet, playwright, and musician, but it was as an educator that he most influenced American literature. He studied literature at Columbia University, where he earned his B.A., M.A., and Ph.D., and where he taught for much of his university career, which also includes teaching at Amherst, and, from 1928 to 1937, serving as president of the Julliard School of Music.

E. enjoyed early success as a poet; his poem, "Actaeon," won a *Century* magazine poetry contest judged by the renowned editor Richard Watson Gilder in 1901. As a scholar, E. remains admired for salvaging the lectures of Lafcadio HEARN, the American author who taught at the University of Tokyo; although Hearn's notes were destroyed, E. carefully collected and published the lectures from student notes.

The Private Life of Helen of Troy (1925) is written in the form of a humorous dialogue between Helen, who has returned home from her adventures in Troy, and her daughter Hermione, who is shocked by her mother and who leads a more conventional, conservative life in Sparta. Not only did critics receive the modern allegory warmly, but it was the best selling book of 1926. Although E. would write more novels in this form, including *Galahad: Enough of His Life to Explain His Reputation* (1926), *Adam and Eve: Though He Knew Better* (1927), and *Penelope's Man: The Homing Instinct* (1928), they were not nearly as successful by popular and critical standards. Among his later novels are *Unfinished Business* (1930), which follows Richard Ormer as he dies and returns to the world to complete all his ambitions, both noble and base, and *The Brief Hour of François Villion* (1937), the first of three historical novels.

As an educator, E. countered the university trend toward specialized education by championing the "Great Books" curriculum for universities, known as "General Honors" at Columbia, where students read seventy-five works over four semesters. Although the majority of authors declared "great" were European, E. also promoted the development of American literary traditions, especially through his coeditorship of *Great American Writers* (1912) and the landmark *The Cambridge History of American Literature* (3 vols., 1917–21). His approach to prescribing and reading the great books of Western literature—at once dogmatic and subjective—also influenced popular self-education movements, which E. reached through speaking on lecture tours, and writing magazine articles and books such as *The Moral Obligation to be Intelligent* (1915). In *The Delight of Great Books* (1928), he explains, "The method I should advise in reading great books is a simple one. I should try, first of all, not to be awed by their greatness. Then I should read without any other preparation than life has given me—I should open the pages and find out how much they mean to me." As evidenced by best-selling books such as E. D. Hirsch's *Dictionary of Cultural Literacy* (1988) and Allan Bloom's *Closing of the American*

Mind (1987), his approach continues to spark debate about what is now known as the literary canon.

BIBLIOGRAPHY: Graff, G., *Professing Literature* (1987); Rubin, J. S., *The Making of Middlebrow Culture* (1992)

                                                    MONIQUE DUFOUR

ESSAY, The

Though the essay has been a popular form of writing in British and American periodicals since the 18th c., until recently its status in the literary canon has been, at best, uncertain. Relegated to the composition class, frequently dismissed as mere journalism, and generally ignored as an object for serious academic study, the essay has sat, in James THURBER's phrase, "on the edge of the chair of Literature." In recent years, however, prompted by both a renewed interest in rhetoric and by poststructuralist redefinitions of literature itself, the essay—as well as such related forms of "literary nonfiction" as biography, autobiography, and travel and nature writing—has begun to attract increasing critical attention and respect.

Since Montaigne adopted the term in 1571 to describe his "attempts" at self-portrayal, essay has served to designate works of remarkable diversity. In its broadest sense, essay may denote virtually any short piece of nonfiction: a newspaper editorial, a critical article, even an excerpt from a book-length study. However, a literary definition of the term is generally more exclusive, insistent on a rough distinction between articles, which are read primarily for the information they contain, and essays, in which the pleasures of reading take precedence over the reception of opinion or fact. Equally problematic are conventional divisions of the essay into formal and informal, impersonal and familiar, expository and conversational. Though imprecise and potentially contradictory, such labels not only serve as a form of critical shorthand but also point to what is often the most powerful organizing force in the essay: the rhetorical voice or projected character of the essayist.

The essay as written in the U.S. has followed forms established by the essay in England, though with increasingly distinctive differences in tone, content, and language. In Benjamin FRANKLIN's "Silence Dogood Papers," the conventions of Joseph Addison and Richard Steele are modified by the native idiom and distinctive point of view of Franklin's eidolon or fictional persona, Widow Dogood. Lewis Leary's characterization of Franklin as "the ventriloquist writer" might in fact be applied just as accurately to any number of American essayists. Washington IRVING, for example,

though variously imitative of Addison, Jonathan Swift, and Oliver Goldsmith, forged a number of original eidolons in his graceful essays: Jonathan Oldstyle in the *Salmagundi Papers,* Diedrick Knickerbocker in the parodic *History of New York,* and Geoffroy Crayon, Gent. in *The Sketch Book.*

Even Ralph Waldo EMERSON, though commonly perceived as speaking in the singular voice of the sage, is adroit in creating alternative personae in his formal essays on morals and philosophy, notably in *Essays: First Series* and *Second Series.* Contemporary novelist and essayist William H. GASS identifies seven different voices in Emerson's essays, each one indicative of the "constructing posture of the self-defining self." Likewise, in *On the Duty of Civil Disobedience* and the philosophical essays of *Walden,* Henry David THOREAU also tries on various experimental selves. And Oliver Wendall HOLMES's best-known work, *The Autocrat at the Breakfast Table,* consists of a series of witty personal essays cast in the form of breakfast conversations at a boarding house. American authors have been adept practiners of the artful confidence game of the essay.

Of all these impostors and impersonators, none is more protean than Samuel Langhorn CLEMENS. Although critics as well as biographers have explored at length the gap between the private Clemens and the showman Mark Twain, no single Twain persona can be pinned down in his works. From the comic travel essays gathered in *The Innocents Abroad* to his fanciful autobiographical writings and pessimistic late essays, collected in *Mark Twain on the Damned Human Race,* Clemens experiments with a gallery of poses, shifting masks as he shifts levels of discourse with such ease and frequency that the reader is not always aware of the transformations.

Unfortunately, the power of the rhetorical voice in Clemens's essays was rarely found in the writings of his less disruptive contemporaries. By the end of the 19th c., the genteel familiar essay was a staple of popular literary magazines such as *Harper's, Scribner's,* and the *Atlantic Monthly.* The slightness of this polite form is confirmed by the absence of any significant critical studies of even the most popular and prolific genteel essayists of this era: Agnes Repplier, Logan Pearsall Smith, and Simeon Strunsky. Soon, however, this "little bit of sentiment or observation," as Repplier characterized her chosen form, was reshaped by decidedly ungenteel forces in the world at large.

The modernist era, that period of fragmentation and innovation at the beginning of the 20th c., is best known to students of literature for the radical transformations that occurred in poetry and fiction. But the essay, too, experienced dramatic changes during this time. Divested of its self-conscious literariness and reinvested with the colloquial vigor of popular journalism, the essay was reborn in such cosmopolitan magazines as the *Smart Set,* the *American Mercury,* and the *New Yorker.* This "new" brand of essay—exuberant, witty, and often contentious—was in fact more faithful to the journalistic traditions of Addison and Steele, Lamb, and Hazlitt than the often preciously lambent writings of those who had deliberately mimicked the English essayists. Recognizing the power of a combative narrative voice to attract readers' attention and impose on a journal a distinctive style, magazine editors recruited writers with forceful rhetorical presences. In the popular press, this movement was represented by the "yellow journalism" of publishers such as William Randolph Hearst. In periodicals with a more literary orientation, the uprising against the "genteel tradition" was led by journalist-critics such as Edgar SALTUS in *The Anatomy of Negation,* James Gibbons Huneker in *Promenades of an Impressionist* (1911), and—most famously—H. L. MENCKEN. These professional iconoclasts challenged the "Puritanism" of the cultural establishment by promoting in their essays foreign ideas (symbolism, impressionism, anarchism) in a highly impassioned style.

Following Mencken's fall from favor early in the 1930s, new essayistic voices came to be heard in American journalism, many of them in the pages of the *New Yorker* magazine. In the writings of Robert BENCHLEY, Christopher MORLEY, S. J. PERELMAN, James Thurber, and, most eloquently, E. B. WHITE, the satiric scorn of Mencken gave way to comic perplexity, and hyperbolic claims to preeminence were superseded by rhetorical gestures of conciliation.

A survey of American essayists following World War II would have to consider an exceptionally diverse group of writers. Alongside the humorists at the *New Yorker* were such notable literary journalists as A. J. Liebling, John HERSEY, and Lillian Ross. In addition, a number of novelists of the postwar period enhanced their reputations through works of nonfiction: James BALDWIN in *Notes of a Native Son,* Truman CAPOTE in *Local Color,* John UPDIKE in *Assorted Prose,* and *Hugging the Shore: Essays and Criticism,* and Gore VIDAL in *Homage to Daniel Shays* among them. But the most forceful and disruptive influence on the evolution of the essay came by way of those young feature writers in the early 1960s who were tagged, presumptuously, as the "New Journalists."

The foremost advocate and practitioner of the New Journalism, Tom WOLFE, laid claim to participating in the invention of a new art form: a species of journalism that incorporates such literary devices as symbolism, dialogue, interior meditations, shifting points of view, detailed descriptions of setting, and—frequently—

though not always—a narrator who functions as a character in the "story." Yet the writings of Wolfe, Jimmy Breslin in *The World According to Breslin* (1984), Joan DIDION in *Slouching toward Bethlehem,* and *The White Album,* Norman MAILER in *Advertisements for Myself,* and other "New Journalists"—remarkable as they are—represent not a new art form but merely the latest evolutionary turn on this malleable genre.

Though the novelty of the New Journalism has passed, the essay—revitalized and endlessly reshaped—remains a popular and powerful literary form. Far more important than the problem of definition or taxonomy is the fact that the essay now serves as the primary literary genre for so many talented American writers, among them Edward ABBEY, Russell Baker, Wendell BERRY, Annie DILLARD, Gerald Early, Joseph Epstein, Ian Frazier, Paul Fussell, Ellen Goodman, Stephen Jay Gould, Lawrence Otis Graham, Bob Greene, Edward HOAGLAND, Sue Hubbell, Maxine KUMIN, John MCPHEE, and Richard Selzer.

BIBLIOGRAPHY: Bier, J., *The Rise and Fall of American Humor* (1968); Fishkin, S. F., *From Fact to Fiction* (1985); Gass, W., *Habitations of the Word* (1985); Good, G., *The Observing Self* (1988); Lopate, P., *The Art of the Personal Essay* (1994); Rubin, L., *The Comic Imagination in American Literature* (1973); Wilson, C. P., *The Labor of Words* (1985); Wolfe, T., and E. W. Johnson, *The New Journalism* (1973)

RICHARD NORDQUIST

EVANS, Augusta Jane [Wilson]
b. 8 May 1835, Columbus, Georgia; d. 9 May 1909, Mobile, Alabama

To E. belongs the double distinction of having written the most popular book of the Confederacy, *Macaria* (1863), and of being the first Southern author to sell a million copies of a book, *St. Elmo* (1866). Her fiction was enormously popular, widely and for the most part favorably reviewed, and it earned international fame. She was also a journalist. When the Alabama Hall of Fame opened in 1953, E. was one of two women and nine men on the initial roll of honor. Yet in the mid-20th c. all of her work was out of print and ignored by critics. It is tempting to compare her with Harriet Beecher STOWE: both had strong opinions and won widespread acclaim, and their interests overlapped. Yet Stowe continued to be acknowledged while E. did not. Perhaps the reason is easy: E. wrote for the losing side. She was an ardent Confederate. Moreover, she declined to consider herself in competition with Stowe, to join the throng of Southern ladies who wrote novels in direct rebuttal of *Uncle Tom's Cabin*. Probably her reason was simply disdain. Her aspiration ran higher than pulp fiction, and she considered politics—or so she said—outside a woman's sphere. All of her major novels were reissued in 1992, and recent criticism has attempted to decide whether she can or cannot be deemed a feminist.

E.'s education was private; she was tutored by her mother and then turned loose in libraries wherever the family went. She read extensively and appears to have remembered every single word; her writing is excruciatingly esoteric and allusive, with a curious mixture of ideas. Belonging to the plantation aristocracy of Georgia and Alabama, she firmly believed in a social hierarchy, including slavery and the domestic role of women. On the other hand, her heroines decry the injustice of unequal pay for working women and insist on women's right to full education. E.'s themes are religion, woman's place, and the noble Confederate cause. *Beulah* (1859), which established E. as a writer at age nineteen, draws on *Jane Eyre* in plot, but focuses on the heroine's religious crisis and redemption. *Macaria, or Altars of Sacrifice* (1863) is aimed towards teaching women their duty during war; its heroines Irene and Electra are the Rosie the Riveter of the Confederacy. *Macaria* was smuggled through the lines by blockade runners and became so popular that at least one northern commander banned it among his troops and burned it as enemy propaganda. But it achieved its purpose; it was influential in mobilizing Southern women. E. herself helped establish a hospital and worked in an orphanage in Mobile.

St. Elmo, one of the most widely read books of the 19th c., sold a million copies within four months and went through at least eight editions. It became the center of a cultural fad that lasted into the 20th c.; two movies were made from the book. It is a passionate love story, the central conflict being the clash of ideals and intellect between the would-be lovers: Edna Earl, the heroine, must tame her Byronic suitor St. Elmo Murray before she can collapse into his arms. The novel constitutes a soap box for Edna; one scene will do for an example. Edna, a governess, is invited to dine with the family and their guests. She is politely asked for her opinion of something, and, "Despite her efforts to control it, embarrassment unstrung her nerves, and threw a quiver into her voice as she answered"—with a three page diatribe into which the other guests are allowed to interject only three brief questions. After that, she is called out of the dining room, but leaves on a triumphant note: before she sweeps away, she recites twelve lines of an obscure poem praising the self-effacing woman. For a modern reader, the irony becomes comic, but it is entirely unintentional. E. apparently never acknowledged any inconsistency between her own words and deeds and those of her heroines. She remained unmarried until she had a secure income from her work, continued to publish into old age, and all of her life insisted that a woman should keep to her own, that is, domestic and private, sphere.

BIBLIOGRAPHY: Baym, N., *Woman's Fiction* (1978); Fidler, W. P., *A. E. W., 1835–1909: A Biography* (1951); Harris, S. K., *Nineteenth-Century American Women's Novels* (1990); Kelley, M., *Private Woman, Public Stage* (1984)

CECELIA LAMPP LINTON

EVANS, Donald

b. 24 July 1884, Philadelphia, Pennsylvania; d. 26 May 1921, New York City

E. was a modernist poet best known for his *Sonnets from the Patagonian* (1913) that introduced a new voice into American poetry, successfully combining the mannered aestheticism of the British 1890s with the literary innovations of Gertrude STEIN. E.'s Claire Marie Press published Stein's *Tender Buttons* in 1914. His urbane "Patagonian" persona was able to express intensely felt and delicately nuanced emotions while maintaining an ironic distance by means of a self-consciously idiosyncratic style.

E. is now remembered chiefly as an important influence on his friend Wallace STEVENS. His sonnet "En Monocle" inspired Stevens's "Le Monocle de Mon Oncle," and his spirit pervades Stevens's *Harmonium* (1923). Evans also influenced the young E. E. CUMMINGS and the older William Carlos WILLIAMS who emulated E.'s cosmopolitan, sophisticated voice in parts of *Paterson*. E.'s talent was admired by other poets as diverse as Edwin Arlington ROBINSON, Amy LOWELL, and Ezra POUND.

His other books of poetry are *Discords* (1912), *Two Deaths in the Bronx* (1916), *Nine Poems from a Valetudinarium* (1916), and *Ironica* (1919). He died by suicide.

BIBLIOGRAPHY: Fields, K., "Past Masters: Walter Conrad Arensberg and D. E.," *SoR* 6 (April 1970): 317–39; MacLeod, G., *Wallace Stevens and Company* (1983)

GLEN MACLEOD

EVERSON, William [Oliver]

b. 10 September 1912, Sacramento, California; d. 3 June 1994, Santa Cruz, California

Throughout a prolific literary career spanning almost fifty years, E. achieved a reputation as a central figure in West Coast regional literature, the San Francisco Renaissance, and religious, erotic, and nature poetry. His ongoing concern with the relationships among violence, sexuality, and religion often led to frustration and radical life changes in his search for value and certainty, but it also fueled his dramatic literary career.

Highly influenced by Robinson JEFFERS's poetry while attending Fresno State College, E. dropped out to write poetry and "commune with nature" on a farm in the San Joaquin Valley. In 1946, he went to San Francisco to join the poets surrounding Kenneth REX-ROTH and five years later joined the Dominican order as a lay monk taking the name Brother Antoninus. Popularly known as the "Beat friar," E. spent eighteen years in the order before renouncing his vows at a poetry reading and returning to secular life.

A thoroughly autobiographical poet, E.'s work reflected his evolving personal history. The poetry volumes written prior to his conversion to Catholicism, including *These Are the Ravens* (1935), *The Masculine Dead: Poems, 1938–1940* (1942), and *The Residual Years: Poems, 1940–1941* (1944), are now collected as *The Residual Years: Poems, 1934–1948* (1968). The early poems reflect Jeffers's portrayal of nature's violent indifference to human suffering, but E.'s voice emerges in his search for the "face of God" in the Western landscape and in his exploration of his personal relationship to the violence in nature. As Rexroth announced in 1947, the autobiographical element of E.'s poetry "may outrage academic circles." But while some critics objected to E.'s personalism, obscure syntax, and fondness for obsolete words, most lauded his sincerity, forceful language, and "compulsive cadence."

The poetry written under the name Brother Antoninus, including his three most important works, *The Crooked Lines of God: Poems, 1949–1954* (1959), *The Hazards of Holiness: Poems, 1957–1960* (1962), and *The Rose of Solitude* (1967), are now collected as *The Veritable Years, 1949–1966* (1978). In the collections, he attempted to transcend his obsession with natural violence and sexuality by interfusing religious and erotic imagery. Using Donne-like mannerisms and Christian mystical verse, he drew a storm of criticism for self-righteous emotional, rhetorical, and theological excesses. But Rexroth again came to his defense, claiming that he was the finest contemporary Catholic poet and that his poetry even superseded that of his master, Jeffers.

In the erotic poem E. read before leaving the monastery, "Tendril in the Mesh," he wrestled with his own sexuality and reconsiders his relationship with nature. This poem, as well as others in the volume *Man-Fate: The Swan-Song of Brother Antoninus* (1974), concern his motivations for leaving the order and the emo-

tional, psychological, and spiritual readjustments he faced as he began his new life. They also display E.'s achievements in verse techniques, including a long, quieter line and rhymed iambic verse. His postmonastic works were intended to be included in a final volume of his life trilogy called *The Integral Years,* a title revealing his hope for a final synthesis of his natural and religious impulses.

BIBLIOGRAPHY: Bartlett, L., ed., *Benchmark & Blaze: The Emergence of W. E.* (1979); Kherdian, D., *Six Poets of the San Francisco Renaissance* (1967); Meltzer, D., *The San Francisco Poets* (1971)

LINDA COX

EXLEY, Frederick
b. 28 March 1929, Watertown, New York; d. 17 June 1992, Alexandria Bay, New York

E.'s literary output amounts to only three novels: *A Fan's Notes* (1968), *Pages from a Cold Island* (1975), and *Last Notes from Home* (1988), and a handful of magazine articles that might fill a small volume. His claim as an important American writer rests mainly—some would say solely—on *A Fan's Notes.* This novel, which E. called a "fictional memoir," is the first in a trilogy of works that combine a personal confession mode with a satire on American culture. In a uniquely personal voice, E. fashions a persona of himself as a failed romantic rebel searching for an unattainable ideal amid the shallow materialism and hypocrisy of contemporary American life. This book was a critical success when it appeared and has become an offbeat American classic, with a devoted readership especially among college students. As such, it stands alongside American rebel classics like J. D. SALINGER's *Catcher in the Rye* and Joseph HELLER's *Catch-22.* E. derives all his work, both novels and magazine articles, from his own pain-racked personal life. He uses the metaphor of "the fan" to contrast the failures of his own life with the achievements of people he admired for their "toughness," their courage, strength, and discipline in confronting life. A former athlete, reduced to being a spectator on the sidelines, E.'s only recourse is to live the life of a fan, living through the vicarious admiration of others.

In *A Fan's Notes,* E. depicts "that long malaise, my life," the agonizing story of a romantic idealist who fails at everything. After graduation from the University of Southern California in 1953, he drifted unsuccessfully for a period of fifteen years through a number of jobs. His two marriages ended in divorce and estrangement from his children. All the while, he developed a serious affinity for alcohol, which he admitted eroded his talent. He has become "a fatuous lunatic" associating with other outsiders and outcasts, an alcoholic sponging off his friends in bars and ending his nights in drunken brawls or in strangers' beds. Then, beginning in 1958, he made several stays in mental hospitals. Despite this tale of personal grief, this strangely powerful book is told in such a unique personal style and with such honesty and lack of self pity that the reader is compelled to E.'s side. Both heartbreaking and funny, *A Fan's Notes* blends rage with critical insight, a narrative of human degradation with outrageous humor and sensitive intelligence, and raunchy sex with spiritual longing.

A Fan's Notes embodies the personal vision and themes that run through all his work. It depicts the E. persona's attraction/repulsion in confronting the American dream. He is a sensitive idealist carrying his burden of grief and searching for authentic human connection and love. But fitting society's expectations, for him, inevitably means conformity to America's notion of success. He would like to believe that America fails him, and not the reverse.

Each of his succeeding novels, *Pages from a Cold Island* and *Last Notes from Home,* was anticipated eagerly by E. fans and critics alike. But neither lived up to the promise of *A Fan's Notes,* to which they were inevitably compared. Both books continue in the combined personal memoir-satirical mode with E. in the role of a fan. In *Pages from a Cold Island,* E. profiles several figures who dominated the American cultural landscape of the 1960s: Edmund WILSON, Gloria Steinem, and Norman MAILER. At the center of *Last Notes from Home* is E.'s homage to his dead brother, Colonel William Exley.

Most critics consider *A Fan's Notes* E.'s only clear success. Others, though, value in all his work a sustained and cogent assessment of American life, a stylistic originality, and a courage of self revelation and passion for life that mark him as a significant American writer.

BIBLIOGRAPHY: Adams, M., "F. E.," in Rood, K. L., et al., eds., *DLB Yearbook 1981* (1982): 195–201; Cantwell, M., "The Hungriest Writer: One Fan's Notes on F. E.," *NYT* 13 September 1992: 30–31; Deegan, T., "F. E.," in Giles, J. R., and W. H. Giles, eds., *DLB,* vol. 143, *American Novelists since World War II* (1994): 24–32; Yardley, J., *Misfit: The Strange Life of F. E.* (1997)

THOMAS DEEGAN

EXPATRIATES

Contemporary use of the term "expatriate" in literature usually refers to a person who voluntary withdraws from his or her native country or renounces his or her national allegiance. In the late 18th c., "expatriate" referred to someone driven or banished from his or her native land, and the term is still occasionally used interchangeably with "exile," although the latter now generally refers to this permanent, political condition. Whether the long series of American writers living and writing in foreign lands were exiles or expatriates, they nevertheless formed a distinctive literary tradition characterized by intensely individualistic artists who discover the nature of their Americanism from the perspective of another country.

Expatriation has been an issue in American writing precisely because Americans themselves were expatriates from Europe, bringing European culture with them only to rebel against it. In the earliest phase of American literary history, revolt against Europe was part of American culture, and literature reflected a nationalistic need for a transformed political and intellectual climate. Many American writers were drawn to Europe primarily for radical, revolutionary political reasons, and only secondarily for literary concerns: Gilbert IM-LAY's *The Emigrants* and Joel BARLOW's *The Vision of Columbus* as well as his mock-heroic poem "The Hasty Pudding" were early expatriate works reflecting this revolutionary spirit while targeting a specifically American audience.

In addition to political fervor, the culture of revolution was producing, in Europe and at home, a sense of artistic alienation and separatism, which was often translated into actual expatriation and a quest for cultural enrichment. After the War of 1812, new transatlantic connections enabled writers to study and tour Europe for longer periods, both as social and political critics and as romantic travelers. Washington IRVING, a prototypical romantic traveler, made his Grand Tour from 1804 to 1806 and later returned for a seventeen-year expatriation. His *Sketch Book* reveals his search for the picturesque—ruins, ancient customs, "storied associations"—in the European landscape and his transposition of these elements onto the ostensibly commonplace, unwritten landscapes of America.

While Irving developed a witty and urbane international style through his romantic travels, many intellectuals in the first half of the 19th c. left for Europe struggling with the mounting tension between the vision of equality as a democratic community and the growing ideology that equality meant the potential for individual advancement. How to define a national heritage from these conflicting ideas of the individual and society was a concern for American writers like James Fenimore COOPER, who spent time in Europe and began to see disturbing similarities between European aristocratic privilege and American capitalistic freedom to surpass—and even to own—one's neighbor. Cooper lived in Europe from 1826 to 1833, during the sweeping changes of the Jackson administration, originally intending to proclaim the American democratic message at the expense of European aristocracy. But his novels written during his expatriation instead expose the distances between worthy American democratic principles and their exploitive, aristocratic applications. In particular, *The Bravo, The Heidenmauer,* and *The Headsman,* while satirizing European feudalism, also reveal similarities between European aristocracy and an American government ruled by the interests of private economic groups, the exclusiveness of Jackson's hereditary bureaucracy, the corruption of spiritual institutions, and the insidious naturalization of poverty and slavery. Cooper's increasingly hostile criticisms of American life during and after his expatriation were greeted by an equally hostile press and public who misunderstood the depths of his patriotism during his long European stay.

In addition to the political unrest of the 1830s, the financial panic of 1837 also heralded a period of economic crisis in America comparable to the Great Depression of the 1930s, driving some writers to Europe. In 1839, Herman MELVILLE, after failing to find stable employment, went to Liverpool as a common seaman at age twenty and returned disillusioned by England's exploitive labor system. While disavowing the European feudal tradition that could produce such oppressive conditions, he later recognized similar conditions in the lives of Irish refugees driven by poverty to New York. This experience, as well as his wide exposure to people his society labeled "savages," led him to reexamine American cultural assumptions about the superiority of white Christian civilization. His novel *Redburn,* which depicts a family dying of starvation beneath a New York warehouse, compares modern secular cities Liverpool and New York in an effort to crush the dangerously innocent American belief that evil is located only abroad.

Other writers found expatriation crucial to their search for the roots of American art. After extensive European travel and exploration of transcendental sources in German idealism and English romanticism, Ralph Waldo EMERSON claimed in "The American Scholar" that Americans had listened too long to "the courtly muses of Europe." While this speech did not instantly liberate American writers from their European cultural fetters, it did mark a turning point in the American literary scene, the beginning of the American Renaissance. Similarly, Nathaniel HAWTHORNE's works reveal the struggles within American literature and culture between European Gothic romance and American REALISM, PURITANISM and TRANSCENDENTALISM, and the independent imagination and the community. Hawthorne left for Liverpool in 1853 to serve

as American consul and lived in Rome among American artist expatriates from 1857 to 1860. From his European perspective, America looked like an "infernally disagreeable country," in part for its material culture and rootless spiritual community. According to Henry JAMES, Hawthorne's imagination was limited by the thinness of American culture: "It takes so many things, as Hawthorne must have felt later in life, when he made the acquaintance of the denser, richer, warmer European spectacle—it takes such an accumulation of history and custom, such a complexity of manners and types, to form a fund of suggestion for a novelist." But the Roman Catholic community and rich artistic heritage Hawthorne admired in Italy and England were ultimately at odds with his sense of American individualism. His primary work of this period, *The Marble Faun,* portrays Rome as a magnet for spiritual and artistic impulses, and explores the complex relationship between art and crime, imagination and damnation, the American transcendent individual and the insignificance of the individual in the traditional European community.

For these and other American writers of the late 18th and early 19th cs., including John NEAL, Henry Wadsworth LONGFELLOW, and N. P. WILLIS, Europe was a crucial touchstone from which to explore the meaning of American democracy, individualism, community, religion, and art, in principle and practice, while developing uniquely American literary voices. In the absence of a distinct American literary and cultural tradition, expatriation itself had been incorporated into the American literary tradition.

After the Civil War, literary expatriates arrived in Europe in unprecedented numbers for several reasons: new wealth was driving older patricians of culture to seek European venues to escape American materialism; European art and culture entered the American commodity market, supported by aesthetes and opposed by bohemians; and the steamship made European travel easier than ever. In 1867, Samuel Langhorne CLEMENS, for example, visited the Holy Land by ship as a traveling journalist with conservative members of a Plymouth church in search of self-definition and an acquaintance with their religious history. In his book about the voyage, *The Innocents Abroad: The New Pilgrim's Progress,* he exposes the cultural conditioning of the passengers in their version of Americanism as religious duty, literal-mindedness, and self-righteousness, all of which undermine the innocence of their pilgrimage for discovery. But he also recognized the powerful, reverent American will to believe in the sacredness of the experience, all the while satirizing the commodification of culture—the growing perception of foreign culture as something to be collected mentally or materially—in the burgeoning tourist industry.

Other expatriates of this period included Bret HARTE, Harold FREDERIC, Henry ADAMS, Stephen CRANE, Henry Harland, and, perhaps the most definitive American expatriate of all, Henry James. Growing increasingly detached from modern American materialism, conformism, and hostility toward leisure, James, after extensive European travel in his childhood and youth, returned to Europe for good in 1875. His European novels between 1875 and 1881 confronted the conformist and commercial pressures existing in America, a country that ironically prided itself on individual freedoms and spiritual community. While James is often considered a defender of traditional and gracious European forms of aristocracy, his novels also demonstrate the tragic consequences of forcing European conventions upon the American spirit. He felt that American capitalists' capture of aristocratic privilege without its anchoring traditions produced an exclusive society hostile to more admirable American values such as democratic individualism and moral strength. James's move to London in 1876 increased the complexity and quantity of his art, and in this traditional yet cosmopolitan city he developed his "international" theme, a moral quest for experience using Americans in European settings to express his perceptions of American culture. *The Europeans, Daisy Miller, Washington Square,* and *The Portrait of a Lady* employ "Europe" as a vehicle for making Americans see themselves in relief. *The Portrait of a Lady* is especially rich in its development of the international moral quest: Isabel Archer moves through traditional England, socialite France, and artistic Italy before becoming trapped by the sterility of expatriate American Gilbert Osmond, part of a new, economic aristocracy. But Isabel weathers the Europeanization with an American stoicism and honor, showing that, while the complexity of a rich historical and cultural setting is required for good fiction, it is only a testing ground for the virtues truly important to Americans.

James's last three European novels, *The Wings of the Dove, The Ambassadors,* and *The Golden Bowl,* present thematically and formally a more disordered European society, the problem of the Anglo-Saxon mind alienated from sensuous experience through the pursuit of wealth and success, but occasionally reunited with art through love. This modernistic enterprise paved the way for new expatriates to experience Europe as a cultural dissent from modern American life—both for those who sought new forms through which to express their dissent and for those who sought to remake tradition from its modern rubble.

Edith WHARTON followed James's lead in seeking continuity and tradition in European society. For her, Paris, where she visited extensively and settled permanently in 1913, offered artistic and social freedom from the smothering pressures of marriage and propriety, and, like James, she sought to relate American values to European culture. Her novels set in France—*Madame de Treymes* and *The Reef*—concern American women confronting often inflexible European aristocratic traditions. *The Age of Innocence* draws on her memory of exclusive upper-middle-class New York society of the 1870s from her expatriate perspective, a portrayal of what might have become of her own life had she not escaped to a creative life in Europe.

While Wharton had many artist friends and acquaintances in Europe, her personality was too formal and her style too conservative for many of the modern artists who were swiftly changing the American literary landscape. Like James and Wharton, Ezra POUND and T. S. ELIOT came to Europe to conserve cultural tradition against the effects of capitalistic society, but both were also interested in radical experimentation with form and style. Pound lived in Venice, London, Paris, and Rapallo, Italy, for most of the years between 1908 and his death in 1972. In London, he experimented with his own poetic form in eleven volumes of poetry, including *Personae, Rispostes, Cathay,* and *Lustra.* In the process, he established IMAGISM, an ideogrammic approach to poetry and the main stylistic movement of American MODERNISM. He also promoted the careers of numerous American writers, including Eliot, Robert FROST, Hilda DOOLITTLE, and Marianne MOORE. Pound struggled through numerous posts at literary magazines between 1914 and 1919 before losing his publishing outlets and moving to Paris in 1920 in frustration, just as new group of expatriates were coming toward bohemia. In Paris, while working for *The Dial,* he continued fostering modern writers' careers, including those of James Joyce, Ernest HEMINGWAY, and E. E. CUMMINGS, while devoting more time to *The Cantos,* begun in London. But by 1923 he was fired from his job and was declining in health; he found Paris enervating and moved to Rapallo to become more involved in political and economic matters. His radical commitment to cutting edge conservative political and economic thought initiated his descent to Mussolinian fascism, his subsequent arrest for treason, and his hospitalization for insanity. In *Patria Mia,* published in 1950, he reveals that despite his years in exile, he remained an American all his life, and that it was his intense American patriotism, in fact, that drove him to Europe to save American literature from cultural decline. Pound had come to Europe to seek out and conserve European cultural achievement but ended up an innovative and influential American writer.

Eliot also went to Europe in 1910 with the conservative goal of rediscovering his Anglo-Saxon origins in a less provincial, less democratic, atmosphere than he felt America afforded. Considering himself a displaced elite in a cultural desert, he wanted to begin over on the religious and cultural ground his ancestors had walked—but also, of course, had rejected. He studied philosophy in Germany and at Oxford and wrote relatively dry poetry for the first seven years of his expatriation. Then in 1917, *Prufrock and Other Observations* was published in the *Egoist,* and in 1922, *The Waste Land* was published in the *Criterion* and, in America, *The Dial.* After a period of ill health and financial difficulty, he became a British subject in 1927 and converted to Anglo-Catholicism. But despite his anglicization, Eliot considered himself an American poet, claiming that his poetry's sources and emotional springs came from America.

While Pound and Eliot came to Europe following James's search for value in tradition, Gertrude STEIN followed his quest for experimental form. She lived in Paris from 1903 to 1946 as hostess of a famous salon, collecting modern art, drawing together creative minds, and developing her own cubist literary style in *The Making of Americans,* characterized by repetitious vignettes and abstracted character analyses. The period between World War I and World War II was her most prolific, influential period, during which she discussed literary vision and practice with Hemingway, F. Scott FITZGERALD, Sherwood ANDERSON, and other members of what she coined the Lost Generation, as well as fostering artistic dialogue between European and American artists. Stein valued French tolerance for modern artistic experimentation and was instrumental in transferring modernist principles to the American literary tradition.

The Lost Generation, the most celebrated of all American expatriates, came not as seekers of tradition or experimental form, but in search of evidence of modern disorder and decadence. Pound wrote in 1935, "The new lot of American *emigres* were anything but the Passionate Pilgrims of James's day or the enquirers of my own. *We* came to find something, to learn, possibly to conserve, but this new lot came in disgust." The favorable exchange rate and French tolerance of social freedom and artistic experimentation lured many young Americans—like Fitzgerald—disillusioned with the materialistic, narrow culture they perceived in America. After joining the army in 1917, Fitzgerald moved to Paris in the 1920s more for economic than artistic reasons—to reduce his significant debt while living in relatively high style. His great American novel, *The Great Gatsby,* written in France, concerns the decay of one of America's preeminent

cultural ideals, the Franklinian myth of material success.

Like Fitzgerald, most Lost Generation expatriates were in their twenties, and many were college graduates who had served in World War I and were deeply affected by what they saw and experienced. Among the most famous members of this group were Hemingway and Cummings. Hemingway, a reporter in Europe during World War I, returned to Paris in 1920 to escape the social narrowness of his Oak Park, Michigan, upbringing. His European novels, which deal explicitly with American expatriate subjects, project American culture as overly practical, serious, and unnatural. *The Sun Also Rises* concerns the decay and impotence of "civilization" and the internal motion toward vitality, while *A Farewell to Arms,* like expatriate and friend John DOS PASSOS's *One Man's Initiation: 1917* and *Three Soldiers* portrays the collapse of traditional American values and European culture through and after the war. *Death in the Afternoon* criticizes American culture's failure to accept death, and the loss of individual identity that follows from this failure. Always concerned with life as process and with spontaneously arising values, his novels written in Paris criticize the American social forces that attempt to petrify these processes and to abstract values such as honor and patriotism for political uses.

Cummings, like Hemingway, reveals in his fiction the destructiveness of self-righteous, authoritative culture to the individual. A Cambridge, Massachusetts, scholar, he volunteered as an ambulance driver for World War I to escape the provinciality of his social background. En route to Paris he met Slater Brown, with whom he forged a friendship based on mutual hostility toward power-driven French and American officials. Brown's openly antagonistic letters landed them in a concentration camp, which became the basis for Cummings's *The Enormous Room,* a powerful book exploring his realization that civilization is founded upon the destruction of the individual and the best qualities of human nature in order to preserve hierarchical power, and that a "painful process of Unthinking" is required to dissolve the cultural conditioning that requires us to fear death and insist upon sexual repression. The idea of the French detention camp as a metaphor for American society, as well as the metaphor of the enormous room as a celebration of being, was lost on the reading public, for whom the subject and innovative form was alien. But it contributes to the modern American expatriate tradition in its characteristic note of transcendence and optimism.

The economic and social freedoms that attracted many men to Paris in the 1920s also offered women artists a liberating, encouraging atmosphere. Natalie Barney, the most famous and daring lesbian of the era, held an international literary salon attended by international intellectuals. One of her frequent visitors, Djuna BARNES, satirized the cultural aristocracy of the sapphic salon while confronting the problem of sexual identity in *Ladies Almanack.* Other women sought freedom for artistic experimentation in Paris. Doolittle, known as the "perfect" imagist, was concerned with women's search for self-identity, and sought in Europe a synthesis of life and art despite modern fragmentation. She served as literary editor of the *Egoist,* and published *Sea Garden, Hymen,* and *Palimpsest* in Paris. Margaret Anderson, an ardent defender of IMAGISM, FEMINISM, and anarchism, published frequently in Jane Heap's the *Little Review.* Avant-garde poet Mina Loy, concerned with the nature of consciousness in modern industrial society, wrote *Lunar Baedecker* in Paris in 1923. And Kay BOYLE, during her prolific eighteen-year expatriation, contributed poems, short stories, and novels, frequently on the personal responsibility inherent with privilege, in Eugene Jolas's experimental *transition* magazine.

Black artists also enjoyed unprecedented artistic and social freedoms in 1920s Paris. Countee CULLEN sought in Paris the freedom to write as an American rather than a black poet, and published *The Black Christ and Other Poems* in 1929. Recalling his five months with black American expatriates in Monmartre, Langston HUGHES's *The Big Sea: An Autobiography* describes his menial jobs and dire poverty, but also celebrates the vibrant spirit of black Monmartre. Claude MCKAY spent most of 1919–24 in Europe, restless due to "color-consciousness"; he moved from Paris to Marseilles to work on *Home to Harlem* and *Banjo,* exploring his love for the rough rhythms of American life.

Throughout the decade, the bohemian subculture developed a support system of bookshops, publishers, and salons: Ford Madox Ford's *transatlantic review,* Jolas's *transition,* Pound's the *Exile,* and Harry and Caresse Crosby's Black Sun Press helped to popularize and lend structure to bohemia, as did Sylvia Beach's popular bookshop, Shakespeare and Company. The corporatizing of the bohemian scene, while providing financial and artistic support for experimental art forms, was also a sign that the Parisian movement was reaching its maturity. For many early expatriates of the 1920s, expatriation had become a decisive experience in their perception of American culture and literature. As Louis BROMFIELD argued in "Expatriate—Vintage 1927," published in *Mirrors of the Year,* living in Europe afforded a clearer perspective of America and showed that American culture was no longer in danger of being swallowed by European culture. Hence by the end of the decade, the climate was right for a mass return to America, aided further by the political uneasiness in Europe and the Wall Street Crash. Malcolm COWLEY's *Exile's Return* paints a picture of the Lost Generation's search for artistic sophistication and tradition, and their return to an America more complex and exciting because of their exile, despite the difficulties they faced assimilating to American life.

Paris of the 1930s retained an expatriate scene, but the note of American optimism present in earlier expatriate literature was giving way to a more surrealistic search for disorder. Samuel Putnam's memoir of the later generation of Paris expatriates, *Paris Was Our Mistress* (1947) argues that Hemingway's *The Sun Also Rises* divides the earlier and later groups of exiles by memorializing the spirit of those who came around 1920, many of whom had fought in the war or had seen its repercussions in America. Henry MILLER's *Tropic of Cancer,* by contrast, was representative of the decay of Parisian scene during the second wave of expatriation. Miller sought in Paris the sense of intimate spiritual community he felt as a child in his immigrant neighborhood, but which he believed modern America had lost. *Tropic of Cancer* narrates the Lost Generation's awakening to a European world of violent disintegration, attempting to cut away the cancerous cultural conditioning of order and institutions that destroy the community. Djuna Barnes's *Nightwood,* experimental in its revolt against linear plot development, also portrays the anguish of the alienated American expatriate of the 1920s and 1930s in a European culture losing its own sense of history and tradition. Anaïs NIN, intimate friend of Henry Miller, also began her literary career in Paris after the early expatriates had returned home. Her Jungian prose poem, *The House of Incest,* and her famous diaries present the imperfection and multiplicity of existence she perceived in 1930s Paris. For another 1930s expatriate, Katherine Anne PORTER, the cultural and geographical distance of her native Texas and the Mexico of her 1920s expatriation from 1930s Paris inspired a search for her roots in such stories as "Pale Horse, Pale Rider," "Noon Wine," and "Old Mortality," actually written in Pennsylvania.

World War II provided the clearest boundary to this Parisian expatriate phase. The cultural conditions that led American writers to seek history, artistic tradition, and freedom of expression in Europe no longer existed in the war-torn Europe stained by the holocaust, historical anxiety, and violence. Yet black American postwar writers still used expatriation to reject American racial myths and to reaffirm their individuality and racial heritage. Richard WRIGHT went to Paris, which he called the "city of refuge," in 1946 after publishing *Native Son,* and there gained renown as an important existentialist writer. But despite his European respectability, a trip back to New York proved racially humiliating, and he chose exile in protest of U.S. racial policy and practice. His European novels, like his previous works, are forged by social protest, but they also recognize certain distinctly American values. His first European novel, *The Outsider*, contains Emersonian themes of the need to remake the self before shaping society into an ideal conception of social justice. *Black Power*, published in 1954, poses the ideological call for the use of militarism to fight colonialism against the Whitmanesque spirit of peace and need for spiritual identity in questioning whether aggressive political aims can justify a loss of tribal spirit.

James BALDWIN also felt the divisive, degrading influences that demean the notion of Americanism, yet he wanted to escape the black community's, including Wright's, conception of literature as social protest. In Europe, he instead explored his personal, emotional history and developed his literary craftsmanship. But the deepest level of his work was social protest of another kind, focusing on individual consciousness. While recognizing French respect for artistic freedom and the refuge Paris offered Americans, he also witnessed the poor treatment of Algerians and was himself humiliated when brought to court for receiving a stolen bed sheet. *Giovanni's Room* was written after this terrifying experience, presents the American notion of sin, which denies the heart and natural impulses for the sake of social status, as itself sinful. His sense of alienation from Europe and from his African heritage led him to recognize his own uniqueness as an American. While he was considered by many members of the black community as escapist, he nonetheless considered himself fully American: "I don't consider myself an exile; I don't consider myself an expatriate. I guess I'm a sort of commuter."

The trend in postwar expatriate writing has focused less on externally defining American and individual values from the distance of another country than on internal explorations, beginning with Miller, of radical literary forms, psychological states, and narrative and philosophical mazes. A number of Beat movement bohemians following Henry Miller, including William S. BURROUGHS in Morocco, Jack KEROUAC in Paris, J. P. DONLEAVY in Dublin, and even Lawrence FERLINGHETTI in the new Left Bank, San Francisco, revolted against the conservative patricians of culture like Eliot and Pound and also against the middle-class Parisian Hemingways who allowed their financial and literary success to compromise their art and their exile. Also, postmodern expatriates like Robert COOVER in Kent and American émigré Vladimir NABOKOV are merging the notion of American and European to the extent that the notion of *patria,* and thereby expatriation, loses clear definition.

Whereas American modernist expatriates hoped to leave the narrow provinciality of their homeland and, with a romantic impulse of liberation, to totalize and transcend American life from their new perspective, the postwar global capitalist market and worldwide assimilation of American culture has changed, and perhaps even precludes the possibility of, classical American literary expatriation. American leadership and a modernized, Americanized Western world in fact has led to reverse expatriation—world artists seeking freedom and self-definition in the U.S. But regardless of its current status, expatriation has played a crucial role in defining the American literary tradition by throwing an often isolated American culture into relief and in giving artists the freedom and perspective to discover their American voices.

BIBLIOGRAPHY: Bradbury, M., *The Expatriate Tradition in American Literature* (1982); Eder, D. L., *Three Writers in Exile: Pound, Eliot and Joyce* (1984); Martin, S., *The Great Expatriate Writers* (1992); McCarthy, H. T., *The Expatriate Perspective: American Novelists and the Idea of America* (1974); Rood, K. L., ed., *DLB,* vol. 4, *American Writers in Paris, 1920–1939* (1980)

LINDA COX

F

FARRELL, James T[homas]
b. 27 February 1904, Chicago, Illinois; d. 11 August 1979, New York City

F. is perhaps the most critically neglected American writer to produce major works of fiction in the 20th c. Most of his gigantic output of novels, short stories, and criticism is out of print today and therefore seldom taught and studied. Yet his true place in modern American literature is not a small one, for F. was a pioneer in American ethnic literature and urban fiction, producing a massive series of novels and short stories that were not only exceptionally high in literary quality but also strongly influenced important writers as diverse as Richard WRIGHT, Norman MAILER, and William KENNEDY. Very few American writers knew the city as well as F. and even fewer were able to make better literary use of the city.

Like Theodore DREISER, who deeply influenced F. as a young writer, F. wrote compellingly of his own lived experiences as a person coming from what he called the "plebeian origins" of a working-class family. Like James Joyce, Marcel Proust, and Sherwood ANDERSON, writers who were equally strong influences on F. throughout his career, he centered his work in a rich sense of place and time. The core of F.'s enormous literary output—he published over fifty books during his lifetime and left a score of unpublished manuscripts at his death—is the sequence of his novels envisioning the world of working-class Irish-Catholic people living in Chicago from the early parts of the 20th c. to the middle of the Great Depression. F. handles this critically important slice of American history very differently than his contemporaries. Whereas John DOS PASSOS focused broadly on the nation in his *U.S.A.* trilogy, F. drew a much more sharply focused and intimate portrait, depicting an Irish-Catholic neighborhood on the South Side of Chicago. And whereas Wright described a nearly identical piece of Chicago

geography as a nightmarish racial ghetto, F. drew his picture of the South Side ambivalently, lovingly detailing its many beauties while also being careful to criticize its negative features, most notably its narrowness. More so than any other major American writer, F. understood the ethnic neighborhood, a community held together by a common history rooted in generally accepted religious, social, and political beliefs.

Two especially remarkable features of F.'s novels are their coherence and depth. Written over a fifty-year time span, his four cycles of novels essentially tell one basic story, becoming what F. would describe late in his career as "panels of one work." *Studs Lonigan* is a trilogy that dramatizes the life of a working-class young man who never fully understands his urban environment and therefore is victimized by its worst tendencies. *Studs Lonigan* is balanced by the O'Neill/O'Flaherty pentalogy, which centers on a young man who is from the same environment but who employs his existential consciousness and will both to utilize the best features of that environment and to transcend its liabilities. Whereas Studs Lonigan's narrative is a classic story of American failure, a downward spiral to psychic disintegration and death, Danny O'Neill's story is an archetypal success tale, an ascent from poverty and misunderstanding to the achievement of selfhood. The Bernard Carr trilogy extends O'Neill's narrative, dramatizing his development as a leftist intellectual and writer in New York. F.'s final series of novels, the *Universe of Time* sequence, returns to the Chicago setting of the earlier novels and centers on Eddie Ryan, who in most respects is an autobiographical portrait of F. as a young man.

Taken as a whole, these novels possess exceptional scope and depth. They are densely populated by a richly imagined cast of characters and are set in a fully reified urban setting. Few American realists surpass F. in his depiction of an urban world, which is at once deeply rooted in a particular cultural history and also serves as a resonant metaphor of 20th-c. American life.

Although primarily noted for his novels, F. was also an accomplished short story writer, publishing twenty-two collections of short fiction from *Calico Shoes and Other Stories* (1934) to *Judith and Other Stories* (1973). His stories are often Chekhovian in form and outlook, economically crafted, and rooted in the apparently small details of everyday life. They also may be compared to Joyce's short fiction, for they usually generate surprisingly rich moments of revelation, distilling extraordinary meanings from mundane circumstances.

F. also produced important works of cultural and literary criticism throughout his career, most notably *A Note on Literary Criticism* (1937), *The League of Frightened Philistines* (1947), *Reflections at Fifty and Other Essays* (1956), and *Literary Essays* (1976). F.'s fiercely independent mind saw critical weaknesses in leftist political theory long before other American critics drew away from Stalinism. His integrity as an artist produced throughout his career a healthy suspicion of ideologies from the left and right. It is also notable that he was one of the first American critics to hail William FAULKNER as an important writer and was also one of the first white writers to draw attention to the significance of Richard Wright's work. And his essays on Dreiser are still regarded as important studies.

Like Dos Passos, John STEINBECK, and Thomas WOLFE, who began their careers with much critical praise in the 1930s and 1940s but then were unfairly demoted in importance by later generations of critics who were often blinded by their own agendas and ideologies, F. needs to be reassessed as an artist and thinker. A balanced estimate of his work and place in American literature is long overdue.

BIBLIOGRAPHY: Branch, E. M., *J. T. F.* (1971); Fanning, C., *The Irish Voice in America from the 1760s to the 1980s* (1990); Flynn, D., ed., *On Irish Themes* (1982); Gelfant, B. H., *The American City Novel* (1954); Wald, A. M., *J. T. F.: The Revolutionary Socialist Years* (1978)

ROBERT BUTLER

FAST, Howard [Melvin]
b. 11 November 1914, New York City

F. is one of the most prolific and versatile writers of the 20th c. In a career that spans over sixty years, F. has published contemporary and historical novels, biographies, collections of stories, plays, and movie and television screenplays. His works have been translated into eighty-two languages.

A third generation American of Ukrainian descent, F. achieved success early; his first novel, *Two Valleys* (1933), was published when he was eighteen. In the next ten years, much of F.'s fiction explored America's heritage of freedom and championed the oppressed peoples in America's history: *Conceived in Liberty* (1939) depicts the hardships suffered by the soldiers at Valley Forge; *The Last Frontier* (1941) tells the moving and tragic story of a group of Cheyenne Indians on a desperate journey to reach their homeland in North Dakota. With the publication of such other accomplished works as *The Unvanquished* (1942) and *Citizen Paine* (1943) as well as several novels for adolescents—*Haym Salomon, Son of Liberty* (1941) and *The Tall Hunter* (1942)—F. established his reputation as a noteworthy author of historical novels.

In 1943, F. joined the Communist Party, and his fiction for the next thirteen years was dominated by such issues as government's abuse of power, workers' right to organize unions, racial equality, with emphasis on communism as the basis for an ideal classless society. However, as his fictional voice became increasingly political and shrill, his popularity decreased and he came under critical attack. Although *Freedom Road* (1944) was praised by W. E. B. DU BOIS and other African American leaders for its depiction of black Americans' struggle for liberation during the Reconstruction era in the South and won the Schomberg Award for Race Relations in 1944, he nonetheless found himself a pariah of the publishing world. Unable to find a publishing house willing to accept his manuscripts, he founded Blue Heron Press. In 1950, he was jailed for three months by the House Committee on Un-American Activities for refusing to divulge the names of political associates. While serving his sentence, he completed the major portion of *Sparticus,* whose depiction of the great slave revolt against the Roman empire in the first century B.C.E. created fresh controversy. However, the 1960 movie of the same title made the book a best seller. Ironically, such works as *Clarkton* (1947), *My Glorious Brothers* (1948), *The Proud and the Free* (1950), and *Sparticus* (1951) were so well received behind the Iron Curtain that F. was awarded the Stalin Peace Prize in 1954. By then, F. had become disenchanted with the Communist Party, and in 1956 he withdrew his membership and renounced all former affiliations. F.'s initial enchantment and eventual disillusionment with the Communist Party are detailed in *The Naked God: The Writer and the Communist Party* (1957).

Since the tumultuous years of the 1950s, F. has enjoyed popular, if not always critical, success. For example, *April Morning* (1961) has been standard reading for seventh and eighth graders for many years. In more recent years, F.'s name is most readily recognized as the author of the five-volume Lavette saga—*The Immigrants* (1977), *The Second Generation* (1978), *The Establishment* (1979), *The Legacy* (1980), *The Immigrant's Daughter* (1985)—which chronicles the family history of Barbara Lavette, whose French-Italian fisherman father had built a shipping empire in San Francisco around the turn of the century. F.'s most recent works—*The Dinner Party* (1987), *The Pledge* (1988), *The Confession of Joe Cullen* (1989)—explore religion, culture, and politics from a wide-ranging perspective.

Under the pseudonym Walter Ericson, F. wrote *Fallen Angel* (1951), which was adapted in 1968 as the motion picture *Jigsaw.* Since 1960, F. has also published twenty-one detective novels under the pseudonym E. V. Cunningham. Twelve of these novels have women's names for titles, and many of them feature a fictional Japanese American detective named Masao Masuto. As E. V. Cunningham, F. enjoys great popularity in Europe and won the Prix de la Policia in France. F. finds it amusing that "Critics can't stand [his] mainline books . . . [but] they love Cunningham."

BIBLIOGRAPHY: Macdonald, A., *H. F.: A Critical Companion* (1996); Meyer, H. D., *History and Conscience: The Case of H. F.* (1958); Rideout, W. B., *The Radical Novel in the United States, 1900–1954: Some Interrelations of Literature and Society* (1956)

VICTORIA H. SPANIOL

FAULKNER, William

b. 25 September 1897, New Albany, Mississippi; d. 6 July 1962, Byhalia, Mississippi

F.'s long and distinguished career rests largely on a body of related works of fiction exploring the history of the American South in mythic Yoknapatawpha County, loosely based on Lafayette County in northern Mississippi, from the first settlement by Indians and white pioneers to the present. By looking sharply at a limited locale and a specific population, he was able to extend his investigation back and forth through the events and forces of time; for him, much of the meaning of the South may be found in the battles and ultimate defeat of the Confederacy in the Civil War. Focusing on events and memories of this war, he was able to show the genuine heroism of the Southern people, from the untrained men who went off to protect their native soil to the women who remained behind to manage the plantations, while at the same time admitting that the cause of the war—slavery—was finally to spell the fall of the cherished antebellum

way of Southern life. Exploitation of the land with the cash crop of cotton and the consequent exploitation of the black race to farm it are the twin causes of the South's defeat according to Ike McCaslin; since that time, F.'s Southern aristocrats—the Sartorises, McCaslins, and Compsons—strive gallantly but vainly to recapture the spirit, pride, and position they held before the war while liberated blacks and poor whites come into greater and greater power in the modern world. For F., as for the South generally, aristocracy involves many characteristics that the initial Scots settlers had inherited from English, and especially Scottish, ancestry: authority, taste, manners, leadership, generosity, discipline. Yet each of these attributes has its negative side that can and did cause the downfall of the South as much from corruption within as from Union attacks without. How man can survive defeat and regain his sense of self-worth, how a whole civilization attempts to understand the past and regain lost self-esteem, is the burden of much of his best writing.

F.'s vision of the South was surely strengthened by his own ancestry. His great-grandfather, William C. Faulkner, the Old Colonel, rose almost mythically from rags to riches. Walking into Mississippi from Tennessee, so the story goes, he worked hard and was soon a successful businessman and then the owner and developer of a narrow-gauge railroad; recent indications are that he fostered a mulatto as well as a white line of descendants; his sudden rise and his quick temper caused him to make political, business, and even social enemies; and after an early attempt of those enemies, his rival R. J. Thurmond killed him in the streets of Ripley. F. uses the life of this colorful historic figure as an inspiration for Colonel John Sartoris in *The Unvanquished* (1938); before he was through, F. drew on all facets of family and regional history. And like F. himself, his characters cannot escape their sense of family lineage and family loyalty or their sense of a glorious past now, it would seem, irredeemably lost. History haunts F.'s characters and their memories and often directs and limits their understanding. And just as their pride in their sense of aristocracy corrupted the past, so their dwelling on the past allows a new lower class to corrupt the present with a grosser but no less central sense of greed and power. Many of F.'s protagonists, such as Young Bayard Sartoris, Quentin Compson, or Ike McCaslin, come to face the mistakes of the past or, like Horace Benbow, Gavin Stevens, and Chick Mallison, attempt to rectify present errors. The chief virtues for F. are earned pride, love of man, justice, bravery, and generosity of heart; rapacity, pride, cruelty, and cowardice are the weaknesses. His county therefore serves not only as a parable for the South generally, but for all mankind. His Nobel Prize Address in 1950, in which he urges the old verities and truths of the heart—love and honor and pity and pride and compassion and sacrifice—argues for the soul of man which, as both his glory and his challenge, can insure not only that he will endure but that he will prevail. In a way all of F.'s fiction was a prolegomenon to that vision.

Yoknapatawpha County, meaning in Chickasaw "water runs slow in flat land," is situated in northern Mississippi, bounded roughly by the Tallahatchie River on the north and the Yoknapatawpha River on the south, and bisected from north to south by John Sartoris's railroad. The land varies from low-lying, fertile, and heavily timbered river bottoms in the west (the "delta," or original bed of the Old Man, the Mississippi River) to sandy pine hills in the northeast (the more uncivilized Beat Four). Nearly at the center is Jefferson (based loosely on Oxford, Mississippi), the county seat, surrounded by gently rolling farmland. Like other towns in the region, at the center stands the courthouse with four clocks at the top facing in all four directions; at the entrance (to the south) stands a monument of a Confederate soldier, shielding his eyes and looking south—either for a lost Yankee regiment or additional allies. The buildings around the courthouse square house the main businesses, law offices, and banks as well as a jail—they are two-storeyed, with galleries and outside staircases. The courthouse lawn is a gathering place for older citizens during the week; on Saturdays, a farmer's market in the square brings in many of the people who live in the county to buy or sell their wares. The only other villages of significance are Frenchman's Bend, a hamlet at the southeastern corner of the county, and Mottstown, a slightly larger village, eighteen miles directly south. Memphis, the closest large city, is seventy-five miles northwest of Jefferson and Oxford, in F.'s fiction the location of the state university, is forty miles away. The prosperous center of town is a mile square—Compson's Mile—and just outside is the biggest plantation of one hundred square miles, Sutpen's Hundred. The county itself has 2,400 square miles with a population of about 15,000, more than half of them black.

F.'s portrayal of Yoknapatawpha and Jefferson is consistent and lucid, but it took him some time to discover it. Throughout high school and a diffident two years at college, he concentrated on writing poetry, inspired by Swinburne and A. E. Housman and supported by his friend, the slightly older Phil Stone. F. attempted to serve in World War I by joining the Royal Air Force of Canada but during his pilot training the armistice was declared: he knew frustration in life as in writing. Indeed, this sense of missed opportunity becomes a theme in his first novel, *Soldiers' Pay*, written in 1926 in New Orleans where he had gone to join the bohemian society there. In the French Quar-

ter, he found a room with the artist and architect William Spratling; he supported himself in part writing "Mirrors of Chartres Street," a column for the New Orleans *Times-Picayune* that gave him material for later characters (such as Benjy, Ike Snopes, and Red); and he gathered material for his second novel *Mosquitoes* (1927), full of artists and patrons talking self-consciously about beauty and art. But most importantly he met Sherwood ANDERSON who, during their daily meetings, gave F. encouragement, helped him publish his first novel about the costs of war, and then urged him to return to Mississippi and write about his own "little postage stamp of native soil." It was Anderson's advice that was the turning point of his career.

Flags in the Dust (1973), first published in a shortened version as *Sartoris* (1929), is an ambitious and comprehensive novel that sets out most of the characters and themes F. was to develop over his remaining thirty-three years. The novel is set immediately after World War I, when the young veteran Bayard Sartoris sneaks home, ashamed he has survived when his twin brother John was killed fulfilling the Sartoris tradition of reckless feats of heroism in wartime. In this, Young Bayard is like his namesake Old Bayard, born too young to serve in the Civil War and too old for the Spanish-American War and so doomed to live a life of vicarious glory. The Sartoris tradition is in miniature the tradition of the South itself—and so a burden that even in defeat Young Bayard cannot escape; ultimately this leads to his causing the ignominious death of Old Bayard in a car accident and his own, simulating the death of his brother when flying a dangerous test plane. Running counter to this sense of doomed glory is the sense of glorious doom that the Sartoris women, notably "Aunt" Jenny DuPré, insist gives to the South and to Southern men their essential purpose and dignity. Other young men, metaphorically twinned to Young Bayard, also fail—Horace Benbow finds no solace in substituting art for life and Byron Snopes finds no final satisfaction in voyeurism and robbery. While *Flags in the Dust* remains an important introduction to F.'s work, *The Sound and the Fury* (1929) was his own personal favorite. Surely it is his most hauntingly beautiful when read aloud. It is also, in many ways, his most experimental. Following the aesthetics of cubism, by which independent episodes are juxtaposed to create statements and simulate meanings and the impressionism fostered by streams of consciousness, *The Sound and the Fury* is told from four discrete viewpoints—that of the idiot Benjy (whose language resembles that of Gertrude STEIN), his older brothers Quentin (whose Freudian meanderings imitate the fiction of James Joyce and others) and Jason (whose crude colloquialism suggests that of characters in Sinclair LEWIS) and a final, more distanced style that attempts, from outside, to understand the black servant Dilsey. All four narrators seek to understand what it means to be a Compson by locating the significance of the family and charting its decline. Despite their vast differences in character and values, all three brothers reveal their shared obsession with sex and death and their persistent confusion of the two. The decline of the family, then, into alcoholism (Mr. Compson), hypochondria (Mrs. Compson), pettiness (Jason) and idiocy (Benjy) which, for Quentin, promotes suicide, is due partly to the genetic make-up of the family, partly to their increasing disillusion and despair. The genuine agony of learning that sexuality—living life most fully—is aligned with death—with the termination of life—provides a sense of doom that not even Dilsey's religious belief and transformation during the Easter Sunday sermon can assuage.

But this novel, one of the masterpieces of American literature, was too gloomy and too experimental to succeed at first, and, to finance himself and a new wife, F. went to work in the power plant of the University of Mississippi where his father was treasurer. There, at night, between shifts at stoking fires, he wrote in a white heat of his own, claiming to complete the first draft of *As I Lay Dying* (1930) in six weeks. Like *The Sound and the Fury,* this work centers on family, sex, and death. Unlike the previous novel, the Bundren family is unified under the pressure of burying Addie, the mother, when she dies in middle age hating and fighting the barrenness of her life and the relative poverty of her family. The plot takes the form of a funeral procession from the hamlet of Frenchman's Bend to the cemetery in Jefferson during which the family must cross a flooded river and survive a fire in which an older son attempts to rid the family of the pain and embarrassment of carrying a stinking corpse across the countryside for days. But the novel is fragmented into fifty-nine sections spoken in monologue by fifteen characters; this way of enriching his story allows F. to show the wide range of reactions to a death in the family. There are moments of grotesque comedy, such as when the youngest son cuts holes in his mother's coffin so that she can breathe; or when the single daughter, Dewey Dell, not understanding the implications of her unexpected pregnancy, invites the advances of an enterprising druggist to cure her. The ending is ironically comic, too, for while the family's unity is no longer secure without the force of the mother and the mission of her burial to hold them together, the father, Anse, manages to find a new wife, mother, and cook; he makes good his family belief that man, like nature's crops, continues cyclic life.

What followed in 1931 is F.'s most notorious novel, *Sanctuary.* This outspoken but highly serious novel examines the effect of commercialism on nature—corn fermented into whiskey and illegally sold; young girls taught the life of prostitution—by seeing the modern South as three distinct environments: the brothel district of Memphis; the natural, weed-choked old Frenchman's place; and the town of Jefferson as equivalents of hell, earth, and heaven. But this heaven, signified only by the heaven tree and spirituals sung outside a jail that holds a potential miscarriage of justice, suggests the 20th-c. wasteland, barren of love and justice. *Sanctuary* thus contends that in modern-day Yoknapatawpha there is no justice, no real hope of heaven, no sanctuary. The final scene confirms this emptiness when in Paris, the center of civilization, the hardened Temple Drake, guilty of perjury and freed by her father, a corrupt judge, sits by his side at a manmade reservoir eyeing herself and her makeup in a mirror, listless, self-absorbed.

In *Light in August,* published in 1932, Joe Christmas, whose unknown racial identity robs him of any secure place in Yoknapatawpha County, is juxtaposed to Gail Hightower, a defrocked preacher whose text is Confederate rather than biblical, and Joanna Burden, whose strong allegiance to abolition in the South has taken her past normal marriage and warped her into a frenzied, isolated spinster. The accidental meetings of these three alienated persons—set apart because they are embarrassingly different in a stratified society—result in the certain deaths of two of them and the final madness or death—it is not clear which—of the third. For F., the bigotry of Yoknapatawpha is not only painful but annihilating.

F.'s finest novel, *Absalom, Absalom!* (1936), was for him the most difficult to write and provides the greatest challenge to readers. Part of its difficulty is caused by the painful truth it attempts to skirt, to ignore, or to rationalize before confronting it directly: that in the South of F.'s fiction, miscegenation is worse than incest. This is Quentin Compson's final admission when forced to scour the depths of his knowledge of the South by his Canadian roommate at Harvard; it succeeds and is far more serious than Rosa Coldfield's accusation that Thomas Sutpen—the white man who bred interracially through ignorance and then refused to recognize his error—is a devil incarnate or Mr. Compson's implicit charge that Sutpen mocks all Southern society by achieving his swift establishment of a plantation and aristocratic stature that should by rights be preserved for those of historic breeding. Sutpen's biography serves in the novel both as an intriguing mystery to be solved—where did he come from and how did he manage to get where he did so fast?—and a steel glass, or mirror that tells someone the truth in its reflections whether they wish to see the truth or not.

It is arguable that F. found *Absalom, Absalom!* especially difficult because it reveals wounds that remained particularly painful for him. Miscegenation, perhaps in reaction to his own family heritage, was one of his gravest concerns. F. continues his exploration of Southern history and the legacy of racism in *Go Down, Moses* (1942), in which he traces this theme through four generations of the McCaslin-Beauchamp-Edmonds family. The McCaslins, one of the early families of Yoknapatawpha, bred from nearly the start a separate mulatto line, the Beauchamps, when Lucius Quintus Carothers McCaslin had a daughter by a black concubine and then fathered a son by his own daughter. The female McCaslin line, named Edmonds, refuses to recognize the Beauchamps just as the McCaslins do. Only when Ike McCaslin learns a century later about the sacrament of love from another mulatto named Sam Fathers—a hunter who is part Indian, part white, and part black—is he able to see how each human being, as much as any animal being hunted, is also sacred. His subsequent examination of the McCaslin family ledgers in their plantation commissary—diarylike entries that spell out the purchase, sale, and misuse of black slaves by his ancestors—causes him to seek reparation by paying to his black kin three times their original legacy. But these kin will not be bought off, and Ike learns that restitution—and even reparation—are impossible in a society in which humans are inhumanly treated. While he spends the remaining years in penance, his essential loneliness and his essential blindness are not proven until, years later, a fourth generation mulatto asks him for love and forgiveness and he once more tries to buy her off with a family heirloom, a revered hunting horn for which she has no possible use. His command that she leave his family and return to Chicago to wait one thousand years or more for the races to begin to intermarry suggests that he is really no different from those forebears he chose to dissociate from, and correct.

In 1938, F. published a second novel on the Sartoris family, *The Unvanquished,* which is frequently cited for the accuracy from the Confederate perspective of its fictional portrayal of a South besieged by Civil War and Reconstruction. Young Bayard—the Old Bayard of *Flags in the Dust*—is a victim of the war along with his childhood companion and servant Ringo and his Granny Millard: they watch the great Sartoris plantation house burn to the ground when Yankees invade their land and then set about to fight the war as best they can, by robbing Union troops of mules and selling them back again. But Granny becomes so angry, proud, and greedy in her exploits that she is herself exploited and killed by more experienced thieves. Bayard and

Ringo take vengeance by killing her murderer. This rough sense of justice is urged on Bayard again when, during Reconstruction, his father is killed by a business competitor, but he has learned from his earlier experience that death only engenders death and he goes to challenge his father's killer unarmed. Surprised and humiliated, his opponent flees town and Bayard achieves peace at the cost of challenging the foundation of violence on which the order of the Old South had stood. *The Unvanquished* is thus a transitional novel, moving from a mythic past to a troubled and cloudy present. Yet for F., such essential transitions of the code of true honor was the duty, and the responsibility, of the aristocracy. However problematic Bayard's final action in the novel, it is therefore not only fitting but necessary that a Sartoris be the one to make the change.

Throughout the 1930s and 1940s F. earned his living in large part by writing film scripts for Hollywood, some of which have been reprinted, *The Road to Glory, Today We Live, The Big Sleep, To Have and Have Not, Air Force, Battle Cry,* and *The DeGaulle Story,* among others. At the same time, he was thinking of the corruption of capitalism on the poorer whites of Yoknapatawpha. *Snopes* (1964) is his saga of a redneck family who rise form intimidating farmers by burning their barns to eventually running the bank in Jefferson, and who thus chart and measure the decay of the old verities revered by the aristocracy. *Snopes* is a trilogy composed of *The Hamlet* (1940), *The Town* (1957), and *The Mansion* (1959) in which Flem Snopes seizes an opportunity to take over a general store in Frenchman's Bend and, by subjecting the countryside to submission through credit accounts, earns his way through a restaurant to the Jefferson bank and ultimately its presidency. In the end, he is shot by his cousin Mink whose elemental but resolute sense of family loyalty is permanently disturbed when Flem, on the rise, refused to acknowledge him. There are, however, endless numbers of Snopes, and the trilogy, in its way, is a dire prediction of an unending process of eroding values in Yoknapatawpha.

But the dehumanization of modern-day society and commerce was for F. always a fundamental threat. Two other works of the 1930s also center on this concern. *Pylon* (1935) equates the death-defying fliers of a traveling air circus come to New Orleans with the death-defying celebrants of Mardi Gras. Both groups, beneath their false courage, have a more profound sense of hopelessness and even suicidal instincts; fittingly enough, their stories are told by a newspaper reporter who is himself nameless and likened to a cadaver. *The Wild Palms* (1939) alternates between the fantasy of a woman who would like life to be only a romance with no responsibilities and the fantasy of a prisoner who attempts to rob a train with a water pistol in emulation of the dime novels he has read; together, they show how unbearable the real world can become, and how the commercialism of fiction and romance can provide corrupt fantasies that have no chance of becoming solutions. An even more bitter castigation of man's nature and of the self-deception of hope is *A Fable* (1954), which F. considered his major work. In retelling the story of Christ as that of a corporal in World War I who lays down his rifle and refuses to fight and is necessarily court-martialed and executed for treason, F. shows that even the intentions of a modern-day savior will win no converts and no conversion of human nature among the Pharisees who have come now to inhabit the world.

Go Down, Moses ends with a brief story about a black McCaslin who runs away from Jefferson, becomes involved with a gangster mob in Chicago, and is executed there. F.'s double focus is on the waste of the young black man and the inability of the white people of Jefferson, who would salve their consciences by paying for his burial (but not attending the ceremony), to see how profoundly racism has taken root in the modern South of his fiction. The episode anticipates F.'s personal and urgent struggle for civil rights in his later years. His polemical *Intruder in the Dust* (1948) attempts to make the matter palatable by placing it in a novel that combines racial lynching with a murder mystery and an adventure story. An elderly woman, a young boy, and his black companion attempt to prove innocent a black man accused of killing a white man, believing that racism is what has leveled the charge initially and that it is strong enough to cause a lynching before a fair trial can be held. This situation allows F. an occasion to praise the innocent woman and children whose concern for the aging Lucas Beauchamp outweighs thoughts of their own safety and Gavin, the boy's uncle, an occasion to deliver speeches on the unequal treatment of blacks. Here as elsewhere, however, F. remained an ameliorist, arguing that racial causes would improve over time and urging the North to be less insistent for change while demanding that the South move toward integration more quickly. This liberal viewpoint—liberal in the South for his day—won no strong allies on either side, and F.'s final novel, *The Reivers* (1962), is a delightful but nostalgic return to the past with the story of a child growing up in the days before the Great War and the modern problems of capitalism and racism. It is a novel richly mythic and celebratory of life, but it conspicuously avoids the more serious concerns of F.'s earlier work.

F.'s themes are therefore traditional ones, but his accompanying sense of epistemology has often made his work seem unnecessarily difficult or obscure. For F., there is no single truth as there is no single interpretation of an event, and much of his writing is an attempt to show how events gain meaning only through contemporaneous or subsequent reaction and interpretation. Thus the understanding or memory of something becomes its meaning, and F.'s restless exploration is an attempt to find one or more narrative perspectives that can accommodate or mediate events. His statement that truth is like thirteen ways of looking at a black bird and that one of his novels is the fourteenth way is revealing. Thus, *The Sound and the Fury* attempts to comprehend the decline of the Compson family, as representative of the decline of the South, by examining it from the viewpoint of an idiot—that is, one whose mind is so untrained that it sees and feels things directly—as well as through the eyes of someone who abstracts meaning, one whose viewpoint is nihilistic, and one whose perspective is essentially moralistic. Together, F. implies, they are able to resurrect much of the truth of what caused the decay of Southern aristocracy in Jefferson and in Yoknapatawpha, although he was still dissatisfied that he had not found the whole truth. In 1946, he wrote an appendix that would supplement the novel and help to explain events yet one more time, from a far more distanced viewpoint. That very appendix is revealing, however, for some events recalled there—notably Caddy's climb up the tree to witness Dammed's funeral—is at odds with events in the novel. F. is repeatedly guilty of such inconsistencies from one work to another, as later novels recall and build on earlier ones, but such discrepancies never bothered him because he said such change represented a growth of awareness. Motion was for him living, the lack of change a kind of death. What is true of small inconsistencies is true of reading larger works; the multiple perspectives that F. employs allow new readings, rather than merely rereads, of his work. Just as how and why men and women know is the theme of much of his fiction (and as important as what they know), so his fiction is constructed to force the reader to make his own (limited, revisable) interpretation too. F.'s fiction is thus always complicate; it builds through juxtaposed episodes and commentary that the reader must put together in order to derive his own independent and individual understanding.

In this, F. follows the poetics of many of his predecessors. An avid reader from childhood, he was first inspired to his long Yoknapatawpha saga by the human comedy of Balzac (and, somewhat later, by the Wessex County novels of Thomas Hardy). From them, he learned how a whole career may concentrate on the continuing investigation of a limited region with a relatively stable population by tracing its history over generations and by showing the fluidity of time and the interpenetrating of time and history. But F. also learned techniques from many other writers: the limited point of view from Henry JAMES; the use of spatial associations from Flaubert; the use of interior monologue from James Joyce and others; and the use of doubling from Dostoevsky, to name a few. In *The Sound and the Fury,* for instance, Benjy's apparently inchoate leaps of memory always associate sex and death—and this is clarified by his limited point of view. He also associates himself by spaces—especially inside and outside the Compson house or yard—while his stream of consciousness deliberately replaces his sister Caddy with her daughter Quentin IV. The reader will be helped in understanding the complicated mind of Benjy—or at least its strangeness—when his older brother shares some of the same concerns despite his tendencies to abstract ideas and moralize behavior. While he does not seek maternal love from Caddy as Benjy does, Quentin seeks a kind of incestuous love; as with his younger brother, Caddy is both the source and object of his affection. In fact, his abstracted sense of love and death sees his own affections as suicidal—both the affections he desires and those he thinks he immorally acted on. Jason overcomes such conclusions by commercializing love, and Dilsey by making it metaphysical, religious, and transcendent.

What is true in the novels is also true in F.'s stories—some of them among the finest in American literature. "A Rose for Emily," for instance, easily a story for an omniscient perspective, must for F. be filtered through the narrative consciousness of a townsperson, because it is not Emily Grierson's actions that the story is finally about but the limited understanding of the town in which she lives and the society to which she belongs that causes her to commit the actions she does, however bizarre they may seem. Or in "That Evening Sun," a story about the chasm of ignorance that separates races, it is important to have as narrator a white boy who cannot comprehend the extraordinary fears of the black woman Nancy alongside her understanding of the limitations of his knowledge and her need to resign herself to her fate. "Barn Burning" has as its painful center young Sarty Snopes's recognition of his father Ab's use of intimidation to secure selfishly and wrongfully what is not his and Sarty's further understanding that he must forsake his own father if he is not to forsake the values that he treasures. The ironic significance of "Dry September" lies in the reader's combination of Minnie Copper's hysteria and Will Mayes's fear, but this meaning lies beyond the comprehension of any single person in the story.

That F. designs his fiction for the participatory understanding of his reader is displayed in his own accounts—or the accounts revealed by the drafts of his work. *The Sound and the Fury* began when he had an image of a girl with dirty drawers climbing a tree; how she received a kind of original stain, how she coped with it, and the reactions of others constitute much of the novel. *Absalom, Absalom!,* F. told his publishers, is the story of a man who outraged the land that then turned and destroyed the man's family. But it is always wise to consider F.'s writing by reconsidering it; readers are meant to constitute and reconstitute episodes and images as they read and reread his work, at once combining the events and comments while assembling and reassembling memories of other parts: F.'s poetics is designed for subsequent reading when the whole is known and so the components can be reinvested with new meaning or actively recombined in fresh ways. In *Absalom, Absalom!,* it is possible to see Rosa Coldfield's damnation of Thomas Sutpen as justly deserved, or as the spiteful result of an embittered and lonely woman, or as the attempt to mythologize what was at first merely tawdry, or as an attempt to shade a story so as to invite Quentin to become so absorbed that he will write a book about it. In *Go Down, Moses,* the reader is invited to see Ike McCaslin's hunt for his cousins as the tracking down of game, repeating what Uncle Buck and Uncle Buddy did with Tomey's Turl, their black half-brother; it could also be the only means of repairing the harm done the black line of his family by his white ancestors; it may also, as Fonsiba and her husband point out, be demeaning; it may be, as Lucas claims, unnecessary—it may, that is, show Ike as heroic or as self-deluded. Given the conflicting ingredients of events and the provisionary nature of F.'s narrative consciousnesses, the reader cannot help but be participatory in F.'s fictional acts. By the same token, this multiplicity of possibilities of the narrative text is a good measure of the power of F.'s poetics, and in the later works, where he grows more polemical or nostalgic, and more transparent in meaning—such as in Gavin Stevens's remarks in *Intruder in the Dust* or Temple Drake Stevens's heavy-handed rationalizations in *Requiem for a Nun* (1951) or Lucius Priest's confession to Boss Priest in *The Reivers*—his work has considerably less force. But in his major period, from *Flags in the Dust* to *Go Down, Moses* (1929–42), his work, local in its detailed depiction but universal in its moral commitment, its penetrating analyses of epistemology, and its exploratory and experimental poetics, constitutes one of the signal achievements in American literature.

BIBLIOGRAPHY: Blotner, J., *F.: A Biography* (1974; rev. ed., 1984); Brooks, C., *W. F.: Toward Yoknapatawpha and Beyond* (1978); Gray, R., *The Life of W. F.* (1994); Kinney, A. F., *F.'s Narrative Poetics* (1978); Mathews, J., *The Play of F.'s Language* (1982); Millgate, M., *The Achievement of W. F.* (1965); Minter,

D., *W. F.: His Life and Work* (1980); Parker, R., *F. and the Novelistic Imagination* (1985); Sundquist, E. J., *F.: The House Divided* (1983); Taylor, W., *F.'s Search for a South* (1983); Williamson, J., *W. F. and Southern History* (1993)

ARTHUR KINNEY

FAUSET, Jessie [Redmon]

b. 27 April 1882, Snow Hill Central Township, New Jersey; d. 30 April 1961, Philadelphia, Pennsylvania

Until recently, F.'s impact on African American literature has been overlooked; she has remained best known, as Langston HUGHES noted in *The Big Sea,* as a "midwife" of "New Negro literature." As literary editor of the *Crisis* from 1919 to 1926, F. published work by most of the day's major African American authors, including Jean TOOMER, Countee CULLEN, Nella LARSEN, and Hughes himself. Ironically, F.'s own essays, poetry, and fiction were largely forgotten, perhaps because she resisted the contemporary tendency to exoticize African American individuals and communities in favor of situating her characters in domestic plots. Recently, however, feminist and African American scholars have introduced F.'s work to a newly appreciative public.

The "race problem," especially the particular dilemmas faced by mulatto men and women, lies at the overt center of all of F.'s novels. Frequently, her mixed-race characters must decide whether to pass as white and accept the attendant privileges—in terms of economic, personal, and artistic freedom—whiteness seems to offer, or to remain loyal to the remarkably whole and relatively affluent African American communities F. portrays. These choices figure prominently in heterosexual relationships. Most notably in *There Is Confusion* (1924) and *The Chinaberry Tree* (1931), marriage is not merely a "happy ending" but becomes a site of tension and reckoning with the contemporary effects of national and personal histories of miscegenation on both black and white communities.

Along with race, class is a central concern in F.'s fiction. Each of her novels features established, solidly middle-class African American families who, despite the racism and prejudice that surround them, have attained the success of the "American dream" through careers such as catering or medicine—for the men—and teaching, performing or fashion design—for F.'s female characters. Alongside these established families, F. sets poor but respectable characters who might be said to be struggling upward, and most of whom, by remaining true to their race, achieve financial and emotional stability. F.'s first novel, *There Is Confusion,* personifies these class and race concerns

in Peter Bye, whose promising medical career is temporarily derailed when he learns of his "confused" ancestry of miscegenation. But F. does not limit the confusion's destructive potential to the African American community; Peter's white cousin must die on the battlefield to redeem his family and nation's raced sin and reinstate Peter as the true inheritor of the Bye family name and fortune.

Finally, F. finds connection to other women writers in her focus on women's creativity. The difficulties women, especially visibly raced women, face in combining artistic and economic success are central to her work, especially *Plum Bun* (1929), where Angela Murray's success as a painter depends on her ability to pass for white. Similarly, Joanna Marshall in *There Is Confusion* and Marise Davies in *Comedy American Style* (1933) parley their talents for singing and dancing into professional careers. In these texts, F. pairs her dramatically creative characters with less privileged female characters who develop their own successful businesses in less "fine" arts, in this case hair design and couture. Through these characters, F. claims the possibility for women's economic and personal happiness, and not always through a "happily-ever-after" marriage as her detractors have claimed. Through subtle analyses of the family, race, economic, and artistic concerns of her day, F.'s novels reveal how a racialized history and present impact all Americans, regardless of their race, class, or gender.

BIBLIOGRAPHY: Ammons, E., *Conflicting Stories* (1992); Carby, H. V., *Reconstructing Womanhood* (1987); Sylvander, C., *J. R. F.: Black American Writer* (1981)

BETSY KLIMASMITH

FEARING, Kenneth [Flexner]

b. 28 July 1902, Oak Park, Illinois; d. 26 June 1961, New York City

Though F. was well known in the 1930s for a poetry that responded to the social upheavals of the time, his literary stock had begun to wane even before his death in 1961. The recent issue of his *Complete Poems* (1994), the inclusion of several of his poems in the last edition of the *Heath Anthology of American Literature,* and the appearance of at least one critical study devoted primarily to his work may signal a change in F.'s literary fortune. As the modernist movement is being reconsidered and found to be more heterogeneous than it has often been assumed, a place might be found for F.'s distinctive voice. Like his more high-brow contemporaries T. S. ELIOT and Ezra POUND, F. formulated powerful poetic responses to the rapidly changing conditions that constitute and propel literary MODERNISM.

F.'s poetic lineage goes back through Walt WHITMAN to Carl SANDBERG. In his naturalistic portraits of down and out, desolate characters can be seen the influence of E. A. ROBINSON. Contemporaries with whom he invites comparison include John DOS PASSOS (particularly *Manhattan Transfer* and the *U.S.A.* trilogy), Michael Gold, and Muriel RUKEYSER. F.'s early poetry, first published in the 1920s in journals such as *New Masses* and collected in *Angel Arms* (1929), is marked by a formal rigor and beauty. He wrote sonnets, villanelles, and poems with rhyming couplets in strict iambic pentameter. Gradually, F.'s poetry in later volumes such as *Dead Reckoning* (1938), *Afternoon of a Pawnbroker* (1943) and *Stranger at Coney Island* (1948) became more "modern" in both theme and style. In the 1930s, he was associated with *Dynamo,* poets influenced by the work of Sergey Eisenstein. Kenneth REXROTH once remarked that F. wrote and thought "like a taxi driver reading a billboard while fighting traffic." Indeed, his best-known poetry responds to and incorporates the language and technology of modernity: radio, cinema, skyscrapers, advertisements, and newspaper headlines.

In the 1940s, F. directed his energies more to fiction, perhaps because the opportunities for commercial success were greater. His best-known novel, *The Big Clock,* was published in 1946 and two years later was made into a movie with Ray Milland and Maureen O'Sullivan. Some critics have placed his fiction within the category of psycho-thrillers, comparing his spare, sharp style to Raymond CHANDLER's. His clever plots might call to mind those of Alfred Hitchcock or Patricia Highsmith. In *The Big Clock,* for instance, the murderer, a publications tycoon, in placing one of his own employees, George Stroud, in charge of finding a stranger who might implicate him, unwittingly charges the man with finding himself. Prey and predator become one and the same.

In *The Big Clock,* F. experiments with point of view much in the way William FAULKNER does in *As I Lay Dying,* shifting between various narrators, each telling pertinent sections of the story. Like Nathanael WEST, another contemporary writer with whom he has been compared, F. associates terror with the very circumstances of modern life. Sources of crime, F. suggests, lie in such things as repressed homosexuality, and urban and corporate structures that corrupt and distort desire, creating alienation, loneliness and violence. His novels—such as *The Hospital* (1939), *Clark Gifford's Body* (1942), *Loneliest Girl in the World* (1951), and *The Crozart Story* (1960)—have a film noir quality to them, haunted as they often are with a sense of paranoia or imminent conspiracy.

Edward DAHLBERG, in his introduction to F.'s second volume of poetry entitled *Poems* (1935), celebrated F.'s critique of capitalism noting his "inexorable, Marxist interpretations." The reductive and misleading "communist" label may have affected F.'s reputation over subsequent decades. Critical, sardonic, and pessimistic, F. certainly was; never, though, would he amputate his poetic vision to fit a party line. In the early 1950s, his communist affiliations came to haunt him. When interviewed by the FBI regarding the Rosenberg trials, he was asked (as were many others during this time) if he'd been a party member. "Not yet!" he replied.

While F. may not be a major American writer, he is certainly one of those truly worthy minor writers who enrich the texture of American literature. His poetry, especially, registers the immediate with a bombardment of images, sounds, and words in a way we now might recognize as distinctly postmodern. He employed mass culture, in a kind of bricolage, offering a strong critique of the mechanisms responsible for producing that culture. We may now read him, as one critic suggests, "as a forgotten ancestor, or even as our contemporary."

BIBLIOGRAPHY: Barnard, R., *The Great Depression and the Culture of Abundance: K. F., Nathanael West, and Mass Culture in the 1930s* (1995); Madden, D., ed., *Proletarian Literature of the Thirties* (1968); Santora, A., "The Life of K. F. F.," *CLAJ* 32 (March 1989): 309–22

ALLEN HIBBARD

FEIFFER, Jules
b. 26 January 1929, New York City

Best known as a syndicated cartoonist for the *Village Voice,* whose cartoons have appeared in over one hundred papers worldwide, F. has also been a successful playwright, novelist, and screenplay writer. He is a long-time social satirist whose New York, Jewish, leftist politics, keen eye, and sharp wit have been appreciated by millions of readers for over thirty years.

F. began a long, productive playwriting career in 1961 with *Explainers,* an adaptation of his own cartoons. That same year, writing under the pen name Norton Juster, F. also penned *The Phantom Tollbooth.* For the next several years, along with his cartooning, F. wrote one-act plays with varying degrees of success.

His first full-length play, *Little Murders* (1967), garnered an Outer Critics Circle Award, and in London, where it was produced by the Royal Shakespeare Company, drama critics voted it Best Foreign Play. An Off-Broadway revival two years later received a prestigious Obie Award, as well. Those same traits that made F. a success as a political cartoonist served him well as a playwright, prompting critic Walter Kerr to remark in his review of *Little Murders* that F. has "the alert ears and eyes of a leprechaun on LSD."

F.'s biggest theatrical success came nine years later, with *Knock, Knock* (1976), a comedy about two cantankerous middle-aged recluses who share a cabin in the woods, and whose days are consumed in petty quarrels. The surprise arrival of Joan of Arc promises to reconcile the two men and repair their tenuous relationship. She settles in with the men, cooking for them, and helping them to understand each other better. It is unclear, however, when Joan leaves whether or not she has been successful. Clive Barnes of the *New York Times,* reviewing the Broadway revival later that year, refers to the "simplistic discussions on reality and illusion" that support the play. Critic Leonard Probst described *Knock, Knock* as an "off-beat, goofy, cartoon strip about two Jewish fellows hiding out in the forest, visited by a nutty dame who thinks she is Joan of Arc." While Martin Gottfried noted that the play mixes "liberal intellectualism with healthy, Jewish self-skepticism and farce." This is an apt description of all of F.'s work, especially his cartooning.

In the interim between these two theatrical successes, F. continued his cartooning, contributed sketches to the popular *Oh Calcutta!* (1969), and also scripted the screenplay for the acclaimed film *Carnal Knowledge* (1971). In 1980, he scripted the screenplay for the popular *Popeye* movie.

Still, despite his successes as an author, it is as a political cartoonist that F. is best known and has been most successful. With simple line drawings, F.'s work affects a humorous desensitization to violence, and was described by Jack Kroll as a "rueful dissection of middle-brow idealism." Perhaps the best description of F.'s social commentary came from John Lahr. Writing about *The White House Murder Case* (1970), F.'s Outer Critic Circle Award-winning play, Lahr noted that F. "deals with the process of moral decay in which a society becomes numb to its own homicide."

BIBLIOGRAPHY: DiGaetani, J. L., ed., *A Search for a Postmodern Theater* (1991); Grimes, L. E., "Stepsons of Sam: Re-Visions of the Hard-Boiled Detective Formula in Recent American Fiction," *MFS* 29 (Autumn 1983): 535–44; Lahr, J., *Astonish Me* (1973); Whitfield, S. J., *Hester Street to Hollywood: The Jewish-American Stage and Screen* (1983)

ERIC MARSHALL

FEMINISM AND WOMEN'S WRITING

The term "feminism" is an abstraction of the grassroots organizations and very real women who have dug deep into the collective conscious of America and dedicated their lives to such purposes as ending slavery, gaining the vote, ending the Vietnam War, and receiving equal pay in the workplace. The appellation of feminism in association with women's sovereignty and their parcel of rights as citizens first appeared around 1910 during the women's suffrage movement, known at that time as the National American Woman Suffrage Association, directed by Carrie Chapman Catt. This new platform of feminism furthered the convictions toward, as Catt stated, "a world-wide revolt against all artificial barriers which laws and customs interpose between women and human freedom," and toward women's uprising within all educational, economic, artistic, and sexual realms.

The map of feminism has remained multipurposed, and within its continuum we can locate Anne Hutchinson's cause of religious freedom in the 1600s; the Canienga (Mohawk) Mary Brant's dedication to the rights of Native Americans during Revolutionary times; the African American Sojourner Truth's fight for rights for all blacks and women in the mid 1800s; Anna J. Cooper's struggle for racial equality during the late 1800s and up until her death in 1964, writing what is recognized as one of the early black feminist texts, *A Voice from the South—By a Black Woman of the South* (1892); Tillie OLSON's imprisonment in the early 1930s for her battle to improve factory conditions, and her portrayal in literature of the poor working woman of the earlier 1900s; Lillian HELLMAN's antifascist activity during the 1930s; Zora Neale HURSTON's anthropological work among black communities from New York to the Caribbean during the Harlem Renaissance, dating between the two world wars; Betty Friedan's raising consciousness of middle-class women in the 1960s; Maya ANGELOU's 1970s multivolume autobiography of growing up black; Shulamith Firestone's 1970s call for women to "dare to be bad"; Jill Johnston's promotion for lesbians in *Lesbian Nation: The Feminist Solution* (1973); Camille Paglia's 1990 text *Sexual Personae,* which redefined the woman from victim to "femme fatale"; and Judith Butler's *Gender Trouble* (1990), in which she proposes that gender identity impedes woman's agency.

It is within these differences of ideas and actions that feminism's arms have reached into every sector of society, linking gender and sexuality to not just the literary critique of the late 20th c.—in which feminists have drawn on postmodernism, particularly its aspect of culturally created contexts in which knowledge is relative rather than absolute and in the focus on evolving patterns rather than discrete units—but to tangible acts of social justice and equality in race, class, political, and economic struggles. Yet the very advances women have made in these social and political sectors, including the academy, have provided contemporary feminist scholars with the option to produce more abstruse feminist discourse, rather than the essentialist texts of the early feminists (work that was founded in social history and the idea that there is a universal basis for feminism that exists cross-culturally). Our current condition is certainly in contrast to that of the early female white settlers and African slaves who were partially or wholly enslaved, and during which time the act of a writing woman was a threat to the educated men who held Western culture in their hands.

While there are three broad historical epochs of women's movements in the U.S.—the antebellum period (1830–60); the progressive era (1900-World War I); and the civil rights movement and the student activism of the 1960s and the early 1970s—it is each individual woman—expressing her convictions, her art, her religious beliefs, her right to support herself, to receive public education, and to procure birth control, who elevated the state of being of all women. The little-known doctor Harriot Kezia Hunt, for example, who had been barred from attending medical lectures at Harvard in the early part of the 19th c., battled the medical establishment and throughout her life pioneered the holistic idea that women, and all people, would benefit from an understanding of the functioning of their bodies, including the right to view their medical records, and thus participate in their health and recovery. In 1856, Hunt published an autobiographical volume, *Glances and Glimpses; or, Fifty Years Social, Including Twenty Years Professional Life.* In the latter part of the 1800s, Nellie Bly's tenacity as a journalist also led her to fight on behalf of the rights of female patients in mental asylums, the working conditions of uneducated women, and the treatment of women in prisons. Later in her life, she dedicated herself to homeless children.

In large part, the early American women writers were unlike their English counterparts principally in their interest in religious matters and politics. The American women's cause arrived with the early settlers like Anne Hutchinson, who, in the first half of the 17th c., trod upon the male domain of theology by holding meetings for women in her Massachusetts Bay home. Contrary to the clergy's preaching of a covenant of works, in which grace could only be received by those who had been selected by God, Hutchinson believed that there was a covenant of grace, which could be realized through an individual's inner experience, personal in nature. She was thrown out of the colony. Anne BRADSTREET, another good citizen of the Massachusetts Bay Colony, had eight children and in her spare time wrote poetry that in 1678, six years after her death, became the first volume of pub-

lished poems on American soil. Bradstreet's poetry extends her feelings about her own writing, but she was also concerned with women's autonomy, and she stated that many of her peers wanted to see her wield a needle rather than a pen.

Puritan society did not obstruct white women from receiving an education—in fact, the governing men encouraged it—but ironically frowned upon women who actually did something with it. Governor John WINTHROP of Massachusetts Bay, where Bradstreet resided, made public the idea that an abundance of reading and writing, for a woman, could lead to emotional instability. Still, white women regardless of obstacles could write while black women and men were enslaved. And yet Phillis WHEATLEY, a West African slave brought to Boston at age seven and purchased by John Wheatley, published her first poem in 1767, six years after her arrival in America. She earned fame in England, more than on American soil, and in 1773 her book *Poems on Various Subjects, Religious and Moral* was published in London. Phillis was taught English by Mary, the Wheatley daughter, and was treated more like a child than servant by Susanna, Wheatley's wife. Tragically, when Phillis gained her freedom and married a free black man who ran a grocery business, she also met with poverty and was refused publication of all of her work. She died shortly after her emancipation, aged about thirty-one, after having written the larger part of her poetry before the age of twenty.

In the 18th c., epistolary exchange was a major means of writing for women like Judith Sargent Murray, who among her many publications wrote "On the Equality of the Sexes" (1779), the first methodical feminist proclamation in American literature, and Mercy Otis WARREN, Abigail Adams, and Susanna Haswell ROWSON, who translated their expertise into public discourse and literature. Mercy Otis Warren, who bore five children, wrote in a variety of genres including poetry and drama. Her collection entitled *Poems, Dramatic and Miscellaneous,* published in 1790, included two tragedies on themes of freedom and patriotism, political satire, pamphlets, and newspaper articles. Her most consequential work was her three-volume *History of the Rise, Progress, and Termination of the American Revolution* (1805). Warren corresponded frequently with Abigail Adams, whose convictions on the status and rights of women were explicitly stated to her husband President John Adams, "I cannot say, that I think you are very generous to the ladies; for whilst you are proclaiming peace and good will to men, emancipating all nations, you insist upon retaining absolute power over wives. But you must remember . . . we have it in our power, not only to free ourselves, but to subdue our masters, and without violence, throw both your natural and legal authority at our feet."

In the early part of the 19th c., American women were inspired by the English author and philosopher Mary Wollstonecraft, who wrote the groundbreaking *A Vindication of the Rights of Woman.* Born in Boston, Hannah Mather Crocker moved with Wollstonecraft's ideas, particularly in her advance of women's education. Crocker bore ten children, and in 1818, as a widow of thirteen years, she wrote and published *A Series of Letters on Freemasonry,* advancing that women form self-improvement societies; in 1816, she published *Observations on the Real Rights of Women,* claiming that women were equals to men since God shows no sexual preference in the distribution of grace.

The movement of women's writing gained force during the late 1700s and the first half of the 19th c., owing to an educational system that began to incorporate, for the first time, female writing as part of its curriculum. Sarah Pierce, Mary Vial Holyoke, and Susanna Haswell Rowson founded female academies that gave young women the opportunity to reenvision their potential, a vision that would soon include the renowned 19th-c. writers Emily DICKINSON, Harriet Beecher STOWE, and Louisa May ALCOTT. Stowe is most distinguished for her work *Uncle Tom's Cabin* (which was first serialized in 1851–52 and published as a two-volume book that was rejected in the South and celebrated in the North), in which she forcefully contended against the institution of slavery. Stowe was inspired by her real-life ambition to end slavery, and what prompted this particular work was her anger at the newly passed 1850 Fugitive Slave Law, requiring Northerners to return escaped slaves to their Southern owners. While Alcott was an avid feminist and abolitionist who supported herself by writing, her popular work *Little Women,* although autobiographical in its portrayal of four sisters' coming of age, does not capture the political agenda of Alcott's life, nor does it mirror the other less noted forms of Alcott's writing, such as her down-to-earth narratives of working women as well as her gothic thrillers.

Harriet JACOBS, born on a slave plantation in North Carolina, escaped to the North with her children, and in 1861 her detailed narrative of slavery, *Incidents in the Life of a Slave Girl,* was published under the pseudonym Linda Brent; Jacobs wanted to protect herself and those who helped her to escape. The Southern actress and writer Fanny Kemble left her husband, which also meant she had to leave her children, in order to get away from the large Georgian plantation that her husband owned and ran with slaves. Kemble's later work, *Journal of a Residence on a Georgian Plantation* (1868), fully discloses the brutality of the lives of slave women, put to hard labor in the fields and treated as breeders and sexual slaves in the production of future slaves for masters.

During the early and mid-1800s, another movement of writers and philosophers named the transcendentalists, with Ralph Waldo EMERSON and Henry David THOREAU at the forefront, took center stage and became active in the arts and social political causes, including the abolitionist movement. However, women, apart from the writer and well-respected conversationalist Margaret FULLER were not included within its core. Emerson befriended Fuller, and Fuller used her expertise with oral language, giving lectures in Boston, to help support Emerson. She coedited with Emerson—although it is said that she did the majority of the labor—the transcendental journal, *The Dial* from 1840 to 1844, but her most important work was her book *Woman in the Nineteenth Century,* published in 1845.

In 1848, Elizabeth Cady STANTON and Lucretia Mott, whom Stanton had met at the World Antislavery Convention in London, arranged the historical first Women's Rights Convention held in Seneca Falls. It was at this occasion that Stanton wrote a Declaration of Sentiments and in which the self-freed black slave Sojourner Truth delivered her influential and magnificent speech "Ain't I a Woman." In 1851, Stanton met Susan B. Anthony, and together these two political activists worked for the next fifty years, securing rights for women. In 1859, Anthony led the legislature for a constitutional amendment that would give women the right to vote as well as property and custody rights in marriage.

During the 1910s, feminist activity steered itself in two directions: one led by the influential Swedish writer Ellen Key, whose books *Century of the Child* (1910) and *Love and Marriage* (1911) were published and widely read by feminists in the U.S., founding a movement of sexual liberation; the other heralded by such activists as labor leader Emma Goldman and journalist and author Charlotte Perkins GILMAN, both of whom were proponents of economic independence for women. Although almost all were in favor of Key's transcendence of the Victorian division between motherhood and eroticism and of her championing of rights for unwed mothers, many American feminists strongly believed, as Key did not, in the cause of women's equality in all other walks of life governed by men. The major contention rested upon the belief, as Gilman argued in her articles, that women's potential was not only to be relegated to their bodies, their sexual freedom, and motherhood, but was also necessarily comprised of identical value with men in all reaches of society, including politics and employment: "the main lines of human development have nothing to do with sex ... what women need most is the development of human characteristic."

Although women were still defined by family and did not have voting rights, the 20th c. opened a fuller range of possibilities to women with professional aims. The first minimum wage laws applicable to women and children were passed in 1912, and journalists such as Ida Tarbell and Nellie Bly and social workers like Jane Addams took action and brought to public awareness the problems of urban indigence. Harriot Stanton Blatch, the daughter of Elizabeth Cady Stanton, became a new leader of the suffrage movement, particularly in her fight for the ballot. In this new era, Harriot Stanton Blatch emphasized women's political leadership, education, and professional skill rather than her mother's natural rights polemic. Emma Goldman, anarchist and labor leader, was a charismatic speaker, and her attention to the birth control movement greatly furthered this cause, which, during this period, linked several of the agendas of feminism: progressive social reform, economic independence, sexual and erotic liberation, class oppression, and the crucial issue of a woman's right to govern her reproductive endowment, unfettered by male control of state. Goldman was arrested for providing public lectures on the use of contraceptives, but this did not stop her activity, nor did it prevent Margaret Sanger, who eventually led this movement, from doing her fieldwork in the tenements and fighting for poor women to have the right of birth control instead of dying in illegal abortions. In 1913, Sanger fled U.S. prosecution, but by the spring of 1914, she had established her radical newspaper, the *Woman Rebel,* advancing the rights of women in marriage and motherhood and in expressing their sexuality.

Marie Jenny Howe led a group named Heterodoxy—so named in the purpose of defying orthodox social and cultural laws—in an enormous gathering of feminists in 1914, which included, among the many, Beatrice Forbes-Robertson Hale, author of *What Women Want: An Interpretation of the Feminist Movement* (1914), and Charlotte Perkins Gilman. This group became symbolic of an entire movement, as feminism's objectives deepened to include not only social and political action but also women's inner psychic growth, a morale that in the 1960s became known as consciousness raising.

Changes began to take place for African American women as well, and many black leaders and organizations, including the National Association of Colored People, founded in 1910, the National Federation of Afro-American Women, and the Northeastern Federation of Colored Women's Clubs fought for women's rights, regardless of the racism they faced in so doing. And with the publication of work by writers such as Mary AUSTIN, who chronicled the lives of Native

Americans in a series of books beginning with *Land of Little Rain* (1903), and Mary Antin, who in her book *The Promised Land* (1912) told the stories of the many Eastern and Southern European immigrants who had entered the U.S. during this period, the first wave of what is now known as multiculturalism began to rise.

The writing women began to shape the geography of the land through the women who inhabited it. Willa CATHER, a journalist, novelist, and short story writer, who was reared in the frontier land of Nebraska, wrote five novels focusing on her life there, including *My Antonia* and *One of Ours,* which won the Pulitzer Prize in 1922. Cather maintained friendships with numerous women writers, among them, the writer Sarah Orne JEWETT, whose childhood in the inland seaport of Maine, in a town that was in great economic decline, became the subject of many of her books, including her best-known, *The Country of the Pointed Firs.*

The pragmatic yet venturous evolution of "human characteristics" galvanized the esprit de corps of feminists and women writers during the 20th c., a time in which poetry and literature merged with woman's athios, to actualize herself, and to break free from what the theorists Michel Foucault and Jacques Lacan later named the Law—one only has to remember that in the early part of the 20th c., there was still a prevalent belief that a woman's reproductive organs caused hysteria, and numerous hysterectomies and ovarectomies were performed on women to control emotional disorders. Thus, a union between erotic revelation and political pragmatics was realized, not only through women's fictional accounts but in the lives they led. This writerly preoccupation was captured by the Louisiana based Kate CHOPIN, who in her most widely read book, *The Awakening,* discloses the sensual and artistic hunger of a married woman, with children, who awakens to her dissatisfaction with the mores encoded within her society and subsequently transgresses these social laws. After its initial publication, the scandal that surrounded this novel caused it to be out of print for the next sixty years until it was rediscovered by women writers and critics in the 1970s. In Chopin's short story "The Storm," she tells of an adulterous sexual liaison between two married people, whose unleashing of lust ironically benefits their respective families. Charlotte Perkins Gilman also gave voice to the injury of woman's repression, particularly in her novella *The Yellow Wallpaper,* a story that is loosely based on her own experience of a nervous breakdown; in it she warns of doctors who prescribe, as cure, a life devoid of intellectual and artistic activity for women. Both of these women lived autonomous lives that paralleled the nontraditional actions of their protagonists.

Many women writers refused their own aristocratic upbringing, finding the familial and financial dictates restrictive to their artistic ambitions and their beliefs. Edith WHARTON, Ellen GLASGOW, and Gertrude STEIN all came from wealthy families and all loathed the social values of their time, and their writing reflects this. The contemporary scholar Elaine Showalter dedicated her text *Daughters of Decadence: Women Writers of the Fin de Siècle* (1993) to the many women writers of this era, who, Showalter believes, were diminished by their male counterparts like Joseph Conrad and Oscar Wilde. In addition, Showalter points out that many of these female writers chose the form of the short story because it offered "flexibility and freedom from the traditional plots of the three decker Victorian novel plots, which invariably ended in the heroine's marriage or her death. In contrast to the sprawling three-decker, the short story emphasized psychological intensity and formal innovation." We can see this infraction of literary convention in the work of Gilman, Chopin, Wharton, and Constance Fenimore WOOLSON, all of whom were influenced by the South African writer and political activist Olive Shreiner, whose "Women and Labor" (1911) was considered the "Bible" of the women's movement.

From about 1910 until the 1940s, black women's writing went unrecognized in the larger American literary circles. It was the contemporary African American writer Alice WALKER who led the way to recovering the great black women writers of the Harlem Renaissance, specifically in her interest in the work of Zora Neale Hurston, who had trained in anthropology with Franz Boas at Barnard College and Columbia University. Hurston, herself reared in the small, all-black town of Eatonville, Florida, gathered folklore and history from rural black communities for her non-fiction but also applied this knowledge to her novels, two of which are set in her hometown of Eatonville, including *Jonah's Gourd Vine* and her most celebrated novel, *Their Eyes Were Watching God.* Hurston has gone unparalleled in her rendering of the lifestyles of rural blacks, as she summoned forth the richness of African American oral culture, and in *Their Eyes Were Watching God* produced a work of magnificence that in its reissue in 1978 would become a best-seller. However, other black women writers came to the fore, and the works of prose fiction writers such as Jessie FAUSET, Nella LARSEN, Dorothy West and poets such as Anne Spencer, Georgia Douglas Johnson, Gwendolyn Bennet, and Helene Johnson made their way to the public and to the critics' tables. Later, Gwendolyn BROOKS would become the first African American to win the Pulitzer Prize in poetry for her second collection, *Annie Allen,* and the first black woman to be elected to the National Institute of Arts and Letters.

Brooks also wrote fiction, and her novel *Maud Martha* depicts a black woman's conflict with self identity. In the great tradition that American women writers set forth, Brooks detailed her environment , narrating the stories of black life in Chicago.

But perhaps women writers of the 20th c. faced their largest battle as American literature in this modernist age defined itself by the grand philosophical issues of, for example, Herman MELVILLE, while downgrading subjectivity and experience to a position of emotional triteness. The ruling literati, particularly Ezra POUND and T. S. ELIOT, demanded objectivity while undermining the kind of subjectivity that Foucault would come to call a remembering of "a secret self," named in the 1800s as life writing and adopted by feminists in the 20th c. Some women writers, however, kept to the esteemed style of the times, and in Djuna BARNES's best-known novel, *Nightwood,* for which Eliot wrote a most favorable introduction, her writing is agreeable to the more objective stance, framed within a mordant critique of a decadent Vienna. Other women writers refused to adopt the male voice and wrote fiction that spoke of their worlds and their experiences. The Canadian poet and writer Elizabeth Smart, for example, experimented with language and subjectivity, and broke with the orthodox male masterplot in her book *By Grand Central Station I Sat Down and Wept* (1945), a work that begins in California and ends in New York City. Smart refrained from joining any literary groups of her time, but she was influenced by one of the greatest and most influential writers of the 20th c., Virginia Woolf, and praised Anaïs Nin, the poet and prose writer better known for her diaries.

Mary MCCARTHY developed a practice of writing semiautobiographical fiction, and this can be seen in her collection of stories, *The Company She Keeps* (1942), which centers on her life in New York in the 1930s, and in which McCarthy's probes both her inner-psychic world and the culture around her. The Southern writers Eudora WELTY, born in 1909 in Mississippi, and Flannery O'CONNOR, born in 1925 in Georgia, made their presence felt in literature and the arts throughout the 20th c., particularly in their trenchant irony and humor and brilliant engagement of the vernacular within their culture and locale. O'Connor's first novel *Wise Blood,* published in 1952, is set in her poor white Southern fundamentalist homeland, and in it she earmarked her writerly concerns for Christianity and salvation, and her attendance upon the jocose and tragic occurrences found within everyday American life. On a different shore, in California, Hisaye YAMAMOTO, a child of Japanese immigrants, wrote of the experience of being a first generation Japanese woman living on American soil, a portrayal that can best be seen in her work "Seventeen Syllables" (1949).

Yamamoto was to establish the cultural themes that in the later part of the 20th c.—with Chinese American writers such as Maxine Hong KINGSTON, best known for her novel *The Woman Warrior,* and Amy TAN, whose book *The Joy Luck Club* was made into a film—became an integral part of literature and the American consciousness in understanding multicultural life in the U.S.

Post–World War II America was a hard place for women writers and feminists. As the economy grew, so too did the suburban sentiment, that each nuclear family should own a home, in which a wife raised children while a husband went outside the home to work. While many poor people hungered for this luxury of the new middle-class, in great measure women suffered its more pernicious effects, and writing and professional women dropped down the rungs of the social ladder—this being after women had gained a certain amount of autonomy during World War II, working in place of the men who had gone to war. Thus, the energy, radicalism, and charisma of the women of the earlier part of the 20th c. were, at least in the public realm, somewhat diminished. It was Rosa Parks, in 1955, a black woman who refused to give up her seat on a crowded bus, who incited a series of events, culminating in a nationwide effort for civil rights.

In the 1960s the National Organization for Women (NOW) fought for the passage of the Equal Rights Amendment and, in the next forty or so years, feminist issues of equality and liberation, involving everything from education to sexuality entered the mainstream. Literature paved a path for women to break out of the restrictions of the home and to explore introspectively, in ways that were congruous to the original philosophies of Heterodoxy in the earlier part of the 20th c. Anne SEXTON went from housewife to one of the most admired poets and readers of poetry of her time, and in her book *To Bedlam and Part Way Back,* she established herself as a confessional writer, following in the footsteps of the poet who most influenced her, W. D. SNODGRASS. Sexton received lifelong support from her friend and writer Maxine KUMIN, whom she met at a poetry workshop, and in Robert LOWELL's Boston University seminar Sexton met Sylvia PLATH, who further moved her away from the formalism of modernist writers and toward the subjectivity that would make her so successful. Sylvia Plath's poetry and prose gained prominence with her novel *The Bell Jar,* a book that details a woman's nervous breakdown; like Sexton, Plath suffered from clinical depression, and tragically both women would end their own lives. Toward the end of her life, while she was living in London with her husband, the poet Ted Hughes, Plath wrote her best poetry (she acknowledged this herself),

and this can be seen in *Ariel,* published posthumously in 1965, and in her *Collected Poems,* published in 1981, which won a Pulitzer Prize. Both of these women are critical to understanding the zeitgeist in which women's consciousness was reemerging, but they were in no way mere cultural icons; they were masters at their craft.

Consequential work has continued to come from women writers who have made the genre of life writing a working treatise that embraces the aesthetic needs of great literature, the social condition of women, and the intimacy of the individual. May SARTON has added to this body of work, particularly with her diaries and her novel *As We Are Now,* which reveals the story of an aging woman, dismissed by an American culture that has no place for her. What is important to note is that many of these texts operate more implicitly toward feminist aims, but then all great literature has always functioned in this way and its more subtle message either by the great craft of a woman writer or through the story that is being told becomes a critical part of women's and men's everyday lives.

America in the 1960s and 1970s became a hotbed of ideas, with the civil rights movement and student activism at its zenith, and feminists penetrated American consciousness. Adrienne RICH's first collection *A Change of World* was published in 1951, but it was not until 1966 when she moved to New York that her work took on its more radical political stance. In the 1970s, she would, with her signature poem, "Diving into the Wreck," reinterpret female identity, exploring gender expectations and androgyny, and in her essay "When We Dead Awaken: Writing as Re-Vision," Rich championed the spirit of women in the 1970s and 1980s. Kate Millet's *Sexual Politics* (1969) brought to light the insidious representation of women often created by male authors, like Henry Miller. French feminists Julia Kristeva, Hélène Cixous, and Luce Irigaray based their psychoanalytically inspired theories on women's genital and libidinal difference from men, and Cixous in "Difficult Joys"(1989) asked "What about what I call 'the quarrel,' of sexual difference in writing. It is not simple, it's not men against women, it's one economy versus the other."

The American scholar Elaine Showalter labeled the critical theory, gynocriticism, and her book *A Literature of Their Own* (1977) and Sandra M. Gilbert and Susan Gubar's *The Madwoman in the Attic* (1979) became foundational texts in the practice of women's studies in the U.S. In Toril Moi's *Sexual/Textual Politics: Feminist Literary Theory* (1985), she criticized these very texts in the writers' lack of engagement within poststructuralist conflicts of language, text, and self (the concerns found within French feminism), while honoring Showalter, Gilbert, and Gubar in their

American pragmatism: the insistence upon a textuality that moves outside of literary criticism into the everyday. The writerly deliberation of feminism produced major consequences in interdisciplinary humanities theory, fostering multiculturalism, post-colonialism, linguistics, biologism, social construction, and gender analyses. Writers like the African American theorist bell hooks and poet Audre LORDE have brought forward the concept of otherness and in so doing they have begun to dismantle systems of oppression and in turn foster new methods of education, in which the kind of transactive experience of learning, that education leader Louise Rosenblatt set forth, takes place in classrooms. Thus, institutionalized answers and practices are replaced with interpretation and questions.

By the 1980s, and this has still continued, feminist arguments swelled and some forgot the larger audience, writing convoluted theory for the eyes of the academy. However, women authors of fiction did not fall into this quagmire, and it is they who have continued to write the real stories of women in this country. Toni MORRISON's richly lyrical writing captured the minds of readers and scholars from the emergence of her first novel, *The Bluest Eye*, to her haunting Pulitzer Prize-winner *Beloved*, to her collection of essays *Playing in the Dark*. Morrison takes female and black experience out of the margins, that had been established by patriarchal scholarly tradition, as does Rita DOVE, the 1993 poet laureate of the U.S., who reflects on her background as an African American in her poetry, and the history of Southern blacks in her grandparents' story *Thomas and Beulah*. The Jamaican-born Michelle CLIFF in such essays as "A Journey into Speech" along with her novels portrays herself as a colonized subject and lays bear the "constant pretense of civility against rape." Cliff and the Antiguan writer Jamaica KINCAID (both of whom now reside in the U.S.) uncover the ambivalence found in subjects of oppression, particularly as this schism relates to their writing life: they were educated in the Queen's English in colonial countries; yet they must expel this part of themselves, this part of their culture, in order to reposition themselves within their own truths and subjectivity.

Perhaps Alice Walker, who won the Pulitzer Prize for *The Color Purple*, has done more for the general populace's understanding of women, racism and poverty in the rural South than Judith Butler's more general and shrouded analysis of gender—although this is not to say that we don't benefit from the latter. Still in high school and undergraduate college classes around this country, students now learn about our society and its cultural implications from authors such as Walker, Morrison, Amy Tan, Leslie Marmon SILKO,

and Maxine Hong Kingston—whose *The Woman Warrior: Memoirs of a Girlhood among Ghosts* has become almost a prerequisite for Writing and Literature courses as well as Women Studies. Women's literature in America signifies a transactive relationship between the writer and reader and, in many ways, women's writing has become the vehicle of feminism.

BIBLIOGRAPHY: Cott, N., *The Grounding of Modern Feminism* (1987); Donovan, J., *Feminist Theory: The Intellectual Traditions of American Feminism* (1985; 1992); Harris, S., ed., *American Women Writers to 1800* (1996); Kilcup, K., ed., *Nineteenth-Century American Women Writers* (1997); Rogers, K., ed., *The Meridian Anthology of Early American Writers: From Anne Bradstreet to Louisa May Alcott, 1650–1865* (1991); Roses, L. E., and R. E. Randloph, eds., *Harlem's Glory: Black Women Writing, 1900–1950* (1996); Rossi, A., ed., *The Feminist Papers from Adams to de Beauvoir* (1988); Showalter, E., *Daughters of Decadence* (1993); Wagner-Martin, L., and C. Davidson, *Women's Writing in the United States* (1995); Weaks, M. L., and C. Perry, eds., *Southern Women's Writing Colonial to Contemporary* (1995); Westbrook, A. R., and P. Westbrook, eds., *The Writing Women of New England, 1630–1900;* Wilcox, H., and K. McWatters, eds., *The Body and the Text* (1990)

LISA TOLHURST

FERBER, Edna

b. 15 August 1887, Kalamazoo, Michigan; d. 16 April 1968, New York City

Although her works are rarely taught in schools today, F. was a major short story writer, novelist, and playwright for nearly fifty years. At her peak, she was a member of the Round Table group of the Algonquin Hotel, forming close friendships with William Allen WHITE, Noel Coward, Moss HART, and Katharine Hepburn.

A lack of funds kept F. from attending college. However, she took a job as a newspaper reporter at the age of seventeen (from which she was fired) and remained a journalist until 1909. F.'s earliest publications were short stories in women's magazines in 1910 and 1911, followed by four collections of short stories between 1911 and 1915. National success came during this period with stories of Emma McChesney, a traveling saleswoman. This theme of work in women's lives would appear through many of her stories and novels.

F.'s 1924 novel *So Big* won the Pulitzer Prize, thus establishing her as a major female novelist with contemporaries such as Edith WHARTON, Willa CATHER, and Ellen GLASGOW. So Big, *Show Boat*

(1926) and *Cimarron* (1929) exemplify F.'s use of strong female characters whose work ethic outperforms those of the weak men in their lives, a theme related to F.'s upbringing where her mother took over the family hardware store when F.'s father's health declined. These female characters show personal strength and an individualism that allows them to succeed, although for them success is measured by integrity rather than by money. While F. continuously examines the concept of success in her writing, her characters lack realistic means to achieve it. One seldom sees the toll of hard work that often destroys women; instead F.'s characters are ennobled by poverty, daily labor, and, often, a solitary lifestyle as they are widowed or abandoned.

F.'s novels also celebrate the power of the land as in *Cimarron, Saratoga Trunk* (1941), *Giant* (1952), and *Ice Palace* (1958). While F. is credited with doing historical research about the places used for settings, critics felt that she was not sufficiently steeped in the complexities of these regions to create realistic novels.

Often incorporating themes of race in her works, F.'s own Jewish background shows in *Fanny Herself* (1917) and *A Peculiar Treasure* (1939). *Show Boat* explores miscegenation; *Cimarron* contains Native American issues; *American Beauty* (1931) deals with Polish immigrants; *Saratoga Trunk* uses a Creole heroine; and *Giant* includes prejudice regarding marriage between Anglo and Mexican characters.

Collaborating with George S. KAUFMAN, F. wrote several successful Broadway plays, including *Minick* (1924), *The Royal Family* (1928), *Dinner at Eight* (1932), *Stage Door* (1936), *The Land Is Bright* (1941), and *Bravo!* (1949). F. only wrote plays in collaboration, never by herself. She did, however, negotiate several of her novels into film and stage productions: *Fanny Herself, Show Boat, Saratoga Trunk,* and *Giant.* Perhaps F. will be better remembered for the adaptations of these novels rather than for the novels themselves.

The strengths of F.'s works lie in her consistent use of strong female characters, often from the lower middle or working class, and the detail used for characterization. However, F.'s greatest weakness as a novelist is her inability to develop plot complexity. While she was a best-selling author during the early half of the 20th c., she is considered more of a popular writer than a literary figure.

BIBLIOGRAPHY: Gilbert, J. G., *F.: A Biography* (1978); Reed, P., "E. F.," in Martine, J. J., ed., *DLB,* vol. 9, *American Novelists, 1910–1945* (1981): 306–12; Shaughnessey, M. R., *Women and Success in American Society in the Works of E. F.* (1977)

REBECCA FABER

FERLINGHETTI, Lawrence
b. 24 March 1919, Yonkers, New York

For nearly all of his adult life, F. has wished to be taken for what he calls "a street poet," one who, in the tradition of Walt WHITMAN, not only speaks for the common man, but is one himself. Thomas Parkinson has quoted F. as saying, "The poetry which has been making itself heard here of late is what should be called street poetry. For it amounts to getting the poet out of the inner aesthetic sanctum where he has too long been contemplating his complicated navel. It amounts to getting poetry back into the street where it once was, out of the classroom, out of the speech department, and—in fact—off the printed page." This is quite a peculiar position for someone who is not only a poet, but a publisher of poetry as well. However, despite his association with the Beat writers and the San Francisco school of avant-garde poets, F. is a highly educated man—more highly educated, indeed, than many of the "academic poets" of the 1950s and 1960s whom he chose to see as the literary enemy.

While still an infant, F. was taken to France and raised there by French foster parents; thus, even his Italian surname is misleading, for during his earliest formative years his cultural background was French, not Italian American. F. took his bachelor's degree from the University of North Carolina and served in the Naval Reserve from 1941 to 1945. He worked for *Time* magazine in New York City, earned an M.A. from Columbia University in 1948, and, back in France, won a Doctorat de l'Universite from the Sorbonne in 1951. By the time he became associated with the Beats, he was an urbane and highly educated person.

F.'s first book, *Pictures of the Gone World,* was self-published in 1955 from City Lights Books, the press he founded in association with City Lights Bookstore of San Francisco, which he had purchased the same year. It has ever since remained a major publisher of the literature of the Beat movement.

At first, F. had a true lyric ear. He might have used it to become an excellent traditional poet. Instead, he chose to write prose poems like those of his friend Allen GINSBERG, whose work he published and promoted. F.'s lyric sensibility, which he has usually managed to suppress, manifested itself most clearly in his second book, *A Coney Island of the Mind* (1958), not insignificantly still his most popular book. Poem number "20," usually titled in anthologies from its first line, "The Penny-Candystore Beyond the El," is one of the most appreciated selections from that collection. On the surface, this poem appears to be written in lineated prose, what has come to be called "free verse" in the 20th c. If it is scanned in the traditional way, however, one discovers that it is actually variable iambic verse. A number of F.'s poems can be seen to be constructed in a similar fashion.

Between 1958 and 1986, F. published many books of poetry, including *Starting from San Francisco* (1961; rev. ed., 1967), *Where Is Vietnam* (1965), *Who Are We Now* (1976), *Landscapes of Living and Dying* (1979), *A Trip to Italy and France* (1981), and *Endless Life: The Selected Poems* (1981). In many of these books, F. wrote didactic harangues and speeches that often made their points by the rhetoric of sarcasm and parody, or attempted to get a reaction through the use of startling words. However, in *Over All the Obscene Boundaries: European Boundaries and Traditions* (1984), F. returned to the scenes of his youth in Paris and elsewhere, and in reminiscing, his lyrical ear reasserted itself occasionally.

F. has laid claim to being a mystic as well as a street poet, but his mysticism is elusive, as more than one critic has noticed. Much more in evidence is the deliberate theatricality of the poet's public performance of his work. For example, during a panel presentation in Portland, Oregon, in late March of 1980, when it came time for F. to make his preliminary remarks, he instead began to chant "Light!" from his seat. He grew louder and louder, rose, and began to dance about. One of the other participants, having anticipated such a scene, pulled a handful of balloons out of his pocket, then began blowing them up and jetting them about over the heads of the audience. Another panelist, the surrealist poet Vern Rutsala, donned his sunglasses, flicked on his cigarette lighter, and began to peer about the room as though he, too, were looking for the light.

Later, F. approached the other panelists and said, "I hope you didn't think I was arrogant by doing what I did instead of discussing things as you were doing, but I felt that there was a stance that I was expected to take, and so I did." And so he has continued to do, in his poems as in person. Nevertheless, both in his role as publisher and as poet, F. has been a model and a mentor to more than one generation of antiestablishment writer.

BIBLIOGRAPHY: O'Kane, J., "L. F.: Anarchism and the Poetry Revolution," *Enclitic* 11 (1989): 47–58; Parkinson, T. F., ed., *A Casebook on the Beat* (1961); Silesky, B., *F.: The Artist in His Time* (1990); Smith, L. R., *L. F.: Poet-at-Large* (1983)

LEWIS PUTNAM TURCO

FERNANDEZ, Roberto G.

b. 24 September 1952, Sagua la Grande, Cuba

While F. published his first three works in Spanish, his two novels in English have brought him critical praise as well as provoked scholastic inquiry. His 1975 collection of short stories, *Cuentos sin rumbos* (Aimless Tales), is a humorous assortment of vignettes that parody the Cuban American community in Miami. In 1981, with *La vida es un special* (Life Is a Special), he carried the parody further to challenge the construct of ethnicity as it relates to consumer practices, a central theme in all of his works. Stylistically, F. incorporates newsbriefs, commercial advertisements, game shows, soap operas, radio contests, and beauty pageants to depict life in the U.S. as a world where illusion and reality are indistinguishable because the American media control information systems to project a fixation with image rather than essence.

In all of his works, F. portrays culture as dichotomous: on one hand, it is ordinary and ubiquitous; on the other, it is accessible only to a select few. Generally, his Cuban characters lament the loss of their property during the Castro-led revolution in Cuba, while his southern characters lament their losses at the hands of Yankee marauders. Nearly all of his characters bemoan their reduced class status in the U.S. and he exaggerates their former status in Cuba, as well as antebellum America, because none of them admits to hailing from humble beginnings.

In *La montaña rusa* (The Russian Mountain), published in 1985, F. continues to parody Miami's Cuban diaspora and its condemnation of Cuba's Marxist regime. "Russian mountain" connotes a geographical and political barrier that the exiled community cannot overcome, but denotes the Spanish equivalent for roller coaster, which implies a convoluted wheel of fortune, or misfortune. F. humorously treats the threat of communism as an amusement park attraction that is both frightening and exhilarating in this work. Nevertheless, it is an artificial fear.

In 1988, *Raining Backwards,* his first novel written in English, was published. National critics lauded this work and international scholars soon began to study it in earnest because of its artistic merit and poignant social observations. Prior works serve as a point of departure as F. uses fragmented discourse and intertextuality from diverse sources to challenge the idea of what constitutes being an American. The American and the Cuban flags frame the novel as characters wrap themselves in the fabric of nationalistic symbols in an effort to differentiate themselves from other groups.

Identity and identification converge and diverge as the characters invent their own pasts based on cultural and literary models. *Raining Backwards* laments a lost Cuban heritage and celebrates a new life as Cuban Americans. This dual identity is neither wholly one nor the other. Rather, it is a synthesis of the two. Synthesis is the method by which F. points out individual, cultural, and religious heterogeneity. Examples of this heterogeneity include the mixture of African and European or Hispanic languages, races, and religions in the form of code-switching, Linda Lucia, and Santería. Both Cubans and Americans try to deny this ethnic, linguistic, and religious olio as they proclaim and advocate purity in each. Nevertheless, the author lets the reader infer that everyone is a mixture of races, languages, and religions.

Holy Radishes! (1995) continues F.'s hyperbolic depiction of society's penchant to equate possessions with social identity, social status with culture, and linguistic competence with national identity. He deftly illustrates that such ideas are erroneous. His works subvert these ideas and the authorities who perpetuate them. It is the most politically incorrect of F.'s works where Bernabé pretends to be Jewish, Nellie pretends to be Italian, and Wavene falsifies her Southern heritage. The common denominator among the principal characters and their ethnicity is that everyone is dispossessed of their property by either Nazis, communists, or Yankees. Consequently, they all live in exile in the U.S.

F. is a noteworthy author whose works require the reader to question authority and authors. To appreciate his novels fully, one must be familiar with popular culture and high culture. He appropriates and rewrites whole passages from European, Hispanic, and American literature as he challenges the reader to decipher his message: don't believe anything you hear and only half of what you see.

BIBLIOGRAPHY: Deaver, W. O., Jr., *A Critical Analysis of Raining Backwards by R. G. F.* (1994); Febles, J., "English and Spanish Pop Songs as Part of Character Speech: Cultural Hybridity in R. G. F. *Raining Backwards,*" in Ryan-Ranson, H., ed., *Imagination, Emblems and Expressions* (1993): 99–108; Vásquez, M. S., "Parody, Intertextuality and Cultural Values in R. G. F.'s *Raining Backwards,*" *AmRev* 18 (1990): 92–102

WILLIAM O. DEAVER, JR.

FICKE, Arthur Davidson

b. 10 November 1883, Davenport, Iowa; d. 30 November 1945, Hillsdale, New York

F. is little known today, and editions of his poetry are hard to find. During his career, he published ten volumes of verse, a novel about Mexico, and two treatises on Japanese painting and prints. His poems are traditional, mostly sonnet sequences and formal lyrics. With Witter BYNNER, F. using the pseudonym "Anne Knish" successfully carried off the infamous

Spectra hoax of 1914. The parodies in the volume were designed to vent his antimodernist disdain, though later he dabbled with free verse himself. He practiced law in Iowa for eight years, gave it up for poetry, traveled around the world, and settled in his later years in Hillsdale, New York, nearby his lifelong friend, Edna St. Vincent MILLAY. His most ambitious writing is found in *Sonnets of a Portrait Painter* (1914; rev. ed., 1922) and the *Selected Poems* (1926).

Compared to his fellow *Spectra* collaborator Bynner, F.'s poetry is quieter, more aristocratic. In language and tone, the poems glide with a simple regard for words as they relate to another, with no arresting imagery to slow the poem's argument. Such directness with words does not always work, leaving the language without a pulse, abstracted, tepid and tame, the poet's voice either unheard or too impersonal. Yet it is precisely that—an impersonality of tone—that F. wants to achieve in order to cure poetry of the neurotic state, too pull art out of the mire of private self-pity. His wish is a stating of conclusions in non-exclusive terms, one that is symbolic for all men. This kind of "public" voice is heard in the *Tumultuous Shore* (1942) with its self-titled sonnet sequence.

The fifty-three sonnets in sequence are a bulky and moody meditation on the vast collective folly of mankind and the unattainability of truth and human wisdom. The speaker is out of faith with all that he experiences; he confesses that he wears a mask of secret fear and knows a bitter alienage among his fellow man. Life has been narrowed to the measures of trade and commerce, and profit is all in a world of nightmare. Man has been bewildered by some ancient sorcery, so that his pilgrim steps going to the devil, he now reads life's riddle wrong. The speaker acknowledges that nature's silences is a clearer book of meanings and may hold some credible answers to his bewilderment. And so he broods on the patterns of nature: a vast magnificent chestnut tree, whose grave natural dignity is like a relic of a quieter, simpler age; a little birchwood, whose slim, white, clustering stems young girls of an ancient day on some Greek headland; a weathered quartz-streaked stone, firm, frugal, significant of its own deep self alone. The descriptions are Wordsworthian: rock and man and trees meet in vistas of quiet sublimity and agelessness. The rest of the sequence alternates in moods of hope and distress between such spiritual proximity with nature—feminine, benign, infinite—and man's rebellious separation, his ways tortured, blind, lost. In the end, figure of man is poor waif on a tumultuous shore, a prisoner in the cell of his lust for his own certainty, yet forever seeking in his transient days a kinship with cycles more complete than he. Despite certain lyric moments, the sonnets at times seem too sanctimonious for their own good—man is this, man is that—as F. rants on-ward about the evil than me do. Understandably, they were written around the time of World War II.

F.'s poetry is more palpable when its lectures less, when it presents access into a fleeting thought or feeling. In the titled poem of *Mountain against Mountain* (1928), the poet sits at a sad hour of early evening to look upon the coming darkness and imagine the beauty of the planet Venus glimmering miraculous above the sunset, above the dark crests of mountain ranges. The border vision at sunset returns eloquently in "Joy," a little epistolary poem addressed to Robinson JEFFERS, in which F. pictures the joyous sun shining down in golden mists around the Carmel poet's private tower of grey stone beside the dark blue sea, and commends the interval recompense of flowered hills and the immortal laughter of lovers, soon before silent darkness lends to them its greatness.

BIBLIOGRAPHY: Cheney, A., *Millay in Greenwich Village* (1975); Smith, W. J., *The Spectra Hoax* (1961)

H. S. YOON

FIEDLER, Leslie A[aron]
b. 8 March 1917, Newark, New Jersey

F. received his B.A. from New York University in 1938. Between 1939 and 1941, he earned M.A. and Ph.D. degrees from the University of Wisconsin. After beginning his teaching career at the University of Montana, F. joined the Naval Reserve and worked as an interpreter in occupied Japan. F. received his official discharge from the navy in 1946 at the rank of lieutenant junior grade. He returned to the University of Montana in 1946 and remained there for the next two decades. In 1967, the University of New York at Buffalo appointed F. the Samuel L. Clemens Professor of American Literature.

Throughout the postwar era, F. contributed free-wheeling and broad-gauged essays to *Commentary, Dissent, Partisan Review, The Nation,* and various academic journals. A typical F. essay would correlate themes from Americanist masterworks with political spectacles like the Rosenberg trials and the McCarthy hearings. From the beginning of his career, F. refused to differentiate the collective sentiments informing these mass events from the literary archetypes under writing the national masterworks.

In establishing such correlations, F. discerned nationalist archetypes as the organizing forces underwriting the masterworks of American literature. F.'s career began with the discovery in 1948 of an interethnic male bond as the foundational archetype of the American literary imagination and the popular culture it re-flected. F. interpreted this archetype as a form invested with wishes as well as anxieties. The interethnic bond offered a dream of endless adolescence as well as a fantasized compensation for the guilt over the violent racism at work in actual relations between whites and non whites.

Throughout the remainder of his career, F. elaborated the interpretive allegory that he first proposed in *Love and Death in the American Novel* (1960). By way of this allegory, F. was able to read Americanist masterworks against the grain of the national mythology. F. believes that archetypes govern the way the world is perceived. According to F., the mythical dimensions of the nation's foundational archetype were granted their most ample representations in what he calls boys' books—Herman MELVILLE's *Moby-Dick,* Mark TWAIN's *Adventures of Huckleberry Finn,* and James Fenimore COOPER's Leather-Stocking tales. Arguing that the national mythology associated heterosexual relations with a loss of freedom, F. identified women as the mythic agent men believed responsible for the conquest of nature and the subjection of nonwhites. In their accomplishment of interethnic bonds, white men discovered a realm of freedom in a wilderness far apart from the realm of heterosexual romance. The homosexual factor in this bond participated in a larger sociopsychological complex that involved white men engaing a private expression of love in an effort to overcome their guilt over the cultural oppression of blacks, native Americans and other nonwhites.

When first published and over most of his career, F.'s thesis outraged the Americanist literary establishment. But in the last decade F.'s project has been celebrated as the harbinger of cultural studies. His obsessional theme has also been interpreted against the grain of F.'s mythology as itself a regulatory force designed to police the boundary separating men's from women's Americanist narratives.

In addition to his critical studies, F. has also published three novels—*The Second Stone* (1963), *Back to China* (1965), and *The Messenger Will Come* (1974)—as well as short fiction collected in *Pull Down Vanity and Other Stories* (1962), *The Last Jew in America* (1966), and *Nude Croquet* (1969).

BIBLIOGRAPHY: Chase, R., "L. F. and American Culture," *ChiR* 14 (Autumn-Winter 1960): 8-18; Winchell, M. R., *L. F.* (1985)

DONALD E. PEASE

FIELD, Eugene
b. 2 September 1850, St. Louis, Missouri; d. 4 November 1895, Chicago, Illinois

Like Walt WHITMAN and William Cullen BRYANT, F. was a career journalist better known for his poetry.

He has been called "the first of the columnists," but is more famous for his poetry for children. He was loved by children across America and is remembered for such poems as "Little Boy Blue," "The Little Peach," and "Christmas Treasure."

F. began his newspaper career in 1873 as a reporter for the *St. Louis Evening Journal*. He soon became the city editor and took the liberty of inserting more humorous news items along the serious. A later editorial post at the *St. Louis Times-Journal* was where he launched "Funny Fancies," a column in which he interspersed his reporting with irrelevant and often libelous material. F.'s unique reportage was well received and his column widely mimicked. In 1881, he accepted a managing editor position at the *Denver Tribune* and there created a column, "Current Gossip," the best of which was collected and published as *A Little Book of Western Verse* (1889). Soon newspaper publishers in Chicago and New York were vying for him. F. chose Chicago and reworked his "Current Gossip" column into "Sharps and Flats" for the *Chicago Morning News*. These columns were not gossip columns in the contemporary sense, rather, he used them to parody—often in verse—the foibles and pretensions of politicians and society types. He also wrote of serious matters.

F.'s was a bibliophile and his lifelong sensitivity to literature produced an effective style of writing. He encouraged young writers to perfect their language skills offering this advice: "A young writer cannot be too careful in his choice of words . . . a writer must know his weapons before he can use them with effect"

When F. died on November 4, 1895, his newspaper wrote: "All of the children of the land mourn their laureate." The city of Denver erected a statue in his honor. F. had significantly impacted the lives of his readers. He was a hero to schoolchildren, often receiving letters from them. His newspapers columns were lighthearted reflections of day-to-day events and activities making him everyone's neighbor.

BIBLIOGRAPHY: Taft, W. H., "E. F.," in Ashley, P. J., ed., *DLB*, vol. 23, *American Newspaper Journalists, 1873–1900* (1983): 110–17; Thompson, S., *Life of E. F.: The Poet of Childhood* (1927)

JASON MCMAHON

FILM AND LITERATURE

The relationship between film and American literature has been surprisingly arid, given that both art forms contain dramatic and narrative elements and should mutually influence and inform one another. With few exceptions, the rendering of great American novels and plays has produced mediocre films, or no films at all. Although a work such as William FAULKNER's *The Sound and the Fury*, published in 1929, employs several cinematic devices—elliptical images shifts, cross-cutting, flashforwards, and flashbackwards—the film version of this novel (1959) is a particularly glaring failure of film adaptation. The screen interpretations of Herman MELVILLE's *Moby-Dick* (1930, 1956) and Nathaniel HAWTHORNE's *The Scarlet Letter* (1926, 1934, 1995) have not fared much better, though Wim Wenders directed a lovely version of Hawthorne's work (1972) originally derived from a German play. While many of Tennessee WILLIAMS's dramas have been turned into films, only Elia Kazan's version of *Streetcar Named Desire* (1951) can be credited with successfully exploring cinematic techniques to re-create the stage play. Williams also wrote an original screenplay for Kazan's much publicized *Baby Doll* (1956), an erratic work which, nevertheless, has moments of visual and dramatic potential. A number of undistinguished films have been adapted from Ernest HEMINGWAY's fiction, with the exception of Robert Siodmak's *The Killers* (1946). And none of the attempts at F. Scott FITZGERALD's *The Great Gatsby* (1949, 1974) have produced anything approaching the merits of the novel.

In contrast, several of Henry JAMES's novels and stories have been brought to the screen with skill; these include Jack Clayton's *The Innocents* (1961), based on *The Turn of the Screw*, Peter Bogdanovich's *Daisy Miller* (1974), and the work of James Ivory and Ismail Merchant, *The Europeans* (1979) and *The Bostonians* (1984). Francois Truffaut, who greatly admired American literature and the work of Henry James in particular, created an inventive interpretation of "The Altar of the Dead" in *The Green Room* (1978). Even though James's fiction predates the film revolution, his narrative style anticipates several cinematic techniques: the Jamesian "orbit of consciousness" with its interior perceptual processes lends itself to the panning camera and close-up; James's convoluted structures, from sentence to dialogue to scene, can find rapport in the malleable patterns of film sequencing. No doubt the psychological and dramatic intensity of James's fiction has drawn gifted directors to his work, and they have responded with cinematic craft. Jane Campion's *Portrait of a Lady* (1996) exquisitely captures the psychological nuances of character and atmosphere, matched by brilliant cinematography and decor.

In a few cases, important American novels have actually been enhanced by their reformulation into cinematic narrative. The cumbersome structure of Theodore DREISER's *An American Tragedy*, published in 1925, is sharply cut and refocused in George Stevens's *A Place in the Sun* (1951). Crisp editing and patterned shot composition bring forth Dreiser's themes with an aesthetic elegance foreign to Dreiser's methodical style. Also, Stevens shifts the narrative emphasis to the last section of the novel by focusing on Clyde Griffith's crime, its causes and its consequences. Yet, Dreiser's profound social and psychological insights are not lost in Stevens's compression of the overall work. Elia Kazan's film (1955) of John STEINBECK's *East of Eden* illustrates another successful restructuring of flawed narrative. Kazan, like Stevens, emphasizes the last section of Steinbeck's novel by focusing on the story of the estranged brother, Cal Trask. Through metaphoric camera set-ups, expressive editing, psychological motifs, and brilliant ensemble acting, Kazan adds an aesthetic energy lacking in Steinbeck's prose. Two recent cinematic interpretations of classic American novels, Martin Scorsese's *The Age of Innocence* (1993) and Michael Mann's *The Last of the Mohicans* (1992), show exceptional skill in translating literary texts to the cinematic medium.

One of the most rewarding translations of novel into film exists in John Schlesinger's *Day of the Locust* (1975). Schlesinger capitalizes on Nathanael WEST's use of the grotesque by finding the appropriate visual language to re-create West's apocalyptic vision. While Schlesinger retains the novel's characters and events, he also adds a subtext of symbolic imagery that enriches and expands West's terse style without sacrificing West's sensibility. Schlesinger has found a workable middle ground; he does justice to the novel, but also impresses the work with his own artistic signature. To a less successful degree, Elia Kazan finds the same middle ground in his interpretation (1976) of F. Scott Fitzgerald's *The Last Tycoon*. However, the limitations of the film follow directly from the fact that Fitzgerald did not complete the novel; Kazan's intention seems to incorporate, rather than correct, that fact.

If masterpieces of American literature have, as a rule, failed in their cinematic adaptation, pulp and genre fiction have, in many instances, turned literary "junk" into film art. Psychological thrillers, such as detective fiction or the suspense novel, have proven especially rich sources for the masters of film. Alfred Hitchcock's realization (1951) of Patricia Highsmith's novel *Strangers on a Train* (1951) underscores how film aesthetics coupled with Hitchcock's genius enhance and enrich popular crime fiction. Wim Wenders achieves a similar success in *The American Friend* (1977), based on Highsmith's *Ripley's Game* (1974). Such Stephen KING novels as *Carrie* and *The Shining,* good examples of commercial genre fiction within the mode of horror and the supernatural, are transformed into cinematic masterpieces through Brian De Palma's

(1976) and Stanley Kubrick's (1980) mastery. Both directors impose their own visions and metaphoric vocabulary on the framework of King's novels, providing a texture and complexity not found in the original work.

In the 1940s and 1950s, perhaps the best wedding of film and American literature occurred in the development of film noir, a cinematic style noted for its use of light and shadow, its hardboiled dialogue, its sharp-edged, often expressive editing and shot composition. Cynical in tone, and preoccupied with the criminal, violent, and perverse, the genre paradoxically bears an undercurrent of the sentimental and redemptive. One primary source of film noir was American pulp fiction, where such writers as James M. CAIN, Dashiell HAMMETT, Raymond CHANDLER, and Mickey Spillane transformed hack formula through stylistic craft. Among the best examples of film noir is Robert Aldrich's aesthetic embellishment of Spillane's *Kiss Me Deadly* (1955). A subtext of Christian allusion structures a narrative that turns the conventions of cop and criminal chase into a social, philosophical, and religious investigation of grace and salvation, themes clearly not in Spillane's original work.

Although lucrative salaries have often drawn writers of talent to Hollywood, it should be noted that few American writers have successfully made the transition from fiction, drama, or poetry to the screenplay. Faulkner's brief and dismal encounter with Hollywood is an obvious example of literary genius largely wasted in hack work. In spite of the fact that Faulkner did an admirable job as script doctor on several Howard Hawks's projects, in the end, Faulkner saw his talents compromised by studio production methods. F. Scott Fitzgerald, Thornton WILDER, Dorothy PARKER, and others adapted in various ways to the Hollywood ambience. Though Nathanael West found an outlet for his despair as a contract studio writer in the satiric voice of *Day of the Locust,* he never was able to achieve any autonomy as a film writer. The status of the screenwriter has always been lowly, subservient either to collaborative committee decision or to the director as auteur. The screenplay, as literary form, is rarely read or studied on its own merits; consequently, the screenwriter does not have the same status as the playwright. In much of film theory, it is assumed that the director, and not the scriptwriter, is the author of the film.

However, exceptions do exist, where writer and director have found a collaborative rapport, or where a screenwriter has managed to assert artistic integrity. Vladimir NABOKOV wrote the screenplay for *Lolita* (1962), altering his novel's (1955, 1958) narrative structure in order to complement the cinematic design of Stanley Kubrick's work. Hitchcock's *Shadow of a Doubt* (1943) had a strong screenplay written by Thornton Wilder. Arthur MILLER's collaboration with John Huston on *The Misfits* (1961) demonstrates how a brilliant script, along with a radiant Clark Gable and Marilyn Monroe, carries the burden of flawed cinematic craft. The same might be said of James AGEE's partnership with Huston; if *The African Queen* (1951) has merit, one must credit a good screenplay, for the overall film lacks aesthetic texture and imagination. Indeed, John Huston, both as director and screenwriter, has attempted to film several masterpieces of American literature: Stephen CRANE's *The Red Badge of Courage* (1951), *Moby-Dick* (1956), and Flannery O'CONNOR's *Wise Blood* (1979). However, none bear any cinematic vigor or inspiration.

Sam SHEPARD and David MAMET, perhaps more than other important American writers, move with facility between drama and cinema. Shepard first wrote for the screen in Antonioni's *Zabriski Point* (1969). His play *Fool for Love,* with a screenplay adapted by Shepard himself, achieved forceful realization in the hands of Robert Altman (1986). In the film *Paris, Texas* (1984), Shepard's original screenplay found artistic compatibility in the creation of director Wim Wenders. David Mamet wrote and directed two of the most powerful and well received works of recent film history, *House of Games* (1987) and *Homicide* (1992). Both films explore Mamet's fascination with language, gender, and mystification in a unique reworking of *film noir* style. Jamie Foley's direction of *Glengarry Glen Ross* (1992) showcases brilliant ensemble acting around Mamet's investigation into American constructions of masculinity.

Because of the almost anonymous status of the screenwriter, those scriptwriters who have gained independence sometimes turn to directing. Paul Schrod, who won acclaim for his screenplay of Martin Scorsese's *Taxi Driver* (1976), later directed his own scripts in *American Gigolo* (1980) and *Mishima* (1985). Likewise, Robert Towne, noted for his screenplays of *Chinatown* (1974) and *Shampoo* (1975), has since turned to directing. Unfortunately, in part because of the method of film production in the U.S., few screenplays seem to stand by themselves as works of art. However, the writing of Steve Tesich, *Breaking Away* (1979) and *Four Friends* (1981), exemplifies the unusual situation of a screenwriter known for his craft. Of course, most of the great directors either write their own scripts or supervise them to such a degree that the writer becomes a technical tool for the director, on a par with the cinematographer or film editor.

Despite film's predominant influence, both domestically and internationally, on popular and high culture, it has had surprisingly little influence on American literature. In the early decades of the century, the new medium played a part in the avant garde aesthetic, with its fluidity of time/space, its disjunctive mode, its primacy of the image. Poets such as T. S. ELIOT in *The Waste Land* and Ezra POUND in *The Cantos* were attuned to this new aesthetic and responded with a poetic form that reflected elements of cinematic style. Indeed, passages from either work lend themselves to a filmic analysis. In the 1920s and 1930s John DOS PASSOS saw the possibilities of cinematic narration as something applicable to the novel; and Faulkner's innovative narrative and visual techniques particularly reflected the impact of film aesthetics. In the contemporary period, works such as E. L. DOCTOROW's *Ragtime* and William Wharton's *Birdy* (1979) reflect such film techniques as crosscutting, flashback, and montage. Interestingly, Alan Parker's film version of *Birdy* (1984) is an exquisite adaptation while the rendition of *Ragtime* (1981), originally to be directed by Robert Altman, fell victim to production politics and, as a consequence, the resultant work, under the uninformed direction of Milos Forman, abandoned the novel's intrinsic cinematic style. Overall, the interplay between film and literature in America has been sadly infertile, in contrast to the fruitful exchange of the two arts within the modern European tradition where aesthetic discourse and theoretical debate inform both the artist and the audience.

One emergent area of American literature is, however, finding resources within cinema—mixed-media. The incorporation of film and video into the *mise-en-scene* and text of the play opens up theater, not just to cinema, but to the other arts as well. The work of such companies as Soon 3 and the Magic Theater in San Francisco provides opportunities for the contemporary American playwright to evolve a new kind of drama. Robert Wilson's epic opera/dance/architectural dramas illustrate the inventive ways cinematic techniques can be incorporated into the environment of the play. All this bodes well for the vigor of contemporary American theater.

Because film is capital intensive, filmmaking as an art has often been debased as a mere entertainment commodity, subjected more to the profit than the aesthetic motive. Although American writing has become increasingly debilitated by the "blockbuster mentality" and relative public indifference, the writer, in contrast to the filmmaker, can continue to practice his art whether or not it is immediately published, read, or performed. Film, on the other hand, requires a strong fiscal underpinning. Given the exigencies of American capitalism, perhaps the uneasy relationship between film and American literature can, in part, be explained by economic necessity. One hopes that such extrinsic interference will one day be overcome so that the natural interplay of the dramatic and narrative elements in film and American literature can be mutually and imaginatively realized.

BIBLIOGRAPHY: Beja, M., *Film and Literature* (1979); Bluestone, G., *Novels into Films* (1957); Boyum, J. G., *Theater and Film* (1979); Friedrich, O., *City of Nets* (1987); Manvell, R., *Double Exposure* (1985); Wagner, G. A., *The Novels and the Cinema* (1975)

DIANE M. BORDEN

FINLEY, Martha

b. 26 April 1828, Chillicothe, Ohio; d. 30 January 1909, Elkton, Maryland

With the publication of *Elsie Dinsmore* (1867), one of the most popular 19th-c. novels set in the South, F. launched a series that within the next four decades would number twenty-eight novels and earn her a quarter million dollars. Earlier, she had sold stories to the Presbyterian Board of Publication for its Sunday school series. They appeared, as did most of her works, under her pseudonym Martha Farquharson (Gaelic for Finley). The Elsie books echo the religious and moral content of those stories. F. was not a Southerner, nor had she visited the South when she began the series. Born in Chillicothe, Ohio, she lived also in Indiana, New York, and Pennsylvania before settling in Elkton, Maryland.

Although critics and editors generally ignored F. or found her work inept—one called Elsie "a nauseous little prig"—19th-c. readers found much to admire. Beautiful, wealthy, perfect but motherless, Elsie suffers and weeps under the trials and punishments imposed by superiors. Striving to win her father's love, yet defying him, when necessary, in order to keep God's law, Elsie triumphs. She marries her father's friend Travilla and bears children, but widowed early, she returns to her father. Later volumes carry titles such as *Grandmother Elsie* (1882), *Elsie at Nantucket* (1884), and *Elsie at the World's Fair* (1894). In recent years librarians have removed *Elsie Dinsmore* from the young adult section because Elsie seems to model judgmental and defiant attitudes toward parents.

Post-Freudian readers find the father-daughter relationship fascinating. Ruth SUCKOW argues that Elsie, in her obedience to both earthly and heavenly fathers, demonstrates that "woman craves a master." Other critics counter that, in league with God, Elsie controls everyone around her.

The Elsie Dinsmore series represents only a third of Finley's publications. Other works include the seven-volume, more realistic Mildred Keith series, the Do-

Good Library; the Pewt Nest series; and the Finley series, none so popular as Elsie's.

BIBLIOGRAPHY: Brown, J. E., "The Saga of Elsie Dinsmore," *UBS* 17 (July 1945): 71–131; Hardman, P., "The Steward of Her Soul: Elsie Dinsmore and the Training of a Victorian Child," *AmerS* 29 (Fall 1988): 69–90; Michie, H., "'Dying between Two Laws': Girl Heroines, Their Gods, and Their Fathers in *Uncle Tom's Cabin* and the *Elsie Dinsmore* Series," in Yaeger, P., and B. Koweleski-Wallace, eds., *Refiguring the Father: New Feminist Readings of Patriarchy* (1989): 188–206; Shepherd, A., "Sweet Little Ways: Elsie Dinsmore," *MarkhamR* 11 (Spring 1982): 57–59; Suckow, R., "Elsie Dinsmore: A Study in Perfection or How Fundamentalism Came to Dixie," *Bookman* 66 (October 1927): 126–33

LUCY M. FREIBERT

FISHER, Dorothy Canfield

b. 17 February 1879, Lawrence, Kansas; d. 9 November 1958, Arlington, Vermont

Although she was born in the Midwest and enjoyed a national and international reputation for most of her life, today F. is best remembered as a New England regionalist writer who wrote about Vermont. While many of her novels and short stories are, indeed, set in the Green Mountain State, F.'s themes—the artistry of domestic ritual, gender equality in matters of education and work, modern marriage and the family, and moral responsibility in solving 20th-c. "problems of living" as she termed them—drew her a wide audience in her day, and made her a best-selling author for much of her career. Current critical attention to F.'s life and career and the reprinting of several of her short stories and novels are helping to reinvigorate her early reputation as an important American author.

F. was a true "woman of letters" publishing eleven novels, several short story collections, and twelve books of nonfiction, including general sociological studies of modern educational trends, and popular histories of American heroes and of her beloved Vermont. She was also a panel judge for the Book-of-the-Month Club, and as such was somewhat of a cultural arbiter of literary taste for twenty-five years. But F. wanted to be remembered for her fiction, and her novels represent a fascinating chronicle of the cultural shift from Victorian values and mores to a modern sensibility.

F. was named after the Victorian heroine Dorothea Brook from George Eliot's *Middlemarch,* and her life and work often exhibit a struggle to shake off restrictive Victorian codes of behavior and Victorian plot structures to try on a modern identity, to tell modern stories. The tension between conserving what was valuable from her 19th-c. upbringing and reforming those elements of Victorian culture that were repressive underlies F.'s fictional endeavors and she draws on various turn of the century social movements to restructure family life for modern America, like the Arts and Crafts Movement, the Montessori Method, and Freudian Psychology. For example, in an early novel, *The Squirrel Cage* (1912), F. models her artist figure, Daniel Rankin, after William Morris, a proponent of the Arts and Crafts Movement that argued for art as a domestic, everyday experience. Rankin is the first in a long line of F.'s domestic male characters who argue that the turn-of-the-century male role of "captain of industry" is too limiting. In this novel, F. also shows the devastating effects of separate spheres on young women as well, as Lydia Emery, her protagonist, wants an education and worthwhile work but has been denied these essentials by a social structure that defines her as decorative.

Perhaps her most modern novel, *The Home-Maker* (1924), is a naturalistic experiment in role reversal, as F. shows the effects on the Knapp family when Lester Knapp stays home to raise his children and his wife, Eva, takes a job in a local department store. F.'s argument in this novel is for work that suits individual abilities rather than social prescriptions based on gender. Her connection of private and public spheres is deepened and broadened in her novel about World War I, *The Deepening Stream* (1930). In the first half of the novel, F.'s protagonist Matey Gilbert overcomes an unhappy childhood to achieve domestic artistry and construct her own happy family life. The second half demonstrates the public need of Matey's newly honed domestic skills as she revives daily processes and rituals in war-torn Paris. F's novel argues that the personal is political as she shows how family lives are ruptured and destroyed by a political process that uses war for material gain. Her depiction of family life is truly modernized with this novel, as public and private spheres are collapsed and "women's work" moves into a global context.

BIBLIOGRAPHY: Madigan, M., *D. C. F.* (1996); Madigan, M. J., ed., *Keeping Fires Night and Day: Selected Letters of D. C. F.* (1993); Rubin, J. S., *The Making of Middlebrow Culture* (1992); Washington, I. H., *D. C. F.* (1982)

ANNE M. DOWNEY

FISHER, M[ary] F[rances] K[ennedy]

b. 3 July 1908, Albion, Michigan; d. 22 June 1992, Glen Ellen, California

Although F. chose cooking and eating as the foundation for most of her essays, to call her a food writer is to ignore the breadth and depth of her work. W. H. AUDEN considered her, simply, "America's greatest writer." A prose stylist for whom food was a metaphor for life and its sensual pleasures, F. changed the very concept of gastronomical writing. She once observed that in writing about hunger, she was "really writing about love and the hunger for it, and warmth and the love of it and the hunger for it." Her collected essays have been steadily reissued and continue to win new generations of admirers.

F. was a newspaper publisher's daughter whose Episcopalian family moved to the Quaker town of Whittier, California, when she was two. Being reared there accustomed her to viewing the world as an outside observer—she said she was never invited into a Quaker home. Her favorite place in the house was the kitchen, where the cook gave her lessons and where she established a special place in the household by helping to cook for the family.

F. attended three different colleges briefly and then, in 1929, married Alfred Young Fisher, a doctoral student in literature. They moved to France, where F. gained proficiency in the language and an understanding of French literature, culture, food, and wine. On their return to California in 1932, F. began writing historical essays based on old cookbooks she found. Her neighbor, a painter named Dillwyn Parrish, encouraged her to include personal reminiscences. The essays, originally intended for the amusement of F., her husband, and Parrish, revisited meals and restaurants from F.'s past and later became her first book, *Serve It Forth* (1937).

F. left her husband in 1937 and moved to Switzerland with Parrish, whom she married that same year. He was stricken with illness in 1939, and they returned to California. Parrish's death in 1941 forced F. to turn to writing full-time to support herself. She produced some of her most enduring writing in these years, including the essay collections *Consider the Oyster* (1941), *How to Cook a Wolf* (1942), which urged readers to deal with the shortages of wartime by inviting "the wolf at the door" in and eating him, *The Gastronomical Me* (1943), and *Alphabet for Gourmets* (1949). F., by turns detached and passionate, both soothes and startles the reader with what one reviewer called "the faintly Gothic perversity" of her style.

F. married for a third time in 1945 and worked for the next few years writing articles for women's magazines, publishing a novel, *Not Now but Now* (1947), and finishing her definitive translation of Brillat-Savarin's *Physiology of Taste* (1949). She divorced again, returned with her daughters to the family home until her father's death in 1953, and then took the children to France and Italy for five years. In Provence, F. made a study of folk cures later published as *A Cordiall Water* (1961). She bought a ranch in California where she lived, when not visiting Europe, for the remainder of her life, attracting visitors to a kind of gourmet's literary salon.

In the 1960s, the *New Yorker* bought exclusive rights to her articles, and she wrote a series on memorable meals and recipes. F. also wrote essays about her childhood later collected as *Among Friends* (1971). Her book *Sister Age* (1981) addressed the complexities of growing older. A long struggle with Parkinson's disease narrowed her world and finally left her unable to walk or write, though she continued to compose and dictate pieces until her death and left a body of work for posthumous publication.

For some years, F.'s works were not given serious attention, because, she believed, others felt that her subject matter was "women's stuff, a trifle." She won admirers who saw her as a "poetic voice of the working woman," but F. herself resisted being categorized either as a cookbook writer or a woman's author. Her incisive works are utterly individual. As the *New York Times Book Review* commented, "In a properly-run culture," F. would be recognized as "one of the great writers this country has produced in this century."

BIBLIOGRAPHY: Lazar, D., "The Usable Past of M. F. K. F.: An Essay on Projects," *SWR* 77 (Autumn 1992): 515–31

CAROLYN LENGEL

FISHER, Vardis [Alvero]

b. 31 March 1895, Annis, Idaho; d. 9 July 1968, Jerome, Idaho

Reared in an isolated area near the Snake River in Idaho, F., author of some thirty books, has been called the last authentic writer of the American frontier. He is also credited with creating the first significant literature of the Rocky Mountain region. The material of his own life and the years of his childhood and youth formed the basis for much of his most powerful work.

F. achieved his greatest reputation in the 1930s for an autobiographical tetralogy. His reputation peaked in 1939 when he received the Harper Prize for *Children of God,* an historical novel about the origins and rise of the Mormon church. F.'s reputation since has not been as substantial as it was in the 1930s (even then he was controversial as to both content and art), but he is widely recognized as one of the important writers of the American West.

F.'s first three novels portray the Idaho country of his youth and many of the harsh realities of frontier life. *Toiler of the Hills* (1928) introduces readers to the Hunter family and describes the dry farming meth-

ods that made the hills productive to settlers. His second novel, *Dark Bridwell* (1931), a more haunting story, recounts the progress of Charley Bridwell, whose approach to life was antithetical to that of the toilers of the first novel. A minor character in *Dark Bridwell* was the autobiographical Vridar Hunter, and F. next turned his attention to Vridar in four novels that took their titles and their themes from lines from George Meredith's *Modern Love,* Sonnet XLIII: "I see no sin: / The wrong is mixed. In tragic life, God wot, / No villain need be! Passions spin the plot: / We are betrayed by what is false within." In *In Tragic Life* (1932), Vridar is appalled by the cruelty he finds in the Bridwells and in most dimensions of frontier life. In adolescence, he feels great guilt because of his sexual drive and fears that he is growing insane. But finally he overcomes some of the fuddled teaching that has warped him, and he establishes lofty goals: he wants to be a teacher and a writer. He makes a tragic marriage with his childhood sweetheart in *Passions Spin the Plot* (1934), and he feels responsible for her suicide at the end of *We Are Betrayed* (1935). He pushes to recovery and new vision in the concluding novel of the tetralogy, *No Villain Need Be* (1936).

As Vridar returns to Idaho from New York City at the end of the tetralogy, so did F. *April: A Fable of Love* (1937) is a short work about the dreaming and courtship of a homely but imaginative girl of the Antelope Hills. *Forgive Us Our Virtues* (1938) treats several of the themes of the tetralogy in a satiric mode. Its chief character, Ogden Greb, leaves the intellectual pretense of New York City and accepts a teaching position at a Midwestern university, where he finds just as much sham. So he moves to Idaho, where he meets Sylvia Dale and has the wisdom to accept her love. Idaho is important to the short stories that F. wrote in the 1930s, gathered as *Love and Death* (1956). In the manner of Edwin Arlington ROBINSON, F. added to his rendering of his Idaho heritage by writing several sonnets about people of the Idaho hills.

F.'s ancestors had gone to Idaho to help settle it for the Mormons, and *Children of God* is a part of his effort to understand himself. Although he had abandoned the faith of his fathers by the time he graduated from high school, he knew that Mormonism was an important shaping influence on his world. He tried to be meticulously fair in his novel, recounting the careers of Joseph Smith and Brigham Young as objectively as possible. His method was to dramatize the story as he found it, much as in his autobiographical novels he dramatized the data of his own memory. Thus, F.'s novel differs from most historical novels, which usually cast the major characters of history as minor characters in the fiction. Only in the final third of *Children of God* did F. focus on invented characters as he recounted the church's resolution of the polygamy crisis.

F.'s other novels dealing with the history of the American West also depict dramatizations of recorded history. *City of Illusion* (1941) recounts the heyday of the Comstock lode in Virginia City, Nevada. *The Mothers* (1943) celebrates mother courage in a rendition of the ill-fated Donner edition. *Tale of Valor* (1958) portrays the Lewis and Clark expedition. F. relied less on actual events and personages for his frame in *Pemmican* (1956), about the Hudson's Bay Company, and in his final novel, *Mountain Man* (1965), which, although based on stories about an actual person, dealt with the stuff of legend. F. thought of that book as a symphony to the West. Whereas he wrote the earlier Western novels, except *Children of God,* to support himself while working on the twelve novels known as the Testament of Man, he wrote *Mountain Man* largely to please himself. F. wrote two nonfiction books about the West. *Suicide or Murder? The Strange Death of Governor Meriwether Lewis* (1962) explores alternative possibilities for the mysterious end of one of F.'s heroes. *Gold Rushes and Mining Camps of the Early American West* (1968), written with his wife Opal Laurel Holmes, is encyclopedic and contains nearly 300 pictures.

By 1939, F. was already convinced that he had not adequately explained the autobiographical Vridar of his tetralogy. Believing that the truth bout any person could make sense only if viewed in light of the evolution of the human race, F. immediately embarked on an ambitious reading schedule of history, anthropology, and religion. The deepest truths about human beings, he concluded, resided in their myths. To illustrate his conviction, he wrote the Testament of Man novels, portraying the evolution of human beings from prehistoric times to the present. In them, he was particularly interested in family structures and the development of religious dogma.

Darkness and the Deep (1943) portrays the life of the ape man, especially his fears. In *The Golden Rooms* (1944), Neanderthal man battles ape man and develops notions of ghosts and an afterlife. *Intimations of Eve* (1946) and *Adam and the Serpent* (1947) portray early matriarchal societies and beginnings of farming and other arts. *The Divine Passion* (1948) leaps over many centuries to the era of the early Hebraic culture with its well-developed language system and elaborate patriarchal codes governing land and sexual conduct. *The Valley of Vision* (1951) imagines King Solomon's life, attempting a realistic portrayal of his society and an idealized Solomon wiser than his times. *The Island of the Innocent* (1952) recounts the history of the Maccabees, which F. sees as a pivotal moment in human history, inviting the reader to ponder what his-

tory might be if the Greek ideal had prevailed over the Hebraic. *A Goat for Azazel* (1956) explores the origins of Christianity, finding its basic notion in the concept of Jesus as an offering for sin, as a scapegoat for Azazel. In *Jesus Came Again* (1956), which he subtitled "A Parable," F. imagines what Jesus's life might have been like, though he calls his main character Joshua rather than Jesus. *Peace like a River* (1957) studies the asceticism of early Christianity. *My Holy Satan* (1958) renders the darker side of medieval Christianity and the horrors of the Inquisition. *Orphans in Gethsemane,* the twelfth novel in the series and by far the longest, retells Vridar's story. The first half of the novel is based extensively on the tetralogy; the second half is partly an apologia for the first eleven novels of the Testament, but it also contains much of biographical interest and recounts Vridar's further insights into his heritage and his evaluation of the American scene. It also recounts his struggles to get his own Testament published, reflecting F.'s declining reputation as an American author in the 1940s. Midway through the Testament, F. had found his publishers uninterested in continuing the series. It languished until the mid-1950s when the writer-publisher Alan Swallow agreed to publish the later volumes.

The exact number of F.'s books depends on how one counts the books he oversaw for the Works Projects Administration: *Idaho, A Guide in Word and Picture* (1937), *The Idaho Encyclopedia* (1938), and *Idaho Lore* (1939). There is no reason to think that they are not largely by his hand. He was a writer of immense ambition and drive. Readers have objected to his work for many reasons, sometimes finding his subjects overly grim (he has been compared to Theodore DREISER and other naturalists), sometimes finding him oppressively didactic (parts of the tetralogy and much of the Testament of Man are overburdened with analysis of ideas). He found an avenue for his largely conservative political views in a regular Idaho newspaper column. He railed against the Eastern establishment in his fiction and in other forums. He was often militantly Western. He wished to change the world, and he recognized this wish as a part of his romantic side. He wrote some fine short stories, but these—like poetry—belonged to his early career, when he seemed more interested in the challenges of genre and form. But the didactic intent persisted.

BIBLIOGRAPHY: Chatterton, W., *V. F.: The Frontier and Regional Works* (1972); Day, G., *The Uses of History in the Novels of V. F.* (1976); Flora, J. M., *V. F.* (1965); Grover, D. C., *V. F.: The Novelist as Poet* (1973); Woodward, T., *Tiger on the Road: The Story of V. F.* (1989)

JOSEPH M. FLORA

FITCH, [William] Clyde

b. 2 May 1865, Elmira, New York; d. 4 September 1909, Chalons-Sur-Marne, France

F. was one of the most prolific and successful playwrights of the early 20th c. Although he enjoyed tremendous popular success during his lifetime, he never achieved the critical fame he hoped for. While critics praised his witty dialogue and deft characterizations of the denizens of New York society, they often labeled his plays shallow for not probing contemporary social "problems" as did the European "realists." In spite of this criticism, F. is counted among playwrights who advanced realism on the American stage through his comedies of American manners. His realism can be described as "local color" in that, in his original works, he created characters and situations true to that segment of American society referred to as "genteel." He teased his audiences with what Russell Lynes has called "discreet naughtiness" through well-made plays written to please his public and not to be studied as pieces of literature.

During his college days at Amherst, F. exhibited a preference for theater in spite of his father's desire that he should study architecture. Throughout his college career, F. wrote, produced, and designed costumes and scenery for various student productions. After graduation, he moved to New York determined to find work in theater, while sustaining himself by writing children's stories, a novel (published in *Lippincott's Magazine,* 1891), and tutoring. During this time, he made his first trip to France and Italy, countries that so captured him that he was to return many times during his lifetime. These trips abroad supplied F. with creative inspiration and subject matter as he watched the trends on European stages.

F.'s first big break came as a result of his acquaintance with E. A. Dithmar, drama editor of the *New York Times,* who recommended him to Richard Mansfield, leading man and matinee idol of the day. The result of this meeting was *Beau Brummell* (perf. 1890, pub. 1915), which met with critical success and began F.'s reputation as an established playwright. While F. made no attempt at complete historical accuracy in *Beau Brummell,* he did reveal traits that were to be further developed in his later works: insightful visualizations of social milieu, dramatically absorbing characterizations, and clever dialogue.

F.'s early works from 1890 to 1900 have been called experimental in that he tried various styles: plays of modern society life, *A Modern Match* (perf. 1892), about a vain, selfish woman who deserts her family during a financial crisis; plays based on historical figures or incidents, *His Grace de Grammont* (perf. 1894), a comedy of manners of the court of Charles II; adaptations from the French, *The Masked Ball* (perf. 1892), a farce-comedy, and *An American Duchess* (perf. 1893), a satire of social and political practices; comedy of manners, *Mistress Betty* (perf. 1895); and plays based on American history, *Nathan Hale* (perf. 1898, pub. 1899) and *Barbara Frietchie* (1899). By 1900, F. had hit his stride with *The Climbers* (perf. 1901, pub. 1906), about a family of "social climbers," except for the stalwart Ruth Sterling, who saves her family from scandal and financial ruin, and in the next decade wrote what have been described as his best plays. In 1901, F. had four plays running to capacity audiences on Broadway at the same time: *The Climbers, Barbara Frietchie, Captain Jinks of the Horse Marines* (1901), and *Lovers Lane* (1915). The next season saw three more F. plays. Other important works of this period (all exhibiting the F. trademark "genteel" social strata and character types) include *The Girl with the Green Eyes* (perf. 1902, pub. 1905), about the finely drawn Jinny Austin who lets jealousy almost ruin her marriage; *Her Own Way* (perf. 1903, pub. 1907), about a young woman, Georgiana Carley, who remains true to a man presumed dead in spite of pressures from another suitor; *The Woman in the Case* (perf. 1905, pub. 1915) and *Her Great Match* (1906), both involving strong women characters who defy tradition concerning a woman's role in marriage; and *The Truth* (1907), for some critics the high point of F.'s career. *The Truth* played successfully in major European cities and Russia, firmly establishing F.'s international reputation. During the next three years, F. continued to write light comedies while he formulated what he hoped would be his best work. *The City* (1915), produced shortly after F.'s death while in Europe, traces the influence of city life upon the Rand family formerly leading citizens of a small New England town. Although he did not live to see the success of *The City,* the play was all F. had hoped it would be representing the height of his qualities as a playwright.

F. excelled at creating female characters and created some of the more interesting "new women," a brand new character to emerge on the American stage during the late 19th and early 20th cs. These "new women" stood in contrast to the traditional roles (as wife and mother) assigned to women at the turn of the century. Many of F.'s "new women" are educated, witty, independent, enjoy professional careers, and accept responsibility for making decisions regarding the source of their lives as well as the lives of their families. Good examples of this character are Blanche Sterling in *The Climbers* who must shoulder responsibility for keeping the family together, and Margaret Rolf in *The Woman in the Case,* who puts herself in jeopardy socially and physically, to save her husband's life and reputation.

In spite of the lack of critical success during his lifetime, F. is now recognized as one of the best, most gifted American playwrights. At a time of theatrical dependence on European imports, F. brought to the stage sparkling and dramatically exciting depictions of genteel, educated, unique members of American society.

BIBLIOGRAPHY: Lynes, R., *The Lively Audience: A Social History of the Visual and Performing Arts in America, 1890–1950* (1985); Quinn, A. H., *A History of the American Drama* (1936)

ALMA J. BENNETT

FITZGERALD, F[rancis] Scott

b. 24 September 1896, St. Paul, Minnesota; d. 21 December 1940, Hollywood, California

F., "half black Irish and half old American stock," was born in St. Paul, Minnesota. His father's family had near-links to Colonial patriots—he was named for Francis Scott Key; F.'s great-great-great-grandfather and Key's grandfather were brothers—and well-bred Southerners but was impoverished, his mother's family were "potato famine Irish" but had money. Unsuccessful in St. Paul, his father moved his wife and son to Buffalo in 1898 and in 1899 to Syracuse, where F.'s sister Annabel was born in 1901. Failing in Syracuse, F. moved his family back to Buffalo in 1903 and in 1908 back to St. Paul where he could work for his wife's family.

In St. Paul, the Fitzgeralds moved every year, to better or worse neighborhoods, posher or plainer streets, larger or smaller houses, depending on his father's fortunes. Thanks to the McQuillan family, there was enough money to send F. to private school in St. Paul (St. Paul Academy, 1908–11) and then east to prep school (Newman School, 1911–13) and university (Princeton, 1913–17), but F. felt stigmatized as the poorest boy in his particular class, circle, school. He wasn't, of course, but he frequently felt like Dexter Green in "Winter Dreams" (1922) who, because he couldn't "afford the luxury of proms . . . stood outside the gymnasium and listened" to the romantic music.

At Princeton, F. wrote lyrics for the Triangle Club musicals and poems for the *Nassau Literary Magazine;* his best friends were John Peale Bishop and Edmund WILSON. In the fall of 1917, F., along with many of his classmates, left Princeton to enlist. Stationed at Fort Leavenworth, Kansas, he spent his spare time rewriting the stories, poems, and journal entries he had written and stitching them together into a loose narrative he called *The Romantic Egotist* which Scribner's quickly rejected.

"The worst second lieutenant in the army," F. was transferred to Camp Taylor, Kentucky, in February 1918, to Camp Gordon, Georgia, in April, and to Camp Sheridan, Alabama, in June. On September 7, 1918, he saw Zelda Sayre, a beautiful and vivacious eighteen-year-old, at a country club dance and, he wrote in his Ledger, "fell in love." The war ended in November before F. could be sent overseas; he was discharged in February 1919 and headed immediately for New York to make his fortune, or at least a future sufficiently promising to marry on.

Failing to get a newspaper job, he went to work for an advertising agency writing slogans for streetcar cards ("We Keep You Clean in Muscatine"). At night, he wrote short stories, the kind popular magazines like the *Saturday Evening Post* paid big money for, nineteen of them between April and June (he accumulated one hundred and twenty-two rejection slips). F. wasn't going anywhere, and Zelda got tired of waiting ("She was feeling the pressure of the world outside," F. wrote of Daisy in *The Great Gatsby,* "and she wanted to see him and feel his presence beside her and be reassured that she was doing the right thing after all") and broke their engagement. Nearly twenty-three and "a failure," he recalled in "Early Success" (1931), "mediocre at advertising and unable to get started as a writer," F. quit his job and, having nowhere else to go, returned to St. Paul.

He took *The Romantic Egotist* out of the drawer where it had gathered dust since Scribner's rejected it a year earlier and spent the summer revising it, adding his love affair with Zelda and its demise. In September, F. sent the manuscript, now called *This Side of Paradise,* back to Scribner's—and Scribner's accepted it. In October, his new agent sold a story, "Head and Shoulders," to the *Saturday Evening Post* for $400 and in November he returned to Alabama to woo Zelda again. He had a future now: a novel soon to be published, stories being sold to *Scribner's* and the *Saturday Evening Post*—between September and December he wrote nine stories, one in a single evening. The Sayres announced the engagement on March 20, 1920, *This Side of Paradise* was published on March 26, and on April 3, F. and Zelda were married in the rectory of St. Patrick's Cathedral in New York.

This Side of Paradise sold 40,000 copies in its first six months. Today, it is hard to understand why it had such a success and caused such a sensation. Copiously, sometimes hilariously, overwritten, intellectually pretentious yet undernourished, the novel tells the story of Amory Blain, starting with a fabulously wealthy childhood dominated by a mother the narrator insists is charming but who emerges as mentally unbalanced. When she has a breakdown, Amory is sent to poorer relatives in St. Paul where he loses some of his Eastern snobbisms and acquires a whole new collection of Midwestern ones.

We follow him to prep school in the East and then to Princeton where Amory spends very little time in class but a lot of time drinking and partying, writing inflated poetry, worrying about the Princeton eating clubs, and falling in and out of love with girls but mainly with himself. World War I rescues Amory from aimlessness.

After the war, Amory goes to New York. Since his father's death the family fortune has dwindled alarmingly, and Amory has to go to work. He meets Rosalind Connage, sister of a classmate, and they fall in love, but Amory's salary at the advertising agency won't pay Rosalind's hairdresser. Rosalind, responding to parental pressure but mainly to her own self-knowledge—what her limitations are, what will make her happy, what will preserve and protect her best but perishable qualities (beauty, charm, freshness)—breaks off the engagement.

Amory gets drunk, quits his job, and has a brief fling with an exciting girl so reckless she is suicidal. At the end of the novel, Amory, penniless, bereft of his past and unable to imagine a future, hitchhikes to Princeton, site of former triumphs. Although he has lost everything, Princeton rekindles his idealism and enthusiasm. The novel ends with Amory's arms "stretched out . . . to the crystalline, radiant sky," an optimism and exuberance that seem more willed than earned.

This Side of Paradise, it seems, spoke to and for his generation, "a new generation," F. announced at the end of the novel, "dedicated more than the last to the fear of poverty and the worship of success, "a generation grown up to find all Gods [sic] dead, all wars fought, all faiths in man shaken." The novel is not, however, depressing as is contemporary novels of similar intention—John DOS PASSOS's *One Man's Initiation* and *Three Soldiers,* C. E. Montague's *Disenchantment,* a British counterpart—but is, in fact, about the sunniest and liveliest treatment of disillusionment one can imagine. And the timing was just right: if Scribner's had published *The Romantic Egotist,* which ended with the hero going off to war, it would have been too early in this generation's infancy; if F. had waited much longer, on the other hand, this generation's rejection of the past and its adoption of hedonism would already have been announced.

The novel became famous, and so did its author and his wife. More than celebrities, the Fitzgeralds became epitomes of what was thought to be urbane and sophisticated, this twenty-year-old from a rather sleepy small city in Alabama, this twenty-three-year-old from staid St. Paul. The novel's success prompted Scribner's to publish a collection of stories as quickly as possible: *Flappers and Philosophers* was published in August, not five months after *This Side of Paradise.*

The Fitzgeralds settled in New York. When Zelda became pregnant at the beginning of 1921, they decided that New York was too unstable an atmosphere into which to bring a new life so they moved to St. Paul. Frances Scott Fitzgerald—Scottie—their only child, was born on October 26, 1921.

In April 1922, Scribner's published F.'s second novel, *The Beautiful and Damned,* stylistically and technically a significant improvement over *This Side of Paradise.* In *The Beautiful and Damned,* F.'s narrative control is much surer, his intent is much clearer, characters actually develop and incidents serve thematic and structural purposes. Although occasionally overwritten, *The Beautiful and Damned* has little of the adolescent callowness that characterized *This Side of Paradise.*

Neither, unfortunately, has it any of *Paradise*'s adolescent exuberance. *The Beautiful and Damned* is a sober and somber, almost clinical, study of disintegration. Its hero—though there is nothing heroic about Anthony Patch who isn't even energetic—squanders and dissipates away the promise of a huge inheritance and takes to drink. In an ironic twist, a court finally awards him his thirty million dollars but it comes very late: his youth and what little enthusiasm he had are gone for good and his sanity may be going as well. Damned, however, seems too dramatic to apply to pallid Anthony—rather, he lets things slip away, peter out—and it is hard to find any beauty in him at all, not in anything he says or does, not in anything he is (even his decadence is inelegant).

But Gloria is another matter. The high point of Anthony's life is his infatuation with, rejection by, and finally wooing and winning of Gloria Gilbert, one of the generation's most famous flappers. She deserves the title, for F.—he was thinking of Zelda—successfully conveys her beauty and charm, intelligence and wit—he borrowed liberally from Zelda's diaries for Gloria's—and her susceptibility to love, a fatal recklessness that damns her freshness to a premature death (she could have married an older and wiser man who would have protected her from life's vicissitudes).

Gloria chooses the lover Rosalind rejects. It's easier for Rosalind because Amory has no money: she thinks she's choosing the security of wealth over the uncertainty of poverty. But Anthony has plenty of money and the promise of much, much more, and Gloria knows he is far too self-absorbed and weak, too immature and irresponsible to take care of himself, much less of her. As Anthony weakens, however, Gloria deepens, nourished by an ego and sense of self Anthony never has.

To the extent that F. set out to show the effects of rootlessness and dissipation on the young, careless, beautiful people of his time, *The Beautiful and Damned* is a success, convincing and persuasive in its cumulative detail and in the slow but steady decline that gives the novel its direction. None of these things had happened yet, not to F. or Zelda or their generation—the decade is only a year old, the Fitzgeralds are young and happy, affluent and admired. Because of what we know did eventually happen to the Fitzgeralds and the twenties *The Beautiful and Damned* has the power and fascination of prophecy.

There is one narrative flaw in the novel, one serious structural weakness in point of view: sometimes we feel we are meant to feel sorry for Anthony and yet at the same time we feel it's his own fault, he gets what he deserves. And that is because F. was himself torn between pity and contempt for Anthony, pity and contempt for himself, or for what he feared he would—had already begun to?—become.

It is least successful as the novel of ideas F. so wanted it to be. He had recently read Frank NORRIS and Theodore DREISER and had adopted a naturalistic stance he didn't come to naturally; sometimes in the novel he seems like a small boy trying on clothes too big, too grown up, for him, or a well-brought up boy using bad words to sound adult and tough. And he had come under the influence of H. L. MENCKEN, whose approbation and respect he craved; there are paragraphs of cynical speechifying condemning American culture that sound forced and seem unearned.

Although a much more interesting novel than *This Side of Paradise* and ten years more mature in intent and execution, *The Beautiful and Damned* did not sell as well as F. had hoped it would. He had already begun to live on publisher's advances against his next novel, his next collection of stories—Scribner's published *Tales of the Jazz Age,* F.'s second collection, in September 1922.

The Fitzgeralds moved to Great Neck in October 1922, and lived a fashionable and expensive life. Still under Mencken's influence, F. spent nearly a year on a political satire called *The Vegetable* (1923), which never made it to Broadway. And he wrote stories: in 1924, he published eight stories; in 1925, seven to get ahead, to buy himself an uninterrupted year on his next novel. He called his stories "trash," though among those first forty were "Diamond as Big as the Ritz," "Bernice Bobs Her Hair," "The Ice Palace," "May Day," "Winter Dreams," "The Sensible Thing," and "Absolution." They weren't trashy, not even the insignificant ones. Almost single-handedly he had elevated the level of the popular magazine story; each one, no matter how trite the material, was written with F.'s

customary grace and, although they were predictable, the stories were never formulaic. As F. observed late in his career, "I have asked a lot of my emotions—one hundred and twenty stories. The price was high . . . because there was one little drop of something, not blood, not a tear, not my seed, but me more intimately than these, in every story, it was the extra I had."

In 1924, the Fitzgeralds moved to Europe—to get away from New York, to live more sensibly and frugally and quietly, and to allow F. to work more seriously and more carefully. *This Side of Paradise* and *The Beautiful and Damned* had been written—assembled, in the case of *Paradise*—too quickly. Furthermore, this time he wanted to do something special, something really his own: to call *This Side of Paradise* derivative is too generous—sometimes it seems plagiarized, a paste-pot job, a pastiche—and the most original moments in *The Beautiful and Damned* are provided by Gloria's—Zelda's—diary.

The Great Gatsby (1925) is special but not because of its subject matter. F. knew—and feared—that the material—rich people on Long Island who drink too much and drive too fast and commit adultery and die violently—was sensational, the kind of frivolity and superficiality he was accused of and that the Horatio Algerish rags-to-riches rise and final fall was trite. What made it special is the way it's told—so intensely, so concisely, in such evocative language—and how it's told—F. solved the problems of narrative perspective that plagued *This Side of Paradise* and *The Beautiful and Damned* by employing a first-person narrator, a strategy he learned from Joseph Conrad (Marlow in *Heart of Darkness* and *Lord Jim*).

If Gatsby, a tasteless parvenu in a pink suit who hosts parties and drives vulgar cars, an adulterer who has an affair with one man's wife and is killed by another man who thinks he has had an affair with his wife, a liar and a phony, maybe even a murderer—is great, it is because of his "romantic readiness," his "gift for hope," his fidelity to "an incorruptible dream," his belief "in the green light, the orgiastic [sic: orgastic, F. instructed his editor Maxwell Perkins in 1925, like an orgasm, not orgiastic like an orgy] future that year by year recedes before us. It eluded us then, but that's no matter—tomorrow we will run faster, stretch out our arms farther. . . . And one fine morning—So we beat on, boats against the current, borne back ceaselessly into the past."

But those are Nick Carraway's pronouncements, and they tell us at least as much about Nick as they do about Gatsby: if Gatsby is great, it's because Nick thinks he is. In being able to separate Gatsby ("Gatsby turned out all right at the end," Nick says) from "what foul dust floated in the wake of his dreams," Nick, too, turns out all right at the end, expresses and keeps faith with his own romantic readiness, his own gift for hope, his own belief in an orgastic future. So sensible and ordinary, so cautious and conservative does Nick seem, moreover, that his elevation of Gatsby at the end to national status ("I became aware of the old island here that flowered once for Dutch Sailors' eyes—a fresh green breast of the new world") and Gatsby's dream of Daisy to the Dutch Sailors ("the last and greatest of all human dreams"), his elevation of Gatsby to a historic universal ("for a transitory enchanted moment man must have held his breath in the presence of this continent, compelled into an aesthetic contemplation he neither understood nor desired, face to face for the last time in history with something commensurate to his capacity for wonder"), and, finally, to a continuous universal ("the orgiastic future that year by year recedes before *us, it eluded us* then, tomorrow *we* will run faster, stretch out *our* arms farther, so *we* beat on, boats against the current") do not, by the time they occur, seem forced or sentimental but, rather, earned, even inevitable.

Very few critics attributed this sort of significance to *The Great Gatsby* in 1925. While most critics applauded the beautiful and tight prose and F.'s much improved technique, they also agreed with H. L. Mencken that the story and the characters were fundamentally trivial. Neither did it achieve anything like the commercial success of *This Side of Paradise* and *The Beautiful and Damned.*

But F. was convinced he was a serious and authentic—as opposed to derivative—writer now, and others he met it Paris that year—Gertrude STEIN, Ernest HEMINGWAY—thought so too. Not yet thirty, he was already the author of three novels and three collections of stories. Scribner's published *All the Sad Young Men* (1926) within a year of *Gatsby,* six books in six years. The decade, which he had helped name and for which he had provided, in his literature and his life, much that seemed quintessential, was at its peak, and so was F.

It cannot be said with any precision when it was exactly that the decade began to wind down, when things began to go sour and wrong—as F. seems to have predicted they would in *The Beautiful and Damned* and *The Great Gatsby*—but F.'s own life began to unravel at about the same time. As the decade had buoyed him up, so now its decline seemed to mirror his own.

Perhaps it was the moment F. discovered that Zelda was in love with—or at least attracted to—someone else. They left the Riviera at the end of 1927 and rented an estate outside Washington. Zelda had begun to study ballet and now began to devote herself to it frantically at an age when many ballet dancers start to think of retirement. They returned to Europe in 1929. In April 1930, Zelda suffered a complete nervous collapse and was institutionalized in a Swiss sanitorium from June 1930 to September 1931. They returned to America but she suffered another breakdown in January 1932. Through 1932 and 1933, they lived in Baltimore where Zelda was being treated. She suffered a third collapse in January 1934, after which she remained more or less permanently institutionalized until her death in 1947.

In smaller, less decisive, and less dramatic ways, F. broke too, but he never stopped writing. From 1928 to 1932, he published eight stories a year, most of them in the *Saturday Evening Post,* which, between 1930 and 1931, paid Fitzgerald $4,000 a story. Where he had extolled flaming youth, the "lovely light" the candle of Edna St. Vincent MILLAY's poem gave off as it burned at both ends, now he paid, especially in "The Last of the Belles," "The Rough Crossing," "The Bridal Party," "One Trip Abroad," "Babylon Revisited," "Crazy Sunday," and the five Josephine stories, sad and haunting farewell to what was already a vanished era. Once his generation's most vigorous and vocal celebrant, he now became its rueful eulogizer. In nine stories, he wrote about an adolescent name Basil Duke Lee, he reached back even farther to that time of comparative quiet and innocence just before the 1920s had gotten underway.

In a sense, he had always been rueful. Much of the poignancy and power of F.'s twenties work proceeds from his instinct that his beautiful young men and women were damned, the dreams would die, love wouldn't last, freshness would fade, the diamond mountain would implode. As he put it in a poem he called "Lamp in a Window" (1935), "the end was desolate and unkind: / To turn the calendar at June and find December / On the next leaf."

In 1934, F. finally finished *Tender Is the Night,* a long novel of decline. Because of his fatal attraction to and love for a fabulously wealthy patient, psychiatrist Dick Diver marries Nicole Warren and gives up a promising career to provide her with the kind of care and atmosphere she needs if she is to get well. The son of a clergyman, Dick ministers to the wealthy who are his patients and friends, achieving the esteem he craves by making himself essential to people who, the narrative leads us to believe, are undeserving of his efforts and self-sacrifice. At the end of the novel, Nicole is cured, which means that she no longer needs Dick (in fact, she *must* leave him, declare her independence from him). For Dick, it is too late to retrieve a lost career or go back to the fork in the road and take the road not taken; depleted of vitality he goes back to America to practice general medicine in smaller and yet smaller towns until he disappears altogether. But Dick is no mere victim of Nicole or money or the time. He succumbs to what she promises to bring him—the wealth of a continent—because of an early susceptibility to what he knows to be the superficial, a fatal fascination with the glitter and glamour great wealth can purchase and provide.

There are splendid scenes in *Tender Is the Night,* memorable characters, graceful and beautiful passages, but the judgment of he critics in 1934 seems just: much care and attention, detail and effort, lavished on undeserving material (Dick's failure, in fact). The subject doesn't seem to warrant all that work, the novel suffers from a fatal lack of proportion, much the same lack of proportion the twenties suffered from, which may make *Tender Is the Night* the quintessential twenties novel—too much made of too little, too slender a scaffold to bear all that weight. The novel leads us to the discovery that, deep down, Dick is shallow (in *The Great Gatsby* we discover the opposite: the shallow Gatsby has depth) and that does not deserve four hundred pages, no matter how beautifully written. Twice the length of *The Great Gatsby, Tender Is the Night* seems the slight and trivial anecdote *The Great Gatsby* was accused of being but which, despite its slightness and triteness, it isn't.

Tender Is the Night has no Nick Carraway to provide perspective. The first section, from the point of view of a very young movie actress infatuated with Dick and the life he lives, provides a lush rendering of being rich on the Riviera and an adoring portrait of Dick Diver, but the rest of the novel is third-person omniscient and the two points of view never mesh. F., always a keen critic of his own work, got it right: he had spent too much time delineating the decline of a character that not many people would care about very much.

Nine years had passed since *The Great Gatsby,* and *Tender Is the Night,* though respectfully reviewed and admired for its writing, did not restore F. to the front rank of American novelists, as he had hoped it would. Nor did it sell well enough to rescue him from financial disaster, and neither did the collection of stories published with the year, *Taps at Reveille* (1935), despite its gorgeous title.

He found it harder and harder to write the kind of short story—young love, happy endings—mass-circulation magazines were willing to pay good money for and on which he had come to depend utterly to pay his bills. In June 1937, he went to Hollywood on a six-month contract with MGM, grateful for the chance to earn a living. He did well enough to get a one-year renewal, but in December 1938, MGM did not renew him again. He hung on, however, very much like Pat Hobby, the itinerant and derelict screenwriter F. wrote eighteen stories about for *Esquire* at $250 per. He even fell in love again, with an English woman,

Sheilah Graham, and, an even bigger surprise, started another novel.

There is no knowing how *The Last Tycoon* (1941) would have turned out—F. revised *The Great Gatsby* significantly, omitting the opening section entirely (published as "Absolution," one of his fines stories) and there are 3,500 pages of holograph manuscript and typescript representing seventeen drafts and three versions of *Tender Is the Night*—had he lived to finish it. But we can say about the six chapters (there were to be nine chapters and an epilogue) that were published after his death that F. had not lost his touch, his ability to write both tight and evocative prose and to create memorable moments. Unlike *Tender Is the Night,* and much more like *The Great Gatsby, The Last Tycoon* has intensity and focus, drama and purpose, and it tells a story very much worth telling.

Based on Irving Thalberg, the boy-genius production head of MGM who died young, Monroe Stahr bears a close resemblance to Jay Gatsby. Like Gatsby, he comes from humble beginnings. Like Gatsby, he is a visionary: "out of the corner of his eye Gatsby saw that the blocks of the sidewalk really formed a ladder and mounted to a secret place above the trees—he could climb to it, if he climbed alone, and once there suck on the pap of life, gulp down the incomparable milk of wonder"; when Stahr was young "he had flown up very high to see . . . and while he was up there he had looked on all the kingdoms, with the kind of eyes that can stare straight into the sun . . . and then, remembering all he had seen from his great height of how things were, he had settled gradually to earth."

The significant difference is that Gatsby incarnated his vision in a beautiful girl, but Stahr expends his romantic readiness and his capacity for wonder on an entire industry, an industry that is both peculiarly and significantly American and central to an understanding of American life. Stahr is F.'s first—and only—hero who does something we are made to believe is worth doing, whatever the failure of movies to achieve their full potential.

Which is why, although Stahr is the *last* tycoon and the novel delineates his decline, defeat, and death—and the decline, defeat, and death of the American values he represents—the novel is not, like *Tender Is the Night,* depressing. The novel is about struggle and strife, pursuit and persistence, and it was to end in a final apotheosis in which what Stahr stood for survives. F., it would seem, had emerged from the "crack-up" he wrote about in 1936 and had found a way out of his own despair.

Writing about his friend Ring LARDNER, F. said that "whatever Ring's achievement was, it fell short of the achievement he was capable of." It seemed that way about F., too, when he died in 1940, forty-four and forgotten: not one of his eight books was in print, he had spent too much time and energy and talent on "trash," on material and audiences not worthy of such expenditure. But despite the conventional wisdom that F. wasted or abused his talent, his "gift"—early on in his career he was likened to a foolish woman in whose care and keeping had been left a precious jewel—F. did keep the contract he had made with his personal god. What F. concluded of Lardner was also true of him: "he had served his Fates well, and no other ones could be casually created for him." Nothing that he wrote was without moments of insight or passages of delight and pleasure and in *The Great Gatsby* he wrote an imperishable novel, something fully commensurate to our capacity for wonder.

BIBLIOGRAPHY: Allen, J., *Candles and Carnival Lights: The Catholic Sensibility of F. S. F.* (1978); Bruccoli, M. J., *Some Sort of Epic Grandeur: The Life of F. S. F.* (1981); Callahan, J., *The Illusions of a Nation: Myth and History in the Novels of F. S. F.* (1972); Donaldson, S., *Fool for Love: F. S. F.* (1983); Lehan, R. D., *F. S. F. and the Craft of Fiction* (1966); Mellow, J., *Invented Lives: F. S. and Zelda F.* (1984); Meyers, J., *S. F.: A Biography* (1994); Miller, J., *F. S. F.: His Art and His Technique* (1964); Mizener, A., *The Far Side of Paradise: A Biography of F. S. F.* (1951); Piper, H. D., *F. S. F.: A Literary Portrait* (1965); Sklar, R., *F. S. F.: The Last Laocoon* (1967); Stern, M., *The Golden Moment: The Novels of F. S. F.* (1970); Turnbull, A., *S. F.* (1962)

BARRY GROSS

FITZGERALD, Robert [Stuart]

b. 12 October 1910, Geneva, New York; d. 16 January 1985, New Haven, Connecticut

F. is perhaps the preeminent American translator of Greek and Roman classical poetry. His reputation rests not only on his celebrated versions of epic poetry—Homer's *The Odyssey* (1961) and *The Iliad* (1974), and Virgil's *The Aeneid* (1983)—but also his widely performed renditions of Sophocles and Euripides. Written in a style at once contemporary and timeless, accessible and dignified, these verse translations provided influential models for subsequent versions of ancient poetry.

F. was reared in Springfield, Illinois, where his father was a lawyer with aspirations toward the stage. F.'s early life was scarred by a series of family tragedies. When he was three, his mother died in childbirth. Five years later, his only brother perished in the influenza epidemic. Meanwhile, his father was invalided

by tuberculosis. Eventually dying when the poet was seventeen, his affectionate father, however, provided a critical emotional stability for the young F., who became a model scholar-athlete. His early literary ambitions even received encouragement from his fellow townsman Vachel LINDSAY.

Upon graduation from high school, F. was sent to the Choate School for a year of college preparation. There he met poet Dudley Fitts, who was his Latin master. Fitts soon became his mentor and eventually his collaborator in their celebrated translations of Euripides' *Alcestis* in 1935 and Sophocles' *Antigone* and *Oedipus Rex* in 1939 and 1948 respectively. F. independently translated *Oedipus at Colonus* in 1941. F. attended Harvard where he took honors in English and Greek. Graduating in 1933, he worked first for the *New York Herald Tribune* and later for *Time* (where he shared an office with James AGEE). During World War II, he served in the U.S. Navy in the Pacific front.

In 1949, F. left *Time* and split his life between teaching in America and writing in Italy where he settled his large family. From 1965 to 1981, he served as Boylston Professor of Rhetoric and Oratory at Harvard where his charismatic teaching, especially his popular course on versification, proved decisive to many of the young poets who would later be called the New Formalists.

Although F. achieved fame from his Greek and Roman translations, he was no classics scholar. Instead, he belonged to a now almost vanished tradition of poets deeply schooled in classical languages and literatures. The particular power of F.'s translations came from their specifically literary virtues. His version of *The Odyssey,* which eventually sold nearly two million copies, displays the qualities that distinguish all his epic translations—a clear and compelling narrative line, masterful delineation of character, and expert pacing. He mixes archaic and contemporary diction to achieve a tone at once stately and unpretentious. The flexible blank verse is resonant without ever becoming intrusive. Demonstrating how classical epic and tragedy could be re-created as living poetry, F.'s translations have generally become the standard by which later versions are measured.

F. was also a lyric poet. His first collection, *Poems* (1935), was followed by *A Wreath from the Sea* (1943) and *In the Rose of Time* (1956). His characteristic poems are quietly elegiac. The early "Midsummer" describes the small-town landscapes of his lonely adolescence. "Souls Lake" and "Colorado," both from *A Wreath for the Sea,* use the natural world as avenues for philosophical speculation. F.'s return to Catholicism in 1945 transformed his later work. His spiritual aspirations were now focused in specifically Catholic terms. "Solstitium Saeculare," a meditation on the second half of life (after surviving World War II), is suffused with religious grace. An active critic and reviewer, F. also left a substantial body of prose, much of it collected in *Enlarging the Change* (1985), and *The Third Kind of Knowledge* (1993).

BIBLIOGRAPHY: Carne-Ross, D. S., "On Looking into F.'s Homer," *NYRB* 12 December 1974: 3–8; Honig, E., *The Poet's Other Voice* (1985)

DANA GIOIA

FITZGERALD, Zelda [Sayre]

b. 24 July 1900, Montgomery, Alabama; d. 10 March 1948, Asheville, North Carolina

In addition to commenting extensively on much of her husband F. Scott FITZGERALD's work in progress and providing the model for many of his female characters, F. was also a gifted, underappreciated, and at times uncredited author, as well as a painter and student of ballet. Recent criticism has corrected the tendency to consider her work only in relation to her husband's.

F.'s diaries and letters provided her husband not only with inspiration but also often with passages for his own writings. Her shorter works, occasionally edited by her husband, were often originally published as by both Fitzgeralds, and in some cases attributed only to F. Scott Fitzgerald. Some of her light early essays are available in *The Romantic Egoists* (1974). *Bits of Paradise* (1973) collects her published short stories (1925–33). Imagistic and sometimes bitter, these usually employ a shadowy first-person narrator to describe women whose lives are constricted by the power of a male world. Her later autobiographical essays, "Show Mr. and Mrs. F. to Number—" and "Auction—Model 1934," available in *The Crack-Up* (1945), have an impersonal, ironic tone that belies their subtly dark emotional content.

F.'s most significant work is the bildungsroman *Save Me the Waltz* (1932). The first part details the youth of Southern belle Alabama Beggs and her love of romance and dance. In part two, she leaves the home of her powerful father, Judge Beggs, for marriage to the charming and arrogant painter David Knight. The power struggle in their marriage takes place in New York and France in an atmosphere of casual dissipation and sophisticated wit. In part three, the emptiness of this life spurs Alabama to dedicate herself to the ballet. Part four treats her experience as a professional dancer in Naples, where an injury ends her brief career. The novel ends with the death of the Judge and with Alabama and David's ambivalent reunion. Much of the action is advanced through dialogue, but the novel's

style is most notable for its vivid profusion of metaphors.

F.'s play, *Scandalabra* (1980), an unsuccessful Wildean farce with an oddly moralistic ending, was performed in 1933. At her death, she was at work on a surrealistic novel, *Caesar's Things.*

BIBLIOGRAPHY: Anderson, W. R., "Rivalry and Partnership: The Short Fiction of Z. S. F.," *Fitzgerald/Hemingway Annual* (1977), 19–42; Mellow, J. R., *Invented Lives: F. Scott Fitzgerald and Z. F.* (1984); Milford, N., *Z.: A Biography* (1970)

FRANN MICHEL

FLANNER, Janet

b. 13 March 1892, Indianapolis, Indiana; d. 7 November 1978, New York City

Although she considered herself a journalist, F. achieved rare literary distinction with her 1925–75 "Letter from Paris" column for the *New Yorker.* Her concise, intelligent prose, compassionate, witty, and informative, captured every aspect of French society and culture with candor and brilliance. F. is rightly associated with the Left Bank EXPATRIATES of the 1920s and 1930s, but her half-century of work is a highly unique accomplishment. She was awarded France's Legion of Honor in 1947, and, after her columns and profiles appeared in collected form, America's National Book Award in 1966. She was also a member of the American Academy and Institute of Arts and Letters.

F.'s first aspiration was to be a novelist, and this she achieved with the autobiographical *The Cubicle City* (1926), the story of a New York stage designer with feminist beliefs. F.'s own story involved her 1918 escape from the Midwest to New York by way of a friendly but short-lived marriage. Her important lifelong relationships, however, and those that supported her independent lifestyle and career, were with Solita Solano, Noel Murphy, and Natalia Danesi Murray. F. was living in Paris with Solano in 1925, the year Harold Ross founded the *New Yorker,* when Ross's wife Jane Grant praised her descriptive personal letters. Ross contracted her to write a column under the name "Genet," suggesting that she write not what she thought, but what the French thought. Of course, this was a goal not quite possible, but the result was a new style and scope of journalism. In the early twenties, *Vanity Fair, The Dial,* and *Town and Country* had attempted Paris letters by top writers, but the writing was always too political, personal, or editorial. F. struck a balance, writing about every aspect of French culture, with opinion but also with an open mind, originality, humor, and substance.

In style, she learned, she said, from the "exactitude" of the French language, reading a dozen French newspapers, making her prose less ornate. And she didn't hesitate to use the audacious long French-style sentence, nor to use antithesis to build purpose and suspense. Often, her sentences boldly rendered one sure-handed phrase after another, unveiling layers of meaning, then ended with an impact, both sonorously and intellectually. For example, her 1939 comment about the state of Europe: "France and England, after first acting as if they would fight for anything and then as if they wouldn't fight at all, have finally made it apparent that they will fight for only a few things, but for them will fight to the death."

F.'s powerful post-World War II writing of a wounded, recovering France greatly increased her fame. Her fear that even the best journalistic efforts are destined for the trash can was alleviated by bound works. *Paris Journal* (2 vols., 1965, 1971) and *Paris Was Yesterday* (1972) represent all five decades of her "Letter from Paris." Her profiles are largely collected in *An American in Paris* (1940) and *Men and Monuments* (1957). She also translated *Cheri* and *Claudine at School* by Colette, and *Maeterlinck and I* by Georgette Leblanc.

BIBLIOGRAPHY: Murray, N. D., *Darlinghissima: Letters to a Friend* (1985); Weiss, A., *Paris Was a Woman* (1995); Wineapple, B., *Genet: A Biography of J. F.* (1989)

JERRY ROSCO

FLAVIN, Martin
b. 2 November 1883, San Francisco, California; d. 27 December 1967, Carmel, California

At the age of thirty-five, wallpaper manufacturer F. returned to the passion of his youth and began writing plays. In only five years, he had his first Broadway hit, *Children of the Moon* (1924), a play of symbolic realism that was also produced internationally. In 1929, *The Criminal Code* received the best play award of the New York Theater Club. Even more impressively in 1929, F. had three works running simultaneously on Broadway, a most rare achievement. Unable to match this success in the coming years, F. abandoned plays and turned to novels. All were well received and his third effort, *Journey in the Dark* (1943), won the Pulitzer Prize and the Harper Prize. His total literary output consists of at least thirteen plays, three film scripts, five novels, and two travel books. He was also a contributor to *Harper's Magazine*.

As both a playwright and a novelist, F. had the most success with serious, realistic works in which he created detailed characters and milieus, and explored contemporary social problems. While some critics admired his stories and craftsmanship, others thought that they were too melodramatic or formulaic. F. was able to write plays and novels that appealed to theater and reading audiences of his day, but the work has not stood the test of time.

The Criminal Code takes place in a penitentiary and features Robert Graham, a young man who is enmeshed by two competing codes of justice—that of the legal system and that unspoken code established by the inmates themselves. Both codes require the proverbial "eye for an eye." The code entraps everyone, including a sympathetic warden, who was also the young man's prosecutor. Graham seals his own fate when he kills a prison guard in reprisal for weeks of torture.

Among other plays, *Broken Dishes* (1930) is a domestic farce, and *Cross Roads* (1930) is a serious play about the decisions that youths must make as they prepare for adulthood. Both of these plays ran concurrently on Broadway with *The Criminal Code*. *Amaco* (1933) is a protest drama against the machine age, and *Achilles Had a Heel* (1936) is an allegorical comedy that features a philosophical elephant keeper caught in a moment of weakness.

Published three years after John STEINBECK's *The Grapes of Wrath*, *Journey in the Dark* is similar in feel and intent, though it examines a different segment of the American landscape. It follows the life of a successful businessman through the sixty years preceding World War II. Sam Braden's "humble beginnings"—especially his inferior social and economic status—in a sleepy Iowa town on the Mississippi River are constantly in his mind even after he has become a manufacturer in the bustling, cosmopolitan metropolis of Chicago. Against the background of these two archetypal settings, he juggles family loyalties, social aspirations, moral questions, and business dilemmas.

F.'s first novel, *Mr. Littlejohn* (1940), is a light-hearted chronicle of the cross-continental adventures of a bored, middle-aged man running away from his family and his business. *Corporal Cat* (1941) is a bleak story of a German parachutist who lands by mistake behind his own lines, only to be pursued to his death by the Nazi war machine. *The Enchanted* (1947) is a fantasy that follows seven European refugee children shipwrecked on a remote tropical island. *Cameron Hill* (1957) is a psychological portrait of a man driven to murder by his domineering and manipulative mother.

Of his travel writing, *Black and White: From the Cape to the Congo* (1950) was positively reviewed for its literary qualities, and for its intelligent description of African geography and peoples.

BIBLIOGRAPHY: Adams, M., "M. F.," in Martine, J. J., ed., *DLB,* vol. 9, part 2, *American Novelists, 1910–1945* (1981): 18–21

MAARTEN REILINGH

FLETCHER, John Gould

b. 3 January 1886, Little Rock, Arkansas; d. 19 April 1950, Little Rock, Arkansas

Imagist poet and Southern Agrarian, F. was born in the former home of Albert PIKE. F.'s father was a Little Rock banker, cotton merchant, and politician. Privately educated at home and in the Little Rock public schools, F. attended Phillips Academy at Andover, Massachusetts before entering Harvard. After the death of his father, he left Harvard in 1908 to travel and did not return permanently to the U.S. until 1933. In London, he associated with imagist poets Ezra POUND and Amy LOWELL, and in *Irradiations/Sand and Spray* (1915) introduced IMAGISM into America. However, after 1916 he quarreled with its leaders and broke with the movement. F. attacked urbanization, corporate capitalism, and mass culture with poetry in *Breakers and Granite* (1921), through a biography of Gauguin, and with a comparative history of Russia and America.

In 1927, he became acquainted with the "Fugitive" school of writers working out of Nashville and contributed an essay on the advantages of an aristocratic education to the Agrarian manifesto, *I'll Take My Stand* (1930). F.'s identification with Southern regionalism increased after he divorced his first wife, returned to Arkansas in 1933, settled in the old family house, and married children's writer and folkways enthusiast Charlie May Simon.

Although F. broke formally with the FUGITIVES/AGRARIANS after 1935, his interest in the South continued unabated. In 1936, he wrote an epic ode for Arkansas's Centennial and helped arrange for the Library of Congress recordings of blind folksinger Emma Dusenbury. Two years later, he won the Pulitzer Prize for his *Selected Poems* (1938), but increasingly his poetic work went unpublished. An impressionistic history, *Arkansas* (1947), emphasized the state's great men, notably Albert Pike, and reflected F.'s abhorrence of the treatment accorded the sharecroppers. In 1949, he was appointed writer-in-residence at the University of Arkansas and helped to establish the Ozark Folklore Society, serving as its first president. During a bout of depression, he committed suicide.

F. defies easy characterization. His early poems reflected his wide reading, especially in Oriental symbolism, while his later work was perhaps too easily understood to suit many critics. In his essays and in *Arkansas,* F. reacted against the crassness of the Southern business elite as typified by his father. In his revolt, he came to reject MODERNISM and turned his hopes instead to the persistence in the South of traditional values that he believed were preserved in their original purity by those mountain folk out of touch with modernization. F. called for an aristocracy raised in the traditions of the Old South to reject both business capitalism and racist demagoguery. His autobiography, *Life Is My Song* (1937), reflected parts of his intellectual turmoil. His wife, in *Johnswood* (1953), offered another view of his struggles.

BIBLIOGRAPHY: de Chaska, E. S., *J. G. F. and Imagism* (1978); Johnson, B. F., *Fierce Solitude: A Life of J. G. F.* (1994); Morton, B., *J. G. F.: A Bibliography* (1979); Stephens, E. B., *J. G. F.* (1967)

MICHAEL B. DOUGAN

FOLKLORE

Although the term "folklore" did not appear until 1846 when British antiquarian William J. Thoms introduced it as a "good Saxon compound" to replace the Latinate term "popular antiquities," American literature has always had a close affinity with traditional culture. Some American folklore materials, those that are a part of oral tradition, reveal literary qualities in themselves. Meanwhile, American authors have consciously and unconsciously drawn upon folklore for enhancement of setting, characterization, plot, structure, and theme.

Folklore covers what may be deemed a society's "unofficial culture," especially that which is learned through direct contact with others in a person's immediate reference groups. While folklore as unofficial culture includes aspects of material culture, belief systems, and customary behavior, much folklore also constitutes a kind of "oral literature" and involves an array of forms ranging from pithy figures of speech ("cold as a welldigger's butt") and memorably phrased bits of practical wisdom ("A rolling stone gathers no moss") to complex sung (ballads and epics) and spoken narratives (myths, legends, and folktales).

Most commentators identify verbal material as folklore on the basis of its orality, its performance and dissemination occurring in situations where a speaker or singer and his or her audience enjoy immediate contact. Another characteristic that most folklore, verbal or otherwise, reveals is a life in tradition. In other words, some features of the material are rooted in an ongoing heritage of oral performance. These features may include, for example, the plot of a story, some of its verbal style, the situation in which it is told, and the gestures that accompany its telling. Because verbal folklore passes among individuals in oral encounters, it lacks the fixity that writing or other transmission media may produce, so another trait associated with folklore is its variability. Each performance of a story, song, or proverb has at least some elements that are unique. Meanwhile, though, certain performance features may remain constant, and folklore often evinces considerable formulation on the level of diction, style, and even theme. Another trait that sometimes distinguishes folklore from other kinds of verbal artistic expression is the anonymity of its creator, whose identity may be unknown to the people who tell the story or sing the song.

While verbal folklore possesses other dimensions such as the performative that should be taken into account for a full appreciation, oral literature may be susceptible to some of the analytical perspectives that contribute to understanding and responding to written literature. For example, one may examine the style and structure of written texts that reproduce what might have been said or sung in oral performance. On one hand, then, American folklore relates to literature because some folklore is distinctly literary. Literary theorists, in fact, have often perceived verbal folklore as providing the foundations for other literary expression in a culture. Some authors, trying to establish a distinctly American literary culture, have turned to what they perceive as indigenous folklore for inspiration. Henry Wadsworth LONGFELLOW, for example, based his most famous attempt at an American epic, *The Song of Hiawatha,* principally on the Chippewa oral literature that had been recorded and published by Henry Rowe SCHOOLCRAFT.

In fact, Thoms's coinage of folklore emerged from similar concerns about cultural nationalism in Britain. His neologism appeared in a letter to the London *Athenaeum* encouraging British antiquarians to match the efforts of the Grimm Brothers in recording the indigenous cultural expressions of the "olden time," thus providing a foundation in tradition for British culture analogous to the Germanic heritage harvested by the Grimms. Even though the international provenance of much folklore has long been recognized, a nationalistic emphasis characterized folklore collecting and study throughout the 19th c. and into the 20th c. While folklorists have come to identify folklore not so much in terms of its age as Thoms did, but by its manner of distribution (oral tradition or informal imitation), by its social context (small group), or by its performance situation (face-to-face interaction), they still often stress the traditional nature of the materials of folklore

and of the ways in which those materials are performed. Even American authors whose nationalism is latent or perhaps nonexistent have often incorporated folklore into their works because of a perceived traditionality that connects their work to a specific place or group of people.

One way in which folklore has affected American writing occurs in the realm of setting. Local colorists, for example, have sometimes drawn upon traditional patterns of speech and belief to enhance their works' ties to a particular place. Harriette ARNOW'S use of folk medical beliefs in her fiction, for instance, helps to establish a southern mountain setting. Writers with strong ties to their ethnic heritages may also use folklore as a way of communicating a non-mainstream cultural milieu. The foodways and celebratory occasions of Italian American life, for instance, help to create a sense of ethnic setting in novels such as Pietro Di Donato's *Christ in Concrete* (1939) and Mario PUZO's *The Fortunate Pilgrim* (1965). Folk beliefs about illnesses and their cures characteristic of American Latino culture pervade Rudolfo ANAYA's *Bless Me, Ultima,* helping to establish the intellectual and spiritual setting for that novel of initiation. Even writers whose stature has allowed them to transcend "regionalist" or "ethnic" status may incorporate folklore into their works as a way of suggesting sense of place. William FAULKNER's Yoknapatawpha County becomes more decidedly Southern through its creator's use of the region's folklore.

Folklore has also been used as a device of characterization. Writers may employ folk speech—perhaps a regional or ethnic dialect or an occupational jargon—to establish the identity of a particular character. The backwoods characters in antebellum southern humor or the personas in the poetry written by African Americans in the late 20th c. establish who they are at least partially by the way they speak. A folk belief system may also help an author fully to realize a character. Jim in the *Adventures of Huckleberry Finn* becomes a more richly developed figure through the superstitions to which Mark TWAIN has him subscribe. The protagonist's acceptance of traditions about witchcraft certainly determines his attitude toward his fellow villagers in Nathaniel HAWTHORNE's "Young Goodman Brown."

In terms of plot, some authors have drawn upon traditional narratives as a basis for their own storytelling. In *The Robber Bridegroom,* which derives its title from a widely known Euro-American folktale, for example, Eudora WELTY begins with a traditional plot that she amplifies with materials from folklore as well as her own creative imagination. Parallels in action between folk and written narrative provide a focus for Leslie Marmon SILKO's *Ceremony,* in which Pueblo

Indian creation mythology is reactualized in the experiences of a 20th-c. Native American returned to his community after military service. Some authors—Joel Chandler HARRIS, for example—have attained their literary reputations through relatively straightforward retellings of folk narratives that they encountered in oral tradition.

Some American authors have fashioned works whose structures resemble traditional genres of verbal folklore. The ironic cynicism of the aphorisms in Ambrose BIERCE's *The Devil's Dictionary* attain some of their effect from their similarity to proverbs from folk tradition. Langston HUGHES's poems based on the blues that had emerged from folk expression into popular culture during the 1910s and 1920s have the customary three-line stanzaic form of the blues in oral tradition. The ballad, or stanzaic narrative folk song, has offered a continuing model structurally and in content for poets, some such as Woody Guthrie and Bob DYLAN consciously writing in an idiom appropriate for the creation of poems intended to be sung and others such as John Greenleaf WHITTIER, Longfellow, and other exemplars of American ROMANTICISM more concerned with producing poetry for reading.

Folklore also has provided thematic and symbolic sources for American writers. Such sources may be as vaguely realized as the preservation of the hero versus monster conflict found in the dragon-slayer motif of European folk narrative in such works as Thomas Bangs THORPE's "The Big Bear of Arkansas" and Herman MELVILLE's *Moby-Dick*. Or folklore may more explicitly provide thematic inspiration as it does in Ralph ELLISON's short story "Flying Home," in which the experience of an African American airman who crashes in the southern countryside parallels a folktale from black oral expression. On a symbolic level, the doubloon in *Moby-Dick,* which comes to be all that holds the questing crew together, derives from an oral story about a golden screw in the navel whose removal causes the tale's protagonist to lose his buttocks.

Since its origins in 1888, when the American Folklore Society was founded, the academic study of folklore has also shown clear ties to literature. The Society's first president was Harvard literature professor Francis James Child, and among its charter members were Joel Chandler Harris and Mark Twain. While folklore studies have also been influenced by anthropology and other social science disciplines, the teaching of folklore at colleges and universities in the U.S. remains principally the province of English departments.

Consequently, on several levels and in several ways, folklore has abutted upon American literature. That it continues to do so may be seen in the use of what are called "urban legends," orally transmitted stories that replace the supernatural forces that previously may have dominated such narratives with modern technology and other late 20th-c. concerns, in such diverse works of modern fiction as Thomas PYNCHON's *V,* Tom ROBBINS's *Another Roadside Attraction,* and Carson MCCULLER's *The Heart Is a Lonely Hunter.*

BIBLIOGRAPHY: Bauman, R., ed., *Folklore, Cultural Performances, and Popular Entertainments* (1992); Brunvand, J. H., ed., *American Folklore: An Encyclopedia* (1996); Dorson, R. M., *America in Legend* (1973); Dorson, R. M., ed., *Handbook of American Folklore* (1983); Oring, E., ed., *Folk Groups and Folklore Genres* (1986); Toelken, B., *The Dynamics of Folklore* (1996)

WILLIAM M. CLEMENTS

FOOTE, Horton
b. 14 March 1916, Wharton, Texas

F. is a prolific and versatile dramatist, scriptwriter, and novelist. He is a respected screenwriter, winning an Academy Award for best screenplay adapted from another source for *To Kill a Mockingbird* (1963), and another Academy Award for best original screenplay for *Tender Mercies* (1983). F., who began his literary career as a playwright in 1942, was given the William Inge Award for lifetime achievement in theater in 1989, and was awarded the Pulitzer Prize in drama for his play *The Young Man from Atlanta* (1995).

F. worked as an actor in New York and Los Angeles from 1939 to 1942. His first play, *Texas Town,* was produced in New York City in 1942. Several of his plays were staged in Washington, D.C., and *The Chase* was produced in New York City in 1952. Encouraged by the success of *The Chase,* he began writing well-regarded TV dramas for such shows as *Kraft Television Theatre* and *Playhouse 90.* Several of these dramas were rewritten versions of his stage plays, including *Only the Heart* (1947), *The Traveling Lady* (1954), and *The Dancers* (1963). This established a pattern through which F. would build a remarkably diverse career, writing successfully for stage, television, and film.

The Trip to Bountiful, an original teleplay written in 1953, was quickly revised for the Broadway stage the same year. F. later adapted it into a critically acclaimed screenplay in 1985. One of his original plays, *The Traveling Lady* (1954), was adapted by F. into a teleplay of the same title and also into the screenplay for *Baby the Rain Must Fall* (1964). His only novel, *The Chase* (1956), was adapted from his 1952 stage play; it was later adapted for a film in 1966.

F.'s adaptation of Harper LEE's Pulitzer Prize-winning novel *To Kill a Mockingbird* was followed by several screenplays, including *Baby the Rain Must Fall, Hurry Sundown* (1966, with Thomas Ryan), *Stalking Moon* (1968), and *Tomorrow* (1972). In 1983, F. wrote *Tender Mercies,* an original screenplay that many critics consider to be his finest achievement. The story focuses on a country music singer who is also a recovering alcoholic and his devotion to a young widow and her son.

His stories tend to settle around several universal themes that make them suitable, and quite successful, for the variety of media through which they are presented. His dramatizations are celebrations of and encouragement to humanity's potential for redemption: he explores the ability of families to endure social, political, and personal crises; outmoded sexual conventions; the unjust consequences of bigotry, prejudice, and hate as opposed to the values of courage and integrity; and, in *The Young Man from Atlanta,* the examination of grief, family dynamics, and self-delusion. His work has been lauded as excellent exercises in character development and the examination of the nature of family secrets. His stories present, simply, the stuff of life through the universal continuums of truth and falseness, happiness and sadness, rejection or acceptance. Other critics fault his depiction of American society and its concerns as limited in scope; they criticize his dialogue as uninspired and cliched.

F. suggests that the language we regularly use should be taken as fully adequate to our condition, and that our condition consists precisely of the people we know, the work we do, and the era in which we live.

BIBLIOGRAPHY: Briley, R. L., *You Can Go Home Again: The Focus of Family in the Works of H. F.* (1993); DiGaetani, J. L., ed., *A Search for a Postmodern Theater: Interviews with Contemporary Playwrights* (1991); Smelstor, M., "'The World's an Orphan's Home': H. F.'s Social and Moral History," *SoQ* 29 (Winter 1991): 7–16

JOSEPH FERRANDINO

FOOTE, Mary Hallock

b. 19 November 1847, Milton, New York; d. 25 June 1938, Hingham, Massachusetts

Born into a Quaker family in upstate New York, F. was destined to spend her life in and derive artistic inspiration from a Western landscape that distanced her from Eastern literary culture and other women. Before her marriage, F. trained at the Cooper Union and became known as "the dean of women illustrators" for her black and white images, which graced the pages of *St. Nicholas* and *Century* magazines along with many of the period's lavishly illustrated giftbooks. F.'s marriage to engineer Arthur Foote in 1876 had a dramatic impact on her work, though not what one might expect of a woman whose autobiography was titled by editor Rodman Paul *A Victorian Gentlewoman in the Far West* (1972). Her husband's work took the couple from California to Colorado to Idaho; while these moves isolated F. from the friendships and intellectual circles she had known in New York, this succession of new landscapes also provided settings first for her illustrations and then for the magazine articles and fiction—numerous short stories and twelve novels—she published from 1883 to 1919.

Much of F.'s early fiction, such as *The Led-Horse Claim: A Romance of a Mining Camp* (1883) and *The Last Assembly Ball: A Pseudo-Romance of the Far West* (1889), revolves around courtship plots featuring refined Eastern girls and rugged young Western men. By 1895, in *The Cup of Trembling and Other Stories,* F. began overtly questioning the "happy endings" of these sentimental plots, particularly for couples whose love crossed class or racial divides. Her later novels, notably *The Desert and the Sown* (1902), *Edith Bonham* (1917), and *The Ground-Swell* (1919), are considered by critics her most sophisticated and fully accomplished work.

Literary scholars, particularly Americanists, are at least as indebted to F.'s prolific letter-writing as they are to her talents as an illustrator or professionl writer. Her five hundred and fifty letters to Helena De Kay Gilder—whose husband Richard Gilder, the editor of *Scribner's,* initially encouraged F. to write articles to go with her illustrations—became a primary source both for Carroll Smith-Rosenberg's groundbreaking article "The Female World of Love and Ritual" and for Wallace STEGNER's novel *Angle of Repose.* Readers who have heretofore appreciated the authenticity of Susan Burling Ward's voice in *Angle of Repose* have in fact encountered F., one of few women writing from, and about, the American West in the 19th c.

BIBLIOGRAPHY: Graulich, M., "*Legacy* Profile: M. H. F.," *Legacy* 3 (Fall 1986): 43–50; Johnson, L., *M. H. F.* (1980); Maguire, J., *M. H. F.* (1972)

BETSY KLIMASMITH

FOOTE, Shelby

b. 17 November 1916, Greenville, Mississippi

The career of this distinguished author may be divided into two related spheres: novels, and a multivolume narrative history of the Civil War. The first, comprising

Tournament (1949), *Follow Me Down* (1950), *Love in a Dry Season* (1951), *Shiloh* (1952), *Jordan County* (1954), and *September September* (1978), has as its chief focus the Mississippi Delta. With the exception of *Shiloh,* the novels take place either in the mythical town of Bristol in Jordan County (modeled after F.'s native Greenville, Washington County) or in Memphis, the Delta's "capitol" and F.'s home since 1953. These works are in the tradition of literary REALISM, in which a photographically accurate surface creates through its accretion of details a sense of the concreteness of the world. It is a tangible, solid world, that the reader recognizes.

From the standpoint of technique, F.'s talent of capturing sensory impressions is one of his major strengths. His novels share several themes. A significant one, as stated in *Tournament,* is "that each man, even when pressed closest by other men in their scramble for the things they offer one another with so little grace, is profoundly alone." The theme of loneliness is pervasive in *Follow Me Down,* where it is stated that "Love has failed us. We are essentially, irrevocably alone." The title of the next novel, *Love in a Dry Season,* speaks for itself in showing the difficulty of nurturing the emotion trivialized into lust, pettiness, weakness, and selfishness in a headlong pursuit of hedonism. (What wonder that a major character in the novel is a voyeur.) Here, woman in general becomes a means of questing for the goal of wealth, a perversion of the chivalric tradition through a materialism that is life-denying and can only result in emotionally bankrupt relationships and sterility. Likewise, *Jordan County* explores the sterile landscape, particularly the causes of violence in the failure of love and the desire for exploitation owing to greed.

The naturalistic element is also strong in these works. Characters are fated by environment and heredity to play their roles in a schema over which they have little or no control. *Follow Me Down,* in particular, provides excellent examples of this theme. All its characters in one way or another are victims. In the same way, *Love in a Dry Season* is a complex study in frustration, the doubly effective symbol of which is the aforementioned voyeur's becoming blind during the novel.

A recent critic has seen F.'s major theme to be the discrepancy between the idea and the act, the "contrast between the conception of an action and its execution." However good the plans (whether the ideals of the people of Bristol or the plans for a specific act), they will fail if not executed in a mature or wise manner. In this way, character becomes fate.

Perhaps F.'s most powerful theme is the tragic nature of existence based on the knowledge of man's fallibility. His portrayal of fallen humanity, from Hugh Bart in *Tournament* to Luther Eustis in *Follow Me Down* motivates compassion and leads to a deeper understanding of the human condition. His novels provide a key to that understanding; and herein lies one of the chief values of his writing.

F.'s second sphere, the monumental *Civil War: A Narrative* (3 vols., 1958, 1963, 1974), has been called variously "an American *Iliad,*" "the treatment of the War most likely to last," and "one of the great achievements of American letters." His models were Homer, Proust, Gibbon, Tacitus, and Thucydides; and it is history in the manner of the best of the great classical histories, written with the finest techniques of modern fiction. Its style is beautifully crafted; and throughout is heard the oral narrative voice that one recognizes so well in F.'s fellow Mississippians Eudora WELTY and William FAULKNER. F. never loses sight of the human element; and his historical figures, while engaged in an epic conflict, remain at the same time ordinary human beings placed in extraordinary circumstances. Again, it is F.'s great ability to report sensory impression that helps make this work so memorably "real." His handling of the sweep of action through swift novelistic plotting and his skillful grasp of the various techniques of the literary realist contribute to making this work the masterpiece that it is.

BIBLIOGRAPHY: Phillips, R. L., "S. F.," in Rubin, L., ed., *The History of Southern Literature* (1985): 501–4; Phillips, R. L., Jr., *S. F.: Novelist and Historian* (1992); special F. issue, *Delta* 4 (May 1977); special F. issue, *MissQ* 28 (Winter 1974–75); Tolson, J., ed., *Correspondence of S. F. and Walker Percy* (1996); White, H., and R. Sugg, *S. F.* (1982)

JAMES EVERETT KIBLER, JR.

FORBES, Esther [Louise]

b. 28 June 1891, Westboro, Massachusetts; d. 12 August 1967, Worcester, Massachusetts

Although scores of authors have written more books than F., few have received as much widespread recognition. Her first novel, *O Genteel Lady!* (1926), became the third selection of the Book-of-the-Month Club. Her biography *Paul Revere & the World He Lived In* (1942) earned a Pulitzer Prize in history as well as another berth on the rolls of the Book-of-the-Month Club. She quickly followed this volume with *Johnny Tremain* (1943), which received the Newbery Medal for the most distinguished contribution to American literature for children. A few years later, her historical novel *The Running of the Tide* (1948) garnered not only Book-of-the-Month Club honors again but the Metro-Goldwyn-Mayer novel award. Her last book, *Rainbow on the Road* (1954), was a choice of the Literary Guild.

F. came by her fascination with the early years of the U.S. naturally. Her family's Massachusetts roots date back to the 1600s, making tales of this period more family tradition than local history. One of her great-uncles was Samuel Adams, an organizer of Boston's Sons of Liberty, who would figure prominently in her biography of Paul Revere.

Set in the mid-19th c., F.'s *O Genteel Lady!* is the humorous and poignant story of Lanice Bardeen, the twenty-four-year-old daughter of an Amherst professor. After she meets and tempestuously falls in love with a dashing young English adventurer and roué, she is torn between prevailing standards of Victorian behavior and her own natural impulses and sexual passions.

Bearing little resemblance to the comedy of manners of *O Genteel Lady!, A Mirror for Witches* (1928) is a moving tale of an English girl, Doll Bilby, who sees her parents burned at the stake as witches. After a sea captain and his wife adopt her, they sail for Massachusetts where in 1663 they settle on a farm near Salem. Continually harassed by malicious gossip, the girl gradually accepts the prevailing attitude in the town that she is a witch and ultimately believes herself to be possessed of a demon lover. The book's point of view enhances the stark realism, for while writing the chilling tale, the author deliberately adopted the style of Cotton MATHER and other great Puritan diarists. Many critics regard the novel as F.'s finest piece of fiction, and it has never been out of print. Over the years, it has been made into a ballet, a musical play, a movie, and an opera.

With *Paul Revere & the World He Lived In,* F. concentrated not on the intellectual Paul Revere—which was the focus of many biographies—but on the "workingman," the Paul Revere as artisan, family man, and average person who had led a simple life until the American Revolution. Similarly, she depicted the war years from the point of view of the ordinary citizens of 18th-c. Boston.

While F. was researching *Paul Revere,* she decided to build a story around a silversmith's apprentice and how he and his friends aided the Revolution. *Johnny Tremain* appeals to both adults and children due to its vividly-drawn scenes of daily life in revolutionary Boston and its true-to-life fictional and historical figures. With F.'s mastery of character development and her portrayal of such timeless and universal dilemmas as taking responsibility for one's actions, understanding the difference between pride and arrogance, struggling with a disability, coping with death, believing in a cause, and facing the obligations and pressures of maturity and adulthood, it is not difficult to understand why it has become one of the true classics in children's literature.

F.'s niche in literary history, however, should be based on more than just the strength of this one book. An indefatigable researcher who paid meticulous attention to details, she was also a versatile stylist with a sound artistic power of selection. With her thorough understanding of human nature and strong sense of time and place, she created people, not puppets, and vividly brought to life now-vanished scenes and eras.

BIBLIOGRAPHY: Bales, J., *E. F.: A Bio-Bibliography of the Author of Johnny Tremain* (1997); Erskine, M., *E. F.* (1976); Jennerich, E. J., "E. F.," in Cech, J., ed., *DLB,* vol. 22, *American Writers for Children, 1900–1960* (1983): 176–78

JACK BALES

FORD, Richard
b. 16 February 1944, Jackson, Mississippi

If the National Book Award won by F. for *Independence Day* (1995) is any indication, his most enduring contribution to American fiction thus far is Frank Bascombe, the main character and narrator of this novel and as well of *The Sportswriter* (1986). Often grouped by critics with the American "minimalist" writers of the 1980s, such as Raymond CARVER and Ann BEATTIE, F.'s work has never sat as comfortably as some others' at that particular beer can and ashtray-covered table; as he has published more and more novels, his individuality has become more and more clear and his importance has come to rest more and more on the stooped but sturdy shoulders of Frank Bascombe.

The minimalist label was earned by F. largely on the merits of *The Sportswriter* and even more for the work of what might be called his Montana period: a collection of stories entitled *Rock Springs* (1987) and *Wildlife* (1990), both set in the West and both chronicling working lives filled with everyday detritus and despair. F. published two novels prior to *The Sportswriter,* though. His first, *A Piece of My Heart* (1976), about a law student back in his home state of Mississippi to take care of an old estate and get his life back on track and an Arkansas drifter on a more sordid personal journey, could be characterized as Southern Gothic in its darkness and its drama. His second, *The Ultimate Good Luck* (1981), shifts to Mexico, where a Vietnam veteran trying to win back his ex-girlfriend goes to rescue her brother from prison and encounters layers of drug-running intrigue and murder.

With the publication of *The Sportswriter,* readers first met Frank Bascombe, former short story writer who has abandoned his novel and now writes for a well-known sports magazine in New York City, a job to which he commutes from suburban New Jersey. Frank has lost his son and is divorced from his wife, known as X; he attends the Divorced Men's Club and has a girlfriend, Vicki. His interviews for the magazine, the club, and scattered events like his dinner with Vicki's family allow F. to digress at length, to let Frank observe and comment, which he does with a distinct voice and sensibility, open but not wide-eyed, sharp but not mocking. The knowledge of time and place is for many readers the book's strength; it is a knowledge gained not aside from the main business of the book but because of this business, because of Frank's detached situation and position as an observer.

As with *The Sportswriter, Independence Day* is as much periphery as center, as much what Frank Bascombe observes as what happens to him and what he causes to happen. And, as with *The Sportswriter,* it might be said that because of this somewhat eccentric distribution of attention, the novel seems at times to go on a bit, to ramble around trailing a relatively insubstantial plot. Frank is, at forty-four, six years older than at his last appearance, and is now in real estate, which, as did his previous profession, affords him the opportunity to observe a number of places and events not directly related to the story. That story involves Frank's planned Fourth of July trip with his new girlfriend, Sally, and his fifteen-year-old son, Paul, to the Basketball and Baseball Halls of Fame, a trip that he hopes will bring him closer to Paul, who has been showing signs of trouble. Among these signs are an arrest following his theft of a box of condoms and his habit of barking, ostensibly because of the death of his dog but also, it seems, because of the loss of his brother. The larger context for this trip includes Frank's desire that Paul come live with him rather than his (now properly named) ex-wife, Ann, his mixed feelings about making his relationship with Sally more permanent, and his wish to get back together with Ann, which is paradoxical in relation to his wish to relocate Paul to his home, in relation to Ann's having remarried, and in relation to his feelings for Sally.

F. uses Frank not only as main character but as narrative focalizer who is in a kind of liminal phase, an in-between state in which all of his significant relationships are either in jeopardy of complete disso-lution or in danger of becoming closer. Frank's state is combined with Frank-as-main-character's profes-sion—of which he says, "You don't sell a house, you sell a life"—and with the holiday of the title to under-score the book's overriding concerns. The in-betweenness of Frank's clients is paralleled in his own life and in those close or not-so-close to him, and the investigation of life—which his watchful eye, situ-ation, and narrative position make possible—examines this very in-betweenness, this limbo between indepen-dence and dependence.

F.'s signature character, like John UPDIKE's Harry "Rabbit" Angstrom, thus fills the position of commen-tator on life in contemporary America, at least on that suburban, Northeast portion, similar to Updike's territory. And again, as with Updike, we should not be shocked if Frank Bascombe resurfaces someday in another novel.

BIBLIOGRAPHY: Crouse, D., "Resisting Reduction: Clo-sure in R. F.'s *Rock Springs* and Alice Munro's *Friend of My Youth," CanL* 146 (Autumn 1995): 51–64; Shel-ton, F. W., "R. F.," in Flora, J. M., and R. Bain, eds., *Contemporary Fiction Writers of the South: A Bio-Bibliographic Sourcebook* (1993): 147–55; Trussler, M., "'Famous Times': Historicity in the Short Fiction of R. F. and Raymond Carver," *WascanaR* 28 (Fall 1994): 35–53

SAM COHEN

FORNÉS, María Irene
b. 14 May 1930, Havana, Cuba

F., the prolific Cuban-born playwright, director, and teacher has worked in the Off-Broadway theater since the early 1960s and is highly esteemed for her experi-mental playwriting, which has yielded over thirty plays and five adaptations of other plays, and for her stagings of her own works and those of others. In her own plays, F. does not advance a particular political agenda. Nevertheless, her plays are designed to break down the conventional barrier between art and life, to sug-gest the material nature of human existence, including its structures of power.

Given her desire to disrupt ordinary spectatorship, it is not surprising that F. has succeeded mostly in New York's smaller, more experimental theaters. Her purposes, and hence her approaches, resemble those of Bertolt Brecht, the German socialist playwright, for whom theater served as a teaching tool. Brecht and F. both faced audiences that passively identified with realistic characters in ordinary situations behind the fourth wall. Both of these playwrights called reality into question by using alienation effects to prevent passive observation and to activate the audience mem-ber's critical appraisal. Audiences were invited not only to appraise the theatrical representation of reality, but its own theater-going practice as well. To make audiences more self-consciously voyeurs of, or active participants in, the drama, F. developed a variety of strategies.

F.'s plays are often not directly linear or "well made," but characterized by disruptions and digressions. Meaning often derives more from the juxtaposition of images than from an unfolding action. Often, the person featured in F.'s plays is a female while the society is patriarchal, even when its immediate representatives are all female, as in *Fefu and Her Friends* (1977). Many critics identify F. as a feminist even as they acknowledge her own disinclination to be associated with an ideological movement. Characteristically, F. surprises us with the comic and the grotesque. In *Fefu and Her Friends,* for example, part 2 begins with Emma's line, "Do you think about genitals all the time?" Surprises disrupt the dramatic illusion, preventing the audience from being deceived by "natural" characters or links between realistic causes and effects. F.'s surprises often include the performance event itself, in which an audience, familiar with the passive, fourth-wall conventions of theater, is asked to volunteer some of its members to participate in the play, such as in *The Vietnamese Wedding* (1967), or is asked to split up into groups and walk from diorama-scene to diorama-scene, as in *Fefu.*

Fefu and Her Friends is F.'s best-known work and also shares thematic concerns with many of her other plays. Fefu, an educator, welcomes seven female colleagues to her New England home, where they are to prepare presentations on educational dramatics. Her husband, brother, and a gardener work outdoors and do not appear, though Fefu begins the play by firing a blank shell at her husband, who had loaded her shotgun himself and honors their prior arrangement by falling down. In the play's chief action, Fefu appears to cause the death of her friend Julia with this shotgun. Julia once fought men for her freedom; however, like Brecht's Galileo, she has recanted, she says, in order to live. Stricken with a psychosomatic disability, she sits in a wheelchair, waiting for death, and hallucinating male torture while flinching submissively. As the play concludes, Fefu pulls Julia out of her wheelchair to force her to stand up; when Fefu is stopped by Christina, a self-confessed conformist, Fefu runs from the house with her shotgun and kills a rabbit: Julia dies in the same instant, as though from the same blast. Like Henrik Ibsen's *Hedda Gabler* the action of *Fefu* is structured by shootings, but Fefu's last shot does not, like Hedda's, destroy her. On the contrary, Fefu's indirect slaying of Julia suggests that feminine subordination to patriarchy has been challenged productively by an empowered woman. Yet because the causal connection is tenuous, so is the significance of the play's end. If we consider that F. herself has identified Julia as the play's seer, feminist triumph in *Fefu* is ambivalent at best. Perhaps Julia's death is instead a kind of crisis for female relationships; perhaps, indeed, this conclusion parallels that of F.'s *The Conduct of Life* (1985), in which a woman shoots her abusive

husband and then hands the smoking gun to his young sex slave.

Fefu and her Friends is not linear, despite Fefu's use of the shotgun and her struggle with Julia. The events just described are actions bracketing other actions and relationships: Paula and Cecelia try to patch up a long-standing friendship; Emma is rhapsodic about Fefu, educative dramatics, and genitals; Cindy tells her dream of male violence. The women race to wash the dishes, then playfully assault one another with pots of water. Together these elements are richly textured and complexly related, suggesting on one hand a healthy sisterhood resistant to patriarchy and representing, on the other hand, a sisterhood expressed in "women's work" and riven by painful reproaches, even death.

This complexity in *Fefu* and F.'s other plays shows that F. is not a feminist propagandist, but a writer who is deeply concerned about the materiality of experience, particularly of women, in societies, American or otherwise, that happen to be ruled by men.

BIBLIOGRAPHY: Cummings, S., "Seeing with Clarity: The Visions of M. I. F.," *Theater* 17 (Winter 1985): 51–56; O'Malley, L. D., "Pressing Clothes/Snapping Beans/Reading Books: M. I. F.'s Women's Work," *SAD* 4 (1989): 103–17; Worthen, W. B., "Still Playing Games: Ideology and Performance in the Theater of M. I. F.," in Enoch B., ed., *Feminine Focus: The New Woman* (1989): 167–85; Zinman, T. S., "Hen in a Foxhouse: The Absurdist Plays of M. I. F.," in Brater, E., and R. Cohn, eds., *Around the Absurd: Essays on Modern and Postmodern Drama* (1990): 203–20

KEITH APPLER

FOSTER, Hannah Webster

b. 10 September 1758, Salisbury, Massachusetts; d. 17 April 1840, Montreal, Canada

As the author of *The Coquette; or, The History of Eliza Wharton* (1797), F., who wrote under the pseudonym, "A Lady of Massachusetts," holds a secure place in American literature. *The Coquette* was the best, and, along with Susanna Haswell ROWSON's *Charlotte Temple* and William Hill BROWN's *The Power of Sympathy,* one of the three most popular works of the National Period.

Born in Salisbury, Massachusetts, F. probably attended a boarding school similar to the one she describes in her second book, *The Boarding School; or, Lessons of a Preceptress to Her Pupils* (1798). Later, she lived in Boston, where she wrote political articles for newspapers. After marrying the Reverend John

Foster, she moved to Brighton, bore six children, wrote her two books, and resumed newspaper work.

The Coquette follows the epistolary tradition popularized by Samuel Richardson. Through letters to friends and confidants, F.'s characters tell of Eliza Wharton's seduction by the rake, Peter Sanford, and her death in childbirth—a story based on the experience of Elizabeth Whitman of Hartford, Connecticut, a distant cousin of John Foster. *The Coquette* surpasses other works of its time in its artistic handling of character and voice. Each character speaks in a unique rhythm, tone, and vocabulary. Eliza, intelligent and spirited, rebels against conventional marriage—the "tomb of friendship." Sanford boasts of enjoying Eliza while simultaneously punishing her friends, whereas J. Boyer, Eliza's clerical suitor, evaluates her in terms of his career. Julia Granby and Lucy Sumner offer loving wisdom, which Eliza ignores.

The Boarding School, harder to classify, describes the routine at Harmony-Grove, where Mrs. Williams instructs young women on morals and manners. Letters exchanged by former students, Mrs. Williams, and her daughters combine with the lectures to support traditional values, moderation, industry, and honesty.

BIBLIOGRAPHY: Bolton, C. K., *The Elizabeth Whitman Mystery* (1912); Davidson, C. N., *Revolution and the Word: The Rise of the Novel in America* (1986); Harris, S. M., "H. W. F.'s *The Coquette:* Critiquing Franklin's America," in *Redefining the Political Novel: American Women Writers, 1797–1901* (1995): 1–22; Pettengill, C. C., "H. W. F. (1758–1840)," *Legacy* 12, 2 (1995): 133–141; Waldstreicher, D., "'Fallen under My Observation': Vision and Virtue in *The Coquette*," *EAL* 27, 3 (1992): 204–18

LUCY M. FREIBERT

FOX, William Price [Jr.]

b. 9 April 1926, Waukegan, Illinois

The quintessential chronicler of Southern "redneck" culture, F. was born in Waukegan, Illinois, where his father was serving in the U.S. Navy and his mother was serving as a night club hostess in nearby Chicago. He grew up in South Carolina, which became the subject and setting for much of his work as a writer. He failed the ninth grade and at eighteen ran off to join the Army Air Force, returning eventually to earn a degree from the University of South Carolina in 1950. He was a packaging salesman in New York, when a friend who wrote for the *Village Voice,* suffering from a hangover, asked F. to substitute for him. The result was a comic story, "Moncks Corner," which attracted the attention of readers and editors and

launched him on his literary career. He has taught at the Writers Workshop at the University of Iowa and in 1976 became writer-in-residence at the University of South Carolina in Columbia.

His first book—and still his best known—is a collection of his short stories and sketches, *Southern Fried* (1962), which introduces a typical gallery of F. "ne'er-do-wells" and down-and-out types. The title story is set in a short order cafe, with characters like Fleetwood Driggers and Preacher Watts. Indeed, most of his characters and stories are from Southern low life: moonshiners and bootleggers, pool room loafers, hustlers, and country singers. F. has said that he loves the common people who live ordinary lives, work an eight-hour day, then come home, eat supper, watch television, and have no desire to write the Great American Novel or get on the *Johnny Carson Show.* He applauds people like Wilson Wade Hampton Peeler, the proprietor of the Casablanca Restaurant, who spent eleven years perfecting his special barbecue sauce. His characters love to talk and their long monologues sometime consume the entire story. Their talk has the authenticity of a secretly taped interview.

Critics have sometimes complained that F. overwhelms his loosely constructed stories with too many details and characters. His novel *Ruby Red* (1971) contains at least a dozen major characters, including Virgil Hooper Haynes, Preacher Roebuck Alexander, Ferline Stover Peterson, Thelma Jean Hooker, as well as Ruby Jean Jamison, an aspiring country and Western singer of questionable talent but unquestionable self-confidence. A reviewer for the *New York Times* wrote: "If Mr. F. knows any detail that might tell you just a bit more about Nashville and environs, he'll work it in whether it belongs to his story or not."

Even F. admits to a general lack of planning when he sets out to write a story or novel. He once confessed to critic Matthew J. Bruccoli that *Ruby Red* was originally to have been about an uncle he called Spider Harold Hornsby in the book, but after writing some three hundred pages, Ruby stepped into the book and took it over, so he junked what he had written and went on with his new protagonist. Indeed, his fiction reminds one of certain other Southern storytellers like Thomas WOLFE and Jesse STUART, from whom words stream out with little seeming effort or control. With his eye for detail, his ear for regional dialect, his fondness for folk humor and his talent as a natural storyteller, his work is squarely in the masculine tradition of the Humorists of the Old Southwest, the mid-19th-c. writers from what is now the Southeast and Texas who wrote about the local culture filled with rough and tumble entertainments and energy. Indeed, much of F.'s fiction is based on his relatives and his own life and experiences. He remembers his father, a sometime South Carolina moonshiner and bootlegger, as "a sorry father but a great character."

Few readers will fault his talent as a master teller of stories, with clearly drawn characters, straightforward plots, and his ability to point a large number of characters in a single direction. His characters are also invariably sympathetic. As author and critic George GARRETT has observed, F.'s people—even the losers—are not merely puppets who are controlled by overwhelming social and economic forces, but they see themselves as free men and women who are ultimately responsible for their successes and failures.

In addition to his novels and short stories, F. has also written screenplays and nonfiction articles. His articles, which often read like short stories with characters, setting, and theme, have ranged from a profile of Johnny Cash to a circus in Florida and have been published in such magazines as the *Saturday Evening Post, Holiday, Sports Illustrated,* and *Southern Living.*

In his 1962 review of *Southern Fried* in the *New York Times Book Review,* Pogo creator Walt Kelly summed up F.'s contribution to American literature: "Mr. F.'s collection of interviews, anecdotes and tall tales of South Carolina folk is not so funny as it is humorous, in the sense that it reflects the humor of a whole people—humor in this case meaning the mood, the temper, of the community." Indeed, the works of F. demonstrate that even in the waning years of the 20th c., the South is still different from the rest of the U.S. It looks different. It sounds different. It is a place where annual chitlin struts are held in small towns in Alabama and South Carolina, a place of mobile home communities, bootlegging and moonshining within sight of the town jail, of barbecue contests, of honkytonks—a place where you may find pictures of Jesus and prophylactic dispensers sharing the same public rest rooms. It is a place, F. has shown us in his stories, where there is a strong sense of family life and where its "crazies" are not only tolerated but sometimes even cultivated.

BIBLIOGRAPHY: Bobbit, J., "W. P. F: The Spirit of Character and the Spirit of Place," *SCR* 9 (1976): 30–35; Israel, C., "Fact and Fiction in W. P. F.," *KenR* 1 (Spring 1988): 44–49

                                        WADE HALL

FRANCIS, Robert [Churchill]

b. 12 August 1901, Upland, Pennsylvania; d. 13 or 14 July 1987, Northampton, Massachusetts

Although F. was born in Pennsylvania, his poetry is rooted in the rich poetic tradition of New England. As he writes in the poem "New England Mind," "My

mind matches this understated land," and his writing is an extension of New England writers—Ralph Waldo EMERSON, Henry David THOREAU, Emily DICKINSON, and Robert FROST. F. himself acknowledges the centrality of these connections with references to these writers in such poems as "Thoreau in Italy," "History," "Oh, What Have I to Do with Time?," "On a Theme by Frost," and perhaps most revealingly in "Two Ghosts," where the ghosts of Dickinson and Frost engage in a heated discussion about each others' poetry.

Many critics have focused upon F.'s connections with Frost—a connection that is justified by the fact that Frost was F.'s friend and mentor of F. as well as F.'s *Frost: A Time to Talk: Conversations and Indiscretions Recorded by R. F.* (1972). Unfortunately, F.'s career as a writer has been eclipsed by his connections with Frost. Given that the first few books of poetry by F.—*Stand with Me Here* (1936) and *Valhalla and Other Poems* (1938)—strongly echo Frost, F.'s later books achieve a singularity of voice and vision and demonstrate a whimsicality of language and ideas that are distinctively different from Frost. Nevertheless, both Frost and F. use plain language; adhere strictly to rhyme, poetic form, and rigid free-verse as a vital component of "poetic" meaning; and are preoccupied with the relationship of humanity and nature. Yet F. differs from Frost in two very significant, and distinctive ways. First, F.'s poetry lacks the darkness and pessimism that seethes beneath the surface of a Frost poem; for F. nature is not in an uneasy relationship with humankind and things spotted in nature are not omens of ill will; rather, nature is splendous, bright, and the cause of celebration, and F.'s poetry often documents his delight in his observations of the world around him. The second and most important distinction between Frost and F. is biographical: Frost was affected both as a writer and a human being by his economic responsibilities towards his family; F., in contrast, lived a frugal existence in a secluded one-room house on the outskirts of Amhearst, Massachusetts. Occasionally, F. would teach writing workshops or accept a lectureship, but the majority of his life remained free from economic pressures related to convention, the critical establishment, or the academy, and thereby allowed his poetry to detail honestly his personal reflections of the objects (and occasional people) that surround him and that constitute his world.

Given his relentless individuality, pragmatic existence, and his desire to construct a lifestyle so that he could pursue his writing as fully as possible, the more appropriate comparison with F. would be another "individualistic" New Englander, who chose to live a secluded life away from the fritters of materialism and business—Henry David Thoreau. F. not only refers to Thoreau throughout his poetry, but more importantly, both Thoreau and F. share a primary concern for the connections of language and vision. As F. writes, "obedient to nothing but the pure act of seeing," both F. and Thoreau are meticulous in their attention to details and their faithful transcription of those details into their writing. Consequently, the body of F.'s writing, which not only includes poetry and criticism but also an autobiography entitled *The Trouble with F.* (1971) and a collection of his journals *Travelling in Amherst* (1986), is filled with vibrant, impressionistic aspects of the human and natural landscape.

F. shares a great deal more with his New England transcendental forebearers and Frost than with any of his contemporaries. And even though F. is not well known, the testament of his force as a poet of the intellectual, natural, and spiritual life of New England is evident by the University of Massachusetts Press and their establishment of a poetry prize in honor of F., the Juniper Prize, named after F.'s home, Fort Juniper.

BIBLIOGRAPHY: McNair, W., "The Triumph of R. F.," *HRev* 11 (Fall 1996): 81–90; special F. issue, *Field* 25 (Fall 1981)

DAVID W. CLIPPINGER

FRANK, Waldo

b. 25 August 1889, Long Branch, New Jersey; d. 9 January 1967, White Plains, New York

A prolific and imaginative novelist and cultural critic of the early 20th c., F. nevertheless remains one of the most overlooked voices of American literature. In addition to regularly contributing political and literary articles to magazines such as the *New Yorker* and the *New Masses,* F. published twelve novels and eighteen social histories. In 1923, an early critic of F.'s work declared F. "the most exciting figure in contemporary American letters," and wrongly prophesied that F. was "likely to dominate the field in America for a long time." Today, few of F.'s books are in print.

Reading F., one hears the echoes of Ralph Waldo EMERSON and Walt WHITMAN, Marx, Freud, and Spinoza. Out of these eclectic voices, F. managed to weave a web of literary and cultural insight that relentlessly focuses on one central theme: the development of the individual from ego-driven, fragmented self to a person fully aware of his organic unity with humankind. F. typically sets his protagonists on a spiritual journey where they attempt to peel away the artificially acquired layers of individuality and pursue the person within who is connected to the rest of the cosmic order. F.'s theme of the development of the whole person is best illustrated in *The Birth and Death of David Markand* (1934). The protagonist, David Mar-

kand, experiences a death from his old life as a self-satisfied businessman and is reborn into a life of social action after he witnesses the death of two friends who were killed while trying to help striking coal miners.

In 1920, F. had a mystical experience, recognized his Judaism, and produced four psychological novels for which he is best known: *Rahab* (1922), *City Block* (1922), *Holiday* (1923), and *Chalk Face* (1924). The "Lyric Novels," as F. came to call them, share a propinquity with the modernist fiction of Joyce in their use of stream of consciousness and their emphasis on the inner lives of characters. Although none of the "Lyric Novels" are read today, *Holiday,* a tale of race relations in the Deep South seems a likely candidate for rediscovery. A dark tale of racial tragedy, *Holiday* tells the story of John Cloud, a black man who tries to break out of the separateness of his own existence, and Virginia Hade, a white woman who never recognizes the evil inside her. Virginia happens upon John as he bathes in the open air. There is an awkward conversation and then a sexually symbolic scene where John and Virginia exchange pocket knives. Virginia suffers from a self-inflicted knife wound to the waist, but the white community, upon seeing Virginia's laceration, assumes she has been violated by John. A mob forms, marches into the black community and promptly lynches John. Meanwhile, Virginia lies quietly in her bed, contemplating coming to John's aid. The other "Lyric Novels" follow a similar pattern: suffering characters leading seemingly futile and chaotic lives attempt, with varying degrees of success, to overcome personal isolation and realize themselves as partial elements within the cosmic order.

Had F. continued to hone his fictional skills, he may have acquired the literary reputation he once seemed destined for. But like his character, David Markand, F. committed himself to the kind of social activism that precluded a narrow focus on his literary skills. After the publication of *Chalk Face,* F. did not publish another piece of fiction for ten years. In the meantime, he began writing articles in political magazines, lecturing throughout Latin America and involving himself with groups such as the National Committee for the Defense of Political Prisoners. Throughout his career, F. was alarmed by the drift toward materialism in American life, and his cultural criticism serves as an example of his jeremiadic vision. In *Our America* (1919; repub. as *The New American,* 1922) and *The Rediscovery of America* (1929), F.'s spiritual wake up call for America, F. called the U.S., "a concept to be created" and emphasized the importance of the development of the nation's spiritual side. "Searchlight," F.'s chosen pseudonym for a series of profiles he wrote for the *New Yorker,* is an aptly chosen name for F.'s efforts to rejuvenate the American spirit.

BIBLIOGRAPHY: Bittner, W., *The Novels of W. F.* (1958); Blake, C., "W. F.," in Jay, G. S., ed., *DLB,* vol. 63, *Modern American Critics, 1920–1955* (1988): 122–30; Carter, P., *W. F.* (1967)

ERIC FRETZ

FRANKLIN, Benjamin

b. 17 January 1706, Boston, Massachusetts; d. 17 April 1790, Philadelphia, Pennsylvania

F. is America's most versatile 18th-c. writer. As a periodical essayist, aphorist, political pamphleteer, satirist, letter writer, and autobiographer, F. used his mastery of English prose to define and defend the nation to which he helped give birth. At the end of the 18th c., F. was America's only internationally famous man of letters; however, in the 19th and early 20th cs., F.'s literary reputation suffered a decline as a consequence of the romantic disenchantment with rationalism, the narrowing of critical interest to belles lettres, and the intellectual disdain for the popular image of F. as the quintessential self-made man. In recent years, F. has regained his stature as one of America's foremost writers. The renewal of interest in colonial and early national literature, a concomitant extension of literature to include nontraditional genres, and a fresh appreciation of the complex artistry underlying the apparent simplicity of F.'s writing have deservedly reestablished F.'s literary reputation. He now stands as the American equal of such 18th-c. prose masters as Jonathan Swift and Samuel Johnson.

F.'s life is too well known and too rich in achievement for a detailed recounting. Since, however, aspects of F.'s life have passed into American legend, it is useful to try to separate fact from myth. The son of Josiah and Abiah Folger Franklin, F. was one of eleven living brothers and sisters and the youngest son. His formal education was minimal, consisting of one year at the Boston Grammar School and one year at George Browness's English school. After rejecting other trades, F. was apprenticed as a printer to his brother James at age twelve.

As a youth, F. appears to have been precocious and rebellious. He early rejected the PURITANISM of his pious parents in favor of the Deism he encountered in books by contemporary freethinkers. He had difficulty settling to a trade, and his adolescent satire of Harvard College suggests that he resented those who, despite inferior talents, escaped the drudgery of a tradesman through their wealth. He joined readily in his brother James's attacks on Massachusetts officials, and at age

seventeen he broke his indentures and sailed for New York and Philadelphia.

After an uncertain start, F. settled down to make a success of himself as a printer in Philadelphia. His hard work, business sense, social talents, community service, and literary skill led to prosperity and public favor. As his growing wealth provided free time, F. became interested in science, making discoveries in electricity that earned him international fame, and he promoted philanthropic public service projects. F.'s reputation in the community led him to enter politics; his local political success led in turn to his appointment as agent in England for Pennsylvania. As F.'s fame grew, he became the agent for other colonies that were trying to redress grievances with the mother country. During this period, F. gained international fame not only as a scientist but as a writer and as a spokesman for America.

Most of the remainder of F.'s life was spent in politics and diplomacy, notably in his role in the Second Continental Congress, his service as American minister to France during the Revolutionary War, his part in making the peace with England, and his participation in the Constitutional Convention. In a sense, however, the very magnitude and diversity of F.'s accomplishments, his successes as a philanthropist, scientist, inventor, statesman, and diplomat, have done him a disservice for they have overshadowed his literary achievements.

F.'s literary career began at age sixteen when he pseudonymously wrote a series of essays for his brother James's newspaper, the *New England Courant.* These essays, known as the "Silence Dogood" papers (1722), from the name of the persona F. employed, reveal that F. had thus early mastered the conventions of the 18th-c. periodical essay and learned to adapt them to the American scene. Inspired by Joseph Addison's and Richard Steele's *Spectator* and by the local essayists who wrote for the *Courant,* F. creates a sharply etched persona, the middle-aged widow Silence Dogood, and uses this persona to satirize the follies and vices of Boston. The essays are notable for the distinctive voice of the persona, their easy, colloquial style, and the range of the young F.'s satiric targets. Bostonian education, religion, gossip, elegies, night life, and politics are all viewed by the keen eye and judged by the sharp tongue of Silence Dogood.

After leaving Boston for Philadelphia and establishing himself as a printer, F. used his talent for writing to help himself succeed in business, to advance his philanthropic projects, and to state his views on political and controversial issues. It is during the years in Philadelphia (1724–57) that F. develops his skills as a writer of diverse kinds of prose. In response to the demands placed upon him by a variety of genres and situations, F. develops the control of style, voice, tone, and argument that mark his mature work. F.'s remarkable versatility as a writer springs largely from the various utilitarian uses to which he turned his pen during his years in Philadelphia.

F.'s most popular work during these years was *Poor Richard's Almanac* (1733–58). In this yearly almanac, F. creates another sharply drawn persona, the star gazer Richard Saunders whose poverty and shrewish wife drive him to compose almanacs. He fills his almanacs with wit, bawdiness, moral saws, and prudential advice borrowed from writers of many nations and times. Whatever F. borrows, he improves. F. rephrases the jokes, adages, and aphorisms he borrows in a colloquial style; he condenses wordy saws into concise proverbs; and he uses alliteration, parallelism, and antithesis to give added point to their humor or morality. The *Almanac* helped F. prosper as a printer and spread his name throughout the colonies; it also helped him develop the pithy wit that remained at his service throughout his career as a writer.

Less well known but equally important in developing F.'s prose mastery were the pamphlets he wrote to further philanthropic projects in Philadelphia. In such works as *A Proposal for Promoting Useful Knowledge* (1743), *Proposals Relating to the Education of Youth in Pensilvania* (1749), and the "Appeal for the Hospital" (1751), F. displays his control of voice, structure, and argument in persuasive prose. In the philanthropic essays, F. adopts the role of the public spirited citizen who is interested only in the welfare of his fellows. He begins these essays by establishing principles on which all reasonable men can agree, such as the usefulness of scientific knowledge, the benefits of education, or the necessity of making some provision for the poor who are ill. He then moves gradually to more controversial issues and finally to his own proposal (always disguised as the plan of several public-spirited men) for resolving the problem he is discussing. Throughout the philanthropic essays, F. unites self-interested and altruistic appeals to his audience; he shows his readers the ways in which they can simultaneously benefit themselves and advance the public good. F. also skillfully adapts his overriding persona, the friend of humanity, to the situation he discusses and the audience he addresses. The philanthropic papers are a triumph of unobtrusive persuasive art.

F. employs similar strategies in his clearly political essays. In the political writing, F.'s favorite stance is that of the fair minded observer whose primary goal is not self-promotion or the success of his party but the good of the community. Political works like *A Modest Enquiry into the Nature and Necessity of Pa-*

per Currency (1729) show F. using arguments designed to prove that his proposals will benefit the community as a whole. In situations that demand passion, F. subtly shifts his persona; he transforms the fair-minded lover of humanity into an outraged citizen who demands that the precepts of common sense, justice, and compassion, which his opponents have violated, be adhered to and acted upon. Openly polemic works such as *Plain Truth* (1747) and *A Narrative of the Late Massacres* (1764) reveal the skill with which F. blends passionate outrage with reason and common sense.

During the years in Philadelphia, F. also honed his skills as a periodical essayist and satirist. In the "Busy Body" papers (1729), the emphasis is on moral advice seasoned occasionally with humor and satire. Its persona is a detached friend of virtue who delivers Addisonian observations on vice and virtue. F. further develops his philosophical ideas in such works as "On the Providence of God in the Government of the World" (1730) and "Self-Denial not the Essence of Virtue" (1734–35); these essays, which emphasize the importance of virtue and benevolence, reflect F.'s disenchantment with the philosophical necessitarianism he upheld in his youthful pamphlet *A Dissertation on Liberty and Necessity, Pleasure and Pain* (1725).

The works of greatest literary interest during the Philadelphia years are the satires. The occasional satires F. wrote during this busy period of his life reveal his mastery of the techniques that became his satiric signature: sharply etched, individualized personae, literary hoaxes designed to ensnare the unwary reader, apparently straight-faced reporting of absurd beliefs and actions, and the extension of apparently reasonable arguments into self-serving rationalization. The two best known satires from these years are characteristic. In "A Witch Trial at Mount Holly" (1730), F. uses the mask of a sober reporter to reveal the absurdity of superstition and to unmask the sexual impulses underlying popular tests for witchcraft; in the superb "The Speech of Miss Polly Baker" (1747), F. creates a female speaker whose speech of vindication moves so subtly from justifiable attacks on the double standard of the bastardly laws to self-interested rationalization to absurd self-glorification that many contemporary readers were taken in completely. Polly Baker's speech was praised as proof of the power of uneducated reason to distinguish between artificial social laws and the fundamental laws of natural humanity.

Except for a brief return to America (November 1, 1762 through November 7, 1764), F. spent the years from 1757 to 1775 in England as colonial agent for Pennsylvania and, as his reputation grew and the quarrels of the colonies with England mounted, for other colonies as well. During these years, F. made effective use of the persuasive and satiric skills he had developed in Philadelphia. F. saw his role as agent as including an obligation to inform the British public as well to lobby the government. Writing for the English newspapers under a variety of pseudonyms, F. attempted to counter English ignorance of and prejudice against America and to state as forcefully as possible the case for American rights. The years in London mark the apex of F.'s achievement as a writer of persuasive and especially of satiric prose. As spokesman for the American colonies, F. produced a stream of masterful works. Although many of F.'s pieces were straightforward attempts to counter his opponents's arguments, the hoaxes and satires inevitably drew the most attention. A glance at a few of these satires reveals the range of F.'s satiric talents. In "The Grand Leap of the Whale" (1765), F. creates a gullible English persona who believes everything he reads in the newspapers; by vouching for a series of tall tales about the extent of American industry and commerce, this persona unconsciously displays the absurdity of British fears of American competition. "Rules by Which a Great Empire May Be Reduced to a Small One" (1773) shows F. ironically laying down instructions for easing the burden of empire by dismembering it; the rules he sets forth are precisely the policies being followed by the British government. Perhaps F.'s most complex satire of this period is "An Edict By the King of Prussia" (1773). In this work, F. places his British readers in the position of the Americans by writing an imaginary edict from the King of Prussia in which the Prussian King makes the same claims and demands on England as England imposes upon America. This elaborate hoax allows F. to manipulate his readers' emotional reactions; he first arouses the British reader's anger and indignation at the presumption and arrogance of the Prussian demands and then, as the reader sees through the hoax to its reflection of British behavior, the reader's indignation recoils upon himself. The "Rules" is perhaps the cleverest satire from the London years, but what astonishes about F.'s satire is not any single piece but the versatility of tone, method, and effect of which F. is capable. In these occasional writings F. produced some of his most brilliant work.

Upon his return to America in 1775, F. became immersed in committee work for the Second Continental Congress. Although he served on the committee for drafting the Declaration of Independence, he contributed little to Thomas JEFFERSON's text. During his years as minister to France and as a member of the peace commission (1776–85), F.'s time was taken up by the official and social duties consequent upon his office. He did, however, write his most savage satire,

"The Sale of the Hessians" (1777). Adopting the persona of the Count De Schaumbergh, F. has the Count urge his commander to incite his troops to die bravely in America for the glory of Hesse and the replenishment of his coffers. The patent hypocrisy of the Count's praise of heroic sacrifice, his indifference to the death and suffering of his subjects, and the luxurious triviality of his occupations create a highly charged, ironic portrait of the callous viciousness of which rulers are capable. This work and the similarly bitter "Supplement to the Boston Independent Chronicle, April, 1782" reveal F.'s anger at the potential for savagery and baseness in humanity.

The anger of the "Sale" and the "Supplement" contrasts curiously with the tone of F.'s most characteristic writings during his years in France, the short pieces known collectively as bagatelles. Although the bagatelles vary widely in subject matter and style, the fines of them embody F.'s playful wit and charm at its most sophisticated level. Posing as the elderly sage adulated by the French, F. uses a delicate irony to expose his own and humanity's pretenses and self-deception. Because the persona accepts even while he laughs at human imperfections (including his own) and espouses virtue even as he reveals the impossibility of perfecting it, the effect is humorous rather than bitter. The best of the bagatelles, such as "The Ephemera" (1778) and "Dialogue between the Gout and Mr. F." (1780), are masterpieces of subtle sophistication presented in the guise of naive simplicity. During the years in Paris, F. also wrote two important informative essays on America, "Remarks Concerning the Savages of North-America" (1783) and "Information to Those Who Would Remove to America" (1784). Designed for a European audience, these essays attempt to replace misconceptions about America with F.'s own views of the subject.

In the years after his return to America until his death (1785–90), F. continued, despite ill-health, to invent, to work in science and politics, and to write. As a member of the Constitutional Convention, F. wrote his most famous speech, delivered on the final day of the Convention, September 17, 1787. In the "Speech in the Convention at the Conclusion of its Deliberations," F. uses all his rhetorical skills to urge the delegates to support the Constitution unanimously. Adopting his favorite pose of the worldly, elderly sage, F. argues that the Constitution, despite his disagreement with some things in it, is closer to perfection than he expected, and he urges every member to "doubt a little of his own infallibility and, to make *manifest* our *unanimity,* put his name to this instrument." F.'s stance in this speech is a more sophisticated version of the "well-wisher to all mankind" persona that he developed during his youth in Philadelphia. F.'s final satire, "Sidi Mehemet Ibrahim on the Slave Trade," (1790) belongs to his last year; in this attack on slavery, F. uncovers the absurdity of pro-slave trade arguments by placing them in the mouth of an Algerian who uses them to justify the capture and enslavement of Christians. Fittingly, F.'s last satire uses one of his favorite satiric devices, turning the tables on his opponents, to reveal the absurdity of self-interested rationalization and to promote a benevolent cause.

F.'s public writing displays the range of his talents, the diversity of the forms he mastered, and the variety of his literary achievements. The full impact of F.'s famous charm and wit, however, can only be savored by reading his letters. The letters provide a record of F.'s development as a thinker and writer, and they show the skill with which he adapts his voice, tone, and style to an enormous range of situations and correspondents. Always clear and concise, F. can be grave or humorous, objective or impassioned, apparently candid or formally reserved as circumstances require; yet each letter bears F.'s voice and individual stamp. A master of this minor 18th-c. art, F. treats his letters with as much skill and care as his more formal writing.

The culmination of F.'s career as a writer, the work with the most influence upon later writers, is his *Autobiography*. Worked on at four different times (1771, 1784, 1788, 1789–90) and revised extensively, the *Autobiography* remained incomplete at F.'s death. An outline F. made while writing the first section suggests that the general plan of the work was present in F.'s mind from the beginning, but the sporadic nature of its composition, the changing circumstances in which it was written, and its unfinished state have blurred its structural unity somewhat.

The *Autobiography* divides naturally into three connected sections. The first part, written in 1771, focuses on F.'s childhood and adolescence in Boston and on his young manhood in London and Philadelphia. This section contains most of the scenes and events that have become part of American mythology, such as F.'s first entrance to Philadelphia. It is the most entertaining of the sections because F. treats his younger self essentially as though he were a protagonist in a picaresque novel. Through the amused, tolerant, eyes of the elderly narrator, the reader sees the young F. learn through experience and error the necessity of virtue, hard work, and worldly wisdom in making one's way in the world. As portrayed by the narrator, the young F. has many faults, but he succeeds because of his ability, his industry, and, especially, his talent for learning from his errors. F. contrasts the young F.'s ability to learn through experience with sharply drawn foil characters who fail, despite talent, education, or connections, because they will not learn from their mistakes how to get on in the world. The

sharp distinction in this section between the experienced narrator and the naive protagonist creates the humor and irony that make the story of F.'s rise in the world appealing.

In the second section, F. focuses on his youthful experiment in attempting to achieve moral perfection; he lists the virtues he considered necessary to a useful and happy life and recounts his attempts to achieve them. This section has provoked more critical controversy than any other part of the *Autobiography* because the irony here is so ambiguous that its targets become unclear. Readings of this section range from condemnations of F. for smug self-congratulation to assertions that the entire section is an ironic attack on the 18th-c. belief in moral perfectibility. Structurally the second section serves as a bridge between the first and third parts. It abstracts the principles that the young F. learned through trial and error were necessary for happiness and success and details them for the reader, but it simultaneously uses irony to laugh at the young F.'s naive confidence in his ability to achieve moral perfection and at the human tendency to rationalize one's imperfections. The second section of the *Autobiography* is both serious and ironic; F. is at his most serious when he is most ironic.

The third section, which includes the remainder of the *Autobiography*, portrays the mature F.'s use of the principles of conduct that he learned in the first section and enumerated in the second. In this section, the reader sees F. employing his hard-won knowledge of himself and humanity for his own and others's benefit. F. focuses on his gradual rise to prosperity, on his scientific studies, and, especially, on his work as a promoter of the public good as a philanthropist and politician. Although F. occasionally steps back and views his adult behavior with an ironic eye, for the most part the gap between narrator and protagonist vanishes. By the third section, the naive protagonist has largely been transformed into the experienced narrator; the reader is invited to learn from, and perhaps marvel at, his accomplishments.

F.'s *Autobiography* is his single most important work, and it is certainly his most controversial one. Ever since its initial publication, it has provoked diverse responses. Detractors see it as a classic example of the worst kind of American glorification of materialism and worldly success; defenders view it as a sophisticated autobiographical masterpiece that unites ironic humor with worldly wisdom and self knowledge. The *Autobiography* remains today a widely read, much translated, still provocative classic of 18th-c. American literature. It stands as an inescapable work for Americans. Viewed in the context of F.'s other writings, the *Autobiography* is the culminating literary achievement of America's foremost, multitalented genius.

BIBLIOGRAPHY: Aldridge, A. O., *B. F., Philosopher and Man* (1965); Clark, R. W., *B. F.* (1983); Labaree, L. W., et al., eds., *The Papers of B. F.* (22 vols., 1959–82); Tourtellot, A. B., *B. F.: The Shaping of Genius, The Boston Years* (1977); Van Doren, C., *B. F.* (1938); Wright, E., *F. of Philadelphia* (1986)

DAVID M. LARSON

FREDERIC, Harold

b. 19 August 1856, Utica, New York; d. 19 October 1898, Kenley, Surrey, England

F. is Mark TWAIN without the Mississippi River and Stephen CRANE without the tragic ending. Perhaps because he was viewed as just another local colorist, as just another realist, or as just the penultimate hack, F. fell into obscurity soon after his death. His rediscovery in the late 1950s, however, shows that he deserves critical attention as another important voice in turn-of-the-century letters.

Born and reared in Utica, New York, F. absorbed even the most minute details of his surroundings with his innate camera-eye. Later he recorded the sights and sounds of his home on paper. After he completed high school at fifteen, F. worked for a photographer where he specialized in retouching negatives. In 1873, he went to Boston and continued work as a photographer and even took art courses. His careful observation and his knowledge of picture-taking later served him well as a writer.

F. displays grandly his talent in two pieces. Set against the backdrop of the Civil War, "Marsena" (1894) focuses on photographer Marsena Pulford. In the story, F. examines how war affects Octavius (or Utica) when Marsena and other young men go off to war to please Julia Parmelee, a local siren—a situation that anticipates William Dean HOWELLS in "Editha." F. handles his version as artistically as Howells, but the real strength of "Marsena" lies in its vivid description and its consideration of "art for art's sake," a prevailing concern for writers in the 1890s. Although he uses his camera-eye well in "Marsena," F. masters his technique in *The Damnation of Theron Ware* (1896), the jewel of his crown. Carefully blending colors and sensuous art objects, he creates a memorable scene when Ware encounters Celia Madden one evening and finds his way into her private chamber—a scene that truly testifies to the worth of F.'s crafts.

F. left photography in 1877 to enter newspaper work, beginning as a proofreader for the Utica *Morning Herald* and shortly thereafter moving to the Utica *Observer.* In 1880, he advanced to the editorship of that paper. Clearly F. had established himself solidly as a journalist when he assumed the editorship of the Albany *Evening Journal* in 1882.

That paper's political leanings would prove the catalyst to set him on the way to his career as a fictionist and as an international figure. F.'s alliance to the Democratic Party is undeniable, for he was comfortable with the *Observer's* stance. The Albany paper had a Republican tradition; however, F. changed that ideology when he endorsed Grover Cleveland in 1882; as a result the two formed a friendship. Within two years, however, the *Evening Journal* reverted to its old ways, and F. no longer had a job. After his departure from Albany, he landed a job as London correspondent for the *New York Times* and moved to England with his family in 1884.

Although F. had begun his literary career when the *Observer* published "The Blakeleys of Popular Place: A Legend of the Mohawk" (1877), he began in 1884 publishing stories and novels in earnest and with regularity until his death. When F.'s first sustained work *Seth's Brother's Wife: A Study of Life in the Greater New York* (1887) appeared, the author set a pattern that he would repeat in later novels and stories: the emphasis on people and places. Like the majority of his works, which are set in upstate New York, the first novel is no exception. It explores politicians and the rivalry between brothers; the tension established by the conflict between the moral, upright brother and the degenerate one occupies the development of the novel. Unlike many of his contemporaries, F. offers the happy ending wherein good triumphs.

This realistic novel was succeeded by the historical romance *In the Valley* (1890), set during the American Revolution. As he would do in *The Copperheads* (1893) and *Marsena and Other Stories of the Wartime* (1894), F. analyzes the effects of war on a small community.

One may posit, however, that throughout his career F. studies war-torn characters, whether participating in actual armed combat or not. Both *The Lawton Girl* (1890), the story of a fallen woman who returns to her hometown, and *Damnation* feature characters who must face hostility in small communities in upstate New York. In *March Hares* (1896), *Gloria Mundi* (1898), and *The Market Place* (1899), F. presents similarly torn characters; but he changes the locality to England and approaches high comedy.

Although exhibiting great diversity, F.'s fiction bears the marks common to literature centered on character and place; however, F.'s flair for art and pseudo-psychology add substance to the material. For these reasons, F. commands our attention.

BIBLIOGRAPHY: Briggs, A., Jr., *The Novels of H. F.* (1969); Fortenberry, G. E., et al., eds., *The Correspon-*

dence of H. F. (1977); O'Donnell, T. F., and H. C. Franchere, *H. F.* (1961)

E. KATE STEWART

FREEMAN, Mary E[leanor] Wilkins

b. 31 October 1852, Randolph, Massachusetts; d. 15 March 1930, Metuchen, New Jersey

Widely acclaimed both popularly and critically in her time, the works of F. went into decline in the decades following her death. Recently, however, largely as the result of feminist interest, her distinguished accomplishment is receiving renewed appreciation. A follower of the New England local color school, and therefore under the influence of Rose Terry COOKE and Sarah Orne JEWETT, F. saw a much grimmer world than her predecessors. F.'s New England was spiritually as well as materially impoverished; indeed it is physical and emotional deprivation that drives many of her characters into dogged, obsessive, neurotic behavior, by which they tenaciously affirm their small portion.

F. was a prolific writer. She produced a total of twenty-two volumes of short stories and essays, nearly one hundred uncollected stories, fourteen novels, three volumes of poetry, three plays, eight children's books, and one film script. It is generally agreed that most of her best work was accomplished early in her career. Several of the stories in two early collections, *A Humble Romance and Other Stories* (1887) and *A New England Nun and Other Stories* (1891), along with a few later pieces, deserve indeed to be included among the masterpieces of the genre. Until her marriage in 1902, she published under "Mary E. Wilkins."

F.'s most anthologized and possibly her best story is thematically representative. "A New England Nun"—first published in May 1887 in *Harper's Bazar,* where most of her early stories appeared—concerns the decision a house-bound spinster must make whether to marry a long-absent suitor. The authorial viewpoint in this story, as in much of F.'s work, is ambivalent. On the one hand, Louisa Ellis's loving attachment to her domestic rituals—picking currants from her garden for tea, making essences of rose and peppermint with her still—reflects the obsessiveness of a religious or artistic vocation. On the other hand, her life is as narrow and circumscribed as that of her chained-up dog and caged canary. Her decision not to wed thus expresses fear of a disruptive new experience but also affirmation of a peaceful feminine world of domestic creativity.

The pathos of her characters' prideful attachment to and often obsessive defense of their paltry lot may be seen in several other remarkable early stories, notably "An Honest Soul," "Brakes and White Vi'lets,"

"A Far-Away Melody," "A Mistaken Charity," "An Object of Love," which Sarah Orne Jewett singled out for praise, "A Gatherer of Simples," and "A Patient Waiter," in *Humble Romance;* and "A Village Singer," "Sister Liddy," "A Wayfaring Couple," "A Poetess," "Christmas Jenny," "A Solitary," "A Church Mouse," and "The Revolt of 'Mother,'" the latter F.'s most popular story during her lifetime, in *New England Nun.*

Like other local color writers, one of F.'s strengths is her use of precisely realistic detail; but F. is distinguished by the intensity of passion her characters feel and by the modernist sense of absurdity that informs her greatest work. Stories like "A Patient Waiter" and "A Wayfaring Couple" evince a sense of failure so profound as to have metaphysical dimensions that anticipate the absurdist literature of the 20th c. In the former story, an aging spinster "waits for Godot" by vainly trekking twice-daily to the post office for forty years hoping for a letter from her lover. In the latter story, an impoverished couple walk from town to town unsuccessfully seeking work. The final scene when the wife puts on carriage traces and "like a beast of burden" drags her delirious husband three miles to a doctor has a starkly Sisyphean existentialist tone.

Later stories of special significance include "Old Woman Magoun" (1905), "Arethusa" (1900), "Evelina's Garden" (1896), "The Long Arm" (1895), and "The Tree of Knowledge" (1899).

While F.'s novels are not of the calibre of her stories, they are nevertheless of considerable interest. Many consider *Pembroke* (1894), her second novel, to be her best. In her preface to the 1899 edition, F. called it a "study of the human will . . . in different phases of disease and abnormal development." Like other women local colorists, F. strongly critiqued residual Calvinist tendencies, especially the New Englander's fierce will and stern conscience, which she saw as a character pathology. This is her subject in *Pembroke:* characters' indomitable wills destroy one another; no compassion or negotiation softens their relentless obsessions. The eyes of one "gleamed with warlike energy" as she listened to the Psalms: "she confused King David's enemies with those people who crossed her own will." F. effectively reaches a note of tragedy in this stark work.

The Portion of Labor (1901) also remains an interesting novel. Ostensibly a work of social protest about factory conditions and working-class injustices, it also plots the career course or a "new woman," Ellen Brewster and her various relationships, one with another emancipated woman, Cynthia Lennox. *By the Light of the Soul* (1907), thought to be F.'s most autobiographical work, similarly has as its principal subject a schoolteacher's emotional life, primarily with her half-sister and a dwarf woman she eventually adopts. F.'s last significant novel was *The Shoulders of Atlas*

(1908). It too remains a powerful and intriguing, if overly plotted, work. As in earlier novels, the complex plot includes latent lesbian relationships that are not fully integrated into the various denouements, which thus remain problematic.

F. experimented with a number of unusual forms. Among her most successful attempts are *Understudies* (1901) and *Six Trees* (1903). The former is a collection of twelve stories in which animals or plants relate or correlate to human beings. The latter, which F. thought her best work, follows the same theme but uses trees somewhat more symbolically to express aspects of human characters' traits or concerns. F. also published a collection of ghost stories, *The Wind in the Rose-Bush and Other Stories of the Supernatural* (1903), which also lends itself to symbolic interpretation. In another innovative gesture, F. contributed a chapter to the composite novel *The Whole Family* (1908) written by twelve authors, including William Dean HOWELLS, Henry JAMES, Elizabeth Stuart PHELPS, and others. The final volume in F.'s literary career was *Edgewater People* (1918).

Other works include *Jane Field* (1893), a novel; *Giles Corey, Yeoman* (1893), a play; *Madelon* (1896), a novel; *Jerome, a Poor Man* (1897), a novel; *Silence and Other Stories* (1898); *The Love of Parson Lord and Other Stories* (1900); *The Givers* (1904), stories; *The Debtor* (1905), a novel; *The Fair Lavinia and Others* (1907); and *The Winning Lady and Others* (1909).

BIBLIOGRAPHY: Donovan, J., *New England Local Color Literature: A Women's Tradition* (1983); Donovan, J., *The (Other) American Traditions* (1993); Foster, E., *M. E. W. F.* (1956); Glasser, L., *"In a Closet Hidden": The Life and Works of M. E. W. F.* (1996); Kendrick, B. L., *The Infant Sphinx: Collected Letters of M. E. W. F.* (1985); Marchialonis, S., *Critical Essays on M. W. F.* (1991); Meese, E. A., *Crossing the Double-Cross* (1986); Reichardt, M. R., *A Web of Relationships: Women in the Short Fiction of M. W. F.* (1992); Reichardt, M. R., ed., *The Uncollected Stories of M. W. F.* (1992); Reichardt, M. R., *M. W. F.: A Study of the Short Fiction* (1997); Reichardt, M. R., ed., *A M. W. F. Reader* (1997); Romines, A., *The Home Plot: Women, Writing and Domestic Ritual* (1992); Westbrook, P. D., *M. W. F.* (1967)

JOSEPHINE DONOVAN

FRENCH, Alice

b. 19 March 1850, Andover, Massachusetts; d. 9 January 1934, Davenport, Iowa

F., a local color writer of the late 19th c., who wrote under the pen name of Octave Thanet, was born in Andover, Massachusetts into an old-line New England family. Although her family moved to Davenport, Iowa, she was educated at Abbot Academy. Her literary career began in 1871 when a short story appeared in the Davenport newspaper. After the Haymarket Square riot in 1876, F., whose family owned a manufacturing plant, wrote about labor relations. Her most ambitious effort in this genre, *The Man of the Hour* (1905), rejected unionism but suggested that corporate greed be tempered by Anglo-Saxon racial superiority. F. believed the Social Darwinism of Herbert Spencer culminated in the American middle class. Her rejection of ROMANTICISM led her to embrace, at least in theory, continental REALISM, and her public announcement of this position at the Columbian Exposition attracted much comment.

Since realism meant writing about what the author had actually experienced, F. began researching local color stories about early Davenport. In 1883, she and her lifelong companion, Jane Allen Crawford, visited the Clover Bend plantation in a remote section of eastern Arkansas, which they subsequently made into their winter home. During the next twenty years, F. exploited every literary aspect of remote Southern rural ways in short stories that put her, in Thomas Wentworth HIGGINSON's judgment, "at the head of American writers of fiction." Appearing in *Scribner's Magazine, Century, Harper's Weekly,* and other periodicals, these prolific stories made her one of the best paid writers of the time.

Less successful were her Western stories, and she exceeded her grasp in attempting novels. Her attempt to resolve the conflict between the increasingly strident Southern racism and lingering Northern idealism in *By Inheritance* (1910) found her advocating that blacks give up all hopes of political rights or economic advancement and find work under the protection of aristocratic Southern whites who were their best friends.

F.'s refusal to change her identification with 19th-c. values made her last years tragic and virtually guaranteed her neglect by subsequent students of American literature. However, for the social historian, F. provides a wealth of material on the Southern yeomanry, blacks, and women. She published on Arkansas folklore and in her early stories succeeded more than most readers liked in reproducing local speech patterns. During her lifetime, she became a fictional character in Opie READ's last novel, *The Gold Glaize Veil*.

F. was hardly the stereotypical reclusive woman writer. A friend of Theodore ROOSEVELT, with whom she corresponded on literature and Arkansas Republican party politics, she was warmly remembered by William Allen WHITE, who recalled the gastronomic feasts of the three-hundred-pound gourmand. While much the liberated woman in her private life and a bitter opponent of prohibition, this active member of the Daughters of the American Revolution opposed woman suffrage. Plagued by diabetes and gout, her career was over by 1920 as she became embittered over the collapse of Victorian values.

BIBLIOGRAPHY: Dougan, M. B., and C. W. Dougan, eds., *By the Cypress Swamp: The Arkansas Stories of Octave Thanet* (1980); McMichael, G., *Journey to Obscurity; The Life of Octave Thanet* (1965)

MICHAEL B. DOUGAN

FRENCH, Marilyn

b. 21 November 1929, New York City

F. is known as a feminist in her literary scholarship as well as in her fiction. She is best known to the general public as the author of *The Women's Room* (1977), which exploded onto the marketplace in the 1970s as part of the expanding women's movement. However, her first published work was *The Book as World—James Joyce's "Ulysses"* (1976), which she wrote for her doctorate (Harvard, 1972). FEMINISM and feminist concerns continue to inform both her fiction and her scholarly work.

Feminism, says F., has to do with a moral view of life rather than anatomy. She sees feminism as embodying the life-affirming, nurturing qualities traditionally ascribed to women and believes the world needs to become a feminist world, to stress life and nurturing rather than killing and power. These values lead F. to focus on women in her fiction and to include children in the lives of her female characters. Some critics believe this focus partly accounts for the tremendous popular success of *The Women's Room,* making it accessible to women put off by a more radical feminist perspective. Mira, the novel's central character, is a conventional woman who returns to school (Harvard) after her marriage ends in divorce. The novel includes the stories of the women Mira meets as well as the gradual raising of her own consciousness. The ending, however, shows Mira alone, and there seems to be no possibility of positive, lasting relationship between men and women. The novel depicts women supporting one another and shows them juggling careers and child-rearing. *Her Mother's Daughter* (1987) further develops the theme of mothering. F. strives to show that good mothering is not genetic, but must be learned, passed on from mother to daughter.

F. aims for a style that reflects her politics. Her fictional works weave together stories of many women into a communal experience in a conversational style, "like one woman talking to another woman across the

coffee table." Her fiction is particularly praised for the powerful characterizations of women. It is sometimes criticized for depicting men only as insensitive brutes as well as having a tedious and repetitive style, but her readers, particulary women readers, strongly identify with her female characters and their experiences.

F. brings a similar feminist perspective to her nonfiction. In *Shakespeare's Division of Experience* (1981), she examines the Shakespearean canon to show how Shakespeare himself questioned whether the separate spheres of men and women were biologically or socially determined and concludes that Shakespeare, despite his questioning, did not escape the misogyny of his age. *Beyond Power: On Women, Men, and Morals* (1985) looks at the way women have been treated over the history of the world. F.'s nonfiction has contributed to the feminist "re-visioning" of the traditional literary canon and of history, and her fiction gives voice to and validates women's experience of the world.

BIBLIOGRAPHY: Todd, J., ed., *Women Writers Talking* (1983); Wagner, L. W., "The F. Definition," *ArQ* 38 (Winter 1982): 293–302

HEIDI PRESCHLER

FRENEAU, Philip [Morin]

b. 2 January 1752, New York City; d. 18 December 1832, Freehold, New Jersey

Labeled as the "poet of the American Revolution," F. is remembered for his satirical and patriotic poems directed against the British and the Tories. But the emphasis on the political aspects of F.'s career has eclipsed his larger literary accomplishments and kept him from receiving recognition as one of the most important American poets of the 18th c.

F. was the most voluminous writer at that time, producing over 500 poems, some 1,100 prose pieces, and a few works of short fiction. He wrote on many of the leading issues of the day, most notably, politics, theology, social manners, nature, and aesthetics. In style, he both imitated British literary traditions—in particular those of Pope, Goldsmith, Milton, and Addison—and experimented with forms of his own making.

F. began his literary career during his years at Princeton where, with Hugh Henry BRACKENRIDGE, he coauthored *Fr. Bombo's Pilgrimage* (1770), a farcical novel intended to ridicule a rival club on campus, and "A Poem, on the Rising Glory of America," a millennial vision of America as a "new Jerusalem." He also wrote poems of his own, in particular "The Power of Fancy," which was neoclassical in style but romantic in its emphasis on nature and the imagination.

In the years after graduation, F. taught, studied theology, and wrote several other noteworthy poems, the most famous of which was "The American Village."

F. gained considerable fame in 1775 publishing satirical verse about tyrannical British officers, though not yet in a spirit of revolution. In 1776, he went to the Caribbean, perhaps in search of a more peaceful environment to further his poetry. This exotic clime inspired him again towards personal expression in the romantic mode, as is seen in "The House of Night" with its vision of the demise of Death and "The Beauties of Santa Cruz" which details the natural splendor of the Caribbean and encourages others in America to leave behind "thy bloody plains."

F. returned to join the militia in 1778. Two years later, when in the Caribbean again, he was captured and imprisoned as a privateer. This traumatic event lead him to write "The British Prison Ship," his most venomous indictment of England. Never again would he feel indebted to "this selfish race"; from 1781 to 1784, he devoted himself entirely to writing vitriolic satire while working as editor of Philadelphia's *Freeman's Journal*.

After the war, F. alternated between working as captain of coastal vessels and as editor of various newspapers in New York, Philadelphia, and Monmouth County, New Jersey. Most significant was his post with Philadelphia's *National Gazette* where, because he pressed for Jeffersonian democracy and objected to Federalist leanings towards monarchy, he won himself many enemies, including Washington who dubbed him "that rascal F."

During this period, F.'s poetry changed to a shorter, more symbolic lyric. He also furthered his most resonant theme—the transiency of life and the inevitability of decay—as is strikingly apparent in nature poems such as "To a Caty-Did," "On Observing a Large Red-Streaked Apple," and "The Wild Honeysuckle," often considered his best lyric. In these poems, he observes a small object in nature that captures the brevity of human existence, with a surprisingly accepting tone; F.'s belief in Deism convinced him that natural laws—including those of aging and death—reflect God's plans and are therefore worthy of celebration.

The ephemeral quality of life is also featured in F.'s Indian poems and poems written during his further adventures at sea. For example, "The Dying Indian" depicts the unfortunate but necessary dying off of a noble race while "The Hurricane" anticipates the watery grave of the oceans, suggesting that "ruin is the lot of all."

While F.'s prose has been generally considered far inferior to his verse, it did allow him to develop a related theme concerning the simplicity of nature and the folly of civilization. In his four most successful prose series, F. created the characters of The Pilgrim, Mr. Robert Slender, The Philosopher of the Forest, and Tom Cheeki, the Creek Indian—all either eccentrics or primitivists—to speak of the absurdity of American morals and manners and glorify a more essential way of life.

F.'s dual careers were finished by 1807. Afterwards, he continued to write, especially during the War of 1812 when his patriotic muse was given new tongue. He died in 1832, unappreciated and largely forgotten, even though five collections of his poetry had been published during his life—in 1786, 1788, 1795, 1809, and 1815. F.'s efforts to establish himself as a lyrical poet were continually interrupted by the public's desire to see the issues of their turbulent time set into verse. His political writing successfully lambasted tyranny of many forms (including slavery) but did not grant him long-term fame as more than a Revolutionary War poet. A reconsideration of F.'s finer poems would reveal his significance as a precursor to the romantics, as the nation's first naval lyricist, and as one of the first authors to express a uniquely American voice.

BIBLIOGRAPHY: Axelrad, J., *P. F.: Champion of Democracy* (1967); Bowden, M. W., *P. F.* (1976); Hiltner, J. R., ed., *The Newspaper Verse of P. F.: An Edition and Bibliographic Survey* (1986); Leary, L., *That Rascal F.: A Study in Literary Failure* (1941); Marsh, P. M., *The Works of P. F.: A Critical Study* (1968)

RENEE SCHATTEMAN

FRIEDMAN, Bruce Jay

b. 26 April 1930, Bronx, New York

This author's remove from the urban and mixed cultural environment of New York to the University of Missouri in the late 1940s and a degree in journalism provides the theme of most of his writing, which is comic alienation and the predicaments of absurdity as the city *schlemiel* confronts the country yokel. The identities of America are divided into far more than three parts, and these conflicts of differing cultures, held within the bounds of a single disparate geography with but a simple compound name, drive a leading comic view of what, even for the native-born, is often an adopted or foreign country. This sense of the foreign, the totally absurd spectacle of one dialect confronting another, though apparently understood yet forever at odds, is the essence of F.'s humor.

While he is known as a comedic writer, F.'s first novel, *Stern* (1962), is a fiction of attempted assimilation partially in the realistic vein of Saul BELLOW or much of the work of Bernard MALAMUD. Stern's goal is to happily provide for his family, move them to the new paradise of high mortgages and crab grass, and enjoy plenty on man's nearest equivalent to heaven on earth, the suburb, what one of the characters in *The Dick* (1970) will call a place "picked up during a storm and blown in whole from Wyoming." The titular character eventually survives the assaults to his person by a local anti-Semite, taking a blow in a physical confrontation that proves, paradoxically, to be regenerative. This is a surprising fiction in its canvass, a comedy in the sense of its representation of everyday life, the typical working of a sympathetic *mensch,* suffering as all creatures suffer, so recognizable in a sympathetic commonness. Stern is a comedy in what might be called a European sense, of the human character surviving, despite his frailty, the banalities of evil, and his own fatality. The Jewish newcomer to the wilds of the suburb has no discernible craft except his commute by auto to and from the city; no practical art is within his complete grasp—mere house maintenance is as deep a riddle as the Delphic mysteries. Abiding xenophobia is loosed upon the newcomer; he is isolated by epithet and hounded by nature, his garden always beyond management. He is released to sanity, to urbanity, only with the sale of his suburban dead end.

Such is the nonpratfall comedy of humors F. also elaborates in *The Dick* and in *About Harry Towns* (1974). His books with mixed reviews, such as *The Lonely Guy's Book of Life* (1976) and its sequel, *The Slightly Older Guy* (1995), at times read like scripts for Steve Martin's quasi-serious monologues of failure, of the too earnest *schlemiel,* yet another mutation of the humorous in an older, continental sense.

In *A Mother's Kisses,* published in 1964, the main character, a youngster applying to colleges after his high school graduation in Brooklyn, is so inept that he is accepted only at a Western polytech, where most of the students are but a few paces removed from the corral, practical cattle breeding and branding, cowboy boots, animal husbandry prep, and Stetson hats. His mother, a momism descriptee from Philip Wylie's *Generation of Vipers* (1942), accompanies him to the school, exhibiting her own libido and inhibiting his, commenting on everything and leaving him tongue-tied. She is all the more aggressive as he, because of her disjointedly maternal and erotically syncopated attention, becomes more inhibited and prone to awkward missteps, to stumbling falls, actual and sexual. A burlesque of cultural discontinuities that anticipates Philip ROTH's *Portnoy's Complaint, A Mother's Kisses* deserves a place as one of the best regarded comic novels of this era. F.'s sequel, *A Father's Kisses* (1996), was less successful than the original.

F. has enjoyed some success in the theater and as a writer of movie scripts. His *Scuba Duba* (1968), with its evisceration of cross-cultural entrapments of

race, sex, and status, enjoyed popular theatrical success in the late 1960s. *Steambath,* another play, was published in 1971. F. had considerable success in Hollywood as a collaborative script writer for *Splash* (1984), as well as *The Heartbreak Kid* (1972), *Stir Crazy* (1980), and other films.

BIBLIOGRAPHY: Avery, E., "B. J. F.," in Walden, D., ed., *DLB,* vol. 28, *Twentieth-Century American-Jewish Fiction* (1984): 69–74; Schulze, M., *B. J. F.* (1974); Seed, D., "B. J. F.'s Fiction: Black Humour and After," *Thalia* 10 (Spring-Summer 1988): 14–22

ROBERT MOYNIHAN

FROST, Robert [Lee]

b. 26 March 1874, San Francisco, California; d. 28 January 1963, Boston, Massachusetts

F. continues to prove himself a major American poet. Perhaps Lawrance Thompson's biography provides an essential clue to the unfailing scholarly interest F. generated throughout his lifetime and generates still. Thompson portrays F. as a man easy to dislike but impossible to dismiss; regardless of any revisionist attempts to correct Thompson's meticulous documentation of what he clearly felt to be the poet's personal shortcomings, F. himself is a provocateur. Whether loved or hated, defended or attacked, F. remains an almost palpable presence in his poetry, which issues the complicated challenge of his voice. F. eschews diplomacy in almost all things, but he is not straightforward. The version he offers of himself is a carefully cultivated persona, witty, irascible, politically and intellectually conservative, rhetorically acute. His poetry, like the man, is full of the enigma of the seemingly forthright; it has the sound of code, the irresistible lure of a subtext buried like a murdered lover in the basement.

In "The Witch of Coos," the dead lover's bones climb up to live in the attic, and they clatter chalkily against the barricaded door that keeps them up there. These bones rattle throughout F.'s poetry, in the wind that scraps the skeletal fingers of winter trees against window panes, in the crack of ice as it shatters, in the vertebral walls whose stones topple down. It is small wonder that sometimes there seems to be, in F.'s poetry, a madman in the attic, like the crazed uncle in "A Servant to Servants" who thrums the hickory bars of his upstairs cage as if they are the poet's harp and cries out about love.

F.'s first two books of poetry, *A Boy's Will* (1913) and *North of Boston* (1914), were published in London after F. failed to interest American publishers in his work. During the next forty-eight years, F. published nine more books of new poetry: *Mountain Interval* (1916), *New Hampshire* (1923), *West Running Brook* (1928), *A Further Range* (1936), *A Witness Tree* (1942), *A Masque of Reason* (1945), *A Masque of Mercy* and *Steeple Bush,* both published in 1947, and *In the Clearing* (1962). He received four Pulitzer Prizes, in 1924, 1931, 1937, and 1943. He was, from beginning to end, a public figure, active throughout his life as a teacher, a lecturer, and a visiting personage.

Although recent criticism has linked F. to the poetic "modernity" that is more typically associated with poets like T. S. ELIOT and Ezra POUND, his poetry lacks the difficulty of access that invites the complicity of the reader, who must reconstruct meaning out of the implication that wholeness is a lost illusion. F.'s poetry calls for a particularly complex kind of interplay by withholding such immediate difficulty. Seemingly, it *tells* a great deal. The poetry is frequently narrative, telling an intelligible story about recognizable people in everyday circumstances: wives quarrel with husbands, neighbors talk together, people reminisce. Its allusions tend to be classical or biblical, or from British and American poetry, philosophy, and science, and readily accessible to anyone educated in the Western tradition. The natural world that it represents is recognizable both descriptively and metaphorically: snow, trees, fields, pools, the ocean look as we know them to look within the New England landscape, and they behave metaphorically within a recognizable Puritan tradition so that they can seem on one level comfortably emblematic. The images throughout F.'s poetry are always visually coherent, and although the poems tend to suggest analogous meanings, the immediate specificities of time and place are not merely means to a symbolic or allegorical end. If, for example, "After Apple Picking" may be seen as a poem analogously about writing poetry or about death, it must first be felt as a sensual re-creation of an event and its aftereffects. Emblematically, the saplings in "Birches" embody the resilient youth who dominates them, just as the trees crippled by past ice storms embody the older speaker, but the poem also has primacy as a description of how one swings on birch trees, re-creating the action in rhythms of tension and release: the climb, the flight, the landing; the sapling first taut and then whipping upward; the speaker plodding among underbrush, his memories lofting upward and arching back down.

Far from advocating a disintegrative modernist vision, F. called himself a "synecdochist," a term that suggests his paradoxical fluidity of vision, one that presumes wholeness but implies it through the precise representation of a "part" that is itself in his poetry a discrete and separate other whole. He called synecdoche, evocatively, "skirting the hem of the goddess," an image that in itself suggests a powerful wholeness of form and function. Synecdoche used conventionally has fairly strict limitations: the part, one of a set of generally agreed upon components, must be integral to that whole that it represents. But what wholeness—what god or goddess—is F. implying through synecdoche? In his narrative poetry, F.'s near neighbors enact between themselves, in his own New England idioms, the eternal dialectics of the self-between soul and body, masculine and feminine, passion and control, isolation and community; in the nonnarrative poetry, the natural world articulates pure passion and visceral retributive instincts that resonate with the human capacity for emotional bloodletting. Combined, this close community of New Englanders playing out their natures against each other and in reaction to external natural forces makes up the world's body, with the social superimposed like vulnerable skin over the anti-social. It is a body that derives its wholeness from F. himself, for the tension in his poetic universe is an extension of his own incessant dialectic; this is why, perhaps, he must so often imagine the world as frost-bound, transfixed by the poetic eye that can rule even the power of the sun. The poetic voice is dissuasive of passion, which is for F. disintegrative, but the instincts behind the voice push toward passion; his poetry embodies the dilemma of his corporeality. F. wrote that he wanted his poetry to take readers through delight to wisdom, an ecstatic passage indeed. Such synecdoche as he uses is based on Olympian assumptions, but the god-like elevation that can reveal wisdom is always threatened in F.'s poetry by the gravity of passion. Because he feels himself to be the world, he cannot rise above it.

F.'s spoken wisdoms seem essentially unmysterious, fraught with cautionary tones that suggest always that fools do not prosper in a world where everyone is a potential enemy. One must be careful of one's own worst nature but, more especially, of the weaknesses or ambitions of others. Sentimentality in any of its manifestations opens avenues of invasion. F. has his clearly autobiographical speaker in "New Hampshire" claim an out-of-fashion virtue; he says that he would like to be a "good Greek"—that is, one who is *not* foolish or needy enough to be taken advantage of by a world that has rejected, forgotten, or never known the Greek ideal. F. consciously valorizes control as a form of wisdom and as a prophylactic against the inevitable abuse of such a world. In "Home Burial," F. subtly takes the side of the aggrieved and rejected husband rather than the grieving mother. When the husband asks his wife how she came to be so inconsolable about the loss of a first child, he is merely being a good Greek, demanding logic in the face of despair. But his son is, in death or in life, a subversion of the husband's desires; marital love carries within it the seeds of its own destruction. The world that waits outside is in collusion with his fleeing wife, who is pulled by emotion into the erratic motions of near hysteria. Susceptible to mother-love, susceptible to grief, she is living proof of love's inherent betrayal. In "Mending Wall," the speaker attacks the stupidity of those who speak without hearing what they say and act without examining why; his neighbor fails the test of rationality, his rhetorical woodenness antithetical to the good Greek skill of effective and enlightened argument. Interestingly, however, the speaker, who *has* given the act of wall-building a great deal of thought, who knows that the walls are not to keep the apple trees from marching over into the pines, chooses himself to rebuild the wall each spring and in fact calls the neighbor to the task. In his unspoken consideration, good walls do make good neighbors when even his plodding, cliche-bound companion becomes "an old-stone savage armed" as he hoists a boulder from the ground.

Women in particular can be trusted only to betray the trust of fidelity, because by definition they cannot achieve the rational control of the good Greek and are, in fact, antithetical in nature to rationality. They are almost always in the act of leaving men. Their escapes into nature only accelerate inevitable domestic decay, so that homesteads disintegrate into cellar holes surrounded by weeds and wildflowers; in "The Thatch," for example, ruined love translates into the ruined house whose hundred-year life ends so abruptly when its inmates leave. There are few love poems in this poetic world where women are so dangerously aligned with nature, and, in fact, F.'s intimate association of the two frequently makes women and nature rivals for a man's affections. The sonnet "Putting in the Seed" states this explicitly, as the speaker invites the woman to come to the field and try to seduce him away from his passion for the earth. This tension is never reconciled toward human love; what the woman hears the brook say will always be different from what the man hear. One must look outside of F.'s poetry for a love poem that integrates the bursting fecundity of earth with a woman's body. Instead, nature calls all of F.'s figures into jealous isolation with it. The early poem, "A Dream Pang," which Thompson argues to be a dream related by F. to his wife in their bed, is a clear statement of this rivalry, as it has the man "withdrawn in forest," his song "swallowed up in leaves," while the woman waits jealously at the forest's edge. Passion is always in F.'s poetry an act of exclusion within a triangle as primally interdependent as the mother-son-father triad of "Home Burial." It is impossible to love without endangering oneself, for there is always a wounded party who might seek revenge.

F. seems thus universally suspicious of others: people in his poetry tend to take advantage, like the hired man who presumes to return to a place where his work has fallen off and where he has shown, to his employer's mind, a singular lack of gratitude for kindnesses received. There are notably few poems of friendship, his lament on Edward Thomas's death, "To E. T.," an exception that is only slightly qualified by the subtle mockery of him in "The Road Not Taken." In F.'s poetic world, even his own closest relationships are represented as subversive of self: "The Subverted Flower," a long-withheld poem about his courtship of Elinor White, shows how her Circe-like sexual power transforms him into a helpless beast. Radiating out from that most intimate of betrayals comes poetry of childless unions, disintegrating marriages, and isolation. On a political level, this lack of familial trust becomes the assumption that any form of liberalism invites abuse; on a psychological level, it becomes a distrust of the entire "new school of the pseudo-phallic" that extenuates weakness by calling it determinism of a sort. Ultimately F.'s wisdom is highly cautionary, suggesting that carefully maintained barriers and well-policed perimeters are essential. From "New Hampshire," which is an outspokenly isolationist vision about the speaker's native state, to the more subtle implications of pervasive wall imagery, F.'s poetry consistently confirms that, while earth might be "the right place for love," love itself is dangerous as it involves trust in another, whose own inevitable triangulation ensures a compromised allegiance.

Nature's manifestations are inevitably extensions of the passions of human nature magnified into the grandeur of annihilating snowstorms, snakelike winds, dark and powerful trees. Consistently personified, nature takes on the power to seduce and betray, and, at its most potent, the function of godly retribution and punishment. It is constantly encroaching, with cleared spaces going over to weeds and scrub pine and ultimately back to dark forests, just as passions erode asceticism. Woods already fathomless "fill up with snow" in poems such as "Stopping by Woods on a Snowy Evening" and "Desert Places" as if the whiteness is, as "Design" suggests of another pallor, a "design of darkness to appall." On one level, whiteness is lovely, as death is sometimes momentarily felt to be lovely, and on another it is leprotic, symptomatic of decay. Trees can become goddesses, queens, sibyls, but the ultimate effect for the human observer is abasement; in "On Going Unnoticed" the human figure is reduced to a mean and leafless coral root clinging to the base of sibylline trees whose high heads wave in the wind. In any love affair in F.'s poetry, with women or with nature, male figures are diminished and made vulnerable by their own needs. Prudence suggests that men follow the Drumlin Woodchuck's instinctive thoroughness about their hiding places, out of love's and harm's way.

There are two possible human reactions within F.'s poetry to this complex, synecdochistic nature that is human passion made manifest: conflict, the battle to keep it at bay, or defeat, sometimes envisioned as seduction but more often as subservience. Humans do not fare well against their own natures or against nature externalized as the jealously punitive Mother (Lover) Nature who may at any time effect a home burial to extinguish progeny and undermine homestead. Mother Nature, intrinsically combative even with herself, engenders change through brutal internecine battles: the trees devour pools and flowers in "Spring Pools," the snow smothers animals in "Desert Places," the ocean batters the shore in "Once By the Pacific." F.'s poetry arouses in the reader a taut expectancy, because it envisions a world where anything may be awakened into madness: in "The Black Cottage," there are angry bees in the walls, and in "A Star in a Stoneboat," there is a star embedded in the masonry, waiting to be awakened into revolution. Touch a stone, become a savage, leave a farmhouse, become a "hill wife" subsumed into wildness. As he says in "The Flood," the very power of blood is to release blood; it is not let loose by the devil but by its own deadly, "tidal wave" pressure.

F.'s extraordinary poetic magnetism emerges from this defensive posture that sees a world full of enemies because the world is an extension of himself, a creature of passion, one who is entirely acquainted with the night. Because the connection is so intimate, because he is exactly the synecdochist he claimed himself to be, his poetry is girded by chiaroscuro. F. superimposes black over white to lock meaning within rigorously controlled structure. The omnipresent walls, the bar-like trees, the black branches against a snow-white trunk, are all reiterated in F.'s stylistic and tonal control, in the "sentence sounds" that persuade the ear to hear order while the eye sees a vision of anarchy. F. uses the iambic pentameter as a rope on which to hang intricately precise sounds: an extra syllable in lines of "Home Burial" to indicate hesitation or indecision, two extra syllables in "After Apple Picking" to jut the two-pronged ladder up through the middle of the line. He augments these variations with careful caesurae, placed like the splitting wedge in a piece of firewood, to break sound into units, with alliteration, and with rhymes chosen to clip lines into the closure of perfect masculine rhymes or to soften them into the flow of feminine or slant rhymes. He rings changes on iambic meter but always with its insistent, rising beat as his reference point. He employs all the tools of prosody

to place a net around the anarchic nature that is his theme and his preoccupation.

Because of his self-conscious and unrelenting structural control, F.'s speakers often seem tonally at odds with their stated perceptions. The distinctive Frostian voice that emerges from his aural manipulation of language is reproduced typographically so that a F. poem on the page looks as though it is working within established boundaries and against established obstacles, conforming to his famous metaphor of the tennis court, where only free verse would try to play without a net. In the carefully modulated line lengths, the punctuation, the stanzaic order or, equally noticeable within context, the dreamy, nonstanzaic form of a poem like "After Apple Picking," are the unmistakable edges of a personality that refuses to be trifled with. This assumed invulnerability marks all of F.'s poetry, giving the most lyrical and the most consciously rhetorical poems the same insistent echoes. Thus, "Desert Places," which claims a vast inner bleakness, to some extent refutes itself in its last lines, whose rhymes—"spaces" / "race is" / "places"—reflect the assumed flippancy of one who refuses to be made afraid either by the outer world or even by the blank inner one he details. Frequently, claimed turmoil is counter-balanced by a structural precision so confident that it emerges in puns and word play, devices that often make for a disturbing tonal discrepancy.

One is not left believing that these speakers really *feel* themselves to be empty or bereft or in despair, but the paradox of F.'s voice is that one becomes convinced that they *are* deeply disturbed by their placement in a frightening world. Whether they call the feeling emptiness or fullness, lack of desire or too much desire, hate of love, ice or fire, it all comes around to the same intuition they are about to be violated by nature that encroaches no matter what the efforts to civilize or cultivate it. An unabashedly arrogant poem like "New Hampshire," which takes as its subject the establishment and maintenance of sufficient boundaries, shares the same fearfulness that emerges, half-said, in poems like "Desert Places" or "Bereft" or "Spring Pools": in "New Hampshire," just as elsewhere, the forests are Birnam Woods on the march and ready to encroach on the illusions of civility.

F.'s poetry is as simple as a snowfield, as simple as whiteness. Perhaps for this reason, critical responses have always been widely various. The issue of control is central to any assessment of F.'s poetry, because the importance of control to F. himself is so clearly implied in the very form and sound of the poems. It has been argued that while the poems are embodiments of "landscapes of self," F. always returns to an affirmation of a world outside of the self. Yet finally to see F.'s poetry as spiritually therapeutic for him is to imply an ontology that recognizes and accepts not only the limitations of self but one that produces a concurrent cessation of anxiety: to know where one is powerless is to know that one is absolved of guilt about the naked, raging, love-sick madman that is the world. But F.'s poetry does not, finally, reassure but has, instead, the power to awaken unease and wonder—to take its participant/readers through delight and wisdom. What F. claims consciously to see of the world's body is seldom very close to what he knows from intimate experience is there; the snow storms that throughout his poetry come to blanket empty fields with whiteness are indeed only the very hem of the goddess. F.'s poetry is, finally, a synecdochist's illusion, and the part that it shows is only minutia compared to what it suggests of the whole.

BIBLIOGRAPHY: Brower, R., *The Poetry of R. F.: Constellations of Intention* (1963); Cook, R., ed., *R. F.: A Living Voice* (1974); Cox, H., and E. C. Lathem, eds., *Selected Prose of R. F.* (1966); Gerber, P., ed., *Critical Essays on R. F.* (1982); Lathem, E. C., ed., *The Poetry of R. F.* (1979); Lathem, E. C., and L. Thompson, *R. F.: Poetry and Prose* (1972); Lathem, E. C., ed., *Interviews with R. F.* (1966); Lentricchia, F., *R. F.: Modern Poetics and the Landscapes of Self* (1975); Lynen, J., *The Pastoral Art of R. F.* (1960); Poirier, R., *R. F.: The Work of Knowing* (1977); Untermeyer, L., ed., *The Letters of R. F. to Louis Untermeyer* (1963)

KATHERINE KEARNS

FUCHS, Daniel

b. 25 June 1909, New York City; d. 26 July 1993, Los Angeles, California

As a young man growing up in Manhattan's Lower East Side, F. had two great passions: novels and movies. Both of these interests he would later make into a career, excelling at both but never achieving the status of a major writer. Although considered important within the American Jewish literary tradition, F.'s work is not widely read and rarely critically recognized. Nevertheless, his writings are a serious contribution to 20th-c. American literature, especially within the genre of the urban novel.

F. is generally known for his Williamsburg trilogy, a series of novels set in the multiethnic Williamsburg neighborhood of the Lower East Side. In all of these works, F. portrays the struggles of immigrant and second-generation Jews within the slum environment. *Summer in Williamsburg* (1934), primarily naturalist in tone, is the story of a young writer's attempt to find meaning in his squalid and claustrophobic neighborhood. The life depicted here is raw and stripped of any nostalgic sentiment, filled with corruption, low-lifes, and pained individuals. Although there is a good deal of social criticism in the novel, as there is in the others of the trilogy, this is not a radical work. F. was not a proletarian novelist, unlike many of the writers of his time. Instead, expressing an overt political agenda, he used the novel as a laboratory of human and social exploration, much as his young protagonist does in *Summer in Williamsburg.*

His next two books continue this exploration. *Homage to Blenholt* (1936) is a more comic novel that examines the contradiction between youthful dreams and stark reality. Yet by the end of the narrative, comedy has given way to frustration and feelings of existential entrapment. The darkening tone continues in *Low Company* (1937), considered by critics to be F.'s masterpiece, where empty lives and barren moral landscapes are the norm. As in much late-19th-c. Jewish-Yiddish literature, a central theme in F.'s novel is estrangement brought on by spiritual isolation and the pressures of assimilation. Throughout the Williamsburg trilogy, later collected as *Three Novels by D. F.* (1961), there is the sense that individuals are doomed to failure, and they are powerless to do anything about it.

His fourth novel, *West of the Rockies* (1971), is set in Hollywood, a land where F. spent much of his creative energies. Unhappy with poor book sales and insubstantial reviews, he accepted a screenwriting contract at RKO pictures. Some of his most notable screenplays include *Hollow Triumph* (1948), *Criss Cross* (1949), *Panic in the Streets* (1950), and *Love Me or Leave Me* (1955), for which he received an Academy Award for best original story. His screenplays in many ways reflect the troubles and frustrations born out in his early novels. Similarly, *West of the Rockies* takes the empty and disintegrating world of *Low Company* and transplants it into the dreamlike land of Hollywood.

F.'s last published work was *The Apathetic Bookie Joint* (1979), a collection of short fiction, Chekovian in technique, which includes the previously unpublished Hollywood novella "Triplicate." Like his earlier fiction, "Triplicate" portrays a sense of isolation and misfortune, but unlike the tone in such works as *Summer in Williamsburg* and *Homage to Blenholt,* here F. demonstrates a sense of acceptance for the life around him, regardless of its tragedies. Whether it be in the Jewish slums of the East or the movie fantasy lands in the West, F.'s focus on the ethnic experience is one of the most honest and penetrating of all the early-20th-c. Jewish American writers.

BIBLIOGRAPHY: Buchen, I. H., "D. F.'s *The Williamsburg Trilogy:* The Fantasy of Meaning," *MELUS* 13 (Spring-Summer 1988): 5–12; Howe, I., "D. F's Williamsburg Trilogy: A Cigarette and a Window," in Madden, D., ed., *Proletarian Writers of the Thirties* (1988): 90–105; Michelson, P., "Communal Values in the Fiction of D. F.," *SAJL* 5 (1988): 69–79; Miller, G., *D. F.* (1979)

DEREK PARKER ROYAL

FUGITIVES/AGRARIANS, The

Some scholars date the start of the so-called Southern Renaissance with the founding, in 1922, of a little magazine of verse entitled the *Fugitive.* Originally conceived as the organ of a group of Nashville townspeople and Vanderbilt academics who had been meeting regularly to discuss poetry and philosophy, it soon became an important vehicle for the "new" poetry that was beginning to assert itself following World War I. By the time it ceased publication in 1925, the *Fugitive* had attracted contributions from outsiders such as Hart CRANE, Witter BYNNER, Robert Graves, and Laura RIDING and had earned high marks from reviewers of the calibre of Mark VAN DOREN. Four members of the original "Fugitive Group" were to make important contributions to the shaping of subsequent literary history: John Crowe RANSOM, Donald DAVIDSON, Allen TATE, and Robert Penn WARREN. As poets, literary critics, and social commentators, these men—whatever their differences in temperament and individual points of doctrine—shared a common distrust of scientism and the gospel of technological progress. Their prophetic critique of America's materialism and its impact upon the imaginative life of the nation, once dismissed in some quarters as a kind of cultural Luddism, now receives a more sympathetic treatment at the hands of many intellectual historians. Ransom, Tate, and Warren also became influential pioneers in the development of what came to be called the New Criticism, an approach that would revolutionize the reading and teaching of literature in America.

Natives of Tennessee or Kentucky, the four principal Fugitives were unmistakable products of the border South, though matters of regional identity were only incidental to their early work on the magazine. By the time the decade of the 1920s had drawn to a close, however, the question of "Southerness" had become paramount. Stung by outsiders' attacks upon their re-

gion for its alleged backwardness and provinciality, Ransom, Tate, and Davidson launched a counterattack with the publication of *I'll Take My Stand* (1930), a loosely knit collection of position papers (by "Twelve Southerners") in which the dominant "American" culture was subjected to scathing analysis and the virtues of the South's agrarian and traditionalist society were held up as a bulwark against the alienation resulting from modern man's estrangement from the natural order. Warren contributed what proved to be a controversial essay on the race question, and other contributors included the poet John Gould FLETCHER, the novelist and playwright Stark Young, and Andrew Lytle, novelist and man of letters who, along with Davidson, would keep the Agrarian faith long after Ransom, Tate, and Warren had, to varying degrees, moved beyond it.

The cumulative thrust of *I'll Take My Stand* is unabashedly reactionary and "un-Reconstructed." The South retains a sense of the past and a nurturing tradition, so the argument runs, that stand in sharp contrast to the collective amnesia of the heavily industrialized and urbanized North. Science and technology have conspired to break the bonds that traditionally linked man with his environment. As Ransom puts it in his introductory "Statement of Principles," nature "industrialized, transformed into cities and artificial habitations, manufactured into commodities, is no longer nature but a highly simplified picture of nature. We receive the illusion of having power over nature, and lose the sense of nature as something mysterious and contingent." The individual citizen languishes under an "evil dispensation" in which he "has lost his sense of vocation" and is caught up in a mindless and ever-accelerating process of production and consumption. The much-praised notion of Progress stands convicted of deadening the human spirit and substituting nebulous abstractions in place of concrete and particularized realities. The self is lost in collectivities.

In contrast, the supposed shortcomings of Southern life were more often than not blessings that offered a more humane order than a technocratic state could provide. The South, in Andrew Lytle's view, quite rightly preferred "religion to science, handcrafts to technology, the inertia of the fields to the acceleration of industry, and leisure to nervous prostration" and should therefore "dread industrialism like a pizen snake"—the boosterism of Southern Chambers of Commerce notwithstanding. Davidson put the matter quite succinctly when he wrote that what the South represented was "the possibility of an integrated life." It may be overstating the case to suggest that the Agrarians saw the South more as metaphor than sociohistorical reality and were never pragmatically oriented. They were indeed seeking to establish a psychic homeland where the fractured modern soul might find wholeness, but they also understood the power of image to inform and reshape the social fabric in a real way. Years later, Warren would say that he had believed that the activities of the Agrarians were aimed at discovering a "rational basis" for democracy.

The economic and political chaos that emerged in the early years of the Great Depression served to confirm the Agrarians in the essential rightness of their cause, and they pursued the battle on a number of fronts. Ransom debated the future of the region, publicly and in print, with "progressive" spokesmen who advocated a "new" South more open to industrial diversification, and he defended the religious sensibility against the claims of scientistic reductionism in *God without Thunder* (1930). The rightist *American Review,* edited by Seward Collins, proved a receptive outlet for Agrarian views in the mid-1930s, and Tate worked with Herbert Agar to bring out *Who Owns America?* in 1936. This volume, sometimes regarded as a sequel to *I'll Take My Stand,* is much more than that. In its pages, Southern chauvinism is less important than the framing of a more broadly based critique of monopolistic capitalism on the one hand and socialism on the other. In this symposium, Tate, Ransom, Davidson, and Warren were joined by contributors from a diverse range of backgrounds, including the British distributist Hilaire Belloc. *Who Owns America?* demonstrated the Agrarians' urge to translate ideas into action (however vaguely envisioned).

Nonetheless, Ransom, Tate, and Warren steadily turned from a commitment to politics to a preoccupation with poetics as the 1930s grew to a close. As has been suggested, this movement away from the public arena into the Republic of Letters should not be regarded as a retreat from the traditionalist values set forth in *I'll Take My Stand* so much as a redirecting of interests and energies into an area where the principals had always been more at home and where tangible victories seemed more accessible. The New Deal and developing tensions in Europe took much of the wind out of Agrarian sails, but the efforts of Ransom, Tate, and Warren to counter reductionism with right reason and to bolster an integrated sense of selfhood in the face of self-eroding "modern heresies" remained undiminished. Their subsequent careers might lead these writers along diverging ideological paths, but the basic assumptions about the nature of man, the function of literature, and the desire for a more humane social order that had brought them together in the beginning remained relatively constant. Today, *I'll Take My Stand* and *Who Owns America?* continue to function as a compelling minority report on the status of the American dream.

BIBLIOGRAPHY: Cowan, L., *The Fugitive Group* (1959); Fain, J. T., and T. D. Young, eds., *Literary Correspondence;* Havard, W. C., and W. Sullivan, eds., *A Band of Prophets* (1982); Karanikas, A., *Tillers of a Myth* (1966); Purdy, R. R., *The Fugitives' Reunion* (1959); Rubin, L. D., *The Wary Fugitives* (1978); Stewart, J. L., *The Burden of Time* (1965); Young, T. D., and G. Core, eds., *Selected Letters* (1985); Young, T. D., and E. Sarcone, eds., *Tate-Lytle Letters* (1987)

WILLIAM BEDFORD CLARK

FULLER, Charles [H., Jr.]
b. 5 March 1939, Philadelphia, Pennsylvania

While Ralph ELLISON's *Invisible Man* and Herman MELVILLE's *Billy Budd* have inspired F. as a writer, jazz—specifically, Thelonius Monk and Miles Davis playing "Round Midnight"—has influenced F.'s theatrical aesthetic. In jazz, each instrument tells its own story, and at times all the instruments express their stories together. Initially, the result may sound like a cacophony of chaotic voices, but as the piece progresses, the voices cohesively blend together. F. noted that, unlike theater with its reliance upon blackouts and scene changes, jazz allows these different stories to be told without relying on transitions. In his major plays, F. attempts to translate the fluidity of jazz's instrumental voices and its unifying conclusion to the theatrical voices of his characters and their stories.

In 1976, F. garnered national recognition for *The Brownsville Raid,* based upon Theodore ROOSEVELT's dishonorable discharge of a black regiment for failing to reveal who started a riot in Brownsville, Texas. Through a docudrama technique of interviews and flashbacks, F. achieved a breakthrough in his theatrical vision as he melded voices from the past and present together. An equally important component is F.'s attention to the complexity of race. Rather than relying on simplistic depictions of a racially infused incident, F. reexamines the past with a critical eye on the motives of both races, acknowledging the possibility of black complicity.

The 1980 production *Zooman and the Sign* (1982) won F. two Obie Awards. While the play has its flaws—which F. acknowledges—it still powerfully depicts the ripple effect a black on black murder has on the teenage criminal, the grieving family, and the apathetic community. F.'s talent at avoiding simplicity is illustrated in his characterization of the murderer Zooman. As expected, the audience sympathizes with the murdered girl's family, but unexpectedly, through the teen's monologues, F. humanizes what should be an evil character. The audience cannot simply dismiss Zooman; they must confront him and his violent rage.

F.'s best-known work is *A Soldier's Play* (1982), for which he won the Pulitzer Prize in drama. The film version entitled *A Soldier's Story* received three Oscar nominations, including Best Picture and Best Adapted Screenplay for F. His fluid aesthetic achieves its greatest success here as the characters and the action intertwine between the past and present. Throughout the play, black soldiers recount the incidents surrounding the murder of Sergeant Waters to the investigating black officer Captain Davenport. F. confronts the prejudices of 1944 as well as the present as the mystery format invites the audience to discover the murderer before Davenport does. This technique exposes the audience to their own prejudices as well as F.'s depiction of bigotry and racial self-hatred—Waters provokes the suicide of a black soldier whom he despises. And, in effect, the play asks: can blacks overcome white oppression if there is no unity among their own ranks?

However, Amiri BARAKA, author of *Dutchman,* found F.'s play racially counterproductive. He disdainfully dismissed *A Soldier's Play* and *Zooman and the Sign* because they discredited the African American struggle by emphasizing black on black crime. Baraka argued that F.'s task as a black writer should be to attack the white oppressors rather than depict inner racial disharmony. However, F.'s intention is not to reinforce stereotypes and limit the discussions only to "us versus them." Instead, as William Demastes notes in his response to Baraka, F. acknowledges the greater complexity of assessing blame and because of this distinction his plays have more theatrical, political, and artistic worth than the overtly didactic later works of Baraka.

Since *A Soldier's Play,* F. has continued his examination of the African American experience by examining the Civil War and postbellum period. While these plays have received mixed reviews, F. still continues to hone his theatrical aesthetic of fluidity while confronting the intricacies of race.

BIBLIOGRAPHY: Baraka, A., "The Descent of C. F. into Pulitzerland and the Need for African-American Institutions," *BALF* 27 (1983): 51–54; Carter, S. R., "The Detective as Solution: C. F.'s *A Soldier's Play,*" *Clues* 12 (1991): 33–42; Demastes, W. W., "C. F. and *A Soldier's Play:* Attacking Prejudice, Challenging Form," *SAD* 2 (1987): 43–56; Herriot. E., *American Voices: Five Contemporary Playwrights in Essays and Interviews* (1988)

WILLIAM C. BOLES

FULLER, Henry Blake

b. 9 January 1857, Chicago, Illinois; d. 28 July 1929, Chicago, Illinois

Although F. may not be remembered as a paragon of American literature at the beginning of the 20th c., his writing life, including his struggles with the literary marketplace, tells a story about what it meant to be a writer during his lifetime. From his travel sketches of Europe to his realist novels and anti–imperialist satires, his work mirrors dominant features of the period's literary and social history.

F.'s first two novels, *The Chevalier of Pensieri–Vani* (1890) and *The Chatelaine of La Trinité* (1892), are travel sketches inspired by his trips to Europe throughout 1879–80 and 1883-85, when he kept detailed journals about his experiences. These somewhat allegorical novels dramatize what many literary historians claim are the characteristic tensions of the period, between Europe and America, aristocracy and democracy, the country and the city, tradition and innovation, as well as between the literary genres of classicism, ROMANTICISM, and REALISM. In these early novels, F. turned to the craft of novel writing to dramatize these conflicts that he felt acutely.

These conflicts found a different literary articulation through a masterful use of realistic techniques in his next two novels, *The Cliff Dwellers* (1893) and *With the Procession* (1895), in which he turned his attention to the American city, and responded to the forces that drove its inhabitants to raise buildings, to amass fortunes, and to climb the social ladder, all by reducing life to a series of transactions. Set primarily in a fictional skyscraper called the Clifton, *The Cliff Dwellers* follows the fortunes of George Ogden, whose incessant ambition is undermined by his limited skills, Erastus M. Brainard, whose ruthless business practices have destroyed the rest of his life, and Cornelia McNabb, who rises from waitress to well-married socialite, only to lose her fortune.

In 1928, Theodore DREISER would call *With the Procession* "as sound and agreeable a piece of American realism as that decade, or any since, produced." F. was also encouraged and mentored by one of the leading proponents of realism, the author and editor William Dean HOWELLS. It follows the fortunes of the Marshall family as they struggle with the moral choices and social pressures of living in an increasingly massive, ruthless and socially rigid Chicago. Jane, the oldest daughter of David and Eliza, urges them to "catch up" by entering into fashionable society, conspicuously donating money to appropriate causes, delivering speeches, and building a new home in an exclusive neighborhoods. F. dramatizes these ideals, as well as their implications, by carefully detailing the daily choices and interactions of his characters, and the real prices that they are charged for their choices and ambitions.

F. examines these real prices even more closely in his two satires, *The New Flag* (1899), a pamphlet of poems that protested the brutality of American imperialist policies in the Philippines, and *Under the Skylights* (1901), a collection of three novellas that examines a Chicago changing through the process of "incorporation." There, artists, patrons, and business people alike are subsumed by the power and allure of corporate structures and paychecks. If this was the way of all art, then F. would write no more of it.

A collection of stories, some biographical sketches, and many book reviews would follow over the next eighteen years, and in 1919, F. self-published *Bertram Cope's Year*. Although his contemporaries and later critics would dismiss this novel about homosexuality, recent critical attention has turned to the work, and to the importance of F.'s homosexuality to an understanding of his career and his literary times. Kenneth Scambray's study, *A Varied Harvest* (1987), notes F.'s "profound isolation in his lifelong struggle to break the silence that heterosexual society had forced upon him both as a social being and as a writer."

BIBLIOGRAPHY: Bowron, B. R., *H. B. F. of Chicago* (1974); Howells, W. D., "The Chicago School of Fiction," *NAR* 176 (May 1903): 739–46; Pilkington, J., *H. B. F.* (1970); Scambray, K., *A Varied Harvest: The Life and Works of H. B. F.* (1987)

MONIQUE DUFOUR

FULLER, [Sarah] Margaret [Marchesa D'Ossoli]

b. 23 May 1810, Cambridge, Massachusetts; d. 19 July 1850, off Fire Island, New York

Founding editor with Ralph Waldo EMERSON of the transcendentalist quarterly, *The Dial* (1840), journalist, critic, and social philosopher F. remains the most controversial literary figure of the American Renaissance. As the product of a remarkable private education designed by her father (based upon classical and modern literatures, languages, philosophy, and history), F.'s first publication was a translation from the German of *Ekermann's Conversations with Goethe* (1839). Having taught at Boston's famed Temple School directed by Amos Bronson ALCOTT, F. became acquainted with the circle of intellectuals and reformers clustered about Emerson in the late 1830s, including Henry David THOREAU. Her reputation as a conver-

sationalist grew as she directed weekly women's discussion groups at the home of Elizabeth PEABODY, the most prominent reformist in women's education. While associated with that group known as "transcendentalists," F. remained skeptical towards any single formulation of transcendentalist philosophy as characteristic of her own. With the creation of a quarterly journal devoted to the writings of this circle, F. agreed to oversee its publication. *The Dial* also provided an important forum for her own essays and reviews on a range of subjects. As she noted in the journal's first issue as "The Editor to the Reader" (a text written by F. and revised by Emerson), TRANSCENDENTALISM was best defined as a "spirit of the time" that included political and social reform, "a new scope for literature and art" and "philosophical insight." F. also emphasized a kind of credo for the critical perspective the journal would take: "All criticism should be poetic; unpredictable; superseding, as every new thought does, all foregone thoughts, and making a new light on the whole world. Its brow is not wrinkled with circumspection, but serene, cheerful, adoring. It has all things to say, and no less than all the world for its final audience." F. and her colleagues proclaimed *The Dial* the "one cheerful rational voice amidst the din of mourners and polemics." F. served as editor for two years, relinquishing control to Emerson in the last two year's of the journal's history.

Of F.'s own contributions to the publication's four-year run, the most notable aside from her literary criticism was "The Great Lawsuit: Man Versus Men. Woman Versus Women" (1844). In her argument for a radical revisioning of women's position in society, the core of analysis is a comparison between the condition of contemporary women and the American slave: "As the friend of the negro assumes that one man cannot, by right, hold another in bondage, should the friend of woman assume that man cannot, by right, lay even well-meant restrictions on woman. If the negro be a soul, if the woman be a soul, apparelled in flesh, to one master only are they accountable. There is but one law for all souls, and, if there is to be an interpreter of it, he comes not as man, or son of man, but as Son of God." F. expanded the essay with scholarly, though often pedantic, illustration and published it in book-length form as *Woman in the Nineteenth Century* (1845), a less readable or coherent version of the treatise, but enormously controversial in this country and abroad. Reviled by many, including Nathaniel HAWTHORNE and Orestes Augustus BROWNSON, the work nonetheless secured her reputation as a powerful influence beyond New England. Apart from the work's reception by individual writers and reformers, *Woman in the Nineteenth Century* has been credited as a philosophical cornerstone of the women's rights movement and the Seneca Falls convention of 1848.

During this period, F. also published an eclectic volume of travel notes, poetry and miscellaneous reflections collected during a trip to the upper Midwest as *Summer on the Lakes* (1844). Although hardly a literary success, the book drew the admiration of Horace Greeley, who invited F. to become the literary critic of his *New York Tribune* that year. The book may have also provided the model for Thoreau's *Week on the Concord and Merrimack Rivers.*

F.'s work for the *Tribune* began in New York (leading to publication of selected reviews as *Papers on Literature and Art,* 1846), but shifted to Europe where she became a foreign correspondent in 1846. In addition to meeting the most prominent writers of the period (including the Brownings, Thomas Carlyle, and George Sand), F. made the acquaintance of Italian patriot, Guiseppe Mazzini, a connection that drew her into the politics and revolution for the unification of Italy. While continuing as war correspondent in Rome, F. met and married the Marchese Giovanni Ossoli; their son, "Angelino," was born in 1848. F. also served the revolutionary cause as director of a Roman hospital until the fall of the city to French forces in 1849. The Ossolis were then forced by politics and increasing poverty to flee to England, then to America where F. hoped to resume her writing. When she left Italy, she took with her a completed manuscript for a book-length history of the revolution, a work lost in the shipwreck off Long Island that claimed the lives of F., her husband, and son in the summer of 1850.

While her *Memoirs* were published in 1852, this volume as assembled by Emerson with William Ellery CHANNING and James Freeman Clarke, was heavily censored by its editors and the F. family, and as such offers a highly unreliable and inaccurate portrait of F. in her own words. Because no standardized edition of her complete works has been published, and her reputation as a writer, "transcendentalist" and feminist reformer has remained a controversy for historians and critics, the fullest estimation of F. in American intellectual history is yet to be written.

BIBLIOGRAPHY: Allen, M. V., *The Achievement of M. F.* (1980); Blanchard, P., *M. F.: From Transcendentalist to Revolution* (1978); Chevigny, B. G., *The Woman and the Myth: M. F.'s Life and Writings* (1976); Deiss, J. J., *The Roman Years of M. F.* (1969); Hudspetch, R. N., ed., *The Letters of M. F.* (1984); Miller, P., *M. F.: American Romantic* (1940)

E. SUZANNE OWENS

FURNESS, William Henry

b. 20 April 1802, Boston, Massachusetts; d. 30 January 1896, Philadelphia, Pennsylvania

His life and career dedicated to "the man of Nazareth and the man of Africa," F. was one of a noted generation of Unitarian ministers who, dissatisfied with the religious, political, and literary orthodoxy of the day, helped shape the transcendentalist movement of the 1830s and 1840s. Raised in the progressive atmosphere of Boston and educated at Harvard, striking important friendships with such future leaders of the transcendentalists as Ralph Waldo EMERSON and Frederic Henry Hedge, he served fifty years as pastor of Philadelphia's historic First Unitarian Church.

A skillful hymn-writer and a prolific composer of sermons—he claimed that modesty forced him to "stop counting" at 1,500—F. was a staunch abolitionist, often using his pulpit to voice his anti-slavery sentiments. While he also wrote verse—his poem "The John Brown Song" enjoyed wide circulation during the storm created by Brown's raid at Harpers Ferry—his major contribution to the cultural climate of the era centered on his cultivation and promotion of German literature. F. collaborated with Hedge in publishing *Prose Writers of Germany* (1848), one of the first books of its kind to make American readers familiar with the works of German authors, and later, on his own, published the very popular *Gems of German Verse* (1853). Among his many translations, he is best remembered for those of Gotthilf Heinrich Schubert, Ludwig Uhland, Daniel Schenkel, Heinrich Heine, and Friedrich Schiller.

Of all his accomplishments none proved more controversial than his pioneering scholarly work in biblical criticism, which embroiled him in what was known as the "miracles question." In *Remarks on the Four Gospels,* published in 1836 just as the transcendentalists' revolt from orthodoxy was beginning, F. rejected the premise that biblical miracles were an indisputable basis for religious faith. Shocking Calvinists and conservative Unitarians, despite his personal equanimity and the reasonableness of his argument, he contended that although the miracles occurred they were in reality natural events; religious faith did not require acceptance of supernatural events. Of note, two years later, in his Divinity School Address, Emerson would assume a more strident position by calling miracles "monsters." In a career that remained active for the rest of his long life, F.'s biblical studies continued with a series of books on the life of Jesus, including *Jesus and His Biographers* (1838), *A History of Jesus* (1850), *Thoughts on the Life and Character of Jesus of Nazareth* (1859), and *The Veil Partly Lifted and Jesus Becoming Visible* (1864).

BIBLIOGRAPHY: Eliot, S., *Heralds of a Liberal Faith* (1910), vol. 3: 133–38; Geffen, E., "W. H. F.: Philadelphia Antislavery Preacher," *PMHB* 90 (April 1958): 259–92; Hoffmann, R. J., "W. H. F.: The Transcendentalist Defense of the Gospels," *NEQ* 56 (June 1983): 238–60; Hurth, E., "That 'Grand Model of Humanity': W. H. F. and the Problem of the Historical Jesus," *SAR* (1995): 101–25; Pochmann, H., *German Culture in America* (1957)

LARRY A. CARLSON

GADDIS, William
b. 29 December 1922, New York City; d. 16 December 1998, East Hampton, New York

After years of being ignored by the great number of readers and critics, G. is gradually assuming the status of an American "original." The categorization is not entirely valid, for the narrative difficulties of his novels were anticipated by James Joyce and William FAULK-NER, and the battle of energy and passivity in his stories has antecedents in the frontier conflict so often replayed in American literature between individual spirit and the village establishment. More distinctive than these aspects of G.'s fiction is a frenetic pace established by a surrealistic swirl of events, sentences that their speakers abort in a sudden loss of interest, and abrupt, underdeveloped transpositions. If the whole effect is surprisingly fluid, it is more macabre for that reason.

The Recognitions (1955), G.'s first and most impressive novel, is an encyclopedic, thousand-page work in which the author creates a world of elaborately interlocked fictions and forgeries. Virtually every character is a counterfeiter of some kind. The central character, Wyatt Gwyon, if first a candidate for the priesthood, then an accomplished forger of Flemish old masters, finally a recluse who scrapes masterworks down to the canvas in an attempt to reach a tabula rasa beyond fictions and forgeries alike. There is no single, great recognition to be had by Gwyon's scraping through layered illusions, however, only multiple "recognitions" of a reality so refracted by fictions and forgeries that it is not otherwise perceptible. The fearsome possibility that reality is not otherwise even extant makes *The Recognitions* a metaphysical horror story as well as a comedic tour de force in an altogether engaging mix of genres.

JR (1975) substitutes for the visual forgeries of *The Recognitions* a world of verbal counterfeit. In the seriocomic rise of ambitious, eleven-year-old J. R. Vansant to eminence in the world of high finance, we are afforded a plethora of jargon, clichés, and barbarisms, stupefying in effect, parodic in the author's intent, but more than parodic inasmuch as G. attempts to reconstitute the rhythms and codes of a debased American idiom as a species of poetry. The parody is probably more successful than the poetry, but the deeper failure of *JR* is its rejection of the metaphysical questions that underlie *The Recognitions* in favor of a settled pessimism that fails to ground the whirligig energies of the novel in a credible point of view.

In *Carpenter's Gothic* (1985), a shorter and more accessible novel than its predecessors, G. tells the story of Paul Booth's attempt to build a financial empire with the aid of a mad evangelist, a conservative politician, and his wife's inheritance. As in *JR*, power and ideology refuse to be marshalled coherently in a world so incapable of fine ordering that it treasures the Carpenter's Gothic style, and G. makes clear through his architectural metaphor a theme that develops with increasing pessimism in his novels: that the authenticity, anonymity, and religious conviction of earlier ages have been supplanted by fakery, self-promotion, and cultivated ignorance. In 1994, G. published *A Frolic of His Own: A Novel.*

BIBLIOGRAPHY: Comnes, G., *The Ethics of Indeterminacy in the Novels of W. G.* (1994); Johnston, J., *Carnival of Repetition: G.'s The Recognitions and Postmodern Theory* (1989); Kuehl, J., and S. Moore, eds., *In Recognition of W. G.* (1984); Moore, S., *W. G.* (1989)

ROBERT F. KIERNAN

GAINES, Ernest J.
b. 15 February 1933, Oscar, Louisiana

G. has chosen the South, in which he grew up, as the setting for his novels and the short stories collected in *Bloodline* (1976). The rural community of New Roads, Louisiana, near the plantation on which he was born, is the town of Bayonne in his fiction, and readers can note similarities between William FAULKNER's Yoknapatawpha and this community to which G. returns in book after book. Even though characters do not reappear, ethnic conflict is a continuing theme in each one.

G. writes about a particular section of the South where such tensions involve not only blacks and whites, but also black Creoles and Cajuns. *Catherine Carmier* (1964) depicts the Creoles' destructive prejudice against other blacks, and both *Of Love and Dust* (1967) and *A Gathering of Old Men* (1983) focus, in part, on the antagonism between blacks and Cajuns.

In *The Autobiography of Miss Jane Pittman* (1971), which has received more critical attention than any of the other novels, the community searches for a leader who will bring them freedom. Miss Jane, who throughout a long life has seen rebellious blacks killed, finally realizes the necessity of political protest and agrees to become the figurehead in a nonviolent demonstration in Bayonne. The civil rights movement is also in the background of *In My Father's House* (1979), but it focuses on the rejection by black sons of their fathers' authority. *A Lesson before Dying* (1993), winner of the National Book Critics Circle Award in fiction for 1994, chronicles the journeys to manhood of a young convict sentenced to death for a murder he did not commit and the school teacher who visits him in jail during his final months of life.

G. writes in the realist tradition. He has acknowledged the importance of Chekhov, Turgenev, Mark TWAIN, and Ernest HEMINGWAY in particular in the development of his own style. Yet *The Autobiography of Miss Jane Pittman,* in the form of an oral history supposedly pieced together from interviews, reveals the significant influence that slave narratives and folk storytelling techniques from his own African American heritage have had on his craft of fiction. He was awarded a MacArthur Fellowship in 1993.

BIBLIOGRAPHY: Babb, V. M., *E. G.* (1991); Beavers, H., *Wrestling Angels into Song* (1995); Byerman, K., *Fingering the Jagged Grain: Tradition and Form in Recent Black Fiction* (1985); Estes, D., ed., *Critical Reflections on the Fiction of E. J. G.* (1994); Gayle, A., *The Way of the New World: The Black Novel in America* (1975); Hicks, J., *In the Singer's Temple* (1981); Lowe, J., ed., *Conversations with E. G.* (1995)

DAVID C. ESTES

GALE, Zona

b. 26 August 1874, Portage, Wisconsin; d. 27 December 1938, Chicago, Illinois

A prolific writer, G. is noted for her portrayal of the comforts and confinements of life in small American towns. Her inspiration was Portage, Wisconsin, where she lived most of her life, but her concerns extended well beyond the lively rendering of local color. After a brief career in journalism, she produced twenty-two volumes of novels and short stories, seven plays, four nonfiction works, and a book of poetry. In addition, she was active in the Women's Peace Party during World War I, helped write Wisconsin's Equal Rights Law of 1923, represented Wisconsin at the 1933 International Congress of Women, campaigned for Robert M. La Follette's Progressive Party, and served as regent of the University of Wisconsin. Despite her commitment to pacifism and FEMINISM, her fiction is remarkably free of polemic.

G. consistently wrote in the realist vein, although her early fiction slips into sentimentality and her later work into mysticism. The first phase of her popularity centered on a series of short stories and novels about the inhabitants of Friendship Village: *Friendship Village* (1908), *Friendship Village Love Stories* (1909), the novel *Mothers to Men* (1911), a novella *Christmas* (1912), the memoir *When I Was a Girl* (1913), *Neighborhood Stories* (1914), and the play *The Neighbors* (1914). *Friendship Village,* a 1920 collection of stories about lives touched by the wise and tactful Calliope Marsh, is a rich record of Midwestern idiom and is genuinely funny as often as it is sentimental.

Her finest novels, *Birth* (1918) and *Miss Lulu Bett* (1921), reflect the more somber realism of the middle phase of her career, just after World War I. A cool elegy, *Birth* is infused with a newly discovered sense of human waste and tragedy. Dramatized in 1925 as *Mr. Pitt,* it is the story of an awkward, inarticulate man whose love-starved honesty drives his wife away and humiliates his son. The novel effectively renders the self-forged values and banal yearnings of Marshall Pitt, and captures the peculiarity rootless and impoverished emotional life of a small-town family. What finally comes to "birth" in Pitt's son is true conscience, as opposed to compunction—a kind of conscience that guides him in every enterprise, not merely in distinguishing right from wrong. The picture of American values is bitter without cynicism, and the tenuous hope offered by the ending avoids sentimentality.

Miss Lulu Bett, about a repressed spinster functioning as a domestic in her married sister's home, has come to be G.'s most popular and readable novel. The portraits of the insufferable family members are drawn with delightful malice, but the plot is resolved with a convention of romantic magazine fiction. G. seemed unhappy with the conclusion and changed it without much improvement when she dramatized the novel. Nevertheless, the play *Miss Lulu Bett* won a Pulitzer Prize in 1921.

The theme of G.'s later work is the possibility of birth into a higher form of consciousness. Her articulation of this state can be turgid and obscure, but it expresses her impatience with the deterministic realism that her focus on small-town settings seemed to emphasize. G.'s earlier fiction contained hints of the mystical consciousness that the poetry of *The Secret Way* (1921) explores. In the 1920s, she began to experiment with various New Thought movements. The chief characteristic of the influence of religious cultism on her style is an increasing reliance on synesthesia as a means of rendering psychic sophistication. In *Faint Perfume* (1923), another novel about an unmarried woman forced to accept the crass charity of her relatives, the heroine Leda Perrin's values are so esoteric that her scruples are hard to fathom. *Preface to a Life* (1926) and *Borgia* (1929) increasingly submerge the reader in the opaque abstraction of the initiate's consciousness as it reacts to a world "violently dedicated to the concrete." During the same period, however, she produced a fine collection of short stories, *Bridal Pond* (1930).

G. deserves to be read along with better-known chroniclers of provincial Americans, such as Sinclair LEWIS, Sherwood ANDERSON, and Theodore DREISER.

BIBLIOGRAPHY: Derleth, A., *Still Small Voice: The Biography of Z. G.* (1940); Herron, I. H., *The Small Town in American Literature* (1939); Hoffman, F. J., *The Twenties: American Writing in the Postwar Decade* (1962); Simonson, H. P., *Z. G.,* (1962)

ROBIN BEATY

GALLAGHER, Tess

b. 12 July 1943, Port Angeles, Washington

In her exploration of how poetry functions both in her life and as a medium for the artist, G. posits that to speak of a writer's influences is "to trace the development of a psychic and spiritual history . . . as an invention of who you are becoming." G. draws from a past in Port Angeles, where she was reared in a working-class family with five siblings, a hard but loving father, and a mother, bending over the stove, "turned in hopeless anger." What best expresses G.'s poetry is her passion for the ordinary, the very real world that surrounds and speaks to the writer. As a child, she would sit in the car for hours with her mother while they waited for her father, drinking in the bars. From this position, G. would examine the life of the town, and it is this visual field—and the stories that emanate from it—that commands her language. G.'s literary influences began with her high school English teacher, Margaret Matthieu, who "had us read poetry in the

Atlantic Monthly," and most significantly include the poets Theodore ROETHKE, her college mentor, W. B. Yeats, Pablo Neruda, and Anna Akhmatova—as well as writers Raymond CARVER, her longtime companion, and Flannery O'CONNOR.

G. came into her right as a poet in the 1960s, at a time when women's voices became audible in the world of politics and literature. G.'s poetry accesses viscerally the feminine identity, for her references, rather than the larger social realm, stem from her own very real stirrings when at sixteen, as she states, "I stood somehow in the power of my womanhood . . . I am aware, looking back, that women even more than children often serve a long apprenticeship to physically and psychically inflicted threat and pain." Writing was the means by which "the heart began to take shelter . . . to build an understanding out of words," and to "give these dead and living lives a way to speak." Education was protection as well for it could release her from the social and economic boundaries of her parents' world.

When she met Roethke at the University of Washington, her interest in writing turned toward poetry. A year after leaving the university and marrying her first husband, Lawrence Gallagher, *Stepping Outside* (1974) was published; two years later would come *Instructions to the Double* (1976), her first full-length edition, and one of her most acclaimed works, in which the dimensions of identity and the ambivalence of family are produced and the deeper emotions that entwine themselves around language, as well as the temper of language itself, are searched. G. states, "The double . . . was a way of speaking into the self. I was acknowledging the specific challenge of being a woman in my time."

In *Under Stars* (1978), G. recalls her love for her ancestral homeland in the section entitled "The Ireland Poems," which visually and metaphorically characterize her connection to the landscape, its people, and their predicament. In the second section, "Start Again Somewhere," she moves toward an inmost privacy, revealing, through narrative, feelings that revolve around her relationship with her father and other men in her life. In "3 A.M. Kitchen: My Father Talking," she turns away from the embroiling of poetics into a straight-forward rendering of her father's experience, told in his language. G. comments that "Much of the quality of a life can be suggested quickly in a few gestures of the voice."

This narrative shift continues in her work and is seen to be, at least partly, owing to G.'s intimate relationship with Carver, with whom she lived and worked from 1979 until his death in 1988. This relationship, Carver's terminal illness, and the death of her father make their presence in her writing both in content and style. In *Willingly* (1984), she travels to distant regions, both metaphorically and spatially: themes of loss emerge in "Stepping Outside"; China and its images are rendered in "Eating Sparrows" and "Some Painful Butterflies Pass Through." Poems from *Under Stars, Instructions to the Double,* and *Willingly* are recontextualized in *Amplitude* (1987), which includes fifty pages of new poems.

G.'s desire to speak plainly through narrative takes on a larger dimension in *Amplitude,* imbued with wit and veracity. In this collection, G. explores morality as an intrinsic entity within the poem, endowing language as a place through which our interactions are probed. Quoting from Jean Cocteau from *Past Tense:* "It is likely I would not have devoted myself to poetry in this world / which remains insensitive to it, if poetry were not a morality," G. moves into her poem of the same name "If Poetry Were Not a Morality," beginning with the line "I'm the kind of woman who" and thus entering into dialogue with Anne SEXTON, who immortalized that sentiment in "Her Kind." The narrative story takes shape in "The Story of a Citizen," which begins with a discussion among people about politics, and then in the title poem "Amplitude" becomes a vignette, in which pieces of the past and the present unfold on a Christmas day with her family and "Ray's Mercedes" parked down the street.

G.'s family originated from Collenamore in the west of Ireland and in *The Lover of Horses* (1986), a collection of short stories, she traces her roots with her great grandfather and her then dying father, finding that at the core they are the same. In *Portable Kisses: Love Poems* (1992) and *Portable Kisses: Expanded* (1994), the theme of sensuality of the spirit is carried through images of the kiss, as she states, "kisses, especially as they are written down, seem to carry entire worlds." This exploration of the senses is beautifully expressed in *Moon Crossing Bridge* (1992), which begins with a dedication to Carver, in the words of Paul Celan: "The world is gone, I must carry you." For G., mourning the death of her loved one includes no pity, only an existential reckoning of love and loss, and images of rebirth through nature abound as the senses are alighted with repeated references to water, rain, cedar, jasmine, musk, eucalyptus, and birds. In "Corpse Cradle," "Reading the Waterfall," and "Trace, In Unison," G. caresses the loss that she has experienced and it takes on a physical presence in the world.

G. has written several introductory essays to Carver's work, including *A New Path to the Waterfall, No Heroics Please,* and *Short Cuts: The Screenplay.* G. and Carver collaborated on their own screenplay *Dostoyevsky* (1985). G. writes "In a poem I consecrate all that forgotten life through memory, cast like a light on my life and the lives of others." And in reading

G., we experience her world as a construct of language that imparts beauty, ambivalence, loss, and most poignantly, truth.

BIBLIOGRAPHY: Harris, P., "Poetry Chronicle: An Extravagant Three: New Poetry by Mitchell, Hoagland, and G.," *VQR* 69 (Fall 1993): 690–705; Woodruff, J., ed., *A Piece of Work: Five Writers Discuss Their Revisions* (1993)

LISA TOLHURST

GARCÍA, Cristina
b. 4 July 1958, Havana, Cuba

The critical and popular acclaim received by G.'s first novel *Dreaming in Cuban* (1992) established the author as one of the most gifted Cuban American fiction writers. With the Cuban exile problematic as backdrop, and memory and the construction of history as theme, the novel explores the recuperation of lost history by those marginalized by official historical discourse. In her second novel, *The Agüero Sisters* (1997), G. continues to elaborate her vision of history as invention and of cultural identity that transcends national borders.

G. immigrated with her family to New York in 1960. She received her M.A. in international relations from Johns Hopkins and worked as a journalist until 1990, when she began writing fiction full-time. *Dreaming in Cuban* is noteworthy for its portrayal of Cuban cultural history as a continuum that comprises both pre- and post-Revolution eras and that includes Cubans both on the island and in exile. The novel focuses on three generations of Cuban women: Celia, the grandmother who remains in Cuba after the Revolution; her daughter Lourdes, who lives in New York and dedicates herself to pursuing the American Dream with her Yankee Doodle Bakery; and the granddaughter Pilar, a New York punk artist who seeks to mend the broken connection with her ancestral tradition. This family chronicle foregrounds the ethnic preoccupation with memory, as well as the way traditional history excludes women's stories. The novel thus questions how history is written—how particular events become historically significant—a theme that is encapsulated in Pilar's telling observation, "Who chooses what we should know or what's important?" By problematizing history in this way, the novel calls attention to silenced voices and to the racial diversity of Cuban society. The intense involvement of Celia's other daughter Felicia in *santería,* for example, and episodes involving ceremonial practices in *The Agüero Sisters,* highlight the powerful influence of Afro-Cuban beliefs and practices on Cuban culture.

Like *Dreaming in Cuban, The Agüero Sisters* is a multigenerational novel that spans several decades before and after the Cuban Revolution. The work revolves around passionate pursuits—science, politics—that play themselves out in Cuban and Cuban American history. The text is circular, opening and closing with a diary entry in which Ignacio, the father of the character Constancia Agüero, narrates the ostensibly accidental death of Constancia's mother Blanca. Through an intricate series of tales of love, insanity, and rivalry involving members of the extended family, the novel weaves together an array of disperse cultural threads that meet in Cuba.

Several stylistic features enrich G.'s storytelling in both *Dreaming in Cuban* and *The Agüero Sisters.* Both novels are hybrid texts in which "non-literary" genres, such as letters and diary entries, that supply key information are woven into the central narrative. G.'s use of nonlinear narrative and effective touches of "magical realism," furthermore, subvert conventional notions of history and emphasize the many potential facets of historical "truth." The poetic, evocative prose of these works likewise underscores the multilayered nature of observed reality. With a high level of craftsmanship, G.'s two novels raise important issues about Cuban and Cuban American cultural history.

BIBLIOGRAPHY: Alvarez-Borland, I., "Displacements and Autobiography in Cuban-American Fiction," *WLT* 68 (Winter 1994): 43–48; Lopez, I., "' . . . And There Is Only My Imagination Where Our History Should Be': An Interview with C. G.," *MQR* 33 (Summer 1994): 605–17

KAREN CHRISTIAN

GARDNER, Erle Stanley

b. 17 July 1889, Malden, Massachusetts; d. 11 March 1970, Temecula, California

Creator of Perry Mason, the most famous fictional trial lawyer of the 20th c., G. began his writing career in the early 1920s purely as a means of adding to the family income. Practicing law in Ventura, California, by day and writing by night, G. methodically became a prodigious writer. His first successes were in the pulp fiction market in popular magazines such as *Black Mask*. The first Perry Mason novel, *The Case of the Velvet Claws,* appeared in 1933 and received limited critical notice. However, in the years that followed, Mason, who shared his creator's ability to bend legalities for the sake of justice, earned G. a substantial fortune from book sale and the subsidiary rights from paperback reprints, book clubs, magazine serialization, movies, radio, television, and a comic strip. In addition to the eighty-two Mason novels, which in all have sold more than three hundred million copies, G.'s output also includes twenty-four mysteries featuring Bertha Cool and Donald Lam, written under the pseudonym of A. A. Fair; nine mysteries featuring the district attorney Doug Selby; seven non-series mysteries; four collections of novelettes and short stories; thirteen nonfiction accounts of exploring Baja California, the American desert, and the Sacramento Delta; two nonfiction books concerning crime; and countless short stories in pulp magazines and other journals. With the use of a dictaphone and a secretarial staff, G. could produce a novel in three and a half days.

The Perry Mason novels that began appearing in the 1930s were stylistically an outgrowth of techniques G. followed and polished from his pulp fiction days. Some readers see G.'s place in mystery fiction as one representing the first American hybrid combination of the so-called Golden Age of Detection (as represented by British authors Agatha Christie and Dorothy L. Sayers) and the tougher, newer school of the hardboiled detective fictions (as represented by Dashiell HAMMETT); it is more likely, however, that the Perry Mason novels were the result of techniques G. followed and polished during his self-taught pulp fiction days. While little of Hammett's pulp fiction from the early 1920s is available for comparison, G.'s work at this time draws more from the "pulp adventure" style of Carroll John Daly than from Hammett's style. In *Dead Men's Letters* (1926–29), the Phantom Crook story series written by G. for *Black Mask,* there is an emphasis on imaginative plots, detailed action, barbed dialogue, and a protagonist who works a thin line between law and crime. These elements, with the incorporation of the court scenes, are recognizable in the very successful formula of a Perry Mason book, a formula that retained much of the escapist adventurism of the pulp fiction style.

Although some readers believe the A. A. Fair series is creatively the best work G. has done, no one can doubt the incredible popularity of the Mason books. While the plots are sometimes less than ingenious and description and narration seem at times to border on cliche, the interaction between the characters, the use of dialogue, and the inevitable dramatic courtroom solutions provide the impetus and pleasure of the formula. Much of the interest lies in the expected: the breezy repartee of Mason, Della Street (his secretary) and Paul Drake, the investigating private eye; Della Street's devotion to Mason and the ambiguous nature of their relationship; Mason's ability to hoodwink both the crooks and the law; and the final defeat and exasperation of Lieutenant Tragg of the Los Angeles police and Hamilton Burger, the district attorney. Although Mason himself represents wealth and success, his main concern, as seen in many a canceled fee, is to help people who are involved in confusing and dangerous situations. This dedication to the plight of ordinary people in their struggles with both criminals and the law gives his character an heroic as well as a maverick cast.

The extremely popular *Perry Mason* television series first debuted on September 21, 1957, and ran until May 22, 1966. G. played the judge in the very last episode.

BIBLIOGRAPHY: Bounds, J. D., *Perry Mason: The Authorship and Reproduction of a Popular Hero* (1996); Breen, J., *Novel Verdicts* (1984); Hughes, D., *E. S. G.* (1978); Mundell, E. H., *E. S. G.: A Checklist* (1968)

LYNN RISSER

GARDNER, Isabella [Stewart]

b. 7 September 1915, Newton, Massachusetts; d. 7 July 1981, New York City

G. published four books of poetry between 1955 and 1980, two of which were nominated for the National Book Award and a third for the American Book Award. Respect for her craft, her "calculated ambiguities," and her intelligence has lasted, and in 1990 *The Collected Poems* was issued, containing the verse in all four volumes, the hitherto uncollected poems, and G.'s brief essay "The Fellowship with Essence" as an afterword.

The title of her first collection, *Birthdays from the Ocean* (1955), illustrates G.'s occasionally fanciful syntax, perhaps taking its cue from E. E. CUMMINGS. In the book's opening poem, her encounter with a great blue heron in the desert takes place "birthdays" (instead of years or miles away) from the ocean. Its epigraph from Martin Buber's *I and Thou* makes the poem suggestive also of a human encounter. Juxtaposition of nature and humans also appears elegiacally in the rich and taut poem "To Thoreau on Rereading Walden." And underlining her active relation to other writers of her time, "When a Warlock Dies, *for Dylan Thomas*" combines the Welsh poet's dense diction and alliterative music with her own stately music and characteristic *aabb* rhyme pattern.

G.'s second book, *The Looking Glass* (1961), contains one of her most admired poems, "The Widow's Yard." Critic Paul Carroll discusses this deft dramatic monologue at some length in *The Poem in Its Skin* (1968), comparing its ambiguities with those in FROST's "Mending Wall" and citing contrasting readings of it by Robert BLY and John LOGAN. In *The Looking Glass,* G. ventures into some rhyming techniques similar to those of Marianne MOORE. For instance, G.'s oft-noted *ars poetica,* "Writing Poetry,"

uses "the" as a rhyme word, a strategy reminiscent of Moore's rhyming use of articles in "The Fish." "The Widow's Yard" creates hyphenated syllable rhymes, "yard" being rhymed with "hard-/ly" and "patient" with "gent-/ler," as Moore also did in "The Fish." "Summers Ago," dedicated to Edith Sitwell and echoing some of Sitwell's verbal music, brings the two rhyming words into the beginning and end of the same line, as Moore had done in "A Carriage from Sweden."

Both *West of Childhood* (1965) and *That Was Then* (1980) are volumes of new and selected poems. The first contains only three new poems, including a haunting meditation on love, mortality, and fellow poets, "This Room Is Full of Clocks." Of the sixteen new poems in the 1980 collection, "Who Spilled the Salt?" is a villanelle with some deft rhymes; "The Music Room" is an elegantly morbid sestina; and "Are Poets Ball Players?" is a conversational response to Moore in a style similar to Moore's "Baseball and Writing." The title poem of this volume, "That Was Then," offers a lively nostalgic reminiscence of summers in Michigan with G.'s second husband's extended Jewish family, among whom she was fondly known as "the Shicksa" and for whose dinner she once baked an elaborate ham. *The Collected Poems* adds to these four volumes thirty mostly shorter uncollected or unpublished poems, among them "Two Sapphics," a "Triolet," and two *ballades* translated from François Villon.

Great-niece of the donor of Boston's Isabella Stewart Gardner Museum, a cousin of Robert LOWELL, and for a time the wife of poet Allen TATE, G. served as associate editor of *Poetry* from 1951 to 1956 during Karl SHAPIRO's editorship. She is remembered and honored primarily by those contemporary poets who value her traditional techniques and poetic diction. Critic Robert Huff has remarked that "many lines strike one as isolated emulations of Miss Gardner's favorite contemporaries," but one may also say that these echoes are evidence of her active participation in the poetic conversations of her day.

BIBLIOGRAPHY: Carroll, P., "A Note on I. G.," *Poetry* 101 (December 1962): 215–17; Carroll, P., *The Poem in Its Skin* (1968); Ehrenpreis, I., "Solitude and Isolation," *VQR* 42 (Spring 1966): 332–36; Huff, R., "The Lamb, The Clocks, The Blue Light," *Poetry* 109 (October 1966): 44–48

MARGARET HOLLEY

GARDNER, John [Champlin, Jr.]

b. 21 July 1933, Batavia, New York; d. 14 September 1982, Susquehanna, Pennsylvania

A medieval scholar as well as a successful novelist, G. published more than thirty books, including nine complete novels, two collections of stories, five works of nonfiction, three children's books, two major translations, *The Complete Works of the Gawain-Poet* (1965) and *Gilgamesh* (1984, with John R. Maier), and an epic poem *Jason and Medeia* (1973). Though G.'s works are uncommonly diverse in form, style, setting, and character, they share recurrent themes, most prominently the value of human community and the efficacy of love and art.

In his controversial polemic *On Moral Fiction* (1978), G. expounds the theory that morality or truth is discovered in the process of creating and of reading a piece of fiction. Though sometimes misunderstood as a defense of conservative religious, political, or literary stances, G.'s book received attention for its attacks, not particularly convincing, on the "immoral" literary practices of such fellow novelists as John BARTH, John UPDIKE, and Joyce Carol OATES. The primary value of *On Moral Fiction* ultimately resides in the insights it provides into the questing protagonists of G.'s own novels.

In its treatment of social disruption and intimate confrontations with the fact of mortality, G.'s first novel, *The Resurrection* (1966), foreshadows much of his later work. Though its characterizations are generally flat and its ideas not fully realized, G.'s account of Professor James Chandler's passage from despair to an acceptance of the connectedness of things establishes a precedent for the journeys of his other protagonists. Ultimately realizing the power of compassion and forgiveness, G.'s heroes forge opportunities for renewal—of the community if not for the individual self.

One of G.'s most eccentric works may also be his most enduring—*Grendel* (1971), a retelling of the Old English epic *Beowulf* from the monster's point of view. Much critical attention has been directed toward the novel's metafictional techniques and intricate structural devices, based on the twelve signs of the zodiac and the twelve Aristotelian virtues. Finally, however, what might have been little more than a clever literary exercise is in fact an eloquent meditation on fate that convincingly re-creates the ethos of its source.

The Sunlight Dialogues (1972), considered by many to be G.'s finest work, deploys the conventions of detective fiction and the strategies of the 19th-c. novel to fuse the stories of one man's obsessions and another's fears. The four dialogues of the title—exchanges between Taggert Hodge (the Sunlight Man) and Batavia Police Chief Fred Clumly—focus on the values of ancient Babylon as a potential antidote to the collapse of Western civilization. But the philosophical underpinnings of the novel are embodied in the conflicts of fully realized characters, culminating in a communal epiphany at a Dairy League meeting. *October Light* (1976), accorded the National Book Critics

Circle Award, also moves toward an epiphanic moment by way of multiple stories and multiple points of view. The two central characters, miserly old James L. Page and his equally stubborn older sister, Sally Page Abbott, derive solace from fictions: Page from the legends of Ethan Allen, and Abbot from the "trashy" paperback novel recounted within G.'s novel entitled *The Smugglers of Lost Souls' Rock*.

Critical response to G.'s other novels has been mixed. Perhaps too self-consciously experimental, *The Wreckage of Agathon* (1970) is the first of G.'s "fabulistic" novels, preparing the way for *Grendel* and *The Sunlight Dialogues* in its reliance on ancient history. Originally conceived as a collection of short stories, *Nickel Mountain* (1973) contains some powerful depictions of human loneliness, though for the most part the characters are two-dimensional. *Freddy's Book* (1980) attempts to marry two novellas, one set in 20th-c. Madison, Wisconsin, and the other in 16th-c. Sweden. *Mickelsson's Ghosts* (1982) is the most ambitious of G.'s "lesser" works, a lengthy psychological novel that revisits the central themes and character types of *The Resurrection*. Following G.'s death, his literary executor, Nicholas Delbanco, arranged for the joint publication in 1986 of two never completed works, *Stillness,* a raw, starkly autobiographical story about the complexities of marriage, and *Shadows,* the opening 250 pages of a novel about an alcoholic and amnesiac detective.

A teacher of creative writing at the State University of New York at Binghampton, G. also composed two books on writing technique, *On Becoming a Novelist* (1983) and *The Art of Fiction* (1984). The first book contains detailed accounts of his own creative methods and processes, while the second is a polemical textbook that moves from general theories of fiction to pragmatic advice for young writers.

BIBLIOGRAPHY: Butts, L., *The Novels of J. G.* (1988); Cowart, D., *Arches and Light* (1983); Henderson, J., *J. G.* (1990); McWilliams, D., *J. G.* (1990)

RICHARD NORDQUIST

GARLAND, Hamlin

b. 14 September 1860, New Salem, Wisconsin; d. 5 March 1940, West Salem, Wisconsin

Though he was very successful and prolific as a writer during his long life, G.'s place in American literature seems in decline. In general, the Midwestern autobiographical reminiscences and fiction of G.'s early (1891–95) and late (1917–34) phases are considered his best work; the Far West romantic novels of his middle years (1891–95) are his worst.

From the experiences of his youth on America's rural "Middle Border" in the years following the Civil War and his extensive reading of Charles Darwin, Herbert Spencer, Henry George, and John Fiske, as well as contemporaneous American fiction during his three-year stay in Boston (1884–87), G. found the material for his critical theories, published in *Crumbling Idols* (1894), and fiction. His first autobiographical articles—later published in part in *Boy Life on the Prairie* (1899)—and short stories dealt with farm life. While some of these pieces relied upon the conventions of sentimental local color writing, as did his stories in *Prairie Folks* (1893), G. was eager to expose the truth about rural life. In his own brand of agrarian realism, called "veritism," G. wished to deflate the widely held romantic notions about life on the farm and to shift the focus away from the "smiling aspects of life" embraced by the realists. Instead, he claimed, he wanted to reveal "the ugliness, the endless drudgery, and the loneliness of the farmer's lot"; he also wanted to promote social change. To achieve that end, he published his most successful work of aesthetic populism, a collection of stories entitled *Main-Travelled Roads* (1891), which contained his most anthologized story, "Under the Lion's Paw."

One of the prominent themes in G.'s fiction dealing with the rural Midwest is the plight of the women who faced the tedium and isolation of life there. His finest rendition of this concern is *Rose of Dutcher's Cooly* (1895), G.'s best novel. However, rather than having a female character physically and emotionally beaten down by her harsh environment, as so often happens to the mature women in *Main-Travelled Roads,* Rose Dutcher is able to overcome the narrowness of being reared by her widower father on a Wisconsin farm and is able to achieve intellectual fulfillment by first attending the state university in Madison and then by moving to Chicago to pursue her career as a writer. Rose could not be satisfied by the monotony of farm chores or by the thought of becoming the subservient wife of any man. She is a New Woman, resolute in her convictions and unswerving in her pursuit of her own conditions for happiness.

By the middle of the 1890s, G. turned westward for the subjects of his next fiction. Inspired by his expeditions to California, the Rocky Mountains, and Western Canada, G. decided that he wanted to depict "the mighty West, with its swarming millions," and he did this by again resorting to some of the devices of earlier Western local color writers such as Bret HARTE and Joaquin MILLER—accurate recording of regional dialects, presentation of character "types," vivid portraits of the magnificent natural scenery, and often a conventional love plot. While few of these works continue to be read, some are not without inter-

est. His earliest Far West novel, *The Eagle's Heart* (1900), is the best example of the ROMANTICISM of G.'s work of this period; *The Captain of the Gray-Horse Troop* (1902) sympathetically treats the plight of Native Americans in their dealings with unscrupulous white men; and *Hesper* (1903) tells the story of a miner's strike in Colorado that, in form, is reminiscent of G.'s early economic fiction.

Despite critical acclaim by the influential William Dean HOWELLS for these Far West books, their popularity with the public waned. G. then turned his creative vision eastward, back to his Midwestern roots, and his two finest autobiographical books emerged: *A Son of the Middle Border* (1917) was a narrative of G.'s early farm life and sojourn East from 1865 to 1893; *A Daughter of the Middle Border* (1921) chronicled his literary maturation and marriage from 1894 to 1914. In addition to providing the facts (though occasionally erroneous and nostalgically presented) of G.'s peripatetic and often unsatisfying life, these works chart the intellectual and emotional development of one of America's most significant minor men of letters.

BIBLIOGRAPHY: Gish, R., *H. G.: The Far West* (1976); Holloway, J., *H. G.: A Biography* (1960); McCullough, J. B., *H. G.* (1978); Nagel, J, ed., *Critical Essays on H. G.* (1982); Pizer, D., *H. G.'s Early Work and Career* (1960); Silet, C. L. P., *Henry Blake Fuller and H. G.: A Reference Guide* (1977); Silet, C. L. P., et al., eds., *The Critical Reception of H. G., 1891–1978* (1985)

ROBERT C. LEITZ, III

GARRETT, George [Palmer, Jr.]
b. 11 June 1929, Orlando, Florida

The manifold achievement of G. as a writer of novels, short stories, poetry, literary criticism and more informal essays has constituted almost an affront to the American literary establishment which much prefers writers to fit into quick and easy categories and stay there. One can point to Robert Penn WARREN as one of the few writers who successfully played most of the games at the literary carnival, but in his time contemporary literature wasn't a classroom subject, which meant that there was no need for a consensus view about each writer's achievement or "relevance." G., as the Henry Hoyns Professor of English at the University of Virginia, is there as a teacher of fiction; his poetry, as far as the department is concerned, is a hobby, something he does the way a Milton scholar might grow roses or play golf.

In a simplistic way, their partial view can seem plausible because G. is best known as a novelist, and, more particularly, a writer of historical fiction. In this quirky and challenging genre, *Death of the Fox* (1971), *The Succession* (1983), and *Entered from the Sun* (1990), his Elizabethan and Jacobean trilogy, is all but unrivaled in our generation. One thinks perhaps of Thomas Flanagan's Irish series, consisting of *The Year of the French, The Tenants of Time,* and *The End of the Hunt,* but while those books are finely crafted and altogether serious, they have neither G.'s literary inventiveness nor his idiosyncratic theological fervor. A proper understanding of his fascination with Elizabeth and James must take into account the fact that he is a Christian, and specifically, a devout Episcopalian. For him, then, the religious contentiousness of that time and place resonate in a profoundly spiritual way.

His other fiction, particularly his military fiction, is also Christian. G. attended Sewanee Military Academy and actually liked it there. After a postgraduate year at the Hill School and an undergraduate career at Princeton (where he took his B.A. in 1952), he served in the U.S. Army (field artillery) and for two years was a master sergeant in Trieste and Austria, which provided him with material for *Which Ones Are the Enemy* (1961) and such stories as " The Old Army Game" and "What's the Purpose of the Bayonet?" about which Robert Bausch has perceptively written: "the narrator says the old Nth Field was 'the best outfit I was ever with in every way. You might not think so but I'll tell you why. We were insideout men. All our vices were apparent. Our virtues were disguised.' These are the people who become 'heroes' in G. G.'s work." That modesty and charity, that concern with the possibilities for redemption of fallen mankind is what one finds in all G.'s work from his wildest burlesques *The Magic Striptease* (1973) or *Poison Pen* (1986), to his accomplished poetry, his essays and stories, and, more recently, his essay-stories that explore the territory between fiction and nonfiction.

The writers he reads with interest because their strategies are congenial and perhaps useful are Frederick Buechner and Wright MORRIS. But G. is funnier than Buechner and his jokes are broader than those of Morris, which also mitigates against his success in the as a writer, where the tastemakers, less confident than they would have the rest of us believe, are uncomfortable about what is funny and suspicious that it can't be "serious."

BIBLIOGRAPHY: Dillard, R. H. W., *Understanding G. G.* (1988); Hawkins, S., ed., *Seven Princeton Poets* (1963); Ruffin, P., and S. Wright, eds. *To Come Up Grinning: A Tribute to G. G.* (1989); Wright, S., *G. G.: A Bibliography, 1947–1988* (1989)

DAVID R. SLAVITT

GARRISON, William Lloyd
b. 10 December 1805, Newburyport, Massachusetts; d. 24 May 1879, New York City

G. is best known for the unrelenting antislavery crusade he carried out in the pages of the *Liberator.* The paper's uncompromising language and extreme measures won G. widespread animosity in both the North and the South, but his pronouncements concerning the law "written by the finger of God upon the heart of man" also lured abolitionist supporters. G. therefore delighted in public odium, for it signified his success at "moral suasion" and agitation.

G. began his career when, after a poor and fatherless childhood, he was apprenticed to a printer at the Newburyport *Herald.* There, he taught himself skills needed for editing by composing anonymous essays. After his training, G. took a variety of editing jobs and began to demonstrate the militant tone and autonomous spirit that would mark his work with the *Liberator.*

In 1829, Benjamin Lundy invited G. to Baltimore to coedit *The Genius of Universal Emancipation,* the only antislavery paper at the time. He accepted but soon after rejected Lundy's beliefs in gradual emancipation and the colonization of freed slaves. And so, after having been jailed for libeling a slave ship owner, G. opted to return to Boston where he could produce a paper demanding immediate emancipation without facing legal ramifications. On January 1, 1831, he published the first issue of the *Liberator.* The paper never proved very popular and relied mainly upon freed blacks in the North for its membership, but its effects were tremendous because of G.'s persistence in sending copies to editors in the South. Reprinted in southern papers, the *Liberator*'s radical views provoked extreme reactions; northern readers, in turn, were incensed by the Southern editorials directed at G. In this skillful exploitation of the editorial exchange system, G. accelerated the divisiveness that would lead to the Civil War.

G. also discredited the American Colonization Society with his treatise *Thoughts on American Colonization* (1832) in which he questioned the morality and the feasibility of sending slaves back to Africa. Later that same year, he founded the New England Anti-Slavery Society, followed by the American Anti-Slavery Society in 1833. Dissension from within the national organization, however, sprung up around G.'s more extreme views, including his opinion that the Constitution was a pro-slavery document and his insistence that abolition be linked to other issues of reform, in particular that of women's rights. G.'s firm stance on such issues also contributed to the eventual breakdown of his relationship with famed black abolitionist Frederick DOUGLASS. G.'s rhetoric, following the manner of British abolitionists, was highly vitriolic and moralistic, alienating some readers with gross exaggeration, pointed biblical references, and warnings of impending doom. As an editor, however, G. allowed for a multiplicity of views in his paper, including proslavery opinions. Popular opinion would necessarily change, he believed, if readers could see how slavery fared under the light of free inquiry.

When Civil War finally erupted, G. disregarded his nonresistance policy and supported Abraham LINCOLN, seeing the war as the final retribution of a just God. Once peace was achieved, G.'s followers encouraged him to use the *Liberator* to fight for the rights of the freed slaves, but he felt its work was done. He did, however, continue to campaign for universal emancipation, working for the peace movement, woman's suffrage, the education of the former slaves, and the rights of Native Americans and Chinese immigrants.

There has been much debate about the centrality of G.'s role in the abolitionist movement as well as varied opinions on his uncompromising manner. Some critics have accused him of foolish utopianism while others have applauded him for providing the spark needed for major social change. All would agree that G. was highly successful at making himself heard. As his Russian contemporary Leo Tolstoy said of G., "If at the time he did not attain the pacific liberation of the slaves in America, he indicated the way of liberating men in general from the power of brute force."

BIBLIOGRAPHY: Cain, W. E., ed., *W. L. G. and the Fight Against Slavery: Selections from the Liberator* (1995); Fredrickson, G. M., *Great Lives Observed: W. L. G.* (1968); Rogers, W. B., *"We Are All Together Now": Frederick Douglass, W. L. G., and the Prophetic Tradition* (1995); Stewart, J. B., *W. L. G. and the Challenge of Emancipation* (1992)

RENEE SCHATTEMAN

GASS, William H[oward]

b. 30 July 1924, Fargo, North Dakota

The figure of G. is paradoxical, or anachronistic, according to the angle of perception. He is a preeminent man of letters in the U.S. and yet he is, to the large reading audience, virtually unknown. His stature and accomplishments suggest comparison with the exceptional literary men of the 18th c., wide-ranging and brilliant commentators on the social and political issues of the day who also turned to "fine writing"—men like Joseph Addison or Samuel Johnson, or later, Samuel Taylor Coleridge. G. was trained as a philosopher,

having earned a Ph.D. from Cornell University with a dissertation on "A Philosophical Investigation of Metaphor." The interest in language indicated by that topic has continued throughout his career and is in part responsible for the complexity and playfulness of his prose style. He has taught at the College of Wooster, Purdue University, and since 1969 continuously at Washington University in St. Louis, where he teaches both philosophy and English and is director of the International Writers Center.

G. has published four works of fiction and four collections of essays, as well as one essay published as a chapbook. It is arguable that he is better known for his essays, since before collection in book form, they have usually appeared in periodicals of some circulation at least among the general public and therefore reach a wider audience than his intricate novels and short stories. G.'s fascination with language and its possibilities as a representational medium is apparent from the titles of his collections, notably *The World within the Word* (1978), *Fiction and the Figures of Life* (1979), *Habitations of the Word* (1985), and *Finding a Form* (1996). He goes so far as to devote a whole essay to the word "And," and his book-length essay, *On Being Blue* (1976) is an extended meditation on every imaginable use and combination of the word, the color, the mood, and the obscenity evoked by the title, with reflections on the history of "blue" and the ways in which its meaning has changed or adapted to meet social or historical needs. His own prose style is intricate and allusive; his sentences sometimes seem to stretch out forever, adding appositives and subordinate clauses qualifying and clarifying even minor elements of the main clause as the sentence progresses toward it often comical conclusion. G. plays with language as only a writer who is deeply serious and thoughtful about its possibilities can do.

The writers who have influenced G.—Paul Valéry, Henry JAMES, and Gertrude STEIN, among others—have benefitted from his critical attention while offering clues as to the background of his own fictional practice. His first novel, *Omensetter's Luck* (1966), was published to lavish acclaim but was probably a disappointment to the common reader; the prose was rich and allusive, arguably self-indulgent in the eyes of those who did not appreciate it or found it too precious a vehicle for the story it conveyed. G. has a way of mixing the most arcane and sophisticated language with the crudest slang, even obscenity; in doing this, he creates a layered effect that is consistent with the mind of a highly educated and self-conscious artist. His fictions have a comparable layered effect, since the characters of his early fictions, at least, are rather ordinary, living in ordinary Midwestern places. The gap between the lives constructed and the language doing the construction has seemed problematic to some critics, even though they admire the power of the writing. G.'s novel, *The Tunnel* (1995), has found a less favorable reception. The writing is still brilliant, the subject matter challenging and intriguing, but the length and the cumulative unpleasantness of the novel have caused negative reactions. The narrator is a professor of history who has completed a study of Nazi Germany; instead of writing an introduction to that text, he begins, as he describes it, "to put this prison of my life in language." Even this early statement alerts the reader with its allusion to "the prison house of language," a phrase familiar in the jargon of structuralism; the novel will be a minefield of verbal jokes, tricks and inversions; the narrator seems obsessed, like Jean-Jacques Rousseau, not only with revealing himself in every detail but with assuring that the most negative, even repulsive, details of his life and thought are always in the foreground. While this novel is undeniably brilliant, darkly comic and engrossing, its length and negative tone will probably dissuade most readers just as the complicated prose of the other fictions will have done.

G. continues to publish essays that challenge and infuriate; *Harper's* has published "On Censorship," an essay calculated to offend many interest groups by questioning the motives of some of their stances while, at the same time, requiring their assent because of his convincing demonstration of the destructive effects of any and all forms of censorship. As a defense of all forms of expression, regardless of their potential for offense, it might almost be a defense of his own work, with its mixture of seriousness and grossness. G.'s place in the literary pantheon is probably secure, though he will never please the general public.

BIBLIOGRAPHY: Holloway, W. L., *W. G.* (1990); McCaffery, L., *The Metafictional Muse: The Work of Robert Coover, Donald Barthelme, and W. G.* (1982); Saltzman, A., *The Fiction of W. G.: The Consolation of Language* (1986)

THOMAS F. DILLINGHAM

GATES, Henry Louis, Jr.

b. 16 September 1950, Keyser, West Virginia

Literary scholar, distinguished professor, public critic, and influential editor, G. ranks as one of the leading voices in American letters. G.'s *Thirteen Ways of Looking at a Black Man,* published in 1997, provides telling reference to the diversity of experience and impulse that found his career, drawing its title from the poem "Thirteen Ways of Looking at a Blackbird" by Wallace STEVENS, the Connecticut poet whose leg-

acy no doubt affected G. when the author was at Yale. Although a history student, the fascination with literature and an understanding of imaginative writing's unique ability to reveal and instruct is an aspect of the writer's perspective that G. never discarded. At Yale, G. was exposed to the rigorous and arcane critical practice known as deconstruction, a method of examining texts in light of their complex linguistic and referential patterns. At the same time, G. established his commitment to "literary archaeology," arguing for the importance of reestimating the value of writings by 19th-and 20th-c. African Americans and incorporating these neglected texts in the American literary canon. These two interests, one chiefly aesthetic, the other largely sociopolitical, combined powerfully in G.'s American Book Award-winning *The Signifying Monkey* (1988), in which he proposed a literary theory specifically appropriate to the study of the African American tradition. It is the foundation provided by oral African traditions, G. argued, upon which African American writers base their "speakerly" writings. This emphasis on storytelling as well as story itself makes African American writing particularly suitable for professional readers whose interests are in the form, not just the content, of literature. At a time when the study of literary form was a valued practice in the academy, G. was able to confirm the artistic value of writings whose status as great works of literature was not yet assured.

G.'s role as a canon reformer, demonstrated by his editing of, among other works, the *Norton Anthology of African American Literature* (1996), reached an early pinnacle with his general editorship in 1990 of the Harper Perennial editions of the works of Zora Neale HURSTON, whose novel *Their Eyes Were Watching God* has since become a staple of American literature courses throughout the academy. As a promoter of Hurston's reputation, G. demonstrated the ability to translate his scholarly perceptions for a wider audience, using criticism to remind literary professionals and students of Hurston's importance, and the mass cultural media to introduce her to recreational readers. Occasionally, G.'s participation in cultural debates has gone beyond the literary realm into the arena of public policy.

No more notably than in his appearance as an expert on metaphor in the 1990 obscenity trial of the rap group 2 Live Crew, and subsequent writings on the band's lyrics, did G. fuse his academic training and cultural savvy. In reference to the group's sexually loaded lyrics, and in defense of their artistic choices, G. wrote: "2 Live Crew must be interpreted within the context of black culture generally and signifying specifically." In referring to "signifying," G. relied upon his own theory of African American writing to explain the "coded ways of communicating" employed by black artists.

The ability and the desire to transcend the exclusive environment of higher learning in order to bring ideas directly to the public—an attempt made successfully by only the rarest of academicians—were further demonstrated by the success of G.'s memoir *Colored People* (1995), an account of growing up in segregated Piedmont, West Virginia, his contributions as staff writer to the *New Yorker,* and his authorship, along with leading African American intellectual Cornel West of *The Future of the Race* (1996). With this access to the popular imagination, and the influence on the academy exerted through his chair of the Department of Afro-American Studies at Harvard University, G. continues his conversations about race and culture with both elite and broadly construed audiences. It is with these two readerships in mind that G. frames the narratives of *Thirteen Ways of Looking at a Black Man.* The figures G. selects, from the realms of literature, politics, entertainment, and religion, share the circumstance of having risen to prominence from humble beginnings, much as did G. himself. But it is the differences among black men with which this text is primarily concerned. G., moving easily between the stories of men as disparate as Colin Powell and Louis Farrakhan, demonstrates that the generalized notion of the unitary black man is just as unavailable to us as was a single view of a blackbird to Wallace Stevens. Again, the issue is both aesthetic and political, as G. rereads a poetic conceit in order to remind us that how we view a subject is a reflection of the broadness of our thinking. Always an educator, often an entertainer, profoundly concerned with the ways in which Americans understand each other, G. works towards an expanded consciousness and a more refined conscience in the nation that has been the focus of his life of writing.

BIBLIOGRAPHY: Bucknell, B., "H. L. G., Jr., and the Theory of 'Signifyin(g),'" *Ariel* 21 (January 1990): 65–84; Lubiano, W., "H. L. G., Jr. and African-American Discourse," *NEQ* 62 (December 1989): 561–72; Ward, J. W., Jr., "Interview with H. L. G., Jr.," *NLH* 22 (Autumn 1991): 927–35

NICK SMART

GAY MALE LITERATURE

The category of gay male literature has only recently been recognized in academic circles, but it is hardly a new phenomenon, notwithstanding the fact that open discussion of homosexuality was severely limited until the second half of the 20th c. Gay literature in its simplest definition encompasses both works in which same-sex desire is explicitly evoked or thematized and works in which same-sex attraction is implicit. In addition, however, gay literature also includes texts in which homosexual themes are coded or disguised and works that are—for reasons not limited to authorial intention—particularly susceptible to gay readings. Hence, the category is an expansive one, containing not only works that have been marginalized because of their subject matter but also a surprisingly large number of canonical texts. If Leslie A. FIEDLER's famous assertion of the universality of male homosexuality in American literature is an exaggeration based on the conflation of misogyny with male friendship and of homosociality with homosexuality, it is nevertheless true that homoeroticism is a significant presence in the works of such classic American authors as Ralph Waldo EMERSON, Henry David THOREAU, Walt WHITMAN, Herman MELVILLE, and Henry JAMES, as well as in a host of lesser known artists.

The transcendentalists were the first group in America to explore relations between persons of the same sex in any depth. Emerson and Thoreau, for example, idealize male friendship and conceive it as superior to heterosexual love. Emerson's 1839 essay on friendship and Thoreau's long discourse on the subject in *A Week on the Concord and Merrimack Rivers* both romanticize same-sex relations and betray despair at the impossibility of realizing the ideal in real life. Their meditations on the beauty and pain of same-sex relations resist easy accommodation within the traditional rhetoric of 19th-c. friendship. Still, the transcendentalists tend to devalue the physical in their devotion to neo-Platonic idealization. In contrast, Whitman boldly valorizes the body itself, particularly the working-class masculine body he celebrates throughout *Leaves of Grass,* first published in 1855 and periodically revised and reissued.

Homoeroticism pervades Whitman's poetry, early and late, but it is expressed most clearly in works such as "Song of Myself," "Song of the Open Road," "Starting from Paumanok," and the forty-five poems of the "Calamus" section. The "Calamus" sequence is especially important as an attempt to explore the author's own homosexual subjectivity while simultaneously attempting to create space for homosexual identity and expression within the American republic. Offering a radical vision of the power of "manly love" to unite and revitalize the nation, Whitman defines homosexuality as a peculiarly American social phenomenon that can transcend the boundaries of class, race, and geography. At the same time, however, the "Calamus" section is shadowed by personal doubt and a feeling of isolation. Thus, notwithstanding such exuberant celebrations of homosexual love as "When I

Heard at the Close of the Day," the "Calamus" poems also acknowledge the difficulties of creating community and finding fulfillment in an America that has not realized its potential and that may never do so.

Whitman's poetry at once expressed and helped create an emerging homosexual self-consciousness. Indeed, it is scarcely possible to overstate Whitman's influence on gay literature, both in America and abroad. Whitman's vision of the transforming power of masculine love and his forging of a link between the personal and the political had a profound influence on English writers such as Edward Carpenter and John Addington Symonds, as well as on such American contemporaries as Bayard TAYLOR and Charles Warren STODDARD. Whitman's influence is such that nearly all subsequent gay American poets were to respond to his ideal of gay community. But in Taylor and Stoddard, the search for communion across barriers of class, race, and geography is also propelled by an attempt to identify with the "other," who is the object of desire. This attempt to comprehend the self by understanding the "other" was pioneered by Melville.

Melville's early novels such as *Typee, Omoo,* and *Redburn* raise crucial questions of race and gender by exploring the social organizations and mores of cultures very different from his own and by depicting his protagonists' search for the ideal friend. These themes are brought together in his greatest work, *Moby-Dick,* in which the erotically charged, interracial friendship of Ishmael and Queequeg challenges the hierarchical and racially biased authoritarianism that threatens American democracy. While the "heart's honeymoon" of the two sailors promises at least the possibility of private contentment, that local triumph ends with Queequeg's death. The will to power of authoritarian obsessives like Captain Ahab seems destined to enjoy the ultimate victory. Melville's final treatment of homosexuality is even more pessimistic, in the posthumously published novella, *Billy Budd.* In this work, the villain, Claggart, is a repressed homosexual whose desire for the beautiful eponymous sailor has been twisted into hatred, and the apparently kind Captain Vere sacrifices Billy for his own advancement.

Like Melville's early novels, Stoddard's stories collected in *South Sea Idylls* and *The Island of Tranquil Delights* are set in the Polynesian islands, which are depicted as the embodiment of a natural sexual freedom that contrasts with the repressiveness of Western society. Taylor similarly sought exotic locales for the homoerotic verse of *Poems of the Orient.* While his novel *Joseph and His Friend* is set in America, it is the mythic America of the West. The two heroes of the title finally travel to California in search of their "Happy Valley," an arcadian world where men can find sexual fulfillment with other men without fear of conventional society. The American West also functions as a pastoral site of homoerotic desire in such novels as *John Brent* (1861) by Theodore Winthrop and *The Virginian* by Owen WISTER. Stoddard's diffuse San Francisco novel, *For the Pleasure of His Company,* also deserves mention for its homosexual allusions and homoerotic incidents. Also noteworthy is *The Story of a Life* (1901) by the pseudonymous Claude Hartland, who in effect embraces the emerging medical model of homosexuality in an effort to understand his "aberration."

Henry James's response to Whitman's call for gay community was more ambivalent than other homosexual writers. While he frequently portrayed male homoerotic relationships, especially those between an older man and a younger one, with insightful sympathy, those relationships typically are doomed within the text. This is true even of *Roderick Hudson,* the most celebratory of James's early treatments of homoerotic friendship, as well as of such works as "The Pupil" and *The Beast in the Jungle.* Although it is a coded and allegorical tale, "The Great Good Place" may affirm James's acceptance of his ambiguous sexuality even in the face of the sensational Oscar Wilde scandal of 1895, which seemed to confirm the American's keen awareness of the potential danger of same-sex love and which profoundly affected homosexual consciousness in the U.S. as well as in England.

Among James's circle was the wealthy American expatriate Howard Overing Sturgis, whose novels *Tim: A Story of Eton* (1894) and *Belchamber* (1904) are homoerotic. Published anonymously and dedicated to "the love that surpasses the love of women," *Tim* is a novel about the tragic infatuation of a sensitive schoolboy for an unresponsive classmate. In *Belchamber,* Sturgis presents a curious portrait of a passive male unable to fulfill the gender-role expectations of his society. While the plot has little to do with homosexuality per se, the novel certainly has homosexual implications in its concern with the role of the sensitive outsider. "Paul's Case" by Willa CATHER also depicts a sensitive outsider. Both a moving tale and a thoughtful contribution to the debate about the relationship of the homosexual to society sparked by the Wilde scandal, "Paul's Case" implies that the solution to the homosexual's dilemma in an unaccepting society lies in integration rather than separation and in self-acceptance rather than self-hatred.

Another writer heavily influenced by James is Edward Irenaeus Prime-Stevenson, who, under the pseudonym Xavier Mayne, published at his own expense a "psychological romance" in 1906 entitled *Imre: A Memorandum.* This novel, which recounts the love of a British aristocrat for a Hungarian military officer, is unusual for its happy ending. Other works by Prime-Stevenson include two Horatio ALGER-like schoolboy novels, *White Cockades* (1887) and *Left to Themselves* (1891); a remarkable defense of homosexuality entitled *The Intersexes* (1908); and a collection, *Her Enemy, Some Friends—And Other Personages* (1913), which includes several homoerotic stories. Like *Imre* and *The Intersexes, Bertram Cope's Year* by Henry Blake FULLER was also published at the author's own expense. It deserves recognition as one of the earliest novels by a nationally celebrated writer to deal overtly with homosexuality.

During the 1910s and 1920s, Hart CRANE began publishing poems with strong homosexual implications. His greatest work, *The Bridge,* emphasizes male communion and culminates in the poet's joining hands with Whitman. Other poets who began publishing homoerotic verse in the 1920s include Claude MCKAY, Langston HUGHES, Countee CULLEN, and Robert MCALMON. Members of the Harlem Renaissance, McKay, Cullen, and Hughes tended to veil their homosexual allusions in code, but many of their poems exemplify a brilliant layering of racial and sexual themes, as, for example, Cullen's "The Black Christ." In 1926, Bruce Nugent, also a member of the Harlem Renaissance, published his short story, "Smoke, Lilies and Jade," perhaps the first depiction of black gay male experience in American fiction. McAlmon's novel *Post-Adolescence* and his stories in *A Companion Volume* and *Distinguished Air* also pioneered in their portraits of gay and lesbian characters in the Jazz Age. Clarkson Crane's academic novel *The Western Shore* (1925) is distinctive in the era for its unselfconscious portrayal of a gay English instructor. Less straightforward is the work of Carl VAN VECHTEN, whose campy novels celebrate bohemian culture in 1920s New York.

Homosexual themes became more frequent and more overt in the 1930s, though gay writers still faced serious obstacles to publishing their work. The painter Marsden Hartley wrote several explicitly gay poems, including "Gay World," which were not published until after his death in his *Selected Poems* (1945); and Paul GOODMAN who was later to publish outspokenly bisexual poems, stories, and novels, wrote eight of his autobiographical "Johnson" stories in the 1930s, most of which were not published until 1976. Wallace THURMAN did publish an interesting portrait of the African American subculture in *Infants of the Spring,* a satire of the Harlem Renaissance. Charles Henri Ford and Parker Tyler published their experimental novel *The Young and Evil* (1933) in Paris. Offering a tour of New York's homosexual subculture, the witty and exuberant work gleefully thumbs its nose at conventional values, yet it is shadowed by its consciousness of the repressiveness of American society that constantly threatens

even its bohemian protagonists. Forman Brown, writing under the pseudonym Richard Meeker, published *Better Angel* in 1933. A bildungsroman tracing the development of a sensitive young man to maturity as a successful composer and musician who finds happiness with another man, the rather artless work rises well above the level of the sensational pulp novels featuring homosexuality that began to appear with some frequency in this decade. George SANTAYANA, who had written a set of four tenderly elegiac sonnets in 1894 mourning the death of a classmate, published his subtly homoerotic novel *The Last Puritan* in 1935.

The 1940s saw an exponential increase in the number of literary works overtly dealing with homosexuality, as well as the beginnings of a homosexual emancipation movement, signaled by the establishment of the Mattachine Society in Los Angeles at the end of the decade. In 1944, young poet Robert DUNCAN published a landmark essay, "The Homosexual in Society," in which he not only identified himself as homosexual but called for political organizing by homosexuals as a persecuted minority. By the time of his death in 1988, Duncan was recognized as a significant American poet, and his numerous celebrations of male-male domesticity were honored as an important part of his canon, but in 1944 Duncan's essay led to his being blacklisted by the principal poetic circles of the day, including the *Kenyon Review,* under the editorship of John Crowe RANSOM. More positively, three fictional works concerned with homosexuality were published by mainstream houses to considerable critical acclaim and reached wide audiences.

These three novels—*The Gallery* (1947) by John Horne Burns, *Other Voices, Other Rooms* by Truman CAPOTE, and *The City and the Pillar* by Gore VIDAL—are all products of the post–World War II literary boom. They challenged the widespread contempt for gay people in America, and mirrored the new frankness in sexual matters that can also be seen in two significant nonfiction works of the era, the famous report on *Sexual Behavior in the Human Male* (1948) by Alfred Kinsey and *The Homosexual in America* (1951) by Donald Webster Cory (pseudonym of Edward Sagarin). The novels by Burns and Vidal are particularly interesting for their attempt to "normalize" homosexual behavior even as they provide glimpses into what was then a hidden and exotic sector of American life. *The Gallery* features a memorable scene in a Neapolitan gay bar frequented by U.S. soldiers as well as locals, while *The City and the Pillar* offers an unsensational portrait of the gay subcultures, first of Hollywood and New Orleans, and then of New York, which is described as "a new Sodom," as it traces the coming-out process of a young man as ordinary and American as apple pie.

In the fiction of Capote and his fellow Southerner Tennessee WILLIAMS, whose astonishingly frank collection of short stories *One Arm and Other Stories* was published in a limited edition in 1948, a wide range of extreme character types—sissy boys, mannish women, transvestites, "dirty old men," flamboyant queens, and male hustlers—co-exist with other unconventional, obviously or obscurely wounded characters in a gallery of the dispossessed. The animating theme of the early fiction of Capote and Williams is the universal human need for love, a theme explored most deeply by their predecessor in Southern gothic, Carson MCCULLERS, whose influence on them is palpable and whose own novels frequently feature gay characters and concerns. Although not a Southerner, Paul BOWLES also embraced a gothic vision, as in the haunting short stories of his first collection, *The Delicate Prey.*

The publication of Williams's short stories in a limited edition in 1948—and in 1954, when another collection, *Hard Candy and Other Stories,* appeared—suggests the recognition on the part of at least some publishers of a self-conscious gay readership. This readership was to expand in the 1950s and authors such as James Barr (pseudonym of Arthur Fugaté), Fritz Peters (Arthur Anderson Peters), and Jay Little (pseudonym of Clarence L. Miller) seem to have had a special rapport with it, as did Lonnie Coleman. The novels and stories of these writers sympathetically (and often sentimentally and melodramatically) depict protagonists who are gay; and these authors assume a level of understanding and inside knowledge on the part of their readers. Peters's *Finistere* (1951) and Coleman's *Sam* (1959) are the most sophisticated of these works appealing to a homosexual audience. In addition, the theme of homosexuality, though often treated sensationally and contemptuously, became increasingly common in the 1950s, especially in the potboilers routinely issued by paperback book publishers.

But the two most important publications of the 1950s from a gay perspective are *Howl and Other Poems* by Allen GINSBERG and *Giovanni's Room* by James BALDWIN. Written at the height of the 1950s backlash against homosexuality—when homosexuals were more aggressively and systematically attacked than at any previous time in American history, when they became the chief scapegoats of the Cold War, faced blatant employment discrimination, and suffered widespread harassment by local and national police organizations—these works question American assumptions about homosexuality. A vigorous challenge to Cold War attitudes, *Howl* not only rejected the conformity and complacency of the Eisenhower years, but also embraced countercultural values and the Whitmanesque dream of an America that lived up to its

potential for love. Ginsberg's book, and the publicity attendant on its sensational obscenity trial, brought to the fore other Beat writers, including Jack KEROUAC and William S. BURROUGHS, whose work also featured homosexuality prominently, as in Burroughs's experimental *Naked Lunch.*

Baldwin's *Giovanni's Room* tackles forthrightly the issue of homosexuality that was understated and implicit in his first novel, *Go Tell It on the Mountain,* and that would also figure in his subsequent work. A central text in the American literature of homosexuality, *Giovanni's Room* vividly captures the painful reality of internalized homophobia, as well as the destructive effects of the external homophobia of its era, and creatively translates pain into compassion and suffering into redemption. A powerful and poignant dramatization of ambivalence and its consequences, it is a coming-out story in which the antihero wrestles with the terror within. Other gay writers who emerged in the 1950s are the poets Jack SPICER, Frank O'HARA, Jonathan Williams, and John Wieners, and the fiction writers Alfred CHESTER, John CHEEVER, and James PURDY .

Three British-born naturalized American citizens, Christopher Isherwood, Thom Gunn, and W. H. AUDEN made important contributions to the gay literature of the 1960s. Isherwood's *The World in the Evening* (1954) has the distinction of offering the first sympathetic depiction of a gay activist in American literature, but *Down There on a Visit* (1962), *A Single Man* (1964), and *A Meeting by the River* (1967) bring homosexual issues even more insistently to the fore. *A Single Man* deserves special note for its sustained and moving portrait of homosexual love and for its highly developed minority consciousness. Presaging the gay liberation movement of the 1970s, *A Single Man* presents homosexuality as simply a human variation that should be accorded value and respect and it depicts homosexuals as a group whose grievances should be redressed. A classic of gay literature, *A Single Man* is also a profound meditation on death and decay and on the disparity between the body and the spirit.

Gunn's poetry becomes overtly gay only in the 1970s, but his work in the 1960s, including *My Sad Captains* (1961), subtly limns homosexual attraction and response. Gunn's youthful pose of heroic masculinity yields in his subsequent work to a warmer and more open persona. Although his homosexuality is an important if understated presence in all his work, Auden expressed it more openly in the 1960s than he had previously. His celebration of his long relationship with fellow poet Chester Kallman, "The Common Life," is especially moving. Auden's impact on younger gay poets, including writers as different as Gunn and Ginsberg, has been enormous, involving his personality as well as his poetry. For example, in his series of adventures with the Ouija board, beginning with *Divine Comedies* and continuing in subsequent volumes, James MERRILL presents Auden as a ghostly presence and source of wisdom, the embodiment of a homosexual artistic sensibility. For Richard HOWARD, who twice addresses Auden as Hephaestos, the only one of the Olympian gods who ever worked, the elder poet functioned as a poetic father and prior ego.

Another significant gay writer of the 1960s is John RECHY, who in a series of novels including *City of Night, Numbers,* and *This Day's Death,* documents the sexual underworld of large American cities and traces the emergence of gay identity. The sexual explicitness of Rechy and other writers of the period is indicative of the weakening of censorship and the relaxation of social control in the 1960s, which contributed to the greater visibility of homosexuality in American life. The 1960s also witnessed another phenomenon that added to the visibility of gay men and lesbians, the appearance of books and articles attempting to explain the gay world to the general public. Often these books were inaccurate and openly hostile, yet they nevertheless served to make people aware of the gay subculture and they offered the opportunity for gay men and lesbians to redefine homosexuality away from the traditional configuration of sin, sickness, and crime.

Other noteworthy novels of the decade with significant gay content include *Two People* (1962) by Donald Windham, *Last Exit to Brooklyn* by Hubert SELBY, Jr., *Totempole* (1965) by Sanford Friedman, *Eustace Chisholm and the Works* by James Purdy, and *Another Country* and *Tell Me How Long the Train's Been Gone* by James Baldwin. Emerging gay poets of the period include Harold Norse, James SCHUYLER, Edward Field, James Merrill, John ASHBERY, and Richard Howard, all of whom would write increasingly frank poetry in the ensuing decades. During the 1960s, homosexuality also became an important staple of American drama, coded and discreet in the work of established dramatists like Tennessee Williams, William INGE, and Edward ALBEE, more open and confrontational in the Off-Off Broadway productions of emerging dramatists such as Lanford WILSON, Doric Wilson, and Robert Patrick. The first commercial play to be set in a gay household, *The Boys in the Band* by Mart Crowley has been bitterly criticized for its lack of gay pride, but it memorably portrays the lives of some gay men in the period immediately before the Stonewall Inn Riots.

Although the Stonewall Rebellion of June 27–28, 1969, serves as a convenient marker of the beginning of gay liberation as a mass movement, Stonewall itself was the culmination of decades of activism, and the emergence of gay men and lesbians as a self-conscious minority was a gradual process. Modeled on the African American civil rights struggle, the antiwar movement of the day, and the new wave of FEMINISM, and made possible by the relaxed and more open social attitudes induced by the (hetero)sexual revolution of the 1960s, the gay liberation movement challenged stereotypical ideas about homosexuality and boldly demanded social and political equality for gay men and lesbians. In its wake came a veritable explosion of literature of all kinds focusing on the homosexual experience, ranging in tone from the gloomy *Something You Do in the Dark* (1971) by Daniel Curzon (pseudonym of Daniel Brown) to the more affirmative popular melodrama *The Front Runner* (1974) by Patricia Nell Warren, the painful and disturbing *The Story of Harold* (1974) by the pseudonymous Terry Andrews, and the unsettling experimental novels of Coleman Dowell. Most significantly, there emerged a distinctively gay literary movement, made possible by the establishment and proliferation of gay newspapers, magazines, journals, bookshops, and publishing houses.

Perhaps the most interesting group of writers who helped create the post-Stonewall renaissance of American gay male literature is the so-called Violet (or Lavender) Quill, a circle of gay male writers in Manhattan. This group of friends and rivals helped create a literature that reflected their gay experience and that mirrored the social revolution wrought by gay liberation. Their works chronicle both the headiness of the early years of the movement and the tragedy of the AIDS epidemic. The writers of the Violet Quill who have achieved the greatest renown are Andrew Holleran, Robert Ferro, and Edmund WHITE. Holleran's *Dancer from the Dance* (1978), which chronicles the life of "that tiny subspecies of homosexual, the doomed queen," lyrically portrays the frenetic gay milieu of Manhattan and Fire Island in the mid-1970s. Holleran's other works include his novels *Nights in Aruba* (1983) and *The Beauty of Men* (1996), as well as *Ground Zero* (1988), a collection of articles and vignettes about the AIDS epidemic. Ferro's *The Family of Max Desir* (1983) and *Second Son* (1988) both focus on young gay Italian Americans and their roles in the families they love but feel estranged from by virtue of their sexuality. *The Blue Star* (1985) chronicles the lives of two Americans who meet in Florence and join together to explore the Florentine demimonde. In all three works, magic realism qualifies the narrative logic, and death is a constant presence. White, the most highly acclaimed contemporary gay writer, has published a wide range of fiction and nonfiction. His semiautobiographical novels *A Boy's Own Story* and *The Beautiful Room Is Empty,* conceived as parts of a projected tetralogy, offer not merely accounts of an individual's coming of age but a kind of social history of gay consciousness. Another member of the group, Felice Picano has produced a number of gay novels, poems, stories, and memoirs, and in 1977 founded SeaHorse Press, New York's first gay publishing house.

Other writers who emerged from the gay liberation movement include the short story writer and novelist Richard Hall, the playwright and novelist Larry Kramer, and the novelist and memoirist Paul Monette. An accomplished master of the short story, Hall explores crucial issues of American gay life in the aftermath of liberation with empathy and clarity. Kramer, whose best known work is *Faggots* (1978), a scathing satire of the same milieu that Holleran celebrates in *Dancer from the Dance,* is also an AIDS activist, the cofounder both of Gay Men's Health Crisis in New York, the first community-based AIDS service organization in America, and of ACT UP, a direct action political group. His plays, *The Normal Heart* (1986) and *The Destiny of Me* (1992), focus on the AIDS epidemic, as does the collection of polemical writings gathered in *Reports from the Holocaust: The Making of an AIDS Activist* (1989). AIDS also transformed the life of Monette, whose most important work was in response to the epidemic. The loss of his lover Roger Horowitz to the disease led to a harrowingly personal collection of poetry, *Love Alone: 18 Elegies for Rog* (1988), which conveys both the pain of grief and the ravages of the disease, and to a prose memoir, *Borrowed Time* (1988). Monette also wrote two novels about AIDS, *Afterlife* (1990) and *Halfway Home* (1991), and his memoir, *Becoming a Man* (1992), which focuses on the difficulties of growing up gay in an unaccepting society.

Two West Coast writers whose work reflects a post-Stonewall sensibility, though in very different ways, are Dennis Cooper and Armistead Maupin. Self-consciously adopting a stance of disengagement, Cooper writes novels preoccupied with violence and anomie, as, for example, *Closer* (1989) and *Frisk* (1991). In contrast, Maupin is optimistic and unabashedly sentimental. He is best known for his six-volume series initiated by *Tales of the City* (1976), by far the most popular works of the post-Stonewall publishing boom. Begun as daily columns in the *San Francisco Chronicle,* the series focuses on a group of eccentric, sexually and socially diverse residents of 28 Barbary Lane, and develops into a social history of two tumultuous decades.

In the post-Stonewall era, gay drama has flourished not only Off-Off-Broadway and in regional theater, but on Broadway itself. Among the leading contemporary gay dramatists are Lanford Wilson, Martin Sherman, Harvey Fierstein, and Terrence MCNALLY. Wilson's *The Fifth of July,* part of his trilogy of plays featuring the Talley family, positions a gay couple as the stable center of an alternative family. Sherman's best-known play, *Bent* (1978), depicts the brutal treatment of homosexuals under the Nazi regime, tracing the growth of a young gay man from self-hatred and evasion to acceptance and affirmation in a concentration camp. Fierstein's *Torch Song Trilogy* (1981) focuses on the attempt of a gay Jewish drag queen to find lasting love; the play pioneers by humanizing drag queens, portraying them as characters with whom a conventional audience can empathize rather than as pathetic victims or exotic divas. McNally, the most prolific of gay American dramatists, has placed gay issues at the fore in works as various as *Bad Habits; The Ritz; The Lisbon Traviata; Lips Together, Teeth Apart;* and *Love, Valour, Compassion.*

Some other important writers particularly associated with the gay movement include the mystery novelist Joseph Hansen, the science fiction writer Samuel R. Delany, and the poet Alfred CORN. Hansen, who has also published a considerable body of non-mystery books, including the novels *A Smile in His Lifetime* (1981) and *Living Upstairs* (1993), is best known as the creator of the Dave Brandstetter mystery series. In the twelve-novel Brandstetter series, beginning with *Fade Out* (1970), Hansen presents gay men and lesbians in all their variety, without sensation, as simply men and women with understandable desires, triumphs, and frustrations. The commercial and critical success of the Brandstetter series led to a proliferation of mystery series featuring gay detectives. Perhaps the most noteworthy younger gay mystery writers are Michael Nava and Steven Saylor. Nava's most recent novels have transcended the mystery genre and have positioned him as a significant voice in contemporary gay literature. A leading practitioner of the "new wave" of science fiction, Delany frequently features socially marginalized outsiders as protagonists in his work, which includes stories like "Aye, and Gomorrah . . ." (1967) and novels like his four-volume Neveryon series (1976–19). Corn's *A Call in the Midst of the Crowd* established him as a poet in the visionary tradition of Walt Whitman and Stephen CRANE.

Somewhat less associated with the gay movement itself are two other writers who also depict same-sex relations memorably, Reynolds PRICE and David Plante. While Price's gay themes are understated and implicit, he evinces an idealization of the male body and a particular interest in male friendship, often between homosexual and heterosexual men. Plante writes more openly of gay characters and situations than does Price, but he too employs a low-key approach. A prolific author, he is most noted for his highly acclaimed Francoeur trilogy, *The Family, The Country,* and *The Woods.*

Among younger gay writers the most celebrated are David LEAVITT and Tony KUSHNER. Leavitt, who first came to prominence with his short story collection, *Family Dancing,* is the author of a subsequent collection of stories and three novels. His work is distinguished especially by his ability to integrate gay issues into the ordinary fabric of contemporary life. In his epic play *Angels in America,* which is subtitled "A Gay Fantasia on American Themes," Kushner offers a complex and stunning commentary on the moral and spiritual plight of the nation by examining the conduct of four homosexual men in the face of the AIDS crisis. Other younger writers of note, somewhat arbitrarily selected, include novelists Alan Gurganis, Robert Glück, Mark Merlis, Christopher Bram, Michael Cunningham, Harlan Greene, Paul Russell, Matthew Stadler, Randall Kenan, and Dale Peck; the playwright Paul Rudnick; and the poets J. D. MCCLATCHY and Mark Doty. Among the numerous promising writers whose lives have been cut short by the tragedy of AIDS are, in addition to several mentioned above, the accomplished African American novelist Melvin Dixon, the Chicano writer Arturo Islas, the novelist and journalist George Whitmore, the journalist Randy Shilts, the poet Essex Hemphill, the short story writer Allen Barnett, and the playwright Charles Ludlam.

Another important post-Stonewall development that has affected gay literature has been the new understanding of sexuality in history and culture that emerged in the 1980s and 1990s, especially within the universities. The gay and lesbian studies movement has not only discovered and recovered neglected texts and authors but has also reclaimed mainstream literature, revealing the pertinence and centrality of (frequently disguised) same-sex relationships in canonical works. Although gay literature has frequently been marginalized and dismissed, it is actually surprisingly rich and central. Preoccupied with such themes as self-knowledge, the relationship of the individual to society, the contemplation of forbidden beauty, the experience of otherness, the pain of exclusion, the yearning for escape, the dilemma of the divided self, and the joy of discovery, gay literature is both universal in theme and a significant part of American literature.

BIBLIOGRAPHY: Austen, R., *Playing the Game: The Homosexual Novel in America* (1977); Bergman, D., *Gaiety Transfigured: Gay Self-Representation in American Literature* (1991); Clum, J. M., *Acting Gay: Male Homosexuality in Modern Drama* (1992); Fiedler, L. A., *Love and Death in the American Novel* (1960); Gifford, J., *Dayneford's Library: American Homosexual Writing, 1900–1913* (1995); Malinowski, S., ed. *Gay and Lesbian Literature* (1994); Martin, R. K., *The Homosexual Tradition in American Poetry* (1979); Nelson, E. S., ed., *Contemporary Gay American Novelists* (1993); Summers, C. J., ed., *The Gay and Lesbian Literary Heritage* (1995); Summers, C. J., *Gay Fictions: Wilde to Stonewall* (1990); Woods, G., *Articulate Flesh: Male Homo-eroticism and Modern Poetry* (1987)

CLAUDE J. SUMMERS

GEISEL, Theodor [Seuss]

b. 2 March 1904, Springfield, Massachusetts; d. 24 September 1991, La Jolla, California

In 1957, after thirty years as a political cartoonist and advertising artist, G. embarked on a long desired career as a children's author. Writing under the pseudonym of "Dr. Seuss," he quickly developed enormous popularity, revolutionizing the genre of grade school primers, spawning a school of whimsical artist/authors, and capturing the hearts and minds of two generations of children.

In a departure from the typical primer of the day, the rather turgid and dull Dick and Jane series, the innovative book G. produced, *The Cat in the Hat* (1957), as well as those that followed it, featured a playfully poetic style, nonsense vocabulary, and a creative and witty child-centered perspective that allowed children to learn to read and to love literature at the same time.

Dr. Seuss books run the gamut of topics likely to appeal to children, but never in an ordinary or expected way. The list includes the traditional ABC book—with a twist: what begins with F? "Four fluffy feathers on a Fiffer-feffer-feff"; a counting book, *One Fish Two Fish Red Fish Blue Fish* (1960), that is not a counting book at all, but rather a menagerie of odd creatures: some animal, some human, each with its own distinctive habit, appearance, or attitude, and many with funny nonsense names; a book of adjectives, *The Foot Book* (1968); a book of sounds, *Mr. Brown Can Moo! Can You?* (1970); and many books that act as guides for the simple problems of being a child. What to do when there's nothing to do is the ostensible theme of *The Cat in the Hat,* and *Green Eggs and Ham* (1960) appeals to any child who has looked uncomfortably upon a plate of strange new foods while being implored to just take one bite. This last was written on a dare from a friend to compose a book using no more than fifty words, a feat G accomplished by writing a minor masterpiece.

Although G. is known primarily for his books for beginning readers, he was by no means limited to that category. In his thirty-odd more advanced books for children, G. consistently pursued the same dual purpose. As a writer G. strove to capture the curiosity, excitement, and wonder at the world around, so characteristic of children, but as he saw it, lacking in most adults. At the same time he featured heroes who consistently embodied the qualities of loyalty, courage, and moral conscience. Many of his stories, though written for children, had rather stern messages for adults. His first book, *And to Think That I Saw It on Mulberry Street* (1937), gave parents an unsettling look at how their protectiveness and concern might stultify the creativity of their children. Others had object lessons on the importance of individuality, *Horton Hears a Who!* (1954), and tolerance, *Yertle the Turtle* (1958). His later works tended toward a more preachy, less playful tone. Of these, *The Lorax* (1971), a cautionary tale about the environment, is the most noted. But it was G.'s Christmas story about the spirit of giving, *How the Grinch Stole Christmas* (1957)—immortalized by the characterization of Boris Karloff in an animated television version—that helped move Dr. Seuss from the level of children's author to cultural icon.

G's hallmark style is one of simple rhyming patterns, full of inventive vocabulary, following a pattern of repeated passages, evolving into more and more elaborated syntax, while slowly, inexorably the action (not always plot) mounts to a climax of swirling words and emotional fever pitch, all captured in illustrations that match his vocabulary in inventiveness and that mirror the increasing verbal elaboration.

Ironically, the very qualities that G. is so renowned for, those of inventiveness, playfulness, and childlike exuberance, are the qualities that prevented his innovative books from taking the sphere of education by storm. Administrators and school board officials tend to view G's antiauthoritarian perspective suspiciously and perceive his penchant for amusing nonsense words as counterproductive to the "proper" education of children. Thus, the "Cat in the Hat" books have never been widely used in schools for the purpose of teaching children to read. However, the enormous appeal of G's work to young children has not been missed by their parents, with the result that millions of children have been introduced to Dr. Seuss at a very young age, and many of them learn to read and to enjoy reading before they ever enter a classroom.

BIBLIOGRAPHY: Lurie, A., "The Cabinet of Dr. Seuss," in Nachbar, J., and K. Lause, eds., *Popular Culture: An Introductory Text* (1992): 68–79; Wolf, T., "Imagination, Rejection, and Rescue: Recurrent Themes in Dr. Seuss," *ChildL* 23 (1995): 137–64

GRETA WAGLE

GELBER, Jack
b. 12 April 1932, Chicago, Illinois

Although G. has spent most of his professional life trying to expand the limits of contemporary American theater, he is known primarily for writing one play, *The Connection,* which premiered in 1959 at Julian Beck's Living Theater in New York City.

The Connection garnered major theatrical awards for G.: the Vernon Rice Award, the New York Drama Critics Poll Award, and an Obie Award. By using nontraditional characters, setting, subject matter, and plot line, G. accomplished in America what John Osborne had accomplished in England three years earlier with *Look Back in Anger.* First, he exposed the theatergoing public to a dreary, desolate new world—that of the lower-class, outlaw caste of skid-row junkies waiting for their heroin connection. Second, in depicting this world he developed themes related to the human condition in contemporary society by establishing metaphoric correspondences for the addicts similar to the analogies created by Samuel Beckett in *Waiting for Godot.*

Drama, even when based on a text and literary conventions, is essentially rooted in performance, and in *The Collection* G. exploits this fact. Indeed, part of the appeal of the play is the way in which it reflects the structure of jazz; there are free-flowing ad-lib variations on the theme that run throughout the drama and that vary slightly from performance to performance. Ironically, because the primary action in the play consists of waiting, there is minimal plot development and little action in the traditional dramatic sense as G. explores universal human needs metaphorically expressed as a heroin fix.

Most of G.'s plays have appeared in print. He has translated a play into English, written the screenplay adaptation of *The Connection* (1962), and authored a novel, *On Ice* (1964). Interestingly, the film version of *The Connection* figured in a prominent obscenity case when it was banned by New York state (due primarily to the use of a single word—a slang appellation for dope); the New York State Supreme Court found that the language in the movie was not obscene.

G.'s experimental approach to his themes established him as an innovative force in the American theater. This is epitomized in *The Connection,* for in this play he unified form and content far more successfully than he could have if he had followed the structures of conventional drama. Since the appearance of *The Connection,* G. has had only marginal success with his writing, though even his failures have reflected his goal of expanding theatrical boundaries.

BIBLIOGRAPHY: Gale, S. H., "J. G.: An Annotated Bibliography," *BB* 44 (June 1987): 102–10; Gilman, R.,

Common and Uncommon Masks (1971); King, K., *Ten Modern American Playwrights* (1982); Petronella, V. F., "J. G.," in Kolin, P. C., ed., *American Playwrights since 1945* (1989): 124–32; Vinson, J., ed., *Contemporary Dramatists* (1977); Wellwarth, G. E., *The Theatre of Protest and Paradox* (1964); Wilcox, A., "J. G.," in MacNicholas, J., ed., *DLB*, vol. 7, part 1, *Twentieth-Century American Dramatists* (1981): 192–200

STEVEN H. GALE

GEROULD, Katherine [Fullerton]

b. 6 February 1879, Brockton, Massachusetts; d. 27 July 1944, Princeton, New Jersey

G.'s stories, novels, and essays reflect her Puritan roots, reaching back to William BRADFORD and Nathaniel MORTON. Her essays, collected in *Modes and Morals* (1920) and *Ringside Seats* (1937) and ranging from fashion to the Tunney-Dempsey fight, are deeply influenced by New England conservatism, which won her both praise and blame by contemporary critics. Although they are dated in subject matter, the essays are worth reading for G.'s witty prose. Her best nonfiction are the travel sketches in *Hawaii: Scenes and Impressions* (1916) and *The Aristocratic West* (1925), which focus on the people and culture of those regions. A bright conversational tone and an often irreverent sense of humor characterize her observations. Her conservatism imposed limitations on her ability as literary critic. "Stream of Consciousness," published in the *Saturday Review of Literature* (October 22, 1927), is representative: she compares Henry JAMES's "tender precision" with the "verbal" with the verbal slush" of Virginia Woolf and James Joyce. Her best criticism is found in *Edith Wharton* (n.d., 1922?). G. praises WHARTON for her moral sensibility and her ability to tell a story, the latter quality the key to her popularity. G.'s pamphlet is particularly interesting because she was briefly engaged to Morton Fullerton, once thought to be her brother but actually her first cousin, and with whom Wharton had an affair from 1908 to 1910. G.'s fiction was often favorably compared with Wharton's, though her early work is influenced by Henry James.

G.'s novels—*A Change of Air* (1917), actually related short stories, *Lost Valley* (1922), *Conquistador* (1923), and *The Light That Never Was* (1931)—are her least noteworthy works. Although she skillfully creates a sense of place, her characters are unconvincing and unsatisfying. Her short stories, however, deserve better recognition that currently accorded them. Over half of them are reprinted in *Vain Oblations* (1914), *The Great Tradition* (1915), and *Valiant Dust* (1922). The stories are characterized by a detached

narrator, exotic settings, and a Puritan dedication to self-sacrifice and a sense of duty. "Vain Oblations," for example, chronicles the hero's discovery that his fiancée, a born and bred New England missionary taken captive by an African tribe, has generated into savagery—she is tattooed, bare-breasted, and pregnant with the chieftain's child. She commits suicide, and the protagonist dies of the fever; the narrator is left to ponder Mary Bradford's moral degradation and Saxe's nobility of soul. Although the influence of Wharton and Kipling is most apparent in the short fiction, it is unfair to see G. as a disciple of either author. The tart, ironic tone, the frequently bizarre twists of plot, and the juxtaposition of New England morality in alien settings give her best work a distinctive stamp.

BIBLIOGRAPHY: Hardy, W. S., "K. G.," in L. Mainiero, L., ed., *American Women Writers* (1980): 116–18; James, E. T., ed., *Notable American Women* (1971); Lewis, R. W. B., *Edith Wharton: A Biography* (1975); Walker, W. S., *Twentieth Century Short Story Explication: Interpretations, 1900–1975, of Short Fiction since 1800* (1977): 235; Wright, A. M., *The American Short Story of the Twenties* (1961)

JUDITH E. FUNSTON

GIBSON, William

b. 13 November 1914, New York City

Known primarily as a playwright, G. is also a respected novelist, poet, memoirist, and theatrical producer. His works are permeated by strong poetic and dramatic sensibilities, and an analytical frame of mind. Several of his plays are staples of college and community theater groups.

Reared in and around New York City, G. educated himself after high school, though he did make some half-hearted attempts at college. G.'s authorial aspiration was initially supported by his wife. Early poems published as *Winter Crook* (1948) received mixed reviews, though no critic disputed his potential. His best-selling novel about life in a mental institution, *The Cobweb* (1954), was made into a movie and marked his ascendancy as a self-sustaining writer. With his first two Broadway productions, G. entered the American theatrical scene in a blaze of accomplishment. *Two for the Seesaw* (perf. 1958, pub. 1959) and *The Miracle Worker* (perf. 1959, pub. 1960) represent an early apex in a career that has lasted yet another thirty years.

Two for the Seesaw is a popular "two-hander" that features an improbable relationship between the carefree, city-born-and-bred dancer; Gittel Mosca and Jerry Ryan, a conservative lawyer from Omaha who has recently fled his domineering in-laws. Gittel was the first of many strong female protagonists that inhabited his plays, many of which were first played by Anne Bancroft. *Two for the Seesaw* ran a respectable 750 performances on Broadway in 1958 and was later adapted (by others) for the successful musical, *Seesaw*.

The *Miracle Worker* first saw life as a television play, presented and published in 1957. The stage version came to Broadway in 1959, and was published in 1960. G. also wrote the screenplay for the 1962 movie version. *Miracle Worker* is based upon the true story of the relationship between Helen Keller, noted deaf and blind lecturer; and her tutor and friend, the sightless Anne Sullivan. The play chronicles the events surrounding their first encounters in which Sullivan breaks through the barriers of the young Helen's disabilities and willfulness. In a moment which now stands as an icon of American film, television, and theater; Sullivan drags the kicking and screaming Helen to a well and drenches her with water, at the same time signing "water" into her hands. In a flash of insight, Helen finally understands the significance of the signs and, with great difficulty, articulates the word. Anne Bancroft played Sullivan and Patty Duke, Helen.

G. explores another difficult moment between these remarkable women in *Monday after the Miracle* (1983). Years after "the miracle," Helen is attending Radcliffe and Anne, still Helen's tutor and companion, has married a younger man, thus setting up a domestic triangle which tests the limits of their mutual commitment and aspirations.

Besides those of Keller and Sullivan, G. is noted for other effective stage biographies. *A Cry of Players* (1969) brings William Shakespeare and Anne Hathaway to the stage for an imaginative recreation of their largely undocumented Stratford lives; *American Primitive* (1972) gives John and Abigail Adams in a play based upon their correspondences; *Golda* (1978) portrays Golda Meir through the lens of the Yom Kippur War; and *Goodly Creatures* (1986) presents the gifted Anne Hutchinson at odds with the Puritan authorities. Several plays on religious themes include *I Lay in Zion* (1947), *The Body and the Wheel* (1975), and a collection of Christmas plays published in 1975.

G.'s prose is less well known, though all are thoughtful, substantial works. A strong religious and mystical sensibility is revealed in two book-length memoirs: *A Mass for the Dead* (1968) and *A Season in Heaven* (1974). The former recounts the lives of his parents and the latter documents experiences with Transcendental Meditation. More earth-bound works describe his theatrical life and opinions: *The Seesaw Log* (1959) reveals disillusionment with the Broadway theater, *How to Turn a Phoenix into Ashes* (1978) chronicles the production of *Golda*, and *Shakespeare's*

Game (1978) is a unique analysis of the Bard's dramatic technique.

BIBLIOGRAPHY: Coy, S. C., "W. G.," in MacNicholas, J., ed., *DLB*, vol. 7, part 1, *Twentieth-Century American Dramatists* (1981): 200–208

MAARTEN REILINGH

GIBSON, William [Ford]
b. 17 March 1948, Conway, South Carolina

Best known as one of the originators of "cyberpunk" SCIENCE FICTION and credited with coining the term "cyberspace," G. rose to prominence in the mid-1980s with the publication of his award-winning first novel *Neuromancer* (1984). The son of a contractor who worked at the Oak Ridge facility where the first atomic bomb was built, G. was raised by his widowed mother in Virginia and attended boarding school in Arizona before moving to Vancouver, British Columbia, at age nineteen to avoid the draft for the Vietnam War, where he has lived since 1972.

G.'s earliest short stories, written in the late 1970s and early 1980s, appeared in *Omni* magazine and similar science fiction venues; many were eventually republished in the collection *Burning Chrome* (1986). Like the work of such other cyberpunk writers as Bruce Sterling, Rudy Rucker, Lewis Shiner, and John Shirley, G.'s fiction portrays a near-future world of plastic, glass, and metallic surfaces in a shadowy, neon-lit, decaying urban landscape through which affectless, decentered characters drift, fighting bouts of paranoia and hustling their way through a day-to-day existence. His protagonists are often alienated white male cowboy-hackers for hire, loners who "jack in" to cyberspace, described as a computer-networked "consensual hallucination," in order to break down data-security systems and steal information. G. employs innovative cinematic effects in his narration, using crosscutting and montage sequences to suggest sudden shifts in setting or even the merging of distinct characters' perceptual fields.

Such features of *Neuromancer* as well as of the other two novels in the Sprawl trilogy, *Count Zero* (1986) and *Mona Lisa Overdrive* (1988), indicate both G.'s engagement with traditional thematic issues of science fiction like the relationship between human and machine, as well as his ability to envision those themes through the framework of ongoing developments in culture, technology, and socioeconomic conditions in the contemporary world. These novels depict a world in which multinational corporations wield enormous power in a global capitalist economy, information (in the broadest sense) is the most precious commodity, and advanced technology has molded both new modes of consciousness and, through microsurgery and genetic manipulation, new kinds of bodies. Despite this engagement with issues of postmodern culture and adoption of a punkish, decadent aesthetic, however, G.'s novels rely on remarkably traditional narrative patterns and protagonist types, usually following an antihero detective through a mysterious but nonetheless linear plot to a successful resolution and denouement.

The premise of *The Difference Engine* (1991), co-authored with Bruce Sterling, is that Charles Babbage's plans for a mechanical adding machine were realized in the 19th c., bringing the information age to the Victorian era. An obvious break from the world of the earlier trilogy, it nonetheless confronts similar issues in its focus on the impact of technology on culture. In *Agrippa: A Book of the Dead* (1992), G. enacted his ideas through the form of the publication itself, collaborating with publisher Kevin Begos, Jr. and artist Dennis Ashbaugh to produce a limited-edition electronic text that erased itself as each line was read. A short poetic reflection focusing on the death of his father, it was soon decoded and made available on the World Wide Web. *Virtual Light* (1993), set in San Francisco in the year 2005, is less dark than G.'s earlier cyberpunk novels and takes on such current issues as environmental destruction, AIDS, crime, and racism. Some characters from *Virtual Light* reappear in *Idoru* (1996), G.'s novel that is set in Japan in the 21st c. and deals with a holographic pop star and the virtual world of celebrity culture.

Cyberpunk may eventually be remembered as a phenomenon of the 1980s: certainly many of the concepts and much of the terminology introduced in G.'s work have come to seem commonplace in the years since *Neuromancer* first appeared, and G. himself has moved in new directions with his writing. But the issues of technology, culture, and human subjectivity that G. explores in his novels remain crucial to our times, and to that extent, he remains an important literary figure whose work exceeds the narrow boundaries of genre.

BIBLIOGRAPHY: McCaffery, L., ed., *Storming the Reality Studio* (1991); Olsen, L., *W. G.* (1992); Slusser, G., and T. Shippey, eds., *Fiction 2000: Cyberpunk and the Future of Narrative* (1992); Sponsler, C., "Cyberpunk and the Dilemmas of Postmodern Narrative: The Example of W. G.," *ConL* 33 (1992): 624–44; Tabbi, J., *Postmodern Sublime: Technology and American Writing from Mailer to Cyberpunk* (1995)

BRIAN DONAHUE

GILCHRIST, Ellen
b. 20 February 1935, Vicksburg, Mississippi

Born and reared in Mississippi, G.'s Southern origins run through her work. She is the author of five books of short stories and six novels, as well as several collections of novellas, journals, essays, and poetry.

G. attended Milsaps College, earning a B.A. in 1967, and went on to do postgraduate work at the University of Arkansas. Her first book *The Land Surveyor's Daughter,* published in 1979, is a collection of poetry, a form G. turned away from over the next several years.

In the Land of Dreamy Dreams (1981), a book of fourteen short stories, introduces some of the cast of characters that form the core of her work. The collection provides the reader with a set of interconnected stories of an extended family in Mississippi and New Orleans. *The Annunciation* (1983), a novel, takes many of the same characters and works with them in different scenarios, not always consistent with the stories from G.'s earlier work.

Her next book, *Victory over Japan* (1984), a short story collection, won the American Book Award. The collection is sectioned, by character, into four distinct parts. "Rhoda," the first section, reintroduces a character who figures prominently into G.'s work. In the title story, it is as if Rhoda introduces herself. A first-person narrative by a child, "Victory over Japan" illustrates the perspective of a precocious child during World War II. The war itself is merely background, whereas more immediate concerns figure prominently. This first section ends with Rhoda as an adult—a divorced, self-absorbed woman on the brink of a new life. Later in the collection, the focus is on Crystal Manning, a member of Rhoda's extended family. The main portion of the stories in this last section are told from the distinctive point of view of Traceleen, Crystal's maid. In contrast to Traceleen's perspective is DeDe, another member of the Manning family. Her voice is distinct from Traceleen and her take on the story fills out the reader's knowledge of this family.

Drunk with Love (1986), another collection of short stories, turns again to the extended family her readership is already acquainted with. That same year *Riding out the Tropical Depression,* G.'s second book of poetry, was published.

G.'s next novel, *The Anna Papers* (1988), takes off from the concluding story of *Drunk with Love.* It is a novel about the suicide of Anna, a writer, the causes for her suicide, and effects upon those family members, lovers and friends whom she has left behind.

In *Light Can Be Both Wave and Particle* (1989), G. creates a history and future for characters previously introduced in earlier books of fiction. Norma Jean, a character previously introduced in *Victory over Japan,* takes center stage. In this book of short stories, G. also builds new characters into her landscape.

Like Eudora WELTY and Flannery O'CONNER, G. is undeniably a Southern writer. Her characters are comfortable only at "home," in Arkansas, Louisiana, and Mississippi, though their experiences span the globe. Her writing has aspects to it that are not unlike the writing of the author Colette: strong female characters who speak their minds, eventually take control of their lives (eventually), and often take younger lovers as well.

G.'s fiction can be viewed as a literary building of a community. The author, unwilling to drop any of her characters from book to book, instead creates a recognition for them in the reader.

BIBLIOGRAPHY: Bain, R., "E. G.," in Flora, J. M., and R. Bain, eds., *Contemporary Fiction Writers of the South: A Bio-Biographical Sourcebook* (1993): 169–85; McCay, M. A., *E. G.* (1997)

MARIKA BRUSSEL

GILLETTE, William [Hooker]

b. 24 July 1853, Hartford, Connecticut; d. 29 April 1937, Hartford, Connecticut

G. achieved a level of critical acclaim and popular success as both playwright and actor, a rare combination in American theater. His most successful ventures came as he assumed the leading roles in his own plays. As an actor he furthered naturalistic acting with his cool, imperturbable, thinking-man heroes who could remain calm in the midst of tense situations, such as his Captain Thorne in *Secret Service* (1895). His physique, described by Chicago critic Amy Leslie as "exceedingly tall" with "sympathetic and smoldering" eyes and "altogether cedar-of-Lebanon physical construction," was also a factor in his popularity with mostly female matinee audiences, especially as he played such heroic roles as Sherlock Holmes and Captain Thorne. Although his style as a dramatist can be described as traditional, he took the melodramatic, well-made-play form to a higher level through his use of situation to drive the action and motivate characters, and his attention to detail in setting and action.

G.'s acting career began in 1875 with an amateur production of *Across the Continent* in New Orleans, and a later Boston production of *Faint Hear Ne'er Won Fair Lady.* His first substantial success as a professional actor came at the Madison Square Theater in New York in June 1881, where he enjoyed 151 consecutive performances as the title character in his own play, *The Professor.* After touring in *Young Mrs. Win-*

throp, G. returned to New York as the title character in his adaptation of a German farce that he called *Digby's Secretary* (1884). From 1894, beginning with Augustus Billings in *Too Much Johnson* (1894), until his retirement in 1919, he enjoyed his greatest successes as the leading man in his own plays. After *Too Much Johnson,* G. wrote and starred in the critically acclaimed *Secret Service,* a Civil War drama, and *Sherlock Holmes,* a mystery based on the Arthur Conan Doyle stories. So effective was his portrayal of the lean, handsome, intelligent detective, Holmes, that audiences came to identify G. with the role. All in all, G. acted in nine of his twenty full-length plays. After playing Dr. Carrington in *Clarice* (1905) he mostly revived his earlier, more successful roles. In 1929, he came out of retirement to play Holmes, which elicited a note from Booth TARKINGTON stating: "I would rather see you play Sherlock Holmes than be a child again on Christmas morning."

As a playwright, G. confined himself to no particular style. His first published play was *Esmeralda* (1877), a collaboration with Frances Hodgson BURNETT. Although all his plays fall within the definition of melodrama, he wrote adaptations of German and French comedies, *Digby's Secretary* and *Because She Loved Him So* (1898); farces, *All the Comforts of Home* (1890); light romantic comedies, *Too Much Johnson;* and spy thrillers, *Held By the Enemy* (1886) and *Secret Service.* In spite of the melodramatic structure, the spy dramas still play well to modern audiences because of their tightly constructed plots, intense situations, and believable characters.

His next great success represents another kind of drama for G.—the detective play. For *Sherlock Holmes* (1899), G. took three characters from the Doyle stories—Dr. Watson, Moriarty, and Holmes—added eighteen original characters and an original plot line, and created the play that still defines his career as actor and dramatist. In this play, G. popularized the use of the "fade-out" and the quiet act ending.

After the turn of the century, G. experimented with the one-act form in plays such as *The Painful Predicament of Sherlock Holmes* (1905), *The Red Owl* (1907), and *Among Thieves* (1907). After *Clarice,* his work did not seem to fit the new age in spite of his attempts to draw on new sources, such as in *Electricity* (1910), a romance featuring an electrician as a leading character. *With The Dream Maker* (1921) and *Winnie and the Wolves* (1923), he returned to his favorite theme of a character in difficult circumstances, but these adaptations of short stories were not successful.

The body of G.'s work is comprised of six dramatizations of fiction, two adaptations from German sources, four from French sources, and eight entirely original plays. In his original works, G. used native material and created distinctly American characters of variety, believability, originality, and a naturalness not found in earlier melodramas. His plots were plausible, action-driven, and contained carefully worked out stage business. In his acting and in his play writing, G. can be called the father of the realism of action.

BIBLIOGRAPHY: Cook, D. E., *Sherlock Holmes and Much More; or, Some of the Facts about W. G.* (1970); Quinn, A. H., *A History of the American Drama* (1936)

ALMA J. BENNETT

GILMAN, Caroline Howard

b. 8 October 1794, Boston, Massachusetts; d. 15 September 1888, Washington, D.C.

G. was arguably the best-known female author of the antebellum South and one of the first female magazine editors in the country. Although she wrote a number of volumes of fiction, poetry, and travel literature, her reputation rests on two early semiautobiographical works and her editorship of one of the earliest juvenile magazines in the U.S.

G. was drawn to literary expression at an early age, publishing her first poem at sixteen. In 1819, she moved to Charleston, South Carolina, where her clergyman husband, Samuel Gilman, was appointed rector of the Second Independent Church. Quickly adapting to her new environment, G. immersed herself not only in aiding her husband's religious instruction and in raising their seven children but in shaping a blossoming literary career. In addition to taking an active part in Charleston's intellectual and cultural milieu, she published a number of poems and sketches in local magazines and newspapers.

In 1832, when her children were old enough to give her more free time, G. instituted the *Rose Bud, or Youth Gazette,* a four-page weekly magazine devoted entirely to instruction and amusement for children. One of the first magazines of its type in the country, the *Rose Bud* included simple stories with clear morals, children's poems (though generally written from an adult perspective), local news items, and brief editorials on a variety of subjects. Religious or political controversy, however, was banned. G. wrote most of the contents herself, although she solicited contributions from young readers as well as other adults.

Beginning with the August 31, 1833 issue, she changed the magazine's name to the *Southern Rose Bud* and two years later altered the title again to the *Southern Rose.* The title changes reflected the magazine's movement toward a more mature audience, prompted largely by G.'s desire for a more sophisticated readership for her own poetry and prose. Until

its termination, the magazine continued to be the main outlet for G.'s literary production. In addition to numerous poems, sketches, articles, and editorials (many of which she continued to write herself), she serialized all of her major prose works of the 1830s in its pages. Her first two serials established her reputation as an author of adult works and would remain her most popular titles. *Recollections of a House Keeper,* serialized between December 28, 1833 and November 15, 1834 and published in book form in 1835, was a semi-autobiographical novel detailing with much color and humor the trials of a young married woman in running a house, especially in keeping and training servants. Published in the North, it became an extremely popular domestic novel and demonstrated G.'s proficiency in this genre. *Recollections of a Southern Matron,* serialized irregularly between March 7, 1835 and March 18, 1837 and published in 1838, is essentially a companion piece to her first book, with the setting moved from Boston to a South Carolina plantation. The degree to which G. had become "Southernized" is readily apparent: the Southern plantation is depicted as an idyllic world for master and slave alike. A pointed contrast is made between the happy, well-cared-for slaves and the miserable, exploited factory workers in the North. Never a feminist, G. made clear that the proper role for a woman, North or South, was to be an uncomplaining helpmate to her husband and a moral example to her children.

G. was never to repeat the success of her first two books. Her third adult novel, *Love's Progress; or, Ruth Raymond* (1840), is a short sentimental romance with Gothic elements. Lacking the humor and the attention to domestic detail that made her earlier works so appealing, the novel showed G.'s weakness in constructing extended characterization and plot. In addition to her three novels, G. is represented in several other genres. A group of travel essays and poems, most of them previously printed in her magazine, was collected under the title *The Poetry of Travelling in the United States* (1838). These diverse sketches and poems, divided into "Notes of a Northern Excursion" and "Notes of a Southern Excursion," are competent pieces, revealing G.'s careful detail to description and her clear admiration for monuments of historical significance or great natural beauty. Two volumes of verse—*Tales and Ballads* (1839) and *Verses of a Life Time* (1849)—are largely reprintings of poems that had appeared mainly in the *Southern Rose.* G.'s poems, often on themes of natural beauty or domestic bliss, are generally traditional in form and content. She also authored several collections of stories and poems for children. *Oracles from the Poets: A Fanciful Diversion for the Drawing-Room* (1844), *The Sibyl or New Oracles from the Poets* (1848), and *Oracles for Youth*

(1852) were selections from famous poems organized as fortune-telling games.

After a prolific decade of the 1840s, G. published very little except for several volumes for children. After the death of her husband in 1858 and the unsettling Civil War, she seems to have lost much interest in creative expression. Of four titles she wrote during the 1870s, two were collections of poetry and prose written with her daughter Caroline Howard Jervey, including *Stories and Poems by Mother and Daughter* (1872).

Although G. occasionally wrote poems and short sketches until a few years before her death at age ninety-three, her best work was accomplished in the 1830s. Her editorship of the *Rose-Bud* and her two domestic novels, *Recollections of a House Keeper* and *Recollections of a Southern Matron,* were the supreme achievements of her distinguished literary career.

BIBLIOGRAPHY: Bakker, J., "C. G. and the Issue of Slavery in the Rose Magazines," *SoSt* 24 (Fall 1985): 272–83; Hoole, W. S., "The Gilmans and the Southern Rose," *NCHR* 11 (April 1934): 116–28; McCanndless, A. T., "Concepts of Patriarchy in the Popular Novels of Antebellum Southern Women," *StPC* 10 (1987): 1–16

WILLIAM K. FINLEY

GILMAN, Charlotte Perkins [Stetson]

b. 3 July 1860, Hartford, Connecticut; d. 17 August 1935, Pasadena, California

G., writer and social reformer, was born and raised in Connecticut, but spent the formative years of her career in Pasadena, California. She was related through her father to the great New England clan sired by Lyman Beecher, including great-aunts Harriet Beecher STOWE and Catharine E. Beecher, as well as her uncle, the Unitarian minister and writer, Edward Everett HALE. While trained at the Rhode Island School of Design (1878–79), G. turned to writing as a profession with the publication of her first poem in 1884. Her national reputation was made with the poem "Similar Cases" (1890), a social satire, but it is a semiautobiographical short story, "The Yellow Wallpaper" (1892), that has come to be regarded as her masterwork, and one of the finest 19th-c. studies of psychosocial-sexual politics. Ostensibly a gothic tale of haunting and insanity, scholarship based on the story's reprinting in 1973 has illuminated the more complex connection between the story and G.'s own struggle with postpartum depression following her daughter's birth in 1886. G. had been treated for her breakdown by the famous nerve specialist, S. Weir MITCHELL, named in the story. This background is detailed in her autobiography, *The*

Living of Charlotte Perkins Gilman (1935), a memoir produced during the 1920s and revised by G. shortly before her death. Although contemporary readers of "The Yellow Wallpaper" responded first to the Gothic overtones of its main character's gradual mental deterioration while confined to a hideous, wall-papered room, recent views of the tale focus upon its early stream-of-consciousness technique, and its ultimate critique of the bonds of marriage and motherhood. The story's earliest admirer for both its craft and subject was William Dean HOWELLS.

G.'s prolific writing career flourished alongside her publicly acclaimed role as social activist and lecturer. Sympathetic at first to the goals of the Nationalist movement of the 1890s (particularly as based upon Edward BELLAMY's utopian romance, *Looking Backward*), G. soon evolved her own program, a consistent social philosophy based upon the role of women in the nation's economic progress. Of special interest to G. were alternative methods of childcare and designs for communal living that could relieve the burden of perpetual, ineffective "housework." This vision took shape through numerous articles and books of social philosophy, beginning with *Women and Economics* (1898), translated into seven languages in as many editions, followed by *Concerning Children* (1900), *The Home: Its Work and Influence* (1904), *Human Work* (1904), *Women and Social Service* (1907), and *His Religion and Hers* (1923). Through G.'s monthly magazine, the *Forerunner* (1909–16), dozens of articles, reviews, and serialized fiction were produced that also reflect this philosophy.

Her social "ethic" as described in her autobiography was based upon a "social evolution" defined as the product of "human work, in the crafts, trades, arts and sciences through which we are related, maintained and developed." Ultimate progress for women, G. believed, would be based even more upon their eventual economic "independence" than on the "ballot." G. was acquainted with Susan B. Anthony, Jane Addams, and Lucy Stone, as well as other women reformers of the national Women's Congress movement. She attended the International Socialist and Labor Congress in London in 1896, where she met Bernard Shaw and the Fabians.

Despite G.'s considerable output as a writer of short stories and novels, only one of her utopian romances, *Herland* (1915), has gained critical attention through its reprinting as a "lost" feminist novel in 1979. Its sequel, *With Her in Ourland* (1916), has been more recently noted in reconsiderations of G.'s contribution to women's utopian literature. The two novels trace the story of three male travelers lost in a female world evolved through parthenogenesis, and the return of one of its inhabitants to "our" world of early-20th-c.

America. Other novels—*What Diantha Did* (1910), *The Crux* (1911), *Moving the Mountain* (1911)—have been of interest solely for their connection to her larger social vision rather than for literary merit. The seventeen selections reprinted from *The Forerunner* that accompany "The Yellow Wallpaper" in *The Charlotte Perkins Gilman Reader* (1979) do not equal the innovative craft or powerful effect of that story's subject and central character. G.'s efforts to write drama and at least one detective story have not been published.

BIBLIOGRAPHY: Fleanor, J. E., "The Gothic Prison: C. P. G.'s Gothic Stories and Her Autobiography," in *The Female Gothic* (1983): 227–41; Hill, M. A., *C. P. G.: The Making of a Radical Feminist, 1860–1896* (1980); Kessler, D. G., "Brittle Jars and Brittle Jangles: Light Verse by C. P. G.," *Regionalism and the Female Imagination,* 4 (1979), 35–43; Lane, A. J., "The Fictional World of C. P. G.," *The C. P. Reader* (1979): ix–xlii; Scharnhorst, G., *C. P. G.* (1985)

E. SUZANNE OWENS

GILROY, Frank
b. 13 October 1925, New York City

Educated at Dartmouth College and Yale Drama School, G. has had a writing career that has produced many works but few unqualified successes, despite his evident skill as a playwright. Success for G., in fact, came early with *Who'll Save the Ploughboy?* (1962), the Obie Award-winning play set in New York City two days before Christmas 1959, and G.'s only Broadway triumph, *The Subject Was Roses* (1965), the Pulitzer Prize and Tony Award-winning drama that ran 832 performances. But theatrical success did not come often; most of G.'s many Broadway efforts have been flops.

Set in May 1946, the virtually actionless *The Subject Was Roses* focuses on a mother and father fighting for their son's respect and love upon his return from World War II. After two tension-filled days, the young man, originally played by a very young Martin Sheen, announces he is leaving. Grudgingly, his parents accept his decision. The play was directed by Ulu Grosbard, with whom G. often worked in the early stages of his theatrical career.

This family drama, which has been compared to Eugene O'NEILL's classic *Long Day's Journey into Night,* reveals how close human ties can bind even virtual strangers. The parents don't understand each other's frustrations, and certainly cannot appreciate their son and his desire for independence. In the tradition of O'Neill, and William INGE, the play grapples with issues of alienation, estrangement, and love. It

focuses on small details, and realistic, even uninteresting characters and dialogue. Yet beneath these pedestrian trappings lie much symbolism, such as the roses emotional connections with past happiness, and irony: the roses came from Timmy, the son.

More frequently, however, G.'s plays have not succeeded in New York, despite their local settings. *That Summer—That Fall* (1967), a New York drama, ran for only twelve performances, *Last Licks* (1979), set in Brooklyn, ran for just fifteen, and *Any Given Day* (1993), something of a prequel to *The Subject Was Roses,* ran for forty-three.

G.'s concrete writing style is characterized by an economy of effect, and naturalistic, even mundane dialogue. This "kitchen sink drama," popularized by O'Neill and others from the 1920s to the 1950s, deals with pipe dreams, wasted youth, and shattered hopes, suggesting that the real world is hard and unforgiving. It is a style that today is, perhaps, better suited for the more visually confined medium of television.

Despite his hard luck on the New York stage, G. has enjoyed much success, and has spent most of his career in Hollywood writing for television. He has also written several books, including *About Those Roses; or, How Not to Do a Play and Succeed* (1965), chronicling the making of *The Subject Was Roses* that G. wrote in Hollywood between screenplay-writing jobs. Interesting, particularly, to aspiring playwrights and producers, this production journal includes reviews of the show, and a budget breakdown among its many stories and descriptions.

BIBLIOGRAPHY: Coy, S. C., "F. G.," in MacNicholas, J., ed., *DLB,* vol. 7, part 1, *Twentieth-Century American Dramatists* (1981): 208–15

ERIC MARSHALL

GINSBERG, Allen
b. 3 June 1926, Newark, New Jersey; d. 5 April 1997, New York City

The work of G. has redirected American poetry, enriched American life and culture, and changed the course of history. Born in Newark, New Jersey, of Russian Jewish immigrant parents, G. grew up in nearby Paterson with his older brother Eugene; his father Louis, a college and high school teacher and a published poet; his mother Naomi, a communist whose beliefs conflicted with Louis's socialism, and whose mental anguish brought about extended stays in sanatoriums. Applying to Columbia University, G. prayed that he might "help mankind," and vowed to become an "honest revolutionary labor lawyer." At Columbia, he found academic literary perspectives inadequate in the face of New York street reality and the vast Whitmanesque sensibility he was coming to recognize in himself and others, and so drew inspiration from sympathetic new companions such as Jack KEROUAC and William S. BURROUGHS. But only a few months after his 1948 Columbia graduation, G. was found in the company—not the business—of thieves; in lieu of jail, a spell in a mental hospital followed, where he met fellow inmate and poet Carl Solomon. Solomon's influence would show in G.'s great long poem *Howl* (1956); another prominent influence on his verse beginning in the late 1940s was William Carlos WILLIAMS. Williams's whole approach to poetry, its humble phrasing, its resourceful use of the everyday, its commitment to "no ideas but in things"—had begun to displace the Renaissance models of Ginsberg's college days.

Howl, completed in his twenty-ninth year, brought fame and notoriety. Begun on an impulse "to follow my romantic inspiration—Hebraic Melvillian bardic breath," G. thought he "wouldn't write a *poem,* but just write what I wanted to without fear, let my imagination go, open secrecy, and scribble magic lines from my real mind . . . something I wouldn't be able to show anybody, writ for my own soul's ear and a few other golden ears." The result of a San Francisco summer 1955 afternoon at the typewriter was a draft—seventy-eight long lines—of the first part of what would become a long poem of three parts and a "Footnote": the entire composition would extend over six months. *Howl,* dedicated to Solomon, was brought out by City Lights in 1956. It revitalized American poetry in part by steering it away from T. S. ELIOT's "extinction of personality" and the New Critical confinement of poem to printed page. G.'s long "elastic line with fixed base" (the base being the anaphoric "Who" of part 1), intended for single-breath delivery, restored consciousness of poetry's living oral tradition, as did its many intralinear rhythmical pyrotechnics ("who lit cigarettes in boxcars boxcars boxcars," part 1; "Moloch! Solitude! Filth! Ugliness!," part 2). Its content—the lives, thoughts, actions, Dostoevskian conversations, and prayers of G. and his bohemian colleagues, who collectively became known, in Kerouac's phrasing, as the Beat generation—challenged prevailing norms of poetic self-effacement: from its opening lines *Howl* offered a multitude of personalities brought to startling life through the "I" of the poet.

In so doing, the poet maintained his commitment to "open secrecy": his poem was rich with homoerotic and heterosexual candor that confounded some of its McCarthy-Hoover-Dulles era readers as others rejoiced. An obscenity trial—unsuccessfully prosecuted—followed its publication. Though the poem displays organization in line and overall structure (its four parts consist of lament, cause of lament, litany, and benediction), cries of "formlessness" and "incoherence" were heard from some readers in the early years of its publication. Such complaints have diminished in recent decades, with more than one poet or critic from the academy "converting." Its experiments in form contributed centrally to later "open form" movements in American poetry; its unabashed content helped younger poets accept their own feelings as starting and end points for poetry. Its condensed imagery marked by a syntax that omits connectives in favor of juxtapositon (e.g., "hydrogen jukebox") within an expansive line accounts for some of its considerable power and influence. The multitude of its resonances encourages immensely rich and varied avenues of response, as readers and listeners discern echoes of numerous and disparate influences.

The frequently anthologized mock-heroic monologue "America" and the ruminative proclamation "Sunflower Sutra," contained in *Howl and Other Poems,* extended G.'s experiments with form, but his next major accomplishment was as unpredictable and unique as *Howl. Kaddish* (1961), a poem of five parts ("Proem," "Narrative," "Hymmnn," "Lament," "Litany & Fugue") more than twice the length of *Howl,* represented for G. "finally, completely free composition, the long line breaking up within itself into short staccato breath units." But *Kaddish*'s power far exceeds technique alone, for this "terrible masterpiece," as Robert LOWELL once called it, documents, in detail that is vivid, gruesome, and compassionate, the mental deterioration of G.'s mother Naomi from his first witness as prepubescent son through her numerous later hospital stays and shock treatments and lobotomy, to her death in asylum. Yet it simultaneously does more than that: it glimpses the industrial Northeast preparing for war; records the workaday assimilation, alienation, dreams, hallucinations, and internecine fighting within this immigrant family to the point of myth and archetype; implicitly proposes Naomi as ironic herald of all citizens beleaguered by high-tech spying and information gathering on the part of the state in later decades; and lays bare as perhaps no other elegy in English has a poet's striving to come to terms with death. Large areas of historical detail and present reflection ("Strange now to think of you, gone without corsets & eyes, while I walk on the sunny pavement of Greenwich Village," the "Proem" begins) alternate with stanzas of religious exhortation ("This is the end, the redemption from Wilderness, way for the Wonderer, House sought for All, black handkerchief washed clean by weeping—page beyond Psalm—Last change of mine and Naomi—to God's perfect

Darkness—Death, stay thy phantoms!" the "Proem" ends).

As G. continued to write and publish, he was also becoming an even more visible public figure, speaking and demonstrating for the legalization of marijuana, freedom from censorship, an end to America's war against Vietnam, and numerous other causes; in 1966, he informed a Senate subcommittee of the value of lysergic acid diethylamide (LSD) and cautioned against the passing of rigid drug laws. At the beginning of the 1970s, aiming to alleviate the domestic "law and order" problem and help end the war, he focused on historical and contemporary corruption in the criminalization of narcotics addicts and U.S. support of opium traffickers in Southeast Asia.

His many poems following *Kaddish* ranged widely in topic, tone, and style. Though perceived by the younger generation in America—and, to a degree, Eastern Europe—as one of their major exponents in the 1960s, G. also wrote poems of a particularly private nature. For example, "The Change" (1963) comes to grips with the fifteen-year influence of his empowering 1948 "auditory illumination," a transcendental experience wherein he heard a voice he took to be William Blake's. "The Change," written following his fifteen-month pilgrimage in India and first Zen Buddhist sitting meditation in Japan, replaces vision quest with appreciation of "Ordinary Mind." On the other hand, "Wichita Vortex Sutra" (1966) discovered war—specifically, America's in Vietnam—to be a matter of language and habit. It contains G.'s seminal pronouncement, "I here declare the end of the war."

From 1968—immediately after his return from the Democratic convention in Chicago—G.'s repertoire expanded into the realm of music: an album of Blake songs set to G.'s music in 1971; the publication in 1976 of the lyrics of his own *First Blues;* the release by John Hammond in 1983 of his recorded *First Blues,* with Bob DYLAN a sideman on some of the cuts. Numerous other collaborations followed, from Philip Glass's G.-inspired opera *Hydrogen Jukebox* (1990) to G.'s final return to London's Albert Hall (where he first read three decades earlier in 1965) for a performance with Paul McCartney. Among his many musical compositions, his "September on Jessore Road" (1971), an extended lament for the refugees of Bangladesh based on G.'s own eyewitness experience, may rank with any of his poems for power and compassion. "You can go anywhere with this song," musician John Lennon once told the poet. *Holy Soul Jelly Roll: Poems and Songs, 1949-1993* a four-compact disc selection of poems and songs, appeared in 1994 on Rhino Records; in 1996, a music video of G. performing his "Ballad of the Skeletons" was released under the direction of filmmaker Gus Van Sant.

Other later works pinpoint the overlap of "megastates" (the U.S. and the U.S.S.R.), as in "Birdbrain!" and "Capitol Air" (1980), while poems such as the Virgil-inspired "Ecologues" (1971) and G.'s declamatory "Plutonian Ode" (1978) variously address the themes of ecology and nuclear war. Throughout much of G.'s public-centered poetry, from the 1950s on, the fall of his nation/empire was a central theme, as announced in the title of his 1972 collection and 1974 National Book Award-winner *The Fall of America.* At the same time, G. continued to write poetry of intimacy, including the revealing sexual anthem, "Please Master" (1968) and the next decade's series of erotic poems such as "Lack Love" (1978), "Love Returned" (1978), "Some Love" (1979), and "Maybe Love" (1979). The poems are marked by their Sapphic influence, their simplicity, their candor not only about sex but the poet's own aging, perceived unattractiveness, and approaching impotence: "now I'm an old fairy," he tells himself in the last. A later lyric, "Autumn Leaves" (1992), concludes with the speaker's pronouncing himself "happy not yet / to be a corpse."

Equally important—after meeting his guru-to-be Chögyam Trungpa in 1971 and his taking of Buddhist vows in 1972—was the subject of meditation in his verse, as in the title poem of *Mind Breaths* (1978). G.'s Buddhism proposes compassion, generosity, amusement, and the debunking of sacred cows ("The heart, famous heart's a bag of shit I wrote 25 years ago"); most of all, "Awareness is prized" ("Manifesto," 1974). The potential of meditation to profoundly alter not only the individual but the world is asserted at the close of "Why I Meditate" (1981): "I sit for Jean-Arthur Rimbaud's Christmas on Earth / I sit for world revolution.

Motifs in G.'s works often repeat themselves in different forms. "White Shroud" (1983) is an epilogue or sequel to *Kaddish;* it is also a dream notation, and in its long, plain sentences, an example of the objectivist influence of Charles REZNIKOFF. Loss and particularly Naomi figure significantly in both early and late work; in conversation, he once suggested of *Howl* that "the substrate of emotions expressed in it relate to my mother, then confined in Pilgrim State Hospital, New York." Elsewhere, in his "Ego Confession" (1974), the poet allows that he had "had no subject but himself in many disguises."

As G. continued productive, his critical standing appeared increasingly impressive, if far from unanimous. His commitment, modeled after Kerouac, to spontaneity ("Mind is shapely, Art is shapely," he wrote on the composition of *Howl*) has triggered a number of enduring works of poetry and music, whether or not the original manuscript may, as in the case of *Howl,* be later revised. As earlier noted, the greater openness and diversity of form that has developed in American verse since the 1950s can be credited in part to his example and urgings; likewise, today's freer discussion of numerous topics such as homosexuality and heroin addiction may in good measure be owing to his personal and poetic candor. A shift in attitude and practice of poetic composition so as to include improvisation is in good measure owing to Kerouac (who, in an age dominated by guarded statements, drew sustenance from jazz musicians) and G. Some scholars believe that the inspiration of G. contributed to the downfall of Communist totalitarianism in the Eastern Bloc (in Prague 1965, he was elected King of May by 100,000 citizens, then deported by the government; when he returned in May 1990, the newly crowned king removed his crown and presented it to Ginsberg). Poets and dissidents from Poland, Rumania, the Soviet Union, and other Iron Curtain nations have attested to the influence of G.'s liberating spirit.

Among numerous other honors, he was inducted into the American Academy of Arts and Letters (1974); served as vice-president of the American chapter of PEN (1986); received the Struga [Yugoslavia] Golden Wreath (1986); was voted an honorary member of the Modern Language Association of America (1987); was knighted in the Order of Arts and Letters by the French Ministry of Culture (1993).

Complementing his many creations in poetry and music is his work in photography. As he wrote in the afterword to his first collection, *Photographs* (1990), he and Kerouac and others in their early days together saw themselves, their situations and relationships as sacred or "sacramental," "in 'a one and only' time in eternity": this with his continuing historical awareness and prescience resulted in his taking 80,000 images over the course of some five decades; the tutelage of Robert Frank and association with Berenice Abbott; and exhibits in many parts of the world, from Amsterdam to East Berlin to Tel Aviv.

His gifts at conversation and informal lecturing, as well as literary theorizing and application, are revealed in transcriptions such as *Allen Verbatim* (1974), *Gay Sunshine Interview* (1974), and *Composed on the Tongue* (1982). He was an omnivorous archivist; his collection of his own journals (three volumes were published in his lifetime), letters from other literary figures, ephemera, news clippings concerning the Beat generation and other cultural events and issues, were transferred from deposit at Columbia University to a permanent special collection at Stanford University in 1994.

Before G.'s death in 1997, he saw his work translated into forty-two languages. Cofounder of the Jack Kerouac School of Disembodied Poetics at Naropa Institute in 1974, he taught there every summer and some winters through 1996. He became Distinguished Professor at Brooklyn College in 1986. Though weakened in later years by ill health, he continued extraordinarily active, teaching, reading his work widely, giving benefits for other writers, artists, and causes until the final weeks preceding his death. Observed Gelek Rinpoche, who became G.'s guru after Trungpa's death in 1987, "He lived five lifetimes."

BIBLIOGRAPHY: Hyde, L., ed., *On the Poetry of A. G.* (1984); Kramer, J., *A. G. in America* (1968); Merrill, T. F., *A. G.* (1969); Miles, B., *G.: A Biography* (1989); Morgan, B., *The Works of A. G. 1941-1994: A Descriptive Bibliography* (1995); Morgan, B., *The Response to A. G., 1926-1994: A Bibliography of Secondary Sources* (1996); Morgan, B., and B. Rosenthal, eds., *Best Minds: A Tribute to A. G.* (1986); Portugues, P., *The Visionary Poetics of A. G.* (1978); Schumacher, M., *Dharma Lion: A Critical Biography of A. G.* (1992); Tytell, J., *Naked Angels: The Lives & Literatures of the Beat Generation* (1976)

GORDON BALL

GIOIA, [Michael] Dana
b. 24 December 1950, Los Angeles, California

G. is the most prominent figure associated with the New Formalism, a poetic movement first identified in the early 1980s by free versifiers who vilified it as an unwelcome "conservative" turn by American poets born largely after World War II. Ironically, it has turned out to be the most significant one to emerge in American poetry since the rise of the confessional poets in the 1960s.

G., a poet, critic, and translator, was educated at Stanford University, where the formalist aesthetic of Yvor WINTERS was still influential in the 1970s, and at Harvard, where he studied poetry with Elizabeth BISHOP and versification and the classical epic with Robert FITZGERALD. Ultimately, G. abandoned academia to pursue a career in business, and it is from this unique position as an executive at Kraft General Foods that G. wrote his two collections of poetry, *Daily Horoscope* (1986) and *The Gods of Winter* (1991), and the essays—most importantly "Notes on the New Formalism"—collected in *Can Poetry Matter?* (1992), nominated for the National Book Critics Circle Award in criticism. Taken together, these books both lay out and embody the aesthetic principles of the New Formalism. These encompass rhymed and metered personal lyrics that eschew the emotional extremity of the confessional lyric for a calmer, more elegiac tone, as well as blank verse narratives that, in their employment of fictional characters and stories, regain some of the territory modernist and postmodernist poetry had yielded to prose fiction.

G.'s most anthologized poem is "California Hills in August" from *Daily Horoscope.* Interestingly, this celebration of the muted beauty of the summer landscape of G.'s home state he feels non-natives are likely to overlook, while written in orderly five line stanzas, is actually one of his many free verse lyrics. Still, *Daily Horoscope* is replete with memorable formal lyrics, perhaps none more so than his disarming, autobiographical "Cruising with the Beach Boys," in which a song heard on a car radio by the poet on a business trip brings back memories of his "lovesick" adolescence in Los Angeles in the late 1960s. The free verse "Eastern Standard Time" registers G.'s multiple sense of uneasiness about being a poet in the modern world forced to make a living in business and of being a Californian living through a dark Northeastern fall. "The Man in the Open Doorway" depicts a businessman's addiction to his job, as well as its tediousness and lack of spirituality in the form of its rhymed quatrains and the metrically shortened fourth line of each modified Sapphic stanza. G. reuses this stanza again in "The Sunday News" to convey the sense of loss felt when coming upon the wedding announcement of a former lover. Finally, "In Cheever Country" presents a commuter train ride along the Hudson north of Manhattan—John CHEEVER country—a poem in which G. embraces this landscape as "home."

G. also proves himself a worthy heir to Robert Browning and Robert FROST in "The Room Upstairs," a dramatic monologue spoken by an aging professor reminiscing eerily upon a possibly homoerotic attachment to a student whose consummation occurred, if at all, after the boy's death in a dream. Death is a central theme in the two dramatic monologues that highlight *The Gods of Winter;* indeed, the entire volume is haunted by the crib death of G.'s first son, Michael Jasper, to whom it is dedicated. "Counting the Children," narrated by a Chinese American accountant, is at times a nightmarish meditation on this speaker's daughter's mortality and the nature of paternal love. The death of G.'s son is addressed directly in "Prayer" and "Planting a Sequoia." Eerily, G.'s love lyric addressed to his wife, "The Gods of Winter," appeared in the December 1987 issue *Poetry* the month of his son's death; its words and imagery—"Briefest of joys, our life together"—seem addressed to his son, *gioia* being Italian for joy.

The Gods of Winter also emphasizes the central role translation plays for G. as it includes his versions of poems by Rainer Maria Rilke, Nina Cassian, and Mario Luzi. In addition to coediting two volumes of

Italian poetry, G. has translated Eugenio Montale's *Motetti* (1990) and Seneca's *The Madness of Hercules* (1995). His poems have been set to music by such composers as Paul Salerni and Alva Henderson, the latter for whom he is writing the libretto for an opera based upon F. W. Murnau's silent film, *Nosferatu.*

BIBLIOGRAPHY: Truesdale, C. W., "D. G. on American Poetry," *NDQ* 61 (Summer 1993): 180–91; Turco, L., "D. G.," in Gwynn, R. S., ed., *DLB,* vol. 120, *American Poets since World War II* (1992): 84–90

ROBERT MCPHILLIPS

GIOVANNI, Nikki
b. 7 July 1943, Knoxville, Tennessee

G. has achieved what few living writers can claim, an unequivocal impact and renown while still early in her writing career. Her status as a major figure in 20th-c. literature rests on the publication of over fifteen collections of poetry and prose. Her work is overtly political and clearly female.

Born Yolande Cornelia Giovanni, Jr. in Knoxville, Tennessee, G. was reared in a suburb of Cincinnati, Ohio. In 1960, she entered Fisk University. Suspended, G. left Fisk only to return several years later, graduating magna cum laude in 1967. She then entered the Fisk writing program where she studied with John Oliver KILLENS. During this time, her politics moved away from the extreme right to the more radical left that she eventually championed in her work. In 1967, she planned the first Cincinnati Black Arts Festival. With this, G. became a major figure in the movement to advance black awareness in that city.

G.'s work reflects her political and personal growth. *Black Feelings, Black Talk* (1967) reads as an outspoken call for militant action for all black people. In this work is the first utterance of G.'s allegiance to the civil rights movement and the beginnings of the strong political currents that run all through her work.

Re-Creation (1970) shows a radical edge to G. that is not confined to her work. Throughout the collection is a tone of introspection and self-awareness that confounds a simplistic reading. *Gemini: An Extended Autobiographical Statement on My First Twenty-Five Years at Being a Black Poet* (1971) is a collection of autobiographical essays nominated for the National Book Award, a rare distinction for such a young writer. *My House* (1972), *The Women and the Men* (1972), and *Cotton Candy on a Rainy Day* (1978), subsequent volumes of G.'s poetry, continue in the political/personal realm, revealing the fluidity of human beliefs and perspectives.

Her numerous volumes of prose include *A Dialogue: James Baldwin and N. G.* (1973) a work that reads not only as a discussion between two writers, but of two generations of black Americans. G. has also written over six books of prose and poetry for children.

In 1997, *Love Poems* was published. The collection is a compilation of poems written over the previous two and one half decades. It once again introduces the undeniable connection of politics and intimacy that G. wields with her particular and distinctive voice.

BIBLIOGRAPHY: Bonner, C., "An Interview with N. G.," *BALF* 18 (Spring 1984): 29–30; Fowler, V. C., *N.G.* (1992); Mitchell, M. G., "N. G.," in Harris, T., and T. M. Davis, eds., *DLB* vol. 41, *Afro-American Poets since 1955* (1985): 135–51

MARIKA BRUSSEL

GLASGOW, Ellen [Anderson Gholson]

b. 22 April 1873, Richmond, Virginia; d. 21 November 1945, Richmond, Virginia

G. is a novelist of character and of manners, and her work is distinguished by her ability to blend comedy and tragedy, satire and irony. She wrote nineteen novels, twelve short stories, a volume of poetry, and autobiographical and critical writings. Her primary concern was to show the emptiness of the myths that masked the grimmer realities of life, and her best work focuses on the situation of the Southern woman who confronts and ultimately transcends disillusionment.

From her mother, Anne Jane Gholson Glasgow, a member of the Tidewater aristocracy, she inherited a sense of breeding and tradition; from her father, Francis Thomas Glasgow, of Scotch-Irish pioneer stock, she received a strong determination and business acumen. G. attributed her vision of the world to her mixed heritage. Although she was one of ten children, G. saw herself as essentially isolated, and her deafness at the age of sixteen contributed to her loneliness. Her mother's death when G. was twenty was a serious shock and deepened her alienation from the family. G.'s numerous female character who must cope with serious illness have been attributed to G.'s won ill health as well as that of her mother.

G. never married, although she had prolonged relationships with two men, "Gerald B—," a married man, and "Harold S—" (Henry W. Anderson), a relationship enduring for nearly thirty years, although the course of it was not smooth—she attempted suicide after an early quarrel.

She wrote her first novel, "Sharp Realities," at seventeen, but after an interview with a literary agent (who told her to go home and have babies) she destroyed the manuscript. Shortly thereafter, she wrote *The Descendant,* and although she destroyed that manuscript at her mother's death, she subsequently rewrote it. Her first two novels, *The Descendant* (1897) and *The Phases of an Inferior Planet* (1898), focus on male characters who rebel against convention and on female characters who struggle to become artists. Marked by didacticism and melodrama, these novels nonetheless sketch themes and character types that G. will later develop with greater skill. In contrast to these apprentice works, both of which are set in New York, is *The Voice of the People* (1900), her first Virginia novel, which explores the political aftermath of Reconstruction. This novel, the first of many that G. would write about Virginia's social history, is notable in its evocation of regional atmosphere and its rendering of character and action.

In *The Battle-Ground* (1902), G. looked further into the past to the Civil War. Although the novel describes the aristocracy of prewar Virginia, it does not sentimentalize the harsh realities of the war. The novel traces the fortunes of two aristocratic families in a Virginia torn by war, and focuses on the relationship between Dan Montjoy and Betty Ambler, whose love survives the confection and the destruction of the families's plantations. While the novel may seem dated in comparison with the war fiction that followed, its treatment of the war's romantic and realistic aspects distinguished it from previous Civil War novels.

With *The Deliverance* (1904), G. returns to the Reconstruction to explore the class conflicts dividing Virginia society after the war. That conflict is depicted in the complex relations between two families, the Blakes and the Fletchers, who dispossess the Blakes of their plantation. The novel's hero, Christopher Blake, is driven to murder because of the hatred he bears toward the Fletchers, but after he is freed from prison he returns to his ancestral home and to Maria Fletcher, whom he loves. *The Deliverance* is distinguished by G.'s skill in blending tragic and comic elements and in portraying characters from a range of social classes.

G.'s next two novels, *The Wheel of Life* (1906) and *The Ancient Law* (1908), are more on a level with the apprentice work, and G. excluded them from her collected work, published in 1938. *The Wheel of Life* attempts to re-create New York bohemian life, with which G. was not familiar; *The Ancient Law* is set in Virginia, but relies on melodrama and stereotyped characters. In *The Romance of a Plain Man* (1909), G. wrote a "heroic romance" chronicling the rise of a man from poverty to social acceptance in turn-of-the-century Richmond, with G. relying upon her own childhood memories to describe the city. *The Miller of Old Church* (1911) examines to the conflict between the aristocracy and the yeomanry first sketched in *The Deliverance*. The novel details the lives of a large cast of characters in the rural community of Old Church, focusing on the romantic relationships among them. Molly Merryweather, who brings together in her character the aristocratic and the common, is the novel's center of action and foreshadows G.'s future concern with the Southern woman, a concern that would distinguish her best work.

G.'s next two novels, *Virginia* (1913) and *Life and Gabriella* (1916), do in fact concentrate on the Southern woman. *Virginia* is G.'s portrait of a lady: Virginia Treadwell, who has been reared to the ideal Southern lady, but who must exist in a less than ideal world. She is trapped in an unfulfilling marriage and is ignored by her children, and the novel details her inner desolation; the only way she endures her situation is with selfless devotion. *Life and Gabriella,* in contrast, depicts the New Woman in a changing South. Gabriella is a successful businesswoman who is able to retain her ladylike qualities.

The two novels that follow these "portraits" do not maintain the high level of technical skill of the previous novels. Both *The Builders* (1919) and *One Man in His Time* (1922) are political novels, but G. does not integrate the rhetoric of politics with the novel's plot or development of character, and the characters themselves tend toward stereotype.

In *Barren Ground* (1925) however, generally recognized as G.'s masterpiece, G. returns to her focus on a central female character. Dorinda Oakley is seduced by the man she loves, Jason Greylock, and is abandoned; but she is not defeated by the loss of her love. Rather, she channels her energy into turning the land, which has destroyed her parents, into a successful dairy farm. In the end, Dorinda triumphs over Jason—she buys the Greylocks' farm and takes care of Jason, who dies of alcoholism—and creates a life for herself. Although Dorinda declares herself glad that she is done with love, the novel leaves open the question that in so doing Dorinda has a diminished existence. G.'s rendering of character is skillful, but the novel's genius lies in its unwavering focus on Dorinda, G.'s transformation of the land into a living presence, and her ability to integrate the symbolic overtones of the landscape into the novel's characters.

G. then turned from the novel of character to the novel of manners. Her next three novels, *The Romantic Comedians* (1926), *They Stooped to Folly* (1929), and *The Sheltered Life* (1932) examine Southern manners and morals in the city of Queensborough, clearly modeled on Richmond. In *The Romantic Comedians,* G. sketches a May-December romance, in which Judge Gamaliel Honey marries and is deserted by a girl of twenty-three. The novel closes with the old Judge flirting with the nurse who is taking care of him. In *They Stooped to Folly,* G. focuses on women who have been seduced or have fallen; the novel is told from the perspective of a very conventional couple, Virginius and Victoria Littlepage. In *The Sheltered Life,* the darkest of the comic trilogy, G. traces the members of three generations of Virginians at the turn of the century. Eva Birdsong, one of the most developed characters in the novel, is yet another portrait of the Southern lady; here she devotes her life to maintaining appearances and sacrificing personal happiness. She shoots her unfaithful husband when she discovers him embracing Jenny Blair, the vivacious granddaughter of the Birdsongs' next door neighbor. In all three novels, G.'s concerns are the conflicts between the generations and the problems associated with love relationships. These novels, which are considered to be among G.'s best, explore the comic side of human affairs, in contrast to the novels of character—*Virginia, Life and Gabriella,* and *Barren Ground*—which focus on the tragic dimensions of human nature.

G.'s last two novels, *Vein of Iron* (1935) and *In This Our Life* (1941), return to that tragic dimension. Ada Fincastle, the novel's heroine and primary point-of-view character, is another of G.'s strong women. Although she is subjected to hardship, she is never hardened as is Dorinda Oakley. Ada's "vein of iron" enables her to endure seeing her fiancé married to a woman who traps him in a compromising situation, to bear his child out of wedlock, and to care for him when he is paralyzed in a car accident. The image of a "vein of iron" runs throughout G.'s fiction; in this novel she explicitly dramatizes the endurance and resilience it gives her women characters.

G.'s final completed novel, *In This Our Life,* returns to Queensborough on the eve of the Second World War to depict a family of "happiness-hunters." In many ways this novel brings G.'s social history of Virginia full circle, for she returns to the class conflicts that dominated her early work. The novel details the decline of an upperclass family, the Timberlakes, and the difficulties besetting the Clays, descended from slaves. Although the novel is flawed—G. was ill when she wrote it—it is notable for G.'s fair treatment of blacks at a time when the South was still segregated. The novel was awarded a Pulitzer Prize in 1942, although critical consensus holds that it was given more out of recognition for G.'s work as a whole than for this particular novel. It was made into a successful film starring Olivia de Havilland, Bette Davis, and Dennis Morgan. In 1944, G. wrote a short sequel, *Beyond Defeat,* published in 1966, and that shows the main characters from the 1941 novel creating new lives for themselves in California.

In addition to the novels, G. wrote poetry that she considered revolutionary, but that has only literary interest today. She also wrote short stories throughout her career, which have been collected into a single volume, *The Collected Stories of E. G.* (1963), edited by Richard K. Meeker. Her topics range from the relations between men and women, the supernatural, and moral dilemmas; and although the stories are competent, G.'s talent is best expressed in the novel's larger purview.

G. also wrote nonfiction, most notably her autobiography, *The Woman Within* (1954), and prefaces for her novels, *A Certain Measure: An Interpretation of Prose Fiction* (1943). G.'s autobiography describes her life as a "long tragedy" of family conflicts, disappointment, illness, and isolation. Although it has been dismissed as "some of G.'s best fiction," it has interest for the insight it offers on G.'s ability to deal with deprivation and hardship. The collected prefaces also illuminate G.'s life: as her autobiography describes "the woman within," the prefaces illuminate G. as writer as well as the genesis, purpose, and themes of the novels.

G.'s best work falls into two triads: *Virginia, Barren Ground,* and *Vein of Iron,* the portraits of strong female characters; and *The Romantic Comedians, They Stooped to Folly,* and *The Sheltered Life,* the comedies of manners. As this division suggests, G.'s particular genius lies in her ability to explore the Southern woman and to examine Southern society. Although her fiction is strongly colored by a particular time and place, G. clearly transcends regionalism through her concerns about the relations between classes, generation, and the sexes; and through her skill in depicting the "land as a living personality, and [portraying] its characteristics in the central figures."

BIBLIOGRAPHY: Godbold, E. S., Jr., *Letters of E. G.* (1958); Godbold, E. S., Jr., *E. G. and the Woman Within* (1972); Kelly, W. W., *E. G.: A Bibliography* (1964); MacDonald, E. E., and T. B. Inge, *E. G.: A Reference Guide* (1986); McDowell, P. W., *E. G. and the Ironic Art of Fiction* (1960); Raper, J. R., *Without Shelter: The Early Career of E. G.* (1971); Raper, J. R., *From the Sunken Garden: The Fiction of E. G., 1916–1945* (1980); Richards, M. K., *E. G.'s Development as a Novelist* (1971); Rouse, B., *E. G.* (1962); Santa, J. F., *E. G.'s American Dream* (1965); Seidel, K. L., *The Southern Belle in the American Novel* (1985); Wagner, L. W., *E. G.: Beyond Convention* (1982)

JUDITH E. FUNSTON

GLASPELL, Susan [Keating]

b. 1 July 1876, Davenport, Iowa; d. 27 July 1948, Provincetown, Massachusetts

G. was profoundly affected by her Midwestern roots throughout her writing career, which falls roughly into three periods. As a successor to Alice FRENCH, the local colorist of Davenport, G. began by writing short stories, which appeared in women's magazines at the beginning of this century and some of which were later collected in *Lifted Masks* (1912). Although G. drew realistic subjects from her experiences as a reporter, the stories are flawed by sentimentalism.

G.'s story-writing continued throughout her life, though by 1910 she had written the majority of them. After completing two novels, *The Glory of the Conquered* (1909) and *The Visioning* (1911), she met George Cram Cook, a friend of Floyd Dell and associated with Chicago's "Little Renaissance." Their marriage in 1913 marked the beginning of a successful collaboration in the theater, he organizing the Provincetown Players and she writing a series of one-act satires (1915–19) and four full-length plays (1921–30). Eugene O'NEILL, John Reed, and Edna St. Vincent MILLAY also were active with the Provincetown Players. G.'s work blends European experimental theater with American REALISM, but her distinguishing quality is her focus on the psychological development of character. *Alison's House* (1930), which won a Pulitzer Prize, and which is based on the life of Emily DICKINSON, is typical of her thematic interests and dramatic techniques. In portraying a family torn apart by having to decide whether to publish Alison's poetry, G. depicts the conflict between private, family values and the public obligation as heirs to a poet. Alison, like several of G.'s strong women characters, never appears on the stage.

When the Provincetown Players became commercially successful, and so losing their unique quality as experimental theater, Cook and G. moved to Greece where G. concentrated on novel-writing. During the years from 1928 to 1945, she wrote seven novels, of which four—*Ambrose Holt and Family* (1931), *The Morning Is Near Us* (1939), *Norma Ashe* (1942), and *Judd Rankin's Daughter* (1945)—are considered her best fiction. She returned to the interests of her early fiction, particularly the Midwestern milieu and its mores, but successfully avoided the sentimentality of her short stories. Her later fiction bears the imprint of her play writing experience, including tight, memorable scenes and the dramatic presentation of character through dialogue. *Judd Rankin's Daughter,* her last and most dramatic novel, examines the conflict between tradition and new values through Judd Rankin, a Midwestern newspaper editor, and his daughter Frances. G.'s resolution strikes a balance between the old and the new in a chaotic postwar world, and achieves this through Judd Rankin's idealism.

G.'s fiction is not her strongest work—she tends to overuse flashbacks and the dramatic scene as narrative devices. Nevertheless, her later novels should not be dismissed; G. deftly captures the thought processes of her characters in accessible, sprightly, and colloquial prose. Currently, however, her reputation rests on her dramatic work, both through her connection with the Provincetown Players and her own plays. Her commitment to social realism and experimentation has shaped the course of American drama.

BIBLIOGRAPHY: Bach, G., "S. G.: A Bibliography of Dramatic Criticism," *Great Lakes Review* 3, 2 (1977):1–34; Makowsky, V., *S. G.'s Century of American Women: A Critical Interpretation of Her Work* (1993); McGovern, E., "E. G.," in Mainiero, L., ed., *American Women Writers* (1980): 144–46; Ozieblo, B., "S. G.," in Bloom, C., ed., *American Drama* (1995): 6–20; James, E. T., ed., *Notable American Women* (1971); Waterman, A. E., *S. G.* (1966)

JUDITH E. FUNSTON

GLÜCK, Louise [Elisabeth]

b. 22 April 1943, New York City

Since the publication of her first two books, *Firstborn* (1968) and *The House on Marshland* (1975), G. has been recognized among her peers as one of the leading contemporary poets. With the appearance of her subsequent volumes, *Descending Figure* (1980), *The Triumph of Achilles* (1985), and *Ararat* (1990), her critical reputation is assured—*The Triumph* having won the National Book Critics Circle Award. In addition to having won numerous other prizes, including the Sara Teasdale Memorial Prize, G.'s work has already been included in many of the major contemporary anthologies, as well as having been translated and published in Sweden, Japan, Italy, Spain, and Brazil. Few poets of her age have earned such widespread recognition.

G. was born in New York City, reared on Long Island, and attended Sarah Lawrence College briefly. Later, at Columbia University, she studied with Stanley KUNITZ and has subsequently taught writing herself at a number of institutions, including the University of Iowa, Columbia, Goddard College, Warren Wilson, and Williams College, among others. One of her former students is Jorie GRAHAM, another poet who has already earned a substantial reputation. G. has also served as judge of several poetry competitions, most notably the Lamont Poetry Prize.

While obviously very involved with the writing profession, G. remains in her poetry intensely private. Her most characteristic mode is the confessional lyric, though it is drawn on a hard edge that threatens at once to shatter into cutting truths (*the* truth being consistently and painfully beyond reach) or to dissolve into a nearly macabre beauty. This odd combination not only yields extremely intense verse, but also defines her distinctive tone—dreamy, inviting, and ruthless. The radiance she evokes in poem after poem is always ringed with arrows. Nevertheless, in her later verse G. has achieved something of an intellectual balance that mediates between calculated control and compassion, and her last two volumes are marked by a new vulnerability.

G.'s most characteristic theme is the fact and inevitability of loss, whether in love, life, or language. This theme has a variety of manifestations, most commonly in the figures of alienated mothers, fathers, sisters, children, or simply remembered places. However, her most important theme and image is the wound—in particular the wounding of the feminine by actual male aggression or by a cultural, "phallocentric" inscription. This figuration provides a critical link between her first volume, which includes a poem specifically entitled "The Wound," and her later work, with the "triumph" of Achilles resting precisely in his ability to be wounded, to feel love, to be mortal, and with G.'s overtly stated ability in *Ararat* to be wounded, herself—and to love. While not a feminist poet in the sense that Adrienne RICH is, G. records in her five volumes a particular psychic growth: from the ruthless exposure of sexual wounding, through specifically revisionary poems that (disturbingly) retell famous myths and poems from a woman's perspective, to a point of acceptance, even confirmation, of human (rather than strictly feminine) vulnerability. Her own triumph is that in her latest work she has already achieved in the measure of her verse what Wallace STEVENS would come to call the "finally human."

BIBLIOGRAPHY: Bonds, D. S., "Entering Language in L. G.'s *The House on Marshland:* A Feminist Reading," *ConL* 31 (1990): 58–75; Keller, L., "'Free/of Blossom and Subterfuge': L. G. and the Language of Renunciation," in Trawick, L. M., ed., *World, Self, Poem* (1990): 120–29; Kuzma, G., "Rock Bottom: L. G. and the Poetry of Dispassion," *MQ* 24 (1983): 468–81; Miklitsch, R., "Assembling a Landscape: The Poetry of L. G.," *HC* 19, 4 (1982): 2–13

JACQUELINE VAUGHT BROGAN

GODFREY, Thomas

b. 4 December 1736, Philadelphia, Pennsylvania; d. 3 August 1763, Wilmington, North Carolina

G. was author of *The Prince of Parthia,* the first American play to be staged by professional actors in this country. While living in Wilmington, North Carolina, G., in 1759, sent a copy of the play to his former teacher, William SMITH, provost of the College and Academy of Philadelphia, and asked him to have it produced by the Douglas Company, then in Philadelphia. However, the play was not produced, and G.

died before his tragedy was ever performed. It was not until April 24, 1765, that the drama was acted when the company substituted it for an announced presentation of *The Disappointment; or, The Force of Credulity*. Nathaniel Evans, a friend of G.'s, published the play along with some of his poems in 1767 under the title *Juvenile Poems on Various Subjects with the Prince of Parthia, A Tragedy*.

Set in ancient Parthia, the play tells of the misfortunes of Arsaces, his beloved Evanthe, and of the treachery that brings about their deaths. Arsaces is the target of the king's second wife, Queen Thermusa, because he has killed her only son in battle. The king also turns on Arsaces because he wants Evanthe for himself. Vardanes, brother to Arsaces, hates him as well as the king, and plots their ruin. Vardanes has the king murdered, then is on the point of raping Evanthe when Arsaces arrives to rescue her. During the climatic struggle, Evanthe, mistakenly believing Vardanes has slain Arsaces, takes poison. She dies in the arms of her lover, who, grief stricken, falls on his sword. Gotarzes, young brother to Arsaces, survives to rule the empire.

Although G.'s plot is original, the play reveals indebtedness to Shakespeare's *Hamlet, MacBeth, Othello, Romeo and Juliet, Julius Caesar,* and *King Lear*. Other Shakespearean touches—the themes of brother against brother, father against child, also figure significantly in the work. the structure of the play is simple, the characters without much shading or complexity. Vardanes is most interesting because of his evil plotting. Oddly enough, he sings a love song to Evanthe just before he attempts to ravish. G. makes an attempt at placing his characters and action on a mythic level—part of the action takes place before the Temple of the Sun, and Arsaces and Evanthe represent light and beneficent power, while Vardanes and his cohort Lysias suggest darkness and evil. In his soliloquy in scene 9, act 3, Vardanes sees himself as a Satanlike figure whose acts shake the whole world. At the very least, the power struggle within a noble family that destroys itself, the bizarre sexual undercurrents, and G.'s verse are dramatic elements that give the play some distinction.

BIBLIOGRAPHY: McCarrion, W. E., ed., *A Bicentennial Edition of T. G.'s The Prince of Parthia, A Tragedy* (1976); Meserve, W. J., *An Emerging Entertainment: The Drama of the American People to 1828* (1977)

EDMUND M. HAYES

GODWIN, Gail
b. 18 June 1937, Birmingham, Alabama

From her first published novel entitled *The Perfectionists* (1970) to *The Good Husband* (1994), Southern writer G. has won critical acclaim as she has produced increasingly sophisticated works of fiction that mirror the postmodern dilemmas of the last three decades. Her reputation has grown with the successive publication of her nine novels and two volumes of short stories. Two of the novels, *Violet Clay* (1978) and *A Mother and Two Daughters* (1982), were nominees for the National Book Award, and in 1981, G. received an Award in Literature from the American Institute and Academy of Arts and Letters. While her two volumes of short stories, *Dream Children* (1976) and *Mr. Bedford and the Muses* (1983), traverse the same fictional territory as her novels, it is on these novels that G.'s critical reputation rests.

From the beginning of her career, G. has focused on female characters and problems of self definition in the marriages they make, the families they belong to, the regions and cultures they identify with, and the work they choose. She has continued to resist the postmodern erasure of self and its accompanying minimalist forms, instead adhering to a belief in the possibility of a coherent self realizable in traditional narrative structures. Her first two novels, *The Perfectionists* and *Glass People* (1972), explore the intimacies of the marriage relationship and the problems that arise when the two partners have different expectations of it. Dane and John Empson in *The Perfectionists* intellectualize their relationship as they strive for some textbook version of marriage that is continually marred by the realities around them, not the least of which is John Empson's three-year-old illegitimate son. Similarly, Francesca Bolt in *Glass People* finds herself trapped in a sterile marriage to a wealthy, powerful man who regards her as little more than a beautiful ornament gracing his career. Her largely ineffectual efforts to escape his clutches end in failure, as the novel closes with Francesca back home and pregnant, agreeing to a compromised relationship.

G.'s increasing mastery both of the novel form and her theme of individuation is evident in the next two novels, *The Odd Woman* (1975) and *Violet Clay,* which deal with unmarried professional women affirming their commitment to their work—Jane Clifford in the first novel is a literature teacher in search of "a metaphor of her own," and Violet Clay is an artist. In these novels, female relationships begin to emerge as increasingly important to the heroines' self-definition.

Marking a turning point in G.'s career, *A Mother and Two Daughters* strikes a new chord in its use of multiple points of view, unlike the largely first-person narratives of the previous novels, and in its sharing the dramatic stage with three female protagonists—Nell, the mother, and Cate and Lydia, the daughters. The contemporary South emerges as a powerful presence in this novel through G.'s penetrating analyses of the perennial issues of family, social class, and race. The novel ultimately affirms in Emersonian fashion the importance of connectedness in its delineation of the mother-daughter relationship as well as the sibling relationship of Cate and Lydia.

An important subtext of G.'s novels, beginning with *Violet Clay,* is the relationship of art to life and the choices women artists face as they attempt to mediate between the two. *The Finishing School* (1984) takes up this theme as its artist-heroine, Justin Stokes, narrates the story of her relationship with a powerful older female mentor and her subsequent disenchantment as she matures. As G.'s next novel, *A Southern Family* (1987), makes clear, these earlier attempts at portraying artist heroines were preparatory sketches for her first writer-heroine, Clare Campion who, like G., must wrestle with the limits of narrative. In trying to account for her brother's suicide, Clare must come to terms with her theory of fiction as well as her theories about her own family's story. These metafictional concerns marked a new direction in G.'s oeuvre.

Father Melancholy's Daughter (1991) and *The Good Husband* expand G.'s fictional concerns to include the mystical and spiritual dimensions of individuation. As their titles indicate, these works continue to probe the complex family and personal relationships defining us—the former novel through the character of Margaret Gower, child of a troubled Episcopalian minister whose wife leaves him when Margaret is a schoolgirl; the latter novel, like its suggested predecessor, Ford Madox Ford's *The Good Soldier,* by giving us the tale of two marriages and the writer-figures enmeshed in them. Multiple viewpoints enrich these two narratives as do the numerous intertextual references to writers as varied as George Herbert and William Blake.

Always conscious of herself as part of a community of writers and a distinguished novelistic tradition, G. continues to explore the possibilities of achieving wholeness in a fragmented, postmodern world, as illustrated in *The Good Husband,* which articulates most forcefully her belief in art's ongoing dialogue with and about the self.

BIBLIOGRAPHY: Hill, J., *G. G.* (1992); Wimsatt, M. A., "G. G.," in Flora, J. M., and R. Bain, eds., *Contemporary Fiction Writers of the South: A Bio-Biographical Sourcebook* (1993): 193-201; Xie, L., *The Evolving Self in the Novels of G. G.* (1995)

MARY ANN WILSON

GOLD, Herbert
b. 9 March 1924, Cleveland, Ohio

G. is one of America's most prolific contemporary writers. As a novelist, short story writer, essayist, and journalist, he has written on an impressively wide range of subjects. He has received a Fulbright Fellowship, a Hudson Review Fellowship, a Guggenheim Fellowship, a National Institute of Arts and Letters grant, a Longview Foundation Award, and a Ford Theater Fellowship. Yet for all of his publications, artistic range, and professional recognition, he has never garnered a solid and lasting reputation within the academic community.

The reason behind this may be that G. and his writing are difficult to categorize, which may suggest more about academic practices than it does G.'s work. He has been read as a Jewish American novelist, a naturalist in the tradition of Theodore DREISER and James T. FARRELL, a postwar neorealist, a Californian bohemian writer, and an ethnic autobiographer, all of which pertain to various facets of his writings, but none of which aptly encapsulate his eclectic literary output. Perhaps it is his broad scope, his resistance to be pigeonholed, that has worked against G.'s reputation within academia.

Nonetheless, as a novelist and as a cultural critic, G. deserves respect and attention. His early writings demonstrate acute cultural insight. In novels such as *Birth of a Hero* (1951), *The Prospect before Us* (1954), *The Man Who Was Not with It* (1956), *The Optimist* (1959), and *Salt* (1963), G. explores the personal goals of his generation. He condemns those who mindlessly seek material security and success, and laments the absence of critical introspection. For instance, in *The Man Who Was Not with It,* considered by some to be G.'s best novel, he presents the lives of two carnival men entangled in a life of drugs and torn between the need for gratification and the desire for deeper meaningful relationships. And in *Slave Trade* (1979) and *He/She* (1980), G. looks at the breakdown of marriage as an American institution.

Other works similarly engage in cultural introspection, but do so by contrasting the life of his present generation to that of his parents. Many times, he presents the insecurities of his parents' generation as spawning a more sincere dedication and appreciation of life, especially when compared to the relative comfort of his own. *Fathers: A Novel in the Form of a Memoir* (1967) contrasts the lives of G.'s father, an immigrant survivor who knows how uncertain life can be but is willing to live with it, and G. himself, who wants nothing more than his father to be happy and secure. In *Family: A Novel in the Form of a Memoir* (1981), he explores similar generational attitudes, but this time in terms of his mother. And in *My Last Two Thousand Years* (1972), G. takes a broader look at his ethnic history and tries to discover what it means to be a Jew and a writer in America. Together these three books are both an autobiographical sketch of the writer's life and a larger cultural statement of an individual's place within contemporary America.

Since the late 1960s, G. has shifted his narrative focus to the West Coast. Works such as *The Great American Jackpot* (1969), *Swiftie the Magician* (1974), *Waiting for Cordelia* (1977), *Travels in San Francisco* (1989), and *She Took My Arm As If She Loved Me* (1997) are all set in California and respond to the social concerns there over the past thirty years. *Bohemia: Where Art, Angst, Love, and Coffee Meet* (1993) is a look back at the bohemian meccas of the 1950s—San Francisco, Greenwich Village, Paris, Morocco, even Tel Aviv—that further expands G.'s literary horizons. G.'s growth as a writer is indeed significant, for in many ways he chronicles the changes the nation has undergone in the last half of the 20th c.

BIBLIOGRAPHY: Moore, H. T., "The Fiction of H. G.," in *Contemporary American Novelists* (1964): 170–81; Tooker, D., and R. Hofheins, "H. G.," in *Fiction! Interviews with Northern California Novelists* (1976): 111–23. Wohlgelernter, M., "H. G.: A Boy of Early Autumn," *SAJL* 10 (Fall 1991): 136–71.

DEREK PARKER ROYAL

GOODMAN, Paul

b. 9 September 1911, New York City; d. 2 August 1972, North Stratford, New Hampshire

Although his posthumous reputation is chiefly that of a social critic and educational gadfly, G. himself had hoped that his literary work would be his greatest and most enduring legacy. It is more likely that he will continue to be best remembered as the adopted father-figure of the American student left, with which he shared a mutual admiration, in the 1960s and 1970s. His notoriety as an activist and polemicist has now all but eclipsed the fact that he was a prolific novelist, poet, playwright, and literary critic, and that he had already published over a dozen books of poetry, fiction, and essays in the 1940s and 1950s, long before he became a public figure on the American cultural and political landscape. In the 1950s, he also had four plays produced Off-Broadway. By 1959, he had collected four of his novels into the tetralogy *The Empire City*—among his other novels are *The Grand Piano* (1949) and *Making Do* (1963). Given G.'s role as an educational iconoclast, it is also easy to forget that he held a Ph.D., and that in 1954 his *The Structure of Literature* appeared under the imprint of the University of Chicago Press.

G.'s admirers have long tried to rescue his literary reputation, especially as a writer of short stories—"Iddings Clark" and the experimental "The Wandering Boys" have been singled out in particular. They often cite an affinity with Nathaniel HAWTHORNE, particularly in his sketches and tales. G.'s poetry has its admirers, too, but on balance it is difficult to like or appreciate. It is, in the end, not very "poetic": declarative rather than figurative, declamatory rather than evocative. G. defended his collection *The Lordly Hudson: Collected Poems* (1962) by saying that he was not interested in producing "individual beautiful poems."

G.'s first major venture into social criticism was *Communitas: Means of Livelihood and Ways of Life* (1947), written with his brother Percival. It was the reissue of this book in 1960 that set the stage for G.'s rise to national prominence, and it was a succession of books in the 1960s and 1970s on which his current reputation largely devolves: *Growing Up Absurd* (1960), *The Community of Scholars* (1962), *Utopian Essays and Practical Proposals* (1962), *Compulsory Mis-Education* (1964), *New Reformation: Notes of a Neolithic Conservative* (1970), and *Speaking and Language* (1971), which is somewhat audaciously subtitled *Defense of Poetry*.

To G.'s critics, and they have always been legion, his writings merely gave the young what they wanted to hear: a scathing critique of the established political order and of American education at all levels, packaged in an anarchist/populist rhetoric. Coming from someone well over the then-benchmark age of thirty, G.'s polemics lent an aura of legitimacy to some of the more radical impulses of the protest generation, including its romantic anti intellectual tendencies. Despite the fact that many of these ideas—to abolish national boundaries, for example, or to return the university to its medieval origins—seem in retrospect naive and utopian, they come from a deeply-felt sense of mission and, even G.'s adversaries concede, from a man of great integrity. There is more consistency to G.'s passions than is often acknowledged: his interest in psychotherapy, for example, was evident as early as the 1950s, when, together with Frederick Perls and Ralph Hefferline, he published *Gestalt Therapy* in 1951. Even his infatuation with the theories of Wilhelm Reich had, like most of his enthusiasms, more than a little of Walt WHITMAN and Rousseau about it. G.'s *Collected Stories* (4 vols., 1978–80) and *Collected Poems* (1974), both edited by Taylor Stoehr, were published posthumously. Read in retrospect, his literary work shares with his other writing a praiseworthy vitality and idealism, but also a deep impatience and sense of alienation.

BIBLIOGRAPHY: Nicely, T., and B. I. Weiss, *Adam and his Work: A Bibliography of Sources By and About P. G.* (1979); Parisi, P., ed., *Artist of the Actual: Essays on P. G.* (1986); Stoehr, T., "Graffiti and the Imagination: P. G. in his Short Stories," *HUB* 5 (Fall 1994): 20–37; Widmer, K., *P. G.* (1980)

JOHN BOENING

GORDON, Caroline

b. 6 October 1895, Todd County, Kentucky ; d. 11 April 1981, San Cristóbal de las Casas, Mexico

G. influenced American fiction both through her example and her precepts. Her novels and short stories are models of the sort of writing the New Critics most valued. They are thoroughly rendered, not reported. The narrator is unobtrusive and the style restrained. The dramatic action itself, together with some allusion to classical myth, guides the reader to the meaning of the work. G. herself helped formulate this vision of fiction, which dominated American writing for decades. Building on the work both of her elders, especially her mentor, Ford Maddox Ford, and of her contemporaries, including her husband Allen TATE, she created a theory of fiction and then taught it to younger writers.

G.'s roots were firmly in the "Merriweather connection" of Kentucky, and most of her novels take the South and its burden of history as their subject. One of the circles in which she moved was the FUGITIVES/ AGRARIANS, including Tate, who celebrated the strengths of Southern culture. Her first novel, *Penhally* (1931), describes generations of a Southern family, which is torn between its agrarian traditions and the pressures of the commercial society that is growing up around it. *Aleck Maury, Sportsman* (1934) is in part a portrait of G.'s father, and in part a description of Southern masculinity. *None Shall Look Back* (1937), a historical novel on the Civil War, and *Green Centuries* (1941), a description of pioneer life, delve into the past of the South, while *The Garden and Adonis* (1937) and *The Women on the Porch* (1944) deal with the modern South. Critics have noted that although G. often celebrates male accomplishment on the surface, on a deeper level her work often in fact shows the power of women.

Despite her celebrations of families that are rooted firmly in a particular place and culture, G.'s own life was in many way rootless and bohemian. She moved constantly and lived in Paris, New York, and Princeton as often as she did in any Southern state. Her marriage with Tate was tempestuous, even after their celebrated conversion to Catholicism. (They divorced in 1946, remarried, and divorced again in 1959.) Catholicism, especially as presented by writers such as Jacques Maritain, was all the same a great influence on G.'s work. Her later novels, including *Strange Children* (1951), *The Malefactors* (1957), and even the myth-

laden *Glory of Hera* all deal with Christian themes. *The Malefactors* is also a *roman à clef* describing G.'s circle of friends during the 1920s, including Tate, Hart CRANE, and Dorothy Day.

G. was as influential as a teacher of the craft of fiction as she was as its practitioner. *The House of Fiction* (1950), which she wrote with Tate, and *How to Read a Novel* (1957) present with great clarity the New Critical idea of what a novel should be. She taught creative writing formally at several universities. Most importantly, her encouragement—which sometimes took the form of magisterial correction—aided a number of younger writers, including Flannery O'CONNOR and Walker PERCY.

BIBLIOGRAPHY: Fraistat, R., *C. G. as Novelist and Woman of Letters* (1984); Jonza, J. N., *The Underground Stream: The Life and Art of C. G.* (1995); Waldron, A., *Close Connections: C. G. and the Southern Renaissance* (1987)

BRIAN ABEL RAGEN

GORDON, Mary [Catherine]

b. 8 December 1949, Queens, New York

On the basis of her first novels, G. seemed to be an anatomist of lives distinctively Roman Catholic—a successor to J. F. POWERS. But unlike most novelists in the Catholic tradition, she shows less interest in the mysteries of grace than in a religious mythos that encourages women to honor father, husband, and priest to the neglect of their own needs. This feminist position has gradually displaced the experience of natal Catholicism as her subject.

G.'s first two novels, *Final Payments* (1978) and *The Company of Women* (1980), trace with affecting realism the heroine's gradual disenchantment with intellectualized creeds. From the suzerainty of a devout father on the one hand and a garrulous clergymen on the other, they turn to "companies of women" for understanding. In *Men and Angels* (1985), G. permits her heroine an indifference to the old religious fidelities and suggests more clearly than before than women must break free of masculine domination in all its subtle guises, although they face profound ambiguities in themselves as a consequence.

In a collection of twenty short stories entitled *Temporary Shelter* (1987), G.'s subject is broader than before: the general tendency to seek asylum in "jerry-built" arrangements of love, loyalty, friendship, marriage, and the creative imagination. Yet these "temporary shelters" of the spirit are the best products of our civilization, she suggests. Such paradoxical awareness, wry, delicately nuanced, and precisely articulated, are an impressive achievement of her fiction.

G.'s critical reputation was further enhanced by the publication in 1989 of *The Other Side,* followed by *Good Boys and Dead Girls and Other Essays* (1991), *The Rest of Life: Three Novellas* (1993), *The Shadow Man* (1996), and *Spending: A Utopian Divertimento* (1998).

BIBLIOGRAPHY: Asirvatham, S., "An Interview with M. G.," *P&W* 25 (July-August 1997): 50–61; Lee, D., "About M. G.," *Ploughshares* 23 (Fall 1997): 218–25, Wymward, E. B., "M. G.: Her Religious Sensibility," *Cross Currents* 37 (Summer-Fall 1987)

ROBERT R. KIERNAN

GOTANDA, Philip Kan
b. 17 December 1953, Stockton, California

Playwright and filmmaker G. is a leading figure in the Asian American cultural arts movement and a pioneer in Asian American theater. Beginning in the late 1960s and early 1970s, Asian American artists, influenced by the civil rights and ethnic identity movements, began creating works that reflected the unique cultural and historical experiences of Asian Americans. As part of this movement, small theaters developed throughout the U.S., hungry for plays depicting Asian Americans, and G. was one of the first dramatists whose works were produced by these theaters. G. has consistently written about Japanese Americans and portrayed them not as the simplistic, problem-free "model minority" represented in popular media but as complex individuals impacted by diverse cultural influences.

Although G. is one of the most respected Asian American playwrights, he did not develop an interest in theater until the late 1970s, as on outgrowth of his efforts as a song writer. A Sansei, or third-generation Japanese American, G. was impressed by artists in the early 1970s who articulated an Asian American cultural identity. After graduating from the University of California at Santa Barbara, he spent two years writing and performing songs about his evolving Asian American identity. He found songs limiting, however, and envisioned theatrical methods blended with his music. Not surprisingly, his first play, *The Avocado Kid,* is a musical, based on the Japanese folktale "Momotaro." Between 1979 and 1985, G. transitioned from musicals to dramas, and his plays were regularly produced by Asian American theater companies throughout the country. By the mid-1980s, G.'s work drew the attention of mainstream theaters and audiences.

G. frequently uses Japanese American families to explore societal forces such as racism and their effects on individuals. *Song for a Nisei Fisherman* (1995), for example, chronicles the life of a Nisei (second-generation Japanese American) doctor and distills a generation's struggles and achievements in coping with racism and building a community, while also revealing the internal price of such efforts. *The Wash* (1995) focuses on the break-up of an elderly Nisei couple and the impact of the separation on their two daughters. *The Wash* depicts the power of community expectations and the difficulties of rejecting culturally-defined gender roles, even by those oppressed by them. In *Fish Head Soup* (1995), the oppression against which characters struggle is racism they have internalized into self-hatred. The play explodes the model minority image through its portrayal of a Japanese American family whose problems are exacerbated by the reappearance of an adult son who was presumed to have drowned.

Having worked intimately with Asian American actors, G. had plenty of raw material for *Yankee Dawg You Die* (1995), which examines the struggles of two Asian American actors, a veteran performer and an ambitious younger man. Through the complex relationship between these two characters, G. explores the ethical and artistic dilemmas of people forced to work within a cultural system that often denies the humanity of Asian Americans.

Two of G.'s plays differ from his others in their surrealistic style and themes of regret and guilt. *The Dream of Kitamura* (1983) is a tale of violence that curses a family living in a mythical feudal society. *Day Standing on Its Head* (1994) deals with shame and doubt manifest in the life of a middle-aged law professor haunted by memories of his political activism in the 1970s and plagued by Prufrock-like uncertainties about his unsatisfying life.

Although the characters in G.'s plays confront problems rooted in the particularities of Japanese American history and culture, their conflicts reveal psychological and emotional realities that resonate beyond the Japanese American community.

STAN YOGI

GOYEN, William
b. 24 April 1915, Trinity, Texas; d. 30 August 1983, Los Angeles, California

Among Europeans, G. is recognized as one of the finest American short story writers of the postwar period. Indeed, his work is much better known in France and Germany than in his native America. Hard to catagorize as a writer, G.'s American neglect is unfortunate but understandable. He explored the traditions of magic realism, surrealism, and the Southern grotesque while maintaining a highly stylized early modern approach to writing best exemplified in T. S. ELIOT, James Joyce, and particularly D. H. Lawrence.

Most American critics and readers know G. for his first two novels, *The House of Breath* (1950) and *In a Farther Country: A Romance* (1955), both of which have been popular enough at home and abroad to merit repeated reprintings. These novels, as with all of G.'s novels except *The Fair Sister* (1963), are episodically structured; they are built upon interconnecting stories and thematic tales rather than linear, plot-progressing chapters. G. was not a novelist at heart, but a story-teller.

Born in rural east Texas, G. received his B.A. from Rice University in 1932 and his M.A. in comparative literature there in 1939. He served in the navy from 1940 to 1944 aboard an aircraft carrier in the South Pacific. During this period, he wrote of his wartime experiences and found publication in the *Southwest Review.* Having received a grant from the review in 1948, G. soon published the lyrical *The House of Breath,* which brought him several literary awards.

The House of Breath is a bittersweet autobiographical remembrance of family and childhood that recalls the works of fellow southerners Thomas WOLFE and James AGEE. In what becomes his trademark, the novel evokes a sense of infinite longing, what Shelley so aptly called "the desire of the moth for a star." Rich in poetic imagery, the novel lacks plot and character development in the traditional sense; rather, life in rural Charity, Texas, unfolds through many Joycean "voices," including that of the wind and the river. The focus of the novel is the leaving and returning of the self-exiled "children" of Charity—the interrelatedness of people and place.

In the 1950s, G. received two Guggenheim Fellowships and moved to New York City where he set his second masterpiece, *In a Farther Country.* No less original than his first novel, this surrealistic work is more straightforward and dramatic in its writing style. The well-received novel focuses on Marietta, a Spanish American, who longs for the glorious rise of her native land in the modern world; the isolated individuals she meets in the course of her life also share their own dreams of resurrection.

Over the next thirty years, G. taught at several Ivy League universities and wrote novels, short story collections, and plays, as well as nonfiction, poetry, song lyrics, and television scripts. Though criticized for failing to create a unified vision in his later novels, his *Faces of Blood Kindred* (1960) and *Collected Stories of W. G.* (1975) both solidified his position as a master storyteller.

In an age of novels, G. remarked tellingly: "the unified novel . . . is a series of parts. How could it not

be?" Thus, his later novels, and for some critics his early ones too, are known for their incantatory passages, their fragmented brilliance, but not their seamless design. Written by a fine craftsman with a unique narrative voice, G.'s *The House of Breath, In a Farther Country,* and *If I Had a Hundred Mouths: New & Selected Stories, 1947–1983* (1985) will stand the test of time.

BIBLIOGRAPHY: Horvath, B., et al., eds., *A G. Companion* (1997); Gibbons, R., *W. G.: A Study of the Short Fiction* (1991); Phillips, R. S., *W. G.* (1979)

JON PARRISH PEEDE

GRAHAM, Jorie
b. 9 May 1951, New York City

The subjects that inform most of G.'s poetry are nature, history, myth, and art. In each of her five volumes of poetry, G. experiments with poetic form, especially in her attention to line length. Her selected poems, *The Dream of a Unified Field* (1995), taken from these five volumes, won the Pulitzer Prize in 1996.

The unpredictability in G.'s evolving poetic form, which moves from a short, lyric line to the uncertainty of the longer line, reflects not only a poet who is demanding of her work, but also the restless spirit that is alive in much of her poetry. G.'s use of associative imagery which leads her to a found destination also reflects this restless, but patient spirit. A good example of this is her poem, "I Watched a Snake," from her second volume, *Erosion* (1983). The poem is evidence of G.'s astute ability to find meaning in everything she observes, especially in nature. In the poem, she patiently watches a snake slowly appear and disappear into the grass. The poem then moves from a discussion of the visible and the invisible, to a definition of desire, and then to the discovery that passion has the power to ground us. Much like Walt WHITMAN's "A Noiseless Patient Spider," the poem suggests how G. views the poet's work.

Drawing on images throughout her work that are sensual and mysterious (deepwood lilies, snow owl, mottled shadows), G.'s first two volumes rely heavily on the observation of nature and art, especially European art, to reveal some truth about our human nature. In this sense, her highly philosophical and intelligent verse is frequently associated with the poetry of Wallace STEVENS.

G. is a poet of the world, not just of America. Her European background, more specifically her time spent in Italy, surfaces in poems about European artists, philosophers, and mythology. Her use of mythology, however, is frequently a vehicle to focus on the subject of women's lives. In her collection *The End of Beauty* (1987), she reveals the power and error of Eve, the obliteration of woman through the story of Eurydice, and the healing patience of Penelope. These stories are also about the relationship between men and women and the push and pull of the energy between them, like the action of Penelope's weaving. The darker imagery that creeps up in *The End of Beauty* goes darker still in her collection entitled *Region of Unlikeness* (1991).

In "Fission," from *Region of Unlikeness,* the scene is Dallas, 1963, and every American immediately ties that point in history with the assassination of President John F. Kennedy. G. detects a major shift in the history of America and the world with this one act of violence. In this collection, G. moves away from the close scrutiny of the natural world to one of the human condition. Themes of gas chambers, nursing homes, and suicide populate these poems; and in her poem, "The Region of Unlikeness," G. even doubts the purpose of poetry.

In *Materialism* (1993), G. returns to the restoring properties of nature, which brings her full circle with her earlier work. These poems enter chaos theory, the desire to see order within disorder. In "The Dream of the Unified Field" (the title chosen for her selected poems), G. moves from the ordinary to the extraordinary as she weaves her present and past with the world's history into the blue-black landscape. One cannot help but think of painterly techniques when reading G.'s work. It is clear that her study of art has entered her poetic techniques: she dabbles, splatters, and makes long strokes of imagery. And much like the intention behind Adrienne RICH's *The Dream of a Common Language,* G.'s selected poems from 1974 to 1994, *The Dream of the Unified Field,* seek to find one place, one thought, one moment that might unify us all.

BIBLIOGRAPHY: Costello, B., "J. G.: Art and Erosion," *ConL* 33 (Summer 1992): 373–95; Vendler, H., *The Given and the Made: Strategies of Poetic Redefinition* (1995)

CATHERINE HARDY

GRAU, Shirley Ann

b. 8 July 1929, New Orleans, Louisiana

Although G. has spent most of life in the New Orleans area and her novels and short stories are often set in the South, she objects to being labeled a Southern or regional writer. She especially objects to the term "Southern *woman* writer" for what she considers to be its pejorative connotation.

Black Prince and Other Stories (1955), G.'s first book, is a collection of nine stories. The book was well received and critics praised G. for the precision of her language, her impersonal depiction of nature, and her ability to arrive at a story from divergent points of view. These qualities can be seen even more clearly in *The Hard Blue Sky* (1958), G.'s first novel, which is set on Isle aux Chiens, an island at the mouth of the Mississippi River. The drama of individual inhabitants is played out against the backdrop of an approaching hurricane. The enormous power of nature and its dominance over the characters' lives is described by G. with precision, control, and almost ruthless impersonality. While reviews were generally favorable, some critics found G.'s episodic method of telling the story, which is without a central plot, rather tiresome.

In her second novel, *The House on Coliseum Street* (1961), G. leaves the primitive setting and the isolated islanders of her first novel to tell the story of Joan Caillet, a worldly urbanite. G.'s craftsmanship remains intact in her depiction of Joan's gradual loss of touch with reality after the abortion, which her mother had arranged in order to avoid a family scandal. However, the characters in this novel lack the power and strengths of those in *The Hard Blue Sky* so that at the end of the novel, they seem as insubstantial as the society that has spawned them.

In G.'s Pulitzer Prize-winning novel, *The Keepers of the House* (1964), nature again assumes a key role, and G. once more demonstrates her mastery in the use of the multiple-points-of-view technique. It is the story of William Howland, his black mistress/wife Margaret, and his granddaughter Abigail Mason Tolliver, the protagonist. It is also a story about racial prejudice and intolerance, hypocrisy, political chicanery, revenge, and courage. Instead of the harsh and unforgiving nature that buffets the inhabitants of Isle aux Chiens in *The Hard Blue Sky,* the land on which the Howlands have lived for generations gives Abigail the necessary sense of belonging and courage with which to fend off her attackers. This is the only novel in which G. strikes a perfect balance between a total absence of sentiment with a sympathetic point of view. G. herself says that this novel explores "the whole human plight of how do you cope with evil."

Although a Book-of-the-Month Club selection, G.'s next novel, *The Condor Passes* (1971), received only mixed reviews. While the majority of the critics had praised G.'s detachment in her management of setting and character in her previous books, many are critical of her journalistic approach in the characterizations of the dying Thomas Henry Oliver—the condor—his two daughters, his son-in-law, his grandson, and his black servant, Stanley. Indeed, the symbol contributes little to the overall meaning of the novel, and the ending is unsatisfying.

The Wind Shifting West (1973) is a collection of eighteen stories. While the stories are not uniformly good, "The Wind Shifting West," "The Beach Party," and "The Way Back" are praiseworthy, perhaps because they are told from a feminine point of view. "Eight O'Clock" and "The Other Way," which explore the black-white relationships, are thoroughly competent.

Evidence of Love (1977), explores the relationship between Edward Milton Henley and his son Stephen, which had been first introduced in "The Patriarch," one of the stories in *The Wind Shifting West*. Although G. again uses the multiple-points-of-view technique to advantage, only Lucy, Stephen's wife, is a developed character; the self-portraits of Henley and Stephen seem rather flat. Instead of evidence of love, the novel seems to explore the absence of love.

The unrelenting fatalism, hopelessness, and resignation of the women make G.'s third collection, *Nine Women* (1985), a rather dissatisfying book. The only exception is the highly acclaimed "Letting Go," in which the protagonist escapes the confinement of parents and husband to create a life of her own. However, some critics see the women as passionate and courageous.

Although the title of G.'s novel *Roadwalkers* (1994) refers to the homeless people who wandered across the rural South during the Great Depression, it is the story of two fascinating and remarkable black women, Baby and her daughter Nanda. Again, G. tells her story from multiple points of view: the story of Baby as a roadwalker and Baby as seen through the eyes of the thirty-six-year-old Nanda, who looks back at the magical childhood created by Baby and her teenage experiences in a white Catholic girls' school. With the exception of the inexplicably lengthy and detailed second chapter, the novel is a rich evocation of the black experience in the South.

BIBLIOGRAPHY: Gossett, L. Y., *Violence in Recent Southern Fiction* (1965); Rohrberger, M., "S. A. G. and the Short Story," *SoQ* 21 (Summer 1983): 83–101; Schlueter, P., *S. A. G.* (1981); Wagner-Martin, L., "S. A. G.'s Wise Fictions," in Inge, T. B., ed., *Southern Women Writers: The New Generation* (1990): 143–60
VICTORIA H. SPANIOL

GREEN, Paul [Eliot]

b. 17 March 1894, Lillington, North Carolina; d. 4 May 1981, Chapel Hill, North Carolina

G. is known in modern American drama as the originator of outdoor historical dramas, as an experimental dramatist, and as a champion of black causes. Born on a farm in eastern North Carolina, he wrote about poor working people, black and white, believing in the heroic possibility of the people achieving greatness. Although he won a Pulitzer Prize for his play *In Abraham's Bosom* (1927), and had the opportunity to capitalize on his successes in Hollywood, on the commercial stage, or as a cultural ambassador, he lived mostly in Chapel Hill, his alma mater, where he taught and helped establish Frederick Koch's Carolina Playmakers.

His career can be divided into three stages, beginning in the 1920s with his early, one-act folk plays exposing religious zealots, *Unto Such Glory* (1928) and *The Lord's Will* (1925), racial bigotry, *White Dresses* (1926), and prison cruelty, *Hymn to the Rising Sun* (1936). The latter was set in a Southern prison camp and graphically illustrates the cruelty of incarceration. In his essay collection entitled *Drama and the Weather* (1958), G. explained his folk plays saying "the 'folk' are the people who seem to matter most to me."

G.'s first full-length work, *In Abraham's Bosom,* with an all black cast, was successfully produced in New York. The play is about a self-educated black man who wants to open a school in rural North Carolina. *The Field God* (1927), also produced in New York, features a poor Southern farmer who rejects the puritanical Christianity of his neighbors for his own spirituality. With *The House of Connelly* (1931), the last of his folk plays in the Chekhovian form, G. established the theme adapted by the writers of the Southern Renaissance such as William FAULKNER, Lillian HELLMAN, and Tennessee WILLIAMS. It is the story of the decay of an aristocratic Southern family headed by a weak, guilt-ridden son who finds hope in the love of a tenant girl. During this period G. was ranked second only to Eugene O'NEILL among American playwrights.

In the 1930s, G. entered a highly experimental period. In 1928, he had won a Guggenheim Fellowship, which took him to Europe where he met Alexis Gronowsky and Bertold Brecht. Adapting their form, he produced three plays in New York that incorporated dialogue, dance, pantomime, acrobatics, chorus, narrator, energized props, and music into what he called "symphonic drama," the "sounding together" of these elements. The first of these plays, *Potter's Field: A Symphonic Play for the Negro People* (1931), was revised as *Roll, Sweet Chariot* (1935) and is still a powerful drama with its unsentimentalized portrayal of a black shantytown. *Johnny Johnson: The Biography of a Common Man* (1937), the most successful of these experiments, gave Kurt Weill his first opportunity in America. It was produced by the left-wing

Group Theatre, staged by Lee Strasberg, and satirizes militarism and jingoism.

Although G. had other major productions in New York, such as his dramatization of Richard WRIGHT's *Native Son* for Orson Wells and John Houseman, he had already begun the third and most important part of his career. To celebrate the 350th anniversary of the settlement in Roanoke, G. wrote and produced the first of his regional outdoor historical dramas, *The Lost Colony* (1937). The success of this play marked a turning point in G.'s career. He now had an audience of common people for plays about ordinary folk caught up in historical events, and it allowed him to continue the development of symphonic drama. His regional outdoor dramas include *The Highland Call* (1939), *Wilderness Road* (1955), *The Founders* (1957), *Steven Foster Story* (1959), *Cross and Sword* (1965), *Texas* (1966), *The Lone Star* (1977), and *Palo Duro* (1978). Throughout this later period, G. also wrote several screenplays and radio dramas.

BIBLIOGRAPHY: Flanagan, H., *Arena* (1940); Kenny, V., *P. G.,* 1971; Lazenby, W., *P. G.,* 1971; Overmyer, J., ed., *A Southern Life: Letters of P. G., 1916-1981* (1994)

NEWTON SMITH

GREENE, Asa

b. 11 February 1789, Ashby, Massachusetts; d. 31 December 1838, New York City

G., who spelled his name "Green" prior to his college days, was a satirist and humorist; he served as editor of the *Berkshire American* (1825–27), a Pittsfield, Massachusetts weekly; published the *Socialist* (1828–29), a nonpolitical weekly; and edited the *Constellation* (1829–32), a news and humorous literature publication. According to Walter Blair, *A Yankee among the Nullifiers* (1833), *The Life and Adventures of Dr. Dodimus Duckworth* (1833), and *Travels in America, by George Fibbleton, Esq., Ex-Barber to His Majesty, the King of Great Britain* (1833) are important mileposts in the development of indigenous American humor between 1825 and 1833.

A Yankee among the Nullifiers examines the socioeconomic and political aspects of the American South. Didactic, strongly satirical, and steeped with stereotypical views of the South, this book is the fictional autobiography of Elnathan Elmwood, a Yankee from Massachusetts. Elmwood tutors sixteen year old Henrietta Harrington of South Carolina whose father, Major Harebrain Harrington, is an ardent supporter of states' rights and nullification. Using a mock-heroic style, G.'s brilliant protagonist convinces Major Har-

rington to abandon his misguided views and subscribe to an antinullification, antislavery viewpoint. G. attempts a number of dialects, the use of figurative language, and other forms of wordplay popularized by humorous writers in the 1830s.

G. satirizes medical charlatans and their gullible patients in his two-volume work, *The Life and Adventures of Dr. Dodimus Duckworth*. A precursor of Henry Clay Lewis's *Odd Leaves from the Life of a Louisiana 'Swamp Doctor'* (1850), G.'s work utilizes puns and malapropisms to achieve humor and to expose the large number of medical quacks in early-19th-c. American society.

Travels in America, by George Fibbleton, Esq., Ex-Barber to His Majesty, the King of Great Britain is a satire of the rather biased commentaries and travel books written by British authors about their observations of America. An Englishman George Fibbleton unintentionally reveals his condescension and ignorance by confusing facts relating to his observations of the geography, history, and politics of America.

Although the humor in G.'s works is oftentimes considered unsuccessful, his works are generally recognized for their sociohistorical value. *A Glance at New York* (1837), his final work, is noted for its factual detail and statistics as well as the accuracy of G.'s personal views about the people and institutions of New York.

BIBLIOGRAPHY: Blair, W., *Native American Humor* (1960); Keeler, M. A, "A. G.," in Trachtenberg, S., ed., *DLB*, vol. 11, part 1., *American Humorists, 1800–1950* (1982): 156–59

CHARLENE TAYLOR EVANS

GREY, [Pearl] Zane

b. 31 January 1872, Zanesville, Ohio; d. 23 October 1939, Altadena, California

Few American novelists have been as enthusiastically received by a popular audience as G., who held a remarkably diverse readership with his tales of Western adventure and heroism. His career as a novelist coincided with the formalist and new critical schools of literary scholarship, perspectives that privileged philosophically complex and elusive works of literature. G.'s hardboiled, typically uncomplicated stories found little favor among members of this scholarly community. With the recent rise of cultural criticism, however, the WESTERN has emerged as a genre of tremendous importance to the American imagination. G.'s work is being reconsidered on these grounds, because of its remarkable resonance with a national culture that continually returns to the West as a mytho-poetic region of mind.

G. came to reading and writing early, consuming both popular and classic literature as a boy and writing imitative short stories. He studied dentistry at the University of Pennsylvania, but after graduating in 1896, he continued to dream of a writing career. He completed *Billy Zane* in 1903, a novel that recast in fictional form the lives of his own Ohio ancestors. Although he was romantic by nature, G. firmly believed in the principle of natural selection. *Billy Zane* begins with the basic romance formula of James Fenimore COOPER's Leather-Stocking tales, but it places the main character into a Darwinian register, creating a new hero that retains his basic virtue but is also dark and mysterious.

In order to acquire the necessary materials for fiction, G. traveled west to spend time on a ranch in Arizona. He learned the working particulars of ranch life, and he became enthralled with the mythic potential of the American West. He published a nonfictional account of his Western journey entitled *The Last of the Plainsmen* (1908) and he turned again to fiction with *The Heritage of the Desert* (1910). The latter work established the pattern that much of G.'s novels would later employ: the bildungsroman, the initiation story, the coming of age tale. This motif was employed in G.'s most popular and well-received novel, *Riders of the Purple Sage* (1912). Here, a mysterious gunman Lassiter and the independent Jane Withersteen battle human greed and brutality in the mountains of Utah. Withersteen is the most dynamic of the two characters, as she in part embodies Darwinian theory by matching violence with violence. But her relationship and reconciliation with Lassiter reflects the fundamental paradox in G.'s themes. Lassiter's naturalism softens as the mystery of his past is revealed, as he finds community, romance, and love through the typical plot resolution of the domestic novel. *Riders of the Purple Sage,* clearly a high optative romance, appealed to an audience that craved escape and preferred clean and complete plot resolution. But in this appeal lies the novel's significance as myth, since the work clearly demonstrates the power of the West as an imaginary space where dominant American values are realized in fictional form.

These same generic patterns and mythical undercurrents appear in *The Light of the Western Stars* (1914), *The Lone Star Ranger* (1915), *The Border Legion* (1916), *The U. P. Trail* (1918), and *The Wanderer of the Wasteland* (1923). All of these works place the perennial conflicts between virtue and vice, malevolence and decency, brutality and kindness, within the context of the romance tradition of James Fenimore Cooper. But these narratives present more modern versions of the myth, portraying a violence consistent with the tenets of literary NATURALISM. Critics have pointed to the diverse impulses of romance and "anti-romance" as a basic and unsuccessfully resolved contradiction in G.'s fiction. It is perhaps true that the author's desire to resolve plots with a happy sentimentality undercuts the pathos and power of his naturalist theme. But this tension is precisely what makes G.'s Westerns fascinating to cultural critics and historians, since his novels emerge as revealing examples of American cultural perception and popular imagination.

BIBLIOGRAPHY: Gay, C., *Z. G.: Story-Teller* (1979); Gruber, F., *Z. G.* (1970); Jackson, C., *Z. G.* (1973); Karr, J., *Z. G.: Man of the West* (1949); Ronald, A., *Z. G.* (1975)

STEVEN FRYE

GRIMKÉ, Angelina Weld

b. 27 February 1880, Boston, Massachusetts; d. 10 June 1958, New York City

Though most literary anthologies define G. as a poet, she made substantial contributions to the literature of the Harlem Renaissance period as a dramatist and fiction writer. G. , whose family name was quite well recognized, had established a reputation with her drama *Rachel* (1920), first staged in 1916. Having grown up influenced by a family composed of both black and white members active in the abolitionist movement, she manifested this influence in the themes that dominated her play. Popularly cited by critics as the first successful drama to be written by an African American author and interpreted by African American actors, the play called attention to the racial oppression of African American blacks. G. centered her play on the prejudice as it affected the lives of a middle-class black family: Mrs. Loving, a middle-class widow, her son and daughter, Tom and Rachel. After the father and another relative were lynched, the family fled the South and moved north to face racial prejudices. While there, Rachel and Tom, both of whom were highly educated, directly confronted prejudice in their lives when they both could not find suitable jobs.

Initially, the play was produced by amateurs for audiences in school and church auditoriums and under the sponsorship of such organizations as the NAACP and the YMCA. Once *Rachel* was published, however, it reached a wider audience and began to fulfill some of the original purpose for which it was intended: to evoke the sympathy of white women to the tragically oppressing condition of American blacks. Published as a result of self-subsidized agreement, the play, which has Rachel reject marriage and motherhood, was criticized for promoting black genocide, a charge that G. countered by explaining her intention to appeal to a largely white, not black audience. Many of the reviews, however, were favorable and praised her work as one that had literary value and which profoundly moved whites to understand the tragedy of middle-class blacks.

Though G. received much publicity during the 1920s when she wrote this play, she—like most other women during the Harlem Renaissance—received far less recognition for their literary efforts than the male writers of that era. Her fame rested on the few poems commonly anthologized, which reflected her use of romantic models: in these poems she described her love of nature and revealed its beauty through a clear and precise use of language. Her poetic style is typified in two of her often anthologized poems: "A Mona Lisa," a romantic love poem focusing on the death-wish theme spoken through the voice of one seeking reconciliation with her lover and emphasizing nature images, and "Grass Fingers," a poem underscoring her love of nature and her emotional intensity and fervor. Although she wrote during the Harlem Renaissance, most of her poems were written using conventional forms; few of her poems used the style popularized during the period emphasizing African American-influenced forms of language and music. Some of her unpublished poems, lesbian in nature, were thought to explore her thwarted sexuality.

Themes prevalent in her plays and poems shone through in her prose, as well. Short stories she authored were "Goldie," which focused on lynching, and "The Closing Door," which examined infanticide in the black community, was taken from an early draft of *Rachel*. Overall, G.'s literary accomplishments should best be remembered as influenced by both the romantic and the New Negro movements.

BIBLIOGRAPHY: Barksdale, R. K., and K. Kinnamon, eds., *Black Writers of America* (1972); Hull, G. T., *Color, Sex, and Poetry* (1987); Shockley, A. A., ed., *Afro-American Writers, 1746-1933* (1988)

LENA AMPADU

GRIMKÉ, Sarah Moore

b. 26 November 1792, Charleston, South Carolina; d. 23 December 1873, West Newton, Massachusetts

Born into a large slave-owning family, G. grew up despising the oppression of humans. Along with her sister, Angelina Emily Grimké, G. became a fierce advocate of abolition and women's rights. The sisters were the first women from a slaveholding family to speak against the practice of slavery. Her place in American literary history was secured by a few poignant epistles on the inhumanity of slavery and women's suffrage. While G. is not a popular topic for contemporary criticism, she is seen as a significant, if somewhat minor, figure in the literature of her century.

Through a series of events that included a move to Philadelphia, religious conversion, and dissension, she found herself an officer of the American Anti-Slavery Society, speaking to other women about the evils of slavery by December 1836 in New York City. Later that year, G. published her first piece of public writing: *An Epistle to the Clergy of the Southern States,* in which she tried to raise the sympathy of Southern clergymen by appealing to their understanding of Christianity and the creation of man. G. says that by condoning the act of slavery, one is in effect saying, "I will as far as I am able destroy the image of God;" her rationale here is that Man was created in God's image and even the slaves are Men. The *Epistle* did not have the effect on the clergy that G. desired but it continues to stand as an important document for it was one of the first of its kind and, quite significantly, was written by a fellow Southerner.

While G. was hard at work with her antislavery activities, she was also becoming more involved in the women's movement that was rising simultaneously with the abolitionist movement. She supported petitions to Congress and continued to speak about women's rights. She and her sister were invited to Boston to work with the Female Anti-Slavery Society. The *New England Spectator* published "S. M. G., Letters on the Equality of the Sexes and the Condition of Woman, addressed to Mary S. Parker, President of the Boston Female Anti-Slavery Society" during the latter half of 1837. This series of letters uses some of the same language and makes some of the same points as G. anti-slavery literature signing each "Thine in the bonds of womanhood." G. covers every aspect of womanhood in her letters, from their treatment by the patriarchal societies described in the Bible to "Legal Disabilities" and the relationship between a wife and her husband. She supports women ministers, women's right to property, equality of the sexes, and women's education. True to her antislavery convictions she notes with "feelings of the deepest shame and sorrow" that some women do nothing to stop "the unbridled cruelty and lust" suffered by female slaves and accuses the apathetic women of being guilty for allowing the slave women to be so treated. G. will not pinpoint exactly what she believes are the duties of women but she does say that women must make use of whatever opportunities come their way and must live morally just lives, for "whatsoever it is morally right for a man to do, it is morally right for a woman to do."

G.'s public support for abolition and women's rights was as fierce as it was short-lived. The antislavery and women's conventions to which she belonged disbanded by 1840 and G. settled into life with her sister's family. Her public writing ceased and her private letters from 1840 through the last year of her life do not mention the causes for which she worked so diligently. Although she is rarely discussed in contemporary criticism, G.'s work appears in anthologies and she is recognized as a significant woman writer. Her work is similar to that of Harriet Beecher STOWE and Margaret FULLER, laying a foundation upon which they could build.

BIBLIOGRAPHY: Birney, C. H., *The G. Sisters; S. and Angelina G.: The First American Women Advocates of Abolition and Woman's Rights* (1969); Lerner, G., *The G. Sisters From South Carolina* (1967; rev. ed., 1971)

MARCY L. TANTER

GUARE, John
b. 5 February 1938, Queens, New York

G. is one of the most interesting, innovative, and imaginative dramatists in the history of the American theater. Unfortunately, he has not written a large number of plays, even though his writing career spans a quarter of a century, and he has received little scholarly acclaim. The lack of critical attention to his work at least partly can be attributed to the fact that some of his canon, particularly those early plays that categorized him in critics' minds, is so outrageous in conception that it is clearly outside the mainstream of American drama and not conducive to developing a popular following. Still, in the late 1980s, *The House of Blue Leaves* was successfully revived, fifteen years after it had first been staged, and it was reprinted in 1995.

G.'s first plays to be produced were sketches, *Did You Write My Name in the Snow?* (perf. 1962) and *To Wally Pantoni, We Leave a Credenza* (perf. 1964). In 1966, *The Loveliest Afternoon of the Year* and *Something I'll Tell You Tuesday,* published together in 1967, brought him to the critics' attention when the pieces were staged at the Off-Off-Broadway Caffe Cino. Two years later, the Off-Broadway production of *Muzeeka* (1968) resulted in an Obie Award for G.; the following year, *Variety* named G. the most promising playwright of the year for his first Broadway show, *Cop Out* (1968). A second Obie Award and the New York Drama Critics Circle Award for best new play of the year came in 1971 with the appearance of *The House of Blue Leaves* (1972), and *Two Gentleman from Verona* (1973) received the Tony Award for best

musical—cowritten by G. and Mel Shapiro, with music by Galt MacDermot, the musical was based on Shakespeare's play. It was also at about this time that G. was called the "most successful and promising playwright to forge to the public's attention since Edward Albee."

The House of Blue Leaves is the best and most important of G.'s early plays. Somewhat autobiographical, the drama revolves around the Pope's visit to New York City in 1965. The playwright has admitted that his concern in writing the play was to show how people avoid humiliation, for "avoiding humiliation is the core of tragedy and comedy and probably our lives." The form of the play grew out of G.'s experience in London in 1969: "I saw Laurence Olivier do [August Strindberg's] *Dance of Death* and . . . [Georges Feydeau's] *A Flea in Her Ear.* The savage intensity of the first blended into the maniacal intensity of the second." An interesting combination of influences from the classical theater and popular culture (songs, television programs, films, commercials) results in a picture of contemporary American society in which the dramatist relies upon nonconventional devices to express his insights.

G.'s early works are innovative, characterized by startling plot twists that enliven them and make them unique in American drama—as in the case of the woman-eating stone lion that crouches in front of the library in *A Day for Surprises* (1971). His fantastic images embody the essence of mid-20th-c. American life. Later, as with the bomb in the elevator in *The House of Blue Leaves,* his plays take on a soap opera tone and merely replicate the bizarre surface nature of contemporary American society. Whereas Miss Jepson and Mr. Falanzano are symbolically confronted with a universe in which the laws of nature are violated in *A Day for Surprises,* Ronnie is nothing more than a representation of the deprived childhood cliche. Even more traditional is the trilogy comprised of *Lydie Breeze* (1982), *Gardenia* (1982), and *Women and Water* (perf. 1985, pub. 1990), a Eugene O'NEILL-like attempt to examine American culture in a historical context.

In the 1990s, G.'s activity expanded. He became a contributing editor to the annual *Connections: The New American Theater;* he published an exploration of the life of contemporary artist Chuck Close; several of his dramas were staged—*Four Baboons Adoring the Sun* (1993), *Six Degrees of Separation* (1990), and *Moon under Miami* (1995). Of these, *Six Degrees of Separation* is the most important. In what many critics consider the playwright's best work, G. tells the story of Paul, a young con man who claims to be Sidney Poitier's son, and the effect of his visit in the home of Manhattan art dealers Quisa and Flan Kittredge.

There is a theory that all people are connected through no more than six genetic links. Based on an actual incident, in the play, which is part drawing room comedy, part detective story, this concept and its ramifications are considered in terms of the relationships between the characters. Through the mechanism of fakery, it is revealed how "there are two sides to every story," and how 20th-c. lives are kept fragmented by various degrees of separation that prevent the characters from knowing one another or themselves. Though not as highly acclaimed as his screenplay for *Atlantic City* (1980), the writer's 1993 cinematic adaptation of *Six Degrees of Separation* was well received.

Only Arthur KOPIT in America and Joe Orton in England can match the sense of the fantastic epitomized in flashes of black humor that characterizes G.'s vision of 20th-c. America. If the theatrical impact that his dramas have were contained in longer plays with more fully drawn characters, G. would be ranked among the most important dramatists of his generation.

BIBLIOGRAPHY: Bernstein, S. J., *The Standards Entwined: A New Direction in American Drama* (1980); Carroll, D., "Not-Quite Mainstream Male Playwrights: G., Durang, and Rabe," in King, B., ed., *Contemporary American Theatre* (1991): 41–61; Cohn, R., *New American Dramatists, 1960–1990* (1991); Dasgupta, G., "J. G.," in *American Playwrights: A Critical Survey* (1981): 41–52; Wetzeon, R., "The Coming of Age of J. G.," *New York* 22 February 1982: 35–39

STEVEN H. GALE

GUEST, Barbara

b. 6 September 1920, Wilmington, North Carolina

G. is a poet who has also written plays, art criticism, a novel, *Seeking Air* (1978), and an acclaimed biography of the modernist poet Hilda DOOLITTLE entitled *Herself Defined* (1984). She began writing in the 1950s as one of the group of poets known as the New York school, which also included John ASHBERY, Kenneth KOCH, Frank O'HARA, and James SCHUYLER. Her work, like theirs, is saturated in the visual arts and music, extends the formal experiments of MODERNISM, plays the abstract qualities of language against its sensuousness and materiality, makes the most of the poem as a field of action, and switches effortlessly between the real and the surreal. G. displays an aesthetic kinship with abstract painters that has resulted concretely in poems to, for, and about the work of Robert Motherwell, Grace Hartigan, Mary Abbott, and Helen Frankenthaler, all of whom were friends, and more generally in a audacious style characterized by indirection,

shifts in scale and perspective, syntactic oddity, and a luscious vocabulary, at once bold and delicate.

Although G. believes that subject matter cannot be the "sole urgency" of a poem, the concerns of her poems include the dislocations of change, the poetics of space and place, the dialectics of travel and homecoming, the suspensions and excruciations of romantic love, the sustenance available in friendship, the necessity and possibility of "Work and Joy." She explores the meaning of landscape and weather, ranging the American prairie, the Santa Fe Trail, hurricane-ravaged Florida, Illyria, London, Paris, Greece, and New England, as well as lovingly particular addresses in New York City. She borrows "adventuresses" from classical mythology—Atalanta, Dido, Persephone, Cassandra—remaking them for our time while retaining indispensable aspects of their ancient feminine personalities. Her densely but deftly allusive poetry reveals the range and depth of her cultural knowledge: into her capacious and shimmering postmodern net are drawn Byron, Keats, Strindberg, Miró, Cézanne, Dora Maar, Delacroix, Warren Brandt, Donne, Kandinsky, Mozart, Flaubert, and Gertrude STEIN, among others.

In the work from *The Location of Things* (1960) through *Fair Realism* (1989), G. characteristically produces formally complex and intricately wrought lyrics, at once decorative, passionate, and energetic: "it was a way of steeples of construction / of pilings of verbs," she writes. With few exceptions—two are the Vietnam War allegory/how-to manual "A Handbook of Surfing," and the humorous and profound "Türler Losses" about two wristwatches seemingly filled with the intent to be lost—the poems are mostly short and dense. She also, however, experiments with a looser and longer alternative form that dominates in the later collections, beginning with *Defensive Rapture* (1993). Here, words, phrases, and stanzas float in vast white space, like Sapphic fragments, suggesting lavish erasure, freedom, a break-up of density, rich leisure and comfort, fluidity.

For much of her long career, and despite her constant production, including twelve collections and chapbooks and a *Selected Poems* (1995), G. has been the least remarked of the New York poets, perhaps due to the civility, beauty, difficulty, and privacy of her work in an era more admiring of personal and political stridencies. Recently, however, the Language poets have claimed G. as precursor, finding her work to be similarly resistant to a latter-day romantic, "I"-centered lyrical mode, and similarly attuned to the swiftness with which worlds are made and unmade via language. Also, feminist readers have begun to appreciate her articulations of a feminine aesthetic that seeks not to dispel mystery but to elaborate and perpetuate it.

BIBLIOGRAPHY: DuPlessis, R. B., "All My Vast/Journeying Sensibility," *Sulfur* 39 (Fall 1996): 39–48; Einzig, B., "The Surface as Object," *APR* 25 (January-February 1996): 7–10; Lundquist, S., "Reverence and Resistance: B. G., Ekphrasis, and the Female Gaze," *ConL* 38 (Summer 1997): 260–86

SARA LUNDQUIST

GUINEY, Louise Imogen

b. 7 January 1861, Boston, Massachusetts; d. 2 November 1920, Gloucestershire, England

In a 1911 essay in *Scribner's Magazine,* G. accurately predicted her future obscurity. Although her poetry seems dated to modern readers, she represents an ideal portraiture of the professional woman scholar in the later half of the 19th c.; she was a successful poet and well respected by her contemporaries. As with other women authors of her time, G. lived on her own. She was unmarried, supported herself through literary endeavors (as editor, translator, and author) and some jobs (postmistress, librarian), spent time traveling with friends like author Alice BROWN, met the requirements of an extended family, and expatriated to England in order to pursue research in Catholic poets such as Henry Vaughan and Edmund Campion.

Before leaving for England in 1890, G. established herself in Boston's literary circles with the publication of her first book of poetry, *Songs at the Start* (1884); her second book, *The White Sail and Other Poems* (1887), suffered from this claustrophobic influence. *A Roadside Harp* (1893) was well received and obviously a more mature collection. While established permanently in Oxford, England, G. supported herself through articles published in American magazines; her poetic output depended on her financial security and freedom from other chores, literary and familial. She maintained ties with literary figures such as Sarah Orne JEWETT in America while participating in English literary circles.

G.'s style is at once traditional, erudite, and devout, yet her poems often gratify modern tastes with demonstrations of varied emotions delivered in compact form. As a traditionalist, she wrote sonnets as often as lyrics and used archaic forms of expression. Her growing spiritually led later to religious poems; her Christian mission is clearly announced in lyrics such as "Sanctuary," and her faith is declared through heroic, cavalier figures in poems such as "The Kings" and "The Knight Errant." She rejected Bliss Carman's pleased pronouncement that she wrote "pagan lyrics" in preference for her own term "natural religion."

The tight construction of select poems belies Harriet MONROE's epitaph in *Poetry* (January 1921), where she pronounced G. "old-fashioned" and "incomplete." In "Sunday Chimes in the City," G. describes the bells' sounds as originating from "all their dark throats aching and outblown." In "The Auditor," G. achieves a similarly tight, modern rhythm as she debates if a jester "knowest not aught of this aching vexed planet down-whirling." G.'s literary tastes also kept pace with the modern in her admiration for A. E. Housman, Aubrey Beardsley (both of whom she reviewed favorably), W. B. Yeats, and Gerard Manley Hopkins. In her letters, she may speak with frustration about her difficulties as a writer torn between "bread-winning" and poetry, yet she always maintains her humor even as she strays from "woman's spear." These letters contradict contemporary and current opinion that she was merely a traditionalist and a Victorian. Rather, as a "new woman" she held her own opinions on literary matters and praised women writers and mentors; "our good new poets over here are all women," she writes.

BIBLIOGRAPHY: Brown, A., *L. I. G.* (1921); Fairbanks, H. G., *L. I. G.* (1973); Guiney, G., ed., *The Letters of L. I. G.* (1926): Tenison, E. M., *L. I. G.* (1923); Tulley, S., "Heroic Failures and the Literary Career of L. I. G.," *ATQ* 48 (Fall 1980): 171–86

TAIMI OLSEN

GURNEY, A[lbert] R[amsdell], Jr.

b. 1 November 1930, Buffalo, New York

G.'s dramas concern the eroding plateau of the lower echelons of American wealth and status. As his characters look out upon their usually alcohol-beclouded landscape, they voice concern about changing values in a world so invasive that it does not respect carefully placed barriers against unwelcome intrusion. In the company of G.'s plays, the social scene may be inane, but it still survives on the last crumbs of plutocracy and pharisaic self-interest. His plays survey the final refuge of minds leaking self-indulgent commonplaces as though they were mordant observation. They close themselves to any perception judged out of the ordinary, and all in balanced phrases and attempts at well-schooled wit. G.'s persistent theme is revealed through the dialogue of narcissists who find themselves out of mirror's reach, extemporizing their reactions to the devious intrusions of common social reality and their own foibles. His work is the dramatic translation of the finite but amusing sphere in the fiction of John P. MARQUAND, and at its highest form of expression, the mordant observations in the stories and novels of John CHEEVER, whose work is the subject of G.'s *Cheever Evening* (1994).

G. stylistically is the descendant of Bernard Shaw's description of the "well-made play," though he occasionally brings some experimentation of time and place to bear. Most notably, *The Dining Room* (1982) plays over the passing generations through the action of players from childhood to maturity to old age. The barbarism and infantilism of the present have obviously made a "formal dining room" into a curio of the past: the order of time, status, patriarchy, the survival of the family itself are all compromised. More limited resources in contemporary life, that of middle-class subsistence or lowered expectations, render such places of money, status, and leisure mere reservations of the privileged. The play is a well-crafted and comfortably surreal representation consisting of the passing of different levels of time and their invocation of flashback and temporal succession. The house, and this most utilitarian room for the sharing of common talk and sustenance, are both left for other, and one feels, more limited experiences than the past—for a more barbarous present. This is a recurrent if not one-note fixation of the playwright. His contest is not over deeply destructive anxiety. Whatever problem may arise merely tests the characters' ability to remain persistently aloof in their remove from the mob. They are equal to whatever indignities may arise, such as adultery or the bankruptcy of family members or acquaintances. They successfully resist the insults of those who wish to rise in the American class system but have not, as yet, learned the knack of self-importance with under-statement, alcoholism with the appearance of public sobriety, criticism of other classes masked by limited optimism, and egotism with the appearance of charitable concern.

G. is the first to admit that life is not reflected in a cocktail glass, though that social immersion may be the subject of polite satire. In the introduction to the New American Library edition of *The Cocktail Hour* (1989), G. observes: "These characters struggling to break the bonds of the world they were born into, and these plays pressing against the limitations of their own form, give my work, I hope, a theatricality which undercuts the conventions of realistic drama and the complacencies of the upper-middle-class milieu." What remains constant, however, is that G.'s dramatic form is conventionally well-wrought, and the satire of his plays fails to reach anything more than the catalogue of the relatively harmless foibles of his own class.

Another Antigone (1988), however, convincingly portrays the perils of unwitting confrontation with multiculturalism in any contemporary American academic scene, and that several years before David MAMET's more jugular *Oleana*. Its main character, a professor of classics, eventually is connived out of his profession by a college administration whose wiliness is more than a match for his own ineptitude. The contemporary antagonist in this play is an old friend who happens to have been made an administrator. She answers the call of the new cultural duty, whatever the cost to her old collegiate ally.

Love Letters, published with *The Golden Age* and *What I Did Last Summer* in 1990, is a theatrical biography from childhood to advanced maturity of Andrew Makepeace Ladd, III, and Melissa, daughter of Mr. and Mrs. Gilbert Channing Gardner. It is the most accessible and easily playable of any drama on the contemporary stage. Its elegiac note, persistent in all of G.'s drama, is here unrestrained, and the play is the least satiric and most affecting of the playwright's work. G. is the author of three novels, the recipient of the Award of Merit from the Academy and Institute of Arts and Letters as well as the Drama Desk Award. His numerous plays include *Scenes from American Life* (1970), *Who Killed Richard Cory?* (1976), *Children* (1977), *The Middle Ages* (1978), and *The Perfect Party* (1989).

BIBLIOGRAPHY: DiGaetani, J. L., *A Search for a Postmodern Theater* (1991); Sponberg, A. E., "A. R. G.," in Bryer, J. R., ed., *The Playwright's Art: Conversations with Contemporary American Dramatists* (1995): 86–101

ROBERT MOYNIHAN

GUTHRIE, A[lfred] B[ertram], Jr.

b. 13 January 1901, Bedford, Indiana; d. 26 April 1991, Choteau, Montana

G. is closely associated with Montana, growing up in the small ranch town of Choteau, located on the eastern slope of the Rockies. This land plays a major role in G.'s fiction, interwoven with the fate of his characters. Along with his capacity to portray accurately his region and its past is his ability to convey universal human qualities not restricted to regionalism. He may best be described as a Western realist, having great regard for the actual facts of history, but combining real events with spiritual and poetic qualities and using landscape, sky and space to suggest these qualities. Although G. writes in several genres—short stories, novels, articles, poems—his place in American literature rests upon his series of novels chronicling the opening and development of the West—by any standards a major contribution to Western American literature. These novels have secured him a place as one of America's foremost Western writers.

The Big Sky (1947) the widely acclaimed first novel in the series, is a vivid and accurate portrayal of the American fur trapper in the Rocky Mountain area. This story of the mountain man from 1830 to 1843 centers on three major characters—Boone Caudill, Dick Summers, and Jim Deakins. *The Way West* (1949), gaining G. the Pulitzer Prize in 1950, is about a wagon train of settlers moving from Missouri to Oregon in 1845, with Dick Summers appearing this time as scout and guide for the wagon train. *These Thousand Hills* (1956) is the story of cattle ranching in Montana in the 1880s and concerns the fortunes of Lat Evans, grandson of Lije Evans and son of Brownie Evans, characters from *The Way West*. *Arfive* (1971) depicts life in a small Montana town from the turn of the century to World War I. There are no characters linking this book to the earlier novels, events here focusing on the lives of Benton Collingsworth, the high school principal, and Mort Ewing, a successful rancher. *The Last Valley* (1975) continues the *Arfive* story, covering the time shortly after World War I to shortly after World War II and centering on the problems of Ben Tate, owner and publisher of the town newspaper.

Wishing to fill the time gap (1845 to 1870) left between *The Way West* and *These Thousand Hills,* G. wrote *Fair Land, Fair Land* (1982) as a sequel to *The Way West,* with Dick Summers as the major character, living out his last years with his Indian wife Teal Eye as an anachronism in the beloved land he had roamed as a trapper in earlier days. This novel emphasizes the elegiac tone and the sense of loss that accompanies change, themes that had been present in varying degrees in all the novels. The first value in the West for G. is the priceless asset of space, land, distance. The overall pattern that these novels take is that as civilization expands, the big sky inevitably contracts, and opportunities for experiencing psychological release and freedom through sacred union with land and sky diminish.

Other writings include *The Big It* (1960), a collection of thirteen short stories; *The Blue Hen's Chick* (1965), his autobiography; *Once Upon a Pond* (1973), a collection of animal fables for children. Beginning with *Wild Pitch* (1973), G. wrote the first in a series of minor but entertaining and well-crafted mystery novels. Set in a present-day small Western town, the stories relate the adventures of Chick Charleston, the town sheriff, and his young helper, Jason Beard. The series continued with *the Genuine Article* (1977), *No Second Wind* (1980), *Playing Catch-up* (1985). The last novel in the series, *Murder in the Cotswolds* (1989), has the Western sheriff sleuthing in the English

Cotswolds. *Big Sky, Fair Land: The Environmental Essays of A. B. G., Jr.* (1988) is a collection of twenty-two of G.'s socioenvironmental essays, book excerpts, and speech texts that address the problems of conservation of the wilderness and its wildlife.

BIBLIOGRAPHY: Chatterton, W., "A. B. G., Jr.," in Taylor, J. G., et al., eds., *A Literary History of the American West* (1987): 912–34; Erisman, F., "A. B. G., Jr.," in Erisman, F., and R.W. Etulain, eds., *Fifty Western Writers* (1982): 162–71; Etulain, R.W., *A Bibliographical Guide to the Study of Western American Literature* (1982); Folsom, J. K., *The American Western Novel* (1966): 64–76; Ford, T. W., *A. B. G., Jr.* (1981); Milton, J. R., *The Novel of the American West* (1980); Petersen, D., "The Evolution and Expression of Environmental Themes in the Life and Literature of A. B. G., Jr.," in Petersen, D., ed., *Big Sky, Fair Land: The Environmental Essays of A. B. G., Jr.* (1988): 9–61

THOMAS W. FORD

GUY, Rosa
b. 1 September 1925, Trinidad, West Indies

Best known as a writer of fiction for young adults, G. has also written two full-length adult novels as well as stories for younger children. Drawing on her research of the black experience in the South and her own knowledge of life in Harlem where she grew up, G. published her first novel, *Bird at My Window* in 1966, a work that met with mixed critical reviews. This is an ambitious first novel that revolves around a black family forced by racism in the South to move to Harlem. The conflicts among the adult children in this family, Wade, Faith, and Willie Earl, and between them and their widowed mother are reflected in the larger society and lead to violence and alienation. Almost two decades later, G. published her second adult novel *A Measure of Time* (1983). This work set partly in Harlem during the 1930s and 1940s traces the hectic life of the inimitable Dorine Davis who continually lives just outside the law. With this second novel, again, the critics, while pointing out that on some level the work succeeds, did not feel that the author had quite fulfilled her literary promise.

In the meantime, G. seemed to have found her creative niche in writing stories suitable for young adults, specifically books for young black adults, a literary genre that had been previously largely nonexistent. Between 1973 and 1978, G. published three such works: *The Friends* (1973), *Ruby* (1976), and *Edith Jackson* (1978). Not surprisingly, in this trilogy, G. draws heavily on her own experience as the child of a transplanted Caribbean family. G. introduces the reader to two families. Calvin and Ramona Cathy, the parents of two teenaged daughters, Ruby and Phylissia, head the West Indian family. The Jacksons are an African American family of six young children, an absent father, and no mother. Ironically, the head of this household is sixteen-year-old Edith, the oldest daughter. By focusing on the experiences of these young female characters, Phylissia, Ruby, and Edith, in the home, at school, and in the community, G. highlights a wide range of issues that affects these young women adversely.

These texts can be read as an indictment of the adults with whom these children interact, an indictment because of the unwillingness of the parents and teachers to talk and to listen to the young people. Calvin Cathy fails as a father because he bullies his daughters and abuses them physically. The silent, nameless Jackson father literally turns his back on his children as he sits with his back to the room and his gaze towards the streets. G. also draws attention to the reality of a racist and uncaring school system in which teachers feel free to insult children and their parents with impunity. In addition, G. tackles the issue of bicultural conflicts. Phylissia is constantly at odds with her father whose West Indian values conflict with the new American values. To compound her problems, Phylissia is alienated from her classmates who mock her speech, her dress, and her general attitude. The only constant in Phylissia's world is the friendship offered her by Edith. Unfortunately, because of her own ambivalence about her values and those of her father, she initially spurns Edith's offer. Finally, the author shows us the maturing Phylissia beginning to come to terms with herself, her father, and her environment after much self analysis. G. continues to explore her concern for the welfare of adolescents, focusing

on the social dilemma of young men in such works as *The Disappearance* (1979) and *New Guys around the Block* (1983). Again, she makes the point that young people, male or female, need caring adults in their lives.

G. has also adapted well-known fables for the purpose of creating works of fiction suitable for younger children, especially children of the black diaspora, stories that entertain as well as teach. First, she translated from the French, Birago Diop's African tale entitled *Mother Crocodile* (1981). This work that can be read as a cautionary tale can also be viewed as a retelling of the story of the African continent and its peoples. Another example of G.'s creative use of a popular fable is *My Love, My Love or the Peasant Girl* (1985), a work fashioned after Hans Christian Andersen's fable "The Little Mermaid." Set in the French Caribbean, this work examines symbolically the issues of colonialism, classism, and sexism. G. reshapes this story into a tale of the beautiful peasant girl Desiree Dieu-Donne who falls in love with Daniel Beauxhomme, the scion of a rich and powerful upper class family to make a statement about those who have power and how they wield that power to control others.

G., who has traveled to the Caribbean and to Africa to research materials for her books, has incorporated in some of her stories aspects of the folklore of the African diaspora, which she uses metaphorically often to convey her theme. By using this literary strategy, G. succeeds in doing what one suspects has been one of her goals ever since she started to write, that is to use her stories to bridge the gap between Africa and the New World.

BIBLIOGRAPHY: Norris, J., *Presenting R. G.* (1988); Pollack, S., and D. D. Knight, eds., *Contemporary Lesbian Writers of the United States* (1993)

                                        LEOTA S. LAWRENCE

H

HACKER, Marilyn
b. 27 November 1942, Bronx, New York

H.'s poetry juxtaposes radical politics with strict formalism, and the contradiction puzzles many readers and critics. Since her first full-length book, *Presentation Piece* (1974), won the Lamont Poetry Selection of the Academy of American Poets and the National Book Award in 1975, many have argued for and against both sides of H.'s art. Those who sympathize with her politics are suspicious of her use of form; they question its necessity and occasionally blame it for undermining her serious concerns. Those who admire her brilliant technical achievements in language are often intimidated by what has been called a sense of despair, an overarching negative worldview in her poems. H.'s topics do address at times the darkest aspects of human nature and history, but through her wit and sensitivity to language, especially with the use of complex forms, she imposes meaning, justice, and even beauty onto what can be a random and cruel universe.

H.'s next two books, *Separations* (1976) and *Taking Notice* (1980), continue the style and themes of *Presentation Piece,* so much so that the books have been called a trilogy. The collections increasingly trace personal developments—relationships with the poet's mother and daughter, her lesbianism, instances of love, death, and illness in her own everyday life—in a more public context: feminism, history, myth. She finds the stories of the world replayed in her own life, and her poems turn on the idea of connecting the universal and the personal, each assisting in making sense of the other. Her use of confining forms like sestinas, canzones, and pantoums give her an increased ability to speak the most intimate words; with their restrictive nature comes the suggestion of privacy, of something held in reserve.

With her fourth book entitled *Assumptions* (1985), H. seemed to be reaching a more sympathetic audi-ence. It was suggested that her formal tendencies were not in opposition to her politics after all, but in fact were an avenue to reclaiming a kind of language that had been exclusive of women. As begun in *Taking Notice,* the landscape of France continued to play a role in her work as she spent more time there, residing in Paris for part of the year. Her sense of disharmony with American politics had caused an earlier self-imposed exile in London as well, where she had been an antiquarian book dealer. Her fifth book was likewise a marriage of radical and traditional; *Love, Death, and the Changing of the Seasons* (1986) was a verse novel chronicling the development of a lesbian relationship through a sonnet sequence. Another collection, *Going Back to the River* (1990), also seems to focus on deep friendships and love; one poem addresses the poet James WRIGHT—a likely comparison to H. with his use of gentle tone and lyrical language to describe some of life's harshest realities.

The Hang-Glider's Daughter: New and Selected Poems appeared in 1990, but the more complete *Selected Poems, 1965–1990* was published in 1994, along with *Winter Numbers,* a collection that reflects H.'s steadfast devotion to presenting harsh reality tempered with beauty. She addresses her own mortality and that of her friends in the context of the AIDS crisis and breast cancer, notably in a sonnet sequence about her own fight with the disease. For this volume, H. received the Lenore Marshall/*The Nation* Poetry Prize.

Although her expert craftsmanship may draw the most critical attention and commentary, formalism is only the beginning of H.'s statements. While anyone writing a canzone expects it to be noted as such, her forms always serve the larger purpose of her subject; the two are inseparable.

H. has edited many journals including *Quark: A Quarterly of Speculative Fiction, Ploughshares,* and more recently the *Kenyon Review.* She has taught writing at many institutions and has received many awards and fellowships, including the Jenny McKeen Moore Fellowship for Writers at George Washington University, the New York YWHA Poetry Center Discovery Award, and Guggenheim, NEA, and Ingram Merrill Fellowships. She was one of very few artists to refuse an NEA Fellowship on the basis of its "obscenity restriction."

BIBLIOGRAPHY: Hammond, K., "An Interview with M. H.," *Frontiers* 5 (Fall 1980): 22–27; Mitchell, F., "M. H.," in Gwynn, R. S., ed., *DLB*, vol. 120, *American Poets since World War II* (1992): 102–8

NICOLE SARROCCO

HADAS, Rachel

b. 8 November 1948, New York City

H., the daughter of the late, prominent Columbia University classicist, Moses Hadas, is, along with Dana GIOIA, Brad LEITHAUSER, Mary Jo SALTER, and Molly PEACOCK, among a group of New Formalist poets to have studied at Harvard with another of the 20th c.'s major classicists, Robert FITZGERALD. Upon graduating from Radcliffe in 1969, H. extended her "classical" education through a sojourn in Athens and on the Greek island of Samos. In Greece, she became acquainted with other American poets there, notably James MERRILL, W. H. AUDEN and Chester Kallman, and Alan Ansen. She also met her first husband, Stavros Kondylis, whom she married in 1970. Her experiences in Greece form the subject matter of her first two collections of poetry, *Starting from Troy* (1975) and *Slow Transparency* (1983), as well as of an illuminating autobiographical essay, "Mornings in Ormos," included in her collection of prose and poetry, *Living in Time* (1990). Since returning to the U.S., H. earned an M.F.A. in poetry from the writing workshop at Johns Hopkins (1978) and a Ph.D. in comparative literature from Harvard (1982). She married George Edwards, a composer and professor of music at Columbia, with whom she had a son, Jonathan, in 1984. Since 1981, she has taught English at Rutgers University—Newark.

With the publication of her third collection of poetry, *A Son from Sleep* (1989), H. began to find the subject matter that would animate her most impressive, mature poetry: maternity and medititations upon literature, teaching, and the passing on of knowledge from generation to generation. The best poems in this volume are "That Walk Away as One: A Marriage Brood," a ten-part meditation on marriage, and "The Cistern," on the connection between the intellectual nourishment H. received from her father and the physical nourishment she provides her son through her body. These themes are expanded upon in H.'s fourth book of poems, *Pass It On* (1989), perhaps her strongest and the one that makes clear that her greatest strengths as a poet lie more as a writer of thematically unified sequences than in shorter self-contained lyrics.

In *Pass It On*, H.'s use of conventional poetic meter and rhyme lend increased clarity and verbal richness to her poetry. In "Fix It (Winter)," H. often uses nursery-rhyme-like quatrains to relay the poet's experience of her son's faith in her ability to "fix" the problems in the world. "Horus Concuss (Spring)," on the other hand, recounts, primarily in rhymed couplets, the poet-mother's morning stroll through upper Manhattan. But perhaps the finest poem here is "Teacher between Terms," a finely-sustained lyric about the emotions a professor feels when she is not teaching. Her best poems about her relationship with her young son include "Our First Son's Summer Here," and "Three Silences," the latter about, among other things, the intimacy of breast feeding.

In 1990, H. won an award in literature from the American Academy and Institute of Arts and published a fifth volume of poetry, *Living in Time,* which includes the long, meditative autobiographical poem, "The Dream Machine," written in the manner of William Wordsworth's *The Prelude,* albeit in a far more compact form. Much of H.'s philosophical speculation here arises from her son's questions about the nature of reality, dreams, and language. Similar preoccupations about the interrelationship between domesticity and culture are contained in H.'s sixth book of poetry, *Mirrors of Astonishment* (1992). H.'s work teaching poetry-writing at the Gay Men's Health Crisis has resulted in *Unending Dialogue: Voices from an AIDS Poetry Workshop* (1991), which contains an autobiographical essay by H. about teaching the workshop; a sequence of her own poems that derive from her firsthand confrontation with AIDS; and a selection of poems by students in the workshop.

H. remains one of the strongest women voices to have emerged from the New Formalism, her poems appearing regularly in journals such as the *New Yorker* and *Boulevard.* She has also published a collection of translations from Latin, French (especially Baudelaire), and modern Greek, *Other Worlds Than This* (1994), as well as a verse translation of Seneca's Latin drama, *Oedipus* (1995).

BIBLIOGRAPHY: Benfey, C., "From the Greek," *Parnassus* 16 (1991): 405–14; Rifkin, L., "Language as Gesture: Mourning and the Poetics of AIDS," *MinnR* 40 (Spring-Summer 1993): 133–37

ROBERT MCPHILLIPS

HAGEDORN, Jessica [Tarahata]
b. 1949, Manila, Philippines

H.'s first novel established her as one of the central voices in postcolonial and Asian American literary studies. Although her short fiction, plays, and poetry are widely anthologized, her eclectic allegiance to multiple media and genres may explain her relatively recent acceptance in larger literary circles. While known predominantly as a novelist, poet, and performance artist, H. has been a playwright, periodical reviewer, screenwriter, anthology editor, lead singer and band lyricist, public radio commentator, and is now channeling her creative energies into film and video. Her work in multiple genres has led to a focus on aural and visual aspects within her writing, which is allied to a sense of interactive performance. Similarly, the experience of immigrant living in San Francisco during the heyday of both political radicalism and ethnic revivalism of the 1960s informs much of the work, as do her adventures as a young adult performance artist in New York.

H.'s writing is characterized by powerful language and a politically sharpened wit, achieved by combining English, Tagalog, Spanish, and vernaculars. Critics have expressed both unease and admiration for her graphic prose, which doesn't flinch in the face of the disorder and horror of emotional power struggles. Sex, drugs, and rock and roll may be the foundations for her pieces, but she does not omit the beating, cheating, madness, and murder inherent therein. Critics also respond to her postmodernist narrative technique of building a composite out of shifting narrators and multiple points of view, as well as her eddying, disruptive sequencing of plot. Clearly influenced by poetic conventions, there is a density of meaning in the language that gives her prose a peculiar weight without ponderous length. Her prose is frequently punctuated with such things as poems, songs, news clippings, dictionary entries, historical accounts, or radio transcript excerpts.

Early in her career, H.'s writing drew the attention of poet Kenneth REXROTH, who encouraged her to refine her craft and eventually edited her poetry for inclusion in the anthology *Four Young Women* (1973). *Pet Food and Tropical Apparitions* (1981), a novella that includes a small collection of poems, garnered the American Book Award and brought H. the recognition and financial backing she needed to complete her first full-length novel. *Pet Food and Tropical Apparitions* is an almost cinematic piece with surreal touches in which characters are sketched from the competing social strata of a culture not explicitly identified as the Philippines. Most importantly, it offers an early taste of the skill that H. would later refine: a fine ear

and accurate hand for depicting women caught in the crossfire of family, cultural, political, and personal expectations.

H.'s breakthrough came with *Dogeaters* (1990); the novel's commercial and critical success resulted in a nomination for the National Book Award. Set in the 1950s Philippines, it is populated by an ensemble cast ranging from Rio Gonzago, a wealthy schoolgirl who grows up in a haze of movies and radio soaps and narrates from her adult residence in the U.S.; to Joey, a radio personality and prostitute; to Rainer, a jaded filmmaker in the local spotlight; to Madamme, the actual dictator's wife. The plot hinges on the assassination of an opposition leader who threatens to undermine the dictator's stranglehold on the nation. Depicting the "dog-eat-dog" mentality of Marcos-era Philippine culture, it juxtaposes the seamy appeal and misery of the slums, and the fears and delusions of the upper class, with the material wealth and moral poverty of the dictator's circle.

Set in 1960s San Francisco, *Gangster of Love* (1996) is the fictional account of Raquel "Rocky" Rivera's progression from Filipina adolescent to New York rock scene diva, then to duty-bound daughter with a daughter of her own. There are plenty of autobiographical elements gleaned from H.'s travails with her Gangster Choir band in New York, but they do not overshadow the slow process of Rocky's grudging love and acceptance of the disparate members of her family. Rocky's attempts to negotiate the demands of being a good daughter, sister, mother, and lover clash with her desire to fulfill her own potential as an artist. This is very much a novel about coming to terms with one's family, whether biological or chosen and assembled of friends, lovers, and colleagues. The shifting narration and sympathies, nonlinear sequence of events, and interweaving of songs, flashbacks, definitions, and other genres reveal H. in peak form, acknowledging but making full use of both the diversity and divides of contemporary American culture.

BIBLIOGRAPHY: Corgan, M., "Gangster of Love," *The Nation* 263 (28 October 1996): 64; D'Alpuget, B., "Dogeaters," *NYTBR* 25 March 1990: 1; De Manuel, T. L., "J. H.," in *Encyclopedia of Post-Colonial Writers in English* (1994): 620; San Juan, E., "Mapping the Boundaries: The Filipino Writer in the U.S.A.," *JES* 19 (1991): 117

ELIZABETH BLEICHER

HALE, Edward Everett
b. 3 April 1822, Boston, Massachusetts; d. 10 June 1909, Boston, Massachusetts

The grandnephew of Nathan Hale, the Revolutionary War patriot who was executed as a spy by the British,

H. is best known for three of his short stories, "My Double; And How He Undid Me" (1859), "The Man without a Country" (1863), and "The Brick Moon" (1869): fictions markedly influenced by his personal background, personality, and choice of profession. Graduating from Harvard College at seventeen, he was fortunate to count among his family's friends and his own relations a number of illustrious Boston "Brahmins"—a caste described by Oliver Wendell HOLMES in *Elsie Venner* as New England's hereditary scholarly aristocracy—and other influential personages. Both grandfathers were ministers. His maternal uncle Edward Everett was a minister and famous orator, a classics professor and president of Harvard, governor of Massachusetts, an ambassador, secretary of state, and U.S. senator. H.'s father, Nathan Hale, was an affluent businessman, newspaper publisher, and railroad developer, In 1852, H. married Emily Perkins, granddaughter of Lyman Beecher and niece of Harriet Beecher STOWE.

H.'s lifework was the Christian ministry. He served as minister of Boston's South Congregational Church from 1856 to 1899; from 1903 to 1909 he was chaplain of the U.S. Senate. Highly articulate, he elected to write for publication, becoming a prolific author of patriotic and historical works, homiletic, social-uplift, and other inspirational pieces, and an array of fiction uneven in quality. He was also a magazine publisher and edited a number of periodicals. John R. Adams remarks, "H.'s ambition to publish the universal ideal literary magazine" caused his biggest "journalistic disappointment . . . the failure of *Old and New*"—published from 1870 to 1875. A salient feature of H. as a writer was his creative imagination and whimsical cast of mind.

"My Double; And How He Undid Me" concerns an overworked Sandemanian Protestant minister, Reverend Frederic Ingham, and his employee, a look-alike simpleton to whom he has taught four routine responses, that he might stand in for him at public functions. The witless "double" in this artistically recycled ancient joke eventually misspeaks, and all is lost. The character Frederic Ingham became a role-changing "double" or alter ego for H. in a number of other stories. Captain Frederic Ingham narrates "The Man without a Country," the account of an army officer, Philip Nolan, who had collaborated with Aaron Burr to seize Southwestern territories of the new nation. The conspiracy was discovered, and Nolan was found guilty of treason; damning his country, Nolan said he wished never to hear of it again. As punishment, he was banished forever from the country he repudiated, and was kept in custody at sea on a succession of naval vessels; however, he died deeply repentant. This story, based indirectly on an actual event,

was made into a motion picture in 1925 and a television movie in 1973 starring Cliff Robertson and Robert Ryan.

Narrated by Frederic Ingham, "The Brick Moon"—a fanciful science fiction piece—describes in close technical detail an enormous brick sphere built by Ingham and associates as a guiding star for mariners. As elsewhere in H.'s science fantasy stories, scientific principles are used and discarded at will. The (prophetically described) satellite is accidentally launched prematurely; nevertheless, the imprisoned astronauts manage to communicate with Ingham to tell him how they are faring. Ingham's comments are significant: he can discuss this "brick moon" matter since his "double" is taking his place at a "bored" meeting, and he ponders whether others would not do better being enclosed in such little worlds, merely telegraphing periodically to the rest of the people. "The Last of the Florida" (1864) concerns a special dispatch sent by Frederic Ingham, captain of the *Florida*, in Bahia, Brazil, to his wife. The dispatch is received four years ahead of the mail by circling the globe 1,200 times spirally from Brazil. In "Colonel Ingham's Journey" (1883), H.'s familiar "double" seeks his other self by going to the North Pole, where he encounters that person, a Chinese named Kan-schau. In response to Nathaniel HAWTHORNE's "The Minister's Black Veil," B.'s "The Minister's Black Veil: With Full Particulars" (1889) describes the plight of Reverend Hooper who, unable to work effectively because of his overly demanding congregants, wears the veil so he can move freely in public, incognito. A slightly irreverent tale, "Aunt Caroline's Present" (1885) is a rollicking account of an unsightly wedding gift that cannot be discarded: a painting inspired by the parable of the Prodigal Son.

Noteworthy among the works of nonfiction of this lover and popularizer of history, dabbler in science, and cleric to the last are *James Russell Lowell and His Friends* (1899), *A New England Boyhood* (1893), and *Memories of a Hundred Years* (2 vols., 1902; rev. ed., 1904).

BIBLIOGRAPHY: Adams, J. R., *E. E. H.* (1977); Holloway, J., *E. E. H.: A Biography* (1956)

SAMUEL I. BELLMAN

HALE, Lucretia Peabody

b. 2 September 1820, Boston, Massachusetts; d. 13 June 1900, Boston, Massachusetts

Although involved in a variety of writing modes from early on in life, H.'s fame rests with her accomplishments in the field of CHILDREN'S LITERATURE, most notably her tales of the fictitious Peterkin family. These Peterkin tales were popular with both children and adults of H.'s time; besides telling simple stories, H.'s Peterkin works are in essence witty comedies of manners, poking fun at the whims and eccentricities of the middle class in which H. was reared.

Several of the Peterkin stories were first published in the juvenile magazines *Our Young Folks* and *St. Nicholas* before being collected in book form as *The Peterkin Papers* in 1880. A second collection, *The Last of the Peterkins, with Others of Their Kin,* was published in 1886. The Peterkin tales continue to find an audience in contemporary times. An edition of "The Lady Who Put Salt in Her Coffee," first published in 1868, was reprinted in book form in 1989, certainly a testimony to H.'s transcendence through the ages.

H. also deserves credit for her writing accomplishments earlier in her life. As an adolescent, H., along with the rest of her family, actively helped father Nathan Hale, editor of the *Boston Daily Advertiser,* by writing editorials and other opinion pieces. As she entered adulthood, H., who remained single throughout her life, supported herself continually—and well—with her writing.

H. deserves credit as a novelist, also, though her efforts in this area were collaborative. *Margaret Percival in America,* a collaboration with her brother Edward Everett HALE published in 1850, revolves around themes of religion and morality in modern society. Another effort, *Six of One by Half a Dozen of the Other* (1872), is a six-way collaboration again involving her brother Edward as well as Harriet Beecher STOWE. This work combines the moral and religious aspects of the previous novels with themes of a comedy of manners, all of which served to prepare H. for her later children's works.

Despite H.'s relegation to relative obscurity in literary history, the author's work—especially the Peterkin family tales—deserves recognition for several reasons. H. does present in the tales as much of a social commentary as do her more noted contemporaries and does write clearly and validly in the mode of comedy of manners. This should not be overlooked simply because of her choice of children's literature as genre. That choice of genre is, in fact, another strength in the author's favor. H.'s abilities in her chosen genre must be granted due credit, especially as her tales remain in print and are readily found in children's libraries, with their inherent message ever relevant. Lastly, H.'s status as a single, independent woman making a good living solely by her pen in 19th-c. America gives cause to hail the author as worthy of a less obscure place in literary study.

BIBLIOGRAPHY: Gay, C., "L. P. H.," in Estes, G. E., ed., *DLB,* vol. 42, *American Writers for Children*

before 1900 (1985): 203–7; Mainiero, L., ed., *American Women Writers* (1982)

TERRY D. NOVAK

HALE, Sarah Josepha [Buell]

b. 24 October 1788, Newport, New Hampshire; d. 30 April 1879, Philadelphia, Pennsylvania

An innovative editor and one of the most influential women of the 19th c., H. began her career at age thirty-five when left a widow with several children to support. She used her rural New Hampshire background in writing *Northwood* (1827), a novel that discusses slavery and contrasts life in the North and South. Perhaps more importantly, it is one of the earliest attempts at realistic portrayal of everyday life.

The success of *Northwood* led H. to the editorship of the Boston *Ladies' Magazine* and eventually *Godey's Lady's Book,* published in Philadelphia by Louis Godey. She made the magazine the arbiter of contemporary taste and manners, as circulation climbed from 10,000 in 1837 to an impressive 150,000 in 1860. H.'s editorial achievement stemmed from her desire to "promote the reputation of my own sex and of my own country." Instead of lifting articles from British periodicals, she sought original writings by Americans, women as well as men, on national subjects. She established the domestic departments existing in today's home magazines—cooking, sewing, gardening—and introduced Godey's famous hand-colored fashion plates and steel engravings.

Although H. tended to be pious and conventional and warned her readers not to "encroach on the prerogatives of men," she campaigned vigorously for higher education for women. The seeming contradiction has resulted in widely varying interpretations, some of H.'s biographers calling her a "militant feminist" and others a "true conservative." Actually, she believed that women were born with a superior moral sense; its effective use required education but also restriction to the domestic sphere lest it be contaminated in the realm of public affairs.

While editor of *Godey's Lady's Book,* H. continued to write prolifically, publishing fiction and poetry and editing numerous recipe books, household handbooks, anthologies of women's writings, and works for children. Her monumental biographical encyclopedia, *Women's Record* (1853; rev. eds., 1869, 1876), contains some 2,500 entries. H.'s most important creative work, however, is that done early in her career—*Northwood, Sketches of American Character* (1829), and *Poems for Our Children* (1830), which contains "Mary Had a Little Lamb."

BIBLIOGRAPHY: Bardes, B. A., and S. Gossett, "S. J. H., Selective Promoter of Her Sex," in Albertine, S., ed., *A Living of Words: American Women in Print Culture* (1995); Baym, N., "Onward Christian Women: S. J. H.'s History of the World," *NEQ* 63 (1990): 249–70; Entrikin, I. W., *S. J. H. and "Godey's Lady's Book"* (1946); Finley, R. E., *The Lady of Godey's* (1931); Okker, P., *Our Sister Editors: S. J. H. and the Tradition of Nineteenth Century American Women Editors* (1995); Rogers, S., *S. J. H.* (1985)

BARBARA A. WHITE

HALEY, Alex [Murray Palmer]

b. 11 August 1921, Ithaca, New York; d. 11 February 1992, Seattle, Washington

For a short time, H. may have been the most famous living African American author, but it is not entirely clear which of the many senses of the word "author" best fits H.'s accomplishments.

Embarking in earnest on a writing career only after twenty years in the Coast Guard, H. was down to eighteen cents and a can of sardines when in 1962 he was assigned by *Playboy* to interview jazz virtuoso Miles Davis. This was followed soon after by a feature on Malcolm X, which led in turn to *The Autobiography of Malcolm X,* published in 1965. In one sense, of course, Malcolm was the author of the *Autobiography,* but the job of getting Malcolm's words on paper fell to H. Malcolm was apparently satisfied with the result, and the book has established itself as a classic of AFRICAN AMERICAN LITERATURE, but what sense of "author" may we apply to H.'s role? Most critics grant H. credit for capturing in print the charismatic presence of the subject. Some felt, however, that H., a political moderate, blunted Malcolm's message.

H.'s next important work, *Roots* (1976), was a remarkable cultural phenomenon whose nature remains ambiguous. That the book is in some part the culmination of H.'s genealogical researches into his family history on his mother's side is certainly true, but much else, including whether H.'s quest was successful, remains unsettled. Two separate charges of plagiarism (one certainly settled out of court with folklorist and novelist Harold Courlander, and Crown Publishers) raised further uncertainties. And H.'s classification of the book as "faction"—neither fact nor fiction—made it difficult to approach it critically. None of these problems lessened the impact. The book sold millions of copies, was used as a text in countless classrooms, and was translated into more than two dozen languages. H. received both the Pulitzer Prize and the National Book Award in 1977. But, further clouding H.'s identification as an author, *Roots* was not just a book. It was also, as of 1977, the most widely viewed miniseries

in the history of television, reaching well over thirty million households.

H. would later announce a number of projects never brought to completion. He did team with Norman Lear to develop a television series, *Palmerstown, USA,* in 1980, and he published in 1988 a novella, *A Different Kind of Christmas,* dealing with slave escapes in the 1850s. *Roots* inspired two television sequels, in 1979 and 1988, but H. did not in any precise sense serve as the author of either one.

Before his death in 1992, H. worked with David Stevens, an Australian screenwriter, on *Queen,* intending this time to trace his father's side of the family. A television series aired in 1993, and Stevens in the same year published a book version, based on boxes of notes and a seven-hundred-page outline left by H. Once again, reviewers were uncertain whether to approach the book as fact or fiction. And the question remains: where in this process can we locate the author?

The question remains, but it may not be important. *Roots* remains as well, part of our shared myth of America. If we accept the critic Leslie A. FIEDLER's provocative view of *Roots* as a segment of America's "inadvertent epic," created to no master plan by many hands over many years, the question of individual authorship loses much of its urgency. But H.'s contribution to this creative process must be gratefully acknowledged.

BIBLIOGRAPHY: Fiedler, L. A., *The Inadvertent Epic* (1979); Taylor, H., "The *Griot* from Tennessee: The Saga of A. H.'s *Roots,*" *CritI* 37 (Summer 1995): 46–62

W. P. KENNEY

HALL, Donald

b. 28 September 1928, New Haven, Connecticut

H. has done a great deal to influence the way many readers think about poetry, both by his example and through his extensive critical writings. H. has written in several styles, first very formal verse, then much looser and often surrealist poems, and later a combination of the two. His poems always show both an abiding interest in craft—H. often revises a poem several times even after it has been published—and a continuing preoccupation with several central themes: the struggle to find a place in the natural world (especially as embodied in the farming life of New England), the pleasures and pains of human intimacy, and the relationship between generations. H.'s work as a critic and essayist is just as important as his poetry. Whether writing family memoirs or in the genre he himself calls "literary gossip," he addresses the most serious issues—mortality, responsibility—in readable, even light-hearted, prose.

One striking feature of H.'s work is that it is at once very literary and very earthy. The life that H. has lived shows the fusion of the same two qualities. He grew up in Connecticut but spent summers at his grandfather's farm on Eagle Pond in New Hampshire. The farm and the memory of the generations of his ancestors who worked the land reappear often in both H.'s poems and his prose. He immersed himself in the literary life early on. He met Robert FROST while taking part in the Bread Loaf writer's conference as a sixteen-year-old. At Harvard, as an editor of the *Harvard Advocate,* he met Dylan Thomas and T. S. ELIOT. During his years in Europe (he received a B.Litt. from Oxford in 1953), he met Ezra POUND. All these poets, however, were more role models and subjects for H.'s memoirs than influences on his own verse.

H.'s earlier poems collected in *Exiles and Marriages* (1955) and *The Dark Houses* (1958) are for the most part in tight metrical forms. Several, such as the widely anthologized "My Son My Executioner" and "Christmas Eve in Whiteneyville," discuss the continuity of the generations and the fact of mortality. In others, like "Exile," for which H. won the Newdigate Prize at Oxford, speakers both yearn for and wish to flee from intimacy. The setting is often a homogeneous suburban world that seems stifling.

During the years he taught at the University of Michigan (1957–75), H.'s poetry became less formal, more sensuous, and sometimes even surreal. His collections of poetry include *A Roof of Tiger-Lilies* (1964), *The Yellow Room* (1971), and *The Alligator Bride* (1969), which reprints some earlier poems in heavily revised forms. H.'s later collections, *A Blue Wing Tilts at the Edge of the Sea* (1975), *Kicking the Leaves* (1978), *The Toy Bone* (1979), and *The Happy Man* (1986), contain a variety of styles. H. revised his work again for *Old and New Poems* (1990), sometimes returning to the earlier version of a poem. He has been very active as a reviewer, a critic, and an editor of collections. His observations on poetry are collected in *Goatfoot Milktounge Twinbird* (1978), *The Weather for Poetry* (1982), and *Poetry and Ambition* (1988).

H.'s memoir of his childhood on the farm, *String Too Short to Be Saved: Recollections of Summers on a New England Farm* (1961), is a profoundly touching, elegiac account of farm life and of the virtues of New England. In 1975, H. retired from teaching and returned to live at the farm, and he has since written more essays about that place as the intersection of the human and the natural worlds, notably in *Seasons at Eagle Pond* (1987) and *Here at Eagle Pond* (1990).

Perhaps more importantly, the farm has inspired a series of powerful poems, such as "Names of Horses" and "Great Day in the Cows' House," in which H. considers the links between generations of men and beasts. The bonds between generations is often the subject when H. writes about sports, as in *Fathers Playing Catch with Sons* (1985), and even when he writes about other poets. *Remembering Poets* (1978), revised as *Their Ancient Glittering Eyes* (1992), is a surprisingly touching account of Robert Frost, Ezra Pound, and the other older poets H. met as a young man.

H.'s more recent work has dealt with aging and the prospect of death. In *The One Day* (1988), which won the National Book Critics Circle Award, H. deals explicitly with middle age in a long poem that imitates several forms, from the pastoral to the jeremiad. In the memoir *Life Work* (1993), he confronts his own liver cancer and the impending death of his second wife, the poet Jane Kenyon. The poems on the same subject show the same technical skill and emotional power that has marked all his work.

BIBLIOGRAPHY: Hamilton, D., "D. H.'s *The One Day,*" *GettR* 2 (1989): 268–78; Haskell, D., "The Modern American Poetry of Deep Image," *SoR* 12 (1979): 137–66; Mills, R., "D. H.'s Poetry," *IowaR* 2 (1971): 82–123

BRIAN ABEL RAGEN

HALL, James
b. 29 July 1793, Philadelphia, Pennsylvania; d. 5 July 1868, Cincinnati, Ohio

Born into a family of writers and publishers, H. was reared thinking writing was a part of everyday life. Though his primary occupation was in law and politics, H. was active as a writer, editor, and publisher throughout his life. He held interests in a number of newspapers, writing journalistic pieces on popular issues, but became popular for his letters and short "Western" tales describing life in the Ohio Valley, which was at the time part of the Western frontier.

It was his "Letters from the West," a serial first published in H.'s *Illinois Gazette* and later expanded into the volume *Letters from the West: Containing Sketches of Scenery Manners, and Customs; and Anecdotes Connected with the First Settlements of the Western Sections of the United States* (1828), that earned him his reputation as a Western writer. His travels as a circuit judge dispensing justice throughout a three thousand square mile wilderness area brought him into contact with the frontier and its settlers. This setting and its characters provided material for most of H.'s tales. He became a vocal advocate of the WEST and was devoted to the creation of a wholly Western literature. He conceived and had published a Western anthology entitled *The Western Souvenir: A Christmas and New Years Gift for 1829* (1828) to which he contributed five tales and nineteen poems. H. tales were highly regarded for their evocation of place and believable characters, but were criticized for an inflated style. One of H.'s stories to appear in the collection is noteworthy for the presence of what was to become a stock character in Western fiction—"The Indian Hater." H. was sensitive to the Indians and portrayed those settlers who harbored a murderous hate for them in a less than kind light. He does, however, present the racial issue in all of its complexity—the Indian hater in this story carries the brutal memory of his family's murder by Indians.

In a later collection, *Tales of the Border* (1835), H. includes a story exploring the same theme. "The Pioneer" begins in much the same way as "The Indian Hater," but differs in that the man's sister is abducted after the family is murdered. The protagonist is bent on revenge, but when he finally finds his sister, he discovers her living peacefully and happily within the tribe.

In addition to short fiction, H. wrote many essays, a novel, histories, and biographies. Late in his career he authored *The History of the Indian Tribes of North America*—published in twenty parts from 1836 to 1844—which, though dated in its sociological and ethnological approach, serves as a valuable historical record. H. is a significant figure in American literary history for pioneering Western literature, for providing a look at life on the early frontier, and for introducing examples of Western stereotypes.

BIBLIOGRAPHY: Flanagan, J. T., *J. H.: Literary Pioneer of the Ohio Valley* (1941); Hall, D. G., "J. H.," in Kimbel, B. E., ed., *DLB*, vol. 74, *American Short Story Writers before 1880* (1988): 125–33; Randall, R. C., *J. H.: Spokesman of the New West* (1964)

JASON MCMAHON

HALLECK, Fitz-Greene

b. 8 July 1790, Guilford, Connecticut; d. 19 December 1867, Guilford, Connecticut

H., a self-proclaimed amateur poet, established his literary reputation publishing satires of New York society between 1819 and 1827. Although criticized for his sentimentality and lack of production, H. won the friendship of William Cullen BRYANT and James Fenimore COOPER, who praised H. for his simplicity and lyricism. H. himself admired simplicity, believing

good poetry should be easy to memorize. H. is seldom read or studied today, but he remains significant both as a minor Knickerbocker poet and as a commentator of New York's upper-class society.

In 1811, H. moved from Guilford to New York City, where he worked as a banker and became an intimate friend of Joseph Rodman Drake. In 1819, H. and Drake collaborated on thirty-five satiric poems as *The Croakers*: Drake was "Croaker," H. was "Croaker, Junior," and together they were "Croaker and Company." These poems, published in the *New York Evening Post* and reprinted nationally, reflected the Knickerbocker taste for light social criticism, referring mostly to local politicians. H. and Drake wrote stanzas of mostly end-stopped, rhymed iambic pentameter and tetrameter lines, with H. favoring an *aabccb* stanza form. The two maintained anonymity for a year, receiving praise for their humor and criticism from Edgar Allan POE, who dismissed the poems as "ephemeral" and "carelessly written."

With the popularity of *The Croakers,* H. anonymously published *Fanny* (1819), a satiric poem about a poor merchant and his daughter who suddenly rise into society. Positioning the story between the visionary and the vulgar, H. sympathized with romance while ridiculing the *nouveau riche*. Advertised as an imitation of Byron's "Beppo," the poem uses digressions, enjambments across stanzas, and humorous, heteromerous rhymes, such as "dressed in" / "interesting" and "believe her" / "the beaver." But H.'s speaker never rises above naiveté, and while New York critics lauded the poem for its ease and local relevance, Poe again criticized H.'s work for its banality.

In the 1820s, H. embraced New York's literati, joining Bryant, Cooper, James Kirke PAULDING, Gulian Verplanck, and Samuel F. B. Morse to form the Bread and Cheese Lunch, an informal social organization. During this period, H. wrote few poems, preferring to socialize instead; however, what he did write was more substantial than his earlier light verse. "Marco Bozzaris" (1825), a poem in an unusual *ababccdeeed* stanza, memorializes the Greek revolutionary killed by the Turks in 1823, and "Connecticut" (1826), a poem in *ottava rima,* defies New York social tastes by appraising the Connecticut character without caricature. This work represents most clearly H.'s attempt in his poetry to dramatize conflicts between the real and the ideal, conflicts based on the polarities of his own character: New York Knickerbocker and New England Puritan, man of imaginative romance and man of stern practicality.

After publication of his collected works in *Alnwick Castle and Other Poems* (1827), H.'s only major literary project was editing *The Works of Lord Byron* (1833), the first edition to aim at completeness. Despite the potential significance of this volume, critics found H.'s commentary inadequate, and, in 1872, when the first statue commemorating an American poet was erected for H. in Central Park, it was testament more to his social than his poetic genius.

BIBLIOGRAPHY: Adkins, N. F., *F. H.: An Early Knickerbocker Wit and Poet* (1930); Wilson, J. G., *The Life and Letters of F. H.* (1869)

                                          TODD VERDUN

HALPER, Albert

b. 3 August 1904, Chicago, Illinois; 20 January 1984, Pawling, New York

H. belongs to the ranks of those writers who used their craft primarily as a form of social protest. He began writing in the late 1920s, and his works reflect the social history of the Great Depression era; he wrote about the labor movement—strikes, clashes with authority, the evils of capitalism—but his focus was on the individuals involved. H. was most concerned with the people's thoughts and feelings, their dignity, and their small triumphs in the face of overwhelming adversity.

H.'s first published novel, *Union Square* (1933), centers on the human activity taking place in and around this urban park. The dozen or so characters huddle, strut, and pace as the giant forces of economy and nature's seasons roll through "like giant wagon wheels . . . as stolid as fate." Each of the characters becomes involved somehow in the social and political issues of the day. H. portrays them in all of their strength and weakness as they grapple mainly with loss—loss of employment, loss of nerve, loss of feeling and belief. *Union Square* was well received for its authenticity.

On the Shore, Young Writer Remembering Chicago (1934), a collection of previously published short stories, chronicles the narrator's youth in the streets of Chicago. The stories are arranged to show the teller's growing awareness. Many see this as H.'s strongest writing. Here, his language is at its slangy and poetical best. *The Foundry* (1934) is the first in a series of novels about H.'s family and work experience. In it, he explores the relation of the individual to machinery and the labor movement. The men of the foundry are being replaced by technology and trouble ensues. *The Chute* (1937), based on H.'s experience as an order picker in a mail order house, attacks the "rapacity of big business." *Sons and Fathers* (1940) tells the story of an immigrant father who has left his native land to avoid military service only to have his sons subject to the same obligation in America. The final book of the series, *The Little People* (1942), is set in a clothing store and relates the heroics and foibles of the employers, employees, and customers—"the little people" in this world.

The two novels to follow, *Only an Inch from Glory* (1943) and *Atlantic Avenue* (1956), both concentrate on the interrelations of small groups of friends, exploring their emotional problems and attitudes toward the world and each other. These titles exhibit some of H.'s most polished work. *The Fourth Horseman of Miami Beach* (1966) has Leo Roth seeking his embezzling cousin in Florida. There, he meets a strange trio of retirees, the Horsemen, who invite him to replace their recently deceased fourth member. His adventures with the Horsemen and the recovery of his cousin lead Leo to important discoveries about himself.

H. went on to write more short stories, edit two anthologies of writings about Chicago, and publish a memoir, *Goodbye, Union Square* (1970). His place in the literary canon is controversial. Many critics found him a capable writer, valuable for his authentic and sympathetic characters, while others found his writing unoriginal, uninspired, and, at times, didactic.

BIBLIOGRAPHY: Champney, F., "A. H. and His Little People," *AR* 11 (December 1942): 628–34; Madden, D., ed., *Proletarian Writers of the Thirties* (1968); Hart, J. E., *A. H.* (1980)

                                          JASON MCMAHON

HAMMETT, [Samuel] Dashiell

b. 27 May 1894, St. Mary's County, Maryland; d. 10 January 1961, New York City

From 1922 to 1934, H. was the most talented and influential participant in the evolution of hard-boiled detective fiction. He developed and defined possibilities for art and authenticity within what might have been at best a lively lowbrow genre, setting a standard to which other writers continue to aspire. At its best, his work renders irrelevant the distinction between popular and serious fiction.

H. first made his mark in the pulp magazines that flourished in the 1920s. Aimed at a male mass audience, the pulps stressed action and adventure rather than the genteel artifice and lightweight intellectualism of the British detective story as it had evolved in England. To establish itself in the pulps, detective fiction would have to undergo a transformation: exploiting the American vernacular; riffing on American myths; offering American readers a detective as man of action, confronting murderers who never heard of the code of the English gentleman, in a world in which morality had to be constantly reinvented.

The stories by H. that appeared in the 1920s in *Black Mask,* most respected of the pulps, are distinguished by craft and vision from those of his contemporaries. Extravagant action and wild violence in a H. story are consistently countered by formal discipline and restraint. His hero, the Continental Op, is a nameless functionary who is authentically tough, but whose toughness reveals itself as a measured response, moral as well as physical, above all professional, to the situation at hand, rather than as brutality, callousness, or swagger.

Narrator as well as protagonist of the stories, the Continental Op avoids sentimentality and introspection with equal rigor. Even of himself, he reports what he says and does, rarely revealing what he thinks and feels. This restraint plays against the extravagance of the action, implying by indirection and understatement a tenuous distance between the hero and the world in which he must function. The distance remains tenuous, because, in H.'s complex moral vision, the hero is not immune to corruption or to violence.

Red Harvest and *The Dain Curse,* two novels featuring the Continental Op, were both published in 1929. The following year, H. produced what remains his most admired work, *The Maltese Falcon.* In this novel, H. replaces the first-person narration of the Continental Op stories with a rigorously objective point of view. Sam Spade, the detective protagonist, is viewed, as are all the other characters, from the outside. An effect is to make of the morally ambiguous detective (not necessarily as crooked as he is supposed to be) the most mysterious character in the book. He is, however, not the only memorable character. The conspirators, the police, the women in Spade's life, his mediocre partner, are all vividly drawn.

The Glass Key (1931), apparently H.'s personal favorite among his novels, has divided critics. While many share H.'s high opinion of it, others find that this time H.'s objective style constitutes an obstacle to the reader's involvement. Yet there is no denying the level of ambition; *The Glass Key* is probably H.'s most sustained attempt to write a detective novel that is unquestionably literature. For some, it remains his most impressive achievement.

The Thin Man (1934) was H.'s last novel. Although it was his greatest commercial success, it is a novel of parts, of witty or otherwise arresting passages, that never cohere to form a satisfying whole. It was the basis of a successful film, the first, as it developed, of a series, and Hollywood was to be the primary site of creative activity for H. from this point on. His only screenplay credit, however, is for the film adaptation of his friend and sometime lover Lillian HELLMAN's play *Watch on the Rhine.*

Where the canon of American literature is concerned, H. may remain just this side of paradise. That he was unable to sustain his powers through the last quarter century of his life, however his silence is to be explained, may seem to diminish the stature of his accomplishments. That his accomplishments may all be encompassed within the limits of a popular genre relegates him, for a certain kind of critic, to the category of minor writer. In Europe, especially in France, he is often numbered among the important American writers of the 20th c.; whether that estimate will ever establish itself on this side of the Atlantic remains in doubt. Yet H.'s critical reputation, though limited, seems secure; it may ascend.

BIBLIOGRAPHY: Gregory, S., *Private Investigations: The Novels of D. H.* (1985); Layman, R., *Shadow Man: The Life of D. H.* (1981); Mellen, J., *Hellman and H.* (1996) Symons, J., *D. H.* (1985); Wolfe, P., *Beams Falling: The Art of D. H.* (1980)

W. P. KENNEY

HAMMON, Jupiter
b. 17 October 1722, Long Island, New York; d. between 1790 and 1806, Long Island, New York

In 1787, H., a Long Island slave for most of the 18th c., commented in his essay "An Address to the Negroes in the State of New-York" that "it may be more for our own comfort to remain as we are." Certainly, H. did not mean to imply that *all* slaves were better off as slaves, yet it is exactly this position that his fellow slaves attributed to him. Interestingly, even two centuries have not served to clarify H.'s position, especially in regard to his place in the American literature.

H.'s position in American literature broadly, and AFRICAN AMERICAN LITERATURE specifically, has been a precarious one. Although he was first published in 1760, it was not until 1915 that he was recognized as the first African American poet published in America. Phillis WHEATLEY held this position until Oscar Wegelin's discovery of H.'s earliest broadside published almost a decade before Wheatley's work began appearing in print. But H.'s position was hardly a notable one, for scholar after scholar summarily dismissed H. as an earnest but unskilled poet whose ideas offered little more that an Uncle Tom viewpoint towards freedom for slaves. Recent scholarship, though, suggests a more favorable interpretation, arguing that H.'s place in American literature extends beyond his position as a first and that he is the progenitor of African American literature who skillfully initiated a protest against slavery, albeit one that has been overlooked because it is disguised by seemingly acquiescent biblical rhetoric.

Although H. lived over three-quarters of a century, he did not start writing until he was nearly seventy. During his relatively short writing career, H. managed to write in a variety of genres, including the poem, sermon, and essay. By the end of his life, he published four poems, one sermon, and two essays. While H.'s ouevre seems rather small, there is evidence that he published other pieces—the *Connecticut Courant,* for example, advertised H.'s "An Essay on the Ten Virgins" in 1779. Further, considering his social position and lack of intellectual training, it is truly remarkable that H. published all that he did.

H.'s themes and style are closely related. His literary themes center around religious topics—a problem to some literary critics because it means H. was not interested in the problem of slavery—while stylistically, he employs biblical rhetoric to do so. His themes closely undermine the institution of slavery precisely because they were religious. For example, in "An Evening Thought" (1760), H. addresses the idea of salvation; he repeats the word salvation twenty-three times. But his salvation is not merely spiritual, it is physical freedom, too. In "Dialogue," he juxtaposes the earthly master with God. In so doing, he subtly reveals the earthly master as hypocritical. H. craftily employs the Bible, thematically and stylistically, to communicate and shield his antislavery message.

Even though in his seventy-sixth year H. did not want emancipation, it is incorrect to argue that he did not want it for others; for in the same sermon that he denied his own need for freedom, he wrote, "yet I should be glad if others, especially the young Negroes, were to be free." Perhaps then the controversy surrounding H.'s position is more correctly assessed in that it is similar to that of other African American writers who do not take a stance against African American oppression like "mainstream" protestors would like; nonetheless, it does not make writers like H. less relevant voices in American and African American literature.

BIBLIOGRAPHY: Bloom, H., ed., *Black Poets and Dramatists before the Harlem Renaissance* (1994); O'Neal, S. A., *J. H. and the Biblical Beginnings of African American Literature* (1993); Ransom, S. A., Jr., ed., *America's First Negro Poet: The Complete Works of J. H. of Long Island* (1970)

NANCY M. STAUB

HANSBERRY, Lorraine

b. 19 May 1930, Chicago, Illinois; d. 12 January 1965, New York City

A committed social activist, editor of Paul Robeson's radical monthly *Freedom,* and daughter of the noted social reformer Carl Hansberry, H. sought through the drama a political response to the complacency and

conformity pervading the "silent generation" of the 1950s. Her first and most famous play, *A Raisin in the Sun* (1959), was doubtless influenced by her father's failure to see implemented *Hansberry v. Lee,* the 1943 Supreme Court case against exclusionary housing covenants. Although the play gained quick acceptance from black audiences and the white establishment, in her own mind, it failed to clarify the deeper issues afflicting African American society. Instead of recognizing the play's subject as a challenge to the institutions perpetuating white racism, audiences seemed to accept an interpretation of uncritical optimism, since the plot resolution depicts a reconciled Younger family resolving to move into a white neighborhood. For H. and a few discerning observers, the play's underpinnings left much unresolved, since the family still faced white resistance in their new neighborhood, and, perhaps more importantly, the long-term problems of black American identity, best conveyed in the play by the perplexities of the daughter Beneatha, raised important and disturbing issues. Moreover, the subsequent film version of the play cut controversial dialogue, including Asagai's speech about personal commitment to political change in the colonized world.

Dissatisfied with the inability of New York audiences and reviewers to discern the underlying critique of the American dream in the Broadway production, H. began work on a play that would stand as an unmistakable challenge both to complacent racism and to the facile notion that the long-term effects of segregation would soon disappear. In *Les Blancs* (1972), H. attempted to demonstrate the persistent effects of racism, particularly as they influenced interracial relationships. For H., the subtler—and therefore more unacknowledged—aspects of racist thinking informed the dynamics of American social life. *A Raisin in the Sun* had concerned the effects of white racism on an African American family; still, except for the minor character of Lindner, it represented not whites. *Les Blancs,* the title intended to ironize Jean Genet's recent play, *Les nègres,* was intended as a clarification of black and white relations, even of the most intimate kind. H. regarded Genet's play, despite its title, as "a conversation between white men about themselves." Instead, she sought to present a dramatic locus unmarred by stereotyping and what she took to be Genet's inaccurate abstractions of black nature as "pain, lust, cruelty, ambition." In short, she began a play "wherein we were *all* forced to confrontation and awareness." Unhappily, although a number of drafts were written, *Les Blancs* never achieved a final form before H.'s untimely death from cancer at the age of thirty-four. As literary executor, her husband Robert Nemiroff completed the play.

Intended as one in a series of videodrama commissioned in 1960 by the NBC to commemorate the centennial of the Civil War, *The Drinking Gourd* (1972) concerned the relationships of a slave-owning family and their slaves. H. was given free reign to choose her subject and treatment, and consciously presented a drama that functioned as a foil to the sentimentalized conceptions of slavery typified in Margaret MITCHELL's *Gone with the Wind*. The drama was never produced for television, however, since the NBC executives found it too controversial for their Civil War project, which seemed to take a patriotic and commemorative turn. In *The Drinking Gourd*, the writer aimed to reveal how personality is formed within social institutions, and to uncover the sources of human behavior—for black and white, villainous and virtuous—within slave society. To this extent, H. continued her endeavor, begun in *Les Blancs*, to push her audiences beyond common stereotypical readings of black and white interaction.

What Use Are Flowers? (1972), begun in late 1961 as a videodrama, but never completed as such, H. wrote in part as an answer to Samuel Beckett's *Waiting for Godot*, which had stimulated her reflections upon ultimate human concerns. A departure from her previous subject matter, the drama, later conceived as a stage play, incorporated the abstracted stagecraft of the theatre of the absurd—a vague, generalized locale, generic characterization, fantastic subject, and philosophical trajectories. A grumbling hermit offers long tirades against a group of frenetic juvenile dancers. H. eventually wanted to explore the juxtaposition of the old man's rhetorical soliloquies against the modern dancing of the "wild" children, but her early death prevented further revision. In this drama, H. seemed to be moving toward a more abstracted theater, one wherein the iconography of race could be circumvented in order to expose the human interior, itself limited by racial prejudice and segregation. Universally misunderstood, H.'s sympathy and broad understanding of social structures informed her drama, which, though consistently underestimated by critics throughout the social spectrum, offer a rare combination of fully developed characters and deep social awareness. H.'s critique of American capitalism, a force that she saw as transcending even deep issues of race, never found adequate expression in her drama.

BIBLIOGRAPHY: Carter, S. R., *H.'s Drama: Commitment Amid Complexity* (1991); Cheney, A., *L. H.* (1984); Keppel, B., *The Work of Democracy: Ralph Bunche, Kenneth B. Clark, L. H., and the Cultural Politics of Race* (1995); Nemiroff, R., ed., *To Be Young, Gifted and Black: A Portrait of L. H. in Her Own Words* (1969)

WILLIAM OVER

HANSEN, Ron

b. 8 December 1947, Omaha, Nebraska

Following in a long tradition set by Flannery O'CONNOR and other American Catholic writers, H. writes with Christian faith as his center of gravity. His work demonstrates his versatility as a writer in both subject matter and genre.

Having attended parochial schools and the Jesuit Creighton University, H. studied fiction writing at the Iowa Writers Workshop. Under the tutelage of John IRVING, with whom he became friends, he served as a live-in babysitter for Irving's two sons as he earned his M.F.A. With two unpublished novels haunting him, H. decided to write a WESTERN, figuring the genre might better his chances of placing a novel with a major publisher. Knopf published both of H.'s Westerns, *Desperadoes* (1979) and *The Assassination of Jesse James by the Coward Robert Ford* (1983), which explore the American West through a revisioning of history. *Desperadoes* tells the story of the notorious Dalton Gang, outlaws who defied the West during the late 1800s. Once peace officers in the Indian territories, the Dalton Brothers degenerated to robbing banks and trains. H.'s narrator, Emmett Dalton, the last of the surviving outlaws, tell his story in retrospect as the themes of honor, loyalty, integrity, selfishness, and reckless ambition rise to the surface.

Similarly, in *The Assassination of Jesse James by the Coward Robert Ford*, H. explores themes of sin and redemption and the corruption of crime. The novel focuses on the legendary outlaw, Jesse James, considered a kind of Robin Hood of the West who gave profits of his exploits to the poor. The young Bob Ford befriends James only to betray him for a reward for the outlaw's death. Both of H.'s Westerns expose the age-old truth that crime never pays.

Central to H.'s work is his Catholic faith. He thinks of writing as a "sacrament insofar as it provides graced occasions of encounter between humanity and God." His third novel, *Mariette in Ecstasy* (1992), confronts the mysteries of spirituality directly. Inspired by H.'s reading of *The Autobiography of St. Therese of Le Seur*, the story of a French woman who joined a convent at an early age and realized a passionate relationship with God, the novel depicts seventeen-year-old Mariette Baptiste who enters the Convent of Our Lady of Sorrows and experiences the phenomenon of stigmata. Wounds in the hands, feet, and side like those suffered by Jesus on the cross present Mariette with a crisis of faith and a quest toward an understanding of these signs. The novel's mystery centers on the origin of the physical wounds—whether they are creations of Mariette's sexual and religious hysteria or actual representation of supernatural phenomena.

H.'s novel *Atticus* (1996) further develops Christian themes in a story of forgiveness and absolution. With a nod to Atticus Finch of Harper LEE's *To Kill a Mockingbird,* the novel depicts Atticus Cody whose story was inspired by H.'s own grandfather and the events of his family history. In the novel, the sixty-seven-year-old Colorado rancher and widower learns that his son Scott, an artist and alcoholic responsible for his mother's death in a car accident years earlier, has committed suicide. When Atticus travels to Mexico to recover the body, the novel soon becomes a murder mystery. In a town named Resurrection, Atticus must confront painful memories of his family's past. Through events paralleling the death of H.'s own uncle who was found shot in the head in the middle of the desert outside Las Vegas, the novel explores the boundaries of forgiveness in a family plagued by guilt.

BIBLIOGRAPHY: Choi, D., "Rewriting History, Demystifying Old West: R. H.'s *The Assassination of Jesse James by the Coward Robert Ford,*" in Wright, W., and S. Kaplan, eds., *The Image of the Frontier in Literature, the Media, and Society* (1997): 231–34; Vorda, A., "A Hard Kind of Play: An Interview with R. H.," in *Face to Face: Interviews with Contemporary Novelists* (1993): 107–26

PATRICIA MONTALBANO

HARDWICK, Elizabeth

b. 27 July 1916, Lexington, Kentucky

H.'s literary reputation rests solidly on a body of work that includes three novels and three volumes of collected essays, short stories, and an edition of William JAMES's letters. Shortly after the publication of her first novel, *The Ghostly Lover* (1945), she became a contributor to the *Partisan Review,* effectively beginning her long and successful career as literary and social critic. She helped found the *New York Review of Books* in 1963, and in 1969 became the first woman to receive the George Jean Nathan Award for outstanding drama criticism. Though born a Southerner, she left Kentucky at the age of twenty-three to attend Columbia University and thereafter lived in New York and Europe. She was elected to the American Academy of Arts and Letters in 1989. She continues to observe the American scene and to write for the *New York Review of Books,* thus continuing the tradition of political activism she began during the *Partisan Review* years.

Her three novels—*The Ghostly Lover, The Simple Truth* (1955), and *Sleepless Nights* (1979)—all show her general preoccupation with the mystery of human experience and her specific concern with what Joan DIDION calls the "difference" of being a woman. Stylistically, they are characterized by H.'s irony, wit, and the meticulous, exact, lucid prose that her reviewers would invariably praise. *The Ghostly Lover* is semiautobiographical in that it deals with a lonely, alienated young woman named Marian who extricates herself from her Southern roots and moves to New York to attend graduate school. The novel ends inconclusively as Marian rejects marriage and a return home and instead opts for an uncertain—but free—future. *The Simple Truth* is based on an actual murder trial in which a wealthy young woman is murdered by her lower-class boyfriend. The novel enables H. to examine the network of social class prejudices inherent in such a case as she unravels it from the point of view of its two obsessive observers, a young pseudo-Marxist, and the wife of a college professor who seems bent on a Freudian psychoanalytical reading. Her most experimental novel was *Sleepless Nights,* which was nominated for the National Book Critics Circle Award. Structured as a series of reminiscences in the mind of its female center of consciousness, Elizabeth, the novel deconstructs the notion of human personality as the reader follows the unraveling of memory that focuses on the unhappy, lonely lives of the people Elizabeth has known and on those who survived.

H.'s essays appearing in her three collections—*A View of My Own* (1962), *Seduction and Betrayal: Women and Literature* (1974), and *Bartleby in Manhattan and Other Essays* (1983)—both reflect and expand the concerns of her novels. Taken as a whole, they constitute a remarkable commentary on the literary, cultural and political landscape of post-1945 America. The author's attacks on David Riesman and the sociologists, on Simone de Beauvoir's *The Second Sex,* and on commercialized, shabby Boston in the first volume exemplify the range of her mind and sensibility, while her sensitive analysis of the problems of being a woman and a writer form the subject matter of the aptly named *Seduction and Betrayal.* She treats women as fiction writers, as biographers, and women who merely observed the careers of their male spouses or relatives: the Brontës, Jane Carlyle, Dorothy Wordsworth, Zelda FITZGERALD. Like Virginia Woolf, H. ponders the disparity between strong female heroes in literature and women's actual powerlessness in society. She concludes that even the ravished heroines of male fiction have a kind of grandeur that saves them from being merely victims.

H.'s last volume of essays, *Bartleby in Manhattan,* is a cultural and literary smorgasbord of topics ranging from a Rolling Stones concert to an analysis of Memphis after the Martin Luther King, Jr. assassination to a profile of Lee Harvey Oswald and his family. As an untiring observer of American life at all levels, H. focuses her powerful intelligence on these signs of our cultural moment and reads them like text. She continues to be a powerful force in the New York literary community.

BIBLIOGRAPHY: Aaron, D., *Writers on the Left* (1965); Nobile, P., *Intellectual Skywriting: Literary Politics and the New York Review of Books* (1974)

MARY ANN WILSON

HARDY, Arthur Shelburne

b. 13 August 1847, Andover, Massachusetts; d. 30 March 1930, Woodstock, Connecticut

H. appears as one of those literary figures who is stowed away in the back of the closet, brought out occasionally, dusted off, only to be returned to storage. In his day, H. enjoyed the high praise of the critics and a respectable readership. Unlike many 19th-c. literati, H. could boast acceptance by the three types of magazines dominating the literary marketplace—the intellectual magazines such as the *Atlantic* and the *Century;* the popular magazines such as *Munsey's* and *Cosmopolitan;* and the "little" magazines such as *Chap-Book.* H. also produced fiction aligned with the dominant literary trends—ROMANCE, REALISM, and determinism. H.'s close ties to the times in which he lived doomed him perhaps to obscurity, yet the careful reader and scholar will learn from him.

Had not H. excelled at his several professions, one might be inclined to regard him a ne'er-do-well. During the most successful phase of his literary career, he served as the mathematics professor at Dartmouth, where he distinguished himself as both a scholar and teacher. Besides his classroom duties, he published three mathematics textbooks that established him as a leading scholar in his field.

These fruitful years saw also the publication of H.'s three best novels, *But Yet a Woman* (1883), *The Wind of Destiny* (1886), and *Passe Rose* (1889). Although he also published his narrative poem *Francesca of Rimini* (1878), he is best remembered as a fictionist. The *Manhattan Review* hailed *But Yet a Woman* as the novel of the year, and critics universally praised its fine style. Because he was so taken with the novel, Fred Lewis Pattee admits that he went so far as to enroll in one of H.'s higher mathematics courses so that he could know the artist.

H. left teaching in 1893 to succeed William Dean HOWELLS as editor of *Cosmopolitan,* a post he held for two years. In 1897, he entered the diplomatic service where, in addition to the duties of state, he produced

Song of Two (1900), a collection of lyrics, and *His Daughter First* (1903), a sequel to *The Wind of Destiny.*

Although his plots are predictable, H.'s novels contain several noteworthy features. Several of his works offer keen insights into the philosophical climate of the turn-of-the-century era. Roger Lande, the agnostic hero of *But Yet a Woman,* grapples with the science/religion controversy; and philosopher Schonberg in *The Wind of Destiny* comments extensively on the workings of fate in the human struggle. Coupled with the displays of the survival instinct in the historical novel *Passe Rose,* these characters serve as apt commentary on post-Darwinian impulses.

After he returned from his diplomatic career, H. continued his writing and published regularly in magazines. He tried his hand at detective fiction with *Diane and Her Friends* (1917) and *No. 13 Rue de Bon Diable* (1919); and he studied—satirically at times—diplomatic service and the expatriate life in *Helen* (1916). Throughout his canon, H. retains his fine style and explores human interaction.

The scion of a wealthy Massachusetts family, H. had the advantages that such a background affords—travel, education abroad, and significant friendships. H.'s main flaw is his close alliance to his times, but such a "flaw" makes him an invaluable study of his age.

BIBLIOGRAPHY: Quinn, A. H., *American Fiction* (1936); Smith, H. F., *The Popular American Novel, 1865–1920* (1986)

E. KATE STEWART

HARINGTON, Donald

b. 22 December 1935, Little Rock, Arkansas

Called by some critics the best-kept secret in American literature, H.'s writing career has spanned over three decades. Influenced by such seemingly disparate authors as William AGEE, Gabriel García Márquez, Vladimir NABOKOV, and William STYRON, H. has produced a body of work that combines humor, pathos, and philosophy with elements of postmodern technique and the sensibilities of magic realism.

From his first published novel, *Cherry Pit* (1965), H. has mined the undiscovered riches of the Arkansas Ozarks for setting and theme. *Cherry Pit,* H.'s most realistic work, is set against the backdrop of change in the South during the tension-filled 1960s. The protagonist, Clifford Stone, provides the first-person narration for a tale of a man returning home to the Little Rock of his youth to try and reclaim his vanished past.

The vanished past resurfaces time and again in H.'s work. His second novel, *Lightning Bug* (1971), returns to Arkansas, but this time focuses on the semifictional Ozark village of Stay More, which is at least the partial setting for all of H.'s fiction. *Lightning Bug* also introduces the first overt appearance of the H. persona as a character in the stories he creates, both as the adult narrator of this tale and as a five-year-old visitor to Stay More named Donald, who both observes and participates in the action. In addition, in *Lightning Bug,* H. introduces the structural and narrative experiments that have become hallmarks of his work; the novel is divided into movements instead of chapters, as in his next novel, *Some Other Place, the Right Place* (1972), and third-person narration is juxtaposed with first-person narration. The final sections of *Lightning Bug,* as in all of H.'s subsequent work, shifts to the future tense, which both creates an air of prophesy and ensures that the story never comes to a complete end.

The Architecture of the Arkansas Ozarks (1975), inspired by García Márquez's *One Hundred Years of Solitude,* is widely considered to be H.'s best work. The novel traces the first one-hundred-forty years of Stay More, focusing primarily on the founders of the village, the two Ingeldew brothers, and the generations that follow. The family fortunes are mirrored by the habitations they build, each drawn by H. at the start of each of the novel's chapters.

After more than a decade, H. published *The Cockroaches of Stay More* (1989), a gently satirical tale of unity and love told from the perspective of the cockroaches who inhabit the village that has been all but abandoned by its human families. Unaware of the anthropomorphized insects are Larry Brace, an alcoholic writer who has come to Stay More to research the life of Daniel Lyam Montross—a character who both narrated and appeared in a reincarnated form in *Some Other Place*—and Sharon Ingledew, the granddaughter of Latha Bourne with whom young Donald stayed in *Lightning Bug.* Their early wariness and antagonism transforms into love in part through the machinations of Gregor Samsa Ingeldew, a deaf cockroach who similarly finds love during the course of the story.

Sharon's grandmother, Latha, returns once again in *The Choiring of the Trees* (1991) to share narration duties with the H. persona. This novel, based on a true event, centers on shepherd, moonshiner, and falsely convicted rapist Niall Chism at the beginning of the 20th c., and the attempt on the part of newspaper sketch artist Viridas Munday to uncover the evidence that will overturn Chism's conviction. Latha's involvement in the events is as the alleged victim's best friend, who comes to doubt the veracity of her friend's charges.

H.'s longstanding admiration for the work of Nabokov is most openly expressed in his 1993 novel, *Ekaterina.* Both parodic and original, *Ekaterina* works as an inversion of Nabokov's *Lolita,* if *Lolita* had followed a journey from Pittsburgh to a fictionalized Ozarks called the Bodarks. The eponymous heroine of *Ekaterina,* a refugee from Soviet Georgia, moves into a boarding house inhabited by a twelve-year-old boy named Kenny, as well as a number of professors, one of whom—the overt H. persona in this novel—is a deaf creative writing instructor known as "I." Pursued by a Soviet agent, Ekaterina and Kenny find their way to Stay More.

In 1996, H. published *Butterfly Weed,* which centers on the young Stay More physician Colvin Swain and his miraculous "dream cures." These result in such a loss of income for Swain that he is forced to leave his wife while he takes employment as a hygiene instructor at a nearby school and falls into the hypochondriac arms of a young student named Tenny. The novel is marked by mythic motifs, most importantly the story of Cupid and Psyche, with its themes of love, labor, and the quest for immortality.

BIBLIOGRAPHY: Arnold, E. T., "D. H.," in Giles, J. R., and W. H. Giles, eds., *DLB,* vol. 152, *American Novelists since World War II* (1995): 82–91; special H. issue, *ChiR* 38, 4 (1993)

                                    ELIZABETH HADDRELL

HARJO, Joy
b. 9 May 1951, Tulsa, Oklahoma

Like many mixed-blood writers of our time, H. can cross an amazing scope of boundaries in her poetry. Her Creek and French-Cherokee heritage serves as a fertile foundation of inspiration for a body of poetry that works consciously on the borders of aesthetics, politics, and the private lyric. H. also makes frequent use of the margin between written and oral communication by including chanting rhythms and pause breaks associated with traditional Native American oralities in many of her poems. Additionally, her language often subverts conventional limits of time and space.

Yet H.'s work is equally notable for its accessibility. This effect is achieved through the use of a conversational tone to describe both apparent physical experiences and more imaginative, though no less "real" spiritual experiences. Consequently, her poems convincingly present entire worlds as overlapping. Animal and human, natural and technological, urban and open space realms are depicted as being simultaneously present in our lives, sometimes juxtaposed, sometimes linked to each other. The resulting sense of surrealism becomes not a distortion, but rather a credible account of a reality that is completely and constantly in motion.

The contemporary American city is one of H.'s most important, ongoing tropes. She uses the city as a negative setting to depict the psychological and spiritual bereftness and personal chaos of urban life for contemporary Native American survivors. In her poems, the lives of these survivors resonate with memories of an ongoing history of Eurocentric and genocidal social and political policies. Her speakers are sustained in such an alien environment by memories of ancestral lands, pan-tribal heritage, and traditional spirituality. The development of this city-as-negative motif begins as early as her first chapbook, *The Last Song* (1975).

In her next collection of poems, *What Moon Drove Me to This* (1979), H. deepens her focus on the destructiveness present in contemporary urban life, particularly that related to alcohol and "bar life." This book also features the debut of the speaker Noni Daylight, a character some have called H.'s alter ego. Noni's experiences and observations grow out of a sense of alienation, and she often turns to high-speed interstate driving as an escape into a more soothing, rhythmic state. Throughout H.'s works, travel becomes an important metaphor for the ever-shifting reality of the present, and motion itself becomes a place, a spiritual home. Noni can be seen as a feminist trickster in her persistent survival and independent assertion of self against the opposition of history, self-doubt, race, and gender. Many poems in this book also focus on other women's issues, including marriage and the complexities of mother-love.

Poems about Noni Daylight continue in *She Had Some Horses* (1983), wherein they become a cyclic quest of a voice looking for home. Several poems in this book depict women who experience inarticulation and a crippling state of indecision; this frozenness results from fear, depression, and a societally reinforced oblivion. At the same time, these women do not die, nor do they destroy themselves, although they come close. The earth, and the stories that arise from it, are also presented as being muted—for now. Yet the Native people in these poems, both women and men, persist and continue to build subtle bridges of empathy, if not dialogue, with each other and the land.

Throughout H.'s early work, a circularity emerges between memory, story, history, ancestral voices, and the land. Her collaborative work, *Secrets from the Center of the World* (1989), fleshes out these themes using landscape photographs by Stephen Strom coupled with prose poems. Several of these poems also imply an erasure of boundaries between the textual and the living natural world.

Although most well known as a poet, H. has also worked as a painter, a filmmaker, and a jazz saxophone player with her band, Poetic Justice. Her time spent with jazz music has had an important influence in her poetry, where jazz rhythms often serve as models for phrasing and jazz musicians as poetic subjects. *In Mad Love and War* (1990) contains a number of eulogies to jazz musicians, and many of the prose poems in this collection explore the use of rhythm and melody. Eulogies to victims of racial injustice also appear here. One of the most overtly political poems of the latter category reveals a great deal about H.'s poetics through its title, "For Anna Mae Pictou Aquash, Whose Spirit Is Present Here and in the Dappled Stars (for we remember the story and must tell it again so we may all live)." The subtitle reveals how highly H. values memory, and suggests that bearing historical witness is a personal duty of the greatest urgency: the final phrase relates how the retelling of stories will save our lives. Her use of the words "we" and "all" represents a common technique for this poet, wherein she draws the reader inside the action to create not only a pan-tribal, but a pan-human vision.

In *The Woman Who Fell from the Sky* (1994), a collection of free-verse poems and prose poems, we find the somber themes of loneliness, poverty, and mourning, but we also find the physical presence of healing powers and renewal in symbols such as dawn, butterflies, and birth. Some of the speakers in *The Woman Who Fell from the Sky* also employ a postmodern humor in the form of fools and/or foolish behavior to help subvert the terror and hysteria of their lives, a device common to Native American literatures and used sporadically in H.'s previous books. H. added a written commentary to each poem, which often tells the story of the poem's genesis and lends an autobiographical tone to the book.

H. remains in the forefront of contemporary Native American poets, and her work continues to be widely cited and anthologized. One can find the influences of June JORDAN, Audre LORDE, Carolyn Forché, and Leslie Marmon SILKO in H.'s poetry, which reaches deep into the worlds of the Native and the feminine, and simultaneously encompasses the fundamental American concerns of personal freedom and survival.

H. has been called a poet of myth and the subconscious because of her skill in drawing on the vast stretches of the hidden mind as well as the storied landscape, yet her work contains such clear accounts of the apparent world, and seeks such an intimate connection to the reader, sometimes to the point of assaulting the reader with the reality of urban Native life, that myth and the subconscious seem to constitute only a portion of the pulse of her work. Yet perhaps myth, or rather mythic spirituality, can be said to underlie even the most bleak-toned of her poems; part of the magic of H. is that she manages to continually illustrate the spiritual interconnection of whole universe, even while describing its most sorrowful regions. Using symbols of destruction, such as alcoholism or silence, for her own creative material becomes a way for H.'s voice to survive and thrive as Native American, female, human, and earthly.

BIBLIOGRAPHY: Coltelli, L., *The Spiral of Memory* (1995); Goodman, J., "Politics and the Personal Lyric in the Poetry of J. H. and C. D. Wright," *MELUS* 19 (Summer 1994): 35–56; Holmes, K., "'This Woman Can Cross Any Line': Feminist Tricksters in the Works of Nora Naranjo-Morse and J. H.," *SAIL* 7 (Spring 1995): 45–63; Lang, N., "'Twin Gods Bending Over': J. H. and Poetic Memory," *MELUS* 18 (Fall 1993): 41–49; Leen, M., "An Art of Saying: J. H.'s Poetry and the Survival of Storytelling," *AIQ* 19 (Winter 1995): 1–16; Ruoff, L. B., *American Indian Literatures* (1990); Scarry, J., "Representing Real Worlds: The Evolving Poetry of J. H.," *WLT* 66 (Spring 1992): 286–91

MARÍA MELENDEZ

HARPER, Frances E[llen] W[atkins]

b. 24 September 1825, Baltimore, Maryland; d. 22 February 1911, Philadelphia, Pennsylvania

Best known to present-day readers as the author of *Iola Leroy* (1892), H. had a multifaceted career as poet, novelist, teacher, traveling lecturer, and abolitionist. She was also one of the 19th c.'s most noted feminists, a leader in the temperance movement, and a cofounder of the National Association of Colored Women. Her literary work is best understood as an outgrowth of her activities as a reformist, as firmly politically and religiously committed art.

H.'s first literary achievements were in the field of poetry. Of an early collection of poetry, *Forest Leaves* (ca. 1845), no extant copies are left, but the success of her *Poems on Miscellaneous Subjects* (1854) can be measured by the fact that several editions appeared over the next two decades. H.'s emergence as an author roughly coincides with her decision to leave her career as a teacher and become a lecturer in the cause of ABOLITIONISM. Her first known collection of poetry served that cause by denouncing slavery. Employing iambic rhythms and rhymed quatrains like her contemporaries Henry Wadsworth LONGFELLOW and John Greenleaf WHITTIER, H.'s poems in this and in her later collections, such as *Poems* (1871), *Sketches of Southern Life* (1872), and *Atlanta Offerings, Poems* (1895), are narrative in nature and informed by the sentimental tradition of her time. "A Slave Mother,"

for example, directly involves the reader with direct appeals for compassion and forces the reader to witness the psychological effects on a mother of the cruel separation from her child. H.'s post–Civil War poems, while sometimes looking backwards to the horrors of slavery, also deal with motherhood in a more general sense and with public events. *Moses: A Story of the Nile* (1869), however, embarks on a new poetical course by employing free verse. As other antebellum African American writers, she implicitly parallels the history of the Israelites to that of African Americans. H. focuses not only on the story of deliverance, but also suggests that full liberation must include a liberation of the soul as well, a goal that can only be accomplished by moral fortitude—a theme that she repeatedly returns to in her fiction as well.

"The Two Offers" (1859), possibly the first short story written by an African American woman, exemplifies the use of that theme. The story contrasts the life courses of two white cousins, Laura Lagrange and Janette Alston. Janette chooses a life of intellectual accomplishment and remains unwed when the one man she loves turns away from her, while Laura marries a handsome and wealthy man she does not love for fear of remaining unmarried. Because of her husband's moral weakness and his alcoholism, Laura's life takes an unhappy turn and ends in her early death. The story praises Janette's life as a triumph of will over matter while mourning Laura's wrong choice.

The juxtaposition of materialism and high-minded spirituality becomes even more explicit in *Sowing and Reaping* (1876–77), first published in the *Christian Recorder,* the journal of the African Methodist Episcopal Church. "The Two Offers" may be regarded as a virtual blueprint for *Sowing and Reaping,* which introduces two male protagonists, one—John Anderson—eager to become rich, no matter the moral cost, the other—Paul Clifford—ambitious but of moral rectitude. Focusing on a temperance theme, the novel traces the downward course of John, who marries Jeanette Roland, the equivalent of Laura Lagrange, and the tumultuous but ultimately morally and financially successful lives of Paul and his wife Belle Gordon, who resembles Janette Alston.

Moral strength is also rewarded in *Trial and Triumph* (1888–89), published in the *Christian Recorder.* Focusing on racial relations in the Reconstruction South, the novel chronicles the lives of Annette Harcourt, Clarence Luzerne, Laura Lusette, and Charley Cooper, all members of the emerging African American middle class, whose ambitions are hampered by race prejudice at every turn. Annette and Clarence marry at the end of the novel after having been purified by struggles in which they had to prove their moral steadfastness. The latter quality and the ability for self-sacrifice are also the themes of an earlier serialized novel, *Minnie's Sacrifice* (1869). In many ways a forerunner to *Iola Leroy, Minnie's Sacrifice* has two African American characters—Minnie and Louis—raised by white families so that they do not know of their African American ancestry. Once they learn of it, they reject the possibility of a luxurious life and choose a commitment to African Americans in bondage.

Iola Leroy may be regarded as the culmination of H.'s literary works in that it incorporates most of the themes of her previous fiction and poetry—racial solidarity, spirituality versus materialism, domesticity, female independence, morality, but for women and men, temperance—but elaborates them on a grander and more historically oriented scale. Its title character, like Minnie, grows up in white privilege before the Civil War but is cast into slavery, experiences life among African American troops during the Civil War, decides to cast her lot with African Americans, and devotes her life to educating Southern African Americans after the war. Her most widely read work, it is a befitting closure to the literary career of an author who firmly believed in the power of fiction to change hearts and minds.

BIBLIOGRAPHY: Boyd, M. J., *Discarded Legacy: Politics and Poetics in the Life of F. E. W. H.* (1994); Carby, H., *Reconstructing Womanhood: The Emergence of the Afro-American Woman Novelist* (1987); Christian, B., *Black Women Novelists* (1980); Giddings, P., *When and Where I Enter* (1984)

MARTIN JAPTOK

HARPER, Michael S[teven]

b. 18 March 1938, Brooklyn, New York

Through nine volumes of poetry, H. has emerged as an important contemporary poet responding to the racial, historical, and cultural divisions that haunt America today. We are a country with a short memory, and a profound schism between professed and realized dispositions toward race. Consequently, our country has sustained casualties, on all sides, and with persevering hope, H. sings the songs that draw our attention to the historical and cultural gaps that are near the root of our suffering. Tending the wound at its source, eloquently drawing on efficacious traditions, H.'s voice invites a return to consciousness and conscience.

African American literary antecedents include poets such as Paul Laurence DUNBAR, Countee CULLEN, Robert HAYDEN, and Sterling A. BROWN. Further, H. expresses a desire to do for poetry what Ralph ELLISON did for the novel, and H.'s poetry does indeed carry

a similar complexity of thought and psychological insight. Critically overlooked is the extent to which H. and Yeats are kindred spirits: both take on the project of recovering history, mythology, and the supportive healing vitality of interrupted and forgotten traditions for nations that have suffered deep schisms based on racial oppression. In short, H., drawing on African American, white, and even Native American history and traditions, is truly an American poet, reflecting the complexity of the country as a whole.

More important in influence than any writers have been the blues and jazz musicians who nurtured H. in his youth and sustained him through painful experiences of loss in his adulthood. "My parents weren't rich, but they had a good record collection," relates H. And the strengths that H. found in these musicians and their art infuses his own poetry. An early trademark of his poetry, according to Robert Stepto, is "a terse riff full of attitude." Blues and jazz rhythms, call and response, refrains, and the stylistic mastery that allows the musician improvisorial freedom carry H.'s ear-and-heartfelt songs. At times exquisite, H.'s diction adds resonances to his poems already layered by music, narrative, and framing devices such as dedications, epigraphs and of course titles.

Dear John, Dear Coltrane (1970), H.'s first book, is written in the modality of the great jazz musician who epitomizes the heroic spirit's struggle for self-definition, prevailing over pain and restrictive artistic and social conventions. Poems powerful and memorable that treat of soul-searing personal losses, notably "Reuben, Reuben" and "Deathwatch," appear alongside poems that celebrate a transcendent mastery of art embodied in the lives of musicians such as Charlie Parker and Miles Davis. Then there are poems that express manifestly historical/political events, such as "American History" and "Biafra Blues," calling to awareness the cultural schisms in our American heritage. Together, these "sorrow songs" bear witness to a grace that shines through artistic excellence and a heroic spirit, a transcendent grace expressed as "a love supreme, a love supreme."

History Is Your Own Heartbeat (1971) again connects the personal with broader historical and cultural associations. American historical amnesia is not an abstraction, but lived by individuals, and is as near and intimately felt as one's own heartbeat. Symptoms of bodily disorder reveal the historical lapses perniciously (invisibly) at work in American consciousness. The book emphasizes the continuity in and across personal and kinship ties, through African American traditions, and in the ignored events of American history. Further along these lines, *Song: I Want a Witness* (1972) continues to relate the personal to the historical and testifies to the diverse ancestors integral to the definition of America. H.'s next book of poetry, *Debridement* (1973), named for "the cutting away of dead or contaminated tissue from a wound to prevent infection," considers the historical figure John Brown, the novelist Richard WRIGHT, and a murdered African American Congressional Medal of Honor winner. One of the book's implications is that America—with all the technological precision and scientific neutrality of an operation in a sterile field—sacrifices its black brothers.

The rich and stylistically varied *Nightmare Begins Responsibility* (1975) celebrates H.'s many "kin": living and dead family members, African American writers, friends, and heroes, essentially acknowledging a community within which action—"waking up"—is the correct response to nightmare, the American dream gone bad.

With the publication of *Images of Kin* (1977), a superb collection of poems culled from the preceding books, along with fourteen new poems, H.'s stature as a major talent has become increasingly evident. Critically acclaimed, the book garnered the Melville-Cane Award and was a finalist for the National Book Award. The title of one section of the book, "Healing Songs," gave birth to the title of his next book, *Healing Songs for the Inner Ear* (1985), and continuity with earlier work is evident. In the manner of the jazz musician who returns to earlier themes only to play them sweeter and delight us with novelty, H. includes a return to some of the topics of his earlier poetry.

H.'s ninth book of poetry, *Honorable Amendments* (1995), draws our attention to things that were left out of our Constitution (two fifths of a person) and out of recorded history. H. would amend the story that America has told of itself in the past, for as he sees it, "from an imaginative point of view, the country is still up for grabs, in terms of definition." "It's a wise blues that knows its father," titles one section of the book and implies that healing, affirmative song bears an understanding of history.

Among the volumes that H. has edited are *Chant of Saints* (1979, with Robert Stepto), a pioneering collection of African American scholarship and criticism; and *Every Shut Eye Ain't Asleep* (1994), an important collection of post-1945 African American poetry.

BIBLIOGRAPHY: Brown, J. A., "Their Long Scars Touch Ours: A Reflection on the Poetry of M. H.," *Callaloo* 9 (1986): 209–28; Kitchen, J., "The Ladybug and the Universe," *GaR* 50 (Summer 1996): 386–403; special H. issue, *Callaloo* 13 (1990)

BRIAN A. SPILLANE

HARRIGAN, Edward [Ned]

b. 26 October 1844, New York City; d. 6 June 1911, New York City

The grandson of an Irish immigrant, H. will always be remembered as a chronicler of Irish characters.

Born on New York's Lower East Side, the setting for almost all of his plays, he first got work in the theater as an "Irish singer" on the variety circuit, inventing farcical characters for himself from minstrelsy and Irish comic tradition.

After his 1870, Broadway debut, H. developed the New York characters for which he was famous. Featuring a plethora of urban "types," performed in thick accents and crazy costumes, H.'s sketches were an instant hit with all classes. In 1870, he joined forces with fifteen-year-old boy soprano and reform school runaway Anthony Cannon. Using the stage name Tony Hart, Cannon complemented H.'s wit with a sweet voice and skill at female impersonation. The duo quickly became inseparable in the public mind.

H.'s first successful full-length play, *Old Lavender* (perf. 1877), portrayed a good-hearted waterfront bum; his next hit, *The Lorgaire* (perf. 1878), imitated the popular Irish adventures of Dion BOUCICAULT. But best known were his Mulligan plays—among them *The Mulligan Guard Ball* (perf. 1879, pub. 1966), *The Mulligan Guard Chowder* (perf. 1879), *The Mulligan Guard Picnic* (perf. 1878), *Cordelia's Aspirations* (perf. 1883), and *Dan's Tribulations* (perf. 1884). Starring Irish adventurer Dan Mulligan and his wife Cordelia, these polyglot tales of the city included a cast of carnivalesque characters—Irish, Chinese, Jewish, Italian, and African American—copied directly from the streets of the Lower East Side. The plots were flimsy, often ill-formed structures on which to hang the impersonations, familiar locales, slambang melees, and hilarious stage mechanics—exploding cigars, collapsing ceilings, violins smashed on heads, escaped pigs—that gave them their broad appeal. H. and Hart each played multiple roles, delighting audiences with their ethnic versatility.

In New York of the 1880s, where just under half of the population was foreign-born, H.'s madcap mix of lingos and types captured an essential feature of urban life. Although his plays were comic, they often dealt with political and social realities, such as battles for the African American vote, the women's rights movement, tenement life, social mobility, and the effects of alcohol and gambling on the working classes. His veracity sometimes hinged on real events: *Squatter Sovereignty* (perf. 1882) portrayed events in an actual shanty town discussed in the newspapers.

While drawing on the era's theatricalization of poverty—encouraged both by reformers like Jacob Riis and by titillating "slumming" tours of the Five Points or the Bowery—the plays were written for the working classes who were both subject and audience. The broad stereotyping—dim-witted Germans, conniving Jews, reprobate Irish, and comic African Americans—was never ill-willed, but captured the public nature of emerging identity-formations in urban America, recording the vibrant vernaculars and seething conflicts of the immigrant working classes. In his column in *Harper's,* William Dean HOWELLS accounted H. part of the era's trend toward REALISM.

After H. and Hart's Theater Comique burned down in 1885, the "merry partners" separated. Hart's career ended; H. went on to write and star in his longest running play, *Reilly and the Four Hundred* (perf. 1890), a story about an upwardly mobile pawnbroker trying to help his son break into society. Like all of his plays, its comically treated theme was class conflict.

Compared in his lifetime to Goldoni, Molière, Zola, Hogarth, Balzac, and Dickens, H. wrote over fifty sketches for the stage and forty-two full-length plays. Only one has appeared in print.

BIBLIOGRAPHY: Kahn, E. J., *The Merry Partners* (1955); Moody, R., *N. H.* (1980)

GINGER STRAND

HARRIS, Frank [James Thomas]

b. 14 February 1856, Galway, Ireland; d. 26 August 1931, Nice, France

In the late 19th and early 20th cs., H. was a major force in American letters as editor, critic, biographer, and writer of fiction. As editor first of the *Evening News,* then of the *Fortnightly Review,* and then of the *Saturday Review,* he interacted with the foremost writers and wielded great political influence. After the first decade of the century, his reputation declined rapidly. By the time of his death, he was thought of as a rogue and a liar—as someone so dishonest that anything he wrote was automatically suspect.

His early fiction, *Elder Conklin and Other Stories* (1894), brought him notoriety and fame, as it was praised for its quality and attacked for its sexuality, but, like his later creative work, it now goes unread. His *The Man Shakespeare and His Tragic Life Story* (1909), an attempt to reconstruct Shakespeare's life from his work, is ignored by scholars. His five volumes of *Contemporary Portraits* issued between 1915 and 1927 receive little attention.

H. is remembered primarily as the author of two works, *Oscar Wilde: His Life and Confessions* (1916) and his five-volume *My Life and Loves,* the first volume of which was privately printed in Paris in 1922. Because of its controversial nature, the latter work was not published in its entirety until 1964. The fifth volume, constructed from H.'s papers by Alexander Trocchi, appeared separately in 1958. The value of both works is impaired by H.'s reputation for unreliability.

In fairness to H., it should be said that, for a number of reasons, the extent of his lying has been exaggerated. As an editor, he made many enemies. His pro-German *England or Germany?* (1915) infuriated many readers, and his descriptions of his sex life (and those of other public figures) repelled many. But most of all, the sociopathic personality he reveals makes him untrustworthy. H., with no apparent inkling that the reader might have moral objections, describes how he rustled cattle, and as a mature man, seduced a fifteen-year-old virgin and had intercourse with a twelve-year-old East Indian girl.

His biography of Wilde and autobiography are readable and alive, and much of the information in them has been substantiated. For example, critic Philippa Pullar finds independent verification for some of H.'s claims about Wilde, and Richard Ellmann, in his *Oscar Wilde* (1988) accepts H.'s claim that Wilde had syphilis. But both Pullar and Ellmann distrust H.'s accounts of his conversations with Wilde. In another case, Carlyle's probable impotence has been often discussed, but it is hard to believe that Carlyle's doctor told H. how he forced a medical examination on a menopausing Jane Carlyle, discovered her to be a virgin, and then received a graphic description of Carlyle's wedding night.

Yet if *My Life and Loves* is untrustworthy, this panorama of the times based on H.'s experiences is valuable. H. ran away from an English public school, traveled to the U.S., worked in New York and Chicago, went further west, became a cowboy, and was admitted to the bar in Kansas. As an editor and author in London, he met the most prominent figures in literature, politics, and other fields while mingling with the English aristocracy. Back in the U.S. as editor of *Pearson's* during World War I, he was involved in home front turmoil through his growing socialist and pacificist tendencies.

Much, but fortunately not all, that H. learned from his experiences is sexual. H.'s sexual revelations about himself and others have an emotional obtuseness one seldom finds outside of hard core pornography, and he assumes that to understand anyone's sex life is to understand the person. Yet, for all its monomania and general unreliability, *My Life and Loves* remains a major achievement.

One may or may not believe that an aging George Meredith asked H. to examine the texts for a new edition of his works, and that H. was forced to tell him that nearly all the changes were a sign of failing powers. One may choose to believe that at Monte Carlo, H. entertained the future Edward VII with "naughty" doggerel. And one is free to believe that

Louis Jennings, an estranged political colleague of Randolph Churchill, told H. in detail how Churchill caught syphilis. Trustworthy or not, H. has captured the feeling of an age, and *My Life and Loves* will continue to be read indefinitely.

BIBLIOGRAPHY: Brome, V., *F. H.* (1959); Pullar, P., *F. H.* (1976); Root, E. N., *F. H.* (1947); Roth, S., *The Private Life of F. H.* (1931)

MARYJEAN GROSS and DALTON GROSS

HARRIS, George Washington

b. 20 March 1814, Allegheny City, Pennsylvania; d. 11 December 1869, Lynchburg, Tennessee

H. is considered by many to be the most accomplished humorist of the Old Southwest before Mark TWAIN. H.'s notorious character, Sut Lovingood, reveals a new and startling vision of the world through the use of decadent vernacular speech and nightmarish folk images. Sut's reckless spirit redefined the boundaries of American folk humor.

Leaving Allegheny City, Pennsylvania at an early age, H. remained in Knoxville, Tennessee for most of his life. Apprenticed as a metal worker, H. became an accomplished silversmith and during his lifetime was the captain of the steamboats the *Knoxville* and the *Aida,* respectively. Involved in a variety of occupations, including farming, railroading, politics, surveying, and management, H. was never able to rely solely on his writing for sustenance, but like many humorists of the Southwest, wrote in his leisure time. He first published in the *Knoxville Argus* and soon after in Porter's *Spirit of the Times* under the pseudonym, "Mr. Free." Although he soon dropped the pen name, the concept of "Mr. Free" defines much of what H. attempted to achieve.

H.'s first sketch of significance is "The Knob Dance," appearing in the *Spirit* in August 1845, under the pen name "Sugartail." This description of a traditional backwoods frolic, told in dialect by the semiliterate "Dick Harlan," presents larger-than-life characters who dance, drink, and celebrate to escape from daily drudgery and routine. Beginning with this story, H.'s work increasingly employs the desires of the flesh as a motif for emotional freedom, while bestowing a humbling retribution upon his characters. In 1854, H. contributed "Sut Lovingood's Daddy 'Acting Horse,'" his last installment in the *Spirit*. It is a grotesque yarn involving a father who decides to harness himself to the plow after the family's only horse has died of starvation. The pitiful father figure is made humorous through H.'s use of the vernacular, and Sut, in his first appearance, jeers at his father after the elder is tormented by hornets and is forced to seek refuge in the river. Violence, nudity, and Sut's ever-persistent attempts to escape the bonds of authority are prevalent in this sketch and characterize much of H.'s work.

Prior to the war years, H.'s hatred of Yankees boiled from the mouth of Sut in such sketches as "Sut Lovingood on the Puritan Yankee." Sut testifies: "As the dorg vomits, as the mink sucks blood, as the snail shines, as the possum shams death, so dus the yankee cheat, for every varmit has hits gif." H. goes beyond the tradition of Southwest humor by dispensing with the "frame story," which enables his narrator, Sut Lovingood, to break through the confines of everyday life into what can only be described as surreal. In "Sut Lovingood's Chest Story," Sut seeks revenge upon the lover of Sicily, a femme-fatale for which Sut once lusted, but who now, after marriage, is beginning to show the ravages of time. In a powerful passage of striking intensity, Sut, masquerading his voice to sound like Sicily's, frightens the hidden lover with an apocalyptic dream-vision: "Thar's a 'thousand laig' wum ontu the fence es long es a close line, hits body is red an streaks ove sheet litenin is playin amung hits scales, and hit hev two imiges ove peple in hits mouf, like ontu you and me. I kin see my har a hangin most tu the yearth, an now an then hit gins them a shake an great big drops ove fat comes outen you, an afore they draps tu the ground they ketches fire an burns like tupentine." The world of suffering is seen in mythic proportions as Sut's narration achieves an almost barbaric religious vigor.

In 1867, H. published his one book *Sut Lovingood's Yarns. Spun by a Nat'ral Born Durn'd Fool* (revised and enlarged as *Sut Lovingood's Yarns* by M. Thomas Inge in 1966). During H.'s lifetime, the literary establishment failed to notice this book of disquieting tales, although it remained in print into the 1950s and was noted by novelist William FAULKNER in the 1930s to be one of his favorites.

H. continued to publish in newspapers and had intended to publish *High Times and Hard Times* when he died suddenly on a trip from Lynchburg, Tennessee in 1869. Modern collections of his work include *Sut Lovingood: Travels with Old Abe Lincoln* (1937), *Sut Lovingood* (1954), *The Lovingood Papers* (4 vols., 1962–65), and *High Times and Hard Times* (1967).

BIBLIOGRAPHY: Caron, J. E., and M. T. Inge, eds., *Sut Lovingood's Nat'ral Born Yarnspinner: Essays on G. W. H.* (1996); Rickles, M., *G. W. H.* (1966)

MICHAEL J. PETTENGELL

HARRIS, Joel Chandler

b. 9 December 1948, near Eatonton, Putnam County, Georgia; d. 3 July 1908, Atlanta, Georgia

H. is best remembered as the creator of Uncle Remus. His first collection of Remus folktales, *Uncle Remus:*

His Songs and His Sayings (1880), was enormously popular and has been followed during H.'s lifetime and since by numerous other collections and editions, among them *Nights with Uncle Remus* (1883) and *Uncle Remus and His Friends* (1892).

H.'s treatment of his Remus materials is complex, combining the myth of the old plantation in his narrator's language and attitude toward the child who listens attentively at Remus's knee with folk tales that have deep roots in an African past. These tales, sometimes violent, reveal in the trickster-rabbit's survival parallels to the black endurance in a predominantly white culture. To what degree H. knew the signifiers in the folk tales he had Uncle Remus tell is hard to determine.

He began collecting these plantation fables and listening to black language from slaves during his work from 1862 to1866 on the *Countryman,* a newspaper published on the Georgia plantation Turnwold. He worked for a variety of other newspapers, among them the *Macon Telegraph,* the *New Orleans Crescent Monthly,* and the *Savannah Morning News* before becoming an editor of the *Atlanta Constitution* in 1876. H.'s work on the important *Constitution* continued for the rest of his career, and with his colleague Henry W. Grady, he become one of the best-known voices of the New South after Reconstruction. His editorials on a broad range of social and political issues must be considered in an assessment of his life and work. His feature writing, however, gave him the opportunity to set down the early Remus sketches, and his humorous writing for the paper was immensely popular.

For all his popularity, however, H. remained modest, and he was significantly shy, even insecure in any public notice or forum. His biographer and critic R. Bruce Bickley analyzes both the public and private selves in H.'s identity and shows how H. used his writing to "mend the rift" in his personality. One may recall the famous episode in Mark TWAIN's *Life on the Mississippi* when H. refused to read his Remus stories for a small audience at the home of George Washington CABLE in New Orleans.

H. wrote a number of children's books during his career, mostly in the manner of the Remus stories, but he also confronted a variety of problems in the postwar South in both short fiction and novels. This interesting work includes *Mingo and Other Sketches in Black and White (1884), Free Joe and Other Georgia Sketches* (1887), *On the Plantation* (1892), *Sister Jane: Her Friends and Acquaintances* (1896), and *Gabriel Tolliver: A Story of Reconstruction* (1902). These books indicate that H. looked seriously at black-white relationships and the problem of the Negro, and like the writings of Twain and Cable, they go beyond the sentimental treatment often found in local color writing after 1865.

Modestly, H. referred to himself throughout his career as a "cornfield chronicler," but his Uncle Remus stories have made him one of the best-known writers in American literature. His collections of black folktales have made him a significant figure in the study of American folklore, and he was, after all, a journalist, and his work with the *Atlanta Constitution* was likewise important to the life of the New South after the Civil War. His novels like *Gabriel Tolliver* and collections of short stores like *Free Joe and Other Georgia Sketches,* which looks with some degree of honesty at the problems of Reconstruction and the postwar South, deserve more attention than they have received. In all this, as Bickley says, he assists in easing tensions between North and South, and he becomes an important man of letters in the South after 1865, offering an honest assessment of its present and a hopeful vision for its future. Fundamentally, however, it is his complex voice that makes H. interesting, as the popularity of his Remus materials defines him as an important figure in American literature.

BIBLIOGRAPHY: Bickley, R. B., *Critical Essays on J. C. H.* (1981); Bickley, R. B., *J. C. H.* (1987); Cousins, P., *J. C. H.: A Biography* (1968); Keenan, H. T., ed., "J. C. H.: The Writer in His Time and Ours," *AHJ* 30 (Fall-Winter 1986–87): 3–4; MacKethan, L. H., "J. C. H.," in Bain, R., and J. Flora, eds., *Fifty Southern Writers before 1900* (1987): 227–39

THOMAS J. RICHARDSON

HARRIS, Mark

b. 19 November 1922, Mt. Vernon, New York

H. is a versatile and prolific writer who has produced fiction, edited volumes, drama, biography, autobiography, literary criticism, a screenplay, and social commentary. He is best known for four baseball novels featuring Henry Wiggen, a pitcher for the fictional New York Mammoths. This remarkable tetralogy includes: *The Southpaw* (1953), *Bang the Drum Slowly* (1956), *A Ticket for a Seamstitch* (1957), and *It Looked Like for Ever* (1979). In these novels, Henry Wiggen progresses from an eighteen-year-old rookie to a thirty-nine-year-old veteran who is forced out of the sport and into retirement. Overall, the novels are marked by certain characteristic H. themes and vision: the bittersweet quality of an always conditional life, the meaning of human bonds of love and concern, the ordinariness of life that is its universal quality, the human comedy of failings and frustrated aspirations, the joy of physical activity and the togetherness of a team, and the wisdom of common people in touch with life. The novels are also remarkable for their ability to capture the American vernacular of baseball players and to convey the changes in the sport and American life from the early 1950s to the 1970s.

H. was born Mark Finkelstein and was educated at the University of Denver and received his Ph.D. from the University of Minnesota in American studies. He has crafted scholarly biographical works on Vachel LINDSAY and Saul BELLOW, published articles in a wide variety of journals, and contributed to volumes with subjects ranging from public television to film. Along with this amazing diversity of interests, he has built a substantial body of fiction ranging from Jewish drama like *Friedman and Son* (1962), to novels of college life and academia like *Wake Up, Stupid* (1959) and *The Goy* (1970), to novels about the military like *Trumpet to the World* (1946) and *Something about a Soldier* (1957).

His university teaching experience is truly national, as he has served as a writer-in-residence and visiting professor at over ten universities as well as been a Fulbright professor at the University of Hiroshima (1957–58) and for the Peace Corps in Sierra Leone in 1965. His career has been one of exceptional and devoted service to his country and its educational system and to its cultural institutions. His vision is truly a national one that exhibits a passionate commitment to the cause of humanity, the expansion of the arts and humanities, and the qualities and resources of the national experience that unify the people in a democracy. His social commentary is pointed, insightful, always provoking and challenging. His three autobiographies—*Mark the Glove Boy; or, The Last Days of Richard Nixon* (1964), *Twentyone Twice: A Journal* (1966), and *The Best Father Ever Invented: The Autobiography of M. H.* (1976)—are notable for their shrewd observations on the times, their wit, their humanity and evolving self-knowledge. H. is a remarkable observer and chronicler of American national life, and his writing and commitments have distinguished him as one deeply involved in the life of a nation he has served admirably.

BIBLIOGRAPHY: Cochran, R., "Bang the Drum Differently: The Southpaw Slants of Henry Wiggen," *MFS* 33 (Spring 1987): 151–59; Lavers, N., *M. H.* (1978)

DOUGLAS A. NOVERR

HART, Moss
b. 24 October 1904, New York City; d. 20 December 1961, Palm Springs, California

In the world of Broadway musical theater, collaboration is quite common. In dramatic theater, however, it is the rare exception. Yet despite this relative dearth of partnerships, the names Kaufman and H. are as familiar to theatergoers as Rodgers and Hammerstein, Lerner and Loewe, and Gershwin and Gershwin.

H. began a legendary theatrical career in America's theater capital, New York City. Reared in poverty in the Bronx, this son of a cigar maker, with an eighth-grade education, was introduced to the theater as a young boy by an aunt. As a young man, H. got work as an assistant to theater impresario Augustus Pitou. During this apprenticeship, the aspiring playwright anonymously submitted his own play to Pitou, who bought and produced it. *Beloved Bandit*—also known as *The Hold-Up Man*—was a flop in 1923, but the experience allowed H. entrée into the professional theater scene. Success, however, did not immediately follow this initial failure.

Everything changed, though, in 1929, when producer Sam Harris introduced the young, inexperienced H. to his theatrical idol, playwright George S. KAUFMAN. Fourteen years H.'s senior, and already an established writer, Kaufman was called in to collaborate on rewrites of H.'s play, *Once in a Lifetime* (1930). The collaborative experience was a particularly fruitful, if exhausting one, during which the pair slept little and ate less.

Despite the rigors of this collaborative writing process, the result was a hit. *Once in a Lifetime,* a brilliant spoof of the Hollywood motion picture industry, opened to rave notices at Irving Berlin's Music Box Theatre. The play, which begins in a rundown apartment in New York City at the dawn of the Great Depression, tells the story of a three-person vaudeville team that has fallen on hard times. The team decides to go to Hollywood to make it big in the nascent talking film industry. Things don't quite work out, however, and the trio ends up giving elocution lessons to actors looking to make the transition from silent films. Typical of Kaufman and H., the play is filled with humorous twists and reversals while it spoofs many of Hollywood's most established institutions.

Also typical of Kaufman and H., this Depression-era comedy is filled with hopeful possibilities and true-to-life people in outrageous situations, simultaneously believable and fantastic. It is a light comedy with serious undertones, suggesting the serendipitous nature of success, and privileging the pursuit of happiness over material wealth. *Once in a Lifetime* ran a healthy 401 performances on Broadway, and was sold to Hollywood. During its run, both Kaufman and H. played the role of Lawrence Vail, the New York playwright.

Kaufman and H.'s decade-long reign during Broadway's heyday included such hits as *Merrily We Roll Along* (1934), an Erwin Piscatoresque examination of the career of a disillusioned playwright, employing a unique temporal structure that moved in reverse chronology from the present back to 1916; the Pulitzer Prize-winning *You Can't Take It with You* (1937), which concerns three generations of a kooky family and their unique hobbies; and the flop *The Fabulous Invalid* (1938), a nostalgic look at the always-dying, never-dead American theater, which ran only sixty-five performances.

On advice from his psychoanalyst that he was growing too dependent on Kaufman, H. broke up the partnership in 1940 after completing *George Washington Slept Here.* He returned to solo composition with *Winged Victory* (1943), a wartime play about the air force, which was performed by soldiers to support army charity. As might be expected, H.'s postcollaborative career had its ups and downs. But in 1948, H. rebounded with one of his most successful plays ever. *Light Up the Sky* (1949) is a comedy dealing with the tryout of a new play. Rumored to have satirized major Broadway theater figures, *Light Up the Sky* was described by the eminent critic Brooks Atkinson in his review as a "Shavian comedy with serious overtones about the human frailties of human beings."

H.'s career as a playwright ended with *The Climate of Eden* (1953), an adaptation of Edgar Mittelholzer's *Shadows Move among Them,* which tells of a missionary and his daughters who are confronted by a mentally unstable man.

H. had a gift for superior, wry, literate dialogue, and probing characterization that often leaned toward, and drew from psychoanalysis. He typically wrote about what he knew: the theater, psychoanalysis, and summer homes. His plays have been described as respectfully malicious and irreverently reverent. He favored broad satire, light on plot, underpinned with seriousness.

Personally idiosyncratic and flamboyant, H. was always very much a man of the theater. Besides playwriting, H. also directed many of own plays, as well as several other hits, and occasionally ventured into production. In addition, H. scripted a number of Hollywood screenplays, notably *Frankie and Johnny* (1936), *Gentlemen's Agreement* (1947), *A Star Is Born* (1954). He served as head of both the Authors' League and the Dramatists Guild, speaking out against the blacklisting of actors and directors. Throughout his long career, H. continued to compose libretti, revue sketches, and screenplays, and penned his popular autobiography, *Act One* (1959). H. died, just six months after his mentor, Kaufman.

BIBLIOGRAPHY: Meredith, S., *George S. Kaufman and His Friends* (1974); Ross, W. W., "M. H.," in MacNicholas, J., ed., *DLB,* vol. 7, part 1, *Twentieth-Century American Dramatists* (1981): 254–62

ERIC MARSHALL

HARTE, Bret [Francis or Frank]

b. 25 August 1836, Albany, New York; d. 5 May 1902, Camberly, Surry, England

We are likely today to think of H. as a short story writer who demonstrated the worst aspects of Victorian sentimentality and inflated diction. But however poorly regarded today, H. is also understood to be the first internationally famous writer of short fiction about the American WEST. "The Luck of Roaring Camp," "The Outcasts of Poker Flat," and "Tennessee's Partner," published in the 1860s, earned H. much fame by the nation's popular audience and approval by Ralph Waldo EMERSON, James Russell LOWELL, Henry Wadsworth LONGFELLOW, and William Dean HOWELLS, the leading literary lights of that day. H. also wrote poetry about California topics, was an editor, and penned a variety of examples of literary criticism. After a tremendous initial success, H. lived over a quarter of a century (mostly in England), during which time his fame steadily decreased.

In the late 1870s, having failed once again to achieve financial security as a fiction writer, H. turned to drama, a lifelong interest. He spent much time rewriting into a play the successful story "Two Men of Sandy Bar." This project proved a financial and artistic failure, and as a last hope, H. collaborated with Mark TWAIN on a play—"the swag," in Clemens's words, to be divided on an equal basis. By this time, the two authors' fortunes were reversed. Clemens's old California mentor was down at the heels, while Mark Twain, now a literary success and married to a very wealthy woman, lived in the most splendid house that Hartford, Connecticut, could provide. Their co-authored play, *Ah Sin,* was not only a failure, but the key wrangle that drove the warm and loyal friendship between these two men into angered ruins.

H. typically wrote parables as his serious poetry and fiction. Parables are designed to illustrate truths, reinforce an audience's expectations, or inspire an audience toward achieving an ideal behavior. Parables are not typically critical or ironic, nor are they well-wrought, complex statements that reveal a strong dimension of artistic consciousness. H. recognized his debt to the parable form in the preface to his first *Collected Works* (1882). There, he related that he "will, without claiming to be a religious man or a moralist, but simply as an artist, reverently, and humbly conform to the rules laid down by a Great Poet who created the parable of the 'Prodigal Son' and the 'Good Samaritan.'" Since at least the end of the 19th c., serious literary figures have been waging war with the parable form. As a leading practitioner of parables, H. stood at the enemy's vanguard. H.'s parables are typically dressed in a Christian imagery, but their primary aims are to illustrate that human beings are ultimately good, not depraved, and that a Victorian civilization always triumphs over an anarchistic and self-serving lack of order.

"The Luck of Roaring Camp" (1868), an early story and prototype for H.'s many volumes of parabolic fiction, is the most important story he ever wrote. The story is about a mysterious stranger, regeneration, and redemption. But, sad to say, we very likely find the story filled with ineptly comic pathos, a story smothered by the affected aura of its own diction. H.'s other stories work in similar ways. "The Outcasts of Poker Flat" shows that in a crisis, there is good in even the worst people. This story has a fair sampling of H.'s famous colorful and picturesque characters, including the slick gambler, the whore with a heart of gold, the ingenue, and the innocent, AMERICAN ADAM-like young male. "Brown of Calaveras" is a parable that demonstrates the nobility of duty over desire, a variant of the Good Samaritan parable. This tale marks the first appearance of Jack Hamlin, whose masculine objectivity and laconic stoicism H. used in some twenty other works. "Tennessee's Partner" is a parable about the power of brotherly love, and "How Santa Claus Came to Simpson's Bar" tells a parable with the message of "never give up."

As a comparison between H.'s fiction against his satire and criticism clearly shows, he was more divided, versatile, and talented than has generally been recognized. H.'s attempt to portray the American West as a collection of losers in the wilderness who could, with luck and hard work, aspire to lofty Eastern standards was no doubt wrongheaded. Instead of creating the Victorian liberal consciousness, at least in the process, he did make local color a viable form of writing.

BIBLIOGRAPHY: Barnett, L. D., *B. H.: A Reference Guide* (1980); Duckett, M., *Mark Twain and B. H.* (1964); Morrow, P. D., *B. H., Literary Critic* (1979); Scharnhorst, G., *Selected Letters of B. H.* (1997); Stewart, G. R., *B. H.: Argonaut and Exile* (1931)

PATRICK D. MORROW

HARTMANN, Sadakichi

b. 8 November 1867?, Desima, Japan; d. 21 November 1944, St. Petersberg, Florida

Journalist, playwright, novelist, and poet—"the King of Bohemia" according to a 1915 article in *Greenwich Village* magazine—H. is an intriguing figure. As a young man, he sought and befriended Walt WHITMAN, whose influence was profound. H. became a zealous proponent of his mentor's work; he tried, in 1887, to establish a Walt Whitman Society in Boston. One of

H.'s earliest poems, "To Walt Whitman" (1887) declares: "Walt Whitman, I do not call thee master, but I am bound to thee forever, thy works were to me, except Love and Nature, the grandest lessons of my life." In 1895, H. published his *Conversations with Walt Whitman*.

H.'s travels in Europe, hobnobbing with the literati, exposed him to French symbolism, which was to shape his later work. He became somewhat of a propagandist for the cause, writing, in the Boston based *Weekly Review* and *Art Critic,* articles on the French poets Rimbaud, Mallarmé, Verlaine, and René Ghil. H.'s 1890 collection, *Poems,* echoes these influences. *Naked Ghosts* (1898), H's most ambitious poetic effort to date, was dedicated to Mallarmé. The volume's final poem "To Stéphane Mallarmé: a Strain in Red," praises the French poet's work, likening it to a wine, "the blood of roses," offered in the holy "chalice" of art. By 1904, with the publication of *Drifting Flowers of the Sea,* it was clear that Whitman's influence had disappeared. The language in this collection is less flamboyant and more structured. Here, he experimented with the traditional Japanese *tanka*. That same year he wrote an article for *Reader Magazine* praising the tanka form for its brevity and concentration. The collection to follow, *Bruno Chap Books* (1915), is composed exclusively of tanka and haiku verses. These forms served H. well by controlling the verbosity and sentimentality of his earlier work. His "melancholy musings" were meant simply to suggest emotions and elevate the primacy of human response. H.'s previously published *My Rubaiyat* (1913) was revised and republished in 1916. Here, H. writes of life's dreariness, of fading youth and innocence. In it, too, are poems protesting militarism, poverty, and the bondage of women.

H. also wrote a number of religious dramas. *Christ* (1893), a production of which earned H. a week in jail for its inclusion of an erotic nude scene, was the first in a cycle of four religious, symbolist dramas. The remaining three were *Buddha* (1897), *Mohammed* (completed in 1896, unpublished), and *Confucius* (1923). These plays, with a strong emphasis on the absurd, employed a variety of visual and aural effects.

H. was also an important art critic whose contribution to this field cannot be overstated. He founded a number of art journals and published such titles as *Shakespeare in Art* (1901), *The History of American Art* (1902), *Modern American Sculpture* (1902), and *Japanese Art* (1904). H. was a great advocate of the emerging art of photography. His essays on the subject were collected and published in 1978 in *The Valiant Knights of Daguerre.*

From 1923 on, H. spent his life in and around Los Angeles fraternizing with the likes of John Barrymore and W. C. Fields. He also served as mentor to a group of area artists, expounding his aesthetic philosophy. In 1930, he published a selection of previously published pieces, *Seven Short Stories.* H. lived for part of his remaining years alone in a desert shack, painting and penning his autobiography, yet he was not forgotten. He counted Ezra POUND and George SANTAYANA among his friends and supporters; the former wrote of his friend H. in Canto LXXX of *The Pisan Cantos* as the leader of a "lost legion."

BIBLIOGRAPHY: Bruno, G., and D. Molby, "Notes on H.," *Greenwich Village* 3 (November 1915): 7–10, 18–19; Knox, G., and H. W. Lawton, *The Life and Times of S. H.* (1970); Van Deusen, M., "S. H.," in Quartermain, P., ed., *DLB,* vol. 54, *American Poets, 1880–1945* (1987): 154–63

JASON MCMAHON

HASS, Robert

b. 1 March 1941, San Francisco, California

H.'s appointment as poet laureate of the U.S. from 1995 to 1997 confirmed what most readers and critics of contemporary poetry had already come to recognize: that H. is one of the best poets and critics writing today. In retrospect, H.'s ascension to such an esteemed position seems inevitable. He received the Yale Series of Younger Poets Award for his first book of poetry, *Field Guide* (1973), the National Book Critics Circle Award for his book of criticism entitled *Twentieth Century Pleasures* (1984), and has translated five volumes of poetry by Czeslaw Milosz to much critical acclaim.

Much of H.'s literary tradition consists of poets who present the physical world in images: haiku artists, Keats and Mallarmé, William Carlos WILLIAMS, Wallace STEVENS, and Hilda DOOLITTLE. In H.'s early poetry, he shares with Japanese haiku masters a belief in the spiritual immanence of natural facts. The natural world is fulfilling in itself and poems easily translate its metaphysical significance. In his later poetry, however, H. dramatizes the inability to translate this significance, and his poems resonate with loss and absence. Ultimately, this Stevensian obsession with the relationship between language and the physical world—between word and thing—informs the whole of his poetry.

In 1971, after four years as assistant professor of English at the State University of New York at Buffalo, H. returned to his native California where he completed *Field Guide.* "In Weather," one of the book's best poems, describes an imaginative lull in H.'s poetic vision. Amid the incessant snows of February, H. la-

ments the erasure of the natural world—its catalog of minute particulars and intricate forms—that culminates in a loss of spiritual vision. Most of the poems in this volume, however, record the natural landscape of his home state, thus illustrating the resurrection of H.'s faith in the natural object as divine. In these poems, sensory images of the natural world pass through his mind as through clear glass and are transcribed in their purest state. H. names the flora and fauna of the coastline, of the old-growth forest of the valley, as well as the mountain trail. Characteristic images also include detailed descriptions of regional food and drink—even recipes—offered up to the reader as sacrament. These names of places, objects, and foods are the guideposts that demarcate the poet's natural world as moral map, and exploring the regions of that world is his spiritual discipline.

H.'s cataloging of natural images reveals a debt to Walt WHITMAN and Williams, two poets equally attuned to the particulars of place; his form, however, is much influenced by the technical rigors of haiku and modern American poet and critic Yvor WINTERS. H.'s graduate work at Stanford (1964–71) brought him into contact with Winters, who insisted on a clarity and coherence of form, content, and sound that went beyond the mere exhibition of emotion and ambiguous images. Most of the poems in *Field Guide* and much of *Praise* (1979), H.'s second book, consist of several short stanzas with lines of alternating syllabic rhythm and length. The frequent stanza breaks and irregular line lengths increase the white space, which the poet consciously employs to magnify the images, his spiritual focus.

Praise includes what most critics describe as H.'s touchstone poem, the much anthologized "Meditation at Lagunitas," which announces a shift in H.'s attitude toward the natural imagery he loves. In fact, the opening lines of this poem are so often quoted because they best articulate the single most important aesthetic principle in H.'s most recent poetry: "All the new thinking is about loss. / In this it resembles all the old thinking. / The idea for example, that each particular erases / the luminous clarity of a general idea / . . . a word is elegy to what it signifies." In these poems, the characteristic natural and culinary imagery of his native California remain, but often H. is aware of an epistemological gap between the thing and the language used to describe it. Rather than insisting that his poems record a greater, transcendent reality, his poems acknowledge loss, suffering, and unfulfilled desire. The poet does not, however, fall prey to nihilism; he instead "praises" the natural world that he can no longer translate clearly.

In *Human Wishes* (1989), H. nearly abandons the short lyric poem and its reliance on the natural image in favor of the sentence-length line and prose poem, which gives the associative imagination more play. In place of the objective namer of things is a restless consciousness that instead records the human truth of incessant desire and longing, both intellectual and visceral. In the title poem, H. asserts that all language is charged by desire, which distorts any attempt to define the metaphysical truth of "things." True to this pronouncement, these poems no longer only record the tangible immediacy of a distinct image or experience, but instead explore an ever-widening web of associative ideas and memories rooted in a variety of domestic scenes and personae. When H. does employ his customary natural image, he initiates a broad spectrum of interpretations or represents the sheer strength of human will that crops up amid personal despair.

In poems that combine the sculpted stanza of the lyric and the discursiveness of prose, *Sun under Wood* (1997) traces an unremitting theme: displacement and accompanying feelings of loss and alienation. What is most powerful about these new poems is the poet's ability to eye the most difficult of subjects—an alcoholic parent, a father's death, divorce—without becoming overly sentimental. Further, this landscape of the subjective imagination acts as a counterpressure to the few natural images H. does use. In the deeply private landscape of *Sun under Wood,* natural images take on a new glow. They deliver the fulfillment and transcendence that the natural world in *Field Guide* and *Praise* do not quite deliver and the poems of *Human Wishes* only hope for, and in so doing, distinguish him as one of the truest voices of the postmodern age.

BIBLIOGRAPHY: Altieri, C., *Self and Sensibility in Contemporary American Poetry* (1984); Bond, B., "An Abundance of Lack: The Fullness of Desire in the Poetry of R. H.," *KR* 12 (Fall 1990): 46–53; Doody, T., "From Image to Sentence: The Spiritual Development of R. H.," *APR* 26 (March 1997): 47–56

WILLIAM E. KING

HAWKES, John [Clendennin Burne, Jr.]

b. 17 August 1925, Stamford, Connecticut; d. 15 May 1998, Providence, Rhode Island

Readers familiar with H.'s writings know that he is anything but a traditionalist. He rejects many of the conventional forms of the novel and avoids what he sees as the limitations of REALISM. In fact, he has been quoted as saying, "I began to write fiction on the assumption that the true enemies of the novel were plot, character, setting, and theme." While this assertion may turn off the more general or leisurely

reader—and indeed, keep the author off the bestseller list—H.'s work is deeply respected within the academic community, and he has gained an increasingly strong critical following. Indeed, in 1980, he was elected to the American Academy and Institute of Arts and Letters and the number of critical works devoted to his fiction is impressive.

Though his fiction is largely unconventional, this is not to suggest that H. completely ignores such elements as plot, character, and theme. These can be found in his works, but they are not H.'s primary concern. Instead, he chooses to privilege form. His novels are highly structured and complex works of art that gain coherence through carefully woven patterns of language and imagery. H. belongs to that group of writers—including John BARTH, Thomas PYNCHON, and Donald BARTHELME—who attempt to break out of traditional novelistic assumptions and instead use language to express the disjointed and chaotic nature of reality.

As several of his critics have noted, H.'s fiction is in many ways a wedding between the comic and nightmarish, but the comedy in his novels does not serve as a reconciliation between individual and society. Readers of his novels do not laugh as a form of relief, even in the most absurd of predicaments, as they may find in Joseph HELLER. Instead, the black comedy elicited here is many times born of horrific surprise, where the reader is unsure whether or not laughter is indeed the appropriate response to the novelistic situations. Such strategies are H.'s way of refusing to mask the tragedies or darker sides of human existence.

H.'s first book was *Fiasco Hall* (1943), a work of poetry, but he did not receive much critical attention until 1949 with the publication of "Charivari," a novella, and *The Cannibal.* The latter, a novel that draws upon his traumatic experience as an ambulance driver during World War II, is a tightly constructed work that in many ways underscores his deemphasizing of plot and characterization. It depicts, among other things, an American soldier, a fanatical Nazi, and a cannibalistic duke in postwar Germany all involved in a surrealistic series of twists and turns that end in despair. His next novel, *The Beetle Leg* (1951), is an even more complex work. It is a consciously experimental piece that parodies the WESTERN, that quintessentially American genre, and shows the dark underside of the American dream.

The simultaneous publication in 1954 of *The Goose on the Grave* and *The Owl*—two novellas that continue his exploration into the horrors of the present and their inextricable links to the past—is considered by many critics to be the last chapter of his early career. His major phase began seven years later with *The Lime*

Twig (1961), a detective novel parody that underscores the reader's desires to vicariously experience gratuitous violence and sexual brutality. This novel, along with *Second Skin* (1964), marks a movement for H. towards a more traditional form. Even though he continued to reject strict representationalism, his writing was becoming more accessible when compared to earlier novels such *The Beetle Leg* and *The Goose on the Grave*.

Considered by many to be one of his greatest achievements, *Second Skin* is H.'s first foray into first person narration and one of his most striking statements on the plights of the artistic imagination. In his triad, *The Blood Oranges* (1971), *Death, Sleep & the Traveler* (1974), and *Travesty* (1976), he continues his work in the first person voice and creates a fictional landscape, at times terrifying, that mirrors his narrators' psyche. With *The Passion Artist* (1979), H. again focuses on the artistic imagination, but this time under the guise of one who is neither passionate nor an artist. Konrad Vost, the novel's protagonist, undergoes an unlikely series of initiations into the art of passion, and through him H. explores the Dionysian powers underlying the act of creation.

The links between sex, violence, and art have always been a most fertile territory for H.'s writing, as can even be seen in his more contemporary work such as *Adventures in the Alaskan Skin Trade* (1985) and *An Irish Eye* (1997). This, coupled with his highly stylized use of language and his pursuits of ever changing form, may not make him the most publicly popular novelist, but it has earned him the reputation of being one of the most daring writers in the last half of the 20th c.

BIBLIOGRAPHY: Berry, E., *A Poetry of Love and Darkness: The Fiction of J. H.* (1979); Busch, F., *H.: A Guide to His Fictions* (1973); Ferrari, R., *Innocence, Power, and the Novels of J. H.* (1996); Greiner, D. J., *Comic Terror: The Novels of J. H.* (1973); Greiner, D. J., *Understanding J. H.* (1985)

DEREK PARKER ROYAL

HAWTHORNE, Nathaniel

b. 4 July 1804, Salem, Massachusetts; d. 19 May 1864, Plymouth, New Hampshire

In H., many critics will agree, we sense for the first time in American fiction the full psychic involvement of the artist in his work, fiction as the writer's journey toward the meaning experience has for him. As readers, we continue to explore and to redefine the meaning H.'s achievement has for us. The American past figures importantly in H.'s work. Established patterns of thought, like the compulsive allegorizing of the Puritans, contribute to its shape. And the influences of contemporary cultural and intellectual currents, notably ROMANTICISM and the TRANSCENDENTALISM that is its most significant American manifestation, make themselves felt in H.'s work. Yet his relation to these forces was far from simple, tending often to the ironic, sometimes to the subversive.

H. was the descendant of Puritan worthies with whom he carried on an inner struggle throughout his life. William Hathorne—it was H. himself who added the "w" to the surname—arrived in Salem in 1630. Serving as a colonial magistrate, he participated in the persecution of the Quakers. His son, John Hathorne, interrogated witches in Salem in 1692. Family legend had it that this Hathorne was the target of a curse extended to all his descendants.

H.'s father, a sea captain, died on a voyage in 1808. H.'s widowed mother lived out her years as a semi-recluse, dependent for the support of her three children on the generosity of her brother. H.'s bookishness was clearly established when, at the age of nine, he suffered an injury that left him partially lame for three years, leading him to turn still more to the solitary pleasure of reading. The works of John Milton and Edmund Spenser and John Bunyan's *Pilgrim's Progress* were among his favorites.

After an undistinguished stint at Bowdoin College, from which he graduated in 1825, H. embarked on a period of twelve years of relative isolation in Salem., by no means in seclusion but separated from the mainstream of social and cultural activity of his generation: in fact, becoming a writer. The romance *Fanshawe,* published anonymously at H.'s expense in 1828, was not an auspicious beginning to a literary career; H. later attempted to have all remaining copies destroyed. The collection *Twice-Told Tales,* published in 1837, was more successful and more satisfying to its author. It was well received critically, inspiring a generous, if far from insightful, response from the poet Henry Wadsworth LONGFELLOW, a classmate at Bowdoin.

Critical success has never been a guarantee of income, however, and H. would never be able to support himself with his pen alone. Fortunately, at least from a financial point of view, H. had political connections. His role as an active Democrat led to his appointment in 1839 as measurer of salt and coal in the U.S. Customhouse in Boston, a position he left after two years. He used the money he had managed to save during this period to purchase in 1841 a membership in Brook Farm, a rural Utopian community established in West Roxbury, just outside Boston. He hoped to find within this community an atmosphere more congenial to the literary vocation than that provided by the Customhouse, but the hope was disappointed. A combination of too much brute physical labor and too little time for writing led him to abandon the community after six months.

In 1842, H. married Sophia Peabody, with whom he took up residence at the Old Manse in Concord. They would later live in Lenox and West Newton, before H. purchased "The Wayside," his last American home, in Concord. During his first stay in Concord, H. became acquainted with some of the central figures of the transcendentalist movement, including Ralph Waldo EMERSON, Henry David THOREAU, and Margaret FULLER, but he formed a close friendship only with Thoreau, of all the American writers of the period perhaps the only one of a more retiring temperament than H. himself. During his time in Lenox, Hawthorne was befriended by Herman MELVILLE, who would dedicate *Moby-Dick* to H.

H. continued to depend on political appointments for much of his income. In 1846, he became surveyor of the Customhouse in Salem, a position he held for three years, until electoral defeat for the Democrats led to his ouster. The episode has been immortalized in the introduction to *The Scarlet Letter* (1850). From 1853 to 1857, H. held the lucrative position of U.S. Consul to Liverpool, England. After traveling in Italy, he returned with his family to the Wayside in Concord. His remaining years were marred by failing health. He died in 1864, while on a vacation tour to New Hampshire in the company of his friend and college classmate Franklin Pierce, former President of the U.S. and subject of a campaign biography written by H. in 1852. H. was buried in the Sleepy Hollow Cemetery in Concord.

The tales gathered in a number of collections, from the first *Twice-Told Tales* to *The Snow-Image,* published in 1852, mark the development of many of H.'s themes and strategies, and the best of them rank with the finest works of short fiction in the language. Against a watered-down version of transcendentalism that threatened to become an American orthodoxy, H. affirmed in his fiction the positive existence of evil, the opacity of experience, and the irreducible complexity of the self. His strategy in many of his most powerful works is to introduce oppositions that are superficially of an allegorical simplicity and clarity, only to interrogate, complicate, and at times subvert, the clarity, the simplicity, even the oppositions themselves. In stories like "The Minister's Black Veil" and "Rappaccini's Daughter," the movement is toward increased ambiguity, rather than final clarification. The binary oppositions that organize "Young Goodman Brown"—forest/village, night/day, evil/good—are ultimately exposed as constructs of the mind of the story's flawed protagonist, leaving to the reader the responsibility of resolving questions of meaning.

Obscurity of motive is a common feature of H.'s tales. In some of the best of them, including "My Kinsman, Major Molineux" and "Roger Malvin's Burial," understanding what drives the protagonists to their destiny may be the most important element of the reader's share. But if the world created by H. can seem maddening in its complexity, the drive toward perfection through simplification is truly mad, as in "The Birthmark," in which the scientist Aylmer's obsession with his fair wife's single imperfection leads to her destruction. Again and again in H.'s fiction, we confront the tragic or, at least, ironic consequences of the turn away from the inevitably imperfect but vitally necessary community, a theme more or less central to most of the stories mentioned already in this discussion, as well as to "Wakefield" and "Ethan Brand." The pursuit of the absolute, whether the absolutely good, the absolutely true, or the absolutely beautiful, as in "The Artist of the Beautiful," must for H. end in disaster. That many of the tales are set in the past, while no doubt serving as a distancing device, also implies a preference for a historical, rather than theoretical-intellectual, understanding of the human condition—a further reflection of H.'s oppositional stance toward the transcendentalist currents of what we have come to call the American Renaissance. In short, H. in his tales defines his characteristically critical, ironic posture in regard to mainstream American romanticism. This posture is assumed as well, we may suppose, in the formal, restrained, at times affected, style, reminiscent of the Enlightenment, that becomes H.'s narrative voice.

In *The Scarlet Letter,* the themes and strategies developed in the tales receive their fullest realization. Often regarded as the first American novel to be fully realized as a work of art, *The Scarlet Letter* remains a masterpiece of composition, achieving a formal symmetry all the more impressive because it in no way compromises the human vitality of the narrative. We hear again H.'s familiar narrative voice, while the relationship between voice and narrative reaches new levels of profundity and complexity. If the narrator is permitted in effect to quarrel with the characters, as in observing critically Hester's emerging radicalism, part of the continuing power of the novel resides in our sense that the narrator does not unequivocally get the best of the argument. Set in the past, the Puritan New England of the later 17th c., and set in motion by events that have already occurred before the narrative begins, *The Scarlet Letter* reinforces H.'s assertion of the historical as the basis of human self-understanding. In this context, he explores again the tensions between the demands of nature and those of the spirit—working characteristically not toward a resolution of the tensions, but rather toward an acknowledgment of their inevitability, their necessity in determining the human condition.

The limited but real success of *The Scarlet Letter* in the marketplace was surpassed by that of *The House of the Seven Gables* (1851), which most critics rank just below *The Scarlet Letter* among H.'s longer works. This study of the continuing pressure of the past and of the futility of efforts to escape its influence restates H.'s distance from the strenuous optimism of Emersonian romanticism. The same theme lies at the heart of *The Marble Faun* (1860), the last romance H. completed. In *The Blithedale Romance* (1852), drawing for material on his unsatisfactory sojourn at Brook Farm, H. offers an ironic portrayal of the popular romanticism, the too easy spirituality that seemed to him pervasive in contemporary American culture.

Like his sometime friend Melville, H. was most certainly a critic of romanticism. But his was a criticism from within. His great themes—alienation, isolation, the tensions of nature and culture, the life of the unconscious—are also among the defining themes of romanticism itself. From the point of view of the literary historian, H.'s great achievement was precisely to absorb the main currents of the American romantic movement without being overwhelmed by them. If Emerson may be regarded as the greatest of the American positive romantics, H. is, with Melville, one of the great critical romantics. From the point of view of the general reader, H. is above all an artist, giving form to the moral, spiritual, and psychological tensions that continue to define for us the American character and, ultimately, the human condition.

BIBLIOGRAPHY: Arvin, N., *H.* (1929); Baym, N., *The Shape of H.'s Career* (1976); Colacurcio, M., *The Province of Piety: Moral History in H.'s Early Tales* (1985); Crews, F. C., *The Sins of the Fathers: H.'s Psychological Themes* (1966); Fogle, R., *H.'s Fiction* (1964); Male, R. R., *H.'s Tragic Vision* (1957); Mellow, J. R., *N. H. in His Times* (1979); Miller, E. H., *Salem Is My Dwelling Place: A Life of N. H.* (1992); Millington, R. H., *Practicing Romance: Narrative Form and Cultural Engagement in H.'s Fiction* (1992); Swann, C., *N. H.: Tradition and Revolution* (1992) Turner, A., *N. H.: A Biography* (1979); Waggoner, H. H., *H.: A Critical Study* (1955)

W. P. KENNEY

HAY, John [Milton]

b. 8 October 1838, Salem, Indiana; d. 1 July 1905, Lake Sunapee, New Hampshire

H. had so much talent that he could have become a great poet, a great novelist, or a great historian if he had narrowed his focus. And he might have done so but for marriage into millions, lavish socializing, a devotion to political service, and occasional self-deprecation. He will still remain an important minor literary figure.

H. earned a master's degree at Brown University (1858), studied law in Springfield, Illinois, met and campaigned for Abraham LINCOLN, and was his assistant private secretary (under John G. Nicolay, 1861–65). After diplomatic duty abroad in Paris (1865–67), Vienna (1867–68), and Madrid (1869–70), H. became an intermittent editor of the New York *Tribune,* married Clara Stone, daughter of ruthless Cleveland railroader Amasa Stone, and thereafter alternated literary work and significant diplomatic endeavors as ambassador to England (1897–98), and Secretary of State under William McKinley and then Theodore ROOSEVELT (1898-1905). H. helped to formulate the Open Door policy in China (1900) and was responsible for the first Panama Canal treaties (1900–1903). He was also the revered personal friend of Henry ADAMS, Bret HARTE, William Dean HOWELLS, Henry JAMES, Clarence KING, Mark TWAIN, and many lesser writers.

H.'s literary production is uneven but at its best superb. The poems in *Pike County Ballads and Other Pieces* (1871) combine crude local-color Midwest dialect and appealingly understated sentimentality. The most famous are "Jim Bludso," which features a rough but heroic Mississippi River steamboat engineer, and "Little Breeches," which opts for pragmatic over theoretical theology. H.'s travel book *Castilian Days* (1871), a sprawling collection of essays on Spanish life, history, art, and beliefs, is notable for its vivid style, its pro-democratic statements, and its criticism of Spanish religion and militarism. His controversial novel *The Bread Winners: A Social Study* (1874), which caused a sensation when first published (anonymously), is less the antilabor novel it has regularly been labeled than an elaborate, half-realistic, half-romantic, antianarchistic love story with autobiographical hero, rich girl, carpenter's pretty daughter, and slow but honest laborer. H. also wrote half a dozen disturbing, challenging short stories, the best of which concern American EXPATRIATES in Europe ("Shelby Cabell") and bittersweet Mississippi Valley life ("The Foster Brothers" and "The Blood Seedling"). *Abraham Lincoln: A History* (10 vols., 1890, with Nicolay) is based on two decades of source hunting, successfully counterpoints national history with intimate biography, and treats three main theses: "War and Politics, campaign and statecraft, are Siamese twins, inseparable and interdependent"; events during the Civil War moved "with a steady pace . . . of a tragic fate"; and both sides enlisted the "saving grace" of dark humor in their efforts to explain the titanic ironies of war.

BIBLIOGRAPHY: Clymer, K. J., *J. H.: The Gentleman as Diplomat* (1975); Dennett, T., *J. H.: From Poetry to Politics* (1933); Gale, R. L., *J. H.* (1978); Monteiro, G., *Henry James and J. H.: The Record of a Friendship* (1965); Monteiro, G., "J. H.'s Short Fiction," *SSF* 8 (Fall 1971): 543–52

ROBERT L. GALE

HAYDEN, Robert

b. 4 August 1913, Detroit, Michigan; d. 2 February 1980, Ann Arbor, Michigan

The recognition that H. is one of our foremost African American poets, and one of the considerable American poets of his generation, began to gather force in the middle of the 1960s, ironically just when his refusal to embrace any form of social or aesthetic separatism was making him the target of attacks from black nationalists who questioned the authenticity of H.'s blackness. In 1966, H. was denounced at a writers' conference held at Fisk University, on whose faculty he had served for twenty years. In the same year, he received the Grand Prix de la Poesie conferred by the First World Festival of Negro Arts, held in Dakar, Senegal. Langston HUGHES—who had years before advised a young H. that his poetry was derivative—chaired the committee and made the presentation. It was the first of a series of honors that H. would receive, from within the academy and beyond, for the rest of his life. The last was the day of tribute set aside for him in 1980 at the University of Michigan, whose Department of English he had joined in 1969. Unfortunately, illness made it impossible for him to attend; H. died the following day.

H.'s earlier poems show the influence of the poets of the Harlem Renaissance and are more frequently in the mode of social protest than would be true of his mature work. He later dismissed the contents of his first book, *Heart-Shape in the Dust* (1940), as apprentice work. He would never, however, become indifferent to politics in the broader sense, nor would he deny the political dimension of the poet's art. The influence of the Harlem Renaissance would never be rejected but, combined with other influences, would become an integral part of his own developing identity as a poet.

Instrumental in helping H. find his own voice was the influence of W. H. AUDEN, with whom H. studied at the University of Michigan in the early 1940s. As H. matured, the inheritance of African American folk culture and the traditions of African American poetry entered into a creative tension with the MODERNISM of poets such as Auden and T. S. ELIOT. The develop-

ment can be traced in two pamphlets, *The Lion and the Archer* (1948) and *Figure of Time* (1955). The poet in full maturity emerges in *A Ballad of Remembrance* (1962), revised as *Selected Poems* (1966), representing what H. at that time considered worth preserving in his own work.

This work cannot be categorized as protest poetry, popular poetry, or personal poetry. African American history provides H. with the thematic source of some of his most intensely realized poems. "Middle Passage" deals with the horrors of slavery, but rather than taking a straightforward narrative or polemical approach to this material, H. makes of it a modernist meditation on history, heroism, the inhumanity that is always a human possibility, and the unkillable human wish for freedom. Presenting the historical materials in a non-linear fashion and through a multiplicity of voices, H. reflects modernist methods of fragmentation and montage, modernist strategies of impersonality. But in its underlying affirmations, the poem breaks sharply with the "Waste Land motif" associated with mainstream modernism.

H. also found inspiration in black popular culture, in black religion, and in the folkways of the black community, especially in the urban setting he knew from his childhood. In dealing with these varied materials, H. demonstrated mastery of a range of formal strategies, consistently matching form to theme. His sureness of touch and tone inform the elevated rhetoric of his sonnet "Frederick Douglass," the blues feeling of "Homage to the Empress of the Blues," the baroque elaboration of "A Ballad of Remembrance," and the starkness of statement in "Those Winter Sundays."

Although much of his most memorable work is on African American themes, H. refused to consider himself a racial poet in the narrow sense, and the Baha'i faith, to which he converted in the 1940s, reinforced his rejection of barriers between peoples. While he never ceased to reaffirm the struggle of black people, he saw it as part of what he called "the long human struggle toward freedom."

BIBLIOGRAPHY: Cooke, M., *Afro-American Literature in the Twentieth Century* (1984); Fetrow, F., *R. H.* (1984); Hatcher, J., *From the Auroral Darkness: The Life and Poetry of R. H.* (1984); Williams, P., *R. H.: A Critical Analysis of His Poetry* (1987)

W. P. KENNEY

HAYNE, Paul Hamilton

b. 1 January 1830, Charleston, South Carolina; d. 6 July 1886, Grovetown, Georgia

In his own day, H. was known chiefly as a poet and man of letters. He published six volumes of poems during his career (1852–86) and was cited throughout the nation as the "poet laureate of the South." And H. was indeed the South's most prominent literary spokesman in the 1870s and 1880s. In this position as well as in a breadwinning capacity, he was not able to devote himself solely to poetry. He found it necessary to write prose of all kinds—reviews, criticism, essays, fiction—and to edit periodicals from time to time. In addition, he kept up a voluminous correspondence that now appears to more than match his poems as his major contribution to literature.

Scion of a prominent Carolina family, H. was born in Charleston, educated at the College of Charleston, and prepared for law. The nephew of Senator Robert Y. Hayne, Daniel Webster's redoubtable opponent in the famous Senate debates of 1830, H. could easily have used the law and family connections to win political office and power, but he preferred literature. In 1852, he acquired the *Southern Literary Gazette* and turned to editing and writing criticism and poems. His first collection, *Poems* (1855), reveals him securely in the Anglo-American tradition of romantic poetry as developed by William Wordsworth, Sir Walter Scott, Percy Bysshe Shelley, John Keats, Alfred, Lord Tennyson, Henry Wadsworth LONGFELLOW, and Edgar Allan POE. His subsequent collections published before the Civil War—*Sonnets and Other Poems* (1857) and *Avolio; A Legend of the Island of Cos. With Poems, Lyrical, Miscellaneous and Dramatic* (1860)—demonstrate his interest in a variety of forms and a growing mastery of technique, but the advent of war interrupted his development. H.'s frail health (he had been struggling with lung trouble and liver disorders since he was sixteen), however, prevented lengthy military duty.

After a period of four months' service, he returned to supporting and defending the Confederacy with his pen. He wrote dozens of war poems, but with the exception of a few, his patriotic lyrics, unlike those of his friend Henry TIMROD, did not capture the eye the ear or the mind. His best verse appeared after the war in three volumes—*Legends and Lyrics* (1872), *The Mountain of the Lovers; With Poems of Nature and Tradition* (1875), and the complete edition of H.'s *Poems* (1881). These poems display his continuing interest in the forms and themes of the Anglo-American tradition, but they also reveal a more mature interest in his own natural surroundings and in the "great heart of humanity." The diction and imagery, however, are conventional and often appear to smack of the tradition rather than the world outside. Yet the poems are Southern to the core in their celebration of the land and the virtues of the culture, in the verbal music of the lyrics, and in the notion that heard melodies are the sweetest.

H. also made a contribution to the literature of the period as a critic and an editor. As editor of the *Gazette,* of *Russell's Magazine* (1857–60), and of numerous columns and departments in magazines and newspapers after the war, H. found ways to foster literature in the South, to express his literary views, and to shape the taste of his readers. He took these duties seriously and continued to seek to exert an influence even when he had no natural platform from which to make known his opinions.

In the end, then, H. may have made his most important contribution as a man of letters whose own situation and whose correspondence reveal the plight of the Southern writer of the period. He wrote many of his contemporaries in America and England, and he expressed his social, philosophical, and literary views at times forthrightly, at times diplomatically. His correspondence demonstrates a devotion to the profession of letters hardly equaled by Poe or William Gilmore SIMMS before him or by such contemporaries as William Dean HOWELLS, Henry JAMES, or Samuel Langhorne CLEMENS. His commitment was rare in his own day, and his sense of vocation may be found rarely in ours.

BIBLIOGRAPHY: Anderson, C. R., "Poet of the Pine Barrens," *GaR* 1 (Fall 1947): 280–93; McKeithan, D. W., *A Collection of H. Letters* (1944); Moore, R. S., "H. the Poet: A New Look," *SCR* 2 (November 1969): 4–13; Moore, R. S., ed., *A Man of Letters in the Nineteenth-Century South: Selected Letters of P. H. H.* (1982); Moore, R. S., *P. H. H.* (1972); Moore, R. S., "P. H. H.," in Rathburn, J. W., and M. M. Green, eds., *DLB,* vol. 64, *American Literary Critics and Scholars, 1850–1880* (1988): 100–7

RAYBURN S. MOORE

HAYSLIP, Le Ly
b. 19 December 1949, Ky La, Quang Nam, Vietnam

Recognized for her Vietnamese perspective on the Vietnam War, H. endeavors in her writings to reconcile the differences between Vietnamese and Americans and to facilitate healing and understanding between the two nations. Her memoirs, *When Heaven and Earth Changed Places: A Vietnamese Woman's Journey from War to Peace* (1989, with Jay Wurts) and its sequel, *Child of War, Woman of Peace* (1993, with her son, James Hayslip), move from H.'s experiences in Vietnam during the war to her subsequent immigration to the U.S. and her negotiations as a Vietnamese American citizen. The power of her message for Americans became particularly clear when filmmaker Oliver Stone adapted her memoirs into *Heaven and*

Earth (1994), the third movie in his Vietnam trilogy. H. continued to spread her message with her humanitarian work with the East Meets West Foundation, an organization founded by her and devoted to the rebuilding of Vietnam.

Presented as an account by the "enemy," *When Heaven and Earth Changed Places* is told from alternating chronological perspectives, shifting back and forth from her experiences in Vietnam during the Vietnam War to 1986 when she returns to Vietnam for the first time after having immigrated to the U.S. The story's style serves to underscore H.'s message of reconciliation, a message reviewers praised for its universality and generosity. H. deftly recounts the impossible and often harrowing situations she and her family faced as they are branded traitors by alternately the Republicans and the Viet Cong. Repeatedly imprisoned and tortured by the Republican army, and eventually raped by Viet Cong soldiers, H. tells a story that speaks to the impossible position in which she, her family, and the other villagers are placed. Her later interactions with American soldiers in Saigon again reinforce her ability to negotiate the restrictive forces that determine her position as a victim of the war and of fate itself.

Although not as well received as her first memoir, H.'s second publication, *Child of War, Woman of Peace,* again highlights this message of healing and agency; however, she turns her attention towards the spiritual and moral bankruptcy of Americans and stresses her own Buddhist values as a response to Americans' excessive consumption without corresponding fulfillment. It is divided into three sections that illustrate this move from the status of Vietnamese antagonist to universal conciliator. The first, entitled "Living with the Enemy," focuses on her position as alienated and disenfranchised. Repeating the theme of her first narrative, H. describes her relationships with American men in warlike terms and recounts her efforts to gain independence from them. The second section, "Finding the American Dream," describes her eventual financial success with restaurants and real estate and chronicles her initial forays into America's spiritual environments. Her third section, "Taking the Long Road Back," concludes her journey of redemption. She speaks in this section mainly of spiritual improvement and the fulfilment of her dream of returning to Vietnam and building a medical clinic in her town. While the second portion of the narrative establishes H. as an American, the third section allows her to transcend national boundaries as well as redeem herself to her family. H. rises to the top, psychically, economically, and spiritually, and her narrative follows the trajectory of many immigrant American success stories.

H. combines the universality of her message with the specificity of her position as a Vietnamese American woman living in Vietnam and the U.S. during and after the Vietnam War. Recognized by mainstream American readers as well as Asian American critics for the new viewpoint she brings, H. is representative of the wave of post-Vietnam War writers who offer healing and perspective to their readers while also offering Asian American scholars a new means of documenting the experiences, politics, and positioning of Vietnamese American writers.

BIBLIOGRAPHY: Bow, L., "L. L. H.'s Bad (Girl) Karma: Sexuality, National Allegory, and the Politics of Neutrality," *PSt* 17 (April 1994): 141–60: Nguyen, V. T., "Representing Reconciliation: L. L. H. and the Victimized Body," *Positions* 5 (Fall 1997): 605–42

CHRISTINE SO

HAZZARD, Shirley
b. 30 January 1931, Sydney, Australia

For H., the challenge faced by the contemporary novelist stems from national dislocation, from individual alienation, and from lack of cultural continuity. The traditional social and personal moorings gone, the novelist's task becomes a reconstructive one. So her fiction depicts modern-day travelers, exiles, and emigrants in search of a personal paradise, or an ideal, which they may discover through love, beauty, art, service to fellow humans—and other such abstractions. Sometimes these metaphorical transients do enter a temporal paradise, and each fleeting experience helps to fill their spiritual vacuum. In other cases, external forces dominate, and the characters fail even to glimpse the vague design they pursue or the unattainable paradise they desire.

H.'s own life reflects this preoccupation with dislocation. Born and raised in Australia, she has lived as well in Hong Kong and New Zealand, where her father served in Australia's foreign service. Later, she spent time in England, then moved to New York, where she joined the United Nations Secretariat, a job that took her to Europe for long periods. Since leaving the UN in 1960, she has divided her time between New York and Italy. She is now a citizen of the U.S.

Publishing initially in the *New Yorker,* H. relied on her UN experience for two of her books, *People in Glass Houses* (1967) and *Defeat of an Ideal* (1973). The first is a collection of interrelated short stories that recount the experiences of people working in a vast international bureaucracy, where language turns meaningless, personal relations dissipate, hypocrisy prevails, and individuality is considered subversive.

This work could be read as a fictional preliminary to the factual account of the UN in her 1973 book, subtitled *A Study of the Self-Destruction of the United Nations.* An earlier short story collection, *Cliffs of Fall* (1963), follows several disjointed and lonely travelers through European hotels, pensions, street cafés, and railway stations, as they search in vain for lasting love but engage only in cursory relationships that foreshadow their destruction.

Of H.'s three novels, *The Evening of the Holiday* (1966), *The Bay of Noon* (1970), and *The Transit of Venus* (1980), the third remains the most enduring and the one on which her reputation rests. The novel's title, drawing from an astronomical term for a planet's movement and a planet named after the goddess of love, reflects the complexity and symbolic nature of the narrative. Its setting shifts to all parts of the world, including Europe, the U.S., and Australia; the time span ranges from World War I to the 1960s; and the cast of characters draws from a varied international group. The action revolves around three Australian women who have left home for Europe to seek what the novel describes as "A mystical passage to another life." Like the travelers in the earlier fiction, the women move from one fragmented experience to another and search for the seemingly unattainable ideal of true love in their encounters with a variety of men—all well-educated and sophisticated, some of whom become lovers or husbands and display different degrees of stability. Although the central characters only succeed partially in the process of emotional ripening, the narrative itself succeeds fully in its rendition of their quest, triumphs, and disenchantment. In this most literary of novels, as in all of her work, H. not only writes exquisite prose and handles symbolism with subtlety but also captures each nuance of character.

The Transit of Venus, in particular, has been likened to the work of Jane Austen and Henry JAMES. Perhaps this is too facile a comparison. Although the novel, constructed in a mannered fashion and set in a rarefied world, does bring to mind 19th-c. fiction from the standpoint of style and technique, it is thoroughly contemporary in its thematic treatment of personal displacement. H. has pointed out that in the past, people could depend on some form of continuity, no matter how precarious, but the events of the 20th c. have blown all the old verities to "smithereens." For H., then, the novelist's job is to assemble and identify "these smithereens" in order to grasp the destinies and destinations of those adrift in a disordered universe.

BIBLIOGRAPHY: Baym, N., "Artifice and Romance in S. H.'s Fiction," *TSLL* 25 (1983): 222–48; Colmer, J., "S. H.'s *The Transit of Venus*," *JCL* 19 (1984): 10–21; Priessnitz, H., "Glimpses of Paradise," in Ross, R. L.,

ed., *International Literature in English: Essays on the Major Writers* (1991): 335–50; Taylor, N., "An Introduction to S. H.'s *The Transit of Venus*," *WLWE* 24 (1984): 287–95

ROBERT L. ROSS

HEARN, Lafcadio

b. 27 June 1850, Ionian Island of Lafcadio, Greece; d. 26 September 1904, Tokyo, Japan

H. was most influential in building the bridge between America and Japan in the late 19th c., as Yone Noguchi played a similar role in the early 20th c. Fascinated by the exotic literature and tradition, H. traveled to Japan, married Koizumi Setsu, the daughter of an old samurai family, raised four children, became a naturalized citizen, and changed his name to Koizumi Yakumo. From 1890, when he was sent to Japan by *Harper's Magazine,* he lived there the rest of his life and, while teaching, produced some of his best work.

His earlier life also made a strong impact on his writings. Born to a young Greek woman and an Irish surgeon in the service of the British army, H.'s life was a procession of restless wandering and exotic travels. When he was five, his mother, suffering a depression, left her children and returned to Greece and his father later married an English woman, an event for which H. never forgave him. H. then became the ward of his great-aunt, who tried to educate him for the priesthood. At thirteen, he was sent to a Catholic school in Paris, and while he became fluent in French, as shown by his superb translations of works by Théophile Gautier, Alphonse Daudet, and Pierre Loti, he detested not only the Catholic faith but Christianity in general.

At nineteen, when the Hearn estate was bankrupt, he sailed to America. He first went to Cincinnati and eventually found employment as a journalist. "His Greek temperament and French culture," wrote Noguchi, "became frost-bitten as a flower in the North." So H. sought and found a milder climate in the South. In 1877, he traveled down the Mississippi and settled in New Orleans. In 1882, he translated Gautier's *One of Cleopatra's Nights and Other Fantastic Romances;* he later tried his hand at the Gothic tale, completing *Stray Leaves from Strange Literature* (1884), his first book of legends and stories. In 1885, he made a trip to Florida and published his second book of fiction, *Some Chinese Ghosts* (1887), in which he sought, in his words, "especially for *weird* beauty." He also traveled to Martinique: from this experience came his first novel *Chita* (1889), which brought him instant recognition.

H.'s first books written in Japan are less accomplished than the later ones. "The Red Bridal," published in the *Atlantic Monthly* (July 1894), is an awkward attempt to draw an analogy between the ancient Urashima folktale and contemporary Japanese scenes. But *In Ghostly Japan* (1899) and *Shadowings* (1900), two of his best books, collect horror stories reminiscent of Edgar Allan POE's. "Ingwa-Banashi" (Tales of Fate) depicts an unexpected terror at a death scene where the dead wife's ghost possesses the new bride's body much like Poe's "Ligeia."

H.'s greatest achievement in Japan, *Kwaidan* (1904; Weird Tales), comprises seventeen short stories transformed from medieval Japanese folktales and legends. "The Story of Mimi-Nashi-Hoichi" (The Story of Hoichi the Ear-less) portrays a blind lute player living at a Buddhist temple. The ghosts of vanquished warriors return to hear his music to console their souls. To chase the ghosts away, the priest writes the text of the holy Sutra all over Hoichi's body, except on his ears. The angry ghosts then tear off Hoichi's ears, leaving him in writhing pain. Ironically, the ghosts' vengeance on him immortalizes him. As do many of H.'s exotic tales, this story offers a parable on the primacy of art over life. Suggestive of the artist's extreme position in life, Hoichi's commitment to art is scarcely appreciated by the measure of this world.

In his own life, H. sought extraordinary experiences to make art out of his troubled life. Despite the wide vision and profound philosophy he had acquired in Japan, in many ways he remained a lonely skeptic, as shown by the famous haiku he chose as the epigraph for one of his last travel essays, "Fuji-no-yama," published in *The Writings of L. H.* (1922): "Kité miréba / Sahodo madé nashi / Fuji no yama!" ("Seen on close approach, the mountain of Fuji doesn't come up to expectation"). To H., disillusionment was the catalyst in an unusual search, and while writing in the rise of realism in America, he remained a confirmed romantic.

BIBLIOGRAPHY: Bisland, E., *The Life and Letters of L. H.* (2 vols., 1906); Gould, G. M., *Concerning L. H.* (1908); Hakutani, Y., "L. H.," *ALR* 8 (Summer 1975): 271–74; Noguchi, Y., "L. H.: A Dreamer," *CurL* 38 (June 1905): 521–23; Stevenson, E., *L. H.* (1961); Tinker, E. L., *L. H.'s American Days* (1924); Webb, K. M., *L. H. and His German Critics* (1984); Yu, B., *An Ape of Gods: The Art and Thought of L. H.* (1964)

YOSHINOBU HAKUTANI

HECHT, Anthony [Evan]
b. 16 January 1923, New York City

Considered by most critics as the premier formalist poet of the latter half of the 20th c., H. studied with New Critic John Crowe RANSOM, claims the influence of W. B. Yeats and W. H. AUDEN, and has experienced an academic career strikingly similar to that of Richard WILBUR, his closest contemporary competitor. H.'s elaborate rhyme schemes, exotic diction, and convoluted syntax recall the style of Gerard Manley Hopkins, Algernon Swinburne, and Dylan Thomas.

Because of his lackluster performance early in school, H.'s worried parents sent him to the Pratt Institute for aptitude testing, then tried to keep from him the bleak results. As a college freshman, he announced his desire to be a poet, whereupon his parents called their only literary friend, Theodore GEISEL, better known as Dr. Seuss, who recommended that H. read the biography of Joseph Pulitzer, which the fledgling poet, fearing a discouraging trap, never did. H. won the Pulitzer Prize in 1968 for *The Hard Hours,* his second volume of poetry. H. has also received the Bollingen Prize as well as Guggenheim, Prixe de Rome, Fulbright, and Ford Foundation Fellowships. He has taught at many universities, including Kenyon, Harvard, Yale, the University of Rochester, and Georgetown, and was poetry consultant to the Library of Congress from 1982 to 1984.

After receiving his B.A. from Bard in 1944, H. was inducted into the army. He saw over half his company killed or wounded in action, and his unit liberated an annex to the Buchenwald concentration camp. Of Jewish descent, H. feels the burden of being a survivor common to war veterans. Images of World War II appear in his poems "Japan," "Still Life," and "The Venetian Vespers," where the description of a soldier who has his head blown off is based on H.'s personal experience. Long after the war, in a poem significantly titled "Persistences," from *The Venetian Vespers* (1979), he says, "Mine is the task to find out words / For . . . the burning, voiceless Jews." Images of the Holocaust are the focus of some of his most powerful poems, including "More Light! More Light!" and "Rites and Ceremonies."

More personally, H. has written a number of poems that put him in company with the confessional poets. "Adam," "A Letter," "Message from the City," "It Out-Herods Herod," "The Ghost in the Martini," and "Going the Rounds" air out the dirty laundry of broken relationships, affairs, and drinking, though H. often tries to mediate the pain through humor.

One of H.'s signature techniques is to describe nuances of weather that correspond to the mood or moral condition of a poem's speaker. In "The Odds," from *Millions of Strange Shadows* (1977), the birth of a son is set against the backdrop of a beautiful snowscape and the atrocities of Vietnam. Moralized landscapes also figure in many of H.'s longest poems. In "The Venetian Vespers," an aging, effete aesthete delivers an interior monologue during his last days in

Venice, the decadent city itself an objective correlative for the parasitic and vacuous life of the expatriate persona.

Throughout his career, H.'s poetry evinces his interest in the relationship between poetry and music, poetry and painting, and, more generally, art and morality. In *The Transparent Man* (1990), "A Love for Four Voices" takes its structure from a Haydn quartet. Poems based on paintings include "A Poem for Julia," "Dichtung Und Wahrheit," and "The Deodand." H.'s tour de force in this genre is "Gladness of the Best," whose sinuous syntax, circular rhyme scheme, and baroque diction imitate both polyphony and the vines of the Gobelin tapestry that is the meditative object of the poem. All of these art forms, in turn, are tropes for God's "holy amity."

Early in his career, one can see H. already tampering with a kind of unified field theory of aesthetics, human behavior, human creations, and the natural world. "The Feast of Stephen," for example, dramatizes the connection between sports, sex, and war. In "The Gardens of the Villa d'Este," from *A Summoning of Stones* (1954), H. impeccably fuses form, subject, and theme. "Dichtung und Wahrheit" avers that 18th-c. music, wigs, architecture, and pastries partook of the same principle.

When H. was asked to deliver the Andrew W. Mellon Lectures in the Fine Arts for 1992, which were published as *On the Laws of the Poetic Art* (1995), it was not surprising that he chose to elaborate on these views in the first two chapters: "Poetry and Painting" and "Poetry and Music."

Much of the darkness in H.'s first four volumes of poetry he has attributed to his own genetic or metabolic predisposition to depression. What is striking about the entire body of his verse, however, is the counterbalancing compassion, wit, and humor. He has even created a light verse form called the double dactyl and collected examples in *Jiggery Pokery* (1983), which is replete with a mock-scholarly introduction by H. and John HOLLANDER. While *The Transparent Man* has a miasmic stream of gloom wending through it, there are also many freshets of H.'s inimitable blend of low humor and high art. "Destinations" and "See Naples and Die," for example, transform innuendo and malediction into deliciously vindictive artifice.

H.'s serious translations of Sophocles and Aeschylus, versions of poems by Nobel laureate Joseph BRODSKY, parodies like "The Dover Bitch," and satiric renditions of Voltaire, Du Bellay, and Baudelaire round out his qualifications not only as the quintessential belletrist of his generation but as one of the great moral writers at the end of the 20th c.

BIBLIOGRAPHY: German, N., *A. H.* (1988); Lea, S., ed., *The Burdens of Formality: Essays on the Poetry of A. H.* (1989)

NORMAN GERMAN

HECHT, Ben
b. 28 February 1894, New York City; d. 18 April 1964, New York City

H. is one of the many talented and prolific journalists who successfully made the transition to a literary career. He was a reporter, writing for the Chicago *Journal* and the Chicago *Daily News* from 1910 to 1923, serving as a correspondent in Berlin between 1918 and 1919. He is the author of more than ten novels, written from 1922 to 1947, and five nonfiction books, including two autobiographies, as well as numerous short stories and sketches. H. also authored over twenty plays from 1921 to 1958 and the screenplays for more than sixty films from 1936 to 1964. H. founded and published the *Chicago Literary Times* (1923–24). He won the first Academy Award ever given for best screenplay for *Underworld* (1927), the film that ushered in the extremely popular gangster genre. He won another Academy Award for best screenplay for *The Scoundrel* (1935), and was nominated for an Academy Award for *Viva Villa* (1934), *Wuthering Heights* (1939), *Angels over Broadway* (1940), and *Notorious* (1946). He also founded a motion picture company in 1934 with Charles MacArthur, a writer with whom H. collaborated on many scripts.

H.'s background in journalism was the single most important influence on his work. As a young reporter, he was known for his colorful sketches of Chicago's low-life, specializing in portraits of murder, brothels, and other urban problems. His subjects, though usually grotesque, are well known to journalists and are considered to be models for the well-written human interest story. *The Front Page,* a play written by H. and MacArthur and produced in New York in 1928—it has been adapted to film three times—is the classic depiction of the newspaper business in the heyday of the 1930s.

H.'s newspaper stories were colorful—often they were gaudy—and sometimes they were not true. In his autobiography, *A Child of the Century* (1954), H. states that his reputation as a reporter was "somewhat undeserved, for it was not my talents as a news gatherer that I offered my newspaper, but a sudden fearless flowering as a fictioneer . . . I made them all up."

Critic Marvin Felheim contends that unlike other American novelists who served their apprenticeship as journalists to write important novels, H. was never able to overcome his background. H.'s novels have not survived, for in them, according to Felheim, H. treats his times with shallow contempt. "The reader responds to his novels as they do to newspaper accounts: that's the way of the world. We are left without either intellectual or emotional depth," wrote Felheim.

H. will be best remembered for his screenplays, a medium in which he excelled. Ironically, H. never took his film work seriously; he thought his reputation as a novelist suffered for it. He claims that he completed many of his most entertaining screenplays within two weeks—never more than eight weeks—and saw Hollywood as only a reliable source of money.

Despite his attitude toward Hollywood and film, H.'s screenplays form an important part of American film history. His screenplay *Underworld* was the first of its kind, creating the popular gangster genre. Other films that H. wrote himself or coauthored include *Scarface* (1932), *Gunga Din* (1939), *Spellbound* (1945), *Kiss of Death* (1947), *Miracle in the Rain* (1956), and *A Farewell to Arms* (1957). He collaborated on, but did not receive credit for, *Gone with the Wind* (1939), *Foreign Correspondent* (1940), *The Shop around the Corner* (1940), *Lifeboat* (1943), *Gilda* (1946), and *Rope* (1948). H. died while he was working on the screenplay for *Casino Royale* (1967), another collaboration for which he did not receive screen credit.

BIBLIOGRAPHY: Harrison, G. A., ed., *The Critic as Artist: Essays on Books, 1920–1970* (1972); Newquist, R., *Counterpoint* (1964); Robbins, J. A., ed., *Literary Essays, 1954–1974* (1976)

JOSEPH FERRANDINO

HEINLEIN, Robert [Anson]

b. 7 July 1907, Butler, Missouri; d. 8 May 1988, Carmel, California

H. stands at the top rank of science fiction writers. The sheer volume of his work is astounding: he completed thirty-six novels as well as a large number of short stories. Many critics credit him with singlehandedly bringing SCIENCE FICTION into the mainstream of 20th-c. literature. In fact, the entry of H.'s short stories into the sci-fi "pulps" of the 1940s is credited with causing a marked upgrade in the quality of work printed in these journals.

H. has received a variety of honors and awards. He was a four-time recipient of the prestigious "Hugo," awarded annually for the year's best science fiction, and was a frequent speaker and honoree at sci-fi conferences and conventions. H. was also awarded the first Grand Master Nebula Award by the Science Fiction Writers of America. In October 1988, he was posthumously awarded the Distinguished Public Service Medal.

From an early age, H. maintained a strong interest in science and the military. These twin interests culminated in his commission as an ensign after his graduation from the Naval Academy in 1929. In 1934, H. was granted a physical disability discharge resulting

from tuberculosis. Though his career as a naval officer was thus brief, H.'s military experiences are clearly reflected in his subsequent work.

H.'s literary career can be divided into two distinct periods. During the first period, a considerable body of "juvenile" or "adolescent" fiction was produced. These works include *Rocket Ship Galileo* (1947), *The Star Beast* (1954), *Have Spacesuit Will Travel* (1958), and *Starship Troopers* (1959). Typically, these short novels place adolescent protagonists into highly imaginative situations in which only their plucky self-reliance and knowledge of applied science enables them to survive. Because of their energy and inventiveness, the fiction produced during this period is considered by some critics to be H.'s best work.

During H.'s second literary period, a major shift occurred. Turning to more mature protagonists and themes, H.'s fiction during this period is typified by his most famous work, *Stranger in a Strange Land* (1961). This controversial novel centers on a "Martian" of human ancestry named Valentine Michael Smith. After being discovered and brought to Earth, Smith establishes a Manson-like cult which practices group marriage and ritual cannibalism. *Stranger in a Strange Land* became, in some circles, a manifesto of the sixties counterculture.

H.'s major works during this second phase of his career include *The Moon Is a Harsh Mistress* (1966), *Notebooks of Lazarus Long* (1978), and *The Cat Who Walks through Walls* (1985), all of which are marked by self-conscious attention to the political and social concerns that were often implicit in his earlier work. Not only are the characters more mature, but the evident conflict also reflects a more mature perspective. Rebellion against oppressive social conventions and corrupt government becomes common. A continuing project for H. is his intricate "future history" motif, in which characters travel back and forth through time and space within an elaborate, detailed map of mankind's future. In such stories as "If This Goes On—" (1940), H.'s adventurers range across not only the solar system and the entire known galaxy, but also across the boundaries of time itself.

H.'s political agenda varies little. Government is seldom cast in a favorable light; freedom, competence, and self-reliance are the hallmarks of the successful individual in H.'s world. This self-reliance is expressed in a number of ways: courage and coolness under fire, an astonishing range of technical and scientific know-how, and a stubborn self-confidence. At the same time, H.'s military background moves him to reconcile this love of freedom with patriotism and respect for properly constituted authority—such as the military. Women are generally cast in submissive or subordinate roles, although their roles become more complex in later works. His portrayal of women has frequently led critics to label him as somewhat sexist or even misogynistic.

Overall, H.'s influence on the development of science fiction is immense; many science fiction writers cite him as a major shaping force in their career development. Not only did he bring a fresh burst of creativity and artistic invention to his craft, but he also set an example for addressing in the genre the full range of human experiences.

BIBLIOGRAPHY: Dickinson, D., "What Is One to Make of R. H.?" *MFS* 32 (Spring 1986): 127–31; Franklin, H. B., *R. A. H.: America as Science Fiction* (1980); Heinlein, V., ed., *Grumbles from the Grave: R. H.* (1989); Stover, L. E., *R. A. H.* (1987); Williamson, J., *R. A. H.* (1978)

HENRY L. WILSON

HELLER, Joseph

b. 1 May 1923, Brooklyn, New York

Among the brilliant first novels in American literature, H.'s *Catch-22* (1961) is probably the funniest. Besides being laugh-out-loud hilarious, however, the book is deadly serious in several senses, exploring the dangerous borderland where the comic flips shockingly over into the horrific, and experimenting with narrative form in a borderland of overlapping genres. H. has been criticized for satirizing the military effort in World War II, which takes for granted that *Catch-22* is a war novel and implies that, in waging satire on the allies, H. lets Hitler off the hook. The book is, indeed, a scathing satire of man's (mostly male) inhumane will to power and wealth, the shallow, circular, self-rationalizing thinking that inhumanity demands, and the complicity with the systems and institutions that thinking produces, but the novel uses its World-War-II setting as a metaphor for the modern free enterprise business model that values only profit and getting its way and replicates itself in government and art through means of reductive, manipulated, ultimately meaningless representation. The novel has its own Hitler, anyway: Lieutenant Scheisskopf, who climbs the ranks with such alacrity that H.'s point on the matter is made perfectly clear—not only doesn't he approve of Hitler, he doesn't approve of the Hitler-types he sees running the American military-industrial complex.

The satiric caricatures are so varied and vivid, the wit so vigorous, the narrative events so absurd, they fill the novel with such teeming life that it seems lifelike, the satire cracking with the authenticity of observed wartime realism. The plot, though, is con-

founding, temporally turning back on itself, spiraling surreally down into depths of irrational brutality and madness, structurally demonstrating the functional principle of Catch-22. In war, armies are supposed to move forward or fall back across distinct battle lines, but bomber squadrons, like the one in which H. served with distinction in the war, fly out and return endlessly; Milo Minderbinder contracts with the enemy to bomb his own base to salvage a commodity speculation; the bottle that provides the fluid the nurses feed intravenously to the soldier-in-white is also used to collect the fluids he expels; and finally, H. makes us realize that the deeper structure of war, and of the marketplace that demands it, is a vicious cycle, a Catch-22. The novel's message, as much as its humor, spoke directly to the generation that came of age in the social protests and experiments of the 1960s, a generation of readers that adopted the book's title as a neologism, its surreal joking as an aesthetic, and its last-page political protest—the dropping out of its sturdy, harried antihero, Yossarian—as a lifestyle.

Despite stage directions that call for a timeless setting, *We Bombed in New Haven* (1967) is very much a play of its time. The style is distinctive sixties, its winking, break-the-illusion, address-the-audience stage business, full of broad comedy, song, and self-deflating theatrics, fitting the modernist themes of shifting identity, conflict between the individual and an authoritarian social order, and the devolution of values. The play's pacifist politics are meant to be universal, as the self-conscious stretching of stage time across generations of airmen at war suggests, but the absurdism of the military command structure is right out of the World War II of *Catch-22* and the ironic rationalizing that demands audience response and responsibility for the sacrifice of the young clearly points to the Vietnam War. The craft, characters, and comedy all lack crisp definition and depth and make only intermittent impressions, despite the effort to dramatize in H.'s extensive stage directions. H. also adapted *Catch-22* for the stage (1973) and worked on drafts of a number of produced screenplays, but his interest in drama seems academic on the one hand and sidelong on the other, ending, as it has for so many accomplished American novelists, in Hollywood hack-work. The insight his dramatic writing leaves us with is that it rarely achieves the "dramatic," primarily because, while his seemingly plotless prose can surprise us with a climax that suddenly makes plot apparent around it, audiences are less patient than readers, and H.'s prose is more entertaining than his characters' stage antics. Besides, his dialogue, which H. rightly recognizes as one of his strengths as a novelist, falls strangely flat, though it has its moments, on stage and screen.

Something Happened (1974) was long and anxiously awaited by the reading public eager to see how H. would follow-up on the success of *Catch-22*. It failed to please, largely because it was not nearly so funny, but it has been critically appreciated since as a serious, major work. It is not true that nothing happens in *Something Happened;* it is just impossible to identify what that something is, reducing the identifiable things that happen to nothing of consequence, reducing identity to some unknowable something that seems less like a functioning personality than simply what happens. Interiorizing and domesticating the chaos, cross purposes, and contradictions of war, the narrative reveals similar patterns of obsessive mania, blinding denial, rationalizing self-justification, and schizophrenic disintegration of personality to those found in his previous war-bound works. The first-person narration by a husband, father, company man, whose name, Bob Slocum, is mentioned so rarely that it barely registers, claims general social significance through the literary agency of the psychological case study. The war between genders and generations, among races, classes, colleagues, and codependents devolves into a struggle between/among selves. All the weapons—sex, money, prejudice, knowledge, lying, love—of this messy, pedestrian war fought on two fronts—household and workplace—detach by some subtle linguistic catastrophe—tone change and repetition, contextualization and its collapse—from meaning and power, and the isolated, anomic self drifts in dream, memory, and fantasy, through an ether of disconnected desires and indifferent fears, toward dissolution, an entropic homogeneity of universal alienation. The interior monologue breaks into dialogue as if it were, at once, empirical evidence and hallucination. Observation is so strict that it is, when working at maximum efficiency, both satiric and surreal. This is, God help us, how people think, talk, and live, and it is profoundly irrational.

Good as Gold (1979) contrasts a large Brooklyn Jewish family, originally from Coney Island, H.'s childhood stomping grounds, with a government of the U.S. (no one from Brooklyn need apply) that was originally democratic but is now only patrician. The novel is a full course meal of Jewish family life, served very swiftly and complemented by side orders of savory satire on Jewish intellectuals, the whiter-than-thou male wealth-and-power displays that pass for American politics, and the product of their blending, Henry Kissinger, Harvard professor, media darling, Secretary of State, German Jew. The satire's caricatures, including that of a second-and third-hand Kissinger, are vibrant enough to round into life, but the parents and siblings of Bruce Gold are portraits by a mature master. The literary frame is full of family half

the time, among the most impressive ensemble scenes in American fiction. It helps that H.'s writing is at its best, his sentences turning smartly on themselves, his descriptions vivid in the mind's eye, his language rich in the mind's ear and mouth, his surrealist's jokes spliced in crisply. The circular logic, lunatic fictions, and commitments of convenience that drive H.'s plots and characters into maddening cul-de-sacs fit modern political life as perfectly as they fit war and business in his previous books. The folly of desire, and the folly it makes of morality and history, provokes poignancy and anxiety, furious frustration and giddy thrills, so that in effect Coney Island is not so far from Capitol Hill, except that the old neighborhood is higher ground, its tough guys, schemers, and disappointed women coming off better than, if as mean-spirited as, the privileged eccentrics, racists, and plagiarists in top-level positions of public trust and service. American democracy may have always been oligarchic, but now it is anarchic as well, demonstrating the fundamental principle of modernity in the flesh and in fiction—entropy, or, as Gold puts it in the title of one of his essays that earn him his reputation as a pundit, "Every Change Is for the Worse." Even with the libido- and IQ-driven ego of Gold as the force and filter of events, the world of arguing relatives, rude politics, and affecting memory rushes in to humble, if not humiliate, the protagonist, who not only comes to terms with his past and his identity, but comes of age at middle-age, in the nick of time to end the novel, as Philip ROTH ends another novel of extended Jewish male adolescence, *Portnoy's Complaint,* with a chance to begin.

God Knows (1984) is the first-person account of the biblical figure David. A postmodern portrait, it quotes at length from the Bible while giving its characters contemporary sensibilities and ludicrously anachronistic attributes. When the technique is successful, the interplay of historical imagination and with-it wit makes for a dizzying whimsy set off against an inescapable sadness, and the reader recognizes in David at once the King and the wise fool. At its worse, when the hip punchlines deflate character and the pop-culture referencing weighs down the already weighty sacred text, the novel seems a vanity, a chance to riff, an entertainment. But even when H. is just showing off, the expertise applied to such trademark passions as politics, military history, and passion, and such characteristic peeves as politicians, the reduction of history to repetition, and bourgeois stupidity, greed, and pride, can dazzle. A single well-prepared, well-turned joke can spin-off into profundity, as when David's lack of respect for his son Solomon, reimagined in the novel as empty-headed and amoral, not only deconstructs the Judaeo-Christian type of just wisdom, but, in the King's inability to even patronize his heir, reduces family to a political association and monarchy to a fragile genetic contingency. While roughly chronological, the narrative backs up into eddies, spirals up for perspective, eats its tale, and spits it out. The fundamental structural principle, as in all H.'s work, is the voice, whether in the first-or third-person, the teller's intelligence as wrought and warped by the psyche and life. H. has no compunction about revealing not only his characters but himself in all his limitations and frailties. David the ecstatic, God's poet, never appears because H. is not a poet, and there is no sense, no longer authorial view, in which David can be contextualized, criticized, or judged. The postmodernist method, the voice as vortex, subverts by subsuming all context, all judgment, all the persons of narration. If David earns the reader's sorrow, it is because he tells us how sorrowful he is, and we are left finally with H.'s word, to be taken on H.'s faith, that a long life as a wise guy can make one a wise man.

No Laughing Matter (1986) is a patchwork of H.'s recollections alternating with those of his friend, Speed Vogel, detailing H.'s recovery from the debilitating effects of Guillain-Barre syndrome. In the opening paragraphs he reflects on his good fortune to have never needed a respirator to help him breathe, for he would have gone crazy without the ability to speak. While his months of paralysis give insight into the bedridden old age of David in *God Knows,* the writing of which H.'s paralysis interrupted, the author's fear at the possibility of losing his voice explains much about the narrative technique in all his fiction, the compulsive telling that in accumulating events reveals character, that in digressing discovers theme, and that in incessantly joking mocks the form of the novel itself. The result is an absudist vaudeville fiction, and makes a tradition with the work of Kurt VONNEGUT, John BARTH, Ishmael REED, Tom ROBBINS, T. Corragheson BOYLE, Thomas PYNCHON, and others. But these memoirs are not fiction, and as with many memoirs, what is *not* in *No Laughing Matter* is as interesting as what is made public. The author who imagined the main character's fear of hospitals in *Something Happened* has little to say—in a book that is all talk—about the frustration of an author stricken mid-novel by a total failure of the body, a profoundly absurdist premise, other than as a primarily fiscal inconvenience in the middle of a middling-messy divorce. Even Vogel writes more of his own burgeoning career as a writer than of his good friend's fight to write again. H.'s fear of losing his voice at the beginning of the book and his slurring and speech impediments included as part of his text-ending catalogue of residual deficits left by the syndrome suggest a story, of an artist whose craft is stolen, that remains untold.

Picture This (1988) is a nonnarrative nonfiction novel, an historical fantasia in the form of a collage of research, ironic commentary, and biography, serial literary effusions, thoughtful and fanciful, billowing from a narrator's contemplation of Rembrandt's *Aristotle Contemplating a Bust of Homer*. Scenes of Rembrandt painting the classical "portrait" alternate with episodes set in the historical Greece of Aristotle and his philosophical forebears, Plato and Socrates, who appear as characters, the text peppered throughout with ironic political and cultural parallels and deconstructed "fact" that by implication, and explicit reference, comment on contemporary America. H.'s imagination ranges impressively wide but rarely delves deep, the effect being instructive, intellectual, and bitterly comic, dry and wry, but emotionally flat. The narrator's vocal qualities are less those of a storyteller than of an informed, opinionated, entertaining lecturer, who occasionally reads from Plato's dialogues and shows an educational video on Rembrandt's career with an actor playing the artist. The high, or low, points of Socrates' death, Plato's disenchantment, and Aristotle's amazement at Rembrandt's creative genius, in contrast to his crass commercialism, are bumps along time lines, modulations amid rants and meditations, glimpses of the lives leveled by all the learning. The purpose of the dual perspective is Socratic, to contemplate history and art as inquiries toward the end of a just appreciation of their achievements, and an understanding of our own. Unless it's all a lot of lies, but that's impossible, isn't it?

Closing Time (1994) reads like a last book. Writing a sequel to *Catch-22* is asking for it, but the melancholy sense of the inevitable—or is it the inevitable sense of the melancholy?—the reader experiences is H.'s theme successfully struck home as much as it is the product of an imagination publicly failing to reinvent a popular masterpiece. Often a threadbare grab bag of H.'s old literary tricks forced onto old characters in the service of old themes, the narrative can wear thin, pretentious, wearisome, and shrill. The flush of pleasure at once again meeting Yossarian, the Chaplain, Milo, and others of their comrades-in-arms-and-fiction pales when they caricature their original caricatures. H. repeats himself without recapturing the genius of his first novel, partly at least because he is revisiting *Good as Gold* and *No Laughing Matter* at least as faithfully. His fiction is most successful when it is most faithless, in its new characters, the lifelong Brooklyn buddies Sammy Singer and Lew Rabinowitz, whose first-person histories are among H.'s finest achievements in his realistic mode, and George C. Tilyou, late owner and proprietor of Steeplechase Amusement Park, formerly on Coney Island, now part of the underworld, a level or two above hell, one of the most fantastic examples of H.'s surreal mode. H.'s talent rises, too, to the society wedding held in New York City's Port Authority Bus Terminal and the almost symphonic intonations of encroaching apocalypse that bring the book to its close. As the vapor trails fill the sky, the sun turns black, and the moon turns red, the inveterately venal dive for the shelter of the underworld and the relatively innocent ride off into the millennium affirming whatever life is left.

Now and Then (1998) is a memoir subtitled "From Coney Island to Here," "here" being where he is writing at the moment, the sense of voice always keeping the present spontaneously present as it recalls the past. His remembrances of Brooklyn, of office jobs in Manhattan, of World War II, of Catch-22 when it was Catch-18, give fleeting insights into the works, but as often confound biographical criticism. The *joie de vivre* H. felt in the working world of the 1950s is as absent from *Something Happened* as H. feels it to be in contemporary corporate life. More interesting is his personal life. His father died when he was the Oedipally significant age of "just past five," and the later tales of H.'s psychoanalysis may send critics searching for father figures in his work, though a naive H. was surprised to find his father in his dreams. He does some telling on himself, exposing embarrassments he had labored to keep secret for years, his tone of self-congratulation and enduring humiliation reminding us of his David and his Gold. But most satisfying are the scenes of Coney Island, the amusement park and the neighborhood, in his youth, when his mother noted he had a "twisted brain," and as it passed into national nostalgia, which will always welcome such well-told stories as those of the creation of the hotdog at the first Nathan's, of rites of passage measured in rollercoasters, of a youth spent in the poolrooms of Weepy and Sammy the Pig. After an adult life spent at war, in college, at work, and in fiction, the voice that speaks in almost all of H.'s work speaks from then and there.

BIBLIOGRAPHY: Kiley, F., and W. McDonald, eds., *A Catch-22 Casebook* (1973); Merrill, R., *J. H.* (1987); Nagel, J., ed., *Critical Essays on J. H.* (1984); Ruderman, J., *J. H.* (1991)

DENNIS PAOLI

HELLMAN, Lillian

b. 20 June 1905, New Orleans, Louisiana; d. 30 June 1984, Martha's Vineyard, Massachusetts

H. is among the most important American playwrights whose major work began before World War II. Six of her eight original plays remain important today, and in recent years her reputation as a dramatist has, if

anything, increased. Two of her plays, *Watch on the Rhine* (1941) and *Toys in the Attic* (1960), won Drama Critics Circle Awards. She also wrote adaptations of foreign plays; film scripts; and four books of memoirs, the first two of which, *An Unfinished Woman* (1969) and *Pentimento* (1973), are especially highly regarded.

H. was born in New Orleans and raised partly there and partly in New York. Members of her father's and mother's families formed the models for various characters in her plays, her mother's especially in *The Little Foxes* (1939) and *Another Part of the Forest* (1947), her father's in *Toys in the Attic;* and all her plays except the first two are laid in the South. Though she traveled widely and spent some time as a scriptwriter in Hollywood, most of her adult life was spent in New York City, on a farm she owned for a number of years in upstate New York, and in two homes she owned successively on Martha's Vineyard. A brief marriage with the playwright Arthur Kober failed, and, with interruptions, she spent many years as the companion of the detective novelist Dashiell HAMMETT. She had no children and was herself an only child, though children figure prominently and effectively in two of her major plays, *The Children's Hour* (1934) and *Watch on the Rhine.*

H.'s first play, *The Children's Hour,* was one of her most successful, in spite of its treatment of a subject, lesbianism, which was at the time considered highly shocking and unsuitable for the stage. A malicious and almost surely psychotic child in a private girls' school in New England falsely accuses the two headmistresses and owners of the school. The eventual result is that they lose the school and that one headmistress, coming to realize that for her the accusation is true so far as desires go, commits suicide. What will happen to the surviving headmistress is left uncertain.

H.'s next successful play, after one failure, is the one for which she is best remembered, *The Little Foxes.* It concerns the attempt of three well-to-do siblings, Ben and Oscar Hubbard and Reginal Giddens, to establish themselves as large-scale capitalists in a small Southern town. Ruthless and evil as they are, the attempt, which is successful, involves them in blackmail, theft, and murder. And as H. exposes the evil, she also shows us the victims of it: Regina's murdered husband; Oscar's abused wife; Regina's teenage daughter, horrified at what she learns about the family; and, by implication, the blacks and "poor whites" in the area.

H.'s plays are in the realistic mode, with exposure of evil as a major concern, though of less importance in her last two plays, *The Autumn Garden* (1951) and *Toys in the Attic. Watch on the Rhine* concerns the evil intentions of a would-be Nazi, a visitor in an upperclass American household near Washington before the U.S. entered World War II. *Another Part of* the *Forest* concerns the evil of the Hubbard family a generation earlier. *The Autumn Garden* centers on the mainly hopeless and very personal problems of the owner and guests at a summer guest house on the Gulf Coast. *Toys in the Attic* concerns two sisters and a brother whose lives, largely because of their own temperaments, are, in a somewhat Chekhovian manner, hopelessly without meaning or possibility of change.

BIBLIOGRAPHY: Adler, J. H., *L. H.* (1969); Bryer, J., *Conversations with L. H.* (1986); Falks, D., *L. H.* (1978); Krutch, J. W., *The American Drama since 1918* (1957); Lederer, K., *L. H.* (1979); Moody, R., *L. H., Playwright* (1972)

JACOB H. ADLER

HELPRIN, Mark
b. 28 June 1947, New York City

H. is perhaps one of the most significant post-acculturation voices in JEWISH AMERICAN LITERATURE. Along with other contemporary writers such as Daphne Merkin, Allegra Goodman, and Adam Schwartz, he has helped to define a Jewish ethnic identity at a time when the family's immigrant past is a distant memory and the forces of assimilation are an inevitable matter of fact. And, unlike that of most earlier Jewish American writers, his fiction is just as concerned with Jewish issues in Israel as it is with Jewish identity at home.

At the same time, H. stands out from many of his contemporaries. He served in the British Merchant Navy, served in the Israeli army and air force in 1972–73—an experience that influenced both his writing and his politics—and worked as a speechwriter within the Republican Party—he describes himself as a "Roosevelt Republican." Yet it is his fiction for which H. is best known, winning him much deserved attention such as the O. Henry Prize, a Guggenheim Fellowship, and nominations for the PEN/Faulkner Award and the American Book Award in fiction.

His first book, *A Dove of the East and Other Stories* (1975), is a collection of twenty short stories, many of which establish a theme that H. carries throughout almost all of his writing: the experience of loss and the redemptive power of beauty to survive that loss. In the title story, for instance, Leon Orlovsky, having lost his parents and wife in World War II, finds some solace in caring for a wounded dove. Similarly, in "The Silver Bracelet," a young orphan uses her sense of loss as an inspiration for her musical talents, and likewise uses her music to balance out the grief within herself and to bring joy to others. Many of the characters in these stories are survivors who look to art and nature as a means of moving beyond their sorrows.

Refiner's Fire (1977), H.'s first novel, is a long episodic work in the picaresque tradition. It tells the story of Marshall Pearl, a child orphaned on his way to Palestine, and the many trials and adventures he undergoes as a youth and adult before ending up wounded on an Israeli battlefield in 1973. Pearl is one of H.'s survivors, overcoming life's many tribulations even up to the dying end. His second novel, *Winter's Tale* (1983), is a fantastical tale reminiscent of the 19th-c. romance tradition of Nathaniel HAWTHORNE and Herman MELVILLE. Like *Refiner's Fire,* it reaffirms life through the beauty of nature, yet unlike the earlier novel, it is more metaphysical in scope and presents an ambiguous apocalyptic vision.

Many reviewers of *Winter's Tale* were critical of what they saw as its disjointed sprawl, and pronounced H.'s talents better suited to the short story genre. They may be right, because it is *Ellis Island and Other Stories* (1981) for which H. is best known. This collection of stories established his reputation and won him both the National Jewish Book Award and the Prix de Rome from the American Academy and Institute of Arts and Letters. As in his earlier work, H. here explores the lives of survivors and their need for reaffirmation. The title novella concerns immigrants who arrive at Ellis Island in hopes of being reborn in America, and of one in particular who uses his love of women as a celebration of life. Another important story in the collection, "The Schreuderspitze," focuses on a Munich photographer who loses his wife and child in an auto accident. Herr Wallich, devastated by his loss, undergoes a withdrawal from the physical world at the same time he experiences a symbolic rebirth through a series of dreams. This results in a transcendental reaffirmation of life that will allow him once again to work in his art.

H. continues to write about loss and how individuals attempt to find hope and meaning in that loss. In both *A Soldier of the Great War* (1991) and *Memoir from Antproof Case* (1995), he uses reminiscences and recollections of a past life, much as he did in *Refiner's Fire,* to express the power of human endurance in the face of adversity. This need for affirmation, along with a keen sense of beauty as well as comedy, is one of the most defining characteristics of H.'s fiction.

BIBLIOGRAPHY: Bell, P. K., "New Jewish Voices," *Commentary* 71 (June 1981): 62–66; Field, L., "M. H. and Postmodern Jewish-American Fiction of Fantasy," *Yiddish* 7 (1987): 57–65; Radeljkovic, Z., "M. H. and D'J Pancake: New Bearings in American Fiction," in Jurak, M., ed., *Cross-Cultural Studies: American, Canadian and European Literatures, 1945–1985* (1988): 165–69

DEREK PARKER ROYAL

HEMINGWAY, Ernest [Miller]

b. 21 July 1899, Oak Park, Illinois; d. 2 July 1961, Ketchum, Idaho

H.'s fame depends on his style. The early style that established his reputation is lean, laconic, devoid of strings of adjectives and adverbs or particularly colorful modifiers. The sentences tend to be simple or compound declarative clauses; conjunctions are coordinating, rarely subordinating, so that items are arranged spatially or sequentially, not causally or logically: H.'s world is subject to fate and bad luck more than to causality. The prose depends on nouns (many monosyllabic) for concreteness and on state of being verbs for a sense of inaction and passivity. (In spite of his reputation as a man of action, H.'s characters frequently just endure.) There is a poetic use of repetition (learned in part from the Bible and Gertrude STEIN) and a concentration on surface detail, on suggesting character through things said and done rather than through psychological analysis. Like his Imagist contemporaries, especially Ezra POUND, from whom he also learned, H. sought the concrete detail that would capture the essence of the moment and convey its emotional content to the reader. His bare-bones style is in part a reaction to over-ornate Victorian prose and to the political rhetoric surrounding World War I; it is also an expression of a bare-bones view of the world. Among the elements in his fiction that H. shares with other modernist writers are alienated characters and their rejection of conventional moral standards, a manner of presentation that, in its incomplete and fragmented manner, echoes the surrounding social disintegration, and a foregrounding of his writing technique (a self-conscious style that calls attention to itself).

Born and reared in Oak Park, Illinois—that middle-class, conservative, self-righteous suburb of Chicago that prided itself on plentiful churches and the absence of saloons—H. spent his summers in northern Michigan, the scene of many of his Nick Adams stories. His father, an avid outdoorsman, hunter, and fisherman, was a local obstetrician; he also did much of the family cooking and housework. H.'s mother had been trained as an opera singer but gave up the stage because the lights hurt her congenitally weak eyes that she passed on to her son. Grace Hall Hemingway, through singing lessons, often made more money than her husband, took regular separate vacations from him, had built for herself a separate summer cottage at their summer home at Walloon Lake, and dominated her husband.

H. graduated from Oak Park schools and worked six months as cub reporter for the Kansas City *Star*. He enlisted in 1917 as a Red Cross ambulance driver for service in World War I, saw insufficient action (for his tastes) in northern Italy and requested a transfer to the Eastern front by Fossalta di Piave. There, two weeks before his nineteenth birthday, while he was distributing cigarettes and chocolates in a listening post, he and three Italians were struck by an Austrian trench mortar shell. Two of the Italians were immediately killed; H. had some 227 shell fragments removed from his legs, along with two machine gun bullets, probably acquired while he was being carried to an aid station. His active service of some five weeks over, he was transferred to a hospital in Milan, where he fell in love with an American Red Cross nurse, who later jilted him; the romance forms the core of his *A Farewell to Arms* (1929). Early criticism focused on his wartime wounding as the traumatic event that shaped his very pessimistic view of life, with its emphasis on bad luck, and on the individual's need for a stoic code of self-control in order to maintain dignity in the face of inevitable misfortune. In *The Old Man and the Sea* (1952), H. writes, "a man can be destroyed but not defeated," thus expressing what has been called the H. code, a mode of behavior valuing self-control in the face of disaster; such stoic behavior is the courage that H. defined as grace under pressure. Later critics have seen World War I as less traumatic than the battles at home between his parents and the (for H.) inverted situation with his mother dominant: although he continued to love his father, he lost respect for him and felt antagonistic toward his mother. Other critics identify the jilting as the event that shaped his dark worldview; certainly it figures frequently in his writing.

H., married four times and three times divorced, fathered three boys, and lived in Paris with his first wife while working as a correspondent, then in Key West, Cuba, and Ketchum, Idaho. During his lifetime, he published a satire, six novels, two books of ostensible nonfiction, a book of poems and stories, five overlapping collections of short stories, and a play, as well as journalism and essays. Posthumously, a memoir, two novels, his poetry, his early journalism, an account of bullfighting in Spain in 1959, and his letters have been published. As a newsman, he covered the Greco-Turkish War of 1922, the Spanish Civil War, and World War II, including the war in China. He won the Nobel Prize in literature in 1954, the same year that he had been in two plane crashes in Africa on two successive days. His health deteriorated in the late 1950s—possibly from a depressive disorder and mental instability inherited from his father. Shock treatments at the Mayo Clinic did little good, and H. committed suicide nineteen days before his 62nd birthday, thirty-three years after his father had.

His early short stories were attempts "to put down what really happened in action; what the actual things were which produced the emotion that you experienced . . . the sequence of motion and fact which made the emotion," and such small masterpieces as "Indian Camp," "The Battler," "Soldier's Home," and chapters 2 and 5 of *In Our Time* (1925) do so admirably. H.'s works are also frequently antiromantic initiations. Thus, "Indian Camp" introduces Nick to the brutality of life and death, as well as to his father's insensitivity; "The Killers" shows Nick a hostile world in which neither good intentions nor adolescent heroics matter. In "Big Two-Hearted River," H. well demonstrates his "ice-berg" technique, a technique of leaving vital elements out of a story to force reader rereading and involvement. "River," without mentioning World War I, tells of Nick's attempts to recuperate from physical and mental war wounds by a pastoral retreat and by the physical therapy of fishing; Nick's overreaction to losing a fish and his extraordinary concentration on the simplest of details are the major clues to what has been omitted.

H.'s first novel, *The Sun Also Rises* (1926), is narrated by Jake Barnes, an American journalist working in Paris; a veteran of the war, he was injured in a plane crash that damaged his penis, rendering sexual intercourse impossible. The novel recounts the aimless activities and drunken parties of Jake's friends, Robert Cohn, Bill Gorton, Mike Campbell, and Brett Ashley. They move from Paris to Pamplona, Spain, for the festival of San Fermin and the bullfighting; while there, thirty-four-year-old Brett—who loves Jake, is engaged to Mike, and has had an affair with Robert—takes up with a nineteen-year-old fighter, Pedro Romero. Early response to the novel focused on the epigraph from Stein ("You are all a lost generation") to the exclusion of the quotation from Ecclesiastes 1:4–7 that supplied the title, and praised it as an accurate picture and criticism of dissolute, postwar life. Subsequent readings have seen the novel as an attempt, after the war had exploded the conventional values of the past, to search for a code of values reached inductively, as a quest or pilgrimage for such empirical standards of conduct. The novel thus is parallel to T. S. ELIOT's *The Waste Land,* from which H. takes the image of Jake as Fisher King. Jake needs to learn the self-control practiced most artistically by Romero within the confines of the bullfight arena, where craft and self-discipline allow one to control death and the forces of nature in an aesthetically satisfying display. H. uses Jake's wound as an objective correlative of the individual's impotence to control his fate and as an analog to the social impotence of these deracinated, valueless expatriates.

H. published a collection of short stories, *Men without Women,* in 1927, with no major stylistic or thematic changes from his earlier works; among the better known are the initiation story, "The Killers," and the marvelous "Hills like White Elephants." His next novel, *A Farewell to Arms,* was about the romance of Lt. Frederic Henry and Catherine Barkley in Italy during World War I. It shows that human love is, like life, fragile, and thus no satisfactory escape from war; that the world destroys soldiers and lovers alike. Henry, attached to the ambulance corps of the Italian Army, is wounded and cared for by a loving nurse, as H. was (though the historical nurse denied ever sleeping with the author). After his recuperation, during which he gets Catherine pregnant, Henry goes back to the front in time to take part in the disastrous retreat from Caporetto. In danger of being shot as a spy, Henry deserts, rejoins Catherine, and the two escape to Switzerland for a few idyllic months before a protracted labor, Caesarian delivery of a stillborn child, and multiple hemorrhages kill Catherine. Henry returns to his hotel alone in the rain. The darkest of H.'s novels, *A Farewell to Arms* contains statements denouncing easy, empty political or moral rhetoric: "Abstract words such as glory, honor, courage, or hallow were obscene beside the concrete names of villages"; there are pessimistic statements: "If people bring so much courage to this world the world has to kill them to break them, so of course it kills them," or "They threw you in and told you the rules and the first time they caught you off base they killed you." A romance that is antiromantic, a war novel that is antiwar, it contains marvelous writing in passages such as the retreat from Caporetto, but its ending is open to interpretation.

Concerned about the commercialization and deterioration of classical bullfighting, H. wrote *Death in the Afternoon* (1932), which captured his love for that art/sport/ritual, as well as his self-indulgent opinions on bullfighting and literature. The following year, he published another short story collection, *Winner Take Nothing* (1933), which included "A Clean Well-Lighted Place," a paradigmatic story of man's existential situation. A safari to Africa in December 1933 through February 1934 resulted in *Green Hills of Africa* (1935), an attempt "to write an absolutely true book to see whether the shape of a country and the pattern of a month's action can, if truly presented, compete with a work of the imagination." H. next published *To Have and Have Not* (1937), a poorly constructed novel put together out of two short stories and a novella. It displays for the first time in his fiction what he had shown in a moving diatribe in *The New Masses* of September 17, 1935, his growing social concerns and his criticism about the U.S. government's inability to handle people's needs during the Great Depression. The social criticism is badly grafted to a hard-boiled adventure yarn of rum-runner and smuggler Harry Morgan, named for the Caribbean pirate. *To Have and Have Not* includes imitation *Ulysses*, a Key West *roman á clef,* and some obvious racism.

In H.'s early works, his protagonists are alone and must adjust to misfortune with no outside aid, using only their own inner resources. In the 1930s, H. displayed greater social awareness, whether in response to critics or because of his own growing social consciousness, leading to the didactic message of *To Have and Have Not* and the purposeful group interaction of *For Whom the Bell Tolls* (1940). H. also experimented with style, using shifting points of view, flashbacks, stream of consciousness, and a looser, less laconic style. Among his better stories of this period are the famous "The Short Happy Life of Francis Macomber" and "The Snows of Kilimanjaro," both first collected in *The Fifth Column and the First Forty-Nine Stories* (1938). The first concerns a wealthy American, whose athleticism does not extend to contact sports, and his lovely but unfaithful wife, Margot, on a shooting safari in Africa. The husband bolts from a charging lion; the wife, ashamed of him and of their marriage, cuckolds him with the guide, Wilson. The next day, Macomber takes his anger out on buffalo, acts courageously, and comes of age. Wilson says of him, "More of a change than any loss of virginity. Fear gone like an operation . . . Made him into a man." When a buffalo charges at her husband, Margot, directly in back of him and standing up in Wilson's open car, fires toward the buffalo and kills Francis—whether accidentally, on purpose, or accidentally on purpose, H. leaves ambiguous. For all its exotic setting, the story is about his common theme of control, of self and others. "The Snows of Kilimanjaro" opens with an epigraph describing a leopard near the summit of Mount Kilimanjaro, frozen, but therefore preserved. The leopard in its elevation and permanence is contrasted to a writer, Harry, who has traded his vitality as an author to live off a rich woman. He is rotting on the plain, figuratively, as well as literally from gangrene caused by an ignominious thorn scratch. Harry laments the waste of his talent in not writing and projects his self-hatred into venomous abuse of his caring wife. The end of the story, in a form borrowed from Ambrose BIERCE's "An Occurrence at Owl Creek Bridge," has Harry believing at the moment of death that he, too, will achieve the summit of permanence represented by Kilimanjaro.

Returning to Spain later that decade, H. reported on the Spanish Civil War, participated in making the documentary film *The Spanish Earth* (1938), for which he wrote the narration, wrote short stories and a play, *The Fifth Column* (1938), and gathered material for his epic novel, *For Whom the Bell Tolls*. The title comes from John Donne's sermon that no man is an island, "any man's death diminishes me, because I am involved in mankind; and therefore never send to know for whom the bell tolls; it tolls for thee"—a continuation of the theme of mutual interdependence. *For Whom the Bell Tolls* tells of Robert Jordan, an American Spanish instructor participating on the Loyalist, Republican, side as a guerrilla behind fascist lines. His assignment is to destroy a bridge at the beginning of a Republican attack so that fascist reinforcements cannot come across it, and he is assigned to a partisan band, nominally led by Pablo, who is degenerating into sloth, drunkenness, and fear. The group is actually held together by Pablo's woman Pilar, large, courageous, tough and tender—H.'s most complete woman. He also meets young and lovely Maria, who has been raped by the fascists, and he falls in love with her. *For Whom the Bell Tolls* is an epic, beginning in medias res, detailing the adventures of a hero, with catalogs of arms, and a touch of the supernatural in the fortune-telling abilities of part-gypsy Pilar. It is an adventure story, a warning to America about fascism and forthcoming war, and an antiwar novel, as H. explicitly details the atrocities on both sides and makes patently clear that Jordan's mission is futile since the Republican attack is doomed from the beginning and Jordan's self-sacrifice will make no difference. Pilar knows that Jordan will die, and Jordan suspects it, yet Pilar encourages the romance between Maria and Jordan and commits herself and her band to the destruction of the bridge: life must be lived to the fullest in whatever time one has, and dedication to a cause, if the cause is noble, is what is significant, not the outcome. Despite occasional rhetorical slackness, the novel is tautly constructed, and episodes like the account of Pablo's attack on Pilar's village and of Sordo's last stand are magnificent pieces of writing.

During the 1940s, H. published little. He worked as a war correspondent and edited a volume *Men at War* (1942), war stories by himself and others. The 1950s also saw few publications. First, there was the bad novel *Across the River and into the Trees* (1950), which recounts the mental maunderings of fifty-year-old Colonel Richard Cantwell, his romance with an eighteen-year old girlfriend, Renata, and duck-shooting in the vicinity of Venice, Italy. The colonel is a pompous veteran of three wars, anxious to be catered to, and a self-cast cowboy hero: he must always sit with his back to the wall lest someone creep up on him, and he chides himself that what he does not notice will someday kill him, when in fact he dies of a heart attack. H. had forgotten what Stein had told him: "Remarks are not literature." He recovered, however, with the greatly successful *The Old Man and the Sea,* a fable about man's courage. Santiago has gone without a fish for eighty-four days before he catches a giant marlin far out from shore. It takes him two days to kill the fish, another day to bring it in, and along the way sharks attack and strip the meat from the marlin. It is a story of hubris: Santiago caught the fish by going out beyond the other fisherman, but the extent of his effort make him and his catch more vulnerable to the sharks. Again, winner takes nothing, except for the satisfaction of knowing that in old age he can still catch an eighteen foot, 1,500 pound marlin, the skeleton of which he displays to his fellow fishermen, confirming his catch and pride in the maintenance of his craft. Like *For Whom the Bell Tolls,* this is also a story of interdependencies. H. insists on a biological or ecological community, Santiago identifies with the fish he pursues and is at the mercy of elemental forces just like the migrating warbler in the story. Moreover, Santiago has initiated a boy, Manolin, into the brotherhood of fishermen, and Manolin has become a surrogate son. Others in the community care for Santiago's needs and look for him when he is missing. H. has shifted the code hero from the individual bullfighter Romero to Joe DiMaggio, ultimate team player of a team sport. The style recaptures the flavor of the earlier, less verbose H. Although the Biblical allusions are blatant and obtrusive, and Santiago lacks the depth to make this story a novel with any believable internal conflict, *The Old Man and the Sea* is a moving parable of an individual adrift in a hostile environment, showing the courage that humans are capable of.

In 1959, H. was commissioned by *Life* magazine to follow the Spanish bullfights and a rivalry between the two leading matadors. He couldn't edit his account down to manageable size, and others had to do it for him. A fuller account, still edited by others, has been posthumously published as *The Dangerous Summer* (1986). Nor could H. manage even a few lines for a presentation volume for John F. Kennedy in 1961. The best of his posthumous publications is a memoir of his early days in Paris, *A Moveable Feast* (1964), the only one that he had edited to a form nearly ready for publication. It is autobiographical fiction in which he paints himself as a starving young artist by not mentioning his wife's independent income. H. disparaged those who had been his friends in Paris and who had helped him as a writer, but the writing is sure and evocative. Other works edited by others include *The Nick Adams Stories* (1964), a compilation of previously published fiction with unpublished stories and fragments of stories in a guessed chronological order, two novels—*Islands in the Stream* (1970) and *The Garden of Eden* (1986)—and the *Selected Letters* (1981). Marking the 1999 Hemingway centennial is the publication of *True at First Light,* based on his 1953–54 safaris.

BIBLIOGRAPHY: Baker, C., *E. H.: A Life Story* (1969); Benson, J. J., *New Critical Approaches to the Short Stories of E. H.* (1990); Benson J. J., *The Short Stories of E. H.* (1975); Messent, P., *E. H.* (1992); Reynolds, M., *H.: The American Homecoming* (1993); Reynolds, M., *H.: The Paris Years* (1989); Reynolds, M., *The Young H.* (1986); *The H. Review* (1989); Smith, P., *A Reader's Guide to the Short Stories of E. H.*

PETER L. HAYS

HENDERSON, Alice Corbin

b. 16 April 1881, St. Louis, Missouri; d. 18 July 1949, Santa Fe, New Mexico

H. is best known for her contributions to *Poetry* magazine of Chicago, the foremost of the literary magazines that brought about the modern "poetry renaissance," but her second significant area of interest—the American Southwest—dominated her writing for over thirty years. H., who published her poetry as "Alice Corbin," spent the years from 1912 to 1916 helping to coedit and produce *Poetry*. She discovered or promoted important writers such as Carl SANDBURG and Edgar Lee MASTERS, and wrote articles analyzing and defending IMAGISM, modern free verse, and a particular literary sensibility indigenous to the U.S., which to her mind necessarily included ethnic and regional writers.

A distinctly American literature, H. believed, would accommodate the variegated cultural landscape and would dispense with the reliance on European, notably English, literary models. H.'s defense of free verse called for sustained critical attention to the particularities of metrical development and experimentation, as distinct from many of her contemporaries who dismissed free verse as carelessness. Her own poetry, which at first had been traditional in form, was sharpened through the influence of imagism, and her vivid poetic descriptions and subtle metrical patterns drew praise and respect from other poets, notably Ezra POUND. H. also experimented with replicating the language patterns, themes, and abstract symbolism of Native American and Hispanic cultures. Even after she left Chicago for New Mexico—a move necessitated by illness—she continued to correspond with Harriet MONROE and *Poetry*'s contributors, to write for the magazine for a number of years, and to help coedit the anthologies *The New Poetry* (1917, 1923, 1932).

In New Mexico, H. became absorbed by the landscape's beauty as well as by the area's oral and folk traditions. She actively sponsored the growth of a Southwestern literary community on several fronts: she arranged annual benefit readings at her home; helped to found Writers' Editions, a publishing house specifically for authors in New Mexico; and adapted local themes and imagery in *Red Earth* (1920), her best book of poetry, and *The Sun Turns West* (1933).

H. also edited *The Turquoise Trail: An Anthology of New Mexico Poetry* (1928) and collaborated with her husband, the artist William Penhallow Henderson, to produce other books, notably an illustrated examination of Hispanic Catholic rites and hymns entitled *Brothers of Light: The Penitentes of the Southwest* (1937). H. was active in the movement for Native American rights and supported the folk literatures and art of New Mexico for the rest of her life.

BIBLIOGRAPHY: Marek, J. E., *Women Editing Modernism: "Little" Magazines and Literary History* (1995); Nadel, I. B., ed., *The Letters of Ezra Pound to A. C. H.* (1993); Norwood, V., and J. Monk, eds., *The Desert Is No Lady: Southwest Landscapes in Women's Writing and Art* (1987); Pearce, T. M., *A. C. H.* (1969)

JAYNE MAREK

HENLEY, Beth
b. 8 May 1952, Jackson, Mississippi

In the 1980s, Southern dramatist H. captivated critical and popular audiences with her comic triumphs, *Crimes of the Heart* (1982) and *The Miss Firecracker Contest* (1985). She also had the considerable good fortune of having successful film adaptations of her early works, starring Holly Hunter and other first-tier Hollywood actors. Though H.'s later works have not found wide acceptance on stage, she continues to be recognized as one of the finest active American playwrights in the comic tradition.

H. studied drama and acting at Southern Methodist University as an undergraduate and for one year of graduate school at the University of Illinois. She tried acting in Los Angeles for several years without success and moved to Louisville, Kentucky, in 1979 and brought her evolving work, *Crimes of the Heart,* to stage there. The play, which quickly found a home Off-Broadway in New York, won the 1981 Pulitzer Prize and the New York Drama Critics Circle Award—a stunning feat for a twenty-nine-year-old, first-time playwright whose work had not yet appeared on Broadway.

Crimes of the Heart focuses on the MaGrath sisters of Hazlehurst, Mississippi, over a period of two tumultuous days. The youngest MaGrath sister, Babe, shoots her husband, the best lawyer in town, because she doesn't like "his stinking looks." As her sisters Lenny and Meg rally around her, Babe tells them the complete truth in three acts set in the family kitchen: she shot him after he caught her in a private moment with her young lover. Babe is not alone in her troubles. Lenny learns on her birthday that her horse has been struck by lightning, and Meg confesses to her sisters that she

has abandoned her singing career in California and has been working in a dog food factory. The MaGrath sisters have had scandal enough it would seem: years earlier, their mother hung herself, and the family cat, in the cellar.

The comic-absurdist tone of *Crimes of the Heart* reminds one of Eudora WELTY's "Why I Live at the P. O.," except where Welty uses hyperbole to explode the importance of Sister moving out of her family home, H. uses ironic understatement to implode the seriousness of the matters at hand, such as attempted murder. Though influenced by the works of Chekhov, H.'s eccentric and obsessed characters, colorful vernacular language, and small-town backdrops place her plays in the rich Southern gothic tradition and have led to comparisons to the fiction of Welty, Carson MCCULLERS, and Flannery O'CONNOR.

The Miss Firecracker Contest and *The Debutante Ball* (1991) also address small-town life and families in moments of crisis; both center around Southern women in particular and community perceptions of beauty. But whereas *The Miss Firecracker Contest* is widely viewed as a highly original, lively, and credible work, *The Debutante Ball* has been criticized as being farcical, cryptic, and thematically derivative of her previous works. Whether in response to such criticism, or as a natural progression for the talented artist she is, H. has presented more diversified plays in recent years—setting works in the American West and in the South of earlier historical periods.

Whatever the setting, one does not find nihilistic indifference in the plays of H. Concrete resolution is always sought, and usually found, albeit not in the most normal of channels. Maybe, in the end, there is one common tendency in her "peculiar" characters: they *do* aspire, and therein lies their redemption.

BIBLIOGRAPHY: Harbin, B. J., "Familial Bonds in the Plays of B. H.," *SoQ* 25 (Spring 1987): 81–94; Shepard, A. C., "Aborted Rage in B. H.'s Women," *MD* 36 (March 1993): 96–108

JON PARRISH PEEDE

HENRY, O. See PORTER, William Sydney

HENTZ, Caroline Lee [Whiting]
b. 1 June 1800, Lancaster, Massachusetts; d. 11 February 1856, Marianna, Florida

Although a New Englander, H. became in the 1850s a leading writer of plantation romances and literary champion of the Southern social and economic system.

H. won praise for her ability to introduce distinctive scenic and cultural details into her works, to create a range of rounded characters and to write with spontaneity, freedom, and humor. Her books remained popular to the end of the century, *Linda; or, The Young Pilot of Belle Creole* (1850), ranking among the "best-sellers."

Contemporary readers are most familiar with H.'s *Eoline; or, Magnolia Vale* (1852) and *The Planter's Northern Bride* (1854), reprinted in the 1970s. While moderns admire her criticism of romantic notions, they find her work limited by attempts to fit assertive women characters into the traditional hierarchical structure and marred by her views of slavery.

Where H. acquired her education is unclear; her father's bookstore in Lancaster, Massachusetts, may have served as her academy. In 1824, she married Nicholas Marcellus Hentz, a French linguist and entomologist, and two years later moved with him to Chapel Hill, North Carolina, where he had accepted a university appointment. In 1830, H. and her husband opened a boarding school for young women in Covington, Kentucky, where H. completed *De Lara; or, the Moorish Bride* (1843) for which she won a $500 prize, wrote two other dramas, and sold stories to the *Western Monthly.* The Hentzes transferred the school to Cincinnati, Ohio, in 1832, and the following year H.'s first novel, *Lovell's Folly* appeared.

Subsequently, the Hentzes established similar schools in Florence, Tuscaloosa, and Tuskeegee, Alabama, and Columbus, Georgia. During this period, H. wrote *Aunt Patty's Scrap Bag* (1846) and *Mob Cap* (1848). When her husband's health failed about 1849, H. turned to writing full time, producing, over the next seven years, nine novels and six volumes of shorter pieces, including poems.

H. created heroines with something of her own resilience. As Nina Baym has pointed out, they suffer and sacrifice if necessary, but they also have a capacity for enjoying life. In *Linda; or, The Young Pilot of Belle Creole,* the heroine endures the loss of her mother, escapes a steamboat explosion that kills her father, runs from the badgering of her stepmother and stepbrother, Robert Graham, into numerous adventures, eventually marrying her rescuer, Roland Lee. The sequel, *Robert Graham* (1855), leads Linda and Graham into marriage after the deaths of their respective spouses.

H.'s works regularly feature contrasting characters. In *Rena; or, The Snow Bird* (1851), set in New England, the honest, resourceful black-haired tomboy Rena wins out over the seemingly angelic but conniving blonde Stella. The hero, Sherwood Lindsay, survives his father, an uncontrollably passionate man, who abandons Rena's aunt Debby and Stella's mother,

and kills himself. *Eoline* also pits the reasonable against the passionate man. *Helen and Arthur; or, Miss Thusa's Spinning Wheel* (1853) contrasts the fair and affectionate Helen against her scheming, passionate sister Mittie.

Marcus Warland; or, The Long Moss Spring (1852), probably written before H. read *Uncle Tom's Cabin* (1852), begins her defense of slavery. *The Planter's Northern Bride* develops her argument thoroughly. H. dramatizes the Southern rationale through the story of Eulalia Moreland, a Northerner married to a Southern slave-holder. H. saw herself as a peacemaker, explaining to Northerners a complex situation she thought they did not understand.

H.'s last novel, *Ernest Linwood* (1856), written in the first person, recounts Gabriella Lynn's joys and sorrows as she struggles through marriage to an unreasonably jealous man, much like H.'s husband. Editions published after both Hentzes had died carried the subtitle "The Inner Life of the Author."

BIBLIOGRAPHY: Bakker, J., "Twists of Sentiment in Antelbellum Southern Romance," *SLJ* 26 (1993): 3–13; Barnes, E. L., "Mirroring the Mother Text: Histories of Seduction in the American Domestic Novel," in Singley, C. J., and S. E. Sweeney, eds., *Anxious Power: Reading, Writing, and Ambivalence in Narrative by Women* (1993): 157–71; Baym, N., *Woman's Fiction* (1978); Ellison, R. C., "Mrs. H. and the Green-Eyed Monster," *AL* 22 (May 1950): 345–50; Papashvily, H. W., *All the Happy Endings* (1956): 77–94; Stanessa, J., "C. H.'s Rereading of Southern Paternalism; or, Pastoral Naturalism in *The Planter's Northern Bride*," *SoSt* 3 (1992): 221–52; Wimsatt, M. A., "C. H.'s Balancing Act," in Manning, C. S., ed., *The Female Tradition in Southern Literature* (1993): 161–75

LUCY M. FREIBERT

HERBST, Josephine

b. 5 March 1892, Sioux City, Iowa; d. 28 January 1969, New York City

In an essay she wrote about Sherwood ANDERSON, H. summarizes her theory of fiction: "The artist seeks to tell us what the world is or isn't; what it should be or even what it cannot be outside the realm of some transcendent dream." H.'s words are emblematic of her own career that spanned twenty-six years, a career in which she produced eight novels. She sought honesty in her portrayals of the characters that populate her work, and her novels show the insight of an author who studied the world around her and the social forces which influence humanity.

H. traveled throughout her tumultuous and often controversial life, working as a special correspondent for the *New York Post* in Nazi Germany in 1935, as well as for several periodicals for which she traveled to Cuba, to Spain during its Civil War, and to South America. She won a Guggenheim Fellowship in 1936 and several other awards and grants throughout her career.

Her first novel, *Nothing Is Sacred,* published in 1928, chronicles the bleak middle-class experience of the Norlands family in her native Iowa. Like *Nothing Is Sacred,* her second book, *Money for Love* (1929), also reveals a distinct disillusionment with life, this time through the story of blackmailer Harriett Everist. Both novels demonstrate an element of humor in the telling of middle-class angst, and they offer a modernistic look at the changes in family and society.

H.'s next three novels form the Trexler-Wendel trilogy: *Pity Is Not Enough* (1933), *The Executioner Waits* (1934), and *Rope of Gold* (1939). The triad has often been compared with John DOS PASSOS's *U.S.A.,* as the novels chronicle several generations of one family, beginning after the Civil War and ending in the late 1930s. By designing her trilogy in such a way, H. is able to coherently form her social commentary, pointing to the capitalistic system as the downfall of several generations of an American family. One aspect of the three novels for which critics often praise H. is the strong characterization of women. Another major point of the three novels is that they are not chronologically arranged but filled with a scattered series of narratives; this lack of chronological consistency fortifies the idea that the past, present, and future are all interwoven.

Pity Is Not Enough shows the destructive power of the post-Civil War quest for financial glory through the story of the Trexler brothers: Joe, who dies penniless and insane, and David, who finds success but does not give aid to his impoverished family. *The Executioner Waits* begins during World War I and reveals the difficulty in the life of farmer Amos Wendel, in stark comparison with his brother-in-law and thriving businessman David Trexler. Amos's daughter Vicky becomes a social activist for the plight of the farmers, and she and her husband Jonathan provide the transition into the third novel. In *Rope of Gold,* set in the 1930s, the fight for social reform, which Jonathan abandons, continues to be Vicky's passion, through which she proves her own courage and fortitude.

After publishing three other works, H. began writing her memoirs before her death in 1969. There was much about her own life she found to be too painful to relate, including an abortion, a bisexual affair, and underground connections to the Communist Party that were allegedly revealed to the FBI by her friend and fellow writer, Katherine Anne PORTER. H. never finished her autobiography, perhaps proving that a "writer seeks to tell us what the world is or isn't," unless that writer is telling the story of her own life.

BIBLIOGRAPHY: Bevilacqua, W. F., *J. H.* (1985); Langer, E., *J. H.: The Story She Could Never Tell* (1984); Roberts, N. R., *Three Radical Women Writers* (1996)

KATHERINE L. KELLER

HERLIHY, James Leo

b. 27 February 1927, Detroit, Michigan; d. 21 October 1993, Los Angeles, California

H. is an actor, playwright, novelist, short story writer, and teacher. He is best known as the author of *Midnight Cowboy* (1965), a novel that served as the basis for the extraordinarily successful 1969 United Artist film of the same title. The novel has been overshadowed by the film, but it did not go by unnoticed. Critic Emile Capouya calls the novel "an appalling story, told with great skill." He also states that H. has a taste, and a talent, for drawing human grotesques. The novel is a grim story about two grotesque social rejects: Joe Buck, a simple-minded cowboy who comes to New York to earn a fortune as a hustler; and Ratso Rizzo, a street-hustling cripple who is dying of some tubercular disease. H. depicts their growing friendship in a way that is quite sensitive to Joe and Ratso's basic human needs. They are grotesque, to be sure, but they are also just like us. This quality appears in most of H.'s work.

In his early plays, H. explores the themes of embattled innocence and vulnerable corruption, often shading into one another. The innocent—struggling in a hostile society they seem to threaten—sometimes perish, sometimes triumph, and sometimes become part of the corruption they once challenged, said Burton S. Kendle in an essay on H.'s works.

In *Moon in Capricorn* (1953), a character has an actual star in her heart, a condition that causes pain and prompts envy in the people closest to her, including a psychotic cripple, a recurring character in H.'s dramas, stories, and novels. *Angry October* (1958) focuses on a mother who tyrannizes her simple-minded son who unearths a family skeleton that could destroy her. *Blue Denim* (1958), written in collaboration with William Noble, explores how children manage to inadvertently imitate the behavior of their elders. The blue jeans of the title is a familiar image in H.'s work, symbolizing sexual aggressiveness or commercial availability. *Stop, You're Killing Me* (1968) is a collection of one-act plays in which H. experiments with various ways to use dramatic monologues in an attempt to create a nightmare vision of a violent America.

In *The Sleep of Baby Filbertson and Other Stories* (1959), H. makes clear his interest in the themes of loneliness, crippled emotion, and physical disability. These ideas reach their culmination in the novel *Midnight Cowboy,* where a deluded out-of-towner stumbles into the grotesque world of midtown Manhattan and is befriended by a larcenous cripple. The urban world is an unpleasant place, a cruel and uncertain place suspended between the heaven of success and the hell of failure. Ratso is near death from tuberculosis; Joe Buck cares for him, steals money for him, and takes him on a final journey to Florida. Ratso and Joe are both lonely men, unable to love anyone but themselves until they meet each other and form a friendship. Joe Buck is deluded, a mental disability; Ratso Rizzo limps and drags one foot, a physical disability. They are both social rejects, and when they realize this about each other it becomes the basis of their friendship.

The thematic center of H.'s drama and prose is the respect with which he presents his "twisted characters," characters who, according to David Galloway, "struggle to maintain some shred of human dignity in a world which seems remorseless in its devices for destroying the self." In most of H.'s work, the grotesque, which at first seems so alien, suddenly seems to represent the average guy.

BIBLIOGRAPHY: Griffith, B. W., "Midnight Cowboys and Edwardian Narrators: J. L. H.'s Contrasting Voices," *NConL* 2 (1972): 6–8; Pervy, C. D., "Songs of Innocence and Experience: H.'s *Midnight Cowboy,*" *Forum* 13 (1976): 62–67

JOSEPH FERRANDINO

HERNE, James A.

b. 1 February 1939, Cohoes, New York; d. 2 June 1901, Long Island, New York

As a playwright and actor, H. was instrumental in transforming the American theater's predilection for romantic and sensational melodrama to psychological realism. In a writing career spanning the years 1874 to 1899, H.'s most notable achievements were *Margaret Fleming* (1890) and *Shore Acres* (1892).

Born James Ahern, H. collaborated on his early plays, and with David Belasco wrote *Hearts of Oak* (1879), his first play to gain notoriety. This domestic melodrama without a villain embraced much physical verisimilitude. *The Minute Men of 1774–1775* (1886), H.'s first solo play, featured the "noble savage" and

tableaux of famous battles as it abandoned domesticity for sensation, a direction H. avoided in later work.

With his temperance play *Drifting Apart* (1888), H. returned to domestic themes. He drew increasingly on the contemporary local color of New England, everyday dialogue and the seamy side of life. This play, which included a dream sequence depicting child starvation, horror and madness, attracted the attention Bostonian literary circles. His subsequent association with Hamlin GARLAND, along with the influence of his actress/wife Katharine Corcoran, sparked H.'s interest in the plays of Henrik Ibsen, Émile Zola, and William Dean HOWELLS, in Social Darwinism, and women's rights—all important to the structure and subjects of later H. plays.

Margaret Fleming was seen by few audiences because commercial producers were afraid to risk production of a play they found so radical. In this play, which is often considered his most Ibsenesque as well as the first serious attempt at realism in American drama, H. explored marital infidelity, responsibility for illegitimate children, and the sexual double standard. The subjects were intended to shock, and audiences were especially disturbed when Margaret nursed the baby of her husband's dead mistress.

Although *Shore Acres* was H.'s most popular play, it continued the playwright's penchant for socially relevant realistic detail by exploring the ideas of "free thinkers" at odds with "Down East" traditional values and fundamental religion. The conclusion, however, optimistically reconciled opposing forces, and all of the final action was effected in nearly ten minutes of protracted silence.

Griffith Davenport (1899) and *Sag Harbor* (1899), H.'s final plays, perpetuated his intention to discuss social issues yet secure a popular audience, a combination successfully attained only in *Shore Acres*. His mature work, with its contemporary, naturalistic character and dialogue in serious domestic situations, resembled late 19th-c. European realism. In America, however, H. was a lone voice in the theater unmatched for some fifteen years beyond his death.

BIBLIOGRAPHY: Edwards, H. J., and J. A. Herne, *J. A. H.* (1964); Moody, R., *Dramas from the American Theater* (1966); Perry, J., *J. A. H.: The American Ibsen* (1978); Quinn, A. H., *Representative American Plays* (1953)

RONALD H. WAINSCOTT

HERRICK, Robert

b. 26 April 1868, Cambridge, Massachusetts; d. 23 December, 1938, Charlotte Amalie, Virgin Islands

H., who was related to his namesake, the 17th-c. English poet, and to the Hawthornes, Hales, and Peabodys in New England, was born in Cambridge, Massachusetts and educated at Harvard, but in 1893, he went to teach in the new University of Chicago, where he remained for exactly a generation. Later, he lived in York Village, Maine, but he died in the Virgin Islands, to which he had been appointed government secretary in 1933.

One of the leading American realistic novelists of the early 20th c., H. himself defined his pervasive theme as "the competitive system—its influence upon men and women." Chicago, in its boom years (the Haymarket tragedy, the Pullman strike, the World's Columbian Exposition, and the Panic of 1894 are all mirrored in his pages) furnished an excellent vantage point for the observation of the corruptions of that system, as manifested not only in the industrialists and financiers but even in artists, scholars, and various professionals. Women are importantly involved through their influence upon men, but though H. was merciless in his portrayal of sterile, lazy, selfish females, he was no misogynist. He created many admirable women, nor was he repelled by faults and limitations that might have been expected to antagonize so intellectual, fastidious, and sometimes acerbic a writer. Homely Lilla, in the late, unappreciated novel of that name is not wholly unworthy of comparison with Willa CATHER's Ántonia.

Though a good case could be made that *Waste* (1924) is H.'s masterpiece, the essence of his portrayal and criticism of society and of his message is contained in *The Man Who Was* (1897), *The Gospel of Freedom* (1898), *The Web of Life* (1900), *The Common Lot* (1904), *The Memoirs of an American Citizen* (1905), *Together* (1908), and *One Woman's Life* (1913). Of these, *The Common Lot* is generally regarded as having established his reputation, and *The Memoirs of an American Citizen,* a meat packer's memoirs, is perhaps most often called his best, but *Together,* a study of marriage, was by far the most "successful."

Though realistic in method, H. was idealistic in spirit, and his conception of the good life is virtually indistinguishable from that of the New Testament. Like Nathaniel HAWTHORNE, he saw no hope for the future in science and technology, and fascism, communism, and Freudianism left him equally cold. So far as he could see, society could be improved only by improving human nature, and modern man had found no means of doing this except those known to antiquity. He called *The Real World* (1901), *A Life for a Life* (1910), *The Healer* (1911), *Clark's Field* (1914), and the short piece, "The Master of the Inn" (1908) the "idealistic" works for which he cared most. Of these, *Clark's Field* ranks well up in his oeuvre, but when he attempts or skirts allegory or symbolism, he is not generally successful. He was not an imaginative or

very inventive writer, and his utopia, *Sometime* (1933), with which he ended his career as a novelist, is not one of his best books. Nor was he at all fastidious about method, especially for a teacher of creative writing and one so well read as he was in 19th- and 20th-c. fiction. His situations often seem contrived and his dialogue stiff and unconvincing, nor was he above using melodrama and coincidence freely. But with all his limitations, he not only observed and chronicled but wisely judged an important period in Western culture.

The ordeal with which World War I confronted the writers of its time greatly affected H. At the beginning, he was a "fervid partisan of the Allies and their cause"; there followed a period "of hesitation and doubt," which was succeeded by his becoming a "pacifist, flat and plain." From 1914 to 1923, he published no novels. His final period, beginning with *Homely Lilla* (1923) embraced five titles, of which three have already been referred to. The other two are *Chimes* (1926) and *The End of Desire* (1932). The first is a bitter attack upon the University of Chicago in certain aspects, with devastating portraits of its first two presidents, and the second expresses his disgust over postwar moral laxity with sufficient documentation to mislead imperceptive readers into accusing him of having joined forces with what he deplored.

BIBLIOGRAPHY: Budd, L. J., *R. H.* (1971); Duffey, B. J., *The Chicago Renaissance in American Letters* (1954); Nevius, B., *R. H.: The Development of a Novelist* (1962)

EDWARD WAGENKNECHT

HERSEY, John (Richard)
b. 17 June 1914, Tientsin, China; d. 24 March 1993, Key West, Florida

H.'s reporting for *Time* and *Life* during World War II was followed in 1946 by the extraordinary *Hiroshima,* an account of the atomic bombing based on interviews with six survivors. Such was the impact of this book, first published in the *New Yorker,* that H. remained identified as a journalist during his early efforts to write what he termed "novels of contemporary history." This inclination to take up the central situations of his time in an unusual number of fictional forms produced several highly praised books and denied him the recognition given more personal journalists or novelists with more conspicuous lines of development.

H.'s first novel, *A Bell for Adano* (1944), came from his coverage of the Sicilian campaign. This story of an American military governor who fights authority to help people rebuild their lives proved irresistible to wartime readers and won H. the Pulitzer Prize. *The*

Wall (1950) followed long research on the Warsaw ghetto uprising. Focusing on survivors from a few families, he made a complex narrative possible by inventing Noach Levinson, self-appointed recorder of all ghetto culture, to tell the story with, as H. put it, "an authority my gifts could not evoke." *A Single Pebble* (1956) presents the enlightenment of an American engineer whose dreams of damming the Yangtze fade as he travels upriver on a junk absorbing lessons of infinite patience from the Chinese crew. This novella foreshadows *The Call* (1985), which traces 20th-c. history of the American Protestant mission in China and touches H.'s own roots as the child of missionaries. More than any of H.'s other characters, Homer Treadup, a missionary enamored of technology, is tested past the threshold of survival into the core of his beliefs.

The range and variety of H.'s fiction may be seen in *The Child Buyer* (1960), a dark satire on the fate of a bright child in an American public school; *White Lotus* (1965), a tale of white Americans in some indefinite future enslaved in China and living through events analogous to historical experience of American blacks; and *The Conspiracy* (1972), which dramatizes a writer's political responsibility in the story of Lucan joining an attempt to overthrow Nero. Other novels are *The Marmot Drive* (1953), *The War Lover* (1959), *Too Far to Walk* (1966), *Under the Eye of the Storm* (1967), *My Petition for More Space* (1974), *The Walnut Door* (1977), *Blues* (1987, a dialogue after *The Compleat Angler*), and *Antonietta* (1991, whose heroine is a violin). *Fling and Other Stories* (1990) and *Key West Tales* (1994) are short story collections. Nonfiction besides *Hiroshima* includes *Men on Bataan* (1942), *Into the Valley* (1943), *Here to Stay* (1963), *The Algiers Motel Incident* (1968), *Letter to the Alumni* (1972, written as Master of Pierson College, Yale), *The President* (1975), and *Life Sketches* (1989), a collection of biographical tales. H. edited *The Writer's Craft* and a collection of essays on Ralph ELLISON, both published in 1974.

BIBLIOGRAPHY: Huse, N. L., *J. H. and James Agee: A Research Guide* (1978); Huse, N. L., *The Survival Tales of J. H.* (1983); Sanders, D., *J. H.* (1967); Sanders, D., *J. H. Revisited* (1990)

DAVID SANDERS

HEYWARD, [Edwin] DuBose
b. 31 August 1885, Charleston, South Carolina; d. 16 June 1940, Tryon, North Carolina

Born into Charleston, South Carolina's coveted aristocracy as the direct descendant of Thomas Heyward,

a signer of the Declaration of Independence, H. nevertheless was reared in reduced circumstances, his family plagued by long-lasting economic losses from the War between the States and by his father's early death. Forced to accept menial jobs, crippled by polio at age seventeen, and later collapsing from overwork as an insurance salesman, he perhaps found a measure of comfort in the process of writing.

With his friends Hervey ALLEN and John Bennett, Northerners who had moved to Charleston, H. helped found the Poetry Society of South Carolina, an organization influential in the rise of the southern literary renascence. In 1923, he married Dorothy Hartzell Kuhns, who persuaded him to abandon his insurance agency and who collaborated with him on dramatizations of two of his novels, *Porgy* and *Mamba's Daughters.*

Porgy (1925), a factually based novel of romance and murder among Charleston's Gullah blacks, remains his most famous work. Following its success as a play, composer George Gershwin (with H.'s consultation) transformed *Porgy* into a monumental opera, *Porgy and Bess,* which premiered in Boston in 1935.

H.'s other publications include *Carolina Chansons* (1922, with Hervey Allen); *Skylines and Horizons* (1924); the novels *Angel* (1926) and *Mamba's Daughters* (1929); a short story, "The Half Pint Flask" (1929); *Jasbo Brown and Selected Poems* (1931); and the novels *Peter Ashley* (1932), *Lost Morning* (1936), and *Star Spangled Virgin* (1939). The only play H. wrote on his own, *The Brass Ankle* (perf. 1931), remained unpublished at the time of his death.

A conscientious writer and—like his contemporary fellow South Carolina novelist, Julia PETERKIN—sensitive to the culture of Gullah blacks who lived along the Palmetto State's coast, H. won praise from liberal blacks and scorn from white southern traditionalists. His command of dialect was good, his plots realistic, readable, and uncomplicated. Today, however, his dated work is little read, and his name would go unrecognized except for the continuing popularity of *Porgy and Bess,* whose touching story was inspired by H.'s neatly crafted novel.

BIBLIOGRAPHY: Cox, H. M., *The Charleston Literary Renascence* (1958); Durham, F., *D. H.: The Man Who Wrote Porgy* (1954); Slavick, W. H., *D. H.* (1981)

HARRY MCBRAYER BAYNE

HIGGINSON, Thomas Wentworth
b. 22 December 1823, Cambridge, Massachusetts; d. 9 May 1911, Cambridge, Massachusetts

While his fame in the 20th c. is based on his relationship with Emily DICKINSON, H. was known for far more during his own lifetime. He was a Unitarian minister, was devoted to women's suffrage, helped raise funds for and plan John Brown's raid on Harpers Ferry, and commanded a black regiment during the Civil War. His writings, on a variety of subjects, were popular and he was an integral part of the intellectual circles of Boston. H.'s contributions to 19th-c. literature are recorded in his own texts and through his support of other luminaries.

H.'s intellectual life began with his birth. He grew up among professors, scholars, and literati, was educated at Harvard College, and was very influenced by Emersonian TRANSCENDENTALISM. By profession, he was a preacher, but he also dedicated himself to education for workingmen, ABOLITIONISM, and women's rights.

H.'s first piece of published prose was an 1843 review article on Lydia Maria CHILD's *Letters from New York* in a magazine called the *Present*, "a new magazine dedicated to 'advance the Reign of Heaven on Earth.'" He was becoming an abolitionist and Unitarian about this time and decided to enter Harvard Divinity School. His feelings about the need for change in the U.S. were expressed in many poems during the 1840s, the majority of which were published in the journal *Harbinger*. The poems are not good enough to make H. a significant poet, but they do make plain his intense belief in the need for social change. He had wanted to be a career poet, but the experience of being published made him realize the wish was unrealistic.

While H. was living in Worcester, Massachusetts, in the 1850s, he made an unsuccessful bid for Congress and became fervently involved in the Worcester Anti-Slavery Society to which men such as Wendell Phillips and Frederick DOUGLASS came to speak. During the latter years of the decade, H. was well known for his antislavery work and trying to aid fugitive slaves. He was asked to contribute articles for a new journal, the *Atlantic Monthly*, which he could not have foreseen as one of the most important steps of his career.

H. used the *Atlantic* as a forum to further the causes he championed. In 1861, he published "Nat Turner's Insurrection," a brutally honest article in which he asserts the terror instilled by the insurrection was "softened only by the greater horror of the its suppression by white southerners." After the Civil War and Reconstruction, H. devoted himself to more literary pursuits. His first novel, *Malbone: An Olport Romance*, was serialized in 1869. It is not a particularly memorable novel and was highly criticized but it marks the effort on H.'s part to enter into a new phase of his life. He had been corresponding intermittently with Dickinson for almost seven years, had befriended women writers such as Helen Hunt JACKSON and Harriet SPOFFORD and

became a coeditor of the feminist *Woman's Journal*. In the fall of 1869, H.'s memoir, *Army Life in a Black Regiment*, was published in which the black soldiers are praised for their abilities and bravery but are not seen as quite equal to whites. This view was not unusual among antislavery supporters and the book was well received. H. was soon making a good living writing for several journals, as well as receiving royalties for a high school textbook, *Young Folks' History of the United States*.

H. soon became known for his criticism of poetry and even published some of his own poetry that was kindly received. His writing decreased as he aged, although he continued to support several social causes. After the death of Dickinson in 1886, which ended twenty-four years of correspondence, H. was instrumental in seeing her poems published. Although he had not been supportive of the idea of her publishing during her lifetime, he came to see the true value of her poems once he read over two hundred of them, far more than she had shown him during their friendship. When H. died in 1911, he left behind what may be his second most important literary contribution: seventy-six years' worth of a personal journal.

Modern critics do not mention H. very often. He is rarely included in anthologies and is mostly remembered for his friendship with Dickinson. He does deserve more credit than he is given, however, for he supported women's causes, abolition, universal education and his articles were an important mainstay of several journals. He helped to further the assimilation of black men and women during Reconstruction and wrote biographies and sketches of several 19th-c. writers, including Thomas Carlyle, Edward Everett HALE, Julia Ward HOWE, and Margaret FULLER.

BIBLIOGRAPHY: Edelstein, T. G., *Strange Enthusiasm: A Life of T. W. H.* (1968); Wells, A. M., *Dear Preceptor: Life and Times of T. W. H.* (1963)

MARCY L. TANTER

HIJUELOS, Oscar
b. 24 August 1951, New York City

While attending the City College of New York, where he earned a B.A. (1975) and an M.A. (1976), H. took writing courses taught by Susan SONTAG, Donald BARTHELME, and Joseph HELLER. Following the publication of his first novel, H. was awarded a Rome Fellowship (1985), and in 1990 became the first Cuban American author to win a Pulitzer Prize in fiction for *The Mambo Kings Play Songs of Love* (1989).

Even though H. is categorized as a Hispanic writer of the U.S., his works lack the stylistic tendencies normally associated with authors of that ethnic group. Code-switching, inverted syntax, and narrative based on oral traditions are noticeably absent in his works. The few Spanish expressions that appear in his novels do not always have the proper diacritical marks. Essentially, he employs traditional narrative techniques that deal with Cuban characters who live in the U.S.

Despite his winning critical acclaim, scholars have neglected to analyze and interpret H.'s corpus. Perhaps, this stems from his rather formulaic tendencies. Each of his novels explores the theme of solitude. Nevertheless, it is an individual solitude grounded in gender rather than ethnicity.

In *Our House in the Last World* (1983), Mercedes suffers verbal and physical abuse as well as ostracism throughout the novel. Alejo, her husband, squanders his money and takes a job that he considers beneath his dignity. Nonetheless, he makes a great show of his generosity. Even though this magnanimous spirit helps his friends to succeed, he is financially and socially frustrated; hence, he seeks solace in the bottle. He is the stereotypical macho, while Mercedes is the stereotypical suffering mother. Their children, Horacio and Hector, hate their home life and try to improve their lot in life. H. changes his characters' names and retells this story in his next two novels.

The Mambo Kings Play Songs of Love focuses on the lives of two brothers, Cesar and Nestor, who leave Cuba to be musicians. Nestor, like Hector, is sickly and miraculously survives a childhood illness. Consequently, both characters emerge as physically weak and passive. H. himself was hospitalized for nefritis as a child and probably uses this experience as the basis for the infirm sibling. Cesar is more akin to Alejo. He is a profligate whose sexual and alcoholic binges leave him unsatisfied, but who epitomizes the macho, Latin lover. After his brother's premature death, Cesar joins the Merchant Marine and then becomes the superintendent of his apartment building upon his return. Hence, Cesar, like Alejo, sees his ambitions thwarted and attributes this to bad luck.

H. uses flashbacks, dreams, and omens in *The Mambo Kings Play Songs of Love* to depict Cesar's life and death. The novel takes place in one evening and is divided into an A and a B side, like a record. Music, film, and television strongly affect and influence the characters in each of H.'s works, especially this one. Moreover, each novel has a son who has alleged homosexual traits, an Irish and a Cuban couple, a Cuban man with a deformed arm, a frustrated female poet and scholar, and various degrees of racial prejudice.

The Fourteen Sisters of Emilio Montez O'Brien (1993) portrays the loss of Cuban culture and the Spanish language within one family. H. focuses on two characters: Emilio and his sister Margarita. As in all his works, at least one woman has incestuous feelings toward a male family member. Unlike his other works, here, the male feels isolated in a household of women. The Irish father and the Cuban mother have a second-class berth on a liner that brings them to the U.S. from Cuba. The eldest child, Margarita, is born at sea to this minority couple—a second-class birth as well. Like *Mr. Ives' Christmas* (1995), this novel did not receive favorable critical attention.

H.'s first two novels are his chief works to date. His style, themes, and tone belong to mainstream American literature rather than to Hispanic literature of the U.S. An undertone of sarcasm runs throughout his novels, but they lack the subversive discontent of typical Hispanic literature. Instead, his works convey incommunication among family members, gender isolation, emotional dissatisfaction, and premature death on individual rather than ethnic levels.

BIBLIOGRAPHY: Dworkin y Méndez, K. C., "When Cuban Meets Irish, It's Magic: *The Fourteen Sisters of Emilio Montez O'Brien*," *Lucero* 4 (1993): 76–78; Pérez-Firmat, G., "Rum, Rump, and Rumba: Cuban Contexts for *The Mambo Kings Play Songs of Love*," *Dispositio* 41 (1991): 61–69

WILLIAM O. DEAVER, JR.

HIMES, Chester
b. 29 July 1909, Jefferson City, Missouri.; d. 12 November 1984, Moraira, Spain

H.'s childhood was marked by battling parents who, he believed, represented the opposing slave traditions of the fieldhand and the house servant. The ancestors of his very dark father, a blacksmithing teacher at small southern colleges, had been field workers; those of his mother, a very light-skinned woman deeply convinced of her superiority to darker blacks, including her husband, and of white superiority to blacks, had been servants. H., whose early, naturalistic work often featured a strong autobiographical element, frequently wrote frankly and graphically about interracial relationships and friction between white or light-skinned women and black men. His later work in the detective genre was critically and popularly acclaimed in France; two of his detective books were made into American films, but H. is still little read in his native U.S.

H. was a promising student who went to Ohio State University to prepare for a medical career. Instead, he developed an interest in sex, drinking, and crime and was asked to leave school after one semester. The following year, he was arrested for armed robbery; he was imprisoned in 1929. During the seven years he spent in Ohio State Penitentiary, he became a writer and had several of his short stories published.

After his release, H. continued to write. His first two published novels, *If He Hollers Let Him Go* (1945) and *Lonely Crusade* (1947), concerned labor and race relations in World War II-era Los Angeles. The first, a nihilistic exploration of events in the life of a character much like H., was explosive in its language and its interracial subject matter. The second was dismissed by critics and is still thought to be H.'s weakest work. The third novel published, *Cast the First Stone* (1952), set in prison, was actually the first H. had written. Most of the characters, as in other "raceless" literature of the period, are white, including the protagonist, who otherwise strongly resembles H. At the insistence of his editors, H. toned down the novel's central homosexual affair. H. later said that he had written the piece to "escape [his] past." The advance from this novel enabled H. to move to France, and he remained abroad—except for brief visits—for the rest of his life.

In France, where his work was more appreciated than in the U.S., H. published two autobiographical novels, *The Third Generation* (1954) and *The Primitive* (1955), which would be the last of his naturalistic fiction. In 1955, he met the French translator of *If He Hollers Let Him Go,* who had been impressed with H.'s hard-boiled prose and suggested he write a detective novel in the style of Raymond CHANDLER. H. took the work for money, but discovered that the genre allowed him to express the absurdity of black American life. He wrote nine novels, seven originally published in France, between 1957 and 1969, including *The Real Cool Killers* (1959, first pub. in French translation, 1958), *Cotton Comes to Harlem* (1965; first pub. in French translation, 1964), and *Blind Man with a Pistol* (1969). H.'s earlier fiction had been shocking in its depiction of sex, but the characters, though tempted to violent actions, failed to act. In the detective stories, H. purposefully included the graphic violence he believed was respected in mainstream America, but that he felt black Americans feared to use. The black detectives of all but one of these novels, Grave Digger Jones and Coffin Ed Johnson, provide a semblance of order in their disintegrating urban world. The detective works are thought by many critics to be among H.'s finest work, but although *The Heat's On* (1966; first pub. in French translation, 1961; repub. as *Come Back Charleston Blue*) and *Cotton Comes to Harlem* were made into American films, the books remain little known in the U.S.

After using his life so frequently in fiction, H. finally published a two-volume autobiography, *The Quality of Hurt* (1972) and *My Life of Absurdity* (1976). With the exception of a ribald satire, *Pinktoes*

(1961), in which H. suggests that interracial sex can provide a means of healing the rift between blacks and whites, H.'s writings are characterized by the pain and absurdity that also seem to have marked his life.

BIBLIOGRAPHY: Fabre, M., *C. H.: An Annotated Primary and Secondary Bibliography* (1992); Lundquist, J., *C. H.* (1976); Margolies, E., *The Several Lives of C. H.* (1997)

                                        CAROLYN LENGEL

HINOJOSA-SMITH, Rolando
b. 21 January 1929, Mercedes, Texas

Born of Mexican American and Anglo parentage in the Rio Grande Valley, H. has written in both Spanish and English about the area's distinctly blended culture. His fictional world, "Klail City" in "Belken County, Texas," reflects a specifically Chicano tension between the pressure for assimilation into Anglo society and a need to remain in touch with Mexican American culture. H.'s books evoke the complex social structure of the region through a collage-like narrative style that includes anecdotes, diaries, letters, newspaper articles, police reports, dramatized conversations, and monologues as well as descriptions. This style enacts the multiple, overlapping stories of the characters of Belken County as they struggle to accept their history and define their identities. H.'s novels together constitute what he calls the "Klail City Death Trip" series.

H.'s innovative writing style drew attention from the first; he won the Quinto Sol Award for his first novel, *Estampas del valle y otras obras: Sketches of the Valley and Other Works* (1973), and the Casa de las Américas Prize for his second, *Klail City y sus alrededores* (1976), which was published in a revised version in English as *Klail City* (1987). In these novels, the characters create a mythology of place through their stories, blending history and contemporary events to depict the valley's changing material and social conditions. The structure of the novels is discontinuous, which not only suggests the inhabitants' multiple perspectives but also evades thematic closure in the face of ongoing racial and political dissent. As the novel series progresses through *Rites and Witnesses* (1982), *Dear Rafe* (1985), and *Claros Varones de Belken/Fair Gentlemen of Belken County* (1986), H.'s overall tendency in character development moves toward assimilation into the Anglo community, particularly as depicted through recurrent character Rafe Buenrostro. In the later Klail City novels, from *Becky and Her Friends* (1990) onward, the increasing fragmentation of the Mexican American community as characters move into Anglo society suggests that class distinctions, rather than ethnicity, determine social mobility. The fact that H. ultimately locates his characters' aspirations in Anglo society suggests the strong sense of ambivalence in his work.

Two of H.'s books depart from his usual panoramic mode: *Korean Love Songs* (1980), a book of poems depicting Rafe's Korean War experiences, and *Partners in Crime* (1985), a mystery novel also focused on Rafe. While the latter volume is comic, the book of poetry is striking in its depictions of the futile grotesquerie of war.

H.'s habit of revising and republishing his books, presenting similar materials under different titles, causes a sense of interconnection and pastiche overall that reflects the many voices of Belken County but also points to the limitations of the author's technique. Presenting his Mexican American materials in postmodernist style, H. celebrates "the presence of the Chicano and his endurance" while rejecting any political constraints that the term "Chicano literature" might imply.

BIBLIOGRAPHY: Calderón, H., and J. D. Saldívar, eds., *Criticism in the Borderlands* (1991); Saldívar, J. D., ed., *The R. H. Reader: Essays Historical and Critical* (1985)

JAYNE MAREK

HISTORY AND LITERATURE

The interaction of "history" and "literature" produces, indeed invites diverse interpretation. Most emphasis here is to be placed upon the use of history in literature, predominantly fiction and drama. But questions arise about other possibilities. For example, are histories to be regarded as literature? Does literature itself make history?

The latter question can be answered first. Powerful literature has helped to form trends, to cause changes, to influence society, if not to make history. Critic Harry Levin has noted that literature is not only affected by social causes, it causes social effects; thus, it is both culture-ridden and culture-forming. Three American novels illustrate the point. Harriet Beecher STOWE's *Uncle Tom's Cabin*, published in 1852, influenced slavery and the American Civil War; Upton SINCLAIR's *The Jungle*, published in 1906, depicted practices in Chicago meatpacking plants in such damaging ways that the book caused a national furor and instigated swift passage of the Meat Inspection Act and the Pure Food and Drug Act; Sinclair LEWIS's *Babbitt*, published in 1922, promulgated a disparaging attitude toward the middle-class American businessman that lasted for decades.

The first question implies that histories themselves may convey enough aesthetic power and beauty to qualify as literature. Significant contributions to American history were made in the 19th c. by four accomplished men of letters, all from Massachusetts: Francis PARKMAN, most known for *The Oregon Trail* and *Montcalm and Wolfe;* William Hickling PRESCOTT, best known for *The Conquest of Mexico* and *The Conquest of Peru;* John Lothrop MOTLEY, remembered for *The Rise of the Dutch Republic* on the resistance of the Protestant Netherlands against Spain during the 16th c.; and George Bancroft, founder of the U.S. Naval Academy and author of the ten-volume *History of the United States* (1834–74). All these histories show a romantic attitude, masterful design, grand sweep, and literary skill.

A prolific writer/historian bridging the 19th and 20th cs. is Henry ADAMS, whose most notable books include *The Education of Henry Adams* and *Mont Saint Michel and Chartres.* In the former, an earnest yet often humorous "autobiography," Adams speaks of himself in the third person, making his own life the object of the history that he writes. The book twists its gnarly way through many contradictory images and ideas: among them, Virgin-Dynamo, freedom-discipline, action-thought, science-metaphysics, unity-chaos, constructive and destructive energy. Although valuable as a document tracing the development of American intellectual thought, it is also marked by inconclusiveness. The latter presents Adams's wide-ranging personal interpretations of life in the Middle Ages when the two great cathedrals of his title were built.

Qualities of aesthetic power and beauty hardly accrue to Puritan histories, yet excerpts of them appear often in anthologies of American literature. The reasons are clear: these primary documents live on as valuable sources of information about events of the colonial period, like the Mayflower journey, the settling of Plymouth and Jamestown, religious fervor, and relationships with native Americans. William BRADFORD's *Of Plymouth Plantation* and Cotton MATHER's *Magnalia Christi Americana* are probably the most frequently anthologized histories, along with the journals, letters, diaries, and assorted personal narratives of men such as Michael WIGGLESWORTH, Samuel SEWALL, John WINTHROP, William BYRD, and Jonathan EDWARDS, writing from the two dominant colonies of Massachusetts and Virginia.

In the 20th c., scholar Perry Miller's valuable accounts of PURITANISM have been followed by refreshing new studies by historian John Demos. Bernard De Voto's trilogy, *The Year of Decision: 1846* (1943), *Across the Wide Missouri* (1947), and *The Course of Empire* (1952), explores in depth the age of expansionism in America. Other modern historians include Samuel Eliot Morison, who wrote about the sea and naval operations; Charles and Mary Beard, who cowrote *The Rise of American Civilization* (1949); Barbara W. Tuchman, an authority on World War I; Arthur M. Schlesinger, Jr., commentator on American culture and author of *The Cycles of American History* (1986); and Theodore H. White, a journalist whose reputation rests on a series of books about modern U.S. presidential campaigns, capped by *America in Search of Itself* (1982).

A highly rewarding approach to this subject is history *as* literature. For centuries, creative writers have used actual historical events and real people as sources for novels, plays, and poems. Political incidents, famous trials, warfare, natural catastrophes, shipwrecks, rebellions, crimes and scandals, and careers of celebrated persons such as artists and statesmen have served as both inspiration and fount for fiction, drama, and poetry. The use of historical materials by an inventive writer presents the careful reader or viewer with several challenging tasks. He must ask himself what the writer has done to transcend fact and why. Next, he must consider what happens when historical truth is dramatically altered into fiction. And last, he must critically assess the difference. This last task proves most demanding because to answer it the reader or viewer must have knowledge of both the literary work and the historical accounts upon which it is based.

History may be used in literature in a variety of ways. For instance, in a traditional genre, the historical novel, the writer combines fiction with history in a compelling narrative. This kind of novel reconstructs the lives of historical personages or recreates historical events or provides a historically accurate milieu, or it may present wholly fictional characters and fictional occurrences in a historical background. The earliest successful practitioner of this form was James Fenimore COOPER in novels such as *The Pioneers* and *The Prairie*. The historical novel reached its apex of popularity in America at the publication of Margaret MITCHELL's best-selling *Gone with the Wind*. Its story of the South and the feisty fictional heroine Scarlett O'Hara ranges from pre–Civil War days to the Reconstruction.

Like other fiction, historical novels vary in quality from popular, escapist entertainment to serious, multidimensioned art. Commercial fiction generally places more emphasis on plot and adventure and shows less skill in characterization and use of language. At either end of the spectrum, the historical novelist is expected to exercise care in treatment of historical background. A sampling of America's popular historical novels published in the 20th c. includes Hervey ALLEN's *Anthony Adverse*, a romance dealing loosely with the

Napoleonic period; Kenneth ROBERTS's *Northwest Passage*, an occasionally fanciful handling of Rogers's Rangers in the French and Indian War; Thornton WILDER's *The Ides of March*, on the last crowded days of Julius Caesar's life; Irving STONE's *The Agony and the Ecstasy*, on the painting of the Sistine Chapel by Michelangelo; and Gore VIDAL's *Empire*, on life in Washington during the Theodore ROOSEVELT era and also involving the likes of William Randolph Hearst, William Jennings Bryan, and the Vanderbilts, the Whitneys, and the Astors.

As good as they may be in their own ways, these novels are not as lasting nor as resonant in their artistry as a classical novel like Nathaniel HAWTHORNE's *The Scarlet Letter*, with its unforgettable recreation of Puritan life, or a postmodern one like Thomas PYNCHON's *Gravity's Rainbow*, an encyclopedic, panoramic narrative that starts with V–2 rocket attacks on London in World War II. If similar gauging for fiction were applied to drama, the glib hipness of Jerome Lawrence and Robert E. Lee's *The Night Thoreau Spent in Jail* (1970) or the illusionary profundity of Maxwell ANDERSON's *Anne of the Thousand Days* would suffer by comparison with the genuine emotional power of Arthur MILLER's *The Crucible*, which dramatizes the Salem witchcraft trials of 1692 and their implied relationship to McCarthyism of the early 1950s.

An offshoot form of history as literature is the true-to-life novel or the nonfiction novel. An old tradition leaped to new life in 1966 with the appearance of Truman CAPOTE's *In Cold Blood*. In his gripping story of the murders of the Clutter family in Kansas in 1959 and the subsequent executions of criminals Perry Smith and Dick Hickock, Capote relies on a technique he calls "creative reportage." He claims that only a creative writer can handle the form, not a journalist untrained in the techniques of fiction. Terms vary from writer to writer. "Energized biography" has been used for Norman MAILER's account of the 1967 mass protest march on the Pentagon that serves as the center of his *The Armies of the Night*. In it, the author uses third person *Mailer* or *He* as his means of perception; the book is thus about himself and his actions. However, in *The Executioner's Song*, an overlong, deliberately flat account of the doomed killer Gary Gilmore, Mailer keeps himself out of the way as narrator. Alex HALEY uses the term "faction" for *Roots*, a story that traces seven generations of his black heritage, beginning with a raid upon a West African village by slavehunters. Two other carefully researched "nonfiction" novels are Ron HANSEN's *The Assassination of Jesse James by the Coward Robert Ford* and Jay Cantor's *The Death of Che Guevera* (1983). In all these cases, the writers have used fictional devices such as plotting, suspense, characterization, symbol, and irony to deepen and enrich their stories about real-life events and people, without necessarily sacrificing much historical accuracy.

The same may be said for certain plays and poems. Although no terms like "faction" or "fictual" exist for drama, some modern plays indeed qualify as factual. They put to use various dramatic strategies, but stay quite faithful to actual events and biographical details, including use of real names, as in William GIBSON's *The Miracle Worker,* on the relationship of the deaf, blind, and mute child Helen Keller and her teacher Annie Sullivan, or the ennobling conquest over polio by Franklin D. Roosevelt as a young man in Dore Schary's *Sunrise at Campobello* (1958). Similar authenticity, including use of real names, may be found in a long narrative poem like George Keithley's *The Donner Party* (1972), on the tragedy that occurred when California-bound pioneer families were trapped without provisions in the Sierra in the winter of 1846–47.

On the other hand, writers can change true names and free the reins on imagination while still staying fairly close to facts. The result is *roman à clef,* a work of fiction based on real people and actual events and places but presented in fictional guise. (*Roman à clef* is literally *story with a key;* when the reader finds the key he unlocks the truth behind the novel.) This form did not flourish in the 18th or 19th centuries, but it has many practitioners in the 20th c. In the rise and fall of the fictional demagogue Willie Stark in *All the King's Men,* Robert Penn WARREN reflects Louisiana politics and specifically the career of Louisiana governor-then-senator Huey Long, who was assassinated in the state capitol in 1935. Real-life counterparts abound in Ernest HEMINGWAY's depiction of expatriate life in post–World War I in Paris and Pamplona in *The Sun Also Rises.* For example, Lady Brett Ashley parallels the real Lady Duff Twysden; Robert Cohn/Harold Loeb; Mike Campbell/Pat Guthrie; Harris/"Chink" Dorman Smith; Pedro Romero/Cayetano Ordonez, a.k.a. Nino de la Palma. The decline of F. Scott FITZGERALD drives Budd SCHULBERG's *The Disenchanted.* Besides Fitzgerald as Manley Halliday, Zelda Sayre FITZGERALD is his wife Jere, Sheilah Graham becomes Ann Loeb, and Schulberg, who worked with Fitzgerald as a fellow screenwriter, appears as Shep Stearns. Criminal cases work effectively as subject matter for *roman à clef.* Bernard MALAMUD uses the fictional Yakov Bok as protagonist of *The Fixer,* a retelling of the Mendell Beiliss case involving murder and flagrant anti-Semitism in Czarist Russia. The case that came to be called "The Kentucky Tragedy" is retold in Robert Penn Warren's *World Enough and Time;* in it, fictional lawyer Jeremiah Beaumont parallels Jereboam Beauchamp; his fictional rival Colonel

Cassius Fort is derived from Colonel Solomon Sharp, and Rachel Jorden as Ann Cook completes the deadly triangle. One other famous case involves the murder of a boy of arrogant young intellectuals in Chicago in 1924. In his novel *Compulsion,* Meyer LEVIN retells the story of killer Nathan Leopold (as Judd Steiner) and Richard Loeb (as Artie Straus). The victim of Bobbie Franks is renamed Paulie Kessler; Clarence Darrow, who defended Leopold and Loeb and managed to get them life imprisonment rather than the expected death penalty, appears as Jonathan Wilk; and Levin himself is narrator and reporter Sid Silver.

The techniques of *roman à clef* are commonly adopted in drama. A good example came out of the Scopes case, pitting theories of evolutionism against creationism in Dayton, Tennessee, in 1925. The Monkey Trial, as it came to be called, informs every scene of Lawrence and Lee's *Inherit the Wind* (1955), including use of specific court testimony. In the play, Bertram Cates parallels John Scopes, Matthew Harrison Brady/William Jennings Bryan, Henry Drummond/Clarence Darrow, E. K. Hornbeck/H. L. MENCKEN. Maxwell Anderson's *Winterset* is based loosely on the Sacco-Vanzetti case of the 1920s. In Howard SACKLER's *The Great White Hope,* the black prizefighter Jack (John Arthur) Johnson becomes Jack Jefferson and his white girlfriend Lucy Cameron becomes Ellie Bachman.

Short fiction and brief poetry should not be overlooked. The following three stories represent only a tiny sampling of historically based fiction written in America over the past century. The sinking of the *Commodore* enroute to Cuba in the winter of 1897 inspired the Stephen CRANE story "The Open Boat" that was published six months later. The assassination of NAACP leader Medgar Evers in Jackson, Mississippi, in 1963 prompted Eudora WELTY to write her story "Where Is the Voice Coming From?" almost overnight; it was published in the *New Yorker* only three weeks after the crime. And in a departure from his usual techniques, Raymond CARVER turns to the fact-oriented "Errand" (1987), a tale that compresses the last years of Anton Chekhov's life to his death from consumption in 1904.

A few examples will have to suffice from among many in poetry. On September 15, 1963, four children were killed by a bomb placed alongside a black church in Birmingham, Alabama. This horrible incident provides the basis for Dudley RANDALL's moving and ironical "Ballad of Birmingham," in which a mother insists that her daughter avoid taking part in a dangerous freedom march and instead go to their church, where she will be safe. And Robert LOWELL wrote a number of poems based on historical occurrences and his own life experiences. "For the Union Dead," originally entitled "Colonel Shaw and the Massachusetts 54th," relates the story of the commander of a black regiment killed in an assault during the Civil War. "After the Surprising Conversions" (1946) is based on a letter that Jonathan Edwards wrote describing both religious awakening in his town and the suicide of an uncle. "Memories of West Street and Lepke" (1958) recounts Lowell's brief jail sentence as a conscientious objector when he served time along with "lobotomized" mob "Czar Lepke."

Whereas Lowell and Randall tend to acknowledge their sources, other writers don't. Sometimes they deny that a historical incident gave rise to a particular work. Sometimes they just evade admitting use of sources. Others may acknowledge a source but do not claim accuracy. For example, in describing the only achieved black rebellion in pre–Civil War Virginia, William STYRON speaks of his novel *The Confessions of Nat Turner* as a "meditation on history." A few other typical disclaimers read "[this work] does not pretend to be journalism" or "I have reshaped [historical fact] to fit my purposes." and some writers deliberately play a challenging game by intermixing fact and fiction as if they were the same. They have real people interacting with fictional characters and actual events merging into imaginative ones. Furthermore, unlike the usual historical novel, their real-life personages often play roles that are as important as their fellow fictional characters.

Novelist E. L. DOCTOROW has put these last three strategies to use. By viewing the novel as "a false document,' he chooses not to worry about distinctions among history, journalism, and fiction—for him there is "only narrative." In explanation of his method, he poses a key question: "A society that deifies facts, as we do in America, tends to see every novel as the true story of thinly disguised people. Why not turn that around and write about imaginary events in the lives of undisguised people?" He does just that in *Ragtime.* While presenting a cross section of American life through three fictional groupings—a traditional WASP family, an immigrant father and daughter, and a black couple—he interlaces their stories with famous people of the period from 1906 to the first world war: escape artist Harry Houdini, celebrity-beauty Evelyn Nesbit whose mad husband Harry K. Thaw went to trial for murdering architect Stanford White, anarchist and feminist Emma Goldman, and the duo of financier J. P. Morgan and auto manufacturer Henry Ford. Doctorow also sprinkles in another fifty minor historical figures and he works in such true-to-life incidents as the violent retaliation against strikers at textile mills in Lawrence, Massachusetts, in 1912, the successful expedition to the North Pole commanded by Robert E. Peary in 1908–9, and the sinking of the *Lusitania* in 1915.

When questioned about whether any of his historical personages—say, Goldman and Nesbit or Thaw and Houdini—ever met, he responds, "They have now—they have all met now." Thus, whatever the writer creates in his mind has occurred. Obviously this view alarms purists concerned about how far creative writers should go in manipulating facts.

The problem is not nearly as complicated in a work like the lengthy trilogy *U.S.A.* because its writer John DOS PASSOS avoids the fusing; he merely juxtaposes the imaginative and the real. Over the first thirty years of the 20th c., his hundred fictional characters cross and criss-cross paths, but their lives are not intruded upon by real-life people and situations, as occurs in *Ragtime.* Rather, the real is set apart in "Biographies," in "Newsreels" that establish the climate of the period, and in the auctorial "Camera Eye."

However, fact and fiction do get mixed up in *Water Music.* In this highly charged picaresque novel, T. Coraghessan BOYLE reprises the actual two expeditions of the young Scottish explorer Mungo Park to discover the source of the Niger River in West Africa. For counterpoint, Boyle creates a fictional co-protagonist in Ned Rise, a scalawag-entrepreneur-survivor from the streets of London. Park and Rise will conjoin in Africa until the ill-fated boating attack at Boussa that claimed Park's life. A similar conjoining occurs in William KENNEDY's *Legs,* in which fictional attorney Marcus Gorman narrates the story of his client and friend Jack "Legs" Diamond, the notorious gangster who was shot five separate times and finally died in his early thirties in Albany, New York, in 1931. Diamond's violent career in crime is based in fact, as is his relationship with his wife Alice and his showgirl-mistress Kiki Roberts (born Marion Strasmick). In his surrealistic satire *The Public Burning,* Robert COOVER uses Richard Nixon as narrator of much of the story that lies behind the execution of the spies Julius and Ethel Rosenberg, but he also introduces a mythical character Uncle Sam, who in the last scene rapes Nixon. In *The Nation Thief* (1984), Robert Houston also mixes fictional characterization in with his account of the brilliant young William Walker of Tennessee who tried between 1855 and 1860 to wrest control of Nicaragua. Similarly in Henry Carlisle's *The Land Where the Sun Dies* (1975), fictional characters interact with the famous chief Osceola at the time of the Second Seminole Indian War in Florida. And one other unusual novelistic device is worth mentioning. In *Slaughterhouse-Five,* author Kurt VONNEGUT intrudes himself into a fictional story that is based upon fact, the Dresden fire bombing in the waning months of World War II. A major example from poetry is Stephen Vincent BENÉT's *John Brown's Body,* an epic on the

Civil War, slavery, and the rebellion and death of abolitionist John Brown.

Some events and people seem to have special appeal. They not only continue to receive the attention of writers from generation to generation—like the Salem witchcraft trials and the life of Abraham LIN-COLN—but they also inspire work in different genres. The previously mentioned Rosenberg case also led to Donald Freed's documentary play *Inquest* (1969) and the E. L. Doctorow *roman à clef The Book of Daniel,* which focuses upon the lives of surviving children. Conditions at the hellish military prison for Union POWs at Andersonville, Georgia, impel MacKinley Kantor's novel *Andersonville* (1955). The criminal case brought against the camp leader Captain Henry Wirz is dramatized in Saul Levitt's play *The Andersonville Trial* (1959); Wirz received the death penalty and was hanged. The career of America's sixteenth President has inspired plays like Robert E. SHER-WOOD's *Lincoln in Illinois* and Mark VAN DOREN's *The Last Days of Lincoln,* a novel like Gore Vidal's *Lincoln,* a poem like Vachel LINDSAY's "Abraham Lincoln Walks at Midnight" (1914). The career of actress Marilyn Monroe, who took her life at age thirty-six in 1962, has resulted in more than a dozen serious nonfiction books, as well as *After the Fall* (1964), a play by her former husband Arthur Miller, and Alvah Bessie's novel *The Symbol* (1967). Interestingly, Paddy CHAYEFSKY's screenplay *The Goddess,* published in 1958, anticipates Monroe's troubled career well before her death.

It would seem that at some point, saturation ought to occur in treatment of certain tragic incidents. Consider the sinking of the *Titanic* in 1912, after she struck an iceberg, causing the loss of 1,523 lives. In three quarters of a century since, that tragedy has spawned an opera, some two hundred books, including many novels, and a dozen movies.

Historical events and real people have been portrayed on film with varying degrees of success. Obviously facts will be altered to suit cinematic needs, but the better films manage to remain reasonably accurate when compared with their original sources. Hundreds upon hundreds of movies have their bases in history in various genres. American Academy Award "Best Picture" winners in the 1980s prove the point in subjects ranging from war and biography and music to politics and religion and sports: Oliver Stone's military experiences in Vietnam in his *Platoon* (1986); the experiences in business and romance of Isak Dinesen—then Karen Blixen—on a coffee plantation in Africa in Kurt Luedtke's *Out of Africa* (1985); the careers of composers Mozart and Salieri in Peter Shaffer's *Amadeus* (1984); the career of the famous Indian leader Mahatma Gandhi in John Briley's *Gan-*

dhi (1982); academic and religious life merged with sports during post World War I, starting in England and Scotland and eventuating in the 1924 Paris Olympics in Colin Welland's *Chariots of Fire* (1982).

It is generally conceded that the treatment of history on television has been less than satisfactory. The docudrama, as it has come to be called, attempts to combine the documentary aspects of real life with the fictional ingredients of drama. The results have veered toward drama in ways that badly distort history. As an instrument for education, as well as for entertainment, TV needs to pay more respect to historical veracity and artistic integrity.

BIBLIOGRAPHY: Canary, R. H., and H. Kosicki, eds. *The Writing of History: Literary Form and Historical Understanding* (1978); Hughes, H. S., *History as Art and as Science* (1975); Schulze, L., and W. Wetzels, eds., *History and Literature* (1983); White, H., *Metahistory* (1973)

CHARLES CLERC

HOAGLAND, Edward
b. 21 December 1932, New York City

Perhaps of all contemporary American essayists, H. reminds us the most of Montaigne, who famously declared, "I am myself the matter of my book." This focus on the self has ever since been a basic ingredient and, as every essayist must, H. has found a way to wear well with his steady ability to create the convivial persona. He has the sound of, if not also the bearing of, the compelling man of letters.

H. emerged as an essayist by first having run poorly as a novelist. H.'s early fiction briefly did gather in a bit of positive commentary. In fact, he made a fast start, placing his first novel, *Cat Man* (1954), with Houghton Mifflin shortly before graduating from Harvard. But there followed a series of lukewarm, or cooler, receptions for *The Circle Home* (1960), *The Peacock's Tail* (1965), *Seven Rivers West* (1986), and his short story collection *The Final Fate of Alligators* (1992). The general weakness in these has been ascribed to various aspects of narrative. Some critics have also complained of characters drawn too lightly or otherwise drawn with too much primitivism. But there was no resisting H. after he started coming out with such revelations of himself as in "Strange Perfume," an *Esquire* essay of 1994: "up with the baby twice a night and scribbling ideas, the knack I had fashioned in my travel books for speaking to a reader had turned into my first essays. I was scarcely aware how this happened, but I poured it on, a bookful in just two years—the baby inevitably inventing herself too as we went along."

Not all of his personal unfoldings, of course, have been quite so wholesome seeming. Part of his appeal is that he is among the frankest of our writers: he has more than once confessed that he let his stammer slow him down in his young man's desire to lose his virginity. The compensation for this, at least as he has dealt with it, has been the stammer's effect of endlessly sharpening his writerly capacity for standing attentively by and recording the flow of life. This impression of a battered but resilient psyche also seems to have another of its roots deep down in his relations with his parents. His father was a high-powered attorney for a Manhattan oil company and would not abide his son's bohemian leanings—those of going off and digging up material for his first novel by working for half a year in the Ringling Brothers Circus. And his mother further strained the family when she sailed for Europe on the day before he was to marry a Jewish woman, his second wife, Marion Magid. So clearly snubbed that way before his wedding, he began to entertain the possibility that his abiding passivity with women sprang from his complicated home life.

The difficult background notwithstanding, H. has come on in his essays to bear an expert witness against much of the absurdity of our modern lives. At once deeply critical of our time and just as deeply involved in its preoccupations, H. has written from the belief he set forth in "Heaven and Nature," a *Harper's* essay of 1988: "Life is a matter of cultivating the six senses, and an equilibrium with nature and what I think of as its subdivision, human nature, trusting no one completely but almost everyone at least a little."

This unusually comprehensive view of "nature" has more than likely helped H. to succeed brilliantly with what is conventionally accepted as the "nature essay." The theme of "the end of nature" could well prove itself to be the defining one of our time. And insofar as it does, H.'s stature indisputably will grow. A nature writer in his own right, he has also won appointment as an editor for the sixteen volumes of Penguin's Nature Classics series. His five books in this vein—*Notes from the Century Before: A Journal from British Columbia* (1969), *The Courage of Turtles* (1971), *Walking the Dead Diamond River* (1973), *The Moose on the Wall: Field Notes from the Vermont Wilderness* (1974), and *Red Wolves and Black Bears* (1976)—deserve attention.

But probably the book with which to start reading H. is the excellent sampler of his essays, *Heart's Desire* (1988). The range of his interests is itself impressive, from jury duty to Johnny Appleseed, from boxing to Christianity's Golden Rule. Regardless of which one of these, however, the essence of H.'s essays goes back to the word's origin in *essais*, or "attempts" at understanding. This is not the promise of received wisdom nor even a confidence of opinion. But there is in him a concerted excitement and purity of intention that has made him one of our most infectious essayists.

BIBLIOGRAPHY: Hart, J. A., "E. H.," in Kibler, J. E., Jr., ed., *DLB*, vol. 6, *American Novelists since World War II* (1980): 144–47

J. RUSSELL BURROWS

HOFFMAN, Alice
b. 16 March 1952, New York City

H. earned her B.A. from Adelphi University and her M.A. from Stanford University, where she was awarded a Mirelles Fellowship in 1975. With some eight novels and several screenplays to her credit, H.'s works usher in a new era of women writings in the U.S. During the 1960s, women's writings were characterized by women in crisis—usually of a psychological nature and usually incurable given the societal influences on women. Contemporary writers tend to be either overly commercial and simplicit in their rendering of modern society or overly obscure. H. has arrived in the middle—which, under ordinary circumstances, would not be a coveted place. In this case, it is.

The middle allows freedom to move, to oscillate toward the right and/or the left, to experiment, and to insist upon a dedication to craft—no matter the source of inspiration. To the right is the middle-class American family in a middle-class neighborhood, and into this mix is thrown the eccentric or exotic (the left) with which the measure of normality must emerge. And this is the brilliance of H.—her fiction renders ordinary people facing extraordinary odds/experiments. Her insistence on the mythic, the mystical, the hyperspiritual in everyday life reveals a way of knowing the world that resonates the interconnectedness of the universe, even in these often uninspired times. Critics laud her writing as "mythic," "lyrical," and "magical."

Youthful protagonists and the belief in romantic love abound in her early works. Her first novel, *Property Of* (1977), features an unnamed seventeen-year-old's stormy, year-long love affair with the leader of an urban gang. Urban violence is not new, but H. manages to instill the near heroic into the relationship. Her second novel, *The Drowning Season*, was named one of the Notable Books for 1979. This time focusing on the relationship between a grandmother and granddaughter, tracing a family's line from Russia to Long Island. *Angel Landing* followed in 1980, then *White Horse* in 1982. Both works feature an old-fashioned love story, of sorts, set against modern intrusions—the threat of a nuclear power plant in the first case, and worship bordering on the incestuous in the second case.

Fortune's Daughter (1985), *Illumination Night* (1987), and *At Risk* (1988) might best be seen as transition novels. *Fortune's Daughter* explores pregnancy and childbirth; *Illumination Night* subtly examines the complexities of marriage; *At Risk* is the story of a family touched by the HIV virus. Reviews of these three novels were mixed, with *At Risk* being identified as the work with the least amount of magical elements that so characterize her works. In each, though, the outrageous and tragic tempered by the believable on the fringe of the everyday are brought into clear focus through wit and sheer talent.

By the publication of *Seventh Heaven* (1990), H. had begun to reach her zenith, her genius in both content and characterization, and in her commentary on social phenomena. *Seventh Heaven* begins in 1959, the sixth year of existence for a development community on Long Island. After the death of one of the neighbors, a divorcée moves in with her two children and manages to disrupt the lives of the very closed community into which she has moved. Along the way, a wife leaves her husband and children, a teenage girl dies in a tragic car accident, and the divorcee maintains an affair with the seventeen-year-old son of one of her neighbors.

The story is about middle America—their hopes and dreams; growing up in the 'burbs—and change. It is a commentary on the disruption of the manicured lifestyles of the 1950s. Nora Silk is no ordinary protagonist. She is bright, upbeat, industrious, witty, and a believer in the nonrational world. After her husband leaves her, she refuses to grant him a divorce until after he cosigns the mortgage for her new home. To pay the bills, she works as a manicurists and sells Tupperware. She is a modern-day superwoman with a twist: she admits when she is tired—unlike her model-mother counterparts.

The concern with the appearance of normality in the face of a family of eccentrics continues in *Practical Magic* (1995). Two orphaned sisters are taken in by distant relatives (the aunts) who are well versed in the art of magic and healing. Because of the reputation of the aunts in the small town to which they come to live, the young girls suffer a notoriety that makes growing up all the more painful. The younger girl, Gillian, escapes via elopement, and the older Sally escapes with her two daughters Antonia and Kylie, after the death of her husband.

Sally settles in a small conventional community in New York State with her two girls. Sometime later, Gillian arrives with the body of her dead lover on a night two rings appear around the moon. Sally and Gillian bury the body in the backyard and the lilacs grow out of season, growing as high as the telephone wires while Sally is plagued with dreams of a man

she never knew in life, and Gillian is unable to stop thinking about him. It is the aunts who rid Sally's house of the ghost of Jimmy, and the girls are reconciled with the aunts. Having watched the aunts perform love spells by twilight for desperate women all their lives, the two vow never to fall in love. But things change. Sally loves Gary and Gillian marries Ben Frye, her fourth husband. In the end, Sally learns to let her girls grow and falls in love again. Gillian makes peace with the aunts, and all is well.

This book contains it all. The youthful love of H.'s early works; fully developed notions of the magical which seasons all her works; and the prose style that is compelling, if not intoxicating. H., like her protagonists, is not a run of the mill modern, popular writer. Her stories say more, explore more, and do more than those of her contemporaries. That includes finely honed details of the human condition mixed with a mysticism that well serves her contemporaries.

BIBLIOGRAPHY: Mewshaw, M., "A Review of *Property Of*," *NYTBR* 10 July 1977: 10; Strouse, J., "Esther the White, Esther the Black," *Newsweek* 94 (20 August 1979): 72

ADELE S. NEWSON

HOFFMAN, Charles Fenno

b. 7 February 1806, New York, New York; d. 7 June 1884, Harrisburg, Pennsylvania

H. served as editor of many New York publications in the 1830s and 1840s. He was also a frequent contributor to periodicals, publishing poetry and a large number of short nonfiction pieces including reviews, travel letters, criticism, and material on history and nature. His most successful work was his only completed novel, *Greyslaer: A Romance of the Mohawk* (1840), which went quickly through two editions and was dramatized and performed at New York's Bowery Theater.

H. came from an eminent New York family and attended Columbia University; however, he paid more attention to sports than to his studies, and when he left after two years he was in the bottom fifth of his class. He went to Albany to study law and in 1827 began practicing in New York with his father, in spite of his dislike for the legal profession. While keeping up a desultory practice, H. began writing for the *American*. When his father died, H. abandoned the law altogether and became the newspaper's coeditor and literary reviewer.

In January 1833, H. became the editor of the new literary magazine the *Knickerbacker,* later changed to the *Knickerbocker.* He served only a few months before illness forced his resignation. In the fall, he traveled west for his health and wrote a series of amusing letters to the *American* about his journey; these were later collected as *Winter in the West* (1835). In 1835, he joined the magazine *American Monthly* as coeditor. His first novel, *Vanderlyn,* was serialized occasionally in the magazine, but H. never completed it. He resigned from the *Monthly* after differences with another editor and moved to the New York *Mirror,* where he published a series of nonfiction pieces which would become *Wild Scenes in the Forest and Prairie* (1837).

After the success of *Greyslaer,* a historical romance based on a famous love triangle murder in Kentucky, H. returned to editing, joining Horace Greeley at the *New Yorker* for a year. In 1841, he left editing for a more lucrative position at the New York customs house. H. published a volume of poems in 1842 that was popular in the U.S. but criticized in England as derivative of Thomas Moore. The title of his second volume of poetry, *Echo; or, Borrowed Notes for Home Circulation* (1844), was a humorous response to these critics.

H. contributed regularly to the *Evening Gazette* during his years at the customs house. In 1847, having lost his political position, he accepted the editorship of the *Literary World* magazine and began work on a third novel, *Red Spur of the Ramapo.* Unfortunately, his chambermaid thought that the finished pages were kindling for the fire and burned all but six of them before he discovered her error. In 1848, he checked himself into a hospital in Philadelphia. Within a month he was released. H. then went to Washington to accept a position in the State Department and soon collapsed. He remained hospitalized, suffering from what may have been a manic-depressive illness, until his death in 1884.

BIBLIOGRAPHY: Barnes, H. F., *C. F. H.* (1930); Bergmann, H. F., "C. F. H.," in Myerson, J., ed., *DLB,* vol. 3, *Antebellum Writers in New York and the South* (1979): 159–60

CAROLYN LENGEL

HOGAN, Linda

b. 16 July 1947, Denver, Colorado

H. rehabilitates wildlife, not only in her daily life, but in her poetry. Brimming with the pastoral, with totems and spirit-haunted imagery, her poetry trades in the concrete images of nature, finding its ultimate power in the mystical. Her insights come from clay, red clay, the earth of her native environment and of her Native American traditions.

H., a Chickasaw poet, novelist, and essayist, was born in Denver and reared in Oklahoma. She has received the Oklahoma Book Award in fiction, the Mountain and Plains Bookseller's Association Fiction Award, and an American Book Award from the before Columbus Foundation. She is also the recipient of a Guggenheim Fellowship, the Colorado Writer's Fellowship, and the Five Civilized Tribes Museum playwriting award. H. is an associate professor at the University of Minnesota in American Indian and American studies, and has served on the National Endowment for the Arts poetry panel.

Throughout the corpus of her work, from *Calling Myself Home* (1978) and *Seeing through the Sun* (1985) to *Mean Spirit* (1992), *Solar Storms* (1995), and *Dwellings: Reflections on the Natural* (1995), one recurring thread weaves and warps through her blanket of diverse patterns: exploring the relationship between the human and the garden as well as humanity's responsibility as caretaker, inhabitant, daughter and mother, brother and son of the earth. In *Eclipse* (1983), she quotes the Iroquois Oren Lyons's speech to the UN in 1977, effectively foregrounding this theme: "I do not see a delegation for the four-footed. I see no seat for the eagles. We forget and we consider ourselves superior, but we are after all a mere part of this creation." H.'s poetry is an extended attempt to provide a voice for that delegation, to remind us again and again of our evolutionary heritage and its accompanying debt.

In one poem, she writes of a beached whale, human initials carved into its hide; in another she points out the dark irony of how easily the trunks of black walnuts are turned into rifle butts. Here, she will elegize a nuclear reactor explosion in Idaho Falls where she imagines the atoms of three vaporized men speeding on to feed the light bulbs and heaters of their community; there, she will observe how humanity has grown "away from the earth," the sun, the plants, the animals, how in today's technophilic world we "see only objects" when we turn to face the place we inhabit.

Nevertheless, H. also recognizes that there are those among us, including herself, still aware of the fact that we cannot leave the natural world behind; it is a part of us. She writes of the "dark amphibians" living in her skin, of the birds that "fly through me," of "the red earth" that "passes like light into us and stays." She says, "we are amber, the small animals are gold inside us." Like Leslie Marmon SILKO in *Ceremony,* H. doesn't so much condemn modern technological society as empathize with it. Her poetry and prose is an attempt to reacquaint us with our own "barbaric yawp," with our roots, our families, our various traditions and histories. She is a voice of the Chickasaw Nation, of the American Nation, of the four-footed, the web-footed, the winged and the deeply rooted. Her writing counts America's rings, taking us back to those origins we tend to forget.

BIBLIOGRAPHY: Bruchac, J., ed., *Songs from This Earth on Turtle's Back: Contemporary American Indian Poetry* (1983); Scholer, B., "'A Heart Made Out of Crickets': An Interview with L. H.," *JEthS* 16 (Spring 1988): 107–17; special H. issue, *SAIL* 6 (Fall 1994)

BRYAN D. DIETRICH

HOLLANDER, John
b. 28 October 1929, New York City

Often cited as America's foremost authority on the theory and practice of poetic form, H. possesses a knowledge of poetry that often threatens to overshadow his own outstanding work in that genre. For over forty years, H. has been one of America's most challenging poets.

H. first came to notice when his first collection, *A Crackling of Thorns* (1958), was selected by W. H. AUDEN for the Yale Series of Younger Poets. "The Great Bear," a poem about how the stellar constellations are fictive projections of the human mind, foreshadows H.'s career-long emphasis on both the artifice and the emotion of imaginative form. During the 1960s, H. was often termed a "neoclassical" poet. But this characterization had more to do with H.'s refusal to join in that decade's psychopolitical poetic concerns than it related to the actual qualities of his verse. *Movie-Going* (1962), for instance, displayed H.'s interest in popular culture and his ability to glimpse poetic meaning in various subject matters. *Visions from the Ramble* (1965) is perhaps H.'s most significant book of poetry. The long title poem is a rapturous chronicle of a young boy's coming to imaginative awareness amidst the skyscrapers of New York. Centered in the "bird ramble" of Central Park, the poem's combination of urban tumult and Wordsworthian reverie is expressed in the poem's central image, the three pools of water in the park that partially represent the Graces, but also testify to the fleetingness and quotidian trappings of even the most visionary impulse. "The Ninth of July" is another boyhood story that seeks to mediate between the familiar and the transcendent; set on July 9, 1939, five days apart from both the American Independence Day with its associations of childhood patriotism and the European Bastille Day, with its overtones of adult cosmopolitanism, the poem weaves together innocence and experience, knowledge and joy, in a fashion at once moving and erudite.

Critics often divide H.'s career into two phases, the second beginning in the early 1970s when H. left New York, where he had been teaching, to move to New Haven, where he took up a position at Yale. His work soon took on a new difficulty and opacity. Previously, one could uncover the meaning of a H. poem, no matter how elaborate, through hard work, but H.'s work in *The Night Mirror* (1971) and after is often resistant to conclusive analysis. H. began to explore his Jewishness more overtly and made frequent allusions to Kabbalistic mysticism in his verse. Increasingly, he used his poetry to explore challenges posed by the doctrines of Yale colleagues. *Blue Wine* (1979) seems influenced by the agonistic theories of Harold BLOOM—who began to vigorously advocate H.'s poetry in the 1970s—and *In Time and Place* (1986) interrogates the epistemological unreliability postulated by Paul de Man. In the midst of all this, though, H. found time for some of his most stunning lyrics. *Powers of Thirteen* (1983) is a book of 169 sonnets composed of thirteen lines instead of the standard fourteen. As in so many of his poems, H.'s formal innovation allows him not only to display his matchless craftsmanship but also show how even complex poetry can relate stories of human experience with which readers can identify. This volume, among other things, displays H.'s strengths as a love poet, in a circuitous way recapitulating the ground of the old Elizabethan sonnet-sequences. *Harp Lake* (1988) continues to explore Jewish themes, the central poem being a pantoum about the Sea of Galilee, or Kinnesareth in Hebrew. *Tesserae* (1993) is highlighted by short, almost pure lyrics which show the poet's skill in concentrating meaning into a dense cluster of words.

As important as H. is as a poet, his role as a critic and theorist of poetry may be even more so. H.'s massive knowledge of poetic forms and practices lies behind his critical works, which have two main concerns: to show what poetry is and is not capable of doing, and to talk about how poems exist in themselves yet reveal hidden dimensions beyond their apparent meaning. *The Untuning of the Sky* (1961) was influential in its refutation of the hope that poetry could ever exactly coincide with a primary, musical impulse; H., though, shows how strongly musical poetry still can be, revealing an interest in the relation between poetry and the other arts also expressed in several essays on ekphrastic poetry. *Melodious Guile* (1988) and *The Work of Poetry* (1997) explore how poems relate complicated allegories of their own composition, and are successful in transmuting deconstruction into a new, intricate mode of close reading.

BIBLIOGRAPHY: Howard, R., *Alone with America: Essays on the Art of Poetry in the U.S. since 1950* (1969;

rev. ed., 1980); Prunty, W., *Fallen from The Symboled World: Precedents for the New Formalism* (1990)

NICHOLAS BIRNS

HOLLEY, Marietta

b. 16 July 1836, Bear Creek, New York; d. 1 March 1926, Jefferson County, New York

H. was a popular late-19th-c. humorist as well as the leading writer of upstate New York in her day. Her reputation is one of the many that fell calamitously with the onset of MODERNISM. Curiously, she has not been rehabilitated nearly as much as some of her contemporaries.

H. was reared in Jefferson County, New York, where she was to live all her life. Skirting the western slopes of the Adirondacks and touching the eastern fringes of Lake Ontario, Jefferson County in H.'s youth was as much an untamed "frontier" area as the more storied pioneer regions out West. From *My Opinions and Betsey Bobbet's* (1873) onward, H.'s work was in the tradition of frontier humor that reached its apogee of popularity with the work of Mark TWAIN; H. indeed was often styled "the female Mark Twain." She participated in a tradition of dialect, rustic humor, and understated wisdom that stretched all across America and can even be compared to the "bush" writers of the 1890s in Australia. Like Twain, H. wrote under a pseudonym, "Josiah Allen's Wife." Josiah Allen's wife was also the primary character and narrator in her books. The character of Samantha Allen, a housewife living in the upstate town of Jonesville, served H. well as a vehicle for familiar, rustic observations that carried a great deal of bite beneath their congenial and unobtrusive cloak.

"Josiah Allen's Wife," though, was very different in her life circumstances from H. herself, who never married or had children—the spinster Betsey Bobbet, another recurring character, differed from H. in other ways. This discrepancy helps foreground the crucial role of gender in H.'s work. The fact that Samantha Allen is not referred to as such but only as the wife of Josiah indicates the subordinate position women were forced to assume in the domestic order; but there is more than a degree of irony in H.'s presentation of Samantha's situation, as she is far more vocal and opinionated than the sometimes phlegmatic Josiah. Samantha operates effectively behind the cloak of her husband's nominal authority, mocking him and, at strategic moments, seizing the spotlight for herself. Notably, in the later works of the series, her Christian name is used in the titles, as in *Samantha at the World's Fair* (1893).

Contrary to the sentimental tradition that had largely dominated women's fiction in the U.S., H. wrote connected sketches rather than melodramatic narratives, and her plots do not lead up to marriage but assume it as a given. In their privileging of anecdote over event, Samantha's adventures enable her to observe life and express her own homegrown philosophy—filled with this-worldly acceptance, despite H.'s early conversion to Baptism and lifelong dabbling in spiritualism. Thus, Samantha's meeting with President Arthur in *Sweet Cicely: Josiah Allen as a Politician* (1885) has none of the drama of Jeanie Deans's appeal to the Queen in Sir Walter Scott's *The Heart of Midlothian,* a scene that H. obviously parodies.

H. could have been expected to resurface in the 1980s with the dramatic increase of attention paid to 19th-c. women writers, but this has not occurred, despite the almost single-handed efforts of the critic Kate H. Winter to revive H.'s reputation. H.'s moderate stance—assertively feminist but less interested in social critique than that of her contemporary Rebecca Harding DAVIS—has not helped. Neither has her residence in upstate New York, always given short shrift in considerations of American REGIONALISM.

BIBLIOGRAPHY: Curry, J., *M. H.* (1996); Winter, K. H., *M. H.: Life with "Josiah Allen's Wife"* (1984)

NICHOLAS BIRNS

HOLMES, Oliver Wendell

b. 29 August 1809, Cambridge, Massachusetts; d. 7 October 1894, Boston, Massachusetts

A man of distinguished New England ancestry, H. combined insatiable curiosity, diverse talents put to good use, and intellectual brilliance with a commanding presence in person and on paper. H.—who had studied law for a year, upon his graduation from Harvard College, where he was selected class poet of 1829—was in the course of his lifetime many things: a medical doctor and researcher; professor of anatomy; prizewinning medical essayist; popular poet, essayist, novelist, and biographer of Ralph Waldo EMERSON; lyceum lecturer; humorist; and member both of the intellectually and socially prominent Saturday Club and the group of leading contributors to the *Atlantic Monthly.*

The wit and conversational virtuosity that readers of his prose essays—occasionally sprinkled with his poetry—have remarked on are prominently displayed in his "Autocrat" volumes: *The Autocrat of the Breakfast-Table* (1858), *The Professor at the Breakfast-Table* (1860), *The Poet at the Breakfast-Table* (1872), and *Over the Teacups* (1891). These were assemblages of pieces written for the *Atlantic Monthly,* in which a droll, garrulous, highly intelligent and well-educated boarding house guest presides dazzlingly over the dining table, his fellow boarders serving apparently as props or foils. H.'s three novels—*Elsie Venner* (1861), *The Guardian Angel* (1867), and *A Mortal Antipathy* (1885)—deal not only with medical and psychological conditions in their characters, but with staples of popular fiction: love or lust relationships, sensational and dramatic events. H.'s deep-lying concern with poetry and with his own poetic creations is seen in his amusing treatment of the unpromising would-be poet named Gifted Hopkins, in *The Guardian Angel.*

Though not considered a major or even an outstanding poet of his century, H.—at heart an essential sentimentalist—authored one of the finest inspirational nature poems of the period: "The Chambered Nautilus" (1858); one of the subtlest satiric commentaries on narrow thinking: "The Deacon's Masterpiece; or, The Wonderful One-Hoss-Shay" (1858); and one of the most effective patriotic poems: "Old Ironsides" (1830). He frequently used simple rhyme schemes, ballad rhythms, and a variety of stanzaic and metrical forms; among the simplest patterns were the *aabb* iambic septameter quatrains in "The Ballad of the Oysterman" (1830), and the *abcbefgf* iambics in octaves of alternating tetrameters and trimeters in "My Aunt" (1831) and "Old Ironsides."

H. loved dedications, celebrations, and commemorations: "A Poem (for the) Dedication of the Pittsfield Cemetery" (1850), "A Song for the Centennial Celebration of Harvard College" (1836), "Poem for the Two Hundred and Fiftieth Anniversary of the Founding of Harvard College" (1886), "On the Death of President Garfield" (1881); he hated ultraconservatism, narrow dogmatism, spiritual self-righteousness: "The Deacon's Masterpiece," "The Moral Bully" (1850); he was intensely patriotic: "God Save the Flag" (1865), "One Country" (1865), "At a Dinner to General Grant" (1865); he was playful and broadly satirical: "My Aunt" (1831), "The Last Leaf" (1831), "Contentment" (1858), "The Height of the Ridiculous" (1830); and, among other things, he delighted in good fellowship, class reunions, and get-togethers with his peers: "The Boys" (1859), "At the Saturday Club" (1884). "Welcome to the Chicago Commercial Club" (1880). Considering all of his contributions to American culture in the larger sense, H.—whose son, Oliver Wendell Holmes, Jr., was a distinguished justice of the U.S. Supreme Court—well deserves to be remembered today.

BIBLIOGRAPHY: Hoyt, E. P., *The Improper Bostonian: Dr. O. W. H.* (1979); Small, M. R., *O. W. H.* (1962)

SAMUEL I. BELLMAN

HONGO, Garrett [Kaoru]
b. 30 May 1951, Volcano, Hawai'i

As a Yonsei (fourth-generation Japanese American), H. achieved prominence in the 1980s with his noted volumes *Yellow Light* (1982) and *The River of Heaven* (1988). Recently, his eminent status as a Pulitzer Prize-nominated American poet has been augmented by his published prose work, *Volcano: A Memoir of Hawai'i* (1995). H.'s poetry and prose are expansive, for they touch upon the personal, social, historical, and philosophical. In fact, his most successful poems contain poignant examinations of people, places, nature, heritage, and history—all under the aegis of what Robert Schultz terms "H.'s rich vocabulary and undulant syntax [that] hold his stories of loss and remembrance in a secure, distinctive music."

H. first achieved success as a writer while founder and artistic director (1975–77) of the Asian Exclusion Act theater group in Seattle, Washington. His play *Nisei Bar and Grill* (1976) looks at Korean War veterans and their postwar struggle. At this time, H. collaborated on a poetic volume with Alan Chong Lau and Lawson Fusao Inada entitled *The Buddha Bandits down Highway 99* (1978), in which he contributed the nine-part poem "Cruising 99."

Yellow Light is H.'s first poetry collection. This volume offers tender homages to Japanese American history and the working class. Mainly, he venerates the laborer—exemplified by H.'s own grandfather and father and those in poor neighborhoods who struggle daily to maintain dignity. He also records history through illuminating and bracing personal points of views. One poem entitled "Stepchild" highlights how Japanese American historical exclusion from school textbooks and discussions have affected the speaker. This forgetfulness demonstrates that Japanese Americans are misbegotten because America as a whole has not acknowledged them as Americans. The poem establishes that part of the success of the American past can be attributed to Asian laborers, many of whom were used and then ousted from the country when no longer needed. In other poems, H. explores our need not only to discern our own essences but also to generate a depth of feeling for humanity. "Roots" encourages the location of the deeper self, the dedication to its discovery, and the knowledge that there is a unique signature to all things animate and inanimate.

The need for shared common experiences and the need for dignity and escape from ridicule are themes carried over to *The River of Heaven* (1988), which won the Lamont Poetry Prize and a nomination for the Pulitzer Prize in poetry. H. retrieves memories by reconstructing the past through a collection of viewpoints. He wants to commune with departed elders, and he memorializes those gone by inhabiting specific people and characters in order to tell their stories. As a result, he records their lives so that they may continue to live.

H.'s use of parallel phrasing can be described at times as Whitmanesque; in his poetic narrative, he carefully layers words and images. H. infuses the visual with other sensate details. Also, animal imagery as well as Hawaiian legend inform his poetic impressions. Consequently, memories imbued with cultural and organic resonances display reverence for nature and its power to help people establish their own identities.

H. pays mindful consideration to the amplitude of what makes us human and connected to one another, to the past, and to nature. The need to find music in oneself is significant. His poems ask that we reexamine our detachment from ourselves, from our spirits, from each other. In fact, we sense that the soul can reach magnanimous formulations regarding the preciousness of humanity and nature. As Maxine Hong KINGSTON eloquently states, H. "extends splendor—and the sight and voice and concern of American poetry."

BIBLIOGRAPHY: Evans, A., "A Vicious Kind of Tenderness: An Interview with G. H.," *P & W* 20 (September-October 1992): 36–46; Jarman, M., "The Volcano Inside," *SoR* 32 (Spring 1996): 337-43; Schultz, R., "Passionate Virtuosity," *HudR* 17 (Spring 1989):149–57; Uba, G., "*Yellow Light*," *JEthS* 12 (1985):123–25

SUZANNE K. ARAKAWA

HOOKER, Thomas

b. ca. 7 July 1586, Markfield (Markworth), Leicestershire, England; d. 7 July 1647, Hartford, Connecticut

In recent scholarship, H. has emerged as a key architect of the Puritan Errand in New England, as a founder of congregational churches and communities in Massachusetts and Connecticut, and as a preacher and theologian, whose preparationist theology and ecclesiastical polity represent his lasting contribution to American PURITANISM and letters.

Educated at the nursery of Puritanism, Emmanuel College, Cambridge (1604–11); and appointed Fellow at Emmanuel (1609–18), H. attained a great reputation as a learned scholar, moving preacher, and vociferous nonconformist. Silenced by William Laud, later Archbishop of Canterbury, and escaping to Holland (1631), H. soon found himself at odds with the Dutch Presbyterian classis at Amsterdam and Delft. Unable to work in peace, H. removed to Newtown (Cambridge), Massachusetts (September 1633) where he was installed as pastor to a group of loyal Chelmsford settlers. Two years later, H. and his Newtown congregation left for

Connecticut against the express orders of the Massachusetts magistracy and established a new colony at Hartford (1635), where he died in 1647.

H.'s "Fundamental Orders of Connecticut" (1639) and his *A Survey of the Summe of Church-Discipline* (1648) represent his major contributions to the political development of New England. While the former served as a political compact for Connecticut in the absence of a charter, the latter represented New England's official defense of congregationalism against attacks from abroad. His major achievement, however, rests in his theological contributions to the Puritan Errand. His preparationist theology—shaped by Richard Sibbes and William Ames—received great impetus during his pastoral care at Esher, Surrey (1618–25), and at Chelmsford, Essex (1625–29). Witnessing the emotional trauma of conversion, H. discovered that many sincere believers rejected the slavific efficacy of grace because they deemed themselves irrevocably lost. His most popular sermonic text, *The Poore Doubting Christian Drawn unto Christ* (1629), delineates the contrite soul's spiritual peregrination toward the Celestial City. A milestone in H.'s developing theology of the heart, *Poore Doubting Christian* decisively breaks with Calvin's Pauline mysticism, the passive waiting for grace, by facilitating spiritual regeneration through eight distinct stages. A collected and revised edition of H.'s subsequent series of sermons on each stage appeared as *The Application of Redemption* (1656), representing H.'s consummate achievement as a preparationist.

H.'s preparationism and its influence on American literature have received increasing attention by Frank Shuffelton, Sargent Bush, Michael J. Colacurcio, and others. While Shuffelton traces H.'s influence on such later writers as Jonathan EDWARDS and Timothy DWIGHT, Bush and Colacurcio discover H.'s preparationist psychology in the works of Ralph Waldo EMERSON, Henry David THOREAU, and Nathaniel HAWTHORNE. Yet the most prolific debate still centers on H.'s supposed democratic revolt against the oppressive Puritan order in Massachusetts. Eager to trace America's democratic roots, George Bancroft, Charles Francis Adams, and Vernon L. Parrington portrayed H. as the archetypal American democrat, whose removal to Connecticut anticipated the American War of Independence. However, Perry Miller in *Errand into the Wilderness* (1956) shows that H.'s political ideas on church membership and the franchise were hardly less oppressive than the Bay's policies. Shuffelton and Bush, H.'s most recent biographers, take a middle ground in this debate, both asserting that H. is more important as a preacher and theologian of the heart than as a Puritan politician or seed-time democrat. The development of H.'s conversion morphology and the definition of Puritan orthodoxy have received renewed attention by a number of recent critics who are again probing the assumptions of Miller's *Orthodoxy in Massachusetts* (1933; rev. ed., 1965).

BIBLIOGRAPHY: Ball, J. H., *Chronicling The Soul's Windings: T. H. and His Morphology of Conversion* (1992); Bozeman, T. D., *To Live Ancient Lives: The Primitivist Dimension in Puritanism* (1988); Bush, S., *The Writings of T. H.: Spiritual Adventure in Two Worlds* (1980); Cohen, C. L., *God's Caress: The Psychology of Puritan Religious Experience* (1986); Delbanco, A., *The Puritan Ordeal* (1989); Hall, D. D., *The Antinomian Controversy, 1636–1638: A Documentary History* (1968); Knight, J., *Orthodoxy in Massachusetts: Rereading American Puritanism* (1994); Pettit, N., *The Heart Prepared: Grace and Conversion in Puritan Spiritual Life* (1966, 1989); Shuffelton, F., *T. H.: 1586–1647* (1977); Williams, G. H., et al., eds., *T. H.: Writings in England and Holland, 1626–1633* (1975)

REINER SMOLINSKI

HOOPER, Johnson Jones

b. 9 June 1815, Wilmington, North Carolina; d. 7 June 1862, Richmond, Virginia

The H. canon includes six books of humor, mostly concerned with the adventures of his most illustrious character "Simon Suggs," and a number of uncollected works published in American periodicals. As a humorist, H. has consistently drawn the attention of small numbers of important publishers like William Trotter Porter and critics like Eugene Current-García. His most enduring work remains *Some Adventures of Captain Simon Suggs, Late of the Tallapoosa Volunteers* (1845).

After the financial exigencies of his genteel family left him in straightened circumstances (much like those of his own hero) in Wilmington, H., departed for the flush times of Alabama. In 1843, H. published his humorous story "Taking the Census in Alabama," signing his column "By a Chicken Man of 1840." The article was reprinted by William Trotter Porter on September 9, 1843 in *Spirit of the Times* and later included in *Some Adventures of Captain Simon Suggs*. The latter contains about twelve stories that form a very loose novel based upon the character of Bird H. Young, Tallapoosa County, Alabama.

Simon Suggs is the result of at least three major influences—the picaresque, the frontier, and oral literatures. As a picaro, Suggs provided his creator with an ideal opportunity to satirize the excesses of an American society increasingly well known for its extremes. In particular, the picaresque shape of the novel allowed H. to burlesque the popular campaign biographies of Andrew Jackson by Amos Kendall and John Henry Eaton. In effect, Suggs became the most finely developed trickster in Southern literature before George Washington HARRIS's Sut Luvingood.

Much of the political satire is aimed at Jackson's victory in 1813 over the Creek Indians and over the British in 1815 at the Battle of New Orleans. Both events, to frontiersmen, were baseless propaganda greatly blown out of proportion in order to elect Jackson. Suggs, like Jackson, is a CONFIDENCE MAN who runs for public office (as sheriff), and his episodic adventures constitute his campaign biography.

An appropriate portion of the satire is directed at American life as represented in a frontier ethic where men are "free to act out their impulses, whether good or bad." Suggs learns in his youth that rascality will triumph over "innocence and unsophistication," and every episode demonstrates that ethic, including the best known "Captain Simon Suggs Attends a Camp Meeting," which Samuel Langhorne CLEMENS borrowed as the basis for chapter 20 of *Adventures of Huckleberry Finn*. The satire on religious enthusiasm in the South draws much of its sophistication from Johnathan Swift's "Essay on the Mechanical Operation of the Spirit." The Swiftian satire paves the way for later writers like Flannery O'CONNOR.

Suggs embodies a good deal of the southern spirit in fiction and may, indeed, be the prototype for many later southern characters such as Ty Ty Walden in Erskine CALDWELL's *God's Little Acre* or Miss Amelia Lymon in Carson MCCULLERS's *Ballad of the Sad Cafe*. Such characters move in a nonconventional world, Suggs becoming the major literary figure in his day, not from the Genteel Tradition.

Suggs, moreover, brought Thackeray to judge H. as the most promising contemporary writer in America. Eugene Current-García sees H. as the origin of the best moments of southern writing ever published in *Spirit of the Times*. Suggs himself shares a literary ancestry with the characters of Ring LARDNER and William FAULKNER.

BIBLIOGRAPHY: Hoole, W. S., *Alias Simon Suggs: The Life and Times of J. J. H.* (1952); Hubbell, J. B., *The South in American Literature* (1954); Lynn, K. S., *Mark Twain and Southwestern Humor* (1959); McIlwaine, S., *The Southern Poor-White from Lubberland to Tobacco Road* (1939); Somers, P., Jr., *J. J. H.* (1984)

GEORGE LONGEST

HOPKINS, Pauline [Elizabeth]

b. 1895, Portland, Maine; d. 23 August 1930, Cambridge, Massachusetts

Though she is best known for her serialized novels, H.'s wide-ranging creative efforts also included three plays—*Colored Aristocracy* (1877), *Slaves' Escape; or, The Underground Railroad* (1879), a musical that was also called *Peculiar Sam,* and a biblical drama entitled *One Scene from the Drama of Early Days*—as well as concerts, lectures, and dramatic performances. H. supported her creative and literary efforts by working as a stenographer, and from 1903 to 1904 she worked as literary editor for the *Colored American Magazine.*

In 1900, H. published her short story "The Mystery within Us" in the inaugural issue of *The Colored American,* the first of many contributions she would make to the Boston-based publication. The journal serialized much of the fiction that has recently been published as full-length novels, including *Winona: A Tale of Negro Life in the South and Southwest* (1902); *Of One Blood; or, The Hidden Self* (1902); and *Hagar's Daughter* (1901–2).

Race, blood and complex family relationships occupy central positions in all of H.'s novels. Through the devices of mistaken identity, disguise, renaming and adoption, H. confounds the distinctions between black and white, slave and free, noble and base that might order the societies she depicts, implicitly arguing that the U.S. is a mulatto nation. The consequences of denying this mulatto nationhood explode in all of H.'s novels. For instance, in *Contending Forces* (1900), H.'s only nonserialized novel, the mysterious Sappho cannot escape a past of slavery and rape, while in *Of One Blood,* denying miscegenation means unknowingly participating in incestuous marriages.

While it essentially asserts that the notion of fixed racial identity is untenable, H.'s fiction also contends that qualities like character and class are carried by blood from one generation to the next. Thus, we often see children who demonstrate the class-based tendencies for good or evil that their parents pass along to them, especially in *Winona* and *Hagar's Daughter.*

H's serious and complex treatment of race, class, and gender identity is frequently obscured when she introduces the element of magical psychic connections or meets formulaic demands for happy endings, wronged lovers, and all-too-obvious concealed identities. Yet, as a prolific writer targeting a specifically African American audience, H. produced work that stands as an important contribution to the wide range of popular fiction published in the early 20th c.

BIBLIOGRAPHY: Carby, H. V., *Reconstructing Womanhood* (1987); Shockley, A., "P. E. H.: A Biographical Excursion into Obscurity," *Phylon* 33 (1972): 22–26; Pryse, M., and H. J. Spillers, eds., *Conjuring: Black Women, Fiction, and Literary Tradition* (1985); Washington, M., ed., *Invented Lives* (1987)

                                    BETSY KLIMASMITH

HOPKINSON, Francis

b. 2 October 1737, Philadelphia, Pennsylvania; d. 9 May 1791, Philadelphia, Pennsylvania

While known today primarily for his humorous writings in the Pennsylvania press in support of the American Revolution, H. had a varied career, as public servant, poet, musician, and composer. Many of his writings are collected in *Miscellaneous Essays and Occasional Writings* (1792), which he had assembled at the time of his death.

A member of the first graduating class of the College of Philadelphia (1757), H. was part of a group of friends interested in the arts, including painter Benjamin West and poet Nathaniel Green who had studied there under William SMITH. After traveling to London in 1766 in the hope of obtaining a position, H. returned to Philadelphia, where he worked primarily in the law. H. would become a member of the Continental Congress in 1776, and a signer of the Declaration of Independence; he was judge of the Admiralty for Philadelphia from 1779 to 1789; and he was a federal judge between 1789 and 1791. He remained active in the cultural life of Philadelphia throughout his life, serving as the organist at St. Peter's Church, performing as a musician (he played the harpsichord and the flute), setting up musical evenings, composing songs, and publishing essays on music. His controversial essay, *The Lawfulness of Instrumental Musick* (1763), defended the place of organ music at church services, and was satirized in the Philadelphia Press. His song, "My Days have been so wondrous free" (1759), for which he set music to a poem by Thomas Parnell, was, he would later claim, the first secular music written by an American composer. His *The Temple of Minerva,* which H. called an "oratorial entertainment," has also been labeled the first American opera; it celebrated the American cause and was performed for George Washington in Philadelphia on December 11, 1781. H.'s *Seven Songs* (1788), for which he wrote both music and words, was dedicated to Washington. H. also delivered a paper in front of the American Philosophical Society describing "An Improved Method of Tonguing a Harpsichord," which would appear in the *Columbian* in 1787. Over the years, he published numerous poems in the Philadelphia press, including the *American, Pennsylvania,* and the *Columbian* magazines.

Much of H.'s literary reputation is based on his contributions to the patriotic press during the Revolutionary War and the years immediately following. His satiric sketches, published under such pseudonyms as "Peter Grievous" and "An Old Bachelor," are reminiscent of Benjamin FRANKLIN's revolutionary writings. The first and most well known of these was a short pamphlet that appeared in 1774 entitled *A Pretty Story, Written in the Year of our Lord 1774, by Peter Grievous, Esq., A. B. C. D. E.* This was a humorous allegory in which a treacherous stepmother and her lover, representing Parliament and the prime minister, deceive and cheat a nobleman and his sons, representing the King and the colonies. Another popular lampoon, "British Valour Displayed: The Battle of the Kegs" appeared in the *Pennsylvania Packet* during the occupation of Philadelphia by the British (1778); it mocked the British army's bumbling overreaction to some mines floating down the Delaware River. H. returned to the *Pennsylvania Packet* to defend the new Constitution, most memorably in "A New Roof," another humorous allegory that describes the proposed new government as a piece of architecture.

BIBLIOGRAPHY: Hastings, G. E., *The Life and Works of F. H.* (1965); Silverman, K., *A Cultural History of the American Revolution* (1976); Sonneck, O. G. T., *F. H., the First American Poet-Composer, 1737–1791, and James Lyon, Patriot, Preacher, Psalmalist, 1735-1794* (1905); Zall, P. M., ed., *Comical Spirit of Seventy-Six: The Humor of F. H.* (1976)

LAURA HENIGMAN

HORGAN, Paul

b. 1 August 1903, Buffalo, New York; d. 8 March 1995, Middletown, Connecticut

H.'s long and prolific writing career produced short stories, novels, histories, and biographies. Beginning with the publication of his first novel, *The Fault of Angels* (1933), H. produced on the average a book every eighteen months. He was twice awarded the Pulitzer Prize, first in 1955 for the historical epic, *Great River: The Rio Grande in American History,* then in 1975 for *Lamy of Santa Fe,* the biography of an antislavery, pro-Indian pioneer bishop. His historical works are the result of tireless research and are characterized by a majestic tone and attention to detail.

Early in his life, H.'s family moved from Buffalo, New York to Albuquerque, New Mexico due to his father's tuberculosis. The Southwest, with its strong Spanish-Catholic influence and sparsely populated landscape of sweeping vistas, became to young H. "tierra encantada," the land of enchantment. This region would be his favorite subject and setting.

Viewed by many as primarily a Catholic writer and regionalist—attributes that may account for his being excluded from the list of America's foremost 20th-c. writers—H. was a traditionalist who, as critic John Barkham wrote in the *New York Post* (September 29,

1970), had the "sensibilities of a generation that valued elegance, symmetry, and morality."

His collection of short stories, *The Return of the Weed* (1936), explores the themes of growth, decay, and death with finely wrought characters battling the harsh, unrelenting forces of nature in the American Southwest. They are stories in which families, their efforts, and constructions crumble and disintegrate. "We can learn from the past," H. states in the introduction, "by thinking about its lingering walls, built by men along their way through wilderness. The men are taken by life or death, and their houses stay until the weather and weed render dust." The collection concludes optimistically as the final story, "The Star," sees the protagonist shake off the New Mexico dust and move on.

The collection to follow, *Figures in a Landscape* (1940), similarly juxtaposes the central characters with the malignant figures and harsh environment of the American desert. The wild, unforgiving desert represents an increasingly hectic America and H. seems to express regret at the loss of a simpler, tamer past, a past in which human beings felt for one another. H.'s characters strive to retain their civility and dignity in the midst of cruelty and chaos.

H. further probes these themes in a later collection, *The Peach Stone* (1967), showing starkly realistic characters questing for stability in an ever-changing America. The title story—widely anthologized and considered by many H.'s best—portrays a family grieving over the loss of their young girl killed by burning tumbleweeds. They are accompanied by a Miss Arlene Latcher on the four hour drive to the burial and the characters struggle with issues of solace and repressed emotions. Arlene is stunted in her efforts to comfort the family and becomes herself the object of healing tenderness. In this, she embodies the peach stone—pruned and externally dried, yet possessing the seed of life within. "Black Snowflakes," one of the last major stories in the collection, continues the theme of life and death as a young boy confronts the passing of his grandfather. The presence of youth and old age completes the circle of life.

His regionalism notwithstanding, H.'s formative years in New Mexico served him well as those critics with whom he found favor consider the distinct flavor of his characters an enhancement to his work. His themes are universal and his writings are considered a valuable contribution to the American canon.

BIBLIOGRAPHY: Day, J., *P. H.* (1967); Gish, R., *P. H.* (1983); Morrison, R. W., "P. H.," in Kimbel, B. E., ed., *DLB*, vol. 102, *American Short Story Writers, 1910–1945* (1991): 171–76

JASON MCMAHON

HOROVITZ, Israel
b. 31 March 1939, Wakefield, Massachusetts

After studying at London's prestigious Royal Academy of Dramatic Arts and at the City University of New York, H. embarked on successful and highly prolific writing career, which, thus far, has produced several books, nearly a dozen teleplays, two dozen screenplays, and more than fifty plays in the past forty years.

A precocious author, who penned his first novel at age twenty-three, H. is a versatile playwright with a vast knowledge of the theater. He blends a wide variety of theatrical styles and traditions from the somber realism of Bertolt Brecht to the modernist psychodrama of Eugene O'NEILL to the postmodern absurdism of Samuel Beckett, Harold Pinter, Eugène Ionesco, and Edward ALBEE. He is a highly energetic and competitive playwright—especially competitive with O'Neill, it has often been observed—whose work has grown darker, more realistic and psychoanalytical over time. H.'s work is characterized by superior dialogue, social consciousness, and a tenuous balance between the comic and the terrifying.

Helplessness and alienation are common themes in H.'s plays, as is the notion that violence is the direct result of the futility associated with these sensations. The menacing forces in H.'s works are often everyday objects and jejune colloquial speech, further dislocating both reader and character. His dark allegorical comedy highlights the poignancy of failure and the basic human quest for answers, even as it mythologizes the past and dreads the future. It has engendered comparisons with O'Neill, Beckett, and even Edgar Allan POE. Also in the tradition of Beckett, H. suggests the potentially powerful and disruptive function of memory, and effects a delicate balance between fantasy and reality. In the postmodern tradition, H. has favored self-sustaining fictions in which the characters are functional expressions of social dislocation. Many of his plays focus on Jewish themes, and many more concern his beloved New England.

Early in his career, H. enjoyed much success writing one-act plays such as the minimalistic *Line,* the violent *The Indian Wants the Bronx, Rats,* and *It's Called the Sugar Plum,* collected in *First Season* (1968). His series plays, such as the Wakefield cycle, comprised of *Alfred the Great* (1972), *Our Father's Failing* (1973), and *Alfred Dies* (1977) and the Quanapowitt quartet of *Hopscotch* (1974), *Spared* (1975), *Stage Directions* (1976), and *The 75th* (1976) are also among his best known. In 1975, H. enjoyed much success with *The Primary English Class,* an hilarious linguistic comedy in the absurdist tradition of Beckett and Ionesco. His collaboration with playwrights Terrence MCNALLY and Leonard Melfi has yielded a number of works dating back to *Morning, Noon, and Night* in 1968. *Unexpected Tenderness* (1994), deals with a Jewish blue-collar family living in the shadow of an abusive father in the 1950s.

H.'s works have been produced worldwide and translated into dozens of languages. For his efforts, he has been the recipient of numerous awards, including a Drama Desk, an Obie, and a National Academy of Arts and Letters Literature award. In 1965, he was the Royal Shakespeare Company's playwright in residence. From 1967 through the mid-1970s, H. taught at a number of colleges, and received an honorary doctor of arts degree from Salem State University in 1991. And from 1971 through 1977, he wrote a column for *Magazine Literaire* in Paris. In 1975, H. founded the New York Playwrights Lab to develop new plays, and four years later founded the Gloucester Stage Company in his hometown of Gloucester, Massachusetts.

BIBLIOGRAPHY: Kane, L., ed., *I. H.: A Collection of Critical Essays* (1994); Kovac, K. P., "I. H.," in MacNicholas, J., ed., *DLB,* vol. 7, part 1, *Twentieth-Century American Dramatists* (1981): 301–8

ERIC MARSHALL

HORTON, George Moses
b. 1797?, Northampton County, North Carolina; d. 1883?

H. was a 19th-c. slave poet who appeared on the literary scene over half a century after the first black poet, Phillis WHEATLEY, had her poems published in the late 18th c. H. was born into slavery in Northampton County, North Carolina, where his duties involved farm work. At an early age, he began to display an interest and talent for poetry; and although he had learned to read, H. delivered his verses orally from memory because he still had not mastered the skill of writing.

By the time H. was twenty years old, he was creating love verses and receiving payment for them from students at Chapel Hill. His student clients sometimes paid him with books that introduced H. to the great classical writers, including Shakespeare, Milton, and Lord Byron. H.'s reading of these authors' works proved very influential to the young man who began to compose his poetry in a style reminiscent of the great writers of England.

Eventually, H.'s thirst for the written word resulted in his ability to write. In this, he was assisted by a Chapel Hill professor's wife, Caroline Lee HENTZ, who also enabled him to publish some of his poetry. Thereafter, H. attracted a number of benefactors who encouraged his writing and sought to purchase his freedom.

In 1829, H. became the first African American Southerner to publish a book, and it was titled *The Hope of Liberty*. The collection of poems centers on themes that are mainly romantic and spiritual, but a few of the selections reveal H.'s own emotional struggles. The poem "On Hearing of the Intention of a Gentleman to Purchase a Poet's Freedom" is especially poignant as it demonstrates H.'s deep yearning for freedom.

In the ensuing years, H., with his master's permission, spent his time writing and working at odd jobs; and he was able to author a second book, *The Poetical Works of G. M. H., the Colored Bard of North Carolina* (1845). As in his first publication, H. makes little reference to the evils of slavery and the injustices of Southern prejudice; however, one of the best poems in this new collection describes the slave's inner torment as he is being sold at the auction block.

Near the end of the Civil War, H. was befriended by a Union Army captain who helped him to publish his final volume of poems, *Naked Genius* (1865). Now a free man, H. wrote more openly of the detrimental effects of the recently abolished slave institution. However, although he reflects on his personal feelings in "G. M. H., Myself," most of the poems do not divert from his usually rendered work, which reveals a traditional form and style inspired by the classical mode—comprising elements of mythological allusions, use of personification, and a preference for abstract diction.

In later years, H. resided in Philadelphia. He ceased to publish additional poetry after he gained his freedom, a fact that critics suggest was caused by his identification for so long as the "colored bard of North Carolina." H. is believed to have died in 1883, but the date and place of his death are uncertain.

BIBLIOGRAPHY: Sherman, J. R., *Invisible Poets* (1989); Walser, R., *The Black Poet: The Story of G. M. H., A North Carolina Slave* (1966)

ANGELO COSTANZO

HOUGH, Emerson

b. 28 June 1857, Newton, Iowa; d. 30 April 1923, Evanston, Illinois

With thirty four major works to his name, including children's books, novels, poems, plays, and nonfiction, H. was on of early 20th c.'s most prolific writers. He was a hardworking journalist, novelist, historian, and conservationist whose work not only helped define the Southwest's character and promote western American literature, but literally saved much of the natural landscape and resources. He counted conservationist and President Theodore ROOSEVELT among his friends and his writings persuaded Congress to pass an act protecting Yellowstone Park's buffalo. H. loved and sought to protect the West, the region that captured his romantic imagination. To him, it was an idyllic land of freedom where men's honor kept order. His novels' heroes were mostly cowboys and the like defending against Indian attacks, eastern capitalists, and women's wiles.

In his twenties, H. spent some years in New Mexico. There, he developed an interest in journalism and the West. H. began his writing career as a journalist for San Francisco's *Golden Era* and sent descriptive sporting pieces to periodicals such as *Field and Stream*. He described the West as the place where he got his first impressions of life and this setting would serve as the stage for some of his most popular work.

The Story of the Cowboy (1897), a nonfiction account of those rugged romantic men, describes stampedes, rustlers, and life on the cattle trail. He contributed articles and short stories to many periodicals and became so closely identified with the West, Albert Lee of *Collier's* wrote to H., "we feel as if we could hardly issue our Western number without insisting on having something from you in it."

The Mississippi Bubble (1902), the story of a handsome gambling man and his travails, was H.'s novel to achieve recognition. H.'s formula of interfacing characters with actual historical events and figures worked well and he seldom strayed from it. His themes centered around the principles of honor and character. In *The Magnificent Adventure* (1916), Meriwether Lewis is put to the test—Colonel Burr uses his beautiful daughter to charm the protagonist, to persuade him to abandon his expedition to the Pacific. The protagonist resists temptation, and fulfills his duty to Thomas JEFFERSON. Upon his return, Jefferson congratulates him: "It was honor saved you—your personal honor—that was what brought us success. No country is bigger than the personal honor of its gentlemen."

The Covered Wagon (1922)—a successful novel later adapted to film—explores similar themes as pioneers must not only face struggles against untamed nature and wild Indians, but internal enemies such as greed, egotism, and malice.

H.'s formulaic plots and romanticism of the West at times border on silly, but his status as a key figure in American frontier writing is unquestionable.

BIBLIOGRAPHY: Stone, L. A., *E. H.: His Place in American Letters* (1925); White, P., "E. H.," in Marline, J. J., ed., *DLB,* vol. 9, *American Novelists, 1910–1945* (1981): 141–45; Wylder, D. E., *E. H.* (1981)

JASON MCMAHON

HOUSTON, Velina [Avisa] Hasu
b. 1957, Tokyo, Japan

H. describes her interest in Japanese war brides as "both personal and political." An extremely prolific playwright and screenwriter, she also lectures and writes essays on drama, multiracial identity and Japanese and Japanese American cultures. Her works include *Amerasian Girls* (1983), *The Legend of Bobby Chicago* (1985), *Christmas Cake* (1990), and *Broken English* (1991). Reflecting both artistic and cultural diversity, H.'s plays blend Japanese and Western theater techniques and poetry with historical accuracy and fantasy. Her most well-known plays recount the relationship between her Japanese mother and father, an African and Native American GI; they met and married in Japan while her father was stationed with the U.S. Army. Moving beyond family history, H.'s work encompasses the history of Japanese American relations and confronts issues of multiculturalism, often criticizing the inability to accommodate diversity.

Tea (1987), the last play of a trilogy that includes *Asa Ga Kimashita (Morning Has Broken)* (1980) and *American Dreams* (1983), is her most famous play. Set in 1960s Kansas where H. spent her childhood, it explores the lives of five Japanese "war brides": Setsuko (named after and based on H.'s own mother), Himiko, Chizuye, Teruko, and Atsuko. The women unite after Himiko kills her husband and commits suicide. The play's title refers to the women's ritual of taking tea, which brings them together and forces them to reflect on their common life experiences. While Himiko was alive, all but Setsuko ignored her and the reasons behind her bizarre behavior. To illuminate Himiko's troubled life, H. has each of the women alternately transform into their respective husbands and teenage daughters. Through the dialogue of these family members, H. demonstrates America's inability to embrace and understand other cultures. Finally acknowledging the abuse suffered by Himiko, the surviving women come to recognize it as a reflection of their own emotional alienation and cultural dislocation.

Like *Tea, Asa Ga Kimashita* and *American Dreams* develop H.'s personal experience to encompass larger issues. Against the background of the U.S. post–World War II occupation of Japan, *Asa Ga Kimashita* suggests the problems of imperialism while describing her Japanese mother's decision to marry and leave Japan. Although H. criticizes the Japanese feudal system for oppressing women and the lower classes, she also denounces the insensitivity of Americans when

enforcing economic reforms. The portrayal of Setsuko's father is sympathetic; he relates his daughter's affection for a U.S. serviceman to Japan's defeat and the loss of his material wealth. His inability to accept the loss of power, on personal and national levels, and eventual suicide cast a shadow on the love story. *American Dreams* follows the newlyweds to America where Creed introduces Setsuko to his family in New York. Much to his surprise, his family disapproves of his interracial marriage, making Creed realize the "melting pot" idea is merely a myth. Both plays suggest America's oppression of racial others while exploring the problems inherent in monoracial and monocultural ideologies.

Not all of H.'s plays narrate events directly from her life, nor do they all focus on Japanese Americans. *Necessities,* for example, concerns a white American woman; however, like the rest of H.'s oeuvre, it explores issues of culture and race.

BIBLIOGRAPHY: Kawarazaki, Y., "Women's Struggles in V. H. H.'s *Tea,*" *AALA Journal* 2 (1995): 47–55; Uno, R., ed., *Unbroken Thread* (1993)

LINDA TRINH MOSER

HOVEY, Richard
b. 4 May 1864, Normal, Illinois; d. 24 February 1900, New York City

Though now viewed as a decidedly minor poet, H. was hugely popular during the 1890s, admired for poems about comradeship, convivial drinking, and the carefree life of the vagabond. Largely forgotten today is that H. was also a dramatist, an essayist keenly interested in the craft of poetry, and a translator of French symbolist writers. Moreover, revealed by poems, plays, and letters, he was a supporter of women's rights.

Critics often remark on H.'s indebtedness to Walt WHITMAN. Whitman undoubtedly did influence H., as can be seen in the latter's celebration of free-spirited wandering, masculine fellowship, and broad-minded sexual attitudes, but Whitman's impact was finally less than that of such poets as Sidney LANIER, Algernon Swinburne, Rudyard Kipling, and Thomas William Parsons. It was also less than that of Fabian Society founder Thomas Davidson.

From 1881 to 1885, H. attended Dartmouth College, where he was an honor student and a flamboyant member of the Psi Upsilon fraternity. Out of his experiences here came some of his best-known poems— "Men of Dartmouth," "Hanover Winter Song," and "A Stein Song." Eventually his college verses would be posthumously published as *Dartmouth Lyrics* (1924), and Dartmouth would embrace H. as its poet laureate.

In 1887, H. met Canadian-born poet Bliss Carman and artist Thomas Meteyard, with whom he made a walking tour of New England. Seven years later, in collaboration with Carman, and with Meteyard as cover designer, H. published *Songs from Vagabondia* (1894), his most acclaimed book. This collection was followed by several others containing poems by both H. and Carman: *More Songs from Vagabondia* (1896) and *Last Songs from Vagabondia* (1900). Proclaiming the joys of life along the open road, out in nature, or in the tavern, the poems in these three volumes effectively defied the polite poetic sentiments esteemed by proponents of the genteel tradition.

While working on his *Vagabondia* volumes, H. was also engaged in writing an ambitious cycle of plays entitled *Poem in Dramas*. Based on the Arthurian legends, the cycle would ultimately consist of three trilogies. However, his career cut short by early death, H. was able to complete only four of the nine parts of this verse drama: *Launcelot and Guenevere* (1891), *The Marriage of Guenevere* (1895), *The Birth of Galahad* (1898), and *Taliesin* (1899). Conspicuous in these plays is a conflict between the laws of society and the dictates of the individual conscience. Also prominent is H.'s sympathetic understanding of problems confronting the so-called new woman of 1890s America.

Three other aspects of H.'s career merit attention. Under the influence of Lanier's *The Science of English Verse,* he published in the *Independent,* between 1891 and 1894, a series of essays on poetic technique. While in France in 1895, he met various members of the symbolist movement, these encounters prompting him to publicize the movement in America and to translate plays by Maeterlinck and poems by Mallarmé and Verlaine. Finally, in 1898, he published *Along the Trail.* Featuring an ample selection of his earlier verse as well as late poems touting the Spanish-American War, it is, perhaps, H.'s most representative volume.

Unfortunately, much of H.'s poetry is characterized by heavy reliance on literal statement and an overweening concern with technique. His place in American poetry roughly resembles that of an earlier poet, Philip FRENEAU, for H., like Freneau, was one whose ideas and attitudes were more compelling than the poetic forms in which he expressed them.

BIBLIOGRAPHY: Linneman, W. R., *R. H.* (1976); Macdonald, A. H., *R. H.: Man & Craftsman* (1957)

DONALD D. KUMMINGS

HOWARD, Bronson [Crocker]
b. 7 October 1842, Detroit, Michigan; d. 5 August 1908, New York City

Among H.'s important plays are *Saratoga* (1870), *Hurricanes* (perf. 1878, pub. 1941), *The Banker's Daughter* (perf. 1873, pub. 1878), *Young Mrs. Winthrop* (1882), *The Henrietta* (1887), *Shenandoah* (perf. 1888, pub. 1897), and *Aristocracy* (perf. 1892, pub. 1898). A significant element in H.'s comedies was his interest in how business and social pressures influenced individuals. He was among the first to incorporate into the drama the role of the business man in American society and his impact on those around him. H. broadened his views on business and social pressures to include European and American characters and settings, thus giving his plays an international flavor.

Although not as gifted a writer as Henry JAMES, H., like the novelist, strove to create complex individuals with strong inner lives who were capable of growth in a complex, demanding social environment. Several women in his plays come closest to being examples of such characters: Lilian Westbrook of *The Banker's Daughter,* Ruth Winthrop of *Young Mrs. Winthrop,* Gertrude Ellingham of *Shenandoah.* He was also capable of writing some of the best social satire in our drama. *Saratoga* is a sprightly, early farce, but *The Henrietta* is a forceful and telling satire on the businessman and his machinations on Wall Street.

Although H. was moving in the direction of greater realism, he was not so much a realist as a romantic. his characters are often motivated by sentiment, and he frequently uses children, symbols of innocence unadulterated by social chicanery, to touch the heart of the audience or to move characters to moral action. Nor did he resist melodramatic touches. In *Shenandoah,* a play about the conflict between love and loyalty to one's country, he weaves in a dying child and a melodramatic villain. His strength lay in his ability to create characters who can rise above selfishness and the demands of a materialistic world.

H. is often cited as representing the "profession of dramatist" as opposed to the journeyman playwright. A man who took his craft seriously, he formed the American Dramatist Club (1891), and set forth in *The Autobiography of a Play* (1914) a dramatic theory for what makes a "satisfactory" play. According to H., common sense and honesty are the fundamental guides to effective dramatic construction. The first duty of the playwright is to put on stage the best work he can; he must deal with subjects of universal interest and do so with honesty and sincerity. H.'s works stand as significant advance in the evolution of American social comedy.

BIBLIOGRAPHY: Halline, A. G., *American Plays* (1935); Meserve, W. J., *An Outline History of American Drama* (1965); Quinn, A. H., *A History of the American Drama from the Civil War to the Present Day* (1927)

EDMUND M. HAYES

HOWARD, Richard
b. 13 October 1929, Cleveland, Ohio

Widely known as a distinguished translator, H. has also produced an estimable body of poetry and criticism. In his poems as well as his translations, he has always been disciplined and fastidious about language—perhaps this came from his having begun as a lexicographer. His poems, like Robert Browning's, often dramatize the historicity of voice and knowledge, striving to embody the past in the tone and timbre of his personae, whether these are imaginary or, as is often the case, historical. As a translator, he has succeeded in recasting French literature into English without obscuring the provenance of the originals, or their formal properties. In some ways, one could say that all of H.'s work is "translation," either between one language to another or between past and present. H.'s interest in the relation between past and present also led to his *Preferences: 51 American Poets Choose Poems from Their Own Work and from the Past* (1974, with the photographer Thomas Victor), a collection of essays in which contemporary writers speak of their relations to their poetic forbears, with H.'s own comments on the choices.

H.'s translations—there are over one hundred—include many of the masterworks of 20th-c. French literature, from novels (particularly the *nouveau roman)* to poetry, drama, and criticism. He first made his mark with Alain Robbe-Grillet's *The Voyeur* (1958)—followed by a host of other translations of Robbe-Grillet's fiction and essays over the next three decades—and has since translated such diverse authors as André Breton, Michel Butor, André Gide, Jean Genet, Jean Cocteau, Roland Barthes, Tzvetan Todorov, Marguerite YOURCENAR, and many others. His widely acclaimed English version of Charles Baudelaire's *Les Fleurs du mal* in 1983 won H. the American Book Award.

H.'s poetry, while sometimes overshadowed by his work as a translator, has also been highly praised. His first two books of poems, *Quantities* (1962) and *The Damages* (1967), have been together reissued as *Quantities/Damages: Early Poems* (1984). His next book, *Untitled Subjects* (1969), was awarded the Pulitzer Prize, and he has published seven further collections of poetry. *Untitled Subjects* contains fifteen dramatic monologues spoken by 19th-c. British writers and public figures. In *Two-Part Inventions* (1974), H. gives us imaginary dialogues, often between famous personages: between Walt WHITMAN and Oscar Wilde, for example, or Rodin and a passing stranger. His *Misgivings* (1979) contains, in addition to occasional

poems, poetic commentaries by such figures as Sarah Bernhardt and Victor Hugo as they seem in their portraits by the photographer Nadar. *Lining Up* (1983) and *Like Most Revelations* (1994) continue the Nadar series as well as H.'s experimentation with dramatic monologues and fictional dialogues, exploring the psychology of creation and the biographical dimension of artistic success and failure.

In addition to his work as a poet and translator, H. has served as poetry editor of *New American Review, Shenandoah,* and the *New Republic,* as well as the editor of *Best American Poetry 1995.* He has been an astute observer of the American literary scene, and many of his critical essays have been collected in *Alone with America* (1969; rev. ed., 1980), which reflects H.'s fascination and admiration for the generation of poets including John ASHBERY, James MERRILL, Robert CREELEY, A. R. AMMONS, Kenneth KOCH, Richard HUGO, and Denise LEVERTOV, among others, who were and are, like H. himself, the immediate heirs of Anglo-American high modernism—it is not insignificant that *Alone with America* is dedicated to Ezra POUND and W. H. AUDEN. In his criticism as in his poetry, H. values that which is cerebral, formal, erudite, witty, inventive, and elegant, finding some of these virtues even in work—such as the poems of Allen GINSBERG and Paul GOODMAN—where others might not. It is no coincidence that H., like Ashbery and Frank O'HARA, also has a strong fascination with the visual arts, and has written a number of catalogue essays and introductions, including one for the 1988 Robert Mapplethorpe exhibition at the Whitney Museum in New York.

BIBLIOGRAPHY: Gray, P. H., "A Conversation with R. H.," *LitP* 2 (November 1981): 76–88; Mann, P., "The Translator's Voice: An Interview with R. H.," *TRev* 9 (1982): 5–15; Summers, C. J., and T.-L. Petworth, "'We Join the Fathers': Time and the Maturing of R. H.," *ConP* 3 (1978): 13–35

JOHN BOENING

HOWARD, Sidney [Coe]
b. 26 June 1891, Oakland, California; d. 23 August 1939, Tyringham, Massachusetts

After a youthful string of attempts to write (mostly unpublished, unperformed, and lost) verse drama on such figures as Phaedra and Francis of Assisi, H. fell under the influence of French playwright Charles Vildrac, whose humane and understated realism inspired H. to write *They Knew What They Wanted* (1925), whose compassionate treatment of an Italian vineyard owner who marries a young mail-order bride and accepts her illegitimate offspring as his own impressed its audiences as a distinctively modern step away from traditional codes of poetic justice. The play exhibited the qualities most admired by critics throughout H.'s career; a careful and evocative rendering of its milieu in realistic terms, rich characterizations, and a deft mingling of comic and melodramatic elements. Although highly regarded both as a playwright and screenwriter during his lifetime, most of H.'s work has been forgotten, and he is best known for his screenplay for *Gone with the Wind* (1939). In the theater, his work is now seldom performed, and audiences generally know H. only through Frank Loesser's musical adaptation of *They Knew What They Wanted* entitled *The Most Happy Fella* (1956).

With his "dramatic biography," *Lucky Sam McCarver* (1925), H. not only rejected the well-made dramaturgy that still dominated American realistic drama in favor of an episodic form that demanded that audiences infer what happened between scenes, but also built his drama around two fundamentally unsympathetic characters—a degenerate society lady and a ruthlessly ambitious gangster. With scenes ranging from a speakeasy to a Venetian palazzo, the play remains one of the most unsentimental and least formulaic dramas of the 1920s. Like the gangster McCarver, H.'s most memorable characters share a singlemindedness that is often rendered harshly: the conniving bootlegger in *Ned McCobb's Daughter* (1926), the desperately driven musicians of *Alien Corn* (1933), and most famously, Mrs. Phelps, the monstrously manipulative mother of his most Freudian play, *The Silver Cord* (1926). In these plays, moral absolutism and single-mindedness are usually rejected in favor of pragmatic relativism. The major exception to this is *The Ghost of Yankee Doodle* (1937), in which weak-willed liberals prove no match for single-minded fascists.

On Broadway and in Hollywood, H. was admired for his abilities as an adaptor. He reworked novels both for the stage, such as Sinclair LEWIS's *Dodsworth* (1934), Humphrey Cobb's *Paths of Glory* (1935), and movies, such as Lewis's *Arrowsmith* (1931) and *Gone with the Wind*. He translated or adapted plays by Vildrac, Edmond Rostand, Ferenc Molnár, and Marcel Pagnol for the American stage. His most celebrated effort in this field was a boulevard comedy by Rene Fauchois, *The Late Christopher Bean* (1932), which combines H.'s talent for realistic observation with a lighthearted tone in the story of a long-suffering maid in an obnoxious family who turns out to have been the secret wife of a neglected painter whose paintings have become valuable since his death.

The last years of H.'s life were marked by efforts at historical dramas. Plays about Dred Scott, Thomas JEFFERSON, and Woodrow Wilson were all left in fragments at the time of death. His only produced historical drama, *Yellow Jack* (1934), about the conquest of yellow fever, may give the best indication of the direction in which H. was moving. Severe, highly episodic, and performed on a unit set, the play looks away from realistic scenography toward epic drama.

BIBLIOGRAPHY: Krutch, J. W., *The American Drama since 1918* (1957); White, S. H., *S. H.* (1977)

ROBERT F. GROSS

HOWE, E[dgar] W[atson]

b. 3 May 1853, near Treaty, Indiana; d. 3 October 1937, Atchison, Kansas

H., the acerbic editor of the *Atchison* [Kansas] *Globe,* wrote popular collections of aphorisms in addition to six novels. His literary reputation rests on his first book, the acclaimed early realist text *The Story of a Country Town,* which drew favorable comment from Mark TWAIN and William Dean HOWELLS. It has frequently been reprinted since H.'s self-published 1883 edition and, in spite of a melodramatic plot and stiff dialogue, remains critically admired for its anti–idealistic treatment of small-town life in the American West.

H. was a lifelong resident of the Midwest. Born in Indiana, the oldest child of his father's second marriage, he spent part of his youth accompanying his father on the preaching circuit around Missouri. Before H. reached his teens, he had found work in a print shop in Bethany, Missouri, where his father bought a newspaper. But in 1865, the father deserted the family to take up with another woman. H. left home and worked as a journeyman printer for newspapers in Iowa, Illinois, Nebraska, Wyoming, and Utah.

During a period of employment in Falls City, Nebraska, H. fell in love with Clara Frank, but he left Nebraska after an argument with his employer. In Golden, Colorado, he became co-owner of a newspaper and served as publisher-editor from 1873 to 1875. He returned to Falls City and married Clara during this period. By 1877, the family had settled in Atchison, Kansas, which would be H.'s home for the remainder of his life. He started the *Atchison Globe* that year. In 1882, after a visit from his father, he began *The Story of a Country Town,* a semiautobiographical novel dealing with unhappy lives in a fictional Missouri hamlet. H. worked on the novel at night after days at the newspaper for most of a year. The nearly 200,000-word finished manuscript was rejected several times, so H. printed it himself at the *Globe* office and sent copies to Twain and Howells, whose enthusiastic response sparked the interest of major Eastern publishers.

Though now a celebrity, H. continued to publish the *Globe,* a paper combining boosterism with stories of scandal. In addition, it featured H.'s "paragraphs," epigrammatic comments that entertained the readership while wittily espousing the editor's jaundiced views. His collection of prejudices was enormous, and many of his ideas—particularly his bitter assessments of marriage and organized religion—were not in line with those of his Midwestern audience; nevertheless, the readers overlooked H.'s rancor because he combined it with humor and a genuine fondness for the community.

H.'s later novels failed to live up to the promise of the first book. *Mystery of the Locks* (1885) attracted little attention. His third novel, *A Moonlight Boy* (1886), received some favorable notice, including a positive review from Hamlin GARLAND, whose work would be influenced by H.'s, but nothing like the acclaim awarded his maiden effort. *A Man Story* (1889) and *An Ante-Mortem Statement* (1891) both continued to address H.'s favorite misogamist theme, and *The Confession of John Whitlock, Late Preacher of the Gospel* (1891) documented religious hypocrisy. Critics dismissed all three.

In 1901, H. moved into a cottage on property behind his home, intentionally giving Clara grounds for divorce. In the next few years, he went abroad a number of times and produced several volumes of travel writings. He sold the newspaper in 1910 but began a magazine in 1911. His most successful publications, five volumes of collections of the "paragraphs" he had long written for the newspaper, appeared between 1917 and 1926; H. L. MENCKEN wrote the preface to the 1919 collection. H.'s autobiography, *Plain People,* appeared in 1929. His eyesight failing, he stopped publishing the magazine in 1933. In 1937, H. died two days after learning of the death of his former wife.

BIBLIOGRAPHY: McReynolds, W. I., "E. W. H.," in Ashley, P. J., ed., *DLB,* vol. 25, *American Newspaper Journalists, 1901–1925* (1984): 124–30; Pickett, C. M., *E. H.: Country Town Philosopher* (1968)

CAROLYN LENGEL

HOWE, Irving

b. 11 June 1920, New York City; d. 5 May 1993, New York City

One of the best known members of the so-called New York Intellectuals, H. assumed a number of roles in over forty years as a writer. His abiding interest lay in the critique of literature, especially fiction, and he practiced a criticism that extended beyond hermeneutics to embrace radical political activism. He was unrivaled as a historian of radical politics. A practitioner and promoter of socialism, he was as fierce an opponent of Stalinism and what he felt was the authoritarianism of the 1960s New Left as he was of unbridled laissez-faire politics. A skeptic and realist, he came to believe that capitalism and socialism are potentially compatible. And as a Jew, he was one of the most important memorializers of the disintegrating Jewish culture.

H. first demonstrated his belief that the function of criticism is to envision and realize democracy in his contributions to *Commentary, The Nation, Partisan Review,* and *Dissent* (which he cofounded in 1954). In his biography *Sherwood Anderson* (1951), the introductory *William Faulkner* (1952), and in what is one of his most widely read books of criticism, *Politics and the Novel* (1957), H. refined his cultural and political approach to literature. In the latter, H. attempts not to devise a new genre of fiction, but to examine the relationship between the ideological context and human experience posited in the works of roughly a dozen novelists. Criticism, H. maintained, serves not to analyze the past, but also to aid us in realizing a more humane, democratic future. H. believed that psychoanalysis is valuable in helping the critic understand certain texts, though he maintained that psychoanalysis is only one possible reading within the larger context of cultural criticism. Like others inside and outside the New York school, H. also attacked New Criticism (as well as myth criticism) for its failure to account for the historicism of literature. Like the fictional worlds that his literary criticism addresses, H.'s histories of radicalism, notably *The American Communist Party* (1957, with Lewis Coser), the first published history of the party, and *Leon Trotsky* (1978), a highly acclaimed book-length essay, treat society as a text from which may be distilled a pragmatic design for the future. Though biased by the author's own politics, these books are nonetheless regarded by many as first-rate works of history.

H. was generally ambivalent toward modern literature, which is characteristically conservative and even reactionary, and he held outright disdain for symbolism, which threatened to obliterate artistic representation, but in the 1960s he published three surveys of modernist literature, *A World More Attractive* (1963), *Literary Modernism* (1967), and *The Idea of the Modern in Literature and the Arts* (1968). Throughout these works, H. attempts to reconcile the appeal of high culture with the principles of political idealism. Of the modernists, he most admired James Joyce for affirming life while facing the nihilism and nausea of modern existence. With the other New York Intellectuals, H. was committed to a realistic aesthetic in art and the didactic, democratic function of literature. He ably discusses his own views on criticism, politics, and culture and his career as a thinker and writer in his 1982 "intellectual autobiography," entitled *A Margin of Hope.*

The last of a breed of leftist, New York, Jewish intellectuals, H. had little use for more recent leftist spokespersons such as Herbert Marcuse or for contemporary literary theory in general, which he felt went against the grain of his humanist and democratic projects. Anachronistic by the 1970s, H. nevertheless almost single-handedly kept the New York school of criticism alive throughout the 1980s and into the 1990s.

Though H. was not a "practicing" Jew, throughout his life he acknowledged and celebrated his Jewish roots. He grew up speaking Yiddish and learned English largely in New York City public schools. Beginning with his critical essays in *Partisan Review* and *Commentary* in the late 1940s, H. became one of the most important popularizers of JEWISH AMERICAN LITERATURE. He was instrumental in Isaac Bashevis SINGER's rise to fame among nonreaders of Yiddish. Among his numerous anthologies, H. edited (with Eliezer Greenberg) several anthologies of Yiddish literature, including *A Treasury of Yiddish Stories* (1954), *A Treasury of Yiddish Poetry* (1969), and *Ashes Out of Hope* (1978). His best-selling, National Book Award-winning *World of Our Fathers* (1976) attempts, in part, to recover the vanishing Yiddish sensibility by tracing the history of Eastern European Jewish immigrants to America. Critical of the watering-down of Jewish culture, H. is nevertheless hopeful toward its future.

BIBLIOGRAPHY: Krupnick, M., "I. H.," in Jay, G. S., ed., *DLB,* vol. 67, *Modern American Critics since 1955* (1988): 167–75; Leitch, V., *American Literary Criticism from the 30s to the 80s* (1988)

BRYAN L. MOORE

HOWE, Julia Ward

b. 27 May 1819, New York City; d. 17 October 1910, Newport, Rhode Island

H. fulfilled her dream of producing an important literary work with her 1861 writing of "The Battlehymn of the Republic." Though H. was prolific as a poet, dramatist, and nonfiction writer, her literary reputation has been largely based on the merit of this single poem. "The Battlehymn" became the battle cry of the beleaguered North, which was eager to see the political circumstances of the Civil War recast as a religious cause. H. created the lyrics after being challenged to "write some good words" for the tune of "John Brown's Body." In lines that she claimed were divinely inspired, H. fused the Old Testament violence of a wrathful God with the New Testament promise of a resurrection to assure Northerners that out of the sufferings of the war would come the rebirth of a redeemed nation.

H.'s literary interests were initiated in the private tutoring she received as the child of a wealthy banking family. She became well versed in "the great masters" and relied upon them as a source of inspiration. H.'s own literary ambitions, however, were frustrated after her 1843 marriage to Samuel Gridley Howe, a prominent reformer from Boston who expected his wife to devote herself exclusively to her family. In 1853, he did call on her to edit the *Commonwealth,* an abolitionist periodical, but he resented any personal initiative she took to become a public figure.

As a result, H. wrote only poetry and plays at this time, mainly as a form of self-expression and a release from personal tension. She eventually published an anonymous collection of the verse entitled *Passion Flowers* (1853), which proved to be better received than the two additional volumes—*Words for the Hour* (1857) and *Later Lyrics* (1866)—that were later published under her own name. As in all of her writing, H.'s poetry explores a variety of topics, including religion, literature, patriotism, motherhood, and social problems, and her strength as a poet lies in her ability to fuse themes together in one work. Of particular note are poems such as "Slave Suicide," "The Slave's Eloquence," and "The Sermon of the Spring," all precursors to "The Battlehymn."

H.'s travel sketches—*A Trip to Cuba* (1860) and *From the Oak to the Olive* (1868)—are based on her many trips abroad; they feature an engaging and humorous tone, picturesque imagery, and helpful hints for fellow travelers. *A Trip to Cuba* also includes numerous derogatory remarks about the slaves in the Caribbean, suggesting that H. did not completely embrace an abolitionist stance until shortly before the beginning of the war.

H. similarly did not become fully converted to the women's rights movement until when, at the age of nearly fifty, she was appointed president of the New England Suffrage Association, a position given to her on the basis of her "Battlehymn" popularity. This began a period of intense activism in H.'s life during which she lectured and organized for woman suffrage, the peace movement, and prison reform. It also marked a change in her literary focus as she limited her writing to essays of social criticism and biographies.

H.'s essays are often lacking in clarity and organization, but her biographies are quite readable. They reflect her interest in a subject's intellectual, moral and social development. Her biography of feminist intellectual Margaret FULLER (1883) closely resembles the construction of H.'s own autobiography, *Reminiscences* (1899), though Fuller's account ends early with her tragic death while H.'s life story goes on to chronicle her work with numerous reform movements, thereby providing an historical record of American idealism of that period.

"The Battlehymn" inspired a region in the midst of a civil war, but it also enabled its creator to transform herself from a frustrated writer locked in a difficult marriage into a significant figure in the literary, transcendentalist, and reform circles of 19th-c. New England.

BIBLIOGRAPHY: Clifford, D. P., *Mine Eyes Have Seen the Glory: A Biography of J. W. H.* (1978); Grant, M. H., *Private Woman, Public Person: An Account of the Life of J. W. H. from 1819 to 1868* (1994), Schriber, M. S., "J. W. H. and the Travel Book," *NEQ* 62 (1989): 264–79

RENEE SCHATTEMAN

HOWELLS, William Dean

b. 1 March 1837, Martin's Ferry, Ohio; d. 11 May 1920, New York City

H. has enduring importance for American literature not only as a novelist, but as the leading critical voice for the realist movement and the chief shaper of cultural expectations and critical norms for literature at the turn of the century. Amazingly prolific, H. produced some thirty-five novels, nine volumes of short fiction, eight volumes of criticism in addition to his thirty years of regular monthly columns in *Harper's*, thirty-six plays, ten travel books, five volumes of autobiography, and four volumes of poetry. Most critics believe that his major work is in the novels, the three that are generally agreed to be his best, *A Modern Instance* (1882), *The Rise of Silas Lapham* (1885), and *A Hazard of New Fortunes* (1890), and others that have attracted a good deal of critical interest over the years, including *Their Wedding Journey* (1872), *A Foregone Conclusion* (1875), *The Undiscovered Country* (1880), *Indian Summer* (1886), *The Shadow of a Dream* (1890), *The Landlord at Lion's Head* (1897), and *The Leatherwood God* (1916).

H.'s most enduring impact on American literature may lie in the enormous influence he exerted over American writers in the second half of the 19th c., as an essayist and critic and as editor, primarily of the prestigious *Atlantic Monthly* (1871–81). Famous for encouraging young writers, he could include among those he had reviewed favorably and helped to get published both his lifelong friends Henry JAMES and Mark TWAIN and such writers as Bret HARTE, Sarah Orne JEWETT, Stephen CRANE, Hamlin GARLAND, Paul Laurence DUNBAR, and Mary MURFREE. His real presence as a cultural power began in 1881, when he incurred the wrath of the Anglo-American critical establishment for praising James's realism. In his "Editor's Study" column begun in 1886, he not only championed the cause of a native-born REALISM against what he considered the false and pernicious conventionality of popular sentimental fiction, but rejected the provincialism then pervading Anglo-American letters and provided some of the first American discussions of such writers as Leo Tolstoy, Henrik Ibsen, Fyodor Dostoevsky, Ivan Turgenev, Émile Zola, Armando Palacio Valdes, and H. H. BOYESEN. Throughout his column, as may be seen in the book *Criticism and Fiction* (1891), which he distilled from it, is the enunciation of the principles he believed necessary for realism: the faithful depiction of characters and events, the notion that truth and morality are inseparable, the importance of the artist in "picturing" reality rather than "mapping" it, and the centrality of character in the novel.

H. came to fiction writing through travel writing. As a young newspaper journalist in Ohio, he had written a successful campaign biography of Abraham LINCOLN that eventually paid off in a consulship at Venice (1861–65). Using the opportunity to steep himself in Italian history, culture, and daily life, he proceeded to write a long magazine article on "Recent Italian Comedy" and the travel books *Venetian Life* (1866) and *Italian Journeys* (1867). These books not only won him his first job on the *Atlantic Monthly* and some acclaim as a travel writer, they provided him with a congenial form for narrative. H.'s first novel, *Their Wedding Journey*, uses a trip from Boston to Niagara Falls and Montreal to provide its narrative structure, and introduces Basil and Isabel March, characters based on H. and his wife, Elinor, who were to figure in a number of books before H. finally finished with them in *Their Silver Wedding Journey* (1899). The novel also introduced Kitty Ellison, an unspoiled American girl from upstate New York who was to become the heroine of his next novel, *A Chance Acquaintance* (1873). Although a journey again provided the narrative structure for this book, H. also developed a narrative tension through the relationship between Kitty and the snobbish Boston Brahmin, Miles Arbuton, the beginning of his sustained treatment of the conflict between egalitarian Western values and those of the civilized and artificial society people of the urban East, particularly Boston.

H. continued his study of the American girl and her conflict with the attitudes of Boston and European society in his next two novels, *A Foregone Conclusion* and *The Lady of Aroostook* (1879). *A Foregone Conclusion,* perhaps H.'s most romantic novel, treats the misunderstandings that arise from the differing cultural viewpoints of Florida Vervain, a seventeen-year-old American girl, Don Ippolito, a romantic young Italian priest who falls in love with her, and Henry Ferris, the American consul who finally marries her. Henry James admired *A Foregone Conclusion,* and it was the first of a number of narrative treatments that both he and H. were to make of the irreconcilability of American cultural values and expectations with those of Europe. In *The Lady of Aroostook,* H. takes his heroine Lydia Blood from South Bradfield, Massachusetts to Venice by way of the ship *Aroostook.* On board she meets James Staniford, the Bostonian who is to be her husband, but only after a number of false perceptions and misunderstandings are cleared away, and the Stanifords eventually accept the social exile of life in California. Staniford's inability to place Lydia socially and the mutual shock with which Lydia and Venetian society encounter each other were to become standard themes in what came to be known as "the international novel."

H.'s next four novels mixed the treatment of topical issues and the realistic study of cultural attitudes and social practices with great attention to psychological depth in characterization. In *The Undiscovered Country,* H. wove the current interest in spiritualism and what was to become for him a long term interest in the Shakers into a love story. *Doctor Breen's Practice* (1881) and *A Woman's Reason* (1883) both treat issues arising from the women's movement, the first whether it is acceptable for women to pursue a profession rather than marry, and the second whether women should be raised in a manner that leaves them unable to cope with the exigencies of making their own living.

A Modern Instance was H.'s first major novel. Inspired by his having seen Franz Grillparzer's adaptation of *Medea* and declaring it "an Indiana divorce case," the novel is a study of the ill-fated marriage of Marcia Gaylord and Bartley Hubbard. Skillfully depicting Bartley's self-centered amorality and Marcia's passionate and undisciplined nature, which is constrained in some unfortunate ways by the cold and narrow New England environment in which she is raised, H. chronicles the seemingly inevitable collapse of their marriage, ending with Bartley's desertion and a divorce in an Indiana courtroom. The issue of divorce is debated in the book by Ben Halleck, a puritanical Bostonian who is tortured by his love for Marcia, and Eustace Atherton, a priggish lawyer who holds that divorce is all right for people like the Hubbards, but

that Halleck cannot marry Marcia after the divorce because it is his social duty to show that he is above such a thing. In the end, H. left open the question of whether Halleck marries Marcia, but the novel produced a storm of abuse from critics who condemned either his immorality in treating the subject of divorce at all or his condemnation of divorced people. Subsequent views of the novel have gotten beyond the divorce question, with critics noticing H.'s skillful use of imagery to depict sexuality and to evoke the vast cultural gap between Boston and Equity, Maine, where Marcia is raised, as well as that between Boston and the West.

The Rise of Silas Lapham is probably the best known of H.'s novels. It plays on the popular pattern of the success story to analyze the social situation of the American businessman, contrasting the Vermont farmer turned self-made magnate Silas Lapham and his family with the Boston Brahmin Corey family, who look down on them socially while they haven't nearly as much money. Silas's "rise" actually takes place when he is forced to make a moral decision that could save or ruin his fortune, a fortune that has gradually diminished as a result of a series of bad decisions and bad breaks. Silas makes the decision that squares with his and his wife's New England consciences, and he has to sell the business to pay off his creditors. He retires to the Vermont farm, feeling himself a failure, but satisfied that he has done right. Their daughter Penelope, meanwhile, has married Tom Corey after an agonizing misunderstanding during which she was prepared to sacrifice her happiness because her sister Irene had loved him first. H. was recognized in his day for his perceptive choice of the businessman as the quintessential subject for the American novel as well as his acute study of the Laphams and the Coreys as representative American phenomena. Later critics have objected to the looseness with which the novel's two plots are tied together, but have recognized it as one of H.'s most acute analyses of his society.

H.'s concerns in *Silas Lapham* produced two themes for novels in the 1880s and 1890s. One is his overt criticism of the self-sacrifice idealized by popular love stories in *Indian Summer* and *April Hopes* (1888). The other is his treatment of social and economic issues in the so-called "economic novels," *The Minister's Charge* (1887), *Annie Kilburn* (1889), *A Hazard of New Fortunes, The Quality of Mercy* (1892), *The World of Chance* (1893), and *The Son of Royal Langbrith* (1904). *Indian Summer* has been seen as a tour de force, a deftly handled study of the May-December romance between Theodore Colville, a forty-one-year-old newspaper editor who has returned to Venice to revisit the scene of his youth, and Imogene Graham, a romantic young girl who wants to sacrifice herself by marrying him to make up for the girl who jilted him in his youth. The treatment of Imogene's deluded idealization of self-sacrifice became the central theme in *April Hopes,* which chronicles the romance of Dan Mavering and Alice Pasmer from the day they meet at Harvard Class Day until the day of their wedding. Playing the reality of their relationship overtly against the sentimentalized idealism of the popular novels where Alice has nurtured her expectations, H. used the narrative itself to reverse the expectations that his readers would have derived from the popular novel.

H.'s economic novels grew out of a progressively greater awareness of social evil in the early 1880s and a progressively greater unease at the disparity between his own luxurious situation and his increasingly social-ist principles, culminating in his outspoken defense of the Haymarket anarchists in 1886. *The Minister's Charge* is a more bitter attack on the success myth than *Silas Lapham,* depicting the social forces, institutions, attitudes, and people that make Lemuel Barker's at-tempt to make his fortune in Boston much more diffi-cult than that of the Alger hero. *Annie Kilburn* treats the attempts of a socially minded society girl to find some way of acting on her beliefs that is more signifi-cant than supporting the Indigent Children's Surf-Bathing Society. *The Quality of Mercy* and *The Son of Royal Langbrith* are less sympathetic treatments of the American businessman than *Silas Lapham.* In the first, Milton J. Northwick, an embezzler who has been viewed as a pillar of the community, escapes to Canada on the verge of being discovered, but is brought back in handcuffs and dies in disgrace. In the second, Royal Langbrith, whose memory is being preserved by his son James as the model of the post-Civil War business-man, is revealed as a cruel, abusive predator who stole the manufacturing process that made him wealthy. *An Imperative Duty* (1892) is based on the issue of miscegenation. Rhoda Aldgate finds she is one-eighth black and releases her fiancé from his engagement because of it, but marries a sensible doctor instead.

A Hazard of New Fortunes is H.'s most ambitious treatment of his contemporary society. H. made his most successful use of Basil March in this novel, as a central consciousness representing the middle-class norm from which to consider the conflicting views in the novel. The Marches move from Boston to New York so that Basil can take up the offer of his friend Fulkerson for the editorship of a new magazine, and they are amazed at the extent of poverty and suffering that they have never noticed in previous visits to the city. Among the people with whom the Marches be-come entangled through the magazine are its owner Jacob Dryfoos, a self-made millionaire from Indiana who has his son Conrad run the "business end" of the

magazine; March's old socialist acquaintance Lindau; Colonel Woodburn, who has come North from Virginia to advocate his idea of a neofeudalism as the nation's salvation; Margaret Vance, a young society woman who is socially centered; Angus Beaton, the vain and self-centered art director of the magazine; and Alma Leighton, who has come to New York with her mother to run a boarding house while Alma studies art. Amid various love stories, the novel treats the conflict be-tween Dryfoos and Conrad, who wants to become a minister and serve others; the conflicts arising from the various social viewpoints represented by Colonel Woodburn, Dryfoos, Conrad and Margaret Vance, and Lindau; the attempts of the Dryfoos family, depicted as more elemental and less sympathetic than the La-phams, to get into society; and the attempts of the Marches to reconcile their Boston principles with New York reality. Eventually, Conrad goes to his death in a bloody streetcar strike after his father slaps him in a quarrel, and Lindau dies of a wound inflicted by a policeman's billy club. In the end, Dryfoos takes his daughters to Europe and sells the magazine to Fulker-son and March. The novel's quality cannot be con-veyed in a short summary, for it is H.'s skill in de-picting the broad spectrum of social reality that is the novel's greatest strength, and his discussion of social ideas that gives it its substance.

H.'s social ideas were given a more direct treatment in his two utopian romances, *A Traveler from Alturia* (1894) and its sequel *Through the Eye of the Needle* (1907), but most of H.'s novels as he moved into his sixties and seventies returned to earlier themes and locations. He made use of his experience at various vacation sites as well as Europe and his experience with the Shakers and with the theater to write stories revolving around courtship and marriage. Three of the later novels call for individual comment, however. *The Landlord at Lion's Head,* with its study of the rise to success of the amoral Jeff Durgin and what H. called "two new neurotic types," the overtly sexual Bessie Lynde and her alcoholic brother Alan, who suggest the degeneracy in the idle life of the leisure class, has been called naturalistic by some critics. *The Leath-erwood God* and the earlier *Shadow of a Dream* are the most uncharacteristic of H.'s novels. *The Shadow of a Dream* is a psychological study of the effect that dreams may have on waking life. *The Leatherwood God* is based on an actual occurrence in Ohio during the 1850s, when a man claiming to be God established a following there. The novel treats the effects of reli-gious fanaticism on the village, with its results in bitter personal conflict and mob violence. H.'s portrait of the imposter Dylks also suggests the relation between sexual energy and religious frenzy. The combination of these elemental forces and the Ohio countryside, vividly remembered and depicted in memoirs such as *A Boy's Town* (1890), *My Year in a Log Cabin* (1893), *New Leaf Mills* (1913), and *Years of My Youth* (1916), gives this book a strength and immediacy of effect that is the more admirable when one considers that H. was seventy-nine years old when it was published.

H.'s plays and poems have not received the attention his fiction has. Alhough H. aspired to be a poet at the beginning of his career, his gift was for prose, and precisely for the depiction of character, the representation of psychological conflict, and the writing of dialogue. His plays have been collected in the *Complete Plays* (1960), and together with the sixty pieces of drama criticism he wrote, a selection of which has been published as *A Realist in the American Theater* (1992), have begun to be recognized for the influence they exerted on American playwrights who followed him.

H. was the subject of controversy from very early in his writing career. His first travel writings and novels were praised for their engaging style and for capturing the tone of a place and time through the depiction of colorful details. In 1882, however, when H. published his article on Henry James, British critics castigated him for daring to suggest that the new "Boston realism" could be compared, favorably, with the work of their literary idols, Dickens and Thackeray. Soon after, *A Modern Instance* was criticized both for being luridly immoral and for being a dull chronicle of the trivial concerns of New England life. For H., this was the beginning of a long battle that he waged for the principles of realism and against what he considered the sentimentality and sensationalism of romantics. In 1886, when he took up the "Editor's Study" column in *Harper's Monthly,* he wrote to Edmund Gosse that he enjoyed "banging the babes of Romance about," but his own work was banged about in return by critics who disagreed with the realist poetics he advocated in his column and his other criticism as well as those who simply disliked his novels. His contemporaries continued to make two conflicting criticisms about his novels: that they treated subjects too coarse for a civilized reading public, particularly women and girls, and that they were dull and commonplace. As H., James, and their contemporaries were succeeded by a younger generation of writers such as Frank NORRIS, Stephen Crane, and Theodore DREISER, who were influenced by the naturalism of Zola as well as the realism of H., the work of the older generation began to be dismissed as old-fashioned realism of the surface only, fiction that treated only the concerns of middle-class domestic life and ignored what the naturalists considered the lowest classes and the lowest instincts of humanity. By 1915, H. was writing to James that

he was "a dead cult, with all my statues cut down and the grass growing over them in the pale moonlight."

At the time of World War I, yet another generation of young writers rejected H.'s work, finding in it the essence of the "genteel realism" they were determined to overthrow. During the twenties, H. was criticized for accepting the restraints of Boston gentility in his depiction of sexual passion and marital relations, and for concentrating on the "smiling aspects" of life that he had once remarked were "more American" than the more rigorous conditions of the life depicted by Dostoevsky. The final blow to H.'s reputation, however, came with Sinclair LEWIS's dismissal in his Nobel Prize address: "Mr. H. was one of the gentlest, sweetest, and most honest of men, but he had the code of a pious old maid whose greatest delight was to have tea at the vicarage."

While H.'s notion of realism was falling steadily further out of fashion, there is no doubt that interest in his work continued. The first three critical books by Alexander Harvey (1917), Delmar Cooke (1922), and Oscar W. Firkins (1924) appeared during this period. The resuscitation of his reputation began with the rediscovery of his "social conscience" during the 1930s. The recognition that H. had not only examined social evils in *A Hazard of New Fortunes* and the other "economic novels," but had taken a brave stand on behalf of the anarchists in the Haymarket case and had espoused a Tolstoy-inspired socialism in his columns during the nineties, gained him a new respect among the leftist critics of the thirties, and began a study of H. as a social realist that has continued into the present.

In the period since World War II, critics of H. divide roughly into two camps that John W. Crowley has named the revivalists and the revisionists. The revivalists, in a conservative reaction against the modernist frame of mind, placed H. as spokesman for realism at the center of literary activity in the second half of the 19th c. The realist H. that such critics described was the artist of the commonplace, dedicated to the depiction of "normal life" from a rational, pragmatic, socially responsible, humanistic, and compassionate point of view. The revisionists opposed to this view of H. what Crowley calls "H. Agonistes," a protomodernist man "racked by existential doubts and neurotic vastations." These critics attempted to probe beneath the careful artifice of realism H. constructed, both to reveal the depiction of "forbidden subjects," such as sex and mental instability, that H. encoded metaphorically and metonymically in his texts and to reveal the dark side of his artistic vision, exposing the author's own psychic tension and unresolved ambivalence about his own life, physical and metaphysical. During the 1970s, H. also came under attack for being too much of a romanticist and not enough of a social activist. In keeping with the general directions that literary criticism has taken recently, however, the major concerns of H. critics have been a renewed interest in H.'s treatment of women characters, male-female relations, and marriage; an attempt to assess the effect of H.'s realism on the larger cultural context; and the analysis of H.'s narrative technique and use of language; and his treatment of class, ethnicity, and race.

BIBLIOGRAPHY: Bennett, G. N., *The Realism of W. D. H.* (1973); Cady, E. H., *The Road to Realism* (1956); Cady, E. H., *The Realist at War* (1958); Cady, E. H., and N. W. Cady, eds., *Critical Essays on W. D. H., 1866–1920* (1983); Cady, E. H., and D. L. Frazier, eds., *The War of the Critics over W. D. H.* (1962); Carter, E., *H. and the Age of Realism* (1954); Crowley, J. W., *The Black Heart's Truth* (1985); Eble, K. E., ed., *H.: A Century of Criticism* (1962); Lynn, K.; *W. D. H.: An American Life* (1971); Nettels, E., *Language, Race, and Social Class in His America* (1988); Prioleau, E. S., *The Circle of Eros: Sexuality in the Work of W. D. H.* (1983)

BRENDA MURPHY

HOYT, Charles [Hale]

b. 26 July 1859, Concord, New Hampshire; d. 20 November 1900, Charlestown, New Hampshire

H. was the most successful playwright of his era. The author of eighteen plays, sixteen of them successful, he was known as the creator of boisterous farces filled with with catchy tunes and wholesome hilarity. His skill at entertaining made him a millionaire by the age of thirty, and it obscured the fact that beneath the rowdy antics of his comedies often lay serious social critique.

H.'s first play was a standard melodrama called *Gifford's Luck* (perf. 1881). Soon thereafter, he switched to his signature genre, the farce. Like Edward HARRIGAN, who preceded him, H.'s humor was deeply influenced by blackface minstrelsy. His plots were based on ludicrous situations, heightened by hilarious physical comedy and brought to life by comic local types. Unlike Harrigan, his locales were varied, and included small-town life as well as urban settings. H.'s fisticuffs and slapstick were reminiscent of Harrigan's low-life sketches, but his effervescent, witty lines were his own stylistic strength. His plays were more topical than Harrigan's, focusing on absurd situations rather than comical types.

H. is sometimes accounted part of the "journalistic" school of playwrights because he began his career as a newspaper reporter. In his humorous column "All Sorts," he profiled eccentric characters much like those in his later plays. Like his journalism, his plays were based on shrewd observation, but on stage his characters evolved into caricatures with a pointed satirical aim. H.'s targets were both official abuses and personal foibles such as the love of novelty, hypochondria, or crass competitiveness. *A Bunch of Keys* (perf. 1883, pub. 1941) profiled the lighter side of hotel management; *A Rag Baby* (perf. 1884) skewered small-town life; *The Brass Monkey* (perf. 1888) parodied popular superstition; *A Milk White Flag* (perf. 1894, pub. 1941) poked fun at home militias. Other plays were more topical: *A Texas Steer* (perf. 1890) took up the popular theme of a naive politician overcome by Washington; *A Temperance Town* (perf. 1893, pub. 1941) took on the evils of overzealous prohibition; *A Runaway Colt* (perf. 1895) indicted corruption in the baseball industry; and *A Contented Woman* (perf. 1897) satirized the suffragist movement.

H.'s serious social critique was couched in the hilarity of slapstick; hence his reputation as a "funmaker" who reliably provided an evening's entertainment. In his trademark prefatory apologies and public disclaimers, he always insisted that he aimed only to amuse, and he revised his plays repeatedly in response to audience likes and dislikes. *A Contented Woman* he called on the program "An attempt to furnish material for an evening's entertainment"; *A Parlor Match* (perf. 1884, pub. 1941) he subtitled "Two hours and a half of nothing in particular, jumbled together by C. H. H." While somewhat disingenuous for most of his satires, the disclaimers were appropriate for H.'s most successful play, *A Trip to Chinatown* (perf. 1891, pub. 1941), which set the 19th-c. record for number of consecutive performances. Unlike most of his plays, *A Trip to Chinatown* was every bit as unsubstantial as it purported to be, adhering to pure comedy, rather than blending comic, tragic, and realistic events as did most of H.'s plays.

H.'s only box-office failures were his final play and an operetta, *The Maid and the Moonshiner* (perf. 1886), starring Edward Harrigan's former partner Tony Hart in an unsuccessful attempt to revive his career after parting from Harrigan. The failure of H.'s final play, *A Dog in a Manger* (perf. 1899), and the death of his second wife, actress Caroline Miskell, contributed to his failing mental and physical health. Committed to an asylum against his will by his friends, he was soon released to die insane at the age of forty-one.

BIBLIOGRAPHY: Hunt, D. L., *The Life and Work of C. H.* (1946)

GINGER STRAND

HUGHES, [James] Langston
b. 1 February 1902, Joplin, Missouri; d. 22 May 1967,
New York City

H. was probably the most original of modern black
American poets and the most representative of black
American writers by virtue of his efforts over almost
fifty years in verse, drama, fiction, and journalism.
Although his name came to be associated with Harlem
in New York, where he lived for much of his life, he
grew up mainly in the Midwest—in Lawrence, Kansas,
and in Cleveland, Ohio, where he graduated from high
school in 1920. Not long afterward, H. made two
crucial decisions. He was determined to live exclusively by his writing (no black American had ever
done so), and he would write mainly about the African
American people.

H.'s unusual sense of mission was instilled in him
above all by his maternal grandmother, whose first
husband had died at Harpers Ferry as a member of
John Brown's band, and whose second husband (H.'s
grandfather) had also been a militant abolitionist. Another important family figure was his grandfather's
brother John Mercer Langston, renowned as a lawyer,
a member of Congress, and a consul for the U.S. in
Haiti and Santo Domingo. Inspired by these ancestors,
young H. struggled at the same time with feelings of
loneliness fostered by his father, who abandoned the
family for a business career overseas, and his mother,
whose interest in the stage and in travel often took
her far from home. H. eventually found his deepest
satisfaction, as an individual and an artist, in writing
about and for the black race in America.

As a poet, his major influences toward maturity
were Walt WHITMAN and Carl SANDBURG ("my guiding
star"), as well as the black poets Paul Laurence DUN-
BAR, a master of dialect verse, and Claude MCKAY, a
radical socialist who also wrote touching lyric poetry.
However, Sandburg's free-verse tributes to American
democracy were decisive in leading H. away from the
formal constraints of the Genteel Tradition and the
tyranny of rhyme. A profound love of black music
and an unprecedented determination to fuse black jazz
and blues with traditional verse distinguished his first
two books of verse: *The Weary Blues* (1926) and *Fine
Clothes to the Jew* (1927).

For his choice of blues and jazz and his emphasis
on lower-class black life, he was harshly attacked
in the black press, especially after his second, more
innovative volume. Discerning critics, on the other
hand, hailed his novel additions both to verse forms
in English and to the subject matter of poetry. These
two books were also milestones in the Harlem Renaissance, a movement mainly among the younger black
artists for which H. provided an eloquent manifesto,

his essay "The Negro Artist and the Racial Mountain"
(1926). Here, he pleaded both for artistic freedom and
for an art inspired by a love of and respect for black
culture, without fear of shame.

His attempts at fiction bolstered his reputation as
a writer. In 1930, his first novel, *Not without Laughter,*
about a sensitive, black Midwestern boy and his struggling family, was hailed as an unusually affectionate
and touching portrait of black life. Four years later,
however, his first collection of stories, *The Ways of
White Folks,* was caustic in tone. Responding to the
onset of the Depression, the swift waning of the Harlem Renaissance, and personal pressures, his vision
of American culture had changed. Another result of
this shift was a series of radical socialist poems, some
written during a year spent in the Soviet Union
(1932–33), that excoriated capitalism and called for
revolution. In this vein, he published the collection *A
New Song* (1938), with a preface by Mike Gold.

After his play *Mulatto,* on one of H.'s most keenly
felt themes—miscegenation and the tragedy of parental rejection—opened on Broadway in 1935, H. wrote
other dramas in the 1930s, including comedies such
as *Little Ham* (1936) and an historical drama, *Emperor
of Haiti* (1936). Most of these plays were only moderate successes, with many critics finding H. technically
limited as a playwright, and inclined to farce and even
burlesque in his comedies. He did better when he
turned away from traditional forms of drama. In 1938,
for example, after some months in Madrid during the
Spanish Civil War, his *Don't You Want to Be Free?*
vigorously blended black racial feeling (voiced principally through the recitation of some of his poems of
black life), the blues as poetry and music, and radical
socialist exhortation.

World War II helped to alienate H. from the far
left. Thus, in his book of verse *Shakespeare in Harlem*
(1942), he once again sang the black blues. On the
other hand, this collection, as well as another, his *Jim
Crow's Last Stand* (1943), strongly attacked racial
segregation. After the war, two books of verse, *Fields
of Wonder* (1947), which H. announced as his first
purely "lyric" or nonracial collection, and *One-Way
Ticket* (1949) added little to his fame. But in *Montage
of a Dream Deferred* (1951) he broke new ground with
verse innovatingly accented by the new discordant
elements in jazz and in the temper of black society.
H.'s last volume of verse was the posthumously published *The Panther and the Lash* (1967), mainly about
the struggle for civil rights.

H.'s achievements in prose were also notable. In
The Big Sea (1940), the first of two volumes of autobiography, he eschewed overt self-revelation or radical
social criticism in favor of a genial tone that touched
lightly and yet memorably on suffering and hardship.

The second volume, *I Wonder as I Wander* (1956), was even more reticent about his personal life but gave a richly entertaining account of his travels and adventures between 1931 and 1938. However, perhaps H.'s most admired prose was written as a newspaper columnist when, between 1942 and 1963, he published weekly in the black *Chicago Defender*. By far the most brilliant aspect of his column was the character Jesse B. Semple, or "Simple," and his dialogues with a staid narrator in a neighborhood bar. Always candid, often outrageous, Simple commented on almost all matters but mainly on race, about which he seemed obsessed. He became H.'s most celebrated fictional creation and the subject of five edited collections starting in 1950 with *Simple Speaks His Mind*.

During World War II and in the years immediately afterward, H. devoted much effort to songwriting as a lyricist. This devotion paid off handsomely when he was chosen by Kurt Weill and Elmer RICE to work on their *Street Scene* (1947), which was soon hailed as a breakthrough in uniting Broadway and opera, with H.'s lyrics lauded for their simplicity and power. Other efforts as a lyricist about this time were less successful, but the Simple series inspired a Broadway musical show, *Simply Heavenly,* which facilitated a fresh involvement in the theater in the later stage of H.'s career. In *Tambourines to Glory* (1958), a musical play satirizing corruption in a black storefront church, H. first used black gospel music, which had come to prominence in the 1940s, as the basis of musical theater. Although this play failed on Broadway, in the 1960s gospel provided him with the backbone of widely acclaimed stage efforts, usually mixing words, music, and dance in an atmosphere of improvisation. Notable here were the Christmas show *Black Nativity* (1961) and, inspired by the civil rights movement, *Jericho-Jim Crow* (1964).

H.'s writing for children was another significant aspect of his creativity. Starting with the tale *Popo and Fifina* (1932), set in Haiti and written with Arna BONTEMPS, he published almost a dozen children's books on subjects such as jazz, Africa, and the West Indies. He wrote a commissioned history of the National Association for the Advancement of Colored People and also the text of a much praised pictorial history of black America. His brief but affecting narrative in *The Sweet Flypaper of Life* (1955), where his words explicated photographs of Harlem by Roy DeCarava, was judged masterful, and further confirmed H.'s reputation for literary versatility and an unrivaled command of the nuances of black urban culture.

In addition to his lifelong devotion to writing about and, to some extent, for African Americans, H. believed in an aesthetic of simplicity as an artist. Committed to democracy, he strove to communicate with the largest number of people, and deplored the more elitist elements of modern art. Accordingly, his work has frequently been slighted by academic critics, both black and white. However, the variety and range of his work, as well as the artistic dividends that came from his commitment to and involvement in black culture, almost certainly guarantee him a lasting place of some prominence in American literature.

BIBLIOGRAPHY: Dickinson, D. C., *A Bio-Bibliography of L. H.* (1967); Nichols, C., ed., *Arna Bontemps-L. H. Letters, 1925–1967* (1980); Rampersad, A., *The Life of L. H., Vol. I, 1902–1941* (1986); Rampersad, A., *The Life of L. H., Vol. II, 1941–1967* (1988)

ARNOLD RAMPERSAD

HUGO, Richard
b. 21 December 1923, Seattle, Washington; d. 22 October 1982, Seattle, Washington

Born and reared in Seattle, H. studied with Theodore ROETHKE at the University of Washington. He served in the U.S. Army Air Forces in the Mediterranean theater from 1943 to 1945, for which he was awarded various medals.

H., considered a regional poet of the Great Northwest, although he has also written about the landscape of Italy and Scotland, has a reputation that continues to grow, primarily because of the emotional veracity of his work. His most important books include *The Lady in Kicking Horse Reservoir* (1973), *31 Letters and 13 Dreams* (1977), *Selected Poems* (1979) and posthumously, *Making Certain It Goes On* (1984). His subject matter is sorrow, grief, and loss. Although occasionally a poem is self-pitying, most of the work is a testimony to the readers that someone else has been battered by the worlds but has somehow survived. William E. STAFFORD has said that H.'s work exemplifies the epic dimensions of the individual life.

H.'s poetry is written in free verse, although upon careful scrutiny, it is obvious that it is considerably less free than one supposes on first reading. He sometimes uses slant rhyme, and his lines are often pentameter or tetrameter, their length giving them a solid and substantial look on the page. His language is colloquial and heightened as he tries to capture the rhythm and melody of ordinary Western speech. Because of his use of color, his work has been compared to that of Wallace STEVENS, but H. is much closer to the frontier than Stevens, closer to Walt WHITMAN who sang the great continent and its people. H.'s vision is more concentrated, however, and more realistic, illustrating all the bad luck and broken dreams of America. Yet H.'s world is not like T. S. ELIOT's "waste land." It is infinitely rich and beautiful, despite the disillusionment of the 20th c. H. has said that the reader expects the poet to tell him the truth and both the form of his work and its subject matter attest to his mastery of this standard.

The Real West Marginal Way: A Poet's Autobiography (1986), edited by Ripley S. Hugo, Lois M. Welch, and James Welch, is a posthumous collection of his essays. *The Triggering Town* (1979) is a collection of essays, mostly on poetry and on writing techniques.

BIBLIOGRAPHY: Allen, M. S., *We Are Called Human* (1982); Meyers, J., *A Trout in the Milk: A Composite Portrait of R. H.* (1982); Pinsker, S., *Three Poets of the Pacific Northwest* (1987)

ANN STRUTHERS

HUIE, William Bradford

b. 13 November 1910, Hartselle, Alabama; d. 22 November 1986, Guntersville, Alabama

One of the most successful fiction and investigative nonfiction writers in American literature, H. was born in the unlikely town of Hartselle, in the heart of "redneck" country in north Alabama. His liberal political and social views, as expressed in his novels and documentary books and articles, put him at odds with local laws and customs. During Governor George Wallace's 1964 campaign for the presidency, H. said that "George Wallace stands for all that is ignorant, backward and cruel in the state of Alabama." As a result, he and his family received many threatening telephone calls, and his home in Hartselle was under siege for a number of days. Nevertheless, he remained in the South, he once told an interviewer, because "I'm proud of what is good. It's the demagogues of the South, the hatemongers, I hold in contempt." Indeed, his books and articles about violence during the civil rights movement of the 1950s and 1960s are among the most accurate and balanced reportage to come out of the struggle. But H.'s literary scope was broad enough to include fiction and nonfiction and such subjects as criminal psychology, warfare, and nuclear disarmament, which he was promoting in the 1940s.

After graduation from the University of Alabama in 1930, he spent more than a dozen years in journalism, as a writer for the *Birmingham Post* and as editor of the *American Mercury* and *Alabama Magazine.* During World War II, he served overseas with the U.S. Navy between 1943 and 1945. Throughout his career, he wrote freelance articles for such periodicals as *Time, Look,* the *Saturday Evening Post, True,* and *Cavalier,* which published many of his investigative articles that were rejected as too depressing and downbeat by mainstream magazines. Six of his *Cavalier* articles were published in 1962 as *The Hero of Iwo Jima and Other Stories.* The title story told the tragic life of Ira Hayes, the Pima Indian and war hero who helped raise the flag at Iwo Jima. "A Tale of Two Lynchings" contrasted the media handling of a lynching in Vermont, which went unreported by the national press, and one in Mississippi, which was sensationalized by reporters from around the world.

His first novel was *Mud on the Stars* (1942), a semiautobiographical love story set against the backdrop of the Tennessee Valley as its inhabitants are dislocated to make way for electricity-generating dams. *The Revolt of Mamie Stover* (1951), which sold almost thirty million copies worldwide, features the proprietor of a World War II Hawaiian brothel, which she operates with the efficiency of an assembly line. *The Americanization of Emily* (1959) is a ribald wartime romance about an American lieutenant in London whose mission is to provide good liquor, thick steaks, and pretty girls for an admiral's dinner parties. H.'s favorite book, *The Klansman* (1967), is the story of a war hero's failure of conscience as a small-town Southern sheriff. These four novels, plus several of his nonfiction books, were made into successful motion pictures.

H.'s best-known work of nonfiction is *The Execution of Private Slovick* (1954), the life of the only American soldier executed for desertion during World War II. Other nonfiction works include *Ruby McCollum: Woman in the Suwannee Jail* (1956), the story of a black woman in Florida jailed for killing a white physician; *Three Lives for Mississippi* (1965), an investigation into the cover-up of the murder of three civil rights works in Mississippi; and *He Slew the Dreamer* (1970), a profile of James Earl Ray, the assassin of Martin Luther King, Jr.

H.'s writing techniques were often borrowed from journalism: extensive interviewing of subjects and participants, use of direct quotations from interviews, short, snappy sentences, frequent use of the first person narrator for both fiction and nonfiction, you-are-there descriptions of places of action, and the "fast lead." Although critics sometime accuse him of being little more than a good journalist, he aspired to and achieved a great deal more. His expertly crafted plots, his careful selection of words, his calculated restraint, even when dealing with sensational materials, his insistence on going beyond facts for universal themes and motifs: all these traits raise much of his fiction and nonfiction to the level of literature.

WADE HALL

HUMES, H[arold] L[ouis]

b. 30 April 1926, Douglas, Arizona; d. 10 September 1992, New York City

H. figured prominently and promisingly in American literary life in the 1950s as a founding editor of the influential quarterly *Paris Review* in 1953 and an "impressive" new novelist in 1958. H. studied at the Massachusetts Institute of Technology and completed his schooling at the Sorbonne in Paris, the setting of his first novel, *The Underground City.*

Praised for its "intense drama" and "intellectual content" and greeted as "a tract for the times," this seven-hundred-fifty-page narrative recounts the World War II and early Cold War experiences of John Stone, a New Jersey high school teacher who served with American intelligence and the French Resistance. *Men Die* (1959), H.'s much terser though equally cinematic second novel, which tells the story of black convict sailors and their white commander at a remote Caribbean ammunition dump, also recalls the War. Both works are marked by the paranoid verve and apocalyptic rage that figured in H.'s decision in the 1960s to renounce his literary career to become an itinerant prophet-against-empire, visiting various college campuses where he warned of massive government conspiracies and came to be known as "Doc" H.

From 1973 on, H. lived a precarious existence in and around Boston, Massachusetts. His third novel was never completed.

JAMES D. BLOOM

HUMOR

American humor really begins after the Revolutionary War. For, though people dwelling or traveling in America wrote humorously from the beginnings of European settlement here (and Native Americans presumably said and did funny things even earlier), written humor that can be clearly identified as American has to wait for the clear establishment of American identity. Nevertheless, some of the forerunners are important to mention. The 18th c. saw the writings of William BYRD of Westover, whose *History of the Dividing Line betwixt Virginia and North Carolina* (wr. 1728) is a funny account of a surveying expedition, accompanied by a burlesque of the natives of North Carolina; Sarah Kemble KNIGHT, whose *Private Journal of a Journey from Boston to New York* (wr. 1704–5) contains vivid pictures of humorous characters and situations; numerous periodical essayists, mostly imitating Addison; and most importantly, Benjamin FRANKLIN.

Franklin did and wrote so much that singling out his contribution to the development of American humor is difficult. But that contribution certainly includes his juvenile "Silence Dogood" papers; *Poor Richard's Almanac,* published from 1733 to 1758, filled with witty and pithy sayings; and his occasional *feuilletons* and satires like "The Sale of the Hessians" and the "Speech of Miss Polly Baker," an ironic defense by a woman being prosecuted for bearing a bastard child.

Like the novel, another demotic literary form, American humor developed its own distinctive native form after the revolution, reaching maturity in the 1830s as James Fenimore COOPER was producing the first genuinely American novels. Cooper's own humor, often featuring joke-Irishmen or other stock comic butts, is inferior stuff; and his contemporary Washington IRVING, though he wrote amusingly in *Diedrich Knickerbocker's History of New York,* wrote for the most part in the English tradition. In such tales as "Rip Van Winkle" and "The Legend of Sleepy Hollow" he uses vernacular American materials with good effect and, in the latter work, the Connecticut schoolmaster Ichabod Crane is firmly in the tradition of the Yankee as comic type.

Walter Blair divides the major American humorous writing of the 19th c. into four useful categories: Down East humor, Southwestern humor, the humor of the literary comedians, and local color humor. Down East humor is characterized by a locality—that is, it is about residents of the New England states, sometimes expanded to include upstate New York—and by using Yankee characters as spokespersons rather than as objects of satire. By the 18th c., a Yankee type, a sharp and often unscrupulous traveling peddler with a bony, ill-clad body and a funny name, was current in comic anecdotes even in London. The Down East humorists (usually New Englanders themselves) used a different Yankee figure, a bumpkin (male or female) whose naiveté and ignorant language nevertheless reveal a practical wisdom. Early Down East humor is found in the Jack Downing stories of Seba SMITH, a Maine newspaperman. Jack Downing is a shrewd rube and expresses himself in a lively way. Smith represents Jack as visiting and commenting on the Maine legislature and, later, President Andrew Jackson. This device—of sending the fictional character to odd or sensational places or to meet the president—is a recurrent feature of American humor.

Other practitioners of Down East humor and their Yankee creations were Thomas Chandler Haliburton ("Sam Slick"); James Russell LOWELL ("Hosea Biglow"), in the *Biglow Papers;* B. P. SHILLABER ("Mrs. Partington"), also an important figure because his magazine the *Carpet Bag* published much original American humor including Samuel Langhorne CLEMENS's first sketch; Frances Miriam WHITCHER ("the Widow Bedott, Widow Spriggins, and Aunt Maguire, the best female Yankee figures of the 19th c."); Marietta HOLLEY ("Samantha, Josiah Allen's wife"); and Ann Sophia STEPHENS ("Jonathan Slick").

The best Down East humor uses the Yankee stereotype in a gentle way, though it can be sharp on the characters who surround the spokesperson. It often conveys serious social or political ideas—for instance, Whitcher campaigned sedulously for women's suffrage and against rum; and it uses the wise *naif* persona that is to be so central in American humor of all kinds.

Southwestern humor is also localized, in what would now be called the Southeastern U.S.—Georgia, Alabama, Mississippi, Tennessee, Kentucky, Arkansas. The first important book of Southwestern humor is probably *Georgia Scenes* by Augustus Baldwin LONGSTREET, published in periodical form and then as a book in 1835. Longstreet's book illustrates many of the persistent traits of this vein of humor. The author, and indeed the narrator, is an educated, literary man. His discourse frames scenes and characters both wild and primitive. Southwestern humor is often violent, and it often relies on the comedy of human corruption or even depravity. The people in the scenes are usually illiterate and speak with zestful crudity. The narrator's attitude is often detached, almost anthropological. Especially in the stories of "Kentuckians"—a term that becomes shorthand for backwoods rearers—boasting and exaggeration form an important part. The stories told of Davy CROCKETT and Mike Fink are the best examples of this strain.

Aside from the writings attributed to Crockett, and the many about him and Mike Fink by anonymous writers, the best known creators of Southwestern humor are Johnson Jones HOOPER, author of *Adventures of Simon Suggs;* Thomas Bangs THORPE, author of the best-known Southwestern story, "The Big Bear of Arkansas," whose books were *The Mysteries of the Backwoods* and *The Hive of the Bee Hunter;* Joseph Glover Baldwin, author of *Flush Times of Alabama and Mississippi* (1853); George Washington HARRIS of Tennessee, whose Sut Lovingood tales were collected in 1867. All of these authors were educated men, usually lawyers; the stories and sketches—like most 19th-c. American humor—first appeared in newspapers. The humor is of duality, of contrast between the civilized and decorous standard of the narrator-observer (and by inference the readers) and the rough, exuberant, often violent world of the people and events inside the frame.

The literary comedians also wrote for periodicals, but they differed from the Southwestern humorists in abolishing the frame. Now the spokesman is himself an unlettered person (Brom Weber calls this group "the misspellers"). Much of the humor of their work is derived from comic deformation of the language. Incongruously, the speaker, represented as an illiterate *naif,* is nevertheless usually knowledgeable, and in the case of someone like "Josh Billings," the pseudonym of Henry Wheeler SHAW, is presented as a wise aphorist. The literary comedians thus have something in common with the Down Easters and with Franklin's Poor Richard. Like Franklin, they almost always wrote from behind a pseudonym.

The best examples and their pseudonymous spokesmen are Charles Farrar BROWNE ("Artemus Ward"); David Ross LOCKE ("Petroleum Vesuvius Nasby"); Charles Henry SMITH ("Bill Arp"); Henry Wheeler Shaw ("Josh Billings"); Edgar W. NYE ("Bill Nye"); and Finley Peter DUNNE ("Mr. Dooley"). "Josh Billings," represented as the most illiterate (he routinely misspells "is"), is also a backwoods sage, whose work appeared as *Josh Billings' Farmer's Allminax.* "Artemus Ward" was allegedly a traveling showman, exhibiting moral waxworks and "beests of pray" and writing about his travels. "Petroleum V. Nasby" was different: a Southerner whose creator was a Northerner, he was a more vicious and self-deluded man, an unwitting vehicle of political satire. The literary comedians were usually professional writers, not lawyers or painters dabbling in literature; but they were also more than just writer, deriving much of their fame and income from lecture appearances.

The local colorists appealed to the interest in realistic information about remote places that helped to explain the popularity in the metropolitan areas of Southwestern humor. Their humor, though, is more gentle, sometimes sentimental. The best known are Harriet Beecher STOWE, author of *Oldtown Folks;* Bret HARTE (*The Luck of Roaring Camp and Other Sketches*); Edward EGGLESTON (*The Hoosier Schoolmaster*); and Joel Chandler HARRIS, whose Uncle Remus stories, folktales retold in black dialect, appeared in a series of books between 1881 and 1910.

Some 19th-c. American humorists elude these categories. Ambrose BIERCE, author of macabre stories and the cynical *Devil's Dictionary* wrote in California, but was a bitter classicist, not a local colorist. The most important American humorous writer, Samuel Langhorne Clemens ("Mark Twain"), practiced all these genres and transcended them all. He began by writing humorous sketches for newspapers and lecturing, having received help from "Artemus Ward"; he went on to write comic novels, including *Adventures of Huckleberry Finn,* one of the greatest American books. And, although he thought humor was inferior and was ashamed of his difference from educated New England Brahmin writers, his best work usually includes dialect humor, REGIONALISM, and often the pose of the wise naïf. Clemens proves, even if he did not himself understand, that the supposed distinction between "humorous" and "serious" writing is an illusion.

American humor in the 20th c. is more difficult to classify. The spread of education and the increasing homogenization of America have worked against misspelling humor and regionalism, respectively, though neither has completely died. The greatest modern changes may well be the increasing prominence of women and Jewish writers, and the decline in importance of the daily newspaper.

Humorous fiction has profited from the example of Clemens and from a less stringent expectation of moral profit in fiction. Early-20th-c. writers such as Booth TARKINGTON, William Sidney PORTER ("O. Henry"), Walter D. Edmonds, and George ADE wrote humorous tales and novels colored with the emotions of youth and family life, with "tough" realism coating sentimentality and ending in irony ("O. Henry"), or with satire on human foibles (Ade's "Fables in Slang"). Clarence DAY entertained with stories of his family, later collected as *Life with Father.* Sinclair LEWIS's satiric anatomies of American life contained plentiful infusions of humor, as in his story "The Man Who Knew Coolidge." William FAULKNER's novels and stories about life in Yoknapatawpha County, especially those about the Snopes family, include plenty of Southwestern-style humor.

Of Americans writing fiction in the second half of the 20th c., the one closest to traditional American humor is Garrison KEILLOR, who writes gentle stories about his fictional Lake Woebegon, Minnesota. Peter DE VRIES has published a number of humorous novels. Philip ROTH is not a "humorist," but his novels, particularly *The Breast* and *Portnoy's Complaint,* are extremely funny and rely, in addition to a strongly marked strain of Jewish humor, on such traditional devices as exaggerated language and the tall tale. Erica JONG has shown a feminine, or feminist, use of humor in such novels as *Fear of Flying.*

Humorous poetry, like poetry generally, is not read on the same scale as fiction, but the 20th c. shows several distinguished practitioners, including Don MARQUIS (whose *persona* was "Archy," a cockroach who typed E. E. CUMMINGS-style poems by jumping onto typewriter keys); Dorothy PARKER, who mastered the craft of sardonic light verse; and Ogden NASH, who created humor by comic deformities in the language he used, often in achieving improbable rhymes.

Humorous nonfiction is the predominant 20th-c. form. It is also the *locus classicus* is the *New Yorker,* a new magazine founded in 1925 by Harold Ross. Dorothy Parker and Clarence Day wrote for it; so did Robert BENCHLEY, E. B. WHITE, James THURBER, Frank SULLIVAN (best known for his "Cliché Expert" series), and S. J. PERELMAN. They inaugurated the (still) characteristic *New Yorker* piece, the "casual"—a page or two, sometimes an essay, sometimes a sketch, the masters of which were Benchley and Perelman. Though there are large differences between these writ-

ers, they all share the assumption of urbanity and literacy in the audience. Often their humor turns on the challenges of modern life—challenges to competence, as in Benchley's accounts of a little man's struggles to function successfully—or challenges to sanity, best illustrated in Perelman's anarchic sending up of literary fads, advertising language, and the other assorted *dreck* of our world.

Humorous writers of the first half of the century not associated with the *New Yorker* included H. L. MENCKEN, primarily a literary and social critic, newspaper columnists like Franklin P. Adams and Heywood Broun, and Ring LARDNER. Lardner began as a sportswriter and soon invented his own genres of humor. He used some comic illiteracy, as in his baseball-player letters; his short stories (the classic is "Haircut") are telling anatomies of human failure; he even wrote surrealistic plays of great interest. Lardner was a loner, much admired by the group associated with the Algonquin Club but aloof from other writers.

More recent writers of humorous nonfiction include Harry Golden, whose columns and books combined autobiography with sly arguments for social reform. Recently, Woody ALLEN, better known as a filmmaker, has mastered the "casual" in the vein of the early *New Yorker,* as have Veronica Geng and Roy Blount, among others.

BIBLIOGRAPHY: Bier, J., *The Rise and Fall of American Humor* (1967); Blair, W., and H. Hill, *America's Humor: From Poor Richard to Doonesbury* (1978); Keough, W., *Punchlines: The Violence of American Humor* (1990): Mintz, L., *Humor in America: A Research Guide to Genres and Topics* (1988); Rourke, C., *American Humor* (1931); Rubin, L., ed., *The Comic Imagination in American Literature* (1973); Yates, N., *The American Humorist: Conscience of the Twentieth Century* (1964)

MERRITT MOSELEY

HUMPHREYS, David

b. 10 July 1752, Derby, Connecticut; d. 21 February 1818, New Haven, Connecticut

One of the principal members of the Connecticut Wits, H. was educated at Yale, where he took a B.A. in 1771 and an M.A. in 1774. Not as deeply read as his classmate and literary collaborator John TRUMBULL, H. nonetheless established himself as one of the central writers of the early national period, primarily for the patriotic themes of his poetry. H.'s early career as a soldier in the Revolutionary army provided the background and inspiration for much of his published works. Serving as aide-de-camp of Israel Putnam and George Washington, he became a respected member of the army and later served in diplomatic capacities in France, Spain, and Portugal from 1790 to 1802. Returning to the U.S., H. finished out his life as a successful industrialist.

Profoundly influenced by John Ward's *System of Oratory* in college, H.'s poetry is primarily oratorical in tone. Relying heavily on exclamatory apostrophes and attempts at sublime grandeur, his epideictic verse is also often partitioned into clearly defined exordiums, encomiums and perorations. As critic Leon Howard remarks, H. used poetry as a means of courting favor and advancing his social status. In July 1776, H. sent a poem to Washington entitled "An Ode to His Excellency . . . ," and although it was never delivered, the accompanying letter shows him expecting preferment. Later, in his light "Letter to a Young Lady in Boston," H.'s poet departs from the young Lady with the words, "Tomorrow—(brief then be my story)—I go to WASHINGTON and GLORY; [as] His aide-de-camp." In 1779, H. was accompanying General Putnam when the general suffered a stroke. Taking advantage of the circumstances, H. retired for several months from the war in New Haven, where he revised the poem that began his reputation, "A Poem Addressed to the Armies of the United States of America" (1778–80), which he also sent to Washington. Written in heroic couplets, the poem's dramatic structure pivots on the Battle of Bunker Hill to lament the death of Warren and to celebrate the appearance of a God-like Washington—even though Washington was not there. By June 1780, H. was appointed to Washington's staff and the two became great friends. Critics have remarked that his respect for Washington was so great that he began to look like him.

In 1784, H. was sent to Europe for two years with John Adams and Thomas JEFFERSON to negotiate commercial treaties for the U.S. While in France, he published "A Poem on the Happiness of the U.S." Notable for its restraint from ponderous apostrophe, the poem celebrates the origin, agriculture, and commercial prospects of the young nation. In a later revision, he abbreviated the poem to its first 700 lines and published the second half as "A Poem on the Future Glory of the U.S." Upon his return from Europe, H. was elected to the Connecticut legislature. His concern about the unstable young republic caused him and his fellow Connecticut Wits—John Trumbull, Joel BARLOW, and Lemuel Hopkins—to respond with *The Anarchiad,* published in successive installments from October 1786 to September 1787 in the *New Haven Gazette.* The poem satirizes the stupidity and unruliness of the lower classes from a Federalist standpoint.

In 1787, H. was invited to stay for several weeks at Mt. Vernon to write Washington's biography. Although the project never got beyond a few pages in length, his manuscript is valuable for Washington's personal account of his early education. While at Mt. Vernon, however, H. did finish an essay that began simply as a few anecdotes about his former superior, *An Essay on the Life of the Honorable Major-General Israel Putnam* (1788). Probably his most influential work, H.'s tale of war-time daring is filled with high adventure, bullet-riddled clothing, and precarious escapes. Selections from it were widely anthologized by schoolbook writers of the period, including Noah Webster and Caleb Bingham. Children were brought up reading about "Putnam and the Wolf," where Putnam, his legs fastened to a rope held by his friends, crawled into the narrow cave of a sheep-killing wolf, armed with a torch and a gun. Most importantly for American literary history, the book provided the inspiration for Charles Brockden BROWN's *Edgar Huntley* and James Fenimore COOPER's *Last of the Mohicans.*

BIBLIOGRAPHY: Bigelow, G., *Rhetoric and American Poetry in the Early National Period* (1960); Howard, L., *The Connecticut Wits* (1943); Humphreys, F. L., *Life and Times of D. H.* (1917); Cifelli, E. M., *D. H.* (1982)

GRANVILLE GANTER

HUMPHREYS, Josephine
b. 2 February 1945, Charleston, South Carolina

Widely acclaimed as a strong voice among the writers of the New South, H. follows the legacy of William FAULKNER, Eudora WELTY, and Walker PERCY in dealing with characteristically southern themes of history, place, and family—but H. gives these themes a contemporary, often postmodern twist. While those forebears looked to the traditions and myths of the past as possible keys to understanding themselves, H.'s characters have examined the traditions of the past and found them faulty. While earlier southern writers tried to reconcile their experience with their region's collective history, H.'s approach is more personal: her characters examine their private rather than public histories in order to live successfully. And while for the Southern Renaissance writers the land held restorative power, H. recognizes that the natural landscapes that once fed the spirits of southern writers have been transformed into urban development, no longer able to regenerate the spirit and as likely to confine and limit possibilities for growth.

With Charleston, South Carolina, as both birthplace and chosen residence, H. is firmly located in the historic, low country South. Her three novels, *Dreams of Sleep* (1984), *Rich in Love* (1987), and *Fireman's Fair* (1991), are all set in and around Charleston; all share an examination of marriage and a cast of characters who are vaguely discontented with their lives, feeling that life is somehow "not enough"; and all explore the theme of disintegration—of traditions, of identities, of the landscape—and the need for reconciling imagination with experience.

Dreams of Sleep was hailed as a remarkable first novel, and indeed, it demonstrates acute perception of what Joan Philpott calls the "sorrowful gentility" of white, modern upper class professional lives. In echoes of Percy, H. creates characters who are self-consciously analytical and intellectual—but who are also nostalgic and bewildered. Will Reese, successful gynecologist, wanders without focus or sustained satisfaction through his experiences as son, husband, doctor, lover, and friend; like subsequent H. characters, he and his wife Alice are somnolent, nonparticipants in their own lives, preferring to watch than to take active responsibility.

H. uses the theme of failed racial integration that informs much of public southern experience as a metaphor for personal disintegration. The fragmented Alice has assigned pieces of herself to others: to Will's receptionist Claire, her role as lover; to the babysitter Iris Moon, that of mother. Only through Iris's definitive action does reconciliation become possible, though H. avoids complete closure with the suggestion that these movements toward connection are tentative and uncertain.

H.'s second novel, *Rich in Love,* again deals with marriages and familiar landscapes that are disintegrating. Her first-person narrator is seventeen-year-old Lucille Odom, another precocious adolescent, who tells the story of her family's disintegration and reconfiguration from her unique perspective as the emotional center of the family. Recurring themes include the erosion of natural landscapes to make way for developments like "Oakview," names chosen, Lucille thinks, as "memorials to what had been bulldozed into oblivion." Despite her attempt to hold onto her comfortable notion of her family as traditional, her mother has run away from home, her wildly independent sister returns home married and pregnant with a baby she doesn't want, her father takes up with his hairdresser, and Lucille learns that she is a twin who survived an abortion because "they didn't know [she] was in there." At novel's end, almost no one is where

we might have expected him or her to be, though each is full of hope for an optimistic future.

H.'s third novel, *Fireman's Fair,* again blends natural landscapes with personal ones. Set in Charleston in the aftermath of a hurricane, it offers the perspective of another disillusioned professional white male as he struggles with his personal storms of discontent. Harboring a secret love for Louise Camden, the wife of his law partner, Rob Wyatt has withdrawn from the life of the city, quit his practice, and moved into an outlying section of town to see what will happen next. As a bird watcher, he epitomizes the characteristics of other H. heroes: observers of life rather than active participants. Into this stalled existence comes Billie Poe, the now familiar strong, self-sufficient teenager, who calls him forth from his loneliness into love. The primary subject here is marriage, and H. offers insight into three different versions: Rob's parents have endured infidelities and betrayal but emerge with renewed love and commitment to each other; Louise and Hank Camden hold their brittle vision of marital happiness together, though with little prospects of living happily ever after; and Rob and Billie, an unlikely pair, embark on the adventure with optimism and hope.

Conventional in her use of plot and character development and sense of optimism in conclusions, H. nonetheless revisits traditional themes from a contemporary perspective. She deserves praise for her fully realized characters, her almost poetic style, and her realistic depiction of a distinctive social milieu.

BIBLIOGRAPHY: Drzal, D. A., "Casualties of the Feminine Mystique," *AR* 46 (Fall 1988): 450–61; Jackson, S. M., "J. H. and the Politics of Postmodern Desire," *MissQ* 47 (Spring 1994): 275–85; Walker, E. A., "J. H.'s *Rich in Love:* Redefining Southern Fiction," *MissQ* 47 (Spring 1994): 301–15

MARY MARWITZ

HUNTER, Evan
b. 15 October 1926, New York City

H. defies easy literary classification for two reasons. First, he has mastered numerous literary forms, including several novel genres, short stories, children's books, screenplays—including *The Birds* (1962)—and teleplays. Second, he publishes under at least six pseudonyms: John Abbott, Curt Cannon, Hunt Collins, Ezra Hannon, Richard Marsten, Ed McBain. This last aspect, though, is not surprising, since H. was actually born Salvatore Lombino. However, concerned that his name would not sell books, he officially changed it in the early 1950s to Evan Hunter (from Evander Childs High School and Hunter College). Almost prophetically, his best known work was published shortly thereafter.

H. based *The Blackboard Jungle* (1954) on his experience as a New York City vocational school teacher. The year in the life novel relates the travails of novice instructor Richard Dadier in a school plagued equally by malicious teens and cynical teachers. The novel not only captures the harrowing difficulties of inner city schooling—education courses still assign the book—but also demonstrates H.'s talent for ear perfect dialogue, a distinguishing characteristic of all H. novels. H. gained even more notoriety when *The Blackboard Jungle* was made into a popular film starring Glenn Ford and featuring the song "Rock around the Clock" by Bill Haley and the Comets.

Besides *The Blackboard Jungle,* H. has attained national recognition for *Sons* (1969) and *Streets of Gold* (1974), both of which portray familial generational conflict and the illusive nature of the American dream. Thoroughly researched, H.'s novels place characters in the context of or in contrast to important events in American history. Covering three years, *Sons* focuses on three generations of Tyler men and their respective involvements in World War I, World War II, and the Vietnam War. At the same time, he depicts an America that changes its patriotic perspective on the necessity of sending young men to war. The focus on family continues in *Streets of Gold,* considered to be H.'s best novel. Told by Ignazio Silvio Di Palermo, a successful, blind piano player, the tale covers the entire life of his grandfather, an Italian immigrant, searching for the American dream. Ironically, while Ignazio achieves the mythic success associated with the "streets of gold," his grandfather realizes that even though he lived in poverty most of his life, he still experienced the true American dream.

While H. considers his novels to be serious literature, he has gained far more recognition and success through his shiftier pseudonym of Ed McBain. Under this name, he created the well-respected 87th Precinct series, of which he has currently published forty-nine. These police procedural novels, considered to be the genre's best, center around the cases and personal lives of a group of detectives, including Steve Carella, Meyer Meyer, and Bert Kling. In order to maintain authenticity, McBain visits police departments around the world, and he includes actual police forms and fingerprints in his novels. What also distinguishes his series is the complexity of the storytelling as numerous subplots swirl around the novel's main investigation. Many critics consider *Ice* (1983) as the most successful novel in the series.

Despite his success, H. has received scant critical attention for numerous reasons. His prolific output (over one hundred novels) has produced, at times, less than stellar work. Since 1952, he has published at least one novel a year except for 1955—and in some years, he has published four novels. His most popular books are mysteries, which are considered second tier literary works. His storytelling is playful as he makes self-referential jokes about his name change and his past works—*The Birds* appears in numerous novels. Even though H. is considered to be too mainstream a writer and therefore unworthy of "serious" attention, one cannot dispute that he can tell a story, and one can only hope he keeps telling them for years to come.

BIBLIOGRAPHY: Butts, D., "The Cop and the Machine: Technology and the 87th Precinct Novels of Ed McBain," *Clues* 6 (1985): 99–107; Dove, G. N., *The Boys from Grover Avenue: Ed McBain's 87th Precinct Novels* (1985)

WILLIAM C. BOLES

HURST, Fannie
b. 19 October 1889, Hamilton, Ohio; d. 23 February 1968, New York City

Perhaps best known for the novels on which the movies *Back Street* and *Imitation of Life* are based, H. should more fully be remembered as a prolific writer of popular fiction and a social activist committed to women's causes. During her lifetime, H. was not given serious critical consideration, but her works give us a view of American life between the two world wars.

H.'s childhood was devoted to writing poetry and short stories, so her success as a writer could have been easily predicted. A graduate of Washington University, H. taught briefly before moving to New York in 1911 where she immediately immersed herself as a writer. Upon receiving numerous rejections for her work, she resorted to other occupations, including sales and acting. These experiences gave her insight into the world of working women and would help to shape future female characters such as Ray Schmidt in *Back Street* (1931) as well as H.'s involvement supporting women wage earners.

Soon H. was making a living as a writer, selling stories to magazines as well as having five collections of stories published between 1914 and 1919. During her career, H. wrote three hundred short stories and thirty novels; twenty-nine films were made from her works. Her most common themes centered around women's lives: how they gained financial security, the exploration of male/female relationships (including the sexual aspect), as well as issues of class, aging, and race. *Humoresque* (1919) contains eight stories about Jews in New York City; *Imitation of Life* (1933) is a novel about passing as well as about a woman finding financial independence. H.'s central female characters are often at the mercy of the cruel men in their lives, physically as well as financially.

H.'s interest in social issues extended beyond her fiction. She was chair of the National Housing Commission from 1936 to 1937, a member of the National Advisory Committee to the Works Progress Administration from 1940 to 1941, and a delegate to the World Health Organization Assembly in Geneva in 1952.

From a contemporary perspective, H.'s novels may seem sentimental or simplistic, but they reveal her interest in the plight of women who depended on men and reflect the tastes of the reading public in the first two-thirds of the 20th c.

BIBLIOGRAPHY: Brandimarte, C., *F. H. and Her Fiction: Prescriptions for America's Working Women* (1980); Hapke, L., *Daughters of the Great Depression: Women, Work, and Fiction in the American 1930s* (1995); Koppelman, S., ed., *F. H.: The Woman, the Writer: A Collection of Essays* (1994)

REBECCA FABER

HURSTON, Zora Neale

b. 7 January 1891, Eatonville, Florida; d. 28 January 1960, Saint Lucie County, Florida

A vivid part of the Harlem Renaissance, H. has remained a force in the renaissance of African American fiction from the mid-1970s to the present, particularly that of Ernest J. GAINES, Alice WALKER, and Toni MORRISON. Although H. published many occasional essays and a few short stories, collaborated with Langston HUGHES on a play, wrote an autobiography, *Dust Tracks on a Road* (1942), and a book on Haitian voodoo, *Tell My Horse* (1938), her fame and influence grow from her collection of folklore, *Mules and Men* (1935), and the first three of her four novels—*Jonah's Gourd Vine* (1934), *Their Eyes Were Watching God* (1937), *Moses, Man of the Mountain* (1939), and *Seraph of the Suwanee* (1948). Many of H.'s contemporaries, Richard WRIGHT the most prominent, highlighted the myriad effects of white racism on the black individual and community. While not denying such oppression, H. instead focuses on black experience in all-black or mostly black contexts. Consequently, her work explores a more independent black existence's speech and art forms, such as the SERMON and the FOLKTALE.

H.'s youth in a small, Southern, all-black town (Eatonville, Florida) developed her lifelong interest in the African American folktale. After working with anthropologist Franz Boas, H. returned South to collect the stories she had grown up with. Her publication of *Mules and Men* began a reevaluation of the oral tradition central to African American culture. H.'s emphasis on the context of the storytelling and on the stories' variety, for example, laid the groundwork for modern examination of call-and-response aesthetics (the dynamic of interaction between speaker and audience) and for the understanding of tales as indirect instructions on surviving and prospering under oppression.

H.'s first two novels explore, in rural Southern settings, the protagonists' attempts to define personal identities within their communities. *Jonah's Gourd Vine*'s John Pearson leaves his abusive stepfather and loving mother, becomes a preacher, suffers from his inability to remain faithful to his first wife, and finally dies feeling that he has betrayed both himself and his second wife. John never reconciles his contradictory urges toward traditional spiritual fulfillment (his vocation and his marriages) and toward sensual exploration. In this work consisting primarily of dialogue, H. pioneered a central focus on black speech, her skill culminating in the great set-piece of John's last sermon.

The successful individualization that eludes John comes to Janie Crawford in H.'s most famous and influential novel, *Their Eyes Were Watching God*. Following Janie from adolescent to forty-year-old woman, the novel shows her progress in several interlocking matrices: search for an emotionally and spiritually fulfilling expression of sexuality, aspiration to and rejection of white middle class norms, discovery of and participation in community, the development of her individual voice. When Janie's husband forbids her to join in the communal creation of folktales, he prevents her from participating in the on-going formation of the community's entertainment and self-definition. Janie's voice finally triumphs, however. Although a third-person narrator frames the novel and occasionally provides information unknown to Janie, most of the novel consists of Janie's direct report of her experience to her friend Pheoby. Although the novel presents every critic with some difficulties—feminists, for example, celebrate Janie's sexuality and her voice while remaining dismayed at H.'s acceptance of male-female physical violence—the novel is acclaimed for its depiction of a strong woman discovering her strengths, its portrait of romantic love, and its presentation of folklore as a dynamic process rather than a static art form.

Moses, Man of the Mountain expands this concern with the creation of myth through its treatment of the biblical figure most important to black culture. An Egyptian whose role is determined by both historical prophecy and an Israelite girl's desire to avoid a whipping, Moses's life combines the grand and the bathetic. *Moses* considers the nature of leadership, the mutually creative and influencing interactions of a community and its leader. In its humorous, incisive reinterpretation of the Old Testament—the Israelites speak black English; Moses converses with God but also trains himself as a magician—the novel is a powerful example of what modernists call deconstruction, the critique of a dominant interpretation in order to empower minorities.

Poverty hounded H. all her life, and many see her last novel, *Seraph on the Suwanee,* as a failed, desperate attempt to secure commercial success. *Seraph* focuses on lower-class whites, with black characters present only as stereotypes. The heroine, puny by the standards of Janie Crawford and Moses, remains too frightened by vitality (including her own sexuality) to have a real identity until late in her life. Most readers find her final metamorphosis either unconvincing or "too little, too late." However unheroic, the novel thoroughly documents the erosion of female identity by traditional expectations of women. Historically, most critics have read the novel as an unsuccessful realistic portrayal of the erosion of female identity by traditional expectations of women. Reconsidering the novel's genre, some recent critics present it as a successful satire of the Cult of True Womanhood (lingering 19th-c. expectations for white middle-class women).

H.'s presentation of black culture as largely independent of Euro-American control, her respect for oral tradition, and her feminism make her an important tradition and a contemporary inspiration. Some writers and critics find her works problematic, however, because of her focus on rural experience and folk wisdom as the repository of cultural knowledge. The question of whether this knowledge can be useful to an increasingly urban, differently educated community is central to many critiques of H.

BIBLIOGRAPHY: Awkward, M., *Inspiriting Influences* (1989); Bell, B., *The Afro-American Novel and Its Tradition* (1987); Bloom, H., ed., *Z. N. H.'s Their Eyes Were Watching God* (1987); Christian, B., *Black Women Novelists* (1980); Gates, H. L., Jr., and A. Appiah, eds., *Z. N. H.: Critical Perspectives Past and Present* (1993); Hemenway, R., *Z. N. H.* (1977); Hines, D. C., *Black Women in America: An Historical Encyclopedia* (1994); Lowe, J., *Jump at the Sun: Z. N. H.'s Comic Comedy* (1994)

MISSY DEHN KUBITSCHEK

HWANG, David Henry
b. 11 August 1957, Los Angeles, California

H. is the first Asian American playwright to bring Asian and American themes to Broadway. His *M But-*

terfly (1988), which won the Tony Award for best play, explores the need to maintain illusion rather than acknowledging truth in East-West cultural and sexual stereotypes. The play is based on the story of a French diplomat found guilty of spying who claimed not to know that his Chinese lover of twenty years, to whom he gave information, was a man.

We meet the diplomat, Rene Gallimard, in prison, where he unfolds his story through flashbacks. Gallimard is not unlike Don Quixote, a man out of touch with his reality, trying to maintain an outdated value system in a changing world. We ask: How could Don Quixote really do battle with a windmill? How could Gallimard not know that Song Liling was a man? How could the West maintain its outdated notions of the East as being feminine, weak, and in need of protection? The need to believe, to maintain one's own self-image can be stronger than truth, which necessitates change.

Throughout the play, H. weaves themes of imperialism, stereotypes of gender and race, and East-West relations. He does this by blending elements of both cultures, using not only the music, lyrics, and Puccini's opera *Madama Butterfly,* but capitalizing on Butterfly as the ultimate Asian female stereotype. To this, he adds elements of the Chinese opera, in which male actors play the role of women. He gives the plot a twist—by making the ultimate female a man and the Western male the gullible partner.

This blending of cultural styles was evident in H.'s earlier plays, and is a creative choice of other multicultural writers in prose and poetry. It is as if no one form is sufficient to express the struggle between two cultures. H. also borrows from the postmodern movement in art and absurdist theater, the stark Japanese noh play, and the stylized Chinese Opera.

The struggle with changing perceptions and Asian and American identity was the central in *F.O.B* (1983), which stands for "fresh off the boat" and is slang for an immigrant. H. explores the stages of assimilation—Dale is a second generation Chinese, who is whiter than white. He is contrasted with Steve, an F.O.B. Situated between them, is Grace, a first generation Chinese, who juggles the conflicts of cultural attitudes and perceptions.

In *Golden Child* (1996), H. returns to the themes of the myth of family past and assimilation. Tieng-Bin returns home from a three-year business trip to the Philippines eager to introduce Western traditions, along with Reverend Baines, a man eager to bring Jesus to the village. Tieng-Bin seeks to break with the past and enter into the new world, unaware of the high cost of change for his family, and for himself.

Perhaps this is why we ultimately believe Gallimard, a man so steeped in Western perspectives. He could not help but see Butterfly as anything but an

561

Asian female stereotype. The truth requires change, but without change we still must pay a price.

BIBLIOGRAPHY: Cooperman, R., "Across the Boundaries of Cultural Identity: An Interview with D. H. H.," in Maufort, M., ed., *Staging Differences: Cultural Pluralism in American Theater and Drama* (1995): 182–204; Skloot, R., "Breaking the Butterfly," *MD* 33 (March 1990): 59–66; Street, D., *D. H. H.* (1989)

KATHLEEN MOTOIKE

I

IGNATOW, David
b. 7 February 1914, Brooklyn, New York; d. 17 November 1997, East Hampton, New York

I. is a distinguished American poet and editor who has spent much of his life in New York, a city whose dark side informs much of his work. The city's influence along with the negative impact of his business experiences as a young man are strongly evident in his early work. In 1948, he published his first volume of poetry, *Poems*. His often matter-of-fact comments on everyday life and his rhetorical style show the influence of William Carlos WILLIAMS, a mentor who praised and encouraged I. Among the other strong influences on his work, I. lists the Bible, the great Russian writers, and the American poet Walt WHITMAN.

I.'s typical poem is the short lyric. His work is strongly autobiographical, although he usually adopts a persona. The style is often simple and straightforward, and his use of the American vernacular underscores the horror he sees and feels as he examines the minute details of both his private and his public life. His themes are not easy to categorize, but his unrelenting focus on his personal response, from the guilty to the angry to the wryly humorous, tends to give his work a sense of unity.

The political and social poems reflect I.'s lived experience: the Great Depression of the 1930s, World War II, the Vietnam War, the American lust for money, the violence and insanity of life in the U.S. The personal poems rely on felt experience. These works often contain a tension generated by juxtaposing the difficulties in marital and family relationships with the blighted, crumbling landscapes the speakers of the poems perceive both inside as well as outside their windows.

The Gentle Weight Lifter (1955) contains a number of poems that seem to be experiments in distancing the content from the urban setting and focusing on the isolation and alienation resulting from social decay. The settings are biblical, classical, or timeless. Much of the work is parablelike, especially the social poetry, and this technique is evident in the poems in *Say Pardon* (1961) and *Figures of the Human* (1964). Urban violence and corruption become slightly surreal and I. often moves away from free verse into the less structured narration of the PROSE POEM. The work in the latter volume is considered some of I.'s weakest—short, flat pieces hinting at emotional exhaustion.

His next book, *Rescue the Dead* (1968), represents a personal and a poetic rebirth. Here I. recasts themes from earlier works: parents, romantic and sexual love, marriage, children, the violence of American society, and the personal threat the speaker feels. Other poems hint at themes that will be explored more fully in *Facing the Tree* (1975) and *Tread the Dark* (1978)—the individual's connection with and relationship to nature. In these two volumes, the poet delves into the complexities and contradictions he discovers in exploring his place within the natural world. It might be speculated that since during this period the poet began spending less time in New York City and was living and writing more often in his country home, the poetry begins to reflect both his physical and emotional distance from the city. Paradoxically, there is no comfort in seeing oneself part of a cycle that hints at eternal return. Instead, especially in the poems of *Tread the Dark,* there is a longing for the release that death offers from a blackness within and the void without. Many poems are concerned with suicide and escape from self.

Despair is transformed into joy and a new wisdom in I.'s next collection, *Whisper to the Earth* (1981). The speaker has faced his mortality and come to terms with it—even if it is on its own terms. The struggle to discover the meaning of life is set aside; perhaps the significance of life is merely its existence.

New and Collected Poems, 1970–1985 (1986) allows the reader to trace I.'s emotional and philosophical growth into impending old age. His themes, as in earlier times, are the security of the child versus the isolation of the elderly, the need to make meaning of the probable meaninglessness of life lived without a spiritual dimension, political cruelty, death. Many of the poems are about poetry. In the end, the personae are able for the most part to come to terms with despair through love—the poet makes a conscious choice to love the universe. In *Shadowing the Ground* (1991) and *Despite the Plainness of the Day: Love Poems* (1991), the voices of the speakers are as authentic as they are individual. By 1996, with *I Have a Name,* much of the bitterness has been transmuted into a deeper and more complex moral and intellectual vision. Emotions are strongly felt, beautifully articulated, and fully realized.

BIBLIOGRAPHY: Lipari, J., *The Poetry of D. I.: An Introduction and Bibliography of Primary Sources, 1931–1978* (1983); Terris, V. R., *Meaningful Differences: The Poetry and Prose of D. I.* (1994)

MARGARET D. SULLIVAN

IMAGISM

It was Ezra POUND's invention of the school of "imagism" in 1912 that was the inciting moment in the modernist revolution. Pound evidently took his ideas on the subject from those discussed at meetings of T. E. Hulme's Poet's Club founded in London about 1908. Hulme was a philosopher, a follower of Henri Bergson, who believed that image is the heart of poetry, not mere decoration. Pound added to this precept the "free verse" practice of the French symbolists and of Walt WHITMAN. Furthermore, as one who chose the whole world as his field of poetic expertise, Pound—together with other members of the school—also was influenced by the practices and traditions of the Chinese and Japanese poets.

In the fall of 1912, Pound dubbed his friend Hilda DOOLITTLE, "H. D., Imagiste," which he wrote beneath her poem "Hermes of the Ways" and sent to Harriet MONROE's new Chicago magazine, *Poetry.* Shortly thereafter, in November, Pound used the term for the first time publicly when he included in his book *Ripostes* an appendix, the "Complete Poetical Works" of Hulme, which consisted of five poems. In January, Doolittle's work appeared in *Poetry* with her literary name subjoined.

In the March 1913 issue of *Poetry,* the British poet F. S. Flint, without naming him, quoted Pound's three tenets of Imagisme, the first of which was, in effect,

"No ideas but in things," as William Carlos WILLIAMS would subsequently put it. The second was spareness and condensation of language, the ideal of the haikuist, and the third was the "vers libre" requirement derived from the symbolists and Whitman. A fourth, mysterious, "Doctrine of the Image" also existed, which Flint said the school "had not committed to writing"; however, in the same issue, Pound himself defined the "image" as "that which presents an intellectual and emotional complex in an instant of time," which is technically the definition of the haiku.

The British imagists—the "e" was soon dropped—originally published their poems in two British periodicals, the *New Freewoman* and its successor the *Egoist,* to which the Americans John Gould FLETCHER and Marianne MOORE also contributed. In 1914, Pound published a seminal anthology, *Les Imagistes,* which added Richard Aldington and James Joyce to the British contingent, Williams, Janet Lewis, and Amy LOWELL to the American. Lowell soon assumed leadership of the group, and Pound dropped out—disgustedly dubbing the group "Amygism"—in favor of a never well-defined movement that he called "Vorticism." Lowell kept the "school" alive during 1915–17 by issuing anthologies entitled *Some Imagist Poets,* and in her prefaces she added to the critical and theoretical literature of imagism even as she herself felt that the movement was being vitiated.

Pound and the imagist poets were influenced not only by Walt Whitman's prose poetry but also by Japanese poetry—especially the haiku—but the argument can be made that Williams deliberately invented an American accentual stanza in his "triversen" that is the equivalent of the Japanese haiku or, more exactly, the three-line katauta. In effect, in his earliest poems—those to be found in the first volume of his *Collected Poems*—Williams adapted to American poetry the syllabic prosody of the haiku and katauta.

The imagists, but in particular Williams, were particularly successful in adapting to American poetics not only Japanese metrical theory, but also the spirit of the haiku to the American sensibility. Many Western poets have been notably unsuccessful in writing good image poetry, and this failure has to do with their attempting what Williams did not attempt to do: naturalize Zen Buddhism, of which the haiku is a relatively recent outgrowth.

Haiku translated into English often appear to members of Occidental culture to be overly sentimental. The Zen poet attempts to put the self into the thing perceived, to do more than empathize with it and "become one" with the thing; thus, by extension, with all things. In Western traditions, empathizing with objects is sentimental; there is even a term, "the pathetic fallacy," to describe the state of excessive personification or overempathy. If American poets try to become one with the object of their perception, their work will appear to be self-indulgent and egocentric. It was T. S. ELIOT, though, who produced the theory that Williams put into practice, the theory of "objective correlative": the poet must choose that object which will be the idea, not merely the symbol of the idea.

BIBLIOGRAPHY: Brower, R. H., and E. Miner, *Japanese Court Poetry* (1961); Hoffman, Y., ed., *Japanese Death Poems* (1986); Tapscott, S. *American Beauty: William Carlos Williams and the Modernist Whitman* (1984); Waggoner, H. H., *American Poets from the Puritans to the Present* (1968; rev. ed., 1984)

LEWIS PUTNAM TURCO

IMLAY, Gilbert

b. ca. 1754, Monmouth County, New Jersey; d. 20 November 1828?, Isle of Jersey, England

Soldier, adventurer, and lover of Mary Wollstonecraft, I. wrote two works: *A Topographical Description of the Western Territories of North America* (1792) and an epistolary novel, *The Emigrants; or, The History of an Expatriated Family* (1793), both published in England after I. left America forever to pursue his political and mercantile schemes. His current literary reputation rests entirely on *The Emigrants.*

The Emigrants combines many literary types, both English and American. Its epistolary format and love story recall Samuel Richardson and the sentimental novel. Its description of Pittsburgh and the frontier along the Ohio suggests the border romance. Its commentary on society and marriage verges on satire. Its attack on class makes it, as John Seelye notes, the "one book" by an American in the "Jacobin mode." And its climax revivifies the most popular prose form in colonial America, the INDIAN CAPTIVITY NARRATIVE.

I.'s one fiction succeeds best when he juxtaposes a fluid, organic natural world with a rigid, constrained social world, when he uses plot and place to illuminate the evils attendant upon stultifying divorce laws and social conventions. *The Emigrants* fails when I. allows his correspondents to theorize sententiously about matters moral and amatory. Though *The Emigrants* is often turgid and prolix, I. is able to castigate social evils by contrasting them with the virgin world of the American West.

Little is known about I.'s last years, and the circumstances of his death are ambiguous. However, it is generally accepted that I. died and is buried on the Isle of Jersey.

BIBLIOGRAPHY: Rusk, R. L., *The Adventures of G. I.* (1923); Seelye, J., "The Jacobin Mode in Early

American Fiction: G. I.'s *The Emigrants,*" *EAL* 22 (Fall 1987): 204–12

JOHN ENGELL

INDIAN CAPTIVITY NARRATIVE

Though Europeans called it the "New World," America was, more precisely speaking, a new focus for old dreams no longer realizable in the "Old World." Indeed, many European dreams were unrealizable in any actual world. Long before colonists arrived, North America was Arcadia, El Dorado, the New Jerusalem—a space prefabricated through imagination, history, mythology, and religious vision. Records of early encounters between Europeans and Native Americans include many Indian captivity narratives that illustrate how settlers in North America saw the New World and its indigenous people almost exclusively according to preconceived visions.

An array of Europeans including Spanish explorers, Jesuit missionaries, and Puritan colonials wrote narratives of Indian captivity. Their stories usually lack ethnographic objectivity and reflect instead their narrators' conscious and unconscious urges to explain new and exotic experiences within Western, Christian epistemological schemes. Since the years of first contact between colonists and tribal peoples, stories of Indian captivity have served as religious and moral instruction, as political propaganda, as material for popular fiction such as the penny-dreadful, as models for slave narratives, and always as archetypal expressions of American values and attitudes.

Mary ROWLANDSON wrote the first and best-known captivity narrative published in America, *The Sovereignty & Goodness of God, Together with the Faithfulness of His Promises Displayed; Being a Narrative of the Captivity and Restauration of Mrs. Mary Rowlandson* (1682). Captured in Massachusetts during King Philip's War by a Wampanoag party, Rowlandson spent eleven weeks (from February 20 to May 2, 1676) among the Indians. Typical of captivity narratives written by Puritans during the 17th c., hers presents a primarily typological interpretation of her ordeal. She views her experiences according to a biblical paradigm that defines captivity as God's trial of the spiritually complacent. Indian captivity in the American wilderness becomes a type for Babylonian captivity, just as the Puritan migration to the New World corresponds typologically to the exodus of the Chosen People out of Egypt. For the Puritan, passing God's test meant remaining a Christian despite the influence of the Indians, whom Calvinists considered the instruments of Satan. If the captive survived, the test was followed by deliverance out of captivity—redemption—and the narrative serves thereafter as a parable for those at home who have never endured traumatic separation from the Puritan community. Overall, the ordeal is considered good, for it strengthens the soul.

Rowlandson's widely circulated narrative itself quickly became a model for subsequent stories of captivity. John Williams's *The Redeemed Captive, Returning unto Zion* (1706), for instance, records his experiences as a captive during the French and Indian Wars. He deemphasizes ethnographic information about Native Americans and composes his story more generally according to the established archetypal Puritan pattern of punishment and trial, salvation and redemption. Williams's narrative provides interesting counterpoint to Rowlandson's, however, for this Puritan narrator's trials and tribulations occur not only at the hands of the Indians, but also at those of the Roman Catholics. Moreover, unlike Rowlandson, Williams was carried off to Canada. Recent comparative studies of captives' experiences in Canada versus those of American colonial captives reveal interesting differences in the two countries' respective relationships with the Indians. Recent studies of captivity narrative in general also provide convincing evidence that Rowlandson and others might have been influenced by accounts of white enslavement in North Africa (Barbary captivity narratives) that predated their own by several years; these stories, some speculate, might also have affected colonial attitudes toward African slavery in America.

Others besides Puritans wrote accounts of Indian captivity. Unsurprisingly, their works deviate from the Calvinist pattern. Jesuit Father Isaac Jogues's account of his captivity among the Mohawks reveals differences between the Puritan and Catholic perception of the meaning of captivity. With a Roman Catholic stress upon the value of martyrdom, Father Isaac emphasizes the physical tortures he suffered at the hands of the Indians.

Jesuit persistence in converting the Indians to Catholicism added to the Puritan fear of Indian captivity. Not only was there always the threat that the captives, especially those from the lax second generation, would "turn Indian," but that they might turn Catholic as well. Williams, for example, laments the loss of his daughter, who preferred to stay among the Indians as a "papist and a pagan." Consequently, one particular aim of captivity narratives of the colonial era was to reinforce the fear of straying from the Puritan community and to suppress individualism. Contemporary studies of these narratives sometimes reveal more complex messages at the subtextual level, however. According to some current scholars, for instance, Rowlandson's narrative bears traces of an implicit struggle with the conventional meanings that her experiences

were supposed to carry based on biblical and other authoritative models. Indeed, since approximately the mid-1980s, a wealth of feminist and New Historical criticism has apprised us of the ways in which female subjectivity is uniquely inscribed within Rowlandson's narrative. Such studies have altered the traditional view of captivity narrative as reflecting the ordeal of the soul who merely desires submission to established authority and reintegration into the Puritan community. When we examine subtleties of discourse in Rowlandson's narrative, for example, we see the author's anger and conflict over her own culturally defined self-worth emerge from beneath her apparent orthodoxy. Some scholars observe in Rowlandson's sublimated individualism a source of inspiration for rebellion bequeathed to her readers of the Revolutionary War period.

Though others besides Puritans wrote narratives of captivity, the Puritan narratives were by far the most numerous and widely read. They proffered the message that America, like life in general, offered two alternatives: to reform and transform history through the Puritan mission, or to "turn Indian" or Catholic and thus deliver the world into Satan's power. Written for publication in England, most of the narratives unfold according to the conventions of the Puritan sermon—they begin with a biblical passage that the story proceeds to illustrate, interpret, and apply as a moral lesson. They defend the errand in the wilderness and deliberately contradict positive portrayals of Native American life such as those in Thomas MORTON's anti-Puritan work, *The New English Canaan*. Captivity material was routinely incorporated into Puritan revival sermons and jeremiads by Increase MATHER and, later, Cotton MATHER; even as late as the 18th c. the rhetoric of the captivity narrative is evident in the works of Jonathan EDWARDS. Such language was by this time so familiar to the audience that Edwards and others could expect predictable emotional responses to particular words and phrases.

During the 18th c., especially after 1720, the Indian captivity narrative began to serve nonreligious purposes. During the French and Indian Wars and the American Revolution, the Indians took more prisoners than ever before. These wars fueled greater hatred of the Indians, now for secular as well as spiritual reasons, and the Indian captivity narrative became the vehicle of anti-French and anti-British political messages as well as of anti–Indian sentiment. Moreover, the genre often included propaganda supporting the doctrine of "Manifest Destiny," westward expansion at the expense of the Indians, who were portrayed as worthless, uncivilized, and expendable in the advancement of white civilization. This attitude prevailed during the first half of the 19th c. in the so-called "nativist" movement of the Jacksonian era. Indeed, the ideas propounded in captivity narratives were probably responsible for many barbarous policies toward Native Americans during the 18th and 19th cs.

During the 19th c., the captivity narrative became highly sensationalized for a growing commercial market as the genre was adapted to pulp fiction. The message became more sympathetic to the Indians, for defeated and driven off their land, they were now perceived as less threatening. Popular fiction portrayed the Indian as an inferior sort of "brother," and contact with Indians was popularly conceived as part of an initiation-in-nature experience for American males. Even in works of higher literary status, such as the novels of James Fenimore COOPER, the Native American is a sentimentalized "noble savage," whose best traits are assimilated by the intellectually and morally superior white man. This notion prevails in 20th-c. literature, for example in novels by William FAULKNER, and in popular works like "The Lone Ranger"—tales of a white, male hero dependent upon the native wit of an Indian "sidekick."

The Indian captivity narrative to some extent also served as a model for yet another kind of narrative during the 19th c. Prior to the emancipation of the slaves in the middle of the 19th c., freed or escaped slaves often composed narratives of their ordeal according to the same pattern as that reflected in the Puritan captivity stories: captivity is a trial for the soul, made stronger by the ordeal and eventually redeemed. Throughout the centuries, the Indian captivity narrative retains this archetypal pattern. As perhaps the first truly American story, it formulates and justifies American mores and values. The pattern concerns the archetypal hero, the captive, who suffers the trauma of separation from his own people and who is forced to live among primitive people in a primal realm. Through a death-and-rebirth ordeal, he is transformed and redeemed from naiveté and ignorance into knowledge and wisdom; then he returns with messages of infinite value to share with those without benefit of his experiences.

The various historical transformations in the Indian captivity narrative map the changes in America's beliefs and anxieties about itself. During the 17th and early 18th cs., the narratives underscore the colonists' sense of religious mission in the New World, as well as their fears of failure. During the late 18th and early 19th cs., captivity narratives reveal the shift in America's sense of itself away from a religious utopia to a secular utopia—a utopia free of all foreign and Native American influence. During the 19th c., the captivity narrative exists primarily as an embedded genre within sensationalist fiction. This fiction propounds the American myth of romantic, "Indianized" heroes in the wilderness who have, however, also retained every-

thing of value from their European heritage. The Indian, in turn, has become Christianized, subdued, and content with adjunct cultural status. The perceived disappearance of Native Americans as an autonomous, living culture posing the threat of difference to the white American is, unsurprisingly, accompanied by the submergence of the Indian captivity narrative into other, more dominant generic forms such as the popular novel.

In the last few decades, women's studies and cultural studies in general have profoundly revised our understanding of issues of gender and culture in history and literature, including tales of Indian captivity. Another source of transformation of contemporary views has been the proliferation of fictional and nonfictional writings by native Americans in the U.S. and Canada, accompanied by the rise of Native American (and Canadian) studies, since approximately the late 1960s. Increased knowledge of, and sensitivity to, tribal peoples generated by the people themselves have altered the mainstream cultural perceptions of Indians and the history of the contact between them and Euro-Americans. One especially intriguing work affecting our view of Indian captivity narrative is a poem by Chippewa poet and novelist, Louise ERDRICH. Entitled "Captivity" (in *Jacklight*), the poem appropriates the speaking voice of Mary Rowlandson and represents the story of her captivity. Erdrich's "Rowlandson" presents a sympathetic view of the captors from an imagined "Indian" perspective.

BIBLIOGRAPHY: Barnett, L. K., *The Ignoble Savage* (1975); Fiedler, L. A., *The Return of the Vanishing American* (1968); Heard, J. N., *White into Red* (1973); Levernier, J. A., and H. Cohen, *The Indians and Their Captives* (1977); Van Der Beets, R., *The Indian Captivity Narrative* (1984); Vaughn, A. T., and E. W. Clark, *Puritans among the Indians* (1981)

CATHERINE RAINWATER

INGE, William [Motter]
b. 3 May 1913, Independence, Kansas; d. 10 June 1973, Los Angeles, California

Because his best works are set in the Midwest, usually Kansas, I. is often considered America's "first authentic Midwestern playwright." However, his themes of loneliness, ineffectuality, and frustration, woven with a complex view of love both inside and outside family relationships, transcend regionalism and make him one of America's most important post-World War II playwrights. I. had his greatest successes during the 1950s with four consecutive long-running Broadway plays: *Come Back, Little Sheba* (1950), *Picnic* (1953),

Bus Stop (1955), and *The Dark at the Top of the Stairs* (1957). Subsequent successful films of these plays helped make I.'s name one of the decade's most luminous.

I.'s genre is conventionally staged domestic drama. Like much postwar theater, his work is neither tragedy nor comedy, but realistic and often naturalistic, featuring individuals struggling to find happiness. I.'s people must accept their circumstances and cope as best they can. His intimate knowledge of small towns and their people comes from being the youngest and most sentient child in a mother-dominated home in tiny Independence, Kansas. This environment earns him kinship with such earlier Midwestern "Revolt from the Village" writers as Sherwood ANDERSON, Sinclair LEWIS, and Edgar Lee MASTERS. Today, I.'s work is considered too obviously Freudian and too simplistically resolved in favor of traditional family configurations, the kind of work popular in the placid Eisenhower years. Though such criticism has validity, his achievement has been lasting, and his successful plays still enjoy frequent production, especially among small theater groups. His reputation rests on the 1950s plays and one screenplay, *Splendor in the Grass* (1961), for which he was given an Academy Award.

An irony of I.'s career is that his works are seen as endorsements of traditional marriages and families when he himself never married and concealed his homosexuality. His affirmations of conventional marriage and family were perhaps all that Broadway would tolerate in the 1950s, but they also seemed personal expressions for I.—the way he wished things could be. His longtime battles with alcoholism informed some of his drama, but his equally longtime homosexual shame remained concealed in his work, emerging only in the mostly unpublished writing of his late years.

Come Back, Little Sheba features a deeply disillusioned couple, Doc and Lola Delaney. He became an alcoholic because of his disappointments of having to marry Lola, having to quit medical school for chiropractic, and losing their only child. Lola became an unkempt and overweight natterer because of her disappointments of losing the child and losing her youthful beauty, which she symbolizes in her little lost dog, Sheba, whom she frequently calls. Although Doc is dry thanks to Alcoholics Anonymous when the play begins, events build to a powerful scene in which, dangerously drunk, he threatens Lola's life before passing out. Later, realizing that they need each other and have no one else to turn to, they reconcile.

The play won I. designation as 1950s "most promising playwright," and when his next play, *Picnic,* won him a Pulitzer Prize, he clearly realized that promise. *Picnic* tells of Hal Carter, a handsome drifter who arrives in a small town and creates a great disturbance among the lonely women there. Hal and Madge Owens, the local beauty, fall in love, but not before several incidents triggered by Hal's presence. Hal affects all the women, from Madge's mother to Rosemary, the schoolteacher who boards at the Owens home. He makes them aware of their loneliness and isolation from most opportunities for love. His volatile presence gets him into enough trouble that he must leave the town, and Madge follows him against both her mother's and I.'s wishes: director Joshua Logan insisted on the "young love triumphs" ending that I. thought unrealistic, but agreed to. He later published *Summer Brave* (1962), a revised version in which Madge stays to become another of the lonely and frustrated women in the town.

I.'s third hit, *Bus Stop,* features travelers stranded at a restaurant by a blizzard. Bo Decker, a rowdy young cowboy, is returning from a Kansas City rodeo; he has in tow his mentor, Virgil Blessing, and a showgirl, Cherie, whom he is abducting to be his wife. Cherie protests that she does not want to go with Bo, but the business of the play is to resolve their conflict and reconcile them. Though *Bus Stop* offers a "happy ending" for Bo and Cherie, the experience of the rest of the cast keeps the play from being exclusively romantic comedy: none of the other characters finds love or happiness. These characters are reminders that in I.'s vision, most people must settle for something less than what they want.

The Dark at the Top of the Stairs was I.'s final hit, an autobiographical play featuring the Flood family, which strongly resembles the I. family of the playwright's boyhood. The father, Rubin, is a philandering traveling salesman who has lost his job selling harness that is rapidly becoming obsolete. He fears the future, but his machismo won't let him admit his fears to Cora, his wife. Cora, like I.'s mother, has drawn her children too closely to her in compensation for Rubin's unfaithfulness and absence. Raised to view sex as "animal," Cora fears its enjoyment and fears she might lose Rubin as well. Reenie, their daughter, is painfully shy; and Sonny, their boy, is a piece-reciting "sissy" who has an oedipal fixation on Cora. The Floods' fears, all caused by self-doubts and poor communication, are resolved after a separation between Rubin and Cora results in an honest baring of souls. This formula of family reconciliation was consistent for I. during the 1950s, even though while he was successful he was personally unhappy and undergoing almost constant psychoanalysis.

After I.'s highly successful screenplay, *Splendor in the Grass* (also about young love in small-town Kansas), he never again wrote popular material. Disappointed by the sharp rejection of New York critics after three unsuccessful plays, I. felt equally rejected in Hollywood, where one of his screenplays was changed so much that he had his name removed from its credits. His career slid depressingly downhill, and after publishing two little-noticed novels, he took his own life.

BIBLIOGRAPHY: Burgess, C. E., "An American Experience: W. I. in St. Louis, 1943–1949," *PLL* 12 (Fall 1976): 438–67; Shuman, R. B., *W. I.* (1965); Voss, R. F., *A Life of W. I.: The Strains of Triumph* (1989); Voss, R. F., "W. I. and the Savior/Specter of Celebrity," *KanQ* 18 (Fall 1986): 25–40

RALPH F. VOSS

INGRAHAM, Joseph Holt

b. 26 January 1809, Portland, Maine; d. 18 December 1860, Holly Springs, Mississippi

Although little known in the late 20th c., I. was a prolific and popular author of the antebellum period. He produced some hundred novels; and his essays, tales, and poems appeared in many of America's leading periodicals. These works enjoyed critical acclaim from even so stern a judge as Edgar Allan POE. I. was a pioneer in the fiction of piracy and the Bible. Cecil B. De Mille consulted I.'s *The Pillar of Fire* (1859) for his 1956 epic film *The Ten Commandments.*

Born in Maine, I. moved to Mississippi in 1830 and in that year probably joined the faculty of Jefferson College, near Natchez. Beginning in 1833, he recorded his impressions of the deep South in a series of letters published in the Natchez *Courier.* These were collected in 1835 as *The South-West,* I.'s first book, which offers a good, objective picture of life in New Orleans and Mississippi in the early 19th c.

In 1836, Harper & Brothers published I.'s first novel, *Lafitte: The Pirate of the South.* On the title page, I. quoted from Byron's *The Corsair:* "He left a Corsair's name to other times, / Link'd with one virtue and a thousand crimes." The epigraph is appropriate, since I. portrays Lafitte as a Byronic hero, an attractive villain with a conscience. Many of I.'s later protagonists follow this model. I. also repeatedly returned to the sea for his settings, and he would frequently again draw on American history for the germ of his plots, thus following the popular fiction of Sir Walter Scott and James Fenimore COOPER, though I. conceded in the preface to *Lafitte,* "With the pages of history we have had to do only so far as they could be made subservient to our tale." Love plays a larger role than history in the work.

Burton; or, The Sieges: A Romance (1838) is based on the early life of Aaron Burr, whose death in 1836

and whose trial for treason at Jefferson College probably suggested the subject. Set in the time of the American Revolution, *Burton* portrays Burr as a libertine Byronic hero. With *Captain Kyd; or, The Wizard of the Sea* (1839), I. returned to a romance about pirates and again built his account around a kernel of history embellished with a love story. *The Quadroone,* set in the New Orleans of the 1760s against the background of the Spanish takeover of hte city, followed in 1841. Henry Wadsworth LONGFELLOW, to whom I. had dedicated *Lafitte* without permission, was not impressed with I.'s novels, claiming in the *Portland Transcript* of September 8, 1838 that they were "the worst . . . ever written by anybody." Poe, however, liked *The South-West,* and while he objected to *The Quadroone,* Poe described I. as "one of our most *popular* novelists, if not one of our best."

The Dancing Feather, another pirate tale, began serialization in the *Boston Notion* in December 1841. When it appeared in book form in 1842 it sold 20,000 copies. Unlike I.'s earlier two-volume books published by Harper & Brothers, this and some eighty to follow were short and hastily written. Many of these works dealt with pirates. Others contrasted the virtuous countryside with the vicious city. Over thirty are historical fiction: some twenty are set in America; another dozen transport the reader to Europe. Several anticipate Horatio ALGER, Jr.'s rags-to-riches formula; the hero of *Jemmy Daily* (1843), like so many of Alger's future millionaires, even begins life as a newsboy. As if this output were not enough to occupy him, between 1838 and 1858, I. contributed extensively to at least twenty-six periodicals, including the *Southern Literary Messenger, U.S. Magazine and Democratic Review,* and *Godey's Lady's Book.* In addition to historical fiction, I. contributed criticism, humor, poetry, and travelogues.

In 1847, I. began studying for the Episcopal ministry; he was ordained as a priest in 1852. During this time, he continued to produce his characteristic work, but in 1855, he turned to a new genre reflecting his new vocation, the biblical romance. *The Prince of the House of David,* set in the time of Christ, enjoyed an immediate and continuing popularity, selling over a million copies by the end of the 19th c. and millions more in the 20th. This work, like I.'s two other novels based on the Bible—*The Pillar of Fire* and *The Throne of David* (1860)—are long epistolary works that expand a core of scripture with much description and romance. While drawing on the Bible marked a shift in I.'s fiction, the ornate style, fair young heroes and frail fair heroines, romantic descriptions, the emphasis on action, and the readiness to manufacture or change history to improve an account recall his earlier works.

I.'s final work, like his first, described the South, though he was more defensive in *The Sunny South* (1860) than in *The South-West*. I. again uses letters to tell his story. These are written by "Kate Conyngham," who comes from Maine to serve as a governess on a plantation in Tennessee and later marries a Louisiana plantation owner. I. wrote the letters, which began appearing in the *American Saturday Courier* (Philadelphia) in 1853, as a response to Harriet Beecher STOWE'S *Uncle Tom's Cabin*, and he aimed at the same female readership by emphasizing the sentimental and the romantic. Kate portrays slavery sympathetically and warns of the impending crisis of secession if Northern abolitionists continue their agitation. I. was at work on a fourth biblical novel, *St. Paul the Roman Citizen*, when he accidentally but fatally shot himself.

Kate Conyngham wrote, "I have very little hopes of being immortalized through my pen." Although he produced ten percent of American fiction in the 1840s and was one of the highest paid writers of his day, I., too, failed to immortalize himself. Still, his fiction reveals much about popular reading tastes in the antebellum period, and his work anticipates better known authors such as Alger and Lew WALLACE.

BIBLIOGRAPHY: French, W. G., "A Hundred Years of a Religious Bestseller," *WHR* 10 (Winter 1955–56): 45–54; Gaston, E. W., Jr., *The Early Novels of the Southwest* (1961); Hart, J. D., *The Popular Book: A History of America's Literary Taste* (1961)

JOSEPH ROSENBLUM

IRVING, John
b. 2 March 1942, Exeter, New Hampshire

I. is a popular postmodern novelist whose unusual blend of dark humor with traditional values has established him as a significant humorist. Born and reared in Exeter, New Hampshire, I. early developed interests in wrestling and writing. After short stints at two American colleges, he went to Vienna to study in 1963; the strange old city captivated him so that it became an important setting in most of his novels. He returned to America in 1963 and later took degrees from the University of New Hampshire and the University of Iowa, where he studied under Vincent BOURJAILY and Kurt VONNEGUT, Jr.

His first three novels—*Setting Free the Bears* (1969), *The Water-Method Man* (1972), and *The 158-Pound Marriage* (1974)—reveal the influence of black humorists as well as I.'s search for his own artistic voice. His next novel, *The World According to Garp* (1978), was a popular and critical success and demonstrates his maturing into an accomplished fiction

writer. *The Hotel New Hampshire* (1981) and *The Cider House Rules* (1985) neither achieved the success of *Garp*, though the latter provoked some controversy in its focus on abortion. In 1989, I. published the highly praised *A Prayer for Owen Meany* followed by *A Son of the Circus* (1994), *Trying to Save Piggy Sneed* (1996), and *A Widow for One Year* (1998).

Acknowledged as one of the most significant contemporary American novelists, I. has developed into a master storyteller and a significant humorist, reflecting black humor in favor of affirming traditional ideals such as the imagination, family, and the values of life in general.

BIBLIOGRAPHY: Epstein, J., "Why J. I. Is So Popular," *Commentary* 73 (June 1982): 59–73; Freeland, A., "A Conversation with J. I.," *NER* 18 (Spring 1997): 135–42; Harter, C. C., and J. R. Thompson, *J. I.* (1986); Miller, G., *J. I.* (1982); Reilly, E. C., *Understanding J. I.* (1991)

CRAIG TURNER

IRVING, Washington
b. 3 April 1783, New York City; d. 28 November 1859, Irvington, New York

I. is best described as the first successful professional man of letters in the U.S. This had to mean a risky commitment to a life of the creative imagination, not just an amateur's happenstance endeavors. It also had to mean winning genuine appreciation overseas for London as the literary capital of the English-speaking peoples. Everywhere abroad it meant, once in print, chancing piracy, for there was no international copyright protection. When he broke the sound barrier of transatlantic applause with *The Sketch Book of Geoffrey Crayon, Gent.*, published in seven parts from 1819 to 1820, this was not just a chronological first but, more to the point, a memorable triumph in its own right, both for storytelling expertise and a graceful prose style.

Born in a New York City still not evacuated by British forces and named by his patriotic emigrant parents for the Revolution's victorious hero George Washington, he lived through a succession of truly historic decades, finally seeing the arrival of Abraham LINCOLN on the Union's troubled scene. First in print at nineteen, I. was still writing within months of his death. He was mourned as a patriarchal figure whose tales, histories, essays, and biographies had helped significantly in the emergence of a distinctive American literature.

I.'s first break into printing found him, in disguise, writing in chatty fashion the *Letters of Jonathan Old-*

style, Gent. In 1801–2, he contributed these apprentice pieces to a Manhattan newspaper, which were later published in book form in 1824. Only nineteen, he adopted the persona of an "odd old fellow" and bachelor about town, to comment archly on the passing scene, especially his already cosmopolitan city's busy world of theater. His pen name foreshadowed his future transitional role: the name Oldstyle looked to the storied past while Jonathan, a current Yankee Doodle term, looked ahead.

Knowing a salmagundi to be a spicy, mixed salad dish, the readers of the twenty yellowclad pamphlets of the periodical *Salmagundi; or, The Whim-Whams of Lancelot Langstaff, Esq. and Others* (2 vols., 1807–8) could anticipate a lively, tart issue each time. The perpetrators of this often rollicking satire were the self-appointed censors, James Kirke PAULDING and his brothers-in-law I. and William Irving, the last a prominent merchant and *pro tem* poetaster. The others contributed teasingly allusive anecdotes and essays of social commentary ascribed to alter egos Will Wizzard, Anthony Evergreen, and Langstaff, who wrote exactly what remains a bibliographer's nightmare. As a Gotham gadfly, "old Sal" was a local sensation, but these amateurs carelessly let U.S. copyright slip away, a lesson Washington never forgot.

Had I., barely admitted to the bar in 1806, stuck firmly to the law, these amateurish beginnings would be all but forgotten. Instead, still wary of writing as a viable alternative, he created *Diedrich Knickerbocker's History of New York* (1809), a literary joke that continues to amuse moderns as well. Begun to parody a current "dry-as-dust" guide to his burgeoning birthplace this once-upon-a-time chronicle soon expanded into a whole, long, and bumptious satire. Crotchety old Diedrich, an incurable antiquarian like his young creator, describes the hilarious reigns of three of the actual six Dutch governors of New Netherlands: pipe-puffing, somnolent Wouter Van Twiller, William (The Testy) Kieft, in effect a take-off of President Thomas JEFFERSON, and the best remembered from this distant colonial past, choleric Peter Stuyvesant. Not all descendants of their caricatured 17th-c. subjects appreciated I.'s extravagant handling of New Amsterdam's burghers and dames, but forty years later he could say with relief that "Knickerbocker" had become a complimentary "household" term. Diedrich had already stepped out of these comedic surroundings to become New York City's symbolic "Father Knickerbocker."

By 1818, sent overseas to help the Liverpool end of the family export business, he was stunned to be caught up in the humiliation of a postwar bankruptcy. This tipped the balance and at long last he opted for authorship—still a gamble at best. The result was the *Sketch Book,* a huge best-seller and by far his best-known and most enduring work. Lightly disguised as "Geoffrey Crayon, Gent." the pioneering American author offered his two differing publics, U.S. and United Kingdom, a miscellany of thirty-odd prose pieces. Its familiar essays, descriptive word sketches, and well-crafted tales are so diverse only the high spots can be noted here. Crayon is not I. True, both are musing, peripatetic bachelors and each has a pleasantly nostalgic strain, but in real life, I. could be thin-skinned, often brooding and, paradoxically, a hard-headed businessman. Also, he possessed a warm personal sense of humor, and by now could command an easy and elegant prose style, a hallmark throughout the long career ahead of him.

One of the staples of LITERARY JOURNALISM is the travel sketch. It then depicted far-off places and peoples for fireside and schoolroom readers at a time when adventurous travel was always troublesome and often dangerous. Of those in the *Sketch Book* two first-class examples, "Stratford on Avon" and "Westminster Abbey," merit special praise. In these, the wandering I., clearly visible as someone sentimental but controlled, shared with contemporaries, many unlikely ever to travel there themselves, visits to two awesome historical sights in what Americans still commonly thought of as the Mother Country. Each heartfelt sketch became an invitation to follow as many Victorian tourists did.

The forthright essay "English Writers on America" has perforce become a period piece, useful chiefly to measure the fine impression the entire *Sketch Book* quickly made, at home and abroad. In 1819–20, Britain was an often haughty imperial power while I.'s distant America was, like a strong but maladroit adolescent, searching for a secure identity. Hard feelings between them could quickly run high as I. would see even more closely in ten short years, as a Jacksonian diplomat stationed in London. Beforehand in this piece focused on "literary animosity," he displayed natural peacemaking instincts, as tactfully, if a bit humorlessly, he called for more light and less heat from writers on both sides of the Atlantic. His honest pacific efforts did not go unappreciated near and far.

Year in and out, one of the most delightful elements in Crayon's entire gathering has been its quintet of Christmas sketches. Coming before Charles Dickens, and even Clement Clarke Moore's "A Visit from St. Nicholas," these jovial celebrations of old-fashioned Noel customs, albeit in a merry-old-England setting in an ancestral Bracebridge Hall, brought to countless readers—New World and Old—renewed regard for gracious if antique Yuletide customs.

The skillfully designed indigenous patchquilt of "Rip Van Winkle" was in fact not woven wholly of

I.'s own imagination. As with the "Legend," its twin star, he first happened on a minor source in German eerie folklore to improve upon. Then using surefire storyteller Diedrich as the pretended source for his seemingly homespun fable, I. created his own New World great sleeper, who awakens in another time, with strangers around, and different values to adjust to. This age old yarnspinning technique he fixed in the upriver Kaatskills, a rugged region he then knew more by sight on shipboard than from onshore trekking. Giving hapless, likeable Rip a good Dutch name added surface authenticity. The overseas author carefully worked in a patriotic theme too, witness George Washington on the overpainted inn sign. This classic short story has stageworthy elements, including comedy and mystery, that have attracted stage versions ever since.

For all its Teutonic ancestry "The Legend of Sleepy Hollow" delivered what its title promised, a believably indigenous folktale. Here Crayon, again via gossiping old Diedrich, put the ageless ghost story of a headless horseman to several overlapping uses. The courtship of coy Katrina is combined with up-to-date indictment of Yankee intrusion into the Hollow's Edenic Dutch farm country life. Both prepare for the climactic wild chase of the schoolmaster from Connecticut by local strongboy Brom Bones, both aptly named. Add contagious good humor and on one level this is pure entertainment, as repeated theatrical versions attest. Yet modern critical opinion continues to search for deeper meanings, like an ironic victory of frontier brawn over citified brains. Both model short stories, like "The Spectre Bridegroom," which can be called sportive, or debunking Gothic, proved beyond doubt I.'s literary abilities, especially as a native humorist. His technical artistry would not be lost on successors such as Nathaniel HAWTHORNE and Edgar Allan POE.

In 1822, writing hard against deadlines, I., now a professional author, completed the two-volume *Bracebridge Hall*. Although tempted to produce a novel as his contemporary James Fenimore COOPER was beginning to do, I., an honest judge of his limitations, chose to follow his own recent landmark success with another medley. Familiar would be the pleasantly idiosyncratic British characters in Squire Bracebridge's patrician circle. Patent again was the author's ability, though unshaken republican, to mingle at ease with these rather anachronistic gentry. But the immediate turmoil of the Industrial Revolution was kept offstage, while in "The Author's Farewell," again with deftness and conviction, I. poured oil on other troubled waters.

More than its abundant Crayonesque humor, much more than the customary romantic tugs at the heart, the best of *Bracebridge Hall* is in three tales: "The Stout Gentleman" complete with surprise ending; the

longish, melodramatic "Student of Salamanca"; and thanks to garrulous old Diedrich again the spooky, Dutch-colonial tale of "Dolph Heyliger." The overall result was encouragingly received but has not worn all that well.

Tales of a Traveller (2 vols., 1824), the third Crayon collection in a row, consisted entirely of short fiction. I. thought highly of this experimental volume, but despite its single successes like the rather racy "Bold Dragon," the Gothic-style hoax "The Adventure of the German Student," and the unmistakably homegrown "The Devil and Tom Walker," critical opinion here and abroad often suggested he was in danger of repeating himself. The result for the easily stung and uneasily expatriate author was a personal crisis and a singular career shift toward factual narration—biography and history in the eventually faded fashion of the age. Luckily in 1826, a friend's invitation to come to Spain would provide inspiring new vistas.

As man and as artist, Don Washington, as he would be dubbed, would have a long love affair with Iberia, becoming in short order one of our earliest and most influential Hispanophiles. As Stanley T. Williams put it, "Altogether on Spain I. wrote some three thousand pages and approximately one million words, amounting to about one third of his total writings. Although he is still known as the traditional interpreter in American literature of Old English, he devoted far more space and effort to his books on Spain. Nor are these inferior."

The carefully researched *A History of the Life and Voyages of Christopher Columbus* (3 vols., 1828) was, amazingly, the first full-length biography ever in English of the heroic, and in the end ill-used, "Admiral of the Ocean Sea." The title page was the first to bear I.'s own name, not a pseudonym. *The Conquest of Granada* (2 vols., 1829) told with gusto of the epic Christian victory over the Moors. I.'s return to a persona, fictitious medieval zealot Fray Antonio Agapida, annoyed some readers. Most, however, fastened instead on the dramatic subject, the Reconquest's ultimate Te Deum triumph.

The Alhambra (2 vols., 1832) was saluted as I.'s intriguing Spanish *Sketch Book*. It has retained much of this good reputation since. This quintessentially romantic *colección* was a temporary return to a miscellany, this time as he put it "in the Haroun Alraschid style." *Alhambra's* fiction skillfully adapted Andalusian lore filled with magic spells, buried treasure and star-crossed lovers. The nonfiction, much of it vivid physical descriptions, is still a good preparation for a visit to the centuries old fortress-cum-palace towering over the legendary city of Granada.

After a literally triumphant homecoming in 1832, I. earned a surprisingly different reputation as a chronicler of realistic and rousing aspects of trans-Mississippi life. This, in three works imbued with the pandemic spirit of Manifest Destiny. *A Tour on the Prairies* (1835) was a short, lively but scrubbed-up account of his month of reconnoitering beyond the Southwestern frontier line. *Astoria* (3 vols., 1836) was a wide-ranging history of John Jacob Astor's daring but disastrous Pacific Fur Company (1810–13). The *Adventures of Captain Bonneville* (1837) recounted the recent adventures and misadventures of that transmontane explorer and fur trade entrepreneur. These disparate works were windows on the vast Far West, until the stampede of events left them behind. The latter two remain prime early Western Americana.

Four significant events determined the quality of I.'s later life. Sunnyside, a small estate acquired in 1835, became home and soon a site for literary pilgrimage. From 1842 to 1846, he served as U.S. Minister to Spain, an honor for both the personable man and his chosen calling. Between 1848 and 1851, with ven-turesome George P. Putnam as catalyst, I. labored at a fifteen-volume Author's Revised Edition, the first in our publishing history—and a bonanza. And addressing a longstanding interest he produced from 1855 to 1859 a five-volume *Life of George Washington,* making that enigmatic chieftain more living person than plaster saint.

By the mid-19th c., the cresting of American RO-MANTICISM was imminent. Never gifted with genius, I. had nevertheless helped prepare the way with unique grace, humor, professional integrity, and talent, especially as an innovative teller of tales.

BIBLIOGRAPHY: Hedges, W. L., *W. I.: An American Study* (1965); Myers, A., ed., *A Century of Commentary* (1976); Rubin-Dporsky, J., *Adrift in the Old World* (1988); Wagenknecht, E., *W. I., Moderation Displayed* (1962); Williams, S. T., *The Life of W. I.* (1935)

ANDREW MYERS

JACKSON, Helen Hunt [Fiske]

b. 5 October 1830, Amherst, Massachusetts; d. 12
August 1885, Colorado Springs

J. was hailed in her lifetime as one of the most popular
writers in America. Her poetry and stories showed a
deep concern for humanity and the rights of all peoples. In the 20th c., J.'s reputation has shrunk and
she is rarely taught in college classrooms. J.'s legacy,
however, has left an indelible mark on American literature, for she raised issues few others would dare to
mention and was one of a few woman writers truly
respected by her male peers who dominated the literary profession.

J.'s career was born out of sorrow. The death of
her second son closely followed the accidental death
of his father; his elder brother had died several years
earlier. J. was so overwhelmed with grief she could
not bear to see her friends, but she did express her grief
through writing poetry. She adopted a pseudonym,
Marah, and she sent her poems to Parke Godwin
at the *New York Evening Post* and—on June 9,
1865—"The Key to the Casket" was published. Other
poems soon followed, as did a travel article published
under the name "H. H." Public response to both the
poetry and prose was so positive that J. began to
consider a career in writing. Encouraged by Godwin,
she wrote more articles and moved to Newport, Rhode
Island where Thomas Wentworth HIGGINSON became
her mentor.

By 1866, J. was established as a writer and she
experimented with different forms and topics, including children's stories based on her own childhood. Her
stories, travel articles, editorials, and book reviews
were all well received, and J. was soon recognized as
one of the most significant women writers in the U.S.,
alongside Harriet Beecher STOWE and Louisa May
ALCOTT. A mere five years after she began her writing
career, she enjoyed great financial success with the
publication of her first collection of fictional stories.
Published in January 1877, her first novel, *Mercy Philbrick's Choice,* received mixed reviews but sold out
its first run in less than one month.

While she had fiercely defended Stowe's sympathetic portrayal of slaves, J. was not an activist. She
did not agree with the women's rights movement and
was very vocal about her views. However, when she
heard of the plight of the Ponca Indians in Nebraska
in 1879, she found a cause with which she could not
part. For the last years of her life, J. became "a leader in
the reform movement, helping to organize the Boston
Indian Citizenship Association." She wrote letters and
articles decrying the government's treatment of Native
Americans, and, although many of her friends did not
share her concern, she researched and published *A
Century of Dishonor* (1881), which chronicled government mistreatment of Native Americans. She sent a
copy of the book to every member of Congress at her
own expense, and on March 3, 1881, the government
reached a favorable settlement with the Poncas and J.
was triumphant. Her public was not as generous toward J., however, as general opinions about Native
Americans were marred by prejudice and fear. J. was
criticized for her efforts by some, but this did not
lessen her desire to fight for Native American rights.
J.'s final novel, *Ramona* (1884), is a story about the
Mission Indians of Southern California. Couched
within a romantic tale, *Ramona* is the first novel in
American literature to show the stark realities of Native American life in the U.S.; the effect of this novel
on the public was similar to that of Stowe's novel.

J.'s popularity continued for many years after her
death but waned during the latter half of the 20th c.
Once counted among the most popular writers of her
day, she is now regarded as a minor figure. The significance of her fight for Native Americans should not
be underplayed, however. She fought the government,
newspaper editors, and the public to show the cruel

ways in which Native Americans had been treated and cheated out of what had been rightfully theirs. Her other writings, the poetry and stories especially, have a quality about them that also deserves recognition. J. depicts her experience of the 19th c. with the truth and vividness typical of American women's writing of her time.

BIBLIOGRAPHY: Banning, E. I., *H. H. J.* (1973); Mathes, V. S., *H. H. J. and Her Indian Reform Legacy* (1990)

MARCY L. TANTER

JACKSON, Shirley [Hardie]

b. 14 December 1919, San Francisco, California; d. 8 August 1965, North Bennington, Vermont

J. achieved a rare combination of critical acclaim and popular success during her lifetime, but descended into obscurity upon her death, only to be remembered by a single short story, "The Lottery," which has been widely anthologized. Recently, however, J. has been rediscovered by feminist critics and others, and several of her novels have been reissued. In 1997, two of J.'s children edited a collection of previously unpublished short fiction, *Just an Ordinary Day.*

"The Lottery," a grim but understated fable that set a sacrifice ritual in an American town, announced J.'s interest in the macabre; when published in 1948, it brought the *New Yorker* more mail than any previous story. It describes one typical world of J.'s fiction, a world in which the surreal or supernatural always lies beneath the surface of reality and threatens to erupt. Yet another typical world of J.'s work is the lightly comical world of suburban family life, and the difficulty of reconciling these two may account for J.'s critical neglect. For in addition to her six novels, J. published two humorous and presumably more autobiographical collections. J.'s inclusion of both kinds of stories in her first collection, *The Lottery; or, The Adventures of James Harris* (1949), may indicate that she considered them on equal terms, but her husband, critic Stanley Edgar Hyman, always believed that the humorous books damaged her literary reputation.

Although the sex of the victim in "The Lottery" is presumably determined by chance, J. became increasingly interested in the victimization of women and in female psychology. The typical J. protagonist is a social misfit, a young woman without the charm or beauty to claim a place for herself in society. In *Hangsaman* (1951), Natalie Waite's loneliness during her first months of college generates an imaginary friend. In *The Bird's Nest* (1954), Elizabeth Richmond's confusion, precipitated by sexual assault, generates multiple personalities. In *The Haunting of Hill House*

(1959), Eleanor Vance's feelings of displacement lead her to escape her dull life to join in the psychic adventures at Hill House; when she is sent away, she commits suicide. In *We Have Always Lived in the Castle* (1962), Mary Katherine Blackwood lives with her sister in a state of siege, barricaded against a town's hostility.

The last of these, a best-seller named one of the ten best novels of the year by *Time,* shows J. at her best, combining humor and horror in the understated first-person narration of a young woman who is certainly a murderer, and who may or may not be mad. Perhaps if readers cannot decide how to take this product of J.'s superbly controlled irony, critics may be forgiven their indecision about J.—a respected American novelist who claimed to be the only practicing witch in New England.

BIBLIOGRAPHY: Friedman, L., *S. J.* (1975); Hall, J. W., *S. J.: A Study of the Short Fiction* (1993); Hyman, L. J., and S. H. Stewart, eds., *Just an Ordinary Day* (1997); Hyman, S. E., ed., *The Magic of S. J.* (1966); Oppenheimer, J., *Private Demons: The Life of S. J.* (1988)

LYNETTE CARPENTER

JACOBS, Harriet

b. 1813, Edenton, North Carolina; d. 1897, Washington, D.C.

She crawled into a very small garret measuring only nine feet long, seven feet wide, and three feet high; she was seeking refuge from a master's incessant sexual solicitations and his eventual desire for her concubinage as well as hoping to impede the sale of her children to a neighboring plantation. This small garret, one that prevented her from even standing, turned into her home for seven years. But when she, J., finally emerged and fled to the North, she eventually put her story on paper—*Incidents in the Life of a Slave Girl* (1861)—to help in the antislavery movement. J. also helped in another way, for she left one of the only slave narratives that offers a glimpse into the experiences of a black female slave.

Incidents in the Life of a Slave Girl, J.'s first and only literary work, represents one of many slave narratives published between the 1830s and the 1860s as part of the abolitionist movement. In her narrative, she tells of her badgering master, her conscious decision to seek a relationship with another white slave owner with whom she had two children, her agonizing decision to "leave" her family, and her life in the North that eventually resulted in her being manumitted and reunited with her children. Upon publication of her narrative under the pseudonym of Linda Brent, J. received some notoriety, but her fame was short-lived for the rumblings of the Civil War could be heard. J.'s narrative represents more than just another slave narrative, though. Instead, it is a story that has helped to redefine the traditional definition of the SLAVE NARRATIVE genre, one more accurately described as a male slave narrative. Unlike most of these narratives, which depict a solitary, linear progression from bondage to freedom, J. tells of a journey that is more complex and complicated because of her gender. Her story exposes the harsh realities of being a slave woman: from being the sexual object of the slave master as well as the mistress's object of hatred to the ties the slave woman felt towards her family, especially her children.

While *Incidents in the Life of a Slave Girl* contributes to a reassessment of the slave narrative, J.'s work stands as a testament to her skill as a writer, although when prodded to put her story in writing, J. responded "don't expect much of me . . . you will have truth, but no talent." What resulted, however, was a carefully constructed rhetorical narrative. J.'s story is not simply a chronological ordering of experiences, but rather a carefully constructed story, one in which she consciously chose what to reveal to her audience. J.'s talent further emerges through her astute awareness of her audience—a white, upper-class woman. Knowing her audience and its sexual codes, J.'s narrator, Linda Brent, maintains a necessary level of sexual purity. Then J. capitalizes on the need to maintain these sexual codes and eliminate moral impropriety by arguing that slavery damages not only the slave, but both the white man and woman as well.

While J.'s story reveals her talent as a writer to create a rhetorically astute story, early scholars actually dismissed the text as either abolitionist propaganda or fiction. While one scholar had argued for the merit of the text in 1947, it was not until 1981 that the narrative gained credibility because its authenticity was established.

J. wanted to tell her story to aid the abolitionist movement, and while she did just that, J.'s narrative also contributes significantly to contemporary understanding of the slave narrative, one that had been too long defined by only the slave narrative of males.

BIBLIOGRAPHY: Braxton, J. M., "H. J.'s *Incidents in the Life of a Slave Girl:* The Re-Definition of the Slave Narrative Genre," *MR* 27 (Summer 1986): 379–87; Doherty, T., "H. J.'s Narrative Strategies: *Incidents in the Life of a Slave Girl,*" *SLJ* 19 (Fall 1986): 79–91; Gray, J. L., "Culture, Gender, and the Slave Narrative," *Proteus* 7 (Spring 1990): 37–42; Gates, H. L., Jr., and C. T. Davis, eds., *The Slave's Narrative* (1985); Sekora, J., and D. T. Turner, eds., *The Art of the Slave Narrative: Original Essays in Criticism and Theory* (1982); Yellin, J. F., "H. J.'s Family History," *AL* 66 (December 1994): 765–77

NANCY M. STAUB

JAMES, Alice

b. 7 August 1848, New York City; d. 6 March 1892, London, England

J. was the youngest child and only daughter of the noted James family. Her two oldest brothers, William and Henry, earned lasting fame as psychologist and novelist, respectively. Her literary reputation rests upon her letters and, most particularly, the diary that she kept during the last three years of her life. Her companion Katherine Peabody Loring preserved the diary, and in 1934, a family descendant published a truncated version entitled *A. J.: Her Brothers—Her Journal.* Finally in 1964, seventy-two years after her death, Leon Edel edited and published the full text as *The Diary of A. J.* In its vivid and often sharply ironic comments on political and social issues, family relationships, and the writer's passage toward death, the diary draws a complex psychological portrait of a chronic invalid who lived in the shadow of illustrious male relatives, yet insisted upon shaping her own worldview.

J. described her childhood as "rootless and accidental," reflecting her haphazard education and her European travels with her family. From all accounts, she was an intelligent and spirited girl who struggled to resist her brothers' teasing and her parents' insistence upon quiet domesticity. Her frustrations flared out in nervous disorders that finally resulted in a serious breakdown when she was thirty. She recovered sufficiently to care for her widowed father and, upon his death, keep house briefly for her brother Henry. A significant reason for her newly found energy was her friendship with Loring, upon whose care she became dependent. They traveled to England in 1881 and again in 1884. During the latter trip, J. grew increasingly feeble and felt unable to return to America. The two women settled down in a house on Camden Hill, London. In May 1891, J. was diagnosed with breast cancer; she died ten months later.

J. began her diary on May 31, 1889 as a bulwark against loneliness and despair. The first entry expresses the hope that her writing may be "an outlet to that geyser of emotions, sensations, speculations and reflections which ferments perpetually within my poor old carcass." Although confined to her room, she lived an intense intellectual life through her eclectic reading, letter writing, and visits from American friends. She described her viewpoint as a "microscopic field" upon which "minute events are perpetually taking place illustrative of the broadest facts of human nature." In her daily entries, she adopts different personae, one of which is the political and social radical who caustically satirizes the English, ardently defends the Irish nationalist movement, and sympathizes with the working poor.

The diary also contains numerous entries in her persona as the frail invalid among energetic brothers. She writes of William with a gentle irony; but of Henry, with whom she had a particularly close relationship, she writes tenderly: "I have given him endless care and anxiety but notwithstanding this and the fantastic nature of my troubles, I have never seen an impatient look upon his face or heard an unsympathetic sound cross his lips." Her dependence upon his occasional visits is clear; for when he is absent, she feels a "sentimental homesickness for him." She took great interest in his literary career, particularly his effort to produce a dramatic version of *The American*. He welcomed her opinions and complimented her on her writing. When he read her diary after her death, he found it "heroic in its individuality" and praised its "rich irony and humour," but he felt that "she simplified too much . . . exercised her wondrous vigour of judgment on too small a scrap of what really surrounded her."

Notwithstanding its occasional capriciousness, J.'s diary is a remarkable record of moral courage in dealing with invalidism and death on her own terms. She welcomes the diagnosis of breast cancer and approaching death because she finally has a "palpable disease" that the doctors take seriously. She finds that death's value is doubled by having it to look forward to: "one becomes suddenly picturesque to oneself, and one's wavering little individuality stands out with a cameo effect." In infrequent entries during her last nine months, she notes her funeral arrangements, commenting wryly that since she was "denied baptism by her parents, marriage by obtuse and imperceptive man, it seems not too bad to assist myself in the first and last ceremony of dying." Her last entry, dictated two days before her death, states her refusal to ask for a lethal dose of morphine as she "steps hesitantly along such unaccustomed ways and endures from second to second." This intensely human document concludes with Loring's comment that J. was revising the wording of the diary until a few hours before her death.

BIBLIOGRAPHY: Lewis, R. W. B., *The Jameses: A Family Narrative* (1991); Matthiessen, F. O., *The James Family* (1948); Strouse, J., *A. J.: A Biography* (1980); Yeazell, R. B., *The Death and Letters of A. J.* (1981)

MARGARET CARTER

JAMES, Henry
b. 15 April 1843, New York City; d. 28 February 1916, London, England

J. was a productive, innovative, and influential American man of letters for half a century, and is now widely regarded as one of the greatest of American writers. He is read, studied, and revered mainly because of his twenty-two novels and one hundred and fourteen short stories; but he also wrote the equivalent of ten books of criticism, seven books of travel, fifteen plays, two biographies, three autobiographical works, and more than fifteen thousand personal letters.

J.'s parents were Henry James, Sr., a rich, eccentric Swedenborgian philosopher, and Mary Walsh James, his gentle, loving, more practical wife. The death of J.'s grandfather in 1832 left his father with a fortune. As a result, J.'s father was never obliged to work, but instead could study and travel at will. The other children in his remarkable household were William JAMES, Garth Wilkinson James, Robertson James, and Alice JAMES. William was the brilliant physician, psychologist, philosopher, and teacher. Garth Wilkinson and Robertson James served in the Union Army during the Civil War, then failed as cotton farmers in Florida, and subsequently led uneventful lives. Witty, analytical Alice became neurasthenic in a household of extravagantly chattering males, traveled a little and was much doctored, and after the death of both parents went to England to be near her indulgent brother J., died of breast cancer, and left a remarkably candid diary.

The childhood and youth of J. were most unusual. From late 1843 to early 1845, the parents, together with both William and J., lived in England and France. In the spring of 1844, while at Windsor (near London), the father experienced a disagreeable ghostly visitation, from the effects of which he was able to recover only by devotion to theological studies, writing, and lecturing. For the next decade, the growing family lived in Albany and New York City, where the children either went to day schools or were taught at home by polyglot tutors. In mid-1855, the seven Jameses (plus a maternal aunt) went to Geneva for abortive schooling for the children; then on to London, and the following summer on to France. The year 1858 found the family in Newport, Rhode Island, where a schoolmate persuaded J. to read Honoré de Balzac, Prosper Mérimée, Théophile Gautier, and the best French journals. American schools seeming unsatisfactory to the parents, the family late in 1859 returned to Geneva, where J. was required to study engineering but soon concentrated on languages and literature; he improved his German at Bonn during the following summer. William, J.'s outgoing, talented older brother, now wished to study painting; so late in 1860, the family returned to Newport—and art classes for William. J., passive and observant, tagged along for a while but soon turned to translating some recent French writing, including that of Mérimée, the structure of whose fiction he admired. Then came the Civil War.

William decided upon a scientific career and enrolled at Harvard in 1861. The younger brothers joined the Union Army. J. in October 1861 was trying to put out a fire in some Newport stables when he suffered a severe back injury, which in his autobiography much later he called horrid, obscure, and neglected. He then enrolled in the Harvard law school from 1862–63, where he mostly attended James Russell LOWELL's lectures on literature, made friends with other literary personages, and began to write. The parents moved from Newport to Boston, and J. lived with them off and on, there and later in Cambridge, until 1869. During these years, he developed literary friendships, including a pair with Charles Eliot Norton and William Dean HOWELLS, which lasted a lifetime, and published short stories and reviews in Boston and New York magazines.

But J. was still only an apprentice writer. In February 1869, he embarked on a momentous European tour alone, in the course of which he quickly met numerous writers and artists in and near London (including Edward Burne-Jones, Charles Darwin, George Eliot, William Morris and his wife, Dante Gabriel Rossetti, John Ruskin, and Leslie Stephen), went on to Paris and Switzerland, and finally, for the first time, to Italy, which became his favorite country for relaxation, cultural renewal, and visiting fellow EXPATRIATES. Back in England early in 1870, he learned that his beloved cousin Minnie Temple, with whom he probably was in love, had died of tuberculosis. He later wrote that the event marked the end of his youth.

Something of her exuberant personality may be seen in his later characterizations of Isabel Archer in *The Portrait of a Lady* (1881) and Milly Theale in *The Wings of the Dove* (1902). J.'s next two years, spent in New England and New York, were productive—more short fiction and reviews, travel sketches, and art notices—but not otherwise especially pleasant, because of loneliness and homesickness for Europe. "A Passionate Pilgrim," his best short story to its date, and *Watch and Ward,* his first novel (later repudiated as weak and derivative), both appeared serially in the *Atlantic Monthly* in 1871. In 1872, J. escorted his ailing sister Alice and their aunt on a European tour, waved goodbye to them at Liverpool, and stayed on alone in Paris, Florence, and Rome, firming up more literary friendships (with Lowell, Ralph Waldo EMERSON, the actress Fanny Kemble and her daughter Sarah Butler Wister, and expatriate American sculptor Wil-

liam Wetmore Story and his group) and steadily writing both fiction and nonfictional prose. From November 1873 into the new year, he played host to his brother William in Florence and Rome, but the two seemingly were not good for one another when in close proximity. William was always critical of his younger (and as he later once said "shallower and vainer") brother's writing style. J., who improved once William had departed, followed him back home half a year later. In 1873–74, J. wrote more than fifty items, mostly nonfiction but including seven short stories. Two of the best of these are "The Madonna of the Future" (1873) and "Madame de Mauves" (1874); the first is a fable against artistic procrastination; the second concerns a heroine whose purity drives a philandering husband to suicide and the hero to inexplicable vacillation.

J.'s 1874–75 sojourn in the U.S. was his last for a long period. His apprenticeship was drawing to a close. The young novelist serialized in the *Atlantic Monthly* (in twelve 1875 installments) what he called his first novel, *Roderick Hudson,* begun in Florence, finished in New York, and dramatizing the ultimate clash between Rowland Mallet, a rational American art patron, and Roderick Hudson, a talented but egocentric and unstable American sculptor whose abortive career the patron finances in Italy. The gallery of women in this novel is notable: the sculptor Hudson's ineffectual old mother Sarah, his devoted American fiancée Mary Garland, and Christina Light, the deadly object of his hopeless love. (J. was so intrigued by Miss Light, who marries Prince Casamassima of Naples at novel's end, that he made her the enigmatic heroine of his *Princess Casamassima* ten years later.) Early in 1875, J. saw into print his first two books: *A Passionate Pilgrim and Other Tales,* a collection of six stories, and *Transatlantic Sketches,* a collection of twenty-five travel essays. Even as J. was trying to gain professional and social status for himself in Manhattan, and was in addition writing reviews (more than one a week in 1875) as well as other pieces, he found himself increasingly yearning for Europe. So he made the most significant decision of his life to that date, and November 1875 found him a resident of Paris.

In almost no time, significant things happened. J. cemented a number of important literary friendships. And yet he was treated by many as an outsider, almost as though he were one of his own American innocents abroad. Among his new acquaintances in Paris may be numbered Gustave Flaubert, Edmond de Goncourt, Guy de Maupassant, Ernest Renan, Émile Zola, and especially Alphonse Daudet and Ivan Turgenev. It was through Turgenev, perhaps his closest European confrère, that J. was first able to attend Flaubert's Sunday gatherings during which writers talked shop elegantly.

But J. disliked their relaxed amorality and also the literary NATURALISM that they were fomenting. Nor did he long continue writing an insufficiently chatty gossip column he agreed to send back home to his friend John HAY, assistant editor of the New York *Tribune,* simply for money. So at the end of 1876, he moved to London, which he called "the great grey Babylon" but in which he could be steadily productive—and sociable.

At this time, J. met or renewed his acquaintance with many important persons, including the following: Robert Browning, George Du Maurier, George Eliot, James Anthony Froude, William Gladstone, Andrew Lang, Lord Houghton, Herbert Spencer, Leslie Stephen, Alfred, Lord Tennyson, and Anthony Trollope. A growing reputation made the young American respected, and his impeccable manners, together with uncanny polyglot conversational talents, made him desired as a dinner guest. He regarded the establishment of a position in high society as a worthy ambition. His flattering attentiveness to hostesses and their talkative guests, especially bright, older women, paid off in countless ideas—he called them "wind-blown seeds"—for future novel and short-story character patterns and plots. He soon solidified his reputation with *The American,* published in Boston in 1877 (an unauthorized British edition soon following); *French Poets and Novelists* (1878); *The Europeans* (1878); "Daisy Miller: A Study," which first appeared in Stephen's *Cornhill Magazine* in 1878 and was promptly pirated in America; and *Hawthorne* (1879). *The American* is a novel featuring symbolically named Christopher Newman, a rich ex-businessman who believes that his money will enable him to purchase the best possible French wife, once he descends upon Paris for a little culture. But he misjudges Madame de Bellegarde, the formidable widowed mother of his choice, Claire de Cintré. J. later deplored the excessive romanticism of his plot in this novel, but its dramatic contrast of American gaucherie and European "evil" makes it exciting to read to this day. In *The Europeans,* J. reverses the pattern of *The American* and has Felix Young, a fun-loving artist, and his charming but deceitful sister Baroness Eugenia Münster, both of whom are Americans long resident in Europe, return to their New England family roots, including their rigid old uncle William Wentworth and his assorted offspring. The result is a bittersweet international comedy of manners, with matrimony and alcoholism in the foreground and background. "Daisy Miller," a perennial favorite among Jamesians, remains an enigma: Daisy Miller, American and dazzlingly pretty, travels in Switzerland and then Italy with a mother so uncomprehending and permissive that her child gets into trouble because of different social mores. She flirts both with Frederick Winterbourne, a Europeanized American who is too reserved to respond heartily, and with Giovanelli, an oily Roman fortune-hunter who is quite eager to respond. Daisy seems simply to like the company of attractive young men. But social leaders of the American colony in Rome see her as immoral and calculating, and freeze her out. When Winterbourne turns critical as well, the bewildered girl goes with Giovanelli late at night to the Coliseum in Rome, catches the deadly Roman fever, and dies. Readers to this day are undecided as to whether Daisy was foolish to defy the customs of a foreign land, whether Winterbourne should have interpreted her more emotionally, whether Giovanelli was vengeful. In "Daisy Miller," J. is dramatizing the dangers and responsibilities of innocence.

J.'s collection of essays on French writers (including Balzac, Charles Baudelaire, and George Sand) and his book on Nathaniel HAWTHORNE (the first ever published) made European readers aware of his critical acumen. American readers, however, were a little miffed at allegations of provinciality leveled at the revered author of *The Scarlet Letter* and other New England masterpieces.

Among several other works, long and short, which J. published before 1882, *Washington Square* and *The Portrait of a Lady,* both published in 1881, remain classics. *Washington Square* dramatizes the conflict in a well-to-do Manhattan family between Dr. Austin Sloper, a dour, correct father, and Catherine, his stolid, long-suffering daughter. Dr. Sloper accurately judges that Morris Townsend, the plain girl's suitor, is a fortune hunter; however, the father's ruthlessness triggers passive but tragic rebellion in his child. J.'s excluding this fine little novel from his New York Edition caused the work to be unfairly downgraded for a generation or more. On the other hand, *The Portrait of a Lady* was J.'s first monumental effort in fiction—it is his longest novel—and for more than a century, it has been regarded as his first indisputable masterpiece. It has a fairy-tale plot: Isabel Archer, the poor, bright, lithe American heroine, visits England through the generosity of her rich aunt, Lydia Touchett; Isabel meets a handsome British aristocrat named Lord Warburton and rejects his quick offer of marriage; she declines a renewed proposal from her old friend Caspar Goodwood, a well-to-do, hardy young American manufacturer; she inherits a veritable fortune from her aunt's expatriated banker husband in London; then she travels abroad with Lydia's smooth female friend Madame Merle, who introduces her to Gilbert Osmond, a curiously attractive American dilettante widower living in Italy with his lovely, frail daughter Pansy. Isabel, the "lady" of the title, is victimized by Gilbert, who is J.'s most consummate villain. In an agonizingly short time after she marries him, she discovers that he and Madame Merle were adulterous lovers and that Pansy is their child. Further, she learns too late that Ralph Touchett, her chronically sick cousin, was responsible for her inheritance and has hopelessly loved her all these years. The serialization of *The Portrait of a Lady* in London and Boston earned J. enough money to return to America to visit his ailing parents late in 1881.

Death claimed both parents in 1882. While J. was the guest of Henry ADAMS and his wife in Washington, D.C., in January, he was called back to Cambridge by his mother's death. He returned to England only in May, did research in France for his travel book called *A Little Tour in France,* published in 1884, and was summoned to America again by the illness of his father, who died in December. Curiously, J. was named executor of the father's will, causing an argument with his older brother William. It was not until September 1883 that J. was able to return to his residence in London, but this time it was to be for the following two decades and more.

Through the remainder of the 1880s, J.'s literary and personal activities were incredible. *The Bostonians* began its year-long serial appearance in February 1885, and *The Princess Casamassima* did the same starting in September. While planning and composing these massive novels, J. also managed to publish six short stories in 1884. They include three gems: "The Author of Beltraffio," about a woman who so fears that her husband's allegedly decadent fiction will corrupt their sick little son when he matures that she withholds the boy's medicine and lets him die; "Pandora," about a feisty young socialite in Washington who wheedles the president himself into doing her a favor; and the sensational "Georgina's Reasons," starring an undiscovered bigamist and her unrequited first husband. At this time, J. also produced a few nonfictional items, including his rousing manifesto of literary REALISM, "The Art of Fiction," which pleads the cause of artistic freedom, and urges critics and ordinary readers alike to judge a writer more by his technique than by his subject matter. Meanwhile, J.'s sister Alice, though ill, moved to England, and J. found rooms for her, cared for her, and gossiped with her lovingly. And to his list of friends he added the American painter John Singer Sargent, the French novelist Paul Bourget, the British novelist Robert Louis Stevenson, and many others.

Poor sales of both *The Bostonians* and *The Princess Casamassima* distressed J. But today both novels are much respected. The first concerns the post–Civil War struggle for women's rights centering in Boston and New York. The plot involves a curious triangle: Verena Tarrant, the lovely, redheaded heroine, is an eloquent

speaker at rallies promoting women's rights. Olive Chancellor, a well-to-do, shy, odd activist, wants to finance the pliant girl, and persuades her to leave her sleazy parents for the Chancellor mansion. But Basil Ransom, a sultry, unreconstructed Confederate army veteran, up from Mississippi to seek his fortune as a lawyer, sees Verena at a suffragette meeting, and soon wants her all for himself. Other women (not to mention a couple of men) also attempt to use Verena for their ends. Only old Miss Birdseye, one of J.'s most brilliant creations, is a truly altruistic feminist. The finale of this long novel, dramatizing Basil's and Olive's tug-of-war for Miss Tarrant, is one of J.'s most electrifying scenes. *The Princess Casamassima* highlights international anarchistic activity in London by presenting Hyacinth Robinson, a cultured but impoverished and illegitimate young bookbinder, who solemnly promises his radical superiors, including Paul Muniment, to assassinate a useless aristocrat when ordered to do so. But then young Robinson's world falls apart: his coarse, warm girlfriend Millicent Henning proves fickle, while Princess Casamassima, who has rather led him on, turns to more virile Paul. Feeling lost, poor Hyacinth feels that suicide is the only answer.

Starting late in 1886, J. took a prolonged working vacation in Italy, decorously shared a villa in the hills beyond Florence with Constance Fenimore WOOLSON, a middle-aged American local-color fiction writer who cared for him and his writing more than he could reciprocate. One fruit of J.'s eight-month Italian sojourn was "The Aspern Papers" (1888), one of literature's great nouvelles. It is based on the true story of a man's pursuit in Florence of a niece to give over her aunt's trove of Shelley-Byron papers. J. shifted the scene to Venice, addressed the moral question of scholarly propriety, and suffused the work with ambiguities (for example, are there really any papers?). In 1888, J. published seven other fictional works, including "The Liar" (asking whether lying, protecting a liar, or catching a liar is the worst sin) and "The Lesson of the Master" (contrasting the demands of artistic and marital happiness). Then J. wrote his last huge novel before the advent of the 20th c. It is *The Tragic Muse* (1890), which concerns Nick Dormer, a British politician who prefers to paint, and Miriam Rooth, a Jewish actress who forfeits a brilliant marriage to a diplomat for a stage career. Long live the muse, even though it exacts a tragic price.

The Tragic Muse failed both with the public and with most reviewers; so the discouraged novelist decided to turn playwright in an effort to conquer the British stage. In 1891, J. saw his dramatized version of *The American* open outside Liverpool and later run in London for only seventy unprofitable nights. It starred the young American actress Elizabeth Robins, who also helped J. appreciate Henrik Ibsen's plays and who later became one of J.'s closest friends. J. wrote several more plays, until his most ambitious effort, *Guy Domville,* was devastatingly booed on opening night in London, early in 1895. As for short fiction, "The Pupil," published in 1891, and "The Real Thing," in 1892, are two of J.'s most compelling tales. In "The Pupil," Pemberton is hired to move about Europe with the scarcely reputable Moreen family and to tutor their youngest child, sick little Morgan Moreen. What follows over the measured years is this: too intimate attachment, a reversal of roles—Pemberton is not a brilliant teacher, and Morgan is too wise for his age—the boy's shame in the face of his parents' shoddy behavior, and fatal exposure. "The Real Thing" is a parable on the aesthetic truism that reality is only the starting point for the imaginative artist, in this case, the painter-narrator. This unnamed hero is torn between retaining Oronte and Miss Churm, professional models who inspire him, or using Major and Mrs. Monarch, a pair of stiff amateurs, his sketches of whom resemble posed photographs. His head tells him to dump the Monarchs, but his heart bleeds for their precarious predicament.

This half-decade ending in 1895 was also marked by personal sadness as well for J. Death took three persons closest to him: his sister Alice in 1892, and two years later both Constance Fenimore Woolson and Robert Louis Stevenson.

In the last half of the 1890s, J. returned with new devotion and undiminished energy to fiction, much of it experimental and thus pointing to his subsequent celebrated "major phase." In 1895–99, he published fourteen short stories and four novels. They include several masterpieces. "The Altar of the Dead" (1895) is a rhapsodic reminder not only that we should honor our sacred dead but also that forgiving those who trespass against us will enable us to live more spiritually. "The Figure in the Carpet" (1896) is an insolubly ambiguous fable about what authors put into and what critics take out of literature. The plot of *The Spoils of Poynton* (1896) turns on property law as it applies to widows, family honor (should a son disenfranchise his widowed mother?), good taste with respect to art objects, and love (the heroine loves the bumbling hero but has an overriding regard for honor and the sanctity of his word, pledged to an undeserving woman). *What Maisie Knew* (1897) records the education of a young girl named Maisie Farange whose parents divorce and take a pair of lovers, who then love each other and Maisie. Maisie's ambiguous knowledge has been the subject of critical controversy, but it probably involves decency and renunciation. "The Turn of the Screw" (1898), one of the world's most challenging ghost stories, with labyrinthine convolutions too numerous to list here in full, raises more questions than it answers: Does the strange governess-narrator see ghosts or are they products of her imagination? Do her two little pupils, Miles and his sister Flora, see the ghosts? Is the housekeeper really dumb? Is knowledge always evil? Does Miles really die? *The Awkward Age* (1899), an experimental novel almost entirely in dialogue, not only contrasts modes of rearing young girls—Aggie has been segregated, while Nanda has been exposed—but also dramatizes their being paraded in early maturity by scheming adults before potential husbands as though they were fillies at a horse show. And "Paste" (1899) dramatizes a reversal of the situation in the world-famous short story "The Necklace" by J.'s friend Maupassant.

Two significant personal events marked J.'s late 1890s. The first was turning to composition by dictation in 1897, with a consequent possible thickening of his prose style. The second was his happy purchase of Lamb House, in Rye, Sussex, in 1899. In the only home he ever owned, the lonely, aging novelist became the generous host of hordes of devotees and relatives, was never far by train from London and his clubs there, and produced what many critics regard as his finest works.

The Sacred Fount (1901), which some readers revere as inviting a plunge into darkest J. but which others praise J. for defining as a "fantasticality" and "a consistent joke," is narrated by a psychological detective. He laboriously theorizes that in every love relationship one drains the other's "fount" of energy; then, when challenged, the narrator abandons his theory. Next came *The Wings of the Dove, The Ambassadors* (1903), and *The Golden Bowl* (1904). These three long novels form an intricate triptych of expatriate Americans abroad, and dramatize selfishness, renunciation, moral relativity, and the high cost of love, all against a painterly background of London, Venice, and Paris; further, these three novels represent as fine an achievement in a relatively short span of time as any American writer could ever boast. Each is of primary importance in its own way. *The Wings of the Dove* presents a British couple, Merton Densher and Kate Croy, who scheme to gain the fortune of Milly Theale, an American heiress staying briefly in London and then proceeding to Venice. Though young, Milly is mortally ill. So Kate passionately persuades Merton to make love to Milly (her physician has told her that love would be therapeutic) so as to collar her money when she dies. But Lord Mark also loves Milly and, in frustration at developments while the girl is dying in Venice, tells her of Kate's liaison with Merton. Then poor Milly truly sickens and, as J. poignantly puts it, "turns her face to the wall." Her posthumous generosity to Merton should be interpreted ambivalently. Merton will accept Kate only without Milly's cash. But Kate will accept him only with it. In *The Ambassadors*, which J. called his finest novel, we find Lambert Strether, an aging American, dispatched on a mission to Paris by Mrs. Newsome, his formidable, widowed fiancee, to save her son Chad Newsome from some *femme fatale* over there. But Strether no sooner locates her in Paris—she is the sumptuously depicted Madame Marie de Vionnet—than he surrenders both to her allure and to that of hr iridescent city. Strether is temporarily misled when a friend of Chad's calls Chad's relationship to Marie "a virtuous attachment." Toward the end, Strether has a moral problem: should he encourage Chad, who seems to be tiring of Marie (she is after all only separated from her old brute of a husband), to remain in Paris, or return to New England and all that it implies? *The Golden Bowl*, J.'s most complex fiction, offers a mathematical plot encased in baroque syntax studded with images: rich and widowered American Adam Verver, an avid art collector abroad, follows his daughter Maggie Verver's marriage in London to Prince Amerigo, a selfish Italian aristocrat, by marrying (all unwittingly) his fresh son-in-law's mistress Charlotte Stant. Maggie does not improve her position by spending entirely too much time with her father, because this action throws the Prince and Charlotte back into each other's arms. Maggie tardily discovers the truth and must now so act as to save both marriages and everyone's feelings. Revealing nothing essential, she takes blame upon herself, allows Charlotte to assume that she is in control, bids her astute father and his imperious wife farewell, and responds to her admiring husband's eager offer of a renewing embrace.

Between novels, J. assembled *The Better Sort* (1903), a collection of eleven short stories. They include "The Beldonald Holbein," contrasting skin-deep and profound feminine beauty; "Flickerbridge," "The Birthplace," and "The Papers," all showing that publicity can be a sought-for kiss of death; and especially "The Beast in the Jungle," an incomparable tale about a man so eager to be ready for a momentous event that his future surely holds that he misses everything in the present. Also in between, J. issued as a labor of reluctant love *William Wetmore Story and His Friends* (2 vols., 1903), Story being a Harvard-trained lawyer turned expatriate sculptor, painter, travel essayist, and poet, whose friendship and friends J. had long enjoyed in Rome, but whose work he regarded as second-rate.

The remainder of J.'s life may be quickly told. The novelist, by now intermittently sick with gout and with stomach and heart disorders, revisited America from August 1904 through July 1905. During these months he saw family members again, met Samuel Langhorne

CLEMENS, called upon his admired friend Edith WHARTON, dined with President Theodore ROOSEVELT at the White House, traveled extensively in the U.S. (south to Florida, then into the Middle West, and on to California), and lectured (on speech habits and on Balzac) for fees he regarded as embarrassingly high. Upon his return to England, he wrote *The American Scene* (1907), one of the most penetrating critiques of American life by a major author. From the unique point of view of an inquiring stranger who is also a returning native, J. records sharp views of his altered homeland—its exploited terrain, its noisy cities, its influx of immigrants, its crass and bragging upper classes. Then J. chose for his plum-colored New York Edition (24 vols., 1907–9) some sixty-seven novels and stories, rewrote many of them extensively, and provided eighteen prefaces of vital importance in understanding not only his creative processes but also his critical standards). He also wrote some more fiction, most notably "The Jolly Corner" (1908)—a poignant *alter-ego* story in which the protagonist sees what he would have become had he not expatriated himself in his youth. J. also made colleagues of many in the rising generation of new writers, including Virginia Woolf, Hugh Walpole, and Rupert Brooke. J. traveled a little more, going, for example, with his ailing brother William and his devoted wife Alice, to Germany and then back with them in 1910 to their summer residence in New England, where the philosopher died. Wearily home again in due time to England, J. devoted himself to writing three autobiographical volumes. World War I shattered the world of Anglo-French culture that he revered. In July 1915, he became a British subject, partly to protest continued American neutrality. That December, he suffered a stroke and thought he heard a voice say, "So here it is at last, the distinguished thing." His widowed sister-in-law Alice crossed the Atlantic Ocean in winter and in wartime to stay beside the dying novelist, who in his final delirium dictated a letter to his secretary and signed it Napoleon.

If Napoleon altered Europe, J. did the same for modern fiction and literary criticism. He was a writer's writer and a critic's critic. He always felt that the manner in which a writer of fiction presents an idea is more important than the idea itself. This belief resulted in his concentration on how to represent reality, with the outcome in his case being an evolution from psychological realism toward impressionism and symbolism. His practice illustrates the following techniques: the restricted point of view, phenomenological ambiguity, minuetlike dialogue, subtle humor, pictorial dramatization of conflict, imagistic density, scene as metaphor of character and theme, organic expansion of a form tentatively sketched in advance, and endings usually running counter to Victorian standards. Two of his main themes, endlessly modulated, are the international clash of naive Americans and more experienced Europeans, and the joys and renunciations of artists and writers. His fiction illustrates his criticism, and his criticism—especially "The Art of Fiction," his prefaces, and numerous reviews—elucidates his creative concerns. Balzac, Hawthorne, George Eliot, and Turgenev among creative writers especially inspired him. Matthew Arnold and Charles Augustin Saint-Beuve among critics especially challenged him. J. was an extraordinary man of letters, whose unremitting devotion to his craft was an inspiration to the most knowledgeable of his contemporaries and to many later practitioners as well.

BIBLIOGRAPHY: Edel, L., *H. J.: A Life* (5 vols., 1953–72; pub. in one vol., 1985); Edel, L., and L. H. Powers, eds., *The Complete Notebooks of H. J.* (1987); Fogel, D. M., ed., *A Companion to H. J. Studies* (1993); Gale, R. L., *A H. J. Encyclopedia* (1989); Kaplan, F., *H. J.: The Imagination of Genius, a Biography* (1992); Lewis, R. W. B., *The Jameses: A Family Narrative* (1991); Novick, S. M., *H. J.: The Young Master* (1996); Przybylowitz, D., *Desire and Repression: The Dialectic of Self and Other in the Late Works of H. J.* (1986); Rowe, J. C., *The Theoretical Dimensions of H. J.* (1984); Wagenknecht, E., *The Novels of H. J.* (1983); Wagenknecht, E., *The Tales of H. J.* (1984)

ROBERT L. GALE

JAMES, William

b. 11 January 1842, New York City; d. 26 August 1910, Chocorua, New Hampshire

A philosopher and psychologist, J. is among the leading American thinkers of the early 20th c. He included among his colleagues and friends such American philosophers as Josiah Royce, Charles Sanders Peirce, whose work he championed, George SANTAYANA, and John Dewey as well as Henri Bergson and F. H. Bradley. Since then, J.'s stature as a philosopher has grown to where he is now regarded as one of the major figures in American philosophy.

Son of the American transcendentalist and Swedenborgian theologian Henry James, Sr., J. divided his early attention between art and science. At Harvard he pursued science, including anatomy and physiology under Louis Agassiz, who he accompanied to Brazil on an expedition. Working on a degree in medicine, J. traveled to Europe to study physiology and psychology with luminaries such as Ernst Mach, Herbert Spencer, Wilhelm Wundt, Charles Renouvier, and Jean Martin Charcot. Setting up the first laboratory for experimental psychology in the U. S., J. commenced a career of teaching and research at Harvard from 1872 to 1907.

The product of J.'s research was his monumental *The Principles of Psychology* (1890). Long recognized as a classic, Jacques Barzun called it an American masterpiece, a quest narrative comparable to Herman MELVILLE's *Moby-Dick*. J. begins by denying the possibility of a pure phenomenological description. Description, he argues, is inevitably conceptual in nature and these concepts act according to human interests. Distinguishing mind from brain function, J. describes various brain states and how they condition the corresponding mental states. These mental states are, nevertheless, realities in themselves, and therefore the full range of mental experience must be taken into account. In the famous section on "stream-of-thought," he attacks the classical Cartesian model of consciousness, arguing that thought is part of personal consciousness, that it is always subject to change, and that it is selective, acting towards the interests of the individual. In this model, mind becomes a process, located in time. All of J.'s subsequent work grows out of the insights developed in *The Principles of Psychology*.

The Varieties of Religious Experience (1902) remains one of J.'s most widely read works. Emerging from the Gifford lectures at Edinburgh University, the book reflects an interest in religious and psychic phenomena that stretched back to the influence of his father. J. assembles and surveys various extreme forms of religious expression, such as that of "the sick soul," "the twice-born," and "the conversion" in order to isolate a common underlying religious experience outside of reason. The underlying unity of religious experience, J. suggests, provides evidence in support of the "religious hypothesis."

J.'s reputation as a philosopher rests on his contribution to pragmatism, developed in *Pragmatism: A New Name for Some Old Ways of Thinking* (1907), *The Meaning of Truth* (1909), *A Pluralistic Universe* (1909), and *Essays in Radical Empiricism* (1912). He attributed the basic idea and name to his friend Charles Sanders Peirce—uncomfortable with J.'s relativism, Peirce renamed his own doctrine pragmaticism. J. envisages pragmatism as a radicalization of the empiricism developed by Francis Bacon, John Locke, and David Hume. Drawing on *The Principles of Psychology,* he expands the concept and content of experience, conceiving truth in terms of practical consequences. Given a choice between competing models, one should select the one that offers the most consequences. As a result, truth becomes relative and provisional, a tool for manipulating the world, to be replaced when a better tool comes along, a notion that exercises a direct influence on Dewey's instrumentalism. For J., there is no absolute truth to be discovered, only a succession of tactical adjustments to specific circumstances. Thus—especially with regard to religion and ethics—one may believe whatever one finds sustaining and meaningful.

The older brother of the novelist Henry JAMES, it has often been quipped that Henry wrote fiction like a psychologist while William wrote psychology like a novelist. J.'s writing is noted for its clarity, directness, and vigor. He popularized terms such as "pragmatism," "pluralism," and coined expressions such as "stream of consciousness," and "moral equivalent of war." A brilliant lecturer, most of his later books developed out of public lectures, aimed at a general audience. A dedicated teacher, his students were as diverse as George Santayana and Gertrude STEIN. A profound thinker, his work anticipates and often exceeds much of modern philosophy.

BIBLIOGRAPHY: Allen, G. W., *W. J.* (1967); Barzun, J., *A Stroll with W. J.* (1984); Edie, J. M., *W. J. and Phenomenology* (1987); Perry, R. B., *The Thought and Character of W. J.* (1935); Seigfried, C. H., *W. J.'s Radical Reconstruction of Philosophy* (1990)

THOMAS L. COOKSEY

JANOWITZ, Tama
b. 12 April 1957, New York City

J. began her writing career as a guest editor for *Mademoiselle* magazine in 1979, providing a venue that allowed her to exercise a quick wit and a wry eye. In the same way, the stylistic looseness and facile subject matter associated with magazine writing allowed J. to perfect a vision shared by others in the 1980s. Like her cohorts Jay MCINERNEY, Fran Lebowitz, and Brett Easton ELLIS, J. catalogued the excesses and absurdities of urban life, casting doubt on any possible redemption for the postmodern era. Ultimately, her reputation rests on the phenomenon of the celebrity writer, and not on lasting fictional quality.

The daughter of a poet and psychoanalyst, J.'s eclectic background is essentially reflected in much of her fiction, as is her New York milieu. Her first novel, *American Dad* (1981), draws on autobiographical material, and is essentially an uneven ride through upper middle-class values and anxieties. The story concerns eleven-year-old Earl Przepasniak, and chronicles his early responses to family disintegration. The child of exceptionally permissive parents, Earl becomes a rebel against their open and easy lifestyle. After the accidental killing of his mother, Earl's father is shipped off to jail, and Earl is left to fend for himself. While the novel is uneven in development, J. tries to explore the growth and maturity of the boy while

exhibiting a comic ingenuity and a fine ear for dialogue.

J.'s critical reputation was made after the publication of her collection of short stories, *Slaves of New York* (1986). Set in New York's bohemian Soho, the stories follow the odd relationships of fringe characters and marginal dropouts, who live lives of quiet desperation and genteel poverty. Covering human relations and trend-setting stylists, the stories are both satirical and sociological in tone, mocking the conventions of savvy New Yorkers while implicitly celebrating their bohemian lifestyles. Like *American Dad,* the style is energetic but the work generally lacks substance.

This tendency recurs in *A Cannibal in Manhattan* (1987), which transplants an innocent cannibal, Mgungu, into the wilds of New York social life. Lured away from his seedy paradise of New Burnt Norton by insane millionairess Maria Fishburn, Mgungu undergoes a reeducation into the ways of the west. Following a picaresque plot peopled by wholly cartoonish characters, Mgungu eventually succumbs to American decadence.

In a similar way, *The Male Cross-Dresser Support Group* (1994) continues J.'s dispassionate approach to bizarre characters, exploring the dark side of middle-class America. Trying to avoid her earlier stereotypical characterization, J. attempts to blur gender lines by concentrating on sexual deviance. While the results are sometimes effective, her writing remains too campy and knowing to have any real impact.

Despite her shortfalls, J. remains a comic writer whose subject is the American family and their closets. While her off-center characters serve as vehicles for a sympathetic concern, J.'s world of tedious negation is dependent more on style than substance.

BIBLIOGRAPHY: Hurley, D., "The End of Celebrity," *Psychology Today* 22 (December 1988): 50–53; Kaye, E., "15 Minutes Over Soho," *Esquire* 110 (November 1988): 170–72; Sheppard, R. Z., "Yuppie Lit: Publish or Perish," *Time* 130 (19 October 1987): 77–79

PAUL HANSOM

JARRELL, Randall [Jackson]
b. 6 May 1914, Nashville, Tennessee; d. 14 October 1965, Greensboro, North Carolina

Poet, critic, novelist, and writer of children's books, J. is perhaps the most underappreciated member of the so-called "middle generation" that included Robert LOWELL, John BERRYMAN, Theodore ROETHKE, and Delmore SCHWARTZ among others. Though many readers are willing to accept Helen Vendler's judgment that J. put his talent into his poetry and his genius into his criticism, they do so without full consideration of J.'s significant creative achievement. Because he was instrumental in promoting or salvaging the reputations of writers such as Walt WHITMAN, Robert FROST, Lowell, Elizabeth BISHOP, and William Carlos WILLIAMS, J.'s position as a true American man of letters has suffered, and is only now beginning to recover.

Early on, as a student of John Crowe RANSOM and Robert Penn WARREN, J. developed a reputation s a prodigy; his early, acerbic reviews, collected in *Kipling, Auden, & Co.* (1980), earned him a reputation as the *enfant terrible* of poetry criticism. By comparison, his early poetry, especially that in his first full collection, *Blood for a Stranger* (1942), was apprentice work modeled on W. H. AUDEN, Allen TATE, and Ransom. J.'s transformation from imitator to creator resembles the similar transformation of the protagonist of his children's book *The Bat-Poet* (1964), in that he came to find his own voice slowly, by trial and error. The war poems of *Little Friend, Little Friend* (1945), which included J.'s most anthologized poem "The Death of the Ball-Turret Gunner," improved his reputation considerably. With its portraits of adolescent soldiers who seem to have gone directly from the womb to the horrors of modern warfare, J. first began to discover in this volume his empathetic voice, one that would identify with society's victims, particularly children and women. *Losses* (1948) contained J.'s first dramatic monologues in women's voices, and also provoked a controversy in *Poetry* magazine between Hayden CARRUTH and W. R. Moses over whether or not J.'s work was sentimental, a controversy very much alive today. In 1951, *The Seven-League Crutches* appeared, the first of three volumes that led Karl SHAPIRO to call J. the poet of *Kinder*. Haunted by his own difficult youth, J. turned increasingly to childhood as his major subject, a subject Lowell called a "governing and transcendent vision."

During the 1950s, J. suffered from a poetry-writing block. Paradoxically, he was at the height of his fame as a poet, serving as poetry consultant at the Library of Congress from 1956 to 1958. During this time, however, he published his best-known volume of criticism, *Poetry and the Age* (1953), a best-selling satirical novel for adults, *Pictures from an Institution* (1954), polemical and literary essays collected in *A Sad Heart at the Supermarket* (1962) and *The Third Book of Criticism* (1969), and a number of translations of writers such as Rilke. J.'s *Selected Poems* (1955) contained only two new poems, and over a third of his National Book Award-winning collection, *The Woman at the Washington Zoo* (1960), were translations. During the 1950s, J. also translated *Faust, Part I* (1976) and Chekhov's *The Three Sisters* (1969), the

latter of which has been produced often and successfully.

J. is said to have complained to his second wife, Mary, that a wicked fairy had turned him into a prose writer. But in 1961, the then junior editor Michael di Capua encouraged the forty-seven-year-old J. to write for children. In addition to writing four children's books—*The Bat-Poet, The Gingerbread Rabbit* (1964), *The Animal Family* (1965), and *Fly by Night* (1976)—J. also found himself again as a poet, writing the poems that appeared in what Lowell called J.'s "last and best book," *The Lost World* (1965). Particularly striking in this volume are a long poem in terza rima, "The Lost World," and its companion-piece, "Thinking of the Lost World," in which J. draws on a period of his boyhood (1925–26) spent with his paternal grandparents in Hollywood. In these poems, J. confronts his own bittersweet childhood in order to understand and to forgive the failures of his broken family. By recalling and letting go of his adoptive grandparental family, J. comes to realize that families do not just happen, but that they must be made, as a poet makes a poem. In doing so, he admits to his own identification with humanity as "something that there's something wrong with."

BIBLIOGRAPHY: Ferguson, S., ed., *Critical Essays on R. J.* (1983); Griswold, J., *The Children's Book of R. J.* (1988); Jarrell, M., *R. J.'s Letters* (1985); Pritchard, W. H., *R. J.: A Literary Life* (1990); Quinn, M. B., *R. J.* (1981); Taylor, P., R. P. Warren, and R. Lowell, eds., *R. J., 1914–1965* (1967)

RICHARD FLYNN

JEFFERS, [John] Robinson

b. 10 January 1887, Pittsburgh, Pennsylvania; d. 20 January 1962, Carmel, California

"Undoubtedly . . . one of the great poets of this century"—thus Nobel laureate Czeslaw Milosz described J. In contrast, Kenneth REXROTH called J.'s philosophy "a mass of contradictions" and considered his "high-flown statements" melodramatic and "often essentially meaningless." So goes the divided reaction to J.'s poetic achievement.

The son of a theology professor, J. grew up in a scholarly, disciplined atmosphere, learned several languages, and gained a thorough background in the bible and Greek classics. The family traveled extensively in Europe where he attended schools in Germany and Switzerland. After the professor retired, the family moved to Southern California; there J. graduated from Occidental College. He then half-heartedly followed graduate studies in forestry and medicine both in the U.S. and abroad. After inheriting money from his uncle, he pursued what he considered his true vocation, poetry. In 1914, J. and his wife Una settled near Carmel along California's central coast, known as the Big Sur, and remained there the rest of their lives. On a bluff overlooking Carmel Bay, J. himself built a house from the native granite and later erected an observation tower as a place to write. Most of his poetry is set in the magnificent landscape he could view from the tower placed between mountains and sea.

In 1912, he published his first volume of poetry, *Flagons and Apples,* followed by *Californians* in 1916; neither received much attention, favorable or otherwise. However, eight years later when *Tamar and Other Poems* appeared critics took notice at last. The title work marks the first of his long narrative poems for which he became best known. Based on a figure from II Samuel in the Old Testament, "Tamar" borrows from Greek tragedy as well and takes California as its setting. The tale of the contemporary Tamar Cauldwell recounts her doomed relations with three lovers—two of the affairs incestuous—and concludes with her setting fire to the house while they are all present. The house itself assumes a life of its own—a place of hatred, bitterness, and deceit.

Tamar and Other Poems introduces most of the sources, themes, and techniques that figure prominently in the subsequent narrative poems. J. continued to draw heavily from both the Bible—the Old Testament in particular—and from Greek tragedy, most often recasting the ancient stories into modern times. Incest, along with castration and parricide, continues to play a role as do the strong women whose desires lead them headlong into a tragic destiny. The other narrative in the collection, "The Tower beyond Tragedy," presents J.'s version of the Orestes and Electra story in which Orestes attains salvation by turning his back on humanity and embracing his physical surroundings. Here J. introduces a central philosophical concept that he expresses variously during his decades of writing. Calling his philosophy "inhumanism," he explained it as "a shifting of emphasis from man to not man." In J.'s world, an uncaring God had deserted humanity, so the individual should set aside emotion and look toward an abstract god found in nature, which far surpasses humankind. This near-pantheistic stance has alienated many readers, even some of those who admire the poetic art. Others find "inhumanism" a contradiction to J.'s reliance on the Bible and the Greek classics, and conclude that he understood neither. The early volume is also distinguished by a maturing of free verse, which has been said to contain the very rhythms of the sea. Still, opinion splits over J.'s technical accomplishment, some critics finding his free verse

original and influential, others describing it as hackneyed and flat.

Roan Stallion, Tamar and Other Poems appeared a year later in 1925, the first of his books to come from a major publisher. The title poem, probably J.'s best-known work, tells the story of a woman named California who develops an overpowering sexual desire for a roan stallion. This venture into bestiality has been said to represent the tragic consequences of seeking the purity inherent in the natural world when the individual has been corrupted by society. As the years passed, J. continued to publish both short poems and narratives, the latter in particular gaining him a wide reputation as one of America's premier poets. Some critics believe, however, that too much emphasis has been placed on the narratives and not enough attention paid to the other poems.

His adaptation of Euripides' *Medea* brought him popular acclaim when the actress Judith Anderson performed the lead role in a 1947 Broadway production. Although described as a triumph by most critics, the reaction was still uneven with one reviewer commenting that the verse sounded "as if Walt WHITMAN were playing at being Sophocles."

Even before his death in 1962, J.'s reputation had begun to sag. The detractors find his work old-fashioned, bombastic, too negative in its intellectual stance. The admirers—who have published extensively in recent years to shore up the poet's standing—excuse the excesses, justify the cruel strains, and call him a prophet who in a brilliantly chiseled language foresaw and warned against the "inhumanism" that has dominated the 20th c.

BIBLIOGRAPHY: Brophy, R., ed., *R. J.: Dimensions of a Poet* (1995); Everson, W., *The Excesses of God: R. J. as a Religious Figure* (1988); Karman, J., ed., *Critical Essays on R. J.* (1990); Karman, J., *R. J.: Poet of California* (1987); Zaller, R., *The Cliffs of Solitude: A Reading of R. J.* (1983); Zaller, R., ed., *Centennial Essays for R. J.* (1991)

ROBERT L. ROSS

JEFFERSON, Thomas

b. 13 April 1743, Goochland (now Albemarle) County, Virginia, d. 4 July 1826, Monticello, Virginia

America's third president, J. was a quintessential man of the Enlightenment. He combined lives of public service and scholarship, and indeed his great achievement was to incorporate philosophical principles and educational theory into the public life of the young U.S. Probably the best-read American of his generation, he was also a voluminous writer whose collected

Papers would fill sixty volumes. Of the three accomplishments he directed to be engraved on his tomb, two are documents—the Declaration of Independence and the Statute of Virginia for Religious Freedom; the third accomplishment was founding the University of Virginia.

J.'s first important literary work was *A Summary View of the Rights of British America* (1774), which laid the philosophical basis for the Declaration of Independence two years later. It shows J.'s legal training as well as his extensive reading in philosophy, leading to his basic doctrine of natural rights. These rights are evoked in the first sentence of the Declaration. J. was chosen by the five-man committee, including Benjamin FRANKLIN and John Adams, to prepare the first draft, and the final document is almost entirely his work, despite excisions following debate in the Continental Congress. The changes, which J. describes in his *Autobiography,* included an attack on slavery—though J. owned slaves—and a lament for the "unfeeling" British people, who receive final blame for the breach of peoples. The Declaration's statement of principles has become, as Abraham LINCOLN recognized, the founding doctrine of American union.

Elected governor of Virginia in 1779, J. drafted the *Act for Establishing Religious Freedom,* one long cumulative sentence building from natural law to recognition of individual conscience as its highest manifestation. In 1785, he published *Notes on the State of Virginia.* Moving from topography and natural history to government, education, and religion, Jefferson's only book epitomizes the mind of the Enlightenment but also, in its evocation of sublimity in the landscape, anticipates romantic views: the historian Howard Mumford Jones credited J. with inventing for American culture the "panoramic landscape organized in aesthetic principles." The *Notes on the State of Virginia* also struggle, much less successfully, to deal with the future of African slaves in American life. Written in a vigorous colloquial style, the book shows, more even than his formal public documents, J.'s gift for the memorable phrase.

J.'s voluminous correspondence shows his philosophical and stylistic powers in a form he found particularly congenial. His extensive correspondence with John Adams has long been recognized as a major contribution to American literature; and there are important letters to friends and family that speak masterfully on education, religious liberty, and other topics close to J.'s heart. In his late seventies, J. worked on his *Autobiography,* which was published posthumously in 1829. Living out his long life at Monticello, the architectural jewel that is perhaps the single best index to his diverse talents and interests, J. died fifty years to the day after the signing of the Declaration of Independence. His personal library of ten thousand volumes became the basis of the Library of Congress.

BIBLIOGRAPHY: Fliegelman, J., *Declaring Independence* (1993); Malone, D., *J. and His Time* (1948); Onuf, P. S., ed., *Jeffersonian Legacies* (1993); Peterson, M. D., *T. J. and the New Nation* (1970); Wills, G., *Inventing America* (1978)

GLEN M. JOHNSON

JEWETT, Sarah Orne

b. 3 September 1849, South Berwick, Maine; d. 24 June 1909, South Berwick, Maine

The most celebrated of the New England local color writers, J. is best known for her fictional sketches of Maine seacoast life in the late 19th c. J. combines sympathy, humor, and, occasionally, irony in her portraits of individuals, many middle-aged or elderly, who persevere in a region largely in decline because of Civil War losses, urban development, and western expansion. J.'s narrative style is uncluttered, often lyrical: she captures the rhythms and idioms of rural New England speech without heavy use of dialect. J. avoids sentimentality but often conveys nostalgia and compassion for her subjects. Her best work focuses on the redeeming qualities of late-19th-c. rural New England life: the beauty and healing properties of nature, the personal dignity of even the most humble folk, and the social and spiritual bondings of women. Her fictional world is often based on conflict—between generations, men and women, and urban and rural values—that are resolved by the creation of a symbolic and mythic world that allows harmonies with nature and maternal forces to be recaptured and preserved.

J. dedicated herself to writing at an early age, producing poetry as well as fiction. Her early stories were written under three pseudonyms: Alice Eliot, A. C. Eliot, and Sarah O. Sweet. In 1868, at age eighteen, she published her first story, "Jenny Garrow's Lovers," in the Boston periodical, the *Flag of Our Union.* A melodrama set in England, this story is unlike the indigenous fiction that soon was accepted by the *Atlantic Monthly, Riverside, Our Young Folks,* the *Independent,* and later, *Harper's* and *Scribner's.* J.'s first book, *Deephaven,* appeared in 1877. Over the course of her lifetime, she published five novels, nine collections of stories and sketches, a history of the Normans, and three children's books. With the exception of a few stories with urban, southern, or Irish settings, and *The Tory Lover* (1901), a historical romance set during the American Revolution, J. wrote about late-19th-c. New England, the region and period she knew intimately.

J. was born, reared, and spent most of life in South Berwick, Maine. Although well educated at Miss Rayne's School and Berwick Academy, she claimed that she acquired her real education—and materials for future stories—from driving around the countryside with her physician father as he made his calls. J.'s world was in no way limited to South Berwick, however. She traveled widely throughout the U.S., Europe, and the West Indies. She also established a close, enduring relationship with Annie Fields, wife of James T. Fields, owner of the *Atlantic Monthly*. After James T. Fields's death, J. spent long periods of time at Annie's Boston and Manchester-by-the-Sea homes, taking part in a lively literary and social community that included many of the most prominent male and female writers of New England. She also knew and corresponded with other important women writers of her day. J. was particularly influenced by Harriet Beecher STOWE's *The Pearl of Orr's Island,* which showed her the value of faithful depictions of rural life.

J. achieves these realistic portrayals in her first novel, *Deephaven* (1877), drawn from sketches that had appeared in the *Atlantic Monthly.* Appointing herself the "mission" of "teach[ing] the world that country people were not the awkward, ignorant set" that city dwellers thought them to be, J. offers an episodic story of female summer adventure and friendship in a quaint New England coastal town. Kate and the narrator Helen, on a retreat from busy Boston life, learn to appreciate how a town "utterly out of fashion" bestows rich gifts of the past on the present. Though its narrative focus is divided between the girls' developing relationship and the town itself, *Deephaven* contains skillfully detailed sketches and memorable characters, at least one of whom, Mrs. Bonny, is a comic forerunner of Almira Todd in *The Country of the Pointed Firs* (1896).

In her second novel, *A Country Doctor* (1884), J. turns her attention to the roles and opportunities open to women. Her most feminist work, *A Country Doctor* is a bildungsroman about a courageous young girl who realizes her dream of becoming a doctor by standing up to a disapproving aunt and by refusing marriage to an attractive suitor. J.'s special interest in the maturation of girls is clearly evident in this novel, as it is in her children's books, where she freely mixes moral lessons with her usual themes. In the stories in *Play Days* (1878), for example, J. writes imaginatively of talking buttons, spools, kittens, and dolls to help children learn the virtues of obedience, kindness, and honesty. In *Betty Leicester* (1890) and *Betty Leicester's English Xmas* (1894), she describes an assertive adolescent girl's struggles to learn self-reliance and responsibility. J.'s third novel, *A Marsh Island* (1855), is a pastoral romance about a country youth and a young man from the city who compete for the hand of a country woman. J. resolves the conflict by having each character decide in favor of what is familiar: the young man returns to the city and the country couple marry with the town's enthusiastic approval.

It is widely agreed that J.'s finest short story is "A White Heron," published in 1886 in a collection by the same name. Young Sylvia, isolated with her grandmother on an idyllic farm, becomes infatuated with a young ornithologist who is hunting for an elusive white heron. When Sylvia decides to climb a tall pine tree to learn the heron's whereabouts, her bravery is rewarded with wide vistas and a glimpse of the majestic heron with its mate. In this powerful communion with nature, Sylvia achieves a spiritual transcendence that gives her courage not to disclose the bird's whereabouts. The story concludes with J.'s celebration of Sylvia's integrity and the triumph of nature over culture, female over male, and rural over urban, but it is a celebration tinged with regret for the human isolation that Sylvia's choice entails.

In the book that is considered her masterpiece, *The Country of the Pointed Firs*, J. weaves her themes into a powerfully evocative fictional account of an old-fashioned Maine seacoast town, Dunnet Landing. In 1925, Willa CATHER edited and wrote a preface for a J. collection that included *The Country of the Pointed Firs.* Noting the "inherent, individual beauty" of J.'s writing, she listed *Pointed Firs,* along with *The Scarlet Letter* and *Adventures of Huckleberry Finn,* as the "three American books which have the possibility of a long, long, life," adding, "I can think of no others that confront time and change so serenely." Today, the work has a secure place in American literature, although J. herself is still often relegated to the category of "regional writer."

The episodic sketches that comprise *The Country of the Pointed Firs* are unified thematically and structurally through the use of a first-person narrator from the city on a summer visit in a New England town. By interlacing the townspeople's accounts with the narrator's own, J. leads the reader gradually to understand and appreciate the customs and values of a town still living in the past. The loss of shipping and seafaring was permanently disabling to New England, evident in J.'s depiction of Captain Littlepage, a disoriented seaman whose tale of the living dead "up north beyond the ice" parallels his own displacement. But J. makes it clear that the loss is partly off-set by the vital community established by women. Mrs. Todd, the narrator's hostess and J.'s most memorable character, is an herbal healer—"a renewal of some historic soul"—whose connections with the land, the sea, and her family facilitate the narrator's own induction into the "sacred and mystic rites" of Dunnet Landing. At

Blackett Island, home of Mrs. Todd's mother, this sense of spiritual community and enduring matrilineal bonds reaches its climax. Throughout *The Country of Pointed Firs,* J. also shows that pathos and sadness need not be tragic. Even the self-exile of "poor Joanna," forsaken in love, and the widowhood and domestication of another seaman, Elijah Tilley, establish a greater understanding of the human condition, of the "place remote and islanded" in each of us "given to endless regret or secret happiness." J.'s organic style permits an impressive fusion of structure and theme—a vision of life as cyclical, nourishing, and enduring—created by endless rounds of visits, reunions, and funerals; the natural cycles of the tides and seasons; and, at the end of the novel, the narrator's own return to the city.

J.'s fiction abounds with women either making their own way or depending on one another without the traditional supports of men. She has a special affinity for the elderly, once telling Willa Cather "that her head was full of dear old houses and dear old women, and that when they came together in her brain with a click, she knew that a story was under way." Often the issues are independence, as in "The Flight of Betsey Lane"; or unexpected friendship, as in "Miss Tempy's Watchers," in which women of different social classes achieve intimacy as they sit watch over their deceased friend. J. carries the theme of female bonding into the supernatural and occult in "Lady Ferry," "The Foreigner," and "The Green Bowl." Romance and marriage do figure in J.'s fiction, but many of her women are widowed or remain single after an early disappointment in love. J. explores the pathos of abandonment in "Marsh Rosemary," the mutuality of separation in *A Marsh Island,* and the comic as well as serious sides of gender roles and reversals in "Tom's Husband" and "Farmer Finch." Her good natured humor and chiding are also evident in tales of affectation or self-delusion such as "The Dulham Ladies" and "The Queen's Twin."

Setting and character figure more prominently in J.'s fiction than plot and dramatic action. Although encouraged by her contemporaries to write more boldly and of larger issues, J. chose to follow her own course, firm in the belief that her fictions were "bright and real and [had] an individuality." Today, her narrative structures are increasingly valued for their obvious breaks with the mainstream male literary traditions. Critics continue to find J.'s delineation of New England and treatment of the past a fertile ground for study; there is also recent interest in her religious and folklore motifs, her representations of women, and her literary and personal relationships with women. The nature of J.'s realism—variously described as regionalist, pastoral, and impressionistic—is open to schol-

arly debate, as is the generic classification of her fiction, which combines elements of the sketch, novel, short story, and memoir. Recent scholarship, especially by feminists, as well as the substantial J. studies over the past century, assures J.'s continued importance in American literature.

BIBLIOGRAPHY: Cary, R., *Appreciation of S. O. J.* (1973); Donovan, J., *S. O. J.* (1980); Howard, J., *New Essays on "The Country of the Pointed Firs"* (1994); Mobley, M. S., *Folk Roots and Mythic Wings in S. O. J. and Toni Morrison* (1991); Nagel, G. L., *Critical Essays on S. O. J.* (1984); Nagel, G. L., and J. Nagel, *S. O. J.: A Reference Guide* (1978); Sherman, S. W., *S. O. J., an American Persephone* (1989); Weber, C. C., and C. J. Weber, *A Bibliography of the Published Writings of S. O. J.* (1949)

CAROL J. SINGLEY

JEWISH AMERICAN LITERATURE

Over the past hundred years, with the gradual liberalization of American culture and the decline of overt anti-Semitism after the Holocaust, Jewish American literature has become a major current in the mainstream of 20th-c. American letters. Two Nobel Prizes in literature and numerous other book awards have been awarded to Jewish American authors. Although fiction predominates, these authors have published in all major genres; Howard NEMEROV became poet laureate of the U.S., and plays by Clifford ODETS and Arthur MILLER have long been standards in the theater repertoire. In the broad field of literary and cultural criticism, the New York Intellectuals—predominantly Jewish—played a major role earlier in the century, most notably during the Marxist period of the 1930s and afterwards into the 1960s.

Nevertheless, fiction has steadily prevailed, especially after World War II, with the works of Saul BELLOW and Isaac Bashevis SINGER (both Nobel laureates), Philip ROTH, Bernard MALAMUD, Grace PALEY, Cynthia OZICK, Chaim POTOK, and many others. Although all of these authors have lived for many years in the U.S., not all were American born, and despite their Jewish roots, each depicts American life in his or her unique manner.

Before the contributions of individual authors are discussed, however, it would be useful to identify two features of Jewish American literature that help distinguish it from the writing of non-Jewish contemporaries. First, in the words of Jules Chametzky, is its essential support for "the liberal, pluralistic and egalitarian aspects of American life." As the target of persistent discrimination over centuries and continents, Jews have learned that to support ethnic or religious prejudice and hostility toward others is eventually to attract similar antipathy to themselves. Conversely, to foster tolerance toward others is indirectly to protect themselves. Perhaps no better illustration of this tendency appears than in one of the earliest and most enduring Jewish American poems, "The New Colossus," engraved in a bronze plaque beside the entrance of the Statue of Liberty. Written by Emma Lazarus in 1883 to help fund the pedestal of this immense French gift, "The New Colossus" epitomizes the liberal democracy that enabled countless numbers of the poor, "homeless," "huddled masses" from foreign lands to find their way to freedom and in many cases prosperity in America despite the hardship and difficulty that most immigrants of the period met in the New World.

The other predominant characteristic of Jewish American writing is *yidishkayt,* the inescapable residue of Eastern European life in the *shtetlakh* (villages to which Jews were restricted). By the time that the doors were closed to new immigrants in 1924, some two million Jews had entered the U.S., chiefly from Eastern Europe, in less than half a century. Emma Lazarus herself was born in the U.S., a well-to-do New Yorker of Sephardic stock. But once awakened to the oppression in the Jewish Pale of (Russo-Polish) settlement and the pogroms of the early 1880s in Czarist Russia, she shifted her attention from the classicism that characterizes her poetry of the 1860s and 1870s to the Jewish themes that prevail in *Songs of a Semite* (1882), the first significant book of Jewish American poetry and of a genuine Jewish American literature. In consequence of her new calling as the poet of her people, Old World Judaism and the Zionism that evolved from European oppression find their way into her life and writing. To this extent the opening lines of "The New Colossus" may be taken autobiographically as she shifts from "the brazen giant of Greek fame" to "A mighty woman with a torch, . . . / Mother of Exiles." Thus begins Jewish American literature as we know it today.

The same year that saw the publication of *Songs of a Semite* also marked the American immigration of Abraham Cahan, whose life and writing over the nearly seven decades that followed exemplify most of the ideas which concerned American Jews during that long period and expose the rapid transformation that occurred in less than three generations. Socialist, journalist, editor, ghetto leader, and novelist, Cahan's contribution to the Americanization of Jewish immigrants from 1882 to his death in 1951 cannot be overestimated. His early life in Russia resembled that of many young Jewish males in the last half of the 19th c. After spending his boyhood years at the *kheder* (Hebrew

school), Cahan attended secular public schools in Vilna and became a teacher himself. However, he soon became involved in revolutionary politics to the extent that he found his life jeopardized and fled to America. Shortly after his arrival, Cahan started writing articles for Russian newspapers and the flourishing Jewish press in the U.S.

In New York, numerous socialist, communist, and other political-economic newspapers were being published for the burgeoning working class. These dailies and weeklies, however, were being printed chiefly in German and Russian, languages that few of the immigrant Jewish laborers could read. As the first reformer to begin addressing the Jewish immigrants in Yiddish, their native tongue, Cahan quickly became a ghetto leader. Moreover, he had rapidly gained fluency in his adoptive language as well. After his stories in English began to appear in the mid-1890s, his first novel, *Yekl: A Tale of the New York Ghetto,* was published in 1896; William Dean HOWELLS's highly favorable review of its realism commenced to establish Cahan as a promising literary figure in America. Although Cahan continued to publish fiction in English during the next decade, he is best known as a novelist for *The Rise of David Levinsky* (1917), in which Levinsky emigrates to America and becomes a wealthy, faithless, lonely man.

Still regarded by many scholars as the most important novel about American immigration around the turn of the century, *The Rise of David Levinsky* combines many characteristic themes of Jewish American literature as a result of Cahan's broadly sharing the immigrant experience of which he was writing, though the novel is only vaguely autobiographical. If Levinsky confronts issues similar to those which Cahan faced, the differences between author and character in terms of the way those issues were met are far more pronounced and, from a literary perspective, more important.

First in a baker's dozen of common themes between *Levinsky* and much other Jewish American fiction is the immigrant experience itself, especially life in the ghetto. Second is *yidishkayt,* the knowledge of belonging to a covenantal people with, in the words of Bonnie Lyons, "a distinct sense of uniqueness, purpose, and calling" toward survival and thus salvation of the vulnerable but closely knit group rather than of any individual within it. Third is the quest for identity as American or Jew: assimilation or isolation? Fourth is the internecine conflict between the liberalized uptown German and Sephardic Jews of earlier immigrant generations in America and the mostly Orthodox Eastern Europeans who settled downtown on New York's Lower East Side and later in Williamsburg, Brownsville, and the Bronx. Fifth is the press by socialists and communists to organize labor in the ghetto, particularly among the sweatshop and factory workers in the rapidly expanding garment trade. Sixth is Zionism, which had been carried from Europe to the U.S. with the immigrants. Seventh is the "streets of gold" motif that proved at once so attractive to the poor, hungry "huddled masses" of Emma Lazarus's sonnet, and yet so elusive to countless thousands of immigrants once trapped in the ghetto. Eighth is the yearning for education and culture in conflict with the quest for riches. Ninth is the crucial role of language in acculturation. Tenth is the fading bond of family among the assimilated. Eleventh is the social and economic impact of the Jewish *nouveaux riches.* Twelfth is the phenomenon of the Jewish businessman in an heretofore WASP-ish domain. Thirteenth and finally is anti-Semitism, overt and implicit. Some of these themes, especially those related to economics and family disintegration, become more pronounced later in the century, whereas others, such as anti-Semitism and FEMINISM, inevitably evolved with shifting social patterns and the attitudinal changes in America consequent to the Holocaust. But *The Rise of David Levinsky* introduced most of them broadly and effectively when literary naturalism was at its apex in the U.S., and as a vibrant representation of Jewish immigrant life a hundred years ago, it has never been superseded.

Other authors of the following two decades published fiction that centered on one or more of these themes as well. Anzia Yezierska, for example, the first woman to write Jewish American fiction of note, also arrived on the Lower East Side late in the 19th c. from the Russian Pale. Unwilling to endure her father's authoritarian Orthodox rule over an impoverished ghetto home to which he added only spiritual sustenance, she fled to make her own way in the New World. Her fiction constitutes an imaginative rendering of her youthful anger, suffering, and flight to independence. Her first volume of collected tales, *Hungry Hearts* (1920), brought her fame through Hollywood, but her best novel, *Bread Givers* (1925), represents the difficulty of a permanent escape from the ghetto, which seems to have captured her soul. Yezierska's work constitutes a useful base of comparison with Mary Antin's *The Promised Land* (1912), an autobiography that details the emigration of another young Jewish girl from the Pale and her subsequent relinquishing of Judaism in favor of Americanism as a religion. Ultimately, Antin's adopted faith was insufficient to sustain the joy of belonging in her "promised land."

A distressing novel of the same period focuses on political and legal corruption in the ghetto. Published anonymously, Samuel Ornitz's *Haunch Paunch and Jowl* (1923) traces the career of Meyer Hirsch from his shrewd, manipulative boyhood through his years as a malignant politician and jurist. At the end of the decade Michael Gold (born Irwin Granich) brought out *Jews without Money* (1930), the best-known Jewish American proletarian novel. Gold represented the Lower East Side as an interethnic war zone in which his Hebrew upbringing was an anachronism; the novel ends with a rhapsodic plea for communism.

Four years later, the publication of Henry ROTH's extraordinary *Call It Sleep* explored the psycho-emotional development of young David Schearl. Roth's sensitivity to nuances of the polyglot ghetto enabled him to represent families and neighborhoods with remarkable authenticity yet with a lyricism that has still not been matched in Jewish American fiction. Through Roth's highly sensuous pictorializing, one lives and suffers the ghetto experience with David, whose initiation carries him through episodes of frightful violence and anti-Semitism as he ventures tentatively away from the warm, loving aura of his mother. Shortly before his death he brought out the first two volumes of *Mercy of a Rude Stream,* a projected six–volume autobiographical novel that he had been writing for decades and had finally completed in manuscript.

More prolific, but less enduring than Roth was Meyer LEVIN, whose first novel, *Reporter,* appeared five years earlier than *Call It Sleep,* and whose last one, *The Architect,* based on the life of Frank Lloyd Wright, was published the year of his death, more than half a century later. In well over a dozen novels, Levin incorporated most of the themes evident in Cahan's magnum opus, though his initial focus is broader, and his setting of his naturalistic fiction is Chicago rather than New York. In *The Old Bunch,* his richest portrait of second-generation Jewish neighborhood life on the West Side, Levin creates a chronological tapestry depicting a group of recent high school graduates drifting in various directions away from their families; the old traditions are no longer vital, and Levin reveals that nothing has evolved to replace them. At the end of his next important novel, *Citizens,* published in 1940, labor unrest threatens American stability, a warning that lost its efficacy with America's entry into World War II the following year. More successful in sales than either *The Old Bunch* or *Citizens,* however, was *Compulsion,* a fictionalized account of the Bobby Franks murder on Chicago's South Side in 1924; Levin's reportorial approach anticipated the contemporary New Journalists in his imaginative yet authentic rendering of a historic crime.

Levin is one of the few prominent Jewish American authors whose writings spanned the war years with a sizable margin before and after. Edna FERBER and Isaac Bashevis Singer are two others. After publishing her first novel in 1911, Ferber continued writing until her death in 1968. Often considered a western regionalist because of best-sellers like *Cimarron* and *Giant,* her range was too broad for such categorization. Indeed, among her most enduring works is *Showboat,* adapted for the stage as a musical by Jerome Kern, who composed the music, and Oscar Hammerstein, II who provided the memorable lyrics. A year before its first publication, Ferber received the Pulitzer Prize for her novel *So Big.* Whereas Ferber's Judaism had little apparent impact on her writing, Singer's fiction is governed by his Jewish background and faith. Yiddish, not Polish, was his native language, and when he emigrated to the U.S. from Warsaw in 1935, he discovered that although he had not been writing for long in Europe, Jewish readers in New York were already familiar with his stories through their publication in the *Jewish Daily Forward,* edited in New York by Abraham Cahan for fifty years. But unlike Cahan, Singer centered his fiction on Old World Judaism, on *yidishkayt* and life in the *shtetl;* moreover, he continued to write only in Yiddish because of his conviction that the vitality of the Jewish culture depended upon it. Yiddish was Singer's weapon against the assimilation that he perceived as the gradual erosion of Judaism in America.

After the war, achievements in Jewish American literature, especially fiction, reached a peak. Undoubtedly the Holocaust both stimulated sympathy and generated curiosity among gentiles about Jews. Whatever the reasons behind the rapid acceptance of Jewish authors writing about Jewish people on Jewish themes in the U.S., a major new force in American literature evolved as a result of them. It would be naive to suggest that anti-Semitism simply disappeared as Jewish American authors gained a large gentile readership, but both its obtrusiveness and its impact rapidly diminished, and assimilation to an unprecedented extent in America was the result.

In consequence, themes Cahan introduced in *The Rise of David Levinsky* also evolved rather than passed into literary history. With the emergence of second-and third-generation Jewish American authors, *yidishkayt* became largely a warm, sweet memory from a childhood spent among grandparents and parents in a family setting. Many of the traditions disappeared with the dying of the older generation and the moving of parents and siblings first from the ghetto to more respectable parts of the city, then to the suburbs; and the rituals that remained were often hollow, the faith behind them gone, leaving only nostalgia.

The resultant loss and the struggle to accommodate it again brought the quest for identity to the center of much Jewish American fiction, though the need to gain external social acceptance transformed to a psy-chological battle between the fact of assimilation through acculturation and the guilt that accompanies a broken ages-old promise. Saul Bellow's fiction from the publication of his first novels in the 1940s, *Dangling Man* and *The Victim,* through much of his work of the 1970s, especially *Mr. Sammler's Planet* and *Humboldt's Gift,* explore this question of identity as an American and a Jew, and in a recent novelette, the slight but amusing *The Bellarosa Connection,* the same idea is central. Even in *The Adventures of Augie March,* the eponymous hero identifies himself with Columbus while others compare him with Walt WHITMAN and Samuel Langhorne CLEMENS's Huck Finn, yet Augie emerges from an Orthodox home and retains his Jewish consciousness without a gnawing Jewish conscience as he cavorts across the continent finding himself as he goes.

In contrast, many of Bernard Malamud's characters, and Philip Roth's, are plagued by conscience. Both authors began publishing their stories in the 1950s, and among their earliest, the impact of a Jewish past on an acculturated American present drives their characters to action, distraction, or both. Malamud's stories in *The Magic Barrel* and *Idiots First* are characterized by unresolvable conflicts, and in his second novel, *The Assistant,* a Catholic paradoxically becomes the suffering Jew. In Malamud's later fiction, however, the author's frustration and bitterness dominate; in *The Tenants,* for example, black and Jew destroy each other, and in *God's Grace* atomic holocaust brings all human life to an end, though a respite among the apes briefly delays the remnant's death. Malamud's fiction achieved popularity not for the author's increasingly dark world view but for his colorful, nostalgic representation of Old World Jewry in a New World setting, evident in such stories as "Angel Levine," "The Jewbird," "The Magic Barrel," "The Mourners," and many others, especially from his early collections.

Similarly, Philip Roth's early stories, such as "Eli the Fanatic" and "Defender of the Faith," that were collected and published with *Goodbye, Columbus* quickly gained him a book award and a striking literary reputation while he was still in his mid-twenties. In *Goodbye, Columbus* the breakdown in traditional morality and the garish display of new money among Jews only one or two generations from the ghetto anticipate most of the conflicts that would remain central in Roth's fiction to follow, though with each new title his work became more outrageous to many readers, from *Portnoy's Complaint* and *The Breast* to *The Professor of Desire* and the *Zuckerman Bound* trilogy. *The Counterlife,* perhaps his best novel to date, brilliantly combines many of his earlier themes with personal responses to numerous critical complaints heretofore inadequately attended, including charges of pornography and Jewish self-hatred.

More than any other major Jewish American author at present, Roth has become preoccupied with the role of critical theory in the creation of a novel, as is evident in *The Counterlife* and his more recent work, including his semiautobiographical *The Facts, Deception,* and *Operation Shylock,* the latter two being his most enigmatic novels to date, and the erotic *Sabbath's Theater.* As Jules Chametzky has suggested, Jewish American writers usually have been more concerned with exploring moral and social values than the creative process in their fiction, though in many cases, especially in recent years, the impact of poststructuralism is increasingly evident. Even before the postmodernist mentality became influential on the writing of young novelists, anticipations of it were evident in the fiction of Edward Lewis WALLANT, especially in the surrealistic segments of *The Pawnbroker,* dominated by terrifying recollections of the Holocaust in relation to the contemporary dehumanization of life in the inner-city. E. L. DOCTOROW's *The Book of Daniel* offers a more sophisticated—and more complex—weaving of text and subtext in its representation of the Rosenbergs, their family, and their trial for espionage. Doctorow has continued to explore the intimate, at times indistinguishable relation between history and imagination, but never with the telling effect that he achieved in this novel.

Three altogether different approaches to contemporary Jewish American fiction appear in the work of Grace Paley, Chaim Potok, and Cynthia Ozick. Paley, an outspoken advocate of liberal causes, has published only three major collections of stories from 1957 to the present, yet she has acquired a sizable following because of the open, earthy honesty with which she represents life, especially the lives of women with relatively low incomes in New York City. Her stories bring the repetitious patterns of Gertrude STEIN in *Three Lives* and the acid wit of Dorothy PARKER, two earlier Jewish American authors, together with the picturesque vernacular of Damon RUNYON, but the resulting story-dialogues and monologues are pure Paley, often disclosed through the persona of Faith, a writer. And it is by virtue of Faith that Paley's own faith emanates—faith in people, in action, in life itself.

In Potok's fiction, the faith is more explicit. Potok is at once an ordained rabbi, a scholar in philosophy (with a Ph.D.), a talented painter, and, of course, an author with seven novels to his credit as well as at least three produced plays. Whereas Paley's stories are generally secular, Potok's fiction is heavily Judaic, saturated with evidence of the author's background in Hebrew theology, mysticism, art, and philosophy. From *The Chosen* and its sequel, *The Promise,* through

nearly all of his later works, Potok has been presenting variations of the basic conflict within closely guarded and essentially closed ultrareligious communities, the struggle among American Jews between strict adherence to Hebrew law with its complex social ramifications and liberalized Judaism in which the faith is retained but not necessarily by the letter of the law.

In contrast to both Paley and Potok, Cynthia Ozick adapts traditional and scriptural Jewish materials and employs them as the core of her fiction. Ozick's essays confirm the depth of her commitment to the living truths of historic Judaism, truths that infuse, color, and dramatize such stories as "The Pagan Rabbi" and "Puttermesser and Xanthippe." Whereas Bellow, Malamud, P. Roth, and others are irked with being labeled as Jewish authors, Ozick "embraces the designation, and seeks to express her artistic vision in Jewish terms, overtly illuminating her fiction with the wisdom of Jewish sources." Moreover, she writes with compelling, almost visionary power on the Holocaust, especially in such works as "The Shawl" and *The Messiah of Stockholm,* in which her Jamesian critical acumen confronts the horrors of Nazi barbarism.

Potok, Paley, and Ozick are three very different contemporary voices, and any thoughtful look at Jewish American fiction from its earliest period late in the last century through the work being published currently will disclose a variety of other fictive approaches and concerns that cannot be examined here because of spatial limitations. For several of these writers, the Holocaust has gained greater prominence as a theme than it had in the first quarter century after the war, perhaps because Jewish American authors found it difficult to address the inhumanity of the *Shoah* toward Jews like themselves as the subject of fiction at that time. Among many other writers whose fiction should be considered for a fuller understanding of the field, the most important are: Ludwig Lewisohn, Nathanael WEST, Daniel FUCHS, Edward DAHLBERG, Tillie OLSEN, Budd SCHULBERG, Norman MAILER, Leslie A. FIEDLER, Herman WOUK, J. D. SALINGER, Joseph HELLER, Norma Rosen, Leon URIS, Herbert GOLD, Johanna Kaplan, Arthur Cohen, Hugh Nissenson, Jay Neugeboren, and Susan Fromberg Schaeffer.

Spatial limitations also preclude more than a few remarks on Jewish American literary criticism, the best known of which as an entity is associated with a broad group called the New York Intellectuals. When the group originated early in the century, the members had a strong socialist orientation, and Jewish leadership was minimal. However, the establishment in 1925 of the *New Masses,* a communist journal, saw the Jewish role become dominant with editorial views largely shaped by the immigrant experiences of the participants or their families. With the advent of the

Partisan Review in 1934 under a fully Jewish editorial board, the role of the intellectuals was generally bifurcated as each journal represented a different facet of Jewish interest. Whereas the *New Masses* supported communism and strong social criticism during the Proletarian 1930s, the *Partisan Review* advocated literary modernism and showed little interest in matters related to the Judaism of its editors. As Hitler's anti-Semitic influence gained strength in Europe, however, it awakened the "intellectuals" more fully to their own identity as Jews. Apart from Isaac Rosenfeld, one of their preeminent voices, who died young in 1956, the New York Intellectuals continued to write authoritatively during the 1950s and 1960s under the leadership of Lionel TRILLING, Philip Rahv, Irving HOWE, and Alfred KAZIN. Though all four have been historically and culturally oriented in their critical approach to literature and therefore may be contrasted to the prevailing New Critics of those years, they differ considerably among themselves in the way that their Judaism affected their critical views as individuals.

A great many volumes have been published by Jewish American poets and dramatists, but one seeks in vain a unified school or movement of either. Much of their writing includes no allusion, direct or implicit, to Jewish themes, characters, sources, or ideas, and for many, explicit Jewish references in their work are exceptional. Whereas some readers believe that they may recognize or sense the operation of a Jewish consciousness behind the writing of an apparently secular poem or play, to identify or characterize that consciousness with convincing specifics often demands more imagination—or faith—than acute perception. To be sure, common ethnic revelations occur at times in this writing—the sense of belonging or not belonging; the awareness of being an object or victim of anti-Semitic hostility; the desire to understand one's relation to the Holocaust as survivor, witness, or descendant—but the isolating individualistic nature of poetry in particular renders it less suitable than fiction for generalization unless it has been written for a specific cause and is thus easily susceptible to categorization and paraphrase. Nevertheless, even a hasty panoramic view of Jewish American literature would not be complete without some representation of the principal poets and dramatists.

In his introduction to *Poems of a Jew,* an early collection of his poetry, Karl SHAPIRO addresses the question of a Jewish consciousness, which he believes has its "central meaning" in the inability to define the term *Jew* specifically. "For to be a Jew," he writes, "is to be in a certain state of consciousness which is inescapable. . . . Being a Jew is the consciousness of being a Jew, and the Jewish identity, with or without religion, with or without history, is the significant fact." It is, also, in his view, obsessional, so "the theme of the Jew" underlies most of his own early poetry.

In contrast to Shapiro's understanding of the psychological thrust behind the writing of Jewish poetry, Louis Harap assesses the Jewishness of the poetry by quantifying a poet's scriptural imagery and traditional Judaic references. Clearly, both approaches may be used to illuminate the work of most Jewish American poets. In the poems of Emma Lazarus, for example, neither her Jewish consciousness nor significant Hebrew references appeared until she published *Songs of a Semite* in 1882. Until then her poetry was secular and steeped in classicism, but her reading of *Daniel Deronda* (1876), by George Eliot (to whom she dedicated the volume), awakened her faith as a Jew and inspired her to write in support of her own people. Revealing her new Zionist vitality, she writes: "Wake, Israel, wake! . . . / Let but an Ezra rise anew; / To lift the banner of the Jew." In "The Dance to Death" she portrays the martyrdom of persecuted Jews in 14th-c. Germany, thus reflecting the anti-Semitic pogroms her people were currently facing in Europe.

After Emma Lazarus, one of the most influential figures associated with Jewish American poetry was Louis Untermeyer; he is better known now as an editor than as a poet in that his anthology, *Modern American Poetry,* passed through numerous editions since its original publication in 1919, each of which included several Jewish poets. The first identifiable group of Jewish American poets were the objectivists—Carl Rakosi, George OPPEN, Louis ZUKOFSKY, and Charles REZNIKOFF. The last two named were of particular influence and importance. Broadly, the objectivist poem is a self-contained reality in which both the imagery and language are clear and precise. R. Barbara Gitenstein, who notes that a strong sense of exile characterizes Reznikoff's poetry, assesses his book-length poem *Holocaust,* a brutally realistic depiction, as "the most successful extended American comment on the Holocaust."

Near mid-century one of the most promising Jewish American poets was Delmore SCHWARTZ, whose work, however, shows evidence of an increasingly damaging self-conflict over his identity as a Jew reared amid the traditional faith of his family and as an assimilated, acculturated American living in a predominantly secular modern world. For instance, though ostensibly writing of a Russian past, his own turmoil is apparent in such lines from "The Ballad of the Children of the Czar" as: "I am my father's father, / You are your children's guilt. / . . . / Child labor! The child must carry / His father on his back." And from "Father and Son": "Guilt, guilt of time, nameless guilt. . . . / Face yourself, constantly go back / To what you were, your own history. / You are always in debt." The titles alone of such poems as "Socrates' Ghost Must Haunt Me Now" and "Abraham and Orpheus" patently expose Schwartz's self-conflict, and "The Fulfillment" reveals the extent to which his despair inexorably carries him as he presents a terrifying recognition in the afterlife of the intrinsic beauty in mortality that, unaware of its value during his lifetime, he strove to overcome. Schwartz's breakdown became the subject of fictive treatment by Saul Bellow in *Humboldt's Gift.*

Perhaps the best-known Jewish American poet of the 1950s and 1960s is Allen GINSBERG, whose career took him from an alienated Beat to acceptance and influence as a member of the Establishment. No one more effectively than Ginsberg adapted the techniques of Walt Whitman to the modern age. His radical views of contemporary American life as a Jew, an American, and an emotionally wrought youth during a period of American peace and prosperity were exposed in *Howl* and *Kaddish,* both of which proved electrifying in both shock and appeal to rebellious young readers across the country.

Another contemporary is Jerome ROTHENBERG, who has brought out over two dozen volumes of poetry and translations during the last three decades. Rothenberg writes in a variety of styles, and his subject matter encompasses not only Jewish materials from his own background but other ethnic themes as well, notably from traditional Native American sources. *Poland/1931,* brought out serially over a period of years, and *Vienna Blood,* incorporate some of his best work on Jewish themes. The first, which is heavily autobiographical, employs Poland as a kind of "deep image" or objective correlative for his Jewish motifs, and *Vienna Blood* deals with the theme of Jewish messianism. In such secular poems as "A Valentine, No a Valedictory to Gertrude Stein" and "Words," Rothenberg illustrates the influence of Stein, for whom the sounds, repetitions, and unexpected placement of words constitute major poetic values in themselves rather than only signifiers toward some larger contextual purpose. "She be blesst," he writes of Stein; "This woman who speaks without breath has opened the ring for me."

Other important American poets who have used Jewish themes and sources significantly are Anthony HECHT, Irving Feldman, Hyam Plutzik, David IGNATOW, John HOLLANDER, David MELTZER, Gerald Stern, and past poet laureate Howard Nemerov. Adrienne RICH and Denise LEVERTOV are often categorized as Jewish poets though they are of mixed background; whereas Rich gives limited attention to Judaism in her work (excepting her translations from the Yiddish), Levertov clearly identifies with the Hasidic blood of her family past, though she does consider herself Jewish.

A Jewish American drama is more difficult yet to ascertain and identify than a Jewish American poem. Whereas a poet can publicize his or her work with minimal assistance, a dramatist requires at least a few readers and preferably a stage with an audience for meaningful exposure. Consequently, if a dramatist is to have a play produced and staged successfully, it must have audience appeal; though it may be based on social controversy, sentiment, ethnic interests, comedy, or any number of other possibilities, without a decided attraction, a play has little chance of reaching the theater, and theater is its *raison d'etre.*

With this in mind it should be clear that a play based on Jewish themes or centered on Jewish characters could not be produced in a social context of antiSemitism unless it were written in a hostile manner to attack or satirize the Jews, or in a sympathetic manner to appeal chiefly if not only to a Jewish audience. An example of the latter is the Yiddish theater that flourished during the period of mass immigration late in the 19th c. and early in the 20th.

Although there were Jewish dramatists who wrote plays in English in 19th-c. America—one of the earliest and best of whom was Mordechai Noah—it was not until after World War One that Jewish American drama truly began. When Elmer RICE became the first Jew to receive a Pulitzer Prize in drama, in recognition of *Street Scene,* it reached a major stage of maturity. His play presented a microcosmic view of tenement life among assorted ethnic groups, including Jews, and two years later his *Counsellor-at-Law* objectively but sympathetically depicted contemporary Jewish life. According to Ellen Schiff, Rice's social realism "set the mood and the tone for subsequent Jewish American playwriting." His realistic portraiture was in striking contrast to most earlier stage depictions of Jews, which were generally comic and heavily stereotyped—the only kind of Jewish character that could be presented with a reasonable expectation of success among gentile audiences. George F. KAUFMAN, S. N. BEHRMAN, and such later comedy writers as Jules FEIFFER, Neil SIMON, and Woody ALLEN are among the many who have capitalized on the Jewish inclination toward stage humor that evolved from the Yiddish theater and vaudeville.

In the 1930s, Clifford Odets achieved his great success with plays centering on the American lower-middle class. His interest in union labor is evident in *Waiting for Lefty,* his first produced play. The "decaying Jewish middle-class" of the 1930s is the subject of *Awake and Sing,* which quickly followed, and *Golden Boy,* his most successful play, exposes Odets's own destructive self-conflict between art and money.

Although Odets's best plays were commercially successful and critically well received, no Jewish

American playwright has been more widely acclaimed over a longer period of time than Arthur Miller. Neither *Death of a Salesman* nor *The Crucible* shows overt evidence of his Judaism, though inevitably, a Jewish consciousness has been identified in the making of them—one secular and the other psychological with a fanatical Christian (Puritan) orientation—but the strength of both as pure drama enables them to transcend interpretations based on so tenuous and reductive a critical approach. Miller has dealt explicitly with a Jewish theme, however, in *Incident at Vichy,* which portrays characters caught in the struggle between salvation and self-sacrifice upon being questioned by the Nazis pending incarceration as Jews during the Holocaust.

Ellen Schiff has focused on three major themes—Judaism, assimilation, and family life of the postwar decades—in a recent essay emphasizing the vitality of contemporary Jewish American drama. Among the most promising of the current playwrights she discusses are Norma Rosen, Wendy WASSERSTEIN, and David MAMET.

A brief survey of Jewish American literature reveals its diversity and exposes the danger of inaccurate generalizations about it as a unique field—apart from the clear fact that it is heavily dominated by fiction. In addition, traditional Judaism and the immigrant experience in the backgrounds of most of its adherents provide significant common ground for these authors of the past century. Ethnically involved and culturally oriented, often victimized by anti-Semitism as children or adults or both, Jewish American authors are simultaneously drawn back to the heritage of their people as Jews and propelled outward as free agents in the secular culture of contemporary America. A major result of this internal conflict is its dramatization in fiction, poetry, and plays as well as literary and broadly cultural criticism written by American Jews. Having taken roughly half a century, Jewish American literature came of age in the 1950s and 1960s, but whether it will continue to ripen or lose touch with the traditional forces that originally inspired and nourished it, only time will tell.

BIBLIOGRAPHY: Aarons, V., *A Measure of Memory: Storytelling and Identity in American Jewish Fiction* (1996); Alter, R., *After the Tradition: Essays on Modern Jewish Writing* (1969); Berger, A. L., *Crisis and Covenant* (1985); Bilik, D., *Immigrant-Survivors: Post-Holocaust Consciousness in Recent American-Jewish Fiction* (1981); Bloom, A., *Prodigal Sons* (1986); Cohen, S. B., ed., *Jewish Wry: Essays on Jewish Humor* (1987); Dembo, L. S., *The Monological Jew* (1988); Fine, D., *The City, the Immigrant, and American Fiction, 1880–1920* (1977); Girgus, S., *The New Covenant: Jewish Writers and the American Idea* (1984); Gitenstein, R. B., *Apocalyptic Messianism and Contemporary Jewish American Poetry* (1986); Guttmann, A., *The Jewish Writer in America: Assimilation and the Crisis of Identity* (1971); Harap, L., *The Image of the Jew in American Literature: From Early Republic to Mass Immigration* (1974); Harap, L., *Dramatic Encounters: The Jewish Presence in Twentieth-Century American Drama, Poetry, and Humor and the Black-Jewish Literary Relationship* (1987); Howe, I., *World of Our Fathers* (1976); Kremer, S. L., *Witness through the Imagination* (1989); Lifson, D. S., *The Yiddish Theater in America* (1966); Liptzin, S., *The Jew in American Literature* (1966); Pinsker, S., *The Schlemiel as Metaphor: Studies in the Yiddish and American Jewish Novel* (1971); Schiff, E., ed., *Awake and Singing* (1995); Schulz, M., *Radical Sophistication: Studies in Contemporary Jewish-American Novelists* (1969); Sherman, B., *The Invention of the Jew: Jewish-American Education Novels, 1916–1964* (1969); Walden, D., ed., *DLB,* vol. 28, *Twentieth-Century American-Jewish Fiction Writers* (1984)

SANFORD E. MAROVITZ

JOHNSON, Charles [Richard]
b. 23 April 1948, Evanston, Illinois

Receiving the National Book Award for *Middle Passage* (1990), J. read a prepared tribute to Ralph EL-LISON, who was in the audience. J. thus staked a claim as Ellison's heir in one tradition of the African American novel, a tradition that roots black experience firmly within American experience, including American literary experience. Like Ellison, J. has applied a contemporary political and cultural sensibility to historical circumstances, specifically slavery; he has experimented with genres and language, yet kept his main emphasis on the growth of consciousness. In J.'s case, consciousness is defined by his studies in phenomenology and refined by an interest in Eastern religion and martial arts. Fiction was not J.'s first career—he began as a cartoonist and journalist—and he has maintained wide interests, writing and appearing in television productions, teaching creative writing, and publishing provocative theoretical and critical writings.

J.'s first published novel, *Faith and the Good Thing* (1974), was written under the influence of John GARD-NER, his mentor at Southern Illinois University. A fable based on folklore, it tells the story of Faith Cross's developing consciousness through a physical journey, from Georgia to Chicago, interacting with a spiritual journey that is incorporated in an alternate, magical world and characters. Despite Faith's physical degradation and death in a brothel, her spirit returns, in a metaphysical form, to her home in Georgia. *Oxherding Tale* (1982) was rejected by more than twenty-five publishers, but it became J.'s breakthrough novel. Deliberately set against the "narrow" protest novels and "up from the ghetto" naturalism popular at the time, *Oxherding Tale* is a "neo slave narrative," told paradoxically in a comic mode—beginning when the protagonist is conceived, not in the rape of a slave woman by a plantation master, but as the result of a bizarre drunken joke when a master and his butler switch wives for an evening. The novel draws upon the Buddhist Platform Sutra and was also intended as a "reply" to Herman Hesse's *Siddhartha,* an earlier attempt to "thematize Eastern thought."

Between his first two novels, J. did doctoral study in philosophy. His dissertation, on phenomenology and black literature, was never completed, but it led to the theoretical half of *Being and Race: Black Writing since 1970* (1988). A manifesto, probably inspired in part by Gardner's *On Moral Fiction, Being and Race* draws upon the philosophical tradition of Husserl, Heidegger, and Merleau-Ponty to present a traditionalist platform for black fiction, emphasizing "cross-cultural fertilization," particularly in the form of experimentation with genres. The critical half of *Being and Race* is divided into "The Men" and "The Women": J. has seen himself as a proponent of work by black males, to the extent of criticizing the success of some black female contemporaries.

The Sorcerer's Apprentice: Tales and Conjurations (1985) is a collection of stories, several, like the title work, mixing realism and fantasy in the fable form. However, it was the publication of *Middle Passage* that brought J. wide recognition. Treating a slaving voyage as a multicultural encounter, the novel mixes together an "unreliable" black narrator with a mad sea captain reminiscent of Herman MELVILLE's, an unruly crew, and a cargo of African magicians. The book's title, besides referring to the route of slave ships, depicts the developing of consciousness through a middle course between conflicting philosophical approaches. *Middle Passage* brings together its two concerns, with racism and philosophy, by seeing slavery as a product of the Western split into mutually exclusive categories like black/white and flesh/spirit. Widely reviewed and honored, *Middle Passage* has established J., with his friend Ishmael REED, as the predominant black male voices in contemporary American literature. C.'s reputation was further enhanced by the publication in 1998 of *Dreamer,* an imagined account of the last days of Martin Luther King, Jr.

BIBLIOGRAPHY: Boccia, M., "An Interview with C. J.," *AAR* 30 (Winter 1996): 611–18; Little, J., "From the Comic Book to the Comic: C. J.'s Variations on Creative Expression," *AAR* 30 (Winter 1996): 519–601

GLEN M. JOHNSON

JOHNSON, Denis
b. 1 July 1949, Munich, Germany

J. is a major voice for the social reprobates whom we scurry to avoid. Yet, he succeeds in demonstrating that one life comprises many lives and that a person's sternest task is to forgive oneself for mistakes in the past. Since 1969, J. has published four books of poetry, four acclaimed novels, and one collection of short stories, *Jesus' Son* (1992), which violates and amends all that is associated with the genre. Critics praise J.'s distinctive hard-driving style and his eerie vision as a brutally honest interpreter of contemporary American life.

The transience that is so apparent in J.'s poetry and fiction is likely drawn from his personal background. He was born in Munich, spent his childhood in Tokyo, his adolescence in Manila, and his teen years in Alexandria, Virginia. After high school, he attended the University of Iowa and later drifted for three years in and out of the Iowa Writers' Workshop while earning his M.F.A. degree. He tried teaching in Chicago and working odd jobs in and around Seattle. In 1978–79, he rescued himself from alcohol and drug addiction, discovering that "To go on living and to understand the past is like taking up another life." Since then, J. has lived in remote places such as Wellfleet, Massachusetts, and Good Grief, Idaho, which takes its name from a tavern along a local highway. To date, his novels *Fiskadoro* (1985), *The Stars at Noon* (1986), and *Resuscitation of a Hanged Man* (1991) rank as his finest work.

Memory, time, myth, and courage are the focal points in *Fiskadoro,* J.'s second novel. Set eighty years into an apocalyptic future, J. transforms Key West, Florida, into a postnuclear waste land of phony messiahs, voodoo cults, pirates dealing in radioactive goods, and ragged cripples deformed by war. Fiskadoro (*pescador* meaning fisherman and *flagador* meaning harpooner) is the book's adolescent hero, and after his father drowns at sea, Fiskadoro walks through a door labeled "fear" to meet himself anew. During a bizarre "subincision" ceremony while among a group of swamp people, Fiskadoro passes from life to death and then back again to life. Although he loses all memory of what he has endured, he becomes a true chosen son and the only person in "Quarantine" who is ready for the inevitable invasion of the future. Surviving loss and surviving pain are inscribed in the grail message that J. extends into the next millennium.

Whereas in *Fiskadoro* J. reinvents a futuristic locale, in *Stars at Noon,* he searches the political terrain in Central America and finds gruesome reminders of Orwell and Dante. The year is 1984, and Managua is the nadir of the world. For her sins, the unnamed American narrator is condemned "just to watch" as Nicaragua sinks further into squalor. When she sells out her British lover who has been trading in industrial secrets, she completes her transformation from journalist to prostitute to betrayer. By way of an epigraph from the poetry of W. S. MERWIN, J. questions what people are looking for in each other—atonement, understanding, forgiveness, hope—if anything at all.

Obsession veers out of control for Leonard English, J.'s protagonist in *Resuscitation of a Hanged Man.* English has tried once to escape from a gritty psychological labyrinth by hanging himself, but he failed. In 1980, he moves to Provincetown in the off-season and doubles as a disc jockey and private investigator. His efforts to connect with others and with himself take several unexpected turns. He falls in love with a woman who loves other women; he finds the body of Gerald Twinbrook—artist, "twin," and Truth Infantry activist—dangling from a tree; he dresses up in his lover's clothing and halfheartedly tries to assassinate a prominent Bishop during the spring Blessing of the Fleet. Whether English's cross-dressing is the expression of an attitude or a disguise, J. sentences him to prison where he can try to get to the bottom of his faith.

In his path from poet to novelist and short story writer, J. has maintained an abiding interest in artistic diversity and maturity. His images are "ferocious" and his vision is "menacing." In seeking the mystery of salvation from violence, addiction, and self-abuse, J. is a daring writer who strives, as Annie DILLARD would say, to do "nothing less than to hold up the universe."

BIBLIOGRAPHY: Hull, L., and D. Wojahn, "The Kind of Light I'm Seeing: An Interview with D. J.," *Ironwood* 13 (Spring 1985): 31–44; Reitenbach, G., "Foreign Exchange in D. J.'s *The Stars at Noon,*" *ArQ* 47 (Winter 1991): 27–47

JOE NORDGREN

JOHNSON, Edward

b. ca. September 1598, Canterbury, England; d. 23 April 1672, Woburn, Massachusetts

J. is remembered exclusively for his *History of New England* (1654), known by its running head, *Wonder-Working Providence of Sions Saviour in New-England, 1628–1651.* The book is often faulted for its historical inaccuracies, yet it deserves praise for its literary merit and its coherent report of early New England. Divided chronologically into three books of seven years each, the work relates the Puritan settle-ment of the colonies, describes the colonists' recent victories over the antinomians, the Pequots, and describes other calamities while it laments the deaths of the colony's prominent leaders.

Recent criticism insists that rather than a legitimate history such as John WINTHROP's or William BRADFORD's, J.'s work should be considered a mythic history of the struggle of New England's Christian saints against Satan's armies. J. is somewhat atypical of Puritan writers in that he makes use of classical as well as biblical allusions and depends heavily on religious allegory. He does not necessarily concentrate on the accurate retelling of historical events; rather he recounts Puritan New England's divine mission. His history is written as a hopeful reassurance to troubled Puritans, worried that their errand to New England has been in vain. J. also offers opinions on relations with Native Americans, reiterating the colonists' superior moral view, but also expressing compassion. The history includes over sixty poems, many of which are worthy of individual critical attention.

BIBLIOGRAPHY: Arch, S., "The Edifying History of E. J.'s *Wonder-Working Providence,*" *EAL* 28 (1993): 42–59; Gallagher, E., "An Overview of E. J.'s *Wonder-Working Providence,*" *EAL* 5 (1971), 30–49; Jameson, J. F., ed., *J.'s Wonder-Working Providence* (1910)

LEE SCHWENNINGER

JOHNSON, James Weldon

b. 17 June 1871, Jacksonville, Florida; d. 26 June 1938, Wiscasset, Maine

J.'s influence upon AFRICAN AMERICAN LITERATURE, culture, and politics is well nigh immeasurable. As an editor, musician, lyricist, author, critic, ambassador, professor, patron of the arts, and civil rights leader, J.'s talents reached into nearly as many realms within the public sphere as his contemporary W. E. B. DU BOIS. The son of middle-class parents and brother to J. Rosamond Johnson, J.'s life was nothing if not one of stellar achievement. As founder of the first public school for African Americans in Florida, the first African American to pass the Florida bar exam, a founding member of the American Society of Composers, Authors and Publishers (ASCAP), and field secretary for the National Association for the Advancement of Colored People (NAACP), J.'s place and importance in American history are assured. If he were remembered solely for his novel *The Autobiography of an Ex-Coloured Man,* published anonymously in 1912 and reprinted in 1927, at the height of the Harlem Renaissance, J. would certainly be guaranteed a permanent tier in African American and American literature.

A complex, frequently ironic novel centering on racism, self-hatred, and the absurdities of racial classifications, *The Autobiography of an Ex-Coloured Man* functioned as one of the primary literary blueprints for the writers of the Harlem Renaissance. Its anonymous narrator, a Black man who could, and eventually does, pass for white, relates many of the horrors and duplicities necessary to live on both sides of the country's color line, especially in the Jim Crow South. His adventures simultaneously provide a glimpse of a wide cross-section of African American life around the turn of the century and allow J. to mix his opinions of racial problems with those of his narrator.

J.'s textual strategies, including the narrator who agonizes over his racial and social status, resounded strongly among the literati of the Harlem Renaissance, as did his work as a poet, which has been widely published and anthologized. J.'s influence was even more strongly felt through his patronage of Harlem Renaissance artists, especially when he was based in Harlem while working for the NAACP. As one of the Harlem Renaissance's patron's, J. underwrote and published the work of many of the period's most talented artists.

It was J.'s ability to represent folk life and the quandaries of African American identity in his works, however, that made the greatest impact on those who followed him. *The Autobiography of an Ex-Coloured Man,* with its biracial narrator and depiction of several levels of African American society, is itself a metaphor for black life. J.'s poetry was heavily influenced by the rhythms and cadences of the blues and the black church in his collection *God's Trombones;* this influence and J.'s general desire to valorize black folk culture guides his selections within *The Book of American Negro Poetry,* one of the best early anthologies of African American poetry, which includes, in its final edition, African American poets from Phillis WHEATLEY to the Harlem Renaissance.

Furthermore, J.'s autobiography, *Along This Way* (1927), is widely considered one of the finest examples of autobiographical writing in the 20th c. and an excellent history of African American life in the early part of the century. J.'s adventures, similar to those of his protagonist in *The Autobiography of an Ex-Coloured Man,* reveal strong opinions about African American politics. More important, however, are J.'s arguments for celebrating the richness of African American literature, especially its folk roots. Given his position as one of the patrons of early-20th-c. literature, J.'s championing of this idea encouraged several generations of African American writers to take the time to appreciate African American folk forms, and stands as perhaps his most admirable contribution to the African American literary tradition.

BIBLIOGRAPHY: Fleming, R. E., *J. W. J.* (1987); Levy, E. D., *J. W. J.: Black Leader, Black Voice* (1973); Smith, V., L. Baechler, and A. W. Litz, eds., *African American Writers* (1991)

DARRYL B. DICKSON-CARR

JOHNSON, Owen [McMahon]

b. 27 August 1878, New York City; d. 27 January 1952, Vineyard Haven, Massachusetts

J. is an unfairly neglected novelist and short story writer of the early 20th c., one of the few American authors since Mark TWAIN who could capture through diversified character types the "feel" of a healthy, adventuresome boyhood: its emotional highs and lows, constraints and rebellions, and hope springing eternal. When he first appeared in print with a story in the *St. Nicholas* magazine, he was about six years old, and at age twelve he was an associate editor of a publication raising funds for the Washington Memorial Arch. After this experience, he aspired to someday become "a real editor-in-chief." Paternal influence may have helped guide his literary career. His father, Robert Underwood Johnson, a poet, was on the staff of the prestigious *Century* magazine, in time moving from associate editor to editor-in-chief.

The inspiration for his best writing, however, was his schoolboy experience, first at the elite Lawrenceville School, near Princeton, New Jersey, then at Yale. His well-crafted stories about student life at Lawrenceville were based on active participation, personal friendships, and the recognition of the opening up of a world of marvelous opportunities for social and intellectual growth. These narratives, rich in social commentary and satire, effectively revealing character development in lively, playful youngsters (who gave each other whimsical nicknames and habitually sought relief from schoolwork), appeared in the *Saturday Evening Post* and then in book form: *The Eternal Boy: Being the Story of The Prodigious Hickey* (1909), *The Varmint* (1910), and *The Tennessee Shad: Chronicling the Rise and Fall of the Firm of Doc Macnooder and the Tennessee Shad* (1911). A literary interlude, the novelette titled *The Hummingbird* (1910), allows a very young Lawrenceville boy who is an avid baseball fan, Dennis de Brian de Boru Finnegan, to show what he could do, not by being allowed to play with the big boys, but by being given the opportunity to be a baseball reporter. Probably the most important group of novels for young males since Twain's *Tom Sawyer* and *Huckleberry Finn,* J.'s Lawrenceville trilogy, cited above, were dramatized on television as American Playhouse productions during 1986–87. Noteworthy also is J.'s varsity novel *Stover at Yale* (1912), which combines the exciting adventures of a college boy beginning to grow up and know himself, with a serious critique of one of the very top universities in the land.

J.'s most important work of fiction, aside from the three Lawrenceville novels and *Stover at Yale,* is *The Salamander* (1914), a novel dealing with an unorganized group of pleasure-seeking young women in a New York boarding house. With or without a vocation, these designing females—"salamanders" in their own special lingo—make a practice of getting the most out of their ardent suitors, while not getting burned in the fire (of close sexual involvement) and giving the least in return. J.'s exploration of the sociology of this type of pre-World War I, New York bachelorette is the subject of the highly informative foreword to the book. A number of J.'s other fictions were novels of social consciousness or society life: *Arrows of the Almighty* (1901), an early-19th-c. period piece; *The Woman Gives: A Story of Regeneration* (1916), an account of odd bohemian types living in Manhattan's Lincoln Square; *The Wasted Generation* (1921), a World War I romantic drama; and *Sacrifice* (1929), a novel of a divorce avoided, despite compelling circumstances, for the children's sake.

Though J. wrote of schoolboy life and the urban jungles from personal experience, there was a regrettable superficiality in this treatment of the latter category of subject matter. An additional indication of his seemingly deeper commitment, as a writer, to the education of American youth was his five-part series of magazine articles on improving conditions in academia: "The Social Usurpation of Our Colleges," which appeared in *Collier's* (May 18–June 22, 1912). An unusually well-rounded man with wide-ranging curiosity and interests, he clearly had the makings of a major literary force.

BIBLIOGRAPHY: Bellman, S. I., "O. J.," in Brook, J. M., ed., *DLB Yearbook: 1987* (1988): 316–25; Maurice, A. B., "O. J.," *Bookman* 39 (June 1914): 416–20; Tunis, J. R., "A Man of Distinction," *NYTBR* 24 September 1967: 8

SAMUEL I. BELLMAN

JOHNSTON, Mary

b. 21 November 1870, Buchanan, Virginia; d. 9 May 1936, near Warm Springs, Virginia

J. achieved fame with the revival of interest in historical romances that occurred in the 1890s and early 1900s and also involved such writers as Charles Major, Paul Leicester Ford, Winston CHURCHILL, and Maurice THOMPSON. She earned critical recognition with *Prisoners of Hope* (1898), and *To Have and To Hold* (1900) was one of the most successful novels of its time. In her treatment of romantic adventure, she would later importantly influence Rafael Sabatini. But the exuberant romanticism of such fiction did not long satisfy her. Her father, John William Johnston, had been a major in the Confederate army, and General Joseph E. Johnston was a relative. In 1911 and 1912, she published two long, serious, carefully researched Civil War novels, *The Long Roll* and *Cease Firing,* which anticipated tendencies in later historical fiction and which, together with *Lewis Rand* (1908), remain the greatest achievements of her first period.

J. published twenty-three novels. Fifteen were concerned, wholly or in part, with her native Virginia, seven of these with colonial Virginia. *Silver Cross* (1922) is set in Henry VII's England and *The Witch* (1914) in the 17th c. *Sir Mortimer* (1904) deals with the Elizabethan sea-rovers, and the narrator of *1492* (1922) sails with Columbus. *Foes* (1918) and portions of *The Slave Ship* (1924) are set in Scotland. *The Fortunes of Garin* (1915) involves a picture of the breakup of the feudal system in 12th-c. France. *The Wanderers* (1917) studies the changing relations between men and women in a series of episodes stretching from prehistoric times to the French Revolution. The suffrage novel, *Hagar* (1913), and *Sweet Rocket* (1920) have contemporary settings, and *The Exile* (1927) reaches into what was then the future. J.'s one play, *The Goddess of Reason* (1907), a poetic drama of the French Revolution, was acted by Julia Marlowe. She also contributed *Pioneers of the Old South* (1918) to the Yale "Chronicles of America" series.

This daughter of the old South came to the end of her life a socialist, pacifist, and mystic, and the development she experienced as a woman importantly influenced her work. She seldom propagandized in behalf of her ideas, but she increasingly concerned herself with characters who shared them. Though her later tendencies were present in her work almost from the beginning, they were strongly accelerated around 1920, when they shaped not only her themes but her style, which became notably more taut, less detailed, more suggestive and impressionistic. She began to think of herself and her characters as pioneers in the field of an expanding human consciousness: "A part of the world is passing beyond old powers into new." Old barriers of space and time were breaking down, to be replaced by a new sense of the unity of all life and all humankind. Like William FAULKNER in his final phase, she came to feel that there was something in man that was undefeatable. As the narrator of *1492* expresses it, "Surely they who serve large purposes are cared for! Though they should die in prison, yet are they cared for!"

Naturally not all readers of *To Have and To Hold* were able to keep pace with its author. The sales of her later books never approached those of her early days. But to readers capable of meeting her on her own ground, such novels as *The Slave Ship, The Great Valley* (1926)—which in some ways anticipates Elizabeth Madox ROBERTS's *The Great Meadow—Miss Delicia Allen* (1933) and *Drury Randall* (1934) are J. at the top of her form.

BIBLIOGRAPHY: Cella, C. R., *M. J.* (1981); Wagenknecht, E., ed., *The Fireside Book of Ghost Stories* (1947); Wagenknecht, E., "The World and M. J.," *SR* 44 (April 1936): 188–206; Woodbridge, A., and H. C. Woodbridge, eds., *The Collected Short Stories of M. J.* (1982)

EDWARD WAGENKNECHT

JOHNSTON, Richard Malcolm

b. 8 March 1822, "Oak Grove," Powelton, Georgia; d. 23 September 1898, Baltimore, Maryland

J.'s reputation was made, in large part, by the American vogue for local color, and he continues to be read and studied as a gauge to literary, cultural, and intellectual life in America during and after the Civil War. More importantly, J. represents the confluence of traditions from earlier Southwestern humorists like Augustus Baldwin LONGSTREET, William Tappan THOMPSON, and Johnson Jones HOOPER as well as later American local colorists like Joel Chandler HARRIS and Thomas Nelson PAGE.

J., moreover, is admired primarily for his sixteen stories collected into *Dukesborough Tales* (1883). The other sixty-six stories in his canon, as noted by Bert Hitchcock, are at best imitative of the sixteen earlier ones. In those sixteen stories, the strongest and most appealing elements are J.'s emphasis on character, especially local eccentrics, and a comic spirit reminiscent of the Southwest humorists before him. Unlike the plantation tradition configuring so prominently in the fiction of Harris or Page, J.'s works rarely ever exploit blacks as either the medium of tale telling or the victims of humor.

Much of what J. wrote about, characteristic of popular realism in the day, was based on his own experiences on the family plantation in Powelton. Educated in field schools—those generally built by plantation owners on nonproductive lands—and academies, J. was well prepared to satirize tyrannical schoolmasters. His knowledge of the rigors and harsh routines at such schools and his own preparation in law enabled him to write some of his best sketches and stories of school and legal life in Middle Georgia at the end of the 19th c.

The real center of J.'s collection is the little village of Dukesborough, the eye of J.'s fictional world, a triangle formed from seventeen counties by the more populous towns of Macon, Athens, and Augusta. "The Goosepond School," J.'s best story, details the defeat of a very unlikable school master, Israel Meadows, by one of his own students, Brinkley Glisson, much to the delight of Glisson's widowed mother. "How Mr. Bill Williams Took the Responsibility" appeared in every edition of *Dukesborough Tales* through the 1892 edition. Following the lead of Washington IRVING in the physical description of his lead character, J. creates a brutal but cowardly pedagogue Josiah Lorriby, who receives, much like Ichabod Crane, his just desserts.

Ten Tales of Middle Georgia: The Primes and Their Neighbors (1891) draws heavily on the established components of local color—eccentric characters, a strong sense of setting, and a heavy dialect. All but one tale in the collection had been previously published in magazines like *Harper's* and the *Century*. Largely ignored today, these stories share a critical fate with the author's four novels published in 1884 through 1898.

BIBLIOGRAPHY: Hitchcock, B., *R. M. J.* (1978); Hubbell, J. B., *The South in American Literature: 1607–1900* (1954); Parks, E. W., *Segments of Southern Thought* (1938); Pattee, F. L., *A History of American Literature since 1870* (1915)

GEORGE LONGEST

JONES, Gayl

b. 23 November 1949, Lexington, Kentucky

Though J. started her career as a writer of fiction, her last three published books have been volumes of poetry, and since 1985, she has enveloped herself in silence. J.'s peculiar publishing history mirrors her singular status as a writer: no one has explored the linkage between language, love, sex, and violence in such searching, even brutal, ways.

J. developed her ear for dialogue in her years in Kentucky listening to her family, but the fact that both her grandmother and mother wrote church plays and short stories, respectively, had a formative influence as well. J. left Kentucky to study at Connecticut College and at Brown University, where Michael S. HARPER became her mentor and where, while still a student, she published her first novel.

J.'s novels probably remain her best-known work. Her first, *Corregidora* (1975), anticipated the wave of novels exploring the connections between slavery and the African American present. Ursa Corregidora, the novel's protagonist, is the great-grandchild of the Portuguese Brazilian slaveholder Simon Corregidora, who also raped her grandmother. Both Ursa's mother and grandmother make it their lives' purpose to keep alive the history of their abuse and torture, and by extension that of African slaves in the New World. But their obsession with the past burdens Ursa, who struggles, as a singer, to find her own purpose in life. Even as she attempts to do so, she herself is trapped in abusive relationships. Sparse in language, relying on terse dialogue and haunting interior monologues, the novel stands in the naturalist tradition as it shows individuals fighting with historical forces beyond their control. However, the end of the novel justifies its status as a "blues" narrative exploring both the pain and the beauty of relationships by implying that psychological struggle and an unsparing confrontation of the past may lead to recovery.

Eva's Man (1976), J.'s second novel, expands on the pain between African American women and men, but it does so with an even greater sense of hopelessness. Like *Corregidora, Eva's Man* relies on minimalist dialogue and on interior monologues, but the latter play an even more important role in J.'s second novel, letting the reader see Eva Medina Canada's past and her descent into mental illness, indicated through repetition of key scenes with variations, implying that Eva's memory disintegrates. The reader encounters Eva in a prison for the criminally insane at the beginning of the story, to which she has been committed for poisoning and castrating her lover. Her flashbacks reveal a life of relentless sexual objectification by men, starting with Freddy, a neighborhood boy who wants to play doctor, to Tyrone, her mother's lover who molests her, to her cousin, who propositions her. The men she encounters regard her as sexual property and react with violence if she rejects their approaches. Davis, the lover she kills, epitomizes this tendency by imprisoning her in a room to which he only comes to sleep with her. By killing him, she rebels against male tyranny, but her descent into insanity indicates that she is unable to construct a new role for herself.

The stories in J.'s excellent short story collection *White Rat* (1977), written between 1970 and 1977, deal largely with the same themes as her novels—communication or the lack of it, insanity, and difficult relationships. *Song for Anninho* (1981), a long narrative poem, covers new ground. Situated in 17th-c. Brazil, the poem tells the story of Almeyda, the narrator, and her husband Anninho, who are residents of Palmares, a historical settlement by fugitive slaves, when it is overrun by Portuguese soldiers, separating husband and wife. Though Almeyda can only find her husband through memory and through art once they

are separated, the poem focuses on desire as a positive theme, and it shows the possibility of love.

J. has described herself as an improvisor, and her work bears out that statement: like a jazz or blues musician, J. plays upon a specific set of themes, varying them and exploring their possible permutations. Though her fiction has been called "Gothic" in its exploration of madness, violence, and sexuality, musical metaphors might make for a more apt categorization.

BIBLIOGRAPHY: Byerman, K., "Black Vortex: The Gothic Structure of *Eva's Man*," *MELUS* 7 (1980): 93–101; Coser, S., *Bridging the Americas* (1995); Harris, T., "A Spiritual Journey: G. J.'s *Song for Anninho, Callaloo* 5 (October 1982): 105–11

MARTIN JAPTOK

JONES, James [Ramon]

b. 6 November 1921, Robinson, Illinois; d. 9 May 1977, Southampton, New York

With the publication of his first and finest novel, *From Here to Eternity* (1951), twenty-nine-year-old J. enjoyed instant commercial success and critical distinction as one of the most promising new writers of postwar America. Although he followed this achievement over the next twenty-five years with seven more novels, a collection of short stories, essays, and two works of nonfiction, J. was unable to sustain serious critical interest in his writing. His reading public, however, better appreciated his work for its uncompromising honesty and graphic realism, perhaps best remembered in his best-selling World War II trilogy: *From Here to Eternity, The Thin Red Line* (1962), and *Whistle* (1978).

The publicity generated by *From Here to Eternity* depicted J. as a self-educated, working-class literary unknown, giving his sudden success a rags-to-riches quality. During his junior year in Robinson, Illinois, his prominent middle-class family collapsed into near poverty during the Great Depression, humiliating circumstances prompting J. to go "on the bum" after high school and then join the army in 1939. Experiencing America from the economic margins no doubt heightened J.'s social conscience, which in turn forged his artistic perspective as champion of the underdog. While stationed at Schofield Barracks, Hawai'i—the setting of *From Here to Eternity*—he wrote short stories and took English courses at the University of Hawai'i where he received initial encouragement and some formal training in writing. J. also undertook a thorough study of late-19th and early-20th-c. novelists, but Thomas WOLFE's *Look Homeward, Angel* affected

J. most profoundly, crystallizing his determination to write professionally.

Despite J.'s professed dislike of army life, his World War II experiences provided raw material for his war trilogy, which progresses from peacetime duty to active combat on through homecoming of the wounded. *From Here to Eternity,* a National Book Award-winner, is the story of America's ill-educated, marginalized men who claim the prewar army as both home and "profession," but are soon disillusioned by its rigid caste system and flagrant opportunism of its officers. Private Prewitt, the novel's romantic rebel and artist figure, tries to play by army rules, yet he stubbornly resists any external conflict with his inner moral gyroscope, insisting on his exclusive right—not the army's—to decide whether to bugle and box for his Company. The Company's First Sergeant Warden, however, survives the army's squandering of human life and energy by outflanking his inept, self-serving captain. Warden negotiates an uneasy compromise between personal integrity and the demands of the system, something Prewitt is unwilling to do, which orchestrates the events leading to his death. *From Here to Eternity* was unique among contemporary war novels for its viewpoint of the enlisted man and its experiments with language and style. Besides ignoring conventional rules of grammar and syntax and writing in a loose, sprawling prose, J. produced a startling realism with colloquial dialogue, vulgar language, and a new sexual frankness—stylistic devices generating critical controversy and reproach from some who called J. "primitive."

J.'s preoccupation with the erosion of individuality, unfailingly identified with masculinity in his fiction, turned to bleak NATURALISM in the trilogy's second and third novels. In *The Thin Red Line,* the grisly, degrading, squalid business of hand-to-hand combat on Guadalcanal engulfs Charlie Company's foot soldiers in relentless suffering and the fear of death. War produces no real heroes or glorious adventures, only an insensate combat numbness as each man is increasingly dehumanized by modern warfare. In *Whistle,* four wounded infantrymen, confronting their bitterness and despair in a Tennessee military hospital, fail to reconnect to the seemingly coherent world of mainstream America or even to one another. Death finally is preferable to a dreary life of habitual drinking and meaningless sex.

Although J. published three novels on nonmilitary subjects in the 1960s and 1970s, his literary reputation was cemented by his devotion to the exclusively male world of the army, with its masculine values and inviolable male bonds, causing some critics to accuse J. of being unable to write convincingly about civilian life or male-female relationships. His refusal to inject political themes or motives into his fiction, particularly when collective politics and protest movements commanded national attention, brought charges of anachronism. His literary response to his own proletarian sympathies posited individualistic resilience and often futile assertion as the worthiest course of action. Although J.'s work underwent reappraisal in the 1980s, it is little considered in the academy. Perhaps his contribution as a 20th-c. novelist is cultural rather than "literary," significant for its richly detailed, authentic portrait of an entire generation of men whose lives were profoundly transformed by the war. Yet J.'s work signifies beyond the military. As a chronicler of those estranged from America's mainstream, he joins Wolfe, Sherwood ANDERSON, John DOS PASSOS, and Theodore DREISER in documenting the collision of bankrupt promises with middle-class prosperity and innocence.

BIBLIOGRAPHY: Garrett, G., *J. J.* (1984); Giles, J. R., *J. J.* (1981); Hendrick, G., ed., *To Reach Eternity: The Letters of J. J.* (1989); MacShane, F., *Into Eternity: The Life of J. J.* (1985)

JANE E. HENDLER

JONES, Madison

b. 21 March 1925, Nashville, Tennessee

J. is a prose fiction writer described by Allen TATE as a Southern Thomas Hardy. Born and reared in Nashville, Tennessee, he has lived in and written almost exclusively about the South. His major themes are the influence of evil on the human soul, the destruction of innocence by social, historical and psychological forces, and the corruption of modern society by its own past.

His first novel, *The Innocent* (1957), narrates the return of Duncan Welsh to his homeland in rural Tennessee after years of wandering in the North. He is a kind of Adam before the fall trying to return to Eden after the fall. Welsh's attempts to reestablish himself on his forefather's land and to live an idealized pastoral life are thwarted both by the evil Aaron McCool, and his own darkening soul.

The theme of corrupt innocence is also a major one in *Forest of the Night* (1960), an historical novel about a naive follower of Rousseau who refuses to believe that evil is not merely the absence of good, but a separate force in the world.

Arguably J.'s best book, *A Buried Land* (1963) is a portrait of the Tennessee River Valley and the changes that come to it with the arrival of the Tennessee Valley Authority (TVA). Percy Youngblood's failure comes about because of his denial of the past and his subsequent attempts to live without a sense of moral order.

An Exile (1970) is also about a man without a sense of morality, a country sheriff who loses soul in a vain attempt to deny the passing of time and the physical changes it brings. In *A Cry of Absence* (1971), J's best-selling novel to date, the civil rights movement is the backdrop of a tragedy brought on by self-delusion. This was followed by a very different sort of book, *Passage through Gehenna* (1978), an allegory about good and evil. The protagonist, Jud Rivers, must find passage out of a Gehenna created by his own pride. *Season of the Strangler* (1982) is a collection of related short stories, twelve gripping, beautifully crafted character portrayals of men and women caught in the tensions of a town in which an unknown strangler kills five elderly women. *Last Things* (1989) investigates the disintegration of society in the new South by greed, drugs, moral relativism, and cynicism.

A powerful writer, J. has been concerned throughout his career not just with the potential for iniquity in the human soul, but with the nature of good and evil. Some of his secondary themes are the inadequacy of human morality, the corruption of innocence, the loss of faith, and the need for unmerited Grace.

BIBLIOGRAPHY: Bradford, M. E., *The History of Southern Literature* (1985); Cohen, S., "Images of Allegory: M. J.'s *Passage through Gehenna*," *SoAR* 53, 1 (1988): 67–81; Jeffrey, D. K., and D. R. Noble, "M. J., an Interview," *SoQ* 21, 3 (1983): 15–26

SANDY COHEN

JONG, Erica
b. 26 March 1942, New York City

After achieving celebrity, financial success, and critical praise as well as denigration for *Fear of Flying* (1973), J.'s works receded from the limelight. The groundbreaking novel is now sometimes criticized for confusing women's liberation with sexual liberation. The success of her first novel also led some to consider J.'s work as popular rather than literary; however, the recent appearance of several critical studies and dissertations indicate that her work may be being reevaluated.

Most critical attention focuses on J.'s novels, but she began as a poet rather than as a novelist and has continued to write poetry throughout her career. She had won numerous prizes for her poetry—*Fruits & Vegetables* (1971) and *Half-Lives* (1973)—when *Fear of Flying* became a huge best-seller and unofficial manifesto of the women's liberation movement. The protagonist, Isadora Wing, is a young poet who travels to Vienna with her Chinese American second husband to attend a psychoanalytic convention. Feeling unful-

filled after several years of marriage, she has been fantasizing about the "zipless fuck"—a passionate, anonymous, brief sexual encounter. At the convention, she meets analyst Adrian Goodlove and, believing she has found her fantasy, romps with him through Europe. Isadora gradually realizes that the often impotent Adrian fails to deliver good love and that the zipless fuck will remain forever a fantasy. The novel's frank and humorous treatment of women's sexuality, using equally frank and earthy language, shocked many and earned the novel generally negative reviews, but readers quickly made it number one on the *New York Times* best-seller list. Isadora Wing resurfaces in *How to Save Your Own Life* (1977) and in *Parachutes and Kisses* (1984) and is the fictional author of *Any Woman's Blues* (1990).

Negative criticism of J.'s work sometimes degenerates into personal invective, for J., like Isadora Wing, is a Jewish poet born and reared in New York City who attended Barnard (B.A., 1963) and Columbia (M.A., 1965) and whose second husband was a Chinese American psychoanalyst. Feminists, however, praised *Fear of Flying,* as did authors such as John UPDIKE and Henry MILLER, who foresaw that it would open the taboo subjects of sexuality and eroticism to women writers.

In 1980, J. published *Fanny, Being the True History of the Adventures of Fanny Hackabout-Jones.* This novel is characteristic of J.'s feminist themes and her confessional, highly literary style. Fanny claims to be the historical figure behind John Cleland's *Fanny Hill* who writes her memoirs to give the "true" account of her adventures. *Fanny* parodies the 18th-c. novel in plot and language as well as spelling, capitalization, and punctuation, all the while re-creating the 18th c. from a 20th-c. feminist point of view.

Evaluations of J.'s work have consistently been at the two extremes. Much of the negative criticism stems perhaps from mistaking J.'s essentially comic vision. Her works are highly literary reworkings of personal experience that make extensive use of irony, satire, and parody. Critics often focus on the theme of sexuality in her work without noting that sex is also the source of creativity. From *Fear of Flying* to *Any Woman's Blues,* J.'s protagonists are artists. *Fear of Flying* can be seen as a künstlerroman in the tradition of Joyce's *A Portrait of the Artist as a Young Man.* The artist's struggle to find his voice and his muse has historically been more difficult for women than for men, and J.'s works detail her protagonists' and her own struggle to find her voice and her muse as a woman writer.

BIBLIOGRAPHY: Martin, W., "E. J.," in Todd, J., ed., *Women Writers Talking* (1983): 21–32; Templin, C., *Feminism and the Politics of Literary Reputation: The Example of E. J.* (1995)

HEIDI PRESCHLER

JORDAN, June

b. 9 July 1936, New York City

With an exceptionally powerful and dynamic voice, J. uses poetry to combat the injustices of racism and sexism in the U.S. Transforming pain into anger and anger into self-determination, J. fervently urges public awareness and personal and political change.

Born in Harlem to working-class parents, J. had what some would consider a privileged education. J. attended Midwood High School in Brooklyn, New York, where she was the only black student, and the exclusive Northfield School for Girls in Massachusetts; she later went on to Barnard College where she discovered that the social, political, and economic concerns of African American people were largely ignored. J. married a white Columbia student; the couple had one son and divorced shortly after. Working as a freelance journalist, J. became the sole supporter of her only child. Her experiences as a black female in a white dominated world, a member of an interracial relationship, and a single working mother were to significantly shape her future work.

After publishing several stories and poems in *Esquire, The Nation,* and the *New York Times* magazine, J. published *Who Look at Me* (1969), a long poem accompanied by twenty-seven paintings that portray African American life. *Who Look at Me,* a project originally begun by Langston HUGHES before his death, focuses on black and white relations and white misperceptions of race. In 1970, J. edited two African American anthologies, *Soulscript* and *The Voice of Children,* whose aim was to inspire young people to use the written word as a vehicle for voice and survival. Throughout her career, J. has written several works for and about children. *His Own Where* (1971) was nominated for a National Book Award in 1971 and was selected as one of the year's outstanding young adult novels by the *New York Times.*

In J.'s first collection of poetry, *Some Changes* (1971), she applies traditional poetic techniques of William Shakespeare, T. S. ELIOT, and Emily DICKINSON to issues concerning African American life. J. revises the sonnet exposing the flaws of idealized love, incorporates Eiliot's witty comedy of manners with images of black urban life, and revives Dickinson's sparse yet intense verse. J.'s focus ranges from parent-children relationships and sexual celebration to the assassination of Martin Luther King, Jr., the rise of Malcolm X, and the senselessness of the Vietnam War. J.'s second collection of poetry, *New Days: Poems of Exile and Return* (1974), focuses largely on racial alienation. Utilizing both standard and "Black English," J. speaks out against the mythologies of race inscribed by white America and talks directly to political figures like Daniel Patrick Moynihan, who described the African American family as pathological because of its matriarchal family structure. J.'s voice is self-contained yet verges on the explosiveness evident in her later works.

Things That I Do in the Dark (1977), a selection of old and new poems edited by Toni MORRISON, and *Passion: New Poems, 1977–1980* (1980) explore violence as a means for revolution. J. urges her oppressors to "be afraid" as she will no longer walk silently behind them. J. confronts police violence, rape, South African apartheid, and parental abuse and promotes the expression of anger as a catalyst for social change. J. continues to explore these issues in *Civil Wars* (1981), a profound collection of political and personal essays, articles, letters, and journals entries that detail her life as an African American woman, her development as a poet, her early experiences as a mother, and her commitment to world change.

J. continues to write both poetry and prose. Later works, which include *Living Room: New Poems, 1980–1984* (1985), *Naming Our Destiny: New and Selected Poems* (1989), and *Kissing God Goodbye: Poems, 1991–1997* (1997), emphasize the emergence of J.'s militant feminist voice.

BIBLIOGRAPHY: Erickson, P., "The Love Poetry of J. J.," *Callaloo* 9 (Winter 1986): 221–34; Erickson, P., "Putting Her Life on the Line: The Poetry of J. J.," *Hurricane Alice* 7 (Winter-Spring 1990): 1–2, 4–5; Harjo, J., "An Interview with J. J.," *HPLR* 3 (Fall 1988): 60–76

SALINDA LEWIS

JUSTICE, Donald [Rodney]

b. 12 August 1925, Miami, Florida

J.'s first volume of poetry, *The Summer Anniversaries* (1960), was the Lamont Poetry Selection for 1959. He has also published *Night Light* (1967), *Departures* (1973) and *Selected Poems* (1979), which was awarded the Pulitzer Prize the following year. In 1987, J. published *The Sunset Maker* (1987), which includes poetry and personal essays. J.'s *New and Selected Poems* appeared in 1995, followed by *Oblivion: On Writers and Writing* (1998) and *Orpheus Hesitated beside the Black River* (1998).

J.'s place in American poetry has not yet been fully established, but if the New Formalism becomes a robust movement, future critics will most likely point to J.'s work as one of its major precursors. His work is low-key, carefully crafted, and has an ironic undertone that has been little noted.

J. is a remarkably versatile poet who is equally competent with both free and metered verse. But even in his free verse there is always a formal distancing. The work is not without emotion, but rather the emotion is always carefully controlled. This control is exemplified in the diction and the phrasing, which is always musical (due perhaps to J. having studied musical composition with Carl Ruggles). Although J. has written some poems that are spare (one has even been called a minimalist poem), many of his finest poems have always had a faintly sub-tropical tone, lush, languid, suggestive of much more than they say. This is a tone almost impossible to define and even more difficult to produce. Emily Grosholz says in the *Hudson Review,* "any young American poet must come to J.'s work sooner or later to learn the state of the art."

J. edited with Paul ENGLE and Henri Coulette *The Collected Poems of Weldon Kees* (1960) and with Alexander Aspel edited *Contemporary French Poetry* (1965). His *Platonic Scripts* (1984) contains various interviews that allow him to explain his aesthetics as well as several of his essays.

BIBLIOGRAPHY: Gioia, D., "D. J.: An Interview," *APR* 25 (January-February 1996): 37–46; Ryan, M., "Flaubert in Florida," *NER* 7 (1984 Winter), 218–32

ANN STRUTHERS

K

KANG, Younghill
b. 1903, Hamkyong Province, Korea (now North Korea); d. 11 December 1972, Satellite Beach, Florida

K. was initially educated in the Confucian tradition and later attended Christian schools, which were established throughout Korea in the second half of the 19th c. by American missionaries. At an early age, K. was sent to a traditional Korean school to study Confucian classics. Later, he attended a Japanese-run school, which emphasized "modern" education and science. He was encouraged by a Korean teacher to continue his higher education in the U.S. In 1919, K. joined the pacifist Korean revolution for independence from Japanese rule. When this movement failed, K. was imprisoned for a brief period.

K. reached New York City in 1921, at the age of eighteen, with only a limited command of English, yet a wide reading knowledge. He worked as a cook's helper, secretary, salesman, and waiter. K. wrote in both Korean and Japanese before 1928, at which time he began writing in English with the help of his wife, Frances Keeley. As a lecturer in the English Department at New York University, K. became close friends with author Thomas WOLFE, who brought the manuscript of K.'s first novel to the attention of Maxwell Perkins at Scribner's. Published in 1931, *The Grass Roof* is an autobiographical novel about a young man's life in Korea up to the point of his departure for America. *The Happy Grove,* his second autobiographical novel that also depicts preimmigrant life in Korea, was published in 1933, and in 1937, *East Goes West: The Making of an Oriental Yankee,* K.'s final novel, was published. Although K. is best known for these works, he also published translations of Korean literature, such as *Meditations of the Lover* and *Murder in the Royal Palace,* along with a number of book reviews in the *New York Times* on Asian culture.

In 1946, K. was sent to Korea as chief of publications for the American Military Government, and for a while, served as the head of the literature department at Seoul National University. He returned permanently to the U.S. in 1948.

The recipient of France's Le Prix Halperine Kaminsky and the Louis S. Weiss Memorial Prize, K. was the first Korean American to achieve widespread recognition as an author.

ALICE SCHARPER

KAUFMAN, George S.
b. 16 November 1889, Pittsburgh, Pennsylvania; d. 2 June 1961, New York City

K. was supremely a man of the theater. For over four decades, he wrote and directed plays. In addition to writing several screenplays, he sold over twenty of his own plays to movie companies. His forte was satirical comedy (theater itself was a favorite topic), and his plays helped give American drama a stature in world theater that it had not previously had. Through his plays, he reflected the cultural and political changes in the U.S. and helped a nation to learn to laugh at itself. By most reckonings, his contribution to American theater is major. One of the wits of the Algonquin Round Table, his skill at repartee is well documented.

But his fame, like that of the other Algonquin wits (except perhaps that of Dorothy PARKER) is fading. K. is not regularly taught in colleges and universities. He no longer makes the anthologies. Despite the fact that K. authored two Pulitzer Prize-wining plays, his work is the subject of critical scrutiny only infrequently.

Nevertheless, K.'s work is most visible where he would most wish it—on stage. Classics such as *You Can't Take It with You* (1937) and *The Man Who Came to Dinner* (1939) are frequently stage throughout the world. Play reading groups continue to be drawn to K.'s works; even amateur readings quickly reveal his ability to delight. Several of K.'s titles are more famous than his own name.

No one understood better than K. that collaboration is the essence of theater. Playwrights work with directors and actors and sometimes with musicians—K.'s musicals were planned with the likes of Deems Taylor, George and Ira Gershwin, Richard Rodgers, Arthur Schwartz, and Cole Porter. Frequently called upon to help others to improve their plays, he was admired as a play director. K.'s plays were nearly all written in collaboration. He worked with over seventeen playwrights, including Marc CONNELLY, Edna FERBER, Laurence STALLINGS, Herman Mankiewicz, Ring LARDNER, Moss HART, Morrie Ryskind, Alexander Woollcott, John P. MARQUAND, and his second wife Leuenn MacGrath. The most extended and most successful collaborations were with Connelly (nine plays) and Hart (nine plays). For good reason, K.'s contemporaries dubbed him "The Great Collaborator."

Nevertheless, the collaborative nature of so much of K.'s work has mitigated against his reputation, making him less inviting as a subject for critical inquiry. Nor does social satire—that dates fairly quickly—usually invite continuing commentary. It may produce delightful theater, but not necessarily scholarly attention.

Representative of K.'s work is the now unjustly neglected *Beggar on Horseback* (1925). Like many of his efforts, this Kaufman-Connelly play is itself based on another work, Paul Appel's German satire *Hans Sonnenstossers Hollenfahrt* (1911). The American playwrights followed Appel's plot and method, but transformed the play into a fully American work, effectively satirizing American notions of conformity, especially as regards art. Deems Taylor composed the incidental music for the play. The action is fast paced; the stage busy; the dialogue clever. The play is one of the high points of expressionism in American drama.

K. exemplifies the tradition of the Jewish comedian, skilled with the wisecrack. (He always let his collaborators handle the love scenes.) He has a keen sense of the possibilities of the stage for comedy and farce.

BIBLIOGRAPHY: Goldstein, M., *G. S. K.: His Life, His Theater* (1979); Mason, J. D., *Wisecracks: The Farces of G. S. K.* (1988); Meredith, S., *G. S. K. and His Friends* (1974); Pollack, R. G., *G. S. K.* (1988); Teichmann, H., *G. S. K.: An Intimate Portrait* (1972)

JOSEPH M. FLORA

KAZIN, Alfred

b. 5 June 1915, Brooklyn, New York; d. 4 June 1998, New York City

K. is a modernist, until recently best known for his critical work. The most famous of his criticism is his analysis of American literature, *On Native Grounds,* published in 1942 when he was only twenty-seven. Regarded by many as the quintessential New York man of letters, K. was born of Eastern European immigrants and was one of a school of New York Intellectuals who came of age during the Great Depression, a group that included socialists Norman Thomas and Max EASTMAN and the playwright James AGEE. He graduated from the City College of New York and during the 1940s worked as an editor at several periodicals based in New York, including the *New Republic* and *Fortune.* From 1955 to 1958, he was professor of American studies at Amherst College, and from 1963 to 1973 a distinguished professor of English at the State University of New York at Stony Brook.

What made *On Native Grounds* unique is that in this work K. examined American literature as a distinct phenomenon, quite independent of its European counterpart. For example, he found that American REALISM and NATURALISM were generated by purely American forces, especially the questioning of the American identity that occurred during the Depression. This questioning, he maintained, contributed to the popularity of the biography as a literary form, citing as proof such works as Carl SANDBURG's multivolume biography of Abraham LINCOLN and Joseph Wood Krutch's exhaustive psychological analysis of Edgar Allan POE. He also found that photography influenced the great American works written during this period, whether directly in a book consisting almost entirely of photographs, such as Agee's and Walker Evan's *Let Us Now Praise Famous Men,* or indirectly, as contributor to the random, almost accidental, encyclopedism found in the works of Thomas WOLFE. This generous encyclopedism he saw as a virtue; in a similar way, he preferred William FAULKNER's impassioned recognition of man's essential powerlessness before the urgency and irrationality of the passions to what he saw as Ernest HEMINGWAY's ultimate self-limitation and narrowness, his refusal to step outside what he knew he could write about.

As a literary critic, K. saw his role as a marketer of literature, one who, as he pointed out in "The Function of Criticism Today" (1961), may also stimulate the production of new works of art by revealing "the hidden issues that give a writer a hint of new subjects." He also maintained that a critic must not present great art respectfully, urging instead that he reveal the sassiness and lightheartedness that went into its creation. To him, in *Lolita,* Vladimir NABOKOV epitomized the artist as iconoclast. In *Bright Book of Life* (1971), he contrasted Nabokov with Poe, saying that, although, like Nabokov, Poe had his own nymphet, Poe did not know how to make comedy out of this obsession. Holding the characteristic modernist stance that a work of art must be judged only by its own aesthetic goals, K. felt that Nabokov's triumph in *Lolita* was to make the reader comfortable with something he or she does not accept intellectually, namely the idea that a middle-aged man lusts after a preteen.

In "The Function of Criticism Today" (1961), K. also warned critics to avoid writing for literary periodicals and to write instead for general magazines. Such conditions, he said, make writers take the trouble to write well, like the English writers Samuel Taylor Coleridge and William Hazlitt, who wrote for newspapers, and Poe, who wrote his greatest critical essays for general magazines.

Although in books like *F. Scott Fitzgerald: The Man and His Work* (1951) and *The Stature of Theodore Dreiser* (1955), K. has produced well-written and insightful studies, perhaps reflecting the diminished role of the literary critic in American life, today K. is better known for his autobiographical works than for his criticism. For example, throughout his life, K. has maintained a love affair with New York. It is this love that he celebrates in *A Walker in the City* (1951) and *Starting Out in the Thirties* (1962). Indeed, critics maintain that his best work may well be *A Walker in the City,* an account of the price paid for success in the lost innocence of K.'s youth in Brooklyn. Critics point to his powers of observation and analysis, his eye for psychological significant detail, and the semi-novelistic sense of milieu that made him such an effective reviewer and critic of fiction. What becomes most clear in *A Lifetime Burning in Every Moment* (1996), excerpts taken from his journal from 1938 to 1955, is that both in critical pieces and in autobiography, K. is a celebrator of literature itself. For him, it is a means of availing himself of loneliness by plunging or being plunged into the depths of personal experience and exploring its meaning, uniqueness and exceptionality. In do doing, literature can be useful, he said in "The Function of Criticism," in providing ideas "central to social policy and moral behavior."

BIBLIOGRAPHY: Rubin, L. D., "A. K.'s American Procession," *SR* 93 (Spring 1985): 250–65; Schneider, R., "A. K.: Americanist," *JAC* 13 (Fall 1990): 61–69

SUSAN HARRINGTON

KEILLOR, Garrison [Gary Edward]

b. 7 August 1942, Anoka, Minnesota

Often compared to Mark TWAIN and to Will ROGERS, as well as to fellow Midwesterner James THURBER, K. is a storyteller, humorist, and mythmaker—on radio and tape and in print. The host of public radio's popular *A Prairie Home Companion,* K. began his radio career

in 1960 as a freshman at the University of Minnesota. Inspired in part by his 1973 *New Yorker* piece on "The Grand Ole Opry," he developed his own radio variety show. The show's highlight became "The News from Lake Wobegon," K.'s oral narrative about his invented Minnesota hometown. In 1987, K. ended his show and moved to Denmark and then to Manhattan, there resuming the program two years later as *G. K.'s American Radio Company of the Air* and restoring its original name in 1993.

K.'s first book draws material mostly from the radio monologues. The main character of *Lake Wobegon Days* (1985) is the eponymous small town itself. Essentially the town's biography, the book places the town's history, geography, and a community of characters within a seasonal structure. In tall tale fashion, pages of evidence document a nonexistent town. A charming ordinariness is distinguishing trait of the town whose motto is "Sumus Quod Sumus" ("We Are What We Are"). Virtues of patience and self-denial prepare the Wobegonians for the banalities of Ralph's Pretty Good Grocery or the Chatterbox Cafe, "where the coffee pot is always on, which is why it tastes that way."

K.'s sequel, *Leaving Home: A Collection of Lake Wobegon Stories* (1987), is a collection of elegiac radio monologues—between script and story in form—concerning evanescence. Structurally, the stories about Wobegonians who leave the town give the appearance of artlessness, usually beginning, like local conversation, with remarks on the weather and then moving circuitously to the main stories. "The Matter of Minnesota" stresses the power of love: husbands and wives quarrel but usually reconcile. And even on the prairie, transcendence is attainable: early in the morning the narrator is entranced by "this little town is so shining and perfect, so fresh, so still." Or, as Myrtle Krebsbach says while looking at the fall foliage, "If this don't prove to them there's an Almighty, I don't know what the hell will." While K.'s affectionate memory of the American hamlet answers earlier fiction such as Sherwood ANDERSON's *Winesburg, Ohio* and Sinclair LEWIS's *Main Street* critical of Midwestern village life, nostalgia is tempered by satire, the realistic depiction of village banality and ineptitude, and the prominent theme of the lonely boy—the sensitive adolescent who yearns to escape provincial dreariness.

Happy to Be Here (1983) collects various pieces published originally in the *New Yorker* and the *Atlantic Monthly;* these show K.'s debt to the urbane sophistication of *New Yorker* writers like E. B. WHITE and S. J. PERELMAN and show a virtuoso parodist in such varied genres as SCIENCE FICTION, rock criticism, and grant writing.

609

With its postmodern sensibility, *WLT: A Radio Romance* (1991) turns away from both the genial if qualified optimism of *A Prairie Home Companion* and the urbane wit of the sketches and parodies; *WLT* is a scatological and jaundiced version of the Horatio AL-GER plot detailing the adventures of Francis With, a Midwestern boy voted "most anonymous" by his high school classmates. Through luck and pluck, he becomes radio personality Frank White, the action ending in the early 1950s as the ambitious Frank gets his first television job. An "Epilogue" revisits White in 1991, by then an elderly television mogul whose own biographer tries unsuccessfully to murder him.

If *A Prairie Home Companion* pays tribute to a pre-television culture, K.'s radio novel depicts that culture in near anarchy with profit as the only rule, epitomized by the often-realized fear of its owners that obscenities will get on the air and ruin their business: performers on WLT (With Lettuce and Tomato) include a foul-mouthed child actress and a debauched gospel quartet. Laced with obscene practical jokes, alcoholism, adultery and sexual obsession, suicide, and catastrophic death, this novel contains K.'s darkest vision of American culture.

K.'s Lake Wobegon stories have attracted millions of listeners and readers. Few American humorists since Twain have so successfully united the poetic and the popular; a United States fragmented after Vietnam responds to K.'s wistful humor, his appreciation of local color and community, and his theme of quiet timelessness in the town that "time forgot and the decades cannot improve."

BIBLIOGRAPHY: Lee, J. V., *G. K.: A Voice of America* (1991); Wilbers, S., "Lake Wobegon: Mythical Place and the American Imagination," *AmerS* 30 (Spring 1989): 5–20

VICTOR K. LASSETER

KELLEY, William Melvin

b. 1 November 1937, New York City

In the preface to his short story collection *Dancers on the Shore* (1964), K. writes that as an author he "should depict people, not symbols or ideas disguised as people," a notion that K. has successfully adhered to throughout his literary efforts. Born and raised in the mostly white North Bronx, K. later received the support of fellowships from the Bread Loaf Writers' and New York Writers conferences, won a grant from the John Hay Whitney Foundation, and taught at the New School for Social Research. *Dancers on the Shore* contains narratives that reflect his lifelong ambivalence toward and criticisms of prevailing racial ortho-

doxies, in addition to providing foundations for his most accomplished novels. Perhaps because K. began his career before the Black Power movement began to inform the politics of prominent African American authors, his works do not fit easily, if at all, into the tenets put forth by the proponents of the Black Aesthetic of the 1960s, who tended to bridle at narratives told from a white point of view, even if done so ironically as K. did on several occasions. K. is more concerned with reflecting the influence of his immediate predecessor, Ralph ELLISON. This refusal to fit wholly into a particular aesthetic may help explain why K.'s works are not taught with the same frequency as other African American authors, but does not make him any less important to the overarching tradition of AFRICAN AMERICAN LITERATURE.

K.'s renown as an author may be most easily attributed to two of his most famous novels, *A Different Drummer* (1962) and *dem* (1967), each of which examines and satirizes white America's dependence upon both white supremacy and the continued presence and labor of African Americans.

A Different Drummer, K.'s first novel, earned him the Richard and Hinda Rosenthal Award of the National Institute of Arts and Letters in 1963. Set in a mythical southern state "bounded on the north by Tennessee; east by Alabama; south by the Gulf of Mexico; west by Mississippi"; this state is, therefore, an amalgamation of the entire Deep South and its history. The narrative revolves around the history of the protagonist, Tucker Caliban, a black sharecropper and descendant of an African chieftan. Caliban indirectly causes the migration of all African Americans from the state when he salts his fields, burns his farmhouses, and leaves the state. The departure of the state's black population leads to the inevitable confusion that follows when an essential labor force disappears. Confronted with their own oppressive practices, the state's whites are forced to contemplate the history that led to Caliban's departure, thus allowing us meditated insights into both the thoughts of the white characters and into the African history that informs the lives of most African Americans. The history of the Dunsford family, introduced in *A Different Drummer*, is continued in *Dunsfords Travels Everywheres* (1970), which also parodies the modernistic methods of James Joyce's *Finnegans Wake*, beginning with its title and continuing through the narrative's circular pattern, style and characters. As in *A Different Drummer*, the theme of *Dunsfords Travels Everywhere* is the inability of most Americans, white and black, to completely understand the complicated nature of race relations well enough to begin working toward ending social inequalities. In addition, the novel explores the occasionally spiteful actions driven by intraracial bigotries and taboos, most notably the taboos against interracial sex and romance. In both novels, the prevailing theme is that independent thinking is the foundation for both the individual and society. In the absence of such thought, racial ignorance and hatred have no choice but to fester and grow.

While *A Drop of Patience* (1965) centers upon jazz and the continually undervalued status of the music and its artists in American culture, *dem,* based on "The Servant Problem," a short story from *Dancers on the Shore,* clearly does not fit into the sort of proscriptions set forth by K.'s other novels. K. sublimates overt racial themes and references for a significant portion of the plot in order to focus on the lives of white primary characters, especially the protagonist, Mitchell Pierce, an advertising executive who apparently epitomizes much of the American Dream (a comfortable home, attractive wife, steady employment, and an ample income), yet is quickly exposed as the antithesis of American ideals via his marked racial chauvinism and inept ability to detect either his bigotries or his own romanticization of his experiences as a white American. More specifically, the novel addresses the American obsession with miscegenation through Mitchell's eyes. When twins, one black and one white, are born to his wife Tam, Mitchell is forced to confront his impotence within his home and, perhaps most devastating, the possibility that African Americans have always been successful subversives within American society.

At least partially a reflection of K.'s reluctance to utilize a single narrative form to "address himself to the Afro-American," *dem* is simultaneously his "dual commitment . . . to his craft and to black people." The novel's satire exposes the degree to which white America's overconfidence in its racial hegemony prevents it from perceiving its own subversion by those it would keep oppressed. It many ways, it is perhaps the best representative of K.'s oeuvre, inasmuch as it consistently exposes the problem of blindness to racial issues that perpetuates systematic racism. K.'s frustration with this blindness forms the basis of many of his works and leads us to investigate American culture's reluctance to consider African Americans human beings fully deserving of equality. Appropriately, it is K.'s novels that provide a beam with which to eliminate that blindness.

BIBLIOGRAPHY: Adams, C. H., "Imagination and Community in W. M. K.'s *A Different Drummer," Crit* 26 (Fall 1984): 26–35; Bell, B. W., *The Afro-American Novel and Its Tradition* (1987); Faulkner, H. J., "A Vanishing Race," *CLAJ* 37 (March 1994): 274–92

DARRYL B. DICKSON-CARR

KELLY, George [Edward]
b. 16 February 1887, Schuykill Falls, Pennsylvania;
d. 18 June 1974, Bryn Mawr, Pennsylvania

Best known for meticulously crafted realistic comedies of middle-class life, K. was often more respected than liked by audiences and critics. Three substantial successes early in his playwriting career—*The Torchbearers* (1922), *The Show-Off* (1924), and *Craig's Wife* (1925)—quickly moved K. to the front ranks of American comic playwrights, but his tendency to pass severe moral judgments on his characters later led to box office failures and critical attacks. After 1946, K. never brought another play to Broadway, although he left behind four, still unpublished plays at his death. Today, only *The Show-Off* enjoys revivals, and his work is generally ignored by scholars. Yet, as those who take the time to seek out his work can attest, it remains some of the most strongly individual and uncompromising work written for the American stage.

K. began as an actor in vaudeville, and progressed from sketches to one-act plays, and then to full-length works. He had very set ideas about how his plays should be produced, and directed the Broadway premieres of all his plays, demonstrating each piece of business for the cast. His attacks on theatrical dilettantism were inspired and vitriolic—*The Torchbearers* juxtaposes hilarious farcical sequences in which we see an inept amateur theater in action with an angry denunciation of its vanity. On the other hand, *Reflected Glory* (1936) presents the heights of professional theater as an exalted vocation that nothing—not even marriage—should compromise.

K.'s plays are often built around vain, self-deluded characters—the amateur thespians of *The Torchbearers,* the domineering and manipulative Harriet Craig, the untalented young playwright of *Philip Goes Forth* (1931), and the self-proclaimed "intuitive" title character in *The Deep Mrs. Sykes* (1945). The puncturing of these delusions can be fatal, as in K.'s one tragedy, *Behold the Bridegroom* (1927) in which a shallow young society woman discovers her moral inadequacy and pines away. These plays have often been criticized for the Jonsonian relish with which they mete out punishments far in excess of the offenses; there is no forgiveness in K.'s dramatic universe. At times, the plays seem coldly efficient machines designed to bring people to unpleasant realizations.

Yet it is wrong to overemphasize K.'s moralistic bent. No previous American playwright had so unsentimentally and painstakingly charted the trivial rivalries, habitual evasions, financial irritations and commodity fetishes of middle-class domesticity. His plots often become slight and elliptical as they make way for this rich detailing. In his last two produced play,

The Deep Mrs. Sykes and *The Fatal Weakness* (1946), the plots seem inconsequential under the amassing of details. Without headlines, topical jokes, political debates or metaphysical reflections, a K. play can seem at once both very familiar and disconcertingly bizarre—as if all the most petty and compulsive moments of domesticity have been allowed to constitute the entire world. Harriet Craig of *Craig's Wife* is K.'s most memorable depiction of domestic authoritarianism, for whom an immaculate house is a consuming passion. A K. household either bristles with irritation or survives by elaborate strategies of evasion; *Daisy Mayme* (1926) may pin her hopes on a home, but the play gives the audience no reason to believe happiness can be found there. K.'s vision is too severe to win vast audiences, yet it remains sharply etched and theatrically vivid.

BIBLIOGRAPHY: Hirsch, F., *G. K.* (1975); Krutch, J. W., *American Drama since 1918* (1939); McCarthy, M., *Theater Chronicles, 1937–1962* (1963)

ROBERT F. GROSS

KELLY, Robert

b. 24 September 1935, Brooklyn, New York

There is little doubt that K. is the most prolific major poet in contemporary American poetry, with over sixty books of poetry and seven collections of prose. He also edited three distinguished journals: *Torbar, Chelsea Review,* and *Matter.* He and poet Jerome ROTHENBERG also founded and named a uniquely American school of poetry called deep imagism.

K. was raised in a typical middle-class family and was educated at Brooklyn Prep, an excellent Jesuit secondary school, which gave its students a thorough grounding in Latin and Greek, knowledge that he used throughout his writing career. Although he experienced some teenage alienation—skipping school—his parents decided to enroll him at the age of sixteen in the City College of New York, where he steeped himself in the works of those writers who became the major influences on his poetry and prose for the rest of his life: Samuel Taylor Coleridge, Apollinaire, Rainer Maria Rilke, T. S. ELIOT, and Ezra POUND. He also began an intense involvement with the musical sources that have also influenced his work: Anton Bruckner, Richard Wagner, Gustav Mahler, Richard Strauss, Alban Berg, and the operas of Vincenzo Bellini and Gaetano Donizetti. After graduating from the City College of New York, he began graduate work at Columbia University, and completed a master's degree and all of the work towards his Ph.D. in medieval literature under

Professor Roger Loomis, but did not complete his dissertation.

K. attributes his commitment to the life of poetry to a visionary event in October 1958; and as a result of this overwhelming experience, he vowed to devote his life to writing: "to write every day . . . To attend to what is said. To listen. To prepare myself by learning everything I could." His early book *Armed Descent* (1961) probes, in a surrealistic mode, the deep images of his own private world and those of the collective unconscious. However, in *Axon Dendron Tree* (1967), he moves away from deep image to exploring the way language creates rather than records experience. The figure of the tree—specifically a linguistic tree—reappears throughout his poetry. What many critics consider one of K.'s most significant collections of poetry is *Finding the Measure* (1968), a volume that extends his examination of language as the most reliable method of understanding reality.

The Common Shore (1969) is an epic poem that came out of his attempt to order the chaos of the turbulent 1960s. Charles OLSON's massive *Maximus Poems* heavily influenced K.'s poetic methodology in *The Common Shore,* especially Olson's geographical mappings of America's spiritual history. But it is in K.'s *The Mill of Particulars* (1973) that K. investigates painting, music, and mythology as "languages"; that is , as linguistic structures. He opens the volume with a line that becomes a crucial key in understanding K.'s sophisticated poetics: "Language is the only genetics." But it is in his next long poem, *The Loom,* in which he brings together and synthesizes his spiritual, mythological, and linguistic sources by interweaving them with the many spiritual and intellectual traditions that make up his life in poetry. The "text"—as in a woven textile—composed of a cast of hundreds, includes the Blessed Virgin Mary, Jesus Christ, Odysseus, Siegfried, Kali, Kore, Arjuna, and many other mythological figures.

Because of the breakup of his second marriage, some of the poems in his next two volumes, *The Convections* (1978) and *Kill the Messenger Who Brings Bad News* (1979), teeter on the edge of despair. Much of *Kill the Messenger* examines archetypal women in both their sacred and profane aspects. But his next major volume *Spiritual Exercises* (1981) shows K. delving into the way language and text interact to become a guide to the imagination rather than a product of the imagination's control.

Because K. became a Tibetan Buddhist in 1981, his poetry moved deeper into what lay beneath their linguistic surface, a process that *Under Words* (1983) and *Not This Island Music* (1987) explore in highly innovative ways. K. explains that he became more interested in "what lay beneath . . . the things I said and meant and used . . . to build poems." Though he found refuge in the consolations of Buddhism, many of the poems in his next volume *A Strange Market* (1992) record his great sorrow over the deaths of both his parents and the woman he had lived with for five years, Mary Moore Godlett. The crowning achievement of K.'s work is *Red Actions: The Selected Poems, 1960–1993* (1995), a four-hundred page selection from over sixty books of poetry, an accomplishment that resulted in his receiving an honorary Doctor of Letters degree from the State University of New York in 1994.

BIBLIOGRAPHY: Blevins, R., "R. K.," in Meanor, P., ed., *DLB*, vol. 130, *American Short-Story Writers since World War II* (1993): 207–16; McCaffery, L., ed., *Some Other Fluency: Interviews with Innovative American Authors* (1996); Rasula, J., "Ten Different Fruits on One Different Tree," *Credences* 3 (Spring 1984): 127–65

PATRICK MEANOR

KENNEDY, Adrienne [Lita]

b. 13 September 1931, Pittsburgh, Pennsylvania.

After decades of distinguished obscurity, K.'s drama has gained increasing recognition in the 1990s. With two major theater festivals showcasing her works, including a seven-play series at New York's Joseph Papp Public Theatre in 1996, along with two collected editions of her plays and a place among just five playwrights in the 1989 *Norton Anthology of American Literature,* K.'s brief but emotionally charged, technically challenging plays are now being acknowledged as important achievements in American theater.

This delayed recognition stems from the difficulty of categorizing K.'s work, her exclusive devotion to the short play form, and her defiance of conventional notions of plot, character, and setting. An African American woman, K. writes plays that deal boldly with elements of race, gender, and culture without pronouncing themselves distinctly "black," "feminist," or "progressive." Unlike other black playwrights, such as her contemporaries Lorraine HANSBERRY, Charles Gordone, and Ed BULLINS who have favored social realism, K. explores the dynamics of race and identity through a highly personal mythology of symbols that draws equally from dreams and private experiences as from the cultures of America, Africa, and Europe.

The 1996 New York festival allowed audiences to become immersed in K.'s densely symbolic, frequently violent and blood-stained drama in a way that seeing or reading individual plays does not permit. But her

1987 scrapbook-style memoir, *People Who Led to My Plays,* had already offered a frank and fascinating glimpse into K.'s highly varied iconography. Beginning with her earliest Off-Broadway plays in the 1960s, she has portrayed her own middle-class, African American background with ruthless attention to its African and its European influences. Beethoven, Jesus, Bette Davis, Marlon Brando, Queen Victoria, Patrice Lumumba, Anne Boleyn, and William Shakespeare all figure in her plays, merging directly with a private life and dreams in a fluid dramaturgy that recalls the expressionist and surrealist art of the 1920s, as well as "confessional" American poetry of later decades, but without ever losing its focus on the struggles of African American cultural identity in the latter half of this century.

If one theme may be said to dominate K.'s plays, and perhaps to account for their difficult, "writerly" texture, it is the transformative, even redemptive, effect of the act of writing itself. Her first and best-known play, *Funnyhouse of a Negro* (1964), was completed and produced with the encouragement of Edward ALBEE, whose playwriting workshop K. attended in 1961, but was spurred by her voyage with her husband to West Africa and London, a trip of stark cultural contrasts that decisively awakened her creative energies. *Funnyhouse of a Negro* ends with the suicide of its heroine, Sarah, who is both fascinated and haunted by dominating images of whiteness such as a large plaster statue of Queen Victoria while struggling to find a coherent place in the world for herself beyond the "funnyhouse" of her own internalized psychic conflicts and fragmented selves. However, her next play, *The Owl Answers* (1965), features a heroine named "She who is Clara Passmore who is the Virgin Mary who is the Bastard who is the Owl," a manifold identity given coherence and strength in the process of transformation itself.

In the late 1960s, K. wrote several more short plays, including *Sun: A Poem for Malcolm X* (1968), *A Lesson in a Dead Language* (1968), and *The Lennon Play: In His Own Write* (1967), adapted from musician John Lennon's informal poems and stories. With *A Movie Star Has to Star in Black and White* (1976), K.'s plays begin to show a more straightforward, self-referential faith in the redemptive power of writing. Using three Hollywood films as a medium for expressing the heroine Clara's family relationships and self-conception, the play dramatizes Clara's emergence from white-dominated Hollywood imagery by writing her own plays, which are clearly two of K.'s own previous works. Likewise, the semiautobiographical Suzanne Alexander of *The Ohio State Murders* (1992) is a writer who, giving a lecture on the violence in her work, traces it to her traumatic life as a university

English major, while overcoming that trauma in the very act of communicating it.

In *Sleep Deprivation Chamber* (a work that premiered at the 1996 New York Festival), K. has collaborated with her son Adam in an attempt to come to terms with a police beating that Adam suffered outside his father's house in 1991. Here K.'s heroine Suzanne Alexander again turns to writing as a means of discovering hard truths about American racism, violence, and family relationships. If this play suggests a growing concern with social realism, perhaps it will also serve as a bridge to K.'s earlier works that, despite their brevity, have illuminated hidden, troubling places in the American psyche.

BIBLIOGRAPHY: Bryant-Jackson, P., and L. Overbeck, *Intersecting Boundaries: The Theater of A. K.* (1991); Robinson, M., *The Other American Drama* (1994)

KURT EISEN

KENNEDY, John Pendleton

b. 25 October 1795, Baltimore, Maryland.; d. 18 August 1870, Newport, Rhode Island

A lawyer by profession, K. is remembered for his four extended major works of fiction and, in particular, for his plantation romance entitled *Swallow Barn* (1832), which is the prototype for the many popular "plantation novels" of the 19th and early 20th cs. His many American historical romances were motivated, in large part, by the changes he saw taking place in American life and, in the case of *Swallow Barn,* those moral changes sweeping the South in its fervor for religious evangelism. Such moral changes fostered by the continuing spread of religion were, he believed, greatly leveling the luxuries and excesses of an older, more gracious and sophisticated life style.

The publication of *Swallow Barn* in 1832 marks a movement of Southern literature from the classics and chivalry to addressing the younger writers of the Northeast. Certainly, in terms of its publication history, the romance was carefully timed to coincide with major moments in cultural and political conflict regarding plantation life and the institution of slavery.

Early reviewers saw the romance as emanating from an idyllic tradition earlier fostered by Washington IRVING in his *Sketch Book* and in *Bracebridge Hall.* The former accounted for a nostalgic love of recording social history and preserving the picturesque. The latter idealized a manorial estate complete with a munificent squire devoted to his people, who are tied to working his land. That illusion of master-servant relations is not altogether different from K.'s romanticizing of Tidewater Virginia plantation domestic life and slavery.

The loose-leaf novel or fictional notebook is really a synthesis of Addisonian essays and character sketches narrated by a pleasure-loving outsider, Mark Littleton, a visitor to the plantation. In terms of characterization, K.'s favorite teacher at Baltimore College, William Sinclair, became the basis of his satirical portrait for Parson Chub. The good-natured but conservative master of Swallow Barn, Frank Meriwether, is K. himself; and in Meriwether is the virtual archetype of the fictional Southern plantation hero—middle-aged, charming but hot tempered, dogmatic but benevolent, democratic but opposed to change and cities of any kind.

With all its inadequacies, *Swallow Barn* remains K.'s best work, for he writes of a life he knew well through summers spent with his mother's Virginia family. The great theme of the work, however, is cautionary—the danger of living an agrarian illusion in order to combat time, a theme which places K. in the company of William FAULKNER, Thomas WOLFE, Ellen GLASGOW, William STYRON, and Eudora WELTY. In that illusion of agrarian paradise, K. saw slavery as waste and extravagance, an institution with, unfortunately, no immediate or easy solution.

Horse-Shoe Robinson (1835), a colonial romance set during the American Revolution, is well known for its depiction of the Battle of King's Mountain. The protagonist is comparable to James Fenimore COOPER's Leather-Stocking, a hardy, vital, likeable but rudely educated man embodying the best of indigenous South Carolina character. Thematically, K. focuses on the painful divided loyalties besetting many colonials in the period.

The romance *Rob of the Bowl: A Legend of St. Inigoe's* (1838) is set in colonial Maryland and depicts the dramatic moment when King Charles ordered all Roman Catholic officers replaced by Protestants in 1621. The colonial romance seems particularly influenced by Sir Walter Scott.

K.'s novel *Quodlibet* (1840) is set in contemporary 19th-c. America and is extremely critical of Jacksonian democracy, including American faith in the majority vote. The novel may be one of America's most powerful early political satires.

BIBLIOGRAPHY: Bohner, C. H., *J. P. K.: A Gentleman from Baltimore* (1961); Cowie, A., *The Rise of the American Novel* (1951); Leisy, E. E., *The American Historical Novel* (1950); Ridgely, J. V., *J. P. K.* (1966)

GEORGE LONGEST

KENNEDY, William

b. 16 January 1928, Albany, New York

K. is an interesting anomaly in American literary tradition. Whereas a classic pattern in American letters is for young writers to produce their best work early in their careers and then to either die young, stop publishing, or produce a long string of disappointing later work, K. did not publish his first book until he was forty-one and did not produce a book of uncontestably high literary quality until he was fifty. Since that time, however, he has produced his best work, *Ironweed* (1983) and *The Flaming Corsage* (1996), becoming in his late sixties one of America's foremost living novelists.

All of K.'s writings are deeply rooted in a particular time and place, Albany, New York from the early parts of the 19th c. to the mid-1960s. K. himself, except for a seven year period where he lived in Puerto Rico and Miami, Florida, has spent his life in Albany. Reared in predominantly Irish-Catholic North Albany, he is a member of a family that had been closely tied to Democratic politics in Albany for generations. If K.'s upbringing provided him with a vivid sense of Albany's political culture, history, and folklore, his work as a journalist enabled him to deepen his understanding of these matters over a long period of time. As a reporter for the *Albany Times Union* from 1952 to 1956 and again from 1963 until recent years, he observed the life of his city closely on a daily basis and also engaged in sustained research on Albany's past, gaining knowledge of this place that was both broad and intimate. As he pointed out in his book on Albany history, *O Albany!* (1983), he regards himself "as a person whose imagination has become fused with a single place, and in that place finds all the elements that a man needs for the life of the soul."

K.'s cycle of novels includes six books that examine that city from a wide variety of perspectives and in a number of time settings. Beginning with *The Ink Truck* (1969), a fictionalized version of the 1964 strike at the *Albany Times Union,* and moving to *The Flaming Corsage,* set between 1884 and 1912, these novels become for K. what the Yoknapatawpha novels were for William FAULKNER, a fictive universe that enabled him to develop a broad, profound, and finally affirmative understanding of his personal background, region and nation as they developed in time. As these novels mature, the Albany setting becomes progressively more important and richly imagined, helping K. to probe more deeply into his complex themes and characters. *The Ink Truck* is only superficially about Albany and *Legs* (1976) is centered on a character who was not an Albany native and whose overall story has little to do with Albany. But beginning with *Billy Phelan's Greatest Game* (1978), a pivotal novel about Democratic machine politics in Albany, K. found his authentic literary subject and voice. Originating in research on Irish-Democratic politics that K. was doing for a series of articles in the *Times Union,* the novel plunged K. deeply into his region's history and

myth that in turn enabled him to see the lives of his characters in fresh, resonant ways.

Ironweed (1983), which K. regards as his best book, is a multilayered novel that invites favorable comparison with American masterworks such as Faulkner's *Light in August,* Sherwood ANDERSON's *Winesburg, Ohio,* and James T. FARRELL's *Studs Lonigan.* Focusing on Francis Phelan, a minor character from K.'s previous book, it probes deeply into the working class world of Albany from the turn of the century to the end of the Great Depression. *Quinn's Book* (1988) reaches further back in time, between 1849 and 1864, when the ancestors of K.'s 20th-c. characters were driven out of Ireland and came to America to start new lives. *Very Old Bones* (1992) takes place in the Albany of the late 1950s but flashes back at several key points to the Albany of 1813.

Common to all of these books is a tough-minded and qualifiedly affirmative vision that testifies to the depth and resiliency of the human spirit. K.'s characters, whether imagined as criminals like Legs Diamond or saints like Annie Phelan, are vivid embodiments of Francis Phelan's belief that "the trick was to live, beat the bastard, survive the mob and that fateful chaos, and show them all what a man can do once he has a mind to do it." K.'s characters typically experience tragic downfalls in which they lose everything that makes life meaningful to them and they experience journeys that clearly resemble Dante's descent into hell. However, they develop spiritual and psychological resources that enable them to recover and rebound, turning hell into a kind of purgatory leading perhaps to "salvation." What makes K. such a remarkable writer is his ability to dramatize such conversion stories in powerfully realistic and altogether convincing terms, never resorting to the sentimentality and melodrama that mar the work of lesser writers.

Throughout his career, K. has employed a wide variety of styles. *The Ink Truck* uses hard-boiled realism to achieve its staccato effects while *Legs* employs surrealistic methods and a complicated point of view to achieve subtler effects. Perhaps K. is at his best when blending realistic and surrealistic styles as he does in *Ironweed.* Alternating between chillingly realistic descriptions of violence and highly evocative surrealistic passages that enable him to probe the wonderfully rich inward lives of his outwardly devastated characters, K. has produced fiction that is only rarely surpassed by post-World War II American novelists.

But K.'s achievement as a writer can best be explained by his ability to use myth and symbol as a way of lifting his materials well beyond their sociological significance. His Albany, like Gogol's Petersburg, James Joyce's Dublin, or Theodore DREISER's Chicago, is both a powerfully rendered actual place with its own unique geography and history and also a resonant symbol of the human condition. Equally at home in describing Albany as a 20th-c. American city in decline or connecting it with Dante's Dis and Augustine's city of God, K. has fashioned novels that at once powerfully describe the modern descent into hell and the universal desire for purgation and transcendence.

BIBLIOGRAPHY: Fanning, C., *The Irish Voice in America: Irish-American Fiction from the 1760s to the 1980s* (1990); Reilly, E. C., *W. K.* (1991); Van Dover, J. K., *Understanding W. K.* (1991)

ROBERT BUTLER

KEROUAC, Jack [Jean-Louis]

b. 12 March 1922, Lowell, Massachusetts; d. 21 October 1969, St. Petersburg, Florida

Despite having written a half dozen books, K. had no literary standing until *On the Road* (1957) catapulted him into celebrity status. Within weeks, he was being lauded by the media as *the* voice of the Beat generation, a label he affixed to young Americans like himself who aimed to discredit materialism and conformity in their search for a new spirit. Although K. was by no means a one-book author, *On the Road*'s exuberance for life and spontaneous prose style have sustained his exceptional popular appeal.

In a brief note to *Big Sur* (1962), K. mentions that all of his writings were meant to "comprise one vast book like Proust's." Late in his career, he intended to revise and connect his fourteen published novels so each would be a separate chapter in an "enormous comedy" to be entitled "The Duluoz Legend," Jack Duluoz being the name K. selected for himself. Thus, to read the K. canon is to read the legend of his life, in which he is both a participant and an observer.

The son of French-Canadian parents, K. grew up in a Catholic working-class household where he learned firsthand about suffering. His older "saintly" brother, Gerard, died at the age of nine, and a 1936 Merrimack River flood ruined his father's printing business and led to his family's slide toward poverty. Between 1940 and 1944, K. walked away from a football scholarship at Columbia University, was discharged from navy boot camp on psychiatric grounds, was jailed as a material witness to murder, and had his first marriage annulled. When his father died of cancer in 1946, K. turned to the friends he had made in New York City and to his writing.

K., Allen GINSBERG, and William S. BURROUGHS had shared their literary interests dating from K.'s days at Columbia, and in December 1946, he was introduced to Neal Cassady. During the next four years, their group established the core of the Beat generation and compelled K., on several occasions, to crisscross the U.S. and Mexico, experiences that he details in *On the Road*. In the novel, Carlo Marx (Ginsberg), Old Bull Lee (Burroughs), Dean Moriarty (Cassady), and Sal Paradise (K.) wear Beat clothes, work Beat jobs, sleep in Beat cold water flats, and roam Beat midnight city streets. K. uses the term "Beat" to describe both things that are worn out and people who are down on their luck and exhausted by the pressure to surrender to middle-class values. His characters seek for "Beatific" meaning in lifestyles that will allow them to transcend suffering.

Sal narrates events. His travels begin, symbolically, in the spring of 1947 when he hitchhikes west to San Francisco, and they end in the fall of 1950 when he returns to New York after succumbing to dysentery and being abandoned by Dean in Mexico City. Sal is attracted to Dean's "natural" intelligence and his "wild yea-saying overburst of American joy." He sees Moriarty as a new kind of hero possessing unlimited energy and doing things merely for the sake of having done them. Dean accelerates across the continent at 110 m.p.h., with one hand on the steering wheel and the other pounding out a bop rhythm on the dashboard of any car he can buy, borrow or steal. Sal goes along for the ride. He accepts everything—alcohol, drugs, betrayal, infidelity, suspicious hipsters, and con men—for he believes that along some far stretch of highway the "pearl" of total knowledge and insight will be handed to him. In their pursuit of "IT," Dean and he dig jazz pianist George Shearing and are bummed by square Washington bureaucrats; they ache for the "blank tranced end of all innumerable riotous angelic particulars lurking in their souls," yet they scoff at wage-earning married couples who sit asylum-like in front of their television sets. Thematically, Dean lives for the road and for bursting through frontiers. In doing so, he punishes his cars, friends, lovers, and wives, naively assuming that his wreckage will be repaired and forgiven. Sal keeps free his emotional responses to life, but from time to time he forsakes the road and goes home to write. In Sal, K. portrays the inner struggle between the claims of independence and stability, of the urge to wander and the urge to settle.

K. did not articulate his principles of spontaneous prose until after *On the Road* was published, yet the intensity of the book's language corresponds to the energy of the narrative itself. Wanting to convey an uncensored flow of speech and thought, on April 5, 1951, K. made a one-hundred-foot-long scroll and sat down to type. Aided by benzedrine and coffee, in three weeks he completed the original 175,000-word single paragraph draft of the novel. While finding his mark of confessional honesty, K. surely has had his detractors, most notably Truman CAPOTE, Norman Podhoretz, and David Dempsey, who considered the Beat generation to be a ruse perpetrated by "rebellious freaks."

K. did create a mystique for himself and his group. Fame and public criticism, however, destroyed his personality and talent as he alienated his friends and deteriorated into alcoholism. Nonetheless, critic Robert A. Hipkiss argues, "Because he was so quintessentially Beat himself, *On the Road, The Dharma Bums* (1958), *The Subterraneans* (1958), and *Big Sur* remain as living testimony to the angst of the lost generation of World War II."

BIBLIOGRAPHY: Charters, A., *K.* (1973); Clark, T., *J. K.* (1984); French, W., *J. K.* (1986); Foster, E. H., *Understanding the Beats* (1992); Hipkiss, R. A., *J. K., Prophet of the New Romanticism* (1976); McNally, D., *Desolation Angel* (1979); Tytell, J., *Naked Angels: The Lives & Literature of the Beat Generation* (1976)

JOE NORDGREN

KESEY, Ken [Elton]

17 September 1935, La Junta, Colorado

K. is a consummate performer who has been fascinated with magic, ventriloquism, hypnotism, and drama since his high school years in Springfield, Oregon. The ultimate role that he has chosen to assume and has also assigned to his protagonists is a counterculture rebel battling a corrupt, mechanistic, conformist society. K. has delighted in his public persona as a bad boy—a pioneer of hippy culture in the bohemian community of Perry Lane in Menlo Park, California, in the early 1960s; the leader of the Merry Pranksters, whose exploits were celebrated in Tom WOLFE's *The Electric Kool-Aid Acid Test;* an outlaw from the FBI in 1966, who bragged about being "salt in J. Edgar Hoover's wound"; and most recently, a stage actor playing the part of the Wizard of Oz in a wild multimedia version of L. Frank Baum's classic tale K. wrote entitled *Twister.*

Yet for all his public posturing, K. should not be pigeonholed into the category of pop culture figures overzealous of attention. For K. is a serious writer who has carefully studied lessons from such masters as Ralph Waldo EMERSON, Henry David THOREAU, Ernest HEMINGWAY, and William FAULKNER. Influenced by his reading of Zane GREY Westerns and comic books, he is the champion of the disenfranchised in American society, such as Native Americans and the mentally ill; and he is an astute social critic exposing the problems of racism, materialism, and ecological destruction. Moreover, he is a pilgrim on a lifelong quest for spiritual transcendence—a journey that has led him to explore the Bible and works of Eastern mysticism, to experiment with altered consciousness through the use of hallucinogenic drugs, to trek to the pyramids of Egypt, and to conceive of his role as a writer as that of a "parabolist."

K.'s critical reputation as well as his popularity among high school and college readers rests primarily upon his first published novel, *One Flew over the Cuckoo's Nest* (1962). In this seminal text of the 1960s, K. pits his hero of individualism, spontaneity, and unbridled sexuality, Randle Patrick McMurphy, against Nurse Ratched, the inhibitor of responsibility, freedom, and adult sexuality and chief representative of an ominous all-powerful bureaucracy K. labels the Combine. Heavily influenced by the Gospels, *One Flew over the Cuckoo's Nest* ultimately casts McMurphy in the role of scapegoat hero as he undergoes a crucifixion of electroshock therapy and a lobotomy in order to empower his disciples, the formerly subjugated men on the mental ward, many of whom eventually gain the courage to leave the hospital.

K.'s first published novel is particularly notable for its elaborate imagery patterns, including images of hands, animals, and electronics, and for the author's decision to render his story through the consciousness of Chief Bromden, K.'s six-foot-eight-inch Native American, made small by matriarchal and racial oppression. Through nightmare hallucinations of wires, transistors, and dynamos and fearful retreats from fog machines, K. masterfully captures Bromden's schizophrenia—a schizophrenia further elucidated by a fragmented chronology through which as Bromden relates McMurphy's exploits, he reveals pieces of his early life that clarify why is on the psychiatric ward.

Even more psychologically probing and technically brilliant than its predecessor is K.'s second published novel, *Sometimes a Great Notion* (1964), in which the writer radically experiments with the time scheme, point of view, and imagery as he celebrates the frontier values of courage, self-reliance, and determination. *Sometimes a Great Notion* focuses on three generations of males in the Stamper Family as they battle against pressures to conform to the demands of a logging union as well as against the wild forests, torrential rains, and raging rivers of western Oregon. However, the most difficult battle the characters in the novel face is coping with psychic wounds created from loneliness and resentments between lovers, brothers, father and son, and husband and wife. Indeed, the title underscores the psychic pain of those contemplating suicide, for it comes from the following lines from the song "Good Night, Irene": "Sometimes I get a great notion / To jump into the river . . . an' drown." Yet ultimately the novel is uplifting as K. asserts the importance of self-reliance, brotherly love, forgiveness, and affirming life.

In *Sometimes a Great Notion,* K. makes great demands upon his readers. Believing that "Time overlaps itself," K. intersperses narrating an event in the present with depicting a closely related event from the past. He also adapts the cinematic technique of spatial simultaneity by revealing what characters in various locales were doing at the same moment. Even more challenging is K.'s use of multiple points of view. These include the author's or persona's direct addresses to the reader at the beginnings of chapters, third person omniscient narration, and the use of various first person narrators, with the most significant being the brothers Hank and Lee Stamper. Furthermore, K. employs the epistolary method in presenting letters that Lee Stamper writes from Oregon to his former Harvard roommate. Adding to the novel's complexity is K.'s intriguing combination of vernacular and academic idioms as he explores the frontiersman dimension of his personality through Hank Stamper and his intellectual side through the younger brother Lee.

Since the early 1970s, K. has pursued an array of projects—publishing two miscellanies, *K.'s Garage Sale* (1973) and *Demon Box* (1986), writing several screenplays, coediting *The Last Supplement to the Whole Earth Catalogue* (1971), and publishing two children books, *Little Tricker the Squirrel Meets Big Double the Bear* (1990) and *The Sea Lion: A Story of the Sea Cliff People* (1991), both celebrating the triumphs of underdog characters.

In 1992, K. published *Sailor Song,* a novel of epic scope set in the early 21st c. Through his portrayal of the small community of Kuinak, Alaska, K. graphically presents the loss of vital fishing grounds, the effects of ozone depletion, the decline in the number of male high school students, and the development of gigantic mutated sea creatures. Ultimately through an apocalyptic final scene indebted to Herman MELVILLE's *Moby-Dick,* K. suggests, "The End of the World is just around the corner." Equally as disturbing as the environmental devastation to K. is the moral decline he exposes as the "Hollywood Dream Machine" invades the sleepy town of Kuinak seeking a suitable movie locale. Inspired by a text from Ecclesiastes: "And as fishes that are taken in an evil net, and as birds that are caught in the snare; so are the sons of man snared in an evil time," K. reveals a host of horrors, including drug dependency, murder, and incest. Yet, as in *Sometimes a Great Notion,* K. does not wish to leave his readers in despair. Thus, he concludes his work with a reenactment of Noah's and his family's salvation from the Flood in which he suggests that through love, individual acts of heroism, and unselfish community spirit, Kuinak—and perhaps the world—may survive.

A lighter mood characterizes K.'s most recent novel, *Last Go Round* (1994), which he wrote with his friend Ken Babbs. In this book, K. returns to the oral tradition he learned to appreciate as a child in listening to the stories of his Grandmother Smith, his Grandpa Kesey, and his father, all master raconteurs. Indeed, the novel grew from K.'s recollection of a story his father told him around a campfire when he was fourteen. Based upon the 1911 Pendleton Roundup, K. and Babbs depict the battle for the title of World Champion Broncobuster between George Fletcher, a black former rodeo clown; Jackson Sundown, a Nez Perce Indian; and Johnathan E. Lee Spain, a Caucasian youth from Tennessee, from the perspective of a nearly ninety-year-old Spain, who travels the rails of his memory to recall his literal journey by rail from Denver to Pendleton, where he became a bronco celebrity at the age of seventeen. In *Last Go Round,* K. and Babbs combine the riproaring entertainment of what they label "A Real Western" with a thought-provoking expose of racial and gender discrimination in Western society.

K. has contended that the greatest sin an artist can commit is causing boredom. In his absorption of both literary and pop culture influences, his constant technical experimentation, and his self-awareness as a performer whether on stage, on film, or in fiction, K. faces little risk of being such a sinner.

BIBLIOGRAPHY: Carnes, B., *K. K.* (1974), Leeds, B. H., *K. K.* (1981), Pratt, J. C., ed., *One Flew over the Cuckoo's Nest: Text and Criticism* (1973), Tanner, S. L., *K. K.* (1983)

LYNNE SHACKELFORD

KILLENS, John Oliver
b. 14 January 1916, Macon, Georgia; d. 27 October 1987, Brooklyn, New York

K. has importance in literary history not just for his novels, which were acclaimed more for their themes than for the author's style, but for his encouragement of other African American writers and his leadership role in protesting the inequalities in African American life. He led writers' workshops both within and outside of academic circles and helped to found the Harlem Writers' Guild of the 1940s. K. was also influential as a driving force behind the Black Arts movement that grew out of the Black Power movement in the

1960s and 1970s. The political and social views that led K. from labor activism to the civil rights movement and black nationalism are inextricable from his writings.

His youth in the South during the early part of the 20th c. made K. all too familiar with the gross injustice of the Jim Crow laws. Incidents he recalled found their way into his later fiction. His family's church in Macon served as the headquarters of a labor campaign called "Operation Dixie," a drive to organize black and white workers together, and K. observed white opposition to the movement and heroic black support for it. K. moved to Washington, D.C. at twenty and took a position on the National Labor Relations Board. He served there except during World War II (when he fought in the Pacific Amphibian Forces of the U.S. Army) until he was disillusioned with the movement for its inability to overcome racial differences.

In the 1950s, K. became known for his literary efforts. He cofounded the Harlem Writers' Guild, a group that provided a forum for many illustrious African American writers early in that decade. There he began to polish what would become his first novel, *Youngblood* (1954). *Youngblood* tells the story of a black Southern family during Jim Crow and the struggles of its members to receive fair treatment. The father, Joe Youngblood, eventually dies as a civil rights martyr, but K. allows his characters to demonstrate their creator's faith that whites and blacks could come to recognize their common humanity. Drawing on K.'s experiences, the novel suggests that organized labor provides the best hope for racial brotherhood. Critics generally admired the novel, though not all were taken with K.'s vernacular style. His second novel aimed self-consciously to be "the great American war novel." *And Then We Heard the Thunder* (1963) again incorporates parts of K.'s past to describe the experiences of a segregated amphibious Army unit. K. shows the bitter irony for African American soldiers of being asked to defend a democracy in which their participation is limited. The novel ends in the middle of a battle—based on historical events—that breaks out between black and white American soldiers; the unresolved ending offers evidence of K.'s artistic growth. Critics observed that some characters are mere mouthpieces for the author's views, a charge repeatedly leveled against K. and generally accepted as a fair critique of his style, but the writing more often transcends this occasional didacticism and the work is considered K.'s finest.

K. threw his efforts into the civil rights movement beginning in 1954, but he gradually moved from supporting Martin Luther King, Jr., to working with Malcolm X and embracing the cause of black nationalism.

His essay collection, *Black Man's Burden* (1965), traces this shift in his political views. In the late 1960s, K. worked as a writer-in-residence at Fisk University in Nashville, where he finished *'Sippi* (1967). K.'s new militance is everywhere evident in this work, including the title, based on a civil rights joke about a black Southerner's refusal to address Mississippi with undue respect. The novel received mixed reviews; K. himself valued it less than its predecessors. His fourth novel, the last published in his lifetime, was a biting satire of absurdities in the black community entitled *Cotillion; or, One Good Bull is Half the Herd* (1971). The book ridicules African Americans who are out of touch with their culture while simultaneously affirming K.'s respect for the beauty and vitality of that culture. *Cotillion* ranked as K.'s second major success as a writer.

The significance of K.'s novels continues to be debated; as a stylist, he often allows his interest in social protest to triumph over his interest in the characters. As a leader, however, his importance is scarcely questioned; his reputation as an activist and an inspiration to writers of his own and succeeding generations seems assured.

BIBLIOGRAPHY: Bell, B. W., *The Afro-American Novel and Its Tradition* (1987): 245–53; Harris, N., *Connecting Times: The Sixties in Afro-American Fiction* (1988): 140–65; Wiggins, W., "Structure and Dynamics of Folklore: The Case of J. O. K.," *KFQ* 17 (1972): 92–118

CAROLYN LENGEL

KILMER, [Alfred] Joyce
b. 6 December 1886, New Brunswick, New Jersey; d. 30 July 1918, Seringe, France

After finishing his undergraduate education at Rutgers and Columbia, K. began a conventional career in journalism and publishing, employed at various times by the *Standard Dictionary,* the *Churchman,* and the *New York Times.* He wrote a number of essays, reviews, and articles, including an appreciation of Thomas Hardy's *The Mayor of Casterbridge.* Volumes of his poetry began appearing: *Summer of Love* (1911), *Trees and Other Poems* (1914), and *Main Street and Other Poems* (1917).

When the U.S. entered World War I in 1917, K. enlisted with the 7th Regiment of the New York National Guard, later transferring to the 165th Regiment (formerly the "Fighting 69th"). A convert to Catholicism, K. served with a group of Irishmen whose problems and exploits were dramatized in the popular movie *The Fighting 69th,* in which K. was a minor character. K. served gallantly and was killed in action within four months of the end of the war, receiving a posthumous Croix de Guerre from the French government.

If he had survived the war, K. might have gone on to continue work as a minor poet and marginal literary journalist with an admirable character but no particular distinction. His death at thirty-one, however, subjected his reputation to a cruel fate. He was inflated into a hero, a martyr, and a great and noble poet for whom national forests would be named. Hero and martyr he may well have been, but he was not a great poet, and his works could not stand up under very probing scrutiny. "Trees" was set to music and made into a literary scapegoat for generations of critics and teachers reluctant to tackle a worthier target. The poem had been published in *Poetry,* and it expresses a fairly uncomplicated sentiment in favor of natural objects that everybody likes. The problem seems to be that K. has applied human anatomy to a tree, with grotesque results: the mouth is pressed against the earth's breast, but the eye looks at God and the arms are lifted in prayer, the hair meanwhile being distributed between (or under) the arms and eyes, also the location of the bosom. Never has a poem once so admired been so bitterly denounced.

K. had little respect for consistency or authenticity, so that he would bend the truth to fit an expedient emotion. It is to his credit that he wrote poems in praise of such fellow poets as Gerard Manley Hopkins, Rupert Brooke, and Lionel Johnson, but it is not to his credit that he had to falsify so many facts about them. Even so, he was paying attention to Hopkins before Robert Bridges finally got around to publishing the long-delayed *Collected Poems* in 1918, twenty-nine years after Hopkins's death.

A further distinction is that K. served as an irritant or catalyst for the creation of what most agree is one of the greatest modern poems, William Butler Yeats's "Easter 1916." Yeats's "September 1913" ridiculed the morally costive Irish. With the failure of the insurrection in 1916, K.'s "Easter Week" spoke to Yeats directly and stridently: "'Romantic Ireland's dead and gone, / It's with O'Leary in the grave.' / Then, Yeats, what gave that Eastern dawn / A hue so radiantly brave?" When Yeats prepared his poem on the subject, he seems not to have considered K.'s challenge, but he did borrow the manner of K.'s "Apology," another poem in the same volume as "Easter Week": "Lord Byron and Shelley and Plunkett, / McDonough and Hunt and Pearse / See now why their hatred of tyrants / Was so insistently fierce." It is almost inconceivable that Yeats could have hammered out the resonant roll-call in "Easter 1916" —"MacDonagh and MacBride /

And Connolly and Pearse"—without the provocation and example furnished by K.

BIBLIOGRAPHY: Holliday, R. C., *J. K.: Poems, Essays, and Letters* (2 vols., 1918, 1921); McGinty, B., "J. K.: Soldier and Poet," *AHI* 22 (May 1987): 46–47

WILLIAM HARMON

KIM, Richard

b. 13 March 1932, Hamhung City, Korea (now North Korea)

K. was born in Korea in 1932 and for the first seven years of his life, he lived in Japanese-controlled Manchuria. K.'s father had been jailed repeatedly for anti-Japanese activities, and lived the life of a political exile for over a decade, often having to move. K. attended a Christian missionary kindergarten and later a Japanese elementary school, where he, along with all other students, was forbidden to speak Korean.

At the age of eighteen, K. joined the South Korean forces as a liaison officer to the United National forces, assigned to an English-speaking unit. At the end of the war in 1953, K. came to the U.S. to complete his studies at Middlebury College, Vermont. Later, he held a University Fellowship at Johns Hopkins, a Writers' Workshop Fellowship at the University of Iowa, and a Ford Foundation Foreign Area Fellowship at Harvard. K. received a master's degree in Far Eastern literature at Harvard University, and taught at the University of Massachusetts from 1969 to 1990.

Published in 1964, K.'s first novel entitled *The Martyred* is a story of spiritual heroism set against the background of the Korean War. His second autobiographical novel, *Lost Names* (1970), draws on the themes of his early years in exile in Manchuria, and a young boy's adoration of his hero-father, who resists British rule with strength and integrity. His last novel, *The Innocent,* received high critical acclaim, and was published in 1972. K. is also the author of a children's book entitled *A Blue Bird* (1983) as well as two collections of essays, *In Search of Lost Years* (1985) and *In Search of Lost Koreans in China and Russia* (1989).

BIBLIOGRAPHY:, Goar, R. J., "The Humanism of R. K.," *MQ* 21 (1980): 450–69; Valdes, M. J., "Faith and Despair: A Comparative Study of Narrative Theme," *Hispania* 49 (1966): 373–79

ALICE SCHARPER

KIM, Ronyoung

b. 28 March 1926, Los Angeles, California; d. 3 February 1987, Marin County, California

K., also known as Gloria Hahn, is widely recognized by Asian American critics for her novel chronicling

Korean American experiences between the two world wars, a story that has largely remained untold. Published in 1986, *Clay Walls* poignantly recalls the limited residential, educational, and employment opportunities afforded to Korean Americans in the U.S. as well as their own frustrated efforts to free Korea from Japanese colonization. Drawing on themes common to Asian American literature, K. explores the complex history of Korean Americans as well as the shifting boundaries of identity as they come to terms with the loss of family, home, and nation.

Based on the experiences of K.'s parents and of her own adolescence, the novel tells a multilayered story that revolves around numerous conflicts surrounding issues of race, class, and gender. The first of three sections is told from the point of view of Haesu, a Korean woman of the "yangban," a privileged class in Korea. Her efforts, and ultimately her failure, to maintain that identity in the U.S. is the basis for much of the story's progression, and K. documents the racial discrimination that defeats Haesu's efforts to rent an apartment, buy a home, or enroll her children in an exclusive military school. The challenges to Haesu's definitions and her identity continue when Haesu returns to Korea. Its colonization by Japan, the suppression of Korean language and culture, and the abuses done to the Korean peoples further leave Haesu bereft of home and self.

In the second section, K. contrasts Haesu's crumbling "clay walls" with her husband Chun's more fatalistic existence, and constructs his character as a foil to Haesu's in terms of class and gender. His farming background is the target for much of Haesu's contempt, while his raping of her and his control over the family's finances asserts his patriarchal power. K.'s naturalistic treatment of Chun emphasizes his lack of control and the inevitability of his demise. He ultimately loses the family's business and life savings to a gambler, who many suspect of cheating, and accepts the outcome as part of a fate that has relegated him to the losing side of a lifelong game. K. contrasts this passivity with Haesu's will to succeed and highlights the futility of both characters' efforts to control their destinies in the U.S. The last section is devoted to their daughter's Faye's grappling with the legacies that her parents have left her. Chun has died far from home while trying to find work, while Haesu has been restricted to working within the home. K. begins here to explore the notion of an Asian American versus a Korean American identity, a distinction all the more significant with the advent of World War II and the struggle by other Asian Americans to distinguish and distance themselves from Japanese Americans.

Although K. died shortly after *Clay Walls* was finished, her writing stands as testament to the triumph involved in breaking through the "clay walls" that have traditionally defined and restricted Korean Americans. Her novel links Haesu's, Chun's, and Faye's stories into a complex whole that articulates the desires, frustrations, and contradictions that distinguish the experiences of Korean Americans in the U.S.

BIBLIOGRAPHY: Lee, A. R., "Eat a Bowl of Tea: Asian American in the Novels of Gish Jen, Cynthia Kadohata, K. R., Jessica Hagedorn, and Tian Van Dinh," *YES* 24 (1994): 263–80; Yun, Chung-Hei, "Beyond 'Clay Walls': Korean American Literature," in Lim, S. G.-L., and A. Ling, eds., *Reading the Literatures of Asian America* (1992): 79–96

CHRISTINE SO

KINCAID, Jamaica
b. 25 May 1949, St. Johns, Antigua

As a self-exile of her Caribbean homeland, K. transgresses the boundaries of language and culture and delivers the words that unmask her truth: the impossible longing for freedom. Hélène Cixous has stated that there are certain writers who locate themselves in places "to which we do have difficulties traveling," but as we must do with K.'s writing, "it's our work, our mission, all of us who are readers, to go to that country." The site that K. claims and to which we go is her childhood in Antigua, a time in which her protagonists battle with ambivalence. K. has stated that she writes fiction that is autobiographical because she "started to write out of this need . . . to settle demons and settle scores."

In her early collection of dreamlike stories, *At the Bottom of the River* (1983), and in her best-known novel, *Annie John* (1985), K.'s vision is fixed on the coming of age of a young girl, a time in which K. frames self-affirmation and development as an ominous act that bears the backlash of deprivation: the loss of innocence, that once symbiotically bound a daughter to her mother and her country, and the rage that follows. Therefore, K.'s journey takes her back to the family, at the core of which is the mystical powers of the mother and the desire of a young girl to return to the womb, to safety and wholeness. However, K. shows us that there is danger residing within this return.

In *Annie John,* the reader is presented with the effects of female identification seen through the eyes of an extraordinarily shrewd and imaginative young girl, fraught with guilt, who aligns herself with the figure of Lucifer, the fallen angel. Annie's growing need for independence eventually leads to a debilitating union of pride, self-loathing, and shame as she begins to fight the colonial structure and that part of her mother which is fastened to that system. This conflict leads K.'s protagonist, at the age of fifteen, to a nervous breakdown, named by the character as a "condition," which endures for a period of three and a half months. It is her grandmother, Ma Chess, who comes to take care of her, somehow knowing that Annie needs to be remothered: "Sometimes at night, when I would feel that I was all locked up in the warm falling soot and could not find my way out, Ma Chess would come into my bed with me and stay until I was myself—whatever that had come to be by then—again."

At the Bottom of the River, which contains her signature piece "Girl," is a less explicit mining—than that in *Annie John*—of female identity and Antiguan culture. In these stories, K. uses tropes, such as the wingless pupa in "Wingless," to embody the psychic life of the young girl, powerless in the face of her mother upon whom she is dependent. In "Blackness," she constructs a ghostly language that traces itself out of the dreams and fear of a young girl emotionally paralyzed, unable to find solace and constancy from her family. Yet it is ironically this same fear that drives K.'s protagonists, and in "Blackness" writing becomes the means towards deliverance, while in *Annie John,* our last image of this young girl, leaving for England by boat, is quite promising. In a radio interview, K. said, "By the transforming powers of the imagination, what appears to have been irretrievably lost may be recuperated—indeed in the very energy involved in violent and destructive acts reside the seeds of creativity."

K.'s writing is ground within paradox, looking towards the past yet moving towards expectation, and in *At the Bottom of the River* the young women we encounter are dangerously ensnared within the confusion of their conflicting needs. In both "Blackness" and *Annie John,* the protagonists have nervous breakdowns, but in "Blackness" the brutality of the character's condition is imparted through a much more pronounced textual atmosphere of fragmentation and loss in which K. ushers forth poetic imagery and rhythm. As the nameless character states, "In the blackness, then, I have been erased. I can no longer say my own name. I can no longer point to myself and say 'I.'"

"Girl," in *At the Bottom of the River,* functions as an interior monologue (not a dreamscape like the other stories in this collection), in which we hear the incessant demands of a mother, warning her daughter to conform. It is here that K. intersects the language and authority of imperialism through an outpour of words, letting loose the subject in process in a kind of innocence that overturns, and so manipulates syntax and semantics. This kind of polemic is reinvented in *A Small Place* (1988), a substantial essay that is concerned with the political and social identity of Antigua

and its deterioration under first British rule and then self-rule, which K. saw as being littered with a corrupt government that continued to undermine its majority. In the first of four sections, K. focuses on the role of tourism in her native land. Seeking her reader out, she speaks in second person (as a kind of threatening superego), exclaiming, "You disembark from your plane. You go through customs. Since you are a tourist, a North American or European—to be frank, white—and not an Antiguan black returning to Antigua from Europe or North America with much needed cheap clothes and food for relatives, you move through customs with ease." Later in the text, K. exposes herself as the speaker; thus, accepting her own accountability as she takes the reader on a historical and cultural tour of her country, one in which stark truth and images replace illusions of Caribbean paradise.

Lucy (1990) sees K.'s authorial persona in New York, a speaker and representative of the silenced others; Lucy is a continuation of Annie, a young woman of nineteen who has come to work as an au pair in the household of a wealthy family, as did K. when she arrived in New York. Similar to *A Small Place,* K. sets Lucy up as a means through which others come to face themselves through her gaze. What we see begin in *At the Bottom of the River* and continue in *Annie John* is the individuation of a young woman, and this is most certainly advanced in *Lucy,* who has gained autonomy. Yet again we return to the allusion of Lucifer, for as Lucy states, with her autonomy she is left with no certainty of place; she has cast herself out of paradise and now has no home. In this struggle, Lucy yearns for her mother but knows that she cannot allow herself to return. But K. does return, at least in her writing, to her mother in the *Autobiography of My Mother* (1994).

K. has won numerous prizes, among them the Morton Dauwen Zabel Award of the American Academy and Institute of Arts and Letters for *At the Bottom of the River.* Her storytelling is exciting, her language poetic, and she is a writer who captures readers within her experience, rendering a transaction that frames all the selves within the discourse of her texts.

BIBLIOGRAPHY: Dutton, W., "Merge and Separate: J. K.'s Fiction," *WLT* 63 (Summer 1989): 406–10; Ferguson, M., *J. K.: Where the Land Meets the Body* (1994); Simmons, D., *J. K.* (1994)

LISA TOLHURST

KING, Clarence [Rivers]

b. 6 January 1842, Newport, Rhode Island; d. 24 December 1901, Phoenix, Arizona

The modern reputation of K. is less that of a writer of American literature than that of a colorful friend to such writers of the period as Henry ADAMS and John HAY. Time has served K. poorly—in large part, because his most significant and substantial literary contributions dealt with scientific geology; and that geology, sophisticated enough in its day, has been largely superseded in the years since K. wrote. In this way, K. has been made a victim of the very forces of scientific change that he welcomed avidly in his work and life. At present, then, it is his life, and especially the unanswered questions concerning the secret life that never entered his books and essays, that continues to interest us.

On the surface, K. was the magical American of his generation, a brilliant conversationalist whose wealthy lifestyle invited envy from those who knew him or merely knew of him. His vivid personality and advanced scientific training offered a special blend of charm and erudition that marked K. out as a symbolic representative of a consciously modern, post–Civil War age. His presence was welcomed in society—high and low—in the West, back East, and in the capital cities of Europe. Little did the women and men who met him suspect that K. had reason to keep much of his life, especially the details of his personal life, a secret from even his closest friends, including Henry and Marian Adams. In truth, K. lived a double life, and he used both his writing and his science to create the public image that shielded his marriage and his private life from observation and criticism. For his peers, he was a virtuoso—as a scientific leader, mining engineer, nature writer, mountaineer, art critic, and trusted adviser to men and women in high places.

Today, K. is remembered chiefly as the friend of Henry Adams whose story becomes a modern parable of failure, in the pages of *The Education of Henry Adams*. That best-selling book, published some seventeen years after K.'s death, has served K. badly. Neither his literary talent nor the fact of his international renown receives adequate recognition, even though, at the time of K.'s death in 1901, he was far better known to the general public than was Adams, who had yet to write his two famous books, *The Education of Henry Adams* and *Mont-Saint-Michel and Chartres*.

K. himself was born in 1842—an eighth-generation son in a prominent Rhode Island family that boasted a long history in the China trade. His father, James Rivers King, died when K. was six; and the child grew up under the strongest kind of maternal influence, which can be traced into K.'s middle age, at least until he reached forty-five. And even then, his biographer concedes, "the anxious demands of a doting mother" continued to determine the course of her son's life.

Already, Mrs. K. had succeeded in thwarting her son's intentions to marry a Virginian City, Colorado, school teacher, of whom she did not approve; and up to the moment of K.'s death, her influence remained strong as she outlived him. K.'s mother attempted to manage large portions of K.'s life, directing his attention, for example, to polite literature rather than to science as a proper path for his career. Yet, while his interest in writing did grow with his knowledge of the world, especially the exciting new world of post-Darwinian science, K. never really accepted literature as an adequate vocation, any more than he limited himself to pure science in the form of scientific research. Instead, he insisted on making practical (and commercial) applications of his geologic knowledge, as a consultant and participant, in mining and engineering. K. was a spectacular (if not always successful) performer in both.

Except for the traumatic interlude cased by his father's death, there is little evidence of an exceptional childhood in K.'s life history. He did show early promise in science, but also in languages and English composition. The first real decision of his life was made in 1860, when the boy turned his back on mother and Yale, choosing instead to attend the briefer course of instruction at the Sheffield School—at that time, a much less prestigious part of Yale. On balance, however, except for those two years at Sheffield and a later set of lectures from famed geologist Louis Agassiz, K.'s formal education remained overwhelmingly classical and traditional. Not surprisingly then, his writing style throughout his career owed much to old models and forms, and little to any scientific novelty. What his years in the exciting environment at Sheffield actually provided the young man was a network of important friendships—a valuable membership in the rather exclusive club of Sheffield students and faculty who looked after each other professionally, as together they set about putting forces of state and national government to work in developing science.

With the coming of the Civil War, in 1863, K. went West, instead of to the War. Using his Sheffield connections, he joined the California Geological Survey, then under the leadership of Josiah Dwight Whitney. The next five years in the West would prove crucial in K.'s career. What he saw and did from the time he left the East until he completed field work on the Geological Exploration of the Fortieth Parallel (often called the Fortieth Parallel Survey), in 1869, provided the colorful material for the writings that made K.'s literary reputation. Appointed in 1867 by President Andrew Johnson as U.S. Geologist in charge of the Fortieth Parallel Survey, K. rapidly became aware that he had secured a political and scientific plum at an unusually early age. Yet there was a price to pay: soon, all too soon in his view, he had to leave the exciting life of outdoor exploration, and take up the more routine literary duties that would prove he had done his Western work in a manner acceptable to his profession, his family, and his Eastern friends. In the 1870s, this meant organizing and editing all of the many publications deriving from the Survey. But in a larger way, the practical geologist-turned-writer also seized the opportunity to become a public figure. With skillful publicity, K. made himself the representative Westerner. He became both author and hero of a personal saga of exploration. Even in scientific writing, K. found room for romance.

First, K. gathered together all the incidental essays he had published since he began writing about the West; then, he added some new material, and printed *Mountaineering in the Sierra Nevada* (1872). This book has since become a classic of both mountaineering and western life, largely because, in his descriptions, K. managed to combine the expert knowledge of a keen geologist with the romantic artist's feelings about the grandeur of Western topography; to this mix, he added skillful storytelling. In *Mountaineering,* each chapter is an individual gem, and readers have responded enthusiastically to the author's invitation to admire each one of them as he does—in the same way they might admire the picture on a postcard. In fact, such visual appeal provides the key ingredient in K.'s literary success here.

Despite the fact that K.'s next important book did not appear as the first volume published from the survey, his *Systematic Geology* (1878) is designated on the spine as volume one. In that thick volume (now little read), there is evidence of the author's imaginative leadership among his scientific peers. Since so much has happened in geology and geological theory in more than one hundred years, however, *Systematic Geology* must now be regarded as a neglected touchstone in geological history. Yet, at the time of its publication, K.'s book excited reviewers and scientists alike; it offered the reader a masterful demonstration of the author's broad scientific learning; and it represented "the highest point yet reached by government publishing in America." Today, the book remains important as a monument—primarily, to the value of the Survey, but also to the clear-sighted intelligence and easy grace of its author. Unfortunately, K. never again reached the heights of professional and public acclaim that he knew in 1879.

What the public learned of K. during the years after *Systematic Geology* can be described as a succession of brief personal triumphs and longer-term financial failures. Simply, he made and lost fortunes in cattle ranching and mining—playing always for life's big prizes, and spurning such quiet academic retreats as the professorships constantly being offered by American universities. Such friends as the Adamses welcomed his irregular appearances among them, and everyone wondered what K. was doing when he disappeared from view. In answer to questions, he always claimed to be at work on a sensational literary project—perhaps a novel to rival in popularity John Hay's *The Bread-Winners* or Henry Adams's *Democracy,* or possibly another masterwork of geology to compare with *Systematic Geology.* Yet, except for a single magazine article, "The Helmet of Mambrino" (1886), nothing appeared from K.'s pen to justify the promise he had shown in the 1870s. Still, when that piece reached readers of the *Century,* they were treated to a classic bit of travel writing, in the manner of Washington IRVING, based on K.'s European wanderings in 1882. Like Irving, K. fell in love with Spain; and, instead of geologizing in the mining country around Rio Tinto and Bilbao, he followed his fancy, to write this chapter as a continuation of Cervantes's *Don Quixote.* Mambrino's helmet, in reality, was nothing more than a barber's basin; and K. sent just such a basin to his Spanish friend, Don Hortio Cutter, along with the manuscript chapter. Brief though the essay is, K.'s claim to talent remains unmistakable.

A much sadder story describes K.'s life after 1888, even though it was largely unknown at the time even to his friends, his mother, and the public. That story tells of a secret marriage to Ada Todd, a Negro nursemaid more than twenty-five years K.'s junior, with whom he maintained a residence in New York State, where their marriage was legally valid. In view of K.'s unusual personality, it is hardly surprising to find that the relationship was kept secret; but the additional fact, that Ada Todd King did not learn—until after her husband's death in 1901—the true identity of the husband who fathered her five children, makes the description almost incredible. No wonder Henry Adams was led to declare: "One C. K. only exited in the world."

For K. himself, the burdens of supporting this secret New York household contributed to the financial and personal crisis that sent the geologist to Bloomingdale Asylum in 1893, for recovery from a "mental disturbance" (certified by his physicians). From that time until his lonely death in 1901, K. wavered between hope and despair. His best years as a scientist and a writer were long past, and he confessed that his life had created a record of failures.

Yet, like his talent for brilliant conversation, K. also retained, almost to the end, that playful optimism that had marked his earlier life. In one of the last letters he was to write, K. declared: "I am fuller of geological ideas than ever, and I shall mass and publish them if I get a reprieve." No reprieve was ever granted K.; so it was left to Henry Adams to compose the final portrait that has kept K. alive in the pages of *The Education of Henry Adams.*

BIBLIOGRAPHY: Wilkins, T., *C. K.: A Biography* (1958); Young, B., *Frontier Scientist: C. K.* (1968)

EARL N. HARBERT

KING, Grace [Elizabeth]

b. 29 November 1852, New Orleans, Louisiana; d. 12 January 1932, New Orleans, Louisiana

Long recognized as a Southern apologist and Louisiana local colorist, K. has more recently been viewed as a postbellum writer of surprising subtlety and versatility, the author of fiction as well as history, biography, and a graceful, if reticent, autobiography, *Memories of a Southern Woman of Letters* (1932).

K. was the daughter of a prominent Protestant family in New Orleans, and her loyalties and fiction were deeply etched by the upheavals of the Civil War. Indeed, she began her first story, "Monsieur Motte" (1888), in response to a casual challenge from editor Richard Watson Gilder to "write better" of her time and place than she and other offended Southerners felt that George Washington CABLE had done.

Though her plots and characters typically rely on local color, K. often imbues this material with interesting social and sexual undercurrents. In both *Tales of a Time and Place* (1892) and *Balcony Stories* (1893), her best-known volume, K. consistently focuses on the intricate relationships that race, class and culture both foster and inhibit, especially among women. In stories like "The Little Convent Girl" (1893), which reveals the devastating consequences of a child's discovery that her mother is black, K. unsettles her conventional perspectives with delicate understatement and a style whose lightness and irony bear the marks of her French education and reading. A structural diffuseness sometimes obscures her impressionistic effects, especially in longer works, like her episodic novel, *The Pleasant Ways of St. Medard* (1916).

Recent criticism of K.'s achievement—her rather oblique narratives, her descriptive nuances, and her intimate focus on women's lives—has given new impetus to her reputation. Though she worked in genres and from a perspective of gender, race, and class that encouraged a nostalgic propriety, the fineness of her perceptions and craft produced a sensitive and complex portrait of her era.

BIBLIOGRAPHY: Bush, R., *G. K.: A Southern Destiny* (1983); Elfenbein, A. S., *Women on the Color Line* (1989); Kirby, D., *G. K.* (1980); Taylor, H., *Gender, Race, and Region in the Writings of G. K., Ruth McEnery Stuart, and Kate Chopin* (1989)

BARBARA C. EWELL

KING, Stephen

b. 21 September 1947, Portland, Maine

If one were to look in a recent American dictionary under the heading "best-seller," one might well find a picture of K. His works—which include more than twenty novels, dozens of short stories, a nonfiction discussion of horror, and screenplays—have sold millions of copies and have been translated into numerous languages. He has probably single-handedly done more to popularize the horror genre than any other 20th-c. American writer; and, in many ways, he may be regarded as a modern Edgar Allan POE. Yet while K. is indisputably a major figure in contemporary American letters, no one—including, probably, K. himself—would argue that he is a great literary artist. He is, ultimately, a highly talented storyteller with an uncanny ability to tap into the fears of people in modern society.

K.'s standard formula places ordinary people—people like us—in extraordinary, terrifying situations. His first novel, *Carrie* (1974), tells of a repressed high school girl with telekinetic powers, who is tormented by both her peers and her zealously religious mother, and who ultimately takes brutal revenge at her senior prom. *Carrie* was followed by *Salem's Lot* (1975), a tale of vampires in rural Maine. A native of Maine himself, K. uses New England locales—particularly the town of Derry, Maine—in many of his works.

K.'s third novel, *The Shining* (1977), is a classic modern horror story. Accompanied by his wife and their young son Danny, Jack Torrance, a novelist and recovering alcoholic, is hired as the winter caretaker of The Overlook, a mountain resort. As one might expect in a K. novel, the hotel is haunted by numerous lost souls, chief among which is the former caretaker, who, years earlier, went insane and killed his own wife and daughters. The spirits of the hotel, the isolation of the wintry landscape, and a maddening case of writer's block all take their toll on Jack, who, by the end of the novel, is ready to follow in the footsteps of his murderous ghostly predecessor. K.'s description of Jack's gradual descent into madness is terrifying, and many readers consider *The Shining* K.'s masterpiece.

The Shining was followed by *The Stand* (1978; rev. ed., 1990), an epic novel in which some ninety-five percent of the population of the U.S. (and presumably the world) is wiped out by the accidental release of a government-created "superflu." The survivors divide into two camps ("good" and "evil"), and the book describes the inevitable final conflict between these two forces. Despite the rather simplistic themes, *The Stand* features some vintage K. writing—particularly in his descriptions of the devastation caused by the superflu and in his engaging portraits of a large cast of characters.

In K.'s next novel, *The Dead Zone* (1979), a schoolteacher named Johnny Smith awakes from a coma after more than four years to discover that he has developed telepathic powers. This enables him to see a future in which the U.S. is ruled by a fascist dictator who unleashes a nuclear holocaust, which Johnny determines to prevent by killing the dictator before he can be elected president. Many critics consider *The Dead Zone* among K.'s finest work, particularly because of its skillful characterizations.

K.'s subsequent works have continued to be successful, although he has not produced anything—at least in the genre of horror—to compare to his earlier works. *Different Seasons* (1982) is a collection of four novellas which—with the exception of the final story—cannot be labeled "horror"; most noteworthy are "The Body"—a semiautobiographical story of a group of teenage boys who undertake a journey to see a dead body—and "Rita Hayworth and the Shawshank Redemption"—about a man wrongly imprisoned for murder—both of which were adapted into enormously successful films. Another of K.'s best works that does not strictly fit the horror label is *Misery* (1987), about a writer who is badly injured in an auto accident and then held hostage by his "number one fan," a psychotic nurse. K. has also produced an ongoing "serial novel," *The Dark Tower,* of which four volumes—*The Gunslinger* (1982), *The Drawing of the Three* (1989), *The Waste Lands* (1992), and *Wizard and Glass* (1996) —have so far been published. This is a fantasy about the adventures of a gunslinger, Roland, and his companions as they travel through a sort of parallel universe in an attempt to unravel the secrets of the Dark Tower.

In addition to novels, K. has also published numerous short stories, many of which have been collected in *Night Shift* (1978), *Skeleton Crew* (1985), and *Nightmares and Dreamscapes* (1993); *Four Past Midnight* (1990) is another collection of novellas. *S. K.'s Danse Macabre* (1981) is a nonfiction book about the art and craft of horror; in it, K. proves to be a skillful and engaging essayist. K. also produced several novels under the pseudonym Richard Bachman, four of which—*Rage, Road Work, The Long Walk,* and *The Running Man*—are collected in *The Bachman Books* (1985), and another two—*Thinner* (1984) and *The Regulators* (1996)—which were published in separate volumes (after Bachman's true identity had been revealed). K. has also produced screenplays for several

of his works. K.'s best-selling *Bag of Bones* (1998) was followed by a 1999 publication, *Hearts of Atlantis*.

The practically nonstop pace of K.'s writing suggests that he will produce many more novels in his lifetime. Whether he ever manages to gain widespread critical acceptance remains to be seen. But whatever the final judgment of his works turns out to be, K. is among the most popular literary figures in late-20th-c. American writing.

BIBLIOGRAPHY: Hoppenstand, G., and R. B. Browne, eds., *The Gothic World of S. K.* (1987); Magistrale, A. S., *Landscape of Fear: S. K.'s American Gothic* (1988); Schweitzer, D., ed., *Discovering S. K.* (1985); Underwood, T., and C. Miller, *Fear Itself: The Horror Fiction of S. K.* (1982); Underwood, T., and C. Miller, *Kingdom of Fear: The World of S. K.* (1986)

JASON BERNER

KINGSLEY, Sidney [Kirschner]

b. 22 October 1906, Philadelphia, Pennsylvania; d. 20 March 1995, Oakland, New Jersey

A leading American playwright in the years surrounding World War II, K. was known for his richly detailed dramas of social concerns. His dramaturgy favored realism, though his stagings ranged from the actual to the abstract. In his plays, K. used debate between an idealist and a cynic to explore the action's larger implications. K.'s best work features complex characters caught in difficult, compelling situations that, though often commonplace, reverberate with greater significance. With time his style has grown dated, but the issues in his plays still ring true.

K.'s first successful work was *Men in White* (1933), a hospital drama that explored the issues of medicine and abortion. Produced by the Group Theatre, *Men in White* gained recognition for its fine acting and its careful reenactment of hospital procedure, including an onstage operation. The close attention to detail, the naturalistic style and themes, the sharply conflicted characterizations all became hallmarks of K.'s writing. *Men in White* won the Pulitzer Prize.

K. followed two years later with *Dead End* (1935), which portrayed a New York City street gang. Tough, insightful, and compelling, *Dead End* depicts children's lives with a sociological understanding and a carefully placed compassion. The children of the tenements are juxtaposed in sharp and telling contrast against a backdrop of affluent high-rise apartments. They are both victims and victimizers, caught in a vicious, devolving cycle. Though dated, the characters are memorable and the play demonstrates K.'s ability to create powerful and convincing drama.

Ten Million Ghosts (1936) and *The World We Make* (1939) both proved failures. The former, an antiwar piece, centered on a conflict during World War I within the French and German branches of a family of arms manufacturers. K. made great use of multimedia to accompany his story. The latter play, an adaptation of Millen Brand's novel *The Outward Room* (1937), recounted the efforts of a mental patient trying to live a normal life.

While serving in the army, K. wrote *The Patriots* (1943), which portrayed the rivalry between Thomas JEFFERSON and Alexander Hamilton and the process by which Jefferson was elected President. The author preserved the characters' mythic stature, yet imbued them with a comfortable humanity. *The Patriots* won the prestigious New York Critics Circle Award.

K. wrote from extensive and thorough research. For *Men in White,* he spent considerable time in New York hospitals observing procedures and also studied the history of medicine. In the case of *Dead End,* he observed street children in New York, and drew upon studies in the "biology of the environment" and economics. For *The Patriots,* K. studied the American Revolution and examined the papers of Jefferson and Hamilton. He brought the same careful preparation to his next successful play, *Detective Story* (1949), spending much time in a police station observing the people, setting and events.

Detective Story dealt with a fanatical policemen who, viewing himself as a moral arbiter, placed himself above the law. Distraught after learning his wife once had an abortion, he collapses and is killed by a suspected burglar. K. wrote the melodrama to criticize governmental officials who claimed moral authority when ignoring the law. But the play is largely remembered for its subplots represented by the various criminals brought through the police station.

K. then dramatized Arthur Koestler's novel, *Darkness at Noon* (1951). Critics praised his techniques for enacting the private, solitary thoughts of political prisons in pre-World War II Communist Russia. *Darkness at Noon* won K. his second New York Drama Critics Circle Award.

The frantic comedy *Lunatics and Lovers* (1954) brought K. his final success. The play tells of New York con men, policemen and lovers romping through a hotel. *Lunatics and Lovers* appeared in striking contrast to K.'s previous plays, all serious dramas of deep social concern. The playwright's final play was *Night Life* (1962), which portrayed a bevy of characters who haunt a night spot, all with their various woes.

BIBLIOGRAPHY: Baily, P. M., "S. K.," in MacNicholas, J., ed., *DLB*, vol. 2, part 2, *Twentieth Century American Dramatists* (1981): 31–41; Couch, N. ed., *S. K.: Five Prizewinning Plays* (1995)

STUART J. HECHT

KINGSOLVER, Barbara

b. 8 April 1955, Annapolis, Maryland

K. enjoys the reputation of a best-selling novelist who adeptly manages to combine entertainment with political activism. Although an accomplished poet, journalist, and nonfiction writer, it is her accessible tales of self-formed families and interdependent women living in the American West that have secured her a worldwide readership. Her fiction explores central themes of relationship, responsibility, and community, subjects that have consistently earned her critical acclaim. Although some have taken her to task for promoting such conservative values under the disguise of progressive politics, she is invariably recognized as a gifted narrative voice.

The protagonist of K.'s first novel, *The Bean Trees* (1988), shares some history with her creator; like Taylor Greer, K. is a Kentucky native who moved to Tucson, Arizona. The account of Taylor's trip cross country and the physically and emotionally abused child who is abandoned in her car during a pit stop on a Cherokee reservation form the basis for K.'s most successful novel. Taylor and Turtle, so named for her reptilian grip on her surrogate mother and all other objects of solace, make a home and family with Lou Ann Ruiz, another single parent, and Mattie, a widow who employs Taylor in her automotive garage and shelters Central American refugees as part of the Sanctuary movement.

The Bean Trees recounts Taylor's coming of age, and her dawning awareness of her responsibilities not only for a dependent child, but also for personal risk and individual political action in the face of injustice. In spite of such issues as child abuse, Native American rights, political persecution, and alcoholism, the novel is not a diatribe but a lively and profoundly humorous work that established K.'s light touch with a heavy subject. In *Animal Dreams* (1990), she employs a similar tactic; Codi Noline has returned to Grace, Arizona to care for her estranged and aging father. As she begins to correspond with her sister, an agronomist in Nicaragua aiding the Sandinistas in their fight against the U.S.-backed Contras, she develops a new perspective on her own power and takes action to save her town from an industrial polluter.

The characters who inhabit K.'s fictional world, and the audience whom she is targeting, are neither political radicals nor social dropouts; they are struggling and committed to surviving in their culture. K. repeatedly returns to ordinary, hard-working people, coping with the extraordinary strains of an economy and social system that are forcing more of them below the poverty line and out onto the margins. *Homeland and Other Stories* (1989), a collection of short fiction, is overtly anchored by K.'s commitment to ideas of community; each of the characters is, in some way, trying to find a home.

Pigs in Heaven (1993), the much anticipated sequel to *The Bean Trees,* demonstrates how difficult and demoralizing such a quest for community can be and the near-impossibility of surviving, much less of being a good parent, without one. Set three years later, *Pigs in Heaven* is thematically rooted in the tensions between individual and communal obligations. Taylor discovers that her adoption of Turtle is not legal because permission to adopt a Native American child was never obtained from the Cherokee Nation to which Turtle belongs. When a Cherokee attorney announces her intention to take the child back to her tribe, Taylor flees with her, cutting herself adrift from the social network that has helped her raise Turtle to this point. While struggling to earn enough to feed them, Taylor tries to avoid the judgmental surveillance of the social services system and experiences the bureaucratic tangle of free clinics and the desperate fear of the substandard child care that enables her to go to her low-paying jobs. While many understood the social commentary this offered K., this novel more than any other opened K. to criticism for unrealistically serendipitous circumstances and tidy endings. When Taylor's mother turns out to have relatives on Turtle's reservation, it permits a happy resolution that cements the child's ties to both her mother and her tribal community of birth.

K.'s *High Tide in Tucson* (1995) is a collection of essays that gives her the freedom to engage in social criticism without the fetters or obligations of fiction, and brings her journalistic experience to the fore. Her narrative style is very present even in these works, though, and admirers of her fiction might well enjoy her direct meditations on the same themes and issues that appear in her stories.

BIBLIOGRAPHY: Perry, D., *Backtalk: Women Writers Speak Out* (1993): 143–69; Rubenstein, R., "Homeric Resonances: Longing and Belonging in B. K.'s *Animal Dreams*," in Wiley, C., and F. R. Barnes, eds., *Homemaking: Women Writers and the Politics and Poetics of Home* (1996): 5–22; Ryan, M., "B. K.'s Lowfat Fiction," *JAC* 18 (Winter 1995): 77–82

ELIZABETH BLEICHER

KINGSTON, Maxine Hong
b. 27 October 1940, Stockton, California

The work of K. blurs distinctions between East and West by integrating Chinese tradition with American culture. Weaving together Chinese "talk-story," historical details, autobiography, and Western literary forms, K. "claims America" for those of Chinese ancestry by challenging pervasive stereotypes. K. is one of few Asian Americans whose work has garnered both critical acclaim and popular success. Her first book, *The Woman Warrior* (1976), won the National Book Critics Circle Award in nonfiction; *China Men* (1980) won the National Book Award in nonfiction.

In *Woman Warrior,* K. wades through the contradictions inherent in her dual heritages. Drawing from Chinese legend and details from her family background and childhood, K. depicts the lives of five women, both real and imagined. In telling each woman's story, K. traverses between China and the U.S. to reveal a combination of gender, class, and racial oppression. American life proves to be harsh and oppressive to the narrator's family. The inability of Moon Orchid, a maternal aunt, to adapt to immigrant life leads to insanity. Brave Orchid, the narrator's mother, also finds herself in a less powerful social situation. As a doctor in China, she resisted war, bandits, and superstition to administer to the sick and weak; in America, she operates a Chinese laundry and cannot protect her daughter from racism. Stereotyped as passive and unable to speak English, the narrator is branded an idiot with a "zero IQ." Despite America's indifference to Chinese experience, however, she comes to understand the value and importance of her ancestral culture. Influenced by her mother's "talk-story," the narrator transforms victimized women into agents of revenge. After Brave Orchid tells the story about the "No Name Woman," a paternal aunt who killed herself and the newborn baby she conceived out of wedlock, the narrator moves from imagining the aunt as a victim of rape to an agent of revenge. Elaborating sketchy details, she reconstructs her aunt's actions as a "spite" suicide; by drowning herself in the village drinking water, the aunt forced the community to remember the wrongs committed against her. Taking this story of vengeance as a model, the narrator begins to fight injustices wrought against Chinese Americans. Like the famed woman warrior, Fa Mu Lan, who has wrongs "carved" into her back, the narrator will battle her oppressors. She, too, has "chink" and "gook" words metaphorically written on her back; however, instead of a sword, she will use words to avenge wrongs.

The same daughter-narrator continues her investigation of Chinese experience in *China Men,* a companion text to *Woman Warrior.* Moving from the latter's focus on women, *China Men* describes the lives of the narrator's actual and spiritual "grandfathers" in response to their exclusion from U.S. history. Although Chinese male immigrants were subject to unequal immigration policies, unfair labor practices, separation from family and continual death threats—what K. labels the "Driving Out"—they established and asserted themselves in the U.S. Using "trickster" methods, Bak

Goong, the narrator's great-grandfather, defies a plantation foreman's admonishment to keep quiet; he coughs out his curses against authority. K. also details material contributions to American culture, including the building of the transcontinental railroad, which would not have been built save for Chinese immigrant labor. She furthermore challenges stereotypical Chinese images by portraying Chinese men as masculine, muscular, brave, sensitive, and intellectually acute.

K. continues to resist Chinese stereotypes in *Tripmaster Monkey* (1989), her first novel. Its protagonist, Wittman Ah Sing, is an artist, draft-dodger, and English major graduate of Berkeley. Although Wittman claims to be an "incarnation" of Monkey who, according to Chinese legend, helped bring Buddhist scripture from India, he also invokes Hollywood films and the work of his namesake, Walt WHITMAN, to define his life. Through his dramatization of the Chinese classic, *Shui Hu Chuan* (*The Water Verge*), Wittman is able to protest American involvement in Vietnam. Using his dual heritage, Wittman insists on their compatibility, thus denying attempts to exclude Chinese from the American experience. Wittman is also the protagonist of a work currently in progress that K. describes as not "simply a sequel" but a "nonfiction fiction nonfiction sandwich."

K.'s intermingling of fact and fiction and Eastern and Western art forms has opened her work to criticism. Some critics interpret her revision of Chinese culture and personal history as "selling out" and distortion. They also object to her focus on the subjugation of women in Chinese culture, claiming it reinforces exotic stereotypes of Chinese men. Unrealistically, these critics assume a definitive version of Chinese American reality that does not exist; they also refuse to acknowledge the complexity of K.'s work. While she does expose the negative practices of Chinese patriarchy, she also condemns gender and racial oppression in America by continually drawing parallels between the degradation of Chinese immigrant men and the suppression of woman in Chinese tradition.

BIBLIOGRAPHY: Cheung, K., *Articulate Silences* (1993); Kim, E., *Asian American Literature* (1982); Schroeder, E. J., "As Truthful as Possible: An Interview with M. H. K.," *Writing on the Edge* 7, 2 (1996): 82–96; Wong, S. C., "Necessity and Extravagance in M. H. K.'s *The Woman Warrior:* Art and the Ethnic Experience," *MELUS* 15 (Spring 1988): 3–26

LINDA TRINH MOSER

KINNELL, Galway

b. 1 February 1927, Providence, Rhode Island

In eight volumes of poetry since 1960, in a novel entitled *Black Light* (1966), in various interviews, collected in *Walking Down the Stair* (1978), in his translations of François Villon and others, and in his essays, especially "Poetry, Personality, and Death," the essential artistic concern of K. has been to explore the meaning of death in our time.

Reared in Pawtucket, Rhode Island, K. was educated at Princeton. In 1955–57, on a Fulbright Fellowship in France, K. was influenced by existentialism, and perhaps that body of thought helped him clarify his position that "the subject of the poem is the thing that dies." His first book, *What a Kingdom It Was* (1960), seems predicated on this idea. Its most affecting poems are explicit elegies, and an elegiac tone predominates throughout. This poetry also possesses a vivid, shimmering imagery, beautiful precisely because it is informed with a sense of mortal transience. In "The Avenue Bearing the Initial of Christ into the New World," the culminating poem of *What a Kingdom It Was,* one sees butterfish in a street-market stall. They are spread out before the speaker, their "mouths still open, still trying to eat." Or, in "Spindrift," from K.'s second book, *Flower Herding on Mount Monadnock* (1964), one sees the speaker lift a shell up out of the surf, and then in the next stanza recall how he had "Sat by a dying woman / Her shell of a hand, / Wet and cold in both of mine."

"The Avenue Bearing the Initial of Christ into the New World" marked a formal breakthrough for K. His earliest poems had been relatively strict in their meter, rhyme, and stanzaic arrangements. With "Avenue," K. took Walt WHITMAN as his model and Manhattan as his topic, experimenting with a long, free-verse line that would allow him to accommodate the impulse to catalogue the images of the city. K. also experimented with the structure of the poem. Like "Song of Myself," there is in "Avenue" an open-ended sequence of numbered sections. Each section culminates in an epiphany about the failure of community in the modern era, the Holocaust being only the most horrifying example. Pared down and focused in stanzas with shorter lines and longer sentence structures, the meditational, open-ended sequence would become K.'s preferred form in many subsequent poems.

He would, for instance, come to use it to explore his deeply ambivalent feelings about his own mortality. He has said that death has two aspects for him, "the extinction which we fear, and the flowing away into the universe, which we desire." This is the inner tension that motivates some of K.'s most important poems, including "The Porcupine" and "The Bear," in *Body Rags* (1968). In both of these poems, we see dramatized a speaker's gradual identification with a grotesquely dying animal. As such, each of these poems reads like a parable of coming to terms with one's own mortality, and the process described is both a frightening and liberating death of self.

K.'s next volume, *The Book of Nightmares* (1971), explores a different sort of pain and fear: the possibility that existence itself is nothing but a meaningless and desolate bad dream. Each of the ten meditations that compose this book brings the reader to an image of death without meaning, and, as in a fugue, the images of such deaths echo one another from poem to poem, making for a cumulative horror. But, at the same time, the horror is balanced by a speaker struggling in each poem to affirm that love and human connectedness can provide some shred of significance, however ephemeral. Dedicated to his two children, framed by descriptions of their births, the poem as a whole is, as K. himself has said, deeply affirmative.

To some, *Mortal Acts, Mortal Words* (1980) and *The Past* (1985) represent a falling off from the intensity of vision preceding them. On the other hand, K. seems to have opened new emotional territory in these volumes. Less bardic and apocalyptic, these poems are as vividly imagined as any of K.'s earlier work. Mostly tender reminiscences and brief elegies, the most moving of those is on the death of K.'s mother. The poem ends with lines that seem to distill the wisdom of his entire opus: "It is written in our hearts, the emptiness is all / That is how we have learned, the embrace is all."

BIBLIOGRAPHY: Guimond, J., *Seeing and Healing* (1984); Mills, R., *Cry of the Human* (1975); Molesworth, C., *The Fierce Embrace* (1979); Nelson, C., *Our Last First Poets* (1981); Nelson, H., *On the Poetry of G. K.* (1987); Zimmerman, L., *Intricate and Simple Things* (1987)

FRED MARCHANT

KINSELLA, W[illiam] P[atrick]

b. 25 May 1935, Edmonton, Alberta, Canada

The fiction of K. abounds with enough bizarre plot twists, supernatural incidents, and larger-than-life characters to test the patience of even the most imaginative reader, and yet one cannot read his work without sensing that K.'s vision is focused on the very heart of reality. Constructed with a smooth blend of enchanting fantasy and earthy texture, K.'s stories rival the works of Gabriel García Márquez and other magical realists for sheer fanciful audaciousness and minute attention to the gritty details of everyday life.

Shoeless Joe (1982), K.'s first novel and best-known work, demonstrates his talent for telling a story that simultaneously draws upon central features of Americana, such as Midwestern cornfields and the national pastime, and dares to explore the fantastic, including elements of time travel, the narrator's un-

likely friendship with the reclusive J. D. SALINGER, and the resurrection of the 1919 Chicago White Sox. *Shoeless Joe*'s adaptation as the commercially successful and critically acclaimed motion picture *Field of Dreams* (1989) introduced K.'s vision to an even broader audience and helped to insure the novel's continued popularity.

K. pushes the envelope of the fantastic even further in his next novel, *The Iowa Baseball Confederacy* (1986). Once again he employs the elements of time travel and resurrected historical figures, ranging from the 1908 Chicago Cubs to Leonardo da Vinci, even as he captures the essence of a Midwestern American town, Onamata, Iowa. By the time the narrative concludes, K. leads the reader through a baseball game that lasts over 2,600 innings, the spell-binding nature of which testifies to the author's capacity for engaging his audience.

While K. has achieved his substantial notoriety through his baseball-inspired novels, his short stories are perhaps even better barometers of his virtuosity. A prolific author of short stories—he has published more than ten collections—K. brings to this genre a talent for storytelling that enables him to experiment with his subject matter, narrative point of view, prose style, and structure without sacrificing what is perhaps his major attribute: the skill to entertain.

K. turns to baseball, a true passion for this Canadian-born author, as the focal point for several short stories, many of which exhibit the same magical qualities present in his novels, but he also uses this genre to explore another passion of his—the Cree Indians of Alberta. In these narratives, which constitute more than half a dozen of his collections, including his first two, *Dance Me Outside* (1977) and *Scars* (1978), Silas Ermineskin, a young Cree, describes life in and around the Cree Indian Reservation, mixing starkly realistic accounts of poverty and oppression with life-affirming cultural pride and humor. Because these stories are told through the voice of Silas, complete with his syntactical peculiarities, and because they lack the heavy doses of fantasy present in K.'s other fiction, they almost appear to be the products of another author. But they do contain the one element that is consistent in all of K.'s work: a captivating story.

Occasionally guilty in his fiction of introducing overdoses of the fantastic and perhaps too dependent on a limited range of subjects, K. nevertheless manages, as he states in his introduction to his short story collection *The Thrill of the Grass* (1984), to "liven up the dull" and "tone down the bizarre until it is believable." For K., the "profound, symbolic, or philosophical," while it may be present in a story, must always remain secondary to what is his most fundamental aesthetic principle: "a fiction writer can be anything except boring."

BIBLIOGRAPHY: Cochran, R. W., "A Second Cool Papa: Hemingway to K. and Hays," *Arete* 4 (1987): 27–40; Hamblin, R., "'Magical Realism'; or, The Split-Fingered Fastball of W. P. K.," *Aethlon* 9 (1992): 1–10

ALLEN ALEXANDER

KIRKLAND, Caroline

b. 11 January 1801, New York City; d. 6 April 1864, New York City

K., who wrote under the pseudonyms of Matilda Stansbury and Mrs. Mary Clavers, is best known for her frontier writings, autobiographical tales, essays, sketches, and poems that present frontier life realistically through unique eyes—those of a 19th-c. woman reporting frontier life from the viewpoint of one committed to the preservation of hearth and home, despite her physical surroundings. This viewpoint has been seen as critically important to the study of 19th-c. REALISM.

The epitome of K.'s work is considered to be her 1838 classic, *A New Home—Who'll Follow?*, which records the author's real life experiences in the frontier lands of Michigan, where she had traveled with her husband to start a semblance of a new life. *A New Home—Who'll Follow?* contains much in the way of humor and witticism, aimed at both her own otherwise dreary situation as well as at her new neighbors and new surroundings. In a very significant way, the city-bred K. writes in this work a comedy of manners, censuring what she sees as a lack of manners and civility in her more down-to-earth neighbors. The reader is left with little doubt regarding K.'s utter distaste for her Western experience.

Despite K.'s prejudices, her contemporaries greeted the book enthusiastically. Critics, including Edgar Allan POE, praised *A New Home—Who'll Follow?* highly, citing its originality and interest as remarkable. Such praise and popularity led to K.'s ability to command above-average pay for subsequent writings.

K. capitalized on interest in *A New Home—Who'll Follow?* with both *Western Clearings* (1845) and *Forest Life* (1872). *Western Clearings* comprises articles and essays, while *Forest Life* is a collection of tales, sketches, and poetry; both focus on Western life again, but this time with even more of a focus on home life and with much less of any adventurous overtones. While reviews for these two later works were overwhelmingly good, critics touted them as less interesting than K.'s first work. Such comments continue to hold true in critical circles. Indeed, it is difficult to

not view the later works as capitalization on a successful theme.

With *Western Clearings*, K. largely ended her use of frontier experience as writing topic. She served as an editor and writer for the *Union Magazine of Literature and Art* from 1847 to 1848. In addition, she published *The Evening Book*, a collection of short stories and essays, in 1852. Later works focus on issues of American morality, fulfilling a need K. felt deeply to use her writing talent as a vehicle for social elevation. While these works assuredly prove additional breadth in K.'s work, she will undoubtedly remain best known for her frontier works.

BIBLIOGRAPHY: Fetterley, J., ed., *Provisions: A Reader from Nineteenth-Century American Women* (1985); Mainiero, L., ed., *American Women Writers* (1982); Osborne, W. S., *C. K.* (1972)

TERRY D. NOVAK

KIZER, Carolyn [Ashley]

b. 10 December 1925, Spokane Washington

At the beginning of her career as a poet, K. was considered to be a regionalist, associated with the Pacific Northwest mainly because her first book, *Poems* (1959), was published by the Portland Art Museum in Oregon. Although, her second, *The Ungrateful Garden*, appeared in 1961 from Indiana University Press, a 1964 anthology of poems titled *Five Poets of the Pacific Northwest*, edited by Robin Skelton, was published by the University of Washington Press in Seattle, and K.'s work appeared prominently in it. The book received wide distribution and reinforced the impression that her poetry, though very well written, was nevertheless provincial.

It was not until the 1965 collection *Knock upon Silence*, containing her long poem "Pro Femina," an early feminist document, that her reputation began to evolve rapidly. In "Pro Femina," she speaks "about women of letters, for I'm in the racket," but it is a man's world in which she must make her way and find her place. This poem was a brilliant contribution not only to the genre, but it was considered by many critics simply to be one of the finest poems of any type written by an American poet in the second half of the 20th c.

Midnight Was My Cry: New and Selected Poems appeared in 1971 and offered a broad view of K.'s abilities and poetic range. At the same time, however, the swiftly developing feminist movement seemed to be leaving her behind, for her criticisms of the patriarchal society and of the relationships among men and women, although they were sharp, were perceived to be also, perhaps, too good-humored; clever rather than outraged, literary rather than partisan.

Mermaids in the Basement and *Yin* were published in 1984, and *The Nearness of You* was issued in 1986. In each of these books, the wide horizon of her emotions appeared to be packaged in all sorts of formal bottles—she was an academic poet accused by her critics of using technical skill to "distance herself from pain." However, K. was well aware that humor is a weapon with a sharp edge, keener even than a sharp tongue.

Another element of K.'s success beside her poetic craft was her ability to tell a story. Narration was one of her strong suits, but narrative is underrated in a period that glorifies confession. The poem "Semele Recycled," from *Yin,* is an example of a narrative that is at once topical and timeless. The poet's source was Greek myth, but she made it near, familiar, and compelling, and loaded it with resonance.

Semele was the mother of Dionysus—god of wine and fertility—by Zeus, the supreme father-god. Semele asked Zeus to appear to her in all his majesty, but the apparition was so terrifying that she died. Semele's various body parts were scattered and had undergone transformations and sundry adventures, but then her lover returned, and the body parts, hearing the rumor, "leapt up" and as many as could do so reunited themselves, sought out Zeus, and fell to making violent love. The poem is built from richly concrete language. It is psychologically complex, the narrative embodiment of the war between the sexes, and the eternal truce that is struck again and again.

Although *Mermaids in the Basement* was subtitled *Poems for Women,* for many years K. wrote with real power for an audience that was wider than the special interest audiences that so many contemporary American poets tried to reach during the period following World War II. K. continued her literary balancing act with her 1986 collection, *The Nearness of You,* which was subtitled *Poems for Men.*

BIBLIOGRAPHY: House, E. B., "C. K.," in Greiner, D. J., ed., *DLB,* vol. 5, part 1, *American Poets since World War II* (1980): 402–5; Howard, R., "C. K.," *TriQ* 7 (Fall 1966): 109–17; Rigsbee, D., ed., *An Answering Music: On the Poetry of C. K.* (1990)

LEWIS PUTNAM TURCO

KNIGHT, Etheridge

b. 19 April 1931, Corinth, Mississippi; d. 10 March 1991, Indianapolis, Indiana

K. achieved early acclaim when he burst on the poetry scene in the late 1960s with poems and prose that came out of the Black Aesthetic movement, which taught that social revolution was necessary if African Americans wanted to find justice in the U.S. K. saw his writing as tools to build that revolutionary spirit. His *Poems from Prison* (1968) and *Black Voices from Prison* (1970) established him as a powerful and articulate voice of anger in the recognition of severe racial oppression, and K. consciously pitched his early writing entirely toward an African American audience. Later in his career, K. broadened his focus, reaching for inclusivity; for him the struggles against slavery and for freedom became universal issues, and not a concern only for African Americans.

K. was serving an eight-year prison sentence for robbery when he began to write poetry. Under the guidance and support of Gwendolyn BROOKS, K. polished his work, which grew out of the oral poetic form of the toast—an important part of African American culture—and of which K. was a master. His poetry never lost elements of the oral tradition, with its often heavy reliance on internal rhyming, and occasionally intrusive iambic beat. K. is also noted for his use of the rhythms of blues and black street talk. Although a few of K.'s early poems are frequently anthologized in college textbooks, his critical reputation remains in flux, with many critics reluctant to place him in the first or second rank of poets. Poets such as Brooks, Robert BLY, and Galway KINNELL, on the other hand, speak highly of K., and his *Belly Song and Other Poems* (1973) received nominations for the National Book Award and the Pulitzer Prize. Over his relatively short writing career of eighteen years, K. displayed a maturing process in his poetry, but critics generally look at one or two of the early poems as his best and most significant work.

"The Idea of Ancestry" is one of K.'s most widely anthologized poems. It has been called by several critics the best expression of African American cultural identity. The poem speaks about isolation and oppression, the power of memory, the bonds of family, and the inescapable private demons that add to the danger from the outside world. "Hard Rock Returns to Prison from the Hospital for the Criminal Insane," another early poem appearing in many anthologies, is concerned with the spirit of a black man that is finally broken by the white system through the tools of lobotomy and shock treatment. Both poems address a major theme running through K.'s early work: the importance of a black community for black people, and the effect of that community's degradation on its members from oppressive racist pressures.

In the last book K. published, *Born of a Woman: New and Selected Poems* (1980), the poet acknowledges the universal aspect of his writing, especially in his preface, "The Poet, the Poem, and the People," where he stresses the importance of community that transcends race, and the poet's communion with that larger body. In "The Stretching of the Belly," a remarkable poem from a poet who Brooks once said wrote starkly masculine poems, K. sings a paean to his pregnant wife's changed body. But the poem is also about the stretching of an idea, enlarging the concept of family and responsibility to extend to all peoples. This collection concludes with "Con/tin/u/way/shun Blues," in which K. acknowledges still the imperfect human society, the presence yet of slavery, but also recognizes the possibility of beauty and fleeting freedom. The street argot is stridently present, but the tone of the piece is quietly triumphant and universalizing, a strong African American voice speaking to and about all humanity.

BIBLIOGRAPHY: Hill, P. L., "'The Violent Space': The Function of the New Black Aesthetic in E. K.'s Prison Poetry," *BALF* 14 (Fall 1980): 115–21; Werner, C., "The Poet, the Poem, the People: E. K.'s Aesthetic," *Obsidian II* 7 (Summer-Winter 1981): 7–17

BRIAN ADLER

KNIGHT, Sarah Kemble

b. 19 April 1666, Boston, Massachusetts; d. 25 September 1727, New London, Connecticut

K. has gained a lasting reputation for a slim volume published nearly one hundred years after her death. This record of a journey from Boston to New York in 1704, *The Journal of Madam K.,* may be slight, but its historical and social significance is far-reaching. Through a collection of pithy and abbreviated entries, the perceptive diarist provides a sweeping and sometimes harsh picture of ordinary life in colonial America.

Called "Madam Knight" in respect for her professional and social stature, this remarkable woman still makes a vivid impression as she describes what was then a perilous journey, especially for a woman on horseback. Although biographical details are scarce, what is known about K. proves that she hardly fits the role of the retiring colonial woman. Perhaps she inherited the spirit of independence from her merchant father, who, according to tradition, was once placed in the stocks for "lewd and unseemly conduct"—that is, kissing his wife on their doorstep after a lengthy absence. Shortly before her father's death in 1689, K. married a widower years older than herself, a shipmaster, Captain Richard Knight, who died in London around 1706 during a prolonged stay there, and with whom she had one daughter.

By this time, K. headed the Kemble household, advised her relatives on financial matters, recorded public documents, and engaged in various legal activities, settling estates in particular. In addition, this energetic and resourceful woman operated a boarding house, ran a shop, kept a school, and invested in real estate. Leaving Boston in 1714, she moved to Connecticut where she continued to prosper as a merchant and landowner. Fined in 1718 for selling liquor to Indians, she placed the blame on a servant and retained her public esteem. At the time of her death, she left a considerable estate. K.'s sketchy biography helps to provide background for the journal she kept on her Boston–New York trek. Not taking the trip for pleasure, she set out to look after a widowed boarder's inheritance, a task she completed satisfactorily.

In the 1920 "Introductory Note" to the journal, George Parker Winship describes K. as a "plump mistress" with an "independent mind and energetic, withal somewhat feminist, character." These qualities surface in her responses to the people she meets along the way. Showing little patience toward those who are lazy, ignorant, and slovenly, she encounters many such colonists and describes them mercilessly. She also condemns the provincial attitudes and contentious behavior of those living in the remote countryside or in homely villages. Obviously she prefers the sophistication of Boston, which she considers superior to New York City. Her disparagement of Native Americans, described as "savages," represents the attitudes of the time. Of course, K., who emerges as something of a snob, delights in meeting the occasional "gentlewoman" or "gentleman," such as Governor John WINTHROP and his family. Not only is she a stern critic of human behavior but of architecture, food, house interiors, and the condition of beds as well. The diarist displays the brighter side of her character through her witty accounts of unpleasant situations, a keen appreciation of the human comedy, and the occasional lapse into mock heroic poetry.

Historians assume that K. made notes in shorthand during the five months it took her to go from Boston to New York and back, then refined them into the diary that has survived. Theodore Dwight of New York, the work's first publisher in 1825, obtained the manuscript from the estate of the diarist's daughter. Whether this "neatly copied" book was in K.'s handwriting has never been determined. By 1858, all but a single leaf of the original manuscript had disappeared. In the 1825 introduction, Dwight regrets that "the brevity of the work should have allowed the author so little room for the display of the cultivated mind and the brilliant fancy which frequently betray themselves in the course of the narrative." The modern reader would certainly agree, and would be delighted, as Dwight says, to read more "from the same practised hand."

BIBLIOGRAPHY: Brink, D., "Issues in Early American English: Using Evidence from the Journal of K.," *AJGLL* 6 (1994): 199–210; Bush, S., *Legacy* (1995): 112–20

ROBERT L. ROSS

KNOWLES, John
b. 16 September 1926, Fairmont, West Virginia

Known primarily for his acclaimed and popular novel *A Separate Peace* (1960), so often required reading for junior or senior high school students, K. has in fact published eight other novels, a collection of short stories, and a book of travel writings. His years attending Exeter and Yale University no doubt provided the academic settings found in many of these novels, beginning with *A Separate Peace* but also including *Indian Summer* (1966), *The Paragon* (1971), and *A Stolen Past* (1983).

Published in 1960, *A Separate Peace* received the William Faulkner Award for Outstanding First Novel and the American Academy and Institute of Arts and Letters Richard and Hinda Rosenthal Foundation Award. The book dramatizes a conflict between two young men of different personality types: Phineas is popular and athletic while Gene is more cerebral and introverted. Over time, Phineas's likable nature inspires jealousy, and eventually violence, in Gene, who resents Phineas's ease in the social world of the private academy the boys attend. K. uses the opposing natures of these two characters to demonstrate the moral of the novel, that ignorance and jealousy creates conflict that can only be resolved through recognition and understanding. This theme is a dominant one in K.'s fiction; warmth and acceptance sustain his noble characters and redeem the failing ones. A film version of the novel appeared in 1972.

In his next novel, *Morning in Antibes* (1962), K. portrays wealthy Americans at play abroad. It echoes F. Scott FITZGERALD with its protagonist, a carefree, jaded young man who, though he thinks of himself as a sophisticate, yearns for meaningful human affection. K.'s novels after *A Separate Peace* possibly suffered under the weight of expectation generated by the promise of his first novel, though his third, *Indian Summer,* was also quite well received. Between his second and third novels, K. published a book based on his own travels, *Double Vision: American Thoughts Abroad* (1964), and in 1968, *Phineas,* a book of short stories containing an early version of *A Separate Peace* was published.

During the 1970s, K. produced three novels, *The Paragon, Spreading Fires* (1974), and *A Vein of Riches* (1979). He continued to develop his themes of human acceptance and love in terms of peer relationships, class differences, and sexuality. Particularly the novels set in the Mediterranean, such as *Morning in Antibes* and *Spreading Fires* tend to deal with romantic and sexual relationships, often contrasting American ideas and values with European. Often in K.'s work, ideas are defined in terms of their opposites: if there is a popular athletic character, there is an unpopular, awkward one; if there are free-thinking liberal characters, there are self-conscious conservative ones. The tension between opposites represents the world as K. perceives it, and his answer to tension is acceptance of opposition, not resistance or force.

In 1981, over twenty years after the publication of *A Separate Peace,* K. wrote a sequel entitled *Peace Breaks Out.* Although *Peace Breaks Out* takes place in the same school setting of *A Separate Peace,* the conflicts are more complicated, involving racial and class prejudices as well as differences of character. The action is seen through the eyes of a teacher who, having suffered injury and personal hardship during the war, has lost faith in humanity. K. himself seems to have lost some of his faith as well in this novel; the resolution and sense of equity that plays such a central role in many of his other books is absent and the reader is left to wonder if the characters in this novel gain moral insight or simply find a way to escape blame.

More critical works have been written on *A Separate Peace* as a novel than on K. as a novelist. Written as it was in the early 1960s during the beginnings of the peace movement, the novel can be read as a sign of the times. It will, however, remain a classic for its timeless themes of youthful competition, search for identity, and ultimate self-knowledge.

BIBLIOGRAPHY: Gardner, J., "More Smog from the Dark, Satanic Mills," *SoR* 5 (Winter 1969): 224–44; Nelson, R. M., "J. K.," in Kibler, J. E., Jr., ed., *DLB,* vol. 6, *American Novelists since World War II* (1980): 167–77

NICOLE SARROCCO

KOCH, Kenneth
b. 27 February 1925, Cincinnati, Ohio

As a prolific poet, playwright, fiction writer, essayist, and educator, K. seeks to give uncommon pleasure by igniting the imagination of his audience with a vast repertoire of styles and subjects. While all of his work merits attention, K. is best known for his lyrical, sometimes satiric poems in which disjunctions of thought and seemingly random images cohere in turns both comic and serious. To achieve such effects, K. employs a variety of techniques, including stream of consciousness, monologue, parody, and surrealism, and he values the potential of surprise, drawing mundane objects into his lines with startling analogies. For all that is packed into his lines, K. is never heavy-handed; in fact, his poems seem deceptively simple, even blithely comic, though his persistent metaphysical questioning and concern with form and sound transform such simplicity into serious experimentation.

K.'s interest in poetry began with Shelley, Walt WHITMAN, and the French symbolists, but it was his friendship with John ASHBERY and Frank O'HARA in the 1950s that most influenced his first published poems. This friendship gave rise to what critics have called the New York school, a style opposed to the burden of symbolism and inspired by the abstract expressionist concern with the aesthetic surface. Accordingly, K.'s early poems depend more on the texture of the words than on semantic cohesion. In this style, K.'s first volume, *Poems* (1953), provoked Harry Roskolenko's dismissal, which incited O'Hara's defense of K. as an original thinker.

K.'s second publication, *Ko; or, A Season on Earth* (1960), received more approval. *Ko* is a 3,504-line discursive story about a Japanese baseball player; in ottava rima modeled after Byron's *Don Juan* and Lodovico Ariosto's *Orlando Furioso,* the poem plots the development of a digressing speaker more than it does a narrative. K. returns to this form in *The Duplications* (1977) and in *Seasons on Earth* (1987), perfecting his garrulous speaker and his memorable rhymes, such as "Poseidon's / inside ins / guidance."

With *Thank You and Other Poems* (1962), K. displays further versatility, winning his work critical acclaim. Though his early free verse poems sometimes seem flatly prosaic, several in this volume develop a rhythmic vitality. Of particular note is "Fresh Air," a satire of the academic, establishment poets: "Oh, to be seventeen years old / Once again . . . and not know that poetry / Is ruled with the sceptre of the dumb, the deaf, and the creepy!" Ridiculing the bad poets, makers of hackneyed comparisons, the speaker invokes a creative "fresh air" to break the monotonous conventions of modern poetry.

Through the 1960s and 1970s, K.'s style develops from the obscurity and surrealism of *When the Sun Tries to Go On* (1969) to the clarity of lyricism, structure, and emotion in *The Art of Love* (1975). By the publication of *The Burning Mystery of Anna in 1951* (1977), a reminiscence of his life in 1950s New York, even K.'s long, prosaic lines have become more rhythmic and revealing, as in "To Marina," a disarmingly

direct elegy for lost love and the expression of a memory when "Everything afterwards seemed nowhere near."

K.'s poetry in *One Train* (1994) plots his further experiments with form, from a re-telling of the Io myth in rhymed, heptameter couplets to the rhythmic time changes in the rhymed free verse of "Time Zone." Each of these poems reveals the unperceived behind the perceived, as the title poem announces, "In a poem, one line may hide another."

K.'s numerous plays and short fiction have been largely overlooked by the public. Plays like "The Construction of Boston," produced in 1962, and "The Gold Standard," produced in 1969, contribute significantly to the verse drama tradition, while the short fiction in *Hotel Lambosa and Other Stories* (1993) offers sensual impressions of human relationships in tightly-structured scenes. In all of his writing, K., following his own advice from "The Art of Poetry," inspires an insatiable sense of wonder: "A reader should put your work down puzzled, / Distressed, and illuminated, ready to believe / It is curious to be alive."

BIBLIOGRAPHY: Davis, J., "K. K.," *APR* 25 (November-December 1996): 45–53; O'Hara, F., "Another Word on K. K.," *Poetry* 85 (March 1955): 349–51; Roskolenko, H., "On K. K. Again," *Poetry* 86 (June 1955): 177–78; Tranter, J., "An Interview with K. K.," *Scripsi* 4 (November 1986): 177–85

TODD VERDUN

KOMUNYAKAA, Yusef
b. 29 April 1947, Bogalusa, Louisiana

K. writes with a compelling power, speaking in a variety of voices about racism, death, love, lust, and a poet's experience of the Vietnam War. He does so at once learnedly, invoking classical allusions on occasion, while also invoking the voice of the street, often utilizing jazz and the blues as reference points for his allusions and in the rhythms of his lines. Although not yet widely anthologized, K. is a major poetic presence.

K.'s growing recognition in the world of letters includes his winning the 1994 Pulitzer Prize in poetry. In the same year, he was awarded the Kingsley Tufts Poetry Prize, given by the Claremont Graduate School. In 1991, he was presented with the *Kenyon Review* Award for excellence in poetry, and in 1990, he received the Thomas Forcade Award dedicated to the reconciliation of Vietnam and America given by the William Joiner Foundation. The *Village Voice* chose K.'s *Magic City* (1992) as one of the twenty-five best books published that year.

Many of K.'s poems contain autobiographical overtones, stemming from growing up in a small Southern town located near New Orleans. The son of a carpenter and the grandson of an immigrant from the West Indies who, according to family tradition, brought the Komunyakaa name from West Africa, the poet crafts tightly constructed poems that convey in his earlier works a sense of congestion, secret lives, heat, and madness. There are also the emotions of despair and anger engendered in a black man's perception of himself located in the Deep South. In *Copacetic* (1984), blues and jazz rhythms help to tease out inferences and connections. K. speaks of the hidden motives in the heart as it runs to hide from the pain of exclusion, and of the effects of love and society failing in large and in small, personal ways. These poems carry with them strong poetic force, vitality in life and in jazz, and an ultimately optimistic stance in spite of the pain and contraction of daily living. In *I Apologize for the Eyes in My Head* (1986), the poet speaks about racism and the transitory nature of life, employing violent and blood-soaked images, making reference to frustration, betrayal, and aching longing.

Another major theme in K.'s works concerns his experiences in Vietnam. He served in Vietnam two years, coming home with the Bronze Star. His poetic reactions to the war are primarily found in *Dien Cai Dau* (1988). The claustrophobia of tunnels, the stolen jazz cadences of Hanoi Hannah, the tortured moral questions, and the troubling unethical acts in the war culminate in a nightmarish landscape of blasted idealism. The collection ends with what may be K.'s finest poem, "Facing It," a powerful elegy involving a visit to the Vietnam Veterans Memorial in Washington, D.C.

The two most recent books, *Magic City* and the Pulitzer Prize-winning *Neon Vernacular* (1994), speak of painful disruptions, racial injustices, and incoherence at the center of significant experiences, but also of gifts of self-insight and the possibility of joy. K. is able to distill experience into packed, concrete packages that end in uncertainty, with emotion and the heat of its turmoil staggering through a delicate and finely nuanced sensibility.

Although disdaining the label of jazz poet, K. quite self-consciously employs music in many of his poems as a structural device and as a method for discovery. He speaks of jazz as a method whereby one may approach the emotional mystery behind events and objects. Focusing on that emotional mystery is a major aspect of K.'s poetry, which necessitates indeterminacy. Yet K. strives after hard truth as well, in a significant voice that is clear and distinctive, multilayered, and psychologically complex.

BIBLIOGRAPHY: Aubert, A., "Y. K.: The Unified Vision—Canonization and Humanity," *AAR* 27 (Spring 1993): 119–23; Kelly, R., "Jazz and Poetry: A Conversation," *GaR* 46 (1992): 645–61; Ringnalda, D., "Rejecting 'Sweet Geometry': K.'s Duende," *JAC* 16 (Fall 1993): 21–28

BRIAN ADLER

KOPIT, Arthur

b. 10 May 1937, New York City

K. is one of the most innovative dramatists in the contemporary American theater. While critics and the public alike tend to label him an absurdist because of the nature of his first successful work, *Oh Dad, Poor Dad, Mamma's Hung You in the Closet and I'm Feelin' So Sad* (1960), he has written at least three other important plays that are better than *Oh Dad, Poor Dad*—*Sing to Me through Open Windows, Indians* (one of the major American dramas written in the 1960s), and *Wings* (one of the best American plays written in the 1970s). He has also written television scripts and authored an insightful theoretical essay comparing modern American and European playwrights—"The Vital Matter of Environment" appeared in *Theatre Arts* in April 1961.

K. began his playwriting career while he was a sophomore at Harvard University. *The Questioning of Nick,* the one-act, award-winning play that was his first effort at dramaturgy, was followed by seven additional plays before he graduated in 1959. Among these was *Sing to Me through Open Windows* (1959). The best of his early works, *Sing to Me* shows the influence of Samuel Beckett and the theater of the absurd in its setting, language, use of pauses, minimal plot, and characterization. Symbolically portraying a transitional moment in the life of a boy, Andrew Linden, the drama depicts the movement from childhood into manhood. On the first day of spring each year Andrew has visited the forest home of magician Ottoman Jud and his helper, Loveless the Clown. On Andrew's final visit the symbolic figure, Jud, apparently dies and Andrew must face the world on his own. There is also a suggestion that Jud is in a transitional state, moving from life to death.

Oh Dad, Poor Dad is a Freudian/Oedipal examination of the relationship between a domineering mother and her Milquetoast son—a theme dealt with in numerous other dramas, including Sidney HOWARD's *The Silver Cord* in 1926; there are also thematic and technical connections with Arthur MILLER's *Death of a Salesman* and Joe Orton's *Loot*. Critical reaction has been divided: some scholars claim that K. is metaphorically portraying the neurosis brought about by the tensions of the nuclear age; others see the play as a satire of avant-garde traditions; others find *Oh Dad, Poor Dad* an unsuccessful example of the theater of the absurd.

Indians (1968) represents a fusion of K.'s previous themes and techniques. A study of the source of mythic heroes, the play places words actually spoken by General William Westmoreland, the Commander-in-Chief of American forces in Vietnam, in the mouth of Colonel Forsythe. Since the Colonel utters these words while looking over the site on which a group of Indians had been massacred the day before, K. demonstrates how certain themes run throughout American history. Composed of a series of scenes alternating between Buffalo Bill's Wild West Show and an 1886 Indian Commission hearing, *Indians* depicts the conflict between basic cultural instincts. The fact that the play's chronology is jumbled indicates both that the action is not to be understood on a literal level and that its meaning is to be applied across time.

Wings (1977) is K.'s finest work to date. As in *Indians,* the dramatist combines strong emotional expression with an intellectual context. In this case, his personal experiences stimulated the play. K.'s father suffered a massive stroke in 1976 that left him incapable of speaking. While visiting his father at the Burke Rehabilitation Center in White Plains, New York, K. became intrigued by the question of what if was like, "To what extent was [his father] aware of what had befallen him? *What was it like inside?*" the protagonist in *Wings,* Emily Stilson, was modeled after the elder K. and other patients at the center.

In addition, K. incorporated material from Charles Lindbergh's *The Spirit of St. Louis* (1953), in which the pilot wrote about his feelings of being cut off and unsure of what was real during his transatlantic flight, two books on brain damage, Howard Gardner's *The Shattered Mind* (1975) and A. R. Luria's *The Man with a Shattered World* (1972), and the experience of Jacqueline Doolittle, the center's therapist, herself a former stroke victim.

What sets *Wings* apart form other contemporary dramas is K.'s ability to recreate the world of a stroke victim through a careful combination of logic, nonsense, articulate speech, and babble that parallels the stage effects of live and recorded sound, colored and flashing lights, shifting points of view, a minimal set, overlapping dialogue, and loudspeakers located throughout the theater—all of which coalesce to depict an extraordinary nonverbal sequence of events as the audience follows the protagonist's mind in its movement from fragmentation to integration over the course of the play.

It is ironic that K. is known for *Oh Dad, Poor Dad,* for this early play is one of his weakest. In fact, with the staging of *Indians* and *Wings,* K. has established himself as a master dramatic craftsman and potentially

among the most important American dramatists of his time.

BIBLIOGRAPHY: Auerbach, D., *Sam Shepard, A. K., and the Off Broadway Theatre* (1982); Cohn, R., "Camp, Cruelty, Colloquialism," in Cohen, S. B., ed., *Comic Relief: Humor in Contemporary American Literature* (1978): 281–303; Wellwarth, G. E., *The Theatre of Protest and Paradox* (1971); Wolter, J., "A. K.: Dreams and Nightmares," in Bock, H., and A. Wertheim, eds., *Essays on Contemporary American Drama* (1981): 55–74

STEVEN H. GALE

KOSINSKI, Jerzy

b. 14 June 1933, Lodz, Poland; d. 3 May 1991, New York City

While many novels contain strong echoes of their authors' autobiographical material, K.'s works parallel his life more closely perhaps than any other of his generation. The invasion of K.'s native Poland in 1939 forced his Jewish family into hiding and put K. into the care of a foster mother who died shortly after. K.'s subsequent solitary and horrific childhood wanderings, which would not end until the close of the war, were the basis for his first and most highly regarded novel—*The Painted Bird* (1965)—and were likely factors in the shaping of the events of his adult life in America as well as his eventual suicide in 1991.

When the war in Europe ended, Poland once more came under the control of the former Soviet Union. K. first studied social psychology in Warsaw and Moscow, and when numerous attempts to emigrate to the U.S. were stonewalled, K. hit upon an ingenious scheme. He created four entirely fictional academicians, all of whom were drafted into service to furnish K. with sterling recommendations to study abroad at a similarly fictitious institute in the U.S. Eventually, K. was granted a visa and arrived in New York on a Christmas Day without friends, money, or more than the merest grasp of colloquial English usage.

In short order, however, K. entered a doctoral program and set forth in earnest on his writing career. It was also in these early years that K. met and in 1962 married Mary Hayward Weir, a wealthy art collector, who had caught his attention when she wrote a fan letter for his first nonfiction work (written under the pseudonym Joseph Novak) *The Future Is Ours, Comrade: Conversations with the Russians* (1960).

The Painted Bird, K's first novel, documents the travels of an abandoned child through the villages of Eastern Europe during the World War II. The boy's muteness, which echoed the young K.'s own inability to speak for five years after experiencing the horrors of the war, allow him a unique perspective as an observer of the lives of rural Poles during the years before he is finally able to reunite with his family.

K's second work of fiction also deals in part with the war, although in a far less linear way than his earlier novel. *Steps* (1968) was described by *Newsweek* as "more than a novel . . . a collection of erotic reminiscences." The work draws on many of K's own experiences before emigrating to the U.S., including his work as a ski instructor in the winters during his Eastern European university days.

Being There (1971) is the story of a simple man whose naive engagement with Western pop culture, particularly television, shows him to be a classic "everyman" of his generation. The blank slate of his personality, against which the words and images of contemporary society reverberate, allow him to stand as a faultless political figure—one with no background whatsoever. Not only was *Being There* a popular and critical success in its literary form, but thanks in large part to K.'s screenplay, it was turned into a highly acclaimed film starring Peter Sellers and won the best screenplay of the year award from the Writers Guild of America (1979) and the British Academy of Film and Television Arts (1981).

Despite this early success, K's subsequent works were increasingly less well received. None of his later novels—*The Devil's Tree* (1973), *Cockpit* (1975), *Blind Date* (1977), *Passion Play* (1979), *Pinball* (1982), or *The Hermit of 69th Street:The Working Papers of Norbert Kosky* (1988)—received the accolades which had been awarded his earlier works. In addition, controversy had begun to surround K. First, due in part to his extensive use of copy editors, rumors began to circulate that the novels which had been published in English under his name were not really his work, but were largely the work of his colleagues or, at best, translations of novels which he had only written in Polish. The other allegation was that his two early nonfiction works, *The Future Is Ours, Comrade* and *No Third Path: A Study of Collective Behavior* (1962), also published under the pseudonym of Joseph Novak, were mere anticommunist propaganda pieces which had been sponsored by the CIA. However, although both these controversies were to shadow him throughout the rest of his life, the strength of the earliest novels and the various humanitarian and artistic causes with which K. was associated, have left a generally positive impression of K.'s work in the mind of the reading public.

BIBLIOGRAPHY: Bruss, P., *Victims: Textual Strategies in Recent American Fiction* (1981); Lavers, N., *J. K.* (1982); Sloan, J. P., *J. K.: A Biography* (1996)

ELIZABETH HADDRELL

KOTZWINKLE, William
b. 22 November 1938, Scranton, Pennsylvania

K.'s novelization of the film *E.T.* (1982) sold over three million copies and briefly cast him into a position of public prominence, but for the majority of his exceptionally productive life as a writer working in an unusually diverse variety of forms, he has been relatively invisible, appreciated by the connoisseurs of the genres he employs while remaining indistinct as a figure in American literary life. His wildly comic account of narco-bohemian hippies living on Manhattan's grungy Lower East Side, *The Fan Man* (1974), which became an immediate underground "classic," led Steven Spielberg to invite K. to work with *E.T.* and has gone through four editions since its publication. His children's books, notably *Hearts of Wood* (1986) and the etymological Holmes-Watson stories *Trouble in Bugland* (1983), are a part of a fundamental library for young readers, and his ventures into the realm of science fiction/fantasy—particularly his eco-fable *Dr. Rat* (1976) and his excursions into the surreal and subconscious *The Hot Jazz Trio* (1989) and *The Exile* (1987)—have won awards for excellence in those fields.

Nonetheless, partially due to an aversion to publicity tours, partially due to his proclivity for "lunatic humor" that has unsettled some commentators who mistake a comic vision for a lack of seriousness, and primarily due to the extraordinary versatility that has prevented the formation of a category, style, or even consistent subject for packaging purposes, K. continues to be an elusive, protean artist, favorably reviewed in newspapers like the *New York Times* as each book appears even as his place in American literary life at the close of the 20th c. remains uncertain in spite of his accomplishments.

His first collection of short fiction, *Elephant Bangs Train* (1971), an eclectic mix of lyric evocations of childhood, surreal depictions of contemporary American life, hybrids, oddities, sketches, aspects of the fantastic and explorations of states of consciousness of creatures not necessarily of human origin established a kind of template for a writing career as K. picked up and developed in subsequent work through three decades the motifs initially set out here. *The Fan Man* presents, from a perspective deeply placed in the mind of its very eccentric protagonist Horse Badorties, a vision of existence on the margins of the sixties counterculture but familiar from other portraits of singular men such as Herman MELVILLE's Bartelby and Laurence Sterne's Tristam Shandy. *Fata Morgana* (1977) examines the nature of magic and the power of illusion through a Balzacian re-creation of 19th-c. Europe that provides the setting for a stolid French police detective's pursuit of a master of mind-clouding manipulation. *Jack in the Box* (1980)—which was made into the film *Book of Love* (1991) from K.'s screenplay—is a blue-collar *Catcher in the Rye* in which Jack Twiller, a characteristically "good-natured zany" like many of K.'s protagonists, struggles through adolescence in the 1950s. *E.T.* not only effectively caught the unique appeal of Spielberg's film but placed the narration within E.T.'s mind, widening and complementing the film's version.

Through the mid-1980s, K.'s fascination with the realm of childhood led to an essentially optimistic outlook, but the darker shades of human experience, glimpsed in the poem/librettos of the illustrated *Herr Nightingale and the Satin Woman* (1978) and *Seduction in Berlin* (1985), became the central focus of *The Exile* (1987) in which K. delineated a successful actor drawing a powerful performance from the depths of his psyche while being pulled from modern Hollywood back to the last days of Hitler's Germany. The fusion of the "real" and the "fantastic" in this book was explored further in the three stories of *The Hot Jazz Trio,* while the force of evil that K. confronted in the Nazi empire in *The Exile* was given an absurdist cast in the affectionate parody of tabloid publishing *The Midnight Examiner* (1989) and drawn as a source of the worst human depravity in *The Game of Thirty* (1994), an updating of the hardboiled detective/mystery of the 1930s. The range of K.'s wildly inventive imagination is evident in *The Bear Went Over the Mountain* (1996) in which a literate bear is celebrated as the "author" of a best-seller, a North American version of magical realism that combines K.'s continuing satiric contemplation of late 20th-c. American life with his ongoing interest in conditions of consciousness other than those defined as specifically human.

BIBLIOGRAPHY: Alpert, H., "Mysterious Mirage," *SatR* 4 (30 April 1997): 23–24; Lewis, L., "W. K.," in Giles, J. R., and W. H. Giles, eds., *DLB,* vol. 173, *American Novelists since World War II* (1996): 98–107; Stone, R., "Soft in Tooth and Claw," *Harper's* (June 1976): 97–102

LEON LEWIS

KREYMBORG, Alfred

b. 10 December 1883, New York City; d. 14 August 1966, Milford, Connecticut

K. played a central role in the emergence of MODERNISM in the U.S. in the first two decades of the century through his activities as poet, dramatist, editor and critic. His lasting legacy is his work as an editor, editing some of the most important "little magazines"

of the period, and helping bring into print at early stages of their careers some of the most important modernist writers. K.'s own writing is now little read, most readers concurring with Allen TATE's judgement in *Sixty American Poets,* published in 1945, that his work is "not impressive."

Unable to find a market for his free form verse and experimental prose and drama, K. founded the *Glebe* in 1913, a magazine funded through his contacts with the Greenwich Village avant-garde. The short-lived journal published the first extended collection of poems by the imagists. A subsequent magazine, *Others* (1915–19), included among its contributors Wallace STEVENS, T. S. ELIOT, Ezra POUND, William Carlos WILLIAMS, Sherwood ANDERSON, and Marianne MOORE. As editor of *Broom* from 1921 to 1922, K. helped produce what some critics feel was the most important of the expatriate avant-garde magazines. K. continued his advocacy of new writing with the *American Caravan* series of anthologies (5 volumes, 1927–36), edited in conjunction with Van Wyck BROOKS, Paul Rosenfeld, and Lewis MUMFORD, and his critical history of American poetry entitled *Our Singing Strength* (1929).

K.'s two early novels, *Erna Vitek* (1914) and *Edna: The Girl of the Street* (1915), demonstrate his career-long interest in urban characters and settings. Of his many dramas, the short *Lima Beans* (1916) is one of the most interesting for its whimsical flouting of convention and for its being produced by the Provincetown Players (with whom Eugene O'NEILL put on many of his early plays). K.'s two early volumes of verse, *Mushrooms* (1916) and *Blood of Things* (1920), demonstrate the influence of Pound and Walt WHITMAN, and also his interest in finding verbal equivalents for music. With *Less Lonely* (1923) and subsequent volumes, K.'s verse turned towards rhyme and more traditional forms.

BIBLIOGRAPHY: Murphy, R., "A. K.," in Quartermain, P., ed., *DLB,* vol. 54, *American Poets, 1880–1945* (1987): 192–201; Turco, L., "The Age of Pound," *ConP* 4, 3 (1982): 33–46

CHRISTOPHER MACGOWAN

KUMIN, Maxine [Winokur]

b. 6 June 1925, Philadelphia, Pennsylvania

Whether it be the death of a parent, the relinquishment of children as they leave home, or the sickness of a friend, more than any other postmodern poet, K. is concerned with themes of loss. With her New Hampshire farm as the chief locale for her poetry, as she herself put it, "Practically all of [my poems] have come out of this geography and this state of mind."

K. began her poetic career late in life, a late blooming she attributes to a disparaging remark from a workshop instructor at Radcliffe College in Boston when she was an undergraduate. The instructor wrote on the front of her portfolio, "Say it with flowers, but for God's sake, don't try to write poems." K. says, "I didn't write another poem for six years." Soon though, after a master's degree and three children, she found encouragement at the Boston Center for Adult Education, and by 1961 had produced her first book of poems, *Halfway.* Twelve years later, she was to receive the Pulitzer Prize for *Up Country: Poems of New England* (1972).

Unlike many modernist and postmodern poets, K. does not view the universe as chaotic and meaningless but insists in *To Make a Prairie* (1979) that there is an order to be discovered in both the natural world and the human one. In her poems, the counterpart to an insistence on order has always been an exacting pattern of syllable count and rhyme. In fact, the more psychically difficult the material the more she seems to choose a difficult pattern, finding that such restrictions direct her to be honest and truthful. For example, in "Mother Rosarine," an early poem about the ethnic confusions caused by her education as a Jew attending a Catholic convent school, she uses an intricate pattern of rhymes and half-rhymes counterpointed with lines of identical syllable counts and an extraordinarily complicated series of metaphors. Finally, Mother Rosarine appears as a kind of coach, who rouses students to root for their own side, no matter what that side might be. In this way, the powerful generosity of Mother Rosarine releases K. to validate her own ethnicity as a Jew.

K. has also been labeled as a transcendental poet, perhaps partly because of her view of poem-making, which she holds as sacred and God-given in the sense that the style of composition and the content of a poem are beyond conscious control. For example, she refused to allow entrance to a group of behavioral scientists from Harvard when they requested permission to observe her while she was writing a poem to see whether the mention of key words or carrying out of specific acts would change the way she built a poem. Her poetry is also transcendental because of its emphasis not only on loss but also on recovery. Because this recovery is not a benign fantasy, but rather an assertion of the effort to go on, like 20th-c. German poet, Rainer Maria Rilke, K. confronts nature as it is. In addition, like her fellow New England poet, Robert FROST—she has even been dubbed Roberta Frost—whether tracing the seasonal pattern of nature, the middle-age decrepitude of a horse, or the death of a friend, K. is mentally tough.

Another affiliation, although one she rejects, is her identification with the confessional school of American poets, such as Robert LOWELL and Anne SEXTON. In a similar way to such poets, although without the inclusion of details about herself, K. involves the reader with members of her own family. Specifically, she explores the rich and subtle relationship she enjoys with parents and daughters, especially the phenomenon of parents departing toward death at about the same time that children are going out on their own. In seismographic poems such as "The Pawnbroker," "Family Reunion" and "Changing the Children," K. records the shock of these losses and the necessity of survival and of compassion for oneself and others.

K. has been a prolific writer, producing eleven books of poetry, four novels for adults, a book of short stories, three books of essays, and twenty children's books. Many of the children's books were written with the late poet Anne Sexton, with whom she was friends for eighteen years.

Critics have found that she does her best work when she insists on her individuality, namely her private approach to pastoral themes of loss and recovery, one in which she conveys a sense that after disaster hits, she will be left standing. In cases where she has sought a more public voice, for instance, in *The Long Approach* (1985), in which she wrote poems on such topics as pollution, religious persecution, nuclear holocaust, and famine, critics say she has foundered. Despite this assessment, however, an opinion poem on the gas chambers of World War II called "Chipmunks" is her most anthologized and her most famous piece. Critical assessment of her work must necessarily be inconclusive at this point. Nevertheless, a most important feature of K.'s poetry may turn out to be that it is written in the best feminist tradition. Acknowledging Marianne MOORE as her chief mentor, K. is not depressed or victimized like Sylvia PLATH, as the U.S. has often preferred its woman poets to be. Quite the contrary, she is both realistic and idealist, both private and public, both tough and compassionate. Although critics find some poems seem to have a plot mapped out before they are written, the best are those whose very process produce their own X-ray vision of the world. As John CIARDI put it, "M. K. knows how see things. . . . When she looks at something . . . I see it better. . . . I therefore trust her."

BIBLIOGRAPHY: Arthurs, A., "On Friendship and M. K.," *PrS* 71 (Winter 1997): 111–16; Grosholz, E., ed., *Telling the Barn Swallow: Poets on the Poetry of M. K.* (1997); Shomer, E., "An Interview with M. K.," *MR* 37 (Winter 1996–97): 531–55

SUSAN HARRINGTON

KUNITZ, Stanley [Jasspon]

b. 29 July 1905, Worcester, Massachusetts

K. set forth a literary goal to transform "life into legend," a personal and poetic credo that invites investigation of the biographical sources of his works. The suicide of K.'s father several weeks before K.'s birth led K. to develop his signal poetic themes: the quest for identity and the search for the father. These themes, dealt with obliquely in his early volumes of poetry, *Intellectual Things* (1930) and *Passport to War* (1944), received more explicit treatment in *Selected Poems, 1928–1958* (1958), awarded the Pulitzer Prize in 1959, and *The Testing Tree* (1971). In such poems as "The Portrait," "The Magic Curtain," and "The Testing-Tree," K. returned to the experiences of his Worcester childhood to explore the pain of loss and the anguish of self-examination. His later poems, in K.'s words, displayed a "more open style, based on natural speech rhythms."

After receiving both his B.A. and M.A. from Harvard, K. was informed that "Anglo-Saxon students would resent being taught English literature by a Jew," an encounter with anti-Semitism that caused him to turn to editing, translation, and temporary teaching posts rather than a career in academe. His founding of the *Wilson Library Bulletin* led to collaborations on an extensive *Biographical Series* on American, British, and world authors. A respected mentor to aspiring poets, K. edited the Yale Series of Younger Poets from 1970 to 1977. His fascination with archetypal themes derived from mythology, evident in the imagery of a number of poems, manifests itself in the foreword to *Passing Through: The Later Poems New and Selected* (1995). That interest, as well as his notion that artists share a "struggle to achieve an imaginary order out of the real disorder of life, K. articulates more fully in his collected essays, *A Kind of Order, a Kind of Folly* (1975).

The honors K. has received for his poetry include the Bollingen Prize, the Harriet Monroe Award, and the National Book Award.

BIBLIOGRAPHY: Henault, M., *S. K.* (1980); Moss, S., ed., *Interviews and Encounters with S. K.* (1993); Orr, G., *S. K.* (1985)

KENT LJUNGQUIST

KUSHNER, Tony

b. 16 July 1956, New York City

K. has earned theater credentials since the 1980s as director and playwright, and has become widely recognized following London and Broadway productions of his play *Angels in America: A Gay Fantasia on National Themes* (1993). Many believe that *Angels in America*—a seven-hour, two-part Pulitzer Prize winner—goes beyond the so-called "AIDS Play," exemplified by Larry Kramer's *The Normal Heart* (1985), and Paul Rudnick's *Jeffrey* (1994), and others, to interrogate the American democratic experiment from a materialist and queer perspective. *Angels in America*'s ubiquity during the 1994–95 season, both in the U.S. and abroad, was in part owing to unprecedented promotion, but the play and K. deserve their high recognition for raising the intellectual standards of American drama and giving impetus to plays with a broader range of theatrical and social interest.

K.'s mature art and commitments derive from his study of literature, art, philosophy, and theater at Columbia University and New York University, and from his social activism and experiences within a New York gay community struggling with AIDS, homophobia, and government neglect. His philosophical orientation is materialist, depending on Marxian theory with a "queer" inflection. Bertolt Brecht is K.'s theatrical inspiration, and Brechtian as well as queer theory and performance both concern themselves with identity's theatricality and the politics of seeming, though Brecht's stress is on economics and queer theory stresses questions of gender; K. is concerned with both economics, gender, and, to some extent, race, as he tries to offer a way to think about America's past and future that does not depend upon religious and national myths. K.'s dramaturgy in *Angels in America* is also reminiscent of Shakespeare's in that it depends on the reciprocal play and mutual commentary of character foils to create meaning.

Angels in America was written and often produced in two parts, the first entitled "Millennium Approaches" and the second entitled "Perestroika." These two parts, like their two titles, are related ironically: "Millennium Approaches" holds out the promise of redemption and "Perestroika" concerns what happens when redemption fails to appear, when lives and communities may still be reconstituted—"perestroika" is Russian for "rebuilding." As a matter of playwriting, "Perestroika" fails to fulfill the utopian promise of "Millennium Approaches"; however, that failure is intentional, because it, like other personal and political failures the play enacts, inspires thinking about new, more material, and more productive ways lives that may be lived and the vital communities that may be created.

With their roots in important American traditions, the characters in *Angels in America* inhabit New York City during the AIDS epidemic. Prior Walter, an AIDS victim, is of an ancient English family with plague victims in other centuries. Joe, newly arrived from Utah with Harper, his wife, is a young Mormon attorney. Hannah, Joe's mother, will follow the couple to New York. Louis, a wordprocessor-intellectual, is secular Jewish, as is the notorious lawyer Roy Cohn, and also one of Cohn's most famous capital convictions, the alleged spy Ethel Rosenberg, who appears to Cohn in his hospital room as a mildly vengeful ghost. Cohn, like Prior, is afflicted with AIDS, and is nursed by—and reviled by—Belize, an African American and friend to Prior and Louis. There is also an angel, whose dive through Prior's ceiling concludes "Millennium Approaches." This angel has multiple associations: with Mormon founder Joseph Smith's angelic messenger, with Gabriel of the Christian Rapture and Apocalypse and with other religious annunciators, and with Walter Benjamin's "Angel of History."

The parallel plots of *Angels in America* repeat a pattern of betrayal and rebuilding of betrayal's victims. The pattern is repeated at different levels, ranging from the personal to the political and extending, metaphorically, at least, even to the cosmological. As "Millennium Approaches" begins, Joe is failing to suppress his homosexuality while his wife grapples with New York City life. With Prior, Louis is soon confronted with caring for a lover with full-blown AIDS. Louis and Joe come together, Louis abandoning Prior to his AIDS and Joe abandoning Harper to her insanity. In the end, Joe and Louis try to return to their original partners, but are repulsed by Harper and Prior, respectively. Both Harper and Prior, having been left to themselves, are in some stage of growth beyond the original relationship and neither is willing to resume life on the old basis.

Meanwhile, Cohn, who respects on self-assertive audacity, insists that Joe protect him from disbarment from within the Justice Department. Cohn betrays Joe by using his paternal, mentoring position to warp Joe's pioneer pragmatism into a more Machievellian instrument. More broadly, Cohn represents for K. the betrayals of neoconservatives, whose brazen self-interest, during the Reagan years especially, caused much suffering among AIDS victims and many other people.

But when Cohn dies from AIDS midway through "Perestroika," Louis, with the help of Ethel's ghost, is still able to say a Jewish Kaddish or blessing over his corpse. Louis and Ethel are Cohn's victims; however, their blessing signals a begrudging relatedness to Cohn, and, indeed, all seem implicated in betrayals. And though personal and even political failings may cause real suffering and may be reproached for that reason, morality in the play is decentered. In the play, individuals transform themselves and, in doing so, alter the lives around them. Without forgiving particular sins, the play does suggest that identity, far from fixed, is really transformational, and that events do not always meet our expectations. In *Angels in America,* most projects are failing, or outliving their usefulness, and individuals, if they survive, move onward, assuming new identities suitable to new circumstances. Hence, in the the play's final scene, Hannah, the strictly religious Mormon mother, has become a New Yorker and has joined in with the gay companions Louis, Prior, and Belize, with whom she has shared her most life-altering experiences. As in this case, transformed identities invite new relationships, new allegiances, and new points of view. This insight—that identity and relationships are never fixed or "naturally" anything in particular—is central to Marxist and queer theory. In both of these, normality is a socially constructed code that is violently enforced and one that mediates between individuals and material reality, inhibiting productive transformations, including personal and political "perestroikas." *Angels in America* acknowledges and affirms the contingency of identity and its potential both for creation and destruction.

If material conditions and potentialities are most important to K., active mythologies must be dismantled. Hence, the Angel and its accompanying mythic baggage must be exposed. Prior, like Jonah, has been singled out as a prophet, but he resists his prophetic role, because the failures here are the Angel and a criminally negligent God. As the play closes, a convocation of angels is updating scripture to conform to the material fact of on-going, human struggle and affirmation on Earth. Indeed, if the angel is a multivalent religious entity, it may symbolize any narrative that totalizes human history, be it the Christian narrative of apocalypse, the Judaic Messianic narrative, the modern capitalist narrative of progress, or the Marxist narrative of communist utopia. As an agent favoring any of these historical narratives, the Angel can also be associated with constructions of reality and identity that conform to, and are limited by, an ideological system or master narrative. In place of any of these belief systems or theories, K. substitutes a theory of continual contingency, one in which identity is free, in which sad and happy conclusions are uncertain, and where there is potential for new combinations of transformed identities.

BIBLIOGRAPHY: McNulty, C., "'Angels in America': T. K.'s Theses on the Philosophy of History," *MD* 39 (Spring 1996): 84–96; Posnock, R., "Roy Cohn in America," *Raritan* 13 (Winter 1994): 64–77; Rogoff, G., "Angels in America, Devils in the Wings," *Theater* 24 (1993): 21–29; Savran, D., "T. K.," in Kolin, P. C., and C. H. Kullman, eds., *Speaking on Stage: Interviews with Contemporary American Playwrights* (1996): 291–313

KEITH APPLER

LA FARGE, Oliver

b. 19 December 1901, New York City; d. 2 August 1963, Albuquerque, New Mexico

Trained as both anthropologist and creative writer, L. devoted himself to both callings throughout his career. He produced twenty-four books, including works of fiction—novels and short story collections—and nonfiction treatises in popular anthropology and social history.

Educated at Harvard, where he served on the editorial board of the *Harvard Advocate* and majored in anthropology, L. experienced the American Southwest for the first time on an archeological field trip to northern Arizona. The region, where he spent several summers doing fieldwork during the 1920s, became the setting for his most important novels: *Laughing Boy* (1929), which won the Pulitzer Prize, and *The Enemy Gods* (1937)—both of which deal with Navajos.

Like most 20th-c. novelists who have treated Native American subjects, L. focused on the problems of culture contact. The title character of *Laughing Boy*, his first novel, is a tradition-oriented silversmith who meets a Euro-Americanized woman at a ceremony. Slim Girl's employment as a servant to a missionary's wife and her liaison with an Anglo rancher have exposed her to a way of life that Laughing Boy finds repugnant. Their marriage and his attempts to woo her back to traditional ways seem to be working when she is tragically killed by a bullet meant for him. The novel ends with Laughing Boy's finding solace and harmony (a value especially prized by Navajos) through the ritual of ceremony.

The novel's contemporary appeal probably derived partially from its romantic theme of ill-fated love. But its popularity also stemmed from L.'s exploiting the "vanishing American" image that had long been part of the Euroamerican imagination. Moreover, his apparent sympathy for the traditional way of life of the Navajo allied L. with the enthusiasts for Native Americana who had been major influences on American art and literature, especially that of the Southwest, for a decade or so before his novel was published.

Though two novels separated it from *Laughing Boy, The Enemy Gods* (1937) returned L. to the setting that had brought his original literary success. Again focusing on the problems generated by culture contact, he concentrates more specifically on contemporary problems faced by the Navajo. The novel's development stresses the struggle for a Navajo boy's allegiance between the Protestant missionaries who have adopted him and his uncle, a ceremonial singer. The novel's protagonist, Myron Begay, affords L. a vehicle for presentating many of the conflicts facing Navajos during the 1930s: between Christianity and traditional religion, between Euroamerican education and the heritage of Navajo enculturation, between the urban allurements of Santa Fe and the high desert of the Four Corners region. The novel, while regarded by L. and by some critics as his most significant, did not have the popular appeal of *Laughing Boy*.

Many of L.'s short stories also reflected his commitment to a sympathetic depiction in fiction of Native Americans. These stories have been collected in *Yellow Sun, Bright Sky* (1988).

L. produced little in anthropology that was truly original. He wrote two collaborative works early in his career based on field research in Central America: *Tribes and Temples* (1927, with Frans Blom) and *The Year Bearer's People* (1931, with Douglas Byers). Most of his other nonfiction offered popularized overviews of ethnological topics, especially ones relevant to American Indians, for whom he remained an outspoken advocate throughout his life.

BIBLIOGRAPHY: Gillis, E. A., *O. L.* (1967); McNickle, D., *Indian Man: A Life of O. L.* (1971); Pearce, T., *O. L.* (1972)

WILLIAM M. CLEMENTS

LANGUAGE AND DIALECT

The conundrum of what constitutes a "language" and what constitutes a "dialect" confronts American literature from its very beginning, for the British considered the language spoken and written in the American colonies a substandard dialect. The American version of the English language asserts its identity with the publication in 1919 of H. L. MENCKEN's *The American Language*. The growing body of literature produced in the U.S. in the early 19th c. significantly improved the status of this lowly dialect as did the appearance of Noah Webster's grammar and dictionary. Once the U.S. was politically independent of England, it quickly established its own standard. The many varieties of American English—for there was already significant linguistic variety in the country—came to be seen in their turn as dialects. Many American writers, however, valued this linguistic abundance and included many of the country's dialects in their literary works.

Francis Moore, in 1735, criticized the "barbarous English" that used the word "bluff" to describe a river bank. In 1781, John Witherspoon made up the first collection of grammatical errors and vulgarisms that were peculiarly American, for which he coined the term "Americanisms." A certain Captain Hamilton in 1833 demonstrates the invective the British directed at the language used in America. He claims that his denunciation is "the natural feeling of an Englishman at finding the language of Shakespeare and Milton thus gratuitously degraded. Unless the present progress of change be arrested by an increase of taste and judgment in the more educated classes, there can be no doubt that, in another century, the dialect of the Americans will become utterly unintelligible to an Englishman, and that the nation will be cut off from the advantages arising from their participation in British literature." Hamilton's vituperation exemplifies a purist view of language, which allows only one fixed, immutable, correct version, which sees difference and change as degradation, which links the supposed degradation to inferiority and which arrogantly assumes that the literature in the "true" English will benevolently improve the poor dialectal stepchild.

Fortunately, Americans did not take such British diatribes to heart and simply set to work creating literature with their supposedly degraded form of English. They could do so because of the difference between the purist's definitions of language and dialect and the linguistic reality of what constitutes a dialect versus a language. Purists, in this case the British critics, hold that there is one and only one version of English that is fit for serious purposes like politics, science, theology, and literature and that this version constitutes the language. Since the American version of English was patently different in grammar, vocabulary, and pronunciation from the British version, America's version was incorrect and not a true language, but rather a "dialect," which is, by the purist's definition, an inferior and degraded form of the language. Linguistically speaking, however, the English language is the sum of all the versions as used by all of the people currently using it. No one knows the entire language. Everyone uses a version or dialect of English, or even several versions. And just as one version of language, German for example, is not superior to English because it has three genders or because it has an elaborate case system, and neither is one dialect superior to another because of differences in vocabulary or grammar. The British contempt for the American version of English reflected their contempt for America and their appreciation of their own supposed superiority. The American version of English was nevertheless just as linguistically fit for intellectual and literary expression as its British cousin.

Dialect has thus been part of the American literary tradition from its very beginning. We could argue that all of American literature is written in "dialect," as is all British literature, for a dialect is "a variety of language used by one group with features of pronunciation, vocabulary and grammar that distinguish it from other varieties." What the British considered a barbarous dialect has, however, come to consider itself a language in its own right, thus proving the linguistic adage that a language is a dialect with an army and a navy. Once the American colonies became the U.S., once Webster wrote his grammar and dictionary, once writers used the American dialect and publishing houses published it and readers bought books written in it, that which had been considered barbarous and ungrammatical became a language. Ironically, once the American dialect gained the status of a language, the democratic American soil gave birth to American purists who began leveling and still level the same charges of barbarism and degradation that the British shot at the Americans at speakers and writers of nonstandard American English dialects. Were these dialects to gain a country, a grammar, a dictionary and a literary tradition, so too would they be considered languages in their own right.

Despite the criticism of the British, early American literature quickly made room for varieties of American English. In the earliest American literature, dialect generally indicates the character's inferior or marginal social status. It appears that by the end of the 18th c., at least ten plays included dialect to portray African American characters. These characters are stereotypically contented slaves or comic figures. Early-19th-c. humorous writing often used dialect to comic ends. George Washington HARRIS, in his portrayal of a Tennessee mountain man, Sut Lovingood, uses dialect to mark Sut as a buffoon and laughing stock. Walt WHITMAN saw the greatness of the U.S. in the ordinary people and set out to be the poet of the people, incorporating into his poetry the use of everyday speech. In the late 19th c., the local color movement deliberately sought to render the customs and the ways of thinking and speaking that were particular to different regions of the U.S. In the writings of Bret HARTE, Sarah Orne JEWETT, Marjorie Kinnan RAWLINGS, Kate CHOPIN, and most particularly Samuel Langhorne CLEMENS, the local ways of being and talking were treated very seriously and used to paint a more realistic picture of the variety in American life. In the *Adventures of Huckleberry Finn,* Clemens consciously sets out to include several dialects and several variations of one of those dialects. His use of dialect is not limited to the dialogue, but extends to the novel's narrative voice. Dialect is central to Huck's character as well as Jim's and is a means of social criticism as well as a theme in itself. Huck's language marks him as socially inferior, yet he is more humane and honest than his supposed betters, for truth and humanity are not corollaries of social status or middle-class grammar. Clemens's work was a turning point in the use of nonstandard varieties of English in literature, and dialect has been an important literary technique in much American literature from Stephen CRANE to Langston HUGHES, Zora Neale HURSTON, William FAULKNER, John STEINBECK, and Carson MCCULLERS. Indeed, many authors and works not traditionally considered part of the local color movement could be considered part of this tradition in that they portray settings, customs, ways of thinking and feeling that are particular not to region, but to a class, gender or otherwise distinctive group. We could thus consider the "teenagerese" in J. D. SALINGER's *Catcher in the Rye* as a dialect.

The writer who chooses to include dialect faces particular challenges. Dialects are marked by differences in pronunciation, vocabulary, grammar, intonation, stress, and pitch. Pronunciation, vocabulary, and grammar are the salient differences with pronunciation perhaps being the most varied and most noticeable. Literature rarely includes dialectal differences in stress, tone, and pitch. Early efforts to render dialects tried to include differences in pronunciation, but phonological differences are virtually impossible to render without an accepted standard such as the international phonetic alphabet. Hence, early renditions of dialect are often simply examples of unconventional spelling called eye dialect rather than true records of pronunciation. For example, in "This iz th' way to Mareez," the "s" of "is" and "Marie's" is pronounced as a "z" even in standard speech. These spellings look like dialect to the reader's eye, but actually reflect standard pro-

nunciation. They function simply to indicate that the character's language is somehow not standard. Characters whose words are spelled conventionally are presumed to be speaking whatever version of English is standard in their area. This convention holds even today, for writers use conventional spelling for works set in Los Angeles, New Orleans, Chicago, and London though actual pronunciation varies considerably. After 1850, more and more of the dialect rendered in literature includes actual dialectal pronunciation, but even authors who treat dialect seriously and work hard to convey it accurately limit the amount of unconventional spellings and still often include eye dialect. Many 20th-c. writers, for example Faulkner and Alice WALKER, do not generally try to render phonological differences. They instead convey their characters' particular language through vocabulary, grammar, images, and rhythm.

Literary dialects are then generally inaccurate and incomplete renderings of a particular dialect, for too many nonstandard spellings, too many regional words or grammatical structures make the literary work difficult reading for anyone who does not know the dialect. Writers usually want to reach a wide audience. They tend to select only enough features to give the flavor of dialect and to indicate the character's regional or social background, and they often regularize these dialect features. Speakers of dialect often know standard pronunciation, vocabulary, and grammar, and some of them switch from the nonstandard to the standard as the situation demands. This complex usage is rarely rendered in literature.

Linguistically, to speak about dialect is to speak about language, for a dialect is simply a aversion of the total language. Historically speaking, however, language and dialect have a different meaning as a part of literary studies. Traditionally, the study of language in literary studies has been the careful analysis of rhyme, rhythm, meter, diction, syntax, assonance, alliteration, metaphor, simile, and other tropes and rhetorical figures. Poetry has been the most usual recipient of such careful, word for word scrutiny, but modern criticism has extended such analysis to the language of fiction and drama. This practice of analyzing the language in a literary work has a long tradition in classical rhetoric, and it in fact implicitly recognizes that the language used in literature and particularly in poetry is a distinctive version of the English language. In modern terminology, this literary language is a dialect just like the language used by Clemens. Contemporary approaches to analyzing language in literature, called stylistics, indeed treat both of these varieties as dialects of English. Modern analysts of language do not limit scrutiny of language to literary dialects, but can also treat scientific prose and the language of advertising and television versions of English that are certainly not generally regarded as part of the literary tradition looking at them as distinct dialects of English.

The analysis of language has long been a part of literary studies, but it has generally been limited to the special use of language as found in poetry. The scientific study of language linguistics is a fairly recent science, but it has rejuvenated the study of stylistics in recent years and will undoubtedly continue to contribute to our general understanding of just what constitutes a language and what constitutes a dialect.

BIBLIOGRAPHY: Bolton, W. F., and D. Crystal, eds., *The English Language* (1987); Burkett, E. M., *American English Dialects in Literature* (1978); Dillard, J. L., *Black English: Its History and Usage in the United States* (1972); Mencken, H. L., *The American Language,* 4th rev. ed. (1963); Traugott, E. C., and M. L. Pratt, *Linguistics for Students of Literature* (1980); Wolfram, W., *Dialects and American English* (1990)

HEIDI PRESCHLER

LANIER, Sidney [Clopton]

b. 3 February 1842, Macon, Georgia; d. 7 September 1881, Lynn, North Carolina

L., a Georgia-born writer best known for the musicality of his verse, is the only notable American poet who was also a professional musician. This fact is critical to an appreciation of his poetry, which developed from conventional 19th-c. verse into a highly individual and innovative form. L. came form a genteel tradition that looked with disfavor upon a profession in the arts—especially for a man—and he therefore spent precious years trying to resolve the conflict between what his tradition expected of him and what he desired. This tension appears as one of the major themes in his work, that of the conflict between art and materialism. Other major themes are: the power of nature, science as a progressive force, a deep religious faith, the interrelationship of music and poetry, and music as symbolic of human harmony. This last idea is epitomized in his most often quoted line from "The Symphony": "Music is Love in search of a word."

Many of these themes L. treated in standard conventional poetic form; but as he was increasingly exposed to the new program music of the day, such as the music of Wagner and Liszt, he attempted freer structure and the blending of voices and tones characteristic of symphonic composition. His mature poems—most notably "The Symphony," "The Marshes of Glynn," and "Sunrise"—are designed for their sound as much as for their literal meaning. L.'s creation of synaesthetic verse, in which he merged sound and idea into very musical poetry, ultimately

has secured his reputation, but has also drawn negative criticism from those who have found it lush and overwritten.

In his short life, L. managed to accomplish a great deal: he played first flute in the Peabody Conservatory Orchestra in Baltimore; lectured widely on Shakespeare and on the English novel; wrote an acclaimed study of English prosody, *The Science of English Verse* (1880), a Civil War novel entitled *Tiger-Lilies* (1867), numerous essays on music and on literature, and editions for children of classic tales; and he composed many musical pieces. L. wrote his most important poetry late in a life cut short by tuberculosis, which he contracted in a Civil War prisoner-of-war camp. L.'s intellectual energy, constantly challenged by illness and financial pressures, was directed in many different directions, and he was often forced to waste time and strength in writing "potboilers" to support his young family. The worlds of poetry and music, however, inspired his strongest efforts and works of lasting significance. His work was published in a number of periodicals during his lifetime, and his national reputation was recognized in 1876—the year his first volume of poems was published—when he was commissioned to write the words for a cantata to be performed at the U.S. Centennial Exposition in Philadelphia.

As with any artist dying prematurely, there is the difficulty of assessing an unfulfilled career. L.'s innovative poetic techniques were just being fine-tuned at the time of his death, so much must be left to speculation. Despite his many accomplishments, and great surges of popularity and even adulation, L. has never been accorded more than minor literary status. Yet there is still a prodigious output to consider for a number of reasons: his poetry delights the ear and mind, his versification provides an intriguing contrast to mainstream late 19th-c. poetry, and his prose (particularly the essays and letters) gives us a rich picture of intellectual and artistic life in America in the decade and a half following the Civil War.

BIBLIOGRAPHY: Anderson, C. R., ed., *Centennial Edition of the Works of S. L.* (1945); Bain, R., and J. M. Flora, eds., *Fifty Southern Writers before 1900* (1987); De Bellis, J., *S. L.* (1972); De Bellis, J., *S. L., Henry Timrod, and Paul Hamilton Hayne: A Reference Guide* (1978); Gabin, J. S., *A Living Minstrelsy: The Poetry and Music of S. L.* (1985)

JANE S. GABIN

LARDNER, Ring [Old Wilmer]

b. 6 March 1885, Niles, Michigan; d. 25 September 1933, East Hampton, New York

From the beginning of his career, whose early success rested on the quintessentially American sport of baseball and that most "American" of characters, Jack Keefe of *You Know Me Al* (1916), L. has embodied for critics the paradox of an aristocratic intellect whose most sustained personae were semiliterate "wise boobs." The "wise-boob" figure has many nuances, ranging from the completely self-deluded and unregenerately dumb Jack Keefe to characters who are equally uneducated but acute enough about certain worldly matters, but nowhere among them is there a genuinely wise man. L. was said to have captured the American voice at its most elemental in these characters, and therein lies the persistent critical ambivalence about the value of his work. His vision of a materialistic country peopled by characters who just want to get their share in the American dream threatens to confirm the critic's worst fear: that, as Henry JAMES implied, Americans—and thus American artists—are daisies, open-hearted enough, but flat, common, and without the deepest dyes. Americans took the three dimensional, multifaceted diamond and laid it out on a field, and L. chose to write about it. And this, wrote Virginia Woolf in a statement as noteworthy for its condescension as for its praise, was a fortunate choice, since his "interest in games" gave him "a clue, a centre, a meeting place for the divers activities of people whom a vast continent isolates, whom no tradition controls."

His work has been seen as the product of a chronic underachiever, one who found it easier to satirize venal superficiality than to probe the human condition. Maxwell Perkins and F. Scott FITZGERALD were among the first to beg L. to live up to his talents and write a novel; that L. chose to remain a "miniaturist" maddened even Fitzgerald into writing, "It's a hell of a lot more difficult to build up a long groan than to develop a couple of short coughs." Nicknamed "Old Owl Eyes," L. was reticent, gaunt, by all accounts tragic-looking. The very picture of the tortured artist, he refused to play the role. His career as a journalist, his remarkable financial success, his obdurate refusal ever to take himself seriously as an artist, all have undermined his position in the American canon.

L. published continuously from 1906 until his death in 1933; during long periods, he wrote six newspaper columns a week while continuing to produce stories, sometimes at the rate of ten a year. He also worked tirelessly and without significant success in theatrical collaborations; musical comedy entranced him, perhaps because as a popular, money-making spectacle it embodied in extravagant scale his delight in the ludicrous. His published work amounts to twenty-three books, among them collections of short stories, plays, autobiographical essays, and poetry. *June Moon* (1930), a collaboration with George S. KAUFMAN adapting his story "Some Like Them Cold," was his greatest stage success. His nonsense plays, written in

the 1920s, defy literary classification, although Ernest HEMINGWAY saw "I Gaspiri" (1924) as a corrective to the pretensions of the Dadaists. *Round Up* (1929), published for the Literary Guild, contains thirty-five previously published stories. The posthumous *First and Last* (1934) resurrected much of L.'s journalistic work and many previously uncollected miscellaneous pieces. *The Portable L.* (1946) and *The R. L. Reader* (1963) anthologize his most important work, and *Some Champions* (1976) contains previously unpublished essays and stories.

The semi-literate figures L. brought to life were unmistakably American in the way they sounded: L. transcribed a vernacular so vivid that it came to be called "Ringlish." But at heart all of L.'s characters share a damning impenetrability that is as total for the rich and famous and the intellectually pretentious as it is for brash ballplayers and lowdown, gold digging women. He had a perfect ear—he was able to identify pitch accurately even from the next room—and yet what he recorded were for the most part voices emitted from people completely deaf to their own assertive stupidities. His characters are themselves utterly without intellectual or spiritual resonance; their deficiencies are cautionary, lack resonates with lack. The absurdist non-sequiturs of his nonsense plays are only slight extensions beyond the "dialogue" of the ego-ridden solipsists of his short stories, characters who no more listen to each other than they really hear themselves. Mabelle Gillespie of "Some like Them Cold" brags to her correspondent that "it is as good as a show to hear me talk." The half-mad ballplayer Elliott in "My Roomy" is a superb batter, but he will not field the ball; he sends but does not receive. He tears up unread letters from his fiancee because "she can't tell me nothin' I don't know already." Small wonder that L.'s only endearing characters are children, like the four-year-old narrator of "The Young Immigrunts" (1920), for the child's literal-mindedness and self-centeredness are appropriate to his age. The gap between what the child says and what the reader intuits results not from his arrogance but from his innocence.

L.'s most famous story, "Haircut," is the monologue of a loquacious barber who unwittingly anatomizes not only the vicious prankster Jim Kendall but a whole town full of unleavened consciousness, where only the village half-wit responds with outrage to Kendall's cruelties. "Haircut" epitomizes the dynamics of character for L.: the barber has under his razor a captive audience—a head of hair, a chin to be shaved, a person reduced to component parts. L.'s characters see each other and the world only in fragments, yet they decide immediately who plays in the bush leagues and who plays in the majors—that is, who might be important enough to be used to their advantage. The one-sided epistolary form of *You Know Me Al* underscores L.'s insistence that for his characters, who are at once both vacuous and self-righteous, self is all there is. For despite Keefe's considerable but completely unrefined skills as a pitcher, his letters reveal him as a man so well satisfied with himself that he is impervious to change; his character is even more static than the traditional picaro with whom Keefe shares many similarities, because at the least the picaro becomes streetwise. Friend Al remains a wordless absence, a letter drop, because anything he might say to Keefe, unless it were praise, would remain unheard.

Critics, since Clifton Fadiman's extremist pronouncement in 1933 that L. hated humanity, have been splitting hairs on L.'s alleged misanthropy. But L. communicated something more profound than misanthropy, something that Dorothy PARKER called astutely as "his sad, bitter pity." He implies that isolation is not a choice but the human condition, which one covers up with the sound of one's voice, loud or soft, brash or humble, stupid or smart. At best, one can post a daily letter and hope someone receives and reads it with the forbearance friend Al extends to Everyman Jack Keefe. The messages L.'s characters send are comic, but often poignant with unintended ambiguity: when the foredoomed Danny Warner of *Loss with a Smile* (1933) brags that he runs "like a street" instead of "like a streak" he unknowingly speaks the truth, about himself and all of L.'s locomotive characters who endlessly traverse the undeviating paths of their own spiritual limitations.

L.'s fictional voices are breathless with self-revelation; on this continuum and in the persona of the wise boob, he included himself autobiographically, always with comic self-deprecation. He did not exclude himself from his indictments of humankind's folly. Otto Friedrich called him, "a lonely man of genius pretending to be ordinary and sociable, a man of great perception pretending not to understand things he understood only too well." The flat, uninflected souls within his fiction caricature his own isolation; they cover it up with the persiflage and exacerbate it with arrogance, but they couldn't, even had they L.'s awareness, escape it. *I Gaspari* sums up L.'s vision of character in isolation: when the Second Stranger asks, "Are you married?" the First Stranger answers, "I don't know. There's a woman living with me, but I can't place her."

BIBLIOGRAPHY: Bruccoli, M. J., and R. Layman, eds., *R. L.: A Descriptive Bibliography* (1976); Caruthers, C. M., *Letters from R.* (1979); Caruthers, C. M., ed., *Ring Around Max: The Correspondence of R. L. and Max Perkins* (1973); Elder, D., *R. L.: A Biography* (1956); Evans, E., *R. L.* (1979); Friedrich, O., *R. L.* (1965); Geismar, M., *R. L. and the Portrait of Folly* (1972); Lardner, R., Jr., *The Lardners: My Family Remembered* (1976); Patrick, W. R., *R. L.* (1963); Yardley, J., *R.* (1977)

KATHERINE KEARNS

LARSEN, Nella

b. 13 April 1891, Chicago, Illinois; d. 30 March 1964, New York City

Although she was once seen as one of the best writers of the Harlem Renaissance, little certain information is available about L.'s early and later life. In 1930, she was the first black woman to receive a Guggenheim Fellowship for fiction. Her third novel was never finished, however, and literary historians have speculated that she withdrew from literary life because of charges of plagiarism (later proved unfounded) concerning her short story "Sanctuary" (1930). L.'s two novels initially received favorable reviews and critical praise, but their reputations have since fluctuated with the changing political demands made upon novels by African Americans. Alternately praised and criticized for focusing on the educated black middle class, L.'s work has more recently been recognized as critical of that class. While earlier readers stressed L.'s treatment of racial issues through the figure of the mulatta caught between the worlds of two races, more recent studies have examined L.'s exploration of black female sexuality.

Quicksand (1928) concerns Helga Crane, like her creator the daughter of a white immigrant mother and a black father. With stylistic economy and sharp irony, the novel indicts patronizing whites, concessionist blacks, and organized religion. Driven by a desire for luxury and dignity, by racial, sexual, and economic conflicts, Helga repeatedly throws herself enthusiastically into new situations, only to become dissatisfied and abruptly seek a change of environment. From a teaching position at Naxos, a black school in the South, Helga returns to her native Chicago, breaking her engagement with James Vayle, a conventional fellow teacher. She finds work in New York with Mrs. Hayes-Rore, who lectures on race. To escape the continual discussion of race, Helga visits maternal relatives in Copenhagen, where she rejects a proposition and a proposal from the painter Axel Olsen. Tired of being treated as an exotic artifact, she returns to New York. Rejected by Dr. Robert Anderson, to whom she is powerfully attracted, Helga impulsively marries the Reverend Pleasant Green. The novel ends with Helga trapped in Alabama by having five children in as many years.

With equal irony and economy, *Passing* (1929) also treats the conflict between respectability and passion, as well as the masquerade of the title. The novel is focalized through Irene Westover Redfield, who loves security above all else. By chance, Irene reencounters her childhood friend Clare Kendry Bellew, who has married a racist white man unaware of his wife's black ancestry. Although judgmental of Clare for passing as white, Irene finds herself powerfully drawn to her, as the passionate, sensual Clare finds herself increasingly drawn back to the black community. Irene begins to suspect Clare of having an affair with her husband, Dr. Brian Redfield, and the novel ambiguously implies that Irene pushes Clare out a window to her death.

BIBLIOGRAPHY: Davis, T. M., *N. L., Novelist of the Harlem Renaissance* (1994); Larson, C. R., *Invisible Darkness: Jean Toomer and N. L.* (1993); McLendon, J. Y., *The Politics of Color in the Fiction of Jessie Faust and N. L.* (1995)

FRANN MICHEL

LATINO/A LITERATURE

Latino/a experience in the U.S. continues to deal mainly with issues of identity, assimilation, cultural heritage, and artistic expression. The works of Latinos/as are read with a great deal of interest and passion, for the literature functions as a mirror, a reflection of the way Latinos/as are viewed by the mainstream culture—but not always the majority. Readers and critics alike tend to celebrate the literature. It is rich, diverse, constantly growing, and though with a past history, a literature that at present is being created by its contemporary practitioners.

In essence, there is a boom in the literature that is a being forged in English by people who live and work in the U.S., not in Spanish as is the case with the earlier practitioners of centuries past. This is a key difference and a point of departure. Of course, there are still some very real issues and problems facing Latino/a writers in terms of finding outlets and venues for their work. Although more of the work is being published by major publishing houses, most of the interesting and engaging literature comes from small and independent presses that rely upon federal, private, and university grants for stability. Literary journals and reviews have always been an outlet for Latino/a voices, and some of the best work is coming from such sources. However, with the recognition associated with the country's most prestigious literary awards—the Before Columbus Foundation Award, the National Book Award, and the Pulitzer Prize—Latino/a authors are receiving increasing attention from the publishing establishment. Keeping in mind, of course, that much is owed to the groundbreaking work of the Chicano Arts movement of the late 1960s and early 1970s and the emergence of poets such as Rodolfo Gonzales and Alurista.

The Chicano Arts movement was born out of a social and political movement, itself propelled by grassroots activists like Cesar Chavez and Dolores Huerta who played key roles in the unionization of migrant workers achieved through "huelgas" (strikes and boycotts). The plight of the migrant workers and their struggle for recognition had a direct influence on the arts. For example, Luis VALDEZ and Teatro Campesino, his theater troupe, played a pivotal role in fomenting solidarity and new social consciousness. During the strikes, Teatro Campesino performed from the back of flatbed trucks using striking migrant workers as performers. This is the true theater for the people and by the people.

There has been a resurgence of interest in ethnic literatures in America, and Latino/a literature is no exception, as it follows closely behind AFRICAN AMERICAN and NATIVE AMERICAN LITERATURE, or literature written by women, gay males, and lesbians. For the purpose of focus, Latino/a literature, though possessing a rich literary history that goes back hundreds of years—evident in the work of writers such as Maria Amparo Ruiz de Burton and Félix Varela or the valuable work a press like Arte Público is undergoing in their "Recovering the U.S. Hispanic Literary Heritage Series"—is defined here as the literature written in English, and which mainly concerns itself with life here in the U.S., exemplified by the publication in 1959 of José Antonio VILLARREAL's *Pocho*.

Other works that merit "classic" status are among the Mexican Americans Rudolfo ANAYA's *Bless Me, Ultima,* Sandra CISNERO's *The House on Mango Street,* Denise CHAVEZ's *The Last of the Menu Girls,* Tomás Rivera's *And the Earth Did Not Devour Him* (1987), the poetry of Gary SOTO, Jimmy Santiago BACA, Alberto RÍOS, Lorna Dee CERVANTES, and Leroy V. Quintana. Puerto Ricans are the second largest contributors to the canon of Latino/a literature with works such as Judith ORTIZ COFER's *The Line of the Sun,* Piri THOMAS's *Down These Mean Streets,* Ed Vega's *Casualty Report* (1991), and the poetry of Victor Hernandez CRUZ, Miguel Algarin, Tato Laviera, and Sandra Maria Estevez. The next largest group is represented by the Cuban Americans, making recent additions to the canon with work such as Roberto G. FERNANDEZ's *Raining Backwards,* Elías Miguel MUÑOZ's *The Greatest Performance,* Cristina GARCÍA's *Dreaming in Cuban,* Oscar HIJUELOS's *The Mambo Kings Play Songs of Love,* and the poetry of Gustavo PEREZ FIRMAT, Ricardo PAU-LLOSA, and Carolina Hospital.

Currently there are many excellent anthologies that represent the individual groups serve as a testament to the interest that exists in the reading world. These anthologies mostly gather the established and emerging voices from among the main Latino/a groups in the U.S., at present represented by Mexican Americans, Puerto Rican, and Cuban Americans with new voices emerging from the Dominican, Columbian, and Guatemalan communities, all currently represented by the work of Julia ALVAREZ, author of *How the García Girls Lost Their Accents* and Jaime Manrique's *Twilight at the Equator* (1997), Francisco Goldman's *The Long Night of the White Chickens* (1992), and Junot Diaz's *Drown* (1996).

The diversity of voices is impressive, since more writers are developing and becoming established. Teachers, editors, and readers more than ever have to be sensitive to issues of factionalism along national lines, which is only natural, but which sometimes opens the door to the forced nature of grouping so many distinct and separate cultures under the term *Latino/a*. The danger and negative consequence of such grouping is that, in the eyes of many Anglos, the diverse Latino/a cultures are interchangeable. Thus, Hollywood will create absurdities such as Cubans eating tacos, or Anglo actors cast in Latino/a roles only because they have dark hair and a tan. In gathering together Mexican, Puerto Rican, Cuban, Dominican, Columbian, and Guatemalan American writers the intent is to unite, and in so doing allow an audience to determine for him/herself what is shared between these writers and what sets them apart from one another. Bringing all these cultures together under the one term Latino/a may be comparable to the tension of sharing a meal with distant relatives—there is a separate history and experience, yet there exists a bond of recognition, a family camaraderie.

The central point of unity amongst Latino/a writers is language. While they may speak with different accents and use different expressions, they all share the experience of bilingualism. The ability to communicate in two languages, and more importantly to think and feel in two languages, brings with it the phenomenon of at times being unable to express oneself fully in only one. Linguists term this "interference," and generally view it as a negative trait, or shortcoming. They, as Latino/a writers and readers of Latino/a literature, however, assert that the intermingling of the two languages is an effective means of communicating what otherwise could not be expressed. Thus, many Latino/a writers use Spanish in their work because it is an integral part of their experience.

Many Latino/a authors believe that in the lives of their characters Spanish is not a "foreign" language, but rather a vital part of everyday speech and as such should not be emphasized with the use of italics. They emphasize the importance of Spanish by doing this. So many of the writers express themselves in English—the language of the mainstream (whatever that may mean)—but are resisting the destruction of their culture and thus preserve their identity by using Latino/a expressions, points of reference and experiences. Hopefully this will become accepted not as "exotic," but rather part of the redefined mainstream in the arts. Again, this is a clear distinction between Latino/a literature and Latin American literature, which exists solely in Spanish and in translation in the U.S., written by writers who do not live and work in the U.S.

A second facet that all Latino/a cultures share is the need for cultural survival. This is a controversial issue among Latinos/as, since it deals with the question of assimilation. How much of their culture should Latinos/as be willing to lose or suppress in order to participate in mainstream society? The answers to this important question vary, yet it is an issue that all Latino/a writers tackle either directly or in more subtle ways. There are striking differences between a novel like *Bless Me, Ultima* by Rudolfo Anaya and Sandra Cisnero's *The House on Mango Street,* and between these two and Roberto G. Fernandez's *Raining Backwards,* whole worlds. But that's the beauty of so many voices adding to the canon.

Cultural survival is nothing new to Latino/a culture. It has strong roots even outside the U.S., and must be placed in a historical context. Octavio Paz in his book *The Labyrinth of Solitude* places it as a central factor influencing the Mexican psyche. When the Spanish conquest defeated and literally toppled the Aztec Gods of Tenochtitlán, the Aztec name for today's Mexico City, the indigenous people were forced to adopt aspects of Spanish culture and religion in order to survive. Even today, Paz points out, Mexicans use *el disimulo* or "the process of concealment" in everyday life. Testimony to the strength of the indigenous culture is the fact that a merciless Spanish rule and five hundred years of history have not been able to eradicate indigenous myths, culture, values, and languages. The Mexican Department of Education recently issued a report that revealed that there are to this day fifty-two indigenous languages in use in the country. Thus Mexican Americans carry the legacy as cultural survivors with strong ties to their ancestral roots. Chicanos/as have also proven to be cultural survivors on this side of the border. The Treaty of Guadalupe Hidalgo in 1848, which ceded a large portion of Mexico to the U.S., effectively made, from one moment to another, the inhabitants of this vast region a conquered people.

Only this time, the occupying and subjugating power was the U.S.

During this period, corridos, a ballad form that recounted heroic exploits, became popular. These corridos were also precursors to Chicano/a poetry produced in the 20th c., which in effect wrote a history for a people who had been written out of history. Out of this history emerge poets like Alurista, Sergio Elizondo, Raul Salinas, and Rodolfo Gonzales.

The corrido, which emerges out of this conflict, lays the foundation for a poetics that fuses the oral and the written, an element of Chicano/a poetry that demonstrates the bonds between music and word. In the corrido we begin to see the mixing of the Spanish with the English, thus creating a new language with which to express a new reality. This is the "Spanglish" so many contemporary poets, novelists, and playwrights employ as a tool to convey their cultural legacy. Octavio Paz's term of *el disimulo* can also be applied to other Latino/a cultures in the U.S. Like chameleons, Latinos/as camouflage and adapt to new environments without losing their identity. *El disimulo* entails adopting characteristics of the mainstream; this is an effort to disguise the true self, which might be deemed unacceptable.

Although the ties that bind all Latino/a cultures are strong, there are many significant differences that are at times not obvious to a mainstream American public. For instance, many Mexican Americans have a peasant or *campesino* tradition that is rural and carries with it strong ties to the land, illustrated in *Pocho* and *Bless Me, Ultima.* Puerto Ricans, Dominican, and Cuban Americans, being islanders, have strong ties to water. This is true of the work of poets like Victor Hernandez Cruz, Ricardo Pau-Llosa, and Carolina Hospital.

Urban life in the U.S. has given rise to a new tradition in Latino/a literature, that of the *barrio.* While for Mexican Americans the barrio is likely to be in California, the Southwest, or Chicago as is the case in *The House on Mango Street,* for the Puerto Rican the barrio is in New York and evident in the work of Piri Thomas, Ed Vega, and Judith Ortiz Cofer. For Cuban Americans, being Latino/a in the U.S. means also dealing with the dilemmas and frustrations of political exile. Their characters often feel a yearning and sense of loss for a homeland to which they cannot return. This is most obvious in nostalgic literature set in the idyllic Cuba of the past, as well as those speculating on the Cuba of the future, like in the work of Roberto G. Fernandez and Cristina García.

There are also differences in religion. Although due to the Spanish conquest and colonization, Latin America is predominantly Catholic, each region has its own brand of Catholicism. In Cuba, Dominican Republic, and Puerto Rico the influence is African,

because the natives were subjected to genocide shortly after the discovery of the new world by Christopher Columbus. For Mexicans, the influence is indigenous.

The Latino/a experience has many points of divergence from that of the mainstream, so it follows that the literature does too. However, there are common experiences that we all share as human beings, experiences that transcend cultures and find expression in art, making it universal and timeless. Coming of age, for instance, is a theme commonly explored in literature, as are family relationships, the pursuit of the American dream, and death. Latino/a writers draw from a specifically ethnic experience, giving their work a unique point of view that has been overlooked or ignored in mainstream American literature.

BIBLIOGRAPHY: Augenbraun, H., and I. Stavans, eds., *Growing Up Latino* (1994); deDwyer, C. C., ed., *Chicano Voices* (1975); Gonzalez, R., ed., *Currents from the Dancing River* (1994); Hospital, C., *Los Atrevidos: Cuban American Writer* (1989); Kanellos, N., ed., *Hispanic Literature of the United States* (1995); Milligan, B., et al., eds., *Daughters of The Fifth Sun/Hijas del Quinto Sol* (1995); Poey, D., and V. Suarez, eds., *Iguana Dreams: New Latino Fiction* (1993); Poey, D., and V. Suarez, eds., *Little Havana Blues: A Contemporary Cuban-American Literature Anthology* (1996)

VIRGIL SUAREZ

LAW-YONE, Wendy
b. 1947, Mandalay, Burma

Political turmoil and the pressures of abrupt immigration, prevalent themes in L.-Y.'s fiction, reflect events in her own life. The second of six children, L.-Y. was reared in Rangoon. She lived through a period of Burmese history marked by riots and violence. Burma established its independence from Great Britain in 1948, and in 1962, a military coup upset the parliamentary democracy. The following year, the self-imposed government arrested L.-Y.'s father, E. M. Law-Yone, who founded and published the *Nation,* the foremost English-language newspaper daily. He was imprisoned for five years without charges or a trial. L.-Y. was also arrested when she attempted to escape similar persecution. After a two-week interrogation, she was released and allowed to leave the country.

In 1968, L.-Y. began working as a writer and editor in Southeast Asia, where she married an American journalist. She immigrated to the U.S. in 1973. Her marriage ended in divorce in 1975, the same year she graduated from Eckert College. She met her current husband, lawyer Charles O'Connor, in 1980, when she was writing for the *Washington Post* on a free-lance basis.

Her first novel, *The Coffin Tree,* was published in 1983. The novel is narrated in first person by a young Burmese woman who immigrates to the U.S. from Rangoon with her older half-brother. It is a tumultuous move from the very start; their father, in hiding from the tyrannical government for his guerilla activism, arranges their journey so they can escape persecution. The two are plucked from their sheltered existence and dropped into an alien and inhospitable world. Due to the political circumstances that necessitated their dislocation, they are cut off from their family, whom they presume killed. The shock and stress of adjusting to life in New York take their toll on the two; the narrator witnesses her brother's descent into madness and paranoia until he finally dies of a mysterious illness. The narrator herself suffers a nervous break-down and attempts suicide. As she recovers in an institution, she comes to terms with her brother's disintegration and her own unintentional collaboration. She turns to the legends that had comforted her brother and discovers her own strength and a new sense of purpose.

The tale of resilience is rendered through powerful imagery and clear, sincere language. Its strength lies in L.-Y.'s ability to portray the debilitating sense of alienation and dislocation that is exacerbated by—but not unique to—immigration. The critical success of *The Coffin Tree* enabled L.-Y. to win a National Endowment for the Arts Fellowship in 1987 to support the writing of her second novel, *Irrawaddy Tango,* which she published in 1994. This novel, set in a fictional country and spanning five decades, did not receive as much critical acclaim as *The Coffin Tree.*

L.-Y. currently lives in Washington D.C. with her husband and three children. She remains an active reporter and commentator on Burmese political events as well as a book reviewer for major American newspapers.

BIBLIOGRAPHY: Lee, R. C., "The Erasure of Places and the Re-Siting of Empire in L.-Y.'s *The Coffin Tree,*" *CultCrit* 35 (Winter 1996–97): 149–78; Ling, A., "W. L.," in Davidson, C. N., and L. Wagner-Martin, eds., *The Oxford Companion to Women's Writing in the United States* (1995): 466

VICTORIA ENG

LEA, Sydney
b. 22 December 1942, Chestnut Hill, Pennsylvania

As founding editor of the *New England Review* (1977), poet L. established himself as a prominent figure in the burgeoning narrative and formalist movements of the past two decades. His work evidences a subtle craftsmanship and narrative thrust that calls to mind the work of Robert FROST and Donald JUSTICE. Among his influences, L. lists Wordsworth, Frost, and contemporary poets T. R. Hummer, Mark Jarmon, and Anthony HECHT—on whose work L. edited a collection of critical essays. Unlike several of his neoformalist contemporaries, L. removes himself from the harsh politics and strictures of the movement through a relaxed dependence on tradition.

Raised by moderately affluent parents in the Philadelphia suburb of Chestnut Hill and educated through his Ph.D. at Yale, L. might be expected to produce intellectual, urban fare. His work, however, more often evidences the influence of time spent on his uncle's farm in rural Ambler, Pennsylvania. L. is a dedicated outdoorsman whose poetry shows a healthy respect for nature; hunting and fishing tales abound in his collections. Balanced against this backwoods NATURALISM, though, is the semiotician's struggle with the inadequacies of language, the philosopher's investigation of the human psyche, and the theologian's courtship with the essence of life. These seemingly antipodal characteristics create an extraordinarily accessible art, blending L.'s world and me.

L.'s first collection, *Searching the Drowned Man* (1980), contains several elegies and narratives that introduce a major concern of connectedness to family, place, and idiom that runs throughout this later work. Several of the poems in the collection feature a first person narrator searching for answers in his experiences. The title poem transposes the actual incident of searching for a drowned man's body into the search for what the dead can show the living. Other poems, such as "The Bus to Schenectady," utilize the objectivity of the third person narrator to deliver epiphanies. Often, the poems examine the bounty and treachery of nature, as in "Incantation against Revelation."

Where L.'s first book offers searches, *The Floating Candles* (1982) delivers answers and hope. The poet's elegiac voice takes on confidence and his manipulation of formal elements becomes more adept. From the opening "Dirge for My Brother" to "The New Year: 1980," L. concentrates on signature themes to develop his notion that incidents and individual are like lights that gain significance only through constellation. Heavy symbolism runs throughout the collection reminiscent of Frost—winter as death, nature as life. The poems range in style from the open-ended impressionism of the first section to the lucid narrative of "The Feud," a long blank-verse poem that proves L.'s acuity as a storyteller.

No Sign (1987) moves away from the obvious figurative tropes of the earlier collections toward a subtler and less self-conscious narrative style. The poetry, as in "The Dream of Sickness," takes on a relaxed, conversational pace some critics have called "windy." Throughout the collection, though, L. is less concerned with answers and interpretations and is quite willing to simply exhibit, as in "Fall" where the narrator accepts loss without despair. Tone dominates theme in poems like "High Wind" and "Sereno." Most prominently, though, the level of craft is raised considerably, nowhere more evident than in the closing sonnet sequence, "Annual Report."

The formal accomplishment of *No Sign* foreshadows the direction of L.'s next two volumes, *Prayer for the Little City* (1991) and *The Blainville Testament* (1992). Each book exploits the landscapes of New England, often investing them with religious connotations. In the title poems of both collections, nature becomes a vessel for the spiritual world realized by the narrators of the poems. "Prayer for the Little City" evokes Christian imagery while "The Blainville Testament" is much more Deist in its approach to nature. Ultimately, the power of L.'s poetry, to address heady polemics in plain language and situation, manifests itself in these collections in poems such as "At the Flyfisher's Shack," "Six Sundays toward a Seventh," and "Spite: Her Tale" solidifying his reputation as one of the premier formalists of his generation.

With the publication of a novel entitled *A Place in Mind* (1989), a collection of personal essays, *Hunting the Whole Way Home* (1994), as well as *To the Bone: New and Selected Poems* (1996), L. has proven himself an accessible, entertaining storyteller whose craft and vision celebrates the traditions, both literary and familial, that produced him.

BIOGRAPHY: Engel, B. F., "S. L.'s *The Floating Candles,*" *SSMLN* 13 (Fall 1983): 29–32; German, N. "S. L.," in Gywnn, R. S., ed., *DLB,* vol. 120, *American Poets since World War II* (1992): 180–85

JACK B. BEDELL

LEAVITT, David
b. 23 June 1961, Pittsburgh, Pennsylvania

As a young writer who came into prominence in the early 1980s and has actively published ever since, L. writes carefully crafted, elegantly nuance prose uninterested in zeitgeist skewerings, grunge glamour, or well-moneyed decadence. Like the serious novelists of previous generations, L. explores essential terrain, deep and unchanging concerns: family, love, sexuality, self-identity, illness, the tangles of human interaction. That L. is an openly gay writer—homosexuality and gay culture are thematic fixtures in his work—further

personalizes the intimate nature and texture of his writing.

The gravity of his solemn, pristine style bespeaks a rare, intuitive understanding of yearnings and loss, an empathy that shapes the short stories collected in *Family Dancing* (1984), his first published work. The concerns of these stories range from cancer to the tensions between a suburban, seemingly fully accepting mother and her son when her brings his lover home for the first time. Though L. was fresh out of Yale and only twenty-one, his writing here was already aesthetically and emotionally sophisticated enough to garner both PEN/Faulkner and National Book Award nominations and to establish him as one of the most intriguing literary chroniclers of gay American life.

His next book, the novel *The Lost Language of Cranes* (1986), is his most acclaimed work. In it, a young gay man's romantic failure and subsequent self-reckoning intersect with his father's grappling with his own long-shunned homosexuality. L. conveys as much keenly felt empathy for the older man's struggle as he does for the ostensible young hero's; he also devotes equal consideration to the dilemmas faced by Rose, the wife and mother in this embattled family. Agonized, intellectual young men and strong, complicated mothers are L. signatures. A copy editor, a professional trained to spot anomalies, Rose is for the most part unable to spot the errors in her own life. By the conclusion of the novel, we are left with both hope and piercing sadness.

L. has written steadily and fluidly. *Equal Affections* (1988), a novel in which a dynamic matriarch's death catalyzes angst-ridden soul-grapplings in her adult children, was followed by a collection of short stories entitled *A Place I've Never Been* (1990) and *While England Sleeps* (1993), inspired by the English poet Stephen Spender's memoir *World within World*. L.'s career was publicly interrupted when Spender took him to court, charging plagiarism. The original version of *While England Sleeps* remaindered or burned, L. was forced to rewrite key chunks of the novel. Despite L.'s asseverating that, bitterly resentful of the trial though he is, the rewritten work is in all ways superior to the contested first version, a detached, vaguely aloof quality permeates the novel, leaving the book intermittently compelling and moving yet underfelt and unexciting.

L.'s ability to channel distinct consciousnesses and his wide-reaching interests in various literary forms have served him extremely well. But he appears to be at a crossroads in his career. It will be fascinating to discover if L. will deepen his craft or merely refine it.

DAVID GREVEN

LEE, Harper [Nelle]
b. 28 April 1926, Monroeville, Alabama

L. is one of the few 20th-c. novelists whose reputation rests solely on one book. Her novel, *To Kill a Mockingbird* (1960), was an enormous popular success. It was selected for distribution by the Literary Guild and the Book-of-the-Month Club, and was published in a shortened version as a *Reader's Digest* condensed book. It also remains a standard reading selection in high school English classes. In addition, the novel was critically acclaimed, winning both the Pulitzer Prize in fiction and the Brotherhood Award of the National Conference of Christians and Jews in 1961. Moreover, the novel was made into an Academy Award-winning film in 1962.

The critical reception of the book has been mixed. Some critics view it as a compassionate, moving novel that offers a persuasive plea for racial justice. Others praise L.'s "insight into Southern mores." Negative commentary includes the novel's sermonizing and melodramatic climax. In addition, the first-person narrative of Scout is more fitting of the prose style of an educated adult, not a six-year-old child. Scholars as recently as the 1970s praise L.'s technical skill and concur that the novel deserves its place in literary tradition. Fred Erisman believes the work belongs to the schools of traditional Southern ROMANTICISM and REGIONALISM. However, R. A. Dave contends that the novel moves beyond regionalism to create "an epic canvas . . . of human behavior."

The novel is narrated by Jean Louise "Scout" Finch, a six-year-old girl who lives with Jem, her ten-year-old brother, and Atticus, her lawyer father, in the small town of Maycomb, Alabama. Scout and Jem gain knowledge of the adult world and human nature during the three years covered by the novel. The main cause of their maturation process is the legal defense by their father of Tom Robinson, a black man accused of raping a white girl named Mayella Ewell. In the months preceding the trial, Scout and Jem suffer the taunts of classmates and townspeople who object to Atticus's defending a black man. As the trial nears, the tensions escalate. Ultimately, the jury finds the black man guilty even though Atticus has clearly proven him innocent. Maycomb's racial prejudice is so powerful that the lawyer cannot convince the townspeople to see the truth about an innocent black man who is accused by a white woman.

The second incident that aids in the maturation process of Scout and Jem is the unraveling of the mystery surrounding their neighbor "Boo" Radley, who has been in seclusion since he was arrested several years before for some teenage pranks. At first, Boo is a victim only of his father's rigid religious ideas and family pride, but eventually he becomes a victim of community prejudice. The townspeople think the worst about Boo and blame him for petty crimes in the area. The children imagine the recluse dining on raw squirrels and roaming the neighborhood at night. Finally, they learn that Boo has been a friend to them. He hides gifts for the children in a hollow tree; he mends the pants Jem snags on a fence; and ultimately he rescues Scout and Jem from the drunken, murderous attack of Bob Ewell, the father of Mayella.

Although the narrative is deceptively simple, *To Kill a Mockingbird* contains a number of complex themes in oppositional pairs: ignorance-knowledge, cowardice-heroism, guilt-innocence, and prejudice-tolerance. The ignorance-knowledge theme is highlighted by the character development of the children as they experience Tom's trial and solve the mystery of Boo Radley. Despite the narrow mindedness of the townspeople, Scout and Jem gain insight and true understanding of the negative effects of ignorance. The cowardice-heroism theme is most obvious in Atticus, who has the courage to confront the prejudiced people in Maycomb, and Bob Ewell, who bullies his daughter, Tom, Atticus, Scout, and Jem. The guilt-innocence and prejudice-tolerance themes are evident in the innocent characters, Tom and Boo, who are judged guilty by a prejudiced society. The Finch family members are the most obvious examples of tolerance.

In addition to the oppositional pairs, L. also uses strong symbolism to illuminate the theme of tolerance and acceptance. Atticus and Miss Maudie, a neighbor, tell the children that it is a sin to kill a mockingbird. The bird closely associated with Boo Radley and Tom Robinson represents joy and innocence. Another powerful use of symbolism occurs when Maycomb has a light snowfall. Jem builds a snowman underlaid with mud because of the limited amount of snow. When Miss Maudie's house burns, the snowman melts leaving only a dark colored mudman. Hence, the snowman's color goes from black to white and back again, illuminating how superficial skin color actually is.

L. does indeed embrace the romantic literary tradition, but she does it universally. She is not just a writer reflecting on the South; instead, she portrays, with her depth of theme, the negative side of human nature.

BIBLIOGRAPHY: Dave, R. A., "To Kill a Mockingbird: H. L.'s Tragic Vision," *ISAL* 1974: 311-23; Johnson, C. D., *Understanding "To Kill a Mockingbird"* (1994)

                                        JANET K. TURK

LEE, Li-Young
b. 19 August 1957, Jakarta, Indonesia

The careful reader will certainly appreciate how the extraordinary personal history of L. comes to inform his subject matter, yet also understands his stylistic debt to a large tradition of American verse. L. is one of the most celebrated poets of his generation, and the winner of two major literary prizes for his books of poetry: the Delmore Schwartz Award for *Rose* (1986) and the Lamont Poetry Selection for *The City in Which I Love You* (1990). His 1995 memoir, *The Winged Seed,* won the American Book Award from the Before Columbus Foundation.

The central figure to be reckoned with in L.'s poetry is his own father, whose political affiliations led to a life in exile for him and his family. Once personal physician to Mao and later, medical advisor to Sukarno, L.'s father was jailed in Indonesia before fleeing across Asia to finally arrive in America. There, he settled as a Presbyterian minister in western Pennsylvania, no less a mythic entity to his young son. The stature L. grants his father—that of an immense, godlike being—evolves out of his search to understand him and his tragic life.

Toward this investigation, *Rose* interrogates the meaning of memory, its revelations, its limitations. Memories stand under constant revision, answerable to the immediacy of situation. One strategy revisits the father in humble domestic moments, but these too are infused with higher significance. In "The Gift," the ritual of removing a splinter is metaphor for the absolute power the Reverend L. holds over the son; the father's hands, both tender and violent, elicit only gratitude from the young boy. Indeed, the poems consciously demonstrate the grace of common domestic life. The act of eating is sensuous and yet still holy, one necessary as much for knowledge as for sustenance. The care shown in preparing a family meal in "Eating Together" follows in sequence the urgency and passion of "Always a Rose," in which the narrator eats a rose for memory, understanding, faith, and intimacy. Twin images of flowers and human hair emerge as consistent signifiers of beauty, their cultivation, that of desire.

The City in Which I Love You departs from *Rose* most obviously in form; in his second book L. explores more substantially the possibilities of the long poem. This form grants L. the freedom of a relaxed verse, accessible to the reader in its plainness. Often his exuberant language takes precedence over traditional structure. In this volume, the attempt to understand the father through memory continues while the sense of the search is more pronounced, whether it is for the father, or for other intimacies. The narrator lacks wholeness, a state owing as much to his spiritual as to his spatial displacement as a Chinese immigrant. Motifs of doubling run through the book as L. reckons with the ambiguities of his personal situation with those of his larger cultural community. In the final

poem "The Cleaving," the poet at last understands his soul as split, and so capable of being restored.

L.'s literary debts reflect his background as much as his professional training. T'ang dynasty poetry was an early study, as was the Bible, whose Song of Songs inspired the poem "The City in Which I Love You." His loose, humble form and democratic impulses recall Walt WHITMAN. There are debts to Rainer Maria Rilke and Theodore ROETHKE. Contemporary influences include James WRIGHT, Galway KINNELL, Philip LEVINE, and his most direct mentor, Gerald Stern. L. has achieved his own distinct and innovative style, however, and stands himself as an important influence among young poets today.

BIBLIOGRAPHY: Baker, D., "Culture, Inclusion, Craft," *Poetry* 158 (June 1991): 158–75

DAVID SHIH

LE GUIN, Ursula K(roeber)
b. 21 October 1929, Berkeley, California

The daughter of an anthropologist father and a writer mother, and the wife of a historian, L.'s writing career has ventured not only into the realms of SCIENCE FICTION and fantasy for which she is best known, but also into poetry, essays, and literary criticism.

L.'s earliest novel, *Rocannon's World* (1966), gives her readers their first look at the world of Hain, which is later returned to in *Planet of Exile* (1966), *City of Illusions* (1967), and many of L.'s more recent works of fiction, including *Searoad: Chronicles of Klatsand* (1992).

Without falling into to the trap that says all fantasy—all speculative fiction, in fact—is inherently "juvenile," it should be noted that there is indeed a fine line in L.'s works between literature intended for a juvenile audience and fiction meant for adults. Yet, while often written in deceptively simple styles, the issues dealt with in L.'s fantasy and science fiction works are rich and complex. *A Wizard of Earthsea* (1968), *The Tombs of Atuan* (1970), and *The Farthest Shore* (1972) are the first books in what continues to be known as the "Earthsea Trilogy," despite the appearance of a sequel in 1990 entitled *Tehanu*. The Earthsea books may be read simply as a series of rather magical bildungsromans, yet at other levels, they are speculations on the nature of language and its relationship to essential meanings, conflicting loyalties, and the search for self.

The political and philosophical movements that took hold of the intellectual imagination of the public during the 1960s have also played a role in the shaping of L.'s fiction. *The Left Hand of Darkness* (1969) is still intriguing for its innovative look at a gender neutral society and how an emissary from a federation of planets sent to "court them"—to bring them into a union of worlds—is himself changed by the experience. *The Lathe of Heaven* (1971), later turned into a television film, looks at dream theory and posits the existence of a man whose dreams are more active than most. As the man allows himself to be made part of a study on sleep, a researcher discovers that his subject's dreams have the ability to change the nature of reality and that nobody but the scientist and his subject are ever aware that the world in which they live has ever been different. And L.'s 1974 novel *The Dispossessed* considers the question of how we might best organize our political and social system. Interestingly subtitled "An Ambiguous Utopia," *The Dispossessed* presents a seemingly perfect society that may not in fact be quite as perfect as it first appears. This theme runs through much of L.'s work; in her collection *The Wind's Twelve Quarters* (1975) can be found a short story with which L. is often associated—"The Ones Who Walk Away from Omelas." This very ambiguous utopian vision, which looks at the price that must be paid for a society's happiness, has been consistently anthologized almost since the moment of its publication.

Apart from fiction, L. is also a poet of some note. She has published five volumes of poetry, including *Tillai and Tylissos* with her mother, Theodora K. Quinn, in 1979. In addition, L. is widely known as a feminist, critic, and essayist on myriad subjects. Her two most noteworthy works in these areas are *Language of the Night: Essays on Fantasy and Science Fiction* (1978) and *Dancing at the Edge of the World: Thoughts on Words, Women, Places* (1989).

BIBLIOGRAPHY: Bucknall, B. J., *U. K. L.* (1981); Cummins, T., *Understanding U. K. L.* (1990); Slusser, G. E., *The Farthest Shores of U. K. L.* (1976); Spivack, C., *U. K. L.* (1984)

ELIZABETH HADDRELL

LEITHAUSER, Brad

b. 7 February 1953, Detroit, Michigan

Trained as a lawyer, L. quickly took to the literary world, publishing four volumes of poetry and four novels in less than two decades. L. earned his B.A. at Harvard University in 1975. During his studies, he was awarded the Academy of American Poets Prize, both in 1973 and 1975. He then went on to graduate from Harvard's law school in 1980. That same year he left the U.S. to reside in Japan, at the Kyoto Comparative Law Center, where he spent the next three

years. In 1981, he won the Amy Lowell Traveling Scholarship, and the following year was awarded a Guggenheim Fellowship.

L.'s first collection of poetry, *Hundreds of Fireflies* (1982), was received with an unusual amount of attention for a debut. As a New Formalist poet, L. holds to traditional poetics of language. He adheres to a more technical form of verse than do many of his contemporaries. *Hundreds of Fireflies* was nominated for the National Book Critics Circle Award. L. himself was awarded a Lavan Younger Poets Award in 1983. He was also awarded a MacArthur Fellowship.

In 1985, *Equal Distance,* L.'s first novel, was published. The protagonist of the novel is Danny, a young American law student who has taken a year off from school to live in Japan. The plot orients itself in part as a bildungsroman. In Japan, Danny meets a number of other young Americans who are disillusioned with the life their native country has to offer. Unlike a traditional coming of age story, Danny does not come to any revelation about his life, but rather, he gradually comes to accept the life he has been born into.

Cats of the Temple, L.'s second poetry collection, was published in 1986. Although nominated for a National Book Critics Circle Award, it met with a less enthusiastic response than did his previous collection. The main criticism of this volume and of L.'s work in general is his reliance on clever language and an apparent lack of deeply involved emotion. Like *Equal Distance, Cats of the Temple* seems to be influenced by L.'s years in Japan. There is a simplicity of style in the poems, as well as distinct observations of the country itself. This collection was nominated for a National Book Critics Award.

A second novel, *Hence,* was published in 1989. It is a stylistically complex novel: a novel within a novel. Garner Briggs, the narrator, is brother to Timothy, a chess prodigy who is gearing up to play a match with a computer. L.'s analogy of man against machine proves a useful tool in this work. In many ways, *Hence* is a satirical novel about the state of late-20th-c. man. The novel was praised by critics as an original, intelligent book.

L. was awarded a Fulbright Fellowship to the University of Iceland in 1989. A year later, he published *The Mail from Anywhere,* a volume of poetry. This collection was deemed a clear breakthrough for L. Earlier criticism of L.'s lack of humanity was called to task. The work in this volume shows not only poetic growth, but a growth in the author's depiction of character and of his understanding of depth of emotion.

Seaward, a novel, was published in 1993. In many ways this novel is more traditional and straightforward than L.'s earlier fictional works. Terry Seward, the protagonist, is a lawyer in Washington. Before the start of the narrative, his wife, Betsy, drowned in a supposed accident. A year following her death, she appears to him—an event that shifts the direction of his thinking, and ultimately of his life.

L.'s novel *Friends of Freeland,* published in 1997, came out to less than favorable reviews. Freeland, an imaginary country somewhere near Iceland, is the setting for this novel. The structure of the novel is somewhat complex as it shifts back and forth in time, switching from first person to third. While the novel is very successful in terms of language, the characters are fragmented, almost illusionary.

Despite the mixed criticism of L.'s work, he is clearly a prolific force in the literary community. His work to date is technically vivid and polished, the accomplishments of a developing talent.

BIBLIOGRAPHY: Gurewich, D., "Games Computers Play," *NewC* 7 May 1989: 81–84; Wojahn, D., "'Yes, but . . . ': Some Thoughts on the New Formalism," *Crazyhorse* 32 (Spring 1987): 64–81

MARIKA BRUSSEL

LEONARD, Elmore

b. 11 October 1925, New Orleans, Louisiana

L. started out his literary career by writing stories and novels in the WESTERN genre, and it was not until he exchanged the frontier setting for the urban scene and switched to the hard-boiled mystery genre that he achieved notable success. *City Primeval: High Noon in Detroit* (1980)—urban and frontier motifs meld in the title—is considered his "breakthrough" novel, although he had done a number of earlier works in the same vein in the late 1970s and did not attain true best-seller status until the publication of *Glitz* (1985).

A typical L. novel, usually categorized a "crime suspense" variant, is noted for its intricate plot, its racy, "with-it" dialogue, and its lean, terse, and fast-moving writing style. Deadpan humor is an active ingredient of his technique, lending color to the prose and evoking the edgy argot of contemporary American speech and brilliantly painting the seedy settings of his backgrounds. L.'s knack is in depicting in detail the tastes of no-class characters, conjuring up the feel of cheap glitzy swank in his settings, and packing his stories with secondary characters etched in indelible fashion by his highly individualized prose. A L. novel focuses on a main protagonist who is probably a man of murky morality, a bit frayed around the edges, just trying to make his way in a world that is as flawed as he. Morally, this hero, or antihero, has discovered that there is no true simplistic notion of good and evil, that indeed morality is really an ambiguous quality at

best. His is a kind of existentialist attitude toward life that is shifting and constantly reinventing itself to surmount life's obstacles.

Although L. turned to the urban milieu with *Fifty-Two Pickup* (1974), a story of a man trying to survive blackmail, kidnapping, and murder; followed it with *Swag* (1976), about an auto thief involved in armed robbery; and *Unknown Man No. 89* (1977), about a seedy process server up against a dangerous con man; and then *The Switch* (1978), a kidnap caper that turns sour, it was *City Primeval* that made his name. *Split Images* (1982) followed, about a broken-down ex-cop and a millionaire homicidal maniac with a death-voyeur obsession. *Cat Chaser* (1982) involves a motel owner, a group of corrupt con artists, and the wife of a rich Dominican exile. *Stick* (1983), starring a character originally in *Swaq,* is the story of an ex-con trying desperately to readjust to life outside prison amongst a group of drug dealers and stock manipulators. *LaBrava* (1983) won the Edgar Allan Poe Award of the Mystery Writers of America. In it, an ex-Secret Service agent tries to break up a complex extortion scam involving an over-the-hill film actress. *Glitz* and *Bandits* (1987) both followed the general lines established in the four previous books.

So did *Maximum Bob* (1991), the story of a hit man hired to kill a hanging judge; and *Pronto* (1993), about a sports bookie who flees to the Italian Riviera when the feds and the mob both try to squeeze information from him; and *Riding the Rap* (1995), about the same character in *Pronto* involved now in a Bahamian kidnap plot. But 1990 saw the most highly acclaimed of L.'s recent novels, *Get Shorty*—a satire on Hollywood and the film industry that was made into a hit motion picture of the same name. Hollywood jumped on a number of Leonard books in the nineties, including *Rum Punch* (1992), retitled *Jackie Brown* on-screen, and *Out of Sight* (1996), starring TV's popular actor, George Clooney.

Then, in 1998, L. embarked on a literary voyage to milieus other than those featured in his most recent work. *Cuba Libre* is a mixed breed—half Western novel and half war novel, along with a smidgeon of crime thrown in. The war is the Spanish-American War, and the setting is Cuba, where the protagonist, a cowboy horse trader, becomes seriously involved in collecting payment for the horses he has sold to the Cuban military. It's a very satisfying departure from L.'s usual, one that bares talents as yet unseen to his growing audience. The sequel to *Get Shorty, Be Cool* (1999), is another transcendent L. experience.

In these later works, L. found his voice after years of labor in the literary wilderness. Although his thematic material and his technique of writing are only loosely concerned with the stern and uncompromising

657

precepts of the conventional detective story format, he is a true follower of the Dashiell HAMMETT and Raymond CHANDLER school, the difference being that his protagonist has passed the stage of moral outrage at evil, has made his peace with the world, and has come to a loose constructionist position about other people's virtue. His main concern is staying alive—more observer than doer, but able to act, and act effectively, when it becomes necessary. This attitude strikes a chord in his readers and is the primary reason for L.'s hard-earned but well-deserved literary success.

BIBLIOGRAPHY: Grella, G., in Reilly, J. M., ed., *Twentieth Century Crime and Mystery Writers*, 2nd ed. (1985): 558–59; Yagoda, B., "E. L.'s Rogues' Gallery," *NYTMag* 30 December 1984: 20

BRUCE CASSIDAY

LESBIAN LITERATURE

Anxiety over how to regard women's desire for one another long preceded late-20th-c. debates over what and who count as lesbian and what counts as lesbian literature. The most interesting analyses, however, are not produced in answering whether one can call some 19th-c. passionate female friendships "lesbian"—before the medicalization of sexuality at the turn of the century and the subsequent pathologizing of same-sex relations—but in recognizing that passionate attachments between women have long been received with apprehension, as they subvert assumptions of the "naturalness" of heterosexuality. Various critics and biographers have long recognized that the intense erotic attachment between Susan and Emily DICKINSON, a passion that sustained itself for four decades and about which Emily was self-conscious and guilty as a young woman, does not quite sustain the claims of Carroll Smith-Rosenberg and others that romantic female friendships, however passionate, were acceptable and "innocent" of sexual desire. Though women did not call themselves "lesbian" until the 20th c., more and more work plumbing written histories is revealing that same-sex desire was a major struggle of sexual identity for Dickinson and Margaret FULLER, for example, and was widely enough recognized and feared that 19th-c. conduct books warned against females becoming overly attached to one another physically. Recent collections of lesbian short stories feature works by such authors as Rose Terry COOKE, Elizabeth Stuart Phelps WARD, Constance Fenimore WOOLSON, Alice FRENCH, Mary E. Wilkins FREEMAN, Kate CHOPIN, and Sarah Orne JEWETT.

From protomodernist experimentations with narrative like that of Jewett in *The Country of the Pointed*

Firs to modernist interrogations of genre and technique like those of Djuna BARNES's *Nightwood*, Gertrude STEIN's *Lifting Belly*, and Hilda DOOLITTLE's posthumously published *Paint It Today*, to the literatures of affirmation and political activism written and supported by lesbian publishers such as Barbara Grier, Judy Grahn, and the Daughters of Bilitis, lesbian literature throughout the first two-thirds of the 20th c. exploited the "outlaw" status of the lesbian. Thus, as Bonnie Zimmerman observes, lesbian critics and critics of lesbian texts often pose questions about identity and literary creativity: "How, for example, does the lesbian's sense of outlaw status affect her literary vision? Might lesbian writing, because of the lesbian's position on the boundaries, be characterized by a particular sense of freedom and flexibility or, rather, by images of violently imposed barriers, the closet? Or, in fact, is there a dialectic between freedom and imprisonment that is unique to lesbian writing?" The year 1900 marks the fin-de-siècle, as the turn from the 19th to the 20th c. witnessed the pathologizing of homosexuality by the medical profession, while 1969 heralds the Stonewall rebellion in New York City, widely received as the original moment of gay and lesbian liberation movements. Though Stonewall is certainly a marker for lesbians, readers should be aware that the formation of lesbian presses and periodicals that emerge in the 1940s through the 1970s was as much a result of the women's liberation movement as of that monumental event of gay liberation. Stonewall of course bolstered a lesbian literary movement well underway and, by making gay and lesbian worlds more visible, provided a desperately needed antidote to the homophobia expressed by some of the key leaders of the women's movement, notably Betty Friedan.

Concomitant with this repression of the lesbian within feminist struggles for liberation are debates over what and who count as lesbian and when a situation or character count as lesbian—for, as Catharine Stimpson and other lesbian critics, theorists, and writers have reminded us—*lesbian* is still a term to which one attaches oneself at great risk. To be unambiguously visible as *lesbian* is to challenge the conventions of heterosexual patriarchy on which legal and social orders rest, and therefore position oneself to be received as threatening, menacing, and disruptive to the foundations of culture and society. Thus, it should come as no surprise that many lesbian writers have deftly encoded expressions of lesbian desire and portrayals of lesbian figures, and, constricted by literary traditions, have turned to experimental forms as they attempt to make literature whose very subject matter is new and revolutionary simply because of the fact that lesbian love has been denied as a vital reality of the human heart.

Whatever form it assumes—poetry, prose fiction, political treatise, autobiography, biography, history, criticism, theory—lesbian literature is that which, as Monique Wittig has argued and Marilyn Farwell reiterated, occupies a "space which is 'not-woman,' which is not dependent on the categorization of difference that resides in the dualisms of man and woman. *Lesbian* is a word that denotes, then, a new positioning of female desire, of the lover and the beloved, of the subject and object." This extends even to familiar roles like that of "butch" and "femme" in lesbian pulp fiction, too quickly dismissed by some as a failure of lesbian imagination. As Elizabeth Meese, drawing on the analysis of Judith Roof and Joan Nestle, observes, "Butch-femme relationships are complex erotic statements, not phony heterosexual replicas"; for example, refusing "analogy to the heterosexual gender roles of masculine and feminine," the butch lesbian creates "an original style to signal to other women what she was capable of doing—taking erotic responsibility."

Zami, Audre LORDE's biomythography, describes 1950s Greenwich Village lesbians passing around pulp paperbacks that proliferated during this period such as *The Price of Salt, Odd Girl Out, Women in the Shadows,* and *Strange Are the Ways of Love.* Literature that promised entry into an outcast world of "twilight" love, these novels were, as Lillian Faderman remarks, "generally cautionary tales: 'moral' literature that warned females that lesbianism was sick or evil and that if a woman dared to love another woman she would end up lonely and suicidal." Yet many lesbians avidly read these novels that "could be picked up at newsstands and corner drugstores, even in small towns" because they "helped spread the word about lesbian lifestyles" and offered public images of lesbian "romance and charged eroticism." By the late 1960s, lesbian literature had been tremendously emboldened by the gay male and women's liberation movements and, in contrast to these tales of the outcast, offered more and more stories of a proud and affirmative community bent on changing public discourse and conventional society's reception of lesbian life.

The most well-known literary lesbian of the 20th c. is Stephen Gordon, the hero of British writer Radclyffe Hall's *The Well of Loneliness,* published in 1928. Hall's widely publicized obscenity trial evinced a bigoted general attitude of scorn for lesbians that had a chilling effect on many American lesbian and bisexual writers, especially expatriates like Hilda Doolittle. Though Doolittle was writing explicitly lesbian fiction, none of it was published until after her death. Unpublished until 1992 in "The Cutting Edge: Lesbian Life and Literature" series, *Paint It Today* serves as "the repressed political unconscious of her *Asphodel* and *Midrigal*"—"countering an androcentric social con-

struction of desire" by proposing a "lesbian matrix of sister-love." Thus, this daring probing of myths of psychology has been overshadowed by the more conventionally palatable *Tribute to Freud,* in print since 1956. Similarly, *Lifting Belly,* Gertrude Stein's delicious celebration of lesbian sexuality was not published until after her death, while *Tender Buttons,* her experimental poems collected under the cunningly titled pun on tend-her-buttons, was published but subjected to ruthless critical ridicule. As Stimpson points out, when Hall "represents the lesbian as scandal and the lesbian as woman-who-is-man," she is "making an implicit, perhaps unconscious pact with her culture" as the "lesbian writer who rejects both silence and excessive coding" and claims her "right to write for the public in exchange for adopting the narrative of damnation." A 1939 novel like Diana Frederics's *Diana,* which presents a "kind of lesbian chauvinism"-"a stupid girl would probably never ascertain her abnormality if she were potentially homosexual. . . . No woman could adjust herself to lesbianism without developing exceptional qualities of courage"—is quite the exception in its championing of lesbian life and desire, even as it plainly acknowledges the larger culture's homophobic suppressions.

Yet Shari Benstock contends that if the "critics who confer canonization" took seriously Blanche Wiesen Cook's claim that Virginia Woolf's "imagination was fueled by Sapphic erotic power," then "they would be forced to redefine modernism in ways that acknowledge its Sapphic elements." If this "erotic power were theorized as Sapphic modernism," not only for Woolf but for Barnes, Doolittle, and Stein, "it could profoundly change not only our notions about modernist art, but also redefine the erotic in relation to the creative sources for all art." Understanding lesbian literary experimentation and its challenges to aesthetic, cultural, and historic concepts will, therefore, remap literary history and reconfigure its intellectual values, including that invested in the "Author."

Traditions of literary history enthralled with the autonomous genius producing works of classic literature, women's traditional symbolic function for men as a passive female muse, and a correlation between creative production and procreative reproduction have made the formulation of a literary dynamic as a collaboration of a woman writer with another woman alien to conventional symbology linking heterosexual desire and poetic inspiration. Various female collaborations remain insufficiently examined—the "Boston marriage" of Sarah Orne Jewett and Annie Fields that proved a mainstay for the former's literary production; Willa CATHER's forty-year partnership with Edith Lewis that provided the writer with the stability and freedom necessary to create, Elizabeth BISHOP's founding of a literary magazine at Vassar with Mary MCCAR-THY, whose best-selling novel *The Group* "showed that lesbianism could be an acceptable, even admirable subject," as well as her years-long relationships with Lota Costellat de Macedo Soares and Alice Methfessel, and, as Sandra M. Gilbert and Susan Gubar explore in "'She Meant What I Said'—Lesbian Double Talk," the collaborative lesbian literary relationships like those between Renee Vivien and Natalie Barney, Doolittle and Bryher, and Stein and Toklas are striking markers of the endeavors of expatriate American and British women writers in the early 20th c.

Relationships with audience are also vital considerations begging for more thorough scrutiny. Analyzing Barnes's work, Benstock argues that *Nightwood,* with which general audiences tend to be more familiar, and *Ladies Almanack* are addressed to two markedly different audiences and that it is crucial for readers to be aware of that in order to understand the very different kinds of cultural work the two are doing. While "*Nightwood* carefully conceals the psychosexual premises on which it establishes its social-cultural critique, *Ladies Almanack* reveals Barnes's enormous ambivalence about the sexual and social privilege it satirizes," that of a "small and select audience of lesbians well known to Barnes (members of Natalie Clifford Barney's salon) . . . *Nightwood* invokes the underside of high modernism while *Ladies Almanack* is addressed to the women who are themselves the subjects of its satire." Misunderstanding audience and intention has fostered mischaracterizing receptions that have bolstered dismissals of considering literature as lesbian, of lesbian literature as "special interest," and of lesbian eroticism as an important wellspring for artistic movements.

This question of audience, or of insufficient consideration of audience, has also resulted in dismissals of poetry like that by Angelina Weld GRIMKÉ as "too conventional." African American and probably lesbian, Grimké was confronted with at least three formidable cultural biases (toward women, blacks, and homosexuals), and thus her apparently timid adherence to form and meter might be seen as a strategy for acceptable expression of unacceptable desires. In *Color, Sex, & Poetry: Three Women Writers of the Harlem Renaissance* (1987), Gloria Hull examines how "Grimké handled in her public art what seem to be woman-to-woman romantic situations" by eschewing "third-person pronouns and the usual tendency most readers have to image the other in a love poem as being opposite in sex from the poem's known author." Hull also recovers Alice DUNBAR-NELSON's lesbian attractions and the fact that the few of her poems on this subject that have survived *and* been made available reveal "the existence and operation of an active

black lesbian network" in the 1920s. Also significant in this period are the vibrant songs performed by blues artists like Bessie Jackson and Bessie Smith, which, as Elly Bulkin observes, provide "a rich source of lesbian expression." Jackson performed "B. D. Blues (Bull Dagger Blues) during her career, while Bessie Smith sang several songs with explicitly lesbian lyrics." Perhaps ironically, lower class status may well have enabled these women to be more daring in lesbian expression than the economically privileged Grimké. Chris Albertson's biography of Smith quotes the unequivocal "The Boy in the Boat" (1930): "When you see two women walking hand in hand, / Just look 'em over and try to understand: / They'll go to those parties—have the lights down low— / Only those parties where women can go. / You think I'm lying—just ask Tack Ann— / Took many a broad from many a man."

In fact, women outside culturally advantaged circles (academe, elite literary cliques) have been largely responsible for lesbian literary movements in the 20th c., and influential publications have emerged from middle-class America. *The Ladder,* the newsletter of America's first lesbian emancipation group, the Daughters of Bilitis, and *Vice Versa* both sought assimilation for lesbians into the mainstream. Not surprisingly, then, authors often used pseudonyms like Lisa Ben (anagram of L-E-S-B-I-A-N) or Laurajean Ermayne. It is crucial for lesbian readers, writers, historians, and critics to be aware of this for, as in the case of Ermayne, "she" has been married to the same woman for forty-one years, has spent a lifetime writing about assorted monsters, goblins, ghouls, politicians, wizards, witches, warlocks, and is actually Forrest J. Ackerman, editor of *Famous Monsters of Filmland* magazine, who wrote as a lesbian because he does not believe in "discrimination against gays-blacks-browns-yellows-red-polkadots-Jews." For us to know that an admittedly eccentric but nevertheless sexually "straight" man was writing for a lesbian magazine in the late 1940s, not for self-titillation but for lesbian and gay liberation, is of vital importance. Our allies and supporters have been more numerous than the keepers of society's conventional and repressive editorial practices would have us believe.

The trajectory of lesbian literature for the first two-thirds of the 20th c. can be described as a movement from encrypted strategies for expressions of the love that dare not speak its name to overtly political celebrations of woman-for-woman passion that, by the late 1960s, refuses to be denied, denigrated, or expunged. Since the 1960s, there has been an explosion of lesbian writing—fiction, autobiography, criticism, theory, journalism, and poetry—and its liberatory nature is poignantly exemplified in vast body of works produced by lesbian writers: novelists and short story writers such as Paula Gunn Allen, Dorothy Allison, June Arnold, Blanche McCrary Boyd, Marion Zimmer Bradley, Pat Califia, Tee Corinne, Andrea Dworkin, Jewelle Gomez, Doris Grumbach, Patricia Highsmith, Paula Martinac, Alma Routsong, Joanna Russ, and Ann Allen Shockley; poets such as Gloria Anzaldúa, Chrystos, Cheryl Clarke, Judy Grahn, Joy HARJO, Audre Lorde, Pat Parker, and Adrienne RICH; playwrights like Jane Chambers; children's and young adult authors such as Lesléa Newman and Sandra Scoppettone; journalists like Jill Johnston; and scholarly writers such as Cherríe Moraga, Barbara Smith, and Bonnie Zimmerman.

BIBLIOGRAPHY: Benstock, S., *Women of the Left Bank: Paris, 1900–1940* (1986); Cruikshank, M., ed., *Lesbian Studies: Present and Future* (1982); Faderman, L., *Odd Girls and Twilight Lovers: A History of Lesbian Life in Twentieth-Century America* (1991); Faderman L., *Surpassing the Love of Men: Romantic Friendship and Love between Women from the Renaissance to the Present* (1981); Friedman, E. G., and M. Fuchs, eds., *Breaking the Sequence: Women's Experimental Fiction* (1989); Friedman, S. S., *Penelope's Web: Gender, Modernity. H. D.'s Fiction* (1990); Gilbert, S. M., and S. Gubar, "She Meant What I Said," in *Sexchanges,* vol. 2, *No Man's Land: The Place of the Woman Writer in the Twentieth Century* (1989): 215–57; Hart, E. L., "The Encoding of Homoerotic Desire: Emily Dickinson's Letters and Poems to Susan Dickinson, 1850–1886," *TSWL* 9 (Fall 1990): 251–72; Hull, G. T., *Color, Sex, & Poetry: Three Women Writers of the Harlem Renaissance* (1987); Jay, K., and J. Glasgow, eds., *Lesbian Texts and Contexts, Radical Revisions* (1990); King, K., *Theory in Its Feminist Travels: Conversations in U. S. Women's Movements* (1994); Koppelman, S., ed., *Two Friends and Other Nineteenth-Century Lesbian Stories by American Women Writers* (1994); Meese, E. A., *(Sem)erotics: Theorizing Lesbian: Writing* (1992); Smith, M. N., *Rowing in Eden: Rereading Emily Dickinson* (1992); Smith, M. N., and E. L. Hart, *Sister We Both Are Women: A Book of Susan and Emily Dickinson* (1998); Stimpson., C. R., "Zero Degree Deviancy: The Lesbian Novel in English," in Abel, E., ed., *Writing and Sexual Difference* (1982): 243–59; Stimpson, C. R., and E. S. Person, eds., *Women, Sex, and Sexuality* (1980); Whitlock, G., "'Everything Is Out of Place': Radclyffe Hall and the Lesbian Literary Tradition," *FSt* 13 (1987): 555–82; Wood, M. E., "'With Ready Eye': Margaret Fuller and Lesbianism in Nineteenth-Century American Literature," *AL* 65 (March 1993): 1–18; Zimmerman, B., "What Has Never Been: An Overview of Lesbian Feminist Literary Criticism," *FSt* 7 (1981): 451–75

MARTHA NELL SMITH

LEVERTOV, Denise

b. 24 October 1923, Ilford, England; d. 20 December 1997, Seattle, Washington

L. has long been associated with the antiformalist Black Mountain school of poets but in the minds of many readers since the 1960s she has also been associated with various worthy causes, beginning with the Vietnamese antiwar movement. She was a nurse during World War II, and her first book of poems, *The Double Image,* was published in London in 1946, the year after the war ended. She married in 1947 and immigrated to the U.S. the following year, becoming a naturalized citizen in 1955. Two years later, Lawrence FERLINGHETTI's San Francisco City Lights Press published her second book, *Here and Now.*

Jargon, the official Black Mountain press, issued her third book, *Overland to the Islands,* in 1958, and she has published many books since, including *With Eyes at the Back of Our Heads* (1959), *The Jacob's Ladder* (1961), *O Taste and See* (1964), *A Marigold from North Vietnam* (1968), *Footprints* (1972), *Collected Earlier Poems, 1940–1960* (1979), *Poems, 1960–1967* (1983), and *Poems, 1968–1972* (1987). She edited a major antiwar anthology, *Out of the War Shadow: An Anthology of Current Poetry,* for the War Resisters League in 1967.

If the definition of a "professional poet" is one who dedicates his or her life to writing poetry, and the definition of an "amateur poet" is one who uses poetry primarily as a vehicle for a didactic purpose, then L. is clearly an amateur. M. L. Rosenthal, the foremost apologist for American "avant-garde" poetry during the past forty years, wrote that "her characteristic expression had been, earlier, the indirect formulation of an abstract thought, perhaps set off by a literary allusion, and then its resolution in some concrete piece of narration or image. The obtrusive tendency of the whole Black Mountain group to call attention in their poems to the fact that they are writing poems, or to offer some nugget of aesthetic wisdom as the cream of a poem on a quite different subject, is present in L.'s work as well." This last quality is a feature of a third type of poet other than "amateur" and "professional"—the "agonist," one who writes metapoetry, that is, poetry about poetry, or spends a great deal of time and energy in expressing theories of poetry in prose. However, although she has occasionally published a book of essays including *The Poet in the*

World (1973) and *Light Up the Cave* (1981), L. is not known as a critic or theoretician.

L.'s involvement in antiwar activity during the 1960s and 1970s came close to obscuring everything else about her work. Her book *Footprints* focused largely upon the war in Vietnam, and it raised a greater number of moral issues than perhaps the poet had intended. One of these had to do with the commitment of the antiwar "artist." It had become obligatory during the war for creative people of all sorts to comment, take stands, on many issues, not all of them clearly related. The example of "Hanoi Jane," as the movie actress Jane Fonda was called by her enemies, is perhaps the most memorable of the period. Like other poets before her, including John Greenleaf WHITTIER, Walt WHITMAN, and even Herman MELVILLE, L. became more famous for her activism than for her art.

What is true of most protest poetry of any period was true of L.'s work and of much of the work by others that she promoted—it was more protest than poetry. When the Vietnam War was over at last, L.'s eye wandered to other social issues including the threat of nuclear war, women's rights, racial prejudice. Most of the pieces that appeared in the various ban-the-bomb, anti-war, civil rights, feminist, and other activist anthologies of the past decades cannot be called art, for they tended to be harangues that called attention to the self-righteous stances of the poets rather than to the atrocities at which these occasional pieces were ostensibly directed. Certainly, artlessness was always L.'s long suit—not the strongest suit for an artist to hold.

BIBLIOGRAPHY: Marten, H., *Understanding D. L.* (1988); Mersmann, J. F., *Out of the Vietnam Vortex: A Study of Poets and Poetry against the War* (1974); Rosenthal, M. L., *The New Poets: American and British Poetry since World War II* (1967); Waggoner, H. H., *American Poets from the Puritans to the Present* (1984); Wagner, L. W., *D. L.* (1967)

LEWIS PUTNAM TURCO

LEVIN, Meyer

b. 8 October 1905, Chicago, Illinois; d. 9 July 1981, Jerusalem, Israel

L. was one of the most prominent Jewish American writers during the 20th c. His literary career extended from 1924, when he was a reporter and columnist for the *Chicago Daily News* and published a series of "Sketches of Roosevelt Road" (then a major Jewish neighborhood in Chicago) in the Jewish periodical the *Menorah Journal,* to 1981, when his last novel, *The Architect,* was published. In addition to writing over

a dozen novels, L. has put together a pictorial study: *If I Forget Thee: A Picture Story of Modern Palestine* (1947), has edited, with Charles Angoff, an anthology, *The Rise of American Jewish Literature* (1970), has made translations—one of them being Sholem ASCH's *Tales of My People,* published in 1948—and, more importantly, has written plays and screenplays. Of his five screenplays, at least two were made into documentaries: *My Father's House* (1947), published that same year as a novel, and *The Illegals* (1948); both deal with the painful attempts of Jewish victims of Hitler's Europe to find sanctuary in British-held Palestine.

L.'s literary approach, social realism, was doubtless influenced by the reporter's supposed obligation to "get it all down" without being arty. What sets him apart from other important writers of whatever cultural or religious background is that ironically he seems never to have been at ease in the three regions where he spent his life: the U.S., Palestine-Israel, and (to a lesser extent) Europe. Angoff quotes L.'s definitive self-summary, "From my first contact with Zionism in Palestine in 1925, my writing has been oriented toward an organic view of Jewish life, in which America, Europe and Israel have their place." Angoff adds, "L.'s fascination with the Jewish experience is total."

Out of all of L.'s novels, a few are particularly noteworthy. *The Old Bunch* (1937) is an absorbing chronicle of the lives, loves, failures, and successes of a neighborhood group of Jewish boys and girls in Chicago from 1921 to 1934: children of immigrants, most of them struggling their way out of a lower-middle-class existence. The highly successful 964-page book has been compared, understandably, with James T. FARRELL's Studs Lonigan novels. L.'s highly critically acclaimed bestseller *Compulsion* (1956) is a documentary novel about the 1924 abduction and mutilation-murder of little Bobby Franks by two high IQ upperclass youths, Leopold and Loeb. Some of his subsequent writing, fiction and nonfiction, would deal fairly objectively with particular aspects of the Holocaust experience and life in Eretz Yisroel (the land of Israel). *Eva* (1959) is a personal account of a young woman's escape from Poland under the Nazis, and later from Auschwitz, and her eventual settlement in Israel. *Gore and Igor: An Extravaganza* (1968), an atypical work, is a romping, tasteless tale of two young, hardworking male newcomers to Israel, one American and one Russian, around the time of the 1967 war, both peace activists, fugitives from the government, concerned about their art, and woman-crazy. *The Settlers* (1972) and *The Harvest* (1978) cover the first half of the 20th c. in Eretz Yisroel, chronicling the fortunes of a Russian refugee family, the Chaimov-itches, up to the time of Israeli independence. *The*

Architect, another atypical work, is an absorbing fictional re-creation of the life and career of the extraordinary architectural genius Frank Lloyd Wright, here called Andrew Lane, center of domestic scandal, and victim of personal tragedy. This highly regarded book is enriched by L.'s highly informative background material on the time period covered, and on what Wright's artistic vision and philosophy obliged him to attempt and to achieve.

One of the handful of L.'s most enduring books is the masterfully written first part of his autobiography, *In Search* (1950), covering his early life in Chicago, his involvement in journalism and the plight of Jews overseas, and his subsequent experience as war correspondent with the Jewish Telegraphic Agency and the Overseas News Agency. In this capacity, he accompanied the armed-forces liberators of the Nazi death camps, including Buchenwald and Dachau, and incidentally helped rehabilitate some of the survivors and assist them in trying to gain safe haven in Eretz. In this connection L. discusses his filmmaking of the refugees' struggle, first for the U.S. Office of War Information, then as an independent filmmaker.

Significantly, these experiences impelled L. the writer to seek a personally meaningful expression of the tragic epic of the Holocaust—since he had not been a victim himself. He found it at last, in the Anne Frank story, given in her diary, and became utterly committed to producing a play version of it, faithful in spirit and body to the original text. But he was thwarted repeatedly by the people he attempted to deal with, literary and religious politics, and artistic egos lying at the core of his failures to achieve his aim. Among other frustrations was the fact that the play was taken out of his hands and rewritten, he felt, in a way that would minimize and trivialize its specifically Jewish frame of reference.

L.'s novel *The Fanatic* (1964) reveals the central concern and grievance of his private life and literary career: a burning sense of injustice and betrayal, primarily at the hands of his fellow Jews: that is, mistreatment so outrageous that there can be no real rest until this basic wrong is redressed. As L. explained in the foreword, the novel is "written in the tradition of realistic fiction," and is narrated by a dead man, Leo Kohn, an escapee from a Nazi death camp. Kohn wrote an account of his experiences as a warning for his people back home, but was ignored by them and ultimately died in the same death camp. A sad, inept agnostic, Maury Finkelstein, who has become a rabbi, somehow obtains Kohn's manuscript, called *Good and Evil,* and in the course of trying to get it published and then turned into a play for dramatic production, brings endless trouble on himself and makes his life a shambles.

The second, and last, part of L.'s autobiography, aptly entitled *The Obsession* (1973), is a fascinating but melancholy account of his fruitless and self-punishing struggle over twenty years to do justice to the drama of Anne Frank, in the face of the enormous success of what he considered to be the egregiously false version. Despite or because of all his conflicts with the literary and dramatic establishments, L. as writer, interpreter of human suffering, and artist deserves far more consideration than he has received in his troubled but meritorious career.

BIBLIOGRAPHY: Bellman, S. I., "The Literary Creativity of M. L.," in Steinbach, A. A., ed., *JBA* 33 (1975–76): 111–16; Bernstein, M. M., "M. L.," in Walden, D., ed., *DLB,* vol. 28, *Twentieth-Century American Jewish Fiction Writers* (1984): 136–41; Miller, A. S., "M. L.," in Martine, J. J., ed., *DLB,* vol. 9, part 2, *American Novelists, 1910–1945* (1981): 161–69; Varon, B. W., "The Haunting of M. L.," *Midstream* 22 (1976): 7–23

SAMUEL I. BELLMAN

LEVINE, Philip
b. 10 January 1928, Detroit, Michigan

L. began to write poetry while he was going to night school at Wayne State University in Detroit and working days at one of that city's automobile manufacturing plants. The intersection of brutal factory work with an impulse to poetry formed the imaginative nexus out of which emanated not only L.'s first poems but also to a considerable degree his entire poetic output, to date consisting of over fifteen volumes of poetry, a collection of interviews, *Don't Ask* (1981), and an autobiographical collection of essays, *The Bread of Time* (1994), as well as his highly valued translations of modern Spanish poetry.

In that intersection of two different kinds of labor, L. discovered that few of the fundamental experiences of working class life had rarely, if ever, found expression in the realms of contemporary American poetry. The epiphany that launched L. was his sense that the clang of industrial labor—and all the human spirit that was swallowed up in it—could be a source of a poetry that probed the many forms of alienation found in and among those people he knew best, those who had to work hard for a living. Though he went on to earn an M.F.A. from the Writer's Workshop at the University of Iowa, though he studied with John BERRYMAN and Robert LOWELL, among others, and though he has taught for many years as a creative writing professor himself, the imaginative core of his being is on the assembly line floor. It is there where he first sensed that an exploration of the infinite varieties of loss could be made into poetry.

L.'s working experience lent his poetry a profound skepticism in regard to conventional American ideals. He had seen too many victims of the crushing pressures felt in the lives of the poor, so he quite naturally found within himself an uncanny empathy with the outcast and the despised in general. In L.'s first two books, *On the Edge* (1963) and *Not This Pig* (1968), the poetry dwells on those who suddenly become aware they are trapped in some murderous processes not of their own making. In "Animals Are Passing from Our Lives," for example, the pig trotting off to market intends to keep his dignity, no matter what the charnel house outcome is, as if that kept dignity marks a triumph. The child in "To a Child Trapped in a Barber Shop" is panicky in what the poet says is the first and archetypal encounter with what will be a lifetime of traps and imprisonment.

L.'s poetry developed its distinctive style and subject matter also during the same years as the U.S. was enmeshed in the African American struggle for civil rights. From L.'s point of view, the dehumanization of factory labor was just another example of what had happened over the centuries to racial minorities. Everything human was or would be turned into a commodity. People and all they cared about were bound to be bought, sold, trashed. The American Dream for some had always been a nightmare. Such is the insight that drives L.'s third book, *They Feed, They Lion* (1972). The title poem was inspired by race riots in Detroit in the late 1960s and forms the refrain of a chant that conjures the fury of the thwarted and dispossessed.

If, in his first two books, L. was somewhat traditional in form and relatively constrained in expression, he discovers with his third book an expressive form that will serve him throughout his poetic career. Beginning with *They Feed, They Lion,* L.'s poems are typically free-verse monologues tending toward trimeter or tetrameter. Sometimes he experiments with syllabic verse, while other times even his loose versification gives way to an emotion that demands release. Above all, the music of L.'s poetry comes to depend on a tension between his line-breaks and his syntax. His sentences want to cascade down the page, passing through skeins of modifying clauses and phrases, through enjambment after enjambment until the energy of his sentence is exhausted. For the reader, there is a gathering, vertiginous momentum in the typical L. poem, which leaves the reader feeling slightly out of control, not knowing what's going to happen next, but utterly in the grip of the emotion. The title poem of *1933* (1974), L.'s next book, is as good an example

as any of the typical cascade of clauses and phrases one finds in L.'s poetry.

With *1933,* a significantly surreal element also emerges into the foreground of L.'s work. The surreal had always been implicit in his poetry, but a long stay in Spain in the late 1960s confirmed L. in this direction. Studying Spanish, he also translated Pablo Neruda and César Vallejo, among many others, and incorporated into his own work their unabashed combination of political concerns with the surprising, nonrational, nonrepresentational image or figure of speech. This served L. in subsequent books such as *The Names of the Lost* (1976) and *Ashes* (1979), the primary subject matter of which are elegies for family members. The speakers of these elegies not only explore feelings of loss and vulnerability, but also maintain an imaginative defiance in the face of death. They speak as if time and mortality were the oppressors; and the imagination—with its capacity for the surreal—becomes a way to lessen the fear of death. The surrealism in L.'s poetry is thus an assertion of the vital realm of the spirit. This is especially clear in his poems about the Spanish Civil War in *7 Years from Somewhere* (1979), and most memorably in "To Cipriano, One for the Wind" in *One for the Rose* (1981).

The way in which the soul manages to survive in hostile environs has been the primary concern in L.'s poetry of the last fifteen years, the most productive period in his career. In *Sweet Will* (1985), *A Walk with Tom Jefferson* (1988), the National Book Award-winning *What Work Is* (1991), the Pulitzer Prize-winning *The Simple Truth* (1995), and *The Look of Things* (1996), the poet scans his life and world for the signs of a sturdy, irrepressible survival of the spirit. As earlier, he finds it most often in memory: of co-workers on the auto plant floor, and of family members and friends of his youth. But in his recent work, he also finds it in various religious traditions, especially his own inherited Judaism. He also finds it in certain rebellious artistic traditions, such as Spanish poetry, especially the poetry of the doomed Republican cause in the Spanish Civil War. He also finds it in the contemplation of his own mortality, the mortality of those close to him, a long list of deaths of loved ones, and graveyards, including those American graveyards masquerading as ways of making a living. L.'s mature meditations show no diminishment in passion, moral outrage, or extravagant imagination, but instead reaffirm the poet's restless vision and literary purpose.

BIBLIOGRAPHY: Buckley, C., *On the Poetry of P. L.: Stranger to Nothing* (1989); Mills, R., *The Cry of the Human* (1975); Jackson, R., "The Long Embrace: P.

L.'s Longer Poems," *KR* 11 (Fall 1989): 160–69; Molesworth, C., *The Fierce Embrace* (1979)

FRED MARCHANT

LEWIS, Alfred Henry

b. 20 January 1857, Cleveland, Ohio; d. 23 December 1914, New York City

A prolific journalist of the muckraking era and the author of some twenty works of popular fiction and juvenile biography, L.'s reputation is based mainly on several collections of humorous western dialect stories that appealed to an age still captivated by the myth of the Old West.

After practicing law and serving for two years as city prosecuting attorney in his home town, L. left Cleveland and the law profession in 1881 and migrated west with his parents to Kansas. He subsequently took jobs as a cowboy on several ranches in Kansas. Participating in cattle drives to Dodge City and the Texas Panhandle, he had ample opportunity to experience life on the Western plains with real cowboys and to listen to their colorful anecdotes of a rapidly fading era in the uncivilized West, accounts that he would later utilize in creating a humorous but realistic portrait of Western scenes and characters. After gaining his first editorial experience as reporter and editor of the Mora County *Pioneer* and the Las Vegas *Optic* in New Mexico, L. drifted to Arizona, where he spent some time in and around Tombstone, a region he was to draw upon in much of his western fiction.

After a second attempt at practicing law proved unproductive, L. committed himself to journalism in Kansas City and found a ready reception for several short western sketches he submitted to local newspapers under the pseudonym of Dan Quin. These tales were purportedly recounted by an "Old Cattleman," a picturesque grizzled survivor of the exciting days of the wild West. Told in a colorful, humorous western vernacular, a style that L. admitted was "crude, abrupt, and meagre," the stories recall the Old Cattleman's experiences in the hybrid community of Wolfville, clearly based on Tombstone. Here a mixture of cattlemen, sheepherders, tenderfoot Easterners, Indians, Mexicans, Chinese, and a sprinkling of pioneer women—with colorful names like Cherokee Hall, Faro Nell, Toothpick Johnson, Tucson Jenny, Texas Thompson, Wagon Mound Sal, and Spelling Bee Johnson—inhabit equally colorful meeting places such as the Bird Cage Opera House, the O. K. House "Restauraw," the New York Store, and especially the Red Light Saloon. Although the tales generally center on rough-and-tumble episodes of comic misadventures in a Darwinism world where fights and killings are casual

occurrences, the plots often reveal underlying themes of love, fidelity, justice, integrity, and courage. Although Wolfville appears on the surface to be as uncivilized as its rival Red Dog, where virtue is entirely lacking, its inhabitants have a strong sense of principle and follow a self-imposed code of decency.

Prompted by avid readers to collect his newspaper tales, L. in 1897 published *Wolfville,* a volume illustrated by Frederic REMINGTON and edited in part by Theodore ROOSEVELT, who counted themselves among Wolfville fans. The popularity of this first volume encouraged L.; and in the midst of a burgeoning career as writer and editor of several newspapers and magazines (including William Randolph Hearst's New York *Journal* and *Cosmopolitan*), he continued to publish Wolfville stories. Five more Wolfville collections followed over the next two decades: *Sandburrs* (1900), *Wolfville Days* (1902), *Wolfville Nights* (1902), *Wolfville Folks* (1908), and *Faro Nell and Her Friends* (1913). The stories continued to be narrated by the Old Cattleman and to be built around a core of Wolfville's most colorful personalities, but each collection added new tales and new characters. Although the stories continued in the same style that had made *Wolfville* popular, the later collections lacked the freshness and vigor of L.'s earlier offerings; and new readers were less receptive to the heavy dialect and the unique vocabulary that were the trademarks of the Wolfville canon.

In addition to his Wolfville collections, L. wrote two novels with Western settings—*The Sunset Trail* (1905) and *The Throwback: A Romance of the Southwest* (1906)—but neither achieved the success of his Wolfville tales. Most of his other fiction shifted to the East and, like many of his newspaper and magazine articles, exposed political and business corruption: *The Boss and How He Came to Rule New York* (1903), *The President* (1904), and *The Apaches of New York* (1912). Between 1901 and 1908, L. also found time to write biographies of Richard Croker, John Paul Jones, Andrew Jackson, and Aaron Burr, mainly for a juvenile audience.

In addition to his books, L. from 1898 to 1900 also edited and wrote much of the copy for the *Verdict,* a Democratic weekly much given to political humor. From 1905 to 1910, he edited *Human Life,* a Boston monthly to which he contributed his autobiographical "Confessions of a Newspaperman" (1905–6).

Although L.'s popularity did not survive him, his stories are important for being among the earliest to capture the spirit of the Old West. While other portrayers of the West who were to follow him, such as Owen WISTER and Zane GREY, essentially were novelists, L. was one of the few authors who concentrated on short stories. Along with Bret HARTE, L. helped raise the

Western above the formulaic hack writing that characterized the dime novels so prevalent in the second half of the 19th c. Although the humor and exaggeration featured in the Wolfville plots place the tales in a somewhat different category of local color than the stories of Harte, Wister, or Grey, the verisimilitude of L.'s characters and setting emphasize the primitive, uninhibited western life that so many writers sought to glamorize.

BIBLIOGRAPHY: Brown, R. M., "A. H. L.," in Ashley, P. J., ed., *DLB*, vol. 25, *American Newspaper Journalists, 1901–1925* (1984): 170–73; Filler, L., ed., *Old Wolfville* (1968); Ravitch, A. C., *A. H. L.* (1978)

WILLIAM K. FINLEY

LEWIS, Sinclair [Harry]

b. 7 February 1885, Sauk Centre, Minnesota; d. 10 January 1951, Rome, Italy

L.'s popular satirical novels of the 1920s struck American life with such force that their impact is still felt. No one today talks or writes extensively about the small town as Dullsville without bringing in the Gopher Prairie of L.'s *Main Street* (1920); nor examines the American businessman for long without alluding to L.'s blabbermouth realtor, George F. Babbitt of *Babbitt* (1922); nor remarks the financial and sexual shenanigans of televangelists without comparisons to L.'s rogue preacher, Elmer Gantry of *Elmer Gantry* (1927). If portions of even L.'s best novels seem dated and overstuffed with detail, superficial and shrill, he did excoriate a still observable vulgarity and conformity and added in George F. Babbitt and Elmer Gantry American characters to place beside Rip Van Winkle, Natty Bumppo, and Simon Legree.

Before attaining success, L. served a long apprenticeship trying his hand at many kinds of writing, ranging from pallid romantic verse to science fiction, from a juvenile adventure novel to slick commercial short stories for the *Saturday Evening Post*. His first appearance in print occurred in 1902 in the *Sauk Centre* (Minnesota) *Herald,* printed in his hometown, where his father was a physician. L. later contributed to student publication at Yale, from which he graduated in 1908. After miscellaneous jobs including a stint on a Waterloo, Iowa, newspaper and a California sojourn, where he sold plots to Jack LONDON, L. went to work for New York City publishers and produced his first book *Hike and the Aeroplane* (1912), a juvenile under the pseudonym Tom Graham.

This juvenile shows L.'s concern for contemporary interests. Research for the aviation parts overflowed into L.'s second novel for adults, *The Trail of the Hawk* (1915), in which Hawk Ericson, born in a Minnesota village, goes on to win glory as an aviator before giving it up after the death of a friend in a flying accident. At the close, Hawk is blissfully married to an upperclass, Eastern girl and employed in the Touricar business. Much indebted to H. G. Wells, L.'s first novel for adults, *Our Mr. Wrenn* (1914), tells about a New York office worker who overcomes an inferiority complex by taking a cattleboat trip to England, meeting a variety of people including a bohemian female, and returning to New York City to a better job and a happy marriage.

One L. novel of 1917, *The Innocents,* is blobby sentimentalism about old folks; but the other, *The Job,* deserves reprinting for its authentic depiction of female white collar life. *The Job* concerns Una Golden, a small-town Pennsylvania girl, who after disappointment in office work in New York City and a failed marriage with Julius "Eddie" Schwirtz, a proto-Babbitt, becomes a hotel executive and finds happiness in a renewed romance with a publicity man.

In the last apprentice novel, *Free Air* (1919), L. once more has a romantically beautiful Eastern upperclass girl for a Midwestern boy, here Milt Daggett, garage owner in Schoenstrom, Minnesota, to dream about. Milt in his little car assists and rescues Miss Claire Boltwood and her father and their big car on the hazardous roads of the teens from middle Minnesota to Seattle. At the end Milt will study engineering and get culture and the girl.

With *Main Street* (1920), L. skyrocketed to fame. Although Hamlin GARLAND, Edgar Lee MASTERS, and Sherwood ANDERSON had already roughly handled the American village in what Carl Van Doren labeled "The Revolt from the Village," no one until L. had done the job so thoroughly. Contemporary readers got the impression that Gopher Prairie, Minnesota, was dirty and emotionally stultified, nosy and materialistic, dull and complacently conformist. Defenders of the village were outraged.

Actually *Main Street* is no simplistic denunciation of the small town. The chief critic of Gopher Prairie is youthful Carol Kennicott married to Dr. Will Kennicott, a general practitioner. Much of Carol's struggle is against small-town traits embodied in her husband, a sometimes obtuse and narrow character, but also, sometimes considerate, even heroic, as performs surgery in an isolated farmhouse. Though L.'s sympathies generally remain with Carol, occasionally she is flighty and naive.

Carol's rebellion climaxes the rebellions of Miles Bjornstam, the Red Swede handyman; of young Fern Mullins, the fun-loving schoolteacher, forced out of her job by Ma Bogart, a churchy scandalmonger; of Erik Valborg, aesthete and tailor's helper. Despite exaggerated caricature, overt editorializing, prolix detail, and undue length, the novel retains power.

Shorter and more polished than *Main Street,* S.'s next resounding novel, *Babbitt* (1922), has claim to be his best. Again the central character revolts against an oppressive social environment, but the revolt of George F. Babbitt, the active partner in a real-estate business in the middle-sized Midwestern city of Zenith, is so stifled by his business associates and his own herd instincts that it may almost be overlooked. But like his more frustrated fellow Booster Paul Riesling, violinist turned tar-roofing salesman, Babbitt dreams of a freer life, of moral and political idealism, though little comes of the rebellion except unsatisfactory sex and a hurried return to conformity when his business is threatened by pressure from the Good Citizens League. Possibly dissent may survive in his son Ted Babbitt, who, unlike George, has chosen a bride and work on his own initiative.

L.'s wide knowledge of the businessman's habitat of booster and lunch clubs and hell-raising conventions and the glee with which he pursues his prey contribute to a remarkable achievement. In the opening, L. writes some of his most effective prose, presenting his balding, pudgy businessman in bed dreaming of a fairy child amid routine morning noises: the newspaper with its standardized opinions thumping the front door; a standardized Ford being cranked; a standardized alarm clock ringing.

L.'s *Arrowsmith* (1925) is also full of rebellion. After a start in Elk Mills, Winnemac, Martin Arrowsmith graduates and obtains a medical degree from the University of Winnemac, marries a comradely wife Leora, and gets the inspiration to pursue scientific research from the genius of Max Gottlieb, an unpopular German-Jewish microbiologist. After fumblings as a physician in Wheatsylvania, North Dakota, and as a public health official in Nautilus, Iowa, and as a laboratory specialist in a fashionable clinic in Chicago, Martin finds his real work as a research scientist at the McGurk Institute in New York City. The McGurk Institute is modeled on the Rockefeller Institute and some of its personalities. Even in his research sanctum, commercialism threatens Martin's work and his efforts to test his bacteriophage in the West Indies are only partly successful. There his faithful wife Leora dies of the plague. Returning to New York City, Martin marries a rich wife and almost succumbs to the cult of success, getting to the woods and an isolated research laboratory in just the nick of time.

Praised and popular, awarded the Pulitzer Prize, which L. rejected, *Arrowsmith* nevertheless strikes this observer as weaker than its immediate predecessors. Despite an occasional drinking spree, Arrowsmith is too much the idealized devotee of research rather than a convincing human being. L.'s reliance for scientific data on Dr. Paul de Kruif, a paid microbiologist consultant, perhaps caused L. and de Kruif to block out the plot of the novel too schematically. Many situations seem contrived. Usually the novelist of a subject area, L. had absorbed through his own experience the worlds of the small town and of the businessman better than he could absorb the unfamiliar world of the investigative scientist. Still, the freshness of the material, the scientist as hero, gave the book an immense and continuing readership. After these important novels, L. startled his readers with a potboiler entitled *Mantrap* (1926), the improbable adventures of a New York lawyer who toughens in the Canadian wilderness.

Elmer Gantry, L.'s definitive fictional treatment of exploitive evangelism, followed in 1927. Dedicated to H. L. MENCKEN, the tireless prodder of the "booboisie," and containing a significant reference to the Dayton (Scopes) evolution trial, *Elmer Gantry* draws a grim picture of the menace to art and thought as this power-hungry fundamentalist clergyman extends his range from Paris, Kansas, to Paris, France. Again L. employed a research assistant, but here he was in better control of his less specialized material.

Gantry is portrayed in meticulous detail, beginning with an undergraduate drinking and wenching winging while enrolled in a small Baptist college and continuing to the conclusion where spectacular success beckons him as future pastor of the Yorkville Methodist Church in New York City and as executive secretary of the National Association for the Purification of Art and the Press (Napap). The most memorable part of the novel (and the only part treated in the celebrated motion picture of 1960) is Elmer's love affair and professional association with the glamorous woman evangelist Sharon Falconer. Sharon later perished in the fire that destroyed her oceanside tabernacle with Elmer only narrowly escaping after knocking down a girl who blocked an exit. Gantry's greatest triumphs came after he joined the Methodists and worked his way up with energy and palaver. At that he was almost destroyed by a sexual scandal, but, though guilty, with legal help, he brazened it out. In the latter novel Elmer no longer drinks, substituting for liquor the intoxication of power. A rude, crude, vigorous book, *Elmer Gantry* draws a haunting picture of decadent Protestant fundamentalism. After the thick *Elmer Gantry,* L. published the slender *The Man Who Knew Coolidge* (1928), an unjustly neglected volume, recording the logorrheic monologue of Lowell Schmaltz, a "Constructive and Nordic citizen," a kind of debased Babbitt.

L.'s great decade ended with *Dodsworth* (1929), the most sophisticated of his novels and one of the most autobiographical. In it, Sam Dodsworth, a Midwestern automobile manufacturer, retires at fifty, and travels in Europe with his snobbish, flirtatious, younger wife.

At the conclusion he will divorce his unfaithful, nagging wife and marry an American widow, Mrs. Edith Cortright, who unlike her predecessor, will encourage him in his creativity and acquisition of true culture. The novel is L.'s version of his failed marriage to Grace Hegger and of his courtship with the noted journalist Dorothy Thompson (their marriage lasted from 1928 to 1942). Though L. strove to give psychological depth to this novel, his popular derisive art was not suited to a Henry JAMES subject. Sam Dodsworth is an awkward split between a masterful executive and a hurt adolescent, and Fran Dodsworth is pure bitch.

Ironically, after L. became the first American to receive the Nobel Prize in literature (1930), the quality, though not the quantity of his work, sharply declined. Only three of his later novels—all best sellers—need attention. *It Can't Happen Here* (1935) excited America with its account of a Fascist dictator, Buzz Windrip, a mix of Adolf Hitler and Huey Long, seizing power. However interesting the subject, the novel itself is slam-bang journalism. *Cass Timberlane* (1945) describes the sometimes troubled marriage of a Midwestern judge and his younger wife. Certain astringent interchapters dealing with parallel and contrasting marriages have sometimes been anthologized. Finally *Kingsblood Royal* (1947) has historical value as an attack on prejudice against blacks.

L. is perhaps best seen as a popularizer of important topics for the increasing mass readership of the 1920s, the same decade that witnessed the start of the *Reader's Digest* (1922) and *Time* (1923). L.'s style is characterized by copious detail; contemporary allusions; blunt comparison and contrast; breezy and slangy dialogue; comic names; noisy sound imagery; much use of short sentences, short paragraphs, subchapters, and even capitalization for emphasis; and broad, sometimes overbroad, sarcasm and irony. Despite the slickness and quickness of much of the fiction, there is a core of permanent value. For a long time, the dust will continue to blow on *Main Street,* Babbitt will babble of service, and Elmer Gantry will commit adultery and grow rich and powerful.

BIBLIOGRAPHY: Bucco, M., ed., *Critical Essays on S. L.* (1986); Dooley, D. J., *The Art of S. L.* (1967); Grebstein, S. N., *S. L.* (1962); Light, M., *The Quixotic Vision of S. L.* (1975); Schorer, M., *S. L.: An American Life* (1961); Schorer, M., *S. L.* (1963); Sheean, V., *Dorothy and Red* (1963)

ROBERT L. COARD

LINCOLN, Abraham

b. 12 February 1809, Hardin County, Kentucky; d. 15 April 1865, Washington, D.C.

William Dean HOWELL called Mark TWAIN "the L. of our literature"—an apt comparison, but based on a false distinction between "literature" and other public uses of language. L.'s writing was, except for some youthful poetry, entirely devoted to political uses—speeches, proclamations and similar documents, and public letters. Nevertheless, our greatest political leader is also a central figure in our literature, using the American vernacular with suppleness and unparalleled eloquence. Basically self-taught, L. developed his vocabulary, style, and imagery from authors well known to ordinary Americans of his time: Aesop, Shakespeare, John Bunyan, Daniel Defoe, Robert Burns, and particularly the King James version of the Bible. To this, he added the logical rigor of great works of law such as Blackstone's *Commentaries.* The result, honed in the courtroom and on the stump, was a prose combining logical precision with diction and rhythm derived both from literary tradition and the vernacular of the frontier.

The vigor of L.'s extemporaneous speech is best preserved in the series of seven debates with Stephen Douglas, part of an 1858 Illinois Senate campaign, as well as in the anecdotes and witticisms preserved by those who attended his cabinet meetings and receptions. His prepared speeches and documents, on the other hand, are crafted with great care, with degrees of formality and eloquence appropriate to the occasions. It has often been noticed, for example, that the Emancipation Proclamation of 1862 is flat and legalistic, in line with L.'s position that this extraordinary moment in human history was simply a military measure.

L.'s earliest important speech was delivered before the Young Men's Lyceum of Springfield, Illinois, in 1837. It anticipates a major theme of L. in its filial tribute to the founders—"the patriots of seventy-six"—and its oath on their "blood" to uphold what they created. Biographers have also found interest in the address for its warning against "ambition"—"Towering genius disdains a beaten path"—which has been seen as a reflection of L.'s growing sense of his own powers and destiny. By the time of his February 1860 speech at New York's Cooper Union, L. had connected his tribute to the "fathers" with the unyielding contention "that slavery is wrong." His peroration gained the attention that led to his nomination to the presidency that summer: "Let us have faith that right makes might, and in that faith let us to the end dare to do our duty as we understand it."

The First Inaugural Address, March 4, 1861, combines a plea to the seceding Southern states with assertions of the indissolubility of the Union—an almost mystical L. belief earlier developed in the "House Divided" speech of 1858, built on Jesus's analogy, "A house divided against itself cannot stand." The conclusion of the First Inaugural provides an opportunity to analyze L.'s masterful use of imagery, diction, and rhythm. A draft by Secretary of State William Seward reads: "I close. We are not, we must not be, aliens or enemies, but fellow-countrymen and brethren." In L.'s hands, this became: "I am loth to close. We are not enemies, but friends. We must not be enemies." L.'s final sentence anticipates the swelling grandeur of his later great speeches: "The mystic chords of memory, stretching from every battlefield and patriot grave, to every living heart and hearthstone, all over this broad land, will yet swell the chorus of the union when again touched, as surely they will be, by the better angels of our nature."

The two greatest speeches of L.'s presidency were called forth by the central battle of the Civil War and by the impending end of the conflict. The address delivered at the dedication of the Gettysburg battlefield cemetery, November 19, 1863, is generally regarded as L.'s finest. Garry Wills's book-length study of this 272-word speech connects it to Athenian funeral oratory, the romantic culture of death, American transcendental philosophy, and the tradition of Constitutional jurisprudence. By comparing the address to speeches of Daniel Webster and Edward Everett, Wills also shows a "revolution in style." Uniformly abstract and elevated, the Gettysburg Address moves from the opening biblical motif of "Four score and ten" to its final evocation of "a new birth of freedom": "that government of the people, by the people, for the people, shall not perish from the earth."

The Second Inaugural Address, March 4, 1865, is more revealing of L.'s personal development during the Civil War. Beginning simply, L. recounts the origins of the war in terms of historical inevitability: "And the war came." He acknowledges slavery as, "somehow," the cause of the war, and then—in an extraordinary statement for a victorious leader—attributes the war to "the providence of God": "He gives to both North and South, this terrible war, as the woe due." The address then concludes with a long final sentence that, with its rhythmic balance, biblical echoes, and general human compassion, fittingly represents L. at his best: "With malice toward none, with charity for all; with firmness in the right, as God gives us to see the right, let us strive on to finish the work we are in; to bind up the nation's wounds; to care for him who shall have borne the battle, and for his widow, and his orphan—to do all which may achieve and cherish a just and lasting peace, among ourselves, and with all nations." Six weeks later, L. was assassinated, an event which inspired Walt WHITMAN's great elegy, "When Lilacs Last in the Dooryard Bloom'd."

BIBLIOGRAPHY: Anderson, D., *A. L.* (1970); Donald, D. H., *L.* (1995); Edwards, H., and J. E. Hankins, *L. the Writer* (1962); Fehrenbacher, D., *L. in Text and Context* (1987); Oates, S. B., *A. L.: The Man Behind the Myths* (1984); Wills, G., *L. at Gettysburg* (1992)

GLEN M. JOHNSON

LINDBERGH, Anne Morrow

b. 22 June 1906, Englewood, New Jersey

L.'s celebrity as the daughter of a distinguished American family and, especially, as the wife of the famous aviator ensured that the public would show an interest in her books. Her graceful prose has been able to stand on its own merit—her travel narratives and novels were critically received with respect and even acclaim—but her most widely read works have been the five volumes of the diary detailing the private side of her very public adult life.

L.'s father, a prominent figure in business and politics, and mother, a poet and crusader for women's education, were the core of an insulated and scholarly family whose closeness L. found both rewarding and stifling. In 1927, while a student at Smith College, L. traveled to the family Christmas gathering in Mexico, where her father was serving as ambassador. There she met the American hero, Charles Lindbergh. She married him in 1929 and was instantly thrust into the public eye.

L. learned flying, navigation, and radio operation and became the first woman in the U.S. to earn a glider-pilot's license. The couple flew together frequently in the first years of their marriage, increasing the intense public scrutiny of their lives. In 1930, when their first child was born, the Lindberghs' star grew even brighter. But when the boy was kidnapped and then found dead, L.'s trauma was exacerbated by the continuing publicity.

Encouraged by her husband to write, L. had begun keeping her diary in 1929. Now he prodded her to produce a work for publication—an account of their surveying flight to Asia via the North Pole in 1931. In 1935, *North to the Orient* saw print and received favorable notice. Lindbergh also convinced L. to accompany him on a five-month exploratory Atlantic flight, a resumption of their old routine, to escape the relentless exposure. The story of this trip, *Listen! The Wind* (1938), proved that her first book had been no fluke; the *New York Times Book Review* noted that the work was "historically valuable; in A. L.'s hands it becomes literature."

In 1944, L. published her first novel, *The Steep Ascent,* whose subject, a married couple's dangerous flight, resembled that of the earlier nonfiction stuff of her life. L. then began to work on a series of autobiographical essays. These eventually became her popular study of marriage, *Gift from the Sea* (1955). The essays symbolize the stages of married life as a series of seashells. L.'s focus in this evocative and poetic work is the effect of marriage on a woman: because marital responsibilities can prevent her from achieving her full potential, creativity and occasional solitude are necessary for her life to have balance. L.'s second novel, *Dearly Beloved* (1962), again explored the territory of marriage. This experimental fiction lacks realistic characterization, but reveals the unsentimental, yet hopeful, possibilities such a relationship can offer a couple.

A volume of poetry, *The Unicorn and Other Poems* (1956), attracted both positive and negative attention. Some readers saw these lyrics as a natural outgrowth of the prose style in L.'s essays. One reviewer, however, found the poetry "offensively bad," a critique that infuriated much of his audience.

The publication of L.'s diaries began in 1972 when she had been convinced by her husband's publisher that the unvarnished minutiae of her life were of value to the public. Covering the period from 1929 to 1944, the volumes include *Bring Me a Unicorn* (1972), *Hour of Gold, Hour of Lead* (1973), *Locked Rooms and Open Doors* (1974), *The Flower and the Nettle* (1976), and *War Within and Without* (1980). The candor of her journals, coupled with "a built-in plot and a soul-searching heroine worthy of a Brontë novel," as one reviewer noted, made these works best-sellers. But the artful prose also reminded L.'s readers that she deserves recognition not simply as a celebrity, but as a talented modern writer.

BIBLIOGRAPHY: Mayer, E. F., *My Window on the World: The Works of A. M. L.* (1988); Wurz, T., *A. M. L.: The Literary Reputation* (1988)

CAROLYN LENGEL

LINDSAY, [Nicholas] Vachel
b. 10 November 1879, Springfield, Illinois; d. 5 December 1931, Springfield, Illinois

In 1920, when L.'s reputation stood at its peak, a writer for the *Observer* (London) called L. "easily the most important living American poet." Shortly after L.'s death, Sinclair LEWIS described him as "one of few great poets, a power and a glory in the land." L. published nine volumes of poetry and five of prose, yet his reputation rests on relatively few pieces that exemplify what L. called "The Higher Vaudeville."

These poems draw on native speech patterns and musical rhythms, particularly hymns and syncopated ragtime, combined with hypermetric lines, complex rhyme schemes, and a variety of traditional poetic feet. The musical quality of these works illustrates the influence of Edgar Allan POE, Sidney LANIER, and Algernon Charles Swinburne. "The Kalliope Yell," written in 1913, relies on sound as much as language ("Hoot toot, hoot toot, hoot toot, hoot toot, / Willy willy willy wah Hoo!"). "General William Booth Enters into Heaven" (1913) was published with musical directions for recitation. "The Santa Fe Trail" (1914) contrasts blaring automobile horns with birdsong and wind. L. imagined "The Congo" (1914), probably his best-known work, as containing "Every kind of war-drum ever heard. Then a Minstrel's Heaven, then a glorified Camp Meeting." Six lines of the last stanza are set to the hymn "Hark, Ten Thousand Harps and Voices."

While L.'s poems broke with convention, he did not sympathize with the modernist movement led by Ezra POUND. Whereas the modernists endorsed concentrated, intellectual, understated verse, which L. condemned as "aesthetic aristocracy," he chose a style that is wordy, expansive, demotic; and whereas modernists drew their inspiration from Continental models, L. sought his themes in America. "The Kalliope Yell," inspired by the Illinois State Fair, celebrates American brashness. "The Santa Fe Trail" depicts the American west. L. wrote eight poems about Johnny Appleseed and drew on other American figures such as Andrew Jackson, Abraham LINCOLN, William Jennings Bryan, and Illinois governor John Peter Altgeld for his subject matter. L.'s prose works also focus on America, from his *Adventures While Preaching the Gospel of Beauty* (1914), based on his 1912 expedition through the American West, and *A Handy Guide for Beggars* (1916) describing his travels through the South in 1906 and Mid-Atlantic states in 1908 to his utopian *The Golden Book of Springfield* (1920) and his collection of essays, *The Litany of Washington Street* (1929). Preaching a "new localism," he argued for "Rhymes on Florida moss, Georgia violin, a New Jersey orchard in the spring . . . a California orange grove, a Washington apple orchard." His celebration of American democracy also underlies *The Art of the Motion Picture* (1915), the first book-length study of movies as an art form. L. praised Thomas Edison for bringing culture to all.

Trained as an artist rather than a writer (Chicago Art Institute, 1900–1903; New York School of Art, 1903–8), L. provided illustrations to accompany his poems. Many of these depict personal mythology he created under Swedenborgian influence. Thus, the amaranth vine stands for eternal beauty; mist represents the spiritual life. Beauty is a butterfly, Mammon the soul of the spider, Aladdin's lamp poetic inspiration. Historical figures also assume symbolic significance: John Peter Altgeld is humanitarianism, William Jennings Bryan egalitarianism, Confucius represents equality, Buddha, chastity.

The surrealistic dream visions that contain these symbols constitute the majority of L.'s work. These poems have not endured, nor has the love poetry he wrote to a series of what he called "inspiration girls," almost all of them considerably younger than he, including Elizabeth Conner, whom he married in 1925. Edwin Arlington ROBINSON's prediction that most of L.'s work would be forgotten has proved prescient. Equally true, however, is Robinson's claim that "in the best of L. there appears to exist a nameless quality that vanished cave-dwellers would have understood, and that unborn sophisticates will accept."

BIBLIOGRAPHY: Harris, M., *City of Discontent: An Interpretive Biography of V. L.* (1952); Massa, A., *V. L.* (1970); Ruggles, E., *The West-Going Heart: A Life of V. L.* (1959)

JOSEPH ROSENBLUM

LIPPARD, George

b. 10 April 1822, Chester County, Pennsylvania; d. 9 February 1854, Philadelphia, Pennsylvania

The most popular antebellum American novelist before Harriet Beecher STOWE, L.'s work is little read today, yet its distillation of the underlying cultural beliefs and obsessions of the period best captures the welter of popular thought behind the American Renaissance.

His early experience as a Philadelphia legal clerk and reporter exposed him to the inequities and corruption of 19th-c. urban life. Viewing fiction as a vehicle for reform, he committed himself to exposing the seamy underside of the cities by confronting topics—the abuses of capitalism and the upper class, the corruption of the judicial system, socialism, sexuality, abortion, adultery, occultism, violence, and murder—with a verve and directness remarkable for its time.

Based on a true story, his best-known book, *Quaker City; or, The Monks of Monk Hall* (1845), wove elements of sensation, pornographic, reform, temperance, occultist, and nativist fiction into a labyrinthine plot centered around the seduction of Mary Arlington, a naive young girl, by Gustavus Lorrimer, a wealthy libertine, and the murderous revenge of Byrnewood, her brother. The Monk Hall of the title, once a convent, is now a private club where bankers, clergymen, lawyers, and the wealthy come to remove their pious masks and revel in drink, gambling, and illicit sex, all under the watchful eye of the doorkeeper, Devil-bug. Filled with trap doors and secret passages, the Hall symbolizes both the corruption of contemporary life and its ability to hide behind a genteel facade. Its

many subplots—a hallmark of L.'s narrative method—ranging from social climbing via adultery and murder to the establishment of a religious cult, coupled with the continual appearance of "heaving bosoms," assured the novel's success. Alternately attacked and praised, its lurid rendition of city life prompted a flood of imitative "City" novels.

After *Quaker City,* L. wrote a series of historical novels and stories including *Blanch of Brandywine* (1846), *The Rose of Wissahikon* (1847), and *Washington and His Generals* (1847), mythologizing the exploits of the founding fathers, who he felt best exemplified the true ideals of the republic. While editing and publishing a weekly newspaper, *Quaker City* (1848), and founding, in 1849, the Brotherhood of the Union (a labor organization), he continued writing novels and stories, such as *The Empire City* (1850) and *New York* (1853), steeped in the dark cultural undercurrents of the period and employing sensational plots and topics in the interest of reform.

While cultural historians have often acknowledged his influence, the confused and strained nature of his plots pose difficulties for modern readers. Still, his work remains vital to those interested in understanding the intersections between culture and fiction in 19th-c. America.

BIBLIOGRAPHY: Reynolds, D. S., *G. L.* (1982); Ziff, L., *Literary Democracy* (1981)

DAVID BORDELON

LIPPINCOTT, Sara Jane [Clark]

b. 23 September 1823, Pompey, New York; d. 20 April 1904, New Rochelle, New York

L. is best known in literary circles as "Grace Greenwood," famous for her moralistic and social commentary letters and essays, many of which are compiled in the 1850 *Greenwood Leaves,* L.'s first best-seller. Many of the selections in *Greenwood Leaves,* as well as many subsequent pieces of like quality and theme, were also published in popular periodicals of the 19th c., notably *Godey's Lady's Book,* the *Saturday Evening Post,* and the *New York Times,* among others.

L.'s first published work came in the form of poetry that appeared initially in small local papers; in 1844, her poetry made its way into N. P. WILLIS's *New Mirror.* L.'s poetry as well as her prose follows closely the moralistic themes with which she has been closely associated. Most of L.'s writing focuses on addressing the social ills of her day—including slavery—in an attempt to rile interest in a faithful Christian community to acknowledge and begin correction of such ills. Her interest in and passion for moral issues have been widely credited to L.'s staunch Puritan upbringing, an upbringing which has its roots in ancestor Jonathan EDWARDS. While much has been made of this relationship, it is reasonable to assume that L. possessed her own sense of morality for which she deserves due credit.

This morality that is so deeply intertwined in L.'s writings also is grounded in the cult of true womanhood so popular in middle-class 19th-c. America. L. unabashedly holds the tenets of this cult as closely to her heart as she does any other moral issue in her writings. So interested was she in preaching her ideas of sound social morality that L. wrote several juvenile works with moralistic themes, including *Nelly, the Gypsy Girl* (1863). In addition, she coedited the children's periodical *The Little Pilgrim* from 1853 to 1875.

There is more depth, however, to L.'s work than is evidenced in her Grace Greenwood tales and essays. She is also responsible for the best-selling *Haps and Mishaps of a Tour in Europe* (1854), a travel account of L.'s solitary journey through Europe. Critics have praised this work for its good writing as well as for its straightforward reporting style. *New Life in New Lands* (1873) continues L.'s mastery of the travel genre. This collection of letters originally published in the New York *Times* between 1871 and 1872 records L.'s travels through the western U.S., with special focus on her Colorado visits. In addition, L. served as a Washington correspondent for the New York *Tribune* from 1850 and 1897; many published letters from the latter part of her career focus on the personalities of political figures in Washington. These travel and political writings serve to round out a career that often seems overshadowed by the moralistic agenda of Grace Greenwood.

BIBLIOGRAPHY: Mainiero, L., ed., *American Women Writers* (1982); Thorpe, M. F., *Female Persuasion: Six Strong-Minded Women* (1949)

TERRY D. NOVAK

LISH, Gordon
b. 11 February 1934, Hewlett, New York

L. has earned both a distinctive and distinguished reputation in contemporary American fiction as an author, editor, and teacher of writing. L. first came into national prominence when he became fiction editor at *Esquire* magazine in 1969, where he offered a national forum to the new fiction emerging in the 1970s. He first published the stories of John CHEEVER and Grace PALEY in *Esquire,* thus giving their stories a wider readership. As important, he introduced to *Esquire* readers the stories of new and talented writers such as Barry Hannah, T. Coraghessan BOYLE, Reynolds PRICE, and Cynthia OZICK, among others. Moving from that magazine to an editorial position at the prestigious Alfred A. Knopf publishers in 1977, L. was responsible for publishing and bringing into prominence story collections of Mary ROBISON, Janet Kauffman, Amy Hempel, Michael Martone, David LEAVITT, Bette Pesetsky, and especially Raymond CARVER. Some critics contend that L. discovered Carver and rigorously promoted his early work. Critic Sven Birkerts recognizes L.'s influence in establishing young writers and designates them as belonging to the "School of L."

In addition to his editorial work at Knopf, L. began teaching creative writing classes at Yale University from 1974 to 1980, and at New York University and Columbia during the 1970s and 1980s. Along with his teaching and editorial duties, L. also founded and edited one of contemporary American literature's most progressive literary journals, the *Quarterly,* which gave hundreds of young writers a chance to publish their sometimes highly experimental work. A number of writers got their start in the *Quarterly,* notably Sam Michel, Noy Holland, Yannick Murphy, and Brian Evenson. There is little question that L. is one of the major formulators of the canon of contemporary American fiction.

Most importantly, though, is L.'s own contribution to the body of contemporary literature with seven novels and three collections of short stories. Critic Frank Lentricchia claims that L. is "easily one of the rare original voices in American writing of the last thirty to forty years." What separates L.'s novels from other writers is that each is written in a different form. His first novel, *Dear Mr. Capote* (1983), was an epistolary confession of a serial killer to Truman CAPOTE, offering Capote a chance to write an account of the killer's past and future murders and split the money that will result from book-and-movie deals. Although the first-person narrative voice certainly sounds like the voice of L. himself, he manages to construct a fictive voice that includes echoes of his own, Capote's, and a stand-up comedian's, all at the mercy of the Freudian slips that reveal the actual truth of the narrator's unconscious attitudes and desires.

L.'s next novel, *Peru* (1986), is considered by many critics to be his most accomplished because of the ingenious ways in which the author plays with a long-repressed memory of a murder he committed when he was seven years old. *Peru* brilliantly explores the metafictional relationships between and among actuality, fiction, and memory so convincingly that Stephen Dobyns calls the theme: "the fiction of the fiction itself." *My Romance* (1991) seemingly dispenses with any attempt at creating a fictive voice and records an actual speech L. gave at a writers' conference. It is, however, a 142-page monologue that becomes more hilarious as it moves along; it is a comic masterpiece. Two short story collections, *What I Know So Far* (1984) and *Mourner at the Door* (1988), show L. to be one of contemporary America's most accomplished postmodernist writers. Many of the stories explore the act of writing itself by intertextually experimenting with voices of earlier writers, such as J. D. SALINGER, especially in the story "For Jerome—with Love and Kisses." But his most notable stories from both collections—genuine masterpieces and deeply moving—are "What Is Left to Link Us" and "The Death of Me." Obvious similarities in both structure and substance show the influence of writers such as Ronald SUKE-NICK, Donald BARTHELME, Thomas PYNCHON, and John BARTH on L.'s absorbent imagination.

L.'s most controversial novels are *Zimzum* (1993) and *Epigraph* (1996). The subject of *Zimzum* is a narrative of the last days of his wife's terminal illness; *Epigraph* records his wife's actual death and its aftermath. *Zimzum* interweaves the horror of death and suffering with the agony of sexual guilt and frustration, a unique and quasi-Nietzschean conflict between *eros* and *thanatos*. Harold BLOOM called it: "Outrageous and obsessive, a kind of leap into the primal abyss. . . . A Beckettian neo-pornography. . . . A living wound of a book." And Cynthia Ozick asks if *Epigraph* is not "the most painful, the most anguished, the most self-lacerating book ever written. . . . And—God help us—the funniest?" Both novels test the transgressive boundaries in ways much closer to the Lower East Side world of Kathy ACKER or the subterranean world of William S. BURROUGHS. However, L. moves the existential terror and agony to his own comfortable Upper East Side New York neighborhood.

There is little question that L. is not afraid to violate taboo and to treat subjects that other writers dare not approach, accomplishments which make the body of his work unique in the annals of contemporary American literature.

BIBLIOGRAPHY: Birkets, S., *An Artificial Wilderness: Essays on Twentieth-Century Literature* (1987); Ferrandino, J., "G. L.," in Meanor, P., ed., *DLB,* vol. 130, *American Short-Story Writers since World War II* (1993): 224–31

PATRICK MEANOR

LITERARY CRITICISM BEFORE 1914

Early American literary criticism is intimately connected to national life. That is to say, the early criticism was conducted outside of a professional context: whereas 20th-c. criticism takes place largely within a university environment, complete with academic presses, scholarly journals, literary conferences, and so on, the early criticism is more closely involved with the actual historical development of the nation itself and, in many ways, actually mirrors that development.

The rigors of colonial life did not encourage belles lettres, and thus the earliest works are autobiographical in nature. Puritan authors such as John WINTHROP and William BRADFORD favored such genres as the diary, the ESSAY, the letter, and the SERMON, works that emphasize survival and salvation rather than artistic elegance. Benjamin FRANKLIN, Tom PAINE, Thomas JEFFERSON, and the other major authors of the revolutionary generation focused on politics and philosophy—again, work destined to be read for other than aesthetic reasons.

The generation of Washington IRVING and James Fennimore COOPER, while still writing with an English readership in mind, began to lay claim slowly to American subjects and modes of expression, and a corresponding critical tradition began to form. In the years between 1810 and 1835, there were more than 130 magazines that might be considered literary. But in the absence of a robust literary context, the majority of the reviews and articles were written by lawyers, lawmakers, ministers, physicians, and schoolmasters rather than poets and novelists. The resultant criticism has a judicial and moral flavor that makes most of it forgettable.

It was not until the 1840s, which heralded the explosive appearance of dozens of now-classic works by American romanticists and realists, that a mature criticism began to appear as an accompaniment to the literature itself. Ralph Waldo EMERSON and Edgar Allan POE were the most important critics of the mid-19th c., with the one articulating a theory of literature that looks at its nature, function, and purpose, and the other concerning himself with theory as well but also with poetics or questions of craft. During that remarkable period known as the American Renaissance, several key developments occurred simultaneously: the first generation of professional writers appeared; many of the enduring works of American literature appeared as well; and a criticism appeared that focused on American writing as an independent type rather than a British derivative. This native literary criticism ranges from extremes that are highly idealistic at one pole and almost scientifically practical at the other, thus laying the groundwork for a broad spectrum of criticism to come. Perhaps not surprisingly, Nathaniel HAWTHORNE, Herman MELVILLE, Walt WHITMAN, and Henry JAMES, authors of much of the most enduring criticism of the period, also wrote the most enduring fiction.

The first radical call to arms for writers comes from Emerson, whose essay "The Poet" is a classic of romantic literary theory. Breaking with neoclassical thought, in which formalism curbs fluid expression, Emerson calls for, not meters, but a meter-making argument in poetry, and a precedence of thought over form. He seeks a specifically American poet, one who will not only rival but even exceed Homer and Shakespeare. Admitting that he sees no such poet yet in America, Emerson maintains nonetheless that the next great poet will create his work in New World groves and pastures rather than in the castles of Europe. He also emphasizes the importance of poetry to society as a liberating force that opens the eyes of its readers to new views. In this seminal essay, Emerson also creates a foundation for the type of criticism called theory, which is devoted to the broader purposes of literature, as opposed to poetics, which deals with the mechanics of its composition.

In sharp contrast to Emerson's theoretical criticism, Poe offers a distinctly practical view of poem-making in "The Philosophy of Composition." Rejecting the romantic assumption that the writer is an instrument responding instinctively to stimuli beyond his ken, Poe argues that it is possible and even desirable for a literary work to be constructed with the rigor and precision of a mathematical problem. Taking "The Raven" as his example, Poe describes his search of the perfect length (one hundred lines, though the finished poem turns out to be one hundred and eight), province (beauty), tone (sadness), and artistic effect (the refrain, which, because of its monotony, would be spoken most logically by a nonhuman creature). The point of a raven saying "Nevermore" at the end of each stanza of a melancholy poem of roughly one hundred lines is to dramatize what Poe calls the most poetical topic in the world, namely, the death of a beautiful woman, and to present that topic from the point of view of the perfect narrator, the bereaved lover who is tormented by grief as well as the utterances of the infernal bird. Here Poe espouses a poetics of literature, which, unlike theory, is concerned with craft rather than function. Poe was an eclectic critic rather than a systematic one like Emerson, but clearly he mined important ideas in the American literary psyche: the idea of the death of a beautiful woman, for example, is used by Emily DICKINSON, a poet as different from Poe as possible, in her poem "Because I Could Not Stop for Death."

Emerson and Poe represent the extremes of early American literary criticism, the first positioning art within the broader spectrum of all human endeavor and the latter examining closely a set of finite precepts. As the Industrial Revolution progressed and new technologies made publication easier for an increasingly literate readership, new outlets for literary expression

appeared as well as new voices, both literary and critical, and it was not long before criticism became as diverse as literature itself. The genteel schoolmasterly approach that appealed to the general reader is represented by James Russell LOWELL's "Fable for Critics," with its witty estimates of such contemporaries as Henry Wadsworth LONGFELLOW, Oliver Wendell HOLMES, William Cullen BRYANT, and John Greenleaf WHITTIER. But there was also biographical criticism, as evidenced in Rufus Griswold's scandal-mongering obituary of Poe and an edition of Poe's letters (1850) to which he added passages favorable to himself.

At this time, too, minority and women's voices were heard widely for the first time, though it would be the next century before they achieved their fullest expression. Margaret FULLER's *Woman in the Nineteenth Century* is the first mature consideration of FEMINISM in American life. Her essay "American Literature: Its Position in the Present Time, and Prospects for the Future" laments the lack of an American literature per se but proposes a list of worthy contemporaries, concluding that "the future is glorious . . . for those who do their duty in the present." Magazines such as *Godey's Lady's Book* (1830–98) influenced fashion, manners, and literary taste, thanks to editors such as Sarah Josepha HALE, who, in her forty years with the monthly, published not only Emerson and Poe but Harriet Beecher STOWE as well. Frederick DOUGLASS's *Narrative of the Life of Frederick Douglass* and his later autobiographies as well as Harriet JACOBS's *Incidents in the Life of a Slave Girl,* with its authorial preface and supportive testimonials by Jacobs's defenders, argue the case for minority viewpoints as a significant aspect of American literary expression.

In all of its variety, 19th-c. literary criticism continued to position itself between Emerson's theory and Poe's poetics. Melville, for example, champions American writers almost as loudly as Emerson does, yet his rhetoric is more grounded in the realities of American life. Too, unlike Emerson, Melville has found his ideal native writer, as the title of his essay "Hawthorne and His Mosses" suggests. Melville likens his new hero to an old one, saying that Hawthorne and Shakespeare share a sense of mirth but an even greater sense of tragedy and that the American novelist's work too is characterized by subtleties as fine as any in Shakespeare. Melville insists that present-day Shakespeares are being born this very day on the banks of the Ohio. What is needed, he claims, is a more professional corps of reviewers to assess American genius. Melville is clearly thinking of the generally sorry state of magazine criticism in the early republic as well as the pointedly unkind reception of some of his own writing when he notes that "there are hardly five critics in America; and several of them are asleep!"

Melville's judgement is harsh, but perhaps not entirely undeserved, considering the failure of 19th-c. literary journalists to comprehend the subtleties of much of his own work. The critical writing with the greatest impact continued to come from the literary artists themselves, often in the form of comment on their own work. In his preface to *The House of the Seven Gables,* Hawthorne draws a careful distinction between the novel, with its professed goal of describing faithfully the actual world, and a form much more congenial to himself and other early American writers, the romance. Hawthorne's entire literary output is convoluted with the ecstasy as well as the anxiety of the author who is trying to free himself of the confines of Old World fiction and put a new kind in its place. Accordingly, in his preface he claims a certain authorial latitude toward the reality he wishes to depict. Whereas the novel limits itself to the probable and the ordinary, the romance may concern itself with the possible. Both genres must deal with truth, but the romancer has more freedom as to the circumstances under which truth will be presented and thus, as Hawthorne says, raise or lower the lights or deepen and enrich the shadows in his fictional picture. Hawthorne cautions a moderate use of these authorial privileges and urges the romancer not to season the dish he offers the public with too much of the marvelous, though he suggests that to disregard this advice would not be a literary crime.

If Hawthorne is closer here to the poetics of Poe, then Whitman, like Melville before him, is closer to the theoretical approach of Emerson. This hardly is surprising, for even though Whitman was one of the most radical technical innovators of any literary period, he was also a steward of the transcendental tradition that argued for the preeminence of the individual over the authority of institutions. Indeed, Whitman was the ideal poet that Emerson called for in his own essay, and when he sent the Sage of Concord a copy of the 1855 edition of *Leaves of Grass,* the older writer replied, "I greet you at the beginning of a new career" (in a letter that Whitman reprinted in future editions, to Emerson's considerable annoyance).

In his preface to the 1855 edition, Whitman asserts his belief that the U.S. themselves are their own greatest poem, a nation among nations that is, at the same time, a literary text with as many spaces, as many opposites and contradictions as the soul requires to find its own homelike niche. In a catalog of the sort that typifies "Song of Myself" and other poems, Whitman praises American speech, dress, friendship, love of freedom, curiosity, delight in music, evenness of temper, even Americans' quickness to anger as well as

their shambling walk. Yet unlike Emerson, Whitman sees America as, not rebelling against European ideas, but embracing them and combining them with American ones. Whitman's celebrated "catalogs"—here of geographical features, species of birds, professions—culminate in a paean to political liberty and the poet's eagerness to know all and embrace all, including venereal sores, masturbation, the burst capillaries of alcoholics, the vileness of seducers and prostitutes and sexual perverts. If Whitman's belief that priests will disappear and poets take their place seems like wishful thinking, and if his hope that a poet's country will absorb him as affectionately as he absorbs it is, in his own case, clearly doomed, at least he sets the stage for writers of generations to come and substantiates their freedom of choice as to technique and subject matter.

Henry James, who was to become the first of the truly modern American literary critics, began his career as a student of the famous writers who preceded him, though he distanced himself from both an optimism about American writing that at times bordered on the jingoistic as well as a critical impressionism that often ignored the writer's craft. The most prolific of the authors mentioned thus far, James published, in addition to his many works of fiction, numerous reviews and critical essays, including the book-length *Hawthorne.* Here James echoes both Hawthorne's own regret over the historical thinness of American life as well as his realization that this deficiency can be a goad to the imaginative powers of American writers and readers alike. If America lacks a sovereign, an aristocracy, a centuries-old church, an even older artistic culture, and a venerable political and military along with the palaces and castles that keep that history alive in present-day minds, then the novelist lacks the ready-made advantage of the English writer, who is presented with a preexisting world at birth and needs simply add his own touches to it. By contrast, the American writer must paint his entire novelistic world from the ground up, which, to James, explains the prevalence of whimsy in American writing. The American reader, too, must rely more on his instincts than his English counterpart.

It is essential that the reader read between the lines, complete the writer's suggestions, and aid the writer in constructing his picture. By bringing the reader into the picture and making him an active participant in the writing process, James turned away from the belief shared by critics as different as Emerson and Poe that the writer is a larger-than-life puppet master who controls the reader's responses. William Dean HOW-ELLS, himself a novelist and James's friend and editor as well, also champions readerly independence in

Criticism and Fiction, one chapter of which is entitled "Realism and the Common Man."

James's best-known essay is "The Art of Fiction," initially a response to a lecture by the Victorian novelist Sir Walter Besant. Whereas Besant maintained that fiction was a fine art like painting or music and should be studied in terms of the immutable laws that governed it, James puts much more emphasis on the novelist's powers of imagination, arguing that the writer's job is to pull the unseen out of the seen. The novel is a free and elastic form governed as much by the writer's and reader's depth of mind as by the outside world. A novel has no moral purpose, as claimed by Besant and such American critics as William Crary Brownell and Paul Elmer More, and instead must offer a sense of deeply felt life. James's famous advice to aspiring novelists in "The Art of Fiction" is to "Try to be one of the people on whom nothing is lost!" Taking issue with the aristocratic Besant's insistence that a novelist must know his or her place, James argues that to possess a first-rate mind permits a young woman who lives in a quiet village to write of military life and a blue-collar novelist to write of high society.

Between 1905 and 1909, James wrote the eighteen prefaces to the so-called New York Edition of his collected fiction. In these essays he counters the impressionistic criticism of the day with a craftsman's rigor, contributing ideas and technical terms still used by literary critics today. Among other topics, he discusses the portrayal of time in fiction; the creation of place; the use of indirection and ambiguity; the importance of using dramatic techniques in fiction; and, perhaps most important, the merit of the "center of consciousness" technique in such novels as *The Portrait of a Lady.*

In James's late criticism, with its emphasis on formalism, American literary criticism made a marked advance toward professionalism. Not an academic himself, James set the stage for the academic critical industry that would grow steadily after World War I and then explosively in the midcentury and beyond. If 19th-c. criticism sometimes seems almost overwhelmingly approving of both American life and literature, 20th-c. criticism often seems the opposite as it interrogates, resists, and, in its most extreme forms, attacks not only American culture in general but also its specifically literary artifacts.

As a profession that can, like the creation of literature itself, now be pursued full-time, contemporary American literary criticism is constantly evolving. The varieties of criticism being practiced today are probably countless and are certainly increasing as time passes and methods of reading change. In general, it may be said that so-called "pure" critics, those who embrace such approaches as New Historicism, femi-

nism, and Marxism, concern themselves with both the cultural origin and cultural impact of literature. On the other hand, critics who are also practicing poets, dramatists, and playwrights deal more with practical matters, such as technique. In other words, critics are still working the field that Emerson and Poe laid out for them, with theory at the one end and poetics at the other.

BIBLIOGRAPHY: Charvat, W., *The Origins of American Critical Thought, 1810–1835* (1936); Goldsmith, A. L., *American Literary Criticism, 1905–1965* (1979); Perosa, S., *American Theories of the Novel: 1793–1903* (1983); Rathbun, J., *American Literary Criticism, 1800–1860* (1979); Rathbun, J., and H. Clark, *American Literary Criticism, 1860–1905* (1979)

DAVID KIRBY

LITERARY CRITICISM SINCE 1914

American literary criticism since 1914 has been a collision of forces, an explosion of talent in the essay form, and a constant coming to terms with the direction of modern literature and thought. From the early part of this century, American critics have been embattled and emphatic as they clear a place for themselves by distinguishing their visions from an older "genteel tradition" and from the appreciative, impressionistic criticism of the 19th c. Late-19th-c. criticism—hardly a unitary movement with figures as different as the analytic Henry JAMES and the moralistic William Crary Brownell—was nevertheless a negative point of reference, a strawman for the new writers. Disillusionment, frustration, and rebellion were the attitudes of newcomers like Van Wyck BROOKS and H. L. MENCKEN. American literary culture of the preceding period was characterized as thin, provincial, puritanical, timorous, and refined. A battle of styles and wills had begun—American literary criticism was to become a series of attacks, new agendas for critics, rhetorical defenses of literature or ideals, and original analytic approaches.

Brooks, Mencken, and Randolph BOURNE—a trio of anti-Victorians—worked in the late teens to rouse American criticism from the torpor of fine taste and vague descriptions. Brooks sounded an early note of protest with *The Wine of the Puritans,* a book that distinguishes between the real wine of American culture—our commercial heritage—and the aroma—our highbrow, transcendental yearnings. He was later to argue that American spiritual energies were most often invested in accumulation, while the surplus spiritual life was put on a high shelf by genteel poets who anesthetized the senses of tired businessmen. In "The Critics and Young America" (1917), Walt WHITMAN was portrayed as a safe institution, the "good gray poet" who posed no radical threats. America, Brooks declared, liked to have a tame literature on hand. This none-too-subtle argument was pursued in a different form in *The Ordeal of Mark Twain* (1920) and *The Pilgrimage of Henry James* (1925). Here Brooks turned psychologist and traced the supposed falling off of the novelists' works to the crassness of the Gilded Age. Combining amateur Freudianism with Hipolyte Taine's emphasis on milieu, Brooks evolved a psycho-social criticism that is more concerned with impulses than with literature. While the attitudes of his later books such as *The Flowering of New England* (1936) were less negative, Brooks continued to deal in environment, personalities, and cultural criticism rather than in the texture of books.

Bourne, a radical who wanted to awaken Americans to the idea of a pluralistic society, was an influential social critic of literature. Speaking of the generation disillusioned by World War I, he called for an American literature that was responsive to the dangers of militarism and sensitive to the needs of a diverse populace. In *Youth and Life* (1913), Bourne established himself as a model for later critics of the American power structure. Meanwhile, Mencken had become the scourge of the "boobosie" and its best-parlor ideas of refined literature. A champion of NATURALISM, he was nevertheless capable of discriminating between Theodore DREISER's power and his clumsy sententiousness. Balanced prose and skepticism were the Mencken criteria; his hatred of the sermon made him intolerant of sentimental noise and cant. For some forty years he attacked "bunk" in print and life. An unabashed elitist who wrote on Nietzsche and insulted Middle America, Mencken was more a gadfly for the middle classes than a professional literary critic. His many essays, including the series of *Prejudices* of the 1920s, are notable for their energy, but contain no enduring original ideas.

Another group of critics—also in a quarrel with 19th-c. standards, particularly the romantic idea of self expression—is closely associated with academe: the New Humanists—Irving Babbitt at Harvard, Paul Elmer More at Princeton, and Stuart P. Sherman at Indiana—worked to undermine the influence of instinct in literature and criticism. Distrustful of feelings unchecked by reason and a standard of classical moderation, they wrote with the force of polemicists and the learning of great scholars. Babbitt's *The New Laocoon* (1910) was an early statement of principles; as a Racine scholar, Babbitt deplored the romantic mixing of genres and called for an American literature that would have the classical qualities of moral maturity

and clarity. "The Critic and American Life" (1932) shows no change of position: Mencken is chided for juvenile cynicism; the naturalism of Dreiser and Sinclair LEWIS is a deplorable kind of submission to modern chaos. Babbitt found that the 1920s style freedom from PURITANISM was a matter of being "unbuttoned" rather than emancipated. The spirit of Rousseau—Babbitt's bete noire—threatened the coherence of modern literature. More attacked American writers from the complex position of a Puritan analyzing the problematic legacy of his creed: the Puritan consciousness of evil in the world was salutary for literature, but emphasis on perfection of the self and need for change fostered illusions. More, a critic of civilization, felt that the "demon of the absolute"—uncontrolled rationalism—was damaging the American mind and the national literature. Like Babbitt, he saw the emerging American novel as an offense against order and moral standards; he called John DOS PASSOS's *Manhattan Transfer* "an explosion in a cesspool." During the 1920s, he also took up the sword against the surrealists, "denationalized Americans" of the Lost Generation, and other writers who celebrated the sovereign romantic self and its "bestial desires." Sherman, a one-time Indiana professor turned journalist, dedicated his first book to More and defended the Puritan idea of building a spiritual community, yet he was involved with democratic ideals and the need to address the ordinary American. As an American Arnoldian—his first book was about the Victorian sage—he criticized our rampant Mammon worship, the elitism in our antique republican tradition, and the vulgar boosterism of commercial America. An important part of an emerging criticism of American civilization, the New Humanists were, nevertheless, insensitive to—when not willfully ignorant of—the styles and ideas of the best 20th-c. writers. While they dealt with ideas in literature over the course of time, they were not as influential as intellectual historian Arthur O. Lovejoy, a John Hopkins professor whose study *The Great Chain of Being* (1936) traced the historical unfolding and transformation of an idea in many texts and did so with the dazzling skills of a polymath. Such interdisciplinary work—unlike the essentially moralistic criticism of Babbitt and More—was a legacy to critics of a later period, including figures as dissimilar as Lionel TRILLING and Leslie A. FIEDLER.

It remained for T. S. ELIOT, Ezra POUND, and Edmund WILSON to work though the 1920s to create a new criticism that would register the developments in literature, offer an aesthetic for the times, and show how to escape from moralism and impressionism. Influenced by George SANTAYANA's distrust of New England Puritanism and Babbitt's classical standards and disdain for romantic individualism, Eliot developed a

677

way of viewing tradition and individual talent and also a method of evaluating poetry. In "Tradition and the Individual Talent" (1917), he declared that the great poet must refine personality out of his work and become a carrier of the weight of past writers' phrases, ideas, and standards. Eliot conceived the literary canon as a community of texts, each modifying the other. His criticism closely examines textures of poems and the ways that motifs and ideas change later literature. He becomes a comparative analyst of poetry rather than a critic involved with authors' psychic lives; texts displace personalities as the critic's concern. Eliot—revolting against earlier emphasis on environment rather than literary style—offers the authority of his intimate, wide-ranging knowledge of poetic forms. In "The Function of Criticism" (1923), he argues that interpretations are "only legitimate when it is not interpretation at all, but merely putting the reader in possession of the facts which he would otherwise have missed." Using these facts about the ways writers structure language is Eliot's way of escaping from what he considers the protestant, subjective, chaotic nature of 19th-c. criticism. Ironically referring to poetry as a superior amusement, he manages to separate literary discussion from the errors and prejudices of men like More. In *The Sacred Wood* (1921), he scores Arnold for putting "literature into the corner until he cleaned up the country first."

Eliot's practical criticism is forever intertwined with his gift for phrasing. Several of his terms—especially "objective correlative" and "dissociation of sensibility"—have given his criticism an authority that has extended over scholarly books, a school of interpretation called the New Criticism, and college classrooms in America during the 1940s and 1950s. "Objective correlative" denotes the correspondence of an image to an emotion in poetry: Eliot measured poetes by their ability to evoke feeling through a pattern of imagery rather than through rhetorical insistence. "Dissociation of sensibility" is Eliot's way of describing the split between feeling and thought in poetry since the 17th c. These terms have in part been responsible for the great prestige of Metaphysical poetry and symbolist literature in our century. Eliot helped later critics, poets, and audiences to acquire a taste for nondiscursive literature that conveys ideas and feelings through carefully shaped imagery.

Altogether, Eliot's work has had enormous consequences for American criticism: it has provided a non-technical model of how to read closely; it has shifted attention from abstract themes in literature to language; it has made poems seem like living things rather than mere messages.

Ezra Pound furthered the idea of poems as entities and the study of technique as the central business of the literary critic. His image-centered conception of poetry draws on his knowledge of Chinese characters, Provencal poets, and Dante. Pound's services to American criticism and culture include the informal editing of Eliot's *The Waste Land,* the writing of many small analytic appreciations of style in poetry, the coining of IMAGISM to describe the work of contemporaries, and the nurturing of many writers' talents during the teens and twenties. Pound's later career—marred by his mad excursions into political economy—stands as a tragic departure from his early devotion to craftsmanship and the "luminous detail" of a poem.

Starting out as a literary journalist in the 1920s, Edmund Wilson made his earlier career a response to Eliot's and Pound's writing. His first major book, *Axel's Castle,* brings the news of literary symbolism—including the French poets of the late 19th c., Joyce, Proust, and Gertrude STEIN—to a general American audience. The title suggests the isolation and sovereignty of the modern artist: this theme provides an important conflict in Wilson's career—that between the literary vocation and social commitment. Unlike Eliot and Pound, Wilson combined socialist ideals and a knowledge of American lives with his aestheticism. His books are a reporter's account of writers' environments, inner lives, and complex struggles with political and social pressures. While not as analytic as Eliot, he nevertheless shares the older critic's "avidity and detachment" in evaluating literature; Wilson typically immerses himself in an author or literary problem without losing his rational judgement and progressive conscience. Unlike Eliot, he is much concerned with writers' daily lives and problems; his sense of history is much more firmly grounded in events than Eliot's "tradition." A "literary worker" rather than a theorist or scholar, Wilson used three uniquely adapted approaches—the aesthetic, the psychological, and the social—as he ranged over an array of subjects large enough to daunt a Renaissance humanist. *The Shores of Light,* a collection of essays and reviews from the 1920s and 1930s, evaluates the techniques of F. Scott FITZGERALD and other contemporaries, probes writers' psyches without using jargon, and employs a special kind of analysis of milieu that does not reduce writers to being mere "products."

America in the 1920s and 1930s saw the full development of the three approaches that Wilson used. Vernon L. Parrington's three-volume *Main Currents in American Thought* (1927–30) took a socioeconomic view of the entire American literary tradition, judged writers according to the progressive quality of their ideals, and generally practiced social criticism in a way that anticipated the insensitivity of the less skillful Marxists. Marxist criticism flourished in the crude evaluations of Mike Gold, editor of the *New Masses.*

In a savage 1930 review, Gold hectored Thornton WILDER for not writing about American class conflict in his novels. In *The Great Tradition* (1933), Granville Hicks measured literature by the standards of Marxist orthodoxy. However, the period also had its subtle Marxist critics—Wilson pointing out that Marxist methodology is no substitute for taste or understanding of literary tradition; James T. FARRELL in *A Note on Literary Criticism* (1936) tempering Marxist analysis with common sense and rejecting leftist rhetoric as sentimentality and fuzzy thinking; Philip Rahv, founder of *Partisan Review,* establishing a journal that combined leftist criticism with analysis and appreciation of the conservative and apolitical elements in modern literature. The excesses of Marxism were also avoided by several other critics of the late thirties, forties, and fifties. Coming out of the overhead era of "social significance" in art, F. O. Matthiessen wrote about Ralph Waldo EMERSON, Henry David THOREAU, and Whitman in *American Renaissance* (1941) from the perspective of a sensitive socialist. Like Wilson, Matthiessen was involved with the humanistic outreach of a writer rather than with political consistency; he judged writers by Eliot's "objective correlative" and considered their attitudes toward democratic culture. Even a writer's failure of progressive vision was not a cause for condemnation. Lionel Trilling began a career in the late thirties that was a vital part of this flexible, subtle social criticism. While concerned that he might be out of touch with his generation, he nevertheless wrote his book on Matthew Arnold. His writing life became a model of poise; in *The Liberal Imagination* he positioned himself between the *Partisan Review* leftists and the wider culture of America, thus becoming a liberal critic of the liberal impulse. His specialty as an essayist was the exploration of the enlightened mind, its grasp and limits, and its need to seek subversive possibilities in art and life. Irving HOWE, another product of the 1930s, was a freethinking Socialist who criticized the institutionalization of modern literary ideas and the dangers of mass culture without becoming a predictable leftist spokesman. Alfred KAZIN's career has also been part of the social impulse of the 1930s. *On Native Grounds* and, over forty years later, *An American Procession* are both built on a sociopolitical view of the situation of American writers; neither a Marxist nor an aesthete, Kazin is involved with the judging the styles and quality of authors who react to the American scene.

The second movement that began in the thirties was the New Criticism. Its origins can be traced to the Fugitive group, Vanderbilt University students of the 1920s who came under the influence of Eliot. John Crowe RANSOM and his pupil Allen TATE were the most powerful early New Critics. They shared important social attitudes—affection for the rural South and disdain for the industrial culture of the North and the leftists who opposed it. They championed the organicism of the small community in a famous Agrarian manifesto entitled *I'll Take My Stand* (1930). In *The World's Body* Ransom argued that poetry was not a medium for transferring ideas but rather an immediate experience the value of which inheres in particulars. His volume called *The New Criticism* offers poetry as an alternative to the tyranny of technological society; for Ransom a poem is a democratic state in which the heterogeneous elements retain their integrity.

Tate, followed his mentor in resisting the social will. A poem is a unique form of knowledge that should not be held up to standards of relevance. Although the author of a book entitled *Reactionary Essays,* published in 1936, Tate was not a typical Southern gentleman of the old school; he found the South—"hag ridden with politics"—woefully deficient in literary talent, mostly because of its tradition of insulating itself from reality. Tate was in turn critical of other American escapes from immediate experience—science and abstract notions of progress that kill the mystery and complexity of attitude that produces poetry. Robert Penn WARREN and Cleanth BROOKS, two other Southerners in the New Critical movement, are less theoretical than Ransom and Tate. Warren's influence is principally as a novelist and social essayist with ironic views about the South. Brooks stands as the most practical of the New Critics. *The Well Wrought Urn* carries forward Ransom's ideas about the error of looking for messages in poetry; Brooks illustrates his principles by analyzing the ironies and paradoxes of great poems and avoiding paraphrases about meaning. He sees a poem as a unified artistic achievement, a reconciliation of opposites that is well wrought despite its warring elements. With Warren, Brooks wrote perhaps the most influential poetry textbook in American history, *Understanding Poetry:* the volume leads students through a course in perceiving the ironic texture and organic unity of poems from many centuries.

R. P. BLACKMUR and Yvor WINTERS were outside the milieu of the Southern New Critics, but had much in common with them. Both were close readers who focused on the autonomous work, and both were at odds with the politicizing of literary criticism characteristic of the 1930s. Blackmur's clearest statement of his approach is "A Critic's Job of Work" (1935), a program designed by a somewhat ironic "amateur." Blackmur warns against "succumbing" to concepts rather than employing them with guarded skepticism. Unlike Ransom and Tate, Blackmur is not opposed to Marxist readings or other approaches that have "ulterior purposes" so long as the critic "delights in discriminations" and is wary of universal applications of a theory. An eclectic and supple critic, Blackmur had wide ranging interests—including the European novel, James's craftsmanship, and Henry ADAMS's intellectual development. His abiding concern was for the texture of language—idiom rather than ideology.

Winters combined aspects of the New Criticism with a classical kind of judicial criticism. He emphasized the rational content in poetry, the inner coherence that separates mature art from what he considers to be nonsense. Winters—almost like a late-blooming New Humanist—attacked ROMANTICISM and "passion running undefined." *Primitivism and Decadence* attacked Joyce as adolescent in technique because of his imitation of the flux of daily life. In *Maule's Curse,* Winters traced a degeneration in American literature to the "curse" of being cut off from a moral tradition altogether—became confused by his own poetic theories and produced "an art to delight the soul of a servant girl."

While the New Criticism flourished from the 1930s through the 1950s, critics influenced by Freud and psychoanalysis also worked several veins. Joseph Wood Krutch's early work called *Edgar Allan Poe* (1926) represents a widespread tendency to search out the neurotic components in an artist's work without connecting them clearly to literary talent. Ludwig Lewisohn made more general use of depth psychology in examining the Puritan mentality in American literature; in *Expression in America* (1932), he uses reductive ideas about inhibitions to criticize the "chilled undersexed valetudinarians" Thoreau and Emerson. In *The Wound and The Bow,* Edmund Wilson offers a far subtler account of the relationship of repression to creativity as he shows Edith WHARTON "relieving an emotional strain" by denouncing her society. Lionel Trilling's essay "Art and Neurosis" stands as a model of sensitivity in its rejection of simplistic correspondences between sickness and genius. Elsewhere, Trilling is critical of Freud the distruster of art. Trilling's psychological criticism also is notably on display in many of his essays that analyze ambivalence and the individual's battle with culture. His famous piece on Samuel Langhorne CLEMENS's *Adventures of Huckleberry Finn* deals with the latter conflict.

But perhaps the most powerful and thoroughgoing use of the Freudian approach is to be found in Kenneth BURKE's lifelong exploration of motives in literature and communication. In *The Philosophy of Literary Form* Burke argues that a writer's vocabulary is a "symbolic action," an expression of his own conflicts. But Burke, unlike Freud, does not give primacy to sexuality, and his treatments of motives therefore extends to religious motives. While Burke's use of psychology tends to involve abstract discussions of language, Leslie A. Fiedler uses psychology to analyze the nature of the American self and the impulses behind our national myths and dreams. In *Love and Death in the American Novel,* he deals with sexual and gothic motifs in classic and contemporary fiction and argues that mature sexuality is rarely depicted by our greatest writers, who turn to the destructive, the repressive, and the bizarre in their flight from women.

The three critical tendencies that developed fully in the 1930s the social, the psychological, the New Critical—have flourished in the later part of the century and have continued to produce reactions, both of a practical and of a theoretical kind. A critic like Mary MCCARTHY—an author of theater criticism, social commentary, and informal analysis of the novel form—has emerged from the world of *Partisan Review* with her sociopolitical vision of the late 1930s intact. Ralph ELLISON's body of critical work, published as *The Collected Essays of Ralph Ellison*—including essays that set a tone of reason and urbanity as they explore the literary situation of blacks in America—is essentially involved with ways in which a major writer reacted to politics and maintained his integrity. With the reactionaries and bigots to one side and the leftist ideologues to the other, Ellison championed a yet-to-be-fulfilled kind of American humanism, one that would bring black identity and artistry within the literary tradition. Also on the social front of literary criticism, Malcolm COWLEY was a tireless chronicler of writers' lives and working methods who kept faith with the environmental approach to understanding creativity; his books have studied many American writers, seen them against the backdrops of their generations and locales, and yet never lost sight of their individual natures. Numbers of critics have tracked the lives and literary fortunes of groups and generations of writers—the New York Intellectuals, the Beat generation, the circle of John BERRYMAN and Robert LOWELL, and other cliques, coteries, and currents. Notable in this area of literary-social criticism is William Barrett's *The Truants* (1982), a portrait of meditation on such intellectuals as Lionel Trilling, Delmore SCHWARTZ, and other figures attached to *Partisan Review* and its New York surroundings in the 1940s and 1950s.

On the psychological front, scores of significant critics have looked at the inner lives of writers, the unconscious patterns to be unearthed from literature, and the inner state of the nation. Leon Edel's monumental critical biography of Henry James is a landmark example of the first kind of psychological work. In studying the details of James's personal life, Edel achieved a balanced and artist-centered portrait of his subject; as much cannot be said of recent psychosocial studies of writers' lives that emphasize pathology and sex at the expense of literary understanding. Psycho-analytically oriented critics have been classic Freudians like Steven Marcus, author of works that use the drives and scenes described by Freud to analyze Dickens and other major writers—and post-Freudians, like the notable Norman O. Brown who deals extensively with repressions and the exactions of civilization in *Life against Death* (1959) and *Love's Body* (1966). Marcus and other traditional Freudians accept the master's vision of human limitation and suffering; Brown and his followers are in the 1960s liberation mode—and end in mysticism. Beyond liberation is Lacanian criticism, a brand of postmodern theory that studies ego and id and the phases of human development in their relationship to language and the power that language exerts; its foremost practitioner in America is Shoshana Felman, author of a book on Jacques Lacan. The national psyche has been analyzed by critics as diverse as Leslie A. Fiedler in *An End to Innocence* (1955) and Allan Bloom in *The Closing of the American Mind* (1987): the first book, by a liberal, examines denials and blind spots in the progressive mind; the second, by and archconservative, excoriates Americans for their renunciation of the traditional life of the mind.

On the text-oriented front, William GASS has shown the way to the new theoretical approaches of the 1970s in *Fiction and the Figures of Life*. Gass's involvement with the worlds of language—the self-referential territory of experimental fiction—produced criticism that took leave of Marxist social significance and Freudian analysis alike. Structuralism was the next step for American criticism—one that turned critics to a new kind of European linguistic analysis, made them acutely aware of what the French theoretician Ronald Barthes has called the "erotics" of words in a text, and caused many to abandon plain criticism of themes and ideas forever. Susan SONTAG's *Against Interpretation* is crucial for understanding of this rebellion against messages in literature. Its championing of the pleasures of language brought the spirit of the new kind of criticism beyond academe. Inside the universities, Jonathan D. Culler's *Structuralist Poetics* (1974) and Robert Scholes's *Structuralism in Literature* (1974) did the official job of explaining the movement. The structuralist critic attempted to reveal the underlying patterns, oppositions, and organizing principles of texts, of cultural phenomena—and of cultures themselves. Unlike the New Criticism, structuralism was unconcerned with literary value or unity in text. It went to work on high and low works—the literary and the popular.

The structuralist emphasis on the relational quality of language—that words refer to other words and not to some signified, objective world—became a major

intellectual principal of the new deconstructionist movement. All power—in literature, in politics, and social life—was assigned to discourse and naming rather than to ideas or discoveries. Deconstruction—a term that has become one of the fighting words of the academy and one of the misunderstood words in the general culture in the 1970s and 1980s—is a critical theory and set of practices that challenge the integrity of a literary work (and discourse generally). In practice it takes apart a work in order to dispel illusions about universal truths, writers' intended messages, and ostensible meanings. It turns away from the aesthetic values and ideas of the modern movement; as the critical arm of postmodernism, it rejects the sustaining myths, arresting personae, psychological depths, and enduring symbols of great writers like Yeats and Joyce. It turns to the endless instabilities of language. In the wake of the modernists and their symbols for art and permanence, the postmodernists celebrated a condition—in art and life—of dissolution and multiplicity. The luminous text of a great modernist writer—valorized and stamped with the identity of an author—gave way to a contemporary work, say an experimental novel by John HAWKES or Thomas PYNCHON, with its violations of textual integrity; a story or character or recurring image became less important than language itself. By the 1980s a hypertext—with its shifting contours, its problematic authorship, its interference from the reader who may alter the so-called creation—competed with the relatively stable text known as a poem or novel. Deconstruction has thrived and won a vast following in intellectual communities at just the time when the images of modernism have been displaced by the rippling surfaces of such postmodern literature. The very notion of literature—in the high modernist period of the 1920s and 1930s, myth, and legend, history, artistic heroism set against a philistine world—had changed; film and other electronic media have stepped up the pace of writing, made permanent images give way to dizzying successions of images, and eroded the distinction between the art novel of James Joyce and Virgina Woolf and popular fiction. Deconstruction has been the ideological force accompanying and fostering this destabilized literature.

The philosophical assumptions of deconstruction—a rejection of the essence of literature, the fundamental literary properties in a text, as well as their bedrock themes and truths—are at least as old as Nietzsche and his attacks on idealism and permanent values, and perhaps as old as the medieval nominalists and their negating of absolutes. The French thinkers Jacques Derrida and Michel Foucault are the 20th-c. avatars of the philosophical urge to deconstruct, the movement's foremost exponents, and the two figures who have influenced American critics most profoundly. Through his essays, oddly unclassifiable discourses, and public statements, Derrida has affected a generation of critics, students, and academic scholars with his fiercely independent and terminology-ridden theory and discipline of reading "a text." The latter word became the 1970s and 1980s substitute for book or poem or story. A text is to be scrutinized—much as the New Critics had scrutinized poems—for ambiguities and incompatibilities in its rhetoric and imagery. However, while the New Critics saw a poem as an organic unity—a world of tensions and paradoxes made into a coherent and beautiful entity by a creator—Derrida has insisted that the infinite play of meanings, the struggle between present meanings and implied absent ones, make any text an unstable locale and therefore no place to find resolution or wholeness. His opponents find this enterprise nihilistic; his defenders find it the great creative breakthrough of the late 20th century, a theory of discourse that allows the imaginative critic to strip a text of its surface and latent meanings and pursue a radical course of detective work. Criticism interrogates a text until it breaks down illusions about major themes and messages; it also breaks down the traditional hierarchies and values that are nothing but age-old superstitions. Discovering plays of meaning and resonances between texts (called intertextuality) is the central enterprise of Derridean deconstruction.

Foucault's work as a philosopher of social consciousness is yet another massive contribution to the study of discourse. In *Madness and Civilization,* first published in French in 1961 and in English in 1965, he conducts an inquiry into forms of knowing (which he calls *epistemes*), and into the ways language expresses them, and in turn shapes life in different eras by controlling institutions, establishing hierarchies, and making conceptions of value seem natural rather than invented. Foucault's work is charged with political implications as he analyzes the power within public discourse, the ability of language to order and restrain. He shares certain central ideas with Derrida: the primacy of discourse in human affairs, and the impossibility of transcendence in a world engulfed in discourse. Absolutes and other cherished values are nothing but socially constructed control mechanisms in the form of texts—poems, speeches, decrees, credos. Such texts are indicators of what a given culture or period is able to grasp.

Deconstruction has set itself against the weight of the past. To Derrida and Foucault and their followers, Arnoldian humanism is mere bourgeois ideology: aestheitic value is an incoherent notion because there is no line between literature and ordinary discourse; authors are not shapers of autonomous works but transmitters of cultural codes; language has not and cannot be controlled by such authors; texts are by nature unstable. There are a number of strains of deconstruction and deconstructionist-influenced criticism; they adapt and modify the above propositions and are best understood by referring to their representative men and women. In the case of critic Harold BLOOM, there is reason to believe that this reverence for great authors makes him a very problematic deconstructionist. The strains are the following: the Yale University-based hermeneutical, the reader response, the anticanonical/multicultural, the New Historicist, the neo-Marxist, and—in its later phases—the feminist.

The Yale critics—sometimes facetiously called the "Hermeneutical Mafia"—taught at the University in the 1970s and continued to make literary study at Yale, as it had been since the 1950s, associated with texts and close reading rather than with the history of ideas or the social dimensions of literature. The major critics—Paul de Man, Geoffrey H. Hartman, J. Hillis Miller, and Harold Bloom—have worn their theory in distinctive ways. Paul de Man explored the central deconstructionist tenet—that readers can never get beyond words to any ultimate meaning or any representation of the real world. In *Bindness and Insight* (1971), literature is about itself—about fictionality and artifice. Only blind interpreters imagine that literay discourse can reach truths or penetrate to the essences of things or discover ideals. An anti-romantic because of his rejection of literary symbols as avenues to nature, de Man has also created a castle of poetic discourse shut off from questions about meaning. After his death, a scandal arose involving discoveries about his youthful politics. A cache of anti-Semitic articles, written by de Man in the 1940s for a Belgian newspaper, became the occasion for all-out attacks on the deconstructionist school itself. With such evidence in hand, detractors understandably pointed out that de Man's ideas of unstable meaning in writing seemed like an elaborate rationalization of his dishonorable past work. Anything could mean anything, according to this view of deconstruction. De Man furthermore was charged with corrupting the rising generation with his sophistries. His defenders escaped from the sheer personal history of the critic by pointing to the error of interpreting a life according to one episode. Some also pointed out that deconstruction was the nemesis of totalitarian discourse with its sweeping generalizations and absolutes.

Hartman, more historically oriented as a critic, shows that the deconstructionist discipline can consort with the real world and humanistic values. While writing about unstable texts and indeterminate meaning in *Criticism in the Wilderness* (1980), he also argues that those texts can save us from totalitarianism and consumerism. "In oppressive social systems it [the work of art] has always found a way to create a form of expression." This credo undercuts the charge that deconstruction is necessarily antihumanistic. This apparent reconnection with Matthew Arnold's function of criticism—its clarifying and healing powers—is acompanied by Hartman's own postmodern twist: deconstruction "proposes a type of analysis that has renounced the ambition to master of demystify its subject (text, psyche) by technocratic, predictive, or authoritarian formulas" or, plainly put, the ambition to prove or discredit a given interpretation. Miller shares the antitotalizing views of Hartman and de Man. He champions the "equivocal richness" of literature in terms that resemble his (now former) Yale colleague Bloom's ideas about new literary texts and older, established texts. Bloom puts this intertextual struggle in Freudian terms—sons overcoming fathers; in "The Critic as Host" (1979), Miller uses the imagery of the parasite and the host. A poem is inhabited by "parasitical presences"-"echoes, allusions, guests, ghosts of previous texts." Miller goes on to describe the ways in which the parasite metaphor can characterize the strangeness, the apparent nihilism, of the deconstructionist position: "nihilism is the parasitical stranger within the house of metaphysics." It gives the lie to illusions about univocal interpretations and other truths that deny the indeterminacy of language.

Bloom is the only member of the Yale school who has moved out of the hermetic atmosphere of such discussions. A forceful spokesman for one deconstructionsit position—intertextuality—he has made himself accessible to the general educated public through his later books, which work out a grand idea of strong latter-day authors trying to overcome greats such as Shakespeare and Milton. *The Anxiety of Influence* (1973) is his landmark study that analyzes the specific figure of speech and rhetorical strategies used by writers rewriting their powerful predecessors. His later book, *The Western Canon* (1994), developed the theory of Oedipal conflict in literature in a style suitable for a wide audience; in its treatment of authors as definite forces in history, it seems to turn aside from the death-of-the-author element in deconstruction. Its impact is best discussed under canonical defense and revision.

Reader response criticism is a second strain of deconstruction. Its most famous proponent, Duke Universtiy professor and essayist Stanley Fish, rejects the distinction between an objective text (something definite "out there") and a reader. In a controversial extended essay *Is There a Text in This Class?* (1980), Fish declares his principles: that a text is wrongly taken to be "self-sufficient" by many critics who demote the reader to the status of a mere receiver and that meaning emerges from "interpretive communities" (with their preconceived notions of beauty and sense) rather than

from any pristine well of authorial intention or encoded meaning. Since menaing is not embedded in a literary text, the competent critic has a feeling of "uneasiness" as he encounters even the most familiar text. Fish uses a Milton sonnet to demonstrate how the critic must overcome the inconsistencies to the text and thus, in effect, collaborate with the poet to create an interpretation.

The brouhaha over such radical tampering with "reality" has also greeted another brand of deconstruction—canon revisionism. Here the controversy has reached the press and general public; educators, students, and even public officials and pundits, like William Bennett, have taken stands on the value of the Western canon of great works—what Bloom has called "The Books and School of the Ages"—as it comes into conflict with the claims of new works—be they postmodernist, popular cultural, feminist, minority, or merely neglected. Bloom's own widely read *The Western Canon* is our most up-to-date course in the "Great Books" in that it takes account of all the forces out against the traditional canon, yet continues to read Shakespeare and Joyce and Freud in a way that does brilliant justice to the deconstructionist idea of intertexulity. However, in the same argument for a community of texts, Bloom ridicules the politics of deconstruction and is witheringly ironic about what he calls the School of Resentment: contemporary academics, influenced by Foucault's ideas of powerful discourse, who deny the intrinsic worth of the Great Books and argue that such works are prestigious commodities whose value has been driven up by a white, male-dominated civilization. Bloom's irony turns tragic as he describes the possibilities if the Resenters prevail: "What are now called 'Departments of English' will be renamed departments of 'Cultural Studies' where Batman comics, Mormon theme parks, television, movies, and rock will replace Chaucer, Shakespeare, Milton, Wordsworth, and Stevens. Major, once-elitist universitites and colleges will still offer a few courses in Shakespeare, Milton, and their peers, but these will be taught by departments of three or four scholars, equivalent to teachers of Greek and Latin." In fact the Resenters are a very diversed group—some thinking that "Trivial Pursuit" is as much a worthwhile object of study as Great Books (as cited by Gertrude Himmelfarb in *On Looking into the Abyss,* 1994), some having political and racial agendas larger than their literary ones, and others involved with a complex opening out of the canon on the basis of what they believe to be literary merit.

African American literary critics have differed from each other in principle and practice, but most in the contemporary period have focussed on black texts and the sociopolitical issues that emerge from the canon debate. In the 1960s and 1970s, champions of the Black Aesthetic movement renounced the accommodationist/humanist positions of Ralph Ellison and others from the 1940s and 1950s who sought to reveal the polyglot nature of the Western canon and the profoundly canonical and traditional elements in the work of black writers. As described by Houston A. Baker, Jr., himself a canon reviser, these separatist figures—including Amiri BARAKA and Larry Neal—saw literature as an ideological weapon and the black literary style as something totally divorced from the images and values of white writers. In their clear but unsophisticated efforts to build their own canon, these critics and writers corresponded to 1930s Marxists who loathed bourgeios literary culture.

At a considerable remove from these doctrinaire proponents of black culture is Henry Louis GATES, Jr., a scholar and sometime popular essayist whose involvement with canon revision and post modern theory combines with his fervent desire to see black discourse—whether novels or criticsm—take its place as a feature of world literature and academic study. Gates is a pluralist, and to some extent holds views like Ralph Ellison's: he believes in the creative cross-fertilization between the black tradition and Western classics, yet unlike Ellison he has devoted his energies to studying black literature and fighting in the ranks of those who are at odds with tradition. He can be justly considered a multiculturist rather than Ellison's enthusiastic, anti–ideological kind of comparativist—which is to say that he is active on behalf of African American writers and less involved with the weight of American literature generally. Gates seeks understanding of "the diversity of human culture," yet what this has come down to is very different from old-fashioned curiosity about world literatures: "My task as I see it, is to help guarantee that black and so-called Third World literature is taught to black and Third World and white students by black and Third World and white professors on heretofore white mainstream departments of literature, and to train students to think, to read, and to write clearly, to expose false uses of language, fraudulent claims, and muddled arguments, propaganda, and vicious lies—from all of which our people have suffered just as surely as we have from an economic order in which we were zeros and a metaphysical order in which we were absences." As a product of Yale, he is strongly influenced by theories of language; he believes that race is not a meaningful biological category but rather a trope—and as such must be studied in all its power to contain and restrain. His scholarly study *The Signifying Monkey* examines the play of language used by the African trickster figure and scrutinizes the irony and defiance in the black literary tradition. Houston A. Baker, Jr., author of *Long*

Black Song (1972), is less skeptical about Gate's theory-oriented position; he calls for more attention to folklore and less emphasis on a hermeneutical approach which he perceives as tainted by white consciousness, but Gates has maintained a position that relates abstractions about discourse to the wider cultural scene.

Such high-level multiculturalism—free of cant about "Dead White Males," yet insistent upon looser canons—is similar to that of Edward W. Said, a poststructuralist critc of cultural values in literature. Said, too, is a deconstructor of European categories of social superiority. Nevertheless he is too sensitive and searching to bash great European authors. Instead, he looks beneath the surfaces of major and minor texts to observe ideologies and assumptions about politics. The special focus of Said's work has been the socially constructed otherness of alien peoples as they are represented in literature—the colonized and marginalized. *Orientalism* (1978) is his pioneering study of Western writers looking at the Middle East; there they discover and invent a culture antithetical to European progress, at odds with enlightenment values, and altogether threatening in its temptations. Said's critical territory is the close study of such empowering discourse. His convictions—as a citizen of the world and a critic—emerge clearly: a desire to break down borders between groups and a zealous pursuit of literary pluralism. *Culture and Imperialism* (1993) applies the aesthtics and politics of Orientalism to a larger swathe of world literature; in this wide-ranging attempt to uncover hidden mentalities and study the rhetoric that expresses imperial yearnings and designs, Said argues that writers, including Jane Austen and Charles Dickens, are part of a political culture that purely aesthetic critics have not recognized. In writing about domestic affairs these English writers also produced allegories about wealth abroad and the glories of space and conquered foreign realms. While avoiding the vulgar Marxist attacks on canonical figures, Said nevertheless will not let great literature be sanitized, removed to a realm of disinterestedness and universal values, or detached from the agonics of social suffering. Martha C. Nussbaum, a critic who crosses into public policy and law in *Poetic Justice* (1966), has used a similar approach in her analysis of the moral claims of literary texts. She studies writers who present the rhetoric of class, race, and gender and shows how the creative works question attitudes about desires and drives and thus makes readers more critical citizens.

Frederic Jameson is the foremost contemporary American Marxist critic and shares with Said the project of exposing the ideologies and class interests of writers, but Jameson's Marxism is distinct from Said's pluralism and multiculturalism. In influential books— *The Prison House of Language* (1972) and *The Politi-*

cal Unconscious (1981)—he exposes the cause of the working class, depicts the great modernist authors as opponents of bourgeois culture, and deplores the formalist tendencies of language-oriented criticsm that would obscure class conflict. Two of his now famous essays—"The Politics of Theory" and "Postmodernism; or, The Cultural Logic of Late Capitalism"—not only define the characteristics of the modern and the post moderns, but extract political significance from those great movements of the 20th c. Our own postmodern world is identified with depthlessness, surface effects, fleeting images, and vague attachments of the moment. Such a world—for a committed Marxist—is an umpromising place in which to forge social change. Its literature is either dominated by commercial consideration or sheer escapism. Jameson's thought cannot be easily connected with an older Marxism and its cries for social realism and art as a weapon. Steeped in deconstruction and therefore concerned first and always with the controlling powers of discourse, he seems a world away from Mike Gold and his simpleminded dislike of Thorton Wilder's hothouse subject matter.

The New Historicists are also quite distant in their theory and their prose from the influence-minded historical critics of the past. While old historicists like Van Wyck Brooks concentrated on background and the ways it illuminated literary talents, the New Historicists—most notably the Renaissance scholar Stephen Greenblatt, author of *Renaissance Self-Fashioning* (1980)—are representative of the deconstructive age; they look at "texts" rather than masterpieces, break down the distiction between various kinds narratives, see literature as the political expression and political expressions as kinds of discourse, and look to marginal materials—untold episodes in an era's history or neglected documents—to illuminate well-known works of literature. Like the deconstructionists, they seek to expose hidden intellectual agendas in a text and unravel surface themes. Simon Schama, a historian who experiments with kinds of narration, is a figure whose work embodies some of the New Historicist principles of interpretation. In *Dead Certainties* (1989)—a book about truths, various accounts of two deaths, diverse materials that serve as evidence—Schama tells two basic stories about General James Wolfe and the struggle to take Quebec at the end of the 18th c. Schama—in true Historicist style—immerses the reader in the complications of two cases involving conflicting stories, myths and legends, hearsay—in short the instabilities of postmodern theory.

American feminist critics are a very diverse group—ranging from straightforward advocates of women's rights and observers of women's negative images in "male" literature to deconstructionist-influenced theories of several stamps. The former acknowlege Kate Millet's *Sexual Politics* (1970) as a groundbreaking work of protest and literary analysis; focussing on the language of sexual domination in the fiction of D. H. Lawrence, Henry MILLER, Norman MAILER, the book set this literary-political force in motion. Thereafter, sexism and patriarchy were topics that went everywhere—into popular articles, magazine editorial policy, studies of literature, and general discourse about inequality in the academy and the outside world. In this like of decent, Sandra M. Gilbert and Susan Gubar's *The Madwoman in the Attic* (1979) analyzes the nature of women's entrapment in and reaction to male discourse; the allusion of the title—Mrs. Rochester hidden away from good society—suggests two kinds of feminist criticism that go beyond base-line discussions of oppression: analysis of what has not been recognized in the canon of world authors and what has not been read from a feminist perspective.

Canon revionists such as Carolyn G. Heilbrun in *Toward a Recognition of Androgny* (1973), Patricia Meyer Spacks in *The Female Imagination* (1975), Elaine Showalter in *A Literature of Their Own* (1977), and Nina Auerbach in *Communities of Women* (1978) concentrated on establishing a distinct women's tradition in writing. Out of this enterprise came the fostering of many contemporary literary talents—Grace PALEY, Alice WALKER—the renewed interest in the work of pioneering feminist such as Adrienne RICH, and the rivival of American women writers including Kate CHOPIN, Edith WHARTON, and Willa CATHER. Scholars, critics, historians, creative writers, and activists who wrote about these figures varied enormously in their approaches; from the bread-and-butter treatment of a women writer's life and times to the rarefied regions of discourse about gender identity, the writing about women writers, women's subjectivity, women's marginality has partaken of every current in contemporary criticsm.

In terms of the feminist perspective on reading mentioned above, a critic such as Annette Kolondy has beamed the insights of deconstruction on reading habits, shown how women's literature was discouraged by the male critical power block, and illustrated how women writers have had to create their won traditions—in the manner of Bloom's the anxiety of influence—in an inhospitable American culture. In *Art and Anger: Reading like a Woman* (1988), Jane Marcus has brought a Marxist concern for material conditions into the world of high-tech, often academic theory; she also expands feminism by studying both male writers who deal with women's issues and the women who partake of their protests. Reader response criticism is also congenial to Judith Fetterley, a feminist

685

who calls for a "resisting reader"; such a combative reader interrogates a text in search of patriarchy and other patterns of domination.

Into this complex poststructuralist mix—which includes those who think women have a fundamental identity as women and those who think gender identity is socially contructed—comes the writing of black feminists who are wary of white-dominated theory and lesbian critics who find the terms of much feminist criticsm to be heterosexual and slanted toward stules and conflicts that exclude them. Of equal or greater importance are the voices of women who are not feminists in the contemporary understandings of the term, including Susan SONTAG—a critic and public intellectual who has devoted a career to studying the avant garde in literature and the visual arts—Elizabeth HARDWICK—a cultural commentator, literary journalist and fiction writer who has been at work since the 1940s—and Camille Paglia—an often outrageous and idiosyncratic defender of the literary canon who openly declares that men have created the great works of the West. Diana Trilling began a career as a reviewer in the 1940s, judging many contemporary writers and correcting them for slack prose and ideological obsessions. In the later part of her life, she used a social phenomena as her texts and produced essays on the Columbia University uprising of 1968 and the notorious Jean Harris/Herman Tarnower murder case. *The Beginning of the Journey* (1993) is a portrait of her marriage to Lionel Trilling—and one of the most cool and balanced accounts of a woman's place in American literary and intellectual life. It should be noted that these women—in the context of the culture wars of the 1980s—have little standing with more traditional feminists.

The powerful challenges of poststructuralist criticsm, in its several forms, at the end of the century have not been sufficient to overshadow the work of numbers of humanists, old-fashioned opinon makers, and nontheoretical appreciators of literature. Amid laments for "the death of the public intellectual" and the man of letters—suggesting as they do that America no longer produces learned, rounded critics who reach out to a general audience—the nation still has its supply of such figures. Gore VIDAL's massive collection *United States: Essays, 1952–1992* is a freewheeling attempt to report on some classics and a great many modern and contemporary figures—and to bring the news of his own reading tastes. As he reacts to Montaigne or Mailer, to Edmund Wilson or Susan Sontag, to American political worthies or Howard Hunt, to the larger culture or to an ironic, mischief-making self, Vidal reminds the reader of the fact that Edmund Wilson's kind of book—personal, diverse, well crafted, almost Renaissance in its range of curiosties—is not

impossible in our time. John UPDIKE has also written freely and unpredictably on everything that catches his eye in *Just Looking* (1989) and *Odd Jobs* (1991). Guy DAVENPORT, a scholarly essayist who shares affinities with historically-oriented critics, is a prolific and lucid surveyor of literary images, their antecedents, and their place in the world's civilizations. His essays in *The Geography of the Imagination* give pride of place to the ways time and cultural setting weigh on the writer. In such cases—where the critics "belong" to no definable movement—sheer interest, knowledge, and taste have determined the nature of the writing, not theory or avowed political commitment. Foremost among such essayists—is George Steiner, a naturalized American born in Paris. His work is always conscious of the latest European developments and brings the news of the theory, little known writers, and all-but-forgotten legacies to a wide readership. In his recent collection, *No Passion Spent* (1966), Steiner has studied his deconstructionist contemporaries with care—and states his own positions. In the midst of almost irrefutable arguments about our imprisonment in language, he nevertheless believes in the practical values of reading for sense and the spiritual dimensions of a book. "The bark and ironies of deconstruction resound in the night but the caravan of 'good sense' passes on." And more importantly, when we "read truly" we read "as if the text . . . incarnates . . . a real presence of significant being." Such pious reading—returning us to a world of Harold Bloom and appears in the work of Sven Birkerts and other critics of a new generation who revere books as books and fear the tidal waves of theory and ideology.

At the close of the 20th c., American criticism seems aflame with conflicts—between many women critics and the feminists, between comparative literature scholars and the multiculturalists, betwen traditionalists and canon revisers, between aesthetes and the politicized, between essayists with public outreach and academics with recondite theories. Athough the intensity of disagreement about criticism and its human uses cannot be traced to the era of Van Wyck Brooks and Randolph Bourne, there is still continuity between the earlier part of the century and the 1990s. It is contained in the ceaseless desire of American critics to break out of conventional modes into new stylisitc and theoretical expressions, yet these new ways of being a critic have never quite overwhelmed the older critical practices, the traditional notions of what literature is, or the many styles of critical discourse from the past.

BIBLIOGRAPHY: Aaron, D., *Writers on the Left* (1961); Atlas, J., *The Book Wars* (1990); Berkovitch, S., ed., *The Cambridge History of American Literature*

(1994); Davis, R., and R. Schleifer, *Contemporary Literary Criticism* (1989); Eagleton, T., *Marxism and Literary Criticism* (1976); Frailberg, L., *Psychoanalysis and American Literary Criticism* (1960); Gates, H., *Loose Canons* (1992); Glicksberg, C. I., *American Literary Criticism, 1900–1950* (1952); Graff, G., *Literature against Itself* (1979); Hyman, S., *The Armed Vision* (1948); Jay, G. S., ed., *Modern American Critics, 1920–1955* (1988); Jay, G. S., ed., *Modern American Critics since 1955* (1988); Kimball, R., *Tenured Radicals* (1990); Kris, E., *Psychoanalytic Expressions in Art* (1952); Kurzweil, E., and W. Phillips, eds., *Literature and Psychoanalysis* (1983); Lentricchia, F., *After the New Criticism* (1980); O'Connor, W. V., *An Age of Criticism, 1900–1950* (1952); Richter, D., *The Critical Tradition* (1989); Robison, L., *Sex, Class, and Culture* (1978); Ruland, R., *The Rediscovery of American Literature: Premises of Critical Taste, 1900–1940* (1967); Stovall, F., ed., *The Development of American Literary Criticism* (1955); Trilling, L., *The Liberal Imagination* (1953); Welleck, R., *American Criticism, 1900–1950* (1986); Wilson, E., *The Triple Thinkers* (1948); Zabel, M. D., *Literary Opinion in America* (1962)

DAVID CASTRONOVO

LITERARY JOURNALISM

In its commonly accepted definition, literary journalism is newspaper, magazine or book-length nonfiction that combines solid reporting with the narrative and rhetorical techniques used by writers of fiction. In other words, it is nonfiction that reads like fiction. Attention was most sharply focused on this literary form in more recent years when, in 1973, writer Tom WOLFE described what he termed the New Journalism, an artistic offshoot of feature writing marked by intensive interviewing and observation, or saturation reporting, extended use of dialogue, varied point of view, scene-by-scene construction in the style of storytelling, and emphasis on "color" details regarding people's lives, singly or in groups.

For some years, many students of this genre appeared to regard "literary journalism" and Wolfe's New Journalism as synonymous. More recent observers have demonstrated that the new journalism of the 1960s and 1970s was merely an especially colorful chapter in the full story of literary journalism as it developed in America. In the preface to *A Sourcebook of American Literary Journalism* (1992), for example, editor Thomas B. Connery points to Daniel Defoe, William Hazlitt, and Charles Dickens as important British predecessors who combined fact and fiction, then describes three peak periods of activity in American literary journalism: the 1890s, the 1930s, and the 1960s-1970s. According to Connery, the first of these periods includes George ADE, Stephen CRANE, Richard Harding DAVIS, Theodore DREISER, Hutchins Hapgood, and Lincoln STEFFENS. Literary journalists of the 1930s include James AGEE, John DOS PASSOS, Ernest HEMINGWAY, A. J. Liebling, John O'HARA, Ernie Pyle, and John STEINBECK. Finally, literary journalists of the 1960s and 1970s include Truman CAPOTE, Joan DIDION, Norman MAILER, John MCPHEE, Gay Talese, Hunter S. Thompson and, of course, Wolfe. However, other scholars include among literary journalists such diverse authors as Lafcadio HEARN, Augustus LONGSTREET, Jacob Riis, Jack LONDON, W. E. B. DU BOIS, Mary MCCARTHY, Tillie OLSEN, and Gloria Anzaldua.

Although a number of recent commentators decry Wolfe's efforts, pointing out among other things the self-interest of his ideas and his having ignored the work of Liebling, McPhee, and other literary journalists at the *New Yorker,* Wolfe's comments always loom large in any discussion of the topic. Wolfe's 1973 remarks that stirred such lively interest in literary journalism concerned, in the main, long feature stories in magazines and newspapers, as written by himself, Mailer, Talese, James BALDWIN, Gail Sheehy, Terry Southern, and other contributors to *Esquire* and *New York.* Yet when literature professors address the subject, the talk almost invariably turns to book work: Wolfe's *The Kandy-Kolored Tangerine Flake Streamlined Baby,* Capote's *In Cold Blood,* Mailer's *The Armies of the Night,* McPhee's *A Sense of Where You Are,* Didion's *Slouching toward Bethlehem.* Most literature professors appear more comfortable addressing book work as opposed to shorter writing forms, in part because book-length works offer the fullest possible development of literary treatment and, possibly, due to a vague distrust of the more transitory nature of periodicals and newspapers.

Some of these discussions also evince a more or less monolithic view of journalism, as though all journalism consists of news stories. In point of fact, journalism consists of several forms of newspaper and periodical writing. The heart of journalism—the most necessary and indispensable of its various forms—is indeed the news story: that which relates the who, what, when, where, why and how of current events or recent trends. Other forms of journalism are editorial writing, which gives the paper or magazine's opinion on issues; reviewing, which offers the writer's own criticism of something that has been held out for public consumption; column writing—brief essays that appear on a regular schedule and offer the writer's personal take on a topic; essays or commentaries—columnlike pieces of writing that appear irregularly; feature writing—longer stories used more for their interest value than for their importance as news; and magazine writing—similar to newspaper feature work but somewhat more attuned to entertaining as opposed to the newspaper feature story's slightly greater emphasis on informing.

Of these seven varieties of non-book journalistic writing, only two—newspaper feature stories and magazine articles—are usually identified as "literary journalism," inasmuch as that term is commonly taken to mean nonfiction that employs the customary tropes of the novelist or short story writer. The shortcoming of this definition is that novels and short stories are hardly the only forms of literature. Variously defined as the term "literature" is, it clearly includes poetry, memoir, the essay, dramatic writing, and criticism. Hence, a less restrictive definition of "literary journalism" would seem decidedly reasonable. To support this expanded view, one must pause to take stock of what is meant by "literary."

In brief summary, "literary" is a term applied to writing that: is of high quality—that rises above the ordinary; is usually aimed at an intelligent audience so as to challenge the mind of an educated reader; is done for people's reading pleasure, not strictly for utilitarian or didactic purposes; is imaginative; is heavy in connotative as opposed to denotative meaning; makes frequent use of rhetorical devices; is concerned with feeling and emotion, not simply with rational thought; is of lasting value or interest; tends to be more personal than impersonal; offers rich layers of meaning; tends to invite reflection; packs dense meaning into its phrases and clauses, as does poetry; draws upon themes or motifs; tends to extrapolate universal experience from isolated experience; and contains a greater than usual measure of wit—in the sense of cleverness.

Keeping these aspects of "literary" in mind, one might note that of the various forms of journalistic writing identified above, the least compatible with literary technique is the news story, which, to do its job, depends upon accuracy, clarity, and objectivity. The next least likely venue for literary journalism is the editorial, in which the writer offers not his or her personal view, but that of the writer's employer—a position often decided upon in an editorial conference. As already noted, "literary" is almost invariably limited to two journalistic forms: the newspaper feature story and the magazine article, which offer the most space, hence the greatest latitude for use of literary technique. Even so, the term "literary," in all its rich diversity of meaning, can also be applied to the three remaining journalistic forms: the column, commentary and review.

It is true that only the feature story and magazine article offer sufficient space to accommodate what might be termed the *macro* literary devices: extended dialogue, highly detailed description and scene-by-scene construction—the products of saturation reporting. Still, the columnist, commentator and reviewer are free to employ *micro* literary devices—those that can be used within a single phrase, sentence or paragraph. The columnist, for example, can make skillful use of such rhetorical devices as simile, metaphor, allusion, anaphora, anticlimax, antithesis, polysendeton, chiasmus, enallage, and metaplasmus, devices that can help boost his or her copy to a more nearly literary level. Such writing gains in imagery and wit, becomes more memorable, and invites reflection. Other micro devices increase the writing's interest level via omission: ellipsis, asyndeton, and zeugma, for instance. Still other literary devices, such as irony and hyperbole, can be employed in either macro or micro usage.

Further, some columns, commentaries and reviews are quite personal, are often marked by keen wit, engage their readers' imaginations and provide copy that is more dense and layered in meaning, hence more "poetic" than what one finds in news stories, where such writing would be less appropriate. More than a few columnists—Langston HUGHES, Don MARQUIS, and Mike Royko, for example—have spoken through fictitious literary characters, using the literary device of point of view. Although some scholars would prefer to view the work of our better columnists, commentators and reviewers as "fine writing," a category they have chosen to regard as distinct from "literary journalism," there is much to be said for a broadened view of literary journalism that would include these three shorter journalistic writing forms. Most people having literary interests will recall Alexander Pope's lines: "True wit is nature to advantage dressed / What oft was thought, but ne'er so well expressed," but fewer are likely to remember the point he made a number of lines later in his "An Essay on Criticism": "Words are like leaves; and where they most abound / Much fruit of sense beneath is rarely found." Put more plainly, good writing often can be found in a small "package" and does not require the length of a novel to rise above the level of the ordinary.

BIBLIOGRAPHY: Anderson, C., ed., *Literary Nonfiction* (1989); Connery, T. B., ed., *A Sourcebook of American Literary Journalism* (1992); Fishkin, S.F., *From Fact to Fiction* (1985); Ford, E. H., *A Bibliography of Literary Journalism in America* (1937); Lounsberry, B., *The Art of Fact* (1990); Sims, N., ed., *Literary Journalism in the Twentieth Century* (1990); Weber, R., *The Literature of Fact* (1980); Wolfe, T., *The New Journalism* (1973)

SAM G. RILEY

LITERARY PRIZES AND AWARDS

Established as a means to provide critical recognition as well as financial support to writers of merit, literary prizes and awards have evolved from the early 20th c. to the present as an element of increasing importance in both the literary profession and the publishing industry. Critical recognition influences public awareness, which then impacts on reader selection and appreciation. For the writer, this recognition serves to acknowledge artistic achievement and to enhance critical reputation. For the publisher, this recognition generates interest in the author, which then impacts on the marketability of the author's work.

The majority of literary prizes and awards are given annually, and among the most prestigious annual awards in American literature is the Pulitzer Prize. Endowed by the bequest of newspaper publisher Joseph Pulitzer to Columbia University's School of Journalism, the Pulitzer Prize was originally established in four categories: novel, play, U.S. history, and American biography. The first Pulitzer Prizes were awarded in 1917 to J. J. Jusserand for *With Americans of Past and Present Days* (history) and to Laura E. Richards and Maude H. Elliott, with assistance by Florence H. Hall, for *Julia Ward Howe* (biography). The first novel to be awarded the Pulitzer Prize was Ernest POOLE's *His Family* in 1918, and in that same year Jesse L. Williams's *Why Marry?* was the first play to receive the award. The first Pulitzer Prize in poetry was awarded in 1922 to Edwin Arlington ROBINSON for his *Collected Poems*. In 1947, the novel prize was changed to "fiction in book form," which enabled the award to be given to a collection of short stories, and in the following year the Pulitzer Prize was awarded to James A. MICHENER for *Tales of the South Pacific*. The category of general nonfiction was created in 1962, first awarded to Theodore H. White for *The Making of the President 1960*.

Literary prizes are awarded from private endowments and foundations as well as from city, state, and national organizations. Major prizes in a variety of categories are awarded by the American Academy of Arts and Sciences, the Modern Language Association, the Jewish Book Council, the PEN American Center, and the Poetry Society of America. Literary prizes awarded by the American Academy and Institute of Arts and Letters include the Howells Medal, given every five years for the most distinguished American fiction of the period, first awarded in 1925 to Mary E. Wilkins FREEMAN; the Richard and Hinda Rosenthal Foundation Award for Fiction; and the Mildred and Harold Strauss Livings Award, first presented in 1983 to Cynthia OZICK and Raymond CARVER. Prizes given by the Academy of American Poets include the Fel-

lowship of the Academy of American Poets, first awarded in 1937 to Edwin MARKHAM, and the Lamont Poetry Selection, first awarded in 1954 to Constance Carrier for *The Middle Years*. The Bollingen Prize is given by Yale University to an American writer for a distinguished book of poetry published during the preceding two years, first awarded in 1949 to Wallace STEVENS. Among the most prestigious prizes in American history is the Bancroft Prize, given by Columbia University, first awarded in 1948 to Allan Nevins for *Ordeal of the Union* and Bernard De Voto for *Across the Wide Missouri*.

Established in 1950, the National Book Awards were first awarded to Nelson ALGREN for *The Man with the Golden Arm* (fiction), Ralph L. Rusk for *Ralph Waldo Emerson* (nonfiction), and William Carlos WILLIAMS for *Paterson III, Selected Poems* (poetry). From 1980 to 1986, the awards were renamed the American Book Awards but in 1987 were reestablished as the National Book Awards. The National Book Critics Circle Award was established in 1975, first awarded to E. L. DOCTOROW for *Ragtime* (fiction), John ASHBERY for *Self-Portrait in a Convex Mirror* (poetry), R. W. B. Lewis for *Edith Wharton* (general nonfiction), and Paul Fussell for *The Great War and Modern Memory* (criticism). In DRAMA, the Antoinette Perry (Tony) Award was established in 1947 by the American Theater Wing for excellence in the theater, awarded for the first time for best play in 1948 to Thomas Heggen and Joshua Logan for the stage adaption of Heggen's novel *Mister Roberts*. The *Village Voice* Obie Award is given for excellence in Off- and Off-Off-Broadway and includes annual awards in playwriting, first awarded for best play in 1955–56 to Lionel Abel for *Absolom*. Prizes in drama are also given by the Authors League of America and the New York Drama Critics Circle. For screenwriting, the most prestigious prize is the Academy (Oscar) Award, first presented in 1927–28. Since 1974, categories for screenwriting awards were established for original screenplay and screenplay adapted from other materials.

Awards in CHILDREN'S LITERATURE and YOUNG ADULT LITERATURE are given by a number of organizations and foundations, most notably by the American Library Association. One of the most prestigious prizes in children's literature is the Newbery Medal. Established in 1921 by the publisher Frederic G. Melcher, the Newbery Medal is given annually for the most distinguished contribution to American literature for children, first awarded in 1922 to Hendrik Van Loon for *The Story of Mankind*. In 1937, Melcher established the Caldecott Medal for distinguished illustration of a book for children, first awarded in 1938 to Dorothy Lathrop for Helen Dean Fish's *Animals of the Bible*. The most prestigious international award in children's literature is the Hans Christian Anderson International Medal, given every two years to a living author and a living illustrator for an outstanding body of work that has made a significant contribution to children's literature. American recipients of the award include Meindert DeJong, Maurice Sendak, Scott O'Dell, and Paula Fox.

In SCIENCE FICTION, the Science Fiction Achievement Awards, known as the Hugo Awards, are given annually to individuals and publishing venues for significant contribution to science fiction writing, first awarded for a novel in 1953 to Alfred BESTER for *The Demolished Man*. The Nebula Awards are given annually in a variety of categories for outstanding achievement in science fiction writing, first awarded for a novel in 1965 to Frank Herbert for *Dune*. In 1974, Robert A. HEINLEIN was the first author to receive the Nebula Grand Master Award for lifetime achievement. The Edgar Allan Poe Awards are given annually for outstanding achievement in mystery writing, first awarded in 1946 to Julius Fast for *Watchful at Night*.

Established in 1965, the National Medal for Literature was given annually to a living American writer for distinguished contribution to American letters, first awarded to Thorton WILDER, but the prize was discontinued in 1985. In that same year, however, President Ronald Reagan established the National Medal of Arts, first awarded to Ralph ELLISON. The first American poet laureate (originally consultant in poetry) was Joseph Auslander from 1937 to 1941. The first woman to serve as poet laureate was Louise BOGAN in 1945–46, and Gwendolyn BROOKS became the first African American to serve in the position in 1985–86.

The most prestigious international awards for which American writers are eligible include the Neustadt International Prize for Literature. The first American writer to win the award was Elizabeth BISHOP in 1976. In 1988, Walker PERCY became the first American to be awarded the Ingersoll Prize–T. S. Eliot Award in Creative Writing, established in 1983 by the Ingersoll Foundation. The most important international literary prize is the Nobel Prize in literature, given annually by the Swedish Academy to an author for his or her body of work. The first American to be awarded the Nobel Prize was Sinclair LEWIS in 1930, followed by Eugene O'NEILL (1936), Pearl S. BUCK (1938), American-born T. S. ELIOT (1948), William FAULKNER (1949), Ernest HEMINGWAY (1954), John STEINBECK (1962), Canadian-born Saul BELLOW (1976), Polish-born Isaac Bashevis SINGER (1978), Russian-born Joseph BRODSKY (1987), and Toni MORRISON (1993), the first African American woman to receive it.

BIBLIOGRAPHY: Bonin, J. F., *Prize-Winning American Drama* (1973); Clapp, J., *International Directory of Literary Awards* (1963); French, W. G., *American Winners of the Nobel Literary Prize* (1968); Hohenberg, J., *The Pulitzer Prizes* (1974); Peterson, L. K., *Newbery and Caldecott Medal and Honor Books* (1982); Pribic, R., *Nobel Laureates in Literature* (1990); Weiss, J. S., *Prizewinning Books for Children* (1983)

STEVEN R. SERAFIN

LITERARY PUBLISHING: BOOKS

American literary publishing has developed over three centuries into a hybrid creature suspended between two poles represented by Mammon and the Muse. On the one hand, it is a business that has followed the economic trajectory of American capitalism and is expected, at the least, to make a profit in order to survive, and at its theoretical best to maximize return on investment; on the other hand, literary publishing has been and still is a necessary agent in the cultivation, development, dissemination, and indeed the very creation of belles lettres and literary culture as they came into being in the U.S.

The most important period is the middle decades of the 19th c. bridging the Civil War, during which an artisans' and small shopkeepers' activity was transformed into a big business, manufacturing and marketing products for mass consumption. Concurrent with developments in the way businesses were capitalized and managed were a set of technological advances in printing and book production processes, a revolution in the speed and volume of transportation, and a massive increase in general education and literacy. These developments had their effect on authors, editors, and the reading public—for example, altering the perception of audience and affecting genres. As important as the 19th c. is, however, one cannot neglect the earlier centuries, out of which the changes grew and from which certain expectations about literature and authorship derived.

In the beginning, of course, there was no literary publishing to speak of in America, nor was there an American literature per se distinct from English and European literature. While the New World was being discovered, explored, and colonized, England was enjoying the first great flowering of its modern literature with the Elizabethan and Jacobean dramatists and poets—especially Shakespeare—and such influential prose works as the new English bibles, in particular the version we call King James. Examples of literary style, role models for authors, and printing and bookselling practices were in place on the eve of the Puritan and Cavalier colonization of the North American continent that would persist for some two centuries.

Moreover, in 17th-c. America, books were a precious commodity, by and large printed in England using processes virtually unchanged since Gutenberg and imported to the colonies at great expense. A personal collection of two dozen titles might have been exceptional, and one recalls that Harvard College grew around the nucleus of John Harvard's personal library. Anne BRADSTREET—the "Tenth Muse Lately Sprung Up in America"—who might legitimately be called the first American poet of note, was initially published in 1650 in England. Reflecting the practice of the time, the *Tenth Muse* was printed with the patronage of her brother-in-law and her name does not appear on the book, the author being identified only as a "Gentlewoman of New England."

Although the greater part of literary production and publication took place across the Atlantic, there were printing presses in the New World early on—the first being set up in Cambridge, Massachusetts, in 1638, by Stephen Daye. This press produced the famed *Bay Psalm Book* in 1640, a new translation into English of the psalms by three Puritan clergymen whose names do not appear on the title page—Thomas Weld, John Eliot, and Richard Mather. This is arguably the first "literary" publication in America, although its use of a sing-song common or ballad meter, its inverted syntax, and its forced rhymes might stretch one's definition of the properly literary.

The audience for these volumes and numerous others chronicled elsewhere—such as Michael WIGGLESWORTH's ironically popular *Day of Doom*—was the educated minority, consisting of clergy, educators, professionals, and gentry, almost entirely male, despite Mistress Bradstreet, and decidedly white. This audience could be reached and serviced by the printer/bookseller from his shop in the commercial center of provincial capitols like Boston. Great numbers and great distances to markets were not an issue.

As the American colonies grew in power, self-confidence and wealth, more and more printing and publishing was done on this side of the ocean, particularly in the great towns like Boston, New York, Philadelphia, and Charleston, where the needs of a commercial and mercantile economy gave rise to almanacs, newspapers, and public broadsheets. Such printer/entrepreneurs as Benjamin FRANKLIN in Pennsylvania and Isaiah Thomas in Massachusetts were typical of the 18th c. As the American nation-to-be moved toward agitation for independence and eventually to open rebellion, an extensive network of presses was turned to political purposes and polemic became the literary genre of the day. So influential was the press that the Stamp Act, attempting to control the distribution of paper, became a *cause celebre*. In the period of national consolidation after the Revolution, works

of political analysis and theory, of which Alexander Hamilton, James Madison, and John Jay's *The Federalist Papers* (1788) is the most famous example, were published—works which we now recognize for their considerable literary merit as examples of neoclassical prose. Such works often appeared first in periodicals and later were collected into volumes.

As the 19th c. opened, three features were characteristic of literary publishing in America (and indeed throughout European influenced literary culture) as a heritage from the previous centuries. One was the notion of the author as, essentially, an amateur, who did something else as a vocation and wrote as an avocation, disdaining self-promotion and seeking publication almost as an afterthought. Coordinate with this was the tradition of anonymous or pseudonymous publication, an idea that persisted deep into the 19th c., as for example, when Richard Henry DANA, Jr.—the scion of prerevolutionary gentry—would not permit his name to appear on the extremely popular novelized memoir, *Two Years before the Mast,* published in 1840.

The second characteristic was a limit on the size of the audience/market to the relatively privileged and affluent. Coordinate with this was the publication in local urban centers for consumption by the local elite. A third feature was the production of books by hand craft processes: printing single sheets of handmade paper, on a press powered by human muscle, from hand-set type cast from hand-cut matrices. Each book was an individual craft object, folded, sewn, and bound in leather by one person. Coordinate with that was the conflation of the roles of the printer, publisher, and bookseller in one person at one shop. By the end of the 19th c., all would be changed, and the system we know today, *mutatis mutandis,* would be in place.

As the American republic grew and defined itself in the opening decades of the 19th c., a self-conscious American literary culture began to arise, as evidenced by the Knickerbocker school in New York and the group around the *North American Review* in New England. Although maintaining ties with Europe and thinking in terms of a generally transatlantic culture, American writers began writing for American audiences and reflecting on a specifically American experience. American publishing houses began to form in response to and in service to this new spirit.

Beginning in the 1820s and 1830s and building on bases as booksellers or printers, modern publishing firms began to emerge such as Carey and Lea in Philadelphia, the Harpers in New York, and Ticknor and Fields, Houghton Mifflin, and Little, Brown, in Boston. The concept of publishing as a specialized, creative enterprise and the publisher as the author's partner began to form. Systems for justly sharing the profits of book publication and sales were worked out for the first time, as authorship progressed from an amateur activity to a profession.

If one recalls the anxiety of the classic writers of the American Renaissance as to their role in a commercial culture, and the very real economic problems that they faced, one begins to understand the profound change in the role of the author that was taking place in the 19th c. Ralph Waldo EMERSON gave up the ministry and, living on his wife's money, crafted the persona of the Sage of Concord. Nathaniel HAWTHORNE spent twelve years in his mother's attic in Salem trying to find himself and forge the proper voice. Herman MELVILLE was chronically impecunious and was forced to build his great metaphysical novels around the inherited form of the exotic travel account. Henry David THOREAU became the town eccentric of Concord and had to purchase the greater part of the printrun of his first book, *A Week on the Concord and Merrimack Rivers,* in order to prevent its destruction. Walt WHITMAN typeset and published the first edition of *Leaves of Grass* himself. Edgar Allan POE never quite found his proper niche and died in obscurity in a Baltimore gutter. None was a member of the landed aristocracy. If such could be said to exist in republican America, and each had to find a way to write, publish, and survive with his self-respect intact, in an environment where literature had to make its own way in the world without patronage. By midcentury, writers' names invariably appear on title pages, and writers were on their way to becoming brand names, as they are today.

At this same time, publishers could draw on the resources of a burgeoning commercial economy and the innovations of a technically explosive age to make those brand names available to a national audience. Improvements in transport such as the steam boat, the railroad, the great barge canals, and extended post roads and postal service meant the end of local and provincial publishing and the beginning of national marketing—indeed, the beginning of a homogenized national culture, sealed by the Union victory in the Civil War. Mechanization of printing process exploded in the 19th c., making possible rapidly produced editions of thousands of copies, and tens of thousands of copies in cases like Harriet Beecher STOWE's *Uncle Tom's Cabin,* published by Jewett of Boston in 1852. Steam-driven presses, stereotype plates, rotary presses, machine-made paper, inexpensive wood-pulp paper, cloth-covered cardboard bindings, cheap paper bindings—all were innovations that made possible a veritable flood of relatively inexpensive books. Everyman could now have a library of dozens of books, if so inclined.

And many, many more were so inclined as the level of education and literacy increased markedly, signaled by the imposition of universal education in publically supported common schools, first taking form in Massachusetts in the 1830s. Moreover, more and more potential readers and book purchasers were entering the great American middle class, as businesses and the professions expanded, and were fostering aspiration to cultural status. For those less affluent, large, free public libraries were founded starting with the Boston Public Library, chartered in 1852.

As the readership changed and enlarged, and as the means of production and distribution made literature a commodity as well as an artistic endeavor, the forms of literary expression changed. The novel, that most bourgeois of genres, came to predominate. Whereas earlier the long narrative poem, as practiced by, say, the Connecticut Wits of the early 19th c., or the moralistic essay in the hands, say, of a Mather or an Adams, might have been the preferred vehicle, now the novel—that all-purpose, Protean genre—was the medium of popular choice. Entertainment as well as edification now became important, and writers and publishers developed strategies for meeting both demands, tragically failing in the case of Melville's *Pierre,* triumphantly succeeding in the case of Hawthorne's *The Scarlet Letter.*

An entire system of book and author promotion, building on the popular press, began to emerge suitable for a commercial age. Skilled publishers like James T. Fields of Boston promoted books by carefully engineering reviews in the newspapers and journals and beginning the use of promotional catalogs and sales techniques to exploit retail and wholesale book markets. Willing authors like Emerson were eager to go on the lecture circuit to promote themselves and their wares. Emerson surely sold thousands of copies of his essay collections to upwardly mobile persons in Midwestern cities, who treated them as icons for display but probably never read a word in them.

The post–Civil War years were an era of rationalization and amplification of the methods and techniques forged earlier in the century. Communications became even more rapid, and pools of potential readers grew to include children and women, who had always been an important audience but now had publications aimed directly at them. The professionalization of authorship increased and individuals and publishers worked out equitable means of compensation, so that an author like William Dean HOWELLS could perfect the role of independent man of letters. An effective international copyright agreement—long sought but not sealed until the end of the century—secured the authors' and the publishers' property rights in literary works. Technological improvements like the linotype machine that permitted rapid inexpensive typesetting and automated bookbinding machines—breaking the last bottleneck of the older artisan trade system—and better reproduction of illustrations through half-tone engraving processes made possible cheaper and/or more attractive books.

As the 20th c. opened, perhaps the most significant development was the consolidation and centralization of literary publishing in New York City, the fast growing financial and cultural capitol of the country. This development was best symbolized by the move in 1891 of William Dean Howells from Boston where he had edited the prestigious *Atlantic Monthly* to New York, where he assumed editorship of *Harper's*. Boston, the cultural mecca to which Howells had gone as an awestruck neophyte in 1866, although it remains the second center of publishing to this day, had followed other provincial centers into decline.

In New York City, during the great flowering of modernism after World War I, new literary publishing houses attuned to these trends came into being like Random House and Knopf, and older houses like Scribner's and Harper's altered to meet the changing times. Authors like Ernest HEMINGWAY and F. Scott FITZGERALD were thoroughly comfortable in the role of writer—in fact cultivated and exploited that role as did many modern artists—and at their best were able to serve both Mammon and the Muse. Editors, like Maxwell Perkins who handled both Hemingway and Fitzgerald, exhibited the full development of the suggestions for author nurturance and market development first laid out by Fields in the 1840s and 1850s. Technology made possible mass-market paperback books, during and after World War II, and an object that had been precious and venerated in the 17th c. became essentially disposable in the post-industrial affluence of the 20th c.

Contemporary literary publishing seems more and more—but not exclusively—to be one facet of a larger expressive enterprise that includes mass electronic media, film, and as yet unspecified interactive computer-assisted forms of art and entertainment. Yet at the center and origin of any literary production is still the author and his or her need and inspiration, some previously blank paper (or an electronic surrogate) now filled with a unique arrangement of words, and an empathetic editor and publisher who have their hands on the techniques that will yoke the enormously effective machinery of modern technology to this individual creation, making it available to literally millions of other individuals, and in the process satisfying the demands of a capitalist economy.

BIBLIOGRAPHY: Bailyn, B., and J. Hench, eds., *Printing and Society in Early America* (1983); Buell, L., *New England Literary Culture: From the Revolution to the Renaissance* (1986); Charvat, W., *Literary Publishing in America, 1790–1850* (1959); Coser, L., et al., *Books: The Culture and Commerce of Publishing* (1982); Davidson, C., *Revolution of the Word: The Rise of the Novel in America* (1986); Exman, E., *The House of Harper* (1967); Gilmore, M., *American Romanticism and the Marketplace* (1985); Hall, D., and J. Hench, eds., *Needs and Opportunities in the History of the Book: America, 1639–1876* (1987); Hart, J., *The Popular Book: A History of America's Literary Taste* (1950); Joyce, W., et al., eds., *Printing and Society in Early America* (1983); Mott, F., *American Journalism: A History of Newspapers in the United States Through 250 Years, 1690–1950* (1967); Stern, M., *Imprints on History: Book Publishing and American Frontiers* (1956); Tebbel, J., *A History of Book Publishing in the United States* (4 vols., 1972–81)

PAUL M. WRIGHT

LOCKE, David Ross

b. 20 September 1833, Vestal, New York; d. 15 February 1888, Toledo, Ohio

L. wrote plays, poems, editorials, and novels, but is best known as the Civil War era satirist who created the humorous character "Petroleum V. Nasby," fictional author of a long series of letters-to-the-editor commenting on current events. Nasby's letters were printed nationwide and counted Abraham LINCOLN among a faithful readership. L. used his creation as a vehicle for social criticism portraying Nasby as a drunken, corrupt, and bigoted character so obviously misguided he would be the object of ridicule and his political views discredited. L. was a lifelong Republican and abolitionist dedicated to weakening Democrats and the South.

L. had little formal education, but an apprenticeship at the *Cortland Democrat,* a great deal of ambition, and a keen interest in social issues led to a successful writing and lecturing career. When he was twenty, L. and a partner purchased an Ohio newspaper, the *Plymouth Advertiser.* There he wrote and printed experimental political commentary in the form of humorous letters written in phonetic spelling under the name by J. Augustus Sniggs. Later, L. became publisher of the *Bucyrus Journal*—a Republican paper in a Democratic county—and further refined this literary form writing pieces that ridiculed Southern sympathizers. In 1861, L. became owner of the *Hancock Jeffersonian* and debuted the Nasby character.

Nasby, the heavy drinking crank, opposed the Union, opposed freeing the slaves, opposed civil rights for all but white men, and thought himself larger-than-life. He was prone to highfalutin phrases riddled with erred spelling and word usage. On Lincoln, he wrote:

"We vew with alarm the ackshun uv the President uv the U.S. in recommendin the immejit emansipashun uv the slaves." Such things were read not as attacks on the Lincoln administration, but recognized as mockery of the opposition.

Although Nasby's language and grandiosity are genuinely funny, L. did not refrain from portraying such a hateful character in all his ugliness. The disarming humor pulls readers uncomfortably close to the detestable bigotry and corruption. In so doing, L. meant to promote honesty and equality.

The Nasby character brought L. much success. In addition to his syndicated letters, L. published a number of books including *The Nasby Papers* (1864), *Divers Views, Opinions, and Prophecies of Yoors Trooly Petroleum V. Nasby* (1866), and a commentary on life abroad, *Nasby in Exile* (1882). Interest in Nasby and his creator revived during the civil rights movement of the 1950s and 1960s as the themes, ideas, and attitudes had a measure of relevance. L. is widely regarded as a skilled, insightful author and recognized as being among the foremost American humorists.

BIBLIOGRAPHY: Austin, J. C., *Petroleum V. Nasby* (1965); Harrison, J. M., *The Man Who Made Nasby* (1969); Minor, D. E., "D. R. L.," in Trachtenberg, S., ed., *DLB*, vol. 11, *American Humorists, 1800–1950* (1982): 429–34

JASON MCMAHON

LOCKRIDGE, Ross, Jr.
b. 25 April 1914, Bloomington, Indiana; d. 6 March 1948, Bloomington, Indiana

A number of critics argue that L.'s *Raintree County* (1948) is the personification of the Great American Novel. Described in *Publishers Weekly* as the "publishing sensation of 1948," L.'s massive epic of 19th-c. Indiana quickly rose to the top of national best-seller lists and was later filmed as a big-budget motion picture by Metro-Goldwyn-Mayer (earning the author the then-astronomical sum of $150,000). Yet, despite his tremendous initial success as one of the few contemporary writers to earn both critical and popular acclaim, L. prevented himself the opportunity of fulfilling his promise as one of the greatest American writers of the 20th c. by committing suicide, ironically at a moment when he was in the midst of the publishing triumph of *Raintree County.*

Born in the college town of Bloomington, L. began seriously thinking about writing an important and substantial literary work while attending Indiana University as an undergraduate. Later, as a graduate student at Harvard University, by the end of 1940 he completed

an epic poem entitled "The Dream of the Flesh of Iron." He offered this four-hundred page poem to Houghton Mifflin for publication, but it was rejected. L. then began writing *Raintree County* in his spare time while he taught English at Simmons College in Boston. Displeased with his initial effort, he threw away a two thousand page draft of the novel before starting another draft. When he completed the novel, the manuscript was over 600,000 words in length and weighed twenty pounds; L.'s wife took some eighteen months to type it. He again submitted his work to Houghton Mifflin, and this time they accepted it for publication.

Set in an imaginary county in Indiana, *Raintree County* tells the story of John Wickliff Shawnessy during a single day, July 4, 1892. L. employs a complex and sophisticated flashback narrative technique to recount Shawnessy's coming-of-age in a country that is also coming-of-age. L. makes clear in his novel that Shawnessy's story is America's story. In fact, as did L. with *Raintree County,* L.'s Shawnessy also intends to write a national epic, but ultimately fails to complete his ambition.

Unlike Shawnessy, L. did complete his literary epic, but as some critics have pointed out, L. put so much effort into his life's work that he was unable to deal emotionally and psychologically with the fact of its completion and success with readers, so he took his own life. In retrospect, the tragic story of L. and the triumphant story of *Raintree County* are bittersweet ones. The novel is indeed a major achievement in the history of American literature, but like all "shaggy dog" stories it is afflicted, at times, by its own girth and lofty ambition. It occasionally suffers from a lack of editorial control, lumbering forth as a highly self-conscious and self-proclaimed epic that attempts to be too many things for too many readers. But no great work of literature is without its flaws, and despite the novel's hubris, *Raintree County* still remains the closest anyone has come to writing the Great American Novel.

BIBLIOGRAPHY: Leggett, J., *R. and Tom: Two American Tragedies* (1974), Lockridge, L., *Shade of the Raintree: The Life and Death of R. L., Jr., Author of Raintree County* (1994)

GARY HOPPENSTAND

LOGAN, John [Burton]
b. 23 January 1923, Red Oak, Iowa; d. 6 November 1987, San Francisco, California

As a consummate lyric poet, L. instinctively understood the power of poetic language. Each word was measured and pondered to fit precisely into a poetic context and to deliver a specific emotional response in performance. While reading, his vowel sounds were elongated, and his lines would rise and fall with emotionally charged breath and genuine intensity. L. considered poetry to be a ballet for the ear. His masters were Dylan Thomas, Hart CRANE, and William Butler Yeats, and his peers were Robert BLY and James WRIGHT. L.'s poems often reflected their various influences. L. structured his poems using textbook poetic technique, innovation, and literary music. They had marvelous, sometimes baroque, cadence, rhythm, and rhyme. He employed puns, psychological illusions, and images, as well as colloquial and vulgar phrases, to draw his readers into a private, complex, psychological labyrinth, which was both a literary fun house and haunted abode. To exercise poetic discipline, L. invented a structure of syllabic lines of eight and thirteen syllables that he used in his travelogue and narrative poems. His book length poem, *Poem in Progress* (1975), uses this form exclusively. L. published twelve books of poetry during his career and won numerous literary awards among them the Morton Dawen Zabel Award in poetry from the American Academy and Institute of Arts and Letters and the Lenore Marshall Poetry Prize.

L. was considered to be the most "catholic" of American poets. His first three collections, *Cycle for Mother Cabrini* (1955), *Ghosts of the Heart* (1960), and *Spring of the Thief* (1963), contain many references to orthodox religious themes. His poems explored the spirituality of various saints and reflect upon Catholicism. L. was deeply influenced by the writing of St. Augustine. The title poem of his first collection, "Cycle for Mother Cabrini," announced, prophetically, the weakness of his flesh and his hope that he might be able to transform and transcend his earthly, therefore corrupt, self. There were many apocalyptic moments in his early poems where the poet is struck with illumination. In the poem "The Picnic," an inner understanding or light radiates throughout the poet's body. He interprets this erotic and spiritual moment as beautiful.

As L.'s career progressed, his poems became less imaginative contemplations and more autobiographical and prosaic. His conflict between his flesh and his spirit found flesh the victor. His poem "Heart to Heart Talk with My Liver" relates his struggle with alcoholism. In his books *Zig-Zag Walk* (1969), *The Anonymous Lover* (1973), and *Bridge of Change* (1981), grief and sorrow become poignant themes and the telling line, "I was born on a street called Joy of which I remember nothing," introduces his longest prose piece, *The House That Jack Built* (1974).

L. became increasingly restless and wrote extensive poems about traveling to California, Hawai'i, Ireland, and Greece. He was seeking innocence, peace, transformation, and acceptance. His poems of this late period were confessions and reports. There were orgiastic images of pleasure, delightful memories, joy, insights into complete happiness or contentment, and into grief, sorrow, and hurt. Above all, it was love in its many facets that L. sought: brotherly love, love of God, heterosexual and homosexual physical love. The relationship between father and son became an important theme that he developed in the context of friendship and forgiveness. A victim of his own overwhelming desires, transcendence, forgiveness, and genuine untainted friendship were too often unobtainable. Nevertheless, L. continued the pursuit. In the late poem, "Believe It," which begins with a list of the grotesque oddities at a "Believe It or Not" museum, L. concludes with making a simile of the Chinese lighthouse man who had a lamp in his skull and himself. L. invites the reader to witness the inner light of his own body, his heart, soul and poems, and welcomes each reader in as a guest.

BIBLIOGRAPHY: Poulin, A., ed., *A Ballet for the Ear: Interviews, Essays, and Reviews* (1983); Waters, M., ed., *Dissolve to Island: On the Poetry of J. L.* (1984)

MICHAEL BASINSKI

LONDON, Jack [John Griffith]
b. 12 January 1876, San Francisco, California; d. 22 November 1916, Glen Ellen, California

"The sudden eruption of L., with his talk of red revolution, his glorification of the Nietzschean superman and his assertive narrative style, into this tea-room atmosphere [of turn-of-the-century American literature] was utterly shocking," Kenneth Lynn has astutely observed. "Except for the similar sensation caused by the appearance of Mark TWAIN's mining camp humor in the midst of Victorian America, nothing more disturbing to the forces of gentility had ever happened in our literature, and it decisively changed the course of American fiction."

L. is, indeed, one of the most sensational figures in American literary history, and the stories he wrote were no more "shocking" than the story of his life. Much of his writing was based upon his personal experiences, and the dividing line between fact and fiction is often so thin as to be virtually indiscernible. Born out of wedlock, L. spent most of his childhood in near-poverty and was forced to quit school at the age of fourteen to become a factory "work beast," as he later called himself. Juvenile delinquent ("Prince of the Oyster Pirates" on San Francisco Bay) at the age of fifteen; able-bodied seaman at seventeen; hobo and convict at eighteen; "Boy Socialist" of Oakland at nineteen; Klondike argonaut at twenty-one; "American Kipling" at twenty-four; internationally famous war correspondent at twenty-eight; world-traveler and adventurer at thirty-one; prize-winning stockbreeder and scientific farmer by thirty-five: L. had become a national legend by the time of his death at forty. But it is the quality of his writings, ultimately, rather than the spectacle of his personal legend, that has won him a permanent place in world literature.

Vitality and variety are two salient characteristics of these writings. In a career that spanned less than two decades, he produced some four hundred nonfiction pieces, two hundred short stories, and twenty novels on such varied subjects as adventure, agronomy, alcoholism, animal training, architecture, assassination, astral projection, big business, ecology, economics, folklore, gold hunting, greed, hoboing, love, mental retardation, mythology, penal reform, political corruption, prizefighting, psychology (animal as well as human), racial exploitation, revolution, science, seafaring, slum dwelling, socialism, stockbreeding, war, wildlife, and the writing game. Such was his rigorous self-discipline that once he had mastered his craft, he spent no more than two hours each morning writing his daily minimum of one thousand words. By the time he burned himself out at the age of forty he had produced more than fifty books.

L.'s extraordinary vitality manifested itself not only in the production but also in the product, serving as a key to the universal appeal of his writings. Russian scholar Vil Bykov, comparing L. favorably with Chekhov and Tolstoy, says that it is the "life-asserting force" in his work and his portrayal of "the man of noble spirit" that has "helped L. to find his way into the heart of the Soviet reader." Likewise, Professor Li Shuyan of Beijing University asserts that "Whatever happens in the critical world, L. will go on enjoying the admiration of Chinese readers. Martin Eden and the many heroes in his stories of the North will always be an encouraging force to those who are fighting against the adversities, and who believe the worth of man lies in doing, creating, and achieving." Among a number of contemporary European critics L. is considered "possibly the most powerful of American writers."

This power was evident in L.'s fiction from the outset, as witnessed by the following passage from his early Northland story "The White Silence": "The afternoon wore on, and with the awe, born of the White Silence, the voiceless travelers bent to their work. Nature has many tricks wherewith she convinces man of his finity—the ceaseless flow of the tides, the fury of the storm, the shock of the earthquake, the long roll of heaven's artillery—but the most stupefying of all, is the passive phase of the White Silence. All movement ceases, sky clears, the heavens are as brass; the slightest whisper seems sacrilege, and man becomes timid, affrighted by the sound of his own voice. Sole speck of life journeying across the ghostly wastes of a dead world, he trembles at his audacity, realizes that his is a maggot's life, nothing more. Strange thoughts arise unsummoned, and the mystery of all things strives for utterance. And the fear of death, of God, of the universe, comes over him,—the hope of the Resurrection and the Life, the yearning for immortality, the vain striving of the imprisoned essence,—it is then, if ever, man walks alone with God."

As is evident in this passage—contrary to academic as well as popular misconception—there is considerably more to L.'s fiction than boys' adventure tales and dog stories. His work also comprises more than the "nature-red-in-tooth-and-claw" and survival-of-the-fittest narratives that characterize literary naturalism, the genre with which L. is usually identified. Beyond his dramatization of such typical naturalistic themes as primitivism, atavism, stoicism, and environmental determinism, what distinguishes L.'s work is his fusing of the mythic with the phenomenal. "His gallery of supermen and superwomen has about it the myth atmosphere of the older world," says Fred Lewis Pattee. "It is not the actual North: it is an epic dream of the North, colored by an imagination adolescent in its love of the marvelous, of fighting and action, and of headlong movement."

This blending of naturalism and supernaturalism is nowhere more evident than in L.'s best-known work: *The Call of the Wild* (1903). Read on one level, the story of Buck's transformation from ranch pet to Ghost Dog of the Wilderness is entertaining escape literature, often relegated to the children's sections of libraries. But mere escape novels do not become world classics—and *The Call of the Wild* has been translated into more than eighty different languages. In addition to its crisp narration, sharply delineated characterization, and lyrical style, its plot is animated by one of the most universal of thematic patterns: the myth of the hero. The call to adventure, departure, initiation through ordeal, the perilous journey to the "world navel" or mysterious life center, transformation, and final apotheosis: these are the phases of this archetypal pattern, and all are evident in Buck's progress from the civilized world to the raw frontier of the Klondike gold rush, to the naturalistic world of claw and fang, and, finally, into the mythic dreamland where the hero "may be seen running at the head of the pack through the pale moonlight or glimmering borealis, leaping gigantic above his fellows, his great throat a-bellow as he sings a song of the younger world."

The atavistic theme that motivated Buck's call would also be applied to L.'s human heroes. Shortly after completing *The Call of the Wild,* L. wrote to George Brett, president of the Macmillan Company, describing a new novel he had in mind: "My idea is to take a cultured, refined, super-civilized man and woman (whom the subtleties of artificial, civilized life have blinded to the real facts of life), and throw them into a primitive sea-environment where all is stress & struggle and life expresses itself, simply, in terms of food & shelter; and make this man & woman rise to the situation and come out of it with flying colors." But, as L. shrewdly added, "Of course, this underlying motif, will be *underlying;* it will be subordinated to the love motif. The superficial reader will get the love story & the adventure; while the deeper reader will get all this, plus the bigger thing lying underneath." L.'s genius in fusing the two leading modes of the early 20th-c. novel—the naturalistic and the sentimental—into this one novel was proved by its popularity: *The Sea-Wolf* (1904) was an immediate success. Three generations after its publication, it is still a bestselling classic and has been made into several film versions.

Essentially, *The Sea-Wolf,* like *The Call of the Wild,* is an initiation novel (in the same mode as Kipling's *Captains Courageous*), charting the progress of Humphrey Van Weyden from an effete upper-class sissy who has never worked a day in his life, to full-blooded manhood. The high priest of his initiation is Captain Wolf Larsen, an unforgettable character so powerful that he can squeeze a raw potato (or a man's arm) to a pulp with one quick grasp of his fist—yet whose personal library includes the works of Shakespeare, Milton, Browning, Darwin, and Herbert Spencer. Larsen has been called "the Captain Ahab of American literary naturalism"; he is a brilliant composite of Miltonic Satan, Byronic rebel, and Nietzschean *übermensch* who rules by fear and by force, alone, and who dies for want of compassion and camaraderie. Larsen is a hopeless materialist: "I believe that life is a mess," he asserts. "It is like a yeast, a ferment, a thing that moves and may move for a minute, an hour, a year, or a hundred years, but that in the end will cease to move. The big eat the little that they may continue to move, the strong eat the weak that they may retain their strength. The lucky eat the most and move the longest, that is all."

The character best fitted for survival in *The Sea-Wolf* is not the *superman* but the *whole* man. It is a combination of adaptability, courage (moral as well as physical), enhanced by a vital optimism and the capacity to love, that enables Humphrey Van Weyden to achieve wholeness in the course of his initiation. If Wolf Larsen is the high priest of his initiation, Maud Brewster—the great American poetess rescued from

shipwreck at midpoint in the narrative—serves as priestess, or anima figure. It is through her influence and by means of their escape from Larsen's hell-ship that Van Weyden is able to put his newfound manhood to test. That manhood is confirmed when he manages not only to cope with the forces of nature, in the mode of Robinson Crusoe, on Endeavor Island, but also—and most significantly—to restep the masts of Larsen's derelict ship when it is stranded there with its dying captain after the crew's desertion. The novel ends with the death of Larsen, who has persisted in clinging blindly to his materialistic individualism, and with the salvation of Humphrey and Maud because they have acted according to the principles of cooperation, idealism, and love.

These principles are central to L.'s work, including his "other great dog novel"—*White Fang* (1906). On December 5, 1904, L. wrote to George Platt Brett, proposing a "complete antithesis" and "companion book" to *The Call of the Wild:* "Instead of devolution or decivilization of a dog," he explained, "I'm going to give the evolution, the civilization of a dog—development of domesticity, faithfulness, love, morality, and al the amenities and virtues." Instead of being a true companion piece, however, this work proved to be a completely different kind of book: a sociological fable dramatizing L.'s theory of environmental determinism. As he wrote to George Wharton James, "I am an evolutionist, therefore a broad optimist, hence my love for the human (in the slime though he be) comes from my knowing him as he is and seeing in him the divine possibilities ahead of him. That's the whole motive of my 'White Fang.' Every atom of organic life is plastic. The finest specimens now in existence were once all pulpy infants capable of being moulded this way or that. Let the pressure be one way and we have atavism—the reversion to the wild; the other—domestication, civilization. I have always been impressed by the awful plasticity of life and I feel that I can never lay enough stress upon the marvelous power and influence of environment."

The power of environment is dramatically evident throughout *White Fang* as the young part-wolf cub learns the law of "Eat or be eaten" in his Northland wilderness, then becomes a savage killer under the sadistic bondage of Beauty Smith, and finally is transformed into loyal pet through the loving kindness of Weedon Scott in his new Southland home.

Complementing L.'s belief in the importance of environment was his socialism. An ardent believer in the rights of the working classes, L. wrote and lectured freely on the behalf of the socialist cause, and in 1905 was elected first president of the Intercollegiate Socialist Society (he also ran twice—unsuccessfully—as socialist candidate for mayor of Oakland).

He produced a score of socialist essays and stories, his enthusiasm peaking with the composition of *The Iron Heel* (1908): an apocalyptic novel praised by Philip Foner as "probably the most amazingly prophetic work of the 20th c." and by Robert Spiller as "a terrifying forecast of Fascism and its evils." The novel predicts the ultimate triumph of the Brotherhood of Man, but only after many centuries of economic and political oppression by the "Iron Heel" of capitalism.

L.'s socialistic writing diminished during the last decade of his life as his interests shifted more to other concerns, such as travel, adventure, and ranching. His famous *Snark* voyage to Hawai'i and through the South Seas in 1907–9 generated a half-dozen books, the most significant of which was his autobiographical novel *Martin Eden* (1909), the story of a brilliant young seaman from the lower classes who is driven by the American Dream to become a world-famous author. Unlike L., however, and somewhat like Wolf Larsen, Martin Eden is an unmitigated individualist who dies (by drowning himself in the middle of the Pacific Ocean) because he has no further purpose in life after having achieved success. Despite its obvious flaws in style and minor characterization, *Martin Eden* remains one of L.'s most important books. Franklin Walker has rightly praised it as possessing "great lasting power, having more vitality today than it did the day it issued from the press."

In 1909, forced by multiple tropical ailments to abandon his projected world cruise, L. turned his attention to the development of his celebrated "Beauty Ranch" in the Valley of the Moon (Sonoma County, California). "In the solution of the great economic problems of the present age," he said, "I see a return to the soil. . . . I see my farm in terms of the world, and I see the world in terms of my farm." This agrarian vision is central to L.'s later years, informing a considerable number of his works, among which two novels are particularly noteworthy. *Burning Daylight* (1910) depicts its central character, Elam Harnish, a Klondike "Bonanza King" who returns to the Southland to become a "Captain of Finance"—only to lose his soul to money and then to regain it through his marriage to Dede Mason, a self-determined career woman who persuades him to renounce his wealth and become a yeoman farmer. *The Valley of the Moon* (1913) reinforces L.'s theme of agrarian salvation by dramatizing the pilgrimage of a young working-class couple named Saxon and Billy Roberts, who abandon their miserable life in the ugly, strike-torn city to find happiness, as the Harnishes have done, in the simple, wholesome life of farming. Significantly, it is the women in both these novels who possess the agrarian vision and who guide the heroes to their salvation.

The theme of the strong-willed, independent woman as moral guide and salvational force is pervasive in L.'s writings, recurring throughout his nonfiction as well as his fiction: from the early Klondike stories, in which he extols the virtues of the native women as well as those of his tough Anglo-Saxon females—such as the protagonist of his first novel, *A Daughter of the Snows* (1902), who brags that she can swim, box, fence, and do twenty pull-ups—through *The Kempton-Wace Letters* (his 1903 epistolary dialogue on love written in collaboration with Anna Strunsky), *The Sea-Wolf* and his agrarian works, to his late Hawaiian and South Pacific stories.

A further theme emerges in these later works: the vitalizing power of myth and the unconscious mind. While visiting Hawai'i in an attempt to restore his health in 1916, L. discovered the recently translated work of C. G. Jung and was immediately captivated, exclaiming to his wife Charmian, "I tell you I am standing on the edge of a world so new, so terrible, so wonderful, that I am almost afraid to look over into it!" Suddenly, the Polynesian myths he had listened to with good-natured skepticism for the past decade assumed a new credibility in the light of J.'s theories of racial memory and the power of the collective unconscious. The literary results of L.'s epiphany were a series of extraordinary stories written during the last six months of his life and published posthumously in *The Red One* (1918) and *On the Makaloa Mat* (1919). These tales signified not only an advance in his own work but also a new dimension in 20th-c. literature: L. became the first major writer to make creative use of J.'s theories.

"The Water Baby," L.'s last story, is exemplary. Virtually without physical action, it consists essentially of a dialogue between two characters who are loafing in a fishing boat offshore. John Lakana (the Hawaiian name for L.), the world-weary narrator, listens with half-hearted skepticism to the energetic ramblings of his good-humored companion Kohokumu, an ancient Hawaiian skin-diving fisherman still capable of descending to forty-foot depths into the sea that he claims as his true mother. "But listen, O Young Wise One, to my elderly wisdom," Kohokumu admonishes: "This I know: as I grow old I seek less for the truth from without me, and find more of the truth within me. Why have I thought this thought of my return to my mother and of my rebirth from my mother into the sun? You do not know. I do not know, save that, without whisper of man's voice or printed word, without prompting from otherwhere, this thought has arisen from within me, from the deeps o me that are as deep as the sea. . . . Is this thought that I have thought a dream?"

L. finished "The Water Baby" on October 2, 1916, only six weeks before his death from what attending physicians diagnosed as a "gastro-intestinal type of uraemia." In his copy of Jung, he had underscored the following biblical quotation that epitomizes the central informing theme of his last work: "Think not carnally or thou art carnal, but think symbolically and then thou art spirit." Clearly, after a lifelong insistence that he was an incorrigible "materialistic monist," L. had undergone a spiritual "sea-change" before the end of his remarkable career.

BIBLIOGRAPHY: Cassuto, L., and J. C. Reesman, *Re-reading J. L.* (1996); Hendricks, K., and I. Shepard, eds., *Letters from J. L.* (1965); Johnston, C., *J. L.—An American Radical?* (1984); Kingman, R., *A Pictorial Life of J. L.* (1979); Labor, E., *J. L.* (1974; rev. ed. with J. C. Reesman, 1994); Labor, E., et al., eds., *The Letters of J. L.* (1988); Labor, E., et al., eds., *The Complete Short Stories of J. L. (1993);* London, J., *J. L. and His Times* (1939); Nuernberg, S. M., *The Critical Response to J. L.* (1995); Ownbey, R. W., ed., *J. L.: Essays in Criticism* (1978); Tavernier-Courbin, J., *Critical Essays on J. L.* (1983); Walker, D. L., *The Alien Worlds of J. L.* (1973); Walker, D. L., ed., *Curious Fragments: J. L.'s Tales of Fantasy Fiction* (1975); Walker, D. L., ed., *J. L.: No Mentor but Myself* (1979); Walker, F., *J. L. and the Klondike* (1966); Watson, C. N., Jr., *The Novels of J. L.* (1983); Wilcox, E. J., *The Call of the Wild by J. L.: A Casebook* (1980); Williams, T., *J. L.: The Movies* (1992); Woodbridge, H. C., et al., eds., *J. L.: A Bibliography* (1966; enlarged ed., 1973)

EARLE LABOR

LONGFELLOW, Henry Wadsworth

b. 27 February 1807, Portland, Massachusetts (now Maine); d. 24 March 1882, Cambridge, Massachusetts

The most popular American poet of the 19th c., L. has been largely and unfortunately denigrated in the 20th c. for a variety of reasons. His accessibility and mellifluousness flout modernist preferences for recondite texts, his Christian humanism is read as facile, and his Eurocentric sympathies seem incompatible with the daring American exceptionalism of writers like Walt WHITMAN. But by contemporary standards, it is possible to assess L. more judiciously and appreciate his poetic suppleness. At the very least, he is probably 19th-c. America's most versatile poet whose oeuvre is wide-ranging and ingenious and possesses great aesthetic and cultural interest.

L. painstakingly schooled himself to be a poet, a status he did not in fact attain until he was in his thirties. Crucial to his development were two tours of Europe he made as a young man. He spent three years (1826–29) studying in France, Spain, Italy, and Germany as the prerequisite for assuming a new professorship in modern languages at Bowdoin; in 1835, to prepare himself for an appointment at Harvard as Smith Professor of Modern Languages, he continued his European education in England, Germany, Denmark, Sweden, and Holland. Thus, he learned his craft through sustained engagement with the languages and literatures of Europe, through the numerous translations he made of the multifarious poetry he encountered, and through a variety of prose works that reflected both his travel and his subsequent scholarly responsibilities—*Outre-Mer,* an 1835 Irvingesque account of his first continental tour, textbooks, literary criticism.

Although L. does little in the way of explicit theorizing about his art, he had a clear and constant sense of mission. As he suggests in "The Singers," (from the 1850 collection *The Seaside and the Fireside*), charming, strengthening, and teaching are the fundamental gifts of the poet whose songs "touch the hearts of men, / And bring them back to heaven again." A public poet, he assumed commonalities of belief allied him with his readers and could serve as the basis of the enlargement of their sensibilities. Despite the richly American content of his work, "nationality" alone struck L. as an insufficient poetics, and he aspired to make the indigenous give voice to the universal.

L. played across a spectrum of poetic types from lyrics, psalms, and ballads to sagas, epics, and tragedies. Among his earlier shorter poems, two particularly well-known pieces are "A Psalm of Life" from *Voices of the Night* (1839) and "The Village Blacksmith" from *Ballads and Other Poems* (1841). Wildy popular in its day, "A Psalm of Life" has become a notorious entry in the L. catalogue, an easy mark for his more predictable critics. The original freshness of the poem's earnest injunctions to act and strive may be irrecuperable now, and the illogicality of some of the poem's metaphors may baffle—a shipwrecked man is somehow able to perceive L.'s proverbial yet hardly immutable footsteps on the sands of time. But the poem is not finally representative of L.'s art, and what might be identified as its strategy of deliberative vagueness is germane both to L.'s aesthetic and popularity. If the poem works, it works precisely because L. never specifies how his readers ought to "act" or what exactly they should be "up and doing"; free of the burden of determinate prescriptions, the individual reader can detail these outlines as he or she sees fit.

"The Village Blacksmith" operates similarly, especially in its closing stanza where the smithy is thanked for the unspecified lesson he has taught us; we in turn are expected to work our own fortunes at "the flaming forge of life," a metaphor openended to the point that it can mean almost anything its readers desire. The blacksmith, however, is more than an exemplary toiler, rejoicer, and sorrower. The artfulness of the poem is evident, for example, in the synechdoche of his hands; initially, the sign of his strength and labor, the image is repeated when he thinks of his dead wife in church and wipes a tear away, the working man revised as the feeling man.

Other representatives of L.'s many noteworthy short poems include *Poems on Slavery* (1842), "Mezzo Cammin" (wr. 1842, pub. 1886), "My Lost Youth," and "The Children's Hour" from *Birds of Passage* (1858), and "The Cross of Snow" (wr. 1879, pub. 1886). The slavery poems indicate L.'s capacity for politically-edged poetry; in "The Warning" he even imagines slavery reducing the country to wreck and rubbish. "My Lost Youth" and "The Children's Hour" are good examples of L.'s nostalgia and lyricism. The former, replaying the words from an old Lapland song in its refrain about the "long, long thoughts" of youth, makes for a reminiscence poem of high order almost universally lauded by L.'s commentators; the latter is striking in its presentation of a domestic rather than laboring father whose imagination, like L.'s, leaps from temporal immediacies to eternal vastnesses, from the mischievousness of three daughters to a concluding image of the round-tower of the heart in dust and ruins. "Mezzo Cammin" and "The Cross of Snow" are two of L.'s best sonnets, the first a confession of the poet's fear that he has failed to construct any lofty tower of song, the second a memorial to his second wife; the two poems begin to suggest L.'s often acknowledged preeminence as a sonneteer.

Of his longer poems, it was L.'s extraordinarily successful *Evangeline* (1847) that secured his renown. Historically rooted in the 1755 British expulsion of the French from Novia Scotia, the poem is also indebted to Tegner's *Frithiof's Saga,* a Swedish epic about the Vikings. Much of the interest of the poem derives from its use of unrhymed dactylic hexameter, a difficult meter to execute in English; the distinct music of the poem perhaps prevails over its matter, for despite its narrative frame of the faithful Evangeline's searching across the continent for her lost love Gabriel, and their eventual reunion in a Philadelphia almshouse not long before his death, not much happens in "Evangeline." In the figure of Evangeline, however, L. does manage to synthesize his twin, overarching concerns of domesticity and questing. As a model of active female self-sacrifice, Evangeline incarnates the last line of "A Psalm of Life" about the necessity of laboring and waiting; L. in fact repeats this very language in describing his later heroine. By the end of the poem, moreover, individual destiny is contextual-

ized by the larger, melancholy voice of nature, the "disconsolate" ocean seeming to speak to the "wail of the forest." L. returned to the hexameter form, but with a lighter touch, in "The Courtship of Miles Standish" (1858), a Puritan "pastoral" whose central figure is Priscilla more than Standish or her other suitor John Alden.

In the twenty-two cantos of the *Song of Hiawatha* (1855), L.'s epic intentions are more explicit than in *Evangeline*. Although the poem's principal source was Henry Rowe SCHOOLCRAFT's work on the Native American tribes of the U.S., the poem's special (and easily parodied) meter, its unrhymed trochaic tetrameter, came from the Finnish epic *Kalevala*. Critics have wondered if *Hiawatha* is really about Native Americans at all. For L., Hiawatha comes to embody a fable of the civilizing process, of progress both individual and national. A gentle savage unlike his ferocious father Mudjekeewis, Hiawatha, possibly as L.'s own surrogate, works for tradition, continuity, and inspiration. He invents, for example, a system of picturewriting and by poem's end blesses the missionaries who have arrived to Christianize his people. "Song of Hiawatha," however, might also be understood as an allegory about the power of marvelous story. As the guests at Hiawatha's wedding acknowledge, perhaps like L.'s own avid readership, it is good stories that help to make the feast joyous and pass the time gaily.

L.'s narrative gifts flower in *Tales of a Wayside Inn,* published in three parts in 1863, 1872, and 1874. Chaucerian in its allocation of tales to a group of seven characters gathered together at an inn, the tales themselves are highly varied in subject and meter. The best known of them, "Paul Revere's Ride" (1863), told by the inn's landlord, manifests a prevailing L. interest in his country's visitable past. "Torquemada" (1863), however, told by the theologian, is an almost Hawthornean meditation on obsession and guilt about an old Hidalgo who turns in his own daughters for heresy during the Inquisition and even adds wood to the fires to which they are sentenced. Critic Newton Arvin thought *Tales of a Wayside Inn* to be L.'s major poetic achievement; it is a work that needs to be more widely read and studied.

L. intended *Christus: A Mystery* (1872) to be his crowning work, an elaborate examination in three parts, he began thinking in 1841, of aspects of Christendom in the apostolic, middle, and modern ages. Part 1, "The Divine Tragedy" (1872), poeticizes the life of Jesus; part 2, "The Golden Legend" (1851), recounts the tale of a prince whose leprosy can be cured only by the blood of a virgin; part 3, *The New England Tragedies* (1868), consists of the blank verse dramas "John Endicott," centering on Puritan persecution of the Quakers, and "Giles Corey of the Salem Farms," a distillation of the hysteria of the witch trials.

L. wanted each of these parts, moreover, to correspond to the three chief Christian virtues of faith, hope, and charity. If the work as a whole lacks the magnitude and completeness L. wished for, its parts greater than its sum, the work is nevertheless vital evidence of L.'s ambitiousness and seriousness of purpose even very late in his poetic career.

Although usually and appropriately remembered as a poet, L. also produced a significant body of prose writings. Among these are *Hyperion* (1839), based on his study of German literature, and his one novel, *Kavanagh* (1849). The number and strength of his translations, especially his *Divine Comedy* (1867–70), also deserve underlining. As an anthologist too, especially in *Poets and Poetry of Europe* (1845), L. again proved to be enormously influential. His literary activity remains remarkable for the cultural practice and promotion it encompasses and for the eloquent reciprocity of old and new world artistry it embodies.

BIBLIOGRAPHY: Arvin, N., *L.: His Life and Work from Revolution through Renaissance* (1963); Buell, L., *New England Literary Culture* (1986); Parini, J., ed., *Columbia History of American Poetry* (1993); Thompson, L., *Young L., 1807–1843* (1938); Wagenknecht, E., *H. W. L.: His Poetry and Prose* (1986); Williams, C. B., *H. W. L.* (1964)

MICHAEL BERTHOLD

LONGSTREET, Augustus Baldwin

b. 22 September 1795, Augusta, Georgia; d. 9 July 1870, Oxford, Mississippi

L.'s *Georgia Scenes* (1835) is the earliest example of what became known as "Humor of the Old Southwest." With their emphasis on vernacular dialect and the realistic depiction of characters of low social status, these sketches strongly influenced the great tradition of 19th-c. American humor, including the later Southwestern humorists and local color writers, which culminated in the work of Mark TWAIN. The *Georgia Scenes* are products of L.'s early career: raised as Southern gentry, he attended Yale and law school, then served as a lawyer, circuit court judge, and newspaper publisher in central Georgia. His observations around the legal circuit of people and their talk led to a reputation as a storyteller. At the urging of friends, L. began publishing his sketches in newspapers. When he collected these, as *Georgia Scenes,* he identified himself only as "a native Georgian."

The sketches in *Georgia Scenes* contrasted sharply with the emphasis of L.'s Southern contemporaries, such as William Gilmore SIMMS and John Pendleton KENNEDY, on gracious plantation life. Their origin is not "literary" but performative, tale-telling around the courthouse and town square. L. showed his contemporaries how to preserve qualities of oral humor in print. Beyond that, he wrote his sketches at least partly to preserve an "overlooked" area of social history, which even then was disappearing: "the manners, customs, amusements, wit, [and] dialect" of frontier people in "common walks of life." Focusing on community activities like "Gander Pulling, " "The Shooting Match," and "The Horse Swap," the *Georgia Scenes* bring forward vigorous lowlife characters like Ransy Sniffle, who in "A Fight" provokes a nose-biting, ear-severing battle that overjoys an entire community. L.'s chief accomplishment here is description of the scene through the banter of onlookers, given in dialect. The rollicking vernacular language is framed by an educated narrator who mediates between the reader and the scene. This interplay of proper narrator and vernacular characters, which emphasizes social and linguistic contrasts, was a vital innovation in American humorous writing.

Following *Georgia Scenes,* L. published relatively few humorous sketches, and none at all after 1843. His short works of the early 1840s were collected in 1912 as *Stories with a Moral;* these sketches lack the vigor of *Georgia Scenes* and are, as the volume title indicates, more didactic. In the second half of his life, L. served as president of four institutions of higher learning, including the universities of Mississippi and South Carolina. He apparently believed that vernacular sketches were unworthy of these positions and inappropriate to the tense time leading up to the Civil War. Instead, L. published a series of proslavery articles, collected in 1847 as *A Voice from the South.* His only novel, *Master William Mitten,* appeared in 1864. A sentimental, moralizing satire on the rearing of a spoiled child, the novel is of interest primarily because it may have been based on the early years of the author's nephew, the Civil War general James Longstreet. L.'s reputation rests solely on *Georgia Scenes,* which Walter Blair's influential *Native American Humor* (1937) called the "first and most influential book" of Southwestern humor.

BIBLIOGRAPHY: Fitzgerald, O. P., *Judge L.* (1891); Meriwether, J. B., "A. B. L.," *MissQ* 35 (1982): 351–64; Wade, J., *A. B. L.* (1924)

GLEN M. JOHNSON

LOOS, Anita

b. 26 April 1888, Sissons (now Mt. Shasta), California; d. 18 August 1981, New York City

Today, L. is best known for her 1925 satiric novel *Gentlemen Prefer Blondes,* but many still remember her as the celebrated symbol of both the Jazz Age and the Golden Age of Hollywood. During a career that spanned seventy years, she was a novelist, playwright, and scenarist. At the age of five, she began to earn her own living as a child actress; at nineteen she was writing scenarios for D. W. Griffith's Biograph Company; and, two decades later, as the author of the surprise hit *Gentlemen Prefer Blondes,* she finally achieved international fame and enough money to enjoy it.

Gentlemen Prefer Blondes was acclaimed by the intelligentsia of its day, and fans included William FAULKNER, Aldous Huxley, and James Joyce. Today, many readers still consider it a minor American classic that satirizes the materialistic world of sex of the 1920s. Noting that men of great wealth, power, and intellect (L. specifically had her friend H. L. MENCKEN in mind) were often to be seen escorting blond playmates as ego possessions, L. began a tongue-in-cheek diary of the adventures of a composite of these women, and the character of Lorelie Lee was born. Written in the semi-literate voice of its heroine, *Gentlemen Prefer Blondes* is a comic expose of the breaking down of Puritan values that accompanied the accumulation of wealth in the 1920s. Lorelie, very much a golddigger and a snob, is nonetheless much more than a stereotypical "dumb blonde." Uneducated as she appears, she is cunning and shrewd as she plots to get her way. Lorelie is not a victim of her society; she is its product. The plot follows Lorelie and her wise-cracking companion Dorothy Shaw from their social life in New York through a tour of Europe to Lorelie's marriage to a wealthy, Puritan member of the social register. Lorelie's experiences allow L. to satirize wealth, royalty, and family life as much as Lorelie's relations with men and her obsession with expensive gifts. With Lorelie's strict sense of propriety, there is very little mention of illicit romance or of any material a 1920s audience would have considered immoral. *Gentlemen Prefer Blondes* was adapted into a very successful Broadway play in 1926, a Broadway musical in 1949, and a Hollywood musical in 1953. A companion piece, *But Gentlemen Marry Brunettes* (1928) continues in Lorelie's voice as she gives the romantic history of her friend Dorothy, but this work did not achieve the success of the first.

L.'s work in Hollywood began in 1912 when D. W. Griffith filmed her scenario *The New York Hat.* Later, in collaboration with director John Emerson, whom she eventually married, she wrote tailored screenplays for Douglas Fairbanks and Constance Talmadge and proved that verbal humor could succeed in the subtitles of the silent film. In the 1930s, L. worked for Irving Thalberg at MGM where her sense of comic dialogue was applied to boost the career of Jean Harlow in *Red-Headed Woman* (1932) and to define the film persona of Clark Gable in *San Francisco* (1937) and *Saratoga* (1937).

In the mid-1940s, L. lived in New York and concentrated on playwriting, creating *Happy Birthday* (1946) as an against-character role for her friend Helen Hayes and *Gigi* (1951), adapted from the short story by Colette. Other works of this period include two satiric novels of Hollywood, *A Mouse is Born* (1951) and *No Mother to Guide Her* (1961); two memoirs, *A Girl like I* (1966) and *Kiss Hollywood Goodbye* (1975); and a biography of *The Talmadge Girls* (1978).

BIOGRAPHY: Carey, G., *A. L.* (1988); Douglas, G. H., *Women of the Twenties* (1989)

LYNN RISSER

LORD, William [Wilberforce]
b. 28 October 1819, Madison County, New York; d. 22 April 1907, New York City

Although L.'s first publication, *Poems* (1845), received more favorable than negative reviews—in a letter, William WORDSWORTH described L. as a highly promising young talent whose poems were deeply felt and cast in a style full of vigor and harmony—he seems to be remembered, if at all, not so much by the poems he wrote than the attack his first volume engendered from Edgar Allan POE. L. had gotten in the middle of a quarrel between Poe and the supporters of the *Knickerbocker Magazine*. Additionally, a parody of Poe's poem "The Raven"—the piece "New Castaglia"—did not help matters. Poe viciously attacked L. several times, the kindest comment being that his was "a very ordinary species of talent."

Poems show influences of Wordsworth and Samuel Taylor Coleridge—as well as other poets—and in content, form, and style displays L.'s vast knowledge of both classical and modern languages and literatures. Adaptations from earlier authors are intentionally introduced in the manner of the ancient writers, with L. evidently expecting his readers to appreciate rather than condemn the adaptations.

Son of a Presbyterian minister, L. received a thorough formal and an unusual informal education. After graduating from high school and the now no longer existing University of Western New York (1837), he spent the next four years as a sailor to recover his health before entering Auburn Theological and Princeton Seminary for his theological training. While the classical part of his upbringing heavily influenced his subject matter, images, and style, the years at sea seem to have not entered his poetry, except perhaps in the poem "I know an Isle."

Poe's attack discouraged L., and instead of pursuing a career as a poet, he chose the church. In 1848, he was ordained deacon in the Protestant Episcopal Church and became a priest two years later. During his long career in the ministry, L. distinguished himself wherever he served. His literary output never entirely stopped. In addition to the occasional poems, L. wrote a religious epic, *Christ in Hades* (1851), in which he tried to render Christ's descent into hell to liberate the souls of the saints and to demonstrate his power over evil. The epic with its strong echoes of Milton was reviewed widely but appealed more to the scholar trained in the classics than to popular audiences.

L.'s last publication, *Andre* (1856), a tragedy in blanc verse, dramatizes events surrounding John Andre, a British Army officer hanged as a spy in 1780 for conspiring with Benedict Arnold, an American general during the Revolutionary War, who fled to England in 1781. A critic praised the play's richness of thought, its poetic imagery, and the true feelings it inspired, but chastised L. for a lack of dramatic sense.

After the Civil War, L. wrote a few lyrical poems that seem to give credence to Wordsworth's high esteem of his early work. First collected and published in 1938, these later verses are more direct, simpler, and less burdened by classical allusions.

For the reader interested in rhetoric, L.'s prose writings are worth mentioning, some of which are published. A witty and erudite conversationalist, L. was an original and forceful public speaker and preacher. His interest in evolution was demonstrated in both a lecture, "Man and the Record of his Origin" (1880) and a poem, "The Great Ascidian" (1871–76), the latter taking its prompt from a quotation by Darwin.

It seems appropriate to let L. have the last word. When reminiscing about Poe's criticism of his early work, he is said to have commented to his grandson: "Poe tried to prove I was not a great poet. It was really a compliment." His epitaph reads, "Poet, Priest, and Scholar."

HEIDEMARIE Z. WEIDNER

LORDE, Audre [Geraldine]

b. 18 February 1934, New York City; d. 17 November 1992, St. Croix, Virgin Islands

Self-described as a "black lesbian feminist poet," L. wrote primarily for personal and collective survival. Prolific as well as forceful, L.'s body of work speaks of the importance of voice, self-definition, and truth in a potentially racist, sexist, and homophobic world.

The daughter of West Indian immigrants, L. grew up in New York City, an urban landscape that often appears in her verse. L. attended Hunter High School where she began writing poetry; her first poem was published in *Seventeen* magazine. After earning a B.A. from Hunter College and an M.A. in library science from Columbia University, L. began a short lived career as head librarian at the Town School Library in New York City where she continued to write; her poems served as a means of understanding and affirming the life that was unfolding before her.

In 1968, a year that was to be crucial to her career as a poet, L. received a grant from the National Endowment for the Arts and became poet-in-residence at Tougaloo College in Mississippi. In the next six years, L. published four collections of poetry. *The First Cities* (1968) is an introspective work that employs nature imagery to explore human emotions and relationships. *Cables to Rage* (1970) explores themes of birth, love, and human fallibility through betrayal and includes the highly praised poem "Martha," which revealed L.'s homosexuality. *From a Land Where Other People Live* (1973), which was nominated for the National Book Award in poetry, denounces racial injustices and celebrates African American womanhood. *New York Head Shop and Museum* (1974), L.'s most radical work, boldly reveals the hardships of poverty and urban decay.

Although L. achieved a fair amount of success, it wasn't until Norton's publication of *Coal* in 1976 that L. gained widespread exposure. *Coal* is a compilation of previously published as well as unpublished poems that deal with African American identity. L. uses figurative language often employing metaphors of birth and rejuvenation to create an amalgam of sensuality and self-affirmation. Writing in tight free verse, L.'s language is natural; her meaning is potent. An anger that underlies L.'s earlier poems surfaces more fully as her voice develops. While *Coal* received favorable reviews, *The Black Unicorn* (1978) is considered to be L.'s most poetically mature work. L. returns to her spiritual roots and uses African mythology and history to assert her power as a strong and resilient black woman; L. also revives the bond of black sisterhood shared in the African tradition.

In the late 1970s, L. was diagnosed with cancer and underwent a radical mastectomy. Challenging the perfect picture image of women created by the media, L. refused to wear a prosthesis. In *The Cancer Journals* (1980), L. reveals her pain, anger, and fear as she confronts her own mortality and reasserts her identity as a woman. Like the phoenix, L. descends into despair and emerges with new vitality. *The Cancer Journals,* which won the American Library Association Gay Caucus Book of the Year Award in 1981, serves as a source of inspiration for other women struggling with this potentially debilitating and deadly disease.

In the following years, L. continued to write both prose and poetry. *Zami: A New Spelling of My Name* (1982), a "biomythology," or combination of history, autobiography, and mythology, is a brutally honest and powerful reflection of L.'s early years growing up in New York, her struggles with voice, and her coming out experiences as a young black lesbian woman. Like Rita Mae BROWN's *Ruby Fruit Jungle,* Zami has become somewhat of a cult text in the lesbian community. In *Sister Outsider* (1984), a collection of essays and speeches that has been widely praised by the feminist movement, L. urges us all, black or white, male or female, homo- or heterosexual, to examine our lives and transform ourselves into agents of truth and action. L. denounces Western traditional valuing of the rational over the emotional, and like French feminists Hélène Cixous and Luce Irigaray, L. avers the erotic as a natural source of self-empowerment for women.

In L.'s last two collections of poetry published before her death, *Chosen Poems: Old and New* (1982) and *Our Dead Behind Us* (1986), L. focuses on national and international crises such as the murder of Emmet Hill in the U.S. South and the bloody massacres in South Africa. In *A Burst of Life* (1988), L.'s last collection of essays, L. ponders death and compares her struggles with cancer to worldwide struggles for racial equality and homosexual acceptance.

Fighting against multiple oppressions, L. has been embraced in varying degrees, by the feminist, lesbian, and African American communities; L. curiously, however, remains a minor poet and her work is in danger of obscurity.

BIBLIOGRAPHY: Christian, B., "The Dynamics of Difference: Review of A. L.'s *Sister Outsider,*" in *Black Feminist Criticism: Perspectives on Black Women Writers* (1985): 205–10; Hull, G. T., "Living on the Line: A. L. and *Our Dead Behind Us,*" in Wall, C. A., ed., *Changing Our Own Words: Essays on Criticism, Theory, and Writings by Black Women* (1989): 150–72; Martin, J., "The Unicorn is Black: A. L. in Retrospect," in M. Evans, ed., *Black Women Writers (1950–1980): A Critical Evaluation* (1984): 277–91

SALINDA LEWIS

LOVECRAFT, H[oward] P[hillips]

b. 20 August 1890, Providence, Rhode Island; d. 15 March 1937, Providence, Rhode Island

Frequently compared to Edgar Allan POE, L. is the modern master of the tale of horror and the macabre. Despite disparagement by Edmund WILSON, who thought the comparison of L. to Poe a poor comment

on the discernment of the American reader, the tales are still widely enjoyed, occasionally taking on a cult status, and have influenced such masters of the horror genre as August DERLETH, Stephen KING, and Clive BARKER, as well as figures as diverse as Colin Wilson, Josef Skvorecky, and Umberto Eco. In turn, L.'s stories, themes, and characters have inspired many horror films, from *The Dunwich Horror* (1970) and the *Re-Animator* series (1985 and 1990) to films by John Carpenter.

L. rarely ventured far from the region of his birth, except for a two year stay in Brooklyn, New York, during an abortive marriage. The region, its architecture, and its history provided him with a backdrop for many of his stories. Brown University for instance, became the model for the Miskatonic University, and Salem, Massachusetts, the city of Arkham. When L. was eight, his father died of the effects of tertiary syphilis. He was raised by his mother, herself later institutionalized for neurosis, and his grandfather. Such a background suggests the origins of the recurrent theme of madness and hereditary degeneration in stories such as "The Rats in the Walls," "The Lurking Fear," "The Dunwich Horror," or "The Shadow of Innsmouth."

Interested in writing from an early age, L. joined the United Amateur Press Association in 1913, contributing articles, poems and short stories, as well as revising, editing, and ghostwriting material. In his relatively brief career, he published over a hundred tales, and an equivalent number of poems and pieces of amateur journalism. Despite this output, the first book-length collection of his stories, *The Outsider,* did not appear until 1939, two years after his death. Although L. had played with the genre of horror fiction at an early age, his first published contributions, "The Tomb," and "Dagon" were written in 1917. Thereafter, he contributed stories to a number of journals, including the Chicago-based magazine *Weird Tales* founded in 1923.

Writing in the wake of Freud, Einstein, and the Wright Brothers, L. was devoted to science, publishing many articles of amateur journalism on astronomy and chemistry. A scientific materialist, many of his stories combine horror with SCIENCE FICTION. Thus, fear and horror are predicated on the natural rather then the supernatural. *Herbert West—Reanimator,* a cycle of six tales that appeared in *Home Brew* (February-July 1922), presents a Frankenstein-like scientist engaged in experiments to bring life to dead bodies. The short novel *The Case of Charles Dexter Ward*—written in 1927 and serialized in *Weird Tales* in 1941—tells the tale of a young man obsessed with the necromanic experiments of his ancestor, Joseph Curwin, a wizard forced to flee Puritan Salem.

L. was deeply read in the classics of horror fiction. In his essay "Supernatural Horror in Literature," he identified Poe, his "God of fiction," and especially Lord Dunsany and Arthur Machen as important influences on his writing. Both Dunsany and Machen drew on myth and folklore to construct fantastic dreamscapes for their stories. Inspired by this device, L. created his own mythology to provide a metatext for many of his best stories. In 1926, he wrote, "The Call of Cthuthu," inaugurating the "Cthuthu Mythos." In tales such as "The Dream-Quest of Unknown Kadath," "The Dunwich Horror," "The Colour Out of Space," "The Shadow Over Innsmouth," and "The Shadow Out of Time," among other stories and poems, L. set his narratives against the backdrop of an ancient race of creatures from other dimensions of space and time, a pantheon of "Great Old Ones," lurking in ancient memories or dreams, ready to exercise their will on the present in preparation for their return. Thus, references and allusions to Cthuthu, Ashtoroth, or Azathoth, "the blind, idiot god," recur in L.'s stories, as does the mysterious *Necronomicon,* a book by the 7th-c. Arab mystic Abdul Alhazred, supposedly containing the key to the return of the "Great Old Ones." It is the Cthuthu mythos more than anything, that accounts both for the success and the influence of L.'s stories.

BIBLIOGRAPHY: De Camp, L. S., *L.: A Biography* (1975); Joshi, S. T., ed., *H .P. L.: Four Decades of Criticism* (1980); Lévy, M., *L.: A Study in the Fantastic* (1988); Shreffler, P. A., *The H. P. L. Companion* (1977)

THOMAS L. COOKSEY

LOWELL, Amy

b. 9 February 1874, Brookline, Massachusetts; d. 12 May 1925, Brookline, Massachusetts

L. was a poet, literary critic, lecturer, and exponent of the poetic doctrines of IMAGISM. Her vivid personality and energetic campaign for freedom of poetic expression made her one of the most prominent figures in the literary world between 1914 and 1925. Critics have generally categorized L. as an imagist poet who wrote a number of remarkable poems. Contemporary feminine critics argue, however, that this label does not do justice to her successful experimentation with a wide range of forms and techniques.

As the daughter of a distinguished New England family, L. grew up in a tradition of cultural and civic leadership. She was educated at home, in private schools, and through extensive reading and foreign travel. Throughout her life she was plagued by a glandular disease that caused obesity and severe headaches. Despite her ill health, she led an extremely active life as owner of the family estate Sevenels, international traveler, patron of the theater and other arts, and literary celebrity famous for her eccentric behavior. Her output was prodigious. Over the span of thirteen years, she published eight volumes of poetry and several prose works, including a two-volume biography of John Keats and *Tendencies in Modern American Poetry* (1917), which gave her a solid reputation as a critic. She also published several poetry anthologies, including *Fir-Flower Tablets* (1921), containing her renditions of Chinese poetry. She was also an accomplished public lecturer.

L. chose poetry as her vocation after being captivated by the stage performance of Eleonora Duse, the Italian actress, in Boston in 1902. For the next eight years, L. undertook a poetic apprenticeship marked by close study of Leigh Hunt's anthology of romantic and Victorian poets. When her first volume of poetry, *A Dome of Many-Coloured Glass* (1912), was criticized for its highly derivative style, she began to experiment with the free verse and imagist style of Hilda DOOLITTLE and other new poets appearing in Harriet MONROE's *Poetry.* In 1914, she took over from Ezra POUND the editorship of the imagist anthology. Throughout her career, she was generous in her support of other writers, including D. H. Lawrence and Robert FROST, who were her close friends.

L.'s poetic breakthrough came with her second book *Sword Blades and Poppy Seed* (1914), which included her first poems written in free verse and "polyphonic prose." In the book's preface, she defines free verse as "unrhymed cadence" and compares the elements of polyphonic prose to the voices of an orchestra, thereby reflecting her view of poetry as an art to be heard. She also believed in the deep relationship between material forms and human emotions. In works such as *Can Grande's Castle* (1918) and *Pictures of the Floating World* (1919), vivid sensory perceptions are expressed in brilliant imagery. Many of the images are taken from her own life—her gardens, her travels, and her experiences with music and theater. Her subject matter has great variety, but many of her most successful poems deal with her changing emotional states, from depression and self-doubt over her lack of love and marriage, to contentment and affection for her long-time companion Ada Russell.

L.'s last book of poetry, *What's O'Clock* (1925), finished shortly before her sudden death and published posthumously, was awarded the Pulitzer Prize in 1926. It contains some of her finest poems, including "Lilacs," perhaps her most brilliant use of imagism; "The Anniversary," representative of her most personal love poems; and six sonnets to Eleonora Duse, her artistic inspiration. Also included is "The Sisters," a meditation on her kinship with Sappho, Elizabeth Barrett Browning, and Emily DICKENSON. She wonders what motivates women poets—"a queer lot"—to "scribble down, man-wise, the fragments of ourselves." This late poem reflects L.'s interest in the powerful effects of gender on the art of literary women. In her own efforts to form a new poetic aesthetic, L. not only contributed a body of lyrical and brilliant pictorial poetry, but also played a significant role in the American poetic renaissance.

BIBLIOGRAPHY: Flint, F. C., *A. L.* (1969); Foster, D., *A. L.* (1935); Gould, J., *The World of A. L. and the Imagist Movement* (1975)

MARGARET CARTER

LOWELL, James Russell

b. 22 February 1819, Cambridge, Massachusetts; d. 12 August 1891, Southborough, Massachusetts

Descended from a venerable colonial family, L. attended Harvard College as an undergraduate and stayed on for a degree in law. Having then proposed that it was "better to be a good fellow than a good poet," L. devoted most of his undergraduate years to making good on that boast. His reputation at Harvard involved the infringement of academic rules and the publication of scurrilous verse for which he graduated as class poet in 1838.

Following law school, L. published his undergraduate verse in a first collection of poetry, *A Year's Life,* in 1841. Thereafter, L. worked on establishing a position in a New York literary scene whose major figures were committed to abolitionism and other reform causes. In 1843, he founded the *Pioneer,* a literary journal devoted to advancing the interests of a national literature. This was to be the first of a series of literary journals that mobilized his considerable energies as editor and writer. After the *Pioneer* failed in 1843, he became editor of the *National Anti-Slavery Standard* (1848–52), founding editor of the *Atlantic Monthly* (1857–61), and starting in 1864, the coeditor of the *North American Review.*

His involvement in reform causes brought him the acquaintanceship of the abolitionist Maria White. When they married in 1844, L. and his wife dedicated their marital compact to the antislavery cause. Throughout their marriage, L.'s peculiar combination of political invective, critical judgment and poetic cultivation enabled him to craft opinions about political and literary matters that enjoyed the status of conventional wisdom. L. would vacillate between the production of serious verse and send-ups of what he considered the chief literary faults of his competitors. In *A*

Fable for Critics (1848), L. put all of his gifts into service when he observed famously of the author of "The Raven": "There comes Poe, with his raven, like Barnaby Rudge, / Three fifths of him genius and two fifths sheer fudge."

L.'s talents would receive national attention in 1848 with the publication that year of *The Bigelow Papers* as well as *Poems . . . Second Series, The Vision of Sir Launfal* and *A Fable for Critics. The Bigelow Papers* consisted of two series of verse letters delivered in Yankee dialect and addressed to L.'s fictive alter ego, the New England farmer Hosea Biglow. L. published the first group of nine letters expressing his opposition to the Mexican War in *National Anti-Slavery Standard.* The second series was published in the *Atlantic Monthly* in 1862 to support the Union's cause in the Civil War. Borrowing its themes from Malory and their versification from Tennyson, L.'s *The Vision of Sir Launfal* gave evidence of L.'s having failed to apply to his own poetry the high standards he required of others.

In 1849, there began an unremitting series of personal tragedies that permanently alienated L. from the enthusiasms of his youth. Between 1849 and the death of his wife in 1853, he would bury two of his three daughters and his only son. After he succeeded Henry Wadsworth LONGFELLOW in the Smith Professorship of French and Spanish at Harvard in 1855, L. turned to his earlier notebooks perhaps as much for the consolation they afforded as literary inspiration. In 1857, L. married his daughter's governess and became the editor of the *Atlantic.* After the Civil War, he actively engaged that journal as well as the *North American Review* in the cause of gaining political rights for newly enfranchised blacks.

In between the aftermath of the war and his death in 1891, L. decided that literary clubs and well appointed dining tables proffered the appropriate social spaces for his peculiar gifts. A founding member of Boston's Saturday Club, L. supervised the elevation of that literary society into the cultural capitol of Brahmin Boston. Although he was an elegant lecturer, L. found it increasingly difficult to support the lavish life style of those years on a professor's salary. In 1871, he sold over twenty acres of the family's estate in Elmwood and retired to Europe the following year.

After arriving in London, L. invested his literary capital in the field of international politics, writing satires and delivering high table witticisms on subjects ranging from diplomatic intrigue to political corruption. His satires circulated throughout international circles. When they received the attention of the political elite in Washington D.C., President Rutherford B. Hayes appointed him ambassador to Spain in 1877. He would become ambassador to England in 1880 where, despite his sometimes spectacular mishandling of matters of state, he remained until President Grover Cleveland removed him in 1885. L. died at the age of seventy-two in his daughter's home in Southborough, Massachusetts.

BIBLIOGRAPHY: Duberman, M., *J. R. L.* (1966); Howard, L., *Victorian Knight-Errant: A Study of the Early Literary Career of J. R.. L.* (1952); Wagenknecht, E., *J. R. L.* (1971)

DONALD E. PEASE

LOWELL, Robert [Trail Spence, Jr.]

b. 17 March 1917, Boston, Massachusetts; d. 12 September 1977, New York City

More than any other poet of his generation, L. helped to revolutionize and define 20th-c. American poetry. Particularly in the work of his middle period—in his so-called confessional poetry—L. demonstrated that personal and private materials that previously had been considered unsuitable for poetry could in fact be transformed into significant, moving, and respected poetry. L.'s New England Brahmin heritage, his friendships, three marriages (to Jean STAFFORD, Elizabeth HARDWICK, and Caroline Blackwood), his mental illnesses, and other events of his life were thus chronicled in poetry. His celebrity as well as his poetic authority and authenticity made L. a recognized spokesperson for his age. Throughout his career, he experimented with many poetic styles, from the rhymed sonnet to free verse, from the highly formal to the laconic and chatty. In addition to poetry, L. wrote prose pieces, creative translations, and verse dramas.

L. was only thirty-years old when he won the Pulitzer Prize for *Lord Weary's Castle* (1946), his second book of poetry. The poems in this volume, like those in his earlier *Land of Unlikeness* (1944), are polished, structured, learned, and allusive; they reveal the influence of Allen TATE and John Crowe RANSOM, L.'s mentors, and of such early modernist poets as T. S. ELIOT and Ezra POUND. Although these early poems often camouflage the personal through poetic masks, they nevertheless demonstrate L.'s own concerns at this stage of his career. Poems such as "Concord," "Christmas Eve under Hooker's Statue," "Rebellion," and "At the Indian Killer's Grave" display his rejection of his New England Puritan ancestry as unworkable in the modern era, his conversion to Roman Catholicism, his yearnings for spiritual fulfillment, and his anger at the hypocrisy and violence in the world.

During the 1950s, L. wrote *Mills of the Kavanaughs* (1951), a complex poem centering on the disintegration of a Catholic family, and started his translations

of classical writers (to be published in 1961 as *Imitations*). Also during the 1950s, L. experienced spiritual and psychological turmoil, began what was to be repeated hospitalizations for manic-depression, married his second wife, left the Catholic Church, and recorded these experiences in his best-known work, *Life Studies* (1959). In this volume, a National Book Award-winner and a hallmark of confessional poetry, L. dropped poetic masks and exposed, often in painful detail, actual events of his personal as well as his political and public life. Particularly probed are the details of L.'s family and ancestry. As open in form as it is in content, *Life Studies* combines a prose section, "91 Revere Street," with sections of free verse. The loosening of L.'s poetic style in this volume has been attributed to the influence of Elizabeth BISHOP (to whom one poem in the volume, "Skunk Hour," is dedicated), and of Allen GINSBERG and other Beat poets.

In subsequent volumes, L. extended the examination of American ancestry, both personal and national. The poems in *For the Union Dead* (1964), especially the title poem, and the verse plays (derived from Nathaniel HAWTHORNE and Herman MELVILLE) in *The Old Glory* (1965) record a driving, almost ruthless, need to explore American history, to understand it in all its complexity, and to learn to live with its effects.

L.'s later works, *Near the Ocean* (1967), *Notebook* (1969), *For Lizzie and Harriet* (1973), *The Dolphin* (1973), *History* (1973), and his final volume, *Day by Day* (1977), continue in the confessional vein, displaying, for example, L.'s relationships with wives and children, his troubling mental problems, and his antiwar and other activities. However, these volumes are also marked, first, by a widening of interest (an exploration not only of personal and national history, but also of the history and politics of the Western world from ancient times to the present), and second, by a return in many poems to structured verse, especially, as in *Notebook* and *History,* to the unrhymed sonnet. These works can be seen as forerunners of the Postmodern period in their ironic stance, their questions about the efficacy of language and art, and especially in their revisions and re-orderings of previous poems. L.'s final work is quieter and wiser than the early work; it expresses less rage and less grandiloquent hope. Like all his work, it reflects a deep commitment to art, to human causes, and to the discovery of his American identity. As L. admits in "Epilogue" from *Day by Day,* "all's misalliance." Yet he insists on the artistic and moral value of recording, as accurately as possible, individual moments in human life.

L. died the year *Day by Day* appeared. After his death, his prose works, including significant essays

707

on translation, theater, poets, novelists, and historians, were published as *Collected Prose* (1987).

BIBLIOGRAPHY: Axelrod, S. G., and H. Deese, *R. L.: A Reference Guide* (1982); Bloom, H., ed., *R. L.* (1986); Hamilton, I., *R. L.* (1982); Hart, H., *R. L. and the Sublime* (1995); Mazzaro, J., *The Poetic Themes of R. L.* (1965); Perloff, M., *The Poetic Art of R. L.* (1973); Rudman, M., *R. L.: An Introduction to the Poetry* (1983); Vendler, H., *The Given and the Made: Strategies of Poetic Definition* (1995); Williamson, A., *Pity the Monsters: The Political Vision of R. L.* (1974); Witek, T., *R. L. and Life Studies: Revising the Self* (1993)

LAURA JEHN MENIDES

LUHAN, Mabel Dodge

b. 26 February 1879, Buffalo, New York; d. 13 August 1962, Taos, New Mexico

Wealthy patron of avant-garde movements in art, literature, and politics, L. inspired both admiration and animosity in her contemporaries. Curiosity about her now centers on her memoirs of Gertude STEIN, D. H. Lawrence (*Lorenzo in Taos,* 1932), Robinson JEFFERS (*Una and Robin,* 1976), and many others, as well as on her long-standing admiration of the Pueblo Indians. An indefatigable hostess and intellectual social climber, she created salons in Italy (1902–12) and New York (1913–18) that attracted a combustible mixture of radical thinkers and celebrities such as Stein, John Reed, Max EASTMAN, Eleonora Duse, Lincoln STEFFENS, Carl VAN VECHTEN, and A. A. Brill. In 1918, she moved to Taos, New Mexico, where she married her fourth husband, a Pueblo Indian named Tony Luhan. Together they built the elaborate homestead that at different times sheltered Lawrence, Willa CATHER, Georgia O'Keeffe, Jeffers, and others over the next forty years.

L. was, by turns, graspingly needy and serenely impassive. Her uncertainty about her own identity allowed her to mimic and reinterpret the ideas and emotions of the people to whom she was attracted, and the resulting cross-pollination helped establish new territories of the imagination. She did not think or write systematically, but she exhibited an intuition and aggressive energy often associated with genius. She found her niche as a publicist and used her time and money to promote artists and causes that appealed to her prophetic instincts.

L. published a four-volume autobiography, *Intimate Memories* (1933–37), four volumes of memoirs, numerous essays, two stories, and left behind a cache of personal papers. *Intimate Memories,* which covers

the first quarter of the 20th c., is her richest contribution to American literary history. *Winter in Taos* (1935), in which she celebrates the seasonal changes and perennial comforts of ranch life, reveals her as a poet of everyday sensualities and is her most readable work.

BIBLIOGRAPHY: Crunden, R., *From Self to Society, 1919–1941* (1972); Hahn, E., *M.* (1978); Rudnick, L. P., *M. D. L.: New Woman, New Worlds* (1984)

ROBIN BEATY

LUM, Darrell H. Y.

b. 2 April 1950, Honolulu, Hawai'i

L. is generally acknowledged to be a pioneering, talented prose writer in the pidgin dialect of Hawai'i, a dialect produced out of the contact between plantation laborers of different ethnicities in early-20th-c. Hawai'i. By privileging an oral and regional sensibility in his writing, L. has paved the way for subsequent writing in pidgin dialect and contributed a fresh reconceptualization of the English language. L.'s volume *Sun: Short Stories and Drama* (1980) is the first major collection of short fiction and drama by a "local"—Hawai'i-based—Chinese American writer. L.'s second collection of short stories, *Pass on, No Pass Back!* (1990), was awarded the 1992 Association for Asian American Studies Outstanding Book Award. Several plays by L. have been produced by Kumu Kahua and Honolulu Theater for Youth, including *Oranges Are Lucky, Fighting Fire, A Little Bit like You, My Home Is down the Street,* and *Magic Mango.*

Critic Stephen H. Sumida has called L. "a master of the Hawai'i childhood idyll in short fiction." The typical L. protagonist is a male child or adolescent, often speaking in pidgin. He is caught in networks of childhood power (bullied by a classmate or older brother, or himself bullying another), and may work against injustice by befriending a social "outsider." Some of L.'s short stories focus on the pleasures and anxieties of taboo activity: painting graffiti art, peeking at mildly pornographic material, sniffing paint, buying and smoking cigarettes. They are humorous and poignant in their depiction of the frustration felt by a young person at being placed in absurd situations. Stories told from an adult perspective are more sober, focusing on the narrator's sense of losing control over his body or his environment. An additional focus of L.'s writing is the elder as precious embodiment of family history, sometimes misunderstood or underestimated by the younger generation.

Critic Gayle K. Fujita-Sato uses the term "ecopoetics" to refer to the motifs of exchange, reciprocity, and recycling in L.'s stories, particularly "Beer Can

Hat," "Primo Doesn't Take Back Bottles Anymore," and "The Moiliili Bag Man." "Eco-poetics" may also connote L.'s own "recycling" of those considered the "waste" of society—the "bag man" as scavenger, the mentally retarded, the old or dying—in literary characters that educate the reader about the environmental and historical context in which he or she lives.

In addition to his creative writing, L.'s editorial work is also considered crucial to the development of a local Hawai'i-based sensibility. He was a cofounder, along with Eric Chock, of *Bamboo Ridge: The Hawai'i Writers' Quarterly,* in 1978, and continues to serve as one its editors. *Bamboo Ridge,* which occasionally publishes single-author volumes as special issues, has published more poetry and short fiction than any other literary press in Hawai'i. L. and Chock received the 1997 Hawai'i Award for Literature. L.'s introductions to *The Best of Bamboo Ridge* and *Paké: Writings by Chinese in Hawai'i* articulate the sensibilities of local multiethnic literature in Hawai'i, as well as early 20th-c. Chinese American writing in Hawai'i. In his creative and editorial work, L. has made a major contribution to shaping a distinctively local Hawai'i-based culture, in the process re-formulating "American" English and American literature.

BIBLIOGRAPHY: Fujita-Sato, G. K., "The Island Influence on Chinese American Writers: Wing Tek Lum, D. H. Y. L., and Eric Chock," *AmerasiaJ* 16 (1990): 17–33

JULIANA CHANG

LURIE, Alison [Bishop]

b. 2 September 1926, Chicago, Illinois

Although L. has made a successful career for herself as a critic, college professor, and author of children's books, she is best known for her novels about the vicissitudes of marriage and the unreliability of self-knowledge. Her sharp satire, biting wit, masterful plotting, and detailed description have earned her numerous awards, among them Guggenheim and Rockefeller Foundation grants—1965 and 1967 respectively—and the 1985 Pulitzer Prize in fiction for *Foreign Affairs* (1984). Her most popular works, *The War between the Tates* (1974) and *Foreign Affairs,* were adapted for television along with *Imaginary Friends* (1967); all feature academic couples, a population she has studied intimately since joining the faculty of Cornell University in 1969. Taken together, her fiction offers an incisive and witty commentary on American social, moral, and sexual practices from the 1960s to the present.

L. trained by reading the novels of Charles Dickens, Jane Austen, and Henry JAMES, and critics have often remarked on their stylist influences upon her writing. Some have claimed that her novels are formulaic and heavily reliant on the conventions of comedy, but she is known and most widely praised for her ability to construct intricate yet tight and suspenseful plotting structures, a particularly Dickensian skill. Her satiric, self-conscious wit, and comedies of manners are frequently compared with Austen's. From James, she inherited a taste for the supernatural and a juxtaposition of American decency and European decadence that reappears throughout her works. Admired for her efficient prose and powers of description, L.'s characters are intelligent, well-educated members of the upper-middle class—often of the academic community—who have a habit of cropping up in more than one novel, and frequently bang their carefully controlled hearts, intellects, and egos on the rocks of reality. L.'s fiction is recognized as smart and highly literary but has occasionally been critiqued as elitist and bookish for the same reasons.

There are recurrent themes in L.'s work, the most prominent of which is her unrelenting interrogation of the institution of marriage and its susceptibility to the toxic virulence of extramarital sex. Her first novel, *Love and Friendship* (1962), is an exploration of Southern California culture in the sixties which recounts the disintegration of two marriages and the American dream. Nine years later, L. launched her first best-seller, *The War between the Tates.* Critics were stunned by L.'s intricately woven analogy between the novel's backdrop, the Vietnam War, and the domestic skirmishes among partners, generations, and cultures that ensue after Professor Brian Tate's midlife crisis culminates in an affair with one of his students. His wife Erica's response with sexual, religious, and drug experimentation, and their children's open rebellion offered L. prime targets on which to hone her satirical pen. *Only Children* (1979) dealt with similar conflicts between sexes and generations but is narrated by two eight-year-old girls with, in critical opinion, varying degrees of success.

The slippery boundaries between the real and the imaginary constitute L.'s other most prominent fictional interest. Repeatedly exploring the limitations of self-knowledge, her novels mine the differences between a constructed persona and the self discovered when tested by crisis. L.'s characters frequently lose their sense of self and their ability to distinguish between fact and fantasy. In *Imaginary Friends,* a renowned sociologist falls prey to the cult he is studying; *Real People* (1969) is the satirical account of a deluded woman suffering writer's block at an artist's colony; and *The Truth about Lorin Jones* (1988) centers on a biographer who becomes obsessed with her subject, only to discover the falseness of her preconceptions. *Women and Ghosts* (1994) is a collection of short fiction in which women are haunted by aspects of their own psyches, taking the fragility of individual identity to the extreme.

The two thematic interests came together in L.'s eighth novel, *Foreign Affairs,* in which Vinnie, a plain, aging, self-pitying academic finds unexpected romance with Chuck, a retired sanitation engineer whom she meets while traveling to London for her sabbatical.

The finely crafted counterpointed plot earned her the Pulitzer Prize and a new audience for a body of fiction that has earned the distinction of being both popular and intelligent.

BIBLIOGRAPHY: Costa, R. H., *A. H.* (1992); Parini, J., "The Novelist at Sixty," *Horizon* 29 (March 1986): 21–22; Satz, M., "A Kind of Detachment: An Interview with A. L.," *SWR* 71 (Spring 1986): 194–202

ELIZABETH BLEICHER

MACDONALD, Cynthia
b. 2 February 1928, New York City

Alicia OSTRIKER calls M. "a dazzlingly witty poet who has become a mistress of monsters." Richard HOWARD calls her a poet of the grotesque. M.'s poetry—whether it deals explicitly with hunchbacks, cannibal babies, tightrope-walker amputees, fat ladies, bearded women, the world's largest man, an autonomous mouth, ear, eye, a woman made of glass, or simply with the more common circuses and freak shows inherent in the human heart—is consistently engaged in exploring those moments when what makes us human puts us in the center ring of our own self-consciousness. M.'s work is about the business of uncovering the unconscious, often revealing it to be the wicked ringmaster that it is.

M. received her B.A. from Bennington College and her M.A. from Sarah Lawrence. Her grants and awards include a National Endowment for the Arts Grant, a Guggenheim Fellowship, and a National Academy and Institute of Arts and Letters Award. Aside from publishing five volumes of poetry and appearing in most of the nation's finest journals, she has been an opera singer and has trained in psychoanalysis at the Houston-Galveston Psychoanalytic Institute. Such variousness of experience is not lost on her poetry. Currently, she teaches at the University of Houston in the creative writing program, which she founded.

Even when the subject matter or the voice of her poems is not, technically, "freakish," her poetry transports us into the realm of the absurd. It is in this Boschian nightmare world where M. manages to reacquaint us with the familiar, even among a family of living dolls or when following a couple who, after sex, find themselves turned to stone by a volcano. Whether she is contemplating the universal implications of hats, erythrophobia, suicide, psychology, or the ethical and moral obligations of two brothers who build a woman out of green hay, M. never lets us lose sight of the characters who—though their circumstances may be surreal—must still, strangely but perfectly, remind us of ourselves.

Intensely psychological, often tremendously casual and heartbreakingly funny, M.'s poetry does not take itself too seriously. The personae she creates shape their living narratives out of detritus, platforms, wax men, high wire acts with pianos; they fall in love with plants. They carry their lives in suitcases, pull them out of hatboxes, pack them into dollhouses. They worry about how to go on living, about falling out of love, about the efficacy of their penmanship. The poems themselves turn, often, on puns, on visual eccentricities reminiscent of May SWENSON, on combinations of obscure quotes in the tradition of Marianne MOORE.

Even the titles of her six major volumes suggest a consistent agenda: *Amputations* (1972), *Transplants* (1976), *(W)holes* (1980), *Alternate Means of Transport* (1985), *Living Wills* (1991), and *I Can't Remember* (1997). Each poem and each book is a process *about* the process of loss and accumulation. Ultimately, M.'s work is most concerned with the pebbling and texturing of consciousness, with its lumps and hunches, with collecting it all—all that life—and packing it tightly into the space of the page as if the ink itself were her steamer trunk.

BIBLIOGRAPHY: Gregerson, L., "Unequal Seas," *Parnassus* 8 (1980): 210–28; Ostriker, A. S., *Stealing the Language: The Emergence of Women's Poetry in America* (1986); Widmann, R. L., "The Poetry of C. M.," *CP* 7 (1974): 19–26

BRYAN D. DIETRICH

MACDONALD, Ross
b. 13 December 1913, Los Gatos, California; d. 11 July 1983, Santa Barbara, California

Often regarded as the third member of a triumvirate consisting of Dashiell HAMMETT and Raymond CHAN-

DLER, Ross Macdonald, the pseudonym of Kenneth Millar, made a number of contributions to hard-boiled detective fiction throughout the 1950s and 1960s. Unlike Hammett or Chandler, he repeatedly situates the origins of a crime within the frame of dysfunctional or ruptured families; in the later novels, he also gives increasing emphasis on the tangled human relationships behind criminal activities, leading his detective to feel compassion for other characters. The frequent exile-and-return pattern in M.'s plots have led critics to indicate strains of Oedipal myth, as well as biographical links with M.'s childhood: an abandonment by his father, and an early move from California to Canada to live with his grandparents. While M.'s fiction still cannot be held strictly to standards of literary "art," his treatment of detective fiction excelled that of Hammett and Chandler in bringing the genre closer to this level of excellence.

In *The Moving Target* (1949), M. introduced the private detective Lew Archer, who served as narrator in most of M.'s subsequent novels. Like Chandler's Marlowe, Archer employs an ostensibly cynical tone combined with a deeper melancholy towards the corruption around him. As he investigates the kidnapping of an oil tycoon, Archer gradually uncovers the moral and emotional decay of the man's family: his alcoholism in response to a stepson's death, the consequent greed of his alienated wife, and the rebelliousness of his daughter, whose affair with an employee provides a link to the kidnapping and murder of her father. In *The Drowning Pool* (1950), the pattern of family dissolution continues as Archer wades through currents of adultery (both heterosexual and homosexual), incestuous jealousy, murder, and mistaken paternity in a wealthy family. Like Chandler, M. often relies on vivid similes in depicting the decadent side of the American dream, as when he sardonically refers to the Nopal Valley's growth as like that of "a tumor." Archer's perspective of his prestigious clients is often ambivalent: while repulsed at their pretensions, his exposure to their environment also makes him feel somewhat sympathetic for certain victimized family members. In the Archer novels to come during this decade, this undercurrent of class tension would continue, as well as a reliance on the genre-type of female culprits driven to murder through jealousy of victimization by others.

In *The Galton Case* (1959), which M. considered his "breakthrough novel," the exile-and-return plot arises through Archer's search for Anthony Galton, the heir of a wealthy family. More than the previous novels, this work allowed M. to come to terms more directly with his own past by focusing on the recovery of a son's rightful identity. Like most of M.'s fiction, the novel deals indirectly with the sociological strati-

fication of California, although due to the plot-centered demands of the genre it typically falls short of any fully-achieved social critique. In his subsequent Archer novels of the 1960s, the theme of complex paternity and missing sons and daughters would resurface even more insistently than in the previous decade. Along with *The Galton Case*, the novels of this period—*The Wycherly Woman* (1961), *The Zebra-Striped Hearse* (1962), *The Chill* (1964), *The Far Side of the Dollar* (1965), *The Instant Enemy* (1968), and *The Goodbye Look* (1969)—serve as the most representative novels of M.'s career.

In *The Underground Man* (1971) and *Sleeping Beauty* (1973), the symbolism reflects M.'s interest in ecology: in the first novel, a forest fire serves as an image of the destructive family passions behind a murder; in the second novel, an oil spill in the Pacific figures the pattern of murder that contaminates the wealthy family that owns the well. At this time, a favorable review of *The Underground Man* by Eudora WELTY helped to solidify M.'s reputation, although other critics objected to the merit of M.'s fiction as "art." In his final novel, *The Blue Hammer* (1975), the fifty-year-old Archer, notably more introspective and weary, experiences a short-lived love affair with a young journalist.

While the repeated themes of false fathers, lost or alienated children, and destructive greed sometimes risk becoming formulaic, M. effectively began where Chandler left off, further developing the mythos of the detective-hero even as he further chronicled the decay of other modern American myths.

BIBLIOGRAPHY: Bruccoli, M. J., *R. M.* (1984); Schopen, B., *R. M.* (1990); Speir, J., *R. M.* (1978); Wolfe, P., *Dreamers Who Live Their Dreams: The World of R. M.* (1976)

CHAD TREVITTE

MACKAYE, Percy [Wallace]
b. 16 March 1875, New York City; d. 31 August 1956, Concord, New Hampshire

A prolific, energetic, and versatile poet, essayist, opera librettist, and dramatist, M. will be remembered best for his effort to create an American artistic tradition incorporating American values. His earliest work from 1903 to 1907 reflects his European experience and literary influences after graduating from Harvard: blank verse plays based on classical and historic themes. However, M. did not regard himself as a Euro-American writer, but as an American who would remake European patterns to enhance a democratic ideal.

In public addresses and essays, he asserted repeatedly that the artist and the statesman were equally obliged to serve the Commonweal; to express "for their countless brothers who are dumb and incapable—the excellent beauty of their common mother." He believed that the theater shapes taste, morality, and intelligence. It must, therefore, produce civic-inspiring art, and it must be protected from commercial corruption. He advocated full endowment of a public theater, independent of external pressure.

M.'s most original concept was the civic masque or pageant, a vivid outdoor event on a heroic scale. Although not the first to present masques in this country, M. carried the form farther than anyone had done. The pageant presents a sequence of historical acts; the masque deals with generalized, even allegorical figures. For M., the masque would not be the creation of a single imagination like the European theater of Strindberg and Ibsen, but the sign of democracy expressed "through a drama OF and BY the people, not merely FOR the people." Although hundreds of thousands saw M.'s masques *St. Louis* (1914) and his *Caliban by the Yellow Sands* (1916), the theater critic and historian, Thomas H. Dickinson, nevertheless attacked M.'s aesthetic. He denied vigorously that art could ever be created by "Society," declared that beauty can be the work only of the individual. But M. insisted that if people are to imagine their "life drama" they must not only see and hear it, "they must themselves enact and interpret it." And so they did: for *St. Louis,* 7,500 performers; for *Caliban by the Yellow Sands,* over 2,000. Community social groups, dramatic societies, music groups, and orchestras rehearsed with the few professionals for weeks—even in bad weather. In St. Louis, in New York, and in Boston, the newspapers daily reported on the preparations and the gorgeous achievements of music, lights, and dance spectacle of the masques. There was some haughty criticism of *Caliban* as a work beyond the education or the comprehension of the mass audience.

M. was dedicated to a transformation of that mass audience. For a poet-playwright like M., pageantry and masque greatly expanded the role for art in a modern society. Historical pageantry could be that link with earlier American social and aesthetic forms that might furnish what in 1918 Van Wyck BROOKS called, "a usable past." Like Brooks, M. was willing to yield some of the individualism that pursues commercial success to create the sense of brotherhood that is "the best promise of a national culture."

M.'s opera libretto, *The Immigrants* (1915), for which F. S. Converse wrote the music as he did for *St. Louis,* shows M.'s range and his consistency of thought. The helpless, brutalized, "tempest-tossed" Europeans arrive here to be further exploited, further brutalized by a different immigrant group. M. hoped his opera would awaken "us" to the needs, the emotions, the sympathies and tragedies that are "like our own." The central figure is the earnest, "American" artist, Noel; his antagonist is the Irish scoundrel, "Scammon." This social passion of M. is partly a social naivete not uncharacteristic of young intellectuals early in the 20th c. The transformation of the untutored masses was a worthy effort. And M. believed those masses are eager to be transformed by the superior Anglo-Saxon model. *Caliban by the Yellow Sands* ends with Caliban kneeling before the wise and generous Prospero. The white Knight triumphs in *St. Louis.*

After the war, M. wrote a last masque, *Washington, the Man Who Made Us* (1919), performed in Washington D.C. for Congress. It was not a popular success. During the 1920s, he created a series of folk plays, an Appalachian cycle in which he paid scrupulous attention to dialect voices. M., the pageant-master, was a reformer at heart. He was not a snob about his audience. He accepted cultural naivete without offering less than his best poetic skills, the best his imagination could conjure, the best designers, musicians, and singers he could persuade to join his adventurous work. If Prospero speaks in iambic pentameter, so does Caliban.

BIBLIOGRAPHY: Brock, D. H., and J. W. Welsh, "P. M.: Community Drama and the Masque Tradition," *Comparative Drama* 6 (Spring 1972): 68–84; Dickinson, T. H., *Playwrights of the New American Theater* (1925); Glassberg, D., *American Historical Pageantry* (1990); Macgowan, K., *Footlights across America* (1929)

VILMA RASKIN POTTER

MACLEISH, Archibald
b. 7 May 1892, Glencoe, Illinois; d. 20 April 1982, Boston, Massachusetts

No figure from the modernist era took on a more public role in civic life than M. While the discredited (and often disgraceful) beliefs and private prejudices of his better-known peers are exposed in each new biography, M.'s reputation for democratic activism and intellectual engagement distinguish him as a humanist of rare integrity and conscience. But his artistic stature has diminished greatly since his death, and he is read even less in the academy than is his one-time friend, John DOS PASSOS, another politically active modernist.

A Harvard-educated lawyer, M. served on the front lines in World War I. He began writing poetry in 1916 but did not produce substantial work until his brief expatriation in Paris in the 1920s, where he mingled with other American EXPATRIATES, E. E. CUMMINGS, Ernest HEMINGWAY, and F. Scott FITZGERALD. His first few volumes of poetry, including *The Pot of Earth* (1924) and *The Happy Marriage and Other Poems* (1925), were well received, and by the late 1920s, he was hailed as a leading literary innovator. M.'s best-known poem, from *Streets in the Moon* (1926) is "Ars Poetica," containing the hotly debated modernist dictum, "A poem should not mean / But be"—a prescription for poetic practice M. later rejected. In his finest lyric poem of this period, "You, Andrew Marvell," insights into temporality and eternity are rendered through evocative glimpses of mythic and ancient worlds. "Memorial Rain," a homage to his brother who was slain in World War I, juxtaposes a statesman's cliché—ridden aphorisms on sacrifice with the starkly personal agony of death on a battlefield.

Though much of his poetry is self-consciously aesthetic, often marred by obvious influences, both in content and style, of Charles Swinburne, W. B. Yeats, Ezra POUND, and T. S. ELIOT (including the latter's reliance on the studies of Jessie L. Weston and Sir James Frazer), he produced longer poetic works that were equally inspired by more traditional poetic genres. *The Hamlet of A. M.* (1928), a gloomy symbolist poem in fourteen sections, weaves lines from the Shakespearean play around a retelling of the Grail legend. *New Found Land* (1930) imitates Anglo-Saxon verse, and *Conquistador* (1932), awarded the Pulitzer Prize, is a 2,000-line narrative poem about Cortez's conquest of Mexico told from the unofficial point of view of a minor historical player. This epic combines M.'s love of the Dantean *terza rima* with a Homeric faith in courageous individuality, as he casts a harsh light on the atrocities of New World conquest in shifting, often gorgeous cadences and tones reminiscent (but not purely imitative) of Eliot's *The Waste Land.*

Frescoes for Mr. Rockefeller's *City* (1933), inspired by the American millionaire's aborted efforts to hire the Marxist Diego Rivera to paint a mural, marks his growing preoccupation with political ideology and global politics. Part Whitmanesque rhapsody and partly a lament for a vanishing primordial American essence, the poem begins a long period in which M. the artist is ultimately eclipsed by M. the statesman. Throughout the 1930s, he wrote articles for *Fortune,* decrying the popularity of anti-democratic sentiments, and chaired the League of American Writers, an anti-fascist organization. In 1939, he was appointed librarian of Congress by President Franklin D. Roosevelt and was assistant secretary of state from 1944 to 1945. Works such as *Panic* (1935), *Air Raid* (1938), and *America Was Promises* (1939) combine elements of propaganda with prophetic warnings of the impending world conflicts. *The Irresponsibles* (1940) is a contro-

versial indictment of American poets and writers who routinely coopted the horrors of history for aesthetic ends but neglected the overriding need for active struggle against communism and fascism.

Although his postwar poetry retreats from his life-long struggle between aesthetic sovereignty and social responsibility, he was the most active of American writers who successfully lobbied the U.S. government in the 1950s for the release of his longtime acquaintance, Ezra Pound, from St. Elizabeths Federal Hospital. Pound, for his part, was not only ungrateful to M., but continued to write sarcastic, often contemptuous letters to him.

M.'s Pulitzer Prize-winning *Collected Poems* (1952) included a number of new poems that blend images of old age, declining creative power, and pastoral life with hard-won everyday truths about love and fidelity. In "The Linden Branch," nature and love are sources of strange music, a theme greatly expanded in *Songs for Eve* (1954), where the Edenic myth is studied in short meditative poems about the cultivation of spiritual innocence through childhood and parentage. He also wrote a number of touching eulogies; notable among them are "Cummings" and "Edwin Muir."

M. was also a playwright, though his impact on the history of American theater is negligible. His verse dramas based on classical literature include the philosophical *JB* (1954), which earned a successful run on Broadway and won M. his third Pulitzer Prize. The play, which dramatizes the conflict between religious ideals and secular realities, is an eccentric retelling of the Book of Job with absurdist elements, including an offstage director who doubles as an image of God, a chorus of clowns, and vaudevillian humor. He won an Academy Award for his screenplay of *The Eleanor Roosevelt Story* (1965).

BIBLIOGRAPHY: Donaldson, S., *A. M.: An American Life* (1992); Drabeck, B. A., and H. E. Ellis, eds., *A. M.: Reflections* (1986); Smith, G. C., *A. M.* (1971)

TIM KEANE

MADHUBUTI, Haki R.

b. 23 February 1942, Little Rock, Arkansas

The controversy surrounding the validity of "Black English" as a legitimate medium of communication for a literate American citizen is not likely to be completely settled in the foreseeable future, but the manner in which a "blackening"—as Gwendolyn BROOKS put it—of the English language can result in a powerful poetic statement was clearly demonstrated by M.'s first major collection *Don't Cry, Scream* (1969). M., along with Sonia SANCHEZ, Amiri BARAKA, and several other pioneering black voices took the vernacular of the African American community—its rhythms, images, and syntax—from a vital oral tradition continuing through three centuries and captured its energy, insight, and style with a book of poems that compelled a reassessment of conventional poetic criteria. Combining an imaginative utilization of some of the most supple elements of spoken "Black English" with a deep understanding of significant cultural currents in black American life, M. brought a sensibility previously submerged into the public consciousness.

Recalling his early education, M. comments that "I grew up in white studies. Blacks were not present in the texts of the day other than as slaves." Even after he met Brooks at Wilson Junior College in Chicago, he remembers that "As much as I was reading, I discovered that these writers were telling our story, but they weren't telling my story." He began to self-publish poetry that he sold on streetcorners, gaining the attention of Dudley RANDALL, whose Broadside Press published *Don't Cry, Scream*—the title taken from M.'s anguished reaction to the death of John Coltrane—which eventually sold more than 500,000 copies. M.'s wit, spirit, and dexterous word play in this collection still seems fresh and inventive, especially in comparison to the prevalence of mediocre rap and hip-hop efforts familiar in popular culture that also draw on the rich body of linguistic inspiration M. utilized.

In accordance with his growing sense of self-awareness, M. changed his given name from Don L. Lee ("I didn't know what Don Lee meant"), choosing Haki ("just") Madhubuti ("precise," "accurate," "dependable") from the Swahili language in 1973, the same year he published *From Plan to Planet, Life Studies: The Need for Afrikan Minds and Institutions* with his own Third World Press. Operating at first from his own basement, M.'s commitment to "kill the rat of racism with a pen: writing and publishing" was realized in a series of hybrid books that he designed and produced for his unique publishing venture. *From Plan to Planet* was conceived as a means of moving beyond the purely poetic representations of black life that formed the body of M.'s early work. It covered African American aspects of identity and origins, and crucial items in a black cultural history and set a pattern of probing personal responses linked to a careful study of an area of investigation, which marked M.'s reasonable and accessible approach to issues. It was also the basis for *Earthquakes and Sunrise Mission* (1984), which was the first of M.'s successful efforts to move beyond generic classifications.

Concentrating on the difficulties faced by many black families, *Earthquakes and Sunrise Missions* offered poems celebrating a harmonious partnership between men and women, intermixed with essays explo-

ring directions for "black renewal" and poetic commentary on continuing African American concerns. The fire and energy of the earlier collections was undiminished here, with a softer, more lyric voice providing a widening perspective on relationships. M.'s employment of this multigenre mode was carried further in *Black Men: Obsolete, Single, Dangerous?* (1990), which combined essays, charts, tributes to black activists and artists, and poems, in a powerful, candid and illuminating examination of the state of the African American people in the U.S. in the last decade of the 20th c. Although ignored by most mainstream journals, the book won the American Book Award in 1991 and sold more than 300,000 copies. He followed this with *Claiming Earth: Race, Rage, Rape, Redemption* (1994), in which he celebrated the achievements of the black community while bringing a sharp critical intelligence to failures in the American social system for all races. The book's fourth section, a series of optimistic, spiritually moving assertions shows M.'s skills with language as undiminished, and his ability to make hard but fair judgments continuing to develop.

BIBLIOGRAPHY: Decker, J. L., ed., *The Black Aesthetic Movement* (1991); Henderson, S., *Understanding the New Black Poetry* (1973); Melhem, D. H., *Heroism in the New Black Poetry* (1990); Mosher, M., *New Directions from Don L. Lee* (1975)

LEON LEWIS

MAILER, Norman
b. 31 January 1923, Long Beach, New Jersey

A novelist and essayist, M.'s celebrity has sometimes eclipsed his reputation as a man of letters. Over the years, his name has been in the news more for what he has done than for what he has written. Nevertheless, he has been a highly influential writer of the post-World War II era. His major themes are the nature of God and the devil, mankind's relation to God and the devil, a search for the true source and nature of power, the problem of free will, and, most of all, the close examination of M. as representative American man.

M. was only twenty-five when his first novel, *The Naked and the Dead* (1948), became an international runaway best-seller. It is the story of a campaign to capture a small Pacific island during World War II. Replete with flashbacks reminiscent of John DOS PASSOS, it also explores the psychological, sexual, social, and political sources and abuses of power, themes M. has continued to be fascinated with throughout his career.

This novel was followed by *Barbary Shore* (1951), a very different novel in size and scope. Influenced by the psychological writings of Robert Linder and Wilhelm Reich, he created characters who are little more than thinly disguised symbols of post-World War II society's various elements as M. then saw them: hedonism, narcissism, and the bureaucracy of monopoly capitalism, among others.

With the relatively poor sales of this book, and the poor critical reception of his next, a Hollywood novel, *The Deer Park* (1955), M. turned more successfully, both aesthetically and financially, to nonfiction. In 1959, he published *Advertisements for Myself,* a mixture of earlier prose fiction and nonfiction, new essays, and thoughts about a projected novel he never wrote, unless *Ancient Evenings* (1983), a long, rambling novel basically set in classical Egypt could be considered this "lost" work. *Ancient Evenings* relates modern society to that of ancient Egypt as M. makes a plea for religious vitalism and explores once again the relationships between political, social, sexual, and psychic power.

In 1964, M.'s novel, *An American Dream,* was serialized in *Esquire* magazine, then revised and published in book form in 1965. This narration by ex-congressman turned talk show host Steven Rojack is based on an existentialist theology that attributes to man a share of the power of both God and the devil, M.'s two warring factions of the universe.

He continued his existentialist speculations in *Cannibals and Christians* (1966), a collection of essays, and in the novel, *Why Are We in Vietnam?* (1967), narrated by an eighteen-year-old soldier, D. J. Jethroe, on his way to Vietnam. Jethroe is a metaphorical microcosm of America and its obsessions with hunting, guns, cleanliness, sex, and machines. He describes a hunting trip in which he tries to become intimate with God by sharing what M. calls the "Divine terror" that not only mankind, but God as well, can fail.

In 1968, M. published *Armies of the Night,* a blend of factual and fictive reporting about the anti–Vietnam war movement. His next two books, much in the same vein, *Miami and the Siege of Chicago* (1968) and *Of a Fire on the Moon* (1970), were reportages and M.'s reactions to political conventions and the launching of rockets to the moon.

Executioner's Song (1979) is a work of fiction clearly and closely based upon the life of twice convicted murderer Gary Gilmore. It is a fascinating portrait of a man with absolutely no morals or self-discipline. His books after 1980 have received increasingly diminished critical acclaim: *Tough Guys Don't Dance* (1984), a murder mystery, *Harlot's Ghost* (1991), a suspense novel about the CIA, and *Oswald's Tale* (1995), a review of Lee Harvey Oswald's life and an examination of his murder of John F. Kennedy.

Throughout his career, M. has remained an astute political observer. His special concern has been the

effects of politics and society upon the individual. By the 1960s, M. was as devoted to reporting private fantasies as he was the broader question of destiny. In his later novels, national destiny and private fantasy are combined in a highly arbitrary eschatology. Perhaps taking his clue from the "new" archaeologists, M. has maintained in his latest novels that mankind is best understood not by its great events but by its offal.

BIBLIOGRAPHY: Cohen, S., *N. M.'s Novels* (1979); Foster, R., *N. M.* (1968); Leeds, B., *The Structured Vision of N. M.* (1969); Lennon, J. M., *Critical Essays on N. M.* (1986); Poirier, R., *N. M.* (1972)

SANDY COHEN

MAJOR, Clarence
b. 31 December 1936, Atlanta, Georgia

M.'s widest recognition has been for his role as one of postmodern fiction's radical innovators. M. first gained literary recognition as an artist during the 1960s as an editor, poet, and anthologist. His publication of *The New Black Poetry* (1969), an eclectic anthology of contemporary black poetry, inspired controversy among the black artistic community currently immersed in the debate over implications of the "Black Aesthetic" being espoused by writers such as Ishmael REED and Amiri BARAKA. M. objected to the idea of a single black aesthetic because it limited African America freedom of expression. In his work, M. sought to challenge the limitations of narrative expression through formal experimentation.

M. began his early artistic career as a painter. When he turned to literary expression, his interest in painting and visual art greatly influenced his work. In each of his experimental novels, M. continually reminds the reader of the limitations of the written word as a mode of expression.

With the publication of his highly controversial and sexually explicit novel *All-Night Visitors* (1969), M. established himself among postmodern writers. His antirealistic, metafictional experiments gained him critical attention as a postmodernist but kept him critically removed from other more visible contemporary African American writers working in more conventional social realism. *All-Night Visitors* presents the world of Eli Bolton, a black male struggling to find freedom, identity, and empowerment in an oppressive world through his sexual encounters with various female characters. The novel illuminates the setting of Eli's mind rather than presenting a coherent plot or chronology. Eli's imagination captures the violence of Chicago commingled on the page with the combat of Vietnam.

M.'s middle novels are widely regarded by critics as his most accomplished works. In *Reflex and Bone Structure* (1975), M. experiments with formal innovation to subvert conventions of the detective novel. The narrative becomes a story of the act of creating narrative itself, exploring the ways imagination alters reality to its own making. In *Emergency Exit* (1979), M. constructs the entire novel in blocks of prose, drawing the reader's attention inward toward the novel evolving rather than outward toward any external reality.

M.'s later novels contain more apparent connections to the referential world. His own European travels and lecture tours inspired *My Amputations* (1986), the absurd story of Mason Ellis, an ex-convict who kidnaps author Clarence McKay and usurps his identity. Drawing its Atlanta setting from M.'s early youth, *Such Was the Season* (1987) portrays an old aunt, Annie Eliza, whose voice shapes the narrative as she manipulates the language and events of the novel.

Painted Turtle: Woman with Guitar (1988) and *Some Observations of a Stranger at Zuni in the Latter Part of the Century* (1989) explore the Native American world while continually reminding the reader through textual interruption that depictions of other cultures are always suspect; we are always limited by our reliance on culturally commodified media (texts and language) to understand another perspective.

M.'s novel *Dirty Bird Blues* (1996) echoes themes of violence, confusion, and imagination explored in his earlier work. Manfred Banks, a blues musician in Chicago in the 1940s, grapples with racism and stiff competition in the music world and soon turns to the "dirty bird," Old Crow whiskey, to ease the pain.

M.'s novels continually complicate and subvert our understanding of language, exposing its limited ability to fully describe reality. M.'s work highlights how deeply human life is inscribed by language and how through texts readers can actively construct and create their own world as part of the reading experience.

BIBLIOGRAPHY: McCaffery, L., ed., *Some Other Fluency: Interviews with Innovative American Authors* (1996); special M. issue, *AAR* 28 (Spring 1994); special M. issue, *BALF* 13 (1979)

PATRICIA MONTALBANO

MALAMUD, Bernard

b. 26 April 1914, Brooklyn, New York; d. 18 March 1986, Brooklyn, New York

M. is a Jewish American novelist and short story writer who won both critical and popular acclaim in his lifetime. His major themes are the imprisonment of the human soul, the journey toward self-transcendence, and the individual's need for moral guidance. Many critics feel his unique prose style captures for English readers the essence of Yiddish speech. It is a style well suited to his often playful though always serious combination of mythos and realism.

In some ways, his first novel, *The Natural* (1952), was atypical of his later style because there are no Jewish characters, and because for comic effect he deliberately overrelied on the myths and legends of the Trojan War, the American Dream, baseball, Judeo-Christian culture, and especially, King Arthur, to tell the story of Roy Hobb's rise and fall as a baseball player.

M.'s second novel, *The Assistant* (1963), is far more realistic, using myth, that of the religious, sexual and seasonal cycles of the fall, resurrection and redemption, only as background. As the novel relates the love affair of Frankie Alpine and Helen Bober, it traces Alpine's spiritual growth under the tutelage of Morris Bober, a Jewish grocery store owner who succeeds morally but fails financially. If the Italian-Catholic Frankie Alpine becomes a Jew at the end of the novel, it is not a cause for surprise or shock; Frankie's conversion is really a confirmation of belief not different in kind from the belief of his childhood hero, Francis of Assisi. As always, M. is using Morris's "Jewish Law" as a symbol for the moral objective of any good man.

A New Life (1961) is a satire about academia as well as an exploration of man's social, moral and personal responsibilities, themes examined much more successfully in *The Fixer* (1966), a fictional rendering of the infamous Mendal Beiless blood libel trial that occurred in Russia near the end of Tzar Nicholas II's reign. In this novel, the protagonist, Yakov Bok, is arrested on a charge of murdering a Christian child to use the boy's blood to bake Passover matzo. The novel relates Bok's barbaric imprisonment and spiritual growth during his years of suffering.

Next followed a kind of picaresque novel, *Pictures of Fidelman, an Exhibition* (1969), consisting of six episodes, half of which had already appeared in book form, either in *Idiots First* (1963) or *the Magic Barrel* (1958), both excellent collections of short stories. *Pictures of Fidelman, an Exhibition* followed the hero through his misadventures in Italy as the Jewish artist and critic attempts to attach himself to, yet never becomes part of, Christianity and the Christian art tradition of Italy. He learns to accept his true place, both in history and in the present. This is a major theme in many of M.'s short stories.

The Tenants (1971) represented a departure for M., for it ended with little hope for self-transcendence for either of the protagonists. The urban setting is a metaphor for all of America's cities. Here, Harry Lessor is working on a novel when a young black writer,

Willie Spearming, moves next door. They cooperate at first, but end up destroying each other as their landlord's screams of "Mercy" remind us of what we all need.

Dubin's Lives (1979) depends less upon myth than any of M.'s previous novels. Middle-aged William Dubin gradually learns to separate from reality the illusions he has always held about himself. In *God's Grace* (1982), however, M. returned to theology, mythology, and fantasy in his story of Calvin Cohn, who becomes the last human alive after a nuclear war. He shares the world with assorted simians who first learn from him, then finish the job nuclear war did not. The book is more an extended parable than a novel.

Perhaps M.'s most memorable work was his short stories, the best of which combine whimsy and deep pathos in a style that has been compared to Marc Chagall's in painting. They often end powerfully with the protagonist gaining new insight about himself and about the duties each of us owes to others.

BIBLIOGRAPHY: Cohen, S., *B. M. and the Trial by Love* (1974); Field, L. A., and J. W. Field, *B. M. and the Critics* (1970); Field, L. A., and J. W. Field, *B. M.: A Collection of Critical Essays* (1975); Richman, S. R., *B. M.* (1966); Salzberg, J., ed., *Critical Essays on B. M.* (1987)

SANDY COHEN

MAMET, David [Alan]
b. 30 November 1947, Chicago, Illinois

Although M. began his playwriting career in the early 1970s, he achieved mostly regional recognition until 1977 when four of his plays premiered and a previous play, *American Buffalo* (1975), made it to Broadway. Not all of his efforts were well received at this time, but nonetheless, critics marked him as someone to watch, and he has lived up to his early promise. M. won a Jefferson Award for *Sexual Perversity in Chicago* (perf. 1972, pub. 1978) in 1974, and a second Jefferson for *American Buffalo* (perf. 1975, pub. 1977) in 1976. He won the 1977 New York Drama Critics Circle Award for the latter play, as well as an Obie Award. He was awarded a second Obie in 1982 for *Edmond* (perf. 1982, pub. 1983). M. reached another peak in his career with *Glengarry Glen Ross* (perf. 1983, pub. 1984), for which he won the Pulitzer Prize.

Not all of M.'s works have been critically acclaimed or commercially successful, though his prize-winning efforts have drawn attention to his less known works. In addition to those plays already mentioned, some of his best-known plays are *Duck Variations* (perf. 1972, pub. 1978), *The Water Engine* (perf. 1977, pub. 1978),

The Woods (perf. 1977, pub. 1979), *A Life in the Theatre* (perf. 1977, pub. 1978), *Lakeboat* (perf. 1970, perf. in rev. version, 1979, pub. 1981), *The Shawl* (1985), *Speed the Plow* (1988), and *Oleanna* (1992).

In the late 1970s, M. also turned to screenwriting. He adapted *The Postman always Rings Twice* (1979), wrote the screenplay *Malcolm X* (1984), and collaborated with Shel Silverstein on *Things Change* (1984). He also wrote *The Tell* (1986), and wrote the dialogue for the box office success, *The Untouchables* (1985). In addition, he both wrote and directed *House of Games* (1987). He has several well-received children's plays to his credit, a translation of Anton Chekhov's *The Cherry Orchard* (1986), radio plays, and works of nonfiction, including *Writing in Restaurants* (1986), *Make-Believe Town: Essays and Remembrances* (1996), *The Old Religion* (1997), and *Three Uses of the Knife: On the Nature and Purpose of Drama* (1998). He has also written for television. Obviously, one of M.'s strengths is his versatility.

M.'s work resists pigeon-holing because of its originality and because each play differs in some way from the others. One common element in M.'s works is his masterful handling of the contemporary American idiom. His reproduction of vernacular speech is flawless, but his use of language extends beyond the merely naturalistic or realistic. The rhythm and pattern of his dialogue often says as much as the actual words, and he has sometimes been linked with Harold Pinter in this way.

M.'s plays are full of people telling stories to others as a means of disguising the fact that they really have very little to say. His characters often fail to communicate, and when they come closest to genuine communion with another person, they are nearly incoherent. This lack of communication occurs between the sexes, between men in particular, and even between family members, notably *Sexual Perversity in Chicago, American Buffalo, Glengarry Glen Ross,* and *Reunion* (1979). Another recurring theme in M.'s work is the devaluation of the American Dream and the twisting of pieties and cliches to justify immoral action. M. is quintessentially American in language and themes.

BIBLIOGRAPHY: Bigsby, C. W. E., *D. M.* (1985); Carroll, D., *D. M.* (1987); Dean, A., *D. M.: Language as Dramatic Action* (1990); Kane, L., *D. M.: A Casebook* (1992)

DENNIS KEARNEY

MANFRED, Frederick [Feikema]
b. 6 January 1912, Doon, Iowa; d. 7 September 1994, Luverne, Minnesota

Although some of M.'s autobiographical protagonists experience wanderlust, they eventually return to their upper Midwestern roots. M. believed in the genius of place, that the land chooses people as much as people choose place. He called his terrain—adjoining areas of Minnesota, Iowa, and South Dakota—Siouxland, and he saw himself as a Midwestern counterpart to William FAULKNER, his goal to portray the stories and lore of Siouxland in 19th and 20th-c. America. The label Siouxland is a tribute to the Native Americans who lived there before white Americans came—and through them recognition of the role of primitive instinct to full living. For M., the artist in touch with the elemental (his Old Lizard) is best equipped to create significant art—a theme of his novel *Milk of Wolves* (1976), which contrasts city and country, civilized and primitive.

M. is best known in the upper Midwest and in the far West. He received his greatest national recognition for *This Is the Year* (1947), a novel about farming life, and for *Lord Grizzly* (1954), a rendering of the legend of the mountain man Hugh Glass. The latter novel belongs to his Buckskin Man Tales, five works that portray the history of the West from pre-white man times through the Wyoming cattle wars of 1892. Other titles in order of the history they portray include *Conquering Horse* (1965), *Scarlet Plume* (1964), *King of Spades* (1966), and *Riders of Judgment* (1957). Like *Lord Grizzly, Scarlet Plume* and *Riders of Judgment* are closely based on actual events and persons. *King of Spades,* the least realistic of the tales, borrows from the Oedipus myth. M.'s designation of the Buckskin works as tales suggests the affinity of all of them to the romance. Although not technically part of the Buckskin Man series, *The Manly-Hearted Woman* (1975) may be considered with it. Like *Conquering Horse* and the novella *Arrow of Love* (1961), *The Manly-Hearted Woman* demonstrates M.'s appreciation for the Sioux Indians.

The term romance also applies to *Morning Red* (1956) as well as to *Milk of Wolves,* works with paired characters, double plots, and urban and rural contrasts. M.'s fondness for such pairings is also pronounced in *Sons of Adam* (1982), his novel about a reporter and a pigsticker in a stockyard—the former in search of his twin brother who had died at birth.

But M. is more convincing with his rural than with his urban characters, and his novels of the soil remain an important part of his work. His first novel, *The Golden Bowl* (1944), celebrated those who stayed on the land in the face of the Dust Bowl. Although *Green Earth* (1977) may not have matched the popularity of *This Is the Year,* it presents numerous pictures of rural life in the early years of the 20th c. The novel is highly autobiographical, owing much to the history of the author's parents and his own childhood. Other works set mainly in the country or in a rural community

include *The Chokecherry Tree* (1948), *The Man Who Looked like the Prince of Wales* (1965), *Eden Prairie* (1968), two novellas, "Lew and Luanne" and "Country Love," and numerous short stories.

M.'s last three novels are also set mainly in rural Siouxland. His preferred time is the early years of the 20th c. *No Fun on Sunday* (1990) is a paean to country baseball as well as an exploration of community mores. Sexual themes, always important in M.'s fiction, are even more pronounced in *Flowers of Desire* (1989) and in the panoramic *Of Lizards and Angles* (1992). Both novels show M.'s increased interest in the female perspective.

Several of M.'s works reveal an autobiographical impetus similar to that of Thomas WOLFE. M called his autobiographical novels *rumes,* or ruminations. His second novel, *Boy Almighty* (1945), recounts a struggle against tuberculosis much like his own. His trilogy, known collectively as *World's Wanderer,* was more in the Wolfean mode: *The Primitive* (1949), *The Brother* (1950), *The Giant* (1950). But critical response suggested that post-World War II readers were ready for different fare. Although M. later revised the trilogy as *Wanderlust* (1962), he took a very different turn after *The Giant,* moving from the rumes to his first Western, *Lord Grizzly.* The doubling found in much of his fiction has a dramatic counterpart in his life: he changed his name from Frederick Feikema to Frederick Feikema Manfred. He had published his first seven novels as Feike Feikema. Although some readers will think of Byron's tortured hero, M. was playing with his first name as well as translating his family name. Readers may find his essential spirit in an autobiographical account of his early young manhood, *The Wind Blows Free* (1979). *The Selected Letters of M: 1932–1954* (1988) provides another window on M.'s life and philosophy, as do two collections of essays—*Prime Fathers* (1989) and *Duke's Mixture* (1994).

BIBLIOGRAPHY: Flora, J. M., *F. M.* (1974); Mulder, R. J., and J. H. Timmerman, *F. M.: A Bibliography and Publishing History* (1981); Wright, R. C., *F. M.* (1979)

JOSEPH M. FLORA

MARKHAM, Edwin [Charles Edward Anson]

b. 23 April 1852, Oregon City, Oregon Territory; d. 7 March 1940, New York City

Throughout his career, poet M. was far more esteemed by the general public than by literary critics. As author of "The Man with the Hoe," M. enjoyed national, even international, renown. His fame was such that in 1932, on his eightieth birthday, he was feted at Carnegie Hall, a glitzy event to which thirty-five nations sent representatives. Average readers were much attracted to a poet whose works expressed sympathy for the laboring masses and espoused such themes as beauty, religion, brotherhood, and peace. Critics, however, increasingly complained that his poetry was rhetorical, sentimental, shallow.

Instrumental in shaping M.'s poetry was, first of all, his mother, a religious fanatic and tyrannical parent. Even more influential was Thomas Lake Harris, a spiritualist, trance poet, and utopian socialist. Much of M.'s religious and social thought was derived from Harris. Other influences included such friends as Ambrose BIERCE, Jack LONDON, and Frank NORRIS. Finally, he was profoundly affected by the intellectual and emotional climate of progressivism.

M.'s most acclaimed poems are "The Man with the Hoe" and "Lincoln, the Man of the People." Inspired by Jean-Francois Millet's painting, the first of these censures the "masters, lords and rulers in all lands" for their exploitation and brutalization of laborers. The second pays homage to an American icon, a man possessed of "the tolerance and equity of light / That gives as freely to the shrinking weed / As to the great oak flaring to the wind." These poems provided the titles for M.'s first two volumes: *The Man with the Hoe and Other Poems* (1899) and *Lincoln and Other Poems* (1901). The tribute to Abraham LINCOLN never quite matched the popularity of "The Man with the Hoe." Nevertheless, in 1922, M. was called upon to read his tribute at the dedication of the Lincoln Memorial.

During his lifetime, M. would publish three more volumes of poetry: *The Shoes of Happiness and Other Poems* (1915), *Gates of Paradise and Other Poems* (1920), and *New Poems: Eighty Songs at Eighty* (1932). Featuring homiletic verses on the role of the poet, metrical effusions on the unity of mankind, and rhymed religious stories, these collections were admired by common readers but harshly reviewed by critics. The only late poem that attracted favorable critical notice was "The Ballad of the Gallows Bird," a lengthy, Bierce-inspired narrative published in 1926 in the *American Mercury*.

M. was not appreciably affected by the poetic revolution that was well underway by the end of World War I. While poets such as Ezra POUND, T. S. ELIOT, and William Carlos WILLIAMS were conducting bold experiments in free verse, finding inspiration in modernist movements like IMAGISM, vorticism, and symbolism, M. continued to produce sonnets, conventional quatrains, heroic couplets, and metronomic blank verse. While modernist poets tended, on the whole, toward pessimism, M. clung to an optimistic outlook.

M. lived well into the 20th c., but he is probably best understood in the context of the "age of reform," a period extending roughly from 1900 to 1915. So situated, he seems an imposing figure among those writers who promoted social reforms and humane causes.

BIBLIOGRAPHY: Filler, L., *The Unknown E. M.* (1966); Shields, S. K., *E. M.: A Bibliography* (3 vols., 1952–55)

DONALD D. KUMMINGS

MARQUAND, John P[hillips]

b. 10 November 1893, Wilmington, Delaware; d. 16 July 1960, Newbury, Massachusetts

Called by critic Charles A. Brady a "Martini-Age Victorian," M. is a novelist of manners in the tradition of Edith WHARTON, James Gould COZZENS, Ellen GLASGOW, and Sinclair LEWIS; M., in fact, considered himself "working in [Lewis's] vineyard." The connection with Lewis suggests the strong vein of social satire that permeates M.'s work; however, like Wharton, M. also celebrated the society he satirized.

M.'s parents were well-to-do, but the family fortune was lost in the "Panic of 1907," which forced the couple to move to Panama, where M.'s father worked as an engineer on the Canal. M. was left behind in Curzon's Hill, Massachusetts, where he was raised by maiden aunts and continued the family tradition of attending Harvard, but because of his public school education he was socially disadvantaged.

After graduation from Harvard in 1915, M. worked as a newspaper feature writer; his true apprenticeship as a writer of fiction began, however, with a short story published in the *Saturday Evening Post* in 1921. For the next fifteen years, M. wrote numerous short stories and serials that appeared regularly in *Ladies' Home Journal* and *Collier's,* as well as the *Saturday Evening Post.* This early work was an attempt, according to M., "to reconcile popular writing with art" but he "overstrained" himself in the process; his stories, while well crafted, "lack depth and significance, qualities popular periodicals customarily avoid, and almost inevitably they reach a happy ending."

Dissatisfied with his short stories, M. traveled to the Far East in search of new material. *Ming Yellow* (1935) reflected his fascination with China, where he observed that "form permeated every phase of personal conduct and governed every situation." Though *Ming Yellow* is an adventure story, it showed M.'s interest in the complex relationship between society and the individual. His next novel—which he considered to be his first "serious" work—*The Late George Apley,* is his masterpiece and a significant novel of manners. First serialized in the *Saturday Evening Post* in 1936, it was published in book form in 1937, won the Pulitzer Prize in 1938, and was adapted as a play in 1946.

In *The Late George Apley,* M. draws heavily upon his childhood amid Boston Brahmins. The novel is in the form of a memoir written by Horatio Willing, who has been charged with the task of editing the personal papers of the late George Apley. These papers—and Willing's linking commentaries—provide M. the opportunity to explore the tensions between the demands of a tradition-bound society and the needs of the individual. As a young man, Apley rebels against the strictures imposed by family and social position, but with his father's death he accepts the obligations of being a Boston Apley, and in turn deplores modern excesses. M.'s narrative strategy creates what John J. Gross rightly sees as "the central irony" of M.'s fiction: "his characters' failure to realize aspects of their own natures that are nonetheless apparent enough to the reader."

M. remained a popular and successful author throughout the remainder of his career, although none of his subsequent novels achieved the reputation of *The Late George Apley.* The typical M. hero was a well-to-do professional, with whom M. identified but who also served as a target of M.'s "gentle"—and genteel—satire. Critics have charged M. with writing formulaic, predictable novels, but such accusations fail to recognize that M.'s "Harvard man" novels are attempts to come to terms with the ambivalence with which he regarded his own heritage.

M.'s interest in the Far East was also reflected in the "Mr. Moto" novels, a series depicting the adventures of a Japanese secret agent and that inspired several motion pictures starring Peter Lorre. However, M.'s most significant contribution to American letters is as a novelist of manners, whose trenchant observations of a society forsaking its traditions are tinged with nostalgia, satire, and sympathy.

BIBLIOGRAPHY: Bell, M., *M.: An American Life* (1979); Birmingham, S., *The Late J. M.: A Biography* (1972); Gross, J. P., *J. P. M.* (1963); Kazin, A., *Contemporaries* (1958); Teachout, T., "Justice to J. P. M.," *Commentary* 84 (October 1987): 54–59

JUDITH E. FUNSTON

MARQUIS, Don[ald Robert Perry]

b. 29 July 1878, Walnut, Illinois; d. 29 December 1937, Forest Hills, New York

Although M. was a prolific and versatile writer, he is remembered as a humorist and specifically as the creator of Archy the cockroach and of Archy's friends. His other works include *Danny's Own Story* (1912), a picaresque view of grass roots America; *Dreams and Dust* (1915), a collection of poetry; *The Dark Hours* (1924), a dramatization of the crucifixion of Christ; *The Revolt of the Oyster* (1922) and *When the Turtle Sings* (1928), collections of comic stories; and *Love Sonnets of a Caveman and Other Poems* (1928), a collection of humorous verse.

Born Donald Ronald Perry, M. hit his stride in 1912 with his first signed column, "The Sun Dial" in the *New York Evening Sun,* where he created three very popular series. One group is collected in *Hermione and Her Little Group of Serious Thinkers* (1916), a satire on pretentious Greenwich Villagers. More popular even than Hermione columns was the Clem Hawley series, collected in *The Old Soak and Hail and Farewell* (1921) and *The Old Soak's History of the World* (1924). Hawley, the "old soak," wistfully recounts all of the social and artistic values of the saloon—an institution now destroyed by Prohibition. In the *Old Soak's History of the World,* Hawley tours Paris with his friends Jake Smith and Al the bartender, making comments with the mixture of ignorance and shrewdness common to uncultivated observers in American realism. In 1922, M.'s play *The Old Soak: A Comedy in Three Acts* proved highly successful.

Hermione and Hawley have become dated, but M.'s third creation from the same period, Archy the cockroach, remains fresh. Archy, a reincarnation of a free-verse poet, is driven by his urge to create, but can write only by diving head first painfully onto the keys of M.'s typewriter. He cannot make capital letters, of course, and does not use commas or periods. Although he shifts somehow from one line to the next, he makes some very strange line divisions.

One of Archy's friends, Mehitabel the alley cat, soon eclipses all the others and even overshadows Archy. These stories, like most beast fables, depend on the contrast between the nature of real animals and the personified nature of the animals in the fable, but beyond that they have the ironic, savage, and frenetic qualities one finds in some of the best humor of the 1920s.

Ordinary flappers pale beside Mehitabel. Convinced she is a reincarnation of Cleopatra, her recurring phrases are "wotthehell," "*toujours gai*" and "always the lady archy," as she describes slashing off the eye or nose of one betraying tomcat after another. She is reconciled to having her body float to sea on a garbage scow some day—a small price to pay for freedom. Because she is an artist, she abandons litters of kittens who might interfere with her calling. She makes up a dancing song while cavorting through the winter night to keep from freezing to death. Her adventures and Archy's are recorded in *Archy and Mehitabel* (1927), *Archy's Life of Mehitabel* (1933), and *Archy Does His Part* (1935). An omnibus edition with an introduction by E. B. WHITE, *The Lives and Times of Archy and Mehitabel,* appeared in 1950. Archy and Mehitabel are permanent additions to American literature.

BIBLIOGRAPHY: Anthony, E., *O Rare D. M.* (1962); Lee, L., *M.* (1981)

MARYJEAN GROSS and DALTON GROSS

MARSHALL, Paule

b. 9 April 1929, Brooklyn, New York

M.'s first three novels depict the female life span: *Brown Girl, Brownstones* (1959) covers adolescence; *The Chosen Place, the Timeless People* (1969), middle age; and *Praisesong for the Widow* (1983), late maturity. Her fourth novel, *Daughters* (1991), centers on the relationship between a woman in her thirties and her father, but in the contexts of the mother-daughter relationship and female friendships. This progression suggests not only the varying challenges to female identity but the thematic shifts in much African American fiction of this time span.

In *Brown Girl, Brownstones,* Selina Boyce discovers her identity in the midst of family strife and the racism of New York City. Waged with powerfully rhythmical, metaphorical Bajan English (the language of Barbados), her parents' war centers on money. Selina's father, defeated by racism, squanders money while her mother labors for economic security. To journey beyond the dichotomy of their values, Selina leaves for their homeland, Barbados. Her search for identity reflects that of other 1950s protagonists, notably in Ralph ELLISON's *Invisible Man* and James BALDWIN's *Go Tell It on the Mountain.*

In the 1960s and 1970s, issues of personal identity become inextricably mixed with cultural and political forces. Set on a Caribbean island, *The Chosen Place* uses emblematic characters: social planner Saul Amron, American heir to the imperialist tradition but simultaneously Jewish outsider, confronts Merle Kinbona, a native spokesperson for the oppressed. Saul learns truths about his own character and cultural heritage. Gaining self-esteem, Merle moves toward a more coherent self. Throughout, the strength and continuity of the peasantry contrast with the shallowness of the island bourgeoisie. The interest in cultural construction of personal identity links this novel to Alice WALKER's *The Third Life of Grange Copeland,* James Baldwin's *Another Country,* and John A. WILLIAMS's *The Man Who Cried I Am.*

Diverging from the earlier works' naturalism to use archetypes, *Praisesong for the Widow* explores the individual's place in his/her spiritual tradition. Avey Johnson, her true identity blurred by years of conformity to upper-class norms, leaves a Caribbean cruise to observe a celebration for the "old ones," African ancestors. Avey experiences a symbolic purging and baptism that allow her to recover her cultural heritage by joining in ritual dances. She recognizes herself as a griot, a chronicler of cultural and familial history. The work shares themes with, among others, Alex HALEY's *Roots,* Toni MORRISON's *Song of Soloman* and *Tar Baby,* and Gayl JONES's Corregidora.

Daughters melds the themes of *Brown Girl, Brownstones* and *The Chosen Place.* Ursa Mackenzie's mother is African American; her father, Afro-Caribbean. They are alienated and yet bonded by love. Ursa strives to separate her identity from that of her politically influential father without rejecting him. The novel explores parallels between black experience in the American South and in the postcolonial Caribbean. Like *The Chosen Place,* it opposes the viewpoints and standards of the black bourgeoisie accepted into governmental positions with only token power with those of the struggling poor. Several novels by African American writers, such as Morrison's *The Bluest Eye,* Baldwin's *Just above My Head,* Walker's *The Color Purple,* and Carolivia Herron's *Thereafter Johnnie* (1991), have explored the father-daughter relationship in terms of incest. Rather than accenting physical dominance, M. stresses psychological dominance, which she shows as part of a complicated relationship with more positive aspects, comparable to the presentation in Louise Meriwether's *Daddy Was a Numbers Runner* (1986). M.'s exploration of social class, gender, and postcolonial culture iterates the same theme as the Zimbabwean novelist Tsitsi Dangarembga's *Nervous Conditions.*

M.'s short stories, "Soul Clap Hands and Sing" (1961) and "Reena and Other Stories" (1983), reiterate the novels' themes of identity's connection to cultural context. Her essay "From the Poets in the Kitchen" (1983) emphasizes the female oral tradition's contributions to the contemporary African American woman's novel.

BIBLIOGRAPHY: Coser, S., *Bridging the Americas: The Literature of P. M., Toni Morrison, and Gayl Jones* (1995); Evans, M., ed., *Black Woman Writers (1950–1980)* (1984); Kubitschek, M. D., *Claiming the Heritage* (1991); Pettis, J., *Toward Wholeness in P M.'s Fiction* (1995); Willis, S., *Specifying: Black Women Writing the American Experience* (1987)

MISSY DEHN KUBITSCHEK

MASON, Bobbie Ann
b. 1 May 1940, Mayfield, Kentucky

"Writing is my version of rock 'n' roll," M. once told an interviewer. Just as rock 'n' roll speaks for the common person rather than the highbrow, her writing gives voice to a population not traditionally heard from in the work of the Southern Renaissance—that of the working class of the New South, specifically of Western Kentucky. Rather than decaying aristocracy, intellectual elites, suffering artists, or even enduring racial minorities, M.'s characters are drawn from the majority of the American populace: typically white, blue-collar workers with a high school education who live on the margins of class and even geography (what M. calls "the ruburbs"), where shopping centers and subdivisions are taking over farmlands. They live in the metaphorical borderland between pastoral agrarian ideals and mechanistic technological utopias, working in the mills and at Walmart, watching Phil Donahue and Oprah, and struggling with changing physical landscapes, gender roles, family structures, and economic demands.

Widely recognized as one of the primary writers of the New South, M. is associated with Raymond CARVER, Jayne Anne PHILLIPS, and Lee SMITH in her distinctive minimalist style and her celebration of popular culture. Both of these emphases have placed her in the frame of New Realism—sometimes called "dirty realism," "K-Mart realism," or even "grit lit." Some critics of her work suggest that in her attention to popular culture she fails to get below surface details; but like Vladimir NABOKOV, the substance of her work is in the details themselves. Rejecting the traditional mythologies of the past, she focuses attention on contemporary heroes like Elvis Presley, whose presence is evoked repeatedly in both her short fiction and novels.

Born in western Kentucky and reared on a farm there, M. offers a view of the working class from the inside. Though she pursued advanced academic studies, earning a Ph.D. from the University of Connecticut in 1972 and publishing her dissertation study of Nabokov as her first book, she rejects that elite academic class in favor or more popular culture—a self-proclaimed literary and class rebel. Because she voices concerns of those not in the mainstream of traditional literature, she has been linked with feminist writers.

M.'s first collection of short stories, *Shiloh and Other Stories* (1982), elicited praise for her poignant treatment of the complexity of the lives of so-called ordinary people and introduced her consistent theme: change and what we are to make of it. In the often anthologized title story, Leroy Moffitt is bewildered by the changes that he sees in his wife, Norma Jean, but he is not sure what to do as she prepares to explore her future alone. The story ends, as do most of M.'s, without closure or a neat solution—just the recognition that change brings with it the potential for opportunity and loss. The central story, "Residents and Transients," presents a related and recurring theme, the tension between stasis and flux, in a vivid image of a cat with one red eye and one green, like traffic lights. Her second collection, *Love Life* (1989), continues her perceptive chronicle of the journey that takes her characters from the farms of their parents' generation to the shopping malls and fast food establishments of their own, icons of popular culture that might satisfy their appetites for a larger experience. Unlike writers who have presented elements of popular culture and working-or lower-class members of society as objects of criticism or ridicule, M. refuses to condemn either the culture or those who enjoy it.

Her first novel, *In Country* (1985), was deservedly greeted with widespread critical acclaim. In it, M. plays with shifting gender roles in contemporary culture as she transforms the archetypal male quest for the father into a female one—seventeen-year-old Sam Hughes (even the name is of ambiguous gender) seeks knowledge of her father, who was killed in Vietnam before her birth. In contrast to traditional war mythology, her Uncle Emmett has been emasculated by that which was supposed to "make a man of him." Emmett, a Vietnam veteran, wears skirts, doesn't work outside his home, and suffers from acne that may be induced from Agent Orange exposure. War metaphors play against female experience when Sam perceives the threat of unwanted pregnancy as akin to sniper fire and when, at Cawood's Pond, she feels the nearest thing to combat terror (a traditionally male experience) when she imagines that she may be raped (a traditionally female experience). Sam's struggle to know the truth of her father's experience leads her in the footsteps of literary investigative predecessors Nancy Drew and Trixie Belden, whom M. celebrated in her early study of adolescent detective literature, *Girl Sleuth: A Feminist Guide* (1975).

Though reviews for M.'s novella *Spence + Lila* (1988) were less enthusiastic, the simple story about an older couple facing her breast cancer provides an important paradigm for how her characters construct meaning for themselves, an overriding theme that informs M.'s earlier and later work. In that epistemological framework, men typically construct knowledge by seeking the big picture from a distant vantage point; women, however, find meaning in a context created by the process of placing one event next to the other like pieces of a puzzle.

M.'s novel *Feather Crowns* (1993) represents a departure of almost one hundred years from her typical setting in contemporary popular culture, though it remains located in Western Kentucky. Based on the historical birth of quintuplets to an uneducated farm woman, the story follows Christie and James Wheeler's quest for understanding of this miraculous event. The images of Burger Barns and laundromats that are characteristic of M.'s work are absent from this scene of Americana, but she offers a picture of the relentless, grinding routine of a tobacco farm at the turn of the 20th c.—significant in its lack of nostalgia for the mythical idealism of the agrarian South.

M. continues to write fiction and to contribute regularly to the *New Yorker*. Her considerable skill in presenting accurate, perceptive portraits of both the psychological and social life of working-class America gives both voice and dignity to a people previously silent in Southern letters.

BIBLIOGRAPHY: Brinkmeyer, R. H., "Finding One's History: B. A. M. and Contemporary Southern Literature," *SLJ* 19 (Spring 1987): 20–33; Durham, S. B., "Women and War: B. A. M.'s *In Country*," *SLJ* 22 (Spring 1990): 45–52; Ryan, B. T., "Decentered Authority in B. A. M.'s *In Country*," *Crit* 31 (Spring 1990): 199–212; Wilhelm, A. E., "Making Over or Making Off: The Problem of Identity in B. A. M.'s Short Fiction," *SLJ* 18 (Spring 1986): 76–82

MARY MARWITZ

MASTERS, Edgar Lee

b. 23 August 1868, Garnett, Kansas; d. 5 March 1950, Melrose Park, Pennsylvania

He wrote more than fifty books, but M.'s reputation rests entirely on one of them, *Spoon River Anthology*. While one might hope that there must be an unacknowledged masterpiece somewhere in that vast corpus, in this case received opinion proves essentially sound. Otherwise a largely negligible writer, M. remains the author of one book that represents a significant contribution to the American literary canon.

The poems that became *Spoon River Anthology* began to appear in May 1914, but they were by no means M.'s first. He had been circulating poetry, published pseudonymously in order to protect his standing as a lawyer, for years. No one could have foreseen, however, in the conventional poeticalities of this early work the poet of *Spoon River*.

This is not to suggest that *Spoon River's* genesis is an impenetrable mystery. M.'s friend William Marion Reedy introduced him to J. W. MacKail's *Select Epigrams from the Greek Anthology*, which provided a kind of model for *Spoon River*, and it was in *Reedy's Mirror*, a periodical Reedy published in St. Louis,

Missouri, that the first of the poems appeared. During the gestation of *Spoon River*, M. also formed friendships with Theodore DREISER and Carl SANDBURG, leading figures of the Chicago Renaissance, an emerging force in American culture, with which M. himself would soon be associated in the critical mind. Finally, "The revolt from the village," the contemporary challenge to sentimental pieties about the American small town, provided a congenial context for M.'s work.

The first edition of *Spoon River Anthology* appeared in April 1915, an expanded edition in November 1916. The poems that make up *Spoon River* are written in a free verse that often descends to the prosaic; yet a strength of the book is that the prosaic often seems precisely what is called for. The voices speaking from the grave are those of the inhabitants of an American small town. A powerful structural feature is the interrelationship established among the epitaphs, as the understanding of character and situation we think we have gained at the end of one poem is undermined, complicated, deepened by disclosures in poems found elsewhere in the book. Living in critical memory as an exposure of the deception, repression, and frustration defining life in Spoon River, the *Anthology* provides as well instances of personal integrity, even of personal fulfillment; still, it is undeniably in its subversion of conventional values that *Spoon River* has spoken most eloquently to its readers.

The impact of M.'s book was felt immediately. Ezra POUND discerned in it reason to hope for a genuine American poetry. Critical reaction was not unmixed, but even Amy LOWELL, although she found the book offensive, noted in 1917 that *Spoon River* had been read by everyone who reads.

It is impossible to claim today that *Spoon River Anthology* is read by everyone who reads, but it is certainly read and, perhaps most importantly, read by the general reader, not merely by the specialist. The remainder of M.'s work, on the other hand, is largely forgotten. *The New Spoon River* (1924) holds some interest because of its link to the original, which it fails to equal in concreteness and dramatic intensity. M.'s unreliable autobiography, *Across Spoon River* (1936), which brings his life story only to 1917, is moderately engaging as a personal narrative. The poetic work M. himself sometimes called his best, *Domesday Book* (1920), offers a vividly drawn protagonist, but little else, to whatever readers it may still find.

That M. never managed to rekindle the creative spark suggests that he understood his own accomplishment in *Spoon River Anthology* too little to build on and transcend it. Only a revolution in taste would reawaken interest in most of M.'s work. Yet *Spoon*

River Anthology will survive, a flawed, cranky, provincial, authentic American classic.

BIBLIOGRAPHY: Flanagan, J. T., *E. L. M.: The Spoon River Poet and His Critics* (1974); Lowell, A., *Tendencies in Modern American Poetry* (1917); Primeau, R., *Beyond Spoon River* (1981); Wrenn, J. H., and M. H. Wrenn, *E. L. M.* (1983)

W. P. KENNEY

MATHER, Cotton

b. 12 February 1662/3, Boston, Massachusetts; d. 13 February 1727/8, Boston, Massachusetts

No other American Puritan has fueled both the popular and academic imagination as has M., whose highly complex character has gone largely unappreciated until fairly recently. On one hand, he has been stereotyped as America's "national gargoyle"—an execrable, neurotic, superstitious hunter of witches and persecutor of Quakers; on the other hand, he has been styled "the first unmistakably American figure"—an individualistic, erudite, urbane shaper of the American self. In effect, M. embodies both the best and worst that American PURITANISM has to offer.

The eldest son of New England's leading divine, Increase MATHER, grandson of the colony's spiritual founders Richard Mather and John Cotton, M. was educated at Harvard (B.A. 1678; M.A., 1681), and received an honorary Doctor of Divinity degree from Glasgow University (1710). As pastor of Boston's Second Church (Congregational), he came into the political limelight during America's version of the Glorious Revolution, when the Bostonians deposed their royal governor, Sir Edmund Andros (1689). During the witchcraft debacle (1692–93), M. both warned the Salem judges against admitting "spectral evidence" as grounds for indictment and advocated prayer and fasting to cure the afflicted, but he also produced New England's official defense of the court's procedures on which his modern reputation largely depends: *The Wonders of the Invisible World* (1693). As the Lord's remembrancer and keeper of the Puritan conscience, he wrote the grandest of American jeremiads, his epic church history *Magnalia Christi Americana* (1702). As a staunch defender of Puritan orthodoxy, M. persuaded Elihu Yale, a London merchant and practicing Anglican, to endow Yale University (1703) as the new nursery of Puritanism after Harvard had become too liberal in its teachings and independent in its thinking. M.'s interest in the new sciences and in new medical theories distinguish him from his American contemporaries. Elected a Fellow of the Royal Society of London (1713), M. defended and popularized the scientific

theories of Henry More, William Derham, John Ray, Thomas Burnet, William Whiston, Sir Isaac Newton, and others, and staunchly advocated a new germ theory and inoculation against smallpox in the face of the united opposition of Boston's physicians during the epidemic of 1721. Whereas Increase Mather had never quite made the transition into the Enlightenment, M. came full circle; he represents the best of early Enlightenment thinking in colonial America. His contributions to literature of the New England Errand are as diverse as his publications are prolific and inexhaustible. In all, he published more than four hundred works on all aspects of the contemporary debate: theological, historical, biographical, political, and scientific. It is therefore deplorable that M.'s reputation is still largely overshadowed by the specter of Salem witchcraft.

No single work of M.'s publication record does justice to his long, productive career in New England's foremost pulpit, but several representative types provide a glimpse at his overall achievements. The *Diary of Cotton Mather* (3 vols., 1911, 1912, 1964) provides a better insight into M.'s volatile nature than his recently published autobiography *Paterna* (1976), which contains many passages from his earlier work. M.'s *Diary* is a Puritan document par excellence, for unlike Judge Samuel SEWALL's more mundane daily journal, it focuses on his spiritual growth and pastoral progress—on M. as an instrument of divine providence in the world. It is therefore not surprising that for the early years he consciously recasts and "improves" his "Reserved Memorials" for the purpose of leaving a devotional guide to posterity. Of the forty-three years covered (1681–1725), only twenty-six survive—each beginning at his birthday. M. characteristically fills his early narrative reflections with solitary devotions in his study, with extraordinary visitations of his guardian angel (carefully delineated in Greek and Latin to hide his experience from the uninitiated), with his introspective descriptions of his shortcomings and vexations, counterbalanced with spiritual and mundane blessings—each leading him to renewed hope and specific actions to prove himself worthy of divine favor. The chronological coherence of his *Diary* to 1713 gives way to his grand Pietistic endeavor: to be fruitful and to do good—even to his worst enemies. If M.'s public persona in his sermons is overbearing and bombastic, his private personal in his *Diary* is modest and unostentatious: a doting son, loving father, affectionate husband, and caring *Pastor evengelicus*—fully aware of his own weaknesses.

M.'s mythic image still rests on his involvement in the Salem witchcraft debacle, by European standards a minor episode in New England's history, and on Robert Calef's libeling allegations in *More Wonders of the Invisible World* (1700). M.'s most important publications on the supernatural are *Memorable Providences, Relating to Witchcraft and Possessions* (1689) and *Wonders of the Invisible World.* The former mostly recounts the possessions and antics of the Goodwin children, the eldest of whom M. observed in his own home and eventually cured through fasting, prayer, and patient reassurance. While to modern readers the narrative smacks of singular gullibility, M.'s practical tests, careful observations, and—most important—sanative procedure in indemnifying the girl's excesses speak of his experimental treatment of the case. The latter of the two publications aims at several purposes. On the one hand, *Wonders of the Invisible World* is New England's official defense of the court's verdict and testimony to the power of Satan and his minions; on the other, it is M.'s contribution to pneumatology, with John Gaul, Matthew Hale, John Dee, William Perkins, Joseph Glanville, and Richard Baxter in the lead. Before M. excerpts the six most notorious cases of Salem witchcraft, he buttresses his account with the official endorsement of Lt. Governor William Stoughton, with a disquisition on the devil's machinations and on the best authorities that the subject affords, with a previously delivered sermon at Andover, and with his own experience at first and second hand. M.'s *Wonders of the Invisible World,* however, does not end without a due note of caution. While exposing Satan's plot to overthrow New England's pure churches, M. also recommends his father's caveat *Cases of Conscience Concerning Evil Spirits,* thus effectively rejecting the use of "spectral evidence" as grounds for conviction, and condemning confessions extracted under torture. What ties the various parts together is M.'s millenarian theme of Christ's imminence, of which Satan's plot is the best evidence. Robert Calef's accusation that M. and others incited the hysteria is perhaps unfounded, but Calef's charge of M.'s ambidextrous disposition seems warranted. For while M. defends the court's verdict and the government's position, he also voices his great discomfort with the court's procedure in the matter. *Wonders of the Invisible World* appeared in print just when the trials were halting, but it remains, in M.'s own words, "that reviled Book," a bane to his name.

M.'s most enduring and, at once, most famous legacy is his Puritan epic *Magnalia Christi Americana* (1702), an ecclesiastical history of New England in the contemporary tradition of providence literature. In seven books of uneven length, M. commemorates on an epic scale virtually every aspect of New England's formative period (1620–98): the great migration and early settlement; the political and religious leaders and their achievements; the history of Harvard, its laws, benefactors, and important graduates; the tenets of New England's congregational churches, their polity,

synods, and schisms; the conversion of the Indians and their wars, execution of felons, and supernatural visitations; and finally, the divisive sects from Antinomians, Familists, Anabaptists, and Quakers and their subversion of the established order. From a literary point of view, M.'s Plutarchan biographies of New England's governors and ministers are of greatest interest. Puritan heroes are juxtaposed with heroes of classical and biblical antiquity, with the former surpassing the latter by emulating their outstanding characteristics. Even though each life follows the pattern of medieval hagiography, M. does not fail to mention some of his heroes' shortcomings and how they transcended them. Since its appearance, *Magnalia Christi Americana* has been criticized for its lack of thematic unity, bombastic style, and undigested material. However flawed by modern standards, each of the seven books develops a specific theme, unified by M.'s Virgilian theme of the mighty works of Christ in the Western hemisphere; M.'s baroque style—though outdated by contemporary standards—is entirely consistent with his own stylistic principles delineated in *Manuductio and Ministerium* (1726): to entertain with stylistic flourishes while instructing with pearls of wisdom. Finally, M.'s consistent narrative voice and rhetorical intent unifiy the subject matter as the grandest of jeremiads that American Puritanism has brought forth.

Out of M.'s Pietist impulse and scientific endeavor grew three strands of works, the best examples of which are his civic-minded *Bonifacius* (1710), his compendium of the new science, *The Christian Philosopher* (1720), his medical handbook *The Angel of Bethesda* (wr. 1723/24, pub. 1972), his manual for the ministry *Manuductio ad Ministerium* (1726), and his hermeneutical defense of eschatology The Threefold Paradise "Triparadisus" (wr. 1723, 1720–27; pub. 1995). M.'s *Bonifacius, An Essay . . . to Do Good* represents the most comprehensive expression of his life's purpose: "*Fructuosus,*" to be serviceable to your fellow man. His long interest in the German Pietist movement of his Frederician colleague August Hermann Francke, of Halle (Saxony), convinced M. that specific practical advice rather than pious exhortations could engender social reform. As in his earlier sermon *A Christian at his Calling* (1701), M. opens with a disquisition on the Protestant work ethic, reaffirming the Calvinist tradition that works without grace are futile. His subsequent essays (chapters) address all classes of society and their various occupations: from parents and children to ministers, governs, magistrates, lawyers, physicians, merchants, and schoolmasters, down to servants (including slaves), outlining how each member can be serviceable to the disadvantaged in particular by serving the community as a whole. Among his most influential recommendations delivered in a warm and helpful tone are the benevolent treatment of children, gentle instruction of pupils, education for boys *and* girls, the formation of reform and self-help societies, and the endowment of public institutions by the rich—all of which had some bearing on Benjamin FRANKLIN in the 18th, and Andrew Carnegie, and other self-made men in the 19th and 20th cs. The popularity of *Bonifacius* and the pertinency of its recommendations can be seen not only in the many 19th-c. editions and many more reprints in the 20th c., but also in its many imitators and emulators, most notably Franklin, who acknowledged his indebtedness to this work long after its author's death.

In typical Renaissance fashion, M. was at home in virtually every discipline of human knowledge, ancient and modern. Though a theologian by vocation, he was a virtuoso of science by avocation as illustrated in his "Curiosa Americana" (1712–14) and *The Christian Philosopher* (1720). In the former, M. describes in more than twenty-three separate epistles his pseudo-scientific observations of the American flora and fauna, ornithology, birth defects, rattlesnakes, earthquakes, Indian customs, and many other American curiosities. Perfectly consistent with European standards at the time, "Curiosa Americana" also pioneers theories of psychogenic causes of disease and of plant hybridization, the earliest known account, which became the basis for the Linnaean system of botany. Like Increase Mather's *Illustrious Providences*, M.'s study of nature provides a rational foundation for Christianity, attempting to reconcile Scripture revelation with the new science. But unlike his father's earlier work, *Christian Philosopher* moves with ease between scientific explanations and theological justifications. In fact, M.'s clockwork universe set in motion by a benign creator (rather than the wrathful God of the jeremiads) comes dangerously close to early Deism, from which M.'s text is virtually indistinguishable. In this visible and mechanical universe, the work of Redemption is relegated to an afterthought, and M. on occasion has to reaffirm his own faith in the greater power of the invisible world, that sphere from which God's invisible agents interfere in the affairs of man. Beginning in Aristotalean fashion with astronomy (light, the solar system, comets), followed by meteorology and geology (rain, wind, lightning, gravity, magnetism, minerals), down to botany and biology (plants, reptiles, insects, birds, and man), M. develops his overall theme: the new natural science reaffirms rather than questions the glory of Jehovah. M.'s style is plain and direct, interspersed with his characteristic flourishes, and his tone is exuberant and self-assured. Above all else, *Christian Philosopher* demonstrates the adaptability of Calvinism to a new philosophy in

its progress toward the TRANSCENDENTALISM of the 19th c.

As an experimenter of medicine, M. was as qualified as any medical practitioner in the Old and New World, for he studied medicine at Harvard when his adolescent stammer seemed to render him unsuitable for the ministry. M.'s lifelong interest and solid foundation is apparent in this single, most comprehensive medical handbook in colonial America, *The Angel of Bethesda* (wr. 1723/24, pub. 1972). Its threefold purpose—religious, medical, scientific—is an outgrowth of his practical Pietism: to provide the indigent with a medical handbook in the absence of a physician. Yet M.'s *The Angel of Bethesda* is remarkable not for its singular medical lore, but for its highly advanced theories that are of continuing interest to modern medicine. Among still valuable recommendations are his prophylactic rules of temperate diet, physical exercise, and discouragement of smoking. His most enduring legacy, however, is his method of overcoming stammer, his benevolent treatment of psychiatric cases, his discussion of psychosomatic causes of illness, his immunological recommendations on inoculation against smallpox (eighty years before Edward Jenner developed his vaccine), and his disquisition on germ theory (animalculae)—long before Lister and Pasteur discovered their bacteriological approaches to preventive medicine in the 19th c. The warm, comforting, and understanding tone of M.'s *The Angel of Bethesda*, its clear structure and consistent narrative voice, are embellished in M.'s characteristic fashion by his entertaining wit, nuggets of wisdom, and occasional metaphors and puns.

In light of his scientific achievements, one almost forgets that M. was a pastor and minister first and foremost. Anticipating his imminent departure from this world, he hastened to write his *Manuductio ad Ministerium* (1726), a book-length manual for the ministry. His recommendations for the novice minister are as manifold and explicit as his Pietism is practical in its application and ecumenical in its spirit. Short on sectarian ideology, *Manuductio* embodies M.'s educational principles for the gentleman minister: next to the traditional classical languages, he recommends such modern languages as French and Spanish; he deemphasizes the customary curriculum of rhetoric, logic, and metaphysics in favor of the new Cartesian logic implemented at Harvard, and advises students to spend his time on the study of the Bible, German Pietism, medicine, mathematics, astronomy, the new science, geography, ancient and modern history, and biography, as well as music for refreshment and poetry for recreation. His revealing recommendations on style (not an end in itself but a means to an end), composition of sermons, and polished oratory evince just how far M.

had come in his old age: the minister of the future was to be above all a humane, liberal, erudite gentleman pastor, whose reformed Calvinism, humanistic scholarship, and polished grace did not neglect such practical matters as a balanced diet and physical exercise to offset the stress of his duties. In its tone urbane and convivial, M.'s persona is that of a benign *Pater familias,* whose lifelong devotion to the service of God had taught him many lessons. His theme of enlightened pietism, practical in its application, unifies the manifold recommendations of M.'s *Manuductio ad Ministerium.*

M.'s lifelong preoccupation with millennialism and its significance to his thought and work have only recently attracted full-scale attention. Beginning with *Things to Be Look'd For* (1691), he published more than fifty works in which eschatology played a major role, notably "Problema Theologicum" (wr. 1695–1703; pub. 1994), a ninety-five-page manuscript reflecting the principal issues in M.'s early millennialism; "Triparadisus" (wr. 1712, 1720–27; pub. 1995), his definitive treatment of his millenarian theories in response to the hermeneutical debate in Europe; and his "Biblia Americana," a gargantuan and unfinished critical commentary on the Bible in six folio volumes, fortified with synopses of the best hermeneutical scholarship of the day. Unlike his earlier "Problema Theologicum" in which M. advances an inchoate system of pre and postmillennialist theories, M.'s *Threefold Paradise* ("Triparadisus") is his most comprehensive study of apocalypticism. As a hermeneutical defense of revealed religion, M.'s discourse seeks to negotiate between orthodox exegesis of the prophecies and the new philological and historical-contextual challenges to the Scriptures by such European scholars as Hugo Grotius, Thomas Hobbes, Baruch Spinoza, Richard Simon, Henry Hammond, Thomas Burnet, William Whiston, and Anthony Collins. *Threefold Paradise* marks M.'s decisive break from the hermeneutical positions he had inherited from his intellectual forebears but also represents the culmination of his lifelong interest in eschatology, which lay at the core of his cosmology and which was the fundamental mainspring of his ministerial and theological office.

From 1720 to 1726, M.'s exegesis underwent a radical shift from a futurist interpretation of the prophecies to a preterit position—from arguing that several signs of Christ's return were still to be fulfilled to asserting that all signs had been give several times over. The structure of *Threefold Paradise*—like that of his *Magnalia Christi Americana*—seems hopelessly imbalanced. Part 1 delineates the history and location of the Garden of Eden as evidenced in the Pentateuch, ancient histories, patristic literature, and contemporary travel accounts. Part 2 is largely a refutation of psycho-

pannychism, that is, a rebuttal of the idea that the soul is dormant and a defense of the soul's immortality. Part 3 is by far the longest and most valuable discussion and covers in twelve subsections a variety of topics affected by the hermeneutical revisionism then taking shape in Europe: The tradition of a literal conflagration of the Earth, his defense of a literal New Heavens and the New Earth during the millennium, his allegorization of the conversion of the Jewish people, and his prophetic timetables calculating the millennial reign of Christ. In this late work then, M. emerges as colonial America's greatest theologian before Jonathan EDWARDS.

M.'s popular and academic reputation is still under the sway of his 19th- and early-20th-c. critics who perpetuated Robert Calef's old allegation that M. and others had incited the witchcraft hysteria. Only recently has this record been revised. Now theories for the outbreak of Salem witchcraft emphasize political and economic causes, social pressures, psychosomatic illness, and ergotism as the raison d'être for the Salem phenomenon. So, too, 20th-c. biographers have done much to reinterpret M.'s image and achievements in a more sympathetic light. His baroque style, derided by M.'s detractors, has become the subject of numerous studies; his rhetoric and typology have been appreciated in the context of the Puritan self and the American jeremiad; the influence of Plutarch and Virgil have been discovered in M.'s biographical and historiographical techniques; the continuity of self-promotion and self-construction have been established in the representative characters of M. and of Franklin; his Pietism has been traced to its German roots in Jakob Spener and Francke; his contribution to science and medicine have earned him a place among colonial America's Enlightenment thinkers; his eschatology and hermeneutic revisionism in his late work have been examined in the context of the philological and historical-contextual challenges to the Bible as prophetic literature; the construction of M.'s Puritan past as usable history for writers of the American Renaissance has been established in the works of Nathaniel HAWTHORNE, Harriet Beecher STOWE, and Solomon STODDARD; recent critics have evaluated and published a collection of M.'s verse in English; and finally, the impact of the Deist philosophy on Puritan providentialism operating in M.'s major work has been the focus of recent studies and in a new edition of M.'s *Christian Philosopher.*

BIBLIOGRAPHY: Arch, S. C., *Authorizing the Past: The Rhetoric of History in Seventeenth-Century New England* (1994); Bercovitch, S., *The American Jeremiad* (1978); Bercovitch, S., *The Puritan Origins of the American Self* (1975); Boas, R., and L. Boas, *C. M.:*

Keeper of the Puritan Conscience (1928); Breitweiser, M. R., *C. M. and Benjamin Franklin: The Price of Representative Personality* (1984); Erwin, J. S., *The Millennialism of C. M.: An Historical and Theological Analysis* (1990); Felker, C., *Reinventing C. M. in the American Renaissance: "Magnalia Christi Americana" in Hawthorne, Stowe, and Stoddard* (1993); Holmes, T. J., *M: A Bibliography of his Works* (3 vols., 1940); Knight, D. D., *C. M.'s Verse in Bibliography of his Works* (3 vols., 1940); Levin, D., *C. M.: The Young Life of the Lord's Remembrancer, 1663–1703* (1978); Levy, B. M., *C. M.* (1979); Lovelace, R. F., *The American Pietism of C. M.* (1979); Lowance, M. I., *The Language of Canaan* (1980); Middelkauff, R., *The Mathers: Three Generations of Puritan Intellectuals* (1971); Silverman, K., *The Life and Times of C. M.* (1984); Smolinski, R., *The Threefold Paradise of C. M.: An Edition of "Triparadisus"* (1995); Solberg, W. U., *C. M.: The Christian Philosopher* (1994); Wendell, B., *C. M.* (1891, 1980); Winship, M. P., *Seers of God: Puritan Providentialism in the Restoration and Early Enlightenment* (1996)

REINER SMOLINSKI

MATHER, Increase

b. 21 June 1639, Dorchester, Massachusetts; d. 23 August 1723, Boston, Massachusetts

No doubt, M., even more than his illustrious son Cotton MATHER, is representative of American PURITANISM in 17th-c. New England. As a leader of Boston's ministry, he became the defender of Puritan orthodoxy during its decline; as president of Harvard, he guided the college through its most difficult period; as a political figure, he secured a new charter for Massachusetts when the old had been revoked; and as a voluminous writer, he published widely on virtually every discipline that engaged the contemporary debate at home and abroad.

Born in Dorchester, Massachusetts, and educated at Harvard (B.A., 1656) and Trinity College, Dublin, Ireland (M.A., 1658), M. served during the last years of the Interregnum as a congregational minister in Southern England (1658–61), before the Restoration and his nonconformity to Anglicanism forced him to return to his native New England where he became a controversial spiritual and political leader until the end of his life. As teacher of Boston's Second Church (1664–1723), he staunchly opposed the Half-Way Covenant (1662), governing church admission, and Solomon STODDARD's open-door policy in the Connecticut churches. During his Harvard presidency (1685–1702), he implemented a new curriculum and championed the study of science. As New England's

envoy to the English crown (1688–92), M. negotiated with James II and his successor William III and obtained a new charter securing most of the colony's former privileges. However, the unpopularity of the Second Charter, his controversial involvement in the Salem witchcraft trials (1692–93), and his unpopular support of smallpox inoculation (1721) characterize the gradual decline of the M. dynasty and its waning political power in New England. M.'s wide reading, more than one hundred and thirty-five publications, and his endeavor to reconcile Scripture revelation with natural science evince his dynamic intellect as the "foremost American Puritan" of the second generation.

Of M.'s numerous publications, several representative types can be singled out. Like all Puritan biographical writings, *The Life and Death of That Reverend Man of God, Mr. Richard Mather* (1670) and *The Autobiography of I. M.,* published in 1962, reveal the Puritan penchant for didacticism—the former, a biography of his father as typological exemplar; the latter, M.'s autobiographical reshaping of the events of his life for the moral edification of his posterity. What emerges is a characteristic Puritan hagiography prominently recording those events of God's providence that led to the individual's conversion and visible sainthood, while relegating all other details to insignificance. M.'s *Autobiography* loosely consists of three parts. The first section (1639–85) is an intimate account of M.'s conversion experience—the contrite soul pouring over its sins and attaining inner peace through God's grace. But M. does not merely concern himself with his own spiritual welfare; rather, he juxtaposes his personal sins with those of New England at large and casts himself in the role of the Old Testament Jeremiah who bewails the apostasy of his New English Israel. Much less introspective and meditative is the second section of M.'s *Autobiography.* Here, M. highlights his public mission to England (1688–92) without taking credit for his vital role in procuring the colony's Second Charter. characteristically, the self is completely subordinated to God's providence, which uses M. as an instrument to preserve New England from disaster. The third part consists of fragmented entries (1696–1711) in which M. denounces—like the prophet Jeremiah—the backsliding of New England's rising generation. However, through biblical incantations and thanksgiving, M. rises above the gloom of New England's apostasy and finds solace in his continual reliance on God's providence, thus lending his work thematic unity.

Like most Puritan histories of 17th-c. New England, M.'s *A Brief History of the Warr with the Indians in New-England* (1676) fosters an American mythology born out of crises and rooted in the Old

Testament language of Israel. In M.'s mythology, specific events of the present are cast in analogous patterns of the past, with God's dealing with ancient Israel becoming a blueprint for how He would deal with His New English Israel. M.'s history of New England's war with the Algonquian King Philip (Metacom) is cast in the framework of a divine struggle between good and evil, God's elect warding off Satan's minions. What emerges is less an impartial account of the Indian war (June 1675–August 1676) than a Puritan mythology, couched in Old Testament parallels and shaped in the style of biblical lamentations. M.'s history bewails New England's departure from its original Errand for which apostasy God uses Satan's Indian allies as a punishing rod to chastize His backsliding children. This theme not only unifies the various events in the book but also underscores M.'s didacticism: while the disastrous war signifies divine displeasure, God has not abandoned New England, for he uses both avenger and victim for his own purposes and, perchance, pardons where He seems most to punish.

Closely related to the Puritan histories and in many respects their rivals were the ever popular providence books of the time. M.'s *An Essay for the Recording of Illustrious Providences* (1684) is a case study of natural phenomena, from which he draws epistemological inferences. Covering such topics as lightning, thunder, magnetism, gravity, comets, as well as ghostly apparitions, demons, and possessions, M. develops a physicotheological assessment of natural and supernatural phenomena in an attempt to reconcile the new science with biblical revelation, the book of Nature corroborating the Book of Scripture Revelation. Throughout *An Essay for the Recording of Illustrious Providences,* M. tries to maintain an objective distance toward his subject by systematically classifying and accurately describing each phenomenon. Yet M. never fails to appeal to his audience's sense of mystery: each case is presented in narrative form, with a third-person narrator organizing his sources around the central allegorical theme of man's cosmic struggle in an natural and supernatural universe, sustained by God's providential intervention in man's affairs. M.'s achievement, however, lies less in his attempts to harmonize theological and scientific theories than in popularizing in New England the latest scientific discoveries of the Royal Society of London. Moreover, his discussion of preternatural activities of witches and their apparitions—a widely held belief at the time—cautions his readers not to mistake purely natural for preternatural phenomena. Like his *Cases of Conscience Concerning Evil Spirits* (1693), his discussion of Salem witchcraft, M.'s *An Essay for the Recording of Illustrious Providences* discourages the admission of "spectral evidence" in a court of law and

denounces torture as a means of extracting confessions. Though firmly believing in the existence of witchcraft and its deadly power, M. also warns of the superstitious imagination and its dangerous potential. Thus, both texts can be seen as the last vestiges of medievalism at the verge of New England's transition into the Enlightenment. Yet it is not M. who completed this transition, but his eminent son Cotton Mather, whose *The Christian Philosopher* succeeds where his father's *An Essay for the Recording of Illustrious Providences* fails.

Of his hermeneutical tracts combating the rise of philological criticism and historical contextual interpretations of the Bible, M.'s *The Mystery of Israel's Salvation* (1669) and *A Dissertation Concerning the Future Conversion of the Jewish Nation* (1709) deserve to be singled out. *The Mystery of Israel's Salvation* is his response to the wide-spread expectation of the return of European Ottoman Jews to the Holy Land in the 1660s. M.'s *A Dissertation Concerning the Future Conversion of the Jewish Nation* continues this line of argument, but specifically targets his European colleagues who allegorized St. Paul's prophecy of Israel's conversion by insisting on a preterit fulfillment of this event in the historical past. Any future expectation—so crucial to millennialists of the period—was therefore null and void.

M.'s greatest contribution to the literature of early America is, perhaps, his American Jeremiad, a homiletic lamentation of New England's departure from its original Errand into the Wilderness. M.'s *Ichabod; or, The Glory Departing* (1702) is its most representative type. Characteristically, M. Assumes the persona of the Old Testament prophet Jeremiah, whose chosen people in the New World are the antitype of God's ancient Israel; he reminds the colony of its Federal Covenant with God and threatens the Saints with divine retribution for their backsliding. In spite of its gloomy vision, *Ichabod; or, The Glory Departing*—like all jeremiad sermons—ends on a note of millenarian hope: the Almighty will not abandon His covenanted Saints if only they repent and reform before it is too late. Thus, while holding the rod of punishment in one hand, M. offers God's dove of peace in the other. The jeremiad as a sermon subgenre came to its full flowering in the decades following New England's Half-Way Covenant (1662), a response to the declining numbers of new church communicants. As a means to incite people to action, the jeremiad also flourished during the Great Awakening and beyond the American Revolution and Manifest Destiny into the early 19th c., when the pursuit of the millennium culminated in the Second Great Awakening.

Critics largely agree with Kenneth Murdock that M. is the foremost American Puritan of his generation, but they have questioned M.'s representation of New England's religious decline. The theory of declension of New England's piety was first developed in Perry Miller's *The New England Mind: Form Colony to Province* (1953), but it has been challenged by Robert G. Pope, whose *The Half-Way Covenant: Church Membership in Puritan New England* (1969) demonstrates that many of M.'s contemporaries did not take advantage of the Half-Way Covenant's benefits extended to unconverted children of full members, because they deemed themselves unworthy of its privileges. Not until the excesses of Salem witchcraft loomed on the horizon did virtually all of New England's churches adopt this new admission policy. Likewise, M.'s controversy with Solomon Stoddard over the Lord's Supper has been challenged by J. P. Walsh, who asserts that in their controversy over the Lord's Supper and church membership the two clergymen had much more in common than modern critics tend to allow. More recently, Stephen Arch has extended the arguments of Miller, Sacvan Bercovitch, Emory Elliott, and Mason Lowance by suggesting that M.'s rhetoric created a usable past that could be invoked in his histories to validate his own ideological aims.

BIBLIOGRAPHY: Arch, S. C., *Authorizing the Past: The Rhetoric of History in Seventeenth-Century New England* (1994); Bercovitch, S., *The American Jeremiad* (1978); Bercovitch, S., *The Puritan Origin of the American Self* (1975); Elliott, E., *Power and the Pulpit in Puritan New England* (1975); Hall, M. G., *The Last American Puritan: The Life of I. M.* (1988); Holmes, T. J., *I. M.: A Bibliography of His Works* (1931); Lowance, M. I., *The Language of Canaan* (1980); Lowance, M. I., *I. M.* (1974); Middlekauff, R., *The Mathers: Three Generations of Puritan Intellectuals* (1971); Murdock, K. B., *I. M.: The Foremost American Puritan* (1926)

REINER SMOLINSKI

MATTHEWS, William [Proctor, III]

b. 11 November 1942, Cincinnati, Ohio; d. 12 November 1997, New York City

M. was perhaps the wisest, most honest, and most sophisticated poet of his generation. His work explores the pleasures and pains of experience with wit, clarity, brilliant imagistic associations, and a light self-deprecating irony. His poetry has W. H. AUDEN's intelligence and surprising imagination without the hostility or barbs. M.'s main themes focus on the experience of living, the passage of time, states of consciousness,

ways we deceive ourselves, marriage, his sons, weather, basketball, jazz, wine, and good food. His poetry delights in life's ambiguous pleasures without romanticizing or self-pity. M. was also known for his editing, teaching, and contributions to contemporary poetry. He chaired the literature panel of the National Endowment for the Arts and was president of the Poetry Society of America. In 1996, he won the National Book Critics Circle Award in poetry for *Time and Money* (1995), and in 1997, the Ruth Lilly Award from the Modern Poetry Association.

M. was educated at Yale and the University of North Carolina where, with Russell BANKS and others, he founded the influential magazine *Lillabulero* (1966–74). His early influences were Robert BLY and James WRIGHT and other so-called deep imagists. In *Ruining the New Road* (1970), his first major book, and *Sleek for the Long Flight* (1972), M. explores the unconscious, dreams, memories, and the surrealism of contemporary life. By *Rising and Falling* (1979), M. has expanded his vision, incorporating the facts of this world in a music of survival. The associations in this and later volumes are imaginative yet logical, the result of a meditative intelligence rigorously examining the emotional content of a life and singing in a sure voice despite the shadow of mortality.

In *Flood* (1982), M. explores the long, open, meditative form so popular in modern poetry yet maintains a tight control of his form and materials. Peter Stitt compares his accomplishment to the wit of John Donne because of the balance between the imagination and the intellect. M. translations of Martial, Horace, and Follain, some of which are collected in his *Selected Poems and Translations:1969–1991* (1992), sharpened his lines into an unstrained virtuosity. In *A Happy Childhood* (1985), M. examines "the story of our lives, lumpy with anecdote." He evokes the evasions of Freudian psychology in elegant pieces such as "The Interpretation of Dreams," and "The Psychopathology of Everyday Life," maintaining that all our attempts at describing our inner lives are studies in "self-deception and survival."

In *Foreseeable Futures* (1987), M. continues his examination of time, saying that the poet is "a student of the future and thus of the past." Though much of the book examines mortality, it is never gloomy or self-pitying. In *Blues if You Want* (1989), M. focuses his attention on jazz and music, a specialty developed throughout his career. His last book, *Time and Money,* is his most courageous, gentle, and accomplished. He has reconciled the losses of life with the joys, and like the blues and jazz musicians he admires, he has "hit the note / and the emotion, both, with the one poor / arrow of the voice."

BIBLIOGRAPHY: McCullough, K., "W. M.," in Greiner, D. J., ed., *DLB*, vol. 5, part 2, *American Poets since*

World War II (1980): 38–41; Stitt, P., "Poems in Open Form," *GaR* 36 (Fall 1982): 675–85; Stitt, P., "Wisdom and Being in Contemporary American Poetry," *GaR* 38 (Winter 1984): 857–68

NEWTON SMITH

MATTHIESSEN, Peter
b. 22 May 1927, New York City

M. has achieved significant reputations both as a novelist who experiments with the form and as a travel writer whose works transcend the limitations of the genre as he delves deeply into the political and psychological experiences of the people who inhabit the places and interact with the environments he describes. At times, his fiction partakes of the documentary power of his travel writing, as in *Killing Mister Watson* (1990), which has been praised for its effective evocation of life in Florida's coastal swamps. His ability to evoke human character, however, invests his nonfiction, such as *Men's Lives: The Surfmen and Baymen of the South Fork* (1986) or *In the Spirit of Crazy Horse* (1983) with the dramatic power and insight of the finest fiction.

M. spent much of his early adult life in and around the transatlantic literary world. He earned his B.A. at Yale University, then lived in Paris for a number of years, where he became a founder and fiction editor of the influential *Paris Review.* His early novels, especially *Partisans* (1955), draw on his experiences as an expatriate involved in the literary and political currents of the fifties. *Partisans* has been criticized for its preachy quality, but is representative of its period, evoking the political uncertainties of the early stages of the Cold War. It is arguable that M. undertook his travels, to remote or wild areas of Africa, Asia, and South America, as an effort to break with the social and intellectual milieu he had known. Certainly the experiences of such diverse peoples and places changed the character of his writing, not only broadening its scope but requiring him to explore areas of human experience unthought of in his early fiction.

M.'s nonfiction has developed from experiences in the Amazon, in the Arctic north, in the Himalayas, and in Chesapeake Bay—*The Cloud Forest: A Chronicle of the South American Wilderness* (1961), *Oomingmak: The Expedition to the Musk Ox Island in the Bering Sea* (1967), *The Snow Leopard* (1978), and *Men's Lives: The Surfmen and Baymen of the South Fork,* respectively—as well as Africa, the Caribbean, and the Florida Everglades. Each of these gives special attention to the human lives encountered. In several volumes, especially *The Tree Where Man Was Born* (1972) and *Sand Rivers* (1981), M.'s prose has been linked with the work of photographer Hugo van Lawick, producing books of uncommon visual beauty as well as literary power.

Both *Sal Si Puedes: Cesar Chavez and the New American Revolution* (1969) and *In the Spirit of Crazy Horse* (1983) represent unusual excursions into political conflict; the latter, in particular, created considerable consternation when it was first published. This narrative of the events of June 1975 near Oglala, South Dakota, involving a shoot-out between FBI agents and members of the American Indian Movement, was a result of a number of years of involvement, on M.'s part, in study of Native American religious and spiritual traditions. M.'s account of his efforts to investigate the truth of the events that led to the imprisonment of Leonard Peltier was suppressed as a result of a libel suit against him and his publisher, Viking Press. The matter was settled in 1991 and a new edition of the book was published at a time when many public figures were again taking an interest in the Peltier case.

M. has been especially praised for the power of his evocation of what may be a dying culture in *Men's Lives,* but he is best known, if sales figures are relevant, for his account of his physical and spiritual journey into Nepal, traveling with the naturalist George Schaller in search of the endangered snow leopard. His second wife had died of cancer shortly before the trip and M. was exploring his own spiritual condition as well as his responses to the mountainous world and the Nepalese people. *The Snow Leopard* won a National Book Award in 1979 and has become, along with its companion volume *Nine Headed Dragon River* (1986), a cult work for many spiritual seekers in the 1990s.

Three outstanding and distinctive novels compete for attention as M.'s best fiction. *Killing Mr. Watson* (1990) has most in common with his nonfiction, since it is based on accounts of an actual event, including interviews M. conducted with some survivors of the murder mentioned in the title. This book has seemed to some uncertain of its identity, developed in ways that detract from a sense of novelistic structure, but dependent on fictional characters and events that assure it is not documentary. M. holds a number of mirrors up to the events involved, with the narrative seeming to return upon itself, risking repetition and loss of dramatic force. Suspense is neither possible nor desired, however, in this narrative, and the reader must be prepared to explore with the writer the multiple perspectives that produce either a myth or a pack of lies, or a rousing good story.

At Play in the Fields of the Lord (1965) is the more conventional of the three major novels, reminiscent of Joseph Conrad in its exploration of the corruption of native peoples by the presence of insensitive missionaries; this novel never allows the predictable dichotomies to play out, however, and the complexity of the interactions between the native peoples and the outsiders is an admirable feature of the novel.

By far the most interesting of M.'s fictions is *Far Tortuga* (1975), a narrative that effectively eclipses Ernest HEMINGWAY's *The Old Man and the Sea*—arguably, much of M.'s other writing might be seen as corrective and atonement for the failings of the Hemingway oeuvre—as it explores the doomed lives of a group of men who fish for sea turtles. The narrative is presented in the rich dialect of the Caribbean, which may be daunting for many readers, and the very unusual narrative structure—fragmentary scenes, documents, monologues with very little of the linking materials expected in conventional fiction—adds its own problems. This experiment in representing the lives of people whose experiences do not conform to the Anglophone traditions of language or narrative challenges readers and writers to expand the range of their sensibilities. It is, in many ways, the most rewarding of his books to those who take the trouble to read it.

BIBLIOGRAPHY: Bender, B., "*Far Tortuga* and American Sea Fiction since *Moby-Dick*," *AL* 56 (May 1984): 227–48; Bishop, P., "The Geography of Hope and Despair: P. M.'s *The Snow Leopard*," *Crit* 26 (Summer 1985): 203–16; Dowie, W., *P. M.* (1991)

THOMAS F. DILLINGHAM

MAXWELL, William
b. 16 August 1908, Lincoln, Illinois

Perhaps best known for his long tenure as fiction editor at the *New Yorker*, M. has published six spare, poetical novels while contributing dozens of delicately wrought short stories to the magazine where he worked. M. has never garnered the fame or critical attention accorded the greatest of the writers he edited, including John O'HARA, John CHEEVER, and John UPDIKE. He is generally more valued by his fellow writers than by the reader at-large, a Flaubertian craftsman whose goal is to render the very texture of human experience. In ways, M.'s long association with the *New Yorker* has obscured form critics the singularity of his achievement in evoking the atmosphere of his blighted youth in small-town Illinois and in delineating the simple wonders in his characters' everyday experience in settings like New York, Chicago, and rural France. In his six novels, M. has fashioned an empathic realism of true moral fiber; he has settled his own literary territory, where he adeptly captures the fragileness of human ties and the mystery of love, the inexorability of social change and the strangeness of "ordinary life."

These same themes are exhibited in M.'s collected stories, *All The Days and Nights,* published in 1994 to critical acclaim.

In 1971, M. published *Ancestors,* a memoir tracing both sides of his family from its earliest ancestor, an 18th-c. Scotch Presbyterian settler, to the key event of his own life—his mother's death in 1918 when he was ten years old. The memoir represents M.'s attempt to get straight the facts of his life and his extended past. He has spent his career distilling these same facts through the alembic of his fiction, mixing information and imagination to reveal the truth concealed in his autobiography.

The treatment of family, origins, and loss in *Ancestors* reflects M.'s interest, when writing fiction, to narrate "The Natural History of Home." In M.'s work, the experience of "home," its sensation and its idea, cannot be separated from the sense of its loss, of "home" as eviscerated. The death of M.'s mother works as a structuring theme in four of his novels—*Bright Center of Heaven* (1934), *They Came like Swallows* (1937), *The Folded Leaf* (1945), and *So Long, See You Tomorrow* (1979).

The loss of the mother and its shaping thematic influence on the mood of place is palpably rendered in *The Folded Leaf* and *So Long, See You Tomorrow,* the two M. novels accorded the most critical interest and generally thought his best works.

The Folded Leaf examines life in the Chicago of the 1920s through the grieving sensibility of Lymie Peters, a fifteen-year-old boy whose struggle to come to terms with his mother's death structures his every perception of the world. Lymie forges a friendship with the athletic, admired Spud Latham, a deep, primitive bond cemented by their mutual experience of loss. The boys go on to college where they feud over a girl they both love and Lymie, distraught over losing Spud's friendship, attempts suicide. Hospitalized, he survives, reconciles with Spud, and the novel ends with cautious hope. M. admirably condenses the sensibilities of grief and yearning into a point of view that captures Lymie's ambivalent movement through the rituals of young adulthood.

So Long, See You Tomorrow is a comparatively short, spare work, giving the effect of stark, timeless myth. As in *The Folded Leaf,* yet more intensely so, "home" denotes the precarious domain of trust inhabited by two boys. The setting is Lincoln, Illinois, M.'s hometown. The first person narrator, nameless, is an older man, about the author's age, remembering a time in his youth when he betrayed a friend—Cletus Smith. He tells the intersecting stories of two boys, Cletus and himself. Each tale is tragic. In 1918, the narrator's mother dies in the influenza epidemic. Four years later, Cletus's father, Clarence Smith, murders his wife's lover and then kills himself. Isolated in between these bleak moments is the brief duration of the boys' friendship. Every day they wander the scaffolding of the house being built by the narrator's father for his second wife, the narrator's new stepmother. M. explains their fate by alluding to Giacommetti's surrealist sculpture, "Palace at 4 A.M.," in which two figures gesture from within a cage-like structure of bone and chord. Giacommetti's work implies the ephemerality of "home"; M.'s book is about this too but, further, about the yearning to restore "home." The day Clarence Smith commits murder, Cletus doesn't come to the construction site and the narrator doesn't see him ever again but for once—years later, when they mutely pass in a Chicago high school hallway. To atone for having snubbed his friend in this way, the narrator imagines the story of the Smiths, trying to reveal their inner lives as a means of conferring withheld recognition upon Cletus. Memory enlists imagination to do the work enabling literary redemption.

So Long, See You Tomorrow earned M. the William Dean Howells Medal from the American Academy of Arts and Letters—awarded for the best novel published in the previous five years.

BIBLIOGRAPHY: Bawer, B., "States of Grace: The Novels of W. M.," *NewC* 7 (May 1989): 26–38; Eakin, P. J., "The Referential Aesthetic of Autobiography," *SLitI* 2 (Fall 1990): 129–44; Maxfield, J. F., "The Child, the Adolescent, and the Adult: Stages of Consciousness in Three Early Novels of W. M.," *MQ* 24 (Spring 1983): 315–35; Plimpton, G., and J. Seabrook, "The Art of Fiction: An Interview with W. M.," *Paris Review* 85 (Fall 1982): 106–39

DAVID WOLF

MCALMON, Robert

b. 9 March 1896, Clifton, Kansas; d. 2 February 1956, Hot Springs, California

M. may well be the least known of the American EXPATRIATES who made their famous mass pilgrimage to Paris in the 1920s. Although M. was a prolific writer, he is now remembered less for his own writing than for his publication of avant-garde and unknown works that were initially unrecognized or rejected by American publishers. Aside from a few footnotes in the memoirs of the more famous expatriates, M. is now all but forgotten. Few prominent literary figures have made the transition from fame to oblivion so thoroughly.

M.'s start both as a writer and a publisher began when he moved to Greenwich Village, New York in 1920. There he met up with William Carlos WILLIAMS,

who would remain M.'s loyal lifelong friend and critic. In the same year, M. and Williams started a magazine called *Contact,* a forum for literature that dealt with the "essential contact" between words and local American experience. *Contact* published poetry and criticism by writers such as Ezra POUND, Wallace STEVENS, Marianne MOORE, Hilda DOOLITTLE, and Kay BOYLE, who all later became leaders in the American literary scene. *Contact* magazine was short lived, however; in 1921, M. married the English poet Bryher, the pseudonym of Anne Winifred Ellerman, and left the Greenwich Village scene for Europe. The motivations behind the marriage are still uncertain, as well as the reasons for the sudden annulment, but it was the generous alimony payment Bryher provided that allowed M. to start his own publishing company in Paris in 1923 and to offer financial support to many important expatriate writers.

M.'s move to Paris brought him into another important literary scene, and his acquaintanceship enlarged to include Sylvia Beach, proprietor of the famous bookshop Shakespeare and Company, as well as Pound and Boyle, who both remained constant champions of M.'s writing throughout his career. After M. started the Contact Publishing Company, he became acquainted with Ernest HEMINGWAY and agreed to publish his first book, *Three Stories and Ten Poems,* as well as Gertrude STEIN's *The Making of Americans.* These two authors, along with F. Scott FITZGERALD, however, were later to become M.'s fiercest critics. Part of this negative criticism was a result of M.'s insistence on publishing his own work without regard for strict editing or stylistic consistency. Although M.'s first self publications, *A Hasty Bunch* (1922) and *Village: As It Happened through a Fifteen Year Period* (1924) both received excellent reviews, the majority of M.'s other publications were consistently criticized for sloppy proofreading and lack of a careful editor's review.

M.'s writing covers a vast number of genres including poetry, short fiction, novels, essays, and memoirs. Of these forms, M.'s poetry is certainly the least distinguished. The poetry he included in *Explorations* (1921), a collection of prose pieces, as well as his two poetry collections *The Portrait of a Generation* (1926) and *North America, Continent of Conjecture* (1929), received less than complimentary reviews at the time of their publication. M.'s stories and novels, which have been received more sympathetically despite their inconsistencies in style and voice, alternate thematically between portrayals of his life and friendships in Greenwich Village, as in *The Hasty Bunch* and *Post-Adolescence* (1923), and portraits of life in the small towns of the Dakotas and the Southwest.

M.'s stories and novels are far from idyllic portrayals of American life. His work takes a direct and unapologetic look at its subjects and, in line with most of his expatriate contemporaries, reproaches an American society that blindly follows worn-out ideals. Despite M.'s criticism of his home land and his choice of a Parisian location throughout the majority of his writing career, most of M.'s prose remains explicitly American. The only collection that deviates from an American location is the highly acclaimed *Distinguished Air* (1925), which documents the summer M. spent in Berlin. Almost all of M.'s work adopts an episodic, plotless and fragmentary style, as well as a direct and realistic speech and straightforward treatment of first person narrative that reflect the preference for contact and locality that he and Williams shared during the days of *Contact* magazine.

M.'s most famous work is his rather impersonal memoir, *Being Geniuses Together* (1934). In 1968, Boyle published a successful second edition of this manuscript, including interchapters that document her own memoirs of the Paris days and fill in some of the gaps left by M.'s account. New editions of *Village, The Hasty Bunch, Post-Adolescence,* and *Distinguished Air,* retitled *Miss Knight and Others,* have also recently been released, which is certain evidence for the current critical revival of M.'s literary contributions. This revival, however, has been stilted as a result of the inaccessibility and disappearance of much of M.'s earlier work. Despite this inconvenience, as well as the continuing debates regarding the importance of M.'s own writing, few can argue against his importance as a publisher or ignore his influences on the expatriate writers who turned to Paris as an escape from postwar America.

BIBLIOGRAPHY: Boyle, K., *Afterword to A Hasty Bunch* (1977); Knoll, R. E., *R. M.: Expatriate Publisher and Writer* (1957); Knoll, R. E., ed., *R. M. and the Lost Generation: A Self-Portrait* (1962); Smoller, S. J., *Adrift Among Geniuses: R. M., Writer and Publisher of the Twenties* (1975)

HEATHER C. URSCHEL

MCCARTHY, Cormac [Charles Joseph, Jr.]

b. 20 July 1933, Providence, Rhode Island

Among the many fine contemporary Western writers, M. is simply unsurpassed. His innovative apocalyptic and epiphanic visions of the West, his talent for creating troubled but intriguing characters, his persistence in portraying the isolate's circuitous search for meaning, and his genius for narrative stylistics all make M. the preeminent revisionist of the traditional WESTERN.

Although reviews of his novels may be considered mixed, especially regarding his early work, critics and award committees recognized his talent from the very beginning and responded with serious reviews, writing grants, and literary prizes. M., however, is legendary for his refusal to grant interviews or accept speaking engagements; he allows absolutely nothing to interfere with his writing. Most of his novels take place in Tennessee, Texas, or Mexico and typically feature solitary protagonists on problematic quests; surrealistic and symbolic violence; grotesque twists of fate and character; and narrative language that is, at once, sparse and lyrical, concrete and figurative, familiar and alien, understated and exaggerated, realistic and romantic.

Blood Meridian; or, The Evening Redness in the West (1985), like many of M.'s earlier novels, features an extreme degree of violence for which many readers and critics have criticized him, violence that is characterized by its affinities with the grotesque and the absurd, as well as by its detached pervasiveness and its unquestioned inevitability. The novel follows an unnamed character from age fourteen to forty-three on his almost random ramblings through the southwest, most often in the company of the ruthless Glanton gang on the quest to exterminate all Indians and Mexicans. M.'s protagonist seems helpless in the bloody current of violence in which he finds himself, a participant who is neither willing nor unwilling but compelled and compromised nonetheless by the gang's and his own violent acts. Virtually incapable of responsible action, he seems a puppet moving to the will of Glanton and especially Judge Holden, the novel's central figure of malevolent power, whom he fails to destroy when he has the opportunity and by whose hands he himself eventually dies. *Blood Meridian* runs counter to virtually every traditional code and cliche of the Western, overturning and renovating the genre by deconstructing its conventions.

All the Pretty Horses (1992), *The Crossing* (1994), and *Cities of the Plain* (1998) comprise the the Border trilogy. Winner of the National Book Award and the National Book Critics Circle Award, *All the Pretty Horses* was a best-seller and made M. well known among the general reading public. Less grim and violent than his previous work, the novel nevertheless reflects many of M.'s consistent themes and characteristic style as it tells the story of teenager John Grady Cole's coming-of-age pilgrimage into Mexico with his friend Lacey Rawlins and Jimmy Blevins, a boy who joins them on the trail.

John Grady embodies all the good, old-time values that seem to have disappeared from the contemporary West and becomes a new kind of stoic, self-reliant figure whose conscience and gentleness balance his capacity for violence. *The Crossing,* the account of sixteen-year-old Billy Parham's three journeys to Mexico, parallels *All the Pretty Horses* in many respects, particularly in its coming-of-age theme set against the background of a changing West. Billy's quests embody traditional Western themes such as the search for freedom and justice, but they also demonstrate the impossibility of their transcendent accomplishment. *Cities of the Plain* unites John and Billy in the quest to recuperate Western tradition and lifestyle. For M., transcendence lies along the borders of experience as articulated in the shifting landscapes of language.

BIBLIOGRAPHY: Arnold, E. T., and D. C. Luce, eds., *Perspectives on C. M.* (1993); Bell, V. M., *The Achievement of C. M.* (1988); Hall, W. H., and R. Wallach, eds., *Sacred Violence: A Reader's Companion to C. M.* (1995)

PHILLIP A. SNYDER

MCCARTHY, Mary

b. 21 June 1912, Seattle, Washington; d. 25 October 1989, New York City

Arguably the preeminent woman of letters in the 20th c., M. produced a distinguished body of work in several genres—literary criticism, the novel, social commentary, political journalism, and travel writing. Her life spanned two world wars, the Vietnam War, the women's movement, and Watergate and thus gave her ample opportunity, as an intellectual, to comment on the country she alternately championed and derided. Perhaps the enduring theme of all her works is what Henry JAMES referred to as the complex fate of being an American—a fate she dramatizes in various guises. From her most famous novel *The Group* (1963), which explores the lives of eight Vassar graduates and the discrepancy between their hopes and the realities of their lives, to her last novel *Cannibals and Missionaries* (1979), which satirizes an American messianic liberal expedition to Iran to investigate the Shah's regime, M. examines the manners and mores of her countrymen in lucid and often pointedly satiric prose. Her contributions to American literature were recognized when she was inducted into the National Academy of Arts and Sciences in 1988, a year before her death.

Perhaps the central biographical fact of M.'s life was the death of both of her parents in the influenza epidemic of 1918, ending her idyllic childhood and beginning a life of rootlessness and travel. Subsequent early years spent with grandparents in Minneapolis and Seattle and in Catholic boarding schools gave

M. material for what some believe is her best work, *Memories of a Catholic Girlhood* (1957). In this clearly autobiographical piece, she documents her bleak years as an orphan and her failure to commit wholeheartedly to the Catholicism of her schoolmates. She explores the nature and sources of identity in her life, from the false identities thrust upon her by her friends to the similarly fabricated label the kind but obtuse nuns give her. M.'s often brutal honesty about herself and her characters emerges here as, from the point of view of an outsider, she deconstructs the microcosm of a girls' private school with its often painful social hierarchies—a subject she would revisit in her novel *The Group.*

M. credits the beginning of her fiction writing career to her second husband, eminent critic Edmund WILSON. Her early efforts had been chiefly essays and reviews written when she served as drama critic for the *Partisan Review* in the 1930s; but with the publication of her first novel, *The Company She Keeps* (1942), she launched a distinguished series of novels and short story collections including two of her best-known works, *The Groves of Academe* (1952) and *A Charmed Life* (1955), satires of academic and artistic communities, respectively. *The Groves of Academe,* set in a progressive college in Pennsylvania during the Joseph McCarthy era, concerns the well-intentioned dismissal of a literature professor for his communist leanings and the surprising turn of events a liberal college president does not anticipate. In *A Charmed Life,* the Jocelyn College of *The Groves of Academe* becomes the artistic community of New Leeds, a New England village of hard-drinking, inbred intellectuals some critics saw as a veiled description of the *Partisan Review* crowd M. knew so well. In these two works, M. satirizes the pitfalls of group identity, the shortsightedness and moral failings of the liberalism of her day, and the unconscious elitism of self-appointed academic and artistic utopias.

M. was ahead of her time in her frank and honest treatment of sexuality, and in novels like *The Group,* her analysis of the nature of a female community. Though she resisted the essentializing label of "woman writer" and scorned what she saw as the self-pity and victimization of professed feminists, M. deals sensitively and intelligently with the lives of her young heroines, many of whom echo their creator's own life. Throughout her writing career, she did not hesitate to make public pronouncements on political issues such as our involvement in the Vietnam conflict, and the crisis of confidence marked by Watergate. Her 1987 memoir, *How I Grew,* published two years before her death, documents M.'s long and productive intellectual and artistic life.

BIBLIOGRAPHY: Auchincloss, L., *Pioneers and Caretakers: A Study of Nine American Women Writers*

(1965); Brightman, C., *Writing Dangerously: M. M. and Her World* (1992); Gelderman, C., *M. M.: A Life* (1988); Grumbach, D., *The Company She Kept* (1967); Hardwick, E., *A View of My Own* (1963)

MARY ANN WILSON

McCLATCHY, J[oseph] D[onald, Jr.]
b. 12 August 1945, Bryn Mawr, Pennsylvania

M. is best known as a poet of dazzling literary style, layering complex levels of meaning within sumptuous, learned language and traditional verse forms. While not directly associated with the New Formalist school, M. does share with his models James MERRILL, Robert LOWELL, and John HOLLANDER a desire to give a modern accent to traditional technique. His ornate technical surface invention is often criticized for overwhelming his reflections on deeper human experience, but the observations on life and art that do emerge are usually brilliant.

In his first collection of poems, *Scenes from Another Life* (1981), M. weaves elegantly between natural and imagined landscapes, exploring the boundaries between the real and the poetically-conceived. These poems demonstrate his interest in the capacity of a poem "to depart from itself into formal surprises or layered meanings or into a new topography of image." But while the clever formal artifice in this and his next volume, *Stars Principal* (1986), has been criticized for obscuring many poems' emotional and narrative depths, rich intellectual and emotional layers often arise from their controlling metaphors. "Scenes from Another Life," for example, meditates on art and the power of the imagination from the new perspective a lost love affair affords the speaker, and "At a Reading" considers the aesthetic and emotional relationships among a poet, the characters in his poem, and a deaf member of his audience who receives the poem in translation.

His later volume *The Rest of the Way* (1990) again displays his poetic virtuosity in poems such as "An Alphabet of Anger," a series of rhyming tercets that move through all letters of the alphabet. But this volume also received acclaim for melding formal mastery and narrative subtlety, forging a middle ground between formalism and discursive verse. Using less self-conscious, but no less complex, stylistic techniques, M. achieved a haunting tone in new poems exploring death and power. *"Medea* in Tokyo" employs sophisticated word-play to interweave the real and artistic more fatalistically than he attempted in earlier works, and the sonnet sequence "Kilim," while intricately interlocking lines of individual poems in the form of

a crown, is also a meditation on violence and art set in the terrorism of the Middle East.

M.'s critical work *White Paper: On Contemporary American Poetry* (1989) was heralded by Harold BLOOM as "the most lucid and aesthetically reliable guide to what is most valuable in contemporary American poetry." Through case studies of poets who challenge "middlebrow expectations brought to poetry over the last thirty years," the book argues that *"voice is our most immediate, and may be our most lasting, source of pleasure in a poem."* While critics question M.'s implication that poetry serves as guardian of an abstracted, ahistorical self and his inadequate explanation of the standards of taste that distinguish a "middlebrow" audience from an audience of "right readers," even the book's detractors admit that his studies of diverse mainstream poets offer lucid observations that occasionally upset accepted opinions and categories. M.'s criticism, like his poetry, is always imbued with a sense of tradition, but his concern with the details of language and poetic interpretation keeps his work innovative and surprising.

BIBLIOGRAPHY: Breslin, P., "Poetry, Criticism, and the World," *Poetry* 156 (August 1990), 297–308; Finkelstein, N., "Form-Fitting Criticism," *GaR* 45 (Winter 1991): 787–91

LINDA COX

MCCLURE, Michael
b. 30 October 1932, Marysville, Kansas

M. is one of America's most prolific poets and playwrights. He is considered both a Beat poet and also a member of the San Francisco Renaissance group. He has published well over fifty volumes of poetry, forty plays, five books of essays, and two novels. Though educated at the University of Wichita, the University of Arizona, and San Francisco State, he found his greatest influences in his own reading and his association with certain key literary figures, mostly in San Francisco: Robert CREELEY, Robert DUNCAN, Allen GINSBERG, Charles OLSON, Philip WHALEN, and Gary SNYDER. He made his dramatic public debut as a poet at the Six Gallery on October 13, 1955, alongside of Ginsberg, who first read *Howl* on that evening.

M.'s past spiritual influences include William Blake, Percy Bysshe Shelley, Charles Baudelaire, E. E. CUMMINGS, D. H. Lawrence, and the mystical writings of Emanuel Swedenborg. His interest in science, especially biology, played a crucial role in the formulation of his individualized poetics. In his *Meat Science Essays* (1966), he defines his conception of human nature: "that matter is spirit and the meat is the container." He refuses to dichotomize matter and spirit, and blames such destructive dichotomies for separating human consciousness from its biological origins. It is through mankind's inability to recognize that it is part of nature that has caused the present-day environmental disasters that plague the planet.

M. considers himself a shaman-activist, whose major function is to enact the Dionysian energies that an overly industrialized technology has repressed in human beings. He hoped, by the power of his bardic voice, to release what he calls the "beast spirit" hidden in the human soul. As one of the 20th c.'s most romantic poets, he views his work as a continuation of Blake's project to reawaken the poetic imagination within each human being. And he has consciously employed the bardic voice of Blake's prophetic poems to heighten the seriousness of his poetic purpose. One of M.'s most dramatic demonstrations of the importance of reconnecting human beings with their animal natures was his appearance at the Lion House at the San Francisco Zoo in 1964. He read selections of his *Ghost Tantras* to the lions and they responded with their own unique lion voices. He had created what he called "beast language" poems—a combination of words and animal sounds that somehow engaged the lions' attention. M. then began to organize his poems on the page according to the bilateral symmetry of the skeletal structure of vertebrates, a species that includes human beings. M. combined, in a truly radical way, his beast language with biographological grids to produce his own unique poetic forms.

His poetry was also heavily influenced by some of the "action painters" of the early 1950s, whose drips, spatters, and abstractions gave M. a model for his poetry as a purely spontaneous and symbolic gesture. But all of his poems and plays adhere to his consistent belief that human creativity is grounded in the mammalian animal and that the imagination is, at base, an animistic system. Several of his most popular collections of poetry, *Hymns to St. Geryon and Other Poems* (1979), *Star* (1970), and *September Blackberries* (1974), vividly demonstrate his unique use of biopesis or, what some have called, bioalchemical consciousness. And many of the poems in these collections combine the bardic voice of Blake and Shelley with the mantric voice of Tibetan Buddhism.

But it is in his role as a playwright that has made M. one of the most popular radical artists of the second half of the 20th c. He took as his model the "theater of cruelty" of French dramatist Antonin Artaud. M. also sees Artaud's insanity participating in the "holy madness" of great visionary poets, like Blake and Christopher Smart. His first major production *The Beard* (1965) featured both Billie the Kid and Jean Harlow as authentic American folk heroes. His other absurdist plays *Spider Rabbit* (1971) and *Gorf* (1976) show the unmistakable surrealist influences of Samuel Beckett, Eugène Ionesco, and especially Jean Genet, and are some of contemporary American theater's most powerful biopolitical theater. The main character Gorf, in the play of the same name, is a winged phallus who attempts to help Mert and Gert find their lost child in the spiritual wasteland of American materialism.

M.'s collection called *Star* contains a long poem entitled "The Surge," a work that is more than simply a symbolic gesture; it embodies the activity of its title. The poem becomes the surge of animistic life when read, becoming an object that testifies to the sacredness of genetic material. Few poems of his express so cogently his absolute belief in the mammalian, and therefore, holy substructure of human consciousness.

BIBLIOGRAPHY: Davidson, M., *The San Francisco Renaissance* (1989); French, W., *The San Francisco Poetry Renaissance* (1991); King, W. R., "M. M.," in Charters, A., ed., *DLB*, vol. 16, part 2, *The Beats: Literary Bohemians in Postwar America* (1983): 382–400

PATRICK MEANOR

MCCORKLE, Jill [Collins]

b. 7 July 1958, Lumberton, North Carolina

M. is among a growing number of Southern women writers gaining national recognition for their ability to capture the telling details of ordinary small-town lives that illustrate larger human truths. M.'s stories are generally set in towns similar to the Lumberton in which she grew up, towns in which everyone knows everyone else and in which opportunities for achievement and adventure are limited. Her main characters are people who chafe at the lack of privacy and of opportunities for individual expression that these small communities present. In their mostly rebellious struggles with these circumstances, they usually come to an awareness of the values and support provided by the closeness of the community, finally understanding the positive nature of such an environment.

In something of a literary coup, M.'s first two novels were published simultaneously by Algonquin Press in 1984. Written first, *The Cheer Leader* describes the triumphant senior year in high school of Jo Spencer, followed by her disastrous freshman year in college. In contrast, displaying a literary versatility that many critics admired, *July 7th,* shifts gears and has a male protagonist who is one of many narrative perspectives about events in the town of Marshboro, North Carolina, on July 7, 1983. As an aspiring writer, Sam tries to imagine the lives of the people he meets, a literary device that enables M. to explore the lives of the community. This novel ends more optimistically than *The Cheer Leader,* which was somewhat inconclusive about Jo's future, as Sam has acquired a new sense of the connectedness of community members and a respect for individual differences.

M.'s third novel, *Tending to Virginia* (1987), features a chronologically older main character than Jo or Sam who is, nonetheless, emotionally immature. Virginia Turner Ballard, known as Ginny Sue to her family, chafes under the burden of late pregnancy, complicated by her doubts about the devotion of her husband. Seeking answers, she makes a pilgrimage to her grandmother. During the visit, Ginny is stricken with toxemia and needs to remain bedridden. The women of the family gather to tend to Virginia and to talk about the family's past history. Hearing the women's stories heals Virginia in body and in spirit as she becomes aware of the common threads in their lives and the bonds of love that connect them.

With *Ferris Beach* (1990), M. attempts a broader canvas, following the life of Kate Burns from childhood through adolescence into early adulthood. As with *Tending to Virginia,* this novel spans generations but includes a wider range of women characters. When the Rhodes family moves across the street, Kate finds a best friend in Misty Rhodes. The Rhodes, especially Misty's mother Mo, represent modern lower-middle-class flamboyance in the face of Kate's mother's conservative upper-middle-class traditionalism. This coming of age tale has another dimension in the lure of Ferris Beach, a rather tawdry resort that, in Kate's memories and dreams, assumes magical qualities. A visit to her mysterious cousin Angela disillusions Kate and enables her to reconcile with her mother after the death of her father.

The volume of short stories *Crash Diet* (1992) explores the anxieties and triumphs of women at various stages in their development. Although most of these women are well past adolescence, like adolescents they are working to come to terms with the realities of lives that have turned out in other than fairy tale fashion, reinforcing M.'s persistent theme of the resilience of the individual to develop despite social constraints and personal mistakes.

This theme takes on a somewhat different color in *Carolina Moon* (1996) when M. examines the life of Quee Purdy, in her sixties, from its past mistakes and hopes and its present machinations in the lives of her daughter and other community members. A narrative innovation has Quee tell of her past in letters to a dead lover. The cost of past mistakes loom larger in this story, but M. retains her hopeful tone.

M.'s depictions of ordinary contemporary Southern women continue to ring true as she experiments with the scope of the stories, the methods of narration, and the ages of her protagonists.

BIBLIOGRAPHY: Bloom, L. Z., "J. M.," in Flora, J. M., and R. Bain, eds., *Contemporary Fiction Writers of the South: A Bio-Biographical Sourcebook* (1993): 295–302; Lesserm E., "Voices with Stories to Tell: A Conversation with J. M.," *SoR* 26 (Winter 1990): 53–64

HARRIETTE C. BUCHANAN

MCCULLERS, Carson [Lulu Carson Smith]

b. 19 February 1917, Columbus, Georgia; d. 29 September 1967, Nyack, New York

M. wrote novels, novellas, short stories, plays, and some poetry. She published four novels and the play, *The Member of the Wedding* (1946), in rapid succession between 1940 and 1946. Each of the novels sold over a half-million copies, and the play ran for 501 performances on Broadway and won, in 1950, the New York Drama Critics Circle Award, the Donaldson Annual Award for Best Drama, and the Gold Medal of Theater Club Award for Best Playwright of the Year. Just before she reached the age of thirty, M. was severely disabled by three strokes and heart disease. Fifteen years after her fourth novel appeared, she published the fifth novel, *Clock without Hands* (1961), but essentially her literary career was six years long and gained for her an international reputation while she was in her twenties.

M. set all of her novels in the South and retained a compelling love-hate attachment to this region of her birth. Her frequent use of bizarre situations and grotesque characters, though often referred to as "Southern Gothic," seems deeply associated with D. H. Lawrence and Isak Dinesen. She treats her unusual figures with empathy; and her prisoners, homosexuals, alcoholics, giants, deaf-mutes, and dwarfs symbolically represent any isolated "outsider." Though an outstanding realist, M. moves always toward the allegorical and philosophical ramifications of the conflicts her characters confront or seek to escape. Often humorous, she projects, nevertheless, the cynical probability that the individual can seldom divert the course of perverse human nature or mindless fate.

Her themes center on psychological isolation, flawed communication, and the ambivalent nature of love. Love can be the healing agent for loneliness, but it too often renders the vulnerable to destruction. In her first book, *The Heart Is a Lonely Hunter* (1940), M. planned to show that love can provide the answer to loneliness or psychological isolation, but as the novel developed, it revealed love's failure to do so;

race, sexual preference, age, and class all separate people. She emphasizes flawed communication through her use of two deaf-mutes as important characters. In *Reflections in a Golden Eye* (1941), neurotic fixations, lust, possessiveness, and jealousy expose the destructive nature of what passes for love in an exaggerated picture of life on an army base. *The Member of the Wedding* presents the obsession that the black Berenice Sadie Brown and the adolescent Frankie Addams have—the achieving of a sense of belonging with other people through a mystic union or ideal marriage. For Berenice, this would come from finding a man who could duplicate her wonderful first marriage; for Frankie, it would occur if her brother and his bride would take her to live with them. In the poetic balancing of her treatment of Berenice and Frankie, M. explores the philosophical conflict both feel in their search for a way, on the one hand, to belong or to unite spiritually with humanity, and, on the other, to satisfy their drive to be completely free. In *The Ballad of the Sad Café* (1951), a tale that merges the realistic depiction of a Southern milltown with the supernatural elements of folklore, Miss Amelia (a giant) temporarily builds a sense of community through the cafe's extension of the magic spell that love has cast over her and Cousin Lymon. But her infatuation insidiously makes her vulnerable to his treachery and that of her first husband. She becomes prone to jealousy, fear, and finally, after Lymon's betrayal, to unending grief and isolation. In *Clock without Hands*, M. presents two strands of plot: a community moving toward a crisis of racial hatred, and the personal crisis of Malone, the town druggist, as he faces impending death. In both plot patterns, flawed communication deepens tragic circumstances.

Music influenced all of M.'s writing—characters, events, background, and metaphor. Throughout childhood and adolescence, she practiced the piano six to eight hours daily in preparation for the concert career her family and teachers expected her to have. The short story, "Wunderkind," written when she was sixteen, presents Francie, a girl who performs with technical perfection but who thinks she fails her music teacher. She simply lacks the maturity to interpret fully the feeling in the music. In this story, M. clearly implies her own frustrations. The young girl in *The Heart Is a Lonely Hunter,* Mick Kelley, though not a prodigy like Francie or like M. herself, hides under the windows of neighbors who own radios in order to hear music; she attempts to build a violin from cigar boxes and keeps it hidden under her bed, and she teaches herself to play the piano after school in the deserted gym. Frankie Addams in *The Member of the Wedding* complains about the "sweet sleazy music" on the kitchen radio; she feels she will go mad when the

piano tuner does not finish a scale or when a trombonist in a neighboring house interrupts a compelling phrase in a blues song; and she finds comfort in the rhythm of an old motor she salvaged for her room. The prospectus that M. presented to the publishers of her first novel describes that novel entirely in musical, rather than literary, terms. During the five years that she struggled with the writing of *The Member of the Wedding,* she insisted that it had to possess "precision and harmony" both as novel and as play. Such concern with precision and harmony made M. feel finally that the writing of poetry might be her true calling.

BIBLIOGRAPHY: Carr, V. S., *The Lonely Hunter: A Biography* (1976); Kiernan, R. F., *C. M. and Katherine Anne Porter: A Reference Guide* (1976); McDowell, M. B., *C. M.* (1980)

MARGARET B. MCDOWELL

MCDERMOTT, Alice

b. 27 June 1953, Brooklyn, New York

A graduate of the University of New Hampshire writing program, M. met early success as a writer with the publication of her first novel, *A Bigamist's Daughter* (1982), at the age of twenty-nine. M.'s work carefully and powerfully portrays the honest reality of family life and the bittersweet experience of love.

For *A Bigamist's Daughter,* M. drew on her experience as a clerk typist at a vanity publisher for her depiction of Elizabeth Connelly, a young woman in search of love and answers to the uncertainties about her father's mysterious life. Elizabeth's job of reading summaries of books (not the books themselves), inflating authors' egos by praising their work, and then slapping them with a bill for $5,000, turns her into a cynic who craves the sincerity of genuine human affection. Her encounter with a southern writer whose novel about a bigamist lacks an ending inspires her own critical scrutiny of her childhood memories, sifting through them to try to explain her father's frequent absence from home.

In *A Bigamist's Daughter,* M. used present tense and a chronological structure to tell her story. For her two later novels, she unfolds the narrative while rearranging the chronological order of events. *That Night* (1987), a National Book Award-nominee, is told through the perspective of a young girl who witnesses the disruption to her neighborhood one night when a wronged lover comes to claim his high school sweetheart from the prison her life has become. As the story evolves though the memory of the narrator in retrospect, both the reader and the narrator come to see the love story of Rick and Sheryl as at once poignant and tragic. When Sheryl gets pregnant and sent away to Ohio to have the baby quietly and give it up for adoption, circumstances kept secret from Rick by Sheryl's mother, the lovers must learn to cope with the anger and frustration of circumstance as they mature to adulthood in different worlds. Set in the 1960s in suburban Long Island, the novel evokes a disturbingly real portrait of the period as well as the place. The narrator comes of age as she watches her neighbor's teenage romance break bitterly apart.

In *At Weddings and Wakes* (1992), M. explores the world of an Irish Catholic family from Long Island through the perspective of three small children who witness the pain, resentment, disappointment, love, and loss of their adult relatives. Through their twice-weekly journeys from their suburban home to the cluttered and dingy streets of Brooklyn, the children travel with their mother to visit their step-grandmother and three aunts: Veronica, a reclusive alcoholic; May, an ex-nun; and Agnes, an insecure business woman. In the cramped and stifling city apartment, the children suffer the summer heat and boredom as the afternoon hours wane and their mother seeks comfort from her novel like puzzle pieces which the reader sorts and orders to create a cohesive chronology. Romance finally happens for the spinster Aunt May only to be stripped away by her sudden death shortly after her wedding. The effect of this aunt's romance and tragedy sends emotional ripples through the whole family as the children try to comprehend life's quiet mysteries.

M.'s power as a novelist comes from her precise use of simple language to reveal the honesty and truth of ordinary human life, often leaving the reader touched by the sadness and despair intermingled with the capacity to love.

BIBLIOGRAPHY: Cooper, R. R., "Charming Alice: A Unique Voice in American Fiction," *Commonweal* 125 (27 March 1998): 10–12

PATRICIA MONTALBANO

MCELROY, Joseph [Prince]

b. 21 August 1930, Brooklyn, New York

An advocate of what he has called the "maximalist novel," M.'s fiction is often compared to that of Thomas PYNCHON, Joseph HELLER, William GADDIS, and John BARTH. His fragmented and convoluted fiction has been described as unreadable and painful as often as it has been labeled brilliant and experimental. His style—characterized by time, place, and point of view shifts, a preoccupation with language, and frequent departures into the social and physical sciences—is as boundless as some of the themes he ex-

plores: the structuring and comprehension of reality, the development of consciousness, and the continuities between past and present.

M.'s first novel, *A Smuggler's Bible* (1966), has the narrator, David Brooke, attempting to put in order a group of manuscripts documenting memories from different times in his life. In so doing, he deconstructs, then reconstructs his life. The title refers to a box David purchased to hold the finished, unified story—the final David. The three novels to follow, *Hind's Kidnap* (1969), *Ancient History: A Paraphrase* (1971), and *Lookout Cartridge* (1975), employ the detective motif as a means of exploring reality. *Hind's Kidnap* centers on a man who has become obsessed with an unsolved kidnapping and the clues lead him back to his own past. In *Ancient History: A Paraphrase*, the protagonist slips into the apartment of his deceased friend—apparently a suicide—sits at his typewriter, and proceeds to reflect upon his friend's life and death. *Lookout Cartridge,* in which a film maker is out to discover who destroyed his recently completed documentary, was described by its publisher as "a gigantic mystery," but the plot is subordinate to M.'s characteristic musings on everything from the Mayan calendar to the properties of liquid crystal.

Plus (1976) is M.'s most experimental work. The central figure is a disembodied human brain that has been implanted aboard a space capsule for the purpose of relaying scientific information back to earth. The brain becomes conscious of itself and, uniting itself with algae beds within the capsule, begins to evolve and create its body anew. Admired by critics for its unique virtuosity, *Plus* is nonetheless controversial in that it is, as critic Sheldon Frank stated, "a work approaching terminal unreadability."

Women and Men (1986), set in New York City in 1976–77, revolves around the lives of Grace Kimball and James Mayn, neighbors whose lives overlap, yet never quite meet. Grace is a fiftyish feminist who runs a "Body-Self" workshop. Her clients—women of various ages and circumstances—reveal their thoughts and troubles to Kimball. James is a seasoned journalist investigating, among other things, a multinational conspiracy that he comes to find involves his own daughter. Mayn also ponders his daydream of a place where men and women are joined as one being. Grace and James, though they never meet, become in the reader's mind, the unified being that Mayn imagines. There are a number of subplots and a multitude of minor characters allowing M. to explore this vast topic from a variety of perspectives, making *Women and Men,* as critic Thomas LeClair remarks, "the most comprehensive treatment I know of relations between the sexes," and "the most important novel to appear in

America since Thomas Pynchon's *Gravity's Rainbow* in 1973."

Though widely admired and praised by reviewers, however, M. has not yet achieved the same level of recognition as his literary counterparts.

JASON MCMAHON

MCGUANE, Thomas [Francis, III]

b. 11 December 1939, Wyandotte, Michigan

Few authors in America successfully achieve recognition among literary scholars while maintaining a consistent appeal with popular culture. M., like Mark TWAIN and Ernest HEMINGWAY, is one of these rare authors. His sad and comic portrayal of the American scene from the 1960s forward is firmly rooted in the novel of manners. But the angst experienced by his characters reflects the concerns of the American psychological romance. M. is often mis-characterized as a "regionalist" since his novels are always informed by place. But ironically, it is the fruitless attempt to establish roots that informs and motivates his characters. M.'s novels are intensely personal insofar as they portray the inner dynamics of the human mind. But they do not sacrifice their relationship with the social world. M.'s work explores the human cost of the cultural upheavals of post World War II generation. The radicalization of politics, the fragmentation at mainstream culture, the growth and development of counterculture, are central elements in M.'s world. The primary focus of his fiction is the way these sociohistorical phenomena work to liberate, fragment, reshape, and sometimes debilitate individual people in America.

M. came from humble, working-class roots, but he grew up in the midst of an Irish family fond of storytelling and humor. In his youth, M. spent time in both the Florida Keys and the Northern Rockies, and it was through these excursions that he developed a love for sport and the outdoors. He earned his B.A. at Michigan State University in 1962 and an M.F.A. from Yale in 1965.

M.'s first novel, *The Sporting Club* (1969), is a satirical romp through the "wilds" of Michigan. The novel explores the behaviors and exploits of a group of wealthy "sportsmen" and the strange and comic society they form within the confines of their elaborate hunting and fishing lodge. M. satirizes the pretensions of these highly paid, urbane, would-be "frontiersmen." The novel is replete with comic references to Hemingway type heroes, as the characters attempt to sort out their respective identities in a world that denies even the possibility of heroism. The *Bushwhacked Piano* (1971) and *Ninety-Two in the Shade* (1973) continue

in the same farcical irreverent style. What emerges as quintessentially American in these novels, underneath the wry cynicism and satirical humor, is their linkage to ROMANTICISM and New England TRANSCENDENTALISM. The stark contrast between the foibles of men in society and the power of Nature finds its roots in Ralph Waldo EMERSON and Henry David THOREAU. Emerging out of the 1960s, these novels reflect a remarkable array of cultural influences, and M. reinterprets the concerns of previous generations through a richly varied narrative voice appropriate to and resonant with a contemporary audience.

Similar sets of concerns inform *Panama* (1979), a novel dealing with the decline of a rock musician; *Nobody's Angel* (1982), which is set in the cattle-ranching country of Montana; *Something to Be Desired* (1985), a story dealing with the exploits of a Montana man searching for personal and financial security; *Keep the Change* (1989), the quirky tale of an artist's life; and *Nothing But Blue Skies* (1992), a sad, stark, yet whimsically comic novel about a Montana real estate developer searching for his lost sense of meaning and identity. In *An Outside Chance* (1980), M. collects essays dealing with his interest in sports, and he has written many film scripts, including *Rancho Deluxe* (1974) and *The Missouri Breaks* (1976).

M.'s work is remarkably varied in its manner of expression. His novels are marked by a vivid attention to the manners and behaviors of specific social environments. However, like his predecessors Twain and Hemingway, M.'s work is deceptive. He masks an often deep philosophical complexity with a surface level simplicity. Humor and playful irreverence clothe characters that confront a culture corrupted by human vice, characters who often function in a bleak and twisted world. In a distinctive set of novels, essays, and screenplays, M. attempts to sort out the fluid complexity of the modern American experience. Unlike authors such as Thomas PYNCHON and John BARTH, he is not an "academic" writer. But he is very much informed by literary tradition. His fictions are drawn from the changing lives of recognizable contemporary people, and through imaginative descriptions of nature, references to classical literature, allusions to Western philosophy, M. manages to provide context, meaning, and humor to the chaos of modern existence.

BIBLIOGRAPHY: Klinkowitz, J., *The New American Novel of Manners: The Fiction of Richard Yates, Dan Wakefield, and T. M.* (1986); Morris, G. L., "How Ambivalence Won the West: T. M. and the Fiction of the New West," *Crit* 32 (Spring 1991): 180–89; Wallace J., *The Politics of Style* (1991); Westrum, D., *T. M.* (1992)

STEVEN FRYE

MCINERNEY, Jay
b. 13 January 1955, Hartford, Connecticut

With the 1984 publication of *Bright Lights, Big City,* M. burst upon the literary scene, obtaining fame and critical success rare with a first novel. Set in the big-spending, freewheeling 1980s, the novel chronicles the adventures of an unnamed protagonist and his carousing buddy, Tad Allagash. The narrator appears as a little boy lost, a grown-up Holden Caulfield, and this, juxtaposed against the absurdities of New York City life, creates a novel that is both cynical and poignant as the protagonist attempts to accept the loss of his job, the break-up of his marriage, and the death of his mother.

Following the release of the novel, M. became part of what the popular press deemed the "Literary Brat Pack." M., along with Bret Easton ELLIS and Tama JANOWITZ, became a personality. Representing the self-indulgent excess of the 1980s, they posed for fashion magazines, endorsed products, and provided fodder for the celebrity gossip mill.

In 1985, M. published his much-anticipated second novel, *Ransom.* The protagonist, Christopher Ransom, a Princeton graduate, has moved to Kyoto to teach English to Japanese businessmen. He is numb from his mother's death and the loss of his two traveling companions in separate drug-related incidents. He is also alienated from his controlling father, whom Ransom believes has prostituted himself in abandoning his career as a playwright in favor of television writing. In an attempt to pay penance for a privileged, upper-middle class life, Ransom immerses himself in the austere purity of the martial arts.

In 1988, M. returned to the venue of New York City with his third novel, *The Story of My Life.* While the novel was praised for its fast pace, wit, and knack for dialogue, *The Story of My Life* was criticized for its portrayal of its female protagonists, Alison and her roommate Jeannie, cartoon-like characters, solely governed by their twin obsessions—casual sex and cocaine.

In 1992, at the age of thirty-seven, M. made what many regard as his transition into adulthood. With the publication of *Brightness Falls,* the novel was compared to Tom WOLFE's social critique, *Bonfire of the Vanities,* in its depiction of Manhattan's decay. Set around the time of the stock market crash in 1987, M.'s literary subjects are older now, "thirtysomethings." Russell and Corrine Calloway are a successful editor and disenchanted stockbroker. The novel was generally well received for what was regarded as M.'s caring, though sometimes self-mocking, portrait of the "yuppies" who peopled Manhattan's Wall Street and publishing worlds, a group deemed the latest "Lost Generation."

M.'s *The Last of the Savages* (1996) received mixed reviews. Praised by some for his continued astuteness as a social critic, the novel was likened by one critic to a sitcom. Perhaps the ambiguous reception is in part due to M.'s choice of subject matter. The North meets the South in an elite New England boarding school, as the two protagonists Patrick Keane, a scholarship student, and Will Savage, a southern aristocrat, forge a friendship that spans three decades. With some excessive M. drug use added for good measure, the novel seems too ambitious. While the writer now resides in Franklin, Tennessee, he does not yet seem prepared to take on the burden of the South and all of its nuances.

Aside from his novels, M. is a contributor to numerous periodicals, including *Atlantic Monthly, Esquire, Vanity Fair, London Review of Books,* and *Paris Review.* In addition, he adapted *Bright Lights, Big City* for a film that was released by Metro-Goldwyn-Mayer/United Artists in 1988.

BIBLIOGRAPHY: Faye, J., "Cultural/Familial Estrangement: Self-Exile and Self-Destruction in J. M.'s Novels," in Whitlark, J., and W. Aycock, eds., *The Literature of Emigration and Exile* (1992): 115–30; Pinsker, S., "Soft Lights, Academic Talk: A Conversation with J. M.," *LitR* 30 (Fall 1986): 107–14

DEBORAH KAY FERRELL

MCKAY, Claude [Festus Claudius]
b. 15 September 1890, Sunny Ville, Jamaica; d. 22 May 1948, Chicago, Illinois

Although he died in relative obscurity, the Jamaican American poet and novelist M. is now recognized as a pioneering figure in the Harlem Renaissance of the 1920s. M. gave voice in his poetry to the anger and alienation of black Americans of his generation and helped inspire other writers of the time. A number of his poems—mainly sonnets—survive in anthologies, and his explorations of black experience in poetry and prose have secured him a place in the history of 20th-c. AFRICAN AMERICAN LITERATURE.

M. was born to a prosperous peasant family in a Jamaican farming village. As a young man, he studied philosophy and English poetry but retained a lifelong love of Jamaican peasant life, and his work often idealizes that life as an alternative to the degradation of modern white-dominated urban society. Before leaving Jamaica for the U.S. in 1912, M. published two volumes of dialect poetry, *Constab Ballads* (1912) and *Songs from Jamaica* (1912). These works, though marred by an attachment to Victorian colonial values, include vivid descriptions of Jamaican life and affirm M.'s fidelity to his peasant origins.

In the U.S., M. studied agriculture at Tuskegee Institute and Kansas State University before moving to Harlem, where he observed the deplorable effects of white racism, abandoned his youthful conservatism, and worked as a radical political journalist, serving for a time as an editor of the *Liberator*. As a supporter of communism—but always a critical and questioning one—he traveled to the Soviet Union in the early 1920s and then lived as an expatriate in Europe and North Africa. After his return to America in 1934, M.'s financial and artistic fortunes declined. He repudiated doctrinaire communism but remained a defender of black populism, urging racial solidarity and group improvement rather than integration, a stance that put him at odds with white liberals and members of the black establishment. In his final years, he lost confidence in political solutions and turned to religion, joining the Catholic Church in 1944.

M.'s most important work is *Harlem Shadows* (1922), which includes some of the earliest militant black poetry published in America. Many regard this collection as the first book of the Harlem Renaissance. While the poems are traditional in form, based largely on Elizabethan and English romantic models, their content is revolutionary. "If We Must Die," M.'s best-known poem, is an angry protest and call to action written in response to the nationwide race riots of 1919. Other poems, less well known, are equally passionate outcries against oppression, notably "Mulatto," "The Lynching," "The White City." M. also writes with nostalgia about Jamaica and powerfully evokes the alienation of modern urban life. Although sometimes criticized for his lack of technical skill and formal innovation, M. is widely credited with bringing new emotions and experiences into black poetry.

Following *Harlem Shadows*, M. wrote fiction, producing three novels during his expatriate years. These books explore the struggle of urban blacks to achieve self-realization in a hostile society and affirm the central importance for African Americans of their cultural and racial heritage. The hero of M.'s first novel—a loosely plotted picaresque tale called *Home to Harlem* (1928)—is Jake Brown, a black vagabond, the natural man of passion and physical vitality who lives in Harlem on his wit and courage. His opposite, Ray, is a lonely, self-conscious intellectual struggling for racial self-consciousness. *Home to Harlem* enjoyed popular success, especially among white readers, though it was harshly criticized by W. E. B. DU BOIS and others for dwelling on the sordid, mean side of urban black life and for promoting racial stereotypes. M.'s second novel, *Banjo* (1929), is essentially a sequel to the first,

set in the port city of Marseilles, France, with a cast that includes several West Indian and black American sailors who gather around Banjo Daily, another natural man.

M.'s first two novels are generally regarded as seriously flawed by their formlessness and overt didacticism, with Ray serving largely as a spokesman for M.'s social and political ideas. In his third and best novel, *Banana Bottom* (1933), M. draws his characters more skillfully and dramatizes, rather than preaches, his ideas. The natural "man" in this case is Bita Plant, a black Jamaican woman who, despite her upbringing by English missionaries, succeeds in recovering her "natural" identity, reconciling her black peasant origins with her "educated" English self. In M.'s Edenic rural Jamaica, Bita and her husband achieve a wholeness that is desired but never approached in the urban novels.

During his expatriate years, M. also completed a collection of short stories, *Gingertown* (1932), set mainly in Harlem and Jamaica. His later work is mostly nonfiction: an autobiography, *A Long Way from Home* (1937), which focuses on his public life and opinions, and a social history, *Harlem: Negro Metropolis* (1940). Near the end of his life, he wrote a memoir of his childhood, published posthumously in *My Green Hills of Jamaica and Five Jamaican Short Stories* (1979). A useful gathering of M.'s work appears in *The Passion of C. M.: Selected Poetry and Prose, 1912-1948* (1973).

BIBLIOGRAPHY: Cooper, W. F., *C. M.: Rebel Sojourner in the Harlem Renaissance* (1987); Giles, J. R., *C. M.* (1976); Tillery, T., *C. M.: A Black Poet's Struggle for Identity* (1992)

MICHAEL HENNESSY

MCMILLAN, Terry
b. 18 October 1951, Port Huron, Michigan

With the 1995 Hollywood version of her 1992 novel *Waiting to Exhale,* M.'s name became a household word. One of the first African American writers of popular novels to break into the ranks of top best sellers, M. has established herself firmly as a chronicler of friendships between African American women and (often troubled) relationships between African American women and men.

M. grew up in Michigan but moved to California when she was seventeen and attended the University of California at Berkeley where Ishmael REED encouraged her to explore her literary potential. After graduating, she left for New York City in pursuit of an advanced degree in film at Columbia University, joined the Harlem Writers' Guild, and produced a draft of her first novel. All of her novels to date have strong autobiographical features. Her first, *Mama* (1987), tells the story of a tough working class African American woman, Mildred Peacock, and her attempts at managing to bring up five children while fighting with an alcoholic and abusive husband. Her second novel, *Disappearing Acts* (1989), may well be understood as a transposition of Janie and Teacake's relationship in Zora Neale HURSTON's *Their Eyes Were Watching God* into a 1980s urban environment—the main character's name Zora indicates as much. Marked by the same ecstatic highs and similar (but worse) abusive lows as Hurston's novel's relationship, Zora and Franklin's years together are characterized by a struggle to overcome class differences and the anger built up in Franklin—mostly unloaded on Zora—through his fragile position in a racist job market. Probably her highest artistic achievement to date, *Disappearing Acts* creates complex and conflicted characters and, through frequent use of interior monologue, makes the reader understand their motivations even when one may be appalled by their actions.

Waiting to Exhale, a huge commercial success, focuses on the friendship of four professional women—Savannah Jackson, Bernadine Harris, Robin Stokes, and Gloria Mathews—and, in turn, on their preoccupation with acquiring or changing partners. Savannah and Robin may be described as the central characters, but the story shifts from character to character, exploring their various relationship problems and the way in which their friendship bonds to each other sustain them. Despite its shift in class environment, the novel uses frank and expletive-studded language, a feature of M.'s novels that has been occasionally criticized. Not as psychologically probing as her earlier novels, *Waiting to Exhale* is full of easy conversation and moves from sexual encounter to sexual encounter in a somewhat breathless fashion.

Published in 1996, *How Stella Got Her Groove Back* is the story of Stella Payne, a highly successful securities analyst dissatisfied with her career and her lack of a love life. As a solution to her problems, Stella takes a vacation in Jamaica, meets a much younger Jamaican man named Winston Shakespeare, and after much soul-searching about their age difference and potential societal disapproval of their match, Stella decides to marry Winston. Clearly the most escapist of her works, *How Stella Got Her Groove Back* portrays Stella's dilemma choosing between successful career and an exploration of her artistic abilities, her commitment to being a mother to her son from a first marriage, and her yearning for love, but without offering any deep analysis of the societal or personal context for those dilemmas. But it is exactly this feature that may explain the success of her last two novels: by offering problems familiar to many readers, packaging them skillfully with wit, and adding generous doses of sex and materialism, M. has adopted a similar formula as Hollywood.

M.'s strength as a novelist is her rendering of dialogue, and her ability to probe the thoughts of her characters, allowing the reader to see them searching for solutions to their dilemmas. M. has been unjustly criticized for giving African American male characters only marginal roles in her fiction. Her novels claim the right to explore, from a woman-centered point of view, African American women's worlds of friendship and love.

BIBLIOGRAPHY: Brown, L. M., "T. M.," in Green, C. H., and M. G. Mason, eds., *American Women Writers* (1994): 284–86; Jackson, E. M., "Images of Black Males in T. M.'s *Waiting to Exhale,*" MAWAR 8 (June 1993): 20–26

                                                    MARTIN JAPTOK

MCMURTRY, Larry
b. 3 June 1936, Wichita Falls, Texas

Thanks to film and television miniseries adaptations of his novels, M.'s personal vision of the West may have the largest popular audience of any contemporary Western writer. M. is certainly among the most prolific, having published over twenty books in his career, most of which are set in his native Texas. He tends to write his novels in groups, each with varying degrees of cohesion among its novels, most often in trilogies with additional volumes often added, as the following list illustrates: the Thalia trilogy, including *Horseman, Pass By* (1961), *Leaving Cheyenne* (1963), and *The Last Picture Show* (1966), plus *Texasville* (1987) and *Duane's Depressed* (1998), which reprise *The Last Picture Show;* the Houston trilogy, including *Moving On* (1970), *All My Friends Are Going to Be Strangers* (1972), and *Terms of Endearment* (1975), plus *Some Can Whistle* (1989), which reprise *All My Friends Are Going to Be Strangers* and *Evening Star* (1992), which reprises *Terms of Endearment;* the Trash trilogy, including *Somebody's Darling* (1978), *Cadillac Jack* (1982), and *The Desert Rose* (1983); and the Lonesome Dove trilogy, including *Lonesome Dove* (1985), *Streets of Laredo* (1993), and *Dead Man's Walk* (1995). *Anything for Billy* (1988) and *Buffalo Girls* (1990) may comprise the first two books in a soon to be completed trilogy based on historic Western characters such as Billy the Kid in *Anything for Billy* and Calamity Jane in *Buffalo Girls*. These thematic groupings reflect M.'s preoccupation with making connections between the present and the past and his obsession with exploring multiple facets of his fictional settings, communities, and characters.

Horseman, Pass By, M.'s first novel, later republished under its film adaptation title, *Hud,* serves notice of M.'s revisionist intentions toward the traditional WESTERN and of his sense of ambiguity regarding the myths that inform it. Set in the contemporary West, around the fictional town of Thalia, the novel sets the traditional Western ethos of Homer Bannon against the greedy materialism of his stepson, Hud, who urges the unethical and illegal sale of diseased cattle against all sense of responsibility. M.'s adolescent narrator, Lonnie, Homer's grandson, eventually sides with his grandfather, rejecting Hud and embracing a future existence on the land. The other Thalia novels—*Leaving Cheyenne, The Last Picture Show,* and *Texasville*—also feature the conflict between the traditional and the contemporary West; however, in these novels the conflict seems murkier, especially as the lines separating these two disparate value systems blur and as materialism and carnality dominate the often ludicrous lives of M.'s characters. The Houston trilogy focuses more on the problematics of marriage and of literary expression with some passing connections to Western myth such as Jim Carpenter's rodeo photography in *Moving On* and Uncle L as a humorous, nearly satiric, version of Homer Bannon in *All My Friends Are Going to Be Strangers.*

Lonesome Dove, the 1986 Pulitzer Prize-winner in fiction, may be the great Western American novel, despite various critics having taken M. to task for the novel's supposed flaws, including his stereotypical characters and trail drive plot, his inconsistent narrative voice, and his coincidental subplots. Far from being stereotypes, Woodrow Call and Augustus McCrae, the aging former Texas Ranger captains who are the novel's main male characters, are exceedingly complex characters, despite their correspondences to traditional Western figures. The stoic silence of Call, who lets his actions speak for him, contrasting the amusing banter of McCrae, for example, sets up a binary that M. undercuts by McCrae's own capacity for action and violence. Call and McCrae live in the twilight of the West, frontier warriors in an increasingly civilized Texas who find their skills becoming obsolete and themselves becoming anachronisms. They undertake the trail drive simply because they want one last great adventure, not because they want to establish a cattle empire. As the novel progresses, their traditional male values come under serious scrutiny and are found wanting; indeed, *Lonesome Dove* and its sequel, *Streets of Laredo,* trace the descent of male values as represented by Call and the ascent of female values as represented by Lorena, the former whore. Even *Dead Man's Walk,* the *Lonesome Dove* prequel, features strong women characters on whom the youthful Call and McCrae depend. Throughout the Lonesome Dove trilogy, M. questions traditional Western codes at the same time he reenshrines them; he celebrates their magnificence while acknowledging their limitations.

BIBLIOGRAPHY: Busby, M., *L. M. and the West* (1995); Jones, R. W., *L. M. and the Victorian Novel* (1994); Landess, T., *L. M.* (1969); Lich, L. P. T, *L. M.'s Texas: Evolution of the Myth* (1987); Neinstein, R. L., *The Ghost Country: A Study of the Novels of L. M.* (1976); Peavy, C. D., *L. M.* (1977); Reynolds, C., ed., *Taking Stock: A L. M. Casebook* (1989); Schmidt, D., ed., *L. M.—Unredeemed Dreams: A Collection of Bibliography, Essays, and Interview* (1981)

PHILLIP A. SNYDER

MCNALLY, Terrence

b. 3 November 1939, St. Petersburg, Florida

Often described as a leading gay playwright, M. does write about homosexual characters and life, but that classification is far too limiting. M. has said that there is no gay theater, just good and bad. He has shown versatility in subject matter—from mental institutions to teaching to theater—but where he excels is in his exploration of complex relationships—heterosexual and homosexual. Although M. doesn't like to be classified, he has called playwright Mart Crowley his one hero for opening up the subject of gay experience in *The Boys in the Band* (1968).

M.'s characters reveal human needs, longings, and failings. They want to be heard, accepted, and loved. They so often quibble about words and meaning while at odds and in opposition with each other, missing the very essence of what the other is dying for them to hear, whether it is about the end of a relationship, cancer, or loneliness. Their dialogue combines bursts of biting humor and catty comments with elements of insecurity and obvious denial.

Johnny, in *Frankie and Johnny* (1987), talks incessantly of himself, how he sees Frankie, how they were meant to be together. Mendy, in *The Lisbon Traviata* (1985), obsesses about finding the Maria Callas Lisbon *Traviata* with the same as intensity obsessing about Stephen. Chloe, in *Lips Together, Teeth Apart* (1992), constantly asks if people need coffee or food. They all talk to fill the air, to make their presence known, to get closer to another person.

And yet, Frankie is driven to distraction by Johnny's barrage of speech. She asks if he has heard her. This is a relationship in the starting gates. But nearly the same speech can be heard at the finish line, when Stephen refuses to listen to Mike because it would mean acknowledging that their relationship was over. And like Chloe, Maria Callas, in *Master Class* (1995), is busy directing activity. Maria says she doesn't care if anyone hears, but she is quick to criticize anything different from the Callas way. She is at the end of her career, her relationship with audiences, but denies it. Behind the denials, the protests, the pleas, the ebb and flow of words, heard and unheard, there are silences.

Critics have claimed that M. relies too much on the biting dialogue and the overt sexual jokes. His work has been compared to other dramatists who write about gay issues, such as Crowley, Tony KUSHNER in *Angels in America,* and Oliver Mayer in *Blade to the Heat* (1996). But even before *Love! Valour! Compassion!* and *The Lisbon Traviata,* M. introduced gay themes to heterosexual audiences from the perspective of a mother of a gay son, who regrets not having accepted her homosexual son before he was killed, in *A Perfect Ganesh* (1993), or a mother of a son who has died of AIDS in *Andre's Mother* (1990), or a sister, who inherits her gay brother's beach house on Fire Island in *Lips Together, Teeth Apart.*

In *Love! Valour! Compassion!,* eight male protagonists take turns narrating the events over three all-American holiday weekends—Memorial Day, Fourth of July, and Labor Day. The locale in an isolated Dutchess County summer house provides an insular world for them, and yet, perhaps, shows how it is only by being isolated can they fully be part of society. Their conversations and concerns unfold, echoing heterosexual couples, not unlike Chloe and her husband John, Frankie and Johnny, and Maria Callas and her audiences.

BIBLIOGRAPHY: Bryer, J. R., ed., *The Playwright's Art: Conversations with Contemporary American Dramatists* (1995); DiGaetani, J. L., ed., *A Search for a Postmodern Theatre: Interviews with Contemporary Playwrights* (1991); Kolin, P. C., and C. H. Kullman, eds., *Speaking on Stage: Interviews with Contemporary American Playwrights* (1996)

KATHLEEN MOTOIKE

MCNICKLE, [William] D'Arcy
b. 18 January 1904, Flathead Indian Reservation, Montana; d. 18 October 1977, Albuquerque, New Mexico

Two important components of the fiction written by Native Americans during the late 20th c. are concentration on a mixed-blood protagonist, a "breed" whose bicultural identity produces alienation from both Native American and Euroamerican heritages, and development of the "return of the native" theme, wherein that protagonist tries to become reintegrated into the Native community in which he or she was enculturated after being away for awhile. Published in 1936, M.'s novel *The Surrounded* anticipates both of these components.

M. drew upon uncertainties about his own identity for his novel. Born on the Flathead Reservation in Montana, he was the son of a Metis (French-Canadian and Cree mixed-blood) mother and a Scotch-Irish father. Though biologically not Flathead, M. became an enrolled member of that tribe through a process, sanctioned by Bureau of Indian Affairs guidelines, that allowed tribal adoption of individuals who were "of other Indian blood." This occurred in 1905, and though M.'s parents were determined that he and his sisters not adopt the tribal culture, enrollment provided M. with a land allotment and, more importantly, with a basis for the Native American identity that he asserted during the 1930s, which dominated his professional and personal life thereafter, and which provided the point of departure for his fiction.

That identity had become muted while M. was attending the University of Montana and living in New York City. He had even adopted the surname Dahlberg from his stepfather. But his efforts to forge a literary career caused him to reconsider a personal past that afforded the thematic basis for *The Surrounded.* In the novel, Archilde Leon, son of a Flathead mother and a Spanish father, returns to the reservation to confront his parents' estrangement from one another and the bifurcation of his own identity. His mother Catherine has become a devoted exponent of a Native American way of life for which his father Max has no use. Archilde had intended to come home only for a brief visit, but events over which he has little control bring him closer and closer to his mother. His increasing involvement with her Indian way of life results in his being blamed for two killings—of a game warden and of a sheriff—and the novel ends with his surrender to the authorities.

The novel offers little hope for Archilde and presumably for those like him who are caught between their bicultural identities, but this bleak message did not necessarily reflect M.'s own experience. After a decade of literary frustration in New York City, he found employment with the Bureau of Indian Affairs and was active in the reorganization of federal policy toward Native Americans during the late 1930s and 1940s. During the 1950s and 1960s, he promoted privately administered programs that would enable Native Americans to maintain cultural identity while adapting to the forces of Euroamerican society. He devoted much of his energy to ensuring that the hopelessness of Archilde's situation was not inevitable for Indians trying to maneuver between two cultures. This activism, the posthumous deposition of his papers there, and his nonfiction treating Native American concerns contributed to the Newberry Library's naming its Center for the History of the American Indian in his honor.

Besides *The Surrounded,* M. wrote two other novels. *Runner in the Sun: A Story of Indian Maize,* which appeared in 1954 as part of a fiction series aimed at young readers, and *Wind from an Enemy Sky,* published posthumously in 1978. M.'s short stories were collected as *The Hawk Is Hungry* in 1992. He also wrote several books on Indian history and cultural adjustment as well as a biography of Oliver LA FARGE.

BIBLIOGRAPHY: Parker, D. R., *Singing an Indian Song: A Biography of D. M.* (1992); Purdy, J. L., *Word Ways: The Novels of D. M.* (1990); Purdy, J. L., ed., *The Legacy of D. M.* (1996); Ruppert, J., *D. M.* (1988)

WILLIAM M. CLEMENTS

MCPHEE, John [Angus]

b. 8 March 1931, Princeton, New Jersey

To lay out satisfactorily M.'s career would require a landscape as vast as those he has written about in his many nonfiction works. M. is nothing if not prolific, having published over twenty-five books, starting with *A Sense of Where You Are* in 1965. He is a journalist, a staff writer for the *New Yorker,* and bases most of his books on essays he writes for that magazine. The list of subjects about which he has written is nearly as long as his publications list. His gift is to introduce readers to topics they considered either too difficult (for instance, plate tectonics) or too mundane to make interesting reading, and to prove them wrong.

M. has done this enough times to earn numerous literary awards and honors, among them the American Academy and Institute of Arts and Letters Award in literature (1977) and the Princeton University Woodrow Wilson Award (1982). His greatest achievement is that he continues to win both critical and popular acclaim.

As a bridge between reader and specialist in a number of fields, M. has a way of both elucidating and cutting through technical jargon while driving the narrative forward, often through travelogues, thus taking the reader on a journey both literal and figurative and of both learning and enjoyment. *Coming into the Country* (1977), which many critics agree is one of M.'s best works, offers an intimate look at Alaska, one of America's final frontiers. The three-part work consists of a canoe trip, a helicopter ride, and a stay on the Yukon river.

M. introduces us to experts in the various fields he explores. In *Survival of the Bark Canoe* (1975), we meet craftsman Henri Vaillancourt, who makes birch bark canoes using the methods of Native Americans. The reader witnesses not only the techniques of this nearly lost art, but a subsequent canoe trip that M.

and three others take. *Basin and Range* (1981), *In Suspect Terrain* (1983)—both contained in the two-volume *Annals of the Former World* (1984)—*Rising from the Plains* (1986), and *Assembling California* (1993) expose us to the world of plate tectonics. As M. learns about this science through his mentor in the field, tectonicist Eldridge Moores, so do we. Indeed, one weakness of M.'s work is that he seems to become so enamored of his mentors that he writes them into heroes rather than real people. So his characterizations of them lack the three-dimensional quality, the thoroughness and accuracy that his treatments of the topics themselves possess.

But M.'s fascination with interesting people in interesting fields rubs off on readers and lends his books part of their charm. *A Roomful of Hovings and Other Profiles* (1969) illustrates this fascination. It is a collection of five essays profiling a museum director, a wild food expert, a Wimbledon groundskeeper, and several others.

As several of his titles indicate, notably, *The Pine Barrens* (1968) and *The Control of Nature* (1989), M. has a long-standing interest in the environment, but his books are far from limited to this subject. *A Sense of Where You Are* is a study of basketball player and future senator Bill Bradley, and *Levels of the Game* (1970) offers an "up close and personal" look at a tennis match between Clark Graebner and Arthur Ashe. It reveals how the players' personalities are reflected in their approaches to the game.

At the heart of M.'s work is a contagious enchantment with the work of the world and the characters who dedicate themselves to that work.

BIBLIOGRAPHY: Pearson, M., *J. M.* (1997)

JENNIFER WHEELOCK

MCPHERSON, James Alan

b. 16 September 1943, Savannah, Georgia

Short story writer and essayist M. has been a contributing editor for the *Atlantic Monthly* since 1969 and a professor in the University of Iowa Writers' Workshop and law school. In 1965, M. won the *Atlantic Monthly* Firsts Award for his short story "Gold Coast," and after completing a law degree at Harvard in 1968, he entered the M.F.A. program at the University of Iowa to continue his writing. His first collection of short stories, *Hue and Cry* (1969), won both a National Institute of Writers Award and an *Atlantic Monthly* grant. His second collection, *Elbow Room* (1977), won the 1978 Pulitzer Prize in fiction. Other honors include MacArthur, Rockefeller, and Guggenheim fellowships and the inclusion of his stories in the *Best American*

Short Stories and *O. Henry Prize Stories* anthology series.

Alternately categorized as a black writer or criticized for not identifying himself as a black writer, M., in his introduction to *Hue and Cry,* expressed his hope that his work would be read "as a book about people—all kinds of people: old, young, lonely, discarded, homosexual, confused, used, discarded, wronged. As a matter of fact, certain of these people happen to be black and certain of them happen to be white; but I have tried to keep the color part of them far in the background, where these things should rightly be kept." Thus, while the typical M. narrator is a black male, the narrator often reveals himself as well as the other characters through objective description of appearance, behavior, and speech and through slightly ironic analysis of what he observes; while the conflicts in M.'s stories are often racial—and autobiographical—in origin, they have universal implications. When Ralph ELLISON in 1969 called him "one of the most gifted Americans," Ellison praised the insight, sympathy, and humor in M.'s work—elements that would continue to characterize his writing.

Hue and Cry, largely autobiographical, is informed partly by M.'s experience as a railroad worker. The railroad has inspired much of M.'s work, notably his novella "A Solo Song: for Doc" and his essays published in *Railroad: Trains and People in American Culture* (1976), which he edited with Miller Williams. This collection, which reveals connections between railroads and American music, folk literature, morality and legal history, demonstrates M.'s varied interests that transcend the African American experience alone: among other topics, he discusses the black, Chinese, and Irish road-gang work songs; how trains facilitated the work of abolitionists in the underground railway; and how the removal of a light-skinned black man from an all-white train coach resulted in the case *Plessy v. Ferguson* (1896), which sanctioned almost sixty years of racial segregation. As in his stories, M. in his nonfiction prose combines imaginative excitement with low-key observation of detail and masterful control or prose style.

Elbow Room, like *Hue and Cry,* deals with a wide variety of characters in conflict, but shows M. improving upon his already psychologically complex, sympathetic characterization. Although M. reputedly began writing a full-length novel after *Elbow Room,* he has yet to publish one; his next major work, published some two decades after *Elbow Room,* is his memoir *Crabcakes,* published in 1998. In this work, M. once more treats relationships among people from different cultures and how these relationships break down in

the face of racism—which he comes to identify as "part of the disease that has scooped out our souls."

BIBLIOGRAPHY: Beavers, H., *Wrestling Angels into Song: The Fictions of Ernest J. Gaines and J. A. M.* (1996); Cox, J. T., "J. A. M.," in Flora, J. M., and R. Bain, eds., *Contemporary Fiction Writers of the South: A Bio-Bibliographical Sourcebook* (1993): 311–19; Domnarki, W., "The Voices of Misery and Despair in the Fiction of J. A. M.," *ArQ* 42 (Spring 1986): 37–44

MARGARET B. MCDOWELL

MELTZER, David

b. 17 February 1937, Rochester, New York

M. has called himself a "second generation Beat writer," but is considered by some critics as a member of the San Francisco Renaissance. However, some Beat writers are often included in the San Francisco school: Michael MCCLURE, Philip WHALEN, Jack SPICER, Robert DUNCAN, among many others. Both of M.'s parents were classically trained musicians. His father was a cellist with the Rochester Philharmonic and a faculty member of the prestigious Eastman School of Music, where his mother studied piano and harp.

M.'s father decided to leave the world of classical music and became a professional comedy writer; in 1954, he decided to move his family to Los Angeles where he continued to write for radio and television. M. became an amateur singer and sang on both the *Al Jarvis Show* and *Stairway to the Stars,* but he so detested performing on these programs that he began writing poems at the age of eleven. One of the obsessions M. brought with him to California was his great love for jazz, which his father had fostered by introducing him to the music of Charlie Parker, Duke Ellington, Billie Holiday, Bud Powell, and Miles Davis. M.'s lifelong devotion to modern jazz flowered years later when he edited a critically acclaimed volume entitled *Reading Jazz: The White Invention of Jazz* (1994). That book consists of a polemic anthology of jazz texts that, as he puts it " demonstrated the white construction of jazz as subject and object." A companion volume, *Writing Jazz,* would concentrate on jazz from an African American perspective and examine its black origins. Though he attended Los Angeles City College, he found little to inspire him except for one English teacher who introduced him to the haiku, a topic that led him to further research into Japanese classical drama and *The Tale of Genji.* After dropping out of college, he began reading D. H. Lawrence, Franz Kafka, William FAULKNER, Sherwood ANDERSON, and

Henry MILLER, authors he had heard about from artists and writers in the Los Angeles undergound intellectual set who gathered at the Coronet Louvre Cinema on La Cienaga Boulevard. There, he met his most enduring intellectual influences, and became close to the artist Wallace Berman and his wife Shirley who, in turn, introduced him to other writers and actors. At the studio of artist John Altoon, he was first exposed to the poetry of Duncan, Robert CREELEY, Charles OLSON, and the fiction of Fielding Dawson in the *Black Mountain Review*. M. decided that Los Angeles was not much of a town for poets—though great for jazz—and moved to San Francisco in 1957, a move that allowed him to combine his love for jazz and poetry. He began a series of readings with jazz accompaniment at the "Jazz Cellar" in North Beach, following in the footsteps of Jack KEROUAC, Lawrence FERLINGHETTI, Kenneth PATCHEN, and Kenneth REXROTH, all of whom were known for reading their work with a jazz background. However, M.'s performances differed from the others (who performed from written texts they brought with them): "I improvised . . . On the spot—in context with the music and the idea of the poem." In that way, there was a more immediate exchange between the poet and the musicians. M. made a number of recordings with a jazz group called Serpent Power.

Beginning with *Ragas* (1959), M. published the first of nearly fifty volumes of poetry down to *Arrows: Selected Poetry, 1957–1992* (1994). His subjects cover an enormous range of themes from Mexico to Bela Lugosi to visionary revelations. He became part of an intellectual coterie in San Francisco, which gathered around the poets Duncan and Spicer. He also met McClure, John Wieners, and Lew Welch. Donald Allen included some of M.'s poetry in his groundbreaking anthology, *The New American Poetry,* in 1960. Afterwards, his work was identified with members of the San Francisco Renaissance. M.'s poems also began to appear frequently in nonacademic journals such as *Caterpillar, Big Table,* the *Floating Bear, Beatitude,* and other avant-garde "little" magazines.

In 1964, M. began an in-depth study of the Kabbalah, the principal text of Jewish mysticism. M.'s work in Kabbalisitic studies resulted in *The Secret Garden: An Anthology in the Kabbalah* in 1976. M. wanted "to somehow relate classical Jewish mystical texts to modern and postmodern poetry and prose."

Tired of being broke and trying to raise a family of four, M. started writing a series of pornographic novels for Essex House Press in 1970. The first volume was called *The Brain Plant Tetralogy: Lovely, Healer, Out,* and *Glue Factory.* He confesses that these novels were also political acts and were responses "to the political and moral stress of that time. . . . I thought pornography was the right form of address to the Viet-

nam War, racism, economic immiseration." There have been six additional novels in the series. His outstanding book of interviews called *Golden Gate: Interviews with Five San Francisco Poets* (1976) received great critical acclaim as being one of the most intelligent books of interviews ever published. M. also edited two popular anthologies with North Point Press. *Birth: Hymns, Prayers, Documents, Myths, Amulets* (1981) and *Death: An Anthology of Ancient Texts, Songs, Prayers and Stories* (1985) are collections of relevant texts surrounding birth and death, resembling in their structures, Jerome ROTHENBERG's very popular *A Big Jewish Book* (1978).

M. has, for the past ten years, been on the faculty of the New College of California where he has taught alongside other well-known poets and scholars. He is presently working on two additional erotic novels, *Boff* and *Lamb,* a genre that allows him "room to rant and speculate and criticize outside the shadows of regulating high culture can(n)ons."

BIBLIOGRAPHY: Hawley, R., and A. Charters, " D. M.," in Charters, A., ed., *DLB,* vol. 16, part 2, *The Beats: Literary Bohemians in Postwar America* (1983): 405–10; Gitenstein, R., *Apocalyptic Messianism and Contemporary Jewish-American Poetry* (1986)

PATRICK MEANOR

MELVILLE, Herman

b. 1 August 1819, New York City; d. 28 September 1891, New York City

The author of such classics as *Typee* (1846), *Moby-Dick* (1851), *Pierre* (1852), "Bartleby" (1853), "Benito Cereno" (1855), and *Billy Budd* (wr. 1888, pub. 1924), M. launched his career boldly but soon lapsed into literary oblivion. His actual fame came thirty years after his death during the "M. Revival" of the mid-1920s.

The son of a bankrupt New York importer, M. left home in 1841 on the whaler *Acushnet* and returned four years later on the naval frigate *United States* bearing maritime and Polynesian experiences that would shape most of his prose fiction and some of his poetry. He achieved instant success with his first book *Typee;* however, the following ten years of intense composition, which yielded his most familiar work, brought only declines in his reputation, royalties and great expectations. During the next floundering decade, the author traveled, lectured, and sought with no success diplomatic appointments as well as a Civil War naval commission. He had given up prose and turned exclusively to poetry, but the failure of *Battle-Pieces* (1866) to rejuvenate his career pushed M. into the New York Customs Office. Marital discord, heavy drinking, and the apparent suicide of his teen-aged son Malcolm culminate this disastrous phase of the author's life. Thereafter, he gave up writing as a profession, eschewed literary circles, and tended to his bureaucratic duties as an inspector of imports. Nevertheless, he continued to write, publishing in severely limited editions the massive poem *Clarel* (1876) and two slimmer volumes of poetry. He died virtually forgotten six years after his retirement from Customs, leaving several packets of poems and all of *Billy Budd* in manuscript.

Creator of some of the 19th c.'s most innovative narratives and challenging poems, M. occupies one of the highest stations in the pantheon of world writers. But this acclaim is largely a 20th-c. phenomenon. In his day, M. wrote uniquely American works to fill the call for a national literature, and though that call was issued by sympathetic friends, American readers failed to acknowledge his true contribution to the cause. Ironically, this neglect and M.'s eventual resurrection only added to the author's modern appeal. For today's artists, authors, and composers, for thinkers and academics in diverse fields, for elitists and populists alike, he has become the "Great American Author," and *Moby-Dick* the "Great American Novel." A writer of the 1840s, he was not fully endorsed until the 1940s.

The relative "newness" of M.'s reputation accounts for the problematic shape of M. criticism. Critics tend to gravitate toward *Moby-Dick* treating earlier works as preparatory lessons in narrative and thematic manipulation and the later fictions as evidence of creative deterioration. The notion that M. "peaked" so early (fostered by M.'s first biographers) has encouraged the belief that M. was fatally at odds with readers, that he would or could not write for popular consumption, and that "Dollars damn[ed him]." Moreover, critics have found cause for M.'s presumed aesthetic failures in the author's loss of faith not simply in God but in the power of language itself. And while the "peak theory" of M.'s creativity has some validity, it tends to detract from the intriguing narrative experiments attempted in the later works and to perpetuate neglect of the poetic phase, both the reasons for M.'s turning exclusively to poetry and the technical brilliance of the poems themselves. To grasp the fullness of M.'s achievements, a reader must grow beyond *Moby-Dick*—as did M.—and embrace all phases of the author's artistic development.

Clear indications of the major themes and narrative problems addressed throughout M.'s career can be found in *Typee*. Bored with the routine and petty authoritarianism of whaling life, the first-person protagonist Tommo and his companion Toby jump ship at Nukuhiva into the clutches of the Typees, a seemingly gentle people about whom, however, there are hints of cannibalism. The natives, especially the ever-serviceable Kory-Kory and the lovely Fayaway, attend to the sailors' needs, in particular Tommo's mysteriously wounded leg. Early on, Toby makes his escape, and after some weeks of alternating moods ranging from contentment to midnight panic, Tommo finagles a trip to the shore and makes a dramatic dash for an awaiting ship.

One is hard pressed to call *Typee* a novel, for it blends social and anthropological observations in a travelog format along with minimal characterization and plot. Nevertheless, for all its lush description, the book is a deeply interior research into the sensual encounter between modern mind and primitive "other." Tommo's wound symbolizes the ambivalence of Eden: it mends when he acquiesces to the native's sexual and social freedoms but it flares when he contemplates the mysteries of taboo and primitive mores. On the whole, the Typees are more caring Christians than the emissaries and missionaries of Western culture whose imperialism perverts native ways and natural religion. However, the book's liberalism falters when the threat of savagery paradoxically undercuts native benevolence. But Tommo's rejection of primitivism does not invalidate the book's multiculturalism, especially in the eyes of the American evangelical establishment that so harshly reviewed M.'s attacks on missionaries that M. was forced to expurgate offensive passages in subsequent editions. The discovery in 1983 of three chapters of M.'s working draft manuscript of *Typee* has stimulated new interest in the author's early personal growth and creative process. In addition, new historicists are turning to the book as a valuable reflection of the problems of colonialism, multiculturalism, the "other," and sexuality.

With Tommo, M. established the comic yet reflective first-person tone that would culminate four years later in Ishmael. M. carried that voice to *Omoo* (1847) emphasizing humor more than insight. Like most sequels—M. actually included passages dropped from *Typee*—this book is not fully satisfying: as the title's translation implies, it "wanders." The narrator and his companion, the risible Long Ghost, spend idle weeks jailed for mutiny in the "calaboose," beachcombing Tahiti and other islands, and observing such inhabitants as Queen Pomare. Aside from their incarceration, there is no tense conflict between island and Western minds inherent in the fearsome captivity of the Typees. What remains in *Omoo* is a comic but desultory work that few critics have seriously attempted to comprehend.

The publication of *Mardi* (1849) marked the beginning of a dramatic intellectual and artistic exploration in M.'s life, and yet its poor reception foreshadowed significant future failures in reaching readers. M.'s contacts with the liberal "Young America" group, and in particular Evert Duyckinck, encouraged him to read deeply in the classics. He was, as well, drawn to German and American transcendentalism, but though he could engage Goethe's and Ralph Waldo EMERSON's "yea-saying" sensibility, he remained wary of its too-facile optimism preferring an admixture of darkness typified in Nathaniel HAWTHORNE's work. M. was also concerned by America's reckless expansionism. Thus, philosophy, politics, and art were on M.'s mind when he wrote *Mardi,* and to relate its thin plot details is to detract attention from the book's ultimate thematic impact as a Sergio-comic and allegorical dialogue on contemporary issues.

Nevertheless, the book begins with a familiar Melvillean plot device: bored with life at sea, the protagonist (later identified as Taji) jumps ship and floats about Polynesia with several eccentrics (Jarl, Samoa, and Annatoo). They encounter Aleema, high priest of the Mardian archipelago, his three sons, and his daughter Yillah, whom they are about to sacrifice. Taji kills Aleema, rescues Yillah, and enjoys brief bliss with her until one morning she vanishes. The rest of the romance is Taji's quest for Yillah, which takes him from one allegorical island to the next, each providing an occasion for discussions on ethics, aesthetics, and politics. Taji's discussants are Mohi (the historian), Yoomy (the poet), and proto-Ishmaelite Babbalanja (the philosopher). Their governor, the patient King Media, mediates the three whose ramblings keep Taji intellectually occupied during his emotionally obsessive search for Yillah (ideal truth). Plot tensions return when Taji is distracted by the temptress Hautia (sensuality) whom he resists, and the book ends with him in mad pursuit of his dream.

Part romance, part satire, *Mardi* is a working out of metaphysical and political problems. Here, storytelling gives way to philosophizing, fact to fiction; but with the instinctual Taji and wise Babbalanja, we see the genesis of Ahab and Ishmael, and with the lush floral imagery conjoined to programmatic allegorical devices, we find evidence of M.'s inchoate symbolism. But for all its experimentation, *Mardi* is more than just an artist's notebook best read by scholars. Its intriguing paradox is that despite Babbalanja's early pronouncement that truth is "voiceless," M. continues for over one hundred and fifty chapters to voice truths. The paradox does not, however, detract from the novel's form; rather, it engenders a necessarily openended process of unfolding, a structure of "endless pursuit." In this regard, *Mardi* is as comical as it is brooding, and it is this serio-comic and picturesque tone that aesthetically redeems the patchwork.

M. was not fazed by *Mardi*'s failure: it was a narrative experiment necessary for his art not his reputation, and he immediately returned to erecting more saleable (and sailable) crafts. *Redburn* (1849) and *White-Jacket* (1850) flowed as confidently as they did quickly from the pen. Each he dismissed as a potboiler, but the disclaimer does not diminish their excellence.

Redburn draws upon M.'s first sea voyage, an 1839 journey on the packet *St. Lawrence* to Liverpool and back. The fifteen-year-old title character is painfully wet behind the ears. A destitute aristocrat, he knows nothing of ship life, duty, protocol, or suffering and is forever forced to endure menial jobs and humiliation. He soon learns the ropes on board the *Highlander* but not before witnessing a suicide, sleeping in the dead man's bunk, and withstanding the insults and threats of the inexplicably malevolent mate, Jackson. In England, the maturing lad observes the squalor of Liverpool (including the three-day death of a homeless mother and her three infants in the town's Launcelott's-Hey district) but also the merriment of the countryside where he befriends another penniless aristocrat, the sexually ambivalent Harry Bolton, who later joins Redburn as a shipmate on the *Highlander*'s return home. Liverpool is a shock to the American. Armed with his father's outdated guide book, he quickly learns that change is the world's first principle. He learns, too, that escape from suffering is impossible, for his ship's "cargo" is five hundred seasick, malnourished, and dismayed immigrants trapped below in their own filth for two months. Liverpool's squalor is in the hold. On the same voyage home, a traveler spontaneously combusts, Jackson pitches overboard, and Redburn is cheated out of his wages. The boy-man takes leave of the maritime but Harry, equally ill-suited to sea life, stays on only to be crushed to death by a whale. A bildungsroman, *Redburn* is M.'s first "true" novel in that its controlled philosophizing is kept strictly within the bounds of the central character's development. Like *Typee,* and to some degree better than that earlier work, its narrative objectives and point of view are well defined.

White-Jacket, however, has no discernible plot, nor conventional character development. Rather, it is a fictionalized narrative of facts concerning life on a U.S. man-of-war, and it is a narrative with an ax to grind against the enormity of flogging. Describing all facets of navy codes, routine, and setting, the book invariably returns to its attack on authoritarianism from democratic as well as humanitarian grounds. Incidents such as the teasing of the poet Lemsford, the refusal of a common sailor to address his higher ranking brother who by chance visits his ship, the incarceration of Ushant for refusing to shave, Surgeon Cuticle's murderous, unnecessary amputation of a sailor's leg, Captain Claret's drunken, near-disastrous mishandling of the ship, and the coddling of a slave sailor in front of abused compatriots because he (unlike they) is worth cash—all argue strongly for serious reforms in that peculiar institution known as the Navy. In contrast to the degenerate autocrats is the gallant democrat, Jack Chase. Handsome precursor to Billy Budd, he acts instinctively to defend freedom and the rights of the common sailor, whom M. persistently refers to as "the people." If the man-of-war *Neversink* serves M. as a microcosm of American life, the narrator's talismanic white jacket symbolizes man's necessary isolation in both society and the universe. It takes a fateful plunge from the masthead to force White Jacket to shed his heavy garment, to cast off not only the repression of naval codes but that more insidious repression stemming from other men's scorn of individuality. The narrator's fall and survival become the symbolic replacement of the white jacket. Experience outmatches Object, and while White Jacket is no less isolated existentially, he is free to join humanity on his own terms, and free to write.

After writing five books in as many years and spending nearly three of those years in a New York City townhouse mingling his growing family with that of his brother, M. was ready for a vacation. A trip to Europe would provide rest and allow him time to peddle *White-Jacket* and garner ideas for new books. The author's journal for this four-month jaunt records a busy schedule of parties, literary conversations, and visits to museums and theaters in London and parts of France and Germany, all ending with a spell of Christmas homesickness that sent M. racing back to America ahead of schedule. He returned with the idea of writing a book on whaling and set to the project quickly enough although 1850 brought various interruptions, not the least of which were trips to the Berkshires (an ancestral setting beloved since childhood) and the transplanting of the family to a farm (Arrowhead) in that district. It took eighteen months to write *Moby-Dick; or, The Whale,* during which time M. befriended Hawthorne, residing in nearby Lenox.

Little is known but much is speculated on how M. composed his masterpiece. The cherished assertion that there were "two *Moby-Dick*s,"—i.e., an initial, factual treatment of whaling that gave way to a more metaphysical investigation inspired by Hawthorne—seems simplistic. As Walter Bezanson points out, M. had already taken deep plunges in *Mardi* and *White-Jacket* without having read any Hawthorne. But there is no doubt that *Moby-Dick* is M.'s most Shakespearean enterprise and that it grew concurrently with his feelings (recorded in ten surviving letters) with Hawthorne, whom M. considered to be America's answer to Shakespeare. *Moby-Dick,* fondly dedicated to

Hawthorne, can be taken, then, as a monument to an intense but all-too-brief literary friendship. M.'s appreciation of that author as well as his picturesque aesthetics and literary nationalism are ardently expressed in his review essay "Hawthorne and His *Mosses*" (1850).

Whether M. planned it from the outset or made it up as he went along, *Moby-Dick* is, in fact, two stories in one. There is, of course, the central tale of revenge: having lost a leg (and his love of nature) to a mythic, omniscient, and seemingly malevolent white whale, Ahab manipulates the *Pequod*'s international crew into a self-destructive pursuit of Moby Dick. The hunt is madness to the pragmatic first mate Starbuck, but by allegorizing the whale into an emblem of a malignant universe, Ahab is able to galvanize support among the crew, and readers as well. It seems a logical madness. Various reports of Moby Dick are delivered through encounters (or gams) with other whalers. Finally, though, Ahab tracks the whale by dead reckoning, without compass or sextant, but in the three-day battle that ensues, the *Pequod,* its crew, and captain are destroyed. Only one survives to tell the tale—Ishmael.

Ishmael's development constitutes a second—and perhaps more significant—tale in *Moby-Dick*. He is the narrator and therefore controlling consciousness in the book. An anxious young man caught up in life's "hypoes," he avoids suicide and seeks self-knowledge at sea. He befriends Queequeg, a Polynesian prince and harpooner, in a New Bedford inn and quickly begins to cast aside his puritanical notions of religion and man for a deeper universal and cosmopolitan brotherhood. The opening third of *Moby-Dick* recounts the antics and insights occasioned by Ishmael and Queequeg's search for a whaling ship. We meet various (even ominous) characters (Peter Coffin, Elijah, Bildad and Peleg) and soon recognize that Ishmael is a sensitive thinker capable of drawing astute analogies between natural object and universal truths, even as he recognizes the world as one large practical joke. Like the rest of the crew, Ishmael becomes entranced by Ahab, who does not appear until after the *Pequod* sails out of sight of land. At this point, Ishmael's control of the narrative becomes problematic. In one chapter, normal narration gives way to a play depicting racial hostilities among the crew. At other times, we overhear the thoughts of characters (the jovial Stubb, troubled Starbuck, obsessive yet human Ahab) that Ishmael could not be privy to. Indeed, Ishmael is annihilated as a character in these dramatic (indeed Shakespearean) chapters that develop Ahab's presence. But throughout the vast middle section of the novel—what Howard Vincent called its "cetological center"—Ishmael appears as an omniscient voice anatomizing all parts of the whale, all aspects of whaling, and all corners of his and Ahab's distinctly different minds. Two of the many chapters epitomize the diversity of Ishmael's intellect: there is the parodic send-up of scientific classification in "Cetology" and there is the sublimely poetic investigation of fear in "The Whiteness of the Whale." Despite their cagey narrative irregularities, the divergent chapters—one comic, one tragic—typify Ishmael's comprehensive sensibility. Ultimately, Ishmael's tale dominates Ahab's, not simply because he is allowed to survive the fatal shipwreck but because unlike the single track mind of Ahab, Ishmael can embrace, comprehend, contain and control the fearful awareness of nihility that drives Ahab mad.

And there is more. Beyond plot, character, and tone, *Moby-Dick* engages readers in vital dialogues concerning the promise and limits of transcendental mysticism, the betrayal of democratic leadership, the toll of American capitalism, the value of primitivism set beside the impossibility of faith, and the perversity of racism amidst the hope of universal brotherhood. The book is as well a relentless exposure of the vacancy of being, a daring experiment in symbolism, and an equally daring examination of male sexuality. Despite claims that M. may have had homosexual encounters at sea, or with Hawthorne, no evidence for such speculation exists. Even so, M.'s own orientation is debatable. His heterosexuality was manifested in his conventional married life, but his writing is so intensely sexualized and homoerotic to boot that no reader can or should ignore its powerful homosexual and homosocial elements. Hints of homosexual desire are found in *Typee* and *Redburn* as well as *Moby-Dick* and *Pierre,* and they continue on most famously perhaps to the end in *Billy Budd.* But equally powerful instances of mixed gender love fill the same works, as well as the last, sensual Rose Poems. In all, it may be said that M. loved love; he was "pansexual"—hetero, homo and something in between.

Generally ignored in its own day, *Moby-Dick* now excites Christians, atheists, Marxists, African Americans, gays, feminists, Freudians, Jungians, humorists, and tragedians. The critical book, article, or encyclopedia entry is yet to be written that can ever fully account for this novel's endless angles: it is a world unto itself.

Early M. scholars marked the completion of *Moby-Dick* (and *Pierre*) as the beginning of the end of the author's creative powers, but the remarkable variations in characters, themes, genres, and narrative techniques in his subsequent fictions suggest instead a fertile period of experimentation. At this point, the author focuses more on the confused and isolated victims of society, generally in urban but also at times in rural and domestic settings. Rarely does M. return to the sea. He attempts different forms: the psychological novel, the short story, the biographical-historical pica-

resque, and comedy. But most significant are his experiments with point of view, in particular a variety of unreliable first-person speakers as well as equally problematic third-person narrators. The first of these experiments was *Pierre* (1852).

Even before he had published *Moby-Dick,* M. was planning his seventh book—a novel designed to sell, a "rural bowl of milk," he told Hawthorne, but also a "Kraken." Like this mythical sea beast, *Pierre* would indeed plunge deeply into problems of self, family, and sexuality. Based (it seems likely) on a family rumor that M.'s father had spawned in his pre-marital days an illegitimate daughter, the novel depicts an aristocratic but naive country lad's discovery and cover-up of his deceased father's sexual indiscretion. Intent upon protecting his prideful mother from the knowledge, Pierre abandons home and his fiancee Lucy to live in New York City, pretending to be husband to his newly-discovered, illegitimate half-sister Isabel, to whom he is uncannily drawn and whom he feels obliged to protect. Pierre's mother dies, but Lucy follows the duo and sets up housekeeping with them while Pierre attempts to make a go of it as a writer. The young man's trials with editors constitutes a ripe satire on New York's literary marketplace, including some of M.'s closest associates. Cousin Glen, now heir to Pierre's inheritance, claims Lucy as his bride, but Pierre shoots him dead. Visiting Pierre in jail, Lucy drops dead, and Pierre and Isabel take poison. A central philosophical matter in the novel is Plotinus Plinlimmon's pamphlet on horologicals and chronometricals (social versus ideal truths). M.'s ironies are such that readers are hard-pressed to accept or condemn the attractive but seemingly too pragmatic Plinlimmon (who advocates ethical trimming) as the novel's moral center. Toward the end, Pierre's dream of Enceladus, a titan fated to self-destruction, is a powerful vision of the neglected artist.

As one contemporary reviewer exclaimed, *Pierre* is a "bad book," and though modern critics are excited by its satires, ironies, and pre-Freudian probing of incest and Oedipus, the novel's excessive language (actually parodied in its day), its invalidation of Christian mores, and its schizophrenic third-person narrator who cannot decide whether to exalt or rail against his protagonist, doomed it to certain market failure. In fact, the novel almost ruined M., cutting short a career that was all too short in the end anyway. A spate of magazine writing forestalled failure.

M.'s phase as a writer for *Putnam's* and *Harper's* began with "Bartleby" in 1853 and ended in 1856 with the volume of selected pieces entitled *The Piazza Tales.* This period brought the author a constant income and allowed him the opportunity for further (and, given the problems of *Pierre,* recuperative) narrative experiments. Only recently have critics begun to place these writings in the context of the political and aesthetic ideologies of the magazines in which they appeared. In "The Encantadas," a series of sketches of the Galapagos Islands, "The Lightning-Rod Man," and "I and My Chimney," we find a return to the jaunty insightful voice of Ishmael, but with "Bartleby," "Cock-a-Doodle-Doo!" "The Piazza," and the curious "diptychs" or double tales such as "The Paradise of Bachelors and the Tartarus of Maids," we find a host of impercipient first-person speakers who, when forced to confront society's more impenetrable outcasts, seem carefully poised on the brink of a deeper insight that only begins to dawn as the tales end. There is much humor and sentiment in many of the tales that only ripen the inherent isolation of the various central figures, usually an unnamed or unknowable bachelor or henpecked husband—"isolatoes," to borrow from Ishmael. "The Bell-Tower," a Hawthornesque pastiche, is an exercise in reliable third-person storytelling, but M.'s brilliant rendering of a shipboard slave revolt in "Benito Cereno" is a modern medley of narrative techniques including an unreliable central consciousness perspective and a set of reports from different observers (borrowed from an original source). Surely an enduring classic, "Benito Cereno" (which like several other M. texts has been adapted to the stage) is no longer condemned as a formal and ideological embarrassment (early critics thought it plagiaristic and racist) but has become the exemplary critique of antebellum racism against which others are inevitably measured.

Also a product of this period is *Israel Potter* (1855), M.'s only serialized novel. This neglected picaresque tale of a hapless Revolutionary War hero contains attacks on American life and ideals broader and more direct than even *White-Jacket* or *Moby-Dick*. Captured at Bunker Hill and shipped as a POW to England, Israel escapes, performs various antics in the countryside, and is enlisted by British sympathizers as a courier to America's ambassador to France, Benjamin FRANKLIN. The revered statesman indoctrinates Israel in the ways of espionage and inevitably reveals his feet of clay. He is one of the first of M.'s confidence men. Also on hand are the rapacious John Paul Jones (a symbol of American policy) and the blustering Ethan Allen (symbol of America's frontier). Israel's corrosive life underground does not end with the close of the war. He subsists in London for fifty years in all, an exile and forgotten patriot. Drawn from the published narrative of an actual veteran of the Revolutionary War, *Israel Potter* contains penetrating characterizations, battle scenes, and descriptions of New England and London introducing imagery that more recent poets have also found compelling (see Frost's wood-

pile and Eliot's London Bridge). Although lacking the metaphysical depth of earlier works, the novel exposes but carefully contains M.'s bitterness toward American politics.

M.'s last novel is his most problematic. While it is clearly comic, *The Confidence-Man* (1857) possesses a narrative tone so detached as to evoke for some readers the chilling immorality of today's minimalists. And yet the often recondite and convoluted style suggests the author is attempting a literary confidence game that confronts readers with myriad moral dilemmas but no clear means of sorting them out. Moreover, M.'s most controlled third-person narrator is himself a CONFIDENCE MAN.

The action is tightly contained between sunrise and midnight on board the Mississippi steamboat *Fidèle,* which carries a microcosmic selection of Americans from St. Louis to New Orleans. The first half of the novel presents us with a succession of confidence men, each with a different scam (alms for poor Indians, stocks, charitable donations, personal loans, medicinal herbs) and each setting up customers for the con man to follow. Clearly, there is a conspiracy of some sort, but while some critics argue (with little supporting evidence) that each diddler is an "avatar" or disguise of a single confidence man (the devil), it is also clear that the novel is much more than a comic allegory of the failure of Christianity that such a reading suggests. The central issue is the problematic nature of faith: man cannot live safely with it nor can he live humanely without it. Those who resist being cheated are as damnable as those gullible souls who too freely surrender to belief.

The procession of confidence men in the first half gives way to a single character, Frank Goodman or the cosmopolitan, in the second. Goodman might be another con man; he might be another victim. The evidence is purposefully ambiguous; readers hoping for definitive conclusions learn to settle for irresolution. The novel's final effect is to engage readers in a process of doubt. Although Goodman dresses, speaks, even struts in outlandish con man fashion, he is himself accosted by far more suspicious characters. Each encounter is an occasion for extended dialogs on friendship, humor, irony, misanthropy and geniality. The cosmopolitan's project is to win converts over to having confidence in him, but is his motive genuine or merely the massaging of future victims? The climax to these successive philosophical matters (which includes an attack on the Emersonian view of friendship) is Goodman's diddling of the ship's barber out of a shave. But even here the evidence against the cosmopolitan is not conclusive, for just as Mark TWAIN's Huck Finn must lie to get people to do the right thing, Goodman seems constrained to con people into having faith. The novel ends with Goodman leading an old unconscious hypocrite into the ominous darkness of the ship's hold.

Critics have generally interpreted this novel as a satire on American benevolence, optimism, and Christianity. Accordingly, attempts have been made to identify characters within M.'s social milieu. But the novel, no matter how dark, is as much as a work of humor focusing on the necessary universal folly of belief. It argues that our humanity is as much defined by our instinctive drive to believe as it is by our instinct to hate. Thus Goodman's projection of the age's new man—a "genial misanthrope"—is a serious proposal, one that can be realized only after the reader is able to sustain the contradictions and doubts that the narrative leaves unresolved. In its complex mingling of humor and satire, the novel's structure most resembles Cervantes's *Don Quixote,* which M. reread before writing the book, and which is alluded to directly in the text. Also Cervantine is Goodman's windmill-tilting idealism as well as M.'s digressive chapters on writing fiction and the interpolated tales of Goneril, China Aster, Moredock the merciless Indian hater, and Charlemont.

M. did not publish another book until 1866. The intervening decade was easily the author's most troublesome period. Near mental and physical breakdown brought on by the strain of so much work and so little gain led M. to a recuperative journey to Europe and the Holy Land (1856–57). He visited Hawthorne in Liverpool, saw much of the Mediterranean, and marveled at Jerusalem. Again he kept a journal that would serve him particularly well with *Clarel.* After three futile years back home on the lecture circuit educating lyceum goers on the wonders of the Pacific and the Vatican museum, M. turned exclusively to poetry. Plans in 1860 for a volume of poems were not actualized; however, the Civil War provided the author (living in Gramercy Park since 1863) with suitable subjects for an ambitious collection: *Battle-Pieces* (1866). The poems vary considerably in length from the short, almost imagistic vision of John Brown's body in "The Portent" to rangier narratives such as "The Scout toward Aldie," which draws upon M.'s visit behind the lines. But each piece is remarkable for its compression of line and intense feeling for the "conflict of convictions" that brought brother against brother. In "The Apparition," the uncontrollable malignancy of war in general is epitomized by the unexpected emergence of a volcanic cone in a green field. Unfortunately, a nation otherwise intent upon impeaching its president for adhering to Lincoln's wish for leniency toward the South was not ready to read M.'s antiwar sentiments or his plea for reconciliation. The book, like all but *Typee,* failed.

Civil War seemed a prophecy of M.'s own mid-life crisis. Letters discovered in 1975 revealed for the first time that in 1867 M.'s wife, Elizabeth Shaw Melville (daughter of Massachusetts Supreme Court Chief Justice Lemuel Shaw), seriously considered a separation. M. had become intolerable, perhaps abusive, perhaps "insane." The Shaw family supported the idea of Elizabeth's removal, but in the end, she stuck it out. Six months later their first son, seventeen-year-old Malcolm, committed suicide. The tragedy, it might be said, saved the marriage and surely made its mark throughout such later works as the poem "The Chipmunk" and M.'s final tale of sacrificed innocence, *Billy Budd.*

After *Battle Pieces,* M. did not publish again until *Clarel* (1876), a modern epic longer than *Paradise Lost* and financed largely by contributions from the author's uncle. The title character (whose name rhymes with "barrel") is a divinity student hoping that Jerusalem will help him recapture his lost faith. Instead, he falls in love with Ruth, daughter of Nathan, an American atheist turned Jew now farming the desert. When Arabs kill Nathan, and Ruth goes into mourning, Clarel joins a group of "pilgrims" on a tour of the Dead Sea area. He is accompanied by characters with various world views: Nehemiah the millennialist, Vine the poetic genius, Rolfe the mediator of head and heart. And they in turn meet others in transit including the positivist Margoth, the self-destructive monomaniac Mortmain, and the Confederate veteran Ungar—each continuing the ongoing discussion of material and spiritual values. At the monastery Mar Saba the pilgrims engage in several nights of revelry in which Clarel becomes more attracted to the Hawthornesque Vine. But the shy artist will not reciprocate. The final blow is Ruth's death, but Clarel endures the tragedy becoming a perpetual pilgrim preparing as the epic ends for yet another tour of the Holy Land.

Clarel has the undeserved reputation of being unreadable. True, its grand, pentameter thoughts crammed into unyielding four-beat lines often create elliptical periods and contorted syntax, and yet the graphic wasteland setting, boldly drawn eccentrics, and dramatic quest for belief amidst episodes of failed love and climactic death make the ambitious poem a crucial document of the crisis of faith. Like *Mardi, Moby-Dick,* or *The Confidence-Man,* it is a masterpiece, one of several "peaks" in M.'s long life of writing by which we must measure the author's evolving artistic genius.

Neglected as a poet and virtually forgotten as a writer of fiction, M. (the self-styled "outdoor Customs House Official") did not neglect his poetry or his craft. Returning to familiar sea topics with *John Marr* (1888), he published in a limited edition four nostalgic portraits of sailors and several shorter "sea-pieces" including such important contributions to American verse as "The Berg," "The Maldive Shark," and "The Enviable Isles." *Timoleon* (1891), published in the year of M.'s death, collects numerous poems on art and politics, notably the title piece, which concerns a power struggle between brothers in ancient Greece, the highly sexual "After the Pleasure Party," the oddly truncated sonnet "Art," and such brilliant gems as "Monody" and "Milan Cathedral." Other similar poems not published until thirty years after M.'s death are the "Burgundy Club Sketches" including the dialog on the picturesque in "At the Hostelry" and the remarkably symbolic tableau of art and humor tensely poised beside Italian revolt and oppression in "Naples in the Time of Bomba." Also posthumously published is the volume *Weeds and Wildings* (1924), a collection of love poems and other ditties intended as a valentine for M.'s patient wife. Principal among these pieces is "Rip Van Winkle's Lilac," which, like the poem "John Marr," is an extended prose sketch plus narrative poem. Not only does this work record M.'s enduring appreciation of Irving and his famous character, but its rewriting of Rip's return emphasizes the old loafer as both a lover and neglected but finally victorious artist. But the best of the collection are its Rose Poems, a dozen or so highly sensual studies in various forms concerning the discovery of spiritual transcendence within physical desire.

Like *Weeds and Wildings, Billy Budd, Sailor* (1924) was found in manuscript decades after the author's death. The tragedy (perhaps M.'s most transcendent work) takes place during the Napoleonic wars. A handsome young sailor is pressed into duty aboard the British warship *Bellipotent*. The lad is loved for his innocence by everyone except John Claggart, the ship's inexplicably malicious Master-at-arms. Billy's only "flaw" is his tendency to stutter under stress, and when Claggart pushes too far, the frustrated sailor kills his superior in one instinctive blow of the fist. The too-rational Captain Vere recognizes Billy's innocence but argues that such mutinous acts in war time demand swift reprisals. Billy is hanged the next morning, but with "God bless Captain Vere" on his lips. Vere, a good man fated to compound evil with evil, dies the following year muttering "Billy Budd, Billy Budd" to uncomprehending attendants.

Scholars Harrison Hayford and Merton M. Sealts, Jr., have determined that this tale of innocence, iniquity, and authority began as the simple ballad "Billy in the Darbies" that now concludes the tale but which was probably intended as a separate inclusion in *John Marr*. At first the poem required a brief prose headnote, but that note grew in magnitude with the addition of plot and the characters Claggart and Vere. The

finished work that we know, a novella not a poem, is, in fact, the patient work of editors, not the final polishings of the author. Critics continue to argue whether Billy's fate represents M.'s own "acceptance" of the inherent tragedy of life or his ironic "resistance" to society's "measured forms." Whatever the interpretation and, indeed, because of the diversity of opinion, *Billy Budd* remains one of M.'s best known works. No less important is the role of the novella's discovery and publication, which helped initiate the "M. Revival" of the 1920s and finally reintroduced M.—seaman, novelist, poet, and bureaucrat—to the appreciative audience he had hoped to reach throughout his varied works and troubled days.

BIBLIOGRAPHY: Adler, J. S., *War in M.'s Imagination* (1981); Anderson, C. R., *M. in the South Seas* (1939); Brodhead, R., *Hawthorne, M. and the Novel* (1976); Bryant, J., ed., *The Companion to M. Studies* (1986); Bryant, J., *M. and Repose* (1993); Cohen, H., and D. Yannella, *H. M.'s Malcolm Letter* (1992); Davis, M. R., *M.'s Mardi* (1952); Dillingham, W., *M.'s Short Fiction* (1977); Dryden, E. A., *M.'s Thematics of Form* (1968); Fisher, M., *Going Under* (1977); Garner, S., *The Civil War World of H. M.* (1993); Herbert, T. W., *Marquesan Encounters* (1980); Horth, L., ed., *Correspondence* (1993); Howard, L., *H. M.* (1950); James, C. L. R., *Mariners, Renegades, and Castaways* (1953); Karcher, C. L., *Shadow over the Promised Land* (1980); Leyda, J., *The M. Log* (1951, 1969); Martin, R. K., *Hero, Captain, and Stranger* (1986); Parker, H., *H. M.: A Biography* (1996); Post-Lauria, S., *Correspondent Colorings* (1996); Quirk, T., *M.'s Confidence Man;* Robertson-Lorant, L., *M.: A Biography* (1996); Rogin, M. P., *Subversive Genealogy* (1983); Rosenberry, E., *M.'s Comic Spirit* (1955); Shurr, W., *The Mystery of Iniquity: M. as Poet* (1972); Sundquist, E. J., *To Wake the Nations* (1993); Vincent, H., *The Trying-Out of Moby-Dick* (1948); Wenke, J., *M.'s Muse* (1995)

JOHN BRYANT

MENCKEN, H[enry] L[ouis]

b. 12 September 1880, Baltimore, Maryland; d. 29 January 1956, Baltimore, Maryland

The most influential critic of American literature and culture in the 1920s, M. remains a powerful rhetorical presence in the history of the American essay. The scholarly interest in language that he so ably demonstrated in *The American Language* (1919)—with several revisions followed by two supplements in 1945 and 1948—was matched by the linguistic inventiveness of his own often comically antagonistic prose.

M.'s copious writings for the *Sunpapers* of Baltimore (from 1906 through 1948), the *Smart Set* (from 1908 through 1923), the *American Mercury* (from its establishment in 1923 until M.'s resignation from the editorship in 1933), and the *New Yorker* (from 1935 until 1948) represented a distinctly aggressive form of the journalistic essay. In place of the "elephantine whimsicality" of more conventional columnists and familiar essayists, M. proffered "iconoclastic gaiety, a boyish weakness for tweaking noses and pulling whiskers, [and an] obscene delight in slang." His prose was consistently exuberant and hyperbolic—whether he was promoting his favorite authors—Joseph Conrad, Sinclair LEWIS, Theodore DREISER, Willa CATHER—or denouncing familiar targets, including politicians, preachers, and professors ("academic idiots"); the leaders and followers of cults, religions, and social organizations ("klans and sodalities"); and the general species of what he called *boobus Americanus.* In short, what M. both provided and evoked was a new ethos for the essay, one distinguished by the comically antagonistic stance of his own textual self.

Despite M.'s own admission that a writer's persona is inevitably a "gaudy" fabrication, many readers have overlooked M.'s genuine artistry, praising or damning the man without recognizing how the narrative voice has been created and crafted. By considering how his persona has been fashioned, how his voice evokes a satirical vision of America, and finally how that vision is imposed upon the reader, one may achieve a clearer understanding of M.'s art. Consistent with his aim to "stir up the animals," M. in his most famous essays—those gathered in *A M. Chrestomathy* (1949) and *The Vintage M.* (1955), edited by Alistair Cooke—frequently poses as the fiercely antidemocratic aristocrat who at the same time boasts joyously of his vulgarity and common tastes. A Juvenalian skeptic and Rabelaisian debunker, he ridicules the enemy, which can be identified broadly as M.'s rhetorically forged "America."

This agonistic relationship of persona to environment—represented by the rebel versus the rabble, the "enlightened minority" set against the "anthropoid majority"—is accentuated by the prominence in his rhetoric of antithetical constructions, comic hyperbole, incongruous analogies, ubiquitous lists, and outrageous epithets. His antic prose style is at once self-defining and self-deflating, much as the self-mocking omniscience that M. often feigns in his work is merely the outward sign of an all-pervasive skepticism. Likewise, M.'s combative stance both presumes and establishes solidarity with his audience: the sympathetic reader, of course, is in on the joke.

Nonetheless, while it is unlikely that M.'s reputation will endure primarily on the strength of his ideas—heavily influenced by the writings of T. H. Huxley, Friedrich Nietzsche, and Bernard Shaw—or the quality of his literary criticism (primarily impressionistic and propagandistic), he generally employs humor not as an end in itself but in the service of his ideas. As a result, divisions arise in his texts: outrage coupled with amusement can produce ambiguity. The penchant for self-burlesque threatens to undermine the seriousness of *any* idea set forth, and thus the experience of reading M. may ultimately create in the reader that same skepticism and suspicion of authority that M. himself maintains.

M.'s fall from fashion after his heyday in the 1920s has been well recorded. The increasingly predictable nature of his attacks, the overly familiar prose style, and the painful irrelevance of his anti-democratic pose in the face of the Great Depression all contributed to the decline of the *American Mercury* and to the waning popularity of its editor. But while he may have met the common fate of the celebrity in America, M. soon found new readers through his "excessively subjective" memoirs, gathered eventually in the three *Days* books—*Happy Days* (1940), *Newspaper Days* (1941), and *Heathen Days* (1943). More nostalgic than antagonistic, more "yarning" (he confessed) than fact, M.'s autobiographical essays share with his earlier writings the presence of an antic voice reminding the reader at every turn that "the record of an event is no doubt often "bedizened and adulterated" by the writer's response to it.

Decades after his death, M. continues to "stir up the animals" with his prejudices. Upon publication of both *The Diary of H. L. M.,* edited by Charles A. Fecher, in 1989, and his fourth autobiographical volume, *My Life as Author and Editor,* edited by Jonathan Yardley, in 1993, a number of reviewers expressed dismay at M.'s numerous mean-spirited, racist, and anti-Semitic characterizations. One need not excuse M.'s verbal crudities and cruelties with the simplistic claim that ethnic slurs were commonplace in his day. More likely, M.'s own response to the critics would still be that free expression means nothing unless it entitles a person "to be foolish and even malicious."

BIBLIOGRAPHY: Bode, C., *M.* (1969); Fecher, C. A., *M.: A Study of His Thought* (1978); Hobson, F., *M.: A Life* (1994); Martin, E.A., *H. L. M. and the Debunkers* (1984)

RICHARD NORDQUIST

MEREDITH, William
b. 9 January 1919, New York City

Though not widely anthologized for a long period beginning in 1950, M. went on to win both the Pulitzer

Prize and the National Book Award for his collections *Partial Accounts* (1987) and *Effort at Speech* (1997) respectively.

M. began writing seriously in the early 1940s. Much of his poetry from this time was influenced by his time spent in military service. *Love Letter from an Impossible Land* (1944) conveys the fascination and horror of a world in global conflict. Some of the poems reflect M.'s personal feelings, while others are written in a more formal, codified verse. The latter variety show M.'s fierce reaction to waves created by his contemporaries, T. S. ELIOT and Ezra POUND; he was committed to the traditional forms.

Ships and Other Figures (1948) centers on the thoughts and feelings of a career fighter pilot, now without a war, recalling past glories. This volume included a number of notes, influenced in part by Eliot, explaining military terminology that many readers found cumbersome, and, as M. later admitted, took away from the force of the poetry by focusing too much on meaning. Published in 1961, *The Open Sea and Other Poems* was also received with mixed critical reception. But this only served to strengthen M.'s commitment to what he deemed well-crafted verse. Some critics, James DICKEY among them, praised this volume for its precision, grace, and depth. However, Dickey also wrote that the writing was also "muffled and distant, a kind of thin, organized, slightly academic murmur." *The Wreck of the Thresher* (1964) too received mixed reviews, but seemed to signal M.'s enlarged ambition.

M. loosened considerably in his 1970 collection *Earth Walk,* and in it one finds some of his best writing. This volume emphasizes M.'s variety and quirks. *Hazard, the Painter* (1975) is considered by many his best. Technically, it exhibits a highly evolved voice and personality. Thematically, by focusing on this painter, Hazard, it explores the artist's struggle with potency, ego, and the agony of stunted creativity.

Drawing from previous collections, including *The Cheer* (1980) and unpublished poems from 1958 to 1983, *Effort at Speech* reaffirmed M.'s critical reputation. In this volume's forward, Michael Collier writes of M.'s famed optimism and of the high esteem in which he is held by his peers. Writing in a time of great spiritual malaise, M. offered hope, not by denying the darkness, but by proclaiming his belief in the power of poetry. In "The Cheer," he wrote: "Words addressing evil won't turn evil back / but they can give heart / The cheer is hidden in right words."

BIBLIOGRAPHY: Howard, R., *Alone with America: Essays on the Art of Poetry in the United States since 1950* (1969; rev. ed., 1980); Moul, K., "W. M.," in Greiner, D. J., ed., *DLB,* vol. 9, part 2, *American Poets since World War II* (1980): 46–52

JASON MCMAHON

MERRILL, James

b. 3 March 1926, New York City; d. 6 February 1995, Tucson, Arizona

M. is generally regarded as one of the finest poets in America today. The high finish, technical brilliance, and intricate elaborations of his poetry have earned him two National Book Awards, the Bollington Prize, the Pulitzer Prize in poetry, and—initially—a reputation for somewhat recherché elegance. That reputation has been generally offset since 1962 by gathering strands of narrative and autobiographical candor in his writing. Robert LOWELL's *Life Studies* was an influence upon M., as upon all poets of his generation who permit themselves a cathartic look inward, but Marcel Proust and W. H. AUDEN seem deeper influences, their lessons evident in the circumstantial immediacy of M.'s poems and in his alertness to meanings that unfold themselves from deceptively casual phrases and images.

M.'s essential subject was evident in the early poems collected in *The Black Swan* (1946) and *First Poems* (1951), many of which are about scenes on the brink of symbolic transfiguration, especially in the eyes of children. In the poems collected in *The Country of a Thousand Years of Peace* (1959; rev. ed., 1970), the world still longs for transfiguration, but the center of imaginative awareness is more adult than before and is alert to its role in the transfigurational process. The emergence of autobiographical candor in the poems of *Water Street* (1962) evidences a change in M.'s thinking about the emotional accommodations of verse but no diminution of his interest in the capacity of mind and metaphor to alter private experience into something revelational.

The great work of M.'s maturity is *The Changing Light at Sandover* (1982), an omnibus assemblage of three books, "The Book of Ephraim" in *Divine Comedies* (1976), *Mirabell: Books of Number* (1978), and *Scripts for the Pageant* (1980), together with a coda entitled "The Higher Keys." As a developing story of M.'s adventures with the occult, the trilogy is organized upon the system of the Ouija board and plays host to a number of voices in time and in eternity. It is ultimately both a serious work of reportage and an exercise in camp playfulness. That combination reminds us that M.'s poems have functioned from the first as ritualistic invocations of a meaning that hides behind the scrim of individual experience, bespeaking itself at different points in the oeuvre (and, presumably, in the author's life) through agencies unexpected and odd.

From the First Nine: Poems, 1946–1976, a selection of M.'s poetry, was published in 1982 as a companion volume to The Changing Light at Sandover. Its overview suggests the growth that made Sandover possible—the growth in particular of an instantly recognizable poetic voice, gracefully cadenced and unobtrusively musical, intimate and self-assured. The same may be said for M.'s posthumous collection A Scattering of Salts (1995). From his twenties, M. was a remarkably accomplished poet, but the liberation of narrative and autobiographical elements in his work makes his voice uniquely affecting.

BIBLIOGRAPHY: Bloom, H., ed., J. M. (1985); Lehman, D., and C. Berger, eds., J. M.: Essays in Criticism (1983); McClatchy, J. D., "J. M.," Paris Review, 84 (Summer 1982): 194–219; Moffett, J., J. M. (1984)

ROBERT F. KIERNAN

MERTON, Thomas

b. 31 January 1915, Prades, France; d. 10 December 1968, Bangkok, Thailand

M. is the foremost Roman Catholic clerical writer of modern American literature; Victor Kramer contends that he achieved "the most fruitful career of any priest/poet in American letters." Born in France to artistic parents, M. lived in New York, France, and England before receiving a B.A. (1938) and an M.A. (1939) at Columbia University, where Mark VAN DOREN was a teacher and close friend. He taught English at St. Bonaventure University from 1939 until December 1941, when he entered the Trappist monastery at Gethsemani, Kentucky, receiving ordination to the priesthood eight years later. M. was accidentally fatally electrocuted in 1968 while attending a conference of the Benedictine and Cistercian orders in Asia.

His best-selling autobiographical account of his religious conversion, The Seven Storey Mountain (1948), recalls Augustine's Confessions rewritten for a post-Christian era, as M. recounted his turn away from the successes and satisfactions of his early life as author and teacher and toward the interior life of a monastic. Yet within the cloister, M.'s literary career flowered even more profusely. Poetry, letters, essays, reviews, and books charted his personal struggle to live as a contemporary Christian. His growing eagerness to confront worldly issues—the war in Vietnam, poverty, racial segregation, Third World cultures and religions—forged a link between the life of monasticism and social activism, making him a figure of admiration as well as controversy.

As M. himself acknowledged in an anthology of his work, The T. M. Reader (1964), his life and writings were compounded of contrary ideas: "I have had to accept the fact that my life is almost totally paradoxical." An authority on and practitioner of the tradition of medieval monasticism yet thoroughly engaged with the topical issues of his day, committed to a vow of silence yet devoted to a vigorous dialogue with the world he had ostensibly "rejected," and living his final years as a solitary hermit yet in great demand as a speaker and commentator, M.'s writings defined for many the model of the contemporary, socially aware Christian. His work is grounded in the individual's search for meaning in a relationship with God and the application of this relationship to the world at large, hence his concern for social justice and his growing interest in and affinity for Eastern religions.

His imagistic poetry shares with his prose an intentionally confrontational clarity of expression and emotional intensity; not only social problems but complex theological issues acquire an immediacy and verve in a style that is often gnomic, illustrated in Seeds of Contemplation (1949): "A tree gives glory to God by being a tree." In an age of "totalitarianism," as M. stated in Thoughts in Solitude (1956), he felt it "right to demand a hearing for any and every sane reaction in favor of man's inalienable solitude and interior freedom. The murderous din of materialism cannot be allowed to silence the independent voices of Christian saints, or the Oriental sages like Lao-Tse or the Zen masters, or the voices of men like [Henry David] THOREAU or Martin Buber or Max Picard." The focus of his life and work is best summarized by the title of a collection of his essays, Contemplation in a World of Action (1971).

BIBLIOGRAPHY: Kountz, P., T. M. as Writer and Monk (1991); Kramer, V., T. M. (1984); Mott, M., The Seven Mountains of T. M. (1984)

CHRISTOPHER BAKER

MERWIN, W[illiam] S[tanley]

b. 30 September 1927, New York City

M. is one of the most distinctive and prolific poets currently writing, having published works of poetry, prose, drama and translation. He has won many of the most prestigious awards available to poets: the Harriet Monroe Memorial Prize from Poetry (1967), the Pulitzer Prize in poetry (1971), a Guggenheim Fellowship, the Bollingen Prize, and, more recently, the Tanning Prize from the Academy of American Poets for outstanding and proven mastery in poetry. His semiautobiographical prose work The Lost Upland was distinguished by the *New York Times Book Review* as one of the top nine books of 1992. His many translations include *Poem of the Cid* (1959), *The Song of Roland* (1970), poems by Pablo Neruda, Jean Follain, Osip Mandelstam, and the exquisite *Sun at Midnight* (1989), a book of poems and sermons by Muso Soseki.

In his foreword to M.'s first book, *A Mask for Janus* (1952), winner of the Yale Series of Younger Poets, W. H. AUDEN notes M.'s awareness of both poetic tradition and of myth. Many critics note the role of myth in M.'s work, less the specific role it plays in, for instance, W. B. Yeats's poetry, but instead a process of mythmaking. His poems often have the authority of the ancient while actually being contemporary. Though the human mind and memory play roles in his landscapes, there is more distinctly a sense of the pure object perceived in a nearly secret, almost lost nature. For his trust of the senses and his affinity for nature, M. has drawn comparisons to writers of the romantic movement. His use of nature as his source of images, especially the use of totemic animals who are often the communicative link between man and nature, best illustrates his adaptation of the mythic process. M.'s interest in myth was shared by at least two close associates: Robert Graves, whose son M. tutored in 1950, and longtime friend and neighbor, Joseph Campbell.

M.'s evocative, spiritual poems resist classification within a particular genre or movement. Critics have suggested Yeats, Ezra POUND, Auden, John Keats, John Crowe RANSOM, and the French symbolists as likely influences; M. has even mentioned Anonymous, or the oral tradition in literature, as a debt. His books often mystify critics upon first appearance, maybe because of this impossibility of classifying M., or perhaps because each book represents a new evolution of both poetic style and vision. At a time when the confessional school made self-revelatory poetry expected rather than shocking, M. shocked by producing poems with a deeply intimate tone while managing to leave the identity of the speaker vague or altogether absent. Often epitaphic, often cryptic, his poetry seems to take place outside of time and space. In his early books, *A Mask for Janus*, *The Dancing Bears* (1954), and *Green with Beasts* (1956), critics could address his use of traditional forms. But as M. began to experiment more with both form and tone, he was occasionally accused of being gratuitously inscrutable.

The disorientation we feel when reading M.'s poems, M. might argue, is a result of the fact that he is reintroducing us to the environment to which we have become ignorant, numb and senseless: the natural world. In *The Lice* (1967), possibly M.'s most widely known and certainly most controversial book, M. addresses what he sees as the rift between man and nature. His tone is of bitter disappointment in humanity for its failure to appreciate and care for its environment. In poems like "The Last One," humanity is punished by nature for its abuses. The parablelike narrative's voice seems beyond time or humanity, like a voice from the earth itself. This voice comes in part from M.'s experiments with style; the decrease in punctuation and significance of line breaks placed for emphasis begun most distinctly here in *The Lice* continues through M.'s later poetry.

Writings to an Unfinished Accompaniment (1973) contains more allegories and fables, such as "A Door" and "A Flea's Carrying Words"; poems like "Ballade of Sayings" require the reader to understand dreams and signs. *The Compass Flower* (1977) finds consolation in nature, completing an arc from the pessimism and bitterness of *The Lice*. "Numbered Apartment" and "St. Vincent's" also complete a circle begun in *The Lice*, shifting back to the urban, New York setting abandoned for rural France in the earlier book. A variety of settings in *Opening the Hand* (1983) represent M.'s travels (Los Angeles in "Late Wonders"), his family and past ("Yesterday," "Birdie") and his many homes (Hawai'i in "Tidal Lagoon").

The area of southwestern France described in *The Lice* and the semiautobiographical prose work *The Lost Upland*, and where M. has resided sporadically for many years, is the setting for *The Vixen* (1996). Some describe *The Vixen* as more narrative than previous works, but the narrative poems still retain a deep sense of myth and fable with settings outside linear time. These poems, altogether without punctuation and relying on line arrangement and breaks for emphasis, are more dense with description and detail. Rather than focusing on a single, weighty image, these poems are cinematic in their views of history ("Francois de Maynard 1582–1646"), the French countryside ("White Morning"), and animals ("The Vixen"). The opening poem, "Fox Sleep," may be one of M.'s most personal: a fable in which the speaker encounters and frees a man trapped by magic in the body of a fox. It is language that both entraps and frees him, a question about those who have "wakened to what is really there." The publication in 1998 of M.'s *The Folding Cliffs: A Narrative* was followed in 1999 with M.'s eighteenth book of poems entitled *The River Sound*.

Through poetry, prose and translations, M. wakes us to what is really there. Thus, his poems are both familiar and shocking, comforting and unsettling. Whatever we say of his work, that it is at times bleak, at times joyous, occasionally funny and often magical, we say of our own environment; M. creates a vast mirror through which we perceive our world purely, the way previously lost to us.

BIBLIOGRAPHY: Brunner, E., *Poetry as Labor and Privilege: The Writings of W. S. M.* (1991); Christhilf,

M., *W. S. M., the Mythmaker* (1986); Davis, C., *W. S. M.* (1981); Dickey, J., *From Babel to Byzantium* (1968)

NICOLE SARROCCO

MICHENER, James A[lbert]

b. 3 February 1907, New York City?; d.16 October 1997, Austin, Texas

In both his life and his work, M. has evolved as somewhat of an American icon. Reared in a foster home, he has known neither quite where, nor quite when, nor to whom he was born. Turning such absence of home territory to a singular advantage, M. has adapted successfully to a multiplicity of cultures both within the U.S. and throughout the world—and, through his writings, has rendered other places, other peoples, intimately intelligible to an audience of millions. While the title of his autobiography, *The World Is My Home* (1992), would appear hyperbolic coming from any other writer, for M. the claim is indisputable.

After a series of teaching and editing jobs (and a great deal of hitchhiking around North America and Europe), M. volunteered for the Naval Reserve in 1942, a decision that would ultimately lead to his writing career. His assignment as "naval historian in the South Pacific" resulted in his *Tales of the South Pacific* (1948), a thematically bound collection of stories revolving around America's involvement in the Pacific theater in World War II. After receiving a Pulitzer Prize in fiction, these stories were subsequently adapted for the stage by Richard Rodgers and Oscar Hammerstein as the musical, *South Pacific,* which went on to become a major motion picture in 1958. Others of M.'s war stories and travel sketches—*Return to Paradise* (1951), *The Bridges at Toko-Ri* (1953), and *Sayonara* (1954)—also achieved much popular acclaim as Hollywood films.

With the publication of *Hawaii* in 1959, however, M. established himself as the purveyor of a genre that is unique in American letters. Although *Hawaii* is touted as a "novel," its true identity as not-quite-a-novel is what accounts for the lasting appeal of not only this work, but those that follow in the same mode. In amalgamating history and fiction, M. went beyond the simply "historical" novel, in that his focus was always a surprise: "big" histories others would be wary of fictionalizing, such as *The Source* (1965), or smaller histories that neither history buffs nor novel-readers could have anticipated would interest them in quite that way, such as *Chesapeake* (1978). More important for American letters, perhaps, these works have been devoured by those who never read either history *or* novels, an increasingly widening audience delighting in being instructed about different climes and cultures.

Any airline on its way to Hawai'i, even today, will have among its passengers more than one reader behind the familiar red cover of M.'s *Hawaii* in paperback. Much of the author's subsequent work follows this pattern of heavily researched "fiction," which customarily begins at the primal dawn of a culture—"if it didn't happen quite this way, it's easy to see how it *could* have." Further, many of his works incorporate a query as to how religion has figured in the development of a territory and its peoples.

By his own admission, the author has often turned down requests to write about Ireland, as he has felt he does not know enough about the "roots of the religious tensions." Though often criticized for his "formula"—that of bringing generations of families, with more action than psychology, through centuries of cultural and political history in a given territory—the author has gratified his readers with that formula for over thirty years, producing a canon that includes *The Source,* Israel past and present; *Centennial* (1974), two hundred years of Colorado life originating in prehistory; *The Covenant* (1980), South Africa from early days to the 1980s; *Poland* (1983); *Texas* (1985); *Alaska* (1988); and *Caribbean* (1989). Other works, outside of this famous formula, have also gained a wide readership: *Caravans* (1963), about an American girl in Afghanistan; *The Drifters* (1971), a take on the wandering hippie; and *Space* (1982), the portrait of a handful of astronauts on their way to the other side of the moon. Lesser known are M.'s political works, which include *Kent State: What Happened and Why* (1971), about the disastrous consequences resulting from student uprisings against the Vietnam War; and *Legacy* (1987), a short, thinly disguised novel about the Iran-Contra scandal in the late 1980s, with an idealized Oliver North who "does the right thing."

Beyond the history and the fiction, each of M.'s works contains an implicit moral document—one that urges cross-cultural understanding, human decency, curiosity, attention to detail, and a premium on integrity, loyalty, self-reliance, and compassion. Mirroring this stance are M.'s less publicized philanthropy and public service—his support of a number of writers' groups, his commitment to committees on the arts, his donations of his own art collections, and the generous gift of his time—both to individuals and to those countless peoples about whom he has written and with whom he found his nomadic home.

BIBLIOGRAPHY: Becker, G. J., *J. A. M.* (1983); Day, A. G., *J. A. M.* (1964); Hayes, J. P., *J. A. M.* (1984); Kings, J., *In Search of Centennial* (1978); Newquist, R., *Conversations* (1967); Prescott, O., *In My Opinion:*

An Inquiry into the Contemporary Novel (1952);
Stuckey, W. J., *The Pulitzer Prize Novels* (1966)
                                            GAY SIBLEY

MIDWEST, The

Consisting roughly of the twelve states that comprise
the vast prairie north and west of the Ohio River, south
of the Canadian border, and east of the foothills of
the Rocky Mountains, the Midwest has always struggled in some sense for a distinct identity altogether
independent of the other major literary regions of the
U.S. Large portions of the Midwest's geographical
territory are variously ascribed to the East, South, and
West in literary histories and textbooks as often, it
seems, as the origins of its greatest writers are forgotten. Yet despite such historical impediments, the Midwest enjoys a long and varied tradition in American
literature and a claim to more than its fair share of
America's most celebrated literary figures.

Initially, the Midwest existed in the literary imagination of early-19th-c. New England writers merely
as a part of the expansive American frontier. Together
with large tracts of the South and certainly all that
was known of the far West, the Midwest came to
represent a wilderness region of both exaggerated brutality and idealized independence. This seemingly
paradoxical characterization emerged from the desire
of early American romantic novelists and poets to
portray an ideological contrast to alternately refined
and oppressive (depending on the writer's perspective)
civilized East. Among the earliest works of American
fiction to employ the Midwest as a setting, James
Fenimore COOPER's *The Prairie,* published in 1827,
juxtaposes these competing conceptions of the frontier,
respectively, in the characters of Ishmael Bush, the
brutish and sometimes lawless husbandman, and Natty
Bumppo, Cooper's mythic self-reliant hero. Washington IRVING soon after treated the Midwest in his 1835
travel narrative *A Tour on the Prairies* in corresponding fashion. Irving's account of his own experiences
on the Oklahoma plains in 1832 presents, among other
characters, bands of vindictive frontier "squatters"
who relish any opportunity to abuse the more virtuous
Osage Indians, who conversely possess in the author's
words "glorious independence" and "the secret personal freedom." Functioning fully within the conventions of romantic literature, particularly through celebration of the noble savage, Cooper, Irving, and their
contemporaries envisioned the Midwest chiefly as a
new Eden threatened by both the immigrant farmer
and the westward expansion of Eastern civilization.

By midcentury, after decades of migration had begun to populate the Great Lakes region and the valleys

of the Ohio and Mississippi Rivers, Midwesterners
themselves gradually assumed the mantle of portraying their region in poetry and fiction. And not
coincidentally, depictions of the Midwest at the same
time were growing more sympathetic to the agrarian
society of the frontier. Henry Nash Smith documents
this evolution in his seminal treatment of the American
West, *Virgin Land* (1950), and reports that the brutish
frontier "squatter" of Cooper and Irving was eventually displaced in American literature by the desperate
but mostly admirable Midwestern granger of Alice
Cary and Edward EGGLESTON. A native of Ohio, Cary
is credited by scholars and literary artists alike, including Smith and Eggleston, as the first writer in American
letters to present the Midwest honestly and authentically. Her poetry and prose is most memorable for
its realistic depiction of the harshness of life in an
agricultural society. In novels such as *Married, Not
Mated* (1856) and poems, particularly "The West
Country" (probably composed in the early 1850s),
Cary sketches the lives of Midwestern men and women
whom she calls "poor hard-working folks" with a remarkably controlled authorial tone that occupies the
narrow space of dispassion between the patronizing
sentiment of preceding authors and the unchecked veneration of writers who followed her.

Encouraged by the likes of James Russell LOWELL,
Eggleston, who spent most of his life in southern
Indiana, built on Cary's pioneering efforts in such
novels as *The Hoosier Schoolmaster* and *The Circuit
Rider* as he introduced regional forms of dialect into
Midwestern prose. In addition to the realistic detail that
vernacular afforded his work, Eggleston's experiments
with language also transformed the image of Midwesterners from worn yet persevering frontier farmers into
citizens of a unique rural folk culture by focusing
on larger communities and rooting their dialect in a
common heritage. Though his fiction by no means
ignores the crudeness of frontier life, Eggleston's Midwestern communities, unlike the sparsely populated
homesteads of earlier works, possessed well-defined
histories, oftentimes stretching back several generations, that provided a native tradition for their distinctive speech patterns and rituals. Eggleston's realistic
studies of Midwest village life also initiated what is
now occasionally referred to as the "Hoosier School"
of literature, a minor turn-of-the-century Midwestern
literary movement characterized by works with romantic plots celebrating homely virtues and whose ranks
eventually included Will Carleton, James Whitcomb
RILEY, and Booth TARKINGTON. Ultimately, through
the work of writers such as Cary and Eggleston, the
Midwest defined itself independent of the West as it
developed for the first time the makings of an identity
all its own.

Hamlin GARLAND and the six stories that comprise the first edition of his *Main-Travelled Roads* established the Midwest, once and for all, as a major American literary region. In works such as "Up the Coule," "A Branch Road," and "Under the Lion's Paw," the Midwest and its distinct agrarian society emerge unambiguously heroic in the face of widespread degradation and suffering brought about by successive decades of natural disasters and oppressive economic conditions. Garland's interest in the populist politics of the 1880s and 1890s clearly shaped his artistic vision, and in fiction, poetry, and such autobiographical works as *A Son of the Middle Border* and *A Daughter of the Middle Border,* he sharpened the realistic depictions of hardship characteristic of Cary's work and combined them with the more salient features of Eggleston's experiments in local color partly in an effort to effect social change for the farming communities of the Midwest. Championed by William Dean HOWELLS and other Eastern establishment literati, Garland's brand of REALISM, which he termed "veritism," eventually garnered an international audience for Midwestern literature.

In the years between the publication of Cary's *Clovernook; or, Recollections of Our Neighborhood in the West* (1852) and Hamlin Garland's *Prairie Folks,* the Midwest saw many of its greatest writers leave the region and produce work abroad. Some Midwesterners, however, such as Abraham LINCOLN, always managed to convey a sense of their frontier heritage through a style marked by plain-spoken language and peppered with homespun witticisms. Others including Mark TWAIN occasionally returned to the stuff of their Midwestern origins for the materials of fiction and autobiography. Harriet Beecher STOWE, though born in Connecticut, spent her twenties and thirties in Cincinnati, Ohio, and that experience unquestionably contributed to the conception of *Uncle Tom's Cabin.* A final group departed (a few only temporarily) and forever remained principally associated with other regions of the country, among them Howells and Paul Lawrence DUNBAR in the East, Charles CHESNUTT and Kate CHOPIN in the South, and Ambrose BIERCE, DAN DEQUILLE, and Frank NORRIS in the West.

The Midwestern tradition in American literature, as it had developed throughout the 19th c., culminated early in the 20th c. in the novels of Willa CATHER. Through *O Pioneers!, The Song of the Lark,* and *My Ántonia,* as well as numerous shorter prose pieces, the Midwest actually assumes the aspect of a cosmos writ-small, populated by a full range of completely realized and complex human types. Cather fully humanizes Midwesterners, and in her work they belong to different classes, hold diverse beliefs, and hail from a multitude of origins. Her treatment of the land itself is also far more complicated than that of her predecessors, as the soil of her Nebraska prairie seemingly possesses the ability to redeem as often as it would destroy. In Cather's hands, the Midwest and its inhabitants finally transcend the sometimes stereotyped categories of weary granger or quaint hayseed and embody supple identities that evolve naturally over the course of a narrative.

The story of the Midwest in 20th-c. literature, on the other hand, is threefold. A number of writers, particularly early in the century, present the Midwest in poetry and prose through mainly satiric portraits of small-town life. Edgar Lee MASTERS's *Spoon River Anthology,* for example, documents the spiritual degeneration of Midwestern culture by contrasting the disillusionment of recent generations with the vigor and pioneering spirit of the original settlers to the region. Sherwood ANDERSON's *Winesburg, Ohio* remains perhaps the most enduring chronicle of disconnection and frustration within the seemingly tranquil communities of middle America. In novels such as *Main Street* and *Babbitt,* Sinclair LEWIS stepped up the "attack on the village" and exposed the stultifying effect that the sham culture of small Midwestern towns could have on an individual whose true potential might have been nurtured and realized in larger, more vital metropolitan areas. Ring LARDNER and James THURBER, both natives of the region, also situate any of their sardonic tales of eccentric and warped small-town folk in the rural hamlets of the Midwest.

A second group of writers portray the Midwest as an idyllic refuge or retreat. Ernest HEMINGWAY, for instance, sets the Nick Adams stories of *In Our Time* in the wilds of northern Michigan, where at least his protagonist attempts to search for the semblance of inner peace after his violent war experiences in Europe. Similarly, F. Scott FITZGERALD envisions his Midwestern origins as a place to which Nick Carraway might return after his harrowing summer in New York among Jay Gatsby and the Buchanans. The poety of James WRIGHT at times implies a comparably affirmatives vision of a pastoral Midwest through quasi-romantic descriptions of the natural world in poems such as "Stages on a Journey Westward" (1963), "Arrangement with Earth for Three Dead Friends" (1963), and "Lying in a Hammock at William Duffy's Farm in Pine Island, Minnesota" (1963).

A final cluster of 20th-c. authors depict the Midwest through vast portraits of metropolitan city life. Large sections of Theodore DREISER's *Sister Carrie,* Carl SANDBURG's *Chicago Poems,* Richard WRIGHT's *Native Son,* Saul BELLOW's *The Adventures of Augie March,* Lorraine HANSBERRY's *A Raisin in the Sun,* and David MAMET's *American Buffalo,* to name only a few, are set in large Midwestern urban areas, and together they demonstrate the degree to which the original idea of an agrarian Midwest has diminished in the 20th c.

Recent trends indicate that contemporary authors are utilizing not one or two but the entire range of long-established authorial attitudes toward the Midwest in their work. Midwesterners William GASS, Toni MORRISON, Rita DOVE, and Louise ERDRICH are among those writers who treat the region's various legacies—Native American cultures, agrarian social systems, differing small-town mentalities, larger urban environments—as a collective, wholly integrated heritage by situating the present always in the broader sociohistorical context of the past.

The Midwest has indeed contributed mightily to American literary history. As a setting, it has furnished American writers with an evolving ideological landscape for nearly two hundred years, and as a region it has produced some of the country's finest poets, novelists, and playwrights, including five of the ten Americans awarded the Nobel Prize in literature in the 20th c.

BIBLIOGRAPHY: Cox, J. C., "Regionalism: A Diminished Thing," in Emory, E., ed., *Columbia Literary History of the United States* (1988): 761–84; Holman, D., *A Certain Slant of Light: Regionalism and the Form of Southern and Midwestern Fiction* (1995); *Midwestern Miscellany: A Publication of the Society for the Study of Midwestern Literature;* Smith, H. N., *Virgin Land: The American West as Symbol and Myth* (1950); Smith, H. N., "Western Chroniclers and Literary Pioneers," in Spiller, R. E., et al., eds., *Literary History of The United States* (1948; rev. ed., 1953): 758–70; Stewart, G. R., "The West as Seen from the East," in Spiller, R. E., et al., eds., *Literary History of The United States* (1948; rev. ed., 1953): 771–77; Sundquist, E. J., "Realism and Regionalism," in Emory, E., ed., *Columbia Literary History of the United States* (1988): 501-24; Weber, R., *The Midwestern Ascendancy in American Writing* (1992); Wecter, D., "Literary Culture on the Frontier," in Spiller, R. E., et al., eds., *Literary History of The United States* (1948; rev. ed., 1953): 652–62

JOSEPH CSICSILA

MILES, Josephine [Louise]
b. 11 June 1911, Chicago, Illinois; d. 12 May 1985, Berkeley, California

A scholar, teacher, and editor, M. was a poet above everything, publishing her first poem at the age of eight. Afflicted by severe arthritis all of her life, M. responded by intense self-discipline, and scholarly and creative activity, establishing a distance from which she observed herself and her work. Interested in linguistics, literature, and the philosophy of language, she completed a Ph.D. at the University of California at Berkeley, where she subsequently taught English from 1940 until her retirement in 1978. She continued to write and publish poetry until her death.

M. published her first volume of poetry, *Lines at Intersection* (1939), at the age of twenty-eight. Its success earned her the distinction of having her second volume, *Poems on Several Occasions* (1941), appear as part of the New Directions Poet of the Month Series. Continuing to write poetry, she produced ten more volumes, including *Local Measures* (1946), *Prefabrications* (1955), *Kinds of Affection* (1962), *Civil Poems* (1966), *Saving the Bay* (1967, *Fields of Learning* (1968), and *Coming to Terms* (1979), as well as several collections, and a verse play, *House and Home* (1960).

Throughout her work, M. shows interest in intricate patterns of rhyme and modulation of meter, though as she progresses, she becomes more relaxed and subtle in her use of form and syntax. At the same time, she is interested in ordinary, everyday objects, mundane experiences, and fragments of slang. Observing objects from the "middle-distance perspective," she creates a tension between the individual and the abstract, preserving a distance from the object that sees the world in terms of the relationship of surfaces. Playing the ordinary things and cliches off the formal conventions of poetry, she illuminates the object and revivifies the form. Lawrence R. Smith sees her as part of an American surrealist tradition that begins with Wallace STEVENS and Marianne MOORE and includes Theodore ROETHKE, John BERRYMAN, W. S. MERWIN, and Diane WAKOSKI. Her approach can also be compared to Wordsworth's practice of making the ordinary extraordinary.

Her later poems turn to the fissures in human relationships and a vacillation between faith and doubt. The darkness of these works is modulated by a hope in the creation of new identities related to her use of the metaphor as something that dissolves identities by positing connections between different objects, but at the same time creating new identities in the process. Influenced by the political turbulence at Berkeley in the late 1960s and early 1970s, she also explores the themes of guilt and irony in her later work.

M.'s scholarly writing and her poetry inform each other. As a scholar, she published thirteen books, all deeply concerned with the language of poetry. In her first critical book, *Wordsworth and the Vocabulary of Emotion* (1940), followed by her three-part study *The Primary Language of Poetry* (1948–51) and *Eras and Modes in English Poetry* (1957), M. presents a detailed description of poetic language and how the poem changes in response to the tastes of the time. Her *Pathetic Fallacy in the Nineteenth Century* (1942) offers insight into her concern for the object. Later studies—*Style and Proportion* (1967), *Poetry and Change* (1974), and *Working out Ideas: Prediction and Other Uses of Language* (1979)—treat the nature of the metaphor. In her criticism, as well as her poetry, M. articulates a vision that finds the universal in the local, the extraordinary in the ordinary.

BIBLIOGRAPHY: Beloof, R., "Distance and Surfaces: The Poetry of J. M.," *PrS* 32 (Winter 1958): 276–84; Smith, L.R., "J. M.: Metaphysician of the Irrational," *Pebble* 18–19 (1979): 22-35; Steinman, L.M., "Putting on Knowledge with Power: The Poetry of J. M.," *ChiR* 37 (Winter 1990): 130–40

THOMAS L. COOKSEY

MILLAR, Margaret [Ellis Sturm]

b. 5 February 1915, Kitchener, Ontario, Canada; d. 26 March 1994, Santa Barbara, California

M. has always worked in the format of the detective story, producing novels that usually transcend the genre and approach the literary mainstream. The Mystery Writers of America awarded her the Edgar Allan Poe Award for best mystery novel for *Beast in View* (1955) and named her Grand Master of the Mystery in 1986.

Beginning her career in the 1940s with a number of books written in the traditional format of the detective story, she soon broke away from the established conventions to probe more deeply into the psychological motivations of murder. The theme of vengeance, carefully camouflaged in some cases even from the avenger, runs strongly through her works. Complex crosscurrents of love and hate force her characters into cerebral as well as physical acts of destruction. Her later stories, set mostly in California, show a simpatico and appreciation of the Chicano population in a primarily Anglo environment. She uses background and sociology skillfully to back up and highlight the aberrations of her main characters.

In *Beast in View,* the work that established her as a major writer of psychological suspense novels, the motivation of the principal character is a tangle of conflicts that creates a psychotic individual capable of being both killer *and* victim. *Beyond This Point Are Monsters* (1970) involves an ethnic conflict between Anglo and Chicano that screens the true motive for murder, pointing up the danger of bigotry and prejudice in trying to uncover the truth. In *Ask for Me Tomorrow* (1976), a clever avenger performs her actions in front of the reader's eyes, but with all motiva-

tion carefully out of sight. In *Spider Webs* (1986), a courtroom drama, the avenger is present, seated quietly and waiting to act if the guilty party should be declared not guilty.

While the conventional detective novelist focuses primarily on a detector or pursuer, M., in her later books, focuses on the actions and reactions of a (usually) female protagonist whose psychological twists, conflicts, or aberrations set the story in motion. In the end, the author is concerned with what makes a killer kill, not with how a detective stalks a murderer. Frequently her detectives are surrogates—lawyers, interested parties, and so on. They play a secondary role in the final revelation of the psychological twists and turns of the protagonist's mind.

A typical M. story line frequently violates the straightline narration of mystery-genre convention, circling warily around before finally zeroing in on the source of evil, the killer, at the end—although clues have been liberally strewn throughout to satisfy the traditional detective fan. In fact, without her in-depth psychological study, expertly presented backgrounds, or evocative characters and spritely dialogue, M.'s plots would stand on their own as models of the genre.

BIBLIOGRAPHY: Budd, E., "M. M.: The Evil Within," *13 Mistresses of Murder* (1986): 87–96; Reilly, J. M., ed., *Twentieth Century Crime and Mystery Writers,* 2nd ed. (1985); Reilly, J. M., in Bargainnier, E. F., ed., *Ten Women of Mystery* (1981)

BRUCE CASSIDAY

MILLAY, Edna St. Vincent

b. 22 February 1892, Rockland, Maine; d. 19 October 1950, Austerlitz, New York

M. achieved her greatest praise for her lyrical expression of the hedonistic and defiant spirit of the post-World War I generation. During the 1920s and 1930s, she enjoyed both popular and critical acclaim for the technical competence and sharply felt life of her ballads, lyrics, and sonnets. As her poetry became more philosophical and then intensely political in the 1940s, her readership declined; and critics faulted her for not assimilating the modernist doctrine of Ezra POUND and T. S. ELIOT. Following her death, her work fell into near obscurity. Recently, however, feminist historians have begun reassessing M.'s poetic achievements to show her significance as a strong female voice in American poetry.

M. published sixteen volumes of poetry and five verse plays over a twenty-seven-year span. Her prolific career began with the publication in 1912 of a long poem "Renascence" in the *Lyric Year* when she was a seventeen-year-old student in a Maine coastal town. Her lyrical statement of a young woman's despair, rebirth, and affirmation caught the attention of New York literati, including a sponsor for her college years at Barnard and Vassar. After graduation in 1918, M. settled in Greenwich Village, where she became acquainted with some of the age's most brilliant and radical writers. She had close friends among the feminists, and she joined the Provincetown Players in hopes of a career as playwright and actor. She had an array of suitors, including Edmund WILSON, the literary critic, and Floyd Dell, the playwright; but her most passionate love affair was with the poet Arthur Davison FICKE, who continued to be her close friend and mentor after the affair had ended. During these early lean and hectic years, M. supported herself by writing short stories under the pseudonym of Nancy Boyd, lecturing and reading from her poetry, and working as a European correspondent for *Vanity Fair.*

By 1923, M. had published four volumes of poetry—*Renascence and Other Poems* (1917), *A Few Figs from Thistles* (1920), *Second April* (1921), and *The Harp Weaver and Other Poems* (1923), for which she received the Pulitzer Prize, the first woman to be so honored. The prevailing theme of all the volumes is the mutability of love and life. Although her persona assumes various guises, it is most often the unconventional woman who lives intensely, burning the candle at both ends—perhaps her most famous poetic image. In lines reminiscent of Andrew Marvell and John Donne, she explores the complexities of love. Her alterable moods—gay, defiant, satirical, and cynical—echo those of the free-spirited Jazz Age. Yet certain poems in these early volumes express the sadness underlying her bravado, a sadness arising from her powerlessness to resolve the conflicting demands of love and poetry. She expresses her longing for escape through allusions to classical female poets like Sappho and recurring images of intensely remembered natural beauty and homely pleasure—hunting seashells on the Maine coast, finding a single blue flower in a bog, feeding sparrows at her doorstep. Many of these poems are noteworthy not only for their striking metaphors and precise diction, but also for their metrical experimentation: lyrical quatrains with variable rhyme schemes; ballads, often with a skillful mixture of nursery rhyme; and sonnets, usually in the Petrarchan mode.

M.'s next volumes of poetry—*The Buck in the Snow* (1928) and *Fatal Interview* (1931)—were published after she had married Eugen Boissevain and moved to Steepletop, their home in the Berkshire foothills. Critics praised the 1928 volume as the work of an experienced poet at the peak of her art. Many of these poems are reminiscences of her travel experiences expressed in vivid images and lyrical quatrains—a brief French love affair, a melody played on a Chinese flute, the smell of burning olive tree branches. There is also an important new theme of political engagement arising from M.'s futile efforts to prevent the execution of the anarchists Sacco and Vanzetti. The most notable of these political poems is "Justice Denied in Massachusetts," a powerful lament for the loss of political freedom. "The Dirge" and "Wine from These Grapes" are also moving expressions of political alienation.

Fatal Interview, a sequence of fifty-two Shakespearean sonnets, demonstrates M.'s continued experimentation with the sonnet form. This account of the female's shifting responses to a passionate love affair is an interesting foil to the male point of view in George Meredith's *Modern Love,* and reflects M.'s rejection of sentimental concepts of women and love. Critics expressed reservations about the lack of realistic natural detail, but admired her innovative molding of structure and thought. The traditional three quatrains and concluding couplet are often replaced by stanzas with variable or random rhymes. Through skillful use of run-on lines, M.'s characteristically convoluted sentences are shaped into the fourteen lines, sometimes using only one sentence unit.

M.'s published work in the late 1930s and early 1940s is uneven in quality and increasingly focused upon political-social issues. The long closet drama *Conversation at Midnight* (1937) reflects her anguish over the world's ills and the threat of World War II. She called the poems in *Make the Arrows Bright* (1940) her "posters" urging American preparedness; but her readers were disappointed in her shift away from the earlier finely crafted lyrics. In her final years, M.'s poetic voice was silenced by bitter disillusionment over the war, grief over her husband's death, and her own ill health. Although her poetic accomplishments were obscured following her death, they merit her a permanent place in the development of American poetry.

BIBLIOGRAPHY: Brittin, N. A., *E. St. V. M.* (1962; rev. ed., 1982); Cheney, A., *M. in Greenwich Village,* (1975); Gould, J., *The Poet and Her Book* (1969); Gurko, M., *Restless Spirit: The Life of E. St. V. M.* (1962); Shafter, T., *E. St. V. M.: America's Best-Loved Poet* (1957)

MARGARET CARTER

MILLER, Arthur
b. 17 October 1915, New York City

One of America's most respected playwrights, M.'s critical reputation rests upon a relatively small body of work produced between 1947, with the production of *All My Sons,* and 1968, with the production of *The Price.* Among his most important plays are *Death of a Salesman* (1949), *The Crucible* (1953), and *A View from the Bridge* (1956). Collectively, his works represent his fascination with the struggle between individual conscience and social pressures, the nature of guilt and love, and the importance of the family as a civilizing influence in contemporary society.

In his life and work, M. also shares some remarkable similarities with Eugene O'NEILL, America's most prominent dramatist. While both are grounded in dramatic realism, they experiment with expressionistic techniques—M. in *After the Fall* (1964) and O'Neill in *The Emperor Jones* (1922)—and with ways of capturing the formal power of Greek tragedy in modern settings—M.'s *A View from the Bridge* employs an equivalent of the Greek chorus and a sense of dramatic inevitability in much the same way as O'Neill's *Desire under the Elms* (1924) and *Mourning Becomes Electra* (1932). They both are driven by a dissatisfaction with the materialism of the American dream and with a need to dramatize enormously personal events—O'Neill particularly with *Long Day's Journey into Night* (1956) and M. with *After the Fall,* for which M. was widely criticized for the portrait of his former wife, Marilyn Monroe. Moreover, they both earned international reputations despite long periods in their mature artistic lives when they did not write for the theater.

But M. differs from O'Neill in at least two critical areas, and these differences are important in understanding M.'s art and his contributions to American drama. Unlike O'Neill, whose plays tend to ramble over huge landscapes with lots of character arias, M. is a precise craftsman and his plays are masterful examples of detailed exposition, dramatic irony and obligatory scenes. And while O'Neill was frequently fascinated with the nature of Fate and God, M.'s focus is on ways in which human beings have created their own social structures and paradigms.

M. learned his craft early. After an undistinguished career in high school, he was able to gain conditional acceptance to the University of Michigan in 1934, where he studied playwriting with Professor Kenneth Thorpe Rowe. Rowe, who later published a text on dramatic construction, taught M. about the necessities of creating plays around major dramatic questions that focused the attention of the audience on the central conflict. M. twice won the Hopwood prize for Drama at Michigan, and following his graduation, he worked for the Federal Theatre Project in New York and wrote radio plays for *Cavalcade of America, U.S. Steel Hour,* and *Columbia Workshop.* Although he chafed at the restrictions imposed by the thirty-minute radio format,

he was paid well for his efforts and he learned a dramatic economy free from digressions and extended flights of fancy. The entire dramatic event had to be created in succinct dialogue form, and echoes of this skill are evident in all of M.'s plays.

M. is also indebted to the Norwegian dramatist Henrik Ibsen, whose 1883 play, *An Enemy of the People,* M. adapted for New York production in 1950. M. was particularly impressed with Ibsen's ability to reveal past action through dialogue and with the ways in which he adapted devices of 19th-c. dramaturgy. In fact, M.'s first Broadway success, *All of My Sons,* exhibits a structural similarity to the traditional "well-made play" with its delayed exposition, obligatory scene and late arriving letter. Like Ibsen, M. has continued to experiment with formal structures. Yet it is not his techniques that have earned him an international reputation, but rather his fascination with men and women trying to make ethical choices in complex moral and social circumstances.

All My Sons, which won the Critics Circle Award in drama in 1947 and ran for two hundred and thirty-eight performances on Broadway, is a play about the consequences of past actions invading the present and forcing a conflict between father and son. Joe Keller, who ran a factory that manufactured airplane engines during World War II, covered up a defect in the assembly line in order to keep the plant in business and then blamed the faulty engines on his partner when the scandal came to light. Years later with his partner about to be released from prison, Joe's son, Chris, uncovers the guilty secret and confronts his father with the crime. Joe, who is seen in much of the play as a decent and affable man, justifies his conduct in terms of pressures to keep the plant open, but Chris invokes a moral authority that eventually drives his father to suicide. Chris is overwhelmed by what his righteousness has wrought, but Joe's conduct is revealed as a betrayal of both his society and his family.

M. was fascinated by this complex landscape of social pressure and private integrity, and two years later, he wrote *Death of a Salesman,* which won the Pulitzer Prize in drama for 1949 and became a classic in the American theater. Like *All My Sons, Death of a Salesman* explores the relationship between a father committed to an American dream of success and a son who questions his accomplishments. Willy Loman, the salesman of the title, believes that success is equated with being "well liked," but Biff, his older son, confronts him with the hypocrisy of this idea, and Willy eventually commits suicide. Willy's death, while seen by many as a renunciation of a misguided American Dream, is also an affirmation of love; Willy believed that Biff would now have a chance for success with the insurance money in his pocket. There is considerable controversy about whether Willy ever learns anything in the play, but the redemptive power of love is certainly critical in this as in all of M.'s plays. Over thirty years later in *The Creation of the World* (1982), M. is still exploring the relationship between love and success when Adam and Eve reject Satan because his offer of complete freedom lacks love.

Death of a Salesman stimulated a lively literary debate about whether Willy Loman was a "tragic hero." M. was a Marxist, and the play's materialist analysis was undermined by its Freudian resolution. Like most mature works of art, however, the play is prismatic, and its production history attests to its ongoing power to compel critical attention and popular acclaim.

M.'s first two Broadway successes both featured middle class fathers who were guilty about the past and earnest young sons who refused to compromise. In *The Crucible*, M. combined these figures in John Proctor, a farmer who is guilty about his past adultery but who recognizes the hypocrisy of the Salem witch hunts and finally denounces them. Proctor, who is one of M.'s most articulate heroes, is vulnerable because of his relationship with Abigail and is forced into a conflict with the witch hunters who expose him. However, he is unwilling to implicate others and thus retains some sense of integrity even in the face of powerful social pressures. M. himself would shortly imitate his hero in a celebrated appearance before the House Committee on Un-American Activities when he was questioned about his "leftist" past. Although M. was cited for contempt when he refused to "name names," his conviction was eventually overturned by the Supreme Court and his subsequent election to the American Institute of Arts and Letters and the presidency of PEN testified to the regard with which he was held by his fellow artists and writers.

"Naming names" or informing on one's friend and colleagues was a central issue in the 1950s, and perhaps not coincidentally, M.'s next play, *A View from the Bridge*, continued this debate. Again, M.'s protagonist is a man who violates the code of his social world—the Brooklyn waterfront—by betraying two illegal aliens who have recently entered the country and are living under his protection. Eddie Carbone has been by most standards a good man, but during the course of the play, he becomes enmeshed in a guilt-ridden desire for his niece that eventually leads to his downfall. Eddie dies struggling to preserve his integrity as M. once again explores the oblique terrain between social pressure and individual conscience. Some critics have suggested that the title of the play is a response to the Elia Kazan film, *On The Waterfront*, which proclaimed—in the wake of the McCarthy era—that it was not only permissible to become an informant, but necessary.

M. married the film star Marilyn Monroe in 1956, and for the next eight years, his career became increasingly entwined with hers. As a result, he wrote very little for the theater, although he did create a successful film script for her in 1960 called *The Misfits*. Following their divorce in 1961, M. married the photographer Ingeborg Morath, and in 1964, he returned to the theater with the newly established Lincoln Center Repertory Company, which also reunited him with his former director and friend, Elia Kazan.

Both *Incident at Vichy* (1964) and *After the Fall*, which were written for the new company, are concerned with guilt, and both are effective evocations of the power that guilt has in human relationships. In *After the Fall*, Quentin, a thinly disguised M., is haunted by the self-inflicted death of his second wife, Maggie (modeled quite obviously on Monroe), and the play allows him to preside at what amounts to his own trial. In addition to Maggie's suicide, he is also tormented by the betrayal of other personal relationships as well as his seeming inability to preserve and maintain human love. Quentin is unable to discover why love dies, but he cannot settle for guilt. Finally he realizes that only acceptance and forgiveness can lead to new beginnings.

M. was disappointed with the Lincoln Center experiment, and with the exception of *The Price*, most of his later plays have premiered at regional stages outside of New York City. *The Price* was a Broadway success, but its thoughtful dramaturgy—uncovering past secrets and obligatory scenes—was increasingly at odds with an American theater now wary of rational art forms. While M. was still seeking ways of combining "new insights into social and psychological mechanisms," a younger generation of writers like Sam SHEPARD and John GUARE were creating a visceral, often irrational drama that was not concerned with explaining behavior. Infused with the counter culture and models like Beckett and Pinter, the drama that was now prized was increasingly oblique rather than explanatory and mysterious rather than motivated.

M. continued to work, however, sometimes in collaboration with Inga Morath. He also wrote a successful teleplay, *Playing for Time* (1980), and directed a highly acclaimed Chinese version of *Death of a Salesman* in Beijing in 1983. His most recent plays are one acts and generally evince an interest in experimenting with a dramaturgy that is less traditional than his earlier work. *Some Kind of Love Story* (1982), *Elegy for a Lady* (1982), and *I Can't Remember Anything* (1986) are all vignettes of traumatic experience involving the death or loss of loved ones, but there is no longer the same compulsion to explain. Increasingly, M. seems content to record and reflect upon human experience, freed somewhat from the demands of the well-made play.

M.'s work also includes a novel, *Focus* (1945), a collection of short stories, *I Don't Need You Anymore* (1967), a journalistic account of his visit to army camps during World War II, *Situation Normal* (1944), and his autobiography, *Timebends* (1987). But his reputation as one of America's most influential and successful playwrights rests upon those primarily realistic, family dramas that explore the tension between individual conscience and the crucible of social pressures, plays that he wrote out of the need to articulate a sense of personal integrity in the face of expedient compromise and human failings.

BIBLIOGRAPHY: Bigsby, C. W. E., *Critical Introduction to Twentieth-Century American Drama* (1984); Carson, N., *A. M.* (1982); Martin, R., ed., *Theater Essays of A. M.* (1978); Moss, L., *A. M.* (1967); Nelson, B., *A. M.: Portrait of a Playwright* (1970); Roudane, M., ed., *Conversations with A. M.* (1987); Schlueter, J., and J. Flanagan, *A. M.* (1987); Welland, D., *A. M.: A Study of His Plays* (1979)

BARRY B. WITHAM

MILLER, Henry [Valentine]

b. 26 December 1891, New York City; d. 7 June 1980, Pacific Palisades, California

There are several reasons why M.'s position in the canon of 20th-c. American literature has been and is likely to remain marginal, most notably the quantity and explicitness of descriptions of sexual activity throughout his autobiographical narratives, sufficient to prevent their legal publication in the U.S. until the 1960s and to ensure their continued exclusion from most American literature reading lists. In addition, while the guardians of public morality have taken offense at his subject matter, many critics have found fault with his excessive prose style, which at its worst can drift into seemingly pointless rambling. Such passages often show M.'s propensity toward overwrought generalizations and pronouncements of opinion on a variety of social and philosophical topics, especially in the essays written after his reputation as a literary outlaw-sage gained him a devoted following of acolytes and visitors to his rustic home at Big Sur, California: of the many identities M. takes on in his writing, the preaching, narcissistic guru is perhaps the least appealing.

Despite his position on the fringes of respectable literary culture, however, M. has been one of the most widely read American authors of the 20th c., partly because of his work's reputed sexual content. Of course, if he were merely a pornographer, he would not have garnered the sustained admiration of his readers and the high praise of critics, especially for his autobiographical narratives of the 1930s—*Tropic of Cancer* (1934), *Black Spring* (1936), and *Tropic of Capricorn* (1939)—all written during his expatriate years in Paris. Indeed, many literary intellectuals in the 1930s, including George Orwell, Edmund WILSON, Ezra POUND, and T. S. ELIOT, expressed adulation for M.'s work when it first appeared, and today his Paris writings are regarded not only as his most significant literary achievement but as some of the best work by any American author of that decade.

When M. arrived in Paris in 1930 at age thirty-eight, he had already written several unpublished third-person novels while living in New York City. But the move to Paris signaled a major shift in his life and art, a break from the kind of writer he had been up to that point—separated from his work by the attempt to mold it according to the traditional form of the realistic novel—toward the kind of writer he was to become, the only kind he would deem worthy of the name artist: exuberant and uninhibited, desperately writing the truth of personal experience and exploring the mystery of the creative process. As he writes near the beginning of *Tropic of Cancer,* "I have moved the typewriter into the next room where I can see myself in the mirror as I write."

M. spent the rest of his career trying to represent what he saw in that metaphorical mirror, though he would never again succeed with the sustained brilliance of *Tropic of Cancer.* If his aesthetic goal when he moved to Paris was to erase as much of the border line between life and art as he could, then this first-person, present-tense portrait of a struggling bohemian writer finding sexual and spiritual liberation in the squalid quarters of Depression-era Paris is surely the closest he would come to achieving that goal. *Black Spring,* a series of sketches and stories ranging from surrealistic dream sequences to memoirs of his childhood in New York, also contains some of M.'s best writing, exploring less the cancer of modern urban civilization than the dream-work of memory and the imagination. The last of his Paris books, *Tropic of Capricorn,* already shows some signs of M.'s decline as a writer of fictionalized autobiography. In recounting his childhood, adolescence, and years as an alienated, frustrated young writer in a spiritually impoverished America, he loses not only the immediacy of the present tense but also the full force of the affirmative, creative vision so palpable in *Tropic of Cancer.* In addition, the latter half of the book exhibits some of the uncontrolled rambling that would characterize too much of his later prose, especially *The Rosy*

Crucifixion trilogy—*Sexus* (1949), *Plexus* (1953), and *Nexus* (1960)—which also deals with M.'s experiences in 1920s New York, though the sexual episodes seem more gratuitous and the point less clear than in *Tropic of Capricorn.*

Derided as an egotistical misogynist, exalted as a visionary genius, M. has provoked extreme reactions as a writer and public figure. For all his rebellious individualism and anarchic iconoclasm, he does belong to a Romantic, confessional literary tradition that includes such American precursors as Ralph Waldo EMERSON, Henry David THOREAU, and Walt WHITMAN, as well as such descendants as Jack KEROUAC, William S. BURROUGHS, and Norman MAILER. While no critic would claim that M.'s work is consistently outstanding, there is no question of the importance of his expatriate writings both as brilliant works of autobiographical fiction and as significant influences on the literature of the late 20th c.

BIBLIOGRAPHY: Brown, J. D., *H. M.* (1986); Dearborn, M. V., *The Happiest Man Alive: A Biography of H. M.* (1991); Ferguson, R., *H. M.* (1991); Lewis, L., *H. M.* (1986); Martin, J., *Always Merry and Bright: The Life of H. M.* (1978); Widmer, K., *H. M.* (1990)

BRIAN DONAHUE

MILLER, Joaquin [Cincinnatus Hiner]

b. 8 September 1841?, Liberty, Indiana; d. 17 February 1913, Oakland, California

M.'s intrinsic literary worth is now considered less important than his status as an index to late 19th-c. cultural values. Born in Indiana, M.—his middle name was sometimes rendered "Heine," his year of birth, 1841—early in his life migrated with his family to Oregon, where he became miner and lawyer, adopted the name of a colorful Mexican desperado, and discovered the subject that was to make him among the most famous Western writers and public figures of his time. After an attempt to make a literary living in San Francisco—unsuccessful despite the encouragement of Bret HARTE and Charles Warren STODDARD—M. sailed for England to seek his fortune. There he published *Pacific Poems* (1871)—soon reissued under the title *Songs of the Sierras*—and became the "Poet of the Sierras," "The Byron of Oregon," the darling of London literati struck by his wild Western appearance and manners.

Much of M.'s poetry today seems derivative, overly romantic and sentimental, full of puerile rhymes, more grandiose than grand. *Songs of the Sierras* includes poems that pay tribute to both the vanishing American—"The Last Taschastas"—and the frontiers-man—the popular "Kit Carson's Ride." Other narrative poems in the volume are tender tales of love and loss like "The Arizonian" and "The Tale of the Tall Alcalde." M.'s exotic settings were the main cause of his popularity, a popularity that consequently waned as he continued to celebrate the West in verse and prose. The autobiographical *Life Amongst the Modocs* (1873) describes the author's adventures with the tribe in northern California and pleads for Indian rights (as does the similarly quasi-fictional *Shadows of Shasta* of 1881). *First Fam'lies of the Sierras* (1876) is a novel in the manner of Bret Harte, replete with rustic characters and stilted dialogue paired with uncouth dialect and simple motivation. Rewritten as an action-filled play entitled *The Danites in the Sierras* (1881) and capitalizing on an apparent anti-Mormon sentiment, the work enjoyed long runs on stages in both America and England. Other noteworthy Western plays include *Forty-Nine—An Idyl Drama of the Sierras* (1882) and *An Oregon Idyl* (1910).

M. did write on other subjects. *The One Fair Woman* (1876), for example, treats Americans in Italy in a novel that portrays an artist, quite renowned for a short time, whose longings merge into a vague dream of love and perfection. In *The Destruction of Gotham* (1886), M. ventured a novel of class conflict set in New York. The titles of other volumes of verse indicate his idealistic "singing" of sun-lands, Italy, Mexican seas, and the soul. Although M.'s name has been kept alive in the 20th c. partly by the thousands of school children who had to memorize the optimistic late poem "Columbus," his real significance lies in his contribution to the mythos of the West. The roles he played are signaled by the monuments to John Charles Frémont, Browning, and Moses that he built near his home above Oakland: pioneer, poet, and prophet.

BIBLIOGRAPHY: Frost, O. W., *J. M.* (1967); Lawson, B. S., *J. M.* (1980); Marberry, M. M., *Splendid Poseur: J. M.—American Poet* (1953); Peterson, M. S., *J. M., Literary Frontiersman* (1937)

BENJAMIN S. LAWSON

MILLER, Sue

b. 29 November 1943, Chicago, Illinois

M. has been recognized by critics and readers for her gifted, realistic depiction of love and marriage, parenting, and the changing roles in the middle-class American family. Although many feminist critics feel that her heroines, like Anna in *The Good Mother* (1986), are not heroic enough, M. is acclaimed for her skilled characterization and dialogue, attention to detail, use of imagery and unique narrative devices.

M.'s controversial debut, *The Good Mother,* evidences her objection to "post-feminist novels which suggested that all you need to do is shed your husband and then you enter this glorious new life of accomplishment and ease" as it details life-after-divorce for Anna Dunlap and her four-year-old daughter Molly. With new lover Leo, Anna begins to find herself emotionally, intellectually, and sexually, and in the process, loses her daughter to the more traditional home of her ex-husband. In order to maintain contact with her daughter, Anna leaves Leo, a decision that bothers many feminist critics and readers who wanted a stronger heroine and a happy ending. Other critics interpret Anna's decision to leave Leo to follow her daughter as a sign of strength and character, brought about by her love for her child.

M.'s second publication, *Inventing the Abbots* (1987), is a collection of stories that continues her investigation of complex family relationships and lays the groundwork for the themes in M.'s later novels. In the title story, M. explores class consciousness and conflict and the difficulties of adolescence. In "Appropriate Affect" and "The Birds and the Bees," M. revisits the conflicts of marriage, divorce, and sexual education first examined in *The Good Mother.* In "Slides," "Travel," and "The Quality of Life," M. uses photography to illustrate her themes and experiences.

M. continues this use of photography in *Family Pictures* (1990) to illustrate the experiences of young photographer Nina Eberhardt as she navigates relationships in a family coping with an autistic child. Critics enjoyed the innovative narrative structure that centers around Nina's perspective but also explores the alternate viewpoints of other Eberhardt family members. Also appreciated were M.'s accomplished characterization of the mother-daughter relationship, the sibling relationship, and the relationship between husband and wife.

In her third novel, *For Love* (1993), M. pits the excitement of romantic love against the work and commitment necessary for a successful marriage. Lottie Gardner reminds critics and readers of Emma Bovary and Anna Karenina; she is unsatisfied with her ordinary life and longs for the excitement of an illicit, passionate relationship. As she witnesses her brother's destructive affair with a married woman, Lottie chooses her marriage over her romanticism; she is an Emma or Anna that is capable of growth and happiness in the real world.

The Distinguished Guest (1996) continues M.'s examination of complex family relationships, this time focusing on an elderly mother and her adult son. As reviewers and readers continue to acknowledge M.'s gift for characterization and her realistic depiction of family scenes, she is beginning to be recognized by critics as more than "just a woman writer"; she is a writer that deals with the core of American society—the family.

BIBLIOGRAPHY: Drzal, D. A., "Casualties of the Feminine Mystique," *Antioch* 46 (Fall 1988): 450–61; Miller, L., "The Novelist Hangs Around," *NYTBR* 27 April 1986: 40; Pearlman, M., *Listen to Their Voices. Twenty Interviews with Women Who Write* (1993); Zinman, T. S., "The Good Old Days in *The Good Mother,*" *MFS* 34 (Autumn 1988): 405–12

ASHLEY BROWN

MILLHAUSER, Steven
b. 3 August 1943, New York City

M. writes fiction of the hothouse variety, focused closely on the intense, twisting relationship of a small corps of characters, finely observed in very finely wrought prose, their tale mocked and made new by a postmodern sensibility—"corps" is a Millhauserian pun, suggesting "core" and "corpse." He may cross some line of taste from time to time with an overfondness for adjectives, for darkness, for literature; but when the gears of his prodigious talents of invention, sense-memory, and sheer writing catch, his passages accelerate and exhilarate and his stories hum like the real thing.

His first novel, written while a graduate student, might be his best. The premise of *Edwin Mullhouse: The Life and Death of an American Writer, 1943–1954, by Jeffrey Cartwright* (1972) is absurd on the face of it: a literary biography of an eleven-year-old author by his twelve-year-old Boswell, who is himself a precocious stylist chafing at the role literary history has assigned him. But the plot is pure and profound, the found poetry of childhood. M. received much critical acclaim for rescuing the authentic sensibility of early youth, its desires and dangers, and this he does through immaculate remembering and language lithe with imagination. He achieves the best kind of modernist parody, inherited from James Joyce through Vladimir NABOKOV, that makes fun and admires at once.

His next novel suggests a bizarre chronological order, the protagonist of one book taking up at the age where the protagonist of the previous one left off. We follow Arthur Grumm of *Portrait of a Romantic* (1977) from ages twelve to fifteen, and again M. gained praise for recognizing an aspect of youth usually absent from fiction, in this case boredom. And again, as in *Edwin Mullhouse,* the same strengths save the same lapses from enervating a vital tale of authentic angst and wonder. Characters have almost allegorical roles:

Mainwaring, the Realist; Schoolcraft, the Decadent Romantic; the "Lady" Eleanor, la belle dame sans merci. Perhaps most teenagers are more likely to play sports, go dancing, and lament acne than they are to read incessantly and play Russian Roulette, as M.'s do, but the secret obsessions, covenants, confusions, and death wish that are more romantic realities of adolescent life deserve, perhaps, the considerable art M. has lavished upon them.

M.'s next novel, *From the Realm of Orpheus* (1986), and his four collections of short fiction—*In the Penny Arcade* (1986), *The Barnum Museum* (1990), *Little Kingdoms* (1993), and *The Knife-Thrower* (1998)—veer toward freer fantasy. From a character who, searching for a foul ball, finds a passage to the underworld, to a new voyage of Sinbad, to a "Klassik Komix" adaptation of T. S. ELIOT's "The Love Song of J. Alfred Prufrock," to tours through Borgesian libraries and catalogues, to the creation of a genuine fairy tale of "The Princess, the Dwarf, and the Dragon," M. mines fable after fantastic fiction for tropes and inspiration, from Hoffman to Kafka, from the Brothers Grimm to Italo Calvino. The forms swerve from musing to parody, from Arabian night to tale of terror, the quality of the storytelling from stunning to precious, from enchanting to showing off. M.'s prose once more prevails, shining up such standard Gothic features as the painting come to life and the automaton, while redeeming "vivid detail" as viable critical praise.

His major work to date is the Pulitzer Prize-winning *Martin Dressler* (1996). No author is so well-prepared and positioned as M. to make the claim that 20th-c. American entrepreneurial capitalism and the culture it created is itself fantasy fiction, defining its function as "rivaling the world," abiding desires so expansive only dreams and novels can accommodate them. Martin's rise from son of an immigrant cigarmaker, to bellhop, to inventor of the fast-food restaurant, to America's premier hotelier makes him one of M.'s most energetic characters, but there is an indolence in M.'s writing—not just thematically, but in his surrender to language, the distancing of allegory, his fabulist's fancy—that seduces not only the reader but the character as well. Martin does not struggle so hard to realize his American dream as M. does to dream America. M. marshals his writer's gifts and his favorite themes—the subterranean world, the blurred boundary of art and reality, the character subsumed by the fiction, the dance of the realist and romantic, in this case the sisters Emmeline and Caroline, Martin's business partner and his mysterious wife—to create a monumental fable, or a small epic, of the American imagination.

BIBLIOGRAPHY: Fowler, D., "S. M., Miniaturist," *Crit* 37 (Winter 1996): 139–48; Kinzie, M., "Succeeding Borges, Escaping Kafka: On the Fiction of S. M.," *Salmagundi* 92 (Fall 1992): 115–44; Saltzman, A. M., "In the M. Archives," *Crit* 37 (Winter 1996): 149–60

                                          DENNIS PAOLI

MIRIKITANI, Janice
b. 4 February 1942, Stockton, California

Perhaps best known for her unrelentingly brutal works on the Japanese American concentration camp experience, M. is also acknowledged as one of the Asian American community's most dynamic and outspoken social activists. Her works—brash, sexual, and unapologetically political—reflect her strong commitment to political and social change.

M.'s writing career grew out of the civil rights movements of the 1960s. While pursuing a graduate degree at San Francisco State University, M. began writing poetry about her family's World War II camp experiences—bitter, scathing examinations of U.S. racism and its effects on families and entire communities. These early works were filled with rage toward two "enemies": the political system that created the camps, and what she perceived to be the silence and apathy of the Japanese American community during the internment period. At the same time, M. began drawing connections between her own personal experiences with racism and similar experiences shared by other individuals and communities of color.

In her first two collections of poems, *Awake in the River* (1978) and *Shedding Silence* (1987), M. tackles a variety of social and political issues—South African apartheid, white feminism, the Hiroshima bombing, the Vietnam War—juxtaposing images from these struggles with her own family's memories and experiences in the camps. These early poems reflect M.'s belief that issues of racial and social inequality must be examined both locally as well as on an international scale, and stress that it is the similarity of experiences that binds peoples and communities together, rather than ethnic and national boundaries. With this global perspective, M. incorporates the experiences of women in Hiroshima and Vietnam and Zimbabwe into poems that speak directly to the Asian American experience.

The Japanese American concentration camps form the central motif of much of M.'s early work. But while M. does focus on many elements of the camps themselves—the living conditions, the lack of privacy, the guilt and shame felt within the camp walls—her poems are often much more concerned with the lingering effects of the camps on subsequent generations of Japanese Americans. The most obvious effect, the strained communication between the Issei and Nisei generations and their Sansei children and grandchildren, is often represented as a direct result of the cloud of shame created by the camps. For M., the silence within her own family was almost unbearable. In "For My Father," M.'s anger is directed not only at her father's refusal to speak out against the racist policies of the U.S. during the time, but also the older generation's unwillingness or inability to discuss the camps within their own families, years after the fact.

These silences have played a major role in many of M.'s best-known works. In "Breaking Silence," M. addresses some of the political motives behind the silencing of Japanese Americans during the postwar period. Employing a multivoiced narrative, M. interweaves official government pronouncements and her own mother's testimony before a 1981 federal commission on the camps. While M. describes this silencing as a direct result of U.S. policy, she also acknowledges its use within the community as a survival technique, a response to the deep feelings of anger and humiliation brought on by the camps. For M., "breaking" these silences serves a dual purpose: it becomes a way of defeating the cycle of self-hate within the Japanese American communities, as well as a strategy for attacking the political system that continues to impose these silences on communities of color.

"Yes, We Are *Not* Invisible" continues this theme of breaking silences by attacking many of the more egregious stereotypes about Asians and Asian Americans. The poem also addresses the stereotype of the Asian American as the eternal, unassimilable foreign by laying claim to collective hometowns in Lodi, Stockton, and Chicago, and fleshing out collective experiences within the U.S. At the same time, the poem also implicitly addresses the attempts within the Asian American community to distance itself from its first generation members and its own immigrant past, by also laying claim to its Asian countries of origin.

Many of M.'s poems also address the issue of internalized racism. Her poetry examines two of the fundamental aspects of internalized racism, self-hatred and the "desire to be white," in relation to her own experiences growing up in largely white communities around the U.S. In "Beauty Contest," M. describes scotch taping her eyelids, one of the primary Asian American rituals of assimilation, so that she would look more "white." M.'s other works describe the competing feature of the desire towards white acceptance: trying to look, act, and sound white to blend in, to "disappear" into the mainstream, and the competing desire to trade on one's "Asianness" by playing the role of the "exotic," mysterious Oriental temptress.

Since 1978, M. has served as the president and executive director of Glide Memorial Church, a progressive organization in San Francisco's Tenderloin district. At Glide, M. has developed outreach programs for the city's homeless populations, helped to implement recovery programs for women dealing with a variety of issues from substance abuse to rape, and compiled oral histories of individuals who have experienced childhood incest and abuse.

Many of the poems in her collection *We the Dangerous* (1995) reflect the issues and problems that she deals with at Glide on a daily basis—homelessness, domestic violence, drug addiction—while other works confront the poet's own experiences of childhood sexual abuse. In "Insect Collection," M. uses the images of poisoning and pinning insects to describe her own feelings of silencing and powerlessness as a victim of child abuse. In the poem, the "poison" is silence, the threats and warnings to never speak about the abuse, while the "pinning" is described as a slow, suffocating, and extremely violent "death."

M.'s poems from this period also offer a return to and reexamination of one of her most predominant themes: her parents' "silence" about the camps. While her older poems were filled with rage towards their silence, her newer works exhibit a more understanding and even forgiving examination of what the Nisei generation went through, and some of the reasons why they remained silent for so long.

M.'s works have appeared in anthologies of Asian American literature and poetry, collections of writings by women of color, and various anthologies of American literature. In addition, she has received several literary awards, as well as dozens of awards and commendations for her leadership roles and participation in a variety of social causes M. maintains an exceptionally brisk schedule, juggling her "duties" as poet, performance artist, editor, dancer, and social activist. While recognized as one of the veterans of the Asian American literary canon, M. nevertheless continues to be one of its most outspoken and revolutionary talents.

BIBLIOGRAPHY: Usui, M., "No Hiding Place, New Speaking Place," J. M.'s Poetry of Incest and Abuse," *SALit* 32 (June 1996): 56–65; Yogi, S., "Yearning for the Past: The Dynamics of Memory in Sansei Internment Poetry," in Singh, A., et al., eds., *Memory and Cultural Politics: New Approaches to American Ethnic Literature* (1996): 245–65

ROBERT ITO

MITCHELL, Donald Grant
b. 12 April 1822, Norwich, Connecticut; d. 15 December 1908, New Haven, Connecticut

All of M.'s literary efforts reflect a staid, even archaic character, a fondness for the simple life of older times, and unabashedly sentimental tastes. His gentle humor is often compared to that of the English writer Jerome K. Jerome. Seldom read today, M.'s work was popular among the members of mid-19th-c. New England's fashionable society.

Most successful in writing his own informal essays, M. also held a wide variety of editorial positions for several periodicals. In the mid-1840s, he served as a Washington correspondent for the New York-based *Morning Courier and Enquirer*. With Oliver Wendell HOLMES, M. edited the *Atlantic Almanac* in 1868–69 and he edited *Hearth and Home* in 1869. Befitting his homey persona, he became the first editor of "The Easy Chair" department of *Harper's* magazine. As the subject matter of much of his post-1851 writing indicates, M. was probably more interested in agriculture than he was in being a writer or editor.

M.'s first book, *Fresh Gleanings* (1847), discusses the author's travels in Europe, and his second, *The Battle Summer* (1850), is a treatment of the French Revolution of 1848. Most of his subsequent works are concerned with his native country. His satire on New York society, *The Lorgnette,* originally appeared as a twelve-volume periodical and was published in 1850 in book form under the pseudonym John Timon. M.'s most popular work, *Reveries of a Bachelor* (1850), is a series of sentimental musings on the subjects of love, marriage, and friendship; *Dream Life,* published the following year, follows a similar vein. Both of the latter were published under the pseudonym Ik Marvell, a misprint of the pseudonym J. K. Marvell, which M. had adopted in 1846 for his journalistic pieces. *My Farm of Edgewood* (1863) consists of romantic reveries revolving around M.'s estate, Edgewood, which is located near New Haven. *About Old Story-Tellers* (1878), intended for juvenile readers, is an informal, first-person retelling of well-known stories from Swift, Defoe, the Grimm brothers, and others. Perhaps the most interesting of all M.'s works is his *American Lands and Letters* (1899), a characteristically chatty and non-scholarly covering the history of American literature between James Fenimore COOPER and Edgar Allan POE.

BIBLIOGRAPHY: Dunn, W. H., *The Life of D. G. M.: Ik Marvell* (1922)

BRYAN L. MOORE

MITCHELL, Joseph

b. 27 July 1908, Iona, North Carolina; d. 24 May 1996, New York City

M. was "the *New Yorker* reporter who set the standard," according to his younger colleague Calvin Trillin. One of a near-legendary group of nonfiction writers associated with the magazine during the editorships of Harold Ross and William Shawn—others included E. B. WHITE and M.'s close friend A. J. Liebling—M. specialized in "profiles." These pieces, often quite long, chronicled quotidian life in New York, with an emphasis on eccentrics and marginal figures, including gypsies, circus freaks, a street preacher, the Union League of the Deaf, Mohawk steelworkers, and a nine-year-old mixed-race musical prodigy. M. combined exhaustively observed physical detail with particular attention to patterns of speech—his profiles are often largely in dialogue—to raise reportage to verbal art. In this, he anticipated the New Journalism of the 1960s and 1970s. Unlike many New Journalists, however, M. never used his reportage to strike attitudes. His subjects are allowed to speak for themselves without condescension.

After attending the University of North Carolina, M. arrived in New York in 1929 and spent the Depression decade writing for newspapers: the *Herald Tribune, Morning World,* and *World-Telegram.* In 1938, a collection, *My Ears Are Bent,* appeared, and M. moved to the *New Yorker,* which gave him time and space to develop his distinctive approach. Sometimes spending months or even years with his subjects, he would then devote equally extended periods to composing a profile. Four collections of New Yorker pieces appeared as *McSorley's Wonderful Saloon* (1943), *Old Mr. Flood* (1948), *The Bottom of the Harbor* (1960), and *Joe Gould's Secret* (1965). Joe Gould, first profiled as "Professor Sea Gull" in 1942, inspired M.'s greatest writing—an alcoholic, panhandling Greenwich Village eccentric, a Harvard graduate who claimed to understand sea gull language and to be writing a massive literary project called An Oral History of Our Time. Ironically, after uncovering Joe Gould's Secret—that the Oral History never existed—M. submitted no new writing for the rest of his life, though for over thirty years he went regularly to his New Yorker office. An omnibus volume, *Up in the Old Hotel,* was published in 1992 and secured a new generation of admirers.

A *New Yorker* editorial following M.'s death compared *McSorley's Wonderful Saloon* to James Joyce's *Dubliners* in its generous comic treatment of local characters, primarily through their distinctive rhythms of language. A great admirer of Joyce, M. nevertheless sensed closer kinship with another favorite, Mark TWAIN, particularly in a fondness for "graveyard humor." It was "seeking to rid my mind of thoughts of death and doom," he wrote, that led him to walk at dawn along New York's bustling waterfront and Bowery. Later in life, M. recognized how much he shared this "cast of mind" with his characters: "I didn't know it at the time, but I interviewed people like me."

BIBLIOGRAPHY: Perrin, N., "Paragon of Reporters: J. M.," *SR* 92 (Spring 1983): 167–84; Zinsser, W., "Journeys with J. M.," ASch 62 (Winter 1993): 132–8; special M. issue, *PM* 26 (1994)

GLEN M. JOHNSON

MITCHELL, Margaret
b. 8 November 1900, Atlanta, Georgia; d. 16 August 1949, Atlanta, Georgia

M. had worked for the *Atlanta Journal* for four years during the 1920s, first as reporter and then as feature writer, and in the early days of her career as a writer had attempted doing short fiction, but the publication of *Gone with the Wind* (1936), her only novel, which was awarded the Pulitzer Prize in 1937, secured for M. a permanent place in American literature. Her creative imagination fashioned *Gone with the Wind* slowly, over a decade or so, from her family history and Southern exposure, while technical details of time, place, and events, including the Civil War, were being checked for accuracy. It is difficult to know whether she was sincere when she wrote a friend that *Gone with the Wind* was "just a simple yarn of fairly simple people," short on description and lacking in "fine writing . . . philosophizing . . . grandiose thoughts . . . hidden meanings . . . symbolism . . . [the] sensational" or anything else that makes for a best seller. But as a phenomenally popular novel since its publication with well over twenty-five million copies in print, it retains a prominent position in American popular culture and is a familiar literary work in other English-speaking countries and elsewhere around the globe, where it has been translated into many languages.

Despite its unflagging action and vividly drawn characters, *Gone with the Wind* has missed the critical acclaim of such contemporaneous novels as William FAULKNER's *Absalom, Absalom!*, John DOS PASSOS's *The Big Money,* and John STEINBECK's *Of Mice and Men*. Often criticized for being simplistic in style and thought, the work is in fact extremely complicated, open to widely varying interpretations. To begin, M. herself was a partial rebel against the weak Southern belle stereotype. She appeared at times a self-determined, tough survivalist and at other times as a dependent, physically frail product of her privileged background. She was in a way a Jazz Age girl—unrefined, ribald, flirtatious, and a poor student, although not very interested in physical sex—yet she was a serious researcher and reader—although favoring a

writer such as Thomas Dixon, chronicler of Ku Klux Klan adventures.

Much of M. went into her heroine Scarlett O'Hara, a fighter against the ravaging effects on her family of the defeat of the Confederacy and the ruination of the Tara plantation, yet held in thrall by a longtime infatuation with Ashley Wilkes, the spiritless son of a planter, and later by her much deeper attachment to the formidable, unscrupulous opportunist Rhett Butler. Like Scarlett, Rhett is a complicated, driven creature who creates his own world around him. Because of a certain ladylike appeal and her ability both to endure the devastation wrought on her land by the Civil War and to rebuild, Scarlett has even been compared with the city of Atlanta. Scarlett's first husband, Charles Hamilton, and Ashley Wilkes both appear fictive versions of an army lieutenant, Clifford Henry (a weak, effete man with homosexual tendencies), to whom M. had been secretly engaged. Rhett Butler seems to be drawn from M.'s first husband, Berrien Upshaw, a brutal football player who abused her and once tried to rape her.

Critical response to *Gone with the Wind* has been mixed, with opponents generally objecting to M.'s preservation of "the plantation legend" of white supremacy and black servitude, and her inartistic narrative style. As for the novel's phenomenal popular success, the fast-paced narrative with its clearly focused, suspenseful storyline can be appreciated by a wide, diversified body of readers. There is also a particular force in the novel that sets it apart from other Civil War novels or "moonlight and magnolia" romances of the Old South; that power comes from M.'s painful experiences with the men in her life, set against her own psychic suffering and physical weakness, and her determination to fight back in whatever ways she could.

Some of *Gone with the Wind*'s continuing fame can be attributed to David O. Selznick's 1939 star-studded film version, described by Leonard Maltin as, "if not the greatest movie ever made, certainly one of the greatest examples of storytelling on film, maintaining interest for nearly four hours." It won nine Academy Awards, including best film, best director (Victor Fleming), best actress (Vivien Leigh), best screenplay (Sidney HOWARD, posthumously), best supporting actor (Thomas Mitchell), and best supporting actress (Hattie McDaniel).

BIBLIOGRAPHY: Bellman, S. I., "Popular Writers in the Modern Age: Constance Rourke, Pearl Buck, Marjorie Kinnan Rawlings, and M. M.," in Duke, M., J. R. Bryer, and M. T. Inge, eds, *American Women Writers: Bibliographical Essays* (1983): 353–78; Edwards, A., *Road to Tara: The Life of M. M.* (1983); Harwell, R.,

ed., *Gone with the Wind As Book and Film* (1983);
Pyron, D. A., ed., *Recasting: Gone with the Wind
in American Culture* (1983); Pyron, D. A., *Southern
Daughter: The Life of M. M.* (1991)

SAMUEL I. BELLMAN

MITCHELL, S[ilas] Weir

b. 15 February 1829, Philadelphia, Pennsylvania; d.
4 January 1914, Philadelphia, Pennsylvania

Although he never achieved the towering literary reputation that he would have liked, M., a respected neurologist who was a writer only when on vacation, was
a frequently-published poet, short story writer, and
novelist. On the advice of Oliver Wendell HOLMES, he
published anonymously until he had established his
medical career; his first literary work under his own
name did not appear until 1873. M.'s physician's perspective is apparent in the psychological study of the
characters in many of his works. He also wrote popular
and carefully-researched historical novels, including
the bestselling 1896 *Hugh Wynne*. But his real passion
was his poetry, which now seems more old-fashioned
than his fiction.

M. was the son of a Philadelphia physician who
also loved poetry. He followed in his father's footsteps,
publishing anonymous poetry from 1846 and becoming a doctor in 1850. His most important writings
before 1880 were medical treatises on such topics as
rattlesnake venom, gunshot wounds, and nerve injuries. As a neurologist, he also influenced literature with
his legendary "rest cure" for nervous breakdowns; he
treated a number of writers, including Edith WHARTON,
and was studied by Freud, who later tried to alleviate
the psychological distress inflicted on some patients
by enforced bed rest—memorably depicted in "The
Yellow Wallpaper" by Charlotte Perkins GILMAN.

M. published a number of short stories pseudonymously in the *Atlantic* during the editorship of William
Dean HOWELLS, who especially admired the more scientific aspects of his fiction. The admiration was mutual; the two carried on a correspondence until M.'s
death. M.'s respectable first novel, *In War Time* (1884),
owed a great deal to Howell's realist classic *A Modern
Instance*. *In War Time* tells of the rise and fall of a
Civil War doctor, Ezra Wendell, who exhibits some
of M.'s characteristics. The novel's attention to clinical
detail interferes with its readability, but enhances the
characters' psychological realism.

Roland Blake (1886), M.'s second novel, was another realist Civil War story in which M. tried to
portray a hero (based, like his name, on the French
epic character and William Blake) in a happy romance.
The too-perfect title character, however, seems to have

held little fascination for M.; his attention was caught
instead by the neurotic invalid Octopia Darnell. Octopia is especially interesting to modern scholars as one
of the earliest lesbian characters in American fiction.

M.'s novels are fairly evenly divided between psychological portraits and historical romances. Among
the former, critics have admired *Constance Trescot*
(1905) as his most effective novel and a finely realized
portrait of its obsessively vengeful heroine. Among
the latter is *Hugh Wynne,* by far his most popular
book, a Revolutionary War novel which sold 500,000
copies. It was frequently compared (even by M.) to
William Makepeace Thackeray's *Henry Esmond*. M.'s
own favorite among his novels was the picaresque
French Revolution tale *The Adventures of François*
(1897), a swashbuckling romance.

M.'s fiction still has admirers, in spite of its sometimes uneasy mingling of the author's patrician, romantic views of life with his clinical behavioral observations. But M.'s own great love was poetry, his own
and that of others. He supplied Walt WHITMAN with
a monthly stipend and gave him free medical treatment
for two years, but ended the friendship when he learned
that Whitman had found M.'s poems pedestrian. Criticism of his poetry angered him and wounded his considerable vanity. His poetic works were respected
enough to see frequent publication, and the *Collected
Poems of S. W. M.* appeared in 1896 and later in an
expanded posthumous edition. But with the possible
exception of "Ode on a Lycian Tomb" (1898), an elegy
for M.'s beloved daughter who had died of diphtheria
at twenty-two, critics today generally agree with Whitman's assessment of M.'s poetry.

BIBLIOGRAPHY: Burr, A. R., *W. M.: His Life and Letters*
(1929); Earnest, E. P., *S. W. M.: Novelist and Physician*
(1950); Lovering, J. P., *S. W. M.* (1971)

CAROLYN LENGEL

MODERNISM

The American expatriate Ezra POUND, who always
kept his hand firmly on the Anglo-American modernist
pulse, gave the movement its rallying cry: "Make it
new!" Of course, Pound's pronouncement could have
applied almost as well to any other literary period
from the Renaissance onward; the writers of each succeeding generation usually felt strongly the anxiety of
their predecessors' influence and, consequently, the
desire to remake literature in their own original images. Contemporary critical theory, however, questions the very possibility of originality, given the predetermined structure of language systems, and also
challenges the validity of our constructions of literary

periods as coherent movements, given the pervasive cultural biases that inform those constructions. Nevertheless, the notion of literary movements, such as modernism, persists, largely because it provides a broad framework on which we build generalizations for ordering and understanding literary texts, a framework that we reserve the right to dismantle or replace later. The modernist movement in American literature, then, may be described broadly as follows: flourishing during the time between World War I and II, although many characteristics of modernism were certainly present before 1914 and after 1945; involving an international group of writers from Great Britain and Europe, as well as America, who interacted with one another; reflecting the sociopolitical climate of the time, including the rise of technology, science, socialism, FEMINISM, civil rights, psychoanalysis, sexual freedom, and so forth; questioning traditional modes of literary expression and transmission and shifting its locus away from the center more toward the margins; experimenting with new aesthetic theories and stylistic practices that tend to privilege fragmentation and eschew coherence; redefining, while reaffirming, the cultural role of the alienated, yet socially engaged, artist.

As the chronological bookends for containing modernism, the two world wars served as touchstones for the grim possibilities of civilization's decline and fall over international struggles for economic, political, and social power, making American isolationism impossible and rendering certain ideals of human progress obsolete. The 1929 Stock Market Crash and resulting Great Depression likewise undercut American confidence in its capitalistic system and suddenly made everything in America seem vulnerable, particularly for the masses of working families who believed themselves to be the American mainstream. The rise of unions, with their Marxist ideological associations and willingness to strike violently against management, reflected the distrust working Americans felt toward American companies and corporations that they felt exploited them for profit. Women and various ethnic groups continued to battle the sexism and racism that pervaded American society and conspired to keep them in the margins, despite the passage of the Nineteenth Amendment in 1920 giving women the vote and the flourishing of the Harlem Renaissance in the 1920s. Suddenly, America, that great and noble experiment in democracy and economic opportunity, seemed less able to reconcile the disparity between its ideology and its reality, causing many of its citizens to feel disaffected, or cut off from the rest of society. This sense of individual isolation was reinforced by Freudian psychology with its internal emphasis on a fragmented self composed of various elements—id, ego, superego—in constant conflict with themselves.

American expatriates flocked to London and Paris and elsewhere to gain some distance and relief from the cultural turmoil they felt and together created new, loosely formed communities in which to live and work. Intellectuals and artists, while maintaining a certain degree of social conscience, distanced themselves from the general public by isolating themselves through an elitist mode of discourse that was self-conscious, self-referential, and self-perpetuating—and thus, they often made their work seem impossibly allusive and obscure. The development of college English departments and the study of American literature in the 1920s and 1930s coincided with the ascendance of New Criticism, a formalist mode of textual analysis based on internal empirical evidence, and, combined with these obscure modernist texts, created professional literary criticism on the premise that it takes an elite reader to read an elite text.

Against and with the grain of the above influences, modern writers produced some extraordinary work. For example, T. S. ELIOT's *The Waste Land,* published in 1922, embodies many of the elements of modernist poetry: its juxtaposition of allusions from popular culture as well as from classic Latinate texts; its combination of colloquial and formal languages; its fragmentary, almost arbitrary stanzas set against its thematically rigid five-part organization; its multiplicity of voices and languages speaking in interior monologues that eventually become dialogues as they interact; its preoccupation with mythic and religious symbols as manifested in the modern world; its location in the city, the emblem of the barrenness of the modern world; its obvious sexual content; its dedication to Pound, who edited it; its use of footnotes; and its prophetic character. In short, *The Waste Land* resists its readers at the same time it compels them to read on and almost forces them to create the meaning of the text for themselves. Published in 1929, William FAULKNER's *The Sound and the Fury* affects readers in much the same way and embodies many of the elements of modernist fiction: its narrow focus on the Compson family; its regional setting and reliance on history; its four-part division with each one focusing on the perspective of a different narrator using an entirely different world view and mode of language expression; its stream of consciousness psychology and stylistics; its nonlinear narrative style; its absent center, Caddy, who is spoken of endlessly but who never speaks for herself; its making Dilsey, the socially marginalized African American servant, the moral center of the novel; its critique of southern ideology, particularly notions of southern womanhood; its refusal to moralize directly; and its addition of a "Compson Appendix" in the 1945 Modern Library edition to help explain the cultural and historical context of the novel. Finally, Eugene O'NEILL's play *Desire under the Elms,* first produced in 1925, embodies many of the elements of modernist drama: its expressionistic stage techniques geared to represent externally the internal oppression of the characters; its working out of an Oedipal drama within the Cabot family; its generational conflicts; its revision of the American patriarch in the figure of Ephraim; its novel-like stage directions; its use of a regional setting and colloquial language; its undercutting of the traditional American dream; its relatively frank sexual references and action; its depiction of violence; and its ambiguous conclusion.

However, while Eliot, Faulkner, and O'Neill, all Nobel Prize winners, represent well the phallocentric tradition of "high modernism," they do not comprehend all aspects of modernism or set forth its immutable aesthetic standards for all modernists to follow. Writers from the Harlem Renaissance such as Richard WRIGHT and Zora Neale HURSTON, for example, embody a very different modernist tradition. Wright's *Native Son* and *Black Boy* radically revise the bildungsroman/künstlerroman tradition simply by making an African American the protagonist-apprentice; while the novels do not depart much from the same generic conventions that Charles Dickens uses in *Great Expectations* or that Thomas WOLFE uses in *Look Homeward, Angel,* they are of a very different character because of the extenuating consequences of racism on self-development. Hurston's novel *Their Eyes Were Watching God* and her autobiography, *Dust Tracks on a Road,* revise the bildungs/künstlerroman tradition more fully by privileging folklore and oral narrative traditions from African American culture and by exploring sexism within that community as well as within the larger white community. Wright and Hurston are also caught up in the double bind of ethnic self-expression in autobiography in which their selves and lives become representative of their race. Both Wright and Hurston become significant influences on contemporary African American writers such as Ralph ELLISON, John Edgar WIDEMAN, Toni MORRISON, and Alice WALKER and their respective articulations of African American selves.

Expatriate leader Gertrude STEIN further challenges old notions of selfhood in *The Autobiography of Alice B. Toklas* by making herself the narrator of an autobiography of her companion. Hilda DOOLITTLE, most famous in her day as an imagist poet, explores her interior self/ves in *HERmione,* written in 1927 but not published until 1981; this autobiographical novel illustrates what contemporary French feminists call *écriture féminine,* or feminine writing, in its nonlinear form, its circular motifs, its privileging of narrative gaps, and so forth. As a recovered text, *HERmione*

reminds us that we may not have all the significant modernist texts available to us and that there still may be intriguing additional modernist experiments of which we are unaware. *Black Elk Speaks,* the spiritual autobiography of a Lakota medicine man as told through John G. NEIHARDT, reflects an entirely different mode of autobiographical expression, one constructed according to a vision framework and connected to the community at every turn. John DOS PASSOS, particularly in his *U.S.A* trilogy—*The 42nd Parallel, 1919,* and *The Big Money*—uses narrative forms adapted from popular culture such as his "newsreel" and "camera eye" sections to reflect the fragmented montage quality of the modern world; his many short American profiles represent his attempt to articulate the multitude of American selves.

Finally, modernism is simply too multitudinous to encapsulate easily, its impulse to "make it new" always moving its writers in new directions that both reflect past literary traditions and anticipate future developments. Modern civilization may have been, as Pound once said, "an old bitch gone in the teeth," but the many and diverse writers that that civilization produced were certainly not. Their profound literary productions, in the face of so many negative cultural forces, bear witness of the continuous human drive for self-expression and of the infinite power of language to engage our intellects and sensibilities.

BIBLIOGRAPHY: Altieri, C., *Painterly Abstraction in Modernist American Poetry* (1989); Baker, H. A., *Modernism and the Harlem Renaissance* (1987); Benstock, S., *Women of the Left Bank* (1986); Clark, S., *Sentimental Modernism* (1991); De Jongh, J., *Vicious Modernism: Black Harlem and the Literary Imagination* (1990); DeKoven, M., *Rich and Strange: Gender, History, and Modernism* (1991); Dettmar, K. J. H., ed., *Rereading the New: A Backward Glance at Modernism* (1992); Dickie, M., and T. Travisano, eds., *Gendered Modernisms* (1996); Doreski, W., *The Modern Voice in American Poetry* (1995); Friedman, A. W., *Fictional Death and the Modernist Enterprise* (1995); Gilbert, S. M., and S. Gubar, eds., *The Female Imagination and the Modernist Aesthetic* (1986); Hutchinson, G., *The Harlem Renaissance in Black and White* (1995); Kindelan, N. A., *Shadows of Realism: Dramaturgy and the Theories and Practices of Modernism* (1996); Korg, J., *Ritual and Experiment in Modern Poetry* (1995); Lentricchia, F., *Modernist Quartet* (1994); Marek, J. E., *Women Editing Modernism* (1995); McDonald, G., *Learning to Be Modern* (1993); Michaels, W. B., *Our America: Nativism, Modernism, and Pluralism* (1995); North, M., *The Dialect of Modernism* (1994); Pizer, D., *American Expatriate Writing and the Paris Movement* (1996); Qian, Z., *Orientalism and Modernism* (1995); Rado,

L., ed., *Rereading Modernism* (1994); Schneidau, H. N., *Waking Giants: The Presence of the Past in Modernism* (1991); Scott, B. K., ed., *Gender of Modernism* (1990); Scott, B. K., *Refiguring Modernism* (1995); Steinman, K. M., *Made in America: Science, Technology, and American Modernist Poets* (1987); Strychancz, T. F., *Modernism, Mass Culture, and Professionalism* (1993); Wheeler, K. M., *Modernist Women Writers and Narrative Art* (1994)

PHILLIP A. SNYDER

MOMADAY, N. Scott

b. 27 February 1934, Lawton, Oklahoma

Many believe that M.'s novel *House Made of Dawn* (1968) actually initiated the Native American literary renaissance. The Pulitzer Prize he received for the novel in 1969 is one of several literary honors he has been awarded. Others include the Academy of America Poets Prize (1962), the Western Heritage Award (1974), the Premio Litterario Internazionale Mondelo (1975), the Distinguished Service Award from the Western Literature Association (1983), the Native American Literature Prize (1989), and the Returning the Gift Lifetime Achievement Award (1992).

M.'s first work was in poetry, something common to most of the recent Native American authors. He matriculated at age eighteen at the University of New Mexico. In 1956, he left to study law at the University of Virginia, where he met William FAULKNER, whose influence on M. can be seen vividly in his fiction and poetry. It is the lyrical nature of his prose that owes much to his poetic work.

In 1959, M. won a creative writing scholarship to Stanford University. He was chosen for the scholarship by the poet critic Yvor WINTERS. Winters had a strong influence on M.'s verse, introducing M. to postsymbolist style—a style stressing sharp sensory detail to suggest the meaning. Typical of such verse is the poem "Angle of Geese," in which M. describes two events: the death of a friend's child and the death of a goose that a fellow hunter shot on a hunting trip M. took as a teenager. In the first section, he ponders the adequate response to the death of the child. In the second section, he uses the image of the dying goose to broach a metaphysical point. The goose serves as an archetype, in its death transcending the limits of time.

M. earned his doctorate with a dissertation on Frederick G. TUCKERMAN, a poet who along with Winters had great influence on M.'s style. One of the best of M.'s poems illustrating this influence is "Before an Old Painting of the Crucifixion." The theme of this poem is the existential position of human life in an indifferent universe, a theme Tuckerman seemed occupied with.

M.'s first novel is often considered his masterpiece. *House Made of Dawn* centers around the main character Abel, who returns to the reservation landscape and culture surrounding it at the end of World War II. There he kills an albino. He serves a prison term and is paroled, unrepentant, to a Los Angeles relocation center. Once in the city, he attempts to adjust to his factory job. Abel drinks and attends religious ceremonies. He cannot cope with his job; he manages to fight with a policeman, but returns to the reservation to take care of his dying grandfather. The novel ends with Abel's running in the ancient ritual dawn race against evil and death and praying for good hunting and harvest. As he runs he sings "House Made of Dawn," an old Navajo song. In his running and singing, Abel becomes once again whole. Throughout the novel, M. uses the rhythms and imagery of his poetry in creating a prose style that is extremely lyrical. It takes special poetic talent to show a self-destructive character like Abel as a sympathetic, complex character, or to portray the dry, dusty pueblo of Jemez as a beautiful place.

M.'s next book, *The Way to Rainy Mountain* (1969), is a series of fragments, a literary collection of poems, essays, myths, historical notes, and personal stories. Its theme is the emergence, development, and decline of the Kiowa culture. M. retraces the journey that the tribe made from their ancestral territory in the northern Rocky Mountains of what we today call Yellowstone, to their present home in Oklahoma. Here, on the plains, they became a society of sun priests, fighters, hunters, and thieves, lasting until they were all but destroyed by the U.S. Army.

The bulk of the story consists of short stories written in three different voices: first a myth, then a historical note, and last a personal story. For example, a story about the buffalo, a symbol of the sun to the Native Americans, begins with the myth of a buffalo with horns of steel, killed by a Kiowa warrior. The tone is lofty and bardic. The historical portion is a pathetic picture describing the last Kiowa buffalo hunt. The personal story tells how M. and his father were pursued by a buffalo cow while walking in a game preserve.

In 1976, M. published his second book of verse, *The Gourd Dancer*. It includes prose poems based on Indian themes and poems depicting scenes from his trip to Russia. In *Names* (1977)—a memoir of his childhood—M. returns to autobiographical themes, incorporating specific Native American motifs, such as the sacred nature of the land and of the language, and the relationship of language to being. M.'s quest for his roots takes him back to the hills of his ancestral Kentucky to the high plains of Wyoming, and from there to the Bering Straits. It is a search and a celebration at the same time, a book of identity and of sources. The book attempts to show that M. himself does not feel the conflict of Kiowa and white traditions; he presents himself in the book as their product, an artist, heir of the experiences of his ancestors and conscious of the strong underlying dormant influence on his life.

In his second true novel *The Ancient Child,* M. returns in it to such subjects as the nature of "Indianness," the aesthetics of painting, and the life and death of Billy the Kid. It combines the conventions of the modern novel with the Kiowa myth of Tsoai, the story of a boy who changes into a bear and chases his sisters up a tree. The sisters become the stars of the Big Dipper; the tree becomes Tsoai, known in the Anglo world as Devil's Tower. This novel is a chronicle of the West, using Billy the Kid to represent the best and the worst of the frontier story of "cowboys and Indians." He is a killer, but at times kind, chivalric, courageous and loyal. In one way, Billy is like the bear, more sinned against than sinning. This novel has not received the critical acclaim of the first, but it still presents M. as a Renaissance man, a painter, a poet, a dancer in tune with the universe, and a novelist. Some, in fact, would say that M. is himself the bear of contemporary Native American life.

BIBLIOGRAPHY: Lincoln, K., *Native American Renaissance* (1983); Schubnell, M., *N. S. M.: The Cultural and Literary Background* (1985); Trimble, M. S., *N. S. M.* (1973); Woodard, C., *Ancestral Voice: Conversations with N. S. M.* (1989)

JOHN W. CRAWFORD

MONROE, Harriet

b. 23 December 1860, Chicago, Illinois; d. 26 September 1936, Arequipa, Peru

In 1912, M. founded and edited *Poetry: A Magazine of Verse,* in its first decade probably the most important of the "little magazines" that emerged with the development of modern poetry in the U.S. At a time when poetry was often regarded as a pleasant, escapist pastime, she insisted upon the high importance of the art and dedicated her magazine to publishing the finest of the verse she received, regardless of schools and reputations. As a result, *Poetry* marked the first or early appearances in print of the poetry of Carl SANDBURG, Edgar Lee MASTERS, Marianne MOORE, Wallace STEVENS, and William Carlos WILLIAMS. Her acceptance of Ezra POUND's offer to be "foreign correspondent" led to the publication of important poems by W. B. Yeats, D. H. Lawrence, Hilda DOOLITTLE, and Robert FROST and to lively debate on the developing

poetics of modernist verse (see MODERNISM) in the critical and correspondence pages of the magazine.

M.'s own lyrical, conservative poetry had already won her a small reputation in Chicago by the time she founded *Poetry.* Her late-Victorian taste (evidenced by her own poetry) and her editorial openness led to a large number of derivative and forgettable poems appearing in the magazine alongside those now central to the history of modern poetry. Figures such as Pound and Williams frequently complained about what they viewed as this lack of discrimination, but M. held to her commitment to concentrate on no particular school of verse—although the magazine did put out special issues from time to time that focused upon a particular group.

By its second decade, although the magazine continued to publish important writers, M.'s conservatism (in 1920 Williams refused to send her any further poems unless she stopped changing to upper case the lower case first letters of his lines) led *Poetry* to have something of a staid reputation beside the more radical modernist magazines. By the 1930s, when she rejected the poetry of W. H. AUDEN and Stephen Spender on the grounds of content, M. herself began to realize the necessity of passing on the editorship to younger hands—although she had not brought herself to do so by the time of her death. *Poetry* celebrated its seventy-fifth anniversary in 1987, and today, in the tradition M. served, is an important outlet for the work of new and established writers alike.

BIBLIOGRAPHY: Cahill, D. J., *H. M.* (1973); Williams, E., *H. M. and the Poetry Renaissance* (1977)

CHRISTOPHER MACGOWAN

MOODY, William Vaughn [Stoy]

b. 8 July 1869, Spencer, Indiana; d. 17 October 1910, Colorado Springs, Colorado

When M.'s *Poems and Plays* appeared posthumously in 1912, a reviewer praised M. as "one of the great poets of our day." Similarly, his drama *The Great Divide* (1906) earned him the accolade "The great American playwright." Though regarded in the latter half of the 20th c. as a minor author, M. remains an important transitional figure leading the way for Edwin Arlington ROBINSON, Robert FROST, Eugene O'NEILL, and Edward ALBEE.

M. was well educated, taking a B.A. (1893) and M.A. (1894) from Harvard, teaching English at Harvard and the University of Chicago, editing Milton and other standard British authors, and coauthoring a textbook on English literature. Thus steeped in the poetic tradition, M. used classical diction, verse forms, and syntax, and his poetry is suffused with literary allusions. As Robinson wrote to Josephine Preston PEABODY, "Perhaps Moody's greatest trouble lies in the fact that he has so many things to unlearn." His poetry seems more like the culmination of the Victorian tradition than the beginning of MODERNISM.

M.'s versification reveals great technical virtuosity. "The Daguerrotype," for example, an ode inspired by a picture of his mother taken when she was seventeen, uses iambic lines varying in length from one foot to seven and adroitly handles a complex rhyme scheme. The poem also expresses one of M.'s recurring themes: suffering as a prelude to redemption through love. Most of M.'s poems focus on the individual consciousness, but three in the 1901 volume attack imperialism. The best, and best known, of these, "An Ode in Time of Hesitation," reveals M.'s traditionalism, as he echoes James Russell LOWELL's "Ode Recited at the Harvard Commemoration" and "Memoriae Positum." With rare exceptions, M.'s poems voice an optimism characteristic of pre-World War I America.

M. was among those in America and Europe seeking to revitalize verse drama. By June of 1897 he was working on *The Masque of Judgement* (1900), a work he described as "a kind Hebrew Götterdammerung." M.'s edition of Milton had attacked 17th-c. Puritans who "crushed the joy and poetry of life in England," and M. had objected to Milton's "passion of purification." In his masque, M. uses Milton's blank verse to reject a vindictive Old Testament-Calvinist deity and to celebrate passion.

The first verse drama intended for performance was *The Fire-Bringer* (1904), the first of a trilogy to precede *The Masque of Judgement*. As the title suggests, M. here retells the Prometheus myth, drawing on both Shelley and the Greeks. M. insists on humanity's infinite potential and concludes with a celebration of Apollo as liberator, though M. argues finally that salvation must come from within. Illness prevented the completion of the trilogy; M. wrote only one act of *The Death of Eve* (1912) before his death.

M.'s verse dramas never were staged, but his first prose play, *The Great Divide,* was a critical and popular success. The work was inspired by trips to the Colorado Rockies in 1901 and Arizona in 1904, combined with a tale told to him by his future wife, Harriet Brainerd. Ruth Jordan, an Easterner visiting Arizona, gives herself to the Westerner Stephen Ghent to save herself from two other ruffians. In act 2, she buys her freedom and returns east. Ghent follows her, and in the third act wins her love. M. successfully fuses realism with mythology, individual action with sociological analysis. Like her biblical namesake, Ruth leaves her old world to follow the protomartyr of the new dispensation as she crosses the great divide of Eastern

Puritanism to Western freedom. M.'s other prose play, *The Faith Healer* (1909), suffered from poor acting but also from its controversial subject matter. M. again uses realistic situations—the play was prompted by newspaper clippings about a faith healer named Francis Schlatter, and it draws on M.'s own Midwestern childhood experiences—with Christian symbolism as suggested by such characters' names as Ulrich Michaelis, Mary and Martha Beeler.

M.'s fusion of realism with symbolism and myth anticipates such works as O'Neill's *Long Day's Journey into Night* and Albee's *Who's Afraid of Virginia Woolf.* His attempts to write about contemporary problems in traditional verse forms provided models for later, more successful efforts. A harbinger if not a practitioner of modernism, M. earned a small but important place in literary history.

BIBLIOGRAPHY: Brown, M. F., *Estranging Dawn: The Life and Works of W. V. M.* (1973); Henry, D. D., *W. V. M.* (1934); Halpern, M., *W. V. M.* (1964)

JOSEPH ROSENBLUM

MOORE, Marianne [Craig]
b. 15 November 1887, Kirkwood, Missouri; d. 5 February 1972, New York City

For the first seven years of her life, M., her older brother, and mother lived with her maternal grandfather, John Warner, a Presbyterian pastor in Kirksville, because her father had suffered a nervous breakdown and returned to his own parents' home, never again living with his family. After Reverend Warner's death, M.'s mother took the children to live in Carlisle, Pennsylvania. In 1904, M. entered Bryn Mawr College and graduated in 1909. Always close, M. and her mother moved to Greenwich Village in 1918 and lived there until their move to Brooklyn in 1929, where M. lived for the next thirty-six years. Besides her poetry, the most remarkable achievement in M.'s life was her editorship of *The Dial* from 1926 until its last issue in 1929.

M. belongs to the modernist school of poetry, although she has sometimes been incorrectly identified as an imagist. Her chief contribution to modern poetry lies in her scintillating use of language. She saw language in several different ways. First, she saw the black words on the white page as a work of visual art, and she utilized the shape of poem on the page the way an artist would. Secondly, she explored the possibilities of words by using them as objects in her poems, using a word in all its various meanings, and meaning all the meanings, and thirdly, she utilized the way words work in the sentence, harnessing the tension between questions and answers, between the opposing parts of seeming contradictions, and between polar opposites. Her syntax pulled and tugged at language, extracting its recalcitrant meanings, eliciting its connotations, and defining its echoes. Her work, while full of real things (including real toads in imaginary gardens), documents the way the mind encounters the modern world.

Her contribution to form includes her extensive use of unique syllabic patterns, her penchant for quotations, and her prowess with slant rhyme.

Not only did she make major contributions to the way writers think about form, but she was considered one of the foremost intellectuals of her day, and her work is freighted with meaning and informed by her moral and theological views. Despite the seriousness of some of her subject matter, she does not take herself too seriously. In "The Pangolin," she wrote, "Humor saves a few steps, it saves years." It is no surprise to find in her work the kind of sophisticated wit that was popular in the 17th c., whose writers M. admired greatly.

Many critics have commented on M.'s use of armor and armored animals. Armor is important to M., and so is the secret self that lies beneath it and the secret meaning beneath the surface of the word and the secret emotion beneath the armored form of a poem. She was acutely aware of not only armor but also of a world where armor was necessary. How to claim the beautiful and the useful while avoiding natural dangers is a process that her poems invoke. Writing her poems was M.'s developing experiment (she had been a biology minor in college and felt deeply indebted to science), designed to bring life's dichotomies into as much harmony as they were able to bear.

BIBLIOGRAPHY: Bloom, H., ed., *M. M.* (1986); Costello, B., *M. M.: Imaginary Possessions* (1981); Martin, T., *M. M., Subversive Modernist* (1986); Schulman, G., *M. M.: The Poetry of Engagement* (1986); Stapleton, L., *M. M.: The Poetry of Engagement* (1978)

ANN STRUTHERS

MORGAN, Robert

b. 3 October 1944, near Hendersonville, North Carolina

M., according to Michael McFee in the *Iron Mountain Review,* is "the greatest Appalachian poet of his generation, and probably of all time . . . indeed one of the best poets *period* of his time." Few writers have explored their place of birth with more precision or intensity than M. He was born near Hendersonville, North Carolina, on land settled by his great, great,

grandfather and has examined its history, landscape, objects, people, work, and religion in poetry and fiction throughout his career. He began his education in science but switched to writing, studying under Fred CHAPPELL at the University of North Carolina at Greensboro, where he obtained his M.F.A. He has taught at Cornell since 1971.

Green River: New and Selected Poems (1991) shows the evolution of M.'s poetry from intensely sensory imagistic poems with an incredible attention to common objects to poems encompassing history, family narratives, and science. Throughout, M.'s writing explores the "archetypal acreage" of his North Carolina homeplace discussed in *Good Measure: Essays and Interviews* (1993).

M.'s early poems have a concision and terseness that are as "encompassing as mathematical proofs." His attention to objects and his startling juxtapositions reflect M.'s early interest in symbolism and surrealism. The early books, *Zirconia Poems* (1969) and *Red Owl* (1972), reveal M.'s tightly controlled mastery of free verse, harnessing the freedom by reining in the words.

With *Land Diving* (1976) and *Trunk & Thicket* (1978), M. began exploring narratives, longer and looser poems, formal poetry, and the deeply Appalachian materials of his origins. His most important poem in *Trunk & Thicket* is "Mockingbird," which uncovers his poetic origins in the "anarchic and creative soil" of the high country and in the objects and stories of the mountains. *Groundwork* (1979), his most lyrical and most formal book, is devoted almost exclusively to Appalachian subjects, as if poetic formalism gave him the freedom to use narrative and speak of the myths, superstitions, and family stories of his homeplace. Few books of contemporary poetry can match the achievement of these poems.

M.'s next two books demonstrate that he is neither a regional chauvinist nor a nostalgic Appalachian. In *At the Edge of the Orchard Country* (1987) and *Sigodlin* (1990), M.'s forms include triolets, terza rima, chant royal, and pantoums while undertaking subjects such as plate tectonics, field theory, and shadow matter as well as American history, religion, and the Viet Nam Memorial.

M. signaled his turn toward fiction with *Blue Valleys* (1989), followed by *The Mountains Won't Remember Us* (1991). These stories range from terse tales told out of a historical perspective to trailer park scenes of contemporary America. *Hinterlands: A Mountain Tale in Three Parts* (1994), M.'s first novel is a family saga that traces the story of the Richards family in the mountains of North Carolina from 1772 to 1845.

M.'s novel *The Truest Pleasure* (1995) is a turn of the century love story exploring the conflicts between a practical man whose faith is in work, land, and money and his wife whose passion is for Pentecostal preaching and the ecstasy of "speaking in tongues." Told from her point of view, the novel examines religious possession, its mysteries, gifts, and embarrassments as well as the enduring, restorative power of love.

BIBLIOGRAPHY: Harmon, W., "R. M.'s Pelagian Georgics: Twelve Essays," *Parnassus* 9 (Fall-Winter 1981): 5–30; Liotta, P., "Pieces of the Morgenland: Recent Achievements in R. M.'s Poetry," *SLJ* 22 (Fall 1989): 32–40; Quillen, R., "R. M.," *Looking for Native Ground: Contemporary Appalachian Poetry* (1989)

NEWTON SMITH

MORLEY, Christopher [Darlington]

b. 5 May 1890, Haverford, Pennsylvania; d. 28 March 1957, Roslyn Heights, New York

Critically and commercially popular during his lifetime while largely neglected today, M. is best remembered as a novelist and essayist, though he was also a publisher, editor, and prolific writer of poems, reviews, plays, criticism, and children's stories. In terms of M.'s sheer literary output, his work can only be calculated, not dissected.

M.'s greatest popular success was the sentimental novel *Kitty Foyle* (1939), which, in his own words, provides "an unexpected revelation, told in the person of an Irish American white-collar girl, of the mind and heart and biology of a young woman of the 1930s." More typical, however, were novels such as *Human Being* (1932) and *Thorofare* (1942), which suffer from M.'s essayistic impulse to reiterate (rather than dramatize) his theme that literature is irretrievably tied to life. Though not without flaws, his final novel, *The Man Who Made Friends with Himself* (1949), may also be his finest. Cast as a memoir discovered after the narrator's death, the novel exploits a form that gives free reign to M.'s penchant for word play, fantasy, symbolism, and private enthusiasms for authors and books.

M.'s more natural literary form, the one in which he excelled throughout his career, was the frequently neglected genre of the familiar essay. Indeed, before E. B. WHITE gained critical recognition through his "One Man's Meat" columns in *Harper's Magazine* in the early 1940s, M. was arguably America's most admired familiar essayist. Though best known for his weekly "Bowling Green" columns in the *Saturday Review of Literature* (1924–39), of which he was a founder and editor, M. published sixteen essay collections between 1918 and 1949. In addition, several of his essays—including "Trifles," "On Visiting Bookshops," "On Going to Bed," and "Notes on an Island"—appeared regularly in college composition readers published during this same period. In 1921 and 1924, M. himself edited two such anthologies, *Modern Essays* and *Modern Essays, Second Series.*

In his first volume of essays, *Shandygaff* (1918), M. initiated what was to become a lifelong practice of promoting authors, living and dead, as well as particular books that he felt deserved wider recognition. In addition, his often aphoristic writing style and his manner of mingling light anecdotes with serious reflections are already well developed. M.'s cultivated homeyness—as suggested by the titles of some of his later collections—*Mince Pie* (1919), *Pipefuls* (1920), *Plum Pudding* (1922), *The Ironing Board* (1949) —can undoubtedly be cloying. But frequently satire and self-deprecation balance, even undermine, the whimsy and the tweedy charm.

In addition to his own engaging prose style, one of M.'s main contributions as a literary enthusiast was his emphasis on the reader's need to collaborate with an author. An early advocate of what would later be academically formalized as "reader-response theory," he acknowledged that a reader's personal and cultural experiences must inevitably merge with the experience of the text being read. The "richest revenue of any art," he believed, "is the unearned increment it sometimes acquires from what happens later, of which the artist could have no specific foreboding."

BIBLIOGRAPHY: Lyle, G. R., and H. T. Brown, Jr., *A Bibliography of C. M.* (1952); Wallach, M. I., and J. Bracker, *C. M.* (1976)

RICHARD NORDQUIST

MORRIS, Willie

b. 29 November 1934, Jackson, Mississippi

M. has attained national prominence as a newspaper editor, journalist, nonfiction writer, novelist, autobiographer, and essayist. Having graduated from high school in Yazoo City, Mississippi, in 1952 as valedictorian of his class, he left his familiar Mississippi Delta for the University of Texas at Austin, where he became editor of the student newspaper, the *Daily Texan,* in his senior year. Upon his graduation in 1956 as a member of Phi Beta Kappa, he studied history at Oxford University as a Rhodes scholar, and from 1960 to 1962 edited the liberal *Texas Observer,* a weekly political newspaper.

In 1963, M. became associate editor of *Harper's* magazine and editor-in-chief in 1967, shortly before the publication of his first autobiographical work. In that widely acclaimed account, *North toward Home* (1967), he relates his personal development to that of America itself, paralleling his own experiences to various social and cultural forces that characterized the nation during the 1940s, 1950s, and 1960s. With an acute sense of history, place, and family—significant themes in much of his writing—Southern expatriate M. struggles to understand and come to terms with his own origins and regional identity as he confronts the turbulent complexities of his generation.

As the youngest editor-in-chief in the history of the nation's oldest magazine, M. aggressively transformed the venerable yet stodgy *Harper's* into one of the country's most exciting and influential periodicals, attracting contributions from such well-known writers as William STYRON, Larry L. King, David Halberstam, Robert Penn WARREN, Arthur MILLER, James DICKEY, and Norman MAILER. Such success notwithstanding, he eventually became embroiled in editorial disputes with the publication's owner. M., unwilling to change the focus and content of *Harper's,* left the magazine in 1971—a step that immediately prompted the mass resignations of most of the magazine's contributing editors.

M.'s second work, *Yazoo: Integration in a Deep-Southern Town* (1971), movingly explores how the 1969 Supreme Court-ordered integration of the public schools in Mississippi affected his hometown. Subsequent books include *Good Old Boy: A Delta Boyhood* (1971), an adventure-filled celebration of his youth written for juveniles; *The Last of the Southern Girls* (1973), a novel of a Southern debutante who comes to Washington, D.C.; and *James Jones: A Friendship* (1978), a heartfelt reminiscence about his longtime comrade and fellow author. In 1980, M. returned to Mississippi and wrote *The Courting of Marcus Dupree* (1983), a skillful combination of sports reporting, historical analysis, and biography in which he recounts the madness surrounding the college recruitment of a talented southern black athlete. The award-winning *Homecomings* (1989), with its original artwork, illustrates his precision and eloquence in crafting essays.

Though some of M.'s books were published in the South and drew mainly regional reviews, two recent volumes assure his national reputation. In the triumphant *New York Days* (1993), he reflects on his heady years at *Harper's* and how they mirrored the tumultuous 1960s. The best-seller *My Dog Skip* (1995) is not only a poignant, bittersweet tribute to the canine companion of his boyhood, but a memoir of a bygone era as well.

BIBLIOGRAPHY: Andrews, W. L., "In Search of a Common Identity: The Self and the South in Four Mississippi Autobiographies," *SoR* 24 (Winter 1988): 47–64;

Raper, J. R., "W. M.," in Bain, R., and J. M. Flora, eds., *Contemporary Poets, Dramatists, Essayists, and Novelists of the South* (1994): 377–87

JACK BALES

MORRIS, Wright [Marion]

b. 6 January 1910, Central City, Nebraska

Events in M.'s early life set the stage for his themes of family and transience: six days after he was born, M. lost his mother, and during his childhood, his father frequently left him in care of relatives. In 1919, M. moved with his father to Omaha, and in 1924, M. went to Chicago. Father and son drove to California in 1926, making the first of several cross-country trips that M. would later write about. He began attending classes at Pomona College in 1930 only to withdraw in 1933 to spend a year in Europe. After living in Massachusetts and Pennsylvania, he eventually settled in California to teach and write. His literary career began in 1940, and he has since published more than thirty volumes of novels, stories, essays, memoirs, and photo-texts. Despite being called consistently original and characteristically American, M. remains mostly unread by the general public.

Literary critics have respected his work from the beginning, but he has received relatively little scholarly attention, and today's critics tend to label him as a Midwestern or Nebraska author. M., however, transcends the particulars of setting with his universal themes: the American character, the search for meaning, the potential for transformation, the extraordinary in the ordinary, the relationship between the past and the present, and the interplay between memory and emotion. His characters are a part of the most common humanity; often they are earnestly comic people who wander from one book to another. Likewise, events, many of which are drawn from his life, recur in different books until a familiar story is illuminated in unexpected ways.

The Field of Vision (1956), for which M. received the National Book Award, and its sequel, *Ceremony in Lone Tree* (1960), are often viewed as his most successful and important novels. In *Field of Vision,* Gordon Boyd, a middle-aged author living in Mexico City, meets his childhood friend from Nebraska, Walter McKee, a cattle breeder. Boyd brings McKee, his wife Lois, father-in-law Tom Scanlon, and grandson Gordon to a bullfight. M. confines the present action of his story to the duration of the fight, during which he narrates the thoughts of his characters as they view the same event. Critics have described the effect as a tapestry of collective consciousness that brings the present and the past together. In *Ceremony in Lone*

Tree, some of the same characters reunite in Lone Tree, Nebraska, to celebrate Tom Scanlon's ninetieth birthday. M. introduces additional characters to those from *The Fields of Vision* to create a total of nine points of view set against a backdrop of murderous violence while evoking a strong sense of tension even though much of the action in the novel is comical.

This apparent contradiction is typical of his work. *The Home Place* (1948), perhaps his most frequently examined work, focuses on Clyde Muncy who leaves New York to return to Nebraska with his wife and children in search of a new home and a sense of rootedness only to discover an old home cluttered with artifacts of daily life and inhabited by people with whom he cannot communicate. One of several photo-texts, *The Home Place* combines pictures taken primarily in Central City and Norfolk, Nebraska, with text to suggest the ability of photography to seemingly stop time. Through his photographs, M. examines the shifting nature of memory as well as the stories conveyed by everyday objects that are, as he has said, saturated with emotion, with implications.

According to M., when we remember, "It is the emotion that is strong, not the details." In his fiction and autobiography, he re-creates the details of ordinary lives through his photographs and words to awaken the reader's emotions.

BIBLIOGRAPHY: Bird, R. K., *W. M.: Memory and Imagination* (1985); Crump, G. B., *The Novels of W. M.: A Critical Interpretation* (1978); Howard, L., *W. M.* (1968); Knoll, R. E., ed., *Conversations with W. M.: Critical Views and Responses* (1977); Madden, D., *W. M.* (1965)

ELIZABETH A. TURNER

MORRISON, Toni
b. 18 February 1931, Lorain, Ohio

One of the most important black American women novelists of the 20th c., M.—born Chloe Anthony Wofford—is the author of a series of novels that have earned her critical as well as popular recognition. Published in 1973, *Sula* was nominated for the 1975 National Book Award. Her 1977 novel *Song of Solomon*—the first novel by a black writer to become a main selection of the Book-of-the-Month Club since Richard WRIGHT's *Native Son* in 1940—won the 1978 National Book Critics Circle Award and an American Academy and Institute of Arts and Letters Award. *Tar Baby* (1981) remained on the best-seller list for several months. *Beloved,* a finalist for the National Book Award and the National Book Critics Circle Award in 1987, won the Pulitzer Prize in fiction in 1988, but

was less successfully adapted as a film, which was released ten years later. In 1993, M. became the first African American woman to be awarded the Nobel Prize in literature.

M.'s fiction can be linked with that of other contemporary American black women writers, such as Alice WALKER or Gloria NAYLOR, in her presentation of black families and black neighborhoods, in her revelation of violence as part of the life in the black community, in her confronting of the exploitation of blacks by other blacks, in her general absence of well-developed white characters, in her unwillingness to produce fiction with artificial happy endings, and in her blending of social realism with a heightened imagination that introduces supernatural elements.

She sees her fiction as deriving, in part, from the meandering black oral folk tale and the language, motifs, and narrative structures one finds in the Bible. As in Greek drama, which she has studied with great interest, her characters develop most fully in moments of extremity following long suffering. In her novels as in Greek drama, growth and understanding occur, rather than a simple resolution of complicated problems.

In all of her work, M. seeks to repay a debt to her black ancestors, especially to strong women like her grandmother, who came from Alabama to Ohio with seven children and only fifteen dollars. She hopes to produce in her writing an "authentic" black literature by fusing—at least in certain moments—the facts of black culture with elements of the mythic. Thus, she blends the realistic detail of black families and neighborhoods (usually in an Ohio town that resembles Lorain, her birthplace) with the symbolic, the ambiguous, and the supernatural. The language of the novels is rich in imagery, in hypnotic rhythms, and in highly dramatic dialogue. She expects the reader to accept the credibility of the supernatural elements. For example, Pilate in *Song of Solomon* is a woman of common sense but also one with magical powers, related in some way to her having been born without a navel. She dies, transfigured mysteriously into a beautiful redbird. Beloved, in the novel of that name, is murdered as an infant and returns as a ghost inhabiting the body of a young woman capable of seducing her mother's new lover and manipulating her mother into an almost fatal state of subjection to her. In the animistic background of *Tar Baby,* trees feel pain, fish grow fearful as the characters's anxiety grows, and clouds talk to each other, while in *The Bluest Eye* (1970) no marigolds bloom in the year that Pecola Breedlove is raped by her father, bears a stillborn baby, and sits fantasizing that others see her as beautiful and lovable because she now supposedly has blue eyes and hair like her Shirley Temple doll.

The violence that dooms Pecola in M.'s first book recurs in her other novels. In *Sula,* Shadrack, a mad man shell-shocked in war, invents an annual "Suicide Day"—the only day in the year in which people should kill themselves; and ironically he leads a crowd of townspeople (who only laugh at him) into a death by drowning. Early in the novel, the main characters, Sula Peace and Nel Wright, as children inadvertently cause the drowning of a smaller black child as Shadrack watches. Eva Peace, Sula's grandmother, according to local mythology, has only one leg because she deliberately allowed the wheels of a train to amputate her other leg in order to get insurance money to feed her children. Eva later sets fire to her grown son, Plum, as he sleeps, because his drug addiction will prevent him from becoming independent as a man. Eva's daughter, Hannah, burns to death in the yard where she is canning by an open fire; and in fascination, rather than terror, her daughter Sula watches passively. Hannah's mother, Eva, leaps from an upstairs window in a vain attempt to save her daughter. In *Song of Solomon,* Milkman Dead's father, Macon Dead, fearing his wife's supposed infidelity, cruelly attempts for weeks to induce the abortion of Milkman. In an earlier generation, Macon Dead and his sister, Pilate, had watched the murder by gunfire of their father by whites. As a young man, Milkman discovers that his friend, Guitar Baines, and six others, have formed the Seven Days, conspirators who murder a white person each time they read in the newspaper of the murder of a black. Milkman in a scene of great intensity lies in bed waiting for minutes without moving as his disappointed lover, Hagar, holds the point of a knife at his throat, and in the close of the book Milkman and Guitar face one another in a silent struggle that will bring the death of one of them—a death foreshadowed by the hunting and butchering of a wildcat a few hours earlier. In *Tar Baby,* the violence is psychological rather than physical, but in the following novel, *Beloved*—which goes back further in history than the other novels—the brutality of slave experience and the destructiveness of the memory of that brutality become the entire fabric of the book. Only a few episodes (one evening of Sethe's skating on the lake with her daughters, Denver and Beloved, for example) lighten the pain and horror of the historical reality that haunts every page and is relived in the appearance of the angry ghost, Beloved.

M.'s novels often develop through repetitions, through parallel situations, and through the pairing and contrasting of individuals. In *The Bluest Eye,* young Claudia McTeer tells the story of Pecola Breedlove, who lives in the same housing development. Pauline and Chollie Breedlove, as struggling black parents, contrast with the parents of Claudia and Frieda McTeer

because of the greater love the McTeers give their daughters. Claudia's repetition of monotonous sentences that match those in a Dick-and-Jane primer emphasize the innocence of the three children, who cannot fully understand the tragedy of incest. In *Sula,* the households of Sula Peace and Nel Wright are contrasted—the one is wild and disreputable, the other is stultifying, rigid, and narrowly disciplined because of Nel's mother's hope to distance herself and Nel from the depravity she finds revolting in her own mother's prostitution in New Orleans. The lives of Milkman and Guitar are paralleled throughout *Song of Solomon.* In *Tar Baby,* the struggle of Jadine and Son to build a lasting love from their strong initial attraction to each other is confounded by their differences, which have resulted from her acculturation as a black educated in white Parisian universities and his refusal to move beyond his closed-in black community in a small Florida town. A further contrast is provided in this book between the black characters and the wealthy white employers of Jadine's aunt and uncle in the Caribbean. In the close of the book the differences are exaggerated as Son is seen running "lickety-split" toward a jungle and Jadine, is about to embark on a plane to Paris.

Even more striking is M.'s related use of a device in which several characters are given the same name, scarcely identified separately, and not allowed to develop as single, free individuals—for example, the three little "Deweys" in Sula's household and the three young men on the Sweet Home plantation in *Beloved* who are called Paul A, Paul F, and Paul D. Only Paul D becomes real to us, while Paul A and Paul F remain shadows lost in a dehumanizing society, where slaves do not matter enough to be given distinctive names.

In 1992, M. fascinated readers in her inventive book *Jazz* where she introduced a mysterious narrator who remained in the background almost to the end of the novel, and then, like a jazz musician, shifted easily from the melancholy and violent lives of the aging Joe and Violet Trace to the surprising music that ends in a remarkable and unforgettable love story. This was followed by the publication in 1998 of *Paradise.* Primarily set in Ruby, a town established by blacks in Oklahoma territory after the Civil War, *Paradise* explores the tensions between the descendants of the early settlers and a group of women living in an abandoned mansion that had once been a school for Arapaho girls. The action of the novel moves backwards from the attack on the convent by the men of Ruby as M. recounts the stories of the women who, fleeing the law, abusive husbands, and painful secrets, have found their way to the shelter of the convent. Warmth and excitement grows in the book as in slow succession the women appear, each finding the solace she needs with the dying nun Mary Magna (called "mother") and the fear and hatred of the men of the town grows. As the people of Ruby grapple with the changes time brings to the "paradise" they set out to create, the women of the convent leave, return, fight with one another, and care for one another.

While each of the women who arrive is interesting in her own way, it is Consolata who commands most attention. Smuggled into the country at age nine by Mary Magna who saw her abandoned and playing in the mud, Consolata has become a strong manager of the convent and directs the women she allows to enter the mansion. Most never return to homes or families; having known violence, suffering, and betrayal, they have chosen the crumbling convent, its dangers, and the flat dry land as their own "paradise." M. insists that her readers can "participate" in the construction of the book and imagine their own view of paradise.

M. has also extended her writing to drama, building on her talent for highly dramatic dialogue already developed in the novel. She has created the lyrics for the musical *New Orleans,* produced by the workshop at the Public Theater, New York; she has adapted *Tar Baby* as a screenplay that has not yet been produced; and she has written a surprisingly innovative drama, *Dreaming Emmett,* commissioned by the New York Writing Institute, which premiered January 4, 1986, at Market Theater, New York. In this play, M. expresses her conviction that violence is claiming a new generation of young urban blacks, as the life of Emmett Till, a fourteen-year-old Chicago youth, was lost when he was slain by racists in Mississippi in 1955. Emmett, returned to earth for vengeance, occupies the center of the stage in this play and controls the rotation of platforms of varying levels on which stand actors representing what M. calls "a collision of three or four levels of time." These actors interpret the facts of Emmett's death from varying points of view.

After her career of twenty years as an editor at Random House, M. now devotes her time to writing and to university teaching. In 1989, M. was named the Robert Goheen Professor in the Humanities at Princeton University. The range and extent of her achievement to date is impressive as she takes her place among the most distinguished contemporary novelists.

BIBLIOGRAPHY: Gates, H. L., Jr., and K. A. Appiah, *T. M.: Critical Perspectives Past and Present* (1993); Harris, T., *Fictional Folklore: The Novels of T. M.* (1993); McKay, N. Y., ed., *Critical Essays on T. M.* (1980); Page, P., *Dangerous Freedom: Fusion and Fragmentation in T. M.'s Novels* (1995); Peach, L., *T. M.* (1995); Otten, T., *The Crime of Innocence in the Fiction of T. M.* (1989)

MARGARET B. MCDOWELL

MORTON, Sarah Wentworth [Apthorp]

b. August, 1759, Boston, Massachusetts; d. 14 May 1846, Quincy, Massachusetts

M. was born into the affluence and prestige of an established New England family, and reaped the benefits of an unusually thorough education. She began writing poetry as early as the age of ten, but published little until well after her marriage to Perez Morton in 1781. Her poetry and prose were held in high esteem for the next several decades, gaining her such honorary titles as the "Sappho of America." Yet it is frequently claimed that M. outlived her fame and was "rediscovered" in the 19th c. only because critics wrongfully attributed William Hill BROWN's *The Power of Sympathy* to her pen. M.'s connection to this seminal American novel will always be important, although not authorial, because its plot is based on M.'s own real life family scandal and tragedy—Perez Morton's affair with her sister Frances Apthorp, which ended in an illegitimate birth and the sister's suicide. M.'s poetry has often been judged imitative and overly sentimental because of her preference for neoclassic diction, rhymed couplets and ballad stanzas, and highly emotive expression. While M. appears to have outlived the aesthetic she worked within, her expert deployment of the strategies of sentimentality has recently brought her work under new and less dismissive scrutiny.

M.'s first book-length effort, *Ouâbi; or, The Virtues of Nature, an Indian Tale in Four Cantos,* appeared in 1790, and is noted for its unique treatment of racial issues, especially miscegenation. The basic plot of *Ouâbi* concerns a love triangle involving Ouâbi, an Illinois sachem, his wife Azâkia, and Celario, an aristocratic European. Recognizing that an intense attraction has developed between Azâkia and Celario, Ouâbi ultimately annuls his marriage, handing over Azâkia to Celario as a reward for his heroism and loyalty. Ouâbi's love for both Azâkia and Celario and his sympathy for their emotional predicament moves him to compassionate and selfless actions. M.'s 19th-c. readership identified with Ouâbi through the poem's invocation of paradigmatic sentimentalism, and was itself moved through this emotionalism to acceptance of the story's legitimation of extramarital desires and passions. The poem was very well received and remained quite popular for some time, so popular, in fact, that a portion of it was subsequently set to music (Ouâbi's "Death Song"), and its plot was used as the basis for a contemporary play.

A companion piece to *Ouâbi* entitled *The Virtues of Society: A Tale Founded on Fact* (1799) was drawn from actual events that took place during the American Revolution, a setting that M. also used for her more ambitious *Beacon Hill* (1797). First appearing in the *Columbian Centinal, Beacon Hill* was intended to be the first book of a much longer poetic work, which never fully materialized. In the poem, M. attempted to chronicle the American Revolution in epic terms. Although the subject matter of the poem is specifically nationalistic, M. also takes the opportunity in it to speak out against slavery.

M.'s concern with the racial issues of her time reflects the fact that both she and her husband were outspoken abolitionists. Indeed, her most anthologized piece, "The African Chief," was a favorite in abolitionist literature, and is another notable example of M.'s use of the politics of sentimentalism. In this poem, M. is able to guide her readers to identification with enslaved peoples by focusing on and individualizing one particular captive "deeply freighted" within a slave ship, while demonizing the "white tyrants" who captured him. The protagonist is described in the poem as being not only a leader and a warrior, but as a man of sensibility and compassion—a man who has provided for the hungry. In this way, M. creates for her Anglo-American readership a sympathetic context for her description of a violent revolt led by the protagonist, and moves them towards an emotional response across racial lines. M.'s political deployment of sentimentality becomes clear in the crux of the poem, which occurs in the second to the last stanza. At this point, the narrator chastises "the hard race of *pallid hue,*" who, she claims, are "Unpracticed in the power to feel."

After publishing under the pseudonyms "Constantia" and "Philenia," M. chose to publish her final work, *My Mind and Its Thoughts* (1823), under her real name. The book is a compilation of "fragments" collected over a lifetime, and includes pieces ranging from single "Thoughts," as she calls them, to poems and essays on a variety of subjects. In her concluding "Apology," M. notes that the fragments she presents in *My Mind and Its Thoughts* became a source of solace and comfort to her over the years, and despite advice to the contrary, published them in the hopes that some readers would find similar uses for them. The overall implication of this sad commentary was that M. found the need for comfort and solace often in her life, a suggestion underscored by the general sense of melancholy and resignation that pervades the work. Over and over again, M. returns to the subjects of disappointment and dissimulation in *My Mind and Its Thoughts,* and often in reference to actual events in her life, as in "Momento, for My Infant, Who Lived

but Eighteen Hours" as well as "To the Mansion of My Ancestors, on Seeing It Occupied as a Banking Establishment," a poem that records M.'s dismay over her husband's decision to literally commodify the Apthorp ancestral home. At no time in *My Mind and Its Thoughts* does M. take what could be described as a feminist stance. In fact, M.'s position on women's rights is often quite the contrary, as in the essay "Right and Wrong," where she openly attacks Mary Wollstonecraft's "pernicious precepts" and "restless and unsubdued spirit." Yet M.'s struggle with the disparity between the popular ideologies she subscribed to and her own lifetime of experiences is clearly evident in such pieces as "Thought #107" ("Women") and the essays "Woman" and "Marriage," all of which note in different ways the wide gap between accepted images of male-female relationships and lived reality.

BIBLIOGRAPHY: Cowell, P., ed., *Women Poets in Pre-Revolutionary America, 1650–1775: An Anthology* (1981); Ellison, J., "Race and Sensibility in the Early Republic" *AL* 65 (1993): 445–74; Pendleton, E., and M. Ellis, *Philenia: The Life and Works of S. W. M., 1759–1846* (1931); Watts, E. S., *The Poetry of American Women from 1632 to 1945* (1977)

MARSHA WATSON

MORTON, Thomas

b. 1579?, West Country, England; d. 1647, Agamenticus (now York), Maine

M.'s literary reputation depends solely on his masterpiece, *New English Canaan* (1637), in which the author purposes to describe the "Indians," land, and settlers of New England. Although as history and ethnography the work remains somewhat suspect, M. deserves a place among early American writers for his commendable consideration of the Native Americans and for his successful, biting satire of the New England colonists. M.'s work has also given rise to numerous subsequent literary accounts about Ma-re Mount (or Merrymount) consequent to the work's portrayal of a dramatic battle between establishment and nonconformity.

Although his report is cluttered with historical inaccuracies, M. is important as one of the first colonists to consider the Native Americans as other than an enemy. He provides a detailed account of the Native Americans' beliefs and lifestyle. In the first of the three books that make up *New English Canaan,* he writes that they have no religion, while nevertheless describing their beliefs and burial practices. He maintains that Native American babies are born white but are washed with leaves to tint their skin, and argues that the Native American languages have Greek and Latin roots. He perpetuates the Puritan belief that Native Americans have a special correspondence with the devil. Through all, however, he argues that the Native Americans are noble, honest, and better humanitarians than the English settlers. The second book reads like a typical promotional tract, describing the abundance of vegetable, mineral, and animal commodities in New England. The third book gives an account of the English settlers. The most widely anthologized and best known section concerns his own quarrel with the separatists of Plymouth. Referring to himself as "Mine Host," he describes how "Captain Shrimp" (Miles Standish) and the rest of the nine worthies of New England destroyed his Maypole on Ma-re Mount, burnt his house, and took him prisoner.

Twice the settlers sent M. to England, a sea journey that gave him the opportunity to cast himself as Jonah and warn the Separatists that to avoid the wrath of God, they must repent.

BIBLIOGRAPHY: Adams, C. F., ed., *New English Canaan* (1967); Connors, D. F., *T. M.* (1969); Drinnon, R., "The Maypole of Merry Mount: T. M. and the Puritan Patriarchs," *MR* 21 (1980): 382–410

LEE SCHWENINGER

MOSS, Howard

b. 22 January 1922, New York City; d. 16 September 1987, New York City

Born and reared in New York City, M. embodies what is often considered the consummate New York City poet: his poetry is highly crafted, witty, full of puns, sharp turns of phrases, urban landscapes, and cultural references. Moreover, in 1950, after a brief stint as the fiction editor for the *New Yorker,* M. became the poetry editor—a position that he held until his death in 1987—where he helped to shape and define what was to become the recognizable "*New Yorker*" poem. At the *New Yorker,* M. was vital in the publishing of works by Theodore ROETHKE, Richard WILBUR, Sylvia PLATH, and Anne SEXTON as well as helping to launch the careers of other poets such as James DICKEY, Galway KINNELL, and Mark STRAND. As an editor, M. left an indelible mark upon poetry after World War II mostly because his editorship defined American poetry, and his patronage catalyzed the careers of many young poets. Unfortunately, M.'s own accomplishments as a writer have been eclipsed by his position as the *New Yorker* poetry editor.

Regardless of the waning critical attention given to M., he received a number of prestigious awards for his own poetry during his lifetime, including the 1972 National Book Award in Poetry for *Selected Poems* and the Leonore Marshall/*The Nation* Prize in Poetry in 1986 for *New Selected Poems.* In addition to his body of poetry, which includes fifteen books, M. was also a respected critic, editor, playwright, satirist, and writer of children's books while teaching creative writing at a number of prestigious colleges and universities.

The body of M.'s poetry is very consistent: he always worked within a rigid iambic meter and traditional poetic forms and structures. At its best, M.'s early poetry resembles the stylistic mastery of W. H. AUDEN or the precision of W. B. Yeats, and his early poetry gained him the reputation of an extremely "accomplished" formal poet. M.'s later works are closer in tone and style to Elizabeth BISHOP, a poet he deeply admired, while the narrative structure suggests a number of similarities with such New Critic poets as Yvor WINTERS, Robert Penn WARREN, and John Crowe RANSOM: M. often uses the poem as a theatrical device that presents a number of dialogues between individuals without supplying any overarching meta-commentary. Like the narrative techniques of William FAULKNER, the poem reveals itself and its rhetorical argument through the tension of the dialogues, and the poems often seem to transcribe conversations overhead on a city street or in a cafe.

The body of M.'s poetry often fluctuates between ruminations upon the city, people, society, and culture and an unpeopled natural landscape. M. himself remarks that "[w]hat my poems are really about, I think, is the experience hovering between the forms of nature and the forms of art. My work is the response of someone who is equally moved by nature and art." Frequently, M. discovers similar things in both nature and art—especially the passage of time—and his poetry is deeply preoccupied with the mind and its relationship to the real, the created, and memory. Not surprisingly, as evident from M.'s *The Magic Lantern of Marcel Proust* (1962), M. deeply admired Proust, and M.'s poetry suggests a number of important affinities with Proust—especially the preoccupation with the fluidity of time and the conception of the individual as the webbing that holds a fragile world together through his/her meditations. Like Proust's grandiose *Remembrance of Things Past,* M.'s poems often evolve out of the texture of memories and experiences, and the subject/viewer is the cohesive agent of meaning.

As such, a landscape and the objects of which it is comprised do not exist in and other themselves; rather nature is always mediated by the lens of the viewer, who imbues it with meaning and a narrative. This is perhaps best illustrated by the acclaimed long poem, "Gravel," which presents the world from the perspective of gravel. Interjected throughout the poem, though, are distinctively human concerns and thematic echoes that pervade so much of M.'s poetry—ennui, romantic failure, the inherent tensions between people, the inevitable ebb of time, the importance of friendship, and the unhappiness of everyday life.

M.'s tenure as the poetry editor of the *New Yorker* guarantees him a place in 20th-c. American poetry, but it will remain to be seen if he achieves the stature of many of the poets he was so instrumental in promoting.

BIBLIOGRAPHY: Gioia, D., "The Difficult Case of H. M.," *AR* 45 (Winter 1987): 98–109; Howard, R., *Alone with America* (1969; rev. ed., 1980); Leiter, R., "H. M.: An Interview," *APR* 12 (September-October 1984): 27–31; Lieberman, L., *Unassigned Frequencies* (1977); Packard, W., *The Craft of Poetry* (1974)

DAVID W. CLIPPINGER

MOTLEY, John Lothrop

b. 15 April 1814, Dorchester, Massachusetts; d. 29 May 1877, Dorset, England

M. is probably the least known of the great romantic historians of mid-19th-c. America. The reason for his obscurity is probably that, unlike George Bancroft, William Hickling PRESCOTT, and Francis PARKMAN, he did not write about the history of the Americas, but devoted most of his attention to the history of the Netherlands. M., though, viewed his researches into Dutch history as explorations into ideas of freedom, liberty, and progress that he saw as vital to American identity.

From his college years at Harvard onward, M. was fascinated by Dutch and German culture, buttressing his interest by extensive European travel. M. composed two early New England novels and wrote for journals such as the *North American Review* and was an interesting literary critic, making a differentiation between the artistic goals of Goethe and Balzac worthy of Henry JAMES. But M. soon found that his true genius was for writing prose history. In *The Rise of the Dutch Republic* (1855), the result of many years of primary research in the Netherlands and elsewhere, M. stirringly chronicled the unlikely success of the revolt of the Dutch Protestants led by William of Orange against their oppressive and powerful Spanish overlords. M.'s style is influenced by that of Thomas Babington Macaulay, whom he knew personally, but it is marked by its own dash and vigor. M.'s prose style can stand with that of the best-known American novelists of the period. It is not purely narrative; philosophical asides are mixed in so that the reader can step back from the action and assess the moral implication of the event.

M. continued his history in the extensively researched, four-volume *History of the United Netherlands* (1860–67) and in the particularly well-written *Life of John van Oldebarnevelt* (1874). The latter was a prelude to a planned general history of the Thirty Years War whose production was prevented by M.'s death, and whose loss must be regretted. M.'s great theme in all his books was the rise of Protestantism, and its connection with progress and enlightenment. Dutch republicanism and egalitarianism were for him the precursor of American liberty. M., though, was interested more in the political side effects of the religious wars than their theological content; there is little exploration of Reformation thought in his work, and M. begs off the theological issues of the Synod of Dordrecht, which sealed the victory of a strict Calvinism over the more latitudinarian sort later to flourish in America.

M.'s rendition of pre-Reformation Dutch history in the first fifteen pages of *The Rise of the Dutch Republic* is almost totally fictive and is laden with a sort of aesthetic Teutonism, alleging that the Germanic barbarians of the Dark Ages held popular consultative assemblies and were stanchions of freedom. This clearly indicated a Germanic race-mysticism that, as the critic David Levin accurately comments, is "atavistic." M.'s political Protestantism can be seen in his diplomatic service as minister to the Austrian Empire from 1861 to 1867, where he opposed that empire's scheme to impose the Archduke Maximilian as ruler of Mexico and thus spread a conservative Catholicism to North America. His Teutonism also manifested itself when he cheered Austria's defeat by the Prussia led by Otto von Bismarck, a personal friend of M.'s from his traveling youth.

It is easy, and inaccurate, to castigate M. for Whiggish optimism. M.'s belief in liberty and progress was heartfelt, deep, and idealistic, and representative of the genuine optimism that many Americans then felt about their country's role in history. M.'s Teutonism, though, and his friendship with Bismarck render his ideological stance more complicated, and suggest that yesterday's progress often turns out to be today's reaction.

BIBLIOGRAPHY: Guberman, J., *The Life of J. L. M.* (1973); Levin, D., *History as Romantic Art: Bancroft, Prescott, M., and Parkman* (1959)

NICHOLAS BIRNS

MOTLEY, Willard

b. 14 July 1909, Chicago, Illinois; d. 4 March 1965, Mexico City, Mexico

The child of a middle-class but emotionally unhappy African American household, M. spent a lifetime pursuing self-evidently impossible ideals. Spurning what could have been a comfortably conventional lifestyle, he plunged into the netherworld of Chicago's poorer neighborhoods in search of what he considered more authentic values. Self-educated in terms of literary styles, he adopted a naturalistic approach some critics decried as outdated. Even within the style of NATURAL-ISM, he pushed the form's limits by drenching his narratives in floods of popular culture references, driving editors and permissions agents to despair. Yet, when successful, his exuberant methods produced bestseller classics that themselves became fixtures in the common urban lifestyle M. so admired.

Knock on Any Door (1947) was M.'s first novel and his greatest career success, written after half a lifetime of juvenilia, informal journalism, travel writing, and the occasional publication of short stories. As the story of Nick Romano, a young Italian American who seems destined for destruction by his ideal of wishing to live fast, die young, and leave a good-looking corpse, *Knock on Any Door* espoused M.'s theory that the deplorable social conditions in Chicago's poverty-ridden neighborhoods ground down any chances for virtue or even assured survival. Yet balancing this somewhat obsolete view was the author's technique of motivating his story's progression by fueling it with rich quantities of jukebox music, lowlife speech, and other atmospheric details from the skid row regions M. so relished for their vitality. That it takes over five-hundred pages of closely set type to kill off his hero (in a chillingly accurate electric chair scene for which M. himself paced off the dimension in the Cook County jail) speaks for the power this novel invests in both character and environment.

As a film, *Knock on Any Door* was one of Humphrey Bogart's less memorable credits, but Bogart's fame kept M. in the public eye. Although his next novel, *We Fished All Night* (1951), proved a critical and popular failure in its attempt to combine big city politics with postwar domestic forces, M. recaptured the public imagination once more with *Let No Man Write My Epitaph* (1958). This novel, which was soon after filmed with James Darren starring as Nick Romano, Jr., and other major actors and actresses in supporting roles, served as a sequel to *Knock on Any Door* not just in topicality but as social theory. Here M. was able to expound on his belief that a combination of personal and environmental forces could overwhelm an individual's chances to succeed.

For his entire writing career, M. was viewed somewhat askance for using Caucasian rather than African American characters as protagonists in his works. As civil rights emerged as a struggle in the 1960s, M.'s assimiliationist views made him unpopular with younger writers. To escape the polarizing conditions of race, he had moved to Mexico, and from his home in Cuernavaca, he worked for many years on a novel

published a year after his death, *Let Noon Be Fair* (1966). In writing about how a seaside tourist town is despoiled by American developers, he was for the first time in his career anticipating a popular attitude rather than responding to one. He was also able to employ his genius for social observation in a new way, catching the nuances of different values among three local families: the Espinozas (of Spanish heritage), the Beltrans (whose fortune came from cheating Indians), and the Tizocs (Indian peasants).

In recent years, M.'s critical reputation has been revived, based on the study of his extensive papers and the publication of his lifelong journal, *The Diaries of W. M.* (1979).

BIBLIOGRAPHY: Fleming, R. E., *W. M.* (1978); Giles, J. R., *The Naturalistic Inner-City Novel in America* (1995); Klinkowitz, J., *The Practice of Fiction in America* (1980); Major, C., *The Dark and Feeling: Black American Writers and Their Work* (1974)

                                        JEROME KLINKOWITZ

MOURNING DOVE
See **QUINTASKET, Christine or Christal**

MUKHERJEE, Bharati
b. 27 July 1940, Calcutta, India

M.'s writings narrate the immigrant tradition. Largely autobiographical, her early works reflect her experiences with expatriation: she was twice expatriated, once from India and then from Canada, where she met outright racism. Born to the very educated, high-caste Hindus, she was highly influenced by her strong-willed, dominant father, on whom she modeled the "Tiger" of her earliest novel, *The Tiger's Daughter* (1971), which revolves around her experiences as an exile while she maintains her Indian heritage and identity and fondly remembers her childhood years in Calcutta. Like the author, the novel's central character Tara, after studying abroad, returns without her foreign husband to Calcutta to find India a very changed, fractured country. Similarly, *Days and Nights in Calcutta* (1977), a memoir written with her husband Clark Blaise, examines the exile's preoccupation with an alien country, followed by the unsettling problems with racism that immigrants face in Canadian society.

Her works continue to document the immigrant experience by exploring the condition of women immigrants and the dual condition of being an Indian expatriate and an American immigrant. A recurrent theme in much of M.'s later fiction is women's search for fulfillment through encounters with men outside their cultural group. In *Wife* (1975), her second novel, M.

gives attention to Dimple Dasgupta's psychological transformation: in the book Dimple refashions her life, ultimately liberating herself by having an affair with Milt Glasser, an American white man. In *Jasmine* (1989), the Indian-born protagonist Jasmine, whose character was taken from a short story in *The Middleman and Other Stories* (1988), finds freedom by deserting her live-in lover and having a relationship with an American, and she undergoes transformation assuming several identities, including Jyoti, a Punjab village girl and Jasmine, a loving and devoted Hindu wife. Finally, as Jane, she experiences confusion about her identity when she engages in a relationship with Bud, an American who names her after Tarzan's mate. M.'s characters often undergo violent transformation while in this state of duality. Thus, it is not surprising that Jasmine's journey of self-discovery, for example, is one marked by violent acts that seem to be a necessary recourse to affirm her will to live. Often writing about women of the middle and working classes, M. has been criticized that her privileged background hinders her insight into the reality of the lives of such characters.

M.'s writings resolve the duality of immigrants by celebrating their experiences. Most of the stories in *The Middleman and Other Stories*, the collection for which she won the National Book Critics Circle Award in fiction, focus on the ability of the characters to forge ahead into new territory and fashion lives for themselves in the American pioneer tradition. M.'s works with this celebratory outlook support her stance that immigrants can reinvent and invent themselves through immigration to America by severing ties to their homeland. Her boldest example of this vein of writing occurs in *The Holder of the Word* (1993), in which she redefines an American by emphasizing the cross-cultural connections between North America and South Asia. Beigh Master, the novel's narrator suggests that colonial New England had interaction with Indians. In fact, two of the characters in the novel, who at first appear to have little in common, later delight in their shared kinship.

Critics object to M.'s unrealistic portrayals of Indian women who can so easily assimilate and carve new identities, overlooking the race, gender, and class distinctions that often inhibit such assimilation. Many of her characters, however, attest to M.'s long-held beliefs to which her life has been a testament: the shedding of one's old identity, painful as it may be, allows one to experience a rebirth in order to move from the margins to the mainstream of society.

BIBLIOGRAPHY: Alam, F., *B. M.* (1996); Nelson, E. M., *B. M.: Critical Perspectives* (1993)

LENA AMPADU

MUMFORD, Lewis

b. 19 October 1895, Flushing, New York; d. 26 January 1990, Amenia, New York

Author, editor, lecturer, and educator, M. became one of the 20th c.'s most influential prophets. His acute, firsthand observations of the American urban scene enabled this historian, critic, and philosopher to recognize subtle relationships between man and his environment, both its natural elements and its fabricated ones.

During his formative years, New York City was M.'s laboratory, and the theories of Scottish sociologist-biologist, Patrick Geddes, constituted his textbook. Although he enrolled in an eclectic assemblage of college courses, he employed them as means to a broader end than a mere academic degree. Beginning a prolific literary career with a history and an analysis of imaginary communities in *The Story of Utopias* (1922), M. moved on to studies of the effects American architecture on those whom it shelters in *Sticks and Stones: A Study of American Architecture and Civilization* (1924), the first of several critical examinations of architecture. Areas of his expertise expanded to include literature and art with the publication of *Herman Melville* (1929) and *The Brown Decades: A Study of Art in America, 1864–1895* (1931).

His next book, *Technics and Civilization* (1934), reflects M.'s lifelong interest in the relationship between technology and human communities and institutions. Ultimately, this book became the first volume of the author's "Renewal of Life" series that includes three additional titles: *The Culture of Cities* (1938), *The Condition of Man* (1944), and *The Conduct of Life* (1951). Taken as a whole, the series explores the effects of man's creations, technologies, and institutions on his spirit and promotes the belief first, that man should make ethical and artistic decisions about technology for the advancement of civilization, and in the later books, that man must take control of the machines and systems he devises if civilization is to survive.

The Great Depression, the threat to democracy of totalitarianism, World War II, and the destruction of Hiroshima and Nagasaki with the subsequent nuclear arms race tempered M.'s assessment that technology is a benign, if powerful, influence on civilization. The period from the late 1930s through the 1950s saw the publication of several books that anticipated an eclipse of human freedom and a nuclear holocaust. *Green Memories* (1947) a biography of his son, Geddes, who in 1944 was killed in the Italian campaign was the first of several biographical and autobiographical works.

M.'s ambivalence towards modern technology matures in the two-volume series, *The Myth of the Machine*. The first volume, *Technics and Human Develop-*

ment (1967), calls the dispassionate objectivity of science into question and explores an expanded concept of technology. Identifying the earliest distinctive pattern of a deified ruler and a priestly class with sole possession of specialized knowledge who direct the actions of the masses in ancient Egypt, *Technics and Human Development* traces that pattern through historical eras to the 17th c. In times of its ascendancy, this system, coined the "megamachine," has fostered subjugation and conformity. Periodically, the voices of prophets, who elevated the individual, have broken the power of the megamachine, and artistic creativity has become the technological generator.

The Pentagon of Power (1970), the second volume of the series, advocates a balanced, holistic approach to technological progress. Picking up where the first volume left off, *Pentagon* rejects the objectives of the military-industrial power complex, the priesthood that has produced a technology of destruction in the 20th c. Science for science's sake, M. believes, is irrational, for its creations threaten to destroy the environment and civilization systematically and with indifference.

The insights and ideas contained in M.'s writings have received acclaim nationally and internationally. During his lifetime, he received the National Book Award (1962) for *The City in History* (1961), the British Royal Gold Medal (1961) for his studies in architecture, the Presidential Medal of Freedom (1964), the National Medal for Literature (1972), the Priz Mondial del Duca (1976) for the body of his works, and the National Medal of Arts (1986). M.'s later writings have been soundly criticized as well for their strident didacticism, for their inconsistencies over time, for their repetition of themes, and for their over-simplified portrayal of the scientific community. Predictably, this last criticism has come primarily from academics in the sciences.

BIBLIOGRAPHY: Hughes, T. P., and A. C. Hughes, eds., *L. M.: Public Intellectual* (1990); Miller, D. L., *M.: A Life* (1989); Newman, E. S., *L. M.: A Bibliography, 1914–1970* (1971)

TERESA K. LEHR

MUÑOZ, Elías Miguel
b. 29 September 1954, Ciego de Avila, Camagüey, Cuba

M. writes with equal ease in Spanish and English. Thus far, he has written two novels in English, *Crazy Love* (1989) and *The Greatest Performance* (1990). Moreover, he has published poetry collections, novels, and literary criticism in Spanish. He holds a B.A. in Spanish from California State University and a doctor-ate in Spanish from the University of California at Irvine. This critical training in literature serves as the impetus for his insightful treatment of gender roles in his own works.

Crazy Love focuses on the life of Julian Toledo and his family after they come to the U.S. from Cuba. Structurally, the novel has three major divisions titled "Step One," "Step Two," and "Step Three." The first two steps each have seven chapters and the last one has six. Nearly every chapter begins with Julian telling his thoughts to either his sister Geneia or his lover Erica. They all end with a letter that Geneia writes him over various years. Since the novel deals with Julian's rise to musical stardom, each step could be considered a rite of passage or a dance movement to go along with his music.

"Step One" depicts the slavish manner in which his grandmother had to care for the men of the household. Still, every time the Paul Anka song "Crazy Love" played, she would take the young Julian in her arms and dance while professing her love for him. Music and dance appear to be the only means for her to escape her virtual thraldom. Nevertheless, crazy love may also be a reference to Juan Ruiz's 14th-c. narrative *El libro de buen amor,* which defined homosexuality as crazy love, "el amor loco." As a child, Julian suffers a gang rape by a group of young boys and is seduced by a priest while serving as an altar boy. At times, he sleeps with his parents and one night, his father mistakes the boy for his mother. Because he plays house with little girls and wants to be an artist, his family considers him abnormal—an effeminate, non-macho male.

"Step Two" moves from the sexism of "Step One" to racism. The Toledo family moves to Hawthorne since the father does not want the children to grow up around Mexicans and African-Americans. Uncle Paco contributes to Julian's sexual identity by telling him that he will be a homosexual when he grows up because of his mannerisms. In fact, Julian's cousin blackmails him into performing fellatio and Julian's first agent promises him a record deal if he will concede to sodomy. Hence, this step turns rape and seduction into physical and spiritual prostitution.

"Step Three" brings the gay aspects of Julian's band into open dialogue as the band members discuss their evolution into something other than a Cuban band. Social and sexual identity become confused as they absorb creative and psychological influences from other musicians and lovers.

The Greatest Performance continues the theme of homosexuality, but incorporates lesbianism as well. The work alternates between the narratives of Mario and Rosa, friends who become one at the end: Mari-rosa, Mariposa. "Mariposa" is a slang term in Spanish for a homosexual. The novel is lyrical and centers around image and essence. Rosa reflects on Mario's life and subsequent death by looking at a photo album which has a picture of a boy presumed to be homosexual. She gives him the name Mario to re-create her friend's life. Mario is an artist who depicts his lovers in his paintings. Both mediums show the facade rather than the interior of the person. M. uses this technique to make the reader question the tendency to define a person by appearance alone.

At times, the work gives graphic depictions of sexual acts. These acts are performances. The title, nevertheless, refers not to the best sex act, but to the role that each character must play in terms of gender. M. focuses on societal expectations regarding gender and brings these expectations into dialogue with biological determinants. Consequently, sex is a motif on several levels: it is an act, an organ, and a gender.

M. treats bisexuality and homosexuality as norms rather than deviations. He incorporates intertextuality with poignant social observation and experimental form to create moving, artful depictions of a double minority: the Hispanic homosexual.

BIBLIOGRAPHY: Deaver, W. O., Jr., "Gender Construction in E. M. M.'s *The Greatest Performance*," *RLA* 8 (1996): 439–41; Foster, D. W., ed., *Latin American Writers on Gay and Lesbian Themes* (1994); Rivero, E., "(Re)Writing Sugarcane Memories: Cuban Americans and Literature," *AmRev* 3–4 (1990): 164–82

WILLIAM O. DEAVER, JR.

MURFREE, Mary Noailles

b. 24 Jan. 1850, Murfreesboro, Tennessee; d. 31 July 1922, Murfreesboro, Tennessee

The leading woman writer from the South during the last quarter of the 19th c., M. now receives mixed recognition. Three or four novels and several stories uphold her fame, although portions of many others repay attention. First acclaimed for *In the Tennessee Mountains* (1884), eight stories originally published in the *Atlantic Monthly,* M. typifies local-color authors prominent in late 19th-c. America. While M. was prolific, *The Prophet of the Great Smoky Mountains* (1885), *In the Clouds* (1886), *The Despot of Broomsedge Cove,* and *In the "Stranger People's" Country* (1891) are her best novels.

The chief strengths of M., who published under the pseudonym Charles Egbert Craddock, lie in creating female characters with plausible, if sometimes idealized, psychological makeup; in enhancing her personages's actions and thoughts by means of pictorial backdrops; and in effecting delightful humor. Frequently,

pictorialism overbalances characterization and plot. Her comic scenes indicate an awareness of the Southwest Humorists, although she scants these predecessors's bawdry. She also employs mountaineers's superstitions to achieve good supernatural fiction. Some of her compelling characters seem linked with otherworldliness. The famous story, "The 'Harnt' That Walks Chilhowee" (1884), demonstrates such techniques in the situation of Reuben Crabb. M.'s ghostly fiction often falls within provinces of traditional Christmas-story supernaturalism. Her characters often show a sameness and hasty conclusions to the novels too often hinder adequate character development, but the endings (of the books and of the lives of the principal males) for *The Prophet of the Great Smoky Mountains* and *In the Clouds* are neither implausible nor over-abrupt. In the first, Hi Kelsey's suicidal demise, if melodramatic at the surface, is consistent with his other self-effacement. In the second, Lorey is "mink by name and mink by nature"; thus his sudden, accidental death suggests the rapid and often chance fate of a hunted animal. such qualities make these books better than many later M. publications. Unexpected artistic flashes illuminate her fiction otherwise; for example, the eerie atmosphere of *In the Clouds,* or characters like old Mrs. Guthrie, with her evil eye, from *In the "Stranger People's" Country,* and the grotesque "river-rats" in a later and lesser novel, *The Fair Mississippian* (1980), are memorable.

Even if a single work is not wholly first-rate, such segments are worth knowing. No mere scribbler, M. thoughtfully planned her novels, which generally appeared first as serials, then in hardcover. In this respect, her correspondence and often lively controversies with publishers are revealing. M.'s talents and her position as a leading woman writer ultimately assure her continuing place in American literature.

BIBLIOGRAPHY: Cary, R., *M. N. M.* (1967); Ensor, A. R., "M. N. M. [Charles Egbert Craddock] (1850–1922)," in Bain, R., and J. M. Flora, eds., *Fifty Southern Writers before 1900* (1987): 336–47; Fisher, B. F., IV, "'The Visitants from Yesterday': An Atypical Previously Unpublished Story from the Pen of 'Charles Egbert Craddock,'" *TSL* 26 (1981): 89–100; Parks. E. W., *Charles Egbert Craddock (M. N. M.)* (1941)

BENJAMIN FRANKLIN FISHER, IV

MURRAY, Albert [Lee]

b. 12 May 1916, Nokomis, Alabama

Like the blues musicians on whom he has focused so much of his work, M. is a master of improvisation, an impressive intellectual who moves deftly among various forms of writing. From polemics to fiction to biography to aesthetics, his contributions to our understanding of African American culture and the origins and evolution of the blues have been consistently profound and entertaining. M.'s impressive and far-ranging oeuvre, unique in its blend of variety and cohesion, may be, however, his greatest liability, for it has spread his identity thin, making him appear as a relatively minor player in several genres. Consequently, he has not received the critical attention due to a writer of his talent and breadth.

In *The Omni-Americans: New Perspectives on Black Experience and American Culture* (1970), M. establishes many of the themes he will carry over to later works, including his critique of "a folklore of white supremacy and a fakelore of black pathology" perpetuated by American culture in general and social scientists in particular. He stresses the affirmative in African American experience, arguing that "far from simply struggling in despair, [African Americans] live with gusto and a sense of elegance that has always been downright enviable."

South to a Very Old Place (1971), an intriguing blend of travel writing, autobiography, journalism, and social criticism, is an account of M.'s journey from New York to Tuskegee, his alma mater, to Mobile, where he spent his formative years, and eventually back to the North. Along the way he interviews notable intellectuals and writers, including C. Vann Woodward, Jonathan Daniels, Walker PERCY, and Hodding Carter. And he also treats his readers to his unique prose style, combining high literary language with idiomatic expressions and occasionally interjecting his own coinages.

In *The Hero and the Blues* (1973), M. details his aesthetic theories, building on his notion, introduced in earlier works, that the blues musician, among all contemporary artists, best exemplifies the traits of the epic hero. *The Blue Devils of Nada: A Contemporary American Approach to Aesthetic Statement* (1996) reiterates and expands upon the ideas presented in *The Hero and the Blues*. In this later work, M. compares the blues musician to other heroic American figures: "the frontiersman, the fugitive slave, and the picaresque hero, the survival of each of whom depended largely on an ability to operate on dynamics equivalent to those of the vamp, the riff, and most certainly the break."

M. elaborates on these ideas in *Stomping the Blues* (1976) and *Good Morning Blues: The Autobiography of Count Basie* (1985). In the former work, which combines M.'s evocative prose treatment of blues history and archival photographs of prominent and influential blues musicians, he waxes eloquent on the nature of the blues idiom, highlighting "its unique combination of spontaneity, improvisation, and control." Above all, he stresses that the blues musician, of whom Count Basie serves as an exemplary model in *Good Morning Blues,* is not an artist who with reckless abandon pursues primitive passions but a virtuoso of a formal art with established aesthetic boundaries.

Unlike the average theorist, however, M. has successfully applied his aesthetic principles to his own artistic endeavors, the novels *Train Whistle Guitar* (1974), *The Spyglass Tree* (1991), and *The Seven League Boots* (1996). In his fiction, M. synthesizes elegant prose and "downhome" expressions, autobiography and strikingly imaginative episodes, straightforward first-person narrative and interludes of stream-of-consciousness. Following the lead of Ralph ELLISON and Ernest HEMINGWAY, two writers he acknowledges as masters of the blues idiom in fiction, M. demonstrates his aptitude for translating a story into a work of art built on the tension between freedom and restraint.

BIBLIOGRAPHY: Carson, W., "A. M.: Literary Reconstruction of the Vernacular Community," *AAR* 27 (1993): 287–95; Gates, H. L., Jr., "King of Cats," *New Yorker* 72 (8 April 1996): 70–81

ALLEN ALEXANDER

MUSIC AND LITERATURE

The widespread collaborative interaction between music and literature derives most obviously from their formal similarity: both generate meaning by structuring the perceived flow of time, in contrast to the spatial organization in the static visual arts. The link between music and literature is especially clear in the case of poetry, in which the musical, rhythmic qualities of language are emphasized along with its referential and connotative meanings. Indeed, the numerous oral traditions based on reciting or singing narrative verse to the accompaniment of music indicate that prior to the dominance of print culture and strict specialization in the arts, music and poetry were not viewed as entirely separate artistic practices. This connection is also evident in the names of such traditional poetic forms as ballad, sonnet, ode, and hymn, all of which have a musical origin, as well as in critical evaluations that praise a composition for its lyrical qualities or a poem for its musical overtones. Walter Pater's famous assertion in the late-19th c. that all art aspires to "the condition of music" represents one of the strongest theoretical statements not only on the aesthetic status of music but on the interrelation of different artistic practices. While poetry may claim the closest literary connection to music, prose writers have also imbued their narratives with musical significance, working with such formal structures as the leitmotif and the coda, taking inspiration from specific musical compositions, and incorporating musical themes, characters, and plot situations into their writing. By the same token, many composers have written musical pieces based on literary works.

In the American context, the relation between music and literature predates the arrival of Europeans, of course, with the songs, prayers, and stories of indigenous tribes, chanted to rhythmic musical accompaniment. The establishment of permanent English settlements on this continent in the 17th c. meant the importation of European cultural traditions, and the history of music and literature in America reflects that influence. Specifically, the English colonists brought with them the popular ballads and hymns of the late Renaissance as well as the practice of metrical psalmody, that is, translating biblical psalms into vernacular poetry. In fact, the first collection of verse published in colonial America was the *Bay Psalm Book* (1640), an attempt at a more accurate and metrically satisfactory rendering of the psalms than was available in the two earlier English versions. American poets of the 17th c. notable for the incorporation of music into their poetry include Anne BRADSTREET, the most famous of the early colonial poets, who praises David the psalmist and mentions the elevating effects of music, and Edward TAYLOR, a Puritan minister writing in the tradition of John Donne and the metaphysical poets whose verse shows the greatest degree of musical knowledge in any colonial poetry.

American literature in the 18th c. is usually associated with political essays, satires, and the patriotic verse of Philip FRENEAU. However, despite the prevailing concern of the era with the issue of nationhood, several poets did produce a substantial amount of lyric poetry as well, mainly in Philadelphia and Boston, the primary musical centers of the period. Francis HOPKINSON—poet, musician, and America's first native-born composer—did much to keep the lyric tradition alive in the 18th c., writing not only popular songs and cantata odes—"libretto" verses to be performed with musical accompaniment—but also elegies and pastoral Miltonic imitations as well as several poems in honor of music that show a clear grasp of contemporary forms and techniques. Other poets of the period who show a musical focus in their work include Thomas GODFREY, who wrote pastoral verse in the tradition of Spenser and Milton; Nathaniel Evans, a skilled imitator of Milton who shows signs in his poetry and essays of an early romantic strain in American literature; and Robert Treat Paine, a writer of both neoclassical and lyric verse who made a living writing

songs, satires, and cantata odes for public occasions and helped revive the sonnet form in American literature.

The 19th c. saw an enhanced interest in the synthesis of the arts, spurred on by the philosophical and literary writing of the German and English romantics. Music, especially the increasingly popular instrumental or "pure" music, was highly praised by philosophers like Schlegel, Schopenhauer, and Nietzsche, all of whom attested to its primacy over verbal expression because of its suggestive and ineffable qualities and its ability to embody sheer emotion. In England, Coleridge, Shelley, and Keats were all strongly influenced by music, and American poets of the time likewise found inspiration in the new convergence of music and philosophy, experimenting with less rigid meters and forms than those of their predecessors. William Cullen BRYANT's melodious verse showed Coleridge's influence and attracted the interest of Edgar Allan POE; Bostonian poets Henry Wadsworth LONGFELLOW, Oliver Wendell HOLMES, and James Russell LOWELL were amateur musicians and avid music lovers; and Ralph Waldo EMERSON, though no musician, employed musical imagery and metaphors frequently in his verse.

Particularly noteworthy for having probed the correlation between music and poetry in the 19th c. are Poe, Walt WHITMAN, and Sidney LANIER, all of whom experimented extensively with musical structures and techniques. In his critical theory Poe discusses at length the relationship between music and poetry, and in his fiction he often incorporates descriptions of ephemeral music to help establish mood. Poe's poetry displays various song-like effects, including careful manipulation of rhyme and alliteration to create verbal melody; strategic use of repetition, as in the famous "Nevermore" refrain from "The Raven"; and rhythmic complexity and syncopation resulting from his conception of meter in terms of musical measures. If Poe's musical source was the song, Whitman's was the symphony: Whitman admired Beethoven's music greatly and sought to imitate the "organic" symphonic form in his poetry, repeatedly returning throughout *Leaves of Grass* to the same few themes of love, death, religious transcendence, democracy, sex, nature, and the freedom of the individual. Each theme blends into the others and receives a different treatment whenever it appears, forming a complex and expansive whole, like a Beethoven symphony. Deserving special mention is "Proud Music of the Storm" (1869), certainly Whitman's greatest tribute to music in a single poem. The only 19th-c. American poet who also played music professionally was Lanier, author of *The Science of English Verse,* an exposition of the metrical quantity theory favored by Poe. "The Symphony," his most famous poem, aroused curiosity because of its attempt to follow the structure of a symphony and its personification of instrumental voices, though it is overly sentimental and by no means his best work. The apex of his experimentation with music and poetry came the following year with "The Centennial Meditation of Columbia." A cantata ode written on request for the U.S. Centennial celebration, the "Meditation" shows the influence of Wagner and anticipates the freer verse forms of the 20th c.

The connection between music and literature continued and expanded during the 20th c., even as the distinction between high culture and popular culture became blurred with the development of technology-dependent mass art forms such as film and multitrack recorded music. Early in the century, musical explorations of atonality and dissonance by modernist composers such as Arnold Schoenberg and Igor Stravinsky reflected the general mood of experimentation and upheaval in the arts and intellectual life. The imagist poets, drawing on Poe and the French symbolists, argued for a conception of the poetic line in terms of the musical phrase, writing free verse and arranging line-breaks according to cadence rather than traditional metrics. An early proponent of IMAGISM, Ezra POUND studied medieval European song and wrote a number of poems in Provençal musical forms. T. S. ELIOT used instrumental music as a formal principle, structuring *The Waste Land* on a symphonic model and *Four Quartets* on the patterns of chamber music; in *The Music of Poetry,* he offers his theory of the interrelation of the two arts. Conrad AIKEN also made use of the symphonic model in his verse, introducing, developing, and merging themes as Whitman had done. Another American modernist who made frequent use of musical tropes and structures was Wallace STEVENS, in whose poems music often signifies the idea of process and functions as the model for modern art generally: sensual, yet self-consciously abstract, temporal, and incomplete.

The first half of the 20th c. also saw a true coming of age for American art music. Unlike the popular music tradition represented by such figures as Stephen Foster, whose minstrel-show songs "Camptown Races," "Oh! Susanna," and "Old Folks at Home," among others, remain a prominent part of America's musical identity, serious concert music in the U.S. was long the province of European, especially German, composers or of Americans imitating European models. The work of iconoclastic composer Charles Ives certainly marked a dissolution of the American inferiority complex with respect to European music. A true experimentalist, Ives drew material from a great variety of sources. Most significant in terms of his connection to the American literary tradition is his

Second Piano Sonata (1909–15), subtitled *Concord, Mass. in the 1840s,* the four movements of which are individually titled "Emerson," "Hawthorne," "The Alcotts," and "Thoreau." Another 20th-c. American composer with ties to literature was Virgil Thomson, who collaborated with Gertrude STEIN on two operas: *Four Saints in Three Acts,* written and composed in Paris in 1927–28 and first performed in Hartford, Connecticut, in 1934, and a commissioned work on the life of Susan B. Anthony, *The Mother of Us All,* first performed in 1946. Thomson also composed music for Stein's *Capitals Capitals,* first performed in 1927, as well as numerous choral settings of poems and the score for Pare Lorentz's documentary *The Plow That Broke the Plains* (1936), the first of several film music projects. Aaron Copland likewise did some composing for film, notably the adaptations of John STEINBECK's *Of Mice and Men* and Thornton WILDER's *Our Town.* A student of both Thomson and Copland, Ned Rorem has continued the alliance between composers and literary artists in the 20th c., writing numerous songs and song cycles drawn from literary sources, including *Poems of Love and the Rain* (1963), two versions each of nine poems by W. H. AUDEN, Emily DICKINSON, Theodore ROETHKE, and E. E. CUMMINGS, and *Last Poems of Wallace Stevens* (1971–72), as well as settings of poems by Whitman, Sylvia PLATH, Paul GOODMAN, and others. He has also written several operas, including one with a libretto adapted from Gertrude Stein, *Three Sisters Who Are Not Sisters* (1969). John Adams is another contemporary American composer who fuses literary and musical forms in such works as *Harmonium* (1980), an orchestral and choral setting of poems by John Donne and Emily Dickinson; *The Wound Dresser* (1989), a musical adaptation of a Walt Whitman Civil War poem; and *Nixon in China* (1987), a full-scale contemporary opera.

For a variety of 20th-c. American prose writers and poets, jazz has also proved to be a rich musical source of literary inspiration. Langston HUGHES helped launch the Harlem Renaissance in the 1920s with *The Weary Blues,* a collection of poems celebrating the experiences of African Americans and other disenfranchised members of American society that draws heavily on the jazz and blues traditions. From the very beginnings of his career, Hughes openly embraced jazz and blues as major influences on his work, one of only a few Harlem Renaissance writers to do so. In the 1950s and 1960s, the bebop jazz of musicians like Charlie Parker, John Coltrane, and Dizzy Gillespie served as a stylistic and metaphoric ideal of freedom, improvisation, and emotional authenticity for American Beat writers and poets such as Jack KEROUAC, Allen GINSBERG, Lawrence FERLINGHETTI, and Kenneth REXROTH, whose work celebrated youthful exuberance and sensuality, evoking the myths of the American open road and bohemian street life and decrying "straight" mainstream American culture. In the San Francisco of the late 1950s, Beat poets would frequently perform their work in coffee bars and clubs to improvised jazz accompaniment. Among African American poets of the time, Sterling A. BROWN, Frank Marshall Davis, and to some extent, Gwendolyn BROOKS all showed a jazz and blues influence. Beginning in the 1960s and 1970s, Larry Neal and Amiri BARAKA explored in their poetry, drama, and criticism the history of racial oppression in America from an African American perspective, incorporating the jazz and blues traditions as politically important cultural forces and espousing a black aesthetics and a Pan-African nationalism. In *Jazz,* a novel set in the Harlem of the 1920s, Toni MORRISON uses jazz music as a backdrop for and motivating factor in the development of the narrative, a cultural point of reference among the characters, and an inspiration for her lyrical prose style. Jazz continues to be a strong influence on contemporary poets like Yusef KOMUNYAKAA and William MATTHEWS.

Rock music and the genres that have grown out of it have had their own strong links to literature and have, like jazz, broken down distinctions between academic high culture and popular culture. The 1960s saw a resurgence of romanticism in popular music with performers not only writing their own songs but treating subjects with the lyrical and often musical complexity and sophistication usually associated with high art: the albums by the Beatles from 1965 to 1970 serve as the clearest example. In the American context, poet–musicians such as Bob DYLAN and Paul Simon crossed over from the early 1960s folk scene into studio-oriented rock but maintained their sometimes personal and introspective, sometimes allusive and suggestive lyrical approaches. Dylan in particular was strongly indebted in his early years to the protest folk songs of the 1930s and 1940s by such significant pre-

cursors as Woody Guthrie and Pete Seeger. Also at this time, singer–songwriter Joni Mitchell received admiration for her emotionally forthright lyrics as she helped define the folk-rock aesthetic. Canadian poet and novelist Leonard Cohen likewise made periodic forays into recorded music, earning critical praise for both his literary and his musical work. Many American performers since the 1960s have garnered critical respect for their lyrics as well, including Patti Smith, who started out reading her poetry at gatherings in New York City in the early 1970s; Tom Waits, who in addition to music, has been involved in theater and in film as both composer and actor; and David Byrne, whose introspective, cerebral lyrics are usually combined with emotionally expressive, polyrhythmic musical arrangements. At the same time, some novelists have adopted rock and punk into both the form and content of their work. Kathy ACKER, for example, employs a punk shock-aesthetic in her surrealistic, jarring narratives, and Don DELILLO's novel *Great Jones Street* explores the decadent world of a 1960s–70s rock star. Rap and hip-hop have also received critical praise both for their focus on urban American youth experience and for their innovative use of recording technology. There is still much to be said about the evolving relationship of music and literature in the U.S.: its historical and aesthetic significance is recognized by both literary critics and musicologists, and the popular appeal of the linkage of words and music testifies to its continued social importance as well.

BIBLIOGRAPHY: Baker, H., Jr., *Blues, Ideology, and Afro-American Literature* (1984); Brown, G., *Music and Literature* (1948); Frye, N., ed., *Sound and Poetry* (1957); Hartman, C. O., *Jazz Text* (1991); Kramer, L., *Music and Poetry* (1984); Lenhart, C., *Musical Influence on American Poetry* (1956); Thomas, L., "'Communicating by Horns': Jazz and Redemption in the Poetry of the Beats and the Black Arts Movement," *AAR* 26 (1992): 291–98

BRIAN DONAHUE

NABOKOV, Vladimir [Vladimirovich]

b. 23 April 1899, St. Petersburg, Russia; d. 2 July 1977, Montreux, Switzerland

Poet, novelist, short story writer, critic, translator, as well as a lepidopterist and avid chess master, N. did much to introduce European modernism to American narrative fiction. Deeply influenced by the Russian avant-garde, especially the symbolist writer Andrey Bely, in addition to the writer Franz Kafka, N. was characterized by one biographer as "a conjecture within a conundrum." The work of the perpetual émigré, his art is marked by its irony, allusion, and minute attention to form and language, capturing the modernist sense of displacement and anxiety with a postmodernist sense of wit and playfulness.

Born in St. Petersburg, the Russian Revolution forced the emigration of N.'s aristocratic family to Berlin in 1919. After receiving a degree in Slavic and Romance literatures at Cambridge, N. returned to Berlin to began his literary career that falls into four chronological periods: from 1919 to 1937 in Berlin, from 1937 to 1940 in Paris, from 1940 to 1961 in the U.S., and from 1961 until his death in 1977 in Switzerland.

Publishing in various émigré journals in Berlin, N. completed eight novels in Russian in addition to a large body of poetry and short stories, and supported himself by giving language lessons, translating, and devising chess problems and Russian crossword puzzles. His novels of this period include *Marshen'ka* (1926; *Mary,* 1970), *Korol', dama, valet* (1928; *King, Queen, Knave,* 1968), *Soglyadatai* (1930; *The Eye,* 1965), *Zashchita Luzhina* (1930; *The Defense,* 1964), *Kamera obskura* (1932; *Laughter in the Dark,* 1938), *Podvig* (1933; *Glory,* 1971), *Otchayanie* (1936; *Despair,* 1937; rev. ed., 1966), *Priglashenie na kazn'* (1938; *Invitation to a Beheading,* 1959), and *Dar* (1937–38; *The Gift,* 1963). N.'s reputation as a novelist in Russian rests on these last two. Deeply influenced by Kafka, *Invitation to a Beheading* is the surrealist tale of the teacher Cincinnatus, condemned to death for "gnostical turpitude." *The Gift* explores the artifice of literature by looking at the development of Fyodor, a young Russian émigré living in Berlin, as he works on a biography of 19th-c. writer Chernyshevsky, and wonders about the fate of his missing father, a noted lepidopterist. *The Gift* shows N.'s eye for detail, as he satirizes the intellectual pretensions of the émigré community.

Fleeing to France with the rise of Nazism in Germany, N. began work on a ninth Russian novel, *Solus Rex,* but never completed it. Trilingual, he composed his next work *The Real Life of Sebastian Knight* (1941) in English. Thereafter, escaping the fall of France, he emigrated with his family to the U.S. In America, N. taught language and literature at Wellesley College and Cornell University, and worked as a lepidopterist at the Harvard Museum of Comparative Zoology. During this period, he wrote only three novels, *Bend Sinister* (1947), *Lolita* (1955), and *Pnin* (1957), though he also produced a memoir originally entitled *Conclusive Evidence* (1951) and revised as *Speak, Memory* (1966). As a scholar he produced a number of important translations of Russian classics, including Mikhail Lermontov's *A Hero of Our Time* (1958) and Pushkin's *Eugene Onegin* (4 vols., 1964; rev. ed., 1975), accompanied by an exhaustive and idiosyncratic commentary. He also published a biographical study on Nikolay Gogol in 1944. Many of his lectures have since been published posthumously: *Lectures on Literature* (1980), *Lectures on Russian Literature* (1981), and *Lectures on Don Quixote* (1983). This period was also marked by N.'s temperamental friendship with the critic Edmund WILSON. *The Nabokov-Wilson Letters* (1979) recounts their enthusiasms and disagreements, including the increasingly bitter exchange over N.'s translation of *Eugene Onegin.*

N.'s American novels and short stories are generally more realistic, playing fewer apparent narrative games than his earlier works, and are marked by their trenchant and witty observations of the idiosyncracies of middle-class American culture in the mid-1950s. Drawing on his own experiences, N.'s *Pnin* offers a satirical portrait of American academic life, observed from the perspective of an émigré Russian professor. Perhaps the most important of the American novels, and certainly the most infamous is *Lolita,* in part a parody of Edgar Allan POE. N.'s unreliable narrator, Humbert Humbert, pursues Dolores Haze, the nymphet who becomes the symbol of his unfulfillable erotic obsessions. The pun on her names, suggesting "vague sadness," is indicative of both of N.'s word play and his theme.

With the success of *Lolita,* N. was able to retire from teaching and return to Europe, settling in Montreux, though he retained his American citizenship and continued to write in English. In this final period, he wrote his last four novels, *Pale Fire* (1962), *Ada or Ardor* (1969), *Transparent Things* (1972), and *Look at the Harlequins!* (1974). *Ada,* subtitled *A Family Chronicle,* is N.'s last major work—as well as his longest. A rich interplay of parodies, it combines American Gothic fiction with the sweep of the classical Russian novel, exploring the themes of eroticism, incest, and the family. Perhaps N.'s greatest work, however, is *Pale Fire.* Half poem and half prose, it is presented as the scholar Kinbote's preface and commentary on John Slade's 999-line poem. It is a masterpiece of form and symmetry, as the commentary leads the reader through a web of cross references and discovery, revealing Kinbote's obsessions and insanity.

N. defined his own aesthetic by his rejection of the psychological realism of Dostoevsky, D. H. Lawrence, and Sigmund Freud. At the same time, eroticism, obsession, and neurosis in a precarious world are central to his work, but the angst of such a world is translated into a narrative and cosmic joke. In place of the realistic, he posits a psychological surrealism, an elegantly structured chaos. His passion for chess problems and crossword puzzles contribute to the formal qualities of his novels and stories, both explicitly in works such as *King, Queen, Knave* and *The Defense,* or indirectly as in *The Gift* and *Lolita.* His works are rich in word play, parodies, puns, anagrams, and other intellectual games. Playful, allusive, ironic, N. typically builds his stories around the interaction of several realities, often deliberately misdirecting the reader, anticipating postmodernism.

Supervising the translation of his Russian works into English as well as his English works into Russian (often by his son Dmitri), N. extended his reputation as an important American writer and more recently as a major modern Russian novelist.

BIBLIOGRAPHY: Bader, J., *Crystal Land: Artifice in N.'s English Novels* (1972); Boyd, B., *V. N.: The American Years* (1991); Boyd, B., *V. N.: The Russian Years* (1990); Clancy, L., *The Novels of V. N.* (1984); Field, A., *V. N.: The Life and Art of V. N.* (1986); Foster, J. B., *N.'s Art of Memory and European Modernism* (1993); Pifer, E., *N. and the Novel* (1980); Rampton, D., *V. N.: A Critical Study of the Novels* (1984)

THOMAS L. COOKSEY

NASH, [Frederick] Ogden

b. 19 August 1902, Rye, New York; d. 19 May 1971, Baltimore, Maryland

N. belongs to the brilliant group of writers, including James THURBER, E. B. WHITE, S. J. PERELMAN, and Dorothy PARKER, who congregated around Harold Ross and his magazine, the *New Yorker,* during the 1920s and 1930s. Ross demanded a certain brand of stylish humor, and N. was among those willing and able to supply it. His first poem, "Spring Comes to Murray Hill," appeared in the magazine in 1930, and a prolific record of subsequent publication in such journals as the *Saturday Evening Post, American Magazine,* and the *Saturday Review of Literature* extended his popularity. He proved to be a notable poet, but the reviews of his books reveal that, tagged as a writer of "light verse," he became well known to the general public without earning a reputation in critical and academic circles.

N. claimed that he was mostly influenced by the bad poems of Julia Moore, "the sweet singer of Michigan," but this claim must be discounted as ingenious, since he participates in a long tradition of comic and nonsense verse. Catullus, Martial, Chaucer, Skelton, and Suckling are among his forebears. The comic verse of the 19th c. by Winthrop Mackworth Praed, Charles Calverley, Edward Lear, and Lewis Carroll, and the distinctively American verse of Oliver Wendell HOLMES and James Russell LOWELL, Don MARQUIS, and Samuel Hoffenstein, as well as that of his elders writing for the *New Yorker,* must have played distinctive roles in his literary development.

Light verse, almost a pejorative term, is read with enjoyment but not reverently studied. Serious poetry is considered elevated, sublime, and beautiful; light verse is usually considered low, reductive, and, perhaps, somewhat ugly. Its techniques are the peripheral ones of poetry and include parody, slapstick, farce, and mockery; it is often parasitic, leeching upon the earnestly serious verse that it caricatures. N.'s poetry is well within the tradition of such verse with its asymmetric lines, puns, *bouffe rime,* inverted clichés and adages, vernacular diction, and distorted grammar. Its subjects deliberately avoid elevation; they are the recognizable middle-sized woes of contemporary existence, like diets, incomprehensible serious poems, the odd behavior of the animal kingdom, children, and crowds. They attack parsley, billboards, and little boys, but praise smelts and the ocean.

N. is not gifted with epic vision; his poetic specialty is the epigrammatic two-liner, and even a long poem is unlikely to be much more than a page of observations or reflections. A prolific poet, he collected and recollected his work in a variety of volumes. *Hard Lines* (1931), *I'm a Stranger Here Myself* (1938), and *Good Intentions* (1942) brought together the work of his first decade or so. After a stint in Hollywood, he collaborated with S. J. Perelman and Kurt Weill on a successful musical play, *One Touch of Venus* (1943). His later poems appeared in *Versus* (1949) and *You Can't Get There from Here* (1957), and many of his best pieces were collected in *Verses from 1929 On* (1959). A selection of wry meditations on illness, insomnia, doctors, germs, and dieting appeared in *Bed Riddance: A Posy for the Indisposed* (1970). An attractive posthumous volume, *I Wouldn't Have Missed It* (1975), offers several hundred pages of N.'s best concoctions, with a pertinent and affectionate introduction by Archibald MACLEISH, an appendix of light-hearted "Notes," and an "Index of Last Lines."

N.'s elegant and laughable poetry is neglected by critics, who can, apparently, find little to say about his sensible nonsense. After all, who can argue with the poet who informs us that "He who attempts to tease the cobra / is soon a sadder he, and sobra"? There is no biography; no one has yet made a selection of N.'s letters, though they would undoubtedly cast a bright light upon their period. No book-length critical study has attempted to plumb his art and attitudes, and our better critical minds have found nothing Marxist, psychoanalytic, or phenomenological to say about him. His solitude in the literary firmament has a kind of grandeur about it.

BIBLIOGRAPHY: Arnold, Jr., S. G. T., "O. N.," in Trachtenberg, S., ed., *DLB*, vol. 11, part 2, *American Humorists, 1800–1950* (1982): 331–44; Hasley, L., "The Golden Trashery of Ogden Nashery," *ArQ* 27 (Spring 1971): 241–50

DOUGLAS ROBILLARD

NATHAN, Robert

b. 2 January 1894, New York City; d. 25 May 1985, Los Angeles, California

N. was, next to James Branch CABELL, the major American fantasist of the mid-20th c. Only two of his thirty-nine novels are full-length and in the realistic mode: the first, *Peter Kindred* (1920), which shows

the influence of H. G. Wells, and *A Star in the Wind* (1962), which deals with the establishment of the state of Israel. Though by no means do all the others involve the supernatural—*The Color of Evening* (1960) is one of his best—all are brief and written in a limpid, beautiful prose, suggestive of the fable, parable, or folktale, with cadences reminiscent of the Old Testament, yet adequate to embracing an epic theme if necessary, as in *Road of Ages* (1935). Though his publisher compared one of his novels to *Candide,* their combination of wistful longing and gentle skepticism brings him much closer to Anatole France.

N. most frequently laid his scenes in New York City, where he was born; Cape Cod, where he often sojourned, notably *The Sea-Gull Cry* (1942) and *Long after Summer* (1948); or California, where he died. But *The River Journey* (1949) travels south on the Mississippi from a town in Iowa; *The Fair* (1964) is set in King Arthur's England; ancient Israel gives us *Jonah* (1925); and *There Is Another Heaven* (1929) invades Eternity. God is a character in *Jonah* and *Mr. Whittle and the Morning Star* (1947); Death in *The River Journey;* and the Devil and his angels in *The Innocent Eve* (1951), *The Devil with Love* (1963), and *Heaven and Hell and the Megas Factor* (1975). Dolls behave like human beings in *The Puppet Master* (1923), and there are talking birds, animals, even fish and insects in *The Fiddler in Barley* (1926), *The Woodcutter's House* (1927), the *Tapiola* novels (2 vols., 1938, 1941), and *Sir Henry* (1955).

N.'s most popular novels are *One More Spring* (1933) and *Portrait of Jennie* (1940). That he should have been able to write with charm, humanity, and whimsy about a group of derelicts living in a tool shed in Central Park at the height of the Great Depression made the former his first real popular success, and *Portrait of Jennie* sent people scurrying to the Metropolitan Museum demanding to see the picture the novel said was there. *Portrait of Jennie* is the most important American example of the many, mainly British, literary works about time-traveling that developed in the wake of J. W. Dunne's speculations about "serial time." N. used time-traveling in a number of other novels, notably in *But Gently Day* (1943) and the semiautobiographical *The Wilderness Stone* (1961). In *Mia* (1970), Emmeline Anderson exists simultaneously for her friend as a mature woman and a little girl, and *The Elixir* (1971) gives an American professor on a gorgeous romp through English history with a girl who seems to have lived since Merlin's time.

N.'s fairy tales are far from having been designed for the nursery. He was a fairly learned writer, and even the special admirers of *Portrait of Jennie* often failed to understand its intellectual and structural framework. Nor is it clear just how *Stonecliff* (1967) is a kind of allegory of the creative process. Though a fantasist, N. was by no means an "escapist." No American writer suffered more from the vulturism, cruelty, and madness of contemporary society. The shadow of World War II hangs over both *They Went on Together* (1941) and *The Sea-Gull Cry.* In *Heaven and Hell and the Megas Factor* both heaven and hell are so appalled by what has become of the human condition that they send emissaries to earth to put it back together, but the process is complicated by a love affair between the two representatives.

N. published three plays: *Jezebel's Husband* and *The Sleeping Beauty,* which appeared together in 1953, and *Juliet in Mantua* (1966). Here Shakespeare's model lovers are spared from death, but both grow stout and their love grows cold. Except for *Morning in Iowa* (1944), a tribute to his great friend, Stephen Vincent BENÉT, his poems are mostly lyrics, illustrating the singing quality he thought modern poetry in general had lost. The largest collection is *The Green Leaf* (1950). *Sui generis* in his canon is *The Weans* (1960), which was enormously successful. The Weans are Americans (from U.W.), whose capitol is Pound Laundry. The little book describes the excavation of their land in the remote future, and the author's publisher always listed it under "Archaeology."

All N. cared for were love and God, but there was more longing than assured faith in his treatment of both. What he never forgot was that "it is much better to love than to be loved, to have love to give rather than to be in need of it" and that the fact that the will or intelligence behind the universe is "unknown and unknowable doesn't mean it doesn't exist, that it isn't there." For "God is at the end of everything," N. writes in *But Gently Day,* "If you were to go right out of the world, He's all you'd find. And if you went down deep into your heart, that's where He'd be."

BIBLIOGRAPHY: Coppersmith, J. D., "R. N.," in Martine, J. J., ed., *DLB,* vol. 9, part 2, *American Novelists, 1910–1945* (1981): 233–38; Sanderlin, C. K., *R. N.* (1968)

EDWARD WAGENKNECHT

NATIONALISM

In January 1820, British critic Sydney Smith asked "In the four quarters of the globe, who reads an American book? or goes to an American play? or looks at an American picture or statue?" An answer was not long in coming, for the publication of Washington IRVING's *The Sketch Book,* James Fenimore COOPER's *The Spy,* and William Cullen BRYANT's *Poems* helped establish American letters on the international scene. In addition, Smith's witticism spurred on an ongoing quest for a national American literature that had begun with the Revolutionary War.

Cotton MATHER and other colonial authors had consciously attempted to create a literature that reflected specifically American ideals, but it was the Revolutionary War that solidified interest in establishing a cultural and intellectual independence from England that would match the newly gained political independence. The nationalistic spirit reflected in works by Philip FRENEAU and Hugh Henry BRACKENRIDGE's "The Rising Glory of America" was transformed with the onset of war into patriotic calls for a literary emancipation from England and the building of an American tradition in literature and the arts. For instance, as one of America's most vocal proponents, Noah Webster would insist in 1783 that America must be as independent in literature as she is in politics. The initial nationalistic fervor in the decade after the Treaty of Paris subsided only slightly at the turn of the century, but was reignited with the War of 1812, and remained of central concern for American authors and critics throughout the 19th c.

From the Revolutionary War until the Civil War, virtually every major and minor American author actively promoted the development of a national literature. In the early years of the republic, a strong nationalistic spirit was promoted in the poetry of the Connecticut Wits and the drama of Royall TYLER and James Nelson BARKER. Early American novelists such as Charles Brockden BROWN and Sally S. B. K. WOOD used native materials in their fiction explicitly in order to help create a native tradition. After the American victory in the War of 1812 a host of America's leading intellectuals—Bryant, Edward Everett, W. H. Gardiner, and Edward Tyrrell Channing, among others—collectively promoted the building of a native tradition in literature. Calls for a national American literature filled the pages of periodicals like the *North American Review,* founded in 1815. In fact, dozens of periodicals, such as Brackenridge's *United States Magazine,* John NEAL's *Portico,* and the *New York Mirror,* were founded on the policy of promoting an emerging American literature. Toward the mid-19th c., many American authors—such as Henry Wadsworth LONGFELLOW, James Russell LOWELL, and Edgar Allan POE—while still in favor of the development of a national literature, turned away from what they saw as a merely provincial nationalism, and advocated a universalist literature instead. Nevertheless, this period also saw two landmarks of American literary nationalism: Ralph Waldo EMERSON's "The American Scholar," which Oliver Wendell HOLMES would later call America's "Declaration of Literary Independence"; and Walt WHITMAN's preface to the 1855 edition of *Leaves of Grass.* Herman MELVILLE, meanwhile, would have the boldness in 1850 to claim that Nathaniel HAWTHORNE approached the genius of Shakespeare and that American authors should do away with the "leaven of literary flunkyism towards England" that corrupts American literature.

The will to manufacture a national literature and the actual power to do so were two very different things. While nearly every American author between 1783 and 1855 advocated in spirit or in practice the creation of a national literature, many of these same authors recognized the tremendous obstacles inhibiting the development of a native tradition. Perhaps the single greatest problem was the towering presence of British and European literature. As early as 1788, Freneau would wryly suggest placing a heavy tariff on all "imported authors," with the proceeds going to aid American authors unable to support themselves with their own writing. Walter Channing spoke for many American authors when he complained in 1815 that the American reading public has remained satisfied with foreign literature rather than showing the "intellectual courage" the development of a native tradition requires. According to many antebellum critics, a national literature was not quick in coming because the American people were consumed with other matters. With all their attention focused on politics and the building of wealth, Americans had little energy left over for producing a national literature.

Early American authors complained of several economic obstacles to the building of a native literary tradition. The lack of an international copyright made it cheaper for American booksellers to reprint and sell English books than to underwrite the publication of native works. The ink on the Treaty of Paris was still drying when the calls for an international copyright went up from Webster, Joel BARLOW, Jeremy BELKNAP, and Thomas PAINE, with Cooper and Timothy Flint following close behind. The cry for copyright protection would continue until the first international copyright law was passed in 1891. Aside from the lack of copyright protection, some antebellum authors lamented the absence of a patronage system for the arts in America, and others complained that the American government seemed largely uninterested in the pursuit of a national literature. As Flint charged in 1833, "Our national and state governments do little or nothing for literature by furnishing example, premiums, excitement, money. They have taken no pains to inspire a taste for it, or to cause it to become part and parcel of the national glory."

Whereas American dependence upon English literature and the lack of economic incentive affected the development of a national literature in a general way, the authors who actually wanted to write such a literature had to discover what there was in America worth writing about. Did America have the raw materials necessary for the creation of literary art? Cooper presented the problem this way in *Notions of the Americans:* "There is scarcely an ore which contributes to the wealth of the author, that is found, here, in veins as rich as in Europe. There are no annals for the historian; no follies (beyond the most vulgar and common place) for the satirist; no manners for the dramatist; no obscure fictions for the writer of romance; no gross and hardy offences against decorum for the moralist; nor any of the rich artificial auxiliaries of poetry." The two biggest concerns for most authors were the lack of the dense social milieu associated with manners, and the fact that America had "no shadow, no antiquity, no mystery, no picturesque and gloomy wrong, nor anything but a commonplace prosperity" as Hawthorne would note in 1860. This presumed deficiency in materials was of particular importance for antebellum authors. Influenced by the criticism of Archibald Alison, Friedrich Schlegel, and Madame de Staël, American authors steadfastly believed that a national literature had to grow organically from native material.

The search for uniquely American materials led down several paths. As the *Southern Literary Messenger* proclaimed in 1845, a national literature "must breathe a national spirit, reflect the peculiar habits and character of a people, and derive its ennobling inspiration from the history, institutions, and scenery of its native land." For its "national spirit," what set America apart was its democratic ideals: "The vital principle of an American national literature must be democracy" declared the *Democratic Review* in 1837. As Freneau put it, America's authors were to celebrate democratic virtues, not the virtues of England's "crowned murderers." As for a history, many antebellum critics argued for the literary value of the Puritan past, which Hawthorne exploited with success, and the Revolutionary War, around which William Gilmore SIMMS fashioned a series of seven novels. Others saw literary potential in the history of westward expansion, and the frontier became a recurrent subject in American literature.

When not looking to the past, American authors turned to the distinctive qualities of the American landscape. According to the *Knickerbocker* in 1838, what really separated America from England was her "sublimities of nature." Unlike England, America had "noble rivers; eternal forests; the most stupendous mountains" not to mention "picturesque Indian landscapes of the west." In a similar vein, it was the Native American presence that many authors felt they could rely on for the raw materials of literary art. In fact, Channing would argue that America already possessed a national literature embodied in the oral tradition of the American Indians.

After the Civil War, American authors continued to discuss the best way to build on the nascent national literature. During the later half of the 19th c., the quest for a national American literature became tangled up in the quest for the Great American Novel, and in the development of literary regionalism in the 1880s and 1890s. Although the question of whether or not America would emerge as a literary power had largely been settled by the end of the 19th c., the search for a national American literature continued. As Hamlin GARLAND argued in *Crumbling Idols*—echoing a theme that had been sounded during the Revolutionary War—literary art will only flourish in America if it first rejects the tyranny of European masters.

BIBLIOGRAPHY: Bolwell, R. W., "Concerning the Study of Nationalism in American Literature," *AL* 10 (1939): 405–16; Clark, H. H., "Nationalism in American Literature," *UTQ* 2 (July 1933): 492–519; Dangerfield, G., *The Awakening of American Nationalism* (1965); Nye, R. B., *The Cultural Life of the New Nation* (1960); Ruland, R., ed., *The Native Muse* (1972); Spencer, B. T., *The Quest for Nationality* (1957); Spiller, R. E., ed., *The American Literary Revolution, 1783–1837* (1967); Streeter, R. E., "Association Psychology and Literary Nationalism in the *North American Review*, 1815–1825," *AL* 17 (1945): 243–54

ERIC CARL LINK

NATIVE AMERICAN LITERATURE

The lack of Native American literature in the past was a direct result of the white conception of the Indian. That conception has varied between that of the noble savage and the bloodthirsty savage, but the latter was the dominant one because history books told white Americans that the culture of the Indian was primitive and that battles like that of the Little Big Horn were inspired by savages wanting revenge against white man's laws. More recently, however, as American history is revised to reflect a broader understanding of the Native American perspective, the role of Native American authors in the development of American literature has gained increased recognition as a critical aspect of literary scholarship.

The view of the Indian from a European perspective has been inaccurate from the beginning, evidenced in the incorrect label given the native peoples of America, a true misnomer. American literature as well has provided in the past an inaccurate assessment. Most graduates of American high schools have become acquainted with James Fenimore COOPER's *The Last of the Mohicans* and LONGFELLOW's *Song of Hiawatha*. But few have heard of the Walam Olum or the chronicles of the Delaware and Iroquois tribes entitled the "Rite of the Condoling Council." Even though Cooper and Longfellow may have meant well with their works, they included inaccuracies and attempted to romanticize Native Americans. Natty Bumpo, the white man in Cooper's novel, still sees himself as the superior being and the Indian Chingachgook as a savage.

Prior to the 20th c., there was little opportunity for Native American authors to realize publication of their work. The first novel written by a Native American author was published in 1833, Elias Boudinot's *Poor Sarah; or, The Indian Woman*. Boudinot was also the editor of the *Cherokee Phoenix*, the first tribal newspaper to print in both Native American language and English. This was followed by John Rollin Ridge's *The Life and Adventures of Joaquin Murieta, the Celebrated California Bandit* (1854) and Simon Pokagon's *Queen of the Woods* (1899). The limited number of novels published by Native American authors in the first half of the 20th c. include MOURNING DOVE's *Cogewea, the Half Blood;* three novels by John Milton Oskison in the 1920s and 1930s; John Joseph Mathews's *Sundown;* and D'Arcy MCNICKLE's *The Surrounded* and *Runner in the Sun.*

Other early Native American writers included Charles A. EASTMAN of the Ohiyesa tribe who added a new dimension to the matter when he told the story of his youth in *Indian Boyhood,* followed by *The Soul of the Indian,* an introduction to Native American religion, and by *From the Deep Woods to Civilization,* another autobiography. An interesting dimension that Eastman points out to his readers is in his account of massacres that occurred at the time when the Ghost Dance religion flourished, revealing that the hope of the Ghost Dance was a total peace with the white man. The massacres occurred only after Indian agents outlawed the performance of the dances. Native Americans needed a spokesman at this point in American history. Helen Hunt JACKSON had attempted to speak for the ignored Indian with her book *A Century of Dishonor,* but the reform that resulted ironically turned against Native Americans. The General Allotment Act of 1887 giving each Native American a parcel of land was abused and in the end ninety million of the 138 million acres were stolen through bribery and deceit. Eastman's efforts did little to change the situation.

Zitkala-Sa, a female Native American writer living at the same time as Eastman, also contributed to Indian literature with her *Old Indian Legends* (1901). It was a children's book in that its purpose was to promote understanding between white and red youth. She later published *American Indian Stories* (1921), a collection depicting Indian life with its legends, reminiscences, and stories.

Anthropologists contributed positively toward getting the more accurate view of Native American life accepted after the turn of the 20th c. The sacred songs, chants, and ceremonies, a basic part of the oral tradition of groups close to nature, were recorded. Some Native Americans contributed to this effort. Francis La Flesche worked with Alice C. Fletcher on *The Omaha Tribe* (1911); later, La Flesche published by himself *The Osage Tribe* (1925) and *The War Ceremony and Peace Ceremony of the Osage Indians* (1939). Ella Deloria published *Dakota Texts* (1932) after working with Franz Boas.

After Eastman's autobiography, several more appeared. *The Autobiography of a Fox Woman* by Truman Michelson was published in 1919, and was followed by *Crashing Thunder* by Paul Radin in 1926. Others include John NEIHARDT's *Black Elk Speaks;* Ruth Underhill's *Autobiography of a Papago Woman* (1936); C. J. Nowell's *Smoke from Their Fires* (1940); and Don C. Talayesva's *Sun Chief: Autobiography of a Hopi* (1942).

Many of the autobiographies contain descriptions and explanations of the traditional way of life, and include myths and legends that reveal symbolic significance. For example, the coyote, the raven, and the crow, all very important symbolic animals in Indian legend, appear in a number of songs. The raven and crow are parallel to many biblical birds; the coyote is a figure who shares many traits with other animals like Reynard the Fox or Brer Rabbit. These autobiographies helped to some degree to establish Native American literature as having archetypes along with those accepted in Western literature.

Although Henry David THOREAU and Walt WHITMAN, two 19th-c. American writers well established in the canon, spent much time writing on behalf of Native Americans, they were ignored. After the false impressions established by Cooper and Longfellow, very few major American writers were interested in the cause of the Native American. The best of any recognition came through the fiction of Willa CATHER and William FAULKNER. In the 1930s Oliver LA FARGE's novel *Laughing Boy,* which won a Pulitzer Prize, drew attention for Native Americans, and in the 1940s Frank Waters's *The Man Who Killed the Deer* did likewise.

It was not until 1969, when N. Scott MOMADAY's *House Made of Dawn,* another Pulitzer Prize-winner, was published that Native Americans once more received true positive attention. Momaday's novel came at the right time. A new look at all minorities was about to begin, due to the civil rights movement of the 1960s. Momaday triggered a dormant need among

Native American writers, with the 1970s seeing the publication of novels by Native American authors, including Janet Campbell Hale, Roger Russell, Ted Williams, Hyemeyohsts Storm, James WELCH, Leslie Marmon SILKO, Virginia Driving Hawk Sneve, and Gerald VIZENOR. More recent Native American novelists include Louise ERDRICH, Michael DORRIS, Paula Gunn Allen, Anna Walters, Tom King, Louis Owens, Ray Young-Bear, and Linda HOGAN. This Renaissance has added Native American poets, as well, and appropriately so, for poetry tied to the oral tradition frequently precedes prose. Such new poets include Peter La Farge, Wendy ROSE, Emerson Blackhorse Mitchell, Alonzo Lopez, Liz Sohappy, and Simon ORTIZ.

The purpose of Native American literature, poetry or prose, is never simply to affirm self-expression. It is a communal literature. One's emotions are one's own. The Native American attitude on this subject is that forcing others to imitate others' emotions is imposition on one's integrity. Through song, ceremony, legend, and sacred stories, the Native American writer seeks to embody, articulate, and share reality, to bring the isolated private self into harmony and balance with this reality, to verbalize the sense of the majesty and reverent mystery of all things, and to actualize, in language, those truths that give to humanity its greatest significance and dignity.

The Native American views space as spherical and time as cyclical, not linear and sequential. The universe, then, moves and breathes continuously, unlike the Western idea of fixed and static movement. The notion that nature is somewhere over there, while humanity is over here, or that a great hierarchical ladder of being exists on which ground and trees occupy a very low rung, animals, a slightly higher one, and man a very high one is antithetical to Native American thought. The Native American sees all creatures as relative, as offspring of the Great Mystery, as co-creators, as children of the same Earth Mother, and all as necessary parts of an ordered, balanced, and living whole. Native American thought, reflected strongly in its literature, does not draw a hard and fast line between what is spiritual and what is material, for it regards the two as different expressions of the same reality, both of which are interchangeable. Western thought is basically a diametrical opposite.

In Native American thought, God is known as the All Spirit. Other beings are also spirit. The natural state of existence is whole. Therefore, the sacred chants and ceremonies, spoken and sung, are meant for healing, emphasizing restoration of wholeness. Beauty is wholeness; health is wholeness; goodness is wholeness. This all rests on the basic Indian assumption of the wholeness or unity of the universe. Thus, Native

American literature must consider how it is relevant to the continuing of the harmony of the universe.

Alienation, a moving away from this harmony, thus becomes for much of Native American literature a strong theme. Some of the earliest recognized fiction disguised the outrage at America's genocidal treatment of Indians as a whole. Mourning Dove was one of the first fictive authors to stress a bitter sense of isolation and estrangement felt by the mixed blood in her novel *Cogowea.* The romantic atmosphere seen in Cooper and others begins to disappear with fiction by Mathews and McNickle. Matthews's *Sundown,* for example, is permeated with a feeling of naturalistic despair as the protagonist, Chal, slips into the deracinated "no-Indian's-Land" between Osage and white worlds. McNickel's *The Surrounded* also reflects a grim naturalism with its protagonist Archilde, who never has a real chance within a civilization bent on turning Indians into Anglo-Europeans.

In his Pulitzer Prize-winning *House Made of Dawn,* Momaday continues with his protagonist Abel, echoing the Abel of the Old Testament, as an alienated and fragmented person. Abel is dislocated from his cultural roots as he returns a World War II veteran. Momaday goes a step further: he brings his hero full circle, back home to his native pueblo and a secure knowledge of who he is. Chal and Archilde have no coherent world to return to, but Abel goes back to his grandfather, his roots, and the home of his people. He too focuses upon the agony of the Native American apparently trapped between two worlds pressuring him, but he finds a solution in the return. With this novel, Native American fiction becomes a kind of vision quest, with novels and short stories demonstrating a journey to self-recognition. It reinforces the positive psychological teaching that one must believe in himself/herself for others to have respect for the person. Therefore, it is a direct part of the process of becoming.

Other Native American fiction writers continue this theme in current materials. James Welch demonstrates it in *Winter in the Blood* when he allows his protagonist a glimpse of the meaningful, ordered world of his ancestral Blackfeet. In a later novel entitled *The Death of Jim Loney,* Welch moves nearer the patterns of *Sundown* and *The Surrounded,* creating in his protagonist a mixedblood trapped between identities and worlds. Loney has the knowledge of his Native American heritage, but with it just outside his reach, he drifts toward self-destruction. In a third novel, Welch completes his own act of recovery as he moves all the way back to the traditional Blackfoot world introduced in his first novel. In *Fools Crow,* he remembers his Blackfoot heritage and makes it whole and accessible. In fact, the reader must adapt to a Blackfoot worldview or he/she misses the story. In *The Indian Lawyer,*

Welch's protagonist is a Native American caught up in the kind of sex/politics entanglement familiar to "soap" fans; Indian elements permeate the novel, but his subject is the common, domestic human drama rather than anything especially Native American.

Leslie Marmon Silko writes again of a mixedblood protagonist lost between cultures and identities. In *Ceremony,* she leads her protagonist Tayo through a healing ceremony in mythic time, making it clear for the first time in Native American literature that the mixedblood is a rich source of power and something to be celebrated rather than mourned.

Gerald Vizenor in *Darkness in Saint Louis Bearheart* challenges those insisting upon static definitions of the concept "Indian." He rejects entirely the conventional posture of mourning for the dilemma of the mixedblood. He continues to explore this theme in *Griever* and in *The Trickster of Liberty,* identifying the mixedblood with the visage of trickster, who requires that we reexamine daily all definition and discourse.

Paula Gunn Allen, in *The Woman Who Owned the Shadows* (1983), and Janet Campbell Hale, in *The Jailing of Cecelia Capture* (1985), introduce the first novels since Mourning Dove's *Cogewea* to be both by and about Native American women. Both these novelists follow the theme of male novelists in leading their progatonists through paths of self-discovery.

Louise Erdrich adds to this body of fiction by Native American women with such novels as *Love Medicine, The Beet Queen,* and *Tracks.* In all three of these, fullbloods, mixedbloods, and non-Indians meet and merge. The first remains the best known among general readers, in which she opens the contemporary Chippewa reservation world to plain view. At the center of the novel is her protagonist heroine Lipsha, circling gradually toward self-knowledge that will come in the form of a Chippewa trickster, Nanapush. In all three of these novels, Erdrich goes beyond the pattern of making cultural conflict and mixedblood angst the thematic center. Instead, she writes of the more universal trials of characters who happen to be full or mixedblood Indian.

Erdrich's husband, Michael Dorris, followed a similar path in his first novel, *A Yellow Raft in Blue Water,* with his half-African, half-Indian Rayona on a quest for identity. Anna Walters's *Ghost Singer* (1988) weaves Navajo history and mythology into a story of ghosts and desecration of Indian artifacts. Walters combines the theme of time as cyclical with a woman's search for identity. She is one of the first Native American novelists in several years to make the appropriation of Indian remains a central theme in fiction. More recently, Linda Hogan has taken up the thread of Matthews's subject matter in *Mean Spirit,* writing about dangerous times of oil money and murder among the Osage.

Native American novelists are continually revising the long-cherished, static view of Native American culture held by people around the world. The interest now is intensely in the Native American defined in terms not of Anglo ideas, but of Native American ideas and needs as those have evolved into the late 20th c. Native American characters being put into fiction are not cardboard cliches; they show complexity, depth, and drama of characters who are truly real.

Native American writers affirm their heritage in their individual ways as do writers of all cultures. Some of the authors write about reservation life; others of urban Native Americans trying to make it in Anglo-European society. Still others write of war, of working away from home, of old traditions threatened by the clash with new ways of living. Although the focus may vary, the themes are usually the same. One of the recent Native American writers once said, "Literature is a facet of a culture." There is nothing new about such a statement because it applies to all literatures of the world. As the contemporary Native American writer demonstrates this in poems and stories, he or she is doing the very same thing that all writers have always done, from Sophocles of ancient Greece to John UPDIKE of contemporary America. Literature in all its forms, oral as well as written, is our most durable way of demonstrating the relationships of people, land, and the past. One citation from Native American poetry illustrates: In Linda Hogan's "Celebration: Birth of a Colt," the poet evokes a striking correlative: the act of bringing a colt into the world is shown in the redness of the life-sustaining membrane as it is reflected in the early morning sun: "The sun coming up shines through, / the sky turns bright with morning / and the land / with pollen blowing off the corn, / land that will always own us, / everywhere it is red." The morning sun, the corn pollen, the new colt, the people observing the rite, the land itself—all these things come together celebrating their dependent relationship.

BIBLIOGRAPHY: Allen, P. G., *Studies in American Indian Literature* (1983); Baker, H. A., Jr., ed., *Three American Literatures* (1982); Lincoln, K., *Native American Renaissance* (1983); Owens, L., *Other Destinies* (1992)

JOHN W. CRAWFORD

NATURALISM

Sometimes thought of as an emphasized realism, naturalism applies to literature those concepts that are central to scientific determinism and comes as an outgrowth of the 19th-c. rise of science. It had its beginnings in France, where it was practiced in the novel by Balzac and Flaubert. Émile Zola, using the works of these writers as examples, formulated the genre and named it in his essay *Le roman experimental*. Here the ideal novelist is described in terms usually applied only to a laboratory scientist and writers are advised that a literary work should emulate the objectivity and rigid control of such an experiment. De-emphasizing the imagination and replacing it with direct observation, Zola declared that life itself should furnish plots and themes sufficient for any writer's purpose. The writer's duty essentially was to report the progress of his "experiment" in full and accurate detail, without moralizing or judging. In America the most devoted follower of Zola was Frank NORRIS, who consciously patterned his novels *McTeague, The Octopus,* and *Vandover and the Brute* upon the theories of the French master. Norris was preceded in publication by Stephen CRANE, whose *Maggie: A Girl of the Streets* is regarded as the first significant American naturalistic novel. These two were followed by Theodore DREISER, who became the principal representative of the genre, particularly in his novels *Sister Carrie, The Financier,* and *An American Tragedy.*

It is no accident that these three emerged toward the turn of the century for, born in the 1870s, they were among the first generation capable of absorbing during their youths and then employing in their writing the Darwinian notions which undergird naturalism. Darwin had provided the metaphor of life as a great battleground where individual members of species—as well as species themselves—fought tooth and nail for survival. Organisms were seen as divided into predators and prey. Survival might depend on one's being heavily armed (teeth, claws, keen eyesight) or upon being provided with defenses such as a means of escape (fast legs, wings, burrowing ability) or else with the capacity of protecting oneself through other means of defense, such as shells or color-adaptation. In Darwin's universe the immense power of heredity and environment are everywhere at play as determinants. The most dramatic fictional instance of the Darwinian metaphor occurs in Dreiser's *The Financier* when young Frank Cowperwood observes a fish tank where a lobster and a squid are locked in mortal combat. Heredity has given each its own means of coping. The lobster possesses aggressive weapons (pincers) besides being heavily armored against attack. The squid is provided with speed for rapid escape as well as ink with which to camouflage his presence and his retreat. But neither can escape from the restricted environment of the aquarium. As time goes by, the squid running out of ink and energy, it is inevitable that the powerful lobster will prevail. Cowperwood realizes that the lobster-squid duel parallels precisely what he has already observed to be true of the human struggle. This analogy became known as Social Darwinism: the application of Darwinian principles to human society. The societal struggle, of course, is what most naturalistic writers are concerned with. In particular, they involve themselves with the plight of those who are victimized in an unequal combat. Crane's *Maggie* plays heavily upon the baleful effects of his heroine's environment: first, her improvident and alcoholic parents, then the crowded tenement and ugly, strife-torn neighborhood, finally the ghetto-like area of the metropolis in which she is doomed to earn a sordid living by prostituting herself to the more fortunate inhabitants of affluent surrounding areas of the city. In Eugene O'NEILL's *The Hairy Ape,* Social Darwinism enters the drama. The central figure, Yank, is provided by heredity with massive physical strength, but he is born into an industrialized society in which human strength counts for nothing. Clearly he is doomed. Ostracized alike by those who have proved "fit" for survival (the rich and powerful oligarchs; the intelligent and highly politicized new breed of labor leaders), Yank finds no place in which he can survive, let alone flourish.

For most naturalistic writers life appears grim indeed. The tragic view prevails, and the human being is victimized more often than he triumphs. The course of human events is markedly ironic, and options are few. As an instance, Shirley in Dreiser's "The Second Choice" is shaped by society to perceive marriage as the single option that will assure her escape from the neighborhood she despises. However, she learns that she cannot have the young man with whom she has fallen in love, while the man for whom she no longer cares remains eager to marry her. She sees life as hopeless. Under naturalism, man's relationship with nature, seen by romanticists as overwhelmingly beneficent, alters dramatically. The inherent hostility of the natural world is depicted by Jack LONDON and others, in whose stories natural forces such as blizzard, flood, tornado, drought, fire, and the like, are inimical. Even more depressing is the view put forward by Crane in "The Open Boat." Here nature is viewed as neither cruel nor comforting, but "indifferent, flatly indifferent." Crucial to the naturalistic outlook is the pessimistic stance taken of the question of freedom of the will. Whereas the realist will tend to see his characters as being provided with viable choices of direction and will then feel justified in charging these characters with responsibility for the consequences of their freely made choices, the naturalist will tend more often to present human beings who are deprived of viable options, yet are forced to choose nevertheless.

Because people delude themselves into believing there are genuine choices where none actually exist, the theme of illusion versus reality takes on a special significance.

An important new dimension was added to naturalistic writing with the advent of Freudianism in the early 20th c. To the older influences that act upon the human being, forces such as nature, society, economics, environment, and heredity, was added now the unseen but invincible force exerted by subconscious impulses that may motivate human actions for better or for worse but, in any case, do so without the full comprehension or consent of the individual. Much of Freudian psychology revolves around the primacy of the sexual drive, and this fact aided writers in breaking down the sexual taboos that had restricted the scope of literature in earlier days. Dreiser in *The Hand of the Potter,* published in 1918, attempted the tale of a mentally retarded boy driven by hidden desires to violate and then to murder a neighbor girl, but the first successful presentation of human beings dominated by subconscious sexual motives occurred the following year in Sherwood ANDERSON's *Winesburg, Ohio.* Here the notion of neurosis as the normal human state is advanced under the label of "grotesque": in Anderson's terminology we are, all of us, "different" or grotesque, but in unique directions, and we are pitifully unable to communicate our problems because we do not comprehend them. The early work of John STEINBECK picked up this theme and carried it further, especially in *The Pastures of Heaven* and *Of Mice and Men.* In addition to Steinbeck, authors in whose works naturalism has played an important role, would include Erskine CALDWELL, John DOS PASSOS, James T. FARRELL, William FAULKNER, Ernest HEMINGWAY, James JONES, Norman MAILER, Joyce Carol OATES, John O'HARA, and Tennessee WILLIAMS.

BIBLIOGRAPHY: Ahnebrink, L., *The Beginnings of Naturalism in American Fiction* (1950); Buchesky, C., *The Background of American Literary Naturalism* (1971); Conder, J., *Naturalism in American Fiction* (1984); Hakutani, Y., and L. Fried, eds., *American Naturalism: A Reassessment* (1975); Howard, J., *Form and History in American Literary Naturalism* (1985); Martin, R., *American Literature and the Universe of Force* (1981); Pizer, D., *Twentieth-Century American Literary Naturalism* (1982)

PHILIP L. GERBER

NATURE AND LANDSCAPE

"Space," the poet Charles OLSON observed, "is the central fact to man born in America." This dictum, suggesting a nation more fascinated with space than time, with living in an environment rather than an historical continuum, carries profound implications that extend to the realms of politics, religion, and commerce. The literature of the American landscape has dealt richly with these manifold implications, evidenced in writings by explorers, travelers, settlers, scientists, storytellers, and poets. Whether individual authors have viewed our continent as a source of commercial gain or visionary wonder, a sharp focus on natural landscape as a distinctive American feature has recurred from John SMITH's description of flora and fauna to F. Scott FITZGERALD's evocation of the "fresh, green breast of the new world."

The Puritans, who imbued their errand into the wilderness" with divine sanction, approached the American landscape with a mixture of religious zeal and emotional trepidation. Immersed in the Old Testament from which they derived their avowed roles as New Israelites, they viewed "vast and howling wilderness" of the New World in typological terms. Only through a covenant worked out between God and "His Chosen People" could the wilderness be redeemed into the Promised Land. As significant as the landscape was as typological figure, extended natural descriptions were rare in the major works of the Puritans, William BRADFORD's *Of Plymouth Plantation* or Edward JOHNSON's *Wonder-Working Providences.* Even in Mary ROWLANDSON's famous narrative of captivity among the Indians, the infernal dimensions of the landscape overshadowed attention to its physical features.

The 18th c. marked significant changes in attitudes toward nature and in literary treatments of the landscape. Although students of nature like William BARTRAM often decorated their scenic descriptions with figures from mythology and legend, their scientifically ordered field inquiries tended to banish the demonic qualities of the wilderness. Bartram's studies, informed by a Deist's nonsectarian assumptions, focused on the landscape as a source of knowledge and insight. In the eyes of many 18th-c. rationalists, God was great because his creations were great; accordingly, landscape, rather than the literal words of the Bible, could be "read" as a kind of natural scripture.

Bartram's *Travels,* a record of his search for specimens in the Carolinas, Georgia, and Florida, also marked the first extensive use of the sublime in American literature. Influenced by Edmund Burke's decided preference for sublimity over beauty, writers like Bartram and Thomas JEFFERSON approached natural description with adroit attention to aesthetic possibilities. The Burkean mixture of terror and delight was evident in Bartram's celebrated description of alligators in *Travels* and in Jefferson's artful manipulation of his observer's perspective on the Natural Bridge in *Notes on Virginia.* Jefferson's glorification of his state's natural scenery, included in a wide-ranging discussion of politics, economics, and social issues, reflected his open desire to promote America's most distinctive attribute to a cosmopolitan audience.

As Bartram and Jefferson showed, a perspective that enhanced the appreciation of natural scenery was the panorama, either a fixed vantage point that presented an unobstructed view or a journey that afforded observation of an unfolding procession of scenes, characters, and events. In the 19th c., the transcendentalists transformed such techniques for their own predilections and purposes. In *Nature,* most notably, Ralph Waldo EMERSON's evocation of the "one vast picture" that God paints constitutes a cosmic panorama that allows a sweeping, visionary survey of past occurrences and imminent revelations. His greatest disciple, Henry David THOREAU, used the moving panorama in *A Week on the Concord and Merrimack Rivers,* a work whose heterogeneous mixture of editorializing and observation, of kinetic movement and quiet reflection, reflected the transcendentalist principle of including variety in unity. In *Walden,* Thoreau proved that the so-called fixed panorama, his adoption of a pondside perspective, could help to focus on life's essentials by simultaneously opening one's mind and imagination to eternity. Throughout the works of the transcendentalists, the natural properties of light and motion served to suggest the possibilities of spiritual illumination and moral reform.

Thoreau's adopted perspective at Walden, of course, indicated his sharp break with society, a division between nature and civilization that was addressed by nearly all the American romantics. From hack writings in 19th-c. periodicals to the major works of the American Renaissance, repeated references to America as "nature's nation" reflected an exercise in cultural self-definition. If America lacked historical depth and endured European opprobrium for alleged cultural inferiority, native authors could cite romantic "nature" as a national birthright. In short, nature had supplanted the Bible as a guiding force for the young republic. While the opposition between nature and civilization received perhaps its most orthodox treatment in the poetry of William Cullen BRYANT, the novels of James Fenimore COOPER, most notably his Leather-Stocking Tales, reflected strikingly an alliance between natural landscape and natural virtue. Cooper's heroic Natty Bumppo, while clearly the beneficiary of white, civilized "gifts," served as both a critic of society's arbitrary rules and laws and a reluctant spectator of nature's destruction. With less amplitude than Cooper's, the writings of Herman MELVILLE and Walt WHITMAN reflected what Perry Miller called the "dilemma" facing the American romantics, the anxious sense that nature was being destroyed under the guise of its glorification.

With Cooper and Washington IRVING as exemplars, subsequent writers attempted to put landscape, in the painter Thomas Cole's words, into "the great theater of human events," to develop associations between specific locales and uniquely American achievements. Despite such efforts, however, the American continent continued to be widely viewed as undifferentiated and unvariegated. As the century progressed, travel writers, with their attempts at geographical precision, struggled to give greater definition to the inchoate land mass of the continent. The expeditions of Lewis and Clark, John Charles Frémont, and John Wesley Powell, in particular, were conducted for "literary," noncommercial purposes as well as for acquiring information about soil, vegetation, and climate. The documents deriving from their travels displayed as much interest in sublime and picturesque scenery as they did in scientific discovery.

Influenced by travel writing as much as by the rich particularity of the several regional settings he observed firsthand, Mark TWAIN's works fully developed the nature versus civilization dichotomy that had intrigued so many previous writers. His works, moreover, displayed affinities with a group of writers that came to be identified with the local color movement. Rather than an America diffused into an abstract concept of nationhood, the local colorists—Harriet Beecher STOWE, Mary E. Wilkins FREEMAN, and Sarah Orne JEWETT in New England; George Washington CABLE and Kate CHOPIN in the South; Hamlin GARLAND in the Midwest; and Bret HARTE in the West—focused on landscape as an extension of regional customs, manners, and values. In the early stages of the movement, regional pride suggested that local color fiction required such "texture" and background that it could be written only by a native about his particular place. Stephen CRANE's *Whilomville Stories* and his Western tales, however, provided subtle reworkings of regional techniques that showed how local landscapes could be exploited fictionally by detached, ironic observers. After the turn of the century, moreover, Willa CATHER's novels and stories about the harshness of immigrant life on the Midwestern prairie displayed interesting modifications of the strategies of local color.

The works of Crane and Cather mark a transition from regional writing to NATURALISM, a movement that presented the landscape as and antagonist to man. Naturalists, like the Puritans of centuries before, adopted a deterministic outlook on their environment: nature was wild, uncontrolled, inhuman, and forbidding. Unlike the Puritans, however, the naturalists looked upon nature as an arena of chaotic, random

forces rather than as a locus of demonic energy. A key to understanding literary naturalism is the discordance between nature and any conception of a *supernature,* an absence of spiritual connection undoubtedly influenced by Darwinian biology and its challenge to religious orthodoxy. Just as the new science minimized man's special place in the order of creation, the naturalists presented landscapes so vast and overwhelming as to stress man's puniness. Crane's "The Open Boat" presented a parable of nature's indifference through his impressionistic rendering of the power of the sea. Jack LONDON's fiction dealt similarly with the sea, but his Klondike stories more directly confronted the theme of nature as antagonist. Frank NORRIS's *The Octopus* viewed America's westward expansion in naturalistic terms, though his Darwinism takes on mystical overtones.

In the 20th c., literary responses to nature are as varied as the individual temperaments of the practicing authors; nevertheless, a few cautious generalizations can be made. Since any recourse to natural landscape in an age of technological ruin carries with it a sense of nostalgia, modern and contemporary authors often juxtapose the past and the present. For the atavistic heroes of Ernest HEMINGWAY's hunting and fishing stories, for example, renewed contact with nature restores a saner and simpler world, an alternative to emotional complication and despair. For Robert FROST, pastoral landscape represents an alternative to the psychic tangles of modern life, though his handling of nature is accompanied by wit, irony, and understatement. Any movement toward nostalgia is likely to receive the accusation of escapism or oversimplification, charges leveled at the Agrarian poets—Allen TATE, Robert Penn WARREN, and John Crowe RANSOM—for their obeisance to a Jeffersonian garden world resistant to the forces of industrialization, commercialization, and abstraction. Perhaps because his agricultural interests and activities so authentically match the subject matter of his poetry and fiction, the works of Wendell BERRY present a Jeffersonian vision attractive to our own time.

In some 20th-c. works, the juxtaposition of past and present carries a penetrating irony, as in E. B. WHITE's "Walden," published in 1939, in which a settling of accounts both echoes and contrasts Thoreau's call for subsistence on nature's essentials. Contemporary purveyors of America's last frontier, the West, cast cold eyes on contemporary society as it collides with a natural domain that once sanctioned hardier individualism—Edward ABBEY with *The Brave Cowboy;* greater respect for Native American culture—N. Scott MOMADAY with *House Made of Dawn;* or stronger moral discipline—Wallace STEGNER with *Angle of Repose.* One paradox of 20th-c.

American literature is that the natural history essay, a form pioneered by Thoreau in the 19th c. that might seem alien to our own time, has never had more adherents, many of whom either imitate or extend the techniques or strategies of *Walden,* notably Loren EISELEY, Joseph Wood Krutch, Annie DILLARD, Henry Beston, Edward Abbey, John MCPHEE, Aldo Leopold, and Edwin Way Teale. These writers use the tools of metaphor and analogy to restore broken connections between man and nature, between the depths of nature's geological and biological past and the present moment. Despite the positive insights offered by these authors and others who desire to reaffirm those shattered connections, notably Gary SNYDER and Robert BLY, darker moods dominate much contemporary literature. In much recent fiction and poetry, distortion, nightmare, or grim silence serve as reminders of man's alienation from a natural world that survives in its grotesque decay or disturbing unfamiliarity.

BIBLIOGRAPHY: Fussell, E., *Frontier: American Literature and the American West;* Huth, H., *Nature and the American* (1957); Martin, J., *Harvests of Change* (1967); Marx, L., *The Machine in the Garden* (1964); Mitchell, L. C., *Witnesses to a Vanishing America* (1987); Miller, P., *Nature's Nation* (1967); Nash, R., *Wilderness and the American Mind* (1967); Sanford, C., *Quest for Paradise* (1961); Slotkin, R., *The Fatal Environment* (1985)

KENT P. LJUNGQUIST

NAYLOR, Gloria

b. 25 January 1950, New York City

N. wrote *The Women of Brewster Place: A Novel in Seven Stories* (1982) while still an undergraduate at Brooklyn College, and since that time she has continued to be a consequential voice in American literature, attending to the emotional and spiritual essence of life. Her language resonates with rhythm and poetry while her subjects confront the urgency of existence: surviving racism, rape, war, childhood neglect, and poverty. N. adeptly and simply unearths the defining moments of an individual's existence and we as readers participate in this space that acts as wounds within the soul: as Sweet Esther says in *Bailey's Cafe* (1992), "I am twelve years old and glad that it is dark. He cannot see my face when he calls me to come down into the cellar. I always come when he calls. This is your husband, my brother said. Do whatever he tells you, and you won't be sent away like the others."

While the emotional lives of her characters are trenchantly real, her environments offer the surreal, merging the unfamiliar within the familiar, as well as

alternatives to a Western metaphysics. These features have become more evident with each successive novel: the Judeo-Christian tenet is challenged in *Mama Day* (1988) through sorcery and mysticism, and in *Bailey's Cafe,* N. situates the novel within a dreamlike locale, a street that is somewhere between the living and the dead, a resting place for lost souls to regain dignity.

The history of African Americans is central to N.'s fiction. In her post-slave narratives, individuals have been severed from their ancestral motherland. Emerging from a past of slavery in which black families were torn apart and children were taken from mothers, they must now retrieve wholeness from a more distant history and also create a new culture within a new birthplace, which most definitely still resonates with persecution and hatred and with the more subtler fear of being excluded, rejected, forgotten. N.'s focus on nurturance and motherhood in the black community is a statement about women who know despair but can bring hope and healing through their alliances.

Thus, N.'s commitment is more exclusive to rendering the condition of women, who—as the seven women in *The Women of Brewster Place* embody—have survived a past embedded in social and or familial tragedy in a doubly hostile environment. As African Americans, they have endured the hardships of their people, but as women, their identities have been truncated by men, not just white men, but black men in their own communities. N. has been reproached by some black critics for her refusal to redefine African Americans in a way that would modify past and current racist attitudes; instead, N. tells it like it is. In *The Women of Brewster Place,* many of the women have been abandoned by the men who have fathered their children. If N. typifies a black man, like Luther Nedeed in *Linden Hills* (1985) as "coal black" but desiring light-skinned women, she does it because of her commitment to veracity however contentious. In *Mama Day* and *Bailey's Cafe,* the evil that has been brought upon the women has also emanated from their black community, family, or lovers. Her readers are therefore able to bring into question the binary implications of oppression that exist: the larger social subjugation of her characters has resulted and continues to result from sources outside, but this oppression also issues from inside. In this way, N. secures self-determination for her characters, regardless of the white domination that frames them.

Take, for example, the young Mattie Michael from *The Women of Brewster Place,* who as a young girl is passionately entranced with the seductive Butch, a man her father has warned her to stay away from. After she becomes pregnant and is thrown out of her home, she decides to raise the child on her own. With no money and no protection, particularly as a black woman, Mattie eventually finds herself in a run-down ghetto called Brewster Place and through a will and perseverance that is larger than life sacrifices herself for the good of her son. Her matriarchal love and duty does not secure the results intended and her son ironically becomes a spoiled man who abandons her; however, Mattie becomes the central figure around which all the other women of Brewster Place derive strength and solitude.

In *Linden Hills,* it is ultimately Willa's struggle for identity that emerges as she is literally annihilated by her rich and powerful husband, Luther, who comes from a long patriarchal line of wife abusers, and represents in this allegorical tale of Dante's *Inferno,* a Satanic figure. In this black upper-middle-class community, the Nedeeds reside at the bottom of a V-shaped township, in which a lower position of land designates greater wealth as well as moral decrepitude. It was said that Luther's double great-grandfather had "sold his octoroon wife and six children," in order to purchase the land. All the Nedeeds want light-skinned sons, and after Luther, ironically, takes Willa, a dark-skinned woman, as his wife, she gives birth to a boy who fulfills Luther's ambitions, but in a generational repetition of torture, Luther eventually imprisons his wife and child in the basement of their home. Willa in her last moments becomes an avenging force after reading the lost narratives of the other abused wives, found in the recipe books and Bible hidden in the basement.

Mama Day's dramatic conflict unfolds on a coastal island, between South Carolina and Georgia. In 1823, the island was given to the newly freed slaves of the white slave owner, Bascombe Wade, who willed it to them after marrying the slave Sapphira with whom he had seven sons. Sapphira's life takes on lengendary proportions both in her conjuring arts and her lingering presence as the mother. The culture of this locale is rooted to the land, to black culture, and to Africa, and these roots bring it outside of white culture and Christianity. The great powers of healing sorcery come into conflict with evil hoodoo and become the forces around which a young woman, Cocoa, originally from this island, finds herself embroiled. Ultimately, N. is concerned with the deeper, mythical powers of women, which are explored in *Mama Day,* and that, George, Cocoa's husband, who comes from an urban environment up North, does not understand. Cocoa herself has been disconnected from her matriarchal line and is nearly destroyed by her ignorance of the forces around her.

All the women in *Bailey's Cafe* have survived childhood neglect and abuse in this most penetrating of N.'s works. Their burden is to go on living, torn between the desperate need to forget and the critical need to remember. And remembering is N.'s process for taking us back and bearing witness to the beginnings of a life before it has been dismembered. N. addresses the consequences for continuing to ignore and/or excuse black men's abusive behavior against women and children on the basis of their powerlessness in the face of racism as she makes clear that in the cycle of abuse it is it is not just men who are responsible. What is most conspicuous in this work is the profound absence of the mother, particularly when compared with N.'s other novels. This motherless condition leads to the trope of the power of women—to give birth, to nurture and to love—being negated in a community that sexualizes her as object and disempowers her through silence.

Eve, who runs the boarding house that cares for these abandoned women, was herself told by her godfather, the preacher, that she had no parents and was "found in a patch of ragweed." He emphasizes his point by insisting that she has no birthday, and deepens her loss of identity through his thorough control of her and in her enforced alienation from the community. Suspended in a world that is absent of all love, Eve turns toward the earth as a conviction of her existence: "The earth showed me what my body was for. Sometimes I'd break my fingernails from clawing them into the dirt or bite my arm from crying out."

Sadie heroically survives a childhood in an urban environment of wretched poverty, with an alcoholic mother who constantly reminds her that she is "The One the Coat Hanger Missed." Sadie's mother has her uterine scraped out when she is twelve, so she can prostitute without fear of pregnancy. Yet somehow this most sorrowful and real of all of N.'s characters, desperately continues to dream of a reciprocity between mother and daughter that will never exist. The negative self-image created in the child is also explored in the stories of Esther and the beautiful Mary, both of whom were oppressed and sexualized by men. As the victims who ingest the perpetrators, these young girls begin to loathe themselves, and in so doing, experience disassociation. Esther is sold by her brother into the home of a plantation owner, whose sadistic sexual abuse, leads her to view herself through distanced eyes. The archetype of the "Shadow" becomes the imaginary onlooker of her repeated rape, a paradoxical figure, who is first a possible savior and later implicated in the perverse satisfaction of the violence. Mary, also called Peaches, is so beautiful as a young girl that her father consumes her life, making her the object, both physically and emotionally, of all his male friends. She cannot escape the gaze of men and so tortured by her experience, she can no longer look in the mirror except to see a "whore" who was "always asking for it, asking for it."

Every N. story confronts the pathos of existence, particularly the tension between a present state that has been determined by a history of oppression and violence and a present potential of personal growth, solace, even redemption. N.'s people are real, touchable, and tragically elegant; their triumph is their tragedy, as they cling on, tenuously, to whatever remains of their lives and from this point try to build anew. Perhaps it is N.'s decision to seek for truth rather than resolution that makes her women so genuine: as Eve in *Bailey's Cafe* remarks, "I don't spend a lot of time with the right or wrong, good or bad of what I am—I am."

BIBLIOGRAPHY: Lynch, M. F., "The Wall and the Mirror in the Promised Land: The City in the Novels of G. N.," in Hukutani, Y., and R. Butler, eds., *The City in African-American Literature* (1995): 181–95; Perry, D., *Backtalk: Women Writers Speak Out* (1993); Rowell, G. H., "An Interview with G. N.," *Callaloo* 20 (Winter 1997): 179–92

LISA TOLHURST

NEAL, John

b. 25 August 1793, Falmouth (now Portland), Maine; d. 20 June 1876, Portland, Maine

N., a Quaker, should be but seldom is regarded as among the most significant American writers between the Revolution and 1850. Editor, poet, dramatist, and defender of "radical" causes including female suffrage, N. succeeded best as critic and romancer. His most impressive critical achievement was a series of articles on American literature and culture written for *Blackwood's* in 1824 and 1825. His six finest romances appeared between 1822 and 1828, five within three years, three within twelve months: *Logan* (1822), *Seventy-Six* (2 vols., 1823), *Randolph* (2 vols., 1823), *Errata; or, the Works of Will Adams* (2 vols., 1823), *Brother Jonathan* (3 vols., 1825), and *Rachel Dyer* (1828). Thereafter, N. wrote less and wrote less well. He turned to editing newspapers, proselytizing for causes, and practicing law.

In his critical essays for *Blackwood's* and elsewhere, N. patriotically defends American culture. His pronouncements about individual authors are always opinionated, usually idiosyncratic, frequently contradictory, and occasionally absurd. He has little use for either Washington IRVING or James Fenimore COOPER but praises Charles Brockden BROWN, with whose works N.'s should be compared. Later, N. became the first American writer to praise Edgar Allan POE in print; Poe's insistence on the primacy of "effect" in literature owes much to N.'s critical views. In theory

and practice, N. espouses a national literature more affective, psychological, and subjective than that found in works by his contemporaries including Cooper, William Gilmore SIMMS, and James Kirke PAULDING.

Four of N.'s six fictions published between 1822 and 1828 might be called historical romances. N. mined the major American subjects of the form. *Logan* is a frontier romance written before Cooper's *The Pioneers. Seventy-Six* and *Brother Jonathan* follow the first romance of the Revolutionary War, Cooper's *The Spy,* by two and three years respectively. *Rachel Dyer* details the moral and social travesty of the Salem witch trials, anticipating Nathaniel HAWTHORNE's historical allegories of the early generations of Puritan New Englanders. But none of these romances is written in the manner of Cooper; N. uses chaotic historical periods to explore abnormal psychology rather than social evolution. Though N.'s historical fictions are prolix, undisciplined, and self-indulgent—*Rachel Dyre* less than the others—all contain passages of memorable power.

As thinker and man N. is represented most clearly in his nonhistorical fictions, the epistolary novel *Randolph* and the autobiographical novel *Errata,* and in his actual autobiography, *Wandering Recollections of a Somewhat Busy Life* (1869). Whether speaking as Randolph, Will Adams, or himself, N. displays extraordinary powers of mind allied to extraordinary lapses of common sense; often he can laugh at these lapses; often he misses them entirely. Hawthorne referred to N. as a "wild fellow." Yet Hawthorne, like Poe, was influenced by N. and admired his genius, while deploring his excesses.

BIBLIOGRAPHY: Lease, B., *That Wild Fellow J. N. and the American Literary Revolution* (1972); Sears, D.A., *J. N.* (1978)

JOHN ENGELL

NEAL, Joseph C[lay]

b. 3 February 1807, Greenland, New Hampshire; d. 17 July 1847, Philadelphia, Pennsylvania

N. was a prominent Philadelphia journalist and popular urban humorist; since his death, however, his work has endured obscurity until its rediscovery by scholars in recent years. Brought up in Philadelphia in a bookish home, N. worked in Pottstown, Pennsylvania, during boom times in the coal region; after two years, in 1831, he returned to Philadelphia and became editor of the *Philadelphia Pennsylvanian,* a weekly newspaper that became a daily. He began publishing his humorous sketches here, and also in Charles Alexander's *Gentle-*

man's *Vade Mecum; or, The Sporting and Dramatic Companion* when he became assistant editor of this newspaper in July 1835. He continued publishing his sketches, entitled "City Worthies," in the successor to the *Gentlemen's Vade Mecum,* Louis A. Godey's *Philadelphia Saturday News and Literary Gazette* (July 2, 1836-January 5,1839), a weekly that he co-edited with Morton McMichael. Edgar Allan POE quoted in the July 1836 *Southern Literary Messenger* the positive comments regarding the June number that appeared in the first issue of the *Saturday News.* In fact, McMichael had published Poe's early poetry in the Philadelphia *Saturday Courier,* and the *Saturday News* would continue to offer Poe considerable praise for both his criticism and his fiction. Additionally, N. commented favorably on "The Fall of the House of Usher" and *Tales of the Grotesque and Arabesque* in the *Pennsylvanian.*

Even as he served as editor and critic, N. continued to write his satirical sketches. The great popularity of these sketches led to the publication of a collection, *Charcoal Sketches* (1838). This book went through many editions and was included, unattributed, as volume 2 of *The Pic Nic Papers* (1841), supposedly edited by Charles Dickens. (Dickens denied knowledge of N.'s work's inclusion.) N. soon published a short second collection, *In Town and About* (1843). Writing additional pieces for the *United States Magazine and Democratic Review, Godey's Lady's Book,* and *Graham's Magazine,* N. then published his third book, *Peter Ploddy, and Other Oddities* (1844). He left the *Pennsylvanian* in 1844 and began *N.'s Saturday Gazette and Ladies Literary Museum,* a weekly. When N. died in 1847, his wife continued *N.'s Saturday Gazette,* and soon thereafter Burgess, Stringer published *Charcoal Sketches, Second Series* (1848). Forty-six of his sketches were later published as *N.'s Charcoal Sketches: Three Books Complete in One* (1865). N.'s work is gently satirical; he mildly and amusingly mocked the poseurs and losers of city life. A great strength of his elegant treatment of the inelegant was its close attention to details of speech and scene. Despite its virtues, N.'s work was satirized by Poe in "Peter Pendulum, the Business Man," and criticized by him as repetitive; N. himself Poe considered "unquestionably *small potatoes.*" Poe lauded only N.'s editing and political writing. While Poe's negative views may have been warranted, N.'s sketches still merit interest as an important part of the developing tradition of urban Northeast literary humor, as recent scholarly writing has demonstrated. Perhaps, too, a few of these sketches may be considered important for their relationship to canonical works outside of that tradition—for example, N.'s most renowned sketch, "Peter Brush, the Great Used Up,"

features language and detail in its opening that seems to anticipate language and detail in the opening of Herman MELVILLE's *Moby-Dick.*

BIBLIOGRAPHY: McMichael, M., "J. C. N.," *Graham's Magazine* 25 (February 1844): 49–52; Sloane, D. E. E., "J. C. N.," in Trachtenberg, S., ed., *DLB,* vol 11, part 2, *American Humorists, 1800–1950* (1982): 344–49

RICHARD KOPLEY

NEIHARDT, John G[reenleaf; later changed to Gneisenau]

b. 8 January 1881, Sharpsburg, Illinois; d. 3 November 1973, Columbia, Missouri

N. is now best known for *Black Elk Speaks* (1932), the book in which he presents the life story of a Holy Man of the Oglala Sioux. That book has been embraced in recent decades by readers ranging from Jungian psychologists to the American Indian movement of the 1970s to scholars of world religions. N., however, was much more than Black Elk's amanuensis. He was a man of letters who wrote in many forms, including the most ambitious, always seeking to fuse two worlds: that of high literature and that of the American West. He worked to earn every part of the title bestowed on him by the legislature of Nebraska: Poet Laureate of Nebraska and the Plains.

N. grew up on the Nebraska plains but acquired a classical education. He wrote in many forms, including history, memoir, literary criticism, and prose fiction. He sought to win a reputation, however, primarily as a lyric and narrative poet. While his poems were ambitious and won some critical praise—Harriet MONROE, the editor of *Poetry,* once put his work on the same level as Ezra POUND's—he was working against the current of his time. While his contemporaries were breaking free of traditional forms, he was embracing them, often even using a vocabulary tinged with poetic archaisms. While they celebrated the imagistic and the fragmentary, he wrote narrative verse. And while the tendency of his time was toward disillusionment, his poems were idealistic. N.'s originality was in his subject: the WEST.

Tennyson's *Idylls of the King* was one of N.'s early influences, and in *A Cycle of the West,* completed in 1949, he tried to make the same poetic use of the "matter of the prairies" that earlier poets had of the Arthurian legends. Like Tennyson's *Idylls,* the poems in N.'s *Cycle* were written and published over decades and can be read independently. Cast in the form of heavily enjambed heroic couplets, the five "Songs" begin with the first expeditions of trappers into the plains and conclude with the end of Indian resistance after the massacre at Wounded Knee. The first three tell the stories of Europeans: "The Song of Three Friends" (1919) and "The Song of Hugh Glass" (1915) are, respectively, tales of jealousy and reconciliation, with the larger movement of history only in the background, while "The Song of Jed Smith" (1941) describes a man who sees Providence at work in the blazing of the overland trail to California. The two concluding songs, "The Song of the Indian Wars" (1925) and "The Song of the Messiah" (1935), tell, from the Sioux perspective, the story of final struggles of the Plains Indians with the invading Europeans. N. traveled and researched the songs carefully and produced several prose works in the process, including *The River and I* (1910), an account of his travels in the plains, and *The Splendid Wayfaring* (1920), a life of Jedediah Smith.

Black Elks Speaks: Being the Life Story of a Holy Man of the Oglala Sioux resulted from N.'s research for *The Song of the Messiah* (1935). N. wanted to tell the story of the Messiah—or "Ghost Dance"—movement, and he went to the Pine Ridge Reservation in South Dakota to speak with one of its participants. In Black Elk, he found someone who could not only tell him about the Messiah movement, but also could recount the pivotal events in the history of Plains—the defeat of Custer at the Little Bighorn and the massacre at Wounded Knee—from the Native American perspective. N. interviewed Black Elk and others at Pine Ridge again in 1944 and cast their narratives as a novel, *When the Tree Flowered: An Authentic Tale of the Old Sioux World* (1951).

N. taught at several colleges, including the University of Missouri, and lectured widely. He won a devoted audience, especially in the Plains states, and remained an active man of letters into his nineties. Although his poems are now not much read, *Black Elk Speaks* ensures that his work will continue to hold an important place in American literature.

BIBLIOGRAPHY: Aly, L. F., *J. G. N.: A Critical Biography* (1977); Blair, W., *J. G. N.* (1976); House, J. T., *J. G. N.: Man and Poet* (1920)

BRIAN ABEL RAGEN

NEMEROV, Howard

b. 1 March 1920, New York City; d. 5 July 1991, St. Louis, Missouri

The surfaces of N.'s poems are generally casual, colloquial, often overtly witty, and it is possible to overlook the fact that the poems are usually written in tight, traditionally formed constructions. To a degree seldom equaled by any of his contemporaries, N. was capable of anchoring his cosmic abstractions by linking them with unusually appropriate images based in reality. That the reader is not startled by these figures of speech is owing to the deceptive plainness of his diction and syntax. Thus, he might equate the loneliness of being with an electrical noise, as in "The Dial Tone," and thereby make palpable and familiar the essential pathos of the human condition.

N. was the author of many books of various kinds, fiction and criticism as well as poetry. Although he was understood by most of the literary world to be primarily a poet, he was almost as well known as a critic. His first book of any kind was the collection of poems entitled *The Image and the Law* (1947). This was followed by *Guide to the Ruins* (1950), *The Salt Garden* (1955), *Mirrors and Windows* (1958), *New and Selected Poems* (1960), *The Next Room of the Dream* (1962), *The Blue Swallows* (1967), *The Winter Lightning: Selected Poems* (1968), and *Gnomes and Occasions* (1972). *The Collected Poems* (1977) was followed by *Inside the Onion* (1984) and *War Stories: Poems about Long Ago and Now* (1987) and *Trying Conclusions: New and Selected Poems, 1961–1991* (1991).

His play *Endor* appeared in 1962, and he published the novels *The Melodramatists, Federigo; or, The Power of Love,* and *The Homecoming Game* in 1949, 1954, and 1957 respectively. Short story collections were *A Commodity of Dreams* (1959) and *Stories, Fables, and Other Diversions* (1971). Nonfiction titles included *Poetry and Fiction: Essays* (1963), the very well-received *Journal of the Fictive Life* (1965), *Reflexions on Poetry and Poetics* (1972), *Figures of Thought: Speculations on the Meaning of Poetry and Other Essays* (1978), *New and Selected Essays* (1985), and *The Oak in the Acorn* (1987).

In none of his contemporaries were the elements of craft and reflection, sensation, sound, wit, and sense more completely integrated in a poetry of balance. That this equilibrium expresses the ambivalence and ambiguity of modern man's position in the natural and intellectual worlds rather than affirmations or denials of faith is not a criticism, but a compliment. N.'s quiet poems reconnected the self with the world in which it found itself held hostage to time, to fate, and to the universal consciousness. "The May Day Dancing" is an example. In this poem, a Maypole ritual brings forth the various school classes, beginning with kindergartners, dressed in costumes of various periods and traditions. All generations are but one generation repeated forever. At last, the ritual expands to mythic proportions and becomes a representation of the universal life process as each child dances.

It is tempting to call N. a religious poet, but to do so might be to frighten off the wary reader. Nevertheless, his concerns were, indeed, "religious," or at least metaphysical. If he was an agnostic, his agnosticism was of the kind typified by the "Creation Myth on a Moebius Strip": a narrow length of paper is given a single twist before its two ends are brought together—it has become a paradox, a single-sided object in a three-dimensional world. In this case, N. took an actually physical thing and put an idea to it that is exactly equivalent to the thought he wanted to express. There can be no clearer example of a metaphor, of an anchored abstraction.

Few poets can take a common situation and add to it incrementally as N. did in "The May Day Dancing" until, suddenly, the reader is spinning around the sun, or listening in to the power of eternity, as in "The Dial Tone," or facing the fact of our self-delusion without illusion, as in "The Goose Fish," in which two young people, after making love, discover the grinning skeleton of a fish lying on the beach and attempt to make a totem of it in order to give their act some sort of meaning beyond the sexual act itself. N. was a poet of large thought and, at the same time, of the physical, not merely the metaphysical world. No one has made the existential condition more intelligible.

BIBLIOGRAPHY: Labrie, R., *H. N.* (1980); Meinke, P., *H. N.* (1968); Mills, W., *The Stillness in Moving Things: The World of H. N.* (1975)

LEWIS PUTNAM TURCO

NEWELL, Robert Henry

b. 13 December 1836, New York City; d. July 1901, Brooklyn, New York

Given the notoriety of N. at the end of the 20th c., it is difficult to think that at the height of his career in the 1860s and 1870s he was one of America's most popular and best-known humorists and political satirists. N. owes obscurity, in part, to his having written the majority of his work under the pseudonym, Orpheus C. Kerr, but it is also owing to the shifting tastes of the American public after the Civil War. N.'s best work, the collections of war-time correspondences—released in three volumes as *The Orpheus C. Kerr Papers* (1862–66) and continued under the titles *Avery Glibun* (1867) and *Smoked Glass* (1868)—dealt with the North's actions during the war and early Reconstruction. But as the nation began to turn its attention elsewhere, the public became increasingly disinterested in the hard-hitting and satiric accounts of military and political life N. had written.

Nevertheless, in *The Orpheus C. Kerr Papers* there remains a brilliant comedic voice and satiric vision. Not only was N. a remarkably gifted mimic of the best writers of his day, his humor is a fine example of 19th-c. American wit which some scholars have argued is only surpassed by Mark TWAIN.

N. was born into a well-off New York, but when his father died in 1854 the family fell into financial straits. N.'s education was cut short, and he was forced to choose a profession. He went into journalism and by 1858 had risen with astounding speed to the position of editor at the *Sunday Mercury,* a leading New York City newspaper.

With the outbreak of the Civil War, N. quickly focused his attention on the North's political and military affairs and created his mouthpiece, Orpheus C. Kerr. Kerr was originally intended to lampoon those who were using the war as a means for their own personal political advancement. But what was initially a *Sunday Mercury* series became wildly poplar and went into syndication. Abraham LINCOLN was himself an avid reader of Kerr's work and, according to Carl SANDBURG, said that "anyone who has not read [*The Orpheus C. Kerr Papers*] is a heathen." N. had Kerr enlist as a member of the Mackerel Brigade of the Army of the Accomac, and from this position he assesses the war and its personalities with devastating irony. His own brigade itself wins renown for its "remarkable retrograde advances," and it is only a disguised George B. McClelland who commands it. N.'s treatment of the South is unfailingly harsh, but as the war progresses even his treatment of the North becomes caustic.

The mock-epic battles for possession of chicken coops and broken fences that mark the early *Kerr Papers* disappear as N.'s real concern over the war increased and the distance between author and subject matter diminished. In the later *Papers,* the satire becomes keener and more biting and the humor increasingly acerbic and black. Through Kerr, N. eventually took on the larger moral questions of slavery and civilian obligation to the army, and he remorselessly attacked political and military leaders who demonstrated anything less than the firmest intention to win the war. By the end of the Civil War, N.'s view of the whole affair had become solidly moralistic: the war was fought to free slaves and make them citizens of the U.S. It is not difficult to see how such a position could detract the humor of his writing.

N.'s literary career produced a remarkable collection of writings. In his last few, N. failed to achieve the success with the novel that he clearly hoped for. There remain, however, his early works, often dazzlingly funny in themselves, and which consistently offer a remarkably rarefied lens through which to view—especially Northern—American perspectives on the social and political issues faced in the years during and immediately after the Civil War.

BIBLIOGRAPHY: Butler, M., "R. H. N.," in Trachtenberg, S., ed., *DLB,* vol. 11, part 2, *American Humorists, 1800–1950* (1982): 350–63; Fienberg, L., "Colonel Noland of the *Spirit:* The Voices of a Gentleman in Southwest Humor," *AL* 53 (May 1981): 232–45

JOHN V. GLASS

NEW ENGLAND

It has became a commonplace to speak of the "Puritan origins" of American culture; even those who refer to the concept only to interrogate it thereby acknowledge its importance. The two Puritan settlements of the 17th c., at Plymouth in 1620 and at Boston in 1629, may therefore claim a more than antiquarian interest. We expect to discern in them at least a foreshadowing of defining qualities of the American experience and character.

John WINTHROP's sermon delivered on the *Arbella* prior to the landing at Boston has established itself as one of our cultural reference points, especially in its comparison of the envisioned settlement to a city set upon a hill, standing as an example to the world. From a later perspective, we discover in Winthrop's text themes that will recur throughout our cultural history. We see, before all, the sense, not merely of an arrival after an arduous journey, but of a step in a divinely ordained mission. America was to be no mere event in a historical chain. We hear also the note of exceptionalism. America, having been singled out by Providence for its destiny, need not fall victim to the forces that have destroyed the many secular civilizations of the old world. There is also an affirmation of newness. For all their theology of predestination, implying that all that is important has already been settled, the Puritans felt strongly that their arrival in the new world constituted the beginning of something unprecedented in human history.

That something was the realization in history of an ideal. The establishment of a society in fulfillment at last of divine justice was the sublime promise in these events. The tension between the ideal and the actual would of course work itself out in the years to come. That tension provides the organizing theme of William BRADFORD's *Of Plymouth Plantation.* In the plain style that would become the norm of Puritan prose, Bradford recounts the failure of the real colony to live up to the ideal. The failure must have been more poignantly felt since the promise had seemed so firmly grounded in the will of God.

Literature in the narrower sense was not a priority of the Puritans, but in the course of the 17th c. the Massachusetts Bay Colony gave us our first considerable American poets in Anne BRADSTREET and Edward TAYLOR. In style, the two poets are very different, but both reflect the Puritan practice, theologically justified, of seeking in the commonplace and in the natural environment evidences of God's presence and design. Their works still speak to us today. The same cannot be so confidently affirmed of Michael WIGGLESWORTH, but his *The Day of Doom* must be acknowledged as inspired doggerel, and, unlike Bradstreet and Taylor, Wigglesworth was widely read by his contemporaries. His apocalyptic vision, of divine wrath unleashed, complements what might be called the optimistic millennialism articulated by Bradford and Winthrop. Both belong to the worldview of the 17th-c. Puritan settler.

Perhaps the greatest intellectual and, in the broad sense, literary figure the American Puritans produced emerged, not in the Puritan dominance of the 17th c., but in the Puritan decline of the eighteenth. Jonathan EDWARDS was an eloquent champion of Puritan orthodoxy, but his eloquence was called forth by what proved to be the terminal weakening of the Puritan order. Edwards's great contemporary Benjamin FRANKLIN, primarily associated with Pennsylvania, but born and raised in New England, spoke in accents confident with the promise of the future.

Franklin's was the voice of Enlightenment, the most powerful ideological force driving the American Revolution. Instead of Puritan theocracy, he spoke for republican ideals. Against Puritan religious orthodoxy, he embraced deism, acknowledging a creator whose concern for his creation ended in the perfection of the creative act. In place of original sin, Franklin and his fellow deists affirmed the natural goodness of human beings, capable to be sure of "errata" (Franklin's word), but not the inveterate sinners of Puritan belief.

Franklin left New England at the age of seventeen, but the spirit of Enlightenment was certainly felt there in the founding years of the Republic. In the matter of religion, by way of illustration, of the sixteen Congregational—by tradition, Puritan—churches established in Boston before the Revolution, fourteen had by 1815 adopted Unitarian principles. King's Chapel in Boston, an Episcopal church, had declared itself Unitarian in 1785.

Unitarianism amounted to a reform of PURITANISM in the spirit of Enlightenment. While still considering themselves residually Christian, the Unitarians rejected as opaque to reason the mystery of the trinity, and hence the divinity of Jesus as second person of the trinity. Indeed, all that orthodox Christianity, and by no means only in the Puritan version, had offered in the way of mystery and miracle was jettisoned. Unitarianism offered itself as a Protestantism for reasonable men and women.

But by the end of the first quarter of the 19th c., it became clear, at least to a substantial number of the younger members of the Unitarian Church, that a Protestantism for the reasonable might not satisfy the full range of human spiritual needs. These young radicals saw Unitarianism evolving into one more orthodoxy or complacency. If Unitarianism itself represents a reform of Puritanism in the spirit of Enlightenment, Unitarianism was about to experience its own reformation, this time in the light of the ROMANTICISM beginning to make itself felt on the American continent. In this reform movement can be found the seeds of the TRANSCENDENTALISM that, like the Puritan impulse, has proven a constant in American culture.

It might have been predicted that American romanticism would be a romanticism with a difference, especially as that romanticism took root in the Puritan soil of New England. Ralph Waldo EMERSON, the indispensable figure in the New England renaissance and, indeed, in American literature, was the descendant of Puritan clergymen. He was himself a clergyman in the Unitarian Church, until his dissatisfaction with what he regarded as the empty ritual still tolerated in that institution drove him from the pulpit. The transcendentalism with which he became associated was both a liberation from, and a continuation of, elements of the older tradition.

Why, Emerson asked, must we look for revelation only in the records and observations of our ancestors? Can there not be a revelation original to ourselves? Any Puritan could have given Emerson the orthodox, resoundingly negative answer to that one. But for Emerson, our individual, immediate experience of nature could provide us with authentic revelation. In the minute examination of nature, he believed, we ultimately intuit the unifying vital principle, the soul of nature itself, which we might as well call God. We can also find our way to God through psychic reconnaissance, exuberant introspection, for God is what is deepest within the self. "Know thyself" and "Study nature," Emerson says, are the same precept. The God Emerson proclaims is scarcely the God of the Puritans. The Emersonian God is a God of possibilities, not of limitations. Yet the process of finding this God parallels both the Puritans' effort to read aright the book of nature and their journeys to the spiritual interior in search of assurances that they were among the elect.

It is because God is what is deepest in the self that we may commit ourselves, as Emerson urges, to the severe rule of self-reliance. In "The American Scholar," Emerson celebrates the impending cultural independence of the new world from the old; the address remains a key document in the evolution of a national literature, an evolution to which New Englanders like Royall TYLER—author of *The Contrast,* the first significant work of American drama—and the Connecticut Wits of Tyler's generation had already contributed. Yet even in that oration, and more explicitly in the essay "Self-Reliance," Emerson enunciated a still more radical notion of independence. If, as he insists, to be a man is to be a nonconformist, then the individual self must declare its independence, even from America. But the rejection of conformity, though necessary, is not sufficient; we must also reject consistency. That is, we must not permit ourselves to be bound today by what we thought, said, or did yesterday. We must be at every moment willing to enact our independence from the selves we have been, risking the spiritual isolation this involves. For Emerson, the risk is exhilarating; for others, it could be terrifying. How much of American literature since has explored that risk, that exhilaration, and that terror? More broadly, with how many themes of our literature—some, as we have seen, in clear continuity with the concerns of the Puritans, others in tension with that same tradition—has Emerson provided us?

The pivotal role played by Emerson in forming our literary culture becomes clear when we but list the names of 19th-c. writers of stature who wrote some of their most characteristic and significant works in response or relation, however complex or ambivalent, to Emerson and Emersonian transcendentalism. The names of fellow transcendentalists such as Henry David THOREAU and Margaret FULLER come first to mind, but other New Englanders like Nathaniel HAWTHORNE and Emily DICKINSON must be included, as must the New Yorkers Herman MELVILLE and Walt WHITMAN. Indeed, as we approach the millennium, Emerson remains a felt presence in our culture, turning up sometimes where scarcely expected. *Invisible Man* is a major work of AFRICAN AMERICAN LITERATURE, but it is also possible to regard Ralph ELLISON's masterwork as the finest transcendentalist novel America has yet produced.

Emerson represents what we regard as most vital in the New England literary culture of his time, but we should not forget that New England in the 19th c. also gave us that more domesticated sort of romanticism we associate with the "Schoolroom Poets," also known as the "Fireside Poets" and as the "Household Poets," all titles that suggest to us, somewhat unfairly to be sure, the most deadening kind of respectability. Still, if William Cullen BRYANT, Henry Wadsworth LONGFELLOW, John Greenleaf WHITTIER, Oliver Wendell HOLMES, and James Russell LOWELL no longer speak to us immediately, we should remember at least two things about them. One is that they came close to defining for the American reader of their time what a poem can and ought to be. Another is that they wrote a few fine poems.

Both the transcendentalists and the Schoolroom Poets represent varieties of romantic idealism, but in the years following the Civil War, while a certain sort of romance survived, the more urgent demand was for realism. New England no longer held the dominant position, in both economic and cultural terms, it had enjoyed earlier in the century, but the *Atlantic Monthly,* published in New England, remained the most important American literary magazine. Lowell had been the first editor of the *Atlantic.* At the helm from 1871 to 1881 was William Dean HOWELLS, one of the prime movers of literary realism in the U.S. Howells, an Ohioan by birth, opened the pages of the magazine to many of the most important writers of the day, reaching—as the names Mark TWAIN and Henry JAMES will suggest—well beyond the boundaries of New England to strengthen the relevance to an expanding nation of a New England institution. A novelist of a high order, Howells set some of his best fiction, including *A Modern Instance* and *The Rise of Silas Lapham,* in a New England he had come to know intimately. That this bright young man from Ohio was drawn to New England, living in the region from soon after the end of the Civil War to 1889, suggests the magnetic attraction New England could still exert. On the other hand, Howells's departure for New York in 1889, Boston having become in his view a "death-in-life," tells us in which direction the cultural wind was blowing.

The wind of economic prosperity, at any rate, was not blowing in the direction of northern New England. The state of Maine, once a major shipping center, was in the grip of an economic decline that can be traced back as far as the Embargo Act of 1807. Yet it produced, as the century drew to a close, two of the most gifted representatives of the literary regionalism that had grown up in close association with realism. Like other regionalists Sarah Orne JEWETT and Mary E. Wilkins FREEMAN sought to capture the qualities of life as it was lived in a particular place, and to find hints of the universal in the particular, even as individual regional identities were, it seemed, being swallowed up in a rush to nationhood energized by the Civil War's vindication of Union and by the relentless development of the railroad. The New England tang of Jewett and Freeman is unmistakable and bracing, although both are sensitive as well to the more melancholy implications of their chosen material. A feature of their work that speaks directly to the contemporary reader is their common focus on the situation of women. They are often read today, in fact, less as regionalists than as contributors to the development of a feminist consciousness in our literature.

New England as a separate cultural entity has less meaning in the 20th c. than in earlier periods. Its fundamental importance is that of any region: that it produces a certain number of writers we value. Yet some works and writers of the 20th c. "speak New Englandly" in a way that deserves our attention. Henry ADAMS's *The Education of Henry Adams* was completed in 1906 and circulated privately beginning in 1907; it was published to the general reader in 1918, after the death of the author. Adams was directly descended from two Presidents of the U.S., and the *Education* traces both the formation of a New England consciousness in one of such formidable antecedents, and the growing awareness on his part of the irrelevance of that consciousness to the world coming into being. Like all great books *The Education of Henry Adams* is many things. One of them is an elegy for the New England that has been the subject of these remarks.

Three important poets of the 20th c. retain a strong New England identity. Edwin Arlington ROBINSON, who began to write toward the end of the 19th c., based Tilbury Town, the fictional setting of his most enduring poems, on his home town, Gardner, Maine. He introduces into these poems much of the force of his generation's realism, otherwise associated primarily with prose fiction. Yet the pathos of his poems is intensified by lingering traces of Emersonian idealism. Robert FROST made north of Boston a significant destination in our literary imagination. He acknowledged Emerson, especially in his more subversive aspect, as a literary father, but the Emersonian coexists in Frost with the Puritan, the tension between the two lending the Frostian pastoral no small portion of its strength. Robert LOWELL, of the same family as James Russell Lowell, drew powerfully on the New England past in such early poems as "Mister Edwards and the Spider" and "After the Surprising Conversions," both in *Lord Weary's Castle,* and, even as he moved to the more confessional mode of his later work, never abandoned his fascination with the New England culture that had shaped him.

In a sense, regions, even though often convenient, are ultimately fictions. Yet, if we relate New England to that larger fiction we call literature, its significance must be acknowledged. At least two crucial moments in the development of our literary culture are New England moments: the founding moment of the Puritans and the revolutionary moment of the transcendentalists. Both of these, we have suggested, made central and permanent contributions to our literary culture. The Puritan millennialism, their faith that the good society is at hand, continues to find an echo in the American soul. And what to make of the diminished thing that is the actual continues to be an American question; a lingering faith in the ideal gives it the specifically American accent. The radical individualism given its noblest and most generous expression by Emerson and the transcendentalists remains a blessing and curse of American culture. The so-called culture wars of the late 20th c. involved the continuing struggle to sort out blessing and curse. Familiar thematic motifs of American literature, including its tendency to turn inward and its often symbolic reading of the natural world, can be related to concerns of the New England past, including both Puritan and transcendentalist. One may also discern in the middle style of our literature the offspring of Puritan plainness and transcendentalist organicism. New England retains a vital place in our literary life; or, if one prefers, in our literary myth—which, after all, amounts to pretty much the same thing.

BIBLIOGRAPHY: Buell, L, *New England Literary Culture* (1986); Bercovitch, S., *The Puritan Origins of the American Self* (1975) Brooks, V. W., *The Flowering of New England, 1815–1865* (1936); Delbanco, A., *The Puritan Ordeal* (1989); Donovan, J., *New England Local Color* (1988); Matthiessen, F. O., *American Renaissance* (1941); Miller, P., *The New England Mind; The Seventeenth Century* (1939); Tyler, M. C., *A History of American Literature during the Colonial Period* (1897); Westbrook, P. D., *A Literary History of New England* (1988)

W. P. KENNEY

NICHOLS, John [Treadwell]

b. 23 July 1940, Berkeley, California

Although N. has worked as both a screenwriter and a journalist, his reputation rests primarily on two comic novels: *The Sterile Cuckoo* (1965), which four years later appeared as a popular movie starring Liza Minnelli, and *The Milagro Beanfield War* (1974), which was also adapted for film and produced by Robert Redford.

The two novels are hardly anything alike, however. *The Sterile Cuckoo* is quite clearly the enthusiastic work of a young man. N. was just twenty-five when he published this first novel, and he wrote from the limited experiences of having been an indifferent student at a private college, and afterward, of knocking around Europe for a year. But he was able, nonetheless, to produce a charming, and ultimately, bittersweet story of lost romance.

The very aptly titled *Sterile Cuckoo* follows the madcap adventures of the co-ed Pookie Adams as she leads her boyfriend, Jerry Payne, toward their lovers' suicide pact. Yet theirs is but an extreme of youthful

insouciance, not anything darkly sociopathic, as some critics believe is her case. Pookie has her problems, to be sure. But she is not a danger to herself, nor to her much-put-upon Jerry, who after all must gather what remains of his wits and narrate their story.

The Milagro Beanfield War is the work of a more mature comedian, one capable of looking beyond himself for his material. N. drew, instead, on the antiestablishment attitudes that he found in Taos, New Mexico, the home he adopted after he had gotten tired of New York. There, in the Southwest, N. encountered a rich Chicano lore, and with it he made his humor answer to a much greater necessity than the campus capers he had played with in his first novel.

Set in the fictional mountain town of Milagro, the so-called bean war gets under way when Joe Mondragon cuts a ditch bank and turns the irrigation water back on his family's ancestral farm. The story offers this action as a kind of updated Boston Tea Party, with Chicanos cast as the ones in righteous revolt from bourgeois America. In place of the grandiose condos, ski resorts, and golf courses of the fat and blind *Americanos,* the Chicanos follow what they believe to be the culturally sane course of returning to a subsistence-level agriculture. They will be romantically free of ties to the outside.

In the Southwest, N. found a subject he really cared for, but rather than producing more fiction, he wrote a series of expository books on New Mexico. Most of these, he expertly enhanced with his own photography: *If Mountains Die: A New Mexico Memoir* (1979); *The Last Beautiful Days of Autumn* (1982); *On the Mesa* (1986); *A Fragile Beauty: N.'s Milagro Country* (1987); *The Sky's the Limit: A Defense of the Earth* (1990); and *Keep it Simple: A Defense of the Earth* (1992).

Apart from these celebrations of the Southwest, N. has also released a hard-hitting novel about Vietnam, *American Blood* (1987). This was the successful culmination of many frustrating attempts to complete the novel he had actually started while the war was still raging.

Finally, there are two more romantic novels whose plot lines and resolutions seem to have returned N. to his creative point of origin with *The Sterile Cuckoo: An Elegy for September* (1992) and *Conjugal Bliss* (1994). They are quite a bit alike in that both rely on wry humor to spell out the utter impossibility of lasting relationships.

BIBLIOGRAPHY: Myers, T., "Dispatches from Ghost Country: The Vietnam Veteran in Recent American Fiction," *Genre* 21 (Winter 1988): 409–28; Thompson, P., "J. N.," in Balassi, W., and J. F. Crawford, eds.,

This Is about Vision: Interviews with Southwestern Writers (1990): 119–27; Wild, P., *J. N.* (1986)

J. RUSSELL BURROWS

NIEDECKER, Lorine [Faith]

b. 12 May 1903, Fort Atkinson, Wisconsin; d. 31 December 1970, Fort Atkinson

N. worked for more than forty years in relative isolation, writing poems that distill the experiences of a modest life spent outside the social and literary mainstream. She lived most of her life on Blackhawk Island, near Fort Atkinson, Wisconsin. Her poetry is inseparably tied to this locale, where she owned a small cabin and worked at various jobs, including one as a stenographer and proofreader and another as a cleaning woman in a local hospital.

N. writes of the changing seasons, the actualities of hard work and poverty, the coming of floods, and the presence of trees, flowers, birds, and fish. While her work is often informed by wide reading and careful thinking, it is always grounded in the physical world. She admired such naturalists as John James Audubon and John Muir for their powers of observation and their recording of the world's diversity. N. celebrates that diversity—but with no sense of romantic transcendence. Her observations are tethered firmly to the actual; she looks *at*—not through or beyond—nature, and she finds in earth and water a counterweight to the human desire for dominance.

While N.'s subjects are decidedly ordinary, her style is not. Her small poems, some as brief as twenty words, are sometimes elliptical and fragmentary. In describing her own work, she says, "I learned / to sit at desk / and condense." Her sparse, lightly punctuated poems highlight single words or phrases, moving quickly down the page. She uses white space to suggest emptiness or silence, and her short lines often include oddly juxtaposed images, word play, and wry humor.

While her poetry is sometime reminiscent of Emily DICKINSON's, N.'s strongest affinities are with the American objectivists, especially Louis ZUKOFSKY, whose 1931 objectivist issue of *Poetry* magazine profoundly shaped her development. She and Zukofsky corresponded for forty years, their letters serving as a kind of literary workshop for the two poets. In Zukofsky and other objectivists, N. found confirmation of her own preference for careful, precise observation and her sense of the poem as a made "object." She also corresponded with William Carlos WILLIAMS, and, during the 1960s, with Cid Corman, who published her poems in his magazine *Origin*. Her friendships with these and a small circle of other poets saved N. from literary isolation, giving her an outlet for discussing her work.

Like many experimental poets, N. published in small literary journals, her first book, *New Goose,* not appearing until 1946. This collection and a second one, *My Friend Tree* (1961), show her skill at observation as well as her capacity to write poems in which historical figures (Audubon, Chief Black Hawk) and ordinary people (a sharecropper) serve as subjects, sometimes speaking in their own voices. *North Central* (1968), generally regarded as N.'s best collection, shows her moving in new directions. Her earlier spare objectivity gives way to a greater willingness to assert herself as a presence in her work, intent on suggesting the world's wholeness as well as its particularity. This development is best seen in her poetic sequence "Lake Superior" and in the relatively long poem "Wintergreen Ridge." Near the end of her life, N. published two more collections: *T & G: The Collected Poems (1936–1966)* (1969) and *My Life by Water: Collected Poems, 1936–1968* (1970). A final volume, *Blue Chicory* (1976), appeared posthumously. The standard edition of N.'s work is *From This Condensary: The Complete Writings of L. N.* (1985).

While she lacked a wide audience in her lifetime, N. is now regarded as an important poet in her own right and as a significant figure in the objectivist movement. Her careful observations of nature, her eye for local detail, and her experimental use of language make her a unique, if quiet, voice in modern American poetry.

BIBLIOGRAPHY: Dent, P., ed., *The Full Note: L. N.* (1983); Faranda, L. P., ed., *Between Your House and Mine: The Letters of L. N. to Cid Corman, 1960–1970* (1986); Williams, J., *Epitaphs for L.* (1973)

MICHAEL HENNESSY

NIN, Anaïs

b. 21 February 1903, Paris, France; d. 14 January 1977, Los Angeles, California

N. is known today primarily as a diarist—a view that has led to a focus on her life at the expense of her fiction. Still, her fiction and diaries can be productively read in conjunction with each other as part of a larger project aiming at the presentation of a certain kind of sensibility to the world.

Critical opinion has always been divided over N.'s work. Her harsher critics have found her writing obscure and self-indulgent, while her supporters praise its experimental qualities and emotional sensitivity. Her detractors may be in the majority, perhaps because her fiction lies outside of the more prevalent realistic tradition. This is compounded by her preoccupation with the details of self-reflection and subjective response. Some feminist readers also find that N.'s ideas of womanhood repeat sexist assumptions about the "natural logic" of men and the "natural emotion" of women. Her supporters rightly point out that many of the topics N. wrote of in her fiction and diaries—hetero- and homosexual experimentation, incest, and adultery—were radical for their time, and her novelistic structures and style were likewise experimental. They also justly praise her finely tuned emotional sensitivity, her sensuality, and her ability to record the nuances of affect.

N.'s early fiction, collected in *House of Incest* (1936), is surrealistic, but quickly becomes more expressionistic in style. The distinction may seem a fine one, but it reflects a movement toward trying to describe subjective states rather than to provide archetypal images of them. Her collection of short stories, *Under a Glass Bell* (1944), exemplifies this newer style, and also evinces her tendency to write in terms of vignettes rather than sustained narrative productions.

Her "continuous novel" and major work of fiction, *Cities of the Interior,* was published in its final form in 1974 and comprised five novels that were published separately between 1946 and 1961: *Ladders to Fire* (1946), *Children of the Albatross* (1947), *The Four-Chambered Heart* (1950), *A Spy in the House of Love* (1955), and *Seduction of the Minotaur* (1961). The five novels do not form a coherent narrative sequence—the unity is provided by the three main female characters: Lillian, a pianist, Djuna, a dancer, and Sabina, an actress. The books explore the paths the women follow through a web of emotional attachments and detachments, sexual experiments, personal and societal pressures, and the difficulties they encounter, particularly with male partners, in so doing.

Her last novel, *Collages* (1964), is a series of vignettes largely centered around the figure of Renate, a painter. The tone of this work is considerably lighter and the effect more scattered than in her previous works. Appearing posthumously, her two collections of erotica, *Death of Venus* (1977) and *Little Birds* (1979), are often cited as creating a new possibility for erotic writing, one that escapes male voyeurism and objectification in favor of a sensual subjectification of the genre.

The low current interest in her fiction is surprising, given that her techniques—fluid characters and lack of narrative structure—mesh well with postmodern considerations of the decentered subject and the breakdown of metanarratives. Perhaps because of her diaries—and her resulting reputation as the high priestess of subjectivity—her fiction has been overlooked on this point.

The Diary of A. N. began appearing in 1966 and quickly outpaced her fiction in both popular and critical attention. The volumes led her appropriation by the burgeoning feminist movement and a popular series of lecture tours. N. started keeping a diary in 1914, just after her parents separated—it was originally addressed as a letter to her father. N.'s problematic, and ultimately incestuous, relationship with her father informed much of her writing. The diary grew to include 150 manuscript volumes: over 15,000 typescript pages. The initial set of seven volumes was edited by Gunther Stuhlman and spanned the years between 1931 and 1974. *The Early Diaries of A. N., 1914–1920* appeared posthumously in 1978, and was followed by two more volumes that filled in the intervening years to 1931. N.'s diaries are considered by many to be her major literary achievement, a place where she is free to explore the inner world without the displacements necessitated by fiction. In them, N. reveals herself to be an acute observer of her own thoughts and feelings, a gifted recorder of subjectivity.

The more explicit sections, however, were largely excised. These have recently begun to be published, as *"A Journal of Love": The Unexpurgated Diaries of A. N.* The first three volumes, *Henry and June* (1987), *Incest* (1992), and *Fire* (1995), fill in the years between 1931 and 1937. They record frankly her affairs with June and Henry MILLER, her analysts René Allendy and Otto Rank, and her father, Joaquin Nin y Castellanos. The critical response to their publication has been sharply divided between those who find them too honest or dishonest, too intimate, or too sexist, and those who praise them precisely for their honesty, intimacy, and exploration of a particular woman's sensibility including evasions and deceits. Ultimately, these diaries should prove valuable for the latter reasons—one does not go to diaries for their objectivity, and it is precisely as a writer of the complex workings of subjectivity that N. deserves to be remembered.

BIBLIOGRAPHY: Bair, D., *A. N.: A Biography* (1995); Fitch, N. R., *A.: The Erotic Life of A. N.* (1993); Franklin, B. V., *A. N., A Bibliography* (1974); Jason, P. K., *The Critical Response to A. N.* (1996)

ROBERT C. SPIRKO

NORDHOFF, Charles [Bernard]

b. 1 February 1887, London, England; d. 11 April 1947, Santa Barbara, California

N. will be forever associated with the novel *Mutiny on the Bounty* (1932) and its coauthor, James Norman Hall. The project was the first of the *Bounty Trilogy* and one of twelve published works upon which the two collaborated. Although the team would continue to write novels set in the South Seas for thirteen years after the publication of *Mutiny on the Bounty,* their commercial success and critical acclaim steadily diminished thereafter.

Mutiny on the Bounty was warmly received by contemporary critics and readers alike; the novel and its successive film adaptations have placed the name "Captain Bligh" as a synonym for tyrant in the American lexicon. Critics were impressed by the novel's storytelling and the historical accuracy of its setting, and quickly recognized it as both contributing to and floating above the rising tide of Hollywood's South Seas fad.

N. and Hall had written as a team on three projects when Hall brought the story to N.'s attention in 1929. At that time, both men were living in the South Pacific. The two World War I veterans had moved their families to Tahiti where they found their greatest inspiration: the story of the *Bounty* was popular island lore. While other writers of the Lost Generation were wrestling with the philosophical questions of their day and changing forever the style and function of writing, N. sought solace in the remoteness of these Pacific islands and the resurrection of events buried in history. Rather than make a modernist break from the past, either in style or theme, both N. and Hall delved into it to fictionalize the story of the *H. M. S. Bounty.*

Hall recognized early that the *Bounty* saga broke naturally into a trilogy: the first novel would focus on the dualism captured in the power struggle of Bligh and Christian, while the second, *Men against Sea* (1934), and the third, *Pitcairn's Island* (1934), would explore the stories of each man after the split. By the time the writing team began the first novel, divisions of labor between the two had been successfully addressed: both men passed the manuscripts back to one another, editing each other's words until the writing was essentially that of a single hand. *Mutiny on the Bounty* is perhaps least recognized for its most significant contribution to literature: it stands as an example of one the most successful collaborations on a novel, an art form which remains the dominion of the individual.

But if the early collaboration was successful, N.'s later efforts with Hall indicated the difficulties such a project can face. In *Mutiny on the Bounty,* the team was aided by a strong historical record, recorded by several perspectives. The trail deteriorated somewhat in *Men against Sea,* in that it relied mainly upon the actual defensive testimony of Bligh. But authorial choices multiplied when the two approached *Pitcairn's Island;* no official record existed here, only contradictory rumors, and N.'s artistic inclinations ran counter to Hall's. N. sought a romantic tale of the

passion he found in the islands while Hall was motivated by their serene beauty. Rather than finding inspiration in this tension, their product suffered. Even the most enthusiastic supporters of *Mutiny on the Bounty* recognize the shortcomings of the two later works.

It is lesser known that N. wrote four novels before collaborating with Hall on the *Bounty Trilogy.* In these early works, N.'s voice is distinctly different from that of his Tahitian days. One such novel is *Pícaro* (1921), set in California, where N. was living at the time. Here N. tells a version of the Cain and Abel story with distinctly modernist overtones, leading the reader to wonder what might have been, had the author not sought refuge in Tahiti from the emerging modernity.

BIBLIOGRAPHY: Briand, P. L., *In Search of Paradise: The N.-Hall Story* (1966); Weeks, E., "C. N. and James Norman Hall," *In Friendly Candor* (1946): 65–83

ROBERT E. CUMMINGS

NORMAN, Marsha
b. 21 September 1947, Louisville, Kentucky

As a dramatist, success came early to N.—too early some critics would argue. Her reputation rests squarely on *'night, Mother* (1983), the blockbuster play that garnered her a place at the table of American drama and for which she won the Pulitzer Prize. Her earlier play, *Getting Out* (1979), was also a critical success which merited her the American Theater Critics Association Prize, as well as the John Gassner New Playwrights Medallion and George Oppenheimer-Newsday Award. Although, she has continued to write, no work, with the exception of her adaptation of Frances Hodgson BURNETT's, *The Secret Garden,* for which N. won a Tony Award in 1991, has received the critical acclaim she enjoyed with these two earlier examples of her work.

N.'s writing career began in high school, where she won first prize in a local literary contest for her essay, "Why Do Good Men Suffer?" She later went on to earn an M.A. from the University of Louisville and subsequently took a job at the Kentucky Central State Hospital teaching disturbed adolescents. That experience ultimately became the gist of *Getting Out,* the story of a disturbed young woman, Arlene Holsclaw, who splits herself into two selves rather than deal with the abuse suffered both as a child in a dysfunctional family and later at the hands of various "scum-bum" boyfriends. After *Getting Out,* N. went on to write *Third and Oak: The Laundromat* (perf. 1978, pub. 1980), *Circus Valentine* (perf. 1979), and *The Holdup* (perf. 1983, pub. 1988), all of which received lackluster, and in some cases, down-right scathing reviews.

After moving to New York in the summer of 1981 to write the book and lyrics to *Orphan Train,* she was fired and found herself at loose ends. Angry and disillusioned with the American theater, she consciously decided to write a play which no one might ever see, a play where she would make all the decisions of what to say and when to say it. The result was *'night, Mother,* a play that presents the painful existence of Jessie Cates, a woman who has decided to commit suicide, to "get off the bus," as her character says, and who spends the entire time explaining this decision to her mother, Thelma. The play was an enormous success, and N., once again, found favor in the critics' eyes. Accolades included such compliments as "an authentic playwright," "one who followed the path of Chekhov," "the genuine article," "a playwright following in the tradition of Eugene O'NEILL." Such effusive praise dwindled considerably in the critics' responses to her later works.

N.'s central themes emphasize a character's search for her/his psychic self. Often these searches involve a mother/daughter relationship beginning with Arlene Holsclaw's abusive mother in *Getting Out,* whose neglect initiates the path of pain she experiences in subsequent failed relationships with the men in her life, or Jessie Cate's mother, Thelma, in *'night, Mother,* who finally realizes that Jessie cannot find any food that she likes to appease her psychic hunger and, difficult as it is, does accept her suicide decision. Even in *Third and Oak: The Laundromat,* Alberta serves as a surrogate mother to Deedee, a woman from a much different background but who even shares the same last name. Through their brief encounter Deedee receives validation and empowerment she has not received from her own mother. In *Traveler in the Dark* (perf. 1984, pub. 1988), which features a male protagonist, Sam, the character attempts, to deal with the grief and guilt surrounding his relationship with his dead mother.

Other motifs in later works such as *Sarah and Abraham* (perf. 1992), *Loving Daniel Boone* (perf. 1992), *The Secret Garden,* and *Trudy Blue* (perf. 1995) include a decided mythic approach. In *Sarah and Abraham,* N. retells the myth of the Bible and shifts the story's power to Sarah as a strong matriarch, instead of the traditional patriarchal view. *Loving Daniel Boone* reflects N.'s reformation of the oral tradition of the folktale. Her adaptation of *The Secret Garden* depicts a departure from the Burnett version of the book. Instead of centering around the neglected children, N.'s version focuses the plot on a man exorcising the ghost of his dead wife. *Trudy Blue* does not take place in "real time," but leaps back and forth in time and

presents imaginary characters and situations, often concurrently.

Always, N.'s characters strive to find their voices, to tell their stories to whomever will listen. They hunger for someone to acknowledge their existence. They become survivors—even heroes. They are what Anne Pitoniak terms "doing the best they can with what they have." In the process, they become visible. They exist. Their struggles have meaning. That existential angst of the internal landscape is shared with an audience. Even though some critics contend that N. is "not enough of a feminist," she continues to write plays which depict characters, usually women, trying to find a more cohesive self regardless of the consequences.

BIBLIOGRAPHY: Brown, L. G., ed., *M. N.: A Casebook* (1996); Kintz, L., *The Subject's Tragedy: Political Poetics, Feminist Theory, and Drama* (1992)

LINDA GINTER BROWN

NORRIS, Frank [Benjamin Franklin Norris, Jr.]

b. 5 March 1870, Chicago, Illinois; d. 25 October 1902, San Francisco, California

N.'s fiction, especially *McTeague* (1899) and *The Octopus* (1901), have been identified as primary examples of naturalistic writing in which certain economic, environmental, and biological forces determine an individual's actions and fate. This rather pessimistic philosophy reflected 19th-c. scientific thought, especially the biological determination of Charles Darwin and the economic determinism of Karl Marx: both found in the novels of Zola and Flaubert. N.'s eye for the realistic, less attractive details of life, his penchant for the epic, and his sympathy for the common man have prompted critics to classify him, along with his contemporaries Stephen CRANE and Jack LONDON, as writers who moved literature from the realm of the romantic hero into the world of the natural man.

One early critic called *McTeague* a "study in stinks," while another reviewer stated that such "grossness for the sake of grossness is unpardonable." At worse, critics such as Lars Ahnebrink and Charles Walcutt caused N. to be seen as the "Son of Zola." At best, the identification of N. as a naturalistic writer has enabled his texts to be discussed within the cultural context of his time when science, technology, and other factors influenced the less moralistic and Victorian values and more detached attitudes of a new generation of authors and readers.

One standard evaluation or perhaps apology for N. cites his tragically short life as the reason for his rather substantial, but uneven literary corpus. This approach frequently prompts comparison with Crane, another author of both several memorable and several mediocre works, who lived hard and died young. Critics of the 1930s, including Granville Hicks and John Chamberlain, have labeled him as a "muckraker," a populist who protested the monopolistic acts of the Southern Pacific Railroad against the ranchers in *The Octopus.* Both the apologetic and populist approaches carry merit, but not at the exclusion of other critical approaches which evaluate thematic and stylistic concerns of equal importance. Today, critics discuss N.'s use of humor, narrative technique, and even his artistic sensibility.

N.'s early years did not foretell his later career. His parents, who would eventually divorce, clashed in their aspirations for N. His mother preferred an artistic career, while his father, a self-made success, favored business training. His family's move from Chicago to San Francisco in 1884 and his education in France, at the University of California at Berkeley, and Harvard constitute key biographical events which propelled his foray into fiction. N.'s stay at Julien Atelier's studio in Paris, where he studied printing, stimulated an interest in romantic medievalism that inspired *Yvernelle* (1891), an epic poem set in medieval France with courtly knights and adoring ladies, and a good dash of romantic moralism.

Contemporary readers praised the book's design and illustration; others noted its similarities to the metrical patterns of Sir Walter Raleigh's verse romances. Today, most critics merely note the difference between its immature, imitative weaknesses and the originality and strength of *McTeague,* which N. was writing as a senior at Berkeley.

Four years of study at Berkeley did not result in a degree, but did stimulate significant interest in college football, the novels of Zola, and the theories of evolution espoused by Professor Joseph Le Conte, who attempted to reconcile the science of evolution with the ideals of religion. After N. entered Harvard in 1894, his writing flourished while he was enrolled in an English course under the direction of Professor Lewis Gates. A stint at the San Francisco paper, the *Wave,* enabled him to complete the *McTeague* manuscript and publish his first novel, *Moran of the Lady Letty* (1898), a story of love and adventure between Ross Wilbur and the daughter of a ship's captain. Wilbur, a socialite, gets shanghaied aboard a pirate ship where he meets Moran: another victim of the greedy Captain Kitchell. Eventually, Wilbur adopts to the hardy regimen aboard ship and conquers the amazon-like Moran through a show of physical force and dominance. She surrenders to his love, but their promising future is cut short when a Chinese coolie murders Moran when stealing some ambergris.

The concept of adopting to a hostile environment and the strong-willed young heroine would be utilized in later fiction. The violent physical struggle between Wilbur and Moran constitutes the focus for most discussions of this novel today and parallels a scene in N.'s better-known novel, *McTeague,* which served as a sponge of ideas or a time capsule of what ideas interested N. at this time: Lambroso's cultural anthropological theories of criminal atavism; Le Conte's scientific theses on evolution and dualism; and the Gilded Age of urban progress and materialism.

McTeague, a massive man, practices dentistry in a small office on Polk Street in San Francisco and clings to his pet canary as a memory of his former life as a miner. He meets and marries one of his patients, Trina Sieppe. The apparent good fortune of a lottery prize, however, reveals character flaws of penuriousness and greed in his wife. When stripped of his dentistry practice, McTeague cannot adapt to the modern world of changing life; he beats and eventually murders his wife. Poor boy does not make good in N.'s story. In fact, McTeague's full upward mobility has been achieved at the beginning of the novel. The remainder plots his economic and moral descent, ending appropriately enough with death in Death Valley. Sections of overwritten prose and melodramatic situations involving characters such as Zerkow and Maria and Old Grannis and Miss Baker must be overlooked to appreciate N.'s criticism of the quest for material success as a significant flaw of the Gilded Age.

Blix (1899), which followed the publication of *McTeague,* recounts how Travis Bessimir, known as "Blix," leaves her decadent San Francisco society to pursue a career. She joins reporter Condy Rivers in a series of adventures which culminate in love and his salvation from gambling. Happiness is assured when Condy receives a job from a New York magazine publisher and can join Blix who will attend medical school in New York.

Sometimes called N.'s third (after *Moran* and *Blix*) "Valkyrie fable," *A Man's Woman* (1900) includes a third strong-willed, independent female character: Lloyd Searight, a registered nurse who meets an arctic explorer named Ward Bennett. Eventually, she too capitulates to the mastery of her male companion and underwrites the cost of Bennett's quest to reach the North Pole.

Moran, Blix, and Lloyd all provide promising case studies of women who rebel against society's conventions in pursuit of their personal goals. Eventually, they sacrifice or at least mold their personal goals into those of the men they love. However, too many improbable situations and occurrences weaken these novels that explore the relationship between the sexes and seem to provide the opportunity for interesting feminist scholarships.

The epic quality of N.'s work is best represented in *The Octopus.* Consistent with Homer's epic poems and with classic Western fiction, this frontier drama takes place during the last days of the West in California. The railroad (the octopus of the title) has crossed the country and the freedom of the frontier with its farming and ranching communities is lost forever: a message delivered in the dramatic opening scene when a herd of sheep are slaughtered by a high speed train.

Several critics have labeled *The Octopus* as a populist tract or a muckraking novel aimed at the Southern Pacific railroad: a companion piece to Upton SIN-CLAIR's *The Jungle* and its attack upon the meat-packing industry. However, N.'s novel more clearly parallels John STEINBECK's *The Grapes of Wrath,* which indeed condemns the banking industry, but does not elevate its protagonists onto the pedestal of romantic idealism. Shelgrim, the railroad administrator, Genslinger, the newspaper editor, and Lyman Derrick, the betrayer, all carry heavy-handed traits of commercialism and progress. but the members of the farmers' "protective league," including Magnus Derrick, Annixter, and others, utilize bribes and other similar tactics to influence the state administration. Even Presley, with his revolutionary poem "The Toilers," does not succeed in leading a proletariat revolution.

The ironic and perhaps just death of S. Behrman, buried in an avalanche of wheat, and the successful quest of the aesthetic Vanamee, illustrate N.'s belief that forces larger than men can, in some cases, provide justice or at least a positive outcome. N.'s melodramatic excesses do exist—Minna Hooven's fall into prostitution and the starvation of Mrs. Hooven while guests dine in the lavish quarters of the Gerard mansion. However, N.'s attempt to portray the story of the American West and the forces which shaped the frontier ring true.

The Pit (1903) constitutes the second of a trilogy N. referred to as "Epic of the Wheat." *The Octopus* would describe the producer (California). *The Pit* would describe the distributor (Chicago). *The Wolf* would describe the consumer (Europe), but was never written. In *The Pit,* Curtis Jadwin, a successful businessman, becomes possessed with the concept of controlling the Chicago wheat market. As his obsession strengthens, his wife Laura has an affair with an artist, Sheldon Corthell. Jadwin nearly succeeds in his quest, but unusually favorable weather and the resulting larger than normal crop cannot be cornered and the wheat, as both an economic and biological force, dominates a man's egotistical and materialistic goals. The deterministic forces of nature and man's helplessness to change them are apparent when Jadwin realizes that the wheat has "cornered" him into bankruptcy. Once again, N. creates a strong-willed woman in Laura Dearborn Jadwin, who must learn how to share in a meaningful relationship with her husband. One critic, Warren French, identifies Jadwin's attempt to corner the wheat market as mere "backdrop" for Laura's education process, which he identifies as the central focus in N.'s novel.

The posthumously published collected essays, *The Responsibilities of the Novelist* (1903), provide a source of the novelist's basic, although occasionally fuzzy, literary beliefs. The novelist must tell the "truth" and avoid "falsehoods," states N., although these terms and processes are never carefully described. success, financial gain, and popularity must be sacrificed for the even greater reward of achieving the "truth." "Man," not "men," should be studied to discover the influence of social, biological and other forces which influence "man."

Posthumously published, *Vandover and the Brute* (1914) may have been written before *McTeague* when N. was at Harvard. Certainly, the plot and the themes indicate many similarities. The son of a wealthy owner of San Francisco slum properties, Vandover aspires to a life as a painter, but lacks the discipline to realize his ambition. One day he seduces Ida Wade, a young woman who commits suicide in guilt for the act. Vandover's father dies suddenly, shocked by his son's actions and their results. Unable to cope with his financial independence, Vandover squanders part of his inheritance on gambling and loses the other portion to his treacherous friend, Charlie Geary.

This financial and moral fall, so similar to McTeague's, is dramatized in his physical degeneration into a syphilitic beast complete with attacks of lycanthropy: walking the floor on all fours and howling like a wolf. N.'s deterministic message almost overwhelms the moralism of the novel. Those who cannot adapt to adversity and change will fail: Ida, Mr. Vandover, Vandover, and even his one loyal friend, Dolly Haight, all die. The malevolent Geary gains financially from their failures and receives no just punishment, in a disturbing thrust of realism.

BIBLIOGRAPHY: Crisler, J. S., and J. R. McElreath, *F. N.* (1974); Dillingham, W. B., *F. N.* (1969); French, W., *F. N.* (1962); Graham, D., *Critical Essays on F. N.* (1980); Graham, D., *The Fiction of F. N.* (1978); McElreath, J. R., and K. Knight, *F. N.: The Critical Reception* (1981); Pizer, D., ed., *The Literary Criticism of F. N.* (1964); Pizer, D., *The Novels of F. N.* (1973); Walker, F. D., ed., *The Letters of F. N.* (1956)

GREGORY S. SOJKA

NOVEL, The

The American novel, in all its variety, does not reflect American life so much as it refracts it, concentrating the diffuse light of daily existence into the concentrated radiance of art. Rather than simply mirror what surrounds them, American writers present what they see as though the light rays have been deflected through their own eyes. That angle of refraction often gives the writing a quality of vision, dream, even nightmare. From the beginning, the American novel reveals a sense of personal displacement, though one that is presented more as a fact of life in the New World than as a misfortune. To a large extent, this idea of displacement still characterizes American fiction today.

The English settlers who came to 17th-c. America left behind one concept of identity and, upon arriving, put another in its place. In the London they left, the household of a typical tradesman might consist of a dozen or more persons: father, mother, children, journeymen, apprentices, servants. This basic social unit was no more secure than any that succeeded it, yet the insecurity of the individual members was different from that of their successors. Each adult and child was rooted in a locale and in a family pattern that had changed little, if at all, from what it had been before and what it would be in the next generation, and thus each person knew his or her fixed place both within and outside of the household.

Economic and social upheaval in the Old World changed forever the essentially feudal lot of the tradesman and his family, of course, but while this traditional pattern is still an important part of the English national memory, in America, it never existed at all. America may be the land of the free, but democracy exacts a price for the freedom it confers. New systems of politics, economics, science, technology: these intoxicating changes also left the individual reeling under the effect of forces that seemed beyond his or her control. It is little wonder that the first American novels deal with displacement, misfortune, and even terror.

The June 1798 issue of the Philadelphia *Weekly Magazine* contained a "Recipe for a Modern Romance" that poked fun at the Gothic fiction tradition while, like all satires, it reminded readers of the importance of the object of its comic intentions. Perfected in England by such writers as Horace Walpole and Mrs. Ann Radcliffe, the Gothic tale, macabre, fantastic, and supernatural, was set customarily in graveyards, ruins, and wild landscapes. Indeed, the *Weekly Magazine* invited would-be Gothic writers to take a haunted castle, partially destroy it, people it with aged servants, and send there a young lady who, after seeing skeletons, ghosts, and other apparitions, will be rescued by a handsome lover, whom she will then marry.

Except for the tidy conclusion, the essential ingredients of this "recipe," refined and embellished, are used again and again in major American novels, from Charles Brockden BROWN's *Wieland* to Henry JAMES's *The Turn of the Screw*. Even in the all-male worlds of Edgar Allan POE's *Narrative of Arthur Gordon Pym of Nantucket* and Herman MELVILLE's *Moby-Dick*, phantoms, ghosts, and creatures from the underworld spring from below decks and appear on the masts of the huge creaking ships that, in American fiction, replace the European castles with their dungeons and towers.

The political founders of America, men like Thomas JEFFERSON, Benjamin FRANKLIN, Alexander Hamilton, and John and Samuel Adams, were followers of John Locke and other Enlightenment figures and thought humankind capable of tolerance, democracy, and reason. They were right, of course, if only partially so. The Gothic mindset accounts for everything the Enlightenment overlooks: terror, perversity, strangeness, a sense of not knowing where one is or how one got there. It is a way of viewing the world that continues to affect American fiction and that appears in works by such 20th-c. authors as William FAULKNER, Flannery O'CONNOR, Ralph ELLISON, Truman CAPOTE, Thomas BERGER, and Joyce Carol OATES.

A second strong current in the growing tide of early American literary thinking is the picaresque. The picaro, as seen in novels by writers like Daniel Defoe and Tobias Smollett, is a person of low birth, no particular occupation, and flexible morals. Typically a young man of dubious or unknown parentage, the picaro is pitchforked into the world at an early age and must make his way however he can. His story is a broadly appealing one, since most readers have to do things they dislike, even though they retain an essentially positive self-image, and since most expect to be knocked about and yet prosper in the end.

Hence, despite considerable controversy, the enduring popularity of the premier American picaro, Mark TWAIN's Huckleberry Finn, as well as such kindred as Melville's seafaring narrators and the protagonists of novels as varied as Stephen CRANE's *The Red Badge of Courage*, J. D. SALINGER's *The Catcher in the Rye*, and Russell BANKS's *Rule of the Bone*.

In many novels, early and late, both Gothic and picaresque elements figure, connoting the extremes of enclosure and mobility that often seem the only choices for protagonists whose home lives are haunted yet whose prospects on the open road are menaced by the unknown. Like Gothicism, the picaresque is a European import, and though both influences immediately take on American characteristics, together they show the enduring power of cultural artifacts. Leaving behind one's social and economic life is one thing, but the products of one's culture are not so easily abandoned.

In the uncertain world of the young nation, American authors often favored the romance, with its greater tolerance for authorial fancy, over the more literal novel. Gothic and picaresque elements abound, and characters are sustained by their own self-questioning, believing, often rightly, that the self will find no home in such a world. The English poet Stephen Spender observed once that whereas English writers are self-actualizers, heirs to modes of vision so venerable as to seem impersonal and absolute, American writers are self-creators who always seem to be rubbing their eyes in disbelief and uncertainty. For this reason, perhaps, characters in 19th-c. American fiction often appear to lack confidence in what they should do and be.

In English fiction of this period, works often conclude with marriage, an act which legitimizes sexual relationships, affirms selfhood, and expresses a faith in a future peopled by the children that will result. In American fiction, by contrast, marriage is either out of the question or doomed, as if to say that a future is not possible. Leslie A. FIEDLER points out how many classic American authors depict pairs of male characters, one light-skinned and one dark, who elude women, marriage, and community by fleeing into the wilderness together. Early examples include James Fenimore COOPER's Natty Bumppo and Chingachgook, Melville's Ishmael and Queequeg, and Mark Twain's Huck and Jim, pairings that foreshadow the characterization in such later novels as Ken KESEY's *One Flew Over the Cuckoo's Nest* and Capote's *In Cold Blood.*

When communities do form, often they are foredoomed. Nathaniel HAWTHORNE's *Blithedale Romance* is the chronicle of a utopian community that splinters into a mockery of the ideals it hoped to attain. Where there is closure in fiction of this period, it is often outside of the story proper, as at the end of *The Scarlet Letter,* when the elf-child Pearl is exorcised of New World ghosts only after she flees to Europe. Similarly, the black family that suffers so in Harriet Beecher STOWE's *Uncle Tom's Cabin* must go to Africa to find peace.

This is not to say that these works are pessimistic or cynical about the individual's prospects in America. Rather, they recognize the ambivalent standing of the individual in an unformed culture and, on occasion, even acknowledge opportunities for progress. For example, Hester Prynne may not learn from her scarlet letter the lesson that the Puritans intend, yet Hawthorne goes to great length to describe how, in her isolation from the community, she develops powers of specula-

tion that permit her to predict that, "at some brighter period, when the world should have grown ripe for it . . . a new truth would be revealed, in order to establish the whole relation between man and woman on a surer ground of mutual happiness." There is no progress without violence, and many antebellum works seem bent on clearing away the vestiges of destructive European thinking that have survived the Atlantic crossing.

In the aftermath of the Civil War, the novel, with its emphasis on realism and believability, replaces the romance as the dominant form for long fiction. This was a time of territorial expansion, of new resources, of new inventions, and new industries. This is arguably the most energetic period in the life of the American novel, with book after book reflecting the burgeoning on every front of American life. Before the Civil War, novelists had no reason to suspect the power of human forces yet to come; after World War I, novelists either railed against the monsters of technology and capitalism or gave in to them. In his novelistic autobiography *The Education of Henry Adams,* Henry ADAMS describes himself as lying on the floor before a dynamo at the Great Exposition of 1900, "his historical neck broken by the irruption of forces totally new." Even as refined an artist as Henry James is described by Ezra POUND as having a style that was like a huge engine capable of heaving the novelist out of himself, out of his personal limitations.

The literary REALISM that appeared in this period is best understood in the plural sense, with there being a variety of schools. Mark Twain represents the high point of what frontier realism, with its folksy humor and local color. His two Hannibal novels as well as works such as *Roughing It* show his realism to be the homely variety, a depiction of life at its most bumptious and uncouth. By contrast, James is a pioneer in the field of psychological realism. His groundbreaking novel *The Portrait of a Lady,* with its use of the "center of consciousness" technique, puts the reader within the protagonist's mind in order to ponder that character's thoughts about the action rather than the action itself. William Dean HOWELLS was another type of American realist, one who adapted English realism for an American audience. Such works of his as *A Hazard of New Fortune* is an American story shot through with social concerns and observations on human nature of the kind associated with Dickens, Thackeray, and Trollope. The more refined realism of James and Howells is extended by Edith WHARTON in such novels as *The Age of Innocence,* in which characters who flout convention do so at their peril.

Like the earlier romances, few of the great realist novels end confidently, either, further evidence of the continuing sense of ambivalence felt by American characters as they alternate between stasis and flight.

No novel illustrates this dilemma better than Mark Twain's *Adventures of Huckleberry Finn,* where there seems no choice for the characters except the stifling confinement of "civilization" or the footloose life of the western wanderer. Other works of the period do actually posit faith in the idea of a sustaining common culture, including Sarah Orne JEWETT's local color novel *The Country of the Pointed Firs.* Ironically, this same affirmative possibility, after much turmoil and pain, often marks the conclusion of the slave narrative, such as Harriet JACOBS's *Incidents in the Life of a Slave Girl,* a form echoed in such 20th-c. works as Charles JOHNSON's *Oxherding Tale* and Toni MORRISON's *Beloved.*

As faith in political and religious institutions were eroded by a rising belief in science and such doctrines as Herbert Spencer's Social Darwinism, literature responded with a narrowing of realism, with its promise of objectivity, into a more doctrinaire naturalism. NATURALISM views the individual as confused, helpless, and victimized by social and economic factors beyond his control and understanding. Naturalistic novels include such works as Crane's *Maggie: A Girl of the Streets,* Frank NORRIS's *McTeague,* and Theodore DREISER's *Sister Carrie.*

The naturalistic trend continues in the 20th c., though often in synthesis with the symbolism that shaped the poetry of the day: Ernest HEMINGWAY's *The Sun Also Rises* is the tale of an ineffectual Lost Generation, but Jake Barnes's emasculation is every bit as representative of the decline of the West as is the impotence of the Fisher King in T. S. ELIOT's *The Waste Land.* The essential American ingredients of uncertainty and dislocation that are embodied in the Gothic and picaresque traditions continue to be seen in such novels as Faulkner's *The Sound and the Fury* and *Light in August,* works haunted by psychological rather than supernatural terrors, and F. Scott FITZGERALD's *The Great Gatsby* and *Tender Is the Night,* with their rootless, amoral characters.

Yet if early American life is viewed tragically by novelists of the day, later life is more commonly seen as absurd by contemporary writers. This shift in mode is occasioned by a shift in the individual's view of himself in relation to the larger world. It would have been tragic, in the 18th or 19th c., to be struck by lightning, which might have seemed an act of God to survivors saddened yet comforted in their certainty that life has a divine purpose, however mysterious. By contrast, in more recent times it would be absurd rather than tragic to be killed by a terrorist's blast, because this would be a preventable act perpetrated by one human on another, and for no overarching reason.

Thus, in works as different as Melville's *Benito Cereno,* Hawthorne's *The Marble Faun,* James's *Daisy Miller,* Mark Twain's *A Connecticut Yankee in King Arthur's Court,* and Kate CHOPIN's *The Awakening,* individuals struggle against larger forces that overwhelm and eventually destroy them, as in classical tragedy. Yet in Faulkner's *Sanctuary,* Djuna BARNES's *Nightwood,* John BARTH's *Giles Goat-Boy,* Thomas PYNCHON's *The Crying of Lot 49,* and Saul BELLOW's *The Dean's December,* individuals challenge an indifferent or malevolent world and, when they prove unable to alter it, often do little more than shrug, acknowledge the absurdity of the situation, and go on with their lives.

Now that America has, with other developed nations, largely left the Industrial Age and entered the Age of Information, it remains to be seen how American novels will refract the events of a new way of living. Eternal verities never die, of course; religion, always a subject of scrutiny in John UPDIKE's fiction, receives a particularly full examination in *In the Beauty of the Lilies,* a study of one family's four generations and the effect religion has had on them. Even Pynchon, whose *Gravity's Rainbow* often reads as a monument to conspiracy and paranoia, seems to mellow somewhat in *Vineland,* where he offers hope of ethical relations in a world tired of the aesthetics of postmodernism.

At the same time, change is constant in American writing, and one needs only to look back over a brief period to see potentially significant trends already taking form. Toward the close of the 20th c., for example, writers seemed to be reflecting a widespread concern about personal identity by writing either memoirlike novels or a so-called "creative nonfiction" in which actual memoirs are given shape through fictive techniques. Using this approach, novelists as different as Susan Cheever, Mary GORDON, William STYRON, Geoffrey Wolff, and Tobias WOLFF explore old themes, yet they do so in ways that will only receive ample critical attention in years to come.

At the same time, fresh voices shaped by other cultures are transforming the American novel in exciting ways as works such as Thomas Sánchez's *Zoot Suit Murders* (1978), Maxine Hong KINGSTON's *Tripmaster Monkey: His Fake Book,* Amy TAN's *Joy Luck Club,* Oscar HIJUELOS's *Mambo Kings Play Songs of Love,* and Julia ALVAREZ's *How the García Girls Lost Their Accents* enrich, alter, and, possibly, even replace the traditional elements of American literary culture. Certainly each of these writers is concerned with cultural survival and the question of how much one can submit to the dominant culture without losing one's own identity. This issue has been so fully dramatized, in fact, that mainstream writers are adopting it, as E. Annie PROULX does when she looks at the lives of immigrants from Africa, France, Germany, Norway, Poland, Mexico, and Sicily in *Accordion Crimes.*

Cultural identity is a problem that is further complicated when sexuality enters the picture. Works by gay mainstream writers such as David LEAVITT's *The Lost Language of Cranes* and Allan Gurganus's *Oldest Living Confederate Widow Tells All* (1989) are already part of the contemporary canon, and they are being joined by, for example, new works by Asian lesbians: the appearance of Kitty Tsui's groundbreaking *The Words of a Woman Who Breathes Fire* (1983) makes possible such works as Sky Lee's *Disappearing Moon Cafe* (1990). John RECHY's *City of Night,* already a cult classic because of its depiction of the underground life of homosexuals, paves the way for work by such younger gay Chicanos as Arturo Islas and Michael Nava, writers whose work typically present characters who are doubly marginalized yet defiant.

As immigrants continue to arrive on these shores and alternative lifestyles blend with the mainstream, new literary developments seem likely to reinforce that essential element of displacement that has characterized the American novel since its beginning. In an 1865 essay, Henry James warned that Gothic terrors were no longer to be found in scary old castles but in cheerful country estates. Can there be any doubt at present that those same apparitions have multiplied and invaded our tract houses and condominiums? Too, even though it is now possible to explore every corner of the world at home via computer, it seems doubtful that the picaresque tradition will be abandoned totally. After all, according to author John GARDNER, there are only two plots: a stranger rides into town and a stranger rides out of town. It seems likely that the novelists of tomorrow will tell us that the ancient demons have not disappeared but only changed form, that there is still reason to flee.

BIBLIOGRAPHY: Fiedler, L. A., *Love and Death in the American Novel* (1960); Martin, J., *Harvests of Change: American Literature, 1865–1914* (1967); Matthiessen, F. O., *American Renaissance* (1941); Reynolds, D. S., *Beneath the American Renaissance: The Subversive Imagination in the Age of Emerson and Melville* (1988); Shulman, R., *Social Criticism and Nineteenth-Century American Fictions* (1987); Spender, S., *Love-Hate Relations: English and American Sensibilities* (1974); Young, P., *Three Bags Full: Essays in American Fiction* (1972)

DAVID KIRBY

NUNES, Susan
b. 27 September 1943, Hilo, Hawai'i

As an author, N. transcends categorization. In fact, her literary diversity represents what is expansive and potentially liberating about American literature today. Perhaps best known for her children's books, N.'s *Last Dragon* (1995) was acknowledged as one of the best books of 1995 by the Smithsonian Institute and has been optioned for a film. The story centers on a Chinese American boy who discovers a dragon in Chinatown and with the help of his mother and aunt, restores it to life. Since the 1980s, however, N. has gained ever more exposure for her short stories. Her best-known fiction, *A Small Obligation* (1982), explores the duality of her Portuguese and Japanese background and the confusion involved in remembering and understanding cultural inheritance.

A Small Obligation, a collection of related short stories told chronologically, highlights childhood and adult memories of a particular family in Hawai'i. These portraitures explore loneliness, the need for community and belonging, and how better to understand our relations with family members. N. tries to bring to her fiction "a quality of memoir." Many pieces in the collection focus on character development, memorializing those who would ordinarily have been forgotten if not kept alive in family stories.

Point of view helps to create a layered depiction of this Portuguese and Japanese American family. Use of first-and third-person narration establishes a depth of perspective in the arrangement. Connective fragments between some longer stories include culturally resonant observations of the family and buried memories of their background. As the stories progress, complications are revealed when members try to accommodate both paternal and maternal influences. Thus, N. illustrates the challenge of trying to harmonize two different cultures within one family. In this way, N. reveals her intrigue for "divided households and family secrets, by outsiders, by our longing for a sense of place and common purpose."

In her acclaimed short story "A Moving Day," anthologized in *The Graywolf Annual Seven: Stories from the American Mosaic* (1990) and *Home to Stay* (1990), N.'s narrator speaks lovingly of her Nisei (second-generation Japanese American) mother and her desire to let go of the past by giving away family relics. N. focuses on the need to tell stories to honor and remember one's lineage, and to understand the past. All of this inevitably feeds our present—our own cultural inheritance and our mothers' obligation to preserve it. Sadness results because culture may irretrievably be lost; not enough time may exist to transmit knowledge and memories.

Although critics often list N. as an Asian American writer, she finds this label to be confining, for her subject matter spans many areas. For example, in "Science of Symmetry: A Love Story," anthologized in *Sister Stew* (1992), race and culture are incidental factors, the focus being on science and perfectionist thinking. Ultimately, her flexibility is reflected in the varied genres in which she has published—award winning children's books, educational books, and fiction. Ever the craftsperson, N. says her main motivation is to be able to "say things simply" and "not to say what I don't need to say."

SUZANNE K. ARAKAWA

NYE, Edgar Wilson [Bill]

b. 25 August 1850, Shirley, Maine; d. 22 February 1896, Arden, North Carolina

Journalist, editor, and author of short comic pieces, essays, burlesque histories, and Broadway plays, N. was a humorist whose reputation rivaled that of his contemporary Samuel Langhorne CLEMENS. N. achieved a remarkable level of success in his short life—he died at age forty-five. His columns, books, and lectures earned him celebrity status and substantial monetary rewards.

N. was born in Maine, but moved to Wisconsin with his family at the age of two. It was there that he became interested in writing and held a few jobs at local newspapers. At twenty-six, the adventurous N. headed west. He wound up in Laramie, Wyoming and was soon working at the *Laramie City Sentinel*. Later, he cofounded the *Laramie Boomerang* where he served as editor and weekly humor columnist. N.'s casual tone and spirited humor attracted local attention and word soon spread. Newspapers and periodicals in Texas, Michigan, and Colorado picked up his column. His topics most often related to the American West. He wrote of miners, Indians, Mormons, and of the Western landscape and climate. N.'s humor can be closely identified with the rough, rustic environment of his adopted home. Some of his humor was violent or "sick" and he was known to be bigoted against certain ethnic and religious groups. What attracted readers most, however, were inane observations and use of understatement and anticlimax. N. published two books and started a third while in Laramie. *B. N. and Boomerang* (1881), *Forty Liars, and Other Lies* (1882), and *Baled Hay* (1884) are mainly collections of previously published essays and sketches.

Illness forced N. to leave the West. A three-year stay in Wisconsin produced a few plays, one of which N. would rework for his lecture tour. N. moved to New York in 1887 to write a weekly humor column for the *New York World*. His fame increased both as a writer and lecturer. *Remarks* (1887), his fourth collection of essays and sketches, marks an increased level of maturity and polish. In 1888, N. released three collections—the first written with lecture circuit

friend, James Whitcomb RILEY—designed for the entertaining railway passengers: *N. and Riley's Railway Guide; B. N.'s Chestnuts Old and New;* and *B. N. Thinks.* Of these titles, the last is considered by many N.'s best. N. covers a wide variety of topics, including impressions of Washington, D.C. and New York City, in a lively style.

N.'s talents were at their peak during the last years of his life. He combined his interest in history with his well-honed narrative, descriptive, and satirizing skills to produce two books of burlesque history: *B. N.'s History of the United States* (1894) and *B. N.'s History of England from the Druids to the Reign of Henry VIII* (1896). Both employ exaggeration of historical events to comic effect, but N.'s themes are often serious. He discusses at length the superiority of democracy and takes a rather harsh view of England's social and political system. As tastes changed, N.'s popularity declined, but he remains an important figure in the lineage of American humorists.

BIBLIOGRAPHY: Hasley, L., ed., *The Best of B. N.'s Humor* (1972); Kesterson, D. B., *B. N.: The Western Writings* (1976); Larson, T. A., *B. N.'s Western Humor* (1968)

JASON MCMAHON

NYE, Naomi Shihab

b. 12 March 1952, St. Louis, Missouri

N.'s heritage has been a crucial, determining factor in her development as a writer. Born to a Palestinian father and an American mother, N. has in her poetry explored issues related to her identity as an Arab American. She grew up in St. Louis, has lived in Jerusalem and Texas, and has traveled extensively. Her poetry is a site for bringing coherence and harmony to these various cultural landscapes and strains of being.

Among N.'s best-known collections of poems are *Different Ways to Pray* (1980), *Hugging the Jukebox* (1982), *Yellow Glove* (1986), *Mint* (1992), and *Red Suitcase* (1994), the first three volumes available as *Worlds under the Words: Selected Poems* (1995). In N.'s poetics, one feels the shaping force of a number of modern and contemporary American poets, particularly William Carlos WILLIAMS, William E. STAFFORD, Richard WILBUR, and David IGNATOW. Into the fabric of her poems are woven references to tangible, common objects often taken for granted: buttons, items of clothing, food. These "things of the world" show us the way, defining and giving meaning to our lives. Titles of some of her best-known poems—"The Traveling Onion," "Yellow Glove," "Red Suitcase," "The

Man Who Makes Brooms"—underscore this fundamental concern.

The language of N.'s poetry is simple and direct. In an interview with Bill Moyers, N. elaborates on her notion that poetry is a kind of conversation: "Poetry is a conversation with the world; poetry is a conversation with the words on the page in which you allow those words to speak back to you; and poetry is a conversation with yourself."

There is often a political thrust to N.'s poems, though for her, like most contemporary Arab writers, the personal and the political are inseparable. Political circumstances, especially in the Middle East, have radically affected individual lives. Her Palestinian ancestry has given her direct access to stories of oppression, loss, and tragedy. Writing, for N., seems to be a way of recording and recuperating that loss.

N. has also done a good deal to make available and promote the work of others who share her vision of the world. With May Jayyussi, she translated a group of poems entitled *The Fan of Swords* (1991) by the Syrian poet Mohammad al-Maghut. She collaborated with Paul B. Janeczko in putting together an anthology of poetry, *I Feel a Little Jumpy around You* (1996), in which poems by male and female poets are juxtaposed in a manner meant to deepen our awareness and understanding of the ways gender affects perception. Gregory Orr's "Who'd Want to Be a Man," for instance, is paired with Daisy Zamora's "To Be a Woman." *This Same Sky* (1992), another anthology of poems selected by N., contains poems by 129 poets from sixty-eight different countries. In *The Tree Is Older Than You Are* (1995), N. acknowledges her longtime love of Mexico, bringing together poems and tales by Mexican writers (the original Spanish versions set next to English translations) along with paintings by Mexican artists.

These anthologies are in large measure designed to introduce children to poetry and different cultures. In two children's books, *Benito's Dream Bottle* (1995), with illustrations by Yu Cha Pak, and *Sitti's Secrets* (1994), with illustrations by Nancy Carpenter, N. reaches out quite specifically to an audience of children, underscoring universal themes of childhood which cut across national and ethnic lines. The young girl narrating *Sitti's Secrets* tells of going to visit her grandmother in the Arab world. "Sometimes I think the world is a huge body tumbling in space, all curled up like a child sleeping," she writes. "People are far apart, but connected." Those lines seem to encapsulate N.'s philosophy that guides all her various projects. She seeks to bring together people of different ages, genders, and cultural backgrounds.

BIBLIOGRAPHY: Booth, P., "Loners Whose Voices Move," *GaR* 43 (Spring 1989): 161–78; Milligan, B., "Writing to Save Our Lives: An Interview with N. S. N.," *Paintbrush* 18 (Spring 1991): 31–52; Moyers, B., *The Language of Life: A Festival of Poets* (1995) Orfalea, G., "Doomed by Our Blood to Care: The Poetry of N. S. N.," *Paintbrush* 18 (Spring 1991): 55–66

ALLEN HIBBARD

O

O. HENRY. See PORTER, William Sydney

OAKES, Urian
b. ca. 1631, London, England; d. 25 July 1681, Cambridge, Massachusetts

A Puritan minister, O. is best known for two works: "An Elegy upon the Death of the Reverend Mr. Thomas Shepard, Late Teacher of the Church at Charlestown in New England" (1677) and "The Soveraign Efficacy of Divine Providence; Overruling and Omnipotently Disposing and Ordering All Humane Counsels and Affairs" (1682). The latter is a sermon accounting for the colonists's serious losses in King Philip's War. It reveals much about the gradual changes in the Puritans' confidence in themselves and their mission in the North American wilderness. Both texts reflect O.'s extensive classical and contemporary knowledge, for which he was highly acclaimed even in his own lifetime. O. is famous for Latin witticisms, especially the one affixed as a motto to the Harvard Almanac for 1650, for which he compiled an impressive table of astronomical calculations.

O. was probably born in London; he emigrated with his parents to Cambridge, Massachusetts, in about 1640, and graduated from Harvard in 1649. Around 1652, O. returned to England, but eventually he was forced back to America by the Act of Uniformity of 1662. O. spent the rest of his life involved in Harvard university politics. With the support of the Mathers, he reluctantly held the office of acting president, and then president of Harvard (1675–81). Like his friends, Increase and Cotton MATHER, O. worked to quell religious rebelliousness and to ensure that the rising generations of Puritans in America remained faithful to the ways of the first generation. The elegy on Thomas SHEPARD reveals some of O.'s recurrent concerns. A sermon in verse, it examines Shepard's life according to the conventions of Puritan hagiography. Rich in imagery and verbal complexity reminiscent of the

metaphysical poets, the elegy attempts to open the eye of reason and effect a turning of the heart toward God by evoking the popular memory of Shepard, whose life becomes an index to the spiritual condition of New England at the time. Like the metaphysicals, O. displays a broad knowledge of science and natural philosophy, as well as the profound influence of Ben Jonson and John Milton. During the latter part of his career, his works are developed in an 18th-c. philosophical mode, and indirectly undertake the reconciliation of science and religion.

BIBLIOGRAPHY: Blau, J. L., *The Soveraign Efficacy of Divine Providence* (1955); Rainwater, C., "U. O.," in Ashley, P. J., ed., *DLB*, vol. 24, *American Newspaper Journalists, 1873–1900* (1983): 239–43; Sibley, J. L., *Biographical Sketches of Graduates of Harvard University,* 1 (1873)

CATHERINE RAINWATER

OATES, Joyce Carol
b. 16 June 1938, Lockport, New York

The remarkably prolific and prodigiously talented O. made a meteoric rise on the American literary scene in the 1960s, from her debut collection of short stories, *By the North Gate* (1963), through a series of highly acclaimed novels, *With Shuddering Fall* (1964), the National Book Award-nominated *A Garden of Earthly Delights* (1967) and *Expensive People* (1968), and culminating with *them* (1969), which won the National Book Award in 1970. In the meantime, she established herself as a master of the short story, winning her share of O. Henry Awards as well as making almost annual appearances in the *Best American Stories* anthologies. In addition, she established herself as a firstrate literary critic even as she published volumes of poetry and saw her early plays produced Off-Broadway. By 1970, she had established herself at the forefront of the writers of her generation and, though her critical reputation has fluctuated somewhat over the years, and the quality of her work has been uneven, she remains a major literary figure with seemingly boundless energy.

O. writes about the dark side of the human psyche, about the violence that erupts again and again in American society. She derives, that is, from the American gothic tradition of Edgar Allan POE, Nathaniel HAWTHORNE, William FAULKNER, and Flannery O'CONNOR, on the one hand, and the American NATURALISM of Theodore DREISER, on the other. The landscape of her earliest fiction is Eden County, a mythologized version of the Erie County in rural western New York State where O. was reared. The name is ironic because the mostly poor and uneducated denizens of this world, far from living in a paradise, inhabit a brutal landscape, constantly forced to confront the evil inherent in human nature and society in its least sophisticated state. The strongest of these early stories is "Upon the Sweeping Flood," in which a young man, Stuart, warned by a policeman to seek safe ground because of an incipient storm, irrationally decides to ignore this advice and succumbs to madness as he becomes trapped in the ensuing flood, symbolic of his own inner psychic turmoil.

By the latter part of the 1960s, O.'s fictional landscape expanded; if she did not completely abandon Eden County, she began to focus more and more upon the city of Detroit where she was living, a symbol of the urban violence and decay that typified that era in recent American history, and the wealthy suburbs of the Motor City where auto executives and other white collar professionals lived in what O. satirizes as mock-pastoral splendor. Arguably, O.'s two finest books were written during this period, *them,* her best-known novel, and *The Wheel of Love* (1970), her finest collection of short stories.

A sprawling, naturalistic novel, *them* examines the life of a poor white family, the Wendalls, and their struggle to endure, from the 1930s through the 1960s amid physical and psychic violence and the squalor of their urban environment. In a note prefacing the novel, O. claims, with a postmodernist touch at once ironic and thoroughly believable, merely to be giving shape to material from letters written to her by a former composition student at the University of Detroit, Maureen Wendall, whom O. flunked—two of these letters appear in the novel. The novel opens with Maureen's mother, Loretta, as a teenage girl whose first lover is murdered, while asleep beside her, by her brother, only to be raped by the police officer—whom she marries—whose assistance she sought. O. subsequently presents the parallel tales of Maureen, a studious girl, the class secretary in her parochial school whose life is thrown into chaos when she loses the class notebook, and Maureen's older brother, the By-

ronically spirited Jules. The former embodies stasis, the latter energy, though both of their lives are, in part, determined by their environment. Jules is nearly destroyed several times in the novel, once after being shot by a lover, Nadine Green, whom he first seduced while she was a teenager in suburban Bloomfield Hills; another time during the Detroit riots of 1967. Maureen, herself nearly killed by her stepfather who discovers she is a prostitute, on the other hand, finds herself married to a professor who she lures away from his marriage. As lurid as the plot seems in summary, and however grotesque many of its violent scenes, O. writes with such insight and intensity here that she captures the violence of the U.S. in the 1960s more powerfully and realistically than any other American writer.

The Wheel of Love contains an unusual number of fine stories, the most-anthologized of which are "Where Are You Going, Where Have You Been?" and "How I Contemplated the World from the Detroit House of Correction and Began My Life Over Again." The former, set in Eden County, traces its teenage heroine, Connie's, dangerous initiation into sexuality at the hands of the eerie, diabolical Arnold Friend. It has been made into a successful film, *Smooth Talk,* directed by Joyce Chopra. The latter, told in the fragmented form of notes for a school essay, relates the violent experiences on the streets of Detroit of a wealthy, unnamed teenage girl who flees the sterility of her suburban existence, only to be forced to return there after being beaten by a fellow inmate in prison. Equally impressive are "In the Region of Ice," about the tragic encounter between a Roman Catholic nun teaching Shakespeare at the Jesuit-run University of Detroit (where O. herself taught) and a brilliant but troubled Jewish student of hers.

Since 1970, O. has continued to publish powerful, award-winning short stories. Her novels took an experimental approach in the 1970s, relying more on stream of consciousness than on the hypnotic straightforward narrative pace of her earlier novels. The results, in such books as *The Assassins* (1975) and *Childwold* (1976) were at best problematic. With *Bellefleur* (1980), O. began to play with various forms of 19th-c. genre fiction—the Gothic family chronicle in this case—which many critics, including myself, found wildly ambitious and entertaining, but which others found fault with.

More recently, she has returned to the realm of social realism with such powerful novels as *Because It Is Bitter, and Because It Is My Heart* (1990), a finalist for the National Book Award, which explores racism in upstate New York from the dual perspective of young white woman and a young black man, writing equally convincing from both perspectives. *Black Water* (1992), a finalist for the National Book Critics

Award in fiction convincingly dramatizes an incident similar to that involving Senator Edward Kennedy and Mary Jo Kopechne at Chappaquiddick from the young woman's point of view as she is drowning. More claustrophobic is O.'s finally unconvincing attempt to write from the perspective of an alcoholic, womanizing politician in upstate New York, the lengthy *What I Lived* (1994), nominated for the PEN/Faulkner Award. Much more successful in anatomizing the raw male psyche is her fascinating book-length essay, *On Boxing* (1987). For her best work, O. will be recognized as one of the strongest and certainly most disturbing American writers of the second half of the 20th c.

BIBLIOGRAPHY: Bastian, K., *J. C. O.'s Short Stories: Between Tradition and Innovation* (1983); Bloom, H., ed., *J. C. O.* (1987); Creighton, J. V., *J. C. O.: Novels of the Middle Years* (1992); Grant, M. K., *The Tragic Vision of J. C. O.* (1978); Johnson, G., *J. C. O.: A Study of the Short Fiction* (1994); Wagner, L. W., ed., *Critical Essays on J. C. O.* (1979); Waller, G. F., *Dreaming America: Obsession and Transcendence in the Fiction of J. C. O.* (1979)

ROBERT MCPHILLIPS

O'BRIEN, Fitz-James

b. 1828?, Country Limerick, Ireland; d. 6 April 1862, Cumberland, Virginia

Although he wrote enough fictional material for two substantial short story collections, O.'s literary reputation rests on three or four short supernatural or science fiction stories that he published in American literary journals between 1852 and 1862 and that continue to appear in various American short fiction anthologies. After immigrating from Ireland to New York City in 1852, O. claimed a position among the New York bohemians, who he described, with his typically self-mocking style, as "writers who cultivate literature and debts, and, heedless of the necessities of life, fondly pursue the luxuries." Despite his obscure past in Ireland, his flamboyant lifestyle in New York, and his early death during the Civil War, O. continues to be the only significant 19th-c. American writer of horror and science fiction tales whose literary merits are comparable to those written by his more well-known contemporaries, Edgar Allan POE and Ambrose BIERCE.

Two of O.'s most frequently anthologized tales are "The Diamond Lens" (1858) and "What Was It? A Mystery" (1859). "The Diamond Lens" has been admired both for its 19th-c. scientific accuracy and for its complex allegorical treatment of a scientist tormented and finally driven to madness not only by his perceptions of the limitations of science, but also by

the absurd circumstance of his having fallen in love with his subject—an animalcule who he names "Animula" and who comes to symbolize more, he claims, than any man can comprehend. "What Was It? A Mystery" also stretches the limits of reason, though it is recounted by an ostensibly sane narrator who encounters a dwarfish yet invisible being, one that physically and metaphysically violates, challenges, and ultimately compromises the narrator's fluctuating perceptions and sense of reality.

Other of O.'s critically noteworthy works include "The Lost Room" (1858), "The Wondersmith" (1859), and his only novella *From Hand to Mouth* (1858). Like his other tales, these works utilize elements of the grotesque, the absurd, the bizarre, the horrific, the experimental, and the scientific. "The Lost Room" details a nightmarish experiment in architecture, one in which a narrator finds himself not only in a mathematically puzzling house, but in one inhabited by fellow humans who behave in curiously inhuman ways. "The Wondersmith" is a grotesquely comic tale in which children's toys are brought to life by gypsies and transformed into evil and deadly automatons. The narrator of *From Hand to Mouth* recounts the fantastic state of being surrounded by disembodied hands, feet, eyes, and mouths in such quasi-absurdist chapters as "How I Magnetized My Eye" and "A Stupid Chapter and I Know It."

Critics have partially neglected O.'s unique use of the absurd and the fantastic in his fiction, but his status as a significant albeit minor 19th-c. American short story writer remains secure.

BIBLIOGRAPHY: Clareson, T. D., "F.-J. O.," in Bleiler, E. F., ed., *Supernatural Fiction Writers* (1985); Franklin, H. B., ed., *Future Perfect: American Science-Fiction of the Nineteenth-Century* (1995)

B. A. HUME

O'BRIEN, [William] Tim[othy]

b. 1 October 1946, Austin, Minnesota

Author of six books and numerous essays, short stories, and book reviews, O. began writing while a student at Macalester College in St. Paul, Minnesota, in the late 1960s and published his first work, segments from what would later become his first book, *If I Die in a Combat Zone* (1973), while serving as a foot soldier in Vietnam in 1969–70. After the war, O. pursued graduate studies in government at Harvard University and worked briefly as a national affairs reporter for the *Washington Post* before turning to writing full-time. His works have appeared in numerous magazines, textbooks, and collections, and he has received awards from the National Endowment for the Arts, the Guggenheim Foundation, and the Massachusetts Arts and Humanities Foundation.

While O. has insisted that his experiences in Vietnam merely inspired him to become a writer, his confessional article, "The Vietnam in Me," featured in the October 20, 1994, issue of the *New York Times* magazine, reveals otherwise. Like numerous other Vietnam veterans, O. has had to make an actual return journey to Vietnam in order to deal with his painful war memories, which perhaps explains why the war has so persistently found its way into most of his writing. His second novel, the critically acclaimed *Going after Cacciato* (1978), which received the National Book Award in 1979, is considered by many scholars to be the definitive Vietnam War novel. *The Things They Carried* (1990), which received a Chicago Tribune Heartland Award, includes a foot soldier who also makes a return journey to Vietnam years after the war, and *In the Lake of the Woods* (1994) features a Vietnam veteran who participated in the My Lai massacre. Even *Northern Lights* (1975) and *The Nuclear Age* (1985), two of O.'s least publicized novels, contain characters whose lives have been influenced in some way by the war.

However, in spite of the shadow of Vietnam, O.'s writing transcends that subject. His works move beyond the war to pose significant moral and philosophical concerns. Universal subjects such as love, death, truth, fear, courage, imagination, memory, and the meaning of existence dominate O.'s writing. *Going after Cacciato* examines the issues of social commitment to one's fellow human beings and the quest for personal freedom versus social consciousness; *The Nuclear Age* the potential horror of nuclear war; *The Things They Carried,* fear, courage, and the power of stories to save us; and *In the Lake of the Woods* the danger of hiding the evils of the past and the extent to which a person will go in order to acquire and keep love.

O. is especially concerned with epistemological and ontological issues. His works are open texts that repeatedly probe the nature of knowledge and that deny the existence of a fixed, objective reality. He continually asks, "What happened, and what might have happened?" O. provides no answers or resolutions to the problematic questions he raises in his fiction. It is his refusal to allow his readers final knowledge, his suspension of definite judgments through all of his works, that contributes to his fiction's distinction.

O.'s thematic concerns are further underscored by his postmodernist playing with form and technique. His works cannot be classified as belonging to any one particular genre. *Going after Cacciato,* for example, has been called a combat novel, a fantasy, an architectonic novel, a work of magical realism, metafiction, and a picaresque adventure. *The Things They Carried* is equally as ambiguous, having been referred to as a collection of short fiction, a combat novel, not a combat novel, and a blend of autobiography, nonfiction, narrative fragments, metafiction, and journalism. Its protagonist is also a writer named Tim O'Brien who has written books entitled *If I Die in a Combat Zone* and *Going after Cacciato,* is in his forties and from Minnesota, is a Phi Beta Kappa graduate of Macalester College, a former graduate student at Harvard University, and a former foot soldier who served in Vietnam, all like the real O., who continually perplexes his readers by blurring the boundaries between fiction and reality.

In addition, O. forces readers to sift through his texts in an effort to piece together the events that take place rather than presenting them in a straightforward linear fashion. *Going after Cacciato, The Nuclear Age,* and *In the Lake of the Woods* each contain three types of chapters, which skillfully alternate throughout the books, taunting readers with their unconventional structures and continually offering new angles of vision. In *In the Lake of the Woods,* for instance, the chapters that deal with John and Kathy Wade's lives alternate with sections entitled "Evidence" and "Hypothesis." Readers must sift through the many examples of evidence that O. provides to consider the possibility that John Wade is guilty of murdering his wife. Like E. L. DOCTOROW in *Ragtime,* O. juxtaposes real, historical figures and actual authors with invented personalities, leaving the reader to wonder in some cases which people are real and which are imaginary. The "Hypothesis" chapters consider the "maybes"—what may have happened to Kathy Wade and why. Maybe she grew tired of her marriage. Maybe there was another man. Maybe she just got lost. Maybe she wrecked the boat on a sandbar. As is typical of O., his readers never learn what happened to Kathy Wade. "Anything could've happened," O. admonishes, once again leaving his work open to multiple possibilities.

Storytelling is another important thematic concern of O. This theme is most fully addressed in the chapter entitled "How to Tell a True War Story" of *The Things They Carried,* where O. defines what a true war story is or is not. However, this metafictive theme shows up in much of O.'s writing, especially through the many chapters of O.'s books that have been published separately as short stories prior to the publication of the longer works, sometimes in a different form. For instance, "Spin," a chapter of *The Things They Carried,* was combined with two other stories under its same title and published in the *Quarterly* (Spring 1990). The most problematic short story, though, is

"Speaking of Courage," which O. has revised and published in numerous places. Originally intended to be a chapter of *Going after Cacciato,* "Speaking of Courage" was initially published as a separate story in the *Massachusetts Review* (Summer 1976). In both that copy and the Neville 1980 version, Paul Berlin, the protagonist of *Going after Cacciato* is the main character. "Speaking of Courage" was left out of *Going after Cacciato,* however, and instead became a chapter of *The Things They Carried* fourteen years later with Norman Bowker as the protagonist, not Paul Berlin. In *The Things They Carried* version, O. explains in a metafictive chapter entitled "Notes" why the main character and certain details are different. "Speaking of Courage" has appeared and reappeared in numerous periodicals and anthologies, with various textual variations, attracting much critical debate in the process and serving as a clear thematic example of O.'s belief in the power of storytelling.

BIBLIOGRAPHY: Bates, M. J., "T. O.'s Myth of Courage," *MFS* 33 (Summer 1987): 263–79; Calloway, C., "'How to Tell a True War Story': Metafiction in *The Things They Carried,*" *Crit* 36 (Summer 1995): 249–57; Kaplan, S., *Understanding T. O.* (1995); Smith, L. N., "'The Things Men Do': The Gendered Subtext in T. O.'s *Esquire* Stories," *Crit* 36 (Fall 1994): 16–40

CATHERINE CALLOWAY

O'CONNOR, Flannery [Mary]

b. 25 March 1925, Savannah, Georgia; d. 3 August 1964, Milledgeville, Georgia

As a novelist, short story writer, and essayist, O. has one of the sternest, most independent, and most powerful visions of all American writers. Although her body of work is relatively small—two novels, two collections of stories, and one posthumous volume each of essays, book reviews, and letters—her fierce and uncompromising perspective on man's relationship to God has made her an important and influential writer far greater than the sum of her works alone might indicate.

A staunch Catholic, she nevertheless wrote most often about backwoods Protestants in the Bible Belt of central Georgia whom she heard on the radio and read out in newspapers because, she said, their relative absence of liturgy forced them to confront God more directly. O. saw a genuine cost in the exercise of religious belief, yet, because it was in a God capable of salvation, a genuinely celebratory and fulfilling joy as well. Her work is theological at its center, but the characters and plots often seem secular and, because

of this, her characters may at first appear grotesque. They are indeed grotesque from the perspective of a loving God and caring man, but their very vulnerability also makes them especially eligible for grace if they dare to allow themselves that possibility. Thus her fiction is often distinguished either by moments that are fearful or moments that are funny, her own perspective alternating between mounting concern and high comedy or ironic satire.

O. claimed always to be writing fiction about the extraordinary moments of God's grace, when it touches even the most maimed, deformed, or unregenerate of people. A proper Christian literature, she remarked, is always an invitation to deeper and stranger visions. But O. reserved part of that strangeness for her characters before they confront religion. In O.'s fictional Bible Belt, modeled closely on mid-Georgia where she spent most of her adult life, God seems to spend his grace on the least likely of people. Often they do not appear to deserve His blessing; almost as often they appear to learn nothing from it (or, if they do, it is not readily apparent). Nor is grace for O.'s characters customarily a dazzling toy, a sudden sweep of awareness. Rather, it comes in an act of random violence, a forceful accident, or a blinding pain. It can be unexpected, intrusive, unwanted, ignored, baffling, misidentified, forgotten. It can bring new suffering, wretchedness, or even annihilation just as easily as joy.

Both her novels—*Wise Blood* (1952) and *The Violent Bear It Away* (1960)—involve murder; the later novel adds arson and rape. In some of her best stories, collected in *A Good Man Is Hard to Find* (1955), similar crises merely take different forms: in the title story, O. argues that the grandmother, in a sudden wrench of compassion for a mad killer, shows him grace by calling him one of her children, but then is shot in vengeance; in "The River," that young Harry Ashfield/Bevel, in seeking the kingdom of Christ, joyously drowns himself in an act of suicide the Catholic church could only condemn; in "Good Country People," that Joy/Hulga, left helpless in a barn loft, robbed of her artificial leg and, no longer whole, stranded by a Bible salesman with obscene playing cards and a box of contraceptives, thereby receives her just reward. For O., these are all arresting moments when a person is suddenly accosted by grace, by a harsh moment of estrangement in which he or she can suddenly see his or her own weakness and need for the strength and compassion of God. For O., then, such apparently random shocks of consciousness and spirit reveal man's essential propinquity for grace.

This is an urgent understanding; it gains even more strength because throughout her life, O. seems never really to have questioned fundamental doctrines of the church to whose beliefs she ardently dedicated both her life and her fiction. She grew up in Savannah living in the shadow of the great cathedral and attending its convent school. When she later moved to Milledgeville, in central Georgia, she watched her equally devout parents organize a Catholic parish and contribute significantly to the building of the parish church. Her library, now publicly housed there on the Georgia College campus, has a large collection of books on theology, on Church history, and on interpretations of Catholic dogma; her letters—collected as *The Habit of Being* (1979)—display everywhere a concern with her faith and the state of the soul of the faithless, even more passionately than her vital concerns for fiction. Thus the oddness she feels in those warped by sin or ignorance—which is the same thing—is odd from the reader's perspective, but not from God's. He understands; hence His acts of grace. Her compassion for those who are handicapped by diseased bodies, minds, or souls was reinforced when, at the age of twenty-five, she was suddenly stricken with the rare and progressive lupus erythematosus, a debilitating paralysis which causes the bones to decay. Despite regular treatments, the illness finally forced her to use crutches, and then ate such pain into her hands that she found it nearly impossible to write. Her final story, "Parker's Back" (1964), was nearly left unfinished despite a year's efforts. Meanwhile, the only treatment known—there was then no cure—was by the use of drugs that caused her face to become disfigured. Thus, she also knew personally the high cost of suffering, the agony of spirit and the yearning for individual grace.

O.'s library suggests that she traced her sense of imagery to St. Thomas Aquinas, who argues the uniqueness of each thing, and Augustine, who argues that the bad is not something substantial, but a shadow which seductively imitates (and thus parodies) the good. She knows that part of God's mystery is revealed in His testing mankind through temptation. She knows that the Devil can only appeal to men by encouraging them in the disguise of something or someone good, such as the itinerant Bible salesman in "Good Country People" who tempts the intellectually smug Joy after she has despaired of her handicap and aggressively taken the ugly name Hulga to confirm her physical deformity. Yet this tempter could get nowhere if Hulga did not find his caresses attractive, if she did not feel (sinfully) that she deserved and even earned his attention. She is, then, essentially foolish, as all sinners are. Joy/Hulga's story is of the disdain of grace, of grace offered and stoutly denied. In "A Good Man Is Hard to Find," the smug and selfish grandmother finds a relationship to an insane criminal, The Misfit, and as she senses this kinship, she is enabled suddenly to acknowledge her own maimed sense of love for others—she reaches out in a split second of grace;

but it is just such a sense of love (and its awesome responsibility) that The Misfit is still unable to accept and his own fear and sense of self-worthlessness that causes him to kill her. In "The River," the misused and lonely Bevel finds peace in sinking beneath the surface of the water: what for the reader is an act of drowning is for the boy an act of baptism into a new life.

O.'s fiction thus dramatizes another Augustinian belief—that God so leaves His divine imprint on the soul that it has a kind of homing instinct to return to Him. This homing instinct, and its awful burden, is the theme of both novels. *Wise Blood* opens with Hazel Motes's separation from the army and his return home. But his house is deserted and rotting; his home is gone. Feeling betrayed by God, he seeks revenge by preaching a religion without God, preaching the gospel of godlessness. Not until he loses his following, his girlfriend, his companion-disciple and even the jalopy he uses as a pulpit—not until he is actually alone in the world with only himself to turn to—does he become reawakened to the need for God and the ritual of penance through self-blindness. In a typical O. gesture, the policeman who stops, finds he has no license, and deliberately wrecks his car, is thus in O.'s theophany an angel in disguise. Young Tarwater in *The Violent Bear It Away* also finds the burden of inheriting the gospel from his great uncle, the locally famous old prophet Mason Tarwater, too heavy to bear—he is even unable to bury the man—until he is randomly raped by a boy who gives him a lift: this violation makes his own self-indulgence quickly apparent, and the rapist also a special agent of God.

In all of these instances, God's grace is free and unmerited; but, when confronted, man must choose to cooperate with it. These confrontations are always crucial moments because everything is suddenly at risk, everything is at stake. The right choice needs to be made willingly, freely, cooperatively, absolutely, or everything is lost. Yet because God's unmerited grace, like His unmerited love, is forever available, the state of mind regarding it at the moment of death is, for the unregenerate, the most crucial because it is the last possible moment of cooperation. Death is therefore prominent in O.'s fiction, as in the novels, "The River," "A Good Man Is Hard to Find," or the later "Everything That Rises Must Converge" when Julian's mother, forced to confront her racism, has a sudden heart attack, because in each case the moment of death is the final telling moment.

But O.'s novels and stories persistently contend that if a person can manage to locate his own fate even in the bleakest of situations, in the greatest trials of consequence, then he has shouldered successfully the true burdens of the Christian life. Those who refuse compassion on their part cannot, in turn, recognize it when God intends it for them. In "The Displaced Person," for example, Mrs. McIntyre thinks of her Polish immigrant family, displaced in America and displacing the black help on her farm, as a clever financial and managerial decision until Mr. Guizac begins to plan his own immigration of more foreigners by having them marry American blacks. Then she arranges his "accidental" death. He is crushed by a runaway tractor. She loses her help and the farming goes bad; she herself becomes displaced because her bigotry and greed opposed God's plan. In "The Artificial Nigger," the estrangement and petty jealousy of old Mr. Head and his grandson Nelson is healed when they see the mysterious happiness of a broken plaster statue of a Negro which, they agree, has no right, privilege, or occasion to be happy. This sight suddenly shatters their previous contestation and quarreling as it unites them in seeing their own shallow sanctimony and self-satisfied pride. In "Parker's Back," the protagonist has a tatoo of a Byzantine Christ put on his back so that he too will know the "burden of the Cross." Such an act of subjugation and humiliation is not only misunderstood by his wife, however, but gives her occasion to reveal her own fallen state as it gives rise to her sin of wrath.

O.'s considerable gift at imagery is her creative answer to St. Thomas's call for the accurate naming of the things of God. The characters she draws—their clothes, gestures, words, thoughts—appear as terse and frequently peculiar. What seems superficially unremarkable, then, is always potentially for O. eschatologically crucial, and urgent. The seduction of the secular and sensual world contains, but also requires, perceptual transpositions. Objects and events demand metamorphosis, recognizing higher apprehensions of reality. The burning tree which appears like Moses's burning bush ("Parker's Back"), the stained ceiling that descends irrevocably in the shape of the Pentecostal dove ("The Enduring Chill"), or the Inferno-like Atlanta of "The Artificial Nigger" are all, in O.'s particular alchemy, alive with the power of the miraculous which embattles a more rational world of statistics and probabilities. The reader's leap of faith invites a reciprocal leap of grace. O. views this technique of her fiction as prophetic, often drawing, in such stories as "The Comforts of Home" and "A Circle in the Fire," on the events of the Bible and on acts of Old Testament prophecy. But her method ironically reverses the prophetic: she starts with phenomena and only hints at the noumena they indicate and that give to her fiction what power and significance, what form and function, it has.

O. often constructs her fiction through ironic juxtapositions of images, too; this extends to such characters as fat Alonzo Myers and the freakish hermaphrodite who image holy incarnation to a girl just past puberty ("A Temple of the Holy Ghost"); to such acts as the fire set by the three boys who destroy God's woods to prove that the woods do not belong to Mrs. Cope ("A Circle in the Fire"); and to such events as Rufus Johnson's eating pages of the Bible at the dinner table ("The Lame Shall Enter First"). Often O. intimates her ideas through implied analogies—as the arson alludes to Daniel 3:91 and the Bible-eating to Apocalypse 10:10—but some significations, such as the homosexual rapist in *The Violent Bear It Away* or the treacherous, greedy drifter Mr. Shiftlet in "The Life You Save May Be Your Own," draw surprisingly obvious pictures while others, such as the bull that gores Mrs. May ("Greenleaf") may seem blasphemous. For O. they are all images and events of a glorious similarity, revealing (as she put it) a peculiar crossroads where time and place and eternity somehow meet.

O.'s basic theme, first and always, is thus the separation of nature and grace, the curving arc of her fictions the convergence of the two. Her chief model is Nathaniel HAWTHORNE, whose stories, like hers, tend toward the allegorical. (The very name of Mrs. Hopewell, Mr. Shiftlet, and Mr. Paradise point directly to her conception of stories as parables, and parables as the best form of fiction.) Her sense of the comic and the grotesque she took from Edgar Allan POE, as well as from Kafka, Dostoevsky, and Gogol. From these established resources she added her love of cartoons and of newspaper stories of bizarre incidents and the very surroundings in which she lived—her farm Andalusia, just outside Milledgeville, bordering on a boys's reformatory and the other side of town from a woman's prison and a mental hospital. From an amalgam of such forces, she creates her endless parade of needy souls, her Christian (or proto-Christian) wayfarers marching, trudging, struggling, or slouching toward Bethlehem to be reborn. Together they become, under her harsh discipline, portraits of pained intensity and of urgent honesty.

Near the end or her abbreviated life, O. discovered the work of Pierre Teilhard de Chardin. She collected his work, praised it in letters, and gathered commentary on it for review. Teilhard focuses on a sense of amelioration. In *The Phenomenon of Man* he argues that people who remain true to themselves move toward a greater consciousness and a greater love; at the summit of such awareness all souls are joined. Everything that rises must ultimately meet. The nine stories of O.'s second collection, *Everything That Rises Must Converge* (posthumously in 1965) are arranged to follow the threefold philosophy of Teilhard—preparation, ascent, communion. The images that emerge now are Mr. Fortune's vision of walking trees and Mrs. Turpin's vision of a classless society. The mind that can understand fiction, O. writes, is not necessarily educated, but it is always the kind of mind that is willing to have its sense of mystery deepened by contact with reality, and its sense of reality deepened by contact with mystery. This encounter with Him is the single story she tells with irrevocable force.

Her essays and speeches, collected in *Mystery and Manners* (1969), taken singly and as a whole, are a remarkably coherent and succinct statement of her own poetics and help to explain her theological principles, her sense of the possibilities and limitations of fiction, her particular sense of comedy, and her appreciation of the Southern environment in which she was reared. Her letters, collected as *The Habit of Being,* speak to theological and poetic issues with some attention given to her own personal life, its joys and its difficulties. Published after her death, this collection remains one of the most substantive and significant body of letters of any American writer and, along with the essays, ought to be read alongside her fiction.

BIBLIOGRAPHY: Asals, F., *F. O.: The Imagination of Extremity* (1982); Friedman, M. J., and L. A. Lawson, *The Added Dimension: The Art and Mind of F. O.* (1966); Hendin, J., *The World of F. O.* (1970); Kinney, A. F., *F. O.'s Library* (1985); Kinney, A. F., "In Search of F. O.," *VQR* 59 (Spring 1983): 271–88; Martin, C. W., *The True Country: Themes in the Fiction of F. O.* (1968); McFarland, D. T., *F. O.* (1976); Schloss, C., *F. O.'s Dark Comedies: The Limits of Inference* (1980); Westarp, K. H., and J. N. Gretlund, eds., *Realist of Distances: F. O. Revisited* (1987)

ARTHUR F. KINNEY

ODELL, Jonathan

b. 25 September 1737, Newark, New Jersey; d. 25 November 1818, Fredericton, New Brunswick, British North America (now Canada)

Even to students of the literature surrounding the American Revolution, O.'s memorably caustic but only twice printed satire in verse called "The American Times" is barely known. But with the recovery of his poems from manuscript and the identification of his Brittanicus essays in James Rivington's *Royal Gazette,* we have a Loyalist perspective of the war from a physician and Anglican minister who first served Commander-in-Chief William Howe, then General Henry Clinton, and finally Sir Guy Carleton who oversaw the withdrawal of British Regulars from the colonies in 1783. Himself a refugee from New Jersey living behind protective British lines in garrisoned New York City, he needed to maintain the "approbation" of those who salaried him at the same time that he needed to explain Britain's "Sword and Olive Branch" policy to furious then frantic Loyalists; that is, why Britain's fabled army was unable to quickly secure a military victory over Washington's virtually untrained, heavily outnumbered and poorly supplied Continental Army.

Occasionally in collaboration with Joseph Stansbury, O.—writing as Britannicus—instructed that the Sword and Olive Branch policy should be understood as a father's gracious leniency towards his misguided children rather than as a failure of military prowess. Rather than feel betrayed, Britannicus went on, Loyalists should patiently trust in England's wisdom: the "greedy few" rebel leaders who were herding "gullible millions" to certain ruin would regain reason and repent.

O. worked as one of Clinton's go-betweens to Benedict Arnold in the plot to turn West Point over to the British. During these optimistic months, he wrote "The American Times." The satire outlines Loyalist ideology as well as the dismal present created by the arch villains Congress and Washington: "When Justice, Law, and Truth are in disgrace, / And Treason, Fraud, and Murder / fill their place."

In letters to his wife and in verse meant for colleagues and parishoners, his mood is somber. In despair, he chronicles the breakdown of normal life for the Loyalists—from the Association of 1774 to exile in Canada after the signing of the Provisional Articles of Peace. Carleton tried to persuade Congress to enforce the Fifth Article whereby Loyalists would be allowed to return to their homes. To that end, O., in one of the most revealing loyalist writings that we have, argues for good will between Americans and Loyalists as well as for the need to protect political dissenters. His treatise on sound governments begins: "This Country, so long convulsed by the rage of Civli War." The attempt at reconciliation having failed, O. preached his last sermon in the colonies and then presented his case to the Loyalist Claims Commission in London. He was give the prestigious post as provisional secretary of New Brunswick, Canada—the start of a long and prosperous political career.

Although O.'s poems, essays, and letters are not always interesting as writing, they do bespeak the life of an articulate, highly positioned, and well informed Loyalist. This record, sometimes startling, now furious, now sad, but always provocative brings us closer to an understanding of the Revolution itself.

BIBLIOGRAPHY: Calhoon, R. M., *The Loyalists in Revolutionary American, 1760–1781* (1965); Edelberg, C. D., *J. O.: Loyalist Poet of the American Revolution*

(1987); Sargent, W., *The Loyal Verses of Joseph Stans-bury and Doctor J. O.* (1860)

CYNTHIA DUBIN EDELBERG

ODETS, Clifford

b. 18 July 1906, Philadelphia, Pennsylvania; d. 14 August 1963, Hollywood, California

Long recognized as the major playwright for the political left in the U.S. during the 1930s, O. sought to present a disillusioned but revitalized middle class that confronted the challenge of economic peril during the Great Depression. Within these limits, O. was partially successful, although his dramas fall short of offering clear political perspectives, his characters finally remaining content to work out economic contradictions by relying upon the traditional dynamics of family life and a vague American optimism. Critics in his day expressed a dissatisfaction with what they took to be a deliberate vagueness and at times even unthinking enthusiasm. Harold Clurman, his close friend and mentor, felt that he "possessed a talent that always had an ambiguous character." Perhaps O. rather developed and forthright social sensibility was perplexed by the uncertainties of class consciousness in America during the Depression; in any case, he failed to discover a social locus for his drama. His interest in working-class culture at the same time as he idealized "the rebel" left him tentative and somewhat disaffected. Success soon deterred him, and he finished his career as a formula writer for the Hollywood studio system. Although O. viewed the Hollywood system as complacent and dedicated to art as commodity, his screenplay attacking American filmmaking, *The Big Knife* (1949), seems only an in-house critique.

After acting for the Theatre Guild, O. joined Harold Clurman, Lee Strasberg, and Cheryl Crawford when they formed the seminal Group Theatre in 1931. Dedicated to a more realistic production style, the Group also sought socially engaging plays. For these purposes, O. proved an early protégée. The long one-act play *Waiting for Lefty* (1935) introduced new staging approaches and gained the playwright critical recognition. Recalling the plot of Gerhart Hauptmann's *The Weavers,* its group protagonist declares a strike, motivated by the conditions forced upon New York cab drivers and incited by the death of the union leader, Lefty. Rarely has an American play about class conflict been so unequivocal and forceful. Like Bertolt Brecht's *Lehrstucke,* "teaching plays" of the early 1930s, O. attempted to present a short didactic piece that profiles the human dilemma of capitalism's victims. He included short scenes from the private lives of selected characters that typify the conflict between business creed and human values. These scenes were acted in blackout with the actors cast in shadows by directional lighting. While *Waiting for Lefty* was avowedly propagandistic, calling for group action and social organization in preference to individualistic moralizing, its performance technique was equally revolutionary, incorporating ensemble acting and innovative scenography to underscore its ideology. In order to lengthen the Broadway production of 1935, O. added his one-act play about the anti-Nazi underground in Germany, *Till the Day I Die* (1935).

Hastily refurbished after the success of his first plays, *Awake and Sing!* (1935) became O.'s most admired work. Produced by the Group Theatre Ensemble, its forceful message of optimism was somewhat complicated by its outright indictment of capitalism. "Go out and fight so life shouldn't be printed on dollar bills" became the line most remembered by audiences. Although O. never clarified his political message, the play, somewhat ironically, proved successful boulevard fare, perhaps because of its well-made-play structure, its mixture of humor and pathos, and its focus on an appealing but temporarily distressed ethnic family. Although much of the dialogue functions as debate between characters holding contrasting political sentiments—for example, the bitter war veteran Moe Axelrod versus the rich Uncle Morty—nevertheless, interest centers on the conflict between strong family personalities. Ralph seeks to break loose from his domineering and conventional mother, Bessie, but after the suicide of the idealistic grandfather Jacob, he resolves to abandon his private preoccupations and dedicate himself to political agitation. *Awake and Sing!* is as politically driven as John Howard Lawson's socially conscious plays of the 1920s, yet it circumvents particular prescriptions for group action to explore instead the dynamics of lower-middle-class family life.

O.'s subsequent plays for the Group Theatre offered individuals and families in conflict with the value systems that they endorse. *Paradise Lost* (1936), *Golden Boy* (1937), and *Rocket to the Moon* (1939) presented the harshness of capitalism, but their nugatory social analyses diminished the characters' credibility and the writer's statements. *Clash by Night* (1942) attempted political allegory but became a tepid love triangle. Typically, O. depicts individuals who have succumbed to the seductions of the American dream in its most materialistic forms. Usually, a growing awareness of their bad faith destroys happiness. Thus, with some irony, the young male protagonists in *Golden Boy* and *Rocket to the Moon* lose the promise of love and contentment assumed in the American dream; in *The Big Knife* a young actor's consciousness is corrupted by quick success and money. Although O. would continue writing plays, Hollywood screenwriting work and a more sentimental tenor undermined his earlier commitments.

BIBLIOGRAPHY: Brenman-Gibson, M., *C. O., American Playwright: The Years from 1906 to 1940* (1981); Cantor, H., *C. O., Playwright-Poet* (1978); Clurman, H., *The Fervent Years: The Story of the Group Theater and the Thirties* (1945); Miller, G., ed., *Critical Essays on C. O.* (1991); Murray, E., *C. O.: The Thirties and After* (1968)

WILLIAM OVER

O'HARA, Frank [Francis Russell]
b. 26 June 1926, Baltimore, Maryland; d. 24 July 1966, Mastic Beach, New York

O. is identified with the New York school of poets, including John ASHBERY, Kenneth KOCH, James SCHUYLER, who came into prominence in the 1950s and with the newly prominent Abstract Expressionist and Action painters—among them Willem de Kooning, Robert Motherwell, Helen Frankenthaler, Jasper Johns, Larry Rivers, and Jackson Pollock. O. came to know them all while serving as an editor of *Art News* and as an assistant curator at the Museum of Modern Art. O. received his B.A. from Harvard and his M.A. from the University of Michigan. After two years of wartime and postwar Navy duty, O. showed early promise as a writer by winning the prestigious Hopwood Award in Creative Writing in graduate school. In 1951, O. took his first job at the museum where he was to work, with one brief hiatus, until his death. He was run over by a beach buggy and killed in 1966. At the time of his death, O. had published four collections of poems: *Mediations in an Emergency* (1957), *Second Avenue* (1960), *Odes* (1960), and *Lunch Poems* (1964).

Two erratically compatible strains mark O.'s poetry: the studied influence of the early 20th-c. European avant-garde—the examples of Apollinaire and Vladimir Mayakovsky—and the native tradition of urban pastoral pioneered by Walt WHITMAN and William Carlos WILLIAMS. O.'s voice characteristically displays an insouciant candor, at its best combining cool urbanity with a frankly egocentric—even adolescent—urgency. In a (tongue-in-cheek) 1959 manifesto, O. described his poetic agenda as "personism," which proposes that poetry eschew philosophy, nostalgia, content, and technique. Personism was born, O. claims, from the realization that "I could use the telephone instead of writing the poem." this observation reflects O.'s reaction, which many of his contemporaries shared, against the bias of high modernism and New Criticism toward the poem as well-wrought arti-

fice. Consequently, much of O.'s poetry enacts the poet's discovery of transience and heterogeneity and celebrates the poet's ranging sympathies and cosmopolitan appetites—for affection, sex, conversation, surprising incongruities, and incessant stimulation.

BIBLIOGRAPHY: Gooch, B., *City Poet: The Life and Times of F. O.* (1993); Perloff, M., *F. O.: Poet Among Painters* (1979); Pinsky, R., *The Situation of Poetry* (1976); Vendler, H., *Part of Nature, Part of Us: Modern American Poets* (1980)

JAMES D. BLOOM

O'HARA, John [Henry]
b. 31 January 1905, Pottsville, Pennsylvania; d. 10 April 1970, Princeton, New Jersey

On his tombstone is the epitaph O. wrote for himself: "Better than anyone else, he told the truth about his time, the first half of the 20th c. He was a professional. He wrote honestly and well." It is a fair summary of his life and his work.

O. is little read and considered today. But among the serious American writers of fiction who also appealed to a mass audience in the mid-20th c.—F. Scott FITZGERALD, Ernest HEMINGWAY, Norman MAILER—O. was the most prolific, and by far the most financially successful. Several of his novels sold millions of copies, and hundreds of his short stories filled the pages of the *New Yorker* and the *Saturday Evening Post* from the 1930s until his death.

The son of a prosperous doctor in the eastern Pennsylvania coal town of Pottsville, O. learned the area and its people travelling with his father on his rounds. His early collection of stories, *The Doctor's Son* (1935) and much of his later fiction about the region reflected these trips, and showed an almost compulsive concern for objective detail that would characterize all his work and mark him as perhaps the purest writer of REALISM since Theodore DREISER.

Originally planning to go to Princeton, O. found himself working as a reporter when his father died in debt in 1925. Young O. worked at a variety of jobs—most of them involving writing—for the next eight years, and went through a failed marriage and a near-suicidal depression while he experimented with fiction. By the early 1930s, he was a recognized contributor to the *New Yorker,* and then, in less than four months at the end of 1933 and early 1934, he wrote *Appointment in Samarra* (1934). It was an immediate success, and it marked O. as one of the most promising writers in America.

Many O. readers, and particularly serious critics, still regard *Appointment in Samarra* as O.'s finest work. It is the story of the last two days in the life of

Julian English, a member of the Depression-era jet set of "Gibbsville," the thinly disguised Pottsville of O.'s youth. Nothing of great import happens in the novel: Julian gets drunk and throws a drink in the face of a member of the Gibbsville Country Club, Julian gets drunk and fights with his wife, Julian gets drunk and insults some Polish lawyers, and Julian gets especially drunk and commits suicide. The chronicle of Julian's disintegrating life would be only depressing and sordid, but the keenness of O.'s sense of social nuance, the crisp concision of his style, and his ability to maintain a frenetic pace while giving this brief fiction the impression of great scope in its picture of a whole society gives *Appointment in Samarra* a readability and gravity comparable to Balzac's finest short novels. Further, O. makes clear the causal chain between Julian's death and the empty social rituals which fill his life.

The eastern Pennsylvania of the upper middle class became the locale of much of O.'s later fiction, and he was to return to it for some seven novels and more than fifty short stories. Notable among the novels were *A Rage to Live* (1949), *Ten North Frederick* (1955), and *From the Terrace* (1958), all very large books that chronicled in great depth and detail the world and manners of the dominant American class in the first half of the 20th c. O. was often criticized for his frank treatment of sex in these works, and for his characters, who often seemed emotionally brutal and professionally ruthless.

O. complemented his prolific production of novels with nearly four hundred short stories, many of them published in the *New Yorker;* O. still holds the record for number of contributions to that magazine by a wide margin. Like the novels, they exhibited a trenchant, chiseled realism in style, a keen sense of social nuance, a fine ear for dialogue, and the overall philosophy that man is a wolf unto man, and not a very nice animal in any sense. In many ways, O. is the true heir of the naturalists—although a finer stylist than any of them.

BIBLIOGRAPHY: Bruccoli, M. J., *The O. Concern* (1986); Eppard, B., ed., *Critical Essays on J. O.* (1994); Farr, F., *O.: A Biography* (1973); Grebstein, S. N., *J. O.* (1966); MacShane, F., *J. O.* (1980)

                                        JACK COBBS

OKADA, John
b. September 1923, Seattle, Washington; d. February 1971, Los Angeles, California

To date, no 20th-c. Japanese American author has received so little recognition for one novel and yet made such an important contribution to American lit-

erature as O. Rediscovered in the 1970s, *No-No Boy* (1957) has inspired many Asian American authors in part because it explores the pressure many ethnic Americans face: How to define themselves under the influence of the dominant culture.

No-No Boy depicts a post-World War II Japanese American community in Seattle, already fragmented by the internment camp diaspora, torn apart by self-hatred due to their humiliation. The novel registers divisive, bitter conflicts among families, relatives, and friends experiencing joblessness, alcoholism, divorce, suicide, and early death. Ironically, the need Japanese Americans had felt to dispel their shame by proving their American-ness, forced many to accommodate the dominant culture at the expense of their own. In the novel, we see exemplified a suffering community that concomitantly scapegoats those who challenged the dominant culture and answered negatively on an army questionnaire—the "no-no boys."

The term "no-no" refers to answers on a loyalty questionnaire that the War Relocation Authority required all interned Japanese American males seventeen years and older to answer. The questionnaire asked them if they would serve in the U.S. armed forces and defend the U.S. faithfully and would forswear any allegiance to the Japanese emperor. Apparently, these questions were to determine clearance for combat duty. Yet, they were insulting to Japanese Americans who were asked to profess loyalty when not one had ever committed an act of disloyalty. Ultimately, the questions divided Japanese Americans. Many violently rejected those who did not answer "yes-yes"; they blamed the no-no boys for reflecting negatively on Japanese Americans determined to adapt to the dominant culture at all costs.

O., a Nisei (second-generation Japanese American), served as a sergeant in the U.S. Air Force during World War II. Interestingly, O. developed a main character, Ichiro Yamada, also a Nisei, whose experiences differed from his own. After Ichiro serves a mandatory two-year prison sentence for answering "no-no," he returns to a fragmented home and community. He spends most of the novel dealing with self-loathing and enduring emotional and physical abuse from others. For the most part, Ichiro questions his existence and identity, for he does not feel part of either the dominant culture or his own. Ichiro's reasoning that he has not proven himself as an American becomes obsessive. He enacts warped thinking where all who have answered yes-yes, who have sacrificed body parts in the war, have more right than he to be on American soil. Kenji is the only Japanese American veteran who befriends Ichiro. Ironically, he envies this veteran who has lost part of his leg in combat; Ichiro feels this physical wound proves Kenji's American-ness. Only through Ichiro's physical and philosophical journey where he encounters other outcasts does he begin to break through this reasoning. As a result, he moves away from an inclusionist versus exclusionist rationalizing and alters his role as the community's scapegoat; that is, Ichiro realizes the constructive nature of identity and the warranted role he needs to play in its construction.

O. dismantles myths of identity, community, and belonging while exposing the relativity of rights and laws. We see how the dominant culture not only punished Japanese Americans, but also contributed to their lack of belief in the Constitution. What is more important, O. posits no easy solution to the strains of identity and assimilation. Although some interpretations emphasize the novel's bleakness in that Ichiro may never feel fully American, hope does exist. O. reveals that recomplications of identity can empower and illuminate our understanding of American identity.

BIBLIOGRAPHY: Ling, J., "Race, Power, and Cultural Politics in J. O.'s No-No Boy," AL 67 (June 1995): 359–81; McDonald, D. R., "After Imprisonment: Ichiro's Search for Redemption in No-No Boy," MELUS 6 (1979): 18–26; Yeh, W., "To Belong or Not to Belong: The Liminality of J. O.'s No-No Boy," AmerasiaJ 19 (1993): 121–33

SUZANNE K. ARAKAWA

OLDS, Sharon

b. 19 November 1942, San Francisco, California

As a poet, O.'s work has been lavishly praised and fiercely condemned; she has won major prizes: *The Dead and the Living* (1983) was the Lamont Poetry Selection for that year and it won the National Book Critics Circle Award; *The Gold Cell* (1987) was a finalist for several awards. Her reputation has been enhanced by her numerous public readings, including appearing as part of Bill Moyers's series on PBS, *Power of the Word,* and as part of the American Library Association recorded series, *Poets in Person,* for which she was interviewed by Alicia OSTRIKER.

To her admirers, O. is a poet of direct physicality and painful honesty, depicting aspects of family life and of personal relationships that have rarely been described in such intimate or graphic terms. The same qualities prompt her detractors, most famously the critic Helen Vendler, to describe her work as self-indulgent, sensationalist, and even pornographic. There seems to be little middle ground in the matter. Like other confessional poets, such as W. D. SNODGRASS or Anne SEXTON, O. explores the pain of living in dysfunctional families as well as the sensuous plea-

sures of marital sexual bliss. Her language is explicit and, as she admits herself, may be embarrassing to some readers. In *The Wellspring* (1995), she describes an outdoors act of oral lovemaking, evoking precisely the sights and sensations of exploring her husband's genitals and finally arriving at "another world / I had thought I would have to die to reach." This poem, like many others, forces the question raised by confessional poets—to what extent is the "I" of the poem identical with the poet, and therefore how much of the narrated experience and evoked feeling must be considered autobiographical. But O. insists on the beauty as well as the humor of her references to intimate body parts and activities—she celebrates the sensuous and cherishes the physical, even the parts usually left unmentioned, unrepresented. That this might offend some readers is not her concern; in revealing the repressed, she moves to heal the sick and soothe the injured. It seems likely that some, at least, of the "offence" is because of O.'s gender: many male poets have celebrated their sexuality and their fascination with women's bodies in explicit terms with little resulting condemnation; that a woman would not only treat men's bodies as sexual objects, but would also comment on her children's eroticism and explore the erotic bonds between a mother and her children—and even a daughter's with her father—still has, apparently, greater shock value.

In addition to displaying what is concealed, O. seems to offer dreadful experiences explored in depth as cathartic. Her book length sequence, *The Father* (1992), is devoted entirely to her memories of growing up with a hapless, hurtful alcoholic father and her struggle to reconcile those memories with the impulse to forgive and love the dying man. Her disgust with his life comes through as she encounters a man who is his double: "the pitted, swelled, fruit-sucker / skin cheeks lips of the alcoholic." Her descriptions of his cancerous decline and her relief when he is gone are brutally honest, both about her hatred of his past and her mixed feelings about the love he expresses for her on his deathbed and her own for him: "a while after he died, / I suddenly thought, with amazement, he will always / love me now, and I laughed—he was dead, dead!" While the experience for the reader can be harrowing, the emotional impact probably does achieve the release through recognition that O. seeks in her work. O. has learned, since the calculated shocks of her first book, *Satan Says* (1980), to orchestrate her themes, as she does successfully in her two most recent books, finding variations on themes that serve to conceal to some extent the recapitulations.

Readers have observed an almost cinematic quality to the organization of each of O.'s books; she shifts both time and space as though editing footage from the past and from the present moment, sometimes offering almost painful close-ups, other times long shots that seem to encompass the whole history of humanity. While these tactics provide variety and surprise in her books, some have observed a sameness in them that prompts concern; a poet who is locked in the matter of body and family, whose only connections to the larger world are metaphorical, may soon find the limits of variation. The emotional power and psychological depth of O.'s poetic output are impressive, but the need for new perspectives and techniques is increasingly apparent.

BIBLIOGRAPHY: Dillon, B., "'Never Having Had You, I Cannot Let You Go': S. O.'s Poems of a Father-Daughter Relationship," *LitR* 37 (Fall 1993): 108–18; Parisi, J., ed. *Poets in Person* (1992); Pearlman, M., *Listen to Their Voices: Twenty Interviews with Women Who Write* (1994)

THOMAS F. DILLINGHAM

OLIVER, Mary

b. 10 September 1935, Maple Heights, Ohio

The power of O.'s highly acclaimed poetry rests in its passionate attention to the natural world which she sees as the source of revelation about ultimate things. Like her romantic predecessors, O. locates wisdom in the wilderness she seeks in solitude, where discoveries about the self and nature's otherness can be made. Her poems of thirty years and her recent prose collection, *Blue Pastures* (1995), reveal an art driven by visionary conviction in a manner similar to her claimed influences, William Blake and Walt WHITMAN. Expressed in simple language and familiar imagery, evoking dark and joyous states, this vision of nature is often conveyed in an ecstatic voice that compels. Celebratory and spiritual in her poetic vision, O. is one of America's finest nature poets.

Born in the Midwest, O. attended Ohio University and Vassar but never completed a college degree. Her early poetry bears kinship with fellow Midwesterner, James WRIGHT, and with Edna St. Vincent MILLAY, whose home she visited when assisting the poet's sister. Since 1964, except for teaching residencies and travel, O. has lived in Provincetown, Massachusetts, close to the sea and woods she cherishes. Among her many awards are a National Endowment for the Arts Fellowship, a Guggenheim Fellowship, and the Pulitzer Prize in 1984.

Her first collection, *No Voyage and Other Poems* (1963), is rooted in a mythical sense of the land and exhibits simplicity and a fine mastery of form, though some critics found the poems mannered. Like Robert FROST, her plain language and conventional forms could mask attention to an uncommon vision of nature's forces. The poems in *The River Styx, Ohio and Other Poems* (1972) call up an Ohio heritage and reclaim it through memory and myth, while her chapbooks, *Night Traveler* (1978) and *Sleeping in the Forest* (1978), develop the mythic dimension more fully, using themes of dreams, birth, and death. O. charts a course in the twenty-six poems of *Night Traveler* between two worlds, human and natural, where the individual faces loneliness and yearns to transcend the limited human world. In "Winter Sleep," the speaker voices her affinity with the she-bear who is the night traveler of the book's title and whose image, closely identified with the poet, reappears in later work. This desire to merge with nature's kingdom opens O.'s fourth collection, *Twelve Moons* (1979), in its first poem, "Sleeping in the Forest," a poem where the poet vanishes over and over into the earth. Crafted thematically, *Twelve Moons* presents a wholistic vision of natural cycles, balancing these processes, as she does eloquently in the twelve *moon* poems, with what exists in human experience.

Heralded for its perceptions of the visible world and the lyric intensity of O.'s voice, *American Primitive* (1983), like no other collection before it, celebrates union with the natural world, immersion in wood and swamp, and becoming other: bear, owl, or whale. For O., the desire to become another begins with longing that originates in the body, but the mind presents an opposing impulse and attempts to bring the body to self-consciousness. "Blossom" and "The Plum Tree" capture this battle between body and mind in a series of oppositions, and while the poems have an edge of didacticism, the sensuous images triumph. In "Crossing the Swamp" and "August," the speakers in the poems merge easily with the other; in the former, she becomes the swamp, her body sprouting branches from the swamp's life force; in "August," she is the bear, more animal than human. Through O.'s repeating verbs of desire, *American Primitive,* which was awarded the Pulitzer Prize in 1984, sings its belief that fusion with nature or merging with the non-human releases the self's multiplicity, fluidity, and ultimate joy.

Widening her vision in *Dream Work* (1986), O. expands her subject matter in an increasingly fluid voice, touching on music and the intimate lives of others in "Consequences," "Robert Schumann," and, in the tribute to her mentor, "Stanley Kunitz." This expansion continues in *House of Light* (1990) with "Singapore" and "Ich Bin Der Welt Abhanden Gekommen," a poem about Mahler on his birthday. As before, the ever-present theme, expressed primarily in poems of four or five line stanzas, is still the sensuous world. Spiritual and prophetic, the poems raise philosophical questions, and in revelatory moments, such as the conclusion of "Wild Geese," they signal the importance of the imagination.

In O.'s oeuvre, *New and Selected Poems* (1992), which is structured in reverse chronological order, a prevailing idiom of wonder and awe reigns. Most of the poems bear the unique stamp of an O. poem: the solitary speaker bringing her uneasy, questioning spirit to the woods or fields in search of understanding, instruction, even solace. The stylistic hallmarks of conversational tone, plain diction, and momentous endings, which frequent O.'s past collections, appear in the new poems as well. These poems have their strength, however, in the theme of imagined death, which is the final wedding of human and natural for the poet. Death recurs in the thirty new poems in various manifestations: in the bold images of "When Death Comes," a poem about the poet's own death; in poignant and urgent lines about the lushness of peonies before death; and stoically in the isolating, falling snow of "Lonely, White Fields."

The companion prose works, *A Poetry Handbook* (1994) and *Blue Pastures* (1995), collectively offer O.'s wisdom about the craft of writing, including the analysis of exemplary poems, and reflection on the necessity of solitude and mystery for a writer's life. Chapters on sound, the line, imagery, tone, and form in *A Poetry Handbook* serve as O.'s concise, experienced guide to writing poetry. The observational powers that enrich O.'s poetry surface in the form of soliloquies in *Blue Pastures,* providing insight to O.'s childhood, her poetics, and philosophy of nature. She meditates on Whitman as the brother she never had, on the merciless horned owl in its flight, and on language as a door past the self. Her brilliant, empathetic essay on the complex love affair between Edna St. Vincent Millay and George Dillon provokes the larger human question; how can we know another's life? This collection, transcendent like her best poems, confirms O.'s talent for prose writing, which she began in *White Pine* (1994), a collection of poems and prose poems looser in structure and, according to several critics, somewhat given to commonplace adjectives and adverbs.

The evocative forty pieces of *White Pine* continue the intense appeal to nature's otherness in poems such as "Toad," where the creature's unknowing grace contrasts with the knowing, conscious language spoken above him. In all of O.'s poetry, the otherness of the natural world and her longing to merge with it coexist with doubt about the value of human consciousness from which the language she uses, springs. O. struggles with her doubts and desires in the theater of the poem, creating a world of flora and beasts transformed in their greenery and creatureliness by language. Embued with the mystic's imagery of light and flame,

O.'s poetry is testimony to our worlds, inner and outer, and to the questions that arise where they touch.

BIBLIOGRAPHY: Bonds, D. S., "The Language of Nature in the Poetry of M. O.," *WS* 21 (1992): 1–15; Doty, M., "Natural Science: In Praise of M. O.," *Provincetown Arts* (1995): 26–29; Kitchen, J., "The Woods Around It," *GaR* 47 (Spring 1993): 145–159; Sofield, D., *America,* 174 (13 January 1996): 16–17

ANNETTE ALLEN

OLSEN, Tillie

b. 14 January 1912 or 1913?, Omaha, Nebraska

O.'s essays in *Silences* (1978) and her biographical interpretation of Rebecca Harding DAVIS entitled *Life in the Iron Mills* (1972) express her preoccupations: that a society must nurture creativity, particularly in women and working-class citizens, in order to avoid wasted talent and silencing of art; and that motherhood is the greatest threat to woman's creativity but also woman's most central psychological and social experience. Her own literary achievement was long-deferred while she supported her four children as a typist in San Francisco. O. began her novel, *Yonnondio: From the Thirties* (1974), in 1931 as a nineteen-year-old mother and published a chapter, "The Iron Throat," in *Partisan Review* (1934). As a political journalist and labor organizer at this time, she was jailed briefly for protest activity in Kansas City, she participated in the "longshoreman's strike," and she wrote about the Spanish Civil War. With four chapters and up to fourteen versions of various parts of her novel completed, she "mislaid" the manuscript for thirty-five years.

Returning to fiction in the late 1950s, O. has won numerous fellowships—Ford, Guggenheim, National Endowment for the Arts, National Institute of Arts and Letters, and American Academy; she has received honorary doctorates; and she has held many visiting professorships. In 1981, the city of San Francisco declared an official "T. O. Day."

O. spent five months in "arduous effort," selecting, editing, and organizing fragments of her rediscovered novel but could not add new writing or recover her imaginative vision of the ending she had planned when young. She prefaced the book with words from Walt WHITMAN's "Yonnondino," lamenting the disappearance of Iroquois aborigines: "Yonnondio! Yonnondio!—unlimn'd they disappear / . . . a wailing word is borne through the air for a moment? Then blank and gone and still, and utterly lost." Yet the incomplete novel contributes significancy to the literature of the Great Depression years. It chronicles the experience of Mary and Jim Holbrook's family, seen mostly through the eyes of their daughter, Maizie, as they move form a mining town in Wyoming to a tenant farm in North Dakota and finally to a slum near a Chicago meat-packing plant. Critics acclaimed the book's sensuous imagery and O.'s variation of rhythms as the third section moves from the view of Maizie to that of her mother, dying of malnutrition, frequent childbirth, and exhaustion. Maizie's ecstasy in nature and her discovery of books and Mary and Jim's moments of affection contrast with the misery forced on the struggling family.

Tell Me a Riddle (1962) includes the title novella plus three stories of elegiac tone, written in the late 1950s: "I Stand Here Ironing," "Hey, Sailor! What Ship?," and "O Yes." The novella, which won the "Best in Volume Award" in *O. Henry Prize Stories* (1961), centers on the antagonism that splits the "gnarled roots" of the forty-seven-year marriage of a Jewish immigrant couple, referred to almost entirely as *he* and *she*. Their adult children, embarrassed, bewildered, and angered at their parents's apparent inflexibility and "selfish" demands, provide an ironic chorus that intensifies the discord. Discovery that the woman has terminal cancer further entraps the couple. As she sings in her delirium one midnight during a storm, the ballad they had sung as revolutionaries in 1905 stirs not only agonizing memories for him but also youthful passion: "how we believed, how we belonged." With almost no plot, this novella sweeps the reader into the family's torment, largely through O.'s harshly derogatory dialogue, neutral reporting of the conflict, and insight into the hopes and frustrations of the stubborn, courageous parents.

BIBLIOGRAPHY: Fishkin, S. F., "The Borderlands of Culture: Writing by W. E. B. Du Bois, James Agee, T. O., and Gloria Anzaldua," in Sims, N., ed., *Literary Journalism in the Twentieth Century* (1990): 133–82; Fishkin, S. F., and E. Hedges, eds., *Listening to Silences* (1992); Pearlman, M., and A. H. P. Werlock, *T. O.* (1991)

MARGARET B. MCDOWELL

OLSON, Charles

b. 27 December 1910, Worcester, Massachusetts; d. 10 January 1970, New York City

As a poet, O. was dynamic, variable, and controversial. During his lifetime, some critics dismissed his work as only marginally interesting, while others highly praised its innovations and its influences on postmodernism. O.'s major opus is his three-hundred-page poetic sequence, *The Maximus Poems,* published in sections between 1953 and 1975 and in its entirety in a huge volume edited by George Butterick in 1983. His other poetry was similarly gathered from all previous editions and published as *The Collected Poems of C. O. Excluding the Maximus Poems* (1987). Robert CREELEY's edition of *Selected Poems of C. O.* (1993) has helped to secure O.'s reputation as a major force in 20th-c. poetry. In addition to his poetry, O. was noted for his polemical essays, literary criticism, poetic theory, and for his teaching and performing. As leader of the Black Mountain movement of poetry (named after the experimental Black Mountain College in North Carolina, where he was rector during the 1950s), O. left his mark upon many poets, including Robert Creeley, Denise LEVERTOV, and Robert DUNCAN. O. gave lively public readings, many of them taped and transcribed by his followers; he insisted that the cadences of a poem should be based not on traditional metrics but on the natural breath units of the poet-speaker and that poetic energy should be transferred from its source directly to the listener.

O. outlined his poetic theories in "Projective Verse" (1950) and in other essays, collected in *Selected Writings* (1966); these offer excellent guides to O.'s own prosody in the *Maximus* sequence as well as in important individual poems, such as "The Kingfishers" and "The Distances." O. did not approve of the closure of traditional verse, preferring instead to write in "open" forms, which would allow for more spontaneity and for the possibility of addition or revision. He placed the words of his poems freely on the page, not always beginning at the left margin, so that the typography would mimic the poem's rhythm and emphasis. Using an analogy from electromagnetism, he advocated composition by "field," in which the speaker of a poem begins with the experience of a particular place and moment and then from that place emanate waves of other experiences, facts, memories, and sensations, in an ever-widening process. In the *Maximus* sequence, the "place" is Gloucester, Massachusetts, where O. himself chose to live for many years. In these poems, the speaker Maximus (spokesperson for O.) and the place Gloucester are bound together, each becoming part of the other's history and mythology, each giving definition and identity to the other.

O. also wrote *Call Me Ishmael* (1947), a personal interpretation of Herman MELVILLE; *The Mayan Letters* (1953), on anthropology and language; *The Post Office* (1975), about O.'s boyhood in Worcester, Massachusetts; *The Fiery Hunt and Other Plays* (1977); *Poetry and Truth* (1971); *C. O. and Ezra Pound: An Encounter at St. Elizabeths* (1975); and *Casual Mythology* (1969).

BIBLIOGRAPHY: Boer, C., *C. O. in Connecticut* (1975); Bollobas, E., *C. O.* (1992); Butterick, G., *A Guide to*

The Maximus Poems (1978); Byrd, D., *C. O.'s Maximus* (1980); Christensen, P., *C. O.: Call Him Ishmael* (1975); Clark, T., *C. O.: The Allegory of a Poet's Life* (1991); Maud, R., *C. O.'s Reading: a Biography* (1996); Sherman, P., *O.'s Push* (1978)

LAURA JEHN MENIDES

O'NEILL, Eugene

b. 16 October 1888, New York City; d. 27 November 1953, Boston, Massachusetts

O. was born in a New York hotel while his father was acting in a play. His parents were both of Irish ancestry, but from different social classes: his father, James O., the son of poor Irish immigrants living first in Buffalo, then in Cincinnati, whose father deserted his wife and eight children when James was a child; his mother, Mary Ellen Quinlan, the daughter of a family in Cleveland who were also Irish immigrants but had prospered. O.'s father, who was to become a famous actor, met his future wife in her early teens when he was acting in a Cleveland theater and became acquainted with her father. Later, the actor and daughter met again in New York and were married.

O.'s life was, from his early youth, frequently disastrous—indeed his actual birth was, since the pain his mother suffered after it caused her inept physician to prescribe morphine, to which she became addicted. After a brief period at Princeton University, O. spent time drifting from saloon to saloon in lower-class Manhattan and almost committed suicide. He married a New York girl, left in less than a week to prospect for gold in Central America, and returned to New York but not to his wife, who presently divorced him. They had a son—oddly, under the circumstances, Eugene O'Neill, Jr.—whom he did not even see until the boy was twelve. After working for a while as a reporter in New England, he developed tuberculosis and spent some time in a sanitarium. Some time later, he married Agnes Boulton and had a son, Shane, and a daughter, Oona, the son becoming (as O.'s brother was) a hopeless alcoholic, the daughter becoming, in a successful marriage, the wife of Charlie Chaplin. (O.'s son by his first wife became a professor at Yale and at the age of forty, no longer at Yale, committed suicide.) O.'s second marriage also ended in divorce. His third marriage, to the actress Carlotta Monterey, lasted until his death, and they lived well in many parts of the world, he having by that time become famous and well-to-do; but the couple on occasion separated, to the point that both were once in the same hospital without either realizing that the other was there. He finally died with his wife at his bedside in a Boston hotel, having suffered for years from a debilitating nerve ailment. His last words, or nearly his last, were something like "Born in a hotel room, died in a hotel room, Goddamit!"

O. is, by large majority if not unanimous opinion, the greatest American dramatist. His plays won four Pulitzer Prizes, and he also won the Nobel Prize in literature. After his siege of tuberculosis, he attended a course in playwriting at Harvard, having already learned from working for a time as a minor actor and stagehand in his father's company; and he then joined, and wrote plays for, a theater group on Cape Cod that was to become famous, the Provincetown Players. His early plays were one-acters, the most impressive being those about sailors and their lives (especially "Bound East for Cardiff," "The Long Voyage Home," and "The Moon of the Caribbees"), something he knew about personally since he had spent some time as a seaman himself. Presently, the Players moved to New York, and two of his first longer and still important plays, *The Emperor Jones* (1920) and *The Hairy Ape* (1921), were produced by them. His first truly full-length play, *Beyond the Horizon,* was produced on Broadway in 1920 and won his first Pulitzer.

Beyond the Horizon centers on two brothers, the sons of a New England farmer, whose lives seem in some ways related to the O'Neill brothers', and many of O.'s later plays also reflect his life. In the case of *Beyond the Horizon,* the relationships include the fact that one of the brothers is romantic and imaginative, like O., and the other not; that the romantic brother gets tuberculosis, and in this case dies of it; and that the romantic brother has an unsuccessful marriage. At the beginning, the realistic brother is to marry a girl and stay home and run the farm (at which he would have been successful), while the romantic one is to roam the world; but at the last minute the girl chooses the other brother, who therefore stays home while the other roams; and hence the lives of both brothers are essentially ruined. The play has, with some justice, been considered the first successful American tragedy. But O.'s best plays are, of course, important for other reasons. The first major American playwright, he frequently succeeded in creating memorable characters and effective plots, and he experimented with a variety of modern dramatic modes: REALISM, NATURALISM, and expressionism. He was influenced by ancient Greek drama and especially by two seminal modern playwrights, Henrik Ibsen, and August Strindberg. *Beyond the Horizon* reflects a realism-in-depth typical of Ibsen, and *The Emperor Jones* and *The Hairy Ape* reflect the expressionism invented by Strindberg, though O. professed never to have heard of the term or the idea at the time. *The Emperor Jones,* which presents a sort of scenery which O. had encountered in Central America, concerns a black American prisoner guilty of murder who had escaped to a Caribbean island and become its ruler. The people rebel, and Jones, trying to escape, becomes hysterical as he runs through a jungle, sees (as the audience does) visions of his past life and of the life of his race, and is finally killed by his pursuers. *The Hairy Ape* concerns a feeble-minded sailor who for the first time leaves the dockside neighborhood and goes into upperclass New York and other parts of the city, and is made to feel alien, bewildered, and rejected in a variety of ways, some of them expressionistic. He finally goes to the cage of an ape in the zoo in a desperate search for companionship, and is killed.

Among O.'s subsequent plays, the most important are probably *Anna Christie* (1921), *Desire under the Elms* (1924), *Strange Interlude* (1928), *Mourning Becomes Electra* (1931), *Ah, Wilderness!* (1932), *The Iceman Cometh* (1946), and *Long Day's Journey into Night* (1956). *Anna Christie* concerns a young woman whose father, a barge operator in New York harbor, sent her as a child to be raised by relatives in the Midwest. She returns as a grown woman and, unknown to her father, a prostitute, one of many prostitutes in O.'s plays; and we see her first in a bar much like those O. had inhabited. She then lives aboard her father's vessel, is somehow changed by the sea atmosphere, and falls in love with a friend of her father's. After she confesses her past, the friend presently recovers from the shock, and they will apparently marry. Not one of O.'s great plays, it presents characters and atmospheres well and won his second Pulitzer Prize.

Desire under the Elms is laid on a New England farm at the time of the 1849 Gold Rush, and is one of O.'s plays clearly influenced by Greek tragedy. Plot and character elements in the play bear resemblances to Sophocles' *Oedipus Rex* and Euripides' *Hippolytus* and *Medea*. A son who hates his father falls in love with his stepmother and has a child by her. A stepmother falls in love with her stepson. And a mother kills her child. But the center of the play is the old farmer, who has married three times, had three sons (two of whom leave early in the play for California seeking for gold: one of the various forms of "desire under the elms"), and never loved anyone. Believing himself ruled by a stern God, and believing hard work the only part of life that matters, he is finally left alone on the farm when his latest wife confesses to child-murder and his son, out of love for her, joins in the confession. As uncomprehending as ever, he will go on, somewhat pathetically but deservedly, alone until he dies. A genuinely effective and moving play, the method of *Desire* is Strindbergian naturalism, in the sense that these people cannot help being what they are, and in the sense that it is realism carried to its limits.

Strange Interlude, which won his third Pulitzer Prize, is one of O.'s most experimental plays. A sort of novelistic drama, it carries a woman from her youth through her son's marriage, and is far longer than the normal play, requiring an audience to attend in the afternoon, take a dinner intermission, and return in the evening. And the length is increased by the fact that the characters speak not only the customary dialogue but also, in a different tone, what they have been thinking as they spoke—a sort of modern version of the Shakespearean soliloquy. Not now as popular as in its own day, it is nonetheless an impressively experimental play, the success of which was doubly impressive in view of the need for audiences who were free to come for a whole day and not just for the evening.

Mourning Becomes Electra, in its day considered O.'s masterpiece, is one of the many modern versions of the Electra story, but unusual in that, unlike almost all other modern versions of Greek tragedy, it is laid neither in the Greek past nor in the playwright's present, but in a period between: New England just after the Civil War. A trilogy, it required an even longer time to present than *Strange Interlude* and was nonetheless also successful, being the direct cause of O.'s winning the Nobel Prize.

Like Aeschylus' Electra trilogy (the only Greek trilogy which survives), the first play in O.'s trilogy concerns the return home of a general from war to a wife who has taken a lover, and the conspiracy of the wife and lover to kill the general; and the second concerns the arrangements of the son and daughter to kill the lover, but not, as in Aeschylus, the mother, who in O.'s play commits suicide. But the third play in Aeschylus' trilogy ends affirmatively, with the gods absolving the son from the charge of matricide, while in O.'s third, the son commits suicide, and the daughter closes herself in the gloomy family mansion for the rest of her life: an ending which hardly satisfies Aristotle's desire for *katharsis,* but which is nonetheless a very powerful ending. And as Aeschylus' trilogy center on the gods as influential, O.'s centers on Freudian psychology.

Ah, Wilderness! is O.'s only comedy. Laid in New England at the time of his own adolescence, it presents a sort of idealized, though not flawless, version of his own family, with some additional members: the wise and loving father, a newspaper publisher; the loyal and perceptive mother; the mother's brother, a reporter and alcoholic; the father's sister, an old maid schoolteacher, who loves the reporter but has sternly refused to marry a drunkard; and the four children who are at home, especially Richard, the central character and a version of O. The play centers on Richard's teen-age romance, broken up by the girl's father; Richard's passing safely through a bitter reaction of getting drunk in a bar and almost becoming involved with a prostitute; and the restoration of the romance and arrival of a deeper understanding and affection between father and son.

The Iceman Cometh was the last O. play produced in his lifetime and is now considered one of his two greatest. Laid in one of the saloon-hotels O. had inhabited in his youth, it concerns a group of alcoholics permanently in the saloon, all of whom, as well as the proprietor, have pipe dreams that they will eventually leave and achieve a long-lost goal; and the play displays an idea frequent in modern drama, the need for illusion, an idea which also exists, though less prominently, in other O. plays. The saloon-dwellers are awaiting the arrival of an occasional-alcoholic traveling salesman, Theodore Hickman ("Hickey"), whose coming has always meant being treated to endless free drinks; but his coming this time turns out to be not what it had been. He is a reformed alcoholic who, while he continues to treat them, apparently wants to reform them; and he psychologically forces them out of the saloon to try to achieve their pipe dreams, not in the hope that they will, but in the belief that once they realize the impossibility they will be content as they are. All go out; all return; all are miserable. They then gradually learn that Hickey's change has come about because he murdered his wife, falsely believing it to have been an act of mercy and shocked when he finally realizes otherwise; and as he goes off to jail, they all, except two, return happily to their pipe dreams, believing that Hickey's behavior, in both the murder and the attempts to reform them, was caused by insanity. Of the two exceptions, one, a newcomer to the bar, has committed suicide, and the other, Larry Slade, who may be the suicide's father and is by far the clearest-sighted of the lot and as central a character as Hickey, knows that he is doomed to a lingering life of seeing himself as he really is. An interesting experimental device in the play is that, except for the departures to the outside world and the returns, there are very few entrances and exits in the play. When O. does not need one of his many characters, he has him fall into a drunken sleep onstage. Another interesting and traditional device is O.'s giving some of the characters names which have a meaning. Thus, the name of the proprietor of the saloon is, ironically, Harry Hope: the only hope his roomers have, since he regularly forgives their not paying their bills, and also representative of the hope they all have that they will some day achieve their pipe dreams. Other meaningful names include Hope's brother-in-law, Ed Mosher, decidedly a moocher; Hugo Kalmar, a Marxist whose name resembles Karl Marx; Theodore Hickman, whose first name ironically means "gift of God,"

whose last name recalls that he was originally a hick, and whose nickname is a blot on one's face; and the policemen who come to arrest Hickey, Moran and Lieb, signifying death and love.

Long Day's Journey into Night is O.'s other masterpiece and the winner of his fourth (posthumous) Pulitzer Prize: a day and night in the life of the O. family in their summer home on the Connecticut shore. Oddly, though they sound very different because of the different tone and atmosphere, the setting of *Long Day's Journey* is, as described, exactly the same as that of *Ah, Wilderness!,* and both picture the actual O. home. Not totally factual, the play is very nearly so; and O., his parents, and his brother are presented almost totally as they were, all except Eugene even having their real first names, with O. giving himself the name of a brother who died as a small child. It is the day on which it is learned that O. has tuberculosis, and also one of the many days during which his mother returned to her narcotics addictions. Long conversations between father and sons reveal much about them all—their love, their hate, their conflicts, their weaknesses, beliefs, illusions. A play of tremendous power, it at last enabled O. to see what had been, to record what he sees, and to forgive it. He left orders when he died that the play should be kept private for twenty years, but his widow disobeyed the order, and it was produced to great acclaim.

Other O. plays of some importance include *All God's Chillun Got Wings* (1923), a play about the tragic results of an interracial marriage; *The Great God Brown* (1926), an expressionistic play involving the wearing of, and occasional removal of, masks, and the contrast, as in *Beyond the Horizon,* of the poetic man and the practical man; *Marco Millions* (1928), a play showing scenes in the life of Marco Polo; *A Moon for the Misbegotten* (1957), a play about a nightlong encounter between O.'s brother and a very tall and muscular virginal woman on a New England farm who loves him and craves an affection he cannot provide; *A Touch of the Poet* (1958), laid in prerevolutionary New England, which is one of the two surviving plays in a series O. attempted to write about an American family generation after generation; and "Hughie," a late one-act play about a lonely roomer in a sleazy New York hotel trying late at night to communicate, in what is almost a monologue, with an equally lonely but reticent desk clerk.

O. wrote a number of other, less impressive plays, and his dramatic experiments did not always work; but his best plays are truly masterpieces of modern drama.

BIBLIOGRAPHY: Bogard, T., *Contour in Time: The Plays of E. O.* (1972); Cargill, O., N. B. Fagin, and W. J. Fisher, eds., *O. and His Plays: Four Decades of*

Criticism (1961); Engel, E., *The Haunted Heroes of E. O.* (1953); Falk, D., *E. O. and the Tragic Tension* (1958); Floyd, V., *E. O. at Work: Newly Released Ideas for Plays* (1981); Floyd, V., ed., *The Unfinished Plays: Notes for "The Visit of Malatesta," "The Last Conquest," "Blind Alley Guy"* (1988); Frenz, H., and S. Tuck, eds., *E. O.'s Critics: Voices from Abroad* (1984); Gassner, J., *O.. A Collection of Critical Essays* (1964); Gelb, A., and B. Gelb, *O.* (1960); Manheim, M., *E. O.'s New Language of Kinship* (1982); Martine, J., *Critical Essays on E. O.* (1984); Miller, J. Y., *Playwright's Progress: O. and the Critics* (1965); Sheaffer, L., *O.: Son and Playwright* (1968); Sheaffer, L., *O.: Son and Artist* (1973); Tiusanen, T., *O.'s Scenic Images* (1968); Tornqvist, E., *A Drama of Souls: Studies in O.'s Supernatural Techniques* (1969)

JACOB H. ADLER

OPPEN, George

b. 24 April 1908, New Rochelle, New York; d. 7 July 1984, Sunnyvale, California

O.'s career was remarkable in that his first book appeared twenty-eight years before his second, yet his distinct style has been highly influential in American avant-garde poetics. Often categorized as an "objectivist," O. wrote in an elliptical, concrete style that, while sometimes baffling, emphasized vivid visual impressions coupled with philosophical insights, which together helped push modern American poetry beyond the delicacies of IMAGISM.

Born George Oppenheimer, O. grew up in New York and San Francisco and traveled extensively with his wife Mary, with whom he enjoyed an enduring aesthetic and political partnership. In France, they founded TO, Publishers (1929–33), which printed books by Ezra POUND, William Carlos WILLIAMS, and Louis ZUKOFSKY. O.'s interest in these important poets is reflected in his early poetic style, which was concerned with precise observations and idiosyncratic juxtapositions that create meaning through several modes of relationship—among portions of a poem, between poems in a book, and between O.'s poems and his life. His first book, *Discrete Series* (1934), established O.'s method of constructing meaning through form, revealing the poet's perception in dynamic relationship to the objects it perceives. Despite O.'s difficult syntax—an expression of the demands of his poetic vision—the book demonstrated O.'s sense of congruence between his political and artistic commitments.

After *Discrete Series* appeared, O. and his wife worked for the Communist Party for several years, during which O. did not write; subsequently, he was wounded during service in World War II. Postwar anticommunist investigations prompted the Oppens to live in Mexico between 1950 and 1958. When they returned to the U.S., O. began to write again, in part because of a propitious dream that infused his poetry with themes of survival, return, and renewal.

O.'s next books were *The Materials* (1962), *This in Which* (1965), and *Of Being Numerous* (1968), accompanied by critical essays that articulated his style and values and that helped bring considerable attention to O. and other objectivist writers who were writing again after decades of silence. As O. described it, writing was a process of disorienting, even frightening, self-discovery—a "test of truth," even a "theology," "built out of a few small nouns." Critical of urban life and modern society, yet undeniably collectivist in spirit and structure, O.'s poems suggest the continuing influence of Marxism on his work.

O.'s last books, including *Seascape: Needle's Eye* (1972) and *Primitive* (1978), were more challenging stylistically. His interest in creating a sense of "interpenetration" led him to pair imagery of fluidity and light with a fragmented syntax, thereby representing the dynamics of a consciousness continually in flux. Since his death, O.'s work has continued to influence modern poetry through his stark, urgent language and his insistence on rigorous integrity in one's poetic vision and craft.

BIBLIOGRAPHY: Freeman, J., ed., *Not Comforts/But Vision: Essays on the Poetry of G. O.* (1985); Hatlen, B., "'Feminine Technologies': G. O. Talks at Denise Levertov," *APR* 22 (May-June 1993): 9–14; Hatlen, B., ed., *G. O.: Man and Poet* (1981); Oppen, M., *Meaning a Life* (1978)

JAYNE MAREK

OPPENHEIMER, Joel

b. 18 February 1930, Yonkers, New York; d. 11 October 1988, Henniker, New Hampshire

O. was one of the major poets to come out of the Black Mountain College, when it was under the rectorship of Charles OLSON. Before he went to Black Mountain, he had attended Cornell University and the University of Chicago, but found their competitive atmospheres uncongenial to his budding artistic talents. He did find the influence of some of his Black Mountain teachers highly energizing. He studied writing with Olson, M. C. Richards, and Paul GOODMAN. Olson's innovative teaching methods were exactly what O. had been looking for to inspire him to become a writer. He also began lifelong friendships with other Balck Mountain writers such as Robert CREELEY, Edward DORN, Jonathan Williams, and Fielding Dawson, among others.

After Black Mountain, he moved to New York City where he worked as a printer, typographer, and production manager for fifteen years. He became the director of St. Mark's Poetry Project (1966–68), one of the most important series of poetry readings and workshops on the East Coast. He also became involved in the "Writers in the Schools" project, which gave talented young students a venue in which they could develop their literary skills. From 1969 to 1984, he wrote a regular column for the *Village Voice* on sports—especially baseball, a sport he was obsessed with all of his life—politics, literature, and food. He became poet-in-residence at the City College of New York for about ten years, and spent time teaching at the State University of New York at Oneonta, Buffalo, and the Rochester Institute of Technology. He found a comfortable position at New England College in Henniker, New Hampshire, where he remained until his death in 1988.

O.'s principal subject matter throughout his writing career was the exploration of interpersonal relationships in what he called his made-up space; that is, his place. His recurring themes are his erotic dreams and actual experiences, daily activities, marital relations, and family—especially his children—and friends. Many of his poems delineate how personal, psychological, and, in his late poems, mythological worlds interact.

Besides the overwhelming influence of Olson, his early literary influences include William Carlos WILLIAMS's early poems and *Pictures from Breughel*. The power of Olson's poetry did not affect O.'s work, though Olson the teacher helped him discover his own unique voice. E. E. CUMMINGS's refusal to use uppercase letters was adopted by O. throughout his writing career, though he later admitted that the shift key on his typewriter broke in 1955, which may have helped him make that decision. Creeley's verbal compactness also helped O. evolve a similarly flat line and plain syntax. Both poets avoid verbal over-elaboration of any kind and adhere to their own practice—learned from Williams—of no ideas but in things. Most of the poems in his early books such as *The Dutiful Son* (1956) and *The Love Bit* (1962) contain short, highly evocative sharp images of domestic scenes, and explore the young poet's immediate domestic surroundings of wife and children. But "The Fourth Ark Royal," from the early 1960s, signals a new direction for his poetry because it was his first long poem, a practice he developed in the later serial poems of *The Woman Poems* (1975). Another theme that emerges in these years is that of the house, becoming a favorite image for the poet who had studied architecture at Cornell. That image persists throughout his work and became a metaphor for O.'s private and public self, and the

conflicts that arose in meeting the obligations of both worlds.

In O.'s later and larger collections *On Occasion* (1973) and *In Time* (1969), he demonstrated his mastery of the occasional poem. By writing poems on a friend's birthday or the death of a poet, O. became known for his uncanny ability to write a poem about virtually anything. He answered some critics who trivialized the custom by pointing out Goethe's championing occasional poetry as "the highest form of art." O. added: "occasional poems also indicate, for me a 'usefulness' for poetry as a function of life and a benefit to society."

Besides his poetic homages to Goodman, Frank O'HARA, and LeRoi Jones (now Amiri BARAKA), among others, O. began to address some social and political problems of the 1960s. Some of the poems in *In Time* protest the expansionist politics of the U.S. into Southern Asia and merged with the protests of Olson, Dorn, and Allen GINSBERG in their concern over America's political arrogance.

During a period from the late 1960s to 1984, he wrote for the *Village Voice,* mostly personal essays about the problems of rearing a family in New York, eating in restaurants—he was the *Voice*'s restaurant critic for many years—baseball, and various political and social movements during that time. *The Woman Poems* (1975), one of his most notable collections, was an authentic serial poem, where a number of poems interconnect thematically. His subject is the pain and pleasure of his relationships with his many lovers down through the years. But his treatment is not simply personal. He views them for the first time within their mythological contexts, having been profoundly influenced by Robert BLY's *Sleepers Joining Hands,* and the Jungian archetypes of the Great Mother, Death Mother, and the Castrating Tooth Mother. His homage to Marilyn Monroe in *Marilyn Lives* (1981) expanded his Jungian appreciations of Monroe as more than simply a contemporary erotic object.

One of his most significant volumes, *New Spaces: Poems, 1975–1983* (1985), brought together new poems from his journals and from recent manuscripts, and signify a change in tone from the nostalgia for the past to an acceptance of the pleasures and pains of the present. The natural process of birth and death and the cyclic changes of the seasons become consistent themes in his later poetry. The more specifically personal the poems, the more mythic they became. Helen Oppenheimer, his first wife and mother of his children, becomes, in "Lesson I" and "Lesson II," the mythic Helen of Troy. And in one of his last collections, *Why Not* (1985), O. clarifies his poetic vision: "every poem is an investigation of the world we live in, the way we live, and the way we treat ourselves and others." He later extended his definition of what a poem is: "a poem is the answer to a question I didn't know I asked myself."

Few of O.'s critics or readers will argue that one of his last works, "The Uses of Adversity," may very well be his greatest poem: its subject is chemotherapy. He wrote it after he discovered he had cancer.

O. will be most remembered as America's most famous practitioner of the occasional poem and the greatest love poet since Kenneth PATCHEN. Few poets have so subtly delineated the relationships between people or between themselves and the world of nature.

BIBLIOGRAPHY: Butterick, G. F., "J. O.," in Greiner, D. J., ed., *DLB,* vol. 5, part 2, *American Poets since World War II* (1981): 133–41; Gilmore, L., *Don't Touch the Poet: The Life of J. O.* (1997)

PATRICK MEANOR

ORIENT, The

When Columbus sighted the shores of the Western world at the end of the 15th c., he thought he had found India, and interest in things of the East has occupied Americans from almost the beginning of our settlements in the 17th c., ebbing and flowing in waves through the intervening years. Nor is this interest as foreign as it may seem, for if the West is a product of the Judeo-Christian tradition, as it merged with those of Greece and Rome, the Judeo-Christian tradition itself arose in the Middle East, while early Greece and Rome themselves also experienced much interchange with the Orient.

It is to be expected that America's response to the Orient has never been simple or objective, varying as it selects this facet or that from out of the jumble of holiness, exoticism, poverty, romance, racial stereotypes, and superstition that constitutes its image of "the mysterious East." But we do not turn to literature for simple and objective pictures of reality, nor is "influence" a matter of accurate transmission—it is rather a process of assimilating the strange into the familiar, the familiar into the strange, usually to highlight some ostensible lack in our own culture. It is when the direction is reversed, however, and the intent is to demonstrate our supposed superiority, that we must be especially on guard. Travel, foreign residence, and scholarship may improve—and have improved—the objectivity, if not the simplicity of this image, but there too we need to guard against failures of empathy.

Oriental influences on American literature may thus be seen as dividing mainly into two different streams.

The first, deriving from the ostensible dispersion of India's stories and folktales through Arabia, Syria, and Persia, and their subsequent entry into the West during the Crusades, finds its watersheds in *The Thousand and One Nights* and the fortunes of the Ottoman Empire. This stream flows through the literature of Great Britain beginning as early as Edmund Spenser, and continuing on through the major writers of the 17th and 18th cs.—and one of whose most enduring monument is Edward Fitzgerald's *The Rubáiyát of Omar Khayyám* (1859). Sir Edwin Arnold's *The Light of Asia* (1879), a poem of eight books in blank verse about Buddhism and its founder, must also be mentioned here.

In American literature, it begins as early as Hugh Henry BRACKENRIDGE and Philip FRENEAU, and includes Benjamin FRANKLIN, Washington IRVING, Herman MELVILLE—who actually exemplifies *both* sorts of influence—Nathaniel HAWTHORNE—whose father sailed out of Salem to the Orient—John Greenleaf WHITTIER, and Mark TWAIN.

As L. S. Luedtke points out, this influence represents "the gorgeous East" of adventure, storytelling, and exoticism, as opposed to "the spiritual East" of the transcendentalists, embodying the second main stream of Orientalism in American literature. Although Luedtke sees the former tradition as significant in counteracting the Yankee Puritan insistence on hard work and sexual repression, and in bringing in an historically relativist perspective, it is the latter that emerged as the more enduring homegrown American response to Eastern philosophy, religion, literature, and culture. It is to this second tradition that we now turn.

Ralph Waldo EMERSON, the first major American writer for whom "the spiritual East" was an important preoccupation, is a case in point. TRANSCENDENTALISM, the philosophy most frequently associated with his name, owes something to Neoplatonism—itself a product of the Middle East in the 3rd c.—to the 19th-c. English and Continental post-Kantian romantic movements—also very much attuned to oriental influences—to his discontent with Unitarianism, and to the nondualistic Hindu tradition of *The Vedas*.

"Veda" is Sanskrit for "knowledge," and *The Vedas* comprise the literature of the Aryan (Sanskrit for "stranger," "enemy," "noble") invaders of India, from 1500 B.C., concerning the fire sacrifice. These are the sacred writings of Hindu scripture, and *The Upanishads* ("sitting at the feet of a master")—a collection of around 112 "books" dating from 800 B.C.E. to the 15th c.—contain the last four classes of *Vedas* (the first of which is *The Rig Veda*). "Vedanta," meaning "end of *The Vedas*," is one of the six systems of Vedic philosophy (which also includes Yoga), and is based upon *The Upanishads.* This philosophy takes as its premise the nondualistic belief in the unity and connectedness of all things, expressed in the Sanskrit formula, *Tat tvam asi,* or "That art thou," and in the conviction that the eternal, inner Self (*Atman*) of each person—as distinguished from the temporal, egoistic self—is made of the same stuff as the Universal Soul (*Brahman*).

The pre-Aryan Indus Valley civilization, ca. 2500–1500 B.C.E., whose native core was in the Dravidian region, was characterized, however, by non-Vedic, dualistic beliefs, and these served in turn as the basis for the later emergence in India of such non-Hindu movements as Buddhism. But such is the complexity of developments in religious belief that even Vedanta has its proponents of dualism, and Hinduism and Buddhism influenced one another reciprocally. Buddha means "The Enlightened One," and his given name was Siddhartha, family name Gautama, clan name Sakyamuni. He is also known as Tathagata, meaning "truth winner." He became so obsessed with the frustration of desire by sickness, old age, and death that he could only see the true nature of life as perpetual suffering. The purpose of religious practice, then, as opposed to Hindu metaphysics and ritual, whose goal was to achieve oneness of Atman with Brahman, was to free one from that cycle. Since the cause of suffering is desire, the cure lies in overcoming desire.

Although such distinctions between Hinduism and Buddhism were not yet wholly clear, Emerson grew up in a New England atmosphere already stirring with interest around the turn of the 18th c. over the Yankee clipper ships that were opening up trade routes to the East, and the work of such early scholars as Sir William Jones, a British lawyer assigned to a government post in India, and Raja Rammohun Roy, a Bengali Hindu devoted to bridging the two cultures, who were translating many of the literary and religious classics of India. By the 1830s and 1840s, Emerson was becoming familiar with Indian philosophy, and what he found was remarkably compatible with ideas he was already working out for himself—with the aid, of course, of the other traditions already mentioned—namely, that the world is the garment of God, that He is both transcendent and immanent, and that therefore all things are interconnected.

The Hindu works with which Emerson familiarized himself were chiefly *The Laws of Manu,* probably compiled between 200 B.C.E. and C.E. 200, and containing rules for religious and civil life; *The Upanishads; The Bhagavad Gita* ("Song of the Lord"), written between the 5th and 2nd cs. B.C.E., and expounding devotion to work apart from needing the rewards of work; *The Vishnu Purana,* traditional legendary material concerning one of the three chief Hindu dieties

(the other two being Brahma and Siva); and the *Sakuntala* of Kalidasa, one of the three surviving plays of this 5th-c. C.E. dramatist. The direct influence of these and other Oriental readings—he was also quite interested in the Persian mystical Sufi poets, for example—is to be seen primarily in several of his poems, such as "Brahma" (1857), "Hamatreya" (1847), and "Maia" (n.d.), and in a number of his essays, such as "Plato" (1850), "The Over-Soul" (1841), "Fate" (1860), "Illusions" (1860), and "Immortality" (1870).

It could be said, then, that Emerson was almost a mystic, and likewise that his disciple, Henry David THOREAU, was almost a yogi, arranging his life for two years at Walden Pond as if it were a hermitage where he could penetrate through the appearance of things to the essentials of existence. He read those oriental books even more eagerly than Emerson, and in the fact that the clipper ships were bringing ice from Walden Pond to India he saw an emblem of the mingling of the waters of his pond with those of the Ganges, a realistic symbol of the interconnection of all things. It is surely no accident that his pamphlet *Civil Disobedience* inspired Mahatma Gandhi in developing his doctrine of passive resistance, and that Gandhi in turn inspired Martin Luther King, Jr., and the civil rights movement of the 1960s.

Although Melville's *Moby-Dick* is full, among other things, of Oriental references and allusions, as a whole it is a critique rather than an example of transcendentalism. Ahab is in effect a transcendentalist turned upside down: he indeed sees the material world as embodying the spiritual, except that the spirit, for him, is demonic rather than divine. As in *Billy Budd* also, Melville portrays the ostensible dangers of subsuming the phenomenal world under the aegis of the noumenal: the things of the earth, human things, must be treated in terms of the earth and the human, otherwise we run the risk of fanaticism, madness, and sanctified murder. Tyrants seek heavenly justification for their deeds as well as saints. If anything, Melville is a Taoist or a Zen Buddhist—but more of these matters later.

Whether Walt WHITMAN had actually any knowledge of Vedic texts before the first publication of *Leaves of Grass* in 1855 apparently cannot be definitively established, although it is known that he read some Indian religion and philosophy afterwards. But he had certainly been reading Emerson, to whom he sent a copy. The salient point is that there is a clear affinity with the doctrines of *The Vedas,* and especially in "Song of Myself," a proclamation of identity with the universe and its living principle. And he does indeed make the distinction explicit between the merely egoistic self and the Universal Self in sections 4 and 5 of that poem. "A Passage to India" (1871) is, of course, another specifically relevant poem, in which the bard sees America as a natural and spiritual bridge between West and East.

A peculiarly American art form was being created by these writers, and they were doing so partly under the influence of Orientalism, and partly of the Senecan prose tradition from Plutarch through Montaigne. If all things are interconnected, then the jumps of the mind as it searches for analogues to illuminate the subject at hand form the organic progression of the piece. The style becomes abrupt, epigrammatic, imagistic, and rhapsodic by turns, and meanings emerge as a result of juxtapositions and accumulations rather than logical sequence. It is not too much to say that *The Upanishads,* which are an amalgam of narrative, drama, prayer, exhortation, instruction, and song, are among the formal as well as philosophical influences behind the transcendentalists, and that both in turn are among the influences behind the modernist writers.

Literary MODERNISM received a good portion of its impulse even more explicitly, of course, from those two most prominent American exemplars, Ezra POUND and T. S. ELIOT. Through his involvement in the Imagist movement during the 1910s, Pound developed an interest, along with Amy LOWELL and John Gould FLETCHER, in Chinese and Japanese poetry. It is one of those remarkable coincidences of literary history that he came into the possession of manuscripts containing notes and translations of Chinese and Japanese literature by Ernest Fenollosa, Harvard scholar of philosophy and art history. An heir of the New England transcendentalists, Fenollosa had gone to Japan to study Eastern art and while there was tutored in oriental literature by several Japanese scholars.

Fenollosa died in 1908, and his widow recognized, on seeing some of his work, that Pound would be just the person to receive these notebooks. This was in 1913. By 1915, he had published *Cathay,* a series of translations—primarily of Li Po ("Rihaku" in Japanese), the famous 8th-c. C.E. Chinese poet—based on Fenollosa's notes. Despite the fact that Pound knew no Chinese at the time and committed a number of blunders, these poems did capture the spirit of the originals and made a great impression upon his fellow poets. Primarily about love and war, they struck a poignant note as the clouds of World War I were gathering over the West, and the cleanness and restraint of their language, rhythms, and imagery were exactly suited to the artistic mood of the day.

In 1918, he edited and published Fenollosa's monograph, *The Chinese Written Character as a Medium for Poetry,* and around this time he began studying Confucius in 18th- and 19th-c. Latin and French translations. By 1936, however, he was learning Chinese in earnest and translating Confucius from the original.

He translated into English three of "The Four Books" (*Shih Shu*)—"The Great Digest" (*Ta Hsio*) in 1928, "The Unwobbling Pivot" (*Chung Yung*) in 1947, and "The Analects of Confucius" (*Lun Yu*) in 1950—and one of "The Five Classics" (*Wu Ching*), "The Book of Odes" (*Shi Ching*), in 1958. I. A. Richards, as influential in modernist criticism as Pound was in poetry, translated the fourth book of the *Shih Shu,* "The Book of Mencius," in 1932 (*Mencius on the Mind),* with an introduction pointing out the similarities between the Chinese language and modernist poetry.

The chief artistic fruits of Pound's Confucian endeavors were Cantos XIII (1933), XLIX (1937), LII (1940), and LIII-LXI (the "China" Cantos, 1940) of *The Cantos.* The attraction of the Chinese written character to Pound was that it embodies a language of pictures—or so he and Fenollosa interpreted it—and hence that it reinforces his Imagistic theory that the language of poetry should be vivid, particular, and concrete. And the attraction of Confucius was that the ancient sage's theories of government and economics seemed to support Pound's own: that taxes should be equitable and fair, the currency be based on real resources, the ruler be an example to his people, and the use of language be sincere and accurate. Thus, *The Cantos,* a modernist epic poem containing history and using the method of juxtaposition and accumulation, rummage through traditions, personages, and events East and West, ancient and modern, in search of principles of order to remedy the chaos and violence of the modern world. The China Cantos in particular, following an 18th-c. French history of the Middle Kingdom, which in turn followed prior Chinese histories, trace the rise and fall of good rule in that ancient and harried nation up to the 18th c., and they do so in terms of Confucian values as touchstone.

It can be seen that the story of oriental influences has taken an entirely different track from the Hinduism with which it began, and indeed Pound, who thought of himself as a hard-headed materialist and rationalist, showed no interest whatever in Hinduism, and what explicit notice he did take of Buddhism and Taoism—a belief in the efficacy of unobstructed natural process—was entirely negative. Lao Tzu, the legendary author of the *Tao Te Ching* ("The Way and Its Power"), was supposed to have been a slightly older contemporary of Confucius. The problem is, however, that both Confucius and Pound have, in fact, their mystical side, believing in "process," in the organic order of nature as the criterion of human value, and are therefore not that divergent from Hinduism and Taoism—or from Emerson and Fenollosa—after all.

Although Buddhism had attracted the passing interest of such earlier writers as Emerson, Thoreau, and Melville, it was not until the latter part of the 19th c.

that it engaged the attention of writers, such as Henry ADAMS and Lafcadio HEARN, in any concentrated way, and it was not until T. S. Eliot, who read *The Light of Asia* and Kipling as a youth, that it profoundly affected a major literary artist. This lack did not deter Pound, however, from attempting to render from Fenollosa's notebooks over a dozen Japanese Noh plays—first published in 1916 as *Certain Noble Plays of Japan,* then in 1917 as *"Noh" or Accomplishment,* and finally in 1959 as *The Classic Noh Theatre of Japan*—nor from experimenting with the haiku form of poetry, both of which, flourishing from the 13th and 14th cs., are strongly Buddhist in spirit.

Eliot greeted Pound's early oriental renderings enthusiastically, but he had already been studying Sanskrit and Eastern religions himself at Harvard a half dozen years earlier, and he had been especially impressed by the meditative and ascetic side of Indian thought—particularly Raja Yoga and Buddhism. After the Hun invasion of the 6th c. and the Muslim invasion of the 11th c., Buddhism was practically extinguished in India by the 13th c. It subsequently evolved into a divided tradition, spreading north into Korea, China, and Japan, and south into Sri Lanka, Burma, and Southeast Asia. The northern branch, *mahayana,* or "big raft," became more democratized and thisworldly, while the southern branch, *hinayana,* or "little raft," preferably *theravada,* or "The Way of the Elders," became more priestly and ascetic. Eliot learned his Buddhism at Harvard from the southern texts and was very tempted, as he himself said, in view of the asceticism of his own nature, to become a Buddhist.

Thus, he could juxtapose Buddha and St. Augustine at the end of section 3 of *The Waste Land* as comparable forms of asceticism. That is not all there is to the Orientalism of the poem, however, for the Hindu influence reenters American poetry at the climax of the poem with the Upanishadic *Datta, Dayadvam, Damyata* (give, sympathize, control)—which is what the thunder said (*Da*), and at its close with the thrice repeated *shantih*—which Eliot renders, in his own notes to the poem, as "The Peace which passeth understanding." The allusion to the thunder is still more complex, going back to Jessie L. Weston's *From Ritual to Romance* (1920), upon which Eliot said the plan and symbolism of the poem were based, and which traces one of the sources of the Grail legends to the hymns in *The Rig Veda* celebrating the thunder God, Indra, as the bringer of rain and fertility.

Eliot was not being a transcendentalist here, for the poem concludes rather with the hope of redemption than its accomplishment, but he did ultimately find his way up the winding stair of *Ash-Wednesday,* published in 1930, to achieve a faith that found its home in the Anglo-Catholic Church. He was then able to

approach more closely the illumination of mysticism and, although he ostensibly had given up his Orientalism, felt free in the *Four Quartets* and his later verse dramas of the 1950s to allude a significant number of times to *The Bhagavad Gita.*

By the 1920s, then, spiritual influences from the East had become an established tradition for American writers. Thus, Hart CRANE referred to the airman's "Sanskrit charge" in the "Cape Hatteras" section of *The Bridge,* a poem about the hope and possibility of Unity, and called Whitman a "Vedic Caesar"—nor is the reference to the Yankee clipper ships in the "Cutty Sark" section unrelated. Eugene O'NEILL fought a personal battle between the Western dualism of his Catholic background and a growing interest in Eastern monism in a number of his plays, including *The Iceman Cometh, Long Day's Journey into Night,* and *Hughie.* E. E. CUMMINGS said of himself that he "lived" in China where a painter is a poet, and not only do a number of his poems typographically resemble ideograms and *haiku,* but also his transcendental vision has a Taoist-Zen-Emerson-Whitman quality. Kenneth REXROTH has long been a distinguished representative of Buddhism in American poetry, and the Beat writers—Allen GINSBERG, Jack KEROUAC, and Gary SNYDER—did much to bring Orientalism, in their paradoxically frenetic way, to the fore in the 1960s. Other notable American writers who have shown an important interest in, or in whom one finds parallels to, oriental influences would include Theodore DREISER, John STEINBECK, Henry MILLER, Wallace STEVENS, Thornton WILDER, Tennessee WILLIAMS, Muriel RUKEYSER, Saul BELLOW, and Denise LEVERTOV.

But it is the fiction of J. D. SALINGER that exemplifies the most significant influence of Zen in American literature. "Zen" derives from the Chinese *ch'an,* which in turn derives from the Sanskrit *dhyana,* meaning "meditation." Zen emerged from the northern branch of Buddhism as it made its way to China in the early centuries of the present era, absorbing some influence from Taoism along the path, and into Japan during the 13th c. Basically, it combined the antiritual focus on meditation of Buddhism with the Brahmanis-Atman doctrine of Hinduism. Zen cannot be equated with Buddhism, therefore, despite the fact that it is called "Zen Buddhism," for it in effect repudiates the dualism of Buddhism, as well as its pessimistic vision of the world as a charnel house. The essence of Zen is to find spiritual illumination among the ordinary tasks of life when these are undertaken purely for themselves rather than for any gain, goal, or purpose—an attitude that is closer to *The Bhagavad Gita* than to the Buddha's "Fire Sermon." As one Zen master put it: "When I am hungry, I eat; when I am tired, I sleep."

Beginning with *The Catcher in the Rye,* although it contains no specific allusions to Zen—Phoebe sits on her bed like a yogi, however, when she "instructs" her older brother Holden—and continuing on with *Nine Stories,* which has the famous one-hand-clapping *koan* as its epigraph, *Franny and Zooey, Raise High the Roofbeam, Carpenters,* and *Seymour: An Intro-duction,* Salinger and his characters have become in-creasingly involved in Zen as a solution to—and some-times as an avoidance of—the pain in their lives and times—symbolized by the death of a brilliant and be-loved brother. After *Seymour,* Salinger himself has in effect become a hermit and has ceased to publish; he continues to write, however, if the few public words that have on occasion been drawn out of him can be believed. Whether he is actually doing what Thoreau did—what yogis do—in retiring from the world in order to contact the reality of Being, or whether he is simply unwilling or unable to deal with the world altogether—as Holden was unable before his healing encounter with Phoebe—remains to be seen.

But either way, it seems clear that Kipling's lines about "never the twain shall meet," which were them-selves qualified during the course of the poem "The Ballad of East and West" (1889), are especially inap-plicable to American literature, if the testimony of our writers from Emerson to Salinger is to be taken seriously. There is a natural affinity between our cul-ture and certain aspects of the cultures of the Orient, and it is here that the general tendency of the West toward material accomplishment—if we can speak of such matters apart from stereotypes—can meet the general tendency of the East toward things of the spirit to perhaps create a new form of unified culture, even as Whitman and Crane have prophesied.

BIBLIOGRAPHY: Ames, V. M., *Zen and American Thought* (1962); Ando, S., *Zen and American Tran-scendentalism* (1970); Christy, A., *The Orient and American Transcendentalism* (1932); Jackson, C. T., *The Oriental Religions and American Thought* (1981); Luedtke, L. S., *Nathaniel Hawthorne and the Romance of the Orient* (1989); Reid, J. T., *Indian Influences in American Literature and Thought* (1965); Riepe, D., *The Philosophy of India and Its Impact on American Thought* (1970); Said, E., *Orien-talism* (1978)

NORMAN FRIEDMAN

ORTIZ, Simon [Joseph]

b. 27 May 1941, Albuquerque, New Mexico

O. is both a Native American (Acoma Pueblo) and a Vietnam-era veteran of the U.S. Army. This combina-tion produces a range of tensions and issues. Pulled in different directions by conflicting loyalties, O. carves out in his work a relentlessly honest poetic identity. He is above all a Native American writer who never loses touch with his cultural heritage, but his work also endeavors to speak for all Americans.

O. has won numerous awards, including a National Endowment for the Arts Discovery Award in 1969 and a 1982 Pushcart Prize for *From Sand Creek* (1981). Increasingly, O. has come to be seen as a leading figure in NATIVE AMERICAN LITERATURE. Yet his work stubbornly refuses to be forced into neat, narrow cate-gories.

O. writes both fiction and poetry. His major works of fiction include *Howbah Indians* (1978), *Fightin': New and Collected Stories,* (1983), and *Woven Stone* (1991), which includes both poetry and prose. Most of his stories deal with the theme of displacement and alienation—separation from the land, from family, and from historical roots. This displacement can take many forms, but the basic principle is invariant: people who lose a deeply-rooted, complex sense of place are headed for trouble.

An example of this theme of displacement is "Kai-ser and the War," a story from *Fightin'* in which the Native American title character resists induction into the Army. When agents from the draft board are sent to forcibly induct him, the "crazy" Kaiser flees into the nearby mountains. The ultimate result of this clash of cultures is that Kaiser is unable to function in either the Native American or the "white" culture; after his long-delayed release from prison, Kaiser flees to the mountains wearing the fading gray, ill-fitting " Ameri-can" suit given him by the government.

O. is best known for his poetry. His major collec-tions include *Naked in the Wind* (1971), *A Good Jour-ney* (1977), *Goin' for the Rain* (1976), and *From Sand Creek.* The poetry in these anthologies is terse and charged with tension, and the poet employs sharp, vivid imagery to accomplish his effects. For example, in "The Wisconsin Horse," from *Goin' for the Rain,* a misplaced horse—a recurrent image for O.—locked within a chainlink fence is contrasted with the whirl of modern construction swirling around it.

O.'s poetry often focuses on distinctive Western landscapes, and the wide range of people who inhabit these landscapes. In "The Boy and Coyote," for exam-ple, the poet's attention to detail is at the same time acute and sweeping; images such as "the rippled sand rifts / shallow inches below the surface" of a riverbank, and the "reports of a shotgun / muffled flat by saltcedar thickets," point the way toward a complex of signifi-cance beyond sensory impression. And in "Wind and Glacier Voices," when the "Laguna man" claims to have "heard that glacier scraping / once, thirty thousand years ago," we must take him at his word, for language transcends time.

In fact, language is the source of all power and knowledge for O. Poetry is more than a passive way of representing reality; it is the interface between external reality and the poet's creative consciousness. As a result, language has immense power to create and define an experience. Further, poetry and storytelling are inextricably linked to the oral tradition, as well as to the context that informs storytelling. Thus, a full understanding of a literary work must take into account the totality of its historical and oral context.

O.'s work is relentlessly political. As Andrew Wiget points out, for O. "Language use is fundamentally political . . . it has real social consequences." The essential creative power of language makes the poet's role crucial; as the keeper of such power, it is the poet's sacred responsibility to make language a force for positive change. This change can occur in several venues, ranging from the mind of the individual reader to the realm of government agencies. Along this spectrum, language works to foreground conflicts, making the reader constantly aware of the intrinsic power of the word.

Overall, O.'s work provides a bridge between literary worlds. By mining the rich vein of Native American mythology and culture for subjective thoughts, images, and themes and then connecting this personal heritage with the broader sweep of American culture and traditions, O. creates a unique artistic achievement. In his hands, two major poetic streams are united, and in this new unity lies a blueprint for a guardedly optimistic future.

BIBLIOGRAPHY: Bruchac, J., *Survival This Way: Interviews with American Indian Poets* (1987): 211–29; Gleason, J., "Reclaiming the Valley of the Shadow" *Parnassus* 12 (Fall-Winter 1984): 21–71; Wiget, A., *S. O.* (1986)

HENRY L. WILSON

ORTIZ COFER, Judith
b. 24 February 1952, Hormigueros, Puerto Rico

Considered one of the premier Puerto Rican writers, O. C. published several poetry chapbooks in the 1980s: *Among the Ancestors* (1981), *The Native Dancer* (1981), *Latin Women Pray* (1986), and *Peregrina* (1986). In 1987, she followed with two longer collections of poems, *Reaching for the Mainland* and *Terms of Survival*. These works deal with her own struggles in forging a bicultural identity, particularly issues from her childhood, which was divided between Puerto Rico and the U.S. Her poems also explore her relationships with her family, her parents and grandmother especially. In addition, her works consider male-female relationships from the perspective of the two cultures that have constituted her existence. O. C. has stated that her poetry is a "study of this process of change, assimilation and transformation."

In 1989, O. C. continued her exploration of her family and heritage, and the resultant effects of their migration to the U.S., in her first novel, *The Line of the Sun*. While the family tries to retain their Puerto Rican cultural heritage, the novel shows their attempts to acclimate themselves to life in Paterson, New Jersey, focusing on the young narrator's coming of age in America. As such, *The Line of the Sun* showcases the hardships ethnic minorities endure in the U.S. as they try to forge a life for themselves within the dominant, Anglo culture.

O. C. next published her autobiographical memoirs, *Silent Dancing: A Partial Remembrance of a Puerto Rican Childhood* (1990), a collection of personal essays that reflect on the writer's life. Influenced by Virginia Woolf, O. C. writes in the preface that her goal was "to try to connect myself to the threads of lives that have touched mine and at some point converged into the tapestry that is my memory of childhood." While the memoir illustrates the relationships between people, it focuses on the tensions of the bicultural identity, the cultural struggles that ensue when a Puerto Rican family settles in Paterson, New Jersey. As with her previous works, this memoir serves to illustrate the confusions and contradictions that have shaped her life and identity.

In *The Latin Deli: Prose and Poetry* (1993), O. C. interweaves short stories, poems, and essays to provide a vivid account of her own bicultural coming of age in America. Set in El Building in Paterson, *The Latin Deli* focuses on the lives of a Puerto Rican family, the women especially, who try to maintain a semblance of "Island" life in the housing complex, while making a transition to the American way of life. Interestingly enough, the women in the text struggle to keep their Puerto Rican identities, complete with traditions and customs, while the men grapple in their quest for the American Dream. As such, *The Latin Deli* addresses the roles of women in both Puerto Rican and American cultures. This work further touches on the stereotyping and discrimination that affect ethnic minorities in the U.S. In one of the most poignant examples, the protagonist in "American History," a young girl, is refused participation in the honors courses at school—despite her excellent grades—because English is not her first language.

O. C. has received various prestigious awards for her work, including the Florida Arts Council (1980), the Bread Loaf Writers Conference (1981), and the

National Endowment for the Arts (1989). Now a professor of English at the University of Georgia, O. C. has also coedited an anthology of Latino/a poetry, *Triple Crown: Chicano, Puerto Rican, and Cuban-American Poetry* (1987).

BIBLIOGRAPHY: Bruce-Novoa, J., "J. O. C.'s Rituals of Moment," *AmRev* 19 (Winter 1991): 88–99; Kallet, M., "The Art of Not Forgetting: An Interview with J. O. C.," *PrS* 68 (Winter 1994): 68–75; Kanellos, N., ed., *The Hispanic Almanac: From Columbus to Corporate America* (1994)

JOSEPH M. VIERA

OSGOOD, Frances Sargent [Locke]
b. 18 June 1811, Boston, Massachusetts; d. 12 May 1850, New York City

Well known, highly praised, and prolific in her own day, O. has been largely neglected as a poet during the 20th c., although biographically she has received some attention because of a possible romantic relationship with Edgar Allan POE. Recent work on some women writers has begun to reestablish O. as a poet worth studying for the sake of her own work.

The daughter of a Boston merchant, O. published her first verses in the *Juvenile Miscellany* at the age of fourteen. After her marriage to portrait artist Samuel Osgood, the couple spent five years in England, where she published her first volume of poetry, *A Wreath of Wild Flowers from New England* (1938). Praise from English critics probably influenced her reception when she returned to America, where during the 1840s she became an active participant in New York literary circles, published more volumes of verse as well as some magazine fiction, and received high praise from critics and the public alike.

O.'s published poetry reflects popular poetics of her day: conventional rhymes, forms, and meters. The predominant topics are sentimental: love, children, friendship, flowers. The poems on love explore the variety and nuances of feeling from celebratory to nostalgic, yearning to bitter. The poems on children frequently contrast the innocence of childhood with the cares of adult life, as in "To a Child Playing with a Watch," in which the speaker wistfully notes the child's blithe unawareness of time. Poems on adult themes also celebrate innocence and simplicity, as in "Victoria, on her way to Guildhall," in which the speaker is moved to feel love and respect for the queen by the sincerity of her smile rather than the pomp of her procession.

O. also had a sophisticated side. Critic Joanne Dobson has printed and analyzed some of the poetry O.

did not publish, but rather wrote for reading and circulating among her New York literary circle. In these manuscript poems, O.'s persona is erotic, clever, and satirical. She lampoons the marriage market and sentimental notions of spiritual love. Dobson shows links between the themes of this "private" poetry and O.'s published work, but she also draws attention to the two personae O. presented. This duality is perhaps the most interesting feature of O.'s body of work.

BIBLIOGRAPHY: Dobson, J., "Sex, Wit, and Sentiment: O. and the Poetry of Love," *AL* 65 (December 1993): 631–50; Walker, C., *The Nightingale's Burden* (1982); Walsh, J. E., *Plumes in the Dust* (1980); Watts, E. S., *The Poetry of American Women from 1632 to 1945* (1977)

ANGELA VIETTO

OSTRIKER, Alicia [Suskin]
b. 11 November 1937, Brooklyn, New York

In her volume of poems *The Crack in Everything* (1996), O. writes, "The teacher's job is to give them permission / To gather pain into language," and in two lines gives her readers an important key to understanding the very heart of her work. In this poem, she discusses how one teaches poetry to budding poets, how ultimately the real lessons they learn will be learned internally. The class is to give that experience shape and order, a model into which they will pour their lives. O.'s own poetry is no different. It is a vessel for her life, and her life, as it manifests in each deeply personal, often confessional poem, is about teaching oneself to just keep pouring.

O., internationally recognized as both poet and critic, is the author of eight volumes of poetry as well as several important critical works, including the exhaustive and highly influential *Stealing the Language: The Emergence of Women's Poetry in America* (1986). O.'s 1986 volume *The Imaginary Lover* won the Poetry Society of America's William Carlos Williams Award. Her poetry, translated into French, German, Italian, Japanese, Hebrew, and Arabic, has also garnered grants from the National Endowment for the Arts, the Rockefeller Foundation, and the Guggenheim Foundation. She is a professor of English at Rutgers University in Princeton, New Jersey.

From her first collection, *Songs* (1969), to the most current poems, O.'s work has regularly embraced a formalist tendency, from outright rhyme to regularized stanzaic patterns. It is just such form that echoes her search for workable paradigms for order in a life seemingly little interested in design. The fact that her teaching shows up itself as a subject in much of her poetry suggests that from the classroom to the printed page to the gurney on which she was wheeled to have her mastectomy, O.'s oeuvre is an oeuvre of a living Lyceum. The reader is invited into her life, into the machinations of her lectures, her loves, her marriage bed, into the process of recognizing a middle age quickly come and—perhaps even more quickly—going. But such revelations suggest far more than simple biography; the moments we play witness to—her mastecotomy, her daughter's first lost love, the death of a friend, a rape, a love of Keats—all provide insight into concerns far more universal than incidental. Her poems ask how we teach ourselves to face evolution, the many tiny deaths it must contain.

O.'s work focuses on the family, on marriage, on the fidelity of lovers' desires to remain in love. But this focus extends to the human family as well, to the marriage of nations and ideologies, to the fidelity—sometimes infidelity—of whole cultures toward learning to love. Often her work is political, feminist, atheist, but just as often it turns such easy terms inside out, forcing the reader to wonder about *all* boundaries, all limits to the quest for learning.

O. is third-generation Jewish; her grandparents were Russian and Lithuanian Jews. As such, she herself takes part in a long tradition of interrogating the word, the Word, Torah, law. And though her most overt acknowledgments of such a tendency, of the very tradition in which she participates, only appear in more recent volumes including *Green Age* (1989), all of O.'s work, whether poetic or scholarly, whether *A Woman under the Surface* (1982) or *The Nakedness of the Fathers: Biblical Visions and Revisions* (1994), finally comes down to one word: *midrash*.

BIBLIOGRAPHY: Aal, K. M., "Readings: An Interview with A. O.," *P&W* 12 (November-December 1989): 16–26; Cook, P., "Secrets and Manifestos: A. O.'s Poetry and Politics," *Borderlands* 2 (Spring 1993): 80–86; Heller, J. R., "Exploring the Depths of Relationships in A. O.'s Poetry," *L&P* 38 (1992): 71–83

BRYAN D. DIETRICH

OZICK, Cynthia
b. 11 April 1928, Bronx, New York

The canon of JEWISH AMERICAN LITERATURE has traditionally been composed almost exclusively of male writers, marginalizing such significant female voices as O., E. M. BRONER, Grace PALEY, Tillie OLSEN, Norma Rosen, and Anne Roiphe. Yet of these latter, O. has risen to become the most prominent. Her many awards, including four O. Henry First Prizes, and the impressive number of book-length studies of her work have established O. as the "first lady" of Jewish American letters.

As a New York intellectual, literary critic, essayist, political commentator, translator, educator, poet, and fiction writer, O. can be found all over the American literary map. Yet what distinguishes much of her work is a concern with religious and ethnic sensibilities and their place within a largely secular American society. She writes on a number of subjects, but her most characteristic themes are those of Jewish identity, Jewish history, and Jewish art, many times from a feminist perspective. Unlike Saul BELLOW, she has no problem with considering herself a Jewish writer. And unlike Philip ROTH, she explores Jewish identity not from a primarily cultural or secular standpoint, but from one that constantly highlights the presence of Jewish faith. What further particularizes her work is a curious mixture of realistic and fantastical discourse, a style that approximates that of magic realism.

O.'s first novel, *Trust* (1966), was written largely under the influence of her academic work on Henry JAMES, and in many ways, reads like a Jamesian novel. It is an epic, intricate, and critically underrated work. Much of it centers on the unnamed narrator's quest for self-discovery. This young woman explores both the life of her natural father, a hedonistic seducer of women, and her step father, a wandering soul in search of a virtuous life. In juxtaposing these two characters, O. establishes a thematic pattern that is interwoven throughout most of her subsequent fiction: the struggle between Pan, the pagan embodiment of abandonment, and Moses, the ultimate Jewish law-giver.

"The Pagan Rabbi," collected in *The Pagan Rabbi and Other Stories* (1971), further explores this dichotomy. In this fantastical story, a young rabbi, Isaac Kornfeld, falls prey to the charms of a dryad. Yet while his flesh succumbs to the lures of nature, his soul is anchored in pious study. Unable to resolve this tension, he ends up hanging himself in the very tree the dryad inhabited. Another story from the collection, "Envy; or, Yiddish in America," translates literal pagan idolatry into its more symbolic manifestation of fame and assimilation. Hersheleh Edelshtein, a Yiddish poet, longs to have his work translated and recognized in America. He compares himself with Yankel Ostrover—a character reminiscent of Isaac Bashevis SINGER—a translated and successful Yiddish author who has found fame in the English-speaking world. Edelshtein soon realizes, in a moment of revelation, that dedication to the Yiddish word is perhaps what is most important, and considers rejecting the idols of commercial success.

Despite her early realistic work, O. is considered by many critics to be a postmodern writer. Her fiction stands as one of the most illustrative examples of postmodernism and its relation to Judaic faith. Her narrative structures betray a conflicting series of postulates that refuse any final synthesis. Embedded in such works as "Usurpation (Other People's Stories)," collected in *Bloodshed and Three Novellas* (1976), *The Shawl* (1990), *The Cannibal Galaxy* (1983), *The Messiah of Stockholm* (1987), and *The Puttermesser Papers* (1997) are both a text and a countertext that vie for dominance but that are ultimately suspended in an uneasy—yet highly revealing—state of irresolution. O. takes to heart the Mosaic law against idolatry, yet is torn by her place as a Jewish writer constantly in the act of creating literary "idols" that approximate existence. This strategy of literary negotiation is particularly significant in that O. not only questions the replications of texts, but also places her ethnic subject-position in the very center of this controversy. Many of her novels use a series of ironic countertexts to explore the place and function of literature in relation not only to the world at large, but more precisely, to the world as defined by her Jewish faith.

Although *The Cannibal Galaxy* is an earlier study in post-Holocaust American Jewish assimilation, *The Messiah of Stockholm* stands as a more illustrative example of post-Holocaust and postmodern identity. Lars Andemening, the novel's orphaned protagonist, convinces himself that he is the one and only child of Bruno Schultz, the Polish writer shot dead by the Nazis in 1942, and creates elaborate scenarios to help explain his unlikely lineage. O. uses him to both highlight the arbitrary and constructed nature of identity formation and to illustrate the high stakes involved in ethnic identification. *The Shawl*—made up of two previously published stories, "The Shawl" and "Rosa"—further explores the fragmentation of post-Holocaust identity. Rosa has lost her daughter while in a concentration camp, and is now in America trying to piece together her life. What starts as a tale of subjective disintegration becomes by the end of the collection a tale of ethnic affirmation and consolidation, all centered on the cultural necessity to preserve the Holocaust in collective memory.

The Puttermesser Papers continues the search for an ethnic identity. The first two chapters, "Puttermesser: Her Work History, Her Ancestry, Her Afterlife" and "Puttermesser and Xanthippe," which were first collected as stories in *Levitation: Five Fictions* (1982), explore the ways in which Jewish memory and folklore transform the novel's protagonist, Ruth Puttermesser. But by the end of the novel, Puttermesser begins to deconstruct her ideals, and is left with an unresolved tension between the truths of Judaism and the temptations of Hellenism. Here, as elsewhere, O.'s fiction thrives on this ambiguous relationship between the sacred and the profane. As one of America's most notable postassimilationist Jewish authors, she more than any other living writer highlights the importance of Jewish history, the burdens of the Holocaust, and the place of spiritual significance in our contemporary assimilative culture.

BIBLIOGRAPHY: Bloom, H., ed., *C. O.* (1986); Cohen, S. B., *C. O.'s Comic Art* (1994); Friedman, L. S., *Understanding C. O.* (1991); Kauvar, E. M., *C. O.'s Fiction* (1993); Pinsker, S., *The Uncompromising Fictions of C. O.* (1987); Walden, D., ed., *Studies in American Jewish Literature: The World of C. O.* (1988)

DEREK PARKER ROYAL

PADGETT, Ron

b. 17 June 1942, Tulsa, Oklahoma

P. is one of a second generation—also including Joseph Ceravolo and Ted Berrigan—said to belong to the New York school of post-World War II poets, originally John ASHBERY, Frank O'HARA, Barbara GUEST, James SCHUYLER, and Kenneth KOCH. Like Koch (once his teacher at Columbia), P. embraces the possibilities of the funny poem; rich, nonsatirical comedy runs through his work, from the early *Great Balls of Fire* (1969) through *The Big Something* (1990) and *New and Selected Poems* (1995). Comedy takes the form of tonic self-reference—P. is always inside the poem, commenting wryly or wildly on his own poetic practice and attitude, on his flights of imagination and rhetoric, on his acts of titling, on his persona as a poet. "Yikes! Do I / mean that?" he queries, after delivering a gorgeous O'Haraesque statement of aesthetic commitment and wonder. Transport, transformation, and transcription have provided him with comedic rather than elegiac perspectives on life's inevitable changes: aging is at once like becoming Grandma Moses, and having "your neck extend[ed] into a curve in time-space." Disorientation is a pervasive positive, an access to possibility.

Into the New York school artistic and literary sophistication is stirred a "little bit of wild west, a little bit of old cowboy" that P. traces to his upbringing in Tulsa, the son of a bootlegger. His tone is fresh, rambunctious, light-hearted, companionable, devoid of neurosis or obsession. Light and air are his media; these are interrelated in "Light as Air," where he typically employs awe and appreciation against authoritarian uses of language. He is deft with short prose poems, which—like those he admires by Max Jacob—read "as if a novella had been compressed into a single paragraph." He is given to exclamatory apostrophe—addressing things, cartoon characters, dead poets. He tinkers with form irreverently—one "sonnet" repeats the line "Nothing in that drawer" fourteen times; a sestina is emptied of all but the required six repeated words. Among his most admired poems are the euphoric seed catalog *cum* love poem, "Sweet Pea," an homage to the *Oxford English Dictionary,* "Who and Each," a hilarious and poignant tour though a high school year book, "Wilson '57," and a fractured narrative of sensory overload and escape from ignorance, "Tell Us, Josephine." Recently, a seriousness about death, loss, and loneliness has entered P.'s poetry, revealing the poet of light sometimes hard up against darkness and the irremediable. Mourning the deaths of Berrigan and Edwin Denby, he finds himself unable to transform the New York streets out of their dark, "nude and stupid" look.

The poetry and prose is littered with knowing, precise, unpretentious reference to painting, often to artists he knows or knew: Joe Brainard, Man Ray, R. B. Kitaj, Jasper Johns, Fairfield Porter, Willem de Kooning. There are also are collaborations with other poets and artists—the titles suggest the antic playfulness and intellectual excitement of these interactions: *Bean Spasms* (1967, with Berrigan), *The Adventures of Mr. & Mrs. Jim and Ron* (1970), *Ooh La La* (1973, with Jim Dine), *How to Be Modern Art* (1984, with Trevor Winkfield), and *Supernatural Overtones* (1990, with Clark Coolidge). P.'s immersion in French MODERNISM has left its mark on his poetry, and has also resulted in translations of Apollinaire's *The Poet Assassinated* (1984) and Blaise Cendrars's *Complete Poems* (1992), and in an affectionate homage to Pierre Reverdy, included with other prose pieces on art, travel, translation, and language in *Blood Work: Selected Prose* (1993).

BIBLIOGRAPHY: Foster, E., "An Interview with R. P.," *Talisman* 7 (Fall 1991): 68–82; Shapiro, D. "A Night Painting of R. P." *Talisman* 7 (Fall 1991): 82–87;

Ward, G., *Statutes of Liberty: The New York School of Poets* (1993)

SARA LUNDQUIST

PAGE, Thomas Nelson
b. 23 April 1853, Oakland, Virginia; d. 1 November 1922, Oakland, Virginia

Primarily known for his dialect stories, P. is most often associated with his widely anthologized short story "Marse Chan," which brought him national recognition in 1884 when the *Century Magazine* published it. Although he was a prolific writer, and his works extended beyond his native South, P. found himself a victim of his initial literary success. In 1910, he became disillusioned with the publishing world when his editors only wanted more of his portrayals of the antebellum South.

Considered the literary spokesman for the conservative South during the 1880s and 1890s, P. used his writings to defend the pre–Civil War South. His works perpetuate the notion that this was the South's golden age, a time of self-sufficiency and stability when the white planter ruled an agrarian society with Christian charity and paternalism. P.'s fiction, especially, serves as a forum for these ideas as well as his racial views. He believed that the slave enjoyed a secure place in plantation life as part of the plantation family, and his fiction extols the relationships between whites and blacks in this context, with the hope that such harmony could exist again.

"Marse Chan" perhaps best represents P.'s idealization of the Old South. Through Sam, an old black freeman and "companion" to Marse Chan, the reader becomes acquainted with the Southern nobleman. Marse Chan, killed in a war that he opposed for a society that was already doomed, is eulogized by his servant, who has now been left to fend for himself. While this story is a pointed indictment against the ruination that occurred in the South after the Civil War, and it is clear that there is no place for Sam in a postslavery America, P. never acknowledges the inherent weaknesses of a society founded on the plantation system. This unmitigated nostalgia for the Old South, as well as the cumbersome dialect and overt sentimentality that often characterize much of local color writing, has contributed to the overly simplistic categorization of P. as a regional writer.

While P. wrote prolifically, publishing the novels *Red Rock* (1898), *Gordon Keith* (1903), and *John Marvel, Assistant* (1909) as well as a biography of Robert E. Lee (1911), and was elected to the Academy of Arts and Letters in 1908, he gradually turned away from writing and embraced the world of international

café society that his stature as a writer afforded him. In his later years, he became increasingly concerned with Virginia and its backstage politics. P. supported Woodrow Wilson in his presidential campaign and was rewarded for his loyalty by an appointment as the ambassador to Rome. Eventually, P. became frustrated with politics and returned to live his final years in Virginia, where he prepared a series of lectures on Dante for the University of Virginia and began work on a novel *The Red Riders,* which was completed posthumously by his brother, Rosewell, and published in 1924.

BIBLIOGRAPHY: Gross, T. L., *T. N. P.* (1967); Page, R., *T. N. P.: A Memoir of a Virginia Gentleman* (1969)

DEBORAH KAY FERRELL

PAINE, Thomas
b. 29 January 1737, Thetford, Norfolk, England; d. 8 June 1809, New York City

A journalist and pamphleteer, P. was one of the driving forces of the American Revolution. Born in Britain of working-class parents and living at the edge of poverty, P. possessed a keen sense of injustice and inequality that drove him to advocate American independence and republicanism and later the French Revolution.

For the first thirty-seven years of his life, P. labored as a stay maker, a sailor on a privateer, and an exciseman. With the exception of the rudiments of education received at a free school, he was largely self-educated. Writing a pamphlet in support of higher wages for excisemen, P. lost his job in 1774. He emigrated to the American colony with a letter of introduction from Benjamin FRANKLIN, living in England at the time. By February 1775, P. became editor of the *Pennsylvania Magazine,* beginning a busy career publishing numerous articles, letters, and poems.

In the wake of the battles of Lexington and Concord, and Bunker Hill, P. published the pamphlet *Common Sense* (January 1776)—the title suggested by Dr. Benjamin Rush. While P. was not the first to address the topic of American independence, *Common Sense* is widely regarded as the most important and influential single document in support of it. Writing in a direct and simple prose style, P. argued persuasively for the reasonableness and plausibility of cutting ties with Britain. More to the point, he argued that the American colonists could sustain a war with Britain. *Common Sense* was an immediate success, and despite Tory counterattacks, played a key role in the efforts culminating with the drafting of the Declaration of Independence, ratified six months later on July 4, 1776. P.

continued his efforts as a pamphleteer. Opening with the lines, "these are times that try men's souls," he published the first of thirteen numbered essays between 1776 and 1783, entitled the *American Crisis,* and signed "Common Sense."

After the success of the Revolution, P. visited Europe on business, but was soon caught up by the events in France. Perceiving the French Revolution as a logical continuation of the American, P. responded to Edmund Burke's *Reflections on the French Revolution* with the first part of his *The Rights of Man* (1791), arguing that human rights derived from nature, and that civil government existed only as a contractual arrangement with the majority. Burke replied to P. and others with *An Appeal from the New to the Old Whigs.* P., in turn, replied in the second part of *The Rights of Man* (1792). In England, the controversy over *The Rights of Man* forced P. to flee to France. In the U.S., Thomas JEFFERSON and the emerging Democratic-Republicans praised it, while John Adams and the Federalists condemned it. Thereafter, *The Rights of Man* became the veritable Bible of radicals and revolutionaries.

P.'s stay in France was no more successful. Allied with the losing factions, he was imprisoned in December 1793, barely escaping execution, and released in November 1794 only through the intercession of James Monroe, the new American minister to France. Before entering prison, he had completed the first part of *The Age of Reason* (1794). Disturbed by the atheism he found in many revolutionary circles, P. favored deism. Deeply influenced by John Locke and Isaac Newton, he argued that human reason could know the workings of God in nature, and from that one could deduce one's moral duties. Such a natural theology eliminated superstition, or the need for a priesthood or religious institutions. His most controversial work, P. lost many of his friends and supporters. While completing the second part of *The Age of Reason,* he wrote his last major pamphlet, *Agrarian Justice* (1796), which looked at poverty, attacking the belief that it was a necessary evil.

P. returned to the U.S. in 1802, where, while he continued to write until his death, was largely ignored. His fame rests not so much with the originality of his ideas, many of which can be found in other writers, but with his power of expression, aimed not at intellectual circles, but at the common man.

BIBLIOGRAPHY: Aldridge, A. O., *Man of Reason: The Life of T. P.* (1959); Claeys, G., *T. P.: Social and Political Thought* (1989); Fruchtman, J., *T. P. and the Religion of Nature* (1993); Keane, J., *T. P.: A Political Life* (1995); Wilson, J. D., *T. P.* (1978)

THOMAS L. COOKSEY

PAK, Gary [Yong Ki]
b. 30 April 1952, Honolulu, Hawai'i

As one of Hawai'i's foremost "local" authors, P. captures a tradition of island writing in his short stories. Utilizing a Local sensibility that came into recognition during Hawai'i's literary renaissance of the 1970s, P.'s work incorporates such themes as a working-class consciousness that unites its various peoples; a deep love and respect for the land; a politicized understanding of Local heritage originating in the plantation experience of the late 19th and early 20th cs.; and the legitimization of "pidgin English"—a mixture of several languages—previously perceived as "substandard" English. Highly alert to Hawai'i's long history of construction by outsiders as an isolated paradise or tourist playground, Local literature counteracted this perspective by giving voice to the people of the islands who were hardly the "dumb locals" or "noble savages" they were often depicted to be in literature, film, and other media.

A third-generation Korean American whose grandparents labored on the sugar plantations, P. focuses much of his writing on various aspects of life in Hawai'i under the legacy of colonialism. *The Watcher of Waipuna and Other Stories* (1992) illustrates both positive and negative interactions within multiethnic communities, overturning the simplistic view of Hawai'i as a multicultural paradise. "The Trial of Goro Fukushima," based loosely on the real-life lynching of an outspoken Japanese laborer, is a dark tale of scapegoating, religious corruption, and racial hierarchies. Calling attention to the ways in which plantation society fostered an internalized racism that could not only allow such a murder to take place, but also encourage and support such an event, this story attests to the partnership between economic exploitation and racism in "local" history. In stories such as "The Valley of the Dead Air" and "A Toast to Rosita," the issue of land rights surfaces as equally critical and provides for exploration into the politics of identity and culture. Locals who are not of native Hawaiian descent must come to terms with their relationship to dispossessed Hawaiians and hence find their claims to the land altered, yet significantly, neither devalued nor erased.

As much as P.'s work challenges dominant stereotypes of Hawai'i's land and people, it also playfully celebrates Local culture. This is best seen in the title story, "The Watcher of Waipuna," later adapted for the stage by Keith Kashiwada in 1995 and performed at the Kumu Kahua Theater on O'ahu. The schizophrenia of the main character, Gilbert Sanchez, enables the rescue of Waipuna from development into a world-class tourist resort. Old Man Nakakura, a war veteran considered crazy by those in the community, helps

Gilbert by fighting the war against enemy "frog-men"— "imaginary" villains that ultimately blur the lines between military and economic aggression. The friendship between Gilbert and Old Man Nakakura illustrates the dedication to the land and community that typifies "local" culture. Through his use of the mystic, P. also affirms the integral role of spiritual and supernatural elements in island life.

A Ricepaper Airplane (1998) takes "local" history in a different direction, towards Koreans in Hawai'i. Through the stories of the protagonist Kim Sung Wha, P. demonstrates how Local racial identity is both specific and panethnic. Although Sung Wha clings tightly to his experiences and memories as a Korean national-ist, this does not preclude his contribution to a multi-ethnic "local" history. As Sung Wha grows older, he begins to realize that "local" culture is not static; its intersections of race, class, and generation determine its membership more than any one specific identity. Through this understanding, he comes to appreciate his place in Hawai'i. It is P.'s sensitivity to these nuances of "local" culture that mark him as one of the island's most cherished writers.

BIBLIOGRAPHY: Chock, E., et al., eds., Talk Story: An Anthology of Hawai'i's Local Writers (1978); Okihiro, G. Y., Cane Fires: The Anti-Japanese Movement in Hawai'i, 1865–1945 (1991); Sumida, S., And the View from the Shore: Literary Traditions of Hawai'i (1991)
                                        BRENDA KWON

PALEY, Grace
b. 11 December 1922, Bronx, New York

P. has achieved wide recognition as a unique short story writer, based on three story collections published over a period of nearly thirty years: The Little Distur-bances of Man (1959), Enormous Changes at the Last Minute (1974), and Later the Same Day (1985)—later republished together in The Collected Stories (1994). Because her stories, whether in first-or third-person narration, contain distinctive voices that pinpoint char-acters' ethnic, social, and geographic identities, P. can be viewed as a type of "local colorist" who captures with uncanny precision the traits, concerns, and sur-roundings of New Yorkers, usually politically progres-sive, first-and second-generation Jews.

Like "Faith," the central character in a number of the stories, P. herself was born in New York, the daugh-ter of Russian-Jewish emigrants. Like Faith, she was married twice, had two children from the first mar-riage, lived in Greenwich Village, was active in the antiwar movement of the 1960s, and worked for many social and feminist causes. Although these experiences

circumscribe many of the conflicts in P.'s work, Faith is not so much an autobiographical figure as a compos-ite of women P. knew, who were coping with an array of social and generational gaps in a world of changing values and roles.

Holding the belief that everyone has a story to tell, P. attends carefully not only to the diction but to the idiom, metaphor, chain of association, and field of references that contain and, often, disguise a person's story. She has referred to her stories as "heard" and to herself primarily as a listener. Because she writes her stories only after she feels she hears them clearly enough, her style has a strong vocal quality. "I write with an accent," she has said.

This focus on the heard story creates important innovations in narrative technique by suggesting that the way people construct their narratives is inseparable from the way they identify and situate their lives, in personal, social, or historical contexts. Often her sto-ries reveal conflicts resulting from one person's at-tempt to impose his or her narrative on another person, whether that narrative defines a sex role, a family role, a view of one's personal history, or an historical narrative of, for example, class struggle. These stories of aggression are balanced by those of community and melioration, in the form of friends, parents, children helping people correct their narratives so that they can have a happier, more optimistic, or more principled view of themselves.

"A Conversation with My Father," P.'s most widely anthologized story, particularly foregrounds the im-portance of narrative and its therapeutic potential. In it, Faith visits her dying father who asks her to make up a traditional story with a beginning, middle, and conclusive end. Faith tries to compose the story, revis-ing it twice in an attempt to accommodate her father's criticisms, but in the process recognizes responsibil-ities to her characters that weigh against her desires to please her father. At issue is the power and burden of narrative to construct and supplement lives, to create and deny hope, in a world in which the teller is also the listener, identifying with and identified by his or her own stories.

These themes also emerge in her poetry, Leaning Forward (1985) and In the Bus: New and Collected Poems (1992), which often address specific social is-sues, as do her essays, collected in Long Walks and Intimate Talks (1991) and her short pieces in the calen-dar book 365 Reasons Not to Have Another War (1969). Her work, in other words, explores with care and responsibility the politics of voice as it affects personal power in the social world.

BIBLIOGRAPHY: Arcana, J., G. P.'s Life Stories: A Lit-erary Biography (1993); Bach, G., Conversations with

G. P. (1997); Brinder, W., and H. Breinig, eds., *American Contradictions: Interviews with Nine American Writers* (1995); Isaacs, N. D., *G. P.: A Study of the Short Fiction* (1990); Taylor, J., *G. P.: Illuminating the Dark Lines* (1990)

ALAN NADEL

PARKER, Dorothy [Rothschild]

b. 22 August 1893, West End, New Jersey; d. 7 June 1967, New York City

Although P. is best known for her acidic wit and her quick repartee, she was in fact a highly disciplined writer of poetry, short stories, drama, screenplays, and criticism. Her major themes in poems and stories are loneliness and despair, which in the best of her work, as in the story "Big Blonde," are memorable because of the depths of her compassion or, as in "The Banquet of Crow," indelible because of the biting satire. Her images tend to make the most commonplace ideas, objects, and manners metaphoric, often funereal; her tone can be mordant. But occasionally, her luminous prose is made witty through the hyperbolic self-pity of her characters; at other times, as with Hazel Morse, the big blonde, the thought of death—in her case by attempted suicide—is searingly graphic, the only apparent recourse to a downwardly spiraling life.

Beneath P.'s wit there is always a sense of guilt or inadequacy. Her Jewish father was a successful businessman in the New York garment district (but no relation to the more wealthy Rothschilds), but her Gentile mother died shortly after her birth and she hated her fiercely authoritative stepmother who died when she was ten. P. grew up blaming herself for both deaths. From the beginning of P.'s life, then, most personal relationships were difficult for her. Two of her three marriages ended in bitterness and divorce; all involved quarreling and alcoholism; and the first, not coincidentally to a member of a prominent Hartford insurance family, Edwin Pond Parker II, also involved his addiction to morphine. For P., such defenses against a hostile and insensitive world often lurk behind her poems and stories. Her protagonists tend to be shy women, either young and anxiously flirtatious or, once plain, now aging, also suffer disappointment in love. The world of P.'s imagination is peopled with those who fail, or those who fear failure.

Much of the power of her best writing depends, therefore, on how startlingly different it is from the quips of the witty woman who held her own in the masculine world of 1920s New York journalism, reviewing theater for *Vanity Fair* and *Ainslee's* and, later, plays and books for the *New Yorker* (of which she was an early editor), and living a life both riotous

and promiscuous. But for those who knew her best, much of her imaginative work had from the start other autobiographical roots, charting her own ill fortune in finding a sense of permanent pleasure or peace. Her wit made her famous at the Algonquin Hotel Round Table, but her facility with language there was both spontaneous and ephemeral, and she later disowned her early writings and the artificiality and self-praise that period of life represented to her.

A more reliable picture of P.'s contribution to American letters can be found in her collected poems, *Not So Deep as a Well* (1936), which reprints *Enough Rope* (1926), *Sunset Gun* (1928), and *Death and Taxes* (1931). Here the close attention to clarity and purity of language, which she learned by studying Latin at Miss Dana's School in New Jersey, is always evident. She began writing verse in imitation of Horace and Juvenal under the tutelage of F. P. A. (Franklin Pierce Adams), but later, with the encouragement of Elinor WYLIE and Edna St. Vincent MILLAY, she turned more often to Propertius, Catullus, and especially Martial. These superior poems seem chiseled out of marble; they are brief, even seemingly abrupt, yet every word functions precisely, placed with a particularity that gives sinew to each line. She once said it took her days to write a poem and this is supported by her exactitude in choice of word and control of tone. Historically, she is America's foremost epigrammatist.

Her stories would also take her months to write, in the same painstaking ways. Her early fiction also tends toward first-person narrative; usually the story is told by a woman whose own ignorance of her situation is apparent to the reader but not immediately, if at all, to her. Occasionally, as in "The Waltz," or "From the Diary of a New York Lady," the work is a monologue, the empty clichés accumulating to carry a deeper meaning of surrender or ennui. But others, such as "You Were Perfectly Fine," "Dialogue at Three in the Morning," or "Here We Are," are executed in the dialectic of dialogue in which one character's greater knowledge makes the story ironic from the start. *Laments for the Living* (1930) and *After Such Pleasures* (1933) were assembled in *Here Lies* (1939) and *Collected Stories* (1942). Her early stories catch the tone of the flapper era of the 1920s; her later ones grow more serious, and sad, insinuating an incremental satire. Her acknowledged models for fiction were three friends—Ernest HEMINGWAY, Ring LARDNER, and F. Scott FITZGERALD. Among the best of the mature stories are "Too Bad" (1939), about the dissolution of a marriage, and "Mr. Druant" (1924) about abortion; later fiction includes "The Lovely Leave" (1943), about marital incompatibility, and the sprightly "The Standard of Living" (1941) about economic classes. The best of her stories—"Big Blonde," which won the O. Henry Award as the Best American Short Story in 1929—is a clinical and painful study of alcoholism and attempted suicide; it should be hailed as a classic work of American literature. P. did not write such potent fiction again until the 1950s, when she produced such stories as "I Live on Your Visits," about a divor-cée who lives vicariously on the appearances of her son, and "Lolita," about the slow erosion of the de-fenses against old age.

During the 1930s, P. went to Hollywood to write film scripts with her second husband, Alan Campbell. Many of them were entertaining screwball comedies such as *Nothing Sacred* (1937), notable for her one-liners. Others were more serious; the scripts for *A Star Is Born* (1937) and *Smash-Up* (1947), written without Campbell, were nominated for Academy Awards. In Hollywood, P.'s sense of guilt turned toward her own wealth—she was making $5,200 a week during the Great Depression—and she assuaged her feelings by demonstrating for the poor, helping to form a writers' union, and supporting Communist-front organizations. Her trip to Spain during the Civil War resulted in her best journalism, "Incredible, Fantastic . . . and True," published in *New Masses* (June 27, 1939), and a re-markable story, "Soldiers of the Republic," as well as the more polemical "Clothe the Naked," both of which were published in 1939.

P. was also a dramatist of note; two of her six plays, *The Ladies of the Corridor* (1953, with Arnaud d'Usseau), about the loneliness of single elderly women in a New York residential hotel much like her own, and *The Coast of Illyria* (1949, with Ross Evans), about Charles and Mary Lamb and the relationship of art, drugs, alcohol, and madness, are still exceptionally forceful works, if seldom acted. Her best criticism appeared in her book reviews in *Esquire* (December 1957 through December 1962) where she fought hard for the high literary standards that she claimed seldom to find.

BIBLIOGRAPHY: Cowley, M., ed., *Writers at Work* (1957); Gill, B., ed., *The Portable D. P.* (1944; rev. ed., 1973); Kinney, A. F., *D. P.* (1988); Meade, M., *D. P.* (1978)

ARTHUR F. KINNEY

PARKER, Robert B[rown]

b. 17 September 1932, Springfield, Massachusetts

P., in the creation of "Spenser," his private investigator hero, succeeds in forging a strong and durable link between the original hard-boiled private eye in the Dashiell HAMMETT-Raymond CHANDLER tradition and the literary private eye of the late 20th c.

His is a wise-cracking, irreverent, and witty narrator-hero with the soul of a dreamer and idealist and the body of a street fighter and pragmatist. Thus, P. straddles the world of ivory-towered academe and the world of urban reality, enabling him to stress literary quality and narrative action at one and the same time.

A thinking man's warrior, Spenser as introduced in *The Godwulf Manuscript* (1974) harks back to the frontier qualities of James Fenimore COOPER's Natty Bumppo and the knight-errant morality of Camelot, but operates in a corrupt and self-serving Boston in the latter decades of the 20th c. P. is astute in naming his hero "Spenser," like Chandler's "Marlowe," a name out of English literature (which P. once taught in college).

Stylistically, P. hews closely to the original narra-tive techniques of his models Dashiell Hammett and Raymond Chandler, delivering fast-paced action, witty and evocative descriptions, and humorous and bouncy dialogue. His plots tend to be a bit pat, but are far simpler than the frequently byzantine twists of Chan-dler's story lines.

Characterwise, Spenser is the apex of a triangle of individuals including Hawk, his black counterpart and psychological mirror image, and Susan Silverman, his lover and politically correct counselor on all things humane. Spenser frequently veers from the straight and narrow, but always is enticed back to politically correct nobility by Susan or to grim reality by Hawk.

P. generally chooses themes that touch on sociopo-litical considerations: teenage runaways; homosexual seduction; left-wing terrorism; gambling troubles; drug addiction; and teenage prostitution. For example, *God Save the Child* (1974) involves a runaway, an oedi-pal conflict, a homosexual encounter, a drug and prosti-tution ring, a corrupt cop, and a kidnapping threat.

Spenser is *not* a gunman per se; he tries to *persuade* people rather than force them into actions contrary to their aims, usually by talk. But if talk fails . . . In *The Judas Goat* (1978), he turns an armed terrorist into an honest woman by moral suasion. But in *Mortal Stakes* (1975), he is forced to kill not one but two men to save a baseball player's career. To go *Mortal Stakes* one better, in *A Catskill Eagle* (1985), both Spenser and Hawk indulge in a blood bath of killing that seems to prove that P.'s characters are as unpre-dictable as real people.

In *Ceremony* (1982), Spenser rescues a teenager from a life of prostitution with a sadistic street pimp and sets her up in a more respectable call-girl establish-ment; in *Taming a Sea-Horse* (1986), he rescues her again from the streets and in the end hopes to get her out of the profession altogether.

In 1989, P. was commissioned to write an ending to an unfinished manuscript by Raymond Chandler, which, published as *Poodle Springs,* one reviewer said, sometimes "sounds more like Chandler than Chandler himself." In the following year, he did another Chandler-connected work—a sequel to *The Big Sleep* entitled *Perchance to Dream,* featuring Philip Marlowe.

Spenser reappeared in *Pastime* (1991), followed by *Double Deuce* (1992) and *Paper Doll* (1993). *Walking Shadow* (1994) was the twenty-first Spenser novel—a strong narrative in which Spenser battled a new enemy with true Spenserian zeal—the Asian gangster. After several more Spensers, P. decided to take a flier all on his own and initiated a new mystery series in *Night Passage* (1997) that featured the exploits of a complicated but with-it protagonist, Jesse Stone. Stone is an ex-cop discharged from the Los Angeles police force for alcoholism and engaged as sheriff of a small East Coast town ironically called "Paradise." Good news: P.'s own style shines in this volume, and the wry, quirky, and sometimes annoying Chandlerisms so integral to the Spenser books have vanished, leaving a very readable authorial voice in control. *Trouble in Paradise,* another Stone opus, followed in 1998.

Promised Land (1996) won an Edgar Allan Poe Award from the Mystery Writers of America.

BIBLIOGRAPHY: Geherin, D., *Sons of Sam Spade: The Private Eye Novel in the 70s* (1980); Winks, R. W., ed., *Colloquium on Crime* (1986)

BRUCE CASSIDAY

PARKER, Theodore

b. 24 August 1810, Lexington, Massachusetts; d. 10 May 1860, Florence, Italy

An early member of the Transcendental Club, P. was the movement's most influential preacher and polemicist. Self-educated son of a Lexington farmer, he became a formidable scholar, proficient at twenty languages, and attended the Harvard Divinity School. No sooner was he ordained than he took up the polemical cudgels against his former professor Andrews Norton in defense of Ralph Waldo EMERSON in the controversy following the Divinity School Address. In *The Previous Question between Mr. Andrews Norton and His Alumni . . .* (1840), P. explained the often airy Transcendentalist position in the straightforward language and relentless logic that became his trademark. Religious truth, he maintained, is everywhere the same, and Christianity is "innate in the soul."

These principles underlie his discourse, *The Transient and Permanent in Christianity* (1841), a land-mark transcendentalist document. Like Emerson—but always within the ministry—he held that to view the Bible as the infallible Word of God, and miracles as a special order of knowledge, is inimical to true religion. The truth of Jesus is "permanent," but forms, doctrines, and institutions are "transient." Christianity is simply "pure morality." After many ministers refused to exchange pulpits with the "radical" P., the 28th Congregational Society was formed expressly as a forum for his powerful preaching, which he carried on before huge audiences at the Melodeon and the Boston Music Hall.

P. combined literary ventures such as editing the *Massachusetts Quarterly Review* (1847–50) with tireless writing and lecturing on all kinds of reform. He opposed slavery and the war with Mexico, believing that "Politics are national morals." *T. P.'s Experience as a Minister* (1859), written in the Virgin Islands as P. sought relief from consumption, is a valediction to his church as well as an important retrospect on TRANSCENDENTALISM in New England. He records his own spiritual and intellectual odyssey, outlines the principles of the "newness," and recounts key events in denominational controversy and reform. More than an apologia, the pamphlet was his final declaration of the "perpetual wonder" of all life. Among his admirers, P. was widely mourned as a martyr to conscience when, short of his fiftieth birthday, he died in Florence. Though posthumous collections of his writings exist—notably *The Collected Works* (14 vols., 1863–71) and *The Centenary Edition of the Works of T. P.* (15 vols., 1907–16)—none is a complete or definitive record of this prolific, eloquent, and passionate giant of American TRANSCENDENTALISM.

BIBLIOGRAPHY: Albrecht, R. C., *T. P.* (1971); Chadwick, J. W., *T. P.* (1908); Collison, G. L., "T. P.," in Myerson, J., ed., *The Transcendentalists* (1984): 216–32; Commager, H. S., *T. P.* (1936); Frothingham, O. B., *T. P.* (1874); Weiss, J., *Life and Correspondence of T. P.* (2 vols., 1864)

WESLEY T. MOTT

PARKMAN, Francis

b. 16 September 1823, Boston, Massachusetts; d. 8 November 1893, Boston, Massachusetts

P. was the best narrative historian that 19th-c. America produced, and this in an epoch which could also boast Henry ADAMS, George Bancroft, John Lothrop MOTLEY, and William Hickling PRESCOTT. P. conquered grievous illnesses, both physical and psychosomatic, to produce a multivolumed history of the long French and English struggle for colonial America, his ever-popular book *The Oregon Trail* (1872), and much else.

P. was born into a distinguished Boston family, which enjoyed money, intellectual activities, and mutual devotion. But young P. proved sickly and was therefore rusticated to his maternal grandfather's Medford farm, then attended private schools; next he entered Harvard, traveled widely to improve his health, and graduated in 1844. Between terms at Harvard law school, where he obtained his degree in 1846, he took a rambling trip to Detroit for research on Pontiac, the Ottawa chief. From April to October 1846, P. explored along the California and Oregon Trail, proceeding from St. Louis to the Fort Laramie environs to camp and hunt with the Sioux and to study frontier and Indian life. Once back in the East, he found that both law-office work in New York and writing serial installments of what became *The Oregon Trail* were most trying. His eyesight was so bad that he had to dictate portions of that early masterpiece.

P.'s life from this time on is a tragic but inspiring account of maladies resisted, publications slowed but accomplished, and personal sorrows stoically met. The valiant historian suffered from chronically weak eyes, blinding headaches, rheumatism, indigestion, and insomnia. In 1850, he married a Boston physician's daughter. The couple had a daughter a year later, then a son in 1854. The son died of scarlet fever in 1857. In 1858, P.'s wife died giving birth to their second daughter. By this date, the crippled historian had published his Oregon Trail book and a romantic, semiautobiographical novel, *Vassall Morton* (1856), and was deep into research for his monumental *France and England in North America* (9 vols., 1865–92), prologued by a separate work, *The History of the Conspiracy of Pontiac* (1851), and concluding with *A Half-Century of Conflict* (1892). In all, there are seven titles (some changed upon revision and republication). Combined, they narrate the sweep of history from the 16th-c. French pioneers in America to the epic *Montcalm and Wolfe* (ending with the French surrender of Canada in 1763). P. also kept splendid journals, published in 1947, and wrote humane, detailed letters, also now published (1960). During the Civil War and later, he sought solace in penning patriotic rhetoric, in studying horticulture, and in travel connected with his research (in Europe, along the Eastern seaboard, and in the Midwest, Canada, upstate New York, and the Deep South). He also enjoyed squabbling in print over democracy, extended suffrage, Canadian partisanship, and educational policies. To the end of his life, he continued revising his historical works, in an effort to heighten their overall unity. Shortly after his seventieth birthday, he fought off pleurisy and phlebi-

tis but then succumbed to appendicitis and accompanying peritonitis.

In its final form, *The Oregon Trail* (entitled *The California and Oregon Trail,* 1849, then *Prairie and Rocky Mountain Life,* 1852, before its present title) is valuable for at least three reasons. First, it accurately reports the adventures of a daring, intelligent young man on a Western trek in 1846. Second, it is a fascinating chapter in the life of one of America's foremost historians, depicting freedom from the confining East and exploits on the plains and in the Rockies. The bracing account bears comparison with the best of American nonfictional, book-length narratives. And third, it displays enduring, organic literary art. It has a sonata-like form: the young hero, as in a myth, leaves the known East; crosses the threshold to the unknown, meets several challenges of life with the Indians, observes, becomes experienced, then almost sadly begins his return; and at last tries to go home again. Chapter 14, "The Ogillallah Village," is central to the whole, subtly balanced, twenty-seven-chapter structure. *The Oregon Trail* combines REALISM and ROMANTICISM: P. meticulously records data of real-life Indian camps, rituals, weapons, and hunting methods—in part to prepare himself for his later historical accounts of Indian allies and enemies of the French and the English. More romantically, he lavishly describes the untainted beauty of Western nature. He also admires, perhaps even envies, mountain men, trappers, and guides, not to mention the obligatory Native American. Returning to Eastern reality literally sickened the romantic historian.

It is for *France and England in North America* that P. is most extolled, which consists of *Pioneers of France in the New World* (1865; rev. ed., 1885), *The Jesuits in North America in the Seventeenth Century* (1867), *The Discovery of the Great West* (1869; rev. as *La Salle and the Discovery of the Great West,* 1879), *The Old Regime in Canada* (1874; rev. ed., 1893), *Count Frontenac and New France under Louis XIV* (1877), *Montcalm and Wolfe* (2 vols., 1884), and *A Half-Century of Conflict* (2 vols., 1892). Successive titles, as they appeared, often proved immensely popular, *Pioneers of France* and *The Old Regime,* for example, going into more than twenty editions each before revision. *La Salle, Montcalm and Wolfe,* and *Pontiac* are now especially admired for their scholarly accuracy and painterly descriptions, and for a narrative momentum reminiscent of Sir Walter Scott and James Fenimore COOPER.

Space is lacking for detailed comment on even the brightest stars of P.'s historical constellation. It may be enough to comment here that throughout the series the following aspects are steadily dramatized: physical hardihood challenged by the big woods and subduing military opposition, the first settlers' moral strength overcoming barbaric Indian ferocity, and forward-looking British political liberty defeating reactionary French theocratic absolutism—all against a panoramic backdrop of such sacred coloration that one wonders whether P. was not sorry that Europeans ever found and exploited the early American Eden. But then, he could never have sought out, admired, and memorialized his New World heroes, notably his five favorites—Samuel de Champlain, René-Robert La Salle, Comte de Frontenac, General James Wolfe, and Chief Pontiac.

BIBLIOGRAPHY: Doughty, H., *F. P.* (1962); Gale, R. L., *F. P.* (1973); Levin, D., *History as Romantic Art: Bancroft, Motley, Prescott, and P.* (1959); Vitzhum, R. C., *The American Compromise: Theme and Method in the Histories of Bancroft, P., and Adams* (1974); Wade, M., *F. P.: Heroic Historian* (1942)

ROBERT L. GALE

PARTON, Sara Payson Willis

b. 9 July 1811, Portland, Maine; d. 10 October 1872, New York City

Better known by her pseudonym, "Fanny Fern," P. was famous in 19th-c. America for her amusing newspaper sketches and scandalous novel, *Ruth Hall* (1854). After her death, literary historians mistakenly classified her as a "tearful moralizer," and she is only now regaining a reputation as a talented humorist.

Although P. tended to downplay her preparation for a writing career, she came from a literary family and began contributing at an early age to journals published by her father in Boston. She also received an education at Catharine E. Beecher's renowned seminary, where her witty compositions impressed Harriet Beecher STOWE.

P. could thus turn to journalism in middle age when, shortly after the deaths of her mother and one of her daughters, her beloved husband died. By her account, she was reduced to poverty, with only grudging assistance from her father, and forced to give up a daughter to her in-laws; her brother, N. P. WILLIS, a successful poet and editor, refused to help place her essays, advising her to make shirts instead. But P.'s short pieces for Boston papers gained such a following that her first collection, *Fern Leaves from Fanny's Portfolio* (1853), and a second series the next year became best-sellers.

P.'s early sketches derive from her own experience. They provide humorous domestic advice ("Hungry Husbands," "Hints to Young Wives"), mourn the dead ("The Widow's Trials," "A Night-Watch with a Dead

Infant"), or satirize unsupportive relatives, as in "Apollo Hyacinth," where she portrays her brother as a selfish dandy.

P. used much of this material in the autobiographical *Ruth Hall,* which caused a sensation when the author's true identity was discovered and the characters traced to their originals. While Nathaniel HAWTHORNE admired the novel, critics attacked it for the lack of "female delicacy" involved in revenging oneself on one's relatives and creating a protagonist who evolves from passive victim to assertive and financially independent author. P.'s second novel, *Rose Clark* (1856), enjoyed a more favorable reception but is disjointed and inferior. Thereafter, P. restricted herself to the form she excelled at, the short informal essay that she produced for the New York *Ledger* each week until her death. Collections, such as *Folly as It Flies* (1859), *Ginger-Snaps* (1870), and *Caper-Sauce* (1872), were published periodically.

Modern critics have seen a split in P.'s writing between the rebellious (Fanny) and the sentimental and conventional (Fern). An alternative interpretation is that P.'s work changed over the years. The lachrymosity of her first pieces gave way, as her grief subsided, to the "noisy, rattling" humor, full of italics and exclamation points, and the pointed satire that her brother disliked. Once established professionally and remarried (to the biographer, James Parton), she developed a surer voice and broadened her range of subject matter. Although P. continued to pursue everyday domestic topics, she also satirized urban social and economic conditions and placed her favorite themes—the rights of women and children—in a wider context.

BIBLIOGRAPHY: Harris, S. K., "Inscribing and Defining: The Many Voices of Fanny Fern's *Ruth Hall,*" *Style* 22 (Winter 1988): 612–27; Huf, L., "The Devil and Fanny Fern," *A Portrait of the Artist as a Young Woman* (1983); Parton, J., ed., *Fanny Fern: A Memorial Volume* (1873); Walker, N., *Fanny Fern* (1993); Warren, J. W., *Fanny Fern: An Independent Woman* (1992); Warren, ed., *Ruth Hall and Other Writings* (1986); Wood, A. D., "The 'Scribbling Women' and Fanny Fern," *AQ* 23 (September 1971): 3–14

BARBARA A. WHITE

PATCHEN, Kenneth

b. 13 December 1911, Niles, Ohio; d. 8 January 1972, Palo Alto, California

P. was a prolific poet, painter, novelist, and playwright: during his lifetime, he published thirty-eight books of poetry, four novels, and two plays in addition to countless drawings and paintings. Despite the sheer volume of his writings, P. has always remained somewhat on the fringe of an American literary canon. Nevertheless, P. enjoyed some degree of success during his lifetime in less-institutionalized circles: for example, P. achieved almost cult status within poetry circles in the 1950s for reading his poetry while accompanied by jazz music—thereby serving as the prototype for the stereotyped image of the Beat poet; his anti–World War II poetry documenting the brutality and atrocity of war gained notoriety with the anti–Vietnam War agenda of 1960s American counterculture; and his novel *The Memoirs of a Shy Pornographer* (1945) with its disheveled and dark surrealism was popular with college students.

P.'s body of writing tends to fall into five thematic groupings: the social protest poem, the love lyric, the surrealist narrative/pastiche, the portrait, and the poem/painting or poem/drawing collaboration. In essence, P.'s poetry is broad in its scope and often draws upon his working-class background, the Great Depression, World War II, as well as his love of the visual arts—Salvador Dali and the surrealists in particular. Nonetheless, the predominant mood of P.'s poetry is dark, and his poetry echoes film noir in that the threat of violence, murder, gunshots, and criminals is set against the backdrop of a modern city. The city for P. is the heart of all human villainy: as P. writes, "What was the beginning of this city [the tower of Babel]? What was it but a concourse of thieves, and a sanctuary of criminals?" And his poetry is, in effect, an attack against villainy, criminality, and evil.

The propensity for social-minded, antiwar themes along with jazz-influenced rhythms and repetitions has prompted critics to regard P. as the 20th-c. inception of Walt WHITMAN. Nevertheless, P.'s somewhat bleak perspective regarding humanity lacks the optimism and hope that drives Whitman's poetry and world view. P. primarily is concerned with the horrors of humanity and mankind's propensity to enact evil and violence upon one another. War and murder reside at the core of P.'s world view, and he perceived in war the true face of human beings. Furthermore, P.'s bleak perspective towards mankind may be an extension of the fact that both P. and his father worked in steel mills, which has prompted some critics to label P. a "proletarian" poet. P.'s writing as a whole often returns to themes that seem to extend out of his experiences in the steel mills and the whole context of the depression era of the 1930s, but P.'s poetry is not limited by a "Marxist" worldview or a strictly social agenda.

Whereas murder, war, and mayhem reside at the core of P.'s poetry, the idealized conception of love provides a counter to this darkness. In P.'s view, the only salve to war and inhumanity is love and poetry, which form the only antidote for inhumanity. The

poem must confront and show brutality for what it is, and the chief weapon for the poem in its battle against inhumanity is the universal power of love. As P. writes, "What else is war, war is also a lie / love is not a lie, love is great, O love is greater." Perhaps not surprisingly, most of P.'s poetry is dedicated to Miriam, his wife, whom he married in 1934. P.'s world, though, is divided into murderers and victims, and love falls upon the victim side of such a continuum: the pair of lovers tenuously hold one another while being perpetually threatened by death, inhumanity, and evil. Love is a sanctuary for P. and the loss of love is true human tragedy. P.'s love lyrics often utilize archaic words such as "Thee" and "Thou"—thereby suggesting that love (as embodied by such language) is not well-suited to the 20th c. and is, rather, closer in sensibility of the idyllic setting of the romantic and pre-romantic poets before the industrial era began to deteriorate the core of humanity.

Even though P. remains relatively overlooked by most critics and is often excluded from most poetry anthologies, his poetry addresses many of the problems and ills that continue to plague contemporary society. His poetry brings into uncomfortable relief issues that most poets opt to ignore. P.'s insistence that the poem must reveal cruelty and brutality flies in the face with the idea of the lyric poem as the embodiment of transcendence and beauty, but it is his reluctance to ignore his world that has given his poetry vitality and weight.

BIBLIOGRAPHY: Nelson, R., *K. P. in American Mysticism* (1984); Rexroth, K., *American Poetry in the Twentieth Century* (1971); Smith, L. R., *K. P.* (1978); Walsh, C., *Today's Poets* (1964)

DAVID W. CLIPPINGER

PATTEN, William Gilbert

b. 25 October 1866, Corinna, Maine; d. 16 January 1945, Vista, California

Writing as Burt L. Standish, P. was one of the most successful and prolific writers of popular, mass circulation sports stories for juveniles and adolescents and creator of the Frank Merriwell weekly series that ran from April 18, 1896 to March 6, 1915 in the *Top Top Library* and *Tip Top Weekly*. After he ceased writing the Merriwell saga in July 1912 (with the stories carried on by other writers under the Standish name), P. published a series of fifteen baseball novels from 1914 to 1928, and in 1941 he published a novel about an adult Frank Merriwell hero in *Mr. Frank Merriwell*.

Raised in rural Maine by strict parents who restricted his reading and physical activities, P. ran away from home and found work in a machine shop in the industrial town of Biddeford, but he returned to his home in Corinna and began writing fiction based on his secret passion for dime novels. At the age of seventeen, he began selling fiction and seemed to be headed for a career as a writer of Westerns and detective thrillers for the publishing house of Beadle and Adams. After ten years with this firm, he formed an association with Street and Smith in 1895 and began the series that featured a remarkable athlete who had an inordinately long career at the Fardale Academy and at Yale. P.'s Merriwell series emphasized the values of fair play, self-discipline, high standards of personal conduct on and off the athletic field, and self-control. After Frank moved out into the world of business, the cycle of his career was repeated by his long-lost half-brother, Dick Merriwell.

As a writer, P. made no claims to literary ambitions or talents, but he was a writer who knew his audience and his subliterary mode of fiction. He was forced to write hurriedly to meet deadlines and to meet the plot demands of a weekly publication. The Merriwell stories, while they featured improbable plots and fantasy adventures, emphasized action developing out of character and conflicts based on character, and they reinforced moral values that found approval of parents. P. raised the dime novel to a higher level of respectability and acceptance and had enthusiastic readers in such national figures as Al Smith, Jack Dempsey, Babe Ruth, and Woodrow Wilson. In 1964, P.'s autobiography, *Frank Merriwell's Father,* was published.

BIBLIOGRAPHY: Cutler, J. L., *G. P. and His Frank Merriwell Saga* (1934); Kunitz, S. J., and H. Haycraft, eds., *Twentieth Century Authors* (1942); Messenger, C. K., *Sport and the Spirit of Play in American Fiction* (1981); Oriard, M. V., *Dreaming of Heroes: American Sports Fiction, 1868–1980* (1982)

DOUGLAS A. NOVERR

PAULDING, James Kirke

b. 22 August 1778, Pleasant Valley, New York; d. 6 April 1860, Hyde Park, New York

P.'s career was marked by his ardent NATIONALISM for the U.S. and his, at times viral, hatred of Britain. Currently, P.'s writings—including novels, sketches, essays, plays, and poems—are critically overshadowed by his collaborator, friend and brother-in-law Washington IRVING. Born in the Hudson River Valley, among a mainly Dutch immigrant population, P. grew up in Sleepy Hollow, New York. P.'s early life was spent in poverty, for his father had pledged his property as collateral to back Continental paper money during

the Revolution. The paper money failed after the war and all of the P.'s attempts at procuring reimbursed were denied, and eventually he was sent to debtors prison. Throughout his work, P. would continually return to the theme of the evils of paper currency. His early experiences with poverty led P. to spend his life writing for the marketplace, producing at a rapid rate, and as a result, his work lacks the polish that might have led to critical acclaim.

In 1797, P. moved to New York and boarded with his older sister Julia and her husband William Irving, the older brother of Washington Irving. Lacking a formal education, P. had read voraciously as a child, and was heavily influenced by the satirist Oliver Goldsmith. In New York, P. found an outlet for his intellect and rapidly joined the Debating Society, the influential Calliopean Society, and helped form the loose social fraternity the "lads of Kilkenny." From January 24, 1807 to January 25, 1808, P. joined Washington and William Irving in publishing *Salmagundi,* a series of twenty satirical pamphlets aimed at criticizing the early society of the Republic. Employing Goldsmith's technique of a narrator who is a stranger in a strange land, the pamphlets used humor as the vehicle for social commentary on such topics as Thomas JEFFERSON, the New York social scene, fashion, and gender roles in the emerging American nation. P. went on to write *Salmagundi: Second Series* (1819–20) by himself.

In *The Diverting History of John Bull and Brother Jonathan* (1812), P. employed satire to construct a political allegory that personifies the national characters of England and America in terms of human emotions. This marked P.'s first major contribution to the Anglo-American controversy, which was a theme that would dominate his writing for the course of his career. P.'s *The Lay of the Scottish Fiddle* (1813), a parody of Sir Walter Scott, concerns the burning of Harve de Grace, Maryland by British forces. P. broke with Irving over the issue of liberating American literature from European (specifically British) models. In the last issue of *Salmagundi: Second Series,* P. included an essay "The Wreck of Genius" (later condensed and reprinted as "National Literature"), which argued for a native American literature based on "rational fictions," which anticipates realism. With the two-volume *A Sketch of Old England by a New England Man* (1822), P. attempts to reverse the trend of English travel accounts of America through satirizing their uniformed conclusions; it is starkly anti-British and at best weak satire. P. again returned to themes of British snobbery with *John Bull in America* (1825). P. achieved commercial popularity with the two-volume *The Dutchman's Fireside* (1831), which traces the maturation of Sybrandt Westbrook from an awkward boy to a courageous individual through his interaction with Indians and confrontations with the British in the wilderness of New York. P.'s commercial success continued with *Westward Ho!* (1832), which chronicles the migration of Colonel Dangerfield and his family from Virginia to Kentucky. P.'s *Life of Washington* (1835) was the standard biography of the national hero until it was superseded by Washington Irving's text in 1855. P. was made Secretary of the Navy (1838–41) by President Martin Van Buren for his partisan writings in newspapers and periodicals.

BIBLIOGRAPHY: Herold, A. L., *J. K. P.: Versatile American* (1926), Paulding, W. I., *The Literary Life of J. K. P.* (1867), Reynolds, L. J., *J. K. P.* (1984)

DUNCAN FAHERTY

PAU-LLOSA, Ricardo
b. 17 May 1954, Havana, Cuba

A respected Cuban American poet, short story writer, essayist, art critic, curator, and lecturer, P. began his writing career at the tender age of eighteen when he published a short collection of poems in Spanish, *Veinticinco poemas* (1973). With this collection, P. demonstrated great potential as a wordsmith and poet.

In 1983, P. followed with his first full-length collection of poetry written in English, *Sorting Metaphors.* This book was awarded the Anhinga Prize for Poetry by Florida State University. Although English is the author's second language, a language he acquired after his immigration to the U.S. in 1960, the collection of thirty-six poems showcases the emphasis P. places on language. Of his poems, he said: "One of the satisfactions of writing in English is the ample sonorous range of that language, the result of its lexical diversity and richness." His poems, according to the author, rely on Latin American literary, philosophical, and pictorial traditions. As such, the poems shed light on the bicultural existence of the author, with their images and references to a bygone Cuba. The title poem, "Sorting Metaphors," offers images of Havana, distant images that now only exist in the speaker's memory as he gazes at a map. Although his former homeland is now reduced to a piece of paper, and the city seems so far removed, the speaker can fit half of it under the spread of his hand, symbolizing what Dionisio Martinez called "a tightrope walk between a cold aesthetic eye and an unabashed nostalgia." Continuing in the lyrical tradition he began at the age of eighteen, these poems capture the bicultural intricacies that define Cuban American sensibilities.

Although P.'s work is characterized by a sense of security and ease of transition, his world in Miami is an uneasy, fractured one. In 1988, Anglo Florida seemed intent upon waging war upon the largely Hispanic, mainly Cuban, communities that reside in the state's southern realms. The English Only Proposition won by a landslide in November 1988. While many Cuban American writers seem mired by their status as exiles, P.'s second, full-length collection of poems, *Bread of the Imagined* (1992), forms a cultural link between two diverse Americas, the multiethnic with the Anglo, the present with the past. Fully embracing his new language, *Bread of the Imagined* continues the poet's explorations of a bicultural identity. His poems play with the manner in which the mind interprets sensory images and impressions through the use of metaphors, similes, and tropes. In addition, this collection heralds P.'s transition to narrative poetry.

A professor of English at Miami Dade Community College, P. continues to write poetry and short fiction. He is currently at work on a novel and a third collection of poems, and his writings have appeared in several Latino/a literature anthologies, *Cuban-American Writers: Los Atrevidos* (1989) and *Iguana Dreams: New Latino Fiction* (1992), and various journals, *Poetry Northwest, Michigan Quarterly Review, Partisan Review, Caribbean Review, Carolina Quarterly,* and the *Kenyon Review,* among others. P. has also written books and essays, and has delivered lectures, on 20th c. Latin American art.

In addition to his creative work, P. has produced many art exhibition catalogs. He is also an advisor on Cuban and Latin American art and a contributor to the *Dictionary of Art,* published by Macmillan.

BIBLIOGRAPHY: Ryan, B., ed., *Hispanic Writers: A Selection of Sketches from Contemporary Authors* (1991)

JOSEPH M. VIERA

PAYNE, John Howard
b. 9 June 1791, New York City; d. 9 April 1852, Tunis, North Africa

P. was the first American to achieve international acclaim as a dramatist. While his work was chiefly derivative—he adapted and translated preexisting material—his supreme craftsmanship secured his place in the literary canon. He was a skilled editor who was often able to improve a play's plot and sharpen the dialogue. P. was rather prolific, producing more than sixty plays in approximately twenty years. He has been called, by some, a hack. Others have compared him to a screenwriter and marveled at his ability to rework popular drama so quickly. P. was the product of an age in which the word "plagiarism" had little meaning and his was a welcome service to theater owners, actors, and a hungry 19th-c. audience.

P., a child prodigy, fell in love with the theater as a young boy. At age twelve, he was already submitting critical reviews to newspapers. He founded his own theatrical newspaper at fourteen, the *Thespian Mirror.* This endeavor won him respect and contacts in the literary scene. His first play, *Julia* (1806), written when he was just fifteen, showed enough promise that his friends sponsored his studies at Union College in up-state New York. Later, P. had moderate but short lived success as an actor. During this period, he began writing adaptations for extra money, a talent he drew upon almost exclusively when American theater began to fall away and his acting career stalled.

P. left the U.S. for England and spent the next twenty years adapting French melodrama for London's Drury Lane and Covent Garden theaters. There, he developed a system by which he could complete the adaptation of an entire French production in just four days. Admittedly drawing from at least seven previous plays, P. produced *Brutus* (1818), which was to become one of the most famous tragedies in English during the 19th c.

Among the great number of French dramas P. adapted for English audiences, *Clari* (1823) is the most notable, for it contains one of the best known ballads of the era—"Home Sweet Home." The melody is based on a French or Sicilian air, but the lyrics were P.'s own.

In 1832, P. returned to America and was greeted as a literary hero, a world class man of letters. His fame won him an appointment to the American consul at Tunis, a post he held until his death. In a twist of irony worthy of the stage, P., famous for writing "Home Sweet Home," died penniless in a foreign land. His contribution to American drama is significant as his work nourished the young, developing culture of a new nation.

BIBLIOGRAPHY: Chiles, R. P., *J. H. P.* (1930); Parham, J. B., "J. H. P.," in Elliott, E., ed., *DLB,* vol. 37, *American Writers of the Early Republic* (1985): 248–53

JASON MCMAHON

PEABODY, Elizabeth Palmer

b. 16 May 1804, Billerica, Massachusetts; d. 3 January 1894, Boston, Massachusetts

Her indomitable spirit captured by Henry JAMES in his unforgettable, gently satiric portrait of her as Miss Birdseye, the nostalgic do-gooder of *The Bostonians* (1885), P. is only now emerging from a century of neglect. While P. was well known and esteemed in her time, the lives and careers of her many famous acquaintants have tended to obscure her own accomplishments as a social and cultural reformer. Spending virtually all her life in Boston and Concord, she counted among her friends such luminaries as the Reverend William Ellery CHANNING, Washington Allston, Amos Bronson ALCOTT, Ralph Waldo EMERSON, Theodore PARKER, and Henry Wadsworth LONGFELLOW. Fame ran in her family, too: one sister, Mary, was the wife of Horace Mann; the other, Sophia, was married to Nathaniel HAWTHORNE.

Eccentric, strong-willed, and compassionate, P. had eclectic interests—in philology and language acquisition, history, theology, teaching, and publishing. In addition, she was an active humanitarian, taking up the causes of émigrés, blacks, and American Indians, as well as a strong advocate for women's rights. Following a period of private tutoring, she assisted transcendentalist Amos Bronson Alcott, from 1834 to 1836, in his experimental Temple School and helped publicize his pedagogical theories and practices in *Record of a School* (1835). P. also recorded Alcott's Socratic discussions that appeared in his *Conversations with Children on the Gospels.* Although she eventually moved away from his radical idealism as she adopted more empirical methods, P. continued to share Alcott's belief in the importance of inspiring self-confidence in students. Her most significant achievement in education, however, was helping to establish the German kindergarten system in America. She edited the *Kindergarten Messenger* (1873–77) and wrote several articles and books on the subject, including *Lectures in Training Schools for Kindergarten* (1888). Among her history books are *Key to History* (1832), *The Hebrews* (1833), *The Greeks* (1833), and *Chronological History of the U.S.* (1856). Her research in linguistics, combining transcendentalist belief in the symbolic nature of language with the theories of Herder and Kraitsir, resulted in several publications, the most illuminating being a long essay entitled "Language" (1848).

It was as a member of the transcendentalist circle that P. makes the greatest claim on the attention of students in American literature. The various editions of her translation of Gerando's *Self-Education* (1830, 1832, 1833, 1860) helped make more readily accessible to the transcendentalists a central text for the formulation of their concept of "self-culture." In the decade following her work with Alcott, she ran a celebrated bookstore and lending library at 13 West Street in Boston, which became an informal gathering place for the transcendentalists and where she and Margaret FULLER held their famous conversations for women. And, like Fuller, P. was a member of the

Transcendental Club. She also published *The Dial,* the transcendentalists' major philosophical and literary journal; and, in 1849, she launched her own (unfortunately stillborn) periodical, *Aesthetic Papers,* which included among other notable contributions the first appearance in print of Henry David THOREAU's "Civil Disobedience." As the century drew to a close, P. also participated in Alcott's Concord School of Philosophy (1879–87) and lectured there on literature and education.

P.'s vivid, anecdote-rich memories of her contemporaries, recorded in her journals and letters and selectively published in such widely admired recollections as *Reminiscences of Rev. Wm. Ellery Channing* (1880) and *Last Evening with Allston* (1886), prompted Theodore Parker to call her, fittingly, the "Boswell" of her era.

BIBLIOGRAPHY: Baylor, R. M., *E. P. P.: Kindergarten Pioneer* (1965); Brooks, G., *Three Wise Virgins* (1957); Chielens, E., ed., *American Literary Magazines: The Eighteenth and Nineteenth Centuries* (1986); Myerson, J., *The New England Transcendentalists and "The Dial"* (1980); Myerson, J., ed., *The Transcendentalists: A Review of Research and Criticism* (1984); Ronda, B., *Letters of E. P. P.* (1984); Tharp, L. H., *The Peabody Sisters of Salem* (1950)

LARRY A. CARLSON

PEABODY, Josephine Preston
b. 30 May 1874, Brooklyn, New York; d. 4 December 1922, Cambridge, Massachusetts

From the early lyric poetry she began publishing at fourteen to the historical drama she wrote during her terminal illness, P.'s work expressed her idealism and ardent wish to share with others a sense of the beauty in the world. She was devoted to Shakespeare, whose influence is often evident in her content if not in form. Her reputation was considerable during her lifetime, especially after she won the Stratford-upon-Avon Shakespeare Memorial Prize in 1910 for her poetic drama *The Piper* (1909), but the ethereal ornateness of her style has long been out of fashion and her work has fallen into critical neglect.

Her first book, *Old Greek Folk Stories* (1897), attracted little notice, but her first collection of poems, *The Wayfarers* (1898), was widely acclaimed for the delicacy of youthful sentiment along with a mature craftsmanship. Eyes, wings, heart, and light are frequent references in these graceful effusions that P. herself later found repetitive. Nine of the poems were selected for inclusion in Edmund Clarence Stedman's *American Anthology.*

Fortune and Men's Eyes (1900) included a one-act play of that title, a dramatic monologue entitled "The Wingless Joy," and some new poems. The play incorporates phrases from Shakespeare's sonnets to lend authenticity to the dialogue of "Master W. S." and others who carry on a merry intrigue at the Bear and Angel Tavern. Her next play, *Marlowe* (1901), is a full-length drama treating the Elizabethan dramatist's love life and death in beautiful language but with little dramatic action. *The Piper,* a poetic dramatization of the story of the Pied Piper of Hamelin, suffused with religious sentiment, remains her best known and most popular work. *The Wolf of Gubbio* (1913) is an ambitious play about St. Francis of Assisi. Her last play, *Portrait of Mrs. W* (1922), a feminist's interpretation of the life of Mary Wollstonecraft, reflects the social concerns that appeared also in her late poetry.

The melodic, often subtly humorous poems of *The Singing Leaves* (1903) were extremely popular, as were the child's-eye poems of *The Book of the Little Past* (1908). *The Singing Man* (1911) and, especially, *Harvest Moon* (1916) reveal a newly evident awareness of human suffering. The latter volume contains a cycle of "War and Women poems" calling upon womankind to lead men away from the horror of war.

BIBLIOGRAPHY: Baker, C. H., ed., *The Diary and Letters of J. P. P.* (1925); Rittenhouse, J. B., *The Younger American Poets* (1904)

FELICIA HARDISON LONDRÉ

PEACOCK, Molly
b. 30 June 1947, Buffalo, New York

If P.'s first book, *And Live Apart* (1980), was to prove a misstep, her second, *Raw Heaven* (1984), firmly established her voice as the New Formalist poet most strongly confessional in her approach to the autobiographical content of her lyrics. These include, most prominently, painfully frank looks at her childhood in working-class Buffalo, dominated by a brutal alcoholic father and a passive, ineffectual mother, and equally graphic explorations of female sexuality. If the exuberance underlying her poems sometimes makes them formally a bit sloppy—iambic pentameter lines stretched beyond their limit; poems that seem to want to be sonnets stretching to fifteen or eighteen lines for no discernable thematic reason—it also evokes a powerful emotional response from her readers. She stands before us unabashedly flawed, proud of her hard-won adult wonder with the world, the happiness of a survivor.

In *Raw Heaven,* P. introduces the subject of a parent's alcoholism and the devastating affect it has on family life in "Those Paperweights with Snow Inside" and "Our Room." The former, a sixteen-line poem ending in a couplet, attempts to impose order upon the chaos of family violence by encapsulating it in the image of the glass paperweight that can be held in the hand and by the order of poetic form—here an imperfect sonnet that nonetheless emphasizes closure, control. The latter draws upon P.'s experience as a kindergarten teacher, the classroom shared between teacher and students becoming a shared safe space where issues like alcoholism can be discussed as in an alternative, more nurturing home. In *Take Heart* (1989), P. continues to explore this theme in her two finest poems on the subject. "Buffalo" deals with the oppression the young poet felt when forced to spend time in bars and parking lots waiting for her father while he drank, oblivious to time. "Say You Love Me" presents the poet and her younger sister being abused, in the absence of their mother, by a drunken father who insists the young poet express a love for a father that she clearly cannot feel.

Raw Heaven and *Take Heart* are equally memorable for their unabashedly explicit poems on sexuality. "She Lays," from *Raw Heaven,* is a detailed celebration of masturbation, its sensuous language heightened by P.'s compulsive use of rhyme. In the rhymed tercets and concluding quatrain of "The Surge," from *Take Heart,* P. deals as explicitly with male sexual anatomy as she did with the female body in "She Lays." In this poem, P. makes explicit, as well, the interconnection she recognizes between sexuality and religion. This parallel is made quite jarring in "ChrisEaster," one of a group of poems from *Take Heart* that chronicle the difficult decision the poet and a lover make that she will have an abortion. Here, the poet's ambivalence about this act is reflected in her feeling the occasion a combination of the holidays of Christmas and Easter because her abortion was a conflation of birth and death.

P.'s *Original Love* (1994) is divided into three sections. The first continues her exploration of female sexuality with such poems as "My College Sex Group," another explicit celebration of female genitalia, and "Have You Ever Faked an Orgasm?" Other poems celebrate her marriage to an old high school boyfriend, some, like "The Scare" and "Little Miracle," focusing on the anxiety provoked by her husband's bout with cancer. The second section explores the poet's relation to her mother, during her struggle with, and after her succumbing to, cancer. This yields an unusual comic tour-de-force, "The Fare," expressing the poet's regret at having buried her mother wearing earrings, surely to cause her unnecessary pain in death, as they did in life. In the final section, P. focuses

on sacred love, as in the poems "Religious Instruction," "Subway Vespers," and "Prairie Prayer."

Her formal inventiveness and linguistic exuberance with which she explores a wide range of experience, often yielding unexpected juxtapositions, makes P. an engagingly entertaining poet.

BIBLIOGRAPHY: Allen, A., "M. P.," in Gwynn, R. S., ed., *DLB,* vol. 120, *American Poets since World War II* (1992): 243–47; Wojahn, D., "Four from Prosperp," *GaR* 43 (Fall 1989): 589–601

ROBERT MCPHILLIPS

PEMBERTON, Caroline Hollingsworth

b. 186?, Philadelphia, Pennsylvania; d. 1927

P. is one of the most invisible white authors in American letters. Absent from every printed biographical dictionary, encyclopedia, and bibliography on women in the English-speaking world, the available details of her life are few, but what is on record points to probable causes of her literary obscurity, despite an unusual career.

Born in Philadelphia to an aristocratic family, she spent part of her professional life and personal fortune to advance equal opportunities for blacks and to improve foster care for underprivileged white children—concerns to which she devoted most of her published writings. Her name is unassociated with feminism, in an era when many women concentrated their efforts on attaining female suffrage. From the mid-1890s through the early years of the 20th c., her public activities were devoted to a crusade to help the economically disadvantaged; she was briefly an unremitting voice against the second-class citizenship of blacks, North and South—apart from any national or local organized movement. A well-bred white American woman who took that step alone in a segregated society in her era risked censure from her own race. The independent role P. chose differed from upper-class female social reformers such as Jane Addams, who in 1889 founded Hull House for foreign immigrants in the slums of Chicago. P. founded no organization, although she generously financed the Children's Aid Society of Pennsylvania of which she was volunteer superintendent and spokesperson in the mid-1890s.

But her main instrument was her pen, and she received brief attention for her first novel, *Your Little Brother James* (1896), about a white boy reared as a thief by a prostitute mother in an urban slum and saved by foster parents and religious conversion. Her belief in the importance of environment over heredity was echoed in her magazine articles and a short story, "The

Putting Away of The McPhersons." Her second novel, *Stephen the Black* (1899), racial in content, went unreviewed by critics, ignored by the public, and all but forgotten until 1972 when reprinted by Books for Library Press (with no information about her).

Stephen the Black, with its nonstereotypical black characters, was uncharacteristic of any fiction about race published by a white American author in 1899; for most Caucasian readers, it was undoubtedly realistic, too sympathetic, and its writer too indignant. That it received no critical attention can be attributed not to its stylistic and structural defects (which were fewer than in her first novel reviewed by the *New York Times*), but because the text defied racial boundaries, exposed and satirized the hypocrisy and race paternalism of Northern white philanthropists; attacked the venal sharecropper system that replaced slavery, and assailed the murder by extremists of a black woman wed to a wealthy white man in the South. In an article in the January 1900 issue of *Arena* magazine, "The Barbarism of Civilization," P. impugned lynching, scorned the illogic of illegal interracial marriage, urged literacy for the black and white masses and an end to race discrimination in skilled trades. She went further in the early 1900s by becoming an active socialist. However, when she found some socialists not immune from racism, she broke ranks and dissented in print.

Her progressive political views were far to the left of her Quaker background. In her old-line family of merchants and scholars prominent in Philadelphia from the days of William Penn, the most famous relative was a West Point-educated uncle who joined the Confederacy: John Clifford Pemberton, the defender of Vicksburg, until Grant forced his unconditional surrender. At the Civil War's end, her uncle settled with his wife and children on a farm in Warrenton, Virginia, where as a young girl P. first visited the South, before the ex-general relocated to Philadelphia in 1876. Her father was John's younger brother, Henry, a Unionist, who later made his name as author of *The Path of Evolution through Ancient Thought and Modern Science* (1902), and as member of the American Philosophical Society, the Academy of Natural Sciences, and Historical Society of Pennsylvania. Her mother, who named her only daughter after herself, was born in London, where she died in 1883, while traveling with P. and an elder son, Harry. Mrs. Pemberton's last will and testament made P. sole heir to a fortune valued at nearly one million dollars—in income and property in England and the U.S. The legal will was contested for more than a year by P.'s two older brothers, both physicians, who ultimately lost to her in a New Jersey court. The *New York Times* reported her legal victory with a poignant sidelight of her personal life that is still veiled in mystery, even if it reads like a sketch of a Henry JAMES novel:

"The lady who wins this great legal battle has a romantic history. While traveling with her mother in Europe, Caroline, then a miss of about eighteen, fell in love with a young Jewish gentleman who was a student at one of the Parisian academies. A clandestine marriage was the result. Later, it is said through the influence of the young wife's family, the husband of Caroline left for parts unknown. A child was afterward born to the young wife, but when she—the mother—regained her health, the child was missing. The young mother was told that it had died immediately after birth. After the death of her mother, Caroline, who still kept her maiden name, found herself a wealthy woman. Visiting Europe, the lady with her wealth used every effort to find her husband and child, both of whom she believed to be alive, but without success."

The final decades of her career are unknown, and her private life concealed by a family reluctant to reopen it. Ahead of her time, she left various pieces in newspapers, black church journals, and now defunct magazines like *Lend a Hand,* and other works yet to be discovered.

FAITH BERRY

Adapted from the forthcoming anthology From Bondage to Liberation, *edited and narrated by Faith Berry. New York: The Continuum Publishing Company. Printed by permission.*

PENNELL, Joseph Stanley

b. 4 July 1908, Junction City, Kansas; d. 26 September 1963, Portland Oregon

Novelist and poet, P. was born in Junction City, a small Kansas town three miles from Fort Riley. P.'s father was a local photographer with a regional reputation. P. attended local schools and studies drama for one year at the University of Kansas. In 1927, he attended Pembroke College, Oxford, England, never taking a degree. Returning to the U.S., he learned news reporting at the Denver *Post,* and then worked for the St. Louis *Post-Dispatch,* the Kansas City *Star,* and the Los Angeles *Examiner* and *Post-Record*. P. worked as a farm news announcer and did comedy routines for St. Louis radio station KMOX, taught from 1931 to 1933 at the John Burroughs School, and acted with local theater groups. Rejected by the Canadian military at the outbreak of World War II, he served in the U.S. Army as a second lieutenant in the coastal artillery.

P. authored an article on Americans at Oxford, "Our Own Oxonians," in the *North American Review,* published in 1930, and his first published poems appeared in Harriet MONROE's *Poetry* magazine in 1931. His first novel, *The History of Rome Hanks and Kindred Matters* (1944), was based in part on P.'s own Kansas family and his detailed study of the Civil War. It remains an extraordinary portrayal of the lives of ordinary soldiers. P.'s sprawling manuscript was reduced and edited by Maxwell Perkins, who considered the novel "the finest piece of writing about war in all literary history." Reviewers compared P. to Thomas WOLFE and William FAULKNER, but the book's fixation on excremental functions led to its being banned in Boston. A proposed Metro-Goldwyn-Mayer film never materialized.

P.'s second novel, *The History of Nora Beckham: A Museum of Home Life* (1948), continued the family saga. Highlighted by a dissection of P.'s mother and a devastating depiction of small-town practices and prejudices, it followed Thomas Wolfe in displaying both attraction and repulsion for the late Victorian world. However, the novel failed to win critical acclaim and certainly did not endear P. to Kansas patriots.

Shortly afterwards, P. moved to Seaside, Oregon, where he remained for the remainder of his life. A projected third volume, entitled "The History of Thomas Wagnal," apparently continued the family saga, but was not published, perhaps due to the death of Maxwell Perkins.

P.'s private life was marked by tragedy and possibly accounted for his failure to fulfill his early promise. He married Elizabeth Horton in St Louis in 1945. After she died from an overdose of sleeping pills in 1949, he married her sister, Virginia Horton, who survived him. After moving to Oregon, he published only *Darksome House,* a collection of his poems, in 1959. Nevertheless, his two published novels remain among the finest pieces of writing in the 20th c.

BIBLIOGRAPHY: Robillard, D., "J. S. P., Rome Hanks, and Kindred Matters," *EAS* 13 (September 1984): 83–93

MICHAEL B. DOUGAN

PERCY, Walker

b. 28 May 1916, Birmingham, Alabama; d. 10 May 1990, Covington, Louisiana

P. helped redefine modern Southern fiction through his deeply philosophical, yet comic, investigations of late-20th-c. disillusionment. Influenced particularly by Søren Kierkegaard and Martin Heidegger, P. wrote about protagonists experiencing a sense of crisis who undertake a search for spiritual vitality. P.'s conversion to Catholicism in 1947 also informed the values expressed in his writings; the philosophical basis of his

work has been characterized as "Catholic existentialism," a label that, despite its incongruity, indicates the tenor of the moral and intellectual lessons that P.'s fiction conveys.

P.'s first novel, *The Moviegoer* (1961), won the National Book Award for 1962 and established his thematic concern with the struggle to find coherence within, or despite, a society that seems morally hollow. *The Moviegoer*'s main character, "Binx" Bolling, feels out of place in the traditional world of Southern gentility; his alienation is only overcome when he acknowledges, on Ash Wednesday, his need for meaningful human relationships. *The Last Gentleman* (1966) continues P.'s social critique through the wanderings of the main character, Will Barrett, whose encounters with various lifestyles tempt him to consider suicide. Suicide reappears as a theme in *Love in the Ruins* (1971), in which protagonist Dr. Thomas More attempts to provide spiritual healing by inventing the "Lapsometer," but this absurd device only provokes people to act in extreme ways rather than offering a solution to modern despair. In *Lancelot* (1977), P.'s revision of romantic and Dantean themes revolves around a narrator so obsessed with his wife's sexual infidelity that he commits murder. Throughout these novels, the theme of humanity's desperate need for loving connections and a workable faith is complicated by P.'s writing style, which avoids giving a sense of closure or certainty.

A more fortunate thematic development occurs in *The Second Coming* (1980), wherein P.'s returning protagonist Will Barrett finds love after demanding proof of God's existence. P.'s sixth novel, *The Thanatos Syndrome* (1987), continues to dramatize the struggle to find goodness despite postmodern alienation. Although P. often declined to give interviews during his career, after writing *The Thanatos Syndrome* he spoke extensively with reviewers and writers for religious publications, as if to highlight his concern for humanity in an era of psychological and spiritual malaise.

P.'s fictional technique includes black comedy, satire, and semiotic theory, a distinctive blend that enlivens his characteristic didacticism. The mixture of philosophical influences in P.'s work led some early critics to consider him in effect a "European" writer; later critics stressed P.'s reworking of American, particularly Southern, literary traditions and his satire of popular culture. P.'s thematic repetitions and failure to offer distinct resolutions frustrate some readers, although these aspects also reflect P.'s ongoing concern with the ambiguities of life that necessitate a struggle or an "epiphany in ordeal" toward redemption in Christian terms. His two essay collections, *The Message in the Bottle* (1975) and *Lost in the Cosmos* (1983), present many of the ideas that drive his fiction, particularly the nature of the modern, secular South, the need for an "intersubjective" sensibility that allows meaningful human relationships, and the necessity of finding a workable faith despite individuals' essential isolation.

BIBLIOGRAPHY: Allen, W. R., *W. P.: A Southern Wayfarer* (1986); Crowley, J. D., and S. M. Crowley, eds., *Critical Essays on W. P.* (1989); Lawson, L. A., *Still Following P.* (1996); Lawson, L. A., and E. H. Oleksy, eds., *W. P.'s Feminine Characters* (1995); Quinlan, K., *W. P.: The Last Catholic Novelist* (1991); Samway, P. H., *W. P.: A Life* (1997); Tolson, J., *Pilgrim in the Ruins* (1992)

JAYNE MAREK

PERCY, William Alexander

b. 14 May 1885, Greenville, Mississippi; d. 21 January 1942, Greenville, Mississippi

P. is best known for his autobiography, *Lanterns on the Levee: Recollections of a Planter's Son* (1941). P.'s less important volumes of poetry include *Sappho in Levkas and Other Poems* (1959), *In April Once and Other Poems* (1920), *Enzio's Kingdom and Other Poems* (1924), *Selected Poems* (1930), and *Collected Poems* (1943).

Lanterns on the Levee is a remarkable book, for it tells us much about the profound social change in Mississippi and the South during P.'s life, as well as the quality of the life lived by an extraordinary man. *Lanterns* describes P.'s Delta country and his roots in both place and family, his education at Sewanee and the Harvard Law School, his role as an officer in World War I, and his career as a Delta citizen, detailing his famous resistance to the Ku Klux Klan and his administration of relief efforts in the massive 1927 flood, among other issues.

Perhaps the most difficult problem he faced was the race issue, and his concept of *noblesse oblige* is now seen as patronizing. Yet he advocated education, moral integrity, and compassion, and his life shows us the "good man," whose biography might provide us with a model for living in the modern world. Essentially, his view of life is stoic, as his traditional values encounter overwhelming odds in the forces of racism, the dehumanization of technology, and the darkening clouds of World War II. Yet he is sustained by the power of memory, not only of his personal past but also of his family's history.

BIBLIOGRAPHY: Baker, L., *The Percys of Mississippi: Politics and Literature in the New South* (1983); Wyatt-Brown, B., *The House of Percy: Honor, Melan-*

choly, and Imagination in a Southern Family (1994); Wyatt-Brown, B., *The Literary Percys: Family History, Gender, and the Southern Imagination* (1994)

THOMAS J. RICHARDSON

PERELMAN, S[idney] J[oseph]

b. 1 February 1904, Brooklyn, New York; d. 17 October 1979, New York City

P. may be the purest comic writer of the 20th c. In the course of some fifty-five years as a professional writer, he devoted himself to the short comic piece almost exclusively. Though he wrote for the stage with some success, and toiled as a screenwriter, including work on two Marx Brothers films, it is for his twenty volumes of prose—all of them collections of short parodies, comic essays, travel articles, and satire—that he will be remembered. In a 1963 interview, he defended his chosen form, which he called the *feuilleton*, firmly: "I regard my comic writing as serious . . . I don't believe in the importance of scale; to me the muralist is no more valid than the miniature painter . . . I think the form I work can have its own distinction, and I would like to surpass what I have done in it."

After schooling in Rhode Island and college study at Brown, where he wrote and drew cartoons for the humor magazine, P. wrote for the humor magazines *Judge* and *College Humor*. After joining the *New Yorker* stable of writers in the early thirties, he did most of his work for that magazine, though he also wrote for *Holiday, TV Guide,* and other journals.

P.'s influences include George ADE, Ring LARDNER, Robert BENCHLEY, and other masters of the short comic form—whom he publicly identified as his mentors—but to what he learned from writers like these he added a highly developed linguistic wit that shows the influence of James Joyce. P.'s essays often employ self-deprecation, describing himself, for instance, as "a middle-aged city dweller, as lean and bronzed as a shad's belly," but unlike writers whose forte is in the manipulation of one persona, P. is a chameleon. His work includes short stories, brief plays, and nonsense "scenarios," as well as ruminative explorations of *outré* topics.

The comedy may come from situations—like "Waiting for Santy," in which disgruntled elves imitate Clifford ODETS characters—but the true keynote is the dizzying mastery of language. P. loves puns, foreign references, unusual literary allusions, Yiddish phrases, the *dreck* of advertising and popular culture screwed up a notch to absurdity. It is a rich, heady texture that makes a P. essay unmistakable and makes him an inimitable writer of HUMOR.

BIBLIOGRAPHY: Cole, W., and G. Plimpton, *Writers at Work,* 2nd series (1963); Fowler, D., *S. J. P.* (1983);

Gale, S., *S. J. P.: A Critical Study* (1987); Hermann, D., *S. J. P.: A Life* (1986)

MERRITT MOSELEY

PEREZ FIRMAT, Gustavo
b. 7 March 1949, Havana, Cuba

A survey of the works of P. F. suggests that his family's exile from Cuba in 1961 has exerted a powerful influence on the author's vision as a writer. Through his poetry and prose, P. F. engages in an ongoing literary exploration of the space between Cuban and American cultures in which the identity of bicultural individuals is forged. He portrays this cultural space as "life on the hyphen;" indeed, this term captures a recurring theme in P. F.'s literary production. As one of the most prolific and critically acclaimed Cuban American writers whose poetry in particular has been widely anthologized, P. F. contributes an important ethnic voice to contemporary American literature.

P. F. grew up in Miami's rapidly growing Cuban exile community. Affective implications of his move to North Carolina to become a professor at Duke University resonate in *Carolina Cuban,* a collection of P. F.'s works included in *Triple Crown: Chicano, Puerto Rican, and Cuban American Poetry* (1987). The problematic of the exile who resides far from his cultural home and writes in his second language is a recurring motif in these poems and in his collection *Bilingual Blues* (1995). Also noteworthy is P. F.'s inclusion in *Los Atrevidos: An Anthology of Cuban-American Writers* (1988), the first anthology of Cuban American writers whose works are primarily in English. Like the collection's other *atrevidos,* or "daring ones," P. F. represents a generation of Cuban exiles who grew up in the U.S. and whose literary formation reflects this bicultural status.

P. F.'s widest critical acclaim to date has come from his essays on Cuban American culture and identity in *Life on the Hyphen: The Cuban-American Way* (1994). This controversial work combines memoir and carefully researched cultural criticism, interspersed with brief prose "mambos" that playfully comment on popular culture. P. F. proposes that Cuban American culture is largely a product of the "one-and-a-half" generation of Cuban immigrants who, like the author himself, came to the U.S. "too young to be Cuban and too old to be American." The cultural production of "one-and-a-halfers" such as Desi Arnaz and Gloria Estefan thus reflects constant negotiation between tradition and translation. He continues to explore this negotiation in his memoir, *Next Year in Cuba* (1995); in this text, P. F. presents exile as the structuring factor that has transformed all aspects of his life—his family,

teaching career, personal relationships, and cultural identity.

Content, form, and theme tend to be closely linked in P. F.'s writing. Language play, for example, serves as an apt vehicle for expression of the bicultural experience. In poems such as "Bilingual Blues" and "Filosofías del no," the writer's clever manipulation of Spanish, English, and code-switching effectively conveys the degree to which cultural identity is influenced by the language one chooses (or is impelled) to use. Likewise, the puns and double entendres that pepper P. F.'s poetry and prose suggest that culture and identity are multilayered and can be read in a variety of ways. References to Cuba and Cuban material culture infuse this author's discourse, and lend his works a character that is clearly the result of writing done "on the hyphen."

BIBLIOGRAPHY: Prieto, R. "Feast Beyond the Fringe," *SLAPC* 7 (1988): 315–20; Piedra, J., "His and Her Panics," *Dispositio*16 (1991): 71–93

KAREN CHRISTIAN

PETERKIN, Julia [Alma Mood]
b. 31 October 1880, Laurens County, South Carolina; d. 10 August 1961, Fort Motte, South Carolina

Born the daughter of a physician but reared chiefly in the milieu of black nurses who spoke the Gullah dialect and Methodist preachers after her mother's death, P. possessed a sure gift for storytelling, although she was educated in music—she had earned B.A. and M.A. degrees by the time she was seventeen at Converse College in Spartanburg, South Carolina. In 1903, she married William George Peterkin of Fort Motte, South Carolina, a wealthy planter, and settled down as mistress of Lang Syne Plantation.

When boredom began to set in, P. turned again to music; she began piano lessons with Henry BELLAMANN, dean of fine arts at Chicora College, forty miles away in Columbia. She alternately amused and startled Bellamann, himself a poet, critic, and novelist, with her tales of plantation life. Bellamann requested that she commit her stories to paper, and asked his friend Carl SANDBURG to read what she had written. Favorably impressed when she read to him during a visit to Lang Syne, Sandburg found P. reluctant to seek publication. He then urged her to submit samples to Baltimore critic H. L. MENCKEN, who praised her Gullah-dialect sketches, and published her work in his own little magazine, *Smart Set* (1921).

P. also in 1921 published short pieces in the *Reviewer,* and in 1924 issued a short story collection, *Green Thursday,* a powerful assortment of realistic glimpses into the often-shocking lives of Gullah-speaking blacks who inhabited South Carolina's plantations. Three full-length novels followed: *Black April* (1927); *Bright Skin* (1932); and *Scarlet Sister Mary* (1928), which won the 1929 Pulitzer Prize in fiction and was later adapted into a dreadful Broadway play, featuring Ethel Barrymore in black face. A fascinating sociological study of the Gullahs, with photographs by Doris Ulmann, *Roll, Jordan, Roll,* appeared in 1933. In 1934, her last major literary effort, *A Plantation Christmas,* was published.

All her works, dealing sympathetically with poor Gullah farm workers, ignited significant controversy in the South in the 1920s and 1930s. In some areas, her books were barred from public libraries. The attacks took their toll. Except for a brief teaching stint in imaginative writing at Bennington College and maintaining her association with several literary societies, she published nothing more after 1937. The death of her husband in 1938 and the suicide of her daughter-in-law in 1941, coupled with farming's tribulations and her own declining health, drastically reduced her public activities.

While Alice WALKER's *The Color Purple* has proven that the literary viability of and popular taste for dialect writings have not evaporated, P.'s sometimes patronizing works clearly belong to a different era. Limited in subject matter and occasionally repetitive, P.'s prose is nevertheless important for its brave portrayals of impoverished Southern blacks. Many of her stories depict with genuine skill grotesque occurrences and colorful characters. Her rendering of the gullah dialect is graceful and highly readable; some of her descriptive passages are memorable for their lyrical beauty.

Most worthy of serious examination are her finest novel, *Scarlet Sister Mary,* which details the life of Mary Pinesett, a fallen woman and the mother of nine children, who struggles at the same time with her spiritual obligations; *Roll, Jordan, Roll,* a non fiction study of the Gullah culture; and *The Collected Stories* (1970), edited by Frank Durham, an anthology of some of her best short essays and stories.

BIBLIOGRAPHY: Henry, L. L., *J. P.: A Biographical and Critical Study* (1965); Landess, T. H., *J. P.* (1976); Maddox, M. P., *The Life and Work of J. P.* (1956)

HARRY MCBRAYER BAYNE

PETRY, Ann

b. 12 October 1908, Old Saybrook, Connecticut; d. 28 April 1997, Old Saybrook, Connecticut

Having enjoyed some public recognition in the 1940s and 1950s, P.'s work remains underappreciated today.

Of her three novels, only *The Street* (1946) is still discussed and read, whereas *Country Place* (1949) and her masterpiece, *The Narrows* (1953), have almost been forgotten. Nonetheless, the strength of her writing, its probing insight and stylistic force, will assure her a prominent place among African American writers in particular and American writers in general.

P. was the only African American in her class in Old Saybrook, an experience that has informed much of her fiction. However, she also lived in Harlem for a number of years, and it is Harlem that provides the background for *The Street*. A work in the naturalist tradition, the novel has often been compared to Richard WRIGHT's work, only that it chronicles the fight of a woman—a perspective missing in Wright's novels—against poverty and racism. Lutie Johnson doggedly tries to improve her economic lot, yet, in large part because men attempt to entrap her in their desires, she spirals down to murder and flight from Harlem, leaving her child behind. Praised for its metaphorical language and its absence of overt politicizing, the novel was an immediate success.

Country Place appeared only three years later but did not find a readership, no doubt in large part because it is set in a small New England town with a cast of white characters, thus not conforming to audience expectations of African American authors. Told largely from the point of view of the town's drugstore owner (a perspective P. was familiar with, having grown up in her pharmacist father's drugstore), the novel delves into the conflicts of a small town, exposing the oddities, hypocrisies, and, most of all, the materialism of its inhabitants. Johnnie Roane's return from World War II sets a plot in motion that lays bare the town's faultlines. Climaxing in a storm that coincides with a murder attempt, Johnnie's discovery of his wife's infidelity, and the revelation of her mother's relationship with the same man, the novel's most hopeful moment is the budding relationship between an African American housekeeper and a Portuguese gardener, both looked down upon by the town's less affluent whites. Johnnie's eventual disgusted departure from the town does not leave much hope for change.

P.'s epic novel *The Narrows,* also set in a New England town, explores the relationship between Link Williams, a highly intelligent and articulate but life-weary African American, and Camilla Treadway Sheffield, Anglo-American heiress to ammunition company wealth, and married. Race, class, and marital status intervene in this relationship and ultimately doom it, as both characters become enmeshed in the suspicions of the outside world, the differing frames of reference that their lives provide, and distrust of each other, which ultimately leads both to re-enact stereotypical expectations of their roles: he reverts to macho behavior to protect himself, and she accuses him of rape out of anger at his rejection, thus causing his death. P. shows how all of the participants in this drama, which also consists of a richly textured background providing insights into both African American and white communities, enact their roles based in part on the history that has shaped them. Link Williams, bartender with a never completed academic career, ponders on life as thwarted by narrowing prejudice in the cadences of high theater, and the tension between his elaborate prose and the bar district that provides a background for it as well as the tragic dimensions of all the characters' lives cause the novel's resemblance to Greek tragedy.

BIBLIOGRAPHY: Bell, B. W., "A. P.'s Demythologizing of American Culture and Afro-American Character," in Pryse, M., and H. J. Spillers, eds., *Conjuring* (1985): 105–15; Clark, K., "A Distaff Dream Deferred? A. P. and the Art of Subversion," *AAR* 26 (Fall 1992): 495–505; Ervin, H. A., *A. P.* (1993)

MARTIN JAPTOK

PHELPS, Elizabeth [Wooster] Stuart

b. 13 August 1815, Andover, Massachusetts; d. 29 November 1852, Andover, Massachusetts

A popular author of domestic novels, P.'s importance today lies principally in her influence on her daughter, Elizabeth Stuart Phelps WARD, also a writer, and her short story, "The Angel over the Right Shoulder" (1852), which has been anthologized and analyzed for its feminist themes. P. published under the pseudonym "H. Trusta," an anagram of Stuart, and anonymously.

The daughter and wife of a minister, P.'s central works deal with the hardships endured by clergymen's wives. Her first novel, *The Sunny Side* (1851), which sold several hundred thousand copies, depicted a wife whose life was wholly absorbed in her husband's career to the point where she has no creative space of her own. P. advocates a modest course of self-cultivation for women in such straits. Her second novel, *A Peep at "Number Five"; or, A Chapter in the Life of a City Pastor* (1852), continued this theme. P.'s close attention to the details of domestic ritual anticipates the emergence of REALISM in 19th-c. women's literature.

She also wrote *The Last Leaf from Sunny Side,* which was published posthumously in 1853; several didactic works for children, known as the "Kitty Brown" series, published between 1851 and 1853; *The Tell-Tale; or, Home Secrets Told by Old Travellers*

(1853); and *Little Mary; or, Talks and Tales for Children* (1854).

BIBLIOGRAPHY: Kessler, C. F., *E. S. P.* (1982); Kessler, C. F., "A Literary Legacy: E. S. P., Mother and Daughter," *Frontiers* 5 (Fall 1980): 28–33

JOSEPHINE DONOVAN

PHILLIPS, David Graham

b. 31 October 1867, Madison, Indiana; d. 24 January 1911, New York City

Having disposed of Henry JAMES, Edith WHARTON, and William Dean HOWELLS, H. L. MENCKEN would boldly nominate P. as the "leading American novelist" of pre–World War America. Yet P.'s reputation today rests not with his twenty-three novels, one play, or handful of short stories, but with the *Treason of the Senate,* nine extraordinary acts of investigative journalism, serialized in *Cosmopolitan* in 1906, that uncovered alliances between individual senators and "the Interests." The public controversy that ensued would lead President Theodore ROOSEVELT to call for an end to muckraking.

P., whose career took him through that curious borderland between mass journalism, fiction, and muckraking movements that existed at the turn of the century, began his career as a reporter in Cincinnati in 1897 after graduating from Princeton. He soon moved to New York, where he worked as a reporter and editorial writer for the famous reformist newspapers the New York *Sun* and the *World*. When he resigned from the *World* in 1902 to pursue his literary ambitions, he was filled with opinions about the social and political issues that marked the turbulent 1900s, including the consolidation of capital, the plight of the urban poor, political corruption, and the New Woman.

P.'s early work entitled *The Cost* (1904) reflects the social and political issues that would exercise him throughout his career. The novel traces the diverging fortunes of two men, the incorruptible politician Hampden Scarborough, patterned after Senator Albert J. Beveridge, P.'s Princeton roommate, and the unscrupulous John Dumont, a Wall Street titan. Scarborough's honesty is eventually rewarded when he is elected governor and wins back his college sweetheart after her unhappy marriage to Dumont. Dumont's symbolic fate, like that of Frank NORRIS's corrupt capitalist Behrman, who dies buried under tons of wheat, is strangulation by stock market ticker-tape. Scarborough and Dumont's parallel stories serve to dramatize the corruption of the political establishment and commerce, and, in the social world, the hypocrisy and pretensions of the plutocracy.

Despite his ability to see further and more deeply than many into the sources of political corruption, business consolidation, and class warfare, P.'s fiction is not undergirded by either a consistent socioeconomic theory or a coherent program for reform. He flirted with socialism, most notably in *The Plum Tree* (1905), *The Second Generation* (1907), and *The Conflict* (1911), but he remained skeptical about the possibility of collective action. In *The Plum Tree,* P. continues the story of Hampden Scarborough. Scarborough, incorruptible representative of the people, is on the path to the presidency, but along the way, P. guides the reader through the sinister machinations of party bosses and ward politics. But the central focus of the novel is the career of Harry Sayler, the novel's narrator. Sayler occupies a middle ground between the spotless Scarborough and vicious party bosses. One senses that there is much of P. in Sayler's cynical appraisal of the role the common people are willing and able to play in ousting their oppressors.

P.'s skepticism about reform as initiated by either the masses or the plutocrats lead him to place his progressivist faith in the dominating individual, specifically the hard-working businessman and captain of industry. Typical of P.'s heroes is narrator-protagonist Matt Blacklock in *The Deluge* (1905). As the novel opens, Blacklock has risen from the streets of New York to become one of the most successful Wall Street traders. Unlike the virtuous Scarborough, Blacklock freely admits to the reader that he "has used the methods of the charlatan" to achieve and hold onto his position. But when he tries to penetrate to the inner circle of wealth and respectability as represented by the "Seven," an immensely powerful group of corrupt financiers, they try to destroy the erstwhile bootblack. He in turn unmasks them in a series of press releases, and in the ensuing financial panic the Stock Market crashes. Blacklock's disdain for the corrupt captains of industry is matched only by his distrust of intellectuals and the Common Man. P. suggests through Blacklock that corruption on this scale can only be successfully combatted by the rugged, tough-minded, hard-working individual who remains moral, but whose "morals are practical, not theoretical."

In the second half of his career, P. focused on the issues surrounding the New Woman. Similar to Charlotte Perkins GILMAN, Olive Schreiner, and other feminist reformers, P.'s anatomy of the condition of women focused on their need for meaningful work, but he would approach this issue from a number of different and potentially contradictory perspectives. Both *The Hungry Heart* (1909) and *The Price She Paid* (1912) take up the plight of the dependent, ornamental wife. In *The Hungry Heart,* newly married Courtney Benedict suffers under her husband's neglect, and it is only when he learns of her affair with his research assistant that he regrets his treatment of her and begs her forgiveness. In *Old Wives for New* (1908) and *The Husband's Story* (1910), P. focuses on upper-middle-class marriages, where the hard-working husband is conquering downtown while the wife is stranded in the increasingly leisured sphere of fashionable uptown. In these novels, however, P. gauges the harm done men by the parasitic, social climbing woman. In *The Husband's Story,* P. chronicles the predicament of Godfrey Loring, who marries Edna Wheatlands while they are still poor. As they grow richer and gain entrance to fashionable circles, Loring grows disillusioned with his wife's snobbery and social climbing. Phillips' ideal of American womanhood is suggested in Mary Kirkwood, whom Loring meets halfway through the novel and eventually marries. His first glimpse of Mary is telling: she is wearing men's clothes and using an axe to help a gang of men clear ground. Like Emily Bromfield, the successful journalist in *A Woman Ventures* (1902), this attractive, usefully employed, independent divorcee is the fitting mate for P.'s hard-working male.

His interest in the condition of women culminated in *Susan Lenox,* published posthumously in 1917. Susan's suffering serves to dramatize both New York's corruption and the reality of life in New York for poor women. She begins her life in a small Indiana town and then escapes from a nightmarish marriage to a local farmer. Within a few years, she is reduced from a ballad singer on a showboat to a prostitute in New York, addicted to both alcohol and opium. Ultimately, her relationship with a playwright leads her to the stage, where she becomes a successful actress. P.'s unflinching descriptions of street life lead many reviewers to reject the novel as obscene, but characteristically, social realism coexists uneasily in the novel with treacly sentimentalism. P. clearly intended *Susan Lenox,* begun in 1904, as his magnum opus, and while he had often succeeded in writing one, even two novels a year, he had just finished revising the novel seven years later when he was assassinated outside his Gramercy Park residence in 1911.

BIBLIOGRAPHY: Filler, L., *Voice of Democracy: A Critical Biography of D. G. P.* (1978): Lynn, K., *The Dream of Success* (1955); Marcossen, I., *D. G. P.* (1932); Ravitz, A., *D. G. P.* (1966)

MARY V. MARCHAND

PHILLIPS, Jayne Anne
b. 19 July 1952, Buckhannon, West Virginia

Recognized primarily as a fiction writer, P. began her literary career in college by publishing individual poems in literary magazines. She shifted from poetry to fiction after she graduated from West Virginia University and began studying in the well-known creative writing program at the University of Iowa, publishing two limited editions of short stories, *Sweethearts* (1976) and *Counting* (1978) by the time that she completed her M.F.A. degree.

While P. frequently sets her literary works in her native West Virginia and grounds them in regional American families, she does not consider herself a regional writer. Her subjects are universal ones that transcend specific locales: family relationships, love, war, good and evil, death, sexuality, alienation, and despair, for example. Her use of the grotesque has led critics to compare her work to that of Flannery O'CONNOR, William FAULKNER, and Eudora WELTY, among others. P. has received a Pushcart Prize, a Radcliffe College Bunting Institute Fellowship, and the Sue Kaufman Award for First Fiction, and her work has been translated into fourteen languages.

It is P.'s third anthology of short fiction, *Black Tickets* (1979), endorsed and published by Seymour Lawrence, that first brought her work critical acclaim. A collection of twenty-seven short stories, some so brief as to fall into the contemporary genre of "flash fiction," *Black Tickets* introduces the themes of family relationships and generational conflicts that permeate P.'s later stories, such as those in *Fast Lanes* (1984), and especially her novels.

P.'s cast of characters, many of whom sordidly illustrate her interest in an American dream gone awry, include figures from the margins of society: in "Gemcrack," a mass murderer; in "Lechery," a prostitute; in "Mamasita," a drunkard; in "The Powder of the Angels, I'm Yours," a drug addict; in "Black Tickets," a rapist; in "Stripper," stripteasers; in "Bess," a voyeur; in "How Mickey Made It," juvenile delinquents; in "Under the Boardwalk," incestuous relatives; in "1934" and "Rayme," the mentally ill; and in general, the lost and the lovelorn. Like those characters created by Edgar Lee MASTERS, who influenced P.'s writing, her protagonists suffer alienation, loss, and despair in a society that relegates them to a life of liminality and insecurity.

John IRVING, one of P.'s earliest reviewers, expressed his hope that P. would change genres, moving from the short story to the novel, an expansion that would offer her an even greater chance to demonstrate her fictional expertise. She has done so and has proven to handle this shift quite well. Her first novel, *Machine Dreams* (1984), a study of the impact of history—World War I, Vietnam, and the sixties generation—on the Hampson family (who were introduced briefly in *Fast Lanes*), has been especially well received. What distinguishes P.'s writing is her gifted ability to shift point of view to create a series of

monologues by narrating chapters from different characters' angles of vision. This technique is a strong point of both *Machine Dreams* and P.'s second novel, *Shelter* (1994), where characters either narrate their own reminiscences in the form of monologues or all-knowing narrators give readers information on specific characters in chapters entitled by the characters' names but told from an omniscient third person point of view.

The titles of P.'s novels indicate their thematic concerns. *Machine Dreams* deals with both machines and dreams and the interaction of the two. Machines are particularly important to Mitch Hampson and his son Billy, who dream frequently of trains, construction equipment, planes, and automobiles. Some of their dreams are nightmares, such as those that Mitch dreams upon his return from World War II. In his postwar dreams, Mitch is haunted by the memories of the putrid enemy corpses that he bulldozed into makeshift mass graves and of the possible death of Katie, a frail, loved one, whereas Mitch's wife Jean dreams that while she visits a cemetery dead bodies are being unearthed, not buried. Ironically, Mitch, who thought he would die in a machinery accident in World War II, survives his war, while Billy, who has more faith in machines than his father, becomes missing in action in the Vietnam War when his helicopter crashes. Billy's sister, Danner, dreams of her inability to control the bad events of life, such as the helicopter crash that leaves Billy's family in a perpetual state of limbo. However, Danner and her mother Jean make dreams a regular part of their thought processes and reminiscences, keeping Billy present in memory, if not in reality.

Dreams are also important in P.'s second novel *Shelter,* where again the title reveals major thematic concerns. The book is set in Camp Shelter in Shelter, West Virginia, a world of dreams and secrets, where the characters in the camp seek safe havens to protect them from their pasts as they undergo unsettling initiations from innocence to experience. For Cap, the camp is a sanctuary away from the arguments of her divorcing parents. For Delia, it is an escape from the reality that her father committed suicide. For Parson, an escapee from prison, the woods surrounding the camp are a shelter protecting his real identity. For Mrs. Thompson-Warner, the camp is an escape from widowhood and rumors that her husband killed himself. For Buddy Carmody, camp and his mother are a safe haven away from the physical, emotional, and sexual abuse he is subjected to by his father, a murderer on parole from prison.

As P. points out in many of her works, shelter is never a permanent condition. Changes wrought by time, family divisions, and the Vietnam War intrude upon the Hampson family in *Machine Dreams,* shattering the bond between Danner and her brother and leaving the family in limbo in regard to Billy's fate. In *Shelter,* while at Girl Guides camp, which should offer a secure environment, the girls receive instruction on the gloom and doom of the Cuban missile crisis and the impending threat of communism, and Turtle Creek turns out to be a place where adolescent sexual urges are acknowledged and confronted. "Camp was like being asleep, like a long, long dream," P. writes, but this dream culminates in a nightmare, the death of Carmody, Buddy's father, a death in which Buddy, Parson, and several of the girl campers participate. In order to have shelter, the characters have to do something terrible and live forever with that secret, yet their actions free Buddy Carmody to grow up without the constant threat of an abusive father, providing some thread of hope that the journey from innocence to experience may offer some sunlight beneath the horror.

BIBLIOGRAPHY: Edelstein, D., "The Short Story of J. A. P.: She Transforms Isolation and Dark Obsession Into Exquisite Prose," *Esquire* 104 (December 1985): 106–12; Lassner, P., "Women's Narrative and the Recreation of History," in Pearlman, M., ed., *American Women Writing Fiction* (1989): 193–210; Stanton, D. M., "An Interview with J. A. P., *Croton Review* 9 (Spring-Summer 1986): 41–44

CATHERINE CALLOWAY

PIERCY, Marge
b. 31 March 1936, Detroit, Michigan

P.'s versatility and productivity as a writer place her in a select company among contemporary writers; she is both an accomplished poet and novelist who has published over twenty-five books for which she has received numerous literary awards. In addition, P. has written several essays on writing and on women's issues, among other topics, and has given many readings across the country, including a performance on Garrison KEILLOR's *A Prairie Home Companion.* Although her poems have long been anthologized in collections of contemporary poetry and many of her novels have sold well enough to have stayed in print, only recently has P.'s writing received the serious critical attention it deserves. Her poetry and her fiction reflect her abiding interest in social issues, from politics to religion to feminism to ecology, but her poems seem to be more personal than her novels which may strive to efface her own first-person voice as much as her poems strive to enact it. In her introduction to *Circles on the Water: Selected Poems* (1982), P. writes that her autobiographical impulse manifests itself more in her poetry, where the voice is usually hers.

Circles on the Water includes poems from seven previous volumes, plus seven new poems, and represents well the ingenuity and incongruity of P.'s original poetic vision and voice: immediate and allusive, singular and eclectic, tangible and abstract, quotidian and mythic, contemporary and universal. For example, she writes of cockroaches and language in "Kneeling at the Pipes"; of crab lice and coitus in "Crabs"; of bonsai trees and women in "A Work of Artifice"; of housewives and bees in "The Daily Life of the Worker Bee"; of burning dinners and gender wars in "What's That Smell in the Kitchen?" P. also writes poem sequences that cohere thematically, such as "The Chuppah" poems from *My Mother's Body* (1985), which celebrate her marriage to Ira Wood, who contributes two poems of his own to the sequence, or the "Slides from Our Recent European Trip" poems from *Available Light* (1988), which explore English and French World War II sites P. visited while doing research for her novel *Gone to Soldiers* (1987).

Woman on the Edge of Time (1976) and *He, She, & It* (1991) represent P.'s dystopian experimentation with the science fiction and fantasy genre. *Woman on the Edge of Time* explores the mind of Connie Ramos, who, wrongly institutionalized for insanity, can communicate with the future world of 2137, where two opposing ways of life are competing for dominance, one open and nurturing and the other closed and totalitarian. In *He, She, & It,* P. creates an intriguing future world of artificial intelligences, Jewish myth, and gender revision that calls into question our assumptions about the separation of magic and science or of humanity and technology. *Fly Away Home* (1984) and *The Longings of Women* (1994) represent P.'s interest in the articulating the complexities of the passages women go through in contemporary culture. *Fly Away Home* tells the story of Dalia Walker, a suburban housewife whose divorce forces her into forging an independent self and life of her own. *The Longings of Women* focuses on three women—writer Leila Landsman, accused murderer Becky Burgess, and domestic Mary Burke—all of whom must deal with the loss of the lives they had expected to live.

BIBLIOGRAPHY: Shands, K., *The Repair of the World: The Novels of M. P.* (1994); Thielmann, P., *M. P.'s Women: Visions Captured and Subdued* (1986); Walker, S., and E. Hamner, eds., *Ways of Knowing: Essays on M. P.* (1991)

PHILLIP A. SNYDER

PIKE, Albert
b. 29 December 1809, Boston, Massachusetts; d. 2 April 1891, Washington, D.C.

P., poet, editor, lawyer, and Confederate general, was born in Boston, Massachusetts. Although a descendant of John Pike who came to Massachusetts in 1635 and remotely related to explorer Zebulon Pike, P. had an improvident father. The hardship of his early days culminated when young P. was admitted to Harvard with junior standing but was unable to pay tuition for the two years he had successfully passed by examination. Pike may have attended one session before leaving. However, he received an honorary degree from Harvard in 1859.

After teaching school from 1824 to 1831, P. headed west, and by late 1832 was at Fort Smith, Arkansas. Although he resumed his teaching career, his writing talent came to attention of Whig leader Robert Crittenden who hired P. to edit the Little Rock *Arkansas Advocate* in 1833. Two years later, P. bought the paper, and in 1836, was admitted to the bar. P. edited the first *Arkansas Reports* for the state Supreme Court, supplied notes for the first state digest, and published a form book. At the onset of the Mexican War, he raised a company which saw action at Buena Vista. On returning to Arkansas, he fought a duel with future governor John S. Roane over allegations concerning the conduct of Roane and the Arkansas regiment. Resuming the practice of law, P. became perhaps the richest lawyer in Arkansas, specializing in Indian claims and the liquidation of the state bank. He erected a still-standing Greek Revival mansion in Little Rock and became active in Masonic affairs. One of the organizers of the American (Know-Nothing) Party, P. refused to support Millard Filmore in the 1856 presidential campaign, claiming that the platform was not sufficiently pro-slavery.

While pursuing successfully a political and legal career, P. was also famous as a poet and essayist. His "Hymns to Gods" appeared in *Blackwood's Magazine* in 1839 attracting a favorable notice from Christopher North (Dr. John Wilson) at a time when American writers were customarily ignored. His topical writings, mostly Western travel stories, appeared in Eastern magazines during the antebellum years, and "Anecdotes of the Arkansas Bar," was included by William Trotter Porter in a collection of works by Southwest humorists entitled *The Big Bear of Arkansas* (1843). Although his early poetry was Byronic in style, his subsequent pieces, such as the much-reprinted "Every Year," were maudlin and sentimental. Two thirds of his published poetry was written before he was thirty-five years old. P. was locally famous as a bon vivant, and his poem "Fine Arkansas Gentleman" was a staple of Arkansas parties for many years.

During the 1850s, P. increasingly became identified with the Southern aristocracy, and, repudiating his earlier Unionism, he embraced secession in late 1860. One of his contributions to the war effort was to pen suitable patriotic sentiments replacing the Minstrel verses for the song "Dixie." These were much printed in the South even after the Civil War. In 1861, P. undertook to help negotiate treaties for the Confederacy with the Five Civilized Tribes, and was commissioned a brigadier general. At the Battle of Pea Ridge (March 7–8, 1862), his failure to assume command after the deaths of generals McCulloch and McIntosh contributed to the Confederate defeat. Unjustly blamed for some battlefield atrocities committed by his Indians, he was denounced as a war criminal in the North. Quarrels with his superiors led to his arrest for insubordination. He then wrote an eloquent defense of civil liberties, served on the Arkansas Supreme Court, and began work on *Morals and Dogma of the Ancient and Accepted Scottish Rite of Freemasonry* (1870).

Fearing arrest after the war, P. fled to Canada, but returned after receiving a presidential pardon. Separated from his wife, he edited the Memphis *Appeal* and opposed Republican Reconstruction. In 1868, he moved to Washington, D.C., where he practiced law for the next ten years. His last years were spent working on his revisions of his Masonic writings, although he did write historical sketches for John Hallum's *Biographical and Pictorial History of Arkansas* (1887). A famous gourmand weighing over three hundred pounds, P. died from a stricture of the esophagus that caused him to starve to death.

Although a better than average poet and writer, P. possessed an enigmatic personality. Contemporaries noted his unexpected switching of sides and his inability to accept less than perfection. A pronounced morbid theme was evident in his work. His great Masonic writings, involving research in Sanskrit and other eastern languages, resulted in one of the most important pieces of scholarship produced in 19th-c. America, albeit of a variety obscure then and remote to subsequent ages.

BIBLIOGRAPHY: Allsopp, F. W., *The Life Story of A. P.* (1920); Boyden, W. L., *Bibliography of the Writings of A. P.* (1921); Duncan, R. L., *Reluctant General: The Life and Times of A. P.* (1961); James, A. E., "The 'Plagiarism' of A. P.," *AHQ* 13 (Autumn 1954): 270–77; Riley, S., "An Early Appearance of the Classic-Romantic Ode: A. P.'s 'Hymns to the Gods,'" *ArkHQ* 22 (Winter 1963): 351–64

MICHAEL B. DOUGAN

PIÑERO, Miguel

b. 19 December 1946, Gurabo, Puerto Rico; d. 16 or 17 June 1988, New York City

P.'s *Short Eyes* (1975), which won the New York Drama Critics Circle Award for best American play as well as two Obie Awards in 1974, served as an inspiration and a model for a rapidly increasing number of Puerto Rican and other Hispanic playwrights in the U.S. Though he remained an effective writer and actor, his later work did not achieve the impact of his first, great success.

P. came to New York in 1950. He is self-educated, though he did spend time in city public schools and also in state reform schools. He was incarcerated at Riker's Island Prison in 1964 for burglary and drug possession, and at Ossining Correctional Facility—Sing Sing—in 1971 to 1973 for burglary. While at Sing Sing, he joined a theater workshop and developed his interest in poetry and drama. Upon his release from prison, with a draft of *Short Eyes* already in hand, P. joined a theater group called "The Family," comprised of former inmates and their director. Independently produced at the Theater of the Riverside Church and performed by the Family, the play was noted by Joseph Papp who brought it to his Public Theater and to the attention of national and international audiences. With this success, *Short Eyes* became an emblem of the burgeoning "Nuyorican" arts scene, of which P. was a part. In subsequent years, P. wrote poetry, short plays, television plays, and the well-received screenplay for *Short Eyes* (1977). He coedited *Nuyorican Poetry* (1975), an anthology of poetry and photographs that reflect the experiences of poor Puerto Ricans in New York City. He has acted frequently in theater, film, and television.

Short Eyes is a flawless, naturalistic play. It successfully combines dramatic crafting, strong prison argot, believable and sympathetic characters, a realistic presentation style, and a significant theme. In *Short Eyes*, P. creates a microcosm of society inside the dayroom of an unnamed house of detention. The inmates have created a code that enables them to live under the watchful eyes of their guards and supervisors. Though the action and dialogue seem quite spontaneous, the finely delineated characters embody social roles and dramatic functions. Julio "Cupcakes" Mercado— Puerto Rican—is a beautiful, thoughtful youth who represents a chance for some sort of sane and integrated society, "El Raheem"—African American—represents those who would strive for success and understanding, Murphy—Irishman—has learned to be tough and to be smart in order to survive in a hostile environment, and so forth. The "Short Eyes" of the title refers to one who has been incarcerated for child molestation—a crime that every other inmate and prison official finds detestable, a symbol of a society that has become twisted against itself. The arrival of "Short Eyes" in the dayroom precipitates an inexorable process that leads to his slaughter at the hands of the inmates, abetted by their guards. Before he is dead, however, the others have debated their motives and jockeyed among themselves for both

moral and physical superiority. The strong ethnic and prison overtones of this compelling drama mask questions that reverberate in society at large. It makes us ask how each of us can respond to social stratification and individual alienation in the face of monolithic social and cultural imperatives.

Comparable techniques and purposes can be found in P.'s other plays. The plays move from prison to the cities, but the characters have all been to prison or are engaged in the kinds of activities that would send them there if they got caught. For example, *The Sun Always Shines for the Cool* (perf. 1975, pub. 1984) is an explosive drama set in a bar populated by prostitutes and their handlers. Newly released from prison, the streetwise Viejo returns to the bar and finds that his daughter is beguiled by Cat Eyes, a brash newcomer with dreams of using her to get rich fast. Viejo sacrifices his own life to keep his daughter "out of the game."

BIBLIOGRAPHY: Kanellos, N., and J. Huerta, *Nuevos Pasos: Chicano and Puerto Rican Drama* (1989)

MAARTEN REILINGH

PINSKY, Robert
b. 20 October 1940, Long Branch, New Jersey

As critic, translator, teacher, and artist, P. has sought to transcend the academic categorization of poetry. In his 1968 study, *Landor's Poetry,* he traces the similarities between classical and romantic poetry, and in *Poetry and the World* (1988) advocates a definition of poetic form, "as an appetite for being autonomous and oneself." Although his own poetic voice is characterized as antimodern for its clear, discursive mode and transcendental cadences, his work incorporates a remarkable range of 20th-c. styles, including the allusive methods of T. S. ELIOT, the condensed phrasing of the imagists (an influence he blames for stifling the progression of contemporary American poetry), the egalitarian sweep of the Beat writers, and the autobiographical approaches of the confessional poets of the 1960s.

Compassion and intelligence are the generative forces behind most of P.'s work. The poems ponder the tensions and meanings of modern American life through acute observations, novelistic dialogue, and telling details. Consequently, the notion of "place" figures prominently in many poems, often taking the form of suburban landscapes and the New Jersey shore of his childhood. In the title poem of *History of My Heart* (1984), the speaker evokes picturesque episodes of desire and bliss from his youth and in so doing crystallizes these disparate images into an understanding that the heart itself is a metaphor for memory and perception, and that "happiness / Needs a place." But "place," for P., is a central enigma. Elsewhere, he writes that, "Place itself is always in motion," a theme central to several of his dense, more compressed pieces such as "The Figured Wheel," "Pilgrimage,"and "City Elegies."

Despite the inscrutability of place (or perhaps intrigued by it), P. titled one of his best-known poems *An Explanation of America* (1979), a colloquial yet subdued forty-page poem structured in the form of a Horatian epistle. In it, the speaker assures his young daughter that he will fulfill the obligation implicit in the poem's title, "Because all things have their explanations / True or false." The speaker precedes to "see" America through the sensibilities of its pure products and people—Brownie scouts and Malcolm X, porno films and Ann Landers, an ax murderer in Oregon and strip malls. But the poem seeks its "explanation" in other places and ideas as well, including an immigrant's horrifying suicide in a prairie thresher and the philosophies and histories of the Roman Stoics, coming to rest, finally, on the occasion of his daughter's performance in *A Winter's Tale,* as the speaker settles on a new reality purely constituted of possibility ("Hope") and time ("Fear").

In another long narrative poem, "Essay on Psychiatrists," from *Sadness and Happiness* (1975), the poet compares the imperatives of the psychiatrist with numerous other vocations, including those of painters, musicians, and airplane pilots, interweaving a reading of Euripides's *Bacchae* as the poem examines the nature of wisdom, concluding, among other things that, "psychiatrist is a synonym for human being."

The subject of Jewish identity and the challenges of religious belief are also prominent in P.'s work, as in "From the Childhood of Jesus" and "Jesus and Isolt." In "The Unseen," a sense of deeply personal moral outrage merge with a cinematic unreality as the speaker recalls a visit to a Nazi death camp, while in "Poem about People" P. turns a melodramatic image from a World War II film into an exploration of the tensions between individuality and ethnicity. His numerous prose works include the essays "Some Passages From Isiah" and "Solidarity Days," which deal with issues of national identity and political activism, were inspired by his visit to Eastern Europe in the tumultuous period of the late 1980s.

His overriding concern with the moral impulse in poetry is further reflected in his acclaimed translations of Europe's most formidable philosophical poets, past and present, including *The Separate Notebooks* by Czelsaw Milosz (1983) and *The Inferno of Dante* (1994).

BIBLIOGRAPHY: Longenbach, J., "R. P. And the Language of Our Time," *Salmagundi* 103 (Summer 1994): 157–77; Sorkin, A. J., "An Interview with R. P.," *ConL* 25 (Spring 1984): 1–14

TIM KEANE

PLATH, Sylvia [Victoria Lucas]

b. 27 October 1932, Boston, Massachusetts; d. 11 February 1963, London, England

Few American poets have provoked the literary and biographical debate that P. has since her suicide, a death that validated her work as a poet yet generated commentary about her personal torment and the brilliant final poems. The extraordinary poetry written at the time of her sudden death elicited bold comments that remain part of her critical legacy, such as the one made by A. Alvarez that "poetry of this order is a murderous art." *Ariel* (1965), the posthumous collection containing the acclaimed, startling poems of the last months, eclipsed the work she lived to see published in England—*The Colossus* (1960) and *The Bell Jar* (1963)—and established her literary career.

P.'s poetry with its stark metaphors and vivid, often violent, imagery has been characterized in various ways: as confessional in its fusing of the private and culturally symbolic, thus linking her with Robert LOWELL, Anne SEXTON, and John BERRYMAN; and as extremist in its exploration of the poet's emotions and experiences, regardless of risk, for the intensity of the art. Most of what she wrote is marked by her own kind of romantic extremism, where imagination is crucial to meaningful existence, and kinship between poetry and death prevails. Her poems consider personal and feminine identity, the lack of balance in familial and career desires, oppression and anger, and death's inevitability; this subject matter confirmed her as a voice for feminist concerns as well. While her poetry may be described in these ways, the distinguishing mark of P.'s poetry is its intensely personal appeal to be understood. She asks the reader to care about her willingness to face searing inward experiences, and she renders the experiences in highly imaginative language, using word sounds, metaphor, and syntactical rhythms.

P.'s early poems and stories demonstrate a precocious ability and earned her awards at Smith College, but she suffered a nervous breakdown and attempted suicide during her junior year. After graduating, she attended Cambridge University on a Fullbright Fellowship where she met and married English poet, Ted Hughes, in 1956. Though her interest was primarily in writing poetry, it was during a stay in Boston after her marriage that she wrote the stories that comprise the posthumous short story collection *Johnny Panic and the Bible of Dreams* (1980). There she also attended Lowell's poetry workshop with Sexton and acknowledged later their important influence on her poetry.

P.'s journals reveal that after her father's death when she was eight, her early childhood near the sea was sealed off like a ship in a bottle, beautiful and inaccessible. This traumatic experience, as it is disclosed in her poetry, caused a fundamental division in her self while giving birth to elegies about "the buried male muse," her father, and the sea imagery in the first collection, *The Colossus*. P.'s images of the dead and the sea appear in their lyric strangeness in such poems as "All The Dead Dears," "Lorelei," "Man in Black," and "Full Fathom Five," this last poem prefiguring her final wrathful elegy, "Daddy." The sea, both threatening and seductive, unites with her dead father and represents oblivion or death, something the poet wants and fears. In the title poem, "The Colossus," the dead father is seen as a great broken statue that she labors to put together but cannot. Unable to escape the myth or his shadow, her life is a living death, a theme that repeats itself in her poetry. Influenced by the mythic qualities of W. B. Yeats and the language exploration of Dylan Thomas and Theodore ROETHKE, these subdued poems use more forms, such as odes and villanelles. P.'s unusual skill with imagery and metaphor, as well as her technically controlled stanza-forms, sound repetitions, and rhymes in *The Colossus,* prepared the way for the wonder of *Ariel*.

Living in England, P. wrote *The Bell Jar,* a novel chronicling the circumstances of her mental collapse and subsequent suicide attempt. A bildungsroman, the novel presents Esther Greenwood's search for identity, her disillusionment and rebellion against traditional female roles, and finally her recovery. Powerful images, such as the bell jar, and the repetition of colors, chiefly black and white, lend a symbolic level to the novel published under a pseudonym and originally turned down by American editors.

After the birth of a son in 1962, P. wrote in a frenzy, producing the powerful radio drama, "Three Women," and most of the *Ariel* poems, writing one or two a day in early morning hours after her separation from Hughes. Abandoned by the romantic figure in her life, P. experienced again the feeling of loss she carried for her father. *Ariel,* published by Hughes after her suicide in 1963, presents through symbolic action the poet's battle between life and death, revealing in diction and theme the nature of the struggle. The language of life, evident in her use of color, blood, flowers, babies, and breath, competes with darkness, emptiness, purity, stasis, moon, edges, and snow that represent the pull of death. Red, the color of life's blood, provides a center of energy in poems about flowers, such as "Tulips," "Poppies in October," and "Poppies in July," but the flowers offer a dual significance since the speaker reacts, often negatively, to their vitality. In *Ariel,* the color white connotes both sterility and death while the moon becomes a symbol for death: its light shines in the dark, it uses borrowed light, and it turns things to stone. These qualities of the moon, including its kinship with snow and absence, are stressed in poems such as "Paralytic," "Medusa," "The Rival," and "The Moon and the Yew Tree." In many of the best known *Ariel* poems, P. uses disturbing imagery and repetitious rhythm and rhyme to mediate the tensions and conflicts she confronts. They are testimony to her craft and her ability to say the unsayable. In "Daddy" and "Lady Lazarus," her personae turn against the ties that strangle their identities, adopting various strategies to gain freedom: namecalling, scorn, and violently imagined destruction. While the anger in these poems sometimes overwhelms readers, recent criticism suggests that P. broke the taboo against woman's anger in the exorcising of her father in the elegy, "Daddy," and extended the genre's boundaries for women poets who follow.

In the early 1970s, Hughes published more of P.'s poems in *Crossing the Water* (1971), which contains poems written between the earlier books, and *Winter Trees* (1972), which includes "Three Women," a verse play that suggests the strongest agent for life is the love between mother and child. The poetry of these collections and *Ariel* have interconnecting themes. The poet explores womanhood and motherhood in such poems as "Childless Woman," "By Candlelight," and "Morning Song," and through various personae in the poems of these collections, she probes the nature of self-identity: its fragility, maskings, and misperceptions. Another connecting theme occurs in the bee poems, which unfold the myth she created for the life and death struggle. The five bee poems form a single narrative of the growing dissolution of the marriage and of the dramatic tension between the self and other. "The Bee Meeting" involves a female victim who is persecuted by villagers and in her suffering, the victim convinces them of her courage. The high drama, found in other poems as well, converts the villagers, just as readers of P. become convinced by the intimacy and shared pain of her poems. In these last works, nature, human experience, and the world are questioned for their meaning and symbolic possibilities, but the subject of the poems is always an individual experience. The publication of *Crossing the Water* and *Winter Trees* confirmed P.'s reputation and produced a dramatic growth in public response to her life and work.

Letters Home by S. P. (1975), the only posthumous publication not edited by Hughes, contains the correspondence between P. and her mother from 1950 to 1963. Published by Aurelia Plath, they provide valuable information about P.'s relationship to her family.

In 1976, Hughes published *The Bed Book,* P.'s only book of children's literature, and collected her journals into *The Journals of S. P.* (1982). In the foreword to P.'s journals, Hughes indicated he had destroyed the last two journals written prior to P.'s suicide. His open admission of this action generated more interest, even outrage, and contributed to continuing controversy.

P.'s poetic achievement was fully recognized by the literary community with the publication of *The Collected Poems* (1981), almost two decades after her tragic death. P.'s poetic gift rests in the control of language, a control so unique and compelling, that readers willingly excavate the hurt and irrational with her words. Seen in their totality, the poems return us again and again to the theme of death and love, to the romantic idea that love is completed and perfected by death. Her vision, embodied in a dead woman who appears to have committed suicide in "Edge," possibly the last poem P. wrote, perfects itself in this extraordinary metaphor of a woman who has become her own tombstone, and in the poem's words, "it is over." The acclaim she desired and deserved came in 1982 when *The Collected Poems* received the Pulitzer Prize.

BIBLIOGRAPHY: Alexander, P., ed., *Ariel Ascending: Writings about S. P.* (1984); Alexander, P., *Rough Magic: A Biography of S. P.* (1991); Bassett, S., *S. P.* (1987); Cox, C. B., and A. R. Jones, "After the Tranquilized Fifties," *CritQ* 6 (1994): 107–15; Hughes, T., *Birthday Letters* (1998); Juhasz, S., *Naked and Fiery Forms: Modern American Poetry by Women of a New Tradition* (1976); Kroll, J., *Chapters in a Mythology* (1976); Lane, G., ed., *S. P.* (1978); Newman, C. H., ed., *The Art of S. P.* (1970); Stevenson, A., *Bitter Fame* (1989); Wagner-Martin, L., *S. P.* (1987)

ANNETTE ALLEN

POE, Edgar Allan

b. 19 January 1809, Boston, Massachusetts; d. 7 October 1849, Baltimore, Maryland

Perhaps no other American writer has been subjected to such detrimental critical appraisal as P. His writings, say detractors, stem from drink, drugs, and debauchery, but anyone familiar with the early-19th-c. literary climate can readily understand how deeply imbued with its essences, particularly those of dark ROMANTICISM, are his works. In more recent scholarship, however, a new P. of solid artistic and, moreover, comic abilities has emerged. Wishing to be a poet, he quickly gained recognition as a critic, but his tales of horror and ratiocination contain his most memorable art.

Orphaned and taken into the home of John Allan, a Richmond, Virginia merchant, P. was reared with the cultural ethics of a Southern aristocrat. He left the University of Virginia and then West Point Military Academy without completing a course of study. Determined to be a poet, he published *Tamerlane and Other Poems* (1827), *Al Aaraaf and Minor Poems* (1829), and *Poems* (1831), which echo the British romantic poets. Nevertheless, P.'s renowned visionary art is evident. "To Helen" (1831), or "The City in the Sea" (1831), "Israfel" (1831), "Introduction" (1831), and "Sonnet—To Science" (1829) number among his finer poems. Two long pieces, "Tamerlane" (1827) and "Al Aaraaf" (1829), incorporate narrative techniques, which are muddled in the first and subsumed by lyric and philosophical intrusions in the second. The weird symbols enveloped within hypnotic lyrics to render intense moments in the human condition, which are found in these little books, recur throughout P.'s verse. Later achievements—"To One in Paradise" (1934), "The Raven" (1845), "Ulalume" (1847), "The Bells," "Annabel Lee," and "Eldorado" (1849), this last atypically cheerful—are infused with such traits.

Requiring greater financial support, P. secured employment with a new periodical, the *Southern Literary Messenger.* Thus, he was enabled to marry his thirteen-year-old cousin, Virginia E. Clemm, in 1836. Marriages between older men and younger women being reasonably common at the time, theirs should not be considered startling. P. maintained thereafter a household that included his devoted mother-in-law, Maria Clemm. Editorial stints occupied most of his career, and he was nothing if not a magazinist. In the *Messenger,* he launched himself as a critic by means of reviews that probed literature as art instead of exemplifications of an author's politics or personal morality. His chief critical dicta treat poetry and the short story, concomitants to his own successes in these genres. Poetry, he wrote, aims primarily at pleasure, is the "rhythmical creation of beauty," is by dint of its very essence (its lyric quality) brief, and may incorporate strangeness—thence his conception that the greatest poetic theme is the death of a beautiful woman. His sustained pronouncements about poetry are "Letter to B———" (1836, expanded from 1831), "Ballads and Other Poems" (1842), "The Philosophy of Composition" (1846), and, posthumously, "The Poetic Principle" (1850). Because P.'s own best poems were lyrics, his demand for brevity in a poem is natural. Not widely divergent, his praise of the short story as the greatest form of prose fiction—because it can be read during a single sitting, its impact deriving from unity of impression or effect—is concisely set forth in his reviews of Nathaniel HAWTHORNE's *Twice-Told Tales.* Intermittently a harsh critic, P. repeatedly brought upon himself wrath from America's literary establishment. The "Literati" sketches (1846) hit at well-known

American literary figures, Lewis Gaylord Clark, Charles F. Briggs, and Thomas Dunn English, among them.

Attempts to win popularity led P. into other forms of writing. First, *Politian* (wr. 1835–36), an incomplete play, aligns with melodramatic vestigial Elizabethan drama that filled theaters in his day. Two would-be novels are also bids for literary marketability. *The Narrative of Arthur Gordon Pym* (1838) originated in advice that writing novels, not short stories, of subtly comic proportions no less, might bring financial rewards. *Pym* began serially in the *Messenger* and, extended, appeared in hardcover. Grounded in narratives of South Pole exploration then much admired, this book—neither obvious nor easily defined, as regards meaning—admits many interpretations. Less troublesome, "The Journal of Julius Rodman," a serial in *Burton's Gentleman's Magazine* (January–June 1840), links with Western travel accounts, also popular at the time. P. used landscape aesthetics more seriously in sketches like "The Domain of Arnheim" (1847) and "Landor's Cottage" (1849). A final book, *Eureka* (1848), termed by P. a "prose poem," supposedly treats cosmology, but comedy makes suspect its scientific soundness. Some critics envision *Eureka* as the work toward which P.'s others lead, an opinion challenged by those who see his journalism as promoting heterogeneous writings instead of a consistent corpus.

P.'s tales spring from early imitations, particularly of *Blackwood's* and other periodicals famous for horror fiction. P. modified Gothic tradition in his tales to incorporate more sophistication than in older Gothic productions, where the chief aim was to titillate and frighten. Typically, P.'s narrators are untrustworthy, and their stories abound in clues undercutting unshakable factuality. Thus, the "supernaturalism" that captivates us may emanate from their distorted subjectivity instead of ghostliness. In "The Fall of the House of Usher," for example, Roderick and Madeline Usher are symbolic dual parts of the self—the "soul" mentioned by P., and a favorite subject with him—who suggest the narrator's own potential downfall (that is, the disintegration of his identity) unless he resists forces destructive to the delicate constitution encompassing physical and psychological makeup. Eeriness arises from his fears mated with easy credence toward supernaturalism. "The Masque of the Red Death" likewise unfolds a literal and figurative dream, or nightmare. P. repeatedly uses pits, whirlpools, spiral stairways, or their equivalents (e.g., the dizzying descent in "The Cask of Amontillado," which compounds the bewilderment of Fortunato by Montresor) for symbolizing journeys into violence, hallucination, and madness. Mirror motifs, too, add treasures to P.'s art, as we see in "Silence—A Fable" (1839) and "William

Wilson." Rhythmic pleasures in the prose of the first, like those in the poems, hypnotically enchant us. Implicitly, we may by dint of such appeals be lured into a depersonalizing world. P.'s love of literary hoaxing complicates attempts to oversimplify his accomplishments, however, and humor blended with horror serves mixed purposes in "The Assignation" (1834), or "Silence—A Fable," among others, may appeal simultaneously on comic and serious levels.

These and other early tales featuring discourse prompted by drunkenness or gluttony (or P.'s insinuations at such states) from verbally halting, odd narrators and other characters amidst weird, hallucinatory, perhaps supernatural, situation, lead toward P.'s reworking such materials to create "terror of the soul," which, he maintained, in the preface to *Tales of the Grotesque and Arabesque* (1840), was the aim and the substance in his stories. He eschewed, he said, current modes of "Germanism" (or "Gothicism"). Subtly modified Gothicism may be found in "The Assignation," "Ligeia" (1838), "William Wilson" and "The Fall of the House of Usher" (1839), "Elenora" and "The Masque of the Red Death" (1842), "The Pit and the Pendulum," "The Tell-Tale Heart," and "The Black Cat" (1843), "The System of Dr. Tarr and Professor Fether" (1845), "The Cask of Amontillado" (1846), or "Hop-Frog" (1849). Here and elsewhere, we find that surfaces of seemingly inexplicable horrors and characters ultimately betray psychological and, often, ironic and comic, foundations. "MS. Found in a Bottle," *Pym,* and "A Descent into the Maelstrom" (1841), moreover, take Gothicism from haunted castles, abbeys, and caverns onto the seas.

P.'s detective or ratiocinative tales are another important contribution to literature. In part a hoax, "The Murders in the Rue Morgue" (1841) opens in good Gothic fashion, but we are soon exhorted that this is no "mystery" or "romance." Names of the suspect Le Bon ("the good"), arrested by the unwitting police, and of the sleuth, Dupin ("dupe-ing"), add comedy. Supernaturalism gives way before Dupin's impressive revelations concerning the mysterious murders: they were committed by a non-human, but not supernatural, orangutan. Less sensational, "The Mystery of Marie Roget" (1842–43) and "The Purloined Letter" (1845) recount further adventures of godlike Dupin. "The Gold-Bug" (1843), P.'s most popular tale in his lifetime, presents detective-story mysteries but no detective proper. Not bound by conventions he established, P. burlesqued ratiocinative tales in "Thou Art the Man" (1844).

P.'s contributions to American literature are important. His criticism, notably the concept that underlying suggestiveness makes great literature, draws repeated attention. His verse reveals limited range, but within that range he achieved heights. *Pym* and *Eureka* have won praise. The tales, in anticipating subsequent developments of haunted heroes and wasteland worlds, of detective, fantasy, and science fiction, are considered his greatest achievement, divergent though opinions about them may be. P.'s shadow indeed falls upon wide territories. The tales, in anticipating subsequent developments of haunted heroes and wasteland worlds, of detective, fantasy, and SCIENCE FICTION, are considered his greatest achievement, divergent though opinions about them may be. P.'s shadow indeed falls upon wide territories.

BIBLIOGRAPHY: Davidson, E. H., *P.: A Critical Study* (1957); Fisher, B. F., IV, ed., *P. at Work: Seven Textual Studies* (1978); Jackson, D. K., and D. Thomas, *The P. Log: A Documentary Life of E. A. P., 1809–1849* (1987); Jacobs, R. D., *P.: Journalist and Critic* (1969); Quinn, A. H., *E. A. P.: A Critical Biography* (1941); Thompson, G. R., *P.'s Fiction: Romantic Irony in the Gothic Tales* (1973); Wageknecht, E., *E. A. P.: The Man behind the Legend* (1963); Walker, I. M., ed., *P.: The Critical Heritage* (1986)

BENJAMIN FRANKLIN FISHER IV

POETRY

When the American colonists fled England and the other European countries, they fled for various reasons, but important among those reasons was the issue of religious freedom—that is, freedom for the Puritans, not for everyone. America was a clean slate upon which might be written the Word of God; it was to be the New Jerusalem, dedicated to the establishment of the Kingdom of God on Earth. The land was to be filled with Light, a Light that had been obscured in the corruption of the Old World.

The Puritans of New England especially were intent upon this purpose, and everything possible was to be subordinated to the purpose. "Everything" included literature. The Bible was *the* Book. Art for Art's sake, or for any other than God's sake, was corrupt, like the art of Europe—or, if not corrupt, at best it was frivolous. If language did not serve the purposes of pragmatic communication, it was to serve the purpose of the Church Militant.

In theory, this was all very well and good, but the colonists discovered that it wasn't so easy a practice to sever their relations with England. Britain had its own commercial and political reasons for wanting America colonized, and the English monarch wasn't keen on letting the colonists do just as they pleased. Though the aim of both Puritans and England was to settle the New World, their motives were different, and compromises had to be worked out.

Furthermore, the colonists needed England for supplies and new settlers. Many of these settlers, especially the leaders of the colonists, were educated people, and it was not easy for them to forget what they had read and learned. Literature, therefore, was imported from Europe, and not all of it was religious literature. Likewise, though most literature written in early America was religious in nature, a few scattered pieces were not, and even the religious literature produced in this country was written in the old European forms, out of Continental and British traditions.

But if America were a clean slate, ought not the literature it produced to be written in a new way? How else to differentiate corrupt literature from purified literature? As America grew and PURITANISM was transformed; as other religions came into America, this attitude toward literature was also changed. But a new element worked itself into the fabric of development: The colonists more and more saw themselves as an autonomous body of people. Pride of country demanded that America be identifiably America, not England-in-America. Americans wanted a unique American national personality, separate from that of the mother country.

A distinction may be made between the "amateur" and the "professional" poet. The former is one who uses poetry as a vehicle for a particular purpose, as Edward TAYLOR did. The latter is simply one who dedicates her life to writing poetry. Thus, Anne BRADSTREET was America's first "professional poet." Taylor was the first "amateur" and the first poet to evince what would later be seen as Emersonian qualities.

Bradstreet's *The Tenth Muse, Lately Sprung up in America* was published, significantly, in England, not in America, in 1650. Although Bradstreet did not set out to be America's first professional poet. She had the distinction thrust upon her by well-meaning relatives and friends who took it into their own hands to pamper this harmless vanity of composition. Bradstreet became, at this point, our first *confessional* as well as our first *professional* poet. She was, at least in her later poems, a subjective poet, not a dramatic one, nor even a narrative poet, and another American precedent was set, one that would be broken by Emily DICKINSON and Marianne MOORE, but that would be observed by many other women and not a few men.

Given the national bias in America against the profession of letters, one felt more at ease with our first amateur poet, Edward Taylor. Here, America was no longer in artistic competition with England and her great makers. One might lower one's sights and see that American poetry is all about something other than worldview, craft, and words—it is about vision, soul, and salvation. It is not concerned with communication on any mundane, humane level. There must be no misunderstanding on this point. Taylor was not any kind of great poet. Rather, his importance lay in his foreshadowing Ralph Waldo EMERSON. Taylor used words "roughly." He used them for pragmatic Puritan purposes: poems were "preparatory meditations," aids in achieving the frame of mind in which he composed his real work, his sermons. Taylor would never publish his poems, not even accidentally, until long after his death; not until the 20th c. would they appear in print. Although he was a remarkable preacher, his status as an amateur poet remains indisputable.

By the 18th c. in North America, there was beginning to be a literary culture. The Connecticut Wits, sometimes inappropriately called the Hartford Wits, was a group made up of Joel BARLOW, Timothy DWIGHT, and John TRUMBULL, the three most prominent members, and of others including Richard Alsop, Theodore Dwight, Timothy's brother; Lemuel Hopkins; David HUMPHREYS, and Elihu Hubbard Smith. They were essentially British-style Augustan satirists. The most remarkable work to issue from the group was Barlow's long *Hasty Pudding*.

Phillis WHEATLEY, America's first significant black poet, was born a century after *The Tenth Muse* had "sprung up," but there were many parallels between them. Bradstreet was a native of England. Though Wheatley was born on the west coast of Africa, she was reared in the same rigorous New England climate that had brought her predecessor to bloom. For whatever reason, however, Wheatley's spiritual home was England no less than it had been Bradstreet's. The difference was only that Bradstreet's models were Puritan English; Wheatley's were Augustan English. The parallels continue; Wheatley's first publication, a translation of a story by Ovid, was published at the behest, and with the aid, of friends, and her first full book, *Poems on Various Subjects,* appeared in England in 1773, though a pamphlet of her work was printed in Boston in 1770. Wheatley emulated popular Augustan poetry to the degree that her talent, great as it was, never developed beyond mere competence, and the wonder she caused lasted no longer than her novelty.

Wheatley and Philip FRENEAU were contemporaries, born within a year or two of one another. Freneau's ambivalence was not of the classic American visionary-artistic type; he was a committed artist. Rather, his was an ambivalence of style, neoclassical versus "preromantic." It is odd to see Freneau's Augustan poems standing side by side with poems that obviously presage and parallel the Romantic style that came to prominence at the turn of the 19th c.

If Edward Taylor's imagination was fantastically baroque, that of Manoah BODMAN was simply fantas-

tic, though it showed more in his prose work than in his poetry. To read Bodman's account of his conversations with angels and demons, in *An Oration on Death,* is to step through a mirror darkly into the world of Edgar Allan POE or H. P. LOVECRAFT, except that it comes off as real, not literary in any way; however, both Taylor and Bodman were concerned mainly with religion, which was acceptable to their society, a subject of practical concern. Neither Bradstreet nor Wheatley were particularly religious poets, except in rather conventional ways. Nor was Freneau.

America produced no exemplars in the 17th and 18th cs.—poets who, despite all handicaps, simply towered out of the ranks. All the exemplars were British, and our underprivileged singers could merely reflect the current poetic styles of the mother country. Not that nobody honored our 19th-c. singers, merely that no one paid serious attention to them. At no time in our history were poets more honored. Bibliophiles, in their browsings through second-hand bookstores, have long been amazed to see how many editions of our 19th-c. professional poets there are on the shelves: "Household Editions" of the Schoolroom Poets who were those American poets of the 19th c. whose work, during the early 20th c., was almost exclusively the only American poetry taught in grammar schools and high schools. They included William Cullen BRYANT, John Greenleaf WHITTIER, John Godfrey Saxe, Oliver Wendell HOLMES, Henry Wadsworth LONGFELLOW, James Russell LOWELL, and Ralph Waldo Emerson. The 19th c. cast them in amber; it institutionalized them. Poets like Walt WHITMAN, who were considered either too vulgar or too lightweight by the "schoolmarms" of the period, were not taught in the classroom that generally followed a curriculum that was not at odds with the genteel tradition of literature, that is, literature as moral uplift. Nothing was to be taught that was not acceptable to the "feminine sensibility."

The Knickerbocker school of writers existed during the first part of the 19th c. in New York City. Members included Bryant, James Fenimore COOPER, Joseph Rodman DRAKE, Fitz-Greene HALLECK, and Washington IRVING. The Transcendental Club, founded in Boston in 1836 at the home of George RIPLEY, met thereafter at odd times and informally at the home of Emerson. Members included Amos Bronson ALCOTT, William Ellery CHANNING, Margaret FULLER, Nathaniel HAWTHORNE, and Henry David THOREAU, among others.

Well into the 19th c., however, all the American arts, literature included, continued to be dominated by British and European culture. Though there was at least a fair amount of fiction and poetry being produced in America, and even some drama, a vocal minority of the writers was restive. Individuals wished to be truly New World artists, in form as well as in content, but no one had yet, it seemed, invented new American forms of writing, or formulated a conscious theory of literary creation that was peculiar to America.

William Cullen Bryant, the poet and editor, rather early in the century called for the theory and practice of a truly "American" brand of poetry, and more than a decade later, Emerson, in his essay "The American Scholar," repeated and amplified this manifesto. Then, in another essay, "The Poet," he made specific proposals about what the New World poet should be and how that poet should proceed.

According to Emerson, American poetry is to be visionary, whereas Old World poetry is literary, artful. The American poet is to be a prophet, a seer. In short, Emerson defined American poetry as a "Romantic," a "Platonic" poetry, not a "Classical," "Aristotelian" poetry. Emerson's creed and formula, then, were outgrowths of the original Puritan strictures about the uses of literature, but Emerson's creed was "transcendentalist," not Calvinist. "For it is not metres, but a metre-making argument," Emerson wrote, "that makes a poem—a thought so passionate and alive, that, like the spirit of a plant or an animal, it has an architecture of its own, and adorns nature with a new thing. The thought and the form are equal in the order of time, but in the order of genesis the thought is prior to form." In other words, craft and technique were to be secondary to the poet's "idea" or vision. Furthermore, the poem itself, like a live organism, would choose its own form; the form would not be imposed upon the idea by the poet who was more a vehicle for the transcendental idea existing in the abstract than an artisan manufacturing a literary object to be read and admired. To be even more reductive, Emerson believed that "content" was more important than "form."

With this essay, "The Poet," the battle lines were clearly drawn between those poets who wrote out of the European tradition that poetry is language art, and those who believed that language was the vehicle for philosophic or religious experience. Emerson's essay maintained that American poetry was not to be an end in itself as literary artifact, but merely a means to an end, a vehicle which helped the poet—and the reader—toward transcendental, or visionary, enlightenment.

It was Emerson who laid down the ground rules for the first "great" American poet, perhaps the only great American poet, according to some: Walt Whitman. The "Good Gray Poet," as he was called, was great not necessarily because he wrote great poems, but because he obeyed Emerson's precepts. According to Emersonian critics, until Whitman there had been only two currents in American poetry—imitation British, that is, professional-artistic, and transcendentalist, that is, amateur-theological. But after Whitman, other

lines of development diverge. The Whitman-minus-Emerson line was a phenomenon of the poetic renaissance of 1912 and after. In the 1920s and 1930s particularly, there were poets whose Whitmanism had nothing clearly transcendental or Emersonian about it. Carl SANDBURG is perhaps the clearest example—until his latest work—but Ezra POUND is another.

Emerson had enunciated the theory, but in practice he was still too conditioned by English convention to be able to break away from traditional forms and prosodies. It took Whitman to put Emerson's theory to work in poems that used a "new" American prosody (or "system" of writing poetry). That prosody was derived, appropriately enough under the circumstances, from the Bible. Specifically, Whitman wrote poems in the prose-mode forms of the Bible.

To that point in America, poetry had always been written in verse-mode, that is to say, in metered (or "measured") language, and the British convention had been adhered to that all poetry was to be written in verse. When Whitman, who was an extremely poor versifier, began writing in the "grammatical parallels" of the Hebrew tradition, his mode of composition seemed startlingly new. But it only seemed so, for it was not in fact new; rather, writing in prose—that is, in unmetered language—is the oldest system in the world. Furthermore, English poets had themselves experimented from time to time with prose poetry over the centuries, especially two 18th-c. poets: Christopher Smart and William Blake who was, for eight years, the contemporary of Whitman. A third Englishman, Whitman's contemporary Martin Farquhar Tupper, had published a book of meditative prose poems called *Proverbial Philosophy* when Whitman was nineteen years of age. This book, which was really quite poor, was nevertheless a phenomenal success, a million-copy best-seller in the U.S. in the 19th c. Whitman was certainly aware of Tupper's book, but the 20th c. justifiably forgot about it.

More to the point, Whitman must have been aware of *Eureka, a Prose Poem,* written by his American contemporary Edgar Allan Poe and published in 1848. Nevertheless, Whitman was credited with having "invented" a new American prosody when he published the first edition of his *Leaves of Grass* in 1855, seventeen years after Tupper's volume appeared, and eight years after Poe's long poem. Emerson, the foremost critic of the day, recognized what Whitman had done and wrote him to say, "I greet you at the beginning of a great career."

Because of the old convention that poetry ought to be written in verse, and because people still thought that prose could not be a vehicle for poetry, the 20th c. had to have a new term to apply to prose poems; hence, the confusing term "free verse" was borrowed from the French symbolists of the 19th c. who called nonsyllabic prosodies *vers libre.* Whitman never used the term; probably, he never heard of it. He knew he was writing prose poems. Later American poets, reacting against the pervasive English conventions of the 18th and 19th cs., began inventing various kinds of prose systems during what has come to be called the "modernist" period, which began about 1912 and lasted through the 1920s, and all of these prosodies were called "free verse," though in fact a system is a system, even that of Whitman, and each system can be analyzed, identified, and given a descriptive name. Instead, so many poets wrote to justify prose poetry as a kind of "verse" that "free verse" came to be accepted as a term that actually describes something that exists.

Whitman's influence upon 20th-c. American poetry was not, however, merely prosodic and technical. Like the English romantics, he was the champion of the "common man" and of ordinary speech, and he was the first American poet to speak in prose poetry in what we today would call the "confessional" voice, the subjective first person singular, as Emerson had demanded. Furthermore, he made the egopoetic "I" into a symbol of the New World as a whole—Whitman maintained that he spoke *for* America, not merely for himself. He would have many followers and imitators when the new century began.

Emily Dickinson, though she conducted a literary correspondence, like Edward Taylor and (briefly) her local contemporary Manoah Bodman, was almost wholly unknown as a poet to her own generation. She lived nearly all her life in her native town, Amherst, Massachusetts. Her adult life was passed as a recluse, but it was not an uneventful life, for she lived an extremely active imaginative existence—she wrote poems constantly. Her posthumous first volume of poetry, *Poems [First Series],* was published in 1890. The *Second Series* appeared in 1891, and *Third Series* in 1896. The definitive edition of her *Poems,* however, did not appear until 1958, in three volumes edited by Thomas H. Johnson.

The two greatest influences in Dickinson's life were her Calvinist father and Ralph Waldo Emerson. Her father was the conservative personification of the Old Testament God, and Emerson was the liberal representation of the New Testament God. Almost all of her poems were debates between, or arguments on one side or the other, of these two points of view. Even her method of writing was a sort of compromise between tradition and innovation, for although she wrote in verse and in the standard forms of common measure to be found in the church hymnals of the day, she was extremely loose in her composition, brilliant in her imagery, and apparently slap-dash in her punctuation which consisted largely of dashes.

Dickinson's angle of vision made her unique in her time. She at first felt uncertain that she could believe the dogmas of her father's Puritanism, and she ended by being certain she could not. Her poems, then, don't attempt to present a visionary "whole truth" as Whitman's did, but they record the vacillations of her thinking and of each moment's new revelation, which is partial, not cosmic. Her poems were a diary recording her existence. She first lost the faith of her father, then the faith of Emerson. She is, from poem to poem, inconsistent as to belief, and this, too, was modernistic., for many of the modernists in their poems coped with the existentialist idea of "the death of God." Dickinson presaged and epitomized American poetry before her time and after it as well, whereas Whitman encapsulated and provided the foundation for that strain of American poetry that we think of as both experimental and personal, religious and "free."

Dickinson wasn't much more interested in the subject of traditional form than Whitman was. She didn't take the advice of her literary correspondents, such as Thomas Wentworth HIGGINSON, editor of the *Atlantic Monthly,* at all. She never learned to rhyme neatly or caused her verse to scan more regularly, although subsequently the editor of her collections of poems, Higginson, Mabel Loomis Todd, and Millicent Todd Bingham, tried to neaten her poems by doing two things to the poems themselves that colored our perception of them in the first part of this century.

One thing that they did was to add punctuation—to Dickinson's dashes the editors added periods, colons and so forth. The second thing the editors did was to add titles to the poems, often from the first lines—Dickinson never used titles. In *Bolts of Melody: New Poems,* edited by Todd and Bingham and published in 1945, the poems were numbered, and in the 1960 standard *Complete Poems* edited by Johnson the poems were not only numbered and untitled, but they also lost the added punctuation.

The early editors did a third thing that colored our perception of Dickinson's verse, not to the poems themselves, but to their sequencing: they arranged her poems in categories such as "Life," "Love," "Time and Eternity," "Nature," and so forth, and published them that way in the first collections. Just seeing them put into pigeonholes that way gave Dickinson's early readers an erroneous impression of her work. It wasn't until 1958 that most people could see what Dickinson had originally written. It was at that point that the truly modern quality of her poems became perfectly apparent.

What is meant by "modern"? The idea of "abstract" or "musical syntax," which was first identified and discussed in Donald Davie's book *Articulate Energy* (coincidentally published in 1958) is the same as that which is behind "abstract art": to approach the condition of music in language or in painting. The traditional kinds of syntax are, first, "subjective" syntax, which is to be found in sentences that express personal opinions, as in almost any sentence written by Whitman: "I swear the earth shall surely be complete to him or her who shall be complete, / The earth remains jagged and broken only to him or her who remains jagged and broken." "Objective" syntax is to be found in sentences that express actions, as in Bryant's, "The planets, all the infinite host of heaven, / Are shining on the sad abodes of death." "Dramatic" syntax is to be found in sentences spoken by invented characters, as in Dickinson's, "I died for Beauty—but was scarce / Adjusted in the Tomb / When One who died for Truth, was lain / In an adjoining Room—" which is obviously spoken by a dead person, not by a live poet.

Abstract syntax is the language equivalent of music, which is the most abstract of the arts in that there are no "meanings" attached to notes or musical phrases. There may be a kind of general feeling attached to some aspects of music: for instance, minor keys "feel" sad whereas major keys don't; fast music feels happy, but slow music feels moody. Aside from that sort of thing, no meanings inhere in music, yet we enjoy it because we can perceive musical structures and progressions, harmonies, dissonances, counterpoint, and so forth.

If painting wishes to approach the abstract condition of music, it must get rid of "representational figures," and the same is true for language. Here is a line from one of Dickinson's letters: "The lawn is full of south / and the odours tangle, / and I hear today for the first / the river in the tree." The syntax of that line does not come to a point where one can identify an exact "meaning." It is an approach to music. Another line from a Dickinson letter that is similar in effect is, "Not what the stars have done, / but what they are to do / is what detains the sky." What one is really doing with words when one uses abstract syntax is manipulating connotations, associations and overtones and not their primary meanings, their denotations.

T. S. ELIOT's *The Waste Land* is written partly in abstract syntax, but the major abstract poet of the 20th c. is Wallace STEVENS who was, paradoxically, a message poet who in nearly all of his poems maintained that mankind had to get rid of romanticism, religion, and all that emotional baggage that we ought, as a race, to have worn out by now. We ought to substitute for them an existential viewpoint which would allow us to get through life with dignity, without resorting to the crutches of tradition. Stevens might have said that in so many words, and in a way he did

in some of his poems, but really what he did was to wrap around this idea some amazing tropical images when he was young and, when he was older, images of the arctic. It is often extremely difficult to get down beneath the imagery to the bedrock of statement, to the condition which he called, in his poem "The Snowman," a "mind of winter." It takes a mind of winter for modern men and women to bear up under the weight of mortality and the perception of that mortality.

A fourth 19th-c. American poet, besides Emerson, Whitman, and Dickinson, also had a large effect on modernist and postmodernist American, even British poetry, though that effect was indirect and more difficult to trace. Edgar Allan Poe influenced poetry and all of fiction as well, both Continental and New World, for it was he who invented the genre of the DETECTIVE STORY. His first important influence, however, was on the French symbolists of the 19th c., Paul Verlaine, Arthur Rimbaud, and Stéphane Mallarmé, leader of the group. These were the people who invented the term "vers libre" or "free verse." It was through T. S. Eliot, the American-born British symbolist poet, that Poe worked his influence upon 20th-c. American poetry, and upon the American and British New Criticism as well.

Poe began to publish his books of poetry in 1827, when he was eighteen years of age, thus equaling the feat of William Cullen Bryant who published his most famous poem, "Thanatopsis," when he was eighteen as well. Poe's "The Raven" appeared in 1845, and Mallarmé published a French translation of it, *Le corbeau,* in 1875, with illustrations by the Impressionist painter, Edouard Manet. In 1848, Poe published *Eureka, a Prose Poem,* thus anticipating by seven years Whitman's issuance of *Leaves of Grass,* a fact that is generally overlooked by those who are determined to believe that Whitman was the first American prose poet.

A great deal about Poe is overlooked by literary scholars, some of whom have said that Poe's idea of poetry appears to be a sort of monstrous distortion of Emersonian transcendentalism. Poe believed, as he wrote in "The Poetic Principle" in 1850, that the poet's function was to achieve a moment, a glimpse of "Supernal Beauty," but that term is Poe's closest approach to Emerson, for supernal beauty could only be achieved by considering melancholy subjects, in particular the death of a beautiful woman. Poe was the first American decadent, which is no doubt why the 19th c. held him at arm's length, even though he was ubiquitous in the literature of his period.

In his theories of writing, too, Poe was at the opposite pole from Emerson, after whom Poe was perhaps the second most important American literary critic of the 19th c.; certainly, Poe's literary opinions and views of writing have outlasted those of most of his contemporaries. In his essay "The Philosophy of Composition" (1846), Poe set out an Aristotelian—indeed, an extremely craftsmanly and technical—view of how poets ought to go about writing their poems. It is, in fact, a rationale for the kind of literary approach to writing that Emerson specifically identified as being un-American.

Poe's poetry—all except *Eureka*—is written in verse mode, and it has been criticized for being too "jingly," too hypnotically metrical (though it is certainly not too metrically regular). His subjects are thought to be too abstract, too decadent, too overtly symbolic. It was all of these things that the French symbolists admired. Likewise, it was all of these things that made Poe seem a sort of Old World weed in the transcendentalist herb garden of America. His lifestyle, too, caused people to lift their noses (in this he was like Whitman), and when he died early of what appeared to be alcoholism or drug addiction, no one was surprised.

These, then, were the four poets who were to do most to shape modernist poetry in the 20th c.: Emerson, the transcendentalist theorist or "agonist" of what American poetry should be; Whitman, the "exemplar" of Emerson's theories who went so far as to exchange his professional journalist's garb for workingman's clothes and a luxuriant beard so that he could be in image as well as in his writings the New World's Everyman; Dickinson, the neurotic recluse of Amherst who never went anywhere but who wrote about everything from so many perspectives that her lonely world was almost too intense for her to bear; and Poe, the native mutant, the alien in an ordinary world, who had to have his effect in a roundabout way because he embarrassed his American contemporaries and they ignored him as best they could.

James Weldon JOHNSON and Paul Laurence DUNBAR, at the end of the 19th c. and the beginning of the 20th, wore the mask of Negro gentility that Wheatley had donned in the 18th c., though Dunbar loosened it a bit with his dialect poems. For two centuries, until the end of the first decade of the 20th c., much if not most of American poetry had been derivative and imitative, a subbranch of British poetry. Only four of five poets had been exceptions to this rule. Ever since Bryant, though some of American literati had been kicking against the traces, most had been unable to break away from traditional accentual-syllabic metrics in practice, including Emerson, the agonist for a new poetics. Most of the trouble seemed to be technical—American poets had difficulty in getting personal voices out of the old forms. Emerson prescribed a remedy: invent new forms; cast off the burden of tradition and allow American poems to grow

naturally, like plants; operate through intuition in order to attain Vision, which is poetry's core, and the form will follow "organically."

If Whitman took the medicine, no one else did in Victorian America—but suddenly, at the turn of the 20th c., there didn't seem to be a problem for three poets who continued to write in the old forms. Edwin Arlington ROBINSON began to emerge from the shadows; Robert FROST published a few poems in periodicals; and Ezra Pound issued *A Lume Spento* in Venice in 1908, "A collection of stale creampuffs" he was to call it in 1964. Perhaps it was so, but Pound was gamboling about in medieval Provençal forms like a dolphin in its native element. Not many years later E. E. CUMMINGS could be so confident of sonnets that he would disguise them by means of grammatical dispersion, and he would be considered a modernist by baffled traditionalists, rather than the sentimental romantic he was.

How did it suddenly happen that, after such long agony, Americans could become master technicians who also had developed their own personal, unmistakably American voice? It wasn't because form itself was so difficult to master, for many American poets from Bradstreet on had been adequate technicians. No, it was because Robinson, Frost, Pound, and others had been able to relieve themselves of the burden of tradition associated with formal poetry, but without discarding the forms themselves.

In the succeeding generation of modernists, there were four poets who had a disproportionate effect on their contemporaries of the Lost Generation and on the postmodernist world. The first of these poets was Pound; the second was Eliot; the third was William Carlos WILLIAMS; and the fourth was Wallace Stevens. It was Pound who appears to the contemporary world to have been the galvanizer, if not the inventor, of modernist poetry.

When Chicagoan Harriet MONROE founded her *Poetry* in October of 1912, modernist poetry was given a birth date, for it was in the pages of *Poetry* that the revolution began, and that revolution was owing largely to the foreign editorship of Pound who sent back from London to Monroe the poems not only of important British poets, but also of expatriate American poets, who stayed at home, like Williams and Stevens. It was Pound who organized the first modernist movement, "Les Imagistes," which we now call IMAGISM. Pound made it up out of whole cloth, drafting poets both British and American, giving at least one of them her name: "H. D., Imagiste," for his friend Hilda DOOLITTLE. Women were to play a large role in the movement, for Amy LOWELL took it over from Pound (at which point some people began to call it

"Amygism"), and Doolittle and Marianne Moore were each dubbed, at different times, "the truest Imagist."

The movement discovered its best slogan, perhaps, in the remark by one of its members, William Carlos Williams, that there ought to be "No ideas but in things." Members of the school believed, according to Pound, that the sensory level of poetry was the most important of the four, and it underplayed the sonic level in particular, though Moore and others of the poets used the typographical level to good effect. The ideational level of a poem continued to be of importance even though an idea might never be mentioned, for Eliot's notion of the "objective correlative" was that, if one chose the proper object or vehicle for one's metaphor, one would not need to mention the subject or tenor at all, for one would have chosen that object which is relative to the idea being expressed; the idea would be clearly seen in the image itself.

A movement that is perhaps not clearly distinguished from imagism, impressionism was a style both in art and in literature of the 1870s in France and elsewhere. The term indicates that the sensory level was to be used in such a way as to evoke mood and to suggest rather than to state. The American modernist poet Alfred KREYMBORG in his poem "Nun Snow" was an impressionist, as were Amy Lowell and Hilda Doolittle in much of their work, although they are both thought of as imagists. As soon as imagism was born with *Poetry* and Pound's *Ripostes,* issued in the same year that the magazine was founded, Pound had closer affinities with Dickinson than with Poe, for the sensory level of the poems of "The Belle of Amherst" had always been of greater importance and prominence than the sonic. But if Pound was directly influenced by Dickinson, he never admitted it.

Perhaps Emerson would not have been pleased that Pound was the person who galvanized American poetry out of its derivative ways and gave it, not merely one direction, but many, for Pound was a literary mover and shaker, not a prophet or seer such as Emerson had called for. In fact, he was the opposite. He at first had more in common with Poe than with any of the other three, for his early poems were strictly formal—villanelles, ballades, madrigals—that took as their subjects personae from various historical periods and places, somewhat in the manner of the English Victorian poet Robert Browning. In fact, Pound's second book of poems entitled *Personae* was published in 1909. As soon as he conceived of imagism, however, Pound dropped formal meters and patterns and never looked back.

Simultaneously, Eliot—Pound's close friend and associate in London—was writing poems and reading the work of the French symbolists of the preceding century. If he wasn't aware of it, Poe was influencing his work subliminally. Symbolism, like impressionism and imagism, relied heavily on the sensory level of language, but the tropes created by symbolist poets were "Freudian" in nature. Furthermore, they were vast and abstract as compared with the figures of speech created by the imagists, which were more specific and concrete. But "Freudian" is not quite accurate as a description. Although it is true that symbolist poems were fraught with sexuality, they ranged farther afield than that in their subject materials, and it might be truer to say that symbolist poems were more "Jungian" than Freudian.

Perhaps it is overly reductive to say that the famed pioneer psychiatric scientist Sigmund Freud believed that sex is at the bottom of everything that has to do with the human character, and that his colleague Carl Jung broke with him in 1913 because Jung believed that the libido is a basically nonsexual energy. Jung was of the opinion that the unconscious mind operated on two levels, not one—the personal, in which everyday events of one's life are repressed, and the "collective unconscious."

The latter is considered to be comprised of inherited symbols, a "race memory" of genetic origin. These memories, which go back to the earliest phases of human origin, are "archetypes," or symbolic representations of our basic drives, such as sex, hunger, fear, affection, ambition, authority, and so forth. These archetypes, although they exist in the unconscious mind, manifest themselves as symbols that take various forms in various cultures and in different periods of history.

It was the imagist William Carlos Williams who invented the slogan "No ideas but in things," and it was he who championed Whitman's poetry of the common man. Although his work developed over the years, he remained steadfast in his concentration upon ordinary speech as a vehicle for poetry, and in his dedication to the sensory level as the most important for poetry. He invented a prosody based upon two elements. The first was what he called "the breath pause": a line of poetry was not to contain a specific number of metered syllables; rather, it was to conform to the length of a phrasal breath. A line was to be long enough to utter what the Japanese called a "katauta," a spontaneous, emotive phrase.

The second element of Williams's prosody was what he termed "the variable foot," which had to do with counting stressed syllables only: each line was to contain no fewer than one stress and no more than four. However, no "verse feet" were involved, as in accentual-syllabic prosody that had been the standard in English poetry through the 19th c., so Williams's use of the term "foot" is misleading. Williams's system has been called "free verse" also, but it is not a prose system based on grammatical and variable accentual prosodies, a fact that is not recognized by many of Williams's disciples and followers.

Many years after Eliot published *The Waste Land* in 1922, Williams looked back and said that it had seemed at the time to be a literary "atomic bomb," for it appeared to him that Eliot had betrayed the modernist revolution by taking poetry out of the hands of the people who wanted to create a new and identifiably American kind of poetry for the common folk to read and enjoy, in which they might find their everyday concerns reflected, and handed it back to the scholars of the academy. Eliot had, in Williams's opinion, not only created the poem that was the lodestone of the modernist generation, drawing to itself all of the archetypal emotions and existential "angst" of the period, he had also created an obviously "literary" work and claimed his own descent in letters was from the 17th-c. English metaphysical poets, including John Donne, George Herbert, and Andrew Marvell, as well as from the French symbolists, though he did not acknowledge his indebtedness to Poe.

Eliot had also defected from America to England literally as well as literarily and had settled there permanently. He had established himself not only as the premiere poet of his generation, but as a literary critic as well. It was Eliot's critical precepts that were the seedbed for what was to become known as the New Criticism in the 1930s and afterward, so that Eliot was not only the poetic Messiah of his time, but the chief priest as well in the high temple of literature.

If Eliot's poetry had given voice to the poetics of despair and disillusion, of what the Germans called "weltschmertz" or world-sickness, and of what the French called an awareness of the "le fin-de-siècle" or the end of the Christian historical era, his remedy was astonishing to most of the literary world, for Eliot became a stout member of the Anglican faith and declared himself to be a monarchist and a Tory in politics. Perhaps his conscious embrace of tradition was really the ultimate act of despair, an intellectual act that admitted people must grasp the social order and hold tight to it or the chaos of the archetypal darkness of the human psyche would engulf our species. In other words, perhaps Eliot's reversion to the institutions of the Christian church, models of monarchical government, and the traditions of the literary establishment was an act of will rather than of belief, of mind rather than of spirit.

Williams was considerably discouraged; indeed, Williams would not himself become very well known until MODERNISM was in its declining stages and postmodernism was well established. Wallace Stevens was another modernist poet whose influence would be deferred for many years; he was a symbolist like Eliot

rather than an imagist like Pound and Williams. Stevens was an existentialist as well. Most of his poems were expositions of the proposition that mankind ought by now to have grown out of romantic notions that there is a god who created the universe and looks after everything in it. To believe in such a creator is to blind oneself to the fact that people need to perceive life with "a mind of winter"—as Stevens wrote in his poem "The Snowman" from his first book, *Harmonium* (1923)—and become responsible for their own actions, make their own order out of the chaos of existence.

Stevens was nearly as mysterious a figure as Emily Dickinson. An insurance executive in Hartford, Connecticut, for most of his life, his own literary existence took place almost exclusively in his imagination. Although he corresponded with other writers, he seldom attended public literary events and functions, and, although he was considered by his peers to be of considerable importance, the general public knew little of him and found it difficult to understand his writing. The reasons for this obscurity had to do with Stevens's use of "abstract syntax." Although abstract syntax has always been a part of poetry, it had not, before the 20th c., been anything more than background, an ornament, not the major syntax of a poem, except in the work of Dickinson. With Eliot, and Stevens in particular, abstractionism became an important element of modernist poetry.

The effect of Pound and Eliot on their own and the subsequent generation was immediate, broad, and continuing. The effect of Williams was strong but delayed, while Stevens's effect was almost totally posthumous. In fact, not until the style of the New York school of Frank O'HARA and John ASHBERY began to spread nationwide in the mid-1980s did Stevens begin to shine.

The reaction against modernism began as early as the 1930s in the work of the British-American poet W. H. AUDEN and his Oxford University contemporaries including Stephen Spender and C. Day Lewis, but the reaction was not a revulsion against the poetry of Eliot, Pound, the Irish poet William Butler Yeats, and the other high modernists so much as it was a feeling of frustration with the apparent impossibility of continuing to explore the outer edges of 20th-c. expression. Auden's first collection *Poems* appeared in 1930, and in it can be perceived the beginnings of a postmodernist period style.

Auden and his group in the pre-World War II period blended formal verse structures with an urbane conversational style. By the time Auden left England in 1939 to emigrate to the U.S. and become a naturalized American citizen in 1946, that period style was well developed, and it had strong features of both formalism and socialism. The first generation of postmodernist poets was forced into a "fall-back position." Some of the features of that position were the use of traditionally formal verse structures, at which Auden was an acknowledged master. If readers are to understand the poetry of these writers, then they must understand the techniques of versification that they thought were important and the traditional verse forms in which they wrote. On the ideational level, there was social concern and a personal element that the school of New Critics, which had developed from modernist practice, struggled hard to keep out of poetry. Poems, they believed, ought to be hard-edged and objectively written in a "metaphysical" style—that is, in a highly metaphorical style learned, via Eliot, from the British school of 17th-c. metaphysical poets.

Perhaps Auden was responsible for the postmodernist period style of postwar America; perhaps he brought it with him from England—or it was developed by many in his generation because literary forward motion could no longer be envisioned. This became what was known as "academic poetry" in the U.S., and it persisted even into the so-called "free-verse" (prose) poems of the postwar generations. Some of those poets who were identified as "academic poets" because they taught and were formalists were Theodore ROETHKE, John BERRYMAN, Delmore SCHWARTZ, Richard EBERHART, Richard WILBUR, Elizabeth BISHOP, Howard NEMEROV, Randall JARRELL, and Karl SHAPIRO. A subdivision of these poets whose vanguard consisted of W. D. SNODGRASS, Robert LOWELL, and John BERRYMAN, became known, beginning in 1959, as the confessional school. Women were prominent among these writers, particularly Anne SEXTON, Sylvia PLATH, and Maxine KUMIN. Their hallmark was the extremely personal poem. Snodgrass's lyrics regarding marital breakup and divorce, *Heart's Needle,* led the way back up the aisle.

The Black Mountain school originated at the sometime Black Mountain College of Asheville, North Carolina, in the 1950s and gave rise to an anti-academic academy that was the center of attraction for many of the disaffiliated writers of the period, including many who were known in other contexts as the Beats or the Beat generation and the San Francisco school. Members of the school were Robert CREELEY, Denise LEVERTOV, Robert DUNCAN, and Joel OPPENHEIMER. The Beats, led by Allen GINSBERG, included Jack KEROUAC, Lawrence FERLINGHETTI, and Gregory CORSO. Kenneth REXROTH was the guru of the San Francisco school which also included David MELTZER and Jerome ROTHENBERG. All of these "beatnik" writers stood against the poets of the academy who were seen as rigidly formal and genteelly correct.

Charles OLSON had been a member of the traditional academy, but he reached the peak of his career when he became "Instructor and Rector" of Black Mountain College from 1951 to 1956. A mythology grew up around it that has grown more archetypal over the years. Olson, after the dissolution of Black Mountain College in 1956, could no longer rely on having a captive audience for his work, but when Donald Allen's anthology *The New American Poetry, 1945-1960,* appeared Olson instead began to build a nationwide audience and following, his work appearing particularly in the experimental little magazines of the period. Although it was larger, this audience was less well defined than it had been when his colleagues and disciples contributed their work to Cid Corman's little magazine *Origin* and its sibling the *Black Mountain Review.* However, once "avant-gardist" poets had appeared in these pages they were thereafter identified as members of the group even though they may not have attended the school itself, and they constituted the shock troops of Olson's advance toward literary acceptance.

The members of the movement kept in touch with one another, published each other, followed each other about until Olson landed, finally, at the State University of New York at Buffalo where his former colleague and friend Robert Creeley continued to teach through the 1980s. Though Olson died at the end of the decade of the 1960s, the so-called "Black Mountain College II" continued as a sort of academic unit at the Buffalo university, and it sent out rhizomes to various other schools including the Universities of Connecticut and Maine, the State University of New York at Albany, and various other places in the Eastern and Western U.S., not to mention Canada where the movement eventually practically took over poetic practice by the 1990s.

If Olson was the postmodernist guru of Black Mountain, it was Pound and William Carlos Williams among the modernists who were his idols to the extent that Olson has been characterized by some critics as "the poor man's Pound." His theories of composition were widely circulated, but they were derived from the theories of Williams. The chief essay exposing his "composition by field" theory was entitled "Projective Verse." In it, Olson prepostulated Emerson's "organic poetry" opinions regarding form as an extension of content and fleshed them out with remarks about the association of syllables with "breath."

Prosodics and poetics were never the chief selling points of Black Mountain, however, for in fact the poets associated with it were a heterogeneous group and the school was nothing if it was not a "cult of personality." Olson's main model for his work was *The Cantos* of Ezra Pound. Olson's *The Maximus*

Poems were often imitations. The level of diction is that of a hip wiseguy; the syntax is not much different from that to be found in the Auden style—it is ordinary speech jazzed up in "lineated" prose lines rather than slickly treated in traditional verse forms. The poem is aimed at a particular audience—the in-jokes, arcane references, and sarcasms are set like land mines and tank traps to keep at bay the bourgeois uninitiated: it is clearly a form of caste poetry.

The "War of the Anthologies" took place during the late 1950s and early 1960s when various collections of poems by both the academic and Black Mountain camps were published and all American poets were required to declare their allegiance to one or the other or be branded as either drug addicts and perverts (by the academics) or war mongering members of the "military-industrial complex," a term that had been coined by President Dwight D. Eisenhower in the previous decade. The onset of the Vietnam War caused many of the academic poets, particularly Karl Shapiro, to abdicate their responsibilities as teachers and to join the ranks of the anti–intellectuals so that their students would not perceive them as uncaring reactionaries, a situation that caused great damage to the education of poets for decades.

Another movement of the period was the poetry of protest, which included the civil rights, antiwar, and the feminist movements. Langston HUGHES was the prototypical civil rights poet; others were Gwendolyn BROOKS, Robert HAYDEN, and Amiri BARAKA. Hughes was a professional writer, not a teacher like Brooks or Hayden. Baraka, a member of the Black Mountain school, became the most militant of the black poets. Denise Levertov, also a Black Mountaineer, made her reputation primarily as an antiwar poet, and Adrienne RICH became the paradigmatic feminist poet, although the academic Carolyn KIZER was perhaps the better writer.

The deep image surrealism of the postmodernist Robert BLY (although the term was invented by Black Mountain poet Baraka) was a late development of imagism. Identified as a part of the antiacademic movement, it supplanted formal poetry in the academy and burgeoned for years—throughout the 1970s and 1980s—in the graduate workshops until it at last gave way before the rise of the New Formalism in the 1990s.

The experimentation of the 1950s was carried on into the 1990s by a school calling themselves, after the periodical they established, the Language poets. The modern poet has generally been expected to make leaps of the imagination that surprise the reader, to make associations that others perhaps would not have made. Not everyone is capable of following the poet in these leaps. It is evident that the difficulty readers of contemporary poetry have with John Ashbery and

others of the New York school and of its current successor, the Language poets, both of which are outgrowths of the practice of Wallace Stevens, is that they jump from one association to another without intervening transitions—it is a modernist technique, one that Pound emphasized in the original draft of Eliot's *The Waste Land* by editing out those transitions and leaving only the narrative and dramatic fragments and the abstract syntax that mirror the fragmentation and the technological leaps of the 20th c.

Nevertheless, this new kind of poetry began displacing Bly's deep imagism and the avant-garde movement of the 1980s. It made inroads on the West Coast where most of the Language poets resided, but in 1986, signs of a further spread became evident, through chapbook publications from the alternative press movement, to New England and the South. Currently, these two schools of "abstract" poetry—the New York school and the Language poets—have spread everywhere, and Ashbery is currently the most lionized poet in the U.S. The only other school of poetry vying with the abstract poets for the literary spotlight is the New Formalists led by Dana GIOIA, Marilyn HACKER, and others.

By 1983, there were beginning to be widespread rumors of a return to formalism in American poetry. By 1986, those rumors had turned into a full-fledged movement, for that was a considerable year for what critics and readers had begun to call neoformalism or the New Formalism in American poetry. The Philip Dacey and David Jauss neoformalist anthology *Strong Measures* appeared during the late winter of 1985; it was the first major anthology of formal poetry to be published since the early 1960s.

During the previous score of years before the pivotal year 1986, the *Mississippi Review* had been nearly alone in devoting a special issue to the subject of form in poetry: in 1977, it had published *Freedom and Form: American Poets Respond*. Poets had been asked to submit a poem and then to write a short comment upon its composition and organization. Contributors to that issue included Richard Eberhart, William E. STAFFORD, Vern Rutsala, X. J. Kennedy, and Richard Wilbur. A decade later, in 1987, another formalist book following the same format was published, David Lehman's *Ecstatic Occasions, Expedient Forms*. Contributors included John Ashbery, Robert Creeley, Richard Wilbur, Dana Gioia, Marilyn Hacker, Anthony HECHT, John HOLLANDER, Richard Kenney, Brad LEITHAUSER, Joyce Carol OATES, Molly PEACOCK, Robert PINSKY, Louis SIMPSON, and Mona VAN DUYN—a real potpourri of both the older formalist poets and neoformalists, plus many antiformalists, young and old.

During the decade of the 1990s, the strains of poetry that continued to be dominant included the subjective prose poems that derived from the movement and confessional poetry of the 1960s, the Language poetry that arose out of Wallace Stevens and the New York school of the same period, and the New Formalism that harked back to the academic poets of the post–World War II era.

BIBLIOGRAPHY: Davie, D., *Articulate Energy* (1958); Perkins, D., *A History of Modern Poetry* (2 vols., 1987); Stauffer, D. B., *A Short History of American Poetry* (1974); Turco, L. P., *Visions and Revisions of American Poetry* (1986); Waggoner, H. H., *American Poets from the Puritans to the Present* (1968; rev. ed., 1986)

LEWIS PUTNAM TURCO

POLITICS AND LITERATURE

From its very inception, the idea of America as a work in progress has operated on many levels, weaving together the issues surrounding national identity, political destiny, and the place of individual consciousness. For writers, the clashes between the community ideal and its material expression produced a constant interrogation of political relations, a process that offered vital commentary on the limits and possibilities of democratic principles. While these novels, plays, and poems are not necessarily about figures or institutions per se, they do serve as a measure of national identity, and give a strong sense of the nature of relations between citizens under an exceptional democracy.

The Puritan world view is central to any understanding of the political nature of American writing, primarily because it chose American soil as the focal point of its intellectual vision and experience. As a place of promise and liberation, America was blessed and God-given, a testing ground for new visions and versions of identity. William BRADFORD's *Of Plymouth Plantation* and John Cotton's *Bay Psalme Book* (1640) were the first accounts of the Puritan journey from Europe to the New World, extolling America as a place of liberty and free expression. Here, the ideal communities would radiate the terms and limits of individual identity and purpose, and these members would in their turn influence the direction of the community under the guidance of God.

Yet from the start, the virtuous relations between God and man in the New World would not remain static in their form, but instead became a dynamic register of change. Anne BRADSTREET's *The Tenth Muse, Lately Sprung Up in America* was a crucial antecedent in the transformation of Puritan literature, explicitly questioning American material conditions,

the nature of the bounteous virtues, as well as the problems of being a woman poet. The tug between public issues and private life would erode the Puritan predestined religious world view, and produce instead an early metaphysical approach that defined individual consciousness as an active process. This relation of the self to the social can be seen clearly in Edward TAYLOR's poetry, and Cotton MATHER's *The Christian Philosopher.* Jonathan EDWARDS's "Sinners in the Hands of an Angry God," *Treatise Concerning Religious Affections,* and his *Personal Narrative* outlined the parallels between external and internal conditions, positing a direct link between a politically conscious identity and location. At the same time, William BYRD's frank *Secret Diary* explicitly chronicled the political machinations of local Puritan elites, suggesting that many of the theological debates had more material ramifications.

These struggles over the definitions of community and the place of the individual were essential to the formation of a national consciousness, and provided a direct link between American experience and the shape of its developing political identity. Benjamin FRANKLIN's pamphlet *A Dissertation of Liberty and Necessity* and Thomas PAINE's *Common Sense* hailed America as a place of rational values, where independence and liberty went hand in hand, and to be a free individual was to be a free nation. The merging of the metaphysical and the nationalist ultimately provided a principled rationale for the revolutionary war against the British, placing an active American citizenry at the center of the struggle.

Franklin's work also connected the American struggle with European Enlightenment ideals, fixing liberty, equality, and fraternity into the American foundations. His *Autobiography* was a central document to the intellectual notion of America itself, in which Franklin's life was seen to be a metaphor of American values, a working out of national virtue in the individual. *The Declaration of Independence* (1776), and the *Constitution* of 1787, both epic poems of sorts, concretized the individualistic basis of American democracy, attesting to the unique nature of its community. J. Hector St. John de CREVCOEUR in his *Letters From an American Farmer,* was the first popularizer of the American political myth, outlining the intimate links between values, character, and national identity. Yet ominously, he also recognized the contradictions between dynamic individualism and static declarations, a divergence between actual government and ideology exemplified in James Madison and Alexander Hamilton's collected essay series, *The Federalist Papers* (1787–88).

Despite the problems of limits and definitions, the new nation set about distinguishing itself from Europe by producing a home-grown, celebratory literature. As self-conscious nationalist expressions, these voices explored the politics of place and the promises of liberty, but were tempered by an uncertainty about what was exactly liberated. Washington IRVING's tale "Rip Van Winkle," whose central character is both a sleeper and a visionary, whimsically explored the relation between the American past and its future. Yet Irving had a strong faith in the American environment as a creative edenic paradise: *The Sketchbook of Geoffrey Crayon, Gent; Bracebridge Hall;* and *Tales of a Traveller* all celebrated American exceptionalism and its political expressions. Irving's idealism was also tempered by uncertainty about the American mission, and the problems caused by reckless expansion and entrepreneurial exuberance emerged in *A Tour of the Prairies, Astoria,* and *The Adventures of Captain Bonneville.*

The confusion over American means and ends, and the guilt of betraying the revolution was also reflected in James Fenimore COOPER's work. In *The Pioneers, The Deerslayer, The Last of the Mohicans,* and *The Pathfinder,* the democratic promise of the wilderness, and the independence it nurtured and guaranteed came into question. The growing conflicts between the settlement of the frontier, and the relations between individuals, traditions, and peoples produced irreconcilable conflicts that haunted the idea of new and innocent beginnings. Cooper's disaffection in *Satanstoe, The Chainbearers,* and *The Redskins,* outlined a growing sense of national decay in the face of commercial exploitation and moral opportunism.

This process of historical and political revision was continued by Nathaniel HAWTHORNE, who resurrected the Puritan ideal as a problematic opening chapter in American experience. His pessimistic vision of a nation doomed by its own dark secrets was laid out in *The Scarlet Letter* and *The House of the Seven Gables,* which shuttled between national experience and the demands of history on the American Republic. Herman MELVILLE also typified this clash between American past and present on land and sea, in *Typee, Omoo, Mardi,* and *Moby-Dick.*

Yet other writers continued to see the promise of American potential, and explored the liberatory aspects emerging from this new culture. Henry Wadsworth LONGFELLOW called for a poetry of public aims that would elevate republican values into the hearts of all citizens, and set out to do so in "Voices of the Night," and "The Song of Hiawatha." Similarly, Ralph Waldo EMERSON added his own politics of personal transcendence to the national vision, merging the romantic and liberatory potential of the individual with the national surroundings, providing a truly American form of spiritualism. In *Nature, Representative Man,*

and essays such as "The American Scholar" and "Self Reliance," Emerson argued for a changed relation between the self and the world, producing a new sense of independence through nature. Emerson's ethic opposed the emerging capitalist ethos of self-interest and exploitation, effectively sacramentalizing the ordinary in a quest for the best self. Similarly, Henry David THOREAU's *Walden* and Margaret FULLER's *Woman in the Nineteenth Century* pushed TRANSCENDENTALISM into more political channels by offering critiques of social and sexual relations. By melding the spiritual with questions of personal liberty, these hybrid strains of transcendentalism tried to bridge the gap between idealism and action.

Walt WHITMAN was one of the few writers who maintained an ideal hope for the democratic experiment; in his poems *Leave of Grass,* he envisaged an intense identification between the nation and its people. However, this idea of an American people in itself as a coherence was a chronic oversimplification of the political scene, as the presence of black slaves made clear. The existence of institutionalized inequality within the Republic silenced a community that demanded and deserved its own voice. Frederick DOUGLASS's *Narrative of the Life of Frederick Douglass, an American Slave, Written by Himself* and William Wells BROWN's *Clotel; or, The President's Daughter,* humanized the contradiction, and brought forth a flurry of protest. John Greenleaf WHITTIER explored the abolitionist position in *Poems Written during the Progress of the Abolition Question* and *Voices of Freedom,* placing the inequities of slavery firmly in the public eye. Harriet Beecher STOWE also set popular taste and perception of this divisive issue in *Uncle Tom's Cabin* and *Dred: A Tale of the Dismal Swamp,* elevating it to a moral cause.

As the Republic collapsed into Civil War, the ideal of democratic unity was smashed to pieces, and America was broken into factions. While the war itself produced its own limited, disillusioned commentaries, namely Whitman's *Speciman Days* and *Drum Taps* and Melville's *Battle Pieces,* a sense of innocent hope had been lost. If the national union was saved, it was at the cost of a disorienting industrial transformation that marked a general decay of political consensus, bringing issues of class conflict to the fore. Mark TWAIN's *The Guilded Age, The Adventures of Tom Sawyer,* and the *Adventures of Huckleberry Finn* explored these transformations as an American fall from grace: innocent of wrong doing, and undeniably romantic, the young Republic was tarnished and corrupted by crushing responsibilities. Twain would end his American odyssey with *A Connecticut Yankee in King Arthur's Court,* pitting American pluck against feudal mores, ultimately destroying both in a techno-logical apocalypse.

The profound sense of pessimism resulting from industrialization, massive immigration, and the unspoken institutionalization of the class system, produced new directions in American literature. The bitter experiences of the urban proletariat found expression in Abraham Cahan's *Yekl* (1896), Paul Laurence DUNBAR's *The Uncalled,* Upton SINCLAIR's *The Jungle,* and Kate CHOPIN's *The Awakening.* Here, the Jeffersonian myth of the free American pioneer was finally laid to rest, crushed under the realities of urban life and the inequities of wage labor.

William Dean HOWELLS offered important visions of class dynamics and relations, fearful of a shift away from democratic principles to closed mindedness, and a social Darwinistic siege mentality amongst the middle class. *A Modern Instance, The Rise of Silas Lapham, A Hazard of New Fortunes,* and *Annie Kilburn* illustrated the contradictory fear of the middle class in the face of working-class political activism. The influx of immigrants with strange socialistic politics and revolutionary outlooks, touched on an intellectual panic about the imminent collapse of American ideals. These fears were echoed in Henry ADAMS's *Democracy,* John HAY's *The Breadwinners,* and Hamlin GARLAND's *Spoil of Office.* The insularity and parochialism of the American elites was also satirized in Henry JAMES's *The Bostonians,* and Edith WHARTON's *The House of Mirth,* and *Ethan Frome.*

The realistic portrayals of class positions and political antagonisms were also melded to the irresistible and disorienting forces of American technology and industry. In this age of the machine, the individual as the cardinal political unit became a victim of the machine, engulfed by the inimical laws of science. The determined realities of the disfranchised could be seen in Theodore DREISER's *Sister Carrie,* Stephen CRANE's *Maggie: A Girl of the Streets,* Frank NORRIS's *The Pit* and *The Octopus,* and Jack LONDON's *The Iron Heel.* The natural forces of technology proved irresistible to human action, constructing a new form of slavery around a grim, industrial determinism.

The collapse of American idealism, and the loss of faith in its political credos led to a moral despair and political detachment in the face of rapacious industrial capitalism. While writers like Lincoln STEFFENS continued to keep the faith in Progressive reform, the impact of World War I was a death blow even to die-hard idealists. The fiction that emerged after the war saw the American dream as a cruel hoax, a distant myth that had no place in the present. While T. S. ELIOT's *The Waste Land* struck a chord for aesthetic modernism, the novels of the period offered no redemption. Theodore Dreiser's *An American Tragedy*

and F. Scott FITZGERALD's *The Great Gatsby,* snuffed out all hope of meaning. Similarly, the belief in the virtue of the countryside was cruelly destroyed in Sherwood ANDERSON's *Winesburg, Ohio,* Willa CATHER's *My Antonia,* and Sinclair LEWIS's *Main Street.* The men and women of this lost generation were severed utterly from their past, drifting without historical memory or political affiliation, desperately trying to salvage some meaning. Ernest HEMINGWAY in *The Sun Also Rises* and *In Our Time* symbolized a new political alienation and stagnation, suffering from what Langston HUGHES would call *The Weary Blues.*

While the corruption and hopelessness of American politics seemed borne out in Herbert Hoover's administration, the stock market crash of 1929 and the onset of the depression ironically offered a new hope. While capitalism tottered on the brink of oblivion, the example set by the Soviets after the Bolshevik Revolution (1917) offered a new strain of salvation. The writing in the 1930s engaged in a new political analysis of material conditions, merging scientific Marxism with human potential, reviving the American radical spirit. The forces of capitalism were not iron-clad, but subject to influence, change, and democratic possibility. Edmund WILSON's *Travels in Two Democracies* and *To the Finland Station* showed the potentials of social and political experimentation. Clifford ODETS caught the spirit of this period in his rousing plays *Waiting for Lefty* and *Awake and Sing.* Jack Conroy's *The Disinherited* (1933), James T. FARRELL's *The Young Manhood of Studs Lonigan,* and John STEINBECK's *The Grapes of Wrath* (1939) reinvested the American individual with new possibilities, suggesting new beginnings and the continuation of the democratic experiment.

Of course not all were so positive in their evaluation of the American scene. John DOS PASSOS, in his epic of American modernism *U.S.A.,* illustrated the sinister and rotten trajectory of American politics and culture. Similarly, Richard WRIGHT in *Native Son* and *Black Boy* recognized that dialectics do not necessarily change the racial grain. Nathanael WEST also took on American myths of success and glamor in *Miss Lonelyhearts, A Cool Million,* and *The Day of the Locust.*

The revival of democratic faith continued through World War II, fueled by the threat of fascist aggression. Yet in the wake of victory, the postwar world took on a surreal quality, resulting in a stupefying consumer-boom nihilism. Despite the allied victory, the visions offered by those who had served overseas were less than heroic. Tainted by the racism and class conflict in the military, the war for many merely reinforced America's own totalitarian strains, turning the ideals of democracy into empty propaganda. Saul BELLOW's *Dangling Man,* Norman MAILER's *The Naked and the*

Dead, Herman WOUK's *The Caine Mutiny,* and ultimately Joseph HELLER's *Catch 22* mediated the contradictions between freedom and domination, and the
myths that remained unchanged and unexamined at
the American core.

As the nation settled into prosperity, growing conformity and conservatism, many literary voices were
less than enthusiastic about the deals being offered.
Nelson ALGREN's *The Man with the Golden Arm,* Carson MCCULLER's *The Heart Is a Lonely Hunter,* and
Flannery O'CONNOR's *A Good Man Is Hard to Find,*
explored the new rural and urban sensibilities. What
emerged was a vision of a culture fractured by addiction and psycho-pathology, where political consciousness dissolved into a world of maddening sterility.
Jack KEROUAC caught some of this in *On the Road,*
and Ralph ELLISON's *Invisible Man* laid the foundation
for an existential politics of social and psychic erasure.

The increasing international role played by
America led to an overextension of an already flimsy
democratic ideal, while the McCarthy show trials at
home marked a new low in political tolerance. Similarly, the Korean War and the race to build Hydrogen
super-bombs encouraged a paranoid vision of American institutions. William S. BURROUGHS's *Naked Lunch*
pushed American ideals to the brink of narcotic melt-
down, while Kurt VONNEGUT's *Mother Night* and
Slaughterhouse Five merged fantasy with horrifying
reality. In exploring American complicity with Nazism
and strategies of mass destruction, these writers suggested America was dangerously off-course, rapidly
losing any sense of its original identity.

With American intervention in Vietnam, and the
covert extension of the war into neutral countries,
governmental institutions took on a decidedly sinister
aspect, fostering a backlash among supporters of the
New Left. The conflicts between the realities of propaganda and the ideals of democratic society can be seen
in Mailer's *The Armies of the Night* and *Why Are We
in Vietnam?,* which consciously blended the psychological with the historical, placing the self as the only
true measure of freedom. The discrediting of American
institutions led to a fusion of the physical as the new
political terrain, and both race and gender became new
sites of radical expression and contestation. From the
Black Power poetry of Amiri BARAKA to the explicitly
feminist poetry of Adrienne RICH, the redefinition of
the racial and the sexual as key elements in American
politics and consciousness marked a radical transformation of the American tradition. Toni MORRISON's
Song of Solomon, Alice WALKER's *The Color Purple,*
and Ishmael REED's *Mumbo Jumbo* explored the varieties of racial expression, putting the black body and
speech forward as vital political sites. Similarly, femi-

nist writers such as Marge PIERCY and Kathy ACKER
merged the personal with the political.

The continual shifting of American political identity eventually turned itself inside out, and the postmodern writers returned to the specific forms of language used by American culture. Political meaning
became a site of narrative play and narcissistic expression, opening cultural history to the influence of endless interpretation. Thomas PYNCHON's *V, The Crying
of Lot 49, Gravity's Rainbow,* and *Vineland* showed
American politics as a shadowland, where anything
can and does happen, where all decisions are absurd.
Robert COOVER's *The Public Burning* turned the Nixon
presidency into farce, transforming political legacy
into dark comedy. The merging of politics and unreality seemed complete with the Reagan administration
in the 1980s, where the values of consumption and
existential despair were at their highest. Brett Easton
ELLIS's *Less than Zero* and his later *American Psycho*
typified the American experience at the end of the
20th c., and reduced the American political landscape
to a testing ground for utter nihilism and mental illness
in the thrall of materialism and entrepreneurial activity.

BIBLIOGRAPHY: Aaron, D., *Writers on the Left* (1974);
Beidler, P. D., *American Literature and the Experience
of Vietnam* (1982); Bercovitch, S., M. Jehlen, and L.
Marx, eds., *Ideology and Classic American Literature*
(1986); Bogardus, R. F., and F. Hibson, *Literature at
the Barricades: The American Writer of the 1930s*
(1982); DeLeon, D., *The American as Anarchist: Reflections on Indigenous Radicalism* (1978); Homb-
erger, E., *American Writers and Radical Politics,
1900–1939* (1986); Trachtenburg, A., *Democratic Vistas, 1860–1880* (1970); Ziff, L., *Literary Democracy:
The Declaration of Cultural Independence in America* (1981)

PAUL HANSOM

POOLE, Ernest

b. 23 January 1880, Chicago, Illinois; d. 10 January
1950, Franconia, New Hampshire

P. was the first winner of the Pulitzer Prize in fiction for
His Family (1917). Though he was a prolific novelist,
publishing twenty-four novels before his death in
1950, only his second and third books published, *The
Harbor* (1915) and *His Family* received great critical acclaim.

P. began his writing career as a journalist. His
"muckraking" articles about child labor laws, tenement conditions, tuberculosis, and sweat-shop conditions brought reform to New York City, where he had
moved in 1902. He also traveled to Russia in 1905 to

cover the October Revolution for *Outlook;* these articles are considered by many to be his best short pieces of writing.

A member of the Socialist Party, P. studied the world around him, and was greatly concerned with social ill and class conflict. Many of his works are seen, by critics, to be ripe with autobiographical detail. His second novel, *The Harbor,* which is often compared to Upton SINCLAIR's *The Jungle,* tells the story of Billy, a young man growing up surrounded by comfort and beauty who, by early adulthood, begins to see the inequalities in the social structure around him. After being exposed to the troubled lives of the dock workers of New York, Billy begins to write so that others will see the unevenness of the class system in America and help to bring about social change, an aspiration not unlike that of P. himself.

The Harbor was a radical novel in its time, bringing about great controversy from all sides of its readership, with detractors denouncing it for its leftist and atheistic bent, and supporters—including Theodore ROOSEVELT—who saw it as an insightful American novel. It was with the publication of *The Harbor* that P. began to achieve an important reputation as a novelist.

P.'s third novel, *His Family,* presents the story of Roger Gale, a widower who must reenter the lives of his three grown daughters in order to fulfill his wife's wish at her death, which was that he bring to her news of their children at the time of his own death. In this quest to understand the generation of his daughters and the ways in which their lives differ from his own, as well as their dependency on him, Gale finally comes to see that all people who have lived and died are a part of one large family, and through this epiphany he realizes "a clear sweet thrill of happiness." This novel brought P. the Pulitzer Prize, a powerful recognition for a writer so early in his career and one that very well might have cursed the reception of the rest of his life's writings; he never again found the kind of success he had with this novel.

P.'s next two novels, *His Second Wife* (1918) and *Blind* (1920), continue in the tradition of the previous novels: each deals with a quest for meaning in life, and each holds elements of the writer's own life, his own search for the ways in which man finds meaning in a world so full of transition and uncertainty.

In his later years, P. published several novels of nonfiction, including *Giants Gone* (1943), and *The Great White Hills of New Hampshire* (1946); his 1940 book, *The Bridge,* was P.'s attempt in writing his own autobiography. He never regained the fame and notoriety he found in the publication of his earlier novels, which may be attributed to the inconsistency of his writing and the fact that his thesis of social consciousness often overshadows character and plot development.

BIBLIOGRAPHY: Keefer, T. F., *E. P.* (1966); Marble, A. R., *A Study of the Modern Novel* (1928); Quinn, A. H., *American Fiction* (1936); Van Doren, C., *Contemporary American Novelists, 1900–1920* (1931)

KATHERINE L. KELLER

PORTER, Katherine Anne

b. 15 May 1890, Indian Creek, Texas; d. 18 September 1980, Silver Spring, Maryland

P. is recognized as one of the finest writers of short fiction in American literature. Like William FAULKNER and other Southern Renaissance writers, she wrote about the waning influence of the past upon the present, particularly the weakening ties to community and nature. Her reputation was assured by the short stories and novellas written in the first half of her life. Her *Collected Stories* (1965) was awarded the National Book Award and the Pulitzer Prize. Her one novel, *Ship of Fools* (1962), was a great publishing success, but it received mixed reviews from critics and readers. It did, however, finally provide economic security for the urbane life style that P. had painstakingly cultivated as a best-selling author, accomplished lecturer, and celebrated hostess.

Throughout her career, P. fictionalized the facts of her life both in creating her fiction and in discussing her biography. The actual records show her remarkable transformation from an impoverished Texan childhood to a successful life of letters. She was born Callie Russell, fourth child of a family proud of their Southern heritage. Her mother died after giving birth to a fifth child. Her father proved incapable of providing for his children. P. was reared by her grandmother, from whom she learned genteel deportment, the art of storytelling, and the skills of survival. An uneven student, P. escaped from her convent school by eloping at the age of sixteen. This unhappy marriage, the first of four failed marriages, ended in divorce three years later, freeing her to pursue her vocation as writer.

P.'s apprenticeship was marked by frequent changes of address, low-paying jobs, and bouts of serious illness. After failing to sell her manuscripts in Chicago, she worked as an entertainer on the provincial theatrical circuit in Texas and as a journalist in Colorado, where she nearly died from influenza in the epidemic of 1918. In the 1920s, she was a member of the Greenwich Village community of women writers that included Elinor WYLIE and Josephine HERBST. During an extended visit to Mexico collecting folk art for a projected traveling exhibit, P. acquired the knowledge of Mexican culture and political conflict that informs several of her early short stories, including "Flowering Judas." In this story about Laura, a young woman who came to Mexico as a teacher but has become involved in the revolutionary movement, P. made a significant breakthrough in the use of natural symbolism to depict her protagonist's inner world.

During the 1930s, her most productive years, P. developed her central theme of the survival of the individual, usually the female, in a world upset by moral decadence and war. The publication of her first book, *Flowering Judas and Other Stories* (1930), made her literary reputation. Included in this volume was another of her most successful stories, "The Jilting of Granny Weatherall," notable for its stream-of-consciousness depiction of the old woman's memories as she lies dying. P.'s growing reputation won her a Guggenheim Fellowship to support European travel, during which she collected materials that would coalesce in a novel thirty years later. In her second book, *Pale Horse, Pale Rider* (1939), the young Miranda Gay, whose efforts to escape her ties to the old Southern order and to shape her destiny reflect P.'s own experience, is the central character in two of the finest novellas, "Old Mortality" and "Pale Horse, Pale Rider." A third story, "The Old Order," appearing in *The Leaning Tower and Other Stories* (1944), completes Miranda's search for role models.

Many readers consider "Pale Horse, Pale Rider" the best proof of P.'s mastery of the novella. Based upon her near-fatal experience with influenza, it tells of the love affair between Miranda and Adam Barclay, a soldier about to be sent into battle overseas. Miranda, a drama critic for a Colorado newspaper, has fallen dangerously ill with influenza. Adam selflessly nurses her until a hospital room becomes available. Once admitted, she is quarantined from all visitors. When she is finally out of danger, she learns that Adam has contracted the disease and died. The story is particularly notable for P.'s continued exploration of the psyche, this time through five dream sequences that reveal the undercurrents of Miranda's mind.

P. wrote in brief intense periods of concentration separated by months of hectic social activity, occasional stints as a lecturer, and continuing guilt over her procrastination. After a long period of gestation, *Ship of Fools* was finally published on All Fools Day in 1962. Lacking the carefully balanced plots of her short fiction, it is a long episodic account of the relationships among the passengers abroad the German vessel *Vera* bound from Veracruz, New Mexico, to Bremerhaven, Germany, in the summer of 1931. The unifying theme is the human inability to establish lasting ties, as reflected in the broken love affair of two young Americans and the tensions among the various

national groups on board, including sixteen Germans who are particularly repugnant. Many critics found the novel's tone too pessimistic and its pace too slow; however, they noted the flashes of shrewd character analysis and brilliant prose characteristic of P.'s best writing.

Made wealthy by the publication and later filming of her novel, P. did not produce any new fiction, although she continued to revise older pieces and plan new projects. Although her body of fiction is, therefore, relatively small, it possesses a remarkable range of settings and events. Yet for all its variety, it is unified by a common theme—the exploration of the responsible individual's survival in an essentially evil world.

BIBLIOGRAPHY: Bloom, H., ed., *Modern Critical Views: K. A. P.* (1986); Givner, J., *K. A. P.: A Life* (1982); Liberman, M. M., *K. A. P.'s Fiction* (1971); Lopez, E. H., *Conversations with K. A. P.* (1981); Warren, R. P., ed., *K. A. P.: A Collection of Critical Essays* (1979)

MARGARET CARTER

PORTER, William Sydney

b. 11 September 1862, Greensboro, North Carolina; d. 5 June 1910, New York City

P., who wrote under the pen name of "O. Henry," is acknowledged as one of the most popular American writers of the early 20th c. The setting of P.'s stories—the American South and Southwest, Latin America, prison, and New York City—grew out of his own experiences, which he used extensively in his works.

A sickly youth in North Carolina, where he worked as a pharmacist in his uncle's drugstore, he sought employment on a Texas ranch to improve his health. Soon tiring of the outdoor life, he found a job as a bank clerk in Austin, and when accused of embezzling, he fled to Honduras, returning two years later to his wife's bedside at her death. Tried and convicted, he served three years in an Ohio penitentiary, where he was assigned primarily to the prison pharmacy. Shortly after his release, he made his way to New York City. Always in poor health, he suffered as well from habits of intemperance, being profligate with money and having become a full-fledged alcoholic, eventually died of cirrhosis of the liver.

He was almost exclusively a writer of short stories—although he published one novel, *Cabbages and Kings* (1904), some verse, and a few humorous pieces—at a time when the popularity of the short story was at a peak, and his reputation rests on some one hundred forty stories set in New York City, which he wrote during the last six years of his life. He was under contract to the New York *Sunday World* to produce a weekly story, for which he was well paid by the standards of the day, and he began publishing collections of his stories in 1906 with *The Four Million;* by the time of his death six years later, he had written fourteen volumes of them, several of which were published posthumously.

Despite the ills, misfortunes, and self-inflicted torments of his life, P.'s fiction has a gentle, caring, and optimistic tenor. Much addicted to word play, literary allusion, and a bombastic manner, his stories nevertheless are tightly plotted and fast paced. He was a leader in using characters of humble origin such as shop girls, office workers, and factory hands, and he made use of extensive circumstantial detail to engage his readers. One device—the surprise ending, which features a sharp plot reversal, often based on coincidence and almost always resulting in some sort of good fortune—is the preeminent literary feature on which his reputation and his popularity rest.

His popularity, indeed, was enormous during the latter years of his life and those immediately following, both in America and abroad, with translations into many languages. Interestingly enough, he was one of the few American writers authorized by the Soviet Union for translation and distribution to its subjects, and his place in world literature has remained secure to this day, as has his popularity with the reading public in the U.S.

His critical reputation in America, however, has been much debated through the 20th c., with sensible critics arrayed against each other on the question of his literary merit through every decade since his death. Certain themes recur through much of this critical debate. In the first place, most, whether judging well or ill, compare him with seriously regarded writers: Sir Philip Sidney, William Makepeace Thackeray, Rudyard Kipling, Guy de Maupassant, Honoré de Balzac, as well as Washington IRVING, Nathaniel HAWTHORNE, Edgar Allan POE, Bret HARTE, Stephen CRANE, Mark TWAIN, and Ernest HEMINGWAY. The shape of the debate is similar from his own day to ours. His detractors decry his facile manner, awkward phrasing, and too-easy plot coincidences, while his admirers choose to notice his tight plotting, warm humor, and magical endings. The critics aside, so long as American literature is read, P. will have a place in it.

BIBLIOGRAPHY: Davis, R. H., and A. B. Maurice, *The Caliph of Bagdad: Being Arabian Nights Flashes of the Life, Letters, and Works of O. Henry* (1931); Harris, R. C., *W. S. P. (O. Henry): A Reference Guide* (1980); Langford, G., *Alias O. Henry: A Bibliography of W. S. P.* (1957)

                                        THOMAS K. MEIER

PORTIS, Charles
b. 28 December 1933, El Dorado, Arkansas

A graduate of the University of Arkansas, P. worked as a newspaperman in Tennessee, New York City, and London before leaving a promising career in journalism to write novels.

His first novel, *Norwood* (1966), gave ample proof of his talent for comic writing, a mode he pushed to both higher and deeper limits in *The Dog of the South* (1970) and *Masters of Atlantis* (1985). In his humorous novels, he can be as jolly or as biting as Mark TWAIN or Stephen CRANE and as engaging as the best of the Southwestern humorists in his creation of character and incident. Like his forebears in Southwestern humor, P. honestly confronts the dark side of humanity and exposes the worst vices of the human animal. Thus he depends on black humor, absurdity, and rollicking good times to give his novels both spice and vinegar.

Adept though he is as a humorist, his most celebrated and enduring work is *True Grit* (1968), serialized in the *Saturday Evening Post* before appearing in hardcover and climbing to a spot near the top of the best-seller list against such competition as John UPDIKE's *Couples* and Arthur Hailey's *Airport*. Although *True Grit* has many lighthearted moments, P. delved into some serious themes in this Western novel: fair play, justice, self-reliance, restlessness, adaptability, and human decency. He created two of his best characters in this novel, Mattie Ross and Rooster Cogburn. Naive, vengeful, self-reliant, loving, and demanding, Mattie brings out the best in drunken, slovenly, trigger-happy Rooster Cogburn. The novel can be read, as it has been, as a spoof of Western novels and movies or as a realistically honest tale of initiation reflecting the conservative values of Southern and Southwestern Americans. The screen adaption brought John Wayne his only Oscar for his portrayal of hard-drinking Rooster Cogburn. P. had no part in the sequel to the movie version of *True Grit, Rooster Cogburn.*

P. writes in a clean, lean style, one befitting his training as a journalist. Unlike some modern-day humorists, he can tell a rip-roaringly funny tale without being foul-mouthed. He obviously enjoys the challenge of creating both character and incident and the parody of the language of modern advertising and journalism. He can be as robust and fresh as Ring LARDNER, George Washington HARRIS, or Flannery

O'CONNOR and as capable of depicting memorable characters.

BIBLIOGRAPHY: Connaughton, M. E., "C. P.," in Kibler, J. E., Jr., ed., *DLB,* vol. 6, *American Novelists since World War II* (1980): 264–68; Idol, J. L., Jr., in *Contemporary Fiction of the South: A Biographical and Bibliographical Sourcebook* (1993): 361–70

JOHN L. IDOL, JR.

POTOK, Chaim

b. 17 February 1929, New York City

As a novelist, scholar, biblical translator, educator, and ordained rabbi, P. brings a unique perspective to American literature. Unlike other Jewish American writers who ignore Judaism or who concentrate on the more secular and assimilative side of their Jewishness, P. has created a body of work that highlights Jewish religious issues and their importance in individual lives. Much in the European tradition of Sholem Aleichem and Chaim Nachman Bialick, he uses Judaic instruction along with his gifts as a writer to educate, without being didactic, as well as to entertain.

P. integrates into his novels a variety of intellectual sources, including Jewish history, Talmudic study, and Western philosophy. In what could be read as his fundamental principle of writing, P. has been quoted as saying that "it's a problem of confrontation of ideas which sparks a novel, the people caught up in the confrontation, and then an attempt to take what is essentially abstract thought and translate it in terms of action, flesh, and blood." This confrontation of ideas is usually that between Jewish tradition and the secular 20th c., and it serves as the thematic centerpiece to almost all of his fiction.

For instance, in his first novel, *The Chosen* (1967), two kinds of confrontations evolve. The first takes place within an Orthodox Judaic context and is between traditionalists and Hasidim, and the second is between a more general religious orthodoxy and Western secular humanism. As he does in his second novel, *The Promise* (1969), P. establishes these conflicts by placing together two boys of divergent backgrounds. The author uses the relationship of the boys—Danny Saunders, a Hasid, and Reuven Malter, of Orthodox heritage—along with their relationships with their fathers, as a narrative means by which to explore Judaic faith and its place within contemporary America. *The Promise* is the sequel to this first work, and continues to trace the lives of Saunders and Malter.

P.'s third novel, *My Name Is Asher Lev* (1972), is also structured around the Hasidic community. In it, the titular hero, who wants to become a painter, runs up against the wishes of his family, who believes his

creative desires to have more in common with Christian sympathies than with Judaism. It is in many ways a traditional novel of initiation, with the young Lev constantly reexamining his life and finding himself isolated from family and community. P. returns to his protagonist eighteen years later in *The Gift of Asher Lev* (1990). By this time, Lev is a successful artist living in France, but the death of an uncle brings him back to America and back to past conflicts. Painfully and against his will, Lev once more must choose between the sacred and the worldly.

In the Beginning (1975), an autobiographical novel, again explores relationships within the Jewish community, but this time the primary encounter is between Jew and Gentile. Anti-Semitism and the Holocaust are the focus here, and P. uses them to show not only the darker side of Western civilization, but also the importance of a revitalization of Judaism, both in America and in Israel. P. uses the counterposition of two intelligent young men from different backgrounds once more in *The Book of Lights* (1981). Gershon Loran, an orphaned rabbinical student drawn to Jewish mysticism, undergoes a spiritual quest with Arthur Leiden, who is pursuing a religious life in order to expiate his father's role in atomic bomb research. Loran's journey takes him from Brooklyn, to the Orient, and eventually to Jerusalem, where he eventually commits his life to Judaic studies. The end in many ways typifies P.'s work by demonstrating the importance of a religious ballast against the chaos of modern life.

P. has departed from the familiar Orthodox Jewish milieu in some of his more recent fiction. *I Am the Clay* (1992) revolves around an old Korean couple and the orphan child they take in during the Korean War, and *The Gates of November: Chronicles of the Slepak Family* (1996) is the story of a Jewish father and son in Stalin's Soviet Union. Yet despite these different settings, P.'s message remains constant: even within the violent and morally tumultuous 20th c., an essentially affirmative view of human nature can and must be achieved.

BIBLIOGRAPHY: Abramson, E. A., *C. P.* (1986); Kauvar, E. M., "An Interview with C. P.," *ConL* 27 (Fall 1986): 291–317; Marovitz, S. E., "Freedom, Faith, and Fanaticism: Cultural Conflict in the Novels of C. P.," *SAJL* 5 (1986): 129–40; Purcell, W. F., "P.'s Fathers and Sons," *StAL* 26 (February 1989): 75–92; special P. edition, *SAJL* 4 (1985)

DEREK PARKER ROYAL

POUND, Ezra [Weston Loomis]

b. 30 October 1885, Hailey, Idaho; d. 1 November 1972, Venice, Italy

P. stands as a powerful and monolithic figure of 20th c. literature. His massive literary output, which includes not only his own poetry, but works of translation, letters, and essays and books on theory and criticism, encompasses all of civilization in its polylingual vocabulary, sets of allusions, and synchronic integration of diverse texts. *The Cantos,* begun in 1917 and completed in fragmentary form by 1969, represent the most compelling and significant accomplishment of P.'s career as a poet, a work many critics have come to view as a monumental achievement of such stature that it will be viewed as the central epic of the 20th c. comparable to Dante's *The Divine Comedy* in its era. Though P. lived most of his adult life in Europe, he always spoke from quintessentially American voice and vision: democratic in spirit and aesthetic, fervent in his homage to the doctrines of the Founding Fathers, and committed to the rhythms and colloquial diction of American English.

Not only has P.'s poetry and critical thought had enormous impact on the direction of 20th c. artistic and intellectual life, but P. directly influenced the careers of many of the major authors of this century. Such poets as T. S. ELIOT, William Carlos WILLIAMS, Wallace STEVENS, William Butler Yeats, E. E. CUMMINGS, Charles OLSEN, and Hilda DOOLITTLE all bear the stamp of P.'s advice, support, and friendship. Indeed, Eliot dedicated *The Waste Land* to P., calling him "*il miglior fabbro.*" James Joyce, Wyndham LEWIS, Ernest HEMINGWAY, among many others, were recipients of his artistic, and sometimes financial, beneficence. A rich exchange of letters, articles, and internal comments in *The Cantos,* as well as in the writings of P.'s fellow artists, gives evidence to this mentorial role. Early in his career, P., along with Williams and others, expounded on the theory of IMAGISM with its concern for the grounding of poetic language in the concrete. Later, however, it was with MODERNISM, as an aesthetic and philosophical movement, which included Imagism as well as other more complex concepts, that P.'s work found its strongest affinity and subsequent influence.

Both the work and life of P., often inextricably bound have generated controversy. A whole strain of Poundian debate is given to partisan polemics: one school denounces the man as a politically dangerous bigot whose work is essentially unintelligible; the other school, recognizing poetic genius and placing P.'s political and economic theories within their appropriate context, extol the brilliance, passion, and inventiveness of his work, particularly *The Cantos.* Though controversy remains, the critical analysis has shifted away from the sometimes uninformed judgments of those who attacked P. in the 1940s and 1950s. Often the most vehement assumptions came without a serious reading of the work or adequate comprehension of P.'s idiosyncratic discourse. But enough time has now passed so that the emotional baggage of preconceptions and half-truths that once colored, perhaps understandably, the critical eye during the war and postwar years has been mediated by an open-minded spirit, more concerned with interpretation than with condemnation.

In recent decades there has been an explosive growth in P. scholarship, most of it very useful, both in its attempts to do basic research in texts and to provide a hermeneutic for the sometimes cryptic, though always structured Poundian opus. At the conclusion of *The Cantos,* P. questions if he "can make it all cohere." One consequence of the vigorous investigation of *The Cantos* has been to show just how extraordinarily it does cohere. A seminal influence in this direction has been the publication, since 1972, by the University of Maine, Orono of *Paideuma: A Journal Devoted to Pound Scholarship.* In 1982, the Orono Press began to publish a parallel work, *Sagetrieb: A Journal Devoted to Poets in the Pound-Williams Tradition. The Analyst,* published at Northwestern University, has also been influential in promulgating P. scholarship.

The scope of P.'s writing is enormous. *The Cantos,* published in sections throughout his life, form the substantial core. Other major poetic works include *A Lume Spento* (1908), *Personae* (1909), and *Homage to Sextus Propertius* (1919). *Hugh Selwyn Mauberley* (1920), a work considered second in importance only to *The Cantos,* has often been compared to Eliot's "The Lovesong of J. Alfred Prufrock" (1917). *Mauberley* consists of a medley of eighteen poems divided into two parts written as a dramatic monologue from the point of view of Mauberley, a persona that P. claims reflected the sensibility of Henry JAMES. In *Mauberley,* P. develops much of the mixed diction, syncopated poetic rhythms, and disjunctive images and allusions that characterize *The Cantos.* The important translations included *Sonnets and Ballate of Guido Cavalcanti* (1912), *Cathay* (1915), *The Natural Philosophy of Love,* by Remy de Gourmont, (1922), *Confucius: The Unwobbling Pivot* and *The Great Digest* (1947), and *Sophokles: The Women of Trachis* (1956). These reflect P.'s perennial interest in classical Chinese literature and philosophy as well as the troubadour tradition of French and Italian poetry. The major critical prose includes *The Spirit of Romance* (1910), *Gaudier-Brzeska: A Memoir* (1916), *Make It New* (1934), *Jeffereson and/or Mussolini* (1935), and *Guide to Kulchur* (1938; also pub. as *Culture*). In *ABC of Reading* (1934), P. articulates his aesthetic principles in a lively, distinctive prose that reflects the epiphanic style of the poetry and an American propensity toward the empirical and the concrete. The voluminous letters have been collected in various publications; two significant editions are *P./Joyce: The Letters of P. to James with P.'s Essays on Joyce* (1967) and *The Selected Letters of P., 1907–1941.*

An overview of *The Cantos* presents a challenge to synthesis. Not only long (803 pages in the New Directions edition), the multivalent array of subjects, image and allusion systems, coupled with complex language strategies, resists simplification. P. attempts to redefine the epic by composing a narrative made up of lyric moments. The term "narrative" must be used in a specialized way, for the story to be told is not the kind found in *The Odyssey* or *Paradise Lost;* rather, the story is the "tale of the tribe," no less than a kind of history of the world as engendered by P.'s heroic *dramatis personae.* In a parallel way, it is P.'s own story, a journey through the creative process and through the public and private domains that encompass the poetic source. In this way, *The Cantos* find their echo in such works as Williams's *Paterson* and Eliot's *Four Quartets.* Radical in style and structure, *The Cantos* embody conservatism in the true sense of the word, in keeping with the epic intent: conservation as preservation of the past while "making it new."

Paradoxically, *The Cantos* can best be read as both the poetry of an electronic age and a book of revelation. Mixed diction, subject matter, and tone create an impulsive, disjunctive style that moves from opacity to lucidity in surges and flows of rhythm and meaning. P.'s point of view can shift from bombast to reverie, from curse to incantation, within a series of lines. Elevated diction coexists with colloquialism; the sublime stands with the vulgar. The image of a "beer bottle on a statue's pediment: is juxtaposed, by way of parody, to a 16th-c Portuguese epic about da Gama. "Martin / Van Buren as a bottle of urine" can be followed by an invocation to "Sagetrieb, or the / oral tradition." A compendium of sense and sound, riddled with the collage of associations, P. is not content to "make it new" solely in English (for he is above all democratic). Rather, he incorporates a variety of languages—from Chinese ideograms, Egyptian hieroglyphics, Provencal French, classical Greek, and Church Latin, to the four icons of playing cards and musical notation. To illustrate in Canto XCI: a rendering of the monosyllabic alliterative Early English versification in "Bright hawk whom no hood shall chain" is followed by the Greek *Kadmu Thaugater,* and then interrupted by the colloquial "'get rid of parapernalia'" that suggests a neologism and a pun. An electronic age creates a fulcrum of information overload. And a book of revelation requires hermeneutic detection. One enters the arcanum of *The Cantos* willing to surrender to sensation while passionate for investigation. P. called the poet "the antennae of the race; it is up to the reader to tune in."

The Cantos pay homage to Homer and Dante, and in Canto I, P. opens with a translation from book 11 of *The Odyssey.* The journey to the Underworld provides a transition into Canto II where P. begins to call up his own heroic dead, such as Robert Browning, and later, in Canto VIII, "the great domed head" of Henry James. Simultaneously, P. conjures the spirit of Dionysius in some of the most extraordinary poetry found in *The Cantos.* The god is transformed into a leopard, "void air taking pelt." The Mediterranean world of olive, grape, sea, and sun moves sensuously in P.'s exquisite rendering.

The radiance of Canto II contrasts with the diatribes of the later hell Cantos where P., invoking Dante's model, damns his "sinners." Vivid with scatological imagery, P. denounces bankers, politicians, and journalists and casts them into the "last cesspool of the universe . . . waving condoms full of black beetles." P.'s impassioned language erupts with equal contempt in the later Usura Cantos. In Cantos XLV, the poet rages against usury, its devaluation of goods, its corruption of the material world and human craftsmanship. He sees in usury an absolute evil since it is *contra naturam.* These cantos reflect P.'s economic theories, which are based on the dangers of inflation inherent in corporate finance and political bureaucracy. In further sub-sets of cantos, P. expands his political/economic/philosophical themes by reflection on the Founding Fathers such as Jefferson and Adams (a good example is Canto XXI) and exposition of the Golden Age of Confucius (Cantos XLII–LI, 1937) and (Cantos LII–LXXI, 1940).

In many ways, the next two groups of *The Cantos* illustrate P.'s poetic genius at its fullest. *The Pisan Cantos* LXXIV–LXXXIV (1949) were written while P. was imprisoned in an outdoor cage in a detention camp in Pisa, Italy. Subjected to severe physical and emotional deprivation, accused of treason for his radio broadcasts in Italy, he confronted a possible death sentence. The irony haunts: P., the major American literary figure of his time, now denied basic civil rights, isolated and misunderstood, viewed by many as a crank, by others as a dangerous fascist, rose out of this "dark night of the soul" to create some of the most moving and profound poetry ever written. P., who believed himself a patriot, espoused the ideals of the Founding Fathers, and in his crusty American speech upheld democratic ideals and the efficacy of the individual. Yet, in the Pisa ordeal, he transcends the irony of his indictment. Throughout *The Pisan Cantos* P. builds a complex of repeated images—dream, light, water, eyes, stone, silk, air, wings, mountains, dust—that culminate in a mystical visitation by Aphrodite. Trapped in his cage, the poet confesses his vanity. But then he sees the alternative, and in triumph, proclaims that he has "gathered from the air a live tradition" and that "this is not vanity."

The extraordinary odyssey of P. continued when he was returned to the U.S. and brought before a tribunal for treason; he was judged mentally unfit and confined to St. Elizabeths Federal Hospital in Washington, D.C. where he remained for fourteen years. During this period, P. once again found the inner resources to overcome his difficult situation, and produced the mastery of *Section: Rock-Drill De Los Cantares* LXXXV–XCV (1955). Filled with a majestical radiance, the *Rock-Drill Cantos* illuminates the possibilities of an earthly paradise. The gnomic and geological metaphors that underlie all of *The Cantos* emerge with full effect here. Drilling through rock, in a quarry for precious gems and metals, the geological strata yield their pure and precious lyric moments. Though he probably would not have approved of a psychodynamic reading, surely the occupation of P.'s father partly instrumentalized such a persistent core of metaphor in P.'s opus. Homer Pound had worked at a government mine in Montana, where P. was born, and later moved his family to Philadelphia where he was employed at the federal mint. Out of the gnomic archeology of *The Rock-Drill Cantos,* rock and light combine in the GREAT CRYSTAL. In the transition from cave to the " *'l terzo ciel movete,"* the controlling image of the eye (one that appears throughout *The Cantos*) arrives at ecstatic illumination: *ubi amor ibi oculus est* (where love is there is the eye). The mystical vision of P.'s sensibility manifests itself most exquisitely in this group of cantos.

By contrast, the final Cantos, completed in fragmentary form and published in 1969, reflect P.'s questioning of his life's work. He had returned to his beloved Italy after dismissal from the mental hospital. His attempts to make a "paradiso terrestre" come under scrutiny and we see poetic structures and human gestures of closure. The spirited, bombastic voice of earlier irreverence now speaks in a serene yet humbled and moving finale, asking the Gods to forgive, asking those he has loved to forgive, what he has made. The simplicity of the concluding Canto CXX reverberates with a power appropriate to the majesty of this extraordinary epic work.

P. is a monumental figure in American literature. In the teens and twenties, the early P. personified the flamboyant poet (a pose he eagerly embellished) and the prototypical American (another pose he readily performed for his European cohorts). From the thirties until his death, P. no longer appeared at the forefront of the artistic avant-garde. Sympathetic to both the domain of meditation and the domain of action, he wished to apply the one activity to the other; yet, ultimately, he was silenced. Quite literally, and not by choice, he was in exile both within and outside of his homeland, an exile that seems to be a fundamental

experience of the epic artist—from Virgil and Dante to Joyce and Mann. However, much of P.'s poetry was written during the years of incarceration. At once the target of acrimony and disregard, he also became a cult figure, esteemed by a fervent following of fellow poets, critics, and artists. Now that the old enmity has moderated, history and the critical tradition must ultimately be kind, indeed, more than kind, to P.; for the beauty, passion, scope and power of his literary contribution will demand it.

BIBLIOGRAPHY: Beach, C., *ABC of Influence: E. P. and the Remaking of American Poetic Tradition* (1992); Brooke-Rose, C., *A ZBC of E. P.* (1970); Bush, R., *The Genesis of Ezra E. P.'s Cantos* (1977); Davie, D., *E. P.* (1975); Edwards, J. H., and W. W. Vasse, *Annotated Index to the Cantos of E. P.* (1957); Heymann, C. D., *E. P.: The Last Rower. A Political Profile* (1976); Joseph, T. B., *E. P.'s Epic Variations: The Cantos and Major Long Poems* (1995); Kenner, H., *The P. Era* (1971); Lentricchia, F., *Modernist Quartet* (1994); Nanny, M., *E. P.. Poetics for an Electric Age* (1973); Pearlman, D. D., *The Barb of Time: On the Unity of E. P.'s Cantos* (1969); Perloff, M., *The Dance of the Intellect: Studies in the Poetry of the P. Tradition* (1985); Pound, O., and R. E. Spoo, *Ezra and Dorothy P.: Letters in Captivity, 1945–46* (1999); Rabate, J. M., *Language, Sexuality, and Ideology in E. P.'s Cantos* (1986); Schafer, R. M., *E. P. and Music* (1978); Schulman, G., *E. P.: A Collection of Criticism* (1974); Stock, N., *The Life of E. P.* (1970); Surette, L., *A Light from Eleusis: A Study of P.'s Cantos* (1979); Wilhem, J., *Dante and P.* (1974)

DIANE M. BORDEN

POWERS, J[ames] F[arl]
b. 8 July 1917, Jacksonville, Illinois

Best known for his short stories and novels dealing with Catholic priests, P. is a master of subtle irony who weaves gentle social satire into tales built around the everyday circumstances of unremarkable characters. But his fiction, conservatively peppered with the occasional wry comment or slender theological allusion, is not any less powerful because of his restrained style. Within the pages of his highly polished work lies finely wrought commentaries on the human condition, made all the more effective because of the rather ordinary characters and quotidian settings through which he works his magic.

In his first short story collection, *Prince of Darkness and Other Stories* (1947), the clerical subjects and theological themes that dominate so much of his later fiction are prominent features, especially in the more highly acclaimed selections, "The Valiant Woman," "Lions, Harts, Leaping Does," and the title story. "Lions, Harts, Leaping Does," written when P. was twenty-five, demonstrates his capacity, even at that young age, for crafting stories of considerable thematic depth. However, this story, and indeed the entire collection, lacks the sly humor that makes his later work all the more impressive.

In *The Presence of Grace* (1956), his second collection of short stories, P. takes a more light-hearted approach toward his clerical subjects, who by this time have come to occupy most of his authorial energy. Nine of the eleven stories collected in this work deal with priests, but even though the range of his subject matter narrows, P.'s narrative repertoire expands considerably. For example, in a style reminiscent of Kafka's "Investigations of a Dog" and "The Burrow," P. tells two of his stories, "Death of a Favorite" and "Defection of A Favorite," from an animal's point of view. Fritz, the rectory cat who narrates these tales, is easily one of P.'s most memorable and charming characters, and, ironically, it is Fritz who, more capably than P.'s human narrators, best reveals the humanity of the priests with whom he resides.

With the publication of *Morte d'Urban* (1962), the winner of the 1963 National Book Award, P. firmly established himself as a first-rate novelist. Set primarily in Minnesota in the late 1950s, the novel follows the misadventures of Father Urban, who finds himself consigned to the Order of St. Clement, an isolated retreat far removed from the comparatively glamorous world he had known as a public speaker and radio personality. As the title of the novel suggests, P. alludes to Malory's Arthurian tale, though the comic elements he employs, such as when Father Urban is knocked unconscious by an errant golf ball, are more reminiscent of Mark TWAIN's rollicking *A Connecticut Yankee in King Arthur's Court.*

P. returned to the short story genre in *Look How the Fish Live* (1975), a collection known primarily for its title story, a father's introspective experience with the innocence of his children and the flaws of nature. This collection also contains two stories, "Bill" and "Priestly Fellowship," that form part of the foundation for P.'s second venture as a novelist, *Wheat That Springeth Green* (1988). Though this novel appears a quarter of a century after his first effort in this genre, his narrative skills lose none of their edge, and his keen sense of humor, which first comes to the forefront in *The Presence of Grace,* has never been more apparent. A meticulous writer who values quality over quantity, P. demonstrates in this second novel that his carefully crafted prose, minute attention to the details of

setting, and mature comic vision are well worth the wait.

BIBLIOGRAPHY: Boken, J. B., "J. F. P.," in Meanor, P., ed., *DLB,* vol. 130, *American Short-Story Writers since World War II* (1993): 266–75; Hagopian, J. V., *J. F. P.* (1968)

ALLEN ALEXANDER

POWERS, Richard [Stephen]
b. 18 June 1957, Evanston, Illinois

One of the most cerebral postmodern novelists, P. is also among the most elusive. In the decade following his first intricate, multiplot novel, *Three Farmers on Their Way to a Dance* (1985), a finalist for the National Book Critics Circle Award, he produced steadily, publishing *Prisoner's Dilemma* (1988), *The Goldbug Variations* (1991), *Operation Wandering Soul* (1993), and *Galatea 2.2* (1995).

The Goldbug Variations, his most intellectually demanding book to date, was *Time*'s 1991 book of the year and a finalist for a National Book Critics Circle Award. *Operation Wandering Soul* was among five finalists for the 1993 National Book Award in fiction. In 1986, the American Academy of Arts and Sciences honored P., and in 1989 he was named a MacArthur Fellow.

The structure of P.'s novels mirrors his quintessential aims in writing: to find order in the universe and to understand the 20th c. with its swift shift from agrarianism to industrialism to modernism and the cybersociety. *Three Farmers on Their Way to a Dance,* triggered by an August Sander photograph, traces the history of three Alsatian peasants and their progeny through World War I and after. The book is arranged in sets of three chapters, one carrying on the main story lines, one each focusing on notable historical figures of the period and on a notable event connected with it.

Prisoner's Dilemma and *Galatea 2.2* are P.'s most autobiographical books. The first, set in De Kalb, Illinois, where he spent his adolescence, relates with some factual distortion the story of his family. Interchapters focus on broader topics, such as P.'s fabrication of Walt Disney's constructing a scale model of the U.S. outside De Kalb.

Galatea 2.2 focuses on P.'s later life. The protagonist, named Richard Powers, finishes a master's degree and goes to Boston with C., his former student, to write. The two eventually resettle in the Netherlands, as P. did for six years, before they separated. He returns to the Midwest, loosely attached to a Big Ten university, where he becomes involved in a sophisticated project to create a computer capable of passing the master's comprehensive in literature, an attempt to replicate human intelligence.

The Goldbug Variations, P.'s most ambitious undertaking, is modeled on Johann Sebastian Bach's "Goldberg Variations," to which it corresponds structurally, and to which P. adds elements from Edgar Allan POE's "The Goldbug." P. draws parallels between Bach's counterpoint and the structure of DNA. The book's double love story apes DNA's double helix.

Operation Wandering Soul, set in a pediatric surgery ward inhabited by gravely ill children, touches on problems of illegal immigrants, abandoned children, and children with such rare diseases as progeria. The ward's resident tries to insulate himself from the horrors he faces daily, but a physical therapist who works with the children humanizes this young physician. The novel has P.'s usual interchapters, each detailing an event relating historically to children: the Children's Army during the Crusades, King Herod's slaughter of the Innocents, the Pied Piper of Hamlin, the Peter Pan story.

Clearly a most promising postmodern novelist, P. has in *Galatea 2.2* provided insights into the creation of his earlier novels. P.'s search for the interconnectedness of all things provides the philosophical underpinnings of his novels.

BIBLIOGRAPHY: Baker, J., "R. P.," *PW* 238 (16 August 1991): 37–38; Howard, M., "Semi-Samizdat and Other Matters," *YR* 7 (Winter 1988): 243–58; Saltzman, A., *The Novel in the Balance* (1993); Stites, J., "Bordercrossings: A Conversation in Cyberspace," *Omni* 16 (November 1993): 38–48: 105–13

R. BAIRD SHUMAN

PRESCOTT, William Hickling
b. 4 May 1796, Salem, Massachusetts; d. 29 January 1859, Boston, Massachusetts

With the publication of *The History of the Reign of Ferdinand and Isabella the Catholic* (1837), P., a dedicated scholar and self-taught historian, began an illustrious career that changed American historiography forever, and P. himself is now known as the finest English-language interpreter of the Hispanic world. An aristocratic Boston Brahmin, P. was accidently blinded in one eye in 1812 and suffered extreme rheumatism in the other eye. Physically unable to become a lawyer, as he had originally intended, and temperamentally unwilling to become a merchant, P. decided to pursue the life of the gentleman scholar, and, funded by his father, began a thorough study of Italian literature. In 1824, under the influence of his friend George

TICKNOR and Ticknor's Spanish literature lectures at Harvard, P. shifted his interests to the language and literature of Spain and in 1826 combined his lifelong love of history with his current studies and began a program of research into the reigns of Ferdinand and Isabella. Thanks to the earlier invention of the noctograph, a writing machine for the blind, and with the aid of his wife, family members, and secretary-readers, P. was able to spend the rest of his life writing and researching Hispanic history. Today, he is the most widely translated and frequently published of American historians.

P.'s major accomplishments reside as much in his philosophical approach to historical writing as in his actual works of history. His use of specific documentation, multiarchival research, and extensive bibliographical notes gives the reader reliable, traceable evidence that links historical perspectives to social analysis. Drawing from his earlier appreciation of the Italian epic, P.'s use of the narrative, of vivid characterization, and of picturesque delineation of events imbues his histories with a strong literary quality of an almost heroic cast. His insistence upon organizing his material to point toward an underlying theme, an approach he discovered in the French historian Gabriel Bonnot de Mably, provides a rational means to comprehend human actions and random events in the light of a moral and progressive point of view.

These techniques are easily seen in what many consider to be his classic work, *The Conquest of Mexico* (1843). The work is divided into three parts: a lengthy introduction to the Aztec civilization and its relationships with other neighboring cultures, a discussion of the Conquest itself, and a brief look at the career of Cortes after the Conquest. The focus of the material on the Aztec world provides P.'s organizing theme or moral that the fall of the Aztecs was based on their tyranny over other subjugated cultures, a point of view that is still widely held today. P.'s vivid portrait of Cortes, an example of his use of literary devices, supports a secondary theme that much of Cortes's incredible accomplishments came from the force of his personality. Thus, the third part of the work, Cortes's subsequent career after the conquest, is necessary as a denouement. The highly readable narrative is substantiated by copious and extremely well-documented scholarship.

Equally successful was P.'s next book, *The Conquest of Peru* (1847), which was followed by *History of the Reign of Phillip the Second* (3 vols., 1855–58) and *The Life of Charles the Fifth after His Abdication* (1858). With its focus upon the history of Spanish civilization and culture in both Europe and the Americas, P.'s work has been credited not only with revolutionizing historical methods but also with influencing

American political thought of the time to move beyond blind nationalism and wary isolationism.

BIBLIOGRAPHY: Charvat, W., and M. Kraus, eds., *W. H. P., Representative Selections, with Introduction, Bibliography, and Notes* (1943); Darnell, D. G., *W. H. P.* (1975); Gardiner, C. H., *W. H. P.: A Biography* (1969)

                                        LYNN RISSER

PRICE, [Edward] Reynolds
b. 1 February 1933, Macon, North Carolina

The rural South comes alive in the writing of P., who often selects the area of North Carolina just south of the Virginia border, where he was born, as the setting for his work. The central core of much of P.'s writing is the family. He emphasizes the inevitable determinism of heredity. In his work, the sins of the father are often visited on the next generation. Even when his characters have free choice, they usually make the frequently destructive choices their progenitors would have made.

P.'s career began auspiciously with the publication of *A Long and Happy Life* (1962) both in hardcover and, in its totality, in the April issue of *Harper's*. This story of young love in an isolated and inbred southern town focuses on the Mustian family, who figure also in *A Generous Man* (1966), which centers on the same family nine years before the action of *A Long and Happy Life,* and in *Mustian* (1983).

These early books evoked comparisons with William FAULKNER to whom P. bears a surface similarity, although his style appears to have been more significantly influenced by John Milton, Leo Tolstoy, Ernest HEMINGWAY and the Bible. P. captures with dazzling authenticity the cadences and rhythms of southern speech. He also has a complete grasp of small-town Southern society.

One of his more significant undertakings is his two related novels, *The Surface of Earth* (1975) and *The Source of Light* (1981). These books, more stylistically complex than his earlier writings, examine four generations of the Kendal-Mayfield family and are, in their ambitious scope, reminiscent of Tolstoy's best work.

Stricken with spinal cancer in 1984, P. is a paraplegic. Hypnosis used to relieve his pain, however, unlocked his subconscious and caused him to embark on an exceptionally productive period of writing. Much of this odyssey is related in *A Whole New Life* (1994), which, along with *Clear Pictures: First Loves, First Guides* (1989), provides valuable autobiographical information about P. The fictional *Love and Work* (1968) is also strongly autobiographical, although it is less dependable as autobiography than the later works.

Kate Vaiden (1986), like all of P.'s novels, has autobiographical elements but facts are rearranged to suit the author's artistic purposes. *Kate Vaiden* is interesting because it is at heart a sensational, melodramatic story to which P. lends a dignity and grace by making it, like most of his fiction, focus more on universals than narrowly on particulars.

In *The Tongues of Angels* (1990), the protagonist Bridge Boatner is obsessed with guilt at the thought that thirty-four years earlier, when he was a camp counselor, he might have been responsible for the death of Raphael Noren, the most talented boy in camp. Underlying this story, with its pervasive guilt, is a subtle homosexual theme, also found in some of P.'s other novels.

P.'s fiction about the South is unfailingly authentic, searching, and often witty. His concern with generational matters pervades all of his novels and most of his short stories. His exquisite use of sensory detail makes his writing memorable and credible.

BIBLIOGRAPHY: Drake, R., ed., *The Writer and His Tradition* (1969); Hoffman, F. J., *The Art of Southern Fiction* (1967); Kaufman, W., "A Conversation with R. P.," *Shenandoah* 17 (Spring 1966): 3–25; Rooke, C., *R. P.* (1983); Wright S. T., and J. L. W. West, *R. P.: A Bibliography, 1949–1984* (1986)

                                  R. BAIRD SHUMAN

PROKOSCH, Frederic
b. 17 May 1908, Madison, Wisconsin; d. 2 June 1989, Plan de Grasse, France

Critics who have admired the writing of P. have often considered why it is that P. is not better known today. Not only is there is a distinct foreignness to his name, but his work has a cosmopolitan flavor. He does not often address the American scene so squarely and directly as did his more enduring contemporaries such as John STEINBECK, William FAULKNER, Ernest HEMINGWAY, F. Scott FITZGERALD, and John DOS PASSOS. At times, he consciously chose not to follow dominant American literary fashions, instead adopting a more cosmopolitan stance.

Of his sixteen novels and thirty volumes of verse, his first novel, *The Asiatics* (1935), no doubt remains his best known and most widely acclaimed work. Praised by celebrated writers such as André Gide and Thomas Mann, the novel, written while he was teaching at Yale, has been widely translated and remains in print in the U.S. A kind of imaginary travelogue written in the first person, *The Asiatics* traces the journey of an American young man from Lebanon to China—territory P. had no direct knowledge of. The ideas of the novel tend to be overshadowed by the novel's rich verbal texture and riveting descriptions of landscape, judged by many critics to be P.'s main achievements. Yet, the nameless narrator's relentless wanderings, his pursuit of a phantom happiness, at the heart of the novel, link it to a classic American theme found in such works as Mark TWAIN's *Adventures of Huckleberry Finn,* Paul BOWLES's *The Sheltering Sky,* J. D. SALINGER's *Catcher in the Rye,* Jack KEROUAC's *On the Road,* and Cormac MCCARTHY's *The Crossing.* Try as he may to find meaning, a gnawing emptiness lies at the core of the narrator's life.

Other P. novels depict American protagonists wandering through various continents. Samuel, in *Storm and Echo* (1948), is on a quest in the Congo to find Leonard Speght. David Gilbert in *Nine Days to Mukalla* (1953) survives a plane crash and journeys through the Ras Fartak region of Oman. Philip, in *The Skies of Europe* (1942), travels through a Europe on the brink of war. Henry in *A Ballad of Love* (1960) moves from Austria to the U.S. and back to Paris. Yet other novels—*The Conspirators* (1943), *Age of Thunder* (1945), and *The Idols of the Cave* (1946)—deal with the experience of World War II.

After the publication of *The Seven Who Fled* (1937), selected for the Harper Novel Prize, P.'s critical and popular status waned, until in 1968, he published *The Missolonghi Manuscript,* an historical novel chronicling the last months of Lord Byron's life that might aptly be compared to Herman Broch's *The Death of Virgil.* P. uses the device of a lost manuscript to let Byron tell his own story. Once again, the author's verbal virtuosity shines more brightly than his insight into the romantic poet's life.

P.'s poetry is even less known than his fiction. Among his American influences were Edna St. Vincent MILLAY and Archibald MACLEISH; he acknowledged, as well, his debt to Friedrich Hölderlin. Some critics have noted a kinship between P., W. H. AUDEN, and Dylan Thomas. His style and themes, however, were distinctly classical, such as in "Sunburned Ulysses," and somewhat out of step with the times. Unlike contemporaries such as Ezra POUND, Hilda DOOLITTLE and James Joyce, P. was unable successfully to yoke classical myth to modern experience.

P.'s memoir, *Voices,* published in 1983, portrays a true cosmopolite, a man of letters with rich and varied experience comparable to Vladimir NABOKOV and Lawrence Durrell. In addition to his other literary pursuits, P. tried his hand as translator, an occupation well suited to his talent and temperament. The works he chose to translate—Euripides' *Medea,* the *Love Sonnets* of the 16th-c. French poetess Louise Labé,

and poetry by Hölderlin—say a good deal about his literary values.

BIBLIOGRAPHY: O'Connor, R. H., "F. P.," in Quartermain, P., ed., *DLB,* vol. 48, *American Poets, 1880–1945* (1986): 344–50; Squires, R., *F. P.* (1964)

ALLEN HIBBARD

PROSE POEM, The

Strictly speaking, the prose poem as a distinct genre emerges in response to the strictures of 19th-c. French academicism. At its core, the prose poem is an oppositional form, as one can see in various works of Bertrand, Baudelaire, and Rimbaud. It is also an experimental form, with the primary experiment being one in which conventional expectations of either prose or poetry are thwarted in the interest of saying what could otherwise not be said. In the early 20th c., the French prose poem became for American poets a model of the rebellion and experimentation that characterized what they imagined as the modern in poetry. Throughout the remainder of the century it has remained a genre where avant-garde gesture has upon occasion turned into brilliant and disturbing hybrid forms of writing.

The American imagination was in a sense fertile ground for the prose poem from the beginning. Long before the French revolt against academicism, there had been in this country a tradition of what we might call a prose approaching the condition of poetry. Ironically, the earliest examples might be Puritan sermons and reflections. In a more secular and democratic vein, the essays of Ralph Waldo EMERSON are clearly organized by a poetic sensibility in which refrain and image are more prominent than syllogism and argument. Tocqueville's intuition that in democracies all inherited artistic forms are likely to lose their force of meaning proved true in the imaginative life of this country. Walt WHITMAN was the foremost example of this, and there is little doubt that his prefaces and essays were the true precursor of 20th-c. prose poems. MODERNISM, for all of its conservative biases, had behind it an impulse to declare independence from the dogma of inherited forms. The prose poem then could not help but prove attractive as inspiration. It provided what seemed to be a usable form, one that provided in its very being a way to avoid subservience to the past.

The first self-aware prose poems by an American writer were probably those of Gertrude STEIN in *Tender Buttons.* Ostensibly a sketchbook of verbal still-life portraits, the fundamental poetic strategy of these writings was in her disjunctive syntax and dislocated semantics. The result are prose pieces that are composed

917

out of fragments of perception that rhythmically sound like poems, though they look like prose. Probably inspired by Picasso's cubist experimentation, *Tender Buttons* may very well have been a lightly disguised set of erotic perceptions and lesbian feelings, just barely visible through the dazzling, foregrounded shards of syntax. If so, Stein's aesthetic gestures had indeed joined to an equally rebellious emotional content.

The revolt against the Genteel Tradition was a central energy in the emergence of American modernism, and no writer found more artistic sustenance in that revolt than William Carlos WILLIAMS. The prose poems served Williams very well in his early years of struggle as an artist. In 1918, he wrote *Kora in Hell,* a book-length collection of prose poems that grew out of a daily free-associational writing practice during that last year of World War II. These pieces are in a stream-of-consciousness mode, and many of them have a broken narrative element lurking in the background. There are no or few plot devices, and certainly few clues as to what this book is all about. Nevertheless there is a moment-to-moment vividness in these prose pieces, in which the narrator above all seems delighted by having found a form in which he can represent his inner turmoil. Williams claimed that in the American cultural climate he felt like Persephone being driven underground. This was a metaphor for his psychic distress, but also his artistic uncertainties. *Kora in Hell* was, in effect, an effort at discovering what poetry actually consisted of, once one stripped away the decorative, the consoling, and the traditional. The answer for Williams in this book, and throughout his work, was that the poem was or would be faithful to the moment-by-moment inner or underground life of the psyche.

The work of Stein and Williams included the most important American prose poems of the era, but these writers were not the only Americans to experiment with the form. A partial list would have to include Amy LOWELL, Sherwood ANDERSON, Hilda DOOLITTLE, and T. S. ELIOT among many others. From 1930 to 1960, however, the prose poem in the U.S. went into minor eclipse, overshadowed to a considerable extent by a reification of Modernist concepts by the so-called New Criticism. Emanating mostly from academia during a time when American universities experienced an enormous period of expansion, the New Criticism favored the well made, explicable literary artifact as opposed to the improvisational and more ephemeral hybrid of the prose poem. The genre made a resurgence, however, during the 1960s, a time when rebellion and experimentation once again became virtues unto themselves.

Of the many American poets to reclaim the prose poem in the 1960s and 1970s, the most important

contributions were made by Robert BLY. In a remarkable series of prose poems beginning with *The Morning Glory* and continuing into *This Body Is Made of Camphorwood and Gopherwood,* Bly used the prose poem as a matrix in which images would shuttle back and forth between the unconscious and conscious dimensions of mind. These poems had the crystal clarity of dream, but above all the dynamic of them was to—in Bly's words—"leap" from one domain of thought and feeling to another, once that by virtue of the height, breadth, or depth of the leap would surprise the reader and poet alike into insight and discovery. Bly was also the paradigmatic deep image poet, and one can see how the prose poem facilitated this aspect of his overall poetic project.

Other American poets in the 1970s and the 1980s took the prose poem in the direction of surrealistic narratives. Michael Benedikt, Edwin Honig, David IGNATOW, Kenneth PATCHEN, W. S. MERWIN, and Russell Edson, each published book-length collections of prose poems. Edson alone of this group of poets worked exclusively within the prose poem form, emphasizing the way in which the prose poem narrative can be used for "cracked" fables with bizarre, counterintuitive "morals" attached to them. John ASHBERY, by contrast, in *Three Poems* found the genre congenial to the swirl of the quotidian. He claimed that this novel-length prose poem would include all that a lineated poem would tend to exclude.

The genre continues to supply individual poets with an enduring arena for experimentation, even if as the century closes the opportunities for literary rebellion have diminished. More recently, in *Black Holes, Black Stockings* (1985), Olga Broumas and Jane Miller collaborated on a prose poem in two voices, each charting the course of a lesbian love affair. In the 1980s and 1990s, the work of the so-called Language poets emanates from what seems to be an intersection of critical theory and the prose poem's traditional foregrounding of language processes. The most important practitioner of the prose poem in the 1990s, however, has been Charles SIMIC. Perhaps because he was born in Yugoslavia, Simic has always retained an interest in this genre that has proved to be so useful to Eastern European writers in general. In any case, Simic's *The World Doesn't End* is a collection of prose poems that won the Pulitzer Prize in 1990. Most of Simic's books include a prose poem or two, and the virtue of the form for him seems to be—as it has throughout the century—to be a place where he experiments with whatever he can discern of the enduring psychic energies of poetry, those that somehow have less to do with versification and more with the volcanic resources of the individual and collective unconscious.

BIBLIOGRAPHY: Benedikt, M., *The Prose Poem: An International Anthology* (1976); Bly, R., *Leaping Po-*

etry (1972); Edson, R., "The Prose Poem in America," Parnassus 5 (Fall-Winter 1976): 321–25; Fredman, S., Poet's Prose (1986); Friebert, S., and D. Young, eds., Models of the Universe: An Anthology of the Prose Poem (1995); Monroe, J., A Poverty of Objects (1987); Murphy, M., A Tradition of Subversion (1962)

FRED MARCHANT

PROULX, E[dna] Annie
b. 22 August 1935, Norwich, Connecticut

Rarely has a writer received such critical acclaim and popular success for one novel as P. received for *The Shipping News* (1993). The book won her the Pulitzer Prize, the National Book Award, and the Irish Times International Fiction Award, and sold over a million copies in hardcover and paperback. P.'s ability to tell a startlingly honest story with poetic and powerful language has earned her much deserved acclaim.

A historian and journalist before she became a novelist, P. conducts extensive research and travels widely for each of her books. Her careful depiction of the wilderness of the American landscape testifies to her dedication to the outdoors. New England claims her roots, but P. has traveled the country exploring the land where her protagonists live and work.

P.'s portrait of American life is often violent and tragic, pathetic and poignant. She depicts poor working class families facing the agony of lives that fail to measure up to any semblance of the American dream. *Heart Songs* (1988), P.'s short story collection, paints rural New England with the broad strokes of farm failure, dilapidated trailers, and simmering family turmoil. In the world P. creates, the fates are forever conspiring to test the will of America's downtrodden.

Winner of the 1993 PEN/Faulkner Award, *Postcards* (1992), P.'s first novel, traces members of the Blood family from the turn of the century to the present. New England farmers, the Bloods become victims of agricultural reform that renders their traditions obsolete and their way of life extinct. The Bloods must adapt to change or perish, and the family begins to crumble as one by one each family member leaves the farm for an alternative chance at happiness and survival. Loyal Blood, the eldest son who sets off this chain of leave-taking, journeys across the country only to meet the alienation and loneliness of a wandering existence. Threaded through the novel and structuring its fragments of lives in desolation are postcards from across the map, artifacts of a family whose communication over decades has been reduced to cryptic sentences scribbled on cards.

P.'s sense of place is crucial to her fiction. When P. visited Newfoundland on a fishing trip, its landscape inspired the setting for *The Shipping News*. Quoyle, a third-rate newspaperman, invests love and life in his failure of a marriage but is set free by his wife's accidental death to explore the possibility of hope for himself and his two daughters. He gravitates toward his ancestral Newfoundland where he meets the comfort and quiet joy of another chance at life, discovering happiness for the first time despite the frigid and sparse terrain.

Accordion Crimes (1994) presents a mosaic of ethnic immigrants set in pockets of America as diverse as the immigrants themselves. The characters hail from Sicily, Germany, Mexico, France via Canada, Africa (via slavery), Poland, and Norway, and each faces the delusion of New World promise. Their nine stories are connected by a green accordion that changes hands throughout the novel, making its way from a violent New Orleans ghetto to Iowa farmland, then to Texas, Maine and Louisiana over one hundred years. As if cursed by the accordion's touch, the characters and their descendants meet with random violence and tragic twists of fate, meanwhile surrendering their cultural heritage for the label "American." As the green accordion finally remains discarded on the side of a highway, its hidden treasure of $14,000 undiscovered between its pleats, so too are the dreams and identity of immigrant Americans and their descendants sentenced to disintegration in American society.

PATRICIA MONTALBANO

PROUTY, Olive Higgins
b. 7 January 1882, Worcester, Massachusetts; d. 25 March 1974, Brookline, Massachusetts

Widely read as popular women's fiction in her own lifetime, P.'s novels were eclipsed for many decades by two classic Hollywood film adaptations of her work, *Stella Dallas,* and *Now, Voyager,* produced in 1937 and 1942, respectively. While feminist film critics have used both in extensive theoretical debates over female agency, melodrama, and the "women's picture," only in recent years has feminist literary criticism turned to P.'s original texts.

Stella Dallas (1922) and *Now, Voyager* (1941) both articulate P.'s preoccupations with class, motherhood, and, increasingly, with depression and recovery. Although P. ultimately regarded herself—and was regarded by critics—as a writer of "light fiction," many of her twelve books, spanning *Bobbie, General Manager* (1913) to *Fabia* (1951), attempt to unravel the complex motivations behind seemingly eccentric acts. For critics, these efforts were melodramatic at best, classist at worst; but P.'s reading public continued to buy her work, sending *Lisa Vale* (1938) to the best-seller list. Several of her other popular works also focused on the Vale clan. Her most well known novel, *Stella Dallas* sold steadily for decades and has been reshaped to fit almost all the century's media, from magazine, novel, stage, and radio to three film adaptations (1925, 1937, 1992).

The P. universe is a white, upper-middle class environment where female protagonists struggle to attain personal fulfillment against class and gender odds. An early contemplation of class (im)mobility and motherhood, *Stella Dallas* contrasts the successful social ascent of Laurel Dallas to her mother, Stella's, utter failure. Frequently read as a fable of maternal sacrifice and class snobbery, this novel both suggests that class barriers are insurmountable and critiques such exclusiveness, creating sympathy for Stella as a innocent woman misjudged by a shallow middle class. Such contradictions often mislead today's readers and probably account for P.'s critical dismissal. However, P.'s ultimate emphasis on Stella's unselfish motives and her compassion for her character suggest the same feminism that had guided P.'s novel, *Fifth Wheel* (1916).

Another P. eccentric, *Now Voyager*'s Charlotte Vale, suffers a nervous breakdown due to an overbearing mother and recovery at the hands of an unconventional psychiatrist. Having suffered severe depressions in her own life, P. details Charlotte's recovery and her subsequent creation of an alternative nuclear family in which Charlotte raises her married lover's legitimate child—but severs the extramarital affair on moral grounds. Long dismissed as melodrama, P.'s novel uses romantic genre expectations to confound gender ideology by having Charlotte reject the "normal" family in favor of one of her own making.

Wealthy through both family inheritance and print popularity, P. spent her later years as a philanthropist. She established, among other things, a scholarship at her alma mater, Smith College, that would go to the young Sylvia PLATH. Simultaneously resistant to and ruled by the gender conventions of her social position, P. may never have become the literary writer she had envisioned in her youth. Yet her novels demonstrate how popular women's fiction, long dismissed as simply conservative, can actually negotiate and challenge the class and gender ideals of its time period.

BIBLIOGRAPHY: Chandler, K. M., "Agency and Stella Dallas: Audience, Melodramatic Directives, and Social Determinism in 1920s America," *ArQ* 51 (Winter 1995): 27–44

                                          EDIE THORNTON

PURDY, James [Amos]
b. 17 July 1923, Ohio

P. has described his work as "an underground river which is flowing often undetected through the American landscape"—an apt metaphor in more than one sense. P.'s novels anticipated by a quarter century today's straightforward treatment of outré subjects. He has focused on barely hidden currents beneath the surface of American life—currents of sexuality and perversity, as well as of compassion, love, and spiritual transformation. P. is also "underground" in the sense that he is largely unknown beyond a circle of admirers and devoted readers. He attributes this to the hostility of a "hidebound" literary establishment, with which he has engaged in "a kind of endless open warfare" for thirty years. Despite obscurity, he has been steadily productive, publishing novels, stores, poems, plays, and commentary.

P.'s earliest works, eventually combined as *63: Dream Palace: A Novella and Nine Stories* (1956), were printed by a subsidy publisher in the U.S., but then championed by Dame Edith Sitwell and published by a major London house. His writings continue to be better known and more widely praised in Europe than in the U.S. *63: Dream Palace* also established a major motif: orphaned or abandoned young men who make their way (eventually to death) in a world where everyone is out to exploit them. *Malcolm* (1959), probably P.'s best-known work, treats the adventures of its abandoned young man as a comic picaresque, told in a flat objective style that renders ambiguous events even more disturbing. Its intimations of "pederasty" also emphasize P.'s theme of the exploitation between generations. In *The Nephew* (1961), the eponymous orphan, missing in action, doesn't appear at all; the novel recounts attempts by an aunt in his hometown of Rainbow Center to organize a written tribute to him. Thus, P. emphasizes the difficulties of the memoirist and provides a basis for satire of the American small town—both common motifs in subsequent work.

Two novels of the 1960s elicited extreme reactions from reviewers. *Cabot Wright Begins* combines the objective presentation of a rapist's exploits with harsh satire of the New York literary establishment. *Eustace Chisholm and the Works* (1968) has been compared to Dickens in its rich tapestry of the world of Depression-era Chicago; its straightforward presentation of bisexuality and homosexuality again alienated many reviewers. The novels that followed tended toward small-town settings, satire, and an increasing Gothic strain. *Jeremy's Version* (1970) and *The House of the Solitary Maggot* (1974) were intended to launch a larger satirical project called "Sleepers in Moon-Crowned Valley," but they have been the only two installments. *In a Shallow Grave* (1976), *Narrow Rooms* (1978), and *Mourners Below* (1981) present macabre events in forms approaching fairy tale. They follow from P.'s most overtly fable-like work, *I Am Elijah Thrush* (1974). These allegorical works of the 1970s also develop, amid the horrors of their plots, P.'s theme of the transforming power of love. This is perhaps clearest in *In a Shallow Grave,* where a horribly disfigured veteran is brought back literally and metaphorically to human form by the ministrations of a young drifter with whom he falls in love. The style of this novel reflects the influence of the Bible.

P. has sought to capture "common American speech"; his vernacular style, which has been compared to Mark TWAIN's, is distinctive. *On Glory's Course* (1985) is his most stylistically experimental novel, seeking to capture flamboyant idioms of the American Midwest in the 1930s. Nominated for the PEN/Faulkner Prize, this novel was also widely criticized as stilted and unreadable. P. continues to be productive, publishing *In the Hollow of His Hand* (1986), *Garments the Living Wear* (1989), and *Out with the Stars* (1993), as well as stories, poetry, and plays.

Some of P.'s poems, set to music by Richard Hundley and Robert Helps, have been widely performed. *Malcolm* was successfully dramatized by Edward ALBEE, and *In a Shallow Grave* was filmed. Though he remains a coterie writer, in recent years, P.'s work has begun to attract more critical attention, particularly by critics of gay literature. Although P. rejects the "gay fiction" label—"a writer is a writer"—he nevertheless was pleased when England's Gay Men's Press republished three of his books, since "they do publish only things of literary value."

BIBLIOGRAPHY: Adams, S., *J. P.* (1976); Chupack, H., *J. P.* (1975); Schwarzschild, B., *"The Not Right House": Essays on J. P.* (1968); Tanner, T., *City of Words* (1971)

GLEN M. JOHNSON

PURITANISM

The term "Puritan" was first used in the 16th c. to disparage dissenters who believed that the Church of England had been corrupted by certain rituals and customs that suggested a lingering Catholic influence inimical to Protestant theology. Persecuted for their refusal to use the Book of Common Prayer, wear clerical vestments, submit to a centralized ecclesiastical authority, or adopt any practices that did not have explicit biblical origins, many Puritan ministers and their followers fled England and settled throughout Europe in the early years of the 17th c. Fearing further oppression and despairing of ever purifying the Anglican Church at home, in 1620 a small group of Puritans decided to separate from the Church and emigrate to America. They settled in New England at Plymouth and elected William BRADFORD their first governor. Ten years later, these settlers were joined in America by a larger group of Puritans who formed the Massachusetts Bay Colony under the leadership of John WINTHROP. These communities quickly proliferated as the population increased and as congregations repeatedly split to found new towns and villages throughout the region, each under the guidance of its own minister.

Though not theocracies, most colonies in New England were dominated by Puritan mores and doctrine. To be sure, not all of the English in Massachusetts Bay were Puritans or even sympathetic to the hegira. Even in the earliest waves of immigration, the Puritans were always a minority, surrounded by a variety of religions, European nationalities, and native peoples of the region. Nevertheless, though constantly challenged by the increasingly secular and heterogenous population of the colonies, the Puritans maintained their hegemony by restricting voting and public office to church members and by viciously persecuting dissenters and Indians. Puritanism thus dominated the intellectual and political life of New England throughout the 17th c. It was not until the early years of the 18th c., after a new colonial charter had undermined the political independence of the Colony and after Enlightenment ideas had found their way across the Atlantic, that Puritanism lost its preeminence in the public discourse of New England.

Colonial Puritans seldom agreed about every tenet of their theology, and over the years even some of their most basic principles, such as the basis for church membership, changed significantly. Yet all forms of Puritanism were characterized by doctrines that reflect the Calvinist origins of most Protestant theology: the division of humanity into groups of the Elect and the damned, a belief in free grace as opposed to a doctrine of works, and predestination. In addition, the work of the most important Puritan immigrants is distinguished by the peculiarly American emphasis on a typological vision of history that casts the colonial Puritans as a community of "visible saints" whose lives reflect the patterns of Old Testament "types" and who are joined together in a national covenant between God and New England. As Winthrop put it in a sermon he preached to the colonists just before they landed, "the Lord will be our God and delight to dwell among us, as his own people and will command a blessing upon us in all our ways . . . we shall be as a City upon a Hill." This faith in the exceptional status of the Puritan nation would eventually become a central premise in American nationalism and remains the most influential contribution of Puritanism to American literature and culture. For the Puritans, however, with that privileged status also came a terrible responsibility. As Winthrop warned, "the eyes of all people are upon us; so that if we shall deal falsely with our god in this work . . . and so cause him to withdraw his present help from us, we shall be made a story and a by-word through the world."

This combination of divine promise with the threat of imminent failure characterizes much colonial Puritan writing, especially for the second and third generation of settlers. Most often, it is expressed as a persistent sense of decline from some prior state of spiritual rectitude and as a threat of catastrophe if the original ways are abandoned. The union of promise and threat serves as the distinctive focus of the jeremiad sermon, one of the most powerful and influential genres in New England. It also pervades the greatest history of the Puritan settlement, Bradford's *Of Plymouth Plantation,* and it is the driving force in the most popular poem published in the first century of American literature, Michael WIGGLESWORTH's apocalyptic *Day of Doom.*

Puritan writing was not exclusively theological. The colonial Puritans were a highly literate and well-educated group who shared the tastes and reading habits of most English men and women of their time, and they produced a surprisingly large amount of writing for frontier settlers. Most of the published work is histories and sermons, but colonial Puritans also wrote a prodigious number of biographies, scientific tracts, diaries and journals, and captivity narratives. In addition, they wrote poetry in genres as various as the religious epic, meditative lyrics, public and private elegies, occasional verse, and anagrams and acrostics. Colonial writers seldom if ever succeeded in matching the extraordinary aesthetic accomplishments of the Protestant poets and essayists of the time in England, but their work was published regularly in London and well respected in most literary, theological, and scientific circles.

Despite their participation in this broader literary culture, most Puritan writers in colonial New England subordinated aesthetic refinement to religious instruction. This attitude was especially evident in their poetry. In Wigglesworth's *Day of Doom,* sinners are condemned and the Elect exalted in a crude ballad meter: "It's now high time that ev'rey Crime / be brought to punishment: / Wrath long contain'd, and oft restrain'd, / at last must have a vent." And in the *Bay Psalm Book* (1640), a new translation of Psalms that became the second most popular book of colonial verse, a preface warns the reader "If therefore the

verses are not always so smooth and elegant as some may desire or expect; let them consider that God's Altar needs not our polishings."

This emphasis on what Thomas HOOKER called the "meat" rather than the "sauce" of literary expression discouraged aesthetic pursuits for their own sake, but a few Colonists managed to turn the contradictions and complexities of Puritan theology into poetic works of extraordinary skill and subtlety. The most important of these poets were Anne BRADSTREET and Edward TAYLOR. Bradstreet's *The Tenth Muse Lately Sprung up in America,* published in London, was the first volume of poems written by an English colonist, and its skillful adaptation of British and European poetic forms and topoi was widely admired on both sides of the Atlantic. In her later poems, Bradstreet focused on more intimate details of her personal experience in New England, and she often addressed the inevitable tension between the unyielding rigor of Puritan doctrine and the tragic vagaries of life in the New World. Her elegy on her grandson Simon and the earlier deaths of two other grandchildren puts this conflict starkly in jolting hemistichs that reflect the conflict between emotion and belief: "No sooner come, but gone, and fal'n asleep, / Acquaintance short, yet parting caus'd us weep, / Three flours, two scarcely blown, the last i'th' bud, / Cropt by th' Almighties hand; yet is he good, / With dreadful awe before him let's be mute, / Such was his will, but why, let's not dispute."

Unlike Bradstreet, the Puritan minister Taylor was unknown as a poet during his lifetime because his poetry was not published until the manuscripts were discovered in 1937. His best works are the two lengthy series of "Prepatory Meditations" that he composed to prepare himself for the Lord's Supper. The theme of sacramental transformation consequently figures prominently in these poems, often in association with a plea for God's help in translating the degraded language of human speech into divine song. The poems also rely extensively on typological parallels, scriptural imagery, and the extended metaphors popularized by the metaphysical poets in England, as in this meditation which plays on the image of an old English gold coin known as an "Angel-noble": "Lord, make my Soule thy Plate: thine Image bright / Within the Circle of the same enfoile. / And on its brims in golden Letters write / Thy Superscription in an Holy Style. / Then I shall be thy Money, thou my Hord: / Let me thy Angell bee, bee thou my Lord."

Puritan prose similarly reflected the general styles and tastes of its time, usually focused on theological themes. The SERMON was the most popular prosaic form and made up almost half of all the books published in New England during the first century of settlement. The Puritan sermon was invariable in structure, always proceeding from scriptural citation and commentary to the application of the theological principles to everyday life. It also followed the relentless patterns of Ramist logic in its classification of topics and subdivision of points. What kept the Puritan sermon from being simply an abstract ministerial exercise was the emphasis on a plain style that would be accessible to everyone in the congregation and the strategic use of concrete sensory imagery to drive home the doctrinal points. In the hands of masters such as Hooker, John Cotton, Thomas SHEPARD, and John Norton, the power of the plain style could be formidable, as in this passage from Hooker's *Application of Redemption:* "Suppose that all miseries and sorrows that ever befel all the wicked in / Earth and Hell, should meet together in one soule, as all waters gathered / together in one Sea: Suppose thou heardest the Devils roaring, and sawest / Hell gaping, and the flames of everlasting burnings flashing before thine / eyes; it's certain it were better for thee to be cast into those / inconceivable torments than to commit the least sin against the Lord."

The principal objective of the Puritan sermon was to recall the sinner to Christ and the community to what the minister Samuel Danforth called New England's "errand into the wilderness." The description of that wilderness and the Puritans' journey through it fell to the historians, who began their work in the earliest days of settlement and continued well into the next century. The first history composed by a colonial Puritan was Bradford's *Of Plymouth Plantation,* which he began in 1630. Bradford's purpose was to portray the Puritans' experience at Plymouth as the story of God's providence, but the complexity of events complicated this plan so much that he simply abandoned his project twenty years later without finishing it.

The first published history of New England was Edward JOHNSON's *Wonder-Working Providence of Sions Saviour in New-England.* Part chronicle, part millennialist epic, Johnson's work vacillates—at times wildly—between detailed accounts of life on the American frontier and apocalyptic visions of the Last Judgment. Blithely ignoring the complications that plagued Bradford, Johnson portrays New England as the site of the new Heaven and new Earth foretold by scripture, and he imagines his history to be preparing its readers for that later transformation. A similarly exalted purpose underlies the greatest of all Puritan histories, Cotton MATHER's *Magnalia Christi Americana.* One of the most prolific of all Puritan writers with over 450 publications to his name, Cotton Mather presents the *Magnalia* as an encyclopedia of Christ's great works in America—the literal translation of the title—and as a Virgilian epic that would establish the spiritual and historical identity of New England. The style of the *Magnalia* matches this epic ambition, for in it can be found quotations from classical authors (in Greek and Latin) alongside scriptural quotations (in Hebrew as well as English), descriptions of the most spectacular miracles and wonders, praise for acts of providence and divine deliverance, and extended biographies of Puritan ministers, governors, and most other important people from the first century of colonization. Mather uses these lives to piece together a colonial eschatology in which individuals embody the collective mission of the Puritan enterprise, and together their separate histories reveal the universal shape of God's timeless plan. The revelation of that plan is at hand as the *Magnalia* concludes with Mather's proclamation of "a Revolution and a Reformation at the very door" and with his promise that the *Magnalia*'s metaphorical union between this world and next will soon be realized in the apocalypse.

Many Puritans remained in positions of power and authority well into the 18th c., but their theology was becoming increasingly diverse and so harder to identify as "Puritan" apart from the more general Protestantism of the growing colonies. At the same time, Puritans' influence on the literary and cultural life of the colonies was rapidly displaced by the increasing importance of Enlightenment ideas and neoclassical tastes. Jonathan EDWARDS was the last Puritan to make a significant impact on American intellectual traditions, and his Puritanism is so laden with the assumptions of Lockean empiricism that the barrier between the worlds of flesh and spirit—a defining principle of colonial Puritanism throughout the 17th c.—often collapses as theological concepts are derived from sensible experience. This difference is evident if we read the preceding passage from Hooker's *Application of Redemption* alongside this paragraph from Edward's most famous sermon, "Sinners in the Hands of an Angry God," preached in 1741: "The wrath of God is like great waters that are damned for the present; they increase more and more, and rise higher and higher, till an outlet is given; and the longer the stream is stopped, the more rapid and mighty is its course . . . if God should only withdraw his hand from the flood-gate, it would immediately fly open, and the fiery floods of the fierceness and wrath of God, would rush forth with inconceivable fury . . . and if your strength were ten thousand times greater than it is, yea ten thousand times greater than the strength of the stoutest, sturdiest devil in hell, it would be nothing to withstand or endure it."

Hooker invoked the image of gathering waters simply to illustrate a spiritual concept that exists independently of the simile, and he concludes by insisting on their difference: it is better to experience flood and flames than to sin against the Lord. Edwards, on the other hand, moves quickly from the opening simile to a metaphor in which God's wrath confronts the reader through the sensible experience of the flood, and the rest of the passage conveys the power of God's wrath directly through the empirical sensations evoked by the concrete terms. This faith in the connection between spiritual ideas and physical sensations was antithetical to the earlier Puritans' insistence on the priority of spirit over flesh, and it suggests an interest in human experience and perception that was foreign to the Puritans' sense of themselves and their destiny. In the hands of less careful theologians than Edwards, this interest quickly evolved into the taste for religious enthusiasm and evangelical preaching of the Great Awakenings that parodied the populist objectives of the Puritan plain style and ignored its logical structure. It also found more serious and philosophical expression in rationalist analysis and empirical observation that characterized the American Enlightenment and that finally displaced Puritanism from the center of intellectual life in New England.

BIBLIOGRAPHY: Bercovitch, S., *Puritan Origins of the American Self* (1975); Gay, P., *A Loss of Mastery: Puritan Historians in Colonial America* (1966); Kibbey, A., *The Interpretation of Material Shapes in Puritanism: A Study of Rhetoric, Prejudice, and Violence* (1986); Knight, J., *Orthodoxies in Massachusetts: Rereading American Puritanism* (1994); Miller, P., *The New England Mind: The Seventeenth Century* (1939); Miller, P., *The New England Mind: From Colony to Province* (1953); Scheick, W., *Design in Puritan American Literature* (1992): Schweitzer, I., *The Work of Self-Representation: Lyric Poetry in Colonial New England* (1991); White, P., ed., *Puritan Poets and Poetics* (1985)

MICHAEL P. CLARK

PUZO, Mario
b. 15 October 1920, New York City

P. did more to shape the contemporary paperback best seller than did any other popular American author of the 1960s and 1970s. His novels, when optioned for paperback release, helped to introduce the so-called big money payoffs for those authors who achieved success on the national best seller lists. Even before P.'s fourth novel, *Fools Die,* was published in hardcover in October 1978, the then-astronomical sum of 2.2 million dollars was paid by New American Library for the paperback rights. In addition, in novels such as *The Godfather* (1969), *The Sicilian* (1984), and *The Last Don* (1996), P. reinvented and refined the mythology of the American gangster, elevating the Mafia racketeer to the stature of epic tragic hero. As P. himself proclaims in an interview for the Associated Press published in 1996: "My Mafia is a very romanticized myth." P. also enjoyed success as a Hollywood screenwriter, receiving two Academy Awards for his work on the Francis Ford Coppola films, *The Godfather* (1972) and *The Godfather, Part II* (1974).

Born in the Hell's Kitchen district of New York City's West Side, P.'s accomplishments as a best-selling novelist and an award-winning screenplay writer seem to parallel somewhat the Horatio ALGER "rags to riches" story that P. himself adopts for his Mafia protagonist, Don Vito Corleone, in *The Godfather*. P. served in the U.S. Army Air Force during World War II, and he attended the New School for Social Research in New York City, as well as Columbia University. His first two novels—*The Dark Arena* (1955), a melodrama set in postwar Germany, and *The Fortunate Pilgrim* (1965), a novel about Italian immigrants living in New York City during the Great Depression—generated much critical praise, but little money, so P. decided that for his third novel he would write a book that appealed more to a wide readership than to the literary critics. As P. remarked in a Larry King interview aired on CNN on August 2, 1996, he wanted to become a storyteller first, and then become an artist of the language second. Even his severest detractors agree that P. readily achieved his first objective, though he perhaps failed to reach his second.

The result of P.'s efforts to write a popular story was *The Godfather,* the first of his five best-selling novels, which earned him nearly a half million dollars in paperback advance money. Though frequently described as the quintessential gangster novel, *The Godfather* is actually about the importance of family; it is as much a domestic melodrama as it is a crime melodrama: the story of Michael Corleone's personal tribulations as he assumes leadership of his powerful family's "business." In addition, the novel explores the immigrant experience in the U.S. that was such an important event for so many American families. Ultimately, *The Godfather*'s wide appeal can be attributed to people's fascination with and desire for power. It offers a modern-day fairy tale in which a benevolent tyrant, Don Vito (and later, Don Michael), is able to cut through the bureaucratic "red tape" of American politics and the courts to enact a simple, yet powerful (and often violent), social code of honor. Indeed, the subject of the use and abuse of power is a theme that runs through most of P.'s work, from his Mafia fiction—including *The Sicilian* (1984), which recounts the events surrounding Michael Corleone's two-year exile in Sicily—to his fast-paced political thriller, *The Fourth K* (1991).

BIBLIOGRAPHY: Ferraro, T. J., "Blood in the Marketplace: The Business of Family in the *Godfather* Narratives," in Sollors, W., ed., *The Invention of Ethnicity* (1989): 176–208; Viscusi, R., "Debate in the Dark: Love in Italian-American Fiction," in Massa, A., ed., *American Declarations of Love* (1990): 155–73

GARY HOPPENSTAND

PYNCHON, Thomas
b. 8 May 1937, Glen Cove, New York

The remarkably solid reputation of P. rests on five novels published between 1963 and 1997. Devotees have discovered that the historically based *Mason & Dixon* (1997) is in the tradition of an already acknowledged masterpiece, *Gravity's Rainbow* (1973). Between these two came *Vineland* (1990). P.'s career began with two novels: *V.* (1963) and *The Crying of Lot 49* (1966). In 1984, there appeared a group of five earlier stories, *Slow Learner*. Its primary value is a long introduction in which P. describes the composition of the stories and his critical reaction to them. Amateurish as they may be in places, the reader can see in them the seeds of his later work.

P. was raised in Glen Cove, Long Island, educated at Cornell, and served a hitch in the U.S. Navy. He published stories in his early twenties, worked for the Boeing company in the Pacific Northwest, traveled, and completed his first novel by the time he was twenty-five. His third vaulted him into the front ranks of 20th-c. writers before he was forty. Part of his notoriety—ironically—has come from his extreme reclusiveness. He has not been photographed or interviewed or recognized in public for many years. His family and friends guard his privacy as he himself cherishes it.

V., a fragmented narrative, ranges from America to West Africa to Latin America to Paris to Malta from a "present" of 1955–56 to events within the preceding century. Its major characters, Herbert Stencil, Benny Profane, and "The Whole Sick Crew" remain in flux: involved or uninvolved, "flopped or flipped," yo-yoing or searching, animated or inanimate. The object of Stencil's major pursuit, the mysterious "Lady V.," is never found, and, by novel's end, has metamorphosed into a multifaceted symbol.

In the briefer but equally complex and ambiguous *The Crying of Lot 49,* the protagonist Oedipa Maas explores the background of an estate to which she has been named executrix. In the face of intensifying entropic effects, she tries to sort out many clues emerging from the inheritance of "one Pierce Inverarity, a California real estate mogul." As her awareness grows and her quest deepens, she becomes more disaffected, "either in the orbiting ecstasy of a true paranoia or a real Tristero" (an anarchic underground communica-

tion system containing both positive and negative forces).

Dazzling pyrotechnics followed seven years later with the appearance of his masterpiece *Gravity's Rainbow,* an encyclopedic, panoramic, global novel that deliberately exploits many styles and modes and utilizes, in erudite, allusive ways, multi subjects like war, history, literature, film, engineering, comedy, science, the military-industrial complex, and international cartels. The major historical symbol unifying the novel is the V–2 rocket that couples sex and death and betokens modern civilization's obsession with technology. The parabola of the Rocket that appears first over London in World War II eventuates in a final descent as a mightier missile upon "everybody" at an apocalyptic moment of the present in Los Angeles. From the main action in 1944–45, the novel freely manipulates time, especially to formative events of the 1920s and 1930s. With side excursions to New England, Southwest Africa, Argentina, and the Russian Steppes, the bulk of the action takes place in England, France, Switzerland, Holland, and Germany. The varied plots overflow with schemes, conspiracies, spying, networks, and conglomerates.

Within a huge, moiling cast of more than three hundred, thirteen characters stand out. Touching almost every principal character of four different nationalities is the American protagonist, Lieutenant Tyronerone Slothrop, a comic but affecting antihero. His numerous sexual "conquests," perhaps more fantasized than real, give evidence of his foreknowledge of rocket hits in London. Convinced that authorities are out to get him, Slothrop escapes into the chaotic randomness of central Europe's Zone. His paranoiac flight is combined with his search for the mysterious "quintuple-zero" rocket and its facsimile, which "The Firm" also wants to find. Thus Slothrop becomes both "seeker and sought," both "baited and bait."

P. fixes his complex and recondite vision on the massive gargoyle of modern society malformed by war and political-industrial-technological chicaneries, all extensions of past malaise. Among the novel's major thematic subjects are the pervasiveness of paranoia, the damages wrought by betrayal and conspiracy, the ravages of destructiveness and waste, the potentialities for transformation, the needs for quests and searches, the contingencies of life. And more: the power of survival, the necessity for disorder, the perils of obsessiveness, the consequences of repressiveness, the entrapment of the powerless, loss of identity. These issues emerge out of the brilliant conceptual stroke of creating a war novel that is less about war than it is about how a world was and is wrought.

A change of pace occurred seventeen years later with the appearance of *Vineland*. While not as visionary or as formidable or as multileveled as *Gravity's Rainbow, Vineland* has a charm all its own. It's more accessible and appealing, a satirical, zany, warm-hearted book composed of serious sublayers. Set in a mythical place in timber country of the Northern California coast, it nevertheless contains real towns like Crescent City and Eureka. Present time is 1984 (an obvious link to George Orwell's *1984*), with flash-backs to the 1960s, a period of intense political up-heaval in the U.S., stressing governmental repression of hippies, flower children, protesters against the bur-geoning Vietnam War.

The male protagonist is Zoyd Wheeler, a forty-year-old ex-musician and vagabond, living catch-as-catch-can with his fourteen-year-old daughter Prairie. They have been separated for years from the girl's mother, Frenesi, a radical filmmaker later placed in a witness protection program, with her new husband and son. Troubles began in the 1960s, when Frenesi fell under the sway of villainous Brock Vond, a federal prosecuting attorney, a control freak, a sadistic ma-nipulator. Vond turned Frenesi into a snitch and a traitor, resulting in the murder of her lover, Weed Atman, a campus leader. Ahead to 1984, the obsessive Vond is searching for Frenesi once again. This time he's a narc leader, working for the Reagan administra-tion, bent on busting marijuana growers and ex-hippies living in the redwood country of Vineland.

As a political novel, *Vineland* sets in motion such conflicting thematic tensions as political paranoia, the dominance of the Establishment, the struggles of a counterculture (hippies, the disinherited, the poor, the homeless, the alienated). Within borders of gray, both sides are bedeviled by weaknesses and betrayals. Also, P. reveals the pernicious influence of television in America. his concern is for a populace falling under the power of a corporate state built on business and entertainment and determined to divert and distract its citizens into becoming brainwashed nonentities. P. puts the problem this way: "The ever-dwindling atten-tion span of an ever-more-infantalized population." Thus, if you are a vidiot, a mallrat, a diehard consumer the state has no more worries about you. P. also has great fun satirizing our preoccupation with violence.

In spite of its pessimistic strain as dystopian fiction, *Vineland* takes a surprising turn toward goodness, redemption, and grace. At its close, the novel drama-tizes the importance of family: the strength, domestic-ity, joy, and harmony that may be found within the cohesive bonds of family. One must still be on the alert for the Brock Vonds of the world, but hope glimmers.

The dimensions of *Vineland* are also evident in its varieties of genres and parodies of genres: California detective story, science fiction, comic book action, martial arts-ninja action, mythology, particularly on

the Yuroks, the not-quite-dead—people who have died but refuse to lie down. *Vineland,* like its progenitor *Gravity's Rainbow,* is also filled with songs, puns, bad jokes, and silly names.

In his novel, *Mason & Dixon,* P. tells the story of Charles Mason, British astronomer and geodesist, and Jeremiah Dixon, British surveyor, and of their famous eponymous line through eastern American colonies. In the next century, it defined the schism between North and South, union and secession, freedom and slavery. Although often interlarded with fanciful and surreal elements, *Mason & Dixon* is basically a histori-cal novel, presenting panoramic events in four parts of the world between 1761 and 1786. Narration occurs by a framing device in which the fictional Reverend Wicks Cherrycoke (Mason and Dixon's "Boswell" and "party chaplain") recounts their adventures to children and interested adults at the home of his sister over Christmastide of 1786 in Philadelphia. Written in late 18th-c. prose style, using complex sentence structure and punctuation and capitalization of generalized nouns in the old manner, the novel also divides itself tripartitely: One, "Latitudes and Departures" (En-gland, Transit of Venus observation at Capetown, South Africa, and data gathering at the island of St. Helena); Two, "America" (in which the line is drawn through Pennsylvania, Maryland, Delaware, Virginia, into the Allegheny Mountains from 1763 to 1768); Three; "Last Transit" (brief coda including returns to England and Pennsylvania, another transit of Venus, deaths of the two scientists in the period from 1769 to 1786).

Given P.'s predilection in *Gravity's Rainbow* for shocking acts, profanity, raw sex, this book is remark-ably sanitized and clean. A bodice is ripped here and there and the *F*-word appears sporadically, but other-wise it's *G*-rated. Moreover, there is surprisingly little concern with the previously dominant subject of para-noia. And unlike prior P. fiction, a detectable story thread (call it a picaresque plot) develops out of "the restless progress" of the two scientists. Has P. been defanged? tamed? Hardly. Because he is ingeniously versatile and flexible, he can adapt form to content for an 18th-c. period piece that demands refinement, if not expurgation as in "G-d" or "d-l." Also, he dem-onstrates an amazing knowledge of technical details of astronomy, geodesy, surveying, and mathematics.

As if to assure his readers that he is still up to his old tricks, P. again relies upon trademark tomfooleries: in the appearance of a love-crazed mechanical duck, a Learned English Dog given speech and reason, a giant runway cheese, a werebeaver named Zepho Beck, a huge conquering worm, and many more. Addi-tionally, his narrator makes use of fairy tale (two Chi-nese are transported aloft in a sky-blue kite), ghost story (the widower Mason haunted by his dead wife Rebekah), fantasy (Dixon visits the hollow center of the earth), to mention a few, and P. has fun with cameos of famous people: Benjamin FRANKLIN, wearing sun glasses, George Washington smoking hemp and singing a duet with Martha, Boswell taking down notes of a voluble Dr. Johnson.

But for all the fireworks, the inside jokes (here *joaks*), the songs and poems and puns, the bizarre episodes, this novel conveys appealing depth of characterization and carries substantial thematic weight. Both Mason and Dixon are far more humanized than previous characters. They exhibit distinctly different personalities. While Mason is "Gothically depressive," gloomy, melancholy, introverted, a brooding widower, and aloof scientist, Dixon is "Westeringly manic," cheerful, chummy, extroverted, the jovial "country lout," lapsed Quaker, and true egalitarian. In spite of the "perilous boundaries" that separate them, they make a memorable paired combination.

The novel's profound thematic subjects entail the omnipresence of violence in man, the heartlessness of colonialism, restlessness (Mason and Dixon seem in perpetual motion), the vagaries of friendship, mistreatment of Native Americans, the contradictions built into the Age of Reason (why so much irrationality and stupidity?), the Age of Enlightenment (why so much darkness and ignorance?), the outstanding advances in science, the spoilation of nature, the ills and evils of slavery (William FAULKNER called it the "curse of slavery"; P.'s term is "the worm of slavery").

The last two topics are fraught with paradox and pain. America was an untamed, primitive, virginal land; two European scientists (men of reason and good will) were commissioned by European landowners to establish precise demarcation (again, our "perilous boundaries") in a half-dozen colonies. The scar ("vistos") that they made in the land seared a young nation. Similarly, slavery created scars early in the colonies that have not healed even now in the fifty united states. Dixon's brave reaction against a vicious slave driver anticipates the later actions of abolitionists (like John Brown) all the way to Civil Rights warriors (like Martin Luther King, Jr.).

Mason & Dixon is certainly a masterpiece, and, along with *Gravity's Rainbow,* affords P. the rare distinction of having provided dual candidacy for the "Great American Novel."

BIBLIOGRAPHY: Clerc, C., ed., *Approaches to "Gravity's Rainbow"* (1983); Green, G., ed., *The "Vineland" Papers: Critical Takes on P.'s Novel* (1994); Hume, K., *P.'s Mythography* (1987); O'Donnell, P., *New Essays on "The Crying of Lot 49"* (1991); Weisenburger, S., *A "Gravity's Rainbow" Companion* (1988)

CHARLES CLERC

QUINTASKET, Christine or Christal

b. April 1888?, Bonner's Ferry, Idaho; d. 8 August 1936, Medical Lake, Washington

Considered by many to be the first Native American woman novelist, Q.—who took the pen name Mourning Dove (or "Humishima" in her Salishan tongue)—concentrated on the issues that navigation between their traditional cultures and Euro-American culture raised for Native Americans. In several literary works, most produced in collaboration with Native American enthusiast and amateur ethnographer Lucullus Virgil McWhorter, Q., who made her living primarily as a migrant worker in the northwest, stressed the continuing significance of traditional culture.

The work on which literary historians have based their claims for Q.'s priority as a Native American woman novelist appeared in 1927 with McWhorter's collaboration acknowledged on the title page. *Co-ge-we-a, the Half-Blood: A Depiction of the Great Montana Cattle Range* combines the formulas of the popular western romance with Q.'s concerns about cultural identity. The protagonist, a mixed-blood woman, learns the significance of that cultural identity through her misguided rejection of a mixed-blood suitor in favor of a Euro-American from back east. She ultimately comes to her senses and recognizes the virtues of her mixed-blood beau. Though she herself was a full-blood (her father an Okanogan, her mother a Colvile), Q. also used the novel to explore the tensions that arise from mixed-blood identity, a theme that has pervaded 20th-c. fiction produced by Native Americans. Throughout the novel, Co-ge-we-a finds that she is fully accepted neither as Euro-American nor as Native American.

Q. incorporated a variety of traditional materials from the Okanogan heritage in *Co-ge-we-a, the Half-Blood,* including beliefs and stories. Under McWhorter's urging, she had set herself the task of preserving in print this material. Another book that appeared during her lifetime reflected this effort. Though it also reflects Q.'s tendency to moralize and to expurgate the sometimes bawdy escapades of its central character, *Coyote Stories* (1933) represents what she feared was the vanishing oral literary heritage of her people. Produced with the assistance of journalist Heister Dean Guie and with notes by McWhorter, the book is a collection of traditional narratives similar to those she had grown up hearing from tribal elders.

Two other works by Q., which demonstrate her commitment to recording and thus preserving a knowledge of the traditional way of life of the Okanogans and other Salishan speakers of the Northwest, have appeared posthumously. In 1976, Donald M. Hines edited *Tales of the Okanogans* from texts that had been preserved in McWhorter's papers, and in 1990, Jay Miller edited Q.'s autobiography. The latter provides a view not only of its author's personal experience but of the culture of her people at the time that it was adapting to Euro-American influences.

BIBLIOGRAPHY: Brown, A. K., "Profile: Mourning Dove (Humishuma) 1888–1936," *Legacy* 6 (Spring 1989): 51–58; Miller, J., "Mourning Dove: The Author as Cultural Mediator," in Clifford, J., ed., *Being and Becoming Indian* (1989): 160–82

WILLIAM M. CLEMENTS

R

RABE, David [William]
b. 10 March 1940, Dubuque, Iowa

R. put the Vietnam War before the public at a divisive time in America's history. In fact, his first two plays, *The Basic Training of Pavlo Hummel* (1971) and *Sticks and Bones* (1971), opened within six months of one another. For *Pavlo Hummel,* R. earned the *Village Voice's* Obie Award for distinguished playwriting, and for *Sticks and Bones,* he received the 1972 Tony Award for best play. Since Tennessee WILLIAMS, few dramatists have had such immediate success in their careers.

R. grew up in a middle-class Catholic family, but his Midwestern values later were challenged by the upheaval of war. R. was working toward a master's degree in theater at Villanova University when he was drafted into the Army in January of 1965. He served for two years, spending his final eleven months in a hospital support group in Long Binh, South Vietnam. After being discharged, he went back to Villanova and started writing plays in which he used Vietnam as a backdrop for questions about manhood, racism, sex, and brutality.

The producer Joseph Papp risked bringing *Stick and Bones,* a sardonic updating of "The Adventures of Ozzie and Harriet," and *The Orphan* (1973) to Broadway. Because of R.'s involved connections between Aeschylus' *Oresteia* trilogy, the Charles Manson killings, and the My Lai massacres, *The Orphan* bewildered New York audiences and closed after a limited run. A fourth Vietnam play, *Streamers* (1976), established him as a leading voice in contemporary theater. R. did not conceive his Vietnam plays for any political aim or effect. He writes, "If they address anything, they address the unmooring of our lives, the drift toward cynicism and impulsive violence."

R. most often creates realistic settings in order to test established views about duty, family, and marriage. However, unlike traditional well-made plays that ad-

here to stringent cause and effect relationships to make evident their psychology, his work seeks for deeper, unconscious answers for human behavior. To this end, language generates a heightened theatricality in his writing. R.'s characters not only talk their own jargon, but also frequently jump from one topic to another, assuming that listeners know where the words are taking them. Thus, R.'s characters magically invent themselves and their destinies as they speak.

Many of these destinies end in tragedy. *Streamers* is set in a Virginia military barracks in the 1960s. Billy, a college graduate from Wisconsin, shares a cadre room with a trendy New York homosexual and an African American who hopes to better his life in the Army. Richie half-seriously professes to be attracted to Billy, yet Roger thinks that Richie is just acting "at that stuff." Along social and racial lines, Billy, Richie, and Roger create a balanced friendship until Carlyle throws himself into their mix. In the play's climactic scene, Carlyle rages into a killing spree. Frightened of dying in a jungle, the men attack one another over trivial matters. R. uses the word "streamer" to refer to a paratrooper whose chute does not open. He entwines World War II, Korea and Vietnam through this image, showing one's fall to earth is both beautiful and deadly.

Since the mid-1970s, R. has focused on the cruelty people routinely accept in their lives. In *Hurlyburly* (1984), cocaine and reckless ambitions undermine Eddie, Mickey, and Phil. Failures in their marriages, they denigrate and abuse women for turning their lives upside down. Having been brought up to compete for power and money, they are gruesomely out of place in a world that now expects them to be reserved and sensitive. They pretend to know what they are doing, but make self-destructive choices that ruin their opportunities. In his "Afterword: 1992," R. discusses the feeling of being "flung out" and of the competitive and alchemical themes that slowly evolved during revisions of the play. "Out of accidents," he contends, "is hewn destiny."

R. traverses a wide spectrum that ranges from Greek mythology to the dark underside of the night-club scene. His psychological force and social commentary rank with the best of Arthur MILLER and Eugene O'NEILL. Although critics tie the strength of his reputation to the Vietnam dramas, no other playwright of his generation has portrayed so forcefully the anger and disorientation that undercut people's lives.

BIBLIOGRAPHY: Herman, W., *Understanding Contemporary American Drama* (1987); Kolin, P., *D. R.: A Stage History and A Primary and Secondary Bibliography* (1988); Zinman, T., *D. R.: A Casebook* (1991)

JOE NORDGREN

RAND, Ayn

b. 2 February 1905, St. Petersburg, Russia; d. 6 March 1982; New York City

Born in Russia, R.'s extreme antisocialist views defined her status as a writer of both fiction and philosophical essays. In her fiction, she elevated the creative, rational egoist to almost godlike stature, notably in her most famous title *Atlas Shrugged* (1957). Her rejection of not only collectivist government but also of any form of social altruism evolved into her philosophy of rational self-interest, which she named objectivism. Although marginalized by both literary and philosophical circles, R.'s fiction has enjoyed a certain, enduring popularity, particularly among young adults and in certain conservative political circles.

Educated in Leningrad, R. emigrated to the U.S. in 1926 and worked in Hollywood as a script assistant where her first work, a play entitled *The Night of January 16th* (1936), was staged in 1934. Predating audience participation by half a century, the play ended each night with twelve members of the audience acting as jury, deciding the fate of heroine Karen Andre.

In the four works that followed, R. developed her theme of the individual against society, culminating in a comprehensive novelistic treatment of objectivism in the opus *Atlas Shrugged.* In terms of representing R.'s heroic ideal, her novels are remarkably consistent. Each features a man of incomparable ability and uncompromising individualism, pitted against the evils of collectivism, forced altruism, and mediocrity. All R.'s heroes share an unflinching faith in their own integrity. Even the naive character Equality 7–2521 in R.'s novella *Anthem* (1938) "instinctively" recognizes his outlawed scientific inquiries as an objective good. And in *The Fountainhead* (1943), defiant architect Howard Roark, R.'s most powerfully realized

hero, when asked incredulously if he has always liked being himself, answers with only a smile described as "amused, astonished [at the question] and involuntarily contemptuous."

If R.'s heroes epitomize the virtue of self-esteem, her heroines—though strong in their own right—are noted particularly for their recognition of supreme masculine virtue. In *Anthem,* the young woman Liberty 5–3000 willingly leaves for the Uncharted Forest with a young man she has barely met; *The Fountainhead*'s Dominique Francon is irresistibly drawn to the figure of Roark bent over his work in her father's drafting room; and Dagny Taggart, after having hunted in hatred the man who has stolen all the great minds in *Atlas Shrugged,* takes one look at John Galt and falls in awe.

No less consistent than her vision of the ideal man is R.'s harsh depiction of the evil of collectivism. In all her fiction, villainous collectivists deny the existence of individual achievement expressly in order to crush the spirit of the individual. In the Soviet Russia of R.'s first novel, *We, the Living* (1937), Kira Argounova, who dreams of building skyscrapers, is refused permission to enter engineering school or to leave Russia to pursue her dream elsewhere. In *Anthem,* where the repression of individuality is so complete that the word "I" has been obliterated, Equality 7–2521 is punished for his natural curiosity by being assigned the job of street cleaner for life. And *The Fountainhead* opens with the expulsion of Howard Roark, by committee vote, of course, from architecture school.

The one feature of which R. seemed less certain was the likelihood of triumph for her characters and her ideals. Her first novel, *We the Living,* set in post-revolutionary Russia, is her bleakest. All three of her major characters are destroyed or killed, including Kira, the heroine of this loosely autobiographical work, who is shot attempting to escape across the border at the novel's end. *Anthem* offers a somewhat more hopeful outcome—although its young hero has no hope of changing his closed minded society, at least he can escape, albeit into a mysterious Uncharted Forest.

The Fountainhead is in some respects romantic in its optimism; it not only allows its hero personal triumph—Roark, who has blown up a housing project because the sponsors have altered its design from his original, is exonerated by a jury—but it also shows faith in the good sense of ordinary people—the jury's verdict represents their honest recognition of Roark's virtue in spite of a tremendous media campaign against him. Nevertheless, it is a partial triumph only. Roark does not defeat the collectivists. He only defies them. The mediocre leech, Peter Keating, still benefits from association with Roark, and the malevolent news columnist, Ellsworth Toohey, will continue to decry all that Roark stands for. It will remain for *Atlas Shrugged,* R.'s last and most ambitious novel, to resolve the problem for the true objectivist of benefitting a society that doesn't deserve it.

Atlas Shrugged presents R.'s utopian vision, but the majority of the thousand-page book is concerned with the gradual crumbling of society when all its thinkers, producers, and creative individuals depart, in a "strike of the mind," leaving an unappreciative and incompetent collective that, having no one left to leech off, has no means of survival. The story recounts the odyssey of railroad executive Dagny Taggart and steel industrialist Hank Reardon as they seek to account for the mysterious disappearances guided only by the cryptic clue, "Who is John Galt?"

Atlas Shrugged is at times an exciting and challenging work. However, R.'s philosophical intent produces an overlong, often turgid presentation. At the height of dramatic action, the story is interrupted for a fifty-seven page exegesis (represented as John Galt's ninety-minute radio broadcast) on the theory of objectivism.

After 1957, R. produced no more works of fiction, instead concentrating on philosophical essays, many of which appeared along with excerpts from her fiction and other writings in her collections including *For the New Intellectual* (1961), *The Virtue of Selfishness* (1964), *Capitalism: The Unknown Ideal* (1966), and *The Romantic Manifesto* (1969). She also published the *Objectivist Newsletter* (1966–71), later called the *Objectivist* in conjunction with Nathaniel and Barbara Branden.

R.'s rejection of any form of social altruism has generally left her beyond the pale of a reasonable, compassionate society. Furthermore, her romanticization of rape as a seductive force, and her depiction of strong women whose fulfillment is dependent upon stronger men make her anathema to feminist sensibility.

Nevertheless, it is R.'s essential message of self-worth that accounts for her great attraction for many readers, particularly young women. And her conservative views have always appealed to some segments of society, no less now with the fall of the Iron Curtain and the ascendency of neoconservatives who call for tax reductions and an end to social welfare.

BIBLIOGRAPHY: Branden, B., *The Passion of A. R.* (1986); Merrill, R. E., *The Ideas of A. R.* (1991); Peikoff, L., *Objectivism: The Philosophy of A. R.* (1991); Sciabarra, C. M., *A. R.: The Russian Radical* (1995)

                                    GRETA WAGLE

RANDALL, Dudley [Felker]

b. 14 January 1914, Washington, D.C.

As one of the poets committed to the belief that politics and art should be wed, R. brought to the forefront the ideas that helped to shape the black aesthetic in the 1960s. Thus, much of his poetry sought to effect social insight and change. Entrenched at an early age in both the oral and political traditions of African Americans by his father, a Congregationalist minister, R. created verses reflecting this influence.

R. was not only a creator of poetry but also a founder and editor of the Broadside Press in Detroit, where he produced single sheets or leaflets of poems called broadsides that he printed and sold at a low cost. In addition, his role as editor and founder of the press allowed him to make one of his greatest contributions to the advancement of AFRICAN AMERICAN LITERATURE: he facilitated the publishing of several poets who later had a notable impact on African American poetry, including Haki MADHUBUTI; Sonia SANCHEZ; Nikki GIOVANNI; and Etheridge KNIGHT. His press published first books for both Madhubuti and Knight. Additionally, the Pulitzer Prize-winning Gwendolyn BROOKS, used the services of Broadside to publish her autobiography instead of those of a more established publisher, such as Random House.

Though much of his poetry emphasized a commitment to social and political themes, it had quite an extensive range. One of his first collections of poems, *Poem Counterpoem* (1966), which he wrote with Margaret Danner, used a unique approach, in which pairs of verses by each writer alternately explored common topics. Included in this early volume were such poems as "Ballad of Birmingham," an outcry against the 1963 bombing of the Sixteenth Street Baptist Church in Birmingham, Alabama, where four girls were killed, and "Booker T. and W. E. B.," one of his most famous, representing the two famous leaders' antithetical views on the methods for educating African Americans and for achieving their social and political equality. Both poems skillfully painted ironic and witty portraits to create satirical messages. His first collection of poetry written without a coeditor, *Cities Burning* (1970), reiterated his revolutionary stance on social issues in the chaotic 1960s and probed the violent urban eruptions that took place throughout the country. His second collection, *More to Remember* (1971), helped to establish his versatility as a poet, presenting poems that addressed both political issues and more universal themes, incorporating varied forms, including traditional Western and innovative, culturally inspired ones, like blues poems and haiku.

R.'s later collections, *After the Killing* (1973) and *A Litany of Friends* (1983), continued to display poetry versatile in outlook and themes; but his craftsmanship and skill became more prominent, his poems capturing the syntax and the vibrant rhythms of African American language, while using language plainly, directly, and freshly.

Further evidence of R.'s literary talents surfaced in his editing of the popular anthology *The Black Poets* (1971) and in his contribution as an essayist to the groundbreaking volume that acted as a manifesto for the 1960s movement, *The Black Aesthetic* (1972). Highly fluent in modern languages, R. translated the Russian poems of Pushkin and various French poems into English. Because of the high quality of his literary output and his influence on emerging, young African American poets and writers, R. was named Detroit's first poet laureate in 1981.

BIBLIOGRAPHY: Barksdale, R. K., and K. Kinnamon, eds., *Black Writers of America* (1972); King, W., Jr., ed., *The Forerunners: Black Poets in America* (1981); Miller, R. B., "D. R.," in Harris, T., and T. M. Davis, eds., *DLB*, vol. 41, *Afro-American Poets since 1955* (1985): 265–73

LENA AMPADU

RANSOM, John Crowe

b. 30 April 1888, Pulaski, Tennessee; d. 5 July 1974, Gambier, Ohio

R. made a dual contribution to American letters, and only time will tell whether he is to be remembered chiefly for his critical theory or for his poetry. R. started writing both at about the same time, when he was a young professor of English at Vanderbilt in the 1920s, meeting with a group of graduate students and friends in the evenings to discuss poetry and offer critiques of one another's work. There is no doubt that this experience influenced R. profoundly; his first critical pieces and most of his poems were published first in the group's little magazine, the *Fugitive* (1922–25). R. went on eventually to become founder and long-time editor of the *Kenyon Review* and author of volumes of criticism, but his critical theory changed little in substance over a lifetime from what it had been in those early days at Vanderbilt. He merely expressed it more fully in works such as *The World's Body* (1938) and *The New Criticism* (1941).

R.'s ideas about poetry are essentially that a poem is a form of discourse having two intermingled parts: the structure, or loosely logical sense or message; and the texture, or form and ordering of parts. The two elements pull against each other, producing a desirable tension, or irony, in the poem. Surrender to either element produces weak poetry, either "heart's desire" poetry, which denies the physical world by idealizing it; or entirely "physical" poetry, such as the imagist poems. In essence, the poem is a way of knowing what we cannot know otherwise, for prose, the language of science, denudes experience of much of its meaning. It is the job of the critic to consider the whole poem, as a poem, not as a piece of biography, history, social theory, or anything else.

This theory, which came to be called the New Criticism, after the title of R.'s 1941 book, became the basic approach to teaching and reading poetry in the academic world in the mid-20th c., and its influence is immeasurable. In time, the little band of Vanderbilt FUGITIVES, who, R. tells us, were fleeing from the high-caste Brahmins of the South, became in their turn the high-caste Brahmins of literature, not only in the South but in the literary world at large. It was inevitable that new generations of theorists would speak against the New Criticism, and they have, in numbers, presenting their own ideas about what a poem is. Yet even today, as academics gaze in confusion at the plethora of critical theories, it is easy to see that the New Criticism, with its insistence upon close reading, forms the infrastructure of all of them.

Not only for its relevance to modern thought about poetry, but also for its smooth, witty, urbane style, is R.'s theory still read; his prose delights as it instructs us. More than one critic has found pleasure, for example, in quoting R.'s explanation that the elements of morality and aesthetics are joined in a poem not as lemon and sugar are joined in lemonade, for there you can always still taste the sour and the sweet; the elements of poetry are inextricable. They are joined more like the way in which sodium and chloride join to make salt. The poem is a compound, a new product altogether. This is essentially the same point R. makes about the structure (the logical sense of the poem, which can be paraphrased), and the texture (the order imposed by the poet—the sum of its parts such as meter, rhyme, metaphor, and so forth). The two elements cannot be considered separable.

But however significant R.'s contributions to criticism, in the long run it might well be his poetry that wins him a lasting place in literature, if for no other reason, then because more people read poems than critical theory. R. produced a small body of elegant poetry, mainly during the years of the *Fugitive*. Later in life, he tinkered with his poems rather than writing new ones, republishing them several times with both minor and major changes. In their best forms—and every poet deserves to have his work judged in its best form—the poems are very good indeed. Most of them are small narratives, told by an ironic observer detached from the action. They employ small slices of human experience, which come to symbolize broad themes: a little girl's pet chicken dies, and she cannot be made to comprehend the permanence of death; a group of young ladies walk laughing beside a stream, and the narrator, watching, is suddenly frozen by the sinister similarity between the sound of their laughter and the sound of a scream. Like other poets of his age, R. was in revolt against the facile sentimentality of much turn-of-the-century poetry. But R. never eschews the music of the metered line, the satisfaction of a difficult rhyme scheme well done. His diction has attracted much critical attention; even in his most tough-minded, modernistic poems, one is likely to find such archaisms as "thole," "sward," "wroth." No other poet in memory can use such words with such distinction; they sound exactly right in context. This blending of the old and the new is typical of R., not only in his style but in the themes embodied in the poetry. In "Armageddon," a poem that makes a wry comment on modern relativism, R. chooses the device of presenting Christ and Antichrist as medieval knights so caught up in the quaint rubrics of a chivalric code of honor that it is difficult to tell them apart; they themselves forget their separate identities and causes. This medievalism is a favorite motif of R.'s, along with biblical and mythological imagery. But his themes are those of the 20th c.: the alienation and helplessness of man amid cosmic forces, the necessity for more than courage, for detachment, when one's back is against the wall.

In evaluating R.'s contribution to American poetry, the critic is hard put to point out weaknesses in individual poems; each one is impressive. Then why is R. not among the top names of poets of his time? For one thing, he stood in the shadow of giants like T. S. ELIOT; for another, his poems are few. R.'s choices for his *Selected Poems* (1945) fill only a single thin volume. When R. attended Oxford as a Rhodes Scholar, he was disappointed with his grade; he was not awarded a First. His consolation was that his mark was the top one among the Seconds. So it is with his standing in the list of 20th-c. American poets: he is not among the firsts, but he is first among the seconds.

BIBLIOGRAPHY: Buffington, R., *The Equilibrist* (1967); Knight, K. F., *The Poetry of J. C. R.* (1964); Magner, J. E., *J. C. R.: Critical Principles and Preoccupation* (1971); Quinlan, K., *J. C. R.'s Secular Faith* (1989); Williams, M., *The Poetry of J. C. R.* (1972); Young, T. D., *Gentleman in a Dustcoat: A Biography of J. C. R.* (1976)

CECELIA LAMPP LINTON

RAWLINGS, Marjorie Kinnan

b. 8 August 1896, Washington, D.C.; d. 14 December 1953, St. Augustine, Florida

R. is best known for *The Yearling* (1938), her novel of twelve-year-old Jody Baxter, just coming of age in his parents' solitary cabin in the backwoods of north central Florida during the later 19th c. She is still widely admired for her semiautobiographical pastoral narrative, *Cross Creek* (1942), and is remembered also for her novels and stories about Florida "Cracker folk"—poor whites living mostly in the woodland of the interior—in the latter half of the 19th and the first half of the 20th c. Prominent among these other fiction works are *South Moon Under* (1933), *Golden Apples* (1935), two novelettes, "Jacob's Ladder" (1931) and "Gal Young Un" (1932), and three comic tales narrated by R.'s fat lady of fun, Quincey Dover, "Benny and the Bird Dogs" (1933), "Varmints" (1936), and "Cocks Must Crow" (1939).

"Jacob's Ladder" won second prize in the 1931 Scribner Prize Contest; "Gal Young Un" took first prize in the O. Henry Memorial Award contest, and a story about miscegenation in the South at the turn of the century, "Black Secret" (1945), won another O. Henry Memorial Award in 1945. The high point of her career came in 1939, when she won the Pulitzer Prize in fiction, was awarded membership in the National Institute of Arts and Letters, and received an honorary degree from Rollins College; she gained another honorary degree in 1942 from the University of Tampa. Screen rights to *The Yearling* had been sold to MGM in 1938, but there were production delays; the film, starring Gregory Peck and Jane Wyman as Jody Baxter's parents, and ten-year-old Claude Jarman, Jr. as Jody, was finally completed in 1946. Aside from the arguable casting of the major roles, the movie was a tolerable rendition of the novel, and was a box office success. A fine version of "Gal Young Un" was made by independent filmmaker Victor Nunez in 1980. In 1983, the film *Cross Creek* appeared: an unintended travesty of R.'s life and literary career, allegedly based on her memoirs but grossly distorting her life story and fusing it with Jody's painful loss of his yearling fawn.

In addition to feeling quite at home with the local inhabitants, white and black, R. was deeply responsive to the quiet, enchanting beauty of her adoptive state's watery-woodland interior, particularly the area she made famous in her *Walden*-like memoir. She defined Cross Creek as "a bend in a country road, by land, and the flowing of Lochloosa Lake into Orange Lake, by water." *The Yearling,* because of its rich, evocative descriptions of the wilderness area surrounding the pine clearing—southeast of Cross Creek—where the Baxters made their home, reads like a beautiful prose poem. Largely as a result of her depictions of the Florida backwoods—scrub and hammock growth, abundant and rich in variety—and colorful inhabitants, the old farmhouse she and her first husband, Charles Rawlings, purchased as part of an extensive orange grove property in 1928 became a literary tourist shrine after her death, and remains so today.

Though R. benefitted greatly from the encouragement and guidance of the famous Scribner's editor Maxwell Perkins, her most significant motifs were her own, and the quality of her published fiction ranged from excellent to bad—in the latter case, despite her awareness that she could write what she called "interesting trash instead of literature." A regional writer (despite her repudiation of the term), at least when writing about Crackers and their ways, R., who so hated cities and heavily populated areas, clearly indicated a deep desire for something transcending locale and natural beauty: a little boy all her own (something she would never have). From her early publication, "The Reincarnation of Miss Hetty"—which won second prize in *McCall's* "Child Authorship Contest" (1912)—through such revealing fictions as "A Mother in Mannville" (1936) and its expanded version as a six-part *Saturday Evening Post* serial—"Mountain Prelude" (1947), down to her last novel, *The Sojourner* (1953)—about a lonely Michigan farmer, this motif appears in some form or other. Among R.'s other motifs are the terrible vulnerability to harm of the young and the great difficulty of sustaining a mutually satisfying domestic relationship. As with the finest writers, R. was often at her best when she transmuted her own life experience into fiction, and her audience will likely continue indefinitely.

BIBLIOGRAPHY: Bellman, S. I., "Writing Literature for Young People: M. K. R.'s 'Secret River' of the Imagination," *Costerus* 9 (1973): 19–27; Bellman, S. I., *M. K. R.* (1974); Bigelow, G. L., *Frontier Eden: The Literary Career of M. K. R.* (1966); Silverthorne, E., *M. K. R.: Sojourner at Cross Creek* (1988)

                                    SAMUEL I. BELLMAN

RAY, David

b. 20 May 1932, Sapulpa, Oklahoma

Like many fine American poets born in the 1930s and 1940s, R. has enjoyed less recognition than his work merits. Laboring in the shadow of poets born in the 1920s, younger poets like R. have been neglected by academic criticism. Yet R. is a significant contemporary voice, one who grapples passionately with matters both public and private. Despite his relative obscurity, he has won several significant prizes, and his 1989 book *The Maharani's New Wall* was a Pulitzer Prize nominee.

The son of a Dust Bowl sharecropper-turned-barber, R. endured a childhood marked by poverty and instability: he spent time in an orphanage and in many foster homes. Despite his disadvantages, R. developed a formidable intellect, and earned a B.A. from the University of Chicago in 1952. After a brief stint doing social work, he earned his M.A. from Chicago in 1957. He has taught at a number of colleges and universities, most recently at the University of Missouri at Kansas City, and has spent many years abroad—in Europe, India, and the South Pacific.

R.'s poetry is typically in free verse, and is wide-ranging in subject matter. One of his running concerns is family. Many poems recall the mistreatment he received at his father's hands, but these are neither angry nor overly mournful; poems such as "X-Ray," "Words at Midnight," and "Analysis" are highly self-conscious reflections that manage to evoke pathos while maintaining a level of emotional distance. R.'s childhood experiences provide the basis for his disturbing long poem "Orphans," which graphically details the abuses the children suffered at the hands of the orphanage workers. Much of R.'s work deals with his own children and his attempts to be a better parent than his father. *Sam's Book* (1987) collects poems written to or about his son, who died in 1984.

Unlike many contemporary writers, R. often chooses to address political matters directly; he has little patience with artists concerned entirely with aesthetics. R. protested the Vietnam War with poet Robert BLY and other writers; poems such as "Some Notes on Vietnam" and "Incident in N.Y." grew out of his response to that conflict and the accompanying domestic turmoil. A longtime dissenter on many issues of national policy, R. claims to have been spied on by the FBI. "To a Child of Baghdad," written in the wake of the 1990 Persian Gulf War, strongly echoes his Vietnam poetry with its evocation of an innocent whose life is ruined by an American political, economic, and military juggernaut.

R.'s protests sometimes deal with issues having little claim on the public imagination. He sees a world in which ordinary people are taken advantage of or otherwise poorly served by governments or large corporate interests. Written long before public controversy over smoking became widespread, R.'s "The Cigarette Factory" attacks that industry for what he calls "the trade in coffin nails." "The Eskimo Girl" meditates on a photograph of a girl who has been radiation-poisoned through exposure to nuclear test fallout. In "The Wise Guys," R. attacks the scientists who pursue "pure" knowledge to the exclusion of addressing the practical—and in his view, dire—problems facing humanity.

"The Eskimo Girl" is also typical of R.'s work in another respect—the frequency with which he writes about the visual arts, including photography, sculpture, and painting. Poems such as "Migrant Mother, 1936," "A Midnight Diner by Edward Hopper," and "An Egyptian Couple in the Louvre" all demonstrate his talent for empathy: he often discusses the people depicted as if they were part of a living scene before him. This approach is consistent with his work in general, which tends to deemphasize the boundaries between life and art.

Collections of R.'s poetry other than those already mentioned include *The Touched Life: Selected and New Poems* (1982), *Wool Highways* (1993), and *Kangaroo Paws* (1995). His other literary work includes a story collection, *The Mulberries of Mingo* (1978), as well as years of editing the literary magazine *New Letters.*

BIBLIOGRAPHY: Struthers, A., "Interview with D. R.," *IJAS* 14 (January 1984): 103–17; Trakas, D., "D. R.," in Greiner, D. J., ed., *DLB,* vol. 5, part 2, *American Poets since World War II* (1980): 175–80

ROBERT WEST

READ, Opie Pope

b. 22 December 1852, Nashville, Tennessee; d. 2 November 1939, Chicago, Illinois

R., a prolific local color novelist of the late 19th c., was born in Tennessee and grew up during the Civil War years. After attending Neophogen College for two years, he embarked on a journalism career, inspired by reading Benjamin FRANKLIN's *Autobiography.* Moving to Arkansas, he eventually became the city editor of the venerable *Arkansas Gazette* from 1879 to 1882 and the friend and confidant of the remnants of the state's antebellum elite. These associations helped mold him into what one critic called the "last gentleman of the Old South." His penchant for passing off fiction as news led him in 1883 to found his own comic paper, the *Arkansas Traveler,* in imitation of *Texas Siftings.* In 1887, R. moved his operation to Chicago, remaining as editor until 1893.

In his paper, R. published his short stories and then serialized his novels. After 1893, novels predominated and by the time of his death amounted to fifty-seven titles. *The Jucklins* (1896) sold over a million copies. R.'s audience consisted of "that part of the reading public which was obliged to spend long hours on railroad journeys." Traditional in his plots and moral in his tone, R. was the epitome of a Southern local colorist. He drew heavily on his Tennessee and Arkansas experiences for geographic background and characters, later expanding his interest to touch almost every Southern state. Despite moving to Chicago, he never used an urban setting. Interestingly, he did not embrace the strident racism of the era, continuing in the paternalism tradition he had learned in Arkansas.

R. was much in demand as a stage personality. Early in his career, he teamed up first with Eugene FIELD and then with poet Bruce Amsbary, working the Chautauqua circuits. An active member of the Chicago Press Club, R. inspired this once well-known poem: "Said O. R. to E. P. Roe, / 'How do you like Gaboriau?' / 'I like him very much indeed,' / Said E. P. Roe to O. R."

Although in his lifetime R. was best known as a humorist, several of his novels retain historical value. *Len Gansett* (1888) is one of the first works to cast a newspaper editor as a hero and accurately anticipates what later became the Southern Gothic political novel. *An Arkansas Planter* (1896) deals with race relations and introduced a Southern liberated woman. His last novel, *The Gold Glaize Veil* (1927), is unique in making his contemporary Alice FRENCH (Octave Thanet) one of the characters. His memoir, *I Remember* (1930), is a gracefully written tribute to what Burton Rascoe called an "articulator of the robust spirit of democratic individualism," while full of what Richard M. Dorson called "lusty anecdotes."

BIBLIOGRAPHY: Dougan, M. B., "Local Colorists and the Race Question: O. R. and Octave Thanet," *PAPA* 9 (Fall 1983): 26–34; Morris, R. L., *O. R., American Humorist* (1965)

MICHAEL B. DOUGAN

REALISM

In the years following the Civil War, American literature began to experience the effects of an international movement that emphasized a fidelity to literary representation of the actual experience and consequences of everyday life. Centered largely in the novel, 19th-c. realism gained currency in France with Balzac and in England with the novels of George Eliot, who is indebted to her precursor, Jane Austen. In America, the most notable authors associated with this new direction were William Dean HOWELLS, Henry JAMES, and Samuel Langhorne CLEMENS. These and other realists pointedly avoided the then popular story lines that were dependent on high drama and tragic implication. Instead, they emphasized characterization, giving particular attention to the development of character in confronting complex ethical issues. Largely a movement in reaction to what was perceived as the falseness and sentimentality of ROMANTICISM, realism carefully avoided the symmetry and balance of contrived plots in fiction, and the undue emphasis on idealized settings and social situations in literature in general.

In particular, the advent of realism in the U.S. was marked by a decided shift away from the imaginative sensibility and Emersonian optimism so very evident in much of the writing of the earlier 19th c. The prevailing tenets of the romanticism that characterized American letters from James Fenimore COOPER through Ralph Waldo EMERSON, particularly the freedom of imagination, the value of intuition, the intrinsic integrity of the "noble savage," and the unique independence of the Jeffersonian agrarian, gradually gave way to the spirit of the new industrialism and to commonplace middle-class life and manners. This new direction in literature had taken a firm hold by 1870, and drew philosophical support from the writings of the school of American pragmatists: Charles S. Peirce, who, in 1878 coined the term "pragmatism," William JAMES, the father of American psychology, and later in the century John Dewey, whose pragmatism was the basis of his theories of education and social reconstruction. Peirce's pragmatism in particular emphasized that value and meaning in life are significant only when they are determined with a recognition of ultimate utility or consequences. Idealism or other metaphysical concerns were largely irrelevant, since they rarely had direct connection with consequences or practical concerns of everyday life.

This influence of rational philosophy on the realist movement in literature was further enhanced by significant developments in science and technology, which were instrumental in the demise of the romantic myths associated with the mystery and vastness of the American wilderness. The completion of the transcontinental railroad in 1869 marked the end of both the literal frontier and of the inviolate quality of the mysterious virgin territory that lay beyond. The railroad was particularly instrumental in dispelling the myth of the romantic West, imposing not only commercial opportunity and incentive, but also the realism and sophistication of the industrial East upon the towns and settlements that once constituted the frontier. The effects of this aspect of the transition from romanticism to realism are poignantly and humorously presented in one of the representative short stories of the period, Stephen CRANE's "The Bride Comes to Yellow Sky."

The invention of the telephone in 1876 and the growing popularity of the automobile in the 1890s further enhanced the realistic and practical application of technology in everyday life, as hitherto distant regions of the North American continent were gradually brought closer to one another. The highly imaginative and romantic conceptions of America beyond the Eastern seaboard that were so much a part of earlier literature receded in favor of more accurate and decidedly less romantic depictions by regionalists and local color writers such as Clemens, Bret HARTE, Joel Chandler HARRIS, and Hamlin GARLAND. Garland's delineation of the hardship and drudgery of Midwestern farm life

in *Main-Travelled Roads* foreshadowed the more trenchant realism and implicit social criticism of later works on the region, most notably Sinclair LEWIS's *Main Street*. Clemens and Harris brought to literature verisimilitude in characterization and dialogue, and in so doing reproduced and preserved authentic speech patterns and dialect that would otherwise have been lost to posterity. Twain was particularly adept in combining the humor of authentic native idiom with an underlying but vigorous desire for social justice and egalitarianism.

As realism became a significant force in American literature, the protagonist of American fiction also underwent a profound change, becoming less adventuresome and more conservative. Characters such as Cooper's Natty Bumppo of the Leather-Stocking tales and Clemens's Huck Finn, spiritually and naively at one with the wilderness as representatives of the collective American character, were gradually metamorphosed into figures more in tune with modern industrialized society, men like Henry James's Christopher Newman in *The American* and Howells's Silas Lapham in *The Rise of Silas Lapham*. The energies of these representatives of American realism were directed not to forging new trails westward to escape the strictures of civilization, but to the manufacture of mundane but ultimately useful commonplace objects such as wash tubs and paint. Newman and Lapham were a new breed of self-made men, captains of industry who owed their very material good fortune to a combination of the Puritan Ethic, the industrial revolution, and the abundant opportunities inherent in American democracy.

The credo of American realism owes its inception to Howells, who articulated its basic tenets in *Criticism and Fiction*. Calling for a fiction that would "cease to lie about life," writing that would "forbear to preach pride and revenge, folly and insanity, egotism and prejudice," Howells was adamant in emphasizing the value of fiction that would "not put on literary airs" but would present its view of life in "the language of unaffected people everywhere." The most notable practitioner of American realism was undoubtedly Henry James, frequently referred to as the father of "psychological realism." In novels such as *The Portrait of a Lady* and *The Ambassadors,* James effectively blends the novel of manners with a remarkable insight into the nuances of select social environment and offers a unique psychological perception of character.

In the decade before the turning of the century, realism had to a large degree blended with NATURALISM. Younger writers such as Crane and Frank NORRIS, both of whom were influenced and helped by Howells, presented a more cynical and harsh reality, one in which a scientific determinism governed human affairs in an indifferent universe. A Darwinian "survival of the fittest" was the prevailing rule of existence, and the writer, in the semblance of the detached scientist, was emphasized as the objective recorder of reality rather than the imaginative creator of fiction. Notable examples of this blend of realism and naturalism are Crane's *Maggie: A Girl of the Streets* and somewhat later Theodore DREISER's *Sister Carrie,* both of which emphasized the perils of human struggle in urban environments. By this time, realism in American literature had created fertile ground for the naturalism that had largely derived from European influences such as French novelist Émile Zola's concept of the "experimental" novel and German philosopher Friedrich Nietzsche's theory of the *Übermensch.* In addition, writers such as Crane and Upton SINCLAIR seemed to owe as much to the revelations of social reformers such as Jacob Riis, author of *How the Other Half Lives* (1890) and *The Children of the Poor* (1892), as they did to Howells. In the 20th c., realism continued as the mainstay of writers such as Lewis, John O'HARA, John P. MARQUAND, Louis AUCHINCLOSS, and most notably, Edith WHARTON, whose psychological realism most closely resembles that of her mentor, Henry James.

BIBLIOGRAPHY: Becker, G. J., *Documents of Modern Literary Realism* (1963); Bell, M. D., *The Problem of American Realism: Studies in the Cultural History of a Literary Idea* (1993); Borus, D. H., *Writing Realism: Howells, James, and Norris in the Mass Market* (1989); Kearns, K., *Nineteenth-Century Literary Realism* (1996); Pizer, D., *Realism and Naturalism in Nineteenth-Century American Literature* (1960; rev. ed., 1984); Thomas, B., *American Literary Realism and the Failed Promise of Contract* (1997)

RICHARD KEENAN

RECHY, John [Francisco]
b. 10 March 1934, El Paso, Texas

R. has gained recognition as a trailblazer both in gay fiction and in Chicano literature. Best known for his first novel, *City of Night* (1963), R. said in the introduction to a 1984 edition that he wants to be identified as someone who wrote about homosexual prostitution and the gay experience, not a former hustler who became a writer. Similarly, while acknowledging his background and using it in his work, he disavows the restrictive label of "Chicano writer," insisting in an interview that he is and always has been a "literary writer."

Certainly, *City of Night* strives to be "literary." That perhaps is its weakness, and the weakness of R.'s work

in general. On one level, *City of Night* offers a vivid picture of the gay underworld in America's major cities during the late 1950s. It follows a male prostitute through the sexual labyrinth of street corners, bars, parks, rest rooms, theater balconies, and cheap hotels. There he finds "scores"—men who will pay him for the use of his body. And he remains rigorously faithful to his role as "trade" in this sharply defined world made up of users and the used, of buyers and sellers. The first person narrator—admittedly the author himself—confesses that the money means less to him than the feeding of his narcissism.

R. shows a keen eye for details, narrates at a breathless pace, and records authentic dialogue as this hustler's progress unfolds. Although the protagonist engages in hundreds of sexual acts during the novel's course, his account remains relatively free of graphic details. The narrative falters, though, when he falls into tedious introspection, especially when he revels in guilt for which his Roman Catholic background appears to be largely responsible and when he questions his own homosexual tendencies. *City of Night,* which received negative reviews but became a bestseller when first published, has turned into a modern classic—another of those self-indulgent but important novels from the 1960s, similar to Jack KEROUAC's *On the Road.*

Two later novels focus on the same sexual underground, *Numbers* (1967) and *Rushes* (1979), as does a nonfiction account of the scene, *The Sexual Outlaw: A Documentary* (1977), which examines in a detached manner the universe inhabited by "youngmen," by "scores" who buy them, and by the police who disrupt the indefinable yet almost redemptive order amid chaos that pure sex creates. In the later works, as in *City of Night,* one-sided physical contacts that most often occur in public for money symbolize alienation from society, reveal loneliness and displacement, underline the battle with guilt, and expose the obsession over lost youth. These books are set in Los Angeles, where R. has lived for many years.

In *This Day's Death* (1970), R. returns to his Southwestern roots and takes up his Chicano heritage more fully than in other work. A rich novel, possibly R.'s finest, it has never received the attention accorded to *City of Night,* even though its concerns are similar. Again the narrative grapples with loss of innocence, the desire to break away from meaningless experience, and the inevitability of corruption; but it does so in a more conventional framework.

Marilyn's Daughter (1988), one of R.'s most experimental novels, examines the legend of Marilyn Monroe, not as biography but as allegory. The narrative follows a young woman who attempts to learn whether she is actually the daughter of Marilyn Monroe and Robert Kennedy. Setting the protagonist on a trek through the inverted world of Los Angeles, R. questions the distinction between reality and fiction, between fact and myth, both through the story itself and its disconnected structure. In this book, and in much of his fiction, R. not only deftly depicts all edges of Los Angeles from the tawdry to the glittery but also turns the city into a metaphor that defines displacement and discontent.

R. deserves credit for daring to write openly and honestly about homosexual experience when such books did not appear in the mainstream. As a writer of Chicano descent, he has helped to break racial barriers as well as sexual ones. Yet when his fiction turns bombastic, self-indulgent, and overwrought—as it sometimes does—it seems a shame that he does not consider himself simply a novelist instead of a "literary writer."

BIBLIOGRAPHY: Bredbeck, G. W., "J. R.," *Contemporary Gay American Novelists* (1993): 340–51; Christian, K., "Will the 'Real Chicano' Please Stand Up?" *Américas* 20, 2 (1992): 89-104; Pérez-Torres, R., "The Ambiguous Outlaw: J. R. and Complicitous Homotextuality," *Fictions of Masculinity: Crossing Cultures, Crossing Sexualities* (1994): 204–25; Steuernagel, T., "Contemporary Homosexual Fiction and the Gay Rights Movement," *JPC* 20 (1986): 125–34

                                    ROBERT L. ROSS

REED, Ishmael
b. 22 February 1938, Chattanooga, Tennessee

R.'s literary reputation is based primarily on his novels, a series of allusive, absurdist satires that led one critic to refer to him as "a black Juvenal." He has also written essays and much-admired collections of poetry, including *Conjure* (1972), nominated for a National Book Award. Yet R. considers his work in publishing—devoted to helping young and minority writers bring their work to readers—to be as important as his writing.

R.'s work has attempted to define a black aesthetic whose aim is to provide a non-Western alternative mythos for black and multicultural Americans. This aesthetic is drawn largely from R.'s study of Vodoun and Egyptology. A Haitian amalgam of African tribal cultures, Vodoun particularly serves R. as a metaphor for the American individual's struggle to maintain a specific ethnic identity. But while R. sees his black aesthetic as opposed to the mainstream of modernist literature, the broad satire and parodic play of his most acclaimed works demonstrate their affinity with the novels of contemporary absurdist writers.

R.'s most successful works have been the parodic novels least interested in the black aesthetic. His first novel, *The Free-Lance Pallbearers* (1967), determinedly dismantles expectations of what a black writer's first novel should be; it satirizes the naive and serious narrators of much classic black fiction. In his second novel, *Yellow Back Radio Broke-Down* (1969), he parodies cowboy fiction and the "yellow-backed" dime novels that popularized stories of the American West. *Yellow Back Radio Broke-Down* alludes to Egyptology in its good-guy/bad-guy confrontations, but was a critical success in spite of, rather than because of, those allusions. In 1971, R. published his "Neo-HooDoo Manifesto," outlining his vision of a black aesthetic to replace what he saw as oppressive Judeo-Christian values. His next two novels, *Mumbo Jumbo* (1972) and *The Last Days of Louisiana Red* (1974), feature a voodoo detective hero, Papa LaBas, but have generally been less well received than his other works because they abandon the humorous satirical approach in an attempt to realize the manifesto.

In 1976, R. published the novel usually considered to be his finest work. *Flight to Canada* is a parody of 19th-c. escaped-slave narratives in which R. returns to the style—a combination of satire, allegory, and farce—that had served him so well in his first works. This novel also revisits the theme of a naive hero seeking his identity. *The Terrible Twos* (1982) critiques the economic and political state of the U.S. at the beginning of the Reagan years and, among other targets, satirizes the commercialization of the St. Nicholas legend. This novel, too, has earned wide praise; the mixed reception accorded most of his earlier works seems to have given way to something of a critical consensus of R.'s importance as a writer.

In addition to writing novels, poetry, and essays, R. has worked for newspapers, most notably in naming and helping to shape the direction of New York City's *East Village Other*. He has worked in academia (which he has also satirized) as a teacher of creative writing and as a mentor who has helped his students find outlets for publication. With Al YOUNG, he cofounded and publishes the *Yardbird Reader*. In these capacities, R. has sought to assist writers he sees as underrepresented in American letters. In his own writings, R. has served as a spokesman for black artists. However, he is equally, if not more, important as a talented poet and prose stylist and as a skilled satirist.

BIBLIOGRAPHY: Martin, R., *I. R. and the New Black Aesthetic* (1997); McConnell, F., "I. R.'s Fiction: Da Hoodoo Is Put on America," in Lee, A. R., ed., *Black Fiction: New Studies in the Afro-American Novel since*

1945 (1980): 136–48; McGee, P., *I. R. and the Ends of Race* (1997)

CAROLYN LENGEL

REESE, Lizette Woodworth

b. 9 January 1856, Waverly, Maryland; d. 17 December 1935, Baltimore, Maryland

Although she is largely forgotten today, R. deserves attention in the history of American poetry, standing as a transition figure between the sentimentalism of much popular 19th-c. romantic poetry and the more vigorous attention to telling image and restrained presentation of emotion of 20th-c. poetry. R.'s career spanned the turn of the century, beginning with the publication of "The Deserted House" in the *Southern Magazine* (June 1874) and ending with the posthumous publication of *The Old House in the Country* and *Worleys* (an unfinished novel) in 1936.

One of R.'s main themes is indicated in the titles of both her first poem and her last volume of verse, the transitory value of the man-made in comparison to the eternal beauty of nature. While this sentiment is entirely conventional, R.'s poetry attains distinction from that of other popular 19th-c. poets by her simple, straightforward language and selection of telling imagery. R.'s first poem was well received and she was encouraged to gather her poetry together for publication in *A Branch of May* (1887), which was privately printed through subscriptions from friends. R. established a somewhat wider reputation by sending this volume to several important critics, including Thomas Wentworth HIGGINSON, William Dean HOWELLS, and Clarence Edmund Stedman, the latter of whom became her friend and mentor. Further encouragement resulted in her second volume, *A Handful of Lavender* (1891), being brought out by a national publisher.

R. combined writing poetry with a career teaching in the public school system of Baltimore. The subject matter of R.'s poetry reflected the experiences of her life by focusing on the landscape of the suburban area of Baltimore in which she lived her entire life and on the emotions of love and loss of love, especially the loss of someone dear through death. In these subjects as well as in some of the imagery she uses, R. resembles Emily DICKINSON, whose poetry she came to know only after she had already established her own style and subject matter. The resemblance to Dickinson can be seen in "In Time of Grief," from R.'s third volume, *A Quiet Road* (1896), in which she compares the pain of grief to the scent of boxwood after rain, a scent that is unique and distinct: "As though one spoke a word half meant / That left a sting behind."

A thirteen-year lull fell between the third and fourth volume, *A Wayside Lute* (1909). R. countered questions about the infrequency of her publication by saying, "I had nothing to say, except at long intervals, and therefore did not try to say it." Meanwhile, in November 1899, in *Scribner's Magazine,* she had published the sonnet "Tears," her best-known and most widely anthologized poem. The tears of the title are repudiated as futile grief over the fugitive cares of life. After R.'s retirement in 1921, Western High School in Baltimore, where she had taught, honored her by inscribing "Tears" on a bronze plaque dedicated in 1923.

The majority of R.'s poetry consists of brief lyrics or sonnets. She did, however, publish one volume best described as a cycle of related narrative poems. *Little Henrietta* (1927) commemorates the life and death of R.'s cousin Henrietta who had died when they were both children. In addition to her poetry, R. wrote two volumes of autobiographical reminiscence, *A Victorian Village* (1929) and *The York Road* (1931). Both volumes focus on the world of her childhood in the Victorian village of Waverly with nostalgic memories of a time when people were unhurried and certain of values they shared with everyone in the community.

Overshadowed by the giants of late-19th and early-20th-c. American poetry, R.'s will remain a minor voice, but her significance as a transition figure should insure her place in literary history. The reissue of her 1926 *The Selected Poems* in 1992 will enable scholars to study her work and understand her place in the history of American poetry.

BIBLIOGRAPHY: Buchanan, H. C., "L. W. R.," in Quartermain, P., ed., *DLB,* vol. 54, part 2, *American Poets, 1880–1945* (1987): 344–53; Harriss, R. P., "April Weather: The Poetry of L. W. R.," *SAQ* 29 (April 1930): 200–207; Kindilien, C. T., "The Village World of L. W. R.," *SAQ* 56 (January 1957): 91–104; Milne, W. G., "L. R. Revisited," *SUS* 8 (June 1969): 207–21

HARRIETTE C. BUCHANAN

REGIONALISM

The efforts of American writers to establish a national literature have perennially entailed their describing what was singular about the nation's different geographical regions—their inhabitants' languages, customs, and preoccupations. James Fenimore COOPER's Leather-Stocking tales and Mark TWAIN's *Adventures of Huckleberry Finn* share Sarah Orne JEWETT's *Country of the Pointed Firs* fascination with regional dialects and folkways. Their sensitivity to what D. H. Lawrence once called the "spirit of place" that he believed haunted the nation's disparate geographical regions has been cited as evidence of their writings' "Americanness." Despite the literary sensitivity to "place" that these writers shared, however, anthologists of American literature regularly classify only Jewett under the rubric of "regional literature." In distinguishing their projects from Jewett's, anthologists credit Cooper's Leather-Stocking tales with inventing a national mythology, and they acclaim (or damn) Twain's *Adventures of Huckleberry Finn* for addressing a national shame. What is irrecuperably regional about Jewett's regional works would appear to refer to their resistance to nationalizing themes.

While such resistance is also discernible in the dialect characters of James Russell LOWELL's *The Bigelow Papers* and the humorists of the Southwest, to name but two prominent examples of antebellum region-based literatures, it would become a valuable literary asset only after the Civil War. Hosea Bigelow's colloquial accounts of New England's woods bear comparison with Edward EGGLESTON's heavily accented depiction of Indiana forests in *The Hoosier Schoolmaster*. But unlike Lowell's characters, who denunciated slavery and the Mexican War in a Yankee drawl, Eggleston's never ventured to sound off about matters east of the Indiana backwoods.

While literary regionalism oversaw the rise of writers like Eggleston and Jewett, it also restricted their literary expertise to knowledge of the region. Regionalism denied its practitioners literary authority to represent national questions. Mark Twain could travel from the American Southwest to southern Italy, lecturing en route about subjects ranging from the literary faults of Cooper's Leather-Stocking tales to his opposition to U.S. imperialism. But Jewett was not authorized to move her characters over the Maine border. Jewett's writings had so magnified the cultural significance of Berwick, Maine that it came to represent regional nostalgia of a special kind. However much enhanced, Berwick, Maine had also circumscribed the exercise of Jewett's literary talents.

The subordination of regional literatures to a culturally inferior position within the hierarchy of genres reflected correlative social rankings and divisions of cultural labor. Members of the Northeastern elite had linked literary regionalism with the conspicuous consumption of leisure in spaces set apart from the metropolitan centers where they conducted business. The primary consumers of regional literatures subscribed to the large Northeastern magazines, *Scribner's* and the *Atlantic*. They perused these literatures to discover new recreation spots and possible vacation homes.

Regional literatures also reflected the national culture's gendered criterion for the allocation of power that delegated authority over local and domestic matters to women. In *Uncle Tom's Cabin,* Harriet Beecher STOWE had turned her comprehension of domestic sentiment into the point of entry for deliberation over the national issues of slavery and abolitionism. But after the war, Stowe's abandonment of national issues for the strictly local concerns of *The Minister's Wooing* inaugurated her new career as a New England writer of local color.

As did Stowe and Jewett, Eggleston constructed a literary inventory of dialect characters who were from a backward region of the country and remained more or less untouched by the processes of industrialization and modernity. So would Kate CHOPIN, Hamlin GARLAND, and Bret HARTE to select but a handful of writers whose works would become representative of different regionalisms. However, the literary value associated with these disparate regional literatures was not solely the consequence of their authors' reticence about national issues. It emerged in direct proportion to the dangers that newly industrializing forces posed for these cultural backwaters.

Sometimes regional writers would directly correlate their writings with the work of salvaging a local culture under threat of extinction. Stephen CRANE reinvented his literary identity when he moved from urban New York to write stories like "The Bride Comes to Yellow Sky" as an illustration of the passing of the West. When they did not state the matter explicitly, other regional writers invoked the threat of cultural endangerment to establish a pervasive mood.

As has been observed, the representation of dialect was a staple feature of diverse antebellum literary genres including the fugitive SLAVE NARRATIVE. Stowe's *Uncle Tom's Cabin* included representations of several regional dialects as well as instances of Southwestern humor. But when the nation-making conflict over slavery and the extension of borders subsumed them under its themes, these works lost their regional identities. It was only after the war had accomplished the national unity, that the integrity of the U.S.'s different regions could be acknowledged as culturally valuable.

When juxtaposed with the Civil War, however, a paradoxical dimension of regional literature becomes visible. Regional literatures did not emerge as such until the Civil War had concluded. Yet the centrifugal forces mobilizing these literatures did not disturb the "union" that resulted from the national ordeal. In historical fact, they helped reconstitute it. In *Cultures of Letters,* Richard H. Brodhead has observed that regionalism became a dominant genre in America at the historical moment when local cultural economies felt strong pressure "from a growingly powerful social model that overrode previously autonomous systems and incorporated them into translocal agglomerations." The incorporation of the local by industrializing forces released in the aftermath of the Civil War required the cooperation of storytellers who could remember lost cultures from the perspective of a new literary genre. Their local color stories organized regional cultures into bright packages that attracted the all-consuming interest of industry and modernity.

By composing literary ethnographies of their provincialisms and vernaculars, regional writers facilitated their consolidation within a national manufacture. An additional consideration of Crane's biregional identity might explain how. When Crane changed his regional focus from the urban ghettoes of New York City to the newly disappearing West, he transformed his regional affiliation. But in doing so by way of a literary form that trafficked in character types and local knowledges, Crane also indicated how regional literature and industrial processes activated mutually determining forces. Crane's writings borrowed from industrialism the know-how required to harness massive spaces to more inclusive operations. Modernizing processes depended for their efficiency on literary regionalism's production of fully homogenized local cultures.

In representing fully integrated locales, regional writers like Crane facilitated the imposition of culturally hegemonic representations over an entire geography. If Crane's ability to typify a region is not altogether distinct from industrialization, neither can literary regions be utterly differentiated from the modernity threatening them with extinction. Modernization required the formation of the local knowledges that it also rendered obsolete. Regional cultures may have been endangered by industrialization, but they also provided factories for the production and markets for the consumption of its products. Factory owners deployed local knowledges' knowledge in the management of a region's work force.

But the general interest in regional literatures extended beyond these local usages and cannot finally be dissociated from the cultural anxieties that local knowledges at once aroused and controlled. The desire to annex new territories abroad was not dissociable from the desire to acquire imaginative authority over regional geographies. And these conjoined desires were inextricably linked at that time to "nativist" anxieties over anything "un-American." Regional literatures were believed to represent a quintessentially American way of life. The cultural usage to which "strictly Americanist" values were put in the heyday of U.S. imperialism involved a chauvinist differentiation from "foreigners." By way of a literary apparatus that classified regions according to dialect and type, local colorists represented their territories as either altogether void of "foreign" influence or capable of confining that influence to socially manageable stereo-types. In the imaginative authority they exercised over geographical territories, regional literatures were akin to the nation's colonial administrations abroad. Their power to impose a set of encompassing representations on a region and its inhabitants realized the surveillance ambitions of the immigration police at home.

BIBLIOGRAPHY: Brodhead, R., *Cultures of Letters: Scenes of Reading and Writing in Nineteenth-Century America* (1993); Levine, L., *Highbrow/Lowbrow: The Emergence of Cultural Hierarchy* (1988); Wiebe, R., *The Search for Order, 1877–1920* (1977)

DONALD E. PEASE

REID, [Thomas] Mayne

b. 4 April 1818, Ballyroney, Ireland; d. 22 October 1883, London, England

Born to a father who was a Presbyterian minister and a mother whose father was also a clergyman, R. was educated to serve the church as well. R., however, anxious to travel and experience adventures, sidestepped his family's plans and in 1840 took off for America. Storekeeper, slave master, private tutor, actor, hunter, trader, explorer, soldier against the Indians and Mexicans, and would-be revolutionary in Europe, R. did it all, and his experiences found their way into the more than ninety novels, works for children, poems, and magazine articles he wrote between 1842 and 1880. In addition to this prolific output on both sides of the Atlantic, R. found time and energy to write for the *New York Herald* (1846) and the *Spirit of the Times* (1846), and to publish two magazines, an evening daily, the *Little Times* (1866), and a New York-based magazine, the *Onward* (1869).

R.'s first novel, *The Rifle Rangers* (1850), uses his experiences in Mexico during the Mexican War. In the Battle of Chapultepec, he became badly wounded in the leg, an injury that repeatedly flared up and left him, after 1874, unable to walk without crutches.

The Quadroon (1856) describes R.'s arrival in New Orleans and a steamboat trip up the Mississippi where he makes the acquaintance of a young Creole plantation owner. The plot thickens after he rescues the plantation mistress during the boat's explosion but then falls in love instead with her beautiful slave, the quadroon of the title. After defying Louisiana plantation society by abducting the slave girl, all ends well with the wedding of the lovers. While the novel seems to plead abolitionist causes, it carries, rather conspicuously, its own brand of racism. Dramatized in London, *The Quadroon* later became the basis for Dion BOUCICAULT's play, *The Octoroon*.

The Quadroon is remarkable for its mix of genres: high adventure and passionate romance alternate with detailed factual descriptions of geography, plants, and animals and schoolmasterly analyses of 19th-c. plantation life and river travel. This style, in which journalistic sensationalism competes with scientific observations and the novelist's interest in action is a hallmark of other R. writings as well. *The White Chief* (1859) tells of high adventure, abduction, and bloody revenge and at the same time enlightens readers about the makeup of the Llano Estacado, the Staked Plains. The descriptive and analytical sections interrupting R.'s story lines might bore today's readers, but they must have fascinated the European audiences—British, German, French—for which they were intended. Today, R.'s books are a valuable secondary source for the historian and popular culture analyst interested in 19th-c. frontier life.

BIBLIOGRAPHY: Meyer, R. W., "The Western American Fiction of M. R.," *WAL* 3 (Summer 1968): 115–32; Reid, E., *M. R.: A Memoir of His Life* (1890); Steele, J., *Captain M. R.* (1978)

HEIDEMARIE Z. WEIDNER

RELIGION AND LITERATURE

The traditional choice offered to Americans asked to designate their religious preference—Protestant, Catholic, Jew, or other—has turned out to be a fairly accurate reflection of the influence of the respective religions upon American literature, with Protestantism most prevalent. The first American literary genres were the SERMON and the spiritual AUTOBIOGRAPHY, both employed by the Puritan founders of New England, who were embarked upon a mighty religious enterprise: establishing the City of God in the wilderness. The influence of these writers on American literature has been incalculable; suffice it to say that certain features can be easily traced to them: a predominant Calvinist viewpoint, with its insistence on human depravity and on predestination; an intense focus on the individual soul; and a lively hortatory strain. Forming a countermotif to the major Calvinistic note is a secondary voice that comprises both Catholic and less severe Protestant influences, which can conveniently be called Anglo-Catholic. The briefest comparison of William BYRD's diary with that of one of the New England pilgrims, John WINTHROP for example, will make clear the difference in character between New England Puritans and the Anglican settler of Virginia and other parts of the South. Contrasting with stern Puritan idealism, Byrd's writing shows the more adventurous and free-wheeling spirit of the lower colo-

nies. The Puritans, with their intense inner searching and their disdain of this world as a stumbling block in the path to spiritual perfection, held sway in New England for a century and a half before their children and grandchildren gradually broke up the community of believers; nothing, however, has yet dispelled their influence on American literature.

One could argue that TRANSCENDENTALISM, for example, the religion of major 19th-c. writers such as Ralph Waldo EMERSON, Henry David THOREAU, Emily DICKINSON, Amos Bronson ALCOTT, Margaret FULLER, and William Cullen BRYANT, is neither Protestant, Catholic, nor Jew, but distinctly "other"—a sort of dilettante pantheism. Nevertheless, it belongs in the Protestant philosophical camp, not only because its adherents were literally as well as culturally descended from the founding Puritans, but because its basis is a romantic preoccupation with the spiritual, a submission, to use Emerson's term, to the "Oversoul." The transcendentalists melded the self-directed ponderings of the spiritual autobiography and the other-directed exhortation of the sermon to produce the conflation of these two genres that characterizes their major works. This technique can be observed in the essays of Emerson, the extended monologue of Thoreau, *The Dial* articles, and "conversations" of Alcott and Fuller. The palpable "you" implicit in these authors' works pulls them up short of the relentless self-exposure of, for example, the *Personal Narrative* of Jonathan EDWARDS; at the same time, the first-personal tone powerfully serves the homiletic purpose of these works. These writers were largely Harvard-educated; they constituted an intellectual upper class, the avant-garde thinkers of their day. They were in rebellion against the orthodox Christianity that was their New England legacy; nevertheless, they were pervasively affected by that legacy. The movement appears to have spread out from a center of ordained ministers and children of ministers to those not directly connected to the church, Walt WHITMAN for example. Dickinson was the daughter of a clergyman; her work holds a tissue of protest against the oppression of Calvinism, yet she freely uses the hoard of Christian images bequeathed to her by her stern ancestors. Other great American writers also owe much to the Puritans, either directly or indirectly; Herman MELVILLE came into the circle of strong transcendental influence; Nathaniel HAWTHORNE's critics have claimed that he spent his life expiating in his writing the deeds of his ancestor who helped condemn the accused witches of Salem.

Thus, it is likewise, as the 19th c. continues, with the deterministic writers who followed, though they may have been far from New England. Mark TWAIN's late novel *The Mysterious Stranger,* published in 1916, is an interesting example. The "stranger" comes to three boys apparently to teach them the harsh truth: man is merely a pawn, useless, corrupt, suffering, hopeless, and ultimately nothing, existence itself being merely an illusion. Yet to teach this lesson, Twain structures a parallel to the Christ story. The stranger is a God-like figure who comes to work miracles and to show the way, the truth, and the darkness, then vanishes. The book is filled with Christian images. As important as these, however, is the doctrine underlying the work: free will is nonexistent; man is predestined by a capricious mysterious force, standing in for the Calvinist God, whose influence is ubiquitous in American literature. Even those naturalistic writers who do not draw on Christian imagery extensively show this pervasive influence, Jack LONDON and Stephen CRANE for example. These writers probably did not consciously draw upon anything like Jonathan Edwards's "Sinners in the Hands of an Angry God" (1741); nevertheless, the secular determinism in their work is a direct literary descendant of the theory of predestination espoused by the Puritans. Even into the 20th c., the influence continues, as in John STEINBECK's *Grapes of Wrath* and Peter DE VRIES's *Blood of the Lamb.*

One branch of American literature that shows an interesting selectiveness in admitting Puritan influence is the work of black authors. From such works as autobiographical slave narratives to the homiletics of such preachers as Booker T. WASHINGTON and Martin Luther King, Jr., the genres are easily traced back to the Puritans. Both draw heavily on religion, particularly biblical themes and images such as the mercy of God who grants deliverance, and the crossing of Jordan to the promised land. Like the transcendentalists, a disproportionate number of black writers have been clergymen. These writers have not embraced the deterministic view; on the contrary, they exhort their readers to take action and to take responsibility for their actions. Not all black literature is autobiography or sermon, of course; the use of religion has been prevalent in other genres as well, ever since Phillis WHEATLEY introduced into black writing two elements unusual in American literature as a whole: simple praise of God and comfort in religion. The latter has been repeated in the work of other writers; frequently the same address that incites to action will offer religious consolation for oppression. Some black writers, Alice WALKER for example, deplore this taking of comfort; the tendency among editors of anthologies is to sneer at it as marking the writer stupidly naive. It has also come into line for bitter satire, notably by Ralph ELLISON, among others.

Calvinism went south from New England, meeting the milder religion of the Catholics in Maryland, Anglicans of Virginia, Wesleyan Methodists in Georgia, Free Will Baptists everywhere (these formed a separate sect before the end of the 18th c. in opposition to the doctrine of predestination), and eventually Catholics of the French settlements along the Gulf Coast, most notably New Orleans. These faiths preach free will, reject determinism, and have widely influenced the literature of the SOUTH. This literature, which has dominated American letters in the 20th c. as New England dominated it in the 19th, has a deep vein of humanism. Southern writers have made good use of such Calvinist images as the revivalist preacher in the mildewed tent ranting about God's wrath, but the South has never truly bought the idea of determinism, and its literature focuses on the world at hand. If a character in a Southern novel locks himself into his study to ponder the capricious and absolute tyranny of God, very likely that character is seen as queer and cranky. The Protestantism of the South has absorbed the influence of Anglo-Catholicism; it loves myth in the sense of a good story, and has earned the region the nickname the "Bible Belt." Flannery O'CONNOR's well-known essay, "The Catholic Writer in the Protestant South," expounds her view that Catholicism is the more abstract and intellectual Christian camp, whereas Protestantism is the more earth-centered, myth-based, concrete. This viewpoint is not surprising in O'Connor. Her early years were spent in a place and time when Catholic children were expected to memorize the Creed and the Catechism, while little Protestant boys and girls were expected to attend Bible School, where they learned stirring and colorful stories. When O'Connor moved away from Savannah, the Catholic center of Georgia, and to the country, where Bible reading Protestants predominated, she found a mine of rich imagery for her fiction, far removed from the memorized abstractions of her childhood. Nonetheless, the dichotomy is here reversed; the prevailing overall influence in American letters of the two divisions of Christianity remains: New England Calvinism and its descending line of sects abstract, romantic, individualistic; Catholicism and its close adherents, together with certain dissenting Protestant sects, concrete, earthy, communal. This division is aptly embodied in two William FAULKNER characters, Henry Sutpen and Charles Bon, in *Absalom, Absasom!.* Henry is a good Protestant country boy, visiting Charles in his New Orleans home. "I can imagine him, with his puritan heritage . . . of fierce proud mysticism," the narrator says, "this grim humorless yokel out of a granite heritage where even the houses, let alone clothing and conduct, are built in the image of a jealous and sadistic Jehovah, put suddenly down in a place whose denizens had created their All-Powerful and His supporting hierarchy-chorus of beautiful saints and handsome angels in the image of their [own] . . . voluptuous lives." John Crowe RANSOM recalls in his poem "Address to the Scholars of New England" the indignation of Southern boys at being taught to revere the Pilgrim fathers; they were too proud, he says; they tried to put Pure Idea into a box and fasten him up in a steeple; such Platonism was scandalous. Ransom, along with the other authors of the New Criticism, insisted on the sacredness of what he termed the World's Body—the concrete, the here-and-now. This is also the philosophy of T. S. ELIOT, who hailed from Missouri and found his spiritual home in Anglo-Catholicism. His poetry is a parallel to the ritual, the pageantry, the allusiveness, of his religion. Like the writing of other Americans influenced by the more myth-minded branches of Christianity, it draws freely on Catholic sacramentalism; that is, the belief that the physical is a direct path to the spiritual, and therefore not to be despised.

Judaism has made its contribution to American literature primarily as a cultural background for the stories of such writers as Bernard MALAMUD, Isaac Bashevis SINGER, Saul BELLOW, Philip ROTH, and Chaim POTOK. Sometimes their writing is altogether secular and sometimes it considers religious themes. Aharon Appelfeld, a leading Israeli writer, considers Singer to be the only American who has produced what can truly be called Jewish literature; that is, literature that comes out of the common memory of the Jewish people. That may be true; most American Jews, like most other Americans, produce distinctly American literature. Malamud, for example, has been compared to Hawthorne, with his technique of adjoining the real and the surreal by introducing the supernatural just out of sight, in the corner of the reader's eye, so to speak. One interesting Jewish American theme has been explored by Potok in *The Chosen*. From American colonial beginnings and the quest to establish the new Jerusalem in New England, Americans have felt chosen for the mighty burden of the world on their shoulders, as the price of their privilege. This feeling, combined with the Jews' ancient belief that they are the Chosen of God, bequeaths a double weight of duty on these people. Potok considers what it means to be a Jew, to be an American, to belong to a sort of nation within a nation.

"Other" sects and creeds have appeared as influences on American literature from time to time, but thus far as very minor voices. For example, Black Muslims have contributed a small body of poetry more political than religious; and some native tribal folklore concerning God has recently been published. Across the whole expanse of American literature, religion has furnished authors not only with creeds upon which to base their work, but also with a rich fund of images and themes, and a temple against which to throw bricks, to borrow an image from Stephen Crane. Religion has been frequently derided, yet never abandoned. Probably religion and literature will always overlap, be-

cause they are engaged in the common endeavor of probing the truths and desires recognized by the human heart, and because they speak in the same richly symbolic language.

BIBLIOGRAPHY: Brooks, V. W., *The Flowering of New England, 1815–1865* (1936); Harap, L., *Creative Awakening* (1987); Newlin, C. M., *Philosophy and Religion in Colonial America* (1962); Roth, R. J., *American Religious Philosophy* (1936); Strandberg, V. H., *Religious Psychology in American Literature* (1981); Wieman, H. N., *American Philosophies of Religion* (1936)

CECELIA LAMPP LINTON

REMINGTON, Frederic

b. 4 October 1861, Canton, New York; d. 26 December 1909, New Rochelle, New York

No one did more than R. to create the visual myths of the American WEST. In magazine illustrations, paintings, and sculptures, R. created enduring images of the Old West—soldiers on a vast and demanding frontier, soldiers battling Indians, Indians on the hunt or in their villages. Most important, his visual art helped transform the cowboy into an epic hero.

Although R.'s fame rests foremost on his contribution to the visual arts, he was also a man of words. An avid reader from youth, he exercised the pen as well as the brush. Through the written word, he complemented his work as illustrator, painter, and sculptor. As he began to find success as an illustrator, he was also publishing his first essays on life in the Southwest as he found it in the late 19th c. Essays led to stories—in R.'s hand, one form easily merged into the other since his stories came from the same frontier experience. The stories first appeared in *Harper's Weekly, Harper's Monthly,* and *Century,* giving him a large national audience. The stories were later collected into four volumes, published with his own illustrations. Just as R.'s visual work changed in the course of his career, so did his writing. In painting, he moved closer to impressionism; his writing became more emphatically realistic, even naturalistic. In his last years writing fiction, he had turned to the novel. By then, he was living in the East, essentially a studio artist.

But he never sentimentalized the West. A hunter and horseman from his youth, he grew up fascinated by the military; he effectively described scenes of battle and carnage. But his most striking creation in his short stories is Sun-Down Leflare, a half-breed Indian. In the Sun Down stories, R. reveals the great gulf between the white intruders and Native Americans and the great price Native Americans paid for the Americanization of the West. R. was the first American writer of the West to depict that complexity and to make a Native American the sympathetic center of a story.

In *West of Everything* (1992), Jane Tompkins faults the creators of Westerns for ignoring the Native American. The charge could not be made against R. He wrote his first novel in reaction to the falsification of the West he found in Owen WISTER's *The Virginian*, the quintessential Western novel, which indeed ignored the Native American. R.'s *John Ermine of the Yellowstone*, also published in 1902, did not challenge Wister's novel aesthetically, but it made Native American experience crucial to plot and theme. The protagonist, a white boy reared by Crow Indians, attempts to reclaim his white heritage as a cavalry scout. Intending to murder a rival for a major's daughter, he is himself murdered by a jealous Crow. The protagonist of R.'s second novel, *The Way of an Indian* (1906), is a Cheyenne who finds his world view in marked contrast to that of the whites he encounters. Fire Eater successfully fights General George Crook's troops following the Little Big Horn massacre of 1876, but eventually his "medicine" fails him and the whites destroy his village.

R.'s fiction, now undervalued, is energetic, direct, accessible. He deserves more recognition for this fiction, especially for his portrayal of the Native American.

BIBLIOGRAPHY: Erisman, F., *F. R.* (1975); Hassrick, P. H., *F. R.* (1973); McCracken, H., *F. R.: Artist of the Old West* (1947); Vorpahl, B., *F. R. and the West* (1978)

JOSEPH M. FLORA

REVARD, Carter [Curtis]

b. 25 March 1931, Pawhuska, Oklahoma

R., part Osage, was given his Osage name Nompehwahteh (Fear Inspiring) in 1952, when he became a member of the Thunder Clan. He grew up poor in a mixed-blood family and lived until he was seventeen with relatives on the Osage Reservation. He attended the University of Tulsa, Oxford, and Yale, and he has taught at Amherst College and Washington University in St. Louis, Missouri. In his poetry, short stories, and essays, R. returns to his Native American roots and to the landscape of Oklahoma.

The hill country of R.'s youth, with its lazy and muddied streams, its stands of oak and hickory, scattered through with redbud and dogwood, lives in his poems. In an interview with Native American author Joseph Bruchac, R. acknowledges the strong influence of the Osage writer, John Joseph Mathews, "He helped create Oklahoma for me."

In his poetry, R. seeks to recover and sustain the voice of Oklahoma, the "rhythms and sounds of Osage Country people, Indian and others." R. weaves his accounts—some funny, some sad, some bittersweet—of his boyhood, his immediate and extended family, their experiences, songs, dances, and stories. A sense of narrative and the rhythm of natural speech strengthen these poems. In the sonnet, "Coyote Tells Why He Sings," published in *Ponca War Dancers* (1980), R. traces his Oklahoma voice back to Coyote, the Trickster/Creator, whose tracks he finds while seeking shelter, with his boyhood friends, from a summer storm.

R. says of his voice and its poetic shapes that they are "afloat between cultures and times, between heaven and earth, between North America and Europe." Such a blend calls for the ability of transformation, a dominant theme in R.'s poems, for only through transformation comes survival and interconnectedness. This message is most clearly expressed in the poem, "Dances with Dinosaurs." Here Osage creation stories—ancestors descending from the sky and finding homes in the bodies of birds—merge with new scientific discoveries—"new myths," as R. calls them—of the connection between dinosaurs and birds.

Humor aids transformation and survival. There often is a wry irony at work in R.'s writings—as when in the essay, "Report to the Nation: Claiming Europe," his narrator, Special Agent Wazhazhe No. 2,230, travels through Europe to claim the lands he encounters. This humor turns into a bitter parody in the poem, "The Discovery of the New World," where invasion of earth by space aliens parallels the Europeans' genocidal takeover of North America. But more often humor makes poems, in R.'s words, "user-friendly." Humor brings forth laughter and keeps hope alive.

As a poet, R. likes to see the return of poems that influence readers strongly. Poetry, according to him, has lost its power because it has lost the ability to tell stories—although not so much among minority writers. He pleads for a comeback of stories, of voice, of rhyme, and with them a celebration of wonder and what is good and strong.

BIBLIOGRAPHY: Bruchac, J., *Survival This Way: Interviews with American Indian Poets* (1987); Swann, B., and A. Krupat, eds., *I Tell You Now: Autobiographical Essays by Native American Writers* (1987)

HEIDEMARIE Z. WEIDNER

REXROTH, Kenneth

b. 22 December 1905, South Bend, Indiana; d. 6 June 1982, Santa Barbara, California

A maverick man of letters, R. was one of the most influential figures in American literature through the middle decades of the 20th c. among publishers and poets working beyond the limits of conventional literary channels. His prominent position in countercultural affairs may have drawn attention away from his own work during his lifetime, but his fascinating involvement with many of the more interesting writers in modern American literary history should not detract from his considerable accomplishments as a poet, literary theorist, self-taught classical scholar and superb translator of an international assortment of poets.

R. attracted considerable attention during his lifetime for his iconoclastic opinions about contemporary and classical writers, and in his most incisive essays and reviews—collected in *Bird in the Bush: Obvious Essays* (1959), *Assays* (1961), *Classics Revisited* (1968), and perhaps most impressively, *American Poetry in the Twentieth Century* (1971)—R.'s range of knowledge, personal involvement with his subject, obvious passion for artistic excellence and often quirky but frequently accurate evaluations remain engaging in a nonpedantic way. His ability to equal the erudition and expertise of scholars in a particular field while reaching for an audience beyond the academy makes his examinations of often obscure but singularly successful writers from other epochs a demonstration of how a "classic" might be made accessible and appealing to a contemporary reader.

R.'s real strength, however, stems from his capability as a poet. While not as highly regarded as the dominant voices of the mid-20th c.—William Carlos WILLIAMS, Wallace STEVENS, Marianne MOORE, Robert FROST—and consequently consigned to a kind of poetic limbo with writers such as E. E. CUMMINGS, Hart CRANE, Hilda DOOLITTLE, and George OPPEN, R. wrote poetry throughout his life and established a style and voice that goes beyond the temporary excitement generated by other writers whose brief prominence depended on an ephemeral device or attention-grabbing gimmicks. Longer poetic sequences like *The Dragon and the Unicorn* (1952), which was based on a trek through Europe, effectively captures the vivid features of a specific setting in the framework of a philosophical inquiry, its discursive elements providing a solid ground for the passages of lyric intensity and personal, emotional expression. R.'s commitment to a vision of social justice—a mixture of anarchist politics, environmental awareness and New Deal decency—keeps the longer poems interesting, but their strongest passages are ones that join R.'s central subject, the nature of a consuming erotic relationship, with the main source of his poetic inspiration, the features of the landscape he loved.

The best of his shorter lyric poetry, notably some selections from *In What Hour* (1940) and *Natural Numbers* (1963), indicate what R. could do at his best.

They have a clear, direct style of presentations, the imagery powerful and concise, the language close to what Henry David THOREAU called "healthy speech" and the rhythms fluid and supple. In these poems, R. was moving toward his most enduring achievement, a body of translation that has been described by Nobel laureate Czeslaw Milosz as the work of "one of the great craftsman" whose "many translations and adaptations from French, Chinese, and Japanese are of particularly high quality." The techniques of translation are a matter of constant contention, but Milosz argues that R.'s translations "are already classic" in their adaptation of the poetry to a "modern sensibility." Due to his own interest in the culture of the Asian Pacific region and his fervid curiosity about feminine reality, R. has been able to craft versions of *The Burning Heart: Women Poets of Japan* (1977) and *The Orchid Boat: Women Poets of China* (1972) working with women who knew the original language. However close these may be to the poetry that inspired them, they stand as superb poems in English, conveying the flavor and sensibility of civilizations both distant and often closely recognizable to contemporary American readers.

BIBLIOGRAPHY: Gardiner, G., ed., *For R.* (1980); Gibson, M., *Revolutionary R.: Poet of East-West Wisdom* (1986); Hamalian, L. *A Life of K. R.* (1991)

LEON LEWIS

REYNOLDS, Jeremiah N.

b. 1799, Cumberland County, Pennsylvania; d. 25 August 1858, St. Catharine's Springs, Ontario, Canada

This celebrated advocate of U.S. exploration of the South Seas is chiefly known today for his work's influence on the writing of Edgar Allan POE and Herman MELVILLE. After three years as a student at Ohio University (1819–22) and one year as editor of the *Wilmington Spectator* (1824), R. joined John Cleves Symmes, proponent of the "holes-at-the-poles" theory, lectured extensively with him, and published *Remarks on a Review of Symmes' Theory* (1827). R. also helped organize the expedition of the *Annawan, Seraph,* and *Penguin* into the South Seas (1829-30); his account of an incident occurring on this voyage, "Leaves From an Unpublished Journal," published in the *New York Mirror* (April 21, 1838) was an important influence on the latter portions of Poe's novel *The Narrative of Arthur Gordon Pym.*

After extensive travels in South America, R. joined the U.S. frigate *Potomac* in Valparaiso in 1832, and later published *Journey of the United States Frigate Potomac* (1835), another influence on Poe's novel. He also edited *A Life of George Washington, in Latin Prose* by Francis Glass (1835) and wrote and presented *Address, on the Subject of a Surveying and Exploring Expedition to the Pacific Ocean and South Seas* (1836), yet a third R. text that influenced Poe's novel. When Poe was editor of the *Southern Literary Messenger* from late 1835 to early 1838, a periodical owned by R.'s friend Thomas W. White, Poe reviewed R.'s books and, in light of his comments, might well have met R. His borrowings from R.'s writings for *The Narrative of Arthur Gordon Pym* involve both verisimilar language and detail, and dramatic events. It is generally thought that Poe's deathbed cries "Reynolds! Reynolds!" referred to R., but this view has been challenged.

Unable to participate in the U.S. Exploring Expedition he had promoted, termed the Wilkes Expedition (1838–42), R. continued to write and publish. One of his pieces was "Mocha Dick; or, The White Whale of the Pacific," published in the *Knickerbocker* (May 1839). The tale, heard by R. on board ship off the coast of South America in 1830, was a suggestive one for Melville in his writing *Moby-Dick; or, The Whale.* A comparison of the two works reveals a resonance of both language and incident. R. was later admitted to the New York Bar, entered New York politics, invested in land in Texas, began a bank in Texas, mined for silver in Mexico, and headed the new American Party in New York City. R.'s writing was not distinguished—his narratives, while often vivid and lively, were conventional in their romantic and pious tone. The importance of his writing lies in the light it sheds on the composing techniques of Poe and Melville; it is not as text but as context that R.'s work endures.

BIBLIOGRAPHY: Almy, R. F., "J. N. R.: A Brief Biography With Particular Reference to Poe and Symmes," *Colophon* 2 (Winter 1937): 227–45; Kopley, R., "The Secret of *Arthur Gordon Pym:* The Text and the Source," *SAF* 8 (Autumn 1980): 203–18; Starke, A., "Poe's Friend Reynolds," *AL* 11 (1939): 152–59; Woodbridge, R. G., III, "J. N. R.: Father of American Exploration," *PULC* 45 (Winter 1984): 107–21

RICHARD KOPLEY

REZNIKOFF, Charles

b. 31 August 1894, Brooklyn, New York; d. 22 January 1976, New York City

R. was born in the Jewish enclave of Brownsville in Brooklyn, New York. In 1910, he graduated from Boy's High School in Brooklyn and entered the newly founded School of Journalism at the University of Missouri, where he stayed for one year and contributed some of his earliest verse to the school magazine. R. was disillusioned by his discovery that journalism was less interested in writing than it was in the uncovering of sensational stories; he was more interested in what writing itself could do to raise the ordinary and everyday happening to a larger significance. R. returned to New York in 1911 and decided, citing the example of Heinrich Heine, to study law. He graduated from the New York University Law School in 1915, second in his class, and one year later was admitted to the bar.

He practiced law only briefly and unsuccessfully, finding himself completely unsuited for the histrionics required in the courtroom, but utilized his legal training in the work he did for *Corpus Juris,* an encyclopedia of law for lawyers, and also in the editing work he did on the papers of Louis Marshall, published in 1957 in two volumes.

But the main business of R.'s life was his writing: poetry, history, translation, fiction, and autobiography. He was a distinguished contributor and eventually editor of the *Menorah Journal,* the quarterly that was the predecessor of the better-known monthly *Commentary,* which also published him in some of its early issues. Some of his work he printed on his own press: one little booklet in 1927 he called *Five Groups of Verse;* another in the same year was entitled *Nine Plays* (in verse). Still another, two years later, was the earliest version of *By the Waters of Manhattan.* In 1930, an expansion of this was published in paperback as a novel, which was introduced by the anthologist Louis Untermeyer and elicited an enthusiastic review by Lionel TRILLING. In 1931, R. was starred in the "Objectivist" issue of *Poetry,* guest edited by R.'s friend Louis ZUKOFSKY, at the instigation of Ezra POUND. Several of his works were published in the 1930s by the Objectivist Press, notably *Testimony* and *Jerusalem the Golden,* and for a time, R. served for a time as an assistant to his friend Albert Lewin, a Hollywood writer-director-producer.

He then virtually disappeared from the literary scene for twenty years. Fortunately, however, an insightful review of one of his self-printed booklets, *Inscriptions: 1944–1956,* which appeared in the January 16, 1961 issue of the *New Leader,* marked the beginning of a new literary life for R. In 1962, he enjoyed his first commercial publication since 1930, a slim paperback selection of his poems that used again the title of his earlier novel, and was introduced to the American public by the well-known English novelist C. P. Snow. *By the Waters of Manhattan* was ecstatically reviewed in the pages of *The Nation,* and from this moment, R. was on the American literary map, invited to give poetry reading across the country and turning up in reference works that had hitherto ignored him. But it was not to be an unalloyed triumph.

In 1965, the first installment of a verse *Testimony* (a previous prose *Testimony,* with an introduction by Kenneth BURKE, had been published by the Objectivist Press in 1934) was poorly received even in those quarters that had been enthusiastic about *By the Waters of Manhattan,* and New Directions dropped its option on further installments of what has proved to be an epic in two volumes. However, the option was picked up by John Martin and his Black Sparrow Press in California.

In the last years of R.'s life, Martin published two other titles by R., *By the Well of Living and Seeing* in 1974 and another long poem, *Holocaust,* in 1975, just a year before R.'s death. In 1976, R. was correcting proofs of the first volume of what was eventually to be a two-volume edition of his *Complete Poems,* edited by Seamus Cooney. In 1977, a year after R.'s death, John Martin also brought out an unpublished novel found among R.'s papers, *The Manner MUSIC.*

BIBLIOGRAPHY: Hindus, M., *C. R.: Man and Poet* (1984); Oppen, G., "On R.," *Sulfur* 32 (Spring 1993): 39–40; special R. issue, *Sagetrieb* 13 (Fall-Spring 1994)

MILTON HINDUS

RICE, Anne

b. 4 October 1941, New Orleans, Louisiana

With her novels' baroque sensibility and prose, R. has crafted a place for herself on the border between mainstream fiction and the Gothic romance. R.'s style is influenced in part by the work of her poet husband, Stan Rice—and her themes, by the death of her daughter at the age of six to leukemia.

Under the pseudonym Anne Rampling, R. has published contemporary fiction with a decidedly erotic edge, such as *Exit to Eden* (1985) and *Belinda* (1986), and as A. N. Roquelaure, she has written the "Beauty" series—an uneasy blend of fairy-tale setting and sadomasochism. But R. is best known for her 1976 novel *Interview with the Vampire,* which met with wildly mixed reviews upon publication, characterized as everything from "too superficial, too impersonal, and too obviously made, to touch the sources of real terror and feeling" to the "quite stunning debut of a young woman" praised for the originality brought to the popular "vampire tradition." Yet the Gothic homoeroticism of this tale, and the evocative renderings of its socially and emotionally alienated vampires, have proven to have an enduring pull on the public imagination and have taken each of R.'s subsequent novels that center on vampirism to the best-seller lists.

Interview with the Vampire has as its chief protagonist Louis, initiated as a vampire after the death of his brother by the charismatic vampire Lestat. Louis's guilt over his brother's death and his feelings of isolation finally prompt him to share the story of his "life" with a young journalist. In subsequent "vampire" novels, Lestat takes over both the narration and the focus of the tales. *The Vampire Lestat* (1985) is Lestat's attempt to "set the record straight" for his readership, sharing vampiric lore as he tells of the path that has led him to pursue ever more public avowals of his true nature, ending with his career as a rock star under a widely emulated, but never believed vampire persona. *The Vampire Lestat* was followed by *The Queen of the Damned* (1988), which tracks Lestat's vampiric ancestry; *The Tale of the Body Thief* (1993), which focuses on Lestat's desire to put an end to a life that he believes has ceased to have meaning; and finally *Memnoch the Devil* (1995), in which Lestat is brought into confrontation with God and the devil to choose whom to follow. A sixth novel set in this "universe," but one which features a female vampire is *Pandora* (1998).

Interspersed between the publication of her vampire tales, R. wrote a number of novels also dealing with alienation, but of a more realistic variety, including *Feast of All Saints* (1980), which focuses on the *gens de couleur libre* (free people of color) in pre-Civil War New Orleans, and *Cry to Heaven* (1982), about the castrati in the opera houses of 19th-c. Italy. And in 1990, R. published *The Witching Hour,* a supernatural Southern Gothic about the Mayfairs—a dynasty of witches in New Orleans. Further installments in a series include *Lasher* (1993) and *Taltos* (1995), which focus on the inhuman child of Rowan Mayfair and the demon that haunts the Mayfair family—and the lengths to which the family must go to remain intact.

Critical reception continues to be mixed for R.'s works, exemplified by more recent novels such as *The Servant of the Bones* (1996) and *Violin* (1997), but despite, or perhaps because of the initial controversy surrounding the 1994 release of the film version of *Interview with the Vampire,* R.'s readership continues to grow.

BIBLIOGRAPHY: Hoppenstand, G., and R. B. Browne, *The Gothic World of A. R.* (1996); Ramsland, K., *Prism of the Night: A Biography of A. R.* (1991); Roberts, B. B., *A. R.* (1994)

ELIZABETH HADDRELL

RICE, Elmer

b. 28 September 1892, New York City; d. 8 May 1967, Southampton, England

For half a century, R. was a true man of the American theater. Not only did he write over fifty plays between

1914 and 1963, but he also taught theater and wrote nonfiction on the subject. He even wrote a novel set in the world of Broadway and bought the Belasco Theatre in 1934.

Born Elmer Leopold Reizenstein, R. attended law school but abandoned plans to practice law when he realized that his personal sense of ethics would prevent him from defending those he knew to be guilty. He would, nevertheless, use his legal knowledge to explore ethical issues in the plays *On Trial* (1914) and *Counsellor-at-Law* (1931). The former was a successful first solo work, despite some structural flaws. The latter is a mature, complex play that shows the workings of a successful law office, intertwining a number of characters and subplots. Main character George Simon is a prosperous attorney shown using his skill and power to help clients by tough, yet ethical means. Ironically, his single well-meaning past act of malfeasance is used against him, and his career is threatened at a time he faces various personal crises. R.'s ability to immerse the audience in the world of the high-class attorney helps make this material engaging.

A decade earlier, R. had shown great skill in the nonrealistic realm with his seminal expressionistic play, *The Adding Machine* (1923). Henpecked husband Mr. Zero is a repetitive number cruncher who is fired after twenty-five years of service. Aside from the innovative staging, the language is strangely ungrammatical and slangy. Condemned and executed for killing his former boss, Mr. Zero finds himself in the Elysian Fields, an afterlife setting where he is reunited with former coworker Daisy (who killed herself over his death), only to be returned to the hell of his old job at play's end. *The Adding Machine* shows the devolution of mankind while condemning technology that turns people into robots. It dazzles the audience with its language, offbeat humor, and staging in ways that are easier to appreciate in today's computer age than in the 1920s, when its innovations and themes puzzled many critics.

Later in that decade, R. won the Pulitzer Prize for his naturalistic *Street Scene* (1929), which meticulously re-created life outside a New York tenement on stage. As in *Counsellor-at-Law,* a number of personal stories and subplots intermingle in this microcosm of lower-class society. People reveal their hopes, dreams, and fears, but the hot, oppressive environment seems to control the characters' destinies. Cultures and ideologies clash, but ironically it is a domestic dispute that culminates in murder. R. directed the original production and later wrote the libretto for the 1947 opera adaptation that featured words and music by Langston HUGHES and Kurt Weill, respectively. In both forms, *Street Scene* remains one of R.'s most enduring works.

Although R. had explored Freudian ideas to some degree through expressionism in *The Adding Machine,* his 1945 play *Dream Girl* overtly relies on dreams—or more accurately Walter Mitty-like fantasies. Georgina Allerton is a career woman who speaks in a fresh voice, perhaps inspired by the fact that R. had his wife Betty Field in mind for the role when he wrote it. Unfortunately, the experience led to their divorce, her nervous breakdown, and a shortening of the play's projected run. A very loose musical adaptation titled *Skyscraper* enjoyed little success in 1963.

The Living Theatre (1959) emerged from R.'s experience teaching a seminar at New York University in 1957. The chapters, each inspired by a seminar discussion, cover R.'s view of the theater scene in various countries, the negative effects of commercialism on drama, and various insights gained from a lifetime in the profession. While he would continue to work for several more years, and a 1951 play, *Love among the Ruins,* would finally be produced in 1963, *The Living Theatre* serves as both a useful introduction and fitting culmination to R.'s career.

Although active in liberal politics, several unfavorably received plays, including *Judgment Day* (1934), made some suspect R. was a communist, when in fact he was simply an outspoken idealist devoted to fundamental democratic principles. He also tended to battle critics, for whom he generally had little regard. He should be remembered today not only for the brilliant *Adding Machine* but also as a prolific, conscientious playwright with a gift for writing dialog and creating a realistic setting in which to observe life and explore important issues.

BIBLIOGRAPHY: Durham, F., *E. R.* (1970); Hogan, R. G., *The Independence of E. R.* (1965); Palmieri, A. F. R., *E. R.: A Playwright's Vision of America* (1980)

GARY KONAS

RICH, Adrienne
b. 10 May 1929, Baltimore, Maryland

R. has become one of the most eminent and respected poets of her generation. Her career began on a high note when she won the Yale Series of Younger Poets Award for her first book, *A Change of World* (1951); she has won numerous awards since then, including the National Book Award for *Diving into the Wreck* (1974), two Guggenheim Fellowships, and a prestigious MacArthur Fellowship in 1994. R. is notable not only as a poet who has vigorously explored the possibility of, in her own phrase, "re-visioning the language," but also as an essayist and political activist who has championed human rights, with special attention to women's liberation and homosexual rights.

While she has sometimes been attacked for allowing her political commitment to interfere with her work as a poet, her recent collection of essays effectively explores and rebuts the perennial questions and complaints about the relationship between the artist's work and her political engagement. R. would argue that her political commitment gives her poetry its weight and power, while her imaginative ability to evoke the historical and political dimensions of her deeply felt and precisely observed personal experiences, uniting them through her poetic process to create new visions of life in America, demonstrates the truth of the feminist argument that the personal is political, and vice versa.

R. has, by her own account, lived a privileged life, though not an easy one. Her parents encouraged her artistic and intellectual interests, and she attended Radcliffe College, where she was able to develop so quickly as a poet that W. H. AUDEN chose her manuscript for the Yale award and wrote an enthusiastic introduction hailing R. for working so effectively in the 'tradition' of her male predecessors, notably W. B. Yeats and Robert FROST—praise revealed as unintentionally ironic by the direction of her poetic career since then. The titles of her books, read in succession, reveal the alternation of the personal and the political, the rebellious and the healing in her work: *Snapshots of a Daughter-in-Law* (1963) and *Leaflets: Poems* (1969); *The Will to Change* (1971) and *Twenty-One Love Poems* (1976); the assertion of the unity of the political and the personal might be most explicit in *Your Native Land, Your Life* (1986), while the continuation of her political commitment may be seen in the alternately agonizing and serene *Dark Fields of the Republic* (1995). R. further enhanced her oeuvre with the publication in 1999 of *Midnight Salvage: Poems, 1995–1998.*

R. began her feminist critique both of women's lives and women's use of male-defined language in her 1960s works, especially poems collected in *Necessities of Life* (1966). These poems look at the presence of signs and omens of death in daily life, and quickly demonstrate that she is not primarily concerned with death as an ending to life, but sees evidences of the death of old ways needed to pass beyond to a new life—the end of the world as it has been known in the flowering of a new world where women may have control of their bodies, their lives, their language. The means of transition for herself and all women would be through the process of "re-visioning" explored in her essay, "When We Dead Awaken" (1972), and exemplified in both her poetry and her essays. The best-known and perhaps definitive statement of her rejection of the patriarchal "tradition" Auden praised her for exemplifying is found in the title poem of *Diving Into the Wreck* (1973) and in other poems of that volume. This volume is exemplary both for the praise it has received as an essential poetic statement of the new feminist consciousness and for the condemnation it has suffered as a work too overtly tendentious and "political" to succeed as art. It is a work of transitions and challenges, questioning all relationships and all boundaries, including gender roles and identities. In "From a Survivor," R. contemplates her dead husband, a suicide, and her own survival as a newly defined person; she has moved beyond "the matrix of need and anger," and is forging a new life as a feminist poet and as a lesbian, along with a new kind of poetry that will emerge "in visionary pain and in relief."

R. has earned her reputation with her poetry, but her work as an essayist also constitutes a major contribution to late-20th-c. American literature. Her essays on rethinking women's roles, on devising a woman-centered university, and especially on the necessary connections between poetry and politics, have broadened and deepened the terms of discussion as she has insisted on the essential role of the creative imagination and the central role of poetry in the political debate. Throughout the essays of *What Is Found There* (1993), R. explores the variety of social and political functions that poetry serves—its healing power, its ability to remind us of the power of speaking truth in language, its ability to nourish and to create. She asserts that poetry is not necessarily more necessary than food or shelter, but that it is, in the final scheme of things, just as important and as necessary. Without the ability of poetry constantly to recall to us the sensuous reality of the lives we try to construct, social and political life become cold, dehumanized, destructive; poetry protects public life, in her terms, by countering the forces that would, as she says in "Voices of the Air," "deprive us of language and reduce us to passive sufferers." Her refusal to accept the isolation of the artist from the public role she believes is essential for the health of the society as well as the viability of the art itself, stands as one aspect of her courageous and revolutionary contribution to poetry and to life.

The South African novelist Nadine Gordimer has praised R. as "the Blake of American letters" for her combined "vision of warning and her celebration of life." While some recoil from the anger and rebellion of R.'s work, the constant affirmation and generosity of her vision are what will sustain her reputation and make her work valuable long past the end of the 20th c.

BIBLIOGRAPHY: Cooper, J. R., ed., *Reading A. R.* (1984); Keyes, C., *The Aesthetics of Power: The Poetry of A. R.* (1986); Martin, W., *An American Triptych: Anne Bradstreet, Emily Dickinson, A. R.* (1984); Ostriker, A., *Writing like a Woman* (1983); Vendler,

H., *Part of Nature, Part of Us: Modern American Poets* (1980)

THOMAS F. DILLINGHAM

RICHTER, Conrad

b. 13 October 1890, Pine Grove, Pennsylvania; d. 30 October 1968, Pottsville, Pennsylvania

In his short stories and novels, R. captured the indomitable spirit of the American pioneer, re-created the atmospheres of the primitive American frontier at various times and locations, and examined the transformations that contact of the pioneer with the frontier wrought in each.

R. began his writing career as a journalist, and his earliest short stories were published in popular magazines before he gathered them into collections. Several of the novels were also serialized in periodicals before publication, which may have contributed to their episodic nature. Of R.'s prolific output—two story collections, three book-length essays, and fourteen novels—two trilogies are of special literary merit.

The trilogy set in the American Southwest consists of *The Sea of Grass* (1937), *Tacey Cromwell* (1942), and *The Lady* (1957). The first novel examines the complex interactions between the earliest American settlers in New Mexico, the cattlemen; those who followed them, the farmers; and the land itself. *Tacey Cromwell* chronicles the efforts of a pair of social outcasts to earn the approbation of a small Arizona community. The third novel in the trilogy returns to the New Mexico locale to document power struggles between cattlemen and sheepmen. Of particular interest in these works and others, R.'s narrators act as unsophisticated eyewitnesses, but relate the events years later as memories, thereby allowing the stories to span long periods of time without losing continuity.

The novels of the Ohio trilogy, *The Trees* (1940), *The Fields* (1946), and *The Town* (1950), are linked through characterization as well as through locale and theme. These novels dramatize R.'s concept of "westering"—the process whereby 17th-and 18th-c. Americans transformed the frontier, and whereby the frontier permeated the pioneers—transfiguring their spirit. *The Trees* introduces the Luckett family, led into the Ohio wilderness by their nomadic patriarch, Worth. Sayward, the eldest daughter, gains full responsibility for the family when her mother dies and her father abandons them to continue west. *The Fields* follows Sayward through her marriage to lawyer Portius Wheeler and the rearing of their young family. It concludes with the protagonist's matronal concern with the successes and failures of her adult children and her death. In the trilogy, Sayward Luckett's maturation and rise to

matriarchal status parallels the slow but steady process that cleared the forests of the Western Reserve land in Ohio, that plowed the land, and that established the communities of eastern Ohio. In 1951, R. was awarded the Pulitzer Prize, ostensibly for *The Town,* but in reality the award was for the three novels in the Ohio trilogy.

With few exceptions, R.'s other fictional works have been acknowledged for their rich and glimmering yet subtle settings, for their use of authentic dialogue, for their heroic but complex characterization, for their avoidance of the excesses and sensationalism often associated with chronicles of American westward expansion. The three extended essays, *Human Vibration* (1926), *Principles in Bio-Physics* (1927), and *The Mountain on the Desert* (1955), philosophical examinations of the dynamics of the human spirit, offer some insights into R.'s values and themes. The excellence of R.'s autobiographical novels, *The Waters of Kronos* (1960), which received the National Book Award, and *A Simple Honorable Man* (1962) has also been acknowledged.

BIBLIOGRAPHY: Barnes, R. J., *C. R.* (1968); Gaston, E. W., Jr., *C. R.* (1989); Lahood, M. J., *C. R.'s America* (1975); Richter, H., ed. "Writing To Survive: The Private Notebooks of C. R.," *SDR* 25 (Autumn 1987): 130–67

TERESA K. LEHR

RIDING, Laura [Jackson]

b. 16 January 1901, New York City; d. 2 September 1991, Sebastian, Florida

Poet, critic, and fiction writer during the 1920s and 1930s, and later a writer on language and the failure of poetry, R. began her career in America, where she was a member of the Fugitive group and a contributor to *Poetry* magazine. However, she left in 1925 to live abroad and soon afterward formed a literary partnership with the English poet Robert Graves. Their most important collaboration was a *Survey of Modernist Poetry* (1927), said to have influenced the methodologies of William Empson and of the New Critics. In this, as in their other collaborations, R.'s contribution seems predominant, though Graves received the greater recognition. *Anarchism Is Not Enough* (1928), a noncollaborative work, shows her critical thought and avant-garde style in pure form. Her fiction is best seen in *A Progress of Stories* (1935), a delightful example of children's literature for adults.

Though prolific in prose, R. placed the highest value on poetry during these years. She wrote nine volumes in all, beginning with *The Close Chaplet*

(1926) and ending with *Collected Poems* (1938). R.'s expectations for poetry were enormous. Like other writers of the period, she was looking for a way to reunite a fragmented world and self, but unlike her contemporaries, she did not look to politics or religion for a solution to the problem. Rather, language was the answer. Used in its truest sense, as poetry, language could draw together the world's scattered miscellany of minds into a new union of truth, with each constituent mind shorn of its fallacious, superficial identity but retaining its individual essence. In this way, chaos would give way to communion in truth. R.'s poems foresee the culmination of this process and follow her own progress toward it. Many are concerned with defining what human beings are, what they have been, and what they might become. In addition, many contrast the unsatisfactory temporal world of the present with the prospective timeless world of final truth.

Although R.'s poems deal in generalities, they are remarkably vivid and exact. In part, she achieves this lively precision by confronting the reader with surprising propositions and startling images that link the inner world of mind with the outer physical world in a way that is indelible, though at times difficult to visualize—the surrealistic disembodiment of "Thought looking out on thought / Makes one an eye." The particular mood that suffuses each poem—in some cases humor or certitude, in others bitterness or despair—also helps mitigate the danger of abstraction. A source of difficulty for new readers is R.'s practice of endowing certain key words with unfamiliar meanings or connotations. For example, "death" is frequently a positive word referring to a state of mental perfection. By contrast, "life" is often a negative word implying mere brutish existence. In most cases, these special usages can be defined from context with a careful reading of the poem. "The Quids," The Rugged Black of Anger," "Death as Death," "World's End," "The Map of Places," "Earth," and "After So Much Loss" are among R.'s finest poems. Some can be found in anthologies, but the best sources readily available are *The Poems of Laura Riding* (1980), a reprint of *Collected Poems,* and *Selected Poems* (1973). In terms of recognition and influence, R. can be accounted only a minor poet. However, the magnitude and originality of her work have attracted new attention in recent years, and a revaluation is currently underway.

R.'s literary career ended not long after her return in America in 1939. She remained virtually silent for years and seemed in danger of being forgotten until she suddenly reemerged in the 1960s under her married name, Jackson. But more than her name had changed. Once poetry's greatest advocate, she was now its implacable opponent. She elaborated her reasons in articles for *Chelsea* (nos. 12, 14, 35) and the *Denver Quarterly* (no. 9). In poetry's place substituted a new

linguistic ideal, which is the subject of her last book, *The Telling* (1972).

BIBLIOGRAPHY: Adams, B., "L. R.'s Autobiographical Poetry: 'My Muse Is I,'" *CP* 15 (Fall 1982): 71–87; Masopust, M., "L. R.'s Quarrel Poetry," *SCRev* 2 (Spring 1985): 42–56; Rosenthal, M. L., "L. R.'s Poetry: A Nice Problem," *SoR* 21 (Winter 1985): 89–95; Wexler, J. P., *L. R.: A Bibliography* (1981); Wexler, J. P., *L. R.'s Pursuit of Truth* (1979)

MICHAEL MASOPUST

RILEY, James Whitcomb

b. 7 October 1849, Greenfield, Indiana; d. 22 July 1916, Indianapolis, Indiana

R. enjoyed enormous popularity in his lifetime, but his reputation declined at his death and has never recovered. By the time of the R. centennial in 1949, his books had sold upward of five million copies, and he could be seen as a pioneer in the professions of newspaper poet and touring platform reader. He was also one of the most persistent practitioners of the dialect writing that many readers lapped up during the period between 1850 and 1920, although the taste for such work has fallen off considerably since then. Some of this distortion represents baby-talk or lisping (such as "ist" for "just"); some is just a fortuitous and pointless misspelling (such as "Ponchus Pilut" for "Pontius Pilate"). With almost studied illiteracy, R. called his first book *The Old Swimmin'-Hole and 'Leven More Poems* (1883).

In 1993, Turner Cassity, speaking some final words over the grave of R.'s reputation, dismissed him as a tremendous embarrassment to American literature. R. had been a versifier and not a genuine poet, and now it is as though he practiced an art that few recognize as a legitimate human activity. It is as though he was a phrenologist or a peddler of blotters in a world that had long since quit using ink pens.

Even so, R. deserves to be remembered for certain contributions to popular culture and to more serious art as well. Although his "Little Orphant Annie" concerns an adult woman, the title was taken over for a comic strip child (little in age and not necessarily in stature) that has been a staple of both the comic pages and the musical theater. The same impoverished creature of R.'s rich imagination gave birth to the Raggedy Ann doll, which remains a favorite. At just about any point in the U.S., one is probably within five miles of a Raggedy Ann, a character rather closer to R.'s "Little Orphant Annie" than to Harold Gray's "Little Orphan Annie."

In his huge output—almost 1,000 pages—he usually stuck to familiar patterns and forms, but in a restless mood he discovered the difficult and demanding villanelle and produced "The Best Is Good Enough," the first American poem to try that form. The villanelle has become a favorite design of American writers, including Edwin Arlington ROBINSON, Elizabeth BISHOP, and Marilyn HACKER.

A further tribute to R.'s influence is the testimony of Ezra POUND, who spent part of an abortive academic year in Indiana during R.'s heyday in 1907. Readers have been shocked to find R.'s idiom among the highly sophisticated Confucian discussion of the ideal life in Pound's Canto XIII. Much later, an isolated line in Canto LXXX muses, "and wd / [J.] W. R. be still found in a highbrow anthology"—a question that Pound was later to answer himself by placing R.'s "Good-By er Howdy-Do" in *Confucius to Cummings,* a decidedly highbrow anthology. When T. S. ELIOT titled the fifth section of *The Waste Land* "What the Thunder Said," Pound would probably have remembered that a poem of R.'s is called "What the Wind Said." With Eliot one can be less certain, but he read as widely as Pound and shared Pound's fondness for coarse popular entertainment. In the labored private lingo they developed for their correspondence over many years, Pound and Eliot seem to have adopted some of R.'s dialect, and Pound kept the same odd concoction for many other letters and for his radio broadcasts. For Pound, if for no one else, R. represents a poetry of the people with modest virtues and simple tastes but nonetheless with value in the world.

Martin Gardner has summarized the harshest judgments: "Ambrose BIERCE called R.'s verse a 'ripple of a rill of buttermilk falling into a pig-trough. His pathos is bathos: his sentiment sediment.'" When a ninety-year-old Louis Untermeyer was interviewed by the *New York Times* (September 30, 1975), he was asked what poets in his many anthologies he would now omit. "J. W. R.," he replied. "Why, why, why, why, oh God, why did I ever include him? I guess I was impressed by all the good clean Midwestern corn." At the time of R.'s sesquicentennial, his reputation is holding up better than Untermeyer's.

BIBLIOGRAPHY: Cassity, T., "Out of the Heartland," *Parnassus* 18 (1993): 381–94; Nolan, J. C., *Poet of the People: An Evaluation of J. W. R..* (1951); Revell, P., *J. W. R.* (1970)

WILLIAM HARMON

RINEHART, Mary Roberts

b. 12 August 1876, Pittsburgh, Pennsylvania; d. 22 September 1958, New York City

R. wrote a number of mainstream novels and stories, but found her forte and gained her literary reputation in the composition of detective stories, which she wrote for fifty years corresponding roughly to the first half of the 20th c.

Her career began with a detective novel that hewed closely to the conventional formula of the day—the closed milieu of a country house, a "detective" searching out clues and hidden facts, and the revelation of the murderer in the last scene. For all its haste of composition, *The Circular Staircase* (1908) has remained a classic of the genre. Twelve years after its publication, the story was adapted as *The Bat* for the Broadway stage, where it became a long-running hit.

R.'s literary career blossomed in the 1930s with the development of her own Americanized version of the typically English country-house detective story. Setting her stories in a mansion or country house of the well-to-do, she simply moved the English "cozy" formula to the U.S. and put her own stamp on it by her thematic material and her astonishing ability to work up complex and baffling plots.

Structurally, she spends as much time on the "inner" story of her novel—what has happened in the past to cause the present conflicts—as she does on the "surface" story. To prevent the typical confusion of the end-of-book "revelation," she allows parts of the inner story to appear piece by piece during the narration, until only the salient elements are left to clear up at the end.

Thematically, she builds her plots on complex social and personal conflicts. A favorite is mesalliance, the crossing of class barriers in marriage—the female "nobody" who pretends to be a "somebody" and marries an unsuspecting upper-class male—as in *The Wall* (1938). Repressed emotion, sexual passion, and jealousy frequently serve as building blocks for her plots, as in *The Album* (1933). In that novel she even plays with the theme of amnesia, later a work horse of the soap opera genre; she hints at incest in that same book years before the subject became fashionable. The problem of identity—concealed by amnesia or by deliberation—always fascinated R.

The Great Mistake (1940) has a monumentally complex plot whose murders hinge on past relationships rather than present ones, thus providing a smokescreen to hide the killer's motivation. Once again, the real relationships, revealed at the end, contain a hint of the incestuous. *The Yellow Room* (1945) is a story of a government agency, a mesalliant marriage, and amnesia, plus a suspicion of incest.

Her reputation as the "had I but known" mystery author, while deserved, is essentially unfair. Writing primarily for magazine serialization, she would create suspense by remarking, "Had I but known then what I know now, I would have. . . ." She did not invent the style, but it seems to cling to her in retrospect.

The other cliché of the mystery—"The butler did it"—could just as easily have been applied to her.

BIBLIOGRAPHY: Cohn, J., *Improbable Fiction: The Life of M. R. R.* (1980); MacLeod, C., *Had She but Known: A Biography of M. R. R.* (1994)

BRUCE CASSIDAY

RÍOS, Alberto [Alvaro]

b. 18 September 1952, Nogales, Arizona

R. writes of the languages and places he knows, but in his poems and short stories, words are more than signs; places evoke more than physical reality. Son of a Mexican father and an English mother, R. explores the real and imaginary border country between the U.S. and Mexico, as represented by the towns of Nogales in Arizona and the Mexican Tapachula in the southern state of Chiapas. Here words and images meet, sometimes clashing, but more often shifting shapes, effortlessly, instantly, transcending reality to capture the richness of his characters' multiple dimensions.

In *Whispering to Fool the Wind* (1982), a collection of poetry, R. pays more than lip service to the Chilean poet Pablo Neruda, who claims that the poet's duty is to name and express the nameless and the unknown. In these early poems, R. evokes his family and upbringing in the bordertown of Nogales, Arizona: a grandfather, long dead, communicates with his grandson through a pipe in the ground; Sunday visits and daily chores are remembered; town characters and town events come alive. In sharp images, R. crosses the line between countries, languages, and realities. In "The Pioneer Hotel Fire," for example, the flames engulfing a woman on the hotel's balcony burn as the fire of a secret and unfulfilled love affair; in "Carlos," the name of a distant relative who dies alone becomes the name for the loneliness, the pain, the cold we all suffer.

R.'s next collection of poetry, *The Lime Orchard Woman* (1988), explores words and the places beyond happiness. The poet argues that living on the fence, between cultures, one has to pay attention to words: lemons are yellow or green depending on what side of the fence one is on. These poems speak of new words, of words as echoes of voices, the end of words. There are words that rumble like cars of trains and words whose power makes a small boy cry; words explode like a gun; words stop a tornado, tear down a building, and keep a hat afloat.

Teodoro Luna's Two Kisses (1990) continues R.'s fascination with words and fluid moves between reality and imagination. As he puts it himself, "in that moment of survival beyond the borders of language and land-scape, and in the way the word does change, much of this book resides." The reader meets in these poems dreamers who dream "the inside of the outside." There may be old acquaintances from R.'s short stories and earlier poems—characters, events, and phrases: the whispers of small towns, the dead visiting, beloved Mariquita.

R. brings the poetic quality of powerful images to his short stories as well. A close observer of life, he names the fleeting and often unspeakable, the bizarre and contradictory. In *The Iguana Killer: Twelve Stories of the Heart* (1984), R. paints the secretive and often painful world of children as they struggle with acceptance from family and friends, the bewildering changes of puberty, or the growing away from their family's culture. In the title story, "The Iguana Killer," Sapito, the boy with bulging eyes, gains fame among his friends with the baseball bat from his Arizona grandmother. In other stories, the body of a dead child is used to transport opium across the border; a fat boy's smell attracts a small group of followers to test their stamina; a destructive child finds a friend or brother in the machine bought to cure him; and love notes attached to a cow explore the different worlds of boys and girls.

In *Pig Cookies* (1995), R. pursues what happens to those who live in the spaces between. Remembering his Mexican grandfather, he writes in the introduction, "He kept his family at the edges of the Republic [southern and northern most Mexico] so that, in case his side lost, the family might take one more step quickly into another land." *Pig Cookies,* too, is a book full of stories from the edges, and one moves, as do the characters, in the blink of an eye from one place to another. The boundaries between worlds are fluid: a word, a gesture blurs the line; and behind everyday images and words lie those of dreams. The circus, introduced in the collection's first story, "Saturnino El Magnifico," and remembered in other stories, most definitely represents this world of shifting shapes as does its main character, Lazaro Luna, baker of pig cookies, surrogate husband, friend, lover, and mayor of this imaginary town where "there is no need of wind, not with so many whispers."

Out of his memories, R. shapes a new language to write about the experiences of his Mexican/Chicano background. As one reviewer wrote, his are not Mexican or Anglo stories but a startling blend of both, moving back and forth to create a new life, new realities, and new imaginations.

BIBLIOGRAPHY: Salívan, J. D., "A. R.," in Lomelí, F. A., and C. R. Shirley, eds., *DLB,* vol. 122, *Chicano Writers* (1992): 220–24

HEIDEMARIE Z. WEIDNER

RIPLEY, George
b. 3 October 1802, Greenfield, Massachusetts; d. 4 July 1880, New York City

R. is often cast as a "minor" transcendentalist whose utopian community, Brook Farm, could not lure Ralph Waldo EMERSON though it won dubious immortality as the setting of Nathaniel HAWTHORNE's *The Blithedale Romance*. But R. was one of the first and most articulate spokesmen for TRANSCENDENTALISM, and a tireless promoter of the cause.

A liberal Unitarian minister and a brilliant scholar, R. wrote *Discourses on the Philosophy of Religion* (1836) to allay fears of the radical new theology while definitively asserting the innate divinity of human nature. His edition of *Specimens of Foreign Standard Literature* (14 vols., 1838–42) presented to American readers the European works that most influenced his circle. A founder of the Transcendental Club, he was quick to enter the lists in defense of Emerson when Andrews Norton condemned the Divinity School Address. In *The Latest Form of Infidelity Examined* (1839), R. openly accused the Harvard establishment of obtuse rationalism that hindered true religion, a charge latent in his earlier skirmishes with Norton.

Resigning his pulpit in 1840, R. wrote for and helped edit *The Dial*. Increasingly concerned with social and political reform as opposed to pure individualism, he served as president of the Brook Farm Association from 1841 until its collapse in 1847. Heavily in debt, he moved to New York City, where he continued to edit the Associationist periodical the *Harbinger* (begun at Brook Farm in 1845) until it too expired in 1849. By the 1850s, he had become a highly respected journalist, writing for newspapers such as Horace Greeley's *New-York Tribune* and editing, with Charles A. Dana, *The New American Cyclopedia* (16 vols., 1858–63). At midcareer a failed reformer, R. ended a leading arbiter of American literature and culture, prolific and popular long after many brighter transcendentalist stars had dimmed.

BIBLIOGRAPHY: Crowe, C., *G. R.* (1967); Delano, S., *"The Harbinger" and New England Transcendentalism* (1983); Frothingham, O. B., *G. R.* (1882); Golemba, H. L., *G. R.* (1977); Myerson, J., *Brook Farm* (1978); Myerson, J., ed., *The Transcendentalists* (1984)

WESLEY T. MOTT

RITCHIE, Anna Cora Mowatt
b. 5 March 1819, Bordeaux, France; d. 21 July 1870, Twickenham, England

A playwright, actress, and fiction writer, R. is best remembered for her social comedy *Fashion; or, Life in New York* (1849), which was first produced at the Park Theater in New York on March 24, 1845. R., who was familiar with social life here and abroad, was not the first to satirize Americans who ape foreign customs, manners, and fashions. Suspicion of the high life or "bon ton" was well established and had been treated in Royall TYLER's *The Contrast* as well as several other comedies. However, in *Fashion,* the Tiffany family, their servants, business and social acquaintances, the republican enthusiast, Adam Trueman, and the imposter Count Jolimaitre were all fresh, funny caricatures who reflected the social folly of the times.

Along with the comedy, there is the warning delivered without subtlety by Adam Trueman that "fashion worship" makes "heathens and hypocrites" of all. As he sees it, the danger is that fashion destroys reality and freedom, while creating poverty and unhappiness. This more serious theme is kept from dominating the play, and eventually American common sense and simple virtue overcome deception and foppishness. Not only was this a popular play, it was also important because it marked an advance in American social comedy and pointed ahead to the more sophisticated works of later American dramatists.

Other works by R. include *Armand; or, The Peer and the Peasant* (1847) and nondramatic works such as the *Autobiography of an Actress* (1854) and *Mimic Life; or, Before and behind the Curtain* (1856).

BIBLIOGRAPHY: Meserve, W. J., *Heralds of Promise: The Drama of the American People in the Age of Jackson, 1829–1849* (1986)

EDMUND M. HAYES

RIVES, Amélie [Louise]
b. 23 August 1863, Richmond, Virginia; d. 16 August 1945, Albemarle County, Virginia

When R.'s name is invoked by literary historians, it is almost invariably as the author of *The Quick or the Dead?* (1888). Given that this novel sparked a heated controversy among contemporary critics and moralists, and that it sold some 300,000 copies, it is neither surprising nor inappropriate that she should be seen in this connection. However, to regard *The Quick or the Dead?* and the events surrounding its publication as emblematic of R.'s life and literary accomplishments is to see both in distorted terms.

The descendant of explorers, diplomats, senators, and soldiers, R. spent much of her youth at "Castle Hill," the family estate near Charlottesville, Virginia. She was given free rein of its library and read voraciously; she began writing stories at a precocious age.

In 1886, a house guest found one of these and placed it in the *Atlantic Monthly*. Entitled "A Brother to Dragons," its Elizabethan setting and redactive language suggest the author's eclectic interests. Subsequently her focus shifted to contemporary settings and characters, notably in *Virginia of Virginia* (1888); however, from first to last R.'s fiction features spirited feminine protagonists who exhibit a striking natural beauty, verve, courage, and a capacity to endure adversity. Although such traits are clearly reflections of R. herself, at this stage in her development they likewise indicate a rather sheltered, and on the whole innocent, upbringing.

This was the "Gilded Age," when fiction containing such romantic elements was being vigorously challenged by the rising tide of REALISM. R., who knew little of the public arena of letters, was unwittingly thrust into this controversy by *The Quick or the Dead?* The protagonist, Barbara Pomfret, is a young widow being courted by a cousin of her late husband. Thus, she is forced to choose between the prevailing social pressures of honoring the latter's memory, or submitting to the dictates of her heart. Largely oblivious to the crosscurrents of the romance-realism controversy, R. in her depiction of Barbara's dilemma unintentionally gave ammunition to both camps. Traditionalists, whose tastes ran toward the "moral" dimension of ROMANCE literature, denounced the novel as immoral, in that it made light of a widow's obligation to the dead. Realists, on the other hand, saw it as overwrought. At least two book-length parodies appeared. Letters to the publisher were so vitriolic that they had to be screened before being sent on to R. Positive reviews and published defenses notwithstanding, the author's reaction, in a word, was shock.

As in many cases when the public has overreacted, the storm over *The Quick or the Dead?* soon passed. In 1912, the *Bookman* noted that while the novel had founded the "semi-erotic genre" in the American novel, it "would probably not cause the slightest ripple of excitement" in the present. Moreover, R. soon went on to more impressive accomplishments. In 1888, she married John Armstrong Chanler, a great-grandson of John Jacob Astor, and began the first of many sojourns in Europe. First, she studied painting in Paris with Charles Lazar; later, she met many of the English literati and associated with "The Souls," an elite group consisting of political, social, and literary figures. Europe now became a setting for her work, beginning with *The Witness of the Sun* (1889) and *According to St. John* (1891).

By 1894, her marriage to Chanler now deteriorated, Oscar Wilde introduced her to Prince Pierre Troubetzkoy, a popular portrait painter. Following their marriage in 1896, the Troubetzkoys lived at "Castle Hill," in New York, and in England. Between 1893 and 1898, R. wrote little; however, the second period of her literary career proved quite productive. Drawing upon new experiences and intellectual stimuli, and adopting a decidedly more realistic approach to her fictional materials, she produced work that was far more substantial than in the period 1886–93. This period begins with the narrative aesthete poem *Seléné* (1905) and the closet drama *Augustine the Man* (1906). The best of the later fiction is characterized by her two most accomplished novels, *World's-End* (1914) and *Shadows of Flames* (1915). Both combine the familiar European and American settings that R. had formerly used, and both are autobiographical in sundry ways. For example, *Shadows of Flames* draws upon her first marriage and her early residence in London; there is even a character based upon Oscar Wilde.

R.'s personal and artistic growth is reflected in other genres as well. The poetry collection *As the Wind Blew* (1920), though uneven, contains ample evidence of her ability as a lyric poet. She also enjoyed several successes on the Broadway stage with *The Fear Market* (1916), an adaptation of Mark TWAIN's *The Prince and the Pauper* (1919), and *The Sea-Woman's Cloak* and *November Eve* (1924). What is unquestionably her finest drama, *The Young Elizabeth,* produced by the Little Theatre of St. Louis in 1938, remains unpublished. However, completing the play represented a personal victory for R., as final revisions were made in the wake of Prince Troubetzkoy's death in August 1936. Her final years were made sad by ill health, and flagging literary activity.

A factor—albeit an unintentional one—in the ferment that established realism as a dominant literary mode, R.'s better work is overshadowed by the scandalous success of *The Quick or the Dead?* However, as one of the privileged few American authors who felt equally at home in Europe during the decades prior to World War I, her fictional chronicling of both cultures, no less that her colorful life itself, deserves more attention than it has received from modern readers.

BIBLIOGRAPHY: Bain, R., et al., eds. *Southern Writers: A Biographical Dictionary* (1979); Longest, G., *Three Virginia Writers—Mary Johnston, Thomas Nelson Page, A. R. Troubetzkoy: A Reference Guide* (1978); Taylor, W. D., *A. R. (Princess Troubetzkoy)* (1973)

                     WELFORD DUNAWAY TAYLOR

ROBBINS, Tom [Thomas Eugene]
b. 22 July 1936, Blowing Rock, North Carolina

In his novel *Skinny Legs and All* (1990), R. writes, "Success eliminates as many options as failure." Although R. has failed to get serious critical attention for his body of work, he and his eccentric novels have been successful in other ways. R.'s antiestablishment stance, interest in Eastern philosophy and religion, and emphasis on personal spiritual growth by bucking the system have engaged the interest of high school and college students since the early 1970s. Many of his novels have achieved cult classic status, and R. himself is considered a cult hero. He worked as a newspaper copy editor, an art reviewer and columnist, and as a radio host before "dropping out" of society in the late 1960s to write fiction. He is a self-described student of art and religion and lives in seclusion in Washington State, where many of his novels are set.

The most striking aspect of R.'s writings is his style—an abundance of metaphor, wordplay, wisecracks, and whimsy. R.'s themes center around the triumph of the individual spirit over restrictive social, religious, and political organizations. He sees the possibility of societal change only through the liberation of the individual and by placing the importance of "personal adventure" over "public mission." R. prefers the Eastern religions and philosophies, where spiritual growth is a development of an individual pursuit of "the stuff of higher consciousness."

Critics agree that R. presents his philosophy in clever and inventive ways, but most also agree that his style is self-indulgent, his plots are convoluted and erratic, and his use of metaphors is excessive. These criticisms, however, are the same qualities that have charmed his readers for decades and have given R. such a dedicated following.

R.'s penchant for wild plots, Eastern philosophy, and overabundant metaphor is established in his first novel *Another Roadside Attraction* (1971). Football player Plucky Purcell exposes the folly of Christianity when he discovers Jesus Christ's mummified body after an earthquake and brings it to the giant hot dog stand run by artist John Paul Ziller and his earth-mother wife Amanda. Jaded scientist Marx Marvelous narrates as Ziller, a pet baboon, and Christ's mummified body journey in a hot air balloon to merge with the energy of the sun.

R.'s second and most popular novel, *Even Cowgirls Get the Blues* (1976), pits societal norms versus individual freedom. In this picaresque road story, big-thumbed Sissy Hankshaw bucks the system and follows her hitchhiking destiny to the Rubber Rose Ranch, where she and the other cowgirls fight the government in the Whooping Crane War. The novel also introduces the clock people, an isolated Indian group that has developed elaborate individual rituals in place of societal norms, an Eastern philosopher known as the Chink, and a psychiatrist narrator named Robbins.

In *Jitterbug Perfume* (1984), R. continues his exploration of Eastern philosophy, spiritual growth, and wacky plots as King Alobar and his lover Kudra find the essence of immortal life following the Bandaloop Doctor's principles, and heroine Priscilla and her psychedelic lover Wiggs Dannyboy search for the perfect perfume to attain the highest state of "floral consciousness."

R. has said that his books have plot but do not depend on plot and that his main interest is in "creating a space where language can happen." Language continues to happen in a big way in R.'s works as he continues to imagine eccentric tales that stimulate the quest for self-knowledge among the young and the young at heart.

BIBLIOGRAPHY: Klinkowitz, J., *The Practice of Fiction in America,* (1980); Nadeau, R., *Readings from the New Book on Nature: Physics and Metaphysics in the Modern Novel* (1981); Whissen, T. R., *Classic Cult Fiction: A Companion to Popular Cult Literature* (1992); Whitmer, P. O., *Aquarius Revisited: Seven Who Created the Sixties Counterculture That Changed America* (1987)

ASHLEY BROWN

ROBERTS, Elizabeth Madox

b. 30 October 1881, Perryville, Kentucky; d. 13 March 1941, Orlando, Florida

R. published eight novels, two collections of short stories, and two volumes of poetry between 1926 and her death in 1941. Several of her books were popular and critical successes, but publishers inexplicably have allowed them to go out of print. In consequence, R.'s literary reputation has diminished, and a new generation of American readers has suffered a great loss.

Seventeen years after R. graduated from high school, she left Springfield, Kentucky to enter the University of Chicago. There she developed close friendships in the Poetry Club with students almost twenty years younger than she—Glenway WESCOTT, Yvor WINTERS, Monroe Wheeler, Vincent Sheean, and Janet Lewis. Harriet MONROE, editor of *Poetry,* published R.'s poems, drew her into the circle of authors, and launched her career as a serious writer. Returning to Springfield in 1921, R. began to write more fiction than poetry. She lived in her childhood home for the rest of her life, and this locale and its history became the background for her writings.

When *Time of Man* (1926), her first novel, was published, Ford Madox Ford called it "the most beautiful individual piece of writing that has as yet come out of America." Sherwood ANDERSON also telegraphed Viking Press to express his pleasure at her "wonderful performance" and "very beautiful work." A Book-of-the-Month-Club selection and a best-seller in both American and British editions, it was translated in six other languages and appeared in editions in Sweden,

German, Norway, Denmark, Spain, and France. The setting of the book is near Springfield. The protagonist, Ellen Chesser, develops from childhood to middle age in the course of the novel, but R. measures time psychologically as Ellen reacts with an intense subjectivity to the phenomena of seed time and harvest, birth and death, the passing of generations and the perennial mystery of the starry universe.

R. also organizes her book cyclically, as the image of Ellen seated in a migrant worker's wagon singing in both the beginning and closing pages would signify. She moves from one tenant farm to several others, first with her parents and then with husband and children. In spite of R.'s realism and sense of specific locale, she centers the novel in the internal life of Ellen. The distinction of this novel lies in the understanding of Ellen's mind and heart and in R.'s control of language—its subtle nuances, its rich imagery, and its suggestive use of dialect.

In her fourth book, *The Great Meadow* (1930), set on the Kentucky frontier between 1774 and 1781, R. utilizes the family legends of her pioneer ancestors, the history of the forts near Springfield, and the biographies of figures such as Daniel Boone, Simon Kenton, Benjamin Logan, and James Harrod, some of whom she actually uses as characters in the novel. The principal figures, Berk Jarvis and his bride, Diony, leave Virginia for Kentucky. When Indians later scalp Berk's mother, Elvira, he abandons Diony to avenge the death, whereas Diony develops an understanding of the Indians and their situation. Assuming Berk to be dead, she marries his friend, Evan Muir, only to discover years later that Berk has been a captive of the Shawnees. She decides that her first loyalty must logically be to her first husband. In this psychologically oriented historical novel, R. enlarges her realistic depiction of the Kentucky pioneers with mythic dimensions as the characters and events attain archetypal proportions.

R.'s other notable novels are *My Heart and My Flesh* (1927), *He Sent Forth a Raven* (1935), and *Black Is My True Love's Hair* (1938). They are all psychological studies of a woman protagonist's betrayal by circumstances and by other human beings and of her subsequent regeneration.

BIBLIOGRAPHY: Capbell, H. M., and Foster, R., *E. M. R.* (1956); McDowell, F. P. W., *E. M. R.* (1963); Rovit, E. H., *Herald to Chaos: The Novels of E. M. R.* (1953)

MARGARET B. MCDOWELL

ROBERTS, Kenneth [Lewis]

b. 8 December 1885, Kennebunk, Maine; d. 21 July 1957, Kennebunkport, Maine

Few writers of historical fiction in the mid-20th c. captured the attention of the reading public as widely as R. With his many exhaustively researched novels, he maintained a reputation throughout his lengthy career as an author whose works were not only enjoyable to read, but also models of historical accuracy.

R. first gained international attention in the 1920s for his numerous articles in George Horace Lorimer's *Saturday Evening Post*. In 1928, he left the *Post* so he could write about the dramatic experiences of his ancestors who had played prominent roles in the development of the U.S. In 1775, his great-great-grandfather from Arundel (now Kennebunkport), Maine, marched with Benedict Arnold through the Maine and Canadian wilderness in an ill-fated expedition to capture Quebec. Although *Arundel* (1930) is slightly marred by R.'s meticulous fact-finding and his compulsion to relate everything he knows about a subject, it is a stirring creative accomplishment as he graphically describes with historical accuracy the long and arduous expedition during the first year of the American Revolution. R. also received popular and critical acclaim for the sequel, *Rabble in Arms* (1933), which follows Benedict Arnold and his Northern Army from their defeat at Quebec in 1776 to the second Battle of Saratoga at Bemis Heights in October 1777.

Northwest Passage (1937) traces the career of Major Robert Rogers, who achieved fame as the commander of colonial soldiers—known as Rogers's Rangers—during the French and Indian War. A widely popular best-seller, the novel is also regarded by many critics as the author's finest work artistically. For unlike the hagiographic portrayal of Benedict Arnold in *Arundel* and *Rabble in Arms* as a fearless military leader who was shamefully victimized by his enemies, in *Northwest Passage,* R. creates a balanced and believable three-dimensional protagonist; that is, an ordinary person with human frailties and shortcomings as well as strength and courage.

Because R. never permitted the heroes and heroines of his novels to show any heartfelt feelings for each other, his works have occasionally been criticized for their flat characterization—especially of women—and constrained love plots. But stirring historical novels do not require deep character analysis, and it is R.'s storytelling abilities that place him among America's best-known writers in this genre. Although the majority of his novels are no longer in print, it seems likely that his books will be remembered by those who enjoy reading American history dramatized as rousing adventure fiction.

BIBLIOGRAPHY: Bales, J., *K. R.: The Man and His Works* (1989); Bales, J., *K. R.* (1993); Murphy, P., *K. L. R.: A Bibliography* (1975)

JACK BALES

ROBINSON, Edwin Arlington

b. 22 December 1869, Head Tide, Maine; d. 7 April
1935, New York City

R. was one of the most prolific of American poets,
but he is better known for a few of his short poems
than for the entire body of his work. His career began
in 1891 and ended with his death in 1935.

R. was reared in Gardiner, Maine. His childhood
was unremarkable but not very happy. He showed a
strong interest in literary pursuits while still in grammar school, especially in reading and writing verse.
As a teenager, he was a member of a "club" whose
members wrote poetry, and it was there that he received
his first encouragement for his efforts at poetry.

In 1891, R. was accepted as a special student at
Harvard. He did not much care for either the academic
or social life he found there, though he began several
friendships that lasted most of his life. He was at
Harvard for two years and then did not return to complete a degree—something he later regretted. While
at Harvard, he submitted poems to various University
publications, and this is the starting point of his poetic
career, but none of his submissions were accepted.

Following his time at Harvard, R. returned to Gardiner. Within the next four years, both of R.'s parents
would die and both of his elder brothers would fail
in their occupations. The hardships suffered by R.
during these unhappy years would influence his poetry
both directly and indirectly.

R.'s first volume of poetry, *The Torrent and the
Night Before,* was rejected by two publishers before
he had three hundred and twelve copies printed at his
own expense in 1896. Most of these he sent to friends,
literary critics, and anyone he thought would be interested in poetry. He found very little acceptance for
his work, but he was undeterred. A year later, a Boston
firm published the volume under the new title of *Children of the Night.* It was at this time that R. moved
to New York, which would be his home until his death.

In 1902, *Captain Craig* appeared and caught the
attention of Theodore ROOSEVELT, among others.
Roosevelt was impressed enough by the poem to offer
R. a sinecure with the New York Customs House in
1905. This job allowed R. both the time and finances
to write. Until then, R. had depended mostly on gifts
from friends and admirers. Nonetheless, R. resigned
in 1909.

During those years at the Customs House, R. wrote
two plays, neither of which made him any money. *Van
Zorn* was produced, but as a mediocre comedy did
not survive long. *The Porcupine,* a tragedy, was a
much better play, but it was never produced except
privately. R. considered his attempts at drama a waste
of time.

Although critics had begun to take note of R. after
the publication of *Captain Craig,* only eight years
later did R. achieve any financial success as a poet
when he published *The Town Down the River* (1910).
It was at this time that he began spending his summers
at the McDowell Colony in Peterboro, New
Hampshire.

Beginning in 1915, when *Captain Craig* was reprinted, R. published volumes of poetry regularly. In
1916, it was *The Man against the Sky. Merlin* followed
in 1917, the first book of R.'s Arthurian trilogy. The
second volume of the trilogy, *Lancelot,* appeared in
1920, and in 1925, *Tristram* completed the cycle. Between *Lancelot* and *Tristram,* he published *The Three
Taverns* (1920), *Avon's Harvest* (1921), and *Collected
Poems* (1921), which won him the Pulitzer Prize in
poetry. *Roman Bartholow* came out in 1923 followed
by *The Man Who Died Twice* (1924), for which he
received a second Pulitzer. *Dionysius in Doubt* appeared in 1925 just prior to *Tristram*—the poem that
was R.'s greatest financial success and also won a
third Pulitzer. From 1929 to 1934 R. produced more
than one book per year: *Cavender's House, the Glory
of the Nightingales, Selected Poems, Matthias at the
Door, Nicodemus, Talifer,* and *Amaranth. King Jasper*
appeared posthumously in 1935.

R.'s primary concern in his poetry is man, but it
is the individual, not mankind that draws his eye.
Several of his best know short poems are titled after
their subjects—"Richard Cory," "Miniver Cheevy,"
and "The Man Flammonde," for example—and they
are exemplars of neatly rendered portraits of individuals for which R. is noted. Nor does he do less in his
long poems. The character studies in those retain their
compact tautness though the poems may be looser in
other ways.

But to say that the individual is the concern of R.'s
poetry is still vague. Having seen two elder brothers
fail in their respective manners, it is not surprising to
find that many of R.'s poems deal with men who fail,
or at any rate, fail to reach their potential. R. also
explores the failure of love between a man and a
woman—a theme we might also find in his biographical circumstances. A third angle on failed individuals
appears in his characters who are materialists who
have failed spiritually and can find no solace or peace.
Little wonder then that R. has often been portrayed
as a gloomy man sounding gloomy notes.

His apparent pessimism notwithstanding, a close
reading of R.'s work will show that his failed characters are not always beyond redemption. Not all of his
defeated men and women are saved; some lack the
inner strength of character necessary to make an inward change, and those who do make the change find
grace in the sight of men, not God. But R. did allow
some of his failed characters to achieve societal and

personal value, and it is not accurate to call R. a pessimist. His was a severely tempered optimism. R.'s own estimation of his outlook was that "there is no sense in saying that this world is not a pretty difficult place, but that isn't pessimism."

Another Robinsonian note is sounded in the Arthurian trilogy. In a letter to a young scholar, R. said that *Merlin* and *Lancelot* were suggested by World War I. R. was strongly affected by that war, and he saw in it the fall of the era into which he had been born. R.'s Camelot is also a world in physical and moral disarray collapsing under its own weight.

In terms of form, structure, and diction, R. is a traditionalist. He was not an innovator, though he was "modern" because his poetry deals with characters in psychological terms, and for this reason he has sometimes been linked with Henry JAMES. R.'s style was simple, though his thoughts were often complex. His poems are highly crafted—he often spent months on a few lines, doing what he called "tinkering." If there is a major flaw in his work, it is that some of the poems could have been shorter without doing damage to the poem.

R. has been tagged with many more labels other than pessimist and traditionalist. Yvor WINTERS calls him a "counter-romantic," and like most labels, there is some truth in it. R.'s language is certainly that of "men speaking to men," but it is also the language of the intellect, not the emotions. Some even claim that R. is "unpoetic," but his poetry is not passionless nor prosy—the emotion in his poems is more abstract and less personal, but it is emotion nonetheless. The New England sensibility exhibited by R. is much more that of the Puritan than the transcendentalists.

Another accusation against R. is that he overworked his themes. This may be a valid criticism, but it seems unfair to say that a theme is "overworked" just because an author finds some ideas more compelling and important than others—particularly when these powerful themes seem to be drawn from personal history. R. plays variations on several ideas, and these tend to crop up repeatedly within his larger themes of failure and redemption. R. believed that materialism was detrimental to both the individual and society. Furthermore, in R.'s view, materialism leads to a lack of self-knowledge that is the cause of failure in life; by acquiring self-knowledge life can be given some personal and social value. Certainly R. repeated his themes, but whether he overworked them is clearly a matter of opinion.

R. is perhaps best known by a few of his short poems that have been frequently anthologized, but when we examine *Collected Poems,* we see that one seventh of the large book contains all of his short poetry up to that time. Likewise, of the eleven volumes published after 1921, ten are long narrative poems. Thus, it is a mistake to base our estimate of R. on what we find in popular anthologies.

R. must be regarded as a major American poet both in terms of output and influence. He showed that he was capable of sustained production over a forty year career. Furthermore, he was one of the first American poets to render his characters in psychological terms, showing the American personality in the modern world.

BIBLIOGRAPHY: Barnard, E., *E. A. R.: A Critical Study* (1952); Bloom, H., ed., *E. A. R.* (1988); Kaplan, E., *Philosophy in the Poetry of E. A. R.* (1940); Winters, Y., *E. A. R.* (1946; rev. ed., 1971)

DENNIS KEARNEY

ROBINSON, Marilynne [Summers]
b. 26 November 1944, Sand Point, Idaho

Housekeeping, R.'s 1980 debut as a novelist, impressed several reviewers with its poetic texture and its lyricism. It won both the PEN/Hemingway Award for First Fiction and the Richard and Hinda Rosenthal Award from the American Academy and Institute of Arts and Letters. Reviewers found echoes in R.'s prose of Keats, T. S. ELIOT, Seamus Heaney, Vladimir NABOKOV, John HAWKES, and Toni MORRISON. R. herself, in a 1984 interview, cited Ralph Waldo EMERSON, Edgar Allan POE, Henry David THOREAU, Herman MELVILLE, Emily DICKINSON, and Walt WHITMAN as formative influences. These influences show in both the language and the story of *Housekeeping:* A first person narrator recalls how she and her sister, orphans in a lakeside railroad town in the Mountain West, came of age under the care of the three egregiously unqualified foster-mothers—two nervous maiden great-aunts and their suicidal mother's long-lost vagabond sister.

R. served in 1987 as an "About Books" columnist for the *New York Times Book Review,* where her reviews and essays appear frequently. She also worked on a study of ecology and politics in Britain, selections of which appeared in *Harper's* in 1985, published as *Mother Country* in 1989. A film of *Housekeeping,* by the Scots director Bill Forsyth, was released in 1987. In 1998, R. published *The Death of Adam: Essays on Modern Thought.*

BIBLIOGRAPHY: Kirby, J., "Is There Life after Art?: The Metaphysics of M. R.'s *Housekeeping,*" *TSWL* 5, 1 (1986): 91–109; Meese, E., *Crossing the Double-Cross: The Practice of Feminist Criticism* (1985)

JAMES D. BLOOM

ROBISON, Mary
b. 14 January 1949, Washington, D.C.

R.'s short fiction has often been favorably compared to some older, more established contemporary writers such as Raymond CARVER, Ann BEATTIE, and Andre DUBUS because of its spare, laconic humor and its wry presentation of empty lives mired in a hopelessly materialistic society. She has been called a minimalist writer by some critics. Though her stories embody the cool precision that has come to characterize *New Yorker* short stories, her style is unique and original. Over half of the stories in her first, critically acclaimed collection, *Days* (1977), were first published in the *New Yorker*. Though she has published two novels—*Oh!* (1981) and *Subtraction* (1991)—her reputation rests firmly on her superb skill as one of contemporary America's freshest and most audacious short-story writers. Among her admirers are writers such as John BARTH, Richard Yates, Bobbie Ann MASON, and Gordon LISH, who, as her editor at Alfred A. Knopf, published her first three books. A persistent theme throughout her work is the spiritual torpor at the center of a materialistic American society that is empty, banal, and boring.

The stories in *Days* have been compared to both Anton Chekhov and James Joyce since they are small slices of life viewed from an objective point of view. And, like the stories in Joyce's *Dubliners,* they frequently deal with debilitating stasis in which their inarticulate and dazed characters (dazed by the ennui of their unvarying days—a pun on the title *Days*) seem incapable of significant action because they're terrified of change. Instead, they wait, like Charlie and Don, a couple in their sixties in "Kite and Paint," who are excitedly anticipating a hurricane on the shores of Maryland, and decorate kites to fly into the storm. The numbing stasis of their lives has been broken as the hurricane regenerated their creative impulses, even though their actions may result in their deaths.

Many of the characters in R.'s early stories live their lives completely unaware of their deepest motivations; they literally do not know what they are doing and are often unconscious of their self-destructive impulses. "May Queen" is a vignette about an eighth grade girl, Riva, who is being crowned May Queen at St. Rose of Lima Church in Indianapolis. Her veil accidentally catches fire and, though Riva is not seriously harmed, the ceremony is disastrous. Of course the story can be read as an unconscious reenactment of pre-Christian human sacrifice, and takes on some of the ominous earmarks of Shirley JACKSON's darker narratives like "The Lottery."

The stories in R.'s second collection of stories, *An Amateur's Guide to the Night* (1983), are less dark because their more obvious humor satirizes American values in less sardonic ways. Lindy, a teenager in the title story, has worked out successful defenses to cope with her mother's inability to grow up and finds deep meaning in her fascination with the celestial movements of the stars. In "I Am Twenty-One," a grieving college student, whose parents had been killed in an automobile accident, finds deep consolation in an esoteric art course called "The Transition from Romanesque to Gothic," a title that defines the direction that her life has taken after the traumatic death of her parents.

R.'s third collection, *Believe Them* (1988), contains stories that are longer and less bitter than those in her two earlier collections. And some of the characters are actually enjoying themselves. They are also very humorous. "For Real" combines humor and pathos in the life of Boffo, the female clown who hosts a midday movie on a local television station. She learns to laugh at herself, painfully, as she realizes that her handsome German boyfriend really does not want to marry her after all; she sees herself as a real clown in life's strange revelations. R. is certainly one of America's most perceptive delineators of the sterility at the center of the American Dream. Her impeccable ear for dialogue and telling details makes her one of contemporary America's most trenchant social critics, but her stories never preach or overtly moralize. What saves her vividly human characters from debilitating depression and breakdown is their sense of humor, their lack of self-pity, and their consistent ability to laugh at themselves.

BIBLIOGRAPHY: Birkerts, S., *An Artificial Wilderness: Essays on Twentieth-Century Literature* (1987); McKenna, M., "M. R.," in Meanor, P., ed., *DLB,* vol. 130, *American Short-Story Writers since World War II* (1993): 276–81

PATRICK MEANOR

ROETHKE, Theodore
b. 25 May 1908, Saginaw, Michigan; d. 1 August 1963, Seattle, Washington

R. had a classic mid-20th-c. poet's career. The poetry of his first book, *Open House* (1941), is written in rhymed and accentually metered lines, in the image of W. H. AUDEN's, filled with close observation and clear recollection. His next collection, *The Lost Son and Other Poems* (1947), includes the occasional poem or passage within a poem with applied rhyme and meter, but by this time R. was experimenting with lines as long as Walt WHITMAN's and as short as anybody's, down to a word. Along the way he became a master of slant rhyme and extended his diction to the sledgehammer-heavy and the scalpel-subtle. His focus narrowed further: in "The Minimal," he would "study the lives on a leaf." He delved deeper into his memory, and produced one of his most anthologized pieces, "My Papa's Waltz." In *Praise to the End!* (1951), in the poem "Where Knock Is Open Wide," he speaks in the voice of a child, like James Joyce at the beginning of *A Portrait of the Artist as a Young Man,* but he twists Joyce's impressionism into a surreal apprehension of his father's death. In this volume he develops the terse, dense style of enigmatic epigram that is recognizable R., and writes the first of his important poetic sequences, "The Lost Son." The Pulitzer Prize-winning *The Waking: Poems 1933–1953* (1953) collected poems old and new, including the sequence "Four for Sir John Davies," which takes a more intellectual tone and turn of mind than R.'s previous work. *Words for the Wind* (1957) won the 1958 National Book Award, recollecting *The Waking* with original work, like the accomplished "Meditations of an Old Woman," in which he speaks in a persona not his own, a dramatic leap for R. Posthumously published, *The Far Field* (1964) won another National Book Award; all love poems and deeply felt philosophical sequences, the volume is the sure, mature legacy of a perhaps great poet.

R.'s place in literary history has been difficult to determine. Much of his work is demonstrably derivative, even in vocabulary and vocal quality, of his great contemporaries, especially Auden, T. S. ELIOT, and W. B. Yeats. His notebooks and verse quote openly from many sources and at times seem ventriloquial of literary voices as diverse as William Shakespeare and Samuel Beckett, voices he urged and cajoled his students to hear and appreciate over decades of teaching at universities across the country. The split among his contemporaries between "deep image" and academic poetry is not helpful in describing R.'s work, which partook of both movements without participating in either. His love for poetry and his extensive learning profoundly affected his writing, yet he is arguably an American original. His verse is candidly personal in its remembrances and emotions, and highly individual in its expressive demands on its diction and imagery. For example, the huge greenhouse, the largest in the U.S., where R. spent his youth, became the storehouse of his deepest deep images and was in his memory and his poetry both an Eden and a prison. The stones that in one poem are fundament or mineral death, laugh or speak in the next, leap or become the moon in another. A sensual, erotic line may be followed by a lucid, cerebral one; a word choice may strike a reader as particularly apt, though it may appear in a passage that is obscure, unfathomable. His longer, more discur-

sive poems that conform in the main to the descriptive-meditative mode can pivot in a line or a word, turn back on themselves, fracture then follow the form, as if he made his own mind spin. This idiosyncratic manner arises partly from his composing process, in which nothing—no idea, no image, no memory, no matter how painful—was dismissed, though it may have been momentarily doubted or denied. He strove for vision, outside of time, by going back through his large, rich notebooks for old material that struck him anew, as he strove for atonement with his authoritarian father, who died just before R.'s fifteenth birthday, whose perfectionism awed and alienated his son, while his care for his hybrid roses and his woodsman's ethic inspired young R. and engendered his most profound—his poet's—education.

R.'s poetry has remained popular because he is demonstrably talented and serious, he confronts the largest themes without compromise, and his work rewards varied interpretation. Naturalism, existentialism, mysticism, even Marxism can prevail for a poem or a passage; he can appear in his verse as a questing romantic visionary or the pathetic victim of the Freudian family romance. Critic Kenneth BURKE, one of R.'s earliest champions, felt it necessary to coin a critical term, "vegetal Radicalism," to describe his style. A manic-depressive condition that first appeared when R. was twenty-seven, for which he was hospitalized several times and ultimately given electro-shock treatment, seems to offer structure to interpretation of his work and its autobiographical aspect, but is finally too simplistic to serve. R. was aware of the issue of the effect of his condition on his writing, was as careful and deliberate as one who strove to be a visionary poet could be in the act of composing, and addressed the issue openly in his poetry, sometimes with humor, generally with perspective. His verse does not suffer from it or, perhaps more remarkably, from its treatment. His oeuvre is less uneven than most poets', and his verse is not distorted, damaged, or apparently driven by his manic or depressive states. Besides, all poetry is the product of brain chemistry in some important way, so the point, while interesting, is moot.

For a poetry full of flowers, there is little color in R.'s work. He is a poet of light, of the moon and sun, night and morning, shapes and reflections, of images shedding their sensual accidents as they merge with ideas. When, in the late "North American Sequence," in the poem "The Rose," he identifies himself as a "rose in the sea-wind," the flower has no hue, and more symbolic power for it. This technique is indicative of his visionary aspirations, and leads to a central question: is the poetry, then, a means to a transcendent state, to a mystical end, or a personal end of finding his "true place," or an atonement with a majestically figured father, with God? The many questions that spike or bend R.'s verse can be reduced rhetorically to this central question, whether inquiry or intellect must be overcome to achieve vision or if dialectic cannot simply prompt visionary experience but give it voice, the poet's truth. The rigor R. demands of his vision, the vitality of his doubt, does not inhibit his verse, but creates dialogue, drama, a sense of arduous progress over the course of his poetic career, of slow, organic growth and critical refinement, of going over the same field to make sure nothing is missed, to discover some new detail, some new aspect, some new glint of light. His high standards and insistent ethic make R.'s imagery and syntax, in the end, intensely personal, his voice most meaningful when it most resists interpretation or apparent understanding. It may be best not to isolate and assault the difficult passages in R.'s work, but rather to see the work itself, his life's work, as a difficult passage, from influence to individuality, from question to vision, from loss to light.

BIBLIOGRAPHY: Bloom, H., ed., *Modern Critical Views: T. R.* (1988); Burke, K., "The Vegetal Radicalism of T. R.," *Language as Symbolic Action* (1966): 254–81; La Belle, J., *The Echoing Wood of T. R.* (1976); Seager, A., *The Glass House: The Life of T. R.* (1968); Wolff, G., *T. R.* (1981)

DENNIS PAOLI

ROGERS, Pattiann

b. 23 March 1940, Joplin, Missouri

R. is a poet of the sublime and the supremely natural. Her seven volumes of poetry contain some of the most powerful and distinctive intersections of scientific matters and spiritual concerns in contemporary verse. Generous selections from *The Expectations of Light* (1981), *The Tattooed Lady in the Garden* (1986), *Legendary Performance* (1987), *Splitting and Binding* (1989), and *Geocentric* (1993) are brought together with twenty-seven new poems in *Firekeeper* (1994). Her seventh volume is *Eating Bread and Honey* (1997).

R. has described her experience of learning science as the opposite of Walt WHITMAN's in "When I Heard the Learned Astronomer": her minor in zoology and in particular a course in astronomy at the University of Missouri filled her with wonder and a sense of liberation. From her earliest to her latest poems, she has taken pleasure in reaching from the minutest forms of vegetative and animal life out to the farthest galaxies, as she explores the dimensions of human meaning and the mysteries of the divine.

R.'s individual collections can be elegantly composed. *Splitting and Binding,* for instance, is divided into nine clusters of three related poems each, the whole beginning with morning and ending with lying down to sleep. The book's title phrase comes from a typically loping and chiming passage in its long closing sentence describing the motion of light among windblown grasses, a motion suggesting her own penetrating and synthesizing vision. This volume and poem lie midway in her gradual development toward increasing densities of detail and syntax. But R. has told interviewer Richard McCann that she envisions her work not in a linear arrangement or broken up into books but rather as "interrelated and circular," indeed as transparently spherical, so that each poem may be viewed in the company of other related poems. For this reason, it is possible to enter her oeuvre at almost any point and enjoy its sensuous detail and its speculative vitality in full bloom.

Likewise, motifs and themes travel from book to book—the cats; the imaginative characters of Sonia, Cecil, Albert, Gordon, and Felicia; the artist; the lover; and the portraits of a god far beyond the limits of our usual language for "him." *Firekeeper* opens with the early poem "Hiring the Man Who Builds Fires for a Living." This character "knows with his breath," as the poet, like the creator, knows with her breath, "how to make flame live." And the volume ends with the title figure of the firekeeper, a background figure in Rembrandt's *Philosopher in Meditation,* who "studies" fire and whose task it is to "construct" a controlled and warming blaze. The poems in between are richly textured with naturalistic detail, catalogues, rhythmic parallel phrases and clauses, litanylike repetitions, alliteration and internal rhyme, and startling conceits. Sparsely populated with human figures, the poems nevertheless offer original and provocative perspectives on the human condition and especially on the timeless poetic concerns of love and death.

R.'s collection entitled *Eating Bread and Honey* continues these concerns. It contains, as the second of its four internal "books," the extraordinary poem called "Animals and People: 'The Human Heart in Conflict with Itself,'" the longest work in verse she has published to date.

R. is the recipient of a Guggenheim Fellowship, a Lannan Poetry Fellowship, and two book awards from the Texas Institute of Letters, among other awards. She is moving from strength to strength as a poet. Judith Kitchen puts it gracefully: "Possibly P. R. sees herself as a firekeeper, but her craft is such that these new poems seem to burst into flame from their own internal combustion."

BIBLIOGRAPHY: McCann, R., "An Interview with P. R.," *IowaR* 17 (Spring-Summer 1987): 25-42; Merrill,

C., "Voyages into the Immediate," *NER* 10 (Spring 1988): 368–78

MARGARET HOLLEY

ROGERS, Will[iam Penn Adair]

b. 4 November 1879, Oologah, Indian Territory (now Oklahoma); d. 15 August 1935, Point Barrow, Alaska

When R. died in a plane crash, the cowboy-philosopher was mourned by the entire nation—he was one of the most well-known figures of his day, his recognition as a public figure second only to that of Franklin D. Roosevelt. Though his writing is dated and is rarely read now, R.'s popular image as a gum-chewing, wise-cracking social commentator continues to inhabit the American mind today. He is easily identified with the statement he chose as his epitaph: "I joked about every prominent man of my time, but I have never met a man I didn't like."

R.'s career as "America's fool" began in vaudeville: he accompanied his fancy lariat twirling and rope tricks with a running satirical commentary on current events and public figures. From the stage, he moved into print journalism with his syndicated columns for the McNaught Newspapers from 1922 to 1935. By 1930, R.'s increasing popularity earned him weekly radio broadcasts, which continued until his death. Concurrent with his writing and broadcasting, R. remained true to his vaudeville origins with appearances in several films between 1918 and 1935, including *Hunting for Germans in Berlin with W. R.* (1927) and *A Connecticut Yankee* (1931).

R.'s link with Mark TWAIN was more substantial than simply appearing in a film based on Twain's novel. R. can be considered part of a tradition of American humorists that includes Twain and ARTEMUS WARD. Like his predecessors, R. used poor grammar, misspelled words, puns, malpropisms, and comic similes to create humor. Although his writing seems rapid-fire, off-the-cuff, and spontaneous, he repeatedly revised and polished his work.

The government and administrative ineptitude were the most frequent targets of his satire; his widespread popularity resulted from R.'s ability to portray himself as a common, unsophisticated American bewildered by what he perceived to be the inane intricacies of bureaucracy. In this respect, he was the spokesman for a generation of Americans increasingly confused and threatened by the numerous changes confronting them between the world wars, including rapid technological change and increased global involvement. As a plain-looking, head-scratching man with an Oklahoma drawl, R. could articulate, behind the mask of humor,

the frustration and alienation many felt, particularly those from rural areas.

R. is the master of the aphorism and the sketch; typical of his work is *The Cowboy Philosopher on Prohibition* (1919) and *The Cowboy Philosopher on the Peace Conference* (1919)—collections of aphorisms—and *Letters of a Self-Made Diplomat to His President* (1926) and its sequel, *There's Not a Bathing Suit in Russia* (1927)—both books are compilations taken from his newspaper columns, "W. R. Says," "The Worst Story I Ever Heard," and "The Daily Telegram." Although he has frequently been compared to Twain in his role as satiric commentator on American morals, mores, and idiosyncracies, critics have also noted that R. lacks Twain's depth of social analysis and ability to sustain an argument.

Today, R.'s writings are dated by their topicality and method of humor. R.'s most enduring importance lies in his carefully crafted persona of the homespun American hero.

BIBLIOGRAPHY: Ketchum, R. M., *W. R.: His Life and Times* (1973); O'Brien, J., *W. R.: Ambassador of Good Will* (1976); Robinson, R., *American Original: A Life of W. R.* (1996); Yates, N. W., *The American Humorist: Conscience of the Twentieth Century* (1964)

JUDITH E. FUNSTON

RÖLVAAG, Ole Edvart

b. 22 April 1876, Roelvaag, Helgeland, Norway; d. 5 November 1931, Northfield, Minnesota

American provincialism accounts for failure to include R.'s *Giants in the Earth* (1924; trans. ed., 1927) as one of our dozen or so great American novels because its author was born in Norway and wrote in Norwegian. The title of the novel, taken from Genesis 6:4, indicates the dual nature of the giants, who represent both the heroic and evil natures of the pioneers coming into the Promised Land. The South Dakota setting, where the prairie resembles a frozen sea and recalls the seas of Scandinavia, is the stage for R.'s interweaving of American and Norse myth and folktales with the Bible. Protagonist Per Hansa suggests the AMERICAN ADAM severed from European roots and defeated by his own innocence, pride and materialism. Beret, his wife, represents defeat of another type in her neurotic efforts to restrain her husband and preserve the cultural traditions and spiritual values of the Old World. If the American Adam, Per is as well a version of the Norwegian folk hero Ash Lad, a type of male Cinderella who defeats the trolls in a strange land and wins a princess and a kingdom. At once an epic in scope and a tragedy in characterization, *Giants* ends with the discovery of Per's body, its eyes looking westward, death the result of egotistical overestimation of human capabilities.

R. continued the story of Per Hansa's family in *Peder Victorious* (1928; trans. ed., 1929), and *Their Father's God* (1931). The tragedy of Per's son Peder relates to the lack of a physical frontier where he can develop his potential and is compounded by the erosion in America of Norwegian culture and religion. "A people that has lost its traditions is doomed!" says a minister in the final novel of the trilogy, succinctly expressing R.'s belief in the necessity of remaining true to one's heritage and developing American character through ethnicity.

R. prepared for *Giants* in three earlier novels: *The Third Life of Per Smevik* (1912; trans. ed., 1971), *Pure Gold* (1920; trans. ed., 1930), and *The Boat of Longing* (1921; trans. ed., 1933). The three lives of the first novel are heavily autobiographical, the author describing through letters Per's life in Norway, his journey to South Dakota, and his life as an immigrant, emphasizing the losses of assimilation. *Pure Gold* tells of a second-generation Norwegian American couple who substitute money for heritage and occupy a limbo dehumanized by greed. In *The Boat of Longing,* the Ash Lad folk tale gives Nils Vaag's exploits mythic dimension. The novel begins and ends in poetic Norwegian settings framing starkly realistic scenes of American life, including those of an immigrant ghetto in Minneapolis. Here and in his masterpiece, R. combines the realism and naturalism of his time with myth and folklore to universalize the tensions of immigrant life beyond Norwegian American significance.

BIBLIOGRAPHY: Haugen, E., *O. E. R.* (1983); Moseley, A., *O. E. R.* (1987); Reigstad, P., *R.: His Life and Art* (1972); Simonson, H. P., *Prairies Within: The Tragic Trilogy of O. R.* (1987); Thorson, G., ed., *O. R.: Artist and Cultural Leader* (1975)

JOHN J. MURPHY

ROMANCE

American popular romance has its roots in 18th-and 19th-c. British fiction, most notably novels such as Jane Austen's *Pride and Prejudice,* Charlotte Brontë's *Jane Eyre,* and British Gothic works such as Ann Radcliffe's *The Mysteries of Udolfo.* However, from the very beginning, American romance has also been set apart by distinctly American concerns and interests. Frontier tales, domestic tales, moral tales: all of these and more became part of this genre as it developed. Although a number of works that are categorized as "romance" have entered the American literary canon,

the 20th c. has seen popular romance largely marginalized, in part because literature dealing with issues of family, love, and marriage has been perceived as not masculine, and thus not deserving of serious interest. Today, with individual print-runs regularly in the hundreds of thousands and titles that frequently appear on the national best-seller lists, publishing houses such as Harlequin—which publishes "category romance" consisting predominantly of short contemporary and historical romances—as well as the mainstream publishers who handle single title romance releases, are incredibly successful. However, the stigma of triviality, often unfairly attached to the popular romance, remains.

Romantic fiction was a popular literary import in America from the birth of the novel in England in the 18th c, and American examples of popular romance began to appear at the end of that century. One of the most important early influences on the American popular romance was the Gothic novel. British Gothic novelists such as "Monk" Lewis, Horace Walpole, and Mrs. Ann Radcliffe treated the subjects of courtship and love, but within decidedly fantastic settings, replete with ghosts and supernatural occurrences. After its heyday in England and America, the Gothic would evolve into a variety of other literary forms such as melodrama, SCIENCE FICTION, and the horror story, of which genre Edgar Allan POE with his tales of terror continues to stand as one of the leading American figures. However, in contrast to its European antecedents, the Gothic romance in America generally focused less on the supernatural per se than on stories in which the male and female protagonists face a vast number of external threats that must be overcome if the two are to achieve lasting happiness. However, some American examples in this genre do have the hallmarks of their English "cousins." Sally S. B. K. WOOD was a popular Maine author of Gothic romances like *Julia and the Illuminated Baron* and *Amelia; or, The Influence of Virtue,* which was both melodramatic and fantastic. Also popular at the end of the 18th c. and the start of the 19th c. was Charles Brockden BROWN who has often been looked upon as the first professional author of the U.S. Influenced by the writings of English author William Godwin, Brown wrote a treatise on the rights of women, and then within the space of two years, completed his four most successful novels: *Wieland, Arthur Mervyn, Ormond,* and *Edgar Huntly,* an epistolary romance. These were followed by two other Gothic romances, *Clara Howard* and *Jane Talbot,* both of which were influenced by the works of English authors Godwin, Radcliffe, and Samuel Richardson.

In 1794, Susanna Haswell ROWSON, who had recently left England for the U.S., published the first

American edition of her novel of seduction, *Charlotte Temple*. The novel, which shares with the Gothic novel a melodramatic tone, is a cautionary tale that tells the story of an innocent woman who is seduced and abandoned by a thoughtless military officer and who finally dies after giving birth to a child. The book, modeled in part on Richardson's classic epistolary novel *Clarissa,* became a great success, seeing over two hundred printings, and was still in print at the start of the 20th c. *Charlotte Temple's* popularity spawned many imitators, among which were Hannah Webster FOSTER's *The Coquette* and Eliza Vicery's *Emily Hamilton* (1803). In 1828, Rowson wrote her posthumously published sequel entitled *Charlotte's Daughter; or, The Three Orphans,* more commonly known as *Lucy Temple.* In addition to novels, Rowson also wrote dramatic works for the stage, including a number of melodramatic romances. Also writing in the late 18th c. were authors such as Charlotte Ramsay Lennox, whose works showed the distinct influence of the European literary world. Ramsay's novel *The Female Quixote; or, The Adventures of Arabella* (1752) was a parody of the popular French romances of the day, and was later dramatized as *Angelica; or Quixote in Petticoats* (1758). More straightforward romances by Lennox include *The Life of Harriet Stuart* (1750), *The History of Henrietta* (1758), *Sophia* (1762), and *Euphemia* (1790).

In the early decades of the 19th c., British authors like Sir Walter Scott were having success in Europe and in the U.S. with novels like *Ivanhoe,* which explored the past in a manner more grandly romantic than historically accurate. These British imports were extremely popular in America, but subsequent American examples of historical fiction, and the historical romance in particular, generally abandoned European settings in favor of American ones, even as they took much of their rather florid rhetorical style from the European authors. Beginning in the 1820s, James Fenimore COOPER embarked on a literary career when his wife challenged his claim that he could write a better book than the English novel he was reading to her. His response to this challenge was *Precaution* (1820), a novel of manners. In this, as in much of his other work, particularly in the Leather-Stocking tales, Cooper used the American scene as the background for romance. He had planned to write thirteen national romances, one for each of the original states, but of these finished only *Lionel Lincoln,* which was set in Revolutionary Boston. However, while traveling abroad, he did write romances about America and life on American ships, including *The Water Witch.* Cooper also wrote satires, social criticism, and scholarly histories including *The Two Admirals* about Columbus's first voyage. His novels are particularly noted

for showing the tensions and conflicts between society and the individual and between the settlements and the wilderness.

Also popular and highly regarded as one of the domestic sentimentalists—the group of novelists who wrote books whose main focus was the relationships between men and women—was Catherine Maria SEDGWICK, who wrote conventional romantic novels, such as *Hope Leslie: or, Early Times in the Massachusetts* dealing with colonial settlers' romances and *Clarence:, or, A Tale of Our Own Times,* set mostly in New York. The novels serve to illustrate the author's moral beliefs and are realistic depictions of social customs in the early 19th c.; however, these are also works whose female heroines are not the passive protagonists seen in earlier moralistic seduction novels, but who take active roles in their own adventures, even going so far as to question the necessity of marriage, as in Sedgwick's late novel *Married or Single?* Not surprisingly, all the heroines of Sedgwick's work do marry in the end, but only after they have matured and developed the qualities valued by their eventual mates. Influenced by Sedgewick were Augusta EVANS, whose *St. Elmo* was one of the biggest sellers of the 19th c., and E. D. E. N. SOUTHWORTH, whose use of Gothic conventions, romantic prose, and historical settings brought her great popularity.

Many novelists in the mid-19th c. used Puritan New England as a background for romantic novels and drew on the theme of lovers kept apart by parents or by social and religious differences. However, in these novels, the young heroines generally demonstrate a more liberal outlook and sense of religious tolerance than would have been approved of in Puritan New England. Typical of these authors is James Kirke PAULDING who expressed admiration for American qualities and a general disdain for the English. His novel *The Puritan and His Daughter* features a Puritan heroine, Miriam, who is saved from a death sentence at the last moment by her Cavalier love, Langley Tyringham. Still popular and highly regarded today is Nathaniel HAWTHORNE, whose own Puritan family included a judge in the Witch Trials in Salem, Massachusetts. Much of Hawthorne's work deals with the effect of PURITANISM on American society. He used Puritan New England as a setting for his novels *The Scarlet Letter* and *The House of the Seven Gables* as well as the majority of his short stories, such as "Young Goodman Brown," "Rappaccini's Daughter," and "The Birthmark."

Another American author who wrote popular romances in the mid-19th c. was William Gilmore SIMMS, who began by writing Byronic romantic verse and later turned to novel writing. He is best known for the Border Romances, which are concerned with colonial and 19th-c. life in the South, including *Guy Rivers* (1834) set in Northern Georgia, as well as for a series called the Revolutionary Romances, including *The Partisan* (1835) and *Katherine Walton* (1851). He intended that his works be an accurate, if romantic, portrayal of the South, yet his novels often suffered from Simms's far too uncritical assessment of the society in which he lived. Like Simms, John Easton COOKE looked back to the American South of years past for his inspiration, most notably in his romances of colonial Virginia, which include *Leather Stocking and Silk* (1854), *The Virginia Comedians, Henry St. John, Gentleman* (1859), and *My Lady Pokahontas*. Also writing during this same period was Elizabeth Oakes SMITH, whose works include *The Western Captive* (1842) and *Bald Eagle* (1867), both of which are tales of the American frontier.

Although it may seem as if the majority of the popular authors of American romance were male, this was not the case. In fact, in the 19th c. as today, domestic tales and romances were often considered the special province of women. Louisa May ALCOTT was educated by her father, the noted transcendentalist and philosopher Amos Bronson ALCOTT, as well as by family friends Henry David THOREAU and Ralph Waldo EMERSON. Alcott soon began to publish pseudonymous shorts works and followed this with a job editing a juvenile magazine before she began writing the novels for which she is most famous: *Little Women, Little Men, Eight Cousins,* and *Jo's Boys,* all of which focus on the March family, which is based in part on Alcott's own family. While these novels are primarily "family" stories, courtship and marriage are important in each, as is the need for women to educate themselves and forge their own destinies. This can be seen especially in the character of writer and budding protofeminist Jo March, who most closely resembles Alcott herself—an early participant in the temperance and woman's suffrage reform movements.

In the post–Civil War period, much of the popular romantic fiction was published in dime novels and weekly fiction papers, although hardback versions of works that had been serialized earlier in magazines were sometimes published as well. Romantic novels about working girls, such as those written by Laura Jean Libbey, were also popular, as was historical fiction that followed the mid-19th-c. tradition of using colonial America as a setting, as seen in Mary JOHNSTON's *To Have and to Hold,* a novel set in colonial Virginia and centering on a woman who comes to Virginia in a shipment of brides.

Other lesser known authors of popular American romance at the turn of the century were Irving Bacheller, an author of popular romances that included *Eben Holden* (1900), Owen WISTER, a Harvard-educated Pennsylvanian from a noted family who traveled west for his health and there found the material for a literary career marked most notably by Western romances and a novel set in Charleston entitled *Lady Baltimore* (1906), and Hamlin GARLAND, most of whose works are set in the Midwest, including *Rose of Dutcher's Coolly,* a protofeminist novel whose heroine attends college, decides to become an author, and then discourages suitors since she believes that to become a "mere housewife" would be a betrayal of her essential nature. Rose eventually marries, but only after finding a man who, like her, desires a marriage of true equals.

Frank NORRIS began by writing medieval romances while studying art in Paris, then romantic poetry. His best known work includes *McTeague, Blix,* a semiautobiographical love story, and *The Octopus,* the first section of a never-completed trilogy that is generally considered his finest work. Norris's novels are noted for the way they combine popular romantic realism and a naturalistic attitude. Less well known, Harold Bell WRIGHT's novels are similarly set in the West and Southwest, and his works, especially *The Winning of Barbara Worth* and *The Shepherd of the Hills,* are concerned mostly with love, adventure, and the superiority of the rugged natural man over the over-civilized man of the cities.

Many stories had far more cosmopolitan settings. Henry JAMES, although born in New York, divided his time between Europe and America, and his work demonstrates an interest in the meeting of the European and American points of view, particularly in novels such as *The American, Daisy Miller*—which features a charming, if naive American girl—*The Portrait of a Lady,* and *The Awkward Age.* Also popular at the end of the 19th c. but less well known today is Francis Marion CRAWFORD. His romantic novels—over forty of them—focus primarily on cosmopolitan life and include *Mr. Isaacs, a Tale of Modern India, A Cigarette-Maker's Romance,* and *The Three Fates,* published in 1892. Crawford adapted a number of his novels for the stage, including *Francesca da Rimini* (1902), written for Sarah Bernhardt, and unlike James, Crawford believed fiction should be written purely for entertainment purposes.

Looking at a similar world to that of James, Edith WHARTON first wrote short stories and novelettes before writing *The House of Mirth* with its story of a young woman's attempt to make a "brilliant marriage" and her subsequent ostracism from conventional society. *The House of Mirth* is—like many of the works of James—a study of the false values present in society. Among Wharton's other novels are *Ethan Frome, Summer, The Age of Innocence*—for which she received a Pulitzer Prize—and an unfinished novel, *The Buccaneers,* which deals with the attempt of bourgeois

American girls to enter English society. Also writing at the turn of the century was Anne Douglas SEDGWICK who had been taken to England from New Jersey in 1882 and lived the rest of her life abroad. Like James and Wharton, she focused primarily on social relationships and particularly on the differences between the English and Americans. Her works include *The Rescue* (1902) and *A Fountain Sealed,* which deals with mother-daughter relationships, as well as *Annabel Chance* (1908), *Franklin Winslow Kane,* which contrasts a British and an American couple, and *Philippa* (1930).

Also writing in the first half of the 20th c., James Branch CABELL focused less on realistic portrayals of contemporary issues than on the romanticizing of historical themes. His novel *The Cream of the Jest* is about an escape into the dream world of the past, while *Jurgen* also focuses on an attempt to escape a prosaic life, although in too suggestive a way for the times, for there was an attempt made to suppress this book as obscene. Cabell includes fantasy elements in his fiction, as well as myth and history, most notably in *The King Was in His Counting House* and *Hamlet Had an Uncle,* both published under the name Branch Cabell. Less adventurous, but no less popular, Margaret Culkin Banning's contemporary novels probe matters of love, marriage, and parenthood, and include *This Marrying* (1920) and *The Dowry* (1955), while Faith BALDWIN wrote over seventy-five books—most of which were light romantic fiction—including *Office Wife* (1930), *White Collar Girl* (1933), and *The Lonely Man* (1964).

The early 20th c. also saw an increase in romantic mysteries written by women—examples of which often included gothic elements—and in the 1930s saw the rise of the so-called "anti-romance" in which the elements of romance are intrinsic to the plot, yet the heroine perversely refuses to follow the constricting rules of romantic fictional roles and ends without the "success" of a happy marriage. Probably the most popular example of this type is the Pulitzer Prize-winning *Gone with the Wind* by Margaret MITCHELL. *Gone with the Wind,* set in the South of the American Civil War and Reconstruction periods, was Mitchell's only book and was made into an extremely successful film starring Vivien Leigh and Clark Gable.

One of the biggest changes in the nature of the popular romance in the 20th c. was the mass-market publication of books under various imprints such as Harlequin—originally a Canadian division of the British romance publishers Mills and Boon. Harlequin's original intention was to publish short works of less than 200 pages that featured a young and naive heroine, often orphaned or otherwise forced to fend for herself. In typical early novels of this type of "category

romance," financial necessity leads the heroine to take employment with the hero, often as his secretary, his nurse, or as governess/companion to his child or ward. In the latter example, many elements of the stories mirror English author Charlotte Brontë's novel *Jane Eyre,* including the relative isolation of the home into which the heroine comes to live, and the possibility of the hero being injured in some manner or otherwise brought down from his initial position of arrogant superiority and seeming perfection before the final pages of the book. Even stories in which no directly hierarchical business relationship is in play, the respective ages of the heroine and the hero—and the latter's generally powerful social position and financial status—present an uneven relationship that can only be balanced by the power of the inevitable love that develops between the hero and the heroine, as in one of the earliest British prototypes for this type of fiction, Jane Austen's *Pride and Prejudice,* published in 1813.

After World War II, a revival in the interest in Gothic fiction led to reprints of earlier 20th-c. works, especially by British authors such as Victoria Holt (the pseudonym of Eleanor Burford Hibbert, and also more popularly known as Jean Plaidy) and Barbara Cartland and Georgette Heyer, both of whom set most of their historical fiction in the early-19th-c. British Regency period, as well as Dorothy Eden. Also during this period, Phyllis Whitney stood out as one of the most popular American authors in this genre.

While this Gothic "revival" never died out entirely, it was joined by many other literary styles in the crowded field that is popular romance today and includes many authors whose books are not immediately categorized as "romance" by the critics or by the authors themselves. Anya Seton wrote works that were primarily historical romances, and that include *My Theodosia* (1941), about Aaron Burr's daughter, *The Winthrop Woman* (1958), and *Dragonwyck* (1944) and *The Turquoise* (1946), both of which are set in 19th-c. America. Alice ADAMS focuses on young women and their relations to family, friends, husbands, and lovers in short stories and novels such as *Careless Love* and *Rich Rewards.* And Anne TYLER writes novels in which uneasy romances develop within the equally complex structures of the family and the modern society, such as *Earthly Possessions, Dinner at the Homesick Restaurant, The Accidental Tourist,* and *The Patchwork Planet.*

Attention should also be paid to the increasingly erotic nature of today's straight-to-paperback fiction, a trend that began in the 1960s and 1970s with such authors as Elizabeth Lowell, whose works are often set in the American Civil War era, but whose heroes and heroines seem more suited to the late 20th c. in terms of their behaviors and attitudes. Jayne Ann

Krentz is a highly successful author of contemporary romantic fiction, and her heroines are, as is the case with many heroines in contemporary romance, sexually experienced before they encounter the hero. Even in her historical romances (written under the name of Amanda Quick), Krentz's heroines—who are bright, but are often portrayed as rather refreshingly "naive" about the restrictive social mores of their own centuries-past eras—generally seem willing to give their virginity to the hero almost as a gift. Indeed, one would be hard pressed to find within most contemporary romantic fiction examples of popular romance that feature a heroine who begins the novel as a virgin and remains one until the end of the book. Exceptions to this rule, however, can be found—often within the new subgenre of category romances with a religious theme or Regency romances from publishers such as Harlequin. The heroines in these works may have anachronistically "kept up" with their contemporary counterparts in terms of their interests in the rights of women, their education, and their willingness to speak their minds, but their sexual experience prior to meeting the men who will eventually be their husbands is usually minimal, if not nonexistent. Perhaps some of this is due to the ongoing influence of the works of authors such as the extremely prolific English author Barbara Cartland, who was partly responsible for defining the conventions of the genre. For the Regency heroines in particular, sexual adventures rarely take place except at the most innocent levels, and in fact, being caught so much as kissing the hero is still reason enough for the heroines to find themselves pressured into a marriage, despite the protestations of either or both of the participants. When sexual acts do take place in these books, it is usually the consummation of the marriage, and even these descriptions are laden with euphemistic phrases, often to the point of the total de-eroticization of the sexual act..

However, the increasing eroticism of much category romance was, in fact, a reflection of the times and appeared to be mirroring the new sexual openness of more mainstream fiction authors such as Jacqueline Susann, whose works include the extremely popular *Valley of the Dolls* (1967), and Harold Robbins, many of whose novels like *The Carpetbaggers* (1961) were also turned into films. More recent on the popular romance scene is Danielle Steele, who has sold billions of books and has had over forty novels on the bestseller lists during the 1980s and 1990s. Her novels are primarily contemporary romances, with love stories framed by a variety of settings—such as Vietnam or Hollywood—and difficult situations—such as seeing to the education of a deaf child or recovering from the death of a much-loved spouse.

Even within mainstream romance, another trend in recent years has been the partial disempowering of the hero so that he is no longer the tall, dark, handsome, wealthy, and practically omnipotent hero of the early part of the 20th c. This can, of course, be seen most clearly in category romances or in historical romances of authors like Laura Kinsale, whose heroes, charismatic though they may be, often come complete with what might appear to be contemporary problems, which can rarely be diagnosed or understood by others in their historical time frame, and which include such things as post-traumatic stress syndrome, aphasia brought on by stroke, and the after-effects of repressed childhood sexual abuse. Even with authors whose heroes appear on the surface to be cut from the same cloth as the wealthy, titled heroes of yesteryear, there has been a definite trend of having these men ostracized from their own social class for some reason, with the result that they can only have a successful relationship with strong, independent heroines, instead of with the traditional young, poor heroine in need of rescuing. In fact, in works such as Mary Jo Putney's historical novels, it is often the men who are most in need of rescuing, if only on an emotional level. For example, one of Putney's earlier works, recently reissued as *The Rake* (1998), focuses on an impoverished nobleman who is also an alcoholic, and the way in which he deals with his condition with the support of the heroine. However, while there has been an increase in romances dealing with serious social issues, there has been an equal increase in the number of books with fantastic elements, marking almost a return to the Gothic novels of the 18th c. Category romances in particular abound with supernatural creatures, although unlike the novels of centuries past, these ghosts, vampires, werewolves, invisible men, and unwilling time travelers are cast as the romantic heroes, and all eventually find true love with their very human female counterparts.

Recently, a number of writers of popular American romance have proved less easy to categorize in what is still unfortunately a marginalized genre. Sandra Brown began strictly as a category writer, but her novels like *Fat Tuesday* (1998) have begun to cross over into mainstream popularity. The novelist Diana Gabaldon, while both knowledgable and enthusiastic about the field of romance writing, has long fought against the easy placement of her own extremely popular series of historical novels. Set in 18th-c. Europe and the Americas, and containing elements of fantasy, Gabaldon's books, beginning with *Outlander* (1991), focus on the unlikely relationship between a mid-20th-c. woman, Claire, and her 18th-c. love Jamie Fraser. The historical settings, particularly the Battle of Culloden in Scotland, are seamlessly woven into the love story and are incredibly well researched. Nor is it only female authors whose works are resisting simple categorization. Robert James Waller had a long stay at the top of the best-seller charts with *The Bridges of Madison County* (1994), a bittersweet love story about an all too brief affair between a farmer's wife and a traveling photographer, which was turned into a very successful film starring Clint Eastwood and Meryl Streep. Waller's subsequent novels, however, though also successful, seemed structurally derivative and failed to touch the reader's emotions as readily as *Bridges* had done. A work with a "happy" resolution to the courtship rituals between the sexes is Terry MCMILLAN's novel *Waiting to Exhale,* which has also been turned into a popular film. A number of McMillan's other works, like *Disappearing Acts,* also focus on romance, but in more detailed and realistic ways.

Today, American romance is more popular than ever, yet novels that are categorized purely as romances are given little serious critical attention, even as they climb to the top of the best-seller lists. It might seem incongruous that works that deal with such basic human conditions as love and family have little relative importance in the literary field, yet it should be remembered that the novel itself was—in its early days—often viewed as a somewhat "trivial" form of literature best suited for women and not serious literature that would be capable of attracting the attention of an intelligent, male readership.

BIBLIOGRAPHY: Dekker, G., *The American Historical Romance* (1987); Mussell, K., *Women's Gothic and Romantic Fiction* (1981); Radway, J., *Reading the Romance: Women, Patriarchy, and Popular Literature* (1984)

ELIZABETH HADDRELL

ROMANTICISM

A revolutionary movement in art, literature, music, and philosophy that began in Europe in the early years of the 18th c. and continued well into the 19th c. In America, the romantic movement began with the "pre-romantic" verse of Philip FRENEAU and continued through the advent of Walt WHITMAN. Romanticism has been described as a "protestantism in the arts and letters," an ideological shift on the grand scale from conservative to liberal ideas. In literature, it ultimately placed greater emphasis on the value of intuition and imagination than on objective reason. It was essentially a revolt against the prevailing concepts of the age, in particular neoclassicism, empiricism, and deism. All three contributed to a fixed social establishment founded on faith in Newtonian science and con-

fidence in the universality of reason. With the advent of romanticism, Newtonian science gradually gave way to philosophical idealism, and the confidence in the universality of reason surrendered to a heightened recognition of the diversity of truth.

The Age of Reason embraced the concept of the "Great Chain of Being," which held that the creatures of the world, from the highest angel to the lowest insect, were part of a descending and intricately connected order, a hierarchy of class structure that was divinely ordained. Kings ruled as "God's anointed," nobles and peasants were divinely placed in their positions in life. It was believed that to tamper with such an enduring but delicate mechanism was to invite the inevitable disaster of an unstable society.

The deists of 18th-c. America, most notably Benjamin FRANKLIN, Thomas JEFFERSON, George Washington, and Thomas PAINE, had no difficulty tampering with the Great Chain, nor in effecting an ideological transition from rational individualism to the more romantic variety. Reason made clear to these revolutionaries the radical idea that all men were "created equal," endowed from birth with certain "inalienable rights" that were permanently granted beyond the discretion of any monarchy, particularly one that denied these rights with what was perceived to be an arrogant and irresponsible abuse of authority. This first wave of political liberalism and revolution, culminating in the revolution of 1776, was the vanguard of American romanticism.

In the early years of the 19th c., the full effect of European romanticism, particularly the English and German variety, made its appearance in American arts and letters. Romantic tenets such as the primacy and validity of feeling and emotion, the freedom and value of imagination and intuition, the nobility of the common man (encompassing both the "noble savage" and the Jeffersonian agrarian), the primacy of the subjective view of the individual, the beauty and spirituality of nature, and the evocation of the picturesque American past, complete with its legends and folklore, were the more common aspects of American romanticism.

The first notable fiction writers of the American romantic movement were Washington IRVING and James Fenimore COOPER. Irving's particular contribution was the rendering of the history of Manhattan, albeit with considerable whimsy, in his *Knickerbocker History,* and the folk legends of New York's Catskill Mountains in "Rip Van Winkle" and "The Legend of Sleepy Hollow." Cooper contributed the first romantic American hero in the Character of Natty Bumppo, the protagonist of five novels known collectively as the "Leather-Stocking" tales. At the conclusion of each novel, Bumppo rejects both the cruel savagery of the wilderness (exemplified by renegade Indians) and the corruptive seductions of invasive civilization. In keeping with the romantic dictum "God made the country but man made the town," Cooper's hero moves ever westward, fleeing the encroaching settlements and seeking some ideal world of higher innocence and freedom. The best of the Leather-Stocking novels, *The Last of the Mohicans,* offers the most memorable example of the romantic concept of the "noble savage" in literature: the depiction of Chingachgook and Uncas, unlettered native Americans whose character and virtue are derived from their proximity to nature.

In the 1850 preface to the revised edition of the tales, Cooper described Natty Bumppo as "a being who finds the impress of the Deity in all the works of nature, without any of the blots produced by the expedients, and passion, and mistakes of man." A similar view was initially expressed by the English poet William Wordsworth, who, in his romantic manifesto to the English speaking world, the *Preface to the Lyrical Ballads,* extolled the value of the common man, called for the replacing of neoclassical diction in poetry in favor of a more basic language, and placed particular emphasis on the spiritually regenerative powers of nature.

These views were shared, particularly in regard to nature, by Wordsworth's American disciples, William Cullen BRYANT and Ralph Waldo EMERSON. Bryant was more cautious and restrained in his romanticism than his mentor, but is nonetheless the poet closest to Wordsworth in style and temperament. This influence is evident in Bryant's "Inscription for the Entrance to a Wood," with its emphasis on the healing sympathy of nature, and in "A Forest Hymn," which stresses both tranquil restoration and the sense of a divine presence in nature. Emerson's most significant contribution to American romanticism was *Nature,* in which he outlined the principles of Transcendentalism, an idealistic but loosely structured philosophy that emphasized a mystical unity with nature in which the mind and soul of the individual become one with the universal mind, or "Over-Soul," achieving thereby a form of nirvana, a mystical "oneness."

Emerson's TRANSCENDENTALISM attracted a considerable following of New England intellectuals, writers, and thinkers, among them his friend Henry David THOREAU; but Thoreau stood on the periphery of the group, the perennial nonconformist and self-sufficient, romantic individualist. In *Walden,* Thoreau demonstrated that he could love nature without sentimentalism, and could describe it with great sensitivity. His idealism was centered on the discerning of the true values of human existence and avoiding the pointless quest for material prosperity. Thoreau, a Harvard graduate who enjoyed speaking with the homely simplicity of a Yankee farmer, found the highest value in whatever was wild in nature or in humanity. He was American romanticism's prime example of the natural, untutored nobility of the common man.

Although the romantic movement was largely confined to New England and the northern states of the eastern seaboard, the south made a relatively small but nonetheless significant contribution. Most noteworthy are the nature poems of Henry TIMROD and Sidney LANIER, which captured respectively a Byronic energy and a Wordsworthian sensitivity. In particular, poems such as Lanier's *The Symphony* effectively combined the aversion to modern commercialism with the belief in nature's power to restore and regenerate the human spirit.

The darker side of American romanticism is represented by Nathaniel HAWTHORNE, Herman MELVILLE, and Edgar Allan POE, who share a series of romantic characteristics: a marked interest in the strange and mysterious, a dark, symbolical imagination, and a certain elusive ambiguity in style and content. Hawthorne, in *The Scarlet Letter* and tales such as "Ethan Brand" and "Young Goodman Brown," and Melville, in *Moby-Dick* and *Billy Budd,* focused on the problem of evil in the universe and the nature of sin, troubling issues from the legacy of their puritan heritage. Poe possessed a somber, brooding imagination that inclined to the eerie and supernatural and to all that was strange and remote to the conventional world. Like Keats and Baudelaire, Poe's romantic pursuit of idealized beauty was of a highly refined variety often associated with death and melancholia, notably in stories such as "Ligeia" and "The Fall of the House of Usher."

Others who were part of the romantic movement in America included Henry Wadsworth LONGFELLOW, John Greenleaf WHITTIER, James Russell LOWELL, Oliver Wendell HOLMES, and finally Walt Whitman, the last and possibly the greatest of the American romantics. In the nine editions of *Leaves of Grass,* from 1855 to 1892, Whitman shared with his readers a joyous celebration of the common man that included an intense desire for the beauty of nature, a subjective individualism, and an uncompromising idealism that made him the fitting culmination of the age of American romanticism.

In the years following the Civil War, romanticism gradually gave way to realism as America moved to take its place in the world as a leading industrial society. Transitional figures such as Mark TWAIN wrote good-natured stories such as "The Celebrated Jumping Frog of Calaveras County" early in his career, but ended with the dark pessimism of *The Mysterious Stranger* and "The Man That Corrupted Hadleyburg." Even the *Adventures of Huckleberry Finn,* whose title character, with his promise to abandon civilization and "light out for the territory" is the literary descendant of Cooper's Natty Bumppo, is a disturbing admixture of innocence, pessimism, and general disillusionment regarding human nature and the inferred promise of America.

A strain of romanticism has continued to appear in modern and contemporary American Literature in the form of the hero questing for some vague and seemingly unachievable ideal of the American dream. Among the many examples of this enduring species are F. Scott FITZGERALD's Jay Gatsby in *The Great Gatsby,* J. D. SALINGER's Holden Caulfield in *Catcher in the Rye,* Saul BELLOW's Augie March in *The Adventures of Augie March,* and John UPDIKE's Harry Angstrom, the title character for four novels: *Rabbit, Run; Rabbit Redux; Rabbit Is Rich; Rabbit at Rest.*

BIBLIOGRAPHY: Brooks, V. W., *The Flowering of New England, 1815–1865* (1937); Buell, L., *Literary Transcendentalism* (1973); Feidelson, C., *Symbolism and American Literature* (1959); Fussell, E. S., *Frontier: American Literature and the American West* (1965); Hoffman, D., *Form and Fable in American Fiction* (1961); Horton, R.W., and H. Edwards, *Backgrounds of American Literary Thought* (1952); Person, S., *American Minds: A History of Ideas* (1958); Reising, R. J., *The Unusable Past: Theory and Study of American Literature* (1986)

RICHARD KEENAN

ROOSEVELT, Theodore

b. 27 October 1858, New York City; 6 January 1919, near Oyster Bay, New York

As the twenty-sixth president, succeeding the assassinated William McKinley and anticipating William Howard Taft, concluding his life as an avid opponent of Woodrow Wilson, R. is a unique specimen of American politician and reformer. He is more in the British than American model—despite his ardent NATIONALISM—for he combined a life of energetic if not frenetic political activity with the discipline of a productive writer. After the failure of his ranches in the Dakota territory and the loss of most of his patrimony invested in that Western adventure, a reverse due to the severe winter of 1886–87, he turned to writing during the remainder of his life as his chief means of support. The American myths he created in the four-volume *The Winning of the West* (1889–96) have transformed themselves into the stereotypes of popular entertainment, the views of the "primitive" in his numerous books about adventure and hunting in Africa as well as in North America have passed into ethnocentric commonplaces, and his 1899 account of military braggadocio in the Cuban adventure is the most successful,

if unwitting, campaign biography ever penned—for it brought him to such prominence that he could not be ignored on the national political scene, winning the Republican vice presidential nomination in 1900.

His view of nature was that it was to be closely studied (he was an amateur naturalist), but it must also be "conquered." This typical antithesis reveals the complexity of his personality: for he at once describes nature as the object of will, then defends its primacy, its fragility, against the trepidations and violation of unwise use. He was, by turns in writing and politics, a jingoist as well as a pleader for international understanding, provincial as well as cosmopolitan, subtle and blunt, both peacemaker and warmonger, a consistent reformer but sometime temporizer.

He was the author of some 150,000 personal letters and 2,000 published works. A good many of his books remain in print, and of American presidents, he is the only one aside from Thomas JEFFERSON and Abraham LINCOLN to merit any literary distinction, and the only one, aside from the doubtful case of Wilson, to have earned any amount considerable enough from his writing alone to sustain political adventure. R.'s writing and publishing successes were the sinew of his political life.

His first and most esteemed work was begun while R. was a Harvard undergraduate and first published in 1882, the still well-regarded *The Naval War of 1812.* This germinal work was to form the basis of his later interest in naval affairs as an instrument of international power. It presaged his ultimate success as assistant secretary to the Navy and the eventual alliance with Alfred Thayer Mahan, whose own formative books on naval power were complementary to R.'s earlier work.

R.'s lifelong commitment to democratic reform is recorded in the multiple levels of his writing as polemicist, advocate, and social historian. His descriptions in the *Essays on Practical Politics* of the stupidity and corruption in New York state government, where he began his political apprenticeship at the age of twenty-three, are unequaled in American writing for their precision and humor. Other works on the same subject, collected in *American Ideals and Other Essays* (1897) from writing appearing in the 1890s in the *Atlantic Monthly, Scribner's,* and the *Century* reveal the writer's personal courage, his reforming impulse, his zest. R.'s accounts of politics in action are overlooked American masterpieces of political zoological description: his taxonomy of the self-serving political animals in their profitable lairs deserves wider note, if not fame, in the present social climate.

R.'s autobiography (1913), written too early to completely line his political and temperamental feuds with Wilson, is of serviceable self-promotion, and his biographies of Thomas Hart Benton (1886), Gouverneur Morris (1888), and Oliver Cromwell (1900), though dictated and written in extreme haste, reveal the author's essentially positive and didactic impulse.

BIBLIOGRAPHY: Beale, H. K., *T. R. and the Rise of America to World Power* (1956); Cooke, J. W., "T. R.," in Wilson, C. N., ed., *DLB,* vol. 47, *American Historians, 1866–1912* (1986): 242–49; Harbaugh, W. H., *The Life and Times of T. R.* (1963); Morris, E., *The Rise of T. R.* (1979)

ROBERT MOYNIHAN

ROSE, Wendy [Bronwen]
b. 7 May 1948, Oakland, California

R.'s poetry and essays depict her efforts to create a unified sense of self out of the contradictions of her several heritages. Born of a Scots-Irish-Miwok mother and a Hopi father, R. writes about not feeling at home in either Indian or white society. At the same time, R.'s Native American heritage contrasts sharply with her academic training in anthropology; her complicated position—as a researcher who is related by blood to the humans being studied—adds emotional and intellectual complexity to her poetry. Expressing alienation and pain while moving toward personal integration, R.'s writings enact a wholeness deliberately crafted despite, and through, the conflicts of her own history and that of her people.

In two ways especially, R.'s writings are politically charged. Her work foregrounds the existence and particular concerns of mixed-blood Native Americans, while her status as an anthropologist gives her power to reclaim Native American history and deconstruct academic condescension toward native peoples. She has called herself a "spy" whose presence both demonstrates the human values that "artifacts" represent and asserts the need for accountability in the history of genocide in America, as expressed in her poem "Three Thousand Dollar Death Song."

R.'s two most important collections are *Lost Copper* (1980), which brought together many of the best poems from her early chapbooks and introduced her to a wider audience, and *Bone Dance* (1994), which includes more personal poetry written over the past twenty-five years and selections from earlier books including *The Halfbreed Chronicles and Other Poems* (1985) and *Going to War with All My Relations* (1993). R.'s poems are both archaeological and mythological. Delving into Native American history, R. finds emblems of her own griefs, and her reclamation of the past affirms her survival and growth.

In her introduction to *Bone Dance,* R. notes that her perspective as a mixed-blood artist has changed;

rather than feeling she ought to protect "the old way," she has realized that the old way "is strong, while people like me are the ones who have always been in danger," and that her "true job" is to "keep listening" to her own experiences. Intense, ironic, and empathetic, R.'s poems express recurrent themes of loss, dignity, horror, and renewal. Her books have reflected various stages of her life as she has learned what it means to be Native American in the modern U.S., has gained a global sense of human concerns, and has discovered her personality as a poet while surviving personal crises. Although at one time she felt a need to use a pseudonym ("Chiron Khanshendel"), R. shows in the sequence of her books of poetry the evolution of a distinct and graceful voice. R. is also an artist who has illustrated some of her books.

BIBLIOGRAPHY: Bruchac, J., *Survival This Way: Interviews with American Indian Poets* (1987); Coltelli, L., *Winged Words: American Indian Writers Speak* (1990); Gordon, A. F., and C. Newfield, eds., *Mapping Multiculturalism* (1996); Schöler, B., ed., *Coyote Was Here* (1984)

JAYNE MAREK

ROSSNER, Judith [Perelman]
b. 1 March 1935, New York City

Influenced by writers such as Grace PALEY and Tillie OLSEN, R. says she eventually found her own style expressed as "a tour of the inside of a woman's head." Her distinctive strength as a writer lies in the psychological exploration of her women characters. Her characters are compelling, at once causing inspiring awe and discomfort. R. creates a quasi-therapist-patient relationship with her readers. And it is in the establishment of this relationship, allowing access to the female psyche, which distinguishes her genius. She forcefully enters this world in a way that no other writer has managed.

R.'s life provides ample raw material from which she creates her superbly psychological fiction about the various dalliances of women. R.'s mother, a school teacher, harbored dreams of becoming a writer, an aspiration she passed on to her daughter. R. dropped out of college to marry a teacher and writer, divorced him, married a magazine editor, had two children, and divorced a second time. Relocating to New Hampshire to start a free school, R. later returned to New York to work in a psychiatry department of a hospital. At thirty-seven, she decided to devote her efforts full-time to writing. After publishing her first two novels, R. was asked by *Esquire* to write a story for a women's issue of the magazine about the twenty-seven-year-old school teacher Roseann Quinn who was murdered by a man she invited home from a bar. *Esquire* never ran the story, but R. decided to turn it into a novel. In 1975, *Looking for Mr. Goodbar* was published and R.'s career, if not her reputation, was established for life.

From the canvass of her life come recurring themes and motifs found in her fiction: mother-daughter relationships, self-absorption conflicting with selflessness, sexual freedom and destruction, isolation, the quest for connection in a lonely world, the east-coast west-coast character types, the writer's preoccupation. Her first novel, *To the Precipice* (1966), is described as a coming-of-age story of a young Jewish woman who marries a gentile. Her second novel, *Nine Months in the Life of an Old Maid* (1969), features a young woman who chooses to live a cloistered existence in the mansion of her sister. Her birth comes when she is compelled to live outside of the confines of the mansion. In both *To the Precipice* and *Nine Months in the Life of an Old Maid,* R. explores the tension between altruism and self-absorption. In *Any Minute I Can Split* (1972), communal life provides the landscape for the ties that bind individuals to a community, and as with the first two novels, R.'s understanding of human nature is expertly rendered. Ruth Kossoff, Elizabeth "Beth" Cane, and Margaret Adams are women in crises whose existences are tied to, if not influenced by, larger American values. The characters' desires—the desire for wealth and security, the desire for quiet enjoyment of the security of the home, the desire to belong and negotiate space in a community—reflect the prevalent American values for the setting of each work.

R. addresses these outward desires manifested in her works in the novel *Nine Months in the Life of an Old Maid.* Beth's brother, who had been her hero, her champion in a difficult family, also happens to be a writer. Of his writings he explains: "in the old days every time I published a book some carping little academic bastard made sure to point out that if I did know what my hero looked like I was keeping it a secret. Anyhow. The symbols of the sixties have the purity of the Greek myth—Vietnam, the Blacks—while the symbols of the thirties were tied up in a thousand tricky little arguments and philosophies which only became purified in later years, the Peekskill riots being one of the better examples." Two points are noteworthy here. First, the level of ideas—of the discourse of ideas—is important to R.'s writing. Here we have a "worldly" brother commenting on the America of his parents and contemporary American life to a sister who has never willingly left the confines of the estate. She is the reader against whom the writer sounds his ideas. Second, in this novel, R. seems to be answering her critics, one of whom described *To the Precipice* as "slow-paced and somberly naturalistic

in many long passages of description that were almost Dreiserian."

Her fourth novel, *Looking for Mr. Goodbar,* is by all accounts her most successful novel, critically and popularly. It is a fictionalized account of a real-life murder. Theresa Dunn, a young Italian Catholic girl, is both disfigured and left slightly crippled owing to a bout with polio at age four. After a year's stay in the hospital, during which time her grandmother dies, she returns home and remains some fifteen pounds overweight, with a disfiguring scar down the length of her spine, until she finds unrequited love with her English professor who eventually breaks off the affair whereupon Theresa loses the extra weight and begins a jaded existence of frequenting bars and picking up men. When it seems that she will manage her demons, she is killed by a man whom she picks up at Mr. Goodbar's where she went because she finds she is unable psychologically to reconcile the pains of childhood with her adult life. Outselling the first three novels by leaps and bounds, it was adapted to film in 1977 and brought even wider recognition to R.

Like Beth Cane of her first novel, here we have a central female character in psychological crisis. Where the first novel begins with a literal nightmare, here R. begins with the nightmare of a heinous crime, a confession that has the dreamlike quality of reverie. Beth hates her mom for her abandonment; Theresa Dunn struggles with her mother's abandonment of her after the death of a beloved brother. And in the midst are some interesting asides related to the academy, race relations, free sex, and human longing. Her observations on human nature are at their best.

Attachments (1977), *Emmeline* (1980), *August* (1983), *His Little Women* (1990), *Olivia; or, The Weight of the Past* (1994), and *Perfidia* (1997) followed *Looking for Mr. Goodbar,* and without disappointment. Though they shock, are calculated to shock with improbable plots, and the reviews are largely mixed, as Marge Piercy says of *Emmeline,* "the part we cannot swallow scarcely bothers our enjoyment." *Attachments,* the story of a woman and her friend who marries Siamese twins, is as much the story of the marriage as it is the manipulative relationship between Nadine Tumulty and her friend Diane. *Emmeline,* the story of a 19th-c. woman who sacrifices herself for her family's economic survival, features a mother-son incestuous relationship. *August* features the relationship between a teenage patient Dawn Henley and her analyst Dr. Lulu Shinefeld. The novel is something of an exposé on the field of psychoanalysis. *His Little Women* is the story of Nell Berman and her (half) sister-novelist Louisa Abrams, and develop more fully theme of parental abandonment (and the wonderful potential of consequences) presented in *Nine Months in the Life of an Old Maid. Olivia* is reminiscent of the relationship between Nadine and Carly in *Attachments* where parental abandonment and adolescent revenge meet in singularly suspenseful and surprising ways. *Perfidia* is based on an actual murder account. It is the story of a girl who murders her abusive mother. And the title's reference to deceit and betrayal is not lost in the scheme of the novel.

At the heart of all R.'s novels is the question of being: relationships, expected and unexpected roles, and fidelity or infidelity to ways of being for characters. Her specific genius is the manner in which she enters and shares the interior lives of her various characters with their often surprising shocking twists. Her stories are uncanny, insightful, modern, and always grounded in the human condition, most probably owing to her decided dedication to psychology. The author may well have pronounced early in her career as did Nadine in *Attachments,* "The following year I would take my first psychology course and lose the ability to offer simple answers to simple questions." Often, she obscures the message via the introduction of sex and erotica as lives are disrupted via these means.

BIBLIOGRAPHY: Potoker, E. M., "J. R.: Daughter of Lovers," *The Nation* 29 May 1976: 661-64; Rinzler, C. E., "A Review of *Looking for Mr. Goodbar,*" *NYTBR* 8 June 1975: 25–26

ADELE S. NEWSON

ROTH, Henry

b. 8 February 1906, Tysmenica, Galicia, Austria-Hungary; d. 13 October 1995, Albuquerque, New Mexico

R. may be the most widely read and most influential one-book American novelist of the 20th c. R.'s *Call It Sleep* (1934) was rediscovered and reissued in 1960. It has been praised widely as a masterpiece of proletarian, Jewish, and modernist fiction. R. was born in Austrian-governed Poland and was brought to New York by his parents eighteen months later. R.'s novel draws on his childhood in New York's Jewish ghettos—the Brownsville section of Brooklyn and Manhattan's Lower East Side. With its intermittently stream-of-consciousness third-person narration, though, *Call It Sleep* is more than veiled autobiography. Its narrative subtlety and psychoanalytic sophistication reflect R.'s estrangement, or emancipation, from his ghetto origins.

While a freshman at the City College of New York, R. met Eda Lou Walton, a poet then teaching at New York University. In 1928, R. began living with Walton—twelve years his senior—who introduced him to literary MODERNISM, anthropology, and Freudian

psychology, all of which figure in *Call It Sleep.* R.'s commitment, as a member at the time of the Communist Party, to a proletarian esthetic also figures in the novel. R. tried and failed twice to write another novel. He recounts this failure, along with his courtship of his wife Muriel Parker and their life together as poultry farmers in Maine, in two memoirs published in *Commentary* in 1959 and 1960. Between 1939 and 1969, R. published several stories in the *New Yorker, Atlantic,* and *The Best American Short Stories: 1967.* R. described himself in 1969 as working on "a rambling interminable multivolume work, hopefully 'posthumous' and provisionally entitled *Portrait of the Artist as an Old Fiasco.*"

In 1987, R. published *Shifting Landscape: A Composite, 1925–1987,* a collection of stories, essays, journal entries, and letters. The first novel of R.'s projected six–volume autobiographical series, *Mercy of a Rude Stream,* appeared in 1994 entitled *A Star Shines over Mt. Morris Park,* and was followed by *A Diving Rock on the Hudson* (1995), and the posthumous *From Bondage* (1996) and *Requiem for Harlem* (1998).

BIBLIOGRAPHY: Baumgarten, M., *City Scriptures: Modern Jewish Writing* (1982); Klein, M., *Foreigners: The Making of American Literature, 1900–1940* (1981); Lyons, B., *H. R.: The Man and His Work* (1977); Rideout, W., *The Radical Novel in America* (1956)

JAMES D. BLOOM

ROTH, Philip

b. 19 March 1933, Newark, New Jersey

R.'s distinctive humor has spanned five decades since the publication of his first book, *Goodbye Columbus,* a collection of stories issued in 1959. Only in recent years has his ebulliently satirical humor turned bitter. The change was apparent in the short novel *Deception* (1990) and pronounced in *Sabbath's Theater* (1995). His concerns, however, have stayed remarkably constant—the search for an identity that permits self-mockery and the need for a counterpoint of view no matter how exalted the original portrait. Similarly, his targets have remained generic—the prejudices of wealth, class, ignorance, and unexamined indifferent custom. Yet the differences in tone between R.'s published work in his first forty years of writing activity and his work in the last five are so alien that it is necessary to sum up his significant achievements before embarking on the less certain path of his future work.

Like a number of Jewish American writers of his generation, R. was strongly influenced at an early age by Henry JAMES. The attraction of James for R. may well have been James's subtlety of mystery, his commitment to evasiveness. James raised ambiguity to a height of elegance never trespassed before his advent; R. and other Jewish American writers turned that ambiguity, and its capacity for rewonder, into an uproarious ambivalence about their Jewish past and the continuing role of Jewishness in their lives. The influence of James may be seen most clearly in *The Ghost Writer* (1979), R.'s *roman à clef* about Bernard MALAMUD and R.'s relationship with him. Tied into the thread of a younger writer confronting a revered older one, of both writers exploring their Jewish identity and yet disguising their soul by the refinement of surface voices, is the story of a possible Anne Frank planted in the midst of a Connecticut landscape. R.'s schema of possibilities becomes a Jamesian evolution of character—the portrait of awareness as it can no longer be deterred. In writing a book about Anne Frank who may have miraculously survived the Holocaust and who has come to live with her rescuer in Connecticut, in having two writers in rivalry with each other about the mythic and the putative real Anne Frank, R. is clearly using mystery to illuminate the profound issue of relevance of Judaism to American Jewry.

R.'s concern with Jewish identity is integral to his early fiction, but its expression is more the stuff of detail than a journey of exploration. In his perfectly realized *Goodbye, Columbus,* the bittersweet tale of a poor Jewish young man who ultimately rejects the confining customs of his Jewish American Princess lover, R. laid out his targets and mockingly shot them down. Brenda, the spoiled princess who believes she can transform her impoverished bohemian lover in time into a Jewish bourgeois, is R.'s first *femme foil* and a recurrent satiric ploy in his work. His hero Neil is the first and far from last appearance of R.'s alter ego, a searcher after truths he reaches but does not grasp. Neil gives up Brenda, believing he must pursue a different path, that of the struggling artist, but it is an easy victory for him.

R.'s balancing, or posing, of alternates between the proper Jew and the embarrassing shameful one, between the conventionally successful professional, academic or businessman, and the odd, rebellious and disturbing eccentric, is also sketched in two of his now-famous early stories, "Conversion of the Jews" and "Eli the Fanatic." R. reached the height of his popularity (though not of his artistry) with the publication of *Portnoy's Complaint* (1969), again a tale of a young Jewish man calling attention to his provocative polemics. In this outrageous satire on contemporary America's passion for psychoanalysis as the cure-all for spiritual ills, Portnoy addresses his ironic troubadour's "complaints" to his readers in the form of an

unraveling therapeutic session. Portnoy is trying to free himself from the mother love that has nurtured his talent and his growth; he is trying to free himself from his father's demands and from the impositions of conventional society.

Portnoy's Complaint established R. as a popular satirist, but it also obscured his questioning of American values. Attention was paid more to the comic outlandishness of his fictional situations than to his junior-Job lamentations, for Portnoy is but one more lost young Jewish American man crying in the wilderness for a faith to redeem them. Because R. rejected both Orthodox Judaism and the compromise of Reform Judaism, because he applied his scalpel skills to all his Jewish characters, he laid himself open to attacks as a Jew-baiter and a self-hating Jew. These criticisms have less validity than half-truths to them. R. has chosen as his appointed fiction the portrayal of desire and wanting, and although his characters are Jews and his milieu is Jewish territory, his profound questioning is nondenominational.

R. continued his exploration of unfulfilled desire in such novels as *My Life as a Man* (1974), *The Professor of Desire* (1977), *Zuckerman Unbound* (1981), *The Anatomy Lesson* (1983), and *The Counterlife* (1986). His famous gallery of characters includes Nathan Zuckerman, David Kepesh, Tarnapol, and Carnovsky—all writers and/or public figures or professor who have excited admiration and envy, and whom would-be writers and fannish zealots pretend to be. Since these writers have exploited reality for their making of literature, these would-be writers now steal their creator's personality. All of them resemble R., suspiciously. The *Zuckerman Bound* trilogy (1985) is so named because it is a pun on the binding of three freewheeling novels into one volume, particularly since the first fiction is titled *Zuckerman Unbound.* In *The Counterlife,* which many critics consider R.'s masterpiece, R. plays out death scenes for Zuckerman and his brother Henry in alternating chapters. What R. seems to be seeking in *The Counterlife* is the rhythm of living responses to death. Thus a writer and his dentist brother, their wives and mistresses, are all played before a tune of death and circumstance; the authorial wit of their responsiveness and the counter-responses become a game as sophisticated in its unique manner as any cosmopolitan satire of manners.

R. is more serious about death in his memoir of his father's dying, *Patrimony* (1991); here he forsakes layered counter-memory for the real stuff of sorrow and laughter. The seriousness of his play acting in the Zuckerman fiction, and particularly in *The Counterlife,* becomes all the more apparent when placed beside the realistic treatment of a son watching his father die in *Patrimony.*

R.'s achievement as a significant novelist and major satirist of the 20th c. is secure, but his most recent works have shown a flagging of professional discipline. *Deception* and *Operation Shylock* (1993) have flashes of brilliant Rothian satire but the tales themselves demonstrate more a volume of personal reference than rounded fictional flesh. In *Sabbath's Theater,* he explicitly turns to a middle-aged picaresque rogue. Sabbath is a puppeteer who has never made the big time, who has suffered excruciating marital and romantic losses (in his own estimation), and who has never separated his manipulation of ties between the people with whom he is involved and the puppets too whose strings he is attached. Of immense sexual potency, Sabbath is unable to be satisfied with one wife at a time, and has caused each of his two wives a great deal of pain. R. presents Sabbath as a self-destructive near-genius with all warts showing. Sabbath's first wife disappears and Sabbath believes he is the primary cause; he cheats on his second wife, who after years of cohabitation, becomes a solitary drunk. Sabbath's great love, his mistress, dies on him, killed in her prime by ovarian cancer.

R. is apparently taking on a new hero in *Sabbath's Theater.* He has put finish to the young and confused hero; he is onto the middle-aged failed protagonist. The problem for some critics with this new R.—the book, it should be noted, has its adherents, having won among other honors the coveted National Book Award in fiction in 1995—is that Sabbath turns out to be unlikable rather than magnificently Rabelaisan. His sexual escapades, mammoth and uncompromising in their inventiveness and enthusiasms, are not so joyful when placed against their possible consequences. His telephone sex with one of his students—an "affair" he justifies as educational for the student—is perhaps funny to some but painful to others.

R. ends *Sabbath's Theater* with his hero literally in the dust, begging for rescue from his self-destructiveness. The portrait is circular, beginning with the youthful Portnoy and coming round to the senior puppeteer. Yet, whereas Portnoy's youthful antics had appeal, Sabbath's end on the heap of loss lacks both youthful pathos and the tragic grandeur of a King Lear. It may be a sign of things to come from R.—the end of self-destructive mockery and thus the possibility of a new humor.

BIBLIOGRAPHY: Jones, M. P., and G. A. Nance, *P. R.* (1981); Lee, H., *P. R.* (1982); McDaniel, J. N., *The Fiction of P. R.* (1974); Milbauer, A. Z., and D. G. Watson, eds., *Reading P. R.* (1988); Pinsker, S., ed., *Critical Essays on P. R.* (1982)

MARTIN TUCKER

ROTHENBERG, Jerome

b. 11 December 1931, Brooklyn, New York

R. is one of America's preeminent poets, editors, translators, anthologists, and teachers. His name was linked with that of poet Robert KELLY and a uniquely American school of poets known as the deep image poets. R. actually coined the phrase deep image, a term borrowed from psychology and linguistics that proposed a poetry that avoids the "cult of personality" and the practices of a prevailing poetic establishment that fosters what critic Jed Rasula calls "the enshrinement of private sentiment." R. and other deep imagist writers draw upon the wisdom of ancient "primitive" cultures, especially their concept of the sacred and their connection with nature and the environment.

R.'s early poetic experiments with both Dadaism and surrealism—and their language-based beliefs—led to his belief in poetry as a nonrational expression of the unconscious. Much of R.'s early poetry came out of direct influences from Getrude STEIN, Federico García Lorca and abstract artists like Arshile Gorky. In *The Gorky Poems* (1966), R. creates linguistic analogues to Gorky's experiments with collage and derive their meaning from aural effects. He has published over sixty volumes of poetry from 1960 to 1995, and his most critically acclaimed ones are those that deal with his imaginative reconstruction of his family's Polish-Jewish background: *Esther K. Comes to America, 1931* (1974), *Poland/1931* (1974), *Vienna Blood and Other Poems* (1980), and *That Dada Strain* (1983).

R.'s interest in the nonrational resources of language led him to an examination of native ethnological records from many countries and cultures. He was one of the first major American poets to combine mythic, anthropological, and ethnological concerns and produce a body of poetic and historical work out of these diverse disciplines. One of his best-known collections of such materials, *Technicians of the Sacred: A Range of Poetries from Africa, America, Asia, and Oceania* (1968) stands out as a unique example of a writer's attempt to include the cultural riches of native traditions, including our own. His *Shaking the Pumpkin: Traditional Poetry of the Indian North Americans* (1972) brought together prayers, poems, rituals and other sacred events from Native Americans in the U.S. and Canada. In both of these seminal works, R. hoped to forge relationships and demonstrate parallel elements common to both ancient and contemporary cultures.

R.'s interest in his own family background led to an examination of ancestral poetry and ritual of a Native American tribe, the Seneca. He and his anthropologist wife, Diane, became residents at the Allegheny Seneca Indian Reservation from 1972 to 1974, and their findings resulted in not only *Shaking the Pumpkin,* but in his critically acclaimed *Seneca Journal* (1978), poems of his own that record his initiation into a new culture and his attempt to integrate Senecan rituals and myths with his own Jewish religious tradition.

As a result of his work as a translator, poet, commentator, and interpreter of so-called "primitive" poetry, he and poet George Quasha edited a groundbreaking anthology in 1973 entitled *America: A Prophecy.* Subtitled *A New Reading of American Poetry from Pre-Columbian Times to the Present,* the volume opened up the definition of what constituted American poetry by including substantial collections of Native American poetry, rituals, hymns, and myths from the Eskimo, the Aztec, Mayan, Toltec, Native North American, Central American, and Mexican traditions.

R.'s publication of *Symposium of the Whole: A Range of Discourse toward an Ethnopoetics* (1983) is a collection of carefully edited excerpts on the nature of myth, religion, anthropology, and poetics, and brought together, for comparative purposes, texts as divergent as William Blake, Leo Frobenius, Claude Lévi-Strauss, Roland Barthes, Benjamin Lee Whorf, Gershom Scholem, Robert DUNCAN, and Mircea Eliade, among many others. R. is considered the founder and most articulate champion of ethnopoetics, a discipline that combines mythology, poetry, ritual, religion, anthropology, and linguistics.

In 1995, with poet Pierre Joris, R. edited the two-volume *Poems for the Millennium: The University of California Book of Modern and Postmodern Poetry.* The first volume, entitled *From Fin-de-Siècle to Négritude,* opens the barriers of canonical literature in new and unique ways. Its concerns move from forerunners such as William Blake and Emily DICKINSON, through Mallarmé and Picasso, to the futurists, expressionists, Dadaists, and surrealists up through the objectivists and Negritude writers.

BIBLIOGRAPHY: Fleischman, B., "J. R.," in Greiner, D. J., ed., *DLB,* vol. 5, part 2, *American Poets since World War II* (1980): 214–19; Zalenski, J., "R.'s Continuing Revolution of the Word," *NDQ* 55 (Fall 1987): 202–16

PATRICK MEANOR

ROWLANDSON [Talcott], Mary [White]

b. ca. 1637, Somerset?, England; d. 5 January 1710/1, Wethersfield, Connecticut

R. wrote only one text that survives, an autobiographical narrative of her capture by Native American tribes during King Philip's War. Except for the unusual cir-

cumstances of her life, she would probably not have contributed at all to American literature; instead, her remarkable account has made her one of the best-known colonial American writers. For two centuries after its first publication, the work appealed to a wide popular audience, and it commands considerable critical attention today.

Her journey toward literary fame began on February 10, 1675/6, when R., a minister's wife living in Lancaster, Massachusetts, and her three children were captured by a raiding party of Indians. The youngest child, a six-year-old girl, was wounded in the raid and later died in captivity; the older son and daughter, like their mother, were eventually ransomed. R. spent three months living with her captors and recorded the details of the twenty "removes" of her journey with the tribe when she wrote her narrative, The *Soveraignty and Goodness of God, Together with the Faithfulness of His Promises Displayed; Being a Narrative of the Captivity and Restoration of Mrs. M. R.* (1682).

As the full title of her work indicates, R. not only recounts the facts of her experience, but also interprets them in the light of her religious beliefs. Her preface explains that the narrative was originally written for private circulation among her friends, who persuaded the author that the pious message of the work was so valuable that it should receive wider dissemination. On its first publication in 1682, the inclusion with it of the last sermon preached by R.'s husband, Joseph, who had died in 1678, emphasized the devotional nature of her material.

The devout aspects of her account are inextricably interwoven into the fabric of the narrative. Again and again R. cites the scriptural passages that brought her comfort throughout her ordeal, passages she sees not as metaphorical guides but as descriptions of her own literal reality. She seeks to understand her experience by placing it in a typological framework: her trials in the wilderness are visited upon her in much the same way that misfortunes were sent to Old Testament figures, and for similar purposes. The work is undeniably Puritan in cast, with the author recalling her transgressions before the kidnapping—such sins as excessive enjoyment of tobacco—and coming to the belief that "It is good for me that I have been afflicted."

The unifying theme of R.'s narrative contributes to the modern evaluation of it as the best, as well as the first, of the genre of captivity narratives. The account is also one of the most readable colonial American texts. R. describes the attack, and especially her daughter's death, in passages charged with emotion. She provides valuable and fascinating historical detail as she reports on her daily life in the Indian camp. Although she continues to compare her captors to devils throughout the work, she nevertheless becomes genuinely interested in them almost in spite of herself; she gives more detailed descriptions of their customs and rituals and begins to individualize her formerly anonymous tormentors as her stay among them lengthens.

Finally, the narrative provides us with a fascinating psychological representation of the author, a seemingly ordinary woman of her time to whom extraordinary things happened. With her relatives and friends murdered and her daughter dead, held captive by strangers who view her as a servant, R. does not surrender to grief and simply wait to die, like another of the English captives she meets. Instead, she makes herself valuable through her needlework skills, earning money, food, and respect. Her account shows her to be devout, but it also demonstrates her strength and adaptability. *The Narrative of the Captivity and Restoration of Mrs. M. R.,* as her story is now known, is the portrait of a survivor.

BIBLIOGRAPHY: Breitweiser, M. R., *American Puritanism and the Defense of Mourning* (1990); Greene, D. L., "New Light on M. R.," *EAL* 20 (Spring 1985): 24–38; VanDerBeets, R., "M. R.," in Elliott, E., ed., *DLB*, vol. 24, *American Colonial Writers, 1606–1734* (1984): 766–67

CAROLYN LENGEL

ROWSON, Susanna Haswell

b. 5 February 1762, Portsmouth, England; d. 2 March 1824, Boston, Massachusetts

R., although born in England, holds the title of America's first best-selling novelist. *Charlotte, a Tale of Truth* (London 1791, Philadelphia 1794), which brought her that distinction, appeared as *Charlotte Temple* in 1797 and has since gone through nearly two hundred editions.

R.'s use of 18th-c. literary forms, her standards of morality, and her patriotism, which pleased her contemporaries, drew criticism in the early 20th c. More recent scholars, however, commend her ability to use the sentimental tradition and simultaneously to criticize it.

The hectic nature of R.'s life ironically fostered her development as novelist, actress, playwright, songwriter, poet, educator, and essayist. At R.'s birth, her mother died, and her father, William Haswell, a member of the Royal Navy, moved to America. In 1767, after a second marriage, he brought R. to the colonies. Back in London in 1778, R. worked as a governess, a position providing continental travel and ample social opportunities. Marriage in 1786 to William Rowson, a sometime musician and actor, introduced her to the stage. Despite marital problems, the couple remained

together, and in 1793, theatrical employment brought them to Philadelphia. Better prospects lured them to Boston, where, in 1797, R. opened the Young Ladies' Academy, for which she wrote a variety of textbooks.

Even before leaving England, R. had established herself as a writer with six books published. Experience had taught her about sexism and classism, and, although writing to make money, she hoped also to share that knowledge. She created a wide range of women characters, from passive to daring, from innocent to villainous. Recurring themes include women's oppression, their need for education, and the wisdom of filial piety. She condemned unrealistic plots and happy endings that mislead the young.

By 1794, R. had arranged for American editions of four of her English novels. *The Inquisitor; or, The Invisible Rambler* (1788), a picaresque work patterned on Laurence Sterne's *Sentimental Journey* (1768), follows the male narrator in a world of oppressed women, where he alleviates poverty and thwarts seducers. *Mentoria; or, The Young Ladies' Friend* (1791), combines letters, stories, and an essay, to alert women to society's dangers. *Charlotte Temple* is a story of an English school girl misled by a corrupt French teacher, Madame La Rue, into a liaison with a dashing army officer. Carried off to America and abandoned by Montraville, his traitorous friend, Belcour, and La Rue, Charlotte dies in childbirth. *Rebecca; or, The Fille de Chambre* (1792), also the story of a young Englishwoman, contains scenes reminiscent of R.'s first voyage to America and her Revolutionary War experiences. It became an American "better seller."

Three novels written in America also received significant attention. *Reuben and Rachel; or, Tales of Old Times* (1798) begins with Columbus's discovery of America, and traces the experiences of select descendants, ending with 18th c. Reuben and Rachel, who epitomize American ideals of that time. *Sarah; or, The Exemplary Wife* (1813)—serialized, as *Sincerity,* in the *Boston Weekly* (1803–4)—addresses older readers, encouraging them to make the best of their marriages but promising little reward. *Charlotte's Daughter; or, The Three Orphans* (1828), a sequel to *Charlotte Temple,* follows the lives of three young women, one of whom is Lucy Blakeney (Temple). More complex than *Charlotte,* this work draws power from the impending incest between Lucy and Montraville's son.

R.'s contribution to the theater included patriotic pieces such as *Slaves in Algiers* (1794), which treats Americans captured at sea, and *The Volunteers* (1795), based on the Whiskey Rebellion. R. also wrote sea chanties and lyrics for love songs, the former representing some of her finest work. Her *Miscellaneous Poems* appeared in 1804.

BIBLIOGRAPHY: Castiglia, C., "S. R.'s Reuben and Rachel: Captivity, Colonization, and the Domestication of Columbus," in *Redefining the Political Novel: American Women Writers, 1797-1901* (1995): 23–42; Nason, E., *A Memoir of Mrs. S. R.* (1870); Parker, P. L., *S. R.* (1986); Stern, J., "Working through the Frame: *Charlotte Temple* and the Poetics of Maternal Melancholia," *ArQ* 49, 4 (1993): 1–32; Vail, R. W. G., *S. H. R., the Author of Charlotte Temple. A Bibliographical Study* (1933); Weil, D., *In Defense of Women: S. R.* (1976)

LUCY M. FREIBERT

ROYALL, Anne [Newport]

b. 11 June 1769, near Baltimore, Maryland; d. 1 October 1854, Washington, D.C.

R. is most often remembered as the only woman in the U.S. to be tried and convicted as a common scold. Current assessments view her travel writing as well as her reports on the people and politics in Washington from 1831 to 1854 as important sources for the social and political history of her era. Her vivid and colorful descriptions of public figures and scenes during her travels and her vehement attacks on fraud and graft in government are entertaining examples of personal journalism of the era.

At eighteen, she moved from the frontier in Pennsylvania to the plantation of Captain William Royall where her mother became a domestic in what is now West Virginia. The next ten years under the captain's tutelage, she learned to write and explored his considerable library. At twenty-eight, she married the captain, then in his mid-fifties, and enjoyed a prosperous life until his death sixteen years later. She was to have inherited his estate, but it was contested and eventually lost.

With few resources, R. began writing down her travels, supporting herself with subscription sales of her books. *Sketches of History, Life and Manners in the U.S.* (1826), her first book, is an account of her trip from Alabama to New England and exhibits her clear style, attention to details, and ability to capture the life of cities and personages. She was a fearless traveler, mingling with all sorts, trading gossip, walking, riding trains, coaches, or horseback in all weather without complaint. Consequently, her travel writing is an excellent social commentary of the period and offers a unique female perspective of travel at the time. Her writing was, in most cases, accurate, humorous, and unpretentious.

She next wrote *The Tennessean: A Novel Founded on Facts* (1827), a meritless work, and then returned to her travel writing. She soon became quite well known in every part of the country because of her books: *The Black Book: A Continuation of Travels in the U.S.* (3 vols., 1828–29); *Mrs. Royall's Pennsylvania* (2 vols., 1829); *Mrs. Royall's Southern Tour* (3 vols., 1830–31); and *Letters from Alabama, 1817–1822* (1830). In her travels, she would visit every city, town, and village on the way, creating her verbal pensketches and portraits of the great and near-great. She interviewed every president from Washington to Lincoln and almost every dignitary or politician on her travels.

Befriended by the Masons, she became their champion, staying in their homes on her travels, speaking at meetings, and soon attracting attacks from the anti-Masons and evangelicals. In 1831 she ceased her travel because of age but soon established a newspaper, *Paul Pry,* which she wrote and printed out of her home in Washington, with its successor, *The Huntress.* Her vow to "expose corruption, hypocrisy, and usurpation without favor or affection," coupled with her vituperative style, antagonized politicians, anti-Masons, and evangelicals and led to her trumped up trial. She suffered injustice, ridicule, and poverty, but died an admirable, charitable, and honest example.

BIBLIOGRAPHY: Jackson, G. S., *Uncommon Scold: The Story of A. R.* (1937); James, B. R., *A. R.'s U.S.A.* (1972); Maxwell, A. S., and M. B. Donlevy, *Virago!: The Story of A. N. R. (1769–1854)* (1985); Porter, S. H., *The Life and Times of A. R.* (1909)

NEWTON SMITH

RUKEYSER, MURIEL

b. 15 December 1913, New York City; d. 12 February 1980, New York City.

The beauty and power of R.'s work, as well as its startling variety, have been obscured for many years, even preceding her death. Her work as a poet is probably best remembered, but her reputation has needed rescue just as her work has needed reprinting in order to restore her to her proper place in literary history. Like other women of her generation (Louise BOGAN, for example, or Laura RIDING), she outlived her first impact as a writer while continuing to produce important work and, perhaps more importantly, continuing to have a powerful influence on younger women writers, who found her more than a mother figure, since her work and counsel affected not only their personal lives but their sense of their potential as writers and as women. Adrienne RICH has, in recent years, written eloquently of R.'s achievements and importance, describing her as "our 20th-c. Coleridge" while decrying her disappearance from literary prominence, the result of careless and wasteful disregard, prompted in part by gender prejudice, in part by disapproval of her active role in political life, in part by critical categories drawn too narrowly to accommodate the range and complexity of R.'s achievements.

Critics have emphasized the continuity of R.'s work, the consistency of both subject matter and style from her first book of poetry, *Theory of Flight* (1935), which won publication in the Yale Series of Younger Poets, through ten other volumes of poems, including *The Green Wave* (1948), *Breaking Open* (1973), and her final individual volume, *The Gates* (1976). R.'s style has been described as intellectual and abstract; even in poems where her sharp observations of color and form, of natural objects, provide the occasion, her quick mind tends to link the details to larger themes of time, of history, of social change. She rages against the oppression of peoples and writes often of social injustice, as in "The Tunnel," or the powerful portrayal of the effects of silicosis on miners in "The Book of the Dead." Though she was no manichean, images of darkness pervade her work—as in the titles, *The Speed of Darkness* (1968) and the posthumous *More Night* (1981)—but the contrasts of dark and light, black and white, are more complex in her work than merely evocative of opposites; often they bathe in each other's arms, the one serving as the occasion for the emergence of the other.

R. was active in both the civil rights movement and opposition to the Vietnam War, appearing frequently at readings with other poets, notably Denise LEVERTOV and Anne SEXTON, who shared her commitment if not her unflagging energy in their support. In "Martin Luther King, Malcolm X," she writes of the assassinated leaders, expressing her solidarity in the image of "my black voice bleeding," and in "Don Baty, the Draft Resister," she insists on the identity of herself and all innocent people of good will with those who stand against unjust war. While she reacts often to current events and issues, her poetry is also rich in allusions to mythology, to the arts and to ancient as well as modern history.

As she grew older, her poetry often focused on human relationships, especially her love for women and her hopes for women's lives. In "Song: Lying in Daylight," from *The Gates* (1976), she evokes the power of touch and of gaze, the connections between two lovers that remain unsaid but deeply felt. Whether she explores the physical forces that keep a plane or a bird in flight or remembers and records the moments that precede a devastating stroke, her imagination fo-

cuses surprising connections and offers insights that seem entirely new and yet familiar.

Among R.'s most valuable works are the many translations she performed, introducing the Anglophone world to such great modern poets as Octavio Paz and Gunnar Ekelöf. She also wrote plays, notably *The Middle of the Air* (1945), *The Colors of the Day* (1961), and *Houdini* (1973), as well as several children's books.

R. was primarily a poet, at least in reputation, but she wrote a number of prose works, including a collection of lectures on poetry, *The Life of Poetry* (1949), a manifesto of the poet's task that challenges and contradicts the modernist values of the male poets of her generation as well as the school of New Criticism that prevailed in literary and academic circles through the 1950s and 1960s. It was the New Critics whose disdain for R.'s kind of poetry—a poetry in the manner of William Blake and Walt WHITMAN, personal, expansive, and prophetic from a progressive stance, rather than reactionary and arcane—probably contributed to the decline of her reputation. The narrow values imposed by the modernist schools could not account for or comprehend the wide-ranging interests and quirky experimentation of a writer like R., who wrote unauthorized biographies—*Willard Gibbs* (1942) and *One Life* (1957), a generically complex study of presidential candidate, Wendell Willkie, written both as a prose account and as a sequence of poems—and an unconventional historical study, *Traces of Thomas Hariot* (1971), the cool reception of which caused R. considerable pain; she is quoted in an interview as objecting to one of its reviewer's calling her "a she-poet," but later defiantly accepting the epithet as proper evidence that her contribution, *as a woman,* was what made her study of that Elizabethan explorer most valuable. R. was not alone among women in her own generation, but her ties to many younger women poets and writers, especially Adrienne Rich, and the quality of much of her best poetry, will assure her influence and reputation for generations to come.

BIBLIOGRAPHY: Jarrell, R., *Poetry and the Age* (1953); Kertesz, L. *The Poetic Vision of M. R.* (1979); Rexroth, K., *American Poetry in the Twentieth Century* (1971)

THOMAS F. DILLINGHAM

RUNYON, [Alfred] Damon

b. 8 October 1880, Manhattan, Kansas; d. 10 December 1946, New York City

R. is identified with the stories of Broadway he created between 1929 and his death, but during his lifetime he was as famous for his newspaper columns as for his fiction. For thirty-five years, he wrote for Hearst newspapers, covering sports, crime, New York life, and his pre-New York experiences—experiences that included writing for several Colorado newspapers, serving in the Spanish-American War, and living a few months as a hobo. His early life emerges indirectly in the rich mixture of his Broadway stories. He receives little attention from scholars and critics, but his characters have become a part of American culture, and his stories remain in print.

R.'s Broadway is a Western village. Everyone knows everyone and gossips about everyone else. Most citizens are colorful eccentrics tolerated by other colorful eccentrics. The mind set of his characters, like that of many Wild West characters, and, quite possibly, like R.'s own, is criminal. His characters are gamblers, bootleggers, burglars, armed robbers, hired killers, and sellers of protection. They have their own morality—a morality that R., by implication at least, finds not inferior to that of mainstream society.

They fall in love, take revenge, cheat each other, and shoot each other—and in the midst of everything else reveal gallantry, chivalry, and sportsmanship. Much of R.'s humor depends on the voice and perspective of his narrator who speaks in the present tense with a mixture of slang and pseudo-dignity as he blandly describes the outrageous. In "The Hottest Guy in the World," one of Big Jules's armed robberies "does not count so much" because only one person was killed. In "Dream Street Rose," the Washington law officers have broken up Good Time Charley's New York speakeasy out of ignorance, because they do not know he is protected.

Exploitation of the outrageous is common among local color writers, but few of them have R.'s identification with their material. He exploits the hilarity of his characters, but he is not remote from them, and the reader, too, is with them. In "The Idyll of Miss Sarah Brown," when Sky Masterson wins the love of Sarah Brown by shooting dice and sending the losers to her mission, one laughs with none of the condescension one feels for the denizens of Poker Flat.

R.'s more than eighty stories of Broadway won him phenomenal popularity throughout the 1930s into the 1940s, both in the U.S. and England, and his work was translated into several languages. Seventeen of his works have been made into films, and the musical *Guys and Dolls,* based on his fiction, was highly successful in 1950 and continues to be revived.

Many sophisticated readers are put off by R.'s use of trick endings and coincidence. His characters, though individual, lack complexity. Yet a handful of his best stories, among them "The Idyll of Miss Sarah Brown," "Dream Street Rose," and "All Horse Players Die Broke," make little use of coincidence and are all the more effective for the single-mindedness of their protagonists. R. is almost certain to remain a part of the American scene.

BIBLIOGRAPHY: Breslin, J., *A Life of D. R.* (1991); Clark, T., *The World of D. R.* (1978); Hoyt, E. P., *A Gentleman of Broadway* (1964); Runyon, D., Jr., *Father's Footsteps* (1954); Wagner, J., *Runyonese: The Mind and Craft of D. R.* (1965); Weiner, E. H., *The D. R. Story* (1948)

MARYJEAN GROSS and DALTON GROSS

S

SACKLER, Howard
b. 19 December 1929, New York City; d. 13 or 14 October 1982, Ibiza, Spain

S. worked both as a playwright and a screenwriter from 1950 to his death in 1982. He was also the director of Caedmon Records, New York and London, from 1953 to 1968. He directed television programs, and he wrote the screenplays for such movies as *Fear and Desire* for Stanley Kubrick in 1953, as well as *Bugsy* (1973) and *Jaws 2* (1976).

Though he was diverse with regard to the milieu in which he worked, S. was best known as a playwright. He merged his love for poetry and verse in his first play *Uriel Acosta* (1954), for which the writings of T. S. ELIOT served as inspiration. In this story of a 17th-c. Portuguese Jew, S. introduced a writing style that he would embrace throughout his writing career: merging historical facts and personae with his own creative fiction. S.'s second play, *The Yellow Lovers* (1962), deals with a 19th-c. French poet, Tristan Corbière. With these two plays, S. began to hone his craft; though neither are the measure of the playwright he was to become, they indicate the beginnings of a writer whose talent lay in his ability to show the universality of the human condition, regardless of race or era.

S. departed from his historic style to write *A Few Enquiries* (1965), a series of four one-act plays including *Sarah, The Nine O'Clock Mail, Mr. Welk and Jersey Jim,* and *Skippy.* In his 1966 play *The Pastime of Monsieur Robert,* however, S. again turned to history for inspiration, finding it in the character of the Marquis de Sade, on whom Monsieur Robert is based. Set following the French Revolution, the drama explores the twisted fantasies of its title character, revealing the psyche of a man who had been imprisoned and disillusioned.

S.'s most acclaimed play, *The Great White Hope* (1967), which was written in verse, was based on the life and career of Jack Johnson, an early-20th-c. boxer who was the first black man to become a heavyweight champion. The story of Johnson (called Jefferson in the play) is poignant, with the boxer's character well defined and full of humanity. The play chronicles seven years of the man's life (1908–15), and with its tragic ending, in which the boxer loses more than a fight in the ring, the reader is left to wonder if is the "great white hope" or Jefferson's own pride that defeats him.

For *The Great White Hope,* S. received the triple crown of theatrical awards—the Pulitzer Prize in drama, the New York Drama Critics Circle Award, and a Tony Award—and, at that time, his play was only the fifth in history to do so. This achievement alone could have been enough to place S. in the league of well-known 20th-c. dramatists, but it did not. S. produced only two more plays before his death, *Semmelweiss* (1977) based on the career of a 19th-c. Hungarian physician, and *Goodbye Fidel* (1980), which includes Fidel Castro as one of its characters. He was at work on *Klondike,* an unfinished play set in the gold rush of Alaska, when he died at the age of fifty-two. S.'s talent lay not just in his fusion of history and poetry, but in his ability to draw very real characters, their thoughts, their speech, their actions, as they reflect the glory and tragedy of life.

BIBLIOGRAPHY: Funke, L., *Playwrights Talk about Writing* (1975); Gottfried, M., Introduction to *A Few Inquiries* (1970); Hungerford, R. W., "H. S.," in MacNicholas, J., ed., *DLB,* vol. 7, part 2, *Twentieth-Century American Dramatists* (1981): 198–204

KATHERINE L. KELLER

SALINGER, J[erome] D[avid]
b. 1 January 1919, New York City

S. has gained prominence and cultlike acclaim from a large cross section of the American public on the basis of a rather limited literary output—one novel, three collections of novellas and short stories, and several additional uncollected short stories.

Many of the stories published in various magazines and journals—*Colliers, Saturday Evening Post, Esquire, Story, Kansas Review, New Yorker*—during the 1940s reflect the influence of S.'s experiences in the U.S. Army during World War II. Some of them feature members of the Glass family and the Caulfield family, characters who will appear again in later works.

In 1951, S. published *The Catcher in the Rye,* an extremely popular novel whose sixteen-year-old narrator, Holden Caulfield, has spoken to and for generations of teenagers ever since. Although young readers empathize with Holden, understanding perhaps too well his depression and his hatred of "phonies," his is not merely a tale for the high school set. Many adults have read and then reread the book, finding they are able to appreciate the agonizing struggles of the young boy far better from a more mature perspective. S. captures the essence of his teenage narrator's feelings of alienation and confusion along with his profound mistrust of the adult world. Holden is the quintessential upper-middle-class adolescent; he is typically and heartbreakingly lonely and unsure. His wry cynicism and often dark humor work to underscore his emotional instability. He has recently been expelled from a New England prep school—not the first—and spends two hilarious but tragic days looking for love and truth in all the wrong places in New York City. Holden has grown up in New York and his family is still firmly ensconced in a large Upper East Side apartment. But now he is suddenly a street kid, confronted with the isolation of one cut off from help in the city where he should most feel at home.

The language is slangy and often peppered with profanities that led to the book's being banned in some libraries and schools. But it is S.'s perfect pitch, his ear for the cadence and repetitiveness of the American teenage vernacular that accounts in large measure for Holden's appeal and the depth and breadth of the book's influence.

Nine Stories (1953) is a collection of short stories, eight of which were originally published in the *New Yorker.* Characters in several stories have been broken psychologically by war experiences. The children tend to be extremely smart and oddly fragile. The tone is often cynical and the narrative stance is slightly withdrawn, lending a special sadness to what is often the focus: loss and in some cases the rage that loss can engender. *Franny and Zooey* (1961) contains a short story concerning a young, disillusioned college girl trying to find meaning in her life through reading a spiritual book, and a novella whose central characters are the two youngest of the seven Glass children—each

of whom has performed brilliantly over the years on a radio quiz show called *It's a Wise Child.* The book became a best-seller, attaining first place on the *New York Times* list. *Raise High the Roof Beam, Carpenters and Seymour: An Introduction* also reached the top of the *Times* best-seller list shortly after it was published in 1963. This book consists of two novellas also dealing with the Glass family, each of which was previously published in the *New Yorker* in 1955 and 1959 respectively. It is clear that S. loves this large, brilliant, and often highly entertaining New York City family he has created—the parents are retired vaudeville performers—and his caring adds to the reader's enjoyment of their exploits and their crises.

In 1965, "Hapworth 16, 1924," a fifty-page story appeared in the *New Yorker,* after which S. stopped publishing entirely. Suddenly, in early 1997, it was announced that his last story would be republished in book format by a small press, Orchises Press in Alexandria, Virginia. However, the publication date has been postponed several times; there is, of course, speculation that the work may never be republished. This is yet another story concerning the Glass family in the form of a long letter that seven-year-old Seymour Glass writes to his family from summer camp. Again, S. captures the voice to perfection. Seymour is a highly precocious child who rambles on at great length about camp life and the books he has read and plans to read, having most recently completed Anna Karenina. However, in the Glass family saga, Seymour is the oldest child who, as a seriously disturbed veteran of World War II, commits suicide in the 1948 story, "A Perfect Day for Bananafish," collected in *Nine Stories.* Questions abound as to S.'s reasons for bringing his last published story forward after so many years of silence. For readers encountering S.'s work for the first time, "Hapworth 16, 1924" seems a singularly inaccessible and unappealing introduction. The motivation behind S.'s and his agent's decision is far from clear, possibly contrived to achieve an end not obvious to S.'s general readership, most of whom have long been hoping for additional material from the writer.

During the decades since S. has lived in seclusion in a small, rural New Hampshire village, there has been much speculation about his literary output. Rumor has it that he has completed at least two full-length works, but his agent will neither confirm nor deny the existence of such material. S. has fiercely guarded his privacy, and any attempts to infringe on his rights and his copyrights are met with litigation. His agent even polices the Internet for those who may quote too lavishly from S.'s works.

In a 1974 telephone interview with Lacey Fosburgh of the *New York Times,* S. expressed his anger over the publication of unauthorized editions of his early previously uncollected works. In that conversation, he also commented that he found "a marvelous peace in not publishing," claiming that publishing is "a terrible invasion of my privacy. I like to write. I love to write. But I write just for myself and my own pleasure."

Needless to say, S.'s many fans would like to have more of his work for their own pleasure. It remains to be seen if their wishes will be granted.

BIBLIOGRAPHY: Bloom, H., ed., *Holden Caulfield* (1990); Hamilton, I., *In Search of J. D. S.* (1988); Lundquist, J., *J. D. S.* (1979); Salzberg, J., ed., *Critical Essays on S.'s The Catcher in the Rye* (1990); Seed, D., "Keeping It in the Family: The Novellas of J. D. S.," in Lee, R. A., ed., *The Modern American Novella* (1989): 139–61

MARGARET D. SULLIVAN

SALTER, Mary Jo
b. 15 August 1954, Grand Rapids, Michigan

S. is among the best of the New Formalist poets, one who, like Dana GIOIA, Rachel HADAS, Katha Pollitt, and her husband, poet, novelist, and critic, Brad LEITHAUSER, attended Harvard University in the 1970s and studied either with Robert FITZGERALD or Elizabeth BISHOP or, like S., both. While it would ordinarily be frowned upon to consider a literary couple's work together, in S. and Leithauser's case, it is difficult not to. Not only do they share a formalist poetic aesthetic, their lyric poetry often reflects their shared lives, including their domestic life in South Hadley, Massachusetts, where they share a teaching position at Mount Holyoke College, as well as their frequent sojourns abroad—to Japan, England, Iceland, France. But if the shimmering surfaces of Leithauser's poetry derive from the whimsical side of Marianne MOORE, S. clearly is more influenced by Emily DICKINSON, the Mount Holyoke graduate about whom she's written, and by the serious travel lyrics of Bishop, though some of S.'s best verse is refreshingly light.

The title of S.'s first collection of poems, *Henry Purcell in Japan* (1985), as well as its epigraph from George Herbert, reflects her grounding in Western civilization—specifically, in this case, the 17th-c. England of Purcell's hymns and Herbert's religious verse—and her simultaneous fascination with travel as an opportunity to experience other cultural angles of vision. Her attempt to read Japanese culture from her distinctly Western perspective is evident not only in this collection's title poem, but in its entire third section, nowhere more ambitiously than in "Japanese Characters," a tripartite meditation on the function of Japanese ideographs in comparison to the English alphabet. "Welcome to Hiroshima," by contrast, reflects ironically upon the English-language sign that greets the tourist-poet to this city destroyed by an American atomic bomb and now reconstructed, with its Peace Park, by the Japanese with American economic assistance. "At the Public Baths" observes the contrast between pre- and postwar Japanese values as they are encountered in the form of a older woman bathing her grandson in the Kyoto public baths in 1982. Finally, in "Shisendo," S. sees continuity between classical Chinese and Japanese poetry and her own contemporary American verse.

In her second and best book to date, *Unfinished Painting* (1989), S. alternates sections of poems on domestic and artistic subjects and light verse with two longer elegies. The first of these, "Elegies for Etsuko," poignantly reflects upon the time she shared with a Japanese friend who committed suicide at twenty-eight. The second, "Dead Letters," focuses on her mother's legacy after her prolonged suffering and death from cancer. Her poems in this book's first section on life in South Hadley include a meditation on women and education at Mount Holyoke ("Reading Room") and her homage to Emily Dickinson ("The Upper Story"), whose house she visits in nearby Amherst. The light verse in the volume's penultimate section shows S. at her most playful and formally polished. This combination provides some of her most memorable poems, including a humorous love lyric to her husband, "Aubade for Brad," and a serious meditation on the nuclear threat to the environment, "Chernobyl," all the more powerful for being written as if a nursery rhyme.

In *Sunday Skaters* (1994), S. continues to write polished formal verse on domesticity, art, travel, and light verse, here widening her repertoire with the inclusion of two ambitious narrative poems, "The Hand of Thomas Jefferson" and "Frost at Midnight," the latter on Robert FROST. Among the most engaging poems in this volume is "A Benediction," at once an epithalamion and a witty reflection, in the manner of W. H. AUDEN's verse letters (his "New Year's Letter" provides the book's epigraph), on marriage in general, hers in particular. Among the many successful pieces of light verse included here, "Half a Double Sonnet" and "Brownie Troop #722 Visits the Nursing Home," deserve special note, as do the erotic epigrams, "Two Sketches." The book's title poem is from "Icelandic Almanac," a sequence that, like S.'s Japanese poems, attempts to unravel the natural iconography of the harshly beautiful northern landscape of Iceland. The sequence's title poem captures this atmosphere, in summer and winter, most effectively.

BIBLIOGRAPHY: Darling, R., "M. J. S.," in Gwynn, R. S., ed., *DLB,* vol. 120, *American Poets since World*

War II (1992): 273–75; Lehman, D., "The Not-So-New Formalism," *MQR* 29 (Winter 1990): 140–44

ROBERT MCPHILLIPS

SALTUS, Edgar [Evertson]

b. 8 October 1855, New York City; d. 31 July 1921, New York City

S. remains today as difficult to categorize and critically assess as he was during his lifetime. During the course of his literary career, he produced twenty-six volumes and worked as a biographer, philosopher, novelist, short story writer, essayist, journalist, poet, and dramatist. Over the years there has been no shortage of attention given to S. by noted scholars, among them Arthur Symons, H. L. MENCKEN, Van Wyck BROOKS, and Claire Sprague, but none of these critics agrees on which of S.'s works is his best, or even at what kind of writing S. most excelled. The title that has received the most scholarly attention is *Imperial Purple* (1892), a series of fictionalized historical essays about the extravagances of last rulers of Rome. What is clear from a study of S.'s oeuvre is the fact that he possessed a passionate love for words, a quality that many critics have viewed as artistically debilitating.

S. was born into the social elite of New York City and enjoyed both leisure and privilege in his early life. Indeed, his social position and its advantages lent themselves to the development of his philosophies of negativism and pessimism that he outlined in his early companion pieces, *The Philosophy of Disenchantment* (1885) and *The Anatomy of Negation* (1886), both of which were regarded, respectively, as highly accessible essays on the work of Schopenhauer, and the philosophy of nihilism and decadent aesthetics. S. attended Yale in 1875 but quickly moved on to pursue a European education at Heidelberg, Munich, and Paris. By 1880, he had returned home and received a law degree from Columbia. But instead of law, S. chose to practice a studied life among New York City's socialites and literati and to turn himself to writing.

His first work was a biography of Balzac (1884). His two philosophical essay collections followed, and then his first novel, *Mr. Incoul's Misadventure* (1887), in which S. attempted to dramatize the pessimism he espoused through Incoul, a thinly-veiled persona of the author. This early novel received positive reviews, perhaps encouraging S. to continue to employ protagonist personae. One of his most intriguing is the novelist Alphabet Jones, the hero of *The Pace That Kills* (1889), who journeys through the world of high society in his quest for literary material.

In 1893, S. was involved in a scandalous divorce from his first wife, Helen Sturges Reed, and produced a treatise on the unchastity of women called *Madame Saphira*. S. would marry and divorce two more times, events that further distanced him from the high society in which he had moved and worked. He gained a reputation, popularly exaggerated, though not entirely unfounded, as a decadent aesthete who sought the pleasure and company of multiple younger women in order to find inspiration to write. Many of these stories were doubtless overblown, and his third wife, Marie Giles Saltus—who introduced him to theosophy and the occult and abetted the causes for scandal surrounding her husband's name—wrote a lengthy biography of her former husband. In *E. S.: The Man* (1925), she attempted to defend S. as a supremely gifted artist existing in a world wholly unresponsive to his genius. Though not wholly convincing in its argument, the work does provide interesting insights into S.'s character, works, and talent.

Perhaps the assessment of S. that strikes closest to the heart of the critical debate over him and his work is provided by Eric McKitrick in his 1970 review of Claire Sprague's study of S. McKitrick writes that the tragedy of S. was "a gnawing fear of involvement, a terrible unwillingness to be spiritually, morally, or intellectually engaged, even in the simplest way." This seems a fair consideration leaving readers with either a man who ingeniously defied the optimism of his age, opting for a darker view of mankind, or an artist who lacked the ability to confront the world in any way other than through a disinterested retreat from it.

BIBLIOGRAPHY: Peckham, M., "E. S. and the Heroic Decadence," *TSE* 23 (1978): 61–69; Sprague, C., *E. S.* (1968)

JOHN V. GLASS

SANBORN, Franklin Benjamin

b. 15 December 1831, Hampton Falls, New Hampshire; d. 24 February 1917, Plainfield, New Jersey

A biographer, editor, journalist, poet, and reformer, S. is at once an important chronicler of Concord TRANSCENDENTALISM and the worst butcher of American literature in the 19th c. Full of ambition, by the age of twenty-one, S. had become acquainted with some of the key cultural figures in New England, including Ralph Waldo EMERSON, Harriet Beecher STOWE, Theodore PARKER, Thomas Wentworth HIGGINSON, and John Greenleaf WHITTIER. Thus ingratiated with this literary circle, after graduating from Harvard in 1855, he established residency in Concord, where he opened a private school, boarded with the family of Henry David THOREAU, and lived a life of decorum.

A third-generation transcendentalist, S.'s character is contradictory in respects. He was, like many transcendentalists, active in the abolitionist movement. But unlike most abolitionists, S. promoted armed opposition to slavery. He was one of the "Secret Six" who championed John Brown and knew in advance of Brown's raid on Harpers Ferry. After Brown was hanged for the raid on Harpers Ferry, S. (twice) fled to Canada to escape indictment; upon returning to Concord, he was arrested, but was released a short time afterwards. Unlike other transcendentalists who felt that free trade was the cause of injustices, S. openly endorsed free trade and the division of labor as means of achieving free soil. As head of the Massachusetts Board of Charities, S. in 1866 helped defeat a bill in the state legislature for an eight-hour work day. S. was the center of the social life in Concord, a successful Boston correspondent and then editor for the Springfield *Republican,* and editor of the Boston *Commonwealth,* but his stubborn, opinionated character led to his decline in public stature in the 1880s.

Most critical discussions of S.'s large oeuvre focus on his editorial work, which is consistently attacked for its sloppiness. His two-volume edition of *Walden* is characterized by careless and inconsistent editing, cavalier omissions, and interpolations of "new" material, and S.'s editions of Thoreau's poems that appeared in the Boston *Commonwealth* are so inaccurate that they are almost unrecognizable as Thoreau's work. S.'s own poetry is routinely dismissed by critics as mediocre at best.

S. is more successful as a biographer and essayist. The youngest and last of the antebellum Concord transcendentalists, S.'s biographical work is interesting, if unreliable. His first-person reminiscences of such key figures as Emerson, Thoreau, Parker, Louisa May ALCOTT, and William Ellery CHANNING are valuable, and he is justly credited for demonstrating the value of these writers, but his numerous "literary recollections" are often excessively detailed. His most notable biographies are *The Life of Henry David Thoreau* (1917) and his two-volume autobiography (four were planned) *Recollections of Seventy Years* (1909). S.'s *The Genius and Character of Emerson* (1885) is one of the most important single-volume collections of criticism on Emerson in the 19th c.

BIBLIOGRAPHY: Burkholder, R. E., "F. B. S.," in Myerson, J., ed., *DLB,* vol. 1, *The American Renaissance in New England* (1978): 160–61; Myerson, J., ed., *The Transcendentalists: A Review of Research and Criticism* (1984)

                                    BRYAN L. MOORE

SANCHEZ, Sonia

b. 9 September 1934, Birmingham, Alabama

Born Wilsonia Benita Driver, S. has been one of the most consistently productive and continuously innovative poets among those writers who developed their craft during the social and cultural turmoil of the 1960s, combining from the beginning of her writing life a facility with the nuances of language and a conviction that literature must address issues of injustice. Her first collection of poems, *Homecoming* (1969), was a pioneering effort in which the relatively submerged but historically crucial questions of race and gender were addressed with the confident voice of a woman who had noted with anger and disgust the racial and sexual insults common to African American women in the middle decades of the 20th c. Mixing criticism of the negative aspects of American society with celebrations of the positive elements of her own cultural experience (as in a poem for Malcolm X), S. wrote in the direct, contemporary idiom of poets like Allen GINSBERG, Gary SNYDER, and others who were in the main current of the New American poetry.

Her struggles with nascent black studies curricula and other emerging aspects of the Black Arts movement led to the purposefully angry poetry of *We a BadddDDD People* (1970), which used the tough vernacular, taut rhythms and assertive attitudes of black street talk. S.'s employment of inventive typography, imaginative spelling and a concern for sound as a dramatic device unnerved some commentators who were not prepared for the power and blunt honesty of this kind of writing, but the songs of praise for sources of black pride and the deft humor of poems like "San Francisco Suicide Number" made the collection more than one dimensional. S. indicated that her range was way beyond the invective of some of these poems with her *Love Poems* of 1973 and her *A Blue Book for Blue Black Magical Women* of that same year, in which she began to directly address the circumstances of her own life in a more specific manner, covering her life from the perspective of a society that, she felt, "does not prepare young black women, or women period, to be women." Her involvement and disengagement from the Nation of Islam informs this book as well, leading her toward a history in a poetic sequence of African American women over more than three centuries. Here her facility with various techniques becomes evident as the poems use a musical score, the rhythms of a child's game, elaborate stage direction/commentary and a vocabulary that is highlighted by linked words and compound adjectives that compress units of meaning into intense bursts of energy.

S. introduced the forms of the haiku and the tanka in *A Blue Book for Blue Black Magical Women,* and continued to use new structural arrangements in *Under A Soprano Sky* (1987), where she assumed the position of a kind of spokeswoman for a cultural community, the time-tested, traditional role of the poet since Homer as the mind of a people. Her "elegy (for MOVE and Philadelphia)" is an examination and indictment of governmental authority gone amok and a lament for the victims of various power-mad groups driven by self-interest and lacking a clear moral conscience. The skillful blending of voices in this eight-part poem shows S.'s range beyond the "blackened" English she used in early work, while the balladlike stanzas of "Song No. 2" recall a British "come-all-ye" chantey adapted to a modern situation. In this poem, S. begins each line with "I say" as a means of declaring with confidence her life's wisdom and her recognition that she has earned the obligation of a seer's eloquent summoning of a people's necessities. This is essentially the theme of *Wounded in the House of a Friend* (1995), which includes longer poems, some akin to extended prose narratives, and many versions of haiku that exhibit S.'s able use of the compressed image laden with implication. These short poems express an enduring hope that balances the incidents of viciousness and exploitation that S. feels compelled to describe in the poetry that gives tongue to the suffering of too many members of the social community she lives in.

BIBLIOGRAPHY: Gibson, D. B., ed., *Modern Black Poets: A Collection of Critical Essays* (1973); Melhem, D. H., *Heroism in the New Black Poetry* (1990); Liebowitz, H., "Exploding Myths: An Interview with S. S.," *Parnassus* 12–13 (Spring-Winter, 1985): 357–68; Tate, C., ed. *Black Women Writers at Work* (1983)

LEON LEWIS

SANDBURG, Carl [August]

b. 6 January 1878, Galesburg, Illinois; d. 22 July 1967, Flat Rock, North Carolina

By any account, S. was an unusual man of letters: he was a Renaissance man, distinguishing himself in poetry, biography, history, and music, and would be the first private citizen to address a joint session of Congress. Yet, throughout his life, he eschewed literary pretension, allying himself with the common man and cultivating a folksy, Midwestern persona, both in print and in his public lectures.

Although he attended Lombard College from 1898 to 1902, S.'s true preparation for his writing career came from the array of odd jobs he held, which in-

cluded milk delivery boy, fireman, truck driver, house painter, film salesman, reporter, secretary, editor, political organizer, newspaper columnist, and radio broadcaster—which are detailed in his autobiography, *Always the Young Strangers* (1952). Ralph Waldo EMERSON, whose writings S. "want[ed] in every room" of his house, and Walt WHITMAN, whose poetry embraced the diversity of the American experience, were major influences on S.'s art and thinking. Whitman resonates through much of S.'s poetry in both form and content; S.'s free verse, which some critics deprecated as more an arrangement of lines than as true poetry, provided him with an appropriate vehicle to capture the vitality of industrial America.

S.'s most characteristic and most well-known poems are those he wrote about Chicago, the "City of the Big Shoulders," in which he celebrates every aspect of the city, from its new skyscrapers to its notorious stockyards. The first appearance of these poems in Harriet MONROE's *Poetry* occasioned some controversy; S. was accused of ushering in "the hog butcher school of poetry." His poetry, however, had tremendous popular appeal because of its realistic subject matter and S.'s use of "the living language of modern speech," according to Penelope Niven, one of S.'s biographers. His early volumes of poetry—*Chicago Poems* (1916), *Cornhuskers* (1918), *Smoke and Steel* (1920), and *Good Morning, America* (1928)—brought him popular success and critical recognition, garnering numerous awards. These included the Poetry Society of America Prize in 1919 and 1921 and the Society's Gold Medal in 1953, as well as the Pulitzer Prize in poetry in 1951. In his later years, he continued to write poetry but he poured most of his creative energy into writing biography and fiction; as a result, his poetry did not develop artistically, and was generally considered to be a repetition of his earlier, groundbreaking work.

Along with Emerson and Whitman, Abraham LINCOLN is the third member of the triumvirate that indelibly influenced and shaped S.'s work. S. read and collected Lincoln material for over thirty years; the result of this immersion was his epic two-volume biography of Lincoln, *Abraham Lincoln: The Prairie Years* (1927), and his four-volume *Abraham Lincoln: The War Years* (1939), for which he was awarded the Pulitzer Prize in history in 1939. S.'s goal was to present Lincoln not as a mythic figure but as a man. To this end, S. recreated historical events, using what he called "artistic license" to give the perspectives of various participants. While scholars took S. to task for his "recreations" and for promoting Lincoln stereotypes, the biography is founded squarely on factual information though presented in a readable, accessible narrative form—but as Niven perceptively notes, S.'s "poetic, highly imaginative" version of Lincoln is "more important as creative writing than as a contribution to Lincoln literature." Yet it is important to remember that S. strove to create a moving, vivid portrait of Lincoln and his times for the average reader, not a scholarly analysis for the specialist.

S. was also popular as a writer of children's tales, most notably *Rootabaga Stories* (1922) and *Rootabaga Pigeons* (1923). The "Stories" are distinguished by zany characters and creatures—Bozo the Button-Buster and the Zizzy Bugs, for example—and silly situations—the wedding procession of the rag doll and the broom handle or rabbits jumping over skyscrapers; more importantly, S. uses the stories to play with the sound and sense of language. He also ventured into adult fiction with *Remembrance Rock* (1948), an historical novel detailing the fortunes of a family from the time of the Pilgrims to World War II; reviewers panned it as a "flawed epic," but the novel was enthusiastically received especially by midwestern readers.

S. also left his mark on American music: he edited *The American Songbag* (1927) and *C. S.'s New American Songbag* (1950). He was an immensely popular and professional entertainer as both lecturer and singer, and he was an accomplished guitarist, having studied with Andres Segovia. Ultimately, all of S.'s work—the songs, the stories, the Lincoln biography, and the poetry—served a single purpose: to forge a national identity for the average American.

BIBLIOGRAPHY: Golden, H., *C. S.* (1961); Haas, J., and G. Lovitz, *C. S.: A Pictorial Biography* (1967); Allen, G. W., *C. S.* (1972); Salwak, D., *C. S.: A Reference Guide* (1988); Niven, P., *C. S.* (1991); Yannella, P. R., *The Other S.* (1996)

JUDITH E. FUNSTON

SANDOZ, Mari [Marie Susette]
b. 11 May 1896, Sheridan County, Nebraska; d. 10 March 1966, New York City

Although generally neglected by critics because of the unorthodox nature of her best work, which combines the research techniques of the historian and the narrative voice of fiction, S. has a firm niche in the growing body of distinguished plains writing.

Her formative years in northwestern Nebraska, in the family homestead on the banks of the Niobrara River and later on her father's ranch among the sand hills, influenced her six–volume Great Plains Series, a human history of the plains from the Stone Age to the present. Three volumes of this series represent her best work. *Old Jules* (1935), winner of the 1935

Atlantic nonfiction contest, tells the story of her father, a violent but charismatic pioneer whose friends, fascinating to Mari, included Native Americans, trappers, prospectors, and settlers. *Crazy Horse, the Strange Man of the Oglalas* (1942) carefully plots through Native American voice the inevitable betrayal and death of the classically heroic Sioux leader. Sympathy for the Native American and the implication that the U.S. was guilty of genocide continue in *Cheyenne Autumn* (1953), depicting the journey of a band of Cheyennes from the Oklahoma reservation to their Montana homeland in 1878–79.

S.'s extended works of fiction, of which *Slogum House* (1937) is the most successful, never got beyond the experimental stage. Her best fiction works are three novellas: *Winter Thunder* (1954) relates the adventures of a country schoolteacher and her pupils in a Nebraska blizzard; *The Horsecatcher* (1957) and *The Story Catcher* (1963) trace the growth of a Native American boy and his relationship to his tribe.

BIBLIOGRAPHY: Faulkner, V., ed., *Hostiles and Friendlies: Selected Short Stories of M. S.* (1976); Rippey, B., "Toward a New Paradigm: M. S.'s Study of Red and White Myth in *Cheyenne Autumn*," in Stauffer, H., and S. Rosowski, eds., *Women and Western American Literature* (1982): 257–66; Stauffer, H. W., *M. S.: Story Catcher of the Plains* (1982); Stauffer, H. W., *Letters of M. S.* (1992); Whitaker, R., "An Examination of Violence as Theme in *Old Jules* and *Slogum House*," *WAL* 16 (Fall 1981): 82–91

JOHN J. MURPHY

SANTAYANA, George
b. 16 December 1863, Madrid, Spain; d. 26 September 1952, Rome, Italy

Philosopher, critic, and novelist, S. is, along with Charles Saunders Peirce, William JAMES, and John Dewey, among the leading American philosophers of the first half of the 20th c. As a person and a thinker, he defined himself by his opposition to his culture. Thus, as a Spanish Catholic, he was uncomfortable with the Protestant, New England world he found at Harvard. At the same time, while S. described himself as "attached to Catholicism," his attachment was "entirely divorced from faith." Philosophically he was a metaphysical materialist—in the sense of Epicurus and Lucretius—and a transcendental subjectivist, putting him at odds with the philosophical pragmatism that dominated his American contemporaries. In turn, while much of his philosophy resembles Edmund Husserl's phenomenology, he was disdainful of the methodological obsessions found in both phenomenology

989

and analytic philosophy. Both as a philosopher and writer, S. was dominated by the spirit and the sensibilities of the artist, the aesthetic always in the background.

Born in Spain but educated at the Boston Latin School and Harvard, he was first a student of William James and Josiah Royce, and later their colleague and critic, becoming a member of Harvard's philosophy faculty. Retiring in 1912 when an inheritance allowed him to return to Europe, he eventually settled in Rome. His philosophical development falls into two periods. The first period, as a young professor at Harvard, saw the publication of *The Sense of Beautiful* (1896) and the masterful five-volume *The Life of Reason* (1905–6). Drawing on his doctoral work on the German philosopher Rudolf Lotze, S. proposed to examine the psychology of mental functions. Influenced by Hegel's *Phenomenology,* he conceived *The Life of Reason* as a sort of biography of the mind as its roles evolve in common sense, art, religion, society, and science. Accepting the primacy of matter, and the role of biological evolution, S. argued that the mind emerged as the by-product of the brain. Reason exists, not as something independent of brain, but as a means of harmonizing our various impulses in a way to achieve the greatest enjoyment or happiness. At the same time, the shared mental phenomena posit a transcendental subjectivism.

The second period of S.'s philosophical career included *Scepticism and Animal Faith* (1923), *The Realms of Being* (4 vols., 1927–40), and *Dominations and Powers* (1949). Here he proposed to clarify his earlier views by sharpening the distinction between mind and psychology. There are two realms, one grounded in the flux of matter, and the other in the intuition of an essence derived by arresting some datum of the flux, and associating it with other essences. S. refused to grant primacy to either realm, nor did he see divine significance in essence. The intuition of an essence is an illusion, the way the mind makes sense of things thereby achieving happiness, but simply because the mind makes sense of the world through essences does not imply any real connection with the existent reality. Developing this in *The Realms of Being,* he posits a series of ontological rather than psychological distinctions between the various objects of mental activities. The essences arc what allow us to become aware of something. Thus, in order to perceive the odor of the violet, we must have the capability for perceiving it prior to experiencing the phenomena; in this way the essence creates the object. Thus, for S., the content of the mind takes on a Platonic character, though unlike the Platonic mind, this content represents neither a universal nor ultimate truth.

Throughout his career, S. also produced a large body of critical work, including *Interpretations of Poetry and Religion* (1900), *Three Philosophical Poets* (1910), *Winds of Doctrine* (1913), *Egotism in German Philosophy* (1915), *Character and Opinion in the United States* (1920), *Platonism and the Spiritual Life* (1927), *Some Turns of Thought in Modern Philosophy* (1933), *Obiter Scripta* (1936), and *The Idea of Christ in the Gospels* (1946). In these, he offered various critical studies of philosophical and aesthetic systems, from Dante, Lucretius, and Goethe, to trenchant remarks on what he termed the "genteel tradition in American philosophy."

S. also published several collections of autobiographical essays, including *Persons and Places* (3 vols., 1944–53), as well as a novel, *The Last Puritan* (1936). Subtitled *A Memoir in the Form of a Novel* and based to some degree on a former student named W. Cameron Forbes who died in World War I, *The Last Puritan* is the study of Oliver Alden, who embodies the puritan spirit of duty and gravity, "at enmity with joy." Alden's tormented adherence to duty is played out against the hedonism of his friend Mario.

Standing in opposition to the dominant American intellectual traditions, S. offered a philosophical alternative for many thinkers and artists disenchanted with pragmaticism and commercialism. The young T. S. ELIOT was his protégée at Harvard, and S.'s aestheticization of values was an important influence on Wallace STEVENS and anticipates much of the doctrine of the American formalist critics.

BIBLIOGRAPHY: Arnett, W. E., *S. and the Sense of Beauty* (1955); McCormick, J., *G. S.* (1987); Sprigge, T. L. S., *S: An Examination of His Philosophy* (1974); Woodward, A., *Living in the Eternal: A Critical Study of G. S.* (1988)

THOMAS L. COOKSEY

SANTOS, Bienvenido N.

b. 22 March 1911, Manila, Philippines; d. 7 January 1996, Manila, Philippines

The more that world circumstances forced him to live in the U.S., the more S. memorialized his countrymen back home. World War II found him separated from his wife and children as a *pensionado* studying at Columbia on a government grant, then serving the Philippine government-in-exile as lecturer across America, declaring the resilience of America's Pacific ally determined to have not only peace but promised independence. His audiences often included Filipinos like himself, distant from their loved ones, who wanted assurance that the virtues they remembered—their wife's fidelity, the persistence of family solidarity despite grinding poverty, the dream of rewards for honesty and respect—would survive the Japanese Occupation as these qualities had endured centuries of Spanish and American colonialism.

S.'s identification with those "Pinoys" suffering alienation in America was deep and tight, as well as implicit in story collections such as *You Lovely People* (1955), *Brother, My Brother* (1960), *The Day the Dancers Came* (1967), and *Scent of Apples* (1979). Intimate portraiture remained his most characteristic achievement even in otherwise loosely constructed novels that won him Guggenheim, Rockefeller, Fulbright, and NEA grants from the country where he always felt uneasy even after becoming an American citizen.

Though repatriated after World War II, S. in 1958 gave up the presidency of the University of Nueva Caceres in order to write and teach at the University of Iowa, with only occasional sabbaticals at home. He was concerned about the political instability of Ferdinand Marcos's seemingly endless autocratic presidency. In 1972, just as he and his wife were prepared to return home, Marcos declared martial law. Out of a lifelong friendship with Marcos's predecessor, President Diosdado Macapagal, S. felt endangered, gave up his Philippine citizenship, and became Distinguished Writer-in-Residence at Wichita State University.

His novels were rarely overtly political but always identified with those struggling against feudalism-induced poverty. *The Volcano* (1965) examined the effect of years of condescension from Protestant American missionaries; *Villa Magdalena* (1965), the tendency of economic ambition to corrupt those rising beyond their "assigned" social status; and *The Praying Man* (1982), temptations among self-serving Philippine cronies plundering the national treasury. Marcos could not overlook S.'s sympathy with the underclass subjected to "colonialism from within." Meanwhile, S. wrote critically of generations of Filipino émigrés, in *The Man Who (Thought He) Looked Like Robert Taylor* (1983) and *What the Hell for You Left Your Heart in San Francisco* (1987). Such novels satirized those expatriates, exploitative professionals and businessmen, whose notion of Americanization meant lording over their less fortunate *kababayan* (countrymen) overseas.

That S. has always been, correctly, seen as a heartfelt man-of-the-people is evident also in his "paperboat" poetry, *The Wounded Stag* (1956) and *Distances: in Time* (1983); his retrieved early stories collected in *Dwell in the Wilderness* (1985); and in his late autobiographies, *Memory's Fictions* (1993),

Postscript to a Saintly Life (1994), and *Letters I* (1995).

BIBLIOGRAPHY: Casper, L., *Firewalkers: Literary Concelebrations 1964–1984* (1987); Casper, L., *In Burning Ambush: Essays, 1985–1990* (1991); Cruz, I., and D. J. Bayot, eds., *Reading S.* (1994)

LEONARD CASPER

SAROYAN, William
b. 31 August 1908, Fresno, California; d. 18 May 1981, Fresno, California

Born to Armenian refugees of Turkish genocidal actions, S. throughout his life sought a meeting place where perceptions of difference could be transcended by a shared recognition of human value. First a writer of short stories, then a playwright and novelist, finally an autobiographer, he remained remarkably focused on a quest for life's elusive values within an American culture that seemed preoccupied with materialist acquisition. Confused by the abundance of modern consumer society, S.'s characters sense a loss of meaning. As the Arab repeats throughout *The Time of Your Life* (1939), "No foundation, all the way down." What distinguishes S. from the European Dadaists and surrealists of the previous generation, however, is his determination to find new meaning within the vanishing landscapes of traditional American society. One senses that it is enough for him that his characters only make the effort. Seldom do they find fulfillment, at least not through lasting and socially promising ways. This might be one reason many critics have found S. at worst maudlin and naive, at best sensitive but facile. While it is true that throughout his career he consciously ignored political ideologies—even at a time, the 1930s and 1940s, when systematic social alternatives preoccupied American writers and intellectuals—S.'s fictional writing nonetheless accurately reflected a genuine American optimism that stubbornly resisted the fatalistic and fascistic tendencies of that era.

S. became a model for certain American writers of the following generation. He, along with Henry MILLER, influenced the Beat movement of the 1950s. Writers such as William S. BURROUGHS and Jack KEROUAC followed S. in their depiction of dropouts and misfits, and shared his interest in immediacy and exuberant spontaneity. Like S., they have lost faith in American institutional values and seek new alternatives by the pursuit of highly individualized lifestyles and by a certain unthinking escapism. However, S.'s characters never wish to abandon society, but only desire a more vital means to live harmoniously. S.

never becomes as antisocial as the Beats. Instead of fleeing the inhumanity of American life, his individuals seek common ground, a tolerance of otherness, and a kind of apolitical social progress. S. is always more inclusive than the Beats, and while the latter was entirely a male-oriented movement, S.'s plays and fiction include women along with a variety of nationalities and races. Common to all, however, is a preoccupation with immediate experience, with the sensuous surfaces of life, and the exhibition of a certain unconsciousness. S.'s fictional writing—not his autobiography—lacks self-consciousness, and his characters are never mouthpieces for specific ideas. At times, however, the vagueness of their statements seems deliberate, as though S. has created earnest street-corner ideologues and then expunged all political reference and topical allusion. His commentary also has that quality, as in the "Noted Appended" to *The Time of Your Life,* "Be the inferior of no man, nor of any man be the superior." S. seems to offer alternatives to capitalism, but doesn't want to be too specific, a tendency that seems somewhat reckless, given the seriousness with which his characters seek to shun the false values of their social institutions.

S.'s experiments as a naive writer of a unique American idiom began with the often lyrical collection of short stories, *The Daring Young Man on the Flying Trapeze* (1934). His most well-known work, *The Time of Your Life,* continues his interest in a cross-section of America, with a variety of characters whose most common qualities are a naive exuberance for life motivated by a belief that life can be redemptive. Joe, S.'s central character, is a barfly of means who dispenses money, gifts, and advice to the despised, rejected, and marginalized. Nick the bartender also exhibits a tolerant, live-and-let-live attitude, as does the laconic Arab, and Tom, a large down-and-out man in love with Kitty, a prostitute whose hope for love and integrity persists in spite of cruel treatment. Harry perhaps comes closest to encapsulating the S. prescription for living in a fallen world: "His philosophy is simple and beautiful. The world is sorrowful. The world needs laughter . . . Harry will make the world laugh." Joe as prime mover wants people to overcome their despair (brought about by class, gender, and racial prejudice), and at first cheers them with small but significant gifts—childhood toys, cigars, temporary jobs, better rooming conditions—then offers some of them more lasting gifts. For Tom and Kitty, this means the security and love of marriage, which Joe orchestrates with split-second timing. As a modern Prospero, Joe seeks to tie up all the loose ends of life for people who show promise, that is, reveal their tolerance, respect for others, and basic humanity. Behind this melange of characters is S.'s vision that all can be made well with

good intentions. Whether this is overly sentimental or simply a valid vision of the world as a struggle between social forces of darkness and light may well depend upon the production vision of the stage or screenwriter.

BIBLIOGRAPHY: Floan, H. R., *W. S.* (1966); Lawrence, L., and B. Gifford, *S.: A Biography* (1984); Keyishian, H., ed., *Critical Essays on W. S.* (1995)

WILLIAM OVER

SARTON, May

b. 3 May 1912, Wondelgem, Belgium; d. 16 July 1995, York, Maine

Poet, novelist and autobiographer, S. was born near Ghent, Belgium, to an English artist (Mabel Elwes) and a Belgian historian of science (George Sarton), S. emigrated with them in 1914 to be reared and educated in Cambridge, Massachusetts. Her parents' history and influence upon her own sense of culture have been examined throughout S.'s career. Of her sense of identity, S. has written: "For forty-five years or so . . . I wandered, borrowing other people's lives, other people's families with the nostalgia of the only child; and for many years could not decide whether I was a European or an American at heart."

Initially trained in the theater under Eva LaGallienne, S. began publishing with a collection of poems, *Encounter in April* (1937), recommended to Houghton Mifflin by Conrad AIKEN. During this period, she traveled to Europe where she gained admittance to the most influential literary circle of the time including Elizabeth Bowen, Leonard and Virginia Woolf, James Stephens, Julian Huxley, S. S. Kotleliansky (responsible for publication of her first novel, *The Single Hound,* 1938), and Belgian poet Jean Dominique. S. fictionalized her early experiences at Bowen Court in *A Shower of Summer Days* (1952). Throughout her career across several genres, S. has drawn upon both European and American associations to illuminate the split heritage of her culture.

In her fourteen volumes of poetry, including the *Collected Poems, 1930–1993* (1993), S. has proved herself one of the most skillful of contemporary writers in the use of conventional forms, including the sonnet. And while highly formal, S.'s verse has ranged in subject from the exploration of local landscapes—notably in *As Does New Hampshire* (1967) and *Letters from Maine* (1984)—to mythical treatments of the natural world, political events, art, and personal reflection.

A significant theme of S.'s eighteen novels is the dynamics of personal relationships, whether between family, friends or lovers (heterosexual and lesbian), as in *The Birth of a Grandfather* (1957), *Kinds of*

Love (1970), and *Anger* (1982). The plight of the aging woman as individual and as artist is the focus of *Mrs. Stevens Hears the Mermaids Singing* (1965) and *As We Are Now* (1973). S.'s novels have also played upon political or social events, such as *The Bridge of Years* (1946), which has been termed a pacifist novel, or *Faithful Are the Wounds* (1955) based upon McCarthy-era suppression of political liberals. S.'s fiction also includes fables and children's stories.

S. has become best known, however, through her autobiographical writing contained in the collections of essay portraits *I Knew a Phoenix* (1959) and *A World of Light* (1976), a memoir, *Plant Dreaming Deep* (1968), and journals. With *Journal of a Solitude* (1973), a brilliant if brooding record of the inner life of the artist, S. gained widely popular and critical attention. This interest in her private life led to her choice of the journal created for publication as her main literary form in subsequent efforts. While *The House by the Sea* (1977) tracks her move from New Hampshire to Maine, *Recovering* (1980) illuminates the daily struggles of surviving cancer; a special year is celebrated in *At Seventy* (1984). S.'s second recovery from life-threatening illness is the subject of *After the Stroke* (1988). In addition to their achievements as skillfully crafted prose, this sequence of journals provides rare insights into the contemporary experience of aging.

BIBLIOGRAPHY: Blouin, L., *M. S.: A Bibliography* (1978); Hunting, C., ed., *M. S.: Woman and Poet* (1982); Simpson, M., and M. Wheelock, *M. S.: A Self-Portrait* (1982)

E. SUZANNE OWENS

SCHNACKENBERG, Gjertrud [Cecilia]
b. 27 August 1953, Tacoma, Washington

With her first chapbook of poetry, *Portraits and Elegies* (1982; rev. ed., 1986), S. established herself as one of the finest poets of her generation, a position confirmed by her second and long-awaited third volumes, *The Lamplit Answer* (1985) and *A Gilded Lapse of Time* (1992). Her first two volumes are characterized by erudite and elegantly polished rhymed and metered personal lyrics, historical-cultural narratives, and excursions into light verse, qualities based upon which critics identified her as a New Formalist poet, albeit one with a clear allegiance to such predecessors as Robert LOWELL, Anthony HECHT, and John HOLLANDER. Her third book, even more elevated in tone and concerned almost exclusively with high culture, also notably abandons meter for free verse.

Portraits and Elegies contains two poetic sequences and a narrative, "Darwin in 1881," (reprinted in her second volume), creating the triptych pattern that will also organize her third volume. The lyrics in the first sequence are elegies to her father, a history professor who died when S. was a college student. They combine to form a portrait of the life shared by father and daughter. In "Nightfishing," S. first recognizes the specter of death on her father's face while fishing together in a rowboat. In other poems, they visit the Europe of their family heritage, Germany and Norway, as well as England. Three of the most notable poems in the sequence, all entitled "A Dream," reflect upon the poet's dreams of her father after his death in astonishingly rhymed, metered, and unpunctuated iambic lines that capture the eerie irrationality of dreams.

"Darwin in 1881" is a carefully researched narrative meditation on Charles Darwin's final days, remembering, like the aged Prospero, the voyages and discoveries of his earlier life. This may or may not be an indirect homage to her father's life, which is undoubtedly the case of S.'s most memorable lyric, "Supernatural Love." In this brilliant tour de force in rhymed tercets that seem to float off the page, the young poet watches as her father reads in a dictionary of the Latin and French roots to the word "carnation," which the precocious S. mythopoetically believed to mean "Christ's flowers." In addition to the light verse of "Two Tales of Clumsy" and an unusually confessional sequence of love poems, *The Lamplit Answer* is made up of a number of explorations of historical and artistic figures in addition to Darwin, among them Chopin and Simone Weil. The latter is the subject of S.'s most powerful poem in this vein, "The Heavenly Feast."

These cultural poems set the stage for *A Gilded Lapse of Time,* S.'s most ambitious and challenging collection. Its three sequences form a kind of spiritual autobiography as the poet muses upon the significance of Dante, in the title sequence; Christ's passion, as reflected in paintings and other Christian artifacts, in "Crux of Radiance"; and upon the cruel fate of Osip Mandelstam in "A Monument in Utopia." Many admirers of S. consider this volume, in its abandonment of traditional form and its deployment of esoteric rhetoric and highly specialized, academic knowledge of her intellectual subjects, to be a serious misstep. Yet if the lightness of touch that characterize her best personal, formal lyrics is disappointingly absent here, S. ultimately succeeds in breaking through to a higher lyric plane with this work than virtually any living poet, making a spiritual journey from despair through salvation in poetic language that is frequently sublime.

BIBLIOGRAPHY: Lake, P., "Return to Metaphor: From Deep Imagist to New Formalist," *SWR* 74 (Autumn

1989): 515–29; McPhillips, R., "G. S.," in Gwynn, R. S., ed., *DLB,* vol. 120, *American Poets since World War II* (1992): 276–80

ROBERT MCPHILLIPS

SCHOOLCRAFT, Henry Rowe

b. 28 March 1793, Albany County, New York; d. 10 December 1864, Washington, D.C.

Ethnologist, explorer, and poet, S. was born in Albany County, New York, the son of a glass-works owner. After attending Middlebury College in Vermont, where he specialized in chemistry and mineralogy, he headed west on a tour that took him into Missouri and Arkansas. In 1820, he served as the geologist for the Lewis Cass expedition into Lake Superior. Settling in Michigan, he married Waboogeeg, the European-educated daughter of an Ojibwa chief, founded the Historical Society of Michigan (1828) and the Algic Society of Detroit (1832), traced the source of the Mississippi River (1832), and played an active role in Native American affairs. After the death of his first wife, he married Mary Howard, the South Carolinian author of *Letters of the Condition of the African Race* (1852) and *The Black Gauntlet* (1860). She served as S.'s amanuensis after a stroke left him partially paralyzed.

S. published extensively. *Vitreology* (1817) was followed by *A View of the Lead-Mines of Missouri* (1819) and subsequent accounts of each of his trips. In addition, S. fancied himself a poet. His "Transallegia, or the Groans of the Missouri" (1820) described the New Madrid Earthquake. S. worked hard to preserve Native American lore, *The Myth of Hiawatha and Other Oral Legends* (1856) being but one example of his labors. In 1851, he began his *Historical and Statistical Information Respecting the History, Condition and Prospects of the Indian Tribe of the United States.* Published in six folio volumes by the federal government, this work marks the formal beginning of American ethnology. His travel accounts, written for popular audiences and not of the first rank, have remained valuable historical documents.

BIBLIOGRAPHY: Bremer, R. G., *Indian Agent and Wilderness Scholar: The Life of H. R. S.* (1987); Osborn, C. S., and S. Osborn, *S., Longfellow, Hiawatha* (1942)

MICHAEL B. DOUGAN

SCHULBERG, Budd

b. 27 March 1914, New York City

S. could best be described as a prolific political novelist, whose prime subject matter are the various sick manifestations of the American dream. As a commentator concerned with the replacement of human decency by the inhuman forces generated by success, wealth, and social position, S. draws on a wide variety of types and dispositions to illustrate his vision. From prizefighters to hack writers, S. empathizes with the American underdog, exploring failure as an exemplary force on the American landscape.

S.'s first success came with *What Makes Sammy Run* (1941), a satiric treatment of Hollywood based on his own experience as a screenwriter. The novel traces the rise of Sammy Glick from office boy to mogul, illustrating the corrosive power of ambition and its fulfillment. Glick's easy separation from decency provides a dark commentary on the Hollywood success story by making that success dependent on degeneration. In his exploration of the ironies surrounding the construction of ideal American visions by less than ideal types, S. peels away the myths surrounding Hollywood.

The Harder They Fall (1947) explores the world of boxing, racketeering, and organized crime through the central figure of prizefighter, Primo Carnero. Essentially one of life's innocents, S. follows his manipulation by crooked managers to his inevitable demise as a crushed and broken man. S. intentionally juxtaposes the naive myths of sporting excellence with the aspects of gangsterism and management, to create a story of profound sadness.

S. returned to his Hollywood theme with *The Disenchanted* (1950), a harrowing tale of alcoholic screenwriters and desperate lives. The novel explores the tragic underside of the film industry and highlights the fate of those who are swept aside and forgotten. While trying to maintain a sense of dignity in the face of utter bankruptcy, S.'s heroes are doomed and ultimately destroyed by the forces that made them great.

The fate of the lonely individual against the organizational powers of American business provides S. the materials to create a new American dream. In his collection of short stories, *Some Faces in the Crowd* (1953), and his screenplay *On the Waterfront* (1953), S. never sentimentalizes the failure of the central figures, but simply insists they can only lose.

S. left his usual subject material with *Sanctuary V* (1969), a novel about the nature of political change and the revolutionaries who are responsible for it. Set in Latin America, S. follows the fortunes of an exiled revolutionary who finds himself cut off from his people. In a similar vein, *Everything That Moves* (1980) loosely follows the Jimmy Hoffa story and explores the corrupting influences of power.

Ironically, despite S.'s critical and popular success, his impact as a novelist has been severely limited by his subject matter. Given his explorations of the corruptions behind the core values of American culture and his interrogation of its spokesmen, S. had been deemed too didactic, and consigned to the social realism section of American letters.

BIBLIOGRAPHY: Bonora, D. C., *The Hollywood Novel in the 1930s and 1940s* (1984); Spatz, J., *Hollywood in Fiction* (1969); Wells, W., *Tycoons and Locusts* (1973); Winchell, M., *Fantasy Seen: Hollywood Fiction since West* (1984)

PAUL HANSOM

SCHUYLER, James
b. 9 November 1923, Chicago, Illinois; d. 12 April 1991, New York City

S. was one of a group of American poets, which also includes John ASHBERY, Barbara GUEST, Kenneth KOCH, and Frank O'HARA, who began writing in the 1950s and who are sometimes referred to as the New York school. Known collectively for their celebrations of New York City, their passion for painting, especially abstract expressionism, their sophisticated wit, their experiments in surrealism and other modernisms, their refusal of linguistic and social decorum, and for their poetic "method" of "paying attention," the five nonetheless developed individual styles and subjects. S. is best known for his contributions to the tradition of American autobiographical poetry in the form of four long journal-like poems, published in collections that bear their names: *The Crystal Lithium* (1972), *Hymn to Life* (1974), *The Morning of the Poem* (1980), and *A Few Days* (1985).

In these poems, with their long sweeping lines inspired by Walt WHITMAN, the speaker is identifiably S. himself and the settings are his own dwellings, as likely to be rural as urban—he lived for eleven years in Maine with Fairfield Porter, whose paintings and aesthetic theories informed his work. He notes dates with care; he minutely chronicles the weather's vicissitudes; he reports on meals (a breakfast of watermelon and iced coffee, a lunch of Fresca and ham and cheese on a roll); he narrates his dreams, whether deliriously sexy or death haunted; he indulges or fends off his memories; he reads his mail; he admires flowers of every variety (but particularly roses); he thinks about his friends and lovers; he speculates on the process that is the composition of the poem. S. rivals William Carlos WILLIAMS as a poet of the uncertain clarifications of spring. "Hymn to Life" follows spring from its earliest winter quickenings through eight packed pages of arrival, never neglecting a beguiling digression, until he can assert about late May: "The apples

flower. The pear is past. / Winter is suddenly so far away, behind, ahead." Into these alert, tender, casual, beautiful descriptions S. embeds deftly offhand questionings of self, fate, perception, and the reasons for which we live. He likes to cite a cliché, and then surround it with humble acceptance or straightforward questioning of its core wisdom, always eschewing derision and cynicism.

S.'s many short lyrics qualify him, according to critic Helen Vendler, as an American pastoralist. They also attest to his belief in the literal realness of things, people, nature, life. He resists metaphor and irony. He loves dailiness, the trivial, the return and departure of seasons, domestic routines, gossip, overheard conversations, self-deprecatory anecdotes, home-made objects, paintings made by friends, whatever is available outside one's own window: "Look out / the win-/ dow / cluck: / it's real, / it's there, / it's life." Titles are likely to be dates, or to mention the day, month or season, attesting to his wish to save the otherwise unobserved, undervalued and fleeing "nothing day full of / wild beauty." Bare emotion and intimacy of tone mark his love poems in which homosexuality is taken for granted and unvexed in presentation. The "Payne Whitney" poems directly, and without self-pity narrate his stay at a psychiatric hospital. The ghost of O'Hara flits through the poetry, a much beloved and missed companion, still a stimulant and a challenge. Despite a pervasive sense of loneliness, S.'s work is filled with people—Ashbery, Guest, Koch, Joe Brainard, the Porters, Darragh Park, Anne Dunn, and Robert Dash appear there, not usually as artistic and literary figures, but as friends and fellow observers of S.'s inexhaustibly various world.

BIBLIOGRAPHY: Clark, T., "S.'s Idylls," *APR* 23 (May-June 1994): 7–13; Crase, D., "A Voice like the Day," *Poetry* 163 (January 1994): 225–38; Vendler, H., *Soul Says: On Recent Poetry* (1995); Ward, G., *Statues of Liberty: The New York School of Poets* (1993)

SARA LUNDQUIST

SCHWARTZ, Delmore
b. 8 December 1913, Brooklyn, New York; d. 11 July 1966, New York City

Appearing on the East Coast literary margin, the narrow and egotistically trammeled boundaries between Boston and New York City, S.'s first book of poetry, *In Dreams Begin Responsibilities* (1958) apparently cast him as the new wonder-child of American literary art, a leading successor of poetic modernism. The work was all but universally praised, with William Carlos WILLIAMS, T. S. ELIOT, Allen TATE, John Crowe RAN-

SOM, Mark VAN DOREN, Dudley Fitts, and even Ezra POUND singing an unlikely chorus of positive comment. S.'s extraordinary short story, which gave its title to the book of poetry, was published in the first pages of the inaugural issue of *Partisan Review* the year before. By 1940 and the critical failure of S.'s 1939 translation of Rimbaud's *Une Saison en enfer*, the elements were in place for the self-doubt and eventual paranoia that would finally overwhelm him.

The debacle of his third major piece of writing in 1943, the verse autobiography *Genesis, Book One*, published at the author's insistence over the advice of his publisher, James Laughlin, drove his poetic creation into successive stages of overconfidence, self-doubt, deep suspicion of the critical establishment, and tirades against his own friends, often preceded by clinical depression and followed by remorse, then further stages of delusion. There was to be no part two of *Genesis*.

A reader of S.'s work by turns admires the craft of his early fiction and poetry, learns to fear the inevitable lapses of diction and invention in successive work, particularly in S.'s verse, and becomes reconciled to the inevitable failures of judgment that became morbidly predictable. Within a mere decade, S. had declined from being the young poet of the hour and the author of a fiction called by Vladimir NABOKOV one of the best prose creations of its era, to an untenured writer in the academy living from post to post at institutions including Harvard, Princeton, Kenyon College, the University of Indiana, the New School, and Syracuse University. At the last, he found professional support, economic security, and sympathetic friendship he tragically was unable to recognize.

His brilliant first published story, "The Dreams Which Begin in Responsibilities," provides a formulaic basis for the interaction of the living with characters projected on the screen. In S.'s fiction, it is he, through the thinly concealed persona of the narrator-character, who hopes to reverse the disasters of the parents' lives and their interactive phobias playing before him in the cinema. Part of the inevitable pathos of this fiction is that the process is re-created for the reader of S.'s own work and his biography. At least in fancy, a reader may again and again seek to reach and reverse one professional or personal error after another that the writer himself commits. S. is caught in patterns of self-annihilation and, for all his gifts of self-description, fails to tap or fully create in literary reimagining this deepest and most perplexing of his destructive traits.

S.'s least appreciated but best sustained writing is that of the working critic. He completed a major but unrevised critical analysis of Eliot that has never seen print, and a good deal of his other work has been lost in manuscript. Nonetheless, he wrote both academic and journalistic reviews of the highest caliber that appear in *Partisan Review, Kenyon Review, The Nation, Saturday Review,* and other major journals. His movie reviews for the *New Republic,* where he was poetry editor from 1955 to 1957, are among the best in the genre. His essays on William FAULKNER helped to transform that writer into a recognized magus of American fiction, and the lecture first delivered at Columbia University in 1946, "The Literary Dictatorship of T. S. Eliot," is the first salvo in the revision of this most touted but problematic of English-writing "moderns." His description, during the same period, of the insecure place and inadequate financial support of poets and poetry in America is accurate, and in view of his own end, mordantly poignant: "During two of the past seventeen years . . . I have been given sums of money sufficient to enable me to devote myself entirely to the writing of poetry: but these grants . . . are based precisely on the fact that it is impossible to earn even the most modest livelihood unless . . . one does a good many other things."

BIBLIOGRAPHY: Aiken, C., "D. S.," in Blanshard, R., ed., *A Reviewer's ABC* (1958): 355–58; Atlas, J., *D. S.: The Life of an American Poet* (1977); Goldman, M., "D. S.," in Walden, D., ed., *DLB*, vol. 28, *Twentieth-Century American-Jewish Writers* (1984): 285–91; Rahv, P., *Essays on Literature and Politics, 1932–1972* (1978)

ROBERT MOYNIHAN

SCIENCE AND LITERATURE

Until recently, literary critics, following Matthew Arnold's argument in "Literature and Science," regarded science and literature as two separate disciplines, famously distinguished by C. P. Snow as "the two cultures." Today, we recognize that "science" refers both to a method of acquiring knowledge, often termed "the scientific method," and to the body of knowledge acquired, and we acknowledge that the body of knowledge acquired also constitutes a "literature." In seeing science as both a discourse and a method, literary and cultural critics explore new ways of looking at the theories and practices of science.

Literary and scientific texts are culturally embedded within fields of production and reception. As Katherine Hayles argues, "one must say that both literature and science are cultural products, at once expressing and helping to form the cultural matrix from which they emerge." Thinking along cultural lines allows us to compare literature and science as imaginative endeavors: we can describe both science and literature as discursive and epistemological practices, for scientists, social scientists, and humanists work on the problem of making sense of the world and recognize that science and literature are "modes of discourse." Cultural critics appreciate that discursive strategies and rhetorical practices affect artistic and scientific pursuits and help develop knowledge. Texts describing scientific discoveries and theories as well as explicitly fictional narratives instruct and entertain, but to varying degrees and effects, sometimes speaking directly to one another.

American authors offer diverse representations of the wide-ranging political and social consequences of scientific and technological developments. Many politicians in the colonial period were particularly attracted to innovations that could support positive social, industrial, and governmental change. Thomas JEFFERSON devoted a great deal of time to working out architectural and domestic improvements in his home and public institutions and attempted in *Notes on the State of Virginia* "to write a natural history of the New World." Benjamin FRANKLIN's mixed career as inventor, politician, and author denotes Enlightenment acceptance of science as a valuable means of social improvement as much as it does American appreciation of innovative technologies and techniques. As a result of the increasing influence of science and technology on American society during and after the Industrial Revolution, many writers—from Edward TAYLOR, whose poetry reflects his "medical vision," to Don DELILLO, whose works have been described as "systems novels"—responded to evolving scientific ideas. American national identity has long been linked with ideas of scientific progress and technological innovation, yet an undercurrent of suspicion and regret about such technical changes has also surfaced in the literature.

American Renaissance authors who witnessed the dramatic scientific and technological innovations of the first half of the 19th c. speculated about the moral influence of natural philosophy and critically evaluated the social costs of science. Edgar Allan POE's prose poem *Eureka* offers a cosmogony reflecting the author's privileging of intuition and individual perception as scientifically valid. He also provided early American examples of science fiction, scientific parody, and detective fiction. Reconfiguring Mary Shelley's *Frankenstein,* Nathaniel HAWTHORNE wrote stories considering the somewhat mystical and suspect practices of science and invention, notably "Rappacinni's Daughter," "The Birthmark," "Doctor Heidegger's Experiment," and "The Artist of the Beautiful," and Herman MELVILLE produced "The Bell Tower," a story describing the destruction of an architect within the elaborate mechanism he has designed. Following

in the footsteps of Charles Darwin, Melville wrote "The Encantadas," ten short sketches conveying anthropological impressions of the Galapagos Islands and its inhabitants, including the great tortoises. Melville's *Moby-Dick* combines concerns common to scientific discourse and travel narratives in portraying life aboard a whaling ship. Henry David THOREAU's antipathy toward overweening hopes of engineers and scientists to improve the human condition by means of technological innovation is most evident in his humorous attack "Paradise (To Be) Regained," published in *United States Magazine and Democratic Review* (November 1843), and surfaces occasionally in other prose.

By the end of the 19th c., fictional anxieties about science and technology increased. In *Connecticut Yankee* and other works, Samuel Langhorne CLEMENS reveals a scientific skepticism that humorously tests our appreciation of modern technological innovations. Henry ADAMS's theories of historical change have been linked to his "appropriation" of Willard Gibbs's phase change rule. Adams proposes a more complex relation of science and art in his discussion of the Virgin and the Dynamo in *The Education of Henry Adams.*

Some authors optimistically hoped that cultural values might change in response to scientific discoveries. Chief justice of the supreme court of Rhode Island, Job Durfee claimed in an 1843 oration that "when the arts and sciences become progressive, all social and political institutions become progressive," but he cautioned against substituting human will for divine guidance. Lydia Maria CHILD, reformer and journalist, wrote more radically in "Hilda Silfverling: A Fantasy," of the possibility that cryogenic science might permit a woman to escape from the puritanical and repressive environment into which she was originally born. Edward BELLAMY's Utopian romance *Looking Backward: 2000–1887* describes scientific and social developments that enhance the quality of life for an American city of the future, noting how culture progresses by incorporating technological possibilities. Charlotte Perkins GILMAN also considered how domestic technological innovations could improve women's lives in a number of magazine short stories and in her romance entitled *Herland.*

Whatever the direction of influence marked by science and literature, it is clear that for American authors, scientific theories and practices deserve attention because they influence culture by reinscribing and reconfiguring cultural values. In particular, many American social reformers have demanded changes in medical practice. Dorothea Dix, a teacher and social reformer, inspired wholesale improvement of asylums and prisons by writing tracts detailing abuses, such as her 1843 "Memorial to the Legislature of Massachusetts." In *Illness and Metaphor* and *AIDS and Its Metaphors,* Susan SONTAG outlines the ways in which medical understanding of diseases, particularly cancer and AIDS, the syndrome caused by the human immunodeficiency virus, is affected by associated images and other previously constructed narratives. Cindy Patton's *Inventing AIDS* (1990) links the virus to cultural shifts concerning sexual orientation, race, and power.

The significant body of 1980s and 1990s fictions, memoirs, and dramas focusing on patient and caregiver responses to the AIDS pandemic deserves to be examined by anyone seeking to come to terms with medical knowledge and its cultural consequences. In *And the Band Played On* (1987), Randy Shilts offers a journalistic account of 1980s political and media responses to the emerging AIDS crisis according to assumptions that linked symptoms and syndrome to marginalized groups: gay men, Haitians, and hemophiliacs. Abraham Verghese's *My Own Country* (1994) has been justly celebrated as an inspiring nonfictional account of a doctor's work with PWAs. Alice HOFFMAN's novel *At Risk* is controversially cited as an example of AIDS fiction for the general public, since it describes the last months of a twelve-year-old girl who contracts the disease from a surgical blood transfusion. David B. Feinberg's satiric novel *Eighty-Sixed* (1989) follows a young man's search for a boyfriend in New York. Larry Kramer's *The Normal Heart* (1985), a polemical and political drama, and William M. Hoffman's *As Is* (1985), an emotional and personal play, delineate the difficult circumstances faced by gays coping with AIDS; Craig Lucas's *Long-time Companion* (1988) follows a community of gay men over a period of years in the fashion of a documentary. Tony KUSHNER's *Angels in America* is an epic account of AIDS and social groups.

Medical caregivers are frequently represented in American fiction as heroic protagonists capable of improving physiology and society, perhaps because doctors develop abilities as perspicacious observers and persuasive narrators. There are a number of fictional works reflecting the early prominence of women doctors, including William Dean HOWELLS's *Dr. Breen's Practice* and Sarah Orne JEWETT's *A Country Doctor.* In *Doctor Zay* by Elizabeth Stuart Phelps WARD, the doctor of the title is a female homeopathic practitioner whose professional expertise is accepted by her rural Maine community while her lack of interest in romance is not. Charlotte Perkins Gilman's story "Mr. Peebles' Heart" presents another independent woman physician, one who intervenes in her sister's marriage in order to save it.

A number of 20th-c. fiction writers integrate medical concerns within richly textured narratives appealing to general audiences. Trained as a doctor, Walker

PERCY draws on his personal understanding of scientists in a number of fictional narratives, including *Love in the Ruins* and *The Thanatos Syndrome.* A satiric comedy, *Love in the Ruins* represents a scientist's project to save America from its own mechanistic culture. Richard Selzer has written books that are largely fact-based and often describe episodes alluding to events that took place during his medical school or his professional practice as a surgeon. His second book, *Mortal Lessons* (1976), has been described as a set of "prose poems" that open up the human body to the reader's view. Notwithstanding that he was for some time in a coma, Selzer discusses his own bout with Legionnaire's disease in *Raising the Dead* (1994). His style is poetic and luminous in describing what doctors sometimes do not understand. For example, in the short story "Imelda," published in the collection *Letters to a Young Doctor* (1982), Selzer characterizes the changed life of a surgeon who performs an operation on a corpse; the narrator sympathetically delineates a grieving mother's mystically religious faith in God and the doctor.

Dramatists in the 20th c. have also considered how a medical practitioner's authority might conflict with the patient's desire, a topic that William Carlos WILLIAMS, a medical doctor, poet, and fiction writer, cogently represented in his short story "The Use of Force." David RABE's drama *A Question of Mercy* (1998) is based on Selzer's nonfictional account of whether to assist a terminally ill person in ending his life. David Feldshuh's *Miss Evers' Boys* (1992) and Brian Clark's *Whose Life Is It Anyway?* (1978) similarly focus on the significant issue of the authority of the caregiver to control the patient. A fictionalized story based on sociologist James H. Jones's *Bad Blood: The Tuskegee Syphilis Experiment* (1981), *Miss Evers' Boys* represents participants, caregivers, and medical administrators of the Tuskegee syphilis study, an historical example of medical research without ethical principles. The subjects of the study, two hundred black men in rural Alabama, were denied antibiotic treatments for syphilis so that researchers could study the progress of the disease. *Whose Life Is It Anyway?* presents the arguments of a conscious yet physically paralyzed protagonist who seeks to end his life rather than enduring medical interventions.

A number of science fiction writers, particularly Isaac ASIMOV, have imagined scientific innovations influencing the discoveries of or the directions taken by scientific researchers. Ernest Callenbach has written a number of works exploring the value of environmentalism, including the popular utopian novel *Ecotopia* (1975). Works by Octavia Butler, Ben Bova, and Samuel R. Delany, among others, have considered future technologies that come to pass and their relations to social issues and changes. Butler's science fiction analyzes genetic engineering from the perspectives of race and sex, while Delany's work makes use of reconfigured mythologies and symbols. Michael CRICHTON, best known for *The Andromeda Strain* and *Jurassic Park,* has written many novels that consider how new scientific technologies have pejorative effects for society. Fictions by Thomas PYNCHON and Richard POWERS critique the powers of science and technology to influence the individual and society; their works have achieved notable followings among scientists and humanists. Influenced most by William S. BURROUGHS's fictions and William GIBSON's *Neuromancer,* contemporary cyberfiction is the most recent genre invented in response to developments in computer science and cognitive, notably work in artificial intelligence and information technology.

In addition to considering how science and technology are represented in literary works, we can study science as literature, for example by examining the narrative strategies that writers from William BARTRAM to Stephen Jay Gould employ in presenting scientific ideas. In particular, certain works of Thoreau, including *Walden* and *A Week on the Concord and Merrimack Rivers,* stand out as 19th-c. examples of natural history written for the common reader, while other works by Thoreau, as Laura Dassow Walls argues, hold a place in the history of science. Analyzing literary conventions and genres in relation to scientific practice, theory, and narrative requires understanding how literary discourse and scientific discourse might be similar, how they influence each other, or in what ways they differ.

Like other writers, scientists influence readers by means of their argumentative strategies and other rhetorical practices informed by culture. The discipline of cultural studies has influenced much recent work connecting literature and science. In particular the constructivist work of many scholars in the humanities and social sciences has been profoundly affected by the theory of paradigm shift outlined by Thomas S. Kuhn in *The Structure of Scientific Revolutions* (1962), which explains the history of science as a series of succeeding conceptual revolutions. According to Kuhn, a new paradigm is not built on an old, rather the new theory supplants the previously established one. Cultural critics in science studies who work on American texts and practices have also found inspiration in writings by British and Continental scholars, notably the work of Sigmund Freud, Raymond Williams, Stuart Hall, Jacques Lacan, Jacques Derrida, Michel Foucault, Michel Serres, and Bruno Latour.

Myra Jehlen notes that European explorers navigating the American continent provide the earliest colonial examples of scientific practice based on "an accumulation of observed and verifiable facts"; in the 16th c., navigators shifted from using mappa-mundi that "projected the true nature of the universe" to portolans, charts that "were sketched by sailors continuously revised to incorporate new information." Bartolome de Las Casas, the first Catholic priest in the New World, criticized Spanish colonial policies that harmed the newly discovered paradise in *The Devastation of the Indies,* thereby linking economic gain to environmental injustice. It is possible to trace through the succeeding centuries developments in medicine, linguistics, and natural history and note that Americans imported European theories and practices, as well as contributing knowledge understood in the New World context. Many Puritans, such as Increase MATHER, struggled to incorporate scientific ideas into a theologically orthodox worldview. For example, a number of individuals—Thomas Thacher, Cotton MATHER, Benjamin Franklin—mention smallpox, a widespread disease in Europe, and its effects on American Indians—who had not built up immunities to it—acknowledging the controversial discussion over the effectiveness of inoculation. Laurel Ulrich's edition of a New England midwife's diary is a valuable record of early American medical practices in the domestic realm.

Colonial writers observed native Americans and described their natural landscape and cultural practices. Analysis of language systems and representations of flora and fauna dominate colonial travel narratives by James Adair and others. John Josselyn, William and John Bartram, and John Jay Audobon wrote narratives that cross cultures and disciplinary boundaries by contrasting English species and environments with American examples. Their works blend scientifically accurate and artistically beautiful illustrations with descriptive prose analyzing species within environments. William Bartram influenced romantic writers in Great Britain and America who read his *Travels,* describing his journey in the Southeastern U.S.; Coleridge, Wordsworth, and Carlyle were among readers influenced by this work, the last recommending the book to Ralph Waldo EMERSON for its "floundering eloquence."

Certain travel narratives can also be characterized as natural or even political history. As Daniel Botkin argues, documents from the Lewis and Clark expedition westward, notably journals kept by the principals Meriwether Lewis and William Clark, tell about the landscape, the American Indians who affected it, and contemporary politics. Francis PARKMAN's *The Oregon Trail* notes his experiences during a cross-continental trip to the Rocky Mountains. In *A Lady's Life in the Rocky Mountains,* Isabella Bird, an Englishwoman who traveled all over the world, describes her journey through Colorado and her meetings with men skeptical of her ability to navigate rugged terrain.

In establishing itself as independent of its British cousin, while continuing to be influenced by romantic precepts, American literature has always had a special interest in nature. Emerson's philosophical essays, notably *Nature,* consider the human experience as part of a natural process and underline the need to communicate with the natural world. In *Letters from an American Farmer,* J. Hector St. John CREVECOEUR describes the benefits that accrue to those linked to the land in America; each family can be independent and reap nature's beneficence. N. Scott MOMADAY in *The Way to Rainy Mountain* describes the Kiowa tribe's travels and experiences under colonialism, while celebrating the myths and rituals of the American Indian way of life and its rootedness in nature. Leslie Marmon SILKO in "Landscape, History, and the Imagination" similarly reflects on the unity of Pueblo Indians and nature.

A number of American writers have distinguished themselves as protectors of the natural landscape. Theodore ROOSEVELT famously related his adventures in the wild and promoted the ethical virtues of engaging in sports in natural settings and preserving the landscape. Other government officials—including Gifford Pinchot, Aldo Leopold, and Al Gore—fought for more progressive conservation laws, and a number of nature writers such as John Burroughs and John Muir promote environmentalism with their own careful depictions of landscapes and inhabitants. Rachel CARSON's *Silent Spring* alerts us to the dangers of pesticide use within the fragile natural world; her other books are *Under the Sea Wind, The Sea around Us,* and *Edge of the Sea.* Poetic prose by Wendell BERRY, John MCPHEE, and Annie DILLARD follows in the tradition of Thoreau and Emerson. Berry's essays consider social idealism in conjunction with the joys and hardships of farming. Relying on his own extensive research, McPhee has written about regions from the pine barrens of New Jersey to the Alaskan wilderness as well as about battles between environmentalists and politicians). Dillard explores the spiritual significance of nature from the vantage point of a "pilgrim," as developed in her book *Pilgrim at Tinker Creek.*

Many American poets strongly identify with concepts imported from natural or physical science. William Cullen BRYANT and Walt WHITMAN celebrate nature and human life in nature. Marianne MOORE, Ezra POUND, Wallace STEVENS, and William Carlos Williams incorporate the telling details of nature within poems exploring human existence. As Miriam Marty Clark argues, A. R. AMMONS emphasizes process rather than taxonomy in his concern with natural organisms and groups; she also points to Ammons's significant concern with "technological processes like digital computation" in discerning connections between the gene and the computer as "information processes." Like his Cornell colleague Ammons, Roald Hoffmann, a Nobel Prize-winning chemist, writes poetry affected by scientific understanding, including short prose poems linking technical analysis and aesthetic concerns.

The range of contemporary popular science writing runs the gamut from anthropological and biological sciences, including new research in immunology, primatology, and sociobiology, to physical sciences, articulating shifting paradigms in quantum theory and astronomy. Some scientists who write for journals such as *Science, Nature,* and *Natural History* also contribute on an occasional basis to more general interest news magazines and appear on television talk shows as iconic figures representing "academic" disciplines and scholarly theories. Influential essays and books by women's studies scholars who examine the experiences of women scientists and feminist approaches to science have also helped to popularize scientific practices and ideas.

The prolific Isaac Asimov, self-described as a "lucid" rather than poetic writer, set a standard for ubiquity and name recognition by writing nearly five hundred books ranging from science fiction to science fact. His story "I Robot" has been claimed as the fictional precursor of robotic science, and his best known work, the future-oriented science fiction series *Foundation,* inspired one of the most popular Hollywood film series—George Lucas's *Star Wars.* Brought to the U.S. from Russia at the age of three by his Jewish parents, Asimov was raised in Brooklyn. He earned a Ph.D. in chemistry from Columbia and became an associate professor of biochemistry at Boston University School of Medicine. He was a man of wide-ranging interests who favored Charles Dickens's novels and wrote guides on Shakespeare, the Bible, and Byron's *Don Juan* as well as a biochemistry textbook. Asimov regarded science fiction as a significant achievement of humanism—he served as president of the American Humanist Association until his death—noting in his letters (published posthumously by his brother Stanley) that "To be a science fan . . . means to be concerned with the future of mankind" (September 26, 1966). His autobiography, *I, Asimov* appeared posthumously in 1994. In an obituary of Asimov appearing in *Nature* (May 14, 1992), Carl Sagan eloquently elegized his friend in comparing him with past and present scientists: "Like T. H. Huxley, Asimov was motivated by profoundly democratic impulses to communicate science to the general public. 'Science is too important,' he said in paraphrasing Clemenceau, 'to be left to the scientists.'"

Sagan's own intellectual development and public persona were in part affected by the example set by Asimov, for both men were identified in the public mind as proponents of space study. Until his death professor of astronomy and director of the Laboratory for Planetary Studies at Cornell University, Sagan was an active scientist and public figure advocating on behalf of science. He described his works as dealing with "the evolution of humans, human intelligence, human emotions." He was active in NASA's *Mariner, Viking, Voyager,* and *Galileo* expeditions, and he "carried out research into planetary atmospheres, the greenhouse effect on Venus, the origin of life on earth, and the possibilities of life elsewhere." Sagan's *The Cosmic Connection* (1973), *Broca's Brain* (1979), and *Cosmos* (1980) present the results of his research in popular form; *Cosmos* became a television series and made him a well-known figure on the talk show circuit. He also wrote a novel, *Contact* (1985), about encountering life on another planet, and was a consultant for the Hollywood movie of the same title, as well as authoring numerous journal articles. In interviews, he explicitly linked science to democracy by describing both as skeptical activities. While he noted that most science begins out of a sense of wonder, he explained how making mistakes and then reconfiguring hypotheses was a necessary and valued process. In his last decade Sagan debated fellow physicists, including Edward Teller, who promoted the "safe" application of nuclear technology, and debunked claims from UFOs to repressed memory as examples of how scientific illiteracy allows the human mind to be fooled. Sagan's continued articulation of scientific reason as a requirement of democratic policy became his greatest legacy.

Also a physicist, Richard P. Feynman became well known to the American public for his straightforward demonstration of the O-ring failure causing the Challenger tragedy. He collaborated on two of the 20th-c.'s scientific developments: the atomic bomb and quantum electrodynamics. At Los Alamos, Feynman "led the computational group that made the crucial calculations for the atomic bombs." "Using a revolutionary methodology that remains at the core of all quantum physics," he "solved the difficulties of quantum electrodynamics," "the theory of electromagnetic interaction of charged particles." Feynman demonstrated colorful personal characteristics and an ability to offer brisk and lively descriptions of quantum physics in works like *QED* (1985) and *Six Easy Pieces* (1995), which were originally presented as lectures to general audiences.

Feynman, like Asimov, had a seminal effect on his discipline. Freeman Dyson, who was a colleague of Feynman's and a popularizer of many of Feynman's more complicated ideas, and James Gleick have also written popular works explaining the increasingly complex theories of the physical world. Gleick's biography of Feynman inspired the film *Infinity,* and his *Chaos: Making a New Science* (1987) describes how scientists in different fields worked out a theory explaining the behavior of complex systems. Gleick's biographical focus on scientists like Benoit Mandelbrot and his use of accessible examples concerning weather prediction and heart rhythms help nonscientific readers work through difficult material. Alan P. Lightman, a physicist, has written a number of works that explore cosmology as well as textbooks and works directed toward the general public. He considers the relations of science and art in poetic sketches that focus on Albert Einstein's life in *Einstein's Dreams: A Novel* (1992).

Lewis Thomas trained as a medical doctor and became a medical researcher, but he is more widely remembered as a modern prose stylist of careful and searching essays on the natural world. His pieces are frequently excerpted or collected in anthologies for writing students. Thomas's books include the anthologies *The Lives of a Cell* (1974), *The Medusa and the Snail* (1979) and *The Fragile Species* (1992). Following in the tradition of essayists from Montaigne to E. B. WHITE, Thomas's insightful essays typically move from the telling detail noticed to a consideration of its significance in the larger world. Thomas observes biological processes from a multidisciplinary perspective; he held chairs in pediatrics, pathology, microbiology, and medicine at different times in his life. As Alexander Beam wrote in an obituary published in *Nature* (January 1994), Thomas supported the Gaia hypothesis; he was convinced "that the Earth is ultimately sustained by coherence, cooperation, and complex self-regulatory systems—as he put it, 'the earth is a sort of immense organism.'" His essays often end on an upbeat note, relaying his own optimism about natural processes.

A number of doctors have also written works for a more general audience. Leon Kass has described medicine as grounding human understanding of "the moral relation between knowledge or expertise and the concerns of life." Sherwin Nuland has written about early medical practicioners and about contemporary attitudes toward death. Peri Klass and Mel Konner write nonfictional prose in the modern tradition of the physician able to speak to contemporary issues related to medicine. Both have written popular books about their experiences in medical schools that open up the worlds of student and resident for those unfamiliar with these experiences.

Loren EISELEY, anthropologist and historian, wrote a number of popular works describing contributions of scientists, such as Bacon and Darwin, that personalize scientific discoveries and arguments. Contemporary science journalists Laurie Garrett in *The Coming Plague* (1994) and Richard Preston in *The Hot Zone* (1994) similarly reveal the esoteric practices of virology research by describing how government and university scientists cope and combat newly discovered diseases.

Stephen Jay Gould, professor of geology and zoology at Harvard University, has become "the chief explainer of evolutionary biology to popular audiences." His essays appear on a monthly basis in *Natural History* magazine. He has written or edited fifteen books, many of which are composed of essays. The most controversial subject he has written about is "punctuated equilibrium," which he and Niles Eldredge theorize accounts for the sudden development of new species, a phenomenon that Gould argues cannot be completely accounted for by Darwin's principles of natural selection. Gould does not hesitate to enter into debates that might seem distant from his academic field of paleontology. His interests in baseball, probability, and the history of science often appear in his essays, either in the foreground or as examples and allusions. In *Full House: The Spread of Excellence from Plato to Darwin* (1996), Gould further explores the dangers of summing up populations according to averages or extremes. "Instead, he says, they should look at the whole flowing spectrum of variation—the bell-shaped curve that so often describes populations."

Gould's *The Mismeasure of Man* (1981) is a highly readable study of the history of scientific racism and psychometrics. He describes pseudo-scientific theories in polygeny, craniometry, craniology, and intelligence testing proposed by 19th- and 20th-c. scientists revealing significant racial bias. Revealing ideas about human nature resembling those promulgated by phrenologists Franz Gall, Johann Spurzheim, and Orson Fowler, some American scientists assumed that physiognomy reveals intelligence—or lack of it—and other character traits. Louis Agassiz, originally a disciple of the great Cuvier, immigrated to America in the 1840s and became a professor at Harvard and the director of its Museum of Comparative Zoology. Gould analyzes Agassiz's writings to determine how the scientist's personal repulsion toward people of color affected his theorizing about races being separate species. Samuel Morton, physician and researcher, collected human skulls and measured cranial capacity as a means of assessing probable intelligence of human individuals according to race; Gould argues that Morton's "finagling" his data reflects preconceptions about white superiority. H. H. Goddard's studies of human mental deficiencies similarly suffer from the author's tendency to manipulate facts; Gould reveals that even the photographs included in Goddard's publications

have been photographically manipulated to make the subjects appear "diabolical."

Trained as a neurologist, Oliver Sacks earned degrees in physiology, medicine, and biology from Oxford; although born in London, he has spent most of his professional career in New York. Sacks actively practices medicine and writes anecdotal and subjective narratives linking his perceptions about medical authority with his observation of patients with odd diseases. *A Leg to Stand On* (1984) is an account of an injury he sustained from a fall during a 1976 hiking trip in Norway and his convalescence in hospital. Yet to summarize Sacks's narratives is to diminish them. As he notes, his books offer "a mixture of physiology with poetic and often tragic accounts of the subjective aspects of being ill, of neurological syndromes which fascinate the two halves of me." Sacks has achieved a high profile in popular culture, for a number of his works have been translated into other media. *Awakenings* (1974), details the experiences of Parkinson's patients who briefly "come alive" mentally when treated with L-Dopa; their stories were adapted for a Hollywood movie starring Robin Williams and Robert De Niro. The director Peter Brooks designed a 1995 operatic production of *The Man Who Mistook His Wife for a Hat* (1986), an anthology of pieces describing individuals who experienced rare neurological dysfunctions. *An Anthropologist on Mars* (1995) includes accounts of patients with Tourette's syndrome, color blindness, amnesia, and autism, while *The Island of the Color-Blind* (1996) follows Sacks to Micronesia where he and a color-blind colleague interact with a tribe that has a high proportion of color-blind individuals. Sacks notes that he is fascinated by "conditions which are deep, complex, strange . . . especially if the people who have them are in touch with the impact of this on their thoughts and feelings and can be articulate." Although some critics claim that he focuses on his own breakthroughs rather than the patient's, Sacks encourages the reader to think of patients as people rather than as examples of diseases. This principle resonates with contemporary views of a more egalitarian relationship between patient and doctor and of the revisionary role of the anthropologist as a participant-observer who is subjectively enmeshed with the community under examination as well with the understanding of the scientist as acting within a cultural framework.

Futurism is the field of social prediction and prognostication that theorizes about the influences of science and technology on cultural change. Marshall McLuhan and Alvin and Heidi Toffler have written tracts that might be described as social histories of the future. In a number of important essays and longer prose works, McLuhan acknowledges that society changes rapidly as communication media are developed and disseminated. He coined the term global village and became famous for the sentence "The medium is the message," both foundational concepts for succeeding theories of communication. The Tofflers have worked together on various nonfictional works; he is usually credited as the writer, while she is often described as an equally important collaborator. *Future Shock* (1970), *The Third Wave* (1980), and *Powershift* (1990) have sold millions of copies. These books describe a theory of human history, summarized as a series of three waves or revolutions: the agricultural wave, the Industrial Revolution, and the age of information technology. While McLuhan became a guru to academics, the Tofflers have been more readily accepted by the general public than by journalists and academicians, until their connection with politician Newt Gingrich was publicized.

The work of feminists has offered an important American development in science studies, especially in analyzing theories and practices as affected by gender. Trained as a physicist, Evelyn Fox Keller in *A Feeling for the Organism* (1983) describes how geneticist Barbara McClintock responded to research results in a way different from those of her male peers. Keller relates that McClintock was isolated by the dominantly male scientific community of population geneticists. Their resistance to McClintock's work and her own willingness to listen rather than fight encouraged her to learn more from her colleagues than they learned from her. Keller's most salient point is that McClintock was unable to articulate her ideas using a language commonly accepted by other scientists; in effect, they belonged to another discourse community. Keller's *Reflections on Gender and Science* (1985), *Refiguring Life: Metaphors of Twentieth-Century Biology* (1995), *Secrets of Life, Secrets of Death* (1992) consider how theory relies on culture in its rhetorical argumentation.

Like Keller, Sandra Harding and Helen Longino offer philosophical arguments that explore the impact of gender on scientific theory. Carolyn Merchant's *The Death of Nature: Women, Ecology, and the Scientific Revolution* (1980) and *Ecological Revolutions: Nature, Gender, and Science in New England* (1989) consider the gendered images and language employed by scientists in the elaboration of their theories about nature. Merchant has also written *Radical Ecology: The Search for a Livable World* (1990), which argues for an activist approach to the ecological crisis in considering the values espoused by ecofeminism, ecowarriors, and Deep Ecology.

Sarah Hrdy, trained as a biological anthropologist, has written a number of works that explore the biological and social bases of female sexuality. As a primatologist, Hrdy has developed powerful arguments that

incorporate her fieldwork on Indian monkeys known as "langurs" in *The Langurs of Abu* (1980). Her willingness to rethink assumptions about male-female roles and sexuality in *The Woman That Never Evolved* (1981) has made her a controversial figure. Also a primatologist, Donna Haraway has written on Hrdy's work in *Primate Visions* (1989) and developed significant theories that reconfigure scientific ideologies in *Crystals, Fabrics, Fields* (1976), *Simians, Cyborgs, and Women* (1990), and *Modest Witness and the Second Millennium* (1996).

Writing for both scholarly and popular audiences, Dorothy Nelkin acknowledges the power and possibility of science in the public imagination. Her many works cover a wide range of interests, as their titles indicate: *Controversy: The Politics of Technical Decisions* (1979), *Science as Intellectual Property* (1984), *Selling Science* (1987), *Dangerous Diagnostics: The Social Power of Biological Information* (1989), and *The Creation Controversy: The Animal Rights Crusade* (1992). Nelkin issued a forthright defense of science studies scholars during the so-called "science wars," noting that science needs to be understood, appreciated, analyzed, and criticized by both those who practice it and those whose lives are determined by it.

Just as American society has adapted in different ways at different times to numerous technologies and scientific discoveries by changing individual and group practices, American writers have also adapted to new knowledge by incorporating their hopes, regrets, ideas, and illusions regarding science and technology within poetry, fiction, drama, and nonfiction. Whether celebratory of science or fearful of its power, American writers acknowledge that the languages of science help to make up what we think of as literature and that scientific reports and analyses cannot fail to be illuminated by linguistic, literary, and cultural analyses.

BIBLIOGRAPHY: Clark, M. M., "The Gene, the Computer, and Information Processing in A. R. Ammons," *TCL* 36 (Spring 1990): 1–9; Gould, S. J., *Mismeasure of Man* (1987); Hayles, N. K., *The Cosmic Web* (1984); Hunter, K. M., *Doctors' Stories: The Narrative Structure of Medical Knowledge* (1991); Jehlen, M., and M. Warner, *The English Literatures of America, 1500–1800* (1997); Jenseth, R., and E. F. Lotto, eds., *Constructing Nature: Readings from the American Experience* (1996); Kass, L., *Toward a More Natural Science: Biology and Human Affairs* (1985); Knight, D., *The Age of Science* (1986); Levine, G., ed., *One Culture: Essays in Science and Literature* (1987); Peterfreund, S., ed., *Literature and Science* (1990); Porush, D., *The Soft Machine: Cybernetic Fiction* (1985); Russett, C., *Sexual Science* (1989);

Scholnick, R. J., ed., *American Literature and Science* (1992); Ulrich, L., *Midwife's Tale* (1990); Walls, L. D., *Seeing New Worlds: Henry David Thoreau and Nineteenth-Century Natural Science* (1995)

CAROL COLATRELLA

SCIENCE FICTION

More commonly referred to as "S-F" or the more egregious "Sci-Fi," the genre of science fiction is arguably the oldest literary form. The first storytellers who described alternative universes wherein animals spoke or heroes won the day with weapons fashioned from otherworldly materials were prefiguring the literary science fiction authors. Although acknowledged as a predominantly American art form, authors such as Jonathan Swift predated many of the genre's conventions with the publication of *Gulliver's Travels* in 1726, as did Mary Shelley with *Frankenstein,* published in 1818. Jules Verne—the ostensible "Father of Science Fiction"—produced what most consider the first true modern science fiction novel *Five Weeks in a Balloon* in 1863, even though Edgar Allan POE had preceded this with *Mellonta Tuta* in 1849. However, despite Swift, Verne, Poe, and occasional others, science fiction as the genre unto itself that we identify today can probably be traced back no further than the publication in 1911 of Hugo Gernsback's *Ralph 124C 41.*

Gernsback was a seminal figure in American science fiction. Although he had wide-ranging interests as an inventor and businessman (he founded the world's first radio supply house and designed the first home radio set), his heart seemed to lie in publishing and writing that he viewed as ways to teach the masses about science. Both his one major novel and a series of short stories about "Baron Munchaussen" were really science lessons in the guise of fiction. While his pedantic writing style may have left something to be desired, his work as editor-publisher of over fifty publications—ranging from *Modern Electrics,* founded in 1908, to *Sexology,* founded in 1933—did much to popularize an astonishing number of subjects. But none of his publications had greater impact than *Amazing Stories.* Inaugurated in 1926, *Amazing Stories* was established as arguably the most influential force in the early period of the genre.

The overwhelming majority of science fiction writers who began their careers in the pre-World War II period notably attribute their first fascination with, and desire to write, science fiction to the stories they read in *Amazing Stories* and subsequent works such as *Astounding, Galaxy,* and the still published *Magazine of Fantasy and Science Fiction,* among numerous

other lesser-known and often short-lived periodicals. Although these publications are credited for pioneering the genre, they were also the leading cause of the low literary reputation that science fiction came to hold among the literary establishment and the reading public in general. While the magazines published far more stories of quality than they are given credit for, the vast majority of their tales fell into the lurid and sensational. The effect of this can be seen in the fact that those authors who were using science fiction concepts in serious ways went to great lengths to deny that their works were indeed a part of the genre. Although early science fiction was dominated by the formulistic approach associated with such authors as E. E. "Doc" Smith and Isaac ASIMOV, there emerged a generation of authors whose contribution paved the way for further development, notably Murray Leinster, Manly Wade Wellman, Jack Williamson, Fritz Leiber, and C. L. Moore—one of the few women writers of the "first wave."

In the late 1940s and early 1950s science fiction underwent a transformation from pulp to legitimate works of social commentary. The shift of the genre's literary quality is traceable back to the writers such as A. E. van Vogt, the author of *Slan* (1946) and *The Pawns of Null-A* (1955); Ward Moore, author of *Greener Than You Think* (1946) and *Bring the Jubilee* (1953); Richard Matheson, author of *I Am Legend* (1954) and *The Shrinking Man* (1956); and Edgar Pangborn, author of *a Mirror for Observers* (1954), among others, who, after suffering the traumatic effects of World War II and particularly the bombing of Hiroshima, began to question the future. The disillusionment they experienced, along with the political climate brought on by the cold war, made expressing such sentiments both unpopular and dangerous. Thus, many writers looked to the past for inspiration, and they discovered anew works such as *Gulliver's Travels,* its ploy so simple and devastating that it became a model for the postwar science fiction novel: "Isn't this a terrible world. But it's *obviously* not our world. It's an alternate universe of flying cities and talking horses, sentient giants and slightly less sentient human ants." George Orwell wrote in *1984* not about the horrors of 1948, but the distant future that would soon appear as reality.

In the hands of the field's best practitioners, science fiction became the marketplace for ideas. Jack Finney wrote not about the dangers of conformist thinking in the East and the West, but about our minds and bodies being taken over by outer space pods in *The Invasion of the Body Snatchers* (1978); Robert HEINLEIN wrote not about the absurdity of intolerance in the early 1960s of sexual, political, and moral differences, but of some future world where these ideas were spread by an alien in *Stranger in a Strange Land*. Moreover, in attracting the most creative of literary thinkers, it also achieved the goal of attracting some of the best writers to the field. With writers such as Kurt VONNEGUT and Phillip K. Dick, the best science fiction contains writing that could stand with the best of any mainstream author. Literary qualities such as the lyricism of Ray BRADBURY, the provocative vision of Harlan ELLISON, and the energy of Michael CRICHTON have contributed to the rise of science fiction as an important part of the literary tradition.

Today's science fiction is a phantasmagoria of styles and subgenres that can be grouped into two general branches, although there is much overlapping between definitions. "Hard" science fiction relies heavily on the technological aspects of science with projections into the next generation as seen in the works of such writers as Isaac Asimov, notably in *Fantastic Voyage* (1966; rev. ed., 1990) and the "Robot" novels and stories as well as the "Foundation" series, and Arthur C. Clarke, author of *Prelude to Space* (1951) and *2001: A Space Odyssey* (1968). "Soft" science fiction deals less with technology and more with ideas and concepts of where technology may be leading us, as seen in such works as Ursula K. LE GUIN's *The Dispossessed* and Roger Zelazny's *This Immortal* (1966) and *Lord of Light* (1969). Hard science fiction is further extended when external technology threatens the Earth's well-being, notably in such works as Crichton's *The Andromeda Strain* or in such "doomsday" novels as Eugene Burdick and Harvey Wheeler's *Fail-Safe* (1962) and Peter George's *Red Alert* (1963), both of which are no less hard science fiction for taking place in the relative "present" in what might be considered "everyday" settings, or when our own technologies—computers, genetic experimentation—are the threat. The "soft" style has works arguing against the destruction or promulgation of ideas and lifestyles. Within these divisions lie further branches, categorized by the treatment of science fiction, ranging from poetry to farce. There is also the subgenre "cyberpunk," a trend in 1990s science fiction started by William GIBSON (who coined the term) that includes, among others, Neal Stephenson's *The Diamond Age* (1995), Gregory Benford's *Cosm* (1998), and William Browning Spencer's *Zod Wallop* (1996), as well as the works of many other offspring of the post–Bill Gates generation.

The variety of styles within science fiction is limitless, since the genre is defined by the importance placed on the idea behind the work rather than the writing style of the author. The story must deal with concepts beyond what exists: it must speculate about "the next step," or even the one beyond that, and present-day knowledge must be extended into that next step. Most importantly, the story must be about the idea of what faces us when that next step is taken. Science fiction is the field of the dreamer who dreams of the possibilities and asks that they be considered and acted upon.

BIBLIOGRAPHY: Aldiss, B. W., *Trillion Year Spree: The History of Science Fiction* (1986); Ash, B., ed., *The Visual Encyclopedia of Science Fiction* (1977); Chute, J., and P. Nicholls, eds., *The Encyclopedia of Science Fiction* (1993); Conklin, G., ed., *The Classic Book of Science Fiction* (1982); Gunn, J. E., *Alternate Worlds: The Illustrated History of Science Fiction* (1975); Peithman, S., ed., *The Annotated Tales of Edgar Allan Poe* (1981); Siegel, M., *Hugo Gernsback: Father of Science Fiction* (1982)

STEVE BERNER

SCOTT, Evelyn

b. 17 January 1893, Clarksville, Tennessee; d. 3 August 1963, New York City

Novelist, short story writer, poet, dramatist, autobiographer, S. won considerable fame during the 1920s and 1930s; her work was touted by H. L. MENCKEN, Sinclair LEWIS, Herbert Read, and others. By the late 1930s, her reputation began a marked decline, perhaps because of her attack on the communist mentality. Her iconoclastic spirit and dark vision were better suited to the mood of the 1920s. With her second husband, the English novelist John Metcalfe, she struggled during the World War II years in London, and after the war in New York. She was living near poverty and in almost total neglect when she died, leaving two long novels completed but unpublished.

That S. is not better known today is surprising since her career was ready-made for the women's movement. S. had defied the expectations of her class and sex. A beauty born to prominent Southern families, she might have become a belle. But she was also highly intelligent, a reader, a woman bent on taking her own course. Following her graduation from Sophie Newcomb College and Newcomb Art School, Tulane University, she left New Orleans with the already married dean of Tulane's School of Tropical and Preventative Medicine to establish a common-law marriage in Brazil. The couple marked the step by changing their names. Elsie Dunn became E. S.; Frederick Wellman became Cyril Kay Scott. S.'s autobiography *Escapade* (1923) recounts the struggle of their difficult five years in Brazil. In *Background in Tennessee* (1937), S. describes her youth in Clarksville and her brief against the South. Her rebellion also informed her fiction, especially *Eva Gay* (1933). S.'s abiding subject was the need for individual freedom and development.

S. was not only avant-garde in her themes, but in her techniques. She exemplifies the modernist sensibility. She published poems in *Poetry Journal, The Dial, Others,* and the *Egoist,* gathered as *Precipitations* (1920), her first book. A second collection, *The Winter Alone,* was published a decade later.

But it was for her fiction that S. won her greatest fame. *The Narrow House* (1921), *Narcissus* (1922), and *The Golden Door* (1925) chronicle the story of a neurotic Southern family, the Farleys, through three generations. A second trilogy underscores the range of her MODERNISM, as she utilizes stream of consciousness and a mixture of genres in an ambitious attempt to portray the development of America from 1851 to 1914. *Migrations: An Arabesque in Histories* (1927) portrays westward expansion. In *The Wave* (1931), S. took the Civil War as subject. The novel anticipates the experiments of John DOS PASSOS in *U.S.A.;* characters from the earlier *Migrations* reappear and interact with a large number of characters, fictional and real, from North and South. In the two-volume novel *Calendar of Sin, American Melodramas* (1931), the families from *Migrations* are again fictional subjects as S. exposes false ideas of sin and sexuality that account for the grimness in her first trilogy, a grimness that echoes that of dramatist August Strindberg, whom S. greatly admired. Although S. herself published only a single play, *Love: A Drama in Three Acts* (1921), the drama was an important influence on her work.

In 1985, S. and Caroline GORDON were subjects for a conference on their work at Austin Peay University in Clarksville, Tennessee. But a more encouraging sign for S.'s reputation is the reissuance of her autobiographical works *Escapades* and *Background in Tennessee,* as well as her novel *The Narrow House.*

BIBLIOGRAPHY: Bach, P., "E. S.: From Tennessee to Greenwich Village," *SoQ* 33 (Winter-Spring 1995): 57–63; Callard, D. A., *Pretty Good for a Woman: The Enigmas of E. S.* (1985); Hatcher, H., *Creating the Modern American Novel* (1935): 72–82

JOSEPH M. FLORA

SCOTT, Winfield Townley

b. 30 April 1910, Haverhill, Massachusetts; d. 28 April 1968, Santa Fe, New Mexico

The poets of the 1940s and 1950s in America labored in the dominating shadows of a number of major figures; some seemed only to be footnotes to the reputations of T. S. ELIOT, Ezra POUND, Wallace STEVENS, and Robert FROST; others attempted to remain independent of those influences, or to remain loyal to other American traditions—those associated with Edwin Arlington ROBINSON or even earlier writers like John Greenleaf WHITTIER. S. was one of the latter. He took pride in being independent of modern literary fashions and claimed to be a member of no school or tendency. While this was a respectable stance, the bulk of his work now appears stylistically derivative, though honorably and sometimes successfully ambitious to establish a distinctive voice. His collected work remains readable and engaging, but the rhetoric of W. B. Yeats, the cadences of Eliot, even occasionally the sharp bite of Pound will echo in most readers' ears as they read his lyrics, and the presences of both Robinson and Frost, sometimes Robinson JEFFERS, can be sensed in the scenarios and the language of his narratives..

S. was born in Massachusetts and educated at Brown University. He worked in Rhode Island for the *Providence Journal* after his graduation from Brown in 1931, and was literary editor of that newspaper from 1941 to 1951; subsequently he held the same post with the *New Mexican* in Santa Fe from 1961 until his death. He also spent some years teaching at Brown, New York University, and Pembroke College. His first professional publication, a chapbook, *Elegy for Robinson* (1936), was followed by *Biography for Traman* (1937) and *Wind the Clock* (1941). The elegy echoes Robinson's cadences and pays homage to his style. Many of S.'s narratives, such as "Gert Swasey," a tale of a wealthy but rebellious young woman whose life ends badly, are similar in theme and style to "Richard Cory," "Miniver Cheevy," and other Robinson poems. The elegy declares S.'s loyalty to Robinson and acknowledges the influence, attested to as well by the sketches of schoolboys and school days among the "Traman" poems, sharply observed vignettes of boyhood cruelty and love, seen through the eyes of S.'s alter ego, Traman. Other narrative poets—Samuel Taylor Coleridge, Thomas Hardy, Robert Graves—appear in his writings as ancestors or admired contemporaries. In his lyrics, S. is a sensuous poet of the body, of the sensations of male physicality, as in the early "Easy Nakedness" or the fine poems of married love, "A and B and the Mirror" and "We Are So Fond of One Another, Because Our Ailments Are the Same."

During his lifetime, S. published seven volumes of poetry, including *Collected Poems: 1937–1962* (1962) and *New and Selected Poems* (1967), as well a collection of essays, *Exiles and Fabrications* (1961). *Alpha and Omega* (1971) appeared posthumously, as did *The Literary Notebooks of W. T. S.: "a dirty hand"* (1969), edited by his friend, Merle Armitage.

S. wrote two book-length narratives, *The Sword on the Table: Thomas Dorr's Rebellion* (1942) and *The Dark Sister* (1958). The earlier narrates an event in Rhode Island history when a constitutional crisis led to an effort by Thomas Dorr and his supporters to assert by force the validity of Dorr's election as governor and the simultaneous establishment of a new state constitution. Dorr's outnumbered forces were defeated, and the final section of the poem presents Dorr's defense of his "rebellion" before the court established by the parties against whom he had rebelled. The controversy had begun because only landowners were allowed to vote under the original Rhode Island constitution; Dorr and his supporters therefore challenged the existing power structure in the state and threatened the interests of the landowners. The themes and attitudes of this poem would probably appeal to many of today's private militia members and others of the "patriot" movements, since S. portrays Dorr as one who challenges the hegemony of a government based on power and privilege, in language that asserts the sovereignty of the common people.

S.'s other major narrative poem is *The Dark Sister*, a poem that now seems heavily indebted to the example of Jeffers. The central character is Freydis, daughter of the Viking leader, Eric the Red, and half sister of Leif Erickson. She emerges as a dark and gloomy figure, a cousin, perhaps, of Lady Macbeth, one who publicly espouses the "new" Christianity that has spread among her people, but who behaves according to the codes of the traditional Norse gods. She plans a voyage to Vinland to acquire a supply of timber, but plots from the beginning to destroy her helpers and keep the whole of the valuable cargo to herself, not so much for the wealth it might bring, but for the "honor" that she would gain, proving that she is as great a leader as her father and brothers. A number of powerful scenes culminate in Freydis's monologue, alone late at night in the wilderness, contemplating the foolishness of the men—both her husband and her partners—as she plots her final moves. Incestuous feelings for her half-brother, Leif Erickson, mix with her powerful ambition, but her triumph ends in madness and dismissal from the presence of the man for whose approval she had undertaken the task. While the poem reads smoothly and the narrative is dramatic, S. was unable to establish the driving rhythm in his long narrative lines that would have given the poem aesthetic power consistent with the intensity of the feelings and ideas he was exploring.

One of S.'s best-known works is the title poem from *Mr. Whittier and Other Poems* (1948), which begins "It is so much easier to forget than to have been Mr. Whittier." The poem is one of many S. wrote that contemplate the difficulties and frustrations of being an unfashionable poet; it's hard enough to be a poet at all, but to be condescended to even by one's vocational peers, especially for one who both values

the poet's role and is self-consciously ambitious in that role, must be both frustrating and depressing. The fate of minor poets is often to disappear from sight for a period after their deaths, in spite of the best efforts of their friends and relatives to protect and propagate their memory. S.'s wife and friends prompted posthumous publications that affirmed his reputation, and a biography by Scott Donaldson, *Poet in America: W. T. S.* (1972), provides a basis for future rediscovery. It seems likely that S. will at least sustain a presence in anthologies with several of his best shorter poems, and that may prompt further reading.

BIBLIOGRAPHY: Donaldson, S., *Poet in America: W. T. S.* (1972); Goldstein, L., "The American Poet at the Movies: A Life and Times," *CentR* 24 (1980): 432–52

THOMAS F. DILLINGHAM

SEA, The

No account of American literary history is complete without a substantial consideration of the nation's other frontier, the sea. Like the West, the sea has represented a physical expansion of the nation, an unpredictable, limitless domain, a reaching out to an unknown destiny, a setting upon which democratic ideals, fierce individualism, and mercantile pursuit have coexisted and conflicted. The sea has also been a spiritual frontier—an elemental, ambiguous force of beauty and terror, a place where American poets, writers and artists sought to transcend the limits of society, convention, selfhood, and ordinary consciousness.

Among the earliest literary treatments of the sea are the oral traditions of Native Americans. Pacific Northwest cultures, for instance, told of the mythical Coyote's salmon fishing rituals, and, in the Eskimo tradition, a young girl who was viciously drowned by her father became the goddess of fate, living at the bottom of the sea.

The rich oral tradition of sea literature extends to the songs of the white settlers. The ballad stanza combined with jingoistic fervor in numerous sea songs, including "The Battle of the Kegs," which described, like many such ballads, an image of the heroic seaman that became an American archetype—the hard-scrabble, inscrutable sea-faring individualist. The seafarer's chantey, or work-song, each with differing choral patterns and moods depending on the intensity and duration of the particular task at hand were also immensely popular and are key expository devices in some of the most important sea novels. The sea appears in numerous African American oral traditions as well. "Didn't My Lord Deliver Daniel," is only one of countless African American spirituals and sermons that drew on biblical imagery of the sea as both a cruel and ungovernable force of fate and the site of salvation. Even blues songs (perhaps the most land-centered of oral traditions in terms of subject matter) often allude to the sea when describing the vicissitudes of romantic love, and some African American folktales parallel ancient European and West African lore in which the sea is a magical, beneficent netherworld.

Though the American sea novel has its predecessors the English sea novels of Sir Walter Scott, Tobias Smollett, and Daniel Defoe, its distinctly nationalistic tenor and narrative structure were established by the voluminous, widely circulated accounts of sea voyages to and from the New World, written by explorers, colonists, merchant marines, and tradesman (and their family members) throughout the 17th and 18th cs.

The adventurous, romantic notions of the sea, which still linger in the national consciousness, are entirely absent from colonial era narratives. Instead, highly detailed works such as William Strachey's "True Repertory of the Wracke," (1625), Henry Norwood's "A Voyage to Virginia," (1732), and the letters of Anthony Thacher, present alternately dramatic and tedious accounts of storm-tossed torment, death by water, and Puritanical perseverance on the sea. These sea survival stories were interpreted, expanded and retold, by Cotton MATHER in his *The Ecclesiastical History of New England* and by many other colonial writers and preachers, as testimonies to an abiding belief in the Lord's ferocity and His mercy, which in turn provided evidence of Divine Providence—confirmation that the New World was their divine destiny.

The combined impact of rationalism, Newtonian science, nationalistic bravado, and boom industries like ship building, slave trading, and fishing gradually changed the tenor of sea narratives. By the middle of the 1700s, the sea's unpredictability and overwhelming vastness (and man's deliverance from it), previously viewed as emblematic of God's design, were evolving into increasingly romantic and aesthetic attitudes toward the sea. Always maintaining their essential realism, tales of sea deliverance were also imbued with a spirit of individualism, as in *Mr. Penrose:The Journal of Penrose, Seaman* (ca. 1770s) about a shipwrecked young man which also dramatizes Enlightenment notions of noble savagery, and *The Female Marine* (1816), a narrative about a woman who, having fallen from social grace, escapes to the sea disguised as a man and participates in the War of 1812.

By 1820, U.S. maritime capacities competed with those of Great Britain. Homegrown innovations like the clipper ship as well as a thriving domestic whaling industry made the sea a new, forbidding frontier, and ushered in an era of sea literature unique in world history. James Fenimore COOPER's novel, *The Pilot,*

about an American schooner caught up in the Revolutionary War, was a huge success. The novel presents the sea as an ever-changing, quasi-mystical backdrop upon which an Anglo-American crew struggle with competing allegiances to a merging national identity, a Byronic individualism, and the compelling comforts of female companionship and the settled life of the shore. Its follow-up, *Red Rover,* depicts a young sailor irresistibly drawn to a vessel led by an aggressive, law-defying sea captain. Male competitiveness and potency on the high seas is further treated in Cooper's *Two Admirals,* in which ships are no longer ghostly visions on uncharted waters but massive technological wonders. The distinction between domesticity and the sea often blur in Cooper's later novels, as in *Afloat and Ashore & Milles Wallingford.*

The sea narratives of Richard Henry DANA, Jr., matched the popularity of Cooper's sea fiction, and may well be more important as literary progenitors of the modern sea novel—Cooper himself expressed a debt of gratitude for Dana's work. Dana's influential *Two Years before the Mast,* about a voyage aboard a merchant ship, narrates, in compelling, dramatic detail, the story of a young marine trying to reconcile his own idealism about seafaring with the brutalities and authoritarian codes of life at sea.

This emerging genre of sea narrative—in which an uninitiated shipmate tells of a sea voyage in a reconstructed diary—served as the model for Edgar Allan POE's novella *The Narrative of Arthur Gordon Pym.* Poe had written of the sea previously, in his story "Ms. Found in a Bottle" and the poems "The City in the Sea" and "Annabel Lee," but in *Pym,* the sea is a physical embodiment of the irrational, or what Poe describes as a swirling black "Mare Tenebraum," upon which the narrator journeys. *Pym* tells the bizarre story of a young man and his companion on the open sea who are rescued from near death. While Pym is stowed away in a box for days, the vessel is overrun by mutineers whom the protagonist and his companion ultimately kill, only to find themselves adrift on the ocean, resorting to cannibalism, capsizing in a storm (during which they are attacked by sharks), drifting near Antarctica, and eventually encountering "savages." Poe's use of the sea narrative as an analogue to a psychic voyage probably stemmed, in part, from his belief (popular in the early 1800s) in the "Symmes Hole" theory which held that the earth was hollow at the North and South Poles. Sea navigation was for Poe, as in "Descent into a Maelstrom," both a metaphorical and literal journey *into* dark regions.

The emerging psychological dimensions of the novel combined with the popular picaresque qualities of the sea narrative in the seminal work of Herman MELVILLE, a writer whom British novelist D. H. Lawrence called the greatest poet of the sea. Familiar with seafaring life from his youth, Melville's first novel *Typee* is a fictionalized version of the highly popular 19th-c. travelogue—a narrative about a long sea journey to and from secret, mysterious islands. Interestingly, Melville's first sea novel centers on the escape *from* the sea, as the narrator and a companion flee a tyrannical captain and take up a leafy residence in the sensual world of the Typees. Eventually, the sea becomes a place the narrator desperately longs for once he has been abandoned by his companion, who fled the island aboard a British vessel. In *Ommo,* a quasi-sequel to *Typee,* the symbolic quality of the sea as escape is complicated by the darker theme of mutiny, while in *Mardi,* the familiar sea survival story becomes an allegorical tale of island-hopping, as the sea provides a means of navigating political, religious, and philosophical ideas represented on various Polynesian islands. Melville continued to depict the sea as the ideal testing ground for intellectual, moral and spiritual development; in *Redburn,* a young idealistic marine learns the darker sides of sea life during a transatlantic passage. *White-Jacket,* a harsh critique of the merciless corporal punishments and autocratic cruelties of sea life, extends, in metaphysical terms, the metaphor of the ship as a sovereign world—the sea vessel as an alternate world that nevertheless mirrors the extreme range of failings and feelings found in the world ashore.

Melville's quintessential sea novel, *Moby-Dick; or, The Whale,* has been widely viewed as not only as the finest achievement in American literature but the most important contribution to sea literature since the epics of Virgil and Homer. From the often rhapsodic but carefully plotted opening chapters, the novel is an exhaustive poetic examination of the universal enchantment of "the watery part of the world." The narrator, "Ishmael," sets out in the whaling vessel, *The Pequod,* with the romantic conviction that, "in landlessness alone resides the highest truth, shoreless, indefinite as God." The crew, a seafaring microcosm of American life—including an African American cabin boy and a Native American harpoonist—set out on what is at once a practical communal enterprise and an individual's uncharted search for the essential mystery of being—a search induced by the sublime immensity of the sea. Indeed the sea and life become one as the book declares decisively, "that unbounded ocean you gasp in, is Life." Man's tragic need to journey into the watery unknown is personified by Ishmael, and, later in the novel, by Captain Ahab; in turn, the sea's awesome powers are embodied by the "leviathan," the white whale. Although the novel's complicated, often Manichean depiction of the sea continues to fascinate readers and critics, the underlying realism of its presentation keeps the sea from becoming simply an amorphous literary symbol. Extended tracts on cetology, references to pre-Darwinian biology, and exhaustive annotations on the *techne* of shipping and whale hunting make the novel an unrivaled testimony to the multifaceted essence of the sea.

By the time of the Civil War, America's maritime culture was already changing. Steamships began to replace schooners and overfishing had hurt the whaling industry, which was already fading with the dawn of petroleum drilling. At the same time, the shipping industry was declining as the need to import natural resources diminished with the nation's push westward. An imperialist attitude toward the sea became pervasive, as evidenced by the popularity of Alfred T. Mahan's *The Influence of Sea Power upon History* (1890). As the impersonal, industrial age and evolutionary theory took hold, the sea fiction of both the late 19th c. and 20th c. reflected this demythologizing of the sea. Melville's dark, unfinished final work *Billy Budd* deals with the profound philosophical struggle of the private conscience at odds with the official authority, and marks one of the last images of an idealized sailor struggling to maintain his selfhood on the metaphysical frontier of the sea. Stephen CRANE's "The Open Boat" centers on four shipwrecked men in a brutally unromantic life and death struggle with a sea of Darwinian indifference.

The seafaring life, represented by the decayed legacies of old sailors and shipbuilders, is a pathetic vestige of the past in Sarah Orne JEWETT's novels *Deephaven* and *The Country of the Pointed Firs.* In a feminist reversal of the male-dominated seafaring narrative, Kate CHOPIN's *Awakenings* makes the sea central to the sexual life of Edna Pontellier who, in her final desperation, sets out into the sea alone, without a boat. To a large extent, Jack LONDON's Wolf Larsen in *The Sea-Wolf* along with Ernest HEMINGWAY's Santiago in *The Old Man and the Sea* and Thomas Hudson in *Islands in the Stream* are modernist reinventions of the seafarer for whom the romance of the sea provided a physical testing-ground for male identity in an increasingly antiheroic age. In both books, seaman-hunters take to the sea in a lonely, often deperate effort to live beyond social role and historical time, and struggle violently but vainly with the untiring forces within and upon the sea. Also important were Eugene O'NEILL's first plays, including *Bound East for Cardiff,* all set at sea, which depict the seafaring life as an alienating, dehumanizing existence despite the occasional charms of male camaraderie.

Though the sea figures less centrally in American poetry than it does in prose, it has maintained a strong presence up through the modern and contemporary periods. The sea is a central force in Philip FRENEAU's poetry of the Revolutionary War period. Henry Wadsworth LONGFELLOW's anthology of sea verse, *The Seaside and the Fireside*, was followed by another American anthology of sea poetry called *Thalatta.* The sea verses of James Gate Percival and William Cullen BRYANT often revived ancient fabulist ideals of the sea while Longfellow's own poems display a transcendental attitude toward the sea, as in "The Secret of the Sea" in which the speaker is urged by an old mariner to meditate on a coastal seascape. His poem, "Wreck of Hisperus" deals with human arrogance toward the power of the sea.

Not surprisingly, much of Walt WHITMAN's sea imagery is uplifting. Poems like "Crossing Brooklyn Ferry" view the sea as a means of connecting with humanity, while in "Out of the Cradle Endlessly Rocking" the sea is a power that answers the human longing for a state of being beyond death. In other poems, such as "Sail out for God," "Eidolon Yacht," and "Now Finale to the Shore," Whitman draws stirring analogies between the sea journey and the voyage at the end of life. Ralph Waldo EMERSON, who also frequently alludes to the sea, does so touchingly in his poem "Terminus" in which the decline of the speaker's creative energies at the end of his life is compared with a ship's coming into dock.

The association of the sea with the artistic faculty, creative self-consciousness, and intangible cosmic forces continues to be an interesting theme in American poetry. Longfellow, in "Becalmed," draws a comparison between a poet's lack of inspiration and a sailor stuck in a never-ending calm. Whitman, in the "Sea Drift" section of *Leaves of Grass* finds poetic impetus in the movement of ocean waves, and Emerson likens Henry David THOREAU's alternative world, Walden Pond, to "a small ocean; the Atlantic, a large Walden Pond"; the sea is an important poetic trope in much of Thoreau's writing, especially in *Cape Cod,* "Autumnal Tints" in *Journal,* and "the Conclusion" of *Walden.* In the latter work, Thoreau calls on his readers to voyage to their interior seas, "explore the private sea, the Atlantic and Pacific Ocean of one's being alone." Even Emily DICKINSON, who writes in one of her poems, "I never saw the sea," occasionally alludes to the sea as a metaphysical paradigm, a sea that is neither a male frontier nor a mystical force. For T. S. ELIOT's Prufrock, the sea is a deeply lyrical yet unreachable alternative to his sterile urban life. In Charles OLSON's *Maximus* poems, and his "Archaeologist of Morning," among many other works, the Atlantic Ocean off the New England coast is a gargantuan presence conveying notions of space, history, and timelessness. The Pacific Ocean is depicted throughout Robinson JEFFERS's poetic oeuvre as a dynamic, defining physical force, and for Wallace STEVENS, the sea,

the subject of endlessly varied meditations, epitomizes the aesthetic potency and perfection that is the means and ends of his poetic venture, as in "Sunday Morning" and "The Idea of Order at Key West."

The subject of the sea continues to play a role in much contemporary poetry, most interestingly in the work of Howard NEMEROV, Richard WILBUR, and W. S. MERWIN. Contemporary novelists such as John BARTH, John HAWKES, and Robert STONE have written a number of novels that involve the sea, and nearly all of Peter MATTHIESSEN's books deal with the sea, most notably his masterful revival of the sea voyage archetype, *Far Tortuga,* set in the Caribbean. The sea is also the setting, often with international plots, in the popular historical novels of Herman WOUK, Peter Benchley, and Tom Clancy.

BIBLIOGRAPHY: Bryant, S. W., *The Sea and the States: A Maritime History of the American People* (1947); Carlson, P. A., ed., *Literature and Lore of the Sea* (1986); Philbrick, T., *James Fenimore Cooper and the Development of American Sea Fiction* (1962); Springer, H., ed., *America and the Sea: A Literary History* (1995); Wharton, D. P., ed., *In the Trough of the Sea: Selected American Sea Deliverance Narratives, 1610–1766* (1979)

TIM KEANE

SEABURY, Samuel

b. 30 November 1729, Groton, Connecticut; d. 25 February 1796, New London, Connecticut

The son of a High Anglican churchman, S. quickly became one himself. Although he had an astoundingly varied career that included being, in addition, a physician and a polemicist, it is as an Anglican bishop that he is most remembered; often, in fact, S. is considered the founder of the American Episcopal Church.

S. first became prominent in 1774, when he was living in Westchester County, serving as a priest and practicing medicine. Firmly loyal to Great Britain, he began to pseudonymously publish broadsides against the American rebel position as "A. W. Farmer." S.'s loyalist position did not simply come out of a brute allegiance to existing institutions. He saw the Continental Congress as unjustifiably usurping power from the British Parliament, and, in a long, knowledgeable exposition, he attacked the prospect of political independence as economically disadvantageous, particularly to upper-middle-class landowners such as himself. S.'s broadsides, collected in 1930 as *Letters of a Westchester Farmer,* were wholly secular in content. In many ways, they betrayed a surprising liberalism. S., though a Loyalist, was not particularly a Royalist;

he mocked the pretensions of the rebels that they were opposing not Parliament but King, and pointed out that in England the King had only nominal authority and that Parliament really ruled. In not complaining about this quasi-democratic situation, S. put himself on the Whig side in British politics, although like his fellow Whigs he still saw the franchise as being confined exclusively to aristocrats, men of wealth, and gentleman farmers.

S.'s polemics, of course, did not go without answer; the most eloquent and vociferous came from the young Alexander Hamilton, who was not even eighteen. The middle-aged S. was strenuously challenged by Hamilton's arguments in his pamphlet "A Full Vindication of the Measures of the Congress," and in his response of December 24, 1774, S. attempted to refute them by demonstrating the vanity of any attempt to countermand British military power. Interestingly, whatever S.'s manifest true-blue Britishness, there is a certain indeterminacy in S.'s attitude towards Britain; at times, he speaks of Britain as the rightful ruler of the American colonies and thus the polity of which he himself is a part, at other times it seems a wholly foreign entity.

With the onset of American independence, S.'s social position became precarious, and he was at times interned by the rebels or given asylum by British troops. During this period, he also sought to advance his clerical career, sending emissaries to England in a series of comical escapades that ended up coming to nothing. After the Revolution had succeeded and all his political hopes were shattered, S. prepared to depart in exile to the new Loyalist settlements in Nova Scotia. But then a surprising thing happened; S. was sounded out about being the first bishop of the American Episcopal Church, as the former Church of England in the colonies was now called. Just because the political power of the Crown, with which the church was associated, had now gone away did not mean the church would as well. S. was sent to London in order to be consecrated Bishop of Connecticut and Rhode Island. Although the political authorities in London had come to terms with American independence, the same was not true for senior churchmen: S.'s consecration was put through interminable delays. Finally, S. journeyed north to Scotland to be consecrated by the "nonjuring" church there, headed by Anglican bishops who had refused to swear oaths to the government of England after the 1688 revolution. Ironically, the first American Episcopal bishop was thus consecrated by an ecclesiastical party to the theological "right" of the mainstream, although the Scottish link was not purely happenstance; much of S.'s theology was influenced by the writings of Scottish divines. Once returned to America, S. devoted himself to building his diocese. Although he encountered some contro-

versy when he styled himself "Samuel, by divine permission, Bishop" and was less than reverent toward American governmental authority, by the end of his life he had largely lived down his previous Loyalism and established his denomination, once thought to be wholly linked with England, as a viable American church.

BIBLIOGRAPHY: Rowthorn, A. W., *S. S.* (1983); Steiner, B. E., *S. S., 1729–1796, a Study in the High Church Tradition* (1972); Thoms, H., *S. S.* (1963)

NICHOLAS BIRNS

SEDGWICK, Anne Douglas

b. 28 March 1873, Englewood, New Jersey; d. 19 July 1935, Hampstead, England

The author of seventeen novels, two collections of short stories, and a volume of reminiscences of the Comtesse de Cabarru, *A Childhood in Brittany 80 Years Ago* (1919), S. was regarded in her day as Edith WHARTON's equal and the chief disciple of Henry JAMES.

An expatriate who lived in England from the age of nine and who studied art in Paris for five years, S. demonstrates a good eye for landscape. "Heathside" in Oxfordshire and "Les Chardonnerets" on the Normandy coast in *The Little French Girl* (1924) and the "Manoir" on the cliff overlooking the Dardogne in *The Old Countess* (1927) are perfectly realized. Drawing on her experiences, she renders well the country houses and their surroundings in England and France.

S.'s chief similarity to Henry James lies in her concern with the international theme. In *A Fountain Sealed* (1907), she creates a self-righteous American woman, Imogene Upton, but she is kinder to her native country in *Franklin Winslow Kane* (1910), where the title character is kind, generous, and forgiving. Adrienne Toner, the eponymous heroine of S.'s 1921 novel, begins much like Imogene but learns compassion. Roger Oldmeadow in that work represents England's solid virtues but appreciates American optimism and self-confidence.

The Little French Girl and *The Old Countess* also address the international theme but contrast England and France rather than America and Europe. Despite living in France for five years while studying art and again for four years during and after World War I, S. shows little sympathy with French characters or customs. The Countess de Lamouderie in *The Old Countess,* for example, is evil incarnate.

As this treatment suggests, S.'s characters tend to be stereotypes. Her men often prove chivalric, her artists weak and self-centered, her women completely virtuous or totally wicked, though she can sometimes transcend this limitation: Adrienne Toner matures; Monica Wilmot in *Dark Hester* (1929) learns to appreciate her daughter-in-law.

From James, S. may also have adopted the limited authorial point of view. She relies heavily on dialogue to allow characters to reveal themselves, and she has them comment on each other in the manner of a Greek chorus. Such devices do not, however, create detachment because her principals echo her views.

Sentimental and idealistic, S.'s fiction suited the popular and critical taste of the early 20th c. Anyone seeking to understand the literary mood of that era cannot ignore her work.

BIBLIOGRAPHY: De Selincourt, B., ed., *A. D. S.: A Portrait in Letters* (1936); Overton, G. M., *The Women Who Make Our Novels* (1928); Quinn, A. H., *American Fiction: A Historical and Critical Survey* (1936)

JOSEPH ROSENBLUM

SEDGWICK, Catharine Maria

b. 28 December 1789, Stockbridge, Massachusetts; d. 31 July 1867, West Roxbury, Massachusetts

When S. launched *A New England Tale* (1822), America still awaited the emergence of a national literature. Her second novel, *Redwood* (1824), widely translated, elicited praise on both sides of the Atlantic; *Hope Leslie* (1827), her best-known novel, moved even Frances Trollope to attest to its "great merit." By the time *Clarence* (1830) and *The Linwoods* (1935) appeared, American literature had come of age, and S. was linked with William Cullen BRYANT, Washington IRVING, and James Fenimore COOPER as a major American writer. Nathaniel HAWTHORNE called her "our most truthful novelist."

Occasionally, S. wrote for young adults, and in the mid-1830s, she began writing didactic narratives intended to help working-class people improve their habits and manners. The trilogy *Home* (1835), *The Poor Rich Man and the Rich Poor Man* (1836), and *Live and Let Live* (1837) became household favorites. Literary critics slighted these works, however, and by the turn of the century, S.'s reputation declined. Early-20th-c. scholars belittled her work, but Edward Halsey Foster's study (1974) and a new edition of *Hope Leslie* in 1987 have refocused her image.

S.'s works reflect her background. Born of an aristocratic mother and a politically and financially successful father, S. developed a deep sense of responsibility. Well educated, at home and at school, she became an unorthodox thinker. Like her father, she turned from Calvinist Congregationalism to Unitarianism and adopted abolitionist views. With her brothers,

she espoused Jacksonian democracy. Writing became the center of her life, helping to ward off an inherited tendency to depression. Spending her winters in New York and summers in Stockbridge, she became the social leader of the Berkshires, including among her close friends William Cullen Bryant and actress Fanny Kemble.

S. began *A New England Tale* as a Unitarian tract, but turned it into a novel, telling the story of Jane Elton, an orphan mistreated by her hypocritically pious Calvinist aunt, Mrs. Wilson, but saved by marriage to the Quaker Mr. Lloyd. Although artistically flawed, it uses New England dialect, manners, and characters innovatively.

Redwood, noted for its realism, exposes the inequities caused by social customs and controls. Separated from her wealthy father by his parents who deplore his wife's servile background and from her mother by death, Ellen Bruce grows up among friends and develops into a natural aristocrat. Reunited with her father, she marries the wealthy Southerner Charles Westall, and takes her rightful place in society. The subplot illustrates S.'s opinion of the Shaker religious sect as wise in practical matters but ignorant in matters of the heart.

The frontier romance *Hope Leslie* is S.'s finest work. It explores conflicts between the Puritan settlers and the Mohawk Indians, revealing the injustices that provoked the Indian attacks. The story centers on Hope Leslie's attempts to rescue her sister Faith from Mohawk captors. Subsequently convinced that Faith has been happily assimilated into the tribe, Hope helps Everell Fletcher release from prison the Mohawk princess Magawisca, who earlier lost an arm while saving Fletcher's life. S.'s writing, always clear and direct, is at its best in portraying Hope and Magawisca. S. demonstrated courage in treating the issue of miscegenation, a topic on which James Fenimore Cooper hedged in novels such as *The Last of the Mohicans.*

S.'s last three novels suffer by comparison with *Redwood* and *Hope Leslie*. *Clarence,* a two-volume novel of manners, contains excellent satire of upper-class Americans and British visitors, but moves slowly in illustrating the superiority of rural over urban life. *The Linwoods,* a historical romance of the Revolutionary War, plays out the loyalist-colonial conflict within the Linwood family, and closes with the marriage of the wealthy Isabella Linwood to a poor farmer. *Married or Single?* (1857), designed to illustrate that a woman need not be married to be fulfilled, ends, nevertheless, by providing Grace Herbert a suitable husband in Archibald Lisle. Although S. did not marry, she regarded marriage as a woman's proper place.

BIBLIOGRAPHY: Castiglia, C., "In Praise of Extra-Vagant Women: *Hope Leslie* and the Captivity Romance," *Legacy* 6, 2 (1989): 3–16; Dewey, M. E., ed., *Life and Letters of C. M. S.* (1871); Foster, W. H., *C. M. S.* (1974); Gould, P., "C. S.'s 'Recital' of the Pequot War," *AL* 66, 4 (1994): 641–62; Kelley, M., "Negotiating a Self: The Autobiography and Journals of C. M. S.," *NEQ* 66, 3 (1993): 366–98; Ross, C. L., "(Re)Writing the Feminist Romance: C. M. S.'s *Hope Leslie*," *CLAJ* 39, 3 (1996): 320–40; Singley, C. J., "C. M. S.'s *Hope Leslie*: Radical Frontier Romance," in Heyne, E., ed., *Desert, Garden, Margin, Range: Literature on the American Frontier* (1992): 110–22

LUCY M. FREIBERT

SEEGER, Alan
b. 22 June 1888, New York City; d. 4 July 1916, Belloy-en-Santerre, France

S., a young poet killed in battle during World War I, gave voice to the fervor and romantic idealization of war felt by many early enlistees. While popular with soldiers during the war and respected by contemporary critics, his poems, conventional in form and immature in style, are rarely read today in the wake of modernist skepticism over the chivalric ideals of the war.

After graduating from Harvard in 1910, S. went to New York for two years in a poetic search for beauty, then followed his literary dreams to Paris. He developed an intense love for the city, and a joyful, albeit shallow, exuberance for life colors his poetry of this period. His devotion to Paris, the imperiled "mystic, maternal, personified" city, as well as his fatalistic belief in the naturalness of war, compelled him to enlist in the French Foreign Legion less than three weeks after the outbreak of war in 1914. Unlike his modernist compatriots, S. retained his idealization of war despite his experiences in the trenches. His poem, "I have a Rendezvous with Death," concludes, "And I to my pledged word am true, / I shall not fail that rendezvous," echoing his somewhat arrogant but sincere sentiments of 1915, "Death is nothing terrible after all. It may mean something even more wonderful than life. It cannot possibly mean anything worse to the good soldier."

His last poems are noteworthy for being composed under the actual duress of war. He was awaiting permission to read his crowning work, the "Ode in Memory of the American Volunteers Fallen for France," in front of the statues of Lafayette and Washington in Paris when he was killed at the village of Belloy-en-Santerre. This poem, his least self-appreciative work, contains rare touches of realism gleaned from almost two years' war experience, yet he never mitigated his praise for honor in battle, nor his commitment to France, which afforded young soldiers "that grand

occasion to excel / . . . And that rare privilege of dying well." While his poetry rarely transcended its dependence on abstractions and rigid metrical conventions, it offers insight into S.'s and his idealistic generation's paradoxical quest for beauty in the inhumane trenches of war.

BIBLIOGRAPHY: Hart, J. A., "A. S.," in Quartermain, P., ed., *DLB*, vol. 45, *American Poets, 1880–1945* (1986); Moore, T. S., *Some Soldier Poets* (1919); Werstein, I., *Sound No Trumpet: The Life and Death of A. S.* (1967)

LINDA COX

SELBY, Hubert, Jr.
b. 23 July 1928, Brooklyn, New York

Not many writers have made the impact that S. did in 1964 with the publication of *Last Exit to Brooklyn*, a collection of violent, interrelated stories depicting thugs, prostitutes, homosexuals, gang rape, and other forms of brutality and unwitting self-destruction. These grim and grotesque stories are written with a heartbeat counting cadence, beating to the rhythms and the passion of his prose.

D. C. C. Chambers says that "the world of *Last Exit* is in fact a world of no-exit—an expressway to nowhere." It is a mechanical world, loveless and absurd. It is a world of tension between responsibility and appetite, a world of mumbling "monologues and soliloquies in which there is no communication because no one listens to anyone else." There is sense of movement and action, but it is designed to prevent the recognition of another person; therefore, the movement is nowhere and the action produces no results. It is a world that revolves and spins until it breaks into pieces or simply slows down and stops.

The story of Tralala, considered by many to be the best piece of writing in the book, tells about a teenage psychopath whose constant rage drags her from one dirty street to another, from juvenile delinquency to prostitution to depravity, dereliction, and destruction. Tralala's brief life is the visual metaphor of the central theme of the novel: Tralala, in her way, enticed and aroused the gang rape from which she died, a haunting image of the violent and obsessive rush toward inevitable destruction.

S. introduces the reader to a world of tedium, depravity, drug abuse, violence, self-exploitation, and stupidity, horrifying, yet all too real. S. said that in the novel he was attempting to "portray the horrors of a loveless worlds" and to "overwhelm the reader with truth, like Beethoven, so that weeks, months, or any damn time after he had finished reading the book and whether he liked it or it disgusted him, he will be forced to think."

Richard A. Wertime pointed out that, as S. hoped, the novel does overwhelm: "it denies the reader the distance which usually goes with aesthetic pleasure, and it does so by detailing explicitly the thoughts and actions of its characters." Some critics responded to the novel with outrage or "self-protective sarcasm." *Last Exit to Brooklyn* was the subject of an obscenity trial in England. It was banned in Italy. It received mixed reviews in the U.S. Wertime claims it is proper to consider S. as a moralist primarily and a social critic only secondarily.

S.'s second novel, *The Room* (1971), was greeted enthusiastically by a number of reviewers. The main character is an unnamed prisoner who fantasizes about his savage revenge on his captors and imagines himself as the leader of a judicial reform campaign. This unnamed character appears as everyman because, according to Wertime, "he is made universal by the bewilderment he feels in trying to assess his actions and feelings, a bewilderment which fatally cripples his sense of responsibility as well as his self-esteem." His desire to be acceptable to himself forces him to repress any idea of his wrongdoings, yet he is punished by guilt: another expression of a suffering character running headlong to participate in his own destruction.

The Demon (1976) received very little critical or public attention. In it, S. attempts to portray a man possessed by ambition, lust, and violence who is engaged in larcenous, lecherous, and murderous pursuits. The novel falters seriously because the author could not decide whether the character, Harry White, should be pitied or despised, and the result is a muddled portrait of a young executive that neither achieves dramatic intensity nor psychological coherency. S.'s *Song of the Silent Snow* appeared in 1986, followed by the publication in 1998 of *The Willow Tree.*

BIBLIOGRAPHY: Peavy, C., "The Sin of Pride and S.'s *Last Exit to Brooklyn*," *Crit* 11 (1969): 35–42; Sorrentino, G., "The Art of H. S.," *Kulchur* 13 (Spring 1964): 27–43; Wertime, R. A., "Psychic Vengeance in *Last Exit to Brooklyn*," *L&P* 24 (4 November 1974): 153–66

JOSEPH FERRANDINO

SENTIMENTALITY

The American tradition of sentimentality grows out of the sentimental novel, popular from the late-18th to the mid-19th cs. and surviving into the 20th. A didactic form, generally artless in style, sincere in tone, and melodramatic in plot, it was addressed to an overwhelmingly female readership. Setting is often nonspecific and characterization flat. The language of the sentimental novel is effusive and periphrastic, but hardly more so than that of journalism and belles-lettres at the time. Influenced by 18th-c. British novels of sentiment like Samuel Richardson's *Pamela,* the American tradition was more earnestly propagandistic in an attempt to counter Puritan disapproval of novels and to instill useful moral and social values in the new society of the republic.

"Sentimentality" originally indicated the reliance on feelings as a guide to truth, but current usage defines it as an appeal to shallow, uncomplicated emotions at the expense of reason. The audience of the sentimental novel is widely assumed to have enjoyed indulging in tears as proof of their refined sensibilities. Critics argue that readers' intellects were overwhelmed by sympathy founded on a simplistic faith in the essential goodness of human nature. Because many of the phenomenally popular novels of the 19th c. seem hopelessly dated today, they have been dismissed by most modern critics as unimportant, even embarrassing. However, the orthodox definition of sentimentality as "unwarranted emotionalism," based on subjective judgements and rigid distinctions between feeling and intellect, presents ideological problems. Recent feminist theory has clarified the use of the term as it applies to the genre. Although historical sentimental novels seem to modern readers to promote false ideals and empty piety, revisionist critics argue that different cultural assumptions arising from the oppression of women gave liberating significance to the works' piety and mythical power to the ideals of the heroines.

The first novels published in the U.S. were sentimental: William Hill BROWN's *The Power of Sympathy,* Susanna ROWSON's *Charlotte Temple,* Hannah Webster FOSTER's *The Coquette,* and Charles Brockden BROWN's *Clara Howard* dealt gingerly with such topics as the dangers of seduction, the importance of choosing a reliable marriage partner, the consequences of sexual transgressions, and the need for female education. Cathy N. Davidson argues that the theme of seduction, in a society where women were without legal power and were punished severely for making the wrong sexual choices, was not melodramatic by metonymic for their need to align themselves with male power of one kind or another. Of course, the seduction plot is also titillating, and by 1818, it had fallen victim to the genteel impulse to bowdlerize.

Opinion was divided in the early novels about whether marriage was primarily a matter of wifely subordination, as the Bible commanded, or whether a woman's capacity for moral discrimination made the ideal of mutual affection more compelling. Later, the valorization of motherhood allowed the two camps to reconcile by confining woman's moral power to the cult of domesticity. The 19th-c. sentimental novel, sometimes called the "domestic novel," offered an idealized vision of what the Christian family should be. Novelists such as Harriet Beecher STOWE, Susan WARNER, Maria CUMMINS, Sara Payson Willis PARTON, Elizabeth Stuart PHELPS, Sarah Josepha HALE, Augusta Jane EVANS, and Frances Hodgson BURNETT were characterized by Nathaniel HAWTHORNE as "a damned mob of scribbling women." Works such as Warner's *The Wide, Wide World* transformed female submission into identification with the will of God. They portrayed the kingdom of heaven on earth as a world guided by women and adjudicated by feeling. Such self-absorption may be seen as a commercial appropriation of the inner life or, alternatively, as a variant of the romantic effort to redefine the inner life in the face of an increasingly commercial society.

Abetted by household manuals and evangelical literature, the form grew more airless in the 1820s and 1830s when it helped inculcate the belief that obedience, even if it involved great suffering, was a familial, civic, and religious virtue. By midcentury, at the peak of the genre's popularity, women were more confined to the home and had more leisure to spend reading than had been the case fifty years before. The novel became obsessed with power relations within the family and consequent violations of identity. The heroine was more likely to be an established matron or innocent child than an unmarried young woman. The passionate impulses were increasingly redirected through Christian piety, and themes such as imprisonment and freedom, the holiness of the heart's affections, the moral purity of the disenfranchised, and the power of death to transform suffering into triumph gained ascendance. Alexander Cowie offers a "recipe" for a typical plot in *The Rise of the American Novel:* "First, take a young and not-too-pretty child about ten years old . . . Make sure that the child is, or shortly will be, an orphan. If the mother is still living, put her to death very gradually in a scene of much sorrow and little physical suffering, uttering pious hopes and admonitions to the last. . . . Now put the child under the care of a shrewish aunt. . . . In an emergency a cruel housekeeper will do. The child is now unhappy, undernourished, and underprivileged. . . . Introduce a young woman living not far away, who embodies all Christian virtues, especially humility. Let this lady kiss, pray over, and cry with the heroine at intervals of three to four pages. The lady may or may not be blind; at any rate she has had her sorrows and she is destined to die. . . . [The girl learns] to subdue her pride and then submit graciously to the suffering which is the lot of all mortals." Most plots were variations on this kind

of formula with occasional borrowings from gothic romance or the historical novel.

Sentimental fiction may have been a way of rationalizing pain, but it was seldom escapist. At its best, it attempted to dignify the disenfranchised in order to reform the general understanding of humane social behavior. The superlative example of this impulse is Harriet Beecher Stowe's *Uncle Tom's Cabin,* which depicts a devoted Christian slave who is ultimately beaten to death for his honorable protection of others. It was the most widely read American novel of the century. Its elaborate plot and sentimental tone are enlivened by humor and an unusual amount of carefully researched detail. The death of Little Eva, a relatively subordinate episode in the original, has become a favorite example of overwrought Victorian sentimentalism. The child, powerless to change the slave system, sickens and dies in the approved manner, her "triumphant" death causing her father's conversion from skepticism. Jane Tompkins argues that modern critical contempt for this episode is based on post-Christian assumptions, and that Little Eva's death recalls the redemptive power of Christ's sacrifice for Stowe's audience. *Uncle Tom's Cabin* inspired a rash of antislavery novels in the 1850's.

Louisa May ALCOTT continued the tradition of the sentimental novel after the Civil War, but the form gradually lost its moral authority. It has been argued that the didactic strain of NATURALISM supplanted sentimentality as a form of social criticism. The mythic appeal of self-sacrifice that informs Little Eva's death spoke to its audience's need for something beyond everyday reality to give significance to the injustices they endured. Naturalism, on the other hand, avoids such transforming rationalization by criticizing the injustice of everyday reality in analytic, precisely observed terms. Although arguably as sentimental as *Uncle Tom's Cabin,* novels such as Stephan CRANE's *Maggie, Girl of the Streets* and Theodore DREISER's *Sister Carrie* were directed at a different audience: the authors assume their characters's powerlessness is determined by social forces but imply that the reader is able to exercise moral and political control over those forces nevertheless.

There continues to be an audience for sentimental novels like Herman WOUK's *Marjorie Morningstar* today, but the critical fissure between aesthetic and popular literature has consigned the tradition to insignificance. Nevertheless, many writers well within the modernist canon—Robert FROST, F. Scott FITZGERALD, and Ernest HEMINGWAY, for instance—appeal to the moral imperative of compassion under a veneer of detached irony or cynicism. In the 20th c., the identification of sentimentality in literature is often an expression of distaste disguised as a critical judgement.

Historically, sentimentality expressed the alternative power of the powerless and, as such, will naturally be spurned by modern critics aligned with a power structure that effectively determines cultural values. Paradoxically, however, the suspicion of all tender emotion as unauthentic is itself an evasion that partakes of what Christopher Ricks calls "the sentimentalities of cynicism."

If sentimentality is a form of self-delusion, rationalization, or avoidance of ugly truths, it is a relatively narrow and clearly definable phenomenon that transcends genre. Sentimental writing consists of imposing a familiar understanding or emotional response on a reality that is more complex and disturbing than the interpretation acknowledges.

BIBLIOGRAPHY: Davidson, C. N., *Revolution and the Word* (1986); Douglas, A., *The Feminization of American Culture* (1977); Fiedler, L. A., *Love and Death in the American Novel* (1960); Fisher, P., *Hard Facts: Setting and Form in the American Novel* (1985); Freibert, L. M., and B. A. White, *Hidden Hands* (1985); Papashvily, H. W., *All the Happy Endings* (1956); Tompkins, J., *Sensational Designs: The Cultural Work of American Fiction, 1790–1860* (1985); Reynolds, D. S., *Beneath the American Renaissance* (1988)

ROBIN BEATY

SERMON, The

Early New England Puritan preaching continued the homiletic tradition of Englishmen such as John Dod and Richard Sibbes, which stressed not reform of church polity but such themes as the necessity for conversion, life as a pilgrimage, and the "covenant" status of the divine-human relationship. Social awareness was emphasized by moral directives calling for a "Holy Commonwealth," a utopian directive that envisioned a reformed coalition of state and church where the "saints governed with biblical guidance. Such sermonizing demanded a moral intensity, often coupled with a millennial expectation, that derived from the Calvinist notion of human dependence upon the unmerited grace of God. Thus the Lutheran doctrine of faith over works led to a Calvinist focus on the irresistible regeneration by the Holy Spirit and on predestination. Such beliefs invited sermons on individual salvation and personal piety.

New England Puritan preaching continued the Protestant tradition of the centrality of the word—pulpits often replaced altars at the center of the church sanctuary—and, despite its orientation towards individual salvation and a close examination of the inner life of the soul, included social and political issues of church and state. The sermons of such American immigrants as John Cotton added church controversy to these themes. As "Teacher" of First Church, Boston, Massachusetts, Cotton affirmed that state power should encompass religious matters. The antinomianism of Anne Hutchinson led to her claim of "special revelation"—that God spoke directly to her about specific matters. God could be approached directly, without the particularities of biblical revelation. Hutchinson's "enthusiasm" included divine visions and immediate revelations, exhibitions that motivated her excommunication and banishment form Massachusetts Bay Colony. In sermons, Roger WILLIAMS affirmed the separation of church and state, tolerance in individual and group rights as well as religious matters—he preached against the expropriation of Native American lands—and foreshadowed the rise of democratic sentiments in America with his affirmation that "the Soveraigne, originall, and foundation of civill power lies in the people." In sermons at Newtown, Massachusetts, Thomas HOOKER rebutted Williams's attacks on "the New England way," but revealed his own tolerance by moving to Connecticut to protest the limitation of suffrage to church membership. In the Puritan mainstream were Increase MATHER and Cotton MATHER, son and grandson of Richard Mather. Increase Mather preached the jeremiad style, a complaining tirade against social and individual lapses, and church governance, but valued emerging science, as did Cotton Mather. Both figures dominated Massachusetts religious life. Cotton Mather became a main participant in the Salem witch trials, but later doubted "spectral evidence" and executions.

Failure to establish a single church throughout the colonies, a lack of rigor within most congregations, and very low church membership led to the First Great Awakening, a revival movement that spread to most American colonies. Philosopher and theologian George Berkeley anticipated elements of the movement by demanding an "inner change," not only good works, in his listeners, and scorning "The Pedantry of Courts and Schools." His sermons in America were informative, rationally persuasive, and optimistic of the goodness within society and individuals. In 1720, Theodorus J. Frelinghuysen preached sincerity and spiritual conscientiousness to his Dutch Reformed congregation in New Jersey. Other preaching revivalists summoned a personal crisis in their listeners and demanded individual rededication to Christianity. Gilbert Tennent's sermon, "The Danger of an Unconverted Ministry," which privileged clergy who supported the revivalist necessity, ignited a controversy that led to a schism within Presbyterianism in 1741.

Itinerant ministers preached immediate and overt conversion with or without permission from other clergy in New England and the South. In 1731, the Boston sermon of Jonathan EDWARDS, "God Glorified in Man's Dependence," attracted wide attention. Edwards combined a respect for the new empirical methods of the Enlightenment with Calvinist fervor. Since all knowledge is based on sense experience, revivalist conversions were observable and therefore self-evident manifestations of supernatural contact in human lives. Thus he drew disfavor from both rationalist ministers and traditional clergy. Using psychological explanations, Edwards saw that emotionalist preaching, weeping and shouting were a beneficial response to the awareness of one's damnation. Horrifying sermons awake the "affections," which become a "spring of men's actions." In Boston, Charles Chauncy objected to the over exuberance and disorder of the revival setting and preached "reasonable religion," eventually proclaiming a more liberal and tolerant theology.

George Whitefield followed John Wesley as a missionary to Georgia in 1738. Whitefield gave unity to the movement after visiting the colonies seven times and preaching evangelical revival to crowds of up to twenty thousand. Beginning the practice of preaching outdoors, Whitefield gave impromptu deliveries and sermonized anywhere, believing that everyone should be given the opportunity to achieve salvation: "Had I a thousand lives, had I a thousand tongues, they would be employed in inviting sinners to come to Jesus Christ!" Although he stressed the centrality of the fall, his theology had universalist tendencies—all people could be saved. While focusing on individual conversion, he also attacked the clergy, who were blind, unregenerate, carnal, lukewarm, and unskilful guides." Emphasis on immediate conversion and rebirth led him to devalue book learning and other cultural diversions, although he quoted biblical passages extensively in sermons. Whitefield's refreshing intimacy with his audiences reflected the inward reflection needed for salvation. Thus his sermons included personal anecdotes, self-disclosure, and reminiscences. His pulpit outbursts and pregnant pauses motivated by love were strategies to win personal trust from his audiences. Whitefield typically asked a series of questions and repeated key phrases to his congregants, and his style was not without humor. Although persuaded by Whitefield to preach outdoors, Wesley delivered restrained and dignified homilies in America.

The Second Great Awakening occurred simultaneously in different states in the early 19th c. New England Congregationalists and Methodists practiced revivalism. The Yale College president Timothy DWIGHT's preaching converted one third of the student body in 1802. James McGready inspired revivals in 1797 with fiery preaching to congregants in Gaspar River, Kentucky. Presbyterian and Methodist ministers exhorted listeners to emotional demonstrations. Another revival in 1800 at Gaspar River included makeshift tents for long-term stay, a feature that developed into the "camp meeting." Tens of thousands attended at Cane Ridge, Kentucky in 1801 with emotive preaching by Baptist, Methodist, and Presbyterians. "Exercises" such as running, falling, jerking, and jumping were associated with the Holy Spirit. The last and most sophisticated phrase was begun by the itinerant New York preacher Charles G. Finney, who included emotional displays but sought more inward conversion. His "New Measures" included the anxiety bench, inquiry room, extended church meetings, and praying for sinners by name. Adapting his preaching style to urban areas, he was successful in large cities such as New York and Boston, and later preached abolitionism.

Attacking the excesses of this Awakening was perhaps the most influential 19th-c. preacher, Horace Bushnell, who sought a way beyond the excessive rationalism of mainstream propositional theology, and the emotionalism of revivalism. Hence his preaching used metaphor, gentle persuasion, and intimate illustrations to stimulate the religious imagination of his listeners. Stimulated by a religious revival at Yale College in 1831, Bushnell dedicated his life to overcoming "the indifference amidst this universal earnestness on every side." As lifelong minister of North Church, Hartford, Connecticut, he taught that the instant but short-term conversion experience of revivalism failed to prepare the Christian for life's vicissitudes. It denied the opportunity of growth in faith and the beneficial realities of family, church, and society. In the sermon, "Living to God in Small Things," Bushnell summarized this view: "The importance of living to God, in ordinary and small things, is in its very nature a growth." With a solemn and intense preaching presence, he gently cajoled his listeners to grow in faith. Since many of his theological ideas were derived from sermons, critics charged him with flashes of insight but underdeveloped concepts. Bushnell countered that imaginative preaching, the use of metaphor and other figures, were necessary to overcome the limitations of rationalist literalism. For him, theology was an art akin to poetry rather than science. Accordingly, preaching was an art form inciting the symbolic consciousness to undertake a pilgrimage of faith, not a sudden conversion. Bushnell's eloquence combined vivid imagery with impressive argumentation, characteristics of liberal preachers such as Ralph Waldo EMERSON and William Ellery CHANNING, and the abolitionist Theodore PARKER.

The abolitionist Henry Ward Beecher cultivated an extemporaneous and personal preaching style that won a large following at Brooklyn's Plymouth Church beginning in the 1840s. Encouraging audience interaction, Beecher extended his pulpit into his congregation: "I want the audience to surround me so that I shall be in the centre of the crowd, and have the people surge all about me." Also avoiding notes were women reform preachers such as Lucretia Mott and Abby Kelley. As a Quaker, Mott preached on feminism "as the spirit giveth utterance." Such personal preaching inspired Walt WHITMAN's revolutionary poetry that spoke directly to the reader.

Between 1870 and 1918 the Social Gospel movement attracted preachers who moved Protestant churches from individual acts of charity to reform-minded strategies. Spurred by the depression of 1873 and union battles of 1877, liberal ministers such as Theodore Munger, William Clarke, and J. H. W. Stuckenberg encouraged working people to organize. Massachusetts responded to the progressive sermons of Joseph Cook, who showed the congruence of Darwinism with Christianity, and Washington Gladden, the "father" of the movement, preached a "practical gospel" that stressed the right of labor to organize, but sought cooperation between unions and management, thus rejecting socialism. More radical was George Davis Herron, the exponent of "the Kingdom movement," who preached a restructuring of society and later left Christianity for socialism. The major figure after 1907 was Walter Rauschenbush, a German Baptist who stressed social ethics and attacked corporate greed in the gilded age but rejected secular socialism.

Civil rights, antipoverty, and Vietnam War protest motivated preaching in the 1950s and 1960s and inspired "the secular city" movement as an offshoot. Martin Luther King, Jr. used the social fervor of the Hebrew prophet with Jesus's sensitivity towards the poor and socially rejected to preach nonviolent civil disobedience in American cities. Combining literary erudition and allusions to Abraham LINCOLN's speechmaking with argumentative attacks against both gradualism and violent protest, King succeeded in unifying a disparate civil rights movement.

BIBLIOGRAPHY: Harap, L., *Creative Awakening* (1987); Newlin, C. M., *Philosophy and Religion in Colonial America* (1962); Roth, R. J., *American Religious Philosophy* (1936); Wieman, H. N., *American Philosophies of Religion* (1936)

WILLIAM OVER

SETH, Vikram
b. 20 June 1952, Calcutta, India

S.'s work has surprised the literary world at every turn. He has constantly brought new life to forms that other writers might dismiss as obsolete: the narrative in verse, the rhymed lyric, the multi-plot novel. His work, however, is always more than the technical tour de force. He is able not only to delineate characters movingly, but to describe whole societies—postpartition India of the 1950s as well as yuppie San Francisco of the 1980s. The grace and fluency of his style, whether in prose or in verse, has allowed him to make whatever world he describes seem immediate, and even familiar, to readers of any background.

S. was born into a Hindu family in Calcutta and received an English-style "Public School" education in India. He then attended Corpus Christi College, Oxford, and went on to do graduate work in demography at Stanford, making China his specialty, but also studying poetry with Donald Davie and Timothy STEELE. Both his field research in China and his study of poetry contributed to his first important book, *From Heaven Lake: Travels through Sinkiang and Tibet* (1983), in which he describes hitchhiking home to India through Tibet and Nepal, with poems interspersed.

In *The Golden Gate* (1986), S. sought to write a novel in verse, and his success was not just artistic, but commercial. The book became something of a sensation. Part of the pleasure for readers was that S. was in such command of his verse: the entire poem, from the dedication to the note on the author, is in the stanza of Pushkin's *Eugene Onegin,* complete with its intricate pattern of alternating masculine and feminine rhymes, and S. is able to use it both for Byronic comic effects and to evoke moments of real feeling. The work also owes its power to its fusion of very contemporary images and a thoroughly traditional plot. Despite the computers, the personal ads, and the punk bands on the surface, the story fits the traditional pattern of comedy, building up to not just a marriage, but a christening. And just as in a Victorian novel, there are moments of pathos and tenderness along the way: S. is capable of evoking tears, as well as laughter. The book also deals with public issues, such as the nuclear freeze movement.

S.'s novel *A Suitable Boy* (1993) is again an application of a traditional form, the multi-plot novel of Trollope or Tolstoy, to a new subject, the India of the 1950s. The central plot describes Lata Mehra's search for a husband—who turns out to be the "suitable boy" her mother finds for her in a traditional arranged marriage. But S. weaves a very large tapestry, following the fortunes of two important political families, one Hindu, one Muslim, and taking readers to settings ranging from the faculty meetings of an Anglicized university to a Hindu religious festival. The greatest appeal of the book, however, is in its narrator, who describes almost all his characters, both the good and the bad, with an appealing sympathy. Since one of

Lata's suitors is a poet, S. is also able to include a number of poetic interludes in the course of the novel.

S. has published three books of short poems, which show the same skill and fluency as the longer narratives. *The Humble Administrator's Garden* (1985) and *All You Who Sleep Tonight* (1990) contain a number of poems of great wit, metrical skill, and emotional depth. Throughout them and the longer books, S. shows a deep interest in the natural world and its preservation. That same issue appears in two works S. has addressed—at least on the surface—to children. In *Beastly Tales from Here and There* (1993), a series of fables told in octosyllabic couplets that invoke Jean La Fontaine, and in *Arion and the Dolphin* (1995), a retelling of the myth based on his libretto for an opera composed Alec Roth, S. uses the cleverest language to make clear humankind's responsibilities to the brute creation. In all S.'s work, skillful verse or prose is used, not for self-referential celebrations of art, but to describe the world in all its variety.

BIBLIOGRAPHY: Gupta, S., "The Golden Gate: The First Indian Novel in Verse," in Kirpal, V., ed., *The New Indian Novel in English* (1990): 91–100; Hill, R., "V. S.'s *The Golden Gate*," *LCrit* 21 (1986): 87–90

BRIAN ABEL RAGEN

SETTLE, Mary Lee
b. 29 July 1918, Charleston, West Virginia

The literary world has not yet recognized S.'s achievement in her historical novels. Her eighth novel, *Blood Tie* (1977), laid in contemporary Caramos, a Turkish island, won the 1978 National Book Award. S. began this novel during a three-year residence in Turkey. The novel focuses on seven English-speaking expatriates who want to make a new life in Turkey but get ensnared in repressive political action. Crowded with minor characters, the book focuses on complex major figures, suspenseful events, compelling plot movement, and perceptive creation of cross-cultural responses.

S.'s startling realism, her strong characters, and her deep sense of historical perspective make the Beulah saga her major achievement. Except for *Prisons* (1973), the books are all set in or near Canona, a fictitious city resembling Charleston, West Virginia. Each novel in the series takes place during, or just before, a public conflict or a war. The series ends with *The Killing Ground* (1982), a newly-envisioned novel designed to replace *Fight Night on a Sweet Saturday* (1964), which S. feels her editors spoiled by weakening its connection with the book that precedes it in the saga. Hannah McKarkle in the 1960s (the decade that S. feels "was the most significant revolution")

learns that her brother accidentally has killed a young black man who fell after he hit him in the Canona Jail drunk-tank. Hannah commits herself to understanding *why* the blow was struck. Essentially, S. had committed herself to understanding this fight that existed only in her mind before she wrote the four earlier books in the series to explore the question. The answer that emerges gradually in the first two books and more clearly in *The Scapegoat* (1980) and *The Killing Ground* (and, of course, *Fight Night on a Sweet Saturday*) is that political and economic protest, racial and class conflict, war, and satirical attack on the criminal justice system in American history are all inseparable from the aspirations that motivated Americans throughout their history and that had brought many to America.

In *Prisons,* set in England, young Johnny Church is executed in 1754 in Cromwell's suppression of the Lavalier radicals. Other characters in *Prisons* reach the Virginia Territory and become the ancestors of some of the five or six families who appear throughout the more than two centuries covered by the last five books in the Beulah saga, as well as in some of S.'s other books. Kinship ties of these families (Catletts, Laceys, Kreggs, McKarkles, and Crawfords) and the use of the Canona River country as setting unite the books. The historic figures (Cromwell, General Braddock, Mother Jones), who enter the novel with the fictional characters, heighten the realism and authenticity of the stories.

Hannah McKarckle in the 1960s is the namesake of Hannah McKarckle, the London pickpocket and prostitute in *Prisons,* who appears in *O Beulah Land* (1956) as an army follower who escapes when the massacre defeats General Braddock in 1774. Surviving by hiking alone across the mountains, she is nursed to health by the fanatical settler, Jeremiah Catlett. The novel ends in 1775. *Know Nothing* (1960) chronicles the equalizing of classes and the bitter conflicts between abolitionists and former Virginia aristocrats now on the frontier from 1839 to 1861. *The Scapegoat* (1980) focuses on a 1912 coal miners strike at Lacey Creek, when the mine is sold to an Eastern corporation. The Italian workers, like the Paganos, are subject to violent prejudice from the old Canona families. "Mother Jones" arrives to give socialist support to the miners. Her first speech is given to a meeting of miners' wives, and the next day she makes another persuasive speech to the rallied workers. Her messages of liberation are balanced closely by the regret for the violence and for the loss of respected local and paternalistic management of the mines. In this way, the end of *The Scapegoat* leads to the conclusion that violent confrontation and idealistic aspirations are inseparable in American history, the conclusion reiterated in *The Killing Ground.*

S.'s other books are varied and of high quality. Critics praised her first two books, *The Love Eaters* (1954) and *The Kiss of Kin* (1955), both laid in contemporary Canona or Beulah Land country. Rosamund Lehman called *The Love Eaters,* which centers on a community theater group, "this year's sharpest novel." *The Kiss of Kin,* written first as a playscript, presents a bitter rural homecoming of Canona relatives for a funeral. *The Clam Shell* (1971), based on the author's days at Sweet Briar College, and *All the Brave Promises* (1966), based on her experience in the British Women's Auxiliary Air Force (WAAF) and the Office of War Information in World War II, are good autobiographical fiction in which S. makes use of a first person narrator. In *The Scopes Trial* (1972) S. reconstructs accurately and vividly this event in American history. The dynamics of the confrontation, the record-breaking heat during the days of the trial, the town's commercial exploitation of the crowds that arrived, and the histrionic performances of the participants in the trial make S.'s prose history as compelling as her fiction.

BIBLIOGRAPHY: Dyer, J. C., "M. L. S.'s *Prisons:* Taproots History," *SLJ* 17 (Fall 1984): 26-39; Vance, J. G., "M. L. S.'s *The Beulah Quintet:* History Inherited, History Created," *SLJ* 17 (Fall 1984): 40–53

MARGARET B. MCDOWELL

SEWALL, Samuel

b. 28 March 1652, Bishop Stoke, Hampshire, England; d. 1 January 1730, Boston, Massachusetts

Probably most famous for his participation as a judge in the Salem witch trials and his later public recantation of that involvement, S. deserves also to be remembered as one of the Puritan age's greatest diarists and as an advocate of human rights. In his diary, S. offers a precise record of both his own and the New England Colony's life from the time he graduates from Harvard in 1674 until 1729, a few months before his death. Of his several tracts, S.'s most important deal with the injustice of the institution of slavery and the importance of treating the Native Americans as fellow human beings.

Unlike the journals of many of his fellow Puritans, *The Diary of S. S.,* reprinted in 1973, is neither obviously thematic nor spiritual. In covering more than fifty years, the *Diary* consists of thousands of entries concerning not only the politically important events but also such seemingly minor ones as the weather or what was served for dinner. Because S. recorded events as they occurred, his work seems to have little organization or thematic coherences. Taken as a whole, however, the *Diary* demonstrates the Puritan's concerns with God's favoring New England and the citizen's concerns with everyday life.

The *Diary* may well be best known for the courtship scenes between S. and the women he courted after the death of his first wife. Though S. has been denigrated for his concerns with economics, he has been praised for his humor, honesty, and succinctness. The *Diary* also shows S. to be a sincere family man. He includes touching accounts of his children's births, namings, baptizings, sicknesses, and deaths. As a Puritan, S. portrays his involvement with religion by recounting his frequent and extensive prayers, his reading the Bible, and his participation in many fast days. He worries incessantly about his worthiness in God's eyes as he contemplates punishments and providences. In addition to a religious life, a secular life is important in a busy, mercantile Boston. To this world, he responds by recounting political events, his own excursions, and even his dinners. He also occasionally writes of his dreams. He describes his recantation of his part in the witch trials. Possibly the single most notable subject of the *Diary* is death. Entry after entry recounts his visiting the dying, their deaths, and burials. In its providing innumerable insights into the daily life of prominent Boston citizens, S.'s *Diary* is unsurpassed.

Besides the *Diary,* S.'s important contributions to American letters include his argument against slavery, *The Selling of Joseph* (1700), America's first antislavery tract. S. bases his argument on the premise that, as heirs of Adam, all men and women have an equal right to liberty. S. insists that one's freedom is next to life itself. He uses biblical argument to maintain that slavery is unjust in that God gave the earth to all, in that Joseph was not "rightfully" a slave, and in that God condemns slave traders to death. He refutes the biblical precedent that blacks are rightfully slaves because of war or Noah's curse of Cham, and he disagrees that slavery benefits pagans by providing them Christianity. Anticipating that 19th-c. emancipationist Henry David THOREAU, S. contends that not only does the institution of slavery corrupt the slave holder, but also, in allowing a slave trade, New Englanders in general are guilty of complicity.

Besides some occasional and elegiac poetry, much of S.'s other writings concern issues of human rights. In *Phaenomena Quaedam Apocalyptica* (1697) and *Proposals Touching the Accomplishment of Prophecies* (1713), he purposes that until the American Indians—as God's children—are treated equally as Christians, Christ will refrain from coming. In *A Memorial Relating to the Kennebeck Indians* (1721), S. defends the Native Americans by arguing the fault of recent uprisings lies with the English not the Indians. Finally, in a tract of which only fragments survive, *Talitha*

Cumi, or an Invitation to Women to Look after their Inheritance in the Heavenly Mansions (1725?) S. defends the rights of women.

As a chronicler of his time and as a humanist, S. can certainly be considered a man in many ways ahead of his time. To paraphrase John Greenleaf WHITTIER's poetic comment, S. deserves praise as a staunch Puritan, but one who in many ways far outran the "halting steps of his age."

BIBLIOGRAPHY: Chamberlain, N. H., *S. S. and the World He Lived In* (1897); Kaplan, S., *The Selling of Joseph* (1969); Rosenwald, L., "S.'s *Diary* and the Margins of Puritan Literature," *AL* 58, 3 (1986): 325–41; Strandness, T. B., *S. S.: A Puritan Portrait* (1967); Thomas, M. H., ed., *The Diary of S. S.* (1973); Winslow, O. E., *S. S. of Boston* (1964)

LEE SCHWENINGER

SEXTON, Anne

b. 9 November 1928, Newton, Massachusetts; d. 4 October 1974, Weston, Massachusetts

In S.'s first book of poems, *To Bedlam and Part Way Back* (1960), nominated for the National Book Award, she emerged as a confessional poet, following in the company of her mentors W. D. SNODGRASS and Robert LOWELL and other poets such as Randall JARRELL and Theodore ROETHKE. She had found poetry, in the midst of a continuing dark depression with a suicide attempt at its core, because her psychiatrist had offered it as a way toward recovery and self-worth. This was in 1956 and S. was twenty-eight, married with two children, and living in a wealthy suburb in Massachusetts.

S. played a duet with madness and art. The darker "irrational" forces led her into the arms of poetry; once there, she crafted language to speak of her inner turmoil, and, in turn, touched her readers with collective truths of women's experience and psychological disorder. S. was both an avid learner and intuitively gifted artist and her words, which were elegantly and meticulously crafted, resonate with poetic rhythm and powerful metaphors. Her poetry was welcomed by scholars and critics—she taught at numerous universities, was appointed as a Radcliffe scholar, and became a full professor at Boston University in 1972. In 1966, S. won the Pulitzer Prize for her third book of poetry, *Live or Die*. But her fame was largely based within her audience, who appreciated the urgency, the beauty, and the honesty of her words. Language—as interpreted by S.—fed identity and uncovered meanings in her life. Yet while poetry played a vital therapeutic role for S., she would continue battling depression for the rest of her life until her suicide in 1974 at the age of forty-five.

It is difficult to separate S.'s life from her poetry because the two were infused, in many ways, like no other poet before her. Turning away from the T. S. ELIOT and Ezra POUND tenet that high poetry is not autobiographical, S. took language to its zenith of subjectivity. The body of her work revolves around her family life and her identity as a woman; as a poet, she endowed her own portrait with such force that her life took on mythical status.

With only a high school education, S. ventured into the world of literature and poetry, greatly inspired by Snodgrass's poem "Heart's Needle," which licensed her to write about "loss, neurosis, and madness." Later, Snodgrass stated that S. took after such poets as Lowell, Jarrell, and John BERRYMAN "who cultivated around themselves such emotional turbulence that biographical accounts tend to misrepresent their complexity." In 1958, S. joined Robert Lowell's seminar at Boston University, where she met the poet Sylvia PLATH. By this time, S. had joined forces with Maxine KUMIN—who was to be an influential and important friend for life—George Starbuck, and John Clellon Holmes, all from her previous night school course at Boston Center for Adult Education. Lowell's prominence, guidance, and encouragement was to play a major role in her coming out as poet.

In *To Bedlam and Part Way Back*, S. explores her mental illness, psychoanalytic images of transference, and most importantly her position as woman, mother, and daughter. Male figures were prominent in S.'s poetry and her life. In "For John, Who Begs Me Not to Enquire Further," S. aims her words as a response to the poet John Clellon Holmes, whom S. believed to be her most important influence. Holmes had warned her against telling too much of her experience in her poetry. But this poem is much grander in scheme than mere rhetoric and it universally responds to the act of confession, and the act of poetry as its transport: "And if I tried / to give you something else, / something outside of myself, / you would not know / that the worst of anyone / can be, finally, / an accident of hope." In the poem "Double Image," S. turns the mirror on herself as a woman caught between motherhood and being a daughter. She addresses the guilt of not being fully present for her daughter, Joy, and as Anne, the daughter, she looks to her own mother who, dying from cancer, blamed her illness on her daughter's suicide attempts.

In "Her Kind," which became the signature poem for her public readings, S. developed a mythic direction. "Her Kind" unearths woman as witch—the dominant image in the poem—a primeval force that is caste out of society as other: she is "possessed," a "lonely thing, twelve-fingered, out of mind." The infamous lines that end each of the three stanzas "A woman like that . . . / I have been her kind" point to a woman who is "not a woman," a woman "that is misunderstood," and a woman "that is not ashamed to die." Thus, the words become an emphatic assertion of identity for S.: as this woman (both artist and mad), she is a force that is hated and feared, but she finds an irreverent power within her estrangement. This image is also seen later in *Transformations* (1971), where her visionary voice is prominent and a return of the witch and wisewoman turn into a piercing critique of Western culture.

S.'s second book, *All My Pretty Ones* (1962), advanced the themes began in her first collection, but its focus is on the loss of loved ones in her life, including the experience of abortion. Both of S.'s parents died in 1959, and this experience resonates throughout this collection. In the title poem "All My Pretty Ones," which alludes to a line from *Macbeth*, spoken by Macduff (act 4, sc. 3), S. carries her anger at her father, but through his death there comes resolution: "Whether you are pretty or not, I outlive you, / bend down my strange face to yours and forgive you." In *Live or Die* (1966), for which S. received the Pulitzer Prize, a central theme of desperation emerges: a woman lost in the web of mental darkness, seeking a kind of metaphysics within its catacombs. In her principal work, "Flee on Your Donkey," S. lets loose images of death and resignation; entrapment within mental illness and institutions; her muse, poetry; and her helplessness and anger toward her now dead father and mother: "That was the winter / that my mother died, / half mad on morphine, / blown up, at last, / like a pregnant pig." But in her last poem "Live," there is an ultimatum given "Live or die, but don't poison everything," and in the last lines come hope: "I promise to love more if they come, / because in spite of cruelty / and the stuffed railroad cars for the ovens, / I am not what I expected. Not an Eichmann. / The poison just didn't take. / So I won't hang around in my hospital shift, / repeating The Black Mass and all of it. / I say *Live, Live* because of the sun, / the dream, the excitable gift."

Three years later, S.'s play *Mercy Street* was to echo *Live or Die,* and its subject was a suicidal woman, framed within a fragmented family: a mother who was not emotionally present and a father who was intimately provocative. *Love Poems,* published in 1969, the same year she finished *Mercy Street,* shows S.'s arrival as a survivor of her mental battles and her move toward the analysis of American culture and values. In "The Breast," "In Celebration of My Uterus," and "Song for a Lady," she landscapes the female body as a place that carries cultural meanings

and potency. In "Mr. Mine," she speaks of a woman's body as being constructed by the "industrialist." But *Love Poems* also investigates the role of the "other" woman, and in "For My Lover, Returning to His Wife" and "You All Know the Story of the Other Woman," we see S. echo the spirit of Dorothy PARKER, telling of the woman who, as S. denotes, is a man's "selection, part time."

In *Transformations,* S. changes her theme and style, bringing a surreal vision to her book of modernized fairy tales. Using the Grimm Brothers' tales as her foundation, S. uncovers the sexual subtext of these stories and transforms our cultural expectations and definitions of morality: the virgin in "Snow White and the Seven Dwarfs"; intimacy between two women in "Rapunzel"; regression and intimations of sexual abuse in "Briar Rose. However, while she accomplishes this transgression, she never leaves her own subjectivity as it is the S. universe of experience that is superimposed on the Grimm Brothers' myths.

All critics agree that S.'s later works—*The Book of Folly* (1972), *The Death Notebooks* (1974), and the last collection that she herself edited before her death, *The Awful Rowing toward God* (1975)—revolve around her growing attraction toward death and consequently a need to find spiritual insight. In *The Book of Folly,* S. repeatedly turns toward the Christ figure, but it is clear that Christianity did not afford her fulfillment; in "Jesus Unborn," she writes: "Now we will have a Christ. / He covers her like a heavy door / and shuts her lifetime up / into this dump-faced day." In 1973, S. divorced her husband and her children were away at school. It was at this time that she wrote the poems for *The Death Notebooks* that some critics believe to be her best, particularly "The Death Baby," "The Furies," and the ten-psalm "O Ye Tongues." Where S. is celebrated in her earlier work for openly embracing large themes of loss and alienation, her later works produce a body that is entirely innovative in its treatment of religion.

S. is a woman who journeyed from madness to art and from suburban housewife to highly esteemed literary figure. She is valued and admired as much for her brilliant metaphors as she is for her relentless exploration of the psyche and the spirit. S. leaves a formidable body of poetry that speaks intimately to all those alienated in society, but her voice does not carry victimhood; instead, it bears a tragic heroic stature as she marks such territory as death, mental torment, family life, religion, and the condition of women in our society.

BIBLIOGRAPHY: McClatchy, J. D., ed., *A. S.: The Artist and Her Critics* (1978); Middlebrook, D. W., *A. S.: A Biography* (1992); Morton, R. E., *A. S.'s Poetry of*

Redemption: The Chronology of a Pilgrimage (1988);
Wagner-Martin, L., ed., *Critical Essays on A. S.* (1989)

LISA TOLHURST

SHANGE, Ntozake

b. 18 October 1948, Trenton, New Jersey

Poet, novelist, short story writer, and playwright, S. was catapulted to national and international prominence with the Broadway production in 1976 of *for colored girls who have considered suicide/when the rainbow is enuf.* She is an African American feminist writer whose literary output mainly concerns the experience of being black and female. Her goal is to raise the consciousness of African Americans and other people of color and women.

As a dramatist, S. is an experimentalist and comes to the theater as a poet. In the choreopoem, which she used in *for colored girls* and other theater pieces, she blends poetry, prose, music, song, and dance. She does not use standard English, but prefers the black vernacular and sometimes profanity. In the printed text, she does not follow the standard rules of punctuation, capitalization, and spelling. She abbreviates words and breaks the flow of lines with virgules. As Neal A. Lester has stated, S. manipulates language to achieve raw emotions such as passion, anger, ecstasy, and pain.

Born Paulette Williams, S. changed her name in 1971, choosing the Zulu names Ntozake, which means "she who comes with her own things," and Shange, which means "who walks like a lion." In her name change as in her experiments with playwriting, she was making an effort to do away with European connotations and conventions and to celebrate her blackness. She has advocated that black playwrights forsake European models for their plays and move their theater into the drama of their lives.

The oppression of black women, the realization of their inner spirituality, and the evolution of a sisterhood are the subjects of *for colored girls.* This choreopoem won a variety of awards including an Obie and the Outer Critics Circle Award.

The seven characters of *for colored girls,* all multiple protagonists, are black women whose names correspond to the color of the dress each is wearing. Each dress is a color in the rainbow, except for brown, which is an earth color. While the twenty poems in the work carry the weight of this theater piece by exploring the black women's minds, the dance and music, on one level, aid in creating and intensifying the "emotional environment." On another level, they eventually help to free the women, thus enabling them to rise above their oppression and pass through mental and physical barriers.

The life explored begins with childhood and the women singing playsongs and progresses through the loss of virginity, the initiation into womanhood, and the experiences, mostly painful, that follow: selfish and insensitive lovers, betrayal and rape, abortion, the meanness of the ghetto, unintentional man-sharing among friends, the distress of lost love. Along with the experiences shared by many are the striking poetic vignettes of individual women such as the girl who discovers Toussaint L'Ouverture, the Haitian hero, in books and Toussaint Jones, a young black boy in St. Louis, and Crystal, the Lady in Red, who narrates a shattering story about the crazed Beau Willie Brown, who brutalizes her and eventually murders their two children. With Crystal's story, the climactic moment in the choreopoem is reached, and this terrifying tale stuns the women on stage, purges them, and reaches out to unite them. They share in the discovery that something important is missing in their lives—something to make them whole.

The Lady in Red relates a mystical experience that brings about the recognition of all the women's shared experiences of distress and leads to a solution. They find "god" in themselves and love her fiercely. The choreopoem culminates in a song of joy, marking the women's discovery of the value of self and transcendence over oppression, the oppressors, and the world that bred them. The separate afflicted figures at the beginning of the choreopoem now form a tight circle of women, symbolizing their support of one another—a sisterhood, a community of women. A healing has occurred. There is spiritual affirmation, and the theater piece ends on a note of hope. The rainbow, as S. has pointed out, comes after a storm, not before it. To her it is the possibility to begin again "with the power and beauty of ourselves." After looking deeply inside themselves, the "colored girls" will discover love and beauty.

Spell #7 (1979) also uses the form of the choreopoem and a play-within-a-play structure. The setting is a bar where African American actors and actresses meet and recite poetry delineating the problems of their profession, which offers them degrading stereotypical roles. They also talk about their individual problems, including the lack of love for the black woman. In the beginning of the work, the characters wear grotesque black minstrel show masks that they shed physically and metaphorically before revealing the truths about their lives. They have hidden their true selves behind these masks in order to survive in America. The huge black face mask, which is suspended from the stage ceiling and at intervals is raised and lowered, never fully disappears from the audience's view as a reminder of the oppression faced by blacks. *Spell #7* also concerns blacks learning to love themselves as well as one another. A magician, who serves as a revised interlocutor, aids in this endeavor as he casts a spell on the characters and states that they will love being colored.

Other published plays by S. include *A Photograph: Lovers in Motion* (1979), *Boogie Woogie Landscapes* (1979), and *From Okra to Greens/A Different Kinda Love Story: A Play/With Music & Dance* (1985). Described as a poemplay, *A Photograph* approaches a more conventional form of drama than the playwright's previous offerings. In *Boogie Woogie Landscapes,* dance, music, and poetry are again integral parts of S.'s work. The framework of this theatre piece, which employs expressionism, is one night of dreams, visions, and memories of Layla, a young black woman who has grown up in America. *From Okra to Greens,* a structurally complicated work in choreopoem form, has two voices. Comprised mostly of poems from S.'s earlier poetry collections and presentations, this theater piece concerns a love story between Okra, a black woman, and Greens, a black man, both of whom are poets.

In a novel entitled *Sassafrass, Cypress & Indigo* (1982), S. focuses on two sisters, Sassafrass and Cypress, who approach life differently, one as a feminist and the other as a woman who chooses to spend her life with an abusive lover. *Betsey Brown* (1985), described as a semiautobiographical novel, is the story of a thirteen-year-old African American girl growing up in St. Louis in 1959, the time of school integration in the U.S. *Nappy Edges* (1978) contains for the most part skillfully written woman-centered poems.

Critic Elizabeth Brown-Guillory describes S. as a gifted poet-playwright whose style, "one of dazzling feminist rhetoric and evocative poetry, is fascinating, powerful, and aggressive." To those who have expressed concerns about S.'s limited focus in her writings and her intended audience, Neal A. Lester has written that women as well as people of color "are demanding that their lives be recovered, reexamined, validated and hence documented accurately"; thus S.'s "work is intensely relevant to our American and global perspectives."

BIBLIOGRAPHY: Brown-Guillory, E., *Their Place on the Stage: Black Women Playwrights in America* (1988); Lester, N. A., *N. S.: A Critical Study of Her Plays* (1995)

JEANNE-MARIE A. MILLER

SHAPIRO, Karl [Jay]

b. 10 November 1913, Baltimore, Maryland

S. for many years seemed to blanket the contemporary literary scene as poet, prosodist, editor (of *Poetry* magazine and, later, *Prairie Schooner*), and general satirical gadfly. Like other members of his poetic generation, S. was of two minds, literarily speaking—he grew up during the modernist (see MODERNISM) revolution reading and admiring the great experimental poets of his day, but in the high school and college classrooms he read the traditional British and American poets and was trained in their methods. S. was a stranger neither to formal craft nor prosodic experiment.

S.'s first volume, *Poems,* was published in 1935. During the next ten years, S. wrote four other books, two of which were particularly well received: *V-Letter and Other Poems* (1944) and *Essay on Rime* (1945), both formalist volumes. The latter *tour de force,* in fact, was a study and consideration of the traditional approaches to poetry, the entire volume itself being written in verse rather than in prose mode. Not until 1958 and his *Poems of a Jew* did S. write another book that achieved an equal success.

During the 1960s, some of the formalist poets were persuaded to the new view of the Beat poets and the Black Mountain poets that formalism was no longer relevant to the times, which were becoming oriented to social activism and reform. S. was one of the first of the formalists to adopt the new stance. He gave a lecture in the early 1960s at various universities that resurrected the theories of the 19th-c. British satirical novelist Thomas Love Peacock to the effect that mankind ought to have outgrown poetry that was no more than the nursery rhymes of an infant society. S. said that if poetry was that which was "lost in translation," then he wanted his work to sound as much like translations as possible, for he wanted no part of rhymes and meters and such linguistic tinkletoys any longer.

S. joined the Beats, also, in making the connection between formal poetry and the "military-industrial complex" when he wrote in *College English,* the issue of October 1964, "An overnight collapse of the stanza might be as dangerous as the abolition of the Army. Poets still need close-order drill and the barracks mentality. It's too bad that they do. Novelists don't nor does any other kind of artist I know of. But poets are still the hostages of convention." Kenneth REXROTH had been saying exactly the same thing for years. This was not the same S. to be found in *An Essay on Rime* nor even in *Trial of a Poet.* In his volume of prose poems entitled *The Bourgeois Poet* (1964), S. tried to "out-Beat" Allen GINSBERG; by the standards of the time, however, S.'s prose poetry was quite tame and unrevolutionary.

By the time *White-Haired Lover* appeared in 1968, however, S. had done another about-face and was writing sonnets again, at least part-time, just as Peacock—despite his haranguing on the subject of formal poetry—had sneaked sonnets into his novels. To read through S.'s *Collected Poems, 1940–1978* (1978) is to ride a roller-coaster through the literary fashions of the times, during all of which S. was an academic teaching at various universities and editing periodicals mainly of an academic stripe, including the long-lived magazine that Harriet MONROE founded in Chicago, *Poetry,* originally the showcase of modernist work but, during the decade of the 1960s, one of the last bastions of formalist practice. Thus, one of the earliest of the postmodernist generation of poets, one of the first contemporary formalists, led the parade to the antiformalism in the academy, and then was the earliest of the converted to backslide again to formalism, long before the neoformalist movement got its foothold in the 1980s.

Other books by S. include *New and Selected Poems, 1940–1986* (1987); two plays, *The Tenor,* in collaboration with the composer Hugo Weisgall, produced in 1952 and published five years later, and *The Soldier's Tale* (1968); a novel, *Edsel* (1971), and various books of nonfiction. These range from scholarly books such as *English Prosody and Modern Poetry* (1947) and *A Bibliography of Modern Prosody* (1948); critical essays, such as *In Defense of Ignorance* (1960) and *The Poetry Wreck: Selected Essays, 1950–1970* (1975), a poetry handbook and a "primer for poets," and an autobiography in several volumes.

As noted, S. has been a lively presence on the literary scene for a long time; he has labored in the vineyards as well as scaled the slopes of Parnassus. He has written some poems, such as his perennial anthology piece, "The Fly," which will remain with readers for many years. S. will be remembered as a bright, if at times, erratic, writer of poetry and a fashioner of contemporary literary taste.

BIBLIOGRAPHY: Bartlett, L., *K. S.: A Descriptive Bibliography, 1933–1977* (1979); Reino, J., *K. S.* (1981); White, W., *K. S.: A Bibliography* (1960)

LEWIS PUTNAM TURCO

SHAW, Henry Wheeler

b. 21 April 1818 Lanesboro, Massachusetts; d. 14 October 1885, Monterey California

With his creation of the cracker barrel philosopher and coiner of clever aphorisms, "Josh Billings," S. achieved commercial success and national fame as one of the foremost literary humorists in America. He employed a style of writing that used misspellings and distorted grammar to comic effect in the style of fellow humorists Charles Farrar BROWNE and David Ross LOCKE. Unlike these contemporaries, S. shied away from political commentary favoring topics closer to home, from humorous sketches on human and animal

characteristics to pithy aphorisms conveying general truths. His strength was his originality in creating such graphic, surprising images as "when a feller gits a goin down hil, it dus seem as tho evry thing had bin greased fro the okashun."

Businessman and family man, S. began in midlife writing humorous pieces for local papers as a hobby. "Essa and a Muel, bi Josh Billings" (1864) caught the attention of a Boston newspaper and S. was catapulted to success. With the help of Browne, S. was able to compile and publish his witticisms in a book entitled *Josh Billings, Hiz Sayings* (1865). The book was a success leading to a career as a humor columnist at the *New York Weekly* and publication of close to a dozen more books including the annual *Josh Billings' Farmer's Allminax* (1870–79) and *Everybody's Friend, or Josh Billings' Encyclopedia and Proverbial Philosophy of Wit and Humor* (1874). The former title was S.'s most successful literary venture, selling as many as 100,000 copies per year and never less than 50,000. The *Farmer's Allminax* followed the format of a typical almanac, but satirized the usual contents—weather predictions, horoscopes, farmer's calender, and other miscellany.

S. was a craftsman who labored over his seemingly simple phrases. He wrote, "ginowine proverbs ar like good kambrick needles—short, sharp, and shiny." S.'s humor matched his general philosophy. He was a serious and gifted writer, admired for his use of language, and his unique imagery is considered key in the rise of REALISM in American letters.

BIBLIOGRAPHY: Kesterson, D. B., "H. W. S.," in Trachtenberg, S., ed., *DLB,* vol. 11, *American Humorists, 1800–1950* (1982): 429–32

JASON MCMAHON

SHAW, Irwin

b. 27 February 1913, New York City; d. 16 May 1984, Davos, Switzerland

Although S. is known for his best-selling novels, he began his literary career as an experimental playwright and also produced a body of short fiction impressive in quantity and quality. The prolific S. produced twelve novels, fourteen plays, thirteen volumes of short stories, and three works of nonfiction.

S. was born Irwin Gilbert Shamforoff. After graduating from Brooklyn College in 1934, he wrote brief radio plays (*Dick Tracy* among them), honing his skill at concise, dramatic narrative. His first play earned the twenty-three-year-old S. critical acclaim and a reputation as a social protest playwright, although S. would abandon the theater after World War II. *Bury the Dead* (1936) is a one-act, antiwar fantasy about six soldiers killed in war who rise up and refuse to be buried; it opened on Broadway to considerable critical acclaim. *The Gentle People* (1939) details a conflict between two hard-working Brooklyn fishermen and an extortionist. The gentle, tenacious workingmen prevail, and faith in the goodness of the average American becomes an important S. theme.

In 1937, S. made his first sale to the *New Yorker,* which published many of his stories, notably "Girls in Their Summer Dresses," which depicts, by subtle scenic narration, a marriage breaking up as Michael and Frances Loomis take a Sunday stroll on Fifth Avenue. Another classic is "The Eighty Yard Run," drawing on S.'s experiences as a college football player; Christian Darling tries to revive his sodden life by recalling glories on the football field, but his eighty-yard run occurred in practice. These and other stories depict the shallowness of affluent America. S.'s short fiction, collected in *Short Stories: Five Decades* (1978), is also concerned with anti-Semitism and the rise of fascism, American EXPATRIATES in Europe, the great depression and poverty.

An influence competing with the concision of radio scripts was an eight-volume fictionalized history of the Civil War that S. read, along with *War and Peace,* as a youth. Later, S. served under fire as a combat photographer in France. *The Young Lions* (1948), S.'s first novel and first major commercial success was the result. It is generally regarded as one of the major realist novels of World War II, along with Norman MAILER's *The Naked and the Dead* and James JONES's *From Here to Eternity.*

In the panoramic *Young Lions,* the war is seen through three parallel characters: Noah Ackerman, a Jewish American; Michael Whitacre, a disillusioned Broadway producer; and Christian Diestl, a German soldier. The novel depicts its protagonists before the war and during such events in the war as the Normandy invasion and the liberation of the death camps. Margaret Freemantle, a young American woman, helps unify the three stories; at the end of the novel, Diestl kills Whitacre. S. stresses, as he does elsewhere, the necessity of moral choice, especially when confronted with randomness. As Diestl consciously chooses evil, he becomes increasingly inhuman.

S.'s ninth novel after *The Young Lions* was *Rich Man, Poor Man* (1970), another panoramic novel that sold over 6,500,000 copies and became an immensely popular mini-series on television. This saga of a lower-class family of German immigrants chronicles the Jordache family through three generations, focusing on the second generation of Rudolph, Thomas, and Gretchen. Thematically, S. depicts lower class characters struggling to maintain integrity against the violence and incoherence of American life. A sequel,

Beggarman, Thief followed in 1977. In the meantime, the Cannes Film Festival setting of *Evening in Byzantium* (1973) finds film producer Jesse Craig trying to salvage his career and his integrity in a story of aesthetic concerns conflicting with commercial needs.

In the 1950s, critic John W. Aldridge rejected S. as part of an inferior generation of writers following Ernest HEMINGWAY; and Leslie A. FIEDLER dismissed S.'s work "half art." S. himself remarked that his *New Yorker* fiction initially made him a "cult figure" but that later he was considered "just a popular writer." In general, S. critics praise the short stories for their economy and understatement but deprecate the later commercial fiction. His last two novels show a more reflective S. concerned with vocation and mortality: *Bread upon the Waters* (1981) is concerned with a Brooklyn schoolteacher, and *Acceptable Losses* (1982) tells the story of Roger Damon, a literary agent whose life is threatened by a mysterious caller.

Part of S.'s mass appeal is his portrayal of vivid, believable characters and his highly skilled storytelling, which sometimes competes with improbable melodrama induced by S.'s emphasis on random disaster. S. is a sharp observer of his milieu in the realist tradition, yet he is often regarded as a superficial reporter of American and international society.

BIBLIOGRAPHY: Giles, J. R., *I. S.* (1983); Giles, J. R., *I. S.: A Study of the Short Fiction* (1991); Shnayerson, M., *I. S.: A Biography* (1989)

VICTOR K. LASSETER

SHEED, Wilfred [John Joseph]
b. 27 December 1930, London, England

An Englishman by birth, S. is one of a very few literary figures who was, nevertheless, actually born into the American literary establishment. Masie Ward, his mother, herself an author, came from a long line of English writers and married Francis Joseph Sheed, like her, a writer, publisher, and Roman Catholic intellectual. Together they founded the influential publishing house Sheed and Ward in 1926 (with an American office in 1933); it became an important force on progressive Catholic issues on both sides of the Atlantic.

Early in World War II, S. moved with his parents to Torresdale, a small town in Pennsylvania, and at fourteen he contracted polio. Rural isolation, intellectual parents, and a crippling disease all turned his thoughts to literary pursuits. His parents enrolled him in a British public school, Downside, run by the Benedictines, after which he attended Lincoln College, Oxford, graduating in 1954. A good deal of autobiographical insight can be glimpsed in his *Frank and*

Masie: A Memoir with Parents (1985) and in several of his novels.

A Middle-Class Education (1960) concerns Oxford undergraduate life and its aftermath, and *The Blacking Factory* (1968) draws on his experience at Downside and as a Roman Catholic in the Vatican II era, while *Office Politics* (1967) satirizes the power struggles of a magazine staff. He had been an editor, movie reviewer, drama and book critic for *Jubilee* and *Commonweal* before writing *Office Politics,* and he went on to forge a career in establishment publishing, working for *Esquire* and contributing articles and reviews to *Saturday Evening Post, Life, Sports Illustrated,* and the *New York Times Book Review. The Boys of Winter* (1988) revisits the insider's world of publishing, this time satirizing the book business. He traveled with Senator Eugene McCarthy's campaign for the Democratic presidential nomination, using this experience and his own travails to inform *People Will Always Be Kind* (1973), a novel describing the run of an Irish American senator, who is a polio victim, for the Democratic presidential nomination.

S.'s contribution to English and American letters has been as a stylist. Whether in fiction, journalism, biography, or criticism, his adept use of words has drawn praise from a variety of critics from his earliest writings to the present day. In fact, there is surprising critical accord in the assessment that his prose is masterfully crafted and wonderfully humorous, and as well that he has not yet lived up to his perceived potential of creating a novel of the sustained quality of John O'HARA, John UPDIKE, or Evelyn Waugh.

BIBLIOGRAPHY: Ross, W. W., III, "W. S.," in Kibler, J. E., Jr., ed., *DLB,* vol. 6, *American Novelists since World War II* (1980): 294–96

THOMAS K. MEIER

SHELDON, Charles M[onroe]
b. 26 February 1857, Wellsville, New York; d. 24 February 1946, Topeka, Kansas

S. was a respected minister of a Congregationalist church in Topeka, Kansas, whose journalistic experiments and works of fiction and nonfiction attracted international attention. By the mid-20th c., S.'s *In His Steps: "What Would Jesus Do?,"* published in serial form in 1896 and as a book in 1897, had sold about eight million copies around the world, making it one of America's most impressive best sellers. The origins of the popularity of *In His Steps* can be traced to a faulty copyright that allowed pirated editions, to the Social Gospel movement, and to the popularity of British works such as Mrs. Humphry Ward's *Robert*

Elsmere (1888) and William Stead's *If Christ Came to Chicago* (1894). More personal contexts include S.'s walks through Topeka disguised as an unemployed printer and his attempts to increase church attendance by replacing Sunday evening sermons with readings from his own didactic fictions.

In 1896, S.'s congregation heard the story of the Reverend Henry Maxwell, who is stunned during a service by the appearance of an ill and unwanted unemployed printer. The minister and a small group pledge to ask, "What would Jesus do?" before making everyday decisions. A singer spurns high paying jobs to sing for poor churches. An editor risks financial ruin by banning liquor ads and boxing news from his paper. A prosperous railroad businessman incurs the wrath of his wife and daughter for admitting his rebate practices. Maxwell's applied Christianity spreads to Chicago and elsewhere. A Christian utopia becomes a real possibility. For 19th- and early 20th-c. readers, *In His Steps* offered the appeal of exemplary lives vignettes and a simplified, action-oriented religion. Its emphasis on the necessities and joys of suffering ridicule for Christ also enabled readers to adopt vicariously a mantle of martyrdom.

BIBLIOGRAPHY: Hart, J. D., *The Popular Book* (1950); Mott, F. L., *Golden Multitudes* (1947); Parrington, V. L., Jr., *American Dreams* (1947)

KENNETH M. ROEMER

SHELDON, Edward
b. 4 February, 1886, Chicago, Illinois; d. 1 April 1946, New York City

Though largely forgotten today, S. was regarded in his heyday as the bright young hope of the American theater. A transitional literary figure, S. drew upon conventional Victorian sensibilities when introducing characters and settings of a far more naturalistic sort. His dramaturgy voiced outrage at then-contemporary injustice, seemingly to urge civic improvement if not actual reform. But though his plays evoked the sorts of issues and concerns voiced most forcibly by Ibsen, S.'s plays failed to follow through to the radical conclusions favored by many modernists, invariably concluding instead with outcomes concocted of equal parts melodrama and the romantic. Consequently, S.'s seemingly social conscious outrage served to provide a degree of sensationalism for pre-World War I audiences, careful to stay within the bounds of propriety.

Born in Chicago to well-to-do parents, S. graduated from Harvard, a prize student of legendary playwriting professor, George Pierce Baker. While still a student, S. submitted his *A Family Affair* to the play broker,

Alice Kauser. Although she rejected the play, Kauser encouraged the playwright. S.'s next effort became a great success. *Salvation Nell* (1908) portrayed a down-and-out scrub woman who finds redemption and self-esteem after joining the Salvation Army. The play proved a popular success for its star, Minnie Maddern Fiske. Set first in a run-down bar and later in a tenement apartment, and focusing upon the plight of an unwed mother, the play centered more on Nell's redemption and the rescue of her dissolute husband rather than exploring the realities of tenement life.

S. followed with *The Nigger* (1909) in which a respected segregationist decides to run for governor of a Southern state only to find he is himself partially of African American blood. Again, though portraying powerful scenes of a threatened lynching, in the end the social issue gives way to happy sentimentality. In *The Boss* (1911), S. attacks ward politics, as a corrupt, ambitious politician changes his ways thanks to the efforts of his enemy's daughter whom he loves. Period audiences found both plays hard-hitting and evocative.

S. then shifted away from realism with *Princess Zim-Zim* (1911), a comedy about a Coney Island snake charmer, and then with *Egypt* (1912), a melodrama portraying gypsy life that starred Margaret Anglin. Both plays failed. *The High Road* (1912) featured a return to realism and to commercial success. It told of a woman with a past who had subsequently rebuilt her life, become champion of the women factory workers, then governor's wife. But her past comes to haunt her when her husband becomes a Presidential candidate. Mrs. Fiske again played S.'s heroine. The play stirred controversy over whether a fallen woman ought be portrayed as "respectable."

S.'s major success was *Romance* (1913), that told of the impossible love between an Italian opera diva (again with a tarnished past) and an idealistic, young American minister. He then turned to adaptations, dramatizing Sudermann's *Song of Songs* (1914), then *The Garden of Paradise* (1914), a reworking of Hans Christian Andersen's *The Little Mermaid.*

After contracting a debilitating arthritis that eventually left him paralyzed and blind, S. remained active with the help of others. He coauthored three successful plays. *Lulu Belle* (1926), written with Charles MacArthur, sympathetically portrayed a New York prostitute. With Margaret Ayer BARNES, he wrote both the comedy *Jenny* (1929), and a lurid tale of passion and poison, *Dishonored Lady* (1930). Though bedridden, S. remained a force on Broadway. He was confidante to most of America's leading theatrical figures, and served as unacknowledged play-doctor or advisor to many dramatists, including Thornton WILDER, Robert E. SHERWOOD, and Ruth Gordon.

While S.'s subject matter and attitude now appear superficial and dated, his dramaturgy remains effective. S. created interesting and often compelling characters who, despite their melodramatic context, still ring consistent, original and true. He was a master of situation and plot construction, inventive with language, and demonstrated a genuine and gripping theatrical flare.

BIBLIOGRAPHY: Barnes, E. W., *The Man Who Lived Twice: The Biography of E. A.* (1956); Ruff, L. K., *E. S.* (1982)

STUART J. HECHT

SHEPARD, Sam
b. 5 November 1943, Fort Sheridan Illinois

Hailed by critics as the dramatic voice of his generation's underground yearnings, S. became an ironic icon for America's disaffected youth in the 1960s and 1970s. A persona whose roots were displaced Midwestern dropped into suburban plastic Southern California, S.'s generic hero is an undeniably isolated individual determined to savage the Establishment. Invariably, as well, he does not know where to turn once he has struck his rhetorically pointed blows.

Two features characterize S.'s writings. One is a rhetorical form, what critics and S. himself have called the "manic monologue." This is a freewheeling speech in which a character who has been roiling in his thoughts spews them out in what seems an unstoppable cascade. The manic monologue does not necessarily come at the play's climax, but it directs the action to a summary of theme and authorial attitude, and an associational reflection of the character's thoughts on himself, the society around him, and the life he is presently leading. A second characteristic is one not so much of technique as of thematic relevance, one in which S. presents two brothers in open but irresolute conflict. The quarrel between brothers is at base a contest between two sides of a man, the good and the bad, the irresponsible and the compassionate. S.'s most famous use of this device is found in the uproarious and frightening comedy *True West* (1980), in which two brothers battle each other to the possible murder of one of them. Their duel is cinematic Western myth, with the play closing on a variant of the "shoot-out," in this instance with one brother poised to deal a fatal hand blow to the other. This narrative exploitation is almost obsessive on S.'s part; it may be seen in *The Tooth of Crime* (1972), *Buried Child* (1979), *A Lie of the Mind* (1985), and *Simpatico* (1995), in which two friends cannot break the quasifraternal bond between them and in which, like the placement in *True West,* the brothers exchange their customary roles and take on the other's pattern of behavior.

S. was born Samuel Shepard Rogers III while his father was away on duty as a bomber pilot in Europe. S.'s father never achieved the kind of success in civilian life he enjoyed in his military career, and after moving from the Midwest to Southern California, he drifted into alcoholism. S. grew up in Duarte, a small-town suburb of Pasadena. He joined the Bishop's Company Repertory Players of Burbank, California, soon after graduating from high school; he went on a cross-country tour with the company but disembarked when the group reached New York City, where he went to live with his high school roommate, Charlie Mingus, Jr., in a Lower East Side apartment. Working as a waiter in Greenwich Village, he met Ralph Cook, who produced S.'s first plays. Increasing attention was paid to his work, and in 1966, he changed his name to Sam Shepard. His underground fame was certainly in part a reflection of his identification with the issues and concerns of his largely East Village and Off-Off-Broadway audiences. In the 1970s, his work began to be seen by larger audiences; ironically, his first critical disaster, *Operation Sidewinder,* was produced at his largest venue at the time, the Lincoln Center stage of New York. In 1979, he received the Pulitzer Prize in drama for *Buried Child,* one of his justifiably most popular and impressive plays; in treating the narrative of a family whose dirty secret must be plucked from the ground where they have tried to bury it, S. again relied on the opposition of brothers as his underlying theme and dramatic device. In the mid-1980s, his legendary productivity (he is credited in his early youth with writing a play in a day) slowed, and though for five years he did not produce a playscript, he continued to work as a film actor. In 1991, he broke his writing silence with a new play, *States of Shock,* which was both reminiscent of earlier work and dated in style and tone. What had seemed of cosmic importance in his work in an earlier decade, words and expressions unable to be mannered into reasonableness, now appeared a strained parody of the protestant spirit on Vietnam, drugs, peace demonstrations and the need to shame one's family to an awareness of its past. Fortunately, *States of Shock* proved simply one of his weaker works and not a demonstration of lasting personal damage. His next play, *Simpatico,* proved a dramatic triumph and turnaround.

S. is one of a long line of contemporary American playwrights who have used the material of their unhappy lives for a transmutation into aesthetic presentation. The dysfunctional family is at the root of his plays, notably in the family cycle that includes *Curse of the Starving Class* (1977), *True West,* and *Buried Child.* In these plays, and in his longest and most complex drama, *A Lie of the Mind,* S. presents a now-familiar triangle: the irresponsible alcoholic father who keeps running off to a desert in search of a place

where he cannot be scored; the long-suffering mother who uses a dry wit and a curtain of resignation to pass through her woes; and the sensitive son, manifesting his rebellion but often sinking into the entropy of the familial situation he is decrying. The pattern can be seen as early as his second play, *Rock Garden* (1964). S., however, is not bewailing his sad stories; his most characteristic trait is a humor that finds triumph in laughter at adversity without disguising the sorrow beneath the humor. In his early work, he showed young heroes bereft of literal and/or psychological father figures; these gave way to flaunting and strutting young men—particularly in *Fool for Love*—who found a timelessness of potency within their dated age but who knew there were limits to timelessness as well. In a mid-career play, *The Tooth of Crime,* S. showed that a star is always in danger of losing its reign in the firmament of fame—his hero, Hoss, bows out to a new and more brutal order of stardom. In this play, S. revealed the lack of a fixed order in any scheme of things, but even here he does not surrender to despair. The old order is vanquished, but the new order is not permanent either.

S. enjoyed a revival in the mid-1990s, with an entire season devoted to his work by the Signature Theatre Company in New York. It is likely his work will rekindle passion of a different order from his dramatic encounters, for he has been steadily revising his plays, and new productions in New York and elsewhere reveal a literary artist willing to succumb to thematic closure, a characteristic he avoided in his early and middle work. In the beginning, S. argued against endings as tyrannies of form and vision. Today, while speaking to youthful yearnings, he appears willing to put a measured frame of design on the mysteries of human life. He is also more willing to turn to what has been present but subterranean work—a declaration of poetry and music as the coequal sources of his inspiration and coherence of dramatic unity.

BIBLIOGRAPHY: Auerbach, D., *S. S., Arthur Kopit, and the Off-Broadway Theater* (1982); Marranca, B., ed. *American Dreams: The Imagination of S. S.* (1981); Mottram, R., *Inner Landscapes: The Theater of S. S.* (1984); Oumano, E., *S. S.: The Life and Work of an American Dreamer* (1986); Tucker, M., *S. S.* (1992)

MARTIN TUCKER

SHEPARD, Thomas

b. 5 November 1605, Towchester, Northhamptonshire, England; d. 25 August 1649, Cambridge, Massachusetts

In 1738, Scottish minister James Fraser recorded in his memoirs "I read Shepherds Sincere Convert in one of my calm fits . . . but I had not read four Leaves of him when I was thrown on my Back." Such was the early impact of S., a man now overshadowed for modern readers by such luminaries as John WINTHROP, Jonathan EDWARDS, and Increase and Cotton MATHER, but in his own day a widely influential Puritan author and divine. After earning his M.A. from Emmanuel College, Cambridge, S. was driven from England in 1635 by Anglican Archbishop Laud. He condemned the heresy of Anne Hutchinson, played a role in the organization of Congregational churches in Massachusetts, advocated educational scholarships, helped found Harvard, and engaged in missionary work with the Native Americans. An effective prose stylist, S. reveals in his works the ways in which literary art, personal faith, and social concern worked together within the New England Puritan community.

S.'s devotional works exemplified the Puritan "plain style"; its rhetorical goal was the inspiration and motivation of the reader rather than literary embellishment for the sake of aesthetic pleasure. Such evangelical writing did not forsake metaphor but employed it for an explicitly horatory and instructive purpose, and S.'s own style was known for its direct and familiar tone. Arguing in *The Sincere Convert* (1641) that the path to holiness was more a journey of struggle than a sedentary page-turning of pious tracts, he wrote that "God hath not lined the way to Christ with velvet," and "Jesus Christ is not got with a wet finger." Such functional imagery appears as well in the titles of his works calling for a compassionate and fair treatment of Native Americans, *The Day-Breaking, if Not the Sun-Rising of the Gospell with the Indians in New England* (1647) and *The Clear Sunshine of the Gospel Breaking Forth upon the Indians in New England* (1648). So important was the proper expression and reception of God's word to S. that his *Treatise of Ineffectual Hearing of the Word* (1652) called for a renewed emphasis on the rhetorical effectiveness of sermons, noting that "there is much preaching, but few serious, few heart-breaking Sermons." A collection of his own sermons, *The Parable of the Ten Virgins,* appeared in 1660.

Throughout his own difficult life, S. struggled in good Puritan fashion to see the guiding hand of God. In his *Journal,* not fully published until 1972, he maintained a spiritual record in the tradition of St. Augustine's *Confessions,* but it is in his *Autobiography* (1832) where we learn of his early life as an orphan as well as the death of his first wife during the voyage to Massachusetts and of his first son shortly thereafter. He later married the daughter of Puritan divine Thomas HOOKER, suffered the death of two more sons and later his second wife, and married a third time and had another son, to whom he dedicated the work. S.'s

account frankly depicts his own religious doubts and scruples. The work is intended as an instructive object-lesson based on his efforts to achieve a providential reliance upon God, and offers a useful contrast to the more deistic self-reliance displayed in Benjamin FRANKLIN's *Autobiography.* S.'s account can be read as a personal rendering of his two later significant doctrinal works *The Sincere Convert* (1641) and *The Sound Believer* (1645), the latter emphasizing God's loving mercy toward the converted, the former focusing on the dismal suffering of the unsaved.

In view of the personal trials that tested his own faith, it is perhaps not surprising that S. should have attacked so vigorously the doctrine of Antinomianism, which discounted the authority of all religious laws and strictures apart from those dictated by an individual's personal conviction of faith as imparted by God's grace. Between 1636 and 1638, it caused a theological and political battle in the Bay Colony that resulted in the banishment of Anne Hutchinson to Rhode Island and the resignation of Governor Henry Vane, who was replaced by John Winthrop. S., a key inquisitor at Hutchinson's trial in Boston in March 1638, asserted that "she is of a most dayngerous spirit and likely with her fluent Tounge and forwardnes in Expresssions to seduce and draw away many, Espetially simple Weomen of her owne sex." Clearly, Hutchinson's rhetoric was as effective as his own, but to him, it served heretical ends from which the colony needed protection.

The Puritan experiment had other challenges to which S. responded. In 1636, the English Presbyterian John Ball had published nine questions addressed to the Puritan colonists that were then answered in 1639 by John Davenport. In 1648, S. and John Allin composed *A Defense of the Answer,* which defended Davenport's essay. *A Defense of the Answer* summarized the essentials of Massachusetts church polity and liturgy, and S.'s preface outlined a guiding vision that confirmed him as a key architect of New England Puritanism. In that same year, he contributed to the Cambridge Platform, the defining code of Congregationalism.

S. died in 1649, having lived out the description of the "wayfaring Christian" described in John Milton's *Areopagitica* five years earlier. Always conscious of his own failings, yet always determined to overcome them so as to serve his vocation, he reveals through his sermons, essays, tracts, and personal writings the driven, introspective, visionary Puritanism that helped shaped American culture. In Cotton Mather's words, S.'s life was "a trembling walk with God."

BIBLIOGRAPHY: Gallagher, E. J., and T. Werge, eds., *Early Puritan Writers: A Reference Guide* (1976);

McGiffert, M., ed., *God's Plot: The Paradoxes of Puritan Piety* (1972); Werge, T., *T. S.* (1987)

CHRISTOPHER BAKER

SHERWOOD, Robert E[mmet]

b. 4 April 1896, New Rochelle, New York; d. 14 November 1955, New York City

S. won four Pulitzer Prizes, three in drama for *Idiot's Delight* (1936), *Abe Lincoln in Illinois* (1938), and *There Shall Be No Night* (1940), and one for his two-volume study of the World War II relationship between Franklin D. Roosevelt, for whom S. wrote speeches, and Harry Hopkins, *Roosevelt and Hopkins* (1948). S.'s script *The Best Years of Our Lives* (1946) won the Academy Award.

Over three decades, S. wrote fifteen plays, one novel, twelve screenplays, and the Roosevelt/Hopkins volumes. He also completed *Second Threshold* (1951) after its author, Philip BARRY, died. Although his work was seldom innovative, S. was a competent playwright, nine of whose dramas had runs of over one hundred Broadway performances. *Abe Lincoln in Illinois,* S.'s best-known play, had 472 performances and is still frequently performed.

S. represents a liberal romanticism manifested in the strident pacifism that pervaded his writing until *There Shall Be No Night* (1940). In this play, he spoke out about the despotism sweeping Europe with the rise of Nazi Germany and called for good people to resist such evil.

S. was a facile writer, often writing a play quickly to escape from the financial problems in which he was often immersed. His first play, *The Road to Rome* (1927), which had 392 Broadway performances, was written in three weeks when his wife's extravagance brought him to the brink of bankruptcy. The play poses the question of why Hannibal, after his many conquests, retreated from the gates of Rome, which he could easily have conquered. S.'s answer is that after Amytis, wife of Fabius Maximus, is captured and lures Hannibal into a tryst, Hannibal sees no further glory in conquest, proclaiming, "There is a thing called the human equation."

Waterloo Bridge (1930), examining the effects of war upon young love, was not a Broadway success but succeeded as a film. *The Virtuous Knight* (1931), S.'s only novel, set in the time of the Crusades, is another call for pacifism, as is *Acropolis* (1933), a commercial failure that remains unpublished. *Reunion in Vienna* (1931), written in three weeks, was a successful drawing room drama that diverted audiences from the gloom of the Great Depression and from a deteriorating European political situation. It focuses

on clandestine attempts to keep an exiled nobility alive in the face of a powerful Austrian bourgeoisie.

The Petrified Forest (1935) and *Idiot's Delight* (1936) did much to solidify S.'s dramatic reputation. Both plays create highly confined microcosms in which questions of good and evil are played out. In *The Petrified Forest,* a gangster Duke Mantee holds at bay a ragtag group in an isolated desert roadside cafe, while, in *Idiot's Delight,* the Italian government confines an internationally diverse group to a hotel just over its Swiss/Austrian borders. Both plays call for nonviolence. *Abe Lincoln in Illinois* scrutinizes a thirty-year span in Lincoln's life, from the time he was a young postmaster to his election as president. S. examines the moral dilemmas that constantly haunted Lincoln, basically a man of peace.

In *There Shall Be No Night,* S. could no longer advocate peace at any cost. Hitler's invasion of Poland and its aftermath demanded unequivocally that evil must sometimes be controlled by force, which is the theme of this play set in wartime Finland.

BIBLIOGRAPHY: Brown, J. M., *The Worlds of R. E. S.* (1965); Brown, J. M., *The Ordeal of a Playwright* (1970); Meserve, W. J., *R. E. S.* (1970); Shuman, R. B., *R. E. S.* (1964); Shuman, R. B., "The Shifting Pacifism of R. E. S.," *SAQ* 65 (1966): 382–89

R. BAIRD SHUMAN

SHILLABER, B[enjamin] P[enhallow]

b. 12 July 1814, Portsmouth, New Hampshire; d. 25 November 1892, Chelsea, Massachusetts

Although his literary reputation rests almost entirely on the creation of a single fictional character, S. was a respected 19th-c. humorist (see HUMOR) and editor whose work forms an important link between early American humor and later post–Civil War tradition and who influenced the writing of Samuel Langhorne CLEMENS, Charles Farrar BROWNE, and other significant humorists.

After serving for seven years as a book compositor for the Boston publishing firm of Tuttle and Weeks, S. in 1840 accepted a job as printer for the Boston *Post,* a venerable newspaper that employed a galaxy of local writers whose forte was humor. S.'s daily association with these humorists influenced his early efforts in that genre.

Although his duties remained primarily those of a printer, S. was gradually given the opportunity to write for the paper. His initial contributions were short pieces to a miscellaneous column called "All Sorts of Paragraphs." By 1847, he appears to have become the major contributor to this column, which became a popular feature of the *Post,* printing verse, anecdotes, notes on local cultural and social events, political commentaries, and important national news.

On February 26, 1847, S. took his first step toward national recognition as a humorist when he inserted in "All Sorts of Paragraphs" his first brief "Mrs. Partington" sketch, a passing comment on the bad taste of Boston city water: "Mrs. Partington insists that she will have to put *alkali* into her tea to destroy the taste of the *ile.*" With this brief passage was born one of the most beloved and widely read creations in 19th-c. American humor. Although her first appearance attracted little attention, Ruth Partington captured public notice with her second brief appearance in the *Post* on July 5, commenting on the rising cost of flour: "Mrs. Partington says that she has always noticed that, whether flour is dear or cheap, she invariably had to pay the same money for a half dollar's worth." When a number of newspapers and magazines reprinted this little bit of humor, S. was encouraged to develop Mrs. Partington's character, and she soon became a regular feature of "All Sorts of Paragraphs." Under S.'s pen, she took the character of a prim, proper, sparsely educated but assertive widow from the provinces who couched her freely given opinions on every conceivable subject in a tidal wave of malapropisms.

As these sketches lengthened, S. added a mischievous nephew Ike and a supporting cast of friends and acquaintances of distinct and humorous character whose function basically was to instigate Mrs. Partington's laughable digressions on religion (especially Calvinism), politics, medical trends, and other current topics of the day. Ike Partington may well have influenced Mark Twain's characterization of Tom Sawyer, and more than one critic has identified Ruth Partington herself as the prototype of Tom's Aunt Polly. Her three major props, Dr. Spooner, Old Roger, and Widesworth, represented respectively, S. noted, "the profound, the jolly, and the sentimental."

Despite the almost instant success of Mrs. Partington, S. left the *Post* in 1850 in search of greater independence and income. After a brief stint as editor of the *Pathfinder and Railway Guide,* he joined with John T. Trowbridge, Silas W. Wilder, and Charles G. Halpin in 1851 to found the *Carpet Bag,* the first magazine in America devoted exclusively to humor. With S. as editor, the paper's announced purpose was "to promote cheerfulness . . . affording both amusement and instruction." S. himself helped fulfill this purpose by contributing a variety of humorous sketches, poems, and editorials.

Although the *Carpet Bag* was never a financial success, it is historically important both as a testimony to the nature and direction of early American humor

and as the magazine that published the first significant writings of Charles Farrar Browne ("Artemus Ward"), George Horatio Derby ("John Phoenix"), and especially Samuel Langhorne Clemens, who anonymously submitted "The Dandy Frightening the Squire" for the 1 May 1852 issue. Despite publishing the works of these and other leading humorists, the *Carpet Bag* ceased publication after only two years, and S. reluctantly returned to the Boston *Post* as a reporter.

At the urging of friends, S. in 1853 published his first book, *Rhymes with Reason and Without,* a collection of poems of various modes, most of which he had previously published in the *Post* or the *Carpet Bag.* Although his poetry would never achieve the popularity or reputation of his humorous anecdotes, this first volume was praised by such readers as Oliver Wendell HOLMES and William Cullen BRYANT. A much later compilation, *Lines in Pleasant Places* (1874) did little to enhance his reputation as a poet, although S. would continue to publish poems in magazines and newspapers until his death.

Encouraged by the continuing popularity of his Mrs. Partington sketches, S. collected the best of them for *The Life and Sayings of Mrs. Partington and Others of the Family* (1854). The book quickly sold over 50,000 copies, and its success spawned three new compilations over the next three decades: *Knitting-Work: A Web of Many Textures, Wrought by Ruth Partington* (1859); *Partingtonian Patchwork* (1872), and *Mrs. Partington's New Grip Sack* (1890). As with the first Mrs. Partington book, most of the anecdotes in the later volumes were culled from S.'s newspaper and magazine sketches. None of the later titles, however, matched the popularity or sales of S.'s initial effort.

In addition to his Partington books and his poetry compilations, S. published four books for boys between 1879 and 1888, two of them featuring Ike Partington. They failed to capture a large audience, however; and S. came to realize that his forte was the short, humorous anecdote.

By the time of his death in 1892, S.'s popularity had been supplanted by Clemens, Browne, and other postwar humorists; and the extremely topical nature of Mrs. Partington's humor found no new audience. But through the creation of a truly memorable comic character and through his editorship of the influential *Carpet Bag,* S. earned a place in American literary history.

BIBLIOGRAPHY: Clemens, C., "B. S. and His 'Carpet Bag,'" *NEQ* 14 (September 1941): 519–37; Coleman, R., "Trowbridge and S.," *NEQ* 20 (June 1947): 232–46; Reed, J. Q., *B. P. S.* (1972)

WILLIAM K. FINLEY

SHIRER, William L[awrence]

b. 23 February 1904, Chicago, Illinois; d. 28 December 1993, Boston, Massachusetts

S.'s best-known work, *The Rise and Fall of the Third Reich: A History of Nazi Germany* (1960), demonstrates his special talent: an eye for the significant and an ability to convey that significance in gripping prose. As journalist and author, S. was a major figure in shaping Americans' views of the world abroad because he was, as the historian James McGregor Burns eulogized him, the man "who chronicled some of the most splendid and the most terrifying events of the century."

S.'s career in journalism began during his years at Coe College, Iowa, where he was a sports reporter for the *Cedar Rapids Republican*. After graduation, determined to escape American "prohibition, fundamentalism, puritanism, Coolidgeism, [and] Babbitry," he worked his way to Paris on a cattle boat, and landed a job at the copy desk of the Paris edition of the *Chicago Tribune*, right next to James THURBER. Immersing himself in European history and languages—he became fluent in German, French, and Italian—he was chosen to be the European correspondent for the *Chicago Tribune* and covered such events as Charles Lindbergh's solo flight across the Atlantic and the League of Nations conferences in Geneva. By 1929, he was chief of the *Chicago Tribune*'s central European bureau in Vienna; during the early 1930s he traveled throughout India at Gandhi's side, eventually turning his observations into his *Gandhi: A Memoir* (1980).

As a result of his position as the European correspondent for *Universal News Service* in 1935, S. was posted to Berlin, where for the next eight years he witnessed and reported on Hitler's Third Reich. S.'s skills in observing and interpreting events for his American audience kept him continually in trouble with the German censors and led to denunciations by Josef Goebbels. S.'s daily observations comprise his first book, *Berlin Diary: The Journal of a Foreign Correspondent, 1934–1941* (1941), an eyewitness account of life in prewar Nazi Germany.

S. continued his broadcast and print journalism—during the war years he and Edward R. Murrow anchored CBS's European broadcasts—until he was blacklisted during the McCarthy era for supporting the "Hollywood Ten." At this point, S. was unemployable; his only source of income came from the lecture circuit—"one-night stands" at universities, which S. later described as "the only place in the country that still had some sort of respect for freedom of speech."

Prevented from working in journalism, S. used these years to research and write *The Rise and Fall of the Third Reich*, a massive history based on S.'s

diaries, his own reports, captured German documents, and transcripts of the Nuremberg trials. A Book-of-the-Month Club selection and best-seller, *The Rise and Fall of the Third Reich* combines exhaustive documentation, memorable details, and telling anecdotes into a lively and readable history. While S.'s work has been criticized for its focus on Nazi excesses, it is this very quality of melodrama that makes for such compelling and accessible reading.

Despite charges of sensationalism and superficiality, S.'s nonfiction books for both adult and juvenile audiences are distinguished by his unerring grasp of the importance of an event and his ability to interpret as well as to report; his writing has been described as personal and passionate, but never prejudiced. S.'s work appeals to the scholar and lay reader alike; his particular strength is his talent to capture a vivid sense of presence: the reader becomes eyewitness.

Although S. wrote several novels as well as history for juveniles, his other notable work includes his three-volume autobiography: *Twentieth-Century Journey: A Memoir of a Life and the Times, Volume I: The Start, 1904–1930* (1976); *Volume II: The Nightmare Years, 1930–1940* (1984); and *Volume III: A Native's Return* (1990). As journalist and as historian, S. chronicled world events for over half a century. Even more important, however, he enabled his readers to understand the larger significance of those events he witnessed.

BIBLIOGRAPHY: Henderson, A., "W. L. S.," in Rood, K. L., ed., *DLB*, vol. 4, *American Writers in Paris, 1920–1939* (1980): 353–56; Rosenfeld, G. D., "The Reception of W. L. S.'s *The Rise and Fall of the Third Reich* in the United States and West Germany, 1960–1962," *JCH* 29 (January 1994): 95–128

JUDITH E. FUNSTON

SHORT STORY, The

Most literary historians generally agree that the short story is the unique contribution of America to world literature. Indeed, Frank O'Connor asserted that the short story was America's national art form. Though there were collections of "tales" going back to ancient Greek, Hebrew Bible, and medieval times—called legends, fables, and parables—the earliest manifestation of the short story in America appeared as "sketches" in Washington IRVING's *The Sketch Book of Geoffrey Crayon* (1820). However, these "sketches" did not appear at the time as anything uniquely American. Rather, they came out of Irving's familiarity with the romance novels of Sir Walter Scott and a European folklore tradition brought over by German immigrants who settled in New York state in the 18th c. The most famous of these tales, "Rip Van Winkle" and "The Legend of Sleepy Hollow," became the earliest examples of short prose narratives that evolved gradually into the bedrock of what became the "short story."

It was, however, Edgar Allan POE's role as a critic and short story theorist—not as a short story writer—that unintentionally formulated the earliest characteristics of the short story. It was Poe's 1847 review of Nathaniel HAWTHORNE's *Twice-Told Tales* in *Graham's Magazine* that defined the heart of Hawthorne's genius as his ability to create in his stories "a unique and single effect." Poe added that a story's emotional effect came out of its organic unity—that is, every word, sentence, and paragraph should move towards the establishment of a single powerful effect that the reader will never forget. Poe also stated that the short story—because of its tightly coherent structure—belongs "to the highest regions of art."

Poe's own short stories certainly adhered to his own theory of what constitutes the power of the short story to move the reader. In both Poe's and Hawthorne's stories, spiritual and psychological conflicts take center stage as isolated and guilt-laden souls try to work out their sanity and/or salvation. G. K. Chesterton best characterized such dilemmas as "the morbid life of the lonely mind." Most of Hawthorne's and Poe's characters suffer alone, at the mercy of their own tortured minds. Their stories established loneliness and isolation as permanent themes from the beginning of the American short story up to the present time. If all stories are variations on the theme of isolation versus community—that is, a character moves from a condition of isolation to a condition of community, or from community to isolation, the stories of both Poe and Hawthorne document their characters' inexorable aloneness. But their "fall" from the "grace" of their childlike innocence is that they realize they are alone.

Henry JAMES's European experience, and its older culture, enabled him to explore the themes of loneliness and isolation even more profoundly than Poe and Hawthorne. And though Hawthorne was a major influence on James, James's "The Real Thing" and "The Beast in the Jungle," among many stories, treat even more extensively the agonies of the solipsistic mind that result not from the discovery of evil beneath the surface of everyday life—Hawthorne's traditional territory—but the psychological and spiritual abyss that threatens his characters' identity.

Herman MELVILLE combined the moral dilemmas of Hawthorne with the psychological crises of James in such brilliant stories as "Bartleby the Scrivener," a character who becomes the first antihero in American literature, and whose tortured consciousness is as contemporary as a John CHEEVER or John UPDIKE story.

As America expanded, so too did the boundaries of its writers. The movement from the haunted Calvinism of the East to the invigorating development of the Midwest and the West resulted in what became known as REALISM. Geography—or setting—became much more significant in Bret HARTE's California gold mine stories, Joel Chandler HARRIS's tales of Uncle Remus and, most significantly, the realistic humor of Mark TWAIN. America was developing its own folk tradition as the South, the Midwest, and the West grew due to the effects of the Northeast's industrial expansion, a pattern that culminated in the Civil War in the 1860s. Classic Twain stories such as "The Celebrated Jumping Frog of Calaveras County" became the first examples of tall tales attaining the status of respectable literature. Twain's later pessimistic stories, "The Man Who Corrupted Hadleyburg" and "The Mysterious Stranger," demonstrated his movement from local color humorist to philosophical commentator. A more ominous tone was taken up by other realistic and naturalistic writers such as Stephen CRANE, Jack LONDON, Hamlin GARLAND, Frank NORRIS, and Edith WHARTON in the late 19th and early 20th cs.

Certainly Crane's classic stories such as "The Blue Hotel," "The Open Boat," and "The Bride Comes to Yellow Sky" pushed the boundaries of realism toward a more naturalistic philosophical position, and thus expanded a local bleakness into cosmic indifference. Though Crane never participated in the brutality of the Civil War, his work absorbed its dark lessons and decisively darkened the tone of American literature. No writer combined the realism of Crane and Twain with the psychological depth of Henry James as successfully as Sherwood ANDERSON. And his small-town characters are even more deeply alone that James's sophisticated city dwellers; Anderson's forlorn antiheroes become victims of a society moving from an agrarian to an industrial culture. Anderson's *Winesburg, Ohio* shows sensitive and innocent characters suffering from their stifled sexuality, exacerbated by their inability to articulate their frustration. The stories of O. HENRY reveal the isolated lives of working-class citizens of New York City, though some of his early stories took place in the Southwest. He is most famous for stories of personal redemption, showing lonely characters moving from isolation to community. These tales became part of every high-school short story textbook. "The Last Leaf," "The Gift of the Magi," and "The Ransom of Red Chief" became touchstones of O. Henry's contribution to the American short story: the surprise ending. A highly prolific writer, he published over three hundred stories from 1904 to 1917. By the end of the 19th c. and the early years of the 20th c., short story writers could make a substantial living selling their stories to mass-circulation magazines and Sunday supplements, where James, Crane, London, and Willa CATHER—along with O. Henry—became famous.

There is a little question, though, that World War I had a tremendous influence on themes that postwar writers eventually pursued. Though Ernest HEMINGWAY was strongly influenced by Twain, Crane, and Anderson, his fictionalized wartime experiences and life in Europe internationalized American literature. Though he wrote about European culture, Hemingway's style revolutionized American prose style by the simplicity of his language and the tightness of his narratives. His dialogue became not only a narrative technique but also a revelation of character. And it is clear in his first story collection *In Our Time* that the influences of James Joyce, Guy de Maupassant, Gustave Flaubert, and Gertrude STEIN are clearly operative. Hemingway's influence changed the direction of not only American short fiction, but also English and Irish literature. Irish writers like Frank O'Connor, Liam O'Flaherty, and especially Sean O'Faolain—who called him "the real man"—were irrevocably changed by Hemingway's "American" prose style.

William FAULKNER's short stories explored the sense of loss and despair that the post–Civil War South underwent right up through the early part of the 20th c. The stories in *These Thirteen* also lamented the emergence of a new breed of Southerner, bereft of the civilizing customs of Southern culture. But Faulkner's major contribution to the short story genre was his collection of cycle stories in *The Unvanquished* and *Go Down Moses*. The Gothic mindset of Faulkner's best work spilled over into a later Southern writer, Flannery O'CONNOR, who replaced Faulkner's post–Civil War despair with a surreal grotesqueness set in a world of existential emptiness. Her collection *A Good Man Is Hard to Find* simmers with Faulknerian darkness, but unexpected intrusions of the sacred in the midst of the spiritual tawdriness of the modern world make her religious vision both compelling and disturbing.

F. Scott FITZGERALD's *Tales of the Jazz Age* named the era in which his "sad young men" left their Midwestern roots to lose their innocent dreams in the materialism of Northeastern cities. "The Rich Boy" and "Winter Dreams" are prime examples of Fitzgerald's highly sophisticated and elegant prose, which owes little to the styles of Hemingway or Faulkner. All three writers were influenced by the psychological theories of Freud and Jung, where the unconscious plays decisive roles. Hemingway and Faulkner were also affected by cultural anthropologist G. S. Fraser's *The Golden Bough;* and Fraser's emphasis on the determining importance of myth and ritual found sympa-

thetic ears in virtually all short story writers from the 1920s to the present.

An important female short story writer from the 1930s through the 1950s was Katherine Anne PORTER. Porter's first collection *Flowering Judas* quickly became a favorite with writers, and she came to be regarded as a writer's writer because of the perfection of her craft. She was a stylist of the highest order. She is also considered a member of a Southern Renaissance coterie. Robert Penn WARREN ranked her with Joyce, Hemingway, and Sherwood Anderson as one of modern literature's most trenchant psychological analysts.

Though Eudora WELTY is considered by some as a Southern writer—even a regional writer—her work combines the sophistication of Porter with the depth of the writers she most admires: Joyce, Virginia Woolf, and the Irish writer, Elizabeth Bowen. "Why I Live at the P.O." and "Shower of Gold" demonstrate her ability to deftly create dramatic monologues second to none. Many of her stories reveal a lyrical quality that she uses to highlight the significance of both setting and character, a technique she may very well have picked up from another writer she admired, Willa Cather.

Certainly the two most popular and respected short story writers after World War II are John Cheever and John O'HARA. And the *New Yorker* became the primary vehicle through which these superb writers became famous. Cheever published over one hundred stories there, but O'Hara well over three hundred. O'Hara published a dozen short story collections, most of them set in a mythical eastern Pennsylvania town called Gibbsville, his Yoknapatawpha County. They are ironic tales about social class, and the sexual and drinking habits of the wealthy and not so wealthy. His subtle handling of dialogue reveals both character and class distinctions.

Cheever's early stories in *The Way Some People Live* concern the brutal effects of the Depression and the stifled sexuality of lonely people in New York city. Only with the appearance of his first best-selling collection, *The Enormous Radio and Other Stories,* did he begin his lifelong habit of "mythologizing the commonplace," a method he used to expand his stories and his Westchester settings into the larger contexts of Greek and Roman myths. From 1953 onward, Cheever was one of America's major mythic writers. His later stories also revealed a satirical edge, which he used to condemn the relentless onslaught of a destructive and dehumanizing technology.

From the 1920s through the 1940s and early 1950s, short story writers had been able to make a substantial living writing for major publications like the *Saturday Evening Post*, *Collier's*, *Harper's*, the *Atlantic Monthly, Scribner's*, the *New Yorker,* and many other magazines. However, the growing presence of television, starting in the 1950s, began to undermine the reading habits of many Americans. As a result, the popular market for short fiction shrank dramatically, and most writers could find markets for their stories only in literary journals usually associated with universities. The few mass-market magazines that publish short fiction still pay well for them, but only the *New Yorker* publishes a story a week, whereasas *Esquire, Playboy, Redbook,* the *Atlantic Monthly,* and *Harper's* publish a story a month. Many writers were forced to find employment in the universities to support themselves and their families. The universities established Master of Fine Arts programs and writing workshops based on the earliest model, the Iowa Writers Workshop, which began in the late 1940s. However, a number of writers choose not to identify themselves with academic programs, and instead started their own little magazines such as the *Floating Bear, Big Table, Lillabulero* and other maverick presses. They felt uncomfortable associating themselves with conservative journals like the *Kenyon Review, Sewanee Review,* or *Southern Review,* which were associated with and supported by academic institutions.

After World War II, short fiction writers can be divided into three major categories: realists or neorealists—which included the so-called minimalists; postmodernists, or metafictionists; and those outside any definable categories, who can be called outsiders or mavericks. The largest group are realists or neorealists, and the neorealists' foremost practitioners were sometimes labeled minimalists. Raymond CARVER is considered the figurative father of both the neorealists and the subgroup of minimalists. But behind Carver's powerful impact on both the content and language of contemporary short fiction, is the influence of what one critic called "The School of Gordon Lish." LISH was fiction editor at *Esquire* for many years and a crucially important editor at Alfred A. Knopf after his *Esquire* years. In those positions he fostered new writing and published Carver's early work along with James Salter, Barry Hannah, Mary ROBISON, David LEAVITT, and many other fresh literary and stylistic voices.

Carver influenced many other writers whose work became popular in both academic journals and mass market publication, but whose work, like Carver's, dealt with the lives of working-class or blue-collar workers. Among others, Ann BEATTIE, Andre DUBUS, Russell BANKS, and Richard FORD have been labeled "Dirty Realists" who write "Trailer-Park Fiction." Many of the protagonists in their stories are rootless and poverty-ridden. Typical characters are troubled by alcoholism, drug-addiction, divorce, and other self-destructive behaviors. All of these authors articulate their characters' inability to express themselves—their

inarticulateness—with painful clarity and subtle poignance. And, thus, the stylistic influence of Stein, Joyce, and Hemingway via Carver reemerged in the late 1960s and throughout the 1970s and 1980s. Certainly collections such as Carver's *Will You Please Be Quiet, Please?,* Ford's *Rock Springs,* Banks's *Trailerpark,* Beattie's *Distortions,* and Dubus's *Adultery and Other Choices,* are classic examples of minimalist writing, combined with the content of the "Dirty Realists." And even though these stories are about families, the prevailing condition of the protagonists is one of torpid solitude. It is no wonder that Frank O'Connor's classic text on the short story is called *The Lonely Voice.* From Nathaniel Hawthorne and Henry James down to the present day, the subject of loneliness may be the primary preoccupation of the American short story. And a part of many of these writers' subjects is "the morbid life of the lonely mind."

Because of the postwar influence of Samuel Beckett, Franz Kafka, and André Breton, many American writers chose the path of what became known as postmodernism or metafiction. Certainly Gordon Lish, Donald BARTHELME, John BARTH, Walter ABISH, and Robert KELLY, among others, demonstrate the importance of language as the formulator of perception and, therefore, that which defines or creates "reality." Classic texts from this school of writers are Lish's *Mourner at the Door,* Barthelme's *Come Back, Dr. Caligari,* Abish's *Minds Meet,* and Kelly's *A Transparent Tree.*

There are writers, though, who do not comfortably fit under any category and may be considered mavericks or outsiders. Charles BUKOWSKI, Alfred CHESTER, Wanda Coleman, and Lucia Berlin depict the hopeless lives of alcoholics and drug addicts with stunning and sometimes shocking accuracy in the lives of the Los Angeles homeless (Bukowski), gay men (Chester), African American women (Coleman), and Southwestern housewives (Berlin). Fielding Dawson's experimental stories vividly explore the agonies of struggling artists and writers. And no other short story writer deals with the subject of innocence so luminously as Guy DAVENPORT does in the Fourierist parables of *Apples and Pears and Other Stories* or *The Jules Verne Steam Balloon.* Harold BRODKEY's stories also trace the perils of innocence, but in a predominantly Freudian mode.

Also a Freudian, though a comic one, Stephen DIXON is the busiest experimental realist working in America today. He is certainly the most prolific short story writer today, with over four hundred stories in print. Geographically his stories take place, for the most part, in New York City, and highlight in sometimes surrealist visions the problems and difficulties of living a "normal" life in its chaotic confines. *All*

Gone best embodies the way Dixon experiments with how language creates systems of entrapment.

Charles Baxter writes of middle-class constraints peculiar to the American Midwest, while Leonard Michaels, Elizabeth TALLENT, and Tobias WOLFF detail troubled domestic lives in the West and the Northwest. And certainly Grace PALEY's spare but elegant stories reveal the difficult lives of first-generation New York Jewish immigrant with vivid accuracy. Lee K. Abbott depicts the haunted lives of Vietnam veterans as starkly as Wolff, but in a Southwestern context; while Ellen GILCHRIST and George GARRETT explore the remnants of an Old South that cannot stay buried in a contemporary world bereft of moral values.

There are, however, signs that the short story has gained considerable ground due to the consistent efforts of some universities. The University of Pittsburgh's Drue Heinz Literature Prize for short stories; and the short story prizes given by the University of Missouri, the University of Illinois, and the University of Georgia, all encourage and support short story writers. Prize-winning stories also appear in annual publications such as *Best American Short Stories* and the *O. Henry Prize Annual*, volumes of which are readily available in most large bookstores and keep alive the public's interest in America's unique contribution to literary history.

There are signs that the short story is gaining ground and enjoying a small but definite renaissance due to the efforts of the university presses, the academic quarterlies, the little magazines, and the flourishing writing programs that promote and nurture fresh talent. Though short stories do not sell as well as novels, they are now available to the general public, and maintain a respectable sales margin, proof that America's unique contribution to world literature continues to thrive.

BIBLIOGRAPHY: Klinkowitz, J., *Structuring the Void* (1992); May, C., *The Short Story* (1995); Peden, W., *The American Short Story* (1975); Stevick, P., *The American Short Story, 1900–1945* (1984); Voss, A., *The American Short Story* (1961); Weaver, G., *The American Short Story, 1945–1980* (1983); West, R. B., Jr., *The Short Story in America, 1900–1950* (1952)

PATRICK MEANOR

SIGOURNEY, Lydia [Howard] Huntley

b. 1 September 1791, Norwich, Connecticut; d. 10 June 1865, Hartford, Connecticut

During much of her lifetime, S. was a successful, prolific, and well-known—if not universally admired—writer of poetry and nonfiction prose. In the years before her death, her popularity declined; her ornate, morally uplifting style passed out of fashion, and, although her name was still widely recognized, her books ceased to be much read. Her reputation after her death declined to the extent that she became a figure of fun, remembered chiefly as a prominent practitioner of the so-called graveyard school of elegiac verse. Some recent critical investigations argue that her writings have been unfairly categorized, but these stop short of assigning her a place of importance in 19th-c. American literature.

S. was the child of a Hartford gardener whose wealthy employer, Mrs. Daniel Lathrop, took an interest in the girl's education and literary talents. Mrs. Lathrop's relatives helped her to establish a school and arranged for the publication of her first book, *Moral Pieces,* in 1815. This volume's religious and historical lessons and meditations on death reflected the types of edifying subject matter that were to be her main concerns. Her literary career was temporarily halted in 1819 by her socially-advantageous marriage to hardware merchant Charles Sigourney, who believed that she should confine herself to private writing. But when her husband's financial setbacks in the 1820s provided a release for S.'s pent-up literary ambitions, she produced a flood of material. She eventually published more than sixty volumes of poetry and prose, as well as scores of works in various periodicals—at first anonymously, as her husband desired, and later under her own name.

S. was soon sufficiently marketable for publishers of popular magazines to pay her for the use of her name as an "editor." Literary respect did not necessarily follow her popularity, however. Edgar Allan POE objected that certain of her works were excessively imitative of another poet, a resemblance that had led less critical reviewers to title her "the American Hemans." He was not the last to criticize her frequently verbose, artificial style. On a trip to Europe in 1840, S. eagerly sought audiences and correspondences with literary greats, not all of whom were impressed with her work; her account of here travels, *Pleasant Memories of Pleasant Lands,* nevertheless enhanced her reputation with an American public easily impressed by its descriptions of her "friendships" with European royalty and literary giants.

Death was certainly one of her major topics, and for some years public appetite for elegiac memorials like hers was insatiable. This literary fashion waned before the end of S.'s career, and after her death, she became associated almost exclusively with the kind of tear-stained poetry parodied by Samuel Langhorne CLEMENS in "Ode to Stephen Dowling Bots, Dec'd." This perception does little justice to the range of topics that occupied S. (or to the two-thirds of her published output that was prose); the common thread in her works is more nearly a preoccupation with morality—which led her on occasion to outspoken criticism of "Christian" behavior—than a preoccupation with death.

BIBLIOGRAPHY: Baym, N., "Reinventing L. S.," *AL* 62 (September 1990): 385–404; Bowles, D. A., "L. H. S.," in Riley, S. G., ed., *DLB*, vol. 73, *American Magazine Journalists, 1741–1850* (1988): 266–74; Haight, G. S., *Mrs. S.: The Sweet Singer of Hartford* (1930)

CAROLYN LENGEL

SILKO, Leslie Marmon

b. 5 March 1948, Albuquerque, New Mexico

Even before her critical acclaim as a novelist, S. was recognized as one of the preeminent voices of the Native American literary renaissance with her short fiction and poetry. A descendant of the Laguna tribe, S. first received critical attention in 1977 with her novel *Ceremony,* a novel telling of a mixed-heritage war veteran's struggle for sanity after returning home from World War II. Tayo, the veteran, is haunted by his violent actions of wartime and by his cousin's death. Tayo suffers gradual mental and physical deterioration on the reservation, where his fellow Native American veterans indulge in heavy drinking. Tayo establishes a strong relationship with old Betonie, who counsels him on the importance and value of ceremony in life, teaching him that it is more than ritual, but also a means of living. Tayo learns that ceremony is the means of harmonizing humanity and the universe.

The predominant themes in S.'s writing derive from her family background and from her family's interaction with Euro-American culture. She demonstrates how her Laguna heritage can and must adapt to the 20th c. Her first important publication was the short story "The Man to Send Rain Clouds" (1969), which promotes the mixture of Roman Catholic and Laguna burial rituals. This story established her basic theme of the necessity of Lagunas and other Native Americans of incorporating Euro-American culture so that traditional values could be retained.

When Kenneth Rosen used S.'s story title as the title of his 1974 anthology of short fiction by contemporary Native American writers, along with six more of her stories, S. received national attention. That same year Greenfield Review Press published her collection of poetry entitled *Laguna Woman.* The poems reiterate her theme of the adaptability of Native American traditions, reflecting her roots in Laguna and Southwest culture. Some of the poems trace S.'s mountain experiences in western New Mexico and stress the strong

spiritual associations that much of the landscape still has for Lagunas.

S.'s second novel *Storyteller* (1981) is set in Alaska. The plot deals with an orphaned Inuit girl who lives with an old couple. The girl is eventually sexually exploited by oil workers. The old man with whom she continues to live after his wife's death tells a story about a polar bear's stalking of a hunter in the icy wilderness. As a parallel, the Arctic winter is overpowering the attempts by civilization to deal with the environment. S. produces an integration in this novel by interweaving stories from the Laguna heritage with family stories, photographs, poetry and fiction, all to demonstrate continuity and change.

Developed in part under the auspices of the MacArthur Foundation, *Almanac of the Dead* (1991) is a sprawling work of seven hundred pages, written over a period of ten years. The title refers to a set of notebooks bequeathed to a Yaqui named Yoeme. A granddaughter, Lecha, wants to decipher these books. Another character named Seese agrees to help her, hoping that Lecha's physic powers can help locate a kidnapped child. Another narrative thread involves Menardo Panson, a rich man serving as a foil to the revolutionary army organizing in central Mexico to march northward to reclaim tribal lands. These two principal threads take place against a series of other plot lines, all of which focus on the retaking of a corrupt North America by the tribal peoples from whom it was stolen. All the evils of Euro-American corruption will eventually be expurgated by the recovery and tribal values will be reasserted.

It is perhaps too early to assess the total impact of *Almanac of the Dead;* however, it is interesting that the subject seems to parallel part of what is occurring in American politics, namely, the return to family values and a focus of the importance of tradition. It remains certain regardless of this that S.'s poetry and fiction represent some of the most stimulating of any literary work by a Native American writer in the later part of the 20th c.

BIBLIOGRAPHY: Hobson, G., *The Remembered Earth* (1980); Krupat, A., *Narrative Chance: Postmodern Discourse on Native American Indian Literature* (1989); Lincoln, K., *Native American Renaissance* (1983); Seyersted, P., *L. M. S.* (1980); Velie, A. R., *Four America Indian Literary Masters* (1982)

JOHN W. CRAWFORD

SIMIC, Charles

b. 9 May 1938, Belgrade, Yugoslavia

Poet, essayist, translator, and editor whose oeuvre features short metaphysical poems influenced by European surrealism and the imagist movement. Since the publication of his *Selected Poems* (1985), S.'s poetry has received a level of recognition, publication, and critical attention unique in American letters. His poems are frenetic ruminations on the mundane and macabre which exhibit unabashed affinities with other creative forms, including the work of painters like Max Ernst and Joseph Cornell, American jazz and the blues, philosophical riddles, nursery rhymes, and Balkan folklore. Though barely alluded to in his poetry, World War II was a defining experience. In *The Uncertain Certainty* (1985), he recalls stealing belts and hats off the bodies of dead German soldiers and passing by corpses hung from telephone poles. These grotesque inversions of practical objects and everyday reality, as well as his subsequent resettlements in cities like Paris, Chicago, and finally, New York, have provided much of the material for his work to date.

Beginning with the poems in *What the Grass Says* (1967), commonplace objects are talismans upon which a solitary speaker fixates. "Stone," from his breakthrough *Dismantling the Silence* (1971), is his most emblematic and anthologized poem, in which the reader is invited to go with the speaker *into* the object at hand, and in the process to bear witness to the stone's intricate travels and interactions with other concrete elements. Throughout these early poems, objects metamorphose into other, quite different objects, as impatient speakers grapple with the phenomenology, animism, and *eidos* of the ordinary; in "Fork," the utensil is revealed as not only a "father-confessor" but also an eye, a candle, and, finally, a poem itself.

This theme of unsettling objective identities is central to S.'s work, as the poet catalogues, in abrupt colloquial verse and often gaudy and erotic metaphors, the aspects of brooms, female breasts, watermelons, the top hats of insects, Joseph Stalin's mustache, the haircuts of young soldiers. In "Charles Simic," a poem that combines cheeky humor with exhilarating aestheticism, the "object" is defined as a unit of grammar as well as a blackmailer, a job applicant, and a young girl in love.

Though he shuns the placid tone of much contemporary American poetry in favor of a blunt rhetoric, his poems often strike a variety of emotions in a single poem. In "Baby Pictures of Famous Dictators" images of domestic innocence are undercut by the sinister futures suggested by the poem's title. The poem concludes with an unnerving description of a pregnant family dog. S.'s awareness of the evil lurking beneath the everyday also informs "History Book" in which a young boy chases the blown pages of a school book down to a bridge, "Where they drown kittens. . . . The one they named 'Victory'/ From which a cripple waves."

His book of prose poems, *The World Doesn't End* (1989), which won S. the Pulitzer Prize, contains strange glimpses of contemporary urban life and is stylistically and structurally reminiscent of Baudelaire's *Paris Spleen*.

Though some prominent critics have described S.'s work as limited in range and amoral in tone, the verve and love of language that fuel his best work have been invigorating contributions to American poetry at the end of the 20th c.

BIBLIOGRAPHY: McQuade, M., "Real America: An Interview with C. S.," *ChiR* 41 (1995): 13–18; Weigl, B., "C. S.: The Metaphysician in the Dark," *APR* 20 (September-October 1991): 5-13

TIM KEANE

SIMMS, William Gilmore

b. 17 April 1806, Charleston, South Carolina; d. 11 June 1870, Charleston, South Carolina

Unquestionably the author with the best claim to being the Balzac of American literature, S. was in fact more prolific and wide-ranging than the great Frenchman himself. The page count of work published in book form alone runs to an amazing 25,000. With uncollected stories, poems, essays and reviews, this figure would be increased by half again. (Of his nearly two thousand poems, for example, only half have appeared in collections. The other thousand remain scattered through scores of 19th-c. periodicals, or rest in unpublished manuscripts.) What wonder that at his death in 1870, his fingers could not be straightened from the position of holding the quill.

No author in the history of literature has written so widely in so many different genres. The fact that he did so with skill and competence makes his achievement all the more impressive. In addition to his poems—lyric, narrative, and dramatic, and some of them book length—he wrote twenty-four novels; over hundred short stories; several plays (that were performed in his home of Charleston); more than a thousand book reviews as editor or staff member of a dozen periodicals; scores of essays, some published as pamphlets; four biographies; speeches and lectures; six editions as diverse as a Shakespeare apocrypha and a volume of Southern war poetry; a volume of history; and even a geography book.

The mere fact that S. published so voluminously in all these genres is certainly noteworthy, but he is much more than a writer of great quantity. What is abundantly clear to the reader of S.'s canon is that he did not possess energy alone, but unmistakable genius as well. It was a talent that displayed itself not in understatement, tightness, and polish but in expansiveness, flamboyance, dramatic vitality, the rush of a vigorous prose style of impressive verbal energy, and restless innovations that left their mark on American letters. That S. wrote competently in so many genres, while at the same time editing one periodical or another throughout over half of his career, should insure him a position of high honor in the annals of our early literature, and at least a modest place worldwide. As one of the major American writers of the 19th c., he is without question the author most unfairly neglected in our day. Even though there has been a large and growing recent interest, his continued exclusion from serious consideration in our literary history is unmerited. Unfortunately, such exclusion has been partly the result of sectional bias. The most recent treatment of his short fiction has, in fact, called S. a "national scapegoat." In 1865, the year Northern troops burned his home, an officer under Sherman, in his memoirs, reports that S. now has "no home" and that in the "glorious future of this country," he will likewise have "no name." Some of S.'s neglect seems thus to have been premeditated along sectional and political lines.

Among S.'s chief contributions to American letters, he should be included with Washington IRVING and Edgar Allan POE as one of the fathers of the SHORT STORY, which he did much to define. Thus, the only distinctive American literary form owes some part to his endeavor. Beginning his short story career in the 1820s, he exerted a direct influence upon Poe that was significant and noteworthy. Poe felt that S.'s story "Grayling" (1841) was the finest ghost story ever written. Among S.'s best works are "The Lazy Crow" (1839), "The Arm-Chair of Tustenugee" (1840), "Caloya; or, The Loves of the Driver" (1841), "The Two Camps" (1843), "Maize in Milk" (1847), "Sharp Snaffles" (1870), and "Bald-Head Bauldy" (1870). His story collection, *The Wigwam and the Cabin: Life in America* (1845), is particularly interesting because of its close thematic arrangement that provides a novelistic unity somewhat in the manner of James Joyce's *Dubliners,* Sherwood ANDERSON's *Winesburg, Ohio* and William FAULKNER's *The Unvanquished* and *Go Down, Moses.*

As a novelist, his versatility allowed for writing several different types, from the Gothic tale like *Castle Dismal* (1844) to the novel of manners like *The Golden Christmas* (1852). He composed the short novel told by the first-person narrator, the primary purpose of which was to explore the narrator's psychology, as in *Martin Faber* (1833) and *Carl Werner* (1838). Poe understandably preferred this branch of S.'s fiction career, particularly when S.'s narrator suffered from dementia or was a criminal. S. was better known, however, for his "romances." He was the first writer

to define the genre as distinct from the novel in his preface to *The Yemassee* in 1835, thus predating by sixteen years Nathaniel HAWTHORNE's famous similar definition in *The House of Seven Gables.* (Hawthorne reviewed S., so did not likely develop the idea independently.) Of S.'s romances, the best are *Woodcraft* (1852), *The Cassique of Kiawah* (1859), *The Yemassee,* and *Charlemont* (1842, 1856). *Woodcraft* deserves to be read as part of the great American Renaissance of the 1850s that produced *The Scarlet Letter, Moby-Dick, The House of Seven Gables, Walden,* and *Leaves of Grass.* What is particularly interesting about the novel in this context is that it is the only work of the group that is predominantly humorous. Its literary descendants include such Southern fiction as Mark TWAIN's *Adventures of Huckleberry Finn* and Faulkner's *As I Lay Dying* and *The Hamlet. The Cassique of Kiawah* (1859), another of S.'s great achievements, was reprinted for the first time only in 1989. *The Yemassee* has been long celebrated for its balanced, realistic portrayal of Native Americans, which critics have for decades considered the best in American literature, and a particularly notable achievement when compared to James Fenimore COOPER's less convincing treatment. S. knew Native Americans (Creek, Choctaw, Catawba, and Cherokee) from firsthand experience on the Southern frontier in the 1820s and 1830s. He lived among them in their camps and witnessed them in their degraded condition in the new towns of the border; Cooper got his view from books. S.'s short stories "Indian Sketch" (1828) and "Oakatibbe" (1841), and his little-known poem "The Indian Village" (1837), present even more coolly realistic treatments of Native American character than *The Yemassee.* In all, S. wrote three novels and at least forty-nine poems, twenty-eight stories, and twenty-three essays that treat Native Americans, an accomplishment unmatched in his century.

In the novels as a whole, S. shows an innovativeness that points the way to later fiction. This energy of mind and originality are in fact often the hallmarks of his writing. From his earliest short stories and novels of the 1820s on, there is a strong impulse to graphic realism (including matters of sex and unpleasantly grim particulars) that is far ahead of its time. It was this strain that offended Poe and even made the early Walt WHITMAN uncomfortable. How ironic that Whitman, in an essay in 1846, would call S.'s realism "coarse and indelicate in its details." In these ways, in fact, S. was being more realistic than some of the realists of the 1880s and 1890s—particularly such an author as William Dean HOWELLS, whose dictum was to write noting that might cause a blush. One has to wait until the 20th c. to see again the frank and unflinching realism of parts of such works as "Caloya," *The Yemassee,* and the border romances.

S. peoples his fictional world with a parade of grotesque characters like "Goggle" Blonay, Blodgits, Mother Blonay, and Bostwick, somewhat reminiscent of Charles Dickens's characters, but more closely akin to the physically deformed and spiritually incomplete characters of Flannery O'CONNOR. This creation of the grotesque character is another way that S. stands at the door opening to later fiction—in this instance, the haunted Southern grotesques of Poe, then Faulkner, O'Connor, Carson MCCULLERS, Cormack MCCARTHY, and Harry CREWS.

It is very significant that S. in the 1820s opted to set his stories and novels in America. His philosophy as expressed in periodicals he edited during this period was that America could never establish its own literature until it stopped imitating British models. He called for American literary independence. From 1825 to 1829, S. strongly and consistently voiced a view that only became widespread in the "Young America" journals of New York in 1837. In the 1820s, he had unequivocally stated the principles of "Young America" that a decade later would be regarded as "radical" heresy by the *Knickerbocker, North American Review, New England,* the *New York Review,* and *American Quarterly.* This demand for freedom from the literary bondage to England expressed itself in S.'s choice for his stories and novels of American setting, dialect, distinctively American character, style, and form—a realism that would fit art to place and rely upon local genius. S., therefore, deserves recognition as precursor of the "Young America" movement that he joined and helped to promote through fiction, essays, and criticism.

S., however, took one important step beyond "Young America," and in carefully formulating his reasons for it, he stands as the premiere spokesman for this idea. This important discovery was that *"for one to be National in literature, he must first of necessity be Sectional"*— that an author must write of his *patria,* his own little area that he knows best; and that the literature of various sections, then, when taken collectively, would produce a literature of national "illustration" and universal import. This intense focus on the immediate locale (its peculiar history, traditions, landscape, mood, character, and evocation of place) would yield a quintessentially Southern literature (see the SOUTH), which was to find expression in the Southern local color movement of the late 19th c., and then to blossom in the 20th c. with scores of gifted Southern writers, the most celebrated of which was Faulkner. S.'s famous dictum on sectionalism in literature has been proven prophetic by that Southern Nobel laureate, the American author most celebrated worldwide.

The close similarities between Faulkner and S. are now undergoing intense scholarly scrutiny.

One must give S. credit, likewise, for being the first to create a panoramic complex myth of this land and its people. He in fact called his romances collectively an epic, saga, or fable of the South. S. in his fiction is always engaged in the process of articulating Southern character and Southernness. He attempts to define his region in terms of its past and how that past shapes its present and will carry into its future. His several historical novels, of which *Woodcraft* and *The Cassique* are examples, display that sense of time, mood, and evocation of place and character that the modern reader perhaps understands best through the word "Faulknerian." S.'s character Porgy of *Woodcraft* is himself a representative of the Southern people as a whole, a veritable embodiment of the South, its hospitality, complacency, scorn of materialism, individualism, warmth, neighborliness, occasional self-indulgence, tolerance, and genial good-naturedness. He is one of the means by which S. portrays Southern ideals as set against Southern realties. Porgy, with all his strengths and weaknesses, is at the same time a believable individual, an interesting and richly complex character who is perhaps S.'s finest creation. He is certainly the best known. Further, he is one of the most likeable individuals in the fiction of the American Renaissance. He bustles about as the chivalric middle-aged knight dressing to meet his would-be fiancee. Having but recently returned home from the Revolutionary War to a burned-out plantation, he must wear clothes that are old and shabby. He has also gained weight, and after his ride to court his lady-fair, and in her presence, begins splitting the seams of his pants. This fine figure of a chevalier is thus lightly burlesqued, but his ideals are revered. He is not merely a Don Quixote or a Falstaff, but his own unique self.

All the major characters tolerate one another's foibles with good nature, and the work concludes with the status quo reaffirmed: Porgy remains a bachelor. His intended, the Widow Eveleigh, does not want to remarry. She enjoys the freedom to manage her plantation, which she does efficiently and effectively, having strength of character and intellect superior to any man in the novel. Interestingly, S.'s female characters run the gamut from the fainting damsel known in Cooper to women of such strength as the widow, thus probably attempting to reflect realistically the spectrum of antebellum Southern womanhood. The complexity of the novel's conclusion causes the reader to question whether, despite Porgy's and the Widow's admirable traits, they are really living up to the Southern ideal after all. As recent criticism has pointed out, one of *Woodcraft*'s primary themes is freedom, its value, cost, and meaning. Both Porgy and Widow Eveleigh figure centrally in it. The novel on many counts is quite an achievement.

In *Woodcraft,* as in most of S.'s fiction, one has the sense of the South's being a place where ideals are high-toned, but tempered by down-to-earth simplicity and common sense. Above all, relations are on a personal rather than a business level. Human contact undercuts and replaces abstraction. The practical and utilitarian purpose must be kept in check by a focus on the human and humane element. In other words, "poetry," beauty, spirituality, and all they represent must not be replaced by the starkly practical and materialistic. Place itself becomes spiritualized and humanized and becomes a character in its own right.

The oral quality of saga and epic is strong in S.'s work as a whole. The sense of the tale recounted is responsible for much of the effectiveness of the border romances as well as backwoods-humor stories like "Sharp Snaffles" and "Bill Bauldy." The narrative voice telling the tale looks forward to the best of Southern writing from Mark Twain to Thomas WOLFE, Robert Penn WARREN, Eudora WELTY, Faulkner, Wendell BERRY, and Fred CHAPPELL.

As a literary critic S. deserves more than passing note. He was quite remarkable for the accuracy of his assessments of his contemporaries in both America and Europe. He was among the most widely-read authors in American literary history. His pronouncements upon literary value are closely in line with modern judgements. After a century and a half, his essay on Cooper is still one of the best. He quickly saw the genius of *Wuthering Heights* and valued Emily Brontë over her sisters. He judged Coleridge's talents superior to Wordsworth's, though not disciplined enough to make him greater, preferred Keats to Shelley and Robert Browning to the more popular Elizabeth Barrett, choices all clear enough today, but not so during S.'s own time. He early saw Poe's genius, and aided, defended, and encouraged him when few did. He understood Poe's mysticism, spirituality, and disdain for the concrete perhaps better than any critic of the 19th c. Ralph Waldo EMERSON he did not like so well. Hawthorne he admired. But S. was not perfect: *Moby-Dick* he did not like at all except for its realistic depiction of whaling, and found Ahab and his ravings a "monstrous bore." His essays on Wordsworth are always full of great good sense, as are his comments on Dickens, Scott, Thackeray, George Eliot, Carlyle, and Tennyson. In the periodicals he edited, or as the author of the book column for the Charleston *Courier* and *Mercury,* he commented on nearly two thousand books during his lifetime. What is indeed so very impressive is his ability, even with so large a number, to hit with precision the essential quality of the book and pronounce upon it, even if limited to a sentence

or two. *Walden,* for instance, he summarized as that curious volume of Yankee philosophy written in good prose, one aim of which was to make a virtue of stinginess. His criticism was composed with the wit, dash, flare and verve of his fiction. Many of his critical essays make for very enjoyable reading—as do his formal essays on literature and social matters. Several of the more significant ones are "Sectional Literature," "Americanism in Literature," "The Social Principle," in which he states that if America is to produce great art and a high culture, her people must be rooted, rather than nomadic, and "The Philosophy of the Omnibus," in which, in 1834, he outlined his attack on an industrial, technically-oriented society and criticized Benjamin FRANKLIN's materialism as too heavily influencing Americans to the point that this country has prostituted high art by mating it to the marketplace, thus making money the new measure of all things. He wrote against the "leveling" spirit of the age when that leveling results in the loss of quality. An incisive social and literary critic, S. can hold his own with the best writers of his day.

As editor, S. rivaled if not surpassed in color, energy, competence, and accomplishment the careers of his literary contemporaries. As a formulator of pioneering ideas in American literature in the pages of his journals, he was quite noteworthy. He was excellent as an effective and practical editor, who devoted his time here as a means to further American literature. He received little remuneration from this work, so it was not done for monetary gain. He saw this endeavor clearly as the sacrifice that it was, a kind of missionary service to letters. S., through his other writing, however, did make a living for himself. He was among the first professional authors in America to do so, no small achievement in itself during his day.

Lately, it has been shown that as a poet, he penned some excellent personal lyrics quite modern in concept. He wrote effective narrative poems as well. His verse descriptive of nature is strikingly accurate. As early as the 1820s, his use of the external landscape as mirror and metaphor of the mind of the viewer was an innovative and effective technique. His use of Coleridgean romanticism, particularly, the concept of nature being formed through the consciousness of the man who views it, predated both Emerson's and Poe's, and may possibly be its earliest expression in America. In the study of American romanticism, S. should hold a key place.

S. considered poetry his forte; and no American writer has written more, or has had a grander conception of its value—particularly as spiritual "minister to man," which would free him from the literal and scientifically empirical response to life in an era of increasing technology. It might be added that unlike his contemporaries from New England, he, like Poe, never joined what he called the wrong-minded cult of the didactic. His poems do not have a moral imprinted on their surface. Their subtlety is refreshing when compared to the effusions of John Greenleaf WHITTIER, Henry Wadsworth LONGFELLOW, Emerson, and even William Cullen BRYANT, who was a strong influence and close personal friend of S. S.'s own moving defense of poetry as the most practical of pursuits against a growing empirically utilitarian world is dramatically given in his *Poetry and the Practical,* a work that can be described as no less than a creation of genius. *Poetry and the Practical,* which stands in the line of literary defenses from Spenser to Shelley, has the power to bridge the gap between poetry and a materialistic society like perhaps no other work in American literature. It is among S.'s highest achievements. It remained in manuscript for a century and half until published in 1996.

Prolific author of short stories, novels, essays, speeches, biographies, plays, and poetry, effective and devoted editor and social critic, S. made an important mark on the literary scene that is just now being charted. His innovations and their influence were significant contributions and stand as the fountainhead of many literary traditions that were to develop after him. Within a career in which he never doubted the primary importance of art and its practical value to humankind, he fought hard and long for the creation of a distinctive local, native literature free from the slavish imitation of foreign models, European or Northern. His own literary productions provided examples of the manner in which it could be done; and his magazines supplied him a place to voice such theories, to publish works that exemplified them, and to encourage their widespread production by adventurous new native authors. It was a grand vision, a totally unselfish one, and one that, in the final analysis, triumphed. It is good that he is at last being recognized for his important role in the history of American literature, for as John Guilds concluded in 1992 in his award-winning biography of S.: "He deserves place as a major American writer."

BIBLIOGRAPHY: Butterworth, A. K., and J. Kibler, *W. G. S.: A Reference Guide* (1980); Guilds, J. C., *S.: A Literary Life* (1992); Guilds, J. C., ed., *W. G. S. and the American Frontier* (1997); Kibler, J., *The Poetry of S.: An Introduction and Bibliography* (1979); Kibler, J., "The Major Fiction of W. G. S.," *MQR* 43 (Winter 1989): 85–95; Parks, E. W., *W. G. S. as Literary Critic* (1961); Rubin, L., *The History of Southern Literature* (1985): 108–17; Simms, W. G., *The Letters of W. G. S.* (1952–1982); Wimsatt, M. A., "S.'s Early Short Stories," *Library Chronicle* 41 (Winter 1978): 163–79

JAMES EVERETT KIBLER, JR

SIMON, [Marvin] Neil
b. 4 July 1927, Bronx, New York

When *Lost in Yonkers* won the 1991 Pulitzer Prize in drama, S. finally began to achieve a measure of critical credibility. After thirty years of unmatched success as a commercial American playwright (at one time in the 1960s four of his plays ran simultaneously on Broadway), he was still commonly perceived as being simply king of the one-liner rather than a playwright with serious intentions. Although S.'s thirty plays to date have run the gamut from farcical entertainment to dramatic stories told through comedy, he has earned not only awards, prizes, and profits, but also respect from critics.

S.'s writing has been enriched by his wide-ranging early experiences in show business. From 1946 to 1958, he wrote for nearly every major radio and television comedian, most notably for Sid Caesar in *Your Show of Shows* (1950–54). S. would later dramatize his experience of working with Caesar, Mel Brooks, Larry Gelbart, and other brilliant comic talents in *Laughter on the 23rd Floor* (1993). Although S. has written two dozen screenplays and the books for five musicals, his greatest strength remains in writing plays, where he can imagine stage action and maintain creative control.

S. was reared on the Jewish West Side of Washington Heights in Upper Manhattan. His home environment—which included a strong mother, a frequently absent father, and an older brother, as well as occasional boarders to supplement the family income—would be dramatized in *Brighton Beach Memoirs* (1983) and *Broadway Bound* (1986), while his military basic training would provide material for the middle play of the Brighton Beach trilogy, *Biloxi Blues* (1985).

The trilogy represents a greater commitment by S. to treat social themes. Although *Memoirs* contains considerable humor, the plot revolves around enough serious problems—including life-threatening illnesses, Nazi persecution, and loss of employment during the Great Depression—to fill a Eugene O'NEILL tragedy. *Biloxi Blues,* a humorous coming-of-age play, explores anti-Semitism, homosexuality, and other social issues. *Broadway Bound,* coming as it did after the death of S.'s parents, is the most touching and genuine effort of the three, ranking among his finest works.

If *Biloxi Blues* explored the personal aspects of anti-Semitism within an Army platoon, *Lost in Yonkers* broadens the discussion of this theme by its frequent references, both direct and indirect, to the atrocities of Nazi Germany. It also includes a memorable character, Grandma Kurnitz, who is unique among S.'s creations for her unstinting sternness, bearing no relation to the witty, affably quirky characters who inhabit S.'s other plays.

Although S.'s treatment of Jewish themes has occupied the foreground in some of his most recent plays, his ethnic background has always played an important role in his writing. Even in his first Broadway hit *Come Blow Your Horn* (1961), the family name may be Baker, but the speech inflections are unmistakably Yiddish. In other plays, such as the trilogy and *Lost in Yonkers,* ethnicity is treated more overtly.

Another consistent pattern in S.'s plays is his general preference for two-character scenes rather than group interactions. One need only think about the relationships between newlyweds Corie and Paul Bratter in *Barefoot in the Park* (1962), Oscar and Felix in *The Odd Couple* (1965), Lewis and Clark in *The Sunshine Boys* (1972), and George and Jenny in *Chapter Two* (1977) to appreciate S.'s comfort and skill in dealing with the two-character format. Much of his popularity derives from his ability to create seemingly mismatched pairs of characters, each of whom feels the need to connect with another human being—something to which everyone in the audience can relate.

S., who admires Chekhov above all playwrights after Shakespeare, has declared that he strives in his works to reveal the absurdity of the way we all live our lives. Although comparing him to such absurdists as Pirandello or Ionesco may be unfair, it is useful to keep his aim in mind while viewing his warring roommates, bickering old vaudevillians, and New York couples under siege from a hostile city. Like the practitioners of the theater of the absurd, S. understands that a disturbing truth can often best be presented to the audience through humor. If his comedy sometimes seems to serve merely as an entertaining end, at other times S. employs humor for a more serious purpose, and skillfully so.

BIBLIOGRAPHY: Johnson, R., *N. S.* (1983); Konas, G., ed., *N. S.: A Casebook* (1997); McGovern, E., *Not-So-Simple N. S.: A Critical Study* (1978)

GARY KONAS

SIMPSON, Louis [Aston Marantz]

b. 27 March 1923, Kingston, Jamaica

Since the romantic era and the appearance of the earliest confessional poems, Wordsworth's *The Prelude* and Byron's *Childe Harold's Pilgrimage,* readers have measured the accomplishments of many poets against the known facts of their lives. Despite the preeminence in the 20th c. of the New Criticism's disdain for biography, we have become accustomed to searching poems for autobiographical revelations and poring over biographies in hopes of gaining insight into the poems. Yet when one considers the external events of the lives of those modern poets labeled confessional—Robert LOWELL, John BERRYMAN, Anne SEXTON, Sylvia PLATH, among others—it comes as something of a letdown to discover that the lives that proved such fertile sources of poetry were for the most part constricted by family, academy, and career, all of which pale beside the intensity of the psychodramas enacted in the poems.

S. has rarely been considered a confessional poet, for his poetry displays a reticence and reserve rare in recent times; still, his work has been from the outset resolutely autobiographical. When one considers the barest outline of S.'s life, it is plain that he has not suffered from any shortage of "external events." Consider, first, the sheer number of coincidences it must have taken for S.'s father, a Jamaican lawyer of mixed Scottish and Creole blood, and his mother, a Russian Jew who emigrated at an early age to New York, to arrive at the same place at the same time. In *North of Jamaica* (1972), his autobiography, S. describes how his mother, who could not swim but nevertheless became a member of the Annette Kellerman Bathing Beauties, came to Kingston to make a film, meeting his father there and marrying him. Following his parents' divorce and his father's remarriage to an unsympathetic stepmother, S. came to New York, in time to study briefly at Columbia before being drafted. In World War II, S. saw fighting in Normandy, survived the siege of Bastogne during the Battle of the Bulge with a case of frostbitten feet that sent him to Paris for recuperation, and participated in the capture of Hitler's private retreat in Bavaria. After his return to civilian life, S. suffered a war-related nervous breakdown, studied at the Sorbonne and on his return to New York at Columbia with Mark VAN DOREN (where Allen GINSBERG was one of his contemporaries), worked in the publishing industry, and began a teaching career that led him to Berkeley during the turmoil of the free speech movement. S. gave numerous readings at antiwar rallies during the Vietnam War, became somewhat disillusioned in the process, and eventually settled in the decades since the 1960s into a "normal" life of university teaching, suburban living, and traveling to foreign countries, all of which have proven stimulating to his poetic output.

In the preface to his *Collected Poems* (1988), S. says that he once arranged his poems under five headings: "The Fighting in Europe," "A Discovery of America," "Modern Lives," "Tales of Volhynia," and "Recapitulations." Despite his ultimate decision to arrange his poems chronologically, these groupings remain a useful way of approaching S.'s poetry. In the first group are the ballads "Carentan O Carentan" and "The Bird," the former of which was recited on a network television documentary about the Normandy invasion. S.'s most ambitious war poem is the long blank verse narrative "The Runner," which appeared in his *A Dream of Governors* (1959), but virtually all of S.'s collections have contained war poetry.

"A Discovery of America" comprises some of S.'s most honored work, for *At the End of the Open Road* (1963) received the Pulitzer Prize primarily on the strength of meditative poems like "Walt Whitman at Bear Mountain" and "Lines Written Near San Francisco." In this book, S. experimented with open forms and an idiom more consistently relaxed than that which he employed in his early lyrics.

"Modern Lives" accounts for much of S.'s work in recent decades, poems, as he says, "that described human situations—poems with people in them. I am particularly fond of the narrative element in poetry—in fact can hardly enjoy a poem that is all idea and has no visible place or action." Shorter narratives like "Sway" or the satiric "The Beaded Pear" and long ones like "The Previous Tenant" have explored both S.'s own past and the quotidian vitae of others "born to this middleclass life."

The final two categories gather, respectively, poems re-creating S.'s mother's early life in her Russian village, Volyhnia, and poems of a more mystical bent in which S. attempts "to bring order out of chaos." He says, "I have always felt that there is a power and intelligence in things. I felt it as a boy when I watched the sun setting from the top of a mountain, when I rode a bicycle in the lanes of Kingston or walked along the shore, listening to the sea." In this category may be found the haunting lyric "My Father in the Night Commanding No," which remains one of S.'s best-known anthology pieces, and "Working Late," a poem comparing his own habits to those of his lawyer father where he observes, "Yet, nothing in nature changes, from that day to this, / she is still the mother of us all."

S.'s early poetry is formally polished and betrays influences as diverse as the Elizabethan lyric and the style of W. H. AUDEN. In the 1960s, in manner similar to that of contemporaries and friends such as Robert BLY and James WRIGHT, he turned from meter and rhyme to open form and deep image metaphor. In recent years, he has primarily employed in his narratives and elsewhere a straightforward, unadorned id-

iom in which most of the traditional rhetorical and figurative devices of poetry are kept in the background.

S. has also proved adept at prose. His novel *Riverside Drive* (1962) covers his war experiences and postwar adjustment to civilian life. His criticism, displayed in longer critical studies of modern poets like *Three on the Tower: The Lives and Works of Ezra Pound, T. S. Eliot, and William Carlos Williams* (1975) and *A Revolution in Taste: Studies of Dylan Thomas, Allen Ginsberg, Sylvia Plath, and Robert Lowell* (1978) and in the shorter pieces gathered in *Selected Prose* (1989) and several more recent collections, reveals a levelheadedness that displays little patience with puffery, jargon, and intellectual fraud, whether they be detected in individual poets, university creative writing programs, or the promoters of literary theory occupying the MLA and most contemporary departments of English. Despite his avowed admiration for Chekhov, who once said that it would take the eye of God to distinguish between good and evil, S. is not reluctant to speak his mind, remaining in many ways an old-fashioned moralist in an age that recognizes few moral absolutes.

BIBLIOGRAPHY: Lazer, H., ed., *On L. S.: Depths beyond Happiness* (1991); Lensing, G. S., *Four Poets and the Emotive Imagination: Robert Bly, James Wright, L. S., and William Stafford* (1976); Moran, R., *L. S.* (1972); Roberson, W., *L. S.: A Reference Guide* (1980)

R. S. GWYNN

SIMPSON, Mona
b. 14 June 1957, Green Bay, Wisconsin

In her two novels, *Anywhere but Here* (1987) and *The Lost Father* (1992), S. creates portraits of a world with a hole at its center. As the articulator of the longing for what is ostensibly meant to fill that hole, she has been called a prophet of desire. Her novels have been praised for this articulation and criticized for its formal and emotional ramifications, often simultaneously, but readers seem never to lose sight of the clarity and beauty of her language and the almost tactile texture of her descriptions.

Anywhere but Here is narrated almost entirely by Ann Stevenson, twelve-year-old daughter of the twice-divorced Adele, who as the novel opens picks up sticks and her daughter and heads West from Bay City, Wisconsin to Southern California. The plan, cooked up by the childlike, unreliable, barely sane Adele, is to make Ann a child star, or to meet a rich man, or both. Ann, swept along by an undependable, often hated mother she must depend upon and cannot help but love, spends the trip West learning just how inextricably tangled her love and hate are. A string of broken promises and roadside abandonments that end with trips for ice cream, the plot tracks Ann and Adele to California, Adele looking for glamour and wealth, Ann for her mother.

Aside from the last chapter, which is narrated by Adele, and chapters narrated by Adele's mother and sister, we see her entirely through Ann's eyes—eyes that grow older but not more able to see Adele, to understand her. And although Ann's grandmother and aunt fill in some of the gaps in their chapters, in her chapter Adele offers nothing but the dreams and delusions we already know fill her head. The resulting portrait conveys almost too well the frustrated grasping after understanding that Ann performs: S. presents the charm and beauty of the mother and the fascinating world the daughter moves in when with her, but she also presents her failure to parent as well as her daughter might like without ever really explaining it. Adele's inexplicability is part of what makes her, part of her perpetual "absence," and that absence creates a hole at the center of the novel as well.

The hole in the center of S.'s *The Lost Father* is perhaps too plainly named by its title, but S. makes no bones about the object of her heroine's attention. Ann Stevenson reappears here as Mayan Amneh Stevenson, taking up the name her Egyptian father gave her before he left her and her mother and disappeared. At the start of the novel, Mayan is twenty-eight and in medical school in New York, and obsessed with her absent father, who she knows was once a professor but now, glamorized by his absence, could be anything. What starts as an abiding interest, one present in the first novel, becomes an obsession, as research turns into a cross-country and eventually cross-Atlantic search for this cipher of a father. It begins to take over her life, destroying her schoolwork, friendships, and nearly her life, and it takes over the novel, which alternates between the search and Mayan's memories of her childhood with her father, who left when she was twelve.

As unavailable as Adele is to Ann and to readers in *Anywhere but Here,* Mayan's father is that much more an unknown. And again, this is what makes him who he is, whatever that may be: the essential element of his attraction is this very absence. But the limited understanding of Adele in the first novel is alleviated by Ann's constant contact with her; if Adele is not finally understood, she is known in some sense, and the source of her attraction is obvious. And the rich texture of the first novel, of Ann's observations and S.'s language, make up for much that might be missing. In *The Lost Father,* while readers may understand Mayan's father attraction intellectually, he is not present as Adele was in the first novel, and Mayan's search

for him carries an obsessiveness that Ann's search did not. There is still S.'s language, though, and Mayan's appreciation for the world's beauty, and her understanding of the value of her search, even if what it turns up is a man much smaller and less worth the effort than she imagined. The desire S. re-creates in Ann/Mayan, for lost parents who will never really be found, is one that creates narrative difficulties, but it is a desire that strikes a profound chord.

BIBLIOGRAPHY: Heller, D. A., "Shifting Gears: Transmission and Flight in M. S.'s *Anywhere but Here,*" *UHSL* 21(1989): 37–44; Morse, D. D., "The Difficult Journey Home: M. S.'s *Anywhere but Here,*" in Pearlman, M., ed., *Mother Puzzles: Daughters and Mothers in Contemporary American Literature* (1989): 67–75

SAM COHEN

SINCLAIR, Upton [Beall, Jr.]

b. 20 September 1878, Baltimore, Maryland; d. 25 November 1968, Englewood, New Jersey

S.'s writing focuses more on society than on individuals. His characters are victims, vehicles he uses to illustrate the social inequities that concern him. His over forty novels, strongly infused with the pessimistic determinism of literary NATURALISM, seek to expose the subjection capitalism imposes on working people.

His first four novels unsuccessful, S. wrote journalistic pieces for radical publications to earn money. One such journal, the *Appeal,* impressed by S.'s historical novel, *Manassas* (1904), asked him to write a novel about working conditions in industrial America, likening them to the pre-Emancipation conditions of American blacks.

S. spent two months in Chicago's meat packing houses, sometimes as worker, sometimes as observant visitor. His first commercially successful novel, *The Jungle* (1906), recounts the exploitation of the immigrant Jurgis Rudkus, who works in a meat-packing plant. *The Jungle,* S.'s best-known novel, is more propaganda than literature, as is much of his other writing. S. hoped to tweak the consciences of his readers, and, in the dozen or so pages he devotes to some of the gory, unsanitary conditions uncovered in his investigations, S. aroused readers, among them President Theodore ROOSEVELT, who summoned S. to the White House to discuss the meat-packing industry. This discussion led to Congress's passing the Pure Food and Drug Act of 1906.

S.'s muckraking books about coal mining, *King Coal* (1917); the oil industry, *Oil, A Novel* (1927) and *The Wet Parade* (1931); the Sacco-Vanzetti case,

Boston (1928); Henry Ford and the automobile industry, *The Flivver King* (1937); and the steel industry, *Little Steel* (1938), all emphasize how the technical-industrial complex uses workers shamefully for its economic aggrandizement. Examples of ideal radicalism, these books attempt to entice middle-class Americans into accepting S.'s notions about the brotherhood of humankind.

S.'s Dead Hand series seeks to expose the negative influence capitalism exerts on religion, journalism, the arts, and education. In *The Profits of Religion* (1918), he attacks institutionalized religion in the U.S. as a capitalist tool. In *The Brass Check* (1919), he illustrates how journalism has been compromised by capitalists.

In two subsequent books, he portrays schools as capitalist tools. *The Goose-Step* (1923) focuses on higher education; *The Goslings* (1924) examines elementary and secondary education. *Mannonart* (1925) considers how artists and writers are co-opted by political power structures.

At the outset of World War II, S. started a momentous undertaking that eventuated in the ten-novel Lanny Budd series, historical novels that chronicle the history of the world from 1913 to 1946. The third of these novels, *The Dragon's Teeth* (1942), depicting the effects of Naziism upon Europe, proved extremely timely and brought S. a Pulitzer Prize in fiction.

S.'s literary reputation has been in a downward spiral since his death in 1968. The social idealism of his writing, however, still resonates for the small, dedicated body of readers his writing attracts.

BIBLIOGRAPHY: Bloodworth, W. A., Jr., *U. S.* (1977); Dell, F., *U. S.* (1927); Gottesman, R., *U. S.* (1973); Harris, L., *U. S.* (1975); Mitchell, G., *The Campaign of the Century* (1992); Mordell, A., *Haldeman-Julius and U. S.* (1950); Yoder, J. A., *U. S.* (1975)

R. BAIRD SHUMAN

SINGER, Isaac Bashevis

b. 14 July 1904, Leoncin, Poland; d. 24 July 1991, Surfside, Florida

Much of S.'s work is rooted in the world of his youth, the shtetls of Poland where life was steeped in Jewish culture, history, and folklore. Whether writing about 17th-c. Eastern European Jewry, ghetto life immediately prior to and during World War II, or Poland as remembered by American émigré survivors of the Holocaust, S. time and again turns to his native land as a vital narrative source. Yet he does so in a way that does not limit himself strictly to traditional Jewish subject matters. His thematic breadth and widespread

appeal is evident in the numerous literary awards he has received, including two National Book Awards and the 1978 Nobel Prize in literature.

S. began writing fiction while working for a Yiddish-language newspaper in Warsaw. After emigrating to the U.S. in 1935, he continued to write in Yiddish, this time for the *Jewish Daily Forward,* a publication in which he contributed many stories and serialized a number of his novels before they were translated into English. Since then, he has distinguished himself not only as a short story writer and novelist, but also as a memoirist, a writer of children's stories, and a frequent contributor to such magazines as *Commentary, Esquire,* and the *New Yorker.*

Although commonly, and misleadingly, grouped along with other Jewish writers of the postwar period such as Saul BELLOW, Normal MAILER, Bernard MALAMUD, Philip ROTH, and Chaim POTOK, S. stands out as a unique voice in the American Jewish literary experience. Not only is his primary domain the Old World of Eastern European Jewry and their Yiddish vernacular, but his narratives, especially his short stories, distinguish themselves as a product of a master storyteller. Instead of minutely exploring the layers upon layers of psychological and intellectual conundrums apparent in many of his contemporaries' fiction, S. saw himself as, if anything, a teller of interesting stories. As a result, many of his narratives have a folk tale quality and a deceptively simple structure. Yet the subject matter of his fiction is anything but simple. Issues of assimilation, cultural alienation, love, and spiritual quests work their way into S.'s fiction in a most lively fashion.

S.'s first novel, *Shoten an Goray* (1935; *Satan in Goray,* 1955), a fantastical narrative that explores the cultural powers of traditional Jewish orthodoxy, was completed before he immigrated to the U.S. But it was not until immediately after the war that S. began to establish his reputation as a promising American writer. *The Family Moskat* (1950), the first of S.'s books to be published in English, is in many ways a commemorative to the work of his writer-brother, Israel Joshua Singer. It is a literary chronicle of the Polish Jewish community between the two World Wars, the ways in which two conflicting forces—modern ideas and values of the past—rupture Jewish cohesiveness, and how these communal battles were nonetheless overshadowed by the spread of Nazism. He followed up this narrative with *The Manor* (1967) and *The Estate* (1969), first serialized in Yiddish between 1953 and 1955. Both are epic works that serve as preludes to *The Family Moskat,* covering the period between the Polish Insurrection of 1863 to the end of the 19th c., and both continue the examination of tradition within an increasingly secularized world.

Many of S.'s novels revolve around individuals haunted by the past, obsessed by memories, and visited by fantastic and otherworldly visions. At times these individuals seek to escape, or even quench, their pathologies by plunging headlong into forbidden passions and sexual entanglements. *The Magician of Lublin* (1960), for instance, is the story of Yasha Mazur, a charismatic conjurer-artist passionately involved with five different women. When he is no longer able to deceive them, he loses his talents and powers of imagination and eventually undergoes a self-imposed religious isolation. Herman Broder, the American émigré protagonist in *Enemies: A Love Story* (1972), undergoes a similar sexual conundrum. He seeks to escape his recurrent nightmares of Nazi horrors by abandoning himself to a hedonistic affair with another Holocaust survivor, while at the same time maintaining a life with not one, but two, wives. Unable to make a commitment to any one woman—and in a parallel manner, unable to commit himself completely to Judiasm—Broder resorts to what served him best in the Holocaust: he flees.

Some of S.'s more recent fiction further explores the interrelationship between the sacred and the sexual. In *Scum* (1991), fears of impotence drive Max Barabander to a mindless pursuit of sex. Much like Yasha Mazur, he becomes involved with five women, then begins to feel himself spiritually deteriorate. Sexual triangles and quadrangles recur in *Meshugah* (1994). In a tale that moves from New York to Paris to Israel and back, Aaron Greidinger, a Jewish refugee from Poland, becomes involved with a Holocaust survivor and her lover. It is a novel that revolves around the erotic entaglements of émigré husbands, wives, friends, lovers, and enemies, and describes a assimilative world that lives up to the title's Yiddish title: crazy.

Despite his accomplishments in the novel, it is the short story form in which S. truly excels. He has published an astounding number of short story collections, the first of which was *Gimpel the Fool and Other Stories* (1957), and much as in his novels, these works are populated by an array of demons, ghosts, dybbuks, and eccentrics. It was with his story "Gimple the Fool" that S. began to receive significant critical attention. Translated by Bellow in 1953, published in *Partisan Review,* and championed by critic Irving HOWE, the story helped to make S.'s reputation in the literary establishment. Gimpel, the childlike fool of the story, believes everything that everyone in the shtetl tells him, no matter how fantastic or improbable. His gullibility makes him a fool in the eyes of the townspeople, but it is his unwillingness to disbelieve that makes of him a saintly figure on which the moral of the story

rests. Other short story collections, such as *The Spinoza of Market Street* (1961) and *Short Friday and Other Stories* (1964), similarly draw on the rich Jewish folklore of the shtetl. Many of the stories in his later collections—most notably *Passions and Other Stories* (1975), *Old Love* (1979), and *The Image and Other Stories* (1985)—deal with the subject of love and its many perverse and absurd, but nonetheless redeeming, manifestations.

S. has also mastered the form of CHILDREN'S LITERATURE, contributing such notable works as *Zlateh the Goat and Other Stories* (1966), *When Shlemiel Went to Warsaw and Other Stories* (1968), and *The Golem* (1982). In accepting the National Book Award for *A Day of Pleasure* (1969), S. gave his reasons for why he writes for children, among them, children "love interesting stories. . . . When a book is boring, they yawn openly, without any shame or fear of authority. . . . They don't expect their beloved writer to redeem humanity. Young as they are, they know that it is not in his power. Only the adults have such childish illusions." These are some of the same words he would use in addressing the Nobel academy several years later, and can be read not only as his rationale for writing children's literature, but also as a glimpse into his powers as a master storyteller for all ages.

BIBLIOGRAPHY: Allison, A., *I. B. S.: Children's Stories and Childhood Memoirs* (1996); Alexander, E., *I. B. S.: A Study of the Short Fiction* (1990); Biletzky, I. C., *God, Jew, Satan in the Works of I. B. S.* (1995); Friedman, L. S., *Understanding I. B. S.* (1988); Lee, G. F., *From Exile to Redemption: The Fiction of I. B. S.* (1987); Malin, I., ed., *Critical Views of I. B. S.* (1969); Miller, D. N., ed., *Recovering the Canon: Essays on I. B. S.* (1986)

DEREK PARKER ROYAL

SINGMASTER, Elsie

b. 29 August 1879, Schuylkill Haven, Pennsylvania;
d. 30 September 1958, Gettysburg, Pennsylavania

S. lived at Gettysburg, where her father became president of the Lutheran theological seminary, and several of her books make use of the lore of the battle and its aftermath. Of both German and English ancestry, she seems to have been most attracted by German culture, and her finest novel, *The Magic Mirror* (1934), whose background involves the life of a whole community and the surrounding countryside, includes an impressive picture of the great Bach Festival at Bethlehem.

Although she was most "successful" as a writer of stories for "young adults," S. nevertheless became our leading fictional historian of the ways of the Pennsylvania Germans, and her serious reputation rests on the solid, sympathetic, realistic, completely decent, but always quite honest and unevasive novels that began with *Basil Everman* (1920), a narrative dominated by the personality of a writer of genius who is dead before it begins.

Her most memorable characters are sensitive, eager, ardent young people, generally girls, who struggle for fulfillment against adverse circumstances, narrow, constricting environments, and the limitations and temptations of their own natures; see especially *Ellen Levis* (1921), *The Hidden Road* (1923), and the somewhat slighter *Keller's Anna Ruth* (1926). In her later novels, she turned more and more to history. *A High Wind Rising* (1942) covers the Pennsylvania frontier between 1728 and the French and Indian War, and the last, *I Speak for Thaddeaus Stevens* (1947) is a biographical novel that aims at rehabilitating the Reconstruction political leader who, as Austin Stoneman, had been the villain of D. W. Griffith's epic film *The Birth of a Nation* (1915).

S.'s only marriage to the musician Harold Lewars was terminated by his death three years later, but she signed her letters "E. S. Lewars" as long as she lived.

BIBLIOGRAPHY: Kohler, D., "E. S.," *Bookman* 72 (February 1931): 621–26; Wagenknecht, E., *Cavalcade of the American Novel* (1952)

EDWARD WAGENKNECHT

SLAVE NARRATIVE, The

One of the most influential genres within African American literature and culture, the slave narrative generally refers to a personal account written by a slave or former slave describing his or her life experience, particularly as that experience was shaped by slavery. The most famous of these accounts were published during the decades leading up to the Civil War as a means of demonstrating firsthand experiences with the horrors of slavery. Yet a variety of personal accounts of individuals' experiences with chattel slavery, even accounts not necessarily written by former slaves themselves, have often been considered part of the tradition of the slave narrative. Indeed, in its broad configuration the slave narrative tradition includes a diverse group of approximately six thousand texts, ranging from 18th-c. accounts dictated to white writers by enslaved African speakers to early 20th-c. accounts based on interviews with former slaves.

The earliest slave narratives, published during the 18th c. in London or New England, were similar in many ways to other personal narratives of the era authored by whites such as Indian captivity narratives, travel writing, and religious autobiographies. Like other personal narratives, early slave narratives, both those written by slaves or former slaves and those transcribed by whites, sought to entertain and instruct their predominantly white readership. The earliest prose narrative written by a slave in the present-day U.S., *The Narrative of the Uncommon Sufferings and Surprizing Deliverance of Briton Hammon* (1760), entertained its readers with an engaging tale of Hammon's captivity among Native Americans and Spanish of Florida as it informed its readers of the proper place for servants and slaves within the social order. Like many 18th-c. slave narratives, Hammon's narrative seemed, at least on the surface, to identify with and accept the dominant culture and its institutions—including slavery. Although early narratives might portray slavery negatively, criticism of slavery tended to focus not upon the institution of slavery itself, but upon the slave trade. In fact, the most widely read and most widely reprinted slave narrative of this era both in Britain and in the U.S., *The Interesting Narrative of the Life of Olaudah Equiano,* was written in order to encourage the British Parliament to abolish the slave trade. Olaudah EQUIANO's narrative—part adventure story, part spiritual autobiography, and part abolitionist tract—was published in England, Ireland, and the U.S., was translated into Dutch and German, and went through eight editions within its first five years of publication. Although most early slave narratives were not overtly abolitionist, early interest in slave narratives waned once the slave trade was abolished in the U.S. in 1808.

What has been referred to as the golden age of the slave narrative occurred decades later, between roughly 1830 and 1860, when the strength of the abolitionist movement drove the demand for eyewitness accounts of slavery. Slave narratives were a vital part of the abolitionist movement and served to circulate information about slavery and southern life quite widely; published in 1845, Frederick DOUGLASS's *Narrative of the Life of Frederick Douglass* was an international best-seller and sold more than 30,000 copies within its first five years of circulation. Slave narratives also played a vital role in asserting the humanity of African Americans. The inclusion of the phrase "written by himself" on the title page of many narratives served not only to support the truth claims of the texts, but also to assert the capabilities and humanity of slaves whose illiteracy was often considered a badge of their inferiority.

Although Douglass's narrative was legendary in its popularity, in many ways the conditions of its writing and the conventions it adopted were quite typical of many ante-bellum slave narratives, particularly those written by men. Many important slave narratives of this era, such as those written by Douglass, William Wells BROWN, and Henry Bibb, were written by men who had spent many years on the abolitionist circuit delivering speeches. Douglass's narrative was written in part to prove that he had in fact been a slave; many who listened to his speeches describing his experiences under slavery doubted that such an eloquent speaker had even been enslaved. Like many narratives, Douglass's opened with letters written by well-known abolitionists, letters that authenticated his text as they testified to the character of its author.

Narratives published during this era were strikingly similar to each other, for each narrator sought to portray him or herself as representative of the larger enslaved population while still offering a personal account of slavery. The narrator's story needed to represent every slave's story if it was to serve as an effective argument for the abolition of slavery by demonstrating that the problem was with the institution of slavery itself, not simply with individual problems within the institution. Abolitionist slave narratives usually followed a similar chronological plot line as they traced a slave's journey from slavery in the South to freedom in the North. Although obtaining freedom in the North is generally the goal within each narrative, narrators often note that the freedom available to African Americans in the North was limited by widespread racial prejudice. Narratives modeled the reader's initiation into the world of slavery by tracing the young slave's movement from ignorance of his or her enslavement to recognition of the nature of slavery and, finally, to a decision to rebel against the hated institution. Narrators sought to educate their readers about the inhumanity of slavery by demonstrating not only how it destroyed the family life of slaves but also how it threatened the family life of white owners.

In many ways, the predominantly white readership of the narratives drove their composition. Furthermore, white abolitionists influenced, edited, and in some cases even wrote slave narratives. Ironically, although a central concern regarding all of the slave narratives of this era was authenticity, using conventions that readers accepted as evidence of "truth" clearly was more important than accuracy. The resulting tensions that emerged between black and white abolitionists were addressed in later narratives such as Douglass's autobiography *My Bondage and My Freedom;* there Douglass spoke tellingly of his frustration on the abolitionist circuit when he was encouraged to put "a *little* more of the plantation manner" into his speech and

to present only "the facts" and to leave "the philosophy" (the interpretation of his experiences) up to white abolitionists. Despite the strong influence of white audiences and white abolitionists on the composition of slave narratives, whites did not control the narratives completely and slave narratives were not written only for them. Slave narrators manipulated Anglo-American rhetorical conventions in subtle and indirect ways that allowed them to address their small but important African American audience.

The overwhelming majority of slave narratives were written or dictated by African American men; according to one estimate, less than twelve per cent of all published slave narratives were written by women. It is perhaps not surprising, then, that critics have unwittingly constructed a male paradigm for the narrative, one that depicts male fugitive slaves as heroic individuals, moving independently toward freedom and independence. As critics like Valerie Smith have pointed out, although rugged individualism, geographic mobility, and physical strength might figure prominently in male-authored texts, they tend to play smaller roles in texts written by women. Recent critical attention to texts written by women, particularly to Harriet JACOBS's well-known *Incidents in the Life of a Slave Girl,* has demonstrated that women's narratives often paint a somewhat different picture of slavery than men's narratives. While male narrators often describe slave women as helpless victims of lustful white masters, Jacobs's narrator emphasizes that a female slave can actively respond to sexual threats by her master. Narratives like Jacobs's also suggest that escape from slavery is less the act of an individual than it is the result of the combined efforts of a broad community made up of both black and white men and women.

Slave narratives published after the Civil War, during the post-slavery era, differ significantly from earlier narratives in their themes and their treatment of slavery. The focus of texts such as Elizabeth Keckley's *Behind the Scenes; or, Thirty Years a Slave and Four Years in the White House, as Mrs. Lincoln's Maid* (1868) and Booker T. WASHINGTON's *Up From Slavery* (1901) is not upon life as a slave but upon life as a free man or woman trying to find a satisfactory position in the postwar social and economic order. Slavery, suggested Keckley and Washington, taught them industry, self-reliance, and frugality, qualities that prepared them well for full participation in society. Essentially narratives of racial uplift, post-war texts suggested that hard work and ingenuity were the means by which former slaves might elevate themselves.

The other main type of post-Civil War slave narrative is the composite autobiography, written based upon interviews with former slaves. One of the most important contributions to the slave narrative began during the 1930s when the Works Progress Administration Federal Writers' Project collected interviews from thousands of former slaves and African Americans who had experienced and observed slavery, often during their childhood. Thousands of pages of material transcribed from these interviews were later published in a seventeen-volume collection entitled *Slave Narratives: A Folk History of Slavery* (1941). Although these narratives and others like them arguably represent a wider range of experience than do abolitionist narratives written and published by fugitive slaves prior to the Civil War, they too must be read carefully and understood within their rhetorical context. Most of the interviews were conducted by white interviewers during an era when race relations in the South were strained at best and when many former slaves still occupied a subordinate, dependent relationship to whites in their communities. Although like their 18th- and 19th-c. predecessors, the WPA accounts were shaped variously by their editors, they still offer invaluable information about aspects of slave life about which little might otherwise be known.

The slave narrative clearly dominated African American literary history during the 18th and 19th cs. Although since that time various genres have assumed center stage, the slave narrative continues to capture the imagination of many contemporary African American writers. Drawing inspiration from the experiences of slaves, contemporary African American writers such as Charles JOHNSON, Toni MORRISON, and Sherley Anne Williams have explored a variety of issues emerging from the genre: the nature of white authority over the record of African American experience and the related silences within slave narratives, the horrifying social and ethical conflicts brought about by slavery, and the psychological trauma of enslavement. Like their literary ancestors, contemporary writers continue to explore the meanings of slavery and freedom for both blacks and whites.

BIBLIOGRAPHY: Andrews, W. L., *To Tell a Free Story: The First Century of Afro-American Autobiography, 1760–1865* (1986); Davis, C. T., and H. L. Gates, Jr., eds., *The Slave's Narrative* (1985); Foster, F. S., *Witnessing Slavery* (1979); Jackson, B., *A History of Afro-American Literature* (1989); Starling, M. W., *The Slave Narrative: Its Place in American History* (1988)

AMY WINANS

SMILEY, Jane
b. 26 September 1949, Los Angeles, California

S. goes straight to middle America in its geographical, economic, and familial landscape. Nearly all of her novels are set in the Midwest in middle-upper-class rural communities in which she renders more often than not a discontented vision. What is evocative about her work is her love and knowledge of the land and her piercing portraits of the families that inhabit it; what is absent from her work is all traces of race and poverty issues. Nevertheless, she is a writer who with each turn unravels the cataclysmic within the so-called ordinary human life. Her academic background in medieval literature—seen in her epic novel, *The Greenlanders* (1988), of 14th-c. Scandinavian frontiers people, affixes a brutality to her characters' worlds, depicting personal and everyday adversity—lack of communication, unmet desire, and ambivalence within the family unit—as a force that shapes morality. In *Barn Blind* (1980), it is a mother's unnerving control over her children that leads to disaster; in *The Age of Grief* (1987), it is a husband trying to accept his wife's infidelity; in *Ordinary Love* (1989), it is a mother knowing that she has reshaped her children's lives by following her passion; in *At Paradise Gate* (1981), it is a woman reassessing the sacrifices she has made as a mother; in *A Thousand Acres* (1991), it is a family falling apart after the father gives his land to his three daughters. S.'s other work, *Duplicate Keys* (1984), set in New York, is a suspense story; her novel *Moo* (1995) is a dark comedy exposing the hypocrisy of academic life.

S.'s success as a 1992 Pulitzer Prize-winner for *A Thousand Acres,* her critical acclaim, her inclusion in major anthologies, and her dedicated readership pay testimony to her craft as well as the desire of her readers to be confronted with a mother writing as a mother. In S.'s 1993 essay, "Can Mothers Think," she discusses maternal subjectivity as one of the critical bases of her writing, specifically in her novella, *Ordinary Love*—which appeared in print as a duo with the novella *Good Will,* forming two views, the prior from a mother, the latter from a father—in which, for one example, she moves outside of a linear structure. S. states that since this archetypal female form was not provided in past narratives, she "did not know how to make this unfolding form of secret surprises work. . . . The models for *Ordinary Love* were not within me. I had to think them up as I went along."

In *Ordinary Love,* S.'s fifty-two-year-old female protagonist narrates her experiences as a wife and mother, and as a woman. Rachel Kinsella tells the price of giving her children "the two cruelest gifts I had to give, which are these, the experience of perfect family happiness, and the certain knowledge that it could not last." Early on in the novel, we learn of the younger Rachel's ambivalence toward her role as mother and wife in what appears to be an "idyllic domestic life." In fact, the book is infused with subtle moments in which the longings of women for that something else that has been denied—education, privacy, freedom—urge them to some extreme. As Rachel takes a lover, the consequences of her actions are explosive: the loss of her family as her husband abandons her, taking the children to England and for many years not allowing them any contact with her.

S.'s protagonists convey a strength of character that is sometimes chilling, and in many ways, she creates heroines who through their resolve generate the tragedies that define them. While Rachel in *Ordinary Love* fully acknowledges and willingly bears the responsibility of her actions, which cast her out of the common melodramatic predicament of the fallen woman: that of victim or perpetrator, Kate Karlson in S.'s first novel, *Barn Blind,* is in fact blinded by the expectations she places on her family, and thus it is her unmoving determination that thwarts and ultimately destroys her family as she neglects their individual needs. Kate, like other S. protagonists, is all too human, particularly, within the breadth of this novel set on a horse farm in Illinois, in her desire to shape her children according to her own fixed obsession: in this case, to give to the world a champion horse and rider. Kate, a converted Catholic—coming from S., a self-proclaimed agnostic—has a vision of human endeavor that is dictated by self-directives, yet ironically the self-discipline she expects of her children is governed by the control she places over them, which subsumes her ability to nurture and ultimately brings disaster.

The reflective Anna Robison in *At Paradise Gate* is more akin to Rachel in *Ordinary Love* as she encounters, in her old age, how her subjective life has been veiled by the larger frame of domesticity. However, while Rachel's maternal world is forfeited to her passions as a woman, Anna has never wavered from the role as matriarch and caretaker and must bear a different kind of loss. As Anna cares for her dying husband, she begins to confront the hardships she has faced along with the realization that her embitterment issues from the disparity between her inner existence and her outer existence as wife and mother.

A Thousand Acres, for which S. received the National Book Critics Circle Award as well as the Pulitzer Prize, turns S.'s focus toward the evolution of a family without a mother. Narrated in first-person by Ginny, one of three daughters of Larry Cook, the story intentionally echoes *King Lear,* as a father's kingdom—his one thousand prime unmortgaged acres of farm—is distributed to his daughters and thus begins the dissolution of the family and the farm as well. At the core of this novel is the deleterious results of farming industrialization, but it is also one of S.'s most disturbing portraits of a family as she quite subtly lays bear the anger and abuse that lay between father and daughters and among the daughters themselves.

In *Moo,* S. turns away from the Midwestern family and uses her prowess to probe the inner sanctum of academia. The beginning of the novel sets the scene for intrigue as S.'s long winding sentences lead to the revelation that the fruit from the campus's apricot and peach trees—that is "big peaches swollen with juice"—appear and then disappear without a clue as to where they have gone. S. brings humor and biting wit—in a book called *Moo* that focuses on a certain boar named Earl—that is new to her writing as well as moving toward a more postmodern Thomas PYNCHON-like web of plots and subplots. This novel placed in a Midwestern agricultural college is a satiric expose, setting alight the masks of hypocrisy under which deceit, envy, lust, and general immorality abound within the academic institution. S.'s academic universe and archetypal professorial figures swell with exaggeration but unfortunately ring too many bells of familiarity and truth; for example, Dr. Gift, the renown economics professor, commercializes education using his material intellectualism to fill his pockets; Dr. Bo Jones has made it his life's work to discover how long a hog would live if one kept feeding it and didn't consume it; Timothy Monahan is a creative writing teacher who teaches his students to be unethical in order to be fiction writers.

S. believes that it is the literary voice that comes to give its culture the truths of its people "by bringing what had seemed alien into the realm of what the culture defined, through literary forms, human," and she does not hesitate to place the reader within this truth most pointedly through her intimacy with the nuclear family and the mother at its core. Yet it is this social contradiction that S. masters in her work, as she assails the domain of the family and the mother, showing the web of love and betrayal, and the ties that bind us to comfort, loneliness, or grief.

BIBLIOGRAPHY: Holstad, S. C., "J. S.'s *A Thousand Acres,*" NConL 26 (March 1996): 5–6; Keppel, T., "Goneril's Version: *A Thousand Acres* and *King Lear,*" SDR 33 (Summer 1995): 105–17

LISA TOLHURST

SMITH, Betty [Wehner]

b. 15 December 1896, Brooklyn, New York; d. 17 January 1972, Shelton, Connecticut

S. considered herself part of the naturalist school and emphasized objective narrative, interest in the lower classes, and the environment's effects on the individual. However, S. does not allow the extreme negative forces of naturalism to dominate her novels. Instead, she allows her main characters a degree of free will. Her fiction is ruled by the inner strength of her heroines, not the more impersonal factors of naturalism. Since these heroines succeed because of their strength and determination, S.'s work offers excellent material for feminist studies, which have yet to be attempted.

S. is best known for her first novel, *A Tree Grows in Brooklyn* (1943). It offers an account of tenement life in the Williamsburg district as experienced by the Nolan family, particularly Francie. The novel chronicles her life from the ages of one through nineteen. Scene after scene presents Francie's world: her daily life in the warmth of a close family and the harsher moments she experiences at the hands of others. The most startling view into her life occurs when she is almost raped. Her father douses her thighs with carbolic acid where the would-be rapist's genitals have touched her. Clearly symbolic, the acid causes scars that Francie must carry throughout life.

The "tree," which figures prominently in the title and throughout the book, is a type of Chinese sumac. It produces seeds that grow almost anywhere, including cracks in cement and garbage heaps. The tree that "liked poor people" grows over the fire escape where Francie sits and daydreams, and it symbolizes the hopes and possibilities for the heroine's future.

S.'s second novel, *Tomorrow Will Be Better* (1948), offers a much darker view of life. It presents Margy Shannon as she grows into adulthood, marries a man with homosexual tendencies, and gives birth to a stillborn baby. As a child she tries to explain a fear she has of the gates that surround the street, but her mother cannot comprehend her fear. As an adult, Margy is plagued by dreams of the gates, which represent the barriers that keep her from finding and enjoying love. While this heroine is not as mentally strong as Francis, Margy does possess resourcefulness and perseverance. She refuses to compromise her ideals or her chance for fulfillment. She never loses hope that life will someday be better.

Maggie-Now (1958) continues the somber tone of *Tomorrow Will Be Better*. The novel is a saga set in Brooklyn, detailing the life of Maggie as she waits for life instead of living it. She cares for her young brother, her impossible father, and her ever-disappearing husband, Claude. Maggie-Now, as her name suggests, symbolizes what is present in everyday life. The other characters represent lost dreams and an inability to let go of the past. The lack of hope in this novel makes it unlike the other works by S.. However, it does present a female character in keeping with the other S. heroines. Maggie is a strong woman who is not defeated by life.

S.'s last novel, *Joy in the Morning* (1963), returns to the author's life as a basis for her fiction. Her heroine, Annie McGairy, encounters many of the experiences the author did as the uneducated wife of a university man. Annie marries Carl against the wishes of both families, and the couple have to cope with finding shelter, food, and jobs while Carl finishes law school. When Carl is in class, Annie audits English classes to fulfill her desire to get an education.

Babette Hall criticizes the book for what she believes is its narrow focus because the couple are so caught up in themselves and their struggle to succeed. However, a more obvious flaw is the couple's endless supply of good luck, which makes the story entirely too sentimental. On a more positive note, S. again presents a female character with enough intellect and perseverance to achieve her desires despite life's stumbling blocks.

While S. was not a feminist, she obviously was aware of the changing roles of women in society. Her fiction is timeless and as relevant today as when it was published.

BIBLIOGRAPHY: Gelfant, B. H., *The American City Novel* (1954); Prescott, O., *In My Opinion* (1952)

JANET K. TURK

SMITH, Charles Henry

b. 15 June 1826, Lawrenceville, Georgia; d. 24 August 1903, Cartersville, Georgia

In the 19th c., rural Georgia produced a notable line of humorists, beginning with Augustus B. LONGSTREET, whose *Georgia Scenes* became a benchmark of Old Southwestern humor. S. occupies an important place in this tradition and, like several of his contemporaries, in Georgia and elsewhere, he was a lawyer whose literary career began with a casual foray into local journalism.

Following an aborted undergraduate career at Franklin College (later the University of Georgia), S. read law privately and was admitted to the bar. He was practicing in Rome, Georgia in 1861, when President Abraham LINCOLN issued an appeal to the Southern states for volunteers. Incensed, S. wrote a bitingly satirical letter to "Mr. Abe Linkhorn" that he read to a group of local citizens. One of these, a wag named William Arp, asked that his name be signed to it.

When he published this initial "Bill Arp" letter in the Rome *Southern Confederacy,* S. probably had no idea of its broader significance within the context of American literature, or that the character of Bill Arp would transform his own life and career. By casting the piece in the dialect of a hypothetical Georgia "cracker" of the time, and expressing strongly felt regional sentiments, S. had given personality and recognizable characteristics to what otherwise might have been only a pseudonym. Beginning with Benjamin FRANKLIN's "Silence Dogood," many such satirical characters had appeared in American newspapers, employed as masks through which their creators made similarly charged political statements.

One useful way of regarding the character and aims of "Bill Arp" is by comparing him to David Ross LOCKE's better-known creation, "Petroleum Vesuvius Nasby." Nasby struck the pose of a "Copperhead," a Northerner who sympathized with the South during the Civil War. However, the pose was as ironic as it was transparent, as Locke's loyalties were clearly with the North. Arp, professing to be sympathetic to "Linkhorn" and his need for Southern volunteers, spoke in similarly ironic terms, and continued to do so as the fortunes of the war shifted in favor of the North. Maintaining his conservative Southern stance, the Arp essays gave comfort and a needed touch of humor during the worst of the war experience. As a Savannah newspaper put it, "In the dark days he kept the Southern heart from breaking."

After serving in the Confederate army and as Judge Advocate in Macon, S. continued his legal practice in the post war years while continuing to write Bill Arp pieces. From 1877 on, these writings and his public lectures became his primary vocation. Over time, the ironic posture, along with the illiteracies and deliberate misspellings of the earlier Arp, gave way to more conventional usages that better reflected the educated voice of S. himself. It has been estimated that they appeared in more than seven hundred newspapers, including the *Atlanta Constitution* (where they ran for some twenty-five years). Several collections of the pieces appeared during S.'s lifetime, the last, *Bill Arp, from the Uncivil War to Date,* in 1903, the year S. died. In noting his passing the *Atlanta Constitution* called S. "the best loved man in all the Southland." The thousands who mourned S.'s death and the numerous printed tributes to him are indications not only of his popularity, but of the appeal of the "uneducated but wise, humorous rustic philosopher" types—Hosy Biglow, Mr. Dooley, Abe Martin, and Will ROGERS, among others—who have enriched American HUMOR.

BIBLIOGRAPHY: Austin, J. C., *Bill Arp* (1969); Christie, A., *C. H. S., "Bill Arp": A Biographical and Critical Study of a Nineteenth-Century Georgia Humorist, Politician, Homely Philosopher* (1952); Landrum, L., *C. H. S. (Bill Arp): Georgian Humorist* (1938); Rolan, E., *C. H. S., Alias Bill Arp* (1982); Taylor, W. D.,

The Newsprint Mask: The Tradition of the Fictional Journalist in America (1991)

WELFORD DUNAWAY TAYLOR

SMITH, Dave [David Jeddie]
b. 19 December 1942, Portsmouth, Virginia

S. emerged in the 1970s as one of the most promising young American poets, and the publication of *The Roundhouse Voices: Selected and New Poems* (1985) as well as the widely used *Morrow Anthology of Younger American Poets* (1985)—a text that he edited with David BOTTOMS and that is the cornerstone of most creative writing courses—further confirmed S.'s reputation. S. is a prolific poet—sometimes publishing two or more books in the same year—and he has also written two novels that have been favorably received as well as a number of critical essays, which have been collected in *Local Assays: On Contemporary American Poetry* (1985).

S. is often regarded as predominately a regional poet preoccupied with the Mid-Atlantic and his native Virginia even though his later poems focus upon the Midwest. Nonetheless, S. is often compared with another Southern writer—Robert Penn WARREN—as well as James DICKEY and James WRIGHT. Critics have cited S.'s use of common language and the grounding of his poetry in personal experience as indications of S.'s Southern inheritance. Such comparisons are certainly justified since S. acknowledges that Warren is a major influence upon his poetry, and both Wright and Dickey as well as Richard HUGO are discussed in some detail in *Local Assays*. S.'s poetry often transcribes his immediate place and environment, and his poetry documents the process of rendering or discovering meaning inherent in a particular locale. That is, S. is a poet of personal subjectivity, place, and personal history, and the poem for S. is often the condensation of his experiences and how places and things are laden with memory. As S. explains, the poet should always ask "why the imagination seizes on one image rather than another." S. insists that"[a]ll things exist in a web of relationships," and the poem is the unraveling of that personal webbing. S.'s poetry as a whole is the untiring exploration of his identity as mediated by the explicit relationship of things, objects, places, experiences, memory, history, and the self.

The past and its relationship to the present, more so than any other element, is the predominant theme of S.'s poetry. For S., everything about the past, though, is bitter-sweet, and his poems often present unsavory glimpses of the past through an oddly nostalgic haze. S. sometimes offers glimpses into the idealized relationship between people, as in "The Spinning Wheel in the Attic" where the tender and intricately woven dependency of a man and a woman are symbolized by a spinning wheel that the husband made and the wife used religiously, but more than likely his poems often reveal a more somber tone. For example, "An Antipastoral Memory of One Summer" records S.'s childhood memory of watching a boy and a woman stand in the eye of a hurricane awaiting its terror and force to again return. Danger, disaster, and death lurk at the fringes of S.'s memories, consequently the focus of a S. poem seems to be that moment poised before the threat of some potential disaster or tragedy.

Often praised for his "promise," S. has been equally criticized for the carelessness of his poetry, his tendency of overwriting, the speed with which the poems (and books) are often composed, and the lack of clarity in the presentation of ideas. Critics have remarked that S. seems to eschew revision and have warned that he may be endangering his reputation as a major poet. Ironically, S. puts forth two central tenets for his poetry—the predominance of form (as the manifestation of words and ideas on the page) and the clarity of that representation. Often riddled with ambiguous pronouns and cluttered syntax, the poems are sometimes nearly impossible to unravel. Nonetheless, at his best S.'s poetry offers poignant insights into the tensions between an idealized world and its real inception—a tension that is often symbolized by an incompatibility of nature and industry, tradition and progress, and the very real desire to be somehow better than one is. While nostalgic for the past and its rich tradition, S. refuses to idealize reality in whatever shape or form. In this regard, he is a poet of deep and unwavering realism.

BIBLIOGRAPHY: Suarez, E., "An Interview with D. S.," *ConL* 37 (Fall 1996): 349–69; Yenser, S., "Sea Changes: On D. S." *APR* 11 (January-February 1982): 32–35

DAVID W. CLIPPINGER

SMITH, Elizabeth Oakes [Prince]
b.12 August 1806, North Yarmouth, Maine; d. 15 November 1893, Hollywood, North Carolina

In 1823, at the age of sixteen years, S. was forced by her mother to marry a man twice her age, Seba SMITH, then editor of Portland's the *Eastern Argus*. When her husband lost the family fortune in land speculations during the Panic of 1837, S. embarked on a professional writing career under the pseudonyms Mrs. Seba Smith and Ernest Helfenstein. S.'s prosperity as a regular contributor to the popular journals and magazines of her time, as well as her later stint as a feminist

lyceum lecturer, helped to stabilize her financial situation, but apparently embittered her less successful husband. S. first established her very respectable literary reputation in 1842, when the *Southern Literary Messenger* published what would become one of her best known poems, "The Sinless Child," in two parts.

The poem centers on a child protagonist, "Eva," whose world view, the narrator explains, is filtered through the divine. Unlike her mother, whose vision is unfortunately pedestrian, Eva has the ability to not only discern but to draw out the sublime in everything. The tension created between the ordinary world the mother moves in and the exalted, spiritual world that Eva inhabits drives the fatal trajectory of the poem, and underpins its ultimately tragic conclusion. In the poem's inscription, the narrator asserts that Eva is the personification, the "ideal birth" of her own inner spiritual self. The presence of a protagonist or narrator who has experienced a mysterious and ethereal inner world or has evolved to a higher spiritual existence, constitutes a characteristic thread that runs through S.'s best work. Indeed, S.'s poetry overall suggests that its author had formulated a complex, perhaps even visionary, spiritual philosophy. While works like "The Sinless Child," "Atheism," and "Strength from the Hills" attest to a devout Christianity emerging through and intertwined with a Wordsworthian reverence for the natural world, poems such as S.'s "Death and Resurrection" and "The Drowned Man" reveal her inclination towards an unconventional mysticism. Like many of her contemporaries, S. would also often draw on her knowledge of classical texts and pagan mythologies for the themes and situations of many of her poems, as in the rather dark but compelling pieces "Ode to Sappho" and "Eros and Anteros." S. gestures in the former towards a feminine tradition of poetic genius through a characterization of Sappho, and in the latter, rewrites classical mythology from a radically feminist perspective.

S. fully articulated her revolutionary feminist politics in a series of articles that first appeared in Horace Greeley's *Tribune* between November 1850 and June 1851, and was subsequently collected and published in pamphlet form under the title *Woman and Her Needs* (1851). The argument presented in this work is built upon S.'s analysis of the cultural and economic position of Anglo-American women in the 19th c.—an analysis that leads her to form three fundamental assertions: that women have the right to individuality, the right to own property, and the right to not marry. S. contended that the realization of these rights could not take place until women, "recogniz[ing] their unlikeness," came to understand and accept the needs that emerge from what she saw as their essential and general difference. Frankly acknowledging the complicity of some women in the prevailing social and cultural system of gender inequality, S. argues that the majority of women are intelligent beings desirous of personal and economic independence. Referring explicitly to what she perceived as a large body of middle-class (implicitly Anglo-American), exemplary working women, S. wrote that the lives of such women were "silent, beautiful epics," far more eloquent and functional than the lives of the women who employed them. Like many early feminists, however, S.'s politics were inflected by her firm subscription to contemporary notions about the inherent moral superiority of women, as well as her partial concurrence with the ideology of separate spheres. S. agreed that such a thing as a strictly "woman's sphere" existed, but argued that its boundaries could not be traced until women had the opportunity to explore their feminine differences.

S. endured harsh treatment, if not at times ostracization, from her (female and male) contemporaries for the overtly feminist stand she took in *Woman and Her Needs,* as well as in her lyceum lectures. Yet over the course of a long and prolific career, S. ultimately enjoyed a generous measure of popular and critical success in numerous genres, writing not only poetry, articles, and short stories, but novels, plays, and juvenile literature.

BIBLIOGRAPHY: Walker, C., *The Nightingale's Burden: Women Poets and American Culture before 1900* (1982); Walker, C., ed., *American Women Poets of the Nineteenth Century: An Anthology* (1992); Watts, E. S., ed., *The Poetry of American Women from 1632 to 1945* (1977); Wyman, M. A., *Two American Pioneers: Seba Smith and E. O. S.* (1927)

                                    MARSHA WATSON

SMITH, [Captain] John

b. ca. 9 January 1580, Willoughby, Lincolnshire, England; d. 21 June 1631, London, England

The first major British–American writer, S. wrote of such marvels and feats that he was long dismissed as a liar and braggart. However, recent reassessments have reestablished the importance of the "Admirall of New England" to literary scholars, as well as to historians, folklorists, ethnographers, cartographers, and linguists. His American writings mark the transition from discovery and exploration accounts to settlement and colonization narratives, as the voyage to the New World in search of quick riches is replaced by the process of the colony becoming established. In S.'s practical visions, the dream of golden plunder by aristocratic European treasure-hunters gives way to a plan of social development by free, industrious colonists. For S., the New World is a place where the poor could earn a new social position by exploiting the natural riches and where heroic, self-made men could establish a new democratic society. S.'s egalitarian and economic themes are extraordinary for his day and are the earliest, noblest expressions of a meaning of America as influential as the Puritan religious origins that traditionally have biased early American studies.

Following eight years of adventuring in Europe, S. joined the voyage to Virginia in 1606 and thereafter devoted his life to promoting America. Despite his efforts to obtain food and to manage the quarrelsome gentlemen colonists, Jamestown almost failed, as Roanoke had, because the men went seeking gold ("guilded dirt," says S.) instead of planting crops, but S.'s common sense and leadership saved the colony from self-destruction. On one of his expeditions, he was captured by Powhatan's warriors but saved by Pocahontas. The story of his rescue was part of the first account he sent back to England, published without his knowledge as *A True Relation of Such Occurrences and Accidents of Noate as Hath Hapned in Virginia since the First Planting of That Collony . . .* (1608), which exposed their mismanagement and dissension and defended his own efforts and practicality. The Pocahontas episode was elaborated in his *Generall Historie of Virginia, New-England, and the Summer Isles . . .* (1624), and it grew into one of America's first great legends. After a year as president of the governing Council, S. was critically burned in a gunpowder accident in 1609 and was forced to return to England, where he wrote about his successful efforts to found the first permanent English colony in America, published in *A Map of Virginia. With a Description of the Countrey, the Commodities, People, Government and Religion* (1612), which contained the engraved map that served as the basis of North American cartography along with invaluable firsthand information on native tribes. In addition to sharp observations, S.'s descriptions are remarkable for his objectivity and caution. While other promotional writers idealized the edenic New World, S. combined his visionary ideals of American potential with realistic practicality, emphasizing risks and requirements, hard work as well as hope for wealth.

With his role in Virginia over, his love of America and adventure led him in 1614 to New England, which he named and where he transferred his hopes for a new society. His *A Description of New England . . .* (1616) catalogs the natural riches and recommends the area as a site for a fishing colony. This pamphlet is considered S.'s first solid work, revealing his character as explorer, narrator, and ethnographer, his vision of an American identity, his propagandist rhetoric, and his retrospective self-discovery. If S. is the American Aeneas, *A Description of New England* is his own Aeneid. Although his seafaring was done, he continued to write as a self-proclaimed expert on transatlantic settlement in *New Englands Trials, Declaring the Successe of 26. Ships Employed Thither within These Six Years . . .* (1620; rev. ed., 1622). The second edition is particularly important because it evaluates the Pilgrims' plantation, pointing out how they had gone wrong and how they might yet succeed.

In 1624, he published *The Generall Historie of Virginia,* a compilation in six books of his previous writings, revised and expanded, along with accounts by others, which he edited and made to reflect his own story. Though somewhat limited in originality, it is his most famous and substantial work. While emphasizing the wisdom of his own policies, especially toward the Indians, it is also the first epic of British North America, written to memorialize the colonists, whom S. compares to the greatest figures in history, the Bible, and myth. Refuting the common 17th-c. image of colonists as outcasts and undesirables, his grand vision of an heroic American identity celebrates colonization as one of the greatest achievements a man could undertake.

Following publication of some nautical writings—*An Accidence; or, The Path-way to Experience. Necessary for all Young Sea-men . . .* (1626), a manual of seamanship and nautical dictionary with advice based on anecdotes of his experiences, and *A Sea Grammar, With the Plaine Exposition of Smiths Accidence for Young Sea-men . . .* (1627), an extension of *An Accidence*—S. then wrote his two masterworks: *The True Travels, Adventures, and Observations of Captaine John Smith, in Europe, Asia, Affrica, and America, from Anno Domini 1593 to 1629* (1630) and *Advertisements for the Unexperienced Planters of New-England; or, Any Where* (1631). His marvelous *True Travels,* one of the first secular autobiographies in English, records with unashamed and endearing bravado S.'s adventures in Hungary, Transylvania, Morocco, and the New World. Intended to establish S.'s greatness in his time, the book is so filled with vigor and derring-do that it has made him a legendary hero for all time. Because his life story includes many classical heroic traits and exploits, he has been called America's Odysseus, who was his own Homer. Further, his autobiography can be viewed as representative of the daring seventeenth-c. colonist, a precursor to Benjamin FRANKLIN's autobiography of the self-reliant 18th-c. American. As such, S. stands in significant contrast to the Puritan writers too often taken as representative of the man who established the framework for the "American self." Now showing

genuine literary skill, S. continued his story in the rollicking, rambling, advice-filled, autobiographical *Advertisements,* which looks back philosophically at his adventures and misadventures and looks ahead prophetically to America's potential. Sometimes vaingloriously, sometimes with good-humored raillery, he vividly presents himself as a self-made man, an individualist, a dreamer, and a realist, with forthright opinions plainly and freely given.

Writing to advance his own interests, S. put himself at the center his time, place and all matters about which he wrote, but his writing transcend self-serving promotions because the author identified with America and celebrated himself as part of his celebration of an ideal: his vision of new opportunities for a new people amid the bounty and beauty of the New World. Expressing in his memorable Elizabethan style how much of himself he had put into the colonies, S. called them his "children, for they have bin wife, my hawks, my hounds, my cards, my dice, and in totall my best content," and he claimed that all future developments in British North America would be "but the pigs of my owne sowe." Not only to enjoy such imagery and language but also to understand S.'s importance in his time and ours, we must read S. as part of the current critical reassessment of American literary history.

BIBLIOGRAPHY: Barbour, P. L., *The Three Worlds of Captain J. S.* (1964); Emerson, E. H., *Captain J. S.* (1971; rev. ed., 1993); Lemay, J. A. L., *The American Dream of Captain J. S.* (1991); Vaughan, A. T., *American Genesis: Captain J. S. and the Founding of Virginia* (1975)

RAYMOND F. DOLLE

SMITH, Lee

b. 1 November 1944, Grundy, Virginia

As a regional writer with broad artistic concerns, S. combines the concreteness of precise place with the abstraction of narrative theory to construct a fiction that stands firmly on the native earth of North Carolina and Virginia, primarily, while also occasionally gesturing toward the heavens of literary transcendence. S. understands that her various narrators and characters must speak from a distinct locus that grounds their discourse firmly in the particular and that narrative flirtations with transcendent universals can end as disappointing, maudlin affairs. She also understands that communal narratives that are performed over several generations and through many decades take on a significant cultural and historical substance that can transcend its individual voices at the same time it reaffirms them. Thus, her novels and short stories are narrative performances in the best artistic tradition of folklore: engaging, innovative, individually informed, reflective of community, responsive to audience, reality based, and infinitely renewable with multiple tellings.

Oral History (1983), *Family Linen* (1985), and *Fair and Tender Ladies* (1988) comprise a consecutive series of novels that demonstrates the coalescence of S.'s many powers as a novelist always willing to experiment with lively multivoiced narrative forms. Her earlier work shows the promise that these novels fulfill. *Oral History,* for example, tells the story of the Appalachian-bred Cantrell family over three generations through multiple first-person and third-person narrators, all framed as a collection assignment for a university folklore course, forcing readers to become narrators themselves as they work to pull all the various narratives together into some larger narrative. S.'s virtuosity in creating these rich contrasting narrative styles enervates the novel without self-conscious pretension; her willingness to forgo some overriding narration of her own and to let her characters speak for themselves demonstrates her faith in both her characters and her readers. Winner of the 1983 Sir Walter Raleigh Award for Fiction and the 1984 North Carolina Award for Fiction, *Oral History* has received the most scholarly attention of S.'s books.

Like *Oral History, Family Linen* features multiple narrative perspectives that cover almost a century of family life and that, taken together, promise to solve old family mysteries, particularly those that have taken on significant psychological depth for its members, partly by airing the proverbial dirty old family linen. Beginning with Sybill Hess's desperate visit to a hypnotist for some answers and ending with the Dotson wedding reception that somehow brings all the familial plot threads together, the novel features the humor of flawed but engaging characters who risk potential tragedy of large and small dimensions as they go about trying to find meaning in their lives. An epistolary novel, unlike *Oral History* and *Family Linen, Fair and Tender Ladies* focuses on one character, Ivy Rowe, who narrates the novel through her letters, thus creating herself as both artist and protagonist over the course of her lifetime of letter writing. Even with one voice dominating, *Fair and Tender Ladies* still celebrates the diverse voices within that one voice as Ivy changes over time. S.'s novel *Saving Grace* (1995) also features a central protagonist, Florida Grace Shepherd, who narrates her own retrospective story of the literal and figurative journeys she has taken from her rural religious roots to the point of her narrating her own story to understand those roots, perhaps for the first time.

BIBLIOGRAPHY: Hill, D. C., *L. S.* (1991); Smith, R., *Gender Dynamics in the Fiction of L. S.* (1997)

PHILLIP A. SNYDER

SMITH, Seba

b. 14 September 1792, Buckfield, Maine; d. 28 July 1868, Patchogue, New York

S. is primarily remembered as the creator of Major Jack Downing, whose letters appeared first in the *Portland Courier* (Maine) in January of 1830, and in *The Life and Writings of Major Jack Downing . . . etc.* (1833) and other collections. The fictional Downing, beside providing a model for many a Yankee sharper, embodied the rising "common man" of Jacksonian democracy through a combination of backwoods innocence, country common sense, and an increasing interest in current political affairs. In the character of Jack Downing, S. gave a realistic portrayal of the "typical Yankee," which was to become the predecessor of Uncle Sam. By simplifying the complexities and abstractions of American politics through the ideas of his backwoods philosopher, S. helped to popularize political satire in America.

Upon initial observations, Downing's letters may appear to be simply long-winded anecdotes, but closer examination reveals a refreshing view of American politics and politicians, written in realistic unexaggerated dialect. The popularity of Downing's character and letter format prompted other writers, such as Charles A. Davis of the *New York Daily Advertiser,* to use them in their own work.

S.'s work takes Downing from his small rural Downingville to far-off places where he becomes involved in military skirmishes and corrupt politics, while befriending several presidents. Having eventually become exhausted and seriously ill from his travels and exploits, Jack Downing soon dies, and a splendid funeral is reported in the *Courier* on April 1, 1836. The humor of the letters offered a welcome relief from the tediousness of popular mid-19th-c. prose, but was balanced by the seriousness of S.'s satire of contemporary situations, such as the relationship between political power and criminal advantage. The character of Jack Downing was inserted into actual situations, giving readers a new perspective from which to view their national leaders.

S. graduated with honors from Bowdoin College in 1818 and began a lifelong career of newspaper work. In 1823, he married Elizabeth Oakes SMITH, who became better-known in many literary circles than her husband. Although he never achieved the kind of notoriety and wealth he had hoped for during his lifetime, S.'s reputation as a major American humorist was founded upon the character of Major Jack Downing.

After the demise of Downing, S.'s life also took a turn for the worse after he lost most of his money in land speculation and unsuccessful inventions. He published *Powhatan* (1841), a metrical romance, and *New Elements in Geometry* (1850), an inaccurate study of geometry, both of which were utter failures. S. resurrected Downing for *May-Day in New York* (1843), and began a second series of letters in the New York *Daily Intelligencer* that led to an anthology of Downing material, *My Thirty Years out of the Senate* (1847), the title of which being a parody of a similar title by Thomas Hart Benton. Although this material is interesting in its own right, the later letters lack much of the innovative energy found in the Jacksonian writings. In 1860, in failing health, S. retired from active life to Long Island.

BIBLIOGRAPHY: Rickels, M., and P. Rickels, *S. S.* (1977); Wyman, M. A., *Two American Pioneers* (1927)

                                    MICHAEL J. PETTENGELL

SMITH, William

b. 27 April 1727, Aberdeenshire, Scotland; d. 14 May 1803, Philadelphia, Pennsylvania

S. is perhaps now most often remembered for who he knew and who he taught, rather than for any significant literary achievement. For example, because he moved in their circles, S. appears in the writings of such early American luminaries as George Washington, Benjamin FRANKLIN, and Benjamin Rush. In addition, S. is said to have fostered among his students the formation of the first American literary and artistic circle, which included painter Benjamin West, poet Francis HOPKINSON, and poet-playwright Thomas GODFREY. Although S.'s early writings included poetry, he soon turned primarily to a less metaphoric form of composition, leaving prodigious writings that remain a valuable source for early American historical and cultural scholarship.

Born in Scotland, S. emigrated to Long Island in 1751 as a tutor to Colonel Josiah Martin's two sons. Two years later, S. published a volume of poetry entitled *Indian Songs of Peace* (1753). The poems included in *Indian Songs of Peace* were pastoral than specifically "Indian," as S. had no personal experience with or much actual knowledge of Native American culture or language. More importantly, in the same year, S. published the most significant of his early writings, *A General Idea of the College of Mirania*. By all accounts, S. was an exceptional and committed teacher, and this pamphlet allowed him to lay out clearly his pedagogical theories and visions through the fictional memories of "Evander," a native of the utopian province of Mirania. S. sent a copy of *A General Idea* to Benjamin Franklin, who, impressed with S.'s practical notions about higher education, saw to it that S. was appointed the first provost of the College of Philadelphia two years later.

Over his lifetime, S. produced many philosophical and scientific papers, making valuable contributions to several academic disciplines. Yet he was best known for his more troublesome writings. Something of a curmudgeon, he had a penchant for making enemies, in large part because of his fondness for writing (supposedly anonymous) controversial political pamphlets and articles concerning both local and national issues. S. edited and published the *American Magazine, or Monthly Chronicle* from 1757 to 1758, using his regular column "Philosophical Miscellany" as a forum for a number of such pieces. Always the unswerving Anglican, the bulk of S.'s later written legacy is comprised of various occasional sermons that reflect in general the established theology and the conservative political wisdom of the late-18th-c. Church of England—a deeply rooted perspective that in part triggered S.'s fall into disrepute in postrevolutionary Pennsylvania.

In 1765, S. published what remains one of his most valuable works, *Expedition against the Ohio Indians in the Year 1764*. *Expedition,* a meticulously detailed analysis of Colonel Henry Bouquet's military and political encounters with Native American tribes in Ohio (the Seneca, Delaware, and Shawnee), apparently struck a chord with S.'s contemporaries, for it quickly went through several editions. From its initial publication, S.'s *Expedition* has been regarded as a particularly accurate historical document in part because S.'s sources included not only the "authentic documents" of an unidentified veteran officer, but his own conversations with some of the officers involved in the expedition (one of whom was related to S. by marriage). Besides a thorough account of Bouquet's victory at Bushy Run in 1763 and his subsequent push into Indian territory to retrieve Anglo-European captives in 1764, S. offers in *Expedition* a fascinating examination of the conflict of cultures on military effectiveness. S. argued that Bouquet's success against what had proven until then to be an almost invincible enemy was a direct result of his recognition that it was necessary to understand and use an enemy's own rhetoric and culture to successfully neutralize and conquer them. Perhaps one of S.'s most interesting insights arose when he noted that the American landscape itself was at odds with the prevailing European culture of war. Because Native Americans had adapted all aspects of their culture to that landscape, S. contended that conquering them necessarily involved European armies making a similar adaptation. To that end, then, S. included in *Expedition* schematics for building more defensible forts, layouts of more suitable troop formations, and suggestions for the most appropriate and necessary supplies.

BIBLIOGRAPHY: Corner, G. W., ed., *The Autobiography of Benjamin Rush* (1948); Gegenheimer, A. F., *W. S.:*

Educator and Churchman (1943); Jones, T. F., *A Pair of Lawn Sleeves: A Biography of W. S. (1727–1803)* (1972)

MARSHA WATSON

SMITH, William Jay

b. 22 April 1918, Winnfield, Louisiana

S. is one of America's most modest, most "I-less" poets. His career has spanned more than half of the 20th c. Professor emeritus at Hollins College since 1980, S. has been a Rhodes Scholar, a consultant at the Library of Congress, and a member of the Vermont House of Representatives. S.'s remarkable career includes distinction as a children's writer and editor, with Louise BOGAN, among others, translator, essayist, and playwright. But primarily he is a poet who owns a secure place in our literature, a poet known for his distinctly imagistic style that makes him, as Richard WILBUR proclaims from the dustjacket of *Collected Poems, 1939–1989* (1990), "One of the very few who cannot be confused with anybody else."

Much of the critical discussion of S.'s work centers around his shift from formal to free verse with the publication of *The Tin Can and Other Poems* (1966). The question is one of preference; few would deny the power of the later free-form poems or the earlier formal ones. *Collected Poems, 1939–1989* clearly displays the free-form verse "fault line" because S. has rolled forward cumulatively most of the poems that were in the successive earlier poetry books: *Poems* (1947), *Poems, 1947–1957* (1957), *The Tin Can and Other Poems,* and *New and Selected Poems* (1970). Thus, the critical arguments followed the most recent book into print since it contains the "problematic" long-lined, unrhymed free verse poems that have drawn complaints of looseness of line after the fashion of Walt WHITMAN and Allen GINSBERG, though the tasteful S. would never howl or shout from roof tops. These notable poems are "The Tin Can," "What Train Will Come," "Fishing for Albacore," "Venice in the Fog," and "The Traveler's Tree." Nobody would want these fine poems expurgated. Indeed Thomas H. Landess writing in *Sewanee Review* finds some of the formal poems in *Poems* to lack an adequate "Dionysian impulse," an impulse more fully supplied in these freer, longer poems. S.'s work well showcases the effects of the two ways of writing. He is always the same personality, the same voice. That he is more expansive in free verse and more memorably beautiful in formal verse hardly comes as a revelation, no more than it is with James WRIGHT, Derek Walcott, or others. But S. is so subtly his own man, so temperamentally stable that the formal versus free verse argument can be rewardingly studied in his work.

S. is an imagist, a "lyric poet," as he describes himself, but one more than usually careful about aesthetic distance. His influences have been traced by Daniel Hoffman to early Wallace STEVENS. Ashley Brown links him to W. H. AUDEN's influence in that S., like many other American poets, followed Auden's "example of formal poetry written in a relaxed contemporary idiom." But S.'s imagism, while relaxed, is demanding. His delight in what one can see, hear, smell, taste, touch, presses him almost to the point of opulence, his images often moving metaphysically into other images, leaving the reader to solve the often difficult connections. S. is painterly, rarely direct with emotions. James DICKEY has described him as "a kind of dispossessed court poet among the ruins," an observation all the more cogent as this century ends. S.'s rich syllabification and the lushness of his often natural imagery repay the reader through sometimes difficult switches of setting. John Malcolm Brinnin finds "The Tin Can" "Wholly convincing, without a false syllable in its hundreds of lines, it is a recreation of experience." S. is a master of aesthetic distance. Here he leaves the inaccroachable curve of our century, retaining his fundamental character, dignity, and taste. S.'s autobiographical *Army Brat* (1980) reveals a childhood that could have yielded ample claims to victimhood had S. really followed the 20th c.'s literary winds to the bitter end.

Judson Jerome once called for a more "readable" poetry, meaning a more accessible poetry, rhymed, formal, easy. S.'s poetry for children fits well these criteria. Notable among these are *Puptents and Pebbles* (1959), *Ho for a Hat* (1964), *Mr. Smith and Other Nonsense* (1968), and *Laughting Time: Collected Nonsense* (1990). A number of the poems from these books are included in the larger books and are excellent poetry—for anybody.

BIBLIOGRAPHY: Dickey, J., *Babel to Byzantium* (1968); Group, B., "W. J. S.," in Greiner, D. J., ed., *DLB*, vol. 5, part 2, *American Poets since World War II* (1980): 262–66; Taylor, H., "Enter the Dark Horse," *MQR* 30 (Fall 1991): 732–46

BOB GASKIN

SNODGRASS, W[illiam] D[eWitt]

b. 5 January 1926, Wilkinsburg, Pennsylvania

S. served in the U.S. Navy during World War II and afterwards received B.A., M.A., and M.F.A. degrees from the University of Iowa. The separation from his daughter after his first divorce provided the most important poems in his first book *Heart's Needle* (1959), which won the Pulitzer Prize in 1960.

The general critical view of S.'s work is that he has not yet produced a book that excels his first. A poet who uses traditional rhyme and rhythm patters, whose work is usually intensely lyrical, S. broke with tradition, not in form, but in his early subject matter, writing from what seemed to be intimate personal experiences. As a result, he was labeled a confessional poet. His work, however, differed in several major ways from the other confessional poets. The voice he used in that first volume utilized material based on S.'s own life, but he also used the objective correlative. Three other techniques he utilizes to mask his true self include the following: a pseudonym, adopting personae, and writing about another art. Why he feels the needs for these various protections is a question that has not yet been answered, but because of these subterfuges, it is difficult to label the true S.

In both the first and second book, *After Experience* (1968), S. often used T. S. ELIOT's objective correlative, and he continued it even after he discovered the intention for this device was to hide the writer's true emotion. His third book, *Remains* (1970), appeared under a pseudonym, S. S. Gardons, an anagram of his last name. This technique enabled him to write from a different viewpoint, and freed the work from being judged by Pulitzer standards. In *The Fuehrer Bunker: A Cycle of Poems in Progress* (1977), he assumed the personae of various Nazis, using techniques reminiscent of Robert Browning's soliloquies. This volume and *Heinrich Himmler: Platoons and Files* (1982) were severely criticized because some reviewers thought they humanized the Nazi leaders, and they did provide Freudian explanations for horrendous Nazi behavior. S., however, was actually using other voices to explore the problem of good and evil in the world, and these powerful poems may be his most important ones. *Kinder Capers* (1986) continued an early practice—using the work of painters for entrance to a poem. The new poems, inspired by the paintings of DeLoss McGraw, in which he assumed the mythologized persona of W. D., allowed the poet to write from behind a screen of another art, giving him the freedom of modernist paintings that reject the mimetic. These later poems are often acerbic, even Swiftian in their irony, using a variety of word plays not seen since the work of James Joyce.

S. has published several volumes of translations. *In Radical Pursuit* (1975) includes essays on the genesis of some of his own poems as well as evaluations of other modern poets, and his *Selected Poems* appeared in 1987.

BIBLIOGRAPHY: Gaston, P., *W. D. S.* (1978); Phillips, R., *The Confessional Poets* (1973)

ANN STRUTHERS

SNYDER, Gary
b. 8 May 1930, San Francisco, California

Writing with directness and clarity in a language both colloquial and eloquent, S. has drawn on the central experiences of his life as an environmental visionary, teacher/scholar, and community activist to address some of the crucial issues of the latter decades of the 20th c. in poetry and essays. His work combines a wide-ranging erudition and an original, inquisitive mind with a congenial wit and high-spirited playfulness that has reached and impressed literary professionals and literate citizens across a broad spectrum of interests and political positions, including the rapt audience at Allen GINSBERG's first reading of *Howl* that S. followed effectively with his own lyric poems, and the more staid legislators in the California state senate where he served a term on the Arts Council.

Fascinated by the ecological biodiversity of the Pacific Northwest where he was reared, S. devised an unusual composite major at Reed College joining (actually creating) a program in environmental studies with one in literature and anthropology. S.'s intellectual predisposition toward a rigorous pursuit of the disciplines that captivated him was purposefully reconciled at the beginning of his career as a writer with his conviction that a practical application of the various forms of knowledge he pursued was crucial to his development as a man and an artist. While he was a student, he worked as a forest ranger, fire watcher, logger, merchant seaman, and trail builder, gathering the lore and language of his experiences into his first book of poetry, *Riprap* (1959), a title that refers to the placing of rock on a mountain trail and the placement of the precise work in a line of poetry. The metaphor linking "the work of hands" and the agility of the poet's mind is characteristic of S.'s method of locating artistic consciousness amidst the commonplace things and activities that constitute what for S. are the fundamental facts of existence. As he puts it, "What we want poetry to do is guide lovers toward ecstasy, give witness to the dignity of old people, intensify human bonds, elevate the community and improve the public spirit."

His commitment to "the real work" as he calls it in a collection of interviews using that title published in 1980 has not separated S. from his scholarly interests, and in the second edition of *Riprap* (1965), S. included *Cold Mountain Poems,* his translation of the poems of a Chinese "mountain madman" who lived in the T'ang dynasty of the 7th c. Here, S. celebrates a "ragged hermit" living in comfortable solitude in the wilderness, a man like the laborers he met in the northwest forest, and the Cold Mountain poems continue the striking depictions of landscape of S.'s first book, moving outward in time and space toward a larger conception of the entire planet as an accessible and inspiring realm for proper human habitation. At this same time, S. published *Myths and Texts* (1960) in which his deepening sense of the ways of the natural world was focused in three sections—"Logging"; "Burning"; and "Hunting"— each an attempt to frame a philosophical position with respect to the demands and necessities of the environment. His use of Native American texts in this collections, notably the Haida story of a bear/human union in "This poem is for bear," was the beginning of an evolving effort to unite the thought of the Western literary tradition that he was solidly grounded in with older, perhaps primal modes of apprehension he felt most Americans had become alienated from. His serious study of Zen in Japan during the 1960s contributed to this perspective, but the dominant feature of S.'s major collection *Turtle Island* (1974), which won the Pulitzer Prize and sold over 100,000 copies, was the critique of current American policies set in contrast to ways of wisdom S. regarded as much more beneficial to the maintenance of a sustainable planetary system.

The poems that S. wrote in the next decade were published as *Axe Handles* (1983), a book with a more reflective tone, a turning inward toward the specifics of S.'s family and the community in the Sierra Nevada where he lived and where he wanted to act as a means of transmission of a cultural continuity he regarded as crucial for following generations. The poems in this collection are marked by a compression of imagery in pursuit of the "relentless clarity" he sought in the finest tools and the sharpest minds of their handlers. While he continued work on a "poem of process" that he called *Mountains and Rivers without End* (which he completed in 1996), S. gathered his thoughts on the "etiquette" of the natural world into *The Practice of the Wild* (1990), a teaching text meant to guide people toward an appreciative coexistence with the natural world, and then carried this theme further with some new and older essays in *A Place in Space* (1995), which reemphasized his belief in a world in which he sees everything "interconnected, interpenetrating, mutually reflecting, and mutually embracing"—the universe of his poetic vision.

BIBLIOGRAPHY: Halper, J., ed., *G. S.: Dimensions of a Life* (1991); Molesworth, C., *G. S.'s Vision: Poetry and the Real Work* (1983); Murphy, P. *Understanding G. S.* (1992)

LEON LEWIS

nese immigrants. The work is important to understanding the abominable treatment of Japanese Americans (Nikkei) by the U.S. government during World War II.

S. was born in a Seattle hotel that her parents owned and operated, in a district known as "Skid Road." The second of four children, S.'s Japanese name, Kazuko, was chosen because it meant "peace," an ironic fact in this tale of discord. She begins her narrative with the striking realization at six years old that she is Japanese as well as American. To her, the idea of being both was "like being born with two heads."

Cultural opposition remains a theme throughout S.'s narrative. As hostility mounted between the Japanese and American governments, all Nikkei on the western coast became regarded as potential collaborators with the Japanese government. After Pearl Harbor, the U.S. government passed Executive Order 9066. In 1942, over 100,000 Nikkei were rounded up and interned in concentration camps. S.'s family was sent to the Minidoka Camp in Topaz, Idaho. Because she was an American citizen, S. was allowed to escape the camp, though she had to leave her parents behind. When the interned prisoners were released at the end of the war, they were instructed to renounce Japanese culture and assimilate into the American mainstream. It was this directive that would inform the tone of the work, which has been criticized for its assimilationist stance.

S. entered Wendell College in the Midwest, and then completed her undergraduate education at Hanover College in Hanover, Indiana. She received a master's degree in clinical psychology from Western Reserve University in Cleveland, Ohio, in 1949.

Published in 1953, *Nisei Daughter* was reprinted in 1979 at the beginning of the redress campaign, when Japanese Americans banded together politically and demanded acknowledgment and compensation from the U.S. government. S.'s autobiography is significant as a historical document of government-sanctioned American prejudice.

BIBLIOGRAPHY: Lim, S. G.-L., "Japanese American Women's Life Stories: Maternality in M. S.'s *Nisei Daughter* and Joy Kogawa's *Obasan*," *FSt* 16 (Summer 1990): 288–312; Sumida, S. H., "Protest and Accommodation, Self-Satire and Self-Effacement, and M. S.'s *Nisei Daughter*," in Payne, J. R., ed., *Multicultural Autobiography: American Lives* (1992): 207–47

VICTORIA ENG

SONE, Monica [Itoi]
b. 1919, Seattle, Washington

The title of S.'s autobiography *Nisei Daughter* (1953) refers to her status as an American-born child of Japa-

SONG, Cathy [Cathy-Lynn Song Davenport]
b. 20 August 1955, Honolulu, Hawai'i

In 1982, S. was chosen winner of the Yale Series of Younger Poets competition. Her manuscript of *Picture*

Bride (1983), selected by Richard HUGO, gained significant critical acclaim and demonstrated the sensuous lyricism and sensitivity to detail that would characterize her later work. Widely anthologized in such volumes as *The Best of Bamboo Ridge* (1986), *The Norton Anthology of Modern Poetry* (1988), and *The Heath Anthology of American Literature* (1994), S.'s writing speaks to a variety of audiences by evoking a specificity located in her experiences in Hawai'i and on the East Coast, as well as a tradition drawn from Asian, English, and North American influences.

The granddaughter of Korean and Chinese immigrants to Hawai'i, S. begins *Picture Bride* by reconstructing the past, interrogating a largely masculinized plantation history of the islands through the figure of the speaker's grandmother in the title poem. By focusing on the interaction between liberation and sexual commodification for the wife of a laborer, S. initiates a feminist critique echoed by her juxtaposition of the works of Kitagawa Utamaro and Georgia O'Keeffe, two artists whose evocation establishes S.'s visual affinity. In tribute to, yet exploration of, Utamaro's 19th-c. Japanese prints, poems such as "Beauty and Sadness" and "Ikebana" touch on the voyeuristic role of the artist and the restricted and sometimes vulnerable position of the subject. The subject finds subjectivity, however, in "From the White Place" and "Blue and White Lines after O'Keeffe," as S. gives voice to O'Keeffe, who is both art and artist. The latter poem, divided like *Picture Bride* into five sections, each named after a flower, demonstrates S.'s close identification with the painter: S. explores kinship and the relationships contextualizing the speaker's existence in the same way that O'Keeffe is the artist naming her surroundings. The bonds between family members are intense and unmistakable, like the "jade link/handcuffed to your wrist" in "Lost Sister." As S. pays tribute to these connections in such pieces as "Easter: Wahiawa, 1959" and "Tribe," she also displays frustration and suffocation in others like "The Pale Arrangement of Hands" and "The Youngest Daughter."

S.'s concern with the domestic continues in her later work, as *Frameless Windows, Squares of Light* (1988) focuses on the attachment between parent and child. In addition, the strong presence of Hawai'i seen in *Picture Bride* resurfaces here; history circumscribes relationships in "Living Near the Water," in which the grandmother's "moment of regret" in meeting the man who sent for her gives birth to the speaker's family. In this way, S. identifies these experiences as specifically "Local," hence recognizable to the predominantly Asian population in the islands descended from plantation laborers. S.'s collection, *School Figures* (1994), combines the themes of family, memory, and Local identity within a framework that is self-conscious of its art and process. "The Story of Madeline" works as a narrative of a narrative by retelling the popular children's story, providing a fable of love translated into efficient concern in the figure of Miss Clavel. A number of poems including "A Conservative View" and "Eat," then, become expressions of love from a daughter to her mother, and storytelling becomes the vehicle by which such feelings are transformed and expressed. This notion culminates in the concluding title poem, as the "repetition of school figures" drawn by children practicing their art eventually comes to define the pattern of their lives. This richness and resonance in S.'s writing, along with the commingling of traditions in her work, makes her one of the finest contemporary American poets, and a valued contributor to Hawai'i's body of literature.

BIBLIOGRAPHY: Sumida, S., *And the View from the Shore: Literary Traditions of Hawai'i* (1991); Sumida, S., "Sense of Place, History, and the Concept of the 'Local' in Hawai'i's Asian/Pacific American Literatures," in Lim, S. G., and A. Ling, eds., *Reading the Literatures of Asian America* (1992): 215–37

BRENDA KWON

SONTAG, Susan

b. 16 January 1933, New York City

S. is one of America's foremost critics and champions of MODERNISM. An admirer of European intellectuals such as Antonin Artaud and Walter Benjamin, writers who push beyond the confines of acculturated Western thought, S. pushes boundaries in her own work—critical and theoretical as well as creative. S. is best known for her nonfiction, publishing several collections of essays, including *Against Interpretation and Other Essays* (1966); *On Photography* (1977)—winner of the National Book Critics Circle Award; *Under the Sign of Saturn* (1980); and *A S. S. Reader* (1981), a sampling of essays and fiction—selected by S. herself. She is also the author of two novels, *The Benefactor* (1963) and *Death Kit* (1967); two film scripts, *Duet for Cannibals* (1969) and *Brother Carl* (1971); a collection of stories, *I, etcetera* (1978); a historical romance, *The Volcano Love* (1992); and a closet drama, *Alice in Bed: A Play* (1993). The pivotal theme in all her work stems from her refusal to prescribe external meanings to individual works of art or cultural experiences—a rebuttal of traditional hermeneutics.

This rebuttal is the subject of S.'s best-known essay: "Against Interpretation." In *The Benefactor*, S.'s Hippolyte (when he's not quoting Baudelaire) asks, "Why not take the dreams at face value? Perhaps I did not need to 'interpret' my dreams at all." S. asks the same question about art and culture in "Against Interpretation." She strives to validate an artistic aesthetic that is based on concrete experience and pleasure, arguing that the appropriate response to creative works should not be intellectual. In place of hermeneutics, S. writes as the essay's coda, "we need an erotics of art."

For this seeming call for a new philistinism (though more precisely, an invocation of a new appreciation of "art for art's sake"), S. has been rebuked for being self-indulgent. She is little read in academic circles, having acquired a reputation as a "pop" critic. Though Carlos Fuentes praises S.'s essays as "great interpretations, and even fulfillments of what is really going on," another critic Jay Parini fiercely censures S. for being "too dead-set against interpretation to read the world at all." Still, the world reads S.—one of the most influential writers of our time. Some critics feel that a valuable function in S.'s work has been to introduce American readers to Continental literature. S.'s lucid sense of modernism coupled with her eminent style make even the somewhat unapproachable and contentious Artaud palatable to the American populace, as in "Approaching Artaud" from *Under the Sign of Saturn*. However, some critics, such as Walter Kendrick, feel that S. "perpetuates a tradition of philosophical naivete that has always kept America subservient to Europe and that surely should have run its course by now."

Regarded by many as her most perceptive criticism, *Under the Sign of Saturn* is a lithe and perceptive—S.'s hallmarks—collection of essays published between 1972 and 1980—unified by only the "modernity" of its (mostly European subjects. "On Paul Goodman" and "Remembering Barthes" are brief personal eulogies—S.'s lamentation for Paul GOODMAN and the "terrible, mean American resentment toward someone who tries to do a lot of things" is most probably self-reflective. In two essays on film, S. debunks the "fascist aesthetics" of Leni Riefenstahl and applauds Han-Jürgen Syberberg for presenting images as images; she paints "literary portraits" of Antonin Artaud, Walter Benjamin, and Elias Canetti.

S.'s politics are radical; she has become the spokesperson for what is modern—politics as well as literature. William Phillips writes, "S. has suffered from bad criticism and good publicity. If she could be rescued from all her culture-hungry interpreters, it might be possible to find the writer who has been made into a symbol."

"What I have been writing is not criticism at all, strictly speaking, but case studies for an aesthetic, a theory of my own sensibility," says Walter Kendrick suggests that the *Reader* may, in fact, be S.'s "self-portrait," showing us "an unexpectedly conservative, philosophical retrograde writer whose primary function has always been domestication"—accommodat-

ing obscure artists and avant garde sensibilities—"to a familiar vocabulary of appreciation and evaluation." Parini suggests reading *A Barthes Reader* and the S. *Reader* in tandem: "the real thing looks even more real beside the imitation." The *Reader* is an ardent and lucid one. "But sensitive people are a dime a dozen," comments Alicia OSTRIKER. "The rarer gift Miss S. has to offer is brains." S. is as controversial a figure as the controversy that stems from her gifts.

BIBLIOGRAPHY: Kendrick, W., "Eminent Victorian," *VV* 35 (15–21 October 1980): 44–46; Ostriker, A., "Anti-Critic," *Commentary* 41 (June 1966): 83–84; Parini, J., "Reading the Readers: Barthes and S.," *HudR* 36 (Summer 1983): 411–19; Phillips, W., "Radical Styles," *PR* 36 (1969): 383–400

ZOE RANDALL

SORRENTINO, Gilbert
b. 27 April 1929, Brooklyn, New York

"Novels are cluttered with all kinds of signals, flashing and gesturing so that the author may direct our attention to a particular configuration of character of plot so that his work, such as it is, may be made simpler for him, and for us." S. makes this judgment in his collected essays, *Something Said* (1984), where his target is the socially realistic fiction of writers such as John O'HARA and John CHEEVER. As such, it associates him with the postmodern innovators—Thomas PYNCHON, Ronald SUKENICK, and others—who also attacked the conventions of traditionally mimetic narrative. Yet in doing this, the author's positive model was William Carlos WILLIAMS, whose fiction was far less well known than his poetry but who helped establish a tradition S. follows: that of resisting not just commercial pressures but academic ones as well.

Active in the 1950s as a poet, S. founded the magazine *Neon* and also worked with such similar venues as *Yugen* and *Kulchur*. His first collections, *The Darkness Surrounds Us* (1960) and *Black and White* (1964), also show the influence of Williams, specifically in how poems are shaped as coming directly out of the mind. By the 1960s, his work as an editor for Grove Press—where he advanced the career of his friend and protégé Hubert SELBY, Jr.—brought him into closer touch with the practice of fiction, and beginning with *The Sky Changes* (1964) and *Steelwork* (1970) S. embarked on a novelist's career that would explore with exquisitely fine detail the formalistic qualities of experience.

These initial novels define both themes and techniques the author would pursue for over three decades. In the first, he adopted the practice of not naming characters and of moving them through landscapes where the narrative progress is fragmentary at best and almost always coolly impersonal. For the second, S. chose the apparently static world of street-corner Brooklyn, where a wide array of nicknamed characters much like the friends of his youth explored nuances and attitudes free from the dictates of chronological time and measurable space. In both, the emphasis is on preventing the materials of fiction from being perverted into what S. feels are the mistruths of convention—of the expectations realistic writers feel compelled to fulfill.

Throughout the 1970s, S. pursued a more aggressive strategy of attacking traditional fiction's methodologies. *Imaginative Qualities of Actual Things* (1971) found him not just satirizing the little magazine and art gallery world he himself had graduated from the decade before but speaking directly to readers as he devastated his characters with deliberately overdone invective. The novella *Splendide-Hôtel* (1973) was a much gentler work, freed from overtly narrative consequence by virtue of its structure, a series of improvisations on the successive letters of the alphabet. Yet with *Mulligan Stew* (1979), he quite literally wrote both conventional fiction and literary postmodernism into the ground by using the authorial self-consciousness perfected by Flann O'Brien in *At Swim-Two-Birds* to explode every pretension an author (here the novelist Anthony Lamont) and his characters (who take life to revolt against him) might have.

With his assumption of the prestigious Wallace Stegner Chair in Creative Writing at Stanford University in 1982, S.'s posture as a writer became decidedly more relaxed. No longer a member of the New York underground—as he had been in the 1950s and early 1960s in the company of LeRoi Jones (now Amiri BARAKA) and Frank O'HARA—and a continent removed from what in the 1970s he had seen as the decline and even deterioration of serious publishing, S. turned to calmly mannered reexplorations of earlier successes. Representative of this happy phase are the novels *Odd Number* (1985), in which his art-world characters from *Imaginative Qualities of Actual Things* are interrogated within a continuous dissolving story, and *Red the Fiend* (1995), where a child raised in the Brooklyn world of *Steelwork* is tutored by adversity in the perverse perspectives disjointed reality allows.

BIBLIOGRAPHY: Klinkowitz, J., *The Life of Fiction* (1977); McPheron, W., *G. S.: A Descriptive Bibliography* (1991); Saltzman, A. M., *Designs of Darkness in Contemporary American Fiction* (1990); Waugh, P., *Metafiction* (1984)

JEROME KLINKOWITZ

SOTO, Gary
b. 12 April 1952, Fresno, California

S. is the most mainstream Chicano writer in the U.S., where he was born and educated. He attended California State at Fresno for his B.A. in English and the University of California at Irvine to earn his M.F.A. in creative writing. His experiences are those of a member of an ethnic minority whose language of choice may be Spanish, English, or both; however, English is his primary language rather than his secondary one. Generally, his works depict characters not wholly at ease with their minority status or assimilation to the mainstream.

S.'s works fall into three categories: poetry, short stories, and children's books. He has also produced three short films for Hispanic children. Among his accolades are the ALA Best Book Award for Young Adults, the 1985 Before Columbus Foundation's American Book Award, the Beatty Award (1990), and the American Library Association's Andrew Carnegie Medal for the film version of *The Pool Party* (1993).

S.'s children's collections affirm a sense of worth and foster self-esteem in the Hispanic child. He treats his characters in a sensitive manner as they deal with poverty and racism. Most of his works are autobiographical and depict his own experiences within his family in the environs of a changing neighborhood. *Too Many Tamales* (1993) portrays a group of youngsters who have to eat a massive platter of tamales as they try to find a ring that one of them has lost. The children's solution to their dilemma is humorous, simplistic, and wonderfully illustrated. When the family discovers the reason for the impromptu feast, the parents lovingly laugh rather than punish the sheepish kids.

The Pool Party deals with racism and classism within the Mexican American community. Rudy, whose family provides lawn care, is invited to a pool party at Tiffany's house. His parents want him to make an impression on the wealthier family and they teach him proper social etiquette so that he can avoid embarrassment. While the other children have sporty pool toys, he arrives with a patched truck inner tube that becomes the hit of the party. The work is both humorous and sad as it shows the differences between social and monetary worth in contrast to individual worth.

Included within this genre is *Crazy Weekend* (1994), which entails a comedic adventure to Fresno that results in a triumphant capture of criminals by two adolescents. *Local News* (1993) and *Baseball in April* (1990) are short story collections that are for older children.

Living up the Street (1985), *Small Faces* (1986), and *A Summer Life* (1990) present musings on poverty and material success, reflections on the Korean and the Vietnam Wars through the eyes of a child who has aged into a prospective draftee, and the trials and tribulations of a minority student who has to artfully vary his scant wardrobe in an effort to appear stylish rather than passe. These collections are oriented toward a more mature audience than the previously mentioned works. Nevertheless, the style is simple and straightforward.

S. has published in numerous journals. His poems are collected into seven full-length collections. *The Elements of San Joaquín* (1977) focuses on marginality, poverty, and the migrant worker experience. *The Tale of Sunlight* (1977) continues the same thematic material, but introduces the worker's perspective along with the image of sparrows, a recurrent motif in S.'s works. *Where Sparrows Work Hard* (1981) brings television shows and their influence as role models to the forefront. Principally, *Ozzie and Harriet* and *The Donna Reed Show* depict clean, well-dressed families that never go hungry in contrast to the argumentative families and squalid conditions of the migrant workers who pick plenty of food, yet never have enough to eat.

Black Hair (1985) begins with remembrances of childhood and progresses to young adulthood as S. recalls the death of his father. *Lesser Evils* (1987) involves a simple style that deals with reflections and meditations on sex, desire, pets, fashion, and aging by a sensitive male with a hardened edge. In *Who Will Know Us?* (1990), the chief themes are death, old age, childbirth, and fatherhood written from a nostalgic point of view.

Essentially, S. is a sensitive author who depicts minority culture as worthy while presenting meanness and poverty as intolerable. He incorporates his own life into much of his work to make it genuine to an empathetic reader.

BIBLIOGRAPHY: Erben, R., and U. Erben, "Popular Culture, Mass Media, and Chicano Identity in G. S.'s *Living up the Street* and *Small Faces*," *MELUS* 3 (Fall 1991–92): 43–52; Olivares, J., "The Streets of G. S.," *LALR* 35 (January-June 1990): 32–49; Pérez-Torres, R., *Movements in Chicano Poetry* (1995)

WILLIAM O. DEAVER, JR.

SOUTH, The

Writing in the Southern colonies in the 17th c. was, of course, the work of new or temporary settlers, mostly English, like Captain John SMITH. By the turn of the 18th c., however, native Virginians such as William BYRD and Robert BEVERLEY, though still under the influence of English education and style, were using local materials. With the arrival of the newspaper several decades later and the political unrest that followed

in midcentury, writing became an important factor in colonial culture, despite the fact that belles lettres were still relatively neglected. This situation was partially rectified by 19th-c. publishing firms in New York and Boston that encouraged writing throughout the country. At the same time, ironically, political, social, and cultural tensions made authors in the South conscious of loyalties to state and region. Consequently, calls for a Southern literature in the 1850s led to responses not unlike those to calls for an American literature in the 1830s. The Civil War heightened this consciousness and temporarily interrupted other developments in literature. The aftermath of the war and reconciliation between the sections, however, led to an outpouring of fiction in the South that ebbed only slightly after the turn of the century and regained strength perceptibly after World War I, together with new contributions to poetry, in the Southern Renaissance. More recent work in the region may have failed to reach the high point of the Renaissance in the 1930s and 1940s, but its overall impact on the national scene has been vital and significant.

The extent of intellectual activity in the colonial period has been more carefully estimated and studied recently, and John Smith, Andrew White, George Alsop, John Cotton, William Byrd, Robert Beverley, Hugh Jones, Ebenezer COOKE, Richard Lewis, Samuel Davies, and Thomas JEFFERSON represent in their work the various genres as well as themes political, social, religious, historical, and cultural. Their joint experience suggests the problems faced by writers during the period—the absence of printing presses and, consequently, of newspapers and periodicals until the 1720s and 1730s, the scarcity of publishers until the 19th c., and the small audiences available for colonial literature. It is not strange, then, that much writing of this time was the work of lawyers, politicians, clergymen, physicians, and others whose main line was something else. The result frequently manifested itself in political pamphlets, religious tracts, sermons, history, diaries, and journals, prose seldom of a belletristic stamp. There were a few exceptions—Cotton's poems on Bacon's Rebellion, and Cooke's satire on Maryland, *The Sot-Weed Factor*—but the best work, William Byrd's for example, was not published during the period, and few who wielded the pen thought earnestly about trying to make a living by it.

It was not until well into the 19th c. that a few hardy souls like Edgar Allan POE and William Gilmore SIMMS sought to make writing a profession and committed themselves to belles lettres seriously. Nor did Poe and Simms find it easy to live by literature above or below the Mason and Dixon line. Poe spent much of his career in Philadelphia and New York eking out a living by editing and contributing to periodicals. He had published three slim volumes of poems by the time he was twenty-two, and he subsequently brought out a novel, two collections of tales, and another of poems. But the appearance of "The Raven" in 1845 won him more public attention than any of his books. Simms, on the other hand, spent most of his life in South Carolina devoting himself to similar enterprises and almost to as little avail. At times, however, in the 1830s and occasionally thereafter, his novels and romances, *Guy Rivers, The Yemassee,* and *The Partisan,* among them, published in the North, sold well, but after the early 1840s, his wife's plantations provided much of his livelihood. Other writers of the period fared little better. John Pendleton KENNEDY, though successful with *Swallow Barn* (1832) and *Horse-Shoe Robinson* (1835), never deserted his legal business, and William Alexander CARUTHERS continued to practice medicine in Virginia, New York, and Georgia while writing three novels and other prose. Concurrently, work in forms considered subliterary, humor for instance, led to realistic portrayals of frontier life and character in language native to place and scene, and though such fiction normally paid no better than more "respectable" writing, it led to local color, realism, and to a use of materials that has characterized much Southern writing since—a fascination with place and language, indeed with translating speech and oral narrative into writing. Together with a drift toward rhetoric and an interest in history, the past, the land, the agrarian ideal, the family, and the community associated with writers of the more conventional literary forms, these qualities represent most of those usually considered integral to Southern literature in general. Moreover, it was during this period that political tensions in the 1850s brought about a demand for a Southern literature; and the establishment of the Confederacy, celebrated by Henry TIMROD in "Ethnogenesis" and "The Cotton Boll," led to a brief concentration on the glories and plights of the new nation. Despite the obvious cultural need, economic and military conditions severely limited the range and scope of and compensation for both poetry and prose, and writers, including Simms and Timrod, had to find other ways to support themselves, another result or byproduct at least of the South's attachment to politics. Allen Tate put it more tartly: the South, he maintained, was "hagridden with politics."

It was not until after the Civil War that many authors could consider making a living from books and periodicals. Samuel Langhorne CLEMENS, of course, made several fortunes, but despite his background and his use of Mississippi-River materials in *Tom Sawyer, Life on the Mississippi,* and *Huckleberry Finn,* he was seldom characterized as a Southern writer. On the other hand, George Washington CABLE, Thomas Nel-

son PAGE, Joel Chandler HARRIS, among many who were viewed as Southern, usually turned to lecturing, law, or journalism to supplement their incomes from writing, a situation that frequently obtained for later generations of artists as well; and poets like Paul Hamilton HAYNE and Sidney LANIER had to contribute prose as well as poetry in attempting to scratch a subsistence from literature. Still the literary magazines of this period—the *Atlantic Monthly, Harper's New Monthly, Scribner's Monthly,* the *Century, Lippincott's* and others—became vital factors in the cultural marketplace, as Poe had anticipated, and made it possible for many Southerners, including women such as Mary MURFREE, Grace KING, and Kate CHOPIN, to consider writing as a possible or partial career; and the popularity of local-color fiction created a demand contributors from all sections eagerly sought to supply. Southern periodicals themselves were rarely financially successful, but Northern journals accepted and, by the 1880s, encouraged contributions from the region not limited to mere local color.

Subsequently, literary activities abated somewhat in the early 20th c., a time when H. L. MENCKEN was characterizing the South as the "Sahara of the Bozart," but even then Ellen GLASGOW and James Branch CABELL were significant figures in the national pantheon; and O. HENRY, though dead by 1910, remained one of the most popular storytellers in the country.

Within a few years of Mencken's comment, writing in the South came into its own with the publication of *The Fugitive* and *I'll Take My Stand,* and William FAULKNER, Thomas WOLFE, and Katherine Anne PORTER joined Glasgow and Cabell on the scene with *The Sound and the Fury, Look Homeward, Angel,* and *Flowering Judas.* The Southern Renaissance was under way, and from the 1930s to the 1950s, the South made a rich and lasting contribution to national literature in the work of those already named, including the FUGITIVES/AGRARIANS John Crowe RANSOM, Allen TATE, Donald DAVIDSON, and Robert Penn WARREN, and in the output of Erskine CALDWELL, Eudora WELTY, Caroline GORDON, Andrew Lytle, Tennessee WILLIAMS, Richard WRIGHT, Peter TAYLOR, Shelby FOOTE, Randall JARRELL, Ralph ELLISON, James DICKEY, Elizabeth SPENCER, William STYRON, and Flannery O'CONNOR. Faulkner's publications alone during this period—*As I Lay Dying, Light in August, Absalom, Absalom!, The Hamlet,* and *Go Down, Moses*—suggest the level of achievement, to say nothing of Caldwell's *Tobacco Road,* Tate's *The Fathers,* Wright's *Native Son,* Williams's *The Glass Menagerie* and *A Streetcar Named Desire,* Warren's *All the King's Men,* Welty's *Delta Wedding,* and a host of other significant titles. A vigorous criticism accompanied this production of prose and poetry, and Ransom, Tate,

Warren, Cleanth BROOKS, and others edited important journals like the *Sewanee Review,* the *Southern Review,* and the *Kenyon Review* where they contributed essays that offered insight into and interpretation of the works of their contemporaries and provided impetus to the rise and development of the New Criticism, a literary achievement in itself. There is some critical disagreement about the vitality of the Renaissance in the 1960s and thereafter, but with many of the abovementioned writers still producing important work—Faulkner's *The Reivers,* Porter's *Ship of Fools,* Foote's *The Civil War: A Narrative,* O'Connor's *Everything That Rises Must Converge,* Styron's *The Confessions of Nat Turner,* among others—and with Walker PERCY, A. R. AMMONS, John BARTH, Reynolds PRICE, Ernest J. GAINES, Shirley Ann GRAU, George GARRETT, and Dabney Stuart beginning to establish themselves, the Renaissance may appear to have declined only in overall achievement, but Southern writing continues to flourish; and even if it loses some of its traditional qualities of attachment to the land and community and of fascination with the language, the people, and the past, or if the South fails eventually to establish a literary or publishing center, it still seems likely to thrive into the distant future.

BIBLIOGRAPHY: Bradbury, J. M., *Renaissance in the South: A Critical History of the Literature, 1920–1960* (1963); Davis, R. B., *Intellectual Life in the Colonial South, 1585–1763* (3 vols., 1978); Holman, C. H., *Three Modes of Modern Southern Fiction* (1966); Holman, C. H., *The Roots of Southern Writing* (1972); Hubbell, J. B., *The South in American Literature, 1607-1900* (1954); Jones, A. G., *Tomorrow Is Another Day: The Woman Writer in the South, 1859-1936* (1981); Parks, E. W., *Segments of Southern Thought* (1938); Ridgely, J. V., *Nineteenth-Century Southern Literature* (1980); Rubin, L. D., Jr., et al., eds., *The History of Southern Literature* (1985); Rubin, L. D., *William Elliott Shoots a Bear: Essays on the Southern Literary Imagination* (1975)

RAYBURN S. MOORE

SOUTHWORTH, E[mma] D[orothy] E[liza] N[evitte]

b. 26 November 1819, Washington, D.C.; d. 30 June 1899, Washington, D.C.

S. turned to writing because it was one of the few ways for a woman of her time to earn money respectably. She penned novels that appeared serially in periodicals, hoping at first only to support herself and her children. Instead, she made a fortune. She became one of the best-known American writers of the mid-19th c., with her serials republished so often under so many

different titles that the exact number of her novels—probably about fifty—can only be conjectured. Her literary style, a blend of the sentimental and the melodramatic, eventually fell from favor. Now, however, a new generation of critics has rescued her from obscurity, intrigued by her unusual portrayals of women and their roles in American society.

S. was educated in her stepfather's academy, where she developed an insatiable appetite for reading. She also indulged her interest in the local history and traditions of Maryland, her mother's early home, absorbing from both written and oral sources details about life there that would provide settings for many of her books. She taught school until 1840, when she married Frederick Hamilton Southworth. The couple moved to Prairie du Chien, Wisconsin. In 1844, she returned to Washington with her sick son, pregnant with another child, and without her husband; she never revealed whether she abandoned him or was herself abandoned. Forced to write for newspapers when her return to schoolteaching failed to provide enough income to support her family, she achieved great success with her first serialized novel, *Retribution,* in 1849.

S. thereafter wrote tirelessly, churning out novels that her reading public, composed of both men and women, devoured. To some extent her works are formulaic: the stories rely on melodramatic coincidence, improbable intrigue, and mysterious secrets, combined rather paradoxically in the service of familiar sentiment; each book ends with a promising marriage. But S.'s novels are ambiguous enough to have been viewed as arguments both for and against the cult of domesticity. Her female characters marry and run households, but they also struggle against male oppression, with degrees of success that vary according to the individual heroine's measure of backbone. Some, like Gertrude Lion, the daring, outdoorsy Amazon of *The Mother-in-Law* (1851), S.'s third novel, or Capitola, the cross-dressing, bandit-outwitting "madcap" of her most popular serial, *The Hidden Hand* (1859), are dashing, larger-than-life women whose appeal for modern feminist critics is easy to understand.

BIBLIOGRAPHY: Baym, N., *Woman's Fiction: A Guide to Novels by and about Women in America* (1993); Dobson, J., "The Hidden Hand: Subversion of Cultural Ideology in Three Mid-Nineteenth-Century Women's Novels," *AQ* 38 (1986): 223–42

CAROLYN LENGEL

SPARKS, Jared

b. 10 May 1789, Willington, Connecticut; d. 14 March 1866, Cambridge, Massachusetts

S. is best known as the documentary biographer of George Washington and Benjamin FRANKLIN. An astonishingly hard worker, he also wrote biographies of John Ledyard (1828) and Gouverneur Morris (1832). He also edited the *North American Review* (1817–18; 1824–30), the twelve-volume *Diplomatic Correspondence of the American Revolution* (1829–30), the twenty-five volume *Library of American Biography* (1834–1848), and the four-volume *Correspondence of the American Revolution* (1853). He served as a Unitarian minister from 1818 to 1823 as well as the President of Harvard from 1849 to 1852. Although S. was a tenacious and invaluable collector of American historical documents at home and abroad, his habit of revising historical correspondence prompted controversy in the 1850s.

Born illegitimate and poor, S. coupled his scholarly interests with sound business sense. Most of his books sold very well. He began his *Diplomatic Correspondence* after securing a contract from the government to buy many of the copies. He bought the *North American Review* in 1824 and sold it several years later at nearly double his investment. In an attempt to modify the Anglophilic orientation of the journal, S. encouraged submissions on South America. In 1824–25, he learned Spanish and wrote several *Review* articles on Mexico, Columbia, and South America.

S. published two collections of Franklin's works, the first of which he rushed to press in 1833 when he discovered someone else was working on the same project. His later work, the ten-volume *Life of Franklin* (1836–40), was noteworthy for its revision of contemporary opinion about Franklin. According to John Spencer Basset, it was commonly believed that Franklin was a cunning and rather disingenuous man. S.'s biography emphasized his wisdom, patience, and sincerity. Most importantly, however, S. included hundreds of unpublished letters and more than fifty articles written by Franklin, which had never been published or collected in one volume.

S.'s greatest achievement was his twelve-volume *Writings of George Washington* (1834-37). Like most of his documentary biographies, the first volume contains a biography and the remaining volumes are devoted to Washington's correspondence, public documents, and speeches. Beyond material pertaining directly to Washington, the collection is valuable for its appendices, which contain historical materials such as letters exchanged between Lord North and King George debating the value of an American war. S. illustrates that the colonists were correct to put direct blame on the king rather than on Parliament.

As was his method with all his subjects, S. was interested in protecting the reputation of Washington and he felt that Washington should be remembered as a national leader. He was educated in an age that firmly believed in the harmony of one's character and writings. As a result, S. often edited Washington's correspondence for publication, substituting colloquial phrases like "wouldn't be a flea bite" for "is inconsequential to us." In one case, S. suppressed an entire passage that was derogatory of New England. Eventually, rival historians noticed the changes. In several *New York Evening Post* articles published in early 1851, a writer named "Friar Lubin" charged S. with tampering with history. At the same time, an English historian, Lord Mahon, noticed similar discrepancies between S.'s version of letters sent to Joseph Reed and those of another edition. A great controversy ensued and S. responded in both the *Post* and in pamphlet form. Showing remarkable restraint and generosity toward his accusers, S. discussed the complexity of editorial work, noting that because Washington's copybook often differed from the text of the letters he actually mailed, an editor had to use judgement because publishing houses would not print every word. S. defended his emendations of grammar and colloquialisms by claiming that personal correspondence was often written in haste and prone to slips of the pen. Refuting one of the central allegations, he also showed that his version was correct, and the other version, on which his accusers had staked their claims, didn't exist in Washington's papers. Although it was apparent that S. had shown questionable judgement in some of his decisions, the controversy left his reputation intact and provided a valuable corrective for later historiography.

BIBLIOGRAPHY: Adams, H. S., *The Life and Writings of J. S.* (1893); Basset, J. S., *The Middle Group of American Historians* (1917); Ellis, G., "Memoir of J. S.," *MHSP* 10 (1869): 211–310

GRANVILLE GANTER

SPENCER, Elizabeth
b. 19 July 1921, Carrollton, Mississippi

Coming after the Eudora WELTY-Katherine Anne PORTER generation and before the Anne TYLER-Lee SMITH one in Southern letters, S. is recognized internationally for her distinguished body of short fiction written over five decades. *The Stories of E. S.* (1981) and *Light in the Piazza* (1960) best represent her profuse talent.

Raised in a family whose Mississippi roots date back to the early 1800s, S. received her B.A. from Belhaven College in Jackson and her M.A. from Vanderbilt University, where she studied under Donald DAVIDSON. While teaching at the University of Mississippi, she published her first novel, *Fire in the Morning* (1948). The novel addresses a two-generation feud over property in a small Mississippi town. Using modernist narrative techniques such as multiple points of view and flashbacks, S. holds a strong command over a large cast of characters while maintaining a sharp focus on her protagonist, Kinloch Armstrong. Set in the hill country of Mississippi and with the prevailing sense that violence might erupt at any moment, the novel is clearly in William FAULKNER's fictional realm; to S.'s credit, *Fire in the Morning* invites such comparisons without seeming to be thematically derivative.

Her second novel, *This Crooked Way* (1952), is also set in the hills of Mississippi in the early part of the 20th c., and it led to a writing grant from the National Institute of Arts and Letters. With two widely reviewed novels to her credit, S. received a Guggenheim Fellowship in 1953 and traveled to Italy where she met John Arthur Blackwood Rusher, whom she married. They moved to Canada in 1958, where they have resided since with sojourns abroad and to the U.S. Continuing to write novels while moving more toward short fiction, S. received a *Kenyon Review* Fellowship in 1957 and citations from the American Academy of Arts and Letters in 1956 and again in 1983. After *The Voice at the Back Door* (1956), which concerns racial equality and came out on the heels of the *Brown* decision, S. shifted away from historical novels of the Southern Renaissance tradition.

Having written of the South while in Italy, S. turned her thoughts to Italy while in Canada and found rich literary territory. As did Robert Penn WARREN and Allen TATE in poetry and William STYRON and Pat Conroy in popular novels, S. addresses the subject of Southerners in Italy in several short novels and stories. Her finest such work, *Light in the Piazza,* confronts many of the same issues as Henry JAMES's short masterpiece, *Daisy Miller.* S.'s novel centers on a wealthy American mother and her decision whether or not to let her mentally impaired daughter marry a young Italian man they meet while in Florence. The marriage would grant the daughter happiness and the mother freedom, but it would also be an act of deceit to the young suitor who knows nothing of his love's impairment. After a last-minute negotiation between the American mother and a knowing Italian father, the longevity of the marriage seems assured on the basis of the youths' mutual love, the American girl's dowry, and the useful language barrier.

Beginning her writing career with historical novels set in the hills of Mississippi, then moving to contemporary stories set in Italy and Canada, S. has also written with great insight and sensitivity about the ever-changing Gulf of Mexico coastal towns in *Ship Island and Other Stories* (1968) and *The Salt Line* (1984) among other works.

BIBLIOGRAPHY: Entzminger, B., "An Interview with E. S.," *MissQ* 47 (Fall 1994): 599–618; Prenshaw, P. W., *E. S.* (1985); Prenshaw, P. W., *Conversations with E. S.* (1991)

JON PARRISH PEEDE

SPICER, Jack

b. 30 January 1925, Pasadena, California; d. 17 August 1965, San Francisco, California

S. is best known for his experimental poetry published from the late 1950s through the mid-1960s. His brief, mimeographed books were often distributed on site during readings to small groups of friends. Fortunately, much of the work has been gathered in *The Collected Books of J. S.* (1975), which also includes a detailed and informative critical essay by friend and poet Robin Blaser, and a sample application questionnaire for S.'s Magic Workshop poetry circle.

Primarily associated with the San Francisco Renaissance, S. also played a significant role in the early stages of the Beat movement. Along with several leading California visual artists, he helped establish the Six Gallery in 1953, where the first public reading of Allen GINSBERG's *Howl,* part 1, took place on October 7, 1955; this group reading, which also featured Philip Lamatia, Philip WHALEN, Michael MCCLURE, and Gary SNYDER, is considered by many to mark the beginning of the Beat generation. S. also instituted "Blabbermouth Night" at the Place, a North Beach, San Francisco, Beat "in-spot" during the 1950s and 1960s. Blabbermouth Night was a discourse and sound poem free for all, reminiscent of Dada oral performances. S. also founded the Magic Workshop in 1957, not so much a writing workshop as a popular culture performance collective-mystical society where members discussed esoteric writings and dramatized roles from the *Wizard of Oz.* Members of the Magic Workshop included Helen Adam, George Stanley, Robert DUNCAN, Ebbe Borregaard, Joe Dunn, and Jack Gilbert.

Though S.'s early poetry, collected in *One Night Stand and Other Poems* (1980), is informed by new critical principles of linguistic spareness, imagistic condensation, and the structural integrity and insularity of the individual poem, the later work is quite intriguing from a postmodern point of view and looks forward to experiments of the Language poets in the 1980s and 1990s. "Halfway through *After Lorca,*" S. comments, "I discovered that I was writing a book instead of a series of [isolated] poems"; he developed a serial method of composition in which groups of poems were to be viewed as offering a multiplicity of synchronous interconnections, sequence being intra-transformative rather than accumulative: the idea is to "explore and retreat but never be fully realized (confined) within the boundaries of one poem." In addition to experimenting with this method, S. performed composition as "dictation," a process in which the poet is "transmitting" or setting down, more than composing, messages received in a heightened state of tuned-in attention. By figuring the poet as receiver-transmitter, or "radio," whose "translations" must in turn be received and interpreted by a reader/listener, S. dialogically contends with an expressionist poetics that places primary value on individual experience voiced through a lyrically self-centered "I."

The apparently quirky, eccentric, highly personal, and cryptic quality of many of S.'s poems parody the intensely subjective impulse of contemporary lyric poetry. The key to the difference is in S.'s syntax and diction, which is often terse and direct, like quick transcriptions, without emotionally charged qualifiers. *After Lorca* (1957) and *The Heads of the Town up to the Aether* (1962), both reprinted in *Collected Books,* display S.'s metalinguistic concerns and the self-reflexive, parodic, and dialogic tendencies that characterize his work through the mid-1960s.

BIBLIOGRAPHY: Davidson, M., *The San Francisco Renaissance: Poetics and Community in Mid-Century* (1989); Perelman, B., ed., *Writing Talks* (1985)

                                        TOM LAVAZZI

SPOFFORD, Harriet Prescott

b. 3 April 1835, Calais, Maine; d. 14 August 1921, Deer Island, Massachusetts

Novelist, short story writer, and poet, S. was the most published writer in *Harper's Bazar* and a frequent contributor to numerous other magazines such as the *Atlantic,* the *Knickerbocker,* and *Lippincott's.* Like many other 19th-c. female writers, however, she fell into almost complete obscurity after death, only to receive the relatively recent interest of feminist critics; with the 1989 publication of *"The Amber Gods" and Other Stories,* S. continues to gain scholarly attention, primarily for the stories in this collection.

While S.'s work could be considered sensation fiction—the lurid tales popular in the 1860s—critics typically situate her within the American romance tradition of Nathaniel HAWTHORNE and Edgar Allan POE. Indeed, like these writers, S. often centers her fictions on crime, the supernatural, and madness. Her first critically acclaimed tale, "In a Cellar" (1859), is a detective story about a Parisian diplomat. It so impressed the editor of the *Atlantic* with authoritative detail of European diplomacy, as well as artistic force, that he doubted whether a "demure little Yankee girl" could have written it. "Circumstance" (1860), about a pioneer woman whose songs save her from a fantastic beast, gained the fearful attention of Emily DICKINSON, who commented, "I read Miss Prescott's 'circum-

stance,' but it followed me in the Dark—so I avoided her."

Also employing elements of the supernatural, "The Amber Gods" (1860) is frequently considered S.'s finest work. The narrator, Yone, tells how she and her meek cousin competed with each other for the affections of a young painter. While the supernatural element of the story becomes only fully apparent at the end—where Yone speaks from beyond the grave—demonic imagery is associated with the narrator throughout. "The Amber Gods" reveals a feminist aspect in S.'s work, giving a potent, immortal voice to a character who is far from the 19th-c. True Woman: rather than pious, domestic, and submissive, Yone is sensual, artistic, dangerous, and self-centered.

The mystical—sometimes demonic—female artist of "The Amber Gods" recurs through S.'s work. In another memorable tale, "Her Story" (1872), a Medusa-like, sensual female artist destroys a traditional woman's marriage. "Her Story," like "The Amber Gods" and other S. fictions, places the demonic female artist in contrast with the household "angel." Yet S. often depicts similarities between these supposedly divergent characters and causes them to rely on each other for survival. She thereby belies such 19th-c. feminine cultural binaries as virgins/whores and artists/domestics, while questioning if women must compete for men.

Although undeniably popular, S.'s sensational themes and lush prose style were denounced by the spokesman of American realism. In his review of her 1865 novel *Azarian,* Henry JAMES took S. to task for the "shortcomings, or rather excesses" of her style. A historical perspective may provide explanation: S. wrote in a postbellum era concerned with the material excesses of industrialization; and fictions such as "The Amber Gods," "Her Story," and "Old Madame" (1882) thematically address material as well as sexual extravagance. S.'s own stylistic "excesses" may then be understood as an attempt to inscribe the cultural excesses surrounding her. From this perspective, her style is less aesthetically problematic than revelatory of the context in which she wrote.

BIBLIOGRAPHY: Gold, E., and T. H. Fick, "A Masterpiece of the Educated Eye: Convention, Gaze, and Gender in S.'s 'Her Story,'" *SSF* 30 (1993): 511–23; Halbeisen, E. K., *H. P. S.* (1935); Shinn, T. J., "H. P. S.: A Reconsideration," *TCW* 1 (Summer 1984): 36–45

                                        DEBRA BERNARDI

SPORTS AND LITERATURE

Although incidental references to sports and sporting activities can be found in the journals and letters of the early colonial Southern aristocracy, the first true sports hero in American literature is undoubtedly James Fenimore COOPER's Natty Bumppo. In the five-novel Leather-Stocking saga, Cooper created the paradigm and apotheosis of the American frontiersman who practiced the outdoor sports of hunting, woodsmanship, and resourceful survival with a code of honor and nobility. Bumppo was a natural athlete who exhibited endurance, finely tuned sense and instinctive reactions, comprehensive knowledge of the environment, and a sensibility that bespoke wisdom and integrity. As a sportsman and loner outdoorsman, Leather-Stocking exemplified the romantic ideals and fantasies of a nation rapidly encroaching on the wilderness and unwittingly changing its character and directing it to purposes of settlement and agriculture. The exploits of other nature's athletes such as Daniel Boone, Mike Fink, and Davy CROCKETT reinforced the image of the strong individual who represented backwoods democracy and heroism while adding the elements of the tall tale and woods lore of the interior frontier.

Early sports literature focused on the individual and his exploits—whether he was a huntsman, a horseman, a harnessman, a prizefighter, an endurance runner or walker, or a fisherman. The sporting sketches of Henry William Herbert, writing as "Frank Forester" and publishing in William Trotter Porter's *Spirit of the Times* (the leading sporting journal from 1831 to 1861), popularized outdoor sports and made him the first nationally known sportswriter. Herbert also published a successful series of Frank Forester books on hunting and fishing as well as a two-volume study of thoroughbred and trotting horses in 1857. The development of wide circulation sporting periodicals not only popularized sports and brought increasing acceptance and respectability to sporting activities but also provided an important publishing opportunity for American writers. George Washington HARRIS, Thomas Bangs THORPE, Johnson Jones HOOPER, William Tappan THOMPSON, and others published stories and sketches in Porter's *Spirit of the Times,* establishing what would be an important connection between sports and oral humor, the rural tall tale, and the regional and country character. For many American writers, sportswriting and reporting would prove to be an entree to fame and popularity as a writer as well as a source of stories and characters. The sporting scene was a remarkably rich resource and index of the national character, for it embraced sporting events and sports heroes with approval and unapologetic enthusiasm. By the mid-19th c., sports were firmly established as events and a source of interest that linked the nation and focused its interest in physical skills, performance, and concentration of effort.

The 1870s and 1880s were remarkable decades for the development of sporting journals like Albert Pope's *Outing,* Francis C. Richter's *Sporting Life,* the Spinks's *Sporting News,* William Bleasdell Cameron's *Field and Stream,* Claude King's *Sports Afield,* and Richard Kyle Fox's *National Police Gazette,* which featured sports as well as sex and crime. In the 1890s, newspapers developed their sports sections and expanded sports coverage. Baseball writers became household names as the "scribes" of the sports garnered a loyal reading audience and brought increasing prestige and fame to their profession. Stephen CRANE, Frank NORRIS, and Richard Harding DAVIS all wrote sports journalism and sports stories in the sports ferment of the 1890s.

The turn of the century also saw the inauguration of the juvenile sports books, which have remained popular to this day. In April 1896, William Gilbert PATTEN, writing as Burt L. Standish, began the Frank Merriwell series, which he published weekly in the *Tip Top Library* and then the *Tip Top Weekly* until July 1912 and which was published in paperbound volumes by Street and Smith between 1900 and 1933. Frank Merriwell became the most recognized fictional sports hero in American popular literature. In the early 1900s, sales totaled 500,000 a week as countless readers followed his exploits—his personification of resourceful thinking, unbelievable agility and skills at all sports, command of critical situations, and ability to overcome all adversity or opposition. Frank was the self-disciplined, clean-thinking athlete who advocated fair play and sound judgment and who always thought of the good of the team. While Patten's series became formulaic in its plots and outcomes, the ideals of Merriwell were solid and exemplary. Frank personified the values of his culture: duty, hard work, constancy of purpose, physical preparedness, and a belief in sports as the right preparation for the tests and trials of life. From 1914 to 1928, Patten also published fifteen baseball novels as Burt L. Standish after he gave up the Merriwell stories in 1912, and other writers continued the series for three years. Other notable practitioners of the juvenile sports novel included Ralph Henry Barbour, who published more than one hundred books from 1899 to 1942; William Heyliger, who published from 1911 to 1943; Edward STRATEMEYER, who published under numerous pseudonyms and founded a syndicate that employed numerous writers. These remarkably prolific writers all contributed to juvenile fiction, filling the heads of impressionable young boys with dreams of glory, honor, and fame while at the same time reinforcing the notion that sports not only tested character but formed it. Each writer created distinctive sports heroes with generic names such as "Baseball Joe" or "Lefty Locke."

Following in the footsteps of these entrepreneurs of juvenile sports fiction were such writers as John R. Tunis, Joe Archibald, Clair Bee, Curtis K. Bishop, Matthew F. Christopher, Elmer A. Dawson, C. Paul Jackson, Wilfred McCormick, and Jackson V. Scholz to name a few of the more prolific and successful. Bee was one of the must successful college basketball coaches in history at Long Island University, and Scholz was a great Olympic sprinter and track star. A number of the Tunis novels have recently been reprinted, and this remarkably accomplished and skillful writer is now available to young readers. While these juvenile fiction writers can be faulted for formulaic writing and creation of stock characters and fantasy plots, their contributions are considerable because they provided high interest level reading for young people, inspired young athletes, and kept alive the spirit of amateurism as an ideal and end in itself.

Mainstream American writers have found in sports the same kind of drama and human interest that professional writers dramatized and reported, but have used sports for other purposes. F. Scott FITZGERALD was attracted to sports figures as failures and losers who briefly experienced the American dream of glory and fame but could not sustain it. Ernest HEMINGWAY saw sports as a metaphor for the condition of the perils and difficulties of modern life—a place where a code could still exist and be acted out in an attempt to assert one's dignity and honor in the face of a chaotic, uncertain world. For Hemingway, the sports of fishing, boxing, and bullfighting represented a ritualistic confrontation of danger, defeat, and death; however, for Hemingway, sports are only a "momentary stay against confusion." One can learn from them, and one can measure up to their codes and traditions. But sports do not offer salvation or redemption in an existential world. Literary treatments of sports have emphasized the failed or flawed hero who is seduced by commercialism, illusory success, the corruptions surrounding sports, and the empty adulation and worship of fans. Works like Ring LARDNER's You Know Me Al, Bernard MALAMUD's The Natural, Peter Gent's North Dallas Forty (1973) illustrate this direction and emphasis. Three Pulitzer Prize-winning dramas also take a critical look at sports and their impact on the athlete's life during and afterward. These are: Howard SACKLER's The Great White Hope on Jack Johnson, the black heavyweight boxing champion; Jason Miller's That Championship Season (1973) on high school basketball; and August WILSON's Fences, about a former Negro League baseball player.

While much of American literature has looked at sports as a culturally supported illusion or an endeavor that may limit personal development, many American writers have found sports to be a source of democratic values, a sense of community, and a place where the spirit of lucid play is active. Sports prove to be a humanizing and often humbling experience or an activity of joy and physical sensation. Mark HARRIS's baseball tetralogy featuring Henry Wiggen as the star baseball pitcher for the fictional New York Mammoths was published between 1953 and 1979, taking Wiggen from a nineteen-year-old rookie to a thirty-nine-year-old veteran who is forced to end his career and to accept the fact that he will not be the manager of the Mammoths. Harris's Wiggen series is a remarkable accomplishment and fictional achievement as the novels are infused with humanity, humor, drama, and poignancy. The novels constitute a complete cycle of an athlete's career as well as reflect three decades of change in the sport and American life. Along with Ring Lardner's Jack "Busher" Keefe, Henry Wiggen is one of the two great fictional narrators and voices of sports literature.

One area where baseball literature has excelled is the creation of the comic novel or the fantasy novel. Notable achievements include: Richard Andersen's Muckaluck (1980), Jerome Charyn's The Seventh Babe (1979), Robert COOVER's The Universal Baseball Association Inc., J. Henry Waugh Prop., James F. Donohue's Spitballs and Holy Water (1977), Lamar Herrin's The Rio Lajo Ringmaster (1977), W. P. KINSELLA's Shoeless Joe, Philip ROTH's The Great American Novel, and Douglass Wallop's The Year the Yankees Lost the Pennant (1954). Baseball has been an important source of American humor with its eccentric and unusual characters, its rich oral history, and its practical jokes and hijinks. It has enriched American literature and reflected important elements of the black experience in such novels as William Brashler's The Bingo Long Traveling All-Stars and Motor Kings (1973), John Craig's Chappie and Me (1979), and Jay Neugeboren's Sam's Legacy (1974).

While the baseball novel has dominated sports literature, several excellent novels have documented other sports. In basketball, Jeremy Larner's Drive, He Said (1964), Jay Neugeboren's Big Man (1966), Charles Rosen's Have Jump Shot, Will Travel (1975) and A Mile Above the Rim (1976), Lawrence Shainberg's One on One (1970), and Todd Walton's Inside Moves (1978) are the best of the lot. In football Don DELILLO's End Zone, Frederick EXLEY's A Fan's Notes, Peter Gent's North Dallas Forty and The Franchise (1983), Dan Jenkins's Semi-Tough (1972), Lloyd Pye's That Prosser Kid (1977), and James Whitehead's Joiner (1971) have achieved considerable recognition.

American sports have also enriched poetry as poets such as Marianne MOORE, John UPDIKE, James DICKEY, Donald HALL, Rolfe Humphries, Robert Wallace, and others have captured aspects of sports in verse and reflected their passionate interest in sports.

Sports have also enriched the field of nonfiction and created a host of legendary sportswriters whose style and approach are familiar to millions of readers. These include: Ring Lardner, Damon RUNYON, Irvin S. Cobb, Hugh Fullerton, Frank Graham, Jr., Grantland Rice, Heywood Broun, Westbrook Pegler, and their modern counterparts in Red Smith, Roger Angell, David Halberstam, and Roger Kahn. These men have dedicated their talents to the service of sport and to the craft of sportswriting, often producing some of the best prose writing in American literature. They have captured much of the human drama and interest of sports as well as explained the enduring appeal or sports, and their readers are as devoted as those of novelists and poets. Even the area of autobiography has been enriched by sports with such works as Grantland Rice's *The Tumult and the Shouting* (1954), Jackie Robinson's *I Never Had It Made* (1972), and Bill Bradley's *Life on the Run* (1977) as examples of notable sports autobiographies.

Sports in American literature and sports as a separate branch of literature have served to develop and enrich American literature in terms of types of writing, genres, and narrative modes. It is a rich heritage only recently being anthologized and studied as its own literature. Sports literature has captured the many dimensions of American national identity and aspirations, shaped and influenced American ideals and values, provided entertainment and enlightenment, and captured the meanings of games and play as well as the implications of organized sport.

BIBLIOGRAPHY: Berman, N. D., *Playful Fictions and Fictional Players: Game, Sport and Survival in Contemporary Fiction* (1981); Higgs, R. J., *Laurel & Thorn: The Athlete in American Literature* (1981); Messenger, C. K., *Sports and the Spirit of Play in American Fiction* (1981); Oriard, M., *Dreaming of Heroes: American Sports Fiction, 1868–1980* (1982); Umphlett, W. L., *The Sporting Myth and the American Experience* (1975); Wise, S., *Sports Fiction for Adults: An Annotated Bibliography of Novels, Plays, Short Stories, and Poetry with Sporting Settings* (1986)

DOUGLAS A. NOVERR

STAFFORD, Jean

b. 1 July 1915, Covina, California; d. 26 March 1979, White Plains, New York

In a small but brilliant canon—three novels, over forty short stories, and numerous essays and reviews—S. probes the manners and morals of intricately drawn

characters to illuminate our disaffected, war-ravaged century. Like her contemporary admirer, Joyce Carol OATES, S. uses the personal to illuminate the historical, examining the lives of isolated individuals who reflect the social and cultural histories they are born into. Once known in some circles primarily as the first wife of poet Robert LOWELL, S. has come into her own in critical reputation. Her distinguished career as a novelist and writer of short stories that appeared in the major periodicals of her day, notably the *New Yorker,* culminated in her winning the 1970 Pulitzer Prize for her *Collected Stories.* She is one of only a few women writers to receive that award for short fiction, and it is chiefly for her short stories that she is known.

Perhaps the central biographical fact of S.'s life is her Western upbringing in Colorado, where she moved at the age of five. Yearning for the sophistication she equated with the genteel East, S. left home after college and effectively never returned. Her characters all mirror this geographical rootlessness, and her fiction evokes a strong sense of place. The preface to her *Collected Stories* invokes her two mentors, Mark TWAIN and Henry JAMES, and thus indicates S.'s fictional articulation of the East-West conflict at the heart of much American fiction. Each of the four sections of her *Collected Stories* bears a geographical heading, emphasizing their clearly delineated setting in Europe, Manhattan, Boston, or the West. Yet the fact that S. wrote only nine short stories with boys or men as central characters indicates that she identifies the sense of anomie and alienation most easily in the lives of the female characters she dramatizes. The child heroines such as Emily Vanderpool in her most well-known story "Bad Characters"; the young women like Emma in her first *New Yorker* story, "Children Are Bored on Sunday"; or the aging women like Angelica Early in "The End of a Career" all suffer from a profound isolation that forms the thematic center of S.'s fiction.

S.'s early plans to be a philologist perhaps account for her lifelong fascination with the language and her skillful manipulation of it. Stylistically, she alternates between the literary voices of her mentors Twain and James, giving us in her western stories a breezy vernacular and in her eastern ones a convoluted Jamesian prose sprinkled with archaisms and poetic diction. One of her strengths is capturing both idioms and using the conflict between them for often comic effect, particularly in her Western stories of childhood. But S.'s angle of vision is almost unrelentingly ironic, even in her humorous stories, for she never lets the reader forget the discrepancy between her characters' hopes and dreams and the often bleak reality surrounding them.

S.'s three novels echo the concerns in her short stories—female individuation, social class restraints, human estrangement and alienation. Though largely forgotten today, her first novel, *Boston Adventure* (1944), was a best-seller and made S. a celebrity. A female bildungsroman after the fashion of Charlotte Brontë's *Jane Eyre,* the novel follows the fortunes of Sonie Marburg, an impoverished New England girl who is adopted by a wealthy Bostonian, Miss Pride, and subsequently disenchanted by her cruelty and hypocrisy. S.'s second and best novel, *The Mountain Lion* (1947), is a double bildungsroman treating a brother and sister who grow up out West. But the fourteen-year-old Molly Fawcett is not allowed to grow up, since she is killed accidentally in a hunting accident at the novel's conclusion. In this novel, S. not only clearly depicts the West as inhospitable to females like the brainy Molly, but also reinscribes her own cultural defensiveness. The last novel S. wrote, *The Catherine Wheel* (1952), depicts a lonely, frustrated New England spinster, Katherine Congreve, who was jilted in her youth and remains bitter and vengeful toward the world. In all of these novels, the process of female initiation is complicated by social class, region, and the perennial fact of lost love. S.'s implicit commentary on the fate of women is unalterably grim.

BIBLIOGRAPHY: Goodman, C. M., *J. S.: The Savage Heart* (1990); Hulbert, A., *The Interior Castle: The Art and Life of J. S.* (1992); Roberts, D., *J. S.: A Biography* (1988); Ryan, M., *Innocence and Estrangement in the Fiction of J. S.* (1987); Walsh, M. E. W., *J. S.* (1985); Wilson, M. A., *J. S.: A Study of the Short Fiction* (1996)

MARY ANN WILSON

STAFFORD, William E[dgar]

b. 17 January 1914, Hutchinson, Kansas; d. 23 August 1993, Lake Oswego, Oregon

Although he did not publish his first book of poetry—*West of Your City* (1960)—until he was in his forties, S. was one of the most prolific of the important American poets in the second half of the 20th c. In addition to twelve books of poetry and a score of limited editions, he also published two collections of essays and interviews, *Writing the Australian Crawl* (1978) and *You Must Revise Your Life* (1986). He also published one memoir, *Down Deep in My Heart* (1947), a reminiscence of his experiences as a conscientious objector during World War II. A selection of S.'s poems entitled *The Darkness around Us Is Deep,* edited by Robert BLY, was published in 1994.

S.'s poems are predominantly short, enigmatic lyrics. In his essays and interviews, S. described how these poems grew out of a daily writing practice based on a free-associational meditation. S. said that his writing process is like "going fishing," and that "there is always a nibble." This folksy analogy underscores S.'s implicit opposition to the strictures and metaphysics of the well-made modernist poem. Instead of making verbal icons, S.'s poetry dramatizes its own arrival at insight, its coming into being as a poem. S. may well remind the reader at times of Robert FROST or Emily DICKINSON, but the central activity of his poems, with their emphasis on process, suggests that S.'s art is genuinely postmodern.

If his is a poetry of process, it is also a poetry of place. The typical terrain of his poetry is somewhere west of the Mississippi, with the majority of his poems emanating from the Pacific Northwest, where S. spent most of his adult life supporting himself as a teacher at Lewis and Clark College in Oregon. Often, S.'s poems begin within a relatively pastoral setting. The rural materials that spark his poems, however, allow him to explore a sense of the sacred, the mysterious, the elemental. Nature in S.'s poetry is more often than not a repository of hints and clues, voices and silences, pasts and presents.

One of the enduring mysteries that S.'s poetry strives to address is that of the human capacity for evil. S. often lodges a quiet protest against the technological threats to the ecosystem. But human malevolence comes in many forms, and so too S.'s poetry that investigates it. This is especially visible in the poetry he wrote during the era of the Vietnam War. A lifelong pacifist, S. never adopts a superior or hectoring tone. His antiwar poems are always gentle efforts urging us to see more clearly what we are actually doing. What S. said about *Traveling through the Dark,* his 1963 National Book Award-winning volume, is true of his work as a whole: the book grew out of "the plight I am in as a human being."

S.'s poetry also explores the landscape of personal and cultural memory. Many of his poems recall the Kansas plains of his birth and upbringing. His parents and relatives, his hometown, and his own longing for what is lost are prominent in the poems of *The Rescued Year* (1966) and *Allegiances* (1970).

Beneath the landscape of memory is another core preoccupation of S.'s poetry. In *Someday, Maybe* (1963), S. said that his poems are a "wavery effort" at following what he calls the "line of the authentic." The sign of the authentic for S. is that it will always surprise and perhaps confound, even as it delights. Thus the effort at following it leads to S.'s poetic signature: the sly or very quiet epiphany, the meaning glimpsed out of the corner of one's eye, or discerned with the wide-open eyes of night vision.

S.'s stance in his poems is, ultimately, one of great humility. The poet is neither heroic in his self-assertion, nor does he despair because of his sense of limitation. His apparently artless surface, colloquial diction, and conversational rhythms are signs of his sense that poetry can and should remain part of the public life of people. In *A Glass Face in the Rain* (1982) and *An Oregon Message* (1987), he is inventing messages and listening to them come to him from others across all sorts of boundaries. In *Passwords* (1991), he is indeed moving between the lines, using language as his method of just barely safe conveyance. In his later books, it becomes clear that he conceives of the poet's role in society as deeply responsible citizen rather than high priest of negation. Rhetorically, an elegiac tone always present in his poetry became ever more prominent in the last four of his books, including *My Name Is William Tell* (1992) and the posthumous *Even in Quiet Places* (1996). But the deep sense of loneliness and loss in his poetry is balanced by the ways in which S. is always able to make or discover just enough meaning in life on this earth to keep going. This sustenance was what his daily writing practice provided him, and provides his readers as well.

BIBLIOGRAPHY: Andrews, T., ed., *On W. S.: The Worth of Local Things* (1993); Carpenter, D., *W. S.* (1986); Holden, J., *The Mark to Turn* (1976); Kitchen, J., *Understanding W. S.* (1989); Lensing, G., and R. Moran, *Four Poets and the Emotive Imagination* (1976); Stitt, P., *The World's Hieroglyphic Beauty* (1985)

FRED MARCHANT

STALLINGS, Laurence [Tucker]

b. 25 November 1894, Macon, Georgia; d. 29 February 1968, Whittier, California

The first Southerner to make a major impact on modern American drama, S. is now remembered almost exclusively for *What Price Glory?* (1924), a play he co-authored with Maxwell ANDERSON. After graduating from Wake Forest College (1916), S. began working as a reporter for the *Atlanta Journal*. Long fascinated by the military, he wrote an article on the U.S. Marines for the *Journal* and promptly joined the corps. He was soon in France, where he saw heavy action in World War I and earned a captaincy. He was wounded at the battle of Belleau Woods in 1918 and spent many months in a military hospital. S. fought valiantly not to lose his right leg, but it had to be amputated in 1922 after he reinjured it in a fall. (His left leg was amputated in 1963, also a result of his war wounds.) In 1922, he became drama critic and later book re-

viewer for the *New York World,* where Anderson was an editorial writer.

Breaking with the romantic tradition of war as presented on the American stage, *What Price Glory?* touched the iconoclastic spirit of the 1920s and was seen as kin to such antiwar novels as John DOS PASSOS's *Three Soldiers* and S.'s war novel, *Plumes* (1924), based on his own war experience. The play's action revolves around a long-standing feud between Sergeant Quirt and Captain Flagg. When Flagg goes to Paris on leave, he leaves Quirt in charge. Flagg returns to discover that Quirt has appropriated his French girlfriend. The rivalry for the girl centers the action, which the reality of a grim (but strangely addictive) warfare checks. Contemporary audiences may be more reminded of situation war dramas such as *MASH* than hard-hitting realism; however, in 1924 *What Price Glory?* was a marked departure, bringing to the stage a depiction of military life not previously found on Broadway. The language was freer, saltier than had previously been heard in the theatre. The success of the play made clear that audiences were ready for the change. The play was the basis for a silent motion picture (1926), which S. and Anderson also co-authored.

S. and Anderson quickly followed with two other collaborations, both historical romances, both now forgotten. *First Flight* (1925) recounts an episode in Andrew Jackson's romantic life; *The Buccaneer* (1925) treats the career of the pirate Henry Morgan.

S. wrote the story for *The Big Parade* (1925), the most successful of the silent war films and one of the top three box office attractions of the 1920s. In 1933, he published *The First World War: A Pictorial History.* When at the end of the decade, Paramount was seeking for someone to dramatize Ernest HEMINGWAY's *A Farewell to Arms,* the company chose S. to write the screenplay (Hemingway would have preferred Anderson). S. was eager to take on a war novel that went even further than his own work in the depiction of sex and the use of strong language. His adaptation did not lead to a long Broadway run, but it and the film that followed helped boost Hemingway's fame. Hemingway included S.'s short story "Vale of Tears" in his 1942 anthology *Men at War.*

Although S. wrote numerous short stories, collaboration was a chief component in much of his work. He wrote the libretto for the opera *Deep River* (1926, with a score by Franke Harling), the musical *Rainbow* (1928, with a score by Oscar Hammerstein, II), and the musical spectacle *Virginia* (1937, with a score by Ben Davis). His play depicting the Marines in World War II, *The Streets Are Guarded* (1944), was considered a failure. His last major publication was *The*

Doughboys, a history of American soldiers in World War I.

BIBLIOGRAPHY: Brittain, J. T., *L. S.* (1975); Leff, L., "A Thunderous Reception: Broadway, Hollywood, and *A Farewell to Arms,*" HemR 15 (Spring 1996): 33–51

JOSEPH M. FLORA

STANTON, Elizabeth Cady

b. 12 November 1815, Johnstown, New York; d. 26 October 1902, New York City

S. was a philosopher and writer who helped shape the political activity of woman's suffrage throughout the second half of the 19th c., although she has been overshadowed in more recent times by her contemporary Susan B. Anthony.

The daughter of a conservative jurist and aristocratic mother, she was educated at Emma Willard's Troy Female Seminary but denied a college education. She eloped with Henry Stanton, an abolitionist agent, when she was twenty-five. They reared seven children. Throughout her life, she enjoyed the company of reformers, political personages, and journalists.

S., encouraged by Lucretia MOTT, called to order the Seneca Falls Women's Rights Convention of 1848 and with it the formal beginning of the women's rights movement in America. The suffragists amended and adopted the "Declaration of Sentiments," which S. wrote based on the Declaration of Independence, listing specific grievances against "all men" as Thomas JEFFERSON listed them against "King George." Influenced by the writing of Mary Wollstonecraft in England, she stated that women's first duty is to themselves as rational thinkers.

S. and Susan B. Anthony met three years later and formed a lifelong friendship and political collaboration. They published *The History of Woman Suffrage* (3 vols., 1881–86), with coauthor Matilda Joslyn Gage. At various times over fifty years, they held executive office together in state and national women's rights and temperance societies; all required speeches that S. wrote for both Anthony and herself.

S. also addressed speeches to state and federal legislative bodies arguing for the woman's vote to address her own grievances. Precluding this granting of power, her speeches demanded for women the representation men had promised them, including divorce reform and married women's equal rights to control of the children and property distribution. She wrote articles arguing for the rights of women in the courtroom and for the admission of women to law schools. In the course of the 1870s, she traveled the often arduous lyceum circuit following the railroad into communities throughout the country and delivering speeches as a paid professional, a minor celebrity. Some of her lecture titles announce her themes: "The Subjection of Women," "Coeducation," "Marriage and Divorce," "Marriage and Maternity," "Prison Life," and for Sundays, "Famous Women in the Bible" and "The Bible and Women's Rights."

Her prose is elegant, witty, logical, and impassioned, calculated to entertain, but with barely contained anger she disabuses her listeners of the inferiority of her mind or the seriousness of her cause. Many considered her greatest speech to be "The Solitude of Self," which she delivered in 1892 to the National American Women's Rights Association. Her personal credo that a woman was first and foremost an individual who is not to be denied any of the rights that a man expected, epistemologically shifts from political philosophy to psychological theory and existential philosophy.

She helped found, edited, and wrote for the *Revolution* from 1868 to 1870. At various times, she was a regular contributor to the *Lily,* the *Una,* and the *Women's Tribune,* and to the *New York Tribune* newspaper.

At the end of the 19th c., Anthony, as the chief strategist, recruited younger women to achieve the ultimate target of woman suffrage, and S. forged new feminist ground in publishing *The Women's Bible* (2 vols., 1895, 1898). Her exegesis of the Bible challenges the conclusions of male ministers that women are inferior beings, a view that she saw as being responsible for the origins and justification of women's oppression. In 1898, she published her autobiography, *Eighty Years and More.* A lengthy essay on divorce reform was published by the Hearst syndicate just two weeks before her death. Extant writings also include letters, a diary, and unpublished fragments.

BIBLIOGRAPHY: Banner, L. W., *E. C. S.* (1980); DuBois, E. C., ed., *The E. C. S.—Susan B. Anthony Reader* (1992); Griffith, E., *In Her Own Right* (1984); Lutz, A., *Created Equal* (1940)

KAREN J. PHILLIPS

STEARNS, Harold E.

b. 7 May 1891, Barre, Massachusetts; d. 13 August 1943, Hempstead, New York

S. was a prolific journalist and author during the first few decades of the 20th c., known primarily as a satirist and literary critic as well as for his influence on the expatriate movement of the 1920s. Despite his later, more patriotic works, S. is best known for his important role as the "enfant terrible of American journalism" and as the editor of *Civilization in the*

United States: An Inquiry by Thirty Americans (1922), the book that played a major role in persuading the dissatisfied and disillusioned American youth of that era to go abroad.

S.'s first significant position as the book reviewer for the *Boston Evening Transcript* in 1909 marked the beginning of his successful eight year career as a journalist. In 1917, after S. landed a job at the prestigious New York magazine *The Dial,* he started his first book *Liberalism in America: Its Temporary Collapse, Its Future* (1919), which launched a fervent attack on the liberalism of President Woodrow Wilson. This book received positive reviews by sympathetic American intellectuals, including H. L. MENCKEN, who later contributed a chapter in S.'s manifesto for exiled youth. Soon after the publication of *Liberalism in America,* S. wrote *America and the Young Intellectual* (1921), a defense of the younger generation's disenchantment with the unsatisfactory conditions of postwar America.

After the critical success of his first two books, S. continued to support the endeavors and "moral idealism" of America's youth, a campaign that culminated in *Civilization in the United States.* In addition to Mencken, Stearns secured contributions for this collection from Conrad AIKEN, Lewis MUMFORD, George Jean Nathan, Ring LARDNER, and Van Wyck BROOKS, important figures from almost every field of American life. In the preface, S. sets the goal for the entire book. He calls this collection of essays a harsh but "constructive criticism" of a country that has given birth to a generation of alienated intellectuals who, in order to reject a vulgar and materialistic life in America, were advised to leave the country in order to preserve their creative individuality. S. left for Europe as soon as the collection was published.

Despite S.'s insistence that taking leave to Europe would ensure the creative and intellectual energies of the American artistic youth, S.'s own move to Paris marked a long pause in his prolific and successful writing career. When he first arrived in Montparnasse, S. landed a copy desk position at the European edition of the *New York Herald* and quickly became a central figure in the expatriate circles of Paris. By 1923, however, he had left his position and was thoroughly entrenched in a world of socializing, horseracing, and heavy drinking. S. was soon legendary within the Montparnasse circles for his extravagant taste and his empty pockets, and was known to borrow large amounts of money from his friends. His only work at this point was selling racing tips and working as a forecaster of races. During S.'s almost eleven years in the Montparnasse, he was both intellectually and creatively unproductive.

With the help of loyal friends, S. was able to return to the U.S. in 1932, and his writing career soon began its rebirth. His first notable publication was an essay for *Scribner's,* appropriately entitled, "A Prodigal Returns." Before his death in 1943, S. wrote three more books, including *Rediscovering America* (1934), his autobiography *The Street I Know* (1935), in which he admits his barren creativity during his Paris days, and *America: A Re-Appraisal* (1937), which defends America against Marxist critics. S. also worked as the editor of his last and most notable publication, *America Now: An Inquiry into Civilization in the U.S.* (1938), a collection that explores the whole spectrum of American life in a tone conspicuously more hopeful and optimistic than S.'s earlier collection of essays.

Despite S.'s challenge to the disillusioned intellectual generation of the twenties to seek creativity on foreign grounds, S. himself was most prolific when he was living in the U.S. Although he will always be known for his influence on the mass exodus to Paris and the ways in which he was unfavorably caricatured as a drunk, gambling layabout by his own Montparnasse crowd, one can certainly benefit from a look at S.'s later works that successfully document the transition from disillusionment to hope that occurred in many expatriate minds after the 1920s.

BIBLIOGRAPHY: Cowley, M., *Exile's Return* (1951); Nash, R., *The Nervous Generation: American Thought, 1917–1930* (1970); Wilson, E., *The Twenties* (1975)

HEATHER C. URSCHEL

STEELE, Timothy [Reid]
b. 22 January 1948, Burlington, Vermont

S. is one of the central New Formalist poets , a group that, in the last quarter of the 20th c., returned to the use of poetic meter and forms that had largely been eschewed by American poets in the wake of modernism. In addition to his three volumes of poetry composed almost entirely in rhyme and meter—*Uncertainties and Rest* (1979), *Sapphics against Anger* (1986), and *The Color Wheel* (1994)—S. has written an important critical book, *Missing Measures* (1990), giving scholarly and aesthetic credibility to the movement. In the latter, S. argues that the abandonment of rhyme and meter by such modernists (see MODERNISM) as T. S. ELIOT, Ezra POUND, and William Carlos WILLIAMS was unprecedented among other legitimate poetic revolutions, like that of the romantics, which had been content with revitalizing poetic language while recognizing meter, in particular, to be a defining element of poetry. S.'s critical ideas and poetic practice were, in part, derived from Yvor WINTERS's presence at Stanford University when he first arrived there in the late 1960s and by Winters's friend and protégé, J. V. CUNNINGHAM, with whom S. later studied at Brandeis. Upon returning to Stanford in the mid-1970s, S. became acquainted with two other prominent New Formalists, Dana GIOIA and Vikram SETH. Seth dedicated his seminal verse novel, *The Golden Gate* (1986) to S. who subsequently dedicated *Sapphics Against Anger* to Seth.

Uncertainties and Rest can, in retrospect, be seen to be among the first volumes of poetry published that was later identified as New Formalist. With no such catchy phrase existing when it was published, however, S. made little critical impact with this book. From the beginning of his career, though, he was admired by such older formalists as Richard WILBUR and X. J. Kennedy. The literary climate was quite different when S.'s second book appeared shortly after the sensation elicited earlier in 1986 with the publication of Seth's *Golden Gate* and *Sapphics Against Anger* was subsequently nominated for the National Book Critics Circle Award in poetry.

Among the New Formalists, S.'s work is the most closely associated with the plain style of Ben Jonson and championed in the 20th c. by Winters and Cunningham. S.'s poems, that is, are generally iambic and contain easily paraphrasable poetic arguments; indeed, they often employ the form of the epigram. With few exceptions, S. has limited himself to the brief lyric poem and the epigram and to a quietly decorous emotional range. Within these self-imposed restrictions, however, S. works unusually well, probably because the modesty of his aesthetic reflects his genuine decency as a person, his quiet dignity. In fact, nowhere is the coincidence of his aesthetic and ethical selves reflected more clearly than in "Sapphics Against Anger" where he argues, within the disciplined structure of the Sapphic stanza—a quatrain whose first three lines contain eleven syllables while the fourth is shortened to six—that a good life, like a good poem, is a matter of strong emotion brought under control by reason.

In addition to this ars poetica and his trenchant epigrams, S.'s lyrics focus upon reminiscences of his youth and family life in Vermont ("Learning to Skate" and "The Sheets"); the landscapes of New England ("Timothy" and "Vermont Spring") and California ("Near Olympic" and "At Will Rogers Beach," where he has lived since the mid-1970s. Such gently erotic love poems as "An Aubade" and "Love Poem" are the most impressive and moving of his lyrics. In *The Color Wheel*, S. has extended his range to combine the personal and the political, as in "Pacific Rim," in which the poet, swimming in the ocean off Los Ange-

les, meditates upon global politics at the close of the 20th c.

BIBLIOGRAPHY: King, B., "Postmodernism and Neo-Formalist Poetry: Seth, S., and Strong Measures," *SoR* 23 (Winter 1987): 224–31; Walzer, K., "The Poetry of T. S.," *TennQ* 2 (Winter 1996): 16–30

ROBERT MCPHILLIPS

STEELE, Wilbur Daniel

b. 17 March, 1886, Greensboro, North Carolina; d. 26 May 1970, Essex, Connecticut

One of our most prolific authors, after William Dean HOWELLS, Henry JAMES, and Joyce Carol OATES, S. during approximately half a century published over two hundred short stories (from which seven short story collections were made), ten novels, two plays, and a collection of one-act plays, as well as magazine articles and two pieces of juvenilia. He won over a dozen prizes for his short fiction, mostly in the annuals, notably the Edward J. O'Brien Best American Short Stories and the O. Henry Memorial Award Prize Stories. From the later 1910s to the later 1930s, S.'s high reputation as an American fiction writer placed him in the forefront. In a much-quoted letter from F. Scott FITZGERALD to the anthologist Dayton Kohler, dated March 4, 1938, Fitzgerald angrily dismissed S. as an author "who left no mark whatsoever, invented nothing, created nothing except a habit of being an innocuous part of the O'Brien anthology."

Reasons given for S.'s faded popularity since the Great Depression have been many: his stories were too old-fashioned, in that they were too carefully fashioned, with well-rounded plot, well described setting, and emphasis on action instead of introspection and feeling; they were grimly oppressive, with their morality and struggle motif; they lacked humor; they were too formulaic, romantic, and exotic. S. had a "bag of tricks" approach to writing the short story; however, as a "modern temper" was forming, editorial tastes no longer responded to S.'s genteel approach.

Yet from these very criticisms we can sense, retrospectively, the strengths of S.'s short fictions: the beauty and pleasure to be found in a vibrant, coherent narrative elegantly written, the allure of faraway places, mysterious ports of call. Such settings, brought to life by a natural storyteller, and evocative of such masters as Kipling and Conrad, even Herman MELVILLE, were bound to appeal to the cultivated tastes of intelligent readers during the early decades of the 20th c., when S. was in his prime. Aside from his having a vivid imagination and a strong sense of the dramatic (S. in 1915 was a cofounder of the Provincetown Players), he was a close observer of human behavior, well fitted to write about motley characters in distant climes or closer to home. As a child, S. lived in Germany, as a young would-be artist had painted or sketched in Paris and Italy, and later traveled in the Caribbean, Bermuda, North Africa, France, Switzerland, England, and South America.

"The Man Who Saw through Heaven" (1925) is probably his finest artistic achievement, though inadequately appreciated by literary critics. It is the saga of a missionary clergyman, Reverend Hubert Diana, who, looking through a powerful observatory telescope, under the supervision of a guide, sees the distant reaches of the universe and becomes transformed. Sailing to Africa with his bride and a troop of female missionaries, he casts off his Christian faith in favor of a continually developing idolatrous religion compounded of tenets both suggestive of relativity theory and traceable to the theory of evolution. This haunting, complex tale about Diana, and the object of his veneration and his sculpting: "Our Father Witch" (as the natives call him), is interpretable on different levels, and evokes a number of literary associations including William Blake's "Auguries of Innocence." Probably S.'s second-best story, "How Beautiful with Shoes" (1932), is a tragic pastoral about a simple Carolina farm girl, Amarantha Doggett, her crude fiancé, Ruby Herter, and an escaped homicidal mental patient—Humble Jewett, who beguiles her with streams of love poetry but is shot to death by Ruby's gang of locals.

Other noteworthy stories include "Footfalls" (1920), "The Shame Dance" (1920), "Bubbles" (1926), and "In the Shade of the Tree" (1929). "The Shame Dance" is a sordid tale of a New York hustler named Signet and his exploitative involvement, in the South Seas, with a Marquesan woman. Here, as in other of S.'s writings, in particular "Can't Cross Jordan by Myself" (1930), S. has been accused by some critics of racism because of his depiction of people of color. "In the Shade of the Tree" concerns spousal empowerment before and after death.

The complex nature of S.'s social outlook and commitment as a fiction writer has been aptly summed up by Thomas A. Gullason: to the "romantic realist" S., "the subtleties and intricacies of plotting were far more important . . . than any moral theme or serious issue he may have wished to explore."

BIBLIOGRAPHY: Gullason, T. A., "The 'Lesser' Renaissance: The American Short Story in the 1920s," in P. Stevick, ed., *The American Short Story, 1900–1945* (1984): 81–83; Seesholtz, M., "W. D. S.," in Kimbel,

B. E., ed., *DLB*, vol. 86, *American Short-Story Writers, 1910–1945* (1989): 264–71

                                         SAMUEL I. BELLMAN

STEFFENS, [Joseph] Lincoln
b. 6 April 1866, Sacramento, California; d. 9 August 1936, Carmel, California

As a journalist, autobiographer, essayist, and fiction writer, S.'s life and influence covered the collapse of empires, the emergence of new socialist states, and the gradual transformation of America itself. As the most prominent figure in the "muckraking" movement of the early 20th c., S. managed to blend a keen descriptive eye with a commitment to urban and national politics.

Initially, S. worked as a journalist on his return from Europe in 1892, starting as a reporter for the *New York Evening Post*. Here, the central elements of his intellectual vision were formed around the plight of the new immigrants, slum conditions, and the indifference and corruption of city governments. The social and political nature of his vision were a vital energy in the Progressive movement, and blended outrage with democratic philosophy.

His transfer to *McClure's* in 1901 freed him from the strict deadlines of the daily, and gave him a wider, more cultured audience. It was at *McClure's* that S. became the prime mover of the muckraking movement, and his investigations of urban political corruption were published as a series of articles entitled *The Shame of the Cities* (1904). Here, S. openly criticized the national city bosses and their local organizational machines, and advocated a clean sweep of reforms that would give local power back to the voters. He believed that machine-mentality only served to thwart the active functioning of democratic participation, and only through dispassionate committee control would cities be made to work for all.

S.'s political style avoided sensationalist calls, instead appealing to an informed liberalism he believed was at the heart of the American democratic experience. His other works from this experimental period include *The Struggle for Self Government* (1906) and *Upbuilders* (1909), both offering urban political investigations.

The gradual unraveling of the political reform movement left S. disillusioned, and his departure from *McClure's* in 1911 marked a new stage in his writing and thinking. In the same year, S. teamed up with Clarence Darrow in San Francisco and entered into an active political period. Working with Darrow in San Francisco, S. entered into a bitter struggle with anti-union campaigners and became a staunch defender of labor rights.

S.'s increasing concern for the plight of the American working class effectively alienated his traditional core of reformist readers. In the same way, his outspoken support of the Mexican and Russian revolutions in his journalism, and his enthusiasm for dynamic social change, sealed his popular and political disregard. S. began his retrospective autobiography in 1924, which finally appeared in 1931 as *The Autobiography of L. S.* A document of alternative educations, it was immediately acclaimed as a classic of the genre, and given the more radical turn in American politics, S. was briefly restored to prominence.

Because of his pro-communist stance, S. was effectively erased from American literature in the 1950s, and his work is now read as a political morality tale. S. has come to be seen as a representative figure demonstrating the alternating extremes of idealism and disillusionment, experienced by intellectuals at the beginning of the 20th c. Despite this reappraisal, S. never succumbed to cynicism, but instead maintained his belief in the transformative potential of the American democratic tradition.

BIBLIOGRAPHY: Horning, A., *Autobiography and Democracy: The Case of L. S.* (1990); Morgan, K. O., *The Man with the Muckrake* (1975); Stinson, R., *L. S.* (1979); Whitfield, S., *Muckraking L. S.* (1978)

PAUL HANSOM

STEGNER, Wallace [Earle]

b. 18 February 1909, Lake Mills, Iowa; d. 13 April 1994, Santa Fe, New Mexico

Among the most forceful spokesmen for environmental protection and understanding of environmental problems, S. was concerned in his nonfiction and his fiction with these important issues from the time that he wrote his 1935 doctoral dissertation (Iowa) on Clarence Earl Dutton, a geologist who helped survey the Rocky Mountain region with John Wesley Powell. The dissertation was prelude to *Beyond the Hundredth Meridian* (1945), a biography of Powell. *The Sound of Mountain Water* (1969) includes S.'s famous "Wilderness Letter" as well as other essays polemical and literary. Later essays are gathered in *One Way to Spell Man* (1982). Other nonfiction includes *Mormon Country* (1942) and two books with editors of *Look* magazine: *One Nation* (1945) and *Look at America* (1945).

As these titles reveal, S. has the historian's bent as well as the conservationist's. His *Wolf Willow: A History, A Story, and a Memory of the Last Plains Frontier* (1962) combines personal history with the history of the Saskatchewan-Montana region of his youth. In *The Gathering of Zion: The Story of the Mormon Trail* (1964), S., although not a Mormon, studied the Western migration of the Mormons, the majority culture of Utah, where he lived his young manhood. S.'s disposition towards historical understanding of the West is also evident in the novel *The Preacher and the Slave,* reprinted in 1969 as *Joe Hill: A Biographical Novel.* Later, S. wrote the biography of a different kind of Westerner, a literary mentor who helped fire his own ambitions: *The Uneasy Chair: A Biography of Bernard De Voto* (1974). Like De Voto, S. knew the pull of the East. He looked at the West broadly. Again like De Voto, he was an important scholar about matters Western. S. also edited *The Letters of Bernard De Voto* (1975). With his son Page S., he wrote the text to accompany Eliot Porter's photographs that celebrate *American Places* (1983). The text ends with the plea that Americans "listen to the land, and hear what it says and know what it can and cannot do."

Much of S.'s career involved teaching creative writing (for twenty-six years, he helped make Stanford's program one of the nation's most prestigious), and he edited numerous collections of short stores and other texts, chiefly dealing with American fiction. S. presented his views on teaching creative writing in lectures at Dartmouth, later published as *On the Teaching of Creative Writing* (1988). In the course of his career, he became more adept at incorporating his didactic concerns into the fictional fabric. His later novels have been his most prized. *Angle of Repose* received the Pulitzer Prize in 1971; *The Spectator Bird* won the National Book Award in 1976.

S.'s writing career began auspiciously. He won the 1937 Little Brown Prize for the novelette *Remembering Laughter* (the first word of the title provides an important clue to S.'s literary technique and theme). Three short novels followed: *The Potter's House* (1938), *On a Darkling Plain* (1940), and *Fire and Ice* (1941). His first major novel was in the tradition of the family saga, *The Big Rock Candy Mountain* (1943). It ranges over vast areas of the West, as Bo Mason, a character based on S.'s father, keeps his eye on the big chance, but misses it. The price he and his family pay is high. The family survivor is Bruce, whose prototype is S. S. returned to Bruce, now a mature man, in *Recapitulation* (1979), a tautly structured novel in which Bruce reconsiders his formative past and comes to a reconciliation with his ghosts.

As was the case with his only novel set in the East, *Second Growth* (1947), parts of *Recapitulation* had had earlier embodiment as short stories. S. is a noted practitioner in that genre. His two collections of stories came midcareer: *The Women on the Wall* (1950) and *The City of the Living* (1956).

Contemporary California became an important subject for S.'s fiction in *A Shooting Star* (1961), a study of a young woman's efforts to correct the many mistakes her wealth made easy and to find a worthwhile life. S. found an especially effective voice for approaching the contemporary scene in his creation of retired literary agent Joe Allston, the narrator of *All the Little Live Things* (1967). Joe has an even larger role in *The Spectator Bird,* pondering his own life more directly than he had in the earlier book. The Alston books share with *Angel of Repose* tensions between freedom and responsibility, individualism and conformity, youth and age, creation and waste. In *Angel of Repose,* Lyman Ward, a retired history professor, seeks to understand his own unsatisfactory marriage by studying the careers of his western grandparents, who are based on the Western writer and artist Mary Hallock FOOTE and her engineer husband. S.'s novel sweeps across the nation and juxtaposes past and present—a continuing challenge to a writer who claims history (national and personal) as a suitable partner for the muse of fiction.

Crossing to Safety (1987) finds S. still at the top of his form as he portrays the friendship of two couples—the Morgans from the West and the Langs from the East. They first meet at Wisconsin, where the men are expectant young English professors in the mid-Depression. Despite differences between the couples in wealth and advantage, despite their contrasting successes and failures, the friendship endures. In measured prose, through the voice of the poet-narrator Larry Morgan, S. makes clear his affinity to Robert FROST, whose life was also enriched by awareness of differences between East and West and from whose verse S. borrowed his title.

BIBLIOGRAPHY: Arthur, A., ed., *Critical Essays on W. S.* (1982); Benson, J., *W. S.* (1996); Etulain, R. W., ed., *Conversations with W. S. on Western History and Literature* (1983); Lewis, M., and L. Lewis, *W. S.* (1972); Robinson, F. G., and M. G. Robinson, *W. S.* (1977)

JOSEPH M. FLORA

STEIN, Gertrude

b. 13 February 1874, Allegheny, Pennsylvania; d. 27 July 1946, Neuilly-sur-Seine, France

S. is remembered more for her influence on the significant writers and artists clustered in post–World War I Paris than as the serious writer she was. Her writing is sufficiently avant-garde to bewilder readers and discourage casual reading. S. was daring in her experiments with language and literary structure. She gave words a life beyond meaning, a life in shape and sound. She understood the possibilities of sentence structure better than any writer of her day. Her repetitions moved readers into new perceptions of meaning.

Her line from *Tender Buttons* (1914) illustrates this: "Rose is a rose is a rose." Neither a horticultural description nor a description of the color, this line provides no insights into the character of someone named Rose. Rather, S. invites her readers to tease from their minds everything they know about "rose." S. plants a seed for her readers' imaginations to cultivate.

Three Lives (1909) and *The Autobiography of Alice B. Toklas* (1933) are S.'s two best-known books. Many consider *The Making of Americans* (1925) unreadable, although a close examination of this immense history of three generations of a German American family is important to readers seriously interested in S.

S.'s first book, *Q.E.D.* (1950), written in 1903 and published posthumously, recounts a lesbian triangle in which S. participated during her years as a medical student at Johns Hopkins. Adele, S.'s autobiographical character, reappears in *Three Lives* as a figure in Melanctha Herbert's life. In *Q.E.D.* as well as in *Three Lives,* S. experiments with a form she invented, based upon what French Impressionist artists attempted in their painting. Called "Portraits," S.'s usually brief impressionistic characterizations reflect her belief that characters shape events, a notion wholly counter to the then-current naturalistic dogma, which posited that institutions and events outside people's control determine their lives.

Three Lives captures with utter realism the speech patterns of working-class people. S., a psychology student at Radcliffe, paid close attention to how common people talk. Her dialogue in *Three Lives* is as repetitious and trivial as is the casual dialogue of common people. *Three Lives* broke further from tradition by giving central position in the novel to Melanctha, the first black protagonist in an American novel treated not specifically as a black but as a working-class woman. Following *Three Lives,* in *Geography and Plays* (1922), a collection of short pieces, and *Tender Buttons,* a book of poetry in which S. applied to her writing techniques of CUBISM and expressionism in painting, she ventures surrealistically into exploring language in all its possibilities.

Until 1925, no one would publish *The Making of Americans,* written between 1903 and 1911. The novel, beginning in a conventional, realistic way moves increasingly from depicting people, places, and things to representing the movement of consciousness as S. experienced it while she created the novel. As associative patterning replaces conventional narration, it moves progressively into abstractions. The publication of this book brought S. the opportunity to lecture at Oxford and Cambridge Universities which spawned the publication of *Composition as Explanation* (1926), in which S. attempts to explain what she seeks to achieve in her writing.

The Autobiography of Alice B. Toklas was S.'s first commercial success. S. wrote it because much that TOKLAS, her companion since 1907, had to tell remained untold. It is an engaging book about Parisian artistic and literary circles during the first third of the 20th c. Although not impeccably factual, the book provides striking insights into the artists and writers of the period. Its success prompted S.'s lecture tour in the U.S., out of which grew *Lectures in America* (1935), an updating of the artistic theories earlier espoused in *Composition as Explanation.*

Upon her death in 1946, S. had twenty-three books in print. Thirteen more followed, as did *The Unpublished Works of G. S.* (8 vols., 1951–58) and *G. S.: Writings and Lectures, 1909-1945* (1967).

BIBLIOGRAPHY: Bloom, H., ed., *G. S.* (1986); Bridgman, R., *G. S. in Pieces* (1971); Hemingway, E., *A Moveable Feast* (1964); Hobhouse, J., *Everyone Who Was Anybody* (1975); Hoffman, F., *G. S.* (1961); Mellow, J. R., *Charmed Circle* (1974); Miller, R. S., *G. S.* (1949); Souhami, D., *G. and Alice* (1991); Sprigge, E., *G. S.* (1957)

R. BAIRD SHUMAN

STEINBECK, John

b. 27 February 1902, Salinas, California; d. 20 December 1968, New York City

At the beginning of S.'s first published novel, *Cup of Gold* (1929), the magician Merlin tells the adventuring young hero Henry Morgan: "you will become a great man—if only you remain a little child. All the world's great have been little boys who wanted the moon." This romantic strain in S.'s writing, most fully realized in his first novel about the quest for ultimate fulfillment, never disappears. S., best known as a realist and naturalist, is also a mythopoeist. Curiously, S. mentions the child's perspective before beginning several works. The stark *Of Mice and Men* (1937) was begun with the desire to "recreate a child's world, not of fairies and giants but of colors more clear than they are to adults, of tastes more sharp and of the queer heart-breaking feelings that overwhelm children in a moment. . . . You have to be very honest and very humble to write for children." Both associations that he makes with children—the need to envision a brighter

world and the capacity to inhabit a vividly real world—are the qualities that inform S.'s best work.

But the writer took nearly twenty years to achieve the appropriate balance between what he termed the German and the Irish in his nature. He was born in the farming community of Salinas, California, to a father of German extraction and a mother of Irish blood. In their own ways, both were supportive of their only son, who decided at fourteen to be a writer and never changed his mind. S.'s mother told him tales of fairies and gnomes and encouraged his reading of Sir Thomas Malory, the Arabian Knights, the Bible, and John Milton. And his stern and silent father gave him the emotional and financial support that allowed him to continue in the face of repeated rejections. Neither would live to know S. as a famous writer, for his mother suffered from a stroke in 1934 and his father died in 1936, a year after the moderately successful *Tortilla Flat*. The three novels published before that may be grouped as S.'s apprenticeship works, for none fully achieves that fine balance between surface realism and symbolic texture so characteristically his own.

The first two are highly symbolic novels. *Cup of Gold, a Life of Sir Henry Morgan, Buccaneer, with Occasional Reference to History* was published in August 1929 by Robert M. McBride & Company. S. worked on his version of the Grail quest while at Stanford University, which he attended sporadically from 1919 to 1925 and left without a degree, and after. Although most readers will barely recognize as S.'s the ornate literary prose of this first novel, they will recognize a characteristic theme—the inevitable disappointment that accompanies the quest for fulfillment. In his second novel about ambitious but flawed visionaries, *To a God Unknown* (1933), S. discovers his country, California, as well as his abiding concern for nature as an organic, interconnected whole. In this and in later novels, men attempt to harness, to worship wrongly, or to ignore nature, and any fixed ideology denies nature's fluidity and essential unit.

S.'s mature vision, however, is most clearly evident in the short stories of the early 1930s about commonplace dreamers. Some were published in *The Pastures of Heaven* (1932) and others were collected in the 1938 volume, *The Long Valley*. The first, composed of thematically linked tales, marks a crucial stage in S.'s career, for he locates *The Pastures of Heaven* in the Salinas Valley; he refines his typically firm prose style; and he focuses on simple people. Loosely connected thematically and geographically, these stories are also linked by the presence in each story of the Munroe family, new residents in the valley. In buying the "cursed" Battle farm, the Munroes may spawn, as one resident suggests, "baby curses," but their real threat is not metaphysical but social. They represent varieties of a complacent social norm that S. scorns throughout his fiction, people who carelessly and thoughtless mar others' lives through their own myopia. And this, for S., becomes the greatest evil of which man is capable, and as such a kind of "curse" under which fallen man labors throughout this and subsequent books. But in these tales, it is not always clear whether the "curse" of knowledge, which the Munroes so frequently and inadvertently bring, frees or condemns characters with illusions or obsessions. The story of Shark Wicks, the first after the introductory sketches, introduces a kind of double-edged sword. Wicks clings to the illusion of his own supposed wealth—which sustains him—and the obsession with his daughter's purity—which harms her. When eventually stripped of both, Wicks and his family have no certain prospects for success or happiness. This tale thus introduces the question that reverberates throughout this novel as well as throughout S.'s oeuvre: are illusions sustaining or harmful? In posing it, the author repeatedly asks the reader to empathize with vulnerable people, people easily destroyed by the forces of respectability.

Both objectivity and sensitivity to the social misfit characterize S.'s best work of the 1930s. A balance is struck between a detached, seeming reportorial voice and the empathy and artistry that demand that the author shape his material symbolically, suggesting meaning through mythic parallels, richly textured descriptions of the landscape and reiterated images. Nowhere is this balance more apparent than in the superb tales he wrote in 1933 to 1934 and collected in *The Long Valley:* "The Red Pony," "The Chrysanthemums," "The Harness," "The Murder" (an O. Henry prize winner in 1934), "Flight," and "Johnny Bear." In these stories, the reader may also identify two important ideas that S. develops in subsequent fiction of the 1930s and 1940s: the Phalanx, or group man, theory and non-teleological thinking. The first is more easily defined. Any group, S. observed, assumes an independent personality that subsumes the individual units composing that group. Thus, the aims, methods, and temperament of a group, whether working for a desirable or an undesirable end, may differ from the intentions or desires of the individual members. In "The Vigilante," for example, S. focuses on the aftermath of a lynching (that actually took place in San Jose in 1933) by recording the deflated emotions of a participant who feels increasingly removed from the moments of shared emotional intensity and commitment, the mob violence that gave his bleak life a sense of purpose. The second concept, nonteleological or "is" thinking, focuses on what exists, not on what might be, nor on the end, purpose, or moral lesson to be gleaned from experience. The working title for *Of Mice and Men* was "Something That Happened," a phrase that certainly expresses his theory. S.'s world, notes his biographer Jackson Benson, is "almost from the beginning of his published work a world that was mechanistic and independent of the desires of man and the presence of God." The author has frequently been called a naturalist, a somewhat slippery term at best, not because he writes heightened realism, but because he sees humans buffeted by often indifferent forces—harsh nature, middle-class respectability, political and social turmoil. Yet the possible despair resulting from such a vision is mitigated by that romantic strain that finds a certain energy in recording what is and in recognizing man's interdependence on the whole human and natural environment. That belief in itself becomes an end, the hope for fulfillment. For if persons see themselves and their relation to the whole of nature clearly, they will not be deluded by the false teleologies that trap humans—Christianity, communism, and capitalism, to name a few.

Although both these concepts were S.'s before he met Ed Ricketts, his thinking was undoubtedly influenced by his closest friend. S. met Rickets in 1930, the same year that he married his first wife, Carol Henning, of San Jose, and the couple moved to the S. family's summer home in Pacific Grove. Ricketts, a marine biologist whose business was collecting, preserving, and selling biological samples, was also an environmentalist, a holistic thinker ("nonteleogical" was his term), a fine scientist, and a devoted conversationalist. His lab on Cannery Row attracted a group of artists and writers who found fellowship in wine, music, and talk. Although the extent of Ricketts's influence is still a matter of some critical discussion, it is certainly fair to say that daily intercourse with two fine minds—Ricketts's and his wife's—stimulated the author who had plied his trade for so many years with little literary recognition and few financial rewards. In the mid to late 1930s, S. wrote most of his finest books—*Tortilla Flat, In Dubious Battle* (1936), *Of Mice and Men,* and *The Grapes of Wrath* (1939).

With the first, he achieved some recognition and an advance that allowed him and Carol to take their first trip to Mexico, which had long fascinated him. It is well to keep this trip in mind while reading *Tortilla Flat* and other works set in Mexico—his documentary film about the peasants' resistance to modern medicine, *The Forgotten Village* (1941), *The Pearl* (1947), and the fine film *Viva Zapata!* (1952) about the Mexican revolutionary leader, Emiliano Zapata. Since childhood, S. had lived near, worked with, and studied the Mexicans and their culture, and his subsequent filmstrips and stories ought not be read in the spirit of cultural imperialism. S. always sympathized with the powerless, and this should be evident when his tone is mock heroic and his subject the paisano n'er-do-wells who live in Montery's Tortilla flat. However charming and humorous their rationalizations of theft, greed, and laziness, the paisanos' natural state is not sentimentalized.

The charge of sentimentality could hardly be leveled at his next two novels about the dispossessed. *In Dubious Battle* is S.'s most incisive study of group man, the striking farm workers in California who are manipulated by two powers, the Communist Party and the Growers' Association. The protagonists, communist organizers Mac and Jim, are never really likeable because party goals precede individual needs. S. called this a "brutal" study, and this nonteleological work does seemingly avoid the author's characteristic balance between realism and symbolism. Yet he also wrote that he "used a small strike in an orchard valley as the symbol of man's eternal, bitter warfare with himself," Milton's "Dubious Battle." In fact, both this and his next book, *Of Mice and Men,* tell of dubious battles, unresolved conflicts men wage within themselves and with a callous world. Also evident in both works is a hallmark of S.'s fiction throughout his career: male associations between friends, workers, brothers, and comrades figure more prominently than those between men and women. As is true of other unlikely male pairs in American literature, Lennie and George's uncommon friendship represents a universal need at odds with the dominant culture. The two bindlestiffs dream of owning a farm, where the childlike Lennie can raise rabbits and where George can work his own land. But these two find only temporary harmony in a world where solitary individuals repeatedly sound variations on the theme of loneliness. The work that S. conceived as a new genre, the play-novellete or novel that could also be performed—he wrote two others, *The Moon Is Down* (1942) and *Burning Bright* (1950), neither of which was a critical success—is appropriately claustrophobic, a work of physical interiors or sets where the threatening outside world is discussed, heard, or glimpsed through windows and doors. This stunning novel, which many think is S.'s best, was a popular success, and under George S. KAUFMAN's direction, the play that opened on Broadway in the same year was a hit, winning the New York Drama Critics Award for 1937.

As he finished the novel in 1936, S., then living in Los Gatos, a town near San Jose, was invited by the *San Francisco News* to do a series on migrant workers in California. That fall, he toured both government and private camps, and spent a great deal of time talking to Tom Collins, the first manager of a California government camp and the man to whom the novel is, in part, dedicated. S. was outraged by what he saw, a sentiment clearly evident in the *News* articles called

The Harvest Gypsies and in the novel he began shortly thereafter, *L'affaire Lettuceberg.* Based on a Salinas strike, the first version of his monumental work was a bitter book, so much so that he burned it rather than send it to his editor, Pascal Covici. He began again. From May to December of 1938, S. wrote a new version, where the rage is vented in the interchapters that place the Joads' trek to California in the broader context of human suffering during the decade. As the novel begins, Tom Joad has been released from jail, an event that marks the end of one individual's incarceration and the beginning of a more general entrapment, the Oklahoma migrants' inability to find in California either the dream they envisioned or finally any hope for and end to physical suffering. But this saga of cultural malaise is mitigated by the individual determination of the preacher Casy and the dominant Joads—Ma, Tom and Rose of Sharon. Each suffers a grave loss: Casy of his calling; Ma of her home, parents, and family; Rose of Sharon of husband and child; and Tom of his ideals of equity. Yet each finds consolation in a renewed commitment to an ideal beyond the needs of self. Both Casey and Tom dedicate themselves to the political and moral needs of the masses, Ma embraces the ideal of a human family, and in the controversial ending to the novel, Rose of Sharon nurses a starving man. The home they discover is inner, not outer peace, and it is this discovery that will insure, in S.'s mind, that the common people, not the powers that be, will survive. Although S.'s commitment to nonteleological thinking caused him to resist pat resolutions or patterns imposed on life, he nonetheless suggest the possibility of improved conditions, that the whole could evolve as species to higher forms.

In the history of American letters, only two other novels of social protest, Harriet Beecher STOWE's *Uncle Tom's Cabin* and Upton SINCLAIR's *The Jungle,* have touched off such controversy and have resulted in legislative measures to redress the ills exposed. But S., exhausted both physically and mentally after finishing the work, was emotionally ill-equipped to respond to the vociferous attacks on his book. Leaving his wife, Carol, to answer the correspondence, he fled their Los Gatos ranch and spent weeks in Monterey with Ed Ricketts and in Los Angeles with friends. In 1940, he began serious study of marine biology, a decision that baffled his critics. Why would a champion of the dispossessed at the height of his powers decide to travel to the Gulf of California to catalogue the marine life of the littoral? It was a decision not unlike others he would make throughout his career, decisions to do and to write as he wished and to select his own subjects. Indeed, one of the most appropriate generalizations about S.'s career is that he is a ceaseless experimenter, and this would become increasingly more apparent in the fiction of the 1940 and 1950, fiction that seldom attracted critical acclaim. Although many had viciously attacked *The Grapes of Wrath* because the author "lied" about conditions, degraded the Oklahoma population, and advocated socialist reforms, the tide of intellectual criticism really broke in the 1940s. To S. goes the dubious distinction of being one of the most popular and most frequently derided of modern writers. When it seemed that he no longer championed the cause of the dispossessed in the 1940s, he was tagged as a writer who sold out. When he left California in the mid-1940s to live in New York with his second wife, Gwyn (he divorced Carol in 1943 and married Gwyn Conger a few days later), was said to have lost his source of inspiration. His most experimental works were said to be superficial, sentimental, uninspired. When he won the Nobel Prize in literature in 1962, it was said to be undeserved. S.'s work in the 1930s may indeed be his best, but it is not true that in the next three decades he wrote little worthy of notice.

Nonetheless, it is true that, with a couple of notable exceptions, the work of the 1940s was not so finely balanced. His best work of the next decade was scientific or biological in its thrust—the *Sea of Cortez,* (1941) *The Log from the Sea of Cortez,* (1951) and *Cannery Row* (1945). The first two are composed of narrative, philosophical, journalistic accounts of his 1940 trip to the Gulf with Ed Ricketts and a crew that included his first wife. Although his and Ricketts's desire was to collaborate on a serious scientific study of the littoral of the region, much of the writing is S.'s, a mixture of scientific observation and philosophical musing—his forte. In these two works are found discussions of the ideas that had occupied S.—nonteleological thinking, group man as a separate entity, an ecological consciousness, and a holistic belief in the interrelatedness of all life. Life's interrelatedness becomes the subject of his fine novel *Cannery Row,* a work whose dominant metaphor is the tide pool where all species depend on one another. Although Mack and the boys recall Danny's crew in *Tortilla Flat,* the tone of the later work is more somber and the structure more complex, roughly similar to that of *The Grapes of Wrath,* where the main narrative is punctuated by highly suggestive interchapters. S. once declared that there were as many as four levels to this often rollicking tale, and tidal patterns suggest those multiple levels—varieties of life on the Row; death as a part of that life; the Cannery Row denizens seen through "another peephole" as part of universal patterns; and finally the mystical level, the suggestion of the unutterable at the core of reality, the sea itself and what some "water gazers" envision within.

As Benson observes, other work of the 1940s seems to divide itself between two impulses—the journalistic and the allegorical—and perhaps this fact helps explain S.'s wavering reputation and his difficulty in finding a voice during and after the war. Into the first, one can place contributions to the war effort, *Bombs Away* (1942), written for the U.S. Army Air Force, which tells of the formation and commitment of a bomber crew, and a series of articles written as a foreign correspondent in Britain, Africa, and off the coast of Italy, later collected in *Once There Was a War* (1958). The latter are characterized by fresh observations about daily life during the war, as S. mixes with the common soldier. Indeed, throughout the next two decades, S. would write frequently for journals, and a collection of his contributions would fill a good-sized volume. The allegorical works were less successful, often because critics found the characters unappealingly flat, the tone dispassionate, and the issues fuzzy. His first patriotic work was the quickly conceived play-novelette, *The Moon Is Down,* an insightful study of enemy occupation in a European village and the villagers' attempted resistance. In the midst of war, Americans were in no mood to attend to S.'s observation that it "is always the herd men," the conquering Germans, "who win battles and the free men who win wars," but the novel won supporters in occupied counties, where resistance movements were sustained by S.'s faith in the power of the common man to defeat oppressive ideologies. This work, like so many of S.'s novels, was also made into a movie and a play; both genres fascinated him, and his next three novels—*The Pearl, The Wayward Bus* (1947), and *Burning Bright*—like so many before and after—were similarly envisioned in both written and visual terms or else adapted for film by Hollywood, where S.'s novels were hot properties. By far the most popular, *The Pearl* is a parable about a man who discovers a great pearl, confronts those who would steal it, and finally has it thrown back into the sea, having discovered—too late—that freedom is more precious than financial security. The free conscience is a them that commanded more and more of the novelist's attention.

East of Eden (1952), the book that S. intended as his "big novel," most clearly indicates the major shift in S.'s fictional concerns from early naturalism to dramas of individual consciousness. In the naturalistic works of the 1930s, characters like Jim Noland, George Milton, and Tom Joad are made aware of the individual's need to make tough moral choices, but that awareness seems doomed by the circumstances of their world. By 1950, however, S. was fully prepared to explore individual torment and resolution. In the last years of the previous decade, S. had endured a painful divorce from his second wife, Gwyn; had lost his best friend, Ed Ricketts, in 1948; and had married Elaine Scott, his serene and capable third wife in 1950. *East of Eden,* perhaps S.'s most autobiographical work, acknowledges his own hard won battle for equanimity. This sprawling novel weaves together two family sagas, one historical—the story of his mother's family, the Hamiltons—and one mythic—the Cain and Abel story recast in the Trasks' westward migration. Again, S. strikes a balance between his two fictional impulses. In spite of the novel's popular success, most critics have complained that the two narratives are wrenched together. For many, the naturalistic story of patriarch Sam Hamilton and his family does not serve as a fitting counterpoint to the lurid tale of brother conflict and of Cathy Ames, the embodiment of evil, the monster woman, who murders her parents, deserts her husband Adam Trask and their newborn sons, and subsequently poisons the madame of a brothel in order to supplant her. Recent assessments have been kinder, arguing that S.'s seemingly awkward structure and obvious symbolism (in the Trask tale, characters' names begin with a C, if evil, and an A, if good) are intentional. The novel is concerned with the tools and process of creation and the author introduces pointed contrasts between good and evil, A and C, in order to deconstruct that opposition, to show both through method and message that art can free itself from imposed definitions and that man can escape inherited tendencies. Both self-conscious artist and conscientious character are free to create. The operative term in this text is "Timshel," translated as "thou mayest."

After *East of Eden,* S. did not again attempt a monumental epic that would equal *the Grapes of Wrath.* But he did continue restlessly to experiment. Until his death in 1968, much of his time was spent researching and translating Malory's *Morte D'Arthur,* a fragment of this effort published posthumously as *The Acts of King Arthur* (1976). Immediately after finishing *East of Eden,* he began working with Rodgers and Hammerstein to transform *Cannery Row* into a musical, and from his efforts came the lighthearted novel in which the heretofore lonely Doc falls in love, *Sweet Thursday* (1954), as well as a libretto for the musical *Pipe Dream.* In 1957, he published another uneven work, a satiric novel about the need for French reforms, *The Short Reign of Pippin IV.* And in 1960, he began writing *The Winter of Our Discontent* (1961), the last novel published during his life. Once again examining an individual's ethical awareness, he set this novel in the contemporary of moral decline. Not to act ethically, posited S., is to forfeit humanity; unfortunately, the author's urgent message is more compelling than the fiction that communicates it.

Two of S.'s final creative endeavors were *Travels with Charley* (1962) and *America and Americans* (1966), and perhaps this national perspective is fitting coda for an artist with such an abiding popularity. Both pieces of highly personal nonfiction suggest the roots of S.'s creativity: contact with a purpose that defines them. In 1960, a rather ill man stepped into a truck with his dog, Charley, and drove around America to discover these roots again—to see the people and the landscapes and the images that were the source of his vivid realism and the reason for his continued appeal. And in the mid-1960s, he wrote for the photographic study *America and Americans* essays that comment on America's situation and destiny: "Why are we on this verge of moral and hence nervous collapse? . . . I believe it is because we have reached the end of a road and have no new path to take, no duty to carry out and no purpose to fulfill." S. always recognized the perilousness of the human condition and saw in idealism both its cause and its consolation. This clarity of vision and faith in tentative solutions, whether broadly or narrowly personal, define the contours of S.'s career.

BIBLIOGRAPHY: Astro, R., and T. Hayashi, eds., *S.: The Man and His Work* (1971); Benson, J. J., *The True Adventures of J. S., Writer* (1984); Benson, J. J., *Looking for S.'s Ghost* (1988); DeMott, R., *Working Days: The Journals of The Grapes of Wrath* (1989); Fontenrose, J., *J. S.: An Introduction and Interpretation* (1963); French, W., *J. S.* (1975); Gladstein, M., *The Indestructible Woman in the Works of Faulkner, Hemingway, and S.* (1986); Levant, H., *The Novels of J. S.* (1974); Lisca, P., *J. S.: Nature and Myth* (1978); Marks, L. J., *Thematic Design in the Novels of J. S.* (1969); Owens, L., *J. S.'s Re-Vision of America* (1985); Steinbeck, E., and R. Wallsten, *S.: A Life in Letters* (1975); Timmerman, J. H., *J. S.'s Fiction* (1986)

SUSAN SHILLINGLAW

STEINER, George
b. 23 April 1929, Paris, France

A teacher, cultural journalist, and critic, S. is one of the leading contemporary men-of-letters writing in English. A brilliant polymath, he is the inheritor of the tradition of Edmund WILSON or F. R. Leavis, bringing a European perspective to American and British letters. Born in Paris to Viennese Jewish parents, he was raised in Vienna and then England where his family escaped the rise of Nazism. S. is equally fluent in French, German, and English. He received a B.A. in 1948 from the University of Chicago, an M.A. in 1950 from Harvard, was a Rhodes Scholar in England, and eventually received a Ph.D. from Oxford University in 1955. He has held positions at Williams College, Stanford, Princeton, and Yale, and for many years has been both a fellow at Churchill College, Cambridge and professor of English and comparative literature at the University of Geneva. S.'s background and learning is reminiscent of the lost high cultural heritage of Middle European Jewry, exemplified by figures such as Sigmund Freud, Theodor W. Adorno, Gustav Mahler, György Lukács, Hermann Broch, and Walter Benjamin. Indeed, the themes of survivorship, exile, and a nostalgia for a lost world are recurrent in his work.

S. published his first book, *Tolstoy or Dostoevsky: An Essay in the Old Criticism* in 1959. Reacting against the so-called New Criticism of the day, he argued that Tolstoy was attempting to re-create the epic in his fiction whereas Dostoevsky drew on the tragic. In this—and other early books such as *The Death of Tragedy* (1961), *Language and Silence* (1967), *Extraterritorial: Papers on Literature and the Language Revolution* (1971), and *In Bluebeard's Castle* (1971)—S. brings to bear a double perspective, that of the liberal humanist tradition, with its devotion to the classics, the role of genius, and universality, and that of the high Marxism of Lukács, Adorno, and Benjamin, with its commitment to dialectic, and the sociohistorical critic of philosophy.

The problem that underlies all of S.'s work derives from the crisis of meaning, language, and culture, emerging from the wake of the Holocaust. As a result, his later work has shifted to hermeneutical phenomenology, increasingly influenced by the philosopher Martin Heidegger. *After Babel: Aspects of Language and Translation* (1975) is his fullest examination of the difficulty of meaning and the rupture between language and truth. This is continued in *On Difficulty* (1978), *Martin Heidegger* (1978), *Antigones* (1984), which returns to his earlier interest in classical tragedy, and *Real Presences* (1989). Following Heidegger, S. progressively argues for the presence and transcendence of being in language as a sort of Pascalian wager to ground meaning.

S. has also published many essays and reviews in popular periodicals such as the *New Yorker,* the *Times Literary Supplement,* and *Salmagundi.* Many of these have been collected in *G. S.: A Reader* (1984) and recently in *No Passion Spent: Essays, 1978–1995* (1996), including the controversial "Archives of Eden," a critique of American culture. S. has also produced a small but steady body of fiction, including *Anno Domini: Three Stories* (1964), *The Portage to San Cristóbal of A. H.* (1981), and *Proofs and Three Parables* (1993). His fiction echos the themes and preoccupations of his essays and criticism. *The Por-*

tage, the most controversial, imagines that Hitler is found alive in the jungles of Brazil. The book looks at different interpretations of this discovery and their effect on our understanding of the Holocaust.

A powerful, combative, and articulate writer, S. combines vast erudition and philosophical sophistication. He represents an important moral and intellectual challenge to modern cultural studies and postmodernist sensibilities.

BIBLIOGRAPHY: Scott, N. A., and R. A. Sharp, eds., *Reading G. S.* (1994)

THOMAS L. COOKSEY

STEPHENS, Ann Sophia

b. 30 March 1810, Humphreysville (now Seymore), Connecticut; d. 20 August 1886, Newport, Rhode Island

S. finds a place in literary history for several reasons that at first glance seem unrelated but that in actuality are closely intertwined to present a solid view of the author's true essence as part of 19th-c. American literature. S. is considered the first American woman humorist. She is also the author of the first Beadle dime novel, a paperback series aimed at mainstream American readers. In addition, she edited and wrote for many popular periodicals.

The best example of S.'s humor is found in her 1843 novel *High Life in New York,* which is written under the pseudonym Jonathon Slick and purports to tell the tale of Slick's adventures amid New York high society. The work capitalizes on poking fun at social class as well as at the urban versus rural and the naive versus the sophisticate points of view. While much of S.'s satire is aimed at society women and their whims, S. presents a sympathetic view toward working-class women. At the same time, she uses the immigrant worker as another target of her satire. Besides the humor and satire present in the work, there are also definite shadings of sentimentalism, though this does not make up the crux of the work.

S.'s *High Life in New York* served to secure her place as one of the most eminent and highly paid authors of her day and was followed by *Fashion and Famine* in 1854. *Fashion and Famine* also focuses on city life and the blunders of city people. The praise and economic rewards received from the publication of this work placed S. at the height of her career.

Shortly thereafter, S. was sought out, as the most popular author of her day, to become the first Beadle author. She consented to the 1860 republication of her novel *Malaeska: The Indian Wife of the White Hunter* as the first dime novel. The publishers rightfully reckoned on S.'s theme to be of vast interest to middle-class American society—and so it was. Though replete with stereotypes and sentimental overtones, and though the story was rescued from its obscure initial serialization in the 1839 *Ladies's Companion, Malaeska* served to open the Beadle dime novels' venture quite successfully. S. herself went on to write six additional dime novels, all formula works based on historical romance that would presumably be of interest to upper-class women readers.

In addition to these achievements, S. penned an 1847 thriller titled *Henry Langford* and worked for many periodicals, namely, *Portland,* a direct rival of *Godey's Lady's Book, Peterson's,* the *Ladies' Companion,* and *Graham's,* where Edgar Allan POE was also on staff. All of S.'s literary works combine to portray her as an author concerned with both maintaining a witty look at her society and catering to the tastes of her middle-class readers, an agenda that worked well for her in the 19th c. but that fails to raise much enthusiasm with the modern-day reader.

BIBLIOGRAPHY: Mainiero, L., ed., *American Women Writers* (1982); Morris, L. A., *Women Vernacular Humorists in Nineteenth-Century America* (1988); Stern, M. B., *We the Women* (1974)

                    TERRY D. NOVAK

STERLING, George [Ansel III]
b. 1 December 1869, Sag Harbor, New York; d. 17 November 1926, San Francisco, California

Though his reputation as a poet has continued to wane since his death, S. is often cited for his centrality in California's Bay Area literary circles, and especially for his founding of the art colony at Carmel-by-the-Sea. Because of the derivative nature of most of his work, S.'s poetry is considered anachronistic and has fallen from favor with modern critics. Originally from Long Island, New York, S. moved to Oakland, California, in 1890 to work for his uncle. He soon became acquainted with such literary figures as Edwin MARKHAM, Joaquin MILLER, Jack LONDON, and Ambrose BIERCE, his mentor. His first collection, *The Testimony of the Suns and Other Poems* (1903), reflects S.'s indebtedness to the Victorians, especially Tennyson, for a poetic style that featured formal versification, rhetorical excesses, archaic language, cosmic despair, and nebulous ideas; conversely, this collection also shows his ability to write a kind of pure lyric poetry, reminiscent of the romantics in their neoplatonic pursuit of Absolute Beauty, that had all but disappeared from fin de siècle American poems. The success of *The Testimony of the Suns* made S. a celebrity, especially

among the young writers known as the bohemians, whom S. befriended. In order to pursue his writing career in relative peace and seclusion, S. moved to Carmel-by-the-Sea in 1905. It was here that S. produced the poetry that received national attention, "A Wine of Wizardry" (1907) and "Three Sonnets on Oblivion" (1908), published respectively in *Cosmopolitan* and the *Century* magazines, and *The House of Orchids and Other Poems* (1911). Even as MODERNISM in poetry became established in the second decade of the 20th c., S. chose not to abandon the tradition of 19th-c. Pre-Raphaelite poetry for the *vers libre.* Sensing that his poetry had lost ground to the imagists, S. compromised his aesthetics and began writing salable sentimental verse, collected in *Beyond the Breakers and Other Poems* (1914) and *The Caged Eagle and Other Poems* (1916), occasional odes on such events as the Panama-Pacific Exposition and the opening of the Panama Canal, and chauvinistic war poems, published in *The Binding of the Beast and Other War Verse* (1917); he continued to write sonnets, for which he received some recognition. In the seven years before his suicide, S. turned to writing long, philosophical verse-dramas, characterized by a similar sense of pessimism and despair that appeared in some of his earliest poetry. But the vogue of his genre had passed, and *Lillith* (1919), *Rosamund: A Dramatic Poem* (1920), and *Truth* (1923) faded into the same obscurity as their creator.

BIBLIOGRAPHY: Benediktsson, T. E., *G. S.* (1980); Longtin, R. C., *Three Writers of the Far West: A Reference Guide* (1980); Noel, J., *Footloose in Arcadia: A Personal Record of Jack London, G. S., Ambrose Bierce* (1940); Starr, K., *Californians and the American Dream* (1981); Walker, F. D., *The Seacoast of Bohemia* (1966)

                    ROBERT C. LEITZ, III

STEVENS, Wallace
b. 20 October 1879, Reading, Pennsylvania; d. 2 August 1955, Hartford, Connecticut

S. is generally considered to be one of the greatest American poets of the 20th c. His career is unusual because he was a businessman as well as a poet. During most of his poetic career, he worked for the Hartford Accident and Indemnity Company, where he eventually became vice president. In this respect, he resembles his friend William Carlos WILLIAMS, who was both a poet and a medical doctor. Unlike Williams, however, S. never wrote poems about his work. Although his poems are rooted in basic human experiences, S. seldom writes about ordinary characters or dramatic situations, preferring (like many modern painters) to contemplate landscapes or still lifes, the exotic creatures of his imagination, or the abstract workings of his own mind. His poems—elegant, extremely inventive, and often ironic—are addressed to a well-educated and highly cultured audience. The philosophical intent and intellectual difficulty of his poems have made him a favorite among academics. But he is also a "poet's poet" who attracts readers with his quirky imagination, his rare attention to delicate nuances of perception, and the sheer beauty of his language.

S.'s first book of poems, *Harmonium* (1923), is the best introduction to his work. Poems like "Disillusionment of Ten O'Clock" and "Le Monocle de Mon Oncle" show S.'s debt to the 19th c.: to the aestheticism of the French symbolists and Walter Pater, the dandyism of Baudelaire and Oscar Wilde. But like the modernist painters and poets of the New York avant-garde with whom he was associated in the 1910s, S. was "brought to a boil" by the Armory Show of 1913 (the huge art exhibition that introduced the American public to postimpressionism and cubism) and by the literary experiments of Gertrude STEIN. Poems such as "The Emperor of Ice Cream," with its oblique title, and "Anecdote of the Jar," which raises the most basic questions about art, repay comparison with the art of Marcel Duchamp, whom S. knew. But *Harmonium* is unique in its freshness and vitality, its variety of theme and style, and its technical mastery of free and strict forms. If S. had never written another poem, this book would still assure him an important place in American literary history.

The elements of theme and style most characteristic of S.'s best work are all present in *Harmonium*. The two poles of his poetic world may be exemplified by "Tea at the Palaz of Hoon," a hymn to the pure power of imagination, and "The Snow Man," an unflinching confrontation with the barest reality. S. continued to think of his poetic activity as adjusting the balance between these two poles. "Sunday Morning," which the critic Yvor WINTERS called the "greatest American poem of the 20th c.," introduces the central theme that occupied him for the rest of his career: the failure of traditional religious beliefs in the modern world, and the consequent search for a religious substitute that will satisfy man's undiminished spiritual desires. This poem's meditative intensity and richness of language have reminded readers of Shakespeare or the great English romantic poets. "A High-Toned Old Christian Woman," a shorter poem on the same theme, exemplifies a very different aspect of S.'s style: his irony and humor. In this poem, a somewhat odd narrator shocks the pious matron of the title with the notion

that poetry alone, rather than the Christian myth, is "the supreme fiction." The jaunty tone, peculiar vocabulary, and nonsense-sounds of this poem also characterize such well-known poems from *Harmonium* as "Le Monocle de Mon Oncle," "Bantams in Pine Woods," "Depression before Spring," and the long semiautobiographical narrative "The Comedian as the Letter C." A good example of the way S.'s earlier poems often provided inspiration for his later ones is the fact that he used the phrase "the supreme fiction" in a major poem twenty years later to denote the central goal of his art.

From the very beginning, S. thought in terms of the relations between the arts. Like Baudelaire, he conceived of a "fundamental aesthetic" that underlies all the arts, but particularly the arts of music, painting, and poetry. He had an extensive record collection, and prided himself on his specialized musical knowledge, dedicating several poems, for instance, to the relatively obscure Russian composer Anatol Liadoff. His poetry is full of musical allusions, from the instrumental metaphors and varied rhythms of "Peter Quince at the Clavier" (1915), which he once described as a "libretto," to the transcendent birdsong in "Of Mere Being," one of the last poems he wrote.

Even more important to S.'s poetic world was the analogy of the visual arts, particularly the art of painting. His imagination was primarily visual; early poems in the imagist manner like "Tea" could consist entirely of visual description. His great love in painting was the Impressionist movement of the 19th c., and "Sea Surface Full of Clouds," with its series of nuanced variations on the title scene, has often been compared to Claude Monet's impressionist paintings of water lilies. But he was also interested, throughout his career, in the developments of contemporary painting. When he lived in New York, he was at the heart of American avant-garde painting. After he moved to Hartford in 1916, he kept up with the art world by reading French, English, and American art magazines, and by traveling into New York several times a month to visit galleries and museums. His awareness of contemporary trends in the visual arts is clear in the cubist aspects of "Thirteen Ways of Looking at a Blackbird" (1917), in the surrealist elements of his poetry in the 1930s, and in his experimenting with increasingly greater degrees of abstraction in his later poetry. Sometimes he even adopts the persona of a painter in his studio, as in the poems "Study of Two Pears," "The Poems of Our Climate," "Dry Loaf," and "So-and-So Reclining on Her Couch." His painterly imagination lies behind some of his most characteristic perceptions; for example, he conceives of light in terms of the physical properties of oil paint in two memorable lines: "I have wiped away moonlight like mud"; and "Smeared with the gold of the opulent sun."

S. was always a philosophical poet, a poet of ideas. He was interested in the relations between philosophy and poetry, and once tried to analyze them in an essay, "A Collect of Philosophy." His writings are full of references to philosophers from Democritus, Plato, and Thomas Aquinas to Friedrich Nietzsche, Søren Kierkegaard, and George SANTAYANA. Even in the poems of *Harmonium,* his theme is often some aspect of aesthetic theory. This interest became more central as his career progressed and his own poetic theory developed. Although he repeatedly warned critics not to search for any systematic philosophy in his work, certain basic ideas naturally recur, and part of the pleasure in reading S. is to discover some coherence among them. S.'s essays, *The Necessary Angel: Essays on Reality and the Imagination,* record his own efforts in this direction. Certain of his central ideas will be discussed below. What is most important for the beginning reader to recognize is S.'s belief that certain ideas are *inherently* poetic, that certain concepts can so unite thought and feeling that merely contemplating them produces aesthetic pleasure. This emphasis on content rather than form separates him from most of his poetic contemporaries in English.

Harmonium was a commercial failure when it was first published in 1923, and for the next seven years, S. wrote virtually nothing, devoting his energy instead to his family (his only daughter was born in 1924) and his business career. When he took up poetry again in the 1930s, he found the literary world increasingly hostile to his kind of "pure poetry." A world torn by the Great Depression, by the antagonistic forces of fascism and communism, and by threat of renewed world war, had little time for sophisticated wit and irony. S. attempted to come to terms with this conflict during his Middle Period, from about 1934 to 1942, and in the process he remade himself from a poet of perception to a poet of "the act of the mind," preparing the way for the great poems of his later years. This development has come to seem increasingly important in recent years, as critics have emphasized S.'s active engagement with the major political events of his time.

His shaken confidence at the beginning of his transitional period shows in the poems of *Ideas of Order* (1935), which seem, with few exceptions—like the serenely beautiful "The Idea of Order at Key West"—shopworn or defensive variations on *Harmonium. Owl's Clover* (1936) was a false step in which S. tried to address head-on the political and social issues of the day; it remains a fascinating historical document but an obscure and tedious poem. He regained his stride in "The Man with the Blue Guitar" (1937), a long poem at once serious and playful, in which he successfully balances the rival claims of art and society by boldly identifying with Pablo Picasso, the undisputed leader of modern art. The poems of *Parts of a World* (1942) record his rapid development over the next five years. "Man and Bottle" and "Of Modern Poetry" define his new poetic stance that gains in strength as it confronts the grim reality of World War II. "On the Road Home" and "the Man on the Dump" strive for a sense of existential freedom. His growing interest in the hero is summarized by the final long poem in that book, "Examination of the Hero in Time of War."

S. was concerned with the idea of the hero—an abstract model of nobility for our modern secular culture—from about 1936 through about 1947. This preoccupation climaxed in 1941–42, when he wrote his best and most important prose essay "The Noble Rider and the Sound of Words," and what many regard as his finest long poem, "Notes toward a Supreme Fiction." "Noble Rider" traces the history of the concept of nobility (the hero's defining trait) as it is depicted in Western art and literature from Plato to the present. The essay concludes with S.'s famous definition of nobility as a force: "It is a violence from within that protects us from a violence without." "Notes toward a Supreme Fiction" takes up the problem of how to construct an object of belief that will make this protective force available to modern man. It does so, first of all, by establishing three necessary attributes of such a "supreme fiction": "It Must Be Abstract," "It Must Change," and "It Must Give Pleasure." Under these three comprehensive subtitles, the poem develops more or less casually certain aspects of poetic creation. "Notes" gains its power from the sublimity of its subject, the beauty of individual cantos, and the sheer virtuosity with which S. modulates the balance between intellectual restraint and imaginative exuberance throughout the length of the poem.

Most of the poems in *Transport to Summer* (1947) develop themes from "Notes toward a Supreme Fiction." "Chocorua to Its Neighbor" elaborates S.'s concept of the hero, and "Esthétique du Mal" tests the notion of a "supreme fiction" against the realities of pain and evil. This volume also contains the hymn to fulfillment "Credences of Summer" that recalls, in its bittersweet tone, Keats's ode "To Autumn." A more personal element enters S.'s verse at about this time. He begins including in poems the names of friends (Henry Church, José Rodríguez Feo), of his own ancestors (Blandina, Jacomyntje, John Zeller) and of things and places that have personal associations for him (the Schuylkill and Perkiomen rivers, Mounts Neversink and Chocorua, the towns of Tinicum and Cohansey).

This personal element is evident in the title poem of S.'s next volume, *The Auroras of Autumn* (1950), which abandons the idea of the hero and develops instead a personal mythology (of the mother and the father) against a generalized tragic background (represented by the aurora borealis). Another attempt at a personal "mythology of modern death" is the elegy "The Owl in the Sarcophagus." These poems also represent the increasingly abstract quality of S.'s later poetry. Both are extremely interesting in conception and contain passages of great beauty, but neither can be fully understood without reference to S.'s earlier verse. The same is true of the long "An Ordinary Evening in New Haven," which attempts to get at "the eye's plain version" of things, to make poetry out of the ordinary without romanticizing it. Read in the context of S.'s entire work, this poem has depth and richness surpassing much of his earlier poetry; but read alone, it is often forbiddingly difficult and obscure. Some critics consider such long poems the epitome of S.'s achievement; others find them too abstract and repetitive.

Like William Butler Yeats, S. unquestionably wrote some of his greatest poems in old age. The poems first published in S.'s *Collected Poems* (1954) under the collective title "The Rock" were written when he was over seventy. "To an Old Philosopher in Rome," addressed to the dying philosopher George Santayana whom S. knew when he was a student at Harvard, is so deeply felt a personal statement that it might almost serve as S.'s own extended epitaph. Shorter poems like "Final Soliloquy of the Interior Paramour," "The Course of a Particular," and "The River of Rivers in Connecticut" combine a hard-won simplicity of vision with a new austerity of language. These late lyrics have a transparent beauty that deepens with each reading.

During most of his lifetime, S. was overshadowed by the figures of T. S. ELIOT and Ezra POUND. Since his death in 1955, however, S. has become one of the most important influences on contemporary American poets. Poets such as John ASHBERY, James MERRILL, A. R. AMMONS, and Jorie GRAHAM have acknowledged their considerable debt to S., and testify to his growing stature in the history of American literature.

BIBLIOGRAPHY: Bates, M. J., *W. S.: A Mythology of Self* (1985); Bloom, H., *W. S.: The Poems of Our Climate* (1977); Brazeau, P., *Parts of a World: W. S. Remembered* (1983); Litz, A. W., *Introspective Voyager: The Poetic Development of W. S.* (1972); Longenbach, J., *W. S.: The Plain Sense of Things* (1991); Vendler, H., *W. S.: Words Chosen Out of Desire* (1984)

GLEN MACLEOD

STEWART, Donald Ogden

b. 30 November 1894, Columbus, Ohio; d. 2 August 1980, London, England

A young member of the literary circle known as the Algonquin Round Table in the 1920s and a close friend of such literary figures as Ernest HEMINGWAY, F. Scott FITZGERALD, and Edmund WILSON, humorist and screenwriter S. spent the last thirty years of his life in exile in London.

S. established his reputation as a humorist with *A Parody Outline of History* (1921), a comic retelling of key events in American history "imagining them as they would be narrated by America's most characteristic American authors." In addition to accomplished stylistic parodies of such writers as James Branch CABELL, Sinclair LEWIS, Fitzgerald, Ring LARDNER, Eugene O'NEILL, and Edith WHARTON, S.'s work includes comic references to contemporary figures ranging from Warren G. Harding to H. L. MENCKEN. Several chapters, including "Main Street—Plymouth, Mass.," as recounted by Lewis, and "Custer's Last Stand," in the manner of Wharton, retain their stylistic charm.

Almost thirty years after the publication of *A Parody Outline,* S. again reworked the prose of Lewis, this time for the screenplay adaptation in 1947 of Lewis's *Cass Timberlane.* Indeed, it was as a screenwriter, usually of adaptations of plays or novels, that S. achieved his most enduring successes. His screenwriting credits include *Holiday* (1938), *Prisoner of Zenda* (1938), *Love Affair* (1939), and *The Philadelphia Story* (1940), for which he won an Academy Award. Blacklisted during the anticommunist purges of the early 1950s, S. retired to England, where he published his autobiography, *By a Stroke of Luck,* in 1975.

BIBLIOGRAPHY: McNutt, J. C., "D. O. S.," in Trachtenberg, S., ed., *DLB,* vol. 11, part 2, *American Humorists, 1800–1950* (1982): 466–73; Yates, N. W., *The American Humorist: Conscience of the Twentieth Century* (1964)

RICHARD NORDQUIST

STICKNEY, Trumbull [Joseph]

b. 20 June 1874, Geneva, Switzerland; d. 11 October 1904, Cambridge, Massachusetts

Hailed by some as the most conspicuously neglected of all American poets, T.—saved from obscurity—now enjoys a reputation as a traditionalist who achieved an individual style during his short life. Early reviewers and anthologists had dismissed him as a decadent fin de siècle aesthete, merely representative of the period. No doubt such a response came from a reading of his *Dramatic Verses* (1902), which contains much verse which was then unfashionably direct, full of sentiment and subjective sublimation. Yet it was Edmund WILSON who first praised S.'s sensuous imagery and eloquent emotion, finding in S. a great spareness and accuracy of language, a chaste and classical regard for truthful expression, and a clear minting of syllables resulting in a rocklike record of frustrated passion.

S. approached poetry with high-minded seriousness, was devoted to eliminating rhetoric from his work, and was prototypically interested in the modernist persona of the poet. Mostly educated in Europe, widely traveled, his intellectual interest was classical Greek, particularly Greek tragedy, for which he was the first American to earn a doctorate from the Sorbonne. He wrote perceptive critical essays on literature, art, and philosophy. He developed a growing admiration for the literature and civilization of ancient India and translated the Bhatavad-Gita.

The body of S.'s poetry can be divided between the dramatic—scenes, dramas, and monologues—and the lyric. In terms of tradition, the poems come at the end of the 19th-c. late romantic aesthetic, and show the influences of Keats, Browning, James Thomson, Paul Verlaine, and A. E. Housman. Of the dramatic poems, with their classical themes and lofty diction, "Oneiropolos" (1897), about a spiritual Indian in exile in ancient materialistic Athens, and "Requiescam" (1900), about a sculptor's desire to communicate his art through a painter's, succeed in presenting living portraits of men and women endowed with viable voices. The longer dramas generally fail in this regard. The lyric poems, on the other hand, offer a personal voice that is forcefully human and above; they constitute S.'s great achievement, what he called "pure" expression.

The poems skirt between twin poles of restless rootlessness and stoic resignation. And separating the distance, there is a hovering oppression, an unnamed sense of futility that is as disturbing as the courage to face it is commanding: grief like the swell of tidal darkness that overwhelms the brain matched with an utterance like in the sonnet: "Hencefoward I no longer shall be known" (1900): "But with dispassionate and quiet eyes / Watching my destiny depart from me / Like flushes in lotus after sunrise." Here the poet's assured strength comes from a recognition of the muted vitality of beauty. In other poems, this sense of calm is not as strongly felt, as doubt lingers to the end, yet almost never in a blanketing veil of despair. S. avoids self-pity or the pose of such, presenting despair as a human emotion, so he believed, simple, healthy and so close to the fresh world he lived in.

The reality of personal experience then, rather than metaphysical abstraction or the world of dream, becomes the most important imperative and inspiration for his poetry, as he writes in "Be still. The hanging Gardens were a dream."

S. writes about the memory of love and of landscape, usually fusing a meditation on a lost personage of love or a past ecstasy of vision with an overwhelming, imaginative return to a place, as illustrated in "In a City Garden," "Mnemosyne," and "In Ampezzo." But none is more sustained or spasmodically immediate than "Eride," a long sequence that broods on love's language and memory, as well as the loss and return of both. The varying of stanza, meter, and rhythm coincide with the various emotions involved: yearning, desire, regret, anger, recrimination, and finally, acceptance. As in the true sense of time evaporates, the act of memory dulls the present as the secret of possession is revealed along with its delusion and danger. And throughout the fitful, relentless image of the sea remains a constant.

The poems reveal an obsession with the concept of time and finality of death. Curiously enough, in light of how S. suddenly died of a brain tumor at the age of thirty, many poems, even those much earlier than when he was diagnosed with the disease, refer to a darkness, a plague resounding across the dying brain, and most famously, "the green and climbing eyesight of a cat" nearing the mind's poor birds, as if the poet's "fright of time" of which he wrote so brilliantly was prophetically the man's.

BIBLIOGRAPHY: Haldane, S., *The Fright of Time* (1970); Reeves, J., and S. Haldane, *Homage to T. S.* (1968); Whittle, A. R., *T. S.* (1973)

H. S. YOON

STILL, James [Alexander, Jr.]

b. 16 July 1906, Lafayette, Alabama

Born into the family of a farmer and veterinarian (or "horse doctor," as he was called) near Lafayette in east central Alabama, S. moved in 1932 to Knott County in the mountains of southeastern Kentucky, and quickly made his new home his literary turf for the rest of his life. From a small cabin on Dead Mare Branch near the county seat of Hindman, S. has contributed some of the most authentic poetry and prose to the southern mountaineer's voice in American literature.

With degrees in English and library science from Lincoln Memorial University, Vanderbilt University, and the University of Illinois, S. began his career as a librarian at the Hindman Settlement School, founded in 1902 to educate mountain children not reached by the public schools. His works chronicle the isolated life of the Southern Appalachians, particularly during the two decades between the World Wars. In the foreword to the thirteen stories collected in *The Run for the Elbertas* (1980), critic Cleanth BROOKS stated that "most readers will be startled by the revelations of such primitive life still surviving in the Southern Appalachians at so late a time." Actually, the mountain culture of his new home was not so different from that in which he grew up in Alabama. Although somewhat more remote and less accessible, the region's language and folkways were those of the English and Scotch-Irish who had also settled the rural areas of his native state and had survived well into the middle of the 20th c. They were mostly hard-working people who live in poverty without anger, accusations or despair.

S.'s first short story was published in the *Atlantic Monthly* in 1936, and a book of poems, *Hounds on the Mountain,* followed in 1937. His first novel, *River of Earth* (1940), the story of a poor Kentucky family's struggle for adequate food and shelter on farms and in coal camps, shared with Thomas WOLFE'S *You Can't Go Home Again* the Southern Authors Award that year. A collection of short stories, *On Troublesome Creek,* came out in 1941, and *Jack and the Wonder Beans,* a retelling of the Jack and the Beanstalk story in mountain dialect, was published in 1977. In all of his stories and poems, S. has depicted the life of mountain people with dignity and without apology.

Although he frequently uses archaic words and expressions, his style is simple, restrained, and straightforward. Even in his fiction, S. searches for the *mot juste* with the hungry economy of a poet. He once said that there is not one unnecessary word in his famous comic short story, "The Run for the Elbertas." This passage illustrates his clean, declarative style as well as the dialect and typical subject matter: "The lamp was smothered; we crawled between the covers. Once the light died the window hole turned gray. You see the shoulders of hills through it. Fern and Lark hushed and slept. I lay quiet, listening, and my ears were large with dark, catching midges of sound. The shuck mattress ticked, ticked, ticked. A rooster crowed. Night wore." *Time* magazine called *River of Earth* nothing less than "a work of art." So much could also be said for most of his work. S. is, indeed, the consummate artist without a social agenda. For many of his stories, S. has created a boy narrator who describes and accepts his cultural and economic limitations without self-pity. There is no clarion call for revolution or reform in his books.

S., a lifelong bachelor, once said he learned to cook "because I got hungry." He also wrote for the same reason: "You get hungry for what writing does for you; writing feeds you, nourishes you, sustains you." Another time he describes himself as "simply a writer, as well as a poet, teacher, traveler, and gardener—with an avid interest in herbs, insects, and primitive civilizations."

Although he has published relatively few books, he has been almost universally acclaimed as an important 20th-c. writer whose local color stories and poems transcend their region to become universal. In his review of *The Wolfpen Poems* (1986), James DICKEY called S. "the truest and most remarkable poet that the mountain culture has produced." The Tennessee novelist and historian Wilma Dykeman summed up his work: "J. S. is the excellent Kentucky writer who distills Appalachian language, beliefs and customs into authentic stories and novels that reveal the region's uniqueness with dignity and humor." Indeed, when S. arrived in eastern Kentucky in 1932 and "just sat down," as his neighbors said, he had found his true place on earth. His signature poem is "Heritage," which is a description of and a tribute to the country where he has lived and written for more than sixty years. "Being of these hills," he wrote, "I cannot pass beyond."

BIBLIOGRAPHY: Beattie, L. E., *Conversations with Kentucky Writers* (1996); Chappel, F., "The Seamless Vision of J. S.," *AppalJ* 8 (Spring 1981): 196–202; Hall, W., *Portrait of J. S. as a Boy in Alabama* (1997)

WADE HALL

STITH, William

b. 1707, Charles City County, Virginia; d. 19 September 1755, Williamsburg, Virginia

With the exception of a few official sermons that were published, S.'s place in the literary annals of America derives solely from his *History of the First Discovery and Settlement of Virginia* (1747). Yet, on the basis of this work, S. has earned a preeminent place among the chroniclers of colonial America.

S. had appropriate, and in some instances singular, credentials for writing his history. Having been educated in the Grammar School of the College of William and Mary, S., a Virginia planter's son, matriculated at Queen's College, Oxford in 1724. He was graduated with a B.A. degree in 1728. After his ordination as a minister in the Anglican Church, in 1731, he returned to Virginia, where he was named master in the Grammar School of the College of William and Mary and began to serve as chaplain to the Virginia House of Burgesses. In July 1636, he began a sixteen-year tenure as Rector of Henrico Parish, some forty miles west of Williamsburg. There, freed of his "laborious employment at the College," and able "to enjoy a little leisure," he began work on his history project.

In his preface, he states that he was motivated by the importance of the undertaking; by a perceived lack of reliable histories covering the early years of the Virginia colony; and by a concern that many of the original sources then available might not endure for long. He was descended on his mother's side from the famous Randolphs of Virginia, one of whom, an uncle, Sir John Randolph, had "purposed to write a preface to our laws, and therein to give an historical account of our constitution and government." However, Randolph had apparently got no further than collecting materials before his death. These were made available to S., as were transcripts of certain records of the London Company, made at the behest of the Earl of Southampton, which were loaned to S. by their current owner, William BYRD, II (who lived nearby, at "Westover"). S.'s search for additional sources, especially official records, produced generally disappointing results, as numerous records were missing or else badly preserved. The only valuable secondary source he mentions is Captain John SMITH's *Generall Historie of Virginia, New England and the Summer Isles,* which he thinks "large and good" but nevertheless "vastly confused and perplexed." He also drew upon Robert BEVERLEY's *History and Present State of Virginia.*

Although the scope of the history that S. set out to write is not known, the one volume he completed covers only through 1724. It was published in 1747 in two editions by William Parks in Williamsburg and later, in 1753, in London. However, it is clear that S. intended that the work run to more than one volume. In an appendix, he states his "surprise and mortification, that some of my countrymen (and those too, persons of high fortune and distinction) seemed to be much alarmed, and to grudge, that a complete history of their own country would run to more than one volume and cost them above half a pistole."

Though S.'s "plain and exact history" is generally held in high esteem, he is often accused of being partisan, in that he defends the Sandys-Southampton administrations of the colony against the opposing policies of James I ("that silly monarch"). Unfortunately, little attention has been given to the fact that S.'s history appeared less than thirty years before Lexington and Concord, or that his remarks against the James I's arbitrary use of authority might be read in conjunction with certain criticisms he levels at Charles II in the "Appendix" to the *History.* Here he rails against that monarch's high-handed levy of taxes against the colony and his concurrent "absolute refusal . . . to ratify and confirm the power and authority of

the Grand Assembly, consisting of the Governor, Council and Burgesses."

Such sentiments seem clearly aligned with the growing colonial restiveness over punitive taxation by the crown. They may also help to explain in part the opposition of Governor Dinwiddie to S.'s appointment as third president of the College of William and Mary in 1752. But S. had also opposed the governor's pistole levy for land grants and Dinwiddie, thinking him "unorthodox and a man of turbulent spirit who had tried to stir up the lower classes against the administration," did not appoint him commissary to the Bishop of London or to the governor's council—positions that his predecessors had held. S. died three years later, while still president of the college.

BIBLIOGRAPHY: Bain, R., et al., eds. *Southern Writers: A Biographical Dictionary* (1979); Hubbell, J. B., *The South in American Literature, 1607–1900* (1954)

                                    WELFORD DUNAWAY TAYLOR

ST. JOHN, David
b. 24 July 1949, Fresno, California

An accomplished poet, editor, and educator, S. conceives of a poem as an experience, a drama of movement, a process that posits a model of consciousness. Inspired by a variety of texts, from the poetry of the French symbolists to the theory of contemporary critics, S. entangles his reading with his personal history, distilling from his perceptions a lyrical poetry concerned with the psychology of human relationships. Although he has been criticized for indulging in rhetoric and nostalgia, S. never allows a trope or an emotion to fall static; rather, his poems adeptly interweave the visual and the aural in carefully structured free verse, creating a cinematic succession of images threaded by rhythm in thought.

In his acclaimed first volume, *Hush* (1976), S. tests the balance of motion and stillness, silence and sound, in familial relationships, particularly those most strained by his own experience of loss: the miscarriage of his second son and the divorce of his first wife. This loss is best recorded in "Naming the Unborn" and in the title poem, in which the poet transposes the voice of the unborn to his own: "As you / Cry out, as if calling to a father you conjure / In the paling light, the voice rises, instead in me." But this loss compels new motion, as in "Slow Dance," a series of interrelated dramas in musically phrased long and short lines well-timed to the syntax. The effect is one of controlled spinning, the body in motion, the images moving as one might turn an object to examine its faces. But here the object is the experience itself, and, even when physical objects are ostensibly the focus as in "Dolls," S. gives priority to the experience of the perception instead.

In *The Shore* (1980), S. traces the bounding lines of senses and perceptions, finding inevitably the renewal of desire, even when hearing echoes of loss, as in "The Boathouse": "Even the sea sings one octave in the past." S.'s psychology of relationships becomes mediated by self-projections into the natural world, as in "Until the Sea Is Dead": "Perhaps / I'll draw myself into the landscape, / To hold you closer to it / Then I could alone." The strength of this volume lies in its subtlety: an understated passion for the undisclosed "you" in the supple movement of thought and phrase.

The poems of *No Heaven* (1985) substitute white space for punctuation, allowing the line breaks and internal gaps to set the tempo and still the movement. As in the previous volumes, the poems in this book turn on each other's images, suggesting here that only we can create a heaven by seeing beyond the absences of difference and circumstance. Such sight develops through the interwoven textures of poems like "The Swan at Sheffield Park" and "The Man in the Yellow Gloves." In the former, S. threads a London April, Gibbon's *Decline and Fall,* the wings of a swan, and the legs of a stripper into the impression a moving body leaves on the surface of thought. This impression lingers, even in the postmodern, cinematic images of "Wavelength" and "Meridian."

S.'s recent work experiments with traditional and new forms. In *Terraces of Rain: An Italian Sketchbook* (1991), the architecture and romances of Italy find new articulation in S.'s juxtapositions of person and place, past and present, name and history. In "To Pasolini," a sequence that memorializes the Italian poet and film director who was murdered in 1975, the poet wades precariously into the sentimental but sharpens his images on his terza rima and his variations of the villanelle. The eleven new poems in *Study for the World's Body: New and Selected Poems* (1994) include ten reflections on mostly European-inspired images and the title poem, a long work joining a meditation and an elegy in two columns of differently typeset verse. This form challenges the reader with a visual and acoustic intermixture, and, like all S. poems, it entices the reader to unravel and reentangle the ordinary through the music of experience and through pictures that move.

BIBLIOGRAPHY: Lummis, S., "The Poetics of Light: An Interview with D. S.," *DQ* 25 (Winter 1991): 120–27; Whedon, T., "Three Mannerists," *APR* 17 (May-June 1988): 41–47

TODD VERDUN

STOCKTON, Frank R. [Francis] R[ichard]

b. 5 April 1834, Philadelphia, Pennsylvania; d. 20 April 1902, Washington, D.C.

S. will likely be eternally linked with his provocative story "The Lady or the Tiger?" (1882) and nothing more. This tale reflects aptly many of the author's concerns—fantasy, human conflict, and the faraway setting. S., however, presents us with something of a dilemma. Approaching S. prompts us to ask "What is literature?" Is it pure entertainment, or is it food for elitists and intellectuals? S. proves convincingly that a writer may coexist in both worlds.

As a high school student, S. believed that he was headed for a career in medicine, and he filled his curriculum with science courses. Although writing was his destiny, this early training impacted his work, a fact that Henry L. Golemba notes in S.'s "consistent plots, close observation, and realistic style." *The Great War Syndicate* (1889), *The Great Stone of Sardis* (1898), and numerous short stories bear the marks of training in science, although fantasy became the writer's trademark.

Apparently S.'s father objected to his son's inclinations toward writing; when S. graduated from high school in 1852, he became a wood engraver, a compromise profession that he would ply for the next eight years. Despite his father's objection and numerous rejections from publishers, however, S. pursued writing.

In 1859, the *Southern Literary Messenger* printed "Kate," a story of the misadventures in love of a "shy person." After this initial success, S. enjoyed some modest triumphs as a writer of children's stories in *Ting-a-Ling* (1870), as an essayist, and as a journalist. His real success as a writer came when he assumed an editorship with *Hearth and Home* in 1872.

From 1873 until his health declined in 1878, S. assisted with *St. Nicholas,* a monthly magazine for children. A prolific contributor to the magazine, he would later collect most of his children's stories into volumes: *Roundabout Rambles in Lands of Facts and Fancy* (1872, written with his wife); *Tales out of School* (1875); *A Jolly Fellowship* (1878); and *What Might Have Been Expected* (1874), among others.

In 1879, S. decided to break from juvenile fiction and turn to the adult audience. The result of this change was a light, whimsical saga. *Rudder Grange* depicts the trials and tribulations of newlyweds as they seek their first home. The couple settles on a "fixed" houseboat, an uncommon dwelling for an uncommon story. *Rudder Grange* fits well as the transition piece to S.'s adult works. Descriptions of the *Rudder Grange* echo the Peggotty's houseboat at Yarmouth in *David Copperfield,* another novel that adapts to a juvenile or adult audience.

Several publishers rejected *Rudder Grange* before Scribner's took a chance on it. The novel proved an instant success largely due to the introduction of the zany maid Pomona, who far outshines her employers. Several critics posit that S. in his creation of Pomona comments astutely on the social order of the day, and especially the servant question. Anything but docile and subservient, Pomona quickly dominates the manor. S. satirizes well this social dilemma, but he also anticipates the "dizzy" domestics in James THURBER's humor, in the screwball comedies of the 1930s, and even several television situation comedies.

Eventually S. wrote two sequels to *Rudder Grange*—*The Rudder Grangers Abroad* (1891) and *Pomona's Travels* (1894), which continue the saga of the narrator, his wife Euphemia, and Pomona in foreign settings. Clearly S. capitalized on the popularity of the first of the series, but he also relied on the appeal of travel literature. In the early 1800s, *Blackwood's* proved that taking the reader on mythical journeys to distant lands would sell; and Edgar Allan POE, a powerful influence on S.'s fiction, proved the genre's success in *The Narrative of Arthur Gordon Pym*.

S. did not, however, merely retailor an established artistic mode; he added his own unique flavor of fantasy and jocularity. Combining ill-fated travels and social commentary, S. all but outdoes Poe in *The Casting Away of Mrs. Lecks and Mrs. Aleshine* (1886) and its sequel *The Dusantes* (1888), the tales of two shipwrecked matrons who survive by their wits and brag about their leaving a deserted island in better shape than they found it.

Later in a period that saw an upsurge in the popularity of romance, S. would carry his readers to the land of pirates and buried treasure in *Buccaneers and Pirates of Our Coast* (1989) and *Kate Bonnet* (1902). Yet when one recalls S.'s collections of children's stories, one notes that the writer did not vary much from his initial course. To S.'s credit, he succeeded in maintaining a consistent vision in his juvenile and adult works.

CHILDREN'S LITERATURE, travel adventures, SCIENCE FICTION—whatever mode S. employed, he carefully draws a fine line between reality and fantasy; he never loses the humor of the situation. Perhaps unfortunately for him, he tries techniques that anticipate surrealism in a day of stark realism and determinism. Perhaps the fields are now ripe for the harvest in S. criticism.

BIBLIOGRAPHY: Golemba, H. L., *F. R. S.* (1981); Griffin, M. I. J., *F. S.: A Critical Biography* (1939)

E. KATE STEWART

STODDARD, Charles Warren

b. 7 August 1843, Rochester, New York; d. 23 April 1909, Monterey, California

Best known for his travel narratives, S.'s fame derived more from his subjects than from intrinsic literary merit. After a New York boyhood and brief period writing for the *Overland Monthly* and the *Golden Era* in San Francisco, S. pushed farther west than his California friends Samuel Langhorne CLEMENS, Bret HARTE, Ina Coolbrith, and Joaquin MILLER to make a significant literary discovery of the Hawaiian Islands. The essays of *South-Sea Idyls* (1873), written in his typical archaic poetic style, recount the author's enjoyment of novel scenery and ways of life. *The Lepers of Molokai* (1885) is part description of a voyage and a place, part commemoration of the self-sacrificial service of Father Damien. S.'s characteristic tone of detachment and a certain world-weariness inform his treatment of the many scenes and folkways of *Hawaiian Life: Being Lazy Letters from Low Latitudes* (1894). In chapters on old and new Hawai'i (such as "In a Summer Sea," "In and Out of Eden," and "A Poi-Feed"), he appears at moments as the cultured romantic and sometime sensualist, bemoaning the physical and cultural ills brought by the West. The islands inspire S. to grand effects, sonorous evocations of the exotic: "the green of the grassy hills and the gold of the sunset sea."

The travel letters of *Mashallah! A Flight into Egypt* (1881) are continued with less verve in *A Cruise under the Crescent: From Suez to San Marco* (1898). Other autobiographical narratives take S. *Over the Rocky Mountains to Alaska* (1899) and *In the Footprints of the Padres* (1902). Careful observation of the present is conjoined with references to the past, as in the memorable portrait of San Francisco in the latter volume.

S.'s conversion to Catholicism in 1867 affected both the choice and presentation of his subjects. He also became a professor of English at Notre Dame and the Catholic University of America. *A Troubled Heart and How It Was Comforted at Last* (1885) describes the writer's intellectual and emotional satisfaction with his faith; *The Wonder-Worker of Padua* (1896) reverently tells the story of St. Anthony of Padua. Poems on religious themes alternate with those about faraway lands and seas in the conventional and often vague verse collected by Coolbrith in 1917 (a smaller collection had appeared in 1867). S. turned to his earlier California bohemianism for aspects of the semifictional essays of *Exits and Entrances* (1903) and his unusual autobiographical novel *For the Pleasure of His Company* (1903).

BIBLIOGRAPHY: Gale, R. L., *C. W. S.* (1977); Walker, F., *San Francisco's Literary Frontier* (1939)

BENJAMIN S. LAWSON

STODDARD, Richard Henry

b. 2 July 1825, Hingham, Massachusetts; d. 12 May 1903, New York City

Poet, critic, and editor, S. was perhaps more prolific than brilliant, more important as a literary figure than as a writer. S. spent most of his boyhood in New York City; his father was a sailor, and died at sea when S. was three years old. S. worked as a scrivener, a blacksmith, and an iron molder before embarking on a writing career. In 1845, he submitted a poem to Edgar Allan POE at the *Broadway Journal,* who replied, "We doubt [its] originality . . . for the reason that it is too good at some points to be so bad at others." S. published a volume of verse, *Foot-prints,* at his own expense in 1849. Shortly after its publication, he recognized its inadequacies and destroyed every copy except one, which is currently in the Library of Congress. Despite the failure of *Foot-prints,* his subsequent career as literary reviewer and editor brought him in contact with many of the best writers of his day.

In 1851, S. married Elizabeth Drew Barstow, a writer who S. noted, had "more of the quality called genius than I, who certainly had more talent than she." S. and his wife had three sons, and the parents outlived all of them. S.'s grief at his son Willy's death, at age seven, is evident in his autobiography. He states, "Few poets' children have been more lovingly hymned than little Willy Stoddard . . . except perhaps poor Hartley Coleridge in the frost midnight musings of his erratic father. . . . His death nearly killed his mother, and if the hearts of men *could* break *would* have broken my heart."

In 1853, S. obtained a position as an inspector of customs at the Port of New York through Nathaniel HAWTHORNE, a job he would keep until 1870. Defying Hawthorne's belief that the Customs House killed creativity, S.'s years there were his most prolific. In 1857, he published his second children's book (he noted that "children . . . liked them, though I could never bring myself to do so"), *Town and Country, and the Voices in the Shells,* as well as *Songs of Summer.* In 1860, he published *The Life, Travels, and Books of Alexander von Humboldt,* and in 1861, *The Loves and Heroines of the Poets,* which was well received as was *The King's Bell,* published in 1863. He published five additional books before leaving the Customs House.

During the 1860s, S. was a reviewer for the *New York World;* during the 1870s, he edited the Bric-a-Brac series and the Sans-Souci series, memoirs of literary men and women. From 1880 until his death, he was the literary editor for the *New York Mail* and *Express.* These positions brought S. into contact with many writers, and the S. house became a literary gathering place in the last decades of the 19th c. S.'s autobiography, *Recollections Personal and Literary,* was published after his death in 1903. In it, he reminisces about his relationships with a number of famous figures of his day, including Hawthorne, N. P. WILLIS, Henry Wadsworth LONGFELLOW, Bayard TAYLOR, and John Greenleaf WHITTIER. Although S.'s verse has not stood the test of time, his autobiography is still a fascinating read for any scholar of American literature.

BIBLIOGRAPHY: Harvey, R. D., "R. H. S.," in Rathburn, J. W., and M. M. Grecu, eds., *DLB,* vol. 64, *American Literary Critics and Scholars, 1850–1880* (1988): 230–35

JILL JONES

STODDARD, Solomon

b. 27 September 1643, Boston, Massachusetts; d. 11 February 1729, Northampton, Massachusetts

S. is best known as the father of Congregational evangelism, and the grandfather of Jonathan EDWARDS. During his long ministry in Northampton, Massachusetts, S.'s most enduring contribution to New England religious history was his promotion of an enthusiastic and emotional submission to Christ's will. During his own day, however, S. was famous as an outspoken opponent of Increase and Cotton MATHER's doctrines concerning admission to the church and the Lord's Supper. In a series of sermons and publications between 1679 and 1724, S. defended the individual's right to partake of the Lord's Supper prior to an experience of saving grace.

Upon graduating from Harvard in 1665, S. was troubled by the terms of both the Full and Halfway covenants, which allowed church membership only to those who testified to an experience of grace (Full) or to the children or grandchildren of those who had made such testimony (Halfway). Because of poor health, S. spent two years as chaplain to the governor in Barbados before he accepted a congregation in the frontier town of Northampton in 1672, upon the death of Reverend Eleazar Mather. S. soon married Mather's widow and began allowing any "nonscandalous" person to partake of the Lord's Supper, whether they had testified to grace or not, a breech of the terms of the Synod of 1662. Concerned by the behavior of his in-law, in 1677, Increase Mather published his cautionary *Discourse Concerning the Danger of Apostasy,* which warned of ministers "that have espoused loose, Large principles" concerning church membership and communion. Two years later, S. first attempted to defend his beliefs at a reform synod in Boston, delivering his "Nine Arguments Against Examinations Concerning a Work of Grace," which argued that internal Grace could not be determined by external signs.

It wasn't until eight years later, however, that S. published his first polemic, *The Safety of Appearing at the Day of Judgement in the Righteousness of Christ* (1687). Boldly parting ways with Boston orthodoxy, S. sought to cleanse Congregational practice of a number of non-Scriptural ordinances that had been passed down from the Puritans. S.'s primary defense was to return to Scripture as a means of purging "erroneous Opinions" about church membership. As Philip Gura remarks, many parishioners had chosen not to take communion for fear of accidentally profaning the sacrament through improper participation. S.'s essay was an attempt to make them feel "safe" about participating in communion as long as they felt a strong urge to do so. S. held that since regeneration was not proven in anyone's life, communion was a converting ordinance, not an ordinance of sainthood.

S.'s next major attack on Mather doctrine was his *Doctrine of Instituted Churches* (1700), which argued boldly for a reformation in New England Congregationalism based on a return to the concept of an Old Testament instituted church, and the rejection of the mistakes of the Puritan founders. S. argued that the New England Congregationalism had developed many un-Scriptural practices that had only been adopted to serve provisional historical needs. Central to this reform was the creation of a national Instituted Church, modeled on the Old Testament rather than the New, and which offered prayer, baptism and communion as a means of attaining grace. As Karl Keller has pointed out, S.'s advocacy of a national church was not without contradictions, but S. redefined key terms of his opponent's arguments, such as the definition of church, ordinance, and community, in complicated ways. By accepting the terms of his antagonists, particularly concerning the Covenant with God, but interpreting them differently, S. escaped charges of heresy.

In his later years, S. sought to bypass entirely doctrinal controversy with conservative Boston by promoting a direct relationship with God through evangelism. Although his *Inexcusableness of Neglecting the Worship of God* (1708) and his *An Appeal to the Learned* (1709) still quarreled with the Mathers, S. put his faith in the resurrecting power of evangelical language to regenerate the church and the colonies. By the time he preached *The Efficacy of the Fear of Hell to Restrain Men from Sin* (1713) and *A Guide to Christ* (1714), he believed that yielding to the power of deeply held emotions—and by extension, the language in which those emotions manifested themselves—was a sufficient means for the proper worship of God.

BIBLIOGRAPHY: Coffman, R, *S. S.* (1978); Gura, P., "S. S.'s Irreverent Way," *EAL* 21 (1986): 29–43; Miller, P., "S. S.," *HTR* 34 (October 1941): 277–320; Miller, P., *From Colony to Province* (1943); Keller, K., "The Loose, Large Principles of S. S.," *EAL* 16 (Spring 1981): 27–41

GRANVILLE GANTER

STONE, Irving

b. 14 July 1903, San Francisco, California; d. 26 August 1989, Los Angeles, California

S. is considered a master in the realm of fictional biographers. This California writer has written prolifically in fiction and nonfiction, but it is for his "biohistories," as he called his style of biographical novel, that he has gained his most ardent fans. His vivid prose, careful plotting, and active narrative are often praised. S.'s ability to get inside the head of his subjects has attracted a wide readership and placed him on the best-seller list for long periods at a time.

S.'s success with critics has been sparse in comparison with his popularity with the public. The general lack of respect among the critics for the genre and its tendency to embellish facts is one reason for this. In addition, S. has been criticized for his idealization of his subjects. While critics applaud his meticulous research methods, his novels are sometimes criticized for the weight with which the factual elements overwhelm the story.

Although S. had written many plays and published mystery novels early in his career, he first gained widespread success with his novel *Lust for Life* (1934). This fictionalized biography about the life of Vincent van Gogh was credited with much of the artist's initial popularity in America. In *Lust for Life,* S. found a crucial element to his success: "ready-made character." He discovered his affinity for writing about people wrongly portrayed by history. He was especially drawn to individuals who had overcome great challenges and contributed to society.

Sailor on Horseback (1938), a biography of Jack LONDON, won S. high praise from critics for its "skillful and honest portrait" of the author. S. saw London, in addition to Ernest HEMINGWAY and Sherwood ANDERSON, as important influences in his writing. This identification with London contributed to S.'s success in "getting inside the skin, head, mind, and brain" of his character: an ability he considered crucial to writing historical biographies.

S. yearned to write a novel about Jessie Benton Frémont, the wife of explorer John Charles Frémont, but had doubts about his ability to identify closely with a woman. With the support of his own wife (and editor from 1933), S. wrote the novel *Immortal Wife* (1944). A huge success, especially among women readers, *Immortal Wife* held its position in the top five of the best-seller list for some fifteen months. With this success, S. was encouraged to write other novels with women protagonists, including *Love Is Eternal* (1954) about the life of Mary Todd Lincoln. S. focused on her relationship with husband, Abraham LINCOLN, and her harsh treatment by the public. Well received by both critics and readers alike, *Love Is Eternal* provides an interesting account of the Civil War period through a woman's eyes.

The Agony and the Ecstasy (1961) achieved vast reader support, but was reviled by critics. Among the most widely read biographical novels of the 20th c., most critics saw this story of Michelangelo as simply a bad novel. The work is faulted for not realistically reflecting the man, as well as for S.'s manipulation of factual material.

Another criticism of S. was his tendency, especially in his later novels, to provide "too much history" and "not enough life." His Freud biography, *Passions of the Mind* (1971), is an example of this. In addition to lacking a sense of the complexity of the famous psychoanalyst, S.'s choice of material was also called into question. In one of his last works, *The Origin* (1980), S. redeemed himself by writing an account of Darwin's life that was called by some his best researched and written book. The enduring popularity of many of S.'s novels has prompted their film rendition and translation into some thirty-five languages.

BIBLIOGRAPHY: Jackson, J. H., *I. S. and the Biographical Novel* (1954); Steig, L. F., *I. S.: A Bibliography* (1973)

ANN O'BRIEN FULLER

STONE, John Augustus

b. 15 December 1800, Concord, Massachusetts; d. 29 May 1834, Philadelphia, Pennsylvania

An actor and playwright, S., early in his short career, responded to an advertisement in *Critic* by actor Edwin Forrest who offered $500 for the best tragedy in five acts, the hero of which had to be an "aboriginal of this country." S.'s submission, *Metamora,* won the competition and helped to maintain Forrest's star billing for forty years. *Metamora* (1892) became a landmark in the American theater. A melodrama with sensational scenes, battles, duels, women in distress, two love stories, and the central focus of a "noble savage" who became the tragic victim of white greed, the play was a great success.

Two lasting qualities of this otherwise dated play are its characterization of Metamora and the message of the central plot regarding the determination of the

powerful to corrupt and dominate the weak. In that regard, Metamora is Goliath-like in his stand against the stronger forces of tyranny. His nobility, courage, and selflessness—foils to the selfishness and sneaking machinations of Mordaunt and Lord Fitzarnold—won the admiration of audiences who cherished such independence.

S., who struggled to survive as an actor and playwright, and in spite of the great success of his play, received little financial rewards, suffered from despondency, and committed suicide in 1834. Some of his other dramatic works include: *Restoration; or, The Diamond Cross* (1824), *The Lion of the West* (1831), a revision of James Kirke PAULDING's play, *Tancred, King of Sicily; or, The Archives of Palermo* (1831), acted, but text lost, *The Ancient Briton* (1833), and *The Knight of the Golden Fleece; or, The Yankee of Spain* (1834).

BIBLIOGRAPHY: Meserve, W. J., *Heralds of Promise: The Drama of the American People in the Age of Jackson, 1829–1849* (1986); Quinn, A. H., *History of the American Drama from the Beginning to the Civil War* (1923)

EDMUND M. HAYES

STONE, Robert

b. 21 August 1937, Brooklyn, New York

S.'s novels, screenplays, and short stories mark S. as a philosophical tough-guy contemplating and evoking the apocalyptic tension and fascination widespread in late 20th-c. American culture.

Reviewers have found in S.'s novels compelling appropriations of diverse precursors, including Nathaniel HAWTHORNE, Ralph ELLISON, Flannery O'CONNOR, Lois Lowry, Joseph Conrad, Norman MAILER, John RECHY, Theodore DREISER, Ernest HEMINGWAY, and B. TRAVEN. S.'s first three novels all foreground his apocalyptic prophesying in current politics. *Hall of Mirrors* (1967), winner of the Faulkner Prize, concerns a down-and-out clarinet-player who finds himself involved with a demagogic radio evangelist in New Orleans. *Dog Soldiers* (1974), a 1975 National Book Award-winner based on S.'s experiences as war correspondent, focuses on a Vietnam veteran who brought home both the war and a large quantity of heroin, while *A Flag for Sunrise* (1981) concerns thrill-seeking gunrunners, revolutionary missionaries, and covert U.S. national-security operatives in Central America. Film versions of S.'s first two novels starred well-known Hollywood actors: Paul Newman and Joanne Woodward in *WUSA,* S.'s adaption of *Hall of Mirrors;* Nick Nolte and Tuesday Weld in *Who'll Stop the Ruin,* a screen version of *Dog Soldiers. Children of Light* (1986), S.'s story of a burned-out screenwriter-actor fond of playing King Lear and a psychotic actress who stars in the writer's adaptation of Kate CHOPIN's *The Awakening,* reflects S.'s interest in and his troubled affinity for the movies.

In 1992, S. won the National Book Award for his fourth novel, *Outerbridge Reach,* and during the late 1980s and early 1990s his commentary and criticism began to appear frequently in the *New York Review of Books, Harper's,* and the *New York Times.*

BIBLIOGRAPHY: Karagueuzian, M., "Irony in *Dog Soldiers,*" *Crit* 24 (Winter 1983): 65–73; Shelton, F., "R. S.'s *Dog Soldiers:* Vietnam Comes Home to America," *Crit* 24 (Winter 1983): 74–81; Solotaroff, R., *R. S.* (1994)

                                    JAMES D. BLOOM

STOUT, Rex [Todhunter]
b. 1 December 1886, Noblesville, Indiana; d. 27 October 1975, Danbury, Connecticut

S. was able to sustain a series of novels featuring his detective fiction creation Nero Wolfe for forty-one years, pleasing both critics and readers through thirty-odd novels and a score of novellas and short stories.

S. created his detective, formidable both in bulk and in intellect, at a time when the conventional detective story involved a closed milieu of suspects and a traditional revelation of the killer to that group at its conclusion, and he kept to that format throughout the Nero Wolfe series. But he heeded the American rebellion against the closed milieu and added a streetwise urban loner to his basic format by creating a second detective, Archie Goodwin, to act as narrator *and* investigator, thus Americanizing his format.

Thematically, S. concocts his plots out of tensions and conflicts arising in family situations; his killers are rarely loners or rootless individuals. The plot complications in the first Nero Wolfe novel *Fer-de-Lance* (1934) involve a father-mother-son triangle that is responsible for five deaths. In *The Red Box* (1937), a daughter's search for her true father and her true mother initiates murder. In *Some Buried Caesar* (1939), there are father-son tensions in two separate families, and brother-sister conflicts as well. S. hewed to the family formula in his detective as well: Wolfe's family is composed of Goodwin, his cook, his gardener, and other legmen.

A secondary theme that informs S.'s fiction is politics—cold war in some instances and domestic in others. S. became conflicted politically at times: outside his writings, he supported the Vietnam War, but

attacked the head of the FBI as a villain in *The Doorbell Rang* (1965). In political as well as sociological considerations, Wolfe is the romantic idealist, Goodwin the pragmatist. Together they form a total persona and complete detective.

In technique, S. achieved a smooth, effortless writing style larded with humor, some overt, some covert. Wolfe, admittedly a genius, thinks and talks like a genius. Goodwin narrates the stories with a wisecracking bonhomie that intrigues and impels one to read on.

One of the founders of the Mystery Writers of America, S. was awarded the association's highest honor in 1958, that of Grand Master. Edward Arnold played Nero Wolfe in a motion picture version of *Fer-de-Lance* entitled *Meet Nero Wolfe* (1936), and in 1981, a television series appeared starring William Conrad as Wolfe.

BIBLIOGRAPHY: Anderson, D. R., *R. S.* (1984); McAleer, J., *R. S.: A Biography* (1977)

                                    BRUCE CASSIDAY

STOWE, Harriet [Elizabeth] Beecher
b. 14 June 1811, Litchfield, Connecticut; d. 1 July 1896, Hartford, Connecticut

S. was the fourth daughter of the thirteen children of Lyman Beecher, a Presbyterian minister. Seven of her eight brothers became ministers, she married a minister, and one of her three sons was a minister. Much of her life was spent first trying to reconcile the conservative Calvinism of her father with the experience of her later years and then preaching her newfound faith and its application through the only pulpit available to her: books. As a local color writer, she tried to preserve the past and traditions she saw slipping away; and as a writer of social protest, she argued for change.

S.'s life can be divided into a period of preparation and a period of creation, each defined by her residence. She was born in the time before railroads and telegraphs in Connecticut, living in Litchfield as a child and then in Hartford as first a student and then a teacher at her sister Catharine's school. In 1832, the family moved to Cincinnati, Ohio, where she taught school, married, acquired all of her first hand knowledge of slavery, and began writing.

Membership in a literary group in Cincinnati encouraged her to write, and when an early piece, a sketch of old times in New England, won a prize, she tried to publish more to augment her husband Calvin Stowe's professorial salary. In eighteen years of writing dozens of sentimental, sometimes witty sketches, she developed an eye for detail and an ability to develop character; but because of their brevity, the sketches gave her no training in plotting an extended narrative, a weakness that mars her later work.

In 1850, she returned East with her husband, first to Brunswick, Maine, second to Andover, Massachusetts, and finally, in 1864, back to Hartford, where she died in 1896. In these Eastern years, she wrote the books that brought her fame and fortune.

Uncle Tom's Cabin; or, The Man That Was a Thing, her first novel and most powerful work, shaped much of the rest of her writing both in theme and content. When she began *Uncle Tom's Cabin,* it was to be simply a series of sketches for the Washington, D.C., abolitionist newspaper the *National Era;* she thought it might run for three or four issues. It began on June 5, 1851, and when it concluded thirty-two issues and forty-three chapters later on April 1, 1852, the lack of a grand design was clear. The story wanders from one set of characters to another. In a deus-ex-machina chapter near the end, she reunites several characters separated earlier, and finally simply tells the reader what happened to everybody else. But the characterization is deft and the details of setting vivid, making emotional involvement by the reader almost unavoidable.

Slavery had been an American institution since the 1620s, but the passage of the amendment to the Fugitive Slave Law of 1793 on September 18, 1850, as part of what was called the "Compromise of 1850" in effect declared open season on all black families in the U.S., and S.'s reaction was to try to do something about it.

In terms of its effect on the history of the U.S. and, to a degree, the world, *Uncle Tom's Cabin* is probably the most important American novel ever written. It personalized a political abstraction by making every reader both a slave and a slaveholder. The first novel written against a specific legislative act, it divided a nation. Abraham LINCOLN allegedly called S. "the little lady who started this great war," and he was right.

Uncle Tom's Cabin is clearly against slavery as an institution; it is also clearly not anti-Southern, as some contemporaries said. Simon Legree, the nastiest man in the book, is from Vermont. S.'s point is not that slaveholders, Southerners, are evil people, but rather that slavery brings out the worst in any person, Northerner or Southerner, black or white. The system corrupts, and it can corrupt absolutely.

But it is an interesting book in other ways. The best people, the strongest people, the people on whom the salvation of the country rests are women. The men in the book are all too deeply committed to the business of slavery either to be able to see it as a moral and social wrong or to be able to act. Men find the financial loss too great to give up the system; women, S. argues,

see the moral loss as too great to permit the system to continue. So it will be the Mrs. Shelbys, the Mrs. Birds, the Cassies, and the Elizas, women, white and black, who will stand and say "enough" and, through moral suasion founded on their faith in immediate, attainable perfection, bring an end to slavery. But until that day dawns, the best immediate solution, S. finds, is to send the blacks back to Africa.

Second, S. is clearly racist; she believes blacks, as a race, are inferior. The intellectual ability and initiative of her black characters are in direct proportion to the amount of "white" blood in their veins, Tom excepted. Most blacks are, to S., at best bright children, who love bright colors, music, and big words. They are emotional, devoted, compassionate people, incapable of thinking abstractly. At worst, they are animals. But these views are not surprising; they reflect the age. S. is revolutionary in her very persuasive arguments that blacks have feelings and moral standards like whites. They love their children, believe in the sanctity of marriage, and will die to protect others.

There remain nine important works, novels in intent and structure if not fact, which develop themes and ideas raised in *Uncle Tom's Cabin* and define S.'s attitudes and values after 1852. In 1856, S. continued her assault on slavery with *Dred: A Tale of the Great Dismal Swamp.* This time she centered the narrative on the white characters, attempting again to show how the system corrupts otherwise admirable people. As in *Uncle Tom's Cabin* and later works, she creates characters who are foils to each other and develops the plot through debates, sometimes quite lengthy, among the characters about the problems that arise in the course of the narrative. In England, the book was entitled *Nina Gordon,* and a major problem with the book's coherence is thereby revealed. It is a book without a focus, without a protagonist. Dred's appearances are too occasional and his influence on the rest of the action too vague to qualify him, and Nina Gordon dies long before the book ends. As with so many of S.'s novels, *Dred* is a loosely linked series of scenes populated by a large cast of characters all associated in one way or another with a general theme.

Inspired by her trips to Italy in 1856 and 1859, S. wrote a medieval romance, *Agnes of Sorrento* (1862). Innocent, religious Agnes must choose between romantic love and the church. After too many pages, the church loses. S.'s skill of rendering locations in vivid detail is marred by a very slow-moving story line and the frequent New Englandisms in the speech of her 15th-c. Italians.

The best of her later works occurred when she left Italy and slavery behind and turned to what she knew best, early New England and contemporary American society. In *The Minister's Wooing* (1859), S. explored the Calvinism of an early 19th-c. Connecticut family. Can Mary Scudder, she asks, accept the drowning of her unconverted young lover as part of God's inscrutable plan? Will she marry the elderly, kindly minister, or break her pledge when the young man is miraculously saved? Will the minister let himself be wooed from his harsh faith into a more compassionate theology, or will he hold firm against the rising tide of liberalism? Here, and in the later *Oldtown Folks* (1869), S. presents perhaps the best fictional account ever written of New England Calvinism. As sympathetic as her treatment is, her rejection of it is firm. The terrifying, inscrutable God of her father must make way for Jesus, the loving, forgiving friend of Man. And according to her last books, the most pleasant place to find Him is in the Episcopal Church, where the beauty of the original Roman service survives cleansed of the corruptions of Popery.

The Pearl of Orr's Island (1862) begins as a local color tale of quaint Maine folk including a shipwrecked orphan and two pretty, innocent girls: one who has found God, the other with more secular interests. Half way through, the story becomes Shakespeare's *Tempest,* set in New England. The first part of the book with its fine depiction of Captain Kittredge and the Toothacre sisters and its delightful dialogue is far superior to the conventional romantic triangle of the second.

In *Oldtown Folks,* she retold the adventures of her husband's youth in Natick, Massachusetts; in *Poganuc People,* she starred as Dolly Cushing and relived her youth in Litchfield. In neither book is there any plot to speak of. Characters appear, disappear, and reappear according to little logic and less plan, but for a picture of life in two early 19th-c. small New England towns, the people and events rendered with great accuracy and without the irony of bitterness of later local color writers, these two works are unsurpassed.

Never an active supporter of Elizabeth Cady STANTON, Lucy Stone, or Susan B. Anthony, S., as the author of *Uncle Tom's Cabin,* clearly felt she had a responsibility to speak out on the role of women. In three works, *Pink and White Tyranny* (1871), *My Wife and I* (1871), and *We and Our Neighbors* (1875), she presented her views.

Lillie Ellis in *Pink and White Tyranny,* the best plotted novel of the three, is one example of a bad woman. Influenced by men who want their women to be beautiful and mindless, Lillie thinks of no one but herself. Equally selfish is Audacia Dangereyes in *My Wife and I.* Modeled on Victoria Woodhull, the radical feminist, free-love advocate, and politician, Audacia tries to be a man and so destroys her femininity. She is forward, smokes, drinks, uses slang, and flirts.

Among S.'s good women are strong, self-sufficient characters like those who appeared first in *Uncle Tom's Cabin.* Cassey and Eliza's spiritual sisters include Anne Clayton in *Dred* and Mary Scudder in *The Minister's Wooing,* but it is in the mini-essays that constitute *My Wife and I* and *We and Our Neighbors* that we find five, Caroline Simmons, and Eva, Ida, Alice, and Angelique Van Arsdel, who represent S.'s models for American women in the 1870s. Caroline is unwilling to wait patiently by the fire until some man comes and offers her position and fortune while other male relatives buy more stony pasture with the money she earns. She uses her savings to go out West to a coeducational medical school seeking only "to be able to do as good work as any man's; to be held to be the same account, and receive only what I can fairly win." Ida Van Arsdel pursues the same course, but studies in Paris.

Alice, Angelique, and Eva all find happiness in marriage. Idealistic Angelique marries a crusading Episcopal minister and becomes his helpmate. Alice, a romantic, decides that heroes "seldom carry parcels" and settles for a good, true, noble hearted boy who can both provide for her and have enough money to do good works. Eva Van Arsdel, the most fully developed, is treated as an equal by her husband in their common sphere of operation, their home, but recognizes that his world of business is different from hers and requires skills, attitude and a nature foreign to her. There she plays second fiddle, but "there must be second fiddles in an orchestra . . . and I have precisely the talent for playing one." A woman's proper sphere, says S., is that which best suits her talents without violating her nature. This she should not be denied simply because she is a woman, a stance fully compatible with that which S. had taken on slavery, where the basis of denial was race or religion, where Calvinism held that only the elect could be saved.

Although she is best known for *Uncle Tom's Cabin,* S. wrote thirty-seven other books. She collected some of her early short stories in *The Mayflower* (1843), others in *Uncle Tom's Emancipation* (1853), and expanded the first collection in *The May Flower* (1855), but all of these are clearly ground work for *Uncle Tom's Cabin;* a later collection, *Sam Lawson's Oldtown Fireside Stories* (1872), capitalized on a character created in 1868. These sketches are sentimental, a part of the development of the local color movement that arose after the Civil War, depicting in nostalgic terms a world, now gone, in which everyone knew his place in an ordered society that was better than the present age.

S. also wrote two travel books: *Sunny Memories of Foreign Lands* (1854) and *Palmetto Leaves* (1873). The first is a narrative of her European tour of 1853;

the second describes her adventures in Florida, where, from 1867 to 1883, she spent her winters in Mandarin, outside of Jacksonville. Both reveal as much about the author, a New England intruder, as inform the reader about the places visited.

Nine juveniles, beginning with *Our Charley and What to Do with Him* (1858), written about or for her children, are unexceptional, as is the volume of her poetry, *Religious Poems* (1867).

She wrote two biographical anthologies, *Men of Our Times* (1868) and *Women in Sacred History* (1873); it was easier to identify the strong men than the strong women of her age. In 1869, she wrote "The True Story of Lady Byron's Life" for the *Atlantic Monthly* in response to an attack on her friend, the poet's wife, by one of Byron's mistresses. There she published the open secret that Byron had committed incest with his sister, Augusta Leigh. She presented an expanded case in *Lady Byron Vindicated* (1870), in which she never used the word "incest" or mentioned Mrs. Leigh by name. Both article and book made her infamous, and the article nearly ruined the *Atlantic Monthly;* subscriptions dropped by one half.

House and Home Papers (1865) and *The American Woman's Home* (1869), the latter written with her sister Catherine, present their theories of domestic economy and health. Both are a piece with earlier and later works as they suggest that a woman, if she wishes, can manage not only her home but her life.

S.'s work should be read for the insight it provides into social attitudes in the last half of the 19th c. Unsettled by industrialization and the war, many sought the more peaceful times pictured in her local color works. Most shared her views on the genetic inequality of blacks. Her decision to renounce the rigid Calvinism of her youth paralleled a loosening of theological bonds widespread even before the War. And her emphasis on the family reassured those who saw the rise of the factory system and the elevation of idle woman as a threat to the family.

BIBLIOGRAPHY: Adams, J. R., *H. B. S.* (1963); Ashton, J., *H. B. S.: A Reference Guide* (1977); Crozier, A., *The Novels of H. B. S.* (1969); Foster, C. H., *The Rungless Ladder: H. B. S. and New England Puritanism;* Gossett, T. F., *Uncle Tom's Cabin and American Culture* (1985); Hildreth, M. H., *H. B. S.: A Bibliography* (1976); Kirkham, E. B., *The Building of Uncle Tom's Cabin* (1977); Rugoff, M., *The Beechers* (1981); Stowe, C. E., *The Life of H. B. S.* (1890); Sundquist, E. J., *New Essays on Uncle Tom's Cabin* (1986); Wagenknecht, E., *H. B. S.: The Known and the Unknown* (1965); Wilson, F., *Crusader in Crinoline* (1941).

E. BRUCE KIRKHAM

STRAND, Mark

b. 11 April 1934, Summerside, Prince Edward Island, Canada

S. is considered to be one of the major figures of contemporary poetry. Early on, he became known for a plain-speaking, detached voice, occasionally delving into surrealism; he has maintained a remarkable evenness of tone throughout his career. The distance in this relatively impersonal voice allows his poems to sound more "public," less the production of private ego speaking to itself.

His poems are concerned with spaces, mortality, and art's ability—or lack thereof—to handle them. The natural world exists in his poetry primarily as a backdrop, a canvas on which he paints his particular concerns. S. is more a discursive poet than an imagistic one, and has successfully avoided being identified with either the confessional or deep-image schools that were in vogue during his early career.

His first book of poems, *Sleeping with One Eye Open* (1964), deals in dream states and initiates his preoccupation with the self, its emptiness and mortality. *Reasons for Moving* (1968) continues this thread, but the poems are longer, more crafted, and focus less on dream states and surreal images. *Darker* (1970) first offers writing or art as a possible solution to S.'s preoccupation with mortality and self-emptiness, a way of alleviating his uneasiness. On the whole, however, it seems even more starkly obsessed with mortality than the first two books.

The poems in *The Story of Our Lives* (1973) are longer—the book comprises only seven poems—and deal more directly with the interpenetration of life and art. "The Story of Our Lives," for example, features two lovers reading a book that describes and even predicts their actions. Yet if this is the solace that art provides, it is a mixed one. The poems themselves achieve varying degrees of success.

The Monument (1978) is an unusual book, a mixture of prose and poetry in an allusive and impersonal voice, addressed to a future translator. This relationship allows S. to meditate on questions of mortality, translation, and the kind of endurance art can provide for the self, three of his classic themes.

Many see *The Late Hour* (1978) as a reaction against the aloofness characteristic of S.'s earlier work and culminating in *The Monument. The Late Hour* certainly shows more affection and a greater degree of domestic detail. "Pot Roast" is perhaps the clearest example of this new orientation, an orientation that carries over into the five "New Poems" in *Selected Poems* (1980). These poems deal with S.'s childhood in a much more direct manner than he had previously done.

It was at this point in S.'s career that he took an interlude from poetry. For some time, S. had been involved in translation and anthologies, including *Another Republic* (1976) with Charles SIMIC. In the 1980s, he published three children's books, two books of art criticism, and a collection of short stories, *Mr. and Mrs. Baby* (1985).

When *The Continuous Life* (1990) appeared, it marked a subtle but important change in S.'s work. The poems and prose poems in *The Continuous Life* are less intimate, perhaps, than the "New Poems," but more so than his previous poems. There is also a sense of humor present in some that was not as prominent in S.'s earlier work. There are important continuities, however, with S.'s earlier use of surrealism, his concern with mortality, and his explorations of the connections between art and life. The change, perhaps, comes from a greater valuing of the quotidian, and a lessening of the sense of isolation that marked S.'s earlier poems; we all die, but we do so in company, and these poems recognize this more clearly.

Dark Harbor (1993) is a long poem made up of a proem and forty-five parts. There is, again, some humor to leaven the morality, but overall, *Dark Harbor* carries on the concerns and approaches of *The Continuous Life*—death, the "salvation" of art, and our relationships to these and to one another. For S., the salvation art provides is always partial and contingent, a momentary stay against dissolution—likewise, that of the human community. Nevertheless, they seem to be all we have.

BIBLIOGRAPHY: Bloom, H., "M. S.," *GettR* 4 (Spring 1991): 247–48; Cooper, P., "The Waiting Dark: Talking to M. S.," *HC* 21 (October 1984): 1–7; Gregerson, L., "Negative Capability," *Parnassus* 9 (1978): 90–114; Kirby, D. K., *M. S. and the Poet's Place in Contemporary Culture* (1990)

ROBERT C. SPIRKO

STRATEMEYER, Edward

b. 4 October 1862, Elizabeth, New Jersey; d. 10 May 1930, Newark, New Jersey

For almost one hundred years, S. and the Stratemeyer Literary Syndicate have been the greatest single influence in the field of popular juvenile fiction. S. created and produced Nancy Drew, the Hardy Boys, the Rover Boys, the Bobbsey Twins, Tom Swift, the Outdoor Girls, and a host of other juvenile series that were the main diet of many American children. His particular importance lies in the impact of his books on the juvenile ethic of the 20th c. His books emphasize, either consciously or unconsciously, his understanding of the reality of the American Dream: the achievement of success through hard work and the virtues of honesty, fair play, imagination, and vigorous enterprise. S. and the Syndicate produced over thirteen hundred titles with sales estimated at over two hundred million copies, and their influence on shaping youthful attitudes and ideals has been both enormous and controversial.

S.'s first published work was *The Tale of a Lumberman* in 1878, although it is doubtful that he personally wrote it. His earliest known story is "Harry's Trial," published in January 1883 in *Our American Boys*. "Victor Horton's Idea," an adventure story for boys written in 1889, launched him into a career writing for young people. In the 1890s, he wrote serials for *Argosy, Golden Days,* and other magazines for young people and also worked for the Street and Smith publishing house, writing dime novels and stories for boys and serving as editor of the juvenile magazine *Good News*. He wrote at least sixty-five dime novels about sports, detectives, adventure, and the Wild West. His first hardcover juvenile books appeared in 1894 as the Bound to Succeed and the Ship and Shore series, and by the end of 1900, he had forty-seven juvenile books in print, written under nine pen names—Arthur M. Winfield, Captain Ralph Bonehill, Roy Rockwood, among others—and published by six different publishers. His Old Glory series, about the Spanish-American War, was very popular with boys, but his thirty-volume Rover Boys series, which started in 1889 and ran until 1926, was even more successful. By the end of 1903, S. had about eighty popular juvenile books in print that he had personally written.

Although he was a tremendously creative writer, he had more ideas, plots, and heroes than time, and in 1904, he created the Stratemeyer Literary Syndicate to produce children's books in high volume at low cost. He also refined the fiction factory approach, spending his time developing ideas for series, creating the general concepts, the plots and the characters, and hiring the writers to write the stories to his specifications. As a matter of good business practice, S. hired competent writers and, while the quality varied, the best of the Stratemeyer Syndicate books were equal or superior to comparable juvenile series. His early series, such as the Bobbsey Twins, which started in 1904, the Motor Boys (1906–24), the Outdoor Girls (1913–33), Ruth Fielding (1913–34), and Tom Swift (1910–41) soon became the principal reading staple for a large percentage of young people. In 1927, S. created the Hardy Boys detective series, and in 1930, the Nancy Drew detective stories. He produced, owned and gave direction to these stories but never personally wrote any of the books. Their popularity can be attributed in large part to their principal authors, Howard

R. Garis and Leslie MacFarlane for the Hardy Boys, and Mildred Wirt Benson for the Nancy Drews.

Although S. personally wrote about one-hundred-fifty juvenile titles, he is best remembered for the millions of Syndicate books, which, for much of the 20th c., played a significant part both in entertaining children and in forming their moral and ethical ideas and values.

BIBLIOGRAPHY: Billman, C., *The Secret of the Stratemeyer Syndicate: Nancy Drew, the Hardy Boys and the Million Dollar Fiction Factory* (1986); Dizer, J. T., *Tom Swift and Company* (1982); Johnson, D., *E. S. and the Stratemeyer Syndicate* (1993)

JOHN T. DIZER

STREETER, Edward

b. 1 August 1891, Chestertown, New York; d. 30 March 1976, New York City

S.'s success as a popular social satirist and novelist was made all the more impressive by the fact that he simultaneously pursued a notable career of some thirty-five years as a banker. A native of Buffalo, S. was educated at Harvard, where he edited the famous *Lampoon* and wrote Hasty Pudding shows. In 1917, while serving in the army, he began writing a series of poignantly satirical letters for the *Gas Attack,* the newspaper of the 27th New York Division. Signed "Bill," they expressed the hopes and fears of the average doughboy called to serve in war time. The letters were addressed to "Mable," the girl back home, their simple candor expressed in a semi–illiterate prose interlarded with frequent misspellings, malapropisms, and wry digs at military authority. The following year S. published a collection of these pieces as *Dere Mable: Love Letters of a Rookie.* In 1919, a sequel, *That's Me All Over, Mable,* sold more than 225,000 copies. These two volumes, plus a third, *Same Old Bill, Eh Mable!* (1919) were published collectively in 1919 as *Love Letters from Bill to Mable.* A reprint, *Dere Mable,* was published in 1941, as America prepared to go to war again.

S. continued to contribute to magazines and newspapers, but it was not until 1938 that he began the most important segment of his writing career. That year he published *Daily Except Sunday,* a novel dealing with the hazards of commuting from the suburbs. In 1947, S.'s elder daughter became engaged, an event he described as being "like the experimental explosion of an atom bomb." This became the basis for his most famous novel, *Father of the Bride* (1949), which became a Book-of-the-Month Club selection and was twice made into motion pictures. *Mr. Hobbs' Vacation* (1954) also became a successful motion picture.

As in the earlier "Dere Mable" sketches, S.'s treatment of the segment of the human comedy he knew best—the substantial urban/suburban middle class—was generous-spirited yet penetrating. Although his fictional milieu has been compared to that of John P. MARQUAND, his depictions are delineated in generally lighter hues and more positive terms that Marquand's. S.'s primary effect is humor, supported by subtexts of mild social satire and gentle tolerance.

Both Stanley Banks and Roger Hobbs, the protagonists of *Father of the Bride* and *Mr. Hobbs' Vacation,* are pillars of the middle class who conscientiously attempt do the best they know how, but whose practical, common-sense approach to life is constantly being challenged by such agents of social pressure as wives and children. As father of the bride, Stanley Banks endures crises ranging from finances to the pathos of seeing one's first-born leave home on the arm of a stranger. Roger Hobbs's "vacation" off the New England coast is a series of predicaments ranging from plumbing disasters, to the visits of unruly grandchildren, to raucous party guests. Yet both adjust with a kind of stoic devotion.

S.'s last novel, *Chairman of the Bored* (1961), involves the hard driving founder of a large investment counseling firm who institutes a policy for mandatory retirement at sixty-five and then has to adhere to it himself. As one reviewer noted, S., in an "urbane and unpretentious way [was saying] that a busy executive—because of the very traits that have made him successful—can never be happy at anything but being a busy executive." Whether or not this could be said of S. himself, since the novel appeared five years after he retired as vice president of the Fifth Avenue Bank (later the Bank of New York), it is clear that his business career was counterbalanced by a number of other interests. In addition to his literary life, which in retrospect surely overshadows his professional one, he served on a number of boards (including the Board of Overseers of Harvard) and enjoyed travel. His European travels became the subject of two books, *Skoal Scandinavia* (1952) and *Along the Ridge: From Northwest Spain to Southern Yugoslavia* (1964).

BIBLIOGRAPHY: Benét, L., *Famous American Humorists* (1959); Masson, T. L., *Our American Humorists* (1922); Taylor, W. D., *The Newsprint Mask: The Tradition of the Fictional Journalist in America* (1991)

WELFORD DUNAWAY TAYLOR

STRIBLING, T[homas] S[igismund]

b. 4 March 1881, Clifton, Tennessee; d. 8 July 1965, Florence, Alabama

Author of sixteen books and numerous works of short fiction, S. was a seminal force in Southern American literature of the 1920s and 1930s. Best known today for his novels of iconoclastic social realism—works set in middle Tennessee and Northern Alabama—S. is significant as a pathbreaker who introduced major themes and a wide array of character types drawn from Southern social history and who treated these materials from a critical-realistic perspective. In assuming this role, S. helped to provide the impetus for several of the South's more prominent and more artistically endowed writers who would exploit a similar subject matter and themes in some of their own novels, albeit at a much higher level of technical sophistication and stylistic innovation.

Born in Clifton, a small town on the Tennessee River in Wayne County, Tennessee, S. enjoyed the special advantage of having a large storehouse of materials at his disposal that he drew on liberally in writing his serious Southern novels. His father had been a Union soldier and his mother's family, who had lived on a small plantation in nearby Gravelly Springs, in Lauderdale County, Alabama, and who had supported the Confederacy during the Civil War, provided him with a fund of legends and stories, some of which he would actually make use of in several of his novels. But S. did not opt to appropriate these materials for fictional use at the outset. Instead he wrote primarily formulaic Sunday school stories, which were sold for publication to denominational magazines, and light adventure stories for some of the popular pulps of the period.

S.'s intent in composing fiction of the light and didactic variety was reflected chiefly in novels with exotic foreign settings, works published between 1917 and 1930, and in detective stories, the latter a mode he would continue to write throughout the remainder of his life. Typically flawed by contrived and sentimentalized plotting, exotic, melodramatic descriptions, overt moralizing, and sometimes wooden characters, S.'s adventure books—*The Cruise of The Dry Dock* (1917), *Fombombo* (1923), *Red Sand* (1924), *East Is East* (1928), *Clues of the Caribbees* (1929), *Strange Moon* (1929), and *Backwater* (1930)—despite their entertainment value, are, with the possible exception of *Clues of the Caribbees*, rarely read today. *Clues,* a collection of five mystery stories set in the Caribbean Islands, features the investigative ingenuity of Henry Poggioli, an amateur American criminologist.

While writing novels and stories of light adventure, S. discovered the mode that would become his principal metier—iconoclastic social realism—which he would apply in *Birthright* (1922), *Teeftallow* (1926), *Bright Metal* (1928), *The Forge* (1931), *The Store* (1932), *Unfinished Cathedral* (1934), *The Sound Wagon* (1935), and *These Bars of Flesh* (1938). The most immediate factor that seems to have stimulated S.'s interest in serious social realism was the impetus

of the "revolt-from-the-village" movement, a widely influential socioliterary trend in American writing during the post-World War I era. Catapulted to national popularity by widely read novels such as Sherwood ANDERSON's *Winesburg, Ohio* and Sinclair LEWIS's *Main Street, Babbitt,* and *Elmer Gantry,* this movement helped to bring to widespread attention many applicable paradigms for delineating small-town experience and provincial attitudes in a disparaging manner, not only in the Midwest, where it originated, but in other sections of the country as well.

Birthright, Teeftallow, and *Bright Metal,* S.'s first three Southern novels, clearly emulate "revolt-from-the village" materials and are closely patterned after Lewis's *Main Street.* Each of these novels has a small-town setting that is based on S.'s intimate familiarity with the villages and people of Wayne County, Tennessee, where he spent his formative years; and each unsparingly debunks reprehensible facets of Southern provincial experience—bigotry, hypocrisy, narrow-mindedness, lawlessness and violence, religious fanaticism, and various other shortcomings—many of which stem from the unethical pursuance of the materialistic ethic. Moreover, these books portray characters who resemble Lewisian village types. Peter Siner, the black protagonist of *Birthright,* and Agatha Pomeroy, the central character of *Bright Metal,* sharply condemn the weaknesses inherent in village life and undertake unsuccessful programs to effect social reform. Both, in fact, exhibit a marked similarity to Carol Kennicott, the principal character in *Main Street.* Other characters in these two novels as well as in *Teeftallow*—dishonest boosters, hideous materialistic bankers, cynics, narrow-minded fundamentalists, pariahs, and gossipy women—seem to share close affinities to Lewis's villagers in *Main Street.* To carry out his iconoclastic purpose in these novels, S., always a propagandist in his serious fictional works, focuses on the unsavory and despicable, accentuating the ugly and disagreeable in setting, characterization, and action, sometimes exaggerating these materials to the extreme of caricature. And in 1928, hoping to capitalize on the popularity of *Teeftallow,* the most controversial of his three Tennessee renditions of *Main Street,* S. collaborated with David Wallace on *Rope,* a dramatized version of this novel.

S.'s major work of the 1930s and his most important and ambitious undertaking as a novelist was *The Forge* (1931), *The Store* (1932), and *Unfinished Cathedral* (1934), a massive trilogy set primarily in Florence, Alabama. As in his three earlier Tennessee novels, S. again assaults the debilitating forces in Southern society, and in so doing covers a time frame from the eve of the Civil War through the boom period of the 1920s. In this trilogy, S. chronicles important changes in Southern social history as they principally affect three generations of the Vaidens, a family of yeoman stock, as well as other social groups, particularly blacks, that comprise the Southern social structure of the period. The central figure is Miltiades Vaiden, who, through brash assertiveness and disreputable and sometimes outright dishonest means, rises from near poverty and obscurity to social and economic prominence. In his adherence to Machiavellian ethics and his acceptance of social and materialistic values over essential human ones, Vaiden demonstrates behavioral patterns and attitudes that anticipate those of William FAULKNER's Flem Snopes of the Snopes trilogy and of Thomas Sutpen of *Absalom, Absalom!* Interestingly, Vaiden's activities and interaction with other characters broadly mirror actual historical developments that occurred in the South, contributing to the demise of the planter-aristocrat after the Civil War and to the ascendancy of a rapacious, opportunistic class whose chief concern was their own materialistic and social aggrandizement in the community.

The first novel of the trilogy, *The Forge,* employs a subject matter that derives mainly from stories about the Civil War and Reconstruction eras that S. had heard from his father, his mother, and members of his mother's family. Using the techniques of critical realism, S. satirically and sometimes ironically examines the passing of the Old South civilization and related developments, including the victimization of blacks, the unheroic side of Confederate and Yankee army life, the nefarious and inhuman activities of guerilla gangs, and the political corruption and materialistic priorities associated with carpetbag Reconstruction in northern Alabama.

S.'s Alabama trilogy continues with *The Store,* which was awarded the Pulitzer Prize in fiction in 1933. Focusing on post-Reconstruction life in northern Alabama, *The Store* presents a denigrating portrait of Miltiades Vaiden's unscrupulous emergence through the theft of his employer's cotton as one of Florence's most influential citizens. Moral integrity and social responsibility, especially among the dominant white class, are no longer viable and operative in the new commercial social order that informs the novel. The principal targets of S.'s satire are disgruntled poor-white sharecroppers, ineffectual and materialist churchmen, and blatantly prejudiced legal officials—all of whom, through their actions to satiate their desires, compromise the standards of basic decency and integrity.

Unfinished Cathedral, the final volume of the trilogy, authentically captures the speculative frenzy of the 1920s as it is manifested in a real estate boom in Florence, Alabama, the consequence of the construction of a government dam on the Tennessee River. Materialism is rampant. In fact, all the novel's princi-

pal white characters succumb to the booster ethic, especially Miltiades Vaiden, now a nonagenarian and the town's wealthiest and most powerful resident, and his nephew, Jerry Catlin II, the assistant minister of a local Methodist church and the principal fund raiser for a vast nonsectarian cathedral that will be more suited for serving the townspeople's secular and corporal interests than their spiritual needs. The cathedral, which is never completed, functions symbolically on two levels: an emblem both of the hypocrisy of the crassly materialistic culture of the New South, whose designs go unrealized, and of the vacuity of Miltiades Vaiden, whose own personal goals also remain unfulfilled. And as in other novels of the trilogy, in *Unfinished Cathedral,* blacks are still victims of racial and economic oppression, but with an important difference: now they have become militant and retaliate with violence.

S.'s final two novels, *The Sound Wagon* and *These Bars of Flesh,* likewise satires, are both set in the North; but neither has elicited any significant critical attention since its publication. After 1938, the year when *These Bars of Flesh* was published, S. mainly concentrated on writing detective stories. In 1940, at the age of fifty-nine, he started his autobiography, *Laughing Stock,* which was posthumously published in 1982.

BIBLIOGRAPHY: Eckley, W., *T. S. S.* (1975); Piacentino, E. J., *T. S. S.: Pioneer Realist in Modern Southern Literature* (1988); Rocks, J. E., "T. S. S.'s Burden of Southern History: The Vaiden Trilogy," *SHR* 6 (Summer 1972): 221–32; Warren, R. P., "T. S. S.: A Paragraph in the History of Critical Realism," *AmerR* 2 (February 1934): 463–86

EDWARD J. PIACENTINO

STUART, Jesse [Hilton]

b. 8 August 1906, near Riverton, Greenup County, Kentucky; d. 17 February 1984, Ironton, Ohio

S.'s sense of place—his home state of Kentucky—permeates his poems, essays, fiction, and children's stories. Kentucky's most prolific writer—of over fifty-five book-length works alone—S. rose from the humblest of beginnings to become, in the words of H. Edward Robinson, "the bardic chronicler of Appalachia—its poet and storyteller."

His love of literature, discovered during his high school years, provided a thirst for education. Even though he struggled, his dogged persistence eventually helped him obtain a bachelor's degree from Lincoln Memorial University in 1929. Upon graduation, he returned home to W-Hollow, the family farm, and taught school while he farmed. Always, he continued to write. He later attended Vanderbilt University but found the academic, theoretical atmosphere stultifying. After his thesis on John Fox, Jr. perished in a dormitory fire, S. took the advice of several professors and returned home to W-Hollow and to the land he loved so well.

His first major publication in 1934, *Man with a Bull-Tongue Plow,* a collection of sonnets, solidly established his reputation as a writer—one often characterized as a regionalist in the pejorative sense of the word. However, to suggest that S.'s outlook as an author is limited to a particular region such as Appalachia is misleading. Max Bogart notes that S. "is a regional writer in the same way Mark TWAIN, William FAULKNER, and Robert FROST may be characterized as regionalists. Each has created a cosmos, using the geographic area as the symbol. While S.'s works center around Appalachia, its people and its land, they have universal implications." H. Edward Richardson elaborates: "under the charm of his regionalism and the uneven and sometimes impromptu quality of [S.'s] work, were the deeps of archetypal and mythopoetic patterns: the earth as mother, father, provider: water images unfolding the evolution of primordial man; an abundance of folklore, myths, and tall tales; recurring allegories and symbols from the racial unconscious of mankind; fears and fantasies, mysticism and superstition emerging in nature images and man in conflict with his own kind."

S.'s themes foreground a love of the land and nature, family, and sense of place. Within those themes, conflicts arise, palpable tensions that fight against injustice, poverty, and the social ills with which S.'s characters struggle. In *Trees of Heaven,* for example, land-hungry Anse Bushman and the carefree, fun-loving squatter Boliver Tussie lock horns. When Bushman buys the five-hundred acres where the Tussies have squatted all their lives, trouble ensues, and Bushman's contract requires much more than the agreement regarding the raising of crops. When the Tussie's cannot keep the unreasonable restrictions, including having parties or having babies, Bushman has them banished from the land. His deathbed religious conversion prompts his repentance, and the Tussies return to their land. Conflict is also present in the love affair between Bushman's son, Tarvin, and Tussie's daughter, Subrinea, who is pregnant with Tarvin's child. The two men of opposing class structure and opposing values eventually must reconcile.

Even with all the dark themes, humor is present in S.'s characters. Max Bogart writes that "In the midst of the pathos in these serious and tragic tales, he sprinkles a unique brand of frontier humor, causing the reader to laugh at many passages. A rich vein of humor, not satire unlike Mark Twain's runs through J. S.'s fiction." Additionally, his command of the rustic speech patterns in the language of the eastern Kentucky hills further enhances the technique S. developed so well. His stories are heard as well as read.

BIBLIOGRAPHY: Blair, E. L., *J. S.: His Life and His Works* (1967); Foster, R. E., *J. S.* (1968); LeMaster, J. R., and M. W. Clarke, eds., *J. S.: Essays on His Work* (1977); Pennington, L., *The Dark Hills of J. S.* (1967)

LINDA GINTER BROWN

STUART, Ruth McEnery

b. 19 February 1852, Marksville, Louisiana; d. 6 May 1917, New York City

S. was a prolific and successful writer of Louisiana local color, including dialect stories and poems. Born to a well-connected family in the Acadian village of Marksville in central Louisiana, S. spent her youth in the cosmopolitan bustle of mid-19th-c. New Orleans. Her early fascination with its diverse cultures provided the fertile material of her more than seventy-five tales and novellas. In stories like her first, "Uncle Mingo's 'Speculations'" (1888), or in the later "Queen o' Sheba's Triumph" (1898) or *Napoleon Jackson: The Gentleman of the Plush Rocker* (1902), S.'s observant renditions of black speech and folkways established the foundation of her considerable popularity, despite a patronizing irony that often diminishes her achievement.

Despite such limitations, S.'s fiction depicts an exceptional diversity of Southern Life, from New Orleans' aristocratic Creoles and exuberant Sicilian and Irish immigrants, as in *Carlotta's Intended* (1891), to the quaintly provincial hill people of southern Arkansas. This latter region, where S. spent her brief married life, is a major focus of her fiction, including one of her best-known volumes, *In Simpkinsville: Character Tales* (1897), with its characteristic themes of romance and marriage, and *Sonny, a Christmas Guest* (1894), an outstanding instance of dialect narrative.

S.'s move to New York City in 1890 brought her into the Northeast literary establishment, where her feminist sympathies flourished, and she soon became the most prominent of the Southern women local colorists, earning a comfortable income from her popular public readings and from her increasingly orthodox versions of regional life. S. was a keen, sympathetic observer of human nature and its social and physical textures, especially among women. Yet her skillful portraits of the humor and quiet dignity of human life, her mastery of dialect and ironic wit, and her strong narrative sense are today somewhat overshadowed by her insistence that art should resolve the moral complexities of life. Even so, in her fidelity to the rich diversity of that life, she emerges as a significant Southern writer.

BIBLIOGRAPHY: Simpson, R., "R. M. S.: The Innocent Grotesque," *Louisiana Literature* 4 (Spring 1987): 57–65; Taylor, H., *Gender, Race and Region in the Writings of Grace King, R. M. S., and Kate Chopin* (1989)

BARBARA C. EWELL

STYRON, William

b. 11 June 1925, Newport News, Virginia

When his mother died in 1938, S.'s father sent him to Christchurch, an Episcopalian preparatory school attended by Tidewater, Virginia's gentry class. S.'s literary apprenticeship was twice interrupted by war. After spending his freshman year at Davidson College, S. joined the marine corps in 1943. He transferred to Duke University two years later where he studied creative writing with William M. Backburn and received his B.A. in 1947. S. then enrolled at the New School for Social Research to study with Hiram Haydn, who oversaw the production of *Lie Down in Darkness.* But after hostilities broke out in Korea in 1950, the marine corps ordered S. to report for boot camp in Camp Lejeune, North Carolina.

S. was released from active duty the following year and returned to Greenwich Village where he helped found the *Paris Review* in 1951. *Lie Down in Darkness* was published that same year when S., then only twenty-six, received the American Academy of Arts and Letters Prix de Rome for the best work of fiction. In 1952, he married Rose Burgunder and they settled in Roxbury, Connecticut.

Considered the most talented writer of his generation, S. was compared favorably with William FAULK-NER. Although he was as indebted to F. Scott FITZGER-ALD for his characters' love of country club settings and the pursuit of luxury, S.'s themes as well as the quasi-allegorical style in which he addressed them encouraged placing him within a Southern storytelling tradition that included Thomas WOLFE and Robert Penn WARREN as well. But the association with Faulkner was perhaps inevitable.

The Sartrean themes that S. added to *Lie Down in Darkness* may have complicated the genre, but its scenes and characters were nevertheless reminiscent of high Southern gothic. After probing the Loftis family history for explanations, the narrator of *Lie Down in Darkness* discovers that Peyton Loftis has traveled to New York City in search of values that she had not found in her Virginia childhood. Before Peyton Loftis throws herself from the window of a Harlem sweatshop, she finds that she does not possess the resources that she needs to resist the vindictiveness and alcoholism she inherited from her parents.

Given the fact that World War II constituted the most important event of S.'s generation and the prominent role that war played during the years of his literary apprenticeship, it is not surprising that S.'s novelistic imagination would vacillate in his first three novels between tracking the intricate ethical quandaries engendered within Southern families and representing the inhumanity of the military. S. published his second novel, *The Long March,* in 1956. The narrative focuses on the bitterness with which Captain Mannix responds to the irrational orders of his military superior Colonel Templeton. Templeton commands Mannix to lead his troops on a thirty-six mile forced march through an impossible geographical terrain. Maddix's undischarged rage might be read within the context of S.'s own anger with the military's institutions.

Neither Mannix nor Peyton Loftis could accommodate their violent passions to a culture that provided them no creative outlet. But in *Set This House on Fire,* which he published in 1960, nine years after *Lie Down in Darkness,* S. constructs an allegory whose protagonist Cass Kinsolving kills a man named Mason Flagg. Flagg represents everything—the racism, the greed, the unreflective pursuit of pleasure—that S.'s other characters found irredeemable about their own family histories. In killing Flagg and then accepting personal responsibility for his death, Cass accepts as well the improbability of a larger social order's coming to appropriate moral terms with this event.

Over the next seven years, S. returned to research he had begun while in Hiram Haydn's class. Rather than urging large claims for the betterment of mankind, S.'s first three novels had attended to the means whereby sensitive characters could maintain their integrity despite the chaos and hypocrisy that surrounded them. But S.'s fourth novel confronted a perennial dilemma of American culture.

In *The Confesssions of Nat Turner* (1967), S. reworked the themes, characters, and events surrounding Nat Turner's 1831 slave rebellion into his masterwork. Set in Tidewater County Virginia, the novel represented the antagonism between the economic necessities of the slave system and the Christian values that the residents pretended to embrace. It also affiliated that historical antagonism with tensions surrounding 1960s civil rights activism. What readers found boldest about *The Confesssions of Nat Turner* entailed S.'s having conjoined the historical record of the event with his own imaginative project. Because the reading public had already associated S.'s novels with the South's history, his project had become symbolic of Southern values and Southern shame.

S. is white and a member of the Virginia's gentry class that had owned slaves. In choosing to identify his narrative voice with Nat Turner's, S. crossed the color line. The novel bore within its pages the South's but also S.'s guilt about the historical fact of slavery. As a consequence, he left every detail of his characterization of Nat Turner open to critical scrutiny for any residual traces of the slave power it might betray. When S. represented Nat Turner's ambivalent emotional response to Margaret Whitehead as his loving her for her sexual purity and despising her for arousing his lust, S. recalled for some readers the accusation of rape that white Southerners had directed against blacks. That accusation had inaugurated the history of lynching that had followed in slavery's wake.

The novel rapidly became a sociopolitical as well as a literary event. *W. S.'s The Confesssions of Nat Turner: Ten Black Writers Respond,* published in 1968, should be numbered among the most thoughtful as well as troubling of the various responses the work elicited. The contributors to this volume charged S. with having misrepresented aspects of the institution of slavery, Turner's life, and even Turner himself. They derided him for his having represented blacks as lacking the energy to defend themselves against slavery's dehumanization. In the defense of S.'s historical research, C. Vann Woodward, who was then acclaimed the dean of Southern history, became an unlikely ally of the Marxist historian Eugene Genovese.

Although *The Confesssions of Nat Turner* received the 1968 Pulitzer Prize, S. remained deeply wounded by the criticism. Perhaps it was out of a need to expiate for the historical guilt critics had associated with his project that S. turned in his next novel *Sophie's Choice* (1979) to the subject of the Nazism and the Holocaust. Although different in many ways, slave plantations and Nazi concentration camps were also remarkably similar, S. believed, in that both of these total institutions utterly demoralized their victims. This novel was published twelve years after *The Confesssions of Nat Turner.* S. recalled its relentless inquiry into "the humanly contrived conditions which cause people to live in wretched unhappiness" in an autobiographical account of his lifelong battle with depression. S. published *Darkness Visible* in 1990.

BIBLIOGRAPHY: Casciato, A., ed., *Critical Essays on W. S.* (1982); Clark, J. H., et al., eds., *W. S.'s Nat Turner: Ten Black Writers Respond* (1968); Morris, R. K., and I. Malin, eds., *The Achievement of W. S.* (1975); Pearce, R., *W. S.* (1971)

DONALD E. PEASE

SUAREZ, Virgil
b. 29 January 1962, Havana, Cuba

Perhaps no other Cuban American writer has been as prolific as S., who has contributed to the canon of Cuban American literature with his novels, short fiction, poetry, and anthologies. Much of the inspiration for S.'s work originates from his own experiences in the U.S. and Cuba. Thematically, his writings deal with life in the U.S., balancing Cuban and cultural identities.

His first novel, *Latin Jazz* (1989), set during the Mariel boatlift, focuses on the lives of the Carrascos and Falcóns as they learn that their relative Hugo, a political prisoner in Cuba, may emigrate to the U.S. While the novel is an indictment of the torturous lives under the Castro regime, it showcases Diego Falcón, a Cuban American twenty-something, and his search for an identity in mainstream American society.

S.'s second novel, *The Cutter* (1991), details the struggles of a young man's desperate attempt to flee post-revolutionary Cuba. Julian Campos has completed the mandatory military service required of all Cuban males and returns to Havana to live with his ailing grandmother as he awaits a permit to exit the country. Instead of receiving the exit permit, he is forced to perform "voluntary" work as a cutter in the "Ten-Million-Ton Sugarcane Program." *The Cutter* captures the painful physical and psychological conditions of these workers, surrendering another strong indictment against the communist state.

Havana Thursdays (1995), S.'s third novel, is less political than his first two. The focus of this work centers on life in the U.S. as the Torres family struggles to retain its Cuban heritage while acclimating to the American way of life. Like most Cuban American writings, this novel contains characters who represent the old and new generations, resulting in a microcosm of the Cuban condition in the new world, the U.S. Centering around the sudden and unexpected death of the patriarch, Zacarías Torres, the novel's plot depicts the family's struggle to pull together from their scattered existences in order to survive this tragedy. One of the work's virtues is that it focuses on a successful Cuban American family. Further, these characters are neither plagued by an exaggerated sense of nostalgia for Cuba nor the paralyzing longing to return to the homeland that characterizes much of Cuban American literature. Instead, *Havana Thursdays* demonstrates S.'s movement toward the portrayal of the bicultural family in the U.S., a movement that suggests ways in which Cuban immigrants and their progeny have fostered and cultivated an identity as both Cuban and American.

Going Under (1996) continues the author's transition to depicting Cuban American life. The novel focuses on Xavier Cuervas as he strives to embrace the American dream. An extremely busy insurance agent, Xavier struggles to keep his life balanced in terms of family and work. As such, Xavier is caught between two cultures. Highly dependent on the metaphor of the highway, this work portrays the cultural clash implicit in the Cuban American identity. In the end, Xavier is abandoned by his family, his American wife, who has opted for a separation, and by his cultures, both American and Cuban. As the title suggests, Xavier is "going under" in his quest for the American dream, a biting indictment of bicultural existence in the U.S.

Apart from these four novels, S., a university professor, has published a collection of short stories, *Welcome to the Oasis and Other Stories* (1992), and has coedited several Latino literature anthologies: *Iguana Dreams: New Latino Fiction* (1993), *Paper Dance: 55 Latino Poets* (1995), and *Little Havana Blues: A Cuban-American Literature Anthology* (1996).

BIBLIOGRAPHY: García, M. C., *Havana USA: Cuban Exiles and Cuban-Americans in South Florida, 1959–1994* (1996); Kanellos, N., ed. *The Hispanic Almanac: From Columbus to Corporate America* (1994)

JOSEPH M. VIERA

SUCKOW, Ruth

b. 6 August 1892, Hawarden, Iowa; d. 23 January 1960, Claremont, California

In the 1920s and 1930s, S. was considered an important writer, her realistic fiction having impressed such contemporaries as Robert FROST and Sinclair LEWIS. Today, she is virtually unknown.

The daughter of an Iowa minister, S. gained an intimate knowledge of rural and small-town life as she accompanied her father on his rounds. She attended Grinnell College and the University of Denver, where she wrote her master's thesis on female novelists and supported herself by beekeeping. She began publishing short stories, acquired a patron in H. L. MENCKEN, and saw her first collection, *Iowa Interiors* (1926), receive enthusiastic reviews.

Nearly all S.'s stories are set in Iowa and about the traditional family, but they appealed to Eastern editors like Mencken because of their lack of provinciality. S. always tried, in her words, to "throw a shadow beyond locality," and she portrays family relationships as reflecting broad social movements. Thus, generational change and the generation gap become important themes in stories such as "Uprooted" and

"Four Generations" and in her first novel, *Country People* (1924). S.'s method is a quiet realism with dramatic incident subordinate to character and atmosphere. Ordinary domestic items, such as household furniture, carry symbolic meaning.

Once she established her literary reputation, S. devoted herself to a series of novels: *The Odyssey of a Nice Girl* (1925), *The Bonney Family* (1928), *Cora* (1929), and *The Kramer Girls* (1930). These bildungsromans share a characteristic S. theme—the conflict between an individual's urge for self-development and the demands of family and small-town tradition. S. viewed the conflict as particularly severe for women, and often portrays women who have lost their identities serving a husband—as in "Resurrection" and "What Have I"—or parent—as in "The Best of the Lot" and "Mrs. Vogel and Ollie."

S.'s second short story collection, *Children and Older People* (1931), contains some excellent stories about women, notably "A Great Mollie" and "Eminence," but does not surpass the achievement of her first. S. did develop as a novelist and in 1934 published her longest and most complex novel, *The Folks*. In her characterization of the Ferguson family, S. adapts Freudian theory to suit her own purposes and provides a panoramic view of social change in the early 20th c., always relating the personal and historical.

Although she lived another twenty-five years, joining her husband in pacifist activities and writing at her leisure, the two novels and several stories she completed are not comparable to her earlier work. This decline may account in part for the dramatic fall in S.'s literary reputation after the 1930s. Her classification as "Midwest regionalist" and the growing unpopularity of feminism and "feminine" subject matter also contributed. S.'s fiction should be better known and more highly regarded.

BIBLIOGRAPHY: DeMarr, M. J., "'The Darkness of the Women': Two Short Stories by R. S.," *Midamerica* 21 (1994): 112–21; Hamblen, A. A., *R. S.* (1978); Kissane, L. M., *R. S.* (1969); Omrcanin, M. S., *R. S.: A Critical Study of Her Fiction* (1972); White, B. A., *Growing Up Female: Adolescent Girlhood in American Fiction* (1985)

BARBARA A. WHITE

SUKENICK, Ronald

b. 14 July 1932, Brooklyn, New York

No other writer enfigures the critical rambunctiousness of 1960s and 1970s innovative fiction so dramatically as does S. Having earned a doctorate in literature from Brandeis University and published his dissertation as

Wallace Stevens: Musing the Obscure (1967), S. promptly turned his back on the safe career track of conventional academics in order to challenge virtually all of its most cherished forms. As something of a scholar-Gypsy, he moved through a series of appointments at physically attractive yet pedagogically volatile colleges before establishing what colleague Steve Katz called his "vast postmodern empire" at the out-of-the-way University of Colorado. In a series of novels, beginning with *Up* (1968), he flamboyantly dismantled the academy's ideals both of what a professor's lifestyle should be and of how respectable fiction should be written. At the same time, he wrote a series of prominently published essays, collected as *In Form: Digressions on the Act of Fiction* (1985), that explicated with brilliant clarity just what he was doing in both his art and his life.

Up is an example of what theorists have called metafiction, fiction that has as its theme an exploration of the conditions of its own making. But in S.'s hands such fiction becomes much more. Although his principal character is named "Ronald Sukenick" and his real-life friends interchange with his cartoonlike creations (such as macho buddy Strop Banally and sexy girlfriend Oolah Wonderleigh), the author is more interested in crafting a narrative that reconnects the energy of experience with the products of art. In this sense, S. is an heir to the tradition of Henry MILLER. To Miller's sense of sexual exuberance, however, he adds a more sophisticated understanding of form, whereby conventions of traditional fiction are not ignored but are rather turned against themselves in the series of liberating additional creative energy.

Throughout the 1970s, S. Devised new forms to incorporate the reader in his strategies of personal and textual liberation. *Out* (1973) locates its narrative within an easily understood structure, that of an East-to-West journey across the U.S. in which characters much like the author (yet with ever-changing names) hope to leave urban clutter for a more pastoral openness. To facilitate this movement the novel itself is printed with ever-quickening chapters, in which lines of print steadily decrease in favor of blank space. *98.6* (1975) combines culturally pertinent dreams with associated narratives set in present-day California commune life and a futuristic, utopian state of Israel (stylized as a "state of consciousness"). Such schemes are taken to their apparent limit in *Long Talking Bad Conditions Blues* (1979), in which an ongoing narrative owes its energy to little more than oral compulsiveness.

Yet by this time S. was beginning to reembrace representable subject matter. *Long Talking Bad Conditions Blues* uses as its occasion for writerly song an ultimately recognizable Paris, where the author had

been spending much of his recent time. An even more recognizable Southern California, including its entertainment industry, appears in *Blown Away* (1986), particularly in the personae of the starlet Clover Bottom and the S.-like "mentist" Boris O. Ccrab, whose probings of creative energy parallel the author's critical statements in *In Form*. With *Doggy Bag* (1994) and *Mosaic Man* (sections of which began appearing in literary magazines during the middle 1990s), readers could locate S.'s interests within a commonly shared universe of interests and values, including such timely issues as Europe's history-bound colonial influence on the U.S. and the need for Jewish Americans to create an identity beyond the self-victimization of Holocaust remembrance that depletes the energy of further creativity.

BIBLIOGRAPHY: Klinkowitz, J., *Structuring the Void* (1992); Kutnik, J., *The Novel as Performance* (1986); McHale, B., *Constructing Postmodernism* (1992); Saltzman, A. M., *The Novel in the Balance* (1993)

JEROME KLINKOWITZ

SULLIVAN, Frank [Francis John]

b. 22 September 1892, Saratoga Springs, New York;
d. 19 February 1976, Saratoga Springs, New York

S. was a humorist mainly associated with the *New Yorker* during its heyday under Harold Ross and William Shawn. His interviews entitled "A Cliché Expert Testifies On . . ." were popular and frequently anthologized, and *New Yorker* readers looked forward to his "Christmas Greetings, Friends!" poems, published annually from 1932 until 1974. Though not a core member of the Algonquin Round Table, he was a close friend of its members and other mid-20th-c. writers such as Russel Crouse, Edna FERBER, George S. KAUFMAN, and Thornton WILDER. His voluminous correspondence, James THURBER's heartfelt dedication of *The Years with Ross* to him, and memoirs by Corey Ford and Joseph Bryan, III, reflect his friends' affection. As a writer, however, he is no longer widely known.

After graduating from Cornell University in 1914, S. worked in Saratoga Springs as a reporter. He served in the U.S. Army during World War I and after discharge worked as a journalist in New York City, notably as a columnist for the *New York World,* until it closed in 1931. By then, he had published four collections of his humorous pieces and was also writing for the *New Yorker* and *College Humor*. He remained a freelance writer for the rest of his life.

Early pieces, such as those in *The Life and Times of Martha Hepplethwaite* (1926), display an antic, almost zany humor, but also a sensitivity to and exploitation of language akin to Groucho Marx's. *Innocent Bystanding* (1928) and *Broccoli and Old Lace* (1931), also collections of previously published pieces, include mild social commentary. In the latter, "The Season at Saratoga" centers on explaining horse track betting, a recurrent topic in S.'s works and a natural one since he was an habitue of the Saratoga track all his life; S. concludes that the Vanderbilts, Whitneys, and their ilk have the best solution to betting: "Be so rich you just don't give a damn whether you win or lose."

In 1934, the cliché expert, Mr. Arbuthnot, appeared in the *New Yorker;* he was interviewed frequently in collections such as *A Pearl in Every Oyster* (1938) and *A Rock in Every Snowball* (1946). The reader of "The Cliché Expert Testifies on the Atom" in the latter expects the cliché, then groans at its arrival: "Q—Where do we stand, Mr. Arbuthnot? A—At the threshold of a new era. Q—And humanity is where? A—At the crossroads. Will civilization survive?"

But in his annual Christmas poems S. delighted readers by cultivating the unexpected. In four lines of the 1967 edition, for example, he rhymed the names of a popular musical group and a carol, then sandwiched the name of an English professor at the local college, Skidmore, between the rhyming names of a famous singer and the well-known chairman of the Columbia Broadcasting System: "Let the tootlers of Tijuana Brass / Tootle a 'Good King Wenceslas' / As a timely treat for Pearl Bailey, / Julia Hysham, and William Paley." He was indeed, as Thurber said, "master of humor."

BIBLIOGRAPHY: Bryan, J., III, *Merry Gentlemen (and One Lady)* (1985); Ford, C., *The Time of Laughter* (1967)

KENNETH A. ROBB

SUPERNATURAL, The

To understand the origins of the supernatural in American literature we must consider the widespread interest in the occult or unseen world during the very inception of the colonies. The first publications in America were almanacs wherein, among other vital information, was always contained an ephemeris describing the influences of astrological forces. In 1672, John Josselyn published his *New England Rarities Discovered,* a detailed empirical account of the unusual plants and creatures endemic to America, which also touched on the metaphysical qualities of remedies found here. And after the Salem witch trials, Cotton MATHER's *The Wonders of the Invisible World* made its debut as

one of the first fundamentalist texts on Satan's and his minions' attempt to dismantle the very fabric of the colonies. Furthermore, Harvard University's department of science and chemistry endorsed alchemical studies throughout the 17th c., producing one of the more renowned alchemists from that period: George Starkey, a.k.a. Eirenaeus Philalethes. Based on this heritage of metaphysical practices and vested beliefs in the supernatural, storytellers of early America did not need to look far for inspiration.

It is misleading to position the supernatural element in American literature within the domain of a single genre because its vestiges can be detected in many works that do not focus solely on the strange. Not only does supernatural literature broach topics such as spiritual activity, monsters, and unexplained phenomenon, but it may also deal with characters displaying psychological aberrations or illogical behavior. Derived from the Latin, the "supernatural" literally denotes that which is above or beyond the natural. Supernatural tales often culminate in tragedy but this rule is not steadfast. In short, many authors of strange tales have adhered to formulas while others have completely defied standardized conventions.

There are several early American writers whose manifold interests included the supernatural such as Charles Brockdon BROWN and Washington IRVING. Brown was clearly influenced by European gothic horror but took it in a new direction. On one hand there is the flavor of Ann Radcliffe in his work, specifically the provision of rational explanations for uncanny events. Such is the case in Brown's *Wieland* wherein the main character, Theodore Wieland, ritually slaughters his wife and five children. He eventually commits suicide upon discovering his supposed divine inspiration is a mere delusion resulting from a hereditary form of madness. And in his *Edgar Huntly; or, Memories of a Sleep Walker,* the narrator wanders the American wilderness after losing his mind while mourning the death of his close friend and losing his life's savings. Brown was preoccupied with man's hardships and search for the self in the literal and mental wilderness.

Irving, on the other hand, wrote several light pieces about spectral phenomenon such as his popular "The Legend of Sleepy Hollow." Even though his "Rip Van Winkle" can be considered a supernatural tale it is more concerned with the political climate of the day. For Irving as well as Brown, the supernatural served as an important backdrop to their greater political and religious concerns.

Nathaniel HAWTHORNE himself produced numerous haunting tales replete with ghosts and otherworldly influences at work in a world of Puritan oppression. "Young Goodman Brown" is reminiscent of Charles

Brockdon Brown's alienated and wandering figures; however, Hawthorne's interest in the supernatural is much more pronounced with the presence of a witch's sabbath and demonic forces in the face of stringent dogmatic Christianity. In *The House of Seven Gables* and *The Marble Faun,* Hawthorne employs an array of traditional Gothic devices and imagery suggestive of Horace Walpole's *The Castle of Otranto* (1760). Yet it would be erroneous to assert Hawthorne's main concern was the spiritual realm in his novels. Rather, the supernatural was woven into his greater concerns with the self, internal strife, and conflict with society's mores.

A close acquaintance of Hawthorne's, Herman MELVILLE, also made prodigious use of supernatural demonic elements in his most famous novel, *Moby-Dick.* As Melville told Hawthorne in a letter, June 1851: "This is the book's motto (the secret one)—*Ego non baptiso te in nomine*—but make out the rest yourself." Subsequently, Melville wrote out this motto in full in chapter 113 where Ahab consecrates the harpoons meant for the white whale: "I baptize thee not in the name of the father but in the name of the devil." And in *Moby-Dick,* the white whale himself comes to epitomize evil incarnate representative of Satan. However, Ahab also partakes of the Satanic persona as he sends himself and his crew into perdition driven by his vengeful bloodlust. In *The Piazza Tales,* vampirism and other haunting disturbances occur. Melville's work overall is concerned with philosophical aspects of human conflict and the search for truth. Yet, like Hawthorne, Melville's tales have had a great impact upon future supernatural authors by demonstrating a multidimensional appropriation of supernatural elements in storytelling.

Even though Edgar Allan POE was also concerned with the human condition, he was truly one of the first major figures in American literature to embrace the bizarre and supernatural as the central focus of his life's work. For instance, Poe was masterful at creating a haunting atmosphere in his *The Narrative of Arthur Gordon Pym of Nantucket.* The denouement of this high seas tale in journal form centers on the whiteness of the Antarctic and the image of a mysterious titan whose skin "was of the perfect whiteness of the snow." Much of the other-worldly sinister nature possessed by Melville's *Moby-Dick,* especially in chapter 42, "The Whiteness of the Whale," appears to be gleaned from Poe's treatment of whiteness as the antithesis of purity. Poe's adroit manipulation of paradox could be attributed to the fact that he "understood so perfectly the very mechanics and physiology of fear and strangeness," as H. P. LOVECRAFT asserted in his "Supernatural Horror in Literature."

Poe's heightened sensitivity to those things man finds most disturbing establishes his work as a cynosure in American literature. Even in his more gruesome tales such as "The Black Cat," Poe almost always explores the psychological dimensions of abnormal behavior. Poe is probably best known for his fascination with dementia as it manifests in his characters that often reaches beyond the grave as in "The Fall of the House of Usher." No matter what other obsessions surface in Poe's stories, the notion of premature burial and especially death are most prevalent. The influence of the classic European gothic of William Beckford, Matthew Gregory Lewis, and Charles Maturin all contributed to Poe's craft. Certain of Poe's stories also convey mysterious abstractions such as "Shadow—A Parable" and "Silence—A Fable." Both of these pieces possess a highly symbolist flavor that may account for the overwhelming popularity of his work in France with the decadents such as Baudelaire and Mallarmé. Furthermore, in his fantastic "The Conversation of Eiros and Charmion," Poe ventures into the realm of SCIENCE FICTION as his two characters discuss their thoughts on this world's destruction and the aftermath. In short, Poe has probably had the greatest impact upon all facets of supernatural literature including murder mysteries, the detective novel, and science fiction.

Much of what makes a supernatural story efficacious in arousing fear is the audience's ability to suspend their beliefs, which becomes paramount in the late 19th c. as the so-called age of reason began to take hold. Early American writers such as Brown and Irving dealt with an audience that did not have to suspend their beliefs of the rational world as much as contemporary readers may need to when contemplating supernatural premises. So by the time of Poe's debut, the general readership had grown more savvy and skeptical of run-of-the-mill psychic and spectral phenomenon in the face of the ongoing scientific and industrial revolutions. The public needed a more enticing and enthralling literature of the strange to elicit the willful suspension of their beliefs, which they found in Poe and his followers.

Even though during the latter half of the 19th c. the traditional ghost story was waning in popularity, it was still employed with some vitality in American texts. In fact, ghosts play an integral part in one of America's best-selling novels ever, *Uncle Tom's Cabin.* Harriet Beecher STOWE interestingly plays upon Simon Legree's fears as he deals with a ghost that supposedly haunts his house. Another female writer whose ghost stories had an even greater influence upon subsequent writers in the supernatural vein was Mary E. Wilkins FREEMAN. Although the bulk of her writings were not concerned with the uncanny, her early collection *The Wind in the Rose-Bush* was. This collection of short stories has not been considered extremely innovative but is important in terms of Freeman's ability to combine the supernatural with social and grassroots issues of the times. For example, in "The Southwest Chamber" the lingering hatred of a deceased apartment dweller wreaks havoc with the tenants and owners of a boarding house by taking advantage of their domestic sensibilities. At one point the ghost of the southwest chamber manipulates the pattern, or at least the new tenant's perception, of a chintz spread hanging over the bed. And in several other ways, Freeman's piece stands as a distant precursor to one of the most haunting pieces ever produced, "The Yellow Wallpaper" by Charlotte Perkins GILMAN.

In the absence of ghosts and otherworldly intervention the short story, "The Yellow Wallpaper" creates a multifaceted atmosphere of dementia and strangeness within a restrictive society. Currently embraced as one of the more important feminist texts, "The Yellow Wallpaper" offers a fascinating look into the Victorian mind-set toward mental health and pathology. At the hand of her husband, the narrator has been sequestered in a small room to help her recover from "temporary nervous depression—a slight hysterical tendency." Forbidden to be active the narrator succumbs to her subsequent delusions from staring at the wallpaper in the room for extended periods. Aside from its feminist appeal, "The Yellow Wallpaper" affords an amazing view of the stark terror and chaos of a self-created world precipitated by sensory deprivation and the horror of ennui. Gilman's story demonstrates that even though an increasingly sophisticated 19th-c. audience sought a more contemporary terrifying story there is one fundamental topic that could still satisfy this penchant for the strange—the mind itself.

Along with the rise of more subtle psychologically oriented tales the public's desire for graphic and egregiously violent horror increased. In many areas of literature, there has often appeared two or more distinct coexisting trends catering to low and high-brow tastes. However, supernatural literature, toward the 20th c., seemed to fall further into disrepute, and was consequently dismissed as an unimportant component of the literary canon. But in many ways, horror literature has long represented one of the vestiges of romanticism attempting to bridge the somatic with the loftier spiritual and rarified realms of awareness.

Ambrose BIERCE, who has been hallowed as one of the more important Victorian authors of the strange, approached the bleakness of war-torn American society with terrifyingly stark and sarcastic portrayals of life. Bierce produced humorous and satirical books such as *The Devil's Dictionary* with its sardonic treatment of euphemisms and off-handed definitions is a classic in its own right. He also produced acerbic

comedies such as "My Favorite Murder," absurdly hyperbolic in its magnitude as well as providing a wry commentary on the macabre. Bierce's works often focus on psychic phenomenon and are considered innovative for the period, such as "An Occurrence at Owl Creek Bridge." The hallmark of Bierce's stories is a violent comeuppance for his villains and a world in which death does not mark the end of torment but merely its beginning.

One of the more pivotal pieces that signals the shift from 19th- to 20th-c. trends in supernatural literature is Robert W. CHAMBERS's collection of stories, *The King in Yellow.* Chambers is one of the first to illustrate that supernatural and inexplicable incidents may no longer involve the individual alone but the collective consciousness of the group and society itself. Chambers, whose style is often characterized as artificial and trite, was prone to occasional flashes of profound insight that earned him the ambivalent respect of H. P. Lovecraft and others. *The King in Yellow* is unique in terms of its self-conscious attention to the act of writing and its dissemination. Prefiguring Lovecraft's fixation with his fictional ancient *grimoire, The Necronomicon,* Chamber's series focuses on a hapless society's perdition that results from their reading a malevolent drama entitled, "The King in Yellow." Chambers effectively touches on every horror writer's fantasy—to create a text that is so terrifying it can literally wreak havoc on its audience.

It was during the mid-1920s that Lovecraft, one of America's greatest avatars of the weird tale, began to first publish his short stories in pulp magazines. Even though he received little recognition or remuneration for his essays and stories during his lifetime, Lovecraft's work has received much exposure and acclaim in recent years. Moreover, in his series of critical essays entitled "Supernatural Horror in Literature," Lovecraft developed his consummate theory of the "weird tale." As Lovecraft adroitly asserts in the opening passages of his study, "the oldest and strongest emotion of mankind is fear . . . of the unknown." What fascinated Lovecraft and his followers the most was the "spectrally macabre," or "cosmic terror" he describes "as an ingredient of the earliest folklore of all races."

For Lovecraft, the otherworldly maintains a paramount role in his literature describing strange beings from outer realms who constantly threaten mankind's consciousness and very existence. "The Call of Cthulu" is the initial short story wherein he establishes his mythos of a race of great old ones who have existed and watched over the earth long before man's appearance. These "deep ones" intermingled with mankind early on, contaminating the species. The Cthulu mythos is reminiscent of various ancient rabbinical lore and texts such as *The Book of Enoch* that hint at man's intercourse with the gods. And in fact, certain modern-day occultists such as Kenneth Grant have posited that Lovecraft unconsciously displayed an awareness of man's primal and atavistic reservoirs through his imaginative tales. Furthermore, Lovecraft attracted a circle of writers who were responsible for various offshoots, some trite, others extremely important to the progression of supernatural literature.

August DERLETH, founder of Arkham House Publishers, started by producing Lovecraft's collections posthumously then moved on to other writers. Subsequently, Arkham House has published the works of Lovecraft's colleagues and various contributors to the pulp magazine *Weird Tales* such as Robert E. Howard, the originator of Conan, Frank Belknap Long, Fritz Leiber, and Joseph Payne Brennan. Many of these authors, and especially Derleth himself, created a myriad of works related directly to Lovecraft's mythos. But out of all of Lovecraft's colleagues the most accomplished both stylistically and in terms of innovation is assuredly Clark Ashton Smith.

Beside being a talented sculptor, painter, and poet of the bizarre, Smith composed some of the more intricate and challenging literature of Lovecraft's circle. Although sometimes prone to an inflated vocabulary and baroque diction Smith's work is still held in high esteem. Many of his tales are set in strange futuristic realms and ancient prehistoric periods as in *Lost Worlds* (1944), *The Double Shadow and Other Fantasies* (1933), and other collections. His stories of Hyporborea are replete with various Lovecraft-isms such as the demon-god Tsathoggua. Smith also explores dimensions of magic and strange creatures that establish him as a precursor of the modern sword and sorcery fantasy genre. However, Smith's work would never fall prey to trite cliches or conventions as many of his followers have in recent years.

Robert Bloch, who also corresponded with Lovecraft, published his first story dealing with cannibalism, "The Feast in the Abbey" (1934) in *Weird Tales* at the age of seventeen. Starting his career with stories in the Lovecraftian vein such as "The Shambler from the Stars" (1935), Bloch gradually veered his focus toward the criminally insane. In his "Yours Truly, Jack, the Ripper" (1943), Bloch adds an extraterrestrial dimension to this murderer endowing him with immortality that facilitates his cyclic appearances on earth. Bloch's most famous story of homicidal pathology, "Psycho" (1959) brought him his long-deserved acclaim with the release of Alfred Hitchcock's film adaptation. Bloch's persistent popularity can probably be attributed to his blend of tried and true horror intermingled with futuristic speculation.

In light of two world wars and increasingly efficient means of exterminating the human race many writers began to take the supernatural tale into the speculative realm often touching on the darker aspects of man's so-called scientific progress. During the 1940s, science fiction began to emerge as a distinct genre. Ray BRADBURY, best know for his serial length collection of speculative fiction, *The Illustrated Man,* started by publishing in *Weird Tales*. Theodore Sturgeon himself, better known for his contribution to science fiction, published a considerable amount of supernatural horror in the pulps, such as "Shottle Bop" (1941), with a strong nightmarish flavor as in his later "It" (1940). Many of Lovecraft's pieces such as "Cool Air," and "The Silver Key" may have served as major inspirations for those writers who began to gradually blend the supernatural with a speculative slant

From the early days of cinema with films such as *Frankenstein* and *Dracula* the mass media has played a powerful role in the shaping and dissemination of supernatural tales. But it was during the 1960s with the appearance of television shows such as Rod Serling's *The Twilight Zone, Outer Limits,* and *Alfred Hitchcock Presents* that the strange tale began to reach a wider audience. For a society that reads less and less as a whole, the mass media has been crucial in sustaining the supernatural writer's acclaim in the world of entertainment. Authors such as T. E. D. Klein and Harlan ELLISON gained popularity through their involvement with these shows. In the wake of the Vietnam War, the sexual revolution, and a growing concern with the emergence of the individual these shows that presented a blend of old-fashioned horror and more contemporary science fiction played upon our past and present fears with ample success.

In the wake of various demonic possession blockbusters like Ira LEVIN's Rosemary's Baby and William Peter Blatty's *The Exorcist* (1971) Stephen KING first made his grand entrance into the horror scene with *Carrie*. The antihero, Carrie, who reaps vengeance upon abusive classmates with her terrific psychic powers was a smash hit as a movie. A strange admixture of films championing the underdog with paranormal powers, and the downfall of others corrupted by all-powerful psychic forces presented us reciprocal views of a bewildering phenomenon. The public had once again become fascinated with the occult and the quest for empowerment cast in a dark light.

Much of Stephen King's popularity with novels such as *Pet Sematary* may lie in his focus on common and rural people whose lives are forever disrupted or controlled by uncanny forces. Not particularly innovative in form or subject matter King's books have a somewhat productionline quality to them often emulating the trashier pulp novels that he grew up reading.

And along with King there have arrived a slew of popular horror writers taking a similar tack aiming for the visceral while employing myriads of conventional forms such as gothic, vampire, and ghost stories. Dean R. Koontz, Michael McDowell, and J. N. Williamson, are some of the more prolific writers today whose works harness almost every cliché of the supernatural-and-slasher genre. In view of the general trends and cycles that the strange tale has been subject to its potential appears in many ways to have become all but exhausted.

It would seem that almost every contemporary horror writer has taken a stab at the age-old legend of the undead who prey upon the living. For instance, through the extremely popular works of Anne RICE and her Vampire Lestat series, the vampire story is thriving better than ever. Rice's *Interview with the Vampire* is presented as factual and the popularity of her novel may be connected with the current mass interest in true crime and police television shows. Poppy Z. Brite is another recent author who is taking the nosferatu into the 1990s with her *Drawing Blood* (1994). The gender of Brite's vampire remains questionable throughout her book that takes some strange erotic twists as do many of her short stories in *Wormwood,* formerly entitled *Swamp Foetus* (1994).

As with so many other genres, the mainstream of supernatural horror has been glutted with formula writers. However, many small presses and magazines, such as Necronomicon Press, which also reprints hard-to-find classic texts of Clark Ashton Smith, along with the more current *Fantasy Book, The Horror Show,* and *Fangoria* are providing a forum for many new authors and movements. For instance, in the anthology *Splatter Punks: Extreme Horror* (1990), edited by Paul Sammon, several featured authors: Joe R. Lansdale, Mick Garris, and Nancy A. Collins to name a few first started publishing in small-press magazines. As a movement in supernatural literature, the Splatterpunk tale has never fully emerged as a distinct entity. The only thread that seems to connect the Splatterpunks is the employment of contemporary settings focusing their attention on the stark cruelty of life on the streets and back-woods of modern America offset by supernatural and occult phenomenon. Splatterpunk is definitely not one-dimensional or specious. The physical violence in Splatterpunk stories can be egregious or completely absent thereby often successfully undermining our expectations. Furthermore, these incongruities are very much a postmodern trait that is becoming increasingly prevalent in the art, music, and literary trends of the 1990s. In short, the open forum that the writers of the 1930s and 1940s found in the small presses and pulp magazines is still an extremely vital artery of supernatural fiction today feeding new

blood into this age-old hybrid tradition as it withstands the rigors of massproduction and the mainstream press.

BIBLIOGRAPHY: Bleiler, E. F., *The Guide to Supernatural Fiction* (1983); Daniels, L., *Living in Fear: A History of Horror in Mass Media* (1975); Grant, K., *Outside the Circles of Time* (1980); Joshi, S. T., *The Weird Tale* (1990); King, S., *Danse Macabre* (1981); Newman, W. R., *Gehennical Fire: The Lives of George Starkey* (1994); Sullivan, J., ed., *The Penguin Encyclopedia of Horror and the Supernatural* (1986)

ROBERT PODGURSKI

SWADOS, Harvey

b. 28 October 1920, Buffalo, New York; d. 11 December 1972, Amherst, Massachusetts

Although self-defined as middle class, S.'s loyalty throughout his career was to the working class. As a young man, he spent time as a merchant marine traveling the globe and, later, as an assembly line worker, which instilled in him a deep devotion to the masses of intelligent and hard-working people, trapped and frustrated, who were unable to realize their ideals. He viewed mind-deadening work as a major source of unhappiness in the world. S. believed socialism could offer the worker a satisfaction and dignity impossible under a capitalist system and used his storytelling skills as a form of political activism, caring little for critical acclaim.

It was with *On the Line* (1957), a collection of short stories about factory life, that S. began to focus on the social and economic factors that shape human lives—themes that would dominate his entire body of work. A second collection, *Nights in the Gardens of Brooklyn* (1961), explores the interrelated lives of people from a variety of social, political, and economic backgrounds. It is here, in his short stories, that S.'s writing is most effective. Stories like "The Dancer," a melancholy tale of a young man's pursuit of his dream and subsequent loss of innocence, are rich in description of people and place.

The three novels to follow dealt with the complexities of family, work, and ideology. *The Will* (1963) involves three brothers' claims to an inheritance and explores their individual socialization experiences and psychologies. *False Coin* (1959) focuses on money's corrupting influence on American art. The protagonist, Ben Warder, is an artist struggling to keep his work meaningful. He seeks to retain his passion and vision in the face of a system that woos the artist with fame and wealth. *Standing Fast* (1970) follows a group of socialists, committed to the labor movement of the 1930s, from their twenties through middle age. The novel spans generations and shifts settings as it tracks the group members and their changing concerns influenced by aging and the forces of history. So many changes occurred between the 1930s and 1960s: the Great Depression gave way to postwar affluence rendering socialism as an economic system irrelevant. The characters play out some of the many possibilities such challenges to an ideology can precipitate. Some continue to embrace the socialist model while others move on to their own higher priorities.

The most well received of S.'s work, published posthumously, was *Celebration* (1975). The ninety-two-year-old protagonist, Samuel Lumen—well known for his radical ideas on child rearing—has begun to take on the public image of a Grand Old Man. He is a bit uncomfortable with this icon status and takes to keeping a diary; he writes about his "real" life so that we will not forget it. He is ill at ease with the public praise as he struggles with the memory of his painful private life. The overall tone is optimistic. Lumen is one whose good deeds, hope, and perseverance outweigh his personal flaws.

S.'s place in the literary canon is somewhat controversial. Proponents cite his depth of feeling and ability to create atmosphere. Others have found his techniques flawed and characterizations clichéd. However, most agree that S.'s work is heartfelt and moving in its exploration of human emotion.

BIBLIOGRAPHY: Kramer, H., "Remembering H. S.," *MR* 14 (1973): 226–28; Marx, P., "H. S.," in Helterman, J., and R. Layman, eds., *DLB,* vol. 2, *American Novelists since World War II* (1978): 475–78; Marx, P., "H. S.," *OntarioR* 1 (Fall 1974): 62–66

JASON MCMAHON

SWENSON, May

b. 28 May 1919, Logan, Utah; d. 4 December 1989, Ocean View, Delaware

S. began publishing her poetry in the early 1950s, and her works regularly appeared in major periodicals such as the *New Yorker* and *Poetry*. The most striking feature of her poetry is its visual design, and she is most often lauded for vivid, accurate, precise, and often very sensual descriptions that make readers see the object described from a fresh perspective. She has been compared to Marianne MOORE for her use of accurate, visual detail, to E. E. CUMMINGS because of the playfulness and visual inventiveness of her poetry, and to Emily DICKINSON for her interest in nature and small creatures. S. acknowledged the influence of these poets as well as that of Elizabeth BISHOP, but she

herself felt more affinity with visual artists such as Georgia O'Keeffe and Marcel Duchamp

Her first book of poetry, *Another Animal* (1954), introduces her major subject matter—nature—and how she uses animals and other objects to reflect upon humans and their relationship to each other and their environment. A hand is contrasted with a wing, leading to the question of which is better. S. does not answer, letting the reader decide. Throughout her career, she wrote of nature in the widest sense of the word, including man, the city, fountains, jets, and needles as well as the more expected natural objects such as trees, lions, snakes, cats and flowers.

S. is best known for the playfulness and visual inventiveness of her poetry, which often leads to unusual arrangements of type and to the use of riddles. In *Iconographs* (1970), nearly each poem's shape in some way mirrors or incorporates the subject of the poem: a poem about a wave marches from left to right across and up the page, with the words building to a crest just as a wave does, and the next line marches across and down, like a breaking wave. The device is not simple decoration, but seeks to build a visual as well as linguistic work of art out of the material of language just as visual artists build their works out of paint or marble or wood.

S.'s works have sometimes been criticized as lacking humans and human relationships, yet "Blood Test," from *In Other Words* (1987), demonstrates how her vivid, intensely visual images capture an ordinary moment in which the small female narrator confronts an African American male nurse and finds a gentle, nurturing professional, revealing how in our daily lives we encounter and overcome stereotypes. S. was undoubtedly familiar with such encounters from her own experiences as a lesbian, which are present in some of her work. S. did not make a secret of her lesbianism, but did not wish to be identified as a lesbian poet, and her works are generally not identified as such. S. did give permission to include some of her work in the anthology *Amazon Poetry* (1975), but declined being included in a later anthology entitled *Lesbian Poetry* (1981) because she saw the title as a label designed to arouse attention rather than to attract good poetry. Her poetry covers the breadth of human experience and strives to make us experience the poem as a thing-in-itself just as nature itself is to be experienced.

BIBLIOGRAPHY: Russell, S., "A Mysterious and Lavish Power: How Things Continue to Take Place in the Work of M. S.," *KR* 16 (Summer 1994): 128–39; Schulman, G., "Life's Miracles: The Poetry of M. S.," *APR* 23 (September–October 1994): 9–13

HEIDI PRESCHLER

TAGGARD, Genevieve

b. 28 November 1894, Waitsburg, Washington; d. 8 November 1948, New York City

T. may now be best known as the author of a ground-breaking study of Emily DICKINSON entitled *The Life and Mind of Emily Dickinson* (1930), but in her own time she was considered an important poet. Her work is divided between evocative lyrics, often celebrations of the natural world, and poems of political protest. Like many writers of her generation, she studied and imitated the metaphysical poets, such as John Donne, but T.'s work also shows a genuinely romantic lushness of imagery, and her celebrations of the character of individual places, whether in tropical islands or rural New England, deserve to find new readers.

Most of T.'s childhood was spent in Hawai'i, where her parents served as missionaries for the Disciples of Christ Church. T. often recalled her Hawaiian years with great fondness, and many of her poems return to the beauty of the tropics. She had no such affection for the periods during which her father's illness forced the family to return to rural Waitsburg, Washington, where T. had been born. The narrowness, insensitivity, and poverty of farm life, especially in contrast to the cosmopolitan society of Hawai'i, were the roots of T.'s lifelong dissatisfaction with American culture and politics.

T. began writing poetry while a student at the Ponahou School in Honolulu. She edited literary magazines both at Ponahou and at the University of California at Berkeley, which she entered in 1914. At Berkeley, T. studied poetry with Witter BYNNER, and her lyrics began appearing in magazines such as *Harper's* and *Poetry* while she was still a student. Her years at Berkeley also shaped her socialist convictions, and after her graduation in 1920, she moved to New York to work on left-wing magazines. T. married her first husband Robert L. Wolf another leftist writer, in 1921,

and both of them served as editors at the *New Masses* during the 1920s. T. was, with Padraic Colum and Maxwell ANDERSON, one of the founders of *Measure: A Magazine of Verse,* which was very influential during its brief existence (1921–26).

T.'s first book, *For Eager Lovers,* appeared in 1922. Most of the poems in that collection are rhymed lyrics that show more interest in the personal than in the political. T.'s succeeding volumes often fuse her political commitments with her growing interest in the importance of place. She returned to her childhood for the setting of *Hawaiian Hilltop* (1923), and during a year in San Francisco, she edited a collection of California poems, *Continent's End* (1925). In her later work, she celebrates the landscape of the South of France (where she lived for a year), of Italy and Spain (where she traveled thanks to a Guggenheim Fellowship in 1931), and most profoundly of New England (where she taught first at Mount Holyoke, then at Bennington, and finally at Sarah Lawrence). T.'s meditations on the natural world, however, often appeared side-by-side with poems of political protest. She edited an anthology of poems from *Liberator* and *New Masses* entitled *May Days* (1925) and many of the pieces in her own collections *Words for the Chisel* (1926), *Not Mine to Finish* (1934), and especially *Calling Western Union* (1936), are explicitly political.

Even in T.'s collection of the 1930s, however, many poems continue to describe the variety of the natural world, and that remains her central subject in her final collections, *Slow Music* (1946) and *Origin: Hawaii* (1947). Many of her poems show the influence of poets like Wallace STEVENS, whose central interest is not political, but art itself. T.'s interest in carefully crafted lyrics is shown in her collection of metaphysical poets entitled *Circumference: Varieties of Metaphysical Verse* (1929) as well as in her own work. The visual evocativeness and verbal music of T.'s poetry was recognized by other artists, including the composer William Schuman, who set her work to music, and the master of woodcuts J. J. Lankes, who illustrated it. While the political element in T.'s work is dated, her evocations of place are still powerful, and in her poems on personal relationships, she has been seen as a precursor of later feminist writers.

BIBLIOGRAPHY: Miller, N., "The Bonds of Free Love: Constructing the Female Bohemian Self," *Genders* 11 (Fall 1991): 37–57; Wilson, M. A., and G. Sell, "Lola Ridge and G. T.: Voices of Resistance," *ArkQ* 2 (Spring 1993): 124–33

BRIAN ABEL RAGEN

TALLENT, Elizabeth
b. 8 August 1954, Washington, D.C.

Prolific T.'s stories are regularly anthologized and appear in literary forums such as *Harper's* and the *New Yorker*. More concerned with the driving force of imagery than narrative, T.'s work embodies an interesting focus on the daydream as adult fantasy, offering an almost anthropological account of human relations. At the same time, T. channels this vision into examining the possibilities and limits of wholly domestic structures, charting the conflicting dynamics between families and generations.

Ironically, T.'s publications began with her *Married Men and Magic Tricks: John Updike's Erotic Heroes* (1982), an academic survey that acts as a template for most of her subsequent fiction. The interplay between the solidity of the marital condition and the extremely arbitrary nature of human identity produces a tension between idealized and actual living. As a result, the loose standards for social and sexual arrangements between men and women produce a rhythm of need that shifts in accordance with the terrain.

T.'s *In Constant Flight* (1983) offers a series of short stories charting the tensions between stability and change, security and risk, rootedness and flight. Essentially focusing on odd and dysfunctional relationships, the men and women in these stories fulfill T.'s basic idea that equilibrium is impossible, and all that is possible is a contingent emotional safety net. While initially mismatched, the couples produce stories of meaning for themselves that adds a stability of sorts and provides a safe haven from which to explore the reasons for failure.

T.'s debut as a novelist came with *Museum Pieces* (1985), which tells the story of a couple struggling for emotional survival under the twin weights of ambition and family. While their marriage is disintegrating, the structure of their derelict house serves as a larger metaphor for their process of personal reconstruction.

As the title suggests, the house they share turns them into oddities, museum pieces as such, preserved as a message for future generations. The centrality of the house itself, long a symbol of familial stability, ironically becomes a container and an instrument of claustrophobic domesticity. The novel engages in a form of domestic archaeology, putting together the fragments of relationships to make a picture grounded in the solidity of family and marriage.

T.'s later work is dependent on exploring the place and function of children within these family structures, and the stories lose the earlier sense of disorientation for a more certain sense of narrative coherence. In *Time with Children* (1987), T. examines the role of the child as a stable marker in parental warring, serving as symbols for the possibility of the future. T., however, never insists on a facile sentimentality, but instead uses the child as a place of unification between the past and the present. In this way, the child is a symbol of potential redemption within the family, and is deployed as a dispassionate commentator on the behavior of adults around them. Much like T.'s use of houses and relationships, the child becomes a focus for the reexamination of the domestic in American life.

BIBLIOGRAPHY: Parini, J., "Honey," *NYTBR* 7 November 1993: 11; Sumnor, C., "In Constant Flight," *TLS* 16 September 1983: 1002

PAUL HANSOM

TALL TALE, The

The tall tale is a comedic form closely connected to the American frontier. In tall tales, a fictive situation is portrayed as factual through a personal narrative or anecdote that challenges the listener with its comic improbability. The teller uses a deliberately exaggerated or an extravagantly understated manner that strains the limits of the listener's credibility, while exposing personal or societal values, customs, behaviors, or character. For comic effect, tall tales rely on the incongruity between their sober narration, realistic detail, literal approach, and common diction, and their implausible narrative. Although humorous even when the listener recognizes that the tale is untrue, the tall tale is most effective when a clever narrator is able to dupe a naive greenhorn, rookie, tenderfoot, or stranger. Traditionally, such stories are associated with the American Southwest prior to the Civil War, an area we currently refer to as the Southeast. Authors, taking advantage of city dwellers, presented wildly imaginative tales as true pictures of life "out West."

While the origins of the American tall tale may be traced to Homer, its debt to the tall tales of German storyteller Baron Münchausen are clearer. R. E. Raspe's collection of the Baron's tales, *Baron Münchausen's Narrative of his Marvelous Travels and Campaigns in Russia* (1786), was so popular that by 1800 it had been translated into five languages and by 1835 had been through twenty-four American editions. American merchants, doctors, lawyers, gamblers, soldiers, and scouts modified and adapted Münchausen's tales to fit their own narrative needs, while inventing new tales of their own. By the early 1800s, the tall tale was a staple of the American frontier, and it began to infiltrate American subliterature in the form of comic plays, almanacs, and newspaper features. Some of these stories were imitations of previously printed American or European tall tales. Examples include the exploits of woodsmen Paul Bunyan and Tony Beaver; or Pecos Bill, the colossal cowboy. However, two of the most famous characters in American tall tales are American frontier scouts Mike Fink and Davy CROCKETT.

The factual details of Mike Fink's life are difficult to separate from his legend. Born on the Western frontier, probably at Fort Pitt (now Pittsburgh, Pennsylvania), Fink is described as a brawling keelboatman on the Mississippi and Ohio rivers and a scout noted for his marksmanship. His exploits first appeared in print in 1829. While many of the stories about Fink were tales he invented and told about himself, his fame caused other authors to make him the hero of their tales. Nevertheless, tales attached to Fink appeared in plays, gift books, and journals including the *Spirit of the Times* and the *Western Review,* as well as several Crocket almanacs.

As popular as Fink was, the most famous American teller of tall tales was the frontier hero, pioneer, and politician, Davy Crockett. Born David Crockett in Greene County, Tennessee, he spent much of his youth as an unlettered frontiersman and backwoods hunter. He served with General Andrew Jackson in 1813, and from 1821 to 1825 he was a member of the Tennessee State legislature. In 1827, he became a member of the U.S. Congress. Crockett went to Texas in 1835, where he joined the struggle against Mexican rule and died defending the Alamo.

During his political career members of the Whig party, making skillful use of his renowned backwoods humor and eccentricities, brought out a number of books attributed to him. These included *A Narrative of the Life of David Crockett, of the State of Tennessee* and *Sketches & Eccentricities of Colonel David Crockett of West Tennessee.* While it is improbable that Crockett was the sole author, it seems likely that he aided in their writing. Popular pamphlets, known as Crockett almanacs, contained tall tales based on oral legends about Crockett and other frontier heroes,

including Daniel Boone and Kit Carson, and were issued by a variety of publishers from 1835 until 1856, twenty-one years after Crockett's death. His fame lived on for the next 100 years in plays, films, songs, and finally, television shows.

The tall tale, which started as an oral genre, mutated into a viable literary genre. The period between 1831 and 1865 was the heyday the American literary tall tale. William Trotter Porter founded the New York journal the *Spirit of the Times* (1831–61), a self-proclaimed "Chronicle of the Turf, Agriculture, Field Sports, Literature, and the Stage." The *Spirit* helped legitimize and popularize the literary tall tale by presenting stories of eccentrics, jokers, and hunters, huge bears, giant insects, and incredible marksmen. With a circulation that ultimately approached 40,000, the *Spirit* demonstrated the public's interest in frontier humor, and paved the way for our greatest authors of literary tall tales.

Although he wrote several books and pamphlets, Augustus Baldwin LONGSTREET is notable for beginning the tradition of the Southern literary tales with *Georgia Scenes.* Longstreet presents anecdotes reclaimed from folktales that are distinguished by a concern for accuracy in dialect and detail, good-natured humor, and a realistic sense of place. His sketches highlight the contrast between rustic and uneducated Georgians and their cultivated, educated, and more aristocratic neighbors. While both groups are satirized, the Yale-educated Longstreet always identifies with the gentry.

However, his friend and associate, William Tappan THOMPSON, writes tales that focus not on Southern aristocrats, but on a depiction of what he called Georgia "crackers." Arguably less interested in humor than in realistically depicting Georgian life, Thompson's created Major Jones, a simple, unsophisticated, middle-class planter and owner of faithful and fun-loving slaves, who provides a quiet picture of upper-middle-class life. *Major Jones' Courtship,* an epistolary novel of twenty-eight letters over two years, describes contemporary plantation life in a series of naive, jovial sketches structured around Jones's attempts to court a neighbor-girl. Jones's impeccable morals and respectable behavior detract from his comic possibilities, but Thompson's ability to create humorous situations, as well as his clever use of spelling and grammatical errors made Jones a favorite of genteel readers.

Joseph Glover Baldwin, a lawyer in Alabama and Mississippi during the 1830s and 1840s, provides both a realistic picture of life on the bench and comic anecdotes of country lawyers, orators, gamblers, and an assortment of liars and storytellers. His *Flush Times of Alabama and Mississippi* (1853) moves away from the stable social order of the old South towards the wide-open excitement of the Southwestern frontier, where the opening of new lands lured thousands of emigrants in search of adventure and wealth. His earthy humor never becomes crude, and his tales of frontier life are marked by a sense of gentility and fair play, demonstrating his ambivalent desire for social order and refinement while recognizing the virtues of a raw and vital populace.

Johnson Jones HOOPER, a lawyer and newspaper editor from Alabama, explores similar territory in *Some Adventures of Simon Suggs, Late of the Tallapoosa Volunteers*. Suggs is a scoundrel, liar, and thief who preys, unrepentantly, on the selfishness, affectation and avarice of his fellow man. Samuel Langhorne CLEMENS uses the comic but conscienceless thief as a model for the King in chapter 20 of *Adventures of Huckleberry Finn*.

George Washington HARRIS, Tennessee silversmith, hunter, journalist, and steamboat captain, created an authentic American comic character in Sut Lovingood. Although *Sut Lovingood Yarns* wasn't published until 1867, Sut first appeared in *Spirit of the Times* in 1845. He is a tall, rough-hewn mountaineer from the Great Smokies who lived to drink whiskey, raise some hell and, whenever possible, have some fun. Harris makes no pretext of offering serious social analysis; he writes to make people laugh. Harris was so successful at creating hilarious and unique American tall tales that *Sut Lovingood Yarns* remained constantly in print for more than seven decades.

Massachusetts-born author Thomas Bangs THORPE lived in Louisiana from 1833 to 1853. During this period, he wrote stories about life on the frontier, including the title story of one of America's most notable collections of tall tales, *The Big Bear of Arkansas*. It is the story of Jim Doggett's attempt to kill an "unhuntable" bear. Thorpe's tall tale is the most anthologized and critically acclaimed work of fiction from the old Southwest. Critics have traced its influence in Herman MELVILLE's *Moby-Dick* and William FAULKNER's "The Bear," and though they admire its literary complexity and significance, it continues to be a superbly humorous narrative.

Clemens is in many ways the culmination of the tradition of Southern tall tales. Although he changed the locale to Nevada for *Roughing It,* California for "The Celebrated Jumping Frog of Calaveras County," and Europe for *A Tramp Abroad,* he retains many of the conventions, rhetorical patterns, and character types of the tall tale.

Despite the popularity of the Southern literary tall tale for a thirty year period, the onset of war in 1861 and the end of mail service between North and South marked the end of the *Spirit of the Times* and national

interest in Southwestern regional literature. But the tall tale remains a vital influence in the work of a variety of American authors.

BIBLIOGRAPHY: Blair, W., and R. I. McDavid, *The Mirth of a Nation* (1983); Brown, C. S., *The Tall Tale in American Folklore and Literature* (1987); Clark, W. B., and W. C. Turner, *Critical Essays on American Humor* (1984); Cohen, H., and W. B. Dillingham, *Humor of the Old Southwest* (1964); Inge, M. T., *The Frontier Humorists* (1975)

KENNETH L. MITCHELL

TAN, Amy
b. 19 February 1952, Oakland, California

Heralded as a major talent with the 1989 publication of her first novel, *The Joy Luck Club,* T. has enjoyed enormous critical and popular success. Although complex in structure, the novel captures the voices of eight women, mothers and daughters, and their conflicts and struggles, while commenting on the past's impact on the present. The principal narrative belongs to Jing-mei Woo, a first-generation Chinese American. It is she who joins her deceased mother's Joy Luck Club, playing mah-jongg in her place. Through one tale skillfully interwoven with another, the reader learns of the struggles of Jing-mei Woo's mother and her three friends, "aunties," Chinese women who have sustained an abiding friendship through their forty years of exile in the U.S. *The Joy Luck Club* is a testimony to these women's survival and a reflection of their daughters' acculturation as they try to balance Chinese female submissiveness with American independence.

T.'s second novel, *The Kitchen God's Wife,* was published in 1991. Much anticipated and widely heralded, the novel continues T.'s exploration of the conflicts that ensue between mothers and daughters when East meets West, when the old collides with the new. While the first two chapters are rather unremarkably narrated by Pearl Brandt, the novel takes flight when her mother, Winnie Louie, begins. *The Kitchen God's Wife* is a transference of family myths and revelation of secrets as Winnie unfolds the details of a life of painful endurance. T. has admitted that much of Winnie's tale is based on her own mother's sufferings in China.

In 1995, T. published her third novel, *The Hundred Secret Senses,* a traversal of time and place from the China of the 1850s to America in the 1990s. The novel is one of ambiguities as the protagonist, Olivia Yee Bishop, must resolve the conflicts of her troubled marriage to Simon Bishop, her guilt over her erroneous belief that she is responsible for her father's death, and her doubts over whether her half-sister's stories of her previous life are real or the result of the shock treatments Kwan received while she was in a mental institution. Ultimately, *The Hundred Secret Senses* is a continuation of T.'s theme of the search for self as Olivia, the daughter of a Chinese father and Anglo-American mother, travels to China upon Kwan's insistence. The novel is also an emotional and spiritual voyage as Olivia must learn to feel with what Kwan calls "the hundred secret senses."

The recipient of many awards and honors, including the National Book Critics Circle Award for best novel for *The Joy Luck Club,* T. has also written short stories, and her work has appeared in *Best American Essays* (1991) as well as the periodicals *Atlantic Monthly, McCall's,* and *Threepenny Review,* among others. In addition, she wrote the children's book *The Moon Lady* (1992) and, with Ronald Bass, coauthored the screenplay for *The Joy Luck Club,* which was released by Hollywood Pictures in 1993. Along with her literary forebearer Maxine Hong KINGSTON, T. is credited with opening up the publishing world for other contemporary Asian American writers.

BIBLIOGRAPHY: Chen, V., "Chinese American Women, Language, and Moving Subjectivity," *W&Lang* 18 (Spring 1995): 3–7; Heung, M., "Daughter-Text/Mother-Text: Matrilineage in A. T.'s *Joy Luck* Club," *FSt* 19 (Fall 1993): 597–616; Wong, S. C., "'Sugar Sisterhood': Situating the A. T. Phenomenon," in Palumbo, L. D., ed., *The Ethnic Canon: Histories, Institutions, and Interventions* (1995): 174–210

DEBORAH KAY FERRELL

TARKINGTON, [Newton] Booth

b. 29 July 1869, Indianapolis, Indiana; d. 19 May 1946, Indianapolis, Indiana.

One of the best-known American writers of the first half of the 20th c., T. was enormously prolific in the production of novels, nouvelles, short stories, full-length and one-act plays, as well as radio dramas and motion picture scenarios. While many of his short stories for the popular magazines of the day appeared also as novels or were reissued as book-length story assortments, his collected works in the Doubleday, Page Doubleday, Doran edition, completed in 1932, number twenty-seven volumes. Despite his longtime concern with literary craftsmanship, his suiting his efforts to the common reader, and his focusing on what he knew and loved well—the Indiana community large or small—the quality of his fiction, to name his more important genre, is quite uneven. This unremark-

able fact, however, highlights the continuing importance and unfortunate neglect of his two major novels, both well-deserving Pulitzer Prize-winners the year following publication: *The Magnificent Ambersons* (1918) and *Alice Adams* (1921). As with a number of his other writings, each of these novels was made into a movie: *The Magnificent Ambersons* in a highly regarded production directed by Orson Welles (1942), and *Alice Adams* in two film versions twelve years apart (1923, 1935).

An early shaping influence on him, aside from his father—a kindly lawyer of strong character—may have been his uncle, Newton Booth, who had gone out West after the gold rush and achieved wealth and power, becoming governor of California in 1871, and later, U.S. senator from California. Booth's financial support enabled his artistically inclined but truant nephew to make up for his wasted high school terms by attending Phillips Exeter Academy, becoming more serious about his studies, including art. A year at Purdue University and—more important—two subsequent years at Princeton brought out his innate versatility, goal-orientation, and group-participation skills. He did sketching and creative writing, was active in college theatricals, joined activity clubs and coteries, and was on the editorial board of the three leading student publications at Princeton.

James Woodress calls T. "a practitioner of the William Dean HOWELLS type of commonplace realism." But that realism is tempered by a sentimentality and a craftsmanly shaping of plot, suited to the mass-circulation periodicals that welcomed his fiction, notably the *Saturday Evening Post, Collier's, Cosmopolitan,* and *Red Book.* T.'s major thematic elements include children at play and at war, young love, sociocultural history including urban and familial growth and decay, and designing women. T.'s interest in historical costume dramas is best shown in his story *Monsieur Beaucaire* (1901), featuring, in an 18th-c. setting, the comic adventures of a barber-in-disguise—actually the Duke of Orleans—bringing woe to the English nobility at England's most prominent spa, Bath. A perennial favorite with the public, *Monsieur Beaucaire* was transmuted into a play, an operetta, and a motion picture: first with Rudolph Valentino in 1924 and later with Bob Hope in 1946.

T.'s recurring motif of small children squabbling, mischief-making, having fun after their fashion, and often disturbing the peace serves as an ironic trademark: much of his raw material was suggested by the antics of his sister's three boys. His famous assemblages of tales of boyhood life in early-20th c. Indiana—*Penrod* (1914), *Penrod and Sam* (1916), and *Penrod Jashber* (1929)—feature a self-willed, imaginative eleven-going-on-twelve-year-old, Penrod Schofield, coping with for him the impossible demands of family, school, and society. His positive relations with his dog Duke and his chum Sam Williams, highly problematical relations with certain little girls in his social group, fair relations with the black twins Herman and Verman, and unsatisfactory relations with the sadistic bully Rupe Collins, still retain some of their earlier reader appeal, especially for youngsters. Of note, T.'s often offensive treatment of African Americans here and elsewhere, may well put today's reader on guard. The motif of young love is prominent in *Penrod* and, inter alia, in *Seventeen* (1916), the saga of seventeen-year-old Willie Baxter and his crush on the enchanting Lola Pratt. Among T.'s many obstreperous "small fry" are eight-year-old Ludlum Thomas in "The Only Child" and nine-year-old Laurence Coy in "Willamilla," both in *The Fascinating Stranger and Other Stories* (1923), and seven-year-old Orvie Stone in the collection *Little Orvie* (1935). *The Magnificent Ambersons* introduces us to another fractious eight-year-old, George Minafer, the novel's protagonist.

T.'s sociocultural history of an Indiana town's gradual enlargement and maturation is traced in his *Growth* trilogy. *The Turmoil* (1914) concerns the Sheridan family, on the rise in the smoke-polluted, money-corrupted, booming Midwestern town (Indianapolis, apparently). *The Magnificent Ambersons* (1918) continues the story of the sprawling urban community, showing how a preeminent pioneering family, the Ambersons, become reduced in social status through the later generations' lack of vision and drive, and their overreliance on the faded glory of the family name. In *The Midlander* (1924), Dan Oliphant, a promoter, real estate developer, and automobile manufacturer, is instrumental in the further expansion of the environmentally unclean city, but his intense efforts bear him bitter fruit. Banking and commercial interests, as well as local officials, obstruct him, in addition to which his disaffected wife and their son abandon him. Among T.'s designing women—opportunistic exploiters, generally heedless of their machinations' effects on others—are Cora Madison in *The Flirt* (1913), Alice Adams in the book bearing her name, Lena Oliphant in *The Midlander,* Mme. Momoro in *The Plutocrat* (1927), Aurelia Hedge in *Young Mrs. Greeley* (1929), and Irene Foote in *The Lorenzo Bunch* (1936).

In contrast to a good deal of T.'s "popular" fiction, which is lacking in style and the finer points of literary craftsmanship, his two Pulitzer Prize-winning novels stand out in bold relief. *The Magnificent Ambersons,* with its single redeeming Amberson descendant, George Minafer—who finally gets over his mother-fixation, gains a sense of purpose and on it, winning the hand of his longtime sweetheart—is graced by a

number of lyrically beautiful passages of first-rate prose. *Alice Adams,* a sad novel but like the other, beautifully and sensitively written, depicts the falling social status of a lower-middle-class family in a small town in the Midwest, and the daughter's pathetic and fruitless attempts to win the affection of a man capable of rescuing her from a lonely, bleak, hopeless existence. At the end of this story of a woman whose designs on men haven't a chance, she has a strikingly insightful philosophical discussion with her father, wherein she faces the reality of having to learn from past experience, as she argues that the idea of a finish to things is all wrong: there is always something beyond, that is to be considered. An excellent treatment of cultural changes and the relaxing of moral standards between 1904 and 1920 is found in the whimsical tale "Jeannette" (1921), included in *The Fascinating Stranger and Other Stories.* As a chronicler of the social and cultural changes occurring in Indiana during the later 1800s and earlier 1900s, a period of sharply increased industrialization and commercialization, T. will retain an important place in American literary history.

BIBLIOGRAPHY: Eugenides, J., Introduction to *The Magnificent Ambersons* (1994); Fennimore, K. J., *B. T.* (1974); Woodress, J. L., *B. T.: Gentleman from Indiana* (1955)

SAMUEL I. BELLMAN

TATE, [John Orley] Allen

b. 19 November 1896, Winchester, Kentucky; d. 9 February 1979, Nashville, Tennessee

T. was always both backward-looking and on the cutting edge of literature. He was always looking to the past—whether to classical culture or to the Old South—not just for inspiration, but for values. All the same, he was a champion of the modernist mode of literature and, as one of the New Critics, changed the way literature was read—and especially the way it was taught—in America. All his works, which range from prose fiction and military biographies to the poems and critical essays for which he is best remembered, use the memory of the heroic past—the Civil War, the wanderings of Aeneas, the passion of Christ—as the lens through which to understand the modern world.

The first turning point in T.'s career was his entry into Vanderbilt University in Nashville in 1918. By that time, he had already begun writing, acquired a thorough grounding in the classics, and read widely in French literature, but there he made several of the literary connections that would shape the rest of his career. He studied under John Crowe RANSOM—who found him more knowledgeable about modernist writing and criticism than many of his own colleagues—and over the years their joint work helped create the New Criticism. Another member of the Vanderbilt faculty, Donald DAVIDSON, invited T. to join the discussion group called the FUGITIVES. In that setting, T. met writers including Robert Penn WARREN—with whom T. roomed for a time—and Laura RIDING. The journal the group produced from 1922 to 1925, *The Fugitive,* became an important forum for modernist thought; T. was an early champion of T. S. ELIOT, and a number of T.'s early poems were published in *The Fugitive.*

T.'s literary circle at Vanderbilt was at once cosmopolitan and intensely regional. Even after many of its members left the South, they continued to celebrate Southern culture and to argue that its values were more genuine than those of the commercial North. T. helped edit the influential manifesto that twelve of them issued in 1930, *I'll Take My Stand: The South and the Agrarian Tradition,* in which he contributed an essay on religion. T. was less interested in the contrast between "agrarian" and "industrial" economic systems than in celebrating a culture based on tradition and loyalty, not just on money. He tried to show how those values had been embodied in several of the great Confederate leaders in his biographies, *Stonewall Jackson: The Good Soldier* (1928) and *Jefferson Davis: His Rise and Fall* (1929). A third biography, one of Robert E. Lee, was never finished. He addressed the Civil War again in his only novel, *The Fathers* (1938). More importantly, the same issues of loyalty and tradition—as opposed to a solipsistic individualism—animate many of T.'s poems, notably "Ode to the Confederate Dead" and "Aeneas in Washington."

T. married the novelist Caroline GORDON in 1924. During the 1920s and 1930s, they moved frequently, sharing a house with Hart CRANE at one point, and taking part in the expatriate literary scene during two long stays in France. T. shared with Gordon both an intense interest in Christianity and firm opinions about the nature of writing. Together, they wrote the highly influential textbook *The House of Fiction* (1950), which summarized the New Critics' view of what novels ought to be. T. continued to write his own highly influential literary essays, publishing collections including *On the Limits of Poetry* (1948) and *The Man of Letters in the Modern World* (1957). Together, they also clarified their religious views and joined the Roman Catholic Church. T.'s conversion in 1950 intensified the religious element already present in his poetry. It did not, however, make his marriage less tempestuous: T. and Gordon divorced, remarried, and divorced again. T. was married twice subsequently.

T. taught at several universities throughout the 1940s to 1960s, including Princeton and the University of Minnesota. He was widely honored for his poems, and his critical theories presented in essays such as "Tension in Poetry" became the basis of American literary criticism during the years of the New Criticism's hegemony.

BIBLIOGRAPHY: Bishop, F., *A. T.* (1967); Dupree, R. S., *A. T. and the Augustinian Imagination* (1983); Squires, R, *A. T.: A Literary Biography* (1971)
BRIAN ABEL RAGEN

TATE, James
b. 8 December 1943, Kansas City, Missouri

T.'s distinctive voice sets him apart from other contemporary poets, leaving him in his own stylistic movement of one. At the same time, throughout a career of twelve full-length books of poetry and at least as many shorter limited editions, T.'s style has not rested. A chronological study of his works reveals continuing experimentation and expansion, particularly impressive from a poet who enjoyed very early success: his first book won him the honor of being the youngest poet ever to receive the Yale Series of Younger Poets Award. With regard to subject matter, T.'s keen focus remains consistently upon the intricate details, the heightened moments of minute experience. Reading T. is transporting, and though the landscape may seem otherworldly, the journey is in fact one into the interior of our own vicinities.

T.'s first full-length book, *The Lost Pilot* (1967), explores personal material, the poet's contemplated relationship with the father he never knew, a World War II pilot whose plane was shot down and never recovered. However, the poet's wild imagery and attention to form quickly earned him a reputation as a poet not of the self, but of an external, projected world. His images come from the natural world, from art, from pop culture—anything accessed by the composing mind—and are fused to create the supernatural landscape of the poems. For the next two decades after the publication of *The Lost Pilot,* books followed at regular intervals: *The Oblivion Ha-Ha* (1970), *Hints to Pilgrims* (1971), *Absences* (1972), *Hottentot Ossuary* (1974), *Viper Jazz* (1976), *Riven Doggeries* (1979), *Constant Defender* (1983), *Reckoner* (1986), and *Distance from Loved Ones* (1990). In addition to the books published and distributed widely during these years, T. published many collections and broadsides with smaller presses. Some of the later collections drew poems from titles brought forth by presses such as Kayak, Black Sparrow, and Unicorn: twelve between 1967 and 1970 alone. Two collaborations with Bill Knott emerged, a book of poems, *Are You Ready Mary Baker Eddy* (1970) and a novel, *Lucky Darryl* (1977). Another small press book, *Apology for Eating Geoffrey Movins' Hyacinth,* came out in 1972, followed in 1981 by *Land of Little Sticks.*

In 1991, T.'s *Selected Poems* chronicled the poet's development; in 1992, it earned both the Pulitzer Prize and the William Carlos Williams Award, interestingly appropriate since William Carlos WILLIAMS is so often mentioned by critics discussing T. Wallace STEVENS's influence is also apparent, not only in a formal sense, as in the tercets employed in *The Lost Pilot,* but in the choice of often exotic imagery, and the heightened sense of sound the poets share. T.'s poems evoke a kind of whimsy and daring found in Williams and Stevens, but for which he has been criticized at times. In the political and confessional context of the 1970, T.'s cleverness and affection for language and sound was quite often dismissed as disingenuous and showy. Others have praised his resistance to the movements of the moment.

Though born in Kansas City, T. has been at home in New England for over twenty-five years; since 1971, he has taught at the University of Massachusetts at Amherst. In 1994, T. was honored again, this time with the National Book Award for *A Worshipful Company of Fletchers,* and in 1995, he was presented with the Tanning Prize from the Academy of American Poets. The publication in 1997 of *Shroud of the Gnome* continued the uninterrupted publishing rhythm of having no more than four years between books over a period of three decades.

BIBLIOGRAPHY: Bellamy, J. D., ed., *American Poetry Observed: Poets on Their Work* (1984); Gardner, S., "J. T.," in Greiner, D. J., ed., *DLB,* vol. 5, part 2, *American Poets since World War II* (1980): 318–22

                                          NICOLE SARROCCO

TAYLOR, Bayard

b. 11 January 1825, Kennett Square, Pennsylvania; d. 19 December 1878, Berlin, Germany

T. is largely forgotten today, but in his time he was a prolific and popular writer of travel narratives and verse. A dabbler in all literary genres, he also experimented with the novel and produced the 19th c.'s most important translation of Goethe's *Faust.* T. acquired and cultivated the good graces of his still-famous literary contemporaries; the Fireside Poets, especially Henry Wadsworth LONGFELLOW and John Greenleaf WHITTIER, praised his travel narratives, and Edgar Allan POE admired his verse.

Born to a poor farming family, T. did not have the means to higher education. Instead, he embarked on a walking tour of Europe as a nineteen-year-old. Ironically, by the time he was twenty-five, he had acquired enough literary fame to provide the Phi Beta Kappa poem to the Harvard graduating class.

Travel narratives, a favorite genre of 19th-c. readers, were T.'s specialty. He traveled extensively through Europe, Africa, Asia, and the U.S., and he produced eleven narratives based on his exotic adventures. Most critics label *Eldorado; or, Adventures in the Path of Empire* (1850), an account of his visit to California during the gold rush of 1949, his best travel book. His experiments with the novel ranged from *Hannah Thurston* (1863), a popular work that took up the question of women's rights, to *Joseph and His Friend* (1870), an abject failure that caused him to give up fiction. T. took up poetry later in his life, and although he produced numerous works of verse, many of which were popular, no one ever accused T. of being unique.

Nevertheless, *The Echo Club and Other Literary Diversions* (1876) will be of interest to any student of American literature. The conceit of the *Echo Club* involves a series of fanciful discussions between members of an imaginary literary club who gather together and "echo" the tone and manner of famous authors. The members, whose personalities range from pretentious to iconoclastic, engage in a series of sometimes enlightening and oftentimes hilarious conversations as they pay homage to as well as make fun of well-known literary giants. Echoing Keats, one member pens an "Ode to a Jar of Pickles." An echo of Swinburne is called "The Lay of the Macaroni." Another member pens a verse that plays off a promissory note Poe apparently wrote to Horace Greeley. The playful tone of the members is peppered with serious discussions of 19th-c. literature. In an Emersonian overture, one member calls for a more analytical form of American literary criticism that elevates the quality of the work over the personal taste of the critic. There is also a great deal of talk about the shortcomings of the American reading public. The members satirize popular literary fashions, and they complain of the indiscriminate public taste that favors the latest trends over the more established literary voices of the literary canon. Finally, the book is not without drama. In one tense moment one of the members threatens to quit the club when another member indicates a desire to "echo" and, perhaps, mimic Whittier. The echo that follows is delightfully hilarious and serves to mollify the devotee of Whittier.

Although there is little chance of a T. revival, he was a popular and well-respected member of the mid- and late-19th-c. literati. As a result, his fiction and verse may be of interest to students of 19th-c. popular culture and his travel narratives may enlighten those interested in 19th-c. American attitudes toward unfamiliar peoples and lands.

BIBLIOGRAPHY: Hansen-Taylor, M., and H. Scudder, *The Life and Letters of B. T.* (1884); Wermuth, P., *B. T.* (1973)

ERIC FRETZ

TAYLOR, EDWARD

b. ca. 1642, Sketchley, Leicestershire, England; d. 24 June 1729, Westfield, Massachusetts

Although T.'s poetry remained undiscovered until the 1930s, today it is appreciated as the most remarkable and brilliant achievement of all New England Puritan literature. T.'s stature as a literary artist steadily increases, and he is on the verge of being recognized as one of the greatest American writers.

Probably born in Sketchley, Leicestershire, England, T. was raised on a farm and received a nonconformist education that was completed, after his immigration to Massachusetts Bay in 1668, at Harvard College. Not long after graduating from Harvard in 1671, he became the minister of Westfield, a frontier settlement in western Massachusetts where he reared a family with Elizabeth Fitch of Norwich, whom he married in 1674, and, three years after the death of his first wife, with Ruth Wyllys of Hartford, whom he married in 1692. Although his residence in Westfield prevented him from actively participating in the intellectual milieu of the coastal towns, T. never lost contact with such leading figures as Increase MATHER and Samuel SEWALL, with whom he corresponded, and he never lost touch with the critical issues of his day. Not merely a physician and an orthodox Congregationalist minister, T. was a genuine product of late Renaissance English culture and, consequently, was fascinated by all fields of knowledge, which is one reason why his poetry is so difficult to understand. He possessed a library of at least two hundred works, and he often copied extensive passages from borrowed books. During the last four years of his life, T. was very ill, and was then ministerially assisted by Nehemiah Bull.

Aside from the fact that T. lived far from Boston, it remains unclear why his poetry (except for stanzas 5 and 7 of "Upon Wedlock and Death of Children" in Cotton MATHER's *Right Thoughts in Sad Hours* [1689]) and his sermons did not appear in print during his lifetime. There is no evidence to support the previously held belief that T. had enjoined his heirs never to publish his verse, and even this notion would not explain why his sermons, which appear to have been prepared for the press, remained unpublished. These works include eight sermons written about 1694 in reply to Solomon STODDARD's liberal interpretation of the Lord's Supper (published in 1966 as *Edward Taylor's Treatise Concerning the Lord's Supper*), thirty-six sermons written between 1693 and 1706 on typology (published in 1989 as *Edward Taylor's upon the Types of the Old Testament*), and fourteen sermons written between 1701 and 1703 on the nature of Christ (published in 1962 as *E. T.'s Christographia*). Although these works, conforming to the Ramist formula for sermons, comprise an important resource for identifying T.'s ideas, no adequate case for their literary merit has yet been made.

Writings also reflecting T.'s varied interests include a few extant letters, a brief diary, an incomplete commentary on the Gospels, a long narrative poem on the history of Christianity, various church records, a few sermons, extracts from or transcriptions of works by others, a long poem on some mastodon bones, and miscellaneous verse (most of these items collected in 1981 in the three volumes of *The Unpublished Writings of E. T.* and in 1982 in *E. T.'s Harmony of the Gospels*). Perhaps the most interesting of these minor works of little artistic accomplishment is T.'s paraphrases of the Psalms, which suggest a source for such features in his poetic meditations as alternation between personal and collective voice; the reliance on a structure developing from lament, to supplication, to thanksgiving; and the use of interrogation, amplification, and antithesis.

The one work of verse that T. almost certainly intended for a public audience is *Gods Determinations Touching His Elect,* a long sequence of doctrinal poetry probably composed around 1682. Apparently it was designed to convince members of the Westfield parish who were reluctant to enter the church as full members. Possible influences upon this series include morality plays, Theocritan song contests, Ignatian meditative practices and homiletic tradition. *Gods Determinations* is particularly noteworthy for its demonstration of T.'s capacity for the dramatic, his relish for paradox, and his ability to organize a long work by means of certain unifying motifs. The most outstanding structural motif in the work is based on a pair of jawbones, the upper extremity of which represents Christ (mercy and the gospel) and the lower extremity of which represents Satan (justice and the law); caught between these two forces are the elect souls, who experience an emotional ebb and flow between despair (Satan) and presumption (Christ) while they, as the church, are conveyed by these jawbone forces from their natural house to a heavenly mansion.

T.'s greatest achievement, however, appears in *Preparatory Meditations before My Approach to the*

Lord's Supper (completely published in 1960 as *The Poems of E. T.),* poetry he wrote in apparent conjunction with certain sermons, particularly the sermons on Christ, the Lord's Supper, and typology. These devotional poems in the 16th- and 17th-c. tradition of meditation were written in preparation for the poet's participation in the Lord's Supper, although evidence suggests that he revised and recast several of them at later times. These poems reflect some traits similar to 17th-c. English "metaphysical" poetry—for example, they occasionally echo George Herbert's verse—but finally they contain such unique features as a deliberately managed decorum of imperfection, an adherence to an exclusionary typological system (at least until late in life), and a management of persona that permits the poet simultaneously to assert self and arrest that assertion, to be at once inside and outside his poem.

Preparatory Meditations has disturbed some critics, and the earliest scholarship on the series tends to emphasize its agreement with Anglican sources and even with Roman Catholic beliefs. In fact, the sacramental features of T.'s poetry do not stand apart from the mainstream of Puritan orthodoxy, which had a greater relish for sacramentality and which was more pluralistic than has been generally acknowledged. If the interest in the alleged Anglican and Roman Catholic characteristics of these poems has subsided, the critical tendency to emphasize theme, theology, intellectual heritage, and aesthetic theory remains strong. Careful attention has especially been given to the Augustinian foundation for T.'s ideas and aesthetic theory as well as to the typological traditions (as exemplified in books by Thomas Taylor and Samuel Mather) informing his verse.

At the moment, two views prevail concerning T.'s use of typology. One holds that T. manages typology very conservatively, presenting an Old Testament type as already completely fulfilled by Christ and therefore excluding the poet, who at best can only place himself, off-center, in a very insignificant corner of a typological picture. The other view holds that whereas T. is initially exegetically conservative and avoids the application of ceremonial types to history and, beyond Christ, to the saint, near the end of his life he moves from typology to allegory, redesigns and personalizes the age-old imagery, and ingeniously attaches his personal pleas for salvation to the typological (figural) development of his meditations.

Such studies of *Preparatory Meditations* yield insights, but several critics have argued for a greater awareness of the artistry of the poetry. T.'s verse has been faulted for an imagistic development that appears to be baroque and free-associative, with the result that each of the poems seems to lack any organization. Reassessments of this poetry, however, have demonstrated an intricate aesthetic integrity, a developmental consistency of imagery, and a logical pattern of transition, albeit all of these characteristics can sometimes be idiosyncratic and private for the poet. Indeed the appearance of internal poetic disorder is often a disguise, a contrived discord appropriate to the inept poet T. pretends to be in order to present himself and the case for his salvation with humility. Beneath this appearance of surface disorder is a real, divinely ordained emblematic cohesion and unity in the poems that T. hopes might indirectly suggest that the beseeching, awkward poet possesses some innate qualities that might be worth divine attention and redemption. The detection (really the *invention*) of this clever poetic demonstration of underlying relationships is the product (the poet hopes) of the remotest recesses of his reason and will, the image of God in him.

Throughout "Meditation 1.8," for instance, there is a proliferation of imagery that gives a surface impression of random image-making; but basically one emblematic configuration binds and interrelates these images, an arch (sky, cage, human body, inverted barrel, God's bowel, rising dough, and overturned crystal bowl) that represents the eventual circular coalescence of microcosm (body and soul) and macrocosm (creation and deity). In "Meditation 1.39," the surface discord of language dramatizes the abject condition of a disoriented ill narrator, whose verbal images nonetheless are integrated, with many subtle poetic interactions, at an underlying level in their appeal for Christ the physician to cure him, for Christ the advocate to plead his case for dereliction of duty (as ministerial shepherd) while he was ill, and for Christ the carpenter to fix once and for all the physical conditions that permit the narrator's failure to tend God's pastoral sheep. In "Meditation 2.3," a stunningly original and difficult poem, T. uses his own aging face as an emblem; at first, the topographical imagery seems wildly out of control—and indeed the associations are nearly cryptic—but finally all of the images in the poem play off each other in a cohesive way that refutes the accusation that in T.'s poetry the worn emblematic tradition makes its last weary appearance and that what emblems he employs fall into utter disorder.

As these examples indicate, the facts of everyday Puritan life as well as the poet's private associations figure importantly in the congruence of the imagery in his meditations. As these examples also indicate, theology provides the fundamental source of T.'s poetic imagery, a source he delights in merger with other, more secular, areas of human interest. Sometimes theology alone provides ample information for detecting the essential integrity of a Taylorian poem; this is the case with "Meditation 2.25" and "Meditation 2.149," in both of which apparent random shifts from image to image actually evince an obscured unity derived from the exegetical traditions of his time. More often, however, T. combines theology and information from numerous other areas of late Renaissance human inquiry, especially science.

In "Meditation 2.61," for example, biblical types and Paracelsian medical theory generate ostensibly discordant images that actually interact coherently to convey a sense of the integration of religion and science, a unifying pattern identical to that informing the seemingly chaotic interface of typology and astronomy in "Meditation 2.10" and "Meditation 2.21." Scientific and folkloric herbalism figures in "Meditation 2.62," in which seemingly confusing references to herbs resolve into an underlying pattern of a thrice-reiterated tripartite progression from purgation, through improving health, to regeneration. And in "Meditation 1.16," apparently contradictory images are reconciled by the poet's unifying vision: that the Aristotelian optical theory of light's reflection in the eye describes the postlapsarian condition of the otherwise sin-blind eye of the soul and that the Platonic optical theory of light's emission from the eye pertains to the fully regenerated state of the rational eye of the soul; so that finally the seeming disorder of the poem resolves into a coherent statement on how, through the alchemy of sunlike grace, the spiritual eye's reflected divine illumination can inflame and refine the entire soul, thereby restoring its eye's capacity to emit its own light.

BIBLIOGRAPHY: Davis, T. M., *A Reading of E. T.* (1992); Gatta, J., *Gracious Laughter: The Meditative Wit of E. T.* (1989); Grabo, N. S., *E. T.* (1961; rev. ed., 1988); Hammond, J., *E. T.: Fifty Years of Scholarship and Criticism* (1993); Keller, K., *The Example of E. T.* (1975); Rowe, K. E., *Saint and Singer: E. T.'s Typology and the Poetics of Meditation* (1986); Scheick, W. J., *The Will and the Word: The Poetry of E. T.* (1974)

WILLIAM J. SCHEICK

TAYLOR, Peter [Hillsman]

b. 8 January 1917, Trenton, Tennessee; d. 2 November 1994, Charlottesville, Virginia

Like many of the characters in his fiction, T. was from the upper-middle-class South, reckoning with a world that was being undermined with the encroachments of modern civilization and its porending loss of manners, gentility, and civilization. Currently recognized as one of the masters of the short story—often compared to Chekhov and Eudora WELTY—T.'s writing career was a meticulous study in craft that also produced plays and novels.

Perhaps part of T.'s success can be attributed to his tutelage under some of the greatest writers of the American South. He studied under Allen TATE, Robert Penn WARREN, and Cleanth BROOKS, and was mentored by John Crowe RANSOM.

In 1948, T. published his acclaimed first collection of short stories, *A Long Fourth and Other Stories,* which heralded the themes that would come to characterize his work: subtle, yet painful, family conflicts; the difficult transition in status and place that accompanied the move from an agrarian setting to that of the city; and T.'s trademark emphasis on what he deemed "the pure story." The title story of this collection, "A Long Fourth," is still regarded as one of his masterpieces because it not only includes T.'s powerful observations of the antagonistic forces implicit in families but also addresses the issues of race, most specifically the relationship between whites and the blacks who served them.

In 1950, T. produced his first novel, *A Woman of Means,* which he referred to as a novelette. It is the touching story of Quint Dudley's loss of heritage and place as he acclimates to life in St. Louis with his rich stepmother. Ann Lauterbach's house, however, is filled with nuances and secrets. Gradually, the stability of Quint's newly formed family is eroded, and Mrs. Lauterbach goes mad. T.'s tightly governed prose carries the reader into the helplessness of childhood as Quint becomes a passive observer in the drama of family life.

From 1954 to 1963, T. continued to secure his place as a modern American master of the short story with his collections *The Widow of Thornton* (1954), *Happy Families Are All Alike: A Collection of Stories* (1959), and *Miss Lenora When Last Seen and Fifteen Other Stories* (1963). The latter contains "Venus, Cupid, Folly, and Time," recipient of an O. Henry Award.

For *The Old Forest and Other Stories,* T. was awarded the 1985 PEN/Faulkner Award in fiction. This collection is most noted for its careful detailing of the losses associated with the disintegration of the patrician South.

In 1987, T. gained further respect with the publication of his Pulitzer Prize-winning novel, *A Summons to Memphis.* A tour de force in the importance of place, the protagonist, Phillip Carver, is summoned from New York City to Memphis, by his two sisters, in order to stop the marriage of his eighty-one year old father. When Carver returns home, he is faced with an intricate web of resentment that is the direct result of his father's controlling nature. The novel is reminiscent of both Henry JAMES and William FAULKNER, especially the latter's use of the South's omnipresent past. Of *A Summons to Memphis,* John UPDIKE wrote that T., "like Faulkner, draws endless inspiration; he stirs and stirs the same waters, watching them darken and deepen, while abstaining from Faulkner's violent modernist gestures. He stirs instead with a Jamesian sort of spoon."

T.'s last novel, *In The Tennessee Country* (1994), is a suitable finale for a career that dwelled on a society haunted by the legacy of the Civil War. Governed by the elusiveness of T.'s prose, the novel details Nathan Longfort's journey from a sheltered childhood to a "dry-as-dust art historian." Like T.'s other works, *In the Tennessee Country* deals with the continuing conflicts the individual faces when confronted with the forces of heritage, place, and family.

Although literary critics and scholars continue to bemoan the fact that T. has never been afforded his due as one of America's preeminent writers, perhaps this gentleman's career progressed just as his life did. Both represent the understated elegance of genteel Tennesseans attempting to hold their own against the intrusions of the 20th c.

BIBLIOGRAPHY: Graham, C. G., *Southern Accents: The Fiction of P. T.* (1994); McAlexander, H. H., ed., *Critical Essays on P. T.* (1993); Robison, J. C., *P. T.: A Study of the Short Fiction* (1988); Stephens, C. R., and L. B. Salamon, eds., *The Craft of P. T.* (1995)

DEBORAH KAY FERRELL

TEASDALE, Sara

b. 8 August 1884, St. Louis, Missouri; d. 29 January 1933, New York City

T. wrote exquisite lyrics, usually in quatrains, within what may be termed the "morbid tradition" of Christian Rossetti, Elizabeth Barrett, and Emily DICKINSON. She informed her voice with past literary tradition: "that white election . . . Despair," the death of beautiful women in love, the cult of "The Lady of Shalott," the internal struggle between Spartan and Sybarite, Pagan and Puritan. Yet in form and meter, and especially in consciousness, she was no staid Victorian resigned to the austere, nunlike moral conventions of her age or of her sex. She sought to push the limits of what was expected of female poets, and her poetic agenda was the resolution through art of troubling emotion. Still, she settled on, in the heyday of modernist free verse, the rhymed, stress-metered brief lyric as her form and endeavored to make it her own. Calling her poems "songs," she worked toward simplicity and naturalness of expression, the rendering of experience rather than the inflating of it. During her career, up to the time of her suicide in 1933, she enjoyed considerable fame and national popularity. T.'s poetry is generally passed over, however, by late 20th-c. academic critics, who may find her lyricism pleasantly bland and her feminism not militant enough. Still, her work is recognized as that of a uniquely gifted and skillful poet. It could be said that even before the Imagist movement, T., despite her tendency to lull the reader with the sing-song of rhythm and rhyme, hammered for concreteness and immediacy—for the striking image.

T.'s first book, *Sonnets to Duse* (1907), written when the poet belonged to a women's arts group in her hometown St. Louis, was a tribute to the then idolized actress, Eleonora Duse, whose feminine beauty was compared to that of Sappho and Venus de Milo. The poems suggest an innocent eroticism and a cautious awakening from chastity toward sensuality. They embark on a theme of self-sufficient womanhood and independence that T. develops further in her next three collections. Romantic love, while yearned for, is viewed with a hazy, often bitterly ironic detachment, with death pursuing at every turn as in the poem, "I Shall Not Care," where the voice speaks imaginatively from beyond the grave to a silent and cold-hearted lover, declaring that in the peace of death her silence and cold-heartedness matches his. Many of the love poems revolve around a single metaphor or simile, as in "The Wave," where the record of love is like a broken wave, ebbed and gone, save the flecks of foam on the sand; or as in "The River," where love, once fresh as a rainfall, runs to meet the sea that makes it bitter. Images of water, stagnant or tempestuous, embody the shapelessness and inconstancy of desire, and love is not a sure escape from sorrow or a complete repose. Only by vanquishing the heart, she writes, is there rest.

With the end of World War I and the publication of *Flame and Shadow* (1920), T. abandoned youthful themes and adopted a more somber tone to reflect the fatalistic mood and shattered ideals of the postwar generation. She took up the study of astronomy and contemplated a religion of star worship. Star imagery is scattered throughout her poems of the 1920s, as in "September Night," with the theme self-sufficiency now likened to that of a star. She admiringly read Yeats. She started to write less, with more skill. As her poetic vision was honed and gathered, her life became increasingly debilitated by illness, physical and mental. Generating the highly rendered style and understated, almost censored, limits of her poetic statements was paradoxically an inner-raging of existential despair, what William Drake describes as a pattern of repressed conflict and self-negation that had plagued the Victorians, combined with the lack of spiritual resources for enduring such torments in the grasping chaos of the modern age. Such insight into her life's daily struggle would suggest that T.'s work reveals a progress of the mind in psychological portraits.

For T., poetry, and the act of writing it was the only safe haven, its fragile and naked walls the sole protection against the onslaughts of her troubled psyche. The poem "Refuge" builds a "house of shining words" to house her frail immortality, the poverty of which is described in "Even To-day" where a small square cottage of the mind is a lonely but cleanly house with shelves too bare to tempt a mouse. Poetry becomes precarious architecture, a small defense, but it nonetheless becomes a power, an art of "Alchemy" capable of changing the lifeless wine of grief to living gold, of lessening the burden of thought down to the unquestioning level of nature. Yet T. found that this power demanded an investment of self that was costly, as she confidently implores in her much anthologized "Barter": that for one white, singing hour of peace, many years of strife are counted well lost, and that for a breath of ecstasy, one must give everything of oneself, past and future.

BIBLIOGRAPHY: Carpenter, M. H., *S. T.: A Biography* (1960); Drake, W., *S. T.: Woman and Poet* (1979); Schoen, C., *S. T.* (1986)

H. S. YOON

TENNEY, Tabitha Gilman
b. 7 April 1762, Exeter, New Hampshire; d. 2 May 1837, Exeter, New Hampshire

With a single novel, *Female Quixotism: Exhibited in the Romantic Opinions and Extravagant Adventures of Dorcasina Sheldon* (1801), T. earned a niche in American literature. Her two-volume satire, one of the best novels and one of the better sellers of the first half of the 19th c., went through at least five editions, one as late as 1841. Prompted by critical attention to the astuteness of T.'s cultural insights, publishers have made several editions available since the 1980s.

T. received her education chiefly under her mother's direction after her father's early death. Her studies included the arts, classics, social practices, and household accomplishments, and probably influenced the content of her first literary venture, *The Pleasing Instructor* (1799), an anthology of poetry and classical pieces combining "instruction with rational amusement" for young women, as well as her 1808 publication *Domestic Cookery.*

When *Female Quixotism* appeared in 1801, T. was living in the nation's capitol, where her husband served in Congress from 1800 to 1807. The young Republic was enjoying a security that encouraged reflexive laughter. *Female Quixotism,* drawing formal inspira-

tion from Cervantes's *Don Quixote* and Charlotte Lennox's *The Female Quixote* (1752), matched that spirit.

T. dedicated *Female Quixotism* "To All Columbian Young Ladies, Who Read Novels and Romances," hoping to win their attention and that of their mentors in order to improve women's education. Her motherless, novel-reading Dorcasina cannot distinguish between reality and fiction. Ignoring the practical advice of her servant Betty, she turns down a model suitor and becomes the victim of every scoundrel she meets. Physical and psychological abuses including beatings, kidnappings, and insults finally convince Dorcasina that happiness does not depend on romantic conduct and that even an ideal marriage includes some suffering. Thus sobered, Dorcas reverts to her biblical name and turns to performing charitable deeds, yet continues reading novels, the only books for which her education has prepared her, the only joy her life affords. Her pathetic image makes T.'s point.

BIBLIOGRAPHY: Bell, C. H., *History of the Town of Exeter, New Hampshire* (1888); Caliskan, S., "The Coded Language of *Female Quixotism," StAH* 3, 2 (1995): 23–35; Davidson, C. N., *Revolution and the Word: The Rise of the Novel in America* (1986); Miecznikowski, C. J., "The Parodic Mode and the Patriarchal Imperative: Reading the Female Reader(s) in T. T.'s *Female Quixotism," EAL* 25, 1 (1990): 34–45; Petter, H., *The Early American Novel* (1971)

LUCY M. FREIBERT

TERKEL, Studs [Louis]
b. 16 May 1912, Bronx, New York

Social historian T. has lived virtually his entire life in Chicago. Earning his law degree from the University of Chicago in 1934 and subsequently becoming involved with the WPA Federal Writers' Project, T. supported himself in the 1930s by acting and dramatic writing, promoting liberal causes both on radio and onstage. During World War II, T. entertained the troops. Returning to Chicago, he advanced in local radio venues, becoming a pioneer of television, and developing a successful talk show program, *Studs' Place.* Despite its popularity, the show fell victim to the House Un-American Activities Committee in the early 1950s. When NBC demanded that T. publicly disavow suspicious charges of any past radicalism, he refused, believing nothing unpatriotic had taken place. Consequently, the network dropped "Studs' Place."

T. performed little during this time but published his first book, *Giants of Jazz,* in 1957, helping him rebound from negative publicity. When he subsequently began working for WFMT radio station, his entertainment program was an almost immediate success, soon gaining a national following. Preparing interviews for his radio broadcast, T. first discovered the usefulness of, and his affinity for, the tape recorder. Over time, he expanded from interviewing musicians to taping interviews with public figures, putting subjects at ease with an empathetic approach that encouraged their candor.

Inspired by his success, T. constructed a book around interviews with the ordinary inhabitants of an American village. The "village" was Chicago, and the resulting book, *Division Street: America,* appeared in 1967. Without a master plan, or even an outline, for his work, T. interviewed subjects scouted from throughout the city. Rarely posing consistent questions, he chose at will which sections of interviews to include and as well as edit. This method of "guerilla journalism" hardly resembles the methodical—and more accountable—techniques of the traditional historian. Critics have argued that T.'s works do not qualify as oral *history* in light of these differences. Further, some suspect that T. gravitates to subjects whose beliefs harmonize with his own, skewing the tenor of his resulting projects. Nevertheless, T.'s gripping accounts of Chicagoans' perceptions of their lives made *Division Street* a commercial success, introducing him to yet another career.

Having uncovered in *Division Street* society's widening class separation, T. devised his next work, *Hard Times: An Oral History of the Great Depression* (1970), as a "memory book" of the era. Aware that critics might scorn his lack of factual precision, T. declared a greater interest with people's personal truths and recollections than with traditional history's fastidious chronicling. His focus on employment and security led to a series of similarly themed oral histories: *Working: People Talk about What They Do All Day and How They Feel about What They Do* (1974); *American Dreams: Lost and Found* (1980); and *The Great Divide: Second Thoughts on the American Dream* (1988). *Working* shattered traditional American perceptions of workers as inspired contributors to the nation's strength, instead portraying disgruntled employees unfulfilled or embittered by their jobs. The latter two studies discuss Americans' shifting goals, finding in this theme, as in *Working,* Americans disillusioned by a system of diminishing returns. While *The Great Divide* inspired the *Chicago Tribune* to hail T. as a "nonfiction John DOS PASSOS," others believed T. chose subjects to resonate with his personal biases and emphasize his message. Though these concerns have validity, *Working,* for example, became one of the most widely-read books about American labor ever published, making the author something of a folk hero. Readers eagerly awaited his memoir, *Talking to Myself*

(1974), an engaging, though meandering, recollection of his life's highlights. A second memoir about his hometown, *Chicago* (1986), received modest attention. The book considered T.'s finest, *The Good War: An Oral History of World War II* (1985), concerned the author's own generation regarding a war whose participants still considered honorable, even exciting. Though never blindly patriotic, the emotionally effective best seller received a Pulitzer Prize in 1985.

Still concerned with the growing chasm in American society, T. focused *Race: How Blacks and Whites Think and Feel about the American Obsession* (1992) on unresolved racial tensions in America. Ironically, *Race* reached stores during the Los Angeles riots subsequent to the Rodney King verdict, demonstrating yet again T.'s uncanny anticipation of trends in Americans' collective psyche.

T. continues to broadcast, research, and lecture, remaining a political progressive who would like his books to positively impact social reform in America. Reflecting on the 20th c. and on his work over that period, octogenarian S. published *Coming of Age: The Story of Our Century by Those Who Lived It* in 1995 and *My American Century* in 1997.

BIBLIOGRAPHY: Baker, J. T., *S. T.* (1992); Parker, T., *S. T.: A Life in Words* (1996)

GINA L. TAGLIERI

TEXTUAL CRITICISM

As the phrase suggests, textual criticism is the critical examination of literary texts. Just like any other a form of criticism, it is inevitably interrogatory, evaluative, and finally speculative, even though textual critics will often use the bibliographical "facts" of a work or document's composition, production, and transmission in making interpretations such as authorial intention and textual corruption. And a "text" is both a network, a tissue, a woven pattern of words or sounds or colors or shapes (with an etymology parallel to the word "textile"), and it is at the same time the text, the authority, the thing itself. With a definition and history as complex—and even contradictory—as this, and with a technical vocabulary and a historical method not easy to master, it is perhaps no surprise that for many general readers, and even for many literary scholars, the response to the complexity of this etymology, terminology, and history is to throw up one's hands and declare that "any text will do"—for casual reading, for assignment in the classroom, and even for citation in a learned article. The problem with this counsel of despair is that, while any text will indeed "do," each text will "do" different things. This range of meaning, cultural function, and interpretation can be understood in some of the best-known "texts" of American literature.

The first edition of Herman MELVILLE's *Typee*, with its overt criticism of the activities of Christian missionaries in the South Seas, is a very different book, in structure, narrative, and ideology, from the second edition, published in the same year, for which Melville removed this culture criticism. While Melville apparently agreed that the cut version was a superior work aesthetically, the editors of the standard Newberry/Northwestern Edition of the work do not take Melville's own critique at its face value, but instead reinsert the cut sections.

The twelve-poem 1855 version of Walt WHITMAN's *Leaves of Grass* is clearly a different collection—in content, organization, intention, and reception—from the growing, evolutive editions of 1860, 1867, 1871, and so on; and, rather like other "versionist" and/or autobiographical works from other literatures, the work could only begin to be considered "finished" with the poet's death.

Those few poems of Emily DICKINSON published during her lifetime—neat, tidy, "correctly" punctuated—are not even the same type of poetic utterance as the untitled, staccato, often brusque and dense statements of the manuscripts. Moreover, recent critical work on the Dickinson fragments and working papers suggests that even the concept of the finished poem may not adequately represent her aesthetic.

T. S. ELIOT's "He Do the Police in Different Voices"—better known as *The Waste Land*—would have been a longer, more sprawling, more personal, and less apocalyptic work without the intervention of Ezra POUND. It might perhaps not have become one of the founding monuments of MODERNISM, and Eliot's poetic and cultural role might have been very different had not Pound "saved" him from "himself."

The *Esquire* version of Norman MAILER's *American Dream* (January–August 1964) not only went through major revisions in the delineation of character and plot before the novel's publication by the Dial Press in 1965, but Mailer also had to contend with the pressures of a changed political situation—between the original writing and setting for the magazine version and the first book edition, President John F. Kennedy had been assassinated, and this had major ramifications for the ironic tone and time scheme of the book: as Hershel Parker puts it, "liberties allowable with a living president [are] in bad taste with a dead one." It may be that Mailer, in attempting his revision, failed to reconcile narrative and psychological states of the two texts, resulting in a fundamentally inconsistent and flawed work.

When William STYRON submitted his first novel, *Lie Down in Darkness,* for publication in 1951, he was obviously not the famous and financially bankable author he was to become, and agreed to accept substantial cuts—especially in the sexual passages—of the novel; and yet, years later, when he was established as a successful novelist, and a uniform edition of his novels was being prepared for Random House—under a changed cultural climate with more liberal attitudes to sexuality—on reflection he decided that, while unwelcome at the time, the original editorial advice he had been given was probably sound and decided not to put back the "censored" parts.

Similarly, both Theodore DREISER's *Sister Carrie*—printed in 1900 but not published until 1907—and Stephen CRANE's *Red Badge of Courage* were subjected to substantial editorial revision before publication; but unlike Styron, neither author lived to be given the second chance to decide whether, in a completely uncensored version—and a different cultural climate—the cuts might or might not be restored. There have thus been longstanding and often passionate disagreements among scholars as to what exactly is the most "authoritative" state of these texts.

Typically, the editions of the papers of the Founding Fathers—Jefferson, Adams, Washington, and so on—do not adhere to the format, punctuation, capitalization of the documents themselves, but rewrite and normalize the styling for the convenience of the modern reader, unlike most editions of the equivalent literary figures in the American pantheon (Nathaniel HAWTHORNE, Melville, Henry David THOREAU, and so on), which usually regard these "surface features" or "accidentals" of an author's text to be a significant and meaningful element of expression.

When given the opportunity to revise his earlier work for the New York Edition (1907–9) of his fiction, Henry JAMES did not simply tinker with a few details; instead he rewrote much of his previously published oeuvre in the light of his current, more developed narrative and aesthetic. In general, those readers who prefer the stylistically, psychologically, and philosophically more complex James will favor the re-sophisticated New York Edition, while those preferring to see an author's corpus as it develops in style and characterization rather than as rewritten by an older man will prefer the first editions.

In a particularly embarrassing case, F. O. Matthiessen took a single phrase from the Constable Standard Edition (1922–23) of Melville's *White-Jacket,* published in 1850, and built an entire aesthetic and compositional theory upon it. Commenting on the locution "soiled fish of the sea," Matthiessen claimed that "hardly anyone but Melville could have created the shudder that results from this frightening vagueness some 'soiled fish of the sea.' The *discordia concors,* the unexpected linking of the medium of cleanliness with filth, could only have sprung from an imagination that had apprehended the terrors of the deep, of the immaterial deep as well as the physical." Unfortunately for Matthiessen's thesis, as Fredson Bowers then pointed out, the *soiled* was in fact a typographical error for *coiled,* and was thus introduced by the compositor, not by the author. Here, a single letter in a text can have enormous critical implications, and a critic's ignorance of—or more likely indifference to—the historical and technical research of textual criticism can produce erroneous implications. Matthiessen committed suicide not long after Bowers's exposure.

Most authors make mistakes of fact—perhaps most famously, Keats's assertion that it was "stout Cortez" rather than Balboa who first saw the Pacific Ocean. In *Billy Budd* (never published by Melville but existing only in manuscript), the author's "error" over the rank of "Vice"—historically "Rear"—Admiral Nelson is corrected in the Hayford-Sealts "reading" or critical edition of the novella. And in a feisty, even polemical, pamphlet, *Getting It Right* (1991), Matthew J. Bruccoli has defended his practice of correcting factual inconsistencies in F. Scott FITZGERALD's *The Great Gatsby* during his tenure as general editor of the Cambridge edition: for example, that one cannot walk *east* from West 158th Street in Manhattan to Central Park, but must proceed *south.*

And a reader's anticipations and understanding of *The Great Gatsby* are subtly changed in an edition that does not use the original illustration on the dustjacket, for Fitzgerald cabled his editor, Maxwell Perkins, that he had been inspired by the design and had incorporated his features into the text of the novel: "For Christ's sake, don't give anyone that jacket. I've written it into the book." The melancholy eyes staring out over strings of carnival lights thus become not an extraneous bibliographical element but part of the composition history of the work. These few samples of what different texts will "do" give some sense of the enormous range of evidence that a textual critic must consider in deciding what it is that is "done" by these texts, and to whom and by whom. Original intention as opposed to final intention; authorial prerogative as opposed to social constraint; external reality and fact as opposed to the fictional and perhaps inconsistent world of the work; fidelity to all aspects of an author's expression versus accessibility to a modern reader; a work that is, in the terms of Roland Barthes, *lisible* or "readerly" (closed, complete, finished) as opposed to one that is *scriptible* or "writerly" (open and hospitable to continual rewriting, by the author or by other agents in the transmission—friends, relatives,

editors, readers, annotators); the technical process of production and the investigation of error introduced during this process; even the function of what Jerome McGann has dubbed the "bibliographical codes" of a text (the format, typography, illustration, as in the case of *Gatsby*) versus the "linguistic codes" (the actual words of the text): all of these matters, and much else beside, must be in the potential intellectual and scholarly armory of the textual critic.

One of protocols written into the establishment of the Modern Language Association's Center for Editions of American Authors (CEAA) was that the texts (re)constructed by the scholarly editions of the canon of American authors be technically transmittable to a more popular format. It was this social agenda that was in part responsible for the decision to favor "clear-text" editions at the CEAA (with all signs of editorial intervention removed from the text-page and instead embedded in a series of apparatuses at the end of the book): such clear-texts could easily be made available for popular consumption, and many volumes of the ongoing Library of America series, presenting the work of both canonical and emergingly canonical American authors in a uniform, accessible, and relatively inexpensive format, have simply co-opted the texts established in the heftier tomes of the CEAA editions.

The CEAA, and its successor the Center for Scholarly Editions, drew its intellectual and methodological inheritance from Anglo-American *analytical biography,* that aspect of the late 19th-c. positivist history of technology that believed in the teleology of the textual enterprise: given enough technical information (about compositorial habits, problems in imposition, and so on) it would eventually be possible to "fix" a text permanently, to create an "ideal" text that represented an authorial intention that was not manifest in the inherently corrupt documents of transmission. The process was from the known and the testable to the unknown and the immanent. This was the Anglo-American tradition, and it was imported into the editing of American literature largely through the enormous personal and institutional influence of Fredson Bowers during the 1950s and 1960s. Arguing that the pragmatic distinction made by W. W. Greg between the relative authority of "accidentals"—those "surface features" of punctuation and so on—and "substantives"—the worlds themselves—in the editing of Renaissance drama could become a systemic, almost a universally valid tool in editing at large, Bowers and his chief proselytizer G. Thomas Tanselle took Greg's thesis of "dual" or "divided" authority between substantives and accidentals and applied the principle to various other fields, most notably American literature.

But where Greg had made his distinction based on the supposition that Renaissance authors had very little control over the accidentals of their texts (and that the authoritative text would therefore be an eclectic mixing of the accidentals of an early stage of transmission as close as possible to likely authorial habits of expression with authorial substantives that could be shown to have been introduced by the author in later stages of the textual transmission) Bowers and Tanselle now confronted the texts of later periods in which the problem was not so much the lack of evidence for authorial preferences but its opposite: in the 19th and 20th cs., we often had multiple authorial stages of vision and revision, and rather than retreat into a single and ideal "text that never was"—supposedly embodying a similarly singular authorial act of composition and volition—some critics of the Greg-Bowers eclectic-text method have declared that it is this very superfluity of documentary evidence that should be celebrated, especially as it might demonstrate the role of collaborative, socialized, and receptional influences on the construction of this later literature.

By deemphasizing the role of editorial "criticism" of the text and by claiming objective historical "fact" for the words on the clear-text pages, those CEAA editions are not only more susceptible to copying in the purely technical sense (there are no editorial symbols to remove from the text), but the more they argue for their "definitiveness" rather than critical provisionality, the more analogous they may become to the objective or mere fact. In such highly uncertain and speculative moments as now, we can observe both in theory and in practice just how embedded textual criticism is in the cultural prejudices and social expectations of its time. Textual criticism has a long history, from the attempts of the Alexandrian librarians in the 3rd c. B.C.E. to establish the text of Homer down to the hypertext publication and dissemination of some contemporary literature and its critique is both reflective of its social circumstances and in part determinative of them.

BIBLIOGRAPHY: Bowers, F., *Textual and Literary Criticism* (1966); Greetham, D. C., ed., *Scholarly Editing: A Guide to Research* (1995); Greg, W. W., "The Rationale of Copy Text," *SB* 3 (1950–51): 19–36; Landow, G. P., *Hypertext: The Convergence of Contemporary Critical Theory and Technology* (1992); Landow, G. P., *Hyper/Text/Theory* (1994); McGann, J. J., ed., *Textual Criticism and Literary Interpretation* (1985); McKenzie, D. F., *Bibliography and the Sociology of Texts* (1986); Parker, H., *Flawed Texts and Verbal Icons: Literary Authority in American Fiction* (1984); Tanselle, G. T., "The Editorial Problem of Final Authorial Intention," *SB* 29 (1976): 167–211; Tanselle, G. T., "External Fact as an Editorial Problem," *SB* 32 (1979): 1–47; Wilson, E., *The Fruits of the MLA* (1986)

DAVID GREETHAM

THAXTER, Celia [Laighton]

b. 29 June 1835, Portsmouth, New Hampshire; d. 26 August 1894, Appledore Island, Isles of Shoals, Maine

Possibly the most widely published woman poet in the latter half of the 19th c., T. is today more admired for her nonfiction prose essays *Among the Isles of Shoals* (1873) and *An Island Garden* (1894), considered masterpieces of realist description.

She was born in the seaport of Portsmouth, New Hampshire, and reared on a rugged, desolate island ten miles off the coast where her father was the lighthouse keeper. T.'s early awareness of the indifference of the elements became a major theme in her poetry, which, unlike sentimentalist verse of the day, provides no religious consolation. At the same time, she appreciated the spare beauty of her locale, which is powerfully transmitted throughout her writings. As an adult, T. became the center of a summer artists' coterie that gathered on the Isles of Shoals. It attracted many of the literary and artistic luminaries of the day, including Nathaniel HAWTHORNE, Henry David THOREAU, Ralph Waldo EMERSON, John Greenleaf WHITTIER, James Russell LOWELL, Samuel Langhorne CLEMENS, Charlotte Cushman, Ole Bull, Lucy Larcom, Sarah Orne JEWETT, Annie and James T. Fields (T.'s primary editor), William Morris Hunt, and Childe Hassam. The latter painted several remarkable impressionist paintings of T., her garden, and the islands, which are now in the Smithsonian. She herself was an accomplished watercolorist.

T.'s first poem, "Land-Locked," appeared in the *Atlantic Monthly* in 1861, and her first collection, *Poems,* was published in 1871 and followed by several revised editions. Other works include *Drift-Weed* (1878), *Poems for Children* (1884), *The Cruise of the Mystery* (1886), *Idyls and Pastorals* (1886), and *My Lighthouse and Other Poems* (1890). Published posthumously were *Stories and Poems for Children* (1895), *The Letters of C. T.* (1895), and *The Heavenly Guest and Other Unpublished Writings* (1935).

BIBLIOGRAPHY: Curry, D. P., *Childe Hassam: An Island Garden Revisited* (1990); Thaxter, R., *Sandpiper: The Life of C. T.* (1962); Vallier, J. E., *Poet on Demand: The Life, Letters and Works of C. T.* (1982); White, B. A., "C. T.," *Legacy* 7 (Spring 1990): 59–64

JOSEPHINE DONOVAN

THEROUX, Paul

b. 10 April 1941, Medford, Massachusetts

Whether as essayist, travel writer, or novelist, most of T.'s published works seem to contain the common thread of being written from the perspective of the outsider looking in. This is not surprising in an author who has lived the greater part of his life as an expatriate, if not quite an exile from his native country—and this outsider status is something that marks many of T.'s fictional characters as well.

T.'s fiction is particularly autobiographical, drawing heavily upon a life spent in one foreign clime after another, beginning with work in the Peace Corps. The time he spent teaching English in Malawi, Africa, ended when T. was falsely branded a spy largely as a result of his friendship with a number of that country's out-of-favor political leaders. However, T. returned to Africa shortly after being expelled from the Peace Corps, this time to teach at Makerere University in Uganda with his wife. In 1966, the author V. S. Naipaul visited Makerere, and as a relationship developed between the two men, Naipaul—who at that time felt himself to be an exile from his native Trinidad in a literal sense—became something of an unofficial mentor for T.

Shortly afterward, T. began his career in fiction with *Waldo* (1967), an episodic novel that earned high praise in many quarters, particularly for its amusing vignettes, yet drew criticism from others for its for "wander[ing] along . . . without much sense of direction." T.'s next three novels—*Fong and the Indians* (1968), *Girls at Play* (1969), and *Jungle Lovers* (1971)—were written after T. had moved to Singapore, and shared a common African setting. Singapore was used as a setting in T.'s 1973 work *Saint Jack,* but only after T. had left his teaching position at the University of Singapore and had relocated to England with his wife and children. *Saint Jack,* a first-person narrative about a middle-aged, expatriate pimp, was later made into a well-received film.

T.'s travel works are, perhaps, more widely read than his fiction, particularly *The Great Railway Bazaar: By Train through Asia* (1975), *The Old Patagonian Express: By Train through the Americas* (1979), which documents travels through Central and South America, *The Kingdom by the Sea: A Journey around Great Britain* (1985), and *The Pillars of Hercules* (1996), T.'s "grand tour" of the Mediterranean. T. looked again at the Far East in works such as *The Imperial Way: By Rail from Peshwar to Chittagong* (1985) and *Riding the Iron Rooster: By Train through China* (1988), and he later returned to consideration of the Americas in the 1986 work *Patagonia Revisited,* which was written with the late Bruce Chatwin, and

later in *Nowhere is a Place: Travels in Patagonia* (1992).

Although T. has developed a strong interest in travel writing and essays—notably in the 1985 collection of "travels and discoveries" entitled *Sunrise with Seamonsters*—he has continued to pursue his work in fiction. Particularly autobiographical works include *The Mosquito Coast* (1982), which was adapted into a well-received 1986 film starring Harrison Ford, and *My Secret History* (1989). T.'s more recent works of fiction, such as *O-Zone* (1986), *Chicago Loop* (1990), and *Milroy the Magician* (1994), have largely abandoned foreign locales as settings, yet still contain the theme of the outsider looking in.

BIBLIOGRAPHY: Coale, S., *P. T.* (1987); Glaser, E., "The Self-Reflexive Traveler: P. T. on the Art of Travel and Travel Writing," *CentR* 33 (1989): 193–206

ELIZABETH HADDRELL

THOMAS, Augustus

b. 8 January 1857, St. Louis, Missouri; d. 12 August 1934, near Nyack, New York

Few, if any, of T.'s thirty-five full-length original plays are found on stages today. To the modern theatergoer, T.'s plots appear melodramatic and his characters altogether conventional. His contribution to American drama, however, was, and in many ways remains, palpable. Certainly the American Society of Arts and Letters believed it to be so when, in 1924, they bestowed on him their gold medal, the highest award for an American playwright. T. was one of the first American dramatists to create thoroughly American plays and insist on American history, characters, and themes as suitable material for the stage. To judge by his nearly continuous successes on stage and off between 1891—the year of his first great success, *Alabama*—and 1924—when he ended his two-year tenure as executive chairman of the Producing Managers' Association—the public and critics in both America and Europe agreed with him.

Like many gifted playwrights, T. acquired an intensely varied education, though he ended his regular schooling at the age of ten and left off even sporadic school attendance by thirteen. He managed, nonetheless, to serve as a page to the Missouri Assembly in 1868 and to the U.S. Congress in 1870–71. He spent nine years working for the St. Louis Railroad, eventually leading—despite being legally underage—the local chapter of the Knights of Labor in their strikes against railroad management. In the early 1880s, he studied law and had a serious intention to go into practice, but he then changed his direction and from

1885 to 1888 worked first as a reporter for the St. Louis *Dispatch,* and then as half-owner and editor of the Kansas City *Mirror.* All through the 1870s and 1880s, T. spent increasing amounts of time working behind-the-scenes in theaters, taking on larger and larger acting roles, touring the country in regionally-produced plays, and writing increasingly complex dramas. In 1899, his play *The Burglar* was produced in New York, and he finally devoted himself entirely to a professional life in the theater, though he remained throughout his life actively involved in politics and an avid traveler both at home and abroad.

T.'s diverse experiences and early theater work helped him to bring two important qualities to bear on his dramas. He possessed both keen interest in and intimate knowledge of regional and political characters and issues, and he developed and consistently promulgated an exacting theory of dramaturgy. As one of his biographers explains, "The play, T. believed, should tap the contemporary collective subconscious of America and express nobility, charity, and other racial ideals embedded in the subconscious. Thus, T. defined the good and successful play as articulating an idea deeply felt by the author and the public." Throughout his career, T. insisted on the idea that drama was principally for the public, that it was the art form best suited to educate and inspire the common individual, and that because of these things the playwright himself had an unavoidable moral obligation to himself, his public, and his craft.

T.'s major successes are also where his theories of drama and love of the common American come across most clearly. A nearly permanent characteristic of T.'s plays is the lack of a distinguishable villain, and sometimes even of a clearly defined hero. It is a signal feature of T.'s plays—one that occasionally caused serious critical debates—that "villains" are merely underdeveloped characters who impede or cannot themselves follow the obviously right, decent, and noble course of action that the play proposes. Heroes are not aggrandized characters, but merely the figures who live decently. This dramatic structure along with the tendency to gravitate in both subject matter and artistic intention toward the lives and needs of the common individual distinguish T., perhaps more than any other American playwright of the late 19th and early 20th cs., as one of the great precursors of the modern age of American drama.

BIBLIOGRAPHY: Bergman, H., "A Forgotten Landmark in Dramatic Realism," *Midamerica* 3 (1976): 92–100; Davis, R. J., *A. T.* (1984)

JOHN V. GLASS

THOMAS, Piri [John Peter]
b. 30 September 1928, New York City

One of the first Puerto Rican writers in the U.S. to achieve critical acclaim, T. is known primarily for his groundbreaking autobiography *Down These Mean Streets* (1967), a candid portrayal of an adolescent Puerto Rican male coming of age on the inner city streets of Spanish Harlem. Taking his readers through a shocking labyrinth of racism, violence, and drug addiction, T. provides firsthand exposure to the tumultuous world of the urban Puerto Rican subculture.

Set in the 1940s and 1950s, *Down These Mean Streets* chronicles T.'s quest for racial identity, dignity, and manhood—themes that recur in T.'s later works and prove central to Puerto Rican literature as a whole. The dark-skinned T., who is often mistaken for African American, becomes increasingly tormented as he questions his place in a racist society. Rejected by his father and longing for a male role model, T. leaves home a strong-willed teenager in search of meaning and purpose. Disillusioned and embittered by the injustices and discrimination he encounters, T. begins using heroin, commits armed robbery, and almost fatally wounds an off-duty police officer. While serving a seven year prison sentence, T. realizes the self-defeating consequences of his actions and undergoes transformation. T. earns his high school diploma, studies philosophy, theology, and psychology; and begins recording his life experiences.

Much controversy surrounded the initial publication of *Down These Mean Streets.* Accused of being obscene, vulgar, and irresponsible, the book was banned by school districts and libraries throughout the U.S. for its use of profanity and its explicit rendering of taboo social topics. Interspersing urban street talk with English dialect peppered with Spanish, T. graphically details the illicit life he knew. Like Claude Brown's *Manchild in the Promised Land* (1965) and Eldridge Cleaver's *Soul on Ice* (1967), *Down These Mean Streets* serves as a powerful testimony of survival despite seemingly insuperable odds.

T.'s subsequent autobiographical narratives, *Saviour, Saviour Hold My Hand* (1972) and *Seven Long Times* (1974), have received far less recognition. T. explores similar themes, yet his later works lack the force and urgency of *Down These Mean Streets.* Both his tone and language are muted, his characters are less developed, and his experience is somewhat distant. *Saviour, Saviour Hold My Hand* chronicles T.'s life as an ex-convict, his decision to marry, and his struggles with Christianity, while *Seven Long Times* is a retelling of his years incarcerated and an argument for prison reform.

T. has also written a collection of short stories for young adults, *Stories from El Barrio* (1978), about growing up in Spanish Harlem; several plays including *The Golden Street,* which was performed in Puerto Rico in 1972; and two television documentaries, *Petey and Johnny* and *The World of P. T.* Through his writings and public service, T. has dedicated his life to reforming inner city youths. Known by many within the Puerto Rican community as the father of Puerto Rican literature in the U.S., T.'s success has inspired a multitude of Puerto Rican American writers.

BIBLIOGRAPHY: Mohr, E. V., "Lives from El Barrio," *RC-R* 8, 4 (1980): 60–79; Stavans, I., "Race and Mercy: A Conversation with P. T.," *MR* 37 (Autumn 1996): 344–54

SALINDA LEWIS

THOMPSON, Jim [James Meyers]

b. 1906, Anadarko, Oklahoma; d. 7 April 1976 or 1977, Hollywood, California

T. is the unequivocal king of the pulp fiction novelists, a title that, unfortunately, has received little attention or respect. His paperback novels feature lurid renderings of violent thoughts and actions common to hardboiled detective fiction, but there is a significant difference: in the detective story, the narrator is usually a "good guy," on the side of law and order and sanity, although he may be a little shady himself or is perceived as being "crooked"; in T.'s thrillers, however, the narrator is usually a "bad guy" and the story is told through the point of view of a miscreant. These characters exhibit criminal and sociopathic behavior that includes murder, sadism, incest, kidnapping, and mutilation. These are the narrators who take us aside, get our confidence, and tell us all about the horrible things they do; the skillful use of the narrative voice is the edge that makes this genre so powerful. It is also an edge honed razor-sharp by T.'s straightforward journalistic style.

Despite his fictionalized autobiography, *Bad Boy* (1953), T.'s background is as mysterious as his novels. He claimed to have been an oil pipeline worker, a steeplejack, a burlesque comedian, and professional gambler. In the early 1930s, he was a reporter for the *New York Daily News* and the *Los Angeles Times-Union.* He was also associated with the Federal Writers' Project during the 1930s. He authored twenty-nine novels, all of which are acknowledged classics of hard-boiled pulp fiction; he authored a collection of short stories, *Fireworks* (1988); and coauthored, with Stanley Kubrick, the screenplay for *The Killing* (1956) adapted from the novel *Clean Break* (1955)

by Lionel White; he also coauthored, with Kubrick and Calder Willingham, the screenplay for *Paths of Glory* (1957) adapted from the novel of the same title by Humphrey Cobb. Several of his novels, *The Getaway* (1972), *The Killer Inside Me* (1976), *Pop. 1280* (for the film *Coup de Torchon* [1981]), *After Dark, My Sweet* (1990), *The Kill-Off* (1990), and *The Grifters* (1990), have been adapted for the screen.

T. produced mystery and suspense novels that are fraught with immorality and exploration of the criminal mind, presenting depraved antagonists who are involved in theft, sadomasochism, and murder. His narratives, however, have drawn favorable comparisons to such writers as James M. CAIN, Raymond CHANDLER, and Dashiell HAMMETT. Lawrence Block, writing for the *New York Times,* said that T. "at his best casts the coldest possible eye on life and death and offers us an unsparing view of the human condition." Meredith Brody, in *Film Comment,* claims that T.'s "body of work may be the most disturbing and the most darkly sadistic of the tough-guy writers." Davis Thomson, a critic for the *New Republic,* states that T. was "one of the finest American writers and the most frightening, the one on best terms with the devil."

Published in 1953, *The Killer Inside Me* is considered to be T.'s best novel. According to R. V. Cassill, Arnold Hano, the editor of Lion Books who commissioned the novel, said that T. wrote the manuscript in two weeks. The novel is "packed with . . . hard breathing clichés of literature for the working man. . . . Yet in T.'s hands the paperback original turns out to be excellently suited to the objectives of the novel of ideas." T., in Cassill's estimation, "makes a hard, scary, Sophoclean statement about American success: Even if you are a rotten, murderous piece of excrement and know it, you're supposed to go on and succeed."

Lou Ford, the central character of *The Killer Inside Me,* is a deputy sheriff in a small and busy Oklahoma city. He is a social success. The townfolk like him and depend on him, and Lou shows them that he has a heart; he does not carry a firearm, his talk is cheerful and optimistic and he laughs a lot, almost too much. Beneath the laughing and jovial surface of the lawman lurks a schizophrenic, sadistic, and murderous personality. T. does not take the easy way and simply present to the reader the bloody course of a murderous, criminal schizophrenic; Cassill states that "T. shows us the meaning of the sort we search for when we ask the meaning of a crucifixion or of the massacre of the innocents." In general, the substance of T.'s work can be summed as the battle between the good and evil in us all, and the particular seduction of the evil.

BIBLIOGRAPHY: Breen, J. L., and M. H. Greenberg, eds., *Murder off the Rack: Critical Studies of Ten*

Paperback Masters (1989); Madden, D., ed., *Tough Guy Writers of the Thirties* (1968); Polito, R., *Savage Art: A Biography of J. T.* (1995)

JOSEPH FERRANDINO

THOMPSON, [James] Maurice

b. 9 September 1844, Fairfield, Indiana; d. 15 February 1901, Crawfordsville, Indiana

Lawyer, editor, naturalist, critic, and poet, T. is now best known as a writer of romances set in Indiana and the South. His life in those parts of the country, his reading of their history and close observation of nature, furnished T. the materials for the many books that have become period pieces in their genteel shunning of the modern, the urban, the foreign, and the realistic. Rendering of scenery and sentiment, dialect and humor, make the early *Hoosier Mosaics* (1875) and *Stories of the Cherokee Hills* (collected in 1898) part of the local color tradition in Indiana and Georgia. In his later works, T. continued to promote the worth of simple, Christian, middle-class American values, defending the romance as the form best suited to presenting images of a better and more heroic life.

Beginning with the somewhat gothic Florida novel *The Mill of God* (1869), T. produced a number or romances dealing with contemporary institutions and manners, always with an emphasis on plot and a conventional love story. Progressive in its praise of the New South, *A Tallahassee Girl* (1882) nonetheless expresses a strong nostalgia for the Old South—and the Southerner gets the girl; in *His Second Campaign* (1883), the Southern heroine marries a Chicagoan. Sectional contrasts are also central to the autobiographical *A Banker of Bankersville* (1886), sometimes considered T.'s best and most realistic novel, in which an ex-Rebel adjusts to life in the North. The Birmingham steel industry is the backdrop for *At Love's Extremes* (1885). The fictional satire *A Fortnight of Folly* (1888) inveighs against the methods and subjects of other American writers, especially the materialism and candor of the realists.

The historical romance allowed T. a greater freedom to indulge his love of adventure and the ideal. *The King of Honey Island* (1893) culminates in the Battle of New Orleans. T.'s national reputation was made late in his life by the best-selling *Alice of Old Vincennes* (1900). The brave and patriotic Alice Roussillon becomes the fictional counterpart to the equally heroic George Rogers Clark. The winning of the Old Northwest Territory from the British, typical of novels of this turn-of-the-century vogue, ironically serves the ethnocentric purpose of praising an Anglo-American tradition; Alice is in the end revealed to be neither

French nor Catholic as she marries Lieutenant Fitzhugh Beverley and settles down with him in aristocratic Virginia.

BIBLIOGRAPHY: Nicholson, M., *The Hoosiers* (1900); Wheeler, O. B., *The Literary Career of M. T.* (1965)

BENJAMIN S. LAWSON

THOMPSON, William Tappan

b. 3 August 1812, Ravenn, Ohio; d. 24 March 1882, Savannah, Georgia

Among the most widely reprinted humorists during the 19th c., T. is today remembered as one of the humorists of the Old Southwest. Yet his preference for domestic incidents that would not offend genteel readers distinguishes him from others in this group, who are generally praised by scholars for their earthy realism and often brutal humor.

T. gained popularity by creating the character of Major Joseph Jones of Pineville, a small planter who sent dialect letters to the Georgia newspapers T. edited in the early 1840s. The *New York Spirit of the Times,* a sporting weekly that promoted regional humor, reprinted them, and T. soon published them in revised form in Carey and Hart's Library of Humorous American Works under the title *Major Jones's Courtship* (1844). The major's letters describe the county militia, his visits to Macon and Madison, and his courtship and eventual marriage to Mary Stallings—activities that provide much material for gentle satire of both contemporary fashions and human nature. Frequently, laughter comes at the expense of Jones himself, who is neither as well educated nor as refined as his bride.

Major Jones did not appear in *Chronicles of Pineville* (1845), a collection of previously published sketches in the tradition of Augustus Baldwin LONGSTREET's *Georgia Scenes*. However, as editor of a newspaper in Baltimore from 1846 to 1848, T. again used the major for a series of letters recounting adventures in the North and Canada. Collected as *Major Jones's Sketches of Travel* (1848), they balance laughter at Jones's unfamiliarity with urban life against the author's respect for his proslavery sentiments. Although a primarily humorous figure, Major Jones displays the rising sectionalism that characterized Southern politics in the 1840s.

BIBLIOGRAPHY: Blair, W., and H. Hill, *America's Humor* (1978); Budd, L. J., "Gentlemanly Humorists of the Old South," *SFQ* 17 (December 1953): 232–40; Miller, H. P., "The Background and Significance of *Major Jones's Courtship,*" *GHQ* 30 (December 1946): 267–96; Osthaus, C. R., "From the Old South to the

New South: The Editorial Career of W. T. T. of the *Savannah Morning News*," *SoQ* 14 (April 1976): 237–60

DAVID C. ESTES

THOMSON, Mortimer [Neal]

b. 2 September 1831, Riga, New York; d. 25 June 1875, New York City

Widely known during the height of his popularity by his pseudonym, Q. K. Philander Doesticks, P. B. (Q. K. for queer kritter and P. B. for perfect brick), T., between 1855 and 1860, enjoyed brief prominence as one of the chief exemplars of literary humor of the urban Northeast. Focusing mainly on the emerging social classes of this region, particularly of New York City, he introduced a series of memorably amusing urban types, whom he consistently portrayed from an unidealized and burlesque perspective. Moreover, he typically exploited in his representative works humorous and clever verbal antics and a narrative strategy featuring a naive persona who functions as a vehicle for exposing shams and hypocrisy. Such techniques would subsequently be adopted by the "Literary Comedians" of the Civil War period, especially Charles Farrar BROWNE and Mark TWAIN.

T. spent his formative years in Ann Arbor, Michigan. His first book, *Doesticks. A Poetical Letter from Q. K. Philander Doesticks, P. B., to His Younger Brother Containing a Thousand and One Lines* (1855), a work that was printed for private circulation by Edwin A. Wales, the owner of the *Detroit Advertiser,* employs a vain and self-confident persona. An extended burlesque employing many hilarious personal allusions, *A Poetical Letter* anticipates the stylistic boldness T. would employ more skillfully in his subsequent works.

After moving to New York City in 1854, T. began writing a series of sketches, likewise under the Doesticks pseudonym, ridiculing many and varied facets of Gotham society. Most of these sketches were first published in the *Detroit Advertiser;* others appeared in the *New York Daily Tribune* and the *Spirit of the Times.* In the summer of 1855, about the time T. joined the *Tribune* as a reporter, he published *Doesticks: What He Says* (1855), his most significant work. A compilation of many of his former newspaper satires, mainly those set in New York, *Doesticks* employs a persona, a simple-minded and naive newcomer through whom T. ridicules a broad range of concerns, some of the more humorous being living conditions in boarding houses, theatrics, popular dramatic productions and other amusements, municipal services, religious fanaticism and spiritualism, and patent medicine remedies. In treating these subjects, T. uses an impressive repertoire of comic strategies, including word play, intentionally mangled syntax and disjointed sentences, farcical descriptions, ironic and sometimes ludicrous comparisons, comic catalogs, and sarcastic asides.

Capitalizing on the popularity of *Doesticks: What He Says,* T., for the next five years, continued to write books exemplifying his spirited and irreverent brand of humor. During this period, he produced five book-length works and a play at the rapid rate of at least one major work per year, while at the same time he was penning shorter pieces for magazines, such as the *New York Picayune* (which he also edited from 1857 to 1858) and the *New Yorker,* as well as writing drama reviews and feature articles for the *Tribune. Plu-ri-bus-tah, A Song That's-By-No-Author* (1856) was a lengthy poem parodying the trochaic metrics of Henry Wadsworth LONGFELLOW's *The Song of Hiawatha* and burlesquing, in the form of a satiric allegory, recognizable aspects of American social history, including the Pilgrim settlers, the Revolutionary War, the slavery controversy, and the Civil War. The common target of T.'s satire is the American love of money and unrelenting pursuance of the materialistic ethic. *The History and Records of the Elephant Club* (1856), a collaboration with Edward F. Underhill, focuses on the comically bizarre misadventures of a group of newcomers to New York City whose chief preoccupation is to explore the "Metropolitan Elephant" as fully as possible. The police-court sketches, characterized by engaging verbal humor and comprised of sketches T. had previously published in the *Tribune,* are the most entertaining sections of the book. *Nothing to Say* (1857), a 306-line poetic parody of William Allen Butler's popular satire on women's fashions, "Nothing to Wear," employs the structure of an allegorical journey of the Spirit of Cant, an impish fellow, and his female guide Charity. T. portrays these characters on their various excursions in a deprecating manner. In response to what he observes in his wanderings, Cant simply has "nothing to say"; his silence, contrary to the claims of Butler's "Nothing to Wear," shows that the wealthy have indeed extended generous assistance to the poor and downtrodden. *The Witches of New York* (1858) graphically debunks the disreputable and criminal activities of Gotham's fortune-tellers, sorceresses, and clairvoyants, all of whom have unflattering traits and hideous appearances, exhibit vulgar mannerisms and duplicity, and issue outrageous and incredible prophesies. *The Great Auction Sale of Slaves at Savannah, Georgia* (1859), T.'s last principal work, was published in the *New York Tribune* under the headline "American Civilization Illustrated: A Great Slave Auction" on March 9, 1859, and was subsequently reprinted as a pamphlet by the American Anti-Slavery Society. Based on an actual sale that T. observed first-hand on March 2 and 3, 1859, *The Great Auction Sale,* a caustic work exposing some of the worst inhumanities of Southern slavery, adroitly uses such devices as consciously crafted stylistic sentences, emotionally charged language (sometimes combined with overt editorializing), caricature, and verbal irony to communicate its message of abolitionist protest.

T.'s only play, *The Lady of the Lake* (1860), a one-act travesty of Sir Walter Scott's 1810 poem by the same title, and characterized by melodrama, caricature, and numerous puns, enjoyed a brief run at Niblo's Garden in New York City. And *The Adventures of Snoozer, a Sleepwalker* (1876), published posthumously, chronicles in an exaggerated manner a series of amusing episodes of a somnambulist, Abijah Jeremia Skillibob Snoozer. In focusing on Snoozer's escapades, T. likewise burlesques selected social concerns of contemporary urban life.

In the late 1860s and 1870s, T. contributed humorous short sketches to various magazines, most notably to Street and Smith's *New York Weekly,* and for a year worked on the *Minneapolis Tribune* before returning to New York to assume the editorship of *Leslie's Illustrated,* a position he held until his death in 1875.

BIBLIOGRAPHY: Lorch, F. W., "'Doesticks' and *Innocents Abroad,*" *AL* 20 (January 1949): 446–49; Piacentino, E. J., "M. N. T.," in Gale, S. H., ed., *Encyclopedia of American Humorists* (1988): 437–41; Piacentino, E. J., "'Seeing the Elephant': Doesticks' Satires of Nineteenth-Century Gotham," *StAH* 5 (Summer-Fall 1986): 134–44; Sloane, D. E. E., "M. T. (Q. K. Philander Doesticks, P. B.)," in Trachtenberg, S., ed., *DLB,* vol. 11, part 2, *American Humorists, 1800–1950* (1982): 491–97

EDWARD J. PIACENTINO

THOREAU, Henry David

b. 12 July 1817, Concord, Massachusetts; d. 6 May 1862, Concord, Massachusetts

T. is best known as the author of *Walden* (1854), the best book in American literature on how to live a deliberate and focused life of material simplicity, intense joy, and perpetual intellectual discovery, and on how best to understand the individual person in the context of nature before—but not in place of—society. He is also remembered as the author of "Civil Disobedience," which rises above being merely a protest against slavery, unjust wars, immoral taxes, and corrupt government to articulate a general principle and thereby to stand as one of the world's preeminent statements of the supremacy of the individual conscience.

T. was a native of Concord, Massachusetts, where he spent almost all of his life. Concord was the center of his world, and it is appropriate that his work teaches us how to find the entire world by staying at home. T. came by his wit and his social conscience from his mother, Cynthia Dunbar, a lively woman active in reform, especially in the antislavery movement. From his father, John Thoreau, T. learned the family business of pencil manufacturing. T. was sent to Harvard, where he showed an interest in classics, in modern languages, and in English poetry. The most valuable thing he gained from college, he later said, was learning how to write.

Graduating from college in 1837, T. began reading Goethe. He met Ralph Waldo EMERSON, and began keeping a journal. The friendship with Emerson was a decisive turning in his life. He read Emerson's *Nature,* and came quickly to share Emerson's philosophical point of view, which is usually called TRANSCENDENTALISM, but which may also be thought of as American idealism, modern Platonism, or American Kantianism. Its central idea, as put by J. A. Saxon in the fifth issue of *The Dial,* is "the recognition in man of the capacity of knowing truth intuitively." Emerson encouraged T. to undertake a life of reading, writing, and lecturing, and persuaded him to start keeping a journal.

The best of T.'s poetry was written early, before he began to work seriously on his prose. T. is not a major poet, though there are a few excellent poems in *Walden,* including "Smoke" and "Haze," and there are a few fine poems in which the usually reticent T. lays bare his innermost feelings. The poem beginning "I am a bundle of vain strivings" is probably his best poem.

In 1842, following the tragic deaths of his older brother and of Emerson's five-year-old son, to whom T. was very close, T. wrote his first important essay, "The Natural History of Massachusetts." Ostensibly a review of four scientific reports, the essay exhibits several of T.'s most characteristic themes: the healthfulness of nature, joy as the most important quality of life, the seasonal cycle of all natural life, the mythical method of nature, and the unexplored wildness of both the world and its inhabitants. The essay is also marked by T.'s characteristically close observation of nature and by his eager interest in science.

"The Natural History of Massachusetts" was published in *The Dial,* the short-lived but influential magazine of the transcendentalists that was edited by Margaret FULLER from 1840 to 1842, and by Emerson from 1842 until its demise in 1844. T. translated Aeschylus' *Prometheus Bound* for *The Dial,* as well as poetry by

Pindar and Anacreon. Throughout his writing life, the classics were to be a source of power for T. He also wrote literary essays—one on Persius, one on Homer, Ossian, and Chaucer—and he edited selections from "ethnical scriptures" outside the Christian tradition, including "The Laws of Menu," "Sayings of Confucius," "Chinese Four Books," and "Hermes Trismegistus," all for *The Dial*.

"A Walk to Wachusett," published in 1843, shows T.'s favorite literary form, the excursion, fully developed. This piece, in the tradition of Virgil and Wordsworth, is a celebration of the countryside, written in a gentle and sociable tone, but with an attractive streak of wildness both in the scenery and in the writing. "A Winter Walk," also published in 1843, is an evocative and lyrical short piece, a miniature excursion containing some of T.'s best natural description.

In 1845, T. built a hut on some land owned by Emerson on the north shore of Walden Pond (actually a sixty-one-acre lake) a mile and a quarter from the Concord railroad station. Here he lived, off and on, for the next two years, a life of experimental primitivism, designed as he said to find out what are the real essentials, the grossest groceries of life. T.'s symbolic withdrawal from family and society in search of his own best self is one of the two events that have consistently attracted attention to the life of T.—a life that is finally, because of the pointedly autobiographical nature of most of his writing, inseparable from his literary achievement. T.'s secular monasticism—he fell in love once but never married—produced an important clarification of the relation of the individual to nature; it also produced an astonishing amount of writing. During the two years and two months T. spent at Walden Pond, he wrote his first book, a first draft of his second book, one third of another book—*The Maine Woods*—his essay on Carlyle, and his famous essay "Civil Disobedience."

A Week on the Concord and Merrimack Rivers, published in 1849, is T.'s first book. It is built around an 1839 river trip T. took with his brother John, and is in some ways an elegy, a prose "Lycidas" for John. The mild New England river trip becomes, in T.'s account, an epic voyage, told with often-humorous detail, from Concord up to a point near Mt. Washington and back. But the book is much more than travelogue. It is loosely organized series of meditations on a wide variety of subjects, including bravery, friendship, the history of colonial New England, the fate of the American Indian, and religion. T.'s interest in Oriental thought and religion (see THE ORIENT) may be seen in *A Week,* where he makes direct use of the Bhagavad Gita and its dialogue between Krishna and Arjoona. Krishna says it is right and proper to fight. Arjoona may be persuaded, T. says, "but the reader is not." A

major aspect of *A Week* is its treatment of religion. T. expresses impatience with the outward forms of Christianity, including the stultifying indolence of keeping the sabbath, and while he says little about Hebrew or Christian Scriptures, he treats Hindu scriptures and Greek pantheism at length and with sympathy. *A Week* is T.'s most diffuse, least focused book, often frustrating as a whole, but made up of many sections that are brilliant or memorable in their own right. There is a splendid account of Asian mythology—treated as a serious and religious analogue to the Hebrew tradition—in T.'s account of *The Laws of Menu* as translated by Sir William Jones. In the "Friday" chapter, there is a superb account and definition of the methods of modern science.

T. took time out from his life at Walden Pond in 1846 to travel to Maine, where he climbed Mt. Katahdin—a trip he quickly wrote up as "Ktaadn." Written in a simple, nonmetaphorical style, with great emphasis on clear description of the land, "Ktaadn" shows T. encountering the *real* wilderness—as opposed to the strictly symbolic wilderness of Walden Pond—and it continues T.'s lifelong interest in Native American, as he wrestles with the problem of their "degradation" and adoption of white ways. "Ktaadn" also marks T.'s rising interest in Pre-Columbian North America, in what the continent and its inhabitants were like before the coming of the white settlers. The piece also contains one of T.'s best treatments of the powerful human drive for contact with what is irreducible and real. T. made a second trip to Maine in 1850 that he wrote up as "Chesuncook," a description of moose-hunting, and a call for the creation of national parks or preserves. He made a third trip in 1857 that he wrote up as "The Allegash and East Branch," a vivid and highly readable account of a difficult canoe trip up around and behind Katahdin in the wilderness of northern Maine, country as wild today as when T. wrote.

In late July 1846, T. spent a night in Concord Jail for refusing to pay his poll tax. T. chose this way to protest slavery and the Mexican War, which he saw not only as aggression against Mexico, but as a war to extend slavery in the U.S. Someone—it is not known who—paid his tax, and T. was released the next day. This symbolic act of civil disobedience and the essay T. wrote as a result have become cornerstones of American social and political activism. Published as "Resistance to Civil Government" in 1849, the essay is usually referred to as "Civil Disobedience." It influenced Gandhi and Martin Luther King, Jr., in the 20th c. The essay is not anarchistic or antigovernment, though it comes close to these positions in its headlong insistence on the absolute primacy of individual conscience. T. takes pains to say that what he wants is not no government, but a better government. He also argues, and this is the practical and usable part of the essay, that if one disagrees with the government one should do more than register one's disapproval by casting a vote. One should clog the system with one's whole weight. T. was willing, on this occasion, to go all the way to active disobedience for his beliefs. In not paying his poll tax, he was concretely removing his support from a government that had become unjust by requiring injustice of its citizens. "In an unjust society, the proper place for a just man is in prison."

T. also wrote the first draft of *Walden* during his time at the pond, which was, after all, a fairly short period. He lived at home with his family most of his life, he lived in Emerson's house for as long as he lived at the pond, and when he was at the pond it was as much a headquarters as a hermitage. *Walden* is generally considered his greatest achievement, though there are a few who would put his journal as high or nearly so. *Walden* describes an experiment in essential living, an effort to conduct his life deliberately, to get the most out of life, "and not, when I came to die, discover that I had not lived." The book expresses T.'s commitment to the Transcendental ideal of self-cultivation or self-development, a task that must be undertaken before other goals become practicable. T.'s description of his beanfield and his chapter on reading showing how he saw cultivating the earth and cultivating the mind as parallel, mutually sustaining activities. *Walden* is also a great modern statement of the perennially attractive philosophy of the stoics, insofar as stoicism is not just keeping a stiff upper lip, but an active concern with the duty of self-rule or self-control. The ancient stoicism of Marcus Aurelius and the modern stoicism of Emerson and T. teaches that one should turn, for the basic rules for a good and just life, not to God, not to the state, not to history, or society, but to nature.

The opening chapter of *Walden,* and the longest, is called "Economy"; it lays out a modern economics of individualism with humorous details that often seems to be a parody of Benjamin FRANKLIN's *The Way to Wealth*. It is also a commentary on classical economic theory. Where the classical economics of Adam Smith approached problems of work, play, money, food, clothing, and shelter from the point of view of the wealth of nations—that is to say, the economic health of the country as a whole—T. approaches all such problems from the point of view of the actual well-being of the individual person. T.'s gestures toward self-sufficiency and his rejection of the blessings of the division of labor grow from his insistence that each person should discover for himself or herself just what he requires in the way of necessaries and just what she prefers to spend her time doing.

T. would have agreed with John CIARDI that "we are what we give our attention to." The "Economics" chapter deals with how to live. The next chapter, "Where I Lived and What I Lived For," deals with the goal or purpose of life. T. finds that most of us either "lead lives of quiet desperation," or are essentially asleep. He calls, with all the racket of a rooster at dawn, for a great awakening, not to Puritan religious feeling, but to the joy and beauty and sufficiency of life itself. Everyone wakes up, every morning, to as fresh and promising a world—to the *same* world—as Moses, Homer, and Shakespeare did.

Walden teaches the imperative of courage. For personal insight and worthy goals are useless unless one can find the courage to put them into practice. T., like his admired Emerson and Goethe, is a great courage teacher. *Walden* is also a major testament to the absolute value of personal freedom. Charles OLSON has pointed out how "to Melville it was not the will to be free but the will to overwhelm nature that is at the bottom of us as individuals." T. maintains the opposite, that personal freedom is the basis of individuality and that it need not lead to a desire to overwhelm or subdue nature. *Walden* reflects T.'s lifelong understanding of Nature as law, human nature being free to chose whether or how to live under nature's law. Many other themes are woven into *Walden,* including a respect for limits—there are some places where humans do not and should not go, life as it is given to us is enough—and a conviction that a well-lived life leads to a felt sense of wholeness or integrity, while a botched life leads to desperation or despair. *Walden* is, in general, addressed to those young enough still to make the right choices.

Structurally, *Walden* condenses the experience of two years and two months into a single cycle of the seasons, ending on a glorious note of rebirth and renewal with the return of spring. The book begins with the economic arrangements of material man, and progresses to the creative rebirth of the inner self. The book is, structurally, what it advocates, a voyage of self-discovery. Stylistically, T. writes a language filled with pith and sinew. His prose is witty, pungent, aphoristic, assertive, and full of metaphor and parable. He rewrote *Walden* at least seven times, working over every sentence many times. Good writing, in his view, should be like conversation folded many times thick. Good writing, he also said, was an inevitable mirror of the person: "The best you can write will be the best you are." No style in the life, no style in the writing.

T. left the pond in 1847 having, as he said, "several more lives to lead." But all his lives, past and to come, were marked by his transcendentalist convictions. He believed that the mind is an active power and not merely a passive receptacle of experience. He believed with Kant and Emerson that the mind possesses structures that are prior to our experience and that in fact help shape that experience. The world we live in, the phenomenal world, is a collaboration between the actual material stuff of the world and the individual active mind. What Virginia Woolf said of Emerson holds true for T. as well: he asserted "that he could not be rejected because he held the universe within him."

T. was also interested in Asian philosophy and religion. It confirmed him in thinking that human nature was the same in all ages and places; it showed him philosophical and religious truths consistent with but culturally broader than Christianity; it emphasized self-discipline and self-rule; and it had as a goal the final liberation of the human mind and spirit. In addition to the Bhagavad Gita and the Laws of Menu, T. read with interest the Vishnu Purana and the Hitopadesa.

In 1849, T. made the first of four walking trips to Cape Cod, three of which were woven into a book published posthumously in 1865 as *Cape Cod*. Full of Ishmaelian humor and topographical detail, it has been described both as T.'s sunniest book and as a serious essay on the inhuman power of nature—in this case, the ocean. It may also be thought of as an extended meditation on the themes of shipwreck, salvation, and daily life. Here, as in "Ktaadn," T. brings the reader face to face with a nature that has no pastoral gentleness, no human kindness in it.

Another trip, in 1850, to Montreal and the Gaspé Peninsula, served as the basis for another long narrative, not quite of book length, called *A Yankee in Canada, with Anti-Slavery and Reform Papers* (1866). Although T. begins this account with the wry comment that what he got by going to Canada was a cold, his experience of the great St. Lawrence estuary and his account of it marks the beginning of a new understanding, for him, of how that river dominates the early, largely French, history of northern North America.

T. did a good deal of public lecturing during his life. Typically, a literary subject appeared first in his journals and progressed next to lecture form. He would revise and try out the idea in repeated lectures and often the idea then became an essay or a book. Another important essay that grew this way was "Life without Principle," which is often regarded as an excellent short summary of T.'s central ideas. Some readers, however, find it too strident, defensive, and humorless to be considered among his best work.

There is no question that his *Journals*, running to over two million words and published in fourteen volumes in 1906, are a major achievement. T.'s *Journals* are not daybooks that record appointments, purchases, and daily transactions; nor are they diaries of his personal feelings; nor are they a reading list of all

the books he has read, valuable though all these different kinds of journals may be. T.'s are a combination of the commonplace book, in which one writes down passages from one's reading, and one's own comments both on life and reading. T.'s journal entries contain innumerable detailed accounts of birds, animals, fish, and insects, accounts of the leafing, flowering, and fruiting of every plant and tree in Concord comprehensively recorded for ten consecutive years. He also included first drafts of ideas and images that later found their way into letters, essays, lectures, and books. His journal also has accounts of his family and friends as well as his views on politics and current events. Above all, the journal records T.'s daily encounters with the natural world. It is the record of a mind, begun probably as a writer's aid, a sort of quarry, but converted sometime in the early 1850s to a work in its own right, having its own artistic integrity. The entire *Journal* repays careful reading. To see how good it can be, the year 1852—"My year of observation," T. once called it—may be recommended. In this part of the *Journal* especially, vignettes of country life, sharply focused passages of close observation of nature, and intense and excited writing show T. at his most passionate and alive.

T. is unusual in that he was interested both in nature—in what is now called the environment—and in social justice. He himself considered the latter interest a natural outgrowth of the former. As he valued his own freedom in nature above everything, he assumed that freedom is of similar value for all human beings. From self-emancipation he moved to active involvement in the abolition movement. He helped slaves toward Canada on occasion, he wrote antislavery speeches, including "Slavery in Massachusetts," and for a brief time he became a major northern defender of John Brown after the latter's raid on Harpers Ferry.

But politics was not the major concern of his life; living in nature was. And just as *Walden* is his best book, so is "Walking" his best essay, and both are on that theme. "Walking" was given many times as a lecture. It shows how the old heroic spirit has been transferred from the knight errant of the Middle Ages to the wilderness seeker of the 19th c. T. insists on the positive value of wildness. "In wildness is the preservation of the world." The essay overcomes the nature-versus-civilization dichotomy in a brilliant way. T. recognizes wildness or wilderness not as the enemy or opposite of civilization, but as the essential raw material out of which all civilization and culture is created.

Among the late essays collected and published posthumously as *Excursions* (1863), "Autumnal Tints" is particularly good. It is an essay on October, on the fall color in New England as the climax and ripening of the year. "Autumnal Tints" also speaks of the natural inevitability of decay and death, but the essay itself is vibrantly alive and intensely visual. It is T.'s best essay on the process of perception.

In "The Succession of Forest Trees" (1860), T. wrote a pioneering essay in technical ecology, showing how it happens that a pine wood will spring up where an oak wood has been cut down and vice versa. This landmark paper, which T. considered a purely scientific effort, was published by itself, although it soon became only a part of a large manuscript, the "Dispersion of Seeds," which occupied T.'s later years, and which has been republished as *Faith in a Seed* (1993). T. became interested in Darwin in his later years, and the more decidedly scientific quality of his late work suggests that his interest in the processes of the natural world increasingly challenged his transcendental belief in the centrality of human perception. But his late work also suggests that this new scientific view did not spell defeat or change of heart for T., but rather provided challenging and puzzling new contexts in which the active human mind willed and created its own world. His late work, like his early, insists that "surely joy is the condition of life." T. was forty-four when he died of tuberculosis. He spent his last days surrounded by his friends and family. He was serene and witty to the last. When an old friend asked him, on his deathbed, if he could see across the river of death, T. summed up his life with his reply. "One world at a time," he said.

BIBLIOGRAPHY: Bode, C., ed., *The Collected Poems of H. T.* (1965); Buell, L., *The Environmental Imagination: T., Nature Writing, and the Formation of American Culture* (1995); Cavell, S., *The Senses of Walden* (1972); Christie, J. A., *T. as World Traveler* (1965); Harding, W., *The Days of H. T.* (1965); Harding, W., and C. Bode, eds., *The Correspondence of H. D. T.* (1958); Harding, W., and M. Meyer, eds., *The New T. Handbook* (1980); Lebeaux, R., *Young Man T.* (1977); Lebeaux, R., *T.'s Seasons* (1984); McIntosh, J., *T. as Romantic Naturalist* (1974); Paul, S., *The Shores of America* (1958); Richardson, R. D., Jr., *H. T.: A Life of the Mind* (1986); Sayre, R. F., *T. and the American Indians* (1977); Seybold, E., *T.: The Quest and the Classics* (1951)

ROBERT D. RICHARDSON, JR.

THORPE, Thomas Bangs

b. 1 March 1815, Westfield, Massachusetts; d. 20 September 1878, New York City

T.'s "Big Bear of Arkansas" (1841), a comic hunting tale of mythic proportions, is the most highly ac-

claimed sketch by any of the humorists of the Old Southwest, those antebellum writers admired for their earthy realism who drew inspiration from backwoods folk humor. T. was reared in New York and did not move to Louisiana until the late 1830s. Yet as editor of numerous local newspapers there throughout the 1840s, he published many of his own sporting and humorous sketches describing the scenery and characters found in the lower Mississippi River valley. The *New York Spirit of the Times,* a weekly sporting paper that promoted regional writers, quickly reprinted his work. T. was widely respected in his own day for the accuracy of his sketches about regional sports.

Although his first collection, *Mysteries of the Backwoods* (1846), contains humorous pieces that would have pleased genteel readers, it is properly classified as a sporting book. T. presents frontier hunters as culture heroes whose bravery and skill are, in his view, representative of the American character. These sketches are important because they helped to Americanize sporting writing by turning away from English game and hunting practices to describe what existed on this side of the Atlantic.

The "Letters from the Far West" series (1843–44) shows T.'s ability to burlesque the conventions of sporting writing that he could handle so capably. In the tradition of Washington IRVING's *A Tour on the Prairies,* these letters by a naive traveler on a sporting expedition humorously record his initiation into nature's harsh realities. T. never reprinted them, but in *The Hive of "The Bee-Hunter"* (1854), he did collect most of his other humorous pieces along with revised material from *Mysteries.* The title refers to the mock-heroic "Tom Owen, the Bee-Hunter," a sketch more popular with T.'s contemporaries than with later readers. Yet over the last fifty years, Jim Doggett's tall tale about chasing the unhuntable "Big Bear of Arkansas" has become a minor classic. T.'s handling of dialect creates a sense of realism, and the scatological humor subverts genteel standards. Symbolically, the Big Bear's ultimate death prophesies the loss of America's untamed wilderness as the nation expanded westward, a change T. lamented also in other sketches.

BIBLIOGRAPHY: Blair, W., "The Technique of 'The Big Bear of Arkansas," *SWR* 28 (Summer 1943): 426–35; Estes, D. C., *A New Collection of T. B. T.'s Sketches of the Old Southwest* (1988); Garner, S., "T. B. T. in the Gilded Age: Shifty in a New Country," *MissQ* 36 (Winter 1982–83): 35–52; Lemay, J. A. L., "The Text, Tradition, and Themes of 'The Big Bear of Arkansas,'" *AL* 47 (November 1975): 321–42; McDermott, J. F., "T. B. T.'s Burlesque of Far West Sporting Travel,"

AQ 10 (Summer 1958): 175–80; Rickels, M., *T. B. T.: Humorist of the Old Southwest* (1962)

DAVID C. ESTES

THURBER, James

b. 8 December 1894, Columbus, Ohio; d. 4 November 1961, New York City

Accidentally blinded in one eye as a child, T. was unable to participate in games and sports with other children; as a result, he spent his time reading and daydreaming and developed a rich fantasy life that served to inspire his later fiction. As a young man, he worked as a reporter for the Paris edition of the *Chicago Tribune*. In 1927, T. was hired as an editor-writer for the then-fledgling *New Yorker* magazine, where he developed the clear, concise prose style for which he would become famous.

In 1929, T. published his first book, *Is Sex Necessary? or, Why You Feel the Way You Do,* with his friend and fellow *New Yorker* staffer E. B. WHITE. *Is Sex Necessary?* is a spoof of contemporary theorists who were attempting to reduce sex to a scientifically and psychologically understandable level. The book instantly established T. as a great comedic talent.

The publication of *My Life and Hard Times* (1933) brought critical acclaim and public recognition of T. as an important American literary figure. *My Life and Hard Times* is a collection of semiautobiographical essays that ostensibly tell of T.'s life while being reared in Ohio. The pieces establish T.'s family as possibly the most eccentric group of relatives in American history, including "Grandfather," a sporadically senile old man who lives half his life in early-20th-c. Columbus and half in the Civil War era. The humor of these essays arises out of T.'s use of irony: the characters are humorously preoccupied with events that are feared but that ultimately never occur.

T.'s fiction generally deals with the themes of man versus woman and imagination vs. reality—and these themes often merge in his short stories. The story that best exemplifies the merging of these themes is "The Secret Life of Walter Mitty" (1939), far and away T.'s most famous short story. In the story, the title character, a meek, mild-mannered, and hopelessly henpecked husband, escapes the tedium of his everyday existence through a series of swashbuckling, escapist fantasies. The terms "Walter Mitty" and "Walter Mittyish" have gained generic status and today can be found in many English dictionaries—denoting an unassuming person with unrealistic, heroic dreams. "Mittyish" characters appear throughout T.'s fiction, in such stories as "The Curb in the Sky" (1931), "The Unicorn in the Garden"

(1939), "The Catbird Seat" (1942), and "The Lady on 142" (1943).

In 1941, T. went totally blind, and, from that point on, he mainly confined his writing to more "simplistic" or childlike forms: fables and children's books, including *Fables for Our Time and Famous Poems Illustrated* (1940–1941), *Many Moons* (1942), *The Great Quillow* (1944), *The White Deer* (1945), *The 13 Clocks* (1950), *Further Fables for Our Time* (1956), and *The Wonderful O* (1957). Despite the seemingly innocent nature of these genres, T.'s fables frequently end with bleak morals of death and/or apocalyptic destruction. His children's tales, although more overtly optimistic, also display a cynical undercurrent, particularly *The White Deer,* whose heroes' "valiant deeds" are undermined by the ironic ease with which they are accomplished and the ultimate absence of any real danger in accomplishing them.

In addition to his fame as a writer, T. was a highly respected artist and cartoonist. His surreal sketches first appeared in *Is Sex Necessary?* and became a regular feature of the *New Yorker,* where they became the prototypes for the cartoons that continue to appear in that magazine to this day. Many of T.'s cartoons were collected in *The Seal in the Bedroom and Other Predicaments* (1932).

BIBLIOGRAPHY: Bernstein, B., *T.: A Biography* (1975); Black, S. A., *J. T., His Masquerades: A Critical Study* (1970); Holmes, C. S., *The Clocks of Columbus: The Literary Career of J. T.* (1972); Holmes, C. S., ed., *T.: A Collection of Critical Essays* (1974); Kenney, C. M., *T.'s Anatomy of Confusion* (1984); Long, R. E., *J. T.* (1988); Morsberger, R. E., *J. T.* (1964); Tobias, R. C., *The Art of J. T.* (1969)

JASON BERNER

THURMAN, Wallace [Henry]

b. 16 August 1902, Salt Lake City, Utah; d. 21 December 1934, New York City

Despite the small number of publications attributed to him, T. emerges as a significant Harlem Renaissance figure primarily because of the influence he had on younger writers and the tension he fomented through his criticism of the Harlem establishment, derisively dubbed the "literati" by young rebels such as T., Langston HUGHES, and Zora Neale HURSTON. T. arrived in Harlem from his native Salt Lake City in 1925 and died in 1934 at the age of thirty-two from tuberculosis probably exacerbated by his bohemian lifestyle. Yet during his brief career, T., described as a brilliant and psychologically complex young man by his contemporaries, gained notice as an author of two novels, *The*

Blacker the Berry (1929) and *Infants of the Spring* (1932), and won notoriety as an iconoclastic "insider" dedicated to exposing the Harlem Renaissance as a propaganda stratagem constructed by well meaning civil rights leaders—black and white—to advance the cause of African Americans.

In *The Blacker the Berry*, T.'s most popular novel, he exposes the raw nerve of Harlem conservatives by undertaking the embarrassing subject of color prejudice against dark-skinned blacks within the African American community. T.'s dramatization of dark-skinned Emma Lou Morgan's struggle against the ridicule of whites and her light-skinned family in Boise, Idaho, and then blacks in 1920s Harlem (an experience closely paralleling the author's own) runs counter to the program of racial uplift as conceived by old-guard leaders. Although unevenly written and portraying a heroine too gullible and too "color struck" to be realistic, the novel's candid presentation of such issues as homosexuality and sexual promiscuity anticipates themes explored more fully by writers in later decades. Of interest also are scenes that capture the "slice-of-life" Harlem of the 1920s, but the protagonist-author's self-contradictory obsession with "color" compresses the novel into a narrow tract.

In November 1926, T. made an important critical impact as editor of *Fire!!*, an avant-garde magazine he founded along with Hughes and Richard Bruce Nugent, all united to declare the younger generation's disdain for the social agenda art advocated by their older, venerated "mentors." With T. as their leader, the young dissenters—including Hurston, Gwendolyn Bennett, Countee CULLEN—repudiated "party-line" ideology for art-for-art's-sake explorations of beauty, vengeance, and erotica. *Fire!!*, surviving only one issue because of financial burdens and an actual fire that incinerated the remaining copies, was ruthlessly attacked by black critics for its alleged irreverence and decadence.

T.'s *roman à clef, Infants of the Spring*, continues his criticism of dissent. As temporary literary editor of the *Messenger* (1925–26), an influential African American publication, and as contributing writer to numerous journals, he condemned the Harlem Renaissance as a collaboration between mediocre black artists and patronizing white supporters who abandoned critical standards when judging the works of black writers. The title, taken from Shakespeare's *Hamlet*, suggests that the writers of the Harlem Renaissance are the "infants" of spring whose immature works received excessive unmerited praise. T., who more than once bitterly conceded his inability to write great works, appears in the novel as Raymond Taylor, the central character, who along with the other effete artists/residents of "Niggeratti Manor," is incapable of creating serious art in a climate saturated with egoism, decadence, and overbearing race consciousness. Thinly disguised Harlem luminaries make their appearances:

Hughes, Hurston, Cullen, Rudolph Fisher, Eric Walrond, and Claude MCKAY. But neither they nor T.'s successful re-creation of the mad tapestry of bohemian Harlem can deliver this novel from the chaos that stems from the author's failure to establish emotional distance between himself and his material.

Although it is tempting to see T. as merely a querulous, cynical critic bent on denigrating the Harlem Renaissance because of his contradictory relationship with the movement and his frustrated attempts to write works of lasting appeal, his contribution to this early-20th-c. movement cannot be discounted. His leadership of young writers and his oppositional critical voice must accord him a place in any meaningful assessment of that period.

BIBLIOGRAPHY: Hamalian, L., and J. V. Hatch, eds., *The Roots of African American Drama* (1991); Haslam, G., "W. T.: A Western Renaissance Man," *WAL* 6 (Spring 1971): 53–59; Lewis, D. L., *When Harlem Was in Vogue* (1979)

BARBARA L. J. GRIFFIN

TICKNOR, George

b. 1 August 1791, Boston, Massachusetts; d. 26 January 1871, Boston, Massachusetts

T.'s importance as a New England literary figure rests more on his patrician ethos than on the quantity of his publications. Although his major work *The History of Spanish Literature* (1849) was a monumental feat of scholarship, T. impressed his peers primarily because he was the living embodiment of a gentleman scholar: educated at several universities, polylingual, disdainful of the marketplace, and interested in politics only to serve as a biographer of great men. He was professor of Spanish and French literature at Harvard from 1819 to 1835.

A young graduate of Dartmouth College, T. returned to Boston in 1807 to participate in the *Monthly Anthology* society and to study law. When he was admitted to the bar in 1813, T.'s education had only begun. In 1815, he went to Europe, studying two years at Göttingen, and traveling through England, France, Italy, and Spain. T.'s trip provided the inspiration for his lifelong interests. In Göttingen, he learned of the importance of a library, and he later became one of the founders of the Boston Public Library. German educational methods also impressed T., inspiring him to recommend a number of unpopular educational reforms at Harvard, requiring greater student discipline, grouping students by ability, the creation of academic departments, elective courses, and non-degree enrollment. Most of all, T. believed students should be taught through close question and answer sessions with professors, rather than through the mind-numbing recitation techniques practiced at Harvard at the time. T.'s reform efforts, discussed in his *Remarks on Changes Lately Proposed or Adopted at Harvard University* (1827) and his *Lecture on the Best Methods of Teaching Living Languages* (1832), were largely opposed during his tenure, and the bitter feelings generated by the controversy caused his early retirement.

After Harvard, T. traveled again to Europe for three years, gathering more information for his three-volume *History of Spanish Literature*. During his research, T. amassed the largest library of Spanish literature in North America, which he eventually donated to the Boston Public Library. Indebted to Germanic theories of national character, as well as to neoclassical ideas of cultural declension, T.'s history describes Spain as a noble culture in decline. Although T. argues the proud Castillian spirit was forged through resistance to the occupation by the Moors, the Inquisition, and the mistakes of a corrupt elite, he suggests even the virtues of Spanish culture tend toward exaggeration and fanaticism. Despite the shortcomings of T.'s national biases and his rather dull narrative tone, the work has extraordinary scope, with detailed treatments of folk ballads and the history of the Spanish theater, as well as studies of Spain's major authors.

T. was also known for his biographies of William Hickling PRESCOTT (1864), historian of Spain, Mexico, and Peru, and Daniel Webster (1831), both of whom were close friends of the author. Citing the example of Prescott, T. disclosed his belief about the moral influence the gentleman scholar. For T., Prescott's life and work illustrated the importance of character. A similar tone of hagiography permeates T.'s work on Webster, a man who T. admired for his plainness, simplicity, and "earnest pursuit of truth for truth's sake." Although T.'s writings are valuable today mostly as monuments of neo-Federalist conservatism, the integration of his life and scholarship was the benchmark of propriety for New England letters during the 19th c.

BIBLIOGRAPHY: Hart, T., "G. T.'s *History of Spanish Literature:* The New England Background," *PMLA* 69 (March 1954): 76–88; Hillard, G. S., ed., *Life, Letters and Journals of G. T.* (1876); Tyack, D. B., *G. T. and the Boston Brahmins* (1967)

GRANVILLE GANTER

TIMROD, Henry

b. 8 December 1828, Charleston, South Carolina; d. 7 October 1867, Columbia, South Carolina

T. was a native of Charleston, South Carolina, and a member of the group of authors and intellectuals, including Paul Hamilton HAYNE, William Gilmore SIMMS, and Basil L. Gildersleeve, who resided there in the years before the Civil War. He attended a good private school where he received a classical education. However, at the University of Georgia, he was an unsuccessful student who remained for only a year and a half. In the following years, he earned his living as a tutor to the children at several plantations, and, during the war, was a newspaper editor. Married in 1864, he survived the war but died in 1867 after a long siege of tuberculosis, his promising career cut off as he was finding Northern markets for his poetry.

Well read in Greek and Latin literature, T. drew some of his poetic inspiration from Horace, Catulus, and Martial. Like most of his contemporaries, he was strongly influenced by the poetry of Wordsworth, Byron, and Shelley, and, on occasion, imitated the poems of Tennyson and Browning. These early, imitative poems remained unpublished during his lifetime. They were brought together in *The Uncollected Poems of H. T.* (1942) with an introduction by Guy A. Cardwell, Jr. T.'s earliest published poems appeared, often pseudonymously, or over his initials, in the *Southern Literary Messenger, Russell's* magazine, and the *Charleston Mercury*. During his brief lifetime, only one volume, *Poems* (1859), was published. As a result, his reputation has been sustained posthumously, first by the efforts of his friends, then by the 20th-c. publications of editors and scholars.

T. had firmly held critical views and was able to voice them in a series of articles for *Russell's* and in a lecture he delivered either in 1863 or 1864 on a "A Theory of Poetry." In the lecture, he attacked Edgar Allan POE's assertion that a long poem is a contradiction in terms. T. cited *Paradise Lost* as his best example of a long poem, though he did concede that any long poem cannot be "all poetry." He dissented, as well, from Poe's view that the subject of poetry is limited to the sense of the beautiful. He added Power and Truth as integral elements of poetry. T. knew the early criticism of Matthew Arnold and praised it, with some reservations. In other essays, he defended the sonnet as a literary form and addressed the question of a distinctively Southern literature that might avoid the dangers of provincialism. His prose pieces have been edited by Edd Winfield Parks as *The Essays of H. T.* (1942).

T.'s earliest poems were conventional in subject and treatment. He addressed love poems to idealized young ladies and wrote nature lyrics that say the expected things about nature; the sonnets tended to the mechanically regular; and a long poem, "A Vision of Poesy," is a didactic allegory. He discovered his individual voice and his most characteristic themes as war threatened, then ravaged, his part of the country. Two of his best poems grew out of his sentiments during the period of secession. In "Ethnogenesis" (1861), a Pindaric ode, he celebrates the meeting of the first Confederate Congress and the establishment, as it then seemed of a new nation. A second ode, "The Cotton Boll" (1861), is a song of praise for the South's most important agricultural product; the poem predicts a peaceful and prosperous Southern nation, after it has defeated the Northern "Goths."

Patriotic poems followed as the war began. In "A Cry to Arms" (1862), the poet urges his countrymen to battle; and "Carolina" (1862), another stirring call to arms, has become the state's official song. But, as the war proceeded, the poems reflect a growing disillusionment. "Charleston" (1862) is a portrait of the city under siege, and "The Unknown Dead" (1863) is a moving elegy for the ordinary soldiers slain in the battle.

T. served briefly in the army before receiving a medical discharge. He was in Columbia South Carolina, working as a newspaper editor when that city was attacked and burned by Federal troops. In the couple of postwar years left to him, he suffered from a combination of poverty and his disease. Several years after his death, Paul Hamilton Hayne was able to bring out an edition of his *The Poems of H. T.* (1873) with an approving introduction; and a "Memorial Edition" of the poems appeared in 1899.

BIBLIOGRAPHY: Hubbell, J. B., *The Last Years of H. T., 1864–1867* (1941); Parks, E. W., *H. T.* (1964); Rubin, L. D., Jr., *The Edge of the Swamp* (1989)

DOUGLAS ROBILLARD

TOKLAS, Alice B.

b. 30 April 1877, San Francisco, California; d. 7 March 1967, Paris, France

T. is the subject, but not the author, of the most famous fictional autobiography of the 20th c. The daughter of an upper-middle-class Jewish family, T. was persuaded by Gertrude STEIN's brother to move to France. In September 1907, T. arrived in Paris, and, as she recalls in her memoir *What Is Remembered* (1963), she was immediately smitten by the "golden brown presence" of Stein. T. immediately devoted herself to encouraging Stein's art, keeping house for the writer, and fulfilling roles as Stein's companion, confidant, and literary agent.

For many years, Stein tried in vain to convince T. to write an autobiography, in part to promote her lively association with writers, painters and free thinkers, and, in 1932, on a whim, Stein wrote T.'s "autobiography" herself. Completed in six weeks and immediately published, it became Stein's breakthrough work, both in Europe and the U.S. It continues to be her most analyzed and widely studied work.

The Autobiography of A. B. T. (1933) records, from the Alice-narrator's point of view, the daily Parisian life of Stein and T. between the two world wars, focusing mostly on their famous ties to the Lost Generation. Written in a conventional syntax and straightforward narrative, both of which were departures from Stein's radically experimental style, it is comprised of amusing encounters, breezy critiques of famous art works, lively gossip, witty observations of manners, and memorable portraits of the titans of MODERNISM, including Ernest HEMINGWAY, Pablo Picasso, and Henry Matisse. T. is portrayed as both a sympathetic naïf and doting caretaker, willing to entertain the wives of the famous while "Gertrude" mingled with their husbands.

For Stein, the success of *Autobiography* was a mixed blessing, bringing her fame and recognition for what had been intended as a joke, thus leaving her with doubts about her own authorial voice and intentions. In recent years, feminist and poststructuralist critics have written convincingly of the *Autobiography* as both a playful act of self-creation, in which she "encoded" her lesbian relationship to T., and an attempt to ease the concomitant pressures of her secret identity.

T., for her part, wrote nothing while Stein was alive. In 1954, at the suggestion of Thorton WILDER, she published the *A. B. T. Cookbook,* consisting of her recipes and brief reminiscences of the prewar era, written in a sturdy, occasionally ironic, anecdotal style. She also contributed pieces to American periodicals, including an earnest defense, in the *New York Times,* of F. Scott FITZGERALD's literary reputation over that of Hemingway, whom she despised. In 1956, she published *The Blue Dog,* a translation of short stories written by a young family friend, and, in 1958 penned an article for the *Atlantic Monthly* on the French designer Pierre Balmain. A second cookbook called *Aromas and Flavors of Past and Present* appeared that same year.

Nearly all of her writing focuses on the golden age in Paris and the creative genius of Stein. T. was so preoccupied with preserving Stein's legacy that a longtime friend abandoned his efforts, in the 1950s, to help T. write her own memoir.

BIBLIOGRAPHY: Burns, E., *Staying on Alone: Letters of A. B. T.* (1973); Simon, L., *The Biography of A. B. T.* (1977); Souhami, D., *Gertrude and A.* (1991)

TIM KEANE

TOLSON, Melvin B[eaunorus]

b. 6 February 1898, Moberly, Missouri; d. 29 August 1966, Guthrie, Oklahoma

T. was a gifted African American poet who remained largely unknown in his lifetime. This is perhaps due to the difficulty of his later verse and to the fact that he lived and taught largely outside of the normal centers of literary production. It was also difficult to classify his work—a "Negro poet" writing modernist poems, alluding to Africa as freely as to the Western canon, incorporating blues lyrics as freely as T. S. ELIOT incorporated the Baghavad Gita. T. also wrote a regular column in the *Washington Tribune* from 1937 to 1944, some of which are collected in *Caviar and Cabbage* (1982).

T.'s first book manuscript, *A Gallery of Harlem Portraits,* was written in the early 1930s, but T. was unable to find a publisher—an edited version was published in 1979. In its original form, *A Gallery of Harlem Portraits* comprised three-hunred-forty separate sketches, brief dramatic poems capturing the wide economic and cultural diversity of Harlem life. These poems are written in plain, direct free verse occasionally intercut with sections of blues lyrics. This manuscript would later be radically reworked into *Harlem Gallery: Book I, the Curator* (1965).

In his first published book, *Rendezvous with America* (1944), T. makes use of more regular rhyme and meter and includes a section of sonnets. The title poem of the collection is Whitmanesque in its compendiousness, but is given an edge by the racial tensions it outlines. In fact, many of the poems in the book have a similar edge to them—they draw on a wide range of historical and cultural metaphors to deal with T.'s vision of contemporary America, and the racial and economic problems that exist.

In 1947, T. was named poet laureate of Liberia. For the country's centennial, he produced his *Libretto for the Republic of Liberia* (1953). The early sections of this long poem define and offer a paean to Liberia; the later ones move to a densely allusive penultimate section placing Africa both in contrast with the West and in the middle of the contemporary conflict between the U.S. and the former Soviet Union. The final section is a dizzying vision of the future of Liberia and Africa, presented in dense verse paragraphs.

Harlem Gallery: Book I, the Curator is generally considered to be T.'s masterwork. The densely allusive style, irregular meter, rhyme, and centering of lines on the page hearken back to the penultimate section of the *Libretto*. The poem deals with questions of art in the African American community, identity in Harlem, and the split between the bourgeoisie and the intellectuals. Thoroughly high-modernist in conception, *Harlem Gallery* revises MODERNISM by including in a sympathetic way nonelite forms of culture—blues lyrics and vernacular language. Where the high modernists went to Asia, T. goes to Africa for his non-Western allusions.

The main characters in the poem represent three distinct positions within the African American intelligentsia: the Curator is a mediator, somewhat ambiguous, although the central figure in the poem; Dr. Nkomo is an African intellectual steeped in the traditions of the West while at the same time mocking them; Hideho Heights is a "people's poet" who entertains secret notions of a more literary career. The other characters in the poem are artists, successful businessmen, musicians, gangsters, and laborers—a cross section of Harlem life.

Harlem Gallery was originally conceived of as a tetralogy of poems in which T. planned to cover the sweep of African American history. Unfortunately, T. did not live to complete his vision; the first section must—and does—stand on its own: a fascinating, complex, often difficult poem, one whose importance remains largely unexplored.

BIBLIOGRAPHY: Berube, M., *Marginal Forces/Cultural Centers* (1992); Farnsworth, R. M., *M. B. T., 1898—1966: Plan Talk and Poetic Prophecy* (1984); Flasch, J., *M. B. T.* (1972)

ROBERT C. SPIRKO

TOOMER, Jean [Nathan Eugene]

b. 26 December 1894, Washington, D.C.; d. 30 March 1967, Doylestown, Pennsylvania

T. is considered to be one of the most influential African American writers. His most well-known work *Cane* (1923), rediscovered in the 1960s, is a literary masterpiece of the Harlem Renaissance. Ironically, shortly after the publication of that work, he emphatically denied any Negro ancestry and chose to be known as a member of a new race, called simply American.

The structure of *Cane* has received much critical attention because it is an unusual mixtures of genres—poems, prose sketches, short stories, and drama. Yet linking the various pieces are repeated natural images, and the sounds of spirituals, blues, and jazz echo throughout in quoted lyrics and in the rhythms of T.'s prose. *Cane*'s experimental style reflects the influence of modernist ideas with which he became acquainted probably through his friend Waldo FRANK. The direct inspiration for the book, however, came while T. worked for several months in rural Georgia and observed, for the first time, black folk culture. He lamented that modernization would soon destroy the spiritual richness of this way of life, and in places *Cane* has an elegiac tone. Nevertheless, emotion did not blind him to social realities, and the book forcefully protests racial discrimination. T. presents the suppression of black women, his most memorable characters, by both white and black men. The prose sketches about these women represent masterful handling of important social themes in a highly experimental lyric style. The drama "Kabnis," with which *Cane* concludes, takes up the question of the black artist's role in relationship to the experiences of his race.

In the 1920s, T. completed several other serious plays that represent pioneering work in folk, symbolist, and expressionist drama. They satirize the black middle-class for rejecting its heritage and also call for the liberation of women, who represent the power of emotion that is all-important in life.

Soon after publishing *Cane,* T. became a disciple of the Eastern mystic Georges Gurdjieff and devoted himself to the spiritual reform of society. The only publication of literary significance during the remainder of his life is the long poem "The Blue Meridian" (1936). In the tradition of Walt WHITMAN's prophetic poetry, it envisions a spiritualized America where all of life is unified. Despite the intensity of T.'s commitment to such a goal, it was not able to inspire writing of artistic merit comparable to the one slim volume on which his reputation rests.

BIBLIOGRAPHY: Jones, R., ed., *J. T.: Selected Essays and Literary Criticism* (1996); Kerman, C. E., and R. Eldridge, *The Lives of J. T.* (1987); McKay, N. Y., *J. T., Artist* (1984); O'Daniel, T. B., ed., *J. T.* (1988); Turner, D. T., ed., *The Wayward and the Seeking* (1980)

DAVID C. ESTES

TORRENCE, Ridgely

b. 27 November 1874, Xenia, Ohio; d. 25 December 1950, New York City

For over fifty years, T. pursued an eclectic literary career as a poet, playwright, essayist, biographer, and editor. He emerged in the first decade of the 20th c. as a poet of great promise, receiving recognition in a 1906 *Atlantic Monthly* article, along with William Vaughn MOODY and Edwin Arlington ROBINSON, as a spiritual descendant of Walt WHITMAN. But in the decades that followed, T. was seen by some critics as slow to develop his own voice, often adapting the form of his writing to his changing literary environments. The themes of his writings, however, were pursued with unflinching consistency, especially spirituality, lost youth and aging, injustice, oppression, and friendship. Despite having his poems regularly anthologized until his death in 1950, his overall small output in verse undoubtedly hindered his sustained critical recognition. Today, his primary accomplishment is seen in his work as poetry editor of the *New*

Republic (1920–34), where he discovered or supported many of the major poets of the day, including Robert FROST. Many of T.'s concerns and images find echoes in Frost's poetry, some of which received open acknowledgment in the form of a dedication.

T.'s first volume of verse, *The House of a Hundred Lights,* appeared in limited edition in 1899 and consisted of a text of 100 quatrains in frank imitation of Omar Khayyám. His second volume of poetry, *Hesperides* (1925), did not appear until two-and-a-half decades later. This volume exhibited the form in which T. excelled: the short lyric, using simple language and complex meter to achieve an overall tone of solemnity. Although T. had rejected his Presbyterian upbringing and traditional, denominational Christianity, his poems such as "Eye-Witness" and "Rituals for the Events of Life," presented secularized treatments of Christian parables and ethics. One of his best-known poems, "The Son," reveals T.'s ability to master a form both demanding and economical. In four stanzas of sixteen short lines, T. deftly juxtaposes a farm wife's emotional responses to an early harvest and the death of her son. Perhaps T.'s finest poem, "The Bird in the Tree," is a monologue by an innocent black man on the verge of lynching by the Ku Klux Klan. *Hesperides* garnished significant critical acclaim, although some found his writings vague and obscure in meaning. T.'s last volume of poetry, *Poems* (1941), was stimulated by the outbreak of World War II. Critics were again puzzled by the scant output of a writer of such promise; the volume contained only fourteen new poems, plus poetry from *Hesperides.* "Lincoln's Dream," the longest of the new poems, details the president's ominous vision of his own corpse in the White House and reflects a similar preoccupation with visions and mysticism found in much of T.'s writing.

In the years between his first two volumes of poetry, T. turned to playwriting, initially in verse and then, after the success of his close friend Moody's drama *The Great Divide,* to prose. In *El Dorado* (1903) and *Abelard and Heloise* (1907), T. tried, like other English-language poets of the time, to elevate the literary merits of theater beyond that of melodrama. But like these other verse dramas, T.'s plays were antiquarian in subject, generalized and unconvincing in character psychology, and too far removed from the tastes of contemporary audiences in their use of blank verse. Much more successful and influential were T.'s *Plays for a Negro Theatre* (1917), which attempted to do for the black community in America what John Millington Synge's dramas had done for the Irish peasantry. Using experiences from his early hometown life in Xenia, Ohio, T. wrote three effective plays capturing the speech, customs, religious beliefs, and racial pride of black Americans. The title character in *Granny*

Maumee nobly embodies a royal African lineage with a spirituality derived from Christianity and voodoo. In *Simon the Cyrenian,* the black cross bearer for Christ forsakes his role as an African revolutionary in Rome in order to follow Christ's nonviolent teachings. T.'s most effective and convincing character of all is Madison Sparrow, who in *The Rider of Dreams* sees his get-rich-quick schemes destroyed by his own incompetence and a world of economic necessities. When produced on Broadway in 1917 with an all-black cast, these plays created a critical sensation in their realistic and sympathetic depiction of black characters and avoidance of traditional dramatic stereotype, prefiguring similar and more widely acknowledged attempts by Eugene O'NEILL in the 1920s.

Late works by T. show his continued concern with racism and the accomplishments of black America. *The Story of John Hope* (1948) is an extensively researched biography of the African American educator. With great sensitivity, the work outlines the psychological and social pressures that provided the background to Hope's achievements, and a review in the *Journal of Negro History* praised T.'s ability as a white writer to recount the black struggle without overt bias. T.'s editorial leadership in the field of American poetry can also be seen in his editions of the *Selected Letters of Edwin Arlington Robinson* (1940) and *Last Poems of Anna Hempstead Branch* (1944). Two years after his death in 1950, his *Poems* was reissued in a revised edition and he was remembered by *Time* magazine as "a poet's poet." T. made an invaluable contribution to the world of American letters and to the foundation of a realistic, African American drama.

BIBLIOGRAPHY: Clum, J. M., *R. T.* (1972); Monteiro, G., "'I Always Keep Seeing a Light as I Talk with Him': Limning the Robert Frost/R. T. Relationship," *SCR* 15 (Fall 1982): 32–43; Thorp, W., "The Achievement of R. T.," *PULC* 12 (Spring 1951): 103–17

JERRY DICKEY

TOURGÉE, Albion [Winegar]

b. 2 May 1838, Williamsfield, Ohio; d. 21 May 1905, Bordeaux, France

Although T. is not widely read by contemporary readers and is generally ignored by critics and scholars, he was a highly controversial figure in late-19th-c. America, both in literature and politics. His involvement in the issues of his time emerges in his best fiction. He left a position as a school principal to become a Union officer in the Civil War and was twice severely wounded in the spine. After the war, he moved to Greensboro, North Carolina, and edited the *Union*

Register, a Republican newspaper that failed in six months. Beginning in 1868, he served six years as a superior court judge in North Carolina and acted as one of three who codified the state's laws. Discouraged by the failure of Reconstruction, he left the U.S. in 1879. In 1897, after a stressful career as a polemicist, he was appointed consul to Bordeaux, where he remained the rest of his life.

The publication in 1879 of *Figs and Thistles* and *A Fool's Errand* initiated a period of heavy literary production. *The Invisible Empire,* which was now published with *A Fool's Errand,* and *Bricks without Straw* appeared in 1880, followed the next year by *A Royal Gentleman,* which had first appeared in 1874 as *'Toinette* under the pen name Henry Churton. In 1882, he published *John Eax and Mamelon* and the following year *Hot Plowshares.* His periodical *Our Continent* ran from 1882 until 1884.

Although T. never stopped writing, most of his best work came in this period. Four of his novels—*A Royal Gentleman, A Fool's Errand, Bricks without Straw,* and *Hot Plowshares*—as well as the factual *The Invisible Empire,* deal with Reconstruction or with attitudes that led to its failure. T. never forsook his principles, but these books reveal an understanding of the Southern position and a condemnation of the national government for its failure to enforce.

A Royal Gentleman deals with Geoffrey Hunter, a Southerner who takes the slave 'Toinette as a mistress, educates her and frees her. After the Civil War, he again wishes to be her lover, but loses her because he cannot accept her as an equal. *A Fool's Errand,* the most popular of his Southern novels, is loosely autobiographical. Its hero, Comfort Servosse, is an idealized portrait of T., defeated by the adamantine convictions of the Southerners and by their ruthless efficiency. The fate of the blacks is sealed by the failure of the federal government to intervene. *Bricks without Straw* examines the same issue from a different point of view, as the black, Nimbus, is forced to abandon the South. *Hot Plowshares* is concerned with underlying racial attitudes. Hilda Hargrove, the daughter of a Southern gentleman, believes mistakenly for a time that she has Negro blood.

These works are sincere but deeply flawed. The characters are wooden, the melodramatic situations trite, the dialogue artificial. The novels are saturated with long political and sociological disquisitions, some directly from T. and some from his characters. The saving virtue of these books is that they are obviously the result of firsthand knowledge.

T.'s later career was a story of financial stress, unrewarding publishing and journalism, and unsuccessful attempts to secure rights for blacks. Representing the National Citizen's Rights Association, he carried the case of *Plessy v. Fergusson* to the Supreme Court, where his defeat confirmed the doctrine of "separate but equal." In his magazine *Basis: A Journal of Good Citizenship* (March 1895 through April 1896), T. promulgated his political views and attacked realists such as William Dean HOWELLS and Henry JAMES for oversubtlety and for a lack of social commitment.

BIBLIOGRAPHY: Dibble, R. F., *A. W. T.* (1921); Gross, T. L., *A. W. T.* (1963); Olsen, O. H., *Carpetbagger's Crusade: The Life of A. W. T.* (1965)

MARYJEAN GROSS and DALTON GROSS

TRANSCENDENTALISM

"Transcendentalism" or "American transcendentalism" or "New England transcendentalism" are somewhat interchangeable designations for an intellectual and social movement dating from the 1830s that is generally identified with Ralph Waldo EMERSON and his circle. The movement was, however, so amorphous in its aims, methods, and members that it is really more a misnomer than a term that can be used with any accuracy to describe a specific group of people or a certain body of thought. In fact, Emerson never applied the title to himself, perhaps because it was the rhetorical tool of the enemies of his romantic agenda who desired to link his work and that of his compatriots with the suspiciously European thought of Immanuel Kant, the philosophical writings of Samuel Taylor Coleridge, and the Germanized English of Thomas Carlyle. Such suspicions of influence and public assertions to the same were potent weapons at a time when blossoming literary and cultural nationalism were aspects of the political arguments for America's claim to status as a great nation.

Emerson, as was often his wont, much preferred to generalize the offensive particulars of what had come to be known as transcendentalism by defining it as "Idealism as it appears in 1842" in his address, "The Transcendentalist." However, when he came to assessing this nominal movement at the end of his life in *Historic Notes of Life and Letters in New England,* published in 1880, he characterized it not as a movement at all, but as "only here and there two or three men or women who read and wrote, each alone, with unusual vivacity." Emerson thought these "two or three men or women" were positively influenced by a number of factors, including the liberal Unitarianism of Dr. William Ellery CHANNING, the rhetorical training grounded in European theory supplied by Edward Everett at Harvard, and the development of modern science. Presumably Emerson and other would-be transcendentalists found in these sources a means of

addressing the problems posed by 18th-c. empiricism and rationalism, the effects of which Emerson described in this most memorable way: "The young men were born with knives in their brain, a tendency to introversion, self-dissection, anatomizing of motives." In contrast, the ideas associated with transcendentalism offered what Emerson called "a new consciousness," a phrase that captures the essence of the movement.

The worldview that we might identify with transcendentalism did meet definite social and political needs. Most of those who have been associated with the movement, like Emerson himself, were Harvard-trained Unitarian ministers affected, no doubt dramatically, by the social upheaval inherent in Jacksonian America. Many of them were the sons of privilege, raised in households where republican ideals were tenuously mixed with conservative Federalism and residual Calvinism. They went off to Harvard to find the truth and found instead a curriculum based on the classics with a generous dose of the empirical philosophy and psychology of John Locke, and the rationalism of French philosophers and Scottish Common-Sense philosophers. The whole was aimed at teaching them their place in a world of structure and surface, at reinforcing their innate sense of the preeminence of reason and order. This was, however, a world that no longer existed. So while most of them passed through Harvard and its Divinity School to accept their places in the social hierarchy by becoming Unitarian ministers, they simultaneously worked to defeat that hierarchy through transcendentalism, with its merging of republican values, European romantic thought, and Puritan nature mysticism.

While Emerson, in "The Transcendentalist," credits the great German philosopher, Immanuel Kant, whose systematic thought was called "Transcendental Idealism," as the founder of the movement, and while one can surely locate ideas that prefigure American transcendentalism in the work of Kant's disciples and refiners, such as Johann Gottlieb Fichte, Johann Gottfried Herder, Friedrich von Schelling, Friedrich Schiller, Friedrich von Schlegel, and Friedrich Schleiermacher, and in the biblical criticism of Johann Eichorn and the Eclecticism of Victor Cousin, the most significant intellectual source is the philosophical works of Coleridge, especially *Aids to Reflection,* published in the U.S. in 1829 under the aegis of James Marsh, then president of the University of Vermont and no transcendentalist himself. The aspect of Coleridge's work that most intrigued and influenced American thinkers was the distinction he made between the epistemological faculties of Reason and Understanding. In suggesting this differentiation, Coleridge was borrowing from Kant, who distinguished *Verstand* (understanding) from *Vernunft* (reason in the narrow sense), but he reversed this Kantian distinction by using "Understanding" to represent rationality or, in a larger sense, all of the negative aspects of 18th-c. logic and science, and "Reason" as a label for ideals and religious beliefs that exist quite apart from scientific empiricism. In arming the would-be transcendentalists with this weapon, Coleridge supplied them with a rationale for denying the validity of Locke's empirical psychology and, by extension, a justification for attacking the rationalism of their own Unitarian mentors at Harvard, whose creedless religion rested firmly on the basis of scientific empiricism. "Religious Sentiment" and "Intuition" could, by using Coleridge, be argued to be superior to rationality in the search for truth. This fact no doubt led to a realignment of those who would become transcendentalists with their American Puritan forebears, such as the catalyst for the Great Awakening, Jonathan EDWARDS, who in his sermon, "Divine and Supernatural Light,' argued for the existence of a transcendent sixth sense, a "sense of the heart," that permits one intuitively to know the reality of God. The mysticism inherent in some Puritan writings may have led the would-be transcendentalists to other works of mysticism as well, such as the writings of the Swedish mystic, Emanuel Swedenborg, to Persian poetry and European Neo-Platonism, and eventually, to the ancient scriptures of India and China.

All of these philosophical and theological antecedents may suggest that transcendentalism was decidedly other-worldly, an undeniable aspect of it that prompted its critics to label it as nothing more than "moonshine." However, in praxis, transcendentalism did have a part in and an effect upon the evolving American society. Almost from the beginning of the historical and critical interest in this movement, there has been curiosity about its manifestation as a social force, contributing to such reforms as antislavery, communitarianism, women's rights, the labor movement, and environmentalism, as well as a range of fringe concerns, from dietary reform and phrenology to a campaign to have Francis Bacon recognized as the author of Shakespeare's plays.

While some transcendentalists were ambivalent in their commitment to the antislavery movement, others like Henry David THOREAU and Theodore PARKER, the firebrand Unitarian minister and member of John Brown's "Secret Six," were unwavering in their support of the cause. Margaret FULLER, who wrote *Woman in the Nineteenth Century,* and Elizabeth Palmer PEABODY, who was a publisher, writer, and owner of the Corner Bookstore, substantially contributed to the fledgling cause of women's rights. George RIPLEY was the driving force behind the utopian community, Brook Farm, whose members included Nathaniel HAW-

THORNE. Amos Bronson ALCOTT, the father of Louisa May ALCOTT, founded Fruitlands, a utopian community based on his own unworkable idealism. Of course, the most famous utopian experiment was the community of one that Thoreau founded on the shores of Walden Pond from 1845 to 1847. Orestes Augustus BROWNSON attacked the wage system and capitalism in general in his important "Laboring Classes" essays of 1840, but stunned and disappointed his transcendentalist colleagues by converting to Roman Catholicism in 1844. Emerson and, most notably, Thoreau, through their focus on man's relationship to nature, are at least in part responsible for the environmentalist movement of the late 19th c. because of the influence their work had on men such as John Burroughs and John Muir.

Certainly the diversity of transcendentalist involvement in reform suggests the difficulty one has in pinning it down. It came closest to being a movement of like-minded individuals for a brief period beginning in 1836—the so-called *Annus Mirabilis* of transcendentalism because of the publication in that year of Emerson's *Nature,* Alcott's *Conversations with Children on the Gospel,* Brownson's *New Views of Christianity, Society, and the Church,* Ripley's *Discourses on the Philosophy of Religion,* and *Remarks on the Four Gospels* by Emerson's childhood friend, the Philadelphia minister, William Henry FURNESS. These works all tended to attack the rationalism and empiricism of the conservative Unitarian position and exacerbated the schism that resulted from a disagreement that took for its focus the validity of miracles as the basis for faith. This so-called Miracles Controversy intensified when the transcendentalists openly attacked conservative positions or methods, as in Emerson's "Divinity School Address" (1838) or Parker's sermon, "The Transient and Permanent in Christianity" (1841).

In practical terms, this schism resulted in the alienation of those identified with the transcendentalist movement from cultural and religious outlets controlled by the conservative Unitarians. It is startling to realize that the preeminent literary journal in Boston, and presumably in the entire U.S., the *North American Review,* ignored Emerson's work until 1847, but this apparent oversight is more understandable in light of the journal's affiliation with the Unitarian establishment and the fact that its editor during those years was John Gorham Palfrey, the man who had been dean of the Harvard Divinity School when Emerson delivered his controversial address there.

Excluded from publishing in established outlets, the transcendentalists were forced to fall back on their own resources and create outlets for the development and publication of their ideas. The earliest of the periodicals linked to the movement, the *Western Messenger,* was published in Cincinnati and Louisville from

June 1835 to April 1841 and was edited by James Freeman Clarke (1836–39), Christopher Pearse Cranch (1837–39), and William Henry Channing (1839–41), all young, Harvard-trained Unitarian ministers. The last was the short-lived *Massachusetts Quarterly Review,* edited by Theodore Parker and published from December 1847 to September 1850. The most famous of the transcendentalist periodicals was unquestionably *The Dial,* published from July 1840 until April 1844 and edited by Margaret Fuller (1840–42) and Emerson (1842–44). As Fuller asserted, *The Dial* provided its contributors the "freedom to say their say, for better or worse," and as such it served as an outlet for some of Emerson's best early poetry and lectures, for John Sullivan Dwight's first attempts at music criticism, Fuller's social criticism, and Thoreau's first essay on natural history, as well as the murky meandering of Alcott's "Orphic Sayings," a work whose eccentricities came to represent the periodical and the movement to its critics. *The Dial* was not a popular success—its subscribers never numbered more than three hundred—but its contents are perhaps the surest way for today's reader to gain some sense of the substance and diversity of transcendentalism.

A second focal point of transcendentalism developed from the same cause as *The Dial.* Since members of the transcendentalist circle found that their "new" ideas were often met with open hostility when uttered publicly, there was a need for a reasonably sympathetic environment for the introduction and discussion of such ideas. Fuller managed to satisfy this need through public "conversations" and Emerson through his lectures, but the most significant development in this vein for all concerned was the Transcendental Club. Founded in 1836, at the suggestion of Emerson, who proposed a "symposium" to discuss the mood of the times, this informal group provided a forum for the dissidents who wished to consider alternative solutions to the theological and moral questions of the time. The Transcendental Club met nearly thirty times between September 1836 and September 1840, when it was disbanded.

With the demise of the Transcendental Club, the end of the publication of *The Dial* in 1844, and the transition of Brook Farm from a transcendentalist to a Fourierist community in 1844, it could be said that as an identifiable movement, transcendentalism ceased to exist in the mid-1840s. Nevertheless, it continued to have a profound effect on American culture for at least the next century through the works of its most influential spokesmen, Emerson, Thoreau, and Fuller, and through the works of those who, like Hawthorne, Herman MELVILLE, and Edgar Allan POE, responded most profoundly to the intellectual challenges presented by the transcendentalists. After the Civil War,

the impulse toward abstract idealism that so characterizes Emerson's thought was supplanted by the social idealism of a group of second-generation transcendentalists such as Franklin Benjamin SANBORN, a pioneer in establishing sociology as an academic discipline, George Willis Cooke, a committed socialist, feminist, and religious reformer, and Moncure Daniel Conway, a philanthropist and proponent of a world religion. Through various social reform movements, transcendentalism, even if it was no longer known by that name, continued to have an impact well into the 20th c.

BIBLIOGRAPHY: Buell, L., *Literary Transcendentalism* (1973); Mott, W. T., ed., *Biographical Dictionary of Transcendentalism* (1996); Mott, W. T., ed., *Encyclopedia of Transcendentalism* (1996); Myerson, J., ed., *The Transcendentalists: A Review of Research and Criticism* (1984); Myerson, J., and P. F. Gura, eds., *Critical Essays on American Transcendentalism* (1982)

ROBERT E. BURKHOLDER

TRAVEN, B.

b. 3 May 1890, Chicago, Illinois; d. 26 March 1969, Mexico City, Mexico

T.'s name was once best known for the 1948 movie version of one of his novels, *The Treasure of the Sierra Madre* (pub. in German, 1927; trans. ed., 1935), directed by John Huston. T. has since been recognized as a major American writer based on his superb storytelling skills, his ironic vision of modern life, and his powerful descriptive narrative of the Mexican landscape and culture. T.'s desire to keep his private life private became so obsessive that he purposely provided false information about his name and his background, and, to date, very little about him is completely verifiable. Nonetheless, many scholars now cautiously accept the information provided by his widow, Rosa Elena Lujan, that T. was born Bewick Traven Torsvan, the son of Norwegian immigrants living in Chicago; that he apparently spent his youth in Germany as an actor and a revolutionary journalist, perhaps using the name Ret Marut; and that he left Germany to live the life of a sailor before he settled in Mexico sometime in the early 1920s and began to write.

It is believed that during T.'s early days in Mexico, he traveled extensively and alone throughout the mountainous and jungle regions of the state of Chiapas, the setting of many of his works. This firsthand experience with the brutal conditions of Indian poverty combined with T.'s anti-industrial, anarchistic political beliefs became the major concerns of his novels and short stories, particularly the six "Jungle novels," published in the 1930s, that detail the oppressive social forces that resulted in the Mexican Revolution. T. is also known for his short stories and novellas, notably "The Night Visitor" (1926), first published in the U.S. in 1934, and "Macario" (1950) in particular. All of T.'s works were first published in Germany, in German.

T.'s most famous novel, *The Treasure of the Sierra Madre,* contains many of the subjects and themes found in other works—the American expatriate in an alien and exotic environment, the vivid use of Mexican landscape and culture, the loss of identity and personal breakdown, the brutalizing effects of poverty. However, this novel is atypical of T.'s work in that the major character, Fred C. Dobbs, lacks any of the redeeming or heroic qualities of T.'s other protagonists. A psychological study with a distinctly ironic and moral tone, Dobbs's descent into paranoia, madness, and death is a dramatic fable that illustrates the effects of greed on three Americans whose own Western culture, represented by the oil corporations, has impoverished and exploited them as much as it has the Indian workers. As Dobbs and Curtin, another jobless drifter, join the old prospector Howard in the search for gold, they agree they will only take what they need, but soon *The Treasure of the Sierra Madre* becomes the old recognizable tale of the three companions whose search for the precious yellow metal ends in death. Curtin and Howard, by clinging to remnants of moral behavior and adjusting to the natural culture of the area, escape Dobbs's fate.

The Bridge in the Jungle (pub. in German, 1929; trans. ed., 1938), is often viewed as T.'s finest work, and it features Gerard Gales who first appears in *The Death Ship.* Built around the simple plot of the death and funeral of a young Indian boy, *The Bridge in the Jungle* is an excellent example of T.'s ability to capture an isolated culture through the point of view of an outsider. The theme of oppression by the industrialized society is again present as the boy's death is caused by both the unsafe bridge built by the railroad company and the boy's clumsiness in the new shoes his brother brings him from Texas. The strength of this work lies in Gale's observations of this society—their extreme poverty but simple dignity, the blend of old Aztec ritual with Christian belief, the seriocomic funeral of the child. Gale's change from outsider to mourner and participant is a personal journey that many critics see as an example of another T. theme, the fantasy of escape into the jungle and away from civilization.

BIBLIOGRAPHY: Baumann, M., *B. T.* (1976); Chankin, D., *Anonymity and Death: The Fiction of B. T.* (1975); Mezo, R., *A Study of T.'s Fiction* (1993); Stone, J., *The Mystery of B. T.* (1977)

LYNN RISSER

TRILLING, Lionel
b. 4 July 1905, New York City; d. 5 November 1975, New York City

A contemporary of the New Critics, the American formalists who dominated the academic study of literature during the mid-20th c., T. shared with them a responsiveness to qualities of tension, ambiguity, and irony in literature. But he differed from them in significant ways as well. Although the New Critics were by no means the art-for-art's-sake aesthetes one hears of in unsympathetic and, too often, uninformed later accounts, they did see tension, ambiguity, and irony as first of all formal qualities, matters of relationships within literary texts. For T., on the other hand, these qualities were before all ethical; they were qualities that, while conveyed and exemplified in the best literature, were essential to a responsible encounter with a reality beyond the bounds of literature. T. consistently valued the literary work precisely for what it contributed to that encounter.

In the 1930s, T. came to be identified with the New York Intellectuals, an informal group of men and women of the left, largely Jewish in ancestry, and, as time went on, emphatically anticommunist in ideology. They clustered especially around *Partisan Review,* which throughout his career remained T.'s preferred outlet.

T.'s first book, *Matthew Arnold* (1939), developed out of his doctoral dissertation. Originally planned as the critique of a Victorian sage from a more or less Marxian perspective, the work in the course of its composition increasingly affirmed Arnoldian over Marxian values. Indeed, many commentators feel that T. had come to see himself as possibly the Arnold of his own generation.

The book was favorably received, and T.'s reputation was enhanced by his *E. M. Forster* (1943), a study of a novelist who at the time seemed to approach T.'s ideal of the man of letters. But it was a gathering of essays published as *The Liberal Imagination* (1950) that confirmed T.'s critical stature; the book probably remains the defining work of T.'s career, as the critical essay proved to be his characteristic form. Although its topics are for the most part literary, the book reveals T., in what most distinguishes him from the New Critics, as a formidable cultural critic, rather than a literary critic in the narrow sense. It positioned him as one of mid-20th-c. American liberalism's most trenchant critics from within. T. rejected what he saw as a blandly optimistic and crudely materialistic liberalism in favor of an ironic or even tragic liberalism. In the light of T.'s moral realism, liberalism is to be embraced, not because it points the way to an ideal future, but because it is, on balance, on the side of justice within a civilization that inevitably entails discontents.

The values articulated in T.'s first three books remain constants of his career. Even *The Middle of the Journey* (1947), the only novel by T., who had once seen himself as a novelist by vocation, is essentially a fictionalized reflection on the same ethical, political, and intellectual concerns. Later books such as *The Opposing Self* (1955), *Beyond Culture* (1965), and *Sincerity and Authenticity* (1972), while inevitably reflecting shifts of emphasis, mark no essential turn. They do, however, suggest T.'s growing unease regarding academic culture as it was reshaped by the upheavals of the 1960s and 1970s. Increasingly, T. found himself in the position of defending at least aspects of the old order. The position seems related to a growing skepticism in the older T. about the power of literature to shape culture, a skepticism which, of course, had disturbing implications for the very literary and cultural values T. had originally championed and never abandoned.

In a way, the skepticism that troubled T. is now celebrated by champions of what we have habituated ourselves to calling postmodernism. If postmodernism truly defines the direction in which cultural criticism is to move in the 21st c., T.'s place in our literary consciousness may diminish to a virtual vanishing point. If, on the other hand, we decide that the postmodern impulse has led us up a blind alley, the sane, ironic, and, in the best sense, liberal intelligence of T. may prove invaluable as we strive to reestablish our bearings.

BIBLIOGRAPHY: Boyers, R., *L. T.: Negative Capability and the Wisdom of Avoidance* (1977); Chace, W., *L. T.: Criticism and Politics* (1980); Krupnick, M., *L. T. and the Fate of Cultural Criticism* (1986); O'Hara, D., *L. T.: The Work of Liberation* (1988); Shoben, E. J., Jr., *L. T.: Mind and Character* (1981); Trilling, D., *The Beginning of the Journey* (1993)

W. P. KENNEY

TRUMBO, Dalton

b. 9 December 1905, Montrose, Colorado; d. 10 September 1976, Los Angeles, California

T. won most of the honors available to screenwriters, including the Academy Award in 1957 for *The Brave One,* the Writer's Guild Laurel Award for lifetime achievement in screenwriting (1970), and the Cannes Film Festival Special Jury Grand Prize in 1971 for *Johnny Got His Gun* as well as many other regional and international prizes. In the decades following his death, however, he has been remembered more for his political activities than his novels and film scripts. During the McCarthy era of the 1950s, T. was the most forthright and articulate of the famous Hollywood Ten, ten screenwriters "blacklisted" by the Hollywood film community after Senator Joseph McCarthy and his House Un-American Activities Committee had maligned them as treasonous communists.

T. had indeed joined the Communist Party in 1943. His sympathies with the communist cause grew out of his memories of the painful spectacle of his father's business failures in his hometown of Grand Junction, Colorado. Later, T. would look to Marxist theory because of the protection it seemed to offer the lower and middle classes against financial disasters such as his father's and the millions of Americans unemployed during the Great Depression. However, he found the Party meetings absurdly unproductive and never participated in any organized Party actions. Nonetheless, when brought before McCarthy's committee in 1947, T. refused to condemn the Party or any of its members, refused either to admit or to express regret that he had ever joined, and refused to name any fellow members. His refusal won him ten months in prison and fourteen years on Hollywood's blacklist. He continued to write during this period, but his scripts were presented to the public under pseudonyms, and under the names of other, non-blacklisted writers who shared in the much reduced fees T. collected for his work during this period. His name did not appear on any of his films again until 1960, when Otto Preminger boldly announced that he had hired T. to write the script for *Spartacus.*

T. had a reputation for leftist politics long before he joined the Communist Party: his novel *Johnny Got His Gun* shocked his readers with its brutally unflinching view of the consequences of war. Again, we can trace the roots of this work to T.'s childhood. T. saw World War I sold to the public as a noble and glamorous affair, and then recoiled from his early enthusiasm as he watched the physically maimed and psychologically scarred young soldiers returning home after their victory. *Johnny Got His Gun* is told from the perspective of a hospitalized veteran trapped within a stump of a body: his participation in World War I has left him limbless, blind, deaf, and unable to speak. The soldier's story unfolds through a series of flashbacks reviewing the events that led him to this plight, interspersed with his ongoing efforts to communicate with his caretakers. The novel ends on a note of silently screaming despair, as the soldier's internal diatribe against war of all kinds finds no sympathetic external audience. One of T.'s reviewers called it "one of the most horrifying books ever written."

T.'s views on war changed with the advent of World War II, which he noted was "not a romantic war" as

World War I had been. Some of T.'s best-known work concerned the bravery of American soldiers during World War II, including the films *A Guy Named Joe,* with Spencer Tracy as the ghost of a combat pilot who returns to guide Van Johnson, a novice flyer, released in 1943, and *Thirty Seconds Over Tokyo* (1944), about America's first air raid on Tokyo. T.'s request that he be allowed to read these works while testifying before the House Un-American Activities Committee in an attempt to show his support for the American government during the war was denied. While the House Un-American Activities Committee muzzled his attempts to include a history of his work in the committee records, they could not stop him from publishing a history of the Committee's own work in his pamphlet, "The Time of the Toad" (1949), a publication that only worsened his political position in Hollywood but that remains one of the clearest analyses of the issues brought before the House Un-American Activities Committee.

After Preminger broke the blacklist by filming T.'s screenplays for *Spartacus* and *Exodus* (1960), T. went on to script such popular films as *The Sandpiper* (1965), *Hawaii* (1966), and *Papillon* (1973), as well as produce the award-winning film version of *Johnny Got His Gun* (1971). Among his colleagues, however, he is remembered not so much for his profitable popular films or his political writings as for his consummate professionalism, his casually artful letters, his gift for friendship, and his grace under pressure.

BIBLIOGRAPHY: Cook, B., *D. T.* (1977); Manfull, H., ed., *Additional Dialogue: Letters of D. T., 1942–1962* (1970); Robb, D., "Naming the Right Names: Amending the Hollywood Blacklist," *Cineaste* 22 (Spring 1996): 24–30; Schickel, R., "Return of the Hollywood Ten," *Film Comment* 17 (March–April 1981): 11–17

GWEN CRANE

TRUMBULL, John

b. 24 April 1750, Westbury Parish, Waterbury, Connecticut; d. 11 May 1831, Detroit, Michigan

As a poet in an age of radical change, T.'s work integrates a variety of philosophical perspectives. He was the son of a congregationalist minister, and at some level he retained the belief that poetry must serve a moral purpose. Drawing from the British neoclassicists, T. felt that poetry must be governed by order, rules, and propriety. He recognized the tyranny of Great Britain in colonial matters, and he used humor as a political weapon and a literary device. In a number of poems and essays including the three-part *The Progress of Dulness* (1772–73), he demonstrated a propensity for satire, and as the American Revolution escalated, he turned his skills to political matters in *M'Fingal* (1776). A member of a celebrated group of young intellectuals centered at Yale called the Connecticut Wits, including such authors as Timothy DWIGHT, David HUMPHREYS, and Joel BARLOW, he was fascinated with the advances of modern literature. Contemporary assessment of T.'s writings suggest that he was more a "thinker" than a "poet." But in an age predating the rise of ROMANTICISM, the two identities were in large part the same. T. the wit, the satirist, the poet, as well as T. the political theorist merged in a set of distinctive and finely wrought early American poems.

T. enjoyed a rather privileged and intellectually stimulating boyhood. His father, like many ministers during the period, was well versed in the classics and valued education. He saw to it that his son was educated at Yale. Although as a young man T. was an intellectual committed to the life of the mind, he was often critical of academic convention and practice. Echoing some of the same concerns as Jonathan Swift, he satirized his college experience in *The Progress of Dulness*. The first part of the poem, entitled "Part First; or, The Rare Adventures of Tom Brainless," follows a comic character, "showing . . . how he went to College, and what he learned there; how he took his degree, and . . . how afterwards he became a Great Man and wore a (clerical) wig." His purpose was to criticize "the state of the times in regard to literature and religion." The poem calls for educational reform and reflects the theory of human nature that the poet developed under the influence of Lord Kames. T. derived his thinking in part from his experience at Yale and in part from his reading of Alexander Pope and Jonathan Swift. He suggests that the greatest flaw in the educational system emanates from an overemphasis upon mathematics and abstract philosophy and an underemphasis upon literature. He advocated the teaching of modern literature and composition as a substitute for the study of ancient languages. Parts 2 and 3 of *The Progress of Dulness* are entitled "Part Second: Or an Essay in the Life and Character of Dick Hairbrain of Finical Memory and "Part Third and Last: Sometimes Called, The Progress of Coquetry, or the Adventures of Mrs. Harriet Simper, of the Colony of Connecticut." These sections continue the same themes, changing characters but maintaining the focus upon educational reform.

T.'s most celebrated poem is *M'Fingal*. This lengthy "epic" is a verse satire that lampoons a 1775 proclamation by General Gage, the British governor of Massachusetts. In high sounding sentence, the proclamation had declared martial law in Boston. *M'Fingal* is designed simply: the persona creates a protagonist for each side of the political argument that lead to Gage's action, and each persona makes speeches intended to incite the audience. The Tory speechmaker is M'Fingal, and the Whig is named Honorius. Both are given to high-blown bombastic arguments, and T. cannot resist the impulse to criticize the manner and presentation of political rhetoric as a whole. But the poem's primary purpose, through the character of M'Fingal, is to dismantle the Tory view and to reveal the false reasoning of the Tory arguments. In *M'Fingal*, the Puritan congregationalist notion of poetry as moral instrument and the neoclassicist emphasis on structure and form merge in a remarkably popular and influential verse satire. Although T. is considered a minor American poet, he is a notable example of a writer of his time, an "intellectual" concerned with creating a literature that alters reality to an ethical and moral purpose.

BIBLIOGRAPHY: Cowie, A., *J. T.: Connecticut Wit* (1936); Gimmestad, V. E., *J. T.* (1974); Howard, L., *The Connecticut Wits* (1943); Parrington, V. L., *The Colonial Mind, 1620–1800* (1927)

STEVEN FRYE

TUCKER, George

b. 20 August 1775, St. George's Island, Bermuda; d. 10 April 1861, Albemarle County, Virginia.

After emigrating from Bermuda to Virginia in 1795, T. served as a competent but undistinguished lawyer and three-term congressman (1819–24) before settling into a twenty-year tenure as a professor at the University of Virginia. As a man of letters, while T.'s most important work was in the field of economics, he was also an accomplished essayist, novelist, and historian. T. began his literary career principally as an essayist, contributing a series of essays entitled "Thoughts of a Hermit"—covering such subjects as literature, art, ethics, and economics—to the *Port Folio* in 1814–15. Another series of essays, *Letters from Virginia* (1816), shortly followed. These letters, allegedly written by a "young Frenchman of ancient family" and subsequently "translated from the French," give a satirical view of the Old Dominion and address such topics as the cruelty of slavery, the dearth of American literature, and Thomas JEFFERSON's views on race. The *Port Folio* essays, with a few additions, were later collected in *Essays on Various Subjects of Taste, Morals, and National Policy* (1822). It was in part this collection that captured the attention of James Madison and Joseph C. Cabell and may have lead them to recommend T. to Jefferson for appointment as professor of moral philosophy at the newly founded University of Virginia.

T. did not accept Jefferson's offer immediately. He waited several months in order to see if his recently published first novel, *The Valley of Shenandoah; or, Memoirs of the Graysons* (1824), would provide enough justification for launching a full-time career as a novelist. Although *The Valley* is arguably the best of T.'s three novels, it did not prove the commercial success T. had hoped. A mixture of sentiment, satire, and manners, *The Valley* is a realistic portrayal of life on a Virginia plantation and a study in seduction and financial ruin. His second novel, *A Voyage to the Moon* (1827), published under the pseudonym Joseph Atterley, appeared three years after *The Valley,* and boasts the distinction of being the first American SCIENCE FICTION novel about interplanetary travel. A Swiftian satire, *A Voyage to the Moon* aims its ridicule at a variety of human foibles, including fashion, useless inventions, and the general incompetencies of intellectuals from physicians to philosophers. A third novel, *A Century Hence; or, A Romance of 1941,* remained unpublished at T.'s death, but has since been brought out in a posthumous edition in 1977. This epistolary romance blends T.'s predictions about American life in the mid-20th c. into a conventional story of love and misunderstanding.

Aside from his important contributions in economics, T.'s significant literary accomplishments in the latter half of his life were in the field of history and biography. T. wrote the first biography of Thomas Jefferson, *The Life of Thomas Jefferson* (2 vols., 1837), still considered, overall, the most balanced 19th-c. treatment of Jefferson. Finally, while living in retirement in Philadelphia, T. wrote the four-volume *A History of the United States* (1856–57). Although T.'s *History* makes for dry reading when compared with the work of other 19th-c. historians such as George Bancroft and Frances PARKMAN, his work does stand out as a model of accuracy and objectivity.

BIBLIOGRAPHY: Helderman, L. C., "A Satirist in Old Virginia," *ASch* 6 (1937): 481–97; Hubbell, J. B., *The South in American Literature* (1954); McLean, R. C., *G. T.: Moral Philosopher and Man of Letters* (1961); Snavely, T. R., *G. T. as Political Economist* (1964)

ERIC CARL LINK

TUCKERMAN, Frederick Goddard

b. 4 February 1821, Boston, Massachusetts; d. 9 May 1873, Greenfield, Massachusetts

The quality and reputation of T.'s poetry was astutely envisioned by his contemporary, Nathaniel HAWTHORNE, when he stated: "I question whether the poems will obtain a very early or wide acceptance from the public ... because their merit does not lie upon the surface, but must be looked for. The great difficulty with you will be to get yourself read at all." Even though T.'s poems have been given little attention, his work warrants our careful consideration in understanding the development of American poetry.

Born into a wealthy family, T.'s formal education culminated with his attending the Dane Law College at Harvard from 1839 to 1842. Soon after his admission to the bar in 1844, he found the legal profession distasteful. T. subsequently retreated to the rural area of Greenfield, Massachusetts. Upon relocating, he met his wife, Anna, whose presence would have the greatest single impact upon his life and work. After her death in 1857, T. began working on his sonnet sequence. While he produced various poems during his life, T. continually worked at this sequence, which culminated in five parts containing one hundred and five sonnets total. He would see only the first two parts published in the four separate editions of his *Poems* during his lifetime, the only edition containing all five being the now out-of-print *Complete Poems of F. G. T.* (1965) with a critical foreword by Yvor WINTERS.

This sonnet sequence has largely been viewed as an elegy in the Tennysonian vein, mourning the loss of his wife Anna and his son. Be this as it may, the sonnets are a multivalent work registering pastoral, visionary, and confessional overtones. The mood throughout the sequence is relatively somber, marked initially by the poet's retreat into the surrounding forests. But by the third part, T. conveys optimism and a full acceptance of oppositional forces reveling in the reciprocity of life and death, decay and growth, darkness and light.

T.'s prosody often exemplifies the tone or subject matter of a given sonnet or poem by occasionally leaving out a foot at the end of a couplet and through the irregular use of partial rhymes. Unlike Donne or Milton, T. did not construct a specific variation and adhere to it consistently. However, most critics now agree that T.'s dynamic play of formal structure and content was deliberately orchestrated much like Emily DICKINSON's verse in her later poems.

Current and past criticism has tended to treat T.'s love of nature as a scientifically fostered interest based upon a devout Christian and Episcopalian stance. However, after T. asks if we have seen Moses's miracle "reversed" in the final sonnet of the fourth part, he offers a brief catalog of nature's other wonders offering to show us "more than these, of nature's secrecies the least." Throughout his work, he never makes explicit references to a Christian God. T.'s meticulous attention to depicting the physical and magical power of nature, which has been not been sufficiently acknowledged, is paramount to his work.

T.'s use of nature imagery is extraordinarily punctilious. His brother Edward was a renowned botanist and did definitive work on New England lichens; in fact, Tuckerman's Ravine in New Hampshire is named after Edward. The poet himself was an enthusiast of botany as well as astronomy. His two chosen areas of natural science converge in the chiasma that opens the poem entitled "Sonnets": "The starry flower, the flowerlike stars that fade." During his first stay in England in 1851, T. made an herbarium that included ground ivy from Gray's grave. In his "A Soul that out of Nature's Deep," T. offers a Whitmanesque catalog of obscure flora and their attributes. He declares that this listing "embodies" and is "emblematic" of "the gleanings of a Life." This taxonomical display of plant species indigenous to the U.S. is a unique aspect of T.'s poetry, and may have been influenced by Tennyson's own close attention to similar details.

In general, T.'s miscellaneous poems are not as consistent as his sonnet series, but many are well executed. For instance, "The Cricket," by far the most popular of the poems, is interesting in terms of its lyrical execution and playful subject matter. Moreover, the subject matter of his mysterious and deeply moving "A Soul That out of Nature's Deep" and several other pieces are directly related to his sonnet sequence. In order for us to appreciate T.'s work as a whole, we need to read it as a contiguous and consciously reflexive body of poetry. When afforded a careful reading, T.'s work is clearly some of the more important and original poetry of the 19th c.

BIBLIOGRAPHY: England, E., *Beyond Romanticism: T.'s Life and Poetry* (1990); Golden, Samuel A., *F. G. T.* (1966); Momaday, N. S., ed., *The Complete Poems of F. G. T.* (1965)

ROBERT PODGURSKI

TURCO, Lewis [Putnam]
b. 2 May 1934, Buffalo, New York

T.'s considerable skills as a poet have perhaps been overshadowed by his reputation as a critic. If T.'s poems have not reached as large an audience as they deserve, *The Book of Forms* (1968) and its successor, *The New Book of Forms: A Handbook of Poetics* (1986), have now influenced two generations of students and poets, most prominently the group known as the New Formalists—a term T. anticipated when he began to write approvingly of neoformalism in the early 1980s. In a period when many American poets grew hostile to meter, stanza, and rhyme, T.'s books remained sources from which younger poets could glean the full possibilities of the poet's craft.

The New Book of Forms is the most complete treatment of poetic techniques currently available, and it has grown far beyond its earlier incarnation, which mainly consisted of a catalog of metrical patterns and rhyme schemes. The first third of the book contains a discussion of the four levels—typographical, sonic, sensory, and ideational—on which poems operate. Useful to the student are T.'s introductory comments on the literary genres and his definition of poetry—as opposed to fiction, drama, or the essay—as "the art of language." T. is equally clear in distinguishing the differences between the four literary genres and the two *modes* of writing—prose ("unmetered language") and verse ("metered language"). Somewhat more controversial is T.'s dismissal of the term "free verse" as self-contradictory: "Either language is metered, or it is not metered; it cannot be both simultaneously." To account for the thousands of poems that employ no consistent metrical system, T. employs terms like "prose poetry" or "triversen" to describe the formal practices of poets as diverse as Walt WHITMAN and William Carlos WILLIAMS. Though many readers may question T.'s conclusions and his occasionally idiosyncratic use of terminology, few will have doubts about the seriousness and thoroughness he has brought to the task of constructing a "handbook" in an age when many American poets and editors gazed on discussions of poetic form with a suspect eye.

As might be expected, T.'s own poetry displays remarkable versatility and formal variety, but the poems collected in *The Shifting Web: New and Selected Poems* (1989) for the most part eschew the more flamboyant formal patterns for syllabic stanzas in the manner of Marianne MOORE or quiet, descriptive poems in, for lack of a better term, free verse. For a number of years, T. has employed an alter-ego, one Wesli Court (an anagram of his name), to construct light verse and formal tours de force, including many of the sample poems in *The New Book of Forms*. His most consistently successful work is found in *American Still Lifes* (1981), a series of verbal portraits of abandoned buildings and places in which the poet's own identity is subsumed in an attempt at objective presentation.

BIBLIOGRAPHY: Doll, M., "L. T.," in Ross, J. W., ed., *DLB Yearbook 1984* (1985): 331–38

R. S. GWYNN

TURELL, Jane [Colman]

b. 25 February 1708, Boston, Massachusetts; d. 26 March 1735, Medford, Massachusetts

Despite her brief life and limited output, T. is known as a significant female poet in prerevolutionary America,

second only to Anne BRADSTREET. Her poetry illustrates the wedding of the spiritual values of the New England Puritan tradition with the newer literary tastes of a more cosmopolitan early-18th-c. Boston.

T. is known to us through a book published as a memorial after her death, *Reliquiae Turellae et Lachrymae Paternae: A Father's Tears over his Daughter's Remains . . . To Which are added some large memoires of her Life and Death* (1735). The book includes two funeral sermons for her written by her father, pastor of the prominent Brattle Street Church in Boston, Benjamin Colman; seven letters from Colman counseling her on her spiritual life; and an appendix compiled by Ebenezer Turell, her husband, printing her poems and other spiritual writings. While most readers have been particularly interested in the poems printed in *Reliquiae Turellae,* its central concern is T.'s spiritual life, including her struggles in deciding to be a communing member at her new church at Medford, under her husband's pastorate.

Ebenezer Turell, acting as his wife's editor, is concerned to depict her as a spiritual exemplar. To that end, he assures his readers that poetry was for her "a *Recreation* not a *Business,*" and he notes that he has omitted from the collection "some pieces of Wit and Humor." These comments have prompted modern readers to argue that T.'s poetic achievements were stifled by her editing relatives. Nevertheless, the book labels T. "pious *and* ingenious," and Ebenezer Turell relates some family stories about her verbal precociousness—she could read at four, and could divert her father's houseguests, including the governor, with her "pertinent remarks"—suggesting that Benjamin Colman encouraged her literary talents from a young age. The book includes a verse paraphrase of Psalm 137 that she wrote as a child, and Colman's encouraging comments to her about it. Other biblical paraphrases provide occasions for T. to meditate on her role as a wife and on the nature of church community. Beyond the paraphrases, poetic paeans to Richard Blackmore and Edmund Waller suggest her literary tastes and English models; Elizabeth Singer Rowe, whom Benjamin Colman had met in London, seems her most important poetic influence. Two poems, "On Reading the Warning by Mrs. Singer" and "To My Muse," praise Singer Rowe and other female poets, making strong claims for the moral authority of a woman's poetic voice.

Other poems of note include an elegy for her mother's death, and the often-anthologized "Lines . . . on childbirth," in which, writing as a pregnant woman, she speaks feelingly of her previous losses, through stillbirth and early death, of two infants, praying this time to be delivered of "a living child / To dedicate to thee."

BIBLIOGRAPHY: Cowell, P., ed., *Women Poets in Pre-Revolutionary America, 1650–1775: An Anthology*

(1981); Watts, E. S., *The Poetry of American Women from 1632 to 1945* (1977)

LAURA HENIGMAN

TWAIN, Mark. See **CLEMENS, Samuel Langhorne**

TY-CASPER, Linda

b. 17 September 1931, Manila, Philippines

Despite earning a law degree in 1957 from Harvard, T. relinquished her legal career to become the foremost historical novelist of the Philippines. Correcting misleading testimonies in the sub-basement of Harvard's Widener Library, T. decided that since "History is the biography of a country, but literature is its autobiography," she would become the advocate for her people through meticulously researched "true fiction." She has said that "Literature is not the place in which to *learn* history, but to *understand* it" through the inner lives of its characters.

The Peninsulars (1964), centered on the Dutch invasion of 18th-c. Manila, set the thematic pattern of self-injury through divisiveness in her later novels. *The Three-Cornered Sun* (1979) dramatized how competing Filipino forces during their Revolution of 1896 against Spain so blunted their own effort at independence that, as recorded in T.'s *Ten Thousand Seeds* (1987), the Americans who came later as expected liberators precipitated the Philippine–American War (1899–1901) and remained as colonial overseers. A final novel in the trilogy, *The Stranded Whale,* about the war's outcome had already been drafted when she was distracted by President Ferdinand Marcos's reign of greed and "crony capitalism" (1965–86).

Dread Empire (1980) exposed a provincial strongman's oppressive tactics paralleling then President Ferdinand Marcos's own; *Hazards of Distance* (1981) pictured how ordinary citizens became caught between the violent demands of communist guerrillas and of reckless government troops; *Fortress in the Plaza* (1985) reenacted the 1972 massacre of opposition party leaders that became Marcos's excuse for martial law. As censorship grew, in order to protect her family still in the Philippines, T. published two novels in London: *Awaiting Trespass* (1985), about the martyrdom of a presumed playboy actually monitoring detainees for their safety, and *Wings of Stone* (1986), the tale of a Filipino expatriate's return from the U.S. during the 1984 election that together with the 1983 public assassination of Benigno Aquino caused widespread uprisings and the exile of Marcos. In 1988, T. published *A Small Party in a Garden,* a novella about murder and rape perpetrated by unknown assailants—predators who could represent either the un-bounded regime of the Marcoses or of President Corazon Aquino whose confusion of popularity left economic overlords in power. *DreamEden* (1996) recounted in detail the People Power Revolution of 1986 as well as the several coups against Aquino for her feeble democratic reforms. All of these works reveal the author's solid commitment to describing a culture too often turned against itself. Narration, therefore, is conveyed typically from a series of revolving points of view.

In three collections of short fiction—*The Transparent Sun* (1963), *Secret Runner* (1974), and *Common Continent* (1990)—T. continued to identify with the struggle of the underclass for self-determination against "colonialism" both foreign and native. Her efforts to picture this disarray have been assisted by fellowships from the Radcliffe Institute, Djerassi, the Massachusetts Artists Foundation, Wheatland, UNESCO/PEN, the Southeast Asia WRITE Foundation, and the Rockeller Center in Bellagio.

BIBLIOGRAPHY: An Lim, J., *Literature and Politics* (1993); Bresnahan, R., *Conversations with Filipino Writers* (1987); Casper, L., *Sunsurfers Seen from Afar* (1996); Montenegro, D., ed., *Points of Departure: International Writers on Writing and Politics* (1991)

LEONARD CASPER

TYLER, Anne

b. 25 October 1941, Minneapolis, Minnesota

In addition to achieving distinction as a short story writer and critic, T. has risen to prominence as a novelist, most notably for *The Accidental Tourist* (1985), which won the American Book Critics Circle Award, and *Breathing Lessons* (1988), which won the Pulitzer Prize. Her earlier novels are: *If Morning Ever Comes* (1964), *The Tin Can Tree* (1965), *A Slipping Down Life* (1970), *The Clock Winder* (1972), *Celestial Navigations* (1974), *Searching for Caleb* (1975), *Earthly Possessions* (1977), *Morgan's Passing* (1980), and *Dinner at the Homesick Restaurant* (1982). Her later novels include *Saint Maybe* (1991), *Ladder of Years* (1995), and *Patchwork Planet* (1998).

Certain themes recur insistently in T.'s novels: nearly all develop the complex relationships existing within a family or among a few friends and neighbors. Repeatedly, her characters struggle between a commitment to family or community, on the one hand, and to individual expression, independence, creativity, or pleasurable solitude on the other. When they adventurously break through inhibitions imposed upon them by childhood experience, they still cling guiltily and sometimes fearfully to family convention.

Like Eudora WELTY, whose work T. considers a formative influence on her own, T. contrasts characters who are naturally "stay-at-homes" with those who are "wanderers" or "humming birds," to use Eudora Welty's terminology. T.'s travelers who seek to escape nearly always return to a familiar place and to the people from who they have fled, but their return is not a dispirited surrender. Despite the circular nature of the journey, the travel has contributed to their understanding of themselves and their situation and has allowed them to make a choice. The travel has sometimes been "enough" when a character has merely checked into a nearby motel or spent a longer than usual time grocery shopping.

Symbols that recur in T.'s novels often relate to such journeys that go nowhere. For example, the antique sleigh bed of Charlotte Emory in *Earthly Possessions* suggests movement but remains in place, as does the merry-go-round that Duncan will operate in the carnival job he is about to take at the close of *Searching for Caleb.* The frequent references to the standardization of popular culture (such as T.'s use of McDonalds or Kentucky Fried Chicken signs) reassure the traveler that he has not left home. Photographs that fix life in a moment of stasis at a significant point become pivotal in several books—Charlotte Emory and her father in *Earthly Possessions* and James in *The Tin Can Tree* are professional photographers; two old photographs are crucial in Justine's search for Caleb, who has left sixty-two years before he is found (*Searching for Caleb*); James's enlargement of a photo recalls the vitality of Janie Rose Pike, the child who decorated the tree with tin cans just before her sudden death (*The Tin Can Tree*); and the photographs that Ezra Tull distributed to his brothers and sisters force them to reconstruct more positively their memories of a turbulent and miserable childhood (*Dinner at the Homesick Restaurant*).

T.'s preoccupation with the analysis of nuclear families and with travel as escape or as a threatening experience may derive from her personal life. She has remarked in interviews that, like Macon Leary in *The Accidental Tourist,* she is a reluctant traveler and that she had a conviction throughout childhood and adolescence that she would become a refugee. She did not live in a typical household until she entered high school, but resided with her family in several Quaker communes.

The novels can be divided into three groups. The first four are early experiments of high quality, with *The Tin Can Tree* the most moving and most complex as it presents the dynamics of three very different households in a three-apartment row house situated in an isolated rural setting. All three families grieve for Janie Rose, whose burial provides the first scene.

The next three novels—*Celestial Navigations, Searching for Caleb,* and *Earthly Possessions*—may comprise T.'s best fiction. In them, she fully probes the psyches of the individual characters and vividly communicates their struggles. Parallels exist among these three novels. All focus on the marriages of a mismatched couple, each of whom is deeply in love with the other. All three novels depict a husband who is impractical, stubborn, imaginative, creative, and willing to ignore the stress that he places upon his spouse, yet he remains a positive or sympathetic character. In *Celestial Navigations,* Mary dares to reach into the fears of the agoraphobic Jeremy Pauling, who becomes during the marriage a notable artist through his creation of collages. Mary forms for him a bridge to the outside world and enables him at least to have the courage to walk to the corner grocery without collapsing and to accompany her to the hospital when their children are about to be born. Though they love one another, they finally surrender to the power of Jeremy's illness, and he will peacefully continue to combine the fragments of cloth, leather, feathers, and paper into art.

In *Searching for Caleb,* Justine and Duncan Peck move every year or two in order to provide the restless Duncan with change in a new job and with stimulus for his inventions. Justine gives herself willingly to Duncan, to her daughter, to her grandfather and to Caleb until she finds that she has lost herself. After a crisis of rebellion, she chooses not to leave Duncan and to wait hopefully for a reconciliation with their conventional daughter, whom they have driven away by constant moving and by incrementally divesting themselves of their worldly goods to make nomadic existence simpler.

Similarly in *Earthly Possessions* the demands of her preacher-husband overburden Charlotte: he tends to ignore her and to give all his love and encouragement to his parishioners and relatives. Again like Justine, Charlotte strips away at her life, systematically putting household furnishings into the trash. Like Justine, she discovers that she has given away her most precious earthly possession, herself, while her husband pursues treasures in heaven. As she stops in the bank to get travelers checks in order to run away, a gently young bank robber captures her. The account of her adventures as a relatively willing hostage for five days alternates with flashbacks to her insecure childhood and the years of her marriage. Like Justine, Charlotte returns to her husband. The plots of these three books are relatively simple, but T.'s skilled use of detail, her resort to comic irony and her deep understanding of the motivation of her characters make these three books outstanding achievements.

The three novels, *Dinner at the Homesick Restaurant, Morgan's Passing,* and *The Accidental Tourist,* exhibit T.'s increasing experimentation with new structures and a fuller use of ironic comedy. Generally speaking, *Dinner at the Homesick Restaurant* maintains a melancholy tone. Each chapter focuses on the point of view of one of the five members of the Tull family, all combining to retell a story of family distress. *Morgan's Passing* excels through the exuberance and volatility of Morgan, but because one never understands his motivation—his need to find a self that seems not to exist as he impersonates several other selves—the book produces no strong emotional or aesthetic effect. Morgan is, as T. comments, a man who "arrived unassembled": his hats, beards, and masks symbolize the many personalities that may exist within any human being. Most successfully, in *The Accidental Tourist* T. creates great suspense in withholding through several tense chapters the final outcome of Macon Leary's love life. Will he return to his long-term wife, Sara, who left him after their young son was shot to death in a fast-food restaurant, or will he defy stultifying propriety and status and marry Muriel Pritchet, the skinny, talkative, warm young woman who, as a veterinarian's assistant, has helped his grotesque dog, Edward, recover from a temporary neurosis aroused by Macon's judgmental relatives. T. miraculously makes Macon Leary, a basically flat and comic character, a highly sympathetic figure in this novel.

BIBLIOGRAPHY: Evans, E., *A. T.* (1993); Petry, A. H., *Understanding A. T.* (1990); Petry, A. H., ed., *Critical Essays on A. T.* (1992); Stephens, C. R., *The Fiction of A. T.* (1990); Voelker, J. C., *Art and the Accidental in A. T.* (1989)

MARGARET B. MCDOWELL

TYLER, Royall

b. 18 July 1757, Boston, Massachusetts; d. 26 August 1826, Brattleboro, Vermont

T. was the first American to write a commercially successful comedy produced in America, *The Contrast* (1790). Though inspired by Richard Brinsley Sheridan's *The School for Scandal, The Contrast* emphasizes American characters and types. Later, T. wrote a satirical picaresque novel in two volumes, *The Algerine Captive* (1797). His reputation rests on these works.

Like his contemporary satirist Hugh Henry BRACKENRIDGE, T. practiced law; in 1807 he was elected Chief Justice of the Vermont Supreme Court. And like Brackenridge, T. wrote in many forms. His works include legal tracts, patriotic operations, sermons, the first American musical drama, at least six additional plays (two of which were performed), two long poems published as pamphlets, and a volume of semifictional travel letters, *The Yankey in London* (1809). With the essayist and editor Joseph Dennie, T. wrote the immensely popular newspaper columns "from the SHOP of Messrs. COLON (Dennie) & SPONDEE (T.)." T.'s contributions to this series were chiefly poetic. Late in life, T. began to rewrite *The Algerine Captive* as *The Bay Boy,* a less satirical, more realistic fiction.

The Contrast was staged first in New York, soon after in Baltimore and Philadelphia. Its popularity can be attributed to T.'s portrayal of three characters: Jonathan, Manly, and Dimple. Jonathan, a plain spoken, simple Yankee, is the comic heart of the play. Manly, an American, and Dimple, an Englishman, are both characterized by their names. They vie for the hand of a New York belle, Maria. The simpering hypocrisies of Dimple are exposed; the native humor of Jonathan and the native integrity of Manly triumph. *The Contrast* has a threadbare plot; act 1 sinks with exposition. But T. displays three dramaturgical gifts: he draws memorable comic types; he writes clear, amusing dialogue; he never overreaches his talents or his audience. *The Contrast* can be produced today.

The Algerine Captive, a more ambitious, complex work, is narrated by Updike Underhill, a callow New England youth. Like Lemuel Gulliver, he is a literalist and a doctor; like Gulliver, he wanders aimlessly. First, Updike travels South, there observing the indignities of slavery. Undaunted he becomes a ship's doctor, sailing to London, then Africa. Too late, Updike learns he has signed on a slaver. He attacks the captain for mistreating blacks and is marooned. In volume two, Updike becomes a slave in Algeria. Much of this volume is undisguised travelogue; T. caters to his readers' fascination with Barbary Coast. But T. does depict slavery as unromantic, brutal, and degrading. Eventually Updike's master allows him to practice medicine. Ever the dupe, Updike is conned by a Jewish merchant and again sold into slavery. A Portuguese ship and an American treaty save him. *The Algerine Captive* is a consistently ironic work of fiction. Updike contrasts American freedom with Algerine slavery; T. satirizes both. He shows how the villainy and innocence of human nature render freedom precarious. Americans, T. suggests, must exercise vigilance and common sense to avoid enslaving themselves.

BIBLIOGRAPHY: Carson, A. L., and H. L. Carson, *R. T.* (1979); Davidson, C. N., *Revolution and the Word: The Rise of the Novel in America* (1986); Tanselle, G. T., *R. T.* (1967)

JOHN ENGELL

UPDIKE, John [Hoyer]
b. 18 March 1932, Shillington, Pennsylvania

As a young man at Harvard working as an illustrator for the *Lampoon,* U.'s first ambition was to become a cartoonist, and the meticulously crafted style that he brought to his cartoons has translated well to his career as writer. U. is considered by most critics to be a master of the well-crafted sentence, using highly selective words that not only crystallize ideas, but whose sound and cadence resonate on the page.

Novelist, short story writer, poet, and essayist, U. is usually viewed as a kind of mannerist realist. His stylistic precision, aesthetic concerns, and focus on a white bourgeois class have placed him in the tradition of Henry JAMES, Ernest HEMINGWAY, and J. D. SALINGER. And, along with John CHEEVER, he has been described as one of the most representative figures in postwar social realism or neorealism. Unlike some of the more radically innovative contemporaries of his early career—notably Donald BARTHELME and Ronald SUKENICK—who privileged exercises in language, U. has tried to maintain above all a sense of story. This attention to stylistic and narrative form has remained a trademark of his writing.

U. had been a contributor and then editor of the *Harvard Lampoon,* but he first received national attention in 1954 when the *New Yorker* published his short story, "Friends from Philadelphia." A year later, he joined the *New Yorker* staff where he contributed to the "Talk of the Town" column. Formally ending his ties with the magazine in 1957 (although continuing to contribute over the next four decades), U. moved to Ipswich, Massachusetts, to concentrate on his writing. His first novel, *The Poorhouse Fair* (1959), is the story of elderly residents of a county poorhouse and their revolt against the institution's overly efficient, sociologically minded administrator. In many ways an allegorical attack on the rampant materialism of

postwar America, this novel introduces several of the themes that U. returns to in later novels.

For instance, *The Centaur* (1963) explores the ways in which individuals attempt to make sense of death, and by association, search for beauty and value in a highly secularized society. Here U. juxtaposes contemporary life with the Chiron myth and creates a tale in which his high school-aged protagonist, Peter Caldwell, learns to overcome his nihilistic fear of living. *Couples* (1968), U.'s fifth novel, concerns the sexual interactions of ten young-to-middle-aged couples in a small New England community. As with many of his novels, a concern with sexual relations between men and women—in this case, the loose lifestyle of spouse swapping—is foregrounded against a backdrop of Calvinistic moralism. The novel illustrates the spiritually decaying effects of lust without love, and shows how there are serious social consequences to certain choices and behaviors.

U. is perhaps most popularly known for his four "Rabbit" novels. Harry "Rabbit" Angstrom, a lower-middle-to-middle-class family man, is the focus of these works, and as his last name suggests, the author uses Rabbit as a gauge by which to measure American culture over a four decade period. *Rabbit, Run* (1960) concerns Rabbit's attempts to find meaning in the highly commercial and secularized 1950s. Much like *The Centaur* and *Couples,* this novel is an exercise in acute social observation that highlights a spiritual quest within an apparently sterilized materialistic world. Rabbit longs for some sort of meaningful stability, but his attempts to escape the barrenness around him make him a social outcast. Unable to maintain his role as husband and father, and unwilling to commit to his adulterous lover, he flees these responsibilities as a way out of his social conundrum.

Each of the succeeding "Rabbit" novels takes as its temporal backdrop the following three decades. *Rabbit Redux* (1971) finds Rabbit caught up in the tumultuous 1960s and all of its cultural phenomena, including radicalism, free love, social protest, racial politics, and space exploration. The critically acclaimed *Rabbit Is Rich* (1981)—winner of the American Book Award, the Pulitzer Prize, and the National Book Critics Circle Award—picks up in the 1970s. Rabbit, by this time, has started to indulge in the materialistic American dream he found so troublesome in the earlier novels. The glory he once found on the basketball court he now finds in owning a Toyota dealership. Still, Rabbit discovers that such economic success is not without its costs to both himself and his family. *Rabbit at Rest* (1990), the tetralogy's final installment, shows an aging and ailing Rabbit who in many ways is a human mirror to the debt-ridden, AIDS-plagued 1980s and an America running out of steam, with nothing but empty patriotism to fall back on. Each of these novels, in addition to chronicling the last half of the 20th c., reiterate U.'s balance of social critique with the desire for personal quest.

Other notable novels of U.'s include a trilogy loosely based on Nathaniel HAWTHRONE's *The Scarlet Letter: A Month of Sundays* (1975), *Roger's Version* (1986), and *S.* (1988). All three of these novels take on, in one way or another, Hawthorne's classic, and as U. himself has pointed out, each is a contemporary retelling of the story from the perspective of the three major figures involved: Arthur Dimmesdale, Roger Chillingworth, and Hester Prynne respectively. *The Coup* (1978) is significant in that it is one of the few times that U. posits his narrative outside of middle-class suburbia. The novel is narrated by Colonel Hakim Felix Ellellôû, former president of the fictional African nation Kush, who labors to explain not only the reasons behind the coup that ousted him, but perhaps more significantly, the private life behind his highly public mask. Later novels are *Memories of the Ford Administration* (1992), *Brazil* (1994), *In the Beauty of the Lillies* (1996), and *Toward the End of Time* (1997).

U. is also known for his work in the short story genre. Early collections such as *The Same Door* (1959), *Pigeon Feathers* (1962), and *The Music School* (1966) helped to establish, along with the novels, U.'s literary reputation. *Museums and Women* (1972) is unique in that it largely deviates from the realist style and indulges in experimental mode of John BARTH. The Bech books—*Bech: A Book* (1970) *Bech Is Back* (1982), and *Bech at Bay* (1998)—are collections of somewhat self-reflexive stories that examine the life of a professional writer and explore the literary marketplace. Henry Bech, a novelist ruined by literary celebrity, in many ways anticipates Philip ROTH's unfortunate Nathan Zuckerman. U.'s inclusion in several short story anthologies published in the 1990s as well as

the reception of his collection *The Afterlife and Other Stories* (1994) indicate his continued success in the genre.

Although not as critically recognized as his work in fiction, U.'s poetry is nonetheless an important facet to his literary career. *The Carpentered Hen and Other Tame Creatures* (1958), his first collection, was largely hailed as the debut of a unique stylized voice. U. called that collection "light verse," much as he did *Midpoint and Other Poems* (1969) eleven years later. But *Midpoint* is highly personal and introspective, and in it he confronts many of the themes and techniques he developed in his fiction. In much of his subsequent poetry, which can be found in his *Collected Poems, 1953–1993* (1993), U. continues the exploration of his favorite themes, and does so as he has in his fiction, with a delicate balance of playfulness and sobriety.

BIBLIOGRAPHY: Bloom, H., ed., *J. U.* (1987); Campbell, J. H., *U.'s Novels* (1987); Macnaughton, W. R., ed., *Critical Essays on J. U.* (1982); O'Connell, M., *U. and the Patriarchal Dilemma* (1996); Plath, J., ed., *Conversations with J. U.* (1994); Ristoff, D. I., *U.'s America* (1988); Schiff, J. A., *U.'s Version* (1992); Tallent, E., *Married Men and Magic Tricks: J. U.'s Erotic Heroes* (1982)

DEREK PARKER ROYAL

URIS, Leon [Marcus]

b. 3 August 1924, Baltimore, Maryland

Having first made a name for himself as an adventure novelist with *Battle Cry* (1953), a story of young Marines in World War II, and *The Angry Hills* (1955), a tale of a noncombatant's immersion in the Greek Underground during the war, U. turned in 1957 to a broader, some would say panoramic, brand of historical fiction with his wildly successful story of the founding of Israel, *Exodus*. While he subsequently wrote other types of fiction—notably *Topaz* (1967), an espionage thriller—since *Exodus* U. has become known for such sprawling novels as *Trinity* (1976), recounting Ireland's struggle for independence from Britain; *The Haj* (1984), telling the story of Israel's founding from the Arab point of view; and *Redemption* (1995), an expansion of the *Trinity* story.

Regardless of the genre, U.'s novels almost always feature a heroic underdog fighting the powers of great nations, industrialists, or evil empires. The odds against his protagonists are huge, usually of global proportions. In *Exodus,* for example, Ari Ben Canaan fights the British blockade of Palestine, the indifference of the postwar world, and the brutality of the Arabs in his quest to establish a Jewish homeland.

Similarly, *Trinity*'s Conor Larkin daringly challenges the British army, Protestant terrorists, and the ruthless greed of Anglo-Irish industrialists as he struggles to bring freedom to his occupied country. Frequently these characters have little more than their ingenuity and a few loyal comrades with which to do battle, and more often than not they are fortified by the undying love of a woman—almost always a woman from the ranks of the enemy. Andrei Androfski, for example, in *Mila 18* (1960), struggles to wrest control of the Warsaw Ghetto from the Nazis with the help of Gabriela Rak, a Polish Catholic.

The historical component of these novels is sweeping, with action often taking place in locales all over the world, and with the occasional appearance of legendary historic characters. David Ben Gurion is featured in both *Exodus* and *The Haj,* as is Sir Winston [Spencer] Churchill in *Redemption.* Often, however, historical figures are fictionalized, such as the egomaniacal French President Pierre LaCroix in *Topaz,* a thinly veiled portrayal of Charles De Gaulle. Sometimes the legendary characters are composites, representing types rather than actual figures. The Irish revolutionary Long Dan Sweeney in *Trinity,* for example, has the precise military mind of a Michael Collins along with the ruthless single-mindedness of an Eamon de Valera. Critics frequently question U.'s historical accuracy, but he is more likely guilty of nothing worse than a sometimes zealous partisanship in recounting historical events. The decidedly partisan point of view of his novels renders their value as historical artifacts neither greater nor less than that of any other historical novel.

U.'s focus on men in battle situations—either fighting in the armed forces in *Battle Cry, Redemption* or as guerrillas in *Mila 18, Trinity*—is reminiscent of Ernest HEMINGWAY. Like Hemingway, U. uses the battlefield as a testing ground for his protagonists, who sustain themselves with alcohol and the love of a devoted woman. The world in which both authors immerse their characters is a distinctively masculine one. What sets U. apart from writers like Hemingway, however, is his treatment of good and evil. While Hemingway and other writers who enjoy a place in the American literary canon present a world filled with ambiguity, in U.'s work the demarcation between good and evil is clearly marked. Good is normally associated with the poor and powerless, evil with the wealthy and powerful. In this regard, U.'s novels sometimes lean toward the melodramatic.

The immense popularity of U.'s fiction can be attributed in part to his flair for melodrama, but his ability to weave several subplots into a fast-paced, cinematic tale set in a volatile historical context also contributes to his reputation with readers. Among writers of popular fiction in the U.S., U. will be remembered primarily as a great storyteller.

BIBLIOGRAPHY: Downey, S. D., and R. A. Kallan, "Semi-Aesthetic Detachment: The Fusing of Fictional and External Worlds in the Situational Literature of L. U.," *ComM* 49 (September 1982): 192–204; Manganero, E. S., "Voicing the Arab: Multivocality and Ideology in L. U.'s *The Hag,*" *MELUS* 15 (Winter 1988): 3–13

KATHLEEN SHINE CAIN

UTOPIA

Imagining better futures is one of America's favorite pastimes. Every generation has conceived of and established its own utopian communities whether they be Puritan townships or ascetic enclaves like Ephrata, 19th-c. secular communes such as Oneida, New Harmony, and Brook Farm, or the hidden urban co-ops and brashly visible Disney Worlds of the late 20th c. Written expressions of utopian contemplation have been at least as varied as the community experiments. Strong utopian elements added intensity to the Declaration of Independence as well as to 20th-c. New Deal and Great Society documents. Utopian episodes and motifs, ranging in tone from exotic romanticism to sharp-edged satire, appear in works written by many of America's best-known novelists. Sections of Herman MELVILLE's *Typee* and *Mardi* demonstrate that one author could express both romantic and satiric extremes. Indeed, several of America's most fascinating works of fiction—Mark TWAIN's *A Connecticut Yankee in King Arthur's Court* and F. Scott FITZGERALD's *The Great Gatsby,* for instance—express ambiguous, even ambivalent, combinations of romantic and satiric utopianism.

There are also fictional utopias: narratives that depict, in some detail, an imaginary, alternative culture that is either much better—a utopia, sometimes called an eutopia—or much worse—a dystopia—than the author's and readers' culture. From the writer's viewpoint, such a text offers opportunities to make their readers think and act differently because the reading experience has altered their perceptions of present realities and future possibilities. From the readers's viewpoint, a fictional utopia invites reevaluation and/or reinforcement of their culture's and their personal values and ideals.

The U.S. has produced more fictional utopias than any other country. Before the publication of Edward BELLAMY's *Looking Backward,* approximately fifty fictional utopias had appeared in America. Between 1888 and World War I, more than two hundred were written. During the 20th c., the primary fictional expressions of utopianism were the hundreds of SCIENCE FICTION dystopias. In every decade, however, readers discovered important American utopias, works as different as Austin T. Wright's agrarian *Islandia* (1942), B. F. Skinner's behaviorist *Walden Two* (1949), Ayn RAND's free-enterprise *Atlas Shrugged,* Robert Rimmer's sexually liberated *Harrad Experiment* (1966), and, in the 1970s and 1980s, the complex and ambiguous works of Samuel R. Delany, Ursula K. LE GUIN, and Marge PIERCY.

The sheer volume, popularity, and diversity of American utopian writing makes it an important topic for literary historians. A highly selective, chronological sampling of this literature also indicates that the study of utopian elements in American nonfiction and fiction and of fully-developed fictional utopias can be crucial to our understanding of particular eras and can raise fundamental questions about the functions of literature in America.

The history of utopian elements in American literature began in European and Native American cultures long before the colonial period. Strains of Christian millennialism and Enlightenment idealism combined with utopian narratives like Sir Thomas More's *Utopia*, published in 1516, and with oral and written tales of Cockayne, the Island of the Blessed, and Lost Continents to create a perceptual climate that emphasized the utopian possibilities in the European discovery of America. And for centuries in America, the "Indians" discovered by the Europeans had expressed tribal concepts of ideality in oral narratives and ceremonial performances—a body of literature ignored by most students of utopia.

There are similarities between the colonial utopian concepts influenced by European traditions and the Native American ceremonial expressions. In "A Model of Christian Charity" (1630), John WINTHROP's emphasis on a lovingly knit and ideally balanced social order can be compared to the stress on restoration of order, after the death of an important leader, in the Iroquois's Ritual of Condolence or to the celebrations of harmony and balance in the nine-day Navajo Nightway ceremony. Nevertheless, whether we examine the idealistic "city upon a hill" passage in Winthrop's lay sermon and the millennialism of Jonathan EDWARDS's series of sermons *A History of the Work of Redemption,* or utopian overtones in travel accounts such as John SMITH's *Description of New England* and Samuel Purchas's *Discourse on Virginia* (1625), or the utopian motifs in Puritan histories at least through Cotton MATHER's *Magnalia Christi Americana,* we are struck by the fundamental differences between the concepts of space and language that support images of ideal places and social orders in Native American and colonial literature.

For example, the Navajo ideal state of harmony-beauty (hózhó) is firmly rooted in an intimate knowledge of and reverence for particular American sacred spaces and in a concept of language that perceives sacred words as generative: words are intrinsic powers that create harmonies reflecting the primal balances experienced by the Navajo Holy Beings. The utopian passages in Euro-American writings tended to elevate American spaces and colonists by comparing them to non-American landscapes and peoples—particularly, though not exclusively, biblical Holy Lands and the Israelites—and to view American land in the abstract terms of a tabula rasa or virgin territory to be used for exciting fresh starts. Language, primarily in writing, was an essential element in attempts to describe, justify, and promote colonial utopian visions, but words in and of themselves did not create idealized states of harmony and order.

An awareness of these striking differences between the verbal constructions of idealized environments and social orders in Native American and Euro-American literatures helps us to understand the nature of the extreme cultural clashes that occurred during the first three centuries of American history. Analyzing utopian expression during the revolutionary years that ended those three centuries can also be illuminating. Key American revolutionary and constitutional writings, which were permeated with dystopian warnings and utopian hopes and influenced by British and European utopias, especially James Harrington's *Common-Wealth of Oceana* (1656), represent a culmination of attempts to define an American utopia by negation and contrast. In American literature, this tradition extends back at least to *A Description of New England,* in which John Smith describes what America should not be—a reenactment of the "bondage, violence, tyranny, ingratitude and . . . double dealing" of the Old World—and what America could and should be—a place of "libertie, profit, honor, and prosperitie." Variations of this form of utopian rhetoric in the Declaration of Independence and Thomas PAINE's *Common Sense* generated the types of personal emotion and group identity necessary to inspire and maintain a revolution. The heritage of this successful revolutionary rhetoric has, however, tended to perpetuate ahistorical and reductionist perspectives that obscure national and international realities. Michel Guillaume Jean de CRÈVE-COEUR's *Letters from an American Farmer* and *Sketches of Eighteenth Century America* offer fascinating examples and critiques of this kind of American utopianism based on inspiring-misleading contrasts to England and Europe.

The late 18th and early to mid-19th cs. offered examples of utopianism in American poetry—such as Joel BARLOW's *The Vision of Columbus* and Timothy DWIGHT's *Greenfield Hill*—and of utopian and dystopian fictions—including Charles Brockden BROWN's *Alcuin* (1798), James Kirke PAULDING's "The Man Machine," published in 1826, Mary Griffith's "Three Hundred Years Hence" (1836), James Fenimore COOPER's *Crater,* and Nathaniel HAWTHORNE's *Blithedale Romance.* It could also be argued that Ralph Waldo EMERSON used revolutionary dystopian and utopian rhetoric in "The American Scholar" and other early lectures and that Henry David THOREAU's *Walden* represented a truly revolutionary form of utopianism, one that defined the good place in terms of a temporary isolation rather than a perpetual society. But it was not until the late 19th c., with the publication of Bellamy's *Looking Backward,* that a significant number of Americans were strongly influenced by a utopian fiction. The response to this book was remarkable: only *Uncle Tom's Cabin* outsold *Looking Backward* during the 19th c., Bellamy Clubs sprung up across the country, a Nationalist Party formed that influenced state legislatures, the Populist movement, and international socialist organizations, and more than two hundred utopian and dystopian fictions appeared between 1888 and the onset of World War I. Many of these were written by the period's most talented and/or most popular authors: William Dean HOWELLS, Mark Twain, Charlotte Perkins GILMAN, Jack LONDON, Charles M. SHELDON, Harold FREDERIC, Upton SINCLAIR—even John Jacob Astor and the inventor of the safety razor, King Camp Gillette, wrote utopian fictions.

Why this period? The old truism is that utopias tend to be written and read during times of turmoil when people are frustrated and seeking solutions. Since, traditionally, utopian literature projects possibilities for coherence, order, and meaning out of the apparent chaos of the present, it is an appealing response to this frustration and seeking. The late 19th and early 20th cs. witnessed sudden economic and demographic shifts, labor strife, rapid urban-industrial growth, a war, and challenges to value systems; the period certainly meets the turmoil criterion. The era did, however, manifest enough signs of hope to make the journey to utopia seem plausible. Thus, significant technological advances and local and national reform movements played key roles in preparing Americans to believe in America as utopia.

Why fiction? By the late 19th c.—primarily because of the efforts of women writers and women readers and technological developments that reduced the cost of books—fiction had become a popular form of entertainment and a powerful social force in America. The

sales and influence of Harriet Beecher STOWE's *Uncle Tom's Cabin* attest to that. Bellamy's use of the conventions of the "sentimental" novel oriented toward domestic setting and characters and charged with melodramatic emotional appeals allowed him to present the traditional utopian plot and visitor-guide dialogues and his Christianized and Americanized socialism in an entertaining and meaningful way for 19th-c. readers.

Until the 1960s, a variety of important utopian fictions continued to be written and read. Despite their diversity, a trend developed that is clearly reflected in one of the most controversial and influential 20th-c. utopias, B. F. Skinner's *Walden Two.* Instead of adopting a class or societal perspective and emphasizing political, economic, or religious reform, Skinner's text focused on a small, harmonious community and on psychological means of conditioning individuals toward being intelligent, lively, and kind people. The scale of the setting implied a rejection of the tradition of grand utopian planning and a repulsion for modern urban life. The emphasis on psychology suggested first that the typical economic and political problems that occupied most pre-20th-c. utopian authors had been or could be controlled by technological and scientific advances, especially if Americans scaled down their material desires, and that the real challenge for the modern utopist was the development of psychological models of better people and better interpersonal relations.

The primary literary evidence of dissatisfaction with traditional pre-20th-c. utopianism was expressed in the hundreds of mid-20th-c. science fiction dystopias. Following the lead of Yevgeny Zamyatin, Aldous Huxley, and George Orwell, science fiction writers in American and England identified potentially disastrous elements in the fictional utopias of the past and in the modern realities of World Wars, totalitarianism, technological dehumanization, industrial pollution, and urban squalor. Popular authors, including Isaac ASIMOV, Ray BRADBURY, John Brunner, Thomas Disch, Harlan ELLISON, and Kurt VONNEGUT, Jr., projected these identifications into dystopian nightmares dominated by authoritarianism, militarism, misused technologies, overpopulation, and manmade catastrophes.

At the beginning of the 1970s, it seemed as if the obsolescence of 19th-c. utopian models, controversies over the ethics of psychological conditioning, the depressing abundance of imitative dystopian science fictions, the agonies of civil rights tensions, the persistent problem of urban and rural poverty, and the failures in Vietnam had all but stifled American utopian fiction. Actually, the mid-1970s witnessed an exciting rebirth of the genre that continued into the 1990s. To some degree, this phenomenon can, like the late-19th-c. outpouring of utopian fiction, be described in terms of the era's combinations of tumultuous signs of despair and exciting signs of hope. In part, the rebirth also reflected interest in "new" issues: Ernest Callenbach's concern about environmental problems and advocacy of steady state economies in *Ecotopia* (1975) exemplify this trend.

Feminism, however, with new and complex literary perspectives and provocative invitations to reconsider basic concepts of gender, was the crucial issue that invigorated the utopian fiction. Before 1970, more than one hundred short and book-length works had been written by American women. Utopian fictions such as Ursula K. Le Guin's "The Ones Who Walk Away from Omelas" (1973), *The Dispossessed,* and *Always Coming Home,* Samuel R. Delany's *Triton* (1976), and Marge Piercy's *Woman on the Edge of Time* (1976) and *He, She, and It* (1991), and Kim Stanley Robinson's *Pacific Edge* (1990) represent significant developments. Not only do they offer provocative examinations of gender related issues—androgyny, sex roles, and paternalistic language—they also use discontinuous and self-reflexive narrative structures that raise fundamental questions about using experimental techniques in a traditionally didactic genre. These literary experiments have begun to sensitize scholars to the importance of literary form and the role of the reader in the study of utopian literature.

As is the case with the study of utopian elements in Euro-American travel accounts or in the Declaration of Independence, it is important to place the rebirth of American utopian fiction within international contexts. Le Guin and Piercy should be read next to Doris Lessing and Margaret Atwood. It might be possible to analyze the nature, though not the impact, of *Looking Backward* by focusing on American contexts. But the late-20th-c. experimental utopias call for an awareness of an international community of writers and readers who are testing the limits of utopian expressions.

BIBLIOGRAPHY: Fogarty, R. S., *Dictionary of American Communal and Utopian History* (1980); Kessler, C. F., *Daring to Dream: Utopian Stories by United States Women before 1950* (1984; rev. ed., 1995); Miller, P., *Errand into the Wilderness* (1956); Parrington, V. L., Jr., *American Dreams* (1947; rev. ed., 1964); Roemer, K. M., ed., *America as Utopia* (1981); Rooney, C. J., *Dreams and Visions: A Study of American Utopias, 1865–1917* (1985); Sargent, L. T., *British and American Utopian Literature, 1516–1985: An Annotated, Chronological Bibliography* (1988); Segal, H., *Technological Utopianism in America* (1985)

KENNETH M. ROEMER

VALDEZ, Luis Miguel
b. 26 June 1940, Delano, California

V. is renowned as the founder and artistic director of El Teatro Campesino. Today, he is perhaps the best known and most influential of all Chicano theater artists. He is a prolific producer, codirector, and writer for both theater and film. *Zoot Suit* (1992), which he wrote, coproduced, and directed, was wildly popular in Los Angeles in 1978 though less successful on Broadway in 1979 where no Chicano play had ever appeared before. A film version that he also directed (1982) recaptures much of the Los Angeles production.

The son of migrant farmworkers and one of ten children, V.'s early education was frequently interrupted as he and his family followed the farmwork. He did well in school, nonetheless, and showed an aptitude for performing. A student activist at San José State College, V. studied political and populist theater, and wrote his first play, *The Shrunken Head of Pancho Villa* (1974), which was produced at the college. He traveled to Cuba in 1964, and then joined the highly political San Francisco Mime Troupe. A year later, he became involved with the United Farmworkers around Delano, and founded El Teatro Campesino, which used worker-actors to rally support for the union. Though it has always remained close to its community, by 1967 the Teatro was expanding its focus to include larger audiences and subjects. In 1971, the company established residence in San Juan Batista, its present home, where it also established a community arts and culture center. V. still lives in San Juan Batista and retains his affiliation with the Teatro.

Together with the Teatro, V. created a series of *Actos* (1971), or brief *commedia*-like agit-prop scenes. Initially, these broadly acted bilingual farces were presented in the fields and in other makeshift locations. The *actos* depicted the plight of farmworkers and declared the union as a viable solution. Later *actos* ex-

plored social problems—assimilation, and military service in Vietnam—experienced by the Chicano community. The Teatro also staged *Shrunken Head* and other V. plays. *Dark Root of a Scream,* first produced in 1971, is the first of several *mitos* or "myth" plays. It is an expressionistic depiction of the wake of a Chicano community leader who died fighting in Vietnam instead of in the barrios where he belonged. *Bernabé* (1990), first produced in 1970, is a historical allegory of a village idiot who desires a union with "la Tierra" (the Earth), symbol of the Mexican Revolution. The *mitos* reflected V.'s "neo-Mayan" philosophy, which he expressed at length in *Pensamiento Serpentinos* (1990), a poetic meditation and arts manifesto. After the company moved to San Juan Batista, V. began to use an old Mexican form known as *corrido,* or ballad, to create dramas with narrated and enacted scenes. A "Signature piece" of the Teatro was *La Gran Carpa de los Rasquachis* (The grand tent of the underdogs) that follows the adventures of a comic, yet resilient, Mexican immigrant in the U.S. *Corridos* (perf. 1982) is a popular musical that utilizes this form. *La Pastorela,* presented each year at Christmastime at San Juan Batista, is a humorous and tender retelling of the *Second Shepherd's Play.* V. adapted and directed film versions of *Corridos* and *Pastorela* for PBS.

Zoot Suit is often described as a piece that brings together all of the elements that V. has explored and refined over the years. It uses the broad performance style and bilingualism of the *acto,* the mythic hero of the *mito,* the narrator and music of the *corrido;* and the political dramaturgy of Bertolt Brecht, the Living Newspapers, and documentary drama. It depicts the one-sided murder trial of Chicano gang-leader Henry Reyna in 1942, in a way that reminds its audiences of the lop-sided justice still faced by the Chicano community. "Zoot suit" refers to a distinctive manner of dress affected by the Chicano gangs, an emblem of self-assertion, worn by "El Pachuco," a quintessential young Chicano and the play's narrator. Stripped of his suit by a gang of U.S. servicemen, the Pachuco is revealed in the loincloth of his Mayan ancestors.

Bandido (perf. 1986, pub. 1992) is a historical play-within-a-play that retells the story of Tiburcio Vásquez, the last man to be legally executed in California in 1875. *I Don't Have to Show You No Stinking Badges* (perf. 1986, pub. 1992) is a realistic examination of a modern Chicano couple that has "made-it" in the entertainment industry, except that they will never be cast in plays that truly reflect Chicano experience. V. also wrote and directed the popular film, *La Bamba* (1987).

BIBLIOGRAPHY: Babcock, G., "Looking for a Third Space: *El Pachuco* and Chicano Nationalism in *Zoot Suit*," in Maufort, M., ed., *Staging Differences* (1995): 215–25; Bagby, B., "El Theatro Campesino: Interviews with L. V.," *TDR* 11 (Summer 1967): 71–80; Huerta, J. A., *Chicano Theater: Themes and Forms* (1982), Kanellos, N., and J. Huerta, *Nuevos Pasos: Chicano and Puerto Rican Drama* (1989)

MAARTEN REILINGH

VAN DOREN, Mark

b. 13 June 1894, Hope, Illinois; d. 10 December 1972, New York City

In an age founded upon the rejection of literary convention, V. embodied tradition. Few literary figures of the 20th c. are so thoroughly linked to scholarly endeavor. Although V. wrote two novels, *The Transients* (1935) and *The Windless Cabins* (1940), he is primarily known as a poet and critic. As editor of *The Nation* and professor of English at Columbia University, he was a minority voice in the age of MODERNISM. He was a leading proponent of highly formalized versification in the English tradition, and his poetry is drawn from nature, partly because of his literary education, which familiarized him with ROMANTICISM and the English pastoral tradition, and partly as a result of his early childhood in rural Illinois. In general, his work is influenced by the pastorals of William Browne and the poetic formalism of Ben Jonson and Robert Herrick.

V. earned both bachelor's and master's degrees at the University of Illinois, emphasizing the liberal arts, and he began writing poetry there, publishing his first poem in 1915 in H. L. MENCKEN's the *Smart Set*. Following his brother Carl, V. moved to New York to continue graduate studies at Columbia University. He studied under John ERSKINE, G. P. Knapp, W. W. Lawrence, and W. P. Trent, who directed his dissertation on John Dryden. His scholarship includes *Henry*

David Thoreau: A Critical Study (1916), *Shakespeare* (1939), *Liberal Education* (1943), and *The Noble Voice: A Study of Ten Great Poems* (1946). Published in numerous collections, his poetry includes *Jonathan Gentry* (1931), *The Mayfield Deer* (1941), and *The Last Look* (1937). His *Collected Poems, 1922–1938* won the Pulitzer Prize in 1940.

Because V. possessed significant connections in the literary world, it was difficult for him to receive unbiased critical examination in his time. His contemporaries recognized V.'s essential lack of innovation but felt compelled, not without reason, to comment on the peculiar originality of a poet that in large part rejected the developing conventions dominant in his age. John Peale Bishop comments on his desire to "integrate" in an age of disintegration, contrasting V. with modernist poets in his rejection of "French influence." V.'s early work, mostly short lyrical poems, appear in *Spring Thunder* (1924), and *7 P.M. and Other Poems* (1926), and *Now the Sky and Other Poems* (1928). These poems make liberal use of pastoral imagery and are drawn perhaps from his early childhood experience in Illinois. Influenced by English romanticism and Thoreauvian NATURALISM, these works explore the integral relationships among natural forms and allude to the supernatural within the natural. In *Jonathan Gentry* and *The Mayfield Deer*, V. made an ambitious attempt at long narrative poetry. *Jonathan Gentry* is a three-part epic narrative dealing with the trials and travails of the Gentry family. V. means for the Gentrys to be examples of the American experience. He follows them through the generations, from their immigration experience in 1800, through the Civil War, into the Great Depression. *Jonathan Gentry* is uneven, alternating powerful moments of prosaic narrative with somewhat verbose description and arbitrary use of poetic diction and form. The same flaws exist in *The Mayfield Deer*, and after an aborted attempt to rewrite this poem years later, V. returned to lyric poetry instead. His best work is lyrical and prosaic. This highly educated critic and scholar is at his best when using common images to explore uncommon materials. *The Last Look* reflects an increasing preoccupation with the role of poet as philosopher and seer. Retaining the aesthetics of romanticism, specifically Shelley's notion of poet as legislator, V. manages, in all his work, to emphasize the integral and productive relationship between lived experience and formal education. A deceptively complicated man, he stood in stark contrast to his contemporaries, and he contributed to the world of letters through a diverse career as poet, cultural critic, teacher, and passionate proponent of humanistic learning.

BIOGRAPHY: Adler, M. J., *Philosopher at Large: An Intellectual Autobiography* (1948); Merton, T., *The*

Seven Storey Mountain (1948); Yearsley, M., "M. V. D.," in Quartermain, P., ed., *DLB,* vol. 45, *American Poets, 1880–1945* (1986): 418–24

STEVEN FRYE

VAN DUYN, Mona

b. 9 May 1921, Waterloo, Iowa

Author of eight critically acclaimed volumes of poetry—from *Valentines to the World* (1959) to *Firefall* (1994)—V. is also recognized as editor and cofounder of the literary quarterly *Perspective* (1947–80) and as a teacher-mentor for younger writers at the universities of Iowa and Louisville and at the University of Washington Writers' Program. She was awarded the Ruth Lilly Prize (1989), the Bollingen Prize (1970), the 1971 National Book Award in poetry for *To See, to Take* (1970), and the 1991 Pulitzer Prize for *Near Changes* (1990). V. served as the first female poet laureate in 1992.

This partial list of her accomplishments and accolades would seem to indicate a poet firmly fixed in the postmodern literary firmament, if not consciousness. Yet this is hardly the case. V.'s work is rarely anthologized, and no critical volume has yet addressed her collective works or her influence on modern letters. This discrepancy is doubly peculiar since her poems regularly appear in influential literary magazines and journals. Although she seems only an afterthought in the judgment of critics like Helen Vendler, other poets have accorded her the great respect of inclusion in their own poems and musings. V.'s work likewise contains ongoing exchanges with Howard NEMEROV, May SWENSON, and John HOLLANDER.

V.'s opus traverses the traditional and innovative. While her early work observes and preserves the order of stanza, structure, and rhyme, her later writings—particularly the minimalist sonnet sequence in *Firefall*—radicalize both line and rhyme. In these sometimes telegraphic poems, she is fearless and jarring in setting up antiphonal responses. In doing so, she not only takes on but also reinterprets some of the most canonical and statically interpreted poems of W. B. Yeats, W. H. AUDEN, T. S. ELIOT, and Robert FROST. Some critics dismiss these sonnets as slight, but such misinterpretation does help illuminate the reason why V.'s poetry is not more widely recognized.

From the moment *Valentines to the World* appeared, V. had chosen her life's themes and images. These poems laud the every day, totaling life's indignities minus love's necessities. And subsequent volumes have continued the poet's need to measure and weigh the ineffable in the language of a finite time and a fallible people. To place V. in her generation is to

understand the double-edge of her being lauded and underestimated simultaneously. Overlooked sometimes because of their quotidian, domestic imagery, her poems reward the reader with their insightful inquiries into love and commitment. In "Remedies, Maladies, Reasons," "Letters from a Father," and "The Stream," the adult child's obeisance to the parent is conflicted, yet love too boils over, searing the couples together in an identification so close as to be claustrophobic: parent and child, poem and reader. While hers is not the clarion cultural voice of her peer Adrienne RICH, neither is she some pedestrian minstrel meant to be shelved as eminent, understood, and forgettable.

From *Firefall,* "The Delivery" quietly exhumes the terrors and alienation of childhood, while "We Are in Your Area" provides exact radiographic imagery of suburbia at the end of the 20th c. It is witty and scathing, wry yet wickedly detailed. Whether in sonnet or sestina, blank verse or couplet, the poems testify to their creator's mastery of form, meter, and rhyme, and her subject matter bears witness to her life as a scholar, a wife, and a poet.

Ultimately, V. is familiar and forgiving of our human existence; she chronicles our often clumsy progress from birth to death, and whether she sees us in Midas or Leda, in hummingbirds or lions, in Paris or in a weed-choked suburban lawn, she looks upon us with an eye more kindly than her unerring ear would seem to allow.

BIBLIOGRAPHY: Hall, J., "Strangers May Run: The Nation's First Woman Poet Laureate," *AR* 52 (Winter 1994): 141–46; Hunting, C., "Methods of Transport," *Parnassus* 16, 2 (1991): 377–88; Logan, W., "Late Callings," *Parnassus* 18, 2 (1993): 317–27

DEIRDRE NEILEN

VAN VECHTEN, Carl

b. 17 June 1880, Cedar Rapids, Iowa; d. 21 December 1964, New York City

Critic, novelist, photographer, and patron of the arts V. grew up in a liberal Midwestern family, receiving as much exposure to the arts as possible. Earning a bachelor's degree in English from the University of Chicago, V. worked briefly as a journalist. In 1907, he moved to New York, where Theodore DREISER, editor of *Broadway,* commissioned him to review the Metropolitan Opera's performance of Strauss's *Salome.* Thereafter, V. became assistant music and performing arts critic for the *New York Times,* promoting the such artists as George Gershwin, Igor Stravinsky, Anna Pavlova, and Isadora Duncan. Through his reviews for the *Times,* V. became America's first serious dance critic.

Inheriting one million dollars from his brother in 1928, V. spent the next several decades encouraging and supporting artist friends with promise and creativity. Blessed with a penchant for recognizing extraordinary talent, V. befriended some of the most promising artists of the period at the New York salon of his friend Mabel Dodge LUHAN and at his own parties. Publication of Langston HUGHES's *Weary Blues* owes much to V.'s intercession, as does Hughes's early career advancement. V. also arranged for Alfred Knopf's publication of early works by Wallace STEVENS, Chester HIMES, and James Weldon JOHNSON. He was a lifelong supporter and friend of Gertrude STEIN, becoming literary executor of Stein's papers.

V. published two books of music criticism, the most influential of which pronounced Stravinsky the next great talent and Arnold Schoenberg the pioneer of dissonance. In reviews and articles as early as 1921, he spearheaded a rediscovery of Herman MELVILLE, rescuing Melville's later works from obscurity. Additionally, V. wrote and edited several books about cats, including a classic study of cats in folklore and literature, *The Tiger in the House* (1920). In numerous publications and reviews, V. expressed admiration for African American music and culture and was an enthusiastic supporter of black culture his entire life. Though some, such as Ralph ELLISON, viewed V.'s patronage and interest warily, others, for example Hughes and Johnson, became lifelong friends.

From 1922 to 1930, V. published seven novels, witty glimpses of society based on his cosmopolitan life in New York and Paris. *Peter Whiffle: His Life and Works* (1922) is a droll autobiography-as-biography in the style of Stein's *Autobiography of Alice B. Toklas.* The most controversial of V.'s novels, *Nigger Heaven* (1926), a bildungsroman set in Harlem, is one of the first modern novels with a black theme written by a white writer. Its title, slang for the uppermost gallery in New York theaters, aroused contempt from blacks and whites, ironically drawing criticism for the man George S. Schuyler once declared had "done more than any single person in this country to create . . . acceptance of the Negro."

In the 1930s, V. focused on archiving collections of friends' letters and papers, as well as portrait photography, begun seriously in 1932. After donating his literary correspondence to Yale University, V. established the James Weldon Johnson Collection of Negro Arts & Letters there in 1941, to which Hughes subsequently donated his papers. V. also contributed letters and/or photographic collections to Fisk and Howard Universities, the New York Public Library, and the Museums of Modern Art and the City of New York.

V.'s second wife, actress Fania Marinoff, shared his passion for culture and the avant-garde; despite rumors of V.'s homosexuality, their union lasted over fifty years. In 1955, V. received an honorary doctorate from Fisk University, and in 1961, along with Langston Hughes, was admitted into the prestigious National Institute of Arts and Letters.

BIBLIOGRAPHY: Kellner, B., *C. V. and the Irreverent Decades* (1968); Lueders, E. G., *C. V.* (1965); Rampersad, A., *The Life of Langston Hughes* (2 vols., 1986)

GINA L. TAGLIERI

VERY, Jones

b. 28 August 1813, Salem, Massachusetts; d. 8 May 1880, Salem, Massachusetts

Although often grouped with the Concord transcendentalists, with whom he associated, V.'s religious poetry is more the combined offspring of Unitarianism, Calvinism, and TRANSCENDENTALISM. Doctrinally, V. is closest to the Unitarians, and he worked from 1843 until his death as a licensed Unitarian minister, writing sermons and acting as a supply preacher along Boston's North Shore and the surrounding area. V.'s tie to earlier Christian Protestantism rests mainly in his ardent conviction—tempered late in life—that mankind was unregenerate and needed to be reborn into the grace of God. He shared with the transcendentalists a strong idealism, a faith in intuition, and a belief in the ability of nature to help guide the individual toward spiritual awareness.

Prior to his long career as a Unitarian minister, V. attended Harvard Divinity school and acted as a Greek tutor. This early phase of his life was capped by several years of religious enthusiasm coupled with intense creative productivity that came to a climax in 1838 when he was institutionalized for a month at the McLean Asylum. A true mystic, V. insisted during the late 1830s that his poetry was literally inspired by the Holy Spirit.

V. published only one book during his lifetime, a slender volume edited by Ralph Waldo EMERSON called *Essays and Poems* (1839) that contains sixty-five poems and three essays. Until recently, the standard edition of V.'s work has been *Poems and Essays* (1883), edited by J. F. Clarke, which contains the majority of V.'s poetic work. This edition has been superseded by *J. V.: The Complete Poems* (1993), edited by Helen Deese. Shakespearean sonnets comprise the majority of V.'s seven-hundred poems, with the remainder consisting of hymns and other lyrics, as well as some blank verse. His subjects are principally religious, urging readers toward spiritual regeneration, and the elements of nature in these poems often act as analogies representing spiritual truths, much in the manner of Jonathan EDWARDS and Emerson. When V. departs from his religious themes he often turns toward the writing of nature poems and the occasional political poem, a few of which deal with the injustice of slavery and the Civil War.

The concept of a "will-less" Christian quietism, in which the subject denies self in order to become completely subsumed within the will of God, is the cornerstone of V.'s religious vision. The paradoxical nature of this vision is expressed in the first two lines of his sonnet "The Hand and the Foot" (1839): "The hand and foot that stir not, they shall find / Sooner than all the rightful place to go." This quietist pietism is also reflected in many of Very's sermons, of which he composed over a hundred. Aside from his sermons, V.'s miscellaneous prose writing includes several essays, written while studying at Harvard, on such topics as "Epic Poetry" and "Shakespeare," as well as a series of three epistles "To the Unborn" that urge the reader toward self denial and spiritual rebirth.

BIBLIOGRAPHY: Bartlett, W. I., *J. V.* (1942); Gittleman, E., *J. V.* (1967); Robinson, D., "J. V., the Transcendentalists, and the Unitarian Tradition," *HTR* 68 (1975): 103–24

ERIC CARL LINK

VIDAL, Gore
b. 3 October 1925, West Point, New York

As the author of numerous historical fictions, scores of essays, and even a series of detective stories published under the pseudonym Edgar Box, V. ranks among the most versatile of contemporary American novelists. Of lasting interest among his early fiction is *The City and the Pillar* (1948; rev. ed., 1965), the carefully understated story of a young man's discovery that he is homosexual and a *succès de scandale* in its day. Radically different in technique is the undervalued *Two Sisters* (1970), an intricate, Chinese box of narrations. *Kalki* (1978) is a doomsday novel that seems the work of a more brooding sensibility, although recognizably Vidalian in some of its flourishes.

The historical novel seems increasingly V.'s best endeavor. *Julian* (1964) and *Creation* (1981) are putative memoirs of the Emperor Julian and an imaginary grandson of Zoroaster—*Julian,* a fascinating account of the 4th-c. defeat of Mithraism by Christianity, and *Creation,* a Cook's Tour of the 5th c., lavish with portraits of the Buddha, Master Li, Confucius, and other luminaries. A sequence of novels that includes *Washington, D.C.* (1967), *Burr* (1973), *1876* (1976),

and *Empire* (1987) is V.'s most impressive work in the historical mode. Linked superficially by the imaginary Schuyler/Sanford dynasty, it is less the story of a family's generations than a gathering story of the American republic and its decay from within. *Lincoln* (1984) belongs to that larger story and rivals *Burr* in both popular and critical esteem as V.'s best novel to date. They share a chiaroscuric interplay of monumentality and intimacy. *Burr* balances a worshipful memoir by Charlie Schuyler, who is Aaron Burr's illegitimate son, with Burr's own, iconoclastic account of the Founding Fathers. With similar effect, the tragic Civil War years of Abraham LINCOLN are rendered through the variously irreverent viewpoints of his family, political rivals, and even his future assassins.

The stature of these historical fictions notwithstanding, it could be argued that V.'s truest gift is for camp extravagance. Indeed, the best parts of the historical novels are often confected moments of high lunacy, as when a matron in *Empire* claims Beowulf as an ancestor.

Such camping is the sustained fun of *Myra Breckinridge* (1968), in which the outrageous title character wages epic battle to realign the sexes in Hollywood as a consequence of her life as Myron before a sex-change operation. In *Myron* (1974), a sequel, the battle is waged between Myra and her earlier self to commandeer the Breckinridge ego, with the stakes nothing less than the integrity of Hollywood's Golden Age. Less successful in this camp mode are *The Season of Comfort* (1949), an overripe exercise in Southern Gothicism, and *Duluth* (1983), a burlesque of law-and-order thinking in Middle America. Estimable in the genre, however is *The Judgment of Paris* (1952; rev. ed., 1965), an updating that is both literate and good fun of a Greek myth.

BIBLIOGRAPHY: Dick, B. F., *The Apostate Angel* (1974); Kiernan, R. F., *G. V.* (1982); Parini, J., ed., *G. V.: Writer against the Grain* (1992); Stanton, R. J., and G. Vidal, eds., *Views from a Window: Conversations with G. V.* (1980)

ROBERT F. KIERNAN

VILLARREAL, José Antonio
b. 30 July 1924, Los Angeles, California

V. has been referred to as the "father" of Chicano letters on the basis of his first novel, which seeks to tell of the Mexican American experience in a novel written in English. *Pocho* (1959) tells the largely autobiographical story of Richard Rubio, a young Mexican American immigrant coming of age in Southern California in the 1930s. Like V., Rubio is the son of a charismatic veteran of the Mexican revolution who forcefully resists the change American culture presents his family. In the Rubio household, this reactionary outlook manifests itself in machismo, and the Rubio matron Consuelo eventually flees after searching in vain for relief from her overbearing husband. Like Rubio, V. grew up in a home where English was forbidden, therefore presenting the future writer with perhaps his greatest obstacle to acclimation in American society. Dealing as it does with themes of a maturing young artist, facing an isolated home life under an overbearing father and examining questions of language, *Pocho* has been compared by favorable critics as a bildungsroman similar to James Joyce's *A Portrait of the Artist as a Young Man.* V. has stated that while writing *Pocho* he was especially influenced by the works of Joyce, Thomas WOLFE and William FAULKNER. Pocho ends with Rubio's decision to enlist in the U. S. Army during World War II, signaling both the final dissolution of the Rubio family and Richard's stand against his father's value of individualism.

If the critical awareness of *Pocho* as a first American novel of the Chicano experience is widespread, it is equally thin. Unlike Joyce's Stephen Dedalus, Richard Rubio has been criticized as unbelievably rendered, directly benefitting too much from his author's wisdom. Others dislike V.'s style, considering the imposition of Spanish speech patterns a distracting and unsuccessful attempt at capturing the language conflict of Richard Rubio's world. While many readers praise V.'s realism in *Pocho,* the novel stood alone for many years as the only acknowledged attempt at fictionalizing the Mexican American experience. And while the Chicano movement of the latter 1960s may have helped revive *Pocho,* a generation gap between V. and the newer, more radical voices is apparent. V. doesn't identify himself as "Chicano," and was himself the focus of much criticism from Chicano activists while he taught at the University of Colorado in the early 1970s. For the new leaders of the Chicano movement, *Pocho* told a traditional immigrant story of obstacles that can be overcome with dedication.

V. has continued to write novels, publishing *The Fifth Horseman* (1974) and *Clemente Chacón* (1984). *The Fifth Horseman* is a historical novel, set in the Mexican revolution, which again split the critics: although most agree that it is a work superior to *Pocho,* Chicano critics were unhappy with its treatment of the war and viewed it as overly simplistic. Plagued by slow sales, the failure of *The Fifth Horseman* at the cash register delayed the publication of *Clemente Chacón* some ten years while V. sought a publisher. This tale of a young Juarez boy who eventually crosses the border to become a successful insurance executive

was viewed by V. as his best work prior to *Grease Korner* (1992), now also out of print.

The passage of time between V.'s works is telling: his writing career has taken second place to the more compelling concerns of raising a family, and his frequent relocations have inevitably taken their toll, leaving critics and readers to speculate that *Pocho* will remain his most important work.

BIBLIOGRAPHY: Carl, S., "*Pocho:* Bildungsroman of a Chicano," *RC-R* 7 (Spring 1974): 63–68; Vallejos, T., "J. A. V.," in Lomelí, F. A., and C. R. Shirley, eds., *DLB,* vol. 82, *Chicano Writers* (1989): 282–88

ROBERT E. CUMMINGS

VIORST, Judith [Stahl]

b. 2 February 1931, Newark, New Jersey

As a writer of books for children, as a mostly humorous poet, as a columnist and editor for *Redbook* magazine, as the creator of television monologues, as the author of the bestselling *Necessary Losses* (1987), and as a novelist, V. has attracted a popular readership in America since the early 1960s.

Born Judith Stahl, V. received her B.A. from Rutgers in 1952, then moved to Greenwich Village and attempted "serious" poetry, with little success. In 1960, she married Milton Viorst, a political reporter and a writer himself, whose support of his wife's writing is documented heavily within her work. In the early years of the decade, her poems began to appear in the Sunday supplements to the *New York Herald Tribune,* and were then accumulated in *The Village Square* (1966). As her three sons arrived and grew, V.'s writing settled almost entirely on the home. In nearly all of her work, the personal becomes the professional: many of her children's stories employ her own children's real names, and the problems her fictional little ones face are those that surfaced and needed solving in the writer's own nest. Not surprisingly, those childhood dilemmas sounded a response in other parents, other children. Among V.'s numerous publications in this genre, *I'll Fix Anthony* (1969) confronts sibling rivalry, *Alexander and the Terrible, Horrible, No Good, Very Bad Day* (1972) eases a case of the baby blues, and *The Tenth Good Thing about Barney* (1971), which won a Silver Pencil Award in 1973, helps build the tiny ego. Other early works, focusing on making science accessible to children, include *Projects: Space* (1962), *One Hundred and Fifty Science Experiments, Step-by-Step* (1963), and *The Changing Earth* (1967). V.'s books of poetry and prose on contemporary marriage and female aging in America employ a more comic take on her life experience, and the titles are illustrative: *It's Hard to Be Hip Over Thirty and Other Trage-dies of Married Life* (1968), *How Did I Get to Be Forty . . . and Other Atrocities* (1976), *When Did I Stop Being Twenty and Other Injustices* (1987), among others. These iconoclastic works demonstrate the au-thor's refusal to be depressed by, and her ability to work around, the domestic responsibilities that have done in many women hankering after their own ca-reers. Both the children's books and the "com-plaints"—the *When Did I*'s and the *If I Were*'s—have managed to suggest to a substantial audience of mod-ern women that the inevitable failures, disappoint-ments, and lost opportunities of housewife life not only can but should be endured with humor.

In 1981, V. enrolled in a six-year stint at the Wash-ington Psychoanalytic Institute and became an active participant at the tail end of America's decades-long love affair with the ideas of Sigmund Freud. Her re-sulting publication, *Necessary Losses: The Loves, Illu-sions, Dependencies, and Impossible Expectations That All of Us Have to Give up in Order to Grow,* adds Freudian theory to the common sense that had characterized her earlier writings. Providing antidote and anodyne for life's passages of grief and grieving, this work became a *New York Times* best-seller. V.'s novel, *Murdering Mr. Monti: A Merry Little Tale of Sex and Violence* (1995), gives its readers a romp through the terrain of a mixed-ethnicity courtship, housewife fantasy, and suburban infidelity.

BIBLIOGRAPHY: Lanes, S. G., *Down the Rabbit Hole* (1971); Street, D., "J. V.," in Estes, G. E., ed., *DLB,* vol. 52, *American Writers for Children since 1960: Fiction* (1986): 368–73

                                          GAY SIBLEY

VIZENOR, Gerald [Robert]

b. 22 October 1934, Minneapolis, Minnesota

Ranked with N. Scott MOMADAY, James WELCH, and Leslie Marmon SILKO, V. is one of the leading figures in modern NATIVE AMERICAN LITERATURE. Translating the materials and methods of traditional Native Ameri-can storytelling through postmodernist theory, V. ex-plores the conditions of the modern Native American in a postmodern world. He challenges the stereotypes of "Indianess"—what he terms "the invented Indian," "terminal thinking," and "the urban reservation"—of-fering in its place visions of "trickster liberation," and "the new earthdivers" or "postindian warriors."

V. is a mixed-blood Chippewa, or Anishinabe, his father's family coming from the White Earth Reserva-tion of Minnesota. When V. was three, his father was brutally murdered. Suffering poverty, abandonment by

his mother, and a succession of foster homes, V. did not discover his intellectual abilities until serving in the army. Returning to civilian life after a tour of duty in Japan, he entered the university to pursue Asian studies. Encouraged by his professors, he composed haiku poetry, publishing his first volume, *Two Wings the Butterfly,* in 1962. Since then, V. has pursued a varied career as a writer, social worker, journalist, editor, and college teacher. To date, he has published twenty-seven books, ranging from poetry, journalism, essays, novels, to collections of short stories and works of mixed genre. He has also edited several collections on Native American literature, and contributed numer-ous additional essays and stories to other collections and periodicals. He has also written several screenplays.

Since *Two Wings the Butterfly,* V. has produced five more volumes of haiku, the most notable being *Matsushima: Pine Islands* (1984). At an early stage, he was struck by the similarity between the language and content of haiku poetry and that of Ojibway dream songs. This led to *Summer in the Spring* (1965), the first of a number books of Ojibway lyric poems and tribal stories. Working as a journalist and social worker, V. observed the conditions of Native Ameri-cans in the modern urban setting. Their stories coupled with his own provided much of the material for his journalism and essays, collected in *Wordarrows: Indi-ans and Whites in the New Fur Trade* (1978), *Crossbloods: Bone Courts, Bingo, and Other Reports* (1990), *Manifest Manners: Postindian Warriors of Survivance* (1994), and in his autobiographical *Earth-divers: Tribal Narratives on Mixed Descent* (1981) and *Interior Landscapes: Autobiographical Myths and Metaphors* (1990).

V. published his first novel, *Darkness in Saint Louis Bearheart,* in 1978. Here he draws on tribal myth and the patterns of spiritual pilgrimage and political confrontation, anticipating the theme of the trickster and "trickster consciousness" that dominates his later fiction. The trickster as a challenger of boundaries offers a vision of transformation and survival. His next novel *Griever: An American Monkey King in China* (1982), which received both the Fiction Collective Award in 1987 and the American Book Award in 1990, develops the theme of the trickster, comparing the Chinese Monkey King Sun Wu-K'ung with the Ojib-way trickster Naanabozho. The success of this novel was followed by *The Trickster of Liberty* (1988), *The Heirs of Columbus* (1991), *Landfill Meditations: Crossblood Stories* (1991), a collection of short sto-ries, and *Dead Voices* (1992). V.'s fiction has grown increasingly experimental, drawing on the irony and narrative techniques of postmodernism in order to cre-ate a literature that challenges the boundaries of culture and language just as his stories and essays have always targeted social hierarchy and the status quo whether that of the white society or that of the Native American.

BIBLIOGRAPHY: Blaeser, K. M., *G. V.: Writing in the Oral Tradition* (1996); Coltelli, L., ed., *Winged Words: American Indian Writers Speak* (1990); Fleck, R. F., ed., *Critical Perspectives on Native American Fiction* (1993); Velie, A. R., *Four American Indian Masters: N. Scott Momaday, James Welch, Leslie Marmon Silko, and G. V.* (1982)

THOMAS L. COOKSEY

VOIGT, Ellen Bryant
b. 9 May 1943, Danville, Virginia

V.'s poetry draws from a variety of influences, literary, geographic, and personal. She was reared in Virginia, and, although currently living in Vermont, returns to the South regularly as part of the faculty of the low-residency M.F.A. program at Warren Wilson College in the mountains of western North Carolina. The region plays an important role in V.'s work; the storytelling aspects and prominence of nature in her poems could place her among other contemporary Southern poets such as Fred CHAPPELL and Pattiann ROGERS. However, she could also be considered as one of the heirs of Sylvia PLATH and Anne SEXTON with her intimate yet not sentimental depictions of domestic life.

V.'s first book, *Claiming Kin* (1976), drew solid critical acclaim and was praised for its perception, language, technique and, somewhat rare in Contemporary poetry, accessibility. This clarity, a constant in V.'s body of work, comes from a combined effect of syntactic order and natural line breaks along with a deliberate rhythm. The controlled pace enhances the sense of loss and mourning, especially in V.'s first two books. The tempo balances the often intensely emotional subject matter and gives the impression of "recollection in tranquility."

The Forces of Plenty (1983) continues V.'s highly personal but carefully crafted style. The poems are still somewhat formal, as with "Liebesgedicht," a modified sonnet. The book's final poems directly address the poet's recent loss of her parents, and in these poems the sense of urgency and sadness that pervades her previous work becomes most isolated and acute. Published in 1987, *The Lotus Flowers* introduced a certain shift in tone. Whereas the poems of the first two books took the form of monologues, spoken only to the self or not at all, the narrative poems of *The Lotus Flowers* look the reader in the eye. Though the subject matter remains personal, with narratives about personal events or family history, the speaker begins in this

book to look beyond the self as well. This speaker is ready to share experiences with others, either to teach, as in "Last Class," to tell a story with personal significance, as in "Short Story," or to record history from an individual perspective, as in "At the Movies, 1956."

V.'s next two books were *Two Trees* in 1992 and *Kyrie* in 1995. Though it addresses a specific, limited topic, it is *Kyrie* that brings together almost all of V.s' earlier interests and talents in one volume. This series of modified sonnets alternates voices as it relates the experiences of a series of victims of the 1918 influenza epidemic. It is structurally one of her most formal books, while at the same time its narrative realistically depicts human speech and emotion. The book has been compared to Edgar Lee MASTERS's *Spoon River Anthology,* but also resembles some of Robert FROST's dramatic monologues, especially with V.'s great attention to natural detail and description.

V.'s poems appear regularly in a variety of literary publications including the *Southern Review,* the *New Yorker, Shenandoah,* the *Atlantic,* and *Poetry.* She has earned grants and fellowships from several organizations such as the Vermont Council on the Arts, the National Endowment for the Arts and the Guggenheim Foundation. In 1995, her book *Kyrie* was selected as a finalist for the National Book Critics Circle Award.

BIBLIOGRAPHY: Hoagland, T., "About E. B. V.," *Ploughshares* 22 (Winter 1996–97): 222–25; Kennelly, L. B., "E. B. V.," in Gwynn, R. S., ed., *DLB,* vol. 120, *American Poets since World War II* (1992): 307–11

NICOLE SARROCCO

VOLLMANN, William T.
b. 28 July 1959, Santa Monica, California

V.'s work eludes definition by the reader, critic, and bibliographer. His themes are as varied as his work is ambitious: to date V. is the author of eleven books, several of them massive thousand page volumes of immense scope.

V.'s first work, *You Bright and Risen Angels* (1987), is typical of both the author's style and the critical reception it has drawn. V. creates a world where the narrator and programmer presses the resurrection button on his computer and thereby creates the novel's central characters. After a lengthy interpretation of the history of electricity—a veiled allegory to the development of first and third world politics—these characters divide into battling factions, all of whom are subsequently engaged in a life and death struggle with the world's insects, who have naturally grown tired of the human race's ceaseless swatting and squashing. V. is clearly an author who's not afraid to risk: *You Bright and Risen Angels* is a huge work by any comparison, and with its multiple plot levels, digressing storylines, and seemingly irrelevant characters, it becomes a precursor of V.'s style.

V.'s next work was *The Rainbow Stories* (1989), inspired by his visitations among the dispossessed street people of San Francisco's Tenderloin district. Explorations of the lifestyles of the dispossessed, especially prostitutes, reoccur in *Whores for Gloria* (1991), *Thirteen Stories and Thirteen Epigraphs* (1991), *The Butterfly Stories* (1994), *Open All Night* (1995), and *The Atlas* (1997). This setting would present itself as a possible handhold on V.'s oeuvre, but for the fact that he has also published three sprawling and well-informed historical novels. V.'s *The Ice Shirt* (1990), *Fathers and Crows* (1992), and *The Rifles* (1994) are volumes one, two, and six, respectively, of a planned seven-volume series entitled *North American Landscapes*. V. has also written *An Afghanistan Picture Show* (1992), a self-deprecating account of his travels among the Mujahadeen rebels of Afghanistan in 1982.

In a 1993 interview with Larry McCaffrey, V. explained the evolution of his seemingly disparate themes. "I wanted to understand what America is like. This fascination I have with the exotic experience was also still very much there—I wanted to look at lost souls and marginal people, with the hope that maybe by understanding them I could help them somehow, as I had done with the Afghans. The experience of writing *The Rainbow Stories* led me to realize that I *still* didn't really understand anything about America and that I probably never would. But it occurred to me that one way of starting to understand would be to see where we as Americans have come from and how we've changed. So it seemed like a nice idea to go back . . . to the first recorded contact between Europeans and Indians and describe everything that's happened since in a series of books that winds up covering roughly a thousand year period."

If critics are unified in their willingness to applaud V.'s bravado, interpretations of the success of these gambles is up for debate. Critic James McManus, in a review of *The Rifles,* summed V.'s developing impact this way: "V. tells us of things we don't know but probably should, and he is expanding the possibilities of his genre, perhaps even forging a new one: the foot-thick documentary prose poem."

BIBLIOGRAPHY: McManus, J., "Captain Subzero and the Lost Expedition," *NYTBR* 27 February 1994: 6; McCaffrey, L., "Moth in the Flame: An Interview with W. V.," in *Some Other Fluency: Interviews with Innovative American Authors* (1996): 310–33; special V. issue, *RCF* 13 (Summer 1993): 9–24

ROBERT E. CUMMINGS

VONNEGUT, Kurt, Jr.
b. 11 November 1922, Indianapolis, Indiana

V. attended Cornell University from 1940 to 1942 and the University of Chicago from 1945 to 1947, eventually receiving an M.A. from the University of Chicago in 1971. He served in the U.S. Army infantry from 1942 to 1945 and, as a prisoner of the Germans, was present at the Allied bombing of Dresden, Germany, in the waning days of World War II. This apparently senseless act of destruction, which served no strategic purpose and resulted in the deaths of some 135,000 civilians—more, V. has pointed out, than were killed at Hiroshima and Nagasaki combined—had a profound effect on V., and it provided the inspiration for his most famous work: the novel *Slaughterhouse Five* (1969).

V. began writing full-time in 1950, publishing his first novel, *Player Piano,* in 1952. For many years, however, V. toiled in relative critical obscurity. This was due largely to V.'s reputation as a SCIENCE FICTION writer. *Player Piano,* for example, depicts a world in which machines have taken over—they perform all of man's chores, including the act of thinking. *The Sirens of Titan* (1959) also employs science fiction conventions, including aliens, space travel, and a Martian invasion. Its basic theme is the essential meaninglessness—in a cosmic sense—of man's endeavors and the consequent necessity for people to simply live their lives, unreliant upon any higher force such as God or cosmic design.

V.'s next novel, *Mother Night* (1962), forsakes science fiction conceits and presents the first-person "confessions" of Howard W. Campbell, Jr., an American expatriate who lived in Germany during World War II and served the Nazis as a radio propagandist; the twist, however, is that—while he was serving the Nazis—Campbell was also sending out coded messages to the Allies. Campbell recounts his story from an Israeli jail cell, where he is awaiting trial for crimes against humanity. Before he can be exonerated by his American former employers, however, Campbell commits suicide to atone not for crimes against humanity but for "crimes against himself." V.'s basic message in this novel, which he states in the preface, is that "We are what we pretend to be, so we must be careful what we pretend to be."

With *Cat's Cradle* (1963), V. began to gain widespread critical notice. On the surface, *Cat's Cradle* appears to be a return to the science fiction genre. The semiautobiographical first-person narrator is a writer recounting the story of the end of the world: Almost all life on Earth is destroyed as a result of the release of "Ice-9"—which instantly freezes water and anything else it touches, including people—into the world's waterways. Despite the destruction of mankind, this is essentially a comic novel, dealing with basic human fallibility. What is perhaps most significant about *Cat's Cradle* is its explication of "Bokononism," a fictional religion, whose central tenet provides the thematic undercurrent of V.'s entire oeuvre: "The one thing sacred is not the mountain, is not the ocean, is not the sun, is not even God. The one thing sacred is man."

This sacredness is put to the test in V.'s next novel, *God Bless You, Mr. Rosewater* (1965), which features possibly the most unattractive and unsympathetic characters V. has ever created. The title character is a millionaire philanthropist who lives among the poor and downtrodden; this noble sounding description, however, is belied by V.'s characterization of Eliot Rosewater as a rather loutish, uncouth slob. Nevertheless, the novel features a quote that sums up V.'s humanistic worldview: "God damn it, you've got to be kind."

Slaughterhouse-Five; or, The Children's Crusade remains V.'s most famous work. Subtitled "The Children's Crusade," this is V.'s long-contemplated "Dresden novel." The protagonist, Billy Pilgrim, possesses a unique view of time—he perceives of his life as a series of crystallized moments without a conventionally linear chronological relationship. Consequently, the novel jumps, seemingly at random, between various episodes in Billy's life: his flight from the Nazis after the Battle of the Bulge; his basically happy middle-class marriage in Ilium, New York; his captivity in a zoo on the planet Tralfamadore; and, climactically, his presence at the bombing of Dresden, which he and a group of fellow POWs survive by sheltering in a meat locker. The novel's chaotic structure may reflect V.'s attitude toward war as an essentially senseless, inhuman endeavor.

After the completion of *Slaughterhouse-Five,* V. fell into a depression, from which he recovered as he approached his fiftieth birthday. *Breakfast of Champions* (1973) has been interpreted as the author's fiftieth birthday present to himself. Characters from previous books reappear—most notably the now-successful science fiction novelist Kilgore Trout, V.'s alter ego who had previously appeared in *God Bless You, Mr. Rosewater* and *Slaughterhouse-Five,* and who is at the end of this novel "set free" by V. himself and presented the Nobel Prize—for medicine—for discovering the "physiological potential of ideas." *Breakfast of Champions* is a sort of "V. sketchbook"—quite

literally, as the author, in addition to expounding on a range of ideas, intersperses doodled "cartoons" throughout the text. V. said of *Slapstick* (1976) that it was "the closest [he would] ever come to writing an autobiography"; the book itself deals obliquely with the relationship between V. and his late sister, Alice. In *Jailbird* (1979), Kilgore Trout—who had been "set free" in *Breakfast of Champions,* returns; he "couldn't make it on the outside," and so he finds himself in jail, unconcernedly serving a life sentence for an accidental crime. As in previous novels, Trout is an authorial figure dispensing philosophical advice to the main character, Walter F. Starbuck, a fellow prisoner in jail for a crime associated with Watergate. As in *Breakfast of Champions,* the images and icons of American pop culture are catalogued and commented upon in V.'s trademark casual-ironic style.

The apparently ubiquitous Trout resurfaces in V.'s next novel, *Galapagos* (1985), in the person of Kilgore's son, Leon Trotsky Trout, who narrates the story. More accurately, Leon's ghost narrates the story—from the vantage point of the Earth of one million years in the future. Leon "haunted" a boat commissioned for the "Nature Cruise of the Century"—the 20th c., that is—to the Galapagos islands. While the tour was meant to be a very high-class affair, a world economic collapse and various other international crises caused the celebrity passengers to cancel, leaving only a small, fairly anonymous and unspectacular cluster of crew and tourists aboard the ship. These people, however, become the genealogical ancestors of all subsequent human life. V. here makes the argument that it is our "big brains" that have gotten us into trouble, and our evolutionary (or devolutionary) successors are much happier with significantly smaller intellectual capacities.

In *Bluebeard* (1987), V. deals with, among other things, the theme of artistry. The main character is Rabo Karabekian, a painter who made his first appearance in *Breakfast of Champions*. Rabo is an ultramodernist who is, throughout the novel, working on his mysterious masterpiece. Through Rabo, V. explores questions of what art is: Is it a classical representation of life as it is? Or is it abstract expressionism? Rabo, who has the ability to paint incredibly lifelike depictions of reality, rejects this approach as too "easy"—instead he produces abstract paintings that people are often hard-pressed to understand. Being true to one's own vision would appear more important than satisfying society's demands.

In addition to novels, V. has also produced short stories, many of which were collected in *Welcome to the Monkey House: A Collection of Short Works* (1968)—which includes the entire contents of the earlier short story collection *Canary in a Cathouse*

(1961), as well as more recent works. Two of the most significant pieces in this volume are "Welcome to the Monkey House" and "Harrison Bergeron," both of which deal with rebellious figures who strike out against a repressive and puritanical society. V. has also written essays, which appear in such volumes as *Wampeters, Foma and Granfalloons: Opinions* (1974) and *Palm Sunday: An Autobiographical Collage* (1981); plays, most notably *Happy Birthday, Wanda June* (1970), which was produced Off-Broadway; and a television play, *Between Time and Timbuktu; or, Prometheus Five: A Space Fantasy* (1972). In 1990, he published another novel, *Hocus Pocus*; V.'s *Bagombo Snuff Box: Uncollected Short Fiction* appeared in 1999.

In the prologue to *Slaughterhouse-Five*, V. recounts a conversation he once had with his father, during which his father commented that V. had never written a book with a villain in it. Indeed, even the Nazis in *Slaughterhouse-Five* are portrayed as basically human and humane compared with some of Billy Pilgrim's fellow American soldiers. In V.'s works there can be no villains, because we are all essentially flawed creatures whose "big brains" and grand ideas always get us into trouble. It is a pessimistic worldview, but one tempered by V.'s offer of a solution to man's ills: "God damn it, you've got to be kind." Though V.'s universe is often a grim one, there is always the possibility, even if unspoken, that we can improve our lot through simple acts of kindness.

BIBLIOGRAPHY: Allen, W. R., *Understanding K. V.* (1991); Goldsmith, D. H., *K. V., Fantasist of Fire and Ice* (1972); Klinkowitz, J., *The V. Statement* (1973); Lundquist, J., *K. V.* (1977); Mayo, C., *K. V.: The Gospel from Outer Space* (1977); Merrill, R., *Critical Essays on K. V.* (1990); Miller, W. J., and B. E. Nelson, *K. V.'s "Slaughterhouse-Five": A Critical Commentary* (1973); Morse, D. E., *K. V.* (1992); Reed, P. J., *K. V., Jr.* (1972); Schatt, S., *K. V., Jr.* (1976)

JASON BERNER

WAGONER, David [Russell]
b. 5 June 1926, Massillon, Ohio

Despite the fact that he is a native Midwesterner, W. has been associated with the regional writers of the Pacific Northwest ever since his work appeared prominently in a widely distributed 1964 anthology of poems entitled *Five Poets of the Pacific Northwest,* edited by Robin Skelton. It was published by the University of Washington Press in Seattle, where W. taught for most of his career and for many years edited the influential and highly regarded periodical *Poetry Northwest.* However, although the Northwest is a prominent physical feature of many of his poems, W.'s work has achieved a national and even an international readership.

In the poet's first book, *Dry Sun, Dry Wind* (1953), there was a promise of more than competence, though the prevalent proficiency of the academic poets of the 1950s was its main feature. One thing was outstanding, however: there was little self-conscious pose. *A Place to Stand* (1958), W.'s next collection, seemed to go in two directions simultaneously, for at the same time that there was greater formality of structure, there was also a loosening-up of language to the point, in certain poems, almost of jazz.

Structurally controlled, yet engaging for their colloquial musicality, the poems of *The Nesting Ground* (1963) were a clear indication of the degree to which W.'s art was developing. The outdoors has been important to W., and it figures prominently in his work, both overtly and inwardly. The brilliant and widely anthologized title poem of *Staying Alive* (1966) was both a handbook about staying alive in the real woods and a parable about how to stay alive as a human being and as a poet in an age increasingly antipoetic and antihuman.

By the time that *New and Selected Poems* was published in 1969, it was apparent that, though W. was, indeed, a regional poet, his work had a very broad range both of subject and technique. His evocative power had grown from book to book, and the range of means he came to command was impressive. The voice had grown surer, subtler, more and more capable of nuance or oddness, of humor, irony, or controlled violence. He was beginning to attract attention abroad, and his *Working against Time* was published in London in 1970.

W.'s *Riverbed* appeared in 1972; two years later, his concerns about the American environment manifested themselves in poems having to do with Native Americans and their lore in "Seven Songs for an Old Voice," which concludes his book *Sleeping in the Woods* (1974). *A Guide to Dungeness Spit* was published the following year, followed in 1976 by *Traveling Light.*

In the same year, W.'s *Collected Poems, 1956–1976* was published. His seemingly informal poems were expressions of a knowledge of pattern and sound so deep that one was unaware of the formalism of these pieces until one went back to reread them with critical eyes. When W. chose to ignore punctuation, as in "The Bad Uncle," he did so for particular reasons—characterization, representation of situation and atmosphere, simulation of people's thought processes—and not out of a programmatic adherence to an idiosyncratic style. The subjects he treated in his books were as wide-ranging as the techniques. Critically, W. did too many things too well to be ignored, but for the same reasons he was not easy to categorize. Although he could write in the northwestern plain style of his fellow regionalists William E. STAFFORD and Richard HUGO when he wished to do so, he could also write in many other styles and on various levels of diction.

In *Who Shall Be the Sun? Poems Based on the Lore, Legends, and Myths of the Northwest Coast and Plateau Indians* (1978), W. personified natural forces and gave them Indian names in his retelling of the mythological narratives of the tribes. *In Broken Country* was issued in 1979 by a Boston publisher, as were *Landfall* in 1981 and *First Light* in 1983; the poems of these collections were crisp and clear, the imagery evocative, the sensibility contemplative. They exhibited a keen sense of narrative, a deep insight into character, a photographer's eye for composition, and a painter's feeling for atmosphere, light, and color. Published in 1987, *Through the Forest: New and Selected Poems, 1977–1987* provided W.'s audience with another overview of his production that showed no dropoff in either quality or range of interest.

BIBLIOGRAPHY: Boyers, R., "The Poetry of D. W.," *KR* 128 (1970): 176–81; Pinsker S., "On D. W.," *Salmagundi* 22–23 (1973): 306–14; McFarland, R., *D. W.* (1989)

LEWIS PUTNAM TURCO

WAKOSKI, Diane

b. 3 August 1937, Whittier, California

W. is one of America's best published, but not always most highly regarded, poets. Though praised for her "fierce imagination" and her ability to weave "gorgeous webs of imagery," she is often criticized for overwriting as well as espousing a self-pitying stance. Her highly personal poems focus on her unhappy childhood, men—including her father—whom she has loved and lost, and her own lack of physical beauty—or what she ascertains as such; they embody a relentless and impassioned search for psychic and physical beauty. This search, however, appears to be located in a pre-feminist world where a woman's sense of self and beauty is validated by the admiration of men. Admittedly not a political poet, she is interested in beauty, music, and in "creating a personal mythology." As certain of the plainness in her life as she is of her body, the poet creates a mythology of "Diane"—a world that is shared with such archetypical characters as the King of Spain and George Washington. Writing since she was seven, the poet says that her poems are a way of "inventing" herself "into a new life."

The poet's first published collections of these "inventions," influenced by Robert LOWELL and Allen GINSBERG and characterized by their sharp imagery, include *Coins and Coffins* (1962), an imaginary tale about a twin brother, David, who committed suicide as a child after they had sex together; *Discrepancies and Apparitions* (1966) and *The George Washington Poems* (1967), continuations of her apocryphal narratives about lost lovers; and *Greed, Parts One and Two* (1968), the beginning of a thirteen-part exploration of

greed as "an unwillingness to give up one thing / for another."

According to W., *Inside the Blood Factory* (1968) marks the turning point of her career as a poet. Exploring themes of reflection and betrayal, W. established a voice that is all her own—the same voice that has been criticized for its self-pity. She dedicates *The Motorcycle Betrayal Poems* (1971) to "all those men who have betrayed [her] at one time or another, in hopes they will fall off their motorcycles and break their necks." In *Virtuoso Literature for Two and Four Hands* (1974), W., who studied piano for fifteen years, sets out to explore "images of fantasy and [her] past"; "My keyboard is now my typewriter," writes the poet.

Waiting for the King of Spain (1976), decidedly her finest book of poems, moves away from speaking about music and rather takes the form of music—a flawlessly orchestrated theme and variation piece. The theme of reflection remains the same—dedicated "To All the Michaels"—but W. is more hopeful here, as in the poem "Precisely, Not Violets": "Violets grow around my lips. Wet with / spring rain. / their blue reminds me / of the beauty / solitary things / can have"; or in "What the Struggle Is All About" where she drinks at the "fountain of life."

By this time, the poet is more indebted to Robert CREELEY, Charles OLSON, and Wallace STEVENS than Lowell and Ginsberg. She plays with Olson and Creeley's structure of "digression"—includes the whole of Steven's "Peter Quince at the Clavier"—in *The Man Who Shook Hands* (1978). *Emerald Ice: Selected Poems, 1962–1987* won the Poetry Society of America's William Carlos Williams Award in 1988. In 1995, she published a collection entitled *The Emerald City of Las Vegas*.

Although primarily known as a poet, W. is also an essayist and critic. Her two controversial volumes of critical work, *Creating a Personal Mythology* (1975) and *Toward a New Poetry* (1979), serve to illuminate the basis for her own highly subjective and personal poetry. Like her poetry, they have been both applauded and denigrated—perhaps the most valid, yet cutting, criticism coming from Robert McDowell: "*Toward a New Poetry* . . . tells you everything you will ever want to know about the author and might better have been called *Wakoski—Why Not?*"

BIBLIOGRAPHY: Harris, M., "D. W.," in Greiner, D. J., ed., *DLB*, vol. 5, part 2, *American Poets since World War II* (1980): 355–66; McDowell, R., "The Mum Generation Was Always Talking," *HudR* 38 (Autumn 1985): 507–19; Ostriker, A., "What Are Patterns For? Anger and Polarization in Women's Poetry," *FSt* 10 (Fall 1984): 485–503

ZOE RANDALL

WALKER, Alice [Malsenior]
b. 9 February 1944, Eatonton, Georgia

W. has published short stories, novels, criticism, and autobiographical pieces. She has served as an editor of *Ms* magazine, edited a book of Zora Neale HURSTON's work, and written several books of poetry. She is among the most versatile and the most outspokenly political of the major voices in late-20th-c. American literature. Most of her work involves several generations of families in the South, the civil rights movement in the 1960s, or the history of the black diaspora. Her work is almost always a validation of black women's lives. This concern has led W. to call herself a "womanist," a word she coined to mean a black woman or woman of color who is a feminist. The word is meant to distinguish her position as a black feminist from that of white feminists. While W. refuses to subscribe to a political agenda set by white feminists, so too does she refuse to write for those who ignore the link between racism and sexism.

Although W.'s work is primarily realist, her stories often concern the spiritual or the supernatural. She tends to see the world, or the "universe" as she sometimes says in her most recent novels, in the venerated tradition of American TRANSCENDENTALISM, which posits within human beings an intuitive and personal mystery that transcends experience. To this theory, W. adds mysticism, her belief that everything is part of god, the Divine Will, or nature. She believes that understanding god necessitates being in a state of oneness with all things. Even an author, in W.'s view, is part of a Divine Will that is capable of sending her messages. Connected to her philosophical concerns is her specific concern with the spiritual survival of black Americans and with a sense of self that resists the battering of racism and sexism. In both her fiction and her essays, W. examines the problem of keeping self-confidence intact in the face of hostility. W.'s sense of what she terms "wholeness" extends to a vision of history in which past and present are merged, an effort that has culminated in her novel *The Temple of My Familiar* (1989), which gives a mythic account of the past 500,000 years.

Before she found her own position as a creative artist, W. realized the importance of literary history and consciously sought artistic models within British and American literature. Among her literary forebears, W. found inspiration in Flannery O'CONNOR, Virginia Woolf, and especially Zora Neale Hurston, who became W.'s favorite author and spiritual mother. Hurston was an important influence on W.'s life, not only because of Hurston's writing but also because of her appreciation of herself. In the dedication to the collection of Hurston's essays *I Love Myself When I Am*

Laughing . . . And then Again When I Am Looking Mean and Impressive (1979), which W. also edited, she praises Hurston for her refusal to be humble or to feel that her work was second-best; Hurston wanted neither to be white nor to be anyone but herself, and valued black folk culture and language, both of which are used very expressively in Hurston's *Their Eyes Were Watching God* (1937). In W.'s collection of speeches and essays *In Search of Our Mothers' Gardens* (1983), she also discusses the importance of the unacknowledged artists of the 19th c. and earlier who maintained a creative tradition through slave narratives, oral accounts of their lives, or traditional stories. W. draws her authority from black folk life, whose forms break with the traditional fiction patterns of the white, male literary tradition.

W.'s concern with spiritual and cultural life came after a long struggle with more volatile social and political issues in her work. The early poetry and fiction deal more often with sharecropper families or other poor families in the South. A second of her major concerns is the role of women in the civil rights struggles of the 1960s and 1970s. W.'s first book of poetry, *Once* (1968), was written during her senior year in college. After suffering from an abortion that year, W. considered suicide because she realized "how alone woman is, because of her body." Many of the poems in *Once* were written during the week immediately after the abortion. Other poems concern the civil rights movement, her experiences living Africa, and the complexity of sexual attraction.

In Love and Trouble: Stories of Black Women (1973) was W.'s first collection of short stories. Each of the thirteen short stories has a black woman as its main interest. Many of them are combating poverty and racism in the South. This collection focuses on the psychology of black women as they struggle to remain unharmed, physically and psychologically, by the racism and sexism in their society. While attending Spelman College in Atlanta, W. became aware of and committed to the struggle in the South for civil rights and other social changes. *Revolutionary Petunias* (1973) examines the isolation and loneliness faced by individuals who choose to fight in the movement. In these stories, W. focuses on black women's relationships with their children and with one another.

In 1970, W. published her first novel, *The Third Life of Grange Copeland* (1970), which deals with three generations of Copelands, a poor sharecropper family in rural Georgia. It juxtaposes the lives of Grange Copeland and his son Brownfield, both of whom experience similar problems. Father and son are tenant farmers and both abuse their wives and children. Grange's wife Margaret kills herself, and Brownfield murders his wife. After escaping to the

North, Grange earns enough money to return home and buy a farm, where he takes his granddaughter Rut. Their life of economic independence and mutual support gives Grange his third life. Grange acknowledges the importance of one of W.'s central ideas, that one must not only survive but survive without being splintered and degraded. Capitulation to white racism makes white men into all-powerful gods, so that taking responsibility for one's actions is a way of demystifying this god. As Grange says: "Survival was not everything. *He* had survived. But to survive *Whole* was what he wanted for Ruth." However, to prevent Brownfield from obtaining custody of Ruth, Grange must kill his son. Grange himself is killed in this confrontation, so that only Ruth remains. There is some hope that she will emerge whole, but W. does not pull back from the costs of this integrity for the Copeland family.

W.'s most significant political and social statement is *Meridian* (1976), a novel that examines the struggles of Meridian Hill to master her self-concept as a daughter, as a woman, and as a member of an oppressed race. W. focuses on Meridian's saintlike capacity for self-sacrifice in the interest of civil rights in the South. But Meridian is unable to make these sacrifices until she survives confrontations with her mother, her own feelings of guilt, and her ambivalence about the treatment of black women by black men.

The structure of the novel departs from the linear narrative of *Grange Copeland*. In *Meridian,* W. places the two major characters, Meridian Hill and Truman Held, in the present of the 1970s. The novel moves back and forth from that present to the 1960s and the beginning of the civil rights movement. Living in the late 1970s, the characters, especially Truman, relive the 1960s in order to discover their meaning. The novel makes impressive use of interior monologue, metaphor, anecdote, oral storytelling, and symbol to convey its message. Particularly powerful are the stories that are interspersed in the novel. Each story relates to the tradition of oral storytelling through which earlier women artists could relate their experiences. Meridian renounces all personal romantic involvement, as well as all material possessions, to live an ascetic life for the betterment of the rural, Southern black people. Despite the destructiveness of her mother, the weakness of her father, and the insensitivity of her husband, Meridian survives her feelings of guilt and achieves the integrity W. seeks in her fiction. Meridian is a deeply spiritual woman, the deepest character W. has created. What the novel achieves is the vision of a human being who has survived to work on behalf of the community. Meridian can define herself as an individual and as part of a group.

W.'s most popular novel is *The Color Purple* (1982), which won the Pulitzer Prize in 1983. In this epistolary novel, the outermost frame is formed through the relationship between Celie and her sister Nettie, two devoted women living in Georgia and Africa, who attempt to communicate through letters. W. deliberately places Celie in the worst position imaginable: when she was a child, Celie's stepfather raped her and forced her to bear his children, whom he then took away from her. Later, claiming that she was not "fresh," Celie's stepfather gave her to a man who married her, beat her, and forced her to raise his children and his crops. Unlike Meridian, who has at least the opportunity to survive her childhood unmolested and to attend college, Celie cannot move toward self-esteem and independence without help. This comes in the unlikely form of Shug Avery, who starts as the mistress of Celie's husband and ends by being Celie's companion and source of strength. With Shug's encouragement, Celie is able to achieve a sense of self-worth and to escape economic dependence on males. She and Shug are intensely spiritual women who have a sense of the universe as a force similar to the force of their own love, one that has more in common with the color purple than with the image of a white male god. At the end of the novel, W. offers a vision of a nonsexist, nonexploitative society in which her home is the center of an extended family.

Equally important is the language in which the novel is written. W. chooses to use letters because they were, along with recipes, diaries, and journals, the type of writing that women were allowed to do in the 19th c. or earlier. The language of Celie's letters is what W. calls "black folk English." It retains the expressiveness of oral storytelling in written form.

Whereas in *The Color Purple* W. achieved the perfect conjunction of historical situation and personal experience, W.'s novel *The Temple of My Familiar* (1989) attempts something more ambitious but is not as successful. W. describes this novel that spans hundreds of thousands of years of black life in the Americas, Europe and Africa as "a romance of the last 500,000 years." The frame of the novel is created from three marriages. One couple consists of a California history professor, Suwelo, and his wife Fanny, a teacher of women's studies who leaves academics to become a masseuse. He and Fanny eventually live in a nonsexist relationship that is symbolized by their house, a structure shaped like a bird and having separate wings for husband and wife. The women in Fanny's consciousness-raising group teach her how to reach her own freedom while Suwelo learns a great deal about human relationships from old friends of his uncle Rafe. Fanny is the granddaughter of Celie and recounts home life with Shug and their family. Second, the rock star Arveyda marries a Latin American refugee Carlotta to then have an affair with her mother, Zede. The last couple is an artist, Harold Jenkins, and a photogenic woman, Lissie, who has been reborn thousands of times and remembers her former lives.

The novel's major interest is what occurs when Suwelo returns east for the funeral of his uncle Rafe and to settle the estate. There he meets Lissie, who comes back to life as a black woman, a black man, the first white man, and even as a lion. In one life, she is a cave woman living with familiars, animals who are the humans' special and individual companions, and in a society where men and women live in separate tribes. She witnesses the founding of patriarchal society, an all-male activity to facilitate warfare that marks the beginning of male insistence that women live in the same tribe with them. Lissie remembers other times in Africa when religion was goddess-centered until domineering males replaced the goddess with images of white men. In showing the reader Lissie's memories, W. is attempting to revise the history of not only the black diaspora but of all history, including the connections between men and women. Her stories are not historically true, but are intended to function as myths that reinvent a history that has been lost. The end of the novel shifts back to the present, where Fanny and Suwelo and Carlotta and Arveyda attempt to deal with the world they find and to search again for the wholeness so important to W. The value of the novel is its attempt to create a mythology that will aid in shoring up the sense of self needed to combat racism, sexism, and violence. W. provides a prescription for the problem of responding to discrimination without becoming oneself violent and filled with hatred.

Characters and concerns from both *The Temple of My Familiar* and *The Color Purple* return in W.'s novel *Possessing the Secret of Joy* (1992). But rather than being a sequel to those works, the latter centers on Tashi, who has been reared in Africa. A middle-aged survivor of her tribe's practice of female genital mutilation, Tashi is put on trial for the murder of M'Lissa, who in attempting to circumcise Dura kills Dura. The novel is perhaps W.'s most overtly political: in the conclusion, the author reveals that a portion of the proceeds from the novel will go to fund programs educating against female genital mutilation. Becoming one such educator herself, W. followed *Possessing the Secret of Joy* one year later by coauthoring, with Pratibha Parmar, the nonfiction work *Warrior Marks: Female Genital Mutilation and the Sexual Blinding of Women*. Female sexuality as well as familial love is further explored in W.'s novel *By the Light of My Father's Smile*, published in 1998.

W.'s most powerful fiction envisions a transformation of destructive human relationships. She proposes a society based not on the model of the nuclear family—which for W. is a product of patriarchy—but on the extended family. In larger groupings, people do no relate to one another on the basis of dominance or economic power but on the basis of shared experiences. The best example of this vision is again *The Color Purple*. The novel proposes an alternative future in which Celie and Shug, two women who love one another, are at the head of a large and comfortable family. The family earns money through a cottage industry, making pants for both sexes, and the agricultural produce of their own land. In giving us this vision, W. places herself in the mainstream of radical feminist thought that argues that inequality will remain constant so long as society is based on concentration of capital, compulsory heterosexuality, and the nuclear, male-dominated, and isolated family. But the real genius of the novel is creating a radical and idealistic vision from the relationship between Shug and Celie, a connection that gives a severely abused woman a sense of herself back, a feat of human psychology that is a spiritual triumph. In this sense, W. is an optimist; she creates a mythology in which women who are denied their full humanity can survive the ordeal if they find strong support from other women.

BIBLIOGRAPHY: Banks, E. D., *A. W.: An Annotated Bibliography (1968–1986)* (1989); Bloom, H., ed., *A. W.* (1989); Howard, L. P., ed., *A. W. and Zora Neale Hurston: The Common Bond* (1993); Gates, H. L., and K. A. Appiah, eds., *A. W.: Critical Perspectives Past and Present* (1993); Winchell, D. H., *A. W.* (1992)

LAURA NIESEN DE ABRUNA

WALKER [ALEXANDER], Margaret [Abigail]

b. 7 July 1915, Birmingham, Alabama; d. 30 November 1998, Chicago, Illinois

W. is a powerful writer whose poems, essays, and fiction document life as an African American in the 19th and 20th cs. Initially recognized for her poetry and most well known for her novel *Jubilee* (1966), W. has emerged in the latter part of the 20th c. as a clear voice singing the lives of her people, their struggles, martyrdom, and hopes. In addition to her poetry and novel, she is also respected as a literary essayist and biographer.

W.'s first publications were poetry. She broke a color barrier when several of her early poems were published in *Poetry* magazine. She collected these and other poems in *For My People* (1942), which won the Yale Series of Younger Poets Award, the first time the award was given to an African American.

After this promising beginning, W. put her literary career on a back burner as she married, reared children, and taught, first in North Carolina and West Virginia before settling in Jackson, Mississippi, to become an important part of the English Department at Jackson State College. During this period, she continued research for a novel based on the life of her maternal great grandmother, begun when she was working on her master's degree. She completed *Jubilee* as her doctoral dissertation from the University of Iowa.

Vyry, the central character in *Jubilee,* is born a slave in Georgia and experiences the abuse and indignity of slavery with stoic fortitude, reinforced by her religious faith and her hope for eventual freedom. When the Civil War ends and Reconstruction begins, Vyry begins the adventure toward her long hoped for freedom. Vyry's hope for personal freedom is sorely tested, but throughout her story, Vyry asserts the need to accept and understand other people while maintaining her own integrity and pride. Because some critics reacted negatively to this book, accusing her of romanticizing or exaggerating life in the 19th-c. South, W. wrote the long essay *How I Wrote Jubilee* (1972) to document the authenticity of her research and to validate the nature of the oral history and folk traditions that form the base of much of that research.

W. sounds a note reflecting the civil rights unrest of the 1960s with most of the poems in *Prophets for a New Day* (1970), which ponder the lives and visions of the martyred Martin Luther King, Jr., and Malcolm X as well as other people and events prominent in the struggle to establish equal rights for black people. In this, as well as subsequent volumes of poetry, W. mixes poems about the struggles of black people with poems about folk characters and topics. Her verse forms include not only variations on traditional forms like sonnets, but also her own blend of rhythms and verse that impart a jazz or blues music to her work.

In addition to her poetry and fiction, W. also engages in literary analysis and has written the controversial literary biography *Richard Wright, Daemonic Genius: A Portrait of the Man, a Critical Look at His Work* (1988). W.'s biography explores flaws in WRIGHT's personality and literature as well as promoting his strengths and his position as a spokesperson about the grim realities of urban life for blacks in the early years of the 20th c.

W.'s poetry and many of her essays have been collected and republished in two valuable books. *This Is My Century: New and Collected Poems* (1989) makes the poems of her earlier volumes available as well as presenting several new poems. As the title indicates, W. takes a poetic view of the 20th c., focusing on the struggles of her people as they prepare for full participation in the 21st c. *How I Wrote Jubilee*

and Other Essays on Life and Literature (1990), edited by Maryemma Graham, reprints the title essay as well as other essays about W.'s life and literary career, focusing on the values of humanism both in individual lives and in the literature of black Americans. W.'s contribution to American literature has yet to be fully appreciated. Continued study should reveal her to be one of the strongest spokespersons for African American history and literature as a force for racial reconciliation and harmony.

BIBLIOGRAPHY: Buckner, B. D., "Folkloric Elements in M. W.'s Poetry," *CLAJ* 33 (June 1990): 367–77; Graham, M., "The Fusion of Ideas: An Interview with M. W. A.," *AAR* 27 (Summer 1993): 279–86; Pettis, J., "M. W.: Black Woman Writer of the South," in Inge, T. B., ed., *Southern Women Writers* (1990): 9–19

HARRIETTE C. BUCHANAN

WALLACE, Lew

b. 10 April 1827, Brookville, Indiana; d. 15 February 1905, Crawfordsville, Indiana

Soldier, lawyer, politician, diplomat, graphic artist, and writer, W. often seems as much a character from an adventure romance as an author of one. Indeed, he has appeared as a character in novels and movies about Billy the Kid and the Apache Wars. Born in Brookville, Indiana, he was the son of the state's governor. At a time when Indiana was still part of the frontier, W. witnessed the Black Hawk Indian Wars, which included among its combatants the young Abraham LINCOLN and Jefferson Davis. Dropping out of school at the age of sixteen, he studied law, but frequently interrupted his practice to pursue adventure. In 1846, he led volunteers in the war with Mexico. During the Civil War, he again volunteered, serving with distinction at the battles of Fort Donelson and Shiloh and later at Monocacy, blunting Confederate General Jubel Early's raid on Washington D.C. Toward the end of the war, he worked as a diplomat to help Juárez oust the Emperor Maximilian. After the war, W. first served as the second-ranking officer on the military commission that tried the conspirators involved in the Lincoln's assassination, and then as the president of the commission that tried Henry Wirz, commander of the Confederate prisoner-of-war camp at Andersonville, Georgia.

Returning to civilian life, he returned to law and politics, and began writing, completing two unproducible plays, *Our English Cousin* (also known as *The Blue and the Gray*) and *Commodus.* He also published his first novel, *The Fair God,* in 1873. From 1878 to 1881, he served as the governor of the New Mexico

Territory, dealing with range wars, Billy the Kid, and the Apache Wars of Geronimo and Victorio. During this period, he completed and published his second and most famous work, *Ben-Hur* (1880). The novel so impressed President James Garfield that he appointed W. to the post of American minister to Turkey, a position he held from 1881 to 1885. Returning to Crawfordsville, the last phase of his life was devoted to writing, politics, and lecturing. In addition to his third and most ambitious novel, *The Prince of India* (1893), he produced *The Boyhood of Christ* (1889), a campaign biography of Benjamin Harrison (1888), several collections of essays, and an autobiography completed by his wife in 1906.

A voracious reader of history and historical fiction all of his life, W. aspired from an early age to be a writer in the spirit of Sir Walter Scott. Inspired by William Hickling PRESCOTT's *Conquest of Mexico,* W. began a novel based on the last days of Montezuma as early as 1843, completing a version of it in 1853 after his experiences in the Mexican War, and publishing the final version in 1873 as *The Fair God,* to critical and popular acclaim. Its success led to work on his most famous novel, *Ben-Hur, A Tale of the Christ.* Set in Judea and Rome, the story traces the life of Judah Ben-Hur through betrayal and triumph. Rich in historical detail, the novel resembles as noted by one critic a combination of *The Count of Monte Cristo* and a Jacobean revenge tragedy, set against the backdrop of the life of Christ. While disparaged by the critics, who favored realistic narrative over historical romance, *Ben-Hur* soon achieved popular success, eventually selling more copies than any other novel in the 19th c., including *Uncle Tom's Cabin.* It was soon adapted for the stage, and eventually inspired two movie versions (1925 and 1959). W.'s final novel, *The Prince of India,* dealt with the fall of Constantinople to the Ottoman Turks, told from the perspective of the Wandering Jew. All of his novels are marked by their elaborate spectacle and attention to detail. They did much to reinvigorate the historical novel at the turn of the century.

BIBLIOGRAPHY: McKee, I., *"Ben-Hur" W.: The Life of General L. W.* (1947); Morsberger, R., *L. W., Militant Romantic* (1980); Russo, D., *Bibliographical Studies of Seven Authors of Crawfordsville, Indiana* (1952)

THOMAS L. COOKSEY

WALLANT, Edward Lewis

b. 19 October 1926, New Haven, Connecticut; d. 5 December 1962, Norwalk, Connecticut

Although his writing career was cut short by his death at age thirty-six of a cerebral aneurysm, W. remains a significant but minor Jewish American writer in post–World War II America. W. anticipates many of the issues that have characterized contemporary American fiction: the revisioning of the Holocaust; the various multicultural urban perspectives; the tension between individual isolation and community integration; and the search for faith and meaning from the margins of the mainstream. Reviewers and critics have commented on W.'s creative use of thematic binaries—such as despair/hope, ignorance/epiphany, victimization/survival, and stasis/progress—with which his characters struggle as they attempt to move from the empty lefthand figure toward some kind of personal and social redemption as represented by the right-hand figure. Indeed, W. situates his narrative conflicts in the space between these binaries.

A commercial artist by profession, W. took creative-writing courses and, in his only published memoir, "The Artist's Eyesight" (1963), lists early influences on his writing, including such diverse writers as Charles Dickens, Edgar Rice BURROUGHS, and John DOS PASSOS. Writing mostly at night after work, he eventually published his first novel, *The Human Season* (1960), which received the Harry and Ethel Daroff Memorial Fiction Award (later renamed for W.) for the best novel of the year on a Jewish theme. W.'s success with *The Pawnbroker* (1961), nominated for the National Book Award, led to his 1962 Guggenheim Fellowship, his growing reputation as a promising new writer, his determination to write full time, and his subsequent job resignation. After his premature death in 1962, his last two novels, *The Tenants of Moonbloom* (1963) and *The Children at the Gate* (1964), were published posthumously.

The Human Season explores the bruised psyche of Joe (Yussel) Berman, a Jewish widower who has isolated himself within the walls of his home and his memory to recover the major losses of his life, particularly his wife, Mary, and his only son, Marvin. W. uses flashbacks to create a counterpoint reverse chronology which emphasizes Berman's struggle to come to terms with the present using touchstones from the past. The persistence of memory and of individual isolation also pervades *The Pawnbroker,* the story of Holocaust survivor Sol Nazerman, an educated Polish Jew who operates a pawn shop in New York City. As the fifteenth anniversary of his family's death approaches, Nazerman's connection with the past intensifies, and he finds Holocaust emblems everywhere he turns, from the resemblance his shop artifacts have to Holocaust booty to the local Mafia's resemblance to concentration camp Nazis. The death of his assistant, Jesus Ortiz, who saves Nazerman's life during a robbery attempt, prompts Nazerman to abandon his isolationism and passive acquiescence and to embrace a more integrated and assertive place in the community.

The Tenants of Moonbloom, the most comic of W.'s novels, concerns the rebirth of Norman Moonbloom, who changes from a slum-lord rent collector into an altruistic tenement renovator and tenant befriender. The novel features a multitude of memorable minor characters who together create a lower-class urban community of diversity and vitality that becomes more and more appealing to Moonbloom, who has hitherto immersed himself in educational, rather than humane, pursuits. *The Children at the Gate,* in contrast, may be W.'s darkest, most fundamentally disturbing novel. Set in an urban hospital, the novel revolves around the attempted rape of a young patient by Lebelov, a hospital orderly, for which another orderly, the eccentric Sammy, attempts to atone by his suicide. Subsequently, Angelo DeMarco, heretofore estranged from his family, suffers a breakdown and returns to his family for recovery.

BIBLIOGRAPHY: Galloway, D. D., *E. L. W.* (1979); Marovitz, S. E., "A Prophet in the Labyrinth: The Urban Romanticism of E. L. W.," *MLS* 15 (Fall 1985): 172–83; Pinsker, S., and J. Fischel, eds., *Literature, the Arts, and the Holocaust* (1987)

PHILLIP A. SNYDER

WAR

The Revolutionary War, which resulted in the dissolution of England's power over the American colonies, was only the first of four major military conflicts that would affect the overall development of the U.S. America's military experiences have served to shape much of its identity. This influence is especially prominent when one examines the literary history of the U.S. Almost all American history textbooks and American literature anthologies are divided by dates that correspond to the Revolutionary War, the Civil War, World War I, and World War II. Considering the extreme impact these conflicts had on the social, economic, and cultural development of the U.S., these divisions are not unexpected.

The U.S. of America began to emerge as more than a philosophical idea in 1774 when the colonists banded together to negotiate their relationship with England. By the time the first shots were fired at Lexington and Concord in 1775, independence from the monarchy had become the major objective. Considering this, it is not surprising that the first "American" literature is primarily composed of political writers. Thomas PAINE's *Common Sense* encouraged the colonists in their struggle to overcome the tyranny of England and

establish an independent country while his series of pamphlets entitled *The American Crisis* rallied both the soldiers and civilians to maintain their allegiance to the cause. Alexander Hamilton, James Madison, and John Jay are the authors of some eighty-five essays that construct *The Federalist* (1787–88), the main goal of which was to encourage the ratification of the proposed new Constitution. The Declaration of Independence, penned by Thomas JEFFERSON, is also one of the lasting literary achievements of the Revolutionary War. The verse of Philip FRENEAU, known as the "Poet of the American Revolution," served to both celebrate military victories and console defeats while Phillis WHEATLEY's poems, such as "To His Excellency General Washington," offer the unique voice and vision of a female, African American writer.

After the war, because Americans were caught up in not only the war effort but the creation of an entirely new nation, they had little time to invest in literary pursuits thus European countries were quick to dismiss American writers as unexceptional. This labeling remained intact until the so-called "Flowering of New England" began in the mid-19th c. when Ralph Waldo EMERSON, Henry David THOREAU, Edgar Allan POE, Nathaniel HAWTHORNE, Herman MELVILLE, Harriet Beecher STOWE, and Walt WHITMAN, among others, began to emerge as the first contingent of "great" American writers. But just as these authors began to establish the literary worth of the U.S., the Civil War began.

Even prior to the Revolutionary War, the issue of slavery in America had been discussed. The tension between those who opposed slavery and those who supported it was evident from the early 1770s when rumblings concerning independence from England began. By 1860, numerous compromises had been reached to alleviate this tension, but these were only temporary abatements. The issue of slavery, combined with the economic and cultural differences between the Northern and Southern states, eventually resulted in the deadliest war in American history.

Abraham LINCOLN forever lionized Harriet Beecher Stowe when he greeted her as "the little lady who wrote the book that made this big war." The victimized characters in her book *Uncle Tom's Cabin; or, The Man That Was a Thing* appealed to the readers' sense of justice, and the audience eagerly responded to Stowe's impassioned plea for moral righteousness.

Walt Whitman, considered by many to be America's greatest poet, has also become a symbol for the Civil War. One of the most powerful sections in his anthology *Leaves of Grass* is *Drum-Taps,* which derived directly from his wartime experience as a wound-dresser in and around Washington, D.C. An ardent admirer of Lincoln, he composed the elegy "When

Lilacs Last in the Dooryard Bloom'd" in honor of the assassinated president.

Although not published until 1893, Stephen CRANE's novel *The Red Badge of Courage* remains one of the standard texts of the Civil War. Other notable Civil War literature of the 19th c. includes Melville's *Battle-pieces and Aspects of the War,* John W. DE FOREST's *Miss Ravenel's Conversion from Secession to Loyalty,* published in 1867, Mark TWAIN's *Adventures of Huckleberry Finn,* Ambrose BIERCE's *Tales of Soldiers and Civilians,* Joel Chandler HARRIS's *On the Plantation: A Story of a Georgia Boy's Adventures during War,* and Bret HARTE's *Clarence.* Some critics claim that the Civil War is the single most influential event in American literary history, but there is a general consensus that there is no great Civil War novel. The reason for this remains obscure although it has been hypothesized that Americans, as a whole, were simply too close and too involved in this conflict to write a "great" novel about it.

The Civil War continues to have ramifications on the literary development of the North and the South. The South is concerned with the past as it relates to the present while the North looks confidently ahead; thus Northern writers of Civil War literature tend to bring the war into focus early in their works while Southerners begin more slowly, usually taking the time to include the antebellum era. Some suspicion still exists between the North and the South as each region retains its own identity.

Following the Civil War, the U.S. progressed rapidly as a nation. The Industrial Revolution was accompanied by increased urbanization, and the nation's population soared as twenty-six million immigrants arrived between 1870–1920 in search of the American Dream. In spite of the depression of the 1890s, America continued to prosper. The outbreak of World War I in 1914 had little affect on the U.S., and most Americans preferred to remain neutral. Woodrow Wilson played on this sentiment and won a second term as president in 1916 by advocating peace and using the campaign slogan, "He Kept Us Out of War." But by 1917, it was obvious that America's isolation from the war could not be maintained.

World War I had a profound affect on the American temperament. Prior to the war, people believed in the basic goodness of humanity and in the progress of democracy, but, in 1919, while the U.S. found itself more secure financially, it also found itself searching frantically for its lost innocence. A new sense of freedom was exemplified by the obvious flaunting of Prohibition, the financial recklessness of Wall Street, and the new, distinctive tone of the literature. But this freedom had an undertone of desperateness. The mass killing, the chemical and trench warfare, the alienation

and disillusionment of the returning soldiers—together they combined to create the Lost Generation. On the surface, the Roaring Twenties were dominated by parties and dancing and liquor, but underneath there was pain and rejection of this superficial society. Ernest HEMINGWAY reveals this paradox in *The Sun Also Rises* as does F. Scott FITZGERALD in *The Great Gatsby.* John DOS PASSOS analyzes the absurdity of the war itself in *Three Soldiers,* a popular as well as critical success, while Hemingway explores the role of the individual in this absurd situation in *An Enormous Room.* Other important works written about World War I include Fitzgerald's *Tender Is the Night,* Hemingway's *A Farewell to Arms* and *For Whom the Bell Tolls,* William FAULKNER's *As I Lay Dying* and *Soldier's Pay,* Willa CATHER's *One of Ours,* and Edith WHARTON's *The Marne* and *A Son at the Front.* Less substantial than the prose, the poetry of World War I does include significant works by Ezra POUND, Alan SEEGER, E. E. CUMMINGS, John Peale Bishop, and John Curtis Underwood.

The modernist movement (see MODERNISM), exemplified by these works, is best known for its experimentation with style. The narrative is no longer restricted to a linear plot; rather, time appears convoluted and whimsical. Nor is there a traditional "story" to be told; instead, readers are offered snippets of information—indicative of the societal and personal fragmentation left by the World War I. Questioning previously accepted values, modernists struggled to create meaning, and this struggle is reflected in the rhetorical tension of their texts, as is their pessimism, disillusionment, and rootlessness.

While a variety of measures were taken to lesson the devastation of the Great Depression, the U.S. did not truly regain its financial equilibrium until the late 1930s. Americans were just beginning to come to some type of acceptance of the horror of World War I when news of the atrocities being enacted against the Jews began to trickle out of Germany. Before World War II ended in 1945, fifty million people would be killed. Technological advancements resulted in mass carnage: 40,000 British were killed in the Blitz; 200,000 citizens were killed in the Warsaw uprising; 78,000 Japanese were killed in Hiroshima. Although the loss of American lives at Pearl Harbor was comparatively low—2,403 killed with an additional 1,178 wounded—the citizens of the U.S. were shocked and scared by this attack on American soil. By the end of the war, 405,399 Americans had died. Even after the war, Americans continued to fear for their safety, and they built bomb shelters in their backyards awaiting attack from the Soviet Union.

Having learned the hard lessons of World War I, the novels of World War II are more intense and personal.

These works reflect the continued disillusionment of the soldiers who are now more brutal and callous and have little sense of who the real enemy is. The wide range of novels about the war reflect its importance as a transitional event between the modernist and postmodernist period. Pragmatism and realism are readily apparent.

Norman MAILER's *The Naked and the Dead* and James JONES's *From Here to Eternity* were the first important novels to come out of World War II. Considered late modernist works, they continue to press the limits of traditional style. Mailer's work was especially experimental as it introduced the new word, "fug," and offered detailed descriptions of the dead and dying soldiers. His manipulation of time is exemplified by his use of the narrative proper, the chorus, and the "Time Machine." Other novels of importance include Joseph HELLER's *Catch-22,* Kurt VONNEGUT's *Slaughterhouse-Five; or, The Children's Crusade,* Thomas PYNCHON's *Gravity's Rainbow,* John HERSEY's *The Wall,* and Saul BELLOW's *Dangling Man.*

While the uniqueness of the prose works of World War II make them hard to categorize, it is even more difficult to generalize about its poetry. The poetry, like the prose, tends to examine not only the war itself but its far-reaching affects on society and the individual. Randall JARRELL is the most widely read and widely published poet of the period, with "Eighth Air Force" and "The Death of the Ball Turret Gunner" being his most popular poems. The poetry of Howard NEMEROV, John CIARDI, Louis SIMPSON, and Karl SHAPIRO is also notable.

Whereas the Revolutionary War, the Civil War, and the two world wars were by far the most influential American conflicts, writers also sought to understand America's other military engagements. *The Bridges of Toko-Ri,* by James A. MICHENER, is one of the few Korean War novels to receive critical attention, but the Vietnam War has had scores of prose and verse written about it. The many notable works of fiction that struggle to come to terms or to make some sense of the American involvement in Vietnam include Tim O'BRIEN's *Going after Cacciato,* Bobbie Ann MASON's *In Country,* Susan Fromberg Schaeffer's *Buffalo Afternoon* (1989), Andre DUBUS's *Bluesman,* Winston Groom's *Better Times than These* (1978), Nicholas Proffitt's *Gardens of Stone* (1983), George Davis's *Coming Home* (1972), Larry Heinemann's *Paco's Story* (1986), and Robert Olen BUTLER's *The Alleys of Eden* and *A Good Scent from a Strange Mountain.* Poets such as Allen GINSBERG, Denise LEVERTOV, Robert BLY, and Robert DUNCAN were outspoken critics of the war as were Eugene McCarthy, W. D. Ehrhart, Walter McDonald, and Yusef KOMUNYAKAA. Notable plays confronting the Vietnam War include Megan Terry's *Viet Rock* (1967), Amlin Gray's *How I Got That Story* (1985), Stephen Metcalfe's *Strange Snow* (1985), and of most importance David RABE's *The Basic Training of Pavlo Hummel* and *Sticks and Bones.*

The impact of war on the development and growth of the U.S. can not be overemphasized. American writers have recognized this and have sought to understand not only the immediate conflict but its wide-ranging social, psychological, and philosophical ramifications. The literature of war, like war itself, continues to challenge old ideas while questioning the perennial issues of individual honor and integrity.

BIBLIOGRAPHY: Colwey, M., *A Second Flowering: Works and Days of the Lost Generation* (1973); Cooperman, S., *World War I and the American Novel* (1967); Fussell, P., *Wartime: Understanding and Behavior in the Second World War* (1989); Hoffman, F. J., *The Twenties: American Writing in the Postwar Decade* (1962); Limon, J., *Writing after War: American War Fiction from Realism to Postmodernism* (1994); Madden, D., and P. Bach, eds., *Classics of Civil War Fiction* (1991); Melley, P. H., *Vietnam in American Literature* (1990); Walsh, J., *American War Literature: 1914 to Vietnam* (1982)

BRENDA GABIOUD BROWN

WARD, Elizabeth Stuart Phelps

b. 3 August 1844, Boston, Massachusetts; d. 28 January 1911, Newton, Massachusetts

The author of one of the bestselling novels of the 19th c., *The Gates Ajar* (1868), W. is read today for her remarkable political novels. Strongly influenced by her Andover, Massachusetts, neighbor Harriet Beecher STOWE, W. believed that art should serve an ethical purpose, a credo spelled out in an essay entitled "Art for Truth's Sake" in her autobiography, *Chapters from a Life* (1896). Among the causes she ardently espoused in her fiction were women's rights, antivivisection, temperance, and homeopathy. Christened Mary Gray, she later adopted her mother's name. Although she married in 1888, most of her fiction was published under Elizabeth Stuart Phelps. A late novel appeared under the pseudonym Mary Adam.

W. said she wrote *The Gates Ajar* as a solace for women bereaved in the Civil War. The underlying philosophy in the work is a kind of "feminized" Christianity, a religion of love, strongly opposed to the harsh doctrines of Calvinism, especially the damnation of the unconverted. It presents a utopian vision of the afterlife, which, admixed with Swedenborgian theosophy, is elaborated in two sequels, *Beyond the Gates* (1883) and *The Gates Between* (1887). In the latter work, W.'s feminism is most apparent in her view of purgatory as a place for the resocialization of an ambitious, insensitive husband.

W. was one of the first American authors to seriously treat urban slum and factory conditions in fiction. Her early story "The Tenth of January" (1868) describes the Pemberton Mill fire, which occurred in Lawrence, Massachusetts, in 1860, the result, W. maintained, of owner negligence. Like much of W.'s work, the story is marred by a hyperbolic sentimentalist style. *Hedged In* (1870), an early novel, similarly deals with life among the underclasses, in particular an unwed adolescent mother named Nixy, herself a victim of alcoholism and abuse, who deserts her baby. W.'s solution here as elsewhere lies in the "social gospel": a good-hearted Christian woman takes Nixy in and provides her with a nurturing environment, and Nixy thus reforms.

The Silent Partner (1871), one of W.'s most interesting novels, connects feminism with reform of factory conditions. The main character is a factory owner—but a "a silent partner" because she is a woman—who takes up the cause of the workers and becomes a sort of settlement worker in their midst. *The Story of Avis* (1877), which remains perhaps W.'s most popular novel, raises the feminist issue of career versus marriage, showing how a woman artist gradually abandons her work because of the pressures of married life. *Dr. Zay* (1882) is more positive in its depiction of a woman physician. W.'s personal favorite among her novels was *A Singular Life* (1895), about a minister whose flock includes prostitutes and derelicts in an urban slum. The temperance theme is central to this work.

In the early years of the 20th c., W.'s primary concern became animal abuse. She wrote several works in which antivivisection was the principal issue; these include *Loveliness* (1899), *Trixy* (1904), *Though Life Do Us Part* (1908), and "'Tammyshanty'" (1908).

W.'s other major literary endeavor was the "Burglars in Paradise" series, including the novels *An Old Maid's Paradise* (1879) and *Burglars in Paradise* (1886), which humorously depict a woman's paradisiacal community before it is destroyed by male intrusion.

BIBLIOGRAPHY: Bennett, M. A., *E. S. P.* (1939); Donovan, J., *New England Local Color Literature: A Women's Tradition* (1983); Kelly, L. D., *The Life and Works of E. S. P., Victorian Feminist Writer* (1983); Kessler, C. F., *E. S. P.* (1982)

JOSEPHINE DONOVAN

WARD, Nathaniel

b. ca. 1578, Haverhill, Suffolk, England; d. ca. 1652, Shenfield, England

Although he spent only twelve years in New England, W. is remembered for writing one of America's first satires, *The Simple Cobler of Aggawam in America* (1647). W. broke with the ordinary Puritan plain style of his contemporaries by using elaborate locutions, elevated diction, neologisms, and an extended metaphor—of a cobbler mending shoes. Despite its uniqueness, however, the work is typical of New England Puritan writing in that it laments the backsliding of a Christian people and calls for their political, religious, and personal reformation and conformity; it reads like a secular jeremiad.

Writing in the context of civil war in England through the persona of an American shoemaker by the name of Theodore de la Guard, W. addresses the English King, arguing from a New England perspective that the empire's duty is to the welfare of the people. The people's duty is to conform religiously and politically. The book is a conservative diatribe against the toleration of any of various sectarians threatening England, old or New. Indicative of the book's satire, subject, and theme is the simple cobbler's declaration that "all Familists, Antinomians, Anabaptists, and other Enthusiasts shall have free Liberty to keepe away from us." Ironically, the perhaps best-known passages, those concerning women's fashions and men's hair styles, are actually short digressions, examples of the dangers of toleration and leniency.

W. also helped draw up the first set of laws for New England, *The Body of Liberties* (1641), laws notable for their incorporating rights of the individual's person and property, but also indicative of W.'s theocratic, aristocratic, and Hebraic values.

BIBLIOGRAPHY: Arner, R. D., "The Simple Cobler of Aggawam: N. W. and the Rhetoric of Satire," *EAL* 5 (1971): 3–16; Morison, S. E., *Builders of the Bay Colony* (1930; rev. ed., 1964); Schieck, W. J., "The Widower Narrator in N. W.'s *The Simple Cobler of Aggawam in America*," *NEQ* 47 (1974): 87–96; Zall, P. M., *The Simple Cobler of Aggawam in America* (1969)

LEE SCHWENINGER

WARNER, Charles Dudley

b. 12 September 1829, Plainsfield, Massachusetts, d. 20 October 1900, Hartford, Connecticut

W. is now best remembered for coauthoring the novel *The Gilded Age* (1873) with Samuel Langhorne CLEMENS. While the idea for the novel appears to have been W.'s, with the character Philip Sterling perceived as a semiautobiographical version of W., the novel's realistic tone and deft comedic touch are distinct aspects of Clemens's style. W. was five when his father died, and although his mother struggled to preserve the family, she finally sent W. in 1837 to live with a family connection in the neighboring town of Charlemont; W.'s semiautobiographical *Being a Boy* (1877) was based on the time he spent on the farm of this guardian in rural Massachusetts. Although raised as a Presbyterian, at age twelve W. moved to his uncle's home in Cazenovia, New York, to attend its renowned Methodist Seminary. From the seminary, W. entered Hamilton College, graduating in 1851. An extended version of his commencement address was published as *The Book of Eloquence for Students* (1853).

After serving as an engineering surveyor for railroad interests in Missouri, W. returned east to take up a career as a lawyer. In 1856, W. married Susan Lee, a former classmate from the Methodist Seminary. In 1860, after several years in Chicago, W. moved his family to Hartford, Connecticut, where he became the editor of the *Hartford Press* (later the *Hartford Courant*). While living in Hartford, W. became friends with several prominent writers, including Clemens, William Dean HOWELLS, Harriet Beecher STOWE, and her siblings Catharine E. Beecher and Henry Ward Beecher.

W.'s first mature work, *My Summer in a Garden* (1870), is his recollection of life at Nook Farm in Hartford. He followed this with a number of collections of essays, childhood recollections, and literary criticism all characterized by his humorous style: *Backlog Studies* (1873), *Baddeck* (1874), *On Horseback* (1888), *As We Were Saying* (1891), *The Relation of Literature to Life* (1897), and the posthumous *Fashions in Literature* (1902). W. wrote a trilogy of novels, *A Little Journey in the World* (1899), *The Golden House* (1894), and *That Fortune* (1899), which focus on the accumulation of an extreme fortune by Rodney Henderson and how his immorality leads to its dissipation. This trilogy is the highlight of W.'s literary career.

BIBLIOGRAPHY: Fields, A., *C. D. W.* (1904); Van Egmond, P., "C. D. W.," in Rathbun, J. W., and M. M. Grecu, eds., *DLB*, vol. 64, *American Literary Critics and Scholars, 1850–1880* (1988): 251–55

DUNCAN FAHERTY

WARNER, Susan

b. 11 July 1819, New York City; d. 17 March 1885, Highland Falls, New York

Writing under the pseudonym Elizabeth Wetherell, W. achieved almost immediate success with publication of her first novel, *The Wide, Wide World* (1851), which vied for popularity with Harriet Beecher STOWE's *Uncle Tom's Cabin* until the end of the 19th c. Her second novel, *Queechy* (1852), sold nearly as well, and the phrase "By the Author of *The Wide, Wide World*" on

the title page of *The Hills of the Shatemuc* (1856) assured first-day sales of 10,000 copies.

W. wrote thirteen novels, some of them for young adults, as well as a number of books on religious topics. With her sister Anna, she coauthored four additional novels. None of her other works, however, matched the first two in quality or popularity. Although Henry JAMES and others admired her realism—James named her favorably in the same breath with Gustave Flaubert—early-20th-c. literary historians classified her books as juvenile reading. Late-20th-c. attention to W.'s work and the publication of a new edition of *The Wide, Wide World* in 1987 offer a reassessment.

W. received the best private education her wealthy New York family could provide. When the panic of 1837 wrecked the family's finances, her father, a lawyer, moved his household—his sister and his two daughters, his wife having died earlier—to Constitution Island, across from West Point, where they spent the remainder of their lives except for a few winters. Stunned by the economic setback and ensuing isolation, the W. sisters turned to religion, which shaped their lives and works. Often forced to sell copyrights to bolster their father's finances and merely to survive, they sacrificed royalty benefits. Only after their father's death did they enjoy relative comfort.

The significance of *The Wide, Wide World* is not limited to its phenomenal sales record. As the prototype of the American female education novel, it inspired seemingly endless successors. The novel tells the story of Ellen Montgomery's spiritual and moral development under a series of guardians. While her parents travel abroad for the mother's health, Ellen struggles under the care of her father's sister, Emerson Fortune, seeks refuge with Alice Humphreys, her spiritual guide, and eventually joins the Humphreys household before going abroad to live with worldly Scottish relatives. Persistently, Ellen endeavors to conform to the wishes of her superiors, whom she sees as God's representatives. In the battle, she weeps copious tears, finding her only consolation in Bible reading and hymning.

The novel's influence derived from its embodiment of the Christian message of sacrifice, voiced by Ellen's mother, "though we *must* sorrow, we must not rebel," the ideal that molded 19th-c. daughters into wives who would endure everything in this world to win a heavenly reward. Ironically, in the final chapter, omitted by Putnam and subsequent publishers, but included in the 1987 edition, Ellen achieves both material and spiritual happiness when John Humphreys brings her back to America to live as his wife in a home filled with art, beautiful furniture, and a desk drawer filled with money—a bit of vicarious wish fulfillment for W.

Queechy follows the educational paradigm, also, but with important differences. The protagonist, Fleda Ringgan, cautioned by her dying mother to keep herself "unspotted from the world," finds herself, more truly than Ellen Montgomery, thrown into the wide, wide world. Exposed to elegant life in Paris, to hard work when her relatives return, penniless, to operate the farm at Queechy and to the jealousy and conniving of self-styled "friends" in New York, Fleda takes responsibility for her adult relatives, as well as for herself. The men in this novel, except for Guy Carleton, the wealthy Englishman whom Fleda eventually marries, are all undependable. Even Carleton, who insists that Fleda educate herself for independence, looks to her for spiritual guidance.

In her later novels such as *Daisy* (1868), *My Desire* (1879), and *The Red Wallflower* (1884), W. continued to create strong women who, after much suffering and injustice, attain happy marriages. These works suffer, however, from excessive commentaries on using one's gifts wisely. They fulfill W.'s personal goal but lack artistry.

BIBLIOGRAPHY: Baker, M., *Light in the Morning: Memories of S. and Anna W.* (1978); Foster, E. H., *S. and Anna Warner* (1978); Stewart, V., "The Wild Side of *The Wide, Wide World*," *Legacy* 11, 1 (1994): 1–16; Stokes, O. E., *Letters and Memoirs of S. and Anna Bartlett W.* (1925); Williams, C. S., "S. W.'s *Queechy* and the *Bildungsroman* Tradition," *Legacy* 7, 2 (1990): 3–16

LUCY M. FREIBERT

WARREN, Mercy Otis
b. 14 September 1728, Barnstable, Massachusetts; d. 19 October 1814, Plymouth, Massachusetts

Best known as a patriot propagandist and historian of the American Revolution, W. exemplifies the Republican woman of letters. According to 18th-c. custom, she received no formal education, but she nevertheless was among the most learned and widely read women of her day, having access through her professionally trained brothers to books and learning. Sister of James Otis, the prominent leader who opposed the Writs of Assistance and the Stamp Act; wife of James Warren, a member of the Massachusetts legislature; and longtime friend of John and Abigail Adams, W. was deeply knowledgeable about Revolutionary politics. She entered enthusiastically into the lively propaganda wars in the Massachusetts press of the 1770s, publishing unsigned satiric plays, intended for reading, not performance, that caricatured the Massachusetts Tories. The most important of these were *The Adulateur: A Trag-*

edy, as It Is Now Acted in Upper Servia, which appeared in the *Massachusetts Spy* in 1773, and *The Group,* published in the *Boston Gazette* in January 1775. In *The Adulateur,* Governor Thomas Hutchinson appears as Rapatio, the tyrant leader of Upper Servia. *The Group* depicts prominent Tories as a corrupt cabal conspiring to suppress liberties not because of principles but from their own cowardice and greed. In discussing their wives, these corrupt Tories admit that these women are much more principled (and patriotic) than they, but boast that they can dominate them by force. Implicitly, then, W. argues that political tyranny has its correlate in domestic.

Poems, Dramatic and Miscellaneous, appeared under W.'s name in 1790. While not commenting directly on contemporary politics, two tragedies, "The Sack of Rome" and "The Ladies of Castille," depict strong female figures, who, like W. herself, do not hesitate to comment on the political turmoil around them; if their principled stands do not avert tragedy, they do establish these women as powerful moral authorities. The volume also includes such occasional poems as "To a Young Lady," "To the Hon. J. Winthrop, Esq.," and "To Fidelio, Long absent on the great public Cause, which agitated all America, in 1776," which comment on the necessity for women to put aside their private desires, whether for foreign luxury goods or the companionship of their politically-involved husbands, for patriotic reasons: "The times demand exertions of the kind / A patriot zeal must warm the female mind."

Taking an unpopular stand in Federalist Massachusetts, W. and her husband opposed the ratification of the Constitution before its amendment, W. publishing *Observations on the New Constitution, and on the Federal and State Conventions* in 1788. For three decades, she worked on her three-volume *History of the Rise, Progress, and Termination of the American Revolution,* which was published under her name in 1805. W.'s *History* has been well known and valued for its firsthand characterizations of the Revolution's principals, many of whom W. knew personally. It is notable for its critique of what W. perceived as Federalist compromising of the principles of liberty in the years following the Revolution, and led to a rift with her lifelong friend, John Adams.

BIBLIOGRAPHY: Anthony, K. S., *First Lady of the Revolution: The Life of M. O. W.* (1958); Silverman, K., *A Cultural History of the American Revolution* (1976); Smith, W. R., *History as Argument: Three Patriotic Historians of the American Revolution* (1966)

LAURA HENIGMAN

WARREN, Robert Penn

b. 24 April 1905, Guthrie, Kentucky; d. 15 September 1989, Stratton, Vermont

In 1986, W. was named the first official poet laureate of the U.S. Congress thus commemorated one of the longest and most versatile careers in American literary history. As a poet, novelist, critic, and social commentator, W. continues to appeal to a wide and varied audience, and his work has earned high praise from fellow critics and common readers alike.

As an undergraduate at Vanderbilt in the early 1920s, W. was welcomed as a junior member of the literary group the FUGITIVES, which included such luminaries as John Crowe RANSOM, Allen TATE, and Donald DAVIDSON. Tate was quick to see the young Kentuckian as the most gifted writer in that charmed circle, and by the time he graduated W. had already assumed important editorial responsibilities on the staff of the *Fugitive,* one of the more significant literary magazines of the decade. W. adopted the Fugitives's commitment to writing that was at once regional and modernist (see MODERNISM), and he contributed an essay to the Fugitive Agrarian symposium *I'll Take My Stand* (1930). Temperamentally, he would share certain of Ransom and Tate's aesthetic and cultural assumptions throughout his career, but from the beginning W. displayed an independence of mind and imagination, informed by a strong strain of pragmatic realism, that set him apart from his supposed mentors. Indeed, one of the most persistent themes underlying W.'s writing is the danger of pat answers and overdetermined worldviews. Armed with this awareness, W. focused upon "the hazards of selfhood" and our need for an "earned vision" that will make self-definition possible in a world where the very concept of "self" is under attack. For W., literature was a way of coming at the self as well as at the world, and therefore a bulwark against those forces of dehumanization that often disguise themselves under the rubric of "progress."

After graduate study at the University of California and Yale and a period at Oxford as a Rhodes scholar, W. assumed a series of academic appointments before joining the faculty of Louisiana State University in the mid-1930s. During his years there, W. gained steady prominence. With Cleanth BROOKS, he edited the prestigious *Southern Review* and began collaboration on a series of textbooks that revolutionized the teaching of literature, bringing New Critical insights into the classroom. However, W.'s primary commitment was to his own writing. His first book of poetry, *Thirty-six Poems* (1935), defined him as a poet in the modernist mold, but his distinctive voice was already present, combining Southern materials and Eliotian "impersonality" in a poetry where colloquialism and erudite diction were often juxtaposed. This "early" period in W.'s career included *Eleven Poems on the Same Theme* (1942), which contained such representative lyrics as "Terror," "Pursuit," and "Original Sin," in which W.'s perennial fascination with the grotesque and macabre plays an informing role. "The Ballad of Billie Potts" (1943), a boldly experimental fusion of folk narrative and densely self-reflexive meditative sections, marked the end of W.'s first stage as a poet, even as it pointed toward things to come.

During this same period, W. was also a prolific writer of fiction, turning out many of the stories that would eventually make up *The Circus in the Attic* (1947) and publishing two novels. The first of these, *Night Rider* (1939), is set during the "tobacco wars" in W.'s native Kentucky and details the gradual destruction of its protagonist, Percy Munn, a man caught between the claims of social justice and the necessity of law and order. *At Heaven's Gate* (1943), based in part on the career of the Tennessee entrepreneur Luke Lea, is among other things an incisive commentary on the inadequacy of characteristic American dreams.

In 1946, W. brought out the novel that most critics agree in his finest, *All the King's Men.* Reviewers immediately drew parallels between the character Willie Stark and the late "kingfish" of Louisiana, Huey P. Long, but W.'s book is anything but a conventional *roman à clef.* In telling the story of Willie, populist idealist turned cynical power-monger, W.'s narrator, Jack Burden, reveals his own tortured flight from selfhood that ends finally with a realization that he cannot secede from moral and social responsibilities. Jack learns that the forces of history may be "blind," but "man is not." Our sins of omission as well as commission define us, but man's free will remains intact and with it a capacity for "good" that is an "index to man's glory and power." W. calls for a higher *Realpolitik,* in which ideals and aspirations must always be balanced against a pragmatic sense of human frailties and limitations. In *All the King's Men,* W. brings together recurrent themes evident in his earlier work—the impact of the past on the present, the human propensity for evil, the ambiguity of human motives, the temptations of self-deception and the terrors of self-awareness—and in doing so demonstrates his own claim to the role of "philosophical novelist," a phrase he used to describe Joseph Conrad. *All the King's Men* is a technical tour de force, operating simultaneously on many levels. It continues to be W.'s best-known and most popular work.

Jack Burden's lesson is replicated in the case of Thomas JEFFERSON, the central figure in *Brother to Dragons* (1953), a book-length "tale in verse and voices" that, like *All the King's Men,* stands as quintessential W. Its centrality to his canon is clear from the fact that W. brought out a substantially reworked "new version" in 1979. Based on an historical episode involving the murder of a slave boy by two of the President's nephews, *Brother to Dragons* pointedly challenges many of the premises about human nature upon which Jeffersonian liberalism is based. Confronted with humankind's capacity for senseless carnage, Jefferson is made to see the inadequacy of the Enlightenment optimism that formed the basis for his democratic vision, but in the end he comes to embrace a new, if more sober, "dream" of America's possibilities, a dream founded upon a realistic assessment of our all-too-human selves. W. himself plays an important role in *Brother to Dragons,* through his "persona" RPW, who acts as something of an interlocutor throughout the poem. This seems to signal the poet's commitment to a more personal and autobiographical brand of verse. Beginning with *Promises* (1957), W.'s poetry increasingly mirrored his own life and feelings, though the poet's respect for form and abiding concern with history saved him from many of the excesses of "confessional" writing.

The immense success of *All the King's Men* has served to overshadow W.'s subsequent novels to varying degrees, yet each of them warrants careful reading on its own terms. *World Enough and Time* (1950) masterfully explores the possibilities of the historical novel, as does *Band of Angels* (1955), which illustrates W.'s ability to put the overworked materials of the popular romance to work for serious purposes. This latter novel also reflects W.'s deep concern with the problem of race, manifested in works of nonfiction like *Segregation* (1956) and *Who Speaks for the Negro?* (1965). In his 1959 novel *The Cave,* an updated and imaginatively heightened version of the Floyd Collins episode, W. comments upon the modern American scene more directly. With the exception of the short novel *Wilderness* (1961), a response to the centennial of the Civil War, W.'s later novels all have more or less contemporary settings. *Flood* (1964) is, as its subtitle indicates, *A Romance of Our Time* in which much of the tawdriness of post–World War II America is subjected to an incisive critique. *Meet Me in the Green Glen* (1971) is notable for its insight into the psychology of love and its meditative lyricism, despite the sensationalistic aspects of its plot—melodrama being a distinctive element of the W. "signature." *A Place to Come To* (1977) has been described as an academic bildungsroman; it is more than that. The self-narrated chronicle of Jed Tewksbury, a scholar who fears the truth about himself and for whom the pursuit of knowledge becomes a technique of self-evasion, it is a summation of those perennial concerns W. wrestled with from the beginning of his career. Taken together, W.'s ten published novels represent a formidable achievement. However unified they may be in terms of thematic motifs and philosophical assumptions, they each represent their author's attempt to meet the demands of a new formal challenge.

W. was never a writer disposed to play it safe, as his later poetry so amply demonstrates. He was fond of quoting Randall JARRELL's advice to those who would practice the poet's risky vocation: "If you want to be struck by lightning, you have to stand out in the rain." W. did just that, aware that on occasion one may be merely soaked for his troubles. *You, Emperors, and Others* (1960), *Incarnations* (1968), and *Or Else* (1974) are generally regarded as uneven collections, and indeed W. was quite conservative in reprinting selections from these and other volumes in the *New and Selected Poems* of 1985. Still, poems like "Mortmain," "Tale of Time," "Masts at Dawn," and "Rattlesnake Country" are likely to last, and W. made two distinguished contributions to the tradition of the American long poem in *Audubon* (1969) and *Chief Joseph of the Nez Perce* (1983). As the poet approached his eighth decade, his poetic output remained unabated, with three remarkable volumes of verse—*Now and Then* (1978), *Being Here* (1980), and *Rumor Verified* (1981)—appearing in rapid succession. Poets of a new generation such as Dave SMITH and T. R. Hummer and critics as diverse as Harold BLOOM and Calvin Bedient have been responsive to W.'s late phase, characterized as it is by a voice that is at once autumnal and authoritative, even as it resists the temptation to be conventionally vatic.

BIBLIOGRAPHY: Burt, J., *R. P. W. and American Idealism* (1988); Casper, L., *R. P. W.* (1960); Cutrer, T. W., *Parnassus on the Mississippi* (1984); Grimshaw, J. A., Jr., *R. P. W.: A Descriptive Bibliography* (1981); Guttenberg, B., *Web of Being* (1975); Justus, J., *The Achievement of R. P. W.* (1981); Strandberg, V., *The Poetic Vision of R. P. W.* (1977); Walker, M., *R. P. W.* (1979); Watkins, F. C., *Then and Now* (1982); Watkins, F. C., and J. T. Hiers, *R. P. W. Talking* (1980)

WILLIAM BEDFORD CLARK

WASHINGTON, Booker T[aliferro]

b. 5 April 1856, Franklin County, Virginia; d. 14 November 1915, Tuskegee, Alabama

Born a slave, emancipated at nine, founder and principal of Tuskegee Industrial College, recipient of an honorary master's degree from Harvard, W. was considered a leader for black Americans of his day, not to mention for many in the 20th c.; further, historians of black America label 1895 to 1915 the "Era of W." Consequently, while it might be argued that his public career eclipsed his literary accomplishments, his works actually augmented his public position. Further, what W. left on paper—namely *Up from Slavery* (1901)—has made a unique contribution to the American and African American literary canon.

Whereas *Up from Slavery* is W.'s most famous work, it represents the second of his two autobiographies; *The Story of My Life and Work* (1900) is the first. Generally, this first autobiography is regarded as unnotable, and whether its poor reception was the fault of the inept black journalist, Edgar Webber, whom W. had hired to write the story, or W.'s absence when the autobiography was being finalized, the work is significant in that it reveals W.'s rhetorical skill, namely in regard to audience. *The Story of My Life and Work* was written for a black audience; hence, some scenes, like when W. recounts seeing his uncle being beaten and hearing him holler for respite, are included in this narrative to build empathy with his readership. Astutely, W. eliminates this less than pleasing scene from his second autobiography, which was written for a white, wealthy readership.

W.'s second book, *Up from Slavery,* fits readily into two genres: the SLAVE NARRATIVE and the AUTOBIOGRAPHY. First, it represents one of the last published slave narratives since these narratives first began appearing in the mid-19th c. Often, W.'s narrative is compared to Frederick DOUGLASS's *Narrative of the Life of Frederick Douglass, an American Slave, Written by Himself* because the two share basic similarities; however, W.'s narrative is significantly different in that it reveals the shift in tone that occurred in many slave narratives published after the Civil War, a tone that abolished any blatant hint of resistance and instead adopted a tone of pragmatism. Further, W.'s text seems to signify, or play off against, Douglass's narrative, an important fact considering it represents a prevalent literary practice in African American literature. Second, *Up from Slavery* is classified as an autobiography, one with didactic intentions. *Up from Slavery* and Benjamin FRANKLIN's 18th-c. *Autobiography* have been compared, for both are fashioned like an exemplary autobiography that illustrates the virtuous steps one takes on the pathway to success.

The debate over the purport of *Up from Slavery* has generated divergent views. Frequently, W.'s narrative is dismissed as a pitiful treatise of accommodationist tactics—an Uncle Tom story. But others argue such criticism misses subtleties of this text written by a rather subtle—and astute—man, for *Up from Slavery* invokes an important African American literary figure known as the trickster—what seems to be acquiescent is covertly subversive. Like the intent of the autobiography, W.'s prose style in this text is more complex than initially evident, for generally, it has been evaluated as little more than straightforward and simple. And,

interestingly, the words W. is most famous for—"In all things that are purely social we can be as separate as the fingers, yet one as the hand in all things essential to mutual progress"—are not from his prose, but from his famous 1895 speech "Atlanta Compromise." W.'s oratorical sentences are much more figurative than his prose, yet his prose style serves a purpose: to construct, not dramatize, his life. Further, W.'s words reveal a writer dexterous in saying one thing but meaning another, a writer knowledgeable in the use of "mother wit."

When W. penned both *The Story of My Life* and *Up from Slavery,* he left a literary record of his rising political dexterity, for both were knowingly constructed as books to garner political and monetary support. At the same time, through *Up from Slavery* he has left a literary contribution that has continued to be read—or misread—long after many slave narratives have become neglected.

BIBLIOGRAPHY: Cox, J. M., "Autobiography and W.," *SR* 85 (Spring 1977): 235–61; Gibson, D. B., "Strategies and Revisions of Self-Representation in B. T. W.'s Autobiographies," *AQ* 45 (September 1993): 370–93; Harland, H. R., *B. T. W.: The Making of a Black Leader, 1856–1901* (1972); McDowell, D., and A. Rampersad, eds., *Slavery and the Literary Imagination* (1989); McElroy, F. L., "B. T. W. as Literary Trickster," *SFQ* 49 (1992): 89–107

NANCY M. STAUB

WASSERSTEIN, Wendy
b. 18 October 1950, Brooklyn, New York

Educated at Mount Holyoke College and Yale Drama School, where she met her friend and occasional collaborator, playwright Christopher Durang, W. began playwriting early and has succeeded often.

As a member of the Baby Boomer generation and a committed feminist, W.'s works often focus on social change and the issues of the times. Through her entertaining, intelligent, and witty dialogue, which betrays a writer of education and sophistication, W. is able to grapple with serious concerns in a comedic framework.

In *Uncommon Women and Others* (1977), set in a restaurant in the present, and then six years earlier at a women's college, W. introduced what has become a familiar theatrical device for her, the flashback, employed to reveal the changes that have taken place over some time period. This device is also central to W.'s first major triumph, *The Heidi Chronicles* (1989), the Pulitzer Prize and Tony Award-winning play that ran for 621 performances.

The play takes place between 1965 and the present, and focuses on Heidi, who lectures on women's matters but is herself unfulfilled and unhappy. She is in love with a political aspirant, who marries someone else. Heidi then befriends a homosexual doctor and adopts a baby. The doctor warns that she will continue to look back at her life and regret her choices. The play contains women's rap session scenes, which have become associated with W., and lend an affectionate, satiric, and insightful look, though time, at women's thoughts and cares. Through these scenes, Wasserstein depicts a balance of anger, unhappiness, self-awareness, and frustration about friendship, loneliness, independence, and achievement.

W. is a shrewdly observant social commentator, yet also deeply personal at the same time. As one critic noted, W. writes about "a generation of women—intelligent, attractive, educated, *uncommon* women—who, while attempting to deal with their fears and disappointments, manage to define and redefine who they are." W. introduced this theme early in her career, returning to it with *Isn't It Romantic* (1981), which focuses on the lives of young women in New York, and continuing to develop on it.

The Sisters Rosensweig (1993), which ran a healthy 142 performances Off-Broadway before transferring to Broadway where it ran for 556 performances, garnered its star Madeline Kahn a Tony Award. The play deals with the very serious issues of anti-Semitism, sexism, assimilation, and child rearing in a thoughtful, yet highly comedic manner, much like Anton Chekhov and Neil SIMON at his hilarious best.

An American Daughter (1997) was something of a departure for W., and was not a critical success. More serious than her previous work, the play focuses on a nominee for U.S. Surgeon General undergoing a grueling confirmation hearing.

Beyond her own playwriting activities, W. has worked as a dramaturg and served on the selection committee of the Young Playwrights Festival at Playwright's Horizons, a theater company with whom W. has had a long relationship. She also contributed material to *Hard Sell* (1980) by Murray Horwitz and to John Tillinger's *Urban Blight* (1988).

In 1990, she published *Bachelor Girls,* a brilliant collection of essays of 1990s pop-feminist satire with titles like "The World's Worst Boyfriends," "My Mother, Then and NOW (yes, that NOW)," "Nails: The Naked and the Red," "Aunt Florence's Bar Mitzvah," and the predictably brief "Perfect Women Who Are Bearable."

BIBLIOGRAPHY: Shapiro, W., "Chronicler of Frayed Feminism," *Time* 133 (27 March 1989): 90–92; Winer, L., "The Art of Theater XIII: W. W. Interview," *Paris Review* 39 (Spring 1997): 164–88

ERIC MARSHALL

WEEMS, Mason Locke

b. 11 October 1759, St. Johns Parish, Maryland; d. 23 May 1825, Beaufort, South Carolina

W. is best remembered for inventing, or at least popularizing, the story of George Washington's chopping down his father's cherry tree, though in W.'s original account the future president kills the tree by damaging the bark. Yet W.'s achievement transcends the retailing of questionable historical anecdotes. His purpose was, he said, "to *Enlighten,* to *dulcify* and *exalt* human nature" by providing books that taught an appreciation for the values embodied in the Declaration of Independence and that promoted material and spiritual well-being. A prolific author and purveyor of moralistic and patriotic works that he sold throughout the South, he introduced books to a new world of readers.

While rector of St. Margaret's in Westminster Parish, Maryland, W. began reprinting and selling sermons of the English divines Robert Russell and Hugh Blair, Hannah Moore's *An Estimate of the Religion of the Fashionable World* (1791), edited by W. in 1793, and chapbooks. Among his first editorial efforts were an expanded version of Luigi Cornaro's *Trattato de la vita sobria* (1558) entitled *A Sure and Certain Method of Attaining a Long and Healthy Life* (1793) and an abridgement in 1794 of George Keate's *Account of the Pelew Islands* (1788). To the former work, W.—who may have studied medicine in Edinburgh—appended "Golden Rules of Health," a compendium of classical advice coupled with his own admonitions.

In 1794, W. began his connection with the Philadelphia publisher Mathew Carey, traveling throughout the South for the next twenty years to sell Carey's publications. W. wrote to Carey that in books for the South "let the moral and religious be as dulcified as possible," an approach that W. took with his own works.

Capitalizing on the popularity of almanacs, W. purloined information from others to create his own versions, such as *The Lover's Almanac* of 1799. Known as the marrying parson, W. here and in many other publications—including his biography of George Washington—urged Americans to marry and multiply. To dulcify his moral he added a portrait of Miss Delia D—of Virginia, the embodiment of ideal American womanhood, and her equally perfect husband, Florio.

The couple reappear in "Hymen's Recruiting Sergeant," first included in W.'s *The Virginia Almanac for the Year of Our Lord 1800* (1799) but also published separately to become what Lewis Leary suggested was America's first best-selling paperback. The work is a quasi-secular, quasi-religious sermon on matrimony, with characters based on biblical parables and 18th-c. periodical essays.

In 1799, W. proposed that Carey publish a series of short biographies on American heroes, beginning with a pamphlet W. was writing about Washington. When W. expanded *A History of the Life and Death, Virtues and Exploits of General George Washington* (1800) into a book, published in 1806, he added anecdotes including that of the cherry tree. W. claimed that all were supplied by those who knew the president, but W. was less concerned with historical truth than with patriotic and moral lessons that could be drawn from Washington's life. He followed this success with biographies of Francis Marion (1809), Benjamin FRANKLIN (1815), and William Penn (1822).

Inspired by engravings of William Hogarth, W. created a series of pamphlets illustrating the dangers of vices such as gambling, drunkenness, and adultery. Again he used characters to make his points, and he repeatedly stressed the need for education. Always the salesman as well as the preacher, he claimed that reading books, especially books like his, would lead to health, wealth, and happiness.

W.'s works were popular in his day, appealing to audiences unlikely to read John Marshall's four-volume life of Washington—which W. also peddled). Though scholars lamented W.'s turning history into romance, in an 1845 essay William Gilmore SIMMS, another fictionalizer of history, summarized W.'s achievement as exercising "a wondrous influence over the young minds of the country."

BIBLIOGRAPHY: Leary, L., *The Book-Peddling Parson* (1984); Skeel, E. E. F., *M. L. W.: His Works and Ways* (1929); Wroth, L. C., *Parson W.: A Biographical and Critical Study* (1911)

JOSEPH ROSENBLUM

WEIDMAN, Jerome
b. 4 April 1913, New York City; d. 6 October 1998, New York City

Although W.'s name may not appear prominently in today's literary canon, Ernest HEMINGWAY once wrote him, "I think you can write better than anybody else that's around." His long, disciplined writing career has produced nearly two dozen novels, six plays and musical libretti, four hundred short stories, and several nonfiction works, including an autobiographical memoir.

Given this impressive output, W. would merit critical note today even if he had abandoned writing after publishing his first novel, *I Can Get It for You Wholesale* (1937) at the age of twenty-four. He produced this classic while working seven days a week in the garment district and attending law school at night. His portrait of amoral hustler Harry Bogen is written in the sort of wisecracking style that such prose stylists as Raymond CHANDLER and Dashiell HAMMETT applied to good effect in their hardboiled detective novels. W.'s novel is memorable for creating a hard-boiled shipping clerk: conniving, manipulative, self-serving, womanizing, yet unabashedly devoted to his mother. The first-person narrative develops a consciousness that lacks a conscience, and Bogan's venomously sarcastic thoughts evoke alternate delight and disgust in the reader.

Bogan would be reincarnated twice: first in a follow-up novel *What's in It for Me?* (1938) and, a quarter century later, in W.'s libretto for the musical adaptation of *Wholesale* (1962), which introduced Barbra Streisand to Broadway. He won the Pulitzer Prize for his libretto for the Jerry Bock-Sheldon Harnick musical *Fiorello!* (1959) based on the life of Fiorello La Guardia. The next year, the same creative team failed with the musical *Tenderlion*. These works all exemplify W.'s attraction to male New Yorkers who are driven to achieve, regardless of means or consequences.

Although not all of his characters are Jewish, W. asserts that everything he has written springs from his experience as a Jew growing up on the Lower East Side, unable to speak English until after he began school. *Fourth Street East* (1970), designated a novel, follows W.'s family life closely, showing both the alienation and assimilation of newly arrived Jewish immigrants. Still, the author prefers selecting and shaping true events as a novelist rather than simply reporting factual truth. As he once put it, in dealing with true events, "Your imagination has to push the scene around and get the essence of it."

W.'s literary influences come from both sides of the Atlantic. He admires, and enjoys rereading, the English classics. The only authors he has acknowledged by name as teaching him about being a writer are Joseph Conrad and James Gould COZZENS.

A survivor of the German air raids in London, W. recalls the philosophic response of a woman with whom he shared a shelter: "One must be able to last it out." W. has adopted this as his personal credo and has lasted it out for over eighty years. His first novel—republished in 1984 with an admiring introduction by Garson Kanin—is likely to endure for many more years.

BIBLIOGRAPHY: Blicksilver, E., "J. W.," in Walden, D., ed., *DLB*, vol. 28, *Twentieth-Century American-Jewish Fiction Writers* (1984): 316–23

GARY KONAS

WEISS, Theodore [Russell]
b. 16 December, 1916, Reading, Pennsylvania

As poet, critic, translator, and longtime coeditor with his wife Renee of the *Quarterly Review of Literature,* W. has played various literary roles and spoken in multiple voices. Influenced by MODERNISM, W. anticipated late 20th-c. poetics, shaping poems whose subjects fluctuate from the commonplace to the sublime, the ancient to the postmodern, and the domestic to the esoteric, as he seeks to bind extremes. After Muhlenburg College, in 1938 he entered Columbia and began writing prolifically. In a preface to *From Princeton One Autumn Afternoon* (1987), his collected poems, he confesses, "From the start I was after a voice that could give voice to the many people inside and out, to the drama of their collision as well as to the larger music of their harmony." These voices are present not only in the dramatic monologues of Caliban in "Caliban Remembers," a World War II soldier undergoing surgery in *Gunsight* (1962), an old woman in her garden in "The Generations," and Eve speaking to the serpent in "The Garden Beyond" in *A Sum of Destructions* (1994). But they are also manifest in W.'s diverse poetic strategies, from concise, poignant assertions about culture and individuality, as in "The Fire at Alexandria," "This Gray Age," "As You Like It," and "Deconstructed," to longer, more intricate narratives, such as "The Storeroom," the book-length *Recoveries* (1982), and "From Princeton One Autumn Afternoon," poems that use from fifteen to sixty pages to unravel their reflections.

Resisting what he considers the prosaic, overly personal language of much postwar verse, W. cultivates the imaginative whimsy he finds in Wallace STEVENS, the rich, inventive rhetoric he admires in Shakespeare, and the unwinding rhythms and open-ended syntax of free verse he adapts from William Carlos WILLIAMS. Homer's mythic reach and epic pacing are also important parameters. Like modern architecture, W.'s early poems nakedly display their scaffolding of heavily enjambed, sometimes crabbed sentence structure, while later poems, though as ornate, tend to be quieter, more self-assured and intimate. Signature poems look closely into Western history, friends' lives, his own past, or artworks (among his favorite subjects), where he typically discovers some small, virtually overlooked detail or phrase around which he constructs a high-minded, if mildly ironic commentary. Williams, a mentor and friend, receives tribute in several poems, notably "The Life Of . . ." and "Yes, But. . . ." "The Ultimate Antientropy," not in *Selected Poems* (1995), concedes that the multifaceted portraits of Helen reveal her inheritance of Zeus's promiscuous nature, yet in a twist suggesting W.'s own poetics, the poem concludes that the more Helen's image varies, the more she is herself. "The Cure" treats the English language in similarly paradoxical fashion. Critics admire W.'s erudition, complex and dramatic phrasing, fragmented polyphony, imaginative speculation, and optimism; some consider his style digressive, obscure, uncompelling or too patrician.

Introducing *The Man from Porlock* (1982), perspicacious essays on poetry, W. invokes the figure who interrupted Coleridge from completing "Kubla Khan" in order to castigate contemporary poets for allowing artistry to succumb to worldly intrusions; at the same time he advocates "the visionary combined with the commonplace, the noble out of the democratic and the colloquial," clearly his own objective. From 1947 to 1987, he taught at Bard and Princeton. Perhaps his most generous contribution to American letters has been his effort since 1943 to discover, publish, and champion poets over several generations.

BIBLIOGRAPHY: Gibbons, R., "The Cure: T. W.'s Poetry," *MPS* 9 (Spring 1978): 18–33; Inez, C., "An Interview with T. W.," *Parnassus* 5 (1977): 161–74; Spiegelman, W., "Reassuring Surprises: T. W.'s Talkies," *Parnassus* 12 (Fall-Winter 1984): 315–29; Stock, R., "A Passion to Equal All Hope: T. W.," *HC* (April 1979): 1–12

JOHN GERY

WELCH, James
b. 18 November 1940, Browning, Montana

W., winner of the 1997 Lifetime Achievement Award of the Native Writer's Circle of the Americas, is a major figure in the Native American literary renaissance. His poetry, fiction, nonfiction, and scriptwriting explore the Native American struggle for identity and survival. W. grew up on the Blackfoot and Fort Belknap reservations and graduated from the University of Montana where Richard HUGO encouraged his poetry and fiction.

His book of poetry, *Riding the Earthboy 40* (1971), was praised for its stark, evocative imagery of the Montana landscape, its unflinching portrait of reservation life, and its mixture of surrealism and existential ambiguity. W. juxtaposes honky-tonk bars, drought, and ranch-hand talk with dreams, vision quests, and a buried history hidden beneath the estranged surface of life.

The Winter in the Blood (1974) is a comic novel of self-discovery. The unnamed narrator begins alienated from himself and his surroundings, flounders through memories in search of identity, and finally returns to the reservation where he discovers his family and tribal origins—a pattern, as critic David Craig notes, that is repeated in all of W.'s novel. The novel's geographical, social, and psychological angst ends with a ritual return to tribal roots in a hilarious epilogue that ambiguously suggests a reconciliation of the narrator with his heritage and the present.

The Death of Jim Loney (1979) is a bleaker tale about a half-breed with no sense of the past or hope for the future and no place in the white or the Indian world. It is another story of alienation, the search for identity, and a quest for a place, not to live but to die. Loney's sister and his white girlfriend try to rescue him from his drunken nihilism, but, haunted by images of a bird and a biblical passage, neither of which he understands, he returns to the reservation and orchestrates his own death.

In *Fools Crow* (1986), his most acclaimed novel, W. examines the Blackfoot massacre by the U.S. Calvary, the smallpox epidemic of the 1870s, and the decimation of the buffalo. The protagonist is White Man's Dog, later called Fools Crow, the leader of a dying culture who sees the future in a dream-vision quest. Though its shifts in perspective and magical-realism are demanding, the book established W. as a major Native American storyteller.

In *Indian Lawyer* (1990), W. explores the shifting identity of a successful Blackfoot corporate lawyer running for Congress who loses his confidence and position because of blackmail and an affair with the wife of an Indian inmate. The protagonist, Sylvester Yellow Calf, used by both Anglos and Indians, eventually chooses a new path that mediates between the two worlds as a lawyer for tribal rights.

Killing Custer: The Battle of Little Bighorn and the Fate of The Plains Indians (1994), a nonfiction collaboration with Paul Stekler, examines the battle and its aftermath from an Indian perspective. The book grew out their earlier Emmy-nominated film, *The Last Stand at Little Bighorn.* His latest publication is another nonfiction collaboration, *Sweet Medicine: Sites of Indian Massacres and Battles* (1995).

BIBLIOGRAPHY: Craig, D., "Beyond Assimilation: J. W. and the Indian Dilemma," *NDQ* 53 (Spring 1985): 182–90; Larson, S., "The Outsider in J. W.'s The Indian Lawyer," *AIQ* 18 (Fall 1994): 495–507; McFarland, R., ed., *J. W.: Interviews and Essays on His Work* (1986); Wild, P., *J. W.* (1983); Viele, A., *Four American Indian Literary Masters* (1982)

NEWTON SMITH

WELLEK, René

b. 22 August 1903, Vienna, Austria; d. 10 November 1995, Hamden, Connecticut

W. was born in Vienna, the son of a Czech father and an Italian mother, and his life spanned the near entirety

of the 20th c., its atrocities, achievements, its changes of taste in literary culture. W. came to the U.S. far earlier than is generally known, in 1927, studying at Princeton University, then teaching German at Smith College, then to Princeton for a short while, returning to Charles University, Prague, where he finished a thesis for his second advanced degree, published as *Immanuel Kant in England, 1793–1838* by Princeton in 1931. After lecturing at London University from 1935 to 1939, W. was invited to the U.S. by colleagues at the University of Iowa, which at that time led the American academy in its notice of contemporary critical method. In 1946, W. moved to Yale, where he spent the next twenty-six years.

W.'s book on Kant sets a standard for his later writing. It is not that crutch of utilitarian critics, a book about "influence" narrowly defined and rigorously administered, though it could be misread as such. Samuel Taylor Coleridge, the main English subject of the work, was after all a compulsive borrower, almost always without attribution. Rather, W. in this work defines literature as an autonomous creation, set afloat in a world of its own definition, not subject to rules or limitations of other subjects judged more pedestrian—such as history, or most particularly, nationalistic history written to a Procrustean economic pattern. Art is to be judged by its aesthetic effect, free of economic and social concerns, and by inference, free of the limitations of influence studies or overt nationalism.

Nonetheless, one can see the clear split in this critic's work between the defense of the autonomous work of art in several essays that were later issued in academically published books (it is sometimes difficult to disentangle the dates of origin, sometimes a full decade before appearing in a critical collection). What is judged his major publication, the eight-volume *A History of Modern Criticism, 1750–1950,* was issued over a period of three decades. The first of these volumes was issued in 1949. This study concerns itself with "The Later Eighteenth Century." For once in English, overdue emphasis is placed on German critics who were to find their place in the aesthetics of the next century, especially Friedrich Schiller, Johann Gottfried von Herder, and the totem of German literature, Goethe. English and French literature follow with approximately sixty pages each, and little relation is adduced between the three spheres. One may feel when reading the pages on Samuel Johnson, for instance, that the arbitrary method of the Victorian selecting of "touchstones" is at work, though with the Great Cham, instead of the Arnoldian superficialities of polished gems pried from the major poets.

It is tempting to claim that W.'s remove to Yale had a dampening influence on his work, that it thereafter blandly describes to encapsulate, to overgeneralize in the styles of the biographical-critical-edition-industry of Tinker to Pottle to Wilmarth Lewis. W.'s technique of commentary may even remove itself to that of a predecessor, the Victorian description of 18th-c. "thought" rendered by Sir Leslie Stephen. The formulaic summary is W.'s method throughout, even in the final volume of the set, which considers American critics from 1900 to 1950, H. L. MENCKEN to W. K. Wimsatt, Jr. Anyone wishing to test W.'s writing need only read extensively in the critic being discussed, then compare the mental notes made with the commentary. W.'s text is repeatedly inadequate or distorted for the expediency of academic summary.

A good deal of this first volume, however, was written before the official remove to Yale: some parts of the book were researched at that unlikely outpost of British colonial rectitude, The Huntington Library in California. At any rate, the same conservatism, the approximate summary as focal explanation, signals other works by W., such as *The Rise of English Literary History* (1941), which pushes British writing forward as more of an autonomous realm than it receives in any of W.'s other work. Mere footnote attention is paid to continental sources. Even Dante is subsumed in anecdote and the dulling succession of disparate references copied with monotonous similarity.

W.'s strongest work remains the book coauthored with Austin Warren, *Theory of Literature* (1949). Whether his assertion in the chapter on "Literary History" survives his own method is moot: "'Romanticism' is not a unitary quality which spreads like an infection or a plague, nor is it . . . merely a verbal label." Nonetheless, the chapter on "The Mode of Existence of a Literary Work of Art" is a source where one may begin the study of the "ontological situs"—the place of moving residence for literary works that have now taken shelter in the least likely places, according to the conservative academic view, in contemporary culture. There, political and sexual activism are brought to the forensic acts of literary commentary. That he rejected notions of the more adventurous recent attacks on "high culture" is to be seen in his much later essay, "The Attack on Literature" (1972; rev. ed., 1982). His distrust of innovation is demonstrable in the artificially circumscribed barriers of his own commentary.

BIBLIOGRAPHY: Bucco, M., *R. W.* (1981); Davidhazi, P., "R. W. and the Originality of American Criticism," in Tibor, F., ed., *The Origins and Originality of American Culture* (1984): 441–52; Demetz, P., "A Conversation with R. W.," *CCur* 9 (1990): 135–45

ROBERT MOYNIHAN

WELTY, Eudora [Alice]
b. 13 April 1909, Jackson, Mississippi

For more than half a century, W. has produced prose fiction in remarkable variety and of unusually consistent high quality, thus establishing for herself a place as one of 20th-c. America's most lasting and successful writers. Her reputation as a versatile and gifted artist has grown with each of her published volumes of fiction and continues to rise under the critical scrutiny that her works have prompted.

W. enjoyed a happy and secure childhood that she has reminisced about in her bestselling autobiographical memoir *One Writer's Beginnings* (1983). Educated in the public schools of Jackson before attending the Mississippi State College for Women for two years, she graduated with a degree in English from the University of Wisconsin in 1929. On the advice of her father, president of a life insurance company, she then studied advertising for a year at the Columbia School of Business in order to prepare for practical employment. In 1931, W. returned to Jackson where she found part-time work with newspapers and radio before taking her most important job as publicity agent for the Works Progress Administration. For three years, she traveled throughout her home state writing about local projects and taking pictures—both literally and figuratively—that were to influence her later life and her career as a writer. Her photographs have been exhibited from New York City to Jackson, and a number of them have been published in *One Time, One Place: Mississippi in the Depression* (1971).

Throughout this period of practical employment, W. wrote fiction that met with rejection on all fronts. Finally, however, in 1936, "Death of a Traveling Salesman" became her first publication in the May–June issue of *Manuscript,* a success that was followed by publication of six of her short stories in the *Southern Review* under the leadership of Cleanth BROOKS, Albert Erskine, and Robert Penn WARREN. Within the next few years, her work was being published regularly and was being championed by such established writers as Ford Madox Ford and Katherine Anne PORTER. By 1941 and the publication of her first collection of short stories, *A Curtain of Green and Other Stories,* W. had won a small but significant national audience for her fiction.

A Curtain of Green (1941) contains a number of W.'s best known and most frequently anthologized stories: in addition to "Death of a Traveling Salesman," it also includes "Keela, the Outcast Indian Maiden," "Petrified Man," "Why I Live at the P.O.," and "A Worn Path." Her second collection, *The Wide Net and Other Stories* (1943), contains such different and challenging pieces as "Livvie," "A Still Moment," and "The Wide Net." Taken together, these two volumes early revealed the depth and breadth of W.'s artistic talents. She herself has designated two different artistic approaches in her fiction: "inside" and "outside" stories. The inside stories are introspective and sensitively probing in their examination of the private mysteries of life; the outside stories are typically more colloquial and comic, frequently invoking satire and focusing on externals as evidence of internal meanings. The stories of these first volumes also demonstrate the hallmarks of W.'s career as a fiction writer: the importance of place, fascination with change, a transfixing lyrical power of description, the significance of family, the complexity of human relationships, and the paradoxical themes of love and separateness.

Her first novella, an historical fantasy entitled *The Robber Bridegroom* (1942), is a curious blend of European fairy tales, American folklore and tall tales, and local legends—all set in Mississippi during its pioneer days. Among its mixture of real and fictional characters are legendary keelboatman Mike Fink, the notorious bandit Harpe brothers, archetypal Southern planter Clement Musgrove and his beautiful daughter, the robber bridegroom Jamie Lockhart, and a variety of others ranging from Natchez Indians to New Orleans merchants. The novella continues the strong strain of humor, much of it heavily indebted to the old Southwestern humorists, that is found in W.'s fiction, as well as her fascination with the theme of doubling.

Her first full-length novel, *Delta Wedding* (1946), is set on the Fairchild plantation in the Mississippi delta in 1923. Though the marriage of Dabney Fairchild to overseer Troy Flavin is the ostensible reason for the extended family's gathering together, the focal event proves to be Uncle George's previous rescue—from being run down by a train—of his simpleminded niece Maureen. *Delta Wedding* continues and expands W.'s exploration of family, her focus on change and its effects, her understanding of local mythmaking, and her technical virtuosity.

The Golden Apples (1949), a cycle of seven short stories that many have read as a novel, concentrates on the leading citizens of the town of Morgana during a forty year span. In it, W. draws heavily on classical mythology to extend the significance of the parochial lives of several generations of the Rainey, MacLain, Morrison, Stark, and Carmichael families. Perhaps the most experimental of her books, *The Golden Apples* demonstrates W.'s remarkable technical skills as she continues to find new methods of sounding her favorite themes: change and its pervasive effects, the importance of family and place, and the tragicomic complex nature of ordinary life.

Her second novella, *The Ponder Heart* (1954), is an extended dramatic monologue in prose delivered by Edna Earle Ponder and focusing on her foolish and naive, but generous and genuinely good-hearted, Uncle Daniel. W.'s talent for rendering Southern dialect and her unerring sense of folk comedy are nowhere better seen than in *The Ponder Heart*. It won the William Dean Howells Medal of the American Academy as the most distinguished work of American fiction between 1950 and 1955.

The Bride of the Innisfallen (1955), another seven story collection, again demonstrates the significance of place in W.'s fiction, though the places here range from New Orleans to Ireland to Italy. These stories grew out of her second Guggenheim Fellowship, during which she traveled through Europe and met Elizabeth Bowen, the Anglo-Irish writer to whom the collection is dedicated and in whom W. found a kindred spirit.

It was fifteen years before W.'s next major work, *Losing Battles* (1970), was published. In it, she returns to her native Mississippi for the setting, but further expands her range of techniques by attempting to convey all thought and feeling through dialogue and action—a completely outside narrative. She again writes about an extended family—the Vaughan-Beecham-Renfro clan—though Judge Moody and Julia Mortimer, the community's late school teacher, are also major forces in the novel. A volatile mixture of comedy and pathos, *Losing Battles* derives its title from such battles as Miss Mortimer's against ignorance and clannishness, from Judge Moody's against a provincial sense of tribal justice, and from the Renfros' against the Depression, the elements, and interference from outsiders. But even in her portrayal of the inevitability of lost battles, W. celebrates love and the mystery and dignity of individual and family spirits.

The Optimist's Daughter (1972), perhaps her most autobiographical fiction, won for W. a much overdue Pulitzer Prize in fiction as well as a Gold Medal for Fiction from the National Institute for Arts and Letters. In this story of the McKelva family of Mt. Salus, Mississippi, she again writes of love in both its constructive and destructive aspects, family, and the inevitability of change, all conveyed through a realistic and tragicomic perspective.

In addition to her fiction, W. has published the autobiographical *One Writer's Beginnings,* a sampling of her photographs in *One Time, One Place,* and *The Eye of the Story* (1978), a collection of essays and book reviews that reveal her skills as a critic.

Though she has achieved international fame and won many honors—including the Hollins Medal, the first annual Award of Excellence by the Mississippi Arts Commission, the M. Carey Thomas Award from Bryn Mawr, two O. Henry Memorial Contest short story awards, the National Medal of Literature, the Medal of Freedom, the Modern Language Association

Commonwealth Award, the American Association of University Women Achievement Award, the National Medal of Arts, and honorary degrees from more than a dozen colleges and universities—W. has remained an essentially private person living in the family home in Jackson. Through more than five decades of writing fiction, she has proven again and again to be one of our most versatile artists with surprises in store at each publication: though most of her fiction derives from the land and the people she knows best, it is diverse and fresh in her varied use of forms, her effective use of both the grotesque and the ordinary, and her continuing discoveries about and celebration of the human spirit. The clarity and lack of pretentiousness in her style, her ability to capture fine nuances of emotion and truth in narrative form, her delicate and yet powerful descriptive powers, and her great courage to extend her range in work after work have made her one of our superb stylists.

BIBLIOGRAPHY: Desmond, J. F., *A Still Moment: Essays on the Art of E. W.* (1978); Devlin, A. J., *W.: A Life in Literature* (1988); Gretlund, J. N., *E. W.'s Aesthetics of Place* (1995); Johnston, C. A., *E. W.: A Study of the Short Fiction* (1997); Kreyling, M., *E. W.'s Achievement of Order* (1979); Trouard, D., *E. W.: Eye of the Storyteller* (1990); Turner, C., and L. Harding, eds., *Critical Essays on E. W.* (1989); Westling, L. H., *E. W.* (1989)

CRAIG TURNER

WESCOTT, Glenway [Gordon]

b. 11 April 1901, Kewaskum, Wisconsin; d. 22 February 1987, Rosemont, New Jersey

W.'s productive early years as a novelist associate him with America's Midwest regional writers and the Paris expatriates of the 1920s. He is also known as an essayist, poet, and critic, and for his literary work with the American Academy and Institute of Arts and Letters, of which he was president from 1960 to 1962. W. is widely regarded as a lyrical prose stylist of impeccable skill, intelligence, and subtlety.

Born on a farm, W. earned a scholarship to the University of Chicago at sixteen. First published in the *Dial, Poetry,* and other journals, he was influenced by Yvor WINTERS and other imagist poets, and produced two poetry collections, *The Bitterns* (1920) and *Natives of Rock* (1925). His first novel, *The Apple of the Eye* (1924), captures with great beauty life on poor Wisconsin farms, but is also an indictment of Midwestern PURITANISM.

First in Villefranche among Jean Cocteau's circle, then in Paris, W. lived nearly a decade in France.

His best-selling Midwest classic, *The Grandmothers* (1927), became a model of the chronicle novel and placed him among the top expatriate writers. Aside from the retrospective chronicle form and the poetic feel of its prose, the novel's success is in its narrative technique. Alwyn Tower, W.'s autobiographical character, is a participating narrator who is sometimes a part of the story, sometimes not, but whose existence makes the overall voice of the novel work.

The stories and title essay in *Goodbye, Wisconsin* (1928) emphasize the harsh realities of the Midwest, though with some humor and irony. W.'s final Midwestern work, *The Babe's Bed* (1930), is the story of expatriate Tower's visit to his family's humble Wisconsin farm. Like his earlier fiction, the story dwells on the poverty and spiritual oppression of the region, but doesn't overlook the natural splendor of the land: "All summer long that country and the sky over it, if any one gaze could have embraced it all at once, would have been seen to be silken, Roman-striped with rainbows."

After a volume of prophetic prewar essays, *Fear and Trembling* (1932), was badly received, W. returned to New York in 1933. The friendship and influence of W. Somerset Maugham, he said, helped counterbalance the years of speaking, reading, and even dreaming in French. With *The Pilgrim Hawk* (1940), W. achieved the height of his literary powers. Universally praised, and included in anthologies of great modern short novels, the story uses the participating narrator technique in the first person and brings it to a higher level. His Alwyn Tower character recalls the events of an afternoon in the Paris of the late 1920s, at the same time commenting upon the universal joys and sorrows of love, marriage, sex, and sexuality—as well as the creative struggle of the artist. In its February 27, 1987 obituary of W., the *Times of London* suggested that *The Pilgrim Hawk* is as perfect as any work in the English language, and stated, "He will be remembered as long as fiction is read."

W.'s only nonautobiographical novel, *Apartment in Athens* (1945) is a highly suspenseful, traditionally-narrated story of a family in Nazi-occupied Greece. It was a best-seller and a Book of the Month Club selection. Between 1932 and 1952, W. abandoned four sizable novel manuscripts, ambitious works that became weighted in technical complexity. The essays in *Images of Truth* (1962) consider the moral purpose of fiction, along with remembrances and criticism of six major writers he knew. W.'s high-profile, lifelong companionship with Museum of Modern Art curator Monroe Wheeler, and his 1950s friendship and work with Dr. Alfred C. Kinsey and the Institute for Sex Research are among the many topics covered in his posthumous journals, *Continual Lessons* (1990).

BIBLIOGRAPHY: Johnson, I. D., *G. W.: The Paradox of Voice* (1971); Rueckert, W. H., *G. W.* (1965)

JERRY ROSCO

WEST, The

As a geographical locale and a mythic region of mind, the West has always exercised a mysterious power over the European and American imagination. For centuries, this power has transcended the boundaries of social class, gender, and ethnicity. Thousands upon thousands of people have dreamed westward: first across the Atlantic, then across the Alleghenies and the wild regions of Appalachia, then across the plains to the Rocky Mountains and the Pacific Coast. The historical experience of westward expansion, together with all the tragic consequences that attended it, was informed by powerful sets of assumptions about human nature, democracy, and human destiny. These ideas were initially conceived by the minds of prophets and poets, and they were implemented in a series of journeys by religious leaders, political activists, ardent capitalists, and common people of humble birth. For all of them, the goal was more than economic. The West was an indescribable region of paradise, possibility, mystery, and promise. Even today, in the minds of new Western writers, the region roughly between the Rocky Mountains and the Pacific Coast possesses its own identity and its own distinctive history. This has led to a powerful and unique literary tradition, which has in turn yielded one of the most rich and various of contemporary literary movements.

The new Western writers, however, are too often considered independent of the tradition that informs them. In American history and literature, the "West" is an evolving concept. For the early settlers, three terms were synonymous: the "West," the "frontier," and the "wilderness." Initially the latter term, with all of its connotations, dominated the colonial mind. The integral nature of these three ideas is first revealed in the explorer narratives of individuals such as Cabeza de Vaca, Christopher Columbus, and Captain John SMITH. In their works, the representation of the wilderness is not merely imaginative but is born of dark and brutal experiences hitherto unimagined. These explorers brought to their journeys certain values, objectives, and dreams that remain the binding element that informs their interpretation of events, and their wilderness experience shaped and reconstituted the European perception of America. *The Narrative of Alvar Nuñez Cabeza de Vaca* (1542) recounts the author's eight-

year odyssey among the Native Americans of Florida, the Gulf Coast, and Northern Mexico. He perceives the wilderness and the frontier as a wild land of Godless barbarism. But paradoxically, he retains a sympathetic view of the Natives that occupy the land. He sees them as a worthy people who must be "won" to the ways of Christianity with "kindness" and "benevolence." To Cabeza de Vaca, the wilderness is a region of dread and brutality, a place that exists to test his spiritual and physical fortitudes. Yet it is also a land of economic possibility and spiritual promise.

The same essential themes find their way into the work of Christopher Columbus, Giovanni de Verrazanno, Pedro de Casteñeda, Richard Hakluyt, Michael Drayton, Samuel de Champlain, and Captain John Smith. In Smith's *The Generall Historie of Virginia, New England, and the Summer Isles,* the Chesapeake Indians under King Powhatan emerge as "savages," but they appear also as a powerful and intelligent people rich in ceremony and religious practice, a people complex in political and social organization. Smith sees the wilderness as a land of potential for colonial expansion, as a place destined to broaden and deepen the European mind.

The darker and more trying aspects of the explorer experience were incorporated into forms of literary expression by the New England Puritans, and they of course interpreted that experience into a more firmly Judeo-Christian context. For individuals such as John WINTHROP William BRADFORD, and Mary ROWLANDSON, the Western frontier could only be seen in scriptural terms, through the use of typology, which was the practice of biblical exegesis that Calvinists drew from the medieval period. Recalling the concept of the "wilderness" as type and antitype, these Puritans saw the frontier as Satan's realm. Like the Israelites in the book of Exodus and like Christ himself, the chosen people of God must enter the wilderness, experience temptation and trial, and emerge redeemed. In *A Model of Christian Charity* and *The History of New England,* Winthrop powerfully argues that the "New Jerusalem," the promised "City on a Hill," can only be born out of this interaction with the savage land, the Western frontier, the wilderness. These assumptions arise also in William Bradford's *Of Plymouth Plantation,* Michael WIGGLESWORTH's *The Day of Doom* and *God's Controversy with New England,* and the poetry of Anne BRADSTREET and Edward TAYLOR. The notion of the Western frontier as "wilderness," as a dark region of trial, temptation, and spiritual transformation, emerges especially in the genre of the captivity narrative. In a series of twenty sections called "removes," Mary Rowlandson recounts the experience in *A Narrative of the Captivity and Restoration of Mrs. Mary Rowlandson.* Here the author again represents the Western frontier as a savage realm of demonic forces, but also as a place ordained as necessary for the refinement and "restoration" of the Christian soul.

The concept of the wilderness as a region of promise and personal transformation continues in the Age of Enlightenment, specifically in the writings of Thomas JEFFERSON and J. Hector St. John DE CRÉVECOEUR. In *Notes on the State of Virginia,* Jefferson sees the Western frontier as a region of ultimate possibility for economic and political utopia. The power resides in the will of enlightened Americans to settle the wild lands, to transform them into pastoral regions of plenty, where agrarian modes of existence may function to reconstitute the moral fibre and identity of the American people. These concerns are expressed also by Crévecoeur in *Letters from an American Farmer,* a treatise powerfully asserting 18th-c. agrarian philosophy and the transformative power of Western lands. For these explorers, settlers, colonists, and early nationalists, the Western frontier was simultaneously a physical locale and a region of mind, a place to project and imagine a personal, spiritual, and national destiny.

This cultural practice continued throughout the 19th c., as the line that divided Eastern civilization from Western frontier shifted and changed. American national identity and mythic self-perception was increasingly defined by the West. Popular heroes emerged, not from the intellectual classes, but from the wilderness, in rogues, adventurers, and frontier heroes such as James Fenimore COOPER's Natty Bumppo, John Filson's Daniel Boone, and the historical yet quasi-fictional personas of Davy CROCKETT, Wild Bill Hickock, Buffalo Bill, Calamity Jane, and Annie Oakley. This pantheon of heroes finds its way into the Western, the most resilient and popular genre in the history of American film.

The power of these myths led serious writers to thoughtfully consider the West as a literary subject, both as a geographical region and an idea in the American imagination. The "regional" literature in the West begins perhaps with the tradition of Southwestern humor in works such as Mark TWAIN 's "The Notorious Jumping Frog of Calaveras County" and *Roughing It.* This appears also in the local color writings of Bret HARTE, the regionally focused naturalist work of Jack LONDON, the historically specific psychological romances of Willa CATHER, and the imaginatively rendered social dramas of John STEINBECK. But in 1893, in an essay entitled "The Significance of the Frontier in American History," Frederick Jackson Turner announced the closing of the frontier. Indeed, at the end of the 19th c., the "wilderness," the "frontier," and the "West" ceased to be synonymous terms. The frontier receded into history, and as exemplified in the concerns of Theodore ROOSEVELT, the wilderness changed from

a land to be settled to a land to be preserved. The West, reduced in size but not in ideological power, became the intimate concern of writers who grew up on the streets of its rugged towns, walked its landscapes, and contemplated its unique identity.

Fiction, travel narratives, oral tales, drama, and poetry emerged from the West throughout the 19th and 20th cs., in the work of literary figures such as Sharlot Hall, H. L. DAVIS, Mary Hunter AUSTIN, J. Frank Dobie, and Wright MORRIS, among many others. But the authors often referred to as the "new Western writers" occupy roughly two generations. The first includes such figures as A. B. GUTHRIE, Jr., Vardis FISHER, Bernard De Voto, Frank Waters, Katherine Anne PORTER, William E. STAFFORD, William EASTLAKE, Walter Van Tilberg CLARK, Wallace STEGNER, and Edward ABBEY. Central to the thematics of all of these writers is the transformative experience of the Western landscape. In works such as *The Big Rock Candy Mountain, Angle of Repose,* and in essay collections such as *Where the Bluebird Sings to the Lemonade Springs ,* Stegner sees the West as a land characterized by aridity and a new civilization shaped by impermanence. The theme of physical transience that informs Stegner's work emerges as a result of the harsh, beautiful, often inhospitable nature of Western lands. In *The Monkey Wrench Gang* and other works, Abbey shares similar concerns. The epic and tragic history of westward expansionism is a central preoccupation of both these writers. The historical experience informed by egalitarian democracy, but marred by the physical and cultural decimation of indigenous peoples and their land, creates a tension that finds its way into the shape and form of characters, themes, and literary styles.

Of primary concern to new Western writers is the relationship between the Western past and the Western present, the process by which five centuries of American history have influenced the direction of the geographically limited region now simply called the "West." This concern with history, historiography, and the formative influence of time and myth continues in the work of contemporary novelists, poets, and essayists, including Sherley Anne Williams, Leslie Marmon SILKO, Joan DIDION, Tillie OLSEN, and Thomas MCGUANE. Particularly notable among recent Western writers, specifically in the way they deal with the West as historical subject, are Larry MCMURTRY and Cormac MCCARTHY. McMurtry has managed to negotiate the boundary between the "popular" and the "literary." In a series of novels including *Leaving Cheyenne, The Last Picture Show, Buffalo Girls, Lonesome Dove, The Streets of Laredo, Dead Man's Walk,* and *Comanche Moon,* McMurtry attempts to explore the nature and structure of Western history. Works set in the present deal with the process by which 19th-c. range values have been interpreted into a 20th-c. world. Historical romances set in the West of the 19th c. reaffirm elements of Western mythology, while expanding the mythohistorical field to explore the darker and more brutal realities behind the "Wild West." This same set of concerns and themes informs the work of Cormac McCarthy, in novels such as *Child of God, Suttree, Blood Meridian; or, The Evening Redness in the West, All the Pretty Horses,* and *The Crossing.* McCarthy's work is remarkable, insofar as he links the concerns of new Western writers with the ideas and aesthetic practices that have informed American literature from its inception. With William FAULKNER's stream-of-consciousness technique and a biblical force that echoes Herman MELVILLE, McCarthy places the historical experience of westward expansionism within the context of Calvinist theology, 19th-c. dark romantic epistemology, and popular Western iconography.

The literature of the "new Western writers" is broad in scope and multiple in its concerns. The complex influences of Native American traditions, the rich literary history of Hispanic, Asian, Scandinavian, and other nationalities, add a depth to Western literature that causes it to transcend the boundaries of the term "regional." Most Western writers are considered by scholars through many perspectives other than region. But the richness and variety of literary expression in the West, the long and various history of Western writing, testify to the transformative power of the West as a place, an idea, and a myth.

BIBLIOGRAPHY: Slotkin, R., *Regeneration through Violence: The Mythology of the American Frontier, 1600–1860* (1973); Slotkin, R., *The Fatal Environment: The Myth of the Frontier in the Age of Industrialization* (1985); Slotkin, R., *Gunfighter Nation: The Myth of the Frontier in Twentieth Century America* (1992); Smith, H. N., *Virginland: The American West as Symbol and Myth* (1958); Taylor J. G., et al., eds. *A Literary History of the American West* (1987)

STEVEN FRYE

WEST, Jessamyn

b. 18 July 1902 or 1903, near North Vernon, Indiana; d. 22 or 23 February 1984, Napa, California

Although she grew up in Yorba Linda, California, the oldest of four "California college educated children," W. laid spiritual claim to southern Indiana, where she was born. Her mother's stories of growing up in Indiana resulted in W.'s feeling "nearer to its climate, its topography, its flowers and trees, and to the farmhouses of my grandparents than to anything in my own state of California." Her family's Indiana roots

and Quaker background fueled some of her best writing, including her "Quaker stories," *The Friendly Persuasion* (1945) and its "companion" piece *Except for Me and Thee* (1969), as well as *Leafy Rivers* (1967) and *The Massacre at Fall Creek* (1975), two bildungsromans that take place on the Indiana frontier.

While W. was pursuing her doctorate in English literature at the University of California, she was diagnosed with bilateral tuberculosis. After a two year stay in the sanatorium, she was sent home to die. Instead, she recovered. In *The Woman Said Yes* (1976), W. chronicles her struggle with tuberculosis and its effect on the rest of her life. She embarked on her writing career during a relapse that sent her back to the sanatorium. She stated, "I am not proud of the manner in which I came to writing; unwilling, until I was backed into a corner by disease, and unable to do anything else except perhaps crochet, to pick up my pen. Talent is helpful in writing, but guts are absolutely necessary." W.'s husband, Harry Maxwell McPherson, sent her first stories out for publication; her first book, *The Friendly Persuasion,* was published in 1945, and the film version was released in 1956. W. coauthored the film script; her book *To See the Dream* (1957) describes W.'s experience in Hollywood.

W.'s work includes novels, short stories, autobiographies, poetry, essays, reviews, screenplays, and an opera. Her writing often deals with girls coming of age, much of her work, both fiction and nonfiction, centers around mother-daughter relationships; W. was strongly influenced by her own mother, "whom," she said "I resemble . . . though I am a pale copy." *A Matter of Time* (1966), one of W.'s finest novels, examines a mother who bestows the gift of strength on her daughters but who inflicts damage as well. Although the approach and style are very different, the subject matter resembles that in *The Woman Said Yes.* Another autobiography, *Double Discovery* (1980), documents not only W.'s experience in England in 1929, but also the discovery of letters her mother had written from Europe some forty years earlier. W. said in an interview, "When [my mother] died . . . I discovered letters which seemed to me from another woman. . . . I was now an older woman, a much older woman, discovering the young woman. . . . It was a young woman's discovery of travel in Europe and the older woman's discovery of the young woman."

Her *Collected Stories,* published two years after her death, demonstrates W.'s versatility as well as her obsessions. The stories include first-and third-person narrators, male and female protagonists, and often focus on everyday experience and coming of age. In 1979, Robert Kirsch concluded his review of *The Life I Really Lived* by stating that it was time to recognize W. as one of the "treasures" of contemporary American llterature; however, W.'s literary contribution, perhaps particularly to autobiography, has yet to be recognized.

BIBLIOGRAPHY: Chapman, J., "J. W.," in Kibler, J. E., Jr., ed., *DLB,* vol. 6, *American Novelists since World War II* (1980): 81–90; Farmer, A. D., *J. W.* (1982); Shivers, A. S., *J. W.* (1972)

                                        JILL JONES

WEST, Nathanael

b. 7 October 1903, New York City; d. 22 December 1940, El Centro, California

Born Nathanael Weinstein, W., in a short career, produced four novels. The first, *The Dream Life of Balso Snell,* appeared in a limited edition in 1931. After this came *Miss Lonelyhearts* (1933), *A Cool Million* (1934), and *The Day of the Locust* (1939).

W.'s works were not well received when they were first published. W. was a sociological writer in the sense that he described what he saw. The mirror he held up to society was the fly-specked mirror of a dingy room in a seedy boarding house, illuminated only by a bare overhead bulb. Nothing softens the harshness of his vision. It may be that he portrayed America accurately, but in the middle of the Great Depression, America was not ready for W.'s bleak outlook and black humor.

The Dream Life of Balso Snell should be considered separately from the other three novels, for it deals more with the self than with society. This short novel, if indeed it can be called a novel, might best be described as surrealistic. It opens with the title character entering a Trojan horse through the anus, and is a bitter attack on Art, portraying the artist as one who must turn to extravagances in order to be heard—if in fact there is any message to hear. Through the novel, W. exemplifies the very thing he mocks. *The Dream Life of Balso Snell* is essentially a private book, and was perhaps not meant for wide exposure.

In *Miss Lonelyhearts,* W.'s severe disillusionment turns outward. The book is more accessible, not only because it is better written than its predecessor, but also because it is easier to understand. W. admits that the artist has a message, even though he says that message is rejected by society. There is a particularly strong religious motif in *Miss Lonelyhearts.* The title character is a man who is the advice columnist for a metropolitan newspaper. He becomes so burdened by the agonies of his correspondents who believe in him that he feels he must somehow save them. His columns of bland optimism are not sufficient for the misery he finds, and he seeks to bring salvation to those around him through Christian love, though he is mocked by his colleagues. The closing scene of the novel shows him with his arms outspread in love, only to be accidentally shot by the man he was trying to help. W. seems to be saying that this is the fate of the artist.

W. savagely satirized the American Dream in his third novel, *A Cool Million.* The book is a parody of the Horatio Alger story that manages to be truly funny as well as biting. Despite the mock heroic style, there is an uneasy sense that W.'s view of the American system—diseased and corrupt—may be close to reality.

W. returns to the theme of *Miss Lonelyhearts* in his final work. *The Day of the Locust* again addresses the theme of the artist trying to help those who do not wish to be helped. The protagonist in the novel is in fact an artist; he wishes to rescue those around him from their disillusionment and sterility, but he is defeated by their apathy and treachery. He finds himself in their condition; he is at work on a picture that he cannot finish. He is able to finish the work only after he has inadvertently started a riot and saved himself from the violence of the mob by resorting to violence.

In addition to this theme of the artist in a society of Philistines, W.'s work also has undercurrents of thwarted sexual desire and a strong element of victimization. Things happen to his protagonists, but the accidents of their lives are always malevolent, never benign. In his last three novels, his heros are passive, and their only actions of consequence come as a response to the actions of others. They are not fighting their way out of the quagmire of life; they are being pulled under precisely because they struggle. Life, in W.'s view, was a discouraging proposition.

W.'s uneven output is small enough to be read in its entirety. Since the publication of his *Complete Works* in 1957, he has gained some of the critical attention that was previously lacking. This is due in part to the fact that we now have some historical perspective on his work. We can hold it up next to his own era and make a judgment. W. provides an alternate American literature of the 1930s and gives us a grotesque angle of vision on questions that are still being asked. W. was working on several film scripts when he died in a car crash at age thirty-seven.

BIBLIOGRAPHY: Madden, D., *N. W.: The Cheaters and the Cheated* (1973); Martin, J., *N. W.: The Art of His Life* (1970); Reed, R., *N. W.: No Redeemer, No Promised Land* (1967)

                                        DENNIS KEARNEY

WESTERN, The

The Western is one of America's two major contributions to world art—the other being jazz. But what is the Western? Though definitions vary, it may reasonably be called a piece of long fiction with all or most of five ingredients in varying degrees of importance. First, it stresses the land—vast, overwhelming, including gardens and deserts, with mountains and storms in between—usually west of the Mississippi River and south of Canada, but often down into Mexico. Second, it features a loner as hero—often tight-lipped about a shadowy past, usually handy with fists, guns, and horses, and always restless. Third, it is filled with violent action, at the end of which evil is usually destroyed. Fourth, it relates, though often only indirectly, to real events in Western history—having to do with pioneering, fighting Indians, crime, ranching, or homesteading. And fifth, it often includes women, but typically in minor roles—for example, schoolteachers, ranchers' daughters, or "soiled doves."

The evolution of the Western has been slow and painful. The popular Western sprang from romantic, even gothic, fiction, with lurid dime novels, many by E. Z. C. Judson (pen name "Ned Buntline") leading the way. More serious Westerns emerged from the early accounts of explorers, pioneers, hunters, scouts, and travelers, with Lewis and Clark pointing the way. The cowboy novel, which until the 1920s captured most of the market, started with *The Virginian* by Owen WISTER; this book sold phenomenally but was consequently so imitated that the genre suffered. More authentic was *The Log of a Cowboy* (1903) by Andy Adams. Many writers followed in the tradition of Adams, including Eugene Manlove Rhodes, also a thoughtful cowboy, whose work is well represented by his *Pasó por Aquí* (1926), which paints the Southwest reverently, and distinguishes between legal and real justice. Of scores of writers capitalizing on Wister's mass appeal and fleshing out his format, the most successful was Zane GREY, whose sales figures were the highest of any such novelist until the advent of the most incredible best-seller of them all, Louis L'Amour. Grey combined romantic plots, a reverence for the redemptive Far West, generalized historical touches, weak characterization, and an often banal style. His *Riders of the Purple Sage* (1912) remains one of the most popular Westerns ever written. L'Amour has written formulaic Westerns, often with a twist—for example, the hero of *The Man Called Noon* (1970) has amnesia—and Westerns resting on historical reality—for example, the hero of *Sitka* (1957) is active at the time of the Alaska Purchase (1867) and even has an audience with Tzar Alexander II of Russia, but L'Amour will be best remembered for his Sackett family saga (17 vols., 1960–85). Three early prolific writers of Westerns almost as renowned with the masses were Frederick Faust (commonest pen name Max Brand), Ernest Haycox, and Frederick Dilley Glidden (pen name Luke Short), all of whom began as "pulp" writers, then graduated to "slicks" and regular

novels. The legendary Faust, who wrote more than three hundred books under nineteen pennames, is perhaps most famous for *Destry Rides Again* (1930), which exemplifies the Western twisted into a detective story. Haycox, who improved on formula fiction by introducing more thoughtful heroes and also heroines in contrasting pairs, is best known for his two fine army Westerns, *The Border Trumpet* (1939) and *Bugles in the Afternoon* (1944), and was moving into Oregon-homesteading fiction when he died early of cancer. Short, preferring to branch out into other genres but trapped by high royalties, infused routine Western action yarns with thematic variety. He is well represented by *Hard Money* (1939), which concerns mining and features a tender-tough hero and contrasting females, and by *And the Wind Blows Free* (1945), which is narrated by a boy who reluctantly sees flaws in his cowboy idol. The best latter-day fictional treatment of cowboys includes works by Edward ABBEY, Ben Capps, Matt Braun, Elmer Kelton, Cormac MCCARTHY, and Larry MCMURTRY.

The legitimate Western may be divided into three main types: formulaic or commercial, historical, and literary. Two recent offshoots are the parody Western and the adult Western.

The recipe for the commercially successful novel includes an exploiting villain who opposes good people—who in turn revere a make-believe West and would build in it—a confused community—in town or camp—and a hero whose permutations are legion. He can ride in, clean up the place, win respect and love, and maybe even settle down. Or he can be a resident to begin with, who leaves on a mission of vengeance, returns, goes into action, and finally either reenters society or departs in disgust—sometimes with the pliant heroine. He can even be a professional "gunny" who comes to fight for money, fun, or excitement, or simply to help good overcome evil. A classic example of the formulaic Western is *Shane* (1949) by Jack Schaefer; it has all the requisite ingredients in its mix, and its remarkable sales figures prove it.

Westerns overtly tied to specific historical events please certain readers by suggesting real-life bases, upset the more sophisticated when they violate historical truth in the interests of melodrama and romance, but please almost all audience levels when they mingle thrilling fictive elements with aspects of verifiable reality from the American past. *The U.P. Trail* (1918) by Zane Grey purports to narrate the career of a young engineer working for the Union Pacific Railroad in 1865; but the story has so few real links to history that, although it was once a bestseller, it is now regarded as too patriotic and sanitary to deserve attention. Worse, Ernest Haycox in *Canyon Passage* (1945) knowingly violated documented history in order to whitewash details of the Rogue War (1855–56) and in the process reflected discredit on the endangered Rogue Indians. Best, on the other hand, is the example of Henry W. Allen (pen names Clay Fisher and Will Henry) who in *I, Tom Horn* (1975) reconstructs the life of the famous cowboy, scout, lawman, and hired killer Tom Horn from his Missouri boyhood and years with the Apaches, including Geronimo, and his work with real-life army scout Al Sieber, to his antirustler range-detective exploits, one of which led to his execution for murder.

The literary Western goes beyond the formula to become enduring art, as vital and unstereotyped as Herman MELVILLE's *Moby-Dick* and Samuel Langhorne CLEMENS's *Adventures of Huckleberry Finn*. Superlative examples abound, including the works of Walter Van Tilburg CLARK, Harvey Fergusson, Vardis FISHER, A. B. GUTHRIE, Jr., Frederic MANFRED, Wallace STEGNER, and Frank Waters, among other too numerous to mention. To call the best works of these writers simply Westerns is a little like calling William FAULKNER a talented local-colorist. Clark's *The Ox-Bow Incident* is a story about lynching but is also a brilliantly modulated allegory on justice. Ferguson's *Wolf Song* (1927) is a mountain-man yarn lyrically presenting the conflict of the wilderness and communities of different racial strains. Fisher's *Children of God: An American Epic* is a well-structured historical novel concerning the founding, heroic move west, and later days of the Mormon church. Guthrie's *The Big Sky* is a sprawling epic, magnificently written, of the mountain men's love and rape of the West. Manfred's *Lord Grizzly* (1954) is a subtly structured redaction of Hugh Glass's real-life 1823 crawl of 150 miles back to "civilization" after being mauled by a bear in the Dakotas. Stegner's *The Big Rock Candy Mountain* chronicles the rebellious life of a pioneer born too late to achieve the American Dream in the latter-day West. Waters's *The Man Who Killed the Deer* (1942) is as sensitive an Indian novel as has been written by a white man (though Waters' father was part Indian); Waters' classic is a mystical, factual study of the connection of people to land, and of diverse cultures, together with their conflicting rituals and laws.

The most notorious parody of the Western is *Little Big Man* by Thomas BERGER, which, among other things, capitalizes on the everlasting appeal of Custer's Last Stand. As for adult Westerns, the less said the better. They feature perverted sex and sadism, and, selling well as a consequence, often crowd worthy Westerns off the paperback racks.

While the Western is usually associated with the novel, several writers of Western novels have also written short stories ranging from competent to excellent. Among the best of many such writers are Allen, Brand, Capps, Clark, Grey, Haycox, Rhodes, Schaefer, and Wister.

The Western has also become a prominent film genre. Any short list of the best of these films would include *The Covered Wagon* (1923), based on the popular 1922 novel by Emerson HOUGH, *Cimarron* (1931), *Stagecoach* (1939), based on a short story by Haycox, *Red River* (1948), *High Noon* (1952), *Hondo* (1953), based on a short story by L'Amour, *Shane* (1953), for which Guthrie wrote the screenplay, *The Searchers* (1956), based on the 1954 novel by Alan Le May, *Gun Fight at the O.K. Corral* (1957), *The Man Who Shot Liberty Valance* (1962), based on a short story by Dorothy M. Johnson, *The Wild Bunch* (1969), *Ulzana's Raid* (1972), *Pale Rider* (1985), *Dances with Wolves* (1990), and *Unforgiven* (1992). With film as with fiction, parody and debasement often enter, for example with *Cat Ballou* (1965), *Blazing Saddles* (1974), and the infamous "spaghetti" Western.

Finally, television has successfully adopted the Western. In 1959, eight of the top ten TV series were Westerns, with *Gunsmoke* (1955–75) leading all others in popularity. Enormously popular later were *Bonanza* (1959–73) and *Little House on the Prairie* (1974–83). By the late 1970s, there were too many such series, often with hackneyed plots; moreover, TV advertisers were aiming their commercials at city dwellers, age 19–50, and this demographic group was turning away from Westerns. The TV Western revived, however, with more sophisticated themes, plots, and acting in series such as *Paradise* (1988–91), *The Young Riders* (1989–92), and *Dr. Quinn, Medicine Woman,* which premiered in 1993. A significant television event was the six-hour miniseries *Lonesome Dove* (1989), based on Larry McMurtry's 1985 novel and budgeted at twenty million dollars.

The popularity of the Western comes and goes. The most recent Western novels seem more self-reflective, more self-conscious, and usually revisionist with respect to history. But as long as "wilderness" is a goal and an ideal, though unattainable, the Western will continue to be an appealing part of American literature.

BIBLIOGRAPHY: Bold, C., *Selling the Wild West: Popular Western Fiction, 1860 to 1960* (1987); Bredahl, A. C., Jr., *New Ground: Western American Narrative and the Literary Canon* (1989); Etulain, R. W., *Reimagining the Modern American West: A Century of Fiction, History, and Art* (1996); Hillerman, T., ed., *The Best of the West: An Anthology of Classic Writing from the American West* (1991); Kowalewski, M., ed., *Reading the West: New Essays on the Literature of the American West* (1996); Mitchell, L. C., *Westerns: Making the Man in Fiction and Film* (1996); Pilkington, W. T., ed., *Critical Essays on the Western American Novel* (1980); Taylor, J. G., et al., eds., *A Literary History of the American West* (1987); Tuska, J., ed., *The American West in Fiction* (1982); Yoggy, G. A., *Riding the Video Range: The Rise and Fall of the Western on Television* (1995)

ROBERT L. GALE

WHALEN, Philip

b. 20 October 1923, Portland, Oregon

Though many young mid-20th-c. writers associated with the Beat movement experiment with unconventional lifestyles, including the use of hallucinogenic drugs, to help maintain a state of mind conducive to their avant-garde style of writing, few lived more completely and unselfconsciously for their art than W., who found that life in its ordinary details could be as intellectually compelling and spiritually satisfying as life lived "on the road." W.'s style is marked by attentiveness to the diurnal and mundane, a self-effacing humor, and avoidance of overtly political content—particular political stances being merely ideological resting places in the complex texture of a life—ballasted by a fine intelligence and acute sense of the spiritual valence of the everyday.

W.'s attention to the passage of the self through everyday reality, adjusting and readjusting moment by moment to changing circumstances, and his attempt to trace the mind in its essential movements, led him away from narrative structure to an elliptical style of composition based on fragments gleaned from notebooks. He began experimenting with the notebook method in the early 1940s during his stint in the Army Air Corps as a radio technician, spending hours in the "greenhouse"—the observation bubble of a B-17; in the mid-1950s, W. took a position as a fire-spotter in Mount Baker National Forest: both jobs gave him the time and altitude to experiment with the contemplative, rhythmic rearranging of notebook jottings that continue to be the driving force in his poems. After his discharge from the army in 1946, W. attended Reed College, meeting Gary SNYDER and Lew Welch. Familiarity with the works and concerns of these poets deepened his sense of sacredness of nature and the essential acts of living—birth, making love, eating, observing, decaying—and the revelatory potential of the immediate environment that continue to figure thematically in his poetry.

In addition to the influence of poets like Snyder, and later Allen GINSBERG, Michael MCCLURE, and Philip Lamantia—these four along with W. formed the historic Six Gallery reading on October 7, 1955—and remaining alert and attuned to his own life as it registered changes in post-World War II culture—mass pro-

duction of products, rhizomatic spread of cities along newly constructed freeways, the emphasis on change and speed in everything from automobile bodies to hamburgers—also drew W. away from a New Critical emphasis on imagistic compression and self-sufficient poetic structures of resolved tensions toward a freer, more dispersed, digressive style. Beginning with the 1955 poem, "If You're So Smart Why Ain't You Rich," we can see W.'s punning, leaping, unconventional style, characteristic of the mind in action, or, as W. phrases it, the poem as "mind graph." W.'s registering of the flux of mind and experience through the montaging of brief, personal phrasings/fragments distinguishes his work from that of a mid-1950s California poet like Jack SPICER, who juxtaposes fragments of thought as "transmissions" or messages "received" from the "outside" and rebroadcast by the poet-as—"radio" functioning according to a depersonalized poetics of "dictation."

Some notoriety followed W. in the wake of the Six Gallery reading; in 1960, he published his best-known works: *Like I Say* and *Memoirs of an Interglacial Age.* Both books demonstrate the notebook montage method of composition and spiritualization of the everyday. It also becomes clear, in these books, that W.'s open form compositions are neither intentionally nor naively apolitical as they may seem, but indirect challenges to behavioral and attitudinal (sexual and intellectual) norms of society. To be open in thought is to be open in both the act and apprehension of living, to rest in no one position—linguistic, intellectual, characterological—longer than its grace, its truth. In 1973, W. became an ordained Zen monk; a nondualistic awareness and collapsing of hierarchies is everywhere evident in his writing. In his poetry, W. allows himself maximum freedom to be, in all its unselfcontradictory complexity: by turns eloquent and bawdy, good-humored and lonely, punning and serious, petty and profound. In the richness of the instant, W. has found the plentitude of the Grail, which is no more nor less than the particular buoyed by a limitless mindfulness, weathered putty crumbling away from the gap between a widow and a wall.

BIBLIOGRAPHY: Allen, D., ed., *Off the Wall: Interviews with P. W.* (1978); Corman, C., *At Their Word: Essays on the Arts of Language* (1978); Kherdian, D., *Six Poets of the San Francisco Renaissance* (1967)

TOM LAVAZZI

WHARTON, Edith

b. 24 January 1862, New York City; d. 11 August 1937, Pavilion Colombe, Saint Brice-Sous-Foret, France

Most critical studies of W. begin by marveling that an upper class girl of late-19th-c. New York society became a writer. This small circumscribed class prided itself on its lack of professions for men, let alone women. Unlike the English nobility who were reared for military or political life or at least squired their land, these affluent New Yorkers considered politics beneath them and owned no estates. And unlike the French aristocracy who enjoyed and fostered the best of their arts, these fashionable New Yorkers saw nights at the opera as one more social event and considered the artists themselves "black labor." Yet W., a daughter of one of the prominent families of this American elite, always had the two conditions that made becoming a writer almost inevitable. She had an unhappy childhood and she had talent.

W. was born in 1862 to George and Lucretia Jones, both descendants of English and Dutch settlers. Her father's inheritance made it unnecessary for him to work, and her mother became one of the elegant hostesses of her set. Born twelve years after her younger brother, W. knew a vain and difficult mother and an adored but ineffectual father. Tutored only at home—unlike her Harvard-educated brothers—but furnished with the surprisingly well-stocked library of her father, W. early became a reader and frequently preferred "making-up" stories to playing with children. Such a lonely regime left her shy and self-conscious and, as she approached womanhood, without the confidence and coy arts needed to succeed in the role most desired by her set, wifehood. Finding herself early an outsider in her own circles where well-connected marriages defined women and served as launching pads for the entertaining that filled their hours, W. never lost that sense of dispossession. Although W. eventually wed a friend of her brother, the marriage, long but never happy, ended in divorce. Her middle-aged extramarital affair with Morton Fullerton, an American journalist residing in Paris, was passionate but brief, and although in her late thirties and after the death of her mother she moved to Paris, began to write prodigiously, and gathered a circle of cultivated friends and writers, she never found enduring intimacy with a man. In her fiction, her heroines' feelings of exclusion from a coveted social world erupt into sexual competitions with other women, and these rivalries become the recurrent structures of their narratives, as if by repeating the search, W. could, in the privilege of the author, win victories for her heroines that she failed to achieve in life. But her artistic courage and honesty permit few happy endings. These fictional personas eventually sabotage imminent successes and in so doing confirm their deepest wounds, their long implanted self-doubts and fears of intimacy.

Several feminist critics read these debacles as Wharton's conscious subverting of the conventional marriage plot, her protest of the traditional American male-centered world with its limited destinies for women. Such indictments bear some social truth and no one can question the cost to women of defining themselves only in relation to men. But marriage remains both in life and fiction a symbolic mode of adulthood and autonomy and potentially one of the defining structures of human communities. Like most male critics, most feminist readers fail to view marriage, as they view the battlefields, sea voyages, and raft journeys of other American fictions, as arenas to test one's worthiness. The aborted intimacies of W.'s heroines mirror deaths at sea, flights into the territory, expirations on the scaffold of famous male narratives. Beneath W.'s novel of manners lies one more version of the now archetypical American romance of doomed searches for affirmation.

What distinguishes W.'s retellings of these quests for succor and validation are the vividly inventoried social worlds backgrounding her narratives. Although W.'s re-creation in two of her best novels, *The House of Mirth* (1905) and *The Age of Innocence* (1920), of her own clannish New York clique has imprinted itself on the American imagination much as Nathaniel HAWTHORNE's evocation of Puritan New England, Wharton's strength as a writer stems as much from the varied milieus, rich and poor, American and European, she used as settings. Further, the power of her retellings draws from the multiplicity of patterns and possibilities of sexual rivalry she retrieves from ordinary reality and literary convention and the rich new insights with which she invests these romantic triangles in the more than twenty novels and over one hundred short stories and ghost tales she wrote.

One of her last short stories, a ghost one at that, "Pomegranate Seed" (1931), set in W.'s New York, contains one of the most understandable rivalries, the second wife who fears she has not won the affections of her widowed husband. When unaddressed letters begin arriving for Kenneth Ashby, the new Mrs. Ashby keeps insisting they are from another woman. When the husband leaves to make arrangements for a reassuring vacation, and never returns, Charlotte Ashby concludes that the letters are from the deceased wife who may have called her husband back to the dead, but equally possible is that the husband has fled his second wife's hysteria that even a dead rival can be more attractive and sexually compelling than her alive presence.

One of W.'s earliest novels, *The Fruit of the Tree* (1907), connects to this late tale with its title again suggesting some primal violation and guilt in the triangles W.'s heroines find necessary for their courtships. Set in the owner-managerial society of a New England mill town, W. draws one of her most Victorian heroines, Justine Brent. Although she is one of few W. women to have a profession, her penniless upper-class family necessitates her becoming a nurse. Justine

Brent prides herself, like George Eliot's Dorothea Brooks, on wanting marriage only with an exceptional man. Discovering one such man in John Amherst, an idealistic plant manager who is married to a former school friend, Bessy, she becomes governess to the latter's child and confidant to the husband's dissatisfaction with his frivolous wife. When Bessy paralyzes herself in a riding accident, Justine, against doctor's orders, administers a fatal sedative. Marrying Amherst and consciously believing herself to have committed euthanasia, Justine still submits to blackmail and when exposed leaves the seemingly insensitive Amherst. Despite the melodramatic, almost lurid situation W. conjures, the novel is a poignant depiction of a woman whose belief in her moral superiority closes her to long denied insecurities and aggressions. Although she returns to her marriage, she now, like Charlotte Ashby, views all her husband's action as attachments to a ghostly presence of his first wife.

That the heroine has resorted to killing the rival, one of the most extreme measures a W. heroine takes to win the hero's affections, is ignored by most critics, partially because the heroine herself never confronts her complicity, but mostly again because literary criticism in general and present feminist criticism in particular expect women protagonists to be, if not victims, models and foils to the meretriciousness surrounding them. Whatever worldly renunciations or defeat they suffer, they emerge in these critics' eyes as spiritually triumphant.

Such are the strange readings emerging for *The Reef* (1912), published after W.'s now renowned liaison with Morton Fullerton. Soon after this affair ended came this most Jamesian novel in which Anna Leath, an emotionally reticent upper-class New Yorker, fortunately finds herself both a widow from an unsatisfactory first marriage and the object of desire by an earlier suitor, George Darrow. Yet as she struggles to surrender to the more sexually exciting man, she discovers his former affair with Sophy, now governess of her child. Viewing this complicated variation of the recurrent triangle from Anna, the older, usually successful rival of the early narratives, W. limns with agonizing detail Anna's slowly awakening sexual jealousy and untapped passion. When Anna decides to resolve her conflicts by offering her lover-to-be back to Sophy, critics see this decision as sign and signifier of her moral superiority. Such a reading ignores the toll her moralizing has taken on herself and all involved and how much such an inappropriate and embarrassing action further closes her to the sexual conflicts she has touched and W. has so courageously articulated.

Although mistaken marriages, painful and unequal unions, thread through W.'s fiction, divorce is never unequivocally taken or suggested. That legal act of separation, W. implies, is fraught with moral and social peroration, an implicit callousness on the part of the divorcing party, and the unsettling loss of status in society, prohibiting frequently another marriage, especially for a woman. Yet in *The Custom of the Country* (1913), W. creates one of her most controversial heroines, Undine Spragg. Born in the Midwest and determined to make the most advantageous marriage she can, this less inhibited heroine couples and uncouples herself as she leaves an upper-class New York marriage for union with French nobility to finally wedding the richest man left on Wall Street who is also her secret first husband. Most critics see Undine's climb as W.'s acerbic critique of a society that considers marriages and women as means of self-aggrandizement. But several women readers see Undine, perhaps more accurately, as W.'s antiheroine, the one who has the courage to act out and act on her desires openly and aggressively, forsaking the deceptions of rivalry, and mimicking to some extent the confidence and self-interest usually only men display in the marriage marketplace of America.

Like most of W.'s characters, these heroines and their rivals, even those fallen on hard times and forced to support themselves, move in upper-class milieus. Yet three of W.'s most poignant works of fiction, the novella entitled *Bunner Sisters* (wr. 1892, pub. 1916) and the novels *Ethan Frome* (1911) and *Summer* (1917), are set among the impoverished in the slums of New York and the villages of New England. In a fragment of unpublished criticism, W. discloses her reasons: "To the student of human nature, poverty is a powerful lens, revealing minute particles of character imperceptible to the prosperous eye. Wealth keeps us at arm's length from life; poverty thrusts us into stifling propinquity." Divorced from the minutiae of social etiquettes, these novels etch more starkly the motif of a woman vying with another woman for the affections of a man and then renouncing her success. Moreover, the final actions of these lower-class women suggest that deeper and more illicit transgressions have been replayed than W. allows her more decorous heroines. These narratives reveal disgust as well as fear of men, the incestuous wishes implied in rivalry, and perhaps the most denied, the homoerotic desire for the rival, the other woman, herself.

Included in the collection *Xingu and Other Stories*, *Bunner Sisters* was initially rejected as too bleak. The narrative tells of Ann Eliza Bunner who with her younger, more frivolous sister, Evalina, lives in the slums of New York and runs a small hat trimming shop. Her dreary routines are upset when a neighboring clockmaker begins to court both sisters. Yet when he proposes to the secretly yearning Ann Eliza, she suddenly demands he marry her sister. Although Ramy proves a wife beater and deserter, the cruelty of men is not so harrowing for the sacrificing Ann Eliza as the returning state of her sister. The young sister's conversion to Catholicism and her attachment to a priest deny to the lonely Ann Eliza the possibility of resumption of their former attachment, the "humble prosperity" of two women living together.

Set in the impoverished hills of Massachusetts, *Ethan Frome,* one of W.'s most famous works, also supposedly exposes an inefficacious man. Frome is seen by most commentators as too cowardly and repressed to leave his tyrannical wife, Zeena, when he falls in love with her cousin the vivacious Mattie Silver, who has come to live with them. But close examination of this spare and concentrated tale reveals that Mattie's own ambivalence of winning a man from his wife and her older cousin has been instrumental in aborting the furtive romance. Never supporting Frome's timid gestures of defiance, even her knowledge that he has considered leaving his wife, she suggests instead a suicidal sled ride that leaves Ethan lamed, herself paralyzed, and both dependent on the controlling wife. Her death wish and mutilation suggest punishments for deeper and more transgressing fantasies.

More open about the power of sex after her own love affair, W. had yet to delineate from the viewpoint of her established heroines their sexual encounters. Only when she chose in *Summer* a heroine both outcast and outsider, Charity Royall, an illegitimate child from a band of outlaws raised as a ward of a debauched lawyer in a small New England town, does W. describe fully a heroine's passionate unfolding. Unfortunately, Charity's tenderly and graphically told affair with a visiting big-town architect ends in the hero's abandoning her to marry a richer, more established woman. But Charity's self-loathing surfaces when, knowing she is pregnant, she writes her seducing lover a note congratulating him on his engagement but never mentioning her condition. Charity's own reluctant marriage at the end to her foster father suggests the incestuous dependence that shadows women who deny themselves sexual success.

The necessity of failure in sexual competitions propels W.'s powerful first novel. In her second and perhaps best novel, *The House of Mirth* (1905), Lily Bart becomes W.'s most subtle and complex portrait of a woman who believes she is searching for marriage to secure her place in society yet sabotages all possibilities, especially to the man she comes closest to loving. Rich in social details and satire that have come to characterize much of W.'s writing, the narrative is set among the gregarious and lavish party-giving set of New Yorkers at the turn of the century. The long country weekends at spacious estates, dinner with elaborate tableaux vivants, trips to the Riviera to consort with royalty, and the philandering of both men and women display the more indulgent living the once more modestly endowed New Yorkers had found in new speculative buying on Wall Street. The heroine, Lily Bart, whose family had once been securely part of this group has because of her father's financial failures and her parents' death been precariously perched for her last ten years on the edge of a world she was groomed to inherit comfortably and effortlessly. Yet what gives this W. heroine her uniqueness is that Lily still has more advantages than the other orphaned and dispossessed women of W.'s fictive worlds. Lily has an allowance from her aunt, knowledge that she is benefactor of this relative's will, and most unusual for a W. heroine, extraordinary physical beauty. Yet the action of this many-chronicled narrative traces the last two years in Lily's life as she pretends to seek marriage yet undermines all such chances. Aware of this narrow destiny for woman that leads many readers to believe that her rejections are conscious feminist protest, Lily expresses a more poignant regret early in her quest. She bemoans the lack of a mother to steer her through the course of courtship. Such yearning implies that her needs are more emotional than monetary and her deprivations less material than internal, the wounds of self-doubts and inhibitions implanted by careless early mothering. Her private refusals or subverting of all her eligible suitors, the rich established New Yorker, Percy Gryce, the newly rich Jew, Simon Rosedale, and the more cultured but less wealthy Lawrence Selden—whom she feels most drawn to—confirm her fears of closeness with men. And the public but never consummated flirtations with the husbands of her close friends' husbands exhibit her rivalry but leave her vulnerable to society's attacks and its eventual desertion of her. The novel achieves its emotional power because W. anchors her story in the consciousness, the inner being, of Lily herself, tracking her desperate battle between her perceived but never expressed longings and her appearance of insouciance, wit, and control. *The House of Mirth* confirms W. as more than a novelist of conflicting manners or a narrator of naturalistic entrapment. This tracing of the psychological disfigurement of a beautiful but insecure and inhibited woman establishes her early and firmly as a psychological writer more in the mode of Hawthorne and Henry JAMES.

That a Hawthornian "romance," an interior psychological drama, is embedded in one of W.'s most overtly realistic and satiric novels is nowhere more clearly illustrated than in The Age *of Innocence* (1920), deservedly one of W.'s most admired novels. The setting is one of imaginative return to her childhood world of affluent but provincial New York in the 1870s, a society whose inhibiting but comforting rituals, prudery, and hypocrisies W. vividly inventories. The narrative traces the threatening disruption to this smug collective by the return of one of its members, the now more worldly Countess Ellen Olenska, estranged from her European husband and trailing clouds of promiscuity. Told mostly from the point of view of one of the younger but conventional men of this class, Newland Archer, the narrative appears to chart the inbred Archer's gradual attraction for the seemingly more sensual and cosmopolitan woman and his disaffection for his established and virginal fiancée, May Welland, Ellen's cousin. Most readers conclude that his eventual marriage to May is the result of his cowardly but inevitable entrapment in the safer prescripts of his class. Although many critical dissections of the inhibiting and bullying tactics of these New Yorkers and the obtuseness and timidity of the hero have been written, little attention is paid to the actions and interactions of Ellen, the ostensibly rejected, seemingly more passionate woman as she first plays the temptress and then becomes the arch voice of conservatism. On the first evening of their meeting, she immediately reminds Archer of his childhood crush on her. Knowing he is engaged to her cousin, she invites him to meet with her alone in her apartment, tantalizes him about her possible scarred past, and later fails to help him get her a divorce. Finally she telegraphs him to pursue her at an upstate rendezvous. Yet when Archer comes to believe he cannot marry May, Ellen suddenly asserts the values of honor and decency and refuses him. After his marriage, when he wants to have an affair with her, Ellen returns to Europe, affirming this time the rights of motherhood, the monogamous structure of society over the fulfillment of the individual. A careful unpacking of this heroine's actions and unstated motives though uncovers the buried text beneath this novel of manners, the recurring propelling "romance" of most of W.'s most potent fiction, the dispossessed and guilty woman's need for affirmation by arranging sexual rivalry, renouncing her victory, and reestablishing her toppled competitor, all in atonement for unacknowledged violations.

The Age of Innocence won the Pulitzer Prize in 1920 and represents one of the apexes of W.'s writing career although she was to write for the next seventeen years, producing eight more novels, four novellas, more than fifty short stories, articles, and an autobiographical memoir, *A Backward Glance* (1936). Yet these later works appear to signal a break from the themes and craft of her earlier years. Many of the novels seem chaotically plotted, the epigrammatic grace of her prose no longer evident, and the narrative patterns of a young, usually unmarried heroine vying for a man and rejecting him less prominent. The protagonists are now older heroines, long married or once married, now frequently estranged from their husbands and abandoned by the lovers for whom they left their families. Most of these novels seem to find these frustrated lonely protagonists yearning for the families, especially the children they neglected, suddenly feeling that only through children, especially daughters, can they find significance. Several critics feel W. had suddenly become preoccupied with a maternal theme; as if disillusioned with the intimacies of heterosexual love, she had turned to the relationships of parents to children, especially mother to daughter. But the involvement of mothers and daughters had always been at the heart of W.'s fiction. Her earlier heroines make that urgency clear each time they renounce their victories and cleave to formidable and competitive mother-surrogates or affirm the claims of matriarchal societies. Now these older women, the once more threatening mother-figures, compete more openly with daughters for a desired man, and are the ones who subvert their own victories, making "sacrifices" for daughters' successes. Such renunciations though frequently cost the loss of relationship with the child.

What becomes clear from these older heroines' scenarios is that the search for motherhood has been, like the narratives of W.'s earlier heroines, a search for the mother of one's lost childhood, a quest for the wholeness of self a mother's absence or indifference once denied. In one of her weakest though still interesting novels, *Glimpses of the Moon* (1922), W. satirically portrays a marriage between a Lily Bart-like figure and an impoverished Lawrence Selden type. When Nick Lansing leaves his wife accusing her of adultery, Suzy Lansing is only redeemed and reunited when she is found working as a governess and surrounded maternally by her five young charges. In a more moving book, *A Son at the Front* (1923), an older philandering artist George Campton eagerly awaits the son he abandoned twenty years ago, but a grown son's own romantic interests and World War I make clear that the kind of intimacy a father wants is no longer possible and a misplaced illusion of parenthood at best. In *Twilight Sleep* (1927), a novel set in the frenzy of the 1920s in New York where Utopian shams appear to abound, Mrs. Manford seems the epitome of the neglectful mother. Her old-fashioned upright daughter needs an appointment to her. The mother's self-preoccupation seems to encourage the daughter to find herself in incestuous competition, first by sympathetically visiting her mother's first husband, then by her own involvement with a married cousin, and finally by attempting to rescue her father from an affair with his daughter-in-law, her sister-in-law. In this seemingly satiric novel, all the marriages are ultimately resumed. Only the confused and inhibited unmarried daughter is left isolated and defeated. W.'s most successful novel of this period and theme is the desolate *The Mother's Recompense* (1925). Having deserted her husband and child for a lover twenty years ago and been exiled from New York society since, Kate Clephane is called back to New York by her now grown daughter. She looks forward to a reunion only to discover that her daughter is about to marry one of her own ex-lovers. Articulating the incestuous competition she feels, she debates whether to tell her daughter, knowing that either option necessitates renouncing the closeness with a daughter for whom she now seems to yearn.

The sacrifice of a mother to assure her daughter's safe and conventional passage into society and marriage is most poignantly explored in *The Old Maid*, the most moving of four novellas W. set in the New York of the mid-1800s and called collectively *Old New York* (1924). Charlotte Lovell's only hope to have the illegitimate daughter she conceived with the forsaken lover of her cousin accepted by society is to let the now married cousin, Delia Ralston, adopt the girl without revealing who the real mother is. The slow wearing down of the unmarried cousin who has moved into the established rival's home and the eventual usurpation of the daughter display the underlying sexual rivalry of all W.'s heroines in one of its most vicious and desperate unfoldings.

The threat of children, the jealousy of the vibrancy of a younger woman, that motivates many of older rivals in these and even some of W.'s earlier novel, is exposed more clearly in *The Children* (1928). Here, Rose Sellars, widowed from a long unsatisfying marriage, finds herself free to marry a man who has quietly courted her during her married ordeal. But again, when her suitor, Martin Boyne, arrives, she finds excuses to delay the marriage. First she claims the proprieties of an old aunt. Then she makes accusations of rivalry, claiming Boyne is in love with a fifteen-year-old girl with whom he struck up a friendship on board ship. Feminist critics, eager to find men unsympathetic and deficient, not complicated and wounded themselves, dismiss the ambivalence and resistance of Rose and dwell only on Boyne's less-than-perfect timidity and confusions. With the rich theme of the older and unfulfilled woman and her jealousy of youth and beauty ignored, *The Children* remains one of W.'s most misread novels.

One last attempted change of direction marked W.'s last three significant works. Perhaps the heart attack she suffered as she turned seventy signaled that death was near and that her last chance to use fiction as wish-fulfillment was approaching. It is both poignant and revealing that this prolific woman writer who won artistic recognition in her lifetime as well as commercial success would still feel incomplete and lonely.

W.'s last works suggest that art, a profession, a career, does not itself complete life, nor satisfy the deepest human longings for more personal intimacy. In her last completed duet of novels, in her fragment for a planned supernatural story, and in her last unfinished manuscript, W. attempted once more to have a woman achieve success with a man, to have him do nothing less than marry her.

In *Hudson River Bracketed* (1929), Halo Tallant makes one of the recurring mistakes of W. heroines: she rejects the passionate artist and marries the respectable man acceptable to her family. But unlike most W. heroines, she finds the courage to run off with the rejected man, the writer, Vance Weston, and the novel ends in triumph with Vance's momentary aloofness the only discordant note. Yet in the sequel, *The Gods Arrive* (1932), which should be read by more readers, W. writes one of her most skillful but neglected novels. This narrative follows Halo and Vance as they live their Bohemian and unmarried life together in Europe, but instead of expected bliss, W. has the courage to expose that the lover one has secretly so long desired may be as obtuse and egocentric as the husband one has deserted. W. depicts with anguished detail the self-abasement of her heroine to the selfishness and philandering of this man. Although Vance's renunciation of his ways and his return to the now pregnant Halo have been read as one of the happier endings in W., it is only the deus-ex machina of the author that has brought about this return. Halo has never analyzed her constant appeasements nor openly confronted her immature and narcissistic lover. The reunion at the end signals W.'s own desperate investment in needing even this vicarious denouement of a romantic coupling.

But with the power and control writing fiction offers, W. was to allow herself an even more forbidden vicarious fantasy than having a man renounce his need for a more sexual woman and accept a more maternal one. Underneath the sexual rivalry of W.'s heroines lay their unacknowledged oedipal struggles, their unresolved competitions with their inadequate mothers for their fathers. Never published in her lifetime but discovered in her long sealed papers at Yale University was a fragment for a planned longer story, to be entitled "Beatrice Palmato." In the fragment W. completed, the heroine comes from an unsatisfying marriage to make love to her father in her mother's drawing room. The graphic and erotic description of their love making conveys the pathology W. knew lay beneath herself and her heroines in their guilt-ridden and self-destructive quests for love.

Yet as writer and woman, W. was still determined, at least in fiction, to enjoy the more satisfying intimacy of an eligible man. In her last incomplete manuscript, *The Buccaneers* (1938), she strives so hopefully for such an alliance. Returning to the time of her own adolescence, the 1880s, but casting the heroine Nan St. George, from an affluent less restricted class, the new entrepreneurs of upstate New York, and giving her a loving mother-surrogate, her governess Laura Testvalley, W. hoped to write and fantasize about that most yearned for human connection, the lasting intimacy of a desired lover. Again she has the heroine marry for the first time mistakenly, here to European nobility, and again like in several of W.'s narratives, the heroine is given her second chance. She is truly attracted to another Englishman who is unattached and attracted to her. In the plot summary W. left, Nan St. George and Guy Thwarte were to run off together to Australia and live happily ever after. The written portion of the novel ends with Nan and Guy only planning her clandestine escape from her marriage. W. never actually wrote that happy ending. Merely to conjecture that possibility was perhaps for W. to commit the most unpardonable offense, to arouse anxiety that could only be quelled by the ultimate atonement of her own death. Her fiction charts to its very last scene the unfulfilled and yearning daughter.

BIBLIOGRAPHY: Bauer, D., *E. W.'s Brave New Politics* (1995); Bell, M., ed., *Cambridge Companion to E. W.* (1995); Bendixen, A., and A. Zilversmit, eds., *E. W.: New Critical Essays* (1992); Benstock, S., *No Gifts from Chance: A Biography of E. W.* (1994); Dwight, E., *E. W.: An Extraordinary Life* (1994); Fedorko, K., *Gender and the Gothic in the Fiction of E. W.* (1994); Goodman, S., *E. W.'s Inner Circle* (1994); Lewis, R. W. B., *E. W.: A Biography* (1975); Singley, C., *E. W.: Matters of Spirit and Mind* (1995); Wolff, C. G., *A Feast of Words: The Triumph of E. W.* (1977)

                                    ANNETTE ZILVERSMIT

WHEATLEY, Phillis [Peters]

b. 1753?, West Africa; d. 5 December 1784, Boston, Massachusetts

The first volume of poetry written by a black American was published in 1773. The author was a young woman who had arrived in Boston in 1761 and was sold to Mrs. Susannah Wheatley, to be her companion. The young woman was named Phillis after the ship that had carried her from Africa, and the family took to her so well that they encouraged her to read and write and raised her to be a pious and devout Christian. W. continues to be a minor yet important figure in American literary history, and selections of her work are staples of anthologies of American literature.

W. began writing poems as her response to the events taking place in Boston, especially with respect to the soldiers she saw on a daily basis. Her patriotism

was so great that in the fall of 1775 she composed and sent a poem to General George Washington, which prompted an eventual meeting. The first volume of poems she tried to publish in Boston was never printed because she could not raise enough subscriptions; with Mrs. Wheatley's help, the volume was printed in London with an attestation in the front signed by many respectable Bostonians, including John Hancock. The volume was a huge success, but while the notices praised W., they also noted the hypocrisy of her owners who fully supported the fame of their servant but did not free her. In October 1772, perhaps prompted by those notices, W. was manumitted.

In 1779, she tried to sell a new volume of poems but inflation was so high in the years following Independence that she again could not get enough subscriptions to publish the volume. She did manage, however, to publish three poems in 1784 in the few months previous to her death: a eulogy for Revered Samuel Cooper, "Liberty and Peace," and "To Mr and Mrs—On the Death of Their Infant Son by P. W." The British volume was published in Philadelphia posthumously in 1786.

True to 18th-c. convention, the majority of W.'s poems are elegies. Their tone is uniformly religious, their form W.'s favorite, the couplet. Other poems celebrate the Imagination or praise her patrons; only a few touch on the condition of slaves in any degree. It is the latter that has caused contention among critics of W.'s work: as a slave, one would expect her to write about slavery and its evils; however, since she was so well treated, was allowed to be fully educated, and had little contact with other slaves, the topic does not seem to have been one that was prevalent in her mind. By the same token, she made no attempt to hide her origins and, to some extent, celebrated them. The public knew she was a "Negro servant," and the fact was published on the title page of her volume of poems. In a famous letter of 1774 to the Rev. Samson Occom, W. deplores the plundering of Africa and, true to her convictions, states that without liberty, those who are being oppressed are being kept from God and that she supports the "vindication of their natural rights."

W.'s humanistic poetry holds its own against other poetry of her time. She is sympathetic and philosophical while also showing great strength and optimism. Her understanding of the poetic movements of the 18th c. is obvious, and she may be recognized as a precursor to the romantic period while also being a significant contributor to the early stages of American literature.

BIBLIOGRAPHY: Mason, J. D., Jr., *The Poems of P. W.* (1989); Robinson, W. H., *P. W. in the Black American Beginnings* (1975)

                                    MARCY L. TANTER

WHEELOCK, John Hall

b. 9 September 1886, Far Rockaway, New York; d. 22 March 1978, New York City

W. was a prolific writer whose poetry ranges from exuberant songs to light verse to satire. Long associated with the publishing house Charles Scribner's Sons, there rising to the rank of senior editor, he generated thirteen collections of verse and a critical book on poetics; he also edited and introduced twenty-four unpublished poets, a volume of excerpts from the writings of Thomas WOLFE, and the letters of Maxwell E. Perkins. His poetry earned him numerous awards, including the Golden Rose and the Bollingen Prize, was praised by many for its uniquely ecstatic nature, lyric power, open consciousness, romantic sensibility, simplicity, accomplished technique, and maturity, all in literary climate favorable to ultrafashionable verse that was dry, oblique, cynical and flat-toned. Despite the sizable recognition he got during his life, his reputation does not fare well today, nor does his work garner much interest.

W.'s collections are littered with "songs," a form in which the poet excels in evoking the lyric voice of a singing moment. The section called "Songs" in the collection *Poems: Old and New* (1956) is a testament to W.'s much favored mode of song. Like Marlowe's shepherd, the lover woos his beloved, praising the rhythm of her body, her breasts arching alternately with every breath, lifting lifeward in long lines of beauty to lapse along the slopes of death. The sensuality here is Keatsian, beauty in life contending with beauty in death. Death, however, does not keep the lovers apart, for the reunion at the grave, whether it is east, west, north or south, will occasion a promised greeting to be sung. And while the lovers may roam in the gray evening over stilled fields and hills, under the restless, pale clouds of night, the thought of love, deep in the heart, is like a thousand stars, thus illuminating their steps. There is quaint pastoral quality to these and other of W.'s songs that breathes into them and makes them viable.

Besides songs, W. wrote convincing "portraits" of life: a modern girl, bizarre, absurd, enchanting, wearing a dear, ridiculous dress swinging a silver satchel, a little dauntless figure, half drowned in the enormous, gay picture-hat tipped forward across her eager face; a West Side morning in New York with its stately buildings looming above the empty streets, a somber and stone desert all around; a lion house at the zoo, the heavy air, the dreadful cage, the low murmur of voices, the tireless footfalls of the caged lion trying the floor and the walls in vain; a fish-hawk and a fish, the predator and prey, that struggle in the rites of survival, the masque of being. He also wrote satires like "Random Reflections on a Cloudless Sunday"

about humans taking the grave view of things, the seriousness with which they consider the present world situation, when the orangutang at the Bronx Zoo loiters with a poker face all day long, very much pleased with his status. Another, "Please Turn Off the Moonlight" is a satire on satire; it parodies the modernist near-decree that poetry should be intellectual and reject the human heart—have profile like that of a Greek monkey.

Religious feeling, usually in Christian terms, enters into W.'s longer philosophical meditations on time and existence, on the unity of experience. These pieces, although fueled by a highly personal attitude of inquiry, are too prosaic, too unabashedly vatic, speaking of and for some faceless multitude, without any felicity of language or remarkable image. The result is that they are not T. S. ELIOT's *Four Quartets,* though certain parts resound.

Dear Men and Women (1966) is likely W.'s best collection, a late work of a mature artist. In it a sequence of eight sonnets revisit the theme of love: a garden and a face, a talk that has been all banter, to-and-fro, the bland of mischief of a smile, conversation about so-and-so, of Eliot and Michelangelo, a sadness suffered years ago, the shapes of clouds, a hand laid in another, a breakfast of bread and wine, love's very presence sitting in a chair, and love's faith amid a wilderness of stars. The book also visits the sea, an image found in countless earlier poems. For W., the sea is washed with memory, a beach place that relentlessly bares the shrouded past. In "Amagansett Beach Revisited," a return to the poet's boyhood haunt by the sea rouses the memory of first desire, the ancient thirst of love first felt near the night sea's dark monotone.

BIBLIOGRAPHY: Hubbell, J. B., "A Major American Poet: J. H. W.," *SAQ* 72 (1973): 295–310; Taylor, H., "Letting in the Darkness: The Poetic Achievement of J. H. W.," *HC* 7 (1970): 1–15; Untermeyer, L., *The New Era in American Poetry* (1919)

H. S. YOON

WHIPPLE, Edwin Percy

b. 8 March 1819, Gloucester, Massachusetts, d. 16 June 1886, Boston, Massachusetts

While no longer considered a prominent figure in the history of American literary criticism, W. was an influential writer who once rivaled Edgar Allan POE and James Russell LOWELL as an authoritative American reviewer. He made his living as a broker in Boston at the Mercantile Exchange until 1860 when he retired to devote himself full time to writing. W. wrote critical essays for newspapers and magazines, notably the *North American Review* and *Harper's,* and was a famous Lyceum lecturer and debater. W.'s first published volumes *Essays and Reviews* (2 vols., 1848–49) were collections of earlier magazine pieces. W.'s *Character and Characteristic Men* (1866) and *Literature and Life* (1871) display his strongly ethical, and somewhat witty, approach to reviewing. His *Recollections of Eminent Men* (1881) and *American Literature and Other Papers* (1887) reflect his strong tendency to craft interpretive pieces rather than criticism.

W. was a strong defender of early American literature, and continually praised the traditional work of Lowell and Henry Wadsworth LONGFELLOW over contemporary writers. His reflections in his reviews were often generous overestimations of writers, praising their moral truths and national virtues. W. had a distaste for Walt WHITMAN, and in a review of *Leaves of Grass* remarked that the volume contained "every leaf but the fig leaf." W. considered Nathaniel HAWTHORNE an important novelist and praised both *The Scarlet Letter* and *The Marble Faun* in reviews. W.'s criticism, though influential in his day, lacks a deep understanding of the literature he reviewed and is seldom considered currently.

BIBLIOGRAPHY: Baker, C., *Emerson among the Eccentrics* (1996); Gerber, G. E., "E. P. W.," in Rathbun, J. W., and M. M. Grecu, eds., *American Literary Critics and Scholars, 1850–1880* (1988): 256–65

DUNCAN FAHERTY

WHITCHER, Frances Miriam
b. 1 November 1811, Whitesboro, New York; d. 4 January 1852, Whitesboro, New York

Writing as "Widow Spriggins," "Widow Bedott," and "Aunt Maguire," W. ranked among the top 19th-c. Yankee humorists, achieving that success in just over five years. Her "Widow Bedott's Table Talk," published under the pseudonym "Frank," appeared in Joseph C. NEAL's *Saturday Gazette* in 1846 and 1847, predating B. P. SHILLABER's creation of Mrs. Partington. The Widow's popularity brought W. an invitation to write for *Godey's Lady's Book* to which she contributed "Aunt Magwire's Experiences" and "Letters from Timberville," three of the latter series appearing over the initials F. M. W.

The Widow Bedott Papers (1856), combining the Bedott and Maguire sketches, sold 100,000 copies within a decade; by 1893 six new editions had appeared. At the turn of the century, W.'s celebrity declined with the vogue for dialect. However, republication of *The Widow Bedott Papers* in 1969 and from 1973 to 1974, plus inclusion of excerpts of her work in recent anthologies, indicates continuing interest in her work.

W. spent most of her life in her native Whitesboro, New York. As a child, her caricatures of relatives and neighbors isolated her, causing loneliness and near despair. In maturity, W. found materials for her humor in the inhabitants of Whitesboro, as well as Elmira, where she and her minister husband lived from 1847 until 1849 when the discovery of her literary identity alienated parishioners who saw themselves mirrored in her works.

The first twenty-one monologues of *The Widow Bedott Papers* follow Prissilly Bedott's thoughts and adventures from the death of her husband Hezekiah through the capture of his successor, the Reverend Shadrack Sniffles. The hatchet-faced Widow, crude and opinionated, who fancies herself "a genyus," a poet and a universal cultural authority, is generally the butt of W.'s humor. The other nine sketches feature Aunt Maguire, a somewhat more compassionate character who, in accounts of the donation party, the Scrabble Hill Sewing Society, and her visits to Slabtown, pokes fun at pretentious smalltown folk, particularly gossips, hypocrites and reformers.

Whitcher concocts her humor from upstate New York dialect, colloquialisms, and malapropisms. Her ambiguous use of patriarchal stereotypes of women marks her as a product of her times. Her uncertainty about women's roles and rights, possibly reflects ambivalence about the use of her literary gift.

Widow Spriggins, Mary Elmer and Other Sketches (1867) brings together other pieces by W. "Widow Spriggins," an early work, burlesques the sentimental novel, specifically Regina Maria Roche's *The Children of the Abbey*. "Mary Elmer, or Trials and Changes," a tale of poverty, suffering and cruelty, intended as a legacy for her daughter, remained unfinished at W.'s death.

BIBLIOGRAPHY: Morris, L. A., *Women's Humor in the Age of Gentility: The Life and Works of F. M. W.* (1992); O'Donnell, T. F., "The Return of the Widow Bedott: Mrs. F. M. Whitcher of Whitesboro and Elmira," *New York History* 55 (January 1974): 5–34; Walker, N. A., *A Very Serious Thing: Women's Humor and American Culture* (1988)

LUCY M. FREIBERT

WHITE, E[lwyn] B[rooks]
b. 11 July 1899, Mount Vernon, New York; d. 1 October 1985, North Brooklin, Maine

W. was a master of the informal personal essay. He is often credited with establishing the crisp, light, and slightly playful style that has long been associated with the *New Yorker*. He began submitting work to the magazine in 1925 and was soon thereafter invited by the editor, Harold Ross, to join the staff. W. wrote and edited the "Talk of the Town" section for more than eleven years. The weekly column was then—and still is—made up several amusing pieces, often slices of New York day-to-day life, as well as serious political commentary in "Notes and Comments." From 1938 to 1943, W. also wrote and edited a column for *Harper's* called "One Man's Meat." He continued to be a regular contributor to the *New Yorker* for the rest of his working life.

W.'s first two books were published in 1929, *The Lady Is Cold,* a collection of light poems, and the humorous *Is Sex Necessary? or, Why You Feel the Way You Do.* The latter he wrote in collaboration with James THURBER, his friend and colleague at the *New Yorker.* W. later published a second volume of poems, *The Fox of Peapack* (1938). His short stories and commentaries are collected in *Alice through the Cellophane* (1933), *Quo Vadimus?* (1939), and *The Second Tree from the Corner* (1954). W. and his wife, Katherine Sergeant Angell, the literary editor of the *New Yorker,* together edited *A Subtreasury of American Humor* (1941).

The enduring popularity of W.'s children's books, *Stuart Little* (1945), *Charlotte's Web* (1952), and *The Trumpet of the Swan* (1970), is a tribute to his ability to empathize with children's emotions. Each new generation of young readers seems to recognize that W. understood the fear, the pain, and the loss they experience in struggling toward maturity.

In 1957, the *New Yorker* published a piece W. had written about his late professor at Cornell, William Strunk, Jr. In this sketch, entitled "Will Strunk," W. discusses *The Elements of Style,* a short rhetoric Strunk had published privately. On the basis of the article, editors at Macmillan asked W. to revise and expand what Strunk had called "the little book." Since its republication in 1959, *The Elements of Style* has been revised and updated several times and is still required reading in many high school and college classes. It is the rare American student who has never heard of what is often referred to as "Strunk and White."

W.'s own writing reflects the fact that he took his former teacher's—and his own—advice. He believed in placing himself in the background, in not taking shortcuts at the cost of clarity, but also in not explaining too much. He often writes from the perspective of the slightly ironic onlooker, but his crisp, direct, and engaging style is never merely superficial. His clear, graceful prose makes him one of America's finest essayists.

W. was an advocate for the right to privacy and always a humane and sensitive spokesman for individual freedom. Although he was a shy, introverted man, the strength of his ethical, moral, and intellectual convictions is always evident, even if just below the surface of his writing. He loved America—the people and the land—and never hesitated to address forces that ignore people's common sense and instinctive intelligence. In 1948, when Truman was elected President in spite of all the polls predicting that Dewey would win, W. wrote: "The total collapse of the public opinion polls shows that the country is in good health.... People are unpredictable by nature, and although you can take a nation's pulse, you can't be sure that the nation hasn't just run up a flight of stairs, and although you can take a nation's blood pressure, you can't be sure that if you come back in twenty minutes you'd get the same reading. This is a damn fine thing.... We are proud of America for clouding up the crystal ball, for telling one thing to a polltaker, another thing to a voting machine. This is an excellent land."

One of America's enduring literary treasures, W. was awarded the Presidential Medal of Freedom in 1963 and the National Medal for Literature in 1971.

BIBLIOGRAPHY: Elledge, S., *E. B. W.: A Biography* (1984); Sampson, E. C., *E. B. W.* (1974); Thurber, J., "E. B. W.," *SatR* 18 (15 October 1938): 8–9; Updike, J., *Hugging the Shore* (1983)

MARGARET D. SULLIVAN

WHITE, Edmund

b. 13 January 1940, Cincinnati, Ohio

The prodigious W. has worked in several literary genres—his output includes novels, plays, short stories, essays, a how-to manual, and even a sociological road journal, *States of Desire* (1980), documenting interviews with and thumbnail sketches of the gay men W. encountered during a fifteen-city tour. Written in pre-AIDS 1977, *The Joy of Gay Sex* seems troublingly outdated now, but in its day, it heralded the new visibility and new excitement of the burgeoning gay rights movement. W.'s oeuvre has been a living chronicle of and testament to this movement. In American gay belles lettres, he is a towering figure.

Although, as he's revealed in interviews, W.'s adolescent years were marked by traumatic struggles with his sexual identity—he was sent to therapy to "reorient" his homosexuality—on completion of his studies in Chinese at the University of Michigan, he set out for New York's Greenwich Village, determined both to write and to connect to his gay identity, goals that have synthesized throughout W.'s career. In the early 1960s, Time, Inc.'s book division hired him as a staff-writer and editor, and his first play, *The Blue Boy in Black* (1963), was produced in New York. After several rounds with publishers, his novel *Forgetting Elena* emerged in 1973, and it was at this point that W. became a literary figure to be reckoned with. Resonant with echoes of 19th-c. American fiction and Franz Kafka, the novel, written in a self-consciously high-toned style, charts the mazy journey of an amnesiac young man, in what is probably New York's Fire Island, towards self-identity. His quest unfolds like a mystery, and it signals what will be a running theme in W.'s work: identity and the individual's grapplings with it. Vladimir NABOKOV hailed the book as "the contemporary American novel I admire most."

Nocturnes for the King of Naples (1978) and *States of Desire*—which some critics labeled "bourgeois" for its chronicling of mainly middle-class gay men—followed, but it was *A Boy's Own Story* (1982) that concretized W.'s early praise into accepted esteem. With this work, his most commercially successful, W. fused both a straight and gay readership into a shared enthusiastic response—one of his most noteworthy accomplishments. Christopher Lehman-Haupt's words are emblematic of the general critical reception: "it is any boy's story, to the marvelous degree that it evokes the inchoate longing of late childhood and adolescence." This deeply autobiographical novel's evocation of adolescent angst circa the 1950s tapped into a mighty vein of nostalgia and regret—the precisely *un*named narrator's pangs registered emotionally and experientially for many readers. His follow-up novel, the equally memoirlike *The Beautiful Room Is Empty* (1988), its title inspired by one of Kafka's letters, was less well received. Though in actuality a more ambitious and interesting novel than its predecessor, it moved to a more personal rather than a universal specificity, and the longings so tenderly explored in the previous novel find no easy fulfillment.

W.'s subsequent work includes *The Darker Proof* (1987, with Adam Mars-Jones), a collection of short stories about the human impact of AIDS—W. has been for may years publicly "out" about his HIV-positive status. *The Burning Library* (1994) includes several of W.'s essays, and was followed by a second collection of short stories, *Skinned Alive* (1995).

"In England," W. has said, "I'm famous writer, in America I'm kind of funny ghettoized marginal writer." But W. is not so much ghettoized writer as he is an unclassifiable writer. His body of work commands great respect, and he writes with authority, but his fiction has not, as a whole, generated the kind of deep affectional loyalty enjoyed by other gay writers such as Alan Hollinghurst, Christopher Isherwood, or Jean Genet, of whom W. has written a vast, highly praised biography. Perhaps the very polymorphousness of his output has paradoxically kept him out of the reach of a larger and sustained readership. Nevertheless, this relentlessly creative and incredibly productive writer has already established himself as a preeminent figure in American letters.

BIBLIOGRAPHY: Bonetti, K., "An Interview with E. W.," *MissR* 13 (1990): 89–110; Radel, N. F., "Self as Other: The Politics of Identity in the Works of E. W.," in Ringer, R. J., ed., *Queer Words, Queer Images: Communication and the Construction of Homosexuality* (1994): 175–92; special W. issue, *RCF* 16 (Fall 1996)

DAVID GREVEN

WHITE, William Allen

b. 10 February 1868, Emporia, Kansas; d. 29 January 1944, Emporia, Kansas

If one could describe an author's theme in one word, for W., the word would undoubtedly be "politics." This tendency to address the political life of America was the direct result of both his main occupation as editor and publisher of the *Emporia Gazette* and his otherwise involvement in the progressive movement of the early 1900s.

W.'s literary fame began in 1896 with the publication of his editorial, "What's the Matter With Kansas." The work was reprinted in nearly every Republican newspaper in America and was used as a political tract by the William McKinley campaign. The essay laments Kansas's decline in population and economic strength and places the blame on the "ordinary clodhopper's" tendency to blame the prosperous for everything and to give them credit for nothing.

W. was clearly at his best when writing nonfiction. Other memorial editorials include "To an Anxious Friend," which received the Pulitzer Prize in 1923. This work was inspired by a local railroad strike and W.'s support for the workers. His willingness to allow them to place a mildly worded placard in his front window brought about his arrest at the order of the Kansas governor. The editorial stands today as a classic defense of First Amendment rights. Another editorial, "Mary White," written on the occasion of his daughter's accidental death is both a father's expression of grief and a celebration of an inspiring life cut short.

Other longer nonfiction works of W. include *The Old Order Changeth* (1910), which consists of articles advancing his proposed political reforms; biographies of Presidents Woodrow Wilson (1924) and Calvin Coolidge (1938); *Masks in a Pageant* (1928), a collection of sketches of important turn-of-the-century politicians; and the *The Martial Adventures of Henry and Me* (1918), a somewhat fictionalized account of his travels as an American Red Cross inspector with Henry Allen in France during World War I. W.'s best-known work of nonfiction is his autobiography published posthumously in 1946, which received the Pulitzer Prize in the same year.

W.'s career in fiction also began in 1896 with the publication of *The Real Issue,* a collection of Kansas stories. The book sold well and obtained favorable reviews. In some ways the stories are like Hamlin GARLAND's *Main Traveled Roads.* However, the characters are not as well developed, and the conflicts do not evoke as strong a reaction as those in Garland's work. The lead story, from which the collection gets its name, is the account of a once idealistic, though now jaded, congressman who sadly admits that the only "real issue" in the upcoming campaign is the continuation of his political life.

Other collections of short stories include *The Court of Boyville* (1889), *In Our Town* (1906), and *Stratagems and Spoils* (1901). Theodore ROOSEVELT, W.'s close friend and political ally, was particularly fond of the latter and praised it for its realistic presentation of political life.

W.'s first experience with novels came in 1909 with *A Certain Rich Man.* The novel records the rise of John Barclay from a poor boy in Sycamore Ridge, Kansas just before the Civil War to a phenomenally wealthy but corrupt businessman in the first decade of the new century. Barclay's wealth comes only at the expense of his friends' reputations and happiness. His own "conversion" takes place after the death of his wife who ironically becomes a victim of one of her husband's crooked schemes. The novel was a great success and sold over 250,000 copies. His next novel, *In the Heart of a Fool* (1927), outlines the career and tragic death of Grant Adams, a labor leader and preacher of progressive reforms. The novel suffers from W.'s tendency to sermonize to the extreme. In both novels, W. relies more on explanation and summary than on actual narration. In addition, there are few memorable descriptions, and the main characters remain, throughout the book, elusive to readers.

BIBLIOGRAPHY: Griffith, S. F., *Home Town News: W. A. W. and the Emporia Gazette* (1989); Jernigan, E. J., *W. A. W.* (1983); McKee, J. D., *W. A. W.* (1975)

MAX L. LOGES

WHITMAN, Albery Allson

b. 30 May 1851, Hart County, Kentucky; d. 29 June 1901, Atlanta, Georgia

In his preface to his poem *The Rape of Florida* (1884), W. mentioned his confident expectation of a poetical revolution; unfortunately, when the revolution came it ensured that W.'s own poetry would remain in obscurity. Twice W. fell victim to the vagaries of fashion in poetry; when he was writing, the world at large had little interest in reading poems by a black man; now that it has such an interest, the world has little taste for book-length, formal, narrative poems such as W. wrote. He has yet to attract critical attention.

Born a slave, W. remained in slavery until the general emancipation. It is undoubtedly true that he did not go to school as a child; it is not true, however, that he was not educated. The one year or so of formal schooling he is known to have received as a young man cannot account for W.'s obvious thorough grounding in the English and American tradition of poetry; one can only speculate as to the extent of private instruction and access to books he must have had as a boy. He became a school teacher, a preacher and pastor in the A.M.E. Church, and the general financial agent of Wilberforce University, as well as a poet.

Except for *Leelah Misled* (1873), the villain and the victim of which are Caucasian, all of W.'s heroes are people of mixed race or Native Americans. Apparently from pictures and descriptions of W., he was himself of mixed ancestry, but he insisted, in the polite terms of his day, that he was a "Negro," a representative of "the up-and-coming colored man." His protagonists are in the romantic mode, larger than life, possessors of all manly virtues; his heroines are beautiful, chaste, modest types of the romantic heroine. W.'s plots are trite: stories of innocent low-caste victims, harried and pursued by high-caste white men and their hillbilly cronies. His narrator is heavily intrusive and digressive; W. freely uses this persona to voice his opinions on race, slavery, freedom, and whatever topic comes to mind. More notable and admirable than his plots, characters, and narrative technique is his adventurousness in trying his hand at the various metrical forms available to the poet in English. His mastery of the heroic couplet, unrhymed trochaic trimeter in the manner of Henry Wadsworth LONGFELLOW, and—most surprising of all—Spenserian stanza, is truly impressive.

Undeniably, W.'s poetry is better than that of many 19th-c. Caucasian poets whose work is widely disseminated while W.'s is ignored, and it would be difficult to find another black poet of his time whose work is as good as W.'s. But the formality and loquaciousness of his style are a hindrance to him today, in an age that likes the terse, the seemingly off-hand, in a poem. Nevertheless, W. is significant for his firsthand experience of "the quarters," his early insistence that slaves had made their contributions to American history, and his refusal to apologize or complain about his background: "I disdain to whine over my previous condition."

BIBLIOGRAPHY: Sherman, J. R., *African American Poetry of the Nineteenth Century* (1992)

CECELIA LAMPP LINTON

WHITMAN, Sarah Helen

b. 19 January 1803, Providence, Rhode Island; d. 27
June 1878, Providence, Rhode Island

Called "Poe's Helen" and the reputed subject of his
poem "To Helen," W.'s place in literary history revolves around two works: *Hours of Life and Other
Poems,* her sole volume of published verse, released
in 1853, and the slender *Edgar Poe and His Critics,*
published in 1860.

Although W.'s poetry is compiled in but one volume, separate poems appeared throughout her writing
career in a variety of periodicals, beginning with "Ret-
rospection," published in *American Ladies' Magazine*
in 1829. This first poem was signed simply "Helen."
W.'s contemporaries found her poetry delightfully romantic and idealistic; they furthermore regarded W.
as the perfect physical embodiment of the ideal lady
poet. Indeed, W.'s poetry overwhelmingly possesses
a romantic flair hinged upon emotions of mild sadness.
In addition, a small collection of her poems work off
of an inspiration by Edgar Allan POE's poetry. For
example, W.'s "The Raven" not only uses the title of
Poe's famous poem but alludes to many of his works.
Likewise, W.'s "Science" becomes a direct companion
piece to Poe's sonnet of the same title. More than
adding to W.'s status as a literary artist, these poems
serve to uplift the work of Poe himself, a task W.
seemed endlessly and tirelessly bound to accomplish.

W.'s idealization of and admiration of Poe culminates in her work *Edgar Poe and His Critics.* Published
eleven years after Poe's untimely death, the volume
serves as W.'s way of defending Poe the man and Poe
the artist to the world at large. W. evidences an intimate
knowledge of Poe's work in this long critical essay;
additionally, she demonstrates her own wide breadth
of knowledge. Though a poet in her own right, W.
seems to be much more remembered for this work
dealing with Poe than she does for any of her own
creative work. Likewise, she seems more remembered
as Poe's fiancée from 1848 to 1849 than she does as
her own person.

W. did break out of the Poe mold somewhat in her
lifetime, though. She was also known as a writer of
scholarly essays and as a news correspondent for both
the *New York Tribune* and the *Providence Journal.*
These accomplishments have long been forgotten in
an effort to focus W.'s work on her Poe commentaries.
This may be unfair to W., whose own poetry can
certainly stand up stylistically to that of any of her
commentaries. Certainly, one must at the very least
acknowledge her critical abilities in *Edgar Poe and His
Critics* as being well developed and as much worthy of
note as is her subject. Still, W.'s writing efforts by
and large have been relegated to the halls of literary

obscurity with her links to Poe and his writings being
the sole vehicle of her fame.

BIBLIOGRAPHY: Mainiero, L., ed., *American Women
Writers* (1982); Walker, C., ed., *American Women
Poets of the Nineteenth Century* (1992)

TERRY D. NOVAK

WHITMAN, Walt

b. 31 May 1819, West Hills, Long Island, New York;
d. 26 March 1892, Camden, New Jersey

Simultaneous "kosmos" and son of Manhattan, W. is
not only the most revolutionary, yet representative, of
American poets, but a central figure of world literature
as well. His masterwork *Leaves of Grass* is the singular
new-world epic he spent his lifetime amplifying and
revising; nine editions of the work appeared from 1855
to 1892. Visionary and liberating, W.'s poetry hazards
to voice unchecked nature, unscrewing literal and proverbial doors from their jambs and launching his readers forward with him to an irresistible "Unknown."
His importance to later American poets such as Ezra
POUND and Allen GINSBERG is well-documented, but
scholars have also argued that he is an informing presence for movements as diverse as French symbolism,
Italian futurism, and German expressionism, and for
writers as diverse as Franz Kafka, Jorge Luis Borges,
and Pablo Neruda.

Although W. has often been read as the incarnation
of Ralph Waldo EMERSON's ideal, unrealized "Poet"
who would take the measure of the incomparable materials and spirit of the American scene, the characterizing, and tremendous, absorptiveness of W.'s verse is
as much experientially rooted as it is the ideological
legacy of a literary forefather. The range of his own
resume—his work, variously, as printer, school
teacher, electioneer, carpenter, newspaperman, and
Civil War nurse—is in many ways the foundation of
the constant attempt of his poetry to assimilate and
transfigure the rich chaos of 19th-c. American life. As
W. argues in his preface to the 1855 *Leaves of Grass,*
the U.S. itself is an inherent and sublime poem, and
it is the American poet's mission to absorb his country
with affection and generosity, gathering and enclosing
its diverse idioms and narratives.

As his country's self-designated bard, W. had inevitably to consider what form of poetry was most appropriate for America. His style generally depends on
experimentation, on taking risks, on determining how
much freedom poetry, and by extension the country,
can in fact bear. Without the staying rhymes and numbers of more traditional poetry, W.'s free verse tends
towards long lines of varying density. The King James

Bible is one important stylistic precursor of this poetry. But W.'s verse is not unrestrainedly "free," deeply dependent on rhythm if not rhyme and regulated by inventive practices of balance and repetition, the most important of which is the parallelism that in its various guises, including the poetry's abundant catalogues, can serve as scaffold for the poet's effusiveness. Musical, if not symphonic, arrangements also underpin the verse, W.'s specific love of opera often resonant in many aria-like passages. W. resists the systematic metrical planning of poets such as Edgar Allan POE, perhaps fearful that such fastidious versification would delegitimize his poetry's authenticity. His own exuberant organicism of form—in the 1855 preface he likens the perfect poem to lilacs, roses, chestnuts, oranges, melons, and pears—suggests rather that the poem needs to be brought precisely to that point where it seems to be bursting out of its own skin.

Leaves of Grass also has to be understood as a sustained linguistic experiment. W.'s language is a heady mix of languages that borrows freely from, for example, French, Italian, Sanskrit, contemporary slang, and phrenology. Intensifying Emerson's idea that words are actions too, W. insists that the poet is capable of making words do anything that man or woman does—sing, dance, kiss, weep, bleed. Reveling in its orality, *Leaves of Grass* in fact demands to be regarded not necessarily as "poetry" at all, but as belching and gabbing and yawping. W., as Ginsberg has observed, gives good mouth.

"Song of Myself" (1855; rev. ed., 1881) is the cornerstone of W.'s emancipatory poetics wherein poet, reader, and country become reciprocating, if not interchangeable, bodies. As is true of much of W.'s poetry, in the fifty-two cantos of "Song of Myself" representations of the open road become paradigmatic of both his philosophy and his verse practice. As W. makes explicit in canto 46, singing the song of the self assumes the tramping of a "perpetual journey." W.'s quest becomes exemplary of the travel that all his readers must undertake themselves, for the only truths he has to offer are antidoctrinal and instigative. He denies the need for any specific church or philosophy, and, if his readers do manage in their quests to become enfolders of earth and heaven like the poet, this accomplishment ought merely to provoke further adventuring. In any case, the poet's song of self, in a fundamental irony of W.'s poetics, must also be a song of self-extinguishment; W. feels his style is most honored when the student destroys the teacher.

Canto 15 is the fullest acknowledgment in "Song of Myself" of the variety and dignity of the lives of the republic. Central to W.'s project is the recognition and celebration of the "people," whom he felt "literature" had historically ignored. In a coinstantaneous present tense, thus, W. provides an extended, inclusive and unmoralized series of succinct portraits of Americans at work and play, among them a duck-shooter, a lunatic, a slave, a factory girl, a new mother, and a canal boy. In a particularly canny (and alliterative) juxtaposition, W. challenges propriety and social divisiveness by setting a prostitute alongside the President.

W. is passionately convinced that his verbal texts have palpable life, that whoever touches *Leaves of Grass* touches a real man. In "Song of Myself," W. casts himself as the conscious poet of both body and soul. Not only does he picture himself throughout the poem in loving detail, from the convolutions of his brain to the aroma of his armpits, but in the hectic canto 5 he arranges a startling marriage of body and soul. In part, as it often pleases W. to do, this stanza advocates a special kind of transcendental loafing as the prelude to the ritualized intensity of union of body and soul that follows. Carnal and mystic, the union climaxes with "soul" plunging its tongue to W.'s very heart, an autoeroticism that in turn generates a swift and intuitive knowledge revealing to W. the hand and spirit of God and the love that binds him to his brother-men and sister-women. Completing the illumination's trajectory, W. at canto's end expresses his renewed appreciation for the most anonymous, unpoeticized objects of this world—a heap of stones, mullein, poke-weed.

Energized by the encounter of body and soul, W. in the next canto begins the elucidation of his poetry's central symbol of the grass. A sustained exercise in democratic symbology, the canto posits the grass variously as the stuff of W.'s own disposition, as God's handkerchief, as a "uniform hieroglyphic" that sprouts alike for all Americans, as the uncut and beautiful hair of graves. What is perhaps most important here is W.'s valuing of the grass's indeterminacy and his insistence that he cannot know finally better than anyone else what it means.

"Song of Myself's" poet of the people and poet of the body is also, as the symbol of the grass suggests, the unflinching poet of death. W. generally attempts to assess death positively, imagining it as a point of departure rather than termination. To die, he suggests in canto 6, might even be construed as a species of luck. The beautiful reminiscence poem "Out of the Cradle Endlessly Rocking" (1859; rev. ed., 1881), describing the maturation of boy to bard, goes on to identify death as the delicious, superior word at the heart of the mystery of W.'s own poetic identity.

Among the earlier editions of *Leaves of Grass,* two of the crucial sections of the whole apart from "Song of Myself" are the "Children of Adam" and "Calamus" clusters. Versions of these groupings first appear in the third edition of the poem in 1860 and are central to any analysis of W.'s sexual politics. Whereas the "Children of Adam" poems are largely public addresses and heterosexually inflected, the "Calamus" poems detail W.'s homosexual desires in much more personal and emotionally complex fashion. Both groups of poems, however, are enmeshed in W.'s overarching concern for the democratic future of the country. Several of the "Children of Adam" poems are songs of procreation. In "A Woman Waits for Me" (1856, 1871), for example, W. abstractly plays the part of robust, undissuadable husband to the woman who will beget perfect men and women for the country. The "Calamus" poems, named for the phallic-shaped plant, are more daring and anguished in their attempts to connect the privacy, and primacy, of W.'s love for men with the larger imperatives and possibilities of democratic culture. If in "Earth, My Likeness" (1860; rev. ed., 1867) W. fears telling in words of his fierce enamoredness with an athlete, in "I Hear It Was Charged against Me" (1860; rev. ed., 1867) he declares his attempt to establish in every city of the union "The institution of the dear love of comrades."

The imminence and eventuality of civil war in America were personal crises for W., and he came to regard the war years as the real "parturition" years of the country. The poems of "Drum-Taps," initially added to the 1867 edition of *Leaves of Grass,* enact the terror and catharsis of the war for W., and he regarded them as essential to the meaning of the whole. Generally, these poems are less philosophical and more regular than W.'s prior work and at points they even approximate a kind of literary REALISM. Although images of amputation recur throughout "Drum-Taps," dismembered bodies the metaphor for W.'s dismembered America, the war also offers an opportunity for the country to test its mettle, to show to the world, as in "Long, Too Long America" (1865; rev. ed., 1881), what its "children enmasse" truly are. In the collection's best-known poem, "The Wound-Dresser" (1865; rev. ed., 1881), W. finds a fulfillment as nurse commensurate to, or perhaps greater than, that of national poet. Moving through the hospitals as a literal soother and pacifier, he gives himself over to a vocation that allows for the imagined dear love of comrades of the "Calamus" poems. The war, and "Drum-Taps," thus become strangely restorative for W. as he comes to reaffirm his sense, as in "Over the Carnage Rose Prophetic, a Voice" (1860; rev. ed., 1867), that "affection" can solve the problems of freedom.

Complementing "Drum-Taps" are W.'s poems about Abraham LINCOLN. W. felt a personal love for the president, who functioned as both comrade and redeemer for him. One of W.'s most popular poems, "O Captain! My Captain!" (1865–66; rev. ed., 1881), melodramatically and conventionally—at least for

W.—mourns the loss of Lincoln. But the great elegy "When Lilacs Last in the Dooryard Bloom'd" (1865–66; rev. ed., 1881), through its carefully modulated entwinement of the symbols of lilac, drooping western star, and solitary thrush, memorably converts the mourning process and death itself into an "outlet" song of life.

Another of W.'s most memorable post–Civil War poems is "Passage to India" (1871; rev. ed., 1881). The poem is based on three 19th-c. engineering marvels: the Suez canal, the transcontinental railroad, and the trans-Atlantic cable. As the bardic container of multitudes, W. refuses to dichotomize science and literature and in fact posits science here as a fair vehicle of global interconnectedness and justification. Consistent with the tropes of earlier W. poems, "Passage to India" culminates in an ode to passage beyond India in which the soul sails farther still; in this heightened rendition of W.'s open road metaphor, the poet with characteristic reassurance promises a voyage of recklessness and daring but of joy and safety too.

The year 1871 also saw the publication of W.'s most important prose piece, the essay "Democratic Vistas." A consummatory rendering of W.'s poetics and politics and the necessary fusion of the two, "Democratic Vistas" provides a trenchant critique of democracy's pretensions and hypocrisies. Surveying a landscape of omnivorous greed and moral bankruptcy, W. actually fears that the American experiment may prove to be history's most colossal failure. Yet he persists in believing that American democracy is religious at its core, that the poet can serve the state as the "divine literatus," and that poetry itself implies a broad and bold program of culture. At the heart of this program is W.'s idea of "Personalism," a regimen for the production of unabashedly transcendental selves. Despite W.'s anger about the country's backsliding, "Democratic Vistas" manages nonetheless to use contemporary depravity as a reminder of ideals unmet and as a spur for future triumphs.

Although W. continued to write until the end of his life, the sixth edition of *Leaves of Grass* (1881–82) is essentially the final *Leaves of Grass;* additional groups of poems, "Sands at Seventy" (1888–89) and "Good-Bye My Fancy" (1891–92), are later annexed to it. The last text of the final 1891–92 edition is the essay "A Backward Glance O'er Travel'd Roads" (originally the preface to the 1888 *November Boughs*), where W. reminds that *Leaves of Grass* is from first to last the attempt to put fully and freely a 19th c. American "Person" on record and admonishes that no one will understand his verse who views it as merely a literary phenomenon; "the strongest and sweetest songs," he concludes "yet remain to be sung." "Crossing Brooklyn Ferry" (1856; rev. ed., 1881), however, may well be W.'s most potent valediction in its deeply felt proclamation that neither the distances of time nor space can sunder W. from generations hence.

BIBLIOGRAPHY: Allen, G. W., *New W. W. Handbook* (1986); Arvin, N., *W.* (1938); Cady, E. H., and L. J. Budd, eds., *On W.* (1987); Chari, V. K., *W. W. in the Light of Vedantic Mysticism* (1965); Erkkila, B., *W.: The Political Poet* (1989); Folsom, E., ed., *W. W.: The Centennial Essays* (1994); Greenspan, E., *W. W. and the American Reader* (1990); Kaplan, J., *W. W.* (1980); Killingsworth, M. J., *W.'s Poetry of the Body* (1989); Larson, K. C., *W.'s Drama of Consensus* (1988); Loving, J. M., *Emerson, W., and the American Muse* (1982); Matthiessen, F. O., *American Renaissance* (1941); Moon, M., *Disseminating W.* (1991); Myerson, J., *W. W.: A Descriptive Bibliography* (1993); Price, K. M., *W. and Tradition* (1990); Reynolds, D. S., *W. W.'s America* (1995); Sill, G. M., ed., *W. W. of Mickle Street* (1994); Thomas, M. W., *The Lunar Light of W.'s Poetry* (1987); Warren, J. P., *W. W.'s Language Experiment* (1990); Zweig, P., *W. W.: The Making of the Poet* (1984)

MICHAEL BERTHOLD

WHITTIER, John Greenleaf

b. 17 December 1807, Haverhill, Massachusetts; d. 7 September 1892, Hampton Falls, New Hampshire

W. was one of the most popular American poets of the 19th c. His nostalgic treatment of the joys of rural life, his talent for making the little known stories of his homeland engaging, his role as the poetic spokesman for the abolitionist movement, and his simple faith in a loving God touched a common cord in the lives of many in his day. However, W.'s poetry was criticized in his day for many of the same reasons it is criticized today. Basically, he failed to edit his work carefully. His rhymes frequently stretched what was allowable, his use of language was often careless, and his repertoire of metrical forms was rather limited.

As a poet, W. was largely influenced by his rural background, his enthusiasm for the poetry of Robert Burns, and his Quaker religion. W. was born on a farm that had been owned by his family for nearly one-hundred-twenty years. This fact gave him an appreciation for family and a place that in turn influenced the subjects of his early poetry, which was mainly concerned with local legends and colonial history. In Burns, W. found a model of what he wanted to express; Burns was, like himself, an unhealthy farm boy who wrote about the ordinary people of his native land. W.'s religious background instilled in him an appreciation for the value of the "inner light," which gave him

the assurance that through his poetry he indeed had something to say. The Quakers' early involvement in the abolitionist movement in America doubtless contributed to his own interest in the cause.

Some of W.'s major collections include *Legends of New England* (1831), *Lays of My Home* (1843), *Voices of Freedom* (1846), *The Tent on the Beach* (1867), and *Among the Hills* (1869). His poetry is normally divided into ballads, abolitionist poetry, nature poetry, religious poetry, and genre poetry.

W.'s ballads are one of his main strengths. They are mainly the products of his early period although some of his best ballads were written later. "Skipper Ireson's Ride" relates the story of a heartless sea captain who refuses to come to the aid of a ship in distress. The drowned sailors' families wreak their anger upon the captain, but the poem goes beyond simply recording the action of a mob as Ireson in his public humiliation realizes the great sin he has committed against his fellow man and understands that, unlike his present distress, this pain will never pass away. In "Telling the Bees," the narrator shares the story of his last visit to his lady love, which occurred one year ago. Upon arriving at her home, he is told through the chore girl's song to the bees that his love has died. Even though the world has gone on and everything is much the same as it was on that tragic day, the news of her death has frozen the narrator in a moment that he cannot get beyond. "Barbara Fritchie," W.'s most famous ballad, is the supposedly true story of the cougeous defense of the Union flag by an old woman during the Confederate invasion of Maryland. Other better known ballads include "Cassandra Southwick," "Kathleen," and "Maud Muller."

Most of W.'s abolitionist poems are little more than propaganda; some, however, have real poetic merit. "Ichabod" laments the fall of Daniel Webster, the former champion of the abolitionist case, with his support for the Fugitive Slave Act. "Massachusetts to Virginia" was written in response to Virginia's attempt to seize George Latimer, a runaway slave living in Massachusetts. W. appeals to Virginia's revolutionary heritage as a reason for the state to mitigate its anger with the refusal to return Latimer. The poem builds to a stirring climax as W., moving from county to county, shows a diverse people united in the resolve to protect freedom for all. "Laus Deo" celebrates the ratification of the constitutional amendment abolishing slavery. In the poem, W. places the struggle for freedom for black Americans within the context of Israel's flight from Egypt in the Old Testament.

W. did not excel in writing nature poetry, largely because of his tendency to use nature as an opportunity to moralize rather than to celebrate the beauty of nature itself. Some of his better nature poems are "Prelude to among the Hills," "The Last Walk in Autumn," and "The Pressed Gentian."

W. is well known for his religious verse, and several of his poems have been converted into hymns. There is a religious undertone in almost every poem he wrote; in fact, some of his most inspiring lines are in poems that are not overtly religious, such as "Snowbound." "The Eternal Goodness," "At Last," "The Meeting," and "Trust" are his most memorable religious poems.

Undoubtedly, the masterpiece of W.'s poetry is the genre piece "Snowbound." The poem's subject is a boyhood memory of a severe blizzard. The first section concerns the arrival of storm and the wondrous changes it brings about. The second section, in a fireside setting, evokes the memories of those family members and friends, now long departed, who shared the experience. The final section returns to the outside world as the neighbors break through the snowdrift. Scattered throughout the poem are sections that sadly reflect upon those times that are no more, but at the same time hope is offered that those days will be renewed in some future state.

W. also wrote several prose works, including *Justice and Expediency* (1833), an abolitionist tract, and *Margaret Smith's Journal* (1849), which records the lengthy visit of an English girl to her relatives in colonial New England. Although W.'s reputation has declined considerably since his death, the very best of his poetry deserves to be placed among America's classics.

BIBLIOGRAPHY: Kribbs, J. K., *Critical Essays on J. G. W.* (1980); Leary, L., *J. G. W.* (1961); Pickard, J. B., *J. G. W.* (1961); Wagenknecht, E., *J. G. W.* (1967); Warren, R. P., *J. G. W.'s Poetry* (1971)

MAX L. LOGES

WIDEMAN, John Edgar
b. 14 June 1941, Washington, D.C.

Unfortunately, W. does not rank among the most popular writers of the latter part of the 20th c. However, he has a very good reputation among critics and readers who know his work, as evidenced by his distinction of being the only writer to win two PEN/Faulkner Awards—for his novels *Sent for You Yesterday* (1984) and *Philadelphia Fire* (1990)—and by his nomination for the National Book Award for his 1995 memoir *Fatheralong: A Meditation on Fathers and Sons, Race and Society.* W.'s publications, which include short story collections in addition to novels and nonfiction, have consistently been of high quality; W. will probably later be judged as one of the major American writers of his time.

In the early phase of his career—from 1967, when he published his first novel, *A Glance Away,* to 1973, when he published his third, *The Lynchers*—W. was influenced by writers such as James Joyce, William FAULKNER, and T. S. ELIOT and modernist and postmodernist literary tradition generally. The subsequent phase of W.'s career, from his 1981 novel *Hiding Place* to his 1998 novel *Two Cities,* shows him combining the early influences with influences from black cultural tradition and also exploring his personal identity as a black man.

Several of W.'s works clearly exemplify his brilliance as a writer. *The Lynchers* is a superb portrayal of black oppression and futility through the framework of modernist stream of consciousness technique, surrealistic form, and thematic pessimism. *Hiding Place* is an example of W. skillfully rendering the effective workings of the black cultural tradition, especially its language rituals. The nonfiction work *Brothers and Keepers* (1984) is a forthright portrayal of W.'s attempt to embrace his black identity. *Rueben* (1987) brings together some of the influences from both phases of W.'s career. *The Stories of J. E. W.,* published in 1992, was followed by *The Homewood Book* (1992), *All Stories Are True* (1993), *The Cattle Killing* (1996), and *Two Cities.*

BIBLIOGRAPHY: Coleman, J. W., *Blackness and Modernism: The Literary Career of J. E. W.* (1989); Harris, T., *Exorcising Blackness* (1984); Mbalia, D. D., *J. E. W.: Reclaiming the African Personality* (1995); TuSmith, B., ed., *Conversations with J. E. W.* (1998)

JAMES W. COLEMAN

WIESEL, Elie
b. 30 September 1928, Sighet, Rumania

Grappling with the profoundly disturbing questions that arise from the extermination of six million Jews during World War II, Auschwitz and Buchenwald survivor W. has produced the most important literature to emerge from the Holocaust. Though he practices the storyteller's art, he writes not merely to entertain; instead, compelled by a moral force, he transmits the horror of what he has seen, the strength and resilience of Jewish tradition, and the questions that when pondered will help modern man steer a course into the future without succumbing to despair, indifference, or hate. That W. has been successful in his project is indicated by literary prizes, political and public recognition, and the 1986 Nobel Peace Prize. His work has been translated into every major language, and both Jews and non-Jews continue to find W. a source of spiritual strength and guidance.

W.'s literary predecessors include Albert Camus and Jean-Paul Sartre, but greater than any individuals, two places—metaphors for poles of existence within which W.'s universe takes shape—Sighet and Auschwitz, have defined W.'s writing.

Sighet, the small Transylvanian town of W.'s childhood, was a center of Jewish thought and tradition. W. was an ardent student, and he relished instruction in the Talmud, Torah, even the Kabbalah. Further, his Hasid grandfather shared the legendary wisdom of Hasidic masters. That tales could convey religious wisdom and address the deepest existential questions established a vocation as tale-teller, a vocation that the young W. would accept only decades later. The paradise of Sighet and W.'s innocence was interrupted when the Nazis arrived in 1944.

W.'s parents and younger sister died in the death camps, and though W. himself survived corporally, the horrors he witnessed penetrated to the depths of his being. Over time, W. had to come to terms with the Holocaust. What meaning was there to these deaths? And to his survival? Where was God, and what kind of God was He? Unfathomable, the holocaust was beyond imagination, and hence beyond words. The dead who had fed the flames of the crematoria could only be betrayed by the inadequacy of words, and hence W. vowed silence for ten years.

When W. finally did put into words his experiences of the death camps, he wrote an eight hundred page work, the immensity of which indicates how poorly words serve the difficult truths of the Holocaust. This work, written in Yiddish, *Un di Velt Hot Geshvign* (1956), was to be the antecedent of the compact yet powerfully disturbing *La Nuit* (1958), translated and published in English as *Night* (1960). A mere 127 pages, *Night* is the stark testimonial to the unending nightmare of the death camps and the humanity that perished there. To read *Night* is to be haunted. A work of nonfiction, *Night* is an outcry conveying horror, aloneness, fear, and endless persecution. In a night sky, we are accustomed to seeing stars, the eyes of God looking down upon us; in this night, however, W. tells us "The stars are only sparks of the fire that devoured us." Night in this account is godless, interminable, a complement to the flames of the crematorium, to the deaths witnessed unto numbness.

The Holocaust casts its shadow in all of W.'s books. In his next book, *L'Aube* (1960; *Dawn*, 1961), the protagonist, a Holocaust survivor, moves beyond the voice of despairing victim to attain the voice of anguished active agent—in this case, a haunted executioner. The seductiveness of hate, the judgement by the dead, and the weight of one's heritage all are thematic in this short novel. *Le Jour* (1961), in English entitled *The Accident* but often referred to as *Day*

(1962), reveals the trap of being caught between the living and the dead, without belonging to either. *Day* concludes hopefully, with the sense that it is possible for a survivor to throw his weight on the side of the living, while still remembering the ashes of the past.

Holocaust issues are further addressed in *La Ville de la chance* (1962; *The Town beyond the Wall*, 1964), which examines the guilt of those who witnessed the Holocaust but did nothing; in W.'s writings, silence, indifference, and inaction allow evil to thrive. Next, the nuanced *Les Portes de la forêt* (1964; *The Gates of the Forest*, 1966) conveys the difficulty of living a relationship to a God who is often silent and may well be delirious, a God who allows—if not sends—the madness of the Holocaust. The novel's resolution conveys existentialist themes: "It's better to sleep on the troden ground, if the ground is real, than to chase mirages," suggests the protagonist, Gregor, for the mirages of the past and our fantasies of the future prevent us from embracing the reality of the present. Later, *Le Cinquième Fils* (1983; *The Fifth Son*, 1985), notes the responsibilities endured by the generation born from Holocaust survivors. The weight on future generations and the anxiety of communicating the Holocaust to them again figures in *L'Oubli* (1989; *The Forgotten*, 1992).

A related focus to W.'s writing is "the eternal Israel," the community of Jewish people across historical epochs and modern events. In this vein is the nonfiction *Les Juifs du silence* (1966; *The Jews of Silence*), a chronicle of anti-Semitism in the former Soviet Union. The oppression of Soviet Jewry is further addressed in the award-winning novel *Le Testament d'un poète juif assassiné* (1980; *The Testament*, 1981). Additionally, W. has received much praise, including the Prix Medicis, for his fictional portrayal of the 1967 Six Day War, *Le Mendiant de Jérusalem* (1968; *A Beggar in Jerusalem*, 1970). Other works, such as *Le Serment de Kolvillàg* (1973; *The Oath*), depict the Jewish community in earlier historical epochs, yet solitude, angst, and trial remain historical constants.

As a faithful messenger of Jewish tradition, W. supports Jewish continuity. Combating the historical events that would destroy faith and leave the Jews exiled not only physically, but spiritually, W.'s writings, like *Célébration hassidique: Portraits et légendes* (1972; *Souls on Fire: Portraits and Legends of Hasidic Masters*), provide sustenance and strength. These delightful stories from the Hasidim help the reader face the difficulties of faith in an unintelligible world; often flustering reason, these tales are themselves a preparation for those sufferings in which reason fails us. Similarly, W. draws on biblical tradition in works such as *Célébration biblique: Portraits et légendes* (1975; *Messengers of God,* 1976), demonstrating a continuity between modern experience and the lives of Old Testament figures, "for Jewish history unfolds in the present."

Several themes and issues recur in W.'s work. Madness, for example, is often embodied in a holy fool or messenger who sees clearly and speaks truthfully but is misunderstood in a mad world; such is the case in *Le Crépuscule au loin* (1987; *Twilight,* 1988). Another recurring theme is silence: the victim's silence that like shame needs to be peeled away, the witness's silence that sustains evil, God's silence that could mean absence, and God's silence in which He communicates between words. In W.'s more than thirty books, including *Tous les Fleuves vont à la mer: mémoires* (1994; *All Rivers Run to the Sea: Memoirs,* 1995), we find the curative and sustaining power of storytelling. The storyteller W. demonstrates the indomitability of the spirit when confronted with madness and silence.

BIBLIOGRAPHY: Berenbaum, M., *Vision of the Void: Theological Reflections on the Works of E. W.* (1979); Brown, R. M., *E. W.: Messenger to All Humanity* (1983); Cargas, H. J., ed., *Responses to E. W.* (1978); Estess, T. L., *E. W.* (1980); Fine, E. S., *Legacy of Night: The Literary Universe of E. W.* (1982); Rittner, C., ed., *E. W.: Between Memory and Hope* (1990); Rosenfeld, A. H., and I. Greenberg, eds. *Confronting the Holocaust: The Impact of E. W.* (1978); Sibelman, S. P., *Silence in the Novels of E. W.* (1995)

BRIAN A. SPILLANE

WIGGIN, Kate Douglas

b. 28 September 1856, Philadelphia, Pennsylvania; d. 24 August 1923, Harrow-on-the Hill, England

In the first two decades of the 20th c., W. was a highly successful fiction writer. She published over fifty volumes, excluding pedagogical works and anthologies of literature for children, and her books were translated into ten languages. Her fan clubs proliferated in the nation's high schools. Yet, although she was well received critically in her own time, she now receives very little notice. The two of her books now generally read, *The Birds' Christmas Carol* (1888) and *Rebecca of Sunnybrook Farm* (1909), are considered children's books.

Although once popular with adult readers, she appealed most strongly to the young, because she deals primarily with the young. She was first of all an educator of children. Influenced by the educational theories of Friedrich Froebel, she began her own kindergarten in Santa Barbara in 1877 and then organized the Silver Street Kindergarten, a free school for the poor in San

Francisco. In 1879, she sought out like-minded transcendentalists, including Amos Bronson ALCOTT, Elizabeth PEABODY, William Ellery CHANNING, and Ralph Waldo EMERSON. The essence of Froebel's approach was the free development of the individual child without the confinement of a rigid structure. In 1880, she began the California Kindergarten Training School and continued to operate her own school as well, while at the same time giving lectures and writing articles about child education. Her kindergarten experience culminated in the three-volume *The Republic of Childhood* (1895–96), written with her sister Nora Archibald Smith.

W. is unusual among highly successful authors in that she was not primarily interested in being an author. She first wrote to raise money for her educational projects, but after her husband died in 1899 turned to writing as a career. Even then, she remained active in various organizations related to her first interest, including the New York Kindergarten Association. Although subjects vary greatly, she often writes about widows with children, and about deprived children.

Carol Bird, the saintly heroine of *The Birds' Christmas Carol,* is deprived physically rather than economically. Always in fragile health, she is dying at the age of ten. She was born on Christmas Day and now dies on Christmas Day after her wealthy family grants her dying wish by giving a dinner party for the several children of poor neighbors, the grateful Ruggles family. The book is as mawkish and heavy-handed as this summary suggests, but continues to remain popular.

More worthy of adult interest is *Rebecca of Sunnybrook Farm,* a realistic picture of Maine life, replete with the speech, the idiosyncrasies, the values, and the prejudices of a small Maine community—the sort of community W. knew well from her childhood. The plot is a variation of a common one. An unwanted child moves into a hostile environment and converts everyone with her charm. But when Rebecca Randall leaves her siblings and widowed mother to live with her aunts Miranda and Jane Sawyer, she performs no miracles. She lives through years of painful conflict with an honorable but harsh and unloving Aunt Miranda, mitigated only slightly by her relationship with a somewhat less repressive Aunt Jane. At seventeen, a freshly graduated Rebecca inherits Miranda's house, but she must also care for a mother incapacitated by a stroke as well as her younger siblings. In the background remains the understated figure of magnanimous Adam Ladd, the Mr. Aladdin of Rebecca's childhood, who seems to be in love with Rebecca. The novels conveys real experience, not wish fulfillment, and is likely to prove W.'s most enduring work.

BIBLIOGRAPHY: Smith, N., *K. D. W. as Her Sister Knew Her* (1925); special W. issue, *UMB* 58 (1956)

MARYJEAN GROSS and DALTON GROSS

WIGGLESWORTH, Michael

b. 18 October 1631, probably Yorkshire, England; d. 10 June 1705, Malden, Massachusetts

Known generally for his important doctrinal poem setting forth the principles and inconsistencies of rigid Calvinism, *The Day of Doom* (1662), W. wrote at least nine other poems that offer contrastive literary worth, a diary, a college declamation, and sermons, of which none was apparently printed. He was born in England but came to the Colonies as a child. He received both Bachelor and Master of Arts degrees from Harvard College, where he remained as fellow and tutor until becoming minister of the church at Malden, at which he was formally ordained on September 7, 1656. Poor health, however, soon interfered with duties, and the years until 1686 saw him unsuccessfully trying to regain his health through a trip to Bermuda, codirecting church activities with a series of colleagues, and producing the poems that we are aware of. He seems to have been offered the presidency of Harvard in 1685, but declined because of ill health. Unexplained is his "wondrous" recovery in 1685, at which time the church was racked with problems due to mismanagement by Thomas Cheever, his co-minister from 1681. He delivered the Massachusetts Election Sermon on May 12, 1686 and the Artillery Election Sermon in 1697. He married three times and fathered eight children. His years from 1686 through 1705 were filled with the duties of his church and his preaching. Cotton MATHER delivered his funeral sermon, entitled "A Faithful Man, Described and Rewarded," at Malden on June 24, 1705; from it we learn some of the information above, as well as other titles of discourses that have disappeared.

W.'s best-known poem, *The Day of Doom,* is subtitled "A Description of the Great and Last Judgment," and is thought to have been published in 1662, its date of composition, although no copy now exists. Five American and two English editions are known before the 1701 "fifth edition," which presents its final, standard form. The editions add, variously, seven of the other known poems. To Mather, the poem "proposed the edification of such Readers as are for plain Truths, dressed up in a *Plain Meeter,*" by which is meant ballad meter, the revision of the fourteener into two lines of eight and six syllables. There are 224 stanzas of eight lines each, each eight-syllable line being rhymed internally and each pair of alternate six-syllable lines rhyming. Jonathan Mitchell in his prefatory poem states the significance of this "versified theology," as *The Day of Doom* has been called: "Truth in Sugar roll'd may taste the sweeter . . . ." W. runs through the gamut of people awaked on Judgment Day and primarily those judged not fit to ascend to the right

hand of God, including "all whining hypocrites," the "Idolators, false worshippers, / Prophaners of Gods Name," and so many others. Each group and each action cited in the full poem is documented by a marginal prooftext from the Bible. Such prooftexts provided the substance of theological compendia and argument in the 17th c., because the Bible as the word of God was irrefutable, needing only, perhaps, some interpretation for humankind. In the poem, Christ openly declares the Calvinistic doctrine of the elect and predestinated: "These Men be those my Father chose / before the worlds foundation, / And to me gave that I should save / from Death and Condemnation." W. denies the growing Arminianism and expansion of both the visible and the invisible churches through the beliefs of numerous schismatic groups. "Others Argue, and not a few, is not God gracious? . . . cannot his mercy great, . . . asswage his angers heat?" But Christ damns them not because they are not elected; it is rather "That man's free-will electing ill, / shall his will to pass." This enormously popular poem provides a strong reactionary statement of a position that was to weaken continuously through the next century, and hear its death knell with the Great Awakening. The poem's origin lies in reaction to the approval of the Half-Way Covenant, written largely by Richard Mather, in 1662.

Other poems indicate why it has been said, thinking only of the previous work, that W.'s religious background stifled his artistic nature. Yet "To the Christian Reader," while using the same ballad meter, does not create a singsong effect or an austerity of distance in the voice. "A Prayer unto Christ, The Judge of the World" in tetrameter couplets, "A Postscript unto the Reader" in pentameter couplets, and "Vanity of Vanities, A Song of Emptiness to Fill up the Empty Pages Following" in quatrains with an alternate rhyme are filled with lines that eschew a preachy tone, though these are poems of faith and orthodoxy: "what is *Beauty,* but a fading Flower?"; "I do much abominate / To call the *Muses* to mine aid"; "The man is lost that this short life mispendeth." The twenty-two stanzas of "A Short Discourse on Eternity" continues the form of the long poem as well as its sermonizing, but its tone is more meditative: "Nought joyn'd to nought can ne're make ought, / nor Cyphers make a Sum"; "ETERNITY! ETERNITY! / thou mak'st hard hearts to bleed."

"Meat Out of the Eater; or, Meditations Concerning the Necessity, End and Usefulness of Afflictions unto God's Children, All Tending to Prepare Them for and Comfort Them under the Cross" (1670) had four editions in ten years, but "God's Controversy with New-England," on the great drought of 1662, had to wait to 1873. The former, in the familiar ballad stanza, is a narrative on the meaning of the cross to comfort those afflicted with troubles and to teach the way to salvation. Its tone is close to that of the shorter poems despite its didacticism. The latter argues the accepted position that the drought was a deliberate act of God, in this case to reduce the prosperity that had led to a less intense life of faith. A warning to "backsliders," the poem would recall for its readers the need for the Mosaic exodus from the security of Egypt and for the flood of Noah. Interestingly, the poem employs the ballad form for the beginning and ending, but when God the Father speaks, the stanza becomes that of George Herbert in "The Church-Porch," five pentameters and an alexandrine, rhyming ababcc. A more majestic, certainly not pedestrian, effect is achieved. To have God speak, of course, was also most unusual in a strictly Puritan poem; it is Christ, as in *The Day of Doom,* who is usually employed to utter divine matter.

The diary, which is owned by the Massachusetts Historical Society, was first published in 1951. Partly in cipher, it covers the period from February 1653 through May 1657. Its concern is sinfulness, seen by W. in his pride and attention to worldly things.

BIBLIOGRAPHY: Cherniavsky, E., *ArQ* 45 (1989): 15–33; Cowder, R., *No Featherbed to Heaven: A Biography of M. W.* (1962); Daly, R. *God's Alter* (1978); Gunmere, R. M., *Seven Wise Men of Colonial America* (1967)

JOHN T. SHAWCROSS

WILBUR, Richard [Purdy]
b. 1 March 1921, New York City

Although W. began writing poetry in earnest while serving in Italy and Germany as a U.S. soldier during World War II, he has never written much about the war itself. For him, poetry is not so much a study of the struggles of life as an adventure in which the intellect and the imagination combine forces in search of beauty. In his first book, *The Beautiful Changes* (1947), for example, it seems to be the imagination that notices how beautiful things alter under changing conditions—as a field of the wildflowers being blown by variable winds beneath a partly cloudy sky—while the intellect notices how beautiful things themselves can alter the reality that surrounds them—as when the poet's beloved walks into the room.

As a young writer, W. was schooled in the rigorous, traditional, neometaphysical style generally advocated by the New Critics. Thus his poems are formal and partake of a sense of ritual, as is indirectly indicated by the title of his second collection, *Ceremony* (1950). When other poets, in the late 1950s especially, began

to abandon the formalism of such traditional techniques as regular rhyme and meter, W. held his ground—so much so that he became almost an avant-garde writer in the 1980s, when sestinas and villanelles were once again the vogue. In terms of content as well, W. has held his turf. So profound is his sense of the world's beauty that he seems to see some sacredness in it. Within the cosmos of his poems, he recognizes in the chaos of the sea and of the dark the existence of a reality unmediated by man's intelligence or—perhaps—God's grace. *Grace* may well be the most important word in W.'s vocabulary, signifying both sanctity and beautiful motion. The one—sanctity—seems cause of the other—beautiful motion—in his poems, as we see in the justly well-known "Love Calls Us to the Things of This World," from his third book, *Things of This World* (1956). As the speaker of this poem gradually emerges from sleep, bringing with him some sense of the spiritual world he has been inhabiting through dream, he becomes aware of the physical world that surrounds him. It is a magical world, a sanctified world, in which intimations of the spirit are carried largely through the motion-giving agency of the wind. Thus, sheets on a clothesline seem ghosts and nuns in their habits seem angels skimming over the earth. W. was presented the Edna St. Vincent Millay Award, the National Book Award, and the Pulitzer Prize in 1957 in honor of *Things of This World.*

At about the time that volume was published, Robert LOWELL began writing the confessional poems later to be gathered in his *Life Studies,* published in 1959. Again, W. resisted this turn to the tormented and the deeply personal, maintaining the elegant objectivity of his own outlook. He did, however, seem to take note of another side of life in his fourth volume, *Advice to a Prophet* (1961), in which he condemns through irony and satire the excesses of a materialistic, valueless, and antispiritual age: here we find lust without love in "Loves of the Puppets," work without workmanship in "Junk," ownership without possession in "A Summer Morning," action without life in "The Undead," shame without guilt in "Shame," dream without belief in "In the Smoking Car," and acquisition without fulfillment in "Ballade for the Duke of Orleans." The entire volume seems constructed to reaffirm T. S. ELIOT's point in *The Waste Land*—that all of man's frenzied physical activity acts only to hide his lack of spiritual belief.

In his later volumes—*Walking to Sleep* (1969) and *The Mind-Reader* (1976)—W. returned to the more gentle approach of his earlier work. The standard edition of his poems is *The Collected Poems of R. W.* (1988). W.'s books of poems generally contain translations in addition to original work—and indeed, translation has been an unusually important component of his career. While living in New Mexico on a Guggenheim Fellowship in 1952–53 and in Italy thanks to the Prix de Rome the following year, W. began his well-known and highly regarded translations of French drama, beginning with Molière's *The Misanthrope*. In 1956, Voltaire's *Candide*—with lyrics by W.—was produced on Broadway. Following the publication of his translation of Molière's *Tartuffe* (1963), W. was awarded the Bolingen Prize for translation. Later, in 1971, W. was awarded the Bolingen Prize in poetry, and from 1987 to 1988 he served as the second poet laureate of the U.S.

BIBLIOGRAPHY: Cummings, P., *R. W.: A Critical Essay* (1971); Hill, D., *R. W.* (1967); Salinger, W., *R. W.'s Creation* (1983); Stitt, P., *The World's Hieroglyphic Beauty* (1985)

PETER STITT

WILDE, Richard Henry

b. 24 September 1789, Dublin, Ireland; d. 10 September 1847, New Orleans, Louisiana

W. is remembered by literary historians for two things, his poetry, much of which remains scattered throughout American periodicals of his day, and his deep interest in the Italian Renaissance. As a writer, he left behind one book of poetry, *Hesperia,* published posthumously in 1867, one published scholarly monograph *Conjectures and Researches Concerning the Love, Madness, and Imprisonment of Torquatto Tasso* (1842), and his unpublished major scholarly treatise *The Italian Lyric Poets.* To literary scholars, W. is a significant Southern lyric poet, author of "The Captive's Lament" and "To the Mocking-Bird."

Although W.'s literary reputation seems most often associated with Augusta, Georgia, his childhood home, and with Southern chivalric verse, his Irish culture and his Roman Catholic faith seem to have fostered strong European leanings in his taste. Indeed, his earliest experiments in romantic poetry are marked by the influence of British authors such as Byron and Thomas Moore. Making his living from law and politics, W. often chose pseudonymous publication, knowing, as he did, the failure of Southern readers to respect poetic endeavor.

In his poetry, imitative of Byron, W. frequently cultivates a persona who is largely unappreciated, sensitive, if not brilliant in his education, and ever listless and alienated. His favorite subjects include the beauty of the fleeting moment—in the manner of the Cavaliers—the exaltation of females—in the "Southern" sense nearly to divinity—praise of those who fight for freedom, and a melancholic fondness for the past that offers a nurturing memory to he who holds the mem-

ory. Like Byron and Moore before him, W. frequently addressed and dedicated his poetry to women. His greatest deficiency as a poet, moreover, was an inability to compress or refine experience into poetry. Characteristically, that failure to refine is manifest as a failure to develop a theme. Ironically, following the same line of reasoning, some of W.'s best moments are those when he translates from Italian to English, following as closely as possible the compression of the original poet.

"The Captive's Lament" has enjoyed a long popularity, W. never claiming authorship for the poem until 1834. Just as the Connecticut Wits had sought to create an American epic, W. hoped to make his fugitive verse part of a larger American epic. Based on W.'s brother James's captivity by the Seminole Indians, the poem was the third stanza of the first fragment, the epic of Spanish Florida never being finished because of James's death in a duel in Savannah. W.'s use of similes in the melodic poem, such as "summer rose," "autumn leaf," and footprints on "Tampa's desert strand," are highly effective in creating the sense of total isolation of the central figure.

A frequently anthologized Italian sonnet "To the Mocking-Bird" is highly effective in terms of viewing that side of natural life that often jests or mimes for the amusement of man. W. sees the mocking-bird as "sophist," "Yorick," "and "Abbot of Misrule."

Searching for a strong, nationalistic theme, much as the Connecticut Wits did, W. called his book of poetry *Hesperia.* The title derives from the Greek goddess Hesperus, when she was goddess of the evening, to imply setting or west to the Greeks as in Italy, the new west to W. being the American landscape. Dedicated to Manfredina di Cosenza, a fictitious name for Mrs. Ellen Adair White-Beatty of Kentucky, the epic begins with Florida. It concludes with Virginia, Acadia, and Louisiana, W. using ancient maps so that "Virginia," for example, includes the area from the Hudson River to the St. John in Florida. Using the ottava rima of Byron's "Don Juan," *Hesperia* is W.'s most sentimental, historical, chivalric poem, well known for its copious descriptions of the American landscape if not American historical figures.

Conjectures and Researches Concerning the Love, Madness, and Imprisonment of Torquatto Tasso (1842) is remembered as early American scholarship. W., who spent much of his life in Italy, dedicated his treatise to his brother John. The monograph was written for those who knew a good deal about Tasso, and is chiefly focused on why Tasso went mad and why he was imprisoned.

W. remains a minor American poet, an exemplar of a developing American ROMANTICISM strongly rooted in the English literary tradition established by

Byron and Leigh Hunt. Within Southern literary studies, W. is a significant semichivalric poet wedded to gentlemanly pseudonymous publication and the dedication of art to females.

BIBLIOGRAPHY: Hubbell, J. B., *The South in American Literature: 1607–1900* (1954); Tucker, E. L., *R. H. W.: His Life and Selected Poems* (1966)

GEORGE LONGEST

WILDER, Laura Ingalls [Elizabeth]
b. 7 February 1867, Pepin, Wisconsin; d. 10 February 1957, Mansfield, Missouri

It may be that no other series of children's books has been as beloved by the American public as W.'s *Little House* series. W. spent her childhood and part of her adulthood as a pioneer, traveling with her family throughout the Midwest and settling on Rocky Ridge Farm with her family; she often told stories of her pioneering days and was encouraged to write about them. Her first book was finally published when she was almost sixty years old, and she was astonished by its popularity. In addition to the books, W. also wrote newspaper and magazine articles about her travels. Her writings serve an important role in literary history, for they chronicle the life of a pioneer family in an engaging, original manner. Children's literature critics often look to W.'s books as a standard by which to judge other texts.

In the last years of the 19th c., W. settled in Mansfield, Missouri, and established a farm. In addition to her chores, W. wrote short articles for a few papers, most notably the Missouri *Ruralist,* for which she wrote about events on local farms in a column called "The Farm Home." Once she had fully developed her writing talent, the editors of the paper created a new column just for her and entitled it "As a Farm Woman Thinks." W.'s articles were popular with the newspaper's readers, perhaps because she wrote on topics with which they could identify: parenting, home life, even occasional pieces about her childhood. As a woman almost sixty years old, she could write from experience and in a way that made her readers trust her.

It was with that spirit of trust that W.'s daughter, who was an established journalist, encouraged her mother to write about growing up in a pioneer family. W. drafted her book in pencil on lined school tablets and in 1932 saw the publication of *Little House in the Big Woods.* Public response overwhelmed W. as she received letter after letter from children asking for more. Twelve years later, she had written eight books, all of which were received with praise from the critics and public alike. She drafted a ninth book in the 1940s

that was published posthumously in 1971 as *The First Four Years* and that also drew praise.

While not extensive, contemporary scholarship focuses on W.'s treatment of the frontier and westward emigration with some discussion of her depictions of familial relationships. The criticism is generally positive and sees W. as an important contributor to both CHILDREN'S LITERATURE and literature of the WEST. W. wrote uncomplicated stories that show both the hardship and the rewards of pioneer life. When she was once asked about slight biographical changes in her books, she replied that she did not realize she had been writing history. Her lack of self-consciousness and simple style assure that W.'s books will remain popular works of American literature.

BIBLIOGRAPHY: Anderson, W., *L. I. W.* (1992); Zochert, D., *L.: The Life of L. I. W.* (1976)

MARCY L. TANTER

WILDER, Thornton
b. 17 April 1897, Madison, Wisconsin; d. 7 December 1975, New Haven, Connecticut

W. ranks as one of the most popular and successful playwrights of the 20th c.: his *Our Town* (1938) has been produced more times than any other American play, and *The Skin of Our Teeth* (1942) is among the most innovative works of the American theater. Also, W. wrote an impressive body of prose fiction that has earned him a place as a significant minor novelist.

W. was born in Madison, Wisconsin, to Isabella Niven Wilder, the daughter of a Presbyterian minister, and Amos Wilder, a newspaper editor with a New England Puritan heritage. In 1905, his father was appointed American Consul General of Hong Kong and moved the family to China. After only six months, Isabella returned to the U.S. and enrolled W. in the public schools of Berkeley, California; she took the children back to China when Amos was reassigned as Consul General of Shanghai. W.'s cosmopolitan education was continued in a German school there, as well as the China Inland Mission School at Chefoo, the Thatcher School of Ojai, California, and Berkeley High School. He began college at Oberlin in 1915 before fulfilling a long-standing dream by enrolling at Yale University two years later.

The literary ambitions that had begun to develop at Oberlin, where he published several pieces in the *Oberlin Literary Magazine,* blossomed in his senior year with the serial publication of his first full-length play, *The Trumpet Shall Sound* (1920), in the *Yale Literary Magazine.* Upon graduating from Yale, W. went to the American Academy in Rome where he sat in on archaeology courses and gathered background material for his first novel, *The Cabala* (1926), set in Rome. He accepted a position teaching French at the Lawrenceville School in New Jersey and earned an M.A. from Princeton University in 1926. The same year, his career as a serious dramatist was formally launched with the production of *The Trumpet Shall Sound* by the American Laboratory Theater. Popular and critical success did not come, however, until the publication of his second novel, *The Bridge of San Luis Rey* (1927), which won him the first of the three Pulitzer Prizes.

The Cabala demonstrates the natural charm and grace that characterize W.'s best prose as well as reflecting his unusually cosmopolitan background. It also thematically points toward the Christian humanism that dominates his later work. *The Bridge of San Luis Rey* is also typical in its long ago and far away setting—1714 in Peru—and in its thematic focus on several different types of love. In both early novels, W. deprecates the modern obsession with scientific, external facts, preferring instead the human significance of internal qualities such as faith, hope, and love.

His next novel, *The Woman of Andros* (1930), based in part on Terence's *Andria,* is indicative of W.'s interest in the classics. Chrysis, a captivating courtesan with a profoundly humanistic spirit, is W.'s archetype of the virtue of hope as she points the way toward the Christian era in her quest for eternal religious truth. W.'s underrated talent for satire is perhaps best demonstrated in *Heaven's My Destination* (1934), his first novel set in America. It focuses on George Brush, an idealistic, fundamentalist, evangelical traveling salesman who embodies the best and the worst of American Christianity: he is a prudish, maddening prig on the one hand, and an attractive, sincere seeker on the other. In *The Ides of March* (1948), W.'s most experimental work of fiction, he returned to classical and historical subjects for his fictional portrayal of the last days of Julius Caesar. This imaginative novel takes the form of letters, diary entries, reports, and proclamations as W. seeks to reproduce creatively the types of source materials that might be used for a genuine biography and to capture the essence of Caesar's character. Nowhere is W.'s penchant for experimentation and his characteristic focus on individuals, rather than ideas or events, better seen than in this novel.

His last two novels, *The Eighth Day* (1967) and *Theophilus North* (1973), reveal W.'s less attractive tendencies toward bookishness and didacticism. His characteristic themes of faith, hope, and love are presented almost as abstract ideas in the mystery of John Ashley, though *The Eighth Day* does insist upon the value and reality of human suffering in the world. The loosely autobiographical story of Ted North stresses

the theme of personal freedom while portraying individual action as the natural and necessary outgrowth of love.

W. won his second Pulitzer Prize and established himself as one of America's leading dramatists with *Our Town* (1938). His best known work, this play is set in Grover's Corners, New Hampshire, and traces the childhood, courtship, and marriage of Emily Webb and George Gibbs through Emily's early death. Though the setting and subjects are, for W., unusually provincial, the dramatic and theatrical techniques he employs—the Stage Manager as a chorus-like commentator, the telescoping of time, and the abandonment of realistic sets and stage properties—are most innovative. Thematically, *Our Town* is humanistic and universal in its assertion of the significance and value of mundane events in the lives of ordinary persons.

The Skin of Our Teeth (1942), his most experimental play in its extension of the expressionistic techniques of *Our Town,* won W. a third Pulitzer Prize. In this remarkable tour de force, heavily indebted to James Joyce's *Finnegans Wake* (1939), W. attempts to merge art and reality by having one of the play's characters, Sabina, at times step out of the dramatic world of the play and directly address the audience. The entire play is something of a dramatized fable of humankind's ability to endure and prevail through its failures and successes.

The Matchmaker (1957), a recasting of *The Merchant of Yonkers* (1938), is W.'s most conventional major play, though even it parodies typical stage comedy. Other, less important W. publications include *The Angel That Troubled the Waters and Other Plays* (1928), *The Long Christmas Dinner & Other Plays in One Act* (1931), *Our Century* (1947), *The Drunken Sisters* (1957), *Plays for Bleecker Street* (1962), *The Alcestiad* (1977), and *American Characteristics and Other Essays* (1979), edited by Donald Gallup.

W. wrote, at his best, in a polished, classical style underlined with objectivity and irony; at his worst, he became didactic, sentimental and somewhat bookish. As novelist, W. is a dramatic tale teller, a significant prose stylist, and an optimistic moralist; as dramatist, he is a careful observer of life, a technical innovator, and a keen analyst of universal human truths. In both fiction and drama, W. is above all an entertainer and a Christian humanist: he compellingly portrays a suffering world in which individuals can achieve qualified happiness through understanding the value and significance of everyday living. He has won a permanent place in the history of American drama with *Our Town* and *The Skin of Our Teeth,* while his graceful prose fiction has earned him a growing appreciation as novelist.

BIBLIOGRAPHY: Burbank, R. J., *T. W.* (1961; rev. ed., 1978); Castronovo, D., *T. W.* (1986); Goldstein, M.,

The Art of T. W. (1965); Haberman, D., *The Plays of T. W.* (1967); Highet, G.A., *The Enthusiast: A Life of T. W.* (1983); Lifton, P., *"Vast Encyclopedia": The Theater of T. W.* (1995); Papajewski, H., *T. W.* (1968); Simon, L., *T. W.: His World* (1979)

CRAIG TURNER

WILLIAMS, C[harles] K[enneth]

b. 4 November 1936, Newark, New Jersey

The power of W.'s poetry comes from his success in creating an ethos of uncompromising honesty; his poetic voice convinces us that every word presents the unfiltered and accurate observations of one who rejects the squeamish evasions and euphemisms of polite conversation or even of the normal day-to-day thoughts of comfortable people who manage to see but not notice the human pain and social hypocrisy that surround them. W. does not flinch from mentioning the blemishes, wounds, grossness, and cruelties large and small that affect us as individuals but that we usually choose not to allow to move us. They are the stuff of our daily lives and we ignore them at great cost, to ourselves as moral beings and to those we ignore because their lives may be diminished by our ignorance. The eye of this poet is merciless and his honesty relentless, but never unfeeling; when he observes and reports the misfortunes of others, the potential anger or contempt is never directed at the unfortunates or sufferers, but always at those who might look without feeling.

In the poem "Hog Heaven," from *With Ignorance* (1977), W. gives the most aggressive statement of his refusal to ignore unpleasantness, opening with a simple, repetitive statement, "It stinks. It stinks and it stinks and it stinks and it stinks" and continuing with a litany of all that is normal and disgusting in all realms of life; he concludes the poem with the same repetition. For some readers, this focus on distasteful sights and emotions may seem excessive, an effort to rub our faces in things we know well enough exist but that need not prevent us from getting on with our daily lives. W. constantly reminds us that our freedom from them is illusory, and our getting on with it may only continue if we forget our own humanity as well as ignore the humanity of others.

It should be said that W. is not a poet of only one note—rage. There are moments of tenderness and love that complement and even justify the anger, especially in poems about his son, such as "Waking Jed," in *Tar* (1983), surely one of the most beautiful and sensuous expressions of fatherly love and fascination with offspring. This fascination is taken up again in several poems included in *Flesh and Blood* (1987), such as "Eight Months" and "War."

In W.'s earlier volumes, including *Lies* (1969) and *I Am the Bitter Name* (1972), he worked in familiar poetic forms, mostly free verse; starting in *With Ignorance* and continuing with *Tar, Flesh and Blood,* and *Vigil* (1997), he has worked most frequently in an unusual long line, sometimes running twenty-one or twenty-four syllables, or more, lines long enough that they cannot be printed continuously on a normal page. These long lines might seem reminiscent of William Blake or Walt WHITMAN, but they are not really comparable to those biblically based forms; W. has devised a line that serves his narrative drive, allowing for a variety of tones, sometimes of bemused interior monologue, sometimes of high oratory or even incantation. The goal would seem to be the same as Milton's stated wish for a metric that flows beyond the line, creating verse paragraphs that are unmistakably poetry, even sometimes lyric, but that take advantage of the spacious rhythms of prose.

In *Flesh and Blood,* W. imposed a seemingly arbitrary stanza length; still written in long lines, each segment is eight lines long, creating vignettes or snapshots, sharp and pointed moments rather than extended narratives, but still intensely focused on remembered relationships or new perceptions that rend consciousness with their power. "The Dream," for example, recreates the terror of a child in 1946 imagining the effects of an atom bomb: "I knew that consciousness itself was dead, the universe shucked clean of mind as I was of my innards," where we experience that phrase "shucked clean" as a moment of almost unbearable force.

W. is capable of manipulating many metrics, however, as he proves in his brilliant translations of Greek tragedy, *Women of Trachis* (1978, with Gregory Dickerson) and *The Bacchae* (1990) and in the surprisingly charming volume, *The Lark, the Thrush, the Starling: Poems From Issa* (1983), a collection of the quirky Japanese poet's observations about nature; they are sometimes as mordant as W.'s own views, but proceed with a kind of humor and resignation not often found in his work; in thinking about a wren's view of the end of the world, Issa—in W.'s words—tells us "it's time to/build your nest, / you build / your nest."

W. has been an editor of the influential *American Poetry Review* and has taught at George Mason University; the evidence of *The Vigil* indicates no diminution of his rage and disgust at human cruelty in all its forms. He remains one of the most morally rigorous and challenging poets in America.

BIBLIOGRAPHY: Keller, L., "An Interview with C. K. W.," *ConL* 29 (Summer 1988): 157–76; Pinsker, S.,

"C. K. W.: Knowing Everything There Is to Know,"
LitR 28 (Fall 1984): 138–44

THOMAS F. DILLINGHAM

WILLIAMS, John A[lfred]

b. 5 December 1925, Jackson, Mississippi

Although born in Jackson, Mississippi, W. was reared
in Syracuse, New York. Following a navy obligation
in 1943, he attended Syracuse University and received
B.A. degrees in English and journalism in 1950. W.'s
various careers numbered positions in both Hollywood
and New York in public relations, television and journalism before the publication of his first novel, *The
Angry Ones* (1960, repub. as *One for New York,* 1975).
As a writer for such magazines as *Newsweek, Holiday,
Jet,* and *Ebony,* W. traveled throughout Africa.

According to his own testimony and that of critics,
W. is an unappreciated artist. Such works as his *Sissie*
(1969), *Sons of Darkness, Sons of Light: A Novel of
Probability* (1969), and *Captain Blackman* (1972),
along with the sixteen or more other books he has
published, are hardly known to most reading audiences.

Contributing to his lack of recognition, perhaps,
has been the fact that publishers and critics, via both
their stated and implicit comparison of W. with Ralph
ELLISON and James BALDWIN, allowed his work to
languish in the shadows of these greats. Additionally,
W.'s abiding interest in developing the psychological
conflicts on the black middle-class loner as well as the
social and political issues embodied in that existence as
he translates these into a complex formal structure
constitute his subjects. Adding to his lack of recognition has been the particular time in history when he
began writing—a period in the 1960's when black
writers were not household names in America to the
degree that Toni MORRISON or Alice WALKER are today.
However, a humanitarian strain runs deeply throughout W.'s art, and his true subject becomes, ultimately,
the complexity of the human condition beyond even
the racial concerns of W.'s surface.

After publishing *The Angry Ones,* W. wrote what
would become his most controversial novel, *Nightsong*
(1962), about a drug-addicted jazz musician other
equally flawed characters, all attempting to make sense
of their lives and their confusion. The American Academy of Arts and Letters notified W. that he would
receive the Prix de Rome—cash and one year in
Rome—for the work. After his interview with one of
the Academy board members, however, the Academy
rescinded its offer, and the explanation for this reversal
was never fully resolved. The award was given instead
to poet Alan DUGAN who, in his acceptance speech,
won W. some small degree of vindication for the Academy's slight.

Fundamentally, W.'s best-known work, *The Man
Who Cried I Am* (1967), embodies the themes and
subjects of black experience, but his formal strategy
incorporates into the complex experiments with design
and pattern for which his work is well known. Indeed,
he uses a missing recording tape to cohere the development of an entire novel. Centering the action on Max
Reddick, a writer, W. sets the stage, initially, for the
enigmatic beginnings of the novel that only the tape
can finally resolve. His character discovers a plan to
incarcerate minorities should a national emergency
arise as well as a host of other politically sensitive
secrets that only Reddick's travel throughout Europe
and America in relation to the tape can resolve.

Captain Blackman equally uses experimental form—
flashbacks and an interwoven retrospective—to tell
the story of the black man in the wars. In fact, as
Bernard W. Bell in *The Afro-American Novel and Its
Tradition* (1987) points out, W. wants to employ the
improvisational style of the jazz musician in his writing where he begins with a standard form and then
spends much of his thematic and structural artistry
improvising on that standard line so that it emerges
quite differently than it appeared initially.

From his beginnings in the many sides of journalism to his varied university positions to mention nothing of the plethora of books he has produced, W. will
endlessly go on being the highly unappreciated but
enormously talented and skillful writer and artist he
has always been.

BIBLIOGRAPHY: Muller, G. H., *J. A. W.* (1984); Nadel,
A., "My Country Too: Time, Place and Afro-American
Identity in the Work of J. A. W.," *Obsidian II* 2
(1987): 25–41

PRISCILLA R. RAMSEY

WILLIAMS, Roger

b. 16 January 1603 or 1604, Cambridge, England; d.
15 March 1683, Providence, Rhode Island

Acclaimed as the architect of the political doctrine of
the separation of Church and State, W.'s life bore
witness to the difficulties of that doctrine's legitimation. W. grew up in the Smithfield district of London,
then notorious as an enclave of separatists. Under
the patronage of Sir William Coke, W. enrolled in
Cambridge in 1623, and after receiving holy orders
in 1628, served as chaplain to Sir William Masham
in the county of Essex. After Archbishop William
Laud required an oath of loyalty to the Church of
England, W. and his wife decided to forsake the

1237

Church and England for America. They boarded the *Lyon* in 1831 and arrived in Cambridge, Massachusetts, that same year.

In the Massachusetts Colony, W. would soon became notorious for his refusal to take part in any service that included unseparated members. In 1833, he declined to serve as minister of the First Church of Boston. Upon explaining that he "durst not officiate to an unseparated people," W. associated his resolve with numerous related beliefs pertaining to the separation of the Church and State. W.'s resolution was thoroughly intertwined with his political conviction that the Church's affairs were utterly different from matters of State. W.'s religious beliefs led him to conclude that the Bay Colony's ministers had violated the principle of separation when, in order to secure Charles I's permission to emigrate, they swore allegiance to the Church of England. His political convictions included the highly controversial claims that Puritan magistrates could not rule on matters of religious conscience, and that, since the colonists had received their title of ownership from the "unseparated" monarch Charles I, the Massachusetts Bay Colony had no legitimate right to territory that properly belonged to the natives.

Unlike W., the leaders of the Massachusetts Bay Colony had not distinguished governmental from pastoral responsibilities. The depth of W.'s commitment to his separatist beliefs and the intellectual rigor with which he expressed them demanded their official response. In answering W.'s tenets of belief, John WINTHROP and William BRADFORD introduced discriminations of a different order. They praised W. for the depth of his learning but denounced him for spreading seeds of political divisiveness. After detecting a "windmill" whirling in W.'s head that he declared liable "to set the entire wilderness on fire," Cotton MATHER added political fuel to the religious controversy. Characterizing him as a threat to the Commonwealth, Governor John Winthrop banished W. on October 9, 1635.

Throughout his exile from the Massachusetts Bay Colony, W. would argue the truth of his religious principles as well the political rights of the Narragansett tribe. Out of respect for the Narragansetts' customs, W. compiled *A Key into the Language of America* in 1643. This work includes translations of native languages along with descriptions of the habitat, the climate and the cultural conditions of the region's native peoples. Despite W.'s expressed admiration for the Narragansetts, *A Key* reveals contradictory attitudes that are referable to their "unbaptized" condition. W. respected the civility that the Narragansetts exercised in their unbaptized state. But he knew that he could not baptize them without alienating them from their culture.

Following his banishment from the Massachusetts Bay Colony, W. purchased land from the Narragansetts and founded the Providence Plantation. This settlement would attract other Puritan dissenters to the Massachusetts Bay Colony's constraints, most famously Anne Hutchinson. But Catholics, Jews, Quakers, Anabaptists, Antinomians, Narragansetts, and political exiles also discovered a haven in the terms of incorporation of the Providence Colony. Within eight years, the newly incorporated settlement expanded to include the territories of Newport and Portsmouth. W. traveled to England in 1643 to request a charter acknowledging the separation of Church and State.

The reputation that W. enjoys as precursor for the doctrine of freedom of conscience can be traced to the argument he conducted in London with John Cotton in 1843. W. had traveled to England to request a patent for the Providence Plantation. Cotton had arrived to argue against it. Entitled *The Bloody Tenent of Persecution,* W. argument with Cotton encompassed religious as well as political rationales for the intertwined principles of religious toleration and freedom of conscience. The 1791 Bill of Rights would enshrine these principles as foundational to American democracy. But the English Parliament found the document's democratic inclinations sufficiently threatening that it published *The Bloody Tenent of Persecution* without attributing authorship and ordering it burned in the year of its publication, 1644.

After King Charles I decreed the Providence Charter invalid in 1651, W. returned to England and received another in 1654. But the colony had to wait until 1663 before Charles II would grant a charter guaranteeing freedom of expression. W. proved significantly less successful in his efforts to negotiate a separate peace for the Narragansetts during King Philip's War. After the tribe burned the Providence settlement, its members were virtually wiped out. At the time of W.'s death in 1683, the principles of tolerance and liberty upon which he had founded the Providence Colony were invoked to defend the colony against attack from surrounding tribes.

BIBLIOGRAPHY: Covey, C., *The Gentle Radical: A Biography of R. W.* (1966); Gilpin, W. C., *The Millenarian Poetry of R. W.* (1979); Miller, P., *R. W.* (1953)

DONALD E. PEASE

WILLIAMS, Tennessee [Thomas Lanier]

b. 26 March 1911, Columbus, Mississippi; d. 25 February 1983, New York City

W. was the second child and first son of parents of long Southern ancestry, including, on his father's side, the poet Sidney LANIER. The father was a traveling salesman, and W. and his sister spent their childhood with their mother in the home of their maternal grandparents, the grandfather being a minister. His father then moved with his family to St. Louis, where he was employed in the headquarters of the firm for which he had traveled. As W.'s *Memoirs* (1975) make clear, the family's financial circumstances in St. Louis ranged from excellent to borderline; and the move and their St. Louis adolescence were traumatic for both W. and his sister, and were at least partly the cause for the sister's psychosis, prefrontal lobotomy, and lifelong institutionalization, and for W.'s lifelong wandering and drinking and probably for his homosexuality.

W. attended the University of Missouri and Washington University, worked in the warehouse of his father's firm, and finally finished a degree at the University of Iowa. He began writing plays, poems, and short stories early, and, later, as the result of winning a contest for a group of one-act plays, attracted the attention and support of a well-known agent, Audrey Wood. His first full-length play, *Battle of Angels* (1940), failed in Boston. His next, and still second most important, *The Glass Menagerie* (1945), opened in Chicago, and as a result of urging by Chicago critics, became a success there and moved to great success in New York. Like Eugene O'NEILL's *Long Day's Journey into Night,* it is at least partly an autobiographical play, though of his family it includes only close parallels of his mother and sister and himself, omitting his father and younger brother; and it presents the family in probably worse circumstances and environment than ever actually occurred. It concerns a time when the young man, Tom, at the persistent urging of his mother, Amanda, brings a friend home—the "gentleman caller," who would become a frequent, almost archetypal, character in W.' plays—to meet his lame and almost pathologically shy and withdrawn sister, Laura. The friend, in a moving scene, succeeds in genuine communication with Laura, which could probably have resulted in her emergence from her shell, and, possibly, as Amanda had fervently hoped, in marriage; but it turns out that the friend is already engaged. It seems clear therefore that Laura's future is hopeless; and Tom, in desperation over his sister's plight, his monotonous life at the warehouse, and his mother's constant nagging, decides to leave home. When he actually does so, a scrim curtain descends, enabling us to see Amanda but not hear her, and hence to see her and Laura in a sort of quintessential, and moving, mother-daughter relationship. The play is clearly Chekhovian in its use of impressionism and symbolism, and Anton Chekhov was to remain the dominant influence on W.'s plays.

W.'s next play, *A Streetcar Named Desire* (1947), completed the establishment of his reputation and remains his most important play and one of the masterpieces of the modern theater. Before the play opens, a young woman of Southern aristocratic ancestry, Blanche Dubois, had become a nymphomaniac and alcoholic as a result of having to take care of a long series of dying relatives, losing the family estate, discovering that her husband was a homosexual, and bitterly reacting to the discovery, resulting in her husband's suicide. A schoolteacher, she has seduced some of her own students, the discovery of which has cost her her job; and as the play opens, she has come to New Orleans to take refuge with her younger sister, Stella, who has married a slumdweller of Polish ancestry, Stanley Kowalski, and lives, to Blanche's horror, in the slum. The play then centers on the relationship among the three as Blanche, having no money and nowhere else to go, remains in the tiny apartment month after month, driving Stanley half crazy and placing Stella, who is pregnant, miserably in the middle between her sister and her husband. One of Stanley's many friends, another "gentleman caller," is attracted to Blanche, and it appears that she might be saved by marrying him until Stanley, having learned of her past as seducer and prostitute, informs his friend out of loyalty to him. Rejected, Blanche moves closer to psychosis, which she reaches, if not before, as a result of Stanley's raping her while Stella is in the hospital having their baby. The play ends with Blanche being escorted to a mental institution by a kindly doctor, and with the relationship between Stanley and Stella—who did not believe Blanche's story of rape—happily restored. One is made in the play to feel sympathy for both Stanley and Blanche as, in a sense, victims; but Stanley, with his many loyal friends, his devotion to his wife—in spite of the rape, which we are perhaps to view as an act of desperation and a result of Blanche's almost subconscious seductive manner—and his ambition to succeed, is the one likely to rise above the victim state and have both a successful career and a successful life as father and husband. And Blanche, ironically, has found her only possible haven.

The symbols in *A Streetcar Named Desire* are admirably effective, the most notable example being the naked light bulb hanging from the ceiling in the Kowalski apartment. When Blanche moves in, she covers the bulb with a shade—a sort of symbol of her hiding from herself and hiding herself from others. As another aspect of this, Stanley's friend has complained that she has never been willing to go out with him in the daytime; and when he comes in after learning of her past, furious and wanting to have sex with her immediately, he pulls the shade off the bulb and thrusts the bulb into her face.

Among W.'s later plays, those most successful were *Summer and Smoke* (1948), *Cat on a Hot Tin Roof* (1955), and *The Night of the Iguana* (1961). Like *A Streetcar Named Desire, Summer and Smoke* concerns the oversensitive Southern girl and the overphysical young man, this time next-door neighbors of the middle class; and when it become clear that the two cannot establish a relationship, the young man marries another woman, and the girl ends by walking out for an assignation with a traveling salesman, possibly facing a future like that of Blanche. Like Blanche and Stanley, the two neighbors seem symbolic respectively of the cultural and the physical, and of the apparent impossibility of combining the two meaningfully—probably a symbol for how W. saw his contemporary South.

Cat on a Hot Tin Roof concerns a wealthy family of poor white origin on its estate in Mississippi, and particularly three of the family members: one of its two sons, Brick, horribly affected, as Blanche was in similar circumstances, by the discovery that his best friend is homosexual, and confronting him with it, resulting in his friend's eventual suicide; the father, "Big Daddy," a huge, complex man whose surface domineering manner and obscenity disguise a basic humor and affection, and who is unaware that he is doomed by cancer; and Brick's wife, Maggie, frustrated by Brick's alcoholism and ignoring of her as a result of shock about his friend and a probably false fear that he too is homosexual. After a long, revealing and highly moving talk between father and son, Big Daddy learns that he is doomed and begins to feel the horrible pain that his doctor had forecast; and it is possible, or even probable, at play's end that the relationship between Brick and Maggie will, because of her determination, be restored—and hence an ending with at least a mild resemblance to that in *A Streetcar Named Desire,* with the future of one of the major characters hopeless and the marriage of the other two back to normal. And as in *A Streetcar Named Desire,* all three characters are vivid, sympathetic in spite of their flaws, and memorable.

The Night of the Iguana takes place at an isolated hotel high on a cliff above the Pacific coast of Mexico, and once again centers on three characters: Shannon, a defrocked minister, and now a tour guide, alcoholic, and seducer of young girls; Maxine, the owner of the hotel, who has recently lost her husband and wants Shannon to stay with her as her lover; and Hannah, a woman who has devoted her life to her now very elderly grandfather, who has in the past acquired some reputation as a poet. The two are penniless, making their bare living by his reciting his poetry and her painting sketches of guests, in hotel dining rooms all over the world. They are allowed to stay at the hotel only through Maxine's grudging generosity. Shannon has brought a tour group there, though it is not on their itinerary, only because that is where he wants to be; and he presently learns that he has been dismissed as a guide. Hannah is almost unique among W.'s female characters both for being a permanent virgin and for being from New England, not from the South. As *Cat* has as its center the long conversation between father and son, so *Iguana* centers on that between Hannah and Shannon, a conversation that leads us finally to believe that he will be freed of his alcoholism, sexual misbehavior, and despair—as the iguana in the play is freed from captivity and probable death—and that he will stay with Maxine, who desperately needs him. Hannah's grandfather finishes a poem that he has been struggling with for years, and after joyfully reciting it, almost immediately dies. Hannah ends the play permanently alone, but with the fortitude to bear both her isolation and her poverty. Hence the play ends more affirmatively than any other W. play.

Among W.'s other plays between *Menagerie* and *Iguana,* the most important may in the long run turn out to be *Camino Real* (1953), in spite of the fact that it, like many other expressionistic plays, has never achieved stage success in the U.S. The work concerns a group of "lost" people, real and fictional, in a mythical and meaningless Central American country, doomed to remain there unless they can recover their self-belief and belief that life and the world have meaning, and hence the courage to risk the hazards of an escape. Some, including Don Quixote, do recover and escape. And the emphasis on achieving meaning also relates the play to existentialism.

Others of W.'s plays that did achieve some stage success include *The Rose Tattoo* (1951), a comedy centering on a Sicilian woman on the Gulf Coast whose husband was killed in a wreck, and who desperately needs, and finally finds, a man to take his place; *Orpheus Descending* (1958), a rewrite of the failed *Battle of Angels; Suddenly Last Summer* (1958), a play involving the psychological disturbance of a young woman who has seen the homosexual man with whom she was traveling killed and eaten by a group of young boys; *Sweet Bird of Youth* (1959), a play centering on a once-important actress traveling in a part of the South that had been the home of the young man who is her lover, a young man who, at the play's end, faces imminent castration; and *Period of Adjustment* (1960), a lightweight, insignificant comedy.

After *Night of the Iguana,* W. continued writing plays for close to twenty years; and while some had at least a degree of quality, none were successful. Continuing all his life to be a wanderer, his main staying place was Key West, where he owned a home;

but he became more and more an eccentric and an addict, and finally choked to death on a medicine bottle cap in a New York hotel.

W.'s best plays are notable for their vividly drawn characters, sensitively drawn relationships, effective and moving dialogue, excellent use of symbol, and, with the exception of *The Night of the Iguana,* their depiction of the American South; and two of them, *A Streetcar Named Desire* and *Cat on a Hot Tin Roof,* won Pulitzer Prizes. His frequent use of extreme violence, such as rape, cannibalism, and castration, is sometimes successful, sometimes not. But his best plays have led to W. being regarded worldwide as one of the great playwrights of the 20th c.

BIBLIOGRAPHY: Griffin, A., *Understanding T. W.* (1995); Gunn, D., *T. W.: A Bibliography* (1980); Hirsh, F., *A Portrait of the Artist: The Plays of T. W.* (1979); Jackson, E., *The Broken World of T. W.* (1965); Lasky, H., *T. W.: A Portrait in Laughter and Lamentation* (1986); McCann, J., *The Critical Reputation of T. W.* (1983); Moore, F., *T. W.* (1979); Murphy, B., *T. W. and Elia Kazan: A Collaboration in the Theater* (1992); Rader, D., *T.: Cry of the Heart* (1985); Savran, D., *Communists, Cowboys, and Queers: The Politics of Masculinity in the Work of Arthur Miller and T. W.* (1992); Spoto, D., *The Kindness of Strangers: The Life of T. W.* (1985); Stanton, S., *T. W.: A Collection of Critical Essays* (1977); Thompson, J. J., *T. W.'s Plays: Memory, Myth, and Symbol* (1989); Tischler, N., *T. W.: Rebellious Puritan* (1961); Williams, E., *Remember Me to Tom* (1963)

JACOB H. ADLER

WILLIAMS, William Carlos

b. 17 September 1883, Rutherford, New Jersey; d. 4 March 1963, Rutherford, New Jersey

For most of his writing career, recognition of W. as a major poet lagged behind the notice accorded to his fellow modernists (see MODERNISM) Ezra POUND, T. S. ELIOT, and Wallace STEVENS. Only with the publication of his long poem *Paterson* (5 vols., 1946–58) did W. begin to receive significant critical attention. In the final decade of his life, his poetry received numerous awards, younger poets started to look to his poetics as an alternative to the neoclassical emphasis of Pound and Eliot, and W.'s fifty years of work began to be discussed on an equal footing with the achievement of his major contemporaries.

In 1902, W. began the study of medicine at the University of Pennsylvania, where he met Pound, and in 1910 set up medical practice in his home town of Rutherford, New Jersey, specializing in pediatrics.

Despite this full-time medical career—which he always regarded as a rich and rare source of material for his writing—W. published more than forty books, including short stories, novels, experimental prose, a history, plays, and even an opera libretto—as well as the poetry upon which his reputation chiefly rests. The nearby city of Paterson is the central focus of W.'s famous long poem, and the subject matter of his shorter poems and his fiction is also often drawn from Rutherford and surrounding towns—and sometimes, too, from New York City, only a short drive from Rutherford.

W.'s first book of verse, *Poems* (1909), reflected the prevailing late romantic sentiments of turn of the century poetry, and was duly blasted by Pound when W. proudly sent a copy to his friend, then established in London. W. took Pound's demands to "modernize" his verse to heart, and his second book, *The Tempers* (1913), reflects Pound's preimagist manner, utilizing unusual verse-forms and short dramatic monologues. Of more lasting impact upon W.'s poetics was Pound's presentation of the principles of IMAGISM in 1913. The central tenets of the short-lived movement remained central to much of W.'s subsequent verse: direct treatment of the "thing," the eschewing of conventional rhythms, and a sparing, concise use of language. W. continued to explore the possibilities of such a poetic long after Pound had moved onto interests closer to the social, historical, and allusive poetic concerns of Eliot. For W., direct treatment of the "thing" matched his demand that American poets present American landscape in nonabstract language, and the throwing out of conventional poetic diction and rhythms paralleled his insistence that American poets develop a distinctive native voice and form. Walt WHITMAN had taken the first important steps, W. often argued, but in his verbosity had failed to discipline his line.

In his books *Al Que Quiere!* (1917) and *Sour Grapes* (1921), W. explored his own brand of imagism, and in 1920 published a book of prose experiments, *Kora in Hell: Improvisations,* containing an important long "Prologue" in which he distinguishes his poetics from the "international" concerns of Pound and Eliot, from the more analytical approach of Stevens, and from what he dismissed as the verbose "local color" efforts of such Chicago poets as Carl SANDBURG.

The radical juxtapositions of *Kora in Hell: Improvisations* find their way into the poetry of *Spring and All* (1923), a book of twenty-seven poems, and loosely associated critical prose, that contains many examples of W.'s finest and most often anthologized poems— shaped around material from encounters with his local world: the mentally retarded house servant Elsie, a baseball game, the coming of spring to the New Jersey swamplands, a red wheelbarrow in a neighbor's garden. An indication of the direction of W.'s reputation for the next twenty years is this book's publication, in France, in an edition of only three hundred—and not reprinted in full until 1970—while Eliot's *The Waste Land*, first published a few months earlier in 1922, quickly came to represent for poets and general public alike the quintessential modernist poem.

W.'s poetry in the first forty years of his writing career is most centrally concerned with the concrete encounter, and the here and now of the moment of perceptual impact. Where the past has a role in his verse, it is as it conditions the quality of the contemporary encounter. On this ground of the important role of the past, W. and Eliot meet, but the resulting emphasis is very different. For Eliot, tradition in the widest sense is a force that must irrevocably be part of the present consciousness, and a force thus to be acknowledged and incorporated into the contemporary poem. For W., on the other hand, the present could free itself of the errors, lies, conventions, and habits rooted in the past—and thus a new American poetic could rid itself of the concerns of the European heritage, and need obey no rules inherited from the traditions associated with another age and another continent. When W. does concern himself with the past, as in sections of *Paterson* and in his series of history essays *In the American Grain* (1925), it is to search for the lost moments of past insight into the unique challenges of the new continent, to trace the suffocation of those moments by fear, greed, and the stultifying force of unthinking acceptance and habit, and to illuminate the open-ended possibilities of change for the present age and the new world—of America and of the poem.

While W. often writes as if the European heritage can be readily ejected from American art and its concerns, some of his work recognizes the difficulty of struggling with a power that offers the haven of the familiar in matters of both form and theme. Poems such as "March" (1916) and "History" (1917), and his first novel, *A Voyage to Pagany* (1928), acknowledge the achievement and seductive power of the European past, and dramatize the struggle to find a contemporary, American form that can promise to match such a heritage. A characteristic motif of the resulting release is that of Madame Curie's discovery of radium in book 5 of *Paterson*, where the powerful essence is released through commitment, courage, and chance—the unpredictable good fortune produced by the venture into the unknown, and at the heart of it, as always in W.'s motifs of birth and discovery, the female principle. A further development of this theme in many of W.'s poems involves a necessary "descent" to bring about renewal—presented, often simultaneously through levels of imagery, as a putting down of roots for future growth, as a necessary failure to achieve success, as

the winter that precedes spring, or as the necessary descent into the body to tap a kind of preconscious self that can engage with the concrete world without the intrusion of the received principles of convention. In his "The Wanderer" (1914), the poet enacts a characteristic gesture, descending into the filthy waters of the local river, the Passaic, and emerging renewed to freshly encounter and articulate the landscape to which with this baptismal act he has dedicated himself to his art.

Until a marked shift in his style and themes in the early 1950s, for the next three decades W.'s poetry continued to demonstrate the general characteristics of the *Spring and All* poems, although his emphasis changes within particular collections. "The Descent of Winter" (1928), also a mix of prose and verse, is a sequence developed from a much more extensive series of notes and diary entries begun in 1927. A ten-poem sequence "Della Primavera Trasportata al Morale," (1930–34) concerns the coming of spring and was originally intended to be part of "The Descent of Winter," both sequences exhibiting W.'s interest in the "Objectivists" movement, particularly its emphasis upon poetry as patterned speech. Following further volumes in the 1930s, *An Early Martyr* and *Adam & Eve & the City*, W. published the first extensive collection of his work, the *Complete Collected Poems*, in 1938, although the collection was not complete—W. refused to reprint his neoromantic 1909 *Poems*.

In the late 1930s, W. began to give serious attention to his long poem centered upon the history and neglected potential of the nearby industrial city of Paterson, a project he had been considering since at least 1927. After a number of false starts in trying to discover a workable form, in 1946, book 1 of the originally projected four books appeared, to be followed by further books in 1948, 1949, and 1951. The alternate prose and poetry sections of book 1 characterize the form of the whole work, the prose sections including material from books, personal letters and historical newspaper accounts. Multiple perspectives, nonlinear juxtapositions, and open-endedness are both themes and characteristics of *Paterson*'s form. The prevailing voice of the poem is sometimes an individual—a poet, a doctor—and sometimes a kind of collective city consciousness, both voices cut across by other individual and collective voices throughout the poem. Within this multiplicity, each of the four books has a central thematic focus. Book 1, "The Delineaments of the Giants," is largely historical, detailing the attraction of the famous Paterson Falls—a central motif of the poem—and the failure to respond to its potential. Book 2, "Sunday in the Park," centers upon the poverty of imagination in the present day populace, whereas book 3, "The Library," finds the poet/city figure searching conventional historical record for an adequate language to express the promise of the landscape as figured in the roar of the falls. That promise is finally released with the destruction by wind, fire, and flood of all the constrictions—literary, historical, perceptual, and emotional—that have characterized the economic, social, and political history of Paterson—and of America—for three hundred years. Book 4 details "The Run to the Sea," and the rebirth out of the sea of a poet figure who turns inland to confront the continent anew, on its own terms. A fifth book, conceived in 1952 after the publication of book 4, and published in 1958, seeks to set some of the major themes of the poems into a wider historical and mythic context represented by the famous Unicorn tapestries at New York's Cloisters Museum, but this later book has as much to do with the themes of W.'s 1950s poetry as with the original conception of *Paterson.*

In 1950 and 1951, W. again collected his poems, this time distinguishing *The Collected Earlier Poems* (1951) from *The Collected Later Poems* (1950). In these years, he also published *The Autobiography of W. C. W.* (1951), finished a prose trilogy begun in 1938 that centered upon the immigrant experience of his wife's family, and undertook a number of reading and teaching assignments that were the result of the increasing critical attention his work was beginning to receive. But in 1951, W. suffered a serious stroke, followed by another in 1952, which together led him to write little verse for almost two years and for his next two books, *The Desert Music* (1954), and *Journey to Love* (1955), to exhibit a very different mood. Many of the poems in the two books are written in the three-step line W. had first used for a part of *Paterson* II. The longest of the poems, "Asphodel, That Greeny Flower," originally conceived as *Paterson* V, is a meditation, in three parts and a coda, upon his marriage, the loss that accompanies old age, and the wisdom and creativity that can come through suffering and love. More accessible than *Paterson* and many of the earlier poems, and centered upon a quiet, ruminative voice that continually juxtaposes memory alongside the present experience, for many readers the poems of these years are among W.'s finest work.

W. tied his three-step line poems to his concept of "the variable foot," and in various critical pieces through the 1950s argued that his line rested upon an underlying poetic geared to the stresses of American speech. Although not completely convincing, the concepts of "the variable foot" and the accompanying concept of "the American idiom" helped a number of younger poets, including Denise LEVERTOV, Robert LOWELL, and Allen GINSBERG, to bring a looser, more colloquial tone to their developing verse. Lowell acknowledged W.'s role in his developing a freer-verse

form for the confessional *Life Studies* poems (1959), while Ginsberg's *Howl* (1956), as the published drafts make clear, was originally conceived in a three-step line similar to that of W.'s 1950s work.

Increasingly handicapped by further strokes through the decade, W.'s final book of verse, *Pictures from Brueghel* (1962), reflects his now circumscribed world—family, letters and postcards received, much loved books, and paintings—in a verse form that in its direct, pared-down nakedness returns to the pictorial focus of his earlier work. A month after his death the book won W. his only Pulitzer Prize.

BIBLIOGRAPHY: Breslin, J. E., *W. C. W.: An American Artist* (1970); Crawford, H. T., *Modernism, Medicine and W. C. W.* (1995); Deese, H., ed., *Critical Essays on W. C. W.* (1994); Dijkstra, B., *The Hieroglyphics of a New Speech* (1969); Larson, K. A., *Guide to the Poetry of W. C. W.* (1995); MacGowan, C., *W. C. W.'s Early Poetry: The Visual Arts Background* (1984); Mariani, P., *W. C. W.: A New World Naked* (1981); Marling, W., *W. C. W. and the Painters, 1909–1923* (1982); Miller, J. H., *Poets of Reality* (1966)

CHRISTOPHER MACGOWAN

WILLINGHAM, Calder [Bayvard] Jr.

b. 23 December 1922, Atlanta, Georgia; d. 19 February 1995, Laconia, New Hampshire

Novelist and screenwriter W. was born and reared in Georgia. He spent one year at the Citadel, in Charleston, South Carolina, (1940–41) and two years at the University of Virginia (1941–43). Almost immediately, he began writing and published his first novel, *End as a Man* (1947), when he was twenty-five. For almost fifty years thereafter, he occupied himself as an uncommonly productive and versatile writer of novels and screenplays, turning out works of satire, science fiction, venereal comedy, medieval adventure, cowboys and Indians, and social melodrama, most vividly in the genre called Southern Gothic, with postdoctoral qualifications in psychosis, retardation, incest, and murder. As credited or uncredited scriptwriter, he was associated with several distinguished movies, including *The Bridge on the River Kwai* (1957), *Paths of Glory* (1957), *The Vikings* (1958), *One-Eyed Jacks* (1961), *The Graduate* (1967), and *Little Big Man* (1970). He also wrote the screen adaptations of *End as a Man,* released as *The Strange One* (1957) and his 1971 novel *Rambling Rose* (1991).

W. has been overshadowed by a number of contemporaries, including J. D. SALINGER, James JONES, and Norman MAILER, to say nothing of such fellow Southerners as William STYRON and Truman CAPOTE. As with several American writers, W. seems doomed to being remembered best for his first book, which happens to be one of the best exemplars of the military school novel, a mode in which the inherent fascination of the military—with all its pageantry, violence, and hypocrisy—is compounded by the inherent fascination of school, especially a single-sex school. W. was a pioneer in territory later explored by such as Lucian K. Truscott IV in *Dress Gray* (1979) and Pat Conroy in *Lords of Discipline* (1980).

In another sort of overshadowing, W.'s work in converting his own *End as a Man* and *Rambling Rose* into screenplays has seemed secondary to his work on several distinguished movies made from novels by others, such as Humphrey Cobb's *Paths of Glory* (1935) and Thomas BERGER's *Little Big Man*—although one can see similarities in these latter works that, like *End As a Man,* involve military hypocrisy and violence.

Aside from reviews in popular periodicals, there has been little in the way of serious critical analysis or judgment of W.'s fiction. One of the earliest appraisals remains the best: Norman Mailer wrote that W. "is a clown with the bite of a ferret, and he suffers from the misapprehension that he is a master mind. He has written what may be the funniest dialogue of our time, and if *Geraldine Bradshaw,* his second novel, had been half as long, it would have been the best short novel any of us did. But it is hard to bet on Calder, for if he ever grows up, where will he go? He lacks ideas, and is as indulgent to his shortcomings as a fat old lady to her Pekinese. This said, it must also by admitted that he is one of the few writers who can man an evening, and once he put me down with the economy of a Zen master. I had just finished *Natural Child,* and happened to run into him at the White Horse Tavern. "Calder," I said, coming on like Max Lerner, "I'd like to talk to you about your book. I liked parts of it and didn't like other parts." "Nawmin," said Calder. "Could you lend me two bucks? I haven't had breakfast yet."

BIBLIOGRAPHY: Mailer, N., *Advertisements for Myself* (1959); Noble, D. R., "C. W., Jr.," in Flora, J.M., and R. Bain, eds., *Contemporary Fiction Writers of the South: A Bio-Biographical Sourcebook* (1993): 494–502

WILLIAM HARMON

WILLIS, N[athaniel] P[arker]

b. 20 January 1806, Portland, Maine; d. 20 January 1867, Idlewild, New York

A prolific journalist, poet, and writer, W. was one of the shapers of popular reading taste in the 19th c.

Discounted in the early 20th c. as a writer of ephemera, W. nonetheless created a journalistic voice that was tremendously influential in the newspaper and magazine industry. Gossipy but well crafted, light but earnest, W.'s writing style sought to amuse, interest, and instruct his middle-class audience. W. also campaigned hard during his entire career to foster American literature through international copyright law and generous payment to journal contributors.

Descended from a line of printer-editors, W. first published religious poems in his father's paper, the *Boston Recorder.* Cultivating his personal appearance and literary interests at Yale, W. returned to Boston determined to make his living as a litterateur. In 1827, he edited the *Token,* and later founded the *American Monthly Magazine* (1829). In November 1829, he recommended Lady Morgan's *Book of the Boudoir,* telling his readers, "We love this rambling familiar gossip. It is the undress of the mind. We would read the grave and dignified authors, but we would do it as we perform the duties of life. There should be a time for lighter things afterward." W.'s fondness for lighter literature, often associated in the minds of his peers with his dandyism and reputation as a lady's man, proved highly saleable.

Moving to New York in 1831, W. became a literary editor for George P. Morris's *New York Mirror,* repudiating his New England roots to become an urbane Knickerbocker. Convincing Morris, with whom he carried on a lifelong partnership, that a series of travel sketches from Europe would sell well, W. embarked on a several year tour of Europe that provided the substance for 139 letters published in the *Mirror* between 1832 and 1836. W. collected and modified these sketches in *Pencillings by the Way* (1835) and *Inklings of an Adventure* (1836). Notable for their tone of familiarity with the reader and their attempt to convey a sense of intimate contact with fashionable European culture, W.'s letters were very popular, but it was felt that he sometimes bordered on indiscretion. Thackeray satirized him as a scandal-mongering dilettante in an article in *Fraser's* (September 1841), and in *Vanity Fair* as Mr. John Paul Jefferson Jones. Although attacked by rival editors from time to time, W. steadfastly refused to indulge in public bickering, generally choosing to accentuate the positive aspects of particular persons and works rather than sensationalize negative criticism. He also believed in paying generously for submissions, an act that helped bring many female writers, such as Fanny Forester, the pseudonym of Emily Chubbock Judson, into prominence. Ironically, W. abruptly terminated editorial sponsorship of his own talented sister, Sara Payson Willis PARTON in 1854. W. went on with his journalistic formula to found the *Corsair* (1839–40), the *New, Weekly,* and

Evening Mirrors (1843–45), to finally settle with the *Home Journal* in 1845, for which he wrote until his death.

Aside from his travel sketches and fiction, which make up the majority of his writing, W. was a competent popular poet. Although he disliked "sentimentality, lack-a-daisical prettyisms, and a morbid depravity of taste," his work often centered around sentimental scenes and death. As biographer Cortland Auser points out, he was greatly influenced by Byron: "Melanie" is an Italian romance tinged by wandering melancholy, and his "Lady Jane" shows him experimenting with Byronic social commentary. His sacred poems, several of which made his reputation in college, rehearse familiar biblical tales such as "The Sacrifice of Abraham," "Absalom," and "Hagar in the Wilderness." W. generally republished his poetry in succeeding volumes, so that his 1850 *Poems of the Early and After Years* encompasses much of the four volumes of poems that preceded it.

W. wrote two marginally successful plays, *Bianca Visconti* (1837), a tragedy, and *Tortesa, the Usurer* (1839), a comedy, both of which were Italian love intrigues. W.'s novel *Paul Fane* (1856), like much of his shorter travel-based fiction, is an attempt to sketch America's relationship to European society. Following an Italian romance, W.'s protagonist comes to value his own self-worth and return to find his fortune in America.

Although W.'s literature itself is seldom studied today, his professional practices and personal example opened up a new literary market for a variety of other American writers, most notably women.

BIBLIOGRAPHY: Auser, C. P., *N. P. W.* (1969); Beers, H. A., *N. P. W.* (1885); Mott, F. L., *A History of American Magazines, 1741–1850* (1930)

                                    GRANVILLE GANTER

WILSON, August

b. 27 April 1945, Pittsburgh, Pennsylvania

Perhaps the most critically respected playwright since the 1980s, W. was a high school dropout who finished his education largely through self-study. Raised in a Pittsburgh slum, his plays are often set in that city on the Midwest. W.'s public library readings exposed him to a spectrum of African American writers, and he became a founder of the Black Horizon Theater in Pittsburgh. Although W. holds to a black nationalist position, and his plays profile the struggle of black individuals and families within the confines of racist institutions and mindsets, specific political agendas are not thematically apparent. Rather, his dramas involve

issues of black identity as their characters face conflicted notions of self-image within a limiting American landscape of racism and neglect. For all their bleakness and hard-edged realism, they uphold an abiding faith in the future and reaffirm traditional black institutions such as the family and jazz music. Significant for the playwright is the connection between the unique values and traditions of African American culture and the ability of his characters to overcome their social and psychological confinement.

Perhaps W.'s importance as a playwright stands upon his ability to sustain compelling characterizations in realistic situations, while offering unstated themes that connect to deep psychological and social causes. His situations almost always involve archetypal endeavors within African American culture. For example, *Ma Rainey's Black Bottom* (1985), his first successful play, depicts the near legendary world of the female jazz singer, a significant source of black American identity. The first in a planned sequence of ten plays intended to reveal the struggle of African Americans in each decade of the 20th c., its plot involves the exploitation of black musicians by white business. The tensive character relationships derive to a great extent from the unjust social structure of segregation—the separate and unequal treatment of musical performers throughout the 19th and 20th cs. Within this delimited circumstance, however, W.'s black musicians reveal individualized responses that further uncover the nuances of racism. Furthermore, their competitive stance towards each other and the music world in general is often more negative than self-affirming; W. thus realistically profiles their natures as creative individuals, but also implies through their misdirected anger the crippling effects of institutional racism. W.'s attempt to disclose the causal relationship between the individual anguish of his characters and their social plight is at times stated explicitly by certain characters, who function as raisonneurs for the others. Ma Rainey herself sings about such anguish while her white producers and audiences, on whom she depends economically, miss the deeper implications of her private sadness, which are derived from the commonality of her racial experience.

Other plays in W.'s planned series include the Pulitzer Prize-winning *Fences* (1986), *The Piano Lesson* (1987), and *Joe Turner's Come and Gone* (1988), each set in his native Pittsburgh. His most family-centered work, *Fences* attempts to lay open the forces that endanger the black American family. Once again, strong individuals are drawn with meticulous detail and depth, but, whereas the musicians of *Ma Rainey* function as competitive individuals, "temperamental artists" tossed together by the strictures of racism, the family members of *Fences* are loving but codependent, desiring more than their strong ties can manage. In this drama also, the disabling effects of racial exclusion both bind the characters closer together and thrust them apart. The ambiguities of the title express this two-way movement, which W. finds a common reality of African American family life. Fences are designed to keep people out but also to keep people in, and deferred dreams often result, paradoxically, in the loss of affirming realities, of the very dreams that are denied by the society.

The Piano Lesson and *Joe Turner's Come and Gone* show the continuing presence of the Old South on contemporary African American lives; it functions ambivalently, as a negative reminder of past disenfranchisement but also as a continuing source of reaffirmation. In these, as in W.'s earlier plays, strong characterizations reveal the resourcefulness of traditional black culture, even in the face of seemingly overwhelming developments. *The Piano Lesson* in particular presents a mixed tone of low comedy structural elements, dramatic character revelation, and musical lyricism. *Two Trains Running* (1992) and *Seven Guitars* (1995) continue to document typical challenges to self-identity in the African American world with great specificity, although the latter drama seems more complex structurally, incorporating more overtly allegorical elements.

Although W. experiments with nonrealistic elements in his dramas, his dramatic form remains well within the limits of American REALISM. Absent is any suggestion of political solutions to the dilemmas that confront his characters; rather, their ability to overcome the longstanding effects of racism and economic inequality are never tested in a political context. Thus far W. has not documented the organized activities of protest and resistance so significant in the political life for black Americans of the 20th c. Rather, his dramas seem to eschew political possibilities, especially of the direct confrontational kind and of specific political movements. Profiles of social activism, either of individuals whose lives are involved in civil rights protest, or of group protagonists, remain unexplored. The playwright depicts the effects of racial institutions on individuals and families, but confines solutions to individualistic notions of courage, determination, and personal integrity. The significance of the civil right movement—actually present in every decade since emancipation—has yet to gain W.'s full attention.

BIBLIOGRAPHY: Elkins, M., *A. W.: A Casebook* (1994); Nadel, A., *May All Your Faces Have Gates: Essays on the Drama of A. W.* (1994); Pereira, K., *A. W. and the African-American Odyssey* (1995); Shannon, S. G., *The Dramatic Vision of A. W.* (1995)

WILLIAM OVER

WILSON, Edmund [Jr.]

b. 8 May 1895, Red Bank, New Jersey; d. 12 June 1972, Talcottville, New York

Among the major American writers of his generation—including Ernest HEMINGWAY, F. Scott FITZGERALD, John DOS PASSOS, Thornton WILDER, Edna St. Vincent MILLAY, and T. S. ELIOT—W. held a special place. His achievement was not quite the creative one of the novelists and poets, but neither was it that of the belletrists or the literary scholars. As a man of letters, he defied categorization by writing literary essays, critical studies, political journalism, cultural reportage, history, contemporary chronicles, polemics, diaries, fiction, and drama. Although he did not create any imaginative works of great originality, he brought a unique kind of authority to 20th-c. American literature. At once learned and keenly aware of the ordinary world, W. poised himself between literary tradition and the enormous upheavals of his era. His lucid prose—a blend of classical and conversational styles—provided a nation of intelligent general readers with the news of MODERNISM and with a daunting number of explorations into literary movements, canonical and neglected writers, social thinkers, and political activists. His primary passion was literature—authors and their creations set against a broad backdrop of historical events and vividly described ideas. Yet his wide culture—acquired before our age of specialization—led him to subjects and controversies that were far from the study of literary texts.

W. spent his early years in an atmosphere of professional distinction and patrician confidence. His father, a lawyer for corporations, was nevertheless involved with good causes and old fashioned republican virtue; the maternal side of the family included rich physicians who were more typical of the Gilded Age mentality. From his days at the austere Hill School in Pottstown, Pennsylvania (1908–12) until the end of his life, W. was the man of privilege who resented privilege. At Hill, he concentrated on reading Greek classics and developing his prose style by editing and writing for the literary magazine; he had no taste for fraternizing with the wealthy. Later at Princeton (1912–16), he took a cool view of eating clubs and was attracted to the bohemianism of his mentor Christian Gauss, a humanist who introduced him to continental writers at a time when the genteel tradition of Anglo-Saxon culture was still prevalent. W.'s college writing includes notable essays on Stendhal and the as yet uncanonical Henry JAMES.

W.'s service in World War I—in a hospital unit and later in the Intelligence Corps—awakened him to the lives of average Americans and Europeans. Like Hemingway and Dos Passos, he became disaffected with the patriotic fervor that separated people into self-protective groups. He thereafter adopted a kind of humane socialism as a protest against the American power drive and the values of the monied class.

In the early 1920s, W. began a journalistic career in New York; with little taste for pedestrian news stories, he focused on contemporary literature, entertainment, and social spectacle. He worked at the upscale and sophisticated *Vanity Fair* in 1920 and soon moved to the more serious liberal *New Republic,* turning out a prodigious number of reviews and essays about major modern writers such as Eliot and James Joyce as well as about supporting players of his era, including Elinor WYLIE, Ring LARDNER, Sherwood ANDERSON, and E. E. CUMMINGS. His cultural criticism led him to speakeasies, cabarets, burlesque shows, films, and Greenwich Village theaters. Never a mere booster of the arts, W. developed a reputation as a severe critic of poor craftsmanship, frivolous experiment, and slickness. "The man in the iron necktie," E. E. Cummings called him. He supplied context and learning in his reviews and held the contemporary world to a standard of excellence that was often in short supply. *The Shores of Light* (1952) brought this work of the 1920s—as well as the continued reviewing of the 1930s—into book form: it stands as an opinionated, scintillating, copious account of a great period in American literature; including English and European writers as well, W. gave American criticism an international flavor and genuine worldliness that even a wit like H. L. MENCKEN or a scholar like Irving Babbitt at Harvard could not provide. W.'s love of the comparative approach found more orderly, if less brilliant, expression in *Axel's Castle* (1931), a book about the symbolist movement that introduced, analyzed, celebrated—yet often was critical of—figures such as Joyce, Eliot, William Butler Yeats, Marcel Proust, and Gertrude STEIN. The mixture of passion and classical restraint makes this book a landmark.

W. lived the life of the Jazz Age: he knew many of the major writers—Fitzgerald, Millay—and led a boozy, disorderly, exciting existence in New York. He married the actress Mary Blair, soon separated after becoming a father, and ended the decade in a sanitarium recovering from a breakdown. His novel *I Thought of Daisy* (1929) is the story of a young intellectual who suffers from an overdose of Greenwich Village aestheticism and uptown cynicism; a jazz baby (read down-to-earth American girl) and an old philosopher (read Christian Gauss) help him to discover vitality and harmony. A finer naturalistic picture of W.'s life is available in *The Twenties* (1975).

During the early 1930s, W. abandoned his vague socialism for a short-term romance with communism. Yet although he voted communist in 1932, he never wrote like a party member. As a social critic, he delivered scathing indictments of American irresponsibility, depictions of mindless materialism and its bitter fruits—the poverty and despair of Americans from Brooklyn to San Diego. In the reportage collected in *American Earthquake* (1958), he used irony and spare description to expose the ugly state of the nation. His own life was no less depressing than the national scene: a two-year marriage to Margaret Canby, a monied Californian, ended with her death in an accident. W. immersed himself in his essay writing—producing an astonishing number of pieces about contemporary writers—and continued his amours and the recording of them in *The Thirties* (1980). In 1934, he started to publish the first chapters of his great leftist epic *To the Finland Station* (1940) in the *New Republic:* this book traced the development of revolutionary thought and action back to its origins in the philosopher Vico and forward to the grand traditions of utopianism and Marxism. Including a vast array of theorists and radical activists—right up to Lenin at the Finland Station—the book is W.'s novelistic rendering of the socialist ideal. By the time it was published, he had little faith in the Soviet experiment. Although he had approved of much that he observed in Russia while on a Guggenheim Fellowship in 1935, he had no taste for Stalinism and no intention of harnessing his career to its ideals. In *The Triple Thinkers* (1938), he disentangled his kind of Marxism from the party line: social analysis in literary study—identification of class conflicts and material circumstances that played a part in literature—was no substitute for taste and humane judgment. By the late 1930s, W. turned away from many of his contemporaries who still believed in the righteous cause of the left; he nevertheless always retained his sharp eye for capitalist injustice and his historical focus. Even the psychological analysis of *The Wound and the Bow* (1941), his pioneering study of neurosis and art, was firmly grounded in an understanding of the social pressures that shaped artists' illnesses and creations.

In 1938, W. married Mary MCCARTHY and began yet another stormy period in his life. The marriage of fine minds was not happy, nor was his relationship with the *New Republic* by the time of the war. W. was against America's involvement and soon turned his career away from public affairs back to his love of books. He became the head reviewer for the *New Yorker*—and as usual built books out of his pieces. *Classics and Commercials* (1950), *The Bit between My Teeth* (1966), and *The Devils and Canon Barham*—published in 1973, a year after his death—are the solid, often quirky, yet always well-crafted results of his reviewing years. Together, they constitute only a part of W.'s post-Depression output. In 1946, W.

reached his limits as a fiction writer with *Memoirs of Hecate County,* a loosely structured novel about his own sexual adventures in suburbia and in the bachelor world of dance halls and clubs.

The 1950s and 1960s saw no abatement of W.'s energies. In a stable marriage with Elena Mumm Thornton, he nevertheless continued to look for conflicts in literature and society. Minorities and misunderstood cultures were obsessions as he wrote *Apologies to the Iroquois* (1960) and later *O Canada* (1965). For years, he investigated ancient Jewish texts and intellectual habits, publishing first the controversial *The Scrolls from the Dead Sea* (1955) and soon after *A Piece of My Mind* (1956). The former book boldly traced the origins of Christian ideals to the Essene sect, and did so in W.'s inimitably readable style. The latter book contains a powerful memoir about W.'s father, a man whose fascination with Abraham LINCOLN ignited his son's interests in the Civil War. The massive *Patriotic Gore* (1962) does for American literature and political rhetoric of the Civil War what *Finland Station* had done for European revolutionary writing and activism: it traces the working out of a seminal idea—the right to shed blood for a cause. W. surveys the writing of fanatics and rationalists—the racist Hinton Helper and the duty-bound Oliver Wendell HOLMES, Jr.—and in the process studies the intellectual climate of the war

In his last decade, W. reflected on his own past and the meaning of American civilization in *Upstate* (1971); he readied his diaries for publication and wrote a broadside against Uncle Sam in *The Cold War and the Income Tax* (1963). Yet neither the political nor the personal kept him from the literary. He told stories about art and artists until the end. *A Window on Russia* (1972), published posthumously, includes a searching essay on Ivan Turgenev's artistry and its relationship to his life and times.

BIBLIOGRAPHY: Berthoff, W., *E. W.* (1968); Castronovo, D., *E. W.* (1984); Douglas, G., *E. W.'s America* (1983); Frank, C., *E. W.* (1970); Groth, J., *E. W.: A Critic for Our Time* (1989); Kriegel, L., *E. W.* (1971); Meyers, J., *E. W., A Biography* (1995); Paul, S., *E. W.* (1965); Wain, J., ed., *E. W.: The Man and His Work* (1978)

DAVID CASTRONOVO

WILSON, Harry Leon

b. 1 May 1867, Oregon, Illinois; d. 28 June 1939, Carmel, California

Although W. had early successes as the editor of *Puck* and as a playwright who collaborated with Booth TAR-KINGTON, he is now best remembered for the group of humorous novels he began in his mid-forties. In 1912, his *Bunker Bean* was serialized in the *Saturday Evening Post* and published in hardback the following year, establishing an association with the magazine that lasted throughout his career. Like most of W.'s subsequent novels, *Bunker Bean* reveals a strong identification with the average American—with his ambitions, limitations, and values.

Bunker Bean gains confidence when he is told he is a reincarnation of Napoleon and of an Egyptian pharaoh. He buys what he believes is a mummy of himself in a former life, marries the boss's daughter and plunges on the stock market. The crisis comes when he discovers the mummy is fraudulent. Bunker Bean, true to the American folk wisdom that permeates W.'s fiction, learns the power of confidence. He now completes his education by learning to draw his confidence from himself.

W.'s two best-known novels are *Ruggles of Red Gap* (1915) and *Merton of the Movies* (1922). The first of these is probably the best of W.'s work. W. was thought of as a popular humorist rather than as someone deserving serious attention, but *Ruggles of Red Gap* brought him letters of praise from the staid William Dean HOWELLS and the iconoclastic H. L. MENCKEN.

Most of the humor derives from a proper English valet's perceptions—and misperceptions—of American culture—of everything from its turns of speech to its most serious values. Marmaduke Ruggles's employer, the Honorable George Augustus Vane-Basingwell, loses him in a poker game to Senator James Knox Floud of Red Gap, whose wife Effie wishes to use Ruggles to improve her uncouth brother-in-law, Egbert Floud. Ruggles is subjected to a series of assaults on his sense of propriety and on his rigid notions of class structure in a community one generation removed from the frontier. Rough, boisterous, extroverted, ostensibly egalitarian—Red Gap society at first shocks him but gradually converts him. Red Gap, however, is really something other than egalitarian. Ruggles is imported for his snob appeal. An inaccurate newspaper story transforms him into Colonel Ruggles, and hostile social sets compete for him. Finally, Ruggles becomes so democratic that he fights these class distinctions.

Soon the English aristocracy feels the influence of Red Gap. The Honorable George Augustus Vane-Basingwell follows his manservant and falls under the spell of the widowed Mrs. Kate Kenner, also known as "Klondike Kate," the leader of the "Bohemian set." The Earl of Brinstead arrives to save his brother George, only to marry Mrs. Kenner himself. By this time Ruggles has become a small businessman, the proprietor of the U.S. Grill.

Ruggles of Red Gap conveys messages that Americans of 1915 liked to hear: American wholesomeness will triumph over English stuffiness. The overly cultivated, given the opportunity, will prefer a life nearly devoid of social inhibition. American democracy will triumph over class distinctions. But these messages have little appeal to modern readers. The well-made film version of 1936, like the novel, has become dated.

Merton of the Movies, too, once had an appeal that is now lost. Merton Gill yearns to be a film star. His serious dramatic efforts are unintentionally funny, and he is tricked into making comedies while he thinks he is making serious films. After he recovers from the trauma of recognizing where his talents lie, he accepts his role as a comedian. Again, W. provides consolation for the common man.

Bits and pieces of W.'s fiction are very funny even today, but the books are seldom read and even at their most successful were considered popular literature. They survive as period pieces rather than as works of art.

BIBLIOGRAPHY: Kummer, G., *H. L. W.: Some Account of the Triumphs and Tribulations of an American Popular Writer* (1963); Rhodes, C., "Twenties Fiction, Mass Culture, and the Modern Subject," AL 68 (June 1996): 385–404

MARYJEAN GROSS and DALTON GROSS

WILSON, John

b. 1588, Windsor, England; d. 7 August 1667, Dorchester, Massachusetts

One of the founders of Massachusetts PURITANISM, W. wrote elegies that significantly contrast with *A Song of Deliverance,* a work he published in 1626 while still in England. An Eton and Cambridge educated divine who had forsaken the Anglican hierarchy, W. arrived in Boston with his wife and children on the wave of the great migration, from 1630 to 1640, which brought some 20,000 settlers from England to Massachusetts, most of them Puritans. His fame as a minister of the First Church in Boston and his propensity to send pious poems to friends and relatives for all occasions have left extant a handful of elegiac poems that, although uninspired, were useful to an audience who spared little time for aesthetics. In contrast, the English audience for W.'s *Song of Deliverance* was treated to a sustained ecclesiastical message grounded on a shared history.

The elegies are anagrams, popular in England throughout the first half of the 17th c.—though disparaged by Ben Jonson—and common in colonial literature. The simple verses are pious and homiletic, often written in the voice of the deceased—a wife, for example, tells of falling asleep to join the church of Christ, the greater bridegroom.

The severity of the tenets and the times of the early Puritans may be seen in the elegy written on the death of W.'s grandson, the first child of his daughter and son-in-law, Samuel Danforth, also a minister and poet. In this elegy, the Old Testament suffering of Job, a favorite theme of W.'s, is judged more worthy than his daughter's laments, were it her fourth child in succession who had died; history went on to record that three of the couple's first four children died. The elegies, although primitive, echo the thematic logic of *A Song of Deliverance* but not its nationalistic spirit. The belief that God had chosen the Puritans of England, as he had once chosen the Jews, to be exemplars of the religious life, is taught in these versus by invoking Old Testament stories to explicate the hand of God in shared current events, such as the 1588 Spanish Armada and the plagues of 1603 and 1625.

Cotton MATHER in *Magnalia Christi Americana* draws W. as a well-loved storyteller and hospitable companion. When W. died, he was eulogized with this anagram of his name, sometimes spelled Willson: Wish no one ill.

BIBLIOGRAPHY: Leverenz, D., *The Language of Puritan Feeling* (1980); Murdock, K. B., ed., *Handkerchiefs from Paul, Being Pious and Consolatory Verse of Puritan Massachusetts* (1927)

KAREN J. PHILLIPS

WILSON, Lanford

b. 13 April 1937, Lebanon, Missouri

In the tradition of Tennessee WILLIAMS, Lillian HELLMAN, and William INGE, W. has explored characters and situations from America's heartland. While his people speak a straightforward language of realism, their musings project a certain lyricism and nostalgia for a past when values seemed stronger and individual choice clearer. Their conflicts generally involve a search for lost meaning, and although they often fail to overcome the perplexities of American life, they often find ways to accommodate lost hopes, usually by arriving at some kind of perception. W. creates characters who through humor and contemplation express an abiding desire for self-fulfillment, hoping to transcend the aimlessness and vacuity of their situations. Although W.'s plays have been criticized for insufficient character motivation and occasional retreats into sentimentality, his ear for human speech patterns, his empathic understanding of a wide range of characters, and his experiments with performance structure, particularly with layered dialogue and choreic commentary, have made his drama eminently stageworthy.

Reared and educated in the Midwest, W. arrived in New York after recognizing a talent for playwriting. At Caffe Cino, he discovered the theater of the absurd, and Joe Cino produced his *So Long at the Fair* in 1963, inspired by Eugène Ionesco's jocose satires against middle-class conventionality. After producing full-length plays at Ellen Stewart's La Mama Experimental Theater, W. and others organized the not-for-profit Circle Repertory Theater in 1969, which became the most appropriate locus for his drama. Profiting from the workshop approach at Circle Repertory Theater, its ensemble rehearsal methods and repertory format, W. gained popular and critical acclaim for *The Hot-L Baltimore* (1973), *The Mound Builders* (1975), and *Talley's Folly* (1980). These dramas involve the effects of a past, distant or recent, upon the individual and collective lives of characters.

Although influenced by William SAROYAN's *The Time of Your Life,* W.'s varied characters in *The Hot-L Baltimore* are generally less sentimentalized, but no less sympathetic for their unconventional lifestyles. Set in the early 1970s in a neglected railway station, the play evokes the golden age of travel, the optimism of adventurers in pursuit of the American dream, yet its people ironize such ideals. The characters are prostitutes, gay partners, the dispossessed, the put-upon, and the despairing who exhibit a spectrum of responses to their lost hopes. Certain characters, especially the street prostitute, show an awareness of what has been lost. W. steers away from the political implications of their plight, however, a tendency that repeats Saroyan and Eugene O'NEILL in *The Iceman Cometh.*

The Mound Builders presents a Midwest locale where two archaeologists and their wives live in a farmhouse, itself now an artifact of nostalgic reflection on America's idyllic past. Structurally the play follows a pattern of parallel-and-contrast between the emptiness of the archaeologists' lives and the vanished society of their dig. During the periodic flashback scenes, photographic slides are projected by August, the senior archaeologist, which show alternately the significant people in his life with short of the decaying glory in the dig site. The wit of the characters, their self-deprecating commentary and ironic perceptions of the futility of civilization's attempts at meaning, accounts for the play's dark humor, and reflects W.'s unique development of Ionesco's themes.

The first of a planned five-play cycle set in Missouri, *Talley's Folly* begins the history of the Talley family from the Civil War to the present. The play demands an unusual narrative device—the main character both opens and closes the stage action with a soliloquy. Requiring only two characters, one setting, and a very restricted time frame—the ninety-six-minute running time of the performance—the plot focuses on the characters' responses to their longstanding relationship. Sally Talley, a member of an old and respected Missouri family, rejects the love promises of Matt, a Jewish American, until she perceives his sincerity. *War in Lebanon* (1980) and *Talley and Son* (1986) became the second and third plays of the Talley cycle.

Burn This (1987) continues W.'s interest in the acerbic chemistry of a romantic odd couple. Anna and Pale are immediately drawn to one another when they meet unexpectedly in Anna's downtown Manhattan loft. They soon digress, however, into frenetic musings brought on by the perplexities of their modern lifestyles and their complicated psychologies. In *Moonshot and Cosmos* (1994), two one-act monologues, W. presents the anguish of an AIDS griever and an adult who was incested as a child. This thematic change may presage a new direction for W.'s drama, one more responsive to social and political issues. W. remains an important force in contemporary American theater, his innovative dialogue, for instance, has clearly influenced David MAMET and other accomplished playwrights, and his choice of Midwestern setting had helped broaden American theater.

BIBLIOGRAPHY: Barnett, G. A., *L. W.* (1987); Dean, A., *Discovery and Invention: The Urban Plays of L. W.* (1994); Williams, P. M., *A Comfortable House* (1993)

                                                    WILLIAM OVER

WILSON, Margaret [Wilhelmina]

b. 16 January 1882, Traer, Iowa; d. 6 October 1973, Droitwich, England

As a Midwestern farmer's daughter turned world traveler, W. enjoyed a unique opportunity to study radically contrasting cultures. She became particularly interested in the shaping influences of religious and legal institutions in the various cultures she observed; she was fascinated by those who presume to stand in for their chosen God as administrators of earthly justice. Her strictly Protestant upbringing, which eventually led her to pursue graduate studies in divinity, did not limit her appreciation of other forms of religious worship nor of the wonders of sexual and romantic passion, whether she was describing the bleak lives of 19th-c. Iowa farmers or the shockingly exotic beauties and tragedies of life in northern India's Punjab region, where she worked as a teacher, medical assistant, and

Presbyterian missionary from 1904 to 1916. She records her trenchant observations with elements of REALISM and NATURALISM that have prompted comparisons with her Midwestern contemporary Theodore DREISER; her characters, however, are more resilient than Dreiser's and more likely to find occasions to celebrate the worlds into which they are born. Her early experiences enriched her later work when, after a midlife marriage to British penal administrator George Douglas Turner, she turned her sociologist's eye on the separate country formed by prisoners and those charged with their punishment and rehabilitation.

She sets her earlier works in the financially and spiritually straitened Scottish Presbyterian community of her own youth. Her most well-received novel *The Able McLaughlins* (1923) presents an unblinking view of the human, and specifically the Presbyterian, desire for vengeance; her main characters, however, are redeemed by their own inherent charity. The novel won the Harper Prize in 1923 and the Pulitzer Prize in 1924. In *The Able McLaughlins, The Kenworthys* (1925), and *The Painted Room* (1926)—the three novels that constitute her American phase—W. examines the role of religion and the human judiciary in shaping the politics of domestic life. While religion is her chief concern, her choice of the domestic mise-en-scène as the site for examining the interactions of divine providence and human legislation makes her work interesting for feminist scholars. W.'s heroines in these works are invariably trapped by their marital standing, and their futures are shaped by the fact or fear of pregnancy.

These same concerns inform the novels of her Indian phase: *Daughters of India* (1928) focuses on the difficulties Indian women face in a polygamous society; *Trousers of Taffeta* (1929) further details the trials women face in a male-dominated culture where women must produce male heirs to prove their own value as members of polygamous households. While working in India, W. wrote to her college friends that she had never been happier, but that she was also witnessing things "so terrible that she would not write home about them." Between her retirement as a missionary in 1916 and her work on *Daughters of India* twelve years later, W. managed to transform her more painful Indian experiences into deeply sympathetic and engaging fiction.

W. began the third phase of her writing career with a nonfiction work, *The Crime of Punishment* (1931), criticizing the harshness of the American penal system. She continued exploring this subject in her next two novels, *The Dark Duty* (1931) and *The Valiant Wife* (1933), melodramatic romances that she constructed around the philosophical and dramatic problems of prison administration and reform. Her final major

work, *The Law and the McLaughlins* (1936), returns to her first subject, religion and frontier justice in 19th-c. Midwestern America. While Wully McLaughlin and his fellow townsmen, resurrected from W.'s first novel, wrestle with the problem of punishing vigilantes involved in a lynching, Wully's sister Jean develops a revolutionary female voice in protesting the severity of the men's judgement.

W.'s novels have been disparaged for a variety of weaknesses: some are too disjointedly episodic for some critics, while others provide inadequate psychological motivation for the characters' actions and choices, and almost all her plots rely too heavily on coincidence. Her sharp sociological observations provide valuable insight for students of cultural history, however; in addition, her strengths as a novelist are evident in the detailed, naturalistic portraits of the daily lives of her characters, and in her inability to involve the reader in the problems her characters face.

BIBLIOGRAPHY: Marathe, S., "M. W.: Introduction to a Worthwhile Witness to Indian History," *LCrit* 22 (1987): 32–40; Wilkie, E. C., Jr., "M. W.," in Martine, J. J., ed., *DLB,* vol. 9, part 3, *American Novelists, 1910–1945* (1981): 159–66

GWEN CRANE

WINTERS, [Arthur] Yvor
b. 17 October 1900, Chicago, Illinois; d. 25 January 1968, Los Altos, California

W. was a contemporary of the New Critics, the American formalists who dominated the academic study of literature in the middle of the 20th c. As long as the New Criticism held sway, W. maintained a position as a provocative and significant outsider. As the direct influence of the New Critics has faded, W.'s position has become ever more marginal, and it is not clear that readers of the 21st c. will find W.'s criticism relevant to their concerns. His poetry, some of it very fine, has never quite been in fashion, and there is no strong reason to expect this to change. He is, in short, a writer whose time may have passed; however, that is not to say he is not worth knowing.

Initially a modernist in his poetic practice, W. in his maturity rejected MODERNISM in favor of a measured classicism characterized by moral reflection and plainness of style. This shift had already occurred by the time he began to write the literary criticism on which his reputation has primarily been based. Although W. shared with the New Critics a distrust of ROMANTICISM and an emphasis on close reading, his distrust of romanticism went further and deeper than theirs, and for him close reading must lead to evaluation, the essential act of criticism. This evaluation, moreover, was in his view moral. Poetry, he notoriously asserted, is a statement in words about a human experience. Its function, the judgment of experience, is a moral function, while the formal resources of poetry permit a precision of judgment transcending the limits of prose.

For over three decades, W. never deviated from the critical principles he had most emphatically stated. His critical project was the justification of those principles and their application to American, English, and, to a lesser degree, French literature. If the application of these principles led to a devaluation of many admired writers of these traditions and to what might strike unsympathetic readers as an eccentric and not always clearly justified enthusiasm for neglected and forgotten poets, those are consequences W. was more than willing to accept. He may forever be remembered as the critic who, having dismissed the likes of Wordsworth, Keats, and Yeats, declared Elizabeth Daryush the greatest English poet since T. Sturge Moore.

W.'s first three books of literary criticism focus on American literature. *Primitivism and Decadence* (1937) defines some of the critical concepts that fundamentally shape W.'s thought. *Maule's Curse* (1938) examines major writers of the American tradition from James Fenimore COOPER through Henry JAMES in the light of W.'s antiromantic attitudes. He can find, for instance, virtually nothing to admire in Ralph Waldo EMERSON, Edgar Allan POE, or Walt WHITMAN, while the poetry of Jones VERY wins at least his partial approval. In fact, no poet ever wins more than partial approval from W. Even Emily DICKINSON, whom he regards as one of the greatest of all lyric poets, managed, according to W., only a handful of successful poems among the more than 1,775 she produced. *The Anatomy of Nonsense* (1943) is a critique both of contemporary American poetry and of the inadequate ideas informing that poetry. The three books were collected as *In Defense of Reason* in 1947.

W. was terminally ill as he worked on his last major book of criticism, *Forms of Discovery* (1967). (He was survived for thirty years by his wife, the poet Janet Lewis.) The book seems at times a compendium of opinions, more or less supported by reasons that may not seem like very good reasons to readers who have not fully accepted W.'s critical principles. It disappointed even many of W.'s admirers. W. was a critic for whom evaluation was everything, but his judgments, when they deviate from the norm, have proven largely unpersuasive to the literary-critical community. Had W. succeeded in his critical project, he would have established an alternative canon of poetry in English. At the end of the 20th c., the very concept of a canon is under attack, and the practice of critical evaluation is called into question. Still, some sort of

canon will survive, and outside the academy people have never lost the habit of evaluating what they read. As long as this is true, a rediscovery of W. remains a possibility. Surely, there will always be readers ready to appreciate the thorny pleasures afforded by this uncompromising literary maverick.

BIBLIOGRAPHY: Hyman, S. E., *The Armed Vision* (1948); Isaacs, E., *An Introduction to the Poetry of Y. W.* (1981); Parkinson, T., *Hart Crane and Y. W.: Their Literary Correspondence* (1978); Powell, G., *Language as Being in the Poetry of Y. W.* (1980); Stanford, D., *Revolution and Convention in Modern Poetry* (1983)

W. P. KENNEY

WINTHROP, John

b. 22 January 1588, near Groton, Suffolk, England;
d. 26 March 1649, Boston, Massachusetts

As first governor of Boston, W. recorded the political and social history of the Massachusetts Bay Colony from its inception in 1630 until his death in 1649. Because he served as elected governor for twelve of his nineteen years in New England and because of the public-record nature of much of his writing, his biography is, to a large extent, New England's history. His journal history of New England is one of America's first histories, and much subsequent scholarship depends on his accounts. W.'s political and ethical savvy enabled the colony to survive the difficult years of its infancy; his vision of a city on a hill as a model Christian commonwealth established a motif that has sparked the American literary imagination for over three centuries.

In 1606 as heir to the Groton Manor estate in Suffolk County, England, as a devout Puritan, and as a husband and new father, W. started a private journal of his spiritual life, *Experiencia* (1864), a journal he kept for some twenty-five years. Like other such diaries of the period, it provides a record of the diarist's personal experiences with faith and his struggles with worldly vanity, a theme that runs throughout. The account also includes an informative and moving narration of the deathbed trials of his second wife, Thomasine, in 1616.

In the late 1620s, W.'s preparations for his migration to the New World left him little time to record his personal experiences. He prepared several drafts and versions of "Arguments for the Plantation of New England" (1629). In his "Arguments," he presents the reasons for settling, answers objections against the settling, and gives reasons justifying the undertaking. Among the many reasons for a Puritan's leaving England, W. discusses corruptions of the church, failure of education, and economic difficulties. Reasons for going to New England include the bounty of animals and plants and the opportunity for the propagation of the gospel to the Indians. W. also provides several personal reasons for his own decision to settle in New England, including the company's dependence on him, his own shortened means, and his desire to do God's will to the best of his ability.

In October 1629, W. was elected governor of the Massachusetts Bay Company and by the following spring he and his constituency were ready to sail. While in port aboard the *Arbella,* W. and several others prepared *The Humble Request* (1630), a document insisting that the departure did not signify a separation from the Church of England. These men, women, and children were leaving England out of love not hatred or bitterness. The *Request* asks those remaining in England to pray for and remember their brothers and sisters across the ocean and to help promote the project.

At sea, W. evidently delivered a sermon in which he outlines the ideals behind the Puritan exodus. This lay-sermon, *A Modell of Christian Charity* (1630), argues that God made rich and poor so that every man would have need of the other, and hence all must work together in a Christian enterprise. W.'s literary figure is that love serves as tendons binding all Christians together. Thus knit into a single body, each part must help the other and thereby help itself. According to W., the colonists were to found "a City upon a Hill," and the eyes of all the world would be upon them. The image has doubtless become an integral part of the American conception of itself as model for and leader of the rest of the world.

Before actually setting sail for the New World, W. began his journal history of New England. Although not published in his lifetime, much of W.'s journal is written as a public record and was first published as *A Journal of the Transactions and Occurrences in the Settlement of Massachusetts and the Other New-England Colonies, from the Year 1630 to 1644* (1790). James Savage later edited a more complete version in two volumes, entitled *The History of New England from 1630 to 1649* (2 vols., 1825, 1826). W. begins his journal with a daily account of the Atlantic crossing, certainly a record he hoped to share with future emigrants. Once W. is established in Massachusetts, he narrates the story of the governing of the infant colony. He describes his political disagreements with Thomas Dudley, the assistant governor, who accuses him of being too lenient with transgressors and of taking too much power for himself. W. also records the colony's fears of and confrontations with the Indians, and its encounters with the potentially dangerous French set-

tlers and sailors to the north. He conscientiously records the patriarchy's struggles to maintain a religiously and politically homogenous group. The journal provides first-hand accounts of his own and the colony's responses to Roger WILLIAMS, Anne Hutchinson, Robert Childs, and Samuel Gorton. Although rarely commenting on daily, mundane events, W. does often mention the severity of the New England weather. He also frequently sets down the colony's experiences with the many providences of God. Storms, accidents, and battles between a snake and a mouse all portend God's favor or disfavor concerning the New England colonies. One important theme running throughout the journal is its author's insistence that regardless of the tribulations the colony undergoes—whether they be internal or international, due to weather or Indian uprising—the text persistently asserts that the city on a hill will overcome all adversity. Each potentially cataclysmic threat is introduced, subdued, and disposed of. Even though Satan is always at work to undermine it, the commonwealth survives.

At times, W. must have considered Roger Williams such a threat. Probably in response to Williams's separatist notions and his refusal to join the congregation at Boston, W. wrote *Reasons to prove a necessitye of reformation from the Corruptions of Antechrist which hath defiled the Christian Churches, and yet without an absolute separation from them . . .* (1631). The tract, usually referred to as "Reformation without Separation," exists only as a fragment, but the surviving text demonstrates that W. saw the churches in England as corrupt but argued nevertheless that because their actual being was not corrupt, the Church of England could be purified from within. W.'s unwritten assumption seems to be that such a purification is the task of the New England Puritans.

Besides the schism threatened by Williams, one of the establishment's greater trials was the threat of civil war caused by the Antinomian controversy. In 1638, W. sat as prosecutor and judge to condemn the Antinomian's spokesperson, Anne Hutchinson, for disrupting the commonwealth and for seditious contempt. First published in London as *Antinomians and Familists condemned by the synod of elders in New-England* (1644), his account is better known by its title in two subsequent editions of the same year, *A Short Story of the Rise, reign, and ruine of the Antinomians, Familists and Libertines.* This document provides the actual courtroom dialogue and W.'s account of Hutchinson's demise. It includes several sections obviously not written by the governor, but W.'s account does provide invaluable firsthand knowledge of the controversy. W. dutifully recounted the proceedings against several of the sectarians, Hutchinson's supporters. The account is one of only two surviving accounts of Hutchinson's actual testimony. The "Short Story" also shows us that W. was to some degree a victim of the biases of his day in that his response to Hutchinson is undoubtedly due partly to his and his age's sexist and intolerant views. In his defense, one can only argue that W. acted in what he felt was the colony's best interest.

In addition to *The Short Story,* the Antinomian Controversy gave rise to W.'s carrying on an early American version of a pamphlet debate, a debate that consisted of the exchange of letters between W. and Henry Vane, a disciple of Hutchinson and one-time governor of the colony. W. defends the court's order to control emigration into the Bay's jurisdiction. In *A Declaration of the Intent and Equitye of the Order made at the last Court* (May 1637) and a subsequent *A Reply to an Answer made to a Declaration . . .* (August 1637), essentially a "Defense of an Order of Court," W. argues that the commonwealth is founded by the free consent of the people and therefore no one may inhabit without their consent. By modern standards, the argument is forthrightly conservative and authoritarian in that it defends the magistrate's right to deny the emigrant the option of settling within the colony's jurisdiction.

The controversy over Anne Hutchinson's promulgation of direct revelation and her doctrine of free grace may also have prompted W. to reexamine and reaffirm the legitimacy of his own conversion experience. W.'s conversion narrative *Christian Experience* (1637) comes across as a traditional, formulaic, public account of a Puritan's progress through the steps of discovering his own saving faith. Recounting the conversion experience was a requisite part of one's becoming a member of the church in New England, and W. accepted the established morphology of conversion. The convert recounts his trials and doubts, his sicknesses and backslidings; he vacillates between conviction and repentance as he passes through the stages from Calivinistic helplessness to assurance in finally closing with Christ.

Besides important religious and civil matters, the Puritan Governor faced the perils of living among the Native Americans. Although conversion of the Indians was early considered a reason for migration, in reality an exchange of arms was much more likely than theological or intellectual exchange. In response to continual troubles with a tribe of Rhode Island Indians, W. wrote a tract to explain the history and current state of the colonists' relation with them: *Declaration of Former Passages and Proceedings Betwixt the English and the Narrowgansets* (1645). In essence the *Declaration* is a justification of the colonists' actions against the Indians and a threat or warning that military action needs to be taken against the Native Americans in certain instances.

In an attempt to retain power and control in governing effectively, W. introduced a law that guaranteed the power of the magistracy. He devised a policy that essentially divided the political body of magistrates and assistants into two houses, insuring that the larger assembly of assistants could not out vote the magistrates simply by virtue of their majority. In a popular court battle over the rightful ownership of a pig, W. defended his conception of negative vote, or power to veto by writing *A Reply to the Answ[er] made to the Discourse about the Neg[ative] vote* (1643). Ironically, this beginning of the bicameral government in the U.S. began as a means to prevent the government from becoming one in which one man had one vote, a "mere democracy," an institution 17th-c. politicians deplored.

In *Arbitrary Government described and the Common mistakes about the same . . . fully cleared* (1644), W. argues that if governors and other magistrates are chosen by the people, the people cannot accuse them of implementing and practicing an arbitrary government. Once elected, officials have absolute power; according to W. in fact, "Judges are Gods upon earth." W.'s statement doubtless indicates his tendency toward theocracy, but it also evidences his faith in himself and other qualified magistrates. As this document makes manifest, W. firmly believed that any judge is absolutely committed to good and has the welfare of the people at heart. Self-interest and corruption do not play a part, and judges will act on good faith, holding forth the wisdom and mercy of God.

Because a group of townspeople from Hingham accused him of overstepping his authority in appointing a militia captain, W. at one point actually had to defend himself before the court. After being cleared of the accusation, W. presented what has become his famous "Little Speech on Liberty" (1645). In the speech, he reiterates his belief that once the people have elected a magistrate they must abide by his decisions; after all, argues W., not only will he judge according to the best of his ability, but he has his authority from God. In this speech, W. also distinguishes between natural and moral liberty. By natural liberty man is free to do as he wishes, but such liberty is incompatible with authority. Through moral liberty, Christians' freedom consists of their enjoying and being satisfied with those liberties God allows. In this sense, W. voices the opinion of the establishment, and the document serves as an indication of the Puritan community's temper and attitude.

W.'s writings are full of the tribulations resulting from the creations and perpetuation of a holy commonwealth, much like the actual life of the governor and the history of the New England colony itself. As evidenced by his written records of the era, surviving and maintaining control was a constant struggle for all members of the community and especially for the one who was elected time and time again to govern, guide, and lead the colonists. Not only was W. the most important early governor of the Massachusetts Bay Colony, but as his journal history, his political writings, and his lay-sermon attest, he is also without a doubt one of the most important colonial writers.

BIBLIOGRAPHY: Dunn, R. S., *Puritans and Yankees: The Winthrop Dynasty of New England* (1962); Dunn, R. S., ed., *The Journal of J. W.* (1996); Hall, D. D., *The Antinomian Controversy* (1968); Mayo, L. S., *The Winthrop Family in America* (1948); Morgan, E. S., *The Puritan Dilemma: The Story of J. W.* (1958); Moseley, J., *J. W.'s World* (1992); Rutman, D. B., *J. W.'s Decision for America* (1975); Schweninger, L., *J. W.* (1990); Winthrop, R. C., *The Life and Letters of J. W.* (2 vols., 1869)

LEE SCHWENINGER

WISTER, Owen

b. 14 July 1860, Philadelphia, Pennsylvania; d. 21 July 1938, near Kingstown, Rhode Island

Although he produced a considerable body of distinguished fiction about the American West, as well as important critical and social commentary, W. is remembered almost exclusively as the author of the 1902 best-seller *The Virginian,* a novel often credited, not inaccurately, with the invention of the WESTERN as an American literary genre. Ironically, this Philadelphia aristocrat, cultivated aesthete, and reactionary critic of democracy and egalitarianism gave America its greatest hero of popular culture—the cowboy.

The Virginian, and W.'s other Western fiction—four short-story collections and another novel, *Lin McLean* (1898)—grew out of a series of trips the Harvard-educated W. made to Wyoming, Washington territory, and Arizona in the 1880s and 1890s, first for his health, then out of a growing fascination with the idea of the West as "the last fair field on which chivalry could have a chance." In 1892, he began writing local color stories for *Harper's* magazine about cowboys within their rough frontier world, stories designed, in his words, to make him "a sagebrush Kipling."

The strength of his stories stems from an effective establishment of character, an eye for social nuance, and a deep sensitivity to both the beauty and the brutality of the raw Western landscape. He sketched a full stable of Western "characters," both comic and dramatic, who form a skillfully-drawn gallery in the local color "character" tradition of Washington IRVING's Ichabod Crane, Mark TWAIN's duke and king, and the

tales of George Washington CABLE, Bret HARTE, Sarah Orne JEWETT, and Harriet Beecher STOWE.

Independently wealthy through his *grande dame* mother, Sarah Butler Wister, who was a close friend of Henry JAMES and a writer herself, W. could afford to work slowly. He was past forty when he began work on *The Virginian* and had a national reputation for his Western stories, but he was hardly a household name. *The Virginian* abruptly made him famous, since for two consecutive years, 1902 to 1903, it was the best-selling book in America. More important, it was the first real Western novel, in the sense that that word has come to define a major genre of popular literature and art. Many of the characteristics of the type as *The Virginian* established then have become clichés: the stolid, laconic code hero, the smarmy saddle-tramp villain, the civilizing school marm heroine, the Eastern greenhorn being initiated into rough Western ways, the walked-off gun duel while the town holds its breath. One of the Virginian's lines—"Smile when you call me that"—became the most famous in Western literature, and the novel has been continuously in print.

Modern readers of *The Virginian* may wonder what all the fuss was about. Three essentially unrelated subplots thread raggedly through the novel. The dominant one concerns the first-person reminiscences of an Eastern tyro learning the ways of the 1880s Wyoming cattle country from an admirable, seasoned cowboy—the nameless "Virginian." Secondly, a sentimental battle-of-the-sexes courtship between the hero and an Eastern schoolmarm-come-West justifies W.'s original subtitle, "A Romance of the Plains." Finally, a subordinated subplot sketches the rivalry between the hero and a devious, eventually criminal, cowboy named Trampas, culminating in the classic gunfight.

Surprisingly, *The Virginian* concentrates less on action than on local color studies of Western society and sketches of Western "characters," the hero included. Disturbing to some early readers was the implicit justification of violence—the hero leads one lynching of rustler, turns down the school marm's pleas to avoid the gunfight—and to a very few the novel's unabashed elitism—"All America is divided into two classes,—the quality and the equality. . . . It was through the Declaration of Independence that we Americans acknowledged the *eternal inequality* of man."

W. lived for twenty-five years after the success of *The Virginian,* but never wrote another Western novel. His short stories in the genre, collected in *Members of the Family* (1911) and *When West Was West* (1928), were increasingly elegiac and bitter, and presented the "modern" West after the turn of the century as a ruined land of lost content, overrun by deceitful riffraff. The true and honorable cowboys of the Virginian's stripe have vanished, and barfly, salesmen, moralistic hypocrites, and opportunists flourish.

W.'s main efforts in the last quarter century of his life consisted of extended essays on the decline of morals, world politics, and the depressing panorama of history Jeremiads intoning, "Turn back, O Man." Late in life, he produced a distinguished memoir of his friend, Theodore ROOSEVELT, *Roosevelt: The Story of a Friendship* (1930) and conservative political and historical essays. He did not return to the West, either in his travels or his writings.

BIBLIOGRAPHY: Cobbs, J. L., *O. W., Chronicler of the West, Gentleman of the East* (1984); Payne, D., *O. W.* (1985); Vorpahl, B. M., *My Dear W.* (1972)

JACK COBBS

WOIWODE, Larry [Alfred]
b. 30 October 1941, Carrington, North Dakota

With the publication of his first novel, *What I'm Going to Do, I Think* (1969)—the story of a newly married, perhaps mismatched couple dealing with an unwanted pregnancy—several reviewers hailed W. as a new Ernest HEMINGWAY. Few authors have received such immediate and remarkable acclaim. He was compared to F. Scott FITZGERALD and D. H. Lawrence for his stylistic precision and ability to evoke emotion through careful observation and sensual rendering of place. Chris, the brooding, self-absorbed protagonist, caused some controversy among critics. Some found him unsympathetic and the novel flawed, while others saw him as embodying the characteristics of a restless, Vietnam War–era generation. Most, however, agreed that this debut novel marked the arrival of major literary talent.

W.'s second novel, *Beyond the Bedroom Wall* (1975), won the author further praise and honors for its serious theme and sophisticated execution. It takes the form of a traditional family chronicle with its large cast of characters and carefully reported details—a form long out of fashion, but in this case quite modern as W. takes liberty with time, place, and point of view. The discontinuity—explained in part by the fact that much of the novel was adapted from previously published short stories—contributes to the overall montage effect; the novel centers on the deaths of four characters in the Neumiller family and tracks the survivors' emotional and psychological responses. Michael E. Connaughton writes that W.'s purpose is "to create a unified family history out of individual, but not isolated, perceptions." The novel's dreamlike, Proustian quality underscores the central concern: human perception and consciousness. Characters are

often found at the twilight of sleep half remembering events, blurring the line between dream and reality.

A conversion to evangelical Christianity in the late 1970s influenced W.'s later works. *Poppa John* (1981) tells the story of an elderly soap opera actor whose Bible-quoting on screen persona—one created out of the actor's own experience—is slowly dying. The actor becomes obsessed with his own mortality and eventually experiences a nervous collapse and subsequent religious conversion. *Born Brothers* (1988), a continuation of the Neumiller family saga, follows the two oldest sons from boyhood to their adult careers, exploring, among other things, the issue of redemption. Critics praised the author's lyricism and sensitive portrayal of childhood. W. envisions *Beyond the Bedroom Wall* and *Born Brothers* as parts of a five-book series.

Published in 1993, *Acts: A Writer's Reflections on the Church, Writing, and His Own Life,* is a collection of meditative essays on the New Testament gospel that further asserts W.'s faith in orthodox Christianity. In that same year, W. released *Silent Passengers,* a collection of short stories.

The award-winning novelist has been translated into eight foreign languages, yet has remained outside the mainstream of American writers. He is widely regarded as a serious thinker, skilled storyteller, and immaculate writer whose best work may yet lie ahead.

BIBLIOGRAPHY: Connaughton, M. E., "L. W.," in Kibler, J. E., Jr., ed., *DLB,* vol. 6, *American Novelists since World War II* (1980): 387–91

JASON MCMAHON

WOLFE, Thomas
b. 3 October 1900, Asheville, North Carolina; d. 15 September 1938, Baltimore, Maryland

William FAULKNER's judgment that W. stood ahead of Ernest HEMINGWAY, John STEINBECK, F. Scott FITZGERALD, and even himself rested more on W.'s potential for greatness and boldness of reach than on achievement. That boldness led W. to attempt to capture the energy, look, shape, sound, and deeds of America, to dream of donning the mantle of Walt WHITMAN and becoming a singer and seer, to aspire to do more than Sinclair LEWIS, H. L. MENCKEN, or Sherwood ANDERSON to set forth the failures and foibles of the American character, to work tirelessly to find ways to understand the loneliness, restlessness, and spiritual emptiness that he discovered in American life, and to record, in both mythic and realistic terms, the struggle of an American artist to realize his power and place in American society. That was a huge order, to be sure, one destined to fall short of fulfillment, not only because of W.'s untimely death caused by tubercular meningitis but also because his Faustian ambitions outstripped his literary grasp.

Lofty as his boldness was and as grand as his potential seemed, his place now rests most securely on a few masterful short stories—"An Angel on the Porch," "The Child by Tiger," "The Lost Boy," "Only the Dead Know Brooklyn," and "Chickamauga"; five superb short novels—*A Portrait of Bascom Hawke* (1932), *The Web of Earth* (1932), *No Door* (1933), *I Have a Thing to Tell You* (1937), and *The Party at Jack's* (1939); and *Look Homeward, Angel* (1929), the only novel largely shaped to W.'s desires and design, the others bearing the imprint of his editors Maxwell Perkins and Edward C. Aswell. Much of what remains forms, published and unpublished, a vast collection of gems and junk, or to be kinder, huge chunks of raw material that awaited a transmutation into something resembling his work at his best. Since W. did not live to transmute those chunks, Aswell partially undertook the job. His efforts to make something of what he came to call the "mess" that W. left behind at his death created a legacy of uncertainty about who wrote what and charges of editorial interference. The outcome for W.'s reputation has left a cloud, one that is being partly removed by the republishing of his work according to modern editorial standards and by such studies as those of Leslie Field, whose *T. W. and His Editors* (1987) examines Aswell's methods of assembling W.'s posthumous novels, *The Web and the Rock* (1939) and *You Can't Go Home Again* (1940).

Editorial problems and failed ambitions aside, W.'s contributions to American letters remains important. That importance does not stem from his work in drama, his earliest love and the art form he studied under master teacher George Pierce Baker at Harvard University, nor from the range and depth of his thought but from his success in adopting the notions of English romantic poets, Walt Whitman, and James Joyce to the uses of autobiographical fiction in America and from his achievement as a writer of novellas. His autobiographical fiction proved an inspiring and liberating model for many American novelist—Jack KEROUAC, James JONES, David Madden, James DICKEY, and Barry Hannah, to name some of the best to acknowledge his presence and force. Even though many of these novelists rejected the sprawl and rhetorical excesses of W.'s writing, they shared with him the belief that the best writing had its roots in the experiences and the emotional, psychic, and intellectual development of the author. W. showed them how to treat their lives and thoughts as either representing or mirroring the American experience.

His truthfulness to the American experience has been much more highly regarded by fellow writers than by the literary establishment in America, which scorns W.'s fiction as formless, undisciplined, and jejune, fit to be read only by youthful readers intent upon wallowing sensuously in W.'s vivid depictions of the sights, sounds, smells, tastes, and textures of American life. For sophisticated readers, the Hegelian cast of mind, his reveling in emotions, his inability to function as an editor of his own work, his failure to control or exorcise his social, cultural, and racial prejudice, and his blend of Southern conservatism and populism with reformatory doctrines of the New Deal all combine to create an almost indelible impression of an eternally sophomoric writer whose lyricism often catches some of the magic and beauty of life but whose murky adjective-and adverb-laden prose proves little better than Southern political poppycock. Heading the list of critics who see no literary value at all in W. is Harold BLOOM, but even for an academician, Bloom's view is extreme.

Now that the kicking season is drawing to a close and W. is being considered among his contemporaries in the Southern Renaissance, the Lost Generation, and the schools of naturalistic or satiric writing led by Theodore DREISER and Sinclair Lewis, W. can be more fairly judged, a process pushed ahead rapidly by the distinguished historian of American culture David Herbert Donald, whose biography of W., *Look Homeward,* convincingly shows how well W. reflects and understands the forces driving American culture during the first third of the 20th c. W.'s reflectors are his fictional surrogates, Eugene Gant and George Webber, and hundreds of men and women from many walks of American life that they both encounter. In a metaphorical sense, they are like clods dropped in a pond, and, like Blakean clods, they are capable of growth, George ultimately more so than Eugene, for George, the center of consciousness in *The Web and the Rock* and *You Can't Go Home Again,* is a more attentive observer and reflective thinker than Eugene. Eugene's problem is that he is a version of a Byronic and Joycean aesthete with traits drawn from village rebels created by Sherwood Anderson and Sinclair Lewis. At least, that is how he came out in *Of Time and the River* (1935), largely because Perkins prevailed upon W. not to introduce revolutionary political leanings, arguing the Eugene as depicted in that novel had yet to reach W.'s stage of political consciousness, which deepened and widened rapidly when W. moved to Brooklyn and became aware of the degree of deprivation and despair among its hungry, jobless, and dispirited masses.

As the son of a middle-class stonecutter and enterprising mother who earned money from her boarding house—called Dixieland in *Look Homeward, Angel*—and wheeling and dealing in real estate in Asheville, North Carolina, W. had enjoyed the advantages of a good education, capped by his studies at Harvard and travels in Europe. He was also helped financially, emotionally, and artistically also by Aline Bernstein, a stage and dress designer from New York who became his mentor, muse, and mistress. Along with members of his family and teachers back in North Carolina and his teachers and fellow aspiring dramatists at Harvard, she would become one of W.'s characters, admired for her charm, wit, creative way with food, beauty, and tales of New York City in her childhood, berated for her association with theatrical people and Jewish blood, and rejected, finally, because her love seemed too possessive and her privileged circle of friends too corrupt and too callous towards the suffering of America's depression-battered middle and lower classes. Intent upon ameliorating the lot of dispossessed, exploited, and weary workers, W. also spoke fervently against the resignation and conservatism of Perkins, depicted as Foxhall Edwards in *You Can't Go Home Again*. W. now wanted to speak as the champion of the family of man, whether the oppression occurred in Nazi Germany or in the slums of Brooklyn or Manhattan.

W. had not always taken the wealth of the privileged or the miseries of the poor as his themes. Instead, he chose to explore the dynamics of family life, the frustrations of a misunderstood and undervalued would-be artist, the greed, boosterism, and provincialism of small-town America, the forces in education awakening or deadening the minds of students, the causes of rootlessness and wandering in America, and the responses of family members to the death of two sons and a father. These are major themes in his first two novels, the Gant cycle, and several of them reappear in the posthumous novels, the Webber cycle. They afforded him the opportunity to draw a lyrical, realistic, satiric, nostalgic, elegiac, pessimistic, and optimistic portrait of America. Even as he was writing about the worst moments of the depressed 1930s, he was able to proclaim, in words still quoted by Republicans and Democrats alike, "I think the true discovery of America is before us. I think the true fulfillment of our spirit, of our people, of our mighty and immortal land, is yet to come."

To capture the essence of the "mighty and immortal land" was his highest hope, his fondest dream. And to that grand task, he brought boundless energy, great love for the shape, scope, and sweep of America, and the drive to get it all down, to make it all vivid, real, memorable, to catch it before time and change ravished it. And to it, he brought a tormented, troubled, distrustful, truculent, memory-haunted spirit, one easily inflamed to wrath when he chose to settle scores, one blind to the merits and concerns of those whom he prejudged. Thus, readers must be prepared to fly to the heights of angels and sink to the vulgarity of fish-

wives in W.'s fiction. For his is indeed a world of opposites, a Hegelian tug of war looking for a synthesis, a manic-depressive realm filled with weal and woe. Despite the canard that W. is best left to callow youth, his fiction demands readers with guts and spirits strong enough to examine his vision of "America the Ugly" alongside "America the Beautiful."

BIBLIOGRAPHY: Bassett, J. E., *T. W.: An Annotated Bibliography* (1996); Donald, D. H., *Look Homeward* (1987); Gurko, L., *T. W.: Beyond the Romantic Ego* (1975); Holman, C. H., *The Loneliness at the Core* (1975); Idol, J. L., *A T. W. Companion* (1987); Johnson, P. H., *Hungry Gulliver: An English Critical Appraisal of T. W.* (1948); Johnston, C., *Of Time and the Artist: T. W., His Novels, and the Critics* (1996); Kennedy, R. S., *The Window of Memory: The Literary Career of T. W.* (1962); Muller, H. J., *T. W.* (1947); Reeves, P., *T. W.'s Albatross: Race and Nationality in America* (1968); Rubin, L. D., *T. W.: The Weather of His Youth* (1955); Walser, R. *T. W.: Undergraduate* (1977); Watkins, F., *T. W.'s Characters: Portraits from Life* (1957)

JOHN L. IDOL, JR.

WOLFE, Tom [Thomas Kennerly, Jr.]

b. 2 March 1931, Richmond, Virginia

As one of the central figures of the so-called New Journalism of the 1960s and 1970s, W. helped transform American LITERARY JOURNALISM. The prevailing pattern for nonfictional prose was that exemplified by the old *New Yorker:* solid research, spare prose, and an objective stance with the author hardly to be seen. W. kept the solid research, but his prose became exuberant and expressive and his authorial presence was one of the great attractions of his work. In one wildly successful novel and a series of books on subjects ranging from stock car racing to art criticism to the space program, W. has analyzed every level of American culture, from the most popular to the most elitist, and created a prose style that is at once elegant and hip. Many of the phrases that define the last three decades are W.'s, such as "radical chic," "the me decade," and "the right stuff."

W. gained a solid background, both academic and journalistic, before beginning his experimental work. After graduating from Washington and Lee College, where he was a sportswriter for the student newspaper, W. entered the graduate program in American studies at Yale. Having earned his Ph.D. in 1957, W. began work as a reporter, first at the *Springfield* (Massachusetts) *Union* and later at the *Washington Post* and the *New York Herald Tribune*. In 1963, he began publishing the series of essays, collected in *The Kandy-*

Kolored Tangerinc-Flake Streamline Baby (1965), that helped create the New Journalism. Using exuberant punctuation, a stream-of-consciousness style, and phrases drawn from his "pop culture" subjects, W. examined many of the distinctive cultural movements of the 1960s—the title essay, for instance, describes California's custom car enthusiasts.

In his succeeding books, W. continued to apply the techniques taken from the novel to nonfictional prose, justifying his method in the anthology he helped edit entitled *The New Journalism* (1973). The power of W.'s writing, however, springs as much from his selection of subjects as from his style. He made the emerging drug culture vivid in *The Electric Kool-Aid Acid Test* (1968), which recounts the activities of the novelist Ken KESEY and his "Merry Pranksters." The stylistic pyrotechnics captured the "psychedelic" mood of the time, as much as the hallucinatory experience itself. W.'s work has been controversial, for he often attacks the icons of the literary establishment. Two essays on the *New Yorker* in 1965 drew sharp criticism from the magazine's admirers. Still more controversial was W.'s account of the party Leonard Bernstein gave to raise money for the Black Panthers, which appeared in *Radical Chic and Mau-Mauing the Flak Catchers* (1970). W.'s satire of liberal pieties, together with his eye for real markers of social class and his ear for varieties of speech, made the essay at once vivid and, for its subjects, infuriating.

W.'s forays into art criticism have also drawn harsh responses—as well as delighted readers who dislike the dominant trends in modern art. In *The Painted Word* (1975), he argues that modern art is essentially textual—the real focus is not on the visual object, but on the theory that has produced it—and that the "art world" is driven primarily by forces that have little to do with the quality of the art. *From Bauhaus to Our House* (1981) makes a similar point about architecture: the undecorated box of the "International Style" has been built so often because of the dogmas of architects, despite the desires of those who live and work in the buildings.

W.'s most successful work of nonfiction, *The Right Stuff* (1979), tells the story of the Mercury astronauts. While undercutting some of the heroic mythology of the space program, W. also makes the astronauts vivid as characters—and as heroic ones at that. In his portraits of Alan Shepard, John Glenn, and especially of Chuck Yeager, who first broke the sound barrier, W. presents the culture of test pilots, and relates their distinctive world to the larger American culture of the time.

In the 1980s, W. turned from nonfiction to the novel. *The Bonfire of the Vanities* was first serialized in *Rolling Stone* in 1984 and 1985 and then revised before its publication as a book in 1987. The novel draws both on W.'s distinctive style and on his skill in research. In telling the story of a bond trader, Sherman McCoy, who finds himself entangled in the criminal courts, W. depicts several layers of modern American culture—all of them corrupt in one way or another. The novel succeeds both as a narrative and as an exploration of the problems—legal, moral, racial—of modern America. W.'s reputation as a novelist was further cnhanced by the publication in 1998 of the much-anticipated *A Man in Full*.

BIBLIOGRAPHY: Crawford, S., "T. W.: Outlaw Gentleman," *JAC* 12 (Summer 1990): 39–50; Kallan, R., *Style and the New Journalism: A Rhetorical Analysis of T. W.* (1979); McKeen, W., *T. W.* (1995)

BRIAN ABEL RAGEN

WOLFF, Tobias [Jonathan Ansell]
b. 19 June 1945, Birmingham, Alabama

With his spare, meticulously-crafted prose, W. has attained a leading position in contemporary American letters as a short-story writer and memoirist. His work in fiction has earned him the 1985 PEN/Faulkner Award for his novella *The Barracks Thief* (1984), O. Henry short story prizes in 1981, 1982, and 1985, the Rea Award in 1989 for his short story "Our Story Begins," and critical plaudits as a writer's writer of telling but ultimately humanistic stories. His memoirs draw on experiences that also find frequent treatment in his fiction: a drifting childhood with an affectionate mother, her disastrous marriage to a martinet, and unhappy time spent serving in Vietnam. *This Boy's Life* (1989), his artistically-embellished childhood memoir, enjoyed best-seller status and was turned into a Hollywood film in 1993.

W. first came to national attention with *In the Garden of the North American Martyrs* (1981), a collection of twelve stories containing many of the stylistic and thematic elements that characterize the bulk of his work: an economical style, a pervading mood of disappointment that is sometimes relieved by humor or by a character's flash of self-recognition, and a cast of characters who fumble toward connection with others and some tentative moral order, often to be frustrated by their self-deceptions or the indifference of those on whom they depend. In addition to occasional journalism and essays, W. has since brought out two further collections of short fiction, *Back in the World* (1985) and *The Night in Question* (1996); a novella, *The Barracks Thief* (1983); and his two memoirs, *This Boy's Life: A Memoir* (1989) and *In*

Pharaoh's Army (1994), a reminiscence of the Vietnam War.

W.'s books show us snapshots of America from the decidedly "uninnocent" 1950s and early 1960s of the author's youth to the present. We see suburban couples snorting cocaine at birthday parties, a book reviewer who gets himself fatally shot by chortling over the clichés of speech used by a bank robber, two hunters sharing superficial confessions while their wounded companion bleeds and freezes to death in the bed of their pickup truck. His work is occasionally brutal, both its revelation of the seamy sides of character and in the physical violence that flares up in it, but W. is generally sympathetic to the struggles of his characters, to their aspirations, and even to the myopia that is the source of much of the pain he chronicles. Indeed, his concern with the effort to discern and honor personal obligations—finding voice, for example, in the humiliated college professor's public call to decency in "In the Garden of the North American Martyrs"—gives his work a recognizable moral content, and though W. is no writer of simple cautionary tales, we can trace much of the tragedy in his work to the "silence in the face of great wrongs" for which one of his characters condemns modern fiction. The massive national self-deceit resulting in the Vietnam conflict is a reflection of this same theme on a larger scale.

W. has sometimes been placed in the schools of dirty realism or minimalism exemplified by the work of Ann BEATTIE and his friend and mentor, Raymond CARVER, and some critics have complained that W.'s work suffers from the faults of those species: that it is too uniformly bleak and too small, that it focuses with discouraging frequency on minor domestic misfortunes, and that the author leaves his tales unresolved and their point unclear. But the metaphorical depth of W.'s stories, the great range of voices—from hippies to college professors to teenage girls—that he is capable of expressing with absolute conviction, the virtuosity of his style, and the not-to-be-denied fact that his books are often very funny, all rescue him from charges of being merely derivative, and contribute to the prevailing critical appreciation of W. as one of the most significant figures in contemporary American literature.

BIBLIOGRAPHY: Hannah, J., *T. W.: A Study of the Short Fiction* (1996); Lyons, B., "An Interview with T. W.," *ConL* 31(Spring 1990): 1–16

CHRISTOPHER J. DEVLIN

WONG, Jade Snow

b. 21 January 1922, San Francisco, California

W. is one of the earliest writers to address the cultural tension that children of Asian immigrants face growing up in America. Her two autobiographies, *Fifth Chinese Daughter* (1950) and *No Chinese Stranger* (1975), chronicle her struggle to balance Chinese and Western values. These reflections of her bicultural heritage expand the idea of what it means to be American.

W. was the fifth child of seven in a household that adhered strictly to traditional Confucian values. Discipline and an appreciation of Chinese culture were the foundations of her upbringing. As a daughter, W. was expected to obey her parents without question and was not afforded as much freedom as her brothers. Through her exposure to Western culture in her public elementary and high schools, she came to view the limitations placed on her within the family structure as oppressive. The importance of education was instilled by her father, though she was not encouraged to pursue a college degree as her brothers were. She attended the prestigious Mills College for women, supporting her education by seeking out domestic work and scholarships. At Mills, she discovered a love for ceramics and writing.

After W. graduated with a B.A., she started her own ceramics business in San Francisco's Chinatown, which became successful enough to establish her as an autonomous businesswoman. In 1950, she published her autobiography, *Fifth Chinese Daughter,* an account of the "collision of worlds" she faced in creating her identity as a Chinese American woman. Cultural tension is marked by her use of third person to refer to herself in accordance to the Chinese tradition of humility, even though she chose to write an autobiography, a genre that focuses on the individual.

Fifth Chinese Daughter became so popular overseas as well as in the U.S. that it was translated into several languages and prompted an invitation from the U.S. State Department to speak about her experiences on a world tour. Her visit to Asia on this journey provided the basis of her second autobiography, *No Chinese Stranger,* as she reflects on her pleasant surprise at finding herself, an American born Chinese, comfortable among the Chinese people as a result of her father's insistence that she learn Chinese language and culture. In this sequel, she also reexamines her childhood relationship to her father and relates it to her own marriage and family life. A parent herself when she wrote *No Chinese Stranger,* she explores the advantages and drawbacks of having been reared in a strict, Confucian household in America.

Though W. considers herself primarily a ceramic artist, her autobiographies remain significant because they introduced a successful integration of Chinese and Western values. Later writers have criticized her for portraying Chinese males unfairly, and of promoting a need to reject Chinese culture, but many have found in her work inspiration and an early model for the evolution of American cultural identity.

BIBLIOGRAPHY: Ling, A., "J. S. W.," in Davidson, C. N., and L. Wagner-Martin, eds., *The Oxford Companion to Women's Writing in the United States* (1995): 942–43; Yung, J., *Unbound Feet: A Social History of Chinese Women in San Francisco* (1995)

VICTORIA ENG

WONG, Nellie
b. 12 September 1934, Oakland, California

Chinese American poet W. knows that history can be burdensome but also liberating. As chronicled in her two books of poetry, *Dreams in Harrison Railroad Park* (1977) and *The Death of Long Steam Lady* (1984), W.'s artistic, personal, and political development has been grounded in an understanding of her own history and its place in the broader histories of Asian Americans, women, and working people.

That W. is an internationally recognized pioneer of Asian American feminist and political poetics belies her upbringing. The fourth of seven children born to parents who immigrated from China, W. was raised like many women of her generation to marry and have children. Nothing in her early life hinted at the literary and activist impulses she would later channel into creative writing and political action.

Reared in Oakland's Chinatown during the assimilationist post-World War II era when ideals of feminine beauty were exclusively European-based, W. was ashamed she was Chinese American. She believed herself unattractive and unlike the glamorous film stars of the 1950s and 1960s, whom she idolized. Although she wanted to attend college, her parents would not allow her. After graduating from high school, she worked as a secretary, her occupation for almost two decades.

In the early 1970s, at the suggestion of a younger sister, W. took a night school writing class that quite literally changed her life. Through this class, W., for the first time, articulated pent up feelings and stories about her family and youth. With encouragement from her writing instructor, W. enrolled as an undergraduate at San Francisco State University. In her thirties at the time, W. took courses in poetry writing, Asian American studies, and feminist studies, and as she learned about the history of discrimination against women and people of color, she developed deep and lasting identities as a feminist and political radical and began writing poems about her concerns. She acknowledged and wrote about how her previous alienation was rooted in racist and sexist expectations for women.

Her early poems are collected in *Dreams in Harrison Railroad Park,* one of the first published books of poetry by an Asian American woman. Her second book, *The Death of Long Steam Lady,* appeared seven years later. The majority of W.'s poems are intensely personal lyrics written in either her own voice or those of other women. Although some of her poems have set rhythms, most of her works are written in free verse and are filled with vivid images of her life in Chinatown and her experiences as a working-class woman.

Thematically, W. returns to similar issues. She writes often about the struggles and strength of her family and other Asian Americans who confront racism. W. also exposes the sexism Chinese American women confront, both from the mainstream society and the Chinese American community. Although the roles offered women in Chinese culture were limited, W. honors the strength of previous generations of Chinese women through many of her poems.

One of these women was W.'s mother, who is the subject of numerous poems. A strong-willed and dominating figure in the poet's life, W.'s mother was both inspiring and frustrating. Like Maxine Hong KINGSTON, W. chronicles the sometimes antagonistic but ultimately reconciled relationship she forged with her Chinese immigrant mother.

Since her transformation from a secretary into a writer and political activist, W. has been fearless in addressing personally and politically sensitive topics to reveal and ultimately eradicate the oppression based on race, gender, and class that she has endured throughout her life.

STAN YOGI

WOOD, Sally S[ayward] B[arrell] K[eating]
b. 1 October 1759, York, Maine; d. 6 January 1855, Kennebunk, Maine

Maine's first novelist, W., or "Madam Wood" as she was often called, made her mark on American literature as a writer of gothic romances tinged with sentiment and suspense. A contemporary of fellow gothic novelist Charles Brockden BROWN, W. published four of her five works between 1800 and 1804. Her first, and best, novel, *Julia and the Illuminated Baron* (1800), is a gothic tale told against the background of the French Revolution and of the dark, subversive, and atheistic activities of the Illuminati. Set principally in France, the novel follows the adventures of Julia as she resists the influence of the evil Baron and suffers through numerous trials, including smallpox, kidnapping, poverty, and attempted rape. Eventually, it is revealed that Julia—unbeknown to her—is of noble birth and heir to a fortune. More than simply a novel of hidden identity, W. claims in her preface to the work that "very many serious truths are interwoven with the story of Julia" and that her motive behind publishing the novel lay in a "wish to do good, or at least to guard against evil." One of these "serious truths" concerns the importance of education. For W., the key to America's "liberty without anarchy and confusion" lies in the Jeffersonian notion of order and freedom through a proper egalitarian education. This American ideal is contrasted with the tyranny of the unenlightened—however "illuminated"—Baron, and with the Reign of Terror, in which order and freedom are lost in chaos.

Julia and the Illuminated Baron was soon followed by *Dorval; or, The Speculator* (1801). Set in America, *Dorval* is the story of land speculation in Georgia. As W. indicates in her preface, in *Dorval* she endeavors "to catch the manners of her native land" and to show "by example, the evils that have arisen from speculation, and that have fallen upon the virtuous and the good, as well as the wicked." In her next two novels, *Amelia; or, The Influence of Virtue* (1802) and *Ferdinand and Elmira: A Russian Story* (1804), W. returns to foreign settings in order to weave moral tales of mystery, adventure, and the relentless triumph of virtue. With her second marriage in 1804 to Abiel Wood, W. stopped writing, only to return to it after her husband's death in 1811. The final work published in her lifetime was a volume of short stories titled *Tales of the Night* (1827). A final novel, *War the Parent of Domestic Calamity: A Tale of the Revolution,* was not published until 1968.

BIBLIOGRAPHY: Petter, H., *The Early American Novel* (1971); Scheick, W. J., "Education, Class, and the French Revolution in S. W.'s *Julia,*" SAF 16 (1988): 111–18

ERIC CARL LINK

WOODWORTH, Samuel

b. 13 January 1784, Scituate, Massachusetts; d. 9 December 1842, New York City

W., a songwriter, editor, and writer, is best known as a playwright. His plays include *The Deed of Gift: A Comic Opera* (1822), *The Forest Rose; or, The American Farmers: A Pastoral Opera* (1825), and *The Cannibals; or, The Massacre Islands* (1833); *The Foundling of the Seas* (1833), written for George H. Hill, has not survived. W.'s career was a short one

because debilitating illness forced him to stop writing by 1835.

W.'s reputation rests primarily on *The Deed of Gift* and *The Forest Rose*. The two plays are distinctly American with native characters and settings—*The Deed of Gift* takes place in Worcester, Massachusetts, while *The Forest Rose* is set in the New Jersey country side. In both plays, W. combines song and dance naturally with the main stories to create unified works. *The Deed of Gift* is a melodramatic piece, but gains a touch of variety when W. introduces the issue of whether or not play-acting is a respectable profession. The heroine, Mary Moreland, becomes a "player" herself as she dons male disguises to turn the tables on the villain of the play and ultimately saves her lover, George Baron, from losing his inheritance.

The two-act pastoral opera *The Forest Rose,* the more important work, was very successful on the stage. Although it has one English character, a fop from New York named Bellamy, it is a native drama about young Americans in love; it honors country living, the American farmer, and simple patriotism. The women in the play, Harriet and Lydia, are spirited figures who depart significantly from the passive women of the typical melodrama. But the most important character, at least from the point of view of American drama, is the Yankee, Jonathan Ploughboy. George H. Hill later took on the part and played him successfully for many years. In doing so, he established the popularity of the Yankee stage character. To many scholars, W. was important because he broke with English models to create native comedies containing original music and songs that salute with pride American scenes and themes.

BIBLIOGRAPHY: Meserve, W. J., *Heralds of Promise: The Drama of the American People in the Age of Jackson (1829-1849)* (1986); Moody, R., *Drama from the American Theatre, 1762–1909* (1969), Quinn, A. H., *A History of the American Drama from the Beginning to the Civil War* (1923)

EDMUND M. HAYES

WOOLMAN, John

b. 19 October 1720, Rancocas, Burlington County, New Jersey; d. 7 October 1772, York, England

W. stands in American literature as the finest example of a life devoted to spiritual purity and love of humanity. The clear, delicate prose in which he recorded that life produced a classic account of a spiritual pilgrimage, *The Journal of J. W.* (1774). In its relation of W.'s rejection of worldliness and convention in favor of a life in accord with the dictates of conscience,

W.'s *Journal* anticipates later American writers, like Henry David THOREAU, but the *Journal*'s uniqueness lies in the perfection with which its lucidly simple prose style reflects the spirit of its writer.

W.'s works spring from his life as a Quaker seeker after purity and benevolence. Born on a farm in West Jersey, W. was the son of prosperous but conservative Quaker farmers. As a boy, he felt the stirrings of the Inner Light within himself, but during his adolescence he found himself tempted by frivolity and underwent a period of spiritual struggle. Emerging from this struggle with renewed faith, W. was recorded as a Quaker minister in 1743, and from that time his life was dedicated to searching for God's voice and will within himself and to following its promptings. W.'s quest for spiritual truth led him to seek to purify both his own life and the practices of the Society of Friends, or Quakers. Because he concluded that his retail business involved him too much in worldliness, W. withdrew from shopkeeping and thereafter earned his living as a tailor; rejecting anything produced through injustice or savoring of luxury, W. became increasingly ascetic throughout his life. His quest for justice and benevolence led him to take a leading role in the movement to abolish slavery in the Society of Friends, to travel to the frontier to experience the privations of the Indians, and to speak out against the burden put upon the poor by the luxurious lives of the rich. Throughout his life, W. traveled widely on Quaker ministerial visits throughout America, and he died during a similar visit to England.

All of W.'s literary works are outgrowths of his life's spiritual quest. In an age when prosperity and power were blurring the Quakers' distinction as a special people, W. adopted for himself and gently urged on others not merely a rededication to the original principles of the Society of Friends but a redefinition of those principles to include benevolence to all living creatures. Rejecting the claims of self-love, W. sought spiritual purity. In this search, he came to identify with all of humanity and concluded that he had an obligation to assume its sufferings as his responsibility and to seek to alleviate them. His pamphlets on slavery, *Some Considerations of the Keeping of Negroes, Part I* (1754) and *Considerations on the Keeping of Negroes, Part II* (1762), emphasize the spiritual cost to both slaves and slave owners of slavery and stress W.'s belief that slave owning is a consequence of preferring one's earthly prosperity to his spiritual welfare. W. came to believe that most injustices had the same root as slavery—a love of self and the world and an indifference to others and the spirit. In his economic essays, W. argues that luxury and its evils also result from selfishness. W. is convinced that God's wisdom has so ordered things that if every one were content

with the necessities of life a moderate amount of labor would be sufficient to provide for all; however, because selfish people desire luxuries, the poor labor excessively and suffer from want. W. sets out his economic ideas in *Considerations on Pure Wisdom and Human Policy* (1758), *A Plea for the Poor* (wr. 1763, pub. 1793), *Considerations on the True Harmony of Mankind* (1770), and *Conversations on the True Harmony of Mankind* (wr. 1772, pub. 1837).

Although his essays have enduring intellectual and historical interest, W.'s masterpiece is *The Journal of J. W.* W. began his journal in 1756 and continued it throughout his life. Written in a clear, simple style that echoes the Bible but always remains uniquely W.'s own, the *Journal* details W.'s spiritual development from childhood through adulthood. At the heart of the *Journal* is W.'s discovery that self-love leads to destruction while spiritual love leads not only to an abandonment of worldliness but also, paradoxically, to a commitment to the creatures in the world. W. believes that a commitment of purity of spirit implies a recognition of the divinity within all people; a rejection of the self results in an altruistic identification with all of God's creatures. The *Journal* traces W.'s gradual recognition of the personal and social implications of his desire for spiritual purity. The dominant tone of the *Journal* is a calm acceptance of God's will as the Inner Light reveals more and more of truth to W.; however, W.'s occasional mention of his personal discomfort at finding himself in disagreement with other Quakers suggests that W. did not achieve his submission of self without strain. The full cost of W.'s suppression of self and identification with others is revealed more clearly in a few of his dream visions, especially a vision in which W., finding himself indissolubly intermixed with all of suffering humanity, is released from pain only on hearing an angelic voice announce "John Woolman is dead." The dream visions and the asceticism of W.'s later years reveal that the quest for spiritual perfection was followed only at the expense of considerable personal suffering. Still, the suffering is transmuted into joy as W. sacrifices self for the spirit. The simple beauty of the prose seems to flow from the tranquility of W.'s soul. The *Journal* remains a classic not only of Quaker but of American literature because it movingly recounts the pilgrimage of its author.

BIBLIOGRAPHY: Cady, E. H., *J. W.* (1965); Gummere, A. M., ed., *The Journal and Essays of J. W.* (1922); Moulton, P. P., ed., *The Journal and Major Essays of J. W.* (1971); Rosenblatt, P., *J. W.* (1969); Whitney, J., *J. W., Quaker* (1942)

DAVID M. LARSON

WOOLSON, Constance Fenimore
b. 5 March 1840, Claremont, New Hampshire; d. 24 January 1894, Venice, Italy

Viewed in her own day as a local colorist and as a realist with interests in psychological analysis and the international scene similar to those of her friends, Henry JAMES and William Dean HOWELLS, W. is still discussed as such by some, though there has been a growing interest in her relations with James and in her work as a whole from a feminist perspective.

Born in New Hampshire and reared and educated in Ohio and New York, W., a grandniece of James Fenimore COOPER, came honestly by her interest in local materials. Beginning in 1870 with sketches describing scenes in Ohio, Michigan, and the Great Lakes, she soon turned out stories based upon similar locales and eventually collected some of them in *Castle Nowhere: Lake-Country Sketches* (1875). In the meantime, she had begun in 1873 to spend part of each year in the South—usually the Carolinas and Georgia, but always Florida—and to write the pieces collected in *Rodman the Keeper: Southern Sketches* (1880). With these fictions, she became the first Northern writer after the war to treat Southern scenes and characters dispassionately. During this period, she was encouraged by Howells to try the novel and the Harper publishing firm. Almost concurrently, she took her first trip to Europe in late 1879, met Henry James in 1880, and thereafter expanded her interests in themes having to do with the impingement of one culture upon another. *Anne* (1882), her first novel, is in some ways a continuation of her interests in locales in the Midwest and New York, but it is also the beginning of her serious efforts to deal with the analysis of character that is so characteristic of her mature work. Though in Europe when *Anne* appeared in *Harper's Monthly,* she continued to use the American scene and her own experience. *For the Major* (1883) is different from *Anne* in length (it is called a novelette) and setting. It is her first long work to take place in the South, a locale important to her later novels. It is like *Anne,* however, in its treatment of character and place and in its use of analysis. The subsequent long fiction—*East Angels* (1886), *Jupiter Lights* (1889), and *Horace Chase* (1894)—concentrates on settings in Florida, Georgia, and North Carolina, respectively, but Northern characters are involved in each instance, and the interest in place and character and the themes of contrasts of culture and self-sacrifice remain prominent.

As for the short story after her move to Europe, W. turned chiefly to Americans in the Old World, not merely because James and Howells were dealing with the international subject so successfully but because it was a natural extension of her interest in such material in her early fiction on the Lake Country and the South. *The Front Yard and Other Italian Stories* (1895) and *Dorothy and Other Italian Stories* (1896), both published posthumously, collect tales that examine Americans in Italy, a land dearly loved by the author, with results that display natives of the New World of various classes frequently resisting the culture and temptations of the Old, but when succumbing to them, as in the case of some artists and others bewitched by the culture, losing their natural gifts and integrity.

W.'s interest in the international theme has led certain critics to conclude that she was a mere follower of Henry James. She had indeed read and reviewed James's fiction before she met him and her examination of Americans in Europe and of similar themes and analysis of character lend some credence to this view. But it should be remembered that her earliest fiction, especially that concerning the Lake country, considers the relationships between cultures—American and French, for example—and that she dealt in character analysis before she read James. It is also clear that her long and close friendship with James not only contributed to and heightened her interest in these matters, but provided James with ideas—"germs" he found in her notebooks—for such tales as "The Beast in the Jungle"—a work affected moreover by his response to her death and his memories of her. In the end, whatever James's influence may have been, W.'s work remains worthy of consideration not just for its contribution to local color, to analysis of character, or to the international theme, but for its realization of place, its treatment of character, its evocation of time in both Old World and New, and for its part in the development of American fiction in the age of realism, minor though it may now seem.

BIBLIOGRAPHY: Dean, S. L., *C. F. W.: Homeward Bound* (1995); Kern, J. D., *C. F. W.: Literary Pioneer* (1934); Moore, R. S., *C. F. W.* (1963); Torsney, C. B., *C. F. W.: The Grief of Artistry* (1989); Torsney, C. B., ed., *Critical Essays on C. F. W.* (1992) Weimer, J. M., "Women Artists as Exiles in the Fiction of C. F. W.," *Legacy* 3 (Fall 1886): 3–15

RAYBURN S. MOORE

WOUK, Herman
b. 27 May 1915, Bronx, New York

Although one of America's best-selling authors throughout his career, W. has a limited literary reputation. He was, however, the first Jewish American novelist to be commercially successful on a wide scale.

He pioneered the acceptability of explicitly Jewish subject matter within "mainstream" American literature, and his work raises important questions about the nature of artistic representation.

W. did not begin to take up writing as a serious vocation until after he had finished serving in World War II. He achieved his career breakthrough with *The Caine Mutiny* (1951). This book won praise and the Pulitzer Prize for its realistic portrayal of discontent aboard a ship that was playing a marginal role in the great war effort. It is W.'s portrayal of the unstable Captain Queeg that has polarized response to the book. W. seems initially to endorse the mutiny against the insecure and unreliable Queeg. Later, though, he seems to do an abrupt swerve, lambasting the mutineers through the ironic means of the Jewish attorney who successfully defended them at their court-martial. The attorney particularly blames a novel-writing officer named Keefer as the insidious, intellectual agent behind the uprising against the legitimate if erratic Queeg, saying accusingly "You are the author of the Caine Mutiny." Although critics have taken this as a straightforward rebuke, the fact remains that W. is the author of *The Caine Mutiny,* and the accusation against Keefer could be considered a form of *Künstlerschuld,* or "artist-guilt." W.'s own status as author could also lend some moral and epistemological ambiguity to the questions of who occasioned the mutiny and whether it was a lawful action.

This ambivalence toward artistry is seen in *Youngblood Hawke* (1962). This novel chronicles the rise and tragic fall of a Southern novelist, who manipulates himself into prominence within the vortex of literary and Hollywood celebrity only to be consumed by it. There is admiration, but also a patronizing condescension, in the book's attitude toward Hawke; his naivete and aesthetic egoism is as censured as his talent is admired. W., the Jewish moralist, may be seen as criticizing Hawke's gullibility and his seeming defiance of his own inevitable tragedy. But there is identification between the two authors, as the similarity in sound between "Hawke" and "Wouk" indicates. W.'s attitude toward art is often dismissed as a combination of conservatism and commercialism. But it participates in a complex Jewish posture towards the idea of representation itself, inherited from the image-ban contained in the Second Commandment. Like later, more critically esteemed Jewish American writers like Cynthia OZICK, W. recognizes the human urge to create and imagine, but calls attention to the danger of seeing human creation as self-sufficient and thus usurping of God's ultimate power.

W.'s Jewishness is most visible in *Marjorie Morningstar* (1955). Again, ironies abound. W. is critical of his eponymous heroine's headlong rush to assimilate into gentile society, and in his portrait of her suitor Noel Airman he indicts the Jew who seeks to enter gentile society as a lightweight poseur-intellectual. But W. himself was writing for a mainly gentile audience, and *Marjorie Morningstar* was the first commercially successful American novel whose themes were essentially, rather than accidentally, Jewish.

W.'s most ambitious work was a long novel about World War II, published in two parts as *The Winds of War* (1971) and *War and Remembrance* (1978). This vast work chronicles the fortunes of the Henrys, an American naval family, against the canvas of the war. At times, it degenerates into a long soap opera, which sometimes seems more set in the 1970s than the 1940s: witness the casual way in which the major characters divorce and remarry. W. provides a captivating plot for entertainment value, but the work's main interest is in terms of genre: calling it a "romance" or a "remembrance" rather than a novel, he avoids the arrogance of the novelist's traditional claims to omnipotence-within-the-book. As a counterpoint to his encyclopedic narrative of war on various fronts and—in a moving and understated rendition—the Holocaust, the comments of a fictive German general are provided. It is a tribute to the work's multiplicity that the general's comments often coincide with the views of the protagonist, Victor Henry, especially regarding the former Soviet Union. The growing Zionist strain towards the end of the work—carried out in two later novels devoted to the subsequent history of Israel—makes clear that W. is aspiring less after historical veracity than to convey the conflict's moral legacy to generations beginning to no longer know the war even as a part of living memory.

BIBLIOGRAPHY: Beichman, A., *H. W.: The Novelist as Social Historian* (1984); Mazzeno, L., *H. W.* (1994)

NICHOLAS BIRNS

WRIGHT, Charles [Penzel, Jr.]
b. 25 August 1935, Pickwick Dam, Tennessee

Condensed, elegiac, and often narratively spare, W.'s poetry investigates the music of eschatology. A master of the meditative lyric, he has published no fiction and only a few prose poems; even his translations, interviews, and essays strictly involve poetry or poetics. Perhaps because of this concentration, a typical W. poem achieves presence not through sentences or extended metaphors, but by the accumulation of images etched onto stone by sound. A highly auditory poet, W. possesses one of the best ears since Ezra POUND, and his poetry, a loosely iambic free verse often written in an extended, two part line, blends euphonious repetitions with subtle musical surprises. Although he uses traditional subjects—"language, landscape, and idea of God"—he does so in reflective, secular, and, ultimately, very distilled ways; his poetry is half seance, half selenography lesson.

W. grew up in the South then after college was stationed in Italy, serving for three years in U.S. Army Intelligence. The sites and memories from both periods remain important sources, enriched by his later returns to Italy as a student and lecturer. A third landscape that informs his poetry is Southern California's, where he lived seventeen years. W.'s Laguna Beach, however, is closer to the Mediterranean than to Mexico, and the "cliff / That Easters down to the ocean" represents not history, politics, chaparral ecology, or confessional autobiography, but instead the pane of glass that separates this life from the next. His poems describe actual places, yet the value of each place rests in how landscape transcends substance, since the textures of the physical world "are an outline of the infinite."

W.'s major publications can be divided into three groups. *The Grave of the Right Hand* (1970), *Hard Freight* (1973), *Bloodlines* (1975), and *China Trace* (1977) constitute the first period, collected in *Country Music* (1982), which won a National Book Award. One achievement of his earlier work is an almost elliptical compression. Diction, narrative, stanza length, emotional expression: all elements receive sober, scrupulous treatment. In *China Trace,* for example, poems range from one to twelve lines—none are longer; in *Bloodlines,* the two most impressive sequences, "Tattoos" and "Skins," each require a following page of explanatory notes. It is entirely characteristic that even then the notes themselves are oblique, and that their presentation in list form creates a semipoem in itself. In interviews, W. has said that the fifty poems of *China Trace* can be read as chapters of one story, an account of a lifetime's pilgrimage; equally true is the observation that they are individual playing cards and can be read in almost any order, telling a different fortune with each dealt hand.

With *The Southern Cross* (1981), a second period takes shape, as W. develops a more relaxed line, one involving a wider range of diction and a looser, more wry sense of humor. Prior thematic concerns remain, but whereas *Hard Freight* opens with four "homage" poems in a row—to Pound, Rimbaud, Baron Corvo, and an algebraic "X"—no poem is longer than a page and a half, and no single line has more than ten syllables. By contrast, "Homage to Paul Cézanne," the first poem of *Southern Cross,* sustains eight brilliant, image-dense pages, and the title poem that closes the book runs twice that length. Along with longer lines and longer overall length, the poems display more

varied spatial compositions. As does *The Other Side of the River* (1984), *Southern Cross* foregrounds exile, pilgrimage, and—in glints and hints—transcendence.

With a cover by Black Mountain graduate Cy Twombly, *Zone Journals* (1988) furthers W.'s maturation into a more discursive, Olsonian line. In ten extended journal entries, the book evokes sacred places and keening memories, using long, two-part lines. To W., the dropped "low rider" is still part of the first line; using it allows him to warp even more slacks and stresses into the weave. *Xionia* (1990) continues to explore journal forms and includes "Language Journal," W.'s rebuttal to the Language poetry movement. *The World of The Ten Thousand Things* (1990) collects work from 1980 to 1990.

W.'s third period is still emerging, marked with two publications, *Chickamauga* (1995) and *Black Zodiac* (1997). In both, when he is at his most first-personal—"I've always liked the view from my mother-in-law's house at night" starts one poem—he seems his most self-effaced; as does Augustine's *Confessions,* these books display the many ways that the particular illuminates the general. *Chickamauga's* poems can be tightly wound or loosely peregrinating, allusive or plain, sly or oak-pew-serious, yet always without the effect seeming mannered or strained. Awarded the Pulitzer Prize in poetry, *Black Zodiac* contrasts "Jesuit Graves" and "Lives of the Saints" with "Lives of the Artists," seeing the three as knots on the same rope. What unifies all of his later works is W.'s persistence in looking into the sun and reporting that "As our bodies rise, / our names turn into light."

BIBLIOGRAPHY: Andrews, T., *The Point Where All Things Meet: Essays on C. W.* (1995); Vendler, H., "C. W.," *The Music of What Happens: Poems, Poets, Critics* (1988): 388–97

                                        CHARLES HOOD

WRIGHT, Harold Bell

b. 4 May 1872, Rome, New York; d. 24 May 1944, San Diego, California

Next to important literary figures of the first half of the 20th c. such as F. Scott FITZGERALD, Ernest HEMINGWAY, and H. L. MENCKEN, popular writers from that era whose books did not record the post-World War I Parisian life of the disillusioned American intellectual have stirred little critical interest or investigation. Although the novels of W. were consistently listed on the best seller lists between 1917 and 1924, they are now virtually ignored by both literary historians and contemporary readers alike. Often compared to other popular writers of the era such as Gene Stratton-

Porter and Zane GREY, W.'s books did not appeal to the intellectual left but to the rural, small town Americans who clung tightly to traditional 19th-c. values, the very values that were being called into question by the Lost Generation. W.'s books, representative of the conservative popular thought of the general public of the 1920s, conveyed old-fashioned messages that fulfilled their readers' demands for comforting, simple messages during confusing times.

In order to reject the solidified doctrines of organized religion, W. escaped the city in 1897 to start a small fundamentalist ministry in a small town in the Ozark Mountains. During his service as minister, W. wrote his first novel, *Shepherd of the Hills* (1907), intending to read it serially to his congregation. The novel circulated beyond the walls of his church, however, and became a surprising best-seller across the entire Midwest. Noting the demand for his fictional lessons on morality, W. quickly followed it with *The Calling of Dan Matthews* (1909), and *The Winning of Barbara Worth* (1911), which became an enormous success, selling over a half-million copies. His last publication before World War I, *The Eyes of the World* (1914), was yet another big seller, but W.'s popularity dropped dramatically after the war. Although W. continued to write a novel every other year for two decades during and after World War I, including two successes, *When a Man's a Man* (1916) and *The Re-Creation of Brian Kent* (1919), his novels were never again as popular as they were between the years 1909 and 1914.

W. wrote only of God, of home and America, of hard work, nature, and morality. The enemies in W.'s novels are urban corruption and industry, although in his novel *The Calling of Dan Matthews* he made sure to offer a solution to the "menace of machinery" in order to remain within the conventions of the romantic novel, which do not allow for pessimistic endings. Most of W.'s novels also contain an autobiographical protagonist, the disillusioned city minister who leaves for the country to rekindle the virtues that were brought into question by harsh city life. The heroic young minister takes his new congregation under his wing and performs miracles; the town and its people are transformed by the minister's virtuous spirit. W.'s female characters are usually "diamonds in the rough," whose rough edges are soon worn smooth by the minister's guidance. W.'s other characters are straightforward allegories of good and evil, symbols of W.'s favorite messages: "the city corrupts," "lost sheep can be found," and "nature restores virtue."

W.'s stereotyped characters and plots, as well as the wooden dialogue and commonplace preaching that remain consistent with every novel, were the constant targets of criticism and ridicule. But W. never pretended to write literature. His intention was to appeal to the popular minds of the twenties, to those who did not want to question their values but rather to take comfort in them. W.'s primary audience was the religious white middle-class rural America, distressed by shifting religious values, industry, and urban anarchy. W.'s audience was looking for comfortable answers, and his first novel fulfilled those needs.

Into the 1930s and 1940s, W. continued to write these wholesome, comforting novels, and despite the wane in his popularity, his conservative religious message never altered. W. was the master of sentimental romance and religious allegory, and his stories were appreciated by millions of rural dwelling Americans. Like Stratton-Porter and other popular writers of the era, W.'s novels are out of print and not recognized as worthwhile subjects of study by the academic community. Although most of W.'s novels have become unavailable and are for the most part forgotten, an exploration into his popularity during the pre-World War I period would expand our understanding of the era we so often only associate with the members of the Lost Generation.

BIBLIOGRAPHY: DeGruson, G., *Kansas Authors of Best Sellers* (1970); Ifkovic, E., "H. B. W. and the Minister of Man: The Domestic Romancer at the End of the Genteel Age," *MarkhamR* 4 (February 1974): 21–25; Nash, R., *The Nervous Generation* (1970); Reynolds, E. W., "H. B. W.: A Biography," in Wright, H., *The Re-Creation of Brian Kent* (1919): 345–52

                                              HEATHER C. URSCHEL

WRIGHT, James [Arlington]

b. 13 December 1927, Martins Ferry, Ohio; d. 25 March 1980, New York City

Enacted in the work of W. are two intense struggles, one for wisdom and one for appropriate song. The poems of his first two collections—*The Green Wall* (1957), which was chosen by W. H. AUDEN for inclusion in the Yale Series of Younger Poets, and *Saint Judas* (1959)—are written in the most traditional poetic forms, nearly always using both meter and rhyme. They also express W.'s preoccupation with human pain and suffering, mostly a result of his intense sensitivity to death and his concern for the social outcast.

With the publication in 1963 of the volume *The Branch Will Not Break,* W. seemed to change both the form and the outlook of his poems. Not only does he seem to find in nature an unusual sense of happiness, even apotheosis as in the justly-famous "A Blessing," but suddenly he is writing free verse poems structured entirely on the images that give them meaning. While the poems in his fourth collection, *Shall We Gather at the River* (1968), continue the imagistic method, they return to the more tortured subject matter of earlier volumes. Here, W.'s speaker undertakes a search for meaning, for solace and understanding, but tragically ends up on the banks of the Ohio River, in which his childhood beloved seems to have perished years earlier.

After the *Collected Poems* (1971), for which he was awarded the Pulitzer Prize, W. produced the highly-controversial volume *Two Citizens* (1973), in which the fierceness of metaphor first introduced in *Shall We Gather at the River* comes to dominate, almost entirely, W.'s vision. *To a Blossoming Pear Tree* (1977), however, returns to the happiness found in *The Branch Will Not Break,* and the posthumous volume *The Journey* (1982) even comes to terms with the fact of death, as seen most strikingly in its central poem, "The Journey." In his later work, W. managed to combine the revolutionary method of his imagistic poems with the traditionalism of his rhymed and metered ones. W.'s reputation has steadily grown since his death, and he is now recognized as the premier American poet of his generation.

BIBLIOGRAPHY: Dougherty, D., *J. W.* (1987); Smith, D., ed., *The Pure Clear Word* (1982); Stein, K., *The Poetry of a Grown Man* (1988); Stitt, P., and F. Graziano, eds., *J. W.* (1987)

PETER STITT

WRIGHT, Jay

b. 25 May 1934, Albuquerque, New Mexico

The awards bestowed upon W., among them a National Endowment for the Arts Award in 1968 and the Academy of American Poets Fellowship for distinguished poetic achievement in 1996, testify to the enduring contribution this writer has made to American poetry. The experiences that fuel W.'s poetry, essays, and plays include growing up in the Southwest; he lived in New Mexico in the care of a couple with whom W.'s father had left him, later joining his father in Los Angeles, playing the bass, playing professional baseball, and serving in the Army, which afforded W. the opportunity to travel throughout Europe.

W.'s first published poetry appeared in the 1967 chapbook *Death as History*. In 1970, Princeton University granted him a Hodder Fellowship in playwriting. However, it was the publication of the collection entitled *The Homecoming Singer* (1971) that firmly evidenced W.'s remarkable ability. Here the almost migratory experience of W.'s childhood and coming of age are addressed by poems that seek to build a bridge between past and present, in which geography

and autobiography depend upon each other's presence as a personal and cultural landscape is mapped. Critical response to the work was admiring. W. was singled out for his ability to fuse disparate thematic elements, as well as for the inventiveness of his form—particularly his use of syntax and rhythm that gave the poems a simultaneous relationship to narrative prose and jazz music.

The Homecoming Singer was written in Mexico, where Mexican, Spanish, and Navajo cultures with which his childhood had brought him in contact were reexamined from a poet's perspective. In 1971, W. spent two years in Scotland before returning to the U.S. and publishing, in 1976, *Soothsayers and Omens* and *Dimensions of History*. In these volumes, W. explores individual and communal links to African history and mythology. His efforts to understand the religions of the Dogon and the Bambari of Mali, as well as the Akan and Nuer tribes provided W. with a background for the clearly realized, yet complex poems. The poetic persona of *Dimensions of History* is a tribal historian—a dyeli—whose role it is to explore the tribe's collective fate. For this work, and the "intellectual biography" *The Double Inventions of Komo* (1980)—a poetic cycle that takes the form of the Komo initiation rights of the Bambara people—W. relied heavily on West African creation myths. The Komo ritual proved an apt vehicle for allegory, as W. applied the ceremony that depicts the creation of the world and articulates the principle values of the tribe to his own poetic process of reflection and instruction. The role of the initiate, the seeker, is one from which W. draws inspiration. W. has identified himself not as a weaver of complex fabrics, but one who strives to reveal the already existing interwoven complexities of our lives.

Even in the more overtly personal *Elaine's Book* (1988), which many critics rate his highest literary achievement, W. uses a polyphonic voice and a multinational geography in the formation of a series of poems written as a birthday gift for his wife's sister. The result is a serious of poems both vexing and soothing; readers grasp for meaning even as they are held in the sway of the speaker's melodious voice. This voice is likely to continue to captivate poetic audiences as W. takes a place in literary history. The consistent excellence of his art has attracted the attention of literary critics as notable as Robert Stepto, John HOLLANDER, and Harold BLOOM, and inspired literary conferences devoted to the discussion of his works.

BIBLIOGRAPHY: Kutzinski, V., *Against the American Grain: Myth and History in William Carlos Williams, J. W., and N.icholas Guillen* (1987); Redmond, E. B., *Drumvoices: The Mission of African-American*

Poetry: A Critical History (1976); Stepto, R. B., *The Chant of Saints: A Gathering of Afro-American Literature, Art and Scholarship* (1979)

NICK SMART

WRIGHT, Richard [Nathaniel]

b. 4 September 1908, Roxie, Mississippi; d. 28 November 1960, Paris, France

It is difficult even today to overestimate the importance of W.'s work since it not only changed the direction of American and African American literary traditions but also helped to transform the ways in which Americans regard race. W. produced, over a relatively short career, several seminal works that emphatically brought something new into American consciousness, a lucid and completely unsentimental vision of the conditions faced by 20th-c. black people who emigrated from the rural South and populated the ghettos of the North.

Like Theodore DREISER, a writer whom he greatly admired and was strongly influenced by, W. lived the experience that his writings so powerfully dramatized. Born on a plantation twenty-two miles east of Natchez, Mississippi, W. grew up in one of the most poverty-stricken and rigidly segregated parts of the Deep South. When he was six years old, his family, despairing of making a living as sharecroppers, moved to Memphis, Tennessee, but their situation only worsened when his father abandoned the family and his mother contracted an illness that reduced her to the status of a chronic invalid. For the next eleven years, W. lived in a bewildering variety of locations in Mississippi and Arkansas, as he, his mother, and brother eked out a marginal living, staying with various relatives. A turning point in his life occurred in November 1925 when W. took up residence in Memphis, where he worked a number of menial jobs and began to read widely in 19th- and 20th-c. literature. His study of H. L. MENCKEN's essays led him to read American naturalists such as Dreiser, Stephen CRANE, and Sherwood ANDERSON, along with European realists such as Fyodor Dostoevsky, Nikolay Gogol, and Henrik Ibsen. Such reading, which he described in *Black Boy* (1945) as "opening up new avenues of seeing and feeling," led to a profound psychological awakening that confirmed his desire to be a writer.

In 1927, W. left the South altogether and moved to Chicago where he lived for ten years. Living in slum housing and working a series of lowly paid jobs as a street sweeper, an insurance agent, a postal clerk, and an aid at a South Side boys club, he developed a firsthand knowledge of the plight of urban blacks during the Great Depression that would serve as a basis for some of his most powerful writing. He continued

to read widely in modern literature and also became strongly involved in leftist politics, becoming a member of the John Reed Club and writing for journals such as *New Masses, Anvil,* and *Left Front.* In 1933, he joined the Communist Party, something that he would later describe as "the first total emotional commitment of my life," embracing a new faith that would replace the traditional beliefs that were shattered by his earlier experience. He also formed important friendships with sociologist St. Clair Drake, poet Margaret WALKER, and novelists James T. FARRELL and Nelson ALGREN. By 1935, he began work on his first novel, *Lawd Today!,* a bitterly naturalistic account of ghetto life that was not published until several years after his death. In 1936, he published "Big Boy Leaves Home," a story that received serious praise in mainstream journals and would later become part of W.'s first published book, *Uncle Tom's Children* (1938).

In 1937, W. moved to New York where he became Harlem editor of the *Daily Worker* and devoted himself to the writing of his masterwork, *Native Son.* This novel, which became a Book of the Month selection in 1940 and sold over 200,000 copies in its first months of existence, established W. as an important new voice in American literature, a writer who almost overnight changed the direction of African American literature by boldly telling a story that no previous American writer had fully revealed. While earlier American fiction about the city either ignored blacks, marginalized their presence, or sentimentalized their condition, *Native Son* examined the life of the black ghetto in a meticulously honest way from the unique perspective of one of its victims. From the dissonant ringing of the alarm clock that opens the novel to the harsh clanging of Bigger Thomas's jail cell that brings the book to such a jarring close, W. provides his readers with a sharp and disturbed awareness of the ravaged world of urban blacks and the grim historical implications of this injustice for all Americans. As one early reviewer put it, *Native Son* packed "a tremendous punch, something like a big fist through the windows of our complacent lives."

While writing *Native Son,* W. experienced serious ideological and personal difficulties as member of the Communist Party and officially resigned from it in 1942. His work from that point on became increasingly existential, rather than Marxist, in outlook. He completed the manuscript version of "The Man Who Lived Underground" in 1942, a darkly surrealistic work that has strong affinities with European existentialists like Dostoevsky and Albert Camus and also served as one of the models for Ralph ELLISON's existential masterpiece, *Invisible Man.* His masterful autobiography *Black Boy* drew sharp criticism from Marxist critics who chided W. for describing his experiences in deeply personal rather than broadly political terms. His later fiction, written after W. had exiled himself in France and had become friends with Jean-Paul Sartre, André Gide, and Simone de Beauvoir, is even more strikingly existential. *The Outsider* (1953), *Savage Holiday* (1954), and *The Long Dream* (1958) are not so much concerned with their central characters' struggles with economic and social forces as they are preoccupied with the recoil from an "absurd" outer universe and the attempt to create meaning by developing existential consciousness and will.

W. died unexpectedly from a heart attack at fifty-two while being treated at a Paris hospital for what might have been the residual effects of a case of amoebic dysentery that he had contracted while traveling in Africa. Although his career as a writer was tragically short, it nevertheless had enormous resonance since his work powerfully influenced several generations of writers. During his lifetime, he inspired a "Wright school" of novelists, which included Ann PETRY, William ATTAWAY, Willard MOTLEY, Lloyd Louis Brown, and Chester HIMES. And Ralph Ellison and James BALDWIN, although they made it clear that they were not part of the "Wright school," were nevertheless greatly in W.'s debt. W.'s pioneering fiction, autobiography, and polemic essays cleared the air of stereotypes and other time-honored misconceptions about race in America, freeing Ellison and Baldwin to pursue their own distinctive visions of African American life. From the mid-1960s onward, when W.'s star began to rise again and he became accepted as a major American writer, figures as diverse as Eldridge Cleaver, Claude Brown, Clarence MAJOR, and Charles JOHNSON have honored W. as a strong influence.

W., who revolutionized African American letters by boldly questioning old taboos that earlier writers dared not to approach, continues to inspire writers and disturb readers. The startling images that he developed to shock his readers into a lucid awareness of the American racial dilemma continue to serve us well, for they are still powerful lenses that correct our vision and force us to see clearly the racial problems that still afflict us.

BIBLIOGRAPHY: Bloom, H., ed., *R. W.* (1987); Butler, R., ed., *The Critical Response to R. W.* (1995); Fabre, M., *The Unfinished Quest of R. W.* (1970); Gates, H. L., and K. A. Appiah, eds., *R. W.: A Critical Perspective Past and Present* (1993); Hakutani, Y., *R. W. and Racial Discourse* (1996); Kinnamon, K., *The Emergence of R. W.* (1969); Reilly, J., *R. W.: The Critical Reception* (1978)

ROBERT BUTLER

WRIGHT, William
b. 9 May 1829, Knox County, Ohio; d. 16 March 1898, West Liberty, Iowa

The reputation of W., best known by his pen name Dan De Quille, long depended on just two events in his long career as a Comstock journalist: he influenced Mark TWAIN when they both worked on the Virginia City, Nevada, *Territorial Enterprise* from 1862 to 1864; and he wrote *The Big Bonanza* (1876), the classic contemporary account of the Comstock lode. With the discovery and publication of lost and forgotten fiction, however, W. has been reestablished as a talented author of serious fiction as well as one of the West's outstanding practitioners of the literary hoax.

Probably the most famous of his many hoaxes is that of the "solar armor" invention, a rubberized suit with a portable air-conditioner that was supposed to enable its wearer to walk comfortably across Death Valley even in mid-summer. His short stories were among the earliest, along with Bret HARTE's and Twain's, to exploit Western settings and characterizations. His last works, especially the novella *Dives and Lazarus* and the long story "Pahnenit," reveal the influence upon him of the classical tradition of literature and mythology, and are among his richest and most literary works of fiction. These works also manifest his populist inclinations, his basic religiosity, and his growing antimaterialism.

BIBLIOGRAPHY: Berkove, L. I., ed., *The Fighting Horse of the Stanislaws: Stories and Essays by Dan De Quille* (1990); Rawls, J. J., ed., *Dan De Quille and the Big Bonanza* (1980)

LAWRENCE I. BERKOVE

WYLIE, Elinor
b. 7 September 1885, Somerville, New Jersey; d. 19 December 1928, New York City

W. was a poet and novelist, and a vivid figure in the literary world of the 1920s. Her work was highly praised by prominent New York intellectuals and critics during her lifetime, but later criticized for its limited variety and lack of development. Most critics now agree that although her techniques have great limitations, she produced a number of lyrics remarkable for their brilliant imagery and musicality.

The daughter of a prominent government official, W. grew up in Philadelphia and Washington. She attended private schools and studied drawing at the Corcoran Gallery. When she took up a literary career in New York in the mid-1920s, she had already gained notoriety as a socially prominent woman who had eloped to Europe with a married man seventeen years her senior, leaving behind her husband of five years and her young son. Six years later, she and her second husband returned to Washington, D.C., and she began to make contacts with prominent literary figures. She received encouragement and support from Edmund WILSON, Sinclair LEWIS, and John DOS PASSOS. In 1923, she moved to New York and married William Rose Bénet, editor of the *Saturday Review of Literature*. Over a period of eight years, she produced four volumes of poetry and four historical novels, and was also a contributing editor of *Vanity Fair*.

W. admired and was influenced by a number of writers. The profusion of images in her poetry suggests that she had studied the metaphysical poets; and her tone often echoes the brittle irony of the late Victorian and Edwardian poets. Her greatest inspiration, however, was the romantic poet Percy Bysshe Shelley. Like him, she viewed poetry as a vehicle for moving beyond the real world into a more perfect mode of existence. She expresses her admiration for Shelley in the four-sonnet sequence "A Red Carpet for Shelley" in *Trivial Breath* (1928). She also alludes to him in many other poems; and figures based upon him are central to two of her four novels. For example, *The Orphan Angel* (1926) is a fantasy of Shelley searching across the expanding American West for a mysterious and beautiful woman.

A strong emphasis upon developing the individual self and maintaining its integrity permeates W.'s poetry. Perhaps this need for self-possession is best expressed in "Let No Charitable Hope," in the lines, "I was, being human, born alone; I am, being woman, hard beset." Closely associated with this self-protective stance are images of entrapment, disguise, and withdrawal. Through the often densely subjective imagery, W. expresses a longing to escape the ugliness and disappointment of the real world. This effort at intellectual and spiritual communion, which W. referred to as her "Platonic cast of mind," achieves mixed results in her published work. Some of the lyrics in her first volume *Nets to Catch the Wind* (1921) are impressive for their artistic perfection. Examples are "Velvet Shoes," which one critic has called her "virtuoso piece," "Atavism," and "Wild Peaches." With each volume, her poetry becomes more complex and introspective. A notable part of the last one, *Angels and Earthly Creatures* (1929), is the sonnet sequence "One Person," an allegorical account of a secret love affair. Like her poems, W.'s novels are rich and intricate accounts of experience in a refined, and at times fantastic, world.

W.'s goal was to make her poems perfectly fashioned, delicately proportioned works of art. They are written in compact forms, such as the sonnet, quatrains, or couplets, with short four-accent, or tetrameter, lines. They have a strong musical quality, and the best of them have a remarkable unity of sound and sense. Many of the images are derived from art—literature, painting, and sculpture. Also common to the poems are images of coldness or colorlessness. The poetic diction, with words like "crystal" and "silver" among her favorites, gives an apparent delicacy to passionate expressions of emotion. Through her mastery of these qualities, W. helped to carry on 19th-c. traditions in feminine lyricism to 20th-c. American poetry.

BIBLIOGRAPHY: Benet, W. R., *The Prose and Poetry of E. W.* (1934); Farr, J., *The Life and Art of E. W.* (1983); Gray, T. A., *E. W.* (1969); Hoyt, N., *E. W.* (1935); Olson, S., *E. W.: A Life Apart* (1979)

MARGARET CARTER

YAMADA, Mitsuye
b. 5 July 1923, Fukuoka, Japan

Blending Japanese folk tales, descriptions of immigration, personal recollections, and dialogue, the poetry of Y. protests racism while insisting on the importance of her heritage. Born in Japan, she was raised in Seattle, Washington until World War II when her family was relocated to a internment camp in Minidoka, Idaho. Y.'s life, mirroring her art, reflects her activism and commitment to multiculturalism. She served on Amnesty International's National Board of Directors and, from 1966 until her retirement in 1989, she taught college English. Y. also supports other ethnic and women writers; she is editor of two ethnic literature collections and founder of the Multi-Cultural Women Writers of Orange County in California.

Using a simple and imagistic style, Y. conveys the complexity of Japanese American experience. Her spare style graphically reflects the humiliation and discomfort of the internment experience, which she describes in *Camp Notes* (1976), a collection that includes some of her earliest poems. Providing intimate details of camp life, the poems depict the physical and psychological control practiced on Japanese Americans who are herded like cattle and treated as if they were unfeeling and unthinking. In "Curfew," the guards admonish the internees to turn out the "light," which refers to both literal and metaphorical illumination. The collection, however, does not merely describe the victimization of Japanese immigrants; Y. aptly demonstrates their strength and bravery. Many poems reinterpret Japanese silence as fortitude rather than passiveness. "Enryo," for example, discusses the practice of holding back complaints and maintaining humility and reserve in unequal power situations. But Y. also demonstrates the inadequacies of this practice when confronted with social injustice. During their removal to internment camps, the evacuees' silence was used against them.

Y. continues to explore the history of Japanese Americans in *Desert Run* (1988), which includes short stories as well as poems. Focused around the motif of returning, to an internment camp's desert location and to Japanese culture, the poems and stories acknowledge both painful and positive aspects of the past. In the work's first section, "Returning," Y. draws connections between desert creatures, plants, and Japanese Americans in order to transform the latter from victims to survivors. Like cactus and creosote bushes, they flourish in bad conditions; like lichen, they resist their host culture (America) in order to survive. In subsequent sections, she finds bravery and beauty in Japanese cultures on both sides of the Pacific. In "I learned to sew," a grandmother denigrates and trivializes her ability to sew. But the irony of her remarks are clear: the skill enables the woman to support three sons after her husband's death. In the last section, aptly entitled "Connecting," Y. reaches beyond her own past to connect with other women. Challenging gender subordination as well as racism, she insists on their shared experience as wives, daughters, mothers, and sisters.

While Y.'s work recounts events from her own experience, it also continually insists on the importance for all Americans to acknowledge the often painful aspects of history. But in remembering, Y. finds moments of resistance and, like the female character in "The Club" who leaves an abusive partner, refuses to be a victim.

BIBLIOGRAPHY: Jaskoski, H., "A *MELUS* Interview: M. Y.," *MELUS* 15 (Spring 1988): 97-108; Schweik, S., "A Needle with Mama's Voice: M. Y.'s *Camp Notes* and the American Canon of War Poetry," in Cooper, E. M., et al., eds., *Arms and the Woman* (1989): 225–43

LINDA TRINH MOSER

YAMAMOTO, Hisaye [DeSoto]
b. 23 August 1921, Redondo Beach, California

Y. began a writing career at an early age; by the time she was fourteen years old, she had already received her first rejection notice. Even as an internee at a Japanese relocation camp during World War II, she wrote for the *Poston Chronicle,* the camp newspaper. After leaving the camp, the *Los Angeles Tribune,* an African American paper, hired her. Despite anti-Japanese sentiment following the war, her short fiction won national recognition; *Arizona Quarterly, Harper's Bazaar,* and *Partisan Review* published her work and, in 1952, "Yoneko's Earthquake" was included in *Best American Short Stories.*

In depicting Japanese American life, Y. typically employs parallel plot lines and a third-person narrator whose naive perspective is often misleading. The central plot deals with universal concerns; like all individuals, her characters grapple with generational conflicts, difficult love relationships and the confusion of adolescence. Against these common experiences, however, Y. uses a latent plot line to depict the particular suffering of Japanese immigrants, often indicting American prejudice. In the title story of *Seventeen Syllables* (1985; rev. ed., 1988), a collection of stories dating from 1948 to 1987, the main plot depicts the adolescent Rosie's growing attraction to Jesus, the son of a Mexican couple who work for her father; the second concerns Rosie's mother, Tome, and her desire to write Japanese haiku. Within the double plot emerges the psychological distance between mother and daughter: Rosie's idealistic love for Jesus blinds her to her parents' incompatible relationship. When her father burns a Hiroshige print, Tome's first place prize in a haiku contest, however, Rosie comes face to face with her mother's discontent. Their stories converge as Tome cautions her daughter against marriage and confesses she wed Rosie's father after becoming pregnant by a man who couldn't marry her. In describing Tome's unhappiness, however, Y. does not only criticize gender subjugation in Japanese culture. The father's inability to appreciate his wife's talent stems largely from the harsh conditions imposed upon him by American prejudice.

"The Legend of Miss Sasagawara" likewise implicates American society while also criticizing aspects of Japanese culture. Through contradictory reports concerning the title character, her fellow inmates at Poston, Arizona, suggest various causes for her deviant behavior. The story ostensibly blames the Japanese American community for failing to embrace Mari Sasagawara. The other inmates, like her religious father, fail to comprehend her need for love and understanding; however, the story also attempts to absolve them.

Through intimate details of camp life, its lack of privacy and material comfort, Y. reveals the connection between an individual's insanity and the insanity of internment. In the end, America's racial fears lead to the entire community's inability to help and understand Miss Sasagawara.

Y. tends to dismiss her importance as a writer in interviews and essays. In "Writing" (1976), for example, she identifies herself as a "housewife." Critics, however, continue to praise her work. In 1986, the Before Columbus Foundation awarded her the American Book Award for lifetime achievement. Her well-executed short stories, although never overtly political, focus on issues of race and gender while accurately portraying the history of the Japanese in America.

BIBLIOGRAPHY: Cheng, M. L., "The Unrepentant Fire," *MELUS* 19 (Winter 1994): 91–107; Cheung, K., *Articulate Silences* (1993); Osborn, W. P., "A Conversation with H. Y.," *ChiR* 39 (1993): 34–38; Yogi, S., *Rebels and Heroines* (1992)

LINDA TRINH MOSER

YAMAUCHI, Wakako [Nakamura]
b. 25 October 1924, Westmoreland, California

Y. was born in California's arid Imperial Valley to Japanese immigrant parents. Legally prohibited from owning land, her family worked as tenant farmers in various towns until moving to Oceanside, where they ran a hotel for other Japanese immigrants. During World War II, she and her parents were interred in a Japanese American relocation camp in Poston, Arizona. Her personal history inspires the majority of her work that focuses on the experience of Japanese immigrant farm workers and the World War II internment experience.

Through powerful descriptions of individuals, Y.'s work typically describes the competing and contradictory aspects of Japanese American life: the contrast between the diverse values of *Issei* (literally, first generation immigrants) and their *Nisei* (second generation) children; the desire to assimilate to American culture despite that culture's hostility; and the opposition between the reality of poverty and dreams of material comfort. Her most widely anthologized work, "And the Soul Shall Dance" (1974), a short story later adapted into a play, exemplifies these themes. In it, the female characters strive to balance their dual cultures. While Masako, the adolescent *Nisei* daughter, weighs filial obligation with a growing desire for independence, her mother dreams of returning to Japan to distract her from the harsh reality of American life. Emiko also dreams of returning; her dancing reenacts life in Japan with a lover whom she was forced to leave. Unlike Masako's mother, however, Emiko dies unable to cope with American life. In life, the dance spiritually releases her from reality and foreshadows the untimely death that releases her soul from unbearable suffering. Although Y. admonishes the Japanese immigrant community for rejecting Emiko, at the same time she implies how the poverty imposed upon them by American culture prevents them from embracing her.

Y.'s work suggests, often subtly, that America is partly to blame for the difficulties faced by Japanese Americans. *The Music Lessons* (1977), a play based on a short story, suggests the impossibility of the American dream in romantic and economic terms. The main plot depicts the generational and cultural conflicts between fifteen-year-old Aki Sakata and her widowed *Issei* mother, Chizuko. Although Aki criticizes her mother for living without romance, the story explains how the poverty of farm life, the premature death of Chizuko's husband, and the responsibilities of raising three children combine to eliminate any possibility of love. The portrayal of Kawaguchi, the middle-aged itinerant worker Aki falls in love with, also suggests the failure of the American dream. A former artist, he is forced into an occupation with a dim future.

Later plays are more direct in their criticism of American practices and policies. The play *12–1–A* (1981), whose title refers to the number of a barrack, indicts the U.S. for incarcerating Japanese Americans during World War II. Y.'s use of irony is at its best as she demonstrates the contradictions faced by the Tanaka family. Although they are American citizens guaranteed the right to freedom, they are incarcerated against their will in a Japanese relocation camp. The Tanaka family, however, like all of Y's characters, endure and survive, a testament to the strength of Japanese Americans.

BIBLIOGRAPHY: Houston, V. H., ed., *Politics of Life* (1993); Uno, R., ed., *Unbroken Thread* (1993); Yogi, S., *Rebels and Heroines* (1992)

LINDA TRINH MOSER

YOUNG, Al[bert James]
b. 31 May 1939, Ocean Springs, Mississippi

Although Y. is an African American writing about the complexities of African American life, his work continually attempts to fathom common humanity. He is especially interested in the poetic power of black vernacular and music, and jazz plays an important role in much of his writing. His novels also explore family relationships, as well as the fates of drifting individuals.

Y. brings to his writing a fund of experience that has served him well. He spent much of his childhood in rural Mississippi where he was born, visiting his grandparents in Pachuta every summer after his father moved the family to Detroit, Michigan. Y. attended the University of Michigan at Ann Arbor from 1957 to 1961, and moved to San Francisco after his graduation. While he was in college, he performed as a freelance guitarist, flute player, and singer, which he continued to do in California. He taught writing at Berkeley and Stanford during the late 1960s and early 1970s, and also wrote scripts for Richard Pryor, Sidney Poitier, and Bill Cosby, who has praised the "wise and musical ear" evident in Y.'s writing.

Y.'s love and knowledge of music permeate his novels and poems. His first novel *Snakes* (1970) is about a young jazz musician called MC, who leaves his home town of Detroit when his first recording entitled "Snakes" does well there. He goes to New York to try and start a musical career, and discovers along the way his true calling as a musician. One of MC's friends, Champ, who has a similar passion for music but lacks the will to act, spends most of his time on drugs, and serves as a dramatic contrast to MC's trajectory of action and self-discovery.

In *Seduction by Light* (1988), Y. portrays the life of a middle-aged black woman named Mamie Franklin, who lives in Santa Monica, California, and takes care of her invalid husband, Burley Cole. She works as a maid in the world of Hollywood producers, and tells her story with ironic distance in a folksy vernacular typical of MC and other Y. protagonists. When Burley dies, and the level of pathos threatens to overflow, Y. upends the convention of the tragic domestic novel by having Burley return as a ghost, with humorous results. Later on, Mamie experiences an earthquake and has an out-of-body experience, in which she encounters the spirit of Benjamin FRANKLIN, her unlikely idol. All of these increasingly strange events create a slightly surreal atmosphere, and give Mamie a platform on which to ruminate on the mysteries of life in her strangely captivating voice.

Y.'s poems share many of the same concerns as his novels, and comment on African American identity, both domestic and political, the power of jazz, and Y.'s own indebtedness to other poets such as Dylan Thomas and W. H. AUDEN. "A Dance for Militant Dilettantes," the first poem in his collection *Heaven: Collected Poems, 1956–1990* (1992) satirizes the advice of a "hip friend" who urges him to write more caustically about race, demonstrating Y.'s refusal to be pigeonholed as an angry protest poet. Although many of his poems are conversational free verse, Y.

also experiments with rhyme in such poems as "Lester Leaps In."

Y.'s collection of memoirs, *Drowning in the Sea of Love* (1994), offers a series of autobiographical reflections on his experiences with the music of John Coltrane, James Brown, Miles Davis, and Charlie Parker. In these essays, as in others, Y. embodies Oscar Wilde's dictum that criticism is the "only civilized form of autobiography," bringing to music criticism the trained ear of a wisely musical poet.

BIBLIOGRAPHY: Harris, W., "Interview with A. Y.," *GaR* 10 (Summer-Fall 1982): 1–19; Mackey, N., "Interview with A. Y.," *MELUS* 5 (Winter 1978): 32–51; O'Brien, J., *Interviews with Black Writers* (1973)

R. A. BENTHALL

YOUNG ADULT LITERATURE

Before the 19th c., few books were written for children, and virtually none for young adult readers. 17th-c. children heard and read the Bible, John Bunyan's *Pilgrim's Progress,* and other works that their elders enjoyed. In the 18th c., children on both sides of the Atlantic read and heard such novels as Daniel Defoe's *Robinson Crusoe,* Samuel Richardson's *Pamela* and *Clarissa,* and Henry Fielding's *Tom Jones* though abridged versions were created for younger readers. These condensed versions sought to inculcate morals: the abridged *Tom Jones,* for example, urged children not to annoy their neighbors. In his *Autobiography,* Benjamin FRANKLIN recorded his delight in Bunyan and in Plutarch's *Lives;* he also bought small, inexpensive chapbooks. Anna Green Winslow, a Boston schoolgirl during the American Revolution, recorded in her diary that for New Year's, 1772, she received a copy of the Bible, *Pilgrim's Progress,* Jonathan Swift's *Gulliver's Travels,* and Fielding's *Joseph Andrews.* From her cousin, she borrowed *The Puzzling-Cap, The Female Orator,* and *The History of Goody Two Shoes.* Both *The Puzzling-Cap* and *Goody Two Shoes* must have come from Britain, since they had not yet been reprinted in America. England remained the source of many books for adults as well as children during this period. In 1753, the New York printer and bookseller Hugh Gaines imported copies of *Robinson Crusoe* from Britain; he did not publish his own edition until 1775. Isaiah Thomas of Worcester, Massachusetts, pirated many volumes first issued by John Newbery, an 18th-c. London publisher who dealt heavily in works for younger readers and who established the first bookshop specializing in such material, yet even the youngest readers continued to pore over books written for their elders.

This practice of appropriation continued into the 19th c.; it is as old as books and will always endure. As Henry Steele Commager noted, "Most of those books which we regard as classics of children's literature were written without children in mind and were taken over by them with cheerful disregard of what they could not understand." Thus, James Fenimore COOPER, Washington IRVING, and Sir Walter Scott enjoyed great popularity among young readers in America and Britain in the early 1800s. At the same time, writers began to focus specifically on children and young adults. Mason Locke WEEMS's biographies sought to teach not just history but also patriotism and morality to the postrevolutionary generation. The American Tract Society, established in 1825 by the merger of the New York Religious Tract Society and the New England Tract Society, undertook a publication program "to counteract the prevailing thirst in the rising generation for the mere entertainment of high-wrought fiction," while at the same time it recognized the need for "something more than didactic discussion." Other religious organizations also began targeting younger readers: the *Children's Magazine* was established by the Episcopal Church in 1828, the *Encourager* by the Methodists, and around midcentury young Catholics might read the *Catholic Youth Magazine.* One important magazine without religious affiliation was the *Juvenile Miscellany* (1827–34), published by John Putnam of Boston and edited initially by Lydia Maria CHILD, succeeded by Sarah Josepha HALE. The stories reveal a New England bias, though no more so than American literature in general in this period. The *Juvenile Miscellany* celebrated American history, with biographies of such figures as Benjamin Franklin and Revolutionary general Israel Putnam. The magazine attracted the leading adult authors of the period, among them Lydia Huntley SIGOURNEY, Eliza Leslie, and Catharine Maria SEDGWICK. Concentrating on American scenes and themes, the periodical broke with English models, thus reflecting the literary nationalism of the era. As the first nonsectarian children's magazine, the *Juvenile Miscellany* served as a model for later children's periodicals.

About 1830, the American Sunday School Union, created in Philadelphia in 1824, began publishing books. It laid down four rules for its writers: books must be of a moral and religious nature; books must be adapted to the age of the reader; the writing must be of good quality; and books should deal with American subjects and be aimed at American readers. One important author the society enlisted was Jacob Abbott, with such titles as the *Young Christian* (1832). Abbott's titles for the society sold tens of thousands of copies. The Ladies Commission of the American Unitarian Society (Boston) did not publish books itself, but it did prepare lists of recommended titles. Many of the authors on these lists were British, including Charles Dickens and Sir Walter Scott, perennial favorites among readers of all ages, but American writers also received recognition.

In 1834, Abbott introduced Rollo, the first popular fictional American boy; by the time of Abbott's death in 1879 he had produced nearly two hundred books for young readers. Abbott grew up in Maine, which serves as the setting for many of his works. Ordained as a minister and trained as a teacher, Abbott provided heavy doses of morality and instruction in his books. An anonymous writer in the *North American Review* in 1866 commented on one of Abbott's characters, "Jonas is an admirable creation—the typical New England boy, such a boy as every one of us has been or know. . . . He is always a wholesome companion who neither intoxicates nor misleads. . . . Jonas is American Democracy in its teens." Abbott's characters are not, however, impossible paragons of virtue. Phonny sets out to work in his garden but then decides to go fishing instead. Nor does Abbott ignore the darker side of life, particularly in his Franconia stories, published from 1850 to 1853. Without sentimentality, these works depict the freedom but also the hardship of childhood and adolescence. Ellen Linn loses her aunt and father in a storm. Mary Erskine must struggle to earn a living for herself and her children.

The prolific publisher and author Samuel Griswold Goodrich created the Peter Parley series. Shunning fiction, he used his books to teach history, science, geography, and biography. *Tales of Peter Parley about America* (1827), the first of 170 Peter Parley books, reflects the patriotic, didactic purpose of Goodrich's writing. Goodrich also founded *Peter Parley's Magazine* (1833–44) and the longer-lived *Merry Museum* (1841–72), the latter edited for a time by Louisa May ALCOTT.

Under the pseudonym of Elizabeth Wetherell, Susan Bogart WARNER produced two popular books for young women, *The Wide, Wide World* and *Queechy,* in which orphans overcome adversity through Christian fortitude. Warner's writing is sentimental, but she provides realistic portraits of life. Caroline M. Hewins, born in 1846, recalled that as a child she enjoyed the works of Eliza Leslie, particularly *Amelia; or, A Young Lady's Vicissitudes* (1848). The story ends with the heroine happily married, but in the course of the novel she is jilted by a suitor and struggles with her family.

The post–Civil War period was the golden age of children's literature, producing classics that still delight young adult readers. This was also the heyday of Beadle's Dime Novels and Munroe's Ten Cent books, inexpensive, action-packed stories that appealed to boys. In 1879, the fourteen-year-old William Lyon

Phelps recorded his voracious reading habits. "I read the entire book of psalms today. This morning I finished [Cherbuliez's] *Jean Têteral's Idea* and in the afternoon and evening read two books of the *Gunboat* series"—books by Charles Austin Fosdick writing under pseudonym of Harry Castlemon. Fosdick served in the navy during the Civil War and drew on his experiences for such books as *Frank on a Gunboat* (1864) and *Frank on the Lower Mississippi* (1867). Franklin P. Adams called Fosdick the "boys' own author," and Fosdick probably was the most read author for boys in the post-Civil War era. He produced some sixty volumes in series dealing with hunting and fishing, war, and the American West. He understood the desires of his audience: "Boys don't like fine writing. What they want is adventure, and the more of it you can get into two-hundred-fifty pages of manuscript, the better fellow you are." Fosdick did not stress the moralistic or the didactic, but his fiction was not without its lessons. He remarked that he sought to show that "success lies in application, and in doing what you can well, and with tenacity of purpose." Elijah Kellogg, though a minister, also avoided explicit didacticism in his stories set in the Maine of the late 18th and early 19th cs. He did, however, illustrate the importance of courage, endurance, and hard work. In his descriptions of Maine, Kellogg was part of the local color movement of his day. More didactic but still immensely popular were Horatio ALGER, Jr.'s various series showing the rise from rags to riches. His *Ragged Dick* was succeeded by over a hundred other titles.

Sophie May—the pen name of Rebecca Sophia Clarke—wrote realistic stories for younger girls, and her Quinnebasset series appealed to young adults, both male and female. Alcott drew on her own experiences, putting herself—as Jo—her sister, parents, and neighbors into realistic fiction showing life in the mid-1800s. Precursors of Alcott's realistic treatment of New England girlhood were Adeline Dutton Train Whitney's *Faith Gartney's Girlhood* (1863) and *A Summer in Leslie Goldthwaite's Life* (1866), though her books have a religious tone absent from Alcott's work. Also reflecting the realistic tendency in children's books of the period and the local color movement, though transcending this genre, were Mark TWAIN's *The Adventures of Tom Sawyer* and *Adventures of Huckleberry Finn.*

The proliferation of literature for younger readers prompted Horace E. Scudder to complain in 1867, "Children have too much reading." This complaint appeared in Scudder's *Riverside* magazine (1867–70), which added to the reading for children. Scudder emphasized the classics, such as Shakespeare, Plutarch, William Blake, and Robert Browning, but he also published Bayard TAYLOR's *Boys of Other Countries,* which appeared in book form in 1876. The *Riverside* was one of a distinguished group of periodicals that appeared after the civil War to appeal to children and young adults. In January 1865, the publishing firm of Ticknor and Field issued the first number of *Our Young Folks* (1865–73), edited by John T. Trowbridge, Gail Hamilton, and Lucy Larcom. This first number included Harriet Beecher STOWE's "Hum, the Son of Buz," a tale of a hummingbird that strayed into her conservatory. The story begins happily, but at the end the bird dies. Whatever facts of life were concealed from young Victorians, death was not one of these. Mayne REID serialized *Afloat in the Forest* in *Our Young Folks* monthly issues for 1865, and Charles C. Coffin contributed *Winning His Way*. Louisa May Alcott, James Russell LOWELL, Henry Wadsworth LONGFELLOW, and John Greenleaf WHITTIER also published here. Trowbridge frequently wrote for his magazine, including *Jack Hazard and His Fortunes,* based on his experiences growing up along the Erie Canal. Lucy Larcom's autobiographical *A New England Girlhood* appeared in the magazine, as did Thomas Bailey ALDRICH's *Story of a Bad Boy,* serialized in 1869. Charles Dickens provided *Holiday Romance* in four installments in 1868 and Lucretia Peabody HALE first introduced the popular Peterkin family in that year through the pages of the periodical.

In 1874, Ticknor and Field sold *Our Young Folks* to Scribner's, which merged the magazine with one even better, *St. Nicholas* (1873–1940). This periodical remains the best ever produced for young readers, and its contents still entertain. Its first editor was Mary Mapes Dodge. In July 1873, Dodge published an unsigned article entitled "Children's Magazines" in *Scribner's.* She observed, "The children's magazine must not be a milk-and-water variety of the periodical for adults. In fact, it needs to be stronger, truer, bolder, more uncompromising than the other." Similarly, in the first issue of *St. Nicholas* (November 1873) she wrote, "Let there be no sermonizing . . . no spinning out of facts, no rattling of dry bones. . . . The ideal children's magazine is a pleasure ground." While including informative articles, the magazine concentrated on stories that would delight young readers. Established authors contributed. Louisa May Alcott serialized *Jo's Boys, An Old-Fashioned Girl,* and *Eight Cousins.* Joel Chandler HARRIS sent Uncle Remus stories. Longfellow, Whittier, William Cullen BRYANT, Sarah Orne JEWETT, Mark Twain, Edward Everett HALE, Thomas Bailey Aldrich, and John T. Trowbridge were among its writers. Howard Pyle first appeared in the pages of *St. Nicholas* in 1877. Later, he serialized his medieval books *Otto of the Silver Hand* and *The Story of King Arthur* in *St. Nicholas.* In 1885, Frances Hodgson BURNETT provided *St. Nicholas* with the first

installment of *Little Lord Fauntleroy.* In the 1890s, John Bennett's *Master Skylark,* set in the reign of Queen Elizabeth, delighted *St. Nicholas* readers; this title, like Pyle's books, illustrates the enduring popularity of historical fiction among young readers. The magazine also published one of the first mysteries for girls, Cecilia Viets Jamison's *Lady Jane* (1891), set in New Orleans. In 1898, the Century Company bought *St. Nicholas,* and Albert Bigelow Paine started the St. Nicholas League to encourage young writers. Among the authors whose careers begin in the pages of *St. Nicholas* were Ring LARDNER, Bennett Cerf, Edmund WILSON, and Edna St. Vincent MILLAY.

Another important magazine of the late 1800s was *Harper's Young People,* later renamed *Harper's Round Table,* which began in 1879 under the editorship of Kirk Munroe and lasted for twenty years. Munroe's *Derrick Sterling* (1888) was one of the first works to present industrial life to young readers, in this case mining. Howard Pyle contributed *The Merry Adventures of Robin Hood,* published in book form in 1883.

As author and illustrator Pyle possessed great skill in presenting old stories in new ways. The retelling of myths for young readers has a long tradition. Earlier in the 19th c., Charles Lamb had written *The Adventures of Ulysses,* and Nathaniel HAWTHORNE had produced *A Wonder-Book* and *Tanglewood Tales.* The end of the century witnessed a proliferation of such books. Alfred J. Church retold the *Odyssey* and *Iliad* (1892). Hamilton Wright Mabie's *Norse Stories Retold from the Eddas* (1894) and Thomas William Hazen Rolleston's *The High Deeds of Finn* (1916) introduced other myths to a new generation. Between 1903 and 1910, Howard Pyle published four volumes, with his own pen and ink drawings, retelling the Arthurian legends of Thomas Malory, and Edith Hamilton's stillpopular *Mythology* (1942) provides a more recent example of this kind of writing.

At the end of the 19th c., girls' fiction tended toward romance, as exemplified by Frances Hodgson Burnett's *Sarah Crewe; or, What Happened at Miss Minchin's,* a delightful but unrealistic portrayal of life in a girls' boarding school. Kate Douglas WIGGIN's *Rebecca of Sunnybrook Farm* resembles the tale of Aladdin and the Princess from the *Arabian Nights,* bowdlerized selections from which Wiggin and her sister, Nora Archibald Smith, published in 1909 with illustrations by Maxfield Parrish. Rebecca's charm lies in her remaining a little girl. Similarly, Eleanor Hodgman Porter's *Pollyanna* (1913) offers its readers an escape from reality. Boys' books, on the other hand, became increasingly realistic, with Aldrich, Mark Twain, and, after the turn of the century, Jack LONDON's *The Call of the Wild,* as dark as any adult fiction of the day.

The 20th c. has seen no decline in historical fiction for young readers. Joseph Alexander Altsheler's *The Horses of the Plains* (1910) and *The Guns of Bull Run* (1914) and Willa CATHER's *Death Comes for the Archbishop* and *Shadows on the Rock* illustrate the genre's continued appeal. Marguerite Henry draws readers to history through animal stories, such as *Justin Morgan Had a Horse* (1945), *Benjamin West and His Cat Grimalkin* (1947), and Newbery Award-winner *King of the Wind* (1948), about the Godolphin Arabian, one of the greatest foundation sires of the thoroughbred. Henry uses the animals' adventures to portray life in Morocco, France, and England in the 18th c. Esther FORBES won the Pulitzer Prize in history in 1942 for *Paul Revere and the World He Lived In* and the Newbery Award in 1943 for *Johnny Tremain,* her novel for young adults based on her research into the Revolutionary period. In both works, historical characters and the past come alive. Leonard Wibberley, who came to the U.S. as an adult, shared Forbes's fascination with the American Revolution. In works like *John Treegate's Musket* (1959), *Peter Treegate's War* (1960), and *Treegate's Raiders* (1962), he sought "not to instruct but to enrich that which is already known; not to distort but to listen to the insistent whispers of forgotten voices penetrating the centuries." The fiction of Cornelia Lynde Meigs shows how the past looked from the perspective of the young, though the naivety of her approach makes her works sound like fairy tales. Elizabeth George Speare has won two Newbery Awards for her historical fiction: *The Witch of Blackbird Pond* (1958), set in 17th-c. Wethersfield—where she lived for some twenty years—and *The Bronze Bow* (1961), set in Israel at the time of Jesus. Theodore Taylor has drawn on his experiences to write about the history of his native South and important naval battles in World War II.

Scott O'Dell has written realistic fiction, but the majority of his works deal with the past; in 1981, he created the Scott O'Dell Award for Historical Fiction. His *Island of the Blue Dolphins* (1960), a Newbery Medal winner, deals with the maturation of Karana as she struggles to survive after raiders expel her tribe and her brother is killed by a wild dog. Karana's story illustrates not only O'Dell's skill as a writer of historical fiction but also his ability to create strong female characters. While setting his stories in the past, O'Dell is concerned with the issues that affect his readers. As he has said, "The problems of isolation, moral decision, greed, need for love and affection are problems of today as well. I am didactic; I do want to teach through books."

This concern with contemporary problems also underlies the historical fiction of Mildred D. Taylor, whose Newbery Award-winning *Roll of Thunder,* *Hear My Cry* (1976), set in the 1930s, confronts the issue of racism. She continued to explore this issue in *Song of the Trees* (1975) and *Let the Circle Be Unbroken* (1981), dealing with recent black history. Carol Ryrie Brink's historical fiction explores family relationships. Her classic *Caddie Woodlawn* (1935), which won a Newbery Medal, is set in Wisconsin during the Civil War, but that conflict plays no role in the book. Drawing on her grandmother's experiences, she does, however, offer a vivid picture of life on the frontier in the 1860s. Jean Fritz, who has eloquently described her own childhood, also has produced books about growing up in mid-19th-c. America, notably, *Brady* (1960) and *I, Adam* (1963), and about Salem, Massachusetts on the eve of the American Revolution in *Early Thunder* (1967).

Fritz's fiction focuses more on the psychology of her characters than on history per se, a characteristic of the "new realism" in young adult fiction. J. D. SALINGER's *The Catcher in the Rye* and John KNOWLES's *A Separate Peace* use first person narrators to express the feelings of young adults. Mary Stolz's *To Tell Your Love* (1950) realistically examines romance from the viewpoint of a seventeen-year-old girl. In that book, Anne loves a young man who no longer loves her. Stolz's *In a Mirror* (1953) shows Bessie Miller coping with obesity. In *Wait for Mr. Michael* (1961), fifteen-year-old Amy falls in love with one of her mother's friends.

Katherine Paterson has written historical fiction set in her native China and in Japan, where she worked for several years as a missionary, but contemporary issues also inform her fiction. In *The Great Gilly Hopkins* (1978), she addressed the pain of foster children. At the end of that book, Mrs. Trotter tells Gilly, "You just fool yourself if you expect good things all the time. They ain't what's regular—don't nobody owe 'em to you." Alice CHILDRESS's *A Hero Ain't Nothin' but a Sandwich* confronts the issue of heroin addiction; maternal neglect underlies her *Rainbow Jordan.* Paul Zindel, Norma Fox Mazer, M. E. Kerr—pen name of Marijane Meaker—Judy Blume, S. E. Hinton, and Cynthia Voigt in her "Crisfield" novels, named for the imaginary town on the eastern shore of Maryland, all exemplify this new and darker realism in children's fiction. Voigt's *Dicey's Song* (1982), one of the Crisfield books, won the Newbery Award.

Though she has written folktales, and though much of her fiction is suffused with the surreal, Virginia Hamilton has sought, in her words, "to shed light on the real concerns of a young people in a world in which survival becomes for them increasingly more difficult." Hamilton's African American heritage underlies her work, but her themes and characters possess universal relevance. As Hamilton has observed, "More than anything, I write about emotions, which are a part of all people."

Other examples of realistic fiction for teenagers of both sexes include Emily Neville's *It's like This, Cat* (1963). This Newbery Award-winner offers a sympathetic yet realistic treatment of fourteen-year old Dave Mitchell's alienation from his father. Neville's second book, *Berries Goodman* (1965), explores anti-Semitism. Robert Cormier's *The Chocolate War* (1974) presents boys who swear and smoke, lust and fight. Cormier paints a grim but truthful portrait of high school life. Barbara Girion in *A Tangle of Roots* (1979) shows how death affects sixteen-year-old Beth and those around her. This title was chosen as one of the Best Books for Young Adults in 1980 and won the Kenneth B. Smilen/*Present Tense* Literary Award for that year. An unsentimental handling of death underlies Paula Fox's *A Place Apart* (1980) and Judy Blume's *Tiger Eyes* (1981). Fox's book is told from the point of view of the adolescent Victoria Flint. In addition to dealing with death, Fox here explores young love, friendship, and the effect of a parent's remarriage.

Not all late-20th-c. works for children and young adults are dark. E. L. Konigsburg's *From the Mixed-up Files of Mrs. Basil E. Frankweiler* (1967), which won the Newbery Award for 1968, shows bright, self-reliant children living comfortably and adventurously in a suburban world. Beverly Cleary, best known for her Ramona stories, has also written for teenagers. Cleary treats her characters with sympathy and humor. Madeleine L'Engle's autobiographical Austin novels do not shun harsh reality; *Meet the Austins* (1960) frankly confronts death. L'Engle is best known, though, for such fantasies as *A Wrinkle in Time* (1962), which won the Newbery Award in 1963. These works combine science, fantasy, and religion, this last element underlying L'Engle's optimism in the power of love to triumph over, indeed to redeem, evil. Jean George combines natural history with her fiction about strong young adults who successfully cope with their problems.

If in general young adult literature has become grittier since World War II, so has life. Young adulthood has always been a period of transition, of adapting to new and unfamiliar situations and settings. Writers for that audience have sought, and continue to seek, to assist in that process.

BIBLIOGRAPHY: Hewins, C., *A Mid-Century Child and Her Books* (1926); Jordan, A. M., *From Rollo to Tom Sawyer and Other Papers* (1948); Lenz, M., *Young Adult Literature and Nonprint Materials* (1994); Meigs, C., et al., *A Critical History of Children's Literature* (1953; rev. ed., 1969); Smith, E. S., *The History of Children's Literature* (1937; rev. ed., Hodges, M., and S. Steinfirst, 1980)

JOSEPH ROSENBLUM

YOURCENAR, Marguerite

b. 8 June 1903, Brussels, Belgium; d. 17 December 1987, Northeast Harbor, Mount Desert Island, Maine

Known primarily as the author of the acclaimed novel *Mémoires d'Hadrien,* published in 1951 and translated as *Memoirs of Hadrian* (1954), Y. was accomplished as well as a poet, short story writer, dramatist, translator, and essayist. Her literary career spanned well over half a century and culminated in the extraordinary distinction when at the age of seventy-six she was elected to the Académie Française, the first woman in the history of the institution to be so honored.

Born Marguerite de Crayencour of a Belgium mother, who died shortly after childbirth, Y. inherited the French citizenship of her father, who assumed responsibility for her upbringing. Y. was encouraged by her father at an early age to pursue her literary interests, and in 1921 he arranged for the private publication of her first book, *Le Jardin des chimères,* a dramatic adaptation of the Icarus legend. This was followed a year later by a collection of poems, *Les Dieux ne sont pas morts.* Her father also assisted in the invention of her anagrammatical pseudonym, which in 1947 she adopted as her legal name.

After her father's death when Y. was twenty-four, she decided to devote herself exclusively to travel, study, and literature. She began to contribute poetry and critical essays to a variety of literary periodicals and in 1929 published her first novel, *Alexis; ou, Le Traité du vain combat,* revised in 1965 and translated as *Alexis* (1984), which earned for her critical as well as popular attention. This was followed by a second novel in 1931, *La Nouvelle Eurydice.* Her emerging literary reputation was further enhanced by the publication in 1934 of *Denier du rêve,* revised and expanded in 1959 and translated as *A Coin in Nine Hands* (1982). Set amid the rise of fascism in prewar Italy, the novel is atypical of Y.'s fiction in utilizing a contemporary setting and an ensemble cast rather than a single, dominant protagonist. It is nonetheless characteristic of thematic concerns that accentuate Y.'s distinct artistic vision, notably the exploration of self, the mystery of human emotion, and the fusion of dream and reality.

In 1936, Y. published a sequence of lyrical prose pieces entitled *Feux,* revised in 1974 and translated as *Fires* (1981), followed by a collection of short stories, *Nouvelles orientales* (1938), revised in 1963 and 1975 and translated as *Oriental Tales* (1985); and a novel titled *Le Coup de grâce* (1939), translated as

Coup de Grâce (1957). She completed the novel while living in Italy, returning to Paris shortly before the outbreak of World War II. Disheartened by the imminent invasion of France, Y. left Europe for the U.S. at the invitation of Grace Frick, an American friend who would become her lifelong companion. The decade that followed was disappointing artistically for Y.; compelled by economic necessity, she turned to translating and teaching as a means to earn her livelihood. In 1942, while living in Hartford, Connecticut, Y. and Frick began to summer in Maine, where in 1950 they purchased what became their permanent residence in Northeast Harbor. In 1947, Y. became a naturalized American citizen.

The turning point of Y.'s literary career was her decision to resume work on a character study of the Roman Emperor Hadrian, a creative impulse that evolved into the novel generally acknowledged to be her most significant achievement. *Memoirs of Hadrian* was the first of Y.'s works to be published in the U.S. Written in the form of a letter to his adopted grandson and future heir, Marcus Aurelius, the novel explores the boundaries of human experience, allowing the protagonist to ruminate on the circumstances of his life while confronting the inevitability of death. The critical reception of *Memoirs of Hadrian* established Y. as an author of international stature, a reputation further solidified by the publication in 1968 of *L'Œuvre au Noir,* translated as *The Abyss* (1976). Similar in context and methodology to *Memoirs of Hadrian, L'Œuvre au noir* is set in northern Europe in the mid-16th c. The protagonist of the novel is the fictitious Zeno, a physician-alchemist-philosopher in search of enlightenment within an age dominated by repression.

The death of Grace Frick after a long illness in 1979 was a tremendous personal loss for Y. Her companion for over fifty years, Frick was both a source of creative inspiration to Y. and her collaborator, translating all of her major works into English. It was shortly after Frick's death that Y. was nominated for membership to the Académie Française. Although her nomination generated heated debate over admission of a woman to the all-male institution, she was elected on March 6, 1980 and inducted on January 22, 1981. Largely the result of becoming France's first académicienne, the demand for her work in the U.S. prompted publication in English of her earlier fiction as well as *Comme l'eau qui coule* (1982), translated as *Two Lives and A Dream* (1987). In addition, her early collection of criticism *Sous bénéfice d'inventaire* (1962) was translated as *The Dark Brain of Piranesi and Other Essays* (1984). This was followed by *Mishima: A Vision of the Void* (1986), first published as *Mishima, ou la vision du vide* (1980), a critical study of the Japanese writer Yukio Mishima. A second collection of criticism, originally published in 1983 as *Le Temps, ce grand sculpteur,* was translated as *That Mighty Sculptor, Time* and published in the U.S. in 1992. *Souvenirs pieux,* the first volume of her semiautobiographical work entitled "Le Labyrinthe du monde," was published in 1973 and translated as *Dear Departed* (1991). The second volume, *Archives du Nord,* published in 1977, appeared as *How Many Years* (1995), and the final volume, "Quoi? l'eternité," was left unfinished.

Y. enjoyed a prolific and diversified career, and she possessed a unique and enduring artistic voice. Merging the past with the present, her fiction evokes a sense of agelessness as well as timely significance.

BIBLIOGRAPHY: Farrell, C. F., and E. R. Farrell, *M. Y. in Counterpoint* (1983); Howard, J. E., *From Violence to Vision: Sacrifice in the Works of M. Y.* (1992); Savigneau, J., *M. Y.: Inventing a Life* (1993)

STEVEN R. SERAFIN

ZUKOFSKY, Louis
b. 23 January 1904, New York City; d. 12 May 1978,
Port Jefferson, New York

Barely and Widely, the title Z. chose for a 1958 collection of his poems, provides the poet's own description of his long career as a "poet's poet" and the subsistance-level conditions under which he lived a brilliant life of the mind. He knew his work was barely available, barely noticed by the general reading public—either his books of poems were self-published in short runs and virtually undistributed or the more commercial editions had been out of print for years—yet, he was widely recognized among U.S.-British poets over three generations—from Ezra POUND, his mentor, and his fellow objectivists, including William Carlos WILLIAMS and Basil Bunting, to Black Mountain poets Robert CREELEY and Robert DUNCAN and their students Joel OPPENHEIMER and Jonathan Williams, and writers as diverse as Cid Corman and Guy DAVENPORT. After taking an M.A. at Columbia, Z. earned his livelihood by teaching English at the Polytechnic Institute of Brooklyn for nearly twenty years and wrote in relative obscurity from the late 1930s to the early 1960s; yet, he produced one of the most important long poems of the 20th c., entitled "*A*"—conceived as a poem-in-progress and written as it was lived from 1928 to 1977—and an innovative volume of Shakespeare commentary, *Bottom: On Shakespeare* (1963), plus many books of lyrical poetry, fiction, drama, translation, and critical essays.

Asked to edit a special edition of *Poetry* in 1931, Z. responded by grouping poets, including Williams, George OPPEN, and Charles REZNIKOFF, Carl Rakosi, and himself, under the term objectivists. His main intentions seem to have been to advance the poetics Pound had codified in IMAGISM, most specifically a verse grounded in close observation and articulated by means of concrete imagery, while adding the inno-vative presence of the poet's discriminating mind. His sense of objectivism begins at the purely objectified recording of things, as he demonstrates in his essay "An Objective," in which he defines first the optical objective, or lens, before he defines the objective of poetry. While objectivism as a movement had its brief life, for Z. it was methodology. Twenty years after the controversial "Objectivist" issue of *Poetry,* he proposed to analyze, in *Bottom: On Shakespeare,* Shakespeare's concept of love by the formula "love is to reason as eyes are to mind"—offering, at once, an objectifying mathematical ratio as well as his personal scale, based on decades of observation while reading and teaching Shakespeare's canon, for developing a critique. By opening *Bottom* with the citation "image in the mind," his stress is clearly on the poet's interior, not Pound's image. For example, the poem "Mantis, An Interpretation," which is a text of mind, is printed following "Mantis," an eye text, in *55 Poems.*

From "Poem Beginning 'The'" (1926), a major early poem written in numbered lines, through "*A*," Z.'s poems are most obviously collages, surfaces of discrete lines and denotative pictures in a democratic eye seemingly in love with all things indiscriminately. Like Walt WHITMAN's "Song of Myself," his is an American construct meant to replace the Old World poetics of association. However, the artist's mind is always present in the poems, too; having arranged and displayed his collage as art, Z. seems to mean, he stands unobtrusively in the gallery, apart, at the apron of the conversation of those who have come to see. "I too have been charged with obscurity," he writes in *Autobiography* (1970), "tho it's a case of listeners wanting to know too much about me, more than the words say." Z. often uses the titles for his books, such as *I's Pronounced "Eyes"* (1963) and *After I's* (1964), to urge us toward his new epistemology.

Z.'s poems are made of images created by a distanced intelligence—elements that echo Pound's prin-

ciples of phanopoeia and logopoeia—but song—melo-
poeia, to Pound—is the linguistic condition of his
poetry. As if his whole canon were necessarily developing toward this realization, *"A"-24* (1972) is
words set to music by his wife Celia, and their son,
Paul, who is a concert violinist and composer. And in
"A"-12, Z. defines "my poetics" in terms of "An inte-
gral/Lower limit speech/Upper limit music." When
Z. and Celia translated Catullus' *Gai Valeri Catulli
Veronensis Liber* (1969), they were meticulous to convey, after the manner of James Joyce, the sound of
the Latin as well as its sense.

Among other critical writings by Z. that are of
major interest are *Le Style Apollinaire* (1934, with
René Taupin) and *A Test of Poetry* (1948). His story
"Ferdinand" and a play, *Arise, Arise* (1973), show a
genuine range in a writer whose signature poems are
developed in short lines of a word or two.

BIBLIOGRAPHY: Ahearn, B., *Z.'s "A"* (1978); Leggott,
M. J., *Reading Z.'s "80 Flowers"* (1989); Perelman,
B., *The Trouble with Genius* (1994); Pound, F., *Polite
Essays* (1937); Stanley, S. K., *L. Z. and the Transfor-
mation of a Modern American Poetics* (1994); Terrell,
C. F., ed., *L. Z.: Man and Poet* (1979); Zukofsky, C.,
A Bibliography of L. Z. (1969)

RICHARD L. BLEVINS

Index

H

1303